melbo[urne]

5th edition

COMPACT STREET DIRECTORY

Proudly Australian
Family Owned Company

by Gregory's

N
UBD
KEY MAP
SCALE 1: 575 000
0 4 8 12 16 20
Kilometres
Clarkefield
MELBOURNE - LANCEFIELD RD
77 78 79 80
Gisborne
CALDER
Jacksons
109 110 111 112 113 114
M79
Sunbury
141 142 143 144
Mickleham
149
Craigieburn
Bulla
GISBORNE MARSH RD
Lerderderg Gorge State Park
MELTON GISBORNE RD
Toolern Vale
SUNBURY RD
187 188 189 190 191 192 193
SOMERTON RD
WESTERN M8 FWY
Lerderderg R
BACCHUS
Diggers Rest
221 222 223 224 225 226 227 228
231 232 233 234 235 236 237
Werribee
WESTERN
MELTON C754 HWY
MELTON
M79 FWY
Melbourne Airport
Bacchus Marsh
263 264 265 266 267 268 269 270
273 274 275 276 277 278 279
Melton Resvr
M8
Kororoit
FWY
St Albans
Essendon
317 318 319 320 321 322 323
WESTERN HWY
Brisbane Ranges National Park
Mt Cottrell
BALLAN RD
Sunshine
363 364 365 366 367
Footscray
Durdidwarrah
Balliang
Tarneit
SAYERS RD
Little
405 406 407 408 409 410 411
Laverton
Altona
DERRIMUT RD
Steiglitz
Brisbane Ranges National Park
445 446 447 448 449 450 451 452
Werribee
Anakie
Wyndham Vale
Point Cook
BACCHUS MARSH - GEELONG
GEELONG - BALLAN RD
487 488
River
You Yangs Regional Park
River
Little River
M1
SOUTH RD
Werribee South
STEIGLITZ RD
Moorabool River
PRINCES
POINT WILSON RD
Lara
MIDLAND HWY
A300
Avalon
BACCHUS MARSH RD
Port Phillip
Gheringhap
Corio
RD
Corio Bay
Portarlington
HAMILTON B140 HWY
GEELONG
HOOD RD
Indented Head
Clifton Springs
Moolap
Barwon
701 702 703 704
C111
Barrabool
PORTARLINGTON RD
MURRADOC RD
RD
St Leonards
BELLARINE
Leopold
Drysdale
705 706
PRINCES A1 HWY
Grovedale
B100
BARWON
River
Lake Connewarre
B110
GRUBB RD
HWY
Swan Bay
707 708 709
MT DUNEED RD
RD
SURFCOAST HWY
HEADS RD
SHELL RD
Queenscliff
HENDY
C135
MAIN RD
ANGLESEA RD
Barwon Heads
710
665 666
Portsea
POINT
Torquay
Bass
The Rip
677 678 679 680
Sorrento
NEPEAN
Rosebud
683
Bellbrae
RD
OCEAN
711 712
Jan Juc
TN
GN
MN
695 696 697 698 699
Rye
BROWNS
GREAT
Anglesea
713 714
Strait
Magnetic Declination approx 11.517 East
Boneo
TRUE NORTH, GRID NORTH AND MAGNETIC NORTH ARE SHOWN DIAGRAMMATICALLY. MAGNETIC NORTH IS CORRECT FOR 2002 AND MOVES EASTERLY APPROX 0.013° EACH YEAR.
COPYRIGHT © UNIVERSAL PRESS PTY LTD (PUBLISHER) 2002

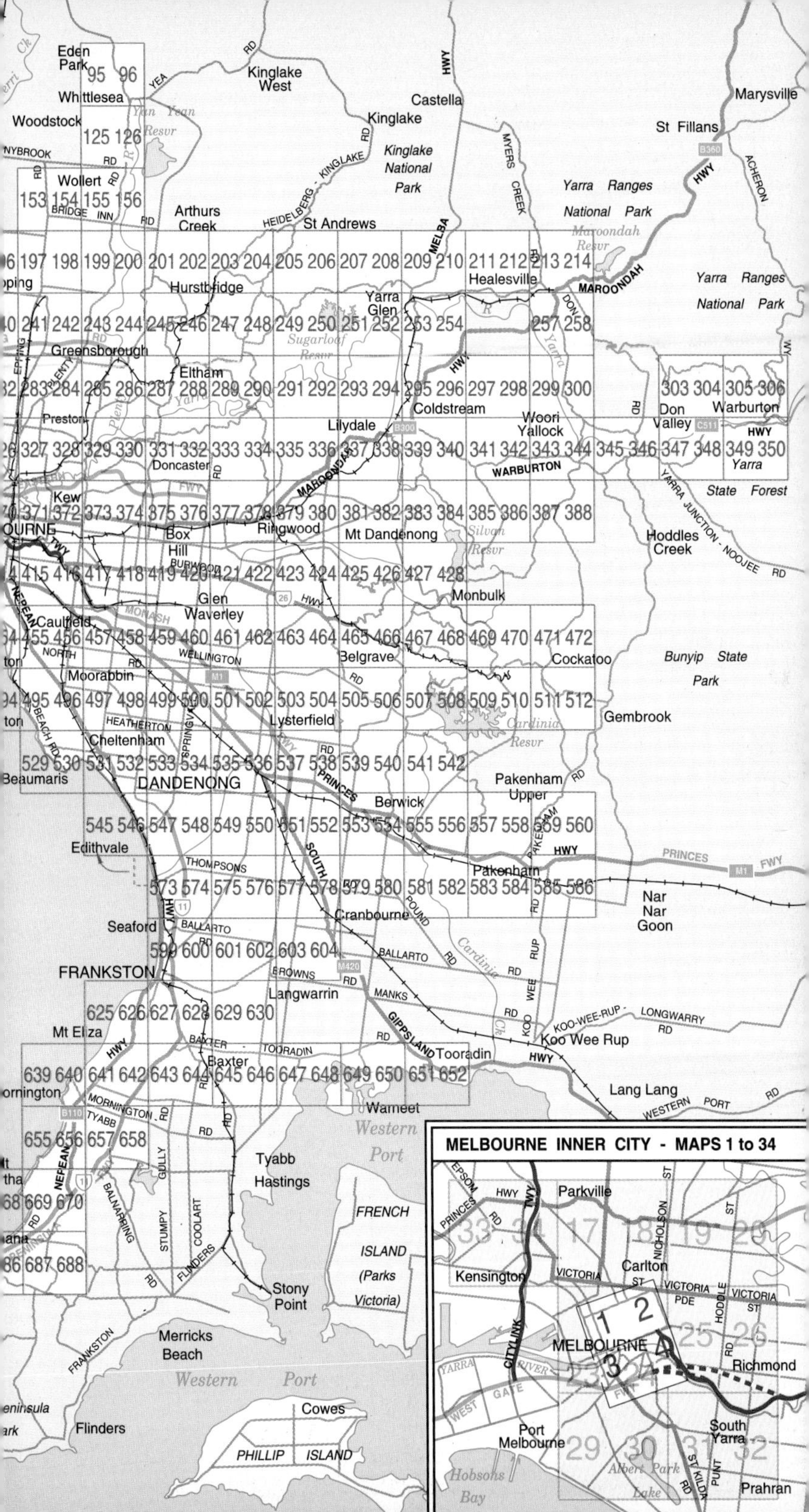
MELBOURNE INNER CITY - MAPS 1 to 34
Eden Park
Whittlesea
Woodstock
Wollert
Arthurs Creek
Kinglake West
Castella
Kinglake
Kinglake National Park
St Andrews
Marysville
St Fillans
Yarra Ranges National Park
Healesville
Hurstbridge
Yarra Glen
Greensborough
Eltham
Coldstream
Preston
Lilydale
Woori Yallock
Don Valley
Warburton
Doncaster
Kew
Box Hill
Ringwood
Mt Dandenong
Hoddles Creek
Yarra State Forest
Monbulk
Caulfield
Glen Waverley
Belgrave
Cockatoo
Bunyip State Park
Moorabbin
Lysterfield
Gembrook
Cheltenham
Beaumaris
DANDENONG
Pakenham Upper
Berwick
Edithvale
Pakenham
Nar Nar Goon
Seaford
Cranbourne
FRANKSTON
Langwarrin
Mt Eliza
Baxter
Tooradin
Koo Wee Rup
Lang Lang
Warneet
Western Port
Tyabb
Hastings
FRENCH ISLAND (Parks Victoria)
Stony Point
Merricks Beach
Flinders
Cowes
PHILLIP ISLAND
Parkville
Carlton
Kensington
MELBOURNE
Richmond
Port Melbourne
South Yarra
Prahran
Hobsons Bay
Albert Park Lake

Cityside Guide

Splash onto Melbourne's exciting aquatic scene. Beaches, boats and boardwalks line the stunning waterways of the city and surrounds, providing a serene, beautiful playground for Melburnians and visitors alike.

Port Phillip Bay is Melbourne's gateway to the rest of the world, and a favourite with locals because of its variety of beaches, scenery and widespread attractions. There's an incredible variety of things to do around this huge body of water. The bay has been amusing Melburnians since the first settlers arrived over 150 years ago.

At the northern end of the bay, the city sits near the mouth of the famous Yarra River. Once bustling with traders, the Yarra is now a peaceful estuary plied by rowers, water taxis, gondolas and scenic cruise vessels. Along its banks, the cyclists, skaters and joggers enjoy the winding trails, while those who just want to relax can settle back on the grassy slopes and watch the world go by.

In the city, at **Southgate Arts & Leisure Precinct (Map 4, Ref C4)** and the **Crown Entertainment Complex (Map 3, Ref B4)**, the Yarra has been turned into a spectacular and exciting waterfront featuring works of art, street theatre and a huge variety of activities.

Beyond the Yarra, the shores of Port Phillip Bay are teeming with picturesque seaside towns like **Brighton (Map 454), Mornington (Map 641)** and **Sorrento (Map 678)**. Brimming with life and atmosphere, every little town along the coast is a great getaway any time of the year. Check out these options!

Arthurs Seat
(Map 685, Ref H14)

Arthurs Seat Road, Dromana
If you want the most breathtaking views of Port Phillip Bay, then Arthurs Seat on the Mornington Peninsula is the number one choice! Treat your honey to the scenic chairlift ride

through the treetops to win some serious points. Nearby, cafés, restaurants and wineries beckon for a Sunday afternoon escape.

Brighton (Map 454, Ref L16)

Brighton Beach (Map 494, Ref G5) is famous for its colourful bathing boxes, a remnant of the beach-goer's style from earlier times. Off the sand, Brighton has an excellent seaside atmosphere with a terrific range of cafés. It's easy to get to — from the city, take the Sandringham train line to Brighton Beach Railway Station and you're right there!

Enterprize (Map 411, Ref H15)

Gem Pier, Williamstown

Catch the train from the city to Williamstown for the opportunity to sail on an awesome replica of the ship that brought the first European settlers to Melbourne — the schooner Enterprize. Put yourself in their shoes as you cruise majestically on the glistening waters of Port Phillip Bay and take in the outstanding views of the city skyline. Ph: (03) 9397 3477

Geelong and Bellarine Peninsula

A little further afield, on the western side of the bay, is the city of Geelong. It boasts a spectacular waterfront with a wide range of restaurants, shopping and outdoor activities. Further south is Victoria's surf coast, featuring legendary beach towns like Torquay and Barwon Heads, along with some of the best surfing and most spectacular coastal scenery in Australia. Trains and buses depart regularly from **Spencer Street Station (Map 23, Ref F11)** in the city.

Golf Highlights

If you fancy a hit of stick, some of Melbourne's best sandbelt courses are situated along the shores of Port Phillip Bay, including the **Royal Melbourne Golf Course (Map 529, J2)**, Cheltenham Road, Black Rock (03) 9598 6755 , site of numerous major tournaments. There are some stunning public courses in the area, including **Sandringham (Map 495, Ref K20)**, the Dunes at **Rye (Map 697, Ref G14)** and **Brighton (Map 495, Ref E3)**.

Sorrento–Portsea
(Maps 677 & 678)

Sorrento was one of Melbourne's first seaside resorts, when paddlesteamers used to transport city folk down to the Sorrento Pier for a day on the beach. Over a hundred years later, Sorrento is still a hugely popular destination and neighbouring Portsea is a fabulous holiday place during the summertime.

St Kilda Foreshore
(Map 413)

Vast green gardens, wide beaches and a canopy of palm trees make St Kilda the vogue capital of Melbourne's waterfront. Home to the famous St Kilda Pier, The Esplanade and Luna Park, the foreshore has a well-deserved reputation for outdoor pleasure. Rollerbladers, cyclists and joggers ply the well-maintained boardwalks endlessly. Windsurfing, sailing, boating and swimming are all popular activities here. Parasailing and jet-skiing are available from St Kilda Marina, Marine Pde, **St Kilda (Map 454, Ref A1)**, plus the hip new sport of kiteboarding is taking off dramatically, with lessons also available at the Marina. The St Kilda Pier, jutting out into Port Phillip Bay, is not only a fantastic place to sit and watch the sunset, it is also the site of a popular café with spectacular panoramic views of the bay.

- **Melbourne River Cruises (Map 4, Ref G3)** Princes Walk, cnr of Princes Bridge and Batman Avenue, City, Ph: (03) 9614 1215
Stuck for a new way to see Melbourne? Relax and soak in the sights of the city with informative commentary in the comfort of a Melbourne River Cruiser. Choose from the 'Scenic River Gardens' upriver cruise, the 'Port & Docklands' downriver cruise, or for the complete city experience, consider the 'Melbourne Highlights' up- and down-river cruise. Cruises depart every half hour daily (except Christmas Day).

When it comes to spoiling yourself, sometimes dinner for two and a movie is just not enough!

Melburnians love to throw the book of convention out the window. Always creative and constantly innovative, the people of Melbourne dare to be different. The result is a fantastic range of alternative activities for those of us who like to veer off the beaten path once in a while.

Whatever takes your fancy — heart-pumping thrills, mouth-watering delights, spectacular scenery or something completely off the wall — Melbourne's got an idea for you!

Here are a few choices for making a special occasion a little more special.

Balloon Sunrise

See Melbourne come to life from a unique perspective, floating quietly above the skyscrapers as you watch the city awaken below. The view is superb, with spectacular morning vistas of prominent landmarks — including Fitzroy Gardens, Botanical Gardens, the Yarra and MCG — followed by a champagne breakfast in Richmond. Ph: (03) 9427-7596

Chocolate Indulgence Walk

For sheer decadence, Suzie Wharton's Chocolate Indulgence Walk is the ultimate. Tastings at Cadbury's, Myer, New Zealand Ice Creamery, Chocolate Box and Darrell Lea will spoil your tastebuds rotten. Go on, you know you want it! Other tours include the Chocolate & Other Desserts Walk, or if coffee is more your scene, rather than chokky, choose the '2Cs' — Coffee & Cakes Walk — Ph: (03) 9815 1228

Colonial Tramcar Restaurant

The only restaurant in Melbourne where the scenery changes every minute! Dazzle your special someone in style with fine dining on a classic W Class Tram. You'll enjoy fantastic food, great wine and some unique city sights while trundling around town in comfort. The Colonial Tramcar Restaurant is ideal for parties, too - you'll find it a moving experience.
Ph: (03) 9696 4000

Day Spas

Pamper yourself and your partner with a special treat – visit one of Melbourne's acclaimed day spas, where super-friendly, super-handy staff utilise massage and aromatherapy to melt away your daily stresses. One of the finest is **Geisha (Map 2, Ref D14)**, Little Collins St, City, (03) 9663 5544 where gorgeous Japanese décor and soothing Oriental delights enhance the pampering experience.

MCG Tours

Sports fans owe it to themselves to take a tour of Australia's most famous sporting venue, the **Melbourne Cricket Ground (Map 25, Ref F12)**, Jolimont. Inside you'll find heaps of memorabilia from our many sporting legends over the years. Stride in the footsteps of our national heroes as you visit the Long Room, the Players' Change Rooms and even take a walk out onto the hallowed turf. Ticketmaster Ph: 136 100

Putting Melbourne in Plane View

Soar above magnificent Melbourne and the spectacular Port Phillip Bay in a seaplane. Scenic Seaplane Flights in Williamstown (Map 411, Ref H15) take off and land in Hobsons Bay, Williamstown. Step out of your plane and straight into one of this village's fantastic waterfront cafes for a day's outing you'll never forget.

Scienceworks

This one's not for nerds — a multitude of cool games awaits you at Scienceworks, 2 Booker St, Spotswood (Map 411, Ref D 2). There's a six million dollar planetarium that will blow your mind, plus a machine that lets you race against Cathy Freeman — don't expect to win! You can also take on a friend in a mechanised rowing contest or test your fitness and learn how technology aids survival in the ocean, desert, Antarctica and outer space. Ph: (03) 9392 4800

Skydive City

For the ultimate thrill there's really nothing that quite compares to diving out of a plane at 10 000+ feet! Skydive City offers you the unique opportunity to tandem skydive into the city of Melbourne. Jump start your day and soar above the city for an adrenaline rush you'll never forget. Ph: (0414) 686 722

The Melbourne Ghost Tour

Smiling city by day, ghosts' playground by night! Melbourne is inhabited by a number of ghosts, and this tour will open your eyes to the city's haunted past.

Your guide is an avid ghosthunter! Get a look at the creepiest parts of Melbourne where the city's first and most recent ghosts have been sighted. This tour has converted many a skeptic — who knows, you might get slimed. 'Who you gonna call?' Ph: (03) 9662 9010

Wine On Sunday

Experience wine and food from various Victorian regions, plus guest speakers & entertainment. Around 60 stalls sell some of Victoria's premium wines, local food can be sampled and wine tasting is available through the purchase of a 'Wine on Sunday' glass. Afterwards, you can catch a classic flick at the Kino Cinema. 'Wine on Sunday' is held the first Sunday of every month from 11am-4pm at **Collins Place (Map 24, Ref J7)**, 45 Collins St, City, Ph: (03) 9655 3600.

Village Gold Class Movies

For the ultimate movie experience, this one's in a class of its own! Sink into the luxurious reclining armchairs, kick your feet up and lounge in first class comfort as you enjoy the latest blockbusters on the big screen. Gold Class also has the ultimate in refreshments available, with a wine bar, a great range of light fare and delicious desserts to add to your viewing pleasure.
Ph: 132 929

village treasures

The CBD is the heart of Melbourne, but the soul and spirit of the city is alive in the urban villages clustered around its perimeter. Diversity is truly defined on the city fringe – experience the colour, the music and the life of Melbourne's inner city suburbs.

Since the end of World War II, Melbourne has hosted a steady stream of immigrants, firstly from Europe, and more recently Asia and the Middle East. The eclectic melting pot of cultures that has evolved is a mix of continental flavours blended with the ubiquitous Aussie persona.

What this means for Melbourne is that the surrounding suburbs offer a mix of ideas and cultural influences, each village marking its territory with its own distinct style.

Each of these areas is just a short sojourn from the city centre, by tram, train, bus or taxi-cab. Though the CBD has plenty to offer, the only way to claim a full Melbourne experience is to get out and about in the thriving inner city suburbs.

carlton (Map 17)

When Italian migrants arrived in Melbourne by the thousands in the post-WWII era, they brought a little piece of Italy with them and planted it just north of the city in Carlton. Melbourne's 'Little Italy' has flourished ever since.

From the time University Cafe opened its doors back in 1951, espresso has been an institution on Lygon Street's vibrant cafe strip, and pizza and pasta are never more than a stone's throw away. In fact, Toto's Pizza House, at 101 Lygon Street, lays claim to being the very first pizzeria in Australia. You'll also find a tremendous variety of other national cuisines, including Thai, Afghan, Malay, Caribbean and Greek.

For a slightly more serene dining environment, try Rathdowne or Grattan Streets for a further range of top quality restaurants, cafes and bars.

Lygon Street's trendy eateries are complemented by a superb range of shopping outlets, including gourmet delicatessens, bookshops and fashion houses. Elegantly presented shopfronts beckon passers-by with a wide range of temptations, from sugar-dusted Mediterranean sweets to the latest in European and Australian fashion.

The Carlton Gardens are home to the Royal Exhibition Building, IMAX Theatre and the new Melbourne Museum.

fitzroy (Map 19)

The lively village of Fitzroy is an eclectic melting pot of expression, individualism and alternative lifestyles. The eccentric, the artistic, and the extroverted converge here in a parade of colour to eat, shop and consume lattes at a frightening rate. A concentration of the city's trendy Bohemian set can be found on Brunswick Street's lively eatery and entertainment strip. If it's zany or esoteric, you'll find it here – from the incredible range of exotic cuisines to original handmade art, and retro clothing that will ensure you stand out from the crowd. This is a place where green hair and a nipple ring will score you smiles, not scowls.

By day, busking poets roam Brunswick Street while the sidewalk cafes are abuzz with activity. By night, the place comes alive as the pubs, bars and live music take centre stage. The available cuisines are as varied and exotic as the clientele they attract, including the best of Thai, Afghan, French, African, Asian, Scandinavian, Malay and Japanese, as well as the standard 'pizza and pasta' type establishments. Brunswick Street is also renowned for its superb vegetarian cuisine, catering to the strictest vegan diets right through to the 'occasional vegetarian' patron. Another Fitzroy icon is the fantastic cooked breakfasts and brunches – great for revitalisation after a big night out at one of the precinct's many bars, pubs and clubs.

port melbourne (Map 29)

Ever since the city was first settled, Port Melbourne has historically provided the first glimpse of Melbourne for visitors, immigrants and sailors arriving by water from destinations all over the world. Nowadays, the re-invented Port has a new appeal, pioneering a hip beachside ambience that's attracting Melburnians and visitors in droves.

Bay Street is the centrepiece of this historic township, beginning at the beach and stretching east to the city skyline. Once the first port of call for goldrush prospectors, international industrialists and hundreds of thousands of European immigrants, Bay Street is now a slick, fashionable enclave for those seeking chic village shopping, dining and lifestyle close to the city.

Bay Street is a shopper's delight – art galleries, gift shops and boutiques line the historical boulevard, combining the traditional and contemporary in elegant fashion. Recently widened footpaths and striking new décor have lifted Bay Street to the status of one of Melbourne's premier shopping promenades.

Gourmet food and wine have found a bright new home on Bay Street. The conventional rules that stipulate what defines a restaurant, café or bar are ignored here – every venue in Port Melbourne, large or small, casual or formal, promises a range of first class cuisine presented with an artistic flair symbolic of Bay Street's passionate devotion to style. Enjoy a sunny light lunch at a superb street cafe, or linger over a long, elegant evening meal with a bottle of fine wine at a first class establishment. Sample one of the many upbeat local pubs, a fortunate legacy of Bay Street's seaside history.

Port Melbourne is just minutes by car or taxi from the heart of the CBD. Alternatively, catch the 109 tram from Collins Street in the city.

richmond (Map 26)

This is one of Melbourne's oldest villages, renowned for its excellent shopping and South-East Asian cuisine. Bridge Road is the mecca of discerning bargain-hunters, with a high concentration of quality designer factory outlets. The neighbouring thoroughfares of Swan Street and Church Street also offer a great range of top class products. Shopping aside, Richmond boasts a thriving social scene with some of Melbourne's finest venues for dancing, drinking and live music.

Victoria Street is now home for many of the post-70s Vietnamese migrants who came to Australia. You'll find many mid-20s returned backpackers attempting their newly acquired Vietnamese at Thang Phong, Quan 88 or Thy Thy. With delicious soups, rice paper rolls, sticky pork buns plus a host of other entrees and main dishes for under $10, you've just discovered the best cheap eats in Melbourne.

south yarra (Map 31)

From fashion to food and furnishings, South Yarra's dedication to class is unparallelled anywhere else in Melbourne. It is the urban playground of choice for Melbourne's celebrities, sports stars and social elite… the place to be seen. South Yarra is Melbourne's heart of sophistication and style. The Chapel Street and Toorak Road shopping precincts exude elegance with countless boutiques, jewellers and exclusive homeware stores. Outlets of world-class designer labels abound, including the likes of Issey Miyake, Helmut Lang, Carla Zampatti, Collette Dinnigan and Bettina Liano.

South Yarra's high-class image is matched by its superb cuisine. Not surprisingly, the city boasts more first-rate dining establishments than any other part of Melbourne. The finest ingredients, the most sophisticated techniques and an overwhelming attention to detail distinguish South Yarra as a forerunner in culinary excellence. Glamorous patrons are drawn to the delectable choices of Japanese, French, Spanish and nouveau gourmet food. The guardians of glamour are in their element in South Yarra at night time, when the stylish clubs and exclusive bars are pumping – offering everything from popular modern beats to jazz and blues.

st kilda (Map 414)

St Kilda is one of Melbourne's favourite bayside villages. In summer, its long sandy beach is inundated with Melburnians lapping up the sunshine or splashing in the marine playground of Port Phillip Bay. The many cafes, restaurants and specialty shops in Acland Street and Fitzroy Street give St Kilda its cosmopolitan ambience. Home to the famous St Kilda Pier, The Esplanade and Luna Park, St Kilda has a well-deserved reputation for outdoor pleasure.

Waterfront activities are something of a speciality in St Kilda with the bay, the marina and easy access to Albert Park Lake. Windsurfing, sailing, boating and swimming are all popular activities here. The St Kilda Pier, jutting out into Port Phillip Bay, is not only a fantastic place to sit and watch the sun set, it is also the site of a cafe with great panoramic views of the bay. On sunny days, you can sit on the pier and watch people playing beach volleyball or rollerblading along the Esplanade. On Sundays, the Upper Esplanade is transformed into an open-air art and craft market. This lively beachfront market specialises in handmade goods such as ceramics, leather goods and jewellery.

Just up from the market is Luna Park, a fun park modelled on New York's Coney Island. Since its opening in 1912, Luna Park's trademark open-mouthed entrance has been a celebrated Melbourne icon, recently refurbished in 2001.

With so much to do, you could almost forget to eat, but that would really be missing out. Fitzroy and Acland Streets are renowned as two of Melbourne's best 'eat streets'. Allow yourself to be tempted by the irresistible aromas of espresso coffee, freshly-baked cakes, breads, muffins and pastries. Pubs and licensed cafes on both Fitzroy and Acland streets ensure that the party continues well after the last dinner guests have left.

williamstown (Map 411)

Williamstown is the oldest continuous post-colonial settlement on the shores of Port Phillip Bay, named in honour of King William IV in 1837. For most of its 150-year history, Williamstown has thrived primarily as a working seaport. Today, however, food, art, gardens, a touch of shopping and weekend tourists lend Williamstown the laid-back ambience of a holiday village.

As is the case with many of Melbourne's eclectic villages, Williamstown has a well-established outdoor cafe culture. 'When in Rome', do as the locals do, enjoying freshly-squeezed juice or lattes over weekend newspapers in the glorious sunshine. Mingle among cyclists, rollerbladers and casual strollers who utilise the gorgeous waterfront. From Williamstown, you have a unique view of Melbourne's skyline and in the late afternoon, the Rialto reflects brilliant sunset colours like a mirror – spectacular hues of pink, red and orange.

Williamstown's dining culture promises an enjoyable outing on any level – a café brunch, elegant fine dining, or a picnic in the park. It's not just the destination, but the journey that matters. If this is true, then Williamstown is an ideal weekend visit. You can choose to drive there, via the panoramic West Gate Bridge, catch a train out of Spencer Street Station, or cruise across the scenic waters of the bay.

retail therapy

The best of the world is on sale in Melbourne's labyrinth of lanes, arcades and major shopping centres. First class international labels including Versace, Cartier, Ferragamo and Max Mara claim retail outlets in Melbourne's CBD. From the Paris end of Collins Street to the Queen Victoria Market, the city is bursting with opportunities. A little exploring divulges a surfeit of options – experience the classic grandeur of the Block and Royal Arcades, or the contemporary elegance of Australia on Collins. Strips of designer boutiques and big brand retailers are peppered with quirky, original and often amusing smaller stores. A day's shopping in Melbourne may reveal many unusual treasures. For instant gratification, you'll soon find everything you need and beyond right in the heart of the city, with three major department stores and several mega-malls offering excellent service, competitive prices and a huge range of merchandise.

Melbourne Central is the colosseum of the consumer. Over 160 specialty shops plus the Daimaru department store surround one of the city's most impressive landmarks. A 20-storey glass cone stretches skyward to envelope the historic Coop's Shot Tower, a 111-year-old heritage building preserved in its original glory beneath the Melbourne Central dome. Inside the atrium, replicas of a hot air balloon and a vintage bi-plane float timelessly overhead, while a gigantic Marionette fob watch chimes to the tune of Waltzing Matilda every hour.

Stretching from Bourke to Lonsdale Streets, the massive Myer and David Jones department stores offer a world of good buys. Featuring an endless variety of items in a wide range of prices, the retail giants provide friendly service and convenience. Out at ground level, tree-lined Collins Street is king with an abundance of premier vogue retailers, but Little Collins, Flinders Lane and Swanston Street also present a remarkable collection of hip fashion outlets.

Across the Yarra River, Southgate Arts & Leisure Centre promises an exciting array of consumer delights with a waterfront promenade housing a range of boutique stores with exotic wares on offer. A little further west, Crown Entertainment Complex displays the finest international labels in opulent fashion beside the Yarra.

The Queen Victoria Market is the largest undercover market in Australia. Established in 1878, the Market is an historic landmark and a Melbourne institution. The variety is eclectic, and bargain opportunities are endless. Open Tuesday through Sunday at various times, this world class shopping destination boasts a vast collection of items, from fresh produce to first-class fashion, as well as homewares, electronics, gifts and much more. Other open markets operating throughout the metropolitan area offer fresh food, flowers, art, giftware and clothing on various days.

beyond the cbd...

From upmarket shops featuring world famous labels to shopping up at the market for a bargain bracelet, Melbourne's metropolitan area offers a multitude of choices. Bridge Road, Richmond, is popular for the huge number of designer outlets available, featuring select labels and garments at affordable prices. There's a blasé, bohemian atmosphere pervading the area – located close to the city, shopping here is casual and fun. For the vogue shopper with a limited budget, Bridge Road in Richmond is a godsend. On this busy inner-city strip, thousands of shoppers converge daily, seeking wide variety and excellent value for money.

Bridge Road is the acknowledged leader of designer outlets in Melbourne – big name brands at bargain prices, plus up-market fashion boutiques, homewares and gift shops. The neighbouring Swan and Church Streets offer a continuation of trendy retail stores and quality items. Situated just beyond the rim of the Central Business District, Richmond is just a short hop away by tram. Catch the number 48 or 75 tram from Flinders Street, and you'll arrive at Bridge Road within minutes. The chic shopping is well catered for by an abundance of hip cafés, cake shops and restaurants – soak in the casual, laid-back atmosphere while seeking a world full of bargains.

In South Yarra, the sophisticated fashion set have stamped a claim on this trendy shopping precinct. Discerning buyers converge on the area daily, arriving in droves by Mercedes, Range Rover or BMW. Ever in vogue, the streets of Chapel, Greville and Toorak Road are lined with prestigious, high-class stores offering the finest in fashion and jewellery. Renowned Melbourne designers proudly call South Yarra home – shopping here can be quite expensive, but it is certainly the best choice on offer.

The wide variety of shopping available is serviced in every location by quality cafes, bars, and restaurants – complete your day with a latte or glass of wine, soaking up Melbourne's cosmopolitan atmosphere in the style of the elite. From fashion to furniture, electronics to elegance, Melbourne boasts unlimited choices at sensational prices, and visitors converge on the city daily as a shopping mecca.

The city pulsates with colour and culture. From innovative 'buskers' amusing crowds on the street to classic symphonies and world class drama, Melbourne's diverse cultural background supplies an abundance of creativity. Magnificent sculptures adorn our streets, parks and promenades. Footpaths and walkways feature attractive murals, lovingly crafted by free-spirited young artists.

Cosmopolitan, fun-loving, and friendly, Melburnians are indeed a mixed breed that draw appeal from visitors throughout the world. Over a third of Melbourne's population has strong ties abroad, creating a multicultural melting pot of ideas, skills and personalities. Ethnic groups delight in celebrating their backgrounds with events including the Antipodes Festival, Oktoberfest and the Chinese New Year. Jazz, film, art, automobiles, flowers and gardens are all highlighted in their own shows and festivals.

art

• National Gallery of Victoria on Russell (Map 2, Ref F5)
285-321 Russell Street, City,
Ph: (03) 9208 0203
The National Gallery features works from the Victorian State Collection in beautiful and historic surrounds. See classic works of art from Australian indigenous artists, and international painting collections as well as special exhibitions.

If you're an art lover, you'll need to explore some of the City's many private galleries, particularly on **Flinders Lane (Map 2, Ref B17-L17)**. This exciting little thoroughfare in the heart of the city reveals a treasure trove of exotic, indigenous and original galleries of painted and sculptured art.

In **South Yarra, Kirkcaldy Davies Galleries (Map 32, Ref G17)**, 467 Malvern Road, Ph: (03) 9827 8790, exhibits a wide variety of works by emerging sculptors, painters and photographers, with solo and group exhibitions changing every month.

In **Richmond, Niagara Galleries (Map 25, Ref L12)** at 245 Punt Road, Ph: (03) 9429 3666, showcases some of Australia's greatest modern artists.

If photography is more your style, shoot down to the **Centre for Contemporary Photography (Map 19, Ref B13)**, located in Johnston St, Fitzroy Ph: (03) 9417 1549, highlighting local and international artists.

classic films

Melbourne boasts several independent theatres serving up classic and contemporary films in an intimate atmosphere. **The Lumiere (Map 24, Ref F3)**, 108 Lonsdale St, City, (03) 9639 1055 , carries the friendly ambience of the times before multiplexes took over, while the **Astor Theatre (Map 414, Ref G13)** at 1 Chapel St, St Kilda (03) 9510 1414, is a classic cinema icon. The old-fashioned kiosk and original 1930s décor is perfect for that nostalgic movie experience.

comedy

Melbourne delivers some of Australia's best comedy — this is why we're home to the International Comedy Festival in April each year. The most consistent laughs are served up at **The Comedy Club (Map 18, Ref F10)** 380 Lygon St, Carlton, Ph: (03) 9348 1622 . There's always a good laugh to be had around town — check the Entertainment Guide in The Age every Friday.

culture

The Koori Heritage Trust (Map 2, Ref C17) 234 Flinders Lane, City, Ph: (03) 9639 6555 was established in 1985 with a commitment to protect, preserve and promote the living culture of the indigenous people of south-east Australia, whose heritage spans more than 40,000 years.

Commemorating those who have journeyed to Melbourne from far-off places, the **Immigration Museum (Map 1, Ref F19)** 400 Flinders St, City, Ph: (03) 9927 2700, is located in the Old Customs House on Flinders St. Visitors can wander through interactive displays of Melbourne's migrant history, featuring graphics, videos and models depicting immigrant life.

dance

The internationally acclaimed Australian Ballet floats into your soul with dance and musical performances at the **State Theatre (Map 4, Ref D9)** St Kilda Road, City, Ph: (03) 9281 8000. If you're after some dance with a little more beat, keep an eye out for **Chunky Move (Map 4, Ref A6)** 35 City Road, Southbank, Ph: (03) 9645 5188. Stylish, sexy and provocative, this troupe will blow you away.

theatre

From summer Shakespearean performances in the Royal Botanic Gardens to the latest Andrew Lloyd Webber production and a host of local talent, the Melbourne stage is set for all seasons.

• Victorian Arts Centre (Map 4, Ref D7) 100 St Kilda Road, Melbourne, Ph: 03 9281 8000
Crowned by the magnificent Spire, one of Melbourne's most distinctive icons, the Arts Centre is the city's hub of visual and performing arts. Explore the centre's many theatres and discover the history of the site on a guided tour.

• CUB Malthouse (Map 3, Ref J15)
113 Sturt Street, Southbank
Ph: (03) 9685 5111
A classic venue for contemporary live theatre, this marvellous old brewery sets the stage for you to enjoy the very best in Australian drama, comedy and satire.

• The Athenaeum (Map 2, Ref G15)
188 Collins Street, City, Ph: 9650 1500
This is an intimate venue, popular with the Bell Shakespeare Company, with the unassuming entrance hiding a 'shabby chic' interior.

In the heart of the city, Melbourne's grand old theatres are unbeatable for character and atmosphere, their ageless Victorian opulence sets the stage for major productions into the new millennium. **The Princess, (Map 24, Ref J3); The Regent, (Map 2, Ref F8); Her Majesty's, (Map 24, Ref G4);** and **The Comedy, (Map 24, Ref H5)** are classic beauties that — in the world of live entertainment — never seem to fade from style. For theatre bookings, Ph: Ticketmaster Bass on 11 500 or Ticketek on 132 849.

pamper your palate

Eating out in Melbourne is an art form. Native 'foodies' know not all is as it seems. Follow the locals and you'll discover that some of the most humble lanes & the most obscure entrances hide the most exquisite dining havens. To truly indulge in the city's food and wine treasures, one must possess a spirit of adventure and embrace the unusual. The maze of laneways criss-crossing Melbourne offers some supreme opportunities.

Dining in the city is a blend of concepts from around the globe… experience a French café on the Riviera… a serene teahouse in a Japanese village… or a Mediterranean tapas bar. Savour a bottle of wine and a gourmet meal in soft-lit intimacy, or gather with friends at a lively bistro for delicious food and a few laughs. Melbourne's eateries cater for all seasons – enjoy warm, moonlit evenings on a terrace during summer; colourful flowers and upbeat ambience in the spring; and cosy, red leather interiors with crackling log fires beckon for an escape from the winter chill.

chinatown (Map 2, H10)

In the heart of the city, lights, lanterns and exotic Asian symbols transform Chinatown into a slice of the Far East. Succulent Oriental cuisine is served in traditional surrounds, using the freshest ingredients and centuries-old recipes to enhance the joy of eating. Surrounding the nearby theatre district is a range of bistros, brasseries and boutique wine bars serving outstanding cuisine in a variety of settings.

- **Empress Of China**
  20 Lt Bourke St, City, Ph: 9663 1883
- **New Lat's**
  15-19 Heffernan La, City
  Ph: 9663 2848
- **Curry Corner**
  Shop 2,188 Russell St, City
  Ph: 9663 4040
- **Bamboo House**
  47 Lt Bourke St, City, Ph: 9662 1565
- **Empress of China**
  120 Lt Bourke St, City, Ph: 9663 1883
- **Jan Bo**
  40 Lt Bourke St, City, Ph: 9662 2884
- **Pepper Chilli**
  85 Lt Bourke St, City, Ph: 9662 9662

southgate (Map 4, B4)

The Yarra River promenade on the south bank, once devoid of restaurants, has become one of Melbourne's premium dining districts. Between Southgate Arts & Leisure Centre and Crown Entertainment Complex, there's an entire world of first-class establishments overlooking the Yarra River and city skyline beyond. Contemporary European, Asian, and Australian restaurants present exotic décor, excellent service and a delectable choice of dishes.

- **Blue Train Café**
  Mid Level, Southgate, Ph: 9696 0111
- **Egusto**
  Shop GR3B, River Level, Southgate
  Ph: 9690 9819
- **Saturne**
  Shop G12/13, River Level, Southgate
  Ph: 9645 9499
- **The River Seafood Grill**
  Shop MR6, Mid Level, Southgate
  Ph: 9690 4699
- **Wolfgang Puck**
  The Beacon, 3 Southgate Avenue, Southbank, Ph: 9686 3511

uptown (Map 2)

In the savvy uptown theatre district on the Spring Street side of town, Melbourne's passion for great food is evident. Local chefs take immense pride in serving up innovative, healthy dishes combining the best international recipes with a touch of Melbourne panache.

- **Becco**
  11-25 Crossley St, City, Ph: 9663 3000
- **Bistro 1**
  126 Lt Collins St, City, Ph: 9654 3343
- **Caffe Cento Venti**
  120 Collins St, City, Ph: 9650 5621
- **Florentino**
  80 Bourke St, City, Ph: 9662 1811
- **Il Bacaro**
  168-170 Lt Collins St, Ph: 9654 6778
- **Il Solito Posto**
  113 Collins St, City, Ph: 9654 4466
- **Punch Lane**
  43 Lt Bourke St, City, Ph: 9639 4944
- **Stella**
  159 Spring St, City, Ph: 9639 1555

the villages

On the northern rim of the CBD, Carlton is one of Australia's best-loved dining precincts. The town's centrepiece, Lygon Street, boasts the finest Italian food outside of Rome, a claim endorsed by Melbourne diners with a unanimous 'Bellissimo!' Ribbons of pasta dance around your fork, the hearty aromas of a million different spices fill the air, and an impressive selection of world class wines will satisfy every connoisseur.

Below the river, South Yarra boasts more first class dining establishments than any other part of Melbourne. Restaurants, cafes and bars clamour to be coolest. Along Chapel Street, Toorak Road, Greville and High Streets, many of the nation's top chefs have carved a special niche. The finest ingredients, the most sophisticated techniques and overwhelming dedication to detail distinguish South Yarra as a forerunner in culinary excellence.

On the edge of the bay, Fitzroy Street in St Kilda plays host to exciting, innovative restaurants and bistros oozing with style, plus a number of classic hotels providing sensational meals with a lively pub atmosphere. Casual ambience, Mediterranean flavours and a great mix of cultures score instantly with diners. By day, adjacent Acland Street indulges the senses with the aroma of freshly-baked cakes, breads, muffins and pastries, and by night it transforms into a chic, contemporary dining strip featuring a range of quality international cuisine.

Just across Port Phillip Bay, the seaside village of Williamstown has reinvented itself as one of Melbourne's most attractive dining destinations. Multiple restaurant venues are enjoying success in recent times, capitalising on panoramic views of the city skyline and an alluring bayside ambience.

living for lattes

During the day, the humble café is the heart and soul of Melbourne, a maelstrom of cappuccinos, lattes, muffins, mochas, and pastries. Enjoy a hot chocolate topped with a mountain of whipped cream high enough to ski on! Relax and read a magazine while sipping a latte with a blackberry muffin chaser... Socialise with other like-minded souls... Devour a turkey and avocado focaccia... You can even buy a cup of coffee!

The evolution of the simple sandwich and cuppa have created a thriving culture that has become a trademark of our city — use your UBD Compact to do a little exploring and see for yourself. Discard the diet for a day and you'll be hooked on Melbourne's café scene.

In other parts of the city, DeGraves Street and Block Place are two more exceptional café enclaves, where visitors can enjoy lattes and light fare in true Melbourne style.

Clarendon Street in South Melbourne is a hotbed of latte lifestyle – celebrities mingle with city workers and coffee lovers in a strip of fantastic cafes, including **Chocolat Champagne (Map 30, Ref A3)** 253 Coventry St and the **Old Paper Shop Deli (Map 3, Ref A4)** 266 Clarendon St.

city

Melbourne is peppered with an amazing assortment of cafes, from dingy dreghouses to refined European eateries. Try the **Medallion Cafe (Map 2, Ref G8)** on Lonsdale St for a Greek flavour, or visit **Guggenheim (Map 24, Ref K7)** on Flinders Lane for the best bagels in town. **Mary Martin Bookshop Café (Map 24, Ref G5)** on Bourke St offers great food, coffee and reading, and the **Hairy Canary Map 2, Ref F13)** on Little Collins St is just downright funky.

Hells Kitchen (Map 2, Ref C17) is a small, New York-style café tucked in off Flinders Lane on Centre Place. **The Paris End (Map 24, Ref K6)** of Collins St hosts many European style cafes, and **Pellegrini's (Map 24, Ref J5)** on Bourke St is a Melbourne institution.

city arcades

Buyers and browsers love roaming Melbourne's labyrinth of arcades, lanes and alleyways, and even the die-hard shopaholics need a place to eat. There's an awesome range of hip cafes filling every spare nook and cranny around town. **DeGraves (Map 2, Ref C18)** is dear to the hearts of many Melburnians, **Block Place (Map 2, Ref C14)** exudes café culture, and **Manchester Lane (Map 2, Ref D17)** sets new standards for café dining. The city's maze of arcades is the ultimate place to get lost.

hardware lane

(Map 1, Ref K 10)

For the latte set, Hardware Lane is the 'in' locale of Melbourne. A myriad of groovy cafes line this unusual bluestone laneway in the heart of the city. Jazz tunes lilt across the pavement during summer, creating a lively, New Orleans-style ambience. Hidden between Bourke and Lonsdale Sts, Hardware Lane boasts an awesome variety of cafés, including Alley Blue, Café Max, Hard Bourke Café and many others. There's a distinct aura about the place, an air of nonchalance oblivious to the pandemonium of the busy city just beyond the lane's entrance.

southgate **(Map 4, Ref C4)**

From it's very beginning, Southgate has had café-goers drooling. The stunning Yarra waterfront and the festive atmosphere provided by crazy street performers and amazing artworks are reason enough to visit, but the cafés are in a class of their own. From simple snacks to delicious main dishes, the food is excellent, and the prices won't punish the purse either. The Blue Train Café is always popular, and the unique Llama Bar is Melbourne's only island café, sitting in the middle of the Yarra River. Every place at Southgate is top notch — a little exploring will be well-rewarded.

villages

Melbourne's café culture is very much alive in the surrounding villages, and each community has blended its own style into the mix. From dawn until dusk, the pursuit of a perfect blend of coffee and food is an irresistible pastime for Melburnians and visitors.

On Brunswick Street in Fitzroy, try cult icons like **Marios (Map 19, Ref C13)**, the **Retro Café (Map 19, Ref C9)** and **Vertigo (Map 19, Ref C12)**.

In Carlton, the **Rathdowne Street Food Store (Map 18, Ref H14)** is a hot favourite with locals, along with Tiamo on **Lygon Street (Map 18, Ref E13)** and many others along this famous stretch of taste treats.

St Kilda is full of beans. Check out **Toasters (Map 414, Ref B14)** at 165 Fitzroy St , and on Acland try **Il Fornaio (Map 414, Ref C18)** and **189 Espresso Bar (Map 414, Ref B18)**. In South Yarra, cafés are all class – sample the best on offer at the **Jam Factory (Map 32, Ref D12)** and all along groovy Chapel Street.

It doesn't matter whether you know the difference between a double decaf French mocha or a plain white tea, every café in Melbourne is a haven where you can sit down with a few friends, relax and simply enjoy the passing parade.

pubs & bars

Step up to any bar in Melbourne, order your first pot or cocktail, and take a look around. Pub culture is as thick in our atmosphere as the air we breathe – if Singapore Slings and sultry lighting get you in the mood, Melbourne has a plethora of hip bars with attitude! Or if tipping a few ales with the boys is more your scene, there's an endless choice of classic hotels that will never, ever go out of style!

No two pubs are alike in Melbourne – there's a broad mix of first class, casual and downright seedy! Whatever appeals, be it cocktails, live music, ambience, or the pursuit of intoxication, you'll find the right venue here!

Only one question left…
'Whose shout?'

a touch of UK

· The Elephant & Wheelbarrow (Map 414, Ref C13)
Fitzroy St, St Kilda
Don't let the name fool you – this pub's full of attractive young people! Friendly, up beat, there's a very English/Irish feel about the place. Knock back a few drinks, then stay while it transforms into a happening dance venue. Also now located at 94-96 Bourke St, City (Map 24, Ref H5) and Bay Street, Port Melbourne (Map 412, Ref K7)

· Bridie O'Reilly's (Map 24, Ref J6)
62 Little Collins Street, City
Live bands offer a combination of local music and traditional Irish jigs to set the night's scene.

· Molly Blooms (Map 412, Ref J7)
39 Bay St, Port Melbourne
Sitting pretty, Molly Blooms is a popular Irish pub close to the beach, ideal for a night of tasty lagers and fine music.

classic jazz

· Night Cat (Map 19, Ref A13)
141 Johnston Street, Fitzroy
Enjoy a vibrant scene with the young trendy crowd and live music lovers.

· Purple Emerald (Map 2, Ref G18)
191 Flinders Lane, City
Retro rules at this hip new bar, featuring live acid jazz, classic 70s furnishings, 16 types of beer and a huge range of cigars.

· Tony Starr's Kitten Club (Map 2, Ref D13)
267 Little Collins Street, City
Sip on the latest martini at this popular venue for those who love to relax to the funky tunes of live jazz.

cocktails and class

· The Saint (Map 414, Ref A14)
54 Fitzroy St, St Kilda
A virtuous name for one of Melbourne's hottest new bars. The Saint is all style and sophistication, frequented by gorgeous ladies and gentlemen enjoying cocktails and fine music.

· One Six One (Map 32, Ref C20)
161 High St, Prahran
As you enter the upper dominion of the bar, the overwhelming glow of red sets the mood whether you seek a sexy place to meet up with friends or a retro bar scene to socialise.

· Gin Palace (Map 2, Ref H13)
190 Lt Collins St, City
A true royal amongst Melbourne's pub scene – sample the 1951 Martini and the industrial revolution, a killer vodka and Sambuca mix!

· Velour (Map 2, Ref L18)
121 Flinders Lane, City
Zone out in the electric blue light of Velour, with killer cocktails and pumping dance music.

designer bars

· Misty (Map 2, Ref H19)
3-5 Hosier Lane, City
Weird, warped and wonderful décor highlight this groovy little hideaway on a cobblestone lane.

· Double O (Map 2, Ref D7)
Sniders Lane, City
The projected logo on the wall is the only external evidence that Double O exists – a cosy, comfortable bar with curvaceous couches, cool cocktails and seductive lighting.

· Troika (Map 24, Ref G2)
106 Lt Lonsdale St, City
It'd make a great 'drop zone' for international spies, yet Troika welcomes everyone to this mysterious cool bar.

· Bond (Map 1, Ref K19)
24 Bond St, City
One of the hottest new additions to Melbourne's bar scene, Bond is slick, cool and a prime venue for both watching and being watched.

live music hotspots

· The Corner Hotel (Map 26, Ref C16)
57 Swan St, Richmond
Specialising in original music from local outfits and overseas bands, the Corner isn't afraid to get a little 'out there'!

· Esplanade Hotel (Map 414, Ref A17)
11 Upper Esplanade, St Kilda
When venturing out of the city grid, the 'Espy' is a Melbourne icon, offering the best local acts in music and comedy and with a prime position overlooking the bay.

· Star Bar (Map 29, Ref L1)
160 Clarendon St, South Melbourne
Best known for fantastic live music, the Star Bar is regularly rocking with a hip young crowd.

· The Punters Club (Map 19, Ref C10)
376 Brunswick St, Fitzroy
Definitely a rocking pub, the 'Punna's' is a cult favourite for Melbourne's alternative live music scene.

on tap

· The Great Britain (Map 26, Ref F18)
447 Church Street, Richmond
From the fireplace in the winter and the textured wall coverings, the 'GB' is an eclectic mix of people just as interesting to be around as the venue itself.

· Terminus (Map 26, Ref L4)
605 Victoria St, Abbotsford
The friendliest of pubs with a focus on the community – Bingo Night is huge, and there's not a grandma in sight!

· Yelza (Map 19, Ref C19)
245 Gertrude Street, Fitzroy
On the city fringe, with a fabulous outdoor setting for when the temperature rises and a luscious venue indoors, this is a bar for all seasons.

· Provincial Hotel (Map 19, Ref B13)
299 Brunswick St, Fitzroy
Everyone knows the Provincial – when you want to go with an 'old faithful', you're always assured a good night out here.

city after hours

Locals know it, visitors love it, others envy it — Melbourne's nightlife is the hottest scene around, a funky tribute to our cosmopolitan people and vibrant lifestyle. When daylight disappears, the city ignites into action, and the party doesn't stop until the sun rises to light the way home. Young revellers flood into town for a pumping, thumping good night!

From jazz to jungle techno, blues to ballroom, retro to rap and grunge to gothic, Melbourne has a hotspot with the groove to get you moving.

clubs

• Candy Bar (Map 32, Ref C18)
162 Greville St, Prahran
Masterful mixes from dynamic DJs all night long.

• Carousel Nightclub (Map 30, Ref F15)
Aughtie Drive, Albert Park
Shake the night away to soulful funk and R'n'B, then cool down on the waterside balcony on Melbourne's famous Albert Park Lake.

• cbd (Map 1, Ref K13)
12 McKillop St, City
Casual, bold and dynamic, the ultimate expression venue.

• Club 383 (Map 1, Ref L9)
383 Lonsdale St, City
Cutting edge sound with multiple dance levels — lots of '80s hits too.

• Club UK (Map 24, Ref H5)
169 Exhibition St, City
The best of British and loads more — a bleedin' good sound and a choice venue.

• Dream (Map 18, Ref B19)
229 Queensberry St, Carlton
A double dose of dance beats with two floors playing different grooves.

• Felix (Map 414, Ref A15)
43 Fitzroy St, St Kilda
Plush lounges, surreal lighting and a sensational cocktail range complement the pumping dance floor at Felix.

• Heat Nightclub(Map 3, Ref B4)
Level 3, Crown Casino, Southbank
A surreal chic club featuring mezzanine levels where you can dance on the main floor to the backdrop of the Melbourne city skyline.

• Khokolat (Map 1, Ref K11)
Hardware Lane, City
A discreet club with a sleek retro interior. Day or night, listen to the grooves of local DJs and bands.

• Laundry (Map 19, Ref A13)
50 Johnston St, Fitzroy
Bold and brash, this place is firing every night of the week.

• Mercury Lounge (Map 3, Ref C5)
Level 3, Crown Casino, Southbank
Funky and upbeat, the Mercury Lounge continues to set temperatures rising.

• Metro (Map 24, Ref J4)
20 Bourke St, City
If bigger is better, the Metro is guaranteed to impress — a staple of the Melbourne nightlife scene for generations.

• Prince of Wales (Map 414, Ref A15)
29 Fitzroy Street, St Kilda
The best local and international DJs spin here as gorgeous people lose themselves amongst disco balls, curvaceous bars and the balcony area.

• QBH (Map 3, Ref F3)
1 Queensbridge Street, South Melbourne
Said to be the largest club in the Southern Hemisphere, take your pick from the seven bars, two dance floors and five DJ booths.

• Revolver (Map 32, Ref D14)
(upstairs) 229 Chapel Street, Prahran
Revolver offers hip-hop, house, UK garage and a concoction of all sorts of beats in the heart of ultra-cool Prahran.

• Salon Rouge (Map 2, Ref D17)
Flinders Lane, City
A funky bar with a happening crowd, cool atmosphere and irresistible dance tunes.

• Silvers (Map 415, Ref C5)
445 Toorak Rd, Toorak
The tempo's always on the move, from R&B and swing to commercial dance.

• Tatou (Map 23, Ref H10)
577 Lt Collins St, City
Classic funky grooves from every era — always a late-night hit.

• The Club (Map 19, Ref F19)
132a Smith St, Collingwood
Offering entertainment several nights a week, you can indulge in a variety of music.

• The Dome (Map 31, Ref J15)
19 Commercial Road, Prahran
Dome provides deep house music and beautiful people to dance and play with.

• The Ivy (Map 2, J18)
cnr Flinders La & Russell St, City
Bright atmosphere, sensational music and an upbeat crowd.

• The Viper Room (Map 32, Ref D15)
371 Chapel St, South Yarra
Style is the domain of the VIper Room — thumbs up from those in the know.

• Twister (Map 414, Ref A18)
Lower Esp, St Kilda
A pumping, thumping humongous dance floor makes Twister a hit every time.

late night munchies

When your body's been in motion for more than a few hours, a fast snack is just what the doctor ordered. Melbourne delivers with a sensational variety of places burning the midnight oil to satisfy your late-night cravings…

• Barflys (Map 24, Ref J5)
16 Bourke St, City
This place not only serves great food, foccaccias and snacks until 5am, it's also a rocking good licensed bar.

• China Bar (Map 2, Ref J9)
235b Russell St, City
Great prices, fast service and a huge menu – the China Bar will fill that hole with great flavours of the Orient.

• Crown Entertainment Complex (Map 3, Ref B4)
8 Whiteman St, Southbank.
Chow down at one of the food courts in between hopping around Crown's awesome clubs.

• Fast Eddy's (Map 24, Ref J5)
32 Bourke St, City
Gobble up nachos, burgers, chips and other tasty snacks at this 24 hour a day saviour.

• The Supper Club (Map 24, Ref J3)
161 Spring Street, City
If you're looking to indulge and impress, wander uptown to the Supper Club for a fine wine, gourmet tapas treats and lush furnishings.

melbourne outdoors

Surrounding the CBD, Melbourne is blessed with a beautiful ring of parkland, an idyllic contrast to the excitement of the city. Constant upkeep ensures the parks are in stunning condition year-round, a menagerie of rich colours and tranquil settings. A variety of native birds and animals have made Melbourne's gardens home, promising sights and sounds to delight those enjoying a stroll, picnic or a quiet, lazy afternoon. Along the Yarra River, the waterfront has been transformed into a spectacular promenade at Southgate and Crown Entertainment Complex, while the Alexandra Gardens and Batman Avenue provide manicured gardens, lawns and trails along the riverbank.

The parks are a haven for recreational activities of all kinds — running, skating, cycling, throwing a frisbee or relaxing the soul through the ancient art of tai chi. If you live in Melbourne and you're not exercising, there's no excuse! Step outside, breathe some fresh air and make the most of our city's green recreational zones.

royal botanic gardens

(Map 31, Ref E2)

At its northern border, South Yarra adjoins the Royal Botanic Gardens and the Yarra River. Established in 1846, Melbourne's Botanic Gardens comprise over 36 hectares of some of the most magnificent landscaped gardens in the world.

Lush green parklands are complemented by marvellous historic buildings, including Government House, the Shrine of Remembrance, the former Melbourne Observatory and La Trobe's cottage. The Royal Botanic Gardens are the emerald jewels of Melbourne. In summer, the Gardens are the site of Melbourne's Moonlight Cinema, an open-air film theatre, featuring classic, cult and arthouse favourites. Visit www.moonlightcinema.com.au . The Royal Botanic Gardens are open every day of the year from 7.30am.

south yarra

Another highlight of South Yarra's parklands is **Fawkner Park (Map 31, Ref F10)** a 19th century landscaped design, featuring shady English Elms and Moreton Bay Fig Trees. Much of the park has been set aside for sporting activities, including tennis. Year-round, cricketers, footballers, softball teams and touch footy players converge on Fawkner Park for both serious and social competition.

carlton

Just a short stroll away from the frenetic activity of Lygon Street is the peaceful **Carlton Gardens (Map 18, Ref H20)** – 16 hectares of landscaped garden featuring floral displays, ornamental lakes and fountains. The centerpiece of the Gardens is the historic Royal Exhibition Building, first built in 1888 and now a splendid backdrop to the ultra-modern Melbourne Museum.

along the yarra banks

Cycling along the Yarra is one of the most relaxing yet exhilarating forms of exercise in Melbourne. The cool breeze, smooth water and green grass generates a sensational feeling of freedom. Whether you're walking, riding or running, the trails winding along the banks of the Yarra River are just a wonderful place to be.

albert park lake

(Map 30, Ref H13)

If you're the type who loves the idea of running but decides they've had enough after a few hundred yards, Albert Park Lake is the place to get you moving! Complete one lap of the lake — 5km — and you'll be taking the first steps towards a healthier lifestyle. You won't be as quick as the Formula One cars in March, but I guarantee you'll feel better.

Located within Albert Park Lake is the **Melbourne Sports and Aquatic Centre**, one of the finest recreational facilities in the city. There's a fantastic pool, plus a gym, numerous basketball courts, table tennis, badminton and much more. It's an outstanding, state-of-the-art venue with just as much emphasis on fun as there is on hardcore training.

city gardens

From the heart of the city, every direction you go will bring you to a haven of greenery in which you can escape for a while. Located close to the CBD, the **Fitzroy and Treasury Gardens (Map 25, Ref D5)** are a popular escape for city workers and students. Possums are everywhere, and while joggers and cyclists plough up-and-down the pathways, the grass areas are a great place to stretch, do a few exercises or throw a frisbee around. In fact, frisbee-golf — the poor-man's version of golf — is a favoured game in the Fitzroy Gardens, where regular 'golfers' have marked out a complex course with pars, tee-off points and obstacles.

Flagstaff Gardens (Map 1, Ref C1) is alive with birds and small animals, while on the banks of the Yarra the **Alexandra Gardens (Map 4, Ref H6)** are the ideal setting for a waterfront picnic, or party central when they host Australia's biggest outdoor festival, Moomba in March. For all their serenity, Melbourne's gardens are a great place to party! Concerts at the **Sidney Myer Music Bowl in Kings Domain (Map 4, Ref L12)** are always a rocking good time too. There's no shortage of great recreational opportunities around here.

Melbourne is a garden city, Melbourne is a sporting city, and Melbourne is a FUN city! If you're not making the most of that, I think it's time you should. Utilise your parks and gardens – call (03) 9658 8713 for more information about Melbourne's parks, including booking areas for functions and events.

Contemporary, protean, always developing and constantly innovating, Melbourne has given rise to an extraordinary number of world class sporting, entertainment, transport, cultural and scientific facilities. Colonial Stadium, the CityLink Expressway, Vodafone Arena and the new Melbourne Museum are just some of the recent additions to the city's landscape. The reinvention of Melbourne's tourism identity continues, and several new developments promise to lift the city even further into the world spotlight.

• Colonial Stadium (Map 23, Ref C9) Footscray Rd, West Melbourne, Ph: (03) 9269 7700
Colonial Stadium, the Docklands' first major development, is a $460 million, high-tech, multi-purpose sports and entertainment venue. It has been one of Australia's most eagerly anticipated projects since construction began in 1997. Used primarily as an AFL venue (home ground for Essendon, St Kilda and the Western Bulldogs), Colonial Stadium is a marvel of engineering. Featuring one of the world's largest retractable roofs, the venue has played host to Barbra Streisand, international cricket and rugby, plus some of the most exciting AFL battles in the history of the sport.

• Melbourne Museum (Map 18, Ref J17) Rathdowne St, Carlton, Ph: 131 102
Situated beside the historical Royal Exhibition Building in the Carlton Gardens, the new Melbourne Museum features the largest exhibition space of any museum in the southern hemisphere. A special children's museum, Aboriginal heritage gallery, special tree garden and many more fascinating features places the Melbourne Museum as one of the city's premier attractions.

• Vodafone Arena (Map 25, Ref E14) Melbourne Park, Swan St, Richmond, Ph: 9286 1234
Melbourne's incredible devotion to sport continues to play a major part in development, with the construction of the new Vodafone Arena at Melbourne Park. This unique, extremely versatile facility is adaptable for tennis, basketball, velodrome cycling, concerts and more. Its retractable roof, along with those of Rod Laver Arena and Colonial Stadium, give Melbourne the distinction of being the only city in the world with three all-weather venues.

Vodafone Arena has been instrumental in making the Australian Open Grand Slam tennis tournament in January the biggest event of its kind in the world.

• Docklands (Map 369, Ref A16)
www.docklands.vic.gov.au
Covering 200 hectares of land and water, Docklands' eight precincts will ultimately feature a diversity of entertainment, waterfront restaurants, promenade shops, residential apartments and townhouses, technology and business centres. Development is staged to meet market demand, with each precinct planned to complement its neighbour and ensure Docklands offers something for everyone.

Melbourne Docklands promises to be the most exciting development since the city was founded in the 19th century, with a brand new area the size of the existing CBD being constructed on the stunning Yarra River waterfront. The new precinct will provide Victorians with significant economic, social and lifestyle benefits over the coming decades.

Development will not occur overnight, but the success of Colonial Stadium has already focused attention on the area. Construction is estimated to take approximately 15 years, spanning a number of economic cycles. Docklands is, after all, six times the size of Sydney's Circular Quay.

Melbourne Docklands will irrevocably change the look and feel of Melbourne. It will become a waterfront destination for an estimated 20 million visitors each year, home for 15,000 people and a workplace for 20,000.

Close monitoring by the government and the critical Melbourne public will ensure good quality design, full public access to Docklands' seven kilometres of waterfront, and integration of public parks, boat moorings, urban art and public transport.

• Eureka Tower (Map 3, Ref K5)
Southbank,
www.eurekatower.com.au
The new Eureka Tower promises to take apartment living to an entirely new level... literally! Rising 88 storeys out of Southbank, Melbourne's premier shopping, dining and entertainment district, Eureka Tower is destined to be the first landmark tower of the 21st century. This exciting development will rank with the construction of the Eiffel Tower or the Empire State Building as a turning point and inspiration for future design ambitions. Eureka Tower will be an extremely high-tech, slick apartment tower designed and built by Australians focusing on quality, technology and environmental responsibility.

Conceptually, the tower is a vertical city. Apartments start on Level 11 and conclude at the penthouses on Level 80 ensuring unimpeded views.

• Federation Square (Map 2, Ref G20)
cnr Swanston & Flinders Streets, City, Ph: (03) 9639 2800
Federation Square is a $260 million project celebrating the centenary of the federation of Australian states. Situated on the corner of Swanston and Flinders Streets, the bold, striking architecture of the Square will propel Melburnians and visitors into the 21st century. Presenting innovative new concepts and designs, this new public space in the heart of Melbourne is set to create cultural, educational and leisure opportunities of a level unlike anything else in Australia. Federation Square will be complemented by the recently refurbished City Square on Swanston Street.

Federation Square is one of the most ambitious and complex projects ever undertaken in Australia. It involves the development of an entire city block, the first ever to physically connect the Melbourne central business district with its Yarra river waterfront. Situated at the heart of central Melbourne, Federation Square will be a fusion of arts and events, leisure, hospitality and promenading. The project is due to open from late 2001.

Melbourne's reputation as a tourist destination has exploded meteorically in the past 10 years. The number of world class attractions available has risen dramatically, confirming the international notion that the city is a highly developed holiday destination. The temperate climate year-round encourages a great deal of activity both indoors and out.

First settled by Europeans in 1835, Melbourne has been a home to indigenous populations for up to 50,000 years. Within three years of their arrival, the Europeans had established the city's rectangular grid pattern, which eventually became known as 'The Golden Mile'. The Gold Rush of the 1850s brought Melbourne enormous prosperity, and many of the grand old buildings that grace our city were erected as a result of these golden years. The riches were also used to build many of Melbourne's magnificent architectural landmarks, including the Melbourne Town Hall, St Paul's Cathedral and 333 Collins St.

In 1901, Australia's federal government was established here in Melbourne and remained headquartered at Parliament House on Spring Street until 1927, when Canberra took over as the seat of national government.

Nowadays, Melbourne is a thriving, cosmopolitan capital with a population of 3.3 million, and visitors can appreciate the clever blend of impressive modern architecture with classic historical landmarks.

Amiable and unpretentious, Melbourne provides a warm welcome with visitors in mind — you'll be amazed how convenient and easy everything is here. The influence of Melbourne's people is everywhere — in our food, our arts, our events and all our passions.

Centred in Australia's most compact mainland state, Melbourne provides day access to all of Victoria's natural wonders — like rainforests, mountain ranges and snowfields. Anywhere and everywhere you turn, Melbourne has something to appeal.

information

• Melbourne Visitor Information Centre (Map 2, Ref F 15)
Melbourne Town Hall, Swanston St, City, Ph: (03) 9658 9955
For new visitors, the first port of call should be the Melbourne Visitor Information Centre, where you can pick up brochures, maps and information on all of Melbourne's secrets.

Friendly staff will gladly answer all your questions – apart from the main headquarters on Swanston Street, there are a number of accredited Visitor Information Centres located throughout Melbourne. Look for the yellow *'i'* on signs during your travels for access to information.

city attractions

With the number of fantastic tourist attractions continuing to grow, visitors to Melbourne now have the opportunity to access the very best of these in one affordable pass. The Melbourne Attractions Pass incorporates the best venues in Melbourne, from sport, to the arts, history and heritage.

Passholders gain entry to a minimum of three and a maximum of six of Melbourne's premier attractions, providing an easy and convenient way to experience the finest of Melbourne's attractions. Contact your local travel agent for further details.

• City Circle tram
The City Circle tram is a completely free way to see the City and learn more about Melbourne. This is the perfect first step to seeing what Melbourne's all about. Visitor brochures are available on board, a running commentary is provided and attendants are happy to answer any questions. Running at 10 minute intervals, the City Circle tram operates between 10am and 6pm, daily.

• Crown Entertainment Complex (Map 3, Ref B4)
8 Whiteman Street, Southbank, Ph: (03) 9292 8888
Crown has become synonymous with entertainment and glamour. There are more than 40 restaurants, bars and cafés to choose from. Add in the casino, cinemas, games arcades, international designer stores, nightclubs, live performance venues, and you've got a cauldron of excitement. Crown hosts film premiers, international conferences and awards ceremonies. Located downstream from Southgate on the banks of the Yarra River, Crown is a world of entertainment.

• Golden Mile Heritage Trail
For a new angle on Melbourne's heritage, the Golden Mile Heritage Trail places the best of Melbourne's historical landmarks on a well-marked path. The trail begins at **Old Customs House (Map 1, Ref F19)**, with decorative plaques set into the pavement marking the route. Along the way, visitors are acquainted with the story of Melbourne's early development and highlighted through a collection of the City's key 'golden era' buildings.

Connect the dots all the way to the **Royal Exhibition Building (Map 18, Ref H18)**, and you'll reveal a marvellous picture of our City's unique historical development, largely thanks to the influx of migrants during the 19th century Gold Rush. Afterwards, the free City Circle tram returns walkers to the city centre.

• IMAX Theatre (Map 18, Ref H17)
Rathdowne Street, Carlton, Ph: (03) 9663 5454
Feel the awe-inspiring convergence of cinema and reality as you watch large format and 3D films on the gargantuan IMAX screen – eight storeys high and 31 metres wide. The visual impact is enhanced by full digital surround sound and hi-tech liquid crystal glasses for 3D movies. Imax films screen daily from 10am until 10pm (late sessions on Fridays and Saturdays).

• Luna Park (Map 414, Ref A18)
Lower Esplanade, St Kilda, Ph: 1902 240 112
Melbourne's Luna Park, based on New York's famous Coney Island, has delighted visitors since its opening in 1912. The bayside theme park has recently undergone a complete refurbishment, and the revamped Luna Park features a host of new state-of-the-art rides and facilities.

Tram No. 96 from Bourke or Spencer Streets, or tram no. 12 from Swanston St, will deliver you from the city to Luna Park and the St Kilda foreshore.

• Melbourne Aquarium (Map 1, Ref B20)
cnr King Street and Queens Wharf Road, City, Ph: (03) 9620 0999
Immerse yourself in the totally interactive marine experience of the Melbourne Aquarium. Travel through billabongs, mangrove swamps, coral atolls, rock pools, a transparent tunnel where sharks and giant stingrays will surround you, and finally right off the deep end into the 2.2 million litre Oceanarium. The City Circle Tram stops right outside.

• Melbourne Museum (Map 18, Ref H17)
Rathdowne Street, Carlton, Ph: 13 11 02 (Map 18, Ref H17)
Walk through a living forest gallery, discover the vibrant story of Melbourne and experience Aboriginal cultural performances in this ultra-modern hands-on museum. Performances, activities and interactive displays make a visit to the Melbourne Museum a truly memorable experience.

• Melbourne Observation Deck (Map 1, Ref B16)
Collins St, City, (03) 9629 8222
For unparalleled views of the City, you naturally have to pick the tallest building in town. The Melbourne Observation Deck offers splendid 360 degree panoramic vistas of the city, Port Phillip Bay, the MCG, Melbourne Park, Colonial Stadium, Southgate and the Crown Entertainment Complex, plus magnificent parkland and beautiful scenery as far as the eye can see.

Up top, a café and bar offer stratospheric dining and drinking while you enjoy the stunning views, and 'Rialto Vision' — a million dollar, award-winning sight and sound extravaganza is free with your Observation Deck admission. Located at the top of Rialto Towers, the Melbourne Observation Deck is near the corner of King and Collins Sts, close to Spencer St railway station and a City Circle tram stop.

• Melbourne Zoo (Map 17, Ref D1)
Elliott Av, Parkville, Ph: (03) 9285 9300
The Melbourne Zoo is world-renowned, and one of the premier features is the amazing gorilla rainforest. In their natural habitat, you'll feel right at home with the gorillas. Or, if you still don't recognize any long-lost family members, try the monkeys, gibbons and orangutans. Plus, there's the tropical butterfly enclosure — just remember to close your mouth. Visit the lions, tigers, bears, reptiles, elephants and giraffes — more creatures than Noah ever dreamed of. The magnificent gardens and scenery are also very attractive.

To get there, take the number 55 tram north from William St in the city.

• Old Melbourne Gaol (Map 2, Ref H2)
Russell St, City, Ph: (03) 9663 7728
Some of Melbourne's most notorious criminals of the past have spent a portion of their lives here, including the legendary bushranger Ned Kelly. The gaol features a fascinating exhibition of 19th century gaol life, and the special night tours with theatrical performances will chill you to the bone.

The free City Circle tram stops at the corner of Russell and La Trobe Streets, very close to the Old Melbourne Gaol.

• Southgate Arts & Leisure Precinct (Map 4, Ref C4)
Southbank, City, Ph: (03) 9699 4311
One of Melbourne's most spectacular showpieces, Southgate is home to more than 20 restaurants, cafés and bars, 41 unique retailers and an innovative food wharf. Lively street theatre, impressive sculptures and artworks, and the magnificent Yarra waterfront make Southgate a wonderful attraction, day or night, year-round.

Southgate is located directly across the Yarra River from Flinders St railway station, with a footbridge conveniently connecting the two.

beyond the city

• Healesville Wildlife Sanctuary (Map 258, Ref C12)
Badger Creek Rd, Healesville, Ph: (03) 5957 2800
Wander among koalas, kangaroos, wombats and countless other native Australian birds and animals at the award-winning Healesville Wildlife Sanctuary. Enjoy a close encounter with an emu, a rare look at a platypus, plus numerous animal presentations by the friendly staff.

If you don't have access to a car, simply catch a train all the way to Lilydale, then jump on a McKenzies coach to Healesville.

• Phillip Island (Maps 725 & 726)
Journey down the Princes Hwy to **Dandenong (Map 536)**, connect with the **South Gippsland Hwy (Map 536, Ref E15)** and follow the signs to Phillip Island — home to the world-famous penguin parade, Seal Rocks Sea Life Centre and numerous other attractions. Check out the fairy penguins as they surf onto the beach and waddle home across the sand every evening. Explore the various wildlife parks on the island that are home to a huge population of fur seals, koalas, kangaroos and other native Australian animals.

• Sovereign Hill
Bradshaw St, Ballarat, Ph: (03) 5331 1944
Follow the Western Freeway through **Melton (Map 269)** all the way to the historic town of **Ballarat** — a 90 minute drive from Melbourne — where you'll see numerous signs guiding you to Sovereign Hill. This living museum is the ultimate goldrush experience, a time warp back to the 1850s, where visitors are immersed in the everyday life at an original gold-mining settlement.

• Victoria's Open Range Zoo (Map 487, Ref J4)
K Rd, Werribee, Ph: (03) 9731 9600
You don't have to go to Africa to enjoy a unique wildlife safari — the Open Range Zoo has an unbelievable range of exotic creatures roaming free within the park. Get up close and personal with rhinos, giraffes, zebras, antelopes, hippos and our own native kangaroos as you tour the savannahs on a special safari bus.

Melburnians love to entertain, and our list of major events is the envy of the world. Roaring crowds… screaming engines… thundering hooves… endless celebrations… experience world-class festivals and events in Melbourne year-round.

Travellers from all over the globe flock to sporting events like the Australian Grand Prix, Australian Open, AFL Grand Final and the Melbourne Cup. Lively festivals adorn the state's calendar throughout the year, including Moomba, the International Comedy Festival, and the Melbourne Festival.

Below is a listing of some of the city's finest, but there's always much more happening each week. For up-to-date information on what's happening in and around the city, visit: www.melbourne.citysearch.com.au.

january

• Australia Day Festival
Various venues, Ph: 9651 5026
In true Aussie fashion, break out the snags and celebrate being part of the greatest country in the world. This fantastic festival will remind you why we're considered the luckiest nation on earth.

• Australian Open Tennis Championships (Map 25, Ref C14)
Melbourne Park, Swan Street, Richmond , Ph: 9286 1175 or visit www.ausopen.org.
The atmosphere is electric and the play is inspirational as the real superstars of tennis put everything on the line for one of the world's biggest Grand Slam tennis competitions. Cheer on your favourite pros, and mingle with one of the biggest international crowds you'll ever see. The combination of Rod Laver Arena and the new Vodafone Arena makes a superb venue.

• Midsumma Festival
Various venues, Ph: 9525 4746 or visit www.midsumma.org.
A gay and lesbian celebration with sensational festivities and art exhibitions — everybody's welcome, gay, straight or just plain curious. There are shows and entertainment to humour all ages, plus a terrific range of stalls offering a collection of the most outrageous products you're ever likely to see in one place.

february

• Woolmark Melbourne Fashion Festival
Various venues, Ph: 9826 9688 or visit www.mff.com.au.
Celebrate style in style with a sensational variety of fashion events and the latest looks for autumn and winter. Gorgeous catwalk models introduce the latest trends, plus there are plenty of social functions and entertainment to amuse even those who can't spot the difference between leather and polyester.

march

• Antipodes Festival
Various city locations, Ph: 9662 2722 or visit ww.antipodesfestival.com.au.
A lively celebration of Melbourne's thriving Greek community, who love to party, love to entertain and love to eat good food. What a combination! Enjoy gourmet Greek cuisine, traditional and contemporary entertainment, and experience the hidden joys of zorba dancing.

• Melbourne Food & Wine Festival
Various venues, Ph: 9628 5008 or visit www.melbfoodwinefest.com.au.
Pay homage to the great tastes of Melbourne and pig out on delicious offerings at this mouth-watering event. Melburnians take enormous pride in their food and wine culture, and this is the occasion where efforts are doubled and competition is fierce to show off the tastiest creations imaginable. Make the most of it - worry about your waistline later!

• Melbourne Moomba Festival (Map 4, Ref L7) Yarra River, Alexandra Gardens and City
Ph: 9699 4022 or visit www.melbournemoombafestival.com.au.
This is the biggest outdoor festival in Australia, featuring carnival rides, entertainment and loads of excitement in the city centre and down by the banks of the Yarra. Highlights of the event include the Tram Parade, Garden Party and the awesome River of Light fireworks spectacular. Thrill to the best water-skiers in the world carving up the Yarra River and soaring over 200 feet through the air at the world's biggest tournament, the Melbourne Masters.

• Fosters Australian Grand Prix (Map 30) Albert Park Lake, Albert Park, Ph: Ticketmaster 131 641 or visit www.grandprix.com.au.
The biggest names in the world of Formula One hurtle around Albert Park Lake at insane speeds during this mammoth international event. Grab your earplugs and join the crowd for one of the biggest parties you'll ever see, a Ferrari-fuelled experience you're never going to forget.

april

• Melbourne International Comedy Festival (Map 2, Ref F15)
Melbourne Town Hall, Swanston Walk, City and various City venues, Ph: Ticketmaster 136 100 or visit www.comedyfestival.com.au.
The funniest April fools from all around the world bombard our City with hilarious entertainment during this major comedy extravaganza. There are more than a hundred acts to choose from every evening throughout the whole month. Warning – Attend too many and you risk dying of laughter!

• Melbourne International Flower & Garden Show (Map 18, Ref H18)
Royal Exhibition Building and Carlton Gardens Ph: 9639 2333 or visit www.melbflowershow.com.au.
To stop and smell the flowers here would take a while. Tens of thousands of cut flowers are under one roof, formed in the most amazing displays your eyes (and your nose) will ever experience. Outside, stroll amidst cool and innovative garden displays that will blow you away, and see incredible sculptures and artwork.

may

• Next Wave Festival
Various venues, Ph: 9417 7544 or visit www.nextwave.org.au.
A showcase of the future, the Next Wave Festival is dedicated to nurturing a culture of contemporary ideas into the 21st Century, supporting the work of a new generation of Australian artists, and encouraging young people to engage with the arts.

• St Kilda Film Festival (Map 414, Ref C17)
National Theatre, Barkly St, St Kilda, Ph: 9209 6711 or visit www.stkildafilmfest.com.au.
A great showing of cool, contemporary Australian short films and videos. The National Theatre's laid-back atmosphere is a tribute to the halcyon days of cinema, before multiplexes and blockbuster special effects blew away the intimate romance of the movies. It's a great chance to see rare, hip films that veer off the mainstream.

• Yarra Valley Expo (Map 253, Ref E1)
Yarra Glen Racecourse, Ph: 9730 1722 or visit www.yarra-valley-expo.com.au.
There's something for everyone here. You'll not only enjoy wine, food and jazz – there are world champion axemen, fashion parades, whipcracking and much more on show at the Yarra Valley Expo. Plenty of stalls offering samples of some of Australia's finest wines – make sure you bring a designated driver!

june

• Mind Body Spirit Festival (Map 23, Ref H17)
Melbourne Exhibition Centre, Ph: 9819 0211, or visit www.mindbodyspiritfest.com.
Nourish your soul at the Mind Body Spirit Festival, where exhibitors present a rare view of holistic pursuits such as Chinese medicine and kinesiology. A truly spiritual experience…

july

• Melbourne International Film Festival
Various cinemas, Ph: 9417 2011 or visit www.melbournefilmfestival.com.au.
Movie fans will go crazy over this showcase of the latest and best films. Take the chance to meet filmmakers, mingle with stars and party in the Festival Club.

august

• The Age Melbourne Writers' Festival
CUB Malthouse, Melbourne Town Hall and various venues, Ph: 9261 4500 or visit www.mwf.com.au.
Lectures and seminars galore with successful writers giving talks and tips on how to make it in the world of writing. Gain inspiration from those who've made it, and learn how you can best launch your writing career.

september

• AFL Grand Final (Map 25, Ref F12)
Melbourne Cricket Ground, Jolimont, Ph: 9643 1999 or visit www.afl.com.au.
Up there Cazaly! Take the top two AFL teams of the season, a crowd of almost 100,000 roaring fans, a skyfull of balloons, a fighter jet, and stir everything into a huge pot called the MCG — this is the recipe for Aussie Rules Football's ultimate clash of the year!

• Melbourne Spring Fashion Week
Various venues, visit www.msfw.org.
A sizzling week of shows and parades that feature the hottest new looks for the spring–summer season, plus a variety of entertainment, competitions and cool seminars. If fashion is your thing and style is your friend, you'd better not miss this event.

• Royal Melbourne Show (Map 323, Ref J20)
Royal Melbourne Showgrounds, Ascot Vale, Ph: 9281 7444 or visit www.royalshow.com.au.
An old favourite with Melburnians, there's always something to entertain everyone at 'The Show'. Carnival rides, animal and agricultural exhibitions, plus fireworks and thrilling entertainment in the arena, the Royal Melbourne Show always puts on a great… show!

october

• Lygon Street Festa (Map 18, Ref E17)
Lygon St, Carlton, Ph: 9348 1299.
Pasta lover or not, you'll have the time of your life at this spirited Italian community festival in one of Melbourne's most-loved streets.

• Melbourne Festival
Various venues, Ph: 9662 4242 or visit www.melbournefestival.com.au.
The very best of our creative culture on show, entertaining you with arts, theatre, music and exhibitions.

• Melbourne Fringe Festival
Various venues, Ph: 9534 0722 or visit www.melbournefringe.org.au.
A three week explosion of fringe art encourages newcomers.
Artists devise, produce and finance their own shows, culminating in the colourful spectacle of the Brunswick Street Parade.

• Melbourne Oktoberfest (Map 323, Ref J20)
Royal Melbourne Showgrounds, Ascot Vale, Ph: 9529 5211.
Why travel to Germany, when you can enjoy the great Bavarian tradition of Oktoberfest right here in Melbourne. A favourite with beerlovers across the city, Oktoberfest is a fantastic weekend.

• QANTAS Australian Motorcycle Grand Prix
Phillip Island Motor Sports Centre, Phillip Island, Ph: Ticketmaster 131 641, or visit www.grandprix.com.au.
At this amazing international event, lives are on the line as the world's top motorcycle racers scream around the premier track at Phillip Island.

november

• Melbourne Cup Day (Map 367, Ref K4)
Flemington Racecourse, Ascot Vale, Ph: 9258 4666, or visit www.racingvictoria.com.au.
Held on the first Tuesday of November, this world famous horse race is an odds-on favourite with everyone throughout Australia. Hats, horses, fashions and flowers will add colour to your day. Only one thing's a sure bet – a photo finish!

december

• Carols By Candlelight (Map 4, Ref L12)
Sidney Myer Music Bowl, City, Ph: 9522 5222 or visit www.avib.org.au.
An Aussie tradition since 1937, thousands of people get together to celebrate Christmas under the stars with live music plus lots and lots of candles.

• Melbourne Boxing Day Test Match (Map 25, Ref F12)
Melbourne Cricket Ground, Jolimont, Ph: 9653 1100 or visit www.viccricket.asn.au.
Cheer on the indomitable Aussies as they clash with international opponents at one of the world's finest cricketing venues — the MCG.

show me the way

Your UBD Compact is the ultimate companion for every journey. Use this key information to get where you need to go in the most efficient way possible. Melbourne's road system and public transport network is world class — trams, trains and buses deliver you virtually to the doorstep of your City destination. There's a vast network of rails, including the underground City Loop, that makes getting into and out of Melbourne a very simple prospect. Read on for all the info you need on Melbourne's transport network.

citylink

The CityLink roadway has been the greatest improvement on Melbourne's traffic situation in many years. The high-tech electronic tolling system allows the uninterrupted flow of traffic, and drivers can travel from one side of the city to the other without stopping, via a network of bridges and tunnels including the scenic Bolte Bridge.

For details call CityLink on 132 629. Alternatively, you can purchase an e-TAG or Day Pass from a CityLink Customer Centre, selected Australia Post Offices or Touch Screen machines at selected Shell outlets. Or you can buy online at www.transurban.com.au.

the met

The Met incorporates all of Melbourne's tram, train and bus services. These services extend from the city in all directions to numerous outer suburbs, with plenty of stops in between to ensure that your destination is accessible as conveniently as possible.

Three different fare zones apply to travelling on the Met. Zone 1 covers the majority of the city and inner suburbs, Zone 2 is the mid-range metropolitan area and Zone 3 applies to the outer suburbs. Each time you pass through a different zone, you pay for a ticket accordingly.

The full range of Met tickets may be purchased from train stations, buses, selected retail outlets and the Met Shop at 103 Elizabeth Street in the city. Aboard trams, only short trip, two-hour and 60+ tickets may be purchased from a machine.

Remember, you must validate your Met ticket before you travel, which means sliding it through one of the validating machines at the train station, or on your bus or tram.

The Met system generally operates between 5am and midnight from Monday to Saturday, and between 8am to 11pm on Sundays. For timetables and route information, call 131 638.

taxis

Over 3000 taxis cruise across all parts of Melbourne day and night, so hailing one usually isn't a problem. But if you're not having any luck, try calling one of the taxi phone numbers (see Fast Facts page 23).

the nightrider bus

You've only got five bucks left and the last train's long gone. Don't panic! Departing hourly from the corner of **Swanston and Collins Sts in the city (Map 2, Ref F15)**, the Nightrider Bus operates between 12.30am and 4.30am on weekends, with routes covering most of the metropolitan area. For further information Ph: 131 638.

train routes

Melbourne has an expansive rail network that heads out from the City in all directions to more than 16 outer suburbs. Here are a few key train routes.

• South Yarra (Map 32, Ref C8)
If you're looking to shop and hang out on Chapel St, you can take your pick from Flinders St railway station – the Sandringham, Frankston, Cranbourne and Pakenham trains all stop at South Yarra.

• Williamstown (Map 411, Ref J18)
This is an easy one! Take the Williamstown line all the way to the last station, then hop off and enjoy life on the Strand.

trams

The green tram is a Melbourne icon, and these much-adored steely beasts dart across the city and suburbs, in all directions, from one stop to the next.

Cars and motorcycles must always give way to trams. If a tram is stopped, no overtaking is permitted – pedestrians may step out unexpectedly when a tram is in the vicinity.

In central Melbourne, many intersections require 'hook turns' for vehicles turning right, which are marked by signs overhead. To make a right turn, you must pull over to the left of the intersection, wait for the light to turn red, and then complete your turn. Though it seems unusual, the system is designed to allow the free flow of cars and trams through the city streets. Here are a few key tram route numbers to remember.

• **70** – From Flinders St in the City, this tram takes you between two of Melbourne's biggest sporting and entertainment venues, Melbourne Park and the **MCG (Map 25, Ref F12)**, before continuing on up Swan St, Richmond.

• **79** – Starting at the corner of **Victoria and Church Sts in Abbotsford (Map 26, Ref H 3)**, No. 79 trundles through Richmond and South Yarra all the way to **St Kilda Beach (Map 413, Ref L17)**.

• **96** – This is the fun tram, touring through some of Melbourne's favourite destinations, splitting the popular villages of Carlton and Fitzroy, down through the city and past Albert Park Lake to another popular hangout, **St Kilda Beach (Map 413, Ref L17)**.

v-line

For travelling further afield to Victoria's regional attractions, V-Line provides convenient, comfortable services to a wide range of destinations across the state. For bookings and further information, contact 136 196 or visit www.vline.vic.gov.au.

emergency services

- **Ambulance–fire–police** – Ph: 000.
- **Centre Against Sexual Assault** Ph: (03) 9344 2210 BH or Ph: (03) 9349 1766 AH.
- **Crisis Line** 24hr general counselling, Ph: (03) 9329 0300.
- **Direct Line** 24hr drug counselling, Ph: (03) 9416 1818.
- **Lifeline** 24hr general counselling, Ph: 131 114.
- **Maternal and child health** After hours service, Ph: (03) 9853 0844.

public hospitals

Each of the hospitals listed below provides 24 Hour Emergency Service.

- **Mercy Hospital for Women (Map 25, Ref G5)** 126 Clarendon Street, East Melbourne Ph: (03) 9270 2222
- **Royal Children's Hospital (Map 17, Ref E10)** Flemington Road, Parkville Ph: (03) 9345 5522
- **Royal Melbourne Hospital (Map 17, Ref H14)** Grattan Street, Parkville Ph: (03) 9342 7000
- **Royal Women's Hospital (Map 18, Ref D14)** 132 Grattan Street, Carlton Ph: (03) 9344 2000
- **Royal Victorian Eye & Ear Hospital (Map 25, Ref A2)** 32 Gisborne Street, East Melbourne Ph: (03) 9929 8666

internet cafés

Immerse yourself in the online world with a cup of coffee and a snack at any one of these great internet havens, where you can chat, send emails or surf the net at very affordable prices.

- **Café Wired (Map 30, Ref B7)** 363 Clarendon Street, South Melbourne Ph: (03) 9686 9555
- **Cybernet Café (Map 372, Ref A14)** 789 Glenferrie Road, Hawthorn Ph: (03) 9818 1288
- **Go Local Internet Lounge (Map 2, Ref E6)** 277 Little Lonsdale Street, City Ph: (03) 9639 6060
- **Internet Café St Kilda (Map 414, Ref B14)** 9 Grey Street, St Kilda Ph: (03) 9534 2666
- **Mary Martin Bookshop Café (Map 2, Ref L11)** 108 Bourke St, City, Ph: (03) 9663 9633
- **Melbourne Central Internet (Map 2, Ref C5)** Level 2, Melbourne Central, Off Swanston Walk, City Ph: (03) 9922 1100
- **Myer RMIT Internet Café (Map 2, Ref D9)** Level 4, 295 Lonsdale Street, City Ph: (03) 9661 1700
- **Net City (Map 414, Ref G12)** 40 Chapel St, Windsor Ph: (03) 9529 1937
- **Net City (Map 19, Ref B12)** 404 Brunswick St, Fitzroy Ph: (03) 9486 0087
- **Net City (Map 414, Ref A15)** 7/63 Fitzroy St, St Kilda Ph: (03) 9525 3411

lost property

- **Melbourne Town Hall (Map 2, Ref F15)** Swanston St, City, Ph: (03) 9658 9463 week days or (03) 9658 9774 w'ends.

movies

Movies always make for a great night out, and Melbourne is a breeding ground for state-of-the-art cinemas.

- **Greater Union (Map 2, Ref J13)** 131 Russell Street, City Ph: (03) 9654 8133
- **IMAX Theatre Melbourne (Map 18, Ref H17)** Rathdowne Street, Carlton Ph: (03) 9663 5454
- **Movieline** Ph:(03) 9685 7111 Just call this number, and enter the location code of your choice from the selections below for information, movie session times and credit card bookings.
- Code 341: **Jam Factory (Map 32, Ref E12)** Chapel Street, South Yarra
- Code 342: **Crown Entertainment Complex (Map 3, Ref C4)** Southbank
- Code 343: **Knox Towerpoint (Map 422, Ref K16)** Burwood Highway, Wantirna
- Code 344: **Sunshine Megaplex 20 (Map 321, Ref C20)** cnr Harvester & Hampshire Rds, Sunshine
- Code 346: **Southland (Map 496, Ref H17)** Nepean Highway, Cheltenham
- Code 347: **City Centre (Map 2, Ref H11)** 206 Bourke Street, City
- Code 348: **Airport West 8 (Map 279, Ref A10)** Westfield Shoppingtown, 29 Louis Street, Airport West
- Code 357: **Glen Waverley 10 (Map 420, Ref D20)** 256 Springvale Road, Glen Waverley
- Code 371: **Highpoint Shopping Centre (Map 323, Ref B16)** Rosamond Road, Maribyrnong
- Code 372: **Cinema Centre (Map 2, Ref L11)** 140 Bourke Street, City
- Code 373: **Greensborough (Map 286, Ref B4)** 25 Main Street, Greensborough
- Code 374: **Chadstone Shopping Centre (Map 457, Ref H5)** 1341 Dandenong Road, Chadstone
- Code 375: **Northland Shopping Centre (Map 283, Ref J19)** 50 Murray Road, Preston
- Code 377: **Croydon (Map 380, Ref B4)** 3 Hewish Road, Croydon
- Code 378: **Forest Hill Chase Shopping Centre (Map 420, Ref C2)** Canterbury Road, Forest Hill
- Code 379: **Broadmeadows (Map 237, Ref L15)** 48-50 Pearcedale Road, Broadmeadows

taxi cabs

When you're stuck for a ride, call one of these numbers and you'll be on your way in no time.

- **Arrow** Ph: 132 211
- **Black Cabs** Ph: 132 227
- **Dandenong Taxis** Ph: (03) 9791 2111
- **Embassy** Ph: 131 755
- **North Suburban** Ph: 131 119
- **Silver Top** Ph: 131 008
- **West Suburban** Ph: (03) 9689 1144

Useful Numbers

Here's some handy phone numbers to have at all times.

- **Melbourne City Council** General inquiries, Ph: (03) 9658 9658
- **Directory assistance** Local, Ph: 12455; International, Ph: 1225
- **Legal Aid Commission** Ph: (03) 9269 0234
- **Met transport info** Ph: 131 638
- **Relationships Australia** Counselling, Ph: (03) 9261 8700
- **Reverse charges** from a public telephone Ph: 12550
- **Time** Ph: 1194 & **Weather** Ph: 1196
- **Traffic hazards** (VicRoads) Ph: 131 170

Useful Websites

Check out these great sites.

- **www.visitmelbourne.com** Informative Melbourne site with a huge range of info and plenty of links.
- **www.whereis.com.au** Type in an address and whereis shows you the location on a map from UBD Melbourne & Surrounds Street Directory.
- **www.beat.com.au** with a finger on Melbourne's pulse, the Beat Magazine website has the latest info on gigs and hotspots around the City.

SUBURBS and LOCALITIES INDEX

Listed below are Melbourne suburbs and localities together with their postcodes and map references. Suburbs and are differentiated in the index as follows:

Altona — Suburb
Hawksburn — Locality shown on maps
Centreville — Local Name
[Map reference indicates approximate location]

Note: Streets are indexed to suburbs only, not localities.

Suburb	Postcode	Map	Ref
Endeavour Hills	3802	537	K5
Epping	3076	197	C18
Essendon	3040	323	G4
Essendon North	3041	279	E20
Essendon West	3033	323	A10
Eumemmerring	3177	537	B14
Exford	3338	267	J18
Fairfield	3078	327	F16
Fawkner	3060	281	J7
Ferntree Gully	3156	464	A9
Ferny Creek	3786	425	L16
Fingal	3941	698	G17
Fishermans Bend	3207	368	A20
Fitzroy	3065	370	B9
Fitzroy North	3068	326	D17
Flemington	3031	367	K3
Footscray	3011	367	D3
Forest Hill	3131	420	C5
Frankston	3199	599	E17
Frankston North	3200	600	G11
Frankston South	3199	626	K11
Fyansford	3221	701	C6
Gardenvale	3185	455	C10
Geelong	3220	703	A9
Geelong West	3218	702	G5
Gembrook	3783	512	J5
Gisborne	3437	78	D10
Gisborne South	3437	109	H17
Gladstone Park	3043	237	A18
Glenferrie	3122	372	A16
Glen Huntly	3163	456	C9
Glen Iris	3146	416	L11
Glenroy	3046	280	F4
Glen Waverley	3150	420	G17
Goonawarra	3429	144	C11
Gowanbrae	3043	279	C7
Greensborough	3088	244	F13
Greenvale	3059	192	G12
Grovedale	3216	706	C18
Gruyere	3770	297	C12
Guys Hill	3807	541	H19
Hadfield	3046	280	K8
Hallam	3803	537	J17
Hampton	3188	495	C7
Hampton East	3188	495	K8
Hampton Park	3976	552	A10
Harkaway	3806	540	L8
Hawksburn	3142	414	J6
Hawthorn	3122	371	G14
Hawthorn East	3123	372	F19
Healesville	3777	257	J8
Heatherton	3202	497	K12
Heathmont	3135	378	H19
Heidelberg	3084	328	J6
Heidelberg Heights	3081	284	F19
Heidelberg West	3081	284	B16
Herne Hill	3218	701	L2
Heyington	3142	415	G3
Highett	3190	496	C14
Highton	3216	705	G9
Hillside	3037	274	D6
Hoddles Creek	3139	388	J14
Holmesglen	3148	417	K19
Hopetoun Park	3340	266	E7
Hoppers Crossing	3029	405	A16
Hughesdale	3166	457	G12
Huntingdale	3166	458	F14
Hurstbridge	3099	202	H16
Ivanhoe	3079	328	C10
Ivanhoe East	3079	328	G15
Jacana	3047	237	G17
Jan Juc	3228	711	C13
Jolimont	3002	370	D15
Junction Village	3977	604	G14
Kallista	3791	467	H6
Kalorama	3766	383	B14
Kananook	3198	599	E8
Kangaroo Ground	3097	247	J12
Karingal	3199	600	E18
Kealba	3021	276	K18
Keilor	3036	277	B8
Keilor Downs	3038	276	D15
Keilor East	3033	321	F3
Keilor Lodge	3038	276	A2
Keilor North	3036	234	D19
Keilor Park	3042	277	J12
Kensington	3031	368	D7
Kew	3101	372	F10
Kew East	3102	372	G4
Keysborough	3173	534	K15
Kilsyth	3137	381	E9
Kilsyth South	3137	381	B17
Kingsbury	3083	283	J10
Kings Park	3021	275	E19
Kingsville	3012	366	J12
Knoxfield	3180	462	K10
Kooyong	3144	416	A5
Kurunjang	3337	227	C7
Lalor	3075	241	H8
Langwarrin	3910	629	J7
Langwarrin South	3910	629	G18
La Trobe University	3083	284	D11
Launching Place	3139	346	E15
Laverton	3028	407	B13
Laverton North	3026	407	E3
Lilydale	3140	338	B12
Long Forest	3340	224	F7
Lower Plenty	3093	286	J17
Lynbrook	3975	551	D20
Lyndhurst	3975	550	H14
Lysterfield	3156	464	G17
Lysterfield South	3156	503	K13
Macaulay	3051	368	H5
Macclesfield	3782	470	J5
Macleod	3085	285	C14
McCrae	3938	684	L13
McKinnon	3204	455	K15
Maddingley	3340	263	J6
Maidstone	3012	366	J3
Malvern	3144	416	B13
Malvern East	3145	457	D3
Mambourin	3024	445	C11
Manifold Heights	3218	702	C3
Mannerim	3222	707	J3
Marcus Hill	3222	707	A12
Maribyrnong	3032	322	H12
Marshall	3216	706	K7
Meadow Heights	3048	237	K1
Melbourne	3000	413	K4
Melbourne Airport	3045	235	B8
Melton	3337	228	B15
Melton South	3338	269	J8
Melton West	3337	224	K14
Mentone	3194	531	J6
Menzies Creek	3159	468	E17
Merlynston	3058	281	C12
Mernda	3754	155	J14
Merricks North	3926	688	L7
Merrimu	3340	223	F11
Mickleham	3064	150	E2
Middle Park	3206	413	F9
Millgrove	3799	348	B3
Mill Park	3082	242	L1
Mitcham	3132	377	E12
Monbulk	3793	428	H13
Mont Albert	3127	374	D14
Mont Albert North	3129	374	D8
Montmorency	3094	286	J11
Montrose	3765	382	E12
Moolap	3221	704	J18
Moonee Ponds	3039	323	J13
Moorabbin	3189	496	F8
Moorabbin Airport	3194	532	C4
Moorooduc	3933	658	D7
Mooroolbark	3138	337	F10
Mordialloc	3195	532	D12
Moreland	3058	325	F7
Mornington	3931	641	C18
Mountain Gate	3156	463	L3
Mt Burnett	3781	511	K17
Mt Dandenong	3767	426	J2
Mt Duneed	3216	705	F19
Mt Eliza	3930	626	A11
Mt Evelyn	3796	383	D2
Mt Martha	3934	656	C6
Mt Toolebewong	3777	300	K6
Mt Waverley	3149	419	E14
Mulgrave	3170	500	J3
Murrumbeena	3163	457	B13
Nangana	3781	472	H1
Nar Nar Goon	3812	586	H7
Nar Nar Goon North	3812	560	H11
Narre Warren	3805	553	G8
Narre Warren East	3804	506	H18
Narre Warren North	3804	538	E1
Narre Warren South	3805	552	F16
Newcomb	3219	704	C10
New Gisborne	3438	79	H3
Newmarket	3031	368	E2
Newport	3015	410	J5
Newtown	3220	702	A11
Niddrie	3042	278	J19
Noble Park	3174	500	J16
Noble Park North	3174	501	B15
Northcote	3070	327	B12

	Postcode	Map	Ref
North Melbourne	3051	368	J8
North Warrandyte	3113	290	B14
Notting Hill	3168	459	D12
Nunawading	3131	376	K16
Nutfield	3099	202	C1
Oaklands Junction	3063	191	H9
Oakleigh	3166	458	D12
Oakleigh East	3166	458	K12
Oakleigh South	3167	498	B4
Oak Park	3046	279	L12
Officer	3809	556	K7
Officer South	3809	582	G15
Olinda	3788	426	K6
Olivers Hill	3199	626	F3
Ormond	3204	456	D12
Pakenham	3810	584	D5
Pakenham Upper	3810	560	B6
Panton Hill	3759	204	G13
Parkdale	3194	531	E10
Park Orchards	3114	333	G15
Parkville	3052	325	C18
Parwan	3340	265	E14
Pascoe Vale	3044	280	E14
Pascoe Vale South	3044	324	K2
Patterson	3189	496	B2
Patterson Lakes	3197	573	G9
Pearcedale	3912	646	F2
Pentland Hills	3341	221	B15
Phillip Island	3922	725	K10
Plenty	3090	244	D7
Plumpton	3037	273	F9
Point Cook	3029	450	F9
Point Lonsdale	3225	707	E10
Port Melbourne	3207	412	A3
Portsea	3944	678	B7
Prahran	3181	414	K10
Preston	3072	326	L2
Princes Hill	3054	325	H20
Queenscliff	3225	708	J17
Ravenhall	3023	317	K12
Red Hill	3937	688	E10
Red Hill South	3937	688	L19
Research	3095	288	J8
Reservoir	3073	282	B8
Richmond	3121	371	C15
Riddells Creek	3431	80	K9
Ringwood	3134	378	G16
Ringwood East	3135	379	A15
Ringwood North	3134	335	C9
Ripponlea	3183	454	J2
Riversdale	3124	373	B20
Rockbank	3335	317	C5
Rosanna	3084	329	C2
Rosebud	3939	684	A18
Rosebud West	3940	683	B17
Rowville	3178	462	J13
Roxburgh Park	3064	194	F12
Rye	3941	696	L4
Safety Beach	3936	669	E16
St Albans	3021	319	J7
St Albans East	3021	276	D19
St Andrews	3761	204	K2
St Andrews Beach	3941	697	H20
St Helena	3088	244	H18
St Kilda	3182	414	F14
St Kilda East	3183	415	A17
St Kilda West	3206	413	L13
Sanctuary Lakes	3029	451	B10
Sandown Park	3171	500	E15
Sandringham	3191	495	F14
Sassafras	3787	426	E17
Scoresby	3179	462	C14
Seabrook	3028	450	J4
Seaford	3198	599	J6
Seaholme	3018	409	K16
Seddon	3011	367	D10
Selby	3159	467	C19
Seville	3139	342	D14
Seville East	3139	343	D14
Sherbrooke	3789	466	J4
Silvan	3795	384	J14
Skye	3977	575	K16
Smiths Gully	3760	205	H7
Somerton	3062	195	B13
Somerville	3912	644	E10
Sorrento	3943	678	F5
Southbank	3006	369	D19
South Geelong	3220	703	C15
South Kingsville	3012	410	F2
South Melbourne	3205	413	E1
South Morang	3752	243	K5
South Yarra	3141	414	C5
Spotswood	3015	411	C3
Springvale	3171	500	B13
Springvale South	3172	533	H2
Steels Creek	3775	208	H2
Strathmore	3041	279	H15
Strathmore Heights	3041	279	E11
Sunbury	3429	144	B3
Sunshine	3020	321	C19
Sunshine North	3020	321	F12
Sunshine West	3020	364	L13
Surrey Hills	3127	373	K19
Swan Bay	3225	707	H15
Swan Island	3225	709	G9
Sydenham	3037	274	J2
Tanti Park	3931	641	A15
Tarneit	3030	405	A8
Tarrawarra	3775	211	F17
Taylors Hill	3037	274	D12
Taylors Lakes	3038	276	C8
Tecoma	3160	466	B12
Templestowe	3106	331	H6
Templestowe Lower	3107	330	F11
The Basin	3154	425	C8
The Patch	3792	468	B4
Thomastown	3074	241	E17
Thomson	3219	703	J16
Thornbury	3071	326	D6
Toolern Vale	3337	227	G1
Tooradin	3980	651	G4
Toorak	3142	415	E4
Tootgarook	3941	698	D4
Torquay	3228	711	G6
Tottenham	3012	366	B13
Travancore	3032	324	H19
Tremont	3785	425	D17
Truganina	3029	406	B14
Tuerong	3933	670	K8
Tullamarine	3043	278	G8
Upper Ferntree Gully	3156	464	K10
Upwey	3158	465	H13
Vermont	3133	421	F2
Vermont South	3133	420	K9
Victoria Dock	3000	368	J16
View Bank	3084	286	A18
Wandana Heights	3216	701	C19
Wandin East	3139	384	H2
Wandin North	3139	340	J12
Wantirna	3152	422	B8
Wantirna South	3152	421	H16
Warburton	3799	349	G4
Warneet	3980	649	G13
Warrandyte	3113	333	F5
Warrandyte South	3134	334	J7
Warranwood	3134	335	B15
Watsonia	3087	285	H7
Watsonia North	3087	285	G1
Wattle Glen	3096	247	F4
Waurn Ponds	3221	705	B15
Werribee	3030	448	C14
Werribee South	3030	488	G6
Wesburn	3799	347	L10
West Footscray	3012	366	F9
Westmeadows	3049	237	D13
West Melbourne	3003	368	B14
Wheelers Hill	3150	460	L9
Whittington	3219	704	A18
Whittlesea	3757	96	J15
Williamstown	3016	411	K18
Williamstown North	3016	410	D11
Windsor	3181	414	E11
Wollert	3750	153	F11
Wonga Park	3115	291	H12
Woodstock	3751	125	C12
Woori Yallock	3139	344	B16
Wyndham Vale	3030	446	A10
Yallambie	3085	285	J14
Yan Yean	3755	125	L15
Yarra Glen	3775	209	D16
Yarra Junction	3797	347	C14
Yarraman	3174	535	C5
Yarrambat	3091	201	G15
Yarraville	3013	367	C19
Yellingbo	3139	387	J11
Yering	3770	252	H17
Yuroke	3063	192	F1

STREET INDEX

[ABBREVIATIONS USED IN THE STREET INDEX]

ABBREVIATIONS FOR DESIGNATIONS

Alley	al
Approach	app
Arcade	arc
Avenue	av
Bend	bnd
Boulevard	bvd
Bowl	bl
Brace	br
Brae	br
Break	brk
Brook	brk
Broadway	bwy
Brow	brw
Bypass	bps
Centre	ctr
Chase	ch
Circle	cir
Circuit	cct
Circus	crc
Close	cl
Common	cmn
Concourse	cnc
Copse	cps
Corner	cnr
Corso	cso
Court	ct
Courtyard	cyd
Cove	cov
Crescent	cr
Crest	cst
Cross	cs
Crossing	csg
Curve	cve
Dale	dle
Down/s	dn
Drive	dr
Driveway	dwy
East	e
Edge	edg
Elbow	elb
End	end
Entrance	ent
Esplanade	esp
Expressway	exp
Fairway	fy
Freeway	fwy
Frontage	fr
Garden/s	gdn
Gate/s	gte
Gateway	gwy
Glade	gld
Glen	gln
Grange	gra
Green	grn
Grove	gr
Grovet	gr
Haven	hvn
Heights	hts
Highway	hwy
Hill	hill
Junction	jnc
Key	key
Lane	la
Link	lk
Loop	lp
Mall	ml
Mead	md
Meander	mdr
Mews	mw
Motorway	mwy
Nook	nk
North	n
Outlook	out
Parade	pde
Park	pk
Parkway	pky
Pass	ps
Pathway	pwy
Place	pl
Plaza	plz
Pocket	pkt
Point/Port	pt
Promenade	prm
Quadrant	qd
Quay/s	qy
Ramble	ra
Reach	rch
Reserve	res
Rest	rst
Retreat	rt
Return	rtn
Ridge	rdg
Rise	ri
Road	rd
Roadway	rdy
Route	rte
Row	row
Serviceway	swy
South	s
Square	sq
Strand	sd
Street	st
Tarn	tn
Terrace	tce
Tollway	twy
Top	top
Tor	tor
Track	tr
Trail	trl
Turn	trn
Underpass	ups
Vale	va
View	vw
Vista	vst
Walk	wk
Walkway	wky
Way	wy
West	w
Wynd	wyn

ABBREVIATIONS FOR SUBURB NAMES

Where it has been necessary to abbreviate the suburb names in the street index the following conventions have been used.
If any difficulty is experienced with the suburban names refer to the SUBURBS and LOCALITIES index.

Airport	Aprt
Basin	Bsn
Bay	B
Beach	Bch
Bridge	Br
Brook	Brk
Central	Ctrl
Chase	Ch
Corner	Cnr
Creek	Ck
Crossing	Csg
Down/s	Dn
East	E
Field/s	Fd
Flat	Fl
Forest	Frst
Garden/s	Gdn
Grove	Gr
Gully	Gly
Harbor/our	Hbr
Head/s	Hd
Headland	Hd
Heights	Ht
Hill/s	Hl
Island	I
Junction	Jctn
Lagoon	Lgn
Lakes	L
Lodge	Ldg
Lookout	Lkt
Lower	Lr
Meadows/s	Mdw
Mount	Mt
Mountain/s	Mtn
North	N
Paradise	Pdse
Park	Pk
Plain/s	Pl
Plateau	Plat
Pocket	Pkt
Point/Port	Pt
Range	Rge
Reach	Rch
Reserve	Res
Ridge	Rdg
River	R
Rocks	Rks
Saint	St
South	S
Terminal	Term
University	Uni
Upper	Up
Valley	Vy
Vale	Va
Village	Vill
Waters	Wtr
West	W

NON-STANDARD ABBREVIATIONS FOR SUBURB NAMES

Bacchus Marsh	Bacchus Msh
Beaconsfield Upper	Beaconsfld Up
Caroline Springs	Caroline Spr
Kangaroo Ground	Kangaroo Grnd
Launching Place	Launching Pl
Melbourne Airport	Melb Airport
Moonee Ponds	Moonee Pnd
Nar Nar Goon	Nr Nr Goon
Nar Nar Goon North	Nr Nr Goon N
Narre Warren East	Nar Warrn E
Narre Warren North	Nar Warrn N
Narre Warren South	Nar Warrn S
Port Melbourne	Port Melb
Strathmore Heights	Strathmr Ht
Templestowe Lower	Templstw Lr
Upper Ferntree Gully	Up Fntree Gly
Williamstown North	Williamstn N

SPECIAL NOTE
The LANES shown in *italics* in the street index are not chartered on the street maps.
For reasons of clarity it is not practical to show them.

A

AANENSEN
ct. Montmorency 287 A11
AARAN
cl. Endeavour Hl 537 G1
AARON
pl. Kilsyth 381 B8
ABASSIA
st. Balwyn N 374 A8
ABBEY
al. Greenvale..........192 J18
cl. Kings Park 319 C2
ct. Frankston S.......628 C15
ct. Gladstone Pk......237 B20
ct. Grovedale 706 C9
ct. Noble Park.........534 K7
ct. Point Cook.........450 F6
ct. Ringwood 379 A3
ct. Wantirna............422 B11
la. McCrae..............685 A14
mw. Eltham 288 A7
pl. Melton W...........226 D17
rd. Nar Warrn S.......578 J3
wk. Vermont 421 K5
ABBEY DALE
ct. Berwick..............554 L19
ABBEYDALE
ct. Mulgrave 501 B5
ABBEYGATE
ct. Frankston...........628 B8
st. Altona North.......410 D7
st. Oakleigh.............457 K15
ABBIN
av. Bentleigh E.........496 G5
rd. Rowville.............502 H2
ABBINGTON
cr. Caroline Spr 318 D4
dr. Truganina 405 F13
ABBOT
ct. Albanvale...........319 E4
ct. Glen Waverley 459 H8
gr. Abbotsford...........20 C11
gr. Clifton Hill 20 F4
st. Abbotsford...........20 D12
ABBOTSFORD
av. Malvern East 457 F3
gr. Ivanhoe..............328 A14
st. Abbotsford...........20 F16
st. N Melbourne 17 A20
st. N Melbourne 34 L20
st. Sorrento 678 K15
st. W Melbourne 17 A19
ABBOTT
ct. Craigieburn 150 C14
ct. Sunbury..............142 J4
ct. Taylors Lakes.....275 J3
rd. Hallam 537 E18
st. Alphington 327 H14
st. Balwyn N 374 B3
st. Dandenong 535 J9
st. Sandringham 494 L13
st. Sandringham 495 A13
st. Spotswood 366 G19
ABBOTTS
rd. Dandenong S 550 B9
rd. Lyndhurst 550 B9
ABBOTTSWOOD
cl. Dingley Village ...533 B9
A'BECKETT
cl. Mt Martha..........656 C15
la. Melbourne 2 A2
rd. Beaconsfld Up....542 J17
rd. Beaconsfld Up....556 K1
rd. Nar Warrn N.......539 E4
rd. Officer...............542 K20
st. Coburg 281 D19
st. Kew...................371 J8
st. Melbourne 1 F2
st. Melbourne 23 J4
st. Prahran..............415 B10
st. St Kilda E 414 K17
st. Seaford..............599 L7
ABELIA
ct. Bundoora............284 K5
ct. Hillside...............274 D3
ct. Meadow Ht 193 K19
ct. Sunbury..............142 G10
ri. Narre Warren 539 D19
st. Doncaster E 332 D19
st. Forest Hill 376 J20
st. Nunawading.......376 J20
wy. Hoppers Csg 405 D14
ABERCAIRN
ct. Deer Park...........318 J11
dr. Nar Warrn S.......552 H18
ABERCARN
av. Craigieburn 194 G4
ABERCORN
av. Ivanhoe.............327 K14
ABERCROMBIE
st. Balwyn..............372 K10
st. Oakleigh S..........497 H5
ABERCROMBY
rd. Blackburn S 419 G2
ABERDEEN
av. Greenvale...........237 D1
cr. Essendon...........323 F8
ct. Epping 198 A18
ct. Narre Warren 539 B18
ct. Wheelers Hill.......460 G14
dr. Dandenong N......501 F13
dr. Lilydale 338 J9
gr. Northcote...........326 F16
hts. Pakenham...........584 K1
rd. Altona 408 F15
rd. Blackburn S 375 E20
rd. Blackburn S 419 E2
rd. Macleod.............285 A15
rd. Prahran................32 K20
rd. Prahran..............414 L10
rd. Prahran..............415 A11
rd. Sandringham 495 K16
st. Aberfeldie...........323 F10
st. Brunswick...........325 J13
st. Geelong West.....702 A6
st. Hawthorn E........372 E20
st. Herne Hill............702 B6
st. Manifold Ht.........702 B6
st. Newtown 702 B6
st. Pascoe Vale S 324 L5
st. Reservoir 283 D4
ABERFELDIE
st. Aberfeldie...........323 G11
st. Moonee Pnd 323 G11
ABERGELDIE
av. Bentleigh............456 F18
av. McKinnon 456 F18
ABERSHAM
ct. Eltham 288 B5
ABEY
rd. Melton S 269 D9
ABINGER
ct. Gladstone Pk......237 C19
pl. Richmond............26 J12
st. Richmond............26 G12
ABLETT
ct. Frankston S.......627 G17
ABOR
ct. Frankston...........600 E19
pl. Melton W...........225 L15
ABOYNE
ct. Mulgrave 501 H5
ABRAHAM
dr. Croydon.............380 J1
ABRAHAMS
ct. Burwood.............419 B7
tr. Lysterfield..........505 G4
ABRAM
ct. Frankston S.......627 H17
ABREHART
rd. Pakenham..........585 K1
st. Eumemmerring ..537 C15
ABRUZZO
cr. Thomastown......241 B18
ACACIA
av. Blackburn 375 G17
av. Kilsyth 381 L6
av. Mentone 531 H8
av. Oakleigh S..........458 A17
av. Seaholme...........409 H18
av. Upwey 466 B9
av. Watsonia 285 C8
cl. Meadow Ht 237 J1
cl. Sunshine W 364 A7
cr. Emerald 510 E5
cr. Melton S 268 G6
cr. Patterson L 573 J8
ct. Briar Hill..............286 L6
ct. Bundoora............284 H6
ct. Croydon S...........379 F11
ct. Delahey..............275 C9
ct. Frankston............628 C4
ct. Gisborne...............78 K9
ct. Pakenham...........584 K9
ct. Ringwood 378 C11
ct. Sunbury..............143 J6
ct. W Footscray........366 F10
ct. Wyndham Va 446 E12
gr. Glen Waverley 420 B14
gr. Pascoe Vale S 324 E5
la. Waurn Ponds 705 D16
pl. Burwood.............418 C5
rd. Ferntree Gly 464 H8
rd. Hurstbridge.........202 K11
rd. Up Fntree Gly 464 H8
rd. Up Fntree Gly 464 H9
st. Box Hill 374 J19
st. Camberwell..........417 G5
st. Carnegie 456 L5
st. Doncaster E 331 G20
st. Doveton..............536 L8
st. Doveton..............537 A8
st. Elsternwick 454 K2
st. Glenroy...............280 C7
st. Mt Martha...........656 F8
st. St Albans 319 F9
st. Thomastown.......241 F14
st. Torquay 711 H11
wyn.Langwarrin 601 J20
ACADEMY
av. Reservoir 282 F13
av. Wheelers Hill......460 D14
dr. Broadmeadows ..238 J12
dr. The Basin............425 B7
ACCESS
rd. Mont Albert N.....374 D11
ACCRA
st. Keysborough 534 K13
ACER
cl. Broadmeadows ..237 L12
st. Doveton..............536 K8
tce. Hoppers Csg 405 F16
ACFOLD
ct. St Albans 275 G17
ACHERON
av. Camberwell.........416 L6
av. Camberwell.........417 A6
av. Mt Eliza..............625 J20
av. Reservoir 283 D13
cl. Hallam 538 C19
cr. Eltham 287 A4
cr. Werribee.............448 C19
ct. Hampton E..........496 B10
ct. Sunbury..............143 C11
st. Doncaster 374 G2
st. Epping 197 G19
st. Tootgarook 698 C5
wy. E Warburton 306 B3
wy. E Warburton 306 E17
wy. Warburton 306 B3
wy. Warburton 306 D17
ACHESON
pl. Coburg N 281 J15
ACHILLES
ct. Lilydale 338 J1
st. Heidelberg W 284 C18
ACLAND
cl. Mulgrave 501 F5
ct. Bundoora............285 D1
ct. Noble Park..........535 B6
st. Albanvale 319 D5
st. St Kilda 414 A15
st. St Kilda 414 B18
st. South Yarra..........31 H4
st. South Yarra.........414 D2
ACLARE
st. Cockatoo 511 H11
ACMENA
ct. Mill Park 243 B8
ACOL
ct. Mulgrave 501 A5
ACORN
ct. Nar Warrn S.......553 E18
ct. Oakleigh S..........498 B9
wy. Baxter................628 D20
ACRE
ct. Narre Warren 538 K14
pl. Malvern 415 L10
ri. Hampton Pk.........552 D12
ACTOAL
dr. Montrose 381 K11
ACTON
cl. Frankston............628 F4
ct. Newcomb 704 B18
pl. Wyndham Va 446 G13
st. Mt Waverley.........458 J8
st. Seddon 367 A12
ACUBA
cl. St Albans 275 J18
ACUNHA
st. Mt Eliza..............641 H3
ACWORTH
ct. Greensborough ..244 E15
ADA
ct. Narre Warren 553 C12
ct. Noble Park..........535 D3
ct. Sunshine W 364 A5
st. Camberwell..........417 G5
st. Doncaster 374 J2
st. Glen Waverley 460 B5
st. Preston 282 C20
st. Rowville...............503 C4
ADAIR
ct. Wantirna.............422 B12
pl. Sunshine W 364 C6
ADALEIGH
ct. Clayton 459 C20
st. Yarraville.............366 H14
ADAM
av. Hallam 537 G14
av. Wheelers Hill.......461 C12
cl. Rowville..............463 K15
cr. Montmorency 287 B10
cr. Roxburgh Pk......194 A9
ct. Cranbourne W....577 F19
ct. Gladstone Pk......237 E18
ct. Pakenham...........584 F2
ct. Reservoir 282 B2
ct. Ringwood N........378 A6
ct. Springvale S........534 A6
ct. View Bank...........285 J19
ct. Werribee.............446 L11
ct. Werribee.............447 A11
dr. Mill Park 243 E6
st. Bentleigh.............455 J19
st. Burnley 371 A20
st. Nunawading........376 J11
st. Rye......................696 E5
wy. Kurunjang 226 G13
ADAMS
av. Rosebud 684 F16
cl. Croydon...............380 F1
ct. Dandenong N......501 J9
ct. E Geelong 703 J8
ct. Sunbury..............143 A16
la. Berwick...............554 D8
la. Mt Evelyn............339 E15
la. Yarra Jctn 347 B16
pl. Glen Waverley 420 B19
pl. Mt Evelyn............338 L14
pl. Port Melb, off Dow St...........412 L5
pl. Geelong, off Little Ryrie St 703 B9
st. Alphington 327 K20
st. Murrumbeena 457 D12
st. Preston 327 E7
st. St Albans 319 F5
st. South Yarra...........31 B7
st. South Yarra.........414 A3
ADAMSON
dr. Endeavour Hl 537 A2
rd. Beaconsfield 554 L16
st. Braybrook...........366 A3
st. Brighton..............454 K19
st. Heidelberg 328 J4
ADARE
cl. Mulgrave 500 L4
cl. Mulgrave 501 A4
pl. Werribee.............447 E13
ri. Roxburgh Pk.......193 K13
ADDERLEY
st. Docklands.............23 C5
st. W Melbourne 23 A2
ADDICOTT
st. Frankston............599 G19
ADDIS
st. Geelong West.....702 D6
ADDISON
ct. Mulgrave 501 H5
pl. Seabrook 450 L5
st. Elwood 454 C3
st. Moonee Pnd 324 E15
wy. Roxburgh Pk......194 A13
ADDLINGTON
ct. Nar Warrn S.......552 K20
ADECROFT
ct. Eltham 288 A8
ADELA
ct. Mulgrave 501 F5
ct. Mulgrave 501 G5
ADELAIDE
av. Kallista................467 C1
av. Mt Waverley.......458 H1
bvd. Gowanbrae 279 E7
cl. Berwick...............553 G3
st. Albion 364 J1
st. Armadale 415 J11
st. Ascot Vale...........324 F16
st. Blairgowrie..........696 C1
st. Cremorne 26 D20
st. Dandenong 535 G2
st. Footscray 367 A7
st. Highton...............701 H17
st. McKinnon 456 D17
st. Mornington..........640 C19
st. Murrumbeena 457 B5
st. Pascoe Vale 280 B15
st. St Albans 319 J3
st. Wantirna S..........422 K16
ADELE
av. Ferntree Gly 463 G5
cl. Narre Warren 538 L18
cl. Wheelers Hill.......461 D12
ct. Hoppers Csg 449 B1
ct. Ringwood 379 A2
ct. Rye......................696 K5
st. Vermont 377 G20
ADELIE
ct. Roxburgh Pk......193 J15
ADELINE
ct. Deer Park...........318 L17
st. Greensborough ..285 J6
st. Preston 326 J4
st. Williamstn N 410 L13
ADELLA
ct. Moolap 704 L18
pl. Templestowe 332 A10
ADELLE
ct. Carrum Downs ...600 K3
ct. Doncaster 330 L18
ADELONG
ct. Berwick...............553 H2
ct. Dandenong N......502 C17
ct. Grovedale 706 D10
ct. Patterson L 573 K9
ADELYN
av. Donvale 376 J7
ADEN
ct. Thomastown.......240 K11
ct. Tootgarook 698 C9
pl. Frankston............600 J15
ADENEY
av. Kew...................372 E10
av. Balwyn N 374 B7
st. Yarraville.............366 D15
ADENEYS
rd. Cannons Creek...649 L5
ADENMORE
ct. Eltham 287 L10
ADIB
ct. Frankston N 600 E11
ADINA
av. Aspendale 546 F4
cl. Bayswater N.......379 L15
cl. Greensborough ..286 H1
ct. Frankston............600 B19
ct. Kurunjang 227 A15
ct. Sunshine W 364 F7
ct. Tullamarine.........278 H9
ct. Yallambie 286 C12
pl. Delahey...............275 B9
pl. Mornington..........641 C15
st. Blackburn N 375 J9
st. Rye......................697 A9
ADIOS
pl. Keilor Dn............275 H11
ADLER
ct. Keilor Dn............276 B15
gr. Coburg N 281 C12
ADLEY
ct. Vermont S 420 G10
pl. Hampton Pk.......551 G4
ADLIN
pl. Roxburgh Pk......194 A12
ADMANS
av. Seaford..............599 E2
st. Pt Lonsdale.........710 G6
ADMIRAL
av. Craigieburn 150 C7
ct. Highton...............701 H10
ct. Lilydale 338 J1
pl. Geelong 703 D9
st. Seddon 367 D10
ADMIRALA
cr. Dandenong N......502 B18
ADMIRALS
cr. Taylors Lakes.....275 G9
ct. Frankston............628 E7
qy. Patterson L 573 J5
ADNETTE
ct. Coburg N 282 B14
ADOBE
ct. Vermont 421 J3
ADOLPH
st. Cremorne 26 D17
ADOLPHSON
av. Ringwood N.......378 B6
ADORI
ct. St Helena 244 K18
ADRIAN
av. Blackburn S 419 L6
av. Vermont S 420 G8
ct. Braybrook...........366 A4
ct. Bundoora............284 H5
ct. Gladstone Pk......237 B18
ct. Heathmont..........378 F18
pl. Rowville..............502 L5
pl. Rowville..............503 A5
rd. Campbellfield 239 E7
ri. Nar Warrn N.......538 B8
st. Bentleigh E..........496 K6
st. Chadstone...........458 C5
st. Cranbourne E 604 K11
st. Glen Iris 417 E10
st. Springvale............500 A16
ADRIENNE
cl. Keilor Park 277 K13
cr. Mt Waverley.......458 H9
ct. Millgrove.............348 F1
ADVANTAGE
dr. Dandenong S 550 F3
rd. Highett...............495 L15

ADZAR
rd. Newcomb....704 A14
AENONE
av. Noble Park....534 F5
AEROS
st. Whittington....704 F19
AFFINITY
cl. Mordialloc....532 D16
AFFLECK
st. South Yarra....31 J15
st. South Yarra....414 E7
wy. Rowville....503 H1
AFFRA
pl. Hampton Pk....551 D4
AFTON
ct. Glen Waverley....460 A10
st. Aberfeldie....323 B10
st. Essendon W....323 B10
st. Research....246 F20
wy. Aspendale....546 D6
AFZAN
ct. Torquay....712 H2
AGANA
av. Noble Park....534 K7
AGATHA
st. Essendon....324 C8
AGATHEA
ct. Frankston N....600 E8
AGE
st. Cheltenham....497 D17
AGG
st. Newport....410 H7
st. Thornbury....327 F11
AGNES
av. Balwyn N....373 L3
av. Blairgowrie....679 G19
ct. Glen Waverley....460 B9
ct. Hillside....274 G2
ct. Kurunjang....227 E11
ct. Langwarrin....629 G7
st. Beaumaris....530 A9
st. Bentleigh E....456 H20
st. E Melbourne....25 D10
st. Mont Albert....374 F15
st. Noble Park....534 F2
st. St Albans....319 F2
st. Thornbury....326 L11
st. Yarraville....367 A13
AGNEW
st. Blackburn S....375 D20
st. Blackburn S....419 D1
st. Brighton East....455 C17
AGONIS
ct. Mill Park....243 C10
ct. Mt Martha....656 G7
ct. Rosebud....684 J14
dr. Taylors Lakes....276 C6
st. Doveton....536 J8
AGORA
bvd. Ferntree Gly....423 L16
AGRA
st. Mitcham....377 B15
AGRICULTURAL
pl. Geelong....703 F10
A H CAPP SCENIC
dr. Bundoora....284 B4
A'HERN
pl. Avondale Ht....322 E16
AHERN
rd. Pakenham....584 L4
st. Noble Park N....501 D10
AHMET
pl. Hillside....274 F3
AIDA
ct. Doncaster E....332 G8
A I F
st. Balwyn....373 E10
AIKMAN
cr. Chadstone....458 A6
AIKSHAW
cl. Hillside....232 D19
AILEEN
av. Caulfield S....455 E8
av. Heidelberg W....284 F16
av. Montrose....382 B11
ct. Hallam....552 C1
AILSA
av. Malvern East....416 K19
ct. Balwyn N....374 A1
ct. Ringwood....379 B3
ct. Sunbury....144 F12
gr. Ivanhoe....328 A12
st. Ascot Vale....324 F19
st. Box Hill S....419 C3
st. Dandenong N....501 L16
st. Keilor....277 D12
st. Laverton....407 A19
st. Mt Martha....655 L16
st.s, Altona Mdw....451 A1

AIMEE
ct. Mornington....657 C3
pl. Rowville....463 A15
AINSDALE
av. Wantirna....422 E8
ct. Sunbury....144 E14
AINSLEIGH
ct. Cranbourne....578 C17
ct. Narre Warren....538 J14
AINSLEY
av. Noble Park....534 K6
AINSLIE
av. Grovedale....706 D11
dr. Wheelers Hill....460 J14
rd. Campbellfield....239 B1
AINSLIE PARK
av. Croydon....379 G3
AINSWORTH
ct. Roxburgh Pk....193 K13
rd. Chum Creek....212 H5
st. Sunshine W....364 H3
AINTREE
av. Doncaster E....376 D1
av. Mulgrave....500 J3
av. Point Cook....450 J9
ct. Greensborough....243 L20
ct. Noble Park N....501 A8
rd. Glen Iris....416 D12
st. Brunswick E....326 A14
st. Mooroolbark....337 B17
AINWICK
cr. Thomastown....240 L11
AIRD
ct. Wonga Park....291 G20
st. Camberwell....416 L2
st. Camberwell....417 A2
st. Ringwood....378 F11
AIRDRIE
ct. Templstw Lr....330 L9
mw. Greenvale....192 J19
rd. Caulfield N....415 F20
AIRDS
rd. Templstw Lr....330 D9
AIREDALE
av. Hawthorn E....416 C4
wy. Rowville....503 F1
AIREY
av. Manifold Ht....702 C5
AIRLEY
ct. Meadow Ht....237 J5
rd. Glen Iris....417 C11
AIRLIE
av. Dandenong....535 G3
av. Prahran....415 B12
ct. Doncaster E....331 J16
ct. Langwarrin....601 L20
ct. Rowville....463 G17
gr. Seaford....573 F16
rd. Healesville....257 H6
rd. Montmorency....286 F12
st. Brighton....454 J7
st. South Yarra....31 J3
st. South Yarra....414 E2
AIRPORT
dr. Melb Airport....235 K12
dr. Tullamarine....278 D8
rd. Mt Duneed....705 J20
AIRSIDE
rd. Melb Airport....235 H11
rd. Melb Airport....235 J10
AIRWAYS
st. Melb Airport....235 A11
AISBETT
av. Camberwell....417 J8
av. Wantirna S....422 K12
AISHA
cr. Dingley Village....533 D2
AITCHISON
av. Ashburton....417 E14
pl. Geelong, off Fenwick St....702 L7
AITKEN
av. Hoppers Csg....449 A2
bvd. Craigieburn....149 E16
cl. Caroline Spr....318 C8
ct. Ferntree Gly....463 H3
dr. Delahey....275 A12
la. Gruyere....298 A10
pl. Gladstone Pk....236 L20
rd. Seville....386 C8
rd. Wandin East....386 C8
st. Clifton Hill....20 G7
st. Gisborne....78 L16
st. Gisborne....79 A8
st. Sunbury....143 K14
st. W Footscray....366 H9
st. Williamstown....411 G15
AJANA
ct. Dandenong N....501 G13
ct. Wheelers Hill....460 H14

la. Frankston S....627 C18
st. Balwyn N....374 A8
AJAX
cl. Keilor Dn....275 L14
ct. Heidelberg W....284 B19
ct. Lilydale....338 J2
ct. Mill Park....242 J12
dr. Wheelers Hill....461 A12
pl. Cranbourne W....577 F17
rd. Altona....408 D14
st. Balwyn N....373 G1
AKARANA
dr. Lilydale....338 F12
rd. Chirnside Pk....337 J6
AKEROA
av. Brunswick E....326 A12
AKERS
ct. Darley....221 H3
AKIMA
cl. Greensborough....244 A17
tce. Mooroolbark....337 E16
AKITA
ct. Berwick....554 D20
ct. Keysborough....534 K14
AKMA
ct. Taylors Lakes....275 L8
AKOONAH
cl. Donvale....332 J15
ct. Burnside....318 H9
AKORA
ct. Frankston....600 H15
AKRANA
ct. Vermont S....421 C14
AKRON
st. Ferntree Gly....424 B19
AKUNA
av. Notting Hill....459 H14
ct. Knoxfield....463 B4
dr. Williamstn N....410 G11
st. Altona....408 K17
st. Warneet....649 G11
ALABAKIS
la. Werribee S....488 K2
ALABAMA
cl. Hoppers Csg....405 C13
ALAIN
av. S Morang....198 J13
ALAMANDA
wy. Cranbourne N....578 J11
ALAMAR
av. Glen Huntly....456 B6
ALAMEDA
av. Maribyrnong....323 C15
av. Mornington....656 F1
pl. Parkdale....531 E13
st. Parkdale....531 E13
ALAMEIN
av. Ashburton....417 F17
av. Croydon....380 K2
av. Kilsyth....380 K2
rd. Heidelberg W....284 B20
st. Noble Park....500 E16
ALAMO
cl. Highton....701 D17
rd. Reservoir....282 D13
ALAN
ct. Alphington....327 J13
ct. Bundoora....285 B2
ct. Noble Park N....501 D8
gr. Woori Yallock....344 F13
pl. Rowville....503 A6
pl. Warrandyte....333 D1
rd. Carrum Downs....574 C17
st. Blackburn S....419 L1
st. Box Hill N....375 C8
st. Croydon....379 L7
st. Kings Park....275 E17
ALANA
ct. Wantirna S....421 L18
ALANAH
pl. Ivanhoe....328 F9
ALANBRAE
tce. Attwood....236 L10
tce. Attwood....237 A10
ALANDALE
av. Balwyn....373 H9
ct. Blackburn....375 L18
rd. Blackburn....375 L18
rd. Eaglemont....328 G11
st. Surrey Hills....418 D3
ALASKA
ct. Werribee....446 H18
ALASTAIR
ct. Kilsyth....381 D3
ct. Surrey Hills....373 L20
dr. Berwick....540 A20
ALASTER
ct. Hampton Pk....551 D11
ALATHEA
ct. Rye....697 E4

ALAWA
ct. Keilor Dn....275 H10
ALAWARA
ct. Burwood E....419 F10
dr. Mooroolbark....337 B15
ALAWARRA
ct. Ringwood N....378 E3
ALBA
ct. Mill Park....243 C8
st. Frankston N....600 E9
wk. Deer Park....319 F12
ALBAN
st. Montmorency....286 J12
st. Richmond....26 F11
ALBANY
av. Point Cook....450 E5
cl. Ringwood N....378 D5
cr. Aspendale....546 E6
cr. Surrey Hills....374 B17
ct. Campbellfield....239 G15
ct. Caulfield N....415 B20
ct. Endeavour Hl....536 L2
ct. Endeavour Hl....537 A2
ct. Macleod....285 J11
ct. Noble Park N....501 D16
ct. Sorrento....678 K9
ct. Taylors Lakes....275 F1
ct. Wantirna....422 H8
ct. Werribee....447 F2
dr. Mulgrave....500 G5
pl. Bulleen....329 G13
pl. Frankston S....627 F9
pl. Mt Martha....656 D8
rd. Oakleigh E....458 H12
rd. Oakleigh E....458 J12
rd. Toorak....415 F6
st. Tullamarine....278 G3
wy. Doncaster E....332 C14
wy. Mornington....641 D19
ALBATROSS
av. Mt Eliza....641 H2
av. Werribee....447 L10
cl. Blind Bight....650 C9
ct. Cannons Creek....649 C8
ct. Keilor....276 K13
dr. Rowville....463 H11
ALBEMARLE
ct. Glen Iris....417 J9
dr. Sunbury....142 L1
st. Williamstn N....410 C11
ALBENCA
st. Cheltenham....531 E7
st. Mentone....531 E7
ALBENS
ct. Narre Warren....553 C1
ALBER
rd. Beaconsfld Up....542 B6
ALBERMARLE
st. Kensington....34 C12
ALBERT
av. Boronia....424 F12
av. Oakleigh....457 L10
av. Rye....696 K2
av. Springvale....499 H15
cr. Mulgrave....499 L4
cr. St Albans....320 A3
cr. Surrey Hills....374 C17
ct. Dromana....685 L10
ct. Epping....197 G14
ct. Frankston....600 B18
ct. Greensborough....243 L20
ct. Greensborough....285 L1
dr. Melton S....268 B12
la. E Melbourne....25 J3
pl. Dingley Village....532 K7
pl. Fitzroy....19 E17
pl. Hoppers Csg....405 A14
pl. S Melbourne....29 H2
pl. Burnley, off Bendigo St....371 C18
rd. Badger Creek....257 J10
rd. Carnegie....456 G12
rd. Clematis....508 J2
rd. Emerald....509 J3
rd. Hallam....537 H15
rd. Healesville....258 A9
rd. Lilydale....338 H7
rd. Melbourne....30 H6
rd. Melbourne....413 K2
rd. N Warrandyte....289 H14
rd. S Melbourne....30 A11
rd. S Melbourne....30 D9
rd. S Melbourne....30 H6
rd. S Melbourne....413 F6
rd. Sunbury....113 D17
rd. Sydenham....274 H2
st. Abbotsford....26 G3
st. Bayswater....423 D4
st. Blackburn....375 K15
st. Brighton....454 F18
st. Brunswick....325 B13
st. Brunswick E....325 L14

st. Brunswick E....326 B14
st. Brunswick W....325 A13
st. Caulfield N....415 H18
st. Coburg N....281 H12
st. Dandenong S....535 K14
st. Darley....221 L6
st. Darley....222 B7
st. E Melbourne....24 L3
st. E Melbourne....25 A3
st. Fawkner....281 H12
st. Footscray....367 E11
st. Geelong West....702 D4
st. Hawthorn E....372 E17
st. Highett....496 B14
st. Malvern East....456 L1
st. Mitcham....377 B13
st. Moolap....704 K16
st. Moonee Pnd....324 B11
st. Mordialloc....531 K18
st. Mornington....640 D14
st. Mt Waverley....459 A3
st. Niddrie....322 L4
st. Northcote....327 A20
st. Oak Park....280 C12
st. Pt Lonsdale....710 F5
st. Port Melb....412 H4
st. Preston....327 E6
st. Reservoir....283 G16
st. Richmond....26 F19
st. Ringwood....378 B14
st. St Kilda....414 B17
st. Seddon....367 E11
st. Sunshine N....321 G18
st. Surrey Hills....417 H2
st. Templestowe....331 J7
st. Up Fntree Gly....465 B8
st. Williamstown....411 D11
st. Windsor....414 E12
tce. Belmont....702 C16
ALBERTA
av. Box Hill N....375 D10
st. W Footscray....366 D7
wy. Berwick....553 G13
ALBERT HILL
rd. Lilydale....337 K7
ALBERTINE
cr. Delahey....275 E9
ALBERT JONES
ct. Eaglemont....328 J10
ALBERTON
av. Roxburgh Pk....194 E6
rd. Selby....467 C16
ALBERT ROAD
dr. Albert Park....30 D9
dr.s, Albert Park....30 B11
ALBION
al. Melbourne....2 D11
al. Melbourne....24 D6
cr. Ardeer....320 D16
cr. Greensborough....244 H19
ct. Hoppers Csg....405 C12
ct. Springvale S....534 B5
pl. Mulgrave....501 H2
rd. Ashburton....417 A14
rd. Box Hill....374 L17
rd. Glen Iris....417 A14
st. Balaclava....414 G20
st. Brunswick....325 F10
st. Brunswick E....325 F10
st. Brunswick W....324 E8
st. Caulfield S....455 H11
st. Essendon....324 E8
st. Kingsville....366 G13
st. South Yarra....31 J12
st. South Yarra....32 A13
st. South Yarra....414 E6
st. Surrey Hills....373 H20
st. Surrey Hills....417 H1
ALBRECHT
av. Berwick....554 F18
ALBURNUM
cr. Templstw Lr....330 L14
ALBURY
av. Altona....407 H15
ct. Croydon N....336 A14
rd. Balwyn N....373 F6
st. Albion....320 J19
ALBYN
cl. Pakenham....584 H3
ct. Mill Park....242 F10
ALBYS
la. Maddingley....263 A15
ALCALA
av. Malvern East....457 F1
ALCHERINGA
cr. Gisborne....78 J20
ALCHESTER
cr. Boronia....424 H5
ct. Thomastown....240 J10
ALCOCK
st. Reservoir....240 C20

ALCON
ct. Langwarrin 629 B2
ct. Vermont 377 D20
ALCOTT
pl. Delahey 275 E15
ALDA
ct. Wheelers Hill 460 F17
ALDBROUGH
rd. Craigieburn 194 H1
ALDEN
ct. Cheltenham 531 E3
st. Sunshine W 364 D2
ALDER
ct. Frankston N 600 F7
ct. Gowanbrae 279 E4
ct. Mill Park 242 D11
ct. Pk Orchards 377 H1
st. Burwood 418 B8
st. Caulfield S 455 F8
st. Langwarrin 628 K1
ALDERBROOK
av. Mulgrave 501 G2
ALDERCRESS
ct. Craigieburn 150 B20
ALDERFORD
ct. Berwick 554 B1
dr. Wantirna 422 G15
ALDERGATE
cr. Kings Park 319 C1
ct. Epping 198 A17
ALDERLEY
ct. Nar Warrn S 579 A5
ct. Chirnside Pk, off Little Chipping Dr. 336 K6
ALDERMAN
cl. Sunbury 142 H14
ALDERNEY
rd. Springvale S 534 C6
ALDERSHOT
dr. Keilor Dn 276 D13
rd. Langwarrin 629 B9
ALDINGA
st. Blackburn S 419 D4
ALDOUS
ct. Epping 197 L20
ALDREN
pl. Bundoora 242 E18
ALDRIDGE
ct. Hampton Pk 552 C8
dr. Sunbury 143 C3
st. Endeavour Hl 536 K3
ALDRIN
ct. Whittington 704 C20
dr. Mt Waverley 419 F12
ALEC
cr. Fawkner 281 J1
ct. View Bank 285 H19
st. Croydon 379 E2
st. Tecoma 466 C11
ALEJA
ct. Noble Park 534 E5
ALEK
ct. Forest Hill 420 B7
ALEMA
ct. Nar Warrn S 552 G15
ALEPPO
cr. Frankston N 600 C8
ALERN
ct. Nunawading 376 K12
ALEX
av. Moorabbin 497 C10
av. Wheelers Hill 461 C13
ct. Greensborough 286 C10
ct. Mooroolbark 337 E17
ALEXANDER
av. Coburg N 281 J17
av. Dandenong 535 E5
av. Mornington 640 E16
av. Oakleigh E 458 K14
av. Rye 696 G2
av. Thomastown 241 C14
av. Upwey 466 A10
av. Upwey 466 A11
av. Upwey 466 A9
cl. Delahey 275 B11
cr. Ferntree Gly 424 H18
cr. Frankston 600 E19
cr. Pt Lonsdale 710 D6
cr. Templstw Lr 330 D11
ct. Aspendale Gdn 546 L4
ct. Broadmeadows 238 E19
ct. Warranwood 334 L12
ct. Warranwood 335 A12
dr. Burwood 418 C11
la. Gisborne S 110 L19
la. Gisborne S 111 A19
pde. McCrae 685 E12
rd. Cockatoo 511 B9
rd. Healesville 213 F17
rd. Warrandyte 332 K3
st. Avondale Ht 322 D13
st. Bentleigh E 496 H1
st. Box Hill 374 J18
st. Brighton East 455 F14
st. Brunswick 325 C12
st. Clifton Hill 20 A9
st. Collingwood 20 A11
st. Cranbourne 578 C20
st. Emerald 469 H20
st. Hallam 537 G16
st. Hampton 495 C9
st. Mitcham 377 A13
st. Montmorency 286 F12
st. Mt Waverley 459 A1
st. Seddon 367 B10
ALEXANDRA
av. Canterbury 373 C16
av. Elsternwick 454 L6
av. Elsternwick 455 A7
av. Geelong 703 E7
av. Hoppers Csg 405 C12
av. Jan Juc 711 C17
av. Melbourne 4 H7
av. Melbourne 24 H13
av. Moonee Pnd 324 D13
av. South Yarra 31 J1
av. South Yarra 414 E1
av. Sunshine 365 E1
av. Toorak 415 B2
cr. Rye 697 K9
cr. Surrey Hills 374 B18
ct. Knoxfield 423 C19
ct. Woori Yallock 344 B13
pde. Clifton Hill 19 B8
pde. Collingwood 19 B8
pde. Fitzroy 19 B8
pde. Fitzroy N 19 A8
pde.e, Clifton Hill 20 D9
rd. Lilydale 338 K5
rd. Lilydale 339 A7
rd. Ringwood E 378 L14
rd. Ringwood E 379 A13
rd. Ringwood E 379 B13
st. Aspendale 546 F11
st. Greensborough 286 A6
st. Melton 226 K19
st. Pascoe Vale 280 J11
st. Reservoir 283 A14
st. St Kilda E 414 L17
st. St Kilda E 415 A14
st. South Yarra 31 J10
st. South Yarra 414 E6
st. Thornbury 326 L11
st. Up Fntree Gly 465 B9
ALEXANDRIA
wy. Werribee 448 D16
ALEXANDRINA
rd. Mt Martha 669 D1
ALEXINA
st. St Albans 320 B2
ALEXIS
ct. Wantirna S 421 L16
ALEX THOMSON
dr. Wandin East 386 B14
ALFA
ct. Ferntree Gly 463 K14
ct. Keilor Dn 276 A16
ct. Lalor 240 K8
ALFADA
st. Caulfield S 455 G10
ALFORD
av. Mooroolbark 337 K20
ri. Croydon N 335 L11
st. Brighton East 455 B17
st. Sunshine N 321 G19
ALFRED
av. Thomastown 241 J14
cl. Nar Warrn N 539 C10
cr. Fitzroy N 19 F1
ct. Bundoora 242 J20
gr. Emerald 470 C17
gr. Oakleigh E 458 J16
la. Prahran 31 E15
pl. Frankston 600 A19
pl. Melbourne 2 L15
pl. Melbourne 24 H7
pl. St Kilda 414 B16
pl. S Melbourne 29 L3
pl. Williamstown 411 G14
rd. Essendon 324 C3
rd. Glen Iris 417 J11
rd. Lilydale 338 H8
rd. Melton S 269 G15
rd. Werribee 446 E20
rd. Werribee 487 A3
sq. St Kilda 413 L16
st. Aspendale 531 L20
st. Balaclava 414 G17
st. Beaumaris 530 G5
st. Blackburn 376 A15
st. Boronia 424 D15
st. Caulfield 455 H4
st. Coburg 325 G5
st. E Geelong 703 G13
st. Fitzroy N 19 C1
st. Hawthorn 372 A16
st. Heidelberg Ht 328 F6
st. Highett 496 G14
st. Kew 372 E11
st. Mornington 640 D13
st. Noble Park 534 G2
st. N Melbourne 34 F7
st. Port Melb 412 J3
st. Prahran 31 H19
st. Prahran 414 D10
st. Preston 327 D6
st. Richmond 26 B13
st. Seddon 367 A10
st. Somerville 645 B14
st. S Melbourne 29 E3
st. Sunshine 365 G5
st. Templstw Lr 330 C10
st. Up Fntree Gly 465 B8
st. Wandin N 340 H15
ALFREDA
av. Bulleen 329 L17
av. Rosanna 329 A1
st. Preston 327 E1
st. Sandringham 495 G12
ALFRED DEAKIN
gr. Skye 575 H15
ALFRED LANGHORNE
cl. Seabrook 450 L6
ALFRICK
rd. Croydon 380 D6
ALFRIEDA
st. St Albans 320 B4
ALFRISTON
st. Elwood 454 F1
ALGONA
ct. St Helena 244 L18
ct. St Helena 245 A18
ALICE
ct. Hallam 537 K13
ct. Noble Park 534 L3
ct. Skye 575 H19
gr. Frankston 599 G20
st. Burwood E 419 K12
st. Cheltenham 531 G4
st. Clayton 458 H19
st. Coburg 325 D3
st. Croydon N 336 A18
st. Malvern 416 B12
st. Moolap 704 K17
st. Mt Evelyn 339 C17
st. Mt Martha 655 L11
st. Mt Waverley 419 A17
st. Sassafras 426 C15
st. Sunshine 365 G2
st. Yarraville 367 B14
ALICIA
ct. Frankston 628 E5
ct. Vermont S 420 J12
st. Hampton 494 L11
st. Hampton 495 A11
ALICK
rd. Tottenham 365 L12
ALICUDI
av. Frankston S 627 D17
ALIDA
ct. Ferntree Gly 464 D9
ALIKI
rd. Wantirna S 422 E19
ALIMAR
ct. Brighton 454 E10
ct. Burwood 419 B11
rd. Glen Waverley 460 G4
ALINGA
pl. Yallambie 286 B12
ALISON
av. Boronia 424 H13
av. Bulleen 330 A11
av. Rye 697 B16
av. Rye 697 B17
cl. Gladstone Pk 237 D19
cl. Pakenham 584 F2
ct. Carrum 573 E10
ct. Langwarrin 629 J5
pl. Aspendale Gdn 546 F1
pl. Attwood 237 D12
st. McKinnon 456 D17
st. Moorabbin 496 D11
st. Mt Waverley 458 L5
st. Thomastown 241 G15
ALISTAIR
cl. Keilor Dn 275 K14
ALISTER
st. Fitzroy N 326 C16
ALIWAL
st. W Footscray 366 D9
ALKEMADE
dr. Melton 268 F1
ALKIRA
cl. Clarinda 498 C7
cl. Wyndham Va 446 H14
ct. Heathmont 379 F19
ct. Patterson L 573 K5
ct. Wantirna 422 B12
ALLA
pl. Mt Eliza 626 J15
pl. Scoresby 462 F11
ALLAMANDA
bvd. Lysterfield 503 K1
cr. S Morang 199 J20
ALLAMBANAN
dr. Bayswater N 380 E20
ALLAMBEE
av. Camberwell 417 D2
av. Grovedale 705 J14
ALLAMBI
av. Rosebud W 699 G2
ct. Clarinda 498 D8
ct. Mt Eliza 626 G16
rd. Chirnside Pk 337 J6
st. Ashwood 418 B18
ALLAMBIE
dr. Eltham 288 D6
pl. Burwood E 419 F9
ALLAN
av. S Morang 243 F2
rd. St Kilda E 414 L19
rd. St Kilda E 415 A19
st. Aberfeldie 323 C10
st. Altona North 409 L8
st. Berwick 555 A9
st. Blairgowrie 695 J1
st. Brunswick 325 J16
st. Fawkner 281 G6
st. Noble Park 500 G20
st. Reservoir 282 D11
ALLANBY
gr. Bentleigh E 496 J1
ALLANDALE
ct. Werribee 447 L19
dr. Deer Park 318 J13
gr. Belgrave 466 F13
rd. Boronia 424 E12
rd. Kings Park 275 A20
rd. Mentone 531 L8
rd. Monbulk 428 H18
ALLANDRY
la. Merrimu 223 B10
ALLANFIELD
cr. Boronia 423 B13
cr. Wantirna S 423 B13
ALLANS
pl. Richmond 26 L9
ALLARA
ct. Donvale 332 J15
st. Rye 696 L6
st. Rye 697 A6
ALLARD
ct. Keilor Dn 276 C15
st. Brighton 454 L13
st. Brighton 455 A13
st. Brunswick W 324 K14
ALLARDICE
pde. Berwick 539 H19
ALLAVILLE
av. Glen Iris 416 E9
ALLAWAH
av. Frankston 599 B14
cl. Keysborough 534 G8
ct. Mill Park 242 D2
ct. Vermont S 420 G11
ALLAWARE
av. Croydon 380 H6
ALLCHIN
av. Mornington 656 L5
av. Mornington 657 A5
cl. Mornington 656 L5
st. Reservoir 282 L16
ALLEE
st. Brighton 454 H15
ALLEFORD
st. Oakleigh S 457 H18
ALLEMBY
dr. Cranbourne W 577 F17
ALLEN
cr. Langwarrin 629 C3
ct. Sunbury 142 K6
dr. Mt Eliza 626 C17
gr. Kew East 372 E6
pl. Port Melb 412 J5
rd. Monbulk 428 C17
st. Anglesea 713 K2
st. Bulleen 329 H16
st. Coburg 325 F7
st. Glen Waverley 460 C5
st. Hawthorn 372 C17
st. Highett 496 B13
st. Laverton 407 C17
st. Newtown 702 B11
st. Oakleigh 457 K6
st. Ringwood 378 G14
ALLENBY
av. Cockatoo 511 D3
av. Glen Iris 416 K15
av. Malvern East 416 K15
av. Reservoir 282 L4
av. Wantirna S 422 L13
av. Wantirna S 423 A13
pl. Gladstone Pk 237 D20
pl. Gladstone Pk 279 D1
rd. Canterbury 372 J16
rd. Hillside 274 C6
rd. Lilydale 338 D18
st. Coburg N 281 E16
st. Frankston 627 E1
ALLENDALE
cr. Wheelers Hill 460 G16
ct. Meadow Ht 238 B6
rd. Croydon 380 G2
rd. Diamond Ck 245 G16
rd. Eltham North 245 G16
rd. Kangaroo Grnd 246 J18
ALLENS
rd. Heathmont 378 L18
rd. Heathmont 379 A18
rd. Montmorency 286 L10
ALLEYNE
av. Armadale 415 G14
av. Bonbeach 547 C20
av. Torquay 711 J9
ALLFREY
ct. Mt Eliza 626 C15
st. Brighton East 455 H13
ALLIANCE
st. Noble Park 535 A6
ALLIE
st. Surrey Hills 418 A1
ALLIED
dr. Carrum Downs 601 E3
dr. Tullamarine 278 F9
ALLIMA
av. Yallambie 286 C12
ALLINGA
pl. Donvale 332 J15
ALLINGTON
pl. Langwarrin 601 L18
pl. Seabrook 450 K5
ALLIPOL
ct. Briar Hill 287 A5
ALLIRA
cl. Berwick 554 K17
ALLISON
av. Eumemmerring 537 B15
av. Glen Iris 417 B16
av. Sassafras 426 J16
cr. Eltham 287 E3
cr. Lilydale 338 G4
ct. Vermont 421 F3
dr. Hillside 274 F3
la. W Melbourne 17 G20
rd. Elsternwick 454 L3
rd. Elsternwick 455 A3
rd. Forest Hill 420 J2
rd. Mont Albert N 374 F9
rd. Mt Eliza 642 J5
rd. Selby 467 D19
st. Mornington 640 K16
st. Sunshine W 364 A5
ALLISTER
av. Knoxfield 462 K2
cl. Knoxfield 462 L6
rd. Noble Park 500 D16
rd. Springvale 500 D16
st. Mt Waverley 418 K16
ALLITT
av. Belmont 706 C2
ALLNUTT
ct. Cheltenham 531 E1
pde. Cheltenham 531 E2
st. Bentleigh 496 B3
ALLORA
av. Ferntree Gly 464 D9
cl. Hoppers Csg 448 E9
ALLOWAH
tce. Richmond 26 D11
ALLSOPS
rd. Launching Pl 344 G12
rd. Launching Pl 345 A13
rd. Woori Yallock 344 G12
ALLUMBA
dr. St Helena 244 J17
ALLUNGA
pde. Berwick 539 J20
ALLURE
ct. Glen Waverley 460 L5
ct. Glen Waverley 461 A5
ALLUVIAL
cl. Menzies Ck 508 A1

ALLUVIAN
wy. Carrum Downs...575 F14

ALLUVIUM
wy. Mt Waverley.......419 G13

ALLWEN
ct. Clarinda.............498 G10

ALLWYN
cr. Mill Park............243 B3
cr. Mill Park............243 C2

ALLY
tce. Chirnside Pk.......336 F6

ALMA
av. Altona Mdw........407 G19
av. Ferntree Gly.......464 D1
av. Laverton............407 A19
cl. Mulgrave............501 H7
cr. Noble Park.........535 D3
ct. Doncaster..........331 D18
ct. Endeavour Hl.....537 D1
ct. Mooroolbark......337 J15
ct. Newcomb...........704 C18
ct. Ringwood..........378 J6
ct. Springvale..........499 J15
gr. St Kilda..............414 F15
la. Kalorama...........383 C11
pl. Carlton.................18 A20
pl. St Kilda..............414 E15
rd. Bundoora............284 H2
rd. Camberwell........416 H3
rd. Caulfield N.........415 A15
rd. Caulfield N.........415 C15
rd. Hampton Pk........551 E7
rd. Panton Hill.........204 E20
rd. Parkdale.............532 A10
rd. St Kilda..............414 D14
rd. St Kilda E...........414 D14
st. Aberfeldie...........323 E9
st. Craigieburn.........150 C17
st. Fitzroy....................18 L20
st. Lower Plenty......286 F13
st. Maidstone...........366 F1
st. Malvern East......457 E4
st. Mornington.........640 B19
st. Tootgarook.........698 C4
st. W Footscray.......366 D5
tce. Newport.............411 C9
tce. Williamstown.....411 C9

ALMA DOEPEL
dr. Altona Mdw........451 L5

ALMANDS
av. Roxburgh Pk......194 E14

ALMAY
gr. Heidelberg.........328 K5

ALMEIDA
cr. South Yarra..........32 D8
cr. South Yarra.........414 H5
ct. Watsonia N........243 G19

ALMER
av. Blackburn..........376 D12
av. Nar Warrn S.......579 D1
av. Nunawading.......376 D12

ALMERIA
ct. Mt Eliza..............626 A12

ALMERTA
pl. Bulleen..............329 K9

ALMIRA
st. Anglesea............713 K2

ALMOND
av. Brooklyn............365 F18
ct. Campbellfield.....239 F11
ct. Thomastown.......240 K14
dr. Doveton.............537 A10
st. Balwyn N...........373 H3
st. Caulfield S..........455 G7
tce. Dingley Village...532 H4

ALMONDBUSH
st. Somerville..........645 E13

ALMONDSBURY
ct. Blackburn..........376 C12

ALMORA
cl. Frankston............600 G19

ALMRAY
pl. Glen Waverley....421 B20

ALMURTA
av. Coolaroo............238 D5
rd. Bentleigh E.........497 A3

ALNUS
ct. Newcomb...........704 C16

ALOAH
st.e, Bayswater N.......379 H18
st.w, Bayswater N.......379 G19

ALOCASIA
cl. Lysterfield..........503 L1

ALOHA
gdn. Templestowe.....331 K10
st. S Kingsville........410 F2

ALOMA
av. Wyndham Va.....446 F10

ALONSO
st. Glen Iris............417 H11

ALONZO
ct. Frankston...........628 F2

ALOOMBA
st. Chadstone..........458 B2

ALOYSIUS
st. Braybrook..........322 C19

ALPHA
cl. Hampton Pk.......551 K15
ct. Mitcham............377 F10
pl. Windsor.............414 F12
st. Balwyn N...........373 J6

ALPHINGTON
st. Alphington.........327 F20
st. Northcote...........327 A16

ALPINA
st. Frankston N.......600 D8

ALPINE
av. Upwey...............466 A10
bvd. Launching Pl......345 F13
cl. Sunbury.............143 A10
cr. Kallista..............467 G4
cr. Noble Park N......501 E10
ct. Badger Creek.....258 G11
ct. Lalor..................240 J10
ct. Vermont S.........420 H9
gdn. Caroline Spr......317 J8
gr. Pascoe Vale.......280 G15
rd. Ferny Creek........425 J17
rd. Ferny Creek........425 J20
st. Ferntree Gly.......464 H2
st. Warburton..........349 E4
wk. Hampton Pk.......551 E12
wy. Kilsyth...............381 H8

ALRAY
dr. Cheltenham........497 C19

ALRENE
ct. Berwick..............554 B1
ct. Vermont S.........420 K8

ALSACE
st. Brunswick E.......325 L10
st. Dandenong........535 E4

ALSOM
pl. Airport W...........278 F16

ALSOP
la. Berwick..............554 J11
la. Melbourne.............1 D6
la. Melbourne...........23 J6
st. Belmont..............702 D18

ALSTON
ct. Nar Warrn S.......552 F19
ct. Thornbury...........327 F7
gr. St Kilda E...........415 A19
st. Thornbury...........327 D7

ALTA
st. Canterbury.........373 D20

ALTAIR
cl. Frankston...........628 F5
ct. Gladstone Pk......278 L2
ct. Gladstone Pk......279 A2
ct. Lilydale..............338 L6
st. Springvale S.......499 G19

ALTARNUN
rd. Langwarrin.........629 J15

ALTER
ct. Skye..................601 D9

ALTHEA
pl. Doncaster..........331 B14

ALTNA
av. Airport W...........278 K15

ALTO
av. Croydon.............379 H1
cl. Bundoora............242 G18

ALTON
av. Brighton.............454 G15
ct. Glen Waverley....461 A1
ct. Narre Warren.....539 A13

ALTONA
ct. Doncaster E.......375 G2
rd. Altona................409 K17
rd. Seaholme...........409 K17
st. Heidelberg Ht.....328 C3
st. Heidelberg W.....328 C3
st. Kensington..........33 H12

ALTSON
la. Melbourne.............1 A7
la. Melbourne...........23 G7
rd. Belgrave S..........506 K10
rd. Belgrave S..........507 A10
rd. Belgrave S..........507 A14

ALTYRE
ct. St Albans...........275 J18

ALUMNUS
ct. Wheelers Hill.....460 D14

ALVA
av. Pk Orchards.......333 H16
cl. Eltham...............287 L10
ct. Fawkner.............239 E20
gr. Coburg...............325 K2

ALVANLEY
ct. Mulgrave...........501 G5

ALVARADO
av. Thomastown......240 F18

ALVASTON
av. Wantirna............422 G15

ALVENA
cr. Heathmont.........378 L16
cr. Heathmont.........379 A16
st. Mentone.............530 L5
st. Mentone.............531 A5

ALVERNA
cl. Greensborough..285 L8
gr. Brighton.............454 L17
gr. Brighton.............455 A17

ALVERSTONE
gr. Mt Eliza..............642 J3

ALVIE
ct. Westmeadows....237 G10
rd. Mt Waverley.......418 K19
st. Malvern East......457 D3

ALVINA
ct. Frankston...........599 E16
st. Ferntree Gly.......464 E1
st. Oakleigh S..........458 E20
st. Sunshine N.........321 B10

ALVIS
cl. Keilor Dn............276 B14

ALWARD
av. Clayton S...........498 K6

ALWYN
ct. Braybrook..........366 B3
ct. Keilor East.........321 K6
ct. Mitcham............377 C18
st. Bayswater..........423 F4
st. Croydon.............380 E4
st. Mitcham............377 A18
st. Pascoe Vale.......280 K14
st. Rye....................697 B12

AMALFI
dr. Endeavour Hl.....536 L4
dr. Endeavour Hl.....537 A4
pl. Epping...............197 E17

AMALIA
cl. Yarra Glen..........208 L19
cl. Yarra Glen..........209 A19

AMANDA
ct. Hallam...............538 A14
ct. Keysborough.....534 J10
ct. Melton...............268 G1
ct. Mt Martha...........655 E18
ct. Mt Martha...........657 A10
ct. Pakenham...........584 G3
ct. Rowville.............503 B8
ct. Seville................341 K12
ct. Yallambie............285 F16
dr. Carrum Downs...600 H1
pl. Frankston...........600 J18
rd. Tottenham.........365 K10

AMANDI
tce. Hoppers Csg......405 D17

AMAR
st. Strathmore.........279 L15

AMARANTH
av. Altona North.......410 A2

AMARINA
cl. Meadow Ht.........194 C20
cr. Grovedale..........705 K12

AMAROO
ct. Berwick..............553 E3
ct. Box Hill N...........375 B6
ct. Burwood E..........419 F10
ct. Diamond Ck.......245 K8
ct. Eltham...............288 D6
dr. Chelsea Ht.........547 D11
rd. Craigieburn........150 J9
st. Chadstone..........458 B2
wy. Yallambie...........286 C11
wyn. Burnside...........318 G8

AMAY
cr. Ferntree Gly.......464 B3

AMAYLA
cr. Carrum Downs...600 F2

AMAZON
ct. Rowville.............462 L17
ct. Rowville.............463 A17
pl. Werribee............447 H4

AMBASSADOR
ri. Research...........288 J1

AMBER
av. Frankston...........600 D16
cl. Brighton.............454 J13
cr. Narre Warren.....539 D13
ct. Altona North......410 C6
ct. Bundoora............284 H5
ct. Cheltenham........531 D4
ct. Kilsyth...............381 K7
ct. Pascoe Vale.......280 K11
ct. S Morang...........199 J19
dr. Hampton Pk.......551 L14

gr. Mt Waverley.......419 B20
pl. Wyndham Va.....446 E9
st. Bayswater..........423 C6
st. Forest Hill..........420 H3

AMBERLEY
av. Aspendale..........546 C4
cr. Dandenong S.....536 A15
cr. Frankston S........626 L8
ct. Bulleen..............330 B18
ct. Highton..............705 K1
ct. Wantirna.............422 H10
dr. Mt Martha...........656 K9
wy. Lower Plenty......286 G19

AMBERLY PARK
dr. Nar Warrn S.......552 F15

AMBERWOOD
ct. Templestowe.....331 D13

AMBLECOTE
cr. Mulgrave............501 F5

AMBLESIDE
cl. Frankston S........627 A15
cl. Mooroolbark......338 A15
cr. Berwick..............554 A9
rd. Greenvale...........193 B19

AMBOINA
av. Mitcham............377 E16

AMBON
av. Deer Park...........319 C9
ct. Heidelberg W.....328 D1
ri. Croydon N..........335 K15
st. Ashburton..........417 F18
st. Preston..............283 H18

AMBRIDGE
gr. Sydenham..........275 B9

AMBRIE
av. Ringwood..........378 K4
cr. Noble Park.........500 H15

AMBROSE
av. Malvern East......417 H20
st. Dallas................238 K9
st. Doncaster..........331 D18
st. Emerald.............509 L5
st. Ivanhoe.............327 J10

AMBROSIA
ct. Endeavour Hl.....537 F6

AMCOR
wy. Campbellfield.....239 D3

AMDURA
rd. Doncaster E.......376 E3

AMEILY
cr. Reservoir...........282 G8

AMELIA
av. Deer Park...........319 D9
av. Essendon............324 C4
av. Healesville..........258 B5
av. Mornington.........640 L13
av. Rye....................697 K5
av. Wheelers Hill......461 F13
cl. Beaconsfield.......555 D13
cr. Doncaster E.......376 D3
ct. Kilsyth...............381 B5
st. Camberwell.........417 G4
st. Caulfield S..........455 L7
st. Knoxfield............423 D20
st. McKinnon...........455 K16

AMERSHAM
av. Springvale S......499 K19
dr. Wantirna............422 C11
dr. Warrandyte........333 A6
dr. Warrandyte........333 B7

AMERY
av. Blackburn..........375 E20
st. Ashburton..........417 B16
st. Reservoir...........282 D1

AMES
av. Carnegie............456 L8
st. Rowville.............503 A1

AMESBURY
av. Craigieburn........194 C4
av. Wantirna............422 F11
ct. Mt Waverley.......458 H4
rd. Mt Eliza..............626 F13

AMESS
st. Brunswick E.......325 L20
st. Carlton N.............18 K3

AMETHYST
av. Glen Waverley....420 G18
cl. St Albans...........320 L9
pl. Werribee............447 F3
wk. Bundoora...........284 G7

AMI
ct. Berwick..............553 L15

AMIEL
st. Springvale..........500 B9

AMIENS
st. Hampton.............495 D5
st. Surrey Hills.........417 L1

AMIET
st. Greensborough..286 B8

AMINGA
av. Doncaster E.......376 E1
ct. Croydon.............336 D18

AMINYA
cr. Yallambie...........286 B15
ct. Wantirna............422 C13
pl. Briar Hill.............286 G3
pl. Camberwell.........417 L3

AMIRIYA
st. Bentleigh E.........496 K2

AMIS
cr. Avondale Ht.......322 B7
cr. Keilor East.........322 B7

AMLEY
ri. Ferntree Gly.......464 D13

AMON
ct. Woori Yallock.....344 E15

AMOORE
av. Highton..............705 K4

AMOS
ct. Clayton S...........499 E16
ct. Nar Warrn S.......552 H18

AMOTT
ct. Aspendale Gdn...546 H3

AMOUR
ct. Wantirna S.........462 D2

AMPHLETT
av. Cockatoo...........511 D5
av. Gembrook..........511 K5

AMPNEY
ct. Kilsyth S............424 K1

AMRON
st. Chelsea Ht..........547 D13

AMSTED
rd. Bayswater..........424 C5

AMSTEL
cl. Darley................221 J2
ct. Hoppers Csg......405 A16
ct. Meadow Ht........237 J4
ct. Mt Waverley.......458 K10
st. Craigieburn........150 G16

AMSTERDAM
st. Richmond............32 F2
st. Richmond...........414 J1

AMUNDSEN
st. Belmont..............702 E19

AMUR
av. Roxburgh Pk......194 E6

AMY
cl. Hoppers Csg......447 L3
cl. Pakenham...........585 C5
ct. Hampton Pk.......552 D13
ct. Mentone.............530 K6
mw. Keysborough.....534 G14
rd. Boronia..............424 F10
st. Camberwell.........417 G4
st. St Albans...........320 A4

AMY MACK
wk. Lynbrook............551 D18

AMYS
gr. Donvale.............377 D8

ANABA
ct. Greensborough..244 G20
ct. Mooroolbark......337 C16
st. Bayswater..........423 B4

ANACONDA
rd. Narre Warren.....539 B17
rd. Nar Warrn N.......539 A15

ANAKIE
ct. Rosebud............700 L5
wk. Delahey.............275 A12

ANAMA
st. Greensborough..285 K3

ANANDA
ct. Donvale.............376 E7
ct. Watsonia............285 C9

ANARTH
st. Bentleigh E.........457 C15
st. Doncaster..........331 C17

ANCHOR
ct. Seabrook...........450 H7
pl. Prahran................32 D19
pl. Prahran..............414 H10
st. Aspendale...........546 B3

ANCHORAGE
av. Williamstown.....411 D17
dr. Blind Bight.........650 D10

ANCONA
ct. Eltham...............288 C4
pl. Keilor Lodge.......275 K4
st. Mentone.............530 L8

ANDACANI
ct. Mt Eliza..............641 L8

ANDELANA
av. Wheelers Hill......460 H17
ct. Sorrento.............679 A14

ANDENE
dr. Narre Warren.....539 C16

ANDERSON
av. Bentleigh E 456 J15
av. Caroline Spr 318 A3
cl. Bayswater N 380 H16
cl. Hampton Pk 551 G7
ct. Endeavour Hl 537 B6
ct. Mentone 530 L6
ct. Richmond 26 E4
ct. Wantirna S 462 F4
dr. Carrum Downs 574 H15
la. N Melbourne 17 H19
pde. Bundoora 285 D1
pl. S Geelong 702 L13
rd. Albion 365 A4
rd. Fawkner 281 E1
rd. Hawthorn E 416 E5
rd. Healesville 258 J4
rd. Keysborough 533 K11
rd. Monbulk 428 G11
rd. Sunbury 143 D14
rd. Sunshine 365 A6
rd. Thornbury 326 B8
rd. W Melbourne 368 C13
st. Ascot Vale 323 H20
st. Bacchus Msh 221 K16
st. Bentleigh 496 B3
st. Caulfield 455 H3
st. Clifton Hill 20 B8
st. E Geelong 703 F13
st. Ferntree Gly 424 K16
st. Frankston 599 F15
st. Heidelberg 329 C4
st. Kallista 467 E3
st. Lalor 241 D7
st. Lilydale 338 F7
st. Malvern East 416 C17
st. Melbourne 31 G4
st. Newport 410 H8
st. Pakenham 584 L5
st. Pascoe Vale S 280 G20
st. Pt Lonsdale 710 G1
st. Port Melb 368 J19
st. St Albans 320 H1
st. S Melbourne 30 A10
st. South Yarra 31 G4
st. South Yarra 414 D2
st. Surrey Hills 373 L20
st. Tecoma 466 D7
st. Templestowe 331 A7
st. Torquay 711 L10
st. Warrandyte 289 K19
st. Werribee 447 J17
st. W Melbourne 34 J19
st. Yarraville 366 K15
st. Geelong West, off Emerald St 702 J7
ANDERSONS
av. Warburton 305 L19
la. N Melbourne 17 A15
ANDERSONS CREEK
rd. Doncaster E 332 C16
ANDES
ct. Lalor 240 H7
ANDLEIGH
dr. Mulgrave 501 E2
ANDLEON
ct. Clayton S 499 C10
wy. Springvale S 533 K7
ANDLON
ct. Tullamarine 278 J2
ANDONOV
dr. Cranbourne W 577 K15
ANDOVER
av. Mitcham 377 A8
ct. Hampton Pk 552 B9
ct. Mulgrave 501 A6
ANDRE
ct. Cranbourne W 577 H19
ANDREA
cr. Cranbourne N 578 H9
cr. Taylors Lakes 275 F5
pde. Ringwood N 378 J2
st. Rye 696 G10
st. St Albans 319 L6
ANDREW
cr. Croydon S 379 E11
cr. Tootgarook 698 G6
ct. Balwyn N 374 C3
ct. Clarinda 498 C9
ct. Doncaster 330 D19
ct. Emerald 470 E16
ct. Narre Warren 539 C17
ct. Pakenham 584 J3
ct. Rowville 503 D2
pl. Bundoora 285 B3
pl. Mornington 640 J20
rd. Gisborne 80 H10
rd. Riddells Ck 80 H10
rd. St Albans 275 G20
rd. Wollert 153 F15
st. Forest Hill 376 H20
st. Glenroy 280 K1
st. Hampton Pk 551 F10
st. Melton S 268 J6
st. Mooroolbark 337 A16
st. Mt Waverley 418 L12
st. Newcomb 704 C13
st. Northcote 326 K16
st. Oakleigh 457 L15
st. Ringwood 378 B10
st. Seaford 599 J9
st. Springvale 499 K17
st. Sunshine 321 F20
st. Sunshine 365 F1
st. Vermont 377 H20
st. Windsor 31 H20
st. Windsor 414 D10
ANDREW CHIRNSIDE
av. Seabrook 450 L6
ANDREWS
av. Reservoir 283 H16
la. Long Forest 224 F2
la. Red Hill 687 K20
st. Burwood 419 A9
st. Eltham 288 A4
st. Geelong West 702 F2
st. Heidelberg 329 A5
st. Spotswood 366 H20
ANDROMEDA
wy. Templstw Lr 330 K16
ANDVAL
ct. Berwick 554 G11
ANEBO
st. Warneet 649 E13
ANEES
ct. Langwarrin 602 B16
ANELIDA
st. Rye 696 D5
ANEMBO
ct. Doncaster 375 D2
ct. Werribee 447 D13
ANERLEY
st. Ivanhoe 328 A17
ANFIELD
ct. Malvern East 457 J1
ANGALA
ct. Frankston S 627 H16
ANGAS
ct. Sunbury 142 L17
ct. Sunbury 143 A17
ANGASTON
ct. Vermont S 421 D11
ANGEL
cl. Nar Warrn S 552 H16
ANGELA
cl. Eltham North 245 C17
ct. Doncaster E 332 G7
ct. Kurunjang 227 D9
ct. Nar Warrn N 539 J9
ct. Rye 696 K4
ct. S Morang 243 H3
dr. Hoppers Csg 405 E20
ANGELICA
cr. Croydon Hills 335 E15
ANGELINA
wy. Somerville 644 J15
ANGELIQUE
gr. Albanvale 319 B7
ANGELO
ct. Melton 268 L1
la. Melbourne 2 C11
la. Melbourne 24 C6
pl. Wonga Park 291 G15
ANGELTOP
tce. Templestowe 331 G5
ANGIE
ct. Aspendale Gdn 546 L5
ANGLE
rd. Balwyn 372 K13
ANGLEMERE
cr. Donvale 376 L5
ANGLER
pde. Ascot Vale 323 G20
ANGLERS
ct. Seabrook 450 H6
ANGLESEA
rd. Waurn Ponds 705 A16
tce. Geelong West 702 J2
ANGLESEY
ct. Mulgrave 501 G5
ANGLISS
st. Yarraville 366 E16
ANGLO
ct. Mooroolbark 337 J18
ANGOURIE
cr. Taylors Lakes 276 A10
ANGUS
av. Altona North 410 B5
av. Croydon 379 E8
av. Ringwood E 379 E8
cl. Wantirna 422 F4
ct. Dandenong N 501 F13
ct. Eltham North 245 C18
ct. Mt Eliza 641 J7
ct. Narre Warren 553 C7
ct. Oakleigh S 498 B9
ct. Pakenham 558 L20
ct. Roxburgh Pk 194 C7
dr. Glen Waverley 420 C17
gr. Doncaster 374 H1
pl. Lilydale 338 J10
rd. Yellingbo 387 G12
st. Belmont 702 C19
st. Hadfield 280 K7
st. Sunshine W 364 G3
ANILE
pl. Williamstn N 410 H13
ANITA
av. Dingley Village 533 C8
ct. Carrum 573 E8
ct. Doncaster E 376 E1
ct. Frankston 627 H4
ct. Mordialloc 532 B10
ct. Mt Martha 657 C7
ct. Taylors Lakes 275 E6
pl. Pakenham 584 G2
st. Beaumaris 530 A11
st. Kilsyth 381 D6
ANJAYA
ct. Blackburn 376 C20
ct. Frankston 600 H15
ANKA
cl. Eltham 288 C7
ANKETELL
st. Coburg 325 D3
ANLEY
mw. Montmorency 287 A8
pl. Sunshine W 364 A6
ANN
cr. Pakenham 584 J9
ct. Aspendale 546 E5
ct. Briar Hill 286 K4
ct. Bundoora 242 C18
ct. Mt Dandenong 426 H1
ct. Mt Waverley 458 J2
ct. Sunshine W 364 D9
pl. Seabrook 450 J4
st. Bayswater 423 G11
st. Beaconsfield 555 C14
st. Brunswick 325 K14
st. Croydon 336 A18
st. Dandenong 535 L5
st. Footscray 367 C9
st. Geelong West 702 D2
st. Pascoe Vale 280 G17
st. Pt Lonsdale 707 H20
st. S Melbourne 29 E2
st. Springvale 499 L17
st. Williamstown 411 J18
st. Windsor 414 J11
ANNA
ct. Narre Warren 538 F17
ct. Pakenham 559 G19
ct. Werribee 447 F4
la. Bonbeach 545 E13
st. Bundoora 242 F16
st. Glen Huntly 456 B7
st. St Albans 319 J5
ANNABELLA
ct. Dandenong N 502 B18
ANNADALE
mw. Greenvale 193 H17
st. Kew 372 D11
ANNAN
ct. Greenvale 237 B3
pl. Templestowe 332 B9
ANNAND
cl. Cranbourne W 577 G20
st. Fitzroy N 19 C2
ANNANDALE
cr. Glen Waverley 420 K19
rd. Keilor 277 F4
rd. Melb Airport 277 F4
rd. Melb Airport 278 A6
rd. Tullamarine 277 F4
ANNASTASIA
wy. Sunshine N 321 B17
ANNE
cl. Somerville 644 F15
cr. Brighton 454 K15
cr. Warburton 349 L6
ct. Cranbourne 603 L3
ct. Heathmont 379 B20
ct. Montrose 382 A8
ct. Tootgarook 698 B8
ct. Yallambie 285 F16
dr. Dromana 686 E10
rd. Knoxfield 462 J6
st. Berwick 554 D7
st. Blackburn N 375 K8
st. Broadmeadows 238 F19
st. Diamond Ck 246 C12
st. Emerald 509 C3
st. Lilydale 339 E9
st. McKinnon 455 L16
st. Menzies Ck 468 H17
st. Newtown 702 H13
st. Reservoir 283 E2
st. Rosebud 700 E3
st. Werribee 447 B18
ANNESLEY
ct. Mt Waverley 458 K3
st. Braybrook 322 A19
ANNETTA
av. Ashburton 417 B18
ct. Albanvale 319 C4
ct. Wheelers Hill 460 H7
ANNETTE
ct. Avondale Ht 322 A16
ct. Endeavour Hl 537 G3
ct. Langwarrin 629 E7
gr. Boronia 423 C14
pl. Templestowe 331 F5
ANNIBA
ct. Melton W 226 B17
ANNIE
ct. Croydon 336 J16
st. Frankston 599 B16
wy. Lilydale 338 H10
ANNIE BORAT
cl. Brunswick, off Eveline St 325 G14
ANNINGIE PARK
pl. Croydon N 336 A13
ANNIVERSARY
pl. Rowville 503 C8
ANNOIS
ct. Sunbury 142 K10
ANOMALY
st. Moolap 704 J16
ANORA
cr. Mulgrave 460 G20
ct. Keilor Dn 276 G15
ANSELM
gr. Glenroy 279 J4
ANSETT
cr. Forest Hill 420 E8
ct. Roxburgh Pk 194 E10
ANSLEY
pl. Truganina 405 J13
ANSON
ct. Ashburton 417 K17
ct. Moorabbin 496 K9
ANSTEE
gr. Bentleigh 455 L20
ANSTEY
av. Reservoir 239 L20
rt. Berwick 554 A3
ANSWER
cl. Sydenham 274 H4
ANTARES
ct. Aberfeldie 323 E11
ct. Torquay 712 D3
ANTHEM
pl. Melton W 226 D17
ANTHLIN
ct. Templestowe 332 B14
ANTHONY
av. Doncaster 330 D15
cl. Lower Plenty 286 H13
cr. Box Hill N 374 J7
ct. Burwood E 419 L8
ct. Hallam 538 C19
ct. Keilor East 322 B6
ct. Kingsbury 283 G9
ct. Melton W 226 A14
ct. Ringwood 378 J7
ct. Rosanna 329 D2
ct. Rye 696 F1
ct. Seaford 599 F3
dr. Chirnside Pk 336 L5
dr. Mt Waverley 459 D6
dr. Rowville 463 K18
gr. Woori Yallock 344 F14
pl. Langwarrin 629 B7
st. Croydon 379 G3
st. Dandenong N 502 A20
st. Dromana 686 B5
st. Glen Iris 416 F13
st. Kensington 33 K6
st. Langwarrin 601 G18
st. Melbourne 1 K2
st. Melbourne 23 L3
st. Newcomb 704 E17
st. Ormond 456 B14
st. Safety Bch 669 A17
st. Sunbury 142 K8
ANTHONYS
la. Langwarrin 629 D12
ANTIBES
st. Parkdale 531 D13
wy. Point Cook 450 G11
ANTIGONE
ct. Templstw Lr 330 K17
ANTIGONI
ct. Warrandyte 333 A5
ANTILL
ct. Mulgrave 460 D16
ANTIOCH
ct. Albanvale 318 L7
ANTIONETTA
wy. Hillside 274 G2
ANTIOPE
ct. Sorrento 679 B13
ANTOINETTE
bvd. Eltham 287 F17
ct. Mt Waverley 458 K2
ANTON
cl. Werribee 448 B15
ct. Chelsea Ht 547 F16
ct. Doncaster 331 D18
ct. Frankston 600 F19
ct. Nar Warrn S 552 E17
gr. Flemington 324 C20
ANTONELLA
ct. Dandenong S 549 J9
ANTONIE
av. Delahey 275 E10
ANTONIETTA
pl. Narre Warren 539 F16
ANTONY
cl. Mill Park 241 L6
ANTRIM
cl. Endeavour Hl 538 A6
ct. Deer Park 318 K10
pl. Langwarrin 629 B9
ANTWERP
dr. Keilor Dn 276 F14
st. Dallas 238 E11
ANVIL
ct. S Morang 199 K17
pl. Attwood 237 A10
ANZAC
av. Coburg N 281 F13
av. Gembrook 512 K10
av. Hurstbridge 203 B14
av. Melbourne 4 E18
av. Melbourne 24 J18
av. Yarra Glen 208 H20
av. Yarra Glen 252 H1
av. Yarra Glen 253 A1
cr. Williamstown 411 A15
rd. Warrandyte S 334 J6
st. Carnegie 457 A5
st. Croydon 379 L4
ANZED
ct. Mulgrave 499 K1
AONACH
st. Clayton S 499 C5
APALOOSA
ct. Belmont 706 B7
APEX
av. Belmont 705 L2
av. Hampton E 495 J8
cr. Bulleen 329 J13
ct. Thomastown 283 K1
st. Dandenong N 502 A16
wy. Montmorency 286 K13
APHRASIA
la. Newport 411 A10
st. Newtown 702 C8
APLIN
pl. Carlton 18 G12
pl. Wantirna S 462 C3
APOINGA
st. Dandenong S 549 J11
APOLLO
cr. Dallas 238 E12
ct. Blackburn 376 B15
ct. Croydon S 380 B11
ct. Doncaster E 332 D17
ct. Frankston 628 F9
ct. Hillside 232 B18
ct. Keysborough 535 A8
ct. Langwarrin 601 L17
ct. Wantirna S 422 B15
ct. Werribee 447 L11
dr. Hallam 537 H20
pl. Sunshine W 363 K5
rd. Taylors Lakes 275 L8
APPERLY
st. Fitzroy N 326 D19
APPIAN
ct. Hoppers Csg 448 H6
dr. Albanvale 319 C6
APPILA
cl. Hallam 538 D20
cl. Hallam 552 D1
APPIN
ct. Meadow Ht 237 J4

PPLE
t. Burwood E.........419 J8
t. Doveton.............536 K8
r. Bayswater..........422 J4
t. Pearcedale.........646 L4
t. Pearcedale.........647 A4
PPLEBERRY
l. Knoxfield............423 A19
l. Ringwood N.......334 J20
l. S Morang...........243 L2
PPLE BLOSSOM
t. Nar Warrn S.......553 C20
t. Templestowe......332 B14
PPLEBLOSSOM
t. View Bank..........329 K1
PPLEBY
r. Brunswick W......325 A8
t. Sunshine...........365 H2
PPLEGUM
l. Croydon Hills.....335 F17
r. Ferntree Gly......423 E10
t. Narre Warren.....538 H14
r. Doncaster E.......332 F12
PPLETON
t. Darley...............222 B10
t. Richmond..........371 B14
PPLETON DOCK
d. W Melbourne.....368 A16
d. W Melbourne.....368 D14
PPLETREE
r. Glen Waverley....461 A2
r. Mill Park............242 D9
PPLEWOOD
t. Doncaster E.......332 C12
r. Knoxfield............423 B20
l. Nar Warrn S.......553 E17
l. Somerville..........645 C20
PREY
l. Eltham...............288 C5
PRIL
l. Albanvale...........319 C7
PSLEY
t. Ferntree Gly.......463 G6
t. Mill Park............242 K12
l. Seaford..............599 J5
rd. Belgrave............466 C17
st. Glenroy..............280 D7
st. Mt Waverley.......459 C7
tce. Berwick.............553 K19
AQUA
st. Langwarrin.........629 H6
AQUAMARINE
ct. Hampton Pk.......551 C10
ct. St Albans...........320 K9
AQUANITA
cr. Keilor Dn...........275 L12
AQUARIUS
ct. Donvale.............377 F2
ct. Lilydale.............338 L7
ct. Lilydale.............339 A7
ct. Wheelers Hill......460 J10
dr. Frankston...........628 D7
AQUATIC
dr. Albert Park..........30 F10
AQUEDUCT
av. Mt Evelyn...........339 F20
la. Diamond Ck.......245 C14
rd. Diamond Ck.......244 K13
rd. Greensborough..244 K13
rd. Langwarrin.........629 J5
rd. Langwarrin.........629 K6
tr. Langwarrin.........629 A13
AQUILA
cr. Endeavour Hl.....536 J2
ct. Wheelers Hill......461 B11
gr. Roxburgh Pk......194 E10
pl. Carrum Downs...575 B14
st. Balwyn N...........329 A20
st. Balwyn N...........373 A1
AQUILLA
av. Torquay.............712 C4
ct. Chelsea Ht..........547 D10
AQUINAS
ct. Hoppers Csg......448 J6
ARABIL
st. Frankston...........599 K19
ARABIN
st. Keilor................277 C13
ARALUEN
dr. Croydon.............380 A10
pde. Belmont.............702 D17
ARAMA
st. Balwyn N...........329 L19
ARANDA
ct. Mulgrave...........500 H5
pl. Epping...............241 K3
ARANDT
rd. Exford...............267 E18
ARANGA
cr. Donvale.............376 F6

ARANMORE
cr. Nar Warrn N.......539 K9
ARAPILLES
dr. Templstw Lr.......330 E12
ARARAT
av. Coburg N...........281 F14
st. Altona North.......410 C6
ARATULA
st. Dandenong........536 D8
ARAWATA
cl. Mornington........657 C3
dr. Doncaster E.......376 D1
pde. Melton..............226 J16
ARAWATTA
st. Carnegie............456 K5
st. Vermont S..........421 E8
ARBON
rd. Mornington........657 A2
ARBOR
av. Belgrave............466 J17
av. Ferntree Gly.......424 L16
av. Nunawading.......376 K12
av. Reservoir...........282 E13
av. Tremont.............425 A16
st. Alphington.........327 K18
tce. Avondale Ht.......322 D13
ARBOUR
gr. Belmont.............706 A5
ARBROATH
ct. Greenvale...........193 E20
rd. Wantirna S.........422 K12
rd. Wantirna S.........423 A12
ARCADE
al. Melbourne.............2 D10
al. Melbourne...........24 C5
rd. Mont Albert N.....374 E10
sq. Keilor East.........321 L4
wy. Avondale Ht.......321 K8
wy. Keilor East.........321 K8
ARCADIA
av. Hallam...............537 F14
av. Malvern East......457 H7
av. Reservoir...........283 F10
av. The Basin...........424 J9
cl. Ringwood N.......378 F3
cl. Taylors Lakes.....275 H1
ct. Glen Waverley....419 L14
ct. Noble Park.........534 C5
st. Box Hill S..........374 L20
st. Carrum Downs...601 C6
st. Hampton............494 L5
st. Hampton............495 A5
wy. Eltham North.....245 G17
wy. Keysborough.....534 G16
ARCADIAN
pl. Hoppers Csg......405 D13
ARCADY
gr. Vermont............421 J4
ARCHBOLD
st. Thornbury..........326 K7
ARCHER
av. Ascot Vale..........323 H19
av. Sunbury.............142 G15
cl. Lilydale..............294 B20
cl. Mt Eliza..............626 C12
ct. Brighton East.....455 D18
ct. Gladstone Pk......279 B1
dr. Kurunjang...........227 E8
dr. Mornington........641 D17
pl. Keilor Dn...........275 K13
pl. Mill Park............242 L10
rd. Diamond Ck.......245 K2
st. Blairgowrie.........679 D18
ARCHERON
ct. Caroline Spr.......318 C6
ARCHIBALD
av. Narre Warren.....539 E18
pl. Langwarrin.........629 D11
st. Box Hill.............374 K14
st. Elsternwick........455 A6
st. Pascoe Vale.......280 F17
ARCH WRIGHT
dr. Reservoir...........282 G5
ARCOLA
ct. Eltham...............287 L11
ARDBLAIR
tce. Nar Warrn S.......553 E20
ARDCLONEY
dr. Sunbury.............143 J10
ARDEA
ct. Endeavour Hl.....536 K2
ARDEER
ct. Meadow Ht.........237 K4
ARDEL
st. Croydon.............335 D20
st. Croydon.............379 E1
ARDEN
cr. Rosanna............285 B20
ct. Kew East............372 H3
ct. Seaford..............599 F3
dr. Noble Park.........534 C6
la. N Melbourne........17 D15
st. Croydon.............336 G19
st. Kensington..........34 A14
st. Kensington..........34 C14
st. N Melbourne........34 F15
ARDENA
ct. Bentleigh E.........456 K18
ct. Keilor Dn............276 H15
ARDENE
ct. Hawthorn...........371 K18
ARDENT
ct. Keilor.................276 K10
ARDGOUR
st. Balwyn N...........373 J3
st. Hughesdale........457 E11
ARDGOWER
ct. Templstw Lr.......330 K8
rd. Noble Park.........500 G16
ARDILL
st. Healesville..........213 E20
st. Healesville..........257 F1
ARDLIE
st. Attwood.............236 L11
st. Attwood.............237 A12
st. Westmeadows....236 L14
st. Westmeadows....237 A14
ARDLUI
dr. Newtown...........701 K11
ARDMERE
pl. Eltham...............288 A6
ARDMILLAN
rd. Moonee Pnd......323 J12
ARDMORE
ct. Macleod.............284 L11
st. Cranbourne........578 C17
st. Mitcham............376 L9
ARDOCH
av. St Kilda E...........414 J14
av. Thomastown......240 G14
ct. Gladstone Pk......237 B17
rd. Sunbury.............143 A6
st. Essendon...........324 B6
ARDOYNE
st. Black Rock.........529 G3
st. Sunshine............365 A8
ARDRIE
rd. Malvern East......456 F1
ARDUINA
ct. Langwarrin.........629 E6
st. Somerville..........645 A13
ARDWELL
ct. St Albans...........275 G19
ARDWICK
st. Bentleigh............496 B4
ARDYNE
st. Murrumbeena....457 B10
ARENA
cl. Flemington...........33 K3
sq. Noble Park.........534 G5
ARGENT
pl. Ringwood..........377 K18
ARGO
st. South Yarra..........31 J13
st. South Yarra........414 E7
ARGONAUT
pl. Altona Mdw........452 A4
ARGONNE
pde. Selby................467 C13
ARGOON
rd. Healesville..........257 F6
ARGUS
cr. Doncaster E.......332 E20
ct. Narre Warren.....553 B12
st. Cheltenham.......496 K17
ARGYLE
av. Chelsea.............547 A20
av. Upwey...............465 K10
cl. Hughesdale........457 E13
cr. Werribee............447 J8
ct. Berwick.............553 H6
ct. Glen Waverley....420 F15
ct. Pakenham...........584 J1
ct. Vermont S.........421 F8
pl. Fitzroy..................19 C12
pl. Lynbrook...........551 H15
pl. Sunbury.............143 H7
pl.e, Carlton..............18 E18
pl.n, Carlton..............18 D16
pl.s, Carlton..............18 D17
rd. Kew..................372 F8
st. Belmont.............702 H20
st. Bentleigh E.........457 C16
st. Donvale.............376 E5
st. Fawkner............281 F11
st. Fitzroy..................19 A12
st. Frankston...........627 C4
st. Glenroy..............280 A6
st. Macleod.............285 B15
st. Moonee Pnd......323 H14
st. New Gisborne......79 B1
st. Reservoir...........283 F5
st. St Kilda..............414 E15
st. W Footscray.......366 H7
st. Geelong, off
Little Ryrie St......703 C9
wy. Wantirna S.........462 D1
ARGYLL
cct. Melton W...........225 K14
cl. Epping...............197 L16
ct. Eltham North......245 C18
st. Malvern East......417 G20
st. Sydenham.........274 H1
ARI
dr. Campbellfield.....239 G10
ARIADNE
av. Murrumbeena....457 A9
ARIANNE
rd. Glen Waverley....420 G20
ARIEL
av. Glen Iris.............417 E11
ct. Keilor Dn............276 B14
ct. Whittington........704 B19
wy. Patterson L........547 G20
ARIES
ch. Kurunjang..........226 L10
ct. Lilydale.............294 H19
ARILPA
ct. Ashwood...........418 C19
ARINGA
av. Highton.............705 G3
ct. Ferntree Gly.......464 E6
ct. Heathmont.........379 B17
ARINYA
cr. Anglesea............713 F4
ARIS
ct. Craigieburn........150 G17
ARISTINES
pl. Sorrento............679 A13
ARISTOC
rd. Glen Waverley....460 A5
ARISTOTLE
ct. Narre Warren.....539 E16
ARJAY
ct. Westmeadows...236 H15
ARKANA
av. Highton.............701 H17
ARKARINGA
cr. Black Rock.........529 E3
ARKARRA
ct. Croydon N.........336 C15
ct. Mooroolbark......337 E12
ARKINDALE
pl. Frankston S........627 H17
ARKINS
st. Pt Lonsdale........710 D5
ARKLE
st. Prahran..............414 L11
st. Prahran..............415 A11
ARKLEY
dr. Greenvale...........237 E1
ARKWELLS
la. Red Hill.............687 H19
ARKWRIGHT
ct. Noble Park N......501 D14
ARLENE
dr. Skye..................601 G5
ARLEON
cr. Cranbourne.........578 F17
ct. Rowville.............463 B14
ct. Somerville..........644 F18
ARLIE
cr. Montrose...........381 J10
ARLINGTON
ct. Dingley Village...532 K6
pl. Nar Warrn S.......579 B3
st. Camberwell.......416 K3
st. Reservoir...........282 L16
st. Ringwood..........378 B14
wk. Vermont............421 K2
wy. Point Cook.........450 G12
ARLUNYA
ct. Aspendale Gdn...546 G3
pl. Templestowe......288 E20
pl. Templestowe......332 E1
rd. Chum Creek.......213 F5
ARMADALE
av. Noble Park.........534 H8
dr. Narre Warren.....553 B10
st. Armadale...........415 F13
st. Melbourne...........31 C11
st. Thornbury..........326 J10
ARMAGH
ct. Belmont.............706 E2
pl. Wantirna S.........422 C19
rd. Frankston S........627 A17

ARMAO
ct. Noble Park.........534 K7
ARMATA
cr. Frankston N.......600 C8
ARMER
ct. Aspendale Gdn...546 H5
ARMFIELD
st. Brighton.............494 L1
ARMIN
st. Scoresby...........462 G5
ARMISTAN
cr. Chelsea Ht..........547 D9
ARMISTEAD
rd. Gruyere.............298 A18
ARMISTON
ct. Endeavour Hl.....538 A5
gr. Altona Mdw........451 L3
gr. Wantirna S.........462 A2
ARMITAGE
ct. Belmont.............706 B6
pl. S Morang...........198 J14
ARMOUR
cl. Glen Waverley....420 L15
ct. Sunshine W......364 J9
ARMSTEAD
av. Coburg..............325 L2
ARMSTRONG
cl. Keilor East..........278 A20
cl. Malvern East......457 F2
ct. Roxburgh Pk......194 F12
ct. Vermont.............421 F1
ct. Whittington........704 C19
dr. Melton S............268 B12
dr. Rowville.............503 D2
gr. Yarra Glen..........209 C19
rd. Bayswater..........423 D2
rd. Beaconsfld Up....542 K17
rd. Heathmont.........379 C20
rd. McCrae..............684 H18
rd. Plenty................244 D1
rd. Seaford..............573 C17
st. Beaumaris..........530 F7
st. Coburg..............281 G18
st. Greensborough..243 K20
st. Laverton............407 D16
st. Middle Park..........30 C20
st. Middle Park........413 G11
st. Mornington........640 D13
st. Mt Waverley.......418 K16
st. Reservoir...........282 H13
st. Springvale..........499 K17
st. Sunshine W.......364 K5
wy. Dandenong N.....501 F12
ARMSTRONGS
rd. Seaford..............573 J17
ARMY
av. Reservoir...........282 E13
rd. Boronia.............424 F3
rd. Lysterfield S.......503 C13
rd. Pakenham..........559 E7
rd. Pakenham..........585 D2
rd. Pakenham Up.....559 E7
tr. Lysterfield S.......503 A11
ARMY SETTLEMENT
rd. Pakenham..........559 H11
rd. Pakenham Up.....559 H11
ARMYTAGE
rd. Officer...............556 B10
ARNA
st. Blackburn..........375 J19
ARNCLIFFE
bvd. Greenvale...........193 C17
ARNDELL
cl. Truganina..........405 J13
st. Thomastown.......241 A11
ARNDT
rd. Pascoe Vale.......280 E12
ARNHEM
ct. Rowville.............463 E15
ARNICA
cl. Hampton Pk.......552 B16
ARNOLD
av. Heidelberg Ht.....328 F1
ct. Bundoora...........242 J20
ct. Dandenong.........536 E9
ct. Hoppers Csg......449 B1
ct. Melton..............268 J1
ct. Pascoe Vale.......280 F13
dr. Chelsea.............547 C14
dr. Donvale.............333 A10
dr. Scoresby...........462 G5
gr. Doncaster..........374 H1
rd. Brighton East.....495 H5
st. Blairgowrie.........695 K3
st. Box Hill.............374 H13
st. Brunswick E.......325 L16
st. Cheltenham.......496 C17
st. Cranbourne........578 G20
st. Kilsyth..............381 F9
st. Mt Waverley.......418 H20
st. Noble Park.........534 L2

st. Preston.............282 L18
st. Princes Hill..........18 C1
st. Princes Hill.........325 G20
st. Ringwood..........378 F7
st. South Yarra..........31 B6
st. South Yarra.......414 A3
st. Sunshine W........364 G3
st. Whittlesea............96 G19

ARNOT
ct. Springvale S.......534 A5
st. Brighton East.....455 D17

ARNOTT
ct. Wheelers Hill......460 J10
pl. Nar Warrn N........539 E9
st. Clayton..............459 D18
st. Cranbourne N.....578 C9
st. Geelong West.....702 F6
st. Mont Albert N.....374 F8
st. Ormond..............456 E13
st. Sorrento.............678 L14

ARNSIDE
cr. Westmeadows...236 F15

AROHA
cr. Camberwell........416 L5
cr. Camberwell........417 A5

AROONA
av. Mitcham............377 D16
ct. Aberfeldie..........323 E12
rd. Caulfield N.........455 D1

ARRAN
cl. Epping...............198 H20
ct. Glen Waverley....419 K14
ct. Sunbury.............144 F11
ct. Sydenham..........274 K2
st. Seddon..............367 D10

ARRANGA
st. Rosebud............684 B19

ARRANMORE
av. Black Rock.........529 G3

ARRAS
st. Spotswood........410 J1

ARRINO
cr. Hallam...............552 C1

ARRUNGA
ct. Patterson L........573 K8

ARSCOTT
cl. Croydon S..........379 H11

ARSENAL
ct. Epping...............242 C1

ARTEMIS
ct. Templstw Lr.......330 L15

ARTHUR
av. Brighton.............494 K3
ct. Bundoora...........284 G2
ct. Noble Park.........534 C2
ct. Skye..................575 G19
pl. Croydon.............336 C18
rd. Chirnside Pk.......336 K4
rd. Cockatoo...........511 D4
st. Aberfeldie..........323 C10
st. Aberfeldie..........323 D10
st. Ashwood...........418 D13
st. Beaconsfield......555 B15
st. Belmont.............706 C1
st. Bentleigh.............456 D20
st. Braybrook..........365 K4
st. Briar Hill..............286 G4
st. Bundoora...........284 D2
st. Burwood............418 D13
st. Burwood E.........419 L8
st. Caulfield N.........415 H17
st. Coburg N...........282 B14
st. Doncaster..........375 A2
st. Dromana............686 A5
st. Eltham...............287 H8
st. Fairfield..............327 E20
st. Footscray...........367 B4
st. Hughesdale.........457 F9
st. Malvern.............416 B7
st. Melbourne...........30 L9
st. Melbourne...........31 A9
st. Melbourne..........414 A5
st. Murrumbeena....457 C7
st. Preston..............326 H2
st. St Albans...........320 B2
st. Sandringham......494 L12
st. Sandringham......495 A12
st. Seaford.............573 D16
st. Selby.................467 C18
st. S Melbourne........29 D3
st. South Yarra..........32 B11
st. South Yarra........414 G6
st. Surrey Hills........374 F18
st. Thornbury..........327 E14
st. Thornbury..........327 F11
st. Wantirna S.........423 B14

ARTHUR PHILLIP
dr. Endeavour Hl.....537 F10
wy. Keilor Lodge.......276 A2
wy. Mill Park............242 D4

ARTHURS
av. McCrae.............685 E12
rd. Dandenong N.....502 E18

ARTHURS CREEK
rd. Doreen...............156 C4
rd. Yan Yean...........156 C4

ARTHURSON
st. Mt Waverley.......419 A20

ARTHURS SEAT
rd. Arthurs Seat.......685 G13
rd. Arthurs Seat.......685 H10
rd. Arthurs Seat.......685 K14
rd. Red Hill..............686 H17
rd. Red Hill..............687 D19

ARTHUR STREETON
dr. Yallambie...........285 J15
pl. Diamond Ck.......245 B13

ARTHURTON
rd. Northcote..........326 D13

ARTISAN
cl. Torquay.............712 C2

ARTISTS
cr. Nar Warrn S.......578 G1

ARTISTS HILL
Eltham North......288 C1

ARUMA
ct. Bundoora...........284 K3
ct. Burwood E.........419 H11
ct. Chelsea.............547 B15
st. Warneet.............649 G11

ARUNDEL
av. Glenroy.............279 K3
av. Reservoir...........283 C1
cl. Springvale S.......499 H20
cr. Surrey Hills........373 K20
cr. Surrey Hills........417 K1
ct. Box Hill S...........418 J5
ct. Hoppers Csg......405 D19
ct. Mt Eliza.............626 K18
ct. Mulgrave............460 F20
rd. Keilor.................276 L1
rd. Keilor.................277 A1
rd. Keilor.................277 B9
rd. Pk Orchards.......333 K16
st. Cranbourne........578 E20
st. Croydon.............335 H19

ARUNGA
dr. Wonga Park.......291 G19

ARUNTA
cr. Clarinda.............498 E4
ct. Eltham...............288 A6
ct. Rye....................696 K11
st. Reservoir...........282 B12

ARURA
ct. Doncaster..........374 G2

ARVERN
av. Avondale Ht.......322 E13

ARVON
rd. Strathmore.........279 K16

ARVONA
av. Sunshine N........321 D12

ARWON
ct. Lilydale.............294 C20
ct. New Gisborne......79 B1
st. Mordialloc..........532 D17

ASCALON
rd. Montrose...........381 L11

ASCOT
av. Bacchus Msh.....221 E14
ct. Broadmeadows..238 A9
ct. Dandenong N.....501 J12
ct. Glen Waverley....459 H7
ct. Nar Warrn N.......539 E9
ct. Oakleigh S.........498 B7
ct. St Albans...........275 G18
ct. Thomastown......241 J16
dr. Keilor Park.........278 B12
dr. Noble Park N......501 B8
pl. Melton W...........226 B15
ri. Berwick..............554 J7
st. Ascot Vale..........324 A20
st. Doncaster E.......332 A20
st. Laverton............407 A19
st. Malvern.............416 A11
st. Newtown............702 F10
st. Preston..............327 A6
st.s, Altona Mdw.......407 A20
st.s, Altona Mdw.......451 A1

ASCOT VALE
rd. Ascot Vale..........324 C19
rd. Flemington...........33 E4
rd. Flemington..........324 C19
rd. Moonee Pnd......324 C19

ASH
cl. Gisborne..............78 K9
cr. Pakenham..........559 A19
ct. Cheltenham........531 F2
ct. Clayton S............498 H8
ct. Donvale.............377 C7
ct. Frankston N........600 F10
ct. Glenroy..............280 C2

ct. Hoppers Csg......405 C16
ct. Pascoe Vale.......280 L11
ct. Waurn Ponds.....705 E16
ct. Wheelers Hill......460 F14
gr. Bayswater..........423 E6
gr. Caulfield............455 L6
gr. Dandenong........535 L2
gr. Keilor East.........322 E6
gr. Malvern East......456 H1
gr. Menzies Ck........468 B19
gr. Montrose...........381 J11
gr. Oak Park............279 K11
gr. Springvale..........499 L15
gr.n, Langwarrin........601 A20
gr.s, Langwarrin........629 A2
pl. Melton S............268 G6
st. Braybrook..........321 L20
st. Cranbourne........604 C2
st. Doveton.............536 K10
st. Lalor..................241 G12
st. Preston..............283 J18
st. Thomastown.......241 G12

ASHBEE
ct. Rowville.............503 F1

ASHBOURNE
pl. Dingley Village...533 D10
st. Herne Hill...........701 K1

ASHBROOK
cct. Bundoora...........242 E18
cl. Rowville.............503 C6
ct. Frankston...........599 L18
ct. Oakleigh S..........498 E1
pl. Mooroolbark.......337 F10

ASHBURN
gr. Ashburton..........417 D20
pl. Blackburn..........376 B14

ASHBURTON
dr. Mitcham............377 G11
rd. Glen Iris.............417 B13

ASHBURY
ct. Mt Waverley.......458 H4

ASHBY
ct. Altona Mdw........451 D4
ct. Balwyn N...........373 D5
ct. Bayswater..........423 D4
st. Chadstone..........458 E4
dr. Dandenong N.....501 L12
gr. Eaglemont..........328 F12
gr. Ivanhoe.............328 F12
la. Caroline Spr.......318 C10
wy. Kilsyth..............381 E7

ASHCOMBE
dr. Ringwood..........335 C19

ASHCROFT
av. Templestowe.....331 H14
gr. Blackburn S.......420 A5

ASHDALE
ct. Hampton Pk........551 E6
ct. Springvale..........499 J7
gr. Eltham...............288 E4

ASHDOWN
ct. Bundoora...........284 K2
ct. Lalor..................241 K6
wy. Wheelers Hill......460 L12

ASHE
cr. Bellfield..............328 C7
gr. Toorak..................32 L14
gr. Toorak................414 L7
gr. Toorak................415 A7

ASHENDEN
sq. Rosebud............699 J1

ASHFIELD
dr. Berwick..............554 B17
dr. Skye..................601 G3
st. Reservoir............282 C6

ASHFORD
cl. Hampton Pk........551 E5
cr. Westmeadows....236 H14
ct. Belmont.............705 L7
ct. Berwick..............554 A2
st. Templstw Lr.......330 J10

ASHKANASY
av. Pascoe Vale.......281 A13

ASHLAR
cr. Blackburn..........376 B12
rd. Moorabbin.........496 D9

ASHLEIGH
av. Frankston...........599 K20
cr. Meadow Ht.........237 K2
ct. Cheltenham........497 B14
ct. Kealba...............276 K17
rd. Armadale............415 D11
st. Frankston...........599 K19
st. Keysborough......534 K12

ASHLENE
gr. Carrum Downs...575 A15

ASHLEY
av. Hoppers Csg......405 A13
cl. Narre Warren.....538 G16
cl. Wheelers Hill......460 J10
ct. Forest Hill...........420 C6

ct. Grovedale...........706 A15
ct. Research............288 G7
ct. Seville.................341 J13
ct. Thomastown.......240 J16
gr. Malvern.............416 B10
rd. Carrum Downs...574 D18
rd. Yarrambat..........200 G13
st. Box Hill N...........375 D11
st. Braybrook..........322 D20
st. Braybrook..........366 C7
st. Maidstone..........322 D19
st. Reservoir............282 J11
st. Wantirna............422 D6
st. W Footscray.......366 C7

ASHLEY PARK
dr. Chelsea Ht.........547 F11

ASHMERE
ct. Caroline Spr.......317 L6

ASHMORE
av. Mordialloc..........531 J16
rd. Bend of Islands..250 L14
rd. Bend of Islands..251 A14
rd. Christmas Hills...250 L14
rd. Forest Hill...........420 K4
st. Brunswick..........325 J11

ASHRIDGE
ct. Wyndham Va.....446 D7

ASHRYE
gld. Nar Warrn S.......552 H7

ASHTED
rd. Box Hill..............374 K17

ASHTON
av. Mooroolbark......337 D10
av. St Albans...........320 L5
av. St Albans...........321 A4
cl. Mill Park.............242 K8
cl. Ringwood...........379 B2
ct. Cranbourne........578 F16
ct. Sunbury.............142 K10
pl. Pakenham..........585 D6
rd. Ferntree Gly.......463 H4
ri. Doncaster E........332 E9
ri. Nar Warrn S.......552 E15
st. Glen Waverley....420 G15
st. Reservoir...........283 E16
st. Yallambie...........285 H15

ASHVIEW
ct. Rowville.............463 H17

ASHWOOD
av. Highett...............495 J13
cl. Gladstone Pk......279 B1
cl. Langwarrin.........629 H1
cl. Wantirna............422 F9
ct. Narre Warren.....538 H19
dr. Ashwood............418 C14
dr. Nunawading.......376 H8
pde. Craigieburn........193 K3

ASHWORTH
av. Wattle Glen........246 J5
dr. Seaford..............599 L1
st. Albert Park...........29 E17
st. Albert Park...........29 G18
st. Middle Park..........29 G18

ASKEW
st. Geelong West.....702 F3

ASLING
st. Brighton.............454 L14
st. Brighton.............455 A13
st. Preston..............282 G19
st. Springvale S.......500 B20

ASPECT
av. Cockatoo...........510 H7

ASPEN
cl. Wantirna S.........422 A15
ct. Frankston N........600 D5
ct. Springvale S.......534 B6
st. Moonee Pnd.......324 B13
st. St Albans...........320 E8

ASPINALL
rd. Box Hill N...........375 B7

ASQUITH
av. Mt Martha..........668 L8
av. Mt Martha..........669 A8
ct. Epping...............197 L16
ct. Wantirna............422 F10
pl. Melton W...........226 B19
st. Box Hill S...........418 K2
st. Kew...................372 C6
st. Kew East............372 C6
st. Reservoir...........283 A2

ASSEMBLY
dr. Tullamarine........278 C9

ASTAIR
av. S Morang...........198 L13

ASTALL
st. Carrum Downs...575 G15

ASTELOT
dr. Donvale.............376 J6

ASTER
av. Carrum Downs...600 F1
cl. Meadow Ht........193 L19

cr. Highett...............496 D1
ct. Mill Park............243 A1
ct. Mt Waverley.......419 C1
st. Dromana............686 F
st. The Basin...........424 K

ASTI
ct. Avondale Ht.......322 D

ASTLEY
ct. Vermont S.........420 K1
st. Montmorency....286 H1
st. Templstw Lr.......330 C
wk. Roxburgh Pk......194 B1

ASTOLAT
av. Murrumbeena....457 C

ASTON
ct. Burwood E.........420 B1
st. Yarraville............367 E1

ASTON HEATH
Glen Waverley....460 L

ASTONS
rd. Yarrambat..........201 J1

ASTOR
ct. Kilsyth...............380 L
pl. Carlton.................18 F1
pl. Melton W...........226 E1

ASTRAN
ct. Endeavour Hl.....537 K
pl. Doncaster..........331 B1

ASTRID
ct. Berwick..............554 G1

ATEN
pl. Tullamarine........278 L

ATHELDENE
dr. Glen Waverley....460 L
dr. St Albans...........275 H1

ATHELLA
ct. Ferntree Gly.......424 H2

ATHELSTAN
rd. Camberwell........416 L7
rd. Camberwell........417 A5

ATHELSTANE
dr. Ringwood N.......378 D2
gr. Ivanhoe.............328 B1

ATHENA
cl. Tullamarine........278 F5
ct. Templstw Lr.......330 K16
pl. Epping...............198 D18

ATHENAEUM
pl. Melbourne.............2 G14
pl. Melbourne...........24 F8

ATHENIUM
ct. Carrum Downs...601 E6

ATHENRY
tce. Templestowe.....332 C4

ATHENS
pl. Oak Park............279 F10

ATHERTON
cl. Aspendale Gdn...546 K7
ct. Kilsyth...............381 J8
rd. Oakleigh.............457 K10

ATHLONE
ct. Endeavour Hl.....537 A1
st. Lilydale.............339 A12

ATHOL
av. Bundoora...........284 G6
av. Coburg N...........281 D13
ct. Blackburn..........375 J13
ct. Langwarrin.........629 E5
ct. Rye....................697 E4
pl. Canterbury.........372 L14
pl. Canterbury.........373 A14
rd. Noble Park.........533 K2
rd. Springvale S.......533 K2
st. Braybrook..........366 C3
st. Moonee Pnd......323 K14
st. Mt Waverley.......458 J2
st. Prahran................31 H16
st. Prahran..............414 E8

ATHORN
ct. Darley................222 A10

ATKIN
st. Melton...............268 K1
st. N Melbourne........17 C18

ATKINS
av. Glen Iris.............416 L8
av. Watsonia N........243 G20
ct. Carrum Downs...575 D15
rd. Pakenham..........585 A4
st. Fyansford...........701 E4
st. Kew...................372 D11
st. Newcomb..........704 A16

ATKINSON
cl. Sunbury.............142 F8
cl. Windsor, off
Hornby St.........414 H12
ct. Aspendale Gdn...546 J3
la. Geelong, off
Ginn St..............702 L3
pl. Reservoir...........283 G4
st. Bentleigh............496 B4

AZAROW
cct. Croydon S 380 A13
AZTEC
ct. Wheelers Hill 461 A13
pl. Thomastown 240 F17
AZURE
ct. Templestowe 331 K6

B

BAAN
cl. Fawkner 281 K11
BABB
st. Maidstone 366 G3
BABINDA
ct. Rowville 463 F15
BABRA
ct. Grovedale 706 D8
BACCHUS
cr. Millgrove 348 E4
ct. Frankston S 627 F13
dr. Croydon S 380 A13
st. Maddingley 221 G20
BACCHUS MARSH
rd. Bacchus Msh 221 E13
rd. Bacchus Msh 265 A1
BACCHUS MARSH-BALLIANG
rd. Maddingley 263 A11
BACCHUS MARSH-GEELONG
rd. Maddingley 264 B3
rd. Maddingley 264 F20
rd. Parwan 264 F20
BACCHUS MARSH-GISBORNE
rd. Bullengarook 77 A7
rd. Darley 222 C9
rd. Gisborne 77 G9
rd. Merrimu 222 C9
BACCHUS MARSH-WERRIBEE
rd. Wyndham Va 446 A2
BACH
la. Fitzroy 18 L16
BACHLI
cl. Mill Park 242 C5
ct. Anglesea 713 A6
ct. Rosanna 284 L20
ct. Rosanna 285 A20
st. Rye 696 J5
BACK
rd. Sherbrooke 466 J2
BACK BEACH
rd. Portsea 677 H6
BACKHAUS
av. Sunbury 142 L17
av. Sunbury 143 A17
st. Hampton 494 L5
BACKOUS
wy. Noble Park 534 F3
BACKSTAIRS
tr. Warburton 348 H6
tr. Warburton 349 A5
BACKWELL
la. Geelong, off Maud St 703 A10
BADEN
cl. Frankston S 626 J11
dr. Hoppers Csg 448 K7
BADENOCH
ct. Highton 701 E16
st. Blackburn 376 C14
BADEN POWELL
dr. Endeavour Hl 502 L18
dr. Endeavour Hl 503 A18
dr. Frankston S 626 J11
dr. Healesville 258 A9
dr. Mt Eliza 626 D15
pl. Mt Eliza 626 C19
BADER
av. Nunawading 376 K12
ct. Frankston S 626 G9
ct. Ringwood 378 L2
BADGE
ct. Laverton 407 B16
BADGER
av. Badger Creek 258 B16
ct. Lilydale 294 J20
ct. Narre Warren 538 J14
ct. Thomastown 240 H14
pl. Mulgrave 501 E5
BADGER CREEK
rd. Badger Creek 258 D10
rd. Healesville 213 K19
rd. Healesville 258 B2
BADGER WEIR
rd. Badger Creek 258 K13
BADMINTON
ct. Wantirna 422 E8
BAEZ
wy. Hampton Pk 551 H12
BAGE
pl. Roxburgh Pk 193 J15
st. Diamond Ck 245 H10
BAGENDON
ct. Kilsyth S 424 K2
BAGGOTT
dr. Hoppers Csg 448 F3
BAGLEY
st. Brighton 494 J2
BAGLEYS
la. Vermont 421 B5
BAGORA
ct. Bayswater N 380 H19
BAGULEY
cr. Kings Park 275 B20
BAHAMA
ct. Vermont 420 L3
ct. Vermont 421 A3
BAHEN
cl. Eltham North 287 K1
ct. Watsonia 285 E8
BAHLOO
ct. Frankston 600 H19
BAILEY
av. Armadale 415 H15
av. Keilor East 278 A17
av. Preston 327 B5
av. St Kilda E 454 K1
ct. Campbellfield 239 G14
ct. Springvale 499 L18
gr. Ivanhoe East 328 G13
gr. Wandin N 340 E15
pl. Mornington 657 E6
rd. Cockatoo 510 J4
rd. Emerald 510 G7
rd. Mt Evelyn 339 F18
rd. Nar Warrn N 539 H4
rd. Wandin N 340 D16
st. Belmont 706 J5
st. Boronia 423 L14
st. Grovedale 706 H12
st. Pt Lonsdale 710 E4
st. St Albans 320 D11
st. Werribee 448 A14
BAILEYANA
dr. Endeavour Hl 502 J19
st. Frankston S 627 D8
BAILEY GULLY
rd. Hurstbridge 203 C19
rd. Wattle Glen 203 C19
rd. Wattle Glen 247 B1
BAILEY JAMES
ct. Rowville 503 C7
BAILEYS
ct. Meadow Ht 238 B3
BAILLIE
ct. Bacchus Msh 221 J16
ct. Frankston 628 C6
st. N Melbourne 17 A16
BAILLIEU
st. Pt Lonsdale 710 F7
BAILY
st. Mt Waverley 419 G17
BAIN
av. Coburg N 281 F12
ct. Newcomb 704 A13
st. Berwick 554 G8
BAINBRIDGE
av. Seaford 599 E12
cl. Craigieburn 150 F20
ct. Carrum Downs 600 L6
ct. Carrum Downs 601 A6
ct. Kilsyth 381 C3
dr. Eltham 288 A7
BAINES
cr. Torquay 711 J7
BAIRD
ct. Blackburn S 419 G2
ct. Rowville 463 C19
st. Ashburton 417 B17
st. Brighton East 495 D5
st. Fawkner 281 J6
st. Greensborough 286 D11
st. Maidstone 366 G3
st. Mulgrave 500 D5
st.e, Doncaster 375 C3
st.n, Doncaster 375 B2
st.s, Doncaster 375 B3
BAKE HOUSE
la. Carlton 18 J15
BAKEHOUSE
la. Fitzroy N 19 C8
rd. Panton Hill 204 J15
BAKER
av. Blairgowrie 679 C19
av. Edithvale 546 K14
av. Glen Waverley 459 K8
av. Kew East 372 B4
ct. Burwood E 419 L11
ct. Meadow Ht 237 L6
la. Prahran 31 F16
pde. Ashburton 417 G13
rd. Bayswater N 379 J15
rd. Harkaway 540 F16
ri. Sunbury 142 G8
st. Anglesea 713 F6
st. Brighton 454 K17
st. Cockatoo 510 L4
st. Geelong West 702 E1
st. Lilydale 337 K4
st. Malvern East 456 K2
st. Moorabbin 496 F7
st. Murrumbeena 457 C14
st. Richmond 26 H4
st. St Kilda 414 B20
st. Sunshine 365 G3
BAKERS
pde. Brunswick W 324 K7
rd. Coburg N 281 B15
rd. Dandenong N 501 E13
rd. Oakleigh S 497 K2
BAKERY
la. N Melbourne 17 C18
sq. Melton 226 L19
st. Brunswick 325 E17
BAKEWELL
ct. Blairgowrie 679 F16
st. Cranbourne 604 E3
st. Tooradin 651 H9
BALACLAVA
av. Altona Mdw 451 G2
rd. Caulfield N 415 F19
rd. St Kilda E 414 L18
rd. St Kilda E 415 A18
BALAKA
av. Aspendale 546 F4
ct. Delahey 275 B11
ct. Rosebud W 699 E2
pl. Bundoora 284 K3
st. Rosebud W 699 E1
st. Warneet 649 D14
BALAM
grn. Sydenham 274 K6
BALAMARA
ct. Frankston S 643 G1
pl. Mornington 641 C16
BALANDA
ct. Bundoora 243 A20
BALANKA
ct. Berwick 580 F1
BALARANG
ct. Patterson L 573 K10
BALBETHAN
dr. Sunbury 144 F3
BALCOMBE
av. Mooroolbark 337 G14
ct. Craigieburn 150 C20
ct. Croydon 379 H6
ct. Donvale 332 L15
ct. Narre Warren 552 G2
dr. Mt Martha 657 B8
dr. Mt Martha 657 C8
pl. Dingley Village 532 L9
pl. Hillside 232 G19
pl. Melbourne 2 B14
pl. Melbourne 24 D8
rd. Beaumaris 529 G5
rd. Black Rock 529 G5
rd. Mentone 530 K7
rd. Newtown 701 L13
st. Frankston 627 E4
st. Mornington 640 K13
st. Sunshine N 321 H19
BALCOMBE CREEK
cl. Mt Martha 656 B14
BALCOMBE PARK
la. Beaumaris 529 L5
BALD HILL
rd. Pakenham 585 A9
rd. Pakenham 586 A14
BALDING
av. Werribee 447 J18
BALDOCK
rd. Mornington 641 J13
BALDWIN
av. Boronia 424 G4
av. Montmorency 286 H8
av. Noble Park 534 H4
av. Sunshine N 321 D7
av. Up Fntree Gly 465 E7
dr. Somerton 194 H10
rd. Altona North 408 K6
rd. Blackburn 375 H20
st. Armadale 415 G12
st. Highett 496 A12
BALDWYN
st. Frankston 599 D13
BALES
st. Ferntree Gly 464 D7
st. Mt Waverley 458 K6
BALFE
cr. Brunswick W 324 J14
BALFOUR
av. Heathmont 378 J17
av. Sunshine N 321 D8
cl. Watsonia N 243 H19
ct. Berwick 554 B2
ct. Glen Waverley 420 D15
pl. Melton W 225 K15
pl. Noble Park N 501 A7
pl. Point Cook 450 E7
st. Brighton East 495 D1
st. Doncaster 374 G3
st. Reservoir 282 K1
st. Toorak 415 G3
BALGONIE
pl. Northcote 326 J14
BALGOWLAH
av. Keysborough 534 G10
BALI
pl. Lalor 241 H7
BALI HI
bvd. Templestowe 331 K11
BALINGA
cl. Skye 601 H2
ct. Doncaster E 332 H10
BALKAN
ct. Dandenong N 502 D17
BALL
rd. Heatherton 497 H15
st. Darley 221 H8
st. Sunshine N 321 F14
BALLABIL
st. Rye 697 F4
BALLADONIA
rd. Rowville 463 G15
BALLAM
cl. Frankston 628 F2
BALLAMORE
cr. Doncaster 331 B13
BALLAN
rd. Werribee 446 J12
rd. Werribee 447 A13
rd. Wyndham Va 445 L1
st.s, Reservoir 282 E1
BALLANDRY
cr. Greensborough 244 K19
BALLANEE
gr. Cranbourne N 578 D9
BALLANTYNE
cr. Kilsyth 381 C3
st. Burwood E 420 B8
st. Southbank 23 J20
st. Southbank 29 K1
st. Thornbury 326 E8
BALLARA
av. Glen Waverley 459 L11
ct. Brighton 454 G13
ct. Highton 705 H5
BALLARAT
rd. Ardeer 319 K16
rd. Braybrook 322 B20
rd. Burnside 318 G12
rd. Deer Park 319 J16
rd. Footscray 367 J6
rd. Maidstone 366 J2
rd. Ravenhall 318 G12
rd. Sunshine 321 F19
rd. Sunshine N 321 F19
st. Brunswick 325 F12
st. Collingwood 19 L11
st. Lalor 241 E6
st. Yarraville 367 C17
BALLARD
av. Coburg N 282 A17
cl. Gladstone Pk 279 D1
ct. Wantirna 422 E13
st. Yarraville 366 E16
BALLART
tr. Lysterfield 505 H2
BALLARTO
rd. Carrum Downs 600 D5
rd. Cranbourne 603 D9
rd. Cranbourne 604 G11
rd. Cranbourne E 604 J11
rd. Cranbourne S 603 D9
rd. Frankston N 600 D5
rd. Junction Vill 604 G11
rd. Skye 601 C6
st. Tooradin 651 K8
BALLATER
av. Newtown 701 K1
st. Essendon 323 G
BALLIANG
st. S Geelong 702 L1
st. S Geelong 703 B1
BALLIN
st. Kings Park 319 E
BALLINA
ct. Deer Park 318 K1
pl. Hampton Pk 552 B
tce. Vermont S 420 L1
BALLINAMONA
st. Fairfield 327 G1
BALLIOL
cmn. Sunbury 144 E1
BALLOAN
st. Coburg 325 E
BALLUK WILLIAM
ct. St Kilda 414 A1
BALLYMORE
ct. Frankston 628 B
BALMAIN
ct. Lalor 240 K
ct. Wantirna 422 F1
dr. Berwick 554 A
dr. Carrum Downs 600 H
st. Cremorne 26 A2
st. Cremorne 32 A
st. Glen Waverley 460 F1
BALMANNO
cr. Strathmore 323 L
BALMER
gra. Brookfield 267 C
st. Brunswick 325 H1
BALMERINO
av. Toorak 415 B
sq. Frankston 628 D
BALMORAL
av. Bentleigh 456 E2
av. Brunswick E 325 L1
av. Bundoora 284 J
av. Dandenong 536 D1
av. Kew 372 J1
av. McKinnon 456 E2
av. Pascoe Vale S 324 J
av. Safety Bch 668 J2
av. Sandringham 495 K1
av. Springvale 499 H1
av. Strathmore 279 H2
av. Templstw Lr 330 E1
av. Wesburn 348 A
cct. Eltham North 245 J1
cct. Sunbury 142 L
cct. Sunbury 143 A
cl. Kings Park 318 L
cl. Wyndham Va 446 C7
cr. Surrey Hills 374 C1
ct. Burwood E 420 A
ct. Frankston S 628 C15
ct. Glen Waverley 459 H1
ct. Hallam 537 E1
ct. Rowville 463 G1
ct. St Kilda E 414 L1
ct. St Kilda E 415 A1
dr. Parkdale 531 K
dr. Point Cook 450 C5
pl. Melton W 226 D15
pl. South Yarra 32 B15
rd. Ringwood N 378 E
st. Braybrook 321 L2
st. Braybrook 365 L1
st. Essendon 323 H6
st. Frankston 599 C1
st. Kilsyth 381 G7
st. Laverton 407 B1
st. South Yarra 32 A15
st. South Yarra 414 G7
st.s, Altona Mdw 407 B2
wy. Pakenham 584 G1
BALNARRING
dr. Kings Park 319 A2
rd. Tuerong 670 L4
BALONNE
cl. Taylors Lakes 233 F18
BALOO
ct. St Helena 244 H17
BALOOK
ct. Cranbourne N 577 L4
ct. Meadow Ht 237 K6
st. Rye 697 B8
BALSAM
ct. Cranbourne N 578 A5
st. Templstw Lr 330 K15
BALSTON
st. Balaclava 414 J18
st. Southbank 3 C10
st. Southbank 24 B17
BALTASER
dr. Pakenham 585 E2

BALTUSROL
cl. Sunbury 144 F12
BALUK
pl. Kurunjang 227 B13
BALWYN
ct. Narre Warren 553 D10
rd. Balwyn 373 E17
rd. Balwyn N 373 G4
rd. Bulleen 329 H17
rd. Canterbury 373 E17
BALYARTA
ct. Forest Hill 420 E6
BAMBA
ct. Scoresby 462 H6
BAMBARA
ct. Greensborough 244 J20
ct. Sunshine W 364 K7
rd. Hurstbridge 203 E13
st. Wantirna 422 C14
BAMBER
cl. Mordialloc 532 E17
BAMBIL
ct. Boronia 424 J6
st. Chadstone 458 B2
BAMBOO
ct. Cranbourne N 577 L6
ct. Doveton 536 H9
ct. Mill Park 242 D11
BAMBRA
ct. Doncaster E 332 C19
ct. Grovedale 705 L14
ct. Mt Waverley 419 E12
ct. Noble Park 534 D2
ct. Seaford 600 B3
ct. Tootgarook 698 F8
ct. Vermont 420 L5
rd. Caulfield 455 K5
rd. Caulfield N 415 K20
rd. Caulfield S 455 J12
st. Croydon 336 J15
st. Mt Eliza 641 L3
st. Geelong, off McKillop St 703 A9
BAMBURGH
st. Jacana 237 J18
BAMBURY
ct. Campbellfield 239 H14
pl. Ferntree Gly 464 F1
st. Boronia 424 E11
BAMFIELD
cl. Templestowe 331 C11
rd. Heidelberg Ht 328 G2
rd. Heidelberg W 284 G20
rd. Mt Evelyn 384 A5
st. Sandringham 494 L12
st. Sandringham 495 A13
st. Sandringham 495 B13
BAMFORD
av. Westmeadows 236 F13
BAMPTON
mw. Craigieburn 194 B3
BANADELL
av. Darley 221 F1
BANANA
al. Melbourne 1 G20
al. Melbourne 24 B12
BANARA
ct. Mulgrave 500 H6
BANBRIDGE
pl. Carlton 18 B16
BANBURY
cr. Craigieburn 149 L15
ct. Somerville 644 J19
rd. Reservoir 282 D9
st. Burwood E 419 L11
BANCELL
st. Campbellfield 239 F16
BANCHORY
av. Hillside 232 D20
st. Essendon 323 H6
BANCROFT
av. Nar Warrn S 579 C5
BANDA
ct. Rye 697 C9
BANDALONG
ct. Bundoora 285 A1
BANDO
rd. Springvale 499 G11
BANEEM
ct. Sydenham 275 A8
BANFF
cl. Mulgrave 500 G1
ct. Balwyn 374 A11
st. Reservoir 283 F5
BANFIELD
ct. Ferntree Gly 463 G9
sq. Mt Waverley 419 D20
BANGALAY
av. Frankston S 626 K10
pl. Berwick 553 H3
BANGALORE
st. Kensington 33 G10
BANGALOW
wy. Aspendale Gdn 547 B4
BANGAMBALANGA
av. Chum Creek 213 A8
BANGERANG
av. Sunshine N 320 L13
av. Sunshine N 321 A13
BANGHOLME
rd. Bangholme 549 C11
rd. Dandenong S 549 A11
BANGOR
ct. Heathmont 422 G2
dr. Frankston 628 E3
BANGS
st. Prahran 32 F20
st. Prahran 414 J10
BANHUL
pl. Bundoora 284 E3
BANJO
bvd. Carrum Downs 575 F18
pl. Officer S 582 B18
BANJO PATERSON
av. Oakleigh E 458 J12
BANJORA
cl. Croydon Hills 335 H15
BANK
pl. Melbourne 1 G15
pl. Melbourne 24 A9
pl. St Kilda 414 D13
pl. S Melbourne 30 B4
pl. Taylors Hill 274 G9
pl. Geelong, off Little Malop St 703 B8
rd. Edithvale 546 G13
st. Alphington 327 K18
st. Ascot Vale 324 D16
st. Box Hill 374 L15
st. Braybrook 366 C5
st. Brunswick 325 H16
st. Bundoora 284 A1
st. Craigieburn 150 C16
st. Northcote 327 C17
st. Oakleigh 457 K13
st. Richmond 26 F9
st. S Melbourne 29 G7
st. S Melbourne 413 E3
st. S Melbourne 413 H2
BANKER
ct. Epping 198 D20
ct. Epping 242 C1
ct. Lilydale 294 A19
BANKS
av. Hampton 495 D11
ct. Belmont 702 E17
pl. Gladstone Pk 237 E16
pl. Keilor 276 L11
rd. Cranbourne 604 A5
rd. Eltham North 287 F1
rd. Mannerim 707 A1
st. McCrae 684 J17
st. Warneet 649 D14
BANKSIA
av. Beaumaris 530 E11
av. Thomastown 240 G14
cct. Wesburn 348 C6
ct. Altona Mdw 451 K1
ct. Bayswater 423 G5
ct. Chelsea 547 B19
ct. Croydon S 379 E11
ct. Frankston S 627 H12
ct. Heathmont 379 B18
ct. Langwarrin 629 J4
ct. Long Forest 224 G10
ct. Newcomb 704 C13
ct. Noble Park 500 K18
ct. Sunbury 143 K6
ct. W Footscray 366 F11
ct. Wheelers Hill 460 E13
gr. Gisborne 78 L9
gr. Mt Martha 669 H1
gr. Sorrento 679 B18
gr. Tullamarine 278 J6
pl. Grovedale 706 E9
pl. Meadow Ht 193 J19
pl. Melton W 226 B15
pl. Rosebud 683 L20
pl. Rosebud 684 A20
rd. Caulfield S 455 F9
ri. Eltham North 245 F19
st. Bellfield 327 L7
st. Bentleigh E 457 E17
st. Blackburn 375 F20
st. Burwood 418 A6
st. Clayton 458 J18
st. Doveton 536 J6
st. Eaglemont 328 A8
st. Eaglemont 328 K8
st. Heidelberg 328 A8
st. Heidelberg 328 K8
st. Heidelberg 329 B9
st. Heidelberg Ht 328 A8
st. Ivanhoe 328 A8
st. Montrose 381 L9
st. St Albans 320 F8
BANKVIEW
wy. Hoppers Csg 405 E15
BANNER
ct. Glen Waverley 420 L18
BANNERMAN
av. Greensborough 286 E4
st. Yarra Jctn 347 E18
BANNIE
la. Mt Martha 657 B10
BANNING
rd. N Warrandyte 290 A15
BANNISTER
av. Anglesea 713 G7
st. Jacana 237 H19
BANNOCKBURN
rd. View Bank 286 B16
BANNON
av. Sunbury 142 H4
ct. Hallam 551 J3
BANNONS
la. Hurstbridge 201 C9
la. Yarrambat 201 B9
la.n, Doreen 202 C8
la.n, Hurstbridge 202 B8
la.n, Nutfield 202 B8
BANOLE
av. Prahran 414 L12
av. Prahran 415 A12
BANOOL
av. Kew 371 H10
av. Mt Evelyn 383 G1
av. Yarraville 367 B18
cr. Mt Eliza 642 E8
ct. Blackburn S 419 J3
ct. Croydon 379 H3
ct. Frankston S 627 E8
qd. Doncaster E 332 C19
rd. Balwyn 373 K12
rd. Selby 467 B15
st. Cheltenham 530 D3
st. Preston 327 D1
st. Surrey Hills 373 K14
BANOON
rd. Eltham 287 G18
BANSKIA
cl. Torquay 711 F11
BANSTEAD
nk. Craigieburn 194 B4
BANTRY
gr. Templestowe 332 D5
BANYALLA
dr. Cranbourne W 577 K16
BANYAN
cl. Carrum Downs 574 L17
ct. Waurn Ponds 705 D15
dr. Frankston 628 C1
st. Chelsea 547 B14
st. St Andrews Bch 697 F20
BANYULE
ct. Frankston S 627 G13
rd. Heidelberg 329 D1
rd. Rosanna 329 C1
rd. View Bank 329 G2
BAPAUME
av. Edithvale 546 G14
BAPTIST
pl. Melbourne 2 G15
pl. Melbourne 24 F7
BARABAND
ct. Diamond Ck 245 D11
BARADINE
ct. Sunbury 142 G10
rd. Mooroolbark 337 D17
st. Chadstone 458 C2
tce. Donvale 332 L14
BARAK
ct. Frankston 600 B18
ct. Glenroy 280 D10
dr. Launching Pl 346 D13
dr. Yarra Jctn 346 G13
la. Healesville 257 E13
rd. Moorooduc 657 K7
rd. Port Melb 412 D5
st. Bulleen 329 G16
BARAKEE
dr. Somerville 644 D19
BARANBALI
dr. Vermont S 420 E12
gr. Greensborough 286 G1
BARAR
ct. Kurunjang 227 A15
BARATTA
st. Blackburn S 419 E3
st. Doncaster E 375 K5
BARB
st. Maribyrnong 323 C14
BARBARA
av. Boronia 423 J11
av. Dandenong N 501 E20
av. Glen Iris 417 J9
av. Glen Waverley 420 C19
cr. Avondale Ht 322 A17
ct. Bacchus Msh 222 B13
ct. Bundoora 285 B2
ct. Heathmont 379 C18
ct. McCrae 685 A14
ct. Mooroolbark 337 B10
ct. Pakenham 584 L1
ct. Thomastown 241 K13
gr. Woori Yallock 344 H14
st. Braybrook 322 C19
st. Doncaster E 375 J3
st. Hadfield 280 J8
st. Mont Albert N 374 F7
st. Moorabbin 496 J8
st. Vermont 377 G20
BARBARY
cr. Taylors Lakes 275 J10
BARBER
ct. Berwick 554 D18
ct. Cheltenham 497 B20
dr. Hoppers Csg 448 C3
BARBERS
rd. Kalorama 382 L13
rd. Kalorama 383 A15
BARBICAN
ct. Rowville 463 B14
BARBISTON
rd. Melb Airport 234 E14
BARCE
pl. Heidelberg W 283 L19
BARCELONA
av. Keilor 277 C11
cl. Thomastown 240 E14
st. Box Hill 375 B17
BARCLAY
av. Croydon 380 E10
av. Frankston 599 H16
av. Up Fntree Gly 465 A5
cl. Gladstone Pk 237 A18
ct. Mulgrave 460 E20
dr. Cheltenham 497 G19
st. Albion 320 L20
st. Albion 364 L1
BARDEN
pl. Thomastown 240 E17
BARDIA
av. Ashburton 417 J15
av. Seaford 599 D5
st. Heidelberg W 328 A4
st. Ringwood 378 F11
BARDOEL
ct. Chelsea 546 L16
ct. Dingley Village 532 J4
BARDOLPH
ct. Bentleigh 456 G20
st. Glen Iris 417 F10
BARDSLEY
ct. Narre Warren 539 A13
st. Sunshine W 364 K5
BARDWELL
av. Frankston 627 K9
BAREENA
av. Rowville 502 F7
dr. Mt Eliza 626 H16
gr. Doncaster E 331 K16
BARELLAN
cl. Rowville 462 K19
cl. St Albans 321 A7
mw. Berwick 554 A3
BARENYA
ct. Kew 372 B11
BARFORD
ct. Sunshine W 363 L5
BARGROVE
ct. Thomastown 240 G11
BARHAM
av. Ferntree Gly 463 F3
BARHOLME
ct. Oakleigh S 457 K19
BARILLA
ct. Burwood E 419 H12
ct. Cranbourne 578 A20
rd. Moorabbin 496 D10
BARINA
av. Mooroolbark 337 E13
cl. Keilor Dn 276 G14
cr. Croydon 336 A20
ct. Berwick 554 C4
rd. Glen Iris 417 A14
rd. Glenroy 280 B10
wy. Mill Park 242 K2
BARINGA
av. Kallista 467 C2
ct. Rowville 463 H13
pl. Eltham 288 C6
rd. Croydon N 336 A15
st. Mt Waverley 419 F19
BARINGA PARK
dr. Nar Warrn S 552 H18
BARINGHUP
st. Cheltenham 496 L20
BARITE
pl. Frankston 600 J20
BARK
av. Rowville 463 K17
BARKALA
cl. Greensborough 244 C19
ct. Frankston 600 F15
st. Rye 697 D8
BARKER
ct. Endeavour Hl 537 H5
dr. Mooroolbark 336 K12
st. Blackburn S 419 D2
st. Cheltenham 496 H19
BARKERS
rd. Chum Creek 213 B11
rd. Hawthorn 371 E13
rd. Hawthorn E 372 A13
rd. Kew 371 E13
st. Heatherton 497 J11
st. Oakleigh S 497 J11
BARKLY
av. Armadale 415 H14
av. Burnley 371 A20
av. Port Melb 29 C5
av. Richmond 26 G20
ct. Brunswick 325 H17
pl. Carlton 18 A17
pl. Footscray 367 E8
pl. Heidelberg 328 H7
st. Box Hill 375 B19
st. Brighton 454 H14
st. Brunswick 325 C17
st. Brunswick E 325 H17
st. Camberwell 417 K8
st. Carlton 18 H15
st. Cranbourne 578 F19
st. E Geelong 703 F13
st. Elwood 454 B3
st. Fitzroy N 326 B18
st. Footscray 366 D6
st. Footscray 367 A8
st. Hughesdale 457 F12
st. Mordialloc 531 K15
st. Mornington 640 D15
st. Mornington 641 A11
st. Ringwood 378 B15
st. St Kilda 414 C19
st. Sunbury 143 G14
st. W Footscray 366 D6
tce. Mitcham 377 C13
BARLBY
ct. Greenvale 237 C4
BARLEY
ct. Delahey 275 A13
BARLEYCORN
pl. Melton W 226 A18
BARLOA
rd. Balwyn 374 C13
rd. Mont Albert 374 C13
BARLOW
av. Cheltenham 497 E17
st. Keysborough 534 L11
st. Keysborough 535 A11
st. Port Melb 412 K5
BARLYN
rd. Mt Waverley 418 H12
BARM
cl. Sydenham 275 A9
BARMAH
cl. Taylors Lakes 276 C7
ct. Frankston S 627 J18
dr. Wantirna 422 A11
st. Mt Eliza 625 J19
BARNABY
pl. Vermont 421 B5
BARNACLE
mw. Templestowe 331 K7
BARNARD
cr. Croydon N 335 K11
ct. Epping 197 J16
ct. Sunshine 365 F3
gr. Kew 371 K3
rd. Toorak 415 H7
BARNATO
gr. Armadale 415 C12
BARN ELMS
pde. Caroline Spr 317 K3

BARNES
av. Burwood 418 B12
cr. Sunshine W 364 G9
dr. Guys Hill 541 L18
gr. Chelsea 546 H17
rd. Altona North 409 E7
wy. Bundoora 284 E15
BARNESDALE
dr. Vermont 421 C4
BARNET
st. Highett 495 L14
st. Yarraville 367 C13
BARNETT
gr. Noble Park 500 K18
pl. Jan Juc 711 E15
pl. Mt Martha 656 C16
st. Hampton 495 F7
st. Kensington 34 B10
st. Sunshine 321 H20
st. Sunshine 365 H1
BARNETTS
pl. Hawthorn 372 D16
BARNEY
ct. Rye 696 L1
BARNFATHER
st. Thomson 703 H16
BARN HILL
cl. View Bank 329 K1
BARNIC
rd. Heathmont 422 K1
BARNINGHAM
st. Brunswick 325 G13
BARNONG
cl. Kurunjang 227 A13
BARNS
st. Blackburn S 375 J20
st. Blackburn S 419 J1
BARNSBURY
cl. Hampton Pk 551 H5
ct. Balwyn 372 L13
rd. Balwyn 372 L12
rd. South Yarra 32 J14
rd. South Yarra 414 K7
BARNSDALE
ct. Wantirna 422 F8
wy. Ringwood N 377 L3
BARNSHAW
la. Emerald 469 F19
BARNSLEY
ct. Kilsyth S 424 K2
dr. Endeavour Hl 538 A4
mw. Westmeadows 237 H12
st. Nunawading 376 E10
BARNSTON
pl. Ringwood 335 C20
BARODA
av. Glen Waverley 460 A10
ct. Keysborough 534 D11
st. Rosebud 684 F15
st. Travancore 324 F18
BARON
ct. Kings Park 318 L2
ct. Ringwood 378 L3
ct. Ringwood 379 A3
ct. Westmeadows 236 F13
BARONDI
av. Narre Warren 538 K17
BARONET
ri. Craigieburn 150 D6
wk. Nar Warrn S 578 G1
BARONGAROOK
ct. Lower Plenty 286 D13
BAROOGA
dr. Wonga Park 291 K15
BAROOK
ct. Ringwood N 378 D3
pl. Greensborough 286 L1
st. Aspendale 546 F6
BAROONA
ct. Brighton 454 K12
st. Mornington 640 J11
BAROSSA
av. Vermont S 421 C10
ct. Mt Martha 656 A15
ct. Waurn Ponds 705 A17
BARQUE
pl. Pt Lonsdale 707 G17
BARR
ct. Pakenham 584 B6
st. Brighton East 495 L6
BARRABOOL
rd. Belmont 702 C16
rd. Highton 701 G17
rd. Wandana Ht 701 A18
st. Doncaster E 331 J17
BARRADINE
cr. Vermont S 420 K9
BARRAGOWA
dr. Rosebud W 699 E2
BARRANI
st. Bentleigh E 457 C16
BARRATT
ct. Noble Park 534 L5
BARREENONG
rd. Cottles Br 203 C5
BARRELL
ct. Delahey 275 E12
BARRETT
ct. Roxburgh Pk 194 F14
ct. Woori Yallock 344 H13
ct. Yarraville 366 J15
la. Albert Park 29 D13
la. Mornington 640 F14
st. Albert Park 29 D13
st. Albert Park 413 B7
st. Cheltenham 530 J2
st. Kensington 34 C13
st. Maidstone 366 E2
st. Up Fntree Gly 464 K9
BARRETTS
rd. Langwarrin S 628 J19
BARRIE
ct. Braybrook 366 A1
rd. Tullamarine 278 G10
BARRIEDALE
ct. Eltham 288 A8
gr. Frankston S 627 H19
BARRIES
rd. Melton 268 F1
rd. Melton W 268 C1
BARRIMAL
wy. Bundoora 284 F3
BARRINA
st. Blackburn S 419 E2
BARRINE
ct. Skye 601 G2
wy. Taylors Lakes 275 L10
BARRINGO
rd. New Gisborne 79 A1
BARRINGTON
av. Kew 372 C10
cl. Keysborough 534 B9
cr. Gladstone Pk 237 C19
ct. Baxter 644 B2
ct. Wantirna 422 J10
dr. Ashwood 418 B16
dr. Pakenham 585 D5
la. Sunbury 142 E14
pl. Hampton Pk 551 D6
ri. Donvale 332 H20
st. Bentleigh E 457 C17
tce. Point Cook 450 H9
BARRINGUN
cr. Clayton S 498 H9
BARRON
ct. Dandenong N 501 F8
st. Reservoir 282 C6
wy. Yallambie 286 A12
BARROT
av. Hoppers Csg 448 K2
BARROW
dr. Heathmont 422 K2
pl. Burnley 371 C20
st. Brunswick 325 J9
st. Coburg 325 J9
st. Mt Martha 669 C2
BARROWBY
av. Woori Yallock 343 L14
BARRUP
st. Carlton 18 K15
BARRY
av. Burwood 418 J8
ct. Scoresby 462 F6
ct. Wonga Park 291 J19
la. Melbourne 1 H9
la. Melbourne 23 L7
rd. Broadmeadows 238 B7
rd. Burwood E 419 K11
rd. Campbellfield 239 A8
rd. Dallas 238 B7
rd. Lalor 239 L10
rd. Meadow Ht 237 H7
rd. New Gisborne 79 D4
rd. Thomastown 239 L10
rd. Westmeadows 237 H7
st. Bayswater 423 L6
st. Bentleigh 496 B5
st. Brunswick 325 C16
st. Carlton 17 L15
st. Kew 371 H9
st. Macleod 285 H10
st. Maddingley 263 G1
st. Mentone 531 C9
st. Northcote 326 G18
st. Reservoir 282 H7
st. Rosebud 684 C16
st. Seaford 599 L7
st. South Yarra 32 C14
st. South Yarra 414 G7
st. Tootgarook 698 H2
st. Watsonia 285 H10
BARRYMORE
rd. Greenvale 236 K4
rd. Greenvale 237 A2
BARRYS
la. Coburg 281 G20
BARTELS
st. McCrae 684 L12
BARTER
cr. Forest Hill 420 D5
BARTLETT
av. Croydon 336 E18
rd. Olinda 427 B1
st. Frankston S 627 J13
st. Hampton E 495 L8
st. Preston 282 F17
tce. Newtown 702 D13
BARTLETTS
la. Kangaroo Grnd 247 K3
la. Panton Hill 247 K3
BARTLEY
pl. Springvale S 499 J18
rd. Belgrave Ht 506 F2
rd. Belgrave S 506 F2
BARTOK
ct. Nar Warrn S 552 G11
BARTOLO
ct. Cranbourne N 578 F9
BARTON
av. Ferntree Gly 464 J3
ct. Bundoora 284 J4
ct. Gladstone Pk 236 L19
ct. Vermont 421 F4
dr. Mt Eliza 626 B14
mw. Berwick 554 H18
rd. Clayton S 498 G4
st. Blairgowrie 679 J20
st. Dandenong N 502 A19
st. Doncaster E 331 L17
st. Hawthorn 371 F16
st. Mt Waverley 418 L14
st. Reservoir 282 H8
st. Sunbury 143 B13
st. Surrey Hills 374 B15
st. W Footscray 366 G5
BARTRAM
ri. View Bank 329 J1
BARTROP
st. Reservoir 282 B2
BARUNAH
ct. Narre Warren 539 A13
st. Hadfield 280 J5
BARWARRE
rd. Grovedale 706 J19
rd. Marshall 706 J19
rd. Marshall 706 K12
BARWISE
st. Laverton 407 E13
st. N Melbourne 34 H15
BARWON
av. Frankston 627 L5
av. Keilor 276 L12
av. Reservoir 283 F13
av. Sunshine N 321 A15
bvd. Highton 701 J12
ct. Clayton S 498 G9
ct. Croydon Hills 335 H14
ct. Donvale 332 L15
ct. Rowville 463 A17
ct. Werribee 447 J7
st. Box Hill N 374 H11
st. Glenroy 279 L7
st. Mentone 531 F6
st. Taylors Hill 274 J15
tce. S Geelong 702 L14
BARWON HEADS
rd. Belmont 702 J17
rd. Marshall 706 L1
BARYN
st. Ashwood 418 C13
st. Cheltenham 497 H18
BASALT
ct. Delahey 275 A15
BASANO
rt. Berwick 539 H18
BASIL
cl. Hallam 538 D18
cr. Wheelers Hill 461 E12
ct. Bayswater 423 B8
st. Dromana 686 E6
st. Fawkner 281 G5
st. Malvern East 417 A18
st. Newport 410 E9
BASIN
ct. The Basin 424 L8
BASINGSTOKE
rd. Mitcham 376 L9
BASIN-OLINDA
rd. Olinda 426 C8
rd. Sassafras 426 C8
rd. The Basin 425 D10
BASS
av. Rosebud 700 E1
ct. Cranbourne N 577 K8
ct. Heathmont 378 D18
ct. Melton S 268 D11
ct. Mt Waverley 419 D12
ct. Sunbury 143 A12
ct. Taylors Lakes 275 J3
ct. Wyndham Va 446 F8
pl. Endeavour Hl 537 G8
rd. Portsea 677 G4
st. Box Hill 374 J19
st. McCrae 685 A16
st. Pascoe Vale 280 C16
BASSETT
rd. Melb Airport 234 G11
BASSETTS
rd. Doreen 156 E18
BASTINGS
ct. Epping 197 K19
st. Northcote 326 J16
BASTOW
ct. Pakenham 584 D2
pl. Mulgrave 499 K1
pl. Richmond 26 C7
rd. Lilydale 338 K6
BATAAN
ct. Lalor 241 H6
BATABA
ct. Clarinda 498 C8
st. Moorabbin 496 C8
BATAVIA
av. Boronia 424 F5
BATE
dr. Braeside 532 K20
BATEMAN
ct. Coburg 282 B19
gr. Hampton Pk 551 E13
gr. Hampton Pk 551 E14
rd. Kensington 33 B11
st. Hampton 495 E7
st. Wantirna 422 B5
BATES
av. Thomastown 241 K14
av. Up Fntree Gly 465 E7
cl. Sunbury 142 K3
ct. Jacana 237 J20
dr. Williamstown 410 L14
rd. Panton Hill 204 C13
st. Cranbourne W 577 G18
st. Malvern East 416 D20
BATESFORD
rd. Chadstone 417 L20
rd. Malvern East 457 J1
BATESLEIGH
rd. Selby 467 D19
BATESON
rd. Wattle Glen 246 L8
BATEY
ct. Bulla 189 G9
BATH
pl. Port Melb 412 K5
pl. Williamstown 411 E14
rd. Glen Iris 417 G11
st. Abbotsford 20 F13
st. Blairgowrie 696 A4
st. Chelsea 546 J18
st. Craigieburn 150 A16
st. Mornington 640 H11
st. St Kilda 414 E16
st. Sandringham 495 B13
BATHE
rd. Pakenham 557 H8
BATHURST
st. Broadmeadows 237 J13
st. Mooroolbark 337 B19
BATMAN
av. Coburg 281 F18
av. Hurstbridge 202 G13
av. Keilor Park 277 J15
av. Melbourne 24 L10
av. Melbourne 25 A10
av. Mt Eliza 642 F5
av. Sunbury 143 B12
cl. Belmont 702 J19
ct. Vermont 421 F5
ct. Werribee 447 E2
gr. Mulgrave 460 F20
rd. Eltham 287 J5
rd. Port Melb 412 B5
st. Aberfeldie 323 C8
st. Altona Mdw 451 G7
st. Fitzroy N 19 C1
st. Footscray 367 B8
st. W Melbourne 1 A1
st. W Melbourne 23 C5
wk. Greensborough 286 F3
BATSKOS
dr. Warrandyte 333 A4
BATTALION
ct. Boronia 424 E3
BATTEN
pl. Aspendale Gdn 546 J5
rd. Marshall 706 L19
st. Glen Waverley 460 B4
st. St Albans 320 C7
BATTERBEE
dr. Mooroolbark 337 C10
BATTERSEA
la. Caroline Spr, off Grove Hall Pl 317 L3
st. Hadfield 281 B8
BATTERY
rd. Panton Hill 204 E15
BATTY
st. Wheelers Hill 461 C20
BAUDELAIRE
av. Wantirna 422 F10
BAULDERSTONE
wk. Kensington 33 E11
BAUM
cr. Highton 701 J16
BAUNTON
ct. Kilsyth S 424 K1
BAWDEN
cl. Watsonia N 243 H20
ct. Pascoe Vale 280 L12
st. Carrum Downs 574 K16
BAWKER
pl. Epping 197 L19
BAXTER
av. Chelsea 547 A15
cl. Gladstone Pk 237 C20
cr. Baxter 644 D2
ct. Chelsea 547 A15
ct. Mt Waverley 418 K14
ct. Thomastown 240 D13
dr. Braeside 532 G17
dr. Waurn Ponds 705 C11
pl. S Melbourne 29 H5
st. Coburg 325 G4
st. Elsternwick 455 D6
st. Eltham 287 C15
st. Frankston 627 C1
st. Toorak 415 C8
BAXTER-TOORADIN
rd. Baxter 644 B1
rd. Blind Bight 650 B1
rd. Cannons Creek 649 B3
rd. Devon Mdw 648 F4
rd. Frankston S 644 B1
rd. Langwarrin S 645 C3
rd. Langwarrin S 646 A3
rd. Pearcedale 645 C3
rd. Pearcedale 646 A3
rd. Warneet 650 B1
BAY
av. Mt Eliza 626 A12
ct. Gladstone Pk 236 L15
rd. Cheltenham 496 A16
rd. Mt Martha 655 J15
rd. Mt Martha 656 B16
rd. Sandringham 495 B15
st. Brighton 454 E13
st. Brighton 455 A14
st. Mordialloc 531 H17
st. Parkdale 531 H17
st. Port Melb 29 A7
st. Port Melb 412 K6
st. Port Melb 413 A3
st. Queenscliff 709 C16
st. Tecoma 466 E8
st.s, Frankston 627 A1
BAYARD
dr. Pakenham Up 559 C1
BAYBREEZE
ct. Rosebud W 699 E3
BAYFIELD
ct. Mt Martha 656 J5
dr. Eltham 288 C3
rd.e, Bayswater N 380 A16
rd.w, Bayswater N 379 J16
BAYLES
ct. Donvale 332 L15
st. Parkville 17 H9
BAYLEY
cl. Heathmont 422 H1
gr. Doncaster 330 J20
gr. Doncaster 374 J1
BAYLEY
st. Geelong 703 A6
BAYLIE
pl. Geelong, off Myers St 703 A9
BAYLISS
av. Hoppers Csg 448 K1
ct. Berwick 553 K3
ct. Cheltenham 531 D3

ct. Pearcedale 646 L2
pl. Vermont 421 B6
rd. Deer Park 318 J17
rd. Lyndhurst 550 G15
rd. Lyndhurst 551 A16
st. Cheltenham 531 D3
st. Preston 282 G17

BAYLON
st. Bentleigh 496 E4

BAYNES PARK
rd. Monbulk 427 L19

BAYNTON
av. Sunshine N 321 A13
cr. Roxburgh Pk 193 L12
st. Oakleigh E 458 H12

BAYONNE
cl. Greensborough 244 G15

BAYPORT
dr. Langwarrin 629 E7

BAY RISE
dr. Mornington 656 H2

BAYSIDE
av. Edithvale 546 J14
av. Port Melb 368 A18
cr. Hampton 495 B11

BAYSTONE
ct. Mt Martha 656 H8
dr. Cranbourne 604 B5
pl. Kurunjang 227 E7
pl. Lilydale 294 B20
rd. Epping 198 C20

BAYSWATER
rd. Bayswater 423 J1
rd. Bayswater N 379 H17
rd. Bayswater N 423 J1
rd. Croydon 379 J9
rd. Croydon S 379 H17
rd. Kensington 33 E10
rd. Newtown 702 C11

BAY VIEW
rd. Seddon 367 A14
rd. Yarraville 367 A14
st. Williamstown 411 A18
tce. Ascot Vale 324 B16

BAYVIEW
av. Aspendale 546 B4
av. Clayton 459 A14
av. Hawthorn E 372 E15
av. Rosebud 700 F4
av. Upwey 465 J13
cr. Black Rock 529 E2
cr. Hoppers Csg 449 B2
cr. The Basin 425 A13
cr. Tremont 425 C13
ct. Highton 701 D15
la. Aspendale, off Bayview Av 546 B4
rd. Beaumaris 530 C6
rd. Belgrave 466 H13
rd. Brighton East 455 H14
rd. Emerald 509 C4
rd. Frankston 627 C5
rd. Glenroy 280 C8
rd. McCrae 685 A14
rd. Mornington 640 F20
rd. Officer 556 E19
rd. Rosebud 700 E2
rd. Tooradin 651 E7
st. Altona 409 E20
st. Bentleigh E 456 K15
st. Elsternwick 455 C3
st. Northcote 326 J17
st. Prahran 32 L20
st. Prahran 414 L10
st. Prahran 415 A10
tce. Kalorama 382 L12
tr. Lysterfield S 503 E13

BAYVILLE
dr. Dingley Village 532 L9

BAYVISTA
ri. Somerville 644 L19
ri. Somerville 645 A19

BAZENTIN
st. Albion 320 K19

BEACH
av. Blairgowrie 679 E20
av. Elwood 454 E5
av. Mordialloc 532 D20
cl. Pt Lonsdale 707 J20
ct. Keysborough 534 C11
gr. Mentone 530 L10
gr. Mentone 531 A10
gr. Mornington 640 D15
gr. Seaford 573 C19
rd. Beaumaris 529 F6
rd. Black Rock 495 D19
rd. Hampton 494 K8
rd. Mentone 530 K10
rd. Mordialloc 531 D13
rd. Parkdale 531 D13
rd. Sandringham 494 L12
rd. Sandringham 495 A12
rd. Torquay 711 J7
st. Dromana 686 C4
st. Frankston 599 A17
st. Frankston 599 C18
st. Port Melb 412 E5
st. Queenscliff 709 C16
st. Seaholme 409 H18

BEACHCOMBER
ct. Patterson L 573 F9
pl. Point Cook 450 L13

BEACHLEY
st. Braybrook 365 K6

BEACHHURST
av. Dromana 686 G3

BEACH VIEW
cr. Torquay 711 H11

BEACHWOOD
cl. Cheltenham 496 J13
dr. Pt Lonsdale 710 E1

BEACON
ct. Templstw Lr 330 K10
dr. Langwarrin 601 K18
rd. Port Melb 412 E5
st. Glen Waverley 460 C4
st. Parkdale 531 H11
st. Vermont S 420 J10

BEACON HILLS
cr. Craigieburn 150 C15

BEACONSFIELD
av. Beaconsfield 555 B16
av. Frankston 627 H4
la. Albert Park 29 B16
pde. Albert Park 29 A15
pde. Albert Park 412 L8
pde. Middle Park 29 A15
pde. Middle Park 413 J13
pde. Northcote 326 E11
pde. Port Melb 412 L8
pde. St Kilda W 413 J13
rd. Briar Hill 286 F5
rd. Hawthorn E 416 E1
st. Doncaster 374 J1

BEACONSFIELD-EMERALD
rd. Beaconsfield 555 B11
rd. Beaconsfld Up 542 B17
rd. Dewhurst 510 C18
rd. Emerald 509 G3
rd. Emerald 510 C18
rd. Guys Hill 555 B11

BEACON VISTA
Port Melb 412 F5

BEAGLE
st. Epping 197 G13

BEAGLEY
st. Kallista 427 A20

BEAL
pl. Mornington 656 J3
st. Mt Waverley 419 F19

BEALE
ct. Templestowe 331 D7
pl. Sunshine N 321 C8

BEALES
la. Greensborough 244 J17
la. St Helena 244 J17
st. Newtown 702 H10
st. Torquay 711 L10

BEALIBA
rd. Caulfield S 455 K8

BEAMISH
ct. Altona Mdw 451 F7
st. Werribee 447 J16

BEAMOND
cl. Langwarrin S 628 K17

BEAMSLEY
st. Malvern 416 A8

BEAN
ct. Keilor Dn 276 B16
ct. Mill Park 243 A2
ct. Whittington 704 D19
dr. Hurstbridge 202 F20
dr. Hurstbridge 246 F1
dr. Wattle Glen 202 F20
st. Geelong 703 C11

BEANEY
la. Melbourne 2 K16
la. Melbourne 24 G8

BEAR
st. Mordialloc 531 K19

BEARD
ct. Heathmont 378 G19
pl. Carlton 18 F15
st. Eltham 288 A6

BEARDSWORTH
av. Chelsea 547 A17

BEASLEY
av. Werribee 447 G13

BEATRICE
av. Aberfeldie 323 B8
av. Heidelberg W 284 E16
av. Surrey Hills 374 B18
ct. Blackburn 376 C20
ct. New Gisborne 79 F6
pl. Ferntree Gly 464 C7
st. Chadstone 418 E19
st. Cheltenham 497 G18
st. Glen Iris 417 G10
st. Kew 371 J9
st. Kilsyth 381 D5
st. Melbourne 31 C17
st. Melbourne 414 B9
st. Noble Park 535 B7
st. Preston 283 G19
st. Yarraville 367 A17

BEATRIX
st. Greensborough 286 D7

BEATTIE
ct. Gisborne 79 A15
st. Montmorency 286 G10

BEATTY
av. Armadale 415 D9
av. Glenroy 280 C5
cr. Ashburton 417 D17
cr. Ormond 456 B10
pde. Cockatoo 511 C3
pde. Mornington 640 H14
st. Ivanhoe 327 K9
st. Mont Albert 374 D14
st. Reservoir 282 F15

BEATTYS
rd. Hillside 273 B5
rd. Plumpton 273 B5
rd. Rockbank 270 C7

BEAU
pl. Pt Lonsdale 707 G17

BEAUCHAMP
st. Preston 282 L19

BEAUFORD
st. Huntingdale 458 E14

BEAUFORT
ct. Ashburton 417 J16
rd. Croydon 379 D4
rd. Ringwood E 379 D4
ri. Warrandyte 332 L5
st. Mitcham 377 D8
st. Mt Waverley 419 C17
st. Preston 327 H7

BEAULIEU
av. Lilydale 338 C15
av. Mooroolbark 338 C15

BEAUMARIS
pde. Highett 496 B16

BEAUMONDE
st. Coburg 326 A7

BEAUMONT
cr. Frankston 600 E17
cr. Lalor 241 K6
ct. Montrose 382 D8
ct. Pakenham 584 E6
ct. Sydenham 274 J1
dr. Point Cook 450 E3
pde. W Footscray 366 E12
pl. Wheelers Hill 461 A8
rd. Berwick 554 G4
st. Canterbury 373 B17
st. Olinda 426 K11
st. Sandringham 495 B13
st. Vermont 421 D3
st. Watsonia 285 C8

BEAUNA VISTA
dr. Rye 697 K5

BEAUTEX
ct. Aspendale Gdn 546 G4

BEAUTY GULLY
rd. Warrandyte 333 H6

BEAUTY POINT
rd. Research 289 B10

BEAUVIEW
pde. Ivanhoe East 328 H14

BEAUVILLE
av. Murrumbeena 457 A12

BEAU VORNO
av. Keysborough 534 B11

BEAVEN
av. Malvern 416 A9

BEAVER
ct. Wheelers Hill 460 J11
st. Aberfeldie 323 F10
st. Box Hill S 419 B2
st. Malvern East 416 C18
st. Point Cook 450 G3
st. St Albans 320 D6

BEAVERS
rd. Northcote 326 D12

BEAVIS
ct. Berwick 554 L8
ct. Templestowe 331 K14
st. Elsternwick 455 B5

BEBINGTON
cl. Ringwood 335 B19

BEBS
ct. Templestowe 331 K8

BECALL
cl. Epping 198 C14

BECCIA
av. Epping 198 F20

BECCIE
ct. Ferntree Gly 464 C6

BECCLES
ct. St Albans 320 E6
st. Fawkner 281 K2

BECK
ct. Noble Park 501 C20
rd. Plenty 244 F9
st. Blackburn 375 E19
st. Keilor Park 278 B14

BECKBURY
ct. Rowville 463 K17

BECKENHAM
dr. Ferntree Gly 463 E3
pl. Langwarrin 629 D5

BECKER
cl. Melton W 225 K18

BECKET
av. Bentleigh E 496 H1
st. Glenroy 279 K2
st. Glenroy 279 K4
st. Rye 696 D4

BECKETT
av. Keilor East 278 A18
ct. Lower Plenty 287 B17
rd. Donvale 377 G8
st. Balwyn 373 K10
st. Chadstone 458 A3

BECKINGTON
cr. Hampton Pk 551 F6
pl. Craigieburn 194 E1

BECKLEY
st. Coburg 326 A5
st. Herne Hill 701 H1

BECKWITH
ct. Taylors Lakes 275 G7
gr. Seaford 599 C2
st. Coburg 325 G1

BEDDOE
av. Bentleigh E 457 B19
av. Brighton East 455 F16
av. Clayton 459 B16
rd. Vermont 421 G2
st. Research 288 H4

BEDDOWS
st. Burwood 418 H10

BEDE
av. Coldstream 295 F15
ct. Gladstone Pk 237 C17

BEDERVALE
dr. Templestowe 331 L7

BEDFORD
av. Surrey Hills 374 A17
ct. Endeavour Hl 536 L2
ct. Heathmont 378 L15
ct. Heidelberg 329 G2
ct. Hoppers Csg 448 K7
ct. Sunbury 142 L2
ct. Sunbury 143 A2
ct. Templstw Lr 330 G11
pl. Mornington 656 F1
pl. N Melbourne 17 H16
rd. Cockatoo 471 K8
rd. Heathmont 378 L14
rd. Ringwood 378 F13
rd. Ringwood E 378 L14
rd. Ringwood E 379 A15
st. Airport W 278 G13
st. Box Hill 375 B19
st. Collingwood 19 G15
st. Hadfield 281 A8
st. Millgrove 304 F20
st. N Melbourne 17 H17
st. Reservoir 283 A11

BEDGGOOD
av. Pt Lonsdale 710 F2
dr. Wesburn 348 E19

BEDINGHAM
dr. Hillside 274 D1

BEDSER
st. Sunshine N 321 G14

BEDWELL
av. Dandenong 535 L3
ct. Endeavour Hl 537 L4
st. Reservoir 240 E20

BEE
ct. Craigieburn 150 H18

BEECH
av. Selby 466 L18
av. Selby 467 A18
ct. Boronia 424 D16
ct. Campbellfield 239 G13
ct. Gisborne 78 L10
ct. Greensborough 244 K20
ct. Greensborough 286 K1
ct. Sunshine W 364 K6
pl. Hallam 552 C2
st. Bentleigh 455 K17
st. Camberwell 417 G5
st. Caulfield S 455 G8
st. Kilsyth 381 L7
st. Langwarrin 628 K3
st. McKinnon 455 K17
st. Malvern East 456 J1
st. Nunawading 376 L20
st. Surrey Hills 418 E2
st. Thomastown 241 D14
st. Whittlesea 96 E18

BEECHER
st. Preston 327 G7

BEECHWOOD
cl. Doncaster E 332 E6
tce. Ashwood 418 C15

BEECROFT
cr. Templestowe 331 G13
dr. Westmeadows 236 H13

BEELA
cl. Greensborough 244 C20
cl. Greensborough 286 C1
ct. Sunshine W 364 F6

BEENA
av. Carnegie 456 L6
ct. Glen Waverley 460 G12

BEENAK
av. Brighton East 495 F1
ct. Doncaster E 332 C19
ct. Forest Hill 420 F4
rd. Seville 385 L2
rd. Seville E 387 A6
rd. Wandin East 341 A17
rd. Wandin East 385 L2
st. Reservoir 283 G7

BEERS
ct. St Albans 320 E13

BEESLEY
pl. Gladstone Pk 237 E17

BEE TENG
ct. Aspendale Gdn 546 H4

BEETHAM
pde. Rosanna 328 L2

BEETHOVEN
ct. Bundoora 242 F17
ct. Mt Martha 656 K9

BEEVERS
st. Altona North 365 K20
st. Footscray 367 J6

BEEWAR
st. Greensborough 285 J6

BEGA
ct. Aspendale 546 F5
ct. Gladstone Pk 278 L2
ct. Gladstone Pk 279 A2
ct. Lalor 240 L7
ct. Lalor 241 A7
ct. Mulgrave 500 J4
ct. Ringwood 379 C1
st. Chadstone 458 C2

BEGG
st. Oakleigh S 497 E1

BEGGS
pl. Rowville 503 B7

BEGONIA
av. Altona North 410 A2
av. Bayswater 423 D7
av. Bayswater 423 E8
ct. Blackburn N 375 H10
ct. Endeavour Hl 537 F5
ct. Lalor 240 K10
ct. Newcomb 704 C13
rd. Gardenvale 455 B11
st. Box Hill S 418 F4
st. Dromana 686 F6
wy. Nar Warrn S 579 E1

BEILBY
cl. Up Fntree Gly 464 H9
st. Bayswater 423 K8
st. Moorabbin 496 F10

BEISSEL
st. Richmond 26 L17
st. Richmond 371 A19

BEITH
st. Brunswick 325 G14

BELAH
av. Altona 452 J1
pl. Endeavour Hl 536 L1
st. Thomastown 241 E14

BELAIR
av. Endeavour Hl 502 K14
av. Endeavour Hl 503 A14
av. Glenroy 279 J5
cl. Seville 341 K13

ct. Bundoora...284 H5
ct. Taylors Lakes...276 A9
ct. Wyndham Va...446 D11
BELALIE
cl. Hampton Pk...552 C16
BELANDRA
dr. Wheelers Hill...460 L15
BELAR
av. Frankston...600 D20
ct. Ferntree Gly...463 F8
ct. Meadow Ht...193 J19
rd. Tootgarook...698 F8
BELBIN
ct. Mill Park...242 A5
BELBROOK
rd. Upwey...465 H8
BELCHER
arc. Geelong, off Little Ryrie St...703 A8
BELCHESTER
av. Coldstream...295 C14
BELCOMBE
ct. Thomastown...240 H14
BELDALE
av. Werribee...446 K20
ct. Berwick...539 G20
ct. Berwick...553 G1
BELDARRY
ct. Mt Martha...657 A10
BELEURA
av. Vermont...421 G5
ct. Taylors Lakes...275 J2
ct. Wantirna...422 J10
gr. Clayton...458 L17
gr. Lower Plenty...286 J14
wy. Seabrook...451 A5
BELEURA HILL
rd. Mornington...640 K10
BELFAST
rd. Brunswick...325 G16
rd. Montrose...382 C6
rd. Mooroolbark...382 C6
st. Broadmeadows..238 E14
st. Newtown...702 E12
BELFIELDS
rd. Cottles Br...204 D6
BELFORD
av. Kew East...372 E7
ct. Keilor...276 F9
rd. Kallista...467 K9
rd. Kew East...372 D7
st. St Kilda...414 C18
BELFORT
st. Dandenong...535 F6
st. St Albans...320 H7
BELFRAYDEN
ct. Mt Waverley...418 L15
BELGIUM
av. Richmond...26 E7
BELGRAVE
av. Belgrave...466 K16
av. Cockatoo...511 D1
cl. Oakleigh S...497 G6
pl. Carrum Downs...575 C20
rd. Malvern East...457 B4
rd. Ringwood...377 L20
rd. Ringwood...421 L1
st. Albanvale...319 C6
st. Coburg...325 K3
st. Hawthorn...372 B20
BELGRAVE-FERNY CREEK
rd. Ferny Creek...466 C3
rd. Tecoma...466 C3
BELGRAVE-GEMBROOK
rd. Avonsleigh...469 J20
rd. Avonsleigh...470 E18
rd. Belgrave...466 J15
rd. Clematis...508 J1
rd. Cockatoo...511 C5
rd. Emerald...469 J20
rd. Emerald...508 J1
rd. Emerald...509 B1
rd. Emerald...509 H1
rd. Gembrook...511 L8
rd. Menzies Ck...467 F14
rd. Menzies Ck...468 A15
rd. Selby...467 A14
rd. Selby...467 F14
BELGRAVE-HALLAM
rd. Belgrave...466 F17
rd. Belgrave S...506 K1
rd. Hallam...538 A15
rd. Nar Warrn E...505 E20
rd. Nar Warrn N...538 E10
BELGRAVIA
av. Mont Albert N...374 D7
st. Burnley, off Swan St...371 B19
BELGROVE
av. Balwyn...373 G9
st. Preston...327 E3
BELINDA
av. Research...288 J6
cl. Kilsyth...381 B11
cl. Kurunjang...226 J13
cr. Doncaster E...331 G19
cr. Wheelers Hill...461 A13
ct. Bentleigh E...497 D7
ct. Dandenong N...502 A15
ct. Springvale S...534 A2
st. Rye...696 D7
BELINDAVALE
dr. Knoxfield...462 K2
BELL
av. Altona...452 E1
ct. Bayswater...423 B3
ct. Keilor Dn...276 A14
ct. Melton...226 G18
ct. Sunbury...143 G9
gr. Braeside...532 J10
la. St Kilda W, off Loch St...414 A14
pl. Melbourne...2 L3
pl. Melbourne...24 F1
pl. Geelong, off Corio St...703 C7
rd. Seville...341 L15
st. Armadale...415 J11
st. Bellfield...328 A4
st. Blackburn...375 K12
st. Blairgowrie...696 B1
st. Box Hill N...374 L8
st. Brunswick...325 G16
st. Clematis...508 K3
st. Coburg...325 A1
st. Cockatoo...511 D6
st. Eltham...287 F13
st. Fitzroy...18 L14
st. Frankston...627 B3
st. Glen Iris...417 C11
st. Hawthorn...372 B15
st. Heidelberg Ht...327 B3
st. Heidelberg Ht...328 A4
st. Heidelberg W...328 A4
st. Montrose...382 C8
st. Pascoe Vale S...324 H1
st. Preston...325 K2
st. Richmond...26 J17
st. Ripponlea...454 J3
st. Seddon...367 E12
st. Sunshine W...364 G3
st. Torquay...712 A12
st. Yarra Glen...209 A20
st. Yarra Glen...253 A2
BELLA
cr. Hallam...552 C2
cr. Hallam...552 D2
ct. Doncaster E...376 E3
ct. St Albans...276 C18
ct. Thomastown...240 G15
ct. Wheelers Hill...460 F14
st. Prahran...32 F18
st. Prahran...414 J9
BELLAIR
av. Up Fntree Gly...464 J10
st. Kensington...33 K5
BELLAIRE
ct. Beaumaris...530 F9
ct. Nar Warrn N...539 E9
ct. Toorak...415 G9
BELLAIRS
av. Seddon...367 D14
av. Yarraville...367 D14
BELLANY
rd. Belgrave S...506 K8
BELLARA
cr. Kealba...276 H18
dr. Croydon...336 G13
dr. Mooroolbark...336 G13
st. Doncaster...375 E3
st. Vermont...420 L6
st. Vermont...421 A6
wy. Wheelers Hill...461 E17
BELLARINE
av. Keilor East...322 B3
ct. Keysborough...534 F11
dr. Cranbourne...578 G17
dr. Lalor...241 B5
hwy.E Geelong...703 G12
hwy.Geelong...703 G12
hwy.Marcus Hill...707 B13
hwy.Moolap...704 C17
hwy.Newcomb...704 C17
hwy.Pt Lonsdale...707 B13
hwy.Queenscliff...707 B13
hwy.Thomson...703 G12
st. Preston...282 G18
BELLA VISTA
Lilydale...338 F12
cr. Olinda...426 L11
cr. Olinda...427 A11
ct. Plenty...244 B4
dr. Tootgarook...698 C6
rd. Caulfield N...415 G17
BELLAVISTA
cr. Clayton S...499 D15
ct. Springvale S...534 A2
pl. Ringwood N...378 C2
rd. Glen Iris...417 C14
BELLBANGRA
av. Rosebud...700 L7
BELL-BANKSIA
lk. Heidelberg...328 G7
BELLBIRD
av. Harkaway...540 D15
av. Launching Pl...345 H14
av. Taylors Lakes...275 G3
cl. Pakenham...559 D15
cr. Emerald...510 C1
cr. Vermont...421 C5
ct. Heathmont...422 D1
ct. Langwarrin...630 E6
ct. Ringwood...422 E1
ct. Springvale S...534 A2
ct. Werribee...448 B6
dr. Bayswater N...423 F1
dr. Craigieburn...149 F17
dr. Wantirna...422 D3
dr. Whittlesea...96 D20
dr. Whittlesea...126 D1
la. Kangaroo Grnd...289 J6
la. Research...289 J6
pl. Lysterfield S...504 D15
rd. Diamond Ck...246 B7
rd. Lilydale...338 H12
rd. Mt Eliza...642 G4
st. Belgrave...466 F18
tr. Lysterfield S...503 D11
BELLBRAE
ct. Meadow Ht...237 L4
BELLBRIDGE
dr. Hoppers Csg...449 B3
BELLBROOK
ct. Clayton S...499 F12
ct. Frankston S...627 A12
dr. Dandenong N...501 K12
BELLE
av. Brighton...454 K20
cr. Mordialloc...532 A12
BELLERINE
st. Geelong...703 B12
st. S Geelong...703 A14
BELLERIVE
av. Mt Waverley...458 L10
BELLETT
st. Camberwell...416 L4
st. Camberwell...417 A4
BELLEVIEW
dr. Sunbury...143 F17
dr. Sunbury...143 F19
BELLE VUE
av. Belmont...705 K4
av. Highton...701 K20
av. Highton...705 K4
BELLEVUE
av. Burwood E...419 L9
av. Doncaster E...332 C18
av. Malvern East...457 F4
av. Point Cook...450 D4
av. Ringwood...378 H15
av. Rosanna...284 K20
bvd. Hillside...231 L20
bvd. Hillside...273 L1
cl. Rosebud W, off Allambi Av...699 E3
cr. Mt Eliza...642 C8
cr. Preston...327 K4
cr. Seaford...600 B4
ct. Boronia...424 D5
ct. Maribyrnong...323 A13
ct. Mickleham...150 C2
ct. Mill Park...242 E12
ct. Mulgrave...500 C4
dr. Berwick...553 J14
dr. Berwick...553 K18
dr. Keilor Dn...275 L14
rd. Balwyn N...329 E19
rd. Bentleigh E...496 K5
rd. Dromana...686 F11
rd. Eltham...287 H5
st. Burnley...371 C18
st. Coburg...325 C2
st. Lilydale...338 G7
BELLFIELD
av. Caroline Spr...318 B7
dr. Ferntree Gly...463 L15
BELLFLOWER
pl. Hampton Pk...552 C17
BELLIN
st. Laverton...407 F13
BELLINGHAM
rd. Arthurs Seat...686 E19
BELLINI
av. Wheelers Hill...460 L14
ct. Grovedale...705 J14
BELLMARE
av. Dromana...686 G4
BELLOWS
st. S Morang...199 K17
BELLS
bvd. Jan Juc...711 A14
ct. Wantirna S...462 A4
BELLS HILL
rd. Research...289 B5
BELLTREES
ct. Pearcedale...646 J3
BELLVIEW
ct. Springvale S...534 A2
BELLVUE
ct. Hampton Pk...551 G8
ct. Noble Park N...501 E12
st. Brunswick E...326 A13
tce. Pascoe Vale...280 E17
BELMAIN
ct. Bulleen...329 E12
BELMAN
pl. Melbourne...2 K9
pl. Melbourne...24 F4
BELMAR
av. Altona...408 H15
st. Cranbourne...578 C16
BELMARINO
ct. Werribee...446 H20
BELMONT
av. Balwyn...373 B12
av. Clayton...498 L3
av. Dandenong N...501 G19
av. Glen Iris...416 E13
av. Keilor Dn...276 A15
av. Kew...372 C10
av. Upwey...465 E11
av.n,Glen Iris...416 E11
cl. Glen Iris...416 E12
cr. Montmorency...287 A12
ct. Carrum Downs...575 D20
ct. Donvale...376 G6
ct. Springvale...500 B17
pl. Gladstone Pk...236 K19
rd. Glen Waverley...420 A14
rd. Ivanhoe...327 K13
rd. Kensington...33 G9
rd.e,Croydon S...380 B12
rd.w,Croydon S...379 J12
st. Belmont...702 G20
st. Preston...282 D20
st. Surrey Hills...374 C20
wy. Mill Park...242 H12
BELMORE
ct. Narre Warren...538 H13
rd. Balwyn...372 L7
rd. Balwyn...373 C8
rd. Balwyn...374 A8
rd. Balwyn N...372 L7
rd. Balwyn N...373 C8
rd. Balwyn N...374 A8
rd. Mont Albert N...374 A8
rd. Sunshine N...321 D13
BELOT
cl. Bayswater...423 B4
BELSAY
pl. Craigieburn...150 E19
BELSHAW
ct. Hillside...232 F18
BELSIZE
av. Carnegie...456 J8
ct. Endeavour Hl...537 A2
BELSON
st. Malvern East...416 D17
BELT
tce. Endeavour Hl...537 J5
BELTANA
ct. Bayswater...423 L9
ct. Vermont...420 L4
ct. Wheelers Hill...460 J19
la. Roxburgh Pk...194 C7
st. Grovedale...706 C13
BELTANE
av. Brighton East...455 H13
BELTON
st. Anglesea...713 A6
BELUGA
st. Mt Eliza...641 G2
BELVEDERE
Kew...371 F8
av. Doncaster E...331 K20
av. Wheelers Hill...460 J9
cl. Maribyrnong...323 D16
cl. Pakenham Up...559 B2
ct. Blackburn N...376 C8
ct. Epping...198 B18
ct. Hampton Pk...551 D7
ct. Highton...705 J6
ct. Noble Park...500 H15
dr. Montrose...382 E8
rd. Seaford...599 K3
BELVOIR
ct. Kilsyth...381 F7
ct. Murrumbeena...457 D12
st. Doncaster E...331 L20
st. Doncaster E...375 L1
BEMBOKA
av. Clayton S...498 F9
ct. Wantirna S...422 C19
ct. Werribee...446 J15
rd. Croydon Hills...335 C16
rd. Warranwood...335 C16
BEMBOOKA
ct. Doncaster...331 F18
BEMBRIDGE
av. Frankston S...626 G6
mw. Craigieburn...194 B3
rd. Somerville...646 L15
rd. Somerville...647 A15
BEMERSYDE
av. Brighton...454 K19
dr. Berwick...554 D16
dr. Berwick...554 D20
BEMM
ct. Croydon Hills...335 J15
ct. Dandenong N...501 L9
ct. Werribee...446 L9
st. Moorabbin...496 H8
BEN
cl. Endeavour Hl...503 L18
ct. Donvale...332 G20
ct. Kalorama...382 L18
ct. Kalorama...383 A18
ct. St Helena...245 C15
dr. Pakenham...559 E18
BENA
ct. Dallas...238 D8
st. Yarraville...366 K19
BENALLA
cl. Endeavour Hl...537 E1
st. Dallas...238 G12
BENALONG
ct. Doncaster...330 J19
BENAMBRA
dr. Templstw Lr...330 F12
st. Broadmeadows..237 H14
st. Mornington...656 G3
st. Oakleigh S...498 A6
st. Preston...282 E18
wy. Hampton Pk...552 C9
BENANEE
dr. Frankston...600 C20
BENARES
st. Mitcham...377 B15
BENARI
ct. Grovedale...706 A12
BENAROON
dr. Lalor...240 D8
BENAUD
cl. Keilor East...278 C20
cl. Meadow Ht...237 J7
pl. Epping...198 H17
pl. Sunbury...142 G15
BENBOW
cr. Boronia...423 H15
ct. Hawthorn E...372 G15
st. Yarraville...366 H18
BENBROOK
av. Mont Albert N...374 G7
BENBURY
cl. St Albans...275 J20
BENCAIRN
ct. Lalor...240 H8
BENCES
rd. Merrimu...223 D1
BENCOOLEN
ct. Epping...198 B17
BEND
rd. Keysborough...534 L16
rd. Keysborough...535 A16
BENDALE
ct. Mill Park...242 C1
BENDALL
st. Kensington...33 G6
BENDEMERE
dr. Bundoora...243 C13
ri. Langwarrin...629 G3
BENDICK
ct. Altona Mdw...451 C3
BENDIGO
av. Bentleigh...496 B2
av. Elwood...454 D5
cct. Caroline Spr...318 E10
cr. Thomastown...240 E13
st. Burnley...371 C19
st. Cheltenham...496 K20
st. Collingwood...20 B11
st. Geelong West...702 E6
st. Hampton...494 L6
st. N Melbourne...17 D17
st. Pascoe Vale...280 H14

st. Prahran....32 F18
st. Prahran....32 F20
st. Prahran....414 J10
st. Reservoir....283 C14
tce. Windsor....414 J13

BENDIX
ct. Mornington....657 B3
dr. Clayton....499 B3

BENDLE
ct. E Geelong....703 K13
st. E Geelong....703 L12

BENDOC
ct. Meadow Ht....238 B6

BENDORAN
cr. Bundoora....284 K6

BENEDIKT
ct. Scoresby....462 H6

BENELONG
cr. Seaford....600 B3

BENGA
av. Dandenong....535 F7

BENGAL
cr. Mt Waverley....419 A15
ct. Cranbourne....577 K10

BENGHAZI
av. Ashburton....417 J17

BEN HOGAN
ct. Mt Waverley....458 K8

BENINA
st. Bentleigh E....496 K2

BENJAMIN
ch. Mooroolbark....337 L18
cl. Bundoora....242 G20
ct. Clarinda....498 C10
ct. Hallam....538 C20
ct. Keysborough....534 D9
ct. Kurunjang....226 G14
ct. Ringwood N....378 J2
ct. Somerville....644 F17
ct. Sydenham....274 H3
la. Melbourne....1 H11
la. Melbourne....24 A8
pde. Blairgowrie....679 K20
st. Box Hill N....375 C7
st. Mt Martha....656 D4
st. Parkville....17 H12
st. Sunshine....365 B6
st. Thornbury....326 J6

BENKEL
av. Cheltenham....531 H1
av. Cheltenham....531 J1

BENMARA
cr. Nar Warrn S....552 G7

BENMORE
pl. Wantirna....422 K6

BENNET
st. Dandenong....535 F9

BENNETT
av. Belgrave....466 G11
av. Heathmont....378 L20
av. Mt Waverley....419 H13
ct. Noble Park....534 L7
ct. Seaford....573 H19
ct. Sunbury....142 H12
ct. Fitzroy N, off Bennett St....326 E19
pde. Kew East....372 J7
pl. Sunshine....365 C2
rd. Gisborne....79 J20
rd. Gisborne....109 K1
st. Alphington....327 J16
st. Bacchus Msh....222 B16
st. Balwyn....372 L11
st. Balwyn....373 A11
st. Boronia....424 G12
st. Burwood....418 H10
st. Fitzroy N....326 E20
st. Forest Hill....420 B3
st. Highton....701 H17
st. Melton S....268 H11
st. Richmond....26 L6
st. Richmond....371 A13
st. Sunshine W....364 H10

BENNETTS
la. Melbourne....2 L6
la. Melbourne....24 F3
rd. Mornington....640 J18

BEN NEVIS
gr. Bulleen....329 F16

BENNIE
st. Brunswick....325 H13

BENNISON
st. Croydon....380 F6

BENNY
pl. Berwick....554 A19

BENO
ct. Thomastown....241 L12

BENONG
pl. Frankston....600 F20

BENOR
ct. Pakenham....584 G1

BENSAM
cl. Rowville....463 E12

BENSON
av. Toorak....415 J8
ct. Narre Warren....539 E18
dr. Yering....252 E20
dr. Yering....294 E1
la. Melbourne....24 H7
rd. Gisborne S....109 E20
st. Belgrave....466 E15
st. Coburg....325 G5
st. Emerald....509 E4
st. Richmond....26 J15
st. Surrey Hills....373 J15
st. Geelong, off Myers St....703 B10

BENSTON
st. Craigieburn....150 H19

BENT
av. Brighton....454 H6
ct. Wantirna S....423 A13
pde. Black Rock....529 E2
rd. Wandana Ht....701 D19
st. Altona....409 D20
st. Bentleigh....456 B18
st. Blackburn....375 H12
st. Brighton....455 B16
st. Brunswick W....324 K11
st. Bundoora....284 H1
st. Caulfield S....455 L8
st. Cremorne....32 A1
st. Cremorne....414 F1
st. Elsternwick....454 K3
st. Kensington....34 D11
st. Malvern East....416 F20
st. Moonee Pnd....324 D11
st. Northcote....326 E12
st. St Albans....320 C10
st. Westmeadows....236 K14

BENTICK
st. Frankston....626 K3

BENTLEY
av. Dandenong N....501 H20
av. Roxburgh Pk....194 B7
cr. Hoppers Csg....448 F3
ct. Mulgrave....500 G2
ct. Warranwood....334 J14
ct. Watsonia N....243 F20
pl. Frankston....627 B4
rd. McCrae....684 H18
st. Surrey Hills....374 E20
st. Wantirna....422 G7
st. Williamstn N....410 C12
wy. Mill Park....243 A2

BENTLY
la. Ringwood....378 E11

BENTON
av. Seaford....599 C11
ct. Doncaster....331 B18
rd. Healesville....214 B17
wy. Taylors Lakes....275 G5

BENTON GRANGE
dr. Mornington....657 E7

BENTONS
rd. Moorooduc....657 H8
rd. Mornington....656 G5
rd. Mornington....657 A6
rd. Mt Martha....656 C4
rd. Mt Martha....656 G5

BENWERREN
la. Yarra Jctn....347 F14

BENWERRIN
dr. Burwood E....419 F10
dr. Wantirna....422 B14
rd. Surrey Hills....374 D18

BENZ
cl. Mill Park....242 L2
cl. Mill Park....243 A2
ct. Keilor Dn....276 B14

BERALA
ct. Keysborough....534 E8
ct. Ringwood....335 B20
pl. Mill Park....242 E1

BERBERIS
cr. Frankston....600 B17
pl. Hoppers Csg....405 E16

BEREA
ct. Ringwood....378 G6

BEREAN
pl. Sorrento....679 B15

BEREMBONG
dr. Keilor East....278 B19

BEREND
st. Hampton E....495 L9

BERENDS
dr. Dandenong S....549 F8

BERENICE
tce. Toorak....415 B3

BERESFORD
cl. Doncaster E....331 H15
cr. Darley....222 C11
cr. Gladstone Pk....237 B17
dr. Boronia....424 J3
rd. Lilydale....338 A3
st. Caulfield N....415 E17
st. Kew East....372 C5
st. Mont Albert....374 B16
st. Pascoe Vale S....324 H6

BERGEN
cl. Keilor Lodge....276 A3
st. Keysborough....534 K13

BERGER
st. Dallas....238 H10

BERGINS
rd. Rowville....502 H4

BERGLUND
rd. Beaconsfld Up....558 B1
rd. Pakenham Up....558 B1

BERGMAN
rd. Langwarrin....629 G15

BERGNER
ct. Lysterfield....464 D19

BERINGA
av. Grovedale....705 L15

BERKEFELD
ct. Cheltenham....497 B20
ct. Templestowe....331 H10

BERKELEY
av. Heidelberg....329 E4
av. Point Cook....450 H8
cl. Broadmeadows....238 J12
cr. Altona North....409 J9
ct. Kew....371 E10
ct. Mt Eliza....626 F16
ct. Seabrook....450 L3
dr. Werribee....447 H2
gr. Brighton East....455 E16
st. Carlton....17 K16
st. Doncaster....331 A20
st. Hawthorn....372 A20
st. Hawthorn....416 A3
st. Huntingdale....458 E14

BERKERLEY
ct. Watsonia N....243 F20

BERKLEY
ct. Endeavour Hl....537 B2
ct. Glen Waverley....460 C3
ct. Greenvale....237 B6
pl. Chirnside Pk....337 J3
pl. Melton W....226 D15
rd. Ringwood....379 A2
st. Wantirna S....422 L14
st. Wantirna S....423 A14

BERKSHIRE
pl. Nar Warrn S....579 A3
rd. Sunshine N....321 D13

BERL
ct. Blackburn S....419 H2

BERMER
ct. Nar Warrn S....552 E17

BERMUDA
ct. Oakleigh S....497 G1
dr. Blackburn S....419 J6

BERNADETTE
ct. Doncaster E....332 H8

BERNARD
cr. Bundoora....285 B1
ct. Keilor East....278 E20
ct. Nar Warrn S....552 H16
ct. Somerville....645 C17
dr. Melton S....268 G5
rd. Rye....696 E9
st. Balwyn N....373 E1
st. Bayswater....423 B7
st. Cheltenham....496 L15
st. Maidstone....366 D3
st. Mt Waverley....458 J5
st. Reservoir....283 A11
st. Spotswood....411 C2

BERNARD HAMILTON
wy. Rowville....462 L20
wy. Rowville....463 A20

BERNARRA
ct. Donvale....333 B11

BERNAY
ct. Springvale S....499 J20

BERNBANKS
av. St Albans....320 J4

BERNBOROUGH
av. Balwyn....373 C8
av. Cranbourne W....577 F18
ct. Bacchus Msh....221 G18
ct. Keilor Dn....275 L13
pl. Mill Park....242 J10

BERNHARDT
av. Hoppers Csg....448 H9

BERNICE
ct. Coburg N....282 B18
st. Doncaster....330 C15

BERRABRI
dr. Scoresby....462 A6

BERRAMONGO
ct. Belmont....706 G2

BERRIDALE
ct. Hampton Pk....551 E11

BERRIE
rd. Gisborne S....110 H16
rd. Gisborne S....141 A1

BERRIGAN
ct. Oakleigh S....498 A8
ct. Werribee....447 J8

BERRIMA
av. Malvern East....456 L3
rd. Donvale....332 K20
rd. Rosanna....329 B2
st. Oakleigh E....458 L11

BERRINGA
ct. Bundoora....243 A20
ct. Meadow Ht....238 C4
rd. Pk Orchards....334 C20
rd. Ringwood N....378 C2
st. Frankston....599 L18
st. Parkdale....531 J9

BERRY
av. Edithvale....546 J15
av. Mitcham....377 E15
av. Somerton....194 G11
cl. Mornington....640 K16
ct. Doveton....536 J8
ct. Highton....705 H3
ct. Keysborough....534 F13
ct. Lilydale....338 J1
ct. Mill Park....242 E9
ct. Safety Bch....669 C11
la. Dandenong....535 K7
rd. Bayswater N....379 G15
rd. Silvan....384 F7
st. Box Hill N....374 J9
st. Clifton Hill....20 E3
st. Coburg....325 D4
st. E Melbourne....25 K11
st. Essendon N....323 G2
st. Fawkner....281 H10
st. Richmond....26 F11
st. Sunshine N....321 C13
st. Yarraville....367 D13

BERRYDALE
ct. Notting Hill....459 K14
rd. Sunbury....144 E7

BERRYS
rd. Emerald....509 D2

BERRYWOOD
wk. Warranwood....335 C16

BERTHA
st. Springvale....499 F16

BERTHANDRA
ct. W Footscray....366 D7

BERTHON
cr. Hillside....232 F18

BERTIE
st. Port Melb....368 H20

BERTRAM
rd. Bayswater....423 J7
st. Elsternwick....455 C10
st. Glen Iris....417 G10
st. Mordialloc....532 A19

BERTRAND
av. Mulgrave....500 K6
cl. Berwick....553 K5
rd. Chelsea....546 L17

BERTY
st. Newport....410 G10

BERWEN
st. Chelsea....546 H16

BERWICK
cl. Frankston....600 G19
ct. Sunshine W....364 L5
pl. Greenvale....193 C20
pl. Melton W....226 D15
rd. Campbellfield....239 D11
rd. Nar Warrn E....506 K17
ri. Templestowe....331 G14
st. Brighton....454 J13
st. Camberwell....372 J18
st. Lilydale....338 F6
st. Reservoir....282 K13

BERWICK-CRANBOURNE
rd. Clyde North....579 L19
rd. Cranbourne....579 L19
rd. Cranbourne E....604 H5
rd. Cranbourne N....579 L19

BERWICK SPRINGS
prm. Nar Warrn S....579 F3

BERWYN
cr. Templestowe....331 H11

BERYL
av. Oakleigh S....457 K20
cl. Greensborough....244 B17
ct. Clarinda....498 C12
ct. Narre Warren....539 F14
ct. Rye....697 A12
ct. Skye....575 H15
pl. Rye....696 H10
st. Croydon....380 E3
st. Essendon W....322 L6
st. Glen Iris....417 H10
st. Nunawading....376 H10

BESANKO
cl. Mordialloc....532 D18

BESANT
st. Hampton E....495 L10

BESGROVE
st. Rosebud....699 K2

BESLEY
st. Dandenong....536 E9

BESS
ct. Dandenong....536 E7

BESSA
ct. Wonga Park....291 J16

BESSAZILE
av. Forest Hill....376 E20

BESSELL
ct. Jacana....237 K18

BESSEMER
rd. Bayswater N....380 H14
st. Springvale....499 L10

BESSIE
st. Oakleigh S....497 G2

BESSIE CREEK
rd. Gembrook....512 K20

BESSIERE
pl. St Kilda....414 A16

BEST
cl. Epping....241 K4
st. Belgrave....466 D16
st. Fitzroy N....19 E1
st. Fitzroy N....326 C20
st. Oakleigh....457 L15
st. Reservoir....282 G9
st. Ringwood....378 G13

BESWICK
st. Clayton S....499 F9
st. Deer Park....318 K17

BESWICKE
ct. Dandenong S....535 H14

BETH
ct. Hampton Pk....552 A9
ct. Rosebud....684 H17

BETHANGA
ct. Taylors Lakes....276 D7
st. Mt Eliza....641 J1

BETHANY
cl. Rye....697 L9
ct. S Morang....199 J19

BETHEL
cl. Nar Warrn N....539 D8

BETHELA
st. Camberwell....417 J7

BETHELL
av. Parkdale....531 F11
st. Ormond....455 K14

BETHELLE
ct. Rowville....463 K17

BETHS
st. Bentleigh....456 F20

BETHUNE
ct. Seaford....573 J18
rd. Gruyere....342 L7
rd.w, Gruyere....342 H7
st. Hawthorn E....416 E5
st. Queenscliff....708 K19

BETHWYN
st. Bentleigh E....456 K16

BETLEIGH
st. Anglesea....713 K1

BETSON
ct. Kealba....276 K17

BETTER BOY
ct. Skye....575 H19

BETTINA
ct. Ascot Vale....323 G17
ct. Berwick....554 K7
ct. Templstw Lr....330 F9
st. Burwood E....419 G11
st. Clayton....459 E19

BETTON
cr. Warrandyte....333 J3

BETTS
wy. Burwood E....420 D13

BETTSONS
ct. Whittington....703 L18

BETTY
av. Mt Eliza 626 B18
cl. Rowville 463 K19
ct. Mt Waverley 459 D5
st. Bulleen 329 H16
st. Rye 696 K7
BETULA
av. Bundoora 242 G14
av. Bundoora 242 H15
av. Mill Park 242 G12
av. Nunawading 376 L20
av. Vermont 376 L20
av. Vermont 420 L1
ri. Hoppers Csg 405 F16
st. Doveton 536 G11
tce. Sunbury 143 E18
BEULAH
st. Broadmeadows 238 G17
BEURON
rd. Altona North 409 H1
BEVAN
av. Clayton S 499 B8
ct. Pakenham 584 E4
st. Albert Park 29 H11
st. Albert Park 413 D5
st. Balwyn 373 C13
st. Ormond 455 J14
BEVERAGE
dr. Tullamarine 278 C12
BEVERIDGE
st. Warrandyte 289 K20
BEVERLEY
cl. Frankston 599 J16
cr. Blackburn 375 G12
ct. Balwyn N 374 A5
ct. Heathmont 379 B19
ct. Hoppers Csg 405 B20
ct. Langwarrin 601 K20
dr. Healesville 213 G15
gr. Mt Waverley 458 K1
pl. Keysborough 534 J10
rd. Heidelberg 329 C7
rd. McCrae 685 A12
rd. Rosanna 329 E3
st. Cheltenham 530 D2
st. Doncaster E 375 K2
st. Dromana 686 C9
st. Glen Huntly 456 C8
st. Kings Park 275 F19
st. Scoresby 462 E9
st. Yarraville 367 C18
BEVERLY
ct. Narre Warren 553 F9
BEVERLY HILLS
dr. Templestowe 332 C7
BEVERSTONE
pl. Werribee 446 L17
BEVINGTON
ct. Highton 701 G13
BEVIS
st. Bentleigh E 456 G19
st. Mulgrave 500 C4
BEVNOL
rd. Langwarrin 629 D10
BEWDLEY
st. Ormond 456 F14
BEWLEY
wy. Berwick 553 H14
BEWSELL
av. Scoresby 462 E7
BEXLEY
cl. Werribee 446 K11
BEXSARM
cr. Rowville 463 B14
BEZZELL
st. Brunswick 325 G14
BHANGOO
ct. Sydenham 274 J4
BIAK
ct. Keilor Park 277 L13
pl. Croydon N 335 L15
BIALA
ct. Mooroolbark 337 D11
BIANCA
ct. Mornington 656 J1
ct. Rowville 503 A4
dr. Aspendale Gdn 546 H4
BIANCHI
cl. Mill Park 242 K1
ct. Keilor Dn 276 A16
BIANCO
ct. Cranbourne N 577 L6
ct. Langwarrin 629 D3
BIARRITZ
av. Beaumaris 530 F4
ct. Frankston 628 D12
BIASIN
ct. Brookfield 268 B5
BIBBY
ct. Albanvale 319 B3
ct. Moorabbin 497 B10

BIBLE
st. Eltham 287 H12
st. Ripponlea 454 J3
BIBURY
ct. Kilsyth S 424 L1
BICENTENNIAL
cr. Meadow Ht 194 B17
ct. Doncaster E 332 K14
BICKERTON
ct. Rowville 502 G1
wy. Roxburgh Pk 193 J13
BICKFORD
cl. Tullamarine 278 K1
ct. Beaumaris 530 G6
pl. Hallam 537 F15
rd. Grovedale 706 A17
BICKHAM
ct. St Kilda E 414 L18
BICKLEIGH
ct. Croydon Hills 335 E17
ct. Glen Iris 416 H9
st. Glen Iris 416 G9
BICKLEIGH-VALE
rd. Mooroolbark 381 H1
BICKLEY
av. Thomastown 241 K14
av. Thomastown 242 A12
ct. Sunshine W 365 B9
BICKNELL
ct. Broadmeadows 237 L20
ct. Broadmeadows 280 A1
BICTON
st. Greensborough 286 E5
st. Mt Waverley 419 C17
BIDDICK
ct. Werribee 448 A12
BIDEY
st. Prahran 414 L12
st. Prahran 415 A12
BIDGEE
st. Frankston 628 B1
BIDSTON
ct. Ringwood 335 A19
BIENIAS
cr. Tootgarook 698 D8
BIESKE
rd. Grovedale 706 D16
BIGELOW
ct. Rye 696 K3
BIGGS
st. St Albans 320 B1
BIGMORE
st. Geelong West 702 G6
BIGNELL
ct. Roxburgh Pk 194 B12
rd. Bentleigh E 497 C5
rd. Moorabbin 497 B10
st. Flemington 34 C1
st. Flemington 324 G20
st. Pascoe Vale 280 K18
BIGOLA
st. Ringwood 378 H7
BIG PATS CREEK
rd. E Warburton 350 K2
BILBUL
av. Rosebud 700 K7
BILBUNGRA
dr. Keysborough 534 C9
BILBY
bnd. Berwick 553 J15
st. Templstw Lr 330 F10
BILGOLA
ct. Mt Eliza 642 A7
BILL
pl. Hampton Pk 552 D12
BILLABONG
cl. Croydon Hills 335 F13
ct. Burnside 318 H6
ct. Greensborough 244 K15
ct. Wantirna S 421 L18
wk. Mornington 656 K2
BILLANOOK
wy. Chirnside Pk 336 H7
BILLARA
cl. Wantirna S 422 L10
cl. Wantirna S 423 A10
BILLAROY
rd. Beaconsfld Up 541 H2
BILLING
pl. Brookfield 267 K10
st. Mt Waverley 458 J1
st. Springvale 500 A18
BILLINGHAM
rd. Deer Park 319 B11
BILLINGSLEYS
rd. Tooradin 652 F9
BILLS
st. Hawthorn 416 B4
tr. Kangaroo Grnd 249 A9

BILLSON
st. Brighton East 455 D20
BILLUNGAH
pl. Burnside 318 G8
BILLY TEA
ct. Greensborough 244 K16
BILOCLA
av. Cockatoo 471 H17
BILSTON
ct. Highton 705 G6
st. Seddon 367 D10
BILTRIS
ct. Jacana 237 J19
BIMBADEEN
cr. Yallambie 286 B13
ct. Bayswater 423 B9
ct. Wheelers Hill 460 J8
dr. Mooroolbark 337 E13
st. Burnside 318 G7
BIMBI
ct. Mooroolbark 337 D13
st. Clayton 499 C2
BIMBIANG
cr. Rye 696 L3
cr. Rye 697 A3
BIMBLE
st. Rye 697 H3
BINALONG
av. Chadstone 418 C20
ct. Burnside 318 F6
ct. Grovedale 705 K12
ct. St Albans 320 L6
ct. St Albans 321 A6
ct. Yallambie 286 B12
BINBROOK
ct. Highton 705 K6
dr. Croydon 335 F18
BINDA
ct. Patterson L 573 K7
BINDEA
rd. Yellingbo 388 C13
BINDI
cl. Frankston 600 D17
cl. Hallam 538 B20
cl. Springvale S 499 H19
cl. Templestowe 332 A13
st. Glenroy 280 C1
st. Wantirna S 422 L13
BINDING
av. Cranbourne 604 C3
BINDTS
rd. Wollert 198 A9
BINDY
st. Blackburn S 420 A4
st. Forest Hill 420 A4
BINGHAM
ct. Bundoora 284 L2
BINGLEY
av. Hurstbridge 202 H9
av. Notting Hill 459 J13
pde. Anglesea 713 H2
BINGO
st. Preston 327 E5
BINNAK
ct. Meadow Ht 194 D19
dr. Watsonia N 243 E19
wy. Baxter 643 H11
BINNIE
st. Brighton East 495 B2
BINNS
st. Altona North 409 E2
st. Montmorency 286 J9
BINOWEE
av. Yallambie 286 C14
BINYA
ct. Dandenong N 501 F14
ct. Sunshine W 364 E7
BIOLOGY
dr. Bundoora, off Science Dr 284 C11
BIRALEE
ct. Berwick 554 G11
BIRAN
ct. Reservoir 283 C8
BIRBANK
ct. Doncaster 331 B14
BIRCH
av. Dandenong N 501 H18
av. Emerald 509 B6
av. Tullamarine 278 J6
av. Wonga Park 336 D6
ct. Bangholme 549 H13
ct. Campbellfield 239 F13
ct. Craigieburn 150 C13
ct. Grovedale 706 B16
ct. Langwarrin 629 J1
ct. Mill Park 242 D9
ct. Narre Warren 553 G9
ct. Pascoe Vale 280 L10

ct. Wyndham Va 446 F10
ct. Wyndham Va 446 F9
gr. Frankston 600 C18
la. Kensington 33 E9
st. Bayswater 423 E6
st. Caulfield S 455 G8
st. Mentone 530 K7
st. Mt Waverley 419 B16
st. Preston 326 C3
st. Springvale 499 J8
BIRCHBANK
cl. Lysterfield S 503 L15
BIRCHFIELD
cr. Wantirna 422 G13
ct. Narre Warren 538 J14
BIRCHGROVE
cr. Templestowe 331 F14
BIRCHMORE
ct. Taylors Lakes 275 F7
BIRCHWOOD
av. Templstw Lr 330 E9
bvd. Deer Park 319 B10
bvd. Hoppers Csg 405 D17
dr. Mooroolbark 337 F9
dr. Preston 283 H18
pl. Sunbury 143 E17
st. Fawkner 239 F20
st. Nar Warrn S 553 E17
wy. Delahey 275 C11
BIRD
av. Thornbury 326 E10
av. Thornbury 326 F10
ct. Williamstown 410 K15
rd. Avonsleigh 470 K12
st. Deer Park 319 A17
st. Eltham 287 D8
st. Mt Eliza 642 E8
st. Springvale 500 D12
BIRDIE
av. Anglesea 713 A6
st. Mt Waverley 459 A6
BIRDROCK
av. Mt Martha 656 C6
BIRDS
rd. Ferny Creek 466 A1
BIRDSALL
pl. Carlton N 18 H4
BIRDSEY
st. Thomson 703 G16
BIRDUM
st. Moorabbin 496 J12
BIRDWOOD
av. Brighton 454 F9
av. Cockatoo 511 D3
av. Dandenong 535 F6
av. Ferntree Gly 424 L20
av. Healesville 212 L15
av. Macleod 285 A14
av. Melbourne 4 F18
av. Melbourne 24 K19
av. Melbourne 30 L1
av. Melbourne 31 A1
av. Melbourne 414 A1
av. Mornington 640 H11
av. Upwey 465 H11
rd. Croydon 380 A6
st. Aspendale 546 E8
st. Balwyn 372 K8
st. Balwyn 373 A8
st. Bentleigh E 457 G15
st. Box Hill S 374 L20
st. Box Hill S 375 A20
st. Box Hill S 418 L2
st. Essendon N 279 D20
st. Frankston 627 E1
st. Kew East 372 E4
st. Maribyrnong 367 A2
st. Parkdale 531 D13
st. Reservoir 282 G16
BIRGITA
ct. Langwarrin 601 J17
BIRKBY
st. Box Hill N 375 C7
BIRKDALE
cl. Anglesea 713 C6
cl. Wantirna 422 B12
ct. Frankston 599 J16
ct. Sunbury 144 F13
BIRKENHEAD
av. Wantirna 422 G11
dr. Grovedale 706 E11
dr. Kilsyth 381 C5
st. Fitzroy N 326 C19
BIRKETT
ct. Altona Mdw 451 J4
BIRKLEY
ct. Noble Park N 501 A7
ct. Rosebud 700 A2
BIRMINGHAM
rd. Mt Evelyn 338 K16
rd. Mt Evelyn 339 A17

st. Spotswood 410 J2
st. Springvale 500 C10
st. Yarraville 367 B15
BIRNAM
ct. Belmont 702 D20
BIRRAKAY
ct. Greensborough 244 B19
BIRRALEE
sq. Keilor Dn 276 G16
st. Mt Waverley 458 K2
st. Wantirna S 422 K12
BIRRARRUNG
ct. Bulleen 329 J8
BIRRELL
ct. Altona Mdw 451 F6
ct. Kew 372 H9
BIRRILEE
ct. Grovedale 706 E9
BIRRONG
av. Noble Park 534 H6
BIRTINYA
ct. Frankston 600 F16
BIRTLES
ct. Balwyn 372 L8
ct. Balwyn 373 A8
st. Balwyn 372 L8
st. Balwyn 373 A8
BIRTLEY
ct. Greenvale 192 K15
BISCAY
ct. Boronia 424 G4
ct. Dingley Village 532 L8
ct. Melton W 226 C12
BISCAYNE
dr. Mt Waverley 419 J15
BISCHOFF
st. Preston 326 D2
BISCOP
rd. Moorabbin 496 E10
BISHOP
av. Diamond Ck 246 C11
ct. Mt Waverley 459 C3
ct. Wantirna 422 E13
pl. Epping 242 A1
pl. Melton W 226 D18
rd. Moorooduc 658 G10
st. Box Hill 375 B15
st. Brunswick 325 H10
st. Coburg 281 B19
st. Kingsville 366 H13
st. Oakleigh 457 L15
st. Yarraville 366 H14
BISHOPS
ct. Seabrook 450 L5
rd. Panton Hill 204 G16
BISLEY
ct. Craigieburn 149 L16
BISMARCK
ct. Bundoora 284 G6
BISSET
ct. Hoppers Csg 448 A2
BITHEL
st. Glen Waverley 420 B19
BITTERN
ct. Werribee 448 B5
dr. Endeavour Hl 536 L4
dr. Endeavour Hl 537 A4
st. Broadmeadows 237 H14
st. Melton 226 F17
BITTERN-DROMANA
rd. Dromana 687 H3
rd. Dromana 688 A4
rd. Red Hill 688 A4
BIZANA
st. W Footscray 366 D9
BIZLEY
st. Mt Waverley 419 G15
BLABY
st. Noble Park 534 L1
BLACK
ct. Avondale Ht 322 G8
ct. Noble Park 534 L3
st. Brighton 454 H17
st. Brunswick 325 E17
st. Chelsea 546 J16
st. Essendon 323 H7
st. Lilydale 338 B7
st. Mont Albert 374 E16
st. Oakleigh E 458 K16
st. Reservoir 283 E8
st. Watsonia 285 D7
st. Westmeadows 237 B14
BLACKBIRD
ri. Avondale Ht 322 E12
BLACKBURN
dr. Cheltenham 531 H1
rd. Blackburn 375 K16
rd. Blackburn S 419 K7
rd. Burwood E 419 K10

rd. Clayton 459 F19
rd. Doncaster E 332 B19
rd. Doncaster E 376 B6
rd. Glen Waverley 459 G10
rd. Mooroolbark 337 J18
rd. Mt Waverley 459 G10
rd. Notting Hill 459 F19
rd. Templestowe 332 B19
st. Lalor 241 G10
st. Surrey Hills 374 B16

BLACKBURNE
sq. Berwick 554 E7

BLACKBUTT
ct. Frankston N 599 K11

BLACK CAMERON
rd. St Andrews 205 H1
rd. Smiths Gly 205 H1

BLACK DOG
dr. Brookfield 268 A3

BLACKERS
la. Yarrambat 201 G14

BLACK FLAT
rd. Whittlesea 96 C16

BLACK FOREST
rd. Werribee 447 A16
rd. Wyndham Va 445 F14

BLACKFRIARS
cl. Toorak 415 C4
cl. Wantirna 422 H10
la. Chirnside Pk 337 E1

BLACKGATE
rd. Torquay 712 G1

BLACKGULLY
rd. Diamond Ck 245 K1
rd. Yarrambat 201 G19
rd. Yarrambat 245 K1

BLACKHEATH
av. Frankston 599 K16

BLACK HILL
pde. Selby 467 E14
rd. Menzies Ck 467 K14
rd. Selby 467 F14
rd. Selby 467 K14

BLACKHILL
rd. Gisborne S 109 L20

BLACKLEY
ct. Deer Park 319 C12

BLACKMAN
av. Mill Park 242 K6
av. Mill Park 243 A7
cl. Sunbury 142 G9
cr. Taylors Lakes 233 A19
cr. Taylors Lakes 233 B20

BLACKMORE
ct. Bundoora 284 H4
st. Chum Creek 212 L11
st. Dandenong N 501 G8
st. Sunshine N 321 E17

BLACK NIGHT
st. Mordialloc 532 C16

BLACKS
rd. Wandin East 386 D10

BLACKSCAMP
rd. Somerville 644 H17

BLACKSHAW
st. Ormond 456 G15

BLACKSHAWS
rd. Altona North 409 C1
rd. S Kingsville 410 C3

BLACKSMITH
av. S Morang 199 L17
dr. Attwood 236 L11
dr. Attwood 237 A11
pl. Sydenham 274 L4

BLACK SPRINGS
rd. Chirnside Pk 336 F5
rd. Wonga Park 336 E5

BLACKSTON
st. Footscray 367 E7

BLACKSTONE
la. Nar Warrn E 506 H15

BLACK WATTLE
pl. Somerville 644 D14
wy. Carrum Downs 575 C14

BLACKWELLS
la. Bulla 190 J15

BLACK WOOD
wk. S Morang 243 L3

BLACKWOOD
av. Mentone 531 G7
av. Warburton 349 K1
cl. Eltham North 245 F18
cr. Campbellfield 239 F13
ct. Frankston S 627 K14
ct. Mt Martha 657 D8
ct. Nunawading 376 K11
ct. St Albans 319 F9
ct. Werribee 447 J9
dr. Hampton Pk 551 L5
dr. Melton S 268 H3
dr. Narre Warren 538 J17
dr. Rosebud W 699 C3
dr. Wheelers Hill 460 E14
dr. Wonga Park 291 K19
pde. Heidelberg W 328 A2
pl. Sunbury 143 F15
ri. Somerville 645 C20
st. Carnegie 456 L5
st. Lalor 241 H12
st. N Melbourne 17 G16
st. Tecoma 466 C8
st. Yarraville 366 L16
wy. Delahey 275 D11

BLACKWOOD PARK
rd. Ferntree Gly 464 B11

BLACKWOODS
rd. Chum Creek 213 C3

BLADEN
av. Brunswick E 325 L11
pl. Gladstone Pk 237 A18
st. Wheelers Hill 461 E16

BLADIN
st. Laverton 407 C17

BLADON
st. Wantirna 422 H14

BLAGDON
st. Cheltenham 530 J2

BLAIR
av. Frankston S 626 L7
ct. Altona North 409 J6
ct. Grovedale 706 E14
ct. Keilor 277 B14
ct. Portsea 677 J2
ct. Thomastown 240 J15
ct. Warranwood 334 L15
pl. N Melbourne 17 E19
rd. Belgrave 466 G16
rd. Glen Waverley 420 C20
rd. Portsea 677 K2
st. Bentleigh 456 A18
st. Broadmeadows 238 D17
st. Brunswick 325 G15
st. Coburg 325 G7
st. Doncaster 375 C1
st. Lilydale 337 K3
st. Maribyrnong 322 J17
st. Moonee Pnd 324 B10
st. Warrandyte 333 J2

BLAIRGOWRIE
av. Blairgowrie 679 H17
ct. Brighton 454 F14
pl. Melton W 226 C17

BLAKE
cl. Delahey 275 F13
ct. Mt Eliza 626 K18
ct. Scoresby 462 A6
ct. Truganina 405 F13
st. Blackburn N 375 F10
st. Caulfield 455 L5
st. Mornington 640 E13
st. Reservoir 283 H16

BLAKENEY
pl. Southbank 23 J20

BLAKEVILLE
dr. Caroline Spr 318 B3

BLAKISTON
av. Mt Evelyn 383 D7
gr. Rye 698 A3

BLAMEY
av. Mill Park 242 J12
ct. Boronia 424 D5
dr. Melton S 268 J13
pl. Mornington 640 F14
rd. Yallambie 285 F12
st. Ascot Vale 324 A19
st. Bentleigh E 497 B7
st. Noble Park 535 C4

BLANCH
st. Preston 326 J3

BLANCHARD
ct. Greensborough 243 J20

BLANCHE
av. Parkdale 531 G12
cl. Cranbourne 578 A14
ct. Coburg N 282 B17
ct. Doncaster E 376 B3
ct. Kilsyth S 381 A19
dr. Vermont 421 G2
st. Ardeer 320 B19
st. Brighton East 455 C16
st. Collingwood 19 H11
st. Cremorne 25 L18
st. Elsternwick 455 D3
st. St Kilda 414 D16
st. Yarraville 367 A15

BLAND
st. Dandenong N 501 H15

BLANDFORD
cr. Bayswater N 380 F19
ct. Carrum Downs 574 H15
st. W Footscray 366 J7

BLANNIN
st. Healesville 213 K20

BLANTON
dr. Mulgrave 501 K6

BLANTYRE
av. Chelsea 546 K18

BLATCH
ct. Forest Hill 420 G1

BLAU
st. Bundoora 242 E16

BLAXLAND
av. Cranbourne N 577 L9
av. Frankston S 627 E10
av. Thomastown 240 E19
ct. Mooroolbark 337 K15
dr. Dandenong N 501 G8
dr. Rowville 463 G16
dr. Sunbury 143 C13
pl. Taylors Lakes 275 K1
rd. Melton S 268 G12
st. Wyndham Va 446 G9

BLAZEY
rd. Croydon S 379 K12
st. Richmond 371 B15

BLEACHES
la. Wesburn 347 K15
la. Yarra Jctn 347 K15

BLEAKHOUSE
la. Albert Park 29 D17

BLEASES
la. Dixons Ck 210 H13
la. Yarra Glen 210 H13

BLEAZBY
av. Brighton 454 K18
st. Bentleigh 456 A19

BLENCAIRN
av. Caulfield N 455 H2
av. Mt Martha 655 H15

BLENDON
av. St Albans 320 H3

BLENHEIM
av. Glen Waverley 460 L1
av. Mont Albert 374 F17
pl. Frankston S 628 C15
rd. Altona North 410 D9
rd. Newport 410 D9
st. Balaclava 414 H18
st. Bentleigh E 457 B15
st. Glenroy 280 A6
st. Heathmont 422 H2
wy. Caroline Spr 317 K4

BLESSINGTON
ct. St Kilda 414 B19
st. Newtown 702 E8
st. St Kilda 414 B19
wy. St Kilda 414 E18

BLETCHLEY
pl. Kealba 276 L20
pl. Kealba 277 A20
rd. Hughesdale 457 G9

BLIBURG
st. Jacana 237 J19

BLIGH
cl. Cranbourne N 578 A9
ct. Endeavour Hl 537 D6
ct. Heathmont 422 G1
ct. Lilydale 338 J2
pl. Melbourne 1 L17
pl. Melbourne 24 C10
pl. Wyndham Va 446 G8
st. Melton S 268 E10

BLIND BIGHT
rd. Blind Bight 650 F8

BLINKER
ri. Endeavour Hl 504 B20

BLISS
st. Burnley 371 A18

BLISSINGTON
st. Springvale 499 L6

BLOCK
ct. Melbourne 2 B15
ct. Melbourne, off Block Pl 24 D8
pl. Melbourne 2 B14
pl. Melbourne 24 D8

BLODORN
ct. Keysborough 534 C11

BLOMBERG
rd. Altona North 409 F9

BLOOM
st. Frankston 627 H3
st. Moonee Pnd 324 A10

BLOOMBURG
st. Abbotsford 26 B1

BLOOMFIELD
av. Maribyrnong 323 A15
av. Nar Warrn S 553 E17
rd. Ascot Vale 324 A17
rd. Gisborne 79 E18
rd. Keysborough 534 J11
rd. Noble Park 534 J11

BLOOMINGDALE
av. Albanvale 319 A5

BLOOMS
rd. N Warrandyte 290 A14

BLOOMSBURY
la. Wyndham Va 446 F9
st. Newtown 702 G13

BLOSSOM
ct. Doncaster 374 H3
ct. Glen Waverley 459 J6
dr. Doveton 536 H10
gr. Knoxfield 423 B19
st. Mitcham 377 J16
st. Parkdale 531 K8
wk. Croydon S 380 C14

BLOSSOM PARK
dr. Mill Park 243 B9
dr. Mill Park 243 C13

BLOXHAM
ct. Hoppers Csg 448 D2

BLUCHER
st. Ferntree Gly 464 E9
st. Glenroy 280 A7
tce. Williamstown 411 F12

BLUEBELL
cr. Gowanbrae 279 C6
ct. Berwick 539 G17
ct. Hoppers Csg 405 C16
ct. Melton W 225 H17
ct. The Patch 467 L6
dr. Epping 198 G19
la. Launching Pl 346 C15

BLUEBERRY
cl. Cranbourne N 578 B10
ct. Bundoora 242 K15
ct. Werribee 447 J10
la. Monbulk 428 G16
rd. Mooroolbark 337 C12

BLUEBIRD
av. Cockatoo 471 D19

BLUEBUSH
ct. Sunbury 143 J7

BLUECHIP
ct. Point Cook 451 B8

BLUEGRASS
cr. Pakenham 585 E7
wk. Frankston 599 L16

BLUE GUM
ct. Chelsea 547 B19
ct. Greensborough 286 K1
ct. Narre Warren 553 G13
mw. Langwarrin 601 H15

BLUEGUM
av. Wheelers Hill 460 L11
cl. Templstw Lr 330 K12
ct. Mill Park 242 F11
ct. Upwey 466 A9
dr. Altona 409 C16
dr. Badger Creek 258 E12
la. Croydon S 379 L14
wy. Hampton Pk 552 A16
wy. Hampton Pk 552 B16
wy. Sunbury 143 F16

BLUE HILLS
av. Mt Waverley 419 F20
av. Nunawading 376 E11
cl. Wantirna 422 C11

BLUE HOUSE
rd. Smiths Gly 205 C8

BLUE JAY
ct. Nar Warrn S 578 K4

BLUE MIST
dr. Croydon S 379 G11

BLUE MOON
wy. Sydenham 275 D8

BLUE RANGE
cr. Lynbrook 551 G17

BLUE RIDGE
dr. Mooroolbark 338 A15
la. Mt Eliza 625 L17
rd. Dewhurst 510 D20

BLUESTAR
ri. Bundoora 284 F9

BLUESTONE
ct. S Morang 199 K16
st. Kensington 33 G5
wk. Delahey 274 L16

BLUE WREN
ct. Mt Evelyn 382 K2
ri. Carrum Downs 601 A7

BLUFF
av. Elwood 454 B4
ct. Highett 495 H13
ct. Rosebud W, off Allambi Av 699 E3
rd. Black Rock 529 F5
rd. Cannons Creek 649 D9
rd. Hampton 495 H12
rd. Sandringham 495 F20
st. Hawthorn E 416 E7
st. Lalor 240 G9

BLUMM
rd. Belgrave S 507 D6

BLUSHING
wy. Bundoora 242 E14

BLYTH
ct. Croydon N 335 K11
ct. Gladstone Pk 279 C4
pl. Mulgrave 500 H1
st. Altona 408 H20
st. Altona 409 A19
st. Altona 452 F1
st. Brunswick 325 G12
st. Brunswick E 325 G12
st. Docklands 23 C13
st. St Albans 320 L6
st. Vermont 377 F20

BLYTHE
av. Boronia 424 G6
ct. Dingley Village 533 B1
st. Murrumbeena 457 D12
st. Thornbury 326 J7

BLYTHES
rd. Mt Dandenong 382 J19

BLYTHSWOOD
ct. Kew 371 E12

BLYTON
cr. Sunbury 142 K9
ct. Highton 705 K9
ct. Templestowe 332 B11

BOA
ct. Sunshine W 364 D6

BOADLE
rd. Bundoora 284 E5

BOAKE
st. Carnegie 456 K13

BOANDYNE
ct. Toorak 415 G3

BOARD
pl. Geelong, off Little Malop St 703 C8
st. Doncaster 331 B17

BOARDMAN
cl. Box Hill S 418 K5
st. Malvern East 416 C20

BOARDWALK
bvd. Point Cook 450 A6

BOASE
st. Brunswick 325 F13

BOATHOUSE
rd. Kew 371 B7

BOB
st. Nar Warrn N 539 B9

BOBBORA
ct. Taylors Lakes 275 H8

BOBERRIT
wyn. Sydenham 274 J6
wyn. Sydenham 274 K7

BODALLA
ct. Frankston 628 E8

BODLEY
st. Beaumaris 530 C11
st. Clarinda 498 H11

BODMIN
ct. Craigieburn 194 C2

BODYCOATS
rd. Wollert 153 C14

BOEING
ct. Forest Hill 420 E9
rd. Strathmr Ht 279 D10

BOGAN
ct. Boronia 424 J6

BOGART
cl. Dingley Village 533 A3

BOGER
rd. Watsonia 285 D8

BOGEY
ct. Dingley Village 533 F9

BOGIE
ct. Anglesea 713 B5

BOGNOR
av. Seaford 573 D17

BOGONG
av. Glen Waverley 460 A5
av. Glen Waverley 460 C2
cl. Hallam 552 B2
ct. Bangholme 549 J13
ct. Broadmeadows 238 A10
ct. Doncaster E 332 D19
ct. Forest Hill 420 D4
ct. Frankston 600 E19
ct. Lalor 240 J8
ct. Reservoir 282 E7

BOHAN
gr. Belmont 702 D20

BOILEAU
st. Keysborough 535 B14

BOISDALE
av. Sunshine N 320 L14
st. Surrey Hills 418 B2
BOKHARA
rd. Caulfield S..........455 K8
BOKISSA
dr. Frankston...........599 L15
BOLAC
pl. Taylors Hill.........274 K12
st. Bayswater..........423 H7
BOLAN
st. Glen Waverley....419 L15
BOLAND
st. Burnley.............371 B17
BOLCH
pl. Oakleigh............458 A8
BOLDEN
st. Heidelberg 328 H6
BOLDREWOOD
pde. Kingsbury 283 F10
pde. Reservoir 283 E12
BOLGER
cr. Hoppers Csg......448 L3
cr. Hoppers Csg......449 A3
BOLINA
ct. Mill Park 242 F10
BOLINDA
pl. Vermont 421 C5
rd. Balwyn N 373 H4
rd. Campbellfield 239 D16
st. Bentleigh............456 D20
BOLINGBROKE
st. Pascoe Vale 280 F17
BOLITHO
st. Sunshine 365 D7
BOLOKA
ct. Patterson L 573 K9
BOLTE
ct. Frankston S........627 H11
BOLTON
av. Hampton............494 J5
ct. Avondale Ht 322 G8
ct. Greenvale...........192 L16
ct. Langwarrin..........629 C7
ct. Mulgrave 460 F20
rd. Selby 467 B20
rd. Wyndham Va 446 G8
st. Beaumaris...........529 K6
st. Box Hill.............375 D14
st. Eltham 287 C15
st. Lower Plenty......287 B18
st. Spotswood 411 A1
BOLWARRA
ct. Cranbourne W....577 K16
st. Chadstone..........458 C2
BOLWELL
st. Werribee............447 H17
BOLYN
ct. Vermont S 420 G10
BON
ct. Nar Warrn N.......539 F9
BONA
av. Healesville..........257 F2
av. Oak Park............279 J11
st. Ashburton..........417 E13
st. Ringwood E 379 B10
st. Tootgarook 698 F2
BON AIR
av. Anglesea............713 H6
BONANG
ct. Meadow Ht 238 A3
BONANZA
la. Beaumaris..........530 G9
rd. Beaumaris..........530 G9
BONAPARTE
pl. Ferntree Gly 463 L12
BONAR
av. Brunswick W......324 L7
ct. Endeavour Hl 503 G17
st. Heidelberg Ht.....328 D2
BONA VISTA
av. Aspendale..........546 C6
av. Surrey Hills........374 A19
rd. Bayswater..........423 C8
BOND
av. Blackburn S 419 K5
av. St Albans 320 F11
ct. Cranbourne........578 A19
ct. Croydon.............380 H5
ct. Keilor East.........322 B3
ct. Lalor..................241 L10
ct. Meadow Ht 238 B2
ct. Montrose............382 E8
dr. Taylors Lakes......275 F5
la. Newport.............411 A10
st. Abbotsford...........26 L3
st. Altona North.......365 J20
st. Caulfield N 456 A1
st. Clayton S............498 G4
st. Doncaster 375 B3
st. Hadfield 281 A9
st. Hoppers Csg......405 A19
st. Ivanhoe.............327 J10
st. Maddingley 264 B2
st. Melbourne 1 K19
st. Melbourne 24 C11
st. Mordialloc..........532 E12
st. Mt Waverley.......459 E2
st. Newtown 702 H11
st. Preston 282 H20
st. Ringwood 378 B12
st. South Yarra..........32 D10
st. South Yarra........414 H5
st.w,Mordialloc 532 C12
BONDI
av. Frankston...........627 G5
rd. Bonbeach...........545 F13
rd. Bonbeach...........573 A3
st. Ringwood E 379 C12
BONDS
ct. Research 288 L5
la. Greenvale...........192 G18
rd. Lower Plenty......330 F6
BONEO
rd. Boneo...............699 H11
rd. Boneo...............699 H20
rd. Rosebud 683 H20
rd. Rosebud 699 H11
rd. Rosebud W........699 H11
BONESHAKER
pl. Carlton.................18 H9
BONFIELD
av. Hawthorn E........416 F6
st. Keilor 277 D14
BONHAM
cr. Oakleigh E.........458 J15
rd. Monbulk 468 D4
rd. The Patch...........468 D4
BONITA
ct. Dandenong N.....502 D19
BONITO
st. Mt Eliza..............641 K4
BONLEIGH
av. Brighton.............454 E9
BONNER
st. Surrey Hills 417 K2
BONNEY
ct. Melb Airport.......235 J12
pl. Roxburgh Pk......194 C10
BONNIE
ct. Ferntree Gly 464 C6
BONNIE DOONE
st. Briar Hill.............286 G3
BONNIE VIEW
rd. Croydon N 336 D16
rd. Mt Dandenong ...426 E1
BONNY
st. Bentleigh E.........496 K5
BONNYBRAE
ct. Sunbury.............144 G13
BONNYVIEW
rd. Mt Eliza.............626 D11
st. Glen Iris 417 J10
BONO
cl. Blackburn S 419 D4
BONSEY
rd. Highton.............705 G2
BONUS
ct. Werribee............446 H19
BONVIEW
av. Herne Hill...........701 H1
av. Ringwood 377 L13
cr. Burwood E 419 H8
ct. Knoxfield............463 C2
ct. Ferny Creek.........465 L2
rd. Malvern 416 A11
st. Reservoir 282 E12
BONVILLE
ct. Camberwell........417 D5
BON VUE
rd. Balwyn N 329 E19
BONWICK
st. Fawkner.............281 G6
BONZA VIEW
Kalorama 382 K13
BOOBYALLA
st. Doveton.............536 J10
BOOKER
st. Cheltenham........530 L4
st. Cheltenham........531 A4
st. Spotswood 411 D2
BOOLARONG
dr. Belmont.............706 H5
BOOLOORA
rd. Springvale..........499 G11
BOOM
pl. Carlton.................18 J9
BOOMERANG
ct. Nar Warrn S.......578 K1
ct. Tootgarook 698 G7
BOONAH
ct. Templstw Lr.......330 K8
st. Springvale..........499 K16
wy. Forest Hill 420 E2
BOONDARA
gr. St Kilda E 414 K15
rd. Mont Albert N.....374 E9
BOONGARRY
av. Blackburn 375 H18
BOONONG
av. Seaford.............599 D11
BOORAHMAN
st. Balwyn N 373 E6
BOORAL
ct. Grovedale 705 L14
dr. Sunshine W 364 J7
BOORAN
av. Glen Waverley 460 B10
pde. Tootgarook 698 D9
rd. Caulfield.............456 A4
rd. Caulfield E..........456 A4
rd. Glen Huntly........456 A12
rd. Ormond 456 A12
BOORLEE
ct. Bundoora...........284 K4
BOORMANII
dr. Mornington........656 J4
BOOROOL
rd. Kew East............372 J7
BOORT
st. Dallas 238 F13
BOOTH
cr. Dandenong N.....501 J17
ct. Eltham...............288 F3
ct. Gladstone Pk......236 L17
ct. Gladstone Pk......237 A17
st. Parkdale.............531 J13
st. Preston..............326 B1
st. Sunshine W 364 L10
st. Sunshine W 365 A10
wy. Taylors Lakes.....275 F6
BOOTHBY
st. Northcote...........327 C15
BOOTIE
ct. Endeavour Hl 537 B6
ct. Roxburgh Pk......194 E15
BOOTTEN
ct. Hoppers Csg......449 E1
BOOYAN
cr. Greensborough ..243 J18
BORADINO
pl. Ferntree Gly 464 A12
BORANG
av. Mt Evelyn...........339 F20
av. Mt Evelyn...........383 F1
av. Selby 467 A14
st. Coburg N 281 J12
BORCHART
st. Guys Hill 541 H15
BORDEAUX
av. Blackburn 375 H11
av. Glen Waverley 460 G11
ct. Frankston...........628 D10
dr. Waurn Ponds......705 E15
st. Avondale Ht 322 C9
st. Doncaster 330 H18
BORDER
bvd. Sunbury.............142 J15
cl. Wantirna S 462 F5
dr. Keilor East..........322 A1
dr. Mill Park 198 G20
dr. Mill Park 242 G1
pl. Meadow Ht 237 K7
BOREE
av. Clarinda 498 E3
ct. Berwick..............553 F4
ct. Frankston...........628 H1
BOREHAM
st. Sunshine 364 L9
st. Sunshine 365 A8
BORELA
ct. Clarinda 498 C8
BORG
cr. Scoresby 462 D8
BORISKA
ct. Glen Waverley 460 A8
BORLASE
st. Yallambie...........285 E17
BORNEO
ct. Heidelberg W 328 C1
BORODA
ct. St Albans 320 H10
BOROLA
ct. Croydon N 336 B16
BORONIA
av. Belgrave Ht 466 J18
av. Croydon S..........379 J13
av. Dandenong N.....501 G18
av. Rosebud W........699 B1
cl. Frankston...........628 A7
cr. Cockatoo 511 C5
ct. Bellfield.............327 L5
ct. Carrum Downs...575 D18
ct. Keysborough 534 A15
ct. Mt Martha..........656 F6
dr. Glen Waverley....420 G19
dr. Hillside..............273 J4
dr. Hillside..............273 J5
gr. Doncaster E 375 L6
rd. Bayswater 422 L9
rd. Bayswater 423 A9
rd. Boronia..............423 J12
rd. Vermont 421 D2
rd. Wantirna.............422 A6
rd. Wantirna S.........423 A9
rd. Warburton 349 K7
st. Bentleigh E.........457 E17
st. Canterbury 373 E17
st. Dromana.............686 F7
st. Newcomb 703 L15
st. Pascoe Vale 281 A19
st. Surrey Hills 418 C1
st. Thomastown......241 G14
wy. Wyndham Va 446 G9
BOROONDARA
rd. Sorrento 678 H7
BORRACK
sq. Altona North.......409 J4
BORRELL
st. Keilor.................277 B11
BORRIE
st. Reservoir 283 E6
BORROWDALE
ct. Cranbourne W....603 H3
ct. Mill Park 242 F5
BORVA
dr. Keilor East..........278 C19
BOSANQUET
av. Newtown 701 J4
BOSC
ct. Templestowe 331 E3
BOSCARNE
av. Torquay 712 F2
BOSCO
cl. Narre Warren 539 B17
st. Chadstone..........458 B3
tce. Keilor Lodge.......276 A4
BOSISTO
st. Richmond............26 E10
BOSQUET
st. Maidstone..........322 H20
st. Maidstone..........366 G1
BOSSINGTON
st. Oakleigh S..........457 H18
BOSTOCK
av. Manifold Ht........702 C1
ct. Ferntree Gly 463 L16
ct. Thomastown......241 F20
BOSTON
av. Malvern East......456 K4
av. Seaford.............600 B5
cr. Keilor Dn............276 C14
ct. Narre Warren 539 G17
ct. Sorrento 678 F6
pl. Fitzroy N 19 B3
rd. Balwyn...............373 D13
rd. Bundoora............243 C20
rd. Lalor..................241 L11
rd. Torquay 711 L9
st. Ashwood 418 F14
st. Fawkner.............281 F3
BOSWELL
av. Newtown 702 H13
ct. Dandenong N.....502 B11
ct. Greenvale...........237 B3
BOTANIC
ct. Bundoora...........284 F6
dr. Cranbourne........604 F15
dr. Doncaster 331 C17
dr. E Geelong 703 G8
dr. Glen Waverley 460 D7
dr. Hillside..............232 B18
dr. Junction Vill.......604 F15
ri. Craigieburn 150 A14
wk. Mont Albert N.....374 G11
wy. Wyndham Va 446 E11
BOTANICA
bvd. Bundoora...........242 F13
bvd. Bundoora...........242 F14
wy. Keysborough 534 G16
BOTANICAL
gr.n,Doveton 536 K5
gr.s,Doveton 536 K5
BOTANY
ct. Clarinda 498 F6
ct. Dingley Village ...533 A8
ct. Wantirna.............422 E4
st. Albanvale 319 D6
wk. Mornington........656 L3
BOTHA
av. Reservoir 282 H5
BOTHERAMBO
st. Richmond............26 B16
BOTHWELL
st. Balaclava............414 G19
st. Pascoe Vale 280 C15
BOTTE
ct. Diamond Ck.......245 F12
BOTTINGS
la. Dixons Ck 210 D4
la. Yarra Glen..........210 D4
BOTTLE
bnd. Forest Hill 420 E2
BOTTLE BRUSH
dr. Doveton.............536 J10
BOTTLEBRUSH
ct. Langwarrin..........601 J14
ct. Sunshine W 363 K8
ct. Wheelers Hill......460 G15
dr. Mill Park 243 B5
BOTTOMLEY
dr. Emerald 469 J19
BOUCHER
la. Olinda................427 B18
BOUGAINVILLE
pl. Princes Hill..........325 J18
BOUGANVILLE
st. Boronia..............424 E3
BOULTON
ct. Greensborough ..286 F2
rd. Blackburn 376 C20
rd. Blackburn 420 C1
st. Springvale..........499 L10
BOUNDARY
rd. Braeside.............532 E19
rd. Carrum Downs...574 G12
rd. Coburg N 281 A11
rd. Coldstream 296 E20
rd. Coldstream 296 F9
rd. Coldstream 340 C10
rd. Derrimut 363 C14
rd. Dingley Village ...498 G20
rd. Dingley Village ...532 G9
rd. Dromana.............686 B8
rd. E Geelong 703 K20
rd. Emerald 510 E3
rd. Grovedale 705 F18
rd. Gruyere..............296 F9
rd. Harkaway............540 L1
rd. Heatherton 498 G20
rd. Kew...................371 G6
rd. Laverton N 363 C14
rd. Lilydale 296 E20
rd. Lilydale 340 C10
rd. Marshall..............706 G19
rd. Moorabbin Aprt...532 G9
rd. Mordialloc..........532 E19
rd. Mt Duneed 705 F18
rd. Nar Warrn E 505 H19
rd. Nar Warrn E 506 E20
rd. Nar Warrn E 540 L1
rd. Nar Warrn E 541 A2
rd. Nar Warrn N........505 J19
rd. Newcomb 703 K20
rd. N Melbourne........34 G10
rd. Olinda 427 G6
rd. Pascoe Vale 280 K11
rd. Sunshine W 364 K16
rd. Thomson 703 K20
rd. Truganina 363 C14
rd. Wandin N............340 C10
rd. Whittington 703 K20
rd. Wollert...............153 A15
rd.e,Emerald 509 D5
rd.w,Emerald 509 C5
st. Southbank 368 J18
st. Port Melb..............29 A1
st. Port Melb............368 J18
st. S Melbourne 368 K20
st. S Melbourne 413 A1
tr. Frankston N 600 F10
tr. Frankston N 600 G14
tr. Warrandyte 334 D3
BOUNTY
ct. Lilydale 338 H3
wy. Berwick..............553 K19
BOURBON
st. Silvan 385 A19
wy. Waurn Ponds.....705 C14
BOURCHIER
st. Glenroy..............280 H4
BOURCHIERS
rd. Kangaroo Grnd...290 K4
rd. Kangaroo Grnd...291 A5

BOURKE
cr. Geelong 703 D11
cr. Hoppers Csg 448 F1
ct. Dandenong N 501 F7
pl. Melbourne 1 B10
pl. Melbourne 23 H9
rd. Clarinda 497 L9
rd. Cranbourne 578 A19
rd. Melton S 268 D12
rd. Oakleigh S 497 L9
rd. Pakenham 585 L20
rd. Red Hill 686 K19
rd. Red Hill 687 A19
st. Brunswick 325 H13
st. Bulla 190 C16
st. Bulleen 329 J11
st. Coburg 281 D20
st. Darley 222 D8
st. Docklands 23 B12
st. Essendon W 323 A8
st. Melbourne 1 B12
st. Melbourne 2 H12
st. Melbourne 2 K12
st. Melbourne 23 G10
st. Melbourne 24 G6
st. Mentone 530 J6
st. Mt Evelyn 339 G15
st. Reservoir 282 E14
st. Ringwood 378 B12
st. Seddon 367 C11
st. Whittlesea 96 K20
BOURKES
rd. Darley 221 A12
rd. Pentland Hl 221 A12
BOURKES CREEK
rd. Dewhurst 510 D20
rd. Pakenham Up 559 J1
BOURKE STREET
ml. Melbourne 24 C7
BOURNE
rd. Glen Iris 416 K12
BOURNEMOUTH
av. Springvale 499 F16
BOURNEVALE
dr. Berwick 554 C3
BOURNEVILLE
av. Brighton East 495 G5
BOURNIAN
av. Strathmore 280 B19
BOUVARDIA
cr. Frankston N 600 E6
BOUVERIE
pl. Carlton 18 A20
pl. Epping 198 B16
pl. Skye 601 G1
st. Carlton 18 A20
BOVEC
ct. Bentleigh E 497 B3
BOW
cr. Camberwell 373 B19
BOWDEN
ct. Wheelers Hill 460 J11
la. Roxburgh Pk 194 E14
st. Ascot Vale 324 A17
st. Preston 283 A17
BOWEN
av. The Basin 425 G13
cl. Melton S 268 C10
cr. Burwood E 419 F12
cr. Carlton N 325 G18
cr. Melbourne 30 K6
cr. Melbourne 413 L3
ct. Berwick 553 H4
ct. Bundoora 284 K1
ct. Mentone 531 G6
ct. Sunbury 142 G11
la. Melbourne 30 K6
la. Melbourne 413 L3
rd. Aspendale Gdn 546 E1
rd. Aspendale Gdn 547 A3
rd. Doncaster E 376 B6
rd. Lilydale 337 K6
rd. Pt Lonsdale 710 J1
rd. Sorrento 678 J11
st. Balaclava 414 G19
st. Camberwell 416 K7
st. Cranbourne 578 E18
st. Ferntree Gly 424 G20
st. Hawthorn 372 A15
st. Hughesdale 457 G13
st. Kew 371 F12
st. McCrae 685 C13
st. Malvern East 457 E5
st. Melbourne 2 G4
st. Melbourne 24 C1
st. Moonee Pnd 323 J15
st. Prahran 414 L12
st. Richmond 26 C8
st. Rye 697 F3
BOWER
ct. Emerald 510 C2
ct. Ferntree Gly 463 K7
ct. Gladstone Pk 236 K20
ct. Langwarrin 629 H1
dr. Werribee 447 K6
st. Northcote 327 A19
BOWERBIRD
pl. Carrum Downs 601 A2
BOWERY
ct. Werribee 448 B15
BOWES
av. Airport W 278 L18
pl. Craigieburn 194 E2
st. Frankston S 626 G9
BOWLER
st. Hawthorn E 372 D19
BOWLERS
av. Geelong West 702 G6
BOWLES
av. Caulfield N 455 L1
BOWLEY
av. Balwyn 373 B13
BOWLING GREEN
la. Mitcham 377 B11
st. Windsor 414 G12
BOWMAN
cl. Nar Warrn S 552 G13
ct. Frankston 600 G17
dr. Mill Park 241 L5
dr. Mill Park 242 A4
dr. Mornington 657 B4
dr. Mornington 657 C4
la. Keysborough 548 E7
rd. Beaconsfield 556 B4
rd. Guys Hill 556 B4
st. Aspendale 545 K1
st. Mt Waverley 419 A18
st. Noble Park 501 B19
st. Werribee 448 A15
BOWMANS
pde. Oakleigh E 458 D10
BOWMORE
av. Pk Orchards 333 L17
rd. Noble Park 500 J17
st. Hughesdale 457 E11
BOWN
ct. Brighton East 455 E19
BOWNANG
st. Sandringham 495 B13
BOWNESS
ct. Croydon Hills 335 H13
BOWOOD
ct. Seabrook 451 B4
BOWRAL
ct. Bundoora 284 K3
BOWRINGS
rd. Red Hill 688 B13
BOWYER
av. Kew 372 G10
BOX
av. Forest Hill 420 F6
cl. Wheelers Hill 460 G14
ct. Altona North 410 C6
ct. Baxter 644 C1
ct. Bentleigh E 496 G1
ct. Kings Park 275 E18
ct. Templstw Lr 330 H13
la. Ringwood N 378 C6
pl. Hoppers Csg 448 A2
pl. Mont Albert 374 E15
rd. Briar Hill 286 J4
st. Dandenong 536 E13
st. Doveton 536 G12
st. Reservoir 283 E7
BOX FOREST
rd. Hadfield 281 B5
BOX HILL
cr. Mont Albert N 374 G9
BOXLEIGH
gr. Box Hill N 375 A6
BOXMOOR
ct. Mt Eliza 642 A4
BOXSHALL
st. Brighton 454 J16
BOXTREE
rd. Montrose 382 A11
BOYANA
cr. Croydon 380 H2
BOYANDA
rd. Glen Iris 416 G13
BOYANICH
ct. Hoppers Csg 405 A19
BOYANNA
rd. Glen Waverley 420 G20
BOYCE
av. Briar Hill 286 J5
rd. Selby 467 E14
BOYD
av. Chelsea 547 C14
av. Oakleigh E 458 K14
cl. Mooroolbark 337 C10
cr. Coburg N 282 A18
cr. Heidelberg W 284 A19
ct. Dandenong N 502 A19
ct. Kealba 277 B20
ct. Melton S 268 K7
ct. Port Melb 411 F6
ct. Scoresby 462 A7
ct. Sunbury 143 A9
ct. Werribee 448 C8
ct. Wheelers Hill 460 G17
la. Dandenong 536 A8
pl. Mill Park 198 K20
pl. Mill Park 242 K1
rd. Gembrook 512 L18
st. Albert Park 29 H18
st. Albert Park 413 D9
st. Altona 408 J18
st. Bacchus Msh 222 B14
st. Blackburn S 419 L3
st. Dandenong N 501 L19
st. Doncaster 374 J4
st. Greensborough 285 J2
st. N Warrandyte 290 A12
st. Richmond 26 L14
st. Richmond 371 A17
st. Thornbury 327 C8
BOYDEN
sq. Roxburgh Pk 194 C10
BOYDS
rd. Hurstbridge 202 D6
rd. Nutfield 202 D6
BOYLAND
ct. Box Hill N 375 B6
BOYLE
cl. Wantirna S 462 F1
cr. Mill Park 242 F8
ct. Sunshine W 364 J10
st. Ashburton 417 C16
st. Forest Hill 376 E19
tce. Burnside 318 D7
BOYNE
av. E Geelong 703 H13
cl. Epping 198 A20
st. Coburg N 282 A17
st. Rowville 463 A18
BOYNTON
pl. Berwick 554 K19
st. Bentleigh E 496 L3
BOYS
rd. Warrandyte 289 D16
BOYSE
ct. Tullamarine 236 G20
BOYS FARM
tr. Lysterfield 504 L5
BOYS FARM HERITAGE
wk. Lysterfield 504 K10
BRABHAM
dr. Mill Park 242 K3
BRACELET
st. Pakenham 584 K4
BRACK
av. Brooklyn 365 G18
ct. Mooroolbark 337 H11
ct. Sunbury 143 A9
BRACKEN
av. Montrose 382 A17
av. Thornbury 326 E7
ct. Ferntree Gly 463 F9
ct. Highton 701 J18
ct. Wheelers Hill 461 B19
gr. Altona 409 G1
rd. Caulfield S 455 F9
rdg. Arthurs Seat 685 K10
rdg. Dromana 685 K10
BRACKENBURY
st. Warrandyte 290 B18
st. Warrandyte 333 J2
BRACKLEY
ct. St Albans 275 H20
BRACKNELL
ct. Vermont S 421 B10
pl. Deer Park 318 J8
st. Keysborough 534 L12
st. Keysborough 535 A12
BRACY
av. Springvale S 534 B2
BRAD
ct. Cranbourne N 578 H11
dr. Mt Martha 655 J17
st. Bentleigh E 496 L5
BRADANO
la. Roxburgh Pk 194 D7
BRADDON
ct. Hillside 274 G1
BRADEN BRAE
dr. Warranwood 335 A12
BRADFIELD
la. Kensington 33 H5
BRADFORD
av. Greenvale 192 K17
av. Kew 372 J11
av. Preston 326 L5
cl. Gladstone Pk 278 L1
ct. Braybrook 322 C20
ct. Braybrook 366 C1
dr. Carrum Downs 575 C14
rd. Mt Martha 668 J8
rd. Mt Martha 669 A8
st. Oakleigh S 497 F3
BRADINA
ct. Chelsea Ht 547 E11
BRADLEY
av. Thornbury 326 E10
av. Vermont 420 L5
ct. Clarinda 498 D11
ct. Hampton Pk 551 L7
dr. Hillside 274 E2
dr. Mill Park 243 B3
pl. Boronia 423 J14
st. Broadmeadows 238 A20
st. Newport 410 G8
st. Pascoe Vale 280 J18
st. Sunshine N 321 D18
tce. Narre Warren 553 C8
wy. Cranbourne W 603 G2
BRADLEYS
la. N Warrandyte 289 F19
BRADMAN
av. Mt Evelyn 339 D14
bvd. Keilor East 322 C1
ct. Boronia 424 F16
dr. Meadow Ht 237 J7
dr. Sunbury 142 G14
dr. Sunbury 142 G15
st. Sunshine N 321 C15
tce. Epping 198 H16
tce. S Morang 198 H16
BRADSHAW
cr. Hillside 232 E17
dr. Healesville 213 K16
st. Essendon 323 C6
st. Essendon 323 C7
st. Frankston 599 F14
st. Kingsbury 283 L10
st. Mordialloc 532 B15
BRADSTREET
rd. Mt Waverley 458 G5
BRADWELL
st. Kealba 276 K20
BRADWORTH
st. Craigieburn 150 A14
BRADY
av. Clayton S 499 D9
cl. Braeside 532 L19
cl. Lynbrook 551 E16
la. Kew 371 H6
rd. Bentleigh E 497 A7
rd. Dandenong N 501 K14
rd. Endeavour Hl 502 E15
rd. Gisborne 109 B1
st. Southbank 23 C19
st. Richmond 26 K13
st. S Melbourne 23 A18
st. S Melbourne 368 L19
BRAE
ct. Chadstone 458 E6
ct. Eltham North 245 B18
ct. Montmorency 287 A9
ct. Rye 697 B2
ct. Sherbrooke 426 L20
ct. Sherbrooke 427 A20
gr. Nunawading 376 G11
rd. Lysterfield 504 H4
BRAEDUKE
la. Hillside 232 E18
BRAELANDS
cl. Caroline Spr 318 D3
BRAEMAR
cl. Gladstone Pk 236 L17
ct. Newtown 702 B13
ct. Sunbury 143 B6
ct. Wheelers Hill 461 D14
st. Croydon 380 F1
st. Essendon 323 F5
st. Mont Albert N 374 E11
st. Pascoe Vale S 324 L4
st. Seaford 599 H10
BRAEMER
ct. Endeavour Hl 503 J19
BRAESIDE
av. Camberwell 417 L7
av. Ringwood E 378 J10
av. Rosanna 284 L17
av. Sherbrooke 426 L20
av. Sherbrooke 427 A20
dr. Braeside 532 H15
dr. Doncaster 330 F19
dr. Launching Pl 345 D16
st. Pascoe Vale 281 B12
tce. Malvern East 457 F1
BRAESWOOD
rd. Kings Park 275 C19
BRAEWOOD
av. Ringwood E 379 C15
pl. Melton W 226 A14
BRAGGE
st. Frankston 599 C15
BRAHAM
st. Donvale 376 F6
BRAHE
pl. E Melbourne 25 L9
BRAHMAN
cl. Belmont 706 B6
ct. Dandenong N 501 E13
BRAHMIN
av. Wheelers Hill 460 J17
BRAID
st. W Footscray 366 J10
BRAIDHILL
rd. Macleod 285 C17
BRAIDWOOD
av. Rosebud 683 F19
av. Rosebud W 683 F19
BRAILSFORD
rd. Bentleigh 496 C5
BRAIM
st. Sunshine N 321 E15
BRAIMTON
cl. Ringwood N 378 D2
BRAITHWAITE
st. Reservoir 282 H3
BRAMBER
ct. Templestowe 331 L7
BRAMBLE
cr. Bundoora 242 D15
cr. Bundoora 242 E15
BRAMBLEBERRY
la. Chirnside Pk 337 C6
BRAMCOTE
dr. Westmeadows 236 L15
BRAMERTON
rd. Caulfield 455 K4
BRAMHAM
dr. Bundoora 284 A6
BRAMLEY
cr. Wheelers Hill 461 F16
ct. Hallam 537 F13
ct. Kew 372 G13
dr. Ringwood N 378 K1
st. Dandenong 535 F10
BRAMPTON
cl. Craigieburn 150 G20
cl. Point Cook 450 G8
ct. Delahey 275 C14
ct. Narre Warren 538 K16
ct. Vermont 421 K1
st. Cheltenham 497 E20
BRAMTON
ct. Mulgrave 500 F1
BRAMWELL
cl. Endeavour Hl 537 H10
st. Lilydale 339 B10
BRANAGAN
dr. Aspendale Gdn 547 A6
BRANCA
ct. Nar Warrn N 538 B12
BRANCH
rd. Bayswater N 379 K15
st. Moonee Pnd 324 G14
BRAND
ct. Melton S 268 H12
dr. Thomastown 241 K19
rd. Knoxfield 463 C9
st. Hampton 495 F11
st. Menzies Ck 468 J17
st. Mt Waverley 418 K15
BRANDON
ct. Briar Hill 286 G3
ct. Craigieburn 194 F2
ct. Endeavour Hl 537 J7
ct. Springvale S 499 H20
rd. Brighton 454 F11
st. Glen Iris 417 E12
wy. Clayton S 499 D11
BRANDON PARK
dr. Wheelers Hill 460 D13
dr. Wheelers Hill 460 F18
dr. Wheelers Hill 460 K19
BRANDT
rd. Lysterfield 505 H13
BRANIGAN
ct. Sunbury 143 D8
BRANKSOME
gr. Blackburn S 375 F20
gr. Blackburn S 419 F1
BRANSDALE
cl. Mooroolbark 338 A16
BRANSGROVE
st. Preston 327 B5
BRANSON
st. Rosebud 699 H3

BRANSTON
rd. St Albans 320 L7
BRANTOME
st. Gisborne 78 K14
BRANTON
dr. Hampton Pk 551 C11
dr. Hampton Pk 551 D12
rd. Hoppers Csg 448 K4
rd. Hoppers Csg 449 A3
BRASSER
av. Dromana 686 J5
ct. Rosebud 700 F4
BRASSEY
av. Highton 705 G1
av. Rosanna 285 B18
BRAVO
cl. Keilor Dn 275 H12
ct. Lilydale 294 B18
BRAW
st. Williamstown 411 E12
BRAY
ct. Bentleigh E 457 A19
ct. Templestowe 332 A9
st. Reservoir 240 B20
st. South Yarra 32 D15
st. South Yarra 414 H8
BRAYFORD
nk. Craigieburn 194 B2
BRAYSHAY
rd. Newcomb 704 B14
BRAYWOOD
dr. Bangholme 549 K13
BRAZEEL
st. Blackburn S 419 K3
BRAZIL
ct. Epping 198 F15
BRAZILIA
av. Kealba 276 K17
dr. Glen Waverley 460 G4
BREAD
st. Geelong West 702 H3
BREADALBANE
ct. Sydenham 274 K1
pl. Newport 411 A11
st. Newcomb 703 L14
BREAKADAY
ps. Chirnside Pk 337 J2
BREAKNECK
rd. Yarra Glen 208 B20
BREAKWATER
rd. Belmont 706 K2
rd. Breakwater 703 D20
rd. Breakwater 703 F19
rd. Breakwater 706 K2
rd. Thomson 703 E19
BREAM
st. Maribyrnong 322 L12
st. Maribyrnong 323 A12
BREAM BAY
Patterson L 573 F7
BREAMLEA
ct. Dandenong N 501 K9
ct. Meadow Ht 237 K6
wy. Cranbourne W 577 F19
BREAR
st. Springvale 499 G10
BREARLEY
ct. Anglesea 713 J1
ct. Rowville 502 J5
pde. Pascoe Vale S 324 J2
pl. Roxburgh Pk 194 D11
BRECHIN
ct. Greenvale 237 A2
dr. Narre Warren 552 L4
BRECON
nk. Craigieburn 194 B3
rd. St Albans 320 J7
BREE
ct. Berwick 553 L18
ct. Kurunjang 226 H14
pl. Rowville 463 E12
BREEN
dr. Brighton East 495 H2
st. Braybrook 366 B5
st. Preston 282 F18
tce. Ferny Creek 426 A15
BREENS
rd. Cranbourne W 577 F13
BREES
rd. Keilor East 322 H3
BREESE
rd. Langwarrin 629 L6
st. Brunswick 325 F11
BREEZE
st. Bonbeach 573 A5
BREEZEWAY
dr. Bangholme 549 J13
BREFFNA
st. Preston 327 B4

BREMEN
ct. Keilor Dn 276 D12
BREMNER
cl. Altona Mdw 451 E5
ct. Mill Park 243 B3
BRENBEAL
ct. Balwyn 373 H12
st. Balwyn 373 H12
BRENCHLEY
pl. Prahran 32 A17
pl. Prahran 414 F9
BRENDA
av. Mt Waverley 419 A12
ct. Croydon 336 K17
ct. Narre Warren 538 K15
ct. Nunawading 376 F16
gr. Tecoma 466 C9
rd. Research 288 J7
st. Nunawading 376 E17
BRENDALE
av. Blackburn N 376 C9
BRENDAN
av. Doncaster 330 J17
ct. Highton 701 H13
rd. Greenvale 192 L15
rd. Greenvale 193 A15
st. Mernda 156 A13
BRENDEL
st. Rosebud W 683 F18
BRENDON
ct. Hallam 538 A15
BRENNAN
av. Beaconsfld Up 541 G13
ct. Altona Mdw 451 G2
ct. Sydenham 274 K4
dr. Wantirna S 462 C4
st. Bentleigh 455 J17
st. McKinnon 455 J17
st. Melton S 268 G9
BRENNAND
st. Fitzroy N 20 C1
BRENS
dr. Parkville 17 A3
dr. Parkville 17 A5
rd. St Andrews 205 L3
rd. Smiths Gly 205 L3
BRENT
cl. Berwick 554 K19
ct. Doncaster E 332 J14
mw. Sunshine W 364 C5
st. Glen Waverley 420 E20
st. Mornington 640 H19
BRENTANI
av. Elsternwick 455 A8
BRENTFIELD
ct. Mill Park 242 E9
BRENTFORD
ct. Noble Park N 501 F17
sq. Forest Hill 420 L2
BRENT LAUREN
ct. Anglesea 713 E3
BRENTLEIGH
ct. Vermont S 420 K8
BRENTLEY
cl. Point Cook 450 G8
BRENTLY
cl. Nar Warrn N 538 K11
BRENTNALL
ct. Hampton Pk 551 E8
rd. Croydon 379 E3
BRENTVALE
ct. Doncaster 331 B12
BRENTWICK
dr. Greensborough ..244 D17
BRENTWOOD
av. Lalor 240 K9
av. Pascoe Vale S 324 F4
cl. Clayton S 498 J6
cl. Dewhurst 510 D20
cr. Frankston 600 B18
dr. Avondale Ht 321 L15
dr. Cranbourne N 578 F10
dr. Glen Waverley 460 F12
dr. Wantirna 422 H12
dr. Werribee 447 G2
ri. Eltham 287 E14
st. Bentleigh 496 E6
wy. Waurn Ponds 705 B16
BRETBY
wy. Montrose 381 J9
BRETONNEUX
sq. Malvern East 456 L3
BRETT
ct. Cheltenham 497 C18
ct. Lalor 240 H4
ct. Sunbury 143 A8
dr. Carrum Downs 574 C16
dr. Keysborough 534 C12
mw. Mt Martha 656 C9
pl. Endeavour Hl 537 K7
pl. Ferntree Gly 464 B5
pl. Wyndham Va 446 C13
rd. Warburton 349 G1
st. Brunswick 325 H13
st. Murrumbeena 457 B14
st. Warrandyte 333 J3
BRETTON
ct. St Albans 275 J19
BREW
rd. Croydon 336 F15
BREWER
ct. Keysborough 534 F14
rd. Bentleigh 495 J1
rd. Brighton East 455 H20
rd. Brighton East 495 J1
BREWIS
la. Geelong 703 B11
BREWSTER
rd. Rye 696 L15
rd. Rye 697 A14
st. Essendon 323 L6
st. Essendon 324 B6
BREX
ct. Reservoir 282 A7
BREYDON
ct. St Albans 320 H6
pl. Hampton Pk 552 D10
BREYLEIGH
dr. Pakenham 559 A17
BREYNIA
wy. Cranbourne W 577 K16
BRIAN
ct. Dingley Village 533 B8
ct. Mt Eliza 642 D2
ct. Niddrie 322 L3
st. Bentleigh E 496 G2
st. Fawkner 281 G1
st. Mitcham 377 A17
st. Safety Bch 668 K19
BRIAR
cl. Gladstone Pk 236 L20
cl. Narre Warren 553 F9
cl. Somerville 644 J13
ct. Doncaster 374 K1
ct. Grovedale 706 C16
ct. Langwarrin 629 H1
ct. S Morang 243 H1
gr. Mulgrave 500 E2
la. Templestowe 331 L1
pl. Pascoe Vale S 324 E6
st. Boronia 424 E18
st. Oakleigh S 497 E1
wk. Blackburn S 420 A5
wy. Sunshine W 364 D8
BRIARCREST
dr. Cranbourne E 578 J20
dr. Cranbourne E 604 J1
BRIARDALE
dr. Werribee 446 L17
BRIARFIELD
ct. Forest Hill 420 J4
ct. Templestowe 331 D13
rd. Noble Park N 501 E17
BRIARHURST
av. Dandenong N 502 D15
BRIARLEY
ct. Hampton Pk 552 C14
BRIAR ROSE
wk. Croydon S 380 B14
BRIARTYS
rd. Gruyere 298 B5
BRIAR VIEW
la. Briar Hill 286 G5
BRIARWOOD
ct. Croydon 336 E17
ct. Doncaster E 332 E12
ct. Sunbury 144 C10
BRICE
av. Mooroolbark 337 B18
av. Newtown 702 B10
gr. Knoxfield 463 A7
BRICK
ct. Pearcedale 646 L3
ct. Pearcedale 647 A3
BRICKENDON
dr. Rosebud W 699 D2
BRICKER
st. Cheltenham 497 D14
BRICKWOOD
st. Brighton 454 J10
BRICKWORKS
la. Northcote 326 L13
BRIDE
av. Hampton Pk 551 F8
st. Malvern 415 K10
BRIDGE
cr. Montmorency 286 K9
ct. Croydon S 379 G12
gr. Kalorama 383 F10
rd. Burnley 371 A16
rd. Keysborough 535 C11
rd. Melton S 268 H13
rd. Richmond 26 B10
rd. Richmond 371 A16
st. Brighton 454 L8
st. Bulleen 329 F9
st. Eltham 287 D10
st. Essendon 324 E3
st. Hampton 494 L11
st. Hampton 495 A11
st. Newtown 702 D14
st. Northcote 326 F17
st. Northcote 326 G17
st. Port Melb 29 A8
st. Port Melb 412 H1
st. Queenscliff 709 C16
st. Spotswood 411 D1
st. Werribee 447 H16
BRIDGEFORD
av. Blackburn N 376 C9
cr. Melton S 268 H12
ct. Heidelberg W 328 D2
BRIDGE INN
rd. Doreen 156 C19
rd. Doreen 201 A1
rd. Mernda 155 A17
rd. Wollert 153 J16
BRIDGES
av. Coburg N 281 B13
av. Edithvale 546 K11
av. Mooroolbark 381 E1
rd. Healesville 212 H15
st. Glen Iris 417 A15
st. Melton S 268 J9
BRIDGET
ct. Kings Park 319 C3
ct. Warranwood 334 K16
st. Glen Waverley 460 B4
BRIDGETON
st. Reservoir 283 G2
BRIDGE VIEW
st. Belmont 702 B18
BRIDGEWATER
ct. Langwarrin 630 B12
dr. Dingley Village 532 L9
gr. Thomastown 241 K16
rd. Craigieburn 194 C5
rd. Roxburgh Pk 194 D8
rd. Seville E 343 A15
tce. Caroline Spr 317 L6
wy. Rowville 462 K20
wy. Truganina 405 E13
BRIDGEWOOD
ct. Wantirna S 423 A16
BRIDLE
ct. Endeavour Hl 503 L19
ct. Epping 198 D19
pl. Pakenham 585 F6
pwy. Chirnside Pk 337 F6
BRIDLINGTON
dr. Greenvale 193 B17
BRIDPORT
st. Albert Park 29 H11
st. Albert Park 413 D6
st. S Melbourne 29 H11
st. S Melbourne 413 D6
st.w, Albert Park 29 D13
st.w, Albert Park 413 B7
BRIEN
la. Melbourne 2 L11
BRIENS
la. Croydon, off Main St 380 A5
BRIERLY
ct. Sunbury 142 K6
BRIGALO
ct. Keysborough 534 G11
BRIGANTINE
ct. Frankston 628 E7
ct. Patterson L 573 H8
BRIGDEN
ct. Mill Park 242 J4
BRIGETTE
ct. Lalor 240 H10
BRIGGS
cr. Noble Park 500 K20
dr. Derrimut 363 G13
st. Caulfield 455 H5
st. Laverton 407 F12
st. Mont Albert N 374 D6
st. Mt Waverley 458 G9
st. Reservoir 283 C2
BRIGHT
cr. Mt Eliza 626 G15
pl. Blackburn S 375 F20
pl. Blackburn S 419 F1
pl. Geelong 703 B9
rd. Montrose 381 L15
st. Brighton East 455 B18
st. Camberwell 417 E8
st. Campbellfield ....239 A[illegible]
st. Kew ....372 C[illegible]
st. Southbank 24 D14
BRIGHTON
av. Preston ....326 L[illegible]
av. Wyndham Va ....446 E[illegible]
cr. Mt Eliza 642 C9
ct. Avondale Ht ....322 C[illegible]
pl. Taylors Hill 274 J8
rd. Balaclava 414 F19
rd. Dandenong 535 G10
rd. Elsternwick ....454 G[illegible]
rd. Elwood ....454 G[illegible]
rd. St Kilda 414 F19
rt. Berwick 539 K16
st. Flemington 33 L2
st. Frankston S 626 G10
st. Glen Waverley 420 G17
st. Oakleigh 458 A15
st. Richmond 32 G3
st. Sandringham 495 D13
BRIGHTS
dr. Rye 697 J8
dr. Tootgarook 698 B7
pl. Melbourne 1 C6
pl. Melbourne 23 H6
BRIGHTWELL
rd. Lilydale 338 L11
rd. Lilydale 339 A11
BRIM
ct. Westmeadows 237 E11
BRIMAR
cl. Diamond Ck 246 A8
ct. Mt Waverley 418 K18
BRIMBANK
bvd. St Albans 275 K18
rd. Keilor East 277 G19
BRIMPTON
gr. Wyndham Va 446 B15
BRINAWA
dr. Greensborough ..243 J17
BRINBAAL
ct. Kurunjang 227 D15
BRINDALEE
dr. Cranbourne E 578 J17
mw. Chadstone 458 D2
pl. Cranbourne E 578 J17
wy. Hillside 274 F5
BRINDISI
st. Mentone 530 L8
st. Mentone 531 A8
BRINDY
cr. Doncaster E 375 F4
ct. Croydon 336 G14
BRINE
st. Hughesdale 457 E15
st. Mt Waverley 459 C2
BRINGA
av. Camberwell 417 C3
BRINKKOTTER
rd. Research 288 G5
BRINSLEY
rd. Camberwell 373 A20
rd. Camberwell 417 A1
BRIODY
dr. Torquay 711 E3
BRISBANE
la. Wantirna, off Capital City Bvd ..422 K17
pde. Warburton 349 H1
rd. Beaconsfld Up 542 G14
rd. Cockatoo 511 F12
st. Albion 320 H19
st. Ascot Vale 324 F16
st. Beaconsfield 555 A16
st. Berwick 554 F6
st. Eltham 287 D9
st. Murrumbeena 457 B5
st. Strathmore 280 B17
tce. Parkdale 531 L11
BRISBANE HILL
rd. Warburton 349 H1
BRISCOE
ct. Endeavour Hl 537 J9
la. Melbourne 1 K14
la. Melbourne 24 B9
pl. Roxburgh Pk 194 C15
BRISLINGTON
st. Sunshine 365 F2
BRISTOL
av. Edithvale 546 H15
cr. Lilydale 338 K10
ct. Epping 197 J17
ct. Forest Hill 420 E9
ct. Glen Iris 416 G7
ct. Glen Waverley 459 H7
ct. Kilsyth 381 G6
ct. Noble Park 534 J7
mw. Craigieburn 194 B4
pl. Rowville 463 E17
rd. Pascoe Vale 280 H10

rd. Torquay.............711 L9
st. Airport W...........279 C16
st. Bentleigh E.........457 C20
st. Heidelberg 329 E3
st. Surrey Hills........417 H1

BRISTOW
cl. Rowville.............463 F17
dr. Forest Hill 376 J20
st. Footscray...........367 F11
st. Seddon..............367 F11

BRITANNIA
st. Geelong West.......702 E1
wy. Lilydale.............338 H3

BRITANNIA CREEK
rd. Wesburn............347 L14
rd. Wesburn............348 E19

BRITANNIA STREET
ml. Mitcham, off Maroondah Hwy...377 B13

BRITISH
pl. Hoppers Csg......448 A1

BRITT
ct. Keilor East..........322 G4
ct. Newport.............410 L6

BRITTEN
ct. Bundoora...........242 H17
st. Glen Iris.............416 K12

BRITTON
rd. Seville................341 L14

BRIXTON
av. Eltham North......287 C2
pl. Melton...............226 K16
rd. Cheltenham.........495 L17
ri. Glen Iris.............416 K13
st. Bonbeach...........545 F15
st. Bonbeach...........573 A4
st. Flemington.........324 E20

BROAD
st. Greensborough..286 A5
st. W Footscray.......366 H6
st. Westmeadows....237 A13
st. Westmeadows....237 B14

BROAD ACRES
rd. Panton Hill.........205 D14
rd. Smiths Gly.........205 D14

BROADACRES
ct. Narre Warren.....538 K20

BROADBEACH
rd. Jan Juc.............711 A20

BROADBENT
ct. Chelsea Ht..........547 E14
wy. Pakenham..........584 D3

BROADCHAPEL
pl. Clarinda............498 D7

BROADFORD
cr. Macleod.............284 K11

BROADGREEN
av. Wantirna............422 A12

BROAD GULLY
rd. Diamond Ck........202 C11
rd. Diamond Ck........245 J8
rd. Hurstbridge.........202 C11
rd. Yarrambat..........202 C11

BROADHURST
av. Reservoir...........282 B6
rd. Pakenham..........585 E4

BROADIES
rd. Coldstream.........295 K10

BROADLAND
wy. Nar Warrn S.......579 B4

BROADLANDS
ct. Hoppers Csg......448 F9
st. Dandenong S.....535 L11

BROADLEA
cr. View Bank..........285 K16

BROADMEADOWS
rd. Gladstone Pk......236 L15
rd. Gladstone Pk......237 A15
rd. Tullamarine.........278 H6
rd. Westmeadows....236 L15
rd. Westmeadows....237 A15

BROADOAK
st. Noble Park.........534 B3
st. Springvale S.......534 B3

BROADWALK
gr. Endeavour Hl.....537 D1

BROADWAY
Belgrave.............466 E17
Bonbeach............545 F12
Bonbeach............573 A2
Camberwell.........372 K18
Camberwell.........372 L18
Camberwell.........373 A18
Elwood...............454 D3
Reservoir............283 B10
Rosebud W.........698 K2
Rosebud W.........699 A1
bvd. Wyndham Va.....446 D11
gdn. Bonbeach...........547 D19

BROADWAY EAST
Point Cook.........450 A5

BROADWAY WEST
Point Cook.........449 L5

BROCK
pl. Richmond............26 C13
st. Thomastown......241 F17

BROCKA
av. Belmont.............702 A19

BROCKENSHIRE
st. Clifton Hill............20 G7

BROCKLEY
rd. Fawkner.............281 G10

BROCKS
rd. Doreen..............201 G1
rd. Nutfield..............202 A1

BRODERICK
rd. Carrum Downs....600 H1

BRODIE
ct. Meadow Ht.........238 D1
mw. Officer................555 J20
st. Seaford..............599 C3

BRODRIBB
st. Bentleigh............495 L4

BROGDEN
ct. Rowville.............503 F2

BROGIL
rd. N Warrandyte.....289 J13
wk. Sydenham 274 K7

BROKEN
ct. Werribee............447 H8

BROLGA
av. Chelsea Ht..........547 G17
cr. Wandana Ht.........701 E20
ct. Carrum Downs....600 J5
ct. Melton................226 H18
ct. Werribee............448 C10
pl. S Morang............243 K4
st. Mt Waverley.......419 A18
st. Westmeadows....236 H14

BROMAGE
cl. Hoppers Csg......405 G20
ct. Grovedale..........706 B10
ct. Wantirna S..........462 C4

BROMBY
st. Gembrook...........512 J11
st. South Yarra..........31 A5
st. South Yarra........414 A3

BROME
st. St Albans...........320 G5

BROMHAM
pl. Richmond.............26 F7

BROMLEY
cl. Chirnside Pk.......336 G7
cl. Ferntree Gly.......463 E3
cl. Heathmont..........379 A20
ct. Toorak................415 G8
pl. Epping................198 F15
st. Rosebud.............699 J2
st. Thomson............703 H16
st. Wyndham Va.....446 F9

BROMPTON
cl. Frankston S........627 G16
ct. Kilsyth...............380 L8

BROMWICH
ct. Mill Park............242 H3

BROMYARD
st. Yarraville............366 G16

BRONALDI
st. Heathmont..........379 C20

BRONCO
ct. Meadow Ht........193 L20

BRONHILL
ct. Cranbourne W....577 G18
rd. Ringwood E.......379 D4

BRONSDON
ct. Mill Park............242 E2

BRONTE
av. Burwood.............418 K7
ct. Croydon N..........336 A11
ct. Delahey..............275 E15
ct. Hampton.............495 G9
ct. Williamstown......411 G12
ct. Wyndham Va......446 E10
ri. Templestowe......332 B11
st. Heidelberg.........328 J4

BRONWYN
ct. Anglesea............713 E9
ct. Blackburn S........419 K4
ct. Clayton S...........499 D16
ct. Deer Park...........319 B11
ct. Research............288 K4
ct. Wheelers Hill......461 C17
st. Coldstream........295 D14

BRONZE WING
ct. Cannons Creek...649 C6

BROOK
cr. Box Hill S...........418 K5
ct. Hampton Pk.......551 H7
dr. Altona................408 K15
st. Hawthorn...........371 E14
st. Jacana...............237 K17
st. Sunbury.............143 H12
st. Yarraville............367 B14

BROOKDALE
av. Emerald.............469 F17

BROOKE
cl. Noble Park.........534 K5
cr. Blairgowrie.........679 G20
ct. Ashwood 418 B15
ct. Eltham North......288 A2
ct. Hoppers Csg.......447 K3
ct. Scoresby 462 C6
dr. Doncaster E.......332 F8
st. Albert Park...........29 F10
st. Albert Park.........413 C5
st. Eaglemont...........328 J13
st. Northcote...........326 K17
st. S Melbourne.........29 F10
st. S Melbourne.......413 C5

BROOKEDGE
ct. Craigieburn........194 A3

BROOKER
ct. Sunshine N.........321 F16

BROOKES
cr. Fitzroy N..............19 A3
ct. Mill Park............242 H4
ct. Mooroolbark.......381 F1
st. Pt Lonsdale........710 F4

BROOKFIELD
av. Brookfield..........267 L6
ct. Berwick..............539 F18
ct. Hawthorn E.........416 G2
pl. Warranwood.......335 C17

BROOKGLEN
ct. Epping...............197 E20

BROOKING
rd. Gisborne............109 A2
st. Upwey...............465 L15

BROOKLAND
ct. Mulgrave............501 D4
gr. Thomastown.......240 J11

BROOKLYN
av. Caulfield S..........455 G9
av. Dandenong S.....535 F13
av. Frankston...........627 J9
ct. Campbellfield.....239 D14
rd. Brookfield...........267 B5

BROOKLYN BAY
cl. Rowville.............502 L7
cl. Rowville.............503 A7

BROOKLYN PARK
dr. Brookfield..........266 L6
dr. Brookfield..........267 A6

BROOKS
av. Blairgowrie.........680 A19
cr. Diamond Ck.......245 K11
dr. Dandenong S.....549 G4
st. Bentleigh E.........457 E18
st. Burnley..............371 C18
st. Fawkner.............281 K6

BROOKSIDE
ct. Caroline Spr.......318 B6
ct. Craigieburn.........150 C14
st. Upwey...............465 J17

BROOKVALE
cl. Beaconsfield......555 A18

BROOKVILLE
av. Werribee............447 G2
dr. Craigieburn.........150 K5
rd. Toorak...............415 B7

BROOKWOOD
dr. Mt Eliza..............626 C9
st. Glen Waverley....460 C8

BROOME
av. Mentone............531 H7
cl. Lynbrook............551 H16
cr. Cranbourne N......578 J9
ct. Epping...............241 J4

BROOMFIELD
av. Alphington.........327 F19
rd. Hawthorn E........372 D20

BROOMHILL
av. Blackburn..........375 G14

BROOMPARK
cr. Olinda...............427 E14

BROSA
av. Bentleigh E.........496 G5

BROSNAN
cr. Strathmore.........280 A15
rd. Bentleigh E.........497 A5

BROTT
ct. Dandenong N.....502 B15
ct. Keysborough......534 D7

BROUGH
st. McKinnon...........456 D17
st. Springvale..........500 F9

BROUGHAM
av. Wyndham Va.....446 C14
cl. Eumemmerring..537 D11
pl. Geelong, off Mercer St............702 L5
sq. Mulgrave............501 D6
st. Box Hill..............374 H16
st. Eltham................287 D11
st. Geelong.............703 A6
st. Kew...................371 J10
st. N Melbourne.........34 J9
st. Richmond.............26 G13

BROUGHTON
av. Croydon.............335 J19
av. Reservoir...........282 J13
dr. Highton..............705 K7
pl. W Melbourne.......23 E5
rd. Surrey Hills........374 C19
st. Seaford..............599 C1

BROULA
ct. Taylors Lakes.....276 B7

BROWN
al. Melbourne..............1 B9
al. Melbourne..............2 C14
al. Melbourne............23 H8
al. Melbourne............24 D8
av. Altona Mdw.........451 F6
av. Ascot Vale..........323 H19
la. N Melbourne.........17 F18
pl. Geelong, off Ginn St...............702 K3
rd. Officer...............556 D14
rd. Officer...............557 C15
rd. Pakenham...........557 C15
st. Avondale Ht........321 L15
st. Boronia..............424 E10
st. Brighton East.....455 D12
st. Coburg...............325 G4
st. Collingwood..........25 K1
st. E Geelong...........703 F12
st. Heidelberg..........328 H5
st. Heidelberg..........329 A6
st. Lilydale..............338 G4
st. Newport..............411 A7
st. Preston..............283 D19

BROWNBILL
st. Geelong.............703 E11

BROWNE
av. St Albans...........320 C12
la. Red Hill..............688 B12
st. McCrae..............685 B11

BROWNELL
rd. Glen Iris.............417 C12

BROWNES
cr. Eltham...............287 J9

BROWNFIELD
st. Cheltenham.........530 L1
st. Cheltenham.........531 A1
st. Mordialloc...........531 L13
st. Parkdale.............531 L13

BROWNHILL
st. Bundoora...........284 F2

BROWNING
av. Clayton S...........499 D8
cr. Avondale Ht.......322 F10
ct. Watsonia N.........285 E3
dr. Glen Waverley....420 H14
dr. Templestowe.....332 A13
rd. Boronia..............423 J10
st. Elwood..............454 E1
st. Kilsyth................380 K6
st. Kingsbury...........283 K11
st. Moonee Pnd.......324 C15
st. Seddon..............367 B12
wk. South Yarra..........32 F15
wk. South Yarra........414 J8

BROWNLEE
cr. Wheelers Hill......460 F17

BROWNLOW
cr. Epping...............198 A20
dr. Diamond Ck........245 K5

BROWNS
av. Ringwood...........378 C11
ct. Clayton..............459 A18
ct. Pk Orchards........378 A1
la. Aspendale...........546 C1
la. Maddingley..........264 L10
la. Parwan...............265 A7
la. Plenty.................244 E3
la. S Melbourne.........29 K2
rd. Bentleigh E..........496 J2
rd. Boneo................698 K14
rd. Boneo................700 K13
rd. Clayton..............499 A3
rd. Cranbourne S.....602 G19
rd. Cranbourne S.....604 J20
rd. Fingal.................697 E13
rd. Keilor.................277 A5
rd. Montrose............382 F12
rd. Noble Park N.......500 K14
rd. N Warrandyte.....289 L16
rd. Nunawading.......376 L19
rd. Rye....................696 G11
rd. Rye....................697 A11
rd. Werribee............446 E20

BROWTOP
rd. Narre Warren.....539 F15
rd. Narre Warren.....539 G16

BROXBOURNE
br. Mornington.........656 L3
br. Mornington.........657 A3

BROXBURN
ct. Berwick..............554 E16

BRUARONG
cr. Frankston S........626 H5

BRUCE
av. Rye....................696 E8
cl. Preston..............326 G1
cr. Ferntree Gly.......464 E2
ct. Berwick..............554 G16
ct. Elsternwick.........455 C6
ct. Gisborne...............79 B15
ct. Pakenham...........558 L20
ct. Ringwood E.........379 C11
ct. Springvale S.......500 B19
ct. Sunbury..............143 F3
dr. Somerville...........644 K16
rd. Frankston............627 G7
rd. Mt Martha...........669 A9
rd. Mt Martha...........669 B11
rd. Safety Bch...........669 A9
rd. Safety Bch...........669 B11
st. Albion.................364 H1
st. Balwyn...............373 K9
st. Beaumaris...........529 K9
st. Bentleigh............456 C18
st. Box Hill...............374 K14
st. Brighton East......455 G13
st. Brunswick...........325 H15
st. Bulleen...............330 B16
st. Coburg...............325 A4
st. Cranbourne.........604 A3
st. Dandenong.........536 B5
st. Diamond Ck.......246 C12
st. Fawkner.............281 J8
st. Greensborough..244 F20
st. Greensborough..286 F1
st. Kensington...........34 C13
st. Lalor..................241 J11
st. Laverton............407 B19
st. Malvern East......457 C4
st. Mitcham.............376 L12
st. Moonee Pnd.......323 G12
st. Mornington.........641 B20
st. Mt Waverley.......459 C1
st. Newport..............410 G4
st. Preston..............326 C1
st. Preston..............326 G1
st. Preston..............326 J2
st. Rye....................697 B14
st. Seaford..............599 H9
st. Strathmore.........324 A2
st. Toorak................415 A4
st. W Footscray.......366 G11
st.s, Altona Mdw.........407 B20
wy. Taylors Lakes.....233 F19

BRUCEDALE
cr. Pk Orchards.......333 K18

BRUFORD
av. Wheelers Hill......461 A15
st. Diamond Ck.......246 A11

BRULU
cl. Mt Eliza..............642 B7

BRUMBY
ct. Cranbourne........578 C15

BRUMBYS
rd. Carrum Downs...575 G18
rd. Warrandyte S.....334 G8

BRUMFIELD
rd. Healesville..........257 J3

BRUNDAGE
ct. Heidelberg W.....328 D2

BRUNDRETT
rd. Nar Warrn N.......539 E10

BRUNEI
cr. Heidelberg W.....284 C18
gr. Frankston...........600 E18

BRUNEL
ct. Aberfeldie...........323 D11
ct. Hampton Pk.......551 D4
rd. Seaford..............573 J20
rd. Seaford..............599 H1
st. Aberfeldie...........323 D11
st. Aberfeldie...........323 D12
st. Malvern East......416 F18
st. S Kingsville........410 F1

BRUNET
st. Dandenong N.....535 L1

BRUNNER
ct. Taylors Lakes.....233 G20

BRUNNING
cr. Frankston N.......600 D8
ct. Somerville..........644 J18

dr. Grovedale 706 H15
dr. Nar Warrn S.......552 F19
dr. Templestowe 331 K13
rd. Melton 226 L15
st. Spotswood 411 B4

BURLES
ct. Kurunjang..........227 F7

BURLEY
ct. Mulgrave 500 H1
st. Montrose...........382 C9

BURLEY GRIFFIN
cl. Avondale Ht 321 L6
pl. Eaglemont..........328 J12

BURLINGTON
ch. Hampton Pk.......552 C11
cl. Wyndham Va 446 E8
cr. Wantirna............422 H9
st. Oakleigh............458 A12

BURLOCK
av. Ringwood N.......378 B6

BURLORN
ct. Carrum Downs...601 D5

BURN
ct. Craigieburn........150 E17

BURNE
ct. Kew...................371 L13

BURNELL
st. Brunswick W......324 L12
st. Mt Eliza.............641 K2

BURNET
ct. Point Cook.........450 F4
st. Mulgrave 460 C18

BURNETT
av. Braybrook...........321 J20
av. Braybrook...........365 K1
cl. Taylors Lakes.....275 F2
cr. Frankston S........626 L12
cr. Reservoir...........283 K3
ct. Altona Mdw.........451 F5
ct. Mill Park 242 H5
ct. Ringwood 378 J15
st. Mitcham 377 D11
st. Mornington.........640 E20
st. St Kilda..............414 C14

BURNEWANG
st. Albion................364 H1

BURNHAM
dr. Hoppers Csg......448 E9
rd. Belgrave............466 C15

BURNIE
st. Toorak...............415 B3

BURNLEIGH
dr. Gladstone Pk......279 A1

BURNLEY
av. Point Cook.........449 L6
ct. Greenvale...........192 L18
ct. Greenvale...........193 A18
gr. Taylors Hill.........274 J8
st. Burnley..............371 A19
st. Frankston...........627 G2
st. Laverton 407 F12
st. Richmond............371 A19

BURNLEY TUNNEL
Melbourne 24 K16
Southbank 24 K16

BURNS
av. Clayton S 499 D8
av. Murrumbeena 457 A9
av. St Albans 320 J2
cl. Dromana.............686 A10
cl. Mt Eliza..............641 L7
ct. Eltham North.......245 D20
ct. Heidelberg Ht 284 F18
ct. Templestowe 332 B12
gr. Kingsbury 283 J11
rd. Altona 407 K11
rd. Dromana.............685 L9
st. Elwood 454 H4
st. Frankston...........627 F2
st. Maidstone...........366 G2
st. Moonee Pnd 323 H13
st. Prahran...............31 K18
st. Prahran..............414 E9
st. Yarraville............367 A13
wy. Delahey.............275 E16
wy. Monbulk 468 K2

BURNSIDE
av. Canterbury.........373 D20
av. Canterbury.........417 D1
ct. Wantirna S.........422 E16
pl. Greenvale...........193 C17
st. Deer Park...........319 C17

BURNT
st. Nunawading.......376 F13

BURONG
ct. Mt Eliza..............641 L3

BURONGA
av. Ringwood E 379 E13

BURR
ct. Laverton N 364 E16
rd. Woori Yallock.....344 A18

BURRAMINE
ct. Frankston S........627 F13
rd. Glen Waverley....460 F4

BURRANEER
cl. Ferntree Gly 463 H8
dr. Keysborough 534 G9

BURRAPIKE
av. Springvale..........500 B16

BURRAWANG
ri. Eltham North......245 F18
tce. Mt Martha..........669 B5

BURRAWONG
av. Seaford..............573 D12

BURREEL
av. Elsternwick 455 D6

BURRELL
st. McCrae..............685 A11

BURR HILL
ct. Berwick..............554 H6

BURRIDGE
cl. Mill Park 242 A8

BURRINDI
rd. Caulfield S..........455 K9

BURROUGHS
rd. Balwyn...............373 K9

BURROW
st. Frankston...........599 F17

BURROWES
st. Ascot Vale..........323 L18

BURROWS
av. Dandenong 536 D5
pl. Geelong, off
Little Malop St ...703 C8
st. Brighton.............454 H20

BURROWYE
cr. Keilor.................276 F8
cr. Taylors Lakes.....276 E9

BURRUMBEET
ct. Wyndham Va 446 C6

BURSARIA
av. Ferntree Gly 423 H19
cr. Frankston N 600 C6

BURSTON
ct. Mt Martha...........656 J6
pl. Brighton.............494 H2
rd. Boronia..............424 J13

BURSWOOD
cl. Frankston S........627 F13
cl. Seabrook 450 L6

BURT
cr. Hampton E.........495 K10
st. Altona................408 K16
st. Northcote............326 L14

BURTON
av. Clayton 498 H3
av. Hawthorn............371 K19
av. Laverton 407 E16
cl. Keilor Dn............276 D13
cr. Ascot Vale...........324 C19
cr. Ivanhoe East 328 J14
cr. Maribyrnong 323 E15
ct. Bayswater 423 J6
ct. Greenvale............192 J16
rd. Beaconsfld Up....542 H12
rd. Lilydale 338 H8
st. Balwyn N 373 J8
st. Chadstone..........418 E20
st. Dromana.............685 D9
st. Lalor...................241 G8
st. Melbourne 24 H2

BURUNDA
rd. Rosebud............684 J19

BURVALE
ct. Tullamarine........278 F3

BURVILLE
cl. Berwick..............554 B1

BURVILLES
rd. Mt Duneed.........706 F20

BURWAH
av. Brighton East 495 G1

BURWOOD
av. Hawthorn E........372 H18
av. Ringwood 378 A13
av. Sunshine N 321 E12
av. Sunshine N 321 E9
ct. Narre Warren 553 A10
ct. Thomastown.......240 H14
hwy.Belgrave 466 A12
hwy.Burwood............418 B9
hwy.Burwood E.........419 B9
hwy.Camberwell........416 E7
hwy.Camberwell........417 H8
hwy.Ferntree Gly 463 J1
hwy.Hawthorn E........416 E7
hwy.Knoxfield 423 A18
hwy.Tecoma 466 B12
hwy.Up Fntree Gly.....465 A7
hwy.Upwey 465 E8
hwy.Vermont S 420 H11
hwy.Vermont S 421 A11
hwy.Wantirna............422 A14
hwy.Wantirna............423 A18
hwy.Wantirna S.........422 A14
hwy.Wantirna S.........422 J17
hwy.Wantirna S.........423 A18
rd. Burwood............418 D8
rd. Burwood E.........419 F9
rd. Hawthorn...........371 E16
rd. Hawthorn...........372 F18
rd. Hawthorn E.........371 F16
rd. Vermont S 421 D12

BUSANA
wy. Nunawading.......376 F9

BUSCH
st. Sunshine N 321 D14
st. W Footscray.......366 H7

BUSH
ct. Frankston...........599 L15
ct. Langwarrin..........629 H1
mw. Gowanbrae 279 D4
pl. Sunbury.............142 J8
st. Coburg N 281 G12

BUSHBURY
ct. Hughesdale........457 F7
ct. Somerville..........644 C19

BUSHBY
ct. Darley 221 G4
ct. Kealba...............276 K20

BUSHFIELD
cr. Coolaroo............238 E7

BUSHLAND
av. Clarinda 498 F10
cl. Eltham 287 D15
ct. Wheelers Hill......460 L10

BUSHLARK
dr. Carrum Downs...600 J1
dr. Carrum Downs...600 K2

BUSHMANS
wy. S Morang...........199 L16

BUSHVIEW
gld. Boronia.............424 E2

BUSHY
ct. Somerville..........645 F18

BUSHY PARK
av. Caroline Spr 317 L3
la. Wantirna S.........421 F17

BUSINESS
dr. Nunawading.......376 K16

BUSINESS PARK
dr. Notting Hill.........459 B12

BUSSELL
ct. S Morang...........243 H4

BUSST
dr. Watsonia N 285 E2

BUSTER
pl. Nar Warrn S.......552 H17

BUTCHER
cr. Laverton 407 D12
ct. Nar Warrn S.......552 D16

BUTE
st. Murrumbeena 457 C9
st. Seddon..............367 D10

BUTLER
av. Mornington........640 L12
av. Mornington........641 A12
ct. Cheltenham........497 B20
ct. Cranbourne........577 K19
ct. Highton..............705 F6
gr. Coburg 326 A6
la. Parkville...............17 H10
la. Roxburgh Pk.......194 C11
pl. Mill Park 198 H20
pl. Mill Park 242 H1
st. Braybrook 321 K19
st. Brighton.............494 J1
st. Camberwell.........416 J1
st. Essendon............324 C4
st. Eumemmerring ..537 A14
st. Northcote...........326 J16
st. Preston..............327 B5
st. Richmond.............26 C3
st. Rye....................680 G20
st. St Albans 319 H2

BUTLERS
cr. Panton Hill 248 K5
rd. Ferntree Gly 464 J3
rd. Plenty 244 H10

BUTMAR
cl. Werribee............446 H16

BUTTERCUP
gr. Bundoora...........242 F15

BUTTERFIELD
rd. Emerald 469 G9

BUTTERFLY
gdn.Doncaster E 332 H14

BUTTERMANS
tr. Christmas Hills...207 E5

BUTTERS
st. Reservoir...........282 H14

BUTTERWICK
tce. Cranbourne E.....578 J17

BUTTERWORTH
cr. Anglesea............713 E4

BUTTLER
st. Kilsyth 381 E11

BUVELOT
ct. Chirnside Pk.......336 K7
pl. Mill Park 243 A8
pl. Sunbury.............143 C8
st. Yallambie 285 K14
wyn.Doncaster E 332 F16

BUXTON
cr. Frankston...........628 D9
ct. Meadow Ht 193 K17
ct. Wheelers Hill......461 B9
ct.n, Mt Martha.........655 L17
ct.s, Mt Martha.........655 K17
pl. Sunbury.............143 D11
rd. Herne Hill 701 J2
rd. Mitcham 377 J14
st. Elsternwick 455 D6
st. W Footscray.......366 J7

BYAHAMEE
st. Rye....................697 A6

BYAMBEE
ct. Grovedale 706 D15

BYFIELD
cl. Gladstone Pk......236 L17
cl. Gladstone Pk......237 A17
st. Reservoir...........282 K10

BYNG
av. Heatherton 497 G14

BYRD
ct. Mt Waverley.......459 C6

BYRNE
av. Elwood 454 C5
cl. Berwick..............539 L20
cr. Watsonia N 243 G19
ct. Campbellfield 239 G11
ct. Cheltenham........497 C19
rd. Bayswater N.......379 G15
st. Belgrave.............467 A16
st. Deer Park...........319 C18
st. Fitzroy N 326 D19
st. Mt Martha...........669 A2
st. Port Melb...........412 H4

BYRON
av. Keilor East..........322 F4
av. Lower Plenty......286 H14
cl. Rye....................696 G3
cl. Templestowe 332 B12
ct. Bundoora...........242 J20
ct. Frankston...........600 D18
ct. Glenroy..............279 F6
ct. Grovedale 706 E11
ct. Heidelberg Ht 284 G20
ct. Mooroolbark.......337 F19
ct. Nar Warrn S.......552 E18
ct. Wyndham Va 446 F10
rd. Christmas Hills...207 H14
rd. Kilsyth 380 K7
st. Blairgowrie..........680 A19
st. Box Hill S 418 G1
st. Brighton.............455 B15
st. Canterbury 373 C20
st. Canterbury 417 C1
st. Carnegie 456 F5
st. Clayton S 498 K6
st. Collingwood..........25 J1
st. Cremorne 26 D17
st. Elwood 454 D2
st. Footscray...........367 F8
st. Kew 372 B12
st. Moonee Pnd 324 C15
st. Mt Martha...........655 K16
st. N Melbourne.........17 D16
st. Ringwood 378 G5
st. Williamstn N 410 C12

BYSOUTH
ct. Pakenham..........584 D3

BYWAYS
dr. Ringwood E 379 D13

C

CABAL
ct. Mulgrave 500 E2

CABARITA
ct. Keysborough 534 F9

CABBAGE TREE
la. Gisborne............110 D16
la. Gisborne S.........110 D16

CABENA
cr. Chadstone..........458 A6
st. Donvale 376 G7

CABERNET
cr. Bundoora...........242 F17
ct. Waurn Ponds.....705 F14

CABINDA
dr. Keysborough 534 J14

CABOT
dr. Epping 198 A18

CADANA
rd. Gisborne S.........110 K17

CADBY
av. Ormond 456 C15
ct. Caulfield.............456 A5
pl. Frankston S........627 H10
st. Brighton.............454 G15

CADD
la. Dandenong 535 J7

CADDICK
gdn. Caroline Spr 318 C5

CADDY
ct. Reservoir...........283 J16

CADELL
ct. Sunbury.............143 A14
pl. Berwick..............553 K13

CADES
rd. Whittlesea..........126 D6
rd. Yan Yean 126 D6

CADIZ
pl. Keilor Dn............276 F13

CADLE
ct. Bayswater 423 J9
st. Dandenong 535 K9

CADLES
rd. Carrum Downs...575 B19

CADMAN
st. Brunswick W......325 A9

CADOGAN
pl. Altona Mdw........451 D5

CADORNA
st. Box Hill S 418 F5

CADOW
st. Kew East............372 F5

CADRONA
ct. Hillside...............274 F1

CADROSS
av. Melton 226 J15

CAERLEON
ct. Eaglemont..........328 K9

CAESAR
st. Mulgrave 500 F5

CAHILL
cl. Mill Park 242 B4
dr. Brookfield 268 A6
st. Bulla 190 C16
st. Dandenong S 549 E6

CAHILLTON
rd. Gruyere.............297 E9
rd. Gruyere.............341 E1

CAIN
av. Keilor East..........278 A19
av. Northcote...........327 A18
ct. Altona 409 F17
ct. Keilor East..........322 F6
rd. Rye....................696 L2
rd. Rye....................697 A2
st. Darley 222 E8
st. Rosebud 699 G1
st. Rosebud W 699 G1
st. Sunbury.............143 E8

CAINE
ct. Endeavour Hl 536 K4

CAIRN
ct. St Albans 320 D12
ct. Frankston...........600 C16
ct. Wyndham Va 446 D13
gr. Glen Waverley.....420 L19
rd. McCrae..............685 A14
rd. Rosebud............685 A14

CAIRNCROFT
av. Launching Pl 345 E15

CAIRN CURRAN
cl. Rowville.............462 J15
tce. Caroline Spr 317 K7

CAIRNES
cr. Brighton.............494 H2
cr. Malvern East 416 L18
gr. Bentleigh............455 K20

CAIRNLEA
dr. Deer Park...........319 K15
dr. St Albans 319 F8

CAIRNS
av. Newtown 702 E12
av. Rosebud 683 G17
dr. Darley 221 L3
pl. Diggers Rest 187 J13
rd. Hampton Pk........551 C11
st. Greensborough ..244 F20
st. Greensborough ..286 F1
st. Rosebud 684 F15

CAIRNVIEW
ct. Launching Pl 345 F14
CAIRO
rd. Mont Albert N 374 G8
CAITHNESS
cl. Sunbury 143 E5
cr. Glen Waverley 460 J5
ct. Jan Juc 711 E13
CAITHWILL
ct. Nar Warrn N 504 E18
CAITLYN
ct. Bundoora 242 D18
ct. Cranbourne N 578 A8
ct. Wantirna S 422 C18
CAKEBREAD
mw. Kensington 33 C9
CALA
st. W Footscray 366 E11
CALADENIA
cct. Frankston S 627 D10
cct.s, Frankston S 627 D11
st. Wesburn 348 B19
CALAIS
ct. Sydenham 274 K4
CALBOURNE
st. Preston 326 C5
CALCUTTA
cl. Altona Mdw 451 L4
st. Mitcham 377 B14
st. Sorrento 679 C13
CALDER
ct. Sunshine W 364 L5
ct. Sunshine W 365 A5
fwy. Airport W 278 D17
fwy. Calder Park 231 L2
fwy. Diggers Rest 141 E2
fwy. Diggers Rest 187 B9
fwy. Gisborne 78 G1
fwy. Gisborne 79 C7
fwy. Gisborne 109 J2
fwy. Gisborne S 110 F13
fwy. Gisborne S 111 A18
fwy. Gisborne S 141 E2
fwy. Keilor 276 G6
fwy. Keilor East 277 D11
fwy. Keilor Lodge 275 L1
fwy. Keilor N 275 L1
fwy. Keilor Park 277 D11
fwy. New Gisborne 78 G1
fwy. Sunbury 111 A18
fwy. Sunbury 141 E2
fwy. Taylors Lakes 233 A13
hwy. Diggers Rest 187 D11
rd. Nangana 472 G3
st. Manifold Ht 702 B6
wy. Wantirna S 422 A19
CALDERA
ct. Mooroolbark 337 C9
CALDER PARK
dr. Calder Park 232 J16
dr. Hillside 232 H20
dr. Sydenham 274 H4
dr. Taylors Hill 274 G9
CALDERWOOD
av. Wheelers Hill 460 L15
st. Bulleen 330 B15
st. Doncaster 330 B15
CALDWELL
cl. Endeavour Hl 538 A6
rd. Arthurs Seat 685 L11
rd. Dromana 685 L11
rd. Vermont 421 J1
st. Glenroy 280 G8
st. Mornington 640 J13
CALEB
st. Bentleigh E 496 J1
CALEDONIA
cr. Mulgrave 500 C4
ct. Berwick 539 H19
CALEDONIAN
ct. Keysborough 534 B8
la. Melbourne 2 E10
la. Melbourne 24 D5
wy. Point Cook 450 G6
CALEMBEENA
av. Hughesdale 457 G14
CALENDONIA
dr. Eltham North 245 D18
CALENDULA
cct. Epping 198 F20
CALEY
st. Frankston N 600 D10
CALGARY
ct. Glen Waverley 461 A2
CALIFORNIA
bvd. Pt Lonsdale 710 E1
cr. Ferntree Gly 423 H16
CALISTA
av. Oakleigh E 458 L13
ct. Elsternwick 455 D3
CALIVIL
st. Dallas 238 F11
CALK
st. Coburg N 282 B15
CALLAGHAN
av. Glen Waverley 459 L9
ct. Cheltenham 531 G2
pl. Frankston 627 B4
st. Noble Park 534 L1
CALLAM
cl. Endeavour Hl 537 E10
CALLAN
ct. Mill Park 242 F1
CALLANAN
dr. Melton S 268 E3
CALLANANS
la. Pearcedale 647 E10
CALLANDER
cl. Sunbury 113 G15
pl. Lysterfield 464 D17
rd. Noble Park 500 J18
rd. Pascoe Vale 280 E12
st. Hughesdale 457 E11
st. Reservoir 240 F20
st. Thomson 703 H17
CALLANDRA
wyn. Upwey 465 G12
CALLANISH
rd. Camberwell 417 H7
CALLANTINA
ct. Frankston 628 C9
rd. Hawthorn 415 K2
CALLAS
st. Dromana 686 F6
CALLEMONDAH
ct. Ferntree Gly 424 A20
CALLENDER
ct. Frankston 628 B6
CALLER
ct. Nunawading 420 J1
CALLIBRIS
ct. Keysborough 534 A15
CALLISTEMON
av. Keysborough 534 A15
cr. Narre Warren 553 C1
cr. Springvale 500 K13
ct. Doncaster E 332 F18
ct. Mt Martha 656 G7
ri. Mill Park 243 B11
CALLUM
av. Somerville 644 F19
CALMSDEN
st. Kilsyth S 424 J1
CALOLA
ct. Ringwood E 379 D6
st. Heidelberg W 328 B2
CALOOLA
av. Oakleigh 457 K7
ct. Rowville 463 G13
dr. N Warrandyte 290 A12
CALROSSIE
av. Montmorency 286 K8
cl. Endeavour Hl 537 G1
rd. Blackburn S 419 F2
CALSHOT
gr. Gladstone Pk 237 B18
CALTHORPE
st. Gisborne 79 A14
wyn. Caroline Spr 317 J2
CALTOWIE
ct. Research 288 G1
CALVERTON
rd. Kealba 276 K20
CALVIN
cr. Doncaster E 375 H2
ct. Watsonia N 285 F1
ct. Wheelers Hill 461 E14
st. Hawthorn 371 E14
CALVO
ct. Werribee 446 H16
CALWELL
ct. Mill Park 242 L5
ct. Mill Park 243 A5
ct. Skye 601 D9
rd. Bend of Islands 249 D18
rd. Christmas Hills 249 G16
rd. Kangaroo Grnd 249 D18
st. Kensington 33 J5
CALYPSO
ct. Forest Hill 420 G6
pl. Thomastown 240 F16
CAM
st. Burwood E 419 E11
st. Greensborough 286 A8
CAMARA
st. St Albans 320 G10
CAMBALA
av. Lalor 240 G9
CAMBARA
ct. Vermont S 420 F9
CAMBDEN PARK
pde. Ferntree Gly 463 E2
pde. Ferntree Gly 463 F4
CAMBER
av. Pk Orchards 334 C19
CAMBERLEY
ri. Ringwood N 334 J20
CAMBERWELL
dr. Narre Warren 553 C9
gr. Hawthorn E, off Burke Av 372 H20
rd. Camberwell 416 J1
rd. Camberwell 417 A5
rd. Hawthorn E 372 F18
CAMBORNE
av. Mt Eliza 625 L16
CAMBRA
rd. Belmont 706 D3
CAMBRIA
rd. Keysborough 535 B11
CAMBRIAN
av. Preston 282 K17
cr. Wheelers Hill 461 A7
ct. Eltham North 287 B1
wy. Melton W 225 L16
CAMBRIDGE
cl. Cranbourne E 578 K17
cl. Croydon Hills 335 D17
cl. Rowville 463 L17
cr. Roxburgh Pk 194 A9
cr. Taylors Lakes 233 D18
cr. Werribee 446 K15
cr. Wyndham Va 446 J12
ct. Thomastown 241 J16
dr. Berwick 554 B1
dr. Glen Waverley 459 H7
dr. Springvale S 533 K7
gdn. Mooroolbark 381 B1
rd. Bentleigh E 456 H18
rd. Kilsyth 381 B1
rd. Montrose 381 J5
rd. Mooroolbark 381 B1
rd. Mt Dandenong 426 F3
rd. Mt Martha 669 K1
st. Armadale 415 E13
st. Belgrave S 506 J1
st. Belmont 706 E1
st. Box Hill 374 J15
st. Brighton East 455 B14
st. Caulfield N 415 C15
st. Collingwood 25 G2
st. Frankston 627 E4
st. Hawthorn E 372 G17
st. Laverton N 364 A16
st. Maidstone 366 G1
st. Oakleigh 457 L13
st. Port Melb 412 J3
st. Seaholme 409 J17
wy. Bundoora 284 J2
wy. Campbellfield 239 G13
wyn. Sorrento 678 D8
wyn. Templstw Lr 330 L13
CAMBRO
rd. Clayton 459 G20
CAMBUS
rd. Yering 253 E19
CAMDALE
cl. Hampton Pk 552 D9
pde. St Albans 275 H19
st. Clarinda 498 H10
CAMDELL
ct. Belmont 706 E6
CAMDEN
ct. Berwick 553 G4
ct. Frankston 600 B18
ct. Glen Waverley 420 L20
rd. Hawthorn 372 A18
rd. Hughesdale 457 G11
rd. Newtown 701 K10
st. Balaclava 414 G17
wy. Wyndham Va 446 J9
CAMDON
gdn. Berwick 554 B3
st. Pascoe Vale 280 F17
CAMEELO
ct. Ferntree Gly 423 K18
CAMELIA
cl. Lalor 240 K10
cr. The Basin 424 K10
ct. Croydon S 379 E11
ct. Doveton 536 J12
ct. Mornington 641 B10
gr. Cheltenham 531 F2
st. Box Hill 375 E14
st. Kings Park 275 E19
CAMELLIA
av. Noble Park N 501 C18
ct. Tarneit 447 J1
ct. Wheelers Hill 460 G13
st. Blackburn N 375 J8
CAMELOT
cl. Research 289 F5
ct. Doncaster E 331 L16
ct. Mooroolbark 337 J14
ct. Mt Eliza 626 K20
dr. Albanvale 319 E4
dr. Glen Waverley 420 J17
dr. Springvale S 499 F19
pl. Hillside 232 B20
CAMEO
ct. Bulleen 329 J11
ct. Narre Warren 553 F9
CAMERON
av. Altona Mdw 407 E19
av. Oakleigh S 497 J2
cl. Bayswater 423 D8
cl. Burwood 418 A5
cl. Donvale 332 J17
ct. Eltham North 246 F20
ct. Eltham North 288 F1
ct. Greenvale 237 B4
ct. Kew 371 G9
ct. Kilsyth 381 A6
ct. Kurunjang 227 F14
ct. Somerville 644 F17
ct. Wantirna 422 G12
la. Dandenong, off Thomas St 535 L10
pde. Bundoora 284 J2
pde. Watsonia 284 J2
pde. Watsonia N 285 A2
pl. Albert Park 29 A15
pl. Albert Park 413 A8
pl. Keysborough 534 K13
rd. Anglesea 713 K3
rd. Box Hill N 375 C11
rd. Croydon 336 J19
rd. Essendon 324 D4
rd. Mt Evelyn 338 K14
rd. Ringwood N 378 D5
st. Airport W 278 L17
st. Brunswick 325 F9
st. Cheltenham 530 K2
st. Coburg 325 F9
st. Cranbourne 604 G7
st. Cranbourne E 604 G7
st. Mt Waverley 419 G19
st. Reservoir 282 H15
st. Richmond 26 D8
st. Rosebud 684 J15
st. Sunshine 365 F2
wy. Mt Eliza 641 K7
wy. Pakenham 585 D7
CAMERONS
rd. Darley 222 A1
rd. Healesville 214 A14
CAMEROUN
ct. Berwick 554 F7
CAMILLE
ct. Avondale Ht 322 D9
CAMINO
ct. Glen Waverley 420 E16
tce. Malvern East 457 D1
CAMINOLE
wyn. Templestowe 332 D6
CAMIRA
cl. Doncaster E 332 G8
ct. Berwick 553 H1
ct. Grovedale 706 D13
st. Malvern East 457 J7
CAMLARNI
cl. Avondale Ht 322 F15
CAMLEY
ct. Berwick 554 D4
CAMMS
rd. Cranbourne 577 L17
rd. Cranbourne W 577 F16
rd. Monbulk 467 K1
rd. The Patch 467 K1
rd. The Patch 468 A1
wy. Meadow Ht 237 J5
CAMP
ct. Mornington 656 G4
rd. Anglesea 713 H2
rd. Broadmeadows 238 B17
rd. Campbellfield 239 B18
rd. Langwarrin S 630 A16
st. Chelsea 546 J18
CAMPASPE
cr. Brookfield 268 D5
cr. Keilor 276 K14
dr. Croydon Hills 335 J15
st. Box Hill N 375 A10
CAMPBELL
arc. Melbourne 2 C20
av. Deer Park 318 K18
av. Mt Dandenong 426 G4
ct. Altona 409 A16
ct. Brookfield 268 A8
ct. Darley 221 F9
ct. Warrandyte 333 B2
dr. Hampton Pk 551 G11
gr. Dingley Village 533 A6
gr. Hawthorn E 416 E2
gr. Mornington 640 H15
gr. Northcote 326 H17
pde. Box Hill S 419 C6
pde. Cranbourne 604 A3
pl. Geelong 703 C12
rd. Balwyn 372 K13
rd. Briar Hill 286 G5
rd. Pakenham 585 D9
rd.s, Hawthorn E 416 G2
st. Bentleigh 495 L1
st. Berwick 554 J8
st. Brighton 454 G11
st. Campbellfield 239 D13
st. Coburg 325 H7
st. Collingwood 19 K18
st. Dandenong 535 F5
st. Diamond Ck 245 G13
st. E Geelong 703 E14
st. Epping 241 J1
st. Frankston 599 J20
st. Glen Waverley 420 F17
st. Healesville 258 C1
st. Heathmont 378 J14
st. Kew 372 F7
st. Kingsbury 283 J11
st. Laverton 407 F13
st. Mooroolbark 337 F20
st. Sandringham 495 C16
st. Tecoma 466 C13
st. Westmeadows 237 D15
st. Yarraville 367 D17
CAMPBELLS
rd. Gisborne 80 G7
rd. Portsea 678 B5
rd. Riddells Ck 80 G7
rd. Sorrento 678 B5
rd. Wandin East 385 D3
CAMPERDOWN
av. Sunshine N 320 K14
st. Brighton East 455 B19
CAMPHOR
cl. Lysterfield 503 L1
ct. Doveton 536 J6
CAMPHORA
ct. Plenty 244 H11
pl. St Albans 320 K8
CAMPUS
ct. Wheelers Hill 460 D15
gte. Chirnside Pk 337 J5
pl. Thomastown 240 J12
CAMRIC
ct. Mt Evelyn 339 E18
CAMROSE
ct. Jan Juc 711 C13
CANADA
la. Carlton 18 C17
CANADIAN
ct. Meadow Ht 238 B5
CANADIAN BAY
rd. Mt Eliza 625 K13
CANANGA
ct. Mill Park 243 C11
CANARA
ct. Bayswater 423 A4
ct. Greensborough 244 K19
st. Doncaster E 375 L4
CANARY
ct. Mill Park 242 B10
CANBERRA
av. Dandenong S 535 J13
av. Hoppers Csg 448 G6
gr. Beaumaris 530 D6
gr. Brighton East 495 C5
gr. Lalor 242 A11
gr. Malvern 416 A14
mw. Port Melb, off Canberra Pde 412 G5
pde. Port Melb 412 H5
rd. Toorak 415 B3
st. Brunswick 325 C9
st. Carrum 573 F7
st. Patterson L 573 F7
CANDLEBARK
cl. Greensborough 245 B15
cl. Hampton Pk 551 L6
cr. Frankston N 600 A9
ct. Research 288 K1
ct. Rosanna 329 E4
la. Nunawading 376 F16
qd. Rowville 502 C5
CANDOVER
st. Geelong West 702 H4
CANDWINDARA
ct. Langwarrin 601 K13
CANDY
cl. Seville 341 K12
st. Northcote 326 H18

CANDYTUFT
cl. Cranbourne N.....578 C10
CANE
av. Seaford....600 B1
mw. Seaford....600 C1
CANES
pl. Geelong....703 D11
CANN
pl. Rowville....463 C17
CANNA
st. Dromana....686 F7
CANNERY
pl. Dingley Village....533 C7
CANNES
av. Avondale Ht....322 E9
av. Bonbeach....573 A4
ct. Greenvale....237 E4
ct. Highton....701 H9
gr. Beaumaris....530 F5
CANNI
ct. Broadmeadows..238 B9
CANNING
dr. Berwick....554 G13
st. Avondale Ht....321 L15
st. Brunswick E....325 L20
st. Carlton....18 J15
st. Carlton N....18 K7
st. Frankston S....626 H11
st. N Melbourne....34 H11
CANNON
ct. Noble Park N....501 D13
st. Sunshine....365 A8
CANNONS CREEK
rd. Cannons Creek...649 E4
CANNY
ct. Altona Mdw....451 F4
CANONBURY
cir. Seabrook....451 A6
CANOPUS
cct. Long Forest....224 C2
cct. Long Forest....224 C3
dr. Doncaster E....332 C17
pl. Melton W....226 B16
CANORA
st. Blackburn S....419 E4
CANOVA
dr. Glen Waverley....420 C14
CANOWINDRA
cl. Vermont S....421 D7
pl. Grovedale....706 D11
CANROBERT
st. Caulfield N....415 F18
CANTALA
av. Caulfield N....415 E16
av. Rosanna....285 D19
cr. Ringwood N....377 L5
ct. Endeavour Hl....538 A7
ct. Vermont S....420 F9
ct. Wheelers Hill....461 B17
dr. Doncaster....331 A16
dr. Jan Juc....711 C18
st. Clayton....459 B19
st. Pascoe Vale S....324 E6
CANTER
st. Rowville....502 D6
CANTERBURY
cl. Melton S....268 B11
cl. Rowville....502 L8
cl. Rowville....503 A8
ct. Bayswater N....379 G20
ct. Wandana Ht....701 D20
dr. Sunbury....142 L1
dr. Sunbury....143 A1
la. Sydenham....275 D8
pl. Brighton....494 F3
pl. Hawthorn E....416 G7
pl. Middle Park....30 A15
pl. Werribee....446 K11
rd. Albert Park....30 A13
rd. Bayswater N....379 K19
rd. Blackburn....375 F20
rd. Blackburn S....420 A1
rd. Box Hill....374 D18
rd. Box Hill S....375 A20
rd. Braeside....532 E19
rd. Camberwell....372 K16
rd. Canterbury....372 K16
rd. Canterbury....373 B17
rd. Forest Hill....420 G2
rd. Heathmont....378 K19
rd. Kilsyth....381 A14
rd. Kilsyth S....381 A14
rd. Middle Park....30 A13
rd. Middle Park....413 G8
rd. Montrose....381 A14
rd. Ringwood....377 L20
rd. Ringwood E....379 C17
rd. St Kilda....413 G8
rd. Surrey Hills....374 D18
rd. Toorak....415 B9
rd. Vermont....377 L20
rd. Vermont....421 A2
st. Cranbourne....578 E19
st. Deer Park....319 C16
st. Flemington....324 D20
st. Hughesdale....457 G13
st. Moonee Pnd....323 L15
st. Mornington....640 D13
st. Richmond....371 A18
st. Sorrento....678 E8
st. Yarraville....367 B15
CANTERBURY JETTY
rd. Blairgowrie....696 C8
rd. Rye....680 D20
rd. Rye....696 C8
CANTLE
cl. Epping....198 F18
cl. Pakenham....585 F5
CANTLEY
la. Vermont....421 B3
CANTON
ct. Eltham North....245 H16
CANTRELL
pl. Nar Warrn S....552 E19
CANTS CREEK
rd. St Andrews....206 B1
rd. Smiths Gly....206 B1
CANTWELL
rd. Nar Warrn N....539 F10
CANTY
la. Pakenham....586 A5
CANUNGRA
cl. Hampton Pk....552 C8
ct. Bundoora....243 B20
CANYON
st. Balwyn....373 A9
CAPE
st. Eaglemont....328 L10
CAPEL
av. Rosebud W....683 D19
pl. N Melbourne....17 G19
st. N Melbourne....17 H20
st. W Melbourne....17 G20
CAPELLA
cl. Doveton....537 C10
cr. Moorabbin....497 D10
pl. Carrum Downs...575 B15
pl. Doncaster E....332 E18
st. Balwyn N....329 B20
st. Balwyn N....373 B1
CAPER
ct. Mulgrave....500 E1
ct. Werribee....447 J10
CAPES
ct. Mill Park....241 L5
CAPITAL
av. Glen Waverley....420 H14
dr. Dandenong S....550 D2
wy. S Morang....198 K13
CAPITAL CITY
bvd. Wantirna S....422 K16
CAPITAL LINK
dr. Campbellfield....239 C2
dr. Campbellfield....239 F3
CAPITOL
arc. Melbourne....2 D14
av. McKinnon....455 K15
CAPLE
pl. Gladstone Pk....237 C17
CAPON
st. Malvern East....457 J6
CAPORN
av. Belgrave....466 H12
CAPP
st. Reservoir....283 D15
CAPPELLA
ct. Glen Waverley....460 D8
CAPRI
cl. Seville....341 J12
cl. S Morang....198 J13
cl. S Morang....198 K14
cr. Avondale Ht....322 E8
ct. Carrum Downs...600 L5
ct. Carrum Downs...601 A5
ct. Deer Park....319 D10
ct. Doncaster....330 D17
ct. Jan Juc....711 B19
ct. Notting Hill....459 H13
ct. Pakenham....584 H4
ct. Reservoir....282 B4
ct. Westmeadows....237 D15
dr. Mt Martha....668 L6
gr. Sorrento....678 H11
wy. Point Cook....450 E8
CAPRICE
av. Port Melb....368 C19
cl. Wantirna....422 H8
ct. Frankston....600 C17
ct. Keilor Dn....275 K14
ct. Templestowe....331 F12
pl. Narre Warren....538 K15
CAPRICORN
av. Doncaster E....332 D18
ct. Taylors Lakes....233 E19
CAPRICORNIA
wy. Aspendale Gdn, off Royal Palms....547 A5
CAPTAIN
st. Aspendale....546 C3
CAPTAIN COOK
cl. Skye....575 H14
CAPTAIN PEARSON
dr. Mickleham....150 B2
CAPULET
st. Moonee Pnd....324 F11
CARA
cr. Berwick....554 L5
ct. Berwick....554 J20
rd. Highton....701 K16
CARAAR CREEK
la. Mornington....640 L7
la. Mornington....641 A8
CARABOTT
pl. Berwick....553 K16
CARADON
dr. Truganina....405 K16
CARAMAR
av. Brighton East....455 G17
dr. Oakleigh S....497 H8
CARAMUT
ct. Warranwood....334 H15
rd. Brighton....455 A13
rd. Ringwood E....379 D5
wy. Seabrook....450 L5
CARAVAN
st. Balwyn....373 L9
CARAVELLE
cr. Strathmr Ht....279 C8
ct. Berwick....540 C20
CARAWA
ct. Bundoora....285 B1
dr. Reservoir....282 A12
pl. Skye....601 G3
st. Cockatoo....471 D20
st. Mooroolbark....337 A15
CARAWAH
rt. St Albans....320 L7
rt. St Albans....321 A7
CARAWATHA
rd. Doncaster....374 H2
CARBEEN
dr. Bundoora....242 G14
CARBEENA
pde. Heidelberg W....328 A2
CARBERRY
dr. Kurunjang....227 D14
CARBERY
ct. Grovedale....706 E10
CARBINE
av. Clarinda....498 D10
cl. Cranbourne W....577 F17
ct. Mill Park....242 K10
ct. New Gisborne....79 C1
pl. Bundoora....284 E4
st. Doncaster E....332 G17
st. Donvale....332 G17
wy. Keilor Dn....275 K15
wy. Mornington....641 D18
CARBON
cr. Mill Park....241 L6
ct. Werribee....447 G12
CARBONI
ct. Mulgrave....501 D4
CARBOOR
st. Tootgarook....698 F9
CARBORA
dle. Greensborough..244 E18
CARBOST
ct. Macleod....284 L11
ct. Macleod....285 A11
CARBURT
ct. Truganina....405 K15
CARCOOLA
ct. Ormond....456 E14
ct. Rosebud....684 F19
rd. Monbulk....428 C16
rd. Ringwood E....379 C5
st. Cockatoo....471 G17
CARDAMON
dr. Hallam....538 C17
CARDER
av. Seaford....599 D12
CARDIFF
cl. View Bank....329 J2
ct. Craigieburn....194 C3
ct. Glen Waverley....459 J7
st. Bentleigh E....457 A20
st. Boronia....423 L10
st. Thomastown....240 C11
st. Vermont....421 H4
CARDIGAN
cl. Melton S....268 C11
cr. Taylors Lakes....275 J2
pl. Albert Park....29 F11
pl. Albert Park....413 C6
rd. Montrose....382 C2
rd. Mooroolbark....337 E20
st. Carlton....18 C20
st. Endeavour Hl....536 K3
st. Geelong....703 B12
st. St Kilda E....414 K16
tce. Carlton....18 C20
CARDINAL
cl. Mill Park....242 K13
ct. Dingley Village...532 L3
ct. Narre Warren....552 F1
rd. Glenroy....280 D10
CARDINIA
cl. Dandenong N....502 F14
cr. Taylors Hill....274 J13
ct. Menzies Ck....468 B12
rd. Officer....583 B19
rd. Officer S....582 G20
rd. Officer S....583 B19
st. Berwick....554 L11
wy. Rowville....463 A18
CARDINIA CREEK
rd. Emerald....507 G14
CARDORE
ct. Noble Park....501 A19
CARDS
la. Olinda....426 K8
CARE
cl. Meadow Ht....194 A19
CAREL
ct. Pk Orchards....333 D19
CAREN
ct. Sunshine W....364 J6
CAREW
ct. Brookfield....268 B5
st. Sandringham....495 A12
CAREY
cl. Grovedale....706 G11
cl. Werribee....446 K11
cr. Bacchus Msh....221 G14
ct. Blackburn....376 A19
ct. Coldstream....295 F12
ct. Keilor East....322 B4
ct. Keysborough....534 D11
ct. Sunbury....144 F10
gr. Preston....327 C5
st. Bentleigh E....456 L15
st. Cranbourne N....578 G10
CARGO
dr. Campbellfield....194 E18
dr. Coolaroo....194 E18
rd. Melb Airport....235 L18
CARIBBEAN
dr. Scoresby....462 B11
CARIBOU
cr. Point Cook....450 E3
cr. Point Cook....450 F3
ct. Wheelers Hill....460 J16
CARINA
cl. Wantirna S....422 K13
ct. Kilsyth....381 G7
dr.s, Melton....226 F19
CARINDA
rd. Canterbury....373 C20
CARINGA
st. Pascoe Vale....281 A11
CARINGAL
av. Doncaster....374 G2
ct. Clayton S....498 H8
CARINISH
rd. Clayton....458 F18
rd. Oakleigh S....458 F18
CARINYA
av. Aspendale....546 E4
av. Newcomb....704 C13
bvd. Burnside....318 G8
cr. Caulfield N....415 E16
ct. Mt Waverley....459 C4
ct. Vermont....421 B1
dr. Gisborne....78 H19
rd. Greensborough..285 L10
rd. Oakleigh S....497 F1
rd. Vermont....377 B20
rd. Vermont....421 B1
CARINZA
av. Altona Mdw....450 J2
CARISBROOK
cr. Lower Plenty....286 D14
ct. Doncaster E....332 D20
ct. Langwarrin....629 H2
CARISBROOKE
ct. Wantirna....422 G13
CARL
ct. Hallam....537 J18
ct. Ringwood....378 H7
pl. Diggers Rest....232 H7
CARLA
ct. Aspendale Gdn...546 K4
ct. Somerville....644 F15
vw. Sunbury....142 E8
CARLING
ct. Altona Mdw....451 J9
CARLINGA
ct. Gladstone Pk....279 B4
dr. Vermont....421 F4
CARLINGFORD
cl. Rowville....503 D6
st. Caulfield S....455 E7
st. Elsternwick....455 B7
CARLISLE
av. Balaclava....414 J18
cr. Hughesdale....457 E10
ct. Campbellfield....239 G13
ct. Frankston....628 B6
dr. Epping....197 J17
dr. Officer....555 H19
rd. Ferntree Gly....463 E1
rd. Hallam....537 E15
st. Balaclava....414 C17
st. Coburg....325 L4
st. Craigieburn....150 G20
st. Preston....327 A6
st. St Kilda....414 C17
tce. Point Cook....450 H9
CARLITA
cl. Mill Park....242 L10
cl. Mill Park....243 A10
CARLO
ct. Greensborough..244 K15
CARLOGIE
ct. Burwood....418 B3
pl. Darley....221 G1
CARLOW
pl. Carlton....18 H14
rd. St Albans....320 J7
st. Bentleigh E....457 B20
CARLSBERG
rd. Eaglemont....328 J11
CARLSON
av. Clayton....459 A13
st. Sunbury....143 C15
CARLSRUHE
pl. Caroline Spr....318 D10
CARLSSON
ct. Brooklyn....365 G19
CARLTON
ct. Braybrook....321 K20
ct. Craigieburn....150 G20
ct. Rye....698 A5
ct. Taylors Hill....274 H8
ct. Templestowe....331 E6
pl. Carlton....18 B18
rd. Dandenong N....501 J16
st. Braybrook....321 J20
st. Carlton....18 H15
st. McKinnon....456 A17
st. Prahran....32 D17
st. Prahran....414 H8
CARLUKE
cl. Berwick....554 C16
CARLY
cl. Nar Warrn S....552 F11
ct. Croydon N....336 E13
pl. Tootgarook....698 B9
tce. Werribee....447 L12
CARLYLE
cl. Hurstbridge....203 D14
cr. Balwyn....374 B12
cr. Bellfield....327 L6
pl. Melton W....226 C18
st. Ashwood....418 A14
st. Croydon....380 H4
st. Hawthorn E....372 H15
st. Maidstone....366 H4
st. Moonee Pnd....324 A10
st. Pakenham....584 E2
wy. Malvern East....416 H18
CARLYON
ct. Springvale....500 E10
st. Ormond....456 C15
CARMANS
la. Geelong....703 D13
CARMARTHEN
cl. Werribee....446 L18
CARMEL
av. Ferntree Gly....424 F17
av. Mt Waverley....418 L20
cl. Greensborough..244 J14
cl. Greenvale....192 J16
ct. Balwyn....373 K10
ct. Bentleigh E....496 K3
ct. Forest Hill....420 A6
ct. Frankston....600 D17
ct. Sydenham....274 H3
CARMELA
cl. Narre Warren....539 E16
wy. Carrum Downs...601 E4

CARMELLA
cl. Chirnside Pk....336 F6
ri. Chirnside Pk....336 F6
CARMELO
av. Malvern East....457 E1
CARMEN
cl. Doncaster E....332 J12
cl. Eltham North....288 A2
cr. Nar Warrn N....538 B6
ct. Glen Waverley....460 E11
ct. Hampton Pk....552 C13
ct. Lilydale....339 A10
ct. Ringwood....379 A2
st. Dandenong....535 E2
st. Newport....410 E8
CARMICHAEL
av. Newtown....701 J4
ct. Glen Waverley....419 L13
rd. Oakleigh E....458 G12
st. Ivanhoe East....328 H14
st. Tootgarook....698 G1
st. W Footscray....366 J8
CARMINE
ct. Carrum Downs....575 F14
CARMODY
dr. Deer Park....319 J10
st. Burwood....418 E12
CARMYLE
av. Toorak....415 G9
ct. Avondale Ht....322 C11
ct. Bundoora....284 H5
CARN
av. Ivanhoe....328 E10
CARNABY
ct. Somerville....645 B18
pl. Wantirna....422 F14
wy. Springvale S....499 J20
CARNARVON
av. Jan Juc....711 F15
av. The Basin....425 A11
cl. Taylors Lakes....233 E19
ct. Sunbury....144 E12
dr. Grovedale....706 A14
pl. Melton W....226 C15
rd. Caulfield N....415 J18
rd. Essendon....323 J2
rd. Strathmore....323 J2
st. Brunswick....325 J12
st. Doncaster....330 K20
st. Hawthorn E....372 E20
CARNATION
ct. Endeavour Hl....537 F5
ct. Springvale S....534 A1
CARNE
rd. Pakenham....558 G1
rd. Pakenham Up....559 D1
CARNEA
cl. Frankston S....627 D10
CARNEGIE
av. Kew East....372 A5
ct. Gisborne....79 D16
pl. Pt Lonsdale....710 G7
CARNELL
pl. Balwyn N....374 A3
CARNEY
ct. Pakenham....584 G6
CARNON
st. Greensborough....244 F20
CARNOUSTIE
av. Jan Juc....711 F16
cr. Chirnside Pk....292 J10
ct. Frankston....599 J15
ct. Rowville....462 D19
dr. Sunbury....144 E12
gr. Mornington....656 D3
pde. Heatherton....497 G16
CARNSWORTH
av. Kew....371 G9
CAROBEN
av. Vermont....421 D5
CAROL
av. Cranbourne....604 C3
ct. Frankston....600 C17
ct. Newcomb....704 A17
ct. Ringwood N....378 H2
ct. Warrandyte....333 E1
gr. Tullamarine....278 J7
st. Mornington....656 F4
st. Scoresby....462 C9
CAROLANNE
ct. Mooroolbark....337 H17
CAROLE
av. Chirnside Pk....336 L6
ct. Aspendale Gdn....546 K7
ct. Cranbourne....577 L16
ct. Seabrook....450 K3
st. Templestowe....331 C6
CAROLE-JOY
av. Reservoir....282 J12
CAROL HANCOCK
pl. Croydon N....335 L13
CAROLINA
st. Mt Waverley....419 F15
CAROLINE
av. Cockatoo....511 C5
cr. Blackburn N....375 G7
cr. Cranbourne W....577 E20
cr. Emerald....469 F16
cr. Hurstbridge....203 G12
cr. Kalorama....382 L18
ct. Bayswater....423 C10
ct. Blairgowrie....680 C19
ct. Preston....327 A5
ct. Rosebud....700 F4
ct. Tootgarook....698 B9
dr. Templstw Lr....330 E12
pl. Hampton Pk....551 K5
ri. Gowanbrae....279 D7
st. Aberfeldie....323 C10
st. Box Hill N....375 D11
st. Clayton....498 F1
st. Clifton Hill....20 F5
st. Dandenong....536 E10
st. Hawthorn E....372 D20
st. Highton....701 K20
st. Kilsyth....381 C5
st. Mt Martha....656 L8
st. Pt Lonsdale....710 E4
st. Ringwood....378 F14
st. Selby....467 F15
st. South Yarra....31 K8
st. South Yarra....414 E4
st. Thomastown....240 L14
st. Thomastown....241 A14
CAROLINE SPRINGS
bvd. Caroline Spr....274 A16
bvd. Caroline Spr....318 A5
CAROLL
ct. Gisborne....79 C16
CAROLYN
cl. Nar Warrn N....538 C6
cr. Bundoora....285 C2
ct. Frankston....600 G18
ct. Keilor Park....278 B13
ct. Langwarrin....629 J5
st. Hampton....495 H9
CAROMAR
st. Croydon....336 K20
CARON
cl. Hallam....537 L14
CAROOL
cl. Tootgarook....698 E7
rd. Ashburton....417 G15
rd. Carnegie....456 L9
CAROUSEL
ct. Epping....198 F17
CARPENTARIA
ct. Aspendale Gdn....547 A4
CARPENTER
ct. Chelsea....547 B19
rd. Beaconsfld Up....557 B1
rd. Officer....557 B1
st. Brighton....454 H18
st. Noble Park....500 L17
CARR
ct. Altona Mdw....451 F3
ct. Bundoora....284 L6
pl. Roxburgh Pk....194 D14
pl. Geelong, off Maud St....702 L10
st. Belmont....706 E1
st. Breakwater....703 F16
st. Brighton East....495 J4
st. Coburg N....281 G17
st. Geelong....702 L11
st. Thomson....703 F16
CARRABIN
ct. Knoxfield....463 B4
CARRAJUNG
st. Rosebud....700 K5
CARRAMAR
av. Camberwell....417 D3
av. Glen Waverley....460 A1
cr. Belgrave....466 L15
ct. Bayswater....423 B9
ct. Emerald....469 J15
ct. Highton....701 G19
ct. Keysborough....534 E8
ct. Rosebud....684 F19
ct. Vermont....421 E6
dr. Frankston....600 E18
rd. Cranbourne S....630 K3
st. Chadstone....458 C1
st. Mornington....641 B16
st. Rye....696 L6
st. Rye....697 A6
CARRANYA
ct. Nar Warrn S....579 A2
CARRARA
rd. Rowville....502 E7
CARRATHOOL
st. Bulleen....329 H11
CARRAWE
ct. Anglesea....713 D4
CARR BOYD
rd. Cranbourne S....602 G15
CARRE
st. Elsternwick....454 L6
st. Elsternwick....455 A6
CARRIBEAN
dr. Keysborough....534 C11
CARRICK
dr. Gladstone Pk....237 B16
dr. Gladstone Pk....278 K5
dr. Gladstone Pk....279 A3
dr. Tullamarine....278 K5
st. Balwyn....374 B11
st. Mont Albert....374 B11
CARRIER
av. Parkdale....531 J14
CARRIGAL
st. Balwyn....374 A9
CARRIGG
st. Dromana....686 D3
CARRINGTON
av. Hawthorn E....372 H18
av. Seaford....599 L3
bvd. Thomastown....240 C14
cl. Chelsea Ht....547 D8
cl. Wyndham Va....446 H12
cr. Carrum Downs....601 F1
ct. Burwood E....420 C13
ct. Chirnside Pk....337 J3
ct. Nar Warrn S....552 H14
ct. Seaford....599 L4
ct. Tecoma....466 D8
dr. Albion....320 F17
dr. Rosebud....700 K3
gr. Brighton East....455 D20
gr. St Kilda E....414 L20
gr. St Kilda E....415 A20
pl. Berwick....553 L5
pl. Point Cook....450 D4
pl. S Melbourne....29 E4
rd. Box Hill....374 H15
rd. Niddrie....279 A20
rd. Niddrie....323 A1
rd. Reservoir....282 D13
st. Balwyn N....373 G8
st. Edithvale....546 F11
st. Hampton E....496 A8
st. Hawthorn....372 A15
st. Pascoe Vale S....324 L6
st. Sydenham....274 J2
st. Thomson....703 F15
CARROL
gr. Mt Waverley....458 F7
st. Reservoir....283 B8
CARROLL
av. Croydon....336 G18
av. Dandenong....536 D5
av. Millgrove....304 G20
cr. Glen Iris....416 D9
cr. Mill Park....242 A7
ct. Greensborough....285 J3
ct. Narre Warren....538 H14
la. Dandenong....535 J10
la. Greenvale....192 F19
rd. Highton....701 G10
rd. Oakleigh S....497 L8
st. Deer Park....318 L16
st. Launching Pl....345 H15
st. N Melbourne....17 A11
st. Richmond....26 C16
st. Woori Yallock....344 B14
CARROLLS
la. N Melbourne....17 A11
rd. Fyansford....701 C7
CARRON
st. Balwyn N....329 J18
st. Coburg....325 F6
CARRONSHORE
cl. Balwyn....373 D14
CARRONVALE
rd. Mooroolbark....337 G18
CARRS
la. N Melbourne....17 A11
CARRUM
cl. Berwick....539 J17
st. Malvern East....457 H7
CARRUM BELLA
dr. Carrum Downs....601 B6
CARRUM WOODS
dr. Carrum Downs....575 C14
CARRUP
pl. Somerville....644 L20
pl. Somerville....645 A19
CARRUTHERS
ct. Altona....409 A16
ct. Altona Mdw....451 D3
ct. Ringwood....378 E20
ct. Thomson....703 H16
CARSHALTON
ct. Hoppers Csg....405 D13
CARSLAKE
av. Blairgowrie....696 C7
CARSON
av. Keysborough....533 K11
av. Mont Albert....374 C13
cr. Hawthorn....371 J18
ct. Rowville....502 K2
ct. Watsonia N....243 F20
ct. Watsonia N....285 F1
la. Roxburgh Pk....194 A14
pl. Melbourne....2 D14
pl. Melbourne....24 D8
rd. Seville....387 B5
st. Dandenong....535 H8
st. Kew....371 E12
st. Mulgrave....500 C3
st. Reservoir....282 K2
CARSONS
rd. Officer....556 J10
CARTER
av. Nunawading....376 J13
av. Werribee....447 J18
cr. Werribee....447 K17
ct. Frankston....628 D3
ct. Portsea....678 A3
dr. Berwick....554 A17
rd. Melton....268 H2
st. Albert Park....29 K15
st. Launching Pl....345 G15
st. Middle Park....29 K15
st. Noble Park....535 B2
st. Sunshine W....364 H4
wy. Dandenong S....550 L5
wy. Dandenong S....551 A5
CARTERS
av. Toorak....415 B6
la. Kangaroo Grnd....248 F17
la. Seville....386 G8
la. Seville....386 J14
CARTHEW
gr. Preston....326 E5
CARTHY
st. Altona North....409 E1
CARTIER
wy. S Morang....198 K12
CARTLEDGE
st. Laverton....407 C16
CARTMELL
st. Heidelberg....328 L7
CARTWRIGHT
st. Oak Park....280 A10
CARUANA
cl. Epping....198 B18
dr. Dingley Village....533 D1
CARVER
st. Burwood E....419 G12
CARVEY
ct. Endeavour Hl....538 A6
dr. Mt Martha....656 J6
CARWARP
st. Macleod....285 A15
CARWEEN
av. Brighton East....455 H13
av. Mitcham....377 A18
av. Upwey....465 K8
CARWELL
ct. Oakleigh S....497 L1
CARY
st. Sunshine N....320 L15
CASABLANCA
ri. Greenvale....237 E5
CASALE
ct. Frankston....628 B12
CASCADE
ct. Montrose....382 H8
ct. Noble Park N....501 E10
dr. Kew East....372 K2
dr. Vermont S....420 F8
dr. Wyndham Va....446 D10
rd. Emerald....469 A19
st. Balwyn N....372 L2
st. Balwyn N....373 A2
st. Frankston....599 G13
st. Oakleigh S....498 A7
wy. Hallam....538 F14
CASCAM
ct. Rowville....463 F13
CASCO
pl. Dingley Village....532 K9
CASDAR
ct. Nar Warrn N....539 C7
CASELLA
st. Mitcham....377 F11
CASERTA
dr. Berwick....540 B20
CASEY
av. Sunbury....143 E6
cl. Springvale S....499 E18
cr. View Bank....285 K17
ct. Clarinda....498 F10
ct. Melton....227 B16
ct. Wantirna....422 F4
dr. Berwick....554 E2
dr. Lalor....241 L10
st. Healesville....258 A8
CASH
cl. Hampton Pk....551 G12
gr. Mt Waverley....458 F7
st. Balwyn N....329 H19
st. Coburg....325 H5
st. Kingsbury....284 A9
CASH FUES
pl. Wantirna....422 A4
CASHIN
ct. Melton....227 B17
CASHINS MILL
pl. Lilydale....338 H10
CASHMERE
cr. Berwick....554 G20
ct. Wyndham Va....446 H9
st. Travancore....324 G18
CASHMORE
ct. Bacchus Msh....221 G16
ct. Bundoora....285 A1
pl. Roxburgh Pk....194 A13
CASINO
ct. Torquay....712 C2
CASLEY
pl. Hoppers Csg....405 B13
CASON
st. Doncaster....330 H17
CASPIAN
pl. Nar Warrn S....552 J20
tce. Williamstown....410 H14
CASS
av. Croydon....336 F19
st. Rosebud....684 D16
CASSAB
mw. Sunbury....142 G7
CASSANDRA
cl. Somerville....644 F13
ct. Ringwood....378 L4
dr. Gladstone Pk....279 B3
CASSAR
pl. Princes Hill....325 J18
CASSAVA
ct. Dingley Village....533 D10
CASSELDEN
pl. Melbourne....24 H2
CASSELL
st. South Yarra....32 K13
st. South Yarra....414 L6
st. Werribee....447 H2
CASSELLS
rd. Research....246 K20
rd. Research....288 K1
rd. Research....289 A1
CASSELS
rd. Brunswick....325 E9
CASSIA
ct. Endeavour Hl....502 L20
ct. Keysborough....534 A15
ct. Mill Park....243 C10
ct. Newcomb....704 D15
ct. St Albans....276 B18
ct. Wantirna....422 B4
gr. Frankston....627 J5
rd. Melton....226 J17
st. Doncaster E....332 E18
st. Doveton....536 H9
st. Notting Hill....459 G12
CASSIN
ct. Dandenong N....502 B13
CASSINIA
av. Ashwood....418 E15
cl. Knoxfield....463 B2
cr. Meadow Ht....237 J2
ct. Delahey....275 C10
ct. Diamond Ck....245 D13
pl. Frankston S....627 G20
rd. Templstw Lr....330 K14
CASSIOBURY
av. Mt Eliza....626 D11
CASSOWARY
av. Werribee....447 K5
cl. Carrum Downs....600 L2
cl. Taylors Lakes....275 G2
st. Doncaster E....375 K4
CASTAWAY
cr. Jan Juc....711 A19
ct. Patterson L....573 G10
ct. Point Cook....451 A13

CASTELLA
ct. Meadow Ht...238 A6
st. Ivanhoe East...328 L17
st. Lilydale...338 E5
CASTILLON
sq. Frankston...628 B9
CASTLE
cl. Eaglemont...328 L9
cl. Glen Waverley...421 A19
ct. Beaconsfield...555 D13
ct. Eltham North...245 C18
rd. N Warrandyte...290 B17
st. Dandenong S...535 L14
st. Eaglemont...328 J9
st. Ferntree Gly...424 B18
st. Williamstown...411 B14
st. Yarraville...366 K16
CASTLEBAR
rd. Malvern East...457 G6
wy. Templestowe...332 A8
CASTLEBURY
pl. Craigieburn...193 L2
CASTLECRAG
cl. Endeavour Hl...537 G3
CASTLEFIELD
sq. Wantirna...422 B10
CASTLEGATE
pl. Berwick...555 A10
CASTLE HILL
dr. Bundoora...243 C13
CASTLEHILL
av. Greenvale...193 F17
ri. Langwarrin...629 H3
CASTLEMAINE
st. Yarraville...367 B14
wy. Caroline Spr...318 F8
CASTLEREAGH
ct. Mt Waverley...418 K12
pl. Watsonia...285 D4
CASTLERIDGE
ct. Nar Warrn S...579 C4
CASTLEROCK
dr. Wyndham Va...446 D7
CASTLES
rd. Bentleigh...496 C6
CASTLETON
ct. Gladstone Pk...237 D17
rd. Herne Hill...701 J2
rd. View Bank...285 J16
CASTLEWELLAN
bvd. Hillside...273 J2
bvd. Hillside...273 K3
CASTLEWOOD
dr. Boronia...424 H14
pl. Templestowe...331 G13
st. Bentleigh E...457 A18
CASTLEY
cr. Braybrook...366 B1
CASTRICUM
pl. Ferntree Gly...423 K17
CASUARINA
av. Boronia...424 J7
av. Torquay...711 G10
cl. Langwarrin...629 J4
cl. Maribyrnong...322 H15
cl. Mornington...656 J3
ct. Hampton Pk...551 C5
ct. Narre Warren...553 D1
ct. Pascoe Vale...280 K10
ct. Sunbury...143 J8
dr. Frankston S...627 F13
rdg. Eltham North...245 G18
tr. Nar Warrn N...504 G19
CASULA
pl. Ringwood N...378 E2
CATALINA
av. Ashburton...417 K17
av. Dromana...686 H5
ct. Eltham...287 D6
ct. Frankston...600 E17
ct. Point Cook...450 A4
dr. Thomastown...240 F14
dr. Tullamarine...236 H19
pl. Melton W...226 C19
st. Heidelberg W...283 L20
CATALPA
pl. Lysterfield...463 K20
st. Doveton...536 J11
CATANI
bvd. Bend of Islands...291 H2
ct. Broadmeadows...237 J14
CATANIA
st. Mentone...530 L8
CATERINA
pl. Carrum Downs...601 F4
CATERPILLAR
dr. Tullamarine...278 L8
CATESBY
cl. Mulgrave...501 K6
ct. Boronia...423 J10

CATHAY
ct. Eltham North...245 F15
la. N Melbourne...17 J20
st. Ferntree Gly...424 L19
st. Ferntree Gly...425 A19
CATHCART
st. Maidstone...366 K1
CATHEDRAL
arc. Melbourne...2 E18
cl. Pakenham...583 L1
pl. E Melbourne...25 A4
CATHERINE
av. Chelsea...547 A18
av. Doncaster E...332 E13
av. Mt Waverley...458 H8
av. Tullamarine...278 G3
ct. Eltham...287 L7
ct. Forest Hill...420 A6
ct. Kilsyth...381 B5
ct. Langwarrin...601 H19
dr. Hillside...274 D5
dr. Hillside...274 E3
pde. Frankston...599 F20
pl. Croydon Hills...335 F15
rd. Bentleigh E...496 H3
rd. Seabrook...450 J4
st. Boronia...424 C10
st. Box Hill...374 K18
st. Canterbury...417 D1
st. Caulfield N...415 H20
st. Coburg N...281 D15
st. Footscray...367 D6
st. Geelong West...702 D3
st. McCrae...684 L13
st. Ringwood...378 B16
st. Southbank...3 A12
st. Southbank...23 L19
wy. Tecoma...466 C14
CATHERINE EDEY
pl. Hampton Pk...552 A12
CATHIE
ct. Narre Warren...539 C19
CATHIES
la. Scoresby...461 L1
la. Wantirna S...421 L16
la.e, Wantirna S...462 A2
CATHRIN
cl. Sunbury...143 C11
CATHY
st. Werribee...448 A11
CATIONS
ct. Altona Mdw...451 C4
CAT JUMP
rd. Donvale...376 H1
CATO
la. Hawthorn E...416 C6
st. Hawthorn E...416 C6
st. Prahran...32 C17
st. Prahran...414 G8
CATON
av. Coburg...326 A6
st. Ferny Creek...465 K3
CATRON
st. Seaford...573 E19
CATTANACH
cr. Werribee...447 L15
CATTERICK
ct. Greenvale...193 C17
CAULFIELD
cr. Roxburgh Pk...194 F14
ct. Narre Warren...553 B9
ct. Wantirna...422 A11
CAULSON
cl. Maribyrnong...322 K16
CAUSON
ct. Noble Park...534 L7
CAVALIER
ct. Epping...198 G16
st. Bentleigh E...457 G17
st. Doncaster E...331 L20
CAVANAGH
rd. Lower Plenty...286 D14
rd. Millgrove...348 B2
rd. Wesburn...347 K8
st. Cheltenham...497 A20
st. Cheltenham...497 B17
CAVE
st. Beaumaris...530 F5
CAVE HILL
rd. Lilydale...338 A7
CAVELL
ct. Beaumaris...530 E6
ct. St Albans...320 F13
st. St Kilda...414 A18
st. Scoresby...462 H5
CAVENDISH
av. Wantirna...422 E14
ct. Endeavour Hl...537 F3
dr. Deer Park...318 L14
dr. Heatherton...497 G14

dr. Point Cook...450 G9
dr. Templstw Lr...330 E9
pl. Brighton...494 K4
pl. South Yarra...32 G16
st. Broadmeadows...237 K14
st. Geelong...702 L5
CAVERSHAM
ct. Nunawading...376 G17
dr. Mornington...656 J3
tce. Lynbrook...551 G17
CAVES
gr. Forest Hill...376 G20
gr. Nunawading...420 G1
CAVESSON
ct. Epping...198 F17
CAVEY
rd. Monbulk...468 L1
rd. Monbulk...469 A1
CAVILL
ct. Vermont S...420 J11
pl. Mt Martha...656 E9
CAWARRA
ct. Doncaster E...331 K15
st. Mornington...656 H3
CAWDOR
av. Pk Orchards...334 B19
CAWKWELL
st. Malvern...416 B12
CAWL
ct. Sunbury...144 F13
CAWLEY
ct. Mill Park...198 G20
ct. Mill Park...242 G1
ct. Wantirna S...462 D3
rd. Yarraville...366 B19
CAWOOD
dr. Sunshine W...364 F10
CAXTON
ct. Kings Park...275 B20
st. Blairgowrie...696 B4
CAYLEYS
rd. Werribee S...488 C17
CAYTRE
cr. N Melbourne...34 G10
CECELIA
dr. Keilor East...321 K5
CECIL
cct. Croydon...379 G7
ct. Mitcham...377 E17
ct. Newcomb...703 L17
ct. S Morang...243 H3
ct. Sydenham...274 K5
ct. Tecoma...466 B8
pl. Prahran...32 D19
pl. Prahran...414 H10
pl. S Melbourne...30 B9
pl. S Melbourne...413 G4
st. Bentleigh E...457 C20
st. Brighton East...455 D18
st. Eltham...287 H7
st. Fitzroy...19 A9
st. Frankston...627 C4
st. Kew...372 F11
st. Sorrento...679 A11
st. Southbank...29 J1
st. Southbank...413 E1
st. S Melbourne...29 J1
st. S Melbourne...413 E1
st. Warburton...349 D4
st. Williamstown...411 F15
st. Wonga Park...336 D7
st. Yarraville...366 K15
CECILIE
ct. Doncaster...374 E2
CECILINA
pl. S Melbourne...30 D4
CECILY
st. Springvale S...533 L6
CEDAR
av. Eltham North...245 H20
cl. Chadstone...458 C6
cl. Deer Park...318 L14
cl. Jan Juc...711 B16
cr. Boronia...424 D17
ct. Altona Mdw...451 K1
ct. Campbellfield...239 F11
ct. Forest Hill...420 G4
ct. Frankston...599 L18
ct. Gisborne...78 K14
ct. Glen Waverley...420 B15
ct. Keysborough...534 F13
ct. Monbulk...468 K2
ct. Oakleigh S...497 L9
ct. Pascoe Vale...280 K11
ct. Werribee...447 E10
dr. Maribyrnong...322 G17
gr. Highton...701 L16
gr. Selby...466 K18
pde. Moolap...704 L16
ri. Warrandyte...332 L8
ri. Warrandyte...333 A8

st. Caulfield S...455 G7
st. Doveton...536 J11
st. Langwarrin...628 K2
st. Mentone...531 F5
st. Thomastown...241 C14
CEDARVIEW
cl. Rowville...463 K17
CEDARWOOD
ct. Mill Park...242 L3
CEDMAR
av. Highton...705 G1
CEDRIC
st. Ivanhoe East...328 G15
st. Mordialloc...531 L14
st. Parkdale...531 K14
CEDUNA
cl. Torquay...712 G1
cl. Wantirna S...422 B16
ct. Doreen...202 B9
ct. Keilor Park...277 L13
CEILTERRE
av. Ringwood N...378 A9
CELEBRATION
ct. Cranbourne W...577 G18
CELESTE
ct. Berwick...553 L5
ct. Chirnside Pk...336 L5
ct. St Kilda E...415 B15
st. Doncaster E...331 J20
CELESTIAL
av. Melbourne...2 G10
av. Melbourne...24 E5
ct. Rowville...463 F16
CELESTINE
pl. Narre Warren...539 D13
CELIA
cl. Yarra Glen...208 L19
cl. Yarra Glen...209 A19
ct. Bangholme...549 H14
ct. Chadstone...458 E4
ct. Doncaster E...332 H8
st. Bentleigh E...496 K6
st. Glen Iris...417 E12
st. Rye...696 L5
CELINA
cl. Whittlesea...96 E17
CELLIBRAND
cl. Seabrook...450 L8
CELTIS
pl. Endeavour Hl...536 K1
CEMALOMA
ct. Highton...705 G2
CEMETERY
la. Bulla...191 A17
rd. Brooklyn...366 B16
rd. Cranbourne...603 L7
rd. Kangaroo Grnd...248 F13
rd. Keilor East...277 K17
rd. Maddingley...263 F3
rd. Pakenham...557 K18
rd. Warrandyte...333 J1
rd. Werribee...448 B11
rd. Yarraville...366 B16
rd.e, Carlton...18 E8
rd.e, Carlton N...18 E8
rd.w, Carlton N...17 L6
rd.w, Parkville...17 L6
tr. Warburton...349 E13
CEMETERY FIRELINE
Warburton...348 K12
Wesburn...348 J12
CENTALLA
grn. Rowville...463 B16
CENTAUR
ct. Bayswater...423 L9
gr. Doncaster E...332 E18
wy. Hoppers Csg...448 G5
CENTAURUS
av. Roxburgh Pk...194 F10
CENTELLA
pl. Launching Pl...345 H13
CENTENARY
av. Kurunjang...226 F14
av. Kurunjang...227 A15
av. Melton...226 F14
av. Melton...227 A15
av. Melton W...226 D14
cr. Werribee...447 F9
ct. Keysborough...535 A11
ct. Kings Park...275 A17
dr. Mill Park...242 J3
dr. Mill Park...243 A4
dr. Port Melb...412 J5
st. Blairgowrie...679 F18
st. Seaford...600 A3
CENTENARY BREAK
Frankston N...600 J11
CENTENNIAL
av. Brunswick W...325 A16
st. W Footscray...366 H10

CENTOFAN
pl. Thomastown...241 J20
CENTRAL
av. Altona Mdw...451 A1
av. Balwyn N...329 G19
av. Bayswater N...379 J13
av. Black Rock...529 H8
av. Blairgowrie...679 E20
av. Boronia...424 B9
av. Box Hill S...374 G19
av. Burwood...418 A8
av. Croydon S...379 J13
av. Dandenong N...501 K15
av. Footscray...367 D6
av. Ivanhoe...328 B16
av. Manifold Ht...702 B5
av. Moorabbin...496 C7
av. Mooroolbark...336 L19
av. Preston...282 L20
av. Seaholme...409 G19
av. Sunshine...365 D8
av. Thomastown...241 A13
av. Torquay...711 L6
bvd. Port Melb...368 B18
dr. Bonbeach...547 E20
gr. Broadmeadows...238 F17
pl. Box Hill...374 J16
rd. Blackburn...375 L16
rd. Hampton Pk...551 E12
rd. Hampton Pk...551 F13
rd. Nunawading...376 C17
CENTRAL PARK
av. Maribyrnong...322 H16
rd. Malvern East...416 C17
CENTRAL PIER
Docklands...368 L15
CENTRE
av. Mt Evelyn...383 C1
av. Port Melb...412 B4
av. Werribee...447 F12
ct. Avondale Ht...322 A7
ct. Burwood...418 J8
ct. Highett...496 G12
ct. Torquay...711 L4
dr. Rye...696 J3
gr. Healesville...213 A16
pl. Melbourne...2 C17
pl. Melbourne...24 E9
rd. Bentleigh...456 A19
rd. Bentleigh E...456 H20
rd. Berwick...553 H15
rd. Brighton East...455 B18
rd. Broadmeadows...238 J16
rd. Carnegie...456 H8
rd. Clarinda...497 H2
rd. Clayton...499 A4
rd. Clayton S...497 H2
rd. Clayton S...499 A4
rd. Hallam...552 A3
rd. Hampton Pk...552 A3
rd. Langwarrin...602 A20
rd. Langwarrin...629 L8
rd. Melb Airport...235 J12
rd. Menzies Ck...467 L16
rd. Monbulk...428 E19
rd. Narre Warren...552 F4
rd. Narre Warren...552 L11
rd. Nar Warrn S...553 A14
rd. Oakleigh S...497 H2
rd. Olinda...383 K19
rd. Scoresby...462 G11
rd. Springvale...499 A4
rd. Upwey...466 A17
rd. Vermont...421 H3
rd. Yellingbo...387 H9
st. Reservoir...283 A12
st. Sunshine...365 E2
st. Seddon, off Windsor St...367 C10
wy. Balwyn N...373 L3
wy. Croydon S...380 F12
wy. Glenroy...279 G6
CENTRE DANDENONG
rd. Cheltenham...496 K20
rd. Dingley Village...533 A5
rd. Heatherton...531 L2
rd. Moorabbin Aprt...531 L2
CENTRE KIRKHAM
rd. Dandenong S...535 E13
CENTREWAY
Bundoora...284 F11
Keilor East...278 D18
Mordialloc...531 K19
Mt Waverley...459 G7
arc. Melbourne...2 C16
CENTURION
ct. Epping...197 K17
CENTURY
dr. Braeside...532 F17
dr. Mt Martha...657 E10
CERAM
ct. Heidelberg W...284 D20

CERBERUS
cr. Williamstn N 410 L13
rd. Baxter 644 A2
st. Donvale 376 E6
CERCIS
ct. Doveton 536 F13
CERES
ct. Meadow Ht 237 L7
st. Rosebud 700 L4
CERISE
ct. Clarinda 498 E10
pl. Mulgrave 501 H6
CERNAN
ct. Whittington 704 D20
CERUTTY
wy. Wantirna S 462 E3
CERVARA
st. Mentone 531 E6
CESUNA
ct. Deer Park 319 D15
CEYLON
st. Nunawading 376 D15
CEZANNE
cr. Wheelers Hill 460 K14
CHABLIS
cl. Croydon 335 E20
cr. Vermont S 421 C9
CHADACRE
pl. Mornington 656 K3
CHADBOURN
pl. Nar Warrn S 552 G19
CHADDESLEY
av. St Kilda E 415 B18
CHADREE
ct. Dingley Village 533 E9
ct. Highton 705 J5
CHADSTONE
rd. Malvern East 457 F5
CHADWELL
gr. Chelsea 545 E12
la. Chelsea, off Chadwell Gr 545 E12
pl. Kings Park 319 A1
CHADWICK
cl. Langwarrin 629 A9
la. Attwood 237 A11
pl. Vermont S 421 C7
rd. Harkaway 540 J5
rd. Harkaway 541 A5
st. Newtown 702 F8
CHAFFER
rd. Chum Creek 212 K11
CHAFFEY
st. Thomastown 240 K19
CHAFFMILL
cl. Sydenham 275 A5
CHAGALL
ct. Scoresby 462 C8
CHAIM
ct. Donvale 377 H8
CHAIN
ct. Nar Warrn S 578 K3
CHALCOT
dr. Endeavour Hl 537 B2
CHALDRON
pl. Dingley Village 533 A2
CHALET
rd. Badger Creek 258 E10
rd. Olinda 427 C9
CHALEYER
st. Glen Iris 417 H13
st. Reservoir 283 E15
CHALICE
ct. Wantirna 422 C14
CHALLAMBRA
cr. Highton 701 H13
CHALLENGE
ct. Frankston 628 F8
CHALLENGER
ct. Chelsea Ht 547 D12
st. Diamond Ck 245 F13
CHALLIS
ct. Rosebud 699 J2
st. Newport 410 G10
CHALLOTE
ct. Keilor Lodge 275 L3
CHALMERS
av. Sandringham 494 L14
av. Sandringham 495 A14
gr. Ferntree Gly 464 G9
gr. Up Fntree Gly 464 G9
pl. Taylors Lakes 233 C17
st. McKinnon 456 E15
CHALON
av. Templstw Lr 331 A12
pl. S Morang 198 J13

CHAMBERLAIN
dr. Kilsyth S 380 K19
st. Ashburton 417 C17
CHAMBERLAINS
la. Sandringham, off Station St 495 A13
CHAMBERLIN
ct. Blackburn S 419 K6
CHAMBERS
ct. Darley 221 E1
rd. Altona North 409 G8
st. Brunswick 325 J18
st. Coburg 325 H4
st. Footscray 367 F8
st. South Yarra 32 D10
st. South Yarra 414 H5
CHAMNEY
pl. Roxburgh Pk 194 C12
CHAMOUNI
ct. Frankston 628 C10
st. Alphington 327 L19
CHAMP
st. Coburg 281 H19
CHAMPAGNE
ri. Chirnside Pk 336 K3
CHAMPION
cr. Bundoora 285 D1
cr. Glen Waverley 421 A18
rd. Newport 410 H10
rd. Williamstn N 410 J11
st. Black Rock 529 H5
st. Blairgowrie 695 K3
st. Brighton 494 L4
st. Brighton 495 A4
st. Doncaster E 331 J20
CHANAK
st. Malvern East 416 B19
CHANCELLOR
dr. Wheelers Hill 460 K19
pl. Highton 701 F20
rd. Airport W 278 J16
CHANDLER
gr. Burwood 418 D12
hwy. Alphington 371 G1
hwy. Kew 371 G1
rd. Boronia 424 D12
rd. Glen Waverley 420 H19
rd. Gruyere 298 F20
rd. Gruyere 342 F6
rd. Keysborough 534 L15
rd. Noble Park 534 L11
st. Blackburn S 419 G1
st. Keilor East 322 D5
st. Parkdale 531 J11
st. Sunshine W 364 C2
st. Williamstown 411 C11
CHANDLERS
la. Kilsyth S 425 C4
rd. Malvern 415 K16
CHANDON
ct. Waurn Ponds 705 C17
CHANDOR
ct. Notting Hill 459 H14
CHANDOS
pl. Attwood 236 L10
pl. Langwarrin 601 F19
st. Cheltenham 496 D17
st. Coburg 325 E5
st. Sydenham 232 J20
CHANDRA
av. Kilsyth S 380 K18
CHANELLE
ct. Springvale S 534 C4
CHANNEL
cr. Blind Bight 650 C8
rd. Mt Evelyn 339 A19
rd. Silvan 384 F9
st. Mornington 640 L11
tr. Lysterfield S 503 D13
wk. Lysterfield S 503 B11
CHANNELLE
cl. Hampton Pk 551 H4
CHANTAL
cl. Thomastown 240 K16
CHANTELL
av. Endeavour Hl 537 K3
CHANTELLE
ct. Skye 575 H19
ri. St Helena 244 L20
ri. St Helena 245 A20
CHANTILLY
av. Avondale Ht 322 C9
ct. Frankston 628 C8
la. Craigieburn 150 B19
st. Mt Waverley 458 J8
CHAPARRAL
ct. Mooroolbark 337 D10
CHAPEAU
tce. Mt Martha 669 G5

CHAPEL
ct. Doncaster 331 E19
la. Nutfield 202 H1
rd. Keysborough 548 B4
rd. Moorabbin 496 F11
st. Blackburn 375 K14
st. Brunswick 325 G15
st. Cremorne 26 D18
st. Fitzroy 19 D14
st. Glen Waverley 420 H18
st. Lilydale 338 E5
st. Prahran 32 C20
st. Prahran 414 G11
st. St Kilda 414 F17
st. South Yarra 32 C20
st. South Yarra 414 H8
st. Windsor 414 G11
CHAPLIN
ct. Templestowe 331 L6
CHAPMAN
av. Glenroy 279 J6
av. Seaford 599 C2
av. Thomastown 241 K15
bvd. Glen Waverley 461 A5
st. Mooroolbark 337 J20
la. N Melbourne 17 C12
rd. Silvan 385 B14
st. Blackburn N 375 G7
st. Brighton East 495 C4
st. Carrum Downs 575 C15
st. Diamond Ck 246 C12
st. Macleod 285 A16
st. Malvern East 457 G4
st. N Melbourne 17 B11
st. Seddon 367 B12
st. Sunshine 365 B6
st. Oakleigh, off Palmerston Gr 457 K10
CHAPPELL
ct. Sunbury 142 G14
dr. Wantirna S 462 F2
dr. Watsonia N 243 D18
pl. Keilor East 322 C1
rtn. Meadow Ht 237 H6
st. Thomastown 241 A12
CHAPROWE
ct. Cheltenham 496 K18
CHAPTER HOUSE
la. Melbourne 2 G19
la. Melbourne 24 F9
CHARDONNAY
cr. Chirnside Pk 336 K4
ct. Waurn Ponds 705 D15
dr. Mt Martha 657 B8
dr. Skye 601 G1
CHARINGA
dr. Werribee 446 K15
CHARING CROSS
pl. Narre Warren 539 C14
pl. Wyndham Va 446 F9
CHARL
cl. Nar Warrn N 539 B10
CHARLBER
la. St Andrews 204 H1
CHARLBURY
gr. St Albans 275 G18
CHARLEMONT
la. Olinda 426 L8
CHARLES
av. Hallam 537 E15
av. Springvale 500 F7
ct. Gisborne 78 J16
ct. Melton S 268 J4
ct. Sydenham 275 B6
ct. Wandin East 384 L4
ct. Wandin East 385 A4
ct. Wantirna S 422 D17
ct. Warranwood 334 K14
dr. Pearcedale 646 K6
la. Torquay 711 K10
pde. Wesburn 348 C18
pl. Fitzroy 19 F17
rd. Altona 408 K13
rd. Lilydale 382 G3
st. Abbotsford 26 C3
st. Anglesea 713 E6
st. Ascot Vale 323 G20
st. Belmont 706 F4
st. Bentleigh E 456 J19
st. Blairgowrie 679 K19
st. Brighton East 455 E13
st. Brunswick 325 G16
st. Carlton 18 J10
st. Cheltenham 530 L3
st. Coburg N 281 B17
st. Dandenong 535 L3
st. Dromana 686 B6
st. E Melbourne 25 E10
st. Elsternwick 455 C4
st. Fitzroy 19 D17
st. Glen Iris 417 K10
st. Greensborough 286 A7
st. Hadfield 280 K7
st. Hampton 495 C9
st. Hawthorn 371 J16
st. Kew 371 L11
st. Kew 371 L13
st. Kew 372 A11
st. Kilsyth 381 D6
st. Lower Plenty 286 K15
st. McCrae 685 A12
st. Mooroolbark 337 A19
st. Mornington 640 C19
st. Mt Waverley 419 D19
st. Newcomb 703 L13
st. Northcote 326 F17
st. Northcote 326 G17
st. Nunawading 376 G10
st. Pakenham 584 L9
st. Prahran 31 L19
st. Prahran 414 F10
st. Preston 282 D19
st. Richmond 26 H17
st. Ringwood E 378 L8
st. Ringwood E 379 A8
st. Rye 697 B5
st. St Albans 276 A20
st. St Kilda 414 D15
st. Seaford 599 E1
st. Seddon 367 A11
st. Selby 467 C15
st. S Melbourne 30 A3
st. Sunshine N 321 C17
st. Surrey Hills 374 F18
st. Thomastown 241 D15
st. Werribee 448 A15
st. Williamstown 411 D15
CHARLES CONDER
pl. Berwick 554 J18
CHARLES FARRER
ct. Mornington 656 J2
CHARLES GREEN
av. Endeavour Hl 537 B7
CHARLES GRIMES
pl. Seabrook 450 L7
CHARLES GRIMES BRIDGE
rd. Docklands 23 C16
CHARLES SMITH
dr. Wonga Park 335 G11
CHARLES STURT
dr. Doreen 201 H10
CHARLES SWANSTON
wy. Seabrook 450 L7
CHARLESVILLE
rd. Plenty 244 B2
CHARLES WILSON
cl. Eltham North 245 F17
CHARLESWORTH
bvd. Burnside 318 E6
pl. Mitcham 377 E9
st. Laverton 407 E15
st. McCrae 685 C11
CHARLEVILLE
ct. Carrum Downs 601 C4
CHARLNET
dr. Vermont S 420 J12
CHARLOTTE
av. Melton W 226 B13
av. Newcomb 704 A16
ct. Cranbourne W 603 G2
ct. Frankston S 627 H14
ct. N Warrandyte 289 L14
pl. St Kilda 414 G13
rd. Beaumaris 530 C7
rd. Boronia 423 C14
rd. Mill Park 242 C3
st. Blackburn S 375 H20
st. Blackburn S 419 H2
st. Brighton East 455 G19
st. Clayton S 498 K7
st. Collingwood 19 K11
st. Glenroy 280 B10
st. Glen Waverley 460 E1
st. Newport 410 E6
st. Richmond 26 G16
st. Springvale S 533 K5
st. Sunshine W 363 L4
st. Yarraville 366 F14
CHARLTON
av. Cheltenham 496 C19
bvd. Darley 222 C5
ct. Reservoir 283 F11
ct. Endeavour Hl 537 K9
ct. Portsea 677 L1
ct. Wantirna S 462 F3
pl. Frankston 627 B4
pl. Point Cook 450 F7
pl. Thomastown 240 E13
rd. Eaglemont 328 G11
st. Bentleigh 495 L1
st. Blackburn N 375 K9
st. Broadmeadows 238 F16
st. Mt Waverley 459 A3
st. Springvale 500 D6
CHARLTONIAN
cl. Bacchus Msh 221 E18
CHARLWOOD
ct. Donvale 376 H1
dr. Mooroolbark 337 L20
CHARM
ct. Mt Martha 669 G4
CHARMAINE
av. Avondale Ht 322 C9
pl. Melton W 226 C17
st. Dromana 686 A9
CHARMAN
av. Emerald 469 F17
rd. Beaumaris 530 H9
rd. Cheltenham 496 J20
rd. Mentone 530 H9
CHARMIAN
cl. Ivanhoe 328 F10
CHARMING
st. Hampton E 495 L7
CHARNFIELD
cr. Noble Park 534 L5
ct. Thomastown 241 E18
CHARNWOOD
cr. St Kilda 414 E14
ct. Narre Warren 552 K1
gr. St Kilda 414 E14
la. Cheltenham 496 L15
rd. St Kilda 414 D13
CHAROLAIS
ct. Belmont 706 B7
CHARON
ct. Frankston 600 D18
CHARTER
cl. Berwick 553 D4
rd. Sunbury 142 J12
rd.e, Sunbury 142 K12
rd.w, Sunbury 142 F12
st. Ringwood 378 B12
CHARTERIS
dr. Ivanhoe East 328 J16
rd. Wandin East 386 A12
CHARTWELL
dr. Wantirna 422 J9
CHASE
la. Woori Yallock 344 L17
rd. Kangaroo Grnd 289 L10
CHASE VIEW
ct. Kangaroo Grnd 290 B8
CHASTA
cr. Mitcham 377 F17
CHASTLETON
av. Toorak 415 C2
CHAT
pl. Werribee 448 C6
CHATEAU
av. Narre Warren 552 J1
cl. Croydon 335 E20
ct. Thomastown 240 E14
gr. Beaumaris 530 G9
ri. Bulleen 329 H9
CHATEAUX
cl. Mt Martha 657 B8
CHATFIELD
av. Balwyn 373 A13
av. Rosebud W 683 D19
st. Kingsville 366 J13
CHATHAM
av. Ferntree Gly 424 G19
pl. Kings Park 319 C1
rd. Canterbury 373 H17
st. Flemington 324 D20
st. Footscray 367 C5
st. Prahran 32 C17
st. Prahran 414 G9
CHATSWOOD
av. Langwarrin 601 B20
cl. Glen Waverley 420 J18
dr. Anglesea 713 D2
dr. Nar Warrn S 578 F3
gr. Chirnside Pk 336 H6
pl. Wyndham Va 446 E8
CHATSWORTH
av. Ardeer 320 C18
av. Brighton 454 F11
cl. Cheltenham 496 K13
ct. Officer 555 J20
ct. Rowville 503 E4
ct. Springvale S 499 F20
qd. Templstw Lr 330 B10
rd. Prahran 415 A11
CHATTAN
ct. Greenvale 237 E1
CHATTERLEY
ct. Frankston 628 E5
dr. Noble Park N 501 C12

CHATTERTON
dr. Delahey 275 E11

CHAUCER
av. Frankston 600 C19
av. Malvern East 456 K2
cl. Delahey 275 C16
cr. Bundoora 242 J20
cr. Canterbury 373 C17
st. Blairgowrie 680 A20
st. Box Hill S 418 G2
st. Moonee Pnd 324 B14
st. Mooroolbark 337 G20
st. St Kilda 414 B18

CHAUMONT
dr. Avondale Ht 322 B8

CHAUNCY
wy. Lynbrook 551 E17

CHAUNDY
rd. Belgrave S 506 B4
st. Ferntree Gly 464 G3

CHAUVEL
pl. S Morang 198 K15
st. Ascot Vale 323 J20
st. Bentleigh E 457 G16
st. Heidelberg Ht 328 G2
st. Melton S 268 J11
st. Reservoir 282 H5

CHAVASSE
st. Brighton 454 H18

CHAVE
ct. Laverton 407 D14

CHEADLE
cr. Bundoora 243 D20

CHEAM
st. Dandenong N 502 C18
wk. Highton 701 H15

CHEASLEY
pl. Altona Mdw 452 A5

CHEDDAR
rd. Reservoir 283 D4
rd.e, Reservoir 283 B8
rd.w, Reservoir 283 B7

CHEDGEY
dr. St Albans 320 E9

CHEDWORTH
ct. Kilsyth S 424 L2

CHEEL
st. Armadale 415 E12
st. Oakleigh E 458 D10

CHEESEMAN
av. Brighton East 455 F15
st. Croydon 336 H18

CHEEVERS
cl. Ringwood E 379 C15

CHEFFERS
st. Moonee Pnd 323 G12

CHEFS
la. Braeside 532 F14

CHELBARA
ct. Chelsea 547 A15

CHELEON
wy. Kings Park 275 B20

CHELMSFORD
av. Newtown 701 J4
av. Templestowe 331 G14
cr. St Albans 320 G6
ct. Craigieburn 194 A1
ct. Ferntree Gly 463 H9
pl. Seabrook 450 L3
st. Balwyn N 373 H4
st. Kensington 34 B12
st. Williamstn N 410 C11
wy. Melton W 226 E18

CHELSEA
av. Mulgrave 501 E7
cl. Wyndham Va 446 E8
cr. Berwick 539 J17
ct. Thomastown 240 D16
ct. Wantirna 422 F8
mw. Mont Albert N 374 F7
rd. Chelsea 546 K18
st. Brighton 454 F16
st. Cheltenham 496 L16

CHELSEA PARK
dr. Chelsea Ht 547 E16

CHELSEY
st. Ardeer 320 B18

CHELSWORTH PARK
la. Lilydale 338 K1
la. Lilydale 339 C5

CHELTENHAM
rd. Black Rock 529 G1
rd. Cheltenham 529 G1
rd. Dandenong 535 B12
rd. Dandenong 535 D11
rd. Dandenong S 535 D11
rd. Keysborough 533 L11
rd. Newcomb 703 L13

CHEMISTRY
dr. Bundoora, off Science Dr 284 C12

CHENIER
st. Rye 696 F8

CHENIES
st. Reservoir 283 H8

CHENIN
mw. Waurn Ponds 705 F13

CHEONG
cl. Carlton N 18 H4
st. Croydon 379 E9
st. Ringwood E 379 E9

CHEPSTOW
ct. Noble Park N 501 C8

CHEQUERS
cl. Wantirna 422 D14
ct. Chirnside Pk 337 H3

CHER
av. Bundoora 242 D20

CHERBOURG
av. Beaumaris 530 F4
ct. Frankston 628 C8

CHERELLE
ct. Eltham North 245 C16

CHERIE
st. Tullamarine 278 H4

CHERITON
ct. Burwood E 419 L11
dr. Mooroolbark 337 H11

CHERRILL
st. Burnley 371 B20

CHERRINGTON
ct. Parkdale 531 J13
sq. Wantirna 422 J12

CHERRY
av. Altona North 409 H3
av. Bayswater 422 J4
cl. Somerville 645 B20
cr. Braybrook 366 B1
ct. Darley 222 B10
ct. Keysborough 534 E13
ct. Lalor 241 G7
ct. Meadow Ht 193 L17
ct. Mitcham 377 D11
gr. Donvale 377 B7
gr. Doveton 536 L12
la. Gisborne 78 K7
la. Laverton N 407 K7
la. Lysterfield S 504 D15
la. Wandin East 385 H4
rd. Avonsleigh 470 E9
rd. Balwyn 373 E13
rd. Gisborne 79 A8
rd. Macclesfield 470 E9
st. Glen Waverley 419 K15
st. Macleod 284 J13
st. Pearcedale 646 K2
st. Werribee 447 K14

CHERRY BLOSSOM
cl. Craigieburn 150 B13
ct. Doncaster E 332 D11
la. Mornington 641 B11

CHERRYBROOK
cl. Nunawading 376 K13
wk. Nunawading 376 K13

CHERRY HILL
wy. Chirnside Pk 293 G20

CHERRY HILLS
ct. Sunbury 144 C11
dr. Cranbourne 603 H6

CHERRYHINTON
st. Box Hill 375 A18

CHERRY ORCHARD
ri. Box Hill N 375 D6

CHERRYPLUM
ct. Cranbourne N 578 C8

CHERRY TREE
ct. Doncaster E 376 D5
gr. Croydon 335 F19
la. Narre Warren 539 E20
la. Narre Warren 553 E1
rd. Hurstbridge 203 F14
rd. Panton Hill 204 A16
ri. Knoxfield 463 C3

CHERRYTREE
la. Box Hill S 419 B6

CHERRYWOOD
ct. Bundoora 284 G5

CHERSTON
ct. Thomastown 240 H11

CHERTSEY
st. Surrey Hills 373 L15

CHERUB
ct. Taylors Lakes 275 H6

CHERWELL
av. Glenroy 279 J4

CHERYL
cr. Belmont 706 F5
cr. Ferntree Gly 463 E7
ct. Hampton Pk 551 K13
gr. View Bank 285 F20
st. Forest Hill 420 G5
st. Kilsyth 381 A9
st. Melton S 268 H9

CHERYLNNE
cr. Kilsyth 381 E8

CHESHIRE
av. Melton S 268 J4
ct. Wantirna 422 H10
pl. Nar Warrn S 579 B3

CHESHUNT
ct. Cranbourne N 578 B8
dr. Hallam 552 A1
st. Pt Lonsdale 710 F5

CHESNEY
ct. Gladstone Pk 279 C2
ct. Thomastown 240 D14
dr. Ringwood 379 C1
rd. Melton 226 G18
st. Keysborough 534 G9

CHESSELL
st. Mont Albert N 374 F5
st. Southbank 3 A15
st. Southbank 23 L20
st. Southbank 29 L1

CHESSY PARK
dr. New Gisborne 79 B2

CHESTER
cl. Greenvale 192 K17
cl. Point Cook 450 J8
cr. Deer Park 318 K8
ct. Endeavour Hl 537 D2
ct. Epping 197 L17
ct. Fawkner 281 H10
ct. Noble Park N 501 C8
ct. Wyndham Va 446 H13
dr. Hampton Pk 551 F12
la. Melbourne 24 J8
pl. Bundoora 284 L1
rd. Altona 408 D16
st. Bentleigh E 497 B1
st. Glen Iris 417 L9
st. Glen Waverley 420 C19
st. Lilydale 294 A19
st. Moonee Pnd 323 L13
st. Newtown 701 K4
st. Oakleigh 457 K11
st. Surrey Hills 418 B1

CHESTERFIELD
av. Malvern 415 L7
ct. Newtown 701 L9
ct. Wantirna 422 G11
dr. Nar Warrn S 578 E2
dr. Wyndham Va 446 E8
rd. Somerville 645 B19

CHESTERTON
rd. Altona Mdw 451 D5

CHESTERVILLE
dr. Bentleigh E 497 A2
dr. Point Cook 449 K6
dr. Point Cook 449 L6
rd. Bentleigh E 496 L6
rd. Cheltenham 496 J18
rd. Glen Waverley 420 B17
rd. Highett 496 J18
rd. Moorabbin 496 J18

CHESTFIELD
ct. Frankston 599 K16

CHESTNUT
av. Ferntree Gly 424 J17
ct. Dingley Village 532 H3
ct. Doncaster E 332 D11
ct. Montrose 381 L8
ct. Wheelers Hill 460 F15
dr. St Albans 320 E8
pl. Chadstone 458 C5
rd. Doveton 536 H12
rd. Mill Park 242 D10
st. Campbellfield 239 E13
st. Carnegie 456 K5
st. Cremorne 26 D20
st. Cremorne 32 D1
st. Surrey Hills 418 F2
wy. Sunbury 143 K17

CHETWYN
ct. Frankston S 627 A18
dr. Kings Park 319 B2

CHETWYND
st. N Melbourne 17 E20
st. W Melbourne 23 E1

CHEVAL
ct. Lower Plenty 286 J15

CHEVALIER
cr. Mooroolbark 337 E10
pl. Frankston 628 F2

CHEVERTON
rd. Lower Plenty 286 G14

CHEVIOT
av. Berwick 554 C15
av. Coldstream 295 E13
cl. Wantirna 422 J6
ct. Melton W 226 A20
rd. Campbellfield 239 E18
rd. Keysborough 534 K10
rd. Mt Waverley 418 L19
rd. Portsea 677 K6

CHEVRON
av. Cranbourne S 602 L12
av. Cranbourne S 603 A12
ct. Jan Juc 711 B19
ct. Seaford 573 B12

CHEVY
ch. Seabrook 450 L3

CHEWTON
st. Braybrook 322 D18
st. Maidstone 322 D18

CHIAM
ct. Langwarrin 600 K18

CHIARA
ct. Glen Waverley 459 H5

CHIARELLA
pl. Altona Mdw 451 F7

CHICAGO
st. Maribyrnong 323 A13

CHICHESTER
dr. Taylors Lakes 275 H6
sq. Wantirna 422 F8

CHICKWEED
st. Newtown 702 G10

CHICOLA
cl. Sunbury 143 D4

CHICQUITA
av. Seaford 599 K3
cl. Keilor Dn 275 L15
ct. Bacchus Msh 221 E16
pl. Mill Park 242 K10

CHIFLEY
av. Altona 409 E17
av. Glenroy 280 C7
cr. Dandenong N 501 J20
ct. Dingley Village 533 B7
ct. Sunbury 143 H4
dr. Maribyrnong 323 B12
dr. Moorabbin Aprt 532 E4
dr. Preston 327 J4
pde. Ringwood N 378 B3
st. Lalor 241 E6

CHILCOTE
av. Malvern 415 L11
ct. Box Hill S 418 H4

CHILDERS
cr. Coolaroo 238 D6
ct. Wyndham Va 446 F13
rd. Malvern 416 B17
st. Cranbourne 604 E4
st. Kensington 33 E14
st. Kew 372 C6
st. Mentone 531 C8

CHILDS
pl. Roxburgh Pk 193 L16
rd. Epping 241 E5
rd. Kalorama 383 D11
rd. Lalor 240 L4
rd. Lalor 241 A4
rd. Lalor 241 E5
rd. Mill Park 242 A6
rd. Sunbury 114 B1
ri. Endeavour Hl 537 E9
st. Melton S 268 E5

CHILE
st. Frankston N 600 A7

CHILLER
ct. Grovedale 705 K17

CHILTERN
ct. Berwick 554 D3
ct. Doncaster E 331 H16
ct. Rowville 502 L8
ct. Rowville 503 A8
ct. Seabrook 450 L3
ri. Langwarrin 629 D12
st. Broadmeadows 238 E14

CHILTERNS
ct. Kealba 276 K20

CHILWELL
ct. Meadow Ht 238 B6

CHINDWIN
pl. Roxburgh Pk 194 F5

CHINGFORD
st. Alphington 327 G14
st. Fairfield 327 F14

CHINNOCK
ct. Craigieburn 150 B18
la. Kensington 33 E9

CHINOOK
cr. Mooroolbark 337 C9
ct. Point Cook 450 E6

CHIPP
ct. Dingley Village 533 A6

CHIPPENDALE
ct. Chirnside Pk 337 F2
ct. Templestowe 331 F13
tce. Burwood E 420 C13

CHIPPEWA
av. Donvale 377 C8

CHIPPING HILL
ct. Wheelers Hill 461 D15

CHIRCOP
cl. Sydenham 274 H4

CHIRNSIDE
av. Werribee 447 L18
cr. Laverton 407 F11
dr. Chirnside Pk 337 D4
rd. Berwick 554 G17
st. Kingsville 366 L13
wk. Berwick 554 D17

CHISHOLM
av. Attwood 237 D10
cl. Gladstone Pk 236 L16
cl. Gladstone Pk 237 A16
cl. Wandana Ht 705 D2
ct. Cranbourne 603 L1
ct. Croydon N 336 D14
ct. Diamond Ck 246 A13
ct. Mill Park 243 A5
ct. Springvale S 499 E18
dr. Caroline Spr 318 C8
dr. Caroline Spr 318 E10
dr. Caroline Spr 318 E9
pl. Melbourne 1 D7
pl. Melbourne 23 J6
pl. Wyndham Va 446 D7
st. Aberfeldie 323 D10

CHISLEHURST
ct. Nar Warrn S 552 H19
rd. Hampton 495 G8

CHISWICK
ct. Endeavour Hl 537 C1
ct. Hampton Pk 551 D5
ct. Pt Lonsdale 707 F18
ct. Rowville 503 G1
ct. Tarneit 405 D12
ct. Templestowe 331 F15
ct. Wantirna 422 E15

CHITRAL
pl. Eltham North 245 G15

CHITTENUP
bnd. Sydenham 274 K8

CHIVALRY
av. Glen Waverley 420 K15

CHIVELL
cl. Endeavour Hl 537 K4

CHIVERS
av. Glen Waverley 459 K8
ct. Dingley Village 533 F10
ct. Warranwood 334 L13
rd. Templestowe 331 G8

CHLOE
cl. Kilsyth S 381 A19
ct. Cranbourne W 577 F17

CHLORIS
cr. Caulfield 455 J6

CHOMLEY
st. Cranbourne 577 K18
st. Prahran 414 L13
st. Prahran 415 A13

CHOPIN
dr. Langwarrin 629 J6

CHORLEY
av. Altona 408 L14
pl. Kings Park 319 B2

CHOSEN
av. Upwey 465 L11

CHOWNE
st. Lalor 241 D9

CHRIS
ct. Aspendale Gdn 546 L5
ct. Cranbourne W 577 K14
ct. Hillside 274 G4
ct. Oak Park 279 G10

CHRISTA
av. Burwood E 419 L9
ct. Lilydale 338 L12

CHRISTEN
ct. Hoppers Csg 448 J7

CHRISTENSEN
st. Cheltenham 497 A14

CHRISTIAN
ct. Rowville 503 A6
gr. Kallista 467 E4
rd. Cottles Br 203 C10
rd. Hurstbridge 203 C10

CHRISTIANS
av. Emerald 470 D16

CHRISTIE
av. Mill Park 242 L5
av. Mill Park 243 A5
ct. Wandana Ht 701 B18

pde. Healesville.........213 G16
st. Deer Park..........319 C17
st. Knoxfield...........462 K8
CHRISTINA
cl. Wheelers Hill.....461 E12
cr. Kurunjang..........227 D10
ct. Avondale Ht.......322 B17
st. Burwood...........418 L7
st. Narre Warren.....538 L14
tce. Dingley Village...533 A4
CHRISTINE
av. Berwick............554 C3
av. Eltham..............288 B7
cr. Richmond...........371 D13
ct. Doncaster..........330 E17
ct. Heathmont..........378 E19
ct. Noble Park.........534 D1
ct. Seaford.............600 B1
pl. Cranbourne N.....577 K6
st. Blackburn S........419 D5
st. Cranbourne........577 L18
st. Millgrove...........304 G19
st. Rye...................696 G11
st. View Bank..........285 H20
CHRISTMAS
st. Alphington.........327 F13
st. Fairfield............327 F13
st. Northcote...........327 A12
CHRISTOPHER
av. The Basin..........425 A10
cl. Pakenham..........559 F19
cr. Melton..............268 G1
cr. Tullamarine........278 H4
ct. Clarinda............498 D7
ct. Hallam..............537 J14
ct. Rye..................698 A6
dr. Frankston S........627 G15
st. Springvale.........499 G14
CHRISTOWEL
st. Camberwell........417 A4
CHRYSLER
ct. Keilor Dn...........276 C13
CHRYSTOBEL
cr. Hawthorn...........371 K15
ct. Coldstream........295 E15
CHUBUT
wy. Roxburgh Pk......194 D6
CHUDLEIGH
cr. Sassafras..........426 F12
CHUM CREEK
rd. Chum Creek.......213 B12
rd. Healesville.........213 B12
CHUMMIE
pl. Carlton...............18 E16
CHUNAR
gr. McCrae.............684 L16
CHURCH
av. Taylors Hill.........274 E9
cr. Cockatoo...........511 B3
hill, Carrum Downs...574 H15
la. Melbourne.............1 C15
la. Melbourne...........23 K10
rd. Carrum.............573 C10
rd. Cottles Br...........204 B8
rd. Doncaster...........375 D4
rd. Keysborough.......534 D15
rd. Menzies Ck.........468 B17
rd. Panton Hill.........204 B8
rd. Templestowe.......331 E15
rd. Woori Yallock......344 A18
sq. St Kilda.............414 A16
st. Abbotsford...........26 H3
st. Bayswater..........423 F2
st. Beaumaris..........530 F6
st. Belmont.............702 G19
st. Berwick.............554 H8
st. Brighton............454 H17
st. Brunswick..........325 K12
st. Burwood............418 A9
st. Campbellfield.....239 D12
st. Canterbury.........373 G19
st. Carlton...............18 B15
st. Clematis............509 C3
st. Coburg..............281 H20
st. Cremorne.............32 E3
st. Cremorne...........414 H1
st. Emerald.............509 C3
st. Epping...............197 E19
st. Fitzroy N..............19 B4
st. Flemington............34 B1
st. Flemington..........324 G20
st. Greensborough...286 A4
st. Grovedale...........706 A11
st. Hawthorn...........371 E16
st. Healesville..........213 H19
st. Kallista..............467 B2
st. Keilor.................277 B13
st. Kilsyth...............381 B7
st. Maidstone...........366 J5
st. Melbourne..............1 C13
st. Melbourne............23 K9
st. Melton...............226 J18
st. Mitcham............377 D14
st. Parkville..............34 H4
st. Port Melb...........412 J6
st. Reservoir...........283 A3
st. Richmond.............32 E3
st. Richmond...........414 H1
st. S Melbourne.........30 A7
st. The Basin...........425 C11
st. Toorak...............415 H9
st. Werribee............447 G18
st. W Footscray.......366 J5
st. Whittlesea............96 E19
st. Bacchus Msh, off Gisborne Rd.......222 A17
CHURCHER
ct. Mt Waverley.......458 F8
CHURCHILL
av. Ascot Vale..........324 A19
av. Braybrook..........366 A2
av. Chadstone..........458 E6
av. Cheltenham........496 G19
av. Maidstone..........366 E1
av. Newtown............702 B7
av. Reservoir...........239 L20
av. Tullamarine........278 F4
cl. Murrumbeena.....456 L13
ct. Brighton East.....495 E4
ct. Dandenong N.....502 C11
ct. Noble Park N.....501 B12
dr. Ferny Creek.......425 F19
dr. Mooroolbark.......337 G10
dr. Tremont.............425 F19
gr. Hawthorn...........372 A14
pl. Maidstone..........366 D2
rd. Croydon.............336 K18
rd. Mt Martha..........669 B8
st. Doncaster E.......376 A1
st. Glenroy.............280 A4
st. Heidelberg Ht.....328 H3
st. Kew..................372 D6
st. Mont Albert........374 E15
st. Ringwood...........378 B11
st. Williamstn N.......410 D12
wy. Kilsyth.............380 K5
wy. Melton W...........226 C15
CHURCHILL PARK
dr. Endeavour Hl.....502 L10
dr. Endeavour Hl.....503 A10
dr. Lysterfield S.......503 A10
CHURCHMEAD
ct. Nar Warrn S.......552 H18
CHURINGA
av. Mitcham............377 G19
CHUSAN
cl. Niddrie..............322 K2
ct. Eltham North......245 H15
st. Balaclava...........414 K17
CHUTE
st. Diamond Ck.......245 H10
st. Mordialloc..........532 A19
CICADA
ct. Carrum Downs...574 L20
ct. Mulgrave...........501 G4
CIMBERWOOD
dr. Craigieburn........150 B17
CINDER
ct. Mulgrave...........500 E1
CINDY
cl. Keysborough.....534 H13
ct. Cheltenham........531 F3
ct. Ferntree Gly.......423 E19
ct. Somerville..........644 F14
CINEL
ct. Truganina..........405 L14
CINERAMA
cr. McCrae.............684 L17
CINEREA
av. Ferntree Gly.......423 F19
gld. Langwarrin.........629 J3
CINNABAR
av. Mt Waverley.......419 G13
CINTRA
av. St Kilda.............414 G13
av. Wheelers Hill.....460 H15
st. Seabrook...........450 L4
CIPORA
ct. Templestowe.....331 D11
pl. Thomastown......240 H12
CIRAI
cr. Cranbourne W....577 H19
CIRCLE
dr.n, Cranbourne.......578 B16
dr.s, Cranbourne.......578 B16
pl. Fitzroy N...........326 D19
rdg. Chirnside Pk.......337 D5
CIRCULAR
dr. Sunbury............143 G17
CIRRUS
cl. Hampton Pk.......551 L15
CITIVIEW
ct. Bulleen.............329 L13
CITRINUS
ct. Narre Warren.....553 C1
CITRIODORA
cct. Sunbury............143 F18
ct. Diamond Ck.......245 D14
wk. Vermont S, off Woodleigh Cr.....421 A10
CITRON
av. Balwyn N..........374 A4
ct. Vermont S.........420 L8
ct. Vermont S.........421 A8
CITRUS
cl. Hoppers Csg......405 E17
cl. Mill Park...........242 E9
ct. Campbellfield.....239 E11
ct. Doncaster..........374 K2
pl. Hillside.............274 C2
st. Braeside............532 F11
st. Vermont S.........420 K11
CITY
pl. Sunshine...........365 C3
rd. Ringwood..........378 D15
rd. Southbank.............3 B9
rd. Southbank...........23 J20
rd. Southbank...........29 E4
rd. S Melbourne........29 E4
rd. S Melbourne......413 C2
vw. Sunbury............142 C7
CITYLINK
twy. Brunswick W......324 J18
twy. Burnley..............32 F4
twy. Cremorne............32 F4
twy. Docklands.........368 F18
twy. Flemington...........34 C20
twy. Flemington.........368 F18
twy. Footscray............34 C20
twy. Footscray..........368 F18
twy. Hawthorn..........416 B5
twy. Kensington...........34 C20
twy. Kensington.........368 F18
twy. Kooyong............416 B5
twy. Moonee Pnd.......324 J18
twy. N Melbourne........34 C20
twy. N Melbourne......368 F18
twy. Parkville............324 J18
twy. Pascoe Vale S.....324 F1
twy. Port Melb..........368 F18
twy. Richmond............32 F4
twy. W Melbourne........34 C20
CITY VIEW
ct. Doncaster..........330 C17
rd. Maribyrnong......322 L13
rd. Maribyrnong......323 A13
CITYVIEW
cl. Taylors Hill........274 G8
ct. Eltham North......246 D20
rd. Balwyn N..........373 E3
CITY VISTA
ct. Plumpton...........273 H14
CIVIC
ctr. Hoppers Csg......448 L6
ctr. Hoppers Csg......449 A6
dr. Epping..............198 J18
dr. Greensborough..244 C17
dr. S Morang...........198 J18
dr. Kew, off Cotham Rd.........371 L10
la. Ringwood, off Civic Pl.............378 D12
pde. Altona...............408 K17
pde. Seaholme..........409 G18
pl. Berwick.............553 L2
pl. Ringwood...........378 D12
sq. Croydon............380 A5
CLABON
ct. Altona Mdw........451 F6
CLACTON
ct. Craigieburn........150 E20
st. St Albans...........320 E6
CLACTON DIVIDE
Rosebud...........683 L19
CLAIR
gr. Tecoma.............466 C10
CLAIRE
cl. Pakenham..........585 F1
ct. Aspendale Gdn...546 E1
ct. Eltham..............287 A4
ct. Langwarrin.........601 K19
ct. Montrose...........381 K9
ct. Narre Warren.....538 L14
ct. Whittlesea...........96 E16
gr. Ringwood E........379 D5
st. Coldstream........295 F12
st. McKinnon...........456 C17
CLAIRMONT
av. Bentleigh...........495 J1
av. Cranbourne........578 A15
cl. Somerville..........644 H13
st. Albion..............320 G19
CLAIRVILLE
st. Anglesea...........713 D6
CLANBRAE
av. Burwood...........418 L7
CLANCY
rd. Mt Evelyn..........339 G19
st. Williamstown.....410 L15
st. Williamstown.....411 A15
CLANCYS
la. Doncaster..........330 L15
CLANGULA
ct. Endeavour Hl.....536 L3
ct. Endeavour Hl.....537 A3
CLANRANALD
wy. Greenvale..........193 C19
CLANSMAN
cl. Hoppers Csg......405 D12
CLAPHAM
av. Springvale.........499 K18
rd. Hughesdale........457 G9
st. Balwyn..............374 A12
st. Thornbury..........326 H9
CLAPPERTON
st. Bentleigh...........455 H20
st. Brighton East.....455 H20
CLAPTON
ct. Cranbourne E.....604 H5
CLARA
ct. Cheltenham........497 C16
ct. Keysborough.....534 H13
st. Brunswick E.......326 B9
st. Fawkner.............281 F8
st. Macleod.............285 G11
st. Preston..............282 G17
st. South Yarra..........32 F10
st. South Yarra..........32 F11
st. South Yarra........414 J6
CLARE
st. Bayswater..........424 B5
st. Blackburn..........375 L14
st. Croydon S.........379 G10
st. Geelong............703 A6
st. Parkdale............531 L11
st. St Albans...........320 E11
st. Yarraville...........366 J16
CLARE BRENNAN
dr. Deer Park..........319 G11
CLAREDALE
av. Gladstone Pk.....237 C16
rd. Dandenong........536 F14
rd. Doveton............536 F14
CLAREMONT
av. Malvern.............415 K16
av. Newtown............702 D9
av. The Basin..........425 F13
cr. Canterbury.........373 E19
cr. Hoppers Csg......448 F7
cr. Keysborough.....535 A9
cr. Reservoir...........282 A1
ct. Langwarrin.........629 D4
gln. Berwick.............553 K17
la. Bulleen.............329 E13
pl. S Melbourne........30 B4
st. Coburg N...........282 A17
st. Fawkner.............281 K2
st. Mt Eliza.............642 F9
st. Pearcedale.........646 K5
st. South Yarra..........32 C9
st. South Yarra........414 H4
wy. Lysterfield.........464 C16
wy. Lysterfield.........464 C17
CLAREMOUNT
ct. Glen Waverley....460 J1
CLARENCE
av. Carnegie............456 J11
av. Keysborough.....534 J9
rd. Wantirna............421 L4
st. Bentleigh E.......496 K4
st. Brunswick E.......325 L11
st. Caulfield S..........455 C8
st. Elsternwick........455 C8
st. Flemington..........33 H4
st. Geelong West.....702 D3
st. Ivanhoe.............328 D14
st. Malvern East......416 C20
st. Reservoir...........282 J16
CLARENDON
av. Oakleigh S.........458 C16
ct. Mooroolbark......337 H18
ct. Seabrook...........451 A2
dr. Melton S............268 C11
dr. Somerville..........644 E17
pde. W Footscray......366 E11
pl. S Melbourne........30 C6
pl. S Melbourne......413 G3
st. Armadale............415 G12
st. Avondale Ht.......322 A13
st. Coburg..............325 B7
st. Cranbourne........604 A1
st. Dromana...........685 F9
st. E Melbourne........25 F8
st. Frankston...........627 E2
st. Maidstone..........366 D1
st. Newtown...........702 H11
st. Southbank...........23 J16
st. Southbank...........29 L1
st. Southbank.........413 F2
st. S Melbourne........23 J16
st. S Melbourne........29 L1
st. Thornbury..........326 K9
st. Yarraville...........367 A17
CLARET
st. Doveton............536 F12
CLARET ASH
dr. Sunbury............143 E16
CLAREVALE
st. Clayton S..........498 L7
CLARICE
cl. St Albans..........320 E11
ct. Donvale............332 H18
rd. Box Hill S..........419 C2
CLARIDGE
av. Roxburgh Pk......194 F14
CLARINDA
ct. Vermont S.........420 G9
dr. Narre Warren.....538 L13
rd. Clarinda............498 B11
rd. Clarinda............498 B8
rd. Clayton S..........498 B8
rd. Heatherton.........498 B11
rd. Oakleigh S.........498 B8
st. Bacchus Msh.....221 K18
st. Caulfield S..........455 E6
st. Essendon...........323 J11
st. Moonee Pnd......323 J11
st. Somerville..........644 L16
st. Somerville..........645 A17
CLARK
av. Warburton.........349 K5
cr. Sorrento...........678 L12
ct. Berwick.............553 J8
ct. Sunbury............114 J11
rd. Ivanhoe.............328 A19
st. Darley...............221 K5
st. Port Melb..........412 G4
st. Reservoir...........283 B11
st. Richmond..........371 C14
st. Sandringham.....495 H17
st. Williamstown.....411 G13
CLARKE
av. Belmont............702 A20
av. Caulfield.............456 A6
av. Flemington.........323 L20
av. St Albans..........320 H5
av. St Albans..........321 A5
av. Warburton.........349 H7
av. Wattle Glen........246 J7
cl. Somerville..........645 F19
cr. Carrum Downs...574 H15
cr. Wantirna S.........462 D3
ct. Mt Waverley.......459 E1
ct. Wheelers Hill......460 L9
dr. Gladstone Pk......237 D17
dr. Ringwood...........422 E1
rd. Caroline Spr.......317 G7
rd. Ferny Creek.......426 A15
rd. Rockbank..........317 G7
rd. Springvale S......499 F18
rd. Yarrambat.........200 C19
st. Abbotsford...........20 H16
st. Blackburn..........375 K16
st. Box Hill S..........374 K19
st. Brunswick E.......325 L16
st. Campbellfield.....239 E13
st. Coburg N...........281 H14
st. Elwood.............454 E2
st. Frankston..........628 A1
st. Glen Iris............416 E10
st. Lilydale.............338 E5
st. Newtown...........702 H10
st. Northcote..........326 E16
st. Northcote..........326 H17
st. Prahran..............32 G17
st. Prahran............414 J9
st. Southbank...........23 L18
st. Southbank...........30 A1
st. S Melbourne........30 A1
st. Sunshine...........365 D2
st. Templestowe......331 C6
st. Thomastown......241 A16
st. W Footscray.......366 J8
CLARKEDALE
ri. Kilsyth S...........381 A20
CLARKES
av. Mt Martha..........656 B8
rd. Brookfield..........267 H12
rd. Fyansford...........701 A5
rd. Whittlesea...........95 H12
CLARKESTOWN
av. Mt Eliza............626 B17
CLARKMONT
rd. Ferny Creek.......426 C18
rd. Sassafras..........426 C18
CLARKS
rd. Keilor East.........278 D20

COATE
av. Alphington 327 G20
COATES
ct. Sunbury..........142 L5
la.e, Melbourne 24 K6
st. Bentleigh...........496 A4
wk. Seaford.............599 C6
COATS
st. Moonee Pnd 324 D12
COB
cl. Broadmeadows..238 A13
pl. Clayton 459 H16
COBAIN
ct. Ringwood 335 B20
sq. Wantirna...........422 H12
st. Clayton 459 C18
st. Keysborough 534 H10
COBAR
ct. Mooroolbark......336 J13
pl. Kings Park.........275 C17
st. Bentleigh E.........457 A15
COBB
jnc. Sydenham 275 A4
rd. Mt Eliza.............641 H8
COBBITTY
ct. Boronia.............424 G3
COBBLER
gra. Lynbrook 551 H18
st. Werribee...........448 C10
COBBLESTONE
av. Nar Warrn S.......553 D16
dr. Attwood............237 A11
dr. S Morang...........199 K17
grn. Caroline Spr.......318 C4
COBBY
ct. Roxburgh Pk......194 E11
st. Laverton 407 B16
COBDEN
cr. Lilydale.............338 F8
st. Campbellfield 238 L9
st. Caulfield N 415 E16
st. Highton..............701 J20
st. Kew....................371 L9
st. N Melbourne........17 J20
st. S Melbourne 30 C7
st. S Melbourne 30 H4
st. S Melbourne 413 G4
COBHAM
ct. Mt Martha..........669 K4
rd. Langwarrin S 629 D19
rd. Mitcham 377 C9
st. Altona...............408 F20
st. Balwyn N 373 C6
st. Cheltenham.........531 A3
st. Reservoir 282 C7
st. St Albans 319 L2
COBRAM
st. Broadmeadows..238 B11
COBREY
st. Sunshine 365 H4
COBUNGRA
ct. Hallam 552 B2
COBURG
st. Coburg 325 J5
COBURN
av. McCrae.............685 A11
COBURNS
rd. Brookfield 268 D8
rd. Kurunjang..........226 F13
rd. Melton 226 E20
rd. Melton S............268 D8
rd. Melton W...........226 F13
COCHRAN
av. Camberwell........416 H4
COCHRANE
av. Keysborough 534 J12
av. Mentone 530 K9
pl. Carlton...............18 F12
st. Brighton.............454 K10
st. Brighton.............454 K13
st. Cranbourne.........604 A1
st. Mitcham 377 F18
COCHRANES
la. Hurstbridge........247 J1
la. Panton Hill 203 K20
la. Panton Hill 204 A18
rd. Moorabbin 497 A10
COCKAIGNE
st. Doncaster 375 C2
COCKATIEL
ct. Diamond Ck.......245 D12
COCKATOO
av. Cockatoo 511 C3
dr. Carrum Downs...600 L4
dr. Whittlesea..........126 C1
COCKER
al. Melbourne 2 E18
al. Melbourne 24 E10
COCKERELL
st. Ferntree Gly 423 K19

COCONUT
gr. Aspendale Gdn...547 B5
COCOPARRA
cr. Taylors Lakes.....275 L9
COCOS
ct. Patterson L 573 F10
CODRINGTON
st. Cranbourne........604 E3
st. Dromana............685 K7
st. Sandringham 495 F15
CODY
av. Hampton Pk.......551 E9
COE
la. Highett..............496 D13
COFFEY
ct. Jan Juc.............711 E13
COGENS
pl. Geelong, off
Corio St 703 D7
COGHILL
st. Bulla 190 D18
st. Westmeadows ...237 A13
COGHLAN
st. Niddrie..............322 L2
st. Niddrie..............323 A2
wy. Kensington 33 F11
wy. Kensington.........368 C6
COHEN
pl. Melbourne 2 L10
pl. Melbourne 24 G4
st. Keilor East..........322 C4
COHUNA
ct. Burwood E.........419 L12
ct. Taylors Lakes.....276 C7
st. Broadmeadows..238 C16
st. Brunswick W......324 J16
COIMADAI
ct. Mornington........641 D13
COLAC
ct. Patterson L 573 K9
gr. Belmont.............706 A5
pl. Thomastown......240 D13
pl. Geelong, off
Maud St............702 L10
rd. Belmont.............705 G11
rd. Highton.............705 G11
st. Dallas 238 H11
COLAN
rd. Kangaroo Grnd...289 K10
COLBERT
ct. Frankston S........628 C17
rd. Campbellfield 239 D10
COLBURN
ct. Hillside..............232 G18
COLBURY
rd. Bayswater N.......380 G18
COLBY
dr. Belgrave Ht 466 F19
dr. Belgrave Ht 506 G1
dr. Belgrave S..........506 G1
gr. Bundoora............242 H15
pl. Hampton Pk.......552 D9
COLCHESTER
ct. Keysborough 534 A9
ct. Somerville..........644 G14
dr. Doncaster E 376 C1
rd. Bayswater N.......380 K16
rd. Boronia..............424 J4
rd. Kilsyth 380 K16
rd. Kilsyth S 424 J4
rd. Rosebud W........699 G5
COLDBLO
rd. Armadale 415 J13
COLDEN
ct. Gladstone Pk......237 E16
COLDRAKE
ct. Carrum Downs...575 A18
COLDSTREAM WEST
rd. Chirnside Pk.......293 F7
rd. Coldstream 293 F7
COLE
av. Belgrave.............466 H10
av. Glen Iris.............416 L12
av. Kew East...........372 C5
cl. Burwood E.........420 D12
cr. Chadstone..........457 K5
cr. Coburg 326 A4
ct. Box Hill N...........374 K7
ct. Bundoora............243 C20
ct. Toorak...............415 E7
row. Doncaster E 332 J14
st. Brighton.............454 E9
st. Brighton.............455 A10
st. Hawthorn E........416 E2
st. Laverton 407 D13
st. Noble Park..........500 H14
st. Richmond 26 L5
st. Williamstown.....411 F19

COLEBROOK
av. Mt Waverley.......418 G20
ct. Mornington........656 L4
rd. Kilsyth 381 F4
st. Brunswick..........325 F9
COLEDALE
cl. Endeavour Hl 537 H3
COLEEN
st. Yallambie...........285 E16
COLEHURST
cr. Sassafras...........426 J14
cr. Sassafras...........426 J15
COLEMAN
av. Kew East...........372 D4
cr. Eltham North......287 K3
cr. Reservoir...........282 H12
cr. Rosebud W........699 G3
ct. Cheltenham........530 K4
ct. Dandenong N.....501 K16
ct. Maidstone..........366 G3
ct. Taylors Lakes.....233 D18
la. Aspendale, off
Coleman Rd........545 L1
mw. Essendon, off
Wheeler Pl 324 C9
pde. Glen Waverley....419 K20
pl. Carlton.................18 J9
rd. Aspendale..........545 L1
rd. Boronia..............423 C12
rd. Wantirna S.........422 K13
rd. Wantirna S.........423 A13
st. Fitzroy N 19 D7
st. Heathmont.........378 L16
st. Heathmont.........379 A16
st. Maidstone..........366 G3
st. Wesburn............347 K15
st. Yarra Jctn 347 K15
COLEMANS
rd. Carrum Downs....574 F18
rd. Dandenong S 550 A12
rd. Lyndhurst 550 A12
COLENSO
st. Carrum 573 B7
COLERAINE
st. Broadmeadows..237 L13
COLERIDGE
ct. Templestowe 331 L12
dr. Delahey.............275 D13
st. Elwood 454 H3
st. Kew..................372 B12
COLES
ct. Beaumaris..........530 F7
ct. Mt Eliza.............626 B13
gr. Carrum Downs...574 H16
tce. Richmond..........371 A12
COLESBOURNE
ct. Kilsyth S 424 L1
COLEUS
st. Dromana...........686 E7
COLGOA
ct. Wattle Glen 246 H9
COLIBAN
cl. Rowville............463 D16
ct. St Albans 320 E12
COLIGNAN
ct. Meadow Ht 238 C3
COLIN
av. Belgrave............466 J16
av. Emerald 469 H16
av. Frankston...........599 E15
av. Pk Orchards.......334 A17
av. Warrandyte 333 G3
ct. Broadmeadows..280 C1
ct. Burwood............418 F12
ct. Dingley Village ...533 E9
ct. Langwarrin.........629 B5
ct. Mernda..............156 B15
rd. Oakleigh S..........458 G18
st. Bentleigh E.........496 H2
st. Caulfield N 415 C15
st. Essendon W.......322 L8
st. Rosebud W........683 F20
st. Sunshine 321 F20
COLINA
ct. Torquay 712 F3
COLING
av. Carnegie 456 L12
COLITE
st. Bulleen 329 K17
COLLACE
st. Brunswick..........325 J13
COLLARD
dr. Diamond Ck.......246 B4
pl. Carrum Downs...575 D15
COLLAROY
cr. Noble Park.........534 H7
COLLEGE
cl. Wantirna S.........422 B16
cr. Carlton N 17 L8
cr. Keysborough 534 E11
cr. Parkville.............17 L8

ct. Glen Waverley....420 A18
ct. Newtown 702 A7
dr. Bundoora...........284 E13
dr. Pakenham..........584 A3
gr. Black Rock.........529 G5
grn. Bacchus Msh 221 F13
pde. Keilor East.........322 H6
pde. Kew..................371 L13
pl. Albanvale 318 K7
pl. Albert Park...........29 J14
pl. Kew...................372 A13
pl. Sunbury............143 J11
rd. Werribee 447 K17
st. Elsternwick 455 B10
st. Hawthorn...........371 G15
st. Williamstown.....411 E13
wy. Burwood...........419 C7
COLLEGIAN
av. Strathmore.........280 C19
COLLEGIUM
av. Wheelers Hill......460 D13
COLLENDINA
cl. Keilor East..........322 A6
cr. Greensborough ..243 G17
cr. Scoresby 462 D6
COLLENSO
st. Sunshine W 364 F4
COLLETT
av. Ringwood 378 G6
av. Roxburgh Pk......194 D14
ri. Endeavour Hl 537 E8
st. Kensington 34 B8
COLLEY
gr. Glen Waverley....459 L9
st. Pearcedale 646 J4
COLLIER
av. Clayton 499 A3
av. Tecoma.............466 A12
cr. Brunswick W......324 L15
cr. Strathmr Ht.......279 A9
cr. Strathmr Ht.......279 B9
ct. Burwood...........418 H10
ct. Strathmr Ht.......279 B9
ct. Taylors Lakes.....233 B20
ct. Wheelers Hill......460 G17
pl. Strathmr Ht.......279 A9
rd. Kilsyth S 380 K20
st. Brunswick..........325 B15
st. Preston.............327 A5
COLLIN
av. Cockatoo 511 E1
COLLINA
st. Mitcham 377 E11
COLLINGS
ct. Mooroolbark......337 E17
ct. Pascoe Vale 281 A12
st. Brunswick W......324 J12
st. Camberwell........417 D7
COLLINGTON
av. Brighton............454 L20
COLLINGWOOD
rd. Newport............411 C7
st. Rye...................697 E3
st. Sandringham 495 D15
COLLINS
av. Altona North.......410 C5
cl. Keilor East..........322 A1
cl. Scoresby 462 H9
cr. Berwick.............553 J9
cr. Balwyn.............373 J9
ct. Chelsea.............547 B13
ct. Bayswater, off
Valma St..........423 E8
gr. Croydon N 336 E13
la. Yarrambat..........201 F17
pde. Sorrento 679 C14
pl. Kew..................371 G5
pl. Kilsyth 381 C6
pl. Ringwood N.......334 H18
pl. Geelong, off
Little Ryrie St 703 B9
rd. Dromana...........686 K9
rd. Dromana...........687 A3
rd. Melton 269 C2
st. Belmont.............702 G17
st. Box Hill 374 L19
st. Brighton.............454 K16
st. Bulleen 329 L12
st. Chadstone..........457 L2
st. Coburg 281 C20
st. Diamond Ck 245 H9
st. Docklands...........23 D13
st. Essendon...........323 H4
st. Geelong West.....702 G2
st. Heidelberg Ht 284 E19
st. Melbourne 1 B16
st. Melbourne 2 C16
st. Melbourne 23 H11
st. Mentone 530 J6
st. Ormond 456 G15
st. Preston 326 E1
st. Red Hill.............687 A18

st. St Albans 320 C4
st. Seddon.............367 C11
st. Sunbury............142 H13
st. Taylors Hill.........274 E9
st. Thomastown......240 H15
st. Thornbury..........326 K7
st. Werribee...........447 H19
st. Williamstown......411 B14
wy. Melbourne 1 K14
wy. Melbourne 24 B9
COLLINSON
st. Keilor Park.........278 A15
COLLIS
st. Brighton East 495 D5
COLLISON
rd. Cranbourne E.....579 E20
rd. Cranbourne E.....604 L6
COLLOCOTT
st. Mordialloc..........531 K16
COLLYER
cl. Brookfield 268 A5
COLMAN
rd. Ringwood N.......334 G11
rd. Warrandyte S.....334 G11
rd. Warranwood......334 G11
COLOMBO
rd. Belgrave............466 K14
st. Mitcham 377 B14
COLONEL
st. Clayton 458 J20
COLONIAL
cl. Wheelers Hill......461 B12
ct. Nar Warrn S.......552 H9
ct. Wantirna...........422 A9
dr. Bangholme 549 K14
dr. Vermont S 421 A12
pl. Kensington 33 F7
COLONSAY
rd. Springvale..........500 B15
st. Templestowe 330 L9
COLORADO
cr. Rowville.............463 D16
ct. Ferntree Gly 423 H16
ct. Werribee...........447 H5
st. Pascoe Vale 280 E12
COLOUR
rd. Diggers Rest......187 A11
COLQUHOUN
ct. Eltham 287 K13
COLRADO
ct. Hallam 552 A1
COLRIC
pl. Eltham..............287 B5
COLSTAN
ct. Mt Eliza.............626 C18
COLSTON
av. Sherbrooke........426 J18
cl. Doncaster...........375 E4
dr. Hillside..............232 E19
pl. Mulgrave............501 A5
COLTAIN
st. Vermont S 420 K8
st. Vermont S 421 A8
COLTHUR
st. Reservoir 282 E7
COLTON
cl. Greenvale..........192 J18
COLUMBA
st. Balwyn N 329 C20
COLUMBAN
av. Strathmore.........324 B2
COLUMBANS
cl. Frankston S........627 K10
COLUMBIA
av. Croydon............379 H3
cct. Broadmeadows..238 L12
cl. Tullamarine.........278 J4
ct. Deer Park..........318 J9
dr. Wheelers Hill......460 L19
dr. Wheelers Hill......461 A17
rd. Lalor.................241 B5
rd. Narre Warren 539 A18
st. Hawthorn...........372 A16
st. Oakleigh S..........497 H7
COLUMBINE
ct. Epping 198 G20
COLVIN
ct. Glen Waverley....460 A11
gr. Hawthorn...........371 G13
COLWYN
cl. Langwarrin.........601 G19
ct. Donvale 376 G6
dr. Nar Warrn S.......552 F18
COMAS
gr. Ashburton.........417 C18
gr. Thornbury..........326 C8
rd. Beaumaris..........530 D4
COMBARTON
st. Box Hill 374 L18

COMBE
ct. Epping 197 L18
COMBEN
dr. Werribee 447 H15
COMBER
st. Noble Park 500 D18
COMBERMERE
st. Aberfeldie 323 G10
COMBIE
st. Preston 327 A2
COMELY BANK
rd. Plenty 244 D12
COMER
st. Brighton East 495 D5
COMERAM
ct. Mill Park 242 G10
COMET
ct. Rosebud 700 J4
COMFORT
cl. Rowville 503 A3
COMIC
ct. Lilydale 294 C19
ct. Melton W 226 D13
ct. New Gisborne 79 C1
COMLEY
st. Sunshine N 321 B14
COMMERCE
ct. Sunbury 143 D15
dr. Hampton Pk 551 J9
la. Hawthorn E, off Evans Pl 372 H20
st. Braybrook 321 J20
wy. Melbourne 1 L18
wy. Melbourne 24 C10
COMMERCIAL
dr. Dandenong S 550 F6
dr. Thomastown 242 A20
pl. Melton 269 D2
pl. Eltham, off Luck St 287 H8
rd. Ferntree Gly 464 A2
rd. Footscray 367 C7
rd. Highett 496 J12
rd. Mentone 531 B9
rd. Mt Evelyn 338 J20
rd. Notting Hill 459 B12
rd. Pk Orchards 333 G12
rd. Prahran 31 D14
rd. Prahran 414 C7
rd. South Yarra 31 E14
rd. South Yarra 414 C7
st. Maidstone 366 F2
COMMERFORD
pl. Chirnside Pk 336 K8
COMMODORE
ct. Taylors Lakes 275 H9
COMMONWEALTH
ct. Craigieburn 150 E16
COMMUNITY
dr. Greensborough 286 F2
pde. Nar Warrn S 578 F2
wy. Lilydale 338 D12
wy. Lilydale 338 D13
COMMUNITY HUB
Hillside 274 C5
Sydenham 274 G5
COMO
av. Rye 698 A8
av. South Yarra 32 K9
av. South Yarra 414 K5
av. Surrey Hills 373 J13
cl. Croydon 380 C10
ct. Dandenong N 502 A16
ct. Dromana 686 J4
ct. Mt Eliza 626 E17
ct. Mt Waverley 458 K9
ct. Springvale 499 J17
ct. Thomastown 240 G15
pde. Maribyrnong 323 D15
pde.e,Mentone 531 C9
pde.e,Parkdale 531 C9
pde.e,Parkdale 531 G13
pde.w,Mentone 531 A7
pde.w,Mordialloc 531 G13
pde.w,Parkdale 531 A7
pl. Campbellfield 239 G12
rd. Lilydale 338 L3
rd. Lilydale 339 A1
st. Alphington 327 K20
st. Alphington 371 K1
st. Doncaster 374 K3
st. Emerald 509 D3
st. Malvern 415 J16
COMONGIN
av. Warburton 305 H20
COMPASS
ct. Somerville 645 E18
COMPORT
st. Beaumaris 530 C12
COMPTON
pde. Sunshine N 321 C15
st. Canterbury 417 G1
st. Glen Waverley 420 F19
st. Mitcham 376 L8
st. Nunawading 376 L8
st. Reservoir 282 J10
COMRIE
ct. Bayswater 423 E7
COMTE
cl. Cranbourne W 577 G19
CONARGO
ct. Greensborough 244 J20
CONCORD
cct. Albanvale 319 A6
cr. Carrum Downs 574 G20
pl. Cranbourne 603 J4
pl. Ferntree Gly 423 J17
ri. Templestowe 332 C2
st. Preston 326 D3
CONCORDE
cr. Werribee 487 H2
CONDAH
ct. Ashwood 418 F17
CONDELL
st. Fitzroy 19 C16
CONDER
av. Burwood 419 B7
cl. Yallambie 286 A14
st. Donvale 376 F6
CONDON
ct. Keysborough 535 A12
CONDONS
la. Darley 221 B11
CONDOR
ct. Frankston 628 F8
ct. Werribee 447 L9
pl. Mill Park 242 L8
pl. Mill Park 243 A8
pl. Sunbury 142 G8
pl. Taylors Lakes 275 J9
st. Hawthorn E 372 F15
CONDOS
ct. Wantirna S 422 E19
CONE
cl. Ringwood N 334 H20
pl. Pakenham 585 K8
st. Bulleen 330 B17
st. Eumemmerring 537 D12
CONEY HURST
cr. Mornington 656 F2
CONFAIT
ct. Berwick 553 L4
CONFERTA
cl. Hillside 274 A4
cr. Doveton 536 K7
ct. Cranbourne W 577 K17
CONGO
ct. Roxburgh Pk 194 F6
CONGRAM
st. Broadmeadows 238 E18
CONIFER
av. Brooklyn 365 G18
cl. Gladstone Pk 279 B1
cl. Hampton Pk 551 E4
cl. Hoppers Csg 405 E16
cl. Mill Park 242 E11
cr. Dingley Village 532 H5
ct. Dandenong N 501 K16
ct. Frankston S 627 J14
ct. Lysterfield 464 A20
ct. Nar Warrn S 553 E20
ct. Ringwood N 334 J20
pl. Hillside 274 D5
pl. Templstw Lr 330 J12
st. Hampton 495 F12
CONISTON
av. Airport W 278 K18
av. Berwick 554 A8
cl. Croydon Hills 335 J13
cl. Springvale S 533 L3
dr. Wheelers Hill 461 C15
st. Diamond Ck 246 A12
CONLEY
st. Noble Park 534 K6
CONN
st. Ferntree Gly 463 K3
CONNAL
dr. Frankston 599 J17
CONNAM
av. Clayton 459 F19
CONNAUGHT
pl. Glen Waverley 461 A3
CONNEL
dr. Melton S 268 F10
CONNELL
av. Oakleigh 458 B13
cl. Dingley Village 533 C8
cl. Hopetoun Park 265 K7
ct. Balwyn 373 L13
st. Glenroy 280 D5
st. Hawthorn 371 G15
st. Mordialloc 531 L18
wk. Roxburgh Pk 194 A10
CONNELLY
st. Brunswick 325 G11
st. Flemington 33 F1
st. Flemington 324 C20
CONNEMARA
cl. Highton 701 B17
CONNERS FLAT
rd. Wandin N 340 K14
CONNEWARRA
av. Aspendale 546 E4
CONNEWARRE
av. Wyndham Va 446 B5
av. Wyndham Va 446 C6
CONNIE
ct. Cranbourne 603 K5
st. Bentleigh E 457 E20
CONNOLLY
av. Coburg 282 A19
cr. Bayswater N 380 A20
CONNOR
pl. Kangaroo Grnd 247 G11
st. Bacchus Msh 221 H16
st. Brighton East 495 D1
st. E Geelong 703 F10
st. Kew East 372 B4
CONNORS
la. N Melbourne 17 K19
la. Seville 386 G4
st. Highett 496 H15
CONOS
ct. Donvale 377 D1
CONQUEST
dr. Werribee 447 L12
wy. Hallam 537 D19
CONRAD
av. Point Cook 450 A5
ct. Blackburn N 376 A7
ct. Pakenham 585 E1
ct. Whittington 704 D19
pl. Wheelers Hill 460 K17
st. St Albans 276 A19
CONRAN
av. Endeavour Hl 537 L6
ct. Box Hill S 419 B5
CONROY
pl. Roxburgh Pk 194 D11
CONSERVATION
dr. Bangholme 549 J14
CONSERVATORY
dr. Burwood 418 A11
CONSIDE
cr. Torquay 712 A2
CONSIDEN
cl. Mill Park 242 E3
CONSIDINE
ct. Bayswater N 379 L15
CONSORT
av. Vermont S 420 G10
pl. Craigieburn 150 F7
CONSTABLE
ct. Scoresby 462 A7
CONSTANCE
cl. Ferntree Gly 464 B14
ct. Healesville 257 F2
ct. Narre Warren 539 E16
st. Alphington 327 L19
st. Blackburn S 419 K2
st. Hawthorn E 416 E4
st. St Albans 319 L1
CONSTELLATION
ct. Taylors Lakes 275 K6
CONSTITUTION HILL
rd. Sorrento 678 K9
CONTESSA
ct. Point Cook 450 G11
CONTI
ct. Mentone 530 J4
CONTINENTAL
wy. Prahran 32 A18
CONTOUR
cl. Research 288 K2
ct. Chirnside Pk 337 F6
CONTURSI
dr. Sydenham 274 H7
CONVENT
ct. Coburg N 281 G16
CONVENTION
av. Belgrave Ht 506 E1
CONVERY
cl. Gladstone Pk 237 D17
CONWAY
av. Donvale 377 A3
cr. Balwyn 373 H13
ct. Altona North 409 J2
ct. Boronia 424 A12
ct. Chelsea Ht 547 D10
ct. Cranbourne 577 L18
ct. Hampton Pk 551 H12
ct. Somerville 644 G15
st. Cranbourne N 578 F9
st. Dandenong S 535 H13
st. Mt Eliza 641 L4
CONYERS
st. The Basin 425 B11
COOBA
ct. Mornington 640 L15
ct. Mornington 641 A15
ct. Mulgrave 500 G2
pl. Frankston 628 C6
st. Canterbury 417 E1
COODE
rd. W Melbourne 367 J12
COOEE
ct. Diamond Ck 244 L13
COOGEE
av. Frankston 627 H6
la. Williamstown 411 D16
pl. Burnside 318 F6
pl. Port Melb 412 E5
st. Boronia 424 C9
wy. Yallambie 286 A13
COOINDA
cl. Burnside 318 G7
cr. Clarinda 498 D7
cr. Watsonia 285 J8
ct. Burwood E 419 F9
ct. Frankston S 627 B6
ct. Mt Waverley 459 C3
dr. Aspendale 546 F5
pl. Malvern East 457 A2
rd. Beaconsfield 555 K7
rd. Woori Yallock 344 K15
rd. Woori Yallock 345 A14
st. Warneet 649 E12
COOK
av. Kealba 277 A20
av. Rosebud 700 D1
ct. Cranbourne N 577 L8
ct. Dandenong N 502 A19
ct. Ferntree Gly 463 E2
ct. Springvale S 534 B1
ct. Sunbury 143 B12
dr. Pakenham 584 L8
pl. Westmeadows 237 E14
rd. Melton S 268 F13
rd. Mitcham 377 F12
st. Blairgowrie 696 C5
st. Brunswick W 325 A11
st. Bundoora 284 G1
st. Hawthorn 371 L17
st. Ivanhoe 327 K9
st. McCrae 685 B17
st. Mornington 640 E11
st. Newtown 702 A10
st. Port Melb 368 D20
st. Port Melb 412 A1
st. Preston 282 K20
st. Southbank 3 J5
st. Southbank 24 D14
st. Sunshine W 364 H14
COOKE
av. Hampton E 495 J10
av. Sunshine N 321 A12
ct. Richmond 26 G4
st. Abbotsford 26 J3
st. Clayton 498 J3
st. Essendon 324 A4
st. Sandringham 495 J18
COOKES
rd. Doreen 156 D17
rd. Doreen 201 B1
rd. Yuroke 192 H1
COOKS
cr. N Warrandyte 289 F14
mw. Point Cook 450 L9
wy. Taylors Hill 274 K12
COOKSON
st. Camberwell 372 J18
COOL
st. Reservoir 282 C14
COOLABAH
av. Glen Waverley 460 A11
cr. Hoppers Csg 405 D17
ct. Kurunjang 227 D15
dr. Eltham North 287 K3
dr. Grovedale 705 L14
gr. Berwick 553 H4
st. Doncaster 375 D2
st. Mentone 531 J8
st. Mooroolbark 337 A15
COOLABINDI
ch. Eltham 287 B6
COOLAC
st. Chadstone 458 E1
st. Cheltenham 497 B20
COOLALIE
ct. Grovedale 705 L13
COOLAMON
st. Albion 320 K20
COOLANGATTA
rd. Mt Martha 655 K12
st. Menzies Ck 468 H18
tce. Dromana 685 L9
COOLARN
st. Mt Waverley 459 G5
COOLAROO
av. Hurstbridge 203 F13
ct. Mooroolbark 337 F12
COOLART
rd. Moorooduc 644 B19
rd. Somerville 644 B19
COOLAVIN
rd. Noble Park N 501 D16
COOLEY
av. Macleod 285 E11
COOLGARDIE
av. Malvern East 456 L1
st. Frankston N 600 A11
COOLIBAH
cr. Bayswater 423 G6
pl. Keysborough 534 F8
COOLIBAR
av. Seaford 573 D14
COOLIDGE
ct. Dandenong N 501 J8
COOLOCK
ct. Rosanna 285 D20
COOLOMON
cl. Wantirna S 422 K11
COOLONG
av. Berwick 553 E4
pl. View Bank 286 C15
COOLOOLI
ct. Ringwood E 379 D14
COOLOONGATTA
rd. Camberwell 417 D5
rd. Sassafras 426 E14
COOLSTORE
rd. Croydon 380 B3
COOLULLAH
av. South Yarra 32 K11
av. South Yarra 414 L6
COOMA
ct. Berwick 553 J1
ct. Dandenong 536 F5
ct. Lalor 240 H8
st. Broadmeadows 238 B10
st. Moorabbin 496 H9
st. Preston 326 L1
COOMALIE
cr. Heidelberg W 328 C4
COOMBAH
ct. Mooroolbark 337 E11
COOMBE
av. Hampton 495 E8
COOMBES
ct. Rye 697 F5
rd. Torquay 711 A1
COOMBS
av. Kew 371 E10
av. Oakleigh S 458 E19
COOMLEIGH
av. Glen Waverley 420 E17
COOMOORA
rd. Springvale S 533 K7
COONAC
pl. Frankston 600 B20
COONAMAR
st. Tullamarine 278 G7
COONAN'S
rd. Pascoe Vale S 324 H6
COONARA
av. Mt Eliza 642 B1
av. Seaford 573 D20
ct. Narre Warren 553 C11
ct. Olinda 427 H17
COONAWARRA
dr. Thomastown 240 G12
dr. Vermont S 421 E9
COONEY
cl. Berwick 554 B17
st. Moolap 704 H17
COONIL
cr. Malvern 415 L15
st. Oakleigh S 498 E2
COOP
rd. Pakenham 586 D17
st. Werribee 447 H14
COOPER
av. Altona North 409 H7
av. Glen Waverley 460 F10
ct. Cranbourne 604 F5
ct. Dandenong 536 D14
ct. Delahey 275 E11

ct. Hallam 538 D15
gr. Sorrento 678 J8
rd. Bulla 232 L3
rd. Bulla 233 A3
rd. Rowville 463 C16
st. Broadmeadows 238 D19
st. Brunswick W 325 B8
st. Campbellfield 195 B18
st. Epping 195 K20
st. Epping 241 A1
st. Epping 241 F1
st. Essendon 323 D7
st. Hoppers Csg 405 B15
st. Melton S 268 F9
st. Preston 282 F18
st. Somerton 195 B18
st. Springvale S 500 B19
st. Sunshine 365 F3
COOPERS
la. Gruyere 341 E1
la. Kensington 33 G7
rd. Macclesfield 471 C2
COOPERS HILL
dr. Westmeadows 236 L14
dr. Westmeadows 237 A14
COORA
ct. Frankston 600 D19
rd. Oakleigh S 458 E18
COORABONG
av. Rosebud 683 J19
COORAMINTA
av. Altona Mdw 450 L1
pl. Diamond Ck 245 H9
rd. Rye 696 L13
st. Brunswick 325 H12
COORIE
av. Bayswater 423 H6
cr. Rosanna 329 C2
COORIGIL
rd. Carnegie 456 J9
COORNONG
ct. Kurunjang 227 D15
COORONG
ct. Meadow Ht 194 B18
ct. Taylors Hill 274 L12
ct. Taylors Lakes 275 L9
ct. Wantirna 422 C13
la. Doncaster 374 H4
pl. Burnside 318 G6
COOROOMBONG
st. Werribee 447 B12
COOTAMUNDRA
av. Rosebud W 699 B3
cr. Blackburn 375 L11
ct. Mornington 656 J4
ct. Werribee 448 G18
dr. Wheelers Hill 460 F13
st. Doveton 536 J6
COOTE
cl. Blairgowrie 695 F1
st. Kensington 33 K7
st. S Melbourne 29 H5
st. S Melbourne 413 D3
COOWARRA
ct. Ferntree Gly 464 C8
wy. Berwick 553 F4
COPE
ct. Wheelers Hill 461 D17
pl. Broadmeadows 238 A8
st. Airport W 278 K12
st. Coburg 281 F19
st. Preston 327 H5
COPELAND
dr. Montrose 382 D9
dr. Point Cook 450 F5
rd. Westmeadows 236 F14
COPELEN
st. South Yarra 32 G6
st. South Yarra 414 J3
COPERNICUS
wy. Keilor Dn 275 J12
COPNAL
ct. Glen Waverley 460 K3
COPPABELLA
wy. Vermont S 420 F11
COPPARD
st. Burwood 418 G9
COPPARDS
rd. Moolap 704 F20
rd. Newcomb 704 F20
COPPEL
ct. Blackburn S 419 J3
COPPELIA
st. Wantirna S 462 B1
COPPELIUS
cl. Sunbury 143 D4
COPPER
la. Clifton Hill 19 L9
COPPERFIELD
dr. Delahey 275 B10
COPPICE
ct. Boronia 424 K5
COPPIN
av. Fitzroy N 20 A1
cl. Hampton Pk 551 K6
cl. Mitcham 377 D15
ct. Glen Waverley 460 B11
ct. Roxburgh Pk 194 B9
gr. Hawthorn 371 E17
rd. Sorrento 678 J11
st. Malvern East 416 C18
st. Richmond 26 J20
st. Richmond 32 J1
COPROSMA
av. Frankston 628 A1
COPSE WOOD
bnd. Caroline Spr 317 L3
COPTFIELD
ct. Glen Waverley 459 K9
COQUETTE
st. Geelong West 702 G6
CORA
av. Altona 407 G15
ct. Mt Waverley 458 K6
CORAL
av. Beaumaris 529 L11
av. Footscray 366 L4
cl. Lilydale 338 L10
cl. Rosebud 700 J5
ct. Avondale Ht 322 A16
ct. Boronia 424 E4
ct. Cheltenham 531 F3
ct. Clarinda 498 F4
ct. Craigieburn 150 E17
ct. Glen Waverley 420 G17
ct. Lalor 241 G6
ct. Lower Plenty 286 H15
ct. Vermont S 420 G13
dr. Hampton Pk 551 K10
mw. Skye 575 J18
rd. Mornington 640 B20
st. Brunswick W 325 B8
st. Frankston 599 K19
st. Heidelberg W 328 C2
CORAL GUM
ct. Narre Warren 538 K19
ri. Diamond Ck 245 C13
CORAL ISLAND
ct. Patterson L 573 H11
CORAM
cl. Nar Warrn N 538 E11
ct. Keysborough 534 D14
ct. Meadow Ht 237 J6
CORAMA
ct. Sydenham 274 L9
CORANDIRK
pl. Yallambie 286 B14
st. Warneet 649 G11
CORANG
av. Grovedale 706 B11
CORBEN
st. Reservoir 282 D15
CORBENS
la. McCrae 685 B11
CORBERT
ct. Ferntree Gly 423 F20
CORBETT
st. Grovedale 706 G10
CORBETTS
rd. Launching Pl 346 C14
CORBIE
pl. Yallambie 285 H14
st. Bentleigh 496 B6
wy. Yallambie 285 H15
CORBIN
pl. Mill Park 242 D2
CORBY
ct. Deer Park 318 L9
st. Balwyn N 373 F3
CORD
cl. Berwick 554 G9
cl. Keilor Dn 276 A13
CORDELIA
gr. St Albans 275 H18
CORDITE
av. Maribyrnong 322 H14
CORDOVA
ct. Dandenong N 501 J10
CORDUROY
rd. Launching Pl 346 J13
rd. Yarra Jctn 346 J13
COREEN
av. Beaumaris 530 D7
st. Croydon 379 D2
CORELLA
av. Melton 226 F15
ct. Carrum Downs 600 L4
ct. Carrum Downs 601 A4
ct. Doncaster 331 C19
ct. Ferntree Gly 464 D8
ct. Mornington 641 C15
dr. Whittlesea 96 C20
dr. Whittlesea 126 C1
pl. Werribee 447 K5
rd. Sunshine W 364 C5
st. Doncaster 331 C19
COREY
av. Dromana 686 H4
CORHAMPTON
rd. Balwyn N 372 L7
rd. Balwyn N 373 A7
CORHANWARRABUL
cl. Rowville 462 F17
CORIANDER
ct. Langwarrin 601 K14
CORINE
ct. Epping 241 L2
CORINELLA
cr. Dallas 238 D9
sq. Wantirna 422 H13
CORINGA
cl. Vermont 377 J20
ct. Knoxfield 463 A6
CORINNE
cl. Springvale S 499 K19
CORIO
av. Frankston 627 F7
dr. Springvale S 499 D18
pl. Geelong 703 F8
st. Belmont 702 G20
st. Geelong 703 A6
st. Geelong 703 C7
st. Glenroy 279 L7
st. Moonee Pnd 323 G11
st. Sunshine 365 C4
CORIS
pl. Epping 198 B16
CORIYULE
ct. Cranbourne N 578 D10
CORK
pl. Mt Martha 657 A9
CORKER
cl. Narre Warren 538 G16
CORLESS
cl. Mt Evelyn 339 J16
CORLETT
st. Frankston 599 E14
st. Mont Albert N 374 F9
CORMAC
st. Preston 327 C4
CORMILIO
dr. Wandin N 340 E5
CORMISTOM
rd. Ringwood N 378 E2
CORMORANT
cl. Blind Bight 650 E8
cl. Endeavour Hl 536 L3
cr. Werribee 448 C10
dr. St Albans 319 G10
pl. Dingley Village 532 L7
pl. Mt Eliza 641 L4
CORNBOROUGH
ct. Frankston S 627 E9
CORNELIA
cl. Kilsyth 381 H8
CORNELIUS
cr. Healesville 213 F14
dr. Wantirna S 422 L19
dr. Wantirna S 423 A19
st. Dandenong 536 E2
CORNELL
ct. Bundoora 284 H4
ct. Frankston 600 B17
pl. Carlton 18 C19
pl. Hampton Pk 552 D12
st. Camberwell 417 J4
st. McCrae 685 B11
st. Mt Waverley 419 F19
CORNER
av. Ferny Creek 425 G19
CORNFIELD
gr. Box Hill S 419 C6
CORNFORTH
wy. Mill Park 242 J1
CORNHILL
st. Ferntree Gly 464 G7
st. St Albans 319 K5
CORNISH
av. Belmont 706 J3
rd. Burwood E 419 G10
rd. Emerald 469 F20
rd. Emerald 509 F1
rd. Healesville 258 A2
rd. Lysterfield 504 C1
rd. Warburton 349 K1
st. Sunbury 143 C10
CORNS
pl. Richmond 26 C10
CORNUS
ct. Narre Warren 539 C20
CORNUTA
wk. Vermont S 420 L11
wk. Vermont S 421 A11
CORNWALL
av. Keysborough 534 K9
cl. Gladstone Pk 237 C18
cr. Mt Martha 669 J1
rd. Pascoe Vale 280 G13
rd. Sunshine 365 F5
st. Avondale Ht 322 A12
st. Blackburn S 420 A2
st. Brunswick W 325 A9
st. Hallam 537 H15
st. Northcote 326 H19
CORNWELL
cr. Cranbourne E 578 J17
COROLLA
av. Bentleigh E 496 H4
COROMANDEL
cr. Knoxfield 463 C4
cr.s, Knoxfield 463 C5
ct. Bulleen 329 H15
pl. Melbourne 2 K13
pl. Melbourne 24 G6
CORONA
ct. Doncaster E 332 E17
pl. Roxburgh Pk 194 F9
st. Balwyn N 373 A1
st. Ivanhoe 328 C14
CORONADO
ct. Highton 705 J5
CORONAL
av. Newtown 701 H5
CORONATA
ct. Narre Warren 553 G11
CORONATION
ct. Bundoora 284 K6
st. Brighton East 455 B12
st. Brunswick W 324 L16
st. Geelong West 702 J7
st. Kingsville 366 K13
st. Mt Waverley 418 L12
st. Sunshine N 321 C17
CORONEL
wy. Beaconsfield 555 E12
CORONET
cl. Epping 198 F18
ct. Cranbourne 603 L4
gr. Beaumaris 529 J9
st. Flemington 33 F4
COROWA
cr. Burnside 318 H7
cr. Greensborough 244 A17
ct. Grovedale 705 L13
ct. Mooroolbark 337 E16
ct. Mt Waverley 419 G13
pl. Frankston 600 H18
CORPORATE
av. Rowville 502 A1
dr. Heatherton 497 G13
CORPORATION
la. Melbourne 2 L18
la. Melbourne 24 H9
la. Ringwood, off Ringwood St 378 D13
CORR
gr. Melton 226 G18
st. Hughesdale 457 G9
st. Moorabbin 497 C9
CORRAN
ct. Endeavour Hl 503 K19
CORREA
av. Cheltenham 496 E19
cl. Delahey 275 C11
cl. Wantirna S 421 L14
ct. Doncaster E 332 E19
ct. Langwarrin 629 K4
ct. Mt Martha 656 G6
ct. W Footscray 366 E11
gr. Frankston S 627 J12
pl. Diamond Ck 245 C11
pl. Endeavour Hl 536 K1
st. Edithvale 546 H15
wy. Sunbury 143 K4
CORRELL
wy. Roxburgh Pk 193 J16
CORRIEDALE
cr. Pk Orchards 333 G18
ct. Belmont 706 C5
rd. Melton W 226 B17
CORRIGAN
av. Brooklyn 365 G17
pl. Attwood 237 B10
pl. Mill Park 242 J9
rd. Keysborough 534 D11
rd. Noble Park 534 D11
rd. Springvale 500 F20
st. Burwood 418 F11
st. Glenroy 279 L4
CORRINGHAM
rd. Beaconsfld Up 542 L15
CORRIS
st. Yarraville 366 J16
CORROBOREE
pl. Templstw Lr 330 D9
CORRONG
cr. Mooroolbark 337 B14
cr. Eltham 288 A15
CORRS
la. Melbourne 2 K10
la. Melbourne 24 F4
CORRYONG
cr. Taylors Lakes 276 D8
CORSAIR
gr. Sorrento 679 A12
rd. The Basin 425 H12
st. Richmond 26 L14
st. Richmond 371 A17
wy. Torquay 712 B3
CORSEWALL
cl. Hawthorn 372 D14
CORSICAN
av. Doncaster E 332 G8
st. Frankston N 600 B7
CORTINA
pl. Avondale Ht 322 D7
CORTLAND
rd. Highton 705 K5
CORUNNA
av. St Albans 275 F19
ct. Glen Waverley 420 C14
CORVETTE
cl. S Morang 198 J14
st. Heidelberg W 284 B20
CORVEY
rd. Reservoir 283 B6
CORVI
ct. Dandenong 535 F4
CORY
ct. Kings Park 275 D17
pl. Berwick 554 L20
CORYULE
av. Mentone 531 A11
rd. Mt Martha 655 J19
COSDOWN
cl. Gladstone Pk 237 C20
COSGRAVE
la. Melbourne 1 A11
la. Melbourne 23 H9
COSGROVE
ct. Meadow Ht 238 A5
st. Rye 696 J6
st. Vermont 421 G3
COSHAM
ct. Greensborough 244 J15
st. Brighton 454 F14
COSIER
dr. Noble Park 534 L7
COSMA
ct. Albanvale 319 B7
COSMO
ct. Kilsyth 380 K9
COSMOS
ct. Doncaster E 332 G13
ct. Whittington 704 E20
st. Dromana 686 E8
st. Glenroy 280 H6
COSSAR
pl. Patterson L 547 H20
COSTAIN
ct. Gladstone Pk 236 L16
ct. Gladstone Pk 237 A16
COSTAS
dr. Hoppers Csg 449 F2
COSTATA
ct. Narre Warren 553 G12
COSTELLO
cl. Bacchus Msh 222 B13
ct. Endeavour Hl 537 K5
la. N Melbourne 34 J11
st. Mont Albert N 374 G8
COSY GUM
rd. Carnegie 456 G4
COSY VALLEY
rd. Langwarrin 629 G6
COTHAM
ct. S Morang 198 J14
rd. Kew 371 K10
sq. Hampton Pk 551 J6
COTONEASTER
ct. Wheelers Hill 460 G15
wy. Langwarrin 601 J15
COTSWOLD
cl. Vermont 421 H5
cr. Springvale S 534 B4

ct. Chirnside Pk.......337 G2
ct. Glen Waverley....459 K4
ct. Grovedale..........706 C13
COTTAGE
cl. Mooroolbark......381 K3
ct. Hampton Pk.......551 H8
pl. Mornington........657 C6
pl. Ringwood N.......334 L20
pl. St Helena...........245 B19
st. Blackburn..........376 A15
COTTER
ct. Berwick.............554 F18
ct. Rowville............462 H17
st. Richmond............32 F1
st. Richmond..........414 J1
COTTERELL
wy. Seabrook...........450 L6
COTTERS
rd. Epping...............196 J14
COTTESLOE
ct. Doncaster E.......332 B16
COTTESMORE
ct. Boronia.............424 G14
COTTINGLEA
Ringwood N.......378 F5
COTTLES BRIDGE-STRATHEWEN
rd. Cottles Br...........203 J1
COTTONWOOD
av. Vermont S.........420 F12
ct. Narre Warren.....553 F10
ct. Templestowe.....331 J5
COTTRELL
ct. Delahey.............275 A12
ct. Nunawading.......376 E8
st. Werribee...........447 F15
st.e, Werribee...........447 G14
COTTSWOLD
av. Narre Warren.....553 D12
pl. Wantirna S.........422 J15
ri. Templestowe.....331 F14
COUANGALT
rd. Gisborne S.........109 B14
rd. Gisborne S.........110 E16
COUCH
st. Sunshine...........365 B6
COULL
av. Boronia.............424 F8
cl. Boronia.............424 G8
COULSON
av. Eumemmerring..536 L15
av. Eumemmerring..537 A15
rd. Monbulk............428 L14
rd. Monbulk............469 G1
COULSTOCK
st. Epping...............197 D20
COULTER
st. Newcomb..........704 F16
COULTON
ct. Werribee...........446 K20
COUNCIL
la. Williamstown.....411 H17
st. Clifton Hill.............19 H7
st. Doncaster...........331 A20
st. Hawthorn E........372 G20
COUNIHAN
st. Sunbury.............142 K10
COUNITHAN
pl. Lysterfield..........464 E17
COUNSEL
ct. Sunbury.............143 D5
COUNTRY
la. View Bank..........285 K20
COUNTRY CLUB
ct. Safety Bch..........669 C19
dr. Chirnside Pk........337 F4
dr. Safety Bch..........686 K2
dr. Safety Bch..........687 A1
COUNTY
cl. Wheelers Hill......461 B14
dr. Berwick.............554 B14
tce. Croydon Hills.....335 H15
tce. Templestowe.....331 G12
COUPER ANGUS
gr. Sunshine...........364 L8
COURAGE
ct. Glen Waverley....420 L15
COURAGEOUS
ct. Frankston...........628 E7
st. Taylors Lakes.....275 H8
COURANG
rd. Glen Iris.............417 B14
COURBRANT
ct. Mont Albert N.....374 F8
COURSE
cl. Forest Hill..........420 E3
COURT
st. Blairgowrie.........696 C2
st. Box Hill.............374 L14
st. Essendon...........323 J9
st. Yarraville...........366 K16
COURTENAY
av. Cranbourne N.....578 B8
COURT HOUSE
pl. Carlton................18 F12
pl. Bacchus Msh, off Bacchus Marsh Rd...........222 A17
COURTIS
st. Williamstown.....411 C12
COURTNAY
pl. Epping...............197 K20
COURTNEY
av. Hoppers Csg......405 B19
pl. N Melbourne........17 E15
sq. Wantirna............422 F9
st. Bundoora...........284 F4
st. Cheltenham........530 K2
st. N Melbourne........17 E14
COURTNEYS
rd. Belgrave S..........506 C12
COUSEN
pl. Gladstone Pk......237 D18
COUSIN
dr. Bayswater..........423 A9
COUTIES
rd. Panton Hill.........248 C4
COUTTS
ct. Blairgowrie.........679 J20
st. Safety Bch..........668 L18
COVAL
ct. Vermont S.........420 K7
COVALA
ct. St Helena...........244 L19
ct. St Helena...........245 A19
COVE
av. Portsea.............666 G20
ct. Endeavour Hl.....503 L19
la. Seaford.............573 F13
pl. Portsea.............666 G19
COVEN
av. Heathmont.........379 E18
COVENTRY
cr. Mill Park............242 L12
ct. Frankston...........599 K16
ct. Grovedale..........706 C12
dr. Werribee...........446 L12
pl. Bayswater..........423 E10
pl. Chirnside Pk........336 H7
pl. Melton S............268 C10
pl. S Melbourne.........29 H4
rd. Narre Warren.....553 C5
st. Burwood E.........420 A13
st. Montmorency.....286 G12
st. Southbank..............3 G20
st. Southbank............30 E1
st. Southbank..........413 H1
st. S Melbourne..........3 A20
st. S Melbourne.........29 E5
st. S Melbourne......413 C3
st. S Melbourne......413 H1
st. Tullamarine........279 A8
COVERLID
pl. Melbourne.............2 K11
pl. Melbourne...........24 G5
COWANS
la. Parwan...............265 H11
rd. Hopetoun Park....223 L20
rd. Hopetoun Park....265 K2
rd. Long Forest.......223 L20
COWARD
st. Footscray...........367 F6
COWDEN
rd. Kangaroo Grnd...289 J10
COWDEROY
pl. St Kilda, off Canterbury Rd....413 L12
st. Hoppers Csg......405 D20
st. St Kilda W.......413 K13
COWELL
st. Fitzroy..................18 L18
COWES
pl. Taylors Lakes.....275 H9
st. Craigieburn........150 A15
COWIE
la. Albert Park...........29 E14
pl. Hoppers Csg......448 B2
COWIN
cl. Rowville.............463 J19
st. Diamond Ck.......245 H9
COWLEY
ct. Mooroolbark.......337 H18
st. Delahey.............275 A11
st. McCrae..............684 J16
COWPER
av. St Albans...........320 K4
cr. Sunbury.............142 K12
ri. Berwick..............554 D3
st. Blairgowrie.........695 K3
st. Brighton.............454 K13
st. Essendon N........279 F20
st. Footscray...........367 F12
st. Footscray...........367 H8
st. Hawthorn E........372 H15
st. Preston..............327 A6
st. St Kilda.............414 B20
st. Sandringham......495 C16
COWRA
av. St Albans...........320 F12
st. Altona...............408 J17
st. Brighton.............455 B14
st. Vermont.............421 F5
COWRIE
ct. Tootgarook........698 F7
rd. Torquay.............711 L6
st. Glen Waverley....460 L5
COX
cr. Carrum Downs...574 H16
ct. Altona Mdw........451 J9
ct. Endeavour Hl.....537 E9
st. Cheltenham........497 D19
st. St Albans...........320 D11
COXS
gdn. Williamstown.....411 F14
COZENS
cl. Frankston S........627 J11
st. Brunswick..........325 F8
CRABAPPLE
cl. Glen Waverley....420 D14
CRABBE
ct. Delahey.............275 D12
CRABILL
wk. Nar Warrn S.......552 F20
CRABTREE
ct. Bundoora...........284 J5
ct. Reservoir...........283 J16
CRACKNELLS
rd. Panton Hill.........248 G3
CRADDOCK
av. Caulfield N.........455 G1
ct. Sunshine N........321 E16
CRADLE
rd. Diggers Rest......187 A10
CRADLEY
av. Kew..................371 F10
ct. Kilsyth...............381 C3
CRAFT
wk. Nar Warrn S.......578 G1
CRAIG
av. Camberwell........372 K19
av. Craigieburn........150 D17
av. Ferntree Gly.......464 F3
av. Mt Dandenong....382 J16
ct. Altona North.......409 E2
ct. Burwood............418 F12
ct. Carrum..............573 E10
ct. Cheltenham........531 G1
ct. Chirnside Pk........337 H6
ct. Heathmont.........378 J20
dr. Berwick.............553 J9
rd. Cranbourne........604 H19
rd. Devon Mdw........648 E3
rd. Donvale.............377 H8
rd. Junction Vill.......604 H19
rd. Pearcedale.........648 E3
rd. Plenty...............244 G10
st. Blackburn S.......375 E20
st. Frankston...........627 J1
st. Keilor East.........322 J4
st. Noble Park.........534 F2
st. Spotswood.........411 B2
CRAIGAVAD
st. Carnegie............456 F4
CRAIG AVON
la. Merricks N.........688 L11
CRAIGAVON
ct. Deer Park...........318 J10
CRAIGDARROCH
av. Anglesea............713 E7
CRAIG HILL
dr. Wheelers Hill......461 D16
CRAIGIE
av. Chelsea.............546 H15
av. Edithvale...........546 H15
ct. Hampton Pk.......551 L9
rd. Mt Martha..........656 A9
rd. Mt Martha..........656 H10
rd. Mt Martha..........657 A11
rd. Newtown............701 K11
CRAIGIEBURN
rd. Oaklands Jctn.....191 E1
rd. Yuroke...............149 A16
rd.e, Craigieburn........150 K19
rd.e, Wollert...............197 B1
rd.w, Craigieburn........149 C16
rd.w, Craigieburn........149 J17
CRAIGIELEA
av. St Albans...........320 C2
CRAIGLEA
ct. Doncaster E.......331 J15
CRAIGMORE
av. Mentone............531 J7
pl. Melton W...........226 C16
CRAIGROSSIE
av. Coburg..............325 D6
rd. Mornington........640 K10
CRAIGS
la. Cannons Creek...648 D7
la. Pearcedale.........648 D7
CRAIGTON
ct. Cranbourne N.....578 D10
CRAIK
rd. Beaconsfld Up....542 H16
CRAILEEN
st. Donvale.............376 F4
CRAINE
st. S Melbourne........30 B2
CRAITHIE
av. Pk Orchards.......334 C17
CRAMER
st. Coburg..............325 B1
st. Preston..............282 D20
wk. Brighton.............454 H16
CRAMOND
pl. Greenvale...........193 F16
CRAMPTON
cr. Mill Park............242 C7
cr. Rosanna............285 A17
ct. Hoppers Csg......405 B18
ct. Rowville.............502 K6
CRANA
ct. Chadstone..........458 A1
ct. Hoppers Csg......405 A17
gr. Greensborough..244 C16
CRANBERRY
pl. Bundoora...........242 D14
CRANBOURNE
av. Sunshine N........321 B15
dr. Cranbourne........604 A2
pl. Cranbourne........578 D17
rd. Frankston...........599 D20
CRANBOURNE-FRANKSTON
rd. Cranbourne........602 H13
rd. Cranbourne S.....602 H13
rd. Cranbourne W....603 A11
rd. Langwarrin.........628 K4
CRANBROOK
ct. Doncaster..........330 J19
ct. Gladstone Pk......237 D20
ct. Gladstone Pk......279 D1
st. Yarraville...........366 H19
CRANHAM
st. Caulfield............455 K5
st. Noble Park.........500 D18
CRANHAVEN
rd. Langwarrin.........629 A4
rd. Langwarrin.........629 D5
CRANLEIGH
gr. Mt Waverley.......458 L2
pl. Craigieburn........150 C20
CRANLEY
ct. Grovedale..........706 A15
pl. Thomastown......240 J11
st. Springvale..........500 A12
CRANMERE
av. Belmont............706 B7
CRANSTON
cl. Nar Warrn N.......539 A6
ct. Rosebud............684 C20
CRANSTOUN
ct. Thomson...........703 K16
CRANSWICK
ct. Mornington........656 L3
ct. Mornington........657 A3
CRANWELL
av. Strathmore........323 J1
ct. Bundoora...........284 K1
ct. Highton.............705 J8
ct. Mulgrave...........500 D1
mw. Skye.................575 J17
st. Braybrook..........321 K19
CRATHIE
ct. Frankston...........627 K8
CRATLOE
rd. Cockatoo...........511 G9
rd. Mt Waverley.......419 A14
CRAVEN
st. Noble Park.........500 G17
st. Prahran.............414 L12
CRAVENS
rd. Mernda.............199 C4
CRAWFORD
av. Dandenong N.....501 E20
rd. Clarinda............498 C5
rd. Doncaster..........330 J16
rd. Gisborne.............78 K8
rd. Templstw Lr.......330 J16
st. Braeside............532 G18
st. Cheltenham........530 F3
st. Moonee Pnd......324 C10
st. Mt Eliza.............626 C12
st. Newport.............411 C9
wy. Sunbury.............142 F9
CRAWLEY
ct. Craigieburn........149 L15
ct. Vermont S.........421 A10
ct. View Bank..........285 J18
gr. Ringwood N.......334 H20
rd. Nar Warrn N.......539 E9
st. Reservoir...........282 J14
CREA
ct. St Helena...........245 A19
CREAN
ct. Mill Park............243 A4
CRECY
ct. Heidelberg W.....284 D18
CREEDMORE
dr. Rye...................697 E8
CREEDON
st. Fawkner.............281 H10
CREEK
ct. Eumemmerring..537 C12
pde. Northcote............20 E1
pl. Clyde North........581 G14
rd. Belgrave............466 J16
rd. Lilydale.............338 E4
rd. Mitcham............377 D15
rd. Mornington........640 J15
st. Melton S............268 H8
st. Ringwood...........378 D11
st. Spotswood........367 A20
CREEKBANK
pl. Caroline Spr.......318 C8
st. Upwey..............465 J17
CREEKVIEW
wy. Wyndham Va.....446 D8
CREEKWOOD
av. Pakenham..........584 A4
dr. Craigieburn........149 L13
CREIGHTON
st. Narre Warren.....538 K13
wy. Doreen.............202 A9
wy. Mornington........657 C3
wy. Nutfield.............202 A9
CRELLIN
av. Laverton............406 J20
av.s, Altona Mdw.......450 J1
cr. Watsonia...........285 F6
gr. Camberwell........417 F5
st. Doncaster E.......331 K18
CREMEAN
av. Ivanhoe.............328 A10
CREMIN
cl. Kew..................371 G4
cl. Mill Park............242 C5
ct. Mt Waverley.......458 L8
ct. Rosanna............284 L20
ct. Rosanna............285 A20
ct. Rowville.............502 L6
ct. Rowville.............503 A6
dr. Pakenham..........559 F15
CREMONA
st. Mentone............531 B9
CREMORNE
ct. Dingley Village...532 L6
pl. Fitzroy..................18 L15
st. Balwyn..............373 E11
st. Braybrook..........322 B20
st. Cremorne............26 A20
st. Cremorne............32 A1
st. Fitzroy..................18 L15
CRERAR
rd. Kallista..............467 K7
rd. The Patch..........467 K7
CRESCENT
la. Ringwood..........378 F12
rd. Camberwell........416 K2
rd. Yarra Jctn..........346 J15
st. Noble Park.........500 F17
CRESMONT
ct. Kings Park.........275 D17
CRESPIN
pl. Roxburgh Pk......194 B11
st. Niddrie..............323 B2
CRESSER
st. Altona North.......409 K5
CRESSIDA
cr. Sydenham.........275 B7
cr. Sydenham.........275 B8
CRESSONIERRE
ct. Hallam...............537 K14

CRESSWELL
cr. Mitcham 377 A8
CRESSWOLD
av. Avondale Ht 322 D13
CRESSY
ct. Broadmeadows ..237 H15
pl. Geelong 703 C8
st. Malvern 416 C10
st. Montmorency 287 A15
CREST
av. Balwyn.............373 B13
av. Hampton E.........495 J9
ct. The Basin...........425 B7
dr. Rosebud 700 K2
gr. Nunawading.......376 K11
rd. Research 247 A20
rd. Research 289 A1
st. Greensborough ..244 G20
CRESTA
ct. Berwick.............554 G20
ct. Keilor East.........322 H5
ct. Lalor..................240 J8
ct. Mulgrave 500 G1
CRESTDALE
rd. Wantirna............422 E12
CRESTHAVEN
ct. Donvale 332 K16
CRESTMONT
ct. Doncaster E 332 G9
ct. Toorak...............415 F5
dr. Glen Waverley 460 J3
dr. Melton S............268 E8
tce. Craigieburn 150 E7
CRESTMOOR
dr. Highton.............705 H5
CRESTVIEW
cl. Montrose 381 K11
ct. Croydon N 336 A14
ct. Frankston S........627 K17
ct. Rye....................697 K7
CRESTWAY
Lilydale 338 C2
CRESWELL
av. Airport W...........279 A18
ct. Altona Mdw........451 E5
rd. Marcus Hill 707 A13
rd. Pt Lonsdale........707 A16
CRESWICK
ct. Point Cook.........450 A5
ct. Roxburgh Pk......194 D12
gr. McKinnon 456 E16
la. Mont Albert........374 F14
st. Balwyn...............372 L11
st. Brighton East 495 E5
st. Donvale 376 H5
st. Footscray...........367 C7
st. Glen Iris 416 D10
st. Glen Waverley 460 L2
st. Hawthorn...........371 D15
st. Laverton 407 F14
CRETE
av. Ashburton.........417 J18
rd. Tremont.............425 C14
CREVELLI
st. Reservoir...........283 H17
CREW
st. Yallambie...........285 G16
CREWE
rd. Hughesdale........457 H9
CREWEN
wk. Keilor Dn............276 F12
CREWS
st. St Kilda E...........414 G16
st. Windsor, off Raleigh St..........414 E11
CRICHTON
av. Port Melb...........412 F3
av. Thomastown......240 A19
la. Kensington 33 E9
rd. Emerald 509 H3
CRICK
st. Braybrook..........365 H5
CRICKLEWOOD
av. Frankston...........599 E16
dr. Templestowe 331 F15
CRIGAN
rd. Pt Lonsdale........710 D6
CRIGHTON
ct. Baxter................644 C3
CRIMEA
cl. Ferntree Gly 463 L13
st. Burnley..............371 B20
st. Caulfield N 415 F18
st. St Kilda...............414 E14
CRIMSON
av. Blackburn S 419 J3
ct. Carrum Downs...575 G15
dr. Doveton.............536 H7
CRINAN
st. Kilsyth 381 A5
CRINNION
rd. Diggers Rest 187 L14
CRISP
av. Brunswick..........325 H10
ct. Bacchus Msh 221 K14
ct. Vermont 421 K3
pl. Burwood............418 E6
st. Essendon...........323 L4
st. Hampton............494 L10
st. Hampton............495 A10
st. Healesville..........257 F1
CRISPE
st. Reservoir 282 G15
CRISPIAN
ct. Thomastown......240 D17
CRISSANE
rd. Bundoora...........284 C15
rd. Heidelberg W 284 C15
CRISTATA
av. Endeavour Hl 502 K20
CROAD
st. Sorrento 678 E6
CROANNA
st. Rye....................697 B6
CROCKERTON
ct. Blackburn S 419 J6
CROCKETT
av. Craigieburn 150 H19
CROCKFORD
st. Port Melb.............29 B6
st. Port Melb............413 A3
CROCUS
cr. Glen Waverley 460 D10
ct. Cheltenham........496 F17
CROFT
al. Melbourne 2 L11
al. Melbourne 24 G5
cr. Reservoir 282 J12
st. Essendon...........323 D4
st. Oakleigh.............458 D14
CROFTON
cl. Wonga Park 335 H11
ct. Eltham 288 E3
ct. Mt Waverley.......419 F15
dr. Williamstown 410 J16
mw. Eltham 288 D4
st. Geelong West.....702 D5
tce. Doncaster E 332 J12
CROFTS
ct. Altona.................452 E1
CROKER
st. Newport.............410 H9
CROM
st. Balwyn...............374 A10
CROMB
av. Beaumaris..........530 D10
CROMBIE
la. Melbourne 1 C10
la. Melbourne 23 J8
rd. Lilydale 340 A8
CROMDALE
st. Mt Martha...........656 D5
CROMER
av. Sunshine N 321 C11
av. Sunshine N 321 C9
cr. Mulgrave 460 G20
ct. Frankston............599 J16
ct. Gladstone Pk......237 B17
pl. Keilor Dn............276 F12
rd. Beaumaris...........530 E11
CROMFORD
cr. Nar Warrn S.......579 A5
CROMPTON
ct. Caulfield S..........456 A10
CROMWELL
cl. Melton S 268 C12
cr. South Yarra..........32 G12
ct. Blackburn 376 C16
ct. Keysborough 534 D9
ct. Lalor..................241 J6
dr. Greenvale...........237 E6
dr. Rowville.............502 H4
pde. W Footscray.......366 C13
pl. Highton..............701 E19
pl. S Melbourne 29 H2
pl. South Yarra...........32 G16
rd. Kings Park 319 B2
rd. South Yarra..........32 H11
rd. South Yarra..........32 H16
rd. South Yarra.........414 K6
rd. Werribee 447 H3
st. Burwood.............418 D9
st. Caulfield N 415 J20
st. Collingwood..........25 L2
st. Eltham 287 D12
st. Glen Iris 417 C11
st. Glenroy..............280 B5
st. Mornington........640 F15
CRONIA
ct. Wheelers Hill......461 G16
CRONIN
ct. Cheltenham........531 G1
CRONULLA
ct. Noble Park 534 G7
CRONUS
ct. Eltham 287 D13
CROOK
st. Bacchus Msh 222 D17
st. Brunswick..........325 D10
CROOKS
rd. Kallista...............427 D19
CROOKSTON
rd. Reservoir 283 D7
CROOM
st. Warburton 349 G3
CROPLEY
cr. Laverton 407 E11
ct. Burwood............418 F7
ct. Seabrook 450 K7
ct. Werribee............447 H10
CROPPER
pl. Williamstown 411 H17
CROPTON
pl. Nar Warrn S.......579 B4
CROSBIE
ct. Sunbury.............143 E8
rd. Murrumbeena 457 A13
CROSBY
cl. Gladstone Pk......237 B15
ct. St Albans 320 K7
dr. Glen Waverley 459 J3
rd. Pakenham Up 559 G2
CROSLEY
st. Healesville..........258 A3
CROSS
rd. Chelsea.............546 K15
st. Braybrook 366 B2
st. Brighton.............454 K8
st. Brunswick E........325 L14
st. Canterbury 373 F19
st. Caulfield S..........455 L11
st. Emerald 469 A20
st. Footscray............366 H8
st. Geelong West.....702 G4
st. Ringwood N......378 E6
st. Toorak 415 J9
st. W Footscray.......366 H8
tce. Glenroy..............279 G3
CROSSAKIEL
ct. Hawthorn...........416 A1
CROSSDALE
ri. Endeavour Hl 537 J1
CROSSLEE
ct. Deer Park...........319 D12
CROSSLEY
cr. Coolaroo 238 F5
ct. Lysterfield 464 B20
rd. Mt Eliza..............642 A6
st. Melbourne 24 J5
CROSSMAN
ct. Box Hill S 418 J4
dr. Croydon Hills 335 D15
st. Doncaster E 375 G2
CROTHERS
st. Braybrook...........366 B4
CROTONHURST
av. Caulfield N 455 F1
CROTTY
rd. Boronia..............423 E12
CROUCH
ct. Dandenong N 536 C1
ct. Doncaster 331 B15
CROW
st. Burwood E.........419 D12
CROWE
ct. Eltham 288 F5
st. Hoppers Csg 448 H4
CROWEA
wy. Mornington........656 J4
CROWFOOT
ct. Clarinda 498 E4
CROWLEY
av. Narre Warren 553 D7
ct. Pascoe Vale 280 F11
rd. Healesville..........257 H2
CROWN
av. Camberwell........416 J6
av. Mordialloc..........532 A18
cl. Oakleigh E..........458 L11
ct. Ferntree Gly 424 E20
ct. Jan Juc...............711 D17
ct. Kings Park 274 L20
pl. Berwick..............539 L19
pl. Melbourne 1 J9
pl. Melbourne 24 A6
pt. Chirnside Pk.......337 H7
pt. Craigieburn 150 F7
rd. Bonbeach...........573 C2
rd. Ivanhoe..............328 A19
st. Flemington...........33 F3
st. Footscray...........367 E7
st. Glen Waverley 419 K17
st. Laverton 407 C19
st. Richmond...........371 B15
st. S Geelong 703 D16
st.s, Altona Mdw........407 C20
tce. Ascot Vale..........323 F15
CROWN POINT
rdg. Chirnside Pk.......337 H5
CROWS
la. Glen Waverley 420 D14
rd. Belmont.............706 K4
CROWTHER
av. Wattle Glen 246 K5
pl. Brighton.............454 H14
CROXLEY
cl. Wyndham Va 446 G11
CROXTETH
wy. Wantirna............422 B11
CROXTON
dr. Kurunjang 227 F9
CROYDON
av. Deer Park...........319 A13
rd. Croydon.............380 B2
rd. Surrey Hills 373 H17
rd. Warrandyte S 334 G8
wy. Croydon.............379 J7
CROYDONDALE
dr. Mooroolbark 337 D17
Croydon HillsS
dr. Croydon Hills 335 F14
CROZIER
ct. McKinnon 455 K17
st. Coburg 326 A5
CRUIKSHANK
pl. Port Melb.............29 C8
st. Port Melb.............29 B10
st. Port Melb...........413 A5
CRUMP
la. Dandenong 536 A9
CRUNDALE
st. Ashwood 418 B15
CRUSADER
cr. Glen Waverley 420 L17
CRUSOE
dr. Ferntree Gly 463 L15
CRYSTAL
cl. Whittlesea............96 E17
ct. Point Cook 451 B6
ct. Wheelers Hill......461 E19
gdn. Cranbourne W....603 G1
CRYSTAL BROOK
ct. Nar Warrn S.......553 D17
CUBBY
pl. Geelong, off Henry St 703 E10
CUBITT
st. Cremorne 32 B2
CUDDLE
ct. Bacchus Msh 221 G15
CUDGEE
ct. Ashwood 418 F17
ct. Research 288 H1
CUDGEWA
pl. Keilor East.........278 B18
CUDMORE
st. Essendon...........323 F2
CUFFE
wk. Kensington 33 F7
CULBARA
dr. Vermont 421 J2
CULBIN
av. Belmont.............702 E17
CULBURRA
av. Frankston...........628 C3
CULCAIRN
ct. Mt Martha..........656 K9
ct. Nar Warrn S.......552 G14
dr. Frankston S........627 E10
CULGOA
ct. Eltham...............287 L5
ct. Keilor.................276 K10
ct. Werribee............447 F8
st. Warneet.............649 D13
CULLA
hill, Eltham 288 A16
CULLAN
pl. Frankston...........600 H20
CULLEN
cl. Berwick..............539 J18
cr. Diamond Ck........245 A3
ct. Albion................320 G18
ct. Chirnside Pk........337 B3
ct. Patterson L 573 K8
ct. Torquay 711 F11
st. Spotswood 410 K2
CULLENS
pl. Geelong, off Little Myers St....703 A9
CULLIMORE
ct. Dandenong S 535 G13
CULLINAN
ct. Ferntree Gly 464 C12
CULLINANE
st. Black Rock.........529 H5
CULLIS
pde. Bayswater 423 H6
CULLITON
rd. Camberwell........417 C5
CULLIVER
av. Eumemmerring..536 L15
CULLODEN
st. Brunswick W......324 K9
CULMA
st. Glen Huntly 456 C8
CULMARA
ct. Berwick..............553 G2
CULOTTA
la. Lynbrook 551 D19
CULSHAW
av. Clayton S 499 F10
st. Toorak 415 C9
CULVERLANDS
rd. Heathmont.........379 C17
st. Heidelberg W 284 G17
CULWELL
av. Mitcham 377 J16
CULZEAN
cr. Highton..............701 H15
CUMBERLAND
av. Balwyn N 374 B7
av. Bayswater 422 J5
av. Noble Park 500 K20
ch. Hampton Pk.........552 B11
ch. Sunbury.............143 D11
cl. Williamstown 411 G18
cr. Chirnside Pk.......337 F1
cr. Thomastown......241 H16
ct. Doncaster E 332 H10
ct. Forest Hill 376 F20
ct. Glen Waverley 460 K1
ct. Preston..............283 G17
ct. Werribee............446 L12
dr. Mt Martha..........656 C16
dr. Seaford.............599 H5
pl. Altona Mdw........451 K4
pl. Carlton.................18 B18
rd. Pascoe Vale 280 H19
rd. Pascoe Vale S 280 H19
rd. Port Melb...........412 C5
st. Eaglemont..........328 L10
st. Newtown 702 E8
st. Sunshine N 321 G18
wy. Endeavour Hl 536 L1
wy. Endeavour Hl 537 A1
CUMBERNAULD
cr. Deer Park...........318 L8
CUMING
pl. Sunbury.............143 J10
st. Yarraville............367 A15
CUMMING
ct. Mornington........656 L1
ct. Mornington........657 A2
st. Brunswick W......324 K10
st. Burwood............418 G11
st. Heathmont.........378 F20
st. Heathmont.........422 F1
CUMMINGS
pl. Geelong, off Corio St 703 C7
rd. Maddingley 264 A20
rd. Parwan 264 A20
rd. Wattle Glen 247 F8
CUMMINS
dr. Somerton...........195 B14
gr. Malvern 416 A16
la. Mt Eliza..............626 L19
rd. Brighton East 495 J5
st. W Melbourne 367 J13
CUMQUAT
ct. Cranbourne N.....578 A6
CUMULUS
ct. Hampton Pk.......552 A15
CUNEATA
cl. Langwarrin.........601 J20
CUNEO
ct. Mill Park 242 C9
CUNNEEN
cr. Berwick.............554 F18
CUNNINGHAM
cl. Aspendale Gdn...546 K6
cl. Darley.................221 J10
cr. Pakenham..........584 G5
ct. Ascot Vale..........324 B20
ct. Melton S 268 F12
ct. Taylors Lakes.....275 E7

dr. Endeavour Hl.....537 L4
dr. Mill Park.....242 J5
pl. Oakleigh S.....498 B10
st. Box Hill.....375 A18
st. Geelong.....703 B6
st. Northcote.....326 G19
st. South Yarra.....32 E11
st. South Yarra.....414 H5

CUNNINGTON
av. Brunswick E.....326 A12

CUPAR
pl. Greenvale.....192 K20

CURDIES
st. Bentleigh E.....496 H6

CURIE
av. Mulgrave.....500 K6
av. Oak Park.....280 B11
ct. Seaford.....574 A19

CURLEW
av. Altona.....408 G19
cl. Maribyrnong.....322 J16
cl. Melton.....226 H16
ct. Carrum Downs...600 K5
ct. Doncaster.....331 C20
ct. Mornington.....640 L17
ct. Pt Lonsdale.....707 H17
ct. Whittlesea.....126 C1
ct. Yallambie.....285 G15
dr. Rosebud W.....699 E4
dr. Whittlesea.....96 C20
dr. Whittlesea.....126 C1
pl. Werribee.....448 A4

CURLEWIS
st. Mont Albert.....374 D13

CURLEW POINT
dr. Patterson L.....573 G10

CURLEY
st. Brighton East.....455 E20

CURNOLA
av. Doncaster.....330 E18
ct. Doncaster.....330 D17

CURNOW
ct. Cranbourne W....577 G19

CURRAJONG
av. Camberwell.....416 H4
av. Mt Evelyn.....383 C4
av. Selby.....466 K18
av. Selby.....467 A17
av. Selby.....467 A19
rd. Hawthorn E.....416 D2
st. Dandenong N.....501 G13
st. Doncaster E.....332 E19
st. Glenroy.....280 A8
st. Oakleigh E.....458 J13
st. St Albans.....320 H9
st. Thomastown.....241 D13
st. Vermont S.....420 J14
st. W Footscray.....366 H10

CURRAL
pl. Elsternwick.....455 B4
rd. Elsternwick.....455 B4

CURRAN
ct. St Albans.....320 D12
la. Dandenong.....535 L10
la. N Melbourne.....34 J8
la. Officer.....556 D18
pl. N Melbourne.....34 K8
st. N Melbourne.....34 J8
st. Oakleigh E.....458 F11
wy. Tootgarook.....698 B8

CURRAWA
dr. Boronia.....424 D16
st. Caulfield.....455 L5

CURRAWEENA
rd. Caulfield S.....455 K9

CURRAWONG
av. Lalor.....241 B5
ct. Rosebud W.....699 F4
ct. Up Fntree Gly.....465 G8
ct. Werribee.....447 J5
dr. Carrum Downs...575 A20
gr. Cannons Creek...649 D7
la. Greensborough...286 D3
rd. Healesville.....258 A1
rd. Montrose.....382 B13
st. Keysborough.....534 K8
st. Mornington.....641 A15

CURRIE
av. Endeavour Hl.....537 H7
av. Tecoma.....466 D11
dr. Delahey.....275 D10
st. Box Hill N.....374 K8
tce. Glen Waverley....461 A6

CURRINGA
cl. Berwick.....553 F6

CURRONG
gr. Croydon.....379 H6

CURRUMBIN
ct. Taylors Lakes.....276 B9
ct. Tootgarook.....698 C6

CURRUNGHI
ct. St Albans.....320 L8
ct. St Albans.....321 A8

CURRY
rd. Pk Orchards.....333 J20

CURTAIN
rd. Hurstbridge.....203 A16
st. Carlton N.....18 G4
st. Kingsbury.....284 A8

CURTAYNE
ct. Noble Park N.....501 E12

CURTIN
av. Brunswick W.....324 H8
av. Hadfield.....280 L7
av. Lalor.....241 E7
cr. Dandenong N.....501 J20
ct. Altona.....409 F17
ct. Maidstone.....366 F2
dr. Sunbury.....143 H4
pl. Fitzroy N.....19 B7
st. Bentleigh E.....457 A17
st. Bundoora.....243 D20
st. Maidstone.....366 E2
st. St Albans.....320 C8

CURTIS
av. Mt Waverley.....458 G7
av. Sunbury.....144 C8
av. Watsonia.....285 C9
cr. Gisborne.....78 L15
ct. Cranbourne.....578 B15
ct. Jan Juc.....711 E15
la. Roxburgh Pk.....194 E15
pl. Brunswick, off Stewart St.....325 G11
rd. Emerald.....509 D6
st. Belmont.....706 K1
st. Essendon.....324 C5

CURZON
av. Healesville.....258 B3
pl. N Melbourne.....17 C18
st. Brighton East.....495 D1
st. Ivanhoe.....327 K8
st. N Melbourne.....17 B20
st. Reservoir.....282 K1
st. W Melbourne.....17 B20

CUSDIN
st. Glen Iris.....417 B9

CUSH
pl. Hampton Pk.....551 G13

CUSHING
av. Bentleigh.....456 E20

CUSTER
gr. Bayswater N.....380 J17

CUSTOM
pl. Werribee.....487 G2
rd. Tullamarine.....278 H1

CUSTOM HOUSE
la. Melbourne.....1 D19
la. Melbourne.....23 L12

CUTHBERT
av. Highton.....705 J2
av. Truganina.....405 G15
ct. Wantirna S.....462 E2
ct. Wheelers Hill.....460 K9
dr. Hillside.....231 K18
dr. Mill Park.....242 E8
pl. Burnside.....318 D7
rd. Reservoir.....283 B10
st. Broadmeadows..238 A16
st. Bulleen.....329 J15
st. Heathmont.....378 F20
st. Heathmont.....422 F1
st. Niddrie.....278 K20
st. Seddon.....367 C10

CUTHBERTSON
ct. Bacchus Msh.....221 K12
ct. Chelsea.....547 B19

CUTLER
cl. Ferntree Gly.....464 A6
ct. Lalor.....241 D7
ct. Ringwood N.....334 J19

CUTTER
st. Burnley.....371 B19

CUTTRISS
rd. Werribee S.....488 G20

CUTTS
av. Croydon.....379 E4
av. Dromana.....685 L10
st. Sunshine N.....321 E17

CUZENS
pl. Geelong, off Fenwick St.....702 L8

CYANAMID
st. Laverton N.....408 B3

CYCADE
av. Altona North.....409 L1

CYCLAMEN
av. Altona North.....409 K1

CYGNET
av. Templstw Lr.....330 A8
ct. Eltham.....287 D8
ct. Frankston.....600 C16
ct. Queenscliff.....707 L19

CYNGA
ct. Grovedale.....706 C10
st. Preston.....327 E3

CYNISCA
ct. Wheelers Hill.....460 J17

CYNTHIA
ct. Hillside.....274 G3
ct. Wantirna S.....423 B14
gr. Woori Yallock.....344 F13

CYPRESS
av. Boronia.....424 C14
av. Brooklyn.....365 H18
av. Burwood.....418 L10
av. Glen Waverley....419 K14
av. Templstw Lr.....330 J12
cl. Hampton Pk.....552 A16
ct. Chelsea.....547 B19
ct. Chirnside Pk.....337 G6
ct. Cranbourne N.....578 E8
ct. Hillside.....273 K3
ct. Noble Park.....500 H17
ct. Oakleigh S.....498 A9
ct. Portsea.....678 B3
gr. Dandenong N.....501 H20
la. Torquay.....711 K3
st. Heidelberg W.....327 L1
wy. Maribyrnong.....322 L12
wy. Maribyrnong.....323 A12

CYPRESS HILL
dr. Nar Warrn S.....553 C19

CYPRESS POINT
ct. Sunbury.....144 B11
dr. Mt Eliza.....626 B9

CYPRUS
av. Nunawading.....376 J10
ct. Bundoora.....284 H6
ct. Wyndham Va.....446 E11
pl. Melton W.....226 A15
pl. Pakenham.....584 H3
st. Eumemmerring..537 C12
st. Lalor.....241 E11

CYRENE
st. Noble Park.....534 F3

CYRIL
ct. Belmont.....706 G2
gr. Noble Park.....535 D5
st. Ashburton.....417 K15
st. Box Hill S.....418 H3
st. Elwood.....454 G2
st. Lilydale.....338 J5
st. Windsor.....414 J12

D

DABCOR
cl. Hallam.....552 B3

DACE
ct. Pascoe Vale S....280 J19

DACELO
av. Broadmeadows...238 A18

DACEY
st. Brighton East.....495 G4

DACTYL
rd. Moorabbin.....496 D9

DADSWELL
ct. Sunbury.....142 L5

DAFF
av. Hampton E.....496 A11

DAFFODIL
ct. Gowanbrae.....279 C6
rd. Boronia.....424 E16
st. Bentleigh E.....496 J2

DAFIELD
ct. Rosanna.....285 C18

DAGOLA
av. Nunawading.....376 K18

DAGONET
st. Strathmore.....279 K16

DAHLEN
pl. Berwick.....553 K14

DAHLENBURG
st. W Melbourne.....367 J12

DAHLIA
ct. Endeavour Hl.....537 E5
ct. Nar Warrn S.....579 D1
st. Dromana.....686 E8
st. Dromana.....686 G7

DAHMEN
st. Carrum.....573 E7

DAI
ct. Mt Waverley.....458 K8

DAIMLER
av. Keilor Dn.....276 A16
ct. Epping.....197 J14
ct. McCrae.....684 K18

DAINA
ct. Diamond Ck.....245 J6
ct. Skye.....601 G4

DAINTREE
av. Pk Orchards.....334 A17
gr. Narre Warren.....539 F20
ri. St Helena.....245 B19

DAIRY
cl. Sydenham.....274 L5
ct. View Bank.....285 K20
la. Ferntree Gly.....463 F6
pl. Skye.....575 G17
rd. Werribee.....448 E14

DAIRYFARM
tce. Hampton Pk.....551 L12

DAISY
ct. Box Hill N.....374 J6
ct. Braybrook.....366 B1
ct. Nar Warrn S.....552 H15
dr. Bundoora.....242 F15
st. Essendon.....323 J8
st. Heathmont.....378 D18
st. Murrumbeena....457 D12
st. Newtown.....702 C11
st. Warranwood.....334 J13
wy. Carrum Downs...574 L19

DAKAR
ct. Keilor Dn.....276 D14

DAKARA
cl. Meadow Ht.....194 C20
ct. Mooroolbark.....337 C16
ct. Wyndham Va.....446 H13
pl. Sunshine W.....364 K7

DAKOTA
ct. Forest Hill.....420 D9
ct. Tullamarine.....236 H20
dr. Thomastown.....240 D17
pl. Point Cook.....450 D4

DALBEATTIE
dr. Clarinda.....498 C7

DALBURY
pl. Mill Park.....242 F10
pl. Narre Warren.....539 F17

DALBY
cl. Rowville.....463 G15

DALE
av. Pascoe Vale.....280 J18
av. Safety Bch.....668 K19
ct. Balwyn N.....374 A1
ct. Blackburn N.....375 F10
ct. Dandenong N.....501 J16
ct. Scoresby.....462 E8
ct. Seville.....341 J12
st. Balwyn.....372 K11
st. Bulleen.....330 A17
st. Cremorne.....32 D3
st. Cremorne.....414 H2
st. Doncaster.....330 A17
st. Eltham North.....287 C2
st. Maribyrnong.....323 A12

DALEGLEN
st. Reservoir.....283 E2

DALEHEAD
ct. Croydon Hills.....335 D16

DALENE
st. Essendon.....324 A3

DALEY
ct. Brookfield.....268 C4
st. Bentleigh.....496 B2
st. Elwood.....454 G4
st. Glenroy.....279 L2
st. Pascoe Vale.....280 H14
st. Preston.....327 F5
st. Sunshine W.....364 E2

DALGAN
st. Oakleigh S.....457 H19

DALGARNO
st. Williamstown.....411 E11

DALGETTY
rd. Beaumaris.....530 B13

DALGETY
la. St Kilda.....414 C14
pl. Carlton.....18 J9
st. Brunswick W.....324 K11
st. Dandenong S.....535 J12
st. Oakleigh.....457 K7
st. Preston.....326 K1
st. St Kilda.....414 C14

DALGLEISH
av. Rosebud.....683 G18
st. Flemington.....324 E20

DALI
ct. Keilor East.....321 K3
ct. Wheelers Hill.....460 L14

DALKEITH
av. Tullamarine.....278 H5
cl. Wheelers Hill.....460 L10
cr. Belgrave.....466 H15
ct. Doncaster E.....332 B16
ct. Frankston.....628 B10
ct. Sunbury.....142 L6
dr. Dromana.....686 K5
dr. Point Cook.....450 G10
rd. Wantirna.....422 K7

DALLAS
av. Hughesdale.....457 F13
cr. Watsonia N.....285 E3
ct. Kilsyth.....381 D4
dr. Dallas.....238 G10
dr. Lalor.....242 A10
st. Emerald.....469 J19
st. Mentone.....532 A7
st. Mt Waverley.....458 J3

DALLAS BROOKS
dr. Melbourne.....31 B4
dr. Melbourne.....414 A2

DALLEY
st. Hawthorn.....372 A19

DALLIMORE
ct. Noble Park.....535 E5

DALLS
rd. Whittlesea.....96 G6

DALLY
st. Clifton Hill.....20 F7
st. Northcote.....326 J12

DALMAHOY
st. Footscray.....367 G8

DALMANY
av. Point Cook.....450 G7

DALMATIA
ct. Rowville.....503 D4

DALMONT
st. Highett.....495 J14

DALMONTE
gr. Kallista.....467 G3

DALMOR
av. Mitcham.....377 D10
av. Ormond.....456 B13
ct. Pakenham.....585 D4
st. Parkdale.....531 G14

DALMORE
dr. Scoresby.....462 A13
rd. Dalmore.....652 J7
rd. Tooradin.....652 J7

DALNY
rd. Murrumbeena....457 A12
st. Malvern.....415 L13

DALPURA
cct. Frankston.....600 F16
ct. Berwick.....553 K3
ct. Notting Hill.....459 J13
ct. Werribee.....446 K15
dr. Bayswater.....423 A4
dr. Sunshine W.....364 G7

DALRAY
cl. Mill Park.....242 J11
cr. Kurunjang.....227 E7
cr. New Gisborne.....79 C2
ct. Cranbourne.....604 B5
ct. Keilor Dn.....275 L15
pl. Lilydale.....294 C20

DALRIADA
st. Toorak.....415 E5

DALROY
cr. Vermont S.....420 G10

DALRY
av. Pk Orchards.....334 C18
cl. Endeavour Hl.....503 K19
ct. Mt Eliza.....641 L4
rd. Badger Creek.....257 J12
rd. Don Valley.....345 F5
rd. Healesville.....257 J12
rd. Launching Pl.....344 F2
rd. Launching Pl.....345 F5
rd. Woori Yallock.....300 B19
rd. Woori Yallock.....344 F2

DALRYMPLE
rd. Gisborne.....110 C6
rd. Sunbury.....110 C6
rd. Sunbury.....111 C8
rd. Sunbury.....111 J13

DALSTEN
gr. Mt Eliza.....626 B17

DALSTON
rd. Hughesdale.....457 G11

DALTON
ct. Meadow Ht.....238 D1
ct. Mulgrave.....500 G2
dr. Melton S.....268 E5
pl. Gladstone Pk.....237 A17
rd. Epping.....197 H17
rd. Lalor.....241 H10
rd. Thomastown.....241 F20

st. Eltham ...287 G13
st. Gisborne ...78 H16
st. S Geelong ...703 E17
st. Sunshine W ...364 F7
DALVANA
ct. Hampton Pk ...551 E5
DALVEEN
rd. Ivanhoe ...327 L9
DALVEY
st. Heidelberg ...329 C5
DALVIDA
ct. Eltham North ...245 D20
DALVISTA
ct. Werribee ...446 H17
DALWOOD
ct. Oakleigh S ...498 B6
ct. Vermont S ...421 E12
pl. Avondale Ht ...322 D12
DALWORTH
av. Dromana ...686 G3
st. Albion ...320 G20
st. Albion ...364 G1
DALY
av. Rye ...697 K3
ct. Darley ...221 L10
ct. Mentone ...531 F5
ct. Rowville ...463 J11
dr. Cannons Creek ...649 F7
pl. Bundoora ...284 H1
rd. Sandringham ...495 E12
st. Brunswick W ...324 L14
st. Doncaster E ...375 F3
st. Frankston ...600 A20
st. Gisborne ...78 H14
st. Oakleigh E ...458 F11
st. S Melbourne ...29 L5
st. South Yarra ...32 D8
st. South Yarra ...414 H4
DALYSTON
st. Grovedale ...706 D10
DALZIEL
la. Northcote ...326 G16
DALZIELL
rd. Cockatoo ...510 E1
DAMALA
ct. Blackburn S ...419 F5
st. Doncaster E ...375 K4
DAMAR
av. Boronia ...424 C8
DAMASK
pl. Niddrie ...322 K4
DAMELIO
ct. Rowville ...503 C5
DAME MARY GILMORE
pl. Oakleigh E, off Baynton St ...458 J12
DAME PATTIE
av. Pakenham ...584 H5
DAMIAN
cl. Mornington ...641 D16
ct. Cranbourne ...578 B17
ct. Dandenong ...535 H9
ct. Glenroy ...279 H2
pl. Wantirna S ...421 L14
st. Melton ...226 G20
DAMIEN
ct. Pakenham ...585 A3
ct. Watsonia N ...243 G19
DAMMANS
rd. Warburton ...349 A3
DAMON
cl. Nar Warrn S ...552 H15
cl. S Morang ...199 K16
ct. Millgrove ...348 D4
rd. Mt Waverley ...458 F4
DAMOSH
av. Carrum Downs ...574 E19
DAMPIER
cl. Skye ...575 G14
ct. Endeavour Hl ...537 E5
ct. Epping ...198 C17
ct. Grovedale ...706 A14
ct. Mornington ...641 E14
ct. Wyndham Va ...446 F8
gr. Mitcham ...377 K12
gr. Ringwood ...377 K12
DAMTE
pl. St Albans ...275 J17
DANA
av. Blairgowrie ...695 J3
ct. Dandenong S ...536 A17
ct. Keilor Lodge ...276 C5
ct. Mulgrave ...500 F2
ct. Rowville ...502 K7
st. Doncaster ...330 E17
DANAE
st. Glenroy ...280 D3
DANBEC
ct. Ferntree Gly ...464 C14
DANDALLO
dr. Eltham North ...245 K20
DANDARRIGA
wy. Delahey ...275 A10
DANDELION
dr. Rowville ...463 H17
dr. Rowville ...503 C1
DANDENONG
av. Olinda ...426 H9
rd. Armadale ...415 A14
rd. Carnegie ...456 F2
rd. Caulfield E ...456 F2
rd. Caulfield N ...415 A14
rd. Clayton ...458 G13
rd. Clayton ...459 B18
rd. Hughesdale ...457 C4
rd. Huntingdale ...458 G13
rd. Malvern ...416 A18
rd. Malvern East ...416 A18
rd. Malvern East ...456 F2
rd. Malvern East ...457 C4
rd. Mulgrave ...499 K4
rd. Murrumbeena ...456 F2
rd. Noble Park ...500 J13
rd. Noble Park N ...500 J13
rd. Oakleigh ...457 C4
rd. Oakleigh ...458 G13
rd. Oakleigh E ...458 G13
rd. Prahran ...414 H13
rd. St Kilda E ...414 H13
rd. Springvale ...499 K4
rd. Windsor ...414 H13
rd.e, Frankston ...599 D17
rd.w, Frankston ...599 D16
st. Dandenong S ...535 G12
DANDENONG-HASTINGS
rd. Cranbourne S ...630 E8
rd. Cranbourne W ...576 J20
rd. Cranbourne W ...602 G16
rd. Langwarrin ...602 G16
rd. Langwarrin ...630 E8
rd. Langwarrin S ...646 C5
rd. Lynbrook ...551 A20
rd. Lyndhurst ...576 L8
rd. Lyndhurst ...577 A2
rd. Pearcedale ...646 C5
rd. Skye ...576 J20
DANDENONG VALLEY
hwy. Bangholme ...549 K16
hwy. Bangholme ...575 C10
hwy. Carrum Downs ...575 C10
hwy. Dandenong ...536 C4
hwy. Dandenong N ...502 D19
hwy. Dandenong S ...536 B19
hwy. Dandenong S ...549 K16
hwy. Frankston ...599 L8
hwy. Frankston N ...599 L8
hwy. Knoxfield ...462 H17
hwy. Rowville ...462 H17
hwy. Rowville ...502 F10
hwy. Scoresby ...462 H17
hwy. Seaford ...599 L8
hwy. Wantirna S ...462 G2
DANDO
st. Richmond ...26 D16
D'ANDREA
ct. Rowville ...463 D20
DANDY
ct. Jan Juc ...711 B18
DANE
ct. Dandenong N ...502 B19
ct. Warrandyte ...333 B6
rd. Hampton E ...495 L9
rd. Moorabbin ...495 L9
st. Box Hill N ...374 L9
st. Seddon ...367 E12
DANEHILL
gr. Berwick ...553 K15
DANENE
ct. Vermont S ...420 J14
DANESON
rt. Cranbourne W ...577 G16
rt. Keilor Dn ...275 J14
DANGERFIELD
dr. Springvale S ...499 L20
DANGLOW
av. Altona ...407 J15
DANI
ct. Rowville ...503 D6
DANIEDA
cr. Ferny Creek ...425 L15
DANIEL
cl. Patterson L ...573 L7
ct. Bundoora ...285 B5
ct. Langwarrin ...629 E8
ct. Mentone ...531 J7
ct. Narre Warren ...539 B14
ct. Pakenham ...584 F2
ct. Pk Orchards ...333 J18
ct. Warranwood ...334 H16
ct. Werribee ...446 K15
dr. Carrum Downs ...600 E2
dr. Langwarrin ...629 J5
dr. Melton S ...268 F5
dr. Moorooduc ...643 G20
st. Burwood ...418 D7
st. Donvale ...332 G19
DANIELA
wy. Seabrook ...450 J5
DANIELL
cr. Caulfield ...456 A4
pl. Kew ...372 E14
DANIELLA
ct. Rowville ...503 A5
DANIELLE
cl. Wheelers Hill ...461 D12
cr. Heathmont ...379 D19
ct. Langwarrin ...629 E7
ct. Vermont S ...421 E8
ct. Wantirna ...422 B12
DANIELS
rd. Oaklands Jctn ...191 D10
DANIEL SOLANDER
dr. Endeavour Hl ...537 B6
DANIEN
st. Glen Waverley ...460 F1
DANIHER
cl. Berwick ...553 L9
DANIN
st. Pascoe Vale ...280 E14
DANITA
dr. Kangaroo Grnd ...289 H12
dr. Research ...289 H12
DANKS
st. Albert Park ...29 A13
st. Albert Park ...29 H18
st. Albert Park ...413 A7
st. Albert Park ...413 D9
st. Middle Park ...29 H18
st. Middle Park ...413 D9
st. Port Melb ...29 A13
st. Port Melb ...412 L7
DANNY
st. Coburg ...326 A6
st. Rye ...697 A12
DANSON
st. Highett ...495 J11
st. View Bank ...285 J18
DANSU
ct. Hallam ...537 D17
DANTHONIA
pl. Yallambie ...286 B11
st. Delahey ...275 A14
DANTUM
gr. Braybrook ...321 L18
DANUBE
ct. Rowville ...463 C16
dr. Werribee ...447 G6
pl. Mulgrave ...460 E20
pl. Roxburgh Pk ...194 D7
DANY
ct. Ferntree Gly ...424 H18
DAOURS
ct. Watsonia ...285 D9
DAPHNE
cl. Aspendale Gdn ...546 G2
cl. Mill Park ...243 A10
cr. Bellfield ...328 A7
cr. Hurstbridge ...203 A16
cr. Werribee ...447 J9
ct. Bayswater ...423 C5
ct. Newcomb ...704 D13
st. Bentleigh E ...456 K19
st. Canterbury ...373 D17
st. Doncaster E ...331 G20
st. Pascoe Vale ...280 L19
st. Sunshine W ...364 B2
wy. Cranbourne N ...578 J8
DAPPLED
wk. Croydon S ...380 B15
DARACOMBE
av. Kew ...372 J11
DARAIO
ct. Ferntree Gly ...464 D9
DARANA
dr. Rye ...697 G9
DARBYSHIRE
ct. Mill Park ...242 K7
rd. Mt Waverley ...418 G13
st. Sunbury ...143 E11
st. Williamstown ...410 A13
D'ARCY
st. Doncaster ...375 E1
st. Maddingley ...263 D4
DARCY
av. Sandringham ...495 J19
ct. Cranbourne ...578 A14
ct. Notting Hill ...459 J12
la. Kensington ...33 G7
st. Mornington ...656 F3
DARCY NILAND
cr. Lynbrook ...551 D19
DARE
st. Coburg ...325 H5
DAREBIN
av. Keilor Dn ...275 J11
bvd. Reservoir ...283 G4
ct. Meadow Ht ...237 J5
dr. Lalor ...241 K7
dr. Thomastown ...241 K14
pl. Caroline Spr ...318 B6
rd. Northcote ...327 B11
rd. Thornbury ...326 J11
st. Heidelberg ...328 H6
st. Heidelberg ...329 A6
DARGAI
rd. Belmont ...706 C1
DARGIE
ct. Dallas ...238 E11
ct. Sunbury ...142 L9
ct. Sunbury ...143 A9
pl. Mooroolbark ...337 C11
DARGO
cl. Croydon Hills ...335 J16
cl. Nar Warrn S ...552 G8
ct. Mt Waverley ...419 C19
ct. Rye ...697 F9
pl. Taylors Hill ...274 L14
DARGON
tr. Lysterfield ...505 C5
DARIAN
rd. Torquay ...712 A5
DARIN
ct. Ringwood E ...379 C5
DARINDA
av. Wandin N ...340 F12
ct. Mt Martha ...656 D8
DARIO
ct. Greensborough ...245 A14
DARIUS
av. Frankston ...628 B11
tce. S Morang ...198 K14
DARK
pde. Sorrento ...678 J11
DARKAN
ct. Eltham North ...288 E1
DARKE
ct. Darley ...222 A7
DARLEY
ct. Frankston N ...600 C7
st. Up Fntree Gly ...465 E7
DARLING
av. Camberwell ...417 L8
av. Upwey ...465 K10
cl. Keilor East ...322 B2
ct. Hampton Pk ...551 J4
ct. Rowville ...463 E19
ct. Sunbury ...143 G6
ct. Taylors Hill ...274 K13
rd. Braeside ...546 J1
rd. Gruyere ...341 D4
rd. Malvern East ...456 J4
rd. Sorrento ...678 J9
st. Alphington ...327 F16
st. E Geelong ...703 F14
st. E Melbourne ...25 L6
st. Fairfield ...327 F16
st. Footscray ...367 C8
st. Hughesdale ...457 F13
st. Mentone ...531 F7
st. Moonee Pnd ...323 J15
st. South Yarra ...32 B8
st. South Yarra ...414 G4
wy. Narre Warren ...553 E9
DARLINGSFORD
bvd. Melton ...269 A3
DARLINGTON
av. Wheelers Hill ...461 A9
gr. Coburg ...325 K6
gr. Sydenham ...232 J18
pde. Richmond ...26 F12
DARLY
gln. Greensborough ...244 B19
pl. Eltham ...287 C8
DARNLEY
ct. Rowville ...463 F19
dr. Skye ...601 C9
dr. Templestowe ...332 C14
gr. Wheelers Hill ...460 G13
pl. Roxburgh Pk ...193 K13
st. Braybrook ...365 K4
DAROOK
st. Blackburn S ...420 A2
DARRACQ
dr. Keilor Dn ...276 B11
DARRANDAUL
dr. Bulleen ...329 H14
DARREN
av. Bundoora ...285 C3
ct. Cheltenham ...496 K15
ct. Clarinda ...498 D6
rd. Keysborough ...534 B8
rd. Springvale S ...534 A7
ri. Doncaster E ...332 G12
DARRI
ct. Glen Waverley ...420 C16
DARRIWELL
ct. Wheelers Hill ...460 H12
DARRIWILL
cl. Delahey ...275 B11
DARRYL
st. Bulleen ...330 B15
st. Scoresby ...462 F9
DART
ct. Mt Waverley ...419 D16
st. Highett ...496 C12
DARTAGOOK
st. Diamond Ck ...245 H7
DARTER
ct. Carrum Downs ...574 L20
DARTFORD
ct. Craigieburn ...194 D4
st. Flemington ...324 D20
DARTMOOR
ct. Craigieburn ...194 C1
ct. Meadow Ht ...238 B6
dr. Highton ...701 B16
DARTMOUTH
ct. Caroline Spr ...318 B7
DARUS
ct. Hoppers Csg ...405 A15
DARVALL
ct. Cheltenham ...496 L14
ct. Werribee ...448 A9
st. Donvale ...376 E7
st. Rosanna ...328 J1
st. Tootgarook ...698 G5
DARVEL
ct. Endeavour Hl ...503 G18
DARVELL
cl. Wheelers Hill ...461 F16
cov. Greensborough ...285 J1
ct. Greenvale ...237 F2
ct. Pakenham ...585 F3
la. Mt Eliza ...626 J14
DARWALA
pl. Greensborough ...286 L1
DARWIN
rd. Boronia ...423 C12
st. Blairgowrie ...696 C7
st. Dandenong N ...501 G17
st. Sunbury ...142 L12
st. Sunbury ...143 A12
st. W Footscray ...366 J10
DARWINIA
ct. Sunshine W ...364 E7
ri. Eltham North ...245 E19
DARYL
av. Glen Waverley ...460 H2
ct. Hampton Pk ...552 A14
ct. Lalor ...240 J5
D'ASSISI
ct. Ringwood N ...334 F14
DAVA
ct. Dandenong N ...501 L16
ct. Ferntree Gly ...463 K6
ct. Gladstone Pk ...237 C20
ct. Gladstone Pk ...279 C1
ct. Kurunjang ...227 F1
ct. Mt Martha ...657 D7
dr. Mornington ...656 C4
DAVANZO
av. Clarinda ...498 D1
DAVELA
ct. Eltham North ...245 B17
DAVENPORT
dr. Sunbury ...142 L17
dr. Sunbury ...143 A16
DAVENTRY
av. Grovedale ...706 C12
dr. Berwick ...580 J1
dr. Berwick ...580 K1
st. Reservoir ...282 J10
DAVERN
st. Pascoe Vale S ...280 F19
DAVEY
av. Brighton East ...455 F14
av. Dromana ...686 D6
av. Oakleigh ...457 J12
ct. Broadmeadows ...238 E19
ct. Springvale ...500 D10
dr. Ringwood E ...379 C9
rd. Emerald ...469 F19
rd. Montmorency ...286 G9
rd. Mt Evelyn ...338 K17
st. Boronia ...423 J1
st. Box Hill ...375 D14

st. E Geelong 703 F11
st. Frankston 599 B20
st. Parkdale 531 K14
st. Sunshine W 364 G2
AVEYS BAY
d. Mt Eliza 626 A8
AVID
av. Cranbourne 577 K17
av. Keilor East 322 E2
cl. Bayswater N 380 H16
cl. Kilsyth 381 H10
cl. Somerville 644 C17
cr. Bundoora 243 A20
ct. Braybrook 365 L4
ct. Cheltenham 531 B3
ct. Darley 222 A8
ct. Mt Waverley 419 B19
ct. Narre Warren 539 B14
ct. Rosebud W 699 G6
ct. Werribee 448 G10
dr. Mooroolbark 337 A10
a. Windsor 414 F11
d. Carrum Downs 574 C16
d. Lilydale 338 J11
d. Lilydale 339 A13
d. Mt Evelyn 338 J11
d. Mt Evelyn 339 A13
d. Templstw Lr 330 C13
d. Warrandyte 290 A19
t. Altona 409 B19
t. Bentleigh E 496 G2
t. Blairgowrie 679 K20
t. Box Hill S 374 K20
t. Brunswick 325 F15
t. Carlton 18 J12
t. Dandenong 535 J4
t. Footscray 367 E6
t. Frankston 599 D16
t. Hadfield 280 L7
t. Hampton 495 D10
t. Hampton Pk 551 E10
t. Knoxfield 463 B5
t. Lalor 241 C10
t. Melton S 268 H6
t. Monbulk 428 F19
t. Mordialloc 532 A16
t. Noble Park 534 H5
t. Preston 326 K2
t. Richmond 371 C14
t. Ringwood 378 G14
t. St Kilda E 415 B19
t. Surrey Hills 373 L16
t.n, Knoxfield 463 B4
AVID COLLINS
r. Endeavour Hl 537 H9
AVID HILL
d. Monbulk 428 E19
d. Monbulk 468 J1
d. Monbulk 469 A2
AVID HOCKNEY
r. Diamond Ck 244 L12
r. Diamond Ck 245 A12
AVID LEE
d. Hallam 537 J20
AVID MUNROE
r. Roxburgh Pk 194 D17
AVIDSON
. Altona Mdw 451 G6
. Attwood 237 D10
r. Torquay 711 L13
. Bellfield 327 L7
. Reservoir 282 C1
. South Yarra 31 K3
. South Yarra 414 E2
. Springvale 500 C10
AVIE
. Cheltenham 496 F17
AVIES
. Brookfield 268 A4
. Mt Eliza 626 B17
. Sunshine N 321 D9
. Wantirna 422 C12
. Sunbury 143 D7
r. Eltham 287 K9
. Yallambie 286 A14
. Altona 409 D19
. Brighton East 455 C18
. Brunswick 325 G8
. Darley 221 K11
. Hadfield 280 L10
. Malvern East 416 G16
. Mentone 530 L8
. Mentone 531 A8
. Moonee Pnd 324 D14
. Newport 411 B8
. Port Melb 29 B7
. Preston 326 G6
. Rosanna 284 J18
. Safety Bch 669 C14
. Sandringham 495 H19
AVIESIA
. Plenty 244 G12

DAVINGTON
ct. Wantirna 422 G14
DAVIS
av. Avondale Ht 322 A10
av. Camberwell 416 H6
av. South Yarra 32 A11
av. South Yarra 414 F5
ct. Altona Mdw 451 G4
dr. Mt Eliza 642 E5
rd. Diggers Rest 187 A9
rd. Wonga Park 291 G11
st. Belmont 706 A3
st. Burwood E 419 G8
st. Carlton N 18 J7
st. Coburg 325 B2
st. Doncaster 374 H4
st. Elsternwick 454 J4
st. Ferntree Gly 464 B3
st. Kensington 34 A6
st. Kew 372 D13
st. Reservoir 283 L17
st. Richmond 26 G19
st. Richmond 414 K1
wy. Springvale 500 C13
DAVIS JOHN
dr. Tarneit 405 C12
DAVISON
cr. Ferntree Gly 464 B7
ct. Maddingley 263 D5
dr. Coldstream 293 L3
pl. South Yarra 32 D12
pl. South Yarra 414 H6
pl. Geelong, off Myers St 703 D10
st. Brunswick 325 D11
st. Mitcham 377 H18
st. Mt Waverley 418 H14
st. Richmond 371 A15
wy. Berwick 554 G17
DAVISONS
pl. Melbourne 2 L6
pl. Melbourne 24 F3
DAVISSON
st. Epping 241 H1
DAVITT
dr. Deer Park 318 L12
DAVOR
ct. Burwood E 419 L8
DAVROSS
ct. Seville 342 K19
DAVY
ct. Nar Warrn S 579 F1
la. Forest Hill 420 G6
DAWAYNE
st. Burwood E 420 B8
DAWE
rd. Mitcham 377 E11
DAWES
ct. Ferntree Gly 464 B6
ct. Mill Park 242 C4
rd. Wonga Park 335 E1
DAWN
av. Dandenong S 535 G13
ct. Epping 198 A19
ct. Glen Waverley 420 C15
ct. Sunbury 142 J7
ct. View Bank 285 J18
dr. Narre Warren 552 G1
st. Boronia 424 G8
st. Highett 496 J15
st. Mt Evelyn 339 E16
st. Rye 696 K8
st. Up Fntree Gly 465 E7
DAWS
ct. Taylors Lakes 233 A20
rd. Doncaster E 331 K19
DAWSON
av. Brighton 454 F8
av. Footscray 367 D5
ct. Aspendale Gdn 546 J3
ct. Clayton 498 F1
ct. Endeavour Hl 537 C4
ct. Noble Park N 501 D9
dr. Glen Iris 416 K11
pl. Roxburgh Pk 194 B13
rd. Briar Hill 286 F6
rd. Kangaroo Grnd 248 B9
rd. Nar Warrn E 507 H18
rd. Panton Hill 248 B9
st. Brunswick 325 A14
st. Brunswick W 324 J14
st. Brunswick W 325 A14
st. Coburg N 281 D18
st. Doncaster 331 E19
st. E Geelong 703 G13
st. Reservoir 282 C1
st. Sunshine 365 D1
st. Tullamarine 278 G4
st. Up Fntree Gly 465 A7
DAWSONS
gln. Heathmont 379 A18

DAX
rd. Panton Hill 248 D6
DAY
cr. Bayswater N 380 G17
rd. Clarinda 498 F12
st. Dandenong 535 K6
st. E Geelong 703 J11
st. South Yarra 31 D5
st. Sunshine W 364 H4
st. Upwey 466 A8
st. Yarraville 366 H16
DAYAN
dr. Wantirna S 422 A17
DAYLESFORD
tce. Caroline Spr 318 C7
DAYMAR
ct. Hillside 274 F1
dr. Mooroolbark 337 E13
DAYS
pl. Geelong, off Garden St 703 F8
DEACON
av. Bundoora 284 C8
DEAKIN
av. Lalor 241 J10
av. Waurn Ponds 705 C10
cr. Baxter 644 C3
cr. Dandenong N 501 K19
ct. Berwick 554 G18
ct. Broadmeadows 238 E16
ct. Mill Park 243 C5
ct. Waurn Ponds, off Deakin Av 705 B10
dr. Mt Martha 655 D18
st. Bentleigh E 456 L17
st. Bentleigh E 457 A17
st. Brunswick E 325 L15
st. Coburg 325 D4
st. Essendon 323 B7
st. Maidstone 366 E3
st. Malvern East 416 C16
st. Mitcham 377 A12
st. Pt Lonsdale 710 E5
st. St Kilda W 413 L13
st. Sunbury 142 L14
st. Sunbury 143 A14
st. Yarraville 366 K14
st.n, Hampton 495 A9
st.s, Hampton 495 A10
DEAKINWOOD
ct. Waurn Ponds 705 E15
DEAKON
ct. Wantirna S 462 L1
ct. Wantirna S 463 A1
DEAL
av. Jan Juc 711 F14
cl. Moorabbin 496 G7
DEALBATA
av. Endeavour Hl 502 K19
pl. Croydon Hills 335 J13
rd. Upwey 465 J7
DEALING
ct. Bundoora 242 F20
dr. Oakleigh S 498 A7
DEALS
rd. Clayton S 498 K13
DEAN
al. Melbourne 2 H11
al. Melbourne 24 F6
av. Hawthorn 372 B18
av. Mt Waverley 459 F2
av. St Kilda E 415 B16
cl. Nar Warrn S 552 G15
cl. Templstw Lr 330 H13
cr. Launching Pl 345 F16
ct. Altona North 409 F2
ct. Carrum Downs 601 D1
ct. Coolaroo 238 D6
ct. Cranbourne W 577 F20
ct. Epping 198 D16
ct. Rowville 503 C2
ct. Sunshine W 364 F8
ct. Wantirna 422 H5
rd. Christmas Hills 207 K14
st. Belmont 706 F1
st. Fitzroy N 326 C18
st. Hoppers Csg 448 J3
st. Kew 372 H14
st. Moonee Pnd 324 E14
st. Preston 283 D20
st. Yarraville 366 L17
DEANE
st. Blackburn N 375 L9
st. Frankston 627 H2
DEANLEA
ct. Hawthorn E 416 C4
DEANS
rd. Upwey 465 H16
st. Coburg 281 H19
DEANSIDE
cl. Seabrook 450 L3

DEANSWOOD
cl. Keysborough 534 F11
cl. Wantirna S 422 J14
ct. Cheltenham 531 G4
dr. Somerville 645 B19
pl. Brookfield 268 A6
rd. Forest Hill 420 B3
rd. Hampton Pk 551 H8
wy. Narre Warren 538 H13
DEANY
st. Springvale 500 B10
DEARING
av. Cranbourne 604 B1
DEARNLEY
st. Manifold Ht 702 B3
DEAUVILLE
ct. Berwick 554 C3
ct. Wantirna 422 J12
st. Beaumaris 530 F10
st. Forest Hill 420 G5
DEAVEY
ct. Altona 408 K14
DEBANNE
ct. Narre Warren 538 L17
DEBBIE
cl. Clarinda 498 C9
cl. Doveton 536 L7
cl. Doveton 537 A7
ct. Dingley Village 533 A6
ct. Mill Park 242 L8
pl. Ringwood N 378 B5
st. Mt Waverley 419 E13
DEBENHAM
dr. St Albans 320 E7
DEBLIN
dr. Narre Warren 552 J6
DEBLONAY
cr. Greensborough 286 C7
DEBORAH
av. Bentleigh E 496 K1
av. Boronia 424 G7
ct. Mt Waverley 459 F8
ct. Noble Park 534 D4
ct. Skye 575 H18
ct. Somerville 644 F17
dr. Baxter 644 C4
st. Kilsyth 381 E9
st. Werribee 447 G11
DEBRA
ct. Berwick 554 B16
ct. Lalor 241 J10
ct. Tootgarook 698 B6
ct. Yallambie 285 E16
st. Rowville 502 C6
wy. Doncaster E 331 G18
DE BRUN
ct. Laverton 407 C16
DEBSON
cl. Boronia 424 D7
DE BURGH
ct. View Bank 285 F20
DE CARLE
la. Brunswick 325 G10
st. Brunswick 325 G11
st. Coburg 325 H7
DE CASTELLA
cl. Mill Park 198 H20
cl. Mill Park 242 H1
DECATHLON
st. Bundoora 284 J3
DE CHENE
pde. Coburg N 281 H16
DECONTRA
cl. Donvale 376 K3
DECOR
dr. Hallam 537 G17
DECORE
dr. S Morang 198 L13
DEDERICK
gr. Braybrook 365 J1
DEDICATION
ct. Carrum Downs 574 H16
DEDRICK
ct. Berwick 554 G19
DEE
ct. Endeavour Hl 503 H19
pl. Rowville 463 E18
rd. Millgrove 303 L18
st. Balwyn 373 E8
st. Heidelberg 328 K4
DEED
ct. Sunshine W 364 J10
dr. Pakenham 584 H2
st. Belmont 706 A5
DEEP CREEK
dr. Doncaster E 332 F7
rd. Mitcham 377 H13
rd. Pakenham 560 B20

DEEPDALE
gr. Mooroolbark 337 D8
st. Dandenong S 535 L15
DEEPDENE
pl. Balwyn 372 K13
rd. Balwyn 372 K13
DEER
st. Deer Park 318 J15
DEERING
av. Badger Creek 258 E19
DEERY
rd. Emerald 509 J10
DEE WY
rd. Nar Warrn S 552 F9
DE FELICE
ct. Forest Hill 420 F3
pl. Wantirna 422 B10
DEFELICE
pl. Mooroolbark 337 K16
DEFENCE
rd. Portsea 665 A15
rd. Portsea 665 J16
DE FEU
st. N Melbourne 34 K16
DE FREDERICKS
la. Yarrambat 201 F13
rd. Yarrambat 201 C15
DEGA
av. Bentleigh E 496 G4
DE GARIS
pl. Werribee 447 B6
DEGARIS
la. Roxburgh Pk 194 E9
DEGAS
ct. Wheelers Hill 460 K16
DEGG
ct. Aspendale Gdn 546 J2
DEGOLDIS
rd. Fyansford 701 A8
DEGRAVES
pl. Melbourne 2 D18
pl. Melbourne, off Degraves St 24 E10
st. Flemington 323 K20
st. Melbourne 2 C19
st. Melbourne 24 E10
st. Parkville 17 J9
DE GRUCHYS
la. N Melbourne 17 A9
DEHAVILAND
av. Forest Hill 420 D9
DE HAVILLAND
av. Strathmr Ht 279 E9
rd. Mordialloc 532 D10
DEHNERT
st. Doncaster E 331 H20
st. Doncaster E 375 H1
DEIDRE
ct. Airport W 278 F15
st. Glen Waverley 459 L3
DEIGHTON
dr. Rosebud 700 B1
DEIRDRE
ct. Montmorency 286 J7
DELACEY
st. Maidstone 366 K2
DELACOMBE
ct. Cheltenham 497 C16
dr. Hampton Pk 551 K7
dr. Vermont S 421 F8
DELAGE
cl. Keilor Dn 276 A13
DELAHUNTY
ct. Altona Mdw 451 L6
DELAMARE
dr. Albanvale 318 L4
DELAMERE
cl. Mulgrave 501 H5
dr. Chirnside Pk 336 J7
mw. Ringwood N 378 G4
DELANCEY
rd. Wandin East 340 K19
rd. Wandin East 341 A17
DELANEY
ct. Keilor 276 G9
DELANEYS
rd. Warranwood 334 K10
DELANY
av. Burwood 418 J8
cl. Canterbury 373 F17
DELATITE
cl. Epping 197 K20
ct. Hallam 538 B19
ct. Rowville 463 E16
ct. Skye 601 G1
ct. Vermont 421 A5
ct. Warranwood 334 H14
ct. Werribee 448 B18

DELAWARE
- dr. Dingley Village...533 D10
- st. Reservoir...283 A12

DELBRIDGE
- dr. Sydenham...274 J5
- st. Fitzroy N...19 H2

DELEWARE
- st. Yarraville...366 J19

DELFI
- ct. Balwyn...373 H10

DELFIN
- cr. Greensborough...286 D1
- ct. Glen Waverley...460 K2
- ct. Rowville...502 G3

DELGANY
- av. Portsea...677 J1
- cr. Point Cook...450 E3
- ri. Langwarrin...629 H4

DELHI
- ct. Travancore...324 J20
- st. Bentleigh...496 F3
- st. Glenroy...280 D3
- st. Mitcham...377 C14

DELHUNTLY
- ri. Nar Warrn S...579 A2

DELIA
- ct. Dandenong N...501 L16
- st. Oakleigh S...457 H20

DE LISLE
- av. Sunbury...143 F2

DELL
- ct. Mt Waverley...419 D13
- *la. Maribyrnong, off William Cooper St...367 C2*
- rd. Frankston...627 D1
- st. Narre Warren...553 F12

DELLA
- cl. St Helena...244 K17
- pl. Sunshine W...364 H7
- st. Scoresby...462 D8

DELLAS
- av. Templestowe...330 K5

DELLA TORRE
- cr. Ivanhoe...327 K13

DELLFIELD
- dr. Templstw Lr...330 J11

DELL VIEW
- cl. Nar Warrn N...538 C1

DELLVIEW
- ct. Donvale...332 K14

DELLWOOD
- ct. Templestowe...331 F13

DELMA
- av. St Albans...319 H8
- st. Bentleigh E...496 H6

DELMAR
- ct. Keilor Lodge...276 C4

DELMARE
- ct. Nar Warrn S...552 H19
- st. Lalor...241 H9

DELMONT
- av. Altona...408 J16
- cl. Epping...241 L2
- ct. Cranbourne...578 B15
- ct. Endeavour Hl...537 J8
- ct. Mooroolbark...381 J4
- st. Albion...320 G20
- st. Werribee...446 L20
- st. Werribee...447 A20

DELMORE
- cr. Glen Waverley...419 K15

DELMUIR
- cl. Eltham...288 B5

DELORAINE
- cl. Doncaster E...332 E8

DELOS
- ct. Endeavour Hl...536 L4
- st. Oakleigh S...457 J20

DELPHIN
- av. Altona North...409 L2
- ct. Narre Warren...553 B12

DELPHINIUS
- cr. Roxburgh Pk...194 F11

DELPURA
- ct. Skye...601 G3
- gln. Greensborough...244 E19

DELTA
- av. Ashwood...418 D12
- av. Coburg N...281 E13
- cl. Lilydale...294 D19
- ct. Cranbourne...604 B5
- ct. Narre Warren...539 B17
- ct. Rowville...502 J2
- ct. Thomastown...241 K14
- pl. Keilor Dn...275 K14
- rd. Greensborough...285 J10
- rd. Macleod...285 J10
- rd. Watsonia...285 K8
- st. Surrey Hills...417 K1

DELVIEW
- dr. Jan Juc...711 B16

DELVILLE
- av. Mentone...531 K6
- st. Mooroolbark...337 B17

DEMBY
- la. N Melbourne...17 H17

DEMINT
- wk. Nar Warrn S...552 G20

DEMOCRAT
- dr. The Basin...424 K9

DEMPSEY
- ct. Epping...197 G17

DEMPSTER
- av. Balwyn N...373 J4
- ct. Donvale...376 L2
- st. Ferntree Gly...464 B4
- st. W Footscray...366 C9

DE MURSKA
- st. Windsor...414 E11

DENA
- ct. Templestowe...331 K7

DENAHY
- ct. Aspendale Gdn...546 J3

DENBIGH
- ct. Keilor...276 F10
- ct. Keysborough...534 G10
- rd. Armadale...415 D13
- rd. Seaford...573 F18
- st. Frankston...627 A3
- st. Moolap...704 L16
- st. Seaholme...409 G16

DENBY
- av. Sorrento...679 C17
- ct. Boronia...424 D6

DENDARYL
- dr. Bundoora...285 D3

DENDLE
- st. Grovedale...706 H9

DEN DULK
- av. Altona...452 G1

DENDY
- ct. Cheltenham...497 A17
- ct. Mulgrave...500 D5
- ct. Roxburgh Pk...194 B13
- la. N Melbourne...17 H19
- st. Brighton...454 F20
- st. Brighton...495 A1
- st. Brighton East...495 B1
- st. Sunshine N...321 E14

DENE
- av. Malvern East...416 J18
- ct. Wheelers Hill...461 A16

DENHAM
- cl. Frankston...599 J14
- cr. Cranbourne N...578 F10
- ct. Highton...701 G13
- ct. Kealba...276 K19
- ct. Scoresby...462 D9
- ct. Templestowe...331 H12
- ct. Westmeadows...236 G14
- pl. Berwick...554 E2
- pl. Mill Park...242 D2
- pl. Toorak...415 H9
- rd. Belgrave S...506 D5
- st. Hawthorn...371 E15

DENHOLM
- st. Rosebud...699 J3

DENHOLME
- ct. Werribee...446 L18

DENIS
- ct. Carrum Downs...601 D5
- st. Mitcham...377 F19

DENISE
- cl. Rowville...462 H17
- ct. Langwarrin...601 L19
- ct. Narre Warren...539 C17
- ct. View Bank...285 J18
- ct. Werribee...447 A12
- pl. Melton W...226 B18
- st. Springvale S...500 B19

DENISON
- cl. Rowville...463 B17
- ct. Sunbury...143 A15
- dr. Yallambie...285 L14
- pl. Roxburgh Pk...193 J15

DENISTOUN
- av. Mt Eliza...626 B8

DENMAN
- av. Edithvale...546 F11
- av. Glen Iris...417 B9
- av. St Kilda E...414 K19
- ct. Sunbury...143 H6
- st. Brunswick...325 C8
- st. E Geelong...703 K11
- st. Kilsyth...381 F7
- st. Mitcham...377 H15

DENMARK
- st. Kew...371 J13

DENMARK HILL
- rd. Hawthorn E...416 G1

DENNETT
- st. Carrum...573 B7
- st. Watsonia...285 G7

DENNING
- ct. Rosebud...700 A2

DENNIS
- av. Keilor East...322 D1
- ct. Bayswater...422 L9
- ct. Bayswater...423 A9
- ct. Keysborough...534 D13
- ct. Mooroolbark...381 E2
- la. Richmond...26 A7
- st. Campbellfield...194 H20
- st. Clayton...459 E19
- st. Croydon...336 J17
- st. Dandenong...536 E14
- st. Footscray...367 F7
- st. Heidelberg Ht...328 G1
- st. Highett...496 J16
- st. Lalor...241 K10
- st. Northcote...326 K12
- st. Reservoir...283 B11

DENNISON
- av. Hoppers Csg...405 B20
- ml. Bundoora...284 G1

DENNY
- cl. Mt Evelyn...338 J14
- pl. Melton S...268 F15

DENNYS
- ct. Grovedale...706 F7
- la. Kensington...33 E11
- *pl. Geelong, off Little Malop St...703 A7*

DENNYSE
- ct. Mt Waverley...419 B14

DENSHAM
- ct. Wantirna S...422 H19
- rd. Armadale...415 E10

DENSLEY
- ct. Darley...221 K3

DENT
- cl. Craigieburn...194 E1
- ct. Thomastown...240 H15
- st. Ashburton...417 B16
- st. Glen Iris...417 B16

DENTON
- av. St Albans...320 C13
- dr. Endeavour Hl...537 L8
- st. Brighton East...495 J5

DENVER
- cr. Elsternwick...455 A8
- cr. Mulgrave...500 H6
- cr. Rowville...462 F19
- ct. Hampton Pk...551 J12
- ct. Meadow Ht...237 K4
- ct. Ringwood N...378 E5
- dr. Narre Warren...539 E17
- st. Bentleigh E...496 K6

DENYS
- st. Fawkner...281 H3

DEPOT
- dr. Melb Airport...235 J13

DEQUIN
- ct. Werribee...487 G1

DERBY
- cr. Caulfield E...456 D2
- ct. Carrum Downs...601 B5
- ct. Wyndham Va...446 H12
- dr. Epping...197 L18
- pde. Bonbeach...547 C20
- pde. Caulfield N...415 H19
- pl. Lynbrook...551 H16
- rd. Boronia...423 D12
- rd. Caulfield E...456 C1
- rd. Herne Hill...701 J2
- rd. Kilsyth...381 E7
- rd. Sunshine...365 B4
- st. Armadale...415 F10
- st. Blackburn...375 F17
- st. Camberwell...372 L20
- st. Camberwell...373 A20
- st. Camberwell...416 L1
- st. Camberwell...417 A1
- st. Collingwood...19 F20
- st. Fawkner...281 K12
- st. Kensington...33 J11
- st. Kew...372 A9
- st. Moonee Pnd...323 J12
- st. Northcote...326 L17
- st. Pascoe Vale...280 L19
- st. Richmond...26 B13
- st. Tullamarine...236 F18
- st. Tullamarine...278 G1
- st. Warburton...349 A2

DERHAM
- dr. Pakenham...585 D8
- st. Mt Waverley...418 J14
- st. Pearcedale...646 J6
- st. Port Melb...412 K2
- st. Spotswood...366 H20

DERING
- st. Diamond Ck...245 J13

DERINYA
- dr. Frankston S...627 B11
- dr. Frankston S...627 B12

DERMOT
- st. Oakleigh S...457 H20
- st. Preston...327 C4

DERNA
- cr. Frankston...600 A17
- cr. Lalor...241 G6
- rd. Ashburton...417 J16
- st. Heidelberg W...328 A3

DERRANE
- pl. Templestowe...332 C5

DERRECK
- av. Bulleen...329 J11

DERRIBONG
- ct. Delahey...275 A10

DERRICK
- cl. Aspendale Gdn...546 L6
- st. Blairgowrie...679 E17
- st. Kew...371 L10
- st. Lalor...241 C10

DERRICKS
- *pl. Geelong, off Bellerine St...703 C11*

DERRIL
- av. Malvern...416 A15
- pl. Frankston...600 D16
- rd. Moorooduc...658 D20
- rd. Moorooduc...658 F17
- rd. Tuerong...658 D20

DERRIMAN
- ct. Mooroolbark...336 K12

DERRIMUT
- rd. Hoppers Csg...448 E6
- rd. Werribee...448 D11
- st. Albion...320 H20
- st. W Footscray...366 G9

DERRY
- cl. Endeavour Hl...537 G5
- st. Aberfeldie...323 E10
- st. Bentleigh E...497 B1

DERRYBEG
- la. Edithvale...546 G13

DERSON
- st. St Albans...320 C10

DERWENT
- cl. Croydon Hills...335 J12
- ct. Berwick...554 B9
- ct. Gladstone Pk...279 B1
- ct. Taylors Lakes...275 E1
- ct. Thomastown...240 E17
- dr. Bayswater...423 E2
- pl. Watsonia N...285 H1
- rd. Werribee...447 F8
- sq. Bulleen...329 F12
- st. Box Hill N...374 H9
- st. Mentone...531 G7
- st. Newport...410 K8
- st. Ringwood N...378 E7

DERWIN
- la. Rye...697 F4
- st. Rye...697 F4

DESCHAMP
- cr. Rowville...462 F20
- ct. Rowville...462 F20

DESCHAMPS
- av. Lilydale...338 F6
- st. Lilydale...338 A5

DESI
- ct. Campbellfield...239 G12

DESLA
- ct. Noble Park...534 J7

DESMOND
- av. Highett...496 B15
- ct. Beaconsfield...555 E18
- ct. Greensborough...286 D9
- st. Highton...701 G9
- st. Maidstone...322 G20
- st. Maidstone...366 G1

DESNA
- pl. Roxburgh Pk...194 G6

DETROIT
- rd. Campbellfield...194 H18

DEUTGAM
- st. Werribee...447 G18

DEUTSCHER
- st. Avondale Ht...322 A10

DEVAS
- ct. Carrum Downs...601 A5

DEVELOPMENT
- bvd. Mill Park...243 E3

DEVENEY
- st. Kensington...33 J5
- st. Pakenham...584 K4

DEVENISH
- av. Montrose...382 B1
- ct. Westmeadows...237 F1
- *ct. Windsor, off Raleigh St...414 E1*
- rd. Boronia...423 J

DEVENPORT
- ct. Altona Mdw...451 J

DEVERALL
- rd. Gisborne...110 E
- rd. Sunbury...110 G1

DE VERE
- ct. Belmont...706 G

DEVERE
- gdn. Vermont S...420 G

DEVEREAUX
- ct. Frankston...628 D1
- st. Oak Park...279 H1

DEVIATION
- rd. Belgrave S...506 J
- rd. Fyansford...701 G
- rd. Herne Hill...701 G
- rd. Newtown...701 G

DE VILLIERS
- dr. Dandenong...535 K

DEVIRA
- ct. Rowville...502 K
- st. Dandenong N...502 A1

DEVITT
- ct. Glen Waverley...461 E
- ct. Mill Park...242 G
- pl. Truganina...405 G1
- st. Burnside...318 E

DEVLAW
- dr. Doncaster E...332 F1

DEVLIN
- ct. Mill Park...242 D
- ct. Rosanna...285 A1
- dr. Hoppers Csg...405 B1
- st. Vermont...421 K

DEVON
- av. Blairgowrie...696 D
- av. Coburg...325 A
- av. Cockatoo...511 C
- av. Heathmont...378 H1
- av. Keilor East...322 G
- cl. Coldstream...293 H
- ct. Bonbeach...573 D
- ct. Dandenong...535 K
- ct. Epping...197 A2
- ct. Frankston...600 C1
- ct. Lower Plenty...286 H1
- ct. Meadow Ht...237 J
- ct. Mt Martha...669 L
- ct. Mt Waverley...459 K
- ct. Rosebud...700 E
- dr. Blackburn N...376 A1
- dr. Doncaster E...375 L
- dr. Springvale S...533 L
- dr. Williamstn N...410 F1
- gr. Oakleigh...458 D
- pl. Footscray...367 D
- pl. Melton W...226 C1
- rd. Pascoe Vale...280 C1
- st. Box Hill S...418 K
- st. Caulfield N...455 H
- st. Cheltenham...530 L
- st. Cheltenham...531 A
- st. Croydon...380 A
- st. Doncaster E...375 L
- st. Dromana...686 D
- st. Eaglemont...328 J1
- st. Kensington...33 G1
- st. Preston...326 K
- st. Rosebud...684 F1
- st. Warburton...305 B2
- wk. Mooroolbark...337 F1

DEVONDALE
- st. Cheltenham...531 G

DEVON PARK
- cl. Sunbury...113 K1

DEVONSHIRE
- ct. Berwick...539 L2
- dr. Keysborough...534 J
- rd. Malvern East...416 C1
- rd. Sunshine...365 D
- rd. Watsonia...285 D
- st. W Footscray...366 E

DEVORA
- rd. Epping...198 A1

DEVORGILLA
- av. Toorak...415 F

DEVOY
- st. Oakleigh S...457 H1

DEW
- st. Geelong...703 B1

DEWAN
- av. Werribee...447 G1

DEWAR
- ct. Ferntree Gly...463 E
- dr. Hurstbridge...203 C1

EWDROP
l. Nar Warrn S.......553 D19
EWEY
t. Keilor Dn............275 H10
EWHURST
l. Emerald.............509 H7
E WINT
t. Scoresby...........462 A8
E WINTER
l. Monbulk............468 F3
EWPOINT
r. Hampton Pk.......551 L15
EWPOND
t. Templestowe.....331 K5
k. Croydon S..........380 B13
EWRANG
Blackburn..........375 F14
Cheltenham........497 B17
EWSBURY
Nar Warrn S.......552 J19
Wantirna............422 G10
EWVALE
Craigieburn........193 L4
AMOND
Albanvale...........319 C4
Glen Waverley.....420 G18
Ferntree Gly.......464 C11
Doncaster E.......332 G12
Hillside..............231 L20
Mornington........641 F14
Narre Warren......539 F13
Sunshine W.......365 A13
Werribee............447 F3
S Morang..........198 H13
Diamond Ck.......245 H10
Eltham..............287 E7
Essendon W.......323 A6
Niddrie...............323 A6
Preston.............327 C1
AMOND BAY
Sorrento............678 L15
AMOND CREEK
Diamond Ck.......244 J13
Greensborough..244 E20
Greensborough..244 J13
Greensborough..286 C2
Plenty...............244 J13
St Helena...........244 E20
AMOND HILLS
Greensborough..244 F17
ANA
Langwarrin.........629 E6
Blackburn N.......376 C11
Werribee............447 F4
Croydon.............379 E5
ANE
The Patch...........467 J4
Pakenham...........585 D5
Croydon.............336 J17
Mooroolbark.......336 J17
View Bank...........329 H1
Somerville...........644 F14
Warrandyte.........333 D3
Mornington.........640 J19
Rye.....................696 E9
ANELLA
Frankston...........628 C5
Narre Warren.......538 F18
W Footscray.......366 F11
Doncaster...........331 C19
ANNA
Hampton Pk.......552 C13
Wheelers Hill......461 C16
ANNE
Craigieburn........150 C17
Cheltenham........497 F20
Cranbourne N.....578 H9
Frankston...........600 A15
Lalor....................240 K5
Springvale S.......533 L2
Tullamarine........278 F7
Vermont S.........420 K8
Melton W...........226 C16
Bayswater..........423 H10
Bundoora...........285 C1
Doncaster E.......376 C4
ANTHUS
Nar Warrn S.......553 F18
B
Tullamarine........278 D12
BERARDINO
Hillside..............274 G7
CELLO
Epping...............198 F15
CK
Eaglemont..........328 G12
CKASONS
Heathmont.........378 K20
Heathmont.........423 A1

DICKENS
cl. Templestowe.....332 C10
ct. Noble Park.........501 C19
rd. Olinda...............426 J4
st. Bentleigh............495 L4
st. Blackburn..........376 B20
st. Burnley..............371 B16
st. Elwood..............414 B20
st. Glen Iris.............417 B9
st. Heidelberg Ht.....284 F18
st. Lalor..................241 A9
st. Moonee Pnd......324 E15
st. Parkdale............531 D11
st. Pascoe Vale S....324 H5
st. St Kilda..............414 F19
st. Yarraville............366 L16
DICKENSON
st. Altona Mdw........451 K5
DICKERSON
av. Mill Park............242 L8
DICKIE
ct. Springvale..........500 B18
rd. Officer................556 G12
rd. Officer................556 K3
st. Bacchus Msh.....222 D15
DICKINSON
gr. Mt Martha..........655 G20
st. Belgrave.............466 E13
st. Hadfield.............280 K10
st. Tecoma..............466 E13
DICKMANN
st. Richmond............26 F16
DICKSON
cr. Ringwood N.......378 G4
ct. Williamstown.....410 L14
la. Portsea.............678 E1
la. Dandenong, off Scott St...........535 L8
st. Avondale Ht.......322 G7
st. Bacchus Msh.....222 B14
st. Kingsville...........366 L11
st. Mt Waverley.......458 F7
st. Sunshine...........365 D3
DIEDRE
st. Dandenong N.....536 C1
DIGBY
av. Belmont.............702 A20
ct. Coolaroo............238 D7
ct. Frankston...........628 G1
ct. Springvale S.......533 K1
DIGGERS
pde. Anglesea............713 H5
pl. Caroline Spr.......318 E10
rd. Werribee S.........488 G19
DIGGINS
ct. Noble Park.........500 E19
DIGGORRA
ct. Pt Lonsdale........710 C3
DIGHT
av. Balwyn N...........373 E6
st. Collingwood.........19 K17
DILIGENT
dr. Bayswater N.......380 A17
DILKARA
av. Bundoora...........284 L5
ct. Doncaster E.......332 J8
ct. Frankston...........600 J15
DILKHOOSA
av. Blind Bight.........650 A8
DILLEY
cl. Noble Park N......501 G15
DILLON
ct. Altona Mdw........451 D3
ct. Bayswater..........423 H8
ct. Diggers Rest......187 L19
gr. Glen Iris.............417 C10
gr. Ringwood N.......378 F4
st. Braybrook..........366 B4
DILLWYNIA
av. Templstw Lr.......330 J14
pl. Meadow Ht.........237 K1
DILOP
dr. Epping...............197 C18
DIMAR
ct. Dingley Village...533 C9
DIMBOOLA
rd. Broadmeadows..237 H12
rd. Westmeadows...237 H12
DINADAN
ct. Glen Waverley....420 L16
DINAH
pde. Keilor East..........322 D3
DINGLE
av. Frankston............627 E1
ct. Berwick...............553 G14
DINGLEY
av. Dandenong S.....535 E13
cl. Gladstone Pk......237 E17
cl. N Warrandyte.....290 C14

ct. Dingley Village...533 F9
la. Mt Dandenong...426 L1
pl. Melton W...........226 C19
st. Templstw Lr.......330 D9
DINGLEY DELL
rd. Healesville..........212 G17
rd. N Warrandyte.....290 B13
DINNELL
st. Sunshine W.......364 D6
DINSDALE
ct. Mooroolbark......337 K15
rd. Boronia..............423 E13
st. Albert Park...........29 F15
st. Albert Park.........413 C8
DION
cl. Lalor..................240 K7
ct. Keilor Dn............276 B13
ct. Narre Warren.....538 G17
dr. Carrum Downs...601 C5
rd. Glen Waverley....460 E8
st. Doncaster..........330 F16
st. Ferntree Gly.......423 L17
st. Glen Iris.............417 G11
DIOR
ct. Cranbourne W....577 G18
DIOSMA
av. Springvale..........500 J11
av. Sunshine W.......363 L8
cr. Nunawading.......376 K19
ct. Cranbourne N.....578 B8
ct. Doncaster..........331 A16
ct. Frankston S........627 C8
ct. Narre Warren.....539 C20
ct. Newcomb..........704 C15
dr. Glen Waverley....460 D9
rd. Eltham...............288 C8
wy. Mill Park............243 C7
DIPLOMAT
dr. Thomastown......240 E15
DIRIGO
dr. Wheelers Hill......460 H17
DIRKALA
av. Heathmont.........422 H2
ct. Mulgrave...........501 F7
rt. Berwick..............554 B3
DIRLETON
cl. Frankston...........599 K15
DIRLTON
cr. Pk Orchards.......333 L18
DISNEY
av. Keilor East..........278 A19
st. Fawkner.............281 E2
st. Heidelberg Ht.....328 D4
DISRAELI
gr. Pascoe Vale S....324 J6
st. Kew....................372 A8
st. St Albans...........319 F4
DISS
ct. St Albans...........320 G6
DISSIK
st. Cheltenham........497 D15
DISTANCE
rd. Melb Airport.......235 F6
DIWAI
cl. Noble Park N......501 B13
DIXIE
cl. Keilor Dn............276 B13
cl. Tootgarook.........698 E7
ct. Meadow Ht........237 K4
DIXON
av. Croydon.............336 E18
av. Werribee............447 K16
ct. Altona Mdw........451 J4
ct. Boronia..............423 F13
ct. Briar Hill..............286 G2
gr. Blackburn...........375 F12
rd. Emerald..............509 E9
rd. Gisborne...............78 B19
st. Clayton..............458 L19
st. Glen Iris.............417 C11
st. Malvern.............416 A15
st. Mentone.............531 C12
st. Noble Park.........500 K15
st. Northcote...........327 C18
st. Pascoe Vale.......281 A12
st. Prahran................32 J17
st. Prahran..............414 K9
DIXONS
rd. The Patch...........468 D6
DJERRIWARRH
ct. Kurunjang..........227 F10
DOBELL
av. Sunbury.............142 H10
cr. Werribee.............448 A8
ct. Dandenong N.....502 B15
ct. Mulgrave............460 C15
ct. Scoresby............462 A8
dr. Chelsea..............547 B14
dr. Eltham North......245 K18
pl. Dallas.................238 E11

pl. Doncaster E.......332 D16
pl. Mooroolbark......337 F12
st. Blackburn S.......419 K5
DOBIES
ct. Westmeadows...237 H11
DOBROYD
ct. Lalor..................240 D9
DOBSON
av. Oakleigh E..........458 L14
av. Rosanna............285 C17
cr. Braybrook..........365 J2
cr. Lynbrook...........551 D16
ct. Dandenong N.....502 D20
ct. Pakenham...........584 E4
rd. Montmorency......286 F8
st. Ferntree Gly.......463 G1
st. South Yarra...........31 K2
st. South Yarra........414 E1
DOCKER
ct. Altona Mdw........451 H4
st. Elwood..............454 E6
st. Richmond............26 E16
DOCKLANDS
dr. Docklands..........368 H15
hwy. Brooklyn...........366 A16
hwy. Footscray...........367 G12
hwy. W Melbourne.....368 B11
hwy. Yarraville...........366 K17
DOCK LINK
rd. W Melbourne.......33 B20
rd. W Melbourne.....368 A12
DOCKSIDE
rd. Port Melb...........411 L5
DOCRELL
la. Portsea.............666 K20
DOCTORS GULLY
rd. Doreen...............156 L19
rd. Doreen...............201 G1
rd. Nutfield..............201 G1
rd. Nutfield..............202 F1
DOD
st. Queenscliff.........708 K18
DODD
la. Caroline Spr.......318 B4
pl. Roxburgh Pk......194 D12
st. Braybrook..........322 A20
st. St Andrews........206 B1
DODDS
rd. Keilor East..........277 J20
rd. Olinda...............426 H8
st. Southbank.............3 H20
st. Southbank...........24 F20
st. Southbank...........30 F1
st. Springvale..........500 C17
DODEMAIDE
cct. Merrimu............223 D1
pl. Brookfield..........268 B6
DODGE
ct. Keilor Dn............276 B14
DODS
st. Brunswick..........325 F16
DOE
st. Rye....................696 F6
DOERY
st. Emerald.............469 A20
DOG TRAP GULLY
rd. Maddingley........263 A4
DOHERTY
st. Deer Park...........318 L16
st. Pakenham..........584 B1
DOHERTYS
rd. Altona North.......408 G2
rd. Laverton N.........407 C1
DOHONEY
rd. Bullengarook........77 C5
DOIDGE
st. Bundoora...........284 H3
DOIG
av. Tootgarook........698 H4
pl. Sunbury.............143 B7
DOLAN
ct. Sunbury.............142 J13
DOLE
av. Reservoir...........283 E3
DOLEEN
rd. N Warrandyte.....289 J12
DOLLMAN
st. Brunswick..........325 D17
DOLPHIN
av. Rye....................696 E3
ct. Gladstone Pk......236 K18
ct. Point Cook.........450 F5
st. Aspendale..........546 D2
st. Mt Eliza..............641 J3
DOMAIN
av. Point Cook.........449 L5
cct. Beaconsfield......555 C11
dr. Berwick..............553 K18
dr. Berwick..............553 L19
dr. Keysborough.....534 G13

mw. Patterson L........547 H19
pky. Langwarrin.........629 H3
pl. Point Cook..........450 F9
rd. Jan Juc.............711 C17
rd. Melbourne...........30 L4
rd. Melbourne...........31 A4
rd. Melbourne.........413 L2
rd. Melbourne.........414 E3
rd. South Yarra..........30 L4
rd. South Yarra..........31 A4
rd. South Yarra........413 L2
ri. Doncaster E.......331 L17
st. Hadfield.............281 B7
st. South Yarra..........31 C7
st. South Yarra........414 B3
tce. S Morang...........198 K14
DOMAINE
gr. Chirnside Pk.......336 K3
DOMAIN TUNNEL
Melbourne...........24 K17
Southbank...........24 K17
DOME
ct. Springvale S.......500 B19
st. Surrey Hills........373 J20
DOMIGAN
ct. Hoppers Csg......448 B1
DOMINIC
pde. Melton...............226 J17
rd. Gruyere.............342 D8
st. Camberwell.........417 G3
DOMINION
av. Glen Waverley....460 L6
rd. Mt Martha..........655 G15
DOMINO
ct. Somerville..........644 F17
ct. Wheelers Hill......460 J9
DOMVILLE
av. Hawthorn...........371 F17
DON
arc. Hawthorn...........372 A16
av. Hoppers Csg......448 H2
ct. Caulfield S..........456 A10
ct. Rye....................696 K5
ct. Wantirna S.........422 L11
ct. Wantirna S.........423 A11
dr. Cranbourne W....603 G1
gr. Greensborough..286 C10
pl. Port Melb...........412 J6
rd. Badger Creek.....258 F7
rd. Don Valley..........346 B5
rd. Healesville..........214 A18
rd. Launching Pl......346 A7
st. Balwyn N...........373 E7
st. Reservoir...........283 J5
DONA
dr. Hoppers Csg......405 E18
DONACH
cr. Bundoora...........285 D2
DONAGHY
st. Geelong West.....702 G3
DONAL
st. Murrumbeena....457 D14
DONALD
av. Anglesea............713 J2
av. Essendon...........324 F7
av. Frankston...........599 D14
cl. Kilsyth...............381 G10
cr. Dromana............686 C6
ct. Boronia..............423 K14
ct. Kurunjang..........227 E11
gr. Chelsea.............546 K16
pl. Doncaster..........331 A15
rd. Burwood............418 A7
rd. Langwarrin.........629 K15
rd. Wheelers Hill......460 L13
st. Ashburton..........417 B18
st. Bacchus Msh.....222 A13
st. Belmont.............706 H2
st. Blackburn S.......375 G20
st. Blackburn S.......419 G1
st. Brunswick..........325 G9
st. Brunswick E.......325 G9
st. Clayton.............498 L1
st. Croydon.............380 E5
st. Dallas...............238 J11
st. E Geelong..........703 G14
st. Footscray...........367 E7
st. Greensborough..286 D6
st. Hadfield.............280 K10
st. Healesville..........258 E4
st. Highett...............496 C14
st. Lalor..................241 K9
st. Laverton............407 C19
st. Mt Waverley.......458 G3
st. Prahran...............31 J19
st. Prahran.............414 E10
st. Preston.............283 F18
st. Rosebud...........683 J18
st. Springvale.........499 G17
st. Sunshine...........365 F4
st.s, Altona Mdw.......407 C20

DONALDA
av. Sorrento 678 G8
DONALD CAMERON
dr. Roxburgh Pk....194 A13
DONALDSON
cr. Menzies Ck 467 J11
la. Melbourne 2 H13
la. Melbourne, off Russell St 24 F6
rd. Kangaroo Grnd...247 A16
rd. Kangaroo Grnd...247 E19
rd. Research 247 E19
st. Bentleigh....456 C18
st. Ivanhoe....328 B11
st. Port Melb....412 J6
DONALDSONS
rd. Red Hill....688 D20
DONAT
ct. Craigieburn 150 E20
DONAVAN
ct. Cheltenham....496 L13
DONBIRN
wy. Vermont S 421 B14
DON BOSCO
dr. Narre Warren 553 E6
DONCASTER
rd. Balwyn N 373 A4
rd. Balwyn N 373 J3
rd. Doncaster 373 K3
rd. Doncaster E 375 J1
st. Ascot Vale....323 F18
DONCASTER EAST
rd. Mitcham 377 C10
DONEGAL
ct. Templestowe 332 D6
wy. Hampton Pk....551 H13
DONELAN
tr. Lysterfield....504 F7
DONELLY
cl. Sunbury....143 H16
ct. Pascoe Vale 280 J10
rd. Hallam....537 E13
DON EVA
ct. Rowville....502 K1
DONGALA
dr. Werribee....446 L17
dr. Werribee....447 A17
DONGOLA
rd. Keilor Dn....276 E16
rd. W Footscray....366 K5
DONHAVEN
ct. Dingley Village ...532 L6
ct. Templestowe 331 J13
DON JUAN
ct. Narre Warren 539 C16
DONN
cl. Frankston S....627 H14
cl. View Bank....285 L15
DONNA
cl. Dingley Village ...533 A4
st. Carrum Downs...600 H1
wy. Doveton....536 K7
DONNA BUANG
rd. Badger Creek 258 E12
rd. Badger Creek 258 K16
rd. Healesville....258 B5
rd. Healesville....303 C4
rd. Warburton 304 B4
rd. Warburton 305 A5
rd. Warburton 306 C5
rd. Warburton 350 A2
rd. Wesburn....303 C4
st. Camberwell....416 L7
st. Camberwell....417 A6
DONNE
ct. Delahey....275 E14
ct. Mooroolbark 337 F20
st. Coburg 325 A7
DONNELLY
ct. Cranbourne....578 B14
ct. Dandenong N....501 K17
ct. Kealba....276 K20
ri. Frankston S....627 J11
DONNELLYS WEIR
rd. Healesville....214 A12
DONNINGTON
ct. Belmont....705 K5
DONNYBROOK
rd. Woodstock 125 A17
rd. Yan Yean 125 G18
DONOVAN
st. Preston....326 J3
DONOVANS
la. N Melbourne....17 A12
rd. Healesville....212 K20
DONVIEW
ct. Croydon....380 G1
DOODSON
ct. Eltham....287 K8
DOOEN
ct. Westmeadows ...237 E12
DOOGA
st. Clayton 499 C1
DOOGAN
st. Blackburn 375 F18
DOOKIE
ct. Broadmeadows ..237 L11
ct. Narre Warren 538 G16
DOOLAN
ct. Rowville....503 D2
st. Maddingley....263 D4
st. Reservoir....283 D15
st. Werribee....447 F19
DOOMBEN
dr. Mill Park 242 K9
DOON
av. Glen Waverley ...419 J18
ct. Briar Hill....286 J3
rd. Launching Pl....346 D12
rd. Yarra Jctn 346 J11
st. Prahran....31 K18
st. Prahran....414 E9
DOONA
av. Kew....372 B11
DOONAHA
rd. Cockatoo 511 G10
DOONBRAE
av. Noble Park N....501 D18
DOONDOO
st. Burwood E....419 F11
DOONE
st. Aberfeldie....323 D9
DOONGA
av. Moorabbin 496 E9
DOONGALLA
rd. Mt Dandenong ...425 L6
rd. The Basin....425 G8
DOONKUNA
av. Camberwell....417 D4
DOONSIDE
dr. Lilydale....338 G12
st. Richmond....371 B14
DOORAWARRAH
ct. Mt Waverley....459 D4
DOOWI
ct. Greensborough ..244 B17
DORA
av. Blackburn 375 E15
ct. Somerville....645 D17
ct. Templestowe 331 E5
st. Braybrook....322 B19
st. Heidelberg 329 B9
wy. Epping....198 F19
DORADO
av. Balwyn N 329 D19
DORAN
ct. Frankston....600 E16
st. Southbank 23 E19
wk. Delahey....275 B12
DORCAS
la. S Melbourne 29 E7
st. Boronia....424 D1
st. Newcomb 704 B12
st. Southbank 30 B4
st. Southbank 413 H1
st. S Melbourne 29 D7
st. S Melbourne 413 C3
DORCHAP
ct. Hoppers Csg 449 B2
DORCHESTER
av. Montrose....382 F8
cr. Carrum Downs...601 B5
ct. Frankston....628 C9
pl. Carlton....18 G15
rd. Cockatoo 511 E10
st. Craigieburn 149 L17
DORE
rd. Nr Nr Goon N....560 E20
rd. Pakenham....560 E20
rd. Tooradin 651 D5
DOREEN
ct. Montrose....381 L8
DOREEN ROGEN
wy. S Morang....243 H2
DORENE
ct. Vermont S 420 H7
DORGAN
ct. Endeavour Hl 503 J20
st. Caulfield N 415 E18
st. Mt Waverley....459 G1
DORIAN
av. Ferntree Gly 464 H3
ct. Berwick....554 F19
DORIS
ct. Scoresby....462 H8
ct. Springvale S....499 G18
ct. Wheelers Hill....460 K16
dr. Hoppers Csg 447 K3
st. Greensborough ..285 H5
st. Murrumbeena 457 D11
DORKING
ct. Craigieburn 150 C19
rd. Box Hill 375 B13
rd. Box Hill N....375 C9
DORLTON
pl. Roxburgh Pk....194 C16
DORMAN
ct. Mill Park 242 A4
DORNIE
mw. Endeavour Hl 503 K18
DORNING
rd. Nar Warrn E....507 E16
DORNOCH
ct. Croydon....336 H20
dr. Sunbury....144 D11
DOROTHEA
cr. Dromana....686 A9
ct. Bundoora....242 F17
st. Canterbury....417 F1
st. Highett....496 A14
DOROTHEA MACKELLAR
av. Oakleigh E....458 H11
DOROTHY
av. Belmont....706 F1
av. Glen Huntly 456 C10
av. Ormond 456 C10
av. Sunshine 365 G1
av. Thomastown....241 C15
cr. Mornington....640 H20
ct. Clayton S 499 E16
ct. Dandenong N....501 K17
ct. Hampton Pk....551 F11
ct. McCrae....685 C14
gr. Ferntree Gly 464 H1
rd. Mt Evelyn....383 L5
st. Brunswick....325 J12
st. Burwood E....419 G10
st. Croydon....380 B9
st. Doveton....537 A8
st. Fawkner....239 G20
st. Healesville....213 G15
st. Pascoe Vale 281 A11
st. Rye....696 E10
st. Tullamarine....278 G4
DORR
ct. Belmont....706 H6
DORRIGO
dr. Boronia....424 K6
DORRINGTON
av. Glen Iris....416 G15
av. Point Cook 450 F6
av. Reservoir....283 F14
ct. Bundoora....243 D19
ct. Dingley Village ...533 G7
ct. Mill Park 242 A2
dr. Mt Waverley....459 E1
DORRIT
st. Carlton....18 E14
st. Springvale S....499 L20
DORSET
av. Heidelberg 329 F4
av. Keilor East....322 G5
ct. Keysborough 534 J8
dr. Greenvale....237 F5
pl. Melton W....226 C15
rd. Bayswater N....380 D19
rd. Boronia....424 D9
rd. Croydon....380 D8
rd. Croydon S....380 D19
rd. Dandenong N....502 C14
rd. Ferntree Gly 464 C3
rd. Mt Martha....655 J19
rd. Pascoe Vale 281 A14
sq. Boronia....424 D12
st. Glen Waverley 459 H11
DORTAD
ct. Hampton Pk....551 H9
DORWARD
av. Newcomb 704 A15
DOTTEREL
cl. Blind Bight....650 B8
cl. Doveton....536 J5
ct. Chelsea Ht....547 D8
ct. Rosebud W....699 E5
ct. Werribee....448 B5
DOUBELL
bvd. Truganina 405 G13
bvd. Truganina 405 G15
cl. Glen Waverley 461 B6
ct. Mill Park 242 G8
DOUCH
st. Williamstown 411 B11
DOUG
ct. Narre Warren 538 L15
DOUGAL
ct. Highton....701 G19
ct. Kurunjang....227 E10
DOUGAND
ct. Dingley Village ...533 B8
DOUGHARTY
rd. Heidelberg Ht 284 B17
rd. Heidelberg W 284 B17
DOUGHERTY
ct. Mulgrave 501 E4
DOUGHTYS
rd. Kalorama 383 A19
rd. Olinda....383 A19
DOUGLAS
av. Box Hill S....418 H2
av. Doncaster E 376 F3
av. Donvale 376 F3
av. St Albans 319 F2
cr. Monbulk 428 F17
ct. Altona Mdw....451 D3
ct. Cranbourne W....577 F19
ct. Nar Warrn N....539 F10
ct. Pt Lonsdale....710 G1
ct. Rye....697 B14
ct. St Helena 244 L19
ct. St Helena 245 A19
ct. Strathmr Ht....279 D9
ct. Thomastown....241 G15
ct. Westmeadows ...236 H15
gr. Frankston....599 D15
pde. Chelsea....546 H17
pde. Croydon....335 L20
pde. Don Valley....346 E9
pde. Newport....411 D8
pde. Spotswood 411 D7
pde. Williamstown 411 D10
pde. Yarra Jctn 347 D18
pl. Geelong, off Maud St....702 K10
ri. Endeavour Hl 503 K18
st. Altona North....409 J8
st. Ashwood 417 L15
st. Balwyn N 373 C6
st. Beaumaris....530 F7
st. Blackburn N 375 L7
st. Boronia....424 D15
st. Malvern East 416 E20
st. Noble Park 500 H20
st. Pascoe Vale 280 C14
st. Port Melb....368 D19
st. Rosanna 328 L1
st. Rosanna 329 A1
st. Southbank 29 G1
st. Southbank 413 D1
st. Sunshine N 321 G13
st. Toorak 415 B4
st. Upwey 466 B9
DOUGLAS MAWSON
dr. Roxburgh Pk....193 J14
DOUGLASS
st. Herne Hill....701 L1
st. Manifold Ht....701 L1
DOULTON
av. Heathmont....378 H18
rd. Blackburn 375 F11
DOUTHIE
rd. Seville....342 K14
rd. Seville....387 E7
rd. Seville E....342 K14
rd. Seville E....387 E7
DOUTNEY
ct. Sunbury....142 J3
DOVAVALLEY
rd. Wandin East....340 H18
DOVE
av. Altona....408 F19
ct. Coolaroo....238 F7
ct. Pakenham....584 L2
ct. Pearcedale 646 K4
ct. Templstw Lr....330 D9
ct. Werribee....448 A8
pl. Burnley, off Type St....371 B17
st. Cremorne 26 A18
st. W Footscray....366 K7
DOVER
ct. Diamond Ck....245 L6
ct. Dromana....686 E9
ct. Ferntree Gly 463 G3
ct. Mulgrave 500 H2
la. Williamstown 411 F12
pl. Melton W....226 E15
pl. Parkdale....531 D12
pl. Geelong, off Little Malop St...703 D8
rd. Williamstown 411 F11
st. Albanvale....319 D4
st. Bentleigh E....457 C20
st. Caulfield S....455 G9
st. Cremorne 32 A2
st. Flemington....33 G1
st. Flemington....324 C20
st. Oakleigh E....458 L15
DOVETON
av. Eumemmerring ..537 C15
DOVETTE
ct. Wheelers Hill....460 K
DOW
st. Port Melb....412
st. S Melbourne 30
DOWD
ct. Pakenham....584
pl. Glenroy....279
rd. Healesville....214 L
DOWDING
cl. Fawkner....281
DOWELL
ct. Dandenong N....502 C
DOWER
st. Camberwell....417
DOWLE
st. Macleod....285 C
DOWLING
av. Springvale....500
ct. Sunbury....142 G
gr. Doncaster E ....332 F
pl. N Melbourne ....17 G
rd. Oakleigh S....498
st. Fawkner....281
st. Kealba....321
DOWMAN
st. Newport....411 D
DOWN
st. Collingwood....19 J
st. Reservoir....282 K
DOWNARD
cr. Dandenong N....501 L
st. Braeside....532 G
DOWNE
pl. Wantirna....422
DOWNES
av. Brighton....454 J
la. Geelong, off Little Malop St....703
pl. Geelong, off Little Malop St....703
st. Strathmore....324
DOWNEY
rd. Dewhurst....510 D
rd. Yarrambat....201 C
DOWNHAM
wy. Wyndham Va ....446 D
DOWNIE
st. Melbourne ....23 H
DOWNING
av. Glen Iris....416 K
st. Blackburn ....375 G
st. Oakleigh....457 L
st. Sunshine N ....321 F
DOWNLAND
pl. Dingley Village ...533
sq. Avondale Ht ....322 D
DOWNS
rd. Lalor....240
rd. Seaford....599
rd. Thomastown....240 C
st. Brunswick....325
st. Pascoe Vale ....280 J
DOWNSHIRE
cl. Wantirna S....422 J
rd. Belmont....702 C
rd. Elsternwick 455
DOWNTON
cr. Pt Lonsdale....707 H
gr. Kew....372 G
DOWNWARD
st. Mornington....640 D
DOWSETT
st. S Geelong ....703 D
DOY
st. Dallas 238
DOYLE
pl. Endeavour Hl 537
rd. Pakenham Up 559
st. Avondale Ht 322
st. Bulleen ....329 J
st. Sunshine N ....321 E
DOYNTON
pde. Hoppers Csg....448
pde. Mt Waverley....459
DOYSAL
av. Ferntree Gly ....424 G
DOZEY
ct. Roxburgh Pk....194 D
pl. Endeavour Hl 537
DRAGON
wy. Kings Park ....274 L
DRAIN RESERVE
rd. South Yarra....32 G
DRAKE
cl. Gladstone Pk....237 A
ct. Avondale Ht ....322 A
ct. Carrum Downs...601
ct. Lilydale 338

ct. Melton......226 L16
pl. Pakenham......584 K8
st. Brighton......454 G10
st. Ferntree Gly......464 E8
st. Mornington......640 E11
st. Newport......411 B5
st. Spotswood......411 B5
st. Sunshine N......321 B14

RAKES
a. N Melbourne......34 K10

RANSFIELD
wy. Epping......198 E15

RAPER
ct. Keilor Dn......276 D12
sq. Wheelers Hill......461 B8
st. McKinnon......456 F16
st. Ormond......456 F16
st. S Melbourne......29 G9
st. S Melbourne......413 D5

RASKA
ct. Oak Park......279 G10

RAYTON
cr. Pk Orchards......333 G18
ct. Baxter......644 B2
ct. Sunshine......365 E5

RAYTONS
pl. Wyndham Va......446 F13

READNOUGHT
ct. Sandringham......495 F15

REAM
pl. Melton S......268 F5

REAMHAVEN
ct. Epping......197 D18

REDGE
ct. Reservoir......282 F1

RESDEN
av. Heathmont......378 H17
ct. Heidelberg Ht......328 G6
wy. Sunshine W......364 C8

RESSAGE
pl. Epping......198 D17

RESS CIRCLE
a. Mooroolbark......337 D7

REW
t. Keilor East......322 E1
t. Yarraville......366 F15

REWE
l. Donvale......332 K17

REWERY
l. Melbourne......2 D7
l. Melbourne......24 C4
a. Melbourne......2 E8
a. Melbourne......24 C4
l. Melbourne......2 D7
l. Melbourne......24 C5

REWETT
t. Surrey Hills......374 D20

REWS
d. Marshall......706 L13

RIFFIELD
r. Sassafras......426 H12

RIFTWOOD
v. Rye......696 E2
l. Seabrook......450 J7
t. Frankston......599 L16
t. Mt Martha......656 K7
t. Narre Warren......538 L20
r. Glen Waverley......460 H1
nw. Carrum Downs......601 D6

RILL
t. Hawthorn......371 J17

RINA
t. Strathmore......280 B17

RINAN
d. Chelsea......546 L17

RINKWATER
r. Sunshine W......364 G7

RISCOLLS
d. Kealba......276 K17
d. Kealba......277 A20

RISHANE
t. Coburg......325 D5

RIVER
. Melbourne......2 B10
. Melbourne......24 C6
t. Kingsbury......283 K8
t. Portsea......678 E2

ROITWICH
r. Deer Park......318 J9

ROMANA
v. Airport W......279 A10
v. Bentleigh E......457 B16
v. Pascoe Vale......280 G17
v. Reservoir......282 D11
de. Safety Bch......686 G2
. Glenroy......279 H8

ROMSALLY
. Warranwood......334 K16

DROOP
st. Footscray......367 D5

DROUIN
ct. Melton S......268 E5
st. Dallas......238 F10

DROVERS
ct. Vermont S......421 B13
la. Somerville......645 F15
rt. Nar Warrn S......552 E17
wk. Chirnside Pk......337 E6

DRUCE
la. N Melbourne......34 J10

DRUITT
st. Oakleigh S......497 G5

DRUM
cl. Frankston......600 H16
st. Rye......696 H9

DRUMDOUNE
dr. Mt Eliza......626 C11

DRUMMARTIN
st. Albion......364 K1

DRUMMER
ct. Hoppers Csg......449 D2
la. Narre Warren......538 J12

DRUMMER HILL
la. Mooroolbark......337 D10

DRUMMOND
cl. Donvale......377 B2
cr. Rowville......462 E19
pl. Carlton......18 F18
rd. Seville......341 K14
st. Blackburn S......420 A2
st. Carlton......18 F20
st. Carlton......18 G9
st. Carlton N......18 G8
st. Chadstone......457 K10
st. Chadstone......457 L3
st. Coburg......325 K1
st. Greenvale......236 L4
st. Greenvale......237 A4
st. Oakleigh......457 K10

DRURY
ct. Noble Park......534 K5
ct. Wantirna S......422 B18
la. Dromana......685 E10
la. Hoppers Csg......448 E5
st. Beaconsfield......554 L16
st. Kensington......33 G6

DRUSHI
ct. Clarinda......498 H11

DRYAD
ct. Chelsea Ht......547 J18

DRYANDRA
av. Epping......198 A19
cr. Keysborough......534 B12

DRYBURGH
pl. Hillside......232 B20
st. N Melbourne......34 L14
st. W Melbourne......34 K19

DRYDEN
cnc. Mooroolbark......381 E2
ct. Berwick......554 J19
ct. Bundoora......242 G17
ct. Keilor......276 G11
st. Canterbury......373 D20
st. Doncaster E......332 A20
st. Elwood......454 E1

DRYSDALE
av. Eltham North......245 K18
av. Frankston......599 J17
av. Nar Warrn N......538 C12
av. Nar Warrn N......538 D10
av. Newcomb......704 A12
av. Taylors Lakes......275 B2
ct. Croydon Hills......335 H16
ct. Hampton Pk......552 D10
ct. Scoresby......462 C8
ct. Thomastown......240 F15
ct. Wheelers Hill......460 E16
pl. Doncaster E......332 F16
pl. Mooroolbark......337 H11
rd. Moolap......704 E12
rd. Newcomb......704 D12
rd. Warrandyte......333 F3
st. Malvern......415 K14
st. Port Melb......412 L6
st. Reservoir......283 E16
st. Sunbury......142 H10
st. Yallambie......285 E16

DRYSTONE
cr. Deer Park......319 E11

DUANE
ct. Altona Mdw......451 H7

DUBAND
st. Burwood E......420 B7

DUBBO
ct. Glen Waverley......420 C16
st. Albion......320 H19

DUBIN
ct. Wantirna S......462 K1

DUBLIN
av. Strathmore......279 H20
dr. Grovedale......705 L13
rd. Ringwood E......378 L8
rd. Ringwood E......379 A8
st. Oakleigh E......458 F12

DUCHESS
ct. Hillside......231 J18

DUCKBOARD
pl. Melbourne......24 J8

DUCKER
st. Yarraville......367 D15

DUCKETT
st. Brunswick......325 F11
st. Doncaster E......375 J5

DUCKHAM
st. Blackburn......375 E19

DUCKMANTON
ct. Bentleigh E......456 G20

DUCKS
la. Seville......342 B17

DUCKWORTH
cl. Berwick......553 L8

DUCOL
ct. Seville......341 J15

DUDLEY
av. Hampton E......496 A9
av. Newtown......701 J4
av. Wantirna......422 E4
ct. Gladstone Pk......236 K19
ct. Somerville......644 F14
gr. Edithvale......546 F12
mw. Pakenham......584 K1
pde. Canterbury......373 C18
rd. Wonga Park......291 J16
st. Belmont......706 H1
st. Brighton......454 E12
st. Caulfield E......456 E2
st. Docklands......23 B5
st. Docklands......368 L13
st. Eltham......287 H9
st. Essendon N......279 C20
st. Fitzroy N......326 C16
st. Footscray......366 L7
st. Ivanhoe......328 A12
st. Mitcham......377 G16
st. Preston......326 D4
st. W Melbourne......23 B5
st. W Melbourne......368 L13

DUDSON
cl. Mt Eliza......626 H19

DUELLS
rd. Rosebud......700 G7

DUERAN
st. Mt Eliza......641 L2

DUERDIN
st. Clayton......459 G15
st. Notting Hill......459 G15

DUFF
pde. View Bank......285 F18
st. Cranbourne W......577 E20
st. Sandringham......495 G19

DUFFIELDS
rd. Jan Juc......711 E10
rd. Jan Juc......711 F15
rd. Torquay......711 E7

DUFFRYN
pl. Toorak......415 F3

DUFFS
rd. Cottles Br......204 G8
rd. Cottles Br......204 L6
rd. Panton Hill......204 G8
rd. Panton Hill......204 L6

DUFFY
av. Elsternwick......455 A9
ct. Sunbury......142 K12
st. Burwood......418 C10
st. Epping......197 E19
st. Epping......241 D1
st. Essendon N......323 F1
st. Maribyrnong......323 D15
st. Portsea......678 C4
st. Reservoir......282 L8

DUFFYS
rd. Emerald......507 J15
rd. Nar Warrn E......507 J15

DUFTON
ct. Greenvale......193 B17

DUGDALE
st. Bacchus Msh......222 B15

DUGGAN
ct. Altona Mdw......451 G9
ct. Highton......701 K18
pl. Gladstone Pk......236 L16
rd. Gisborne......109 A4
st. Balwyn N......373 H5
st. Brunswick W......324 J10
st. Mordialloc......532 C10

DUGONG
ct. St Helena......245 A17

DUIGAN
pl. Roxburgh Pk......194 C11

DUIKER
ct. Langwarrin......600 K17
ct. Nar Warrn N......538 K8

DUKE
ct. Bundoora......284 G4
ct. Skye......575 H19
rt. Eltham......288 F6
st. Abbotsford......26 L3
st. Abbotsford......371 A12
st. Altona North......409 H4
st. Ashburton......417 E14
st. Aspendale......546 E7
st. Avondale Ht......322 A16
st. Braybrook......321 J19
st. Braybrook......365 H4
st. Brunswick E......326 A13
st. Caulfield S......455 E8
st. Emerald......469 B20
st. Fitzroy......25 B1
st. Kew......371 K5
st. Richmond......26 K17
st. St Kilda......414 F17
st. Sunshine......365 H4
st. Sunshine N......321 J19
st. Werribee......447 B14
st. W Footscray......366 G11
st. Windsor......414 H11
st. Yarra Jctn......347 E17

DULCIE
ct. Noble Park N......501 B10
gr. Bentleigh......496 E6
st. Sunshine......365 F1

DULCIE DOMUM
rd. Olinda......426 L5

DULCIFY
ct. Keilor Dn......275 H11
ct. Melton W......226 C13

DULGAI
ct. Frankston......600 F14

DULKARA
pl. Berwick......553 F3

DULLARD
st. Rosebud......700 A1

DULNAIN
cl. Hampton Pk......551 G4
st. Mt Martha......656 D5

DUMARESQ
st. Brighton East......495 K5

DUMAS
av. Avondale Ht......322 D13
st. Cranbourne......578 C15

DUMBARTON
cct. Melton W......225 L15
st. Reservoir......283 G3

DUMBLANE
av. Ascot Vale......323 H20
st. Balwyn N......373 J2
st. Hughesdale......457 E12

DUMFRIES
ct. Glen Waverley......420 K19
ct. Highton......705 K6
ct. Torquay......712 D2
rd. Keysborough......534 G11
st. Deer Park......319 B12
tce. Greenvale......236 J1
wy. Wantirna......422 K6

DUMMETT
av. Hoppers Csg......448 H2
cr. Fitzroy N......20 B3

DUMOSA
av. Croydon......380 D10
ct. Narre Warren......538 J18
ct. St Albans......320 K8

DUMOSSA
av. Bulleen......329 H11

DUNAI
wk. Delahey......275 A15

DUNBAR
av. Caulfield N......455 F2
av. Cranbourne......578 B20
av. Kalorama......382 L16
av. Kalorama......383 A16
av. Sunshine......365 A8
cl. Wheelers Hill......460 K10
ct. Greenvale......236 J3
ct. Keilor Dn......276 E11
ct. Lalor......240 L6
ct. Lalor......241 A6
la. Dandenong, off Thomas St......535 L10

DUNBARTON
av. Hoppers Csg......448 F6
dr. Eltham North......245 B18
dr. Pakenham......585 F5
dr. Wantirna......422 J6

DUNBLANE
rd. Noble Park......500 K19

DUNCAN
av. Boronia......423 K10
av. Greensborough......285 L7
av. Seaford......599 D12
cl. Mt Eliza......641 K6
ct. Kurunjang......227 G8
ct. Noble Park......500 K19
ct. Ringwood......379 B2
ct. Westmeadows......236 H15
dr. Pakenham......584 E4
rd. Lalor......240 L8
rd. Lalor......241 A8
rd. Officer S......582 G20
st. Box Hill S......418 K2
st. Fairfield......327 D17
st. Flemington......33 D2
st. Narre Warren......538 J15
st. Sandringham......495 F13
st. Templstw Lr......330 G6

DUNCANS
la. Diggers Rest......232 B4
la. Ferny Creek......425 H20
rd. Werribee......447 K16

DUNCOMBE
av. Brighton......454 L20
av. Brighton......455 A20

DUNCRAIG
av. Armadale......415 H14
ct. Narre Warren......538 K14
gr. Sunbury......143 B7

DUNDALK
st. Sunshine......364 L8

DUNDAS
av. Sunbury......142 K10
ct. Doncaster E......331 J17
la. Albert Park......29 H12
la. Albert Park......29 J12
pl. Albert Park......29 J11
pl. Albert Park......413 E6
st. Darley......222 B9
st. Diggers Rest......141 L12
st. Frankston......627 E3
st. Glen Iris......417 K10
st. Herne Hill......701 L1
st. Preston......326 K6
st. Rye......697 C18
st. St Andrews Bch......697 C18
st. Thornbury......327 A6

DUNDEE
av. Chadstone......457 L6
cl. Gladstone Pk......236 L16
ct. Endeavour Hl......503 H18
ct. Frankston N......600 A11
ct. Greenvale......236 L4
ct. Pakenham......584 J2
ct. Templestowe......332 B9
pl. Newtown......701 L12
pl. Wantirna......422 L7
st. Balwyn......373 G10
st. Blackburn S......419 D2
st. Reservoir......283 E4
st. St Albans......320 J6
st. Watsonia N......285 E3
wy. Sydenham......274 H3

DUNDONALD
av. Malvern East......416 K19

DUNE
tr. Frankston N......600 J12
tr. Langwarrin......628 J9

DUNEARN
rd. Dandenong N......501 G20

DUNEDIN
st. Maidstone......322 E20

DUNEED
wy. Delahey......275 A12

DUNELL
av. Roxburgh Pk......194 D9

DUNFERMLINE
av. Greenvale......193 E20
av. Greenvale......237 F3

DUNFIELD
av. Mitcham......376 L10
dr. Gladstone Pk......237 C17

DUNHAM
st. Rye......696 K4

DUNHELEN
la. Craigieburn......192 J2
la. Craigieburn......193 A2
la. Greenvale......192 D1
la. Greenvale......193 A2
la. Yuroke......192 D1

DUNK
cl. Mill Park......242 C5

DUN KEITH
av. Jan Juc......711 C16

DUNKELD
av. Sunshine N......320 L14
av. Sunshine N......321 A14
st. Meadow Ht......238 B3

DUNKINSON
st. Narre Warren......553 E7

DUNKIRK
dr. Point Cook 450 F11
DUNKLEY
av. Highett 496 D15
rd. Altona 407 H14
DUNLANE
ct. Rye 697 E5
DUNLAVIN
rd. Mitcham 376 L11
rd. Nunawading 376 L11
DUNLOE
av. Mont Albert N 374 E10
ct. Bentleigh 496 F5
ri. Templestowe 332 C6
DUNLOP
av. Ascot Vale 324 A18
av. Bayswater N 379 H14
av. Hoppers Csg 405 J20
av. Kew 371 G10
av. Ormond 456 D14
cr. Mill Park 242 G2
ct. Bayswater 423 L3
rd. Mulgrave 459 K15
st. Ashburton 416 L17
st. Ashburton 417 A16
st. Malvern East 416 L17
st. Maribyrnong 323 A13
DUNLUCE
ct. View Bank 329 G2
DUNMERA
cr. Nar Warrn S 578 L2
DUNMOOCHIN
rd. Cottles Br 203 G4
DUNMORE
ct. Cranbourne 578 G17
DUNN
av. Ferny Creek 465 J1
cr. Dandenong S 535 D13
cr. Langwarrin 629 B7
ct. Darley 221 H8
st. Broadmeadows 238 A20
st. Cremorne 26 D18
st. Ringwood E 379 D9
st. Watsonia 285 F4
DUNNE
st. Kingsbury 283 F9
st. Reservoir 283 F9
DUNNELL
ri. Berwick 553 K7
DUNNES
la. Coburg, off Sydney Rd 325 H2
DUNNETTS
rd. Yan Yean 126 H18
DUNNINGS
rd. Point Cook 449 H7
rd. Point Cook 450 F8
DUNNS
ct. Wantirna S 422 E17
rd. Mornington 656 G10
rd. Mt Martha 656 F12
rd. Mt Martha 656 G10
DUNNS CREEK
rd. Dromana 687 K4
DUNOLLY
cr. Reservoir 283 E10
DUNOON
ct. Brighton East 455 H17
ct. Mulgrave 500 C5
st. Doncaster 375 D4
st. Mooroolbark 337 A15
st. Mulgrave 500 C5
st. Murrumbeena 457 B8
DUNOWIE
ct. Grovedale 705 J16
DUNRAVEN
av. Toorak 415 D7
ct. Frankston 628 C6
ct. Langwarrin 601 B20
ct. Narre Warren 538 J13
ct. Sydenham 232 J20
ct. Watsonia N 243 E19
dr. Tarneit 447 J2
dr. Werribee 447 J2
DUNROBIN
ct. Carrum Downs 601 C4
DUNROSSIL
cl. Mulgrave 501 G6
ct. Brookfield 267 L6
dr. Kilsyth 381 D3
dr. Sunbury 143 H3
DUNSCOMBE
av. Ashburton 417 K14
av. Glen Waverley 459 J2
cl. Rowville 503 D1
pl. Chelsea Ht 547 D13
DUNSMORE
rd. Highton 705 G1
DUNSMUIR
dr. Mt Waverley 419 D20
dr. Rosebud 700 B1
DUNSTAN
av. Brunswick 325 K10
cr. Tremont 465 H4
dr. Hurstbridge 203 D14
pde. Campbellfield 238 L9
pde. Port Melb 412 B4
rd. Avonsleigh 470 E20
st. Balwyn N 373 J8
st. Clayton 498 H2
st. Frankston S 626 G8
st. Macleod 284 K14
st. Preston 282 C17
DUNSTANS
ct. Reservoir 241 E20
DUNSTER
ct. Endeavour Hl 537 K9
pl. Roxburgh Pk 194 C14
DUNSTERVILLE
cr. Frankston 600 H15
st. Sandringham 495 F12
DUNSTONE
dr. Rosebud 700 A1
DUNTROON
av. Rye 696 E1
dr. Wantirna 422 E14
DUNURE
ct. Balwyn 373 H10
DUNVEGAN
cr. Dandenong 535 H1
cr. Macleod 285 A10
dr. Kurunjang 227 D11
DUNWOLD
wy. Vermont 421 C4
DUOSA
rd. Altona North 365 H20
DURACK
av. Lynbrook 551 C16
ct. Sunbury 143 A15
pl. Mill Park 242 H6
DURANG
ct. Croydon N 335 L14
ct. Endeavour Hl 538 A7
rd. Selby 467 B14
rd. Upwey 466 A9
DURBAN
ct. Epping 198 B16
ct. Grovedale 706 D12
ct. Keilor Dn 276 E14
rd. Emerald 509 J1
st. Bentleigh 496 F3
DURCELL
av. Portsea 678 A4
DURHAM
cl. Craigieburn 150 G20
cr. Hoppers Csg 448 F2
ct. Croydon N 336 A11
ct. Dandenong N 502 D12
ct. Epping 197 L17
ct. Mt Martha 655 L20
ct. Narre Warren 538 K16
ct. Somerville 644 G16
dr. Mornington 657 B5
pl. Clayton S 499 E10
pl. Melton W 225 K14
pl. Rosebud 684 C14
pl. Sorrento 678 D9
rd. Kilsyth 381 D6
rd. Sunshine 365 B3
rd. Surrey Hills 373 J20
rd. Surrey Hills 417 J2
st. Albert Park 29 D11
st. Albert Park 413 B6
st. Eaglemont 328 J10
st. Kensington 33 K11
st. Richmond 32 G3
st. Richmond 414 J2
DURKIN
ct. Templestowe 331 C8
st. Newport 410 K7
DURLEY
cl. Frankston 600 B20
DURNESS
ct. Endeavour Hl 503 K19
DURNSTAN
ct. Wheelers Hill 460 J18
DURRANT
pl. Endeavour Hl 538 A5
st. Brighton 454 L15
st. Brighton 455 A15
DURWARD
av. Glen Waverley 459 K7
rd. Malvern East 457 G3
DUSK
ct. Hampton Pk 552 A15
DUSKY
dr. Safety Bch 669 B16
DUSTER
ct. Brookfield 268 B4
DUSTIN
ct. Sydenham 275 B6
DUTCH
ct. Melton 269 D1
DUTCHMAN
ct. Taylors Lakes 275 H5
DUTON
ct. Wheelers Hill 460 L7
DUTTON
cl. Lynbrook 551 D15
ct. Meadow Ht 237 L2
DUVAL
ct. Albanvale 318 L3
ct. Wheelers Hill 461 E14
DUXSON
dr. Templestowe 331 A9
DWYER
av. Reservoir 282 E13
ct. Donvale 332 K16
pl. Greensborough 243 H18
st. Blackburn 375 F20
st. Clifton Hill 20 H1
st. Macleod 284 K14
DYER
ct. Clarinda 498 G11
ct. Epping 197 K19
st. Hoppers Csg 448 J3
DYFFRYN
ct. Kilsyth 380 L4
DYLAN
ct. Berwick 539 G19
DYMOCK
ct. Craigieburn 194 B4
DYNES
st. Ringwood E 379 C6
DYNON
rd. Footscray 33 H17
rd. W Melbourne 33 A17
rd. W Melbourne 367 L8
DYSART
pl. Mooroolbark 381 H3
DYSON
ct. Mooroolbark 337 F11
dr. Lynbrook 551 E16
dr. Sunbury 142 G10
rd. Carrum 573 D9
st. Dromana 686 D7
st. Reservoir 282 D9
st. W Footscray 366 G12

E

EADES
ct. Templestowe 331 C8
pl. W Melbourne 17 E20
st. E Melbourne 25 D3
st. Laverton 407 F14
EADIE
av. Healesville 214 A16
st. Sunbury 144 A12
EAGLAND
rd. Cheltenham 531 E3
rd. Yarrambat 201 K12
EAGLE
al. Melbourne 1 B6
al. Melbourne 23 H6
av. Anglesea 713 B5
av. Kingsbury 283 K9
ct. Blind Bight 650 C10
ct. Craigieburn 193 L2
ct. Dingley Village 532 L7
ct. Eaglemont 328 H10
ct. Mt Waverley 458 K9
ct. Vermont S 420 G13
dr. Noble Park N 501 D10
dr. Pakenham 584 J2
dr. Pakenham 584 J3
pl. Melton 226 G15
ri. Templstw Lr 330 A8
st. Mornington 641 B11
st. Werribee 447 J18
tce. Taylors Lakes 275 G3
EAGLEFARM
ct. Keilor Park 277 L12
EAGLEMONT
cr. Eaglemont 328 H11
EAGLENEST
rd. Olinda 427 H3
EAGLE RIDGE
ri. Burwood 418 B3
EAGLET
ct. Mill Park 242 J12
EAGLEVIEW
pl. Point Cook 451 B8
wy. Craigieburn 150 C6
EAGLING
st. Keilor 277 B13
EALING
cl. Craigieburn 150 E20
cl. Epping 197 K17
cr. Springvale S 499 H20
ct. Glen Waverley 460 L6
EAMA
ct. Bulleen 330 A15
EAMES
av. Brooklyn 365 H18
EAMON
ct. Kew 371 E10
dr. View Bank 285 H19
EAMONT
cl. Chelsea Ht 547 D9
EARIMIL
dr. Mt Eliza 625 G16
EARL
ct. Hallam 538 B17
ct. Werribee 447 A10
gr. Craigieburn 150 F7
pl. Melton W 226 B14
st. Airport W 279 A16
st. Carlton 18 D20
st. Carlton N 18 K4
st. Doncaster 331 D17
st. Kew 371 K4
st. Kew East 371 K4
st. Upwey 465 G9
st. Windsor 414 H11
st.e, Windsor 414 J11
EARLBY
ct. Greenvale 193 D19
EARLE
cl. Mont Albert 374 C15
cl. Pakenham 559 A17
st. Preston 282 K20
EARLING
cl. Wyndham Va 446 G13
EARLINGTON
bvd. Burnside 318 E7
EARLS
ct. Balwyn N 373 L1
ct. Endeavour Hl 537 D1
ct. Mulgrave 500 D1
ct. Pascoe Vale 280 K12
ct. Wantirna S 422 E18
rd. Moolap 704 H20
EARLSFIELD
ct. Deer Park 319 B11
dr. Berwick 554 K20
dr. Berwick 554 L19
rd. Hampton 495 E8
EARLSTON
cct. Cranbourne 604 F9
sq. Berwick 554 G16
EARLSTOWN
rd. Hughesdale 457 H11
EARLSWOOD
cl. Caroline Spr, off Copse Wood Bnd 317 L3
EARLWOOD
ct. Thomastown 240 K16
dr. Wheelers Hill 460 H15
st. Dingley Village 532 L6
st. Nar Warrn S 578 F2
EARLY
pl. Boronia 424 J4
EARNSHAW
dr. Carrum Downs 601 E3
EARSDON
st. Yarraville 367 E16
EASEY
st. Collingwood 19 G12
EAST
av. Mt Evelyn 383 D1
cct. Sunshine W 364 H11
cnc. Beaumaris 530 B10
cr. Springvale 500 K10
ct. Braybrook 366 C3
ct. Camberwell 417 L4
ct. Keysborough 534 E13
ct. Lalor 241 F9
ct. Mooroolbark 336 K20
ct. Newcomb 703 L16
gwy. Wyndham Va 446 F12
lk. Chirnside Pk 337 D5
rd. Pearcedale 630 L10
rd. Pearcedale 647 B11
rd. Seaford 599 J1
rd. Vermont S 421 G8
st. Ascot Vale 324 E18
st. Coburg 325 L8
st. Hadfield 281 A10
st. Heidelberg W 328 C1
st. Malvern 416 B11
st. Melb Airport 235 K10
st. Northcote 326 K19
st. Reservoir 283 B13
EASTAWAY
st. Elsternwick 455 C
EAST BOUNDARY
rd. Bentleigh E 496 J
rd. Scoresby 462 F1
tr. Lysterfield 505 D1
EASTBOURNE
ct. Frankston 599 J1
ct. Glen Waverley 460 F1
rd. Rosebud 683 J2
rd. Rosebud W 683 D2
st. Windsor 414 H1
wy. Nar Warrn S 579 B
EASTBRIDGE
ct. Nunawading 376 L1
EASTBURY
ct. Nar Warrn S 552 K1
EASTCOTE
ct. Vermont S 420 H1
st. Sunshine N 321 C1
EASTERLEIGH
ct. Dandenong 535 K
EASTERN
av. Doncaster 330 E1
fwy. Abbotsford 20 D1
fwy. Abbotsford 371 B
fwy. Balwyn N 328 J2
fwy. Balwyn N 329 A2
fwy. Blackburn N 375 C
fwy. Box Hill N 375 C
fwy. Clifton Hill 371 B
fwy. Collingwood 20 D1
fwy. Doncaster 374 E
fwy. Donvale 375 C
fwy. Fairfield 371 E
fwy. Kew 371 E
fwy. Kew 372 A
fwy. Kew East 372 A
fwy. Mont Albert N 374 E
fwy. Nunawading 375 C
hwy. Clifton Hill 19 F
hwy. Fitzroy 19 F
hwy. Fitzroy N 19 F
pl. Hawthorn E 372 D1
rd. S Melbourne 3 C2
rd. S Melbourne 30 D
rd. S Melbourne 413 H
rd. S Melbourne 413 J
st. Craigieburn 150 H1
EASTERN BEACH
Geelong 703 C
Geelong 703 D
EASTERN PARK
cct. E Geelong 703 G
sq. Nar Warrn S 553 D2
EAST ESPLANADE
St Albans 275 L1
St Albans 320 E
EASTFIELD
rd. Croydon 379 K1
rd. Croydon S 379 K1
rd. Ringwood E 379 C
EASTGATE
ct. Wantirna S 423 A1
dr. Greensborough 243 G1
rd. Craigieburn 194 G
st. Oakleigh 457 J1
st. Pascoe Vale S 280 G1
EAST GLIDE
rd. Melb Airport 235
EASTHAM
st. Fitzroy N 326 D2
EAST INDIA
av. Nunawading 376 G1
EAST KIRKBY
ct. Highton 705 K
EASTLEIGH
av. Keilor East 321 L
dr. Glen Waverley 460 L
EAST MADDINGLEY
rd. Maddingley 264 A
EASTMEAD
rd. Croydon 380 C
EASTMENT
st. Northcote 326 H1
EASTON
av. Seaford 599
ct. Dandenong N 501 F1
ct. Ferntree Gly 463 K
EAST SPUR
ct. Kilsyth S 381 B1
EAST VIEW
cr. Bentleigh E 496
tce. Jan Juc 711 D1
EASTVIEW
av. Seville E 343 D1
pde. Belmont 702 G1
EASTWAY
av. Donvale 376 K

AST-WEST
brk. Lysterfield.........504 G6
ASTWOOD
av. Preston.............282 H20
cr. Mooroolbark......337 G9
st. Kensington..........33 L5
st. Kensington..........34 A11
st. Seddon.............367 F11
ATON
cl. Diamond Ck.......245 L6
ct. Albanvale..........319 D6
pde. Laverton...........407 D13
pl. Baxter..............644 C2
pl. Narre Warren.....538 F20
pl. Wheelers Hill......461 E14
st. Melton S............268 J5
st. Oakleigh............457 K11
ATONS CUTTING
d. Dromana............687 B11
d. Red Hill.............687 B18
BB
st. Aspendale..........546 C3
BBELS
pde. Olinda...............427 B10
BDALE
st. Frankston...........599 C16
BDEN
v. Black Rock.........529 G5
t. Broadmeadows..237 L9
st. Brighton............454 J6
t. Moorabbin.........497 A9
t. Noble Park N......501 C17
BELI
l. Nar Warrn N.......504 D19
BLANA
v. Mentone............531 B10
BON
t. Doncaster..........374 G3
BONY
r. Bundoora...........242 J15
r. Langwarrin.........601 K14
r. Pakenham..........585 G1
de. Heidelberg W.....328 A2
CCLES
. Mill Park.............242 H2
CHIDNA
S Morang, off Kangaroo Tce.....243 J2
d. Eltham North......288 F2
CHO
v. Balwyn N...........373 G1
t. Whittington........704 F19
CHUCA
d. Greensborough..286 D6
t. Dallas...............238 H9
CHUNGA
. Forest Hill..........420 E7
CKERSALL
t. Brunswick..........325 G11
CKERSLEY
t. Blackburn S.......419 K1
CKFORD
. Dandenong........536 D11
CLIPSE
r. Watsonia...........285 H9
. Hampton Pk.......552 A15
l. Hoppers Csg......405 A13
DALE
l. Kings Park.........319 A2
DAM
. Balwyn...............373 F10
DAN
. Pakenham...........559 A20
DDIE
t. Highett...............496 A15
. Pascoe Vale.......280 H16
. St Albans...........276 H19
DDIE BARRON
e. Pakenham..........558 J20
DDINGTON
l. Endeavour Hl.....537 E1
DDISON
. Altona Mdw........451 K7
DDY
. Abbotsford...........20 B18
. Brunswick E........325 K11
. Camberwell.........417 C8
. Moonee Pnd.......324 B12
DDYS
. Bentleigh...........455 K20
DDYSTONE
l. McCrae..............684 K12
DEBOHLS
l. Nar Warrn E.......506 L18
l. Nar Warrn E.......507 A17
DELMAIER
. Bayswater..........423 K6

EDEN
av. Box Hill S...........419 C5
av. Heathmont.........422 J1
av. Springvale..........500 C17
av. Watsonia...........285 D6
cl. Mulgrave............501 A6
ct. Ascot Vale..........323 G16
ct. Camberwell.........417 K8
ct. Doncaster...........375 C2
ct. Forest Hill...........420 C3
ct. Noble Park..........535 B3
ct. Toorak...............415 H7
gr. Knoxfield.............463 A8
gr. Nar Warrn S.........553 A18
pl. Greenvale............237 F4
st. Cheltenham..........530 K3
st. Croydon..............379 G3
st. Footscray............366 L5
st. Heidelberg Ht.......328 D5
wy. Kilsyth................381 G8
EDENBRIDGE
ct. Carrum Downs...601 B5
EDENHOPE
st. Kilsyth...............381 G7
EDENMONT
rd. Emerald..............468 L20
rd. Emerald..............469 A20
rd. Emerald..............508 L2
EDEN VALLEY
cl. Vermont S...........421 D10
rd. Warranwood.......335 C11
EDEYS RUN
Hampton Pk.........551 K11
EDGAR
av. Wonga Park........335 J6
ct. Ferntree Gly........464 C2
pl. Mt Eliza...............626 B13
st. Brighton..............455 B17
st. Glen Iris...............416 D13
st. Hadfield...............280 L7
st. Heidelberg...........329 A4
st. Kingsville............366 J13
st. Moonee Pnd.........324 B15
st. Reservoir.............282 L16
st. Rye.....................696 G1
st. Werribee..............447 C14
st.n, Glen Iris............416 E9
EDGARS
rd. Lalor...................240 K6
rd. Thomastown.........240 J19
EDGBASTON
cct. Berwick...............554 D19
pde. Caroline Spr.........317 J3
EDGECOMBE
ct. Moorabbin............497 D10
st. Kew.....................371 F11
st. Oak Park..............280 B13
wy. Roxburgh Pk.........194 C13
EDGERTON
ct. Hampton Pk.........551 H4
rd. Mitcham..............377 F11
rd. Mitcham..............377 H12
st. Hawthorn.............371 H13
EDGEVALE
rd. Bulleen................329 J16
rd. Kew....................372 C13
EDGEWARE
cl. Kealba.................276 L19
ct. Wantirna..............422 F14
EDGEWATER
bvd. Maribyrnong.........367 C1
cct. St Albans.............319 H6
cl. Queenscliff............707 L18
EDGEWOOD
av. Burwood E...........419 L12
cl. Thomastown.........240 F15
ct. Wantirna S...........422 J19
rd. Dandenong...........535 G3
st. Carnegie..............456 G5
EDGOOSE
av. Mont Albert N.......374 F10
EDGWARE
ct. Epping.................197 J15
EDI
ct. Coolaroo..............238 E7
EDINA
av. Port Melb.............412 C5
cl. Port Melb.............412 G5
ct. Blairgowrie...........679 L20
gr. Altona Mdw...........452 A3
pl. Torquay...............712 D4
rd. Ferntree Gly.........424 A18
st. Williamstn N.........410 L13
EDINBOROUGH
st. Hallam.................537 J15
EDINBURGH
av. Caulfield...............455 E3
av. Glen Waverley.......420 G18
av. Herne Hill..............701 L4
ct. Frankston S...........628 B15
ct. Greenvale.............237 F6

ct. Werribee.............446 L11
dr. Officer.................555 J20
dr. Skye...................601 H1
pl. Melton W..............226 D16
rd. Bayswater............423 F11
rd. Blackburn S..........419 E3
rd. Lilydale...............338 F20
rd. Springvale............500 F7
st. Bentleigh E...........457 B19
st. Box Hill S.............374 J20
st. Clayton...............458 G18
st. Diamond Ck..........245 F11
st. Flemington.............33 E2
st. Hampton..............495 E10
st. Oakleigh S............458 G18
st. Richmond...............26 L17
st. Richmond.............371 A18
EDINGTON
wy. Craigieburn..........194 D4
EDIS
ct. Endeavour Hl........537 C2
EDITH
av. Croydon...............379 E5
av. Nunawading..........376 J18
ct. Belmont...............706 D6
ct. Bentleigh E...........497 B2
ct. Doncaster.............374 G2
ct. Mt Dandenong......426 G5
ct. Olinda..................426 G5
la. Box Hill N..............375 E10
pl. Dromana...............685 K9
rd. Ferny Creek...........425 K14
ri. Hampton Pk...........552 B12
st. Beaumaris.............530 A10
st. Beaumaris.............530 B9
st. Caulfield N............415 G18
st. Dandenong............536 B6
st. Glen Waverley.......419 K20
st. Heathmont............378 K17
st. Mordialloc.............531 K16
st. Noble Park............534 K4
st. Oak Park...............280 C13
st. Preston................326 J1
EDITHVALE
rd. Aspendale Gdn...547 A10
rd. Chelsea Ht...........547 A10
rd. Edithvale..............546 H12
EDLINGTON
st. Hawthorn..............372 D18
EDMANSON
av. Brighton...............454 K7
EDMENDS
st. Brunswick.............325 G12
EDMILL
ct. Belmont................706 D3
EDMOND
cr. Wandin N..............340 J15
ct. Rowville................503 B5
st. Balwyn..................373 D11
st. Parkdale...............531 H9
st. Springvale.............500 A11
EDMONDS
av. Ashwood..............418 A14
ct. Pascoe Vale..........281 A15
st. Diamond Ck...........245 G9
st. Narre Warren........539 A14
EDMONDSON
st. Lalor....................241 F7
EDMONSON
pl. Geelong, off Fitzroy St..........703 E10
EDMONTON
pl. Doncaster E..........332 F5
EDMUND
rd. Silvan..................385 C19
st. Clifton Hill...............20 K3
st. Dallas...................238 J9
st. Maidstone.............366 H1
EDMUND RICE
pde. Watsonia N..........243 D18
EDMUNDS
rd. Cockatoo..............511 E10
EDNA
av. Dandenong N........501 F20
ct. Melton S...............268 J6
ct. Wantirna...............422 C3
gr. Coburg.................326 A3
st. Frankston..............626 L3
st. Heathmont.............378 H17
st. Malvern East..........457 A3
st. Mt Waverley...........419 H20
st. Sunshine N............321 F16
st. Thomastown...........241 E15
EDNA WALLING
la. Mooroolbark..........381 J1
EDNEY
ct. Noble Park............501 A17
EDRINGTON PARK
dr. Berwick.................554 G12

EDRO
av. Brighton East.......495 B3
ct. Bundoora..............284 H4
EDSALL
cl. Hampton Pk...........551 E5
cl. Rowville.................502 J3
st. Highett.................496 H16
st. Malvern................415 K14
EDWARD
av. Altona North.........409 H2
av. Dandenong...........535 L4
ct. Berwick.................554 L19
ct. Croydon................380 G7
ct. Ivanhoe................327 K13
gr. Mt Martha..............655 C20
pl. Armadale...............415 E9
rd. Chirnside Pk..........293 D16
rd. Chirnside Pk..........337 C5
rd. Wandin East..........384 L3
rd. Wandin East..........385 A4
st. Anglesea...............713 D7
st. Balaclava...............414 G17
st. Bayswater.............423 G10
st. Belgrave................466 E15
st. Brighton East.........455 D13
st. Brunswick..............325 F16
st. Brunswick E...........325 F16
st. Bundoora...............284 F2
st. Camberwell............416 L5
st. Chadstone.............418 E20
st. Cheltenham............530 K2
st. Coburg..................325 H5
st. Deer Park..............319 A18
st. Donvale.................377 C2
st. Elsternwick............455 C4
st. Essendon...............323 K6
st. Fawkner................281 F8
st. Hawthorn...............372 B15
st. Healesville.............213 K20
st. Healesville.............257 K1
st. Kew.......................372 H12
st. Langwarrin.............628 J3
st. Macleod.................285 B13
st. Mitcham.................377 B13
st. Mordialloc..............532 B16
st. Noble Park.............534 D1
st. Northcote...............326 K19
st. Oakleigh.................458 A13
st. Rye.........................696 K2
st. Sandringham..........495 E19
st. Seddon...................367 A10
st. Somerville..............644 K14
st. Toorak....................415 B8
st. Up Fntree Gly.........465 D9
st. Wattle Glen............246 G8
st. Wesburn................348 B9
EDWARDES
st. Berwick.................554 G8
st. Reservoir...............282 C9
EDWARD FREETH
dr. Endeavour Hl.........537 J10
EDWARD HENTY
av. Doreen..................201 E9
EDWARDS
arc. Altona....................409 C19
av. Port Melb...............412 D4
ct. Darley.....................222 A10
dr. Altona Mdw............451 F7
la. Blind Bight.............650 F1
la. Werribee S.............488 G12
rd. Diggers Rest..........232 H6
rd. Werribee................448 C18
st. Burwood.................418 B9
st. Lower Plenty..........286 H15
st. Thomastown...........240 L16
st. Thomastown...........241 A16
EDWARDSTOWN
rd. Wesburn................348 E17
EDWIN
ct. Clarinda.................498 D6
pde. Highett.................496 E13
rd. Templestowe..........331 D5
st. Box Hill N...............374 K7
st. Fairfield..................327 E14
st. Heidelberg Ht.........328 E8
st. Nar Warrn S...........553 G20
st. Preston..................327 D6
EDWINA
ct. Croydon Hills.........335 D15
EDYVEAN
st. Surrey Hills............374 D20
EDZELL
av. Toorak..................415 E2
rd. Menzies Ck............468 H20
EEL RACE
rd. Carrum..................573 B11
EFFIE
av. Upwey..................465 L15
ct. Springvale S..........499 F20
EFFINGHAM
rd. Newport................411 B8

EFFRON
ct. Frankston..............600 E18
EFRON
ct. Box Hill N..............375 D6
st. Dandenong N.........501 J18
st. Nunawading..........376 H10
EGAN
cl. Werribee...............448 A6
ct. Darley..................221 E2
dr. Bulleen.................329 J13
pl. Richmond.................26 C7
rd. Dandenong S........535 D13
st. Brighton East.......455 H15
st. Carnegie..............456 J5
st. Deer Park.............318 J14
st. Diamond Ck..........245 L12
st. Richmond................26 A7
st. Springvale............499 F16
EGANLEE
ct. Wantirna..............422 B10
EGERTON
av. Cheltenham..........531 C2
gr. Epping..................198 G15
rd. Armadale..............415 G15
st. Blairgowrie...........695 K1
st. Pt Lonsdale...........710 D4
wy. Delahey................275 B12
EGGINTON
st. Brunswick W.........324 J10
EGGLETON
ct. Preston.................283 G17
ri. Rowville.................463 F18
EGLINTON
cl. Berwick.................553 H14
st. Kew......................371 K7
st. Moonee Pnd..........323 J14
EGREMONT
st. Fitzroy N...............326 C20
EGRET
cr. St Albans..............319 G6
ct. Blind Bight............650 E8
ct. Mornington............657 B1
ct. Rosebud W............699 E4
ct. Werribee...............447 K6
pl. Whittlesea.............126 D1
EGTON
ct. Craigieburn...........150 E19
EIGHTH
av. Anglesea...............713 E11
av. Chelsea Ht.............547 E13
av. Eden Park................95 A16
av. Rosebud................684 B19
av. Springvale.............500 J9
av. Springvale.............500 L9
av. Springvale.............501 A9
st. Parkdale................531 F11
EILA
cl. Cheltenham...........497 D20
EILDON
av. Wyndham Va.........446 B6
cct. Taylors Hill............274 J14
ct. Meadow Ht...........194 A19
ct. St Albans...............320 C11
ct. St Kilda..................414 B15
dr. Keysborough.........534 C10
pde. Rowville.................463 A18
rd. Ashwood................418 E14
rd. Endeavour Hl.........503 E20
rd. St Kilda..................414 B15
st. Doncaster..............374 K4
st. Ferntree Gly..........463 G1
EILEEN
av. Kalorama...............382 L17
cl. N Warrandyte..........289 L10
ct. Langwarrin.............601 J18
ct. Werribee................447 G13
gr. Woori Yallock.........344 E15
rd. Clayton S...............499 D13
st. Armadale...............415 D10
st. Hadfield.................280 H7
st. Mt Waverley...........458 K10
st. View Bank..............285 F17
EILMONT
dr. Werribee................448 D18
EINSTEIN
av. Mulgrave...............500 K5
EIRENE
st. Yarraville...............366 K18
EISE
ct. Brighton East........455 E20
EISEMANS
rd. Yarrambat.............201 E12
rd. Yarrambat.............201 E13
EISENHOWER
st. Reservoir...............283 G16
EISNER
st. St Albans..............276 F20
EKARI
ct. Yallambie..............286 C12
EKERT
ct. Mt Martha..............657 C8

ELAINE
cl. Epping 241 G5
ct. Bentleigh E 497 D2
ct. Cranbourne 603 K3
ct. Glen Waverley 460 F9
ct. Mooroolbark 336 K13
ct. Richmond 371 D13
ct. Somerville 644 E14
ct. Springvale 500 A17
pl. Rowville 503 B4
rd. Rye 696 F10
st. St Albans 320 B3
ELAMO
rd. Healesville 214 A17
ELANA
ct. Croydon N 336 A14
ct. Langwarrin 629 C7
ct. Langwarrin 629 D7
ELANDRA
ct. Seaford 600 C3
ct. Wantirna 422 F12
wy. Cranbourne W 603 E1
ELANORA
ct. Aspendale 546 E6
ct. Mornington 641 B15
ct. Rosebud W 683 B19
ct. Torquay 712 D3
wy. Hampton Pk 551 E12
ELAROO
av. Camberwell 417 D4
cl. St Helena 244 J17
st. Chadstone 458 A2
ELATA
dr. Tullamarine 278 B10
pl. Endeavour Hl 502 K19
st. Donvale 376 F6
st. Oakleigh S 458 A17
ELBA
cl. Ferntree Gly 463 L12
pl. Keilor Dn 276 F14
ELBE
cl. Werribee 447 H6
ELBENA
gr. Carnegie 456 L8
ELBERTA
av. Templstw Lr 330 G15
ELCAN
av. Cranbourne W 603 J1
EL CENTRO
Chirnside Pk 337 A5
ELCHO
st. Newtown 702 A12
ELDA
ct. Cranbourne N 578 F11
ELDALE
av. Greensborough 286 B5
ct. Wantirna 422 F6
ELDAN
dr. Werribee 447 B13
ELDENE
ct. Toorak 415 F3
ELDER
cl. Hallam 538 C18
cl. Meadow Ht 193 J18
ct. Sunshine N 321 D14
ct. Templstw Lr 330 J14
ct. Thomastown 240 K11
gr. Boronia 423 K15
pde. Essendon 323 H8
st. Blackburn 376 B14
st. Clarinda 498 C12
st. Clarinda 498 D4
st. Greensborough 285 L9
st. Watsonia 285 G8
st.s, Heatherton 498 C12
ELDERBERRY
pl. Frankston S 628 B17
ELDERGREEN
cct. Craigieburn 193 L3
ELDERSHAW
dr. Lynbrook 551 D19
ELDERSLIE
tce. Newtown 702 A5
ELDINE
ct. Grovedale 705 L16
ELDO
st. Keysborough 535 B8
ELDON
ct. Hampton E 496 B10
st. Broadmeadows 239 A19
EL DORADO
ct. Noble Park N 501 D9
ELDORADO
cr. Meadow Ht 237 L4
ct. Frankston 628 C10
ct. Wyndham Va 446 F11
st. Strathmore 279 K14
ELDRIDGE
pl. Belmont 706 H6
st. Footscray 367 C4

ELEANOR
ct. Donvale 376 J3
ct. Pakenham 585 C6
gr. Kallista 468 F13
st. Ashburton 417 G14
st. Broadmeadows 279 K1
st. Footscray 367 A7
st. Jacana 237 K20
st. Preston 326 B2
ELEANORE
cr. Hallam 538 C20
ELECTRA
av. Ashwood 418 E18
ct. Forest Hill 420 D8
st. Williamstown 411 F15
ELECTRIC
av. Glenroy 280 B8
pl. Melbourne 1 H2
pl. Melbourne 23 K3
st. Broadmeadows 237 L20
st. Cremorne 32 D2
st. Cremorne 414 H1
ELEEBANA
av. Hughesdale 457 G14
ELEGAN
ct. Hillside 273 J3
ELEMHEIM
ct. Blackburn S 419 L2
ELENYA
ct. Frankston 600 H16
ELESBURY
av. Brunswick E 326 A13
ELEVA
rd. Healesville 213 A16
ELEVENTH
av. Anglesea 713 C13
av. Eden Park 95 A7
ELEY
rd. Blackburn S 419 A6
rd. Box Hill S 418 K6
rd. Burwood 418 K6
rd. Burwood E 419 A6
ELFIN
ct. Chirnside Pk 337 J2
pl. Kings Park 319 E2
ELGAN
av. Rye 697 C3
ELGAR
av. Kew East 372 J6
ct. Doncaster 374 K1
gr. Portsea 678 A4
rd. Box Hill 374 F20
rd. Box Hill N 374 H9
rd. Box Hill S 374 F20
rd. Box Hill S 418 E8
rd. Burwood 418 E8
rd. Doncaster 374 H9
rd. Mont Albert 374 F20
rd. Mont Albert N 374 H9
rd. Surrey Hills 418 F3
ELGATA
cl. Meadow Ht 238 B1
ct. Diamond Ck 245 F8
ELGIN
av. Armadale 415 C12
cr. Pk Orchards 334 B19
gr. Belgrave S 506 H1
gr. Pt Lonsdale 710 E4
pl. Carlton 18 D12
pl. Hawthorn 371 H16
rd. Greenvale 237 B3
st. Berwick 554 H8
st. Carlton 18 E12
st. Hawthorn 371 H16
st. Newport 411 B8
st. Pascoe Vale S 324 L4
EL GOLEA
mw. Keilor Dn 275 J13
EL GRECO
ct. Scoresby 462 C8
ct. Wheelers Hill 460 L14
ELI
ct. Rowville 502 H1
ELIANA
ct. Kilsyth S 380 L20
ct. Melton W 225 K13
ct. Rowville 503 B4
ct. Warranwood 334 J16
ELIAS
mw. Endeavour Hl 537 J3
ELIDA
pl. Wheelers Hill 460 G17
ELIDON
cr. Point Cook 450 G6
ELIMATTA
rd. Carnegie 456 J13
st. Warneet 649 D14
ELINBANK
dr. Grovedale 706 E11

ELINDA
pl. Reservoir 283 E1
ELINGA
ct. Albanvale 319 A4
ct. Frankston 600 E17
ELIOT
ct. Bundoora 242 K20
ct. Mooroolbark 337 E20
ELISABETH
av. Springvale S 499 L20
ELISDON
dr. Seaford 600 A3
ELISSA
ct. Cheltenham 497 F19
wy. St Albans 275 K18
ELIZA
cl. Bayswater 423 C5
cl. Greensborough 286 K3
cl. Warranwood 334 L12
cl. Williamstn N 410 G12
ct. Gladstone Pk 237 B20
ct. Hillside 232 H18
ct. Nunawading 376 G10
ct. Seaford 600 A4
dr. Mt Eliza 642 C4
pl. Somerville 644 F13
st. Black Rock 495 E20
st. Blairgowrie 679 E18
st. Keilor Park 277 K14
st. Newport 411 B9
st. Rosebud W 698 L2
st. Rosebud W 699 A2
tce. Mt Eliza 626 E11
ELIZABETH
arc. Melbourne 2 A14
av. Dromana 686 E7
av. Nar Warrn S 553 G20
av. Rosebud W 683 A19
av. Rosebud W 699 B4
av. Werribee 447 B14
cr. Carnegie 456 F8
ct. Altona Mdw 451 J7
ct. Dandenong 535 L5
ct. Donvale 377 H4
ct. Emerald 470 A20
ct. Mooroolbark 337 H15
ct. Narre Warren 539 D19
ct. Pakenham 585 A4
ct. Reservoir 283 E2
ct. Ringwood E 379 B5
ct. Rowville 462 G18
dr. Lalor 240 H5
dr. Rosebud 700 F2
dr. Sunbury 142 L14
gr. Bundoora 284 H3
gr. Torquay 711 G11
la. Woori Yallock 344 B15
rd. Portsea 677 J5
rd. Red Hill 687 A19
st. Anglesea 713 K1
st. Bayswater 423 G10
st. Belmont 702 G20
st. Bentleigh E 496 G1
st. Box Hill N 374 K6
st. Braybrook 366 B3
st. Brighton East 455 E15
st. Brunswick 325 H13
st. Bulleen 329 G9
st. Burwood 418 A12
st. Carlton 17 K17
st. Coburg 326 A2
st. Coburg N 282 C17
st. Cranbourne N 578 B8
st. Croydon 380 A1
st. Diamond Ck 245 K10
st. Doncaster E 375 G3
st. Elsternwick 454 K4
st. Fawkner 281 K5
st. Ferntree Gly 464 F4
st. Frankston 627 D1
st. Geelong West 702 E4
st. Glen Iris 417 C9
st. Hawthorn 371 K17
st. Highton 701 J17
st. Kensington 34 B12
st. Kooyong 416 A10
st. Malvern 416 A10
st. Melbourne 2 B16
st. Melbourne 23 L1
st. Melton S 268 J5
st. Mentone 530 L7
st. Mentone 531 A7
st. Mitcham 377 A14
st. Montmorency 286 J12
st. Moonee Pnd 324 D15
st. Mornington 640 G16
st. Mt Evelyn 339 B17
st. Newport 410 J5
st. Newport 410 J6
st. Northcote 326 E17
st. N Melbourne 17 K17
st. Oakleigh E 458 E10
st. Pt Lonsdale 710 G4

st. Richmond 26 B4
st. St Albans 319 J3
st. South Yarra 32 C15
st. South Yarra 414 G7
st. Westmeadows 237 D14
st. Yarraville 366 L16
st.n, Kooyong 416 A5
ELK
trn. Cranbourne 603 J5
ELKA
pl. Frankston 628 G1
rd. Springvale S 533 L4
ELKINS
ct. Wheelers Hill 460 G16
ELLA
cl. Newtown 701 L7
cr. Doncaster 374 F2
cr. Rosebud W 683 E19
ct. Hoppers Csg 405 A14
ct. Kurunjang 227 D12
ct. Lalor 240 L9
ct. Lalor 241 A9
ct. Narre Warren 538 L13
gr. Chelsea 546 L15
gr. Chelsea 547 B12
gr. Edithvale 547 B12
pl. Langwarrin 629 L1
pl. Rowville 463 F19
st. Murrumbeena 457 D8
ELLAD
cl. Vermont 421 F2
ELLAM
ct. Meadow Ht 237 J3
ELLAND
av. Box Hill 374 K14
ELLAROO
ct. Werribee 446 K14
ELLASWOOD
cl. Berwick 554 A2
ct. Hampton Pk 551 G5
ELLBEDE
rdg. Nar Warrn S 552 G7
ELLEMAREE
ct. Keilor East 322 F7
ELLEN
av. Keilor East 322 E6
ct. Burwood 419 A11
ct. Greensborough 286 G2
gr. Don Valley 346 D8
gr. Templestowe 330 J5
rd. Mooroolbark 337 D18
rd. Nar Warrn S 579 G2
st. Balwyn 373 F11
st. Bentleigh E 456 H19
st. Parkdale 531 J11
st. Springvale 499 G16
ELLENDALE
rd. Noble Park 500 L19
st. Balwyn N 373 J2
st. Hughesdale 457 E12
ELLENVALE
av. Pascoe Vale S 324 J4
dr. Narre Warren 539 F15
ELLERINA
rd.w, Mt Martha 698 A9
ELLERSLIE
ct. Bacchus Msh 222 B19
ct. Mill Park 242 K11
ct. Noble Park N 501 B9
pl.e, Toorak 415 A7
st. Kingsbury 284 A10
ELLERTON
ct. Donvale 332 G16
sq. Wantirna 422 H14
ELLERY
ct. Cranbourne N 577 K9
ct. Mulgrave 460 C17
st. Bundoora 284 L1
st. Chadstone 458 A5
ELLESMERE
av. Croydon 379 L3
av. Mt Martha 655 F17
cr. Gladstone Pk 237 B17
ct. Frankston 628 B11
pde. Rosanna 284 K20
rd. Burwood E 419 L10
rd. Windsor 414 K13
st. Blairgowrie 679 L20
st. Northcote 326 L16
st. Oakleigh S 497 H7
ELLESMORE
ct. Kew 371 K8
ELLESSE
cr. Berwick 554 G20
ELLETSON
ct. Dandenong 535 G3
ELLETT
ct. Grovedale 705 G13
ELLIMATTA
rd. Anglesea 714 B1

ELLIMINYA
ct. Clarinda 498 C
ELLIN
st. Doncaster E 376 C
ELLINDALE
av. McKinnon 456 D1
cl. Hampton Pk 552 B1
ELLINGBANK
cr. Mornington 657 C
ELLINGSWORTH
st. Brunswick 325 H1
ELLINGTON
st. Caulfield S 455 F
ELLINGWORTH
pde. Box Hill 374 L1
ELLIOT
cl. Donvale 377 D
ct. Greenvale 237 A
ct. Pt Lonsdale 707 H1
dr. Braeside 532 L1
pl. Ringwood 378 A1
st. Fitzroy 19 E1
st. Kings Park 319 E
st. Knoxfield 462 K
st. Mordialloc 531 L1
st. Parkdale 531 K1
st. Reservoir 282 G
ELLIOTT
av. Balwyn 373 C1
av. Broadmeadows 238 E2
av. Carnegie 456 K
av. Highton 705 J
av. Parkville 34 K
cl. Epping 197 J1
cr. Dingley Village 533 D
ct. Burnside 318 H1
ct. Hoppers Csg 448 F
ct. Whittington 704 C1
la. Melbourne 1 A
la. Melbourne 23 D
rd. Dandenong S 549 J
rd. Upwey 466 A
st. Ascot Vale 323 J2
st. Ashwood 417 L1
st. Boronia 424 E1
st. Cheltenham 531 C
st. Coburg N 281 F1
st. Heidelberg Ht 328 E
st. Seaford 599 H
ELLIS
av. Sassafras 426 E1
ct. Braybrook 366 B
ct. Grovedale 705 J1
ct. Mooroolbark 337 J1
ct. Warburton 306 A2
la. Dandenong 535 H
la. Diamond Ck 246 F1
rd. Glen Iris 416 E1
rd. Yarra Glen 208 L1
rd. Yarra Glen 209 A1
st. Dandenong S 535 L1
st. Frankston 600 A2
st. Richmond 26 D
st. South Yarra 32 D1
ELLISON
st. Blackburn 376 C1
st. Malvern East 417 A1
st. Preston 283 B1
st. Ringwood 378 D1
ELLISYUM
pl. Frankston S 627 G1
ELLSA
cl. Keysborough 534 J1
st. Balwyn N 373 L
ELLT
cr. Noble Park 500 G1
ELLWOOD
dr. Pearcedale 646
ELM
av. Elsternwick 454
av. Elsternwick 455
cr. Eltham 287 D
cr. Emerald 469 H1
cr. Ivanhoe East 328 H1
ct. Altona North 410 D
ct. Coolaroo 238
ct. Frankston N 599 J1
ct. Mt Eliza 626 C
ct. Nar Warrn S 553 C2
ct. Ringwood N 378 C
ct. Rosebud 700 G
ct. Scoresby 462
ct. Templestowe 331 L1
ct. Waurn Ponds 705 E1
ct. Wyndham Va 446 E
gr. Armadale 415 E1
gr. Balaclava 454 J
gr. Brighton 454 K1
gr. Brunswick E 326 A1
gr. Coburg 325 H
gr. Essendon N 279 F2
gr. Kew East 372 D

gr. Langwarrin.........628 K1
gr. McKinnon..........456 B16
gr. Mooroolbark......337 C8
gr. Mt Waverley.......419 H17
gr. Parkdale............531 G13
gr. Richmond...........26 G16
gr. Springvale..........500 A14
pl. N Melbourne........17 A17
pl. Windsor............414 H13
rd. Glen Iris............416 J11
st. Airport W...........278 K17
st. Bayswater..........423 E6
st. Blackburn..........376 B13
st. Elsternwick.........454 K2
st. Flemington...........33 J1
st. Hawthorn...........371 E13
st. Northcote...........326 E13
st. N Melbourne........17 A18
st. N Melbourne........34 L18
st. Preston.............283 J18
st. St Albans...........320 F9
st. Surrey Hills........418 D2
st. Thomastown......241 G12
st. Whittlesea...........96 F17

ELMA
dr. Cheltenham........497 D14
rd. Cheltenham........497 D14
st. Keilor Park.........278 C15

ELMAN
rd. Cheltenham........530 K2

ELMAR
ct. Campbellfield.....239 H11

ELMBANK
dr. Keysborough.....534 J9

ELMDON
dr. Scoresby..........462 C11

ELMES
ct. Hoppers Csg......448 E1

ELM GROVE
ct. Torquay.............712 B3

ELMHURST
ct. Melton S............268 F14
rd. Bayswater N.......423 G1
rd. Blackburn..........375 F13
rd. Caulfield N.........415 G20
rd. Gladstone Pk......278 L1
rd. Gladstone Pk......279 A1
st. Noble Park N......501 E18

ELMIE
st. Hawthorn...........372 C19
tce. Mt Martha..........655 G16

ELMO
rd. Montmorency....287 A7

ELMORE
av. Croydon............336 D18
ct. Endeavour Hl.....537 F3
ct. Ferntree Gly.......463 H9
wk. Blackburn..........375 G15

ELM PARK
dr. Hoppers Csg......449 G1

ELMS
ct. Dandenong N.....502 C16
ct. Gowanbrae........279 B6
rd. Bangholme........575 C2
rd. Mooroolbark......337 G18
rd. Wandin East.......384 H4

ELMSFORD
ct. Keysborough.....534 E14

ELMSTEAD
ct. Ferntree Gly.......423 L19
dr. Wheelers Hill......461 G15

ELM TREE
dr. Dingley Village...532 J7
pl. Carlton.................18 F20

ELMTREE
rd. Doncaster..........375 B3
tce. Chadstone..........458 E3

ELMWOOD
cr. Glen Waverley.....460 A9
pl. Craigieburn........193 L3
pl. Cranbourne W.....603 J2
ri. Eltham North......245 G19

ELNA
ct. Moorabbin.........496 J11

EL NIDO
gr. Carnegie...........456 E7

ELOERA
st. Upwey...............465 H17

ELONARA
ct. Wheelers Hill......460 K8
rd. Vermont S.........420 G9

ELONERA
av. Greensborough..286 B11
av. Yallambie..........286 C11
rd. Noble Park N......501 C17

ELORA
ct. St Albans...........320 C12
rd. Oakleigh S..........497 J3

ELOUERA
cl. Eltham...............288 D5

ELOURA
av. Brighton East.....455 G17

ELPARA
pl. Skye..................601 D7
wy. Hampton Pk.......551 K16

ELPHIN
gr. Canterbury.........417 D1
gr. Hawthorn...........372 C15
st. Ivanhoe.............328 B17
st. Newport.............411 A7

ELPHINSTONE
bvd. Greenvale...........236 K1
ct. Kew...................371 H10
st. W Footscray.......366 G6
wy. Caroline Spr.......318 D10

ELPIS
ct. Oak Park...........279 G10

ELRAY
av. Dandenong........535 E3
ct. Tullamarine........278 L3

EL RENO
cr. Airport W...........278 K16

ELRONA
ct. Pakenham..........585 A3

ELSA
ct. Eltham...............287 H6
pl. Narre Warren.....539 E18
st. Fawkner.............281 K5
st. Templestowe.....330 L8

ELSAN LEA
ct. Langwarrin.........629 D2

ELSEY
rd. Reservoir...........283 B5

ELSIE
av. Seaford.............599 D5
gr. Chelsea.............546 J15
gr. Edithvale...........546 J15
gr. Healesville..........258 A5
gr. Mt Evelyn...........339 A19
mw. Brunswick E, off Elesbury Av.........326 A13
st. Boronia.............424 D10
st. Greensborough..286 A8
st. Wandin East.....340 L20
st. Wandin East.......341 A20

ELSTAR
dr. Carrum Downs...575 E16
rd. Narre Warren.....538 H15

ELSTER
av. Elsternwick........455 B10
av. Gardenvale.........455 B10

ELSTERNWICK
pl. Elsternwick........454 L5

ELSTONE
av. Airport W...........279 A18

ELSTREE
ct. Kealba...............276 K19

ELSUM
av. Bayswater N.......380 A16
av. Deer Park...........319 C8

ELSVERN
av. Belmont.............702 A18

ELSWILL
st. Bentleigh E.........497 A5

ELSWORTHY
ct. Endeavour Hl.....502 L20
ct. Endeavour Hl.....503 A20

ELTHAM
st. Dallas................238 D12
st. Flemington...........33 K1

ELTHAM-YARRA GLEN
rd. Christmas Hills...205 K20
rd. Christmas Hills...249 C8
rd. Eltham...............287 H5
rd. Eltham North.......287 H6
rd. Kangaroo Grnd...247 J20
rd. Kangaroo Grnd...289 H2
rd. Lower Plenty......286 G13
rd. Montmorency.....287 A15
rd. Panton Hill........248 D17
rd. Research...........289 H2
rd. Yarra Glen..........208 C18

ELTON
cl. Watsonia N........243 G19
rd. Ferntree Gly.......463 H6

ELVA
ct. Braybrook..........366 B3
ct. Mitcham............377 C10

ELVARA
ct. Mulgrave...........460 F19

ELVIAN
rd. Woori Yallock.....344 A17

ELVIE
st. Doncaster E.......376 D2
st. Rye...................697 C5

ELVIN
cl. Gladstone Pk......237 C20
st. Macleod.............285 F10

ELWERS
rd. Rosebud............684 G18
st. Watsonia N........285 F2

ELWICK
ct. Noble Park N......501 C7

ELWOOD
av. Sunshine N........321 F10
st. Brighton.............454 G12
st. Notting Hill.........459 H12
st. Surrey Hills........418 C2

ELWYN
st. Bentleigh E.........456 J16

ELY
ct. Dingley Village...533 B7
ct. Keilor East.........277 K16
st. Eltham...............287 C13

ELYSEE
ct. Noble Park N......501 E9
ct. Strathmr Ht........279 D9

ELYSIUM
cr. Oakleigh E..........458 G11

ELYSTAN
rd. Altona Mdw........451 E6

EMANUEL
dr. Seaford.............599 J1

EMARY
ct. Yarra Glen..........208 L17

EMBANK
arc. Melbourne.............2 A16
ct. Kealba...............276 J17

EMBANKMENT
gr. Chelsea.............546 K17

EMBERSON
st. Kallista..............467 B2

EMBLEY
gld. Endeavour Hl.....537 H6

EMBLING
rd. Malvern.............415 K10

EMBREY
ct. Pakenham..........585 E11

EMDEN
cr. Mulgrave...........500 E2
ct. St Albans...........320 H6

EMERALD
cl. Emerald.............469 G20
cl. Mornington........656 L2
ct. Belmont.............706 J1
ct. Boronia..............424 K11
ct. Caroline Spr.......318 E9
ct. Hampton Pk.......551 C10
ct. Langwarrin.........629 G5
ct. Narre Warren.....539 D14
dr. Springvale..........499 H16
pl. Geelong, off Corio St..............703 B7
st. Collingwood.........19 J15
st. Dallas................238 E8
st. Essendon W.......323 A7
st. Geelong West.....702 J7
st. Mt Waverley.......419 C14
st. Oakleigh S.........497 J8
st. Preston.............327 D2
st. Ringwood..........378 G15
st. S Melbourne.........29 H6
st. S Melbourne.......413 D3
tce. Werribee...........447 F3
wk. Bundoora...........284 G8
wy. S Melbourne.........30 C3

EMERALD CREEK
rd. Monbulk............428 F13

EMERALD HILL
pl. S Melbourne........30 A4

EMERALD LAKE
rd. Emerald.............509 H2

EMERALD-MONBULK
rd. Emerald.............469 G19
rd. Kallista..............469 A7
rd. Monbulk............428 C20
rd. Monbulk............468 E1
rd. Monbulk............469 A7

EMERSON
cl. Frankston...........600 F18
ct. Berwick..............553 J3
ct. Roxburgh Pk.......194 C11
pl. Rowville.............503 C3
st. Glen Waverley.....460 B8

EMERY
ct. Altona................408 L16
ct. Altona Mdw........451 D3
dr. Dingley Village...533 F10
la. Montrose............382 B6
st. Port Melb............412 E4
st. Preston.............326 J2

EMIL
ct. Melton...............226 J18

EMILTON
av. St Kilda.............414 C15

EMILY
cl. Pakenham..........559 E19
ct. Burwood E.........419 H7
ct. Clarinda.............498 C11
ct. Coldstream.........295 F15
ct. Cranbourne W....577 F14
ct. Croydon.............336 A20
ct. Mulgrave............500 F4
ct. Springvale S.......499 L20
dr. Hallam...............538 E16
dr. Hallam...............538 F15
dr. Narre Warren.....538 F14
dr. Narre Warren.....538 F17
pl. Aspendale Gdn...546 K2
pl. Mill Park.............243 D5
st. Beaumaris...........530 B10
st. Brighton.............454 J17
st. Carnegie............456 L8
st. Pt Lonsdale........710 C1
st. St Albans...........319 K4

EMMA
av. Reservoir...........282 E9
ct. Berwick..............553 F3
ct. Coburg N............281 H12
ct. Ferntree Gly........463 F7
ct. Hampton Pk.......552 D13
ct. Mt Waverley.......458 H9
ct. Taylors Lakes.....275 E6
ct. Thomastown.......240 E16
ct. Woori Yallock.....344 G15
pl. Dingley Village...532 L3
rd. Croydon.............380 E1
st. Carrum..............573 D9
st. Caulfield S..........456 A8
st. Collingwood.........19 H11
st. Fawkner.............281 K5
st. Seddon..............367 B10

EMMALINE
st. Northcote...........326 E11

EMMAUS
ct. Rye...................697 B14

EMMELINE
dr. Gisborne..............79 J15

EMMERSON
ct. Mill Park............242 H4
la. Croydon.............380 G5
st. Keysborough.....534 D7

EMMERTON
pl. South Yarra..........31 G5

EMMS
st. Bundoora...........284 E1

EMMY
ct. Burwood............418 C5
ct. Grovedale..........705 K13

EMO
ct. Clarinda.............498 F11
rd. Malvern East......456 G3

EMORA
ct. Frankston...........628 A3
st. Croydon.............380 E8

EMOU
cl. Cranbourne........578 G17

EMPEROR
av. Craigieburn........150 D7
pl. Ferntree Gly.......464 B13

EMPERY
ct. Donvale.............332 K18

EMPIRE
av. Jan Juc..............711 D17
ct. Torquay.............712 A3
dr. Hoppers Csg......405 A12
st. Footscray...........367 C4
st. Mornington.........640 E14
st. Preston.............283 D19
wy. Hallam...............551 K1

EMPRESS
av. Kingsville...........366 K13
ct. Sunshine W........363 L5
rd. St Kilda E..........414 K18
rd. Surrey Hills........373 J15
wy. Melton W...........226 B18

EMSLIE
st. Sunshine W.......364 F9

EMU
av. Altona................408 G19
ct. Badger Creek.....258 G12
ct. Dandenong N.....501 H15
ct. Melton...............226 H15
gr. Frankston...........599 A18
pde. Jacana...............237 H18
rd. Maidstone..........322 H19
rd. Mt Eliza.............625 J17
rd. Sunbury.............113 F19

EMVILLE
ct. Cheltenham........497 G19

ENA
rd. Belgrave.............466 G13
st. St Albans...........320 A5

ENBROOK
ct. Grovedale..........706 D9

ENCORE
av. Somerton...........195 A14

ENDEAVOUR
av. Thomastown......240 F15
cr. Endeavour Hl.....537 D3
cr. Westmeadows...237 E14
ct. Bundoora...........284 K6
ct. Keilor Lodge.......276 A3
dr. Chelsea Ht.........547 D13
dr. Cranbourne N.....577 H8
dr. Maribyrnong......322 J15
dr. Torquay.............712 D3
dr. Williamstn N......410 F12
la. Williamstown, off Osborne St.........411 D17
pl. Melton W...........225 J20
pl. Wantirna S.........462 B1
st. Mitcham.............377 D9
wy. Braeside.............532 K16
wy. Wyndham Va.....446 C15

ENDERBY
ct. Boronia..............424 G14
ct. Braybrook..........365 K6

ENDERLY
av. Reservoir...........283 D2

ENDSLEIGH
av. Bundoora...........284 H3

ENEA
pl. Hoppers Csg......448 J1

ENFIELD
av. Pk Orchards.......333 G20
av. Pk Orchards.......377 G1
av. Preston.............327 E1
av. Werribee...........446 K10
cl. Endeavour Hl.....537 J8
ct. Wheelers Hill......461 B7
dr. Bayswater..........423 E9
pl. Craigieburn........150 C19
pl. Forest Hill..........420 E3
rd. Brighton.............455 A13
st. Albanvale...........318 L7
st. Eltham...............287 L8
st. St Kilda.............414 B15

ENGELKE
rd. Belgrave S..........506 G14
rd. Belgrave S..........506 H8
rd. Nar Warrn E.......506 G14

ENGINEERING
rd. Clayton.............459 C15

ENGLAND
rd. Glen Waverley....459 H8
st. Bentleigh E..........496 J2
st. Bulleen..............329 G9
st. Dandenong S.....550 C8
st. Geelong, off Eastern Beach.....703 D7
wk. Nar Warrn S.......552 H20

ENGLEFIELD
ct. Werribee............446 J18

ENGLEWOOD
ct. Belmont.............706 G4
pl. Eltham North......288 F2

ENGLISH
av. Scoresby...........462 F8
ct. Kings Park.........274 L17
st. Airport W...........279 C15
st. Seville...............341 L11

ENID
ct. Heatherton.........497 H15
ct. Hillside..............274 G7
pl. Strathmore.........279 G13

ENMORE
cl. Berwick, off Milparinka Wy....554 F11
ct. Chelsea Ht.........547 E12

ENNERSDALE
ct. Templestowe.....331 L7

ENNGONIA
cr. Clayton S...........498 G9

ENNISMORE
cr. Pk Orchards.......333 K19
dr. Keysborough.....534 A8

ENNISS
av. Bentleigh E.........497 A4

ENOCH
ri. Hallam...............538 B20

ENRICA
pl. Wheelers Hill......460 K16

ENRIGHT
st. Highett...............496 H16

ENROB
ct. Grovedale..........706 E13

ENSAY
ct. Endeavour Hl.....537 E1
ct. Vermont S.........420 K12

ENSBY
st. E Geelong..........703 H15
st. Thomson............703 H15

ENSIGN
cl. Wantirna 422 G9
gr. Taylors Lakes 275 J9
st. Maribyrnong 323 F13
ENTALLY
dr. Albanvale 318 L3
dr. Albanvale 319 A3
dr. Wheelers Hill 460 H11
ENTERPRISE
av. Berwick 554 B10
av. Hampton Pk 551 J9
av. Port Melb 412 B5
ct. Mulgrave 460 C20
pl. Thomastown 241 L18
wy. Bayswater N 380 A17
wy. Mitcham 377 B13
ENTERPRIZE
av. Chelsea Ht 547 D10
dr. Sunbury 113 E12
ENTRANCE
rd. Seaford 573 C19
EOTHEN
la. Kilsyth 381 D6
EPACRIS
ct. Langwarrin 629 K3
ct. Ringwood 379 B2
pl. Keysborough 534 A15
EPALOCK
cr. St Albans 320 D11
EPHCRIS
ct. Endeavour Hl 502 L20
EPPALOCK
cct. Caroline Spr 318 A8
ct. Noble Park N 501 E10
dr. Wyndham Va 446 A5
EPPING
rd. Epping 197 G19
rd. Lalor 241 C6
rd. Thomastown 241 C6
rd. Wollert 197 F14
rd. Woodstock 153 H1
st. Hadfield 281 B5
st. Malvern East 416 E20
EPSOM
av. Epping 198 C18
cl. Bacchus Msh 221 D13
ct. Craigieburn 150 C20
ct. Donvale 376 G5
ct. Fawkner 281 L3
ct. Noble Park N 501 B8
rd. Ascot Vale 323 J16
rd. Flemington 33 B1
rd. Flemington 323 J16
rd. Flemington 368 A1
rd. Kensington 33 B1
rd. Mordialloc 531 J18
st. Caulfield E 456 D3
st. Laverton 407 D19
st.s, Altona Mdw 407 D20
EPSTEIN
st. Reservoir 282 F8
EPWORTH
ct. Glen Waverley 420 A17
EQUITABLE
pl. Melbourne 2 A15
pl. Melbourne 24 C9
ERA
ct. Donvale 332 K13
ERAM
rd. Box Hill N 375 D6
ERAMOSA
rd.e, Somerville 645 B14
rd.w, Baxter 642 K10
rd.w, Baxter 643 B11
rd.w, Moorooduc 642 K10
rd.w, Somerville 644 E13
ERAMU
pl. Kurunjang 227 A14
ERANG
cl. Greensborough 244 E19
ct. Mooroolbark 337 D15
dr. Mt Eliza 626 E12
ERASMUS
st. Surrey Hills 374 E20
ERAWAN
av. Notting Hill 459 H15
ERCILDOUNE
av. Hawthorn 416 C3
st. Caulfield N 415 C17
EREBUS
st. Keilor Park 278 A15
ERIC
av. Mordialloc 531 L15
av. Templstw Lr 329 K7
cr. Mornington 656 F2
ct. Langwarrin 629 B4
ct. Oakleigh S 458 B17
ct. Pearcedale 646 K3
ct. Wheelers Hill 460 H8
st. Belgrave 466 G11
st. Brighton East 455 F13
st. Croydon 336 G14
st. Essendon 324 E7
st. Hawthorn 371 J15
st. Preston 282 C20
ERICA
av. Boronia 424 C13
av. Glen Iris 416 E15
av. St Albans 320 C4
cl. Endeavour Hl 537 F5
cr. Heathmont 378 G19
cr. Kilsyth 381 G6
ct. Bellfield 328 A6
ct. Blackburn N 375 H9
ct. Bundoora 285 A5
ct. Heathmont 378 G19
ct. Hoppers Csg 405 A16
ct. Lalor 240 H8
ct. Langwarrin 629 J3
ct. Mt Martha 656 F8
st. Canterbury 373 E16
st. Dandenong N 501 J15
st. Frankston 627 L7
st. Mt Waverley 458 L6
st. Pascoe Vale 280 L19
st. Springvale 499 F17
st. Windsor 414 K12
ERICKSEN
st. Springvale 499 J9
ERIC McDONALD
ri. Nar Warrn S 552 J13
ERIDEN
cl. Glen Waverley 420 G15
ERIE
av. Rowville 462 K15
av. Rowville 463 A16
ERIKSSON
wy. Nunawading, off Walkers Rd 376 H15
ERILYN
ct. Vermont 377 F20
ct. Vermont 421 F1
ERIN
ct. Coolaroo 238 F7
ct. Doncaster 331 A18
ct. Frankston 627 C4
ct. Hampton Pk 552 B13
pl. Keysborough 534 C7
pl. Wantirna 422 A12
st. Hillside 274 G6
st. Preston 326 F4
st. Richmond 26 A9
ERINBANK
cr. Attwood 237 D11
cr. Westmeadows 237 G12
ERINDALE
av. Deer Park 319 B10
av. Ripponlea 454 H2
ct. Grovedale 706 G14
mw. Point Cook 450 G7
st. Murrumbeena 457 C9
ERINKA
cr. Patterson L 573 K8
ERINNE
ct. St Helena 245 D15
ERINVALE
cl. Gisborne 79 C12
ERITH
la. Kalorama 383 A12
ERLANDSEN
av. Sorrento 679 B12
ERLDUNDA
ct. Lilydale 337 L2
ERLI
ct. Blackburn 375 L13
ERMINGTON
pl. Kew 372 B10
ERNE
st. Balwyn 374 B11
ERNEST
cl. Melton W 225 K20
ct. Portsea 678 B5
pl. Nar Warrn S 552 G18
rd. Croydon 336 D19
rd. Kalorama 383 A17
st. Bayswater 423 B5
st. Blackburn 375 F12
st. Broadmeadows 238 D20
st. Mt Martha 655 L13
st. Sunshine 321 G20
st. Sunshine 365 G1
ERNST
st. Doncaster 330 E16
ERNST WANKE
rd. Berwick 539 E13
rd. Narre Warren 538 G14
rd. Narre Warren 539 E13
rd. Nar Warrn N 539 A12
EROWAL
st. Beaumaris 530 B3
ERRINGTON
rd. St Albans 320 H4
ERROL
av. Brunswick 325 J12
cl. Aspendale Gdn 547 A5
ct. Greensborough 286 D8
pl. N Melbourne 17 C19
st. Braybrook 321 L18
st. Footscray 367 B9
st. N Melbourne 17 C18
st. Prahran 32 L18
st. Prahran 414 L9
st. Prahran 415 A9
ERSKINE
av. Cheltenham 496 E19
av. Reservoir 283 F13
cr. Wheelers Hill 461 C15
ct. Greenvale 237 A1
dr. Rowville 463 B13
la. N Melbourne 17 A10
pl. N Melbourne 34 K10
rd. Emerald 510 D11
rd. Macleod 285 B15
rdg. Mooroolbark 337 A11
st. Albert Park 29 K16
st. Armadale 415 G10
st. Frankston 599 D17
st. Middle Park 29 K16
st. N Melbourne 34 J10
st. Nunawading 376 J17
wy. Sydenham 274 H1
ERSWELL
ct. Montmorency 287 B10
ERUTTA
pl. Frankston S 627 H12
ERVAL
av. Preston 327 B3
ERVIN
rd. Kilsyth 380 L6
rd. Mooroolbark 380 L6
ERVINE
cl. Sunbury 143 F5
ERWIN
dr. Seaford 599 F3
ESCABON
gr. Frankston 600 H19
ESCARPMENT
dr. Frankston S 627 K18
dr. Frankston S 628 A17
ESCOTT
gr. Berwick 554 C15
ESDALE
st. Blackburn 376 B12
st. Nunawading 376 F12
ESHER
ri. Mt Martha 669 J3
ESK
ct. Dandenong 536 F6
ct. Forest Hill 376 E19
ESKAY
rd. Epping 198 A15
rd. Oakleigh S 497 L3
ESKDALE
ct. Eltham North 245 C19
ct. Mornington 657 B4
ct. Narre Warren 539 A15
dr. Croydon Hills 335 H12
rd. Caulfield N 455 H1
ESKHOLME
ri. St Helena 245 B20
ESLA
dr. Roxburgh Pk 194 D7
ESMALE
st. Strathmore 279 L16
ESME
ct. Mt Eliza 642 G1
ESMOND
st. Ardeer 320 A19
st. Preston 282 F18
ESPER
av. Oakleigh S 497 H4
ESPERANCE
av. Brighton 454 G17
rd. Mt Waverley 419 G14
ESPERANTO
ct. Glenroy 280 C9
ESPLANADE
Altona 452 L1
Brighton 454 F18
Brighton 494 G5
Frankston 626 L2
Mitcham 377 C13
Mornington 640 B19
Mornington 640 C13
Mt Martha 655 L11
Mt Martha 656 B6
Mt Martha 668 K4
Mt Martha 668 K9
Mt Martha 669 A2
Queenscliff 708 J19
Seaholme 409 G20
Sorrento 678 K8
Williamstown 411 D18
av. Brighton 494 G4
pl. Port Melb 29 A8
w. Port Melb 412 K7
ESPLANADE EAST
Port Melb 29 A10
Port Melb 412 L7
ESPLANADE WEST
Port Melb 412 L5
ESSEX
cl. Avondale Ht 322 G10
ct. Bayswater 423 G9
ct. Cranbourne E 578 H18
ct. Epping 197 K16
ct. Heidelberg 329 F3
ct. Somerville 644 H16
ct. Templstw Lr 330 G11
dr. Melton 226 L17
pl. Carlton 18 C20
rd. Mt Martha 656 A20
rd. Mt Waverley 418 G14
rd. Surrey Hills 373 K20
rd. Surrey Hills 417 K2
st. Blackburn N 376 B10
st. Box Hill N 375 D9
st. Briar Hill 286 H5
st. Brunswick 325 H16
st. Dandenong N 502 E13
st. Footscray 366 L6
st. Glen Iris 416 J14
st. Moolap 704 J16
st. Pascoe Vale 280 G15
st. Prahran 32 E18
st. Prahran 414 H9
st. Sandringham 494 L13
st. Sandringham 495 A13
st. Sunshine N 321 G18
st. Warburton 305 A20
st. W Footscray 366 D5
ESSEX PARK
dr. Endeavour Hl 536 K1
ESSINGTON
ct. Mulgrave 460 C18
ct. Grovedale 706 G10
ESSUE
ct. Mill Park 242 C2
ESTA
ct. Doncaster 374 H4
st. Blackburn N 375 F7
st. Melton 268 F1
ESTATE
rd. Don Valley 346 B6
ESTEEMED
ct. Tootgarook 698 C9
ESTELLA
ct. Narre Warren 539 F15
st. Glen Iris 416 L15
ESTELLE
ct. Altona North 409 H2
ct. Noble Park N 501 C13
st. Bulleen 329 J17
st. Oakleigh 458 C8
st. Sunshine W 364 F3
ESTER
cl. Endeavour Hl 537 H6
cr. Clayton S 498 F7
dr. Mill Park 242 A3
st. Greensborough 285 L5
ESTHER
cr. Mooroolbark 336 J14
ct. Boronia 424 C17
ct. Fawkner 281 H10
ct. Mt Waverley 458 F4
ct. Noble Park 500 F19
ct. Seabrook 450 J4
st. Preston 326 J4
st. Templstw Lr 330 B11
ETHEL
av. Lalor 241 F9
ct. Pt Lonsdale 707 H19
ct. Springvale 499 H17
gr. Reservoir 283 C15
st. Bentleigh 496 B4
st. Boronia 424 F14
st. Brunswick E 325 L15
st. Greensborough 286 B7
st. Malvern 416 A8
st. Oak Park 279 L14
st. Sunshine 364 J2
st. Thornbury 326 J7
ETKA
av. Keilor East 278 F20
ETNA
cl. Keilor Lodge 276 A4
ct. Coolaroo 238 C7
st. Glen Huntly 456 C7
ETNAM
st. Preston 326 E4
ETON
cl. Sunbury 144 D1
ct. Balwyn 373 J
ct. Dandenong 536 G
ct. Frankston 627 D
ct. Gladstone Pk 237 B1
ct. Heathmont 378 G1
ct. Heidelberg 329 F
ct. Hoppers Csg 405 A1
pl. Portsea 677 L
pl. Springvale S 499 H1
rd. Belmont 702 C2
sq. Wantirna 422 H
st. Mt Waverley 419 C1
st. Preston 327 E
ETTRICK
pl. Berwick 554 F1
ETZEL
st. Airport W 278 G1
EUCALYPT
av. Springvale 500 K1
av. Templstw Lr 330 K1
ct. Altona Mdw 407 L2
ct. Langwarrin 601 L1
dr. Lilydale 338 B1
dr. Mill Park 243 B
EUCALYPTUS
pl. Meadow Ht 194 A1
rd. Eltham 288 B1
rd. Sunshine W 364 C
st. Richmond 26 F1
wk. Carrum Downs 575 D1
EUCRA
st. Hadfield 280 K
EUGENE
st. View Bank 286 A1
tce. Ringwood 378 A1
EUGENIA
ct. Boronia 424 K7
st. Doveton 536 K1
st. Nunawading 376 J1
st. Rye 696 H8
EULA
ct. Chadstone 458 F2
ct. Frankston 628 H1
EULINGA
av. Aspendale 546 B3
rd. Clarinda 498 D5
EUMARELLA
st. Tullamarine 278 H7
EUMEMMERRING
dr. Eumemmerring 537 B12
EUMERALLA
av. Templestowe 330 L11
av. Templstw Lr 330 L11
ct. Frankston S 626 L13
gr. Mt Eliza 642 F8
rd. Caulfield S 455 L11
EUMONG
ct. Mornington 641 C14
EUNEVA
av. Glen Waverley 460 C1
EUNICE
ct. Kilsyth S 381 A19
ct. Pascoe Vale S 280 J19
dr. Cheltenham 531 F1
EUNSON
av. Northcote 326 E16
EURABBIE
ct. Eltham 288 A6
EURAH
pl. Eltham 288 C6
EUREKA
cr. Nar Warrn S 552 G8
ct. Bangholme 549 J13
ct. Kings Park 275 C17
rd. Diggers Rest 187 A10
st. Geelong West 702 E6
st. Richmond 26 H4
st. Rye 698 A6
EURELLA
cr. Rowville 502 E8
EUROA
av. Berwick 539 J20
av. Sunshine N 321 B13
wk. Kurunjang 226 J15
EUROKA
ct. Grovedale 705 K16
st. Chadstone 458 C1
EUROLIE
st. Balwyn N 373 E6
EUROPA
ct. Wheelers Hill 460 J17
EURORA
ct. Taylors Lakes 276 A8
EURYTHMIC
st. Mordialloc 531 K16
EUSTACE
st. Blackburn 375 K19

FAITH
ct. Langwarrin...629 L12
st. Ferntree Gly...463 K6
FAKENHAM
rd. Ashburton...417 G14
FALCON
cl. Blind Bight...650 C10
cst. Craigieburn...149 G17
ct. Carrum Downs...601 B1
ct. Doncaster E...375 K3
dr. Keysborough...535 C8
dr. Melton...226 F15
pl. Pakenham...584 L10
rd. Macleod...285 C17
st. Thomastown...240 E14
st. Werribee...448 C9
wk. Kings Park...319 A1
FALCON CREST
Wheelers Hill...461 C14
FALCONER
cr. Bayswater N...380 F17
ct. Keilor...276 G10
ct. Mornington...641 B15
rd. Boronia...423 H11
rd. Pk Orchards...334 A13
st. Fitzroy N...19 G1
st. Fitzroy N...326 E20
st. Glen Waverley...459 J2
FALCONHURST
ct. Eltham North...245 K19
FALDO
ct. Mill Park...242 B6
ct. Rowville...463 H11
FALFIELD
pl. Templestowe...332 A12
FALK
av. Reservoir...283 B2
rd. Wandin East...340 L19
FALKINER
cr. Dandenong...536 D3
ct. Carrum Downs...574 J20
ct. Carrum Downs...600 J1
st. Eltham...287 E16
FALKINGHAM
rd. Mt Evelyn...339 B20
rd. Mt Evelyn...383 A1
FALLON
st. Brunswick...325 C15
st. Caulfield...455 K6
FALLONS
wy. Bayswater...423 C4
FALLS
rd. Kalorama...382 J16
rd. Kalorama...383 A19
rd. Mt Dandenong...382 J16
rd. Mt Dandenong...426 L1
rd. Mt Dandenong...427 A1
rd. Mt Evelyn...383 C2
rd. Olinda...426 K8
rd. Olinda...426 L1
rd. Olinda...427 A1
rd. Olinda...427 A7
FALMER
pl. Craigieburn...150 D20
FALMOUTH
ct. Craigieburn...194 D4
st. Hawthorn...372 C16
FALSHAM
pl. N Melbourne...17 D15
FALSHAWS
la. N Melbourne...17 C15
FAME
st. Coburg N...281 F16
FAMECHON
rd. Chelsea...547 B13
rd. Edithvale...547 B13
FANECO
rd. Plenty...244 K4
FANKHAUSER
dr. Vermont S...420 H10
FANNING
st. Heidelberg...328 L4
st. Heidelberg...329 A4
st. Southbank...4 A7
st. Southbank...24 E14
FANNY
st. Moonee Pnd...324 F11
FANTAIL
ct. Carrum Downs...600 J5
ct. Taylors Lakes...275 G2
pl. S Morang...243 K3
ri. Warburton...349 J4
tce. Healesville...258 A1
FAORO
ct. Keysborough...534 D12
FARADAY
ct. Glen Waverley...460 L5
la. Carlton...18 E14
rd. Croydon S...379 J12
st. Boronia...423 J12
st. Carlton...18 D13
FAREY
av. Dromana...685 F9
FARLEIGH
av. Burwood...418 K7
gr. Brighton...454 F17
FARLEY
ct. Gladstone Pk...237 C17
FARLEY GREEN
ct. Vermont...421 E1
FARM
cl. Greensborough...286 D10
la. Berwick...540 L17
la. Berwick...541 A17
la. Don Valley...345 L5
rd. Alphington...327 L19
rd. Cheltenham...497 E19
rd. Coburg...281 J19
rd. Cocoroc...487 A18
rd. Heatherton...497 E19
rd. Oakleigh S...498 A2
rd. Werribee...447 C18
st. Newport...411 A6
FARMER
ct. Melton W...226 A17
st. Ashwood...418 E16
st. Brighton East...495 C4
st. Burnley...371 A19
st. St Kilda...414 E16
FARMERS
wy. Narre Warren...552 K5
FARMHOUSE
ct. Nar Warrn N...538 D12
ct. Sydenham...274 L7
FARMILLO
ct. Ferntree Gly...464 B16
FARMINGTON
ct. Wheelers Hill...460 G14
FARNAN
st. Northcote...326 L18
FARNBOROUGH
av. Craigieburn...150 B20
wy. Berwick...553 K19
FARNCOMB
st. Ascot Vale...324 B20
FARNDONS
rd. Mt Dandenong...382 J18
FARNHAM
av. Wheelers Hill...460 H16
cr. Mill Park...242 G2
ct. Bundoora...284 K1
ct. Craigieburn...150 B20
ct. Flemington...324 F20
pl. Mornington...657 A1
rd. Bayswater...423 J7
rd. Healesville...214 B19
st. Caulfield...456 A5
st. Flemington...324 E20
FARNLEY
st. Croydon...380 H5
FARNSWORTH
av. Footscray...367 E4
av. Portsea...677 K4
ct. Berwick...553 L3
st. Sunshine...321 E19
FARQUHARSON
av. Belgrave...466 H15
st. Mt Waverley...419 A19
FARRANT
ct. Altona Mdw...451 J3
FARRAR
wy. Wandin N...340 L13
wy. Wandin N...341 A13
FARRELL
av. Yarra Glen...252 L2
av. Yarra Glen...253 A2
ct. Pakenham...584 G5
ct. Williamstown...411 A16
la. Williamstown...411 A18
mw. Williamstown...411 A18
st. Frankston...599 F13
st. New Gisborne...79 B3
st. Niddrie...322 L1
st. Niddrie...323 A1
st. Port Melb...412 J3
st. Port Melb...412 K4
st. Safety Bch...668 L18
FARRELLY
ct. Epping...197 L19
FARRER
cl. Cranbourne...603 K1
cl. Diamond Ck...246 A12
cl. Wandana Ht...705 D1
ct. Doncaster E...331 H15
ct. Mill Park...242 L6
ct. Mill Park...243 A6
ct. Warranwood...334 K13
pl. Berwick...553 D2
FARRIER EDWARDS
la. Port Melb, off
Rouse St...412 J7
FARRINGDON
rd. Kalorama...383 C12
st. Pascoe Vale...280 D15
FARRINGTON
ct. Rosebud...684 C20
FARSKIENE
pl. Hampton Pk...551 G12
FARVIEW
dr. Rowville...503 A6
st. Glenroy...280 G8
FASAN
ri. Ringwood N...334 F13
FASHION
pde. Broadmeadows...239 A19
FASHODA
st. Hawthorn...371 H15
FASTNET
dr. Taylors Lakes...275 F8
FATIMAH
ct. Torquay...712 J2
FAULKINER
st. Clayton...498 J2
FAULKNER
st. Bentleigh...496 C6
st. Blackburn S...420 A3
st. Forest Hill...420 B3
st. Hampton...495 G6
FAULL
cl. Croydon N...335 L18
FAUNA
av. Badger Creek...258 E12
av. Dingley Village...533 H10
ct. Narre Warren...538 J20
ct. Werribee...447 E6
FAUSSETT
la. Albert Park...29 J12
st. Albert Park...29 H12
st. Albert Park...413 D6
FAVARO
pl. Hillside...274 D3
FAVERSHAM
ct. Greenvale...237 C6
rd. Canterbury...373 G17
sq. Ferntree Gly...463 F4
FAVOURITE HILL
rd. Pearcedale...630 F15
FAVRIL
st. Hampton...495 B6
FAWCETT
pl. Sunbury...143 B11
st. Mitcham...377 C9
st. Sunshine N...321 E15
FAWKNER
av. Blairgowrie...679 F16
cr. Hurstbridge...202 H12
cr. Keilor East...322 C6
ct. Mill Park...242 J4
ct. Mooroolbark...337 K14
la. Southbank...3 L7
rd. Pascoe Vale...280 E16
st. Aberfeldie...323 D11
st. Aberfeldie...323 D12
st. St Kilda...414 B17
st. Southbank...3 G8
st. Southbank...3 K7
st. Southbank...24 C16
st. South Yarra...31 J11
st. South Yarra...414 E6
st. Sunbury...143 A13
st. Sunshine N...321 F18
st. Westmeadows...236 K14
wy. Seabrook...451 A7
FAWN
ct. Langwarrin...629 F3
FAY
ct. Croydon...380 H7
ct. Noble Park...534 C6
ct. Somerville...644 E14
st. Balwyn N...373 J1
st. Brunswick...325 G15
st. Eltham...287 E8
st. Fawkner...281 K4
st. Heidelberg...329 D4
st. Melton...268 H1
st. Scoresby...462 D8
st. Seaford...599 J9
FAYE
cr. Keilor...276 L10
cr. Keilor...276 L9
cr. Keilor...277 A10
cr. Keilor...277 A9
ct. Tootgarook...698 C8
pl. Hampton Pk...551 K6
st. Burwood E...420 B8
st. Moorabbin...496 J8
st. Reservoir...283 H15
FAYETTE
ct. Wheelers Hill...461 E18
FAYGATE
ct. Frankston...628 F4
FEAR
st. Richmond...26 A13
FEATHER
cr. Diamond Ck...245 J13
FEATHERBY
wy. Altona Mdw...451 G9
FEATHERPARK
tce. S Morang...199 J14
FEATHERTOP
av. Templstw Lr...330 D12
ch. Burwood E...419 F12
dr. Keilor...277 B14
dr. Noble Park N...501 D10
dr. Wyndham Va...446 C12
ri. Wheelers Hill...461 D17
FEDERAL
rd. Ringwood E...378 L10
st. Footscray...367 E6
st. Mt Waverley...418 L13
st. Williamstown...411 C12
FEDERATION
ct. Altona...409 A16
ct. Nar Warrn S...553 F20
gln. Croydon Hills...335 K15
la. Berwick...553 L16
st. Ascot Vale...324 A16
st. Box Hill...374 G17
wk. Hughesdale...457 F7
wk. St Albans...319 H7
wy. Caroline Spr...318 A6
wy. Moorabbin Aprt...532 D3
FEDERICO
ct. Ringwood...335 A18
FEDRA
st. Mt Martha...657 A10
FEEHAN
cr. Nar Warrn S...578 E2
FEENEY
ct. Hampton Pk...551 E11
FEHON
st. Yarraville...367 A16
FELDSPAR
cl. St Albans...320 J9
ct. Narre Warren...539 F13
FELECIA
st. Rye...696 J8
FELGATE
cl. Tullamarine...278 K3
pde. Vermont S...420 L7
pde. Vermont S...421 A8
FELICIA
gr. Forest Hill...420 K1
ri. Diamond Ck...246 D9
st. Mordialloc...532 B12
wy. Delahey...275 E9
FELICITY
ct. Narre Warren...552 G1
FELIX
cr. Ringwood N...377 L8
cr. Torquay...712 B7
ct. Woori Yallock...344 E14
gr. Mooroolbark...336 L18
la. St Kilda W, off
Loch St...414 A14
st. Grovedale...706 E13
st. Surrey Hills...373 L20
FELL
cr. Malvern East...416 H19
ct. Altona Mdw...451 G2
rd. Cockatoo...471 F18
FELLMONGERS
rd. Breakwater...703 D20
FELLOWES
ct. Tullamarine...278 G9
st. Seaford...599 K6
FELLOWS
rd. Pt Lonsdale...707 G20
rd. Queenscliff...707 G20
rd. Swan Bay...707 G20
st. Hughesdale...457 F6
st. Kew...371 G7
st. Mitcham...377 B12
FELLOWSHIP
gr. Kilsyth...381 A8
FELSTEAD
av. Sunshine W...364 H10
FELTHAM
ct. Rosebud...699 L1
st. Pearcedale...646 L6
FELTON
av. Sunbury...142 H10
FENACRE
st. Strathmore...280 A17
FENCHURCH
st. Sunbury...144 C9
FENECH
cl. Mill Park...241 L
ct. Hillside...274 F
FENFIELD
st. Altona...408 H1
st. Cranbourne...578 B1
FENLAND
ct. Highton...705 L
FENNELL
st. Port Melb...412 J
FENTON
av. Kew...371 J1
av. Rosebud...700 G
cr. Frankston S...626 J
ct. Keysborough...534 G1
st. Ascot Vale...324 E1
st. Huntingdale...458 F1
st. Mt Dandenong...426 H
wy. Kew, off
High St...371 K1
FENWICK
ct. Bundoora...284 G
pl. Avondale Ht...322 D1
pl. Geelong, off
Little Ryrie St...702 L
st. Carlton N...18 G
st. Clifton Hill...20 G
st. Frankston...627 E
st. Geelong...702 K
st. Kew...371 F1
st. Malvern East...457 E
st. Thornbury...326 K1
FEODORE
st. Caulfield S...456 A1
FERDINAND
av. Balwyn N...373 K
st. Nunawading...376 K
FERDINANDO
la. Sandringham, off
Abbott St...495 A1
FERGIE
st. Fitzroy N...19 F
st. Fitzroy N...326 D2
FERGUS
ct. Sydenham...274 K
FERGUSON
ct. Eumemmerring...537 C1
ct. Ferntree Gly...463 H
rd. Kilsyth...381 E
st. Abbotsford...26 B
st. Albion...320 L1
st. Ascot Vale...323 K1
st. Belgrave...466 H1
st. Black Rock...529 H
st. Brighton East...455 B1
st. Glen Iris...416 J1
st. Kew...371 G
st. Macleod...285 B1
st. Maribyrnong...367 A
st. Mitcham...377 J1
st. Spotswood...366 G1
st. Upwey...465 E1
st. Williamstown...411 D1
FERMANAGH
gr. Sorrento...679 A1
rd. Camberwell...372 K2
FERMONT
ct. Clarinda...498 D
FERMOY
wy. Narre Warren...553 G
FERN
av. Ferny Creek...466 B
av. Guys Hill...556 B
av. Windsor...414 K1
cl. Broadmeadows...238 A1
cl. Seaford...599 L
ct. Campbellfield...239 E1
ct. Craigieburn...150 D1
ct. Eltham...287 B
ct. Launching Pl...345 F1
ct. Mill Park...242 F1
ct. Rosebud...700 H
ct. Werribee...447 B1
gr. Ferny Creek...466 C
gr. Rye...696 E
mw. Langwarrin...601 K1
rd. Up Fntree Gly...464 L
st. Beaconsfld Up...542 G1
st. Black Rock...495 G2
st. Newcomb...703 L1
st. Oakleigh E...458 D1
st. Pearcedale...646 G
st. Sunshine W...364 B
st. The Basin...425 G1
tce. Footscray...367 D
wy. Nar Warrn S...553 C1
FERNALD
av. Anglesea...713 F4
FERNBANK
cr. Mulgrave...501 H
ct. Kilsyth...381 E10
rd. Healesville...212 H16

FERNBERG
l. Melton W 226 C15
FERNBROOK
d. Ferny Creek 466 B2
i. Knoxfield 463 C1
vy. Templestowe 331 D13
FERNCROFT
v. Malvern East 416 H17
t. Berwick 554 K20
t. Cranbourne N 578 C9
t. Vermont 420 L5
FERNDALE
v. Upwey 465 J16
l. Dingley Village 532 K6
l. Werribee 447 B18
r. Dandenong N 501 K16
r. Frankston 628 F5
de. Highton 701 L17
d. Glen Iris 417 B11
d. Sassafras 425 J14
d. Silvan 385 F20
d. Silvan 428 L3
d. Sunshine N 321 C14
d. Up Fntree Gly 464 L9
d. Warburton 306 C19
t. Surrey Hills 418 D3
FERNDELL
r. Templestowe 331 J14
t. Belgrave Ht 506 E3
FERNE
l. Mt Martha 655 E20
FERNEAUX
l. Melton W 226 B16
FERNERY
r. Newtown 702 D9
a. Frankston 626 K2
d. Upwey 465 J16
FERNGLADE
r. Emerald 510 D3
FERNGLEN
v. Mt Dandenong 426 J1
FERNGULLY
r. Kalorama 383 E9
d. Cockatoo 510 L10
d. Don Valley 346 D1
FERNHILL
t. Albanvale 319 A4
r. Dingley Village 532 L4
r. Highton 701 L16
d. Caulfield S 455 E9
d. Mt Evelyn 339 F14
d. Sandringham 495 C15
d.n, Sandringham 495 C14
t. Ascot Vale 324 G18
t. Glen Waverley 420 B20
FERNHURST
l. Keysborough 534 B9
r. Glen Waverley 420 B18
r. Kew 371 H10
FERNIE
l. Attwood 237 D11
FERNLEA
v. Rowville 463 H14
l. Watsonia N 243 G19
r. Doncaster E 332 E5
t. Sunshine W 364 D5
FERNLEIGH
r. Mooroolbark 381 K3
t. Newtown 702 H13
FERNLEY
v. Macleod 285 C12
FERNLY
t. Wheelers Hill 461 F15
FERNSHAW
gdn. Hallam 552 B1
l. Mt Eliza 642 G4
l. Sunbury 143 B10
d. Monbulk 428 D20
t. Thomastown 240 F13
FERNSIDE
v. Briar Hill 286 H5
FERNTREE
v. Warburton 350 B3
t. Ferntree Gly 463 H7
r. Aspendale Gdn 547 C5
vy. Keysborough 534 A9
FERNTREE GULLY
rd. Clayton 459 C10
rd. Ferntree Gly 463 G4
rd. Glen Waverley 459 C10
rd. Knoxfield 463 A8
rd. Mt Waverley 459 C10
rd. Notting Hill 459 C10
rd. Oakleigh 458 B9
rd. Oakleigh E 458 B9
rd. Scoresby 462 A11
rd. Wheelers Hill 459 C10
rd. Wheelers Hill 460 H13
rd. Wheelers Hill 461 B13
FERNVALE
cr. Wheelers Hill 460 H15

FERNWOOD
av. Ringwood E 379 D17
dr. Langwarrin 629 J2
rd. Narre Warren 538 K20
FERNWREN
pl. Carrum Downs 600 E5
FERNY
ct. Bangholme 549 H14
ct. Nar Warrn S 553 E17
FERNY CREEK
av. Up Fntree Gly 465 D7
FERNYHILL
ct. Greenvale 193 D17
FERRARO
cl. Epping 198 F16
FERRARS
pl. S Melbourne 29 K7
pl. S Melbourne 413 E4
st. Albert Park 413 D2
st. Southbank 23 F18
st. Southbank 29 G1
st. Southbank 413 D1
st. S Melbourne 29 G1
st. S Melbourne 413 D1
st. S Melbourne 413 D2
FERRERO
gr. Mt Martha 655 G18
FERRES
bvd. S Morang 198 L19
ct. Glen Waverley 420 J15
rd. Emerald 469 E19
FERRIER
ct. Rosanna 284 L20
ct. Rosanna 285 A19
ct. Rowville 502 J5
rd. New Gisborne 78 H1
FERRIMAN
st. Brunswick W 324 L14
FERRIS
av. Box Hill N 374 J8
av. Deer Park 319 B10
av. Mitcham 377 E17
rd. Melton 269 G8
rd. Melton S 269 F15
FERRY
cl. Wyndham Va 446 G14
cr. Brunswick W 325 A12
gr. Newcomb 703 L16
FERSFIELD
rd. Gisborne 79 A16
FESCUE
pl. Delahey 274 L14
FESTIVAL
cr. Keysborough 535 B10
gr. Lalor 240 L5
pl. The Basin 425 B8
tce. Berwick 553 E2
FETHERSTON
st. Armadale 415 E12
FETLOCK
pl. Epping 198 D16
FETTLING
st. Preston 282 G19
FEVERSHAM
av. Pk Orchards 334 B18
FEWSTER
dr. Wantirna S 462 D3
rd. Hampton 495 D8
FIANDER
av. Glen Waverley 459 J1
FIAT
ct. Keilor Dn 276 C15
FICIFOLIA
dr. Doveton 536 G12
FIDDAN
ct. Altona Mdw 451 J6
FIDDES
st. Moorabbin 496 F8
st. Reservoir 282 D5
FIDGE
cr. Breakwater 703 H20
ct. Jacana 237 J19
FIDLER
av. Burnside 318 E5
ct. Altona Mdw 451 K7
FIELD
av. Edithvale 546 H12
ct. Dandenong N 502 A12
ct. Gladstone Pk 237 D18
ct. Montrose 382 E10
st. Bentleigh 456 C17
st. Caulfield S 455 K6
st. Clifton Hill 20 J8
st. Craigieburn 150 F17
st. Croydon 379 J8
st. Hampton 495 F12
st. McKinnon 456 C17
st. Moonee Pnd 324 A10
st. Rye 697 J4

FIELDEN
cl. Mooroolbark 381 K1
FIELDER
rd. Cockatoo 511 G9
FIELDERS
wk. Westmeadows 236 G15
FIELDING
dr. Chelsea Ht 547 H18
dr. Gisborne S 141 A2
rd. Diamond Ck 245 B8
rd. Rosebud W 683 B20
st. Yarraville 367 B13
wy. Templestowe 331 L9
FIELDLARK
ct. Carrum Downs 600 K3
ct. Werribee 447 L6
FIELDSTONE
bvd. Beaconsfield 555 B12
FIESTA
ct. Thomastown 240 F17
FIFE
ct. Belmont 702 H20
ct. Mulgrave 500 J1
FIFER
ri. Bundoora 242 C20
FIFESHIRE
dr. Hoppers Csg 405 C13
FIFTH
av. Altona North 409 K7
av. Anglesea 713 C11
av. Aspendale 546 F10
av. Brunswick 325 E9
av. Chelsea Ht 547 F13
av. Cockatoo 510 H6
av. Dandenong 535 H7
av. Eden Park 125 A3
av. Edithvale 546 F6
av. Hadfield 281 D9
av. Pakenham 584 L2
av. Rosebud 684 A18
av. Rowville 462 E19
rd. Springvale 500 L10
st. Black Rock 529 H8
st. Parkdale 531 E11
FIG
ct. Cranbourne N 578 C5
st. Dromana 686 E6
FIGTREE
ct. Mill Park 242 C10
gr. Bayswater 422 J5
la. Burwood, off College Wy 419 C7
FIJI
ct. Mulgrave 500 C3
FILBERT
ct. Cranbourne N 577 L4
st. Bentleigh E 456 H20
st. Caulfield S 455 G7
FILER
ct. Keysborough 534 C9
FILIPPIN
ct. Werribee 447 K18
FILLMORE
rd. Dandenong N 501 J10
FILLO
dr. Somerton 195 C16
FILMER
ct. Nar Warrn S 552 G17
ct. Rowville 462 K20
FILOMENA
ct. Cranbourne N 578 E10
FILSON
st. Ascot Vale 324 D18
FINAL
la. Endeavour Hl 502 L17
FINBAR
ct. Nar Warrn S 552 E15
FINCH
ct. Pakenham 584 L2
ct. Point Cook 450 D3
pl. Blackburn S 419 K6
pl. Melton 226 G15
st. Altona 408 F20
st. Bayswater 423 C5
st. Berwick 539 J18
st. Burwood 418 K11
st. Doncaster E 375 K4
st. Frankston 599 D15
st. Glen Iris 416 D15
st. Malvern East 416 C20
st. Mt Martha 656 B8
st. Notting Hill 459 G12
st. Thomastown 240 G16
FINCHAVEN
av. Keysborough 535 A11
st. Herne Hill 701 L4
FINCHFIELD
la. Belmont 706 A7

FINCHLEY
av. Glenroy 279 K5
ct. Endeavour Hl 503 B20
ct. Epping 197 K18
ct. Hawthorn 371 L18
ct. Springvale S 499 K20
pl. Kealba 276 K19
rd. Point Cook 450 J10
FINCHS
rd. Melton 228 B10
FINDEN
ct. Craigieburn 150 B15
FINDLAY
gr. Belmont 702 G17
la. Altona 409 C19
st. Northcote 326 G11
FINDON
av. Caulfield N 415 E16
cr. Kew 371 F12
ct. Berwick 554 H19
ct. Highett 496 D12
ct. Seaford 573 F13
ct. Wantirna S 462 C2
pl. Point Cook 450 F7
rd. Epping 197 G15
rd. S Morang 198 G17
st. Hawthorn 371 F13
st. Malvern East 416 B19
st. S Geelong 703 A14
wy. Melton W 226 D15
FINGAL
dr. Frankston 600 B16
FINHAVEN
ct. Kew 371 D11
FINISTERRE
ct. Frankston 628 D10
dr. Keysborough 534 G12
FINK
ct. Donvale 376 F7
st. Kensington 34 C13
st. Preston 327 H6
st. Williamstn N 410 B12
FINKEL
rd. Harkaway 540 L11
rd. Harkaway 541 A11
FINLAY
al. Melbourne 1 J7
al. Melbourne 23 L5
cl. Gladstone Pk 237 B17
pl. Carlton 18 E18
st. Albert Park 29 G14
st. Albert Park 413 E7
st. Frankston 599 E18
st. Yarraville 366 H17
FINLAYSON
av. Mt Martha 669 B2
st. Doncaster 374 D2
st. Forest Hill 420 C2
st. Malvern 416 A18
st. Ringwood E 379 E17
st. Rosanna 284 L20
st. Rosanna 285 A20
FINLEY
ct. Endeavour Hl 538 B4
ct. Wantirna S 422 D17
rd. Altona 408 K14
FINMERE
cr. Up Fntree Gly 464 J9
FINN
ct. Maddingley 264 E3
ct. Templstw Lr 330 F10
st. Rosanna 329 C2
FINNBAR
wy. Seabrook 450 L6
FINNIGAN
st. Research 288 J5
FINNINGLEY
ct. Highton 705 L7
dr. Tullamarine 278 K2
FINSBURY
cl. Rowville 503 H2
ct. Dandenong N 501 F10
rd. Devon Mdw 604 J20
st. Flemington 33 L2
wy. Camberwell 417 A4
FINSTALL
cl. Caroline Spr 317 K2
FINTON
cl. Glen Waverley 461 A5
ct. Pakenham 585 E4
gr. Gladstone Pk 279 A2
gr. Reservoir 283 C1
FINTONA
ct. Coldstream 295 F13
FINTONIA
rd. Noble Park 501 A19
st. Balwyn N 373 K1
st. Hughesdale 457 E13
FINUCANE
pl. Fawkner 281 F2

FIOCCHI
av. Frankston 599 B15
FIONA
ct. Blairgowrie 679 C18
ct. Cheltenham 531 D1
ct. Eltham North 288 A1
ct. Ferntree Gly 463 E2
ct. Gladstone Pk 279 B2
ct. Glen Waverley 419 K18
ct. Kealba 276 H18
ct. Keysborough 534 F11
ct. Mooroolbark 337 A11
ct. Mt Martha 656 J7
ct. Narre Warren 553 D8
ct. Ringwood 379 B3
ct. St Kilda 414 F16
ct. Somerville 645 B16
ct. Vermont 377 F20
ct. Warrandyte 333 B8
dr. Cranbourne S 603 K20
pl. Pakenham 559 F19
pl. Whittlesea 96 E17
FIR
cl. Broadmeadows 237 L12
ct. Kilsyth 381 K7
ct. Mt Waverley 419 B16
gr. Cheltenham 496 F19
st. Blackburn 376 A13
st. Bulleen 330 A17
st. Dingley Village 532 H6
st. Thomastown 241 C13
st. Whittlesea 96 D18
FIRA
ct. Narre Warren 539 A20
FIRBANK
cl. Langwarrin 601 G19
tce. Albanvale 319 A5
FIREBALL
ct. Taylors Lakes 275 H5
FIREBELL
la. Richmond 26 C13
FIRE STATION
rd. Melb Airport 235 B10
FIRESTONE
ct. Sunbury 144 C10
FIRETAIL
ct. Carrum Downs 600 L1
ct. Carrum Downs 601 A1
FIREWEED
ct. Hillside 231 L16
FIRMAN
st. Springvale S 500 A20
FIRST
av. Altona North 410 A6
av. Anglesea 713 F8
av. Aspendale 546 F9
av. Box Hill N 375 E6
av. Brunswick 325 D8
av. Chelsea Ht 547 D14
av. Cockatoo 510 J4
av. Craigieburn 150 G17
av. Dandenong N 501 J15
av. Eden Park 95 A20
av. Eden Park 125 A1
av. Hadfield 281 E11
av. Hoppers Csg 448 K6
av. Kew 372 H7
av. Melton S 268 E6
av. Moorabbin Apt 531 L4
av. Murrumbeena 457 A11
av. Pakenham 584 K3
av. Rosebud 683 K20
av. Springvale 500 G10
av. Strathmore 279 H19
av. Sunshine 365 E7
cr. Hadfield 281 D9
ct. Cranbourne 603 J6
ct. Preston 282 C19
dr. Springvale 500 G10
st. Black Rock 529 G6
st. Clayton S 499 D6
st. Geelong West 702 H3
st. Moorabbin Apt 532 A5
st. Parkdale 531 D8
st. Warrandyte 333 F1
st. W Footscray 366 F7
FIRST SETTLEMENT
dr. Sorrento 679 C15
FIRTH
la. Doncaster 330 K20
la. Doncaster 374 J1
rd. Moorooduc 643 L16
st. Doncaster 374 J1
FISCHER
st. Coburg 281 C19
st. Torquay 712 A9
FISCOM
ct. Croydon N 336 A14
ct. Mill Park 242 J12
FISHBURN
ct. Mill Park 242 D3
pl. Cranbourne W 603 H3

FISHER
av. Belmont 706 J3
av. Lalor 241 J10
cl. Berwick 554 G16
cr. Dandenong N 535 K1
ct. Altona 409 E17
ct. Bayswater N 380 F17
ct. Bentleigh E 456 L17
ct. Sunbury 143 G4
ct. Werribee 448 A6
gr. Tullamarine 278 E7
mw. Braeside 547 F3
pde. Ascot Vale 367 G3
pde. Flemington 367 G3
pde. Footscray 367 G3
pl. Kurunjang 227 D12
st. Footscray 366 L6
st. Forest Hill 376 H20
st. Gisborne 78 H13
st. Maidstone 322 K18
st. Malvern East 456 J4
FISHERIES
rd. Devon Mdw 649 D2
FISHERMANS
dr. Blind Bight 650 D8
FISHERS
la. Fitzroy 19 B16
FISHLEY
st. S Melbourne 29 L5
FISKEN
pl. Kensington 33 G11
pl. Kensington 368 D6
st. Bacchus Msh 546 F6
st. Maddingley 264 C4
st. Maddingley 264 C6
FITHIE
st. Blackburn N 375 K7
FITTIS
st. Newport 410 G3
FITZGERALD
ct. Mooroolbark 337 G11
ct. S Morang 199 D11
ct. Taylors Lakes 233 E17
rd. Derrimut 363 J12
rd. Essendon 324 D9
rd. Hallam 538 C17
rd. Laverton N 407 H6
rd. Sunshine W 363 J12
rd.n, Hallam 538 C16
st. Balwyn 374 A11
st. Ferntree Gly 464 A3
st. Mornington 641 C15
st. Ringwood E 379 E16
st. South Yarra 32 B12
st. South Yarra 414 G6
FITZGIBBON
av. Brunswick W 324 L15
cr. Caulfield N 455 J1
st. Cremorne 26 B18
st. Parkville 17 J11
FITZJOHNS
ct. Portsea 677 K1
FITZPATRICK
dr. Altona Mdw 450 L1
st. S Melbourne 30 F4
FITZROY
av. Frankston 599 A17
ct. Endeavour Hl 536 L1
ct. Endeavour Hl 537 A1
gr. Chadstone 418 F19
st. Darley 222 C9
st. Fitzroy 24 L1
st. Footscray 367 E7
st. Geelong 703 C13
st. Geelong 703 D12
st. Geelong 703 E9
st. Hadfield 281 B8
st. Laverton 407 D18
st. McKinnon 456 A18
st. Preston 282 F19
st. St Kilda 414 A14
st. Sunbury 142 B12
st.s, Altona Mdw 407 D20
FITZSIMONS
la. Eltham 287 C19
la. Lower Plenty 287 C19
la. Templestowe 331 C4
FITZWILLIAM
st. Kew 372 B12
FIVE CROWN
gr. Doncaster E 332 H12
FIVE MILE
rd. Pakenham 586 L19
FIVEWAYS
bvd. Keysborough 533 J9
FLAG
st. Kingsbury 283 J10
FLAGSTAFF
la. Taylors Hill 274 E9
la. W Melbourne 23 F3

FLAKE
ct. Diggers Rest 187 A12
FLAM
st. Frankston 600 A17
FLAME
cl. Delahey 275 C9
st. Mt Waverley 419 B16
FLAMINGO
ct. Nar Warrn S 552 F14
dr. Wantirna S 422 B17
rd. Rosebud W 698 L2
rd. Rosebud W 699 A1
FLANDERS
la. Geelong, off Swanston St 703 C12
FLANIGAN
la. Melbourne 1 K5
la. Melbourne 23 L4
FLANNERY
av. Bundoora 284 H4
ct. Brunswick W 324 G8
ct. Oak Park 279 G10
ct. Warrandyte 332 L8
ct. Warrandyte 333 A8
FLATROCK
rd. Hurstbridge 203 F15
rd. Kangaroo Grnd 247 J6
rd. Panton Hill 247 H1
FLAVIA
ct. Mt Waverley 459 E3
rd. Keysborough 534 B17
FLAX
ct. Cranbourne N 578 A4
ct. Werribee 447 E12
FLEAY
av. Badger Creek 258 D14
FLECKNEY
ct. Keysborough 534 G8
FLEET
st. Fitzroy 18 L18
st. Laverton N 407 H8
st. Mornington 640 G17
st. Mt Waverley 419 D18
st. Somerton 195 D18
FLEETWOOD
cct. Melton W 225 H19
cct. Melton W 225 H20
cr. Frankston S 626 G7
ct. Gladstone Pk 236 K20
dr. Greenvale 192 L16
dr. Greenvale 193 A16
dr. Narre Warren 553 B11
FLEMING
av. Seabrook 451 A7
cl. Endeavour Hl 538 A6
ct. Oakleigh S 497 H6
ct. Research 288 L5
ct. Seaford 600 A1
gr. Pascoe Vale 281 A15
pl. Melbourne 1 L15
pl. Melbourne 24 B9
pl. Mill Park 242 L6
pl. Mill Park 243 A6
st. Altona 408 K17
st. Brunswick W 324 L16
st. Mornington 640 A17
st. Safety Bch 686 G1
tce. Pakenham 558 K20
FLEMINGTON
cr. Werribee 446 H19
dr. Mill Park 242 H9
rd. Carlton 17 A8
rd. N Melbourne 17 A8
rd. Parkville 34 J5
st. Travancore 324 G20
FLEMMING
av. Burnside 318 D7
av. Maribyrnong 322 H16
ct. Keilor 277 A14
FLETCHER
ct. Mt Waverley 458 J3
pde. Burwood 418 F8
rd. Cranbourne S 603 K20
rd. Dandenong N 502 C17
rd. Frankston 599 B17
rd. Frankston 599 C19
rd. Mooroolbark 337 A8
st. Essendon 324 B8
st. Forest Hill 376 E20
st. Hawthorn E 372 D19
st. Moorabbin 496 G8
FLETE
av. Armadale 415 G11
FLETT
st. Preston 326 L4
FLEUR
av. Tootgarook 698 D9
ct. Boronia 424 H10
ct. Nar Warrn S 552 J17
FLIGHT
ct. Thomastown 240 H17

FLINDERS
av. Canterbury 373 G16
av. Rosebud 700 D3
ch. Pakenham 583 L1
cr. Boronia 424 G7
cr. Wyndham Va 446 G8
ct. Bundoora 242 L20
ct. Cranbourne N 577 L8
ct. Kilsyth 381 J9
ct. Lalor 240 J8
ct. Melbourne 2 A19
ct. Melbourne 24 D10
dr. Mornington 640 D12
la. Glenroy 280 L3
la. Melbourne 1 A17
la. Melbourne 2 D17
la. Melbourne 23 H12
la. Torquay 712 E2
st. Bulleen 329 L12
st. Coburg 281 C20
st. Docklands 23 G14
st. Heidelberg Ht 284 F19
st. Keilor Park 277 K14
st. McCrae 684 K17
st. Melbourne 1 B19
st. Melbourne 2 C19
st. Melbourne 23 G14
st. Melton S 268 D11
st. Mentone 530 J5
st. Mentone 531 A5
st. Mitcham 377 E9
st. Noble Park 500 D16
st. Queenscliff 708 G19
st. Rye 696 H4
st. Sunbury 143 B13
st. Taylors Hill 274 F9
st. Thornbury 326 K7
st. Thornbury 327 C8
wk. Melbourne 24 D12
FLINDERS WAY
arc. Melbourne 2 D17
FLINT
cr. Delahey 275 A16
st. Eltham 287 C13
FLINTOFF
av. Burnside 318 F9
ct. Mill Park 241 L7
st. Greensborough 286 C4
FLINTOFT
av. Toorak 415 C2
FLOCKHART
st. Abbotsford 371 A12
FLODDEN
wy. Briar Hill 286 G4
FLOODS
rd. Kangaroo Grnd 289 K10
rd. N Warrandyte 289 K10
FLORA
av. Badger Creek 258 G13
cl. Cockatoo 511 J1
cr. Smiths Gly 205 E2
ct. Chelsea Ht 547 E16
ct. Cranbourne N 578 B6
ct. Narre Warren 538 J19
ct. Ringwood 379 A4
gr. Forest Hill 420 C3
gr. Ivanhoe East 328 E16
la. Craigieburn 150 F14
rd. Clayton 458 H19
rd. Donvale 333 A20
rd. Donvale 377 B1
rd. Mt Martha 656 G7
st. Keilor 277 D14
st. Ringwood E 379 E14
FLORAL
ct. Warranwood 334 J12
gdn. Nar Warrn S 579 D1
FLORA PARK
wy. Carrum Downs 601 B7
FLOREAT
ct. Glen Waverley 419 L18
pl. Melton W 226 D17
FLORENCE
av. Berwick 553 J5
av. Clayton 459 A13
av. Donvale 376 J7
av. Emerald 469 G17
av. Frankston 599 C20
av. Kew 372 E10
av. Ringwood N 378 E3
av. Rosebud W 698 K1
av. Sassafras 426 G15
av. Upwey 466 B7
cl. Cranbourne 603 K1
cl. Reservoir 282 B3
ct. Dandenong 535 G1
ct. Wandana Ht 701 D20
ct. Werribee 447 F18
dr. Rye 696 G6
la. Sunbury 143 G19
pl. Port Melb 412 K5
rd. Cottles Br 202 K1

rd. Surrey Hills 374 B20
st. Bentleigh E 497 C2
st. Blackburn 376 D19
st. Brighton East 455 F19
st. Brunswick 325 F10
st. Burwood 418 F12
st. Coburg 325 E6
st. Essendon 323 J7
st. Glen Iris 416 L13
st. Glen Waverley 460 A3
st. Kilsyth 381 C5
st. Mentone 530 L8
st. Mentone 531 A8
st. Niddrie 278 H20
st. Noble Park 534 D3
st. Nunawading 376 D19
st. Ormond 456 G13
st. Prahran 415 B11
st. Seddon 367 A12
st. Williamstn N 410 H12
FLORET
pl. Narre Warren 553 D3
FLOREY
cr. Mulgrave 460 C18
pl. Mill Park 242 L6
FLORIANA
av. Doveton 536 J4
FLORIDA
av. Beaumaris 529 L10
av. Dingley Village 533 B8
ct. Mitcham 377 F18
ct. Moorabbin 496 C10
dr. Ferntree Gly 423 H16
st. Mt Waverley 419 H15
wy. Seaford 573 D18
FLORISTON
gr. Eltham 288 C4
rd. Boronia 424 E13
FLORIZEL
st. Ashburton 417 E13
st. Burwood 417 E13
FLOWER
ct. Grovedale 706 E13
st. Essendon 323 L8
st. Ferntree Gly 424 B19
st. Pakenham 584 J8
FLOWERDALE
ct. Nar Warrn S 579 F1
rd. Deer Park 319 F11
rd. Glen Iris 417 C12
rd. Hampton E 496 A10
FLOWERDRUM
cl. Templestowe 332 A6
FLOWERFIELD
dr. Coldstream 294 A11
FLOWERING GUM
gr. S Morang 199 J12
FLOWERS
cl. Roxburgh Pk 194 C14
st. Caulfield S 455 K7
FLOWERVALE
pl. Brookfield 267 L8
rd. Noble Park 534 E2
FLYING FOX
tce. S Morang 199 J13
FLYING STAR
wk. Skye 575 H15
FLYNN
cr. Coolaroo 238 E5
ct. Frankston 628 G1
ct. Nar Warrn S 552 E15
st. Ferntree Gly 424 J19
st. Springvale 500 B12
st. Springvale 500 C10
FOAM
av. Blairgowrie 679 E20
av. Torquay 712 C3
rd. Fingal 697 L20
st. Aspendale 546 C3
st. Elwood 454 F7
st. Hampton 495 B9
st. Mornington 640 G16
st. Parkdale 531 E14
st. Rosebud 684 D20
FOCH
av. Coburg 325 D7
rd. Silvan 384 L9
rd. Silvan 385 A10
st. Box Hill S 418 K3
st. Ormond 456 B11
st. Reservoir 283 B16
FODEN
av. Campbellfield 194 H20
st. Brunswick W 325 A15
FOGARTY
av. Yarraville 366 F19
ct. Oakleigh 458 C9
pde. Blairgowrie 679 H20
st. N Melbourne 34 G14
FOKKER
st. Strathmr Ht 279 D9

FOLEY
av. Preston 327 D
pl. Bentleigh E 497 A
st. Eltham 287 D1
st. Kew 371 H1
FOLEYS
rd. Deer Park 318 J2
FOLKESTONE
cr. Beaumaris 530 F
cr. Springvale S 499 H2
rd. Glen Waverley 419 K1
FOLKSTONE
cr. Ferntree Gly 463 E
FOLLET
st. Torquay 712 B
FOLLETT
ct. Carrum Downs 575 C1
rd. Cheltenham 531 C
FONCECA
st. Mordialloc 532 E1
FONTAIN
ct. Werribee 448 D1
FONTAINE
st. Grovedale 706 B1
st. Pascoe Vale S 324 H
tce. Nar Warrn N 538 D
FONTAYNE
ct. Frankston S 627 B1
FONTEIN
st. W Footscray 366 D
FONTEYN
dr. Wantirna S 462 B
FOORD
la. Dromana 685 D
FOOT
st. Frankston 627 D
st. Frankston S 627 D
st. Frankston S 627 D
FOOTE
la. Albert Park 29 D1
st. Albert Park 29 B1
st. Albert Park 413 A
st. Brighton 454 H1
st. Dromana 685 J
st. Templestowe 330 G
st. Templstw Lr 330 G
FOOTHILLS
av. McCrae 684 K1
FOOTSCRAY
rd. Docklands 23 A1
rd. Docklands 368 K1
rd. W Melbourne 367 L1
rd. W Melbourne 368 K1
FOOTT
rd. Beaconsfld Up 541 G
FORAN
gr. Oakleigh S 458 F1
FORBES
av. Lynbrook 551 D1
cl. Knoxfield 463 C
ct. Attwood 237 E1
ct. Bayswater N 380 E1
ct. Mill Park 242 D
dr. Aspendale Gdn 546 H
gr. Oak Park 280 D1
pl. Balwyn N 374 A
st. Essendon 324 B
st. Rye 697 B1
st. Safety Bch 686 H
st. Warrandyte 289 J1
FORD
av. Oakleigh 458 A1
av. Sunshine N 321 B1
cr. Thornbury 327 H1
ct. Mill Park 242 D7
ct. Noble Park N 501 C1
ct. Truganina 405 G14
rd. Altona 408 K14
rd. Emerald 510 D6
st. Brunswick 325 D11
st. Clifton Hill 20 F6
st. Footscray 367 F7
st. Ivanhoe 327 J11
st. Newport 410 H8
st. Preston 282 F20
st. Ringwood 378 G15
st. Rye 680 F20
st. Southbank 23 D19
FORDE
ct. Narre Warren 539 F16
ct. Sunbury 143 H8
FORDHAM
av. Camberwell 417 C2
ct. Richmond 26 D12
ct. Rowville 503 C1
ct. Springvale S 534 B1
rd. Reservoir 283 C10
st. Newtown 702 B10
FORDHAMS
rd. Eltham 287 G15

FORDHOLM
rd. Hampton Pk...551 D9
rd. Hawthorn...371 K20
rd. Hawthorn...415 K2
FORDS
rd. Gruyere...342 H2
FORDSON
rd. Campbellfield...239 D12
FORDYCE
rd. Mt Dandenong...426 J3
rd. Olinda...426 J3
st. Cheltenham...497 B20
FORE
st. Whittlesea...96 L20
FORENSIC
dr. Macleod...284 H13
FORESHORE
st. Frankston...599 A20
FOREST
ct. Croydon...379 J3
ct. Gladstone Pk...237 A17
ct. Glen Waverley...459 J8
ct. Ringwood...335 A18
ct. Templestowe...332 C13
dr. Frankston N...599 K9
dr. Mt Martha...669 D9
dr. Somerville...644 K17
pl. Templestowe...332 B13
rd. Belgrave...466 J10
rd. Blackburn...376 D20
rd. Boronia...424 H13
rd. Boronia...424 H14
rd. Boronia...424 J13
rd. Ferntree Gly...424 J18
rd. Ferntree Gly...464 G4
rd. Ferntree Gly...464 H2
rd. Forest Hill...376 D20
rd. Mt Evelyn...340 D19
rd. The Basin...425 A12
rd. Wesburn...348 D17
st. Collingwood...20 A11
st. Greensborough...244 H19
st. Monbulk...428 E20
st. Monbulk...468 E1
st. Whittlesea...96 F19
st. Yarra Glen...208 K17
st. Yarra Glen...209 A17
tr. Kallista...467 H9
vw. Bundoora...284 E9
wk. Ringwood N...377 L4
wy. Kilsyth...380 K5
FOREST GLEN
av. Blackburn S...419 L6
FOREST OAK
dr. Up Fntree Gly...464 K7
FOREST PARK
rd. Dingley Village...533 C8
rd. Upwey...465 E13
FOREST RED GUM
dr. Mickleham...149 B3
FORGE
cl. Maribyrnong...322 J16
la. Heidelberg...329 A8
rd. Mt Evelyn...339 G16
FORMAN
st. Westmeadows...236 K14
FORMBY
cl. Wantirna...422 C11
FORMOSA
ct. Narre Warren...553 G11
st. Newtown...702 C8
FORREST
av. Sorrento...679 C16
ct. Anglesea...713 G7
ct. Endeavour Hl...538 A8
ct. Sandringham...495 K17
ct. Toorak...415 G5
hill, South Yarra...32 E7
hill, South Yarra...414 H4
pl. Taylors Lakes...233 D18
st. Albion...364 F1
st. Ardeer...364 A1
st. Ardeer...364 F1
st. Bentleigh E...457 F18
st. Geelong...703 D14
st. Melton S...268 J12
st. Spotswood...411 A1
st. Sunbury...142 L12
st. Sunbury...143 A12
st. Sunshine...364 F1
st. Sunshine...365 A2
st. Sunshine W...364 A1
st. Yarraville...367 A14
FORRESTER
st. Essendon...323 B6
st. Essendon...323 G7
wk. Nar Warrn S...578 H1
FORREST HILL
gr. Lysterfield S...503 L14

FORSTER
av. Frankston N...600 C11
av. Malvern East...416 L20
ct. Bentleigh E...456 L17
ct. Pascoe Vale S...324 F1
ct. Sunbury...143 F2
rd. Mt Waverley...459 B10
st. Heidelberg Ht...328 E7
st. Mitcham...377 J15
st. Noble Park...500 D17
st. South Yarra...32 E11
st. South Yarra...414 H5
st. Williamstown...411 D17
FORSYTH
cl. Burnside...318 D7
ct. Cranbourne N...578 F8
ct. Narre Warren...552 G1
pl. Rowville...502 H4
rd. Hoppers Csg...406 A18
rd. Hoppers Csg...450 B1
rd. Laverton...406 A18
rd. Point Cook...450 B1
rd. Truganina...406 B16
st. Frankston...599 K19
FORT
st. Mt Waverley...419 H16
FORTESCUE
av. Seaford...599 D10
ct. Wantirna...422 F10
gr. Vermont S...420 H11
FORTUNA
av. Balwyn N...373 D3
av. Croydon...379 J8
st. Clayton...459 B19
FORTUNE
av. Lilydale...339 B11
av. Mt Evelyn...339 B11
st. Box Hill N...375 E11
FORUM
pl. Tullamarine...278 K4
FORWOOD
wy. Roxburgh Pk...194 D16
FOSBERY
av. Caulfield N...415 C20
cr. View Bank...285 G16
FOSSICKERS
wy. Warrandyte...333 G3
FOSTER
av. Glen Huntly...456 B9
av. St Kilda...414 C18
cr. Knoxfield...462 L3
cr. Knoxfield...463 A3
ct. Thomastown...240 F13
la. Aspendale, off Foster St...546 D7
pl. Richmond...26 L11
rd. Eltham...288 C4
rd. Olinda...427 J18
st. Anglesea...713 F6
st. Aspendale...546 D7
st. Dallas...238 G10
st. Dandenong...535 K10
st. Dandenong...536 A10
st. Elsternwick...455 C5
st. McKinnon...456 C17
st. St Kilda...414 D17
st. S Geelong...702 L13
st. S Geelong...703 A13
st. Werribee...446 J16
st.e, Dandenong...536 C9
FOSTERS
ct. Cranbourne N...578 G9
rd. Keilor Park...277 K15
FOTINI
gdn. Bundoora...242 L20
FOTIS
ct. Oak Park...279 G11
FOULDS
ct. Berwick...553 L8
ct. Montrose...382 A8
FOULKES
st. Alphington...327 K19
FOUNDRY
la. Maribyrnong...367 C2
rd. Sunshine...321 C19
FOUNTAIN
ct. Kew...371 H5
ct. Werribee...446 H19
dr. Narre Warren...538 H20
FOUNTAINE
av. Malvern East...457 A3
FOURTH
av. Altona North...409 K7
av. Anglesea...713 C10
av. Aspendale...546 F10
av. Brunswick...325 D9
av. Chelsea Ht...547 E13
av. Cockatoo...510 H5
av. Eden Park...95 B20
av. Eden Park...95 C6
av. Hoppers Csg...448 L5
av. Pakenham...584 K2
av. Rosebud...683 L18
av. Rowville...462 E19
av. Sunshine...365 E9
cr. Hadfield...281 C8
cr. Hadfield...281 C10
dr. Springvale...500 J12
st. Beaumaris...529 H7
st. Black Rock...529 H7
st. Parkdale...531 D10
FOWLER
cr. Newport...410 H9
ct. Gisborne...78 K18
ct. Mill Park...242 B5
ct. Rosebud...684 F14
rd. Dandenong S...536 F16
rd. Rowville...502 L7
st. Bonbeach...573 B1
st. Box Hill S...418 G3
st. Breakwater...703 F20
st. Chelsea...547 A19
st. Coburg...325 J3
st. Hoppers Csg...405 A19
FOWLERS
la. Geelong...703 D12
FOX
cl. Hampton Pk...551 D9
cl. Highett...496 E15
ct. Dandenong S...535 J13
ct. Jacana...237 K19
ct. Sunbury...143 B9
ct. Sunshine W...364 G8
rd. Beaconsfld Up...542 L9
rd. Nar Warrn N...538 K9
rd. Smiths Gly...206 G5
st. Dandenong...536 D12
st. St Albans...276 A19
FOXCROFT
ct. Sunshine W...364 B9
FOXEYS
rd. Dromana...670 G11
rd. Tuerong...670 G11
FOXGLOVE
ct. Cranbourne N...578 C5
ct. View Bank...285 K20
la. Craigieburn...150 E14
pl. Epping...198 F20
FOXLEY
st. Glen Waverley...420 F15
FOXTON
la. Melbourne...1 G19
la. Melbourne...24 B11
pl. Roxburgh Pk...194 A13
st. St Albans...320 D5
FOXWOOD
dr. Point Cook...450 E7
pl. Somerville...645 A16
FOXZAMI
cr. Epping...198 C20
cr. Epping...242 C1
FOY
av. Chelsea...546 H16
ct. Glen Waverley...420 J15
la. Chelsea...546 H16
la. Yellingbo...387 F12
FRALLON
cr. Frankston...600 A15
FRAME
av. Tecoma...466 D11
FRAMPTON
st. St Kilda...414 E15
FRAN
cr. View Bank...329 G1
ct. Glen Waverley...420 D19
ct. Ringwood...378 L5
ct. Templstw Lr...330 D7
ct. Werribee...446 K16
st. Glenroy...279 G6
FRANCES
av. Greensborough...286 D10
av. Montrose...382 C11
av. Vermont...421 E2
av. Yarra Glen...209 C19
cr. Cranbourne N...578 F10
ct. Cranbourne...604 B5
dr. Mt Martha...656 G9
dr. Sunshine N...321 A15
st. Heathmont...378 H19
st. Highett...495 H15
st. Springvale S...499 G18
st. The Basin...425 A11
FRANCESCA
ct. Frankston...628 E9
st. Mont Albert N...374 D9
FRANCESCO
dr. Dandenong N...502 B12
st. Bentleigh E...456 J20
FRANCINE
ct. Narre Warren...538 F16

FRANCIS
av. Newcomb...704 B16
bvd. Sunbury...144 D14
cr. Ferntree Gly...424 D19
cr. Glen Iris...417 A16
cr. Mt Evelyn...338 K14
ct. Narre Warren...538 L17
gr. Thornbury...326 L11
gr. Thornbury...327 A11
la. Kensington...33 C10
st. Ascot Vale...324 A18
st. Belmont...706 H6
st. Blackburn...375 L14
st. Brighton East...455 D15
st. Brooklyn...366 A16
st. Clayton...498 L1
st. Coburg...281 B20
st. Cockatoo...471 F17
st. Collingwood...20 A14
st. Dandenong S...535 J13
st. Dromana...686 A7
st. Frankston...599 G17
st. Hadfield...280 J9
st. Heidelberg Ht...328 E6
st. Keilor Park...277 L15
st. Melbourne...1 A15
st. Melbourne...23 G11
st. Melton S...268 H4
st. Mordialloc...532 A16
st. Mt Waverley...419 G20
st. Oak Park...279 K12
st. Prahran...32 H17
st. Prahran...414 K9
st. Richmond...26 K11
st. Rye...696 K10
st. Sandringham...495 C13
st. Seaford...599 H2
st. S Melbourne...29 L4
st. Tecoma...466 D12
st. Warrandyte...333 F2
st. Werribee...447 H17
st. Yarraville...366 A16
st. Yarraville...366 K17
FRANCIS BRIGGS
rd. Melb Airport...235 K14
FRANCISCAN
av. Frankston...628 B12
FRANCIS WALTON
rd. Mill Park...242 D3
FRANCONIA
ct. Mulgrave...501 D5
FRANGIPANI
cl. Endeavour Hl...537 G6
ct. Port Melb...412 H3
la. Maribyrnong...322 H16
wy. Bundoora...242 F14
FRANK
av. Clayton S...498 J4
ct. Rowville...463 K19
st. Balwyn N...373 K5
st. Belmont...702 H16
st. Box Hill S...418 H5
st. Coburg...325 E3
st. Dallas...238 L10
st. Doncaster...374 L3
st. Eltham...288 B5
st. Frankston...599 H18
st. Glen Waverley...460 C5
st. Lalor...241 B8
st. Mornington...640 J19
st. Newtown...702 D12
st. Noble Park...500 H20
st. Safety Bch...686 H1
st. Sunshine W...364 C2
st. Vermont...421 H2
FRANKCOM
st. Blackburn...375 G15
FRANK FORD
st. Northcote...326 J15
FRANKLAND
ct. Wyndham Va...446 G8
FRANKLIN
av. Chelsea...546 J17
av. Roxburgh Pk...194 A10
bvd. Hoppers Csg...449 A4
ct. Craigieburn...150 C17
ct. Frankston...599 G19
ct. Glen Waverley...459 J4
la. Chelsea...546 J17
pl. Caroline Spr...318 B4
pl. Delahey...275 B11
pl. W Melbourne...23 D5
rd. Doncaster E...375 K1
rd. Lalor...240 H10
rd. Portsea...677 L7
st. Coburg...325 K5
st. Eltham...287 G11
st. Maddingley...263 K1
st. Melbourne...1 G1
st. Melbourne...1 K1
st. Melbourne...23 H3
st. Mentone...531 B6
st. Moorabbin...496 H9
st. Mornington...640 F12
st. Newport...411 B9
FRANKLYN
st. Huntingdale...458 G16
st. Oakleigh E...458 G16
FRANKS
gr. Kew...372 A11
wy. Cranbourne N...578 E10
FRANKSTON
dr. Endeavour Hl...502 L12
fwy. Frankston...599 G18
fwy. Frankston N...599 G18
fwy. Seaford...599 G7
st. Reservoir...282 H14
FRANKSTON-DANDENONG
rd. Bangholme...549 K20
rd. Bangholme...575 A14
rd. Carrum Downs...574 J18
rd. Dandenong S...536 A20
rd. Dandenong S...549 K20
rd. Frankston...599 G12
rd. Frankston N...599 G12
rd. Lyndhurst...549 K20
rd. Lyndhurst...575 A14
rd. Seaford...599 G12
FRANKSTON-FLINDERS
rd. Frankston...627 G6
rd. Frankston S...627 G6
rd. Frankston S...627 K17
rd. Somerville...644 G7
FRANKSTON GARDENS
dr. Carrum Downs...574 D19
FRANK WORRELL
dr. Mornington...657 B2
FRANLEIGH
dr. Narre Warren...539 A17
FRASER
av. Anglesea...713 D3
av. Beaconsfld Up...541 G11
av. Edithvale...546 H13
cl. Epping...197 H15
cl. Mill Park...242 F7
cr. Wantirna S...462 E1
ct. Cranbourne N...578 G8
ct. Jacana...237 H16
ct. Sunbury...143 C13
pl. Forest Hill...420 G3
rd. Clayton S...498 J11
st. Airport W...278 K14
st. Airport W...279 A14
st. Bentleigh E...456 L19
st. Brunswick...325 C11
st. Coburg...281 E20
st. Dandenong N...502 C19
st. Diamond Ck...245 K12
st. Glen Waverley...460 A8
st. Herne Hill...701 J3
st. Hoppers Csg...448 J1
st. Malvern...416 A13
st. Melton S...268 J6
st. Middle Park...413 J12
st. Ormond...456 A12
st. Queenscliff...708 G19
st. Richmond...371 A17
st. Sunshine...364 J2
st. Sunshine...365 A2
st. Yarraville...367 D18
FRATER
ct. Doncaster E...332 F16
pl. Mill Park...242 L8
st. Kew East...372 J3
FRAWLEY
rd. Eumemmerring...537 A12
rd. Hallam...537 G14
st. Frankston...599 L20
FRAYNE
ct. Highton...705 K7
FRAZER
av. Altona...408 L14
FREAME
st. Yarraville...366 H17
FREDA
av. Cheltenham...496 L18
ct. Blackburn S...419 G5
ct. Eltham North...245 E19
ct. Narre Warren...539 B14
ct. St Albans...320 F11
ct. Wheelers Hill...460 L17
st. Broadmeadows...238 D19
st. Hughesdale...457 E10
FREDERIC
dr. Ringwood...379 A3
FREDERICK
ct. Werribee...448 H9
ri. Nar Warrn S...552 H7
st. Anglesea...713 E7
st. Balwyn...373 E10
st. Blackburn...375 H14

st. Brunswick 325 E11
st. Bulleen 329 L17
st. Caulfield S 455 L12
st. Croydon 380 C9
st. Dandenong S 536 A14
st. Doncaster 374 L2
st. E Geelong 703 H10
st. Fawkner 281 J8
st. Ferntree Gly 424 J15
st. Heidelberg Ht 328 G5
st. Malvern 416 B12
st. Northcote 326 J15
st. Thomastown 241 D15
st. Tottenham 365 J9
st. Windsor 414 H12
st. Yarraville 367 D17
st. Hawthorn, off Wakefield St 372 A16

FREDERICO
st. Highett 495 J11

FRED McCUBBIN
cl. Diamond Ck 245 A13

FREDMAN
ct. Dingley Village 532 K6

FREE
pl. Sunbury 113 D12
st. Yarraville 367 A15

FREEBURGH
ct. Meadow Ht 238 B4

FREEDMAN
av. Boronia 424 B8

FREELAND
gr. Jacana 237 K20

FREELANDS
dr. Mt Eliza 642 J3

FREEMAN
av. Burnside 318 D7
cr. Mill Park 242 E8
ct. Endeavour Hl 538 A5
dr. Glenroy 280 G10
pl. Langwarrin 629 B6
st. Balwyn 373 D10
st. Campbellfield 239 E4
st. Caulfield 455 K5
st. Fitzroy N 19 A5
st. Hawthorn E 372 F17
st. Richmond 26 A8
st. Ringwood E 378 L10
st. Ringwood E 379 A10
st. Sunshine 365 A7
st. Wheelers Hill 461 A8
st. Yarraville 366 H16

FREEMANS
rd. Altona North 409 F1
rd. Mt Eliza 626 A9

FREEMANTLE
dr. Wantirna S 421 L14

FREESIA
ct. Hoppers Csg 405 D16

FREGON
rd. Clayton 458 L19

FREIGHT
dr. Somerton 195 D15
rd. Tullamarine 278 H1

FREIGHTER
rd. Moorabbin 497 E13

FREMANTLE
rd. Sunbury 142 J12

FREMONT
cl. Bulleen 329 K9
pde. Sunshine W 364 E7
st. Heathmont 378 K15

FRENCH
av. Brunswick E 325 L14
av. Edithvale 546 H12
av. Northcote 327 C15
cl. Mooroolbark 337 J11
ct. Watsonia 285 D8
rd. Greenvale 192 K14
st. Camberwell 417 J6
st. Coburg N 281 E16
st. Croydon 336 G18
st. Elsternwick 454 L3
st. Footscray 367 E9
st. Geelong West 702 D5
st. Lalor 241 D11
st. Mt Waverley 459 B5
st. Noble Park 500 L20
st. Ringwood E 378 L11
st. Rye 696 L7
st. Thomastown 241 D13

FRENSHAM
rd. Macleod 285 F11
rd. Watsonia 285 F11

FRESHFIELD
av. Mooroolbark 337 L16
av. Wantirna 422 A10

FRESNO
st. Altona 409 D17

FREW
av. Frankston 599 L16

FREY
st. Pascoe Vale 280 E18

FREYER
st. Williamstown 411 C13

FREYNE
st. Wonga Park 335 D4

FRIAR
pl. Melton W 226 D17
st. Blairgowrie 696 C6

FRIARS
ct. Doncaster E 331 L19
rd. Moorabbin 496 L12

FRIBOURG
ct. Ivanhoe East 328 K15

FRICKER
av. Greensborough 286 D9

FRIEDA
ct. Ferntree Gly 464 C6
st. Dromana 686 D7

FRIEND
ct. Mill Park 242 L7
st. Mont Albert N 374 C7

FRIENDLY
ct. Kilsyth 381 A8

FRIENDSHIP
av. Mill Park 242 D3
cl. Cranbourne W 603 G2
ct. Keilor Lodge 276 A3
sq. Cheltenham 497 A17

FRIER
av. Reservoir 283 C16

FRIESIAN
ct. Belmont 706 C6

FRIMLEY
rd. Surrey Hills 374 A16

FRIMMELL
wy. Portsea 678 A4

FRINTON
st. Dromana 686 D9

FRIPP
av. Fitzroy N, off Rushall Cr 326 F20

FRISINA
ct. Nunawading 376 D13

FRISWELL
pl. Frankston 627 B4

FRITH
rd. Gisborne 78 K8
st. Brunswick 325 B13

FRITZLAFF
ct. Berwick 554 L9

FROBISHER
ct. Frankston 628 E10
st. Melton 226 L16

FRODSHAM
rd. Ringwood 335 B19

FROGGITTS
la. Werribee 448 C19

FROGLEY
cl. Badger Creek 258 E13

FROGMORE
cr. Pk Orchards 333 H20
rd. Carnegie 456 L9

FROGNAL
dr. Noble Park N 501 D13
mw. Berwick 554 D19

FROGNALL
pl. Canterbury 372 K15

FROME
av. Frankston 627 C4
st. Croydon 336 F20

FROMELLES
ct. Wantirna S 462 F3

FROMER
st. Bentleigh 496 D4

FROMHOLD
dr. Doncaster 331 E18

FROND
dr. The Patch 468 E8

FRONTAGE
wy. Mornington 640 J10

FROST
ct. Bundoora 242 F17
ct. Dandenong N 502 A13
dr. Delahey 275 B15
rd. Gisborne 78 C17

F R SMITH
dr. Burnley 371 F20

FRUDAL
cr. Knoxfield 462 K5

FRUEHAUF
ct. Coolaroo 194 F18

FRY
ct. Clarinda 498 G11

FRYE
st. Watsonia N 285 G3

FRYER
ct. Forest Hill 420 C3

FRYERS
rd. Belmont 705 H4
rd. Highton 705 H4

FUCHSIA
av. Springvale 500 J12
ct. Narre Warren 553 E10
ct. Newcomb 704 C16
ct. Wheelers Hill 460 G14
pl. Meadow Ht 193 H19
st. Blackburn 375 F16
st. Ferntree Gly 423 L18

FUGE
st. Highett 495 K12

FUGOSIA
st. Doveton 536 K13

FUJI
cr. Mornington 640 K18

FULFORD
rd. Wonga Park 291 K13

FULHAM
av. South Yarra 32 K9
av. South Yarra 414 L5
cl. Frankston S 627 F9
cl. Hampton Pk 551 D5
ct. Endeavour Hl 537 C2
ct. Grovedale 706 B10
ct. Hoppers Csg 405 A16
ct. Keysborough 534 D8
gr. Reservoir 282 F14
pl. Melbourne 1 L17
pl. Melbourne 24 C10
rd. Alphington 327 G19
rd. Rowville 462 H18

FULLARD
rd. Narre Warren 552 L7

FULLARTON
rd. Airport W 278 K18
rd. Keilor Park 277 H15

FULLBROOK
dr. Sunbury 142 K3

FULLER
av. Glen Iris 417 B15
ct. Hopetoun Park 265 K8
ct. Sunbury 143 H4
rd. Mt Evelyn 338 L14
rd. Mt Evelyn 339 A14
rd. Ravenhall 318 G14
rd. Ripponlea 454 H2
st. Belgrave 466 G17
st. Bulleen 329 J17
st. Caulfield S 455 D12
st. Diamond Ck 245 F10
st. Essendon 323 L3
st. Mitcham 377 F17

FULLWOOD
dr. Sunbury 142 G8
pde. Doncaster E 332 G15

FULMAR
st. Carrum Downs 600 D5

FULTON
av. Mornington 656 D1
cl. Diamond Ck 246 A6
cr. Burwood 419 B7
ct. Brunswick E 326 C14
dr. Derrimut 363 E13
rd. Blackburn S 419 D5
rd. Mt Eliza 626 F18
rt. Sunshine N 321 A9
st. Armadale 415 C11
st. Clayton 458 F17
st. Oakleigh S 458 F17
st. St Kilda E 414 J14

FULTONS
rd. Baxter 628 F20

FULVIEW
ct. Blackburn 376 C17
ct. Templestowe 331 A5
pl. Springvale S 499 F18

FULWOOD
ct. St Albans 275 J17
pl. Mulgrave 500 L4

FUMINA
ct. Meadow Ht 238 B6

FUNNELL
rd. Beaconsfld Up 542 K14

FUNSTON
ct. Pakenham 584 E4
st. Berwick 554 L10

FURLONG
ct. Endeavour Hl 503 L20
rd. Deer Park 319 E11
rd. St Albans 319 E11
rd. St Albans 319 L10
rd. St Albans 320 C11
rd. Sunshine N 320 H11
rd. Sunshine N 321 A12

FURMSTON
la. Healesville 213 H19

FURNEAUX
ct. Frankston 628 C10
gr. Bulleen 329 G17
gr. St Kilda E 414 L20

FURNELL
ct. Toorak 415 C7
wy. Ringwood N 334 K19

FURNESS
ct. Berwick 554 E11
st. Blackburn 375 K18

FURNEW
st. Springvale 500 A9

FURPHY
ct. Berwick 554 G18

FURY
ct. Clayton S 499 C10

FURZE
ct. Cranbourne W 577 J17

FURZER
st. Preston 282 C15
st. Reservoir 282 C15

FUSCO
tce. Berwick 554 A18

FUSSELL
rd. Montrose 381 F13

FUTURA
rd. Keysborough 535 C9

FYANS
st. Fyansford 701 F4
st. S Geelong 702 K13
st. Yarraville 367 A18

FYANSFORD
st. Newtown 702 C7

FYFE
av. Ringwood 378 G6
dr. Templstw Lr 330 H14
pl.n, Geelong, off Corio St 703 D7
pl.s, Geelong, off Corio St 703 D7
st. Reservoir 283 B6

FYFFE
st. Berwick 554 F11
st. Diamond Ck 245 K12
st. Thornbury 326 B6

G

GABBA
ct. Anglesea 713 F4

GABLE
la. Warburton 349 J4

GABO
ct. Endeavour Hl 537 D3

GABONIA
av. Watsonia 285 G9

GABRIEL
av. Malvern East 457 E1

GABRIELLA
ct. Cranbourne N 578 E10
ct. Ringwood N 378 D6

GABRIELLE
cl. Werribee 448 B17
cr. Gladstone Pk 279 D2
ct. Bayswater N 380 D16
ct. Ferntree Gly 464 B1
ct. Hampton Pk 551 L6

GADD
st. Northcote 326 E11
st. Oakleigh 458 B15

GADSDEN
st. Altona North 365 E20

GAEL
ct. Mernda 156 A13

GAELYNE
ct. Warranwood 334 J15

GAETANA
st. Avondale Ht 322 E15

GAFFNEY
st. Coburg 281 B18
st. Pascoe Vale 280 F17
st. Strathmore 280 C17

GAHAN
ct. Toorak 415 D3

GAHNIA
cl. Ringwood N 334 H19

GAIL
ct. Albion 320 H18
ct. Dingley Village 532 L4
st. Newcomb 704 E16

GAINE
ct. Bayswater N 379 H17
rd. Dandenong S 550 L8

GAINFORD
ct. Greenvale 192 L18
ct. Hoppers Csg 447 L1

GAINSBOROUGH
av. Wheelers Hill 460 L1
pl. Melton W 225 L1
rd. Mentone 531 K
st. Doncaster E 331 L1

GAINSFORD
wy. Burnside 318 E

GAIR
cl. Berwick 554 G1
ct. Glen Iris 417 J1

GAIRLOCH
av. Jan Juc 711 D1
dr. Frankston 599 G1
gr. Newtown 701 K1

GAIRLOCK
ct. Doncaster 331 A1

GAIRNS
ct. Croydon 379 J
rd. Wesburn 347 F

GAIRS
ct. Clayton S 498 H

GALA
pl. Keilor Dn 275 L1

GALADA
wy. Brunswick E 326 B1

GALAGHER
st. Belgrave 466 G1

GALAH
st. Cockatoo 471 H1

GALAHAD
cr. Glen Waverley 420 K1

GALASHIELS
tce. Greenvale 192 J2

GALA SUPREME
cl. Mordialloc 532 C1

GALATEA
st. Diamond Ck 245 G1

GALAXY
ct. Whittington 704 C1
wy. Sunbury 143 E1

GALE
ct. Lysterfield 464 D1
ct. Yarra Glen 209 A1
st. Aspendale 546 C
st. Brunswick E 325 K1

GALEKA
st. Coburg N 281 D1

GALENA
cr. Kings Park 275 A1

GALILEE
bvd. Melton W 226 D1
cr. Mill Park 242 J1
ct. Mt Martha 656 J
ct. New Gisborne 79 D
ct. Rye 697 B1

GALLAGHER
pl. Grovedale 706 G1
pl. Melbourne 1 B1
pl. Melbourne 23 J

GALLAGHERS
rd. Glen Waverley 460 H

GALLANT
st. Footscray 367 E

GALLATLYS
la. Warrandyte 289 E1

GALLEMONDA PARK
rd. Kallista 468 A1
rd. Menzies Ck 468 A1

GALLERY
pl. Mt Waverley 459 B
pl. Point Cook 450 K1

GALLERY GATE
rd. Yallambie 285 L1

GALLI
ct. Dandenong S 550 K
ct. Templstw Lr 330 F

GALLICA
cl. Niddrie 322 K

GALLIPOLI
pde. Croydon 379 L
pde. Pascoe Vale S 324 H

GALLIVAN
rd. New Gisborne 79 E

GALLOWAY
ct. Taylors Lakes 275 H
dr. Nar Warrn S 578 L
gr. Bayswater N 380 E17
pl. Caroline Spr 318 D
st. Dandenong N 501 F1

GALLUS
cl. Vermont 421 G
ct. Bundoora 242 J17

GALOS
pl. Noble Park N 500 L7

GALOVAC
cl. Donvale 332 G1

GALT
st. Box Hill N 374 L7

rd. Cranbourne W....577 H17
st. Frankston S.......627 E8
GENOA
av. Bonbeach..........573 B3
av. Reservoir..........283 F12
ct. Bangholme 549 H14
ct. Coolaroo...........238 D7
ct. Frankston..........600 D18
ct. Mt Waverley......459 G3
ct. Templstw Lr.......329 K8
pl. Deer Park..........319 D11
st. Dandenong N.....502 A10
st. Moorabbin.........496 J10
st. Parkdale............531 D13
wy. Cranbourne W....577 F15
GENT
st. Yarraville...........366 G16
GENTLE
st. Clayton 498 G1
GENTLE ANNIE
dr. Blind Bight.........650 B9
GENTLES
av. Campbellfield 239 A11
GENTZEN
dr. Wyndham Va 446 G15
GEOFFREY
ct. Cranbourne.......577 L17
ct. Frankston..........626 L3
ct. Lower Plenty......287 B17
ct. Narre Warren 538 J13
dr. Kilsyth 381 C9
st. Blairgowrie.........696 C3
st. Thomastown......241 C15
GEOFREY
st. Frankston..........626 L3
GEORDY
cl. Wantirna S.........462 A1
GEORGE
av. Hallam...............537 F14
cct. Bundoora..........283 L4
ct. Greensborough ..286 E7
ct. S Morang............243 G2
la. St Kilda.............414 B14
pde. Melbourne............2 L17
pde. Melbourne...........24 H8
rd. Healesville.........257 K2
rd. Silvan................385 B13
rd. Vermont S 421 C9
st. Anglesea............713 E6
st. Ashwood 417 L14
st. Bacchus Msh 222 B15
st. Beaconsfield 555 C14
st. Belmont.............702 H19
st. Bentleigh E.........456 J15
st. Blackburn 375 L15
st. Brunswick..........325 H14
st. Camberwell........417 D7
st. Caulfield N 415 C16
st. Clifton Hill 20 E3
st. Cockatoo 511 D9
st. Cranbourne.........578 D18
st. Dandenong 535 K9
st. Diamond Ck.......245 L10
st. Doncaster 330 L16
st. Doncaster E 331 G18
st. Dromana............686 A6
st. E Melbourne 25 F8
st. E Warburton 306 L18
st. Ferntree Gly 464 D2
st. Fitzroy..................25 D1
st. Fitzroy N 19 E8
st. Flemington...........33 H1
st. Flemington.........324 D20
st. Frankston...........627 A3
st. Geelong West.....702 D8
st. Glenroy..............279 K9
st. Gruyere..............342 L8
st. Hampton Pk........551 D10
st. Hawthorn...........372 B17
st. Highett...............495 L13
st. Lilydale 338 G5
st. Maidstone..........322 J19
st. Malvern East......416 E19
st. Mont Albert........374 F13
st. Moonee Pnd 323 J11
st. Mooroolbark 337 B19
st. Mordialloc..........531 H17
st. Mornington.........640 C20
st. Mt Evelyn...........338 L18
st. Mt Evelyn...........339 A18
st. Murrumbeena 457 D13
st. Newtown 702 D8
st. Niddrie...............322 L3
st. Noble Park..........500 G19
st. Northcote...........326 G18
st. N Melbourne.........34 H7
st. Oakleigh.............458 C13
st. Olinda 426 H8
st. Preston..............282 C19
st. Reservoir............282 H11
st. Richmond............26 G15
st. Rye....................697 B4
st. Safety Bch..........686 H2
st. St Albans...........276 A18
st. Sandringham 495 K19
st. Scoresby 462 B5
st. Somerton...........194 G17
st. Somerville..........644 K15
st. Sorrento 678 J8
st. S Melbourne 29 F2
st. Spotswood 410 L1
st. Sunshine 365 D1
st. Sunshine 365 D2
st. Templstw Lr........330 J16
st. Up Fntree Gly 465 C10
st. Upwey 466 A15
st. Wandin N...........340 J15
st. Windsor...............31 J20
st. Windsor.............414 D10
st. Yarra Jctn 346 J15
st. Yarraville...........367 A15
GEORGE BASS
av. Endeavour Hl 537 H10
ct. Skye 575 H15
GEORGE BENJAMIN
ct. Seabrook 450 K8
GEORGE CHUDLEIGH
dr. Hallam 538 D14
GEORGE GREEVES
pl. Hoppers Csg......447 K1
GEORGE KNOX
dr. Rowville............502 B6
GEORGE RAE
av. Harkaway...........540 E12
GEORGES
rd. Olinda................427 F3
rd. Ringwood 378 G9
rd. Sherbrooke 466 J1
rd. The Patch...........467 L5
GEORGETTE
cr. Endeavour Hl 537 J3
GEORGIA
ct. Ferntree Gly 463 L6
pl. Kealba...............276 J19
GEORGIA MAE
ct. Rowville.............503 B6
GEORGIAN
ct. Balwyn..............373 D13
ct. Ringwood 334 L20
ct. Ringwood 335 A20
gdn. Wantirna...........422 F12
pl. Melton W 226 B15
GEORGIANA
cl. Chelsea Ht..........547 E12
pl. McCrae 685 A13
st. Sandringham 495 A12
GEORGINA
pde. Camberwell........417 D6
st. Wheelers Hill......461 E12
GEPP
rd. Healesville..........213 H16
GERA
ct. Wantirna S..........421 L19
GERALD
ct. Chelsea Ht..........547 E16
dr. Langwarrin..........629 C2
st. Blackburn 376 D19
st. Ferntree Gly 464 H1
st. Murrumbeena 457 B10
st. Sunshine N 321 C17
st. Werribee 446 L11
st. Werribee 447 A10
GERALDINE
cl. Kilsyth S 424 L2
cl. Wheelers Hill.......461 E19
dr. Hampton Pk........552 C15
st. Rye....................696 G11
GERANG
cl. Rowville.............463 A16
GERARD
ct. Croydon N 336 D13
ct. Pakenham...........585 A3
st. Caulfield..............455 F3
st. Dandenong 535 J2
st. Templstw Lr........330 H14
GERBER
rd. Monbulk 468 H2
GERBERA
ct. Blackburn N 375 J8
GERBERT
st. Broadmeadows ..238 D18
GERDA
st. Scoresby 462 H9
GERLACH
st. Clayton S 498 H9
GERMAIN
ct. Keilor Dn............276 B16
st. Oakleigh S...........458 D16
GERMAN
ct. Thomastown......240 L14
GERMANDER
ct. Hillside..............274 C4
ct. Hoppers Csg......405 C14
ct. Meadow Ht 193 J19
GERONA
ct. Keilor 277 C11
st. Keilor.................277 B10
GERRARD
ct. Glen Waverley....459 H6
st. Watsonia N 243 H19
GERRATTS
av. Upwey 465 L7
GERRY ANNA
ct. Epping...............198 E20
GERTONIA
av. Boronia..............423 F15
GERTRUDE
ct. Noble Park.........535 B7
st. Fitzroy..................18 L19
st. Frankston............627 G1
st. Geelong West.....702 D6
st. Preston 326 J4
st. St Albans 319 K2
st. Sunshine 365 F3
st. Templstw Lr........330 B11
st. Windsor.............414 J12
GERTZ
av. Reservoir 283 H3
GERVASE
av. Glenroy.............279 J2
GERVES
st. Torquay 711 G11
GEUM
st. Hadfield 280 H7
GEZA
ct. Baxter................643 L2
GEZIREH
st. Pascoe Vale S 324 H1
GHAZEEPORE
rd. Grovedale 705 C20
rd. Waurn Ponds.....705 C20
GHERA
ct. Greensborough ..244 C17
GHERINGHAP
st. Geelong 702 L10
GHIRAN
cl. Aspendale Gdn...546 H3
GIANA
ct. Ringwood N.......377 L6
GIANNARELLI
dr. Brunswick E.......325 K18
GIANNI
ct. Keysborough 534 C13
GIBB
ct. Pakenham..........584 F3
rd. Red Hill..............688 C5
st. Berwick..............554 D9
st. Dandenong N.....502 A16
st. Maidstone..........366 F4
GIBBO
ct. Coolaroo............238 G7
GIBBON
av. Vermont S 420 J7
ct. St Albans 275 G18
GIBBONS
dr. Epping...............198 G20
pl. Carlton.................18 D18
st. Richmond............26 F20
st. Sunbury.............142 J13
st. Werribee............447 J16
st. W Melbourne 367 K14
GIBBS
rd. Ferntree Gly 423 L19
rd. Healesville..........258 H4
rd. Montrose............382 G11
rd. Yarra Glen..........209 A11
st. Balaclava............414 G19
st. Balaclava............414 G20
st. Beaumaris...........530 C10
st. Newcomb 703 L16
GIBCOE
st. Greensborough ..286 B6
GIBDON
st. Burnley 371 B20
GIBLIN
la. Melton W...........225 B7
GIBNEY
cl. Roxburgh Pk......194 C12
st. Hawthorn...........371 H17
GIBSON
av. Brunswick W......324 J17
ct. Altona Mdw........451 D3
ct. Essendon...........323 C2
ct. Ringwood 378 D20
ct. Sunbury.............142 G9
ct. Sydenham 274 K4
rd. Ringwood N........335 A10
rd. Warranwood 335 A10
st. Alphington 327 K19
st. Box Hill S...........374 H20
st. Broadmeadows ..238 A19
st. Caulfield E..........456 F3
st. Dromana............686 A5
st. Hallam...............537 J13
st. Lalor..................241 E5
st. Mitcham 376 L16
st. Northcote...........326 L15
GIBSONS
pde. Warburton 349 H1
GIDEON
cl. Boronia..............423 J14
GIDGEE
av. Templstw Lr........330 G13
ct. Cranbourne W....577 K15
ct. Forest Hill 420 F4
ct. Keilor Dn...........276 H15
ct. Wantirna S.........423 B11
GIFFARD
st. Williamstown 411 F18
GIFFORD
av. Ferntree Gly 464 C4
cl. Berwick..............554 E16
rd. Doncaster 375 A2
GIFFORDS
rd. E Warburton 350 C2
rd. Warburton 350 C2
GILARTH
st. Highett...............495 K14
GILBA
pl. Lilydale 338 G17
GILBANK
st. Reservoir 282 F13
GILBERT
ct. Keysborough 534 C11
ct. Lalor..................240 J7
ct. Mt Waverley.......458 F6
ct. Parkdale.............531 J10
ct. Scoresby 462 H7
gr. Bentleigh............495 L1
gr. Carnegie 456 K12
la. Dandenong 535 L10
pde. Camberwell........417 D6
rd. Ivanhoe..............328 D15
rd. Preston..............326 D5
rd. Reservoir............282 E20
st. Braybrook...........321 L19
st. Bulleen 330 B16
st. Coburg 325 D4
st. Mont Albert.........374 G13
st. Torquay 712 B9
GILBERT PARK
dr. Knoxfield............463 C8
GILBERTSON
rd. Laverton N 363 K18
st. Essendon............323 D2
wk. Kensington 33 E8
GILBY
rd. Mt Waverley.......459 E11
GILCHRIST
cr. Sunbury.............143 D9
wy. Aspendale Gdn...547 B7
GILDA
ct. Ringwood 378 K5
ct. Rowville.............503 A5
st. Maidstone..........366 G3
GILDAN
ct. Hoppers Csg......449 C4
st. Balwyn N 373 A7
GILES
ct. Cranbourne N.....577 J8
ct. Frankston S........627 F10
ct. Mill Park 242 L5
ct. Werribee 448 B8
rt. Endeavour Hl 537 J6
GILFORD
gr. Cheltenham........496 G19
GILGA
st. Mornington.........640 L16
st. Mornington.........641 A16
GILGANDRA
st. Warneet.............649 F11
GILJA
ct. Boronia..............424 K7
ct. Cranbourne W....577 J16
GILL
ct. Rowville.............463 J19
pl. Hoppers Csg......405 A14
pl. Mooroolbark 337 D11
pl. Sunbury.............143 C8
rd. Pt Lonsdale........710 A4
st. Belmont..............706 B1
st. Cranbourne.........604 D2
st. Doncaster E 376 E1
st. Reservoir 282 D9
GILLAN
rd. Belgrave S..........506 K10
rd. Belgrave S..........507 B6
GILLARD
pl. Ringwood N........334 K20
st. Brighton East 455 F17
st. Burwood 418 G11
GILLARDS
rd. Mt Eliza..............626 C15
rd. Mt Eliza..............626 E16
GILLESPIE
ct. Cranbourne N.....577 J9
pl. Epping...............241 J5
rd. Kings Park 275 A19
rd. St Albans 275 G20
GILLIAN
rd. Mt Waverley.......419 A16
st. Springvale S.......534 A7
GILLIES
ct. Nar Warrn S.......552 J12
st. Essendon N.........323 G2
st. Fairfield..............327 D17
st. Fairfield..............327 D19
st. Hampton.............495 B10
st. Mitcham 377 A12
st. Thornbury..........327 E10
GILLIGAN
ct. Brunswick W......324 K8
rd. Altona North.......409 L9
rd. Gisborne S.........141 A2
GILLIGANS
ct. Rowville.............502 F2
GILLINGHAM
cr. Craigieburn 150 D20
st. Preston 326 F5
st. Watsonia N 243 G19
GILLIS
ct. Diamond Ck.......246 A16
st. Millgrove.............348 E2
GILLMAN
st. Cheltenham........530 J3
st. Hawthorn E.........372 F18
st. Malvern East 416 C16
GILLON
ct. Oakleigh.............458 D7
ct. St Albans 320 G11
GILLS
al. Melbourne 1 L13
al. Melbourne 24 B8
rd. Christmas Hills ..249 E4
rd. Panton Hill 205 E20
GILLWELL
rd. Lalor..................240 F10
GILMORE
cr. Lynbrook 551 D15
ct. Belgrave S..........506 H3
dr. Attwood.............237 B12
pl. Caroline Spr 318 E10
pl. Gladstone Pk......279 D1
rd. Doncaster 375 B2
GILMOUR
ct. Greensborough ..243 K20
ct. Greensborough ..285 K1
ct. Meadow Ht 237 L2
ct. Pascoe Vale 281 A15
rd. Bentleigh............496 D6
rd. Camberwell.........417 K5
rd. Sunshine N 320 L16
rd. Sunshine N 321 A15
st. Burwood............418 B10
st. Coburg 325 F1
GILROY
cr. Mill Park 242 F2
GILSLAND
rd. Murrumbeena 457 D6
GILSTON
wy. Ringwood 335 A18
GILWAY
ri. Greensborough ..244 B20
GIMCRACK
wy. Mt Martha.........657 C8
GIMLET
cl. Meadow Ht 193 L18
GINA
ct. Doncaster E 332 G5
ct. Hallam 537 H15
GINGHAM
pl. Berwick..............553 J1
GINIFER
av. Altona North.......409 H5
ct. St Albans 320 H12
GINN
cl. Mill Park 242 B6
st. Geelong 702 L3
GINNIE
ct. Mornington.........640 J20
GINNIVANS
rd. Smiths Gly 206 D3
GINO
ct. Diamond Ck.......246 D9
GIPPS
av. Mordialloc..........532 A19
cr. Cranbourne N.....577 H7
ct. Epping...............197 A19
st. Abbotsford...........20 B19
st. Collingwood..........19 J18
st. E Melbourne 25 G6

st. Richmond 26 C15
st. Rosebud 684 C16
GIPPSLAND
rd. Lilydale 339 A9
GIPSON
st. Diamond Ck 245 L9
GIPSY
wy. Sandringham 495 B13
GIRDWOOD
av. Carnegie 456 F4
rd. Boronia 424 D10
GIRGARRE
st. Broadmeadows 238 A9
GIRRALONG
ct. Greensborough 244 D19
GIRRAWEEN
dr. Eltham North 245 K20
GIRTON
cr. Manifold Ht 702 B5
GIRVAN
cct. Endeavour Hl 503 H17
gr. Pt Lonsdale 710 E3
pl. S Morang 199 D10
GISBORNE
cr. Reservoir 283 F11
rd. Bacchus Msh 222 A16
rd. Darley 222 A16
st. Bulleen 329 L10
st. E Melbourne 24 L3
st. Elsternwick 454 L6
st. Elsternwick 455 A6
GISBORNE MELTON
rd. Gisborne 78 D20
GISELLE
av. Wantirna S 462 B1
ct. Frankston 600 F19
GISH
ct. Hadfield 281 A8
GISSARA
ct. Wonga Park 291 F14
GISSING
st. Blackburn S 419 K3
GITTUS
st. S Melbourne 368 K20
GIULIANO
ct. Keilor East 322 G7
GIVERNY
cl. Highton 701 E14
GIVVENS
av. Wantirna S 422 F17
GLADE
av. Altona North 409 F1
av. Craigieburn 150 D18
dr. Bangholme 549 K14
GLADESVILLE
bvd. Patterson L 573 H10
bvd. Patterson L 573 J4
cl. Lysterfield S 504 B15
ct. Dandenong N 501 J16
dr. Bentleigh E 497 D5
dr. Kilsyth 381 F10
GLADESWOOD
dr. Mulgrave 501 D5
GLADHALL
av. Thornbury 327 E8
GLADIGAU
cr. Carrum Downs 575 G14
GLADMAN
st. Greensborough 286 A10
GLADSTONE
av. Armadale 415 G15
av. Aspendale 546 C6
av. Northcote 326 E12
gr. Melton 226 K18
gr. S Melbourne 29 G5
la. S Melbourne 29 B2
pde. Elsternwick 455 B8
pde. Glenroy 279 J7
pl. S Melbourne 29 E2
pl. Werribee 447 K15
rd. Briar Hill 286 E5
rd. Dandenong 535 H3
rd. Dandenong N 501 H20
st. Coburg 325 L3
st. Glen Iris 416 L14
st. Kew 372 B8
st. Lilydale 338 A4
st. Moonee Pnd 324 B14
st. Reservoir 283 A8
st. St Albans 319 F5
st. Sandringham 495 D16
st. Southbank 29 C2
st. Southbank 413 B1
st. S Melbourne 29 C3
st. S Melbourne 413 B1
st. Surrey Hills 374 F18
st. Thomastown 240 G13
st. Windsor 414 D11
st. Yarraville 367 B16
GLADSTONE PARK
dr. Gladstone Pk 236 K19
GLADSWOOD
st. Ascot Vale 324 A17
GLADWELL
st. Rye 696 H7
GLADWYN
av. Bentleigh E 456 J16
av. Frankston 599 J19
ct. Eltham 288 B4
GLADYS
ct. Coburg N 281 J15
ct. Mt Dandenong 426 G4
gr. Croydon 379 G2
st. Nunawading 376 G11
GLAISDALE
ct. Greenvale 237 C5
GLAMA
ct. Roxburgh Pk 194 D6
GLAMIS
av. Hampton 495 F9
ct. Balwyn N 373 L1
ct. Croydon 380 F3
ct. Endeavour Hl 537 L5
ct. Glen Waverley 460 A9
ct. Officer 555 G19
dr. Avondale Ht 321 L8
pl. Melton W 226 D15
rd. W Footscray 366 H11
st. Beaumaris 530 D4
st. Greensborough 285 L2
st. Mt Martha 655 L18
st. Newtown 701 K12
st. Warrandyte 333 A9
GLAMORGAN
av. Werribee 446 L12
av. Werribee 447 A12
cr. Mt Martha 656 A18
GLAN AVON
rd. Hawthorn 371 G18
GLANCE
st. Flemington 33 G4
GLANEUSE
av. Torquay 712 D2
rd. Pt Lonsdale 710 E6
GLANFIELD
ct. Ringwood N 334 H19
st. Northcote 327 A15
GLASGOW
av. Reservoir 282 C5
ct. Endeavour Hl 503 J19
rd. Kilsyth 381 E17
rd. Montrose 381 K19
rd. Mt Dandenong 381 K19
st. Collingwood 25 J1
GLASS
rd. Up Fntree Gly 465 A5
st. Essendon 323 K4
st. Kew East 372 J4
st. N Melbourne 17 C17
st. Richmond 26 L17
st. Richmond 371 A18
GLASSCOCKS
rd. Lyndhurst 575 K1
GLASSFORD
av. Springvale S 533 L5
av. Up Fntree Gly 465 G7
st. Armadale 415 F10
GLASSHOUSE
ct. Berwick 554 G20
rd. Collingwood 19 J19
st. Burnley 371 B17
GLASSON
ct. Greenvale 193 A17
sq. Mt Waverley 419 D20
st. Rosebud 700 A1
GLASTONBURY
cct. Point Cook 450 H9
cct. Point Cook 450 J10
dr. Highton 705 J8
GLAZEBURY
ct. Langwarrin 629 B3
GLEADELL
st. Richmond 26 J10
GLEANMOR
tce. Pakenham 558 J19
GLEBE
av. Cheltenham 530 H2
ct. Wantirna 422 G5
pl. Melton W 226 D17
pl. Thomastown 240 K11
pl. Wheelers Hill 461 E15
st. Forest Hill 420 C1
st. Forest Hill 420 C4
GLEDHAN
cl. Altona Mdw 451 E6
GLEDHILL
st. Seddon 367 C11
GLEDITSIA
wy. Bundoora 242 E13
GLEESON
av. Camberwell 417 L5
av. Lysterfield 464 F18
ct. Langwarrin 602 A19
dr. Bundoora 285 B6
wk. Roxburgh Pk 193 L15
GLEGHORN
rd. Kallista 467 C1
GLEN
av. Belmont 706 K1
av. Croydon 379 K2
av. E Geelong 703 J10
ct. Frankston 627 C4
ct. Glen Waverley 460 F2
ct. Hampton Pk 551 E7
ct. Keilor East 322 H6
ct. Narre Warren 538 K16
ct. Templestowe 331 C12
dr. Eaglemont 328 J12
dr. Rye 697 F7
pl. Healesville 300 C13
rd. Ashburton 417 B20
rd. Belgrave 466 D18
rd. Belgrave Ht 466 D18
rd. Cockatoo 510 K4
rd. Glen Waverley 460 D2
rd. Lysterfield 504 F4
rd. Melton 226 H19
rd. Mitcham 377 C11
rd. Silvan 385 A16
rd. Toorak 415 H5
st. Aspendale 546 E6
st. Blackburn N 376 C10
st. Essendon 323 L6
st. Glenroy 280 D5
st. Hawthorn 371 L20
st. Hawthorn 415 L2
st. Werribee 447 J13
tr. Lysterfield 504 D10
tr. Lysterfield 504 D13
GLENAIR
ct. Templstw Lr 330 G8
st. Templstw Lr 330 G10
GLEN ALLAN
st. Broadmeadows 238 A20
GLENALVA
pde. Cannons Creek 649 D8
GLEN ALVIE
av. Keysborough 533 J10
st. Seaford 599 K8
GLENANN
ct. Boronia 424 A8
GLENARA
ct. Belmont 702 H19
ct. Bundoora 285 A3
ct. Endeavour Hl 537 L8
dr. Bulla 190 E18
GLENARA FORD
Seabrook 451 A2
GLENARD
dr. Eaglemont 329 A11
dr. Heidelberg 328 L11
dr.e, Eaglemont 329 B9
dr.w, Eaglemont 329 A9
GLENARM
pl. Mt Waverley 419 J16
rd. Glen Iris 416 F11
GLENAUBURN
ct. Sunbury 143 B6
rd. Lower Plenty 286 E14
GLEN AVIS
gr. Dingley Village 532 K7
GLENBAR
ct. Kealba 276 L19
ct. Kealba 277 A20
GLENBARRY
rd. Campbellfield 239 C7
rd. Wantirna 422 K6
GLENBERVIE
dr. Somerville 645 B19
rd. Strathmore 323 K1
rd. Toorak 415 K6
GLENBOURNE
rd. Cranbourne 577 L15
GLENBRAE
ct. Belmont 706 G6
ct. Berwick 553 L4
GLENBROOK
av. Bonbeach 547 C20
av. Chelsea 547 C20
av. Clayton 458 L15
av. Malvern East 416 H17
cl. Frankston S 627 G18
cl. Mooroolbark 337 L19
ct. Greenvale 237 F5
gdn. Brookfield 267 L6
rd. Clematis 508 H4
rd. Warburton 349 E5
GLENBRUAR
dr. Hillside 232 F19
dr. Hillside 232 G18
GLENBURN
ct. Bangholme 549 H13
dr. Hallam 538 C19
rd. Boronia 424 H15
st. Newcomb 704 E16
st. Thomastown 240 C13
GLENBURNIE
rd. Eden Park 95 A11
rd. Mitcham 377 E20
rd. Vermont 377 E20
rd. Whittlesea 95 J15
GLENCAIRN
av. Brighton East 495 F5
av. Camberwell 417 F8
av. Coburg 325 D7
av. Deer Park 319 E15
av. Hallam 552 B2
av. Ringwood 378 K6
cr. Broadmeadows 238 A9
ct. Eltham North 245 C17
dr. Greenvale 193 A19
pl. Mill Park 242 F10
st. Mulgrave 500 D4
GLENCANNON
cr. Clayton S 498 H7
GLENCAPEL
ct. Hillside 232 E16
GLENCAPLE
ct. Endeavour Hl 503 H16
GLENCARA
cl. Westmeadows 236 H15
st. Avondale Ht 322 D14
GLEN CENTRE
arc. Hawthorn, off Glenferrie Rd 371 L15
GLENCESTER
ct. Bulleen 329 H12
GLENCOE
av. Truganina 405 L14
cr. Mt Martha 655 L20
ct. Epping 198 C20
dr. Diggers Rest 188 D12
gr. Dandenong N 501 L16
pl. Lilydale 294 D19
pl. W Melbourne 23 B1
st. Caulfield N 455 E2
GLENCROFT
tce. Wheelers Hill 461 B19
GLENDA
cl. Clarinda 498 E11
ct. Boronia 424 J8
ct. Vermont S 420 J8
st. Doncaster 330 C19
st. Werribee 447 G10
GLENDALE
av. Epping 198 D17
av. Templestowe 331 B8
cl. Langwarrin 601 L17
cr. Berwick 553 H3
ct. Boronia 424 G15
ct. Kilsyth 381 D8
ct. Werribee 448 C5
dr. Chirnside Pk 337 A4
gr. Rosebud 684 J15
pl. Gladstone Pk 237 C18
rd. Briar Hill 286 G4
rd. Springvale 499 J7
st. Glen Waverley 460 C2
st. Nunawading 376 G14
st. Surrey Hills 418 B2
GLENDALOUGH
ct. Watsonia N 243 E18
GLENDARRAGH
rd. Templestowe 332 B9
GLENDEARG
gr. Malvern 415 L17
GLENDEN
rt. Cheltenham 496 J13
GLENDENE
av. Kew 372 G10
ct. Doncaster 375 E5
ct. Werribee 447 A19
GLENDENNING
ct. Frankston 628 C13
ri. Templestowe 331 F4
st. St Albans 320 A5
GLEN DHU
rd. Kilsyth 381 A6
GLENDINNING
ri. Mornington 656 G2
GLENDOON
st. Junction Vill 604 H14
GLENDORA
av. Brighton 454 K6
la. Doncaster E 331 L16
GLENDOWAN
rd. Mt Waverley 418 L18
GLENDOWER
ct. Mooroolbark 337 D8
GLENDYE
ct. Toorak 415 F5
GLENEADIE
av. Badger Creek 258 B11
cl. Hampton Pk 552 B9
GLENEAGLE
wy. Eltham 287 B7
GLEN EAGLES
ct. Burwood 418 B3
GLENEAGLES
av. Mornington 656 B1
ct. Croydon 380 J7
ct. Darley 221 G1
ct. Rowville 462 D19
dr. Endeavour Hl 503 J20
dr. Melton W 225 G20
dr. Sunbury 144 F13
GLEN EBOR
av. Blackburn 376 A16
GLEN EIRA
av. Balaclava 454 H1
rd. Caulfield 455 F2
rd. Caulfield N 455 A2
rd. Caulfield S 455 F2
rd. Elsternwick 454 H1
rd. Ripponlea 454 H1
rd. St Kilda E 454 H1
GLENELG
av. Frankston 627 J7
bvd. Taylors Hill 274 K12
ct. Brookfield 268 D6
ct. Dingley Village 532 K7
ct. Rowville 462 J17
dr. Clayton S 498 F8
dr. Mentone 531 F5
pl. Taylors Lakes 233 E18
st. Coolaroo 238 E3
st. Dandenong N 501 K8
wy. Seabrook 450 L5
GLENFERN
av. Doncaster 330 C17
av. Upwey 465 K15
cl. Upwey 466 A14
ct. Blackburn S 419 J7
pl. Glenroy 280 G9
rd. Ferntree Gly 464 E5
rd. Healesville 213 G18
rd. Lysterfield 465 B14
rd. Upwey 465 B14
GLENFERRIE
pl. Hawthorn, off Glenferrie Rd 372 A17
rd. Hawthorn 371 L20
rd. Hawthorn 415 L3
rd. Kew 371 L20
rd. Kooyong 415 K8
rd. Malvern 415 J15
st. Caulfield N 415 J17
GLENFIELD
cl. Deer Park 319 H11
ct. Lalor 240 C9
GLENGALA
ct. Greensborough 286 B10
ct. Mentone 531 L8
dr. Sunshine W 364 H11
rd. Sunshine 364 H4
rd. Sunshine W 363 L3
rd. Sunshine W 364 G4
rd. Sunshine W 365 A3
GLENGARIFF
dr. Mulgrave 500 G2
GLENGARRIFF
cr. Montmorency 286 J8
GLENGARRY
av. Burwood 418 H6
dr. Torquay 712 B2
GLEN GULLY
rd. Eltham North 245 F19
GLENGYLE
st. Coburg 325 K7
GLEN HARROW
rd. Belgrave 466 H10
GLENHAVEN
ct. Gisborne 109 C4
ct. Thomastown 240 E16
rd. Hurstbridge 202 E19
GLENHELEN
pl. Chirnside Pk 336 E8
GLEN HOLME
av. Mt Evelyn 383 E2
GLEN HUNTLY
rd. Carnegie 456 E7
rd. Caulfield 455 B5
rd. Caulfield 456 A6
rd. Caulfield S 455 B5
rd. Elsternwick 454 G4
rd. Elwood 454 C4
rd. Glen Huntly 456 A6
GLENICE
av. Blackburn S 419 D6
st. Greensborough 286 B9

GLENIFER
av. Scoresby 462 G8
GLENIFFER
av. Brighton East 495 L5
GLEN INNES
cl. Chirnside Pk 336 E8
GLEN IRIS
rd. Camberwell 417 A14
rd. Glen Iris 417 A14
GLENISLA
dr. Mt Martha 655 G18
wy. Berwick 553 K14
GLENISTER
dr. Eltham 287 L10
GLEN KATHERINE
dr. St Helena 245 A18
GLENLEA
cl. Rowville 463 J14
ct. Mill Park 242 E10
GLENLEIGH
ct. Cranbourne N 578 G8
ct. Glen Waverley 420 H19
GLENLEITH
av. Geelong 702 K1
ct. Geelong 702 K1
GLENLITTA
av. Broadmeadows 238 L19
GLENLOTH
av. Lilydale 294 B18
ct. Epping 198 D19
GLENLUSS
st. Balwyn 373 K9
st. Werribee 447 J13
GLENLYON
rd. Brunswick 325 H15
rd. Brunswick E 325 H15
GLENMAGGIE
cr. Wyndham Va 446 C7
ct. Meadow Ht 238 B5
ct. Wantirna S 422 B20
dr. St Albans 320 E12
GLENMANOR
cl. Templestowe 332 C8
GLENMARK
av. St Kilda 414 F17
GLENMER
st. Bentleigh 496 F6
GLENMIRE
st. Highton 701 G18
GLENMORE
cr. Black Rock 529 E3
ct. Seaford 600 A5
gr. Mt Waverley 418 K20
pl. Greenvale 237 G1
st. Box Hill 374 L17
st. Macleod 284 L12
GLENMORGAN
cl. Clayton S 499 E13
st. Brunswick E 325 L11
GLENMOYNE
sq. Werribee 447 L20
GLENMURRAY
pl. Chirnside Pk 336 E8
GLENN
cl. Cranbourne W 577 E20
cr. Bundoora 242 B20
cr. Bundoora 284 B1
cr. Clayton S 499 E15
ct. Mooroolbark 336 L13
ct. Rowville 503 D5
dr. Bundoora, off College Dr 284 F12
GLENNDEN
ct. Bundoora 285 D2
GLENN ERIN
wy. Berwick 553 K16
GLENNIE
av. Oakleigh S 497 H4
GLENNIS
st. Frankston 627 H1
GLENNON
la. Carlton 18 G14
GLENOLA
rd. Chelsea 545 F11
rd. Chelsea 547 A20
GLENONE
av. Dromana 685 J9
GLENORA
av. Coburg 325 L5
av. Croydon 379 K3
ct. Frankston 628 C3
dr. Vermont 421 D6
st. Chadstone 458 E2
GLEN ORCHARD
cl. Templestowe 332 B13
GLEN ORME
av. McKinnon 456 B16
av. Ormond 456 B16
GLEN PARK
av. Glenroy 279 H5
dr. Selby 467 H14
rd. Bayswater N 379 J20
rd. Eltham North 287 E1
GLENPARK
dr. Chirnside Pk 336 E8
GLENROBE
st. Deer Park 319 C9
GLENROSA
ct. St Albans 275 H20
GLENROY
rd. Glenroy 280 B6
rd. Hawthorn 371 L20
rd. Hawthorn 415 K1
GLENSCOTT
cr. Strathmr Ht 279 C9
GLENSHEE
dr. Lynbrook 551 F16
GLEN SHIAN
cr. Mt Eliza 625 K12
la. Mt Eliza 625 L12
GLENSIDE
st. Avondale Ht 322 E15
wk. Berwick 539 H18
GLENTHORN
av. Balwyn N 373 L8
GLENTHORNE
dr. Keysborough 534 K12
GLENTILT
rd. Glen Iris 416 F11
GLEN TOWER
dr. Glen Waverley 460 J2
GLENVALE
cr. Mulgrave 460 B20
rd. Donvale 377 K9
rd. Glen Iris 416 H13
rd. Reservoir 282 D12
rd. Ringwood N 377 K9
GLEN VALLEY
ct. Greensborough 285 J3
rd. Forest Hill 376 E20
rd. Nunawading 420 E1
GLENVALLEY
cr. Seville E 343 C13
GLENVERN
rd. Panton Hill 248 D2
rd. Panton Hill 248 J8
GLEN VIEW
ct. Glen Waverley 460 H2
rd. Monbulk 428 L17
rd. Monbulk 469 D1
GLENVIEW
av. Malvern 416 A11
cr. Frankston 628 A4
ct. Avondale Ht 322 F9
ct. Croydon N 335 L12
pl. Ferntree Gly 464 C14
rd. Doncaster E 376 B5
rd. Launching Pl 345 L13
rd. Mt Evelyn 339 D18
rd. Strathmore 280 B19
rd. Yarra Glen 252 D9
GLENVILL
ct. Templestowe 332 B8
GLENVILLE
rd. Glen Waverley 460 L2
rd. Highton 701 G10
rd. Highton 701 H11
GLEN VISTA
dr. Nar Warrn N 538 D10
GLENVISTA
av. Emerald 469 G15
pl. Templestowe 332 C8
GLENVUE
rd. Rye 696 L10
rd. Rye 697 A10
GLENWAY
dr. Dingley Village 532 L7
GLENWERRI
ct. Vermont S 421 A14
GLENWOOD
av. Altona 408 L17
av. Beaumaris 529 L9
av. Dromana 686 A9
av. Glen Waverley 460 A6
cl. Donvale 377 K4
ct. Cranbourne 578 C15
dr. Croydon 379 G7
dr. Greensborough 244 D15
dr. Springvale S 499 L19
gr. Knoxfield 423 B20
rd. Nar Warrn N 538 H11
GLENWRIGHT
av. Woori Yallock 344 G13
GLENYS
av. Airport W 278 G15
ct. Belmont 706 D5
ct. Clarinda 498 E10
ct. Dandenong S 535 L13
ct. Wantirna S 422 E17
GLEW
st. Brunswick E 325 L17
GLIDER
pl. S Morang 243 K2
GLIKA
st. Donvale 376 E4
GLINDEN
av. Ardeer 320 B18
GLISMANN
rd. Beaconsfield 555 E16
GLITTER
rd.n, Diggers Rest 187 D12
rd.s, Diggers Rest 187 C12
GLOAMING
ct. Mill Park 242 L12
GLOAMING RIDE
Kurunjang 226 G11
GLOBAL
dr. Westmeadows 236 H16
dr. Westmeadows 236 H17
GLOBE
al. Melbourne 2 F10
al. Melbourne 24 D5
pl. Epping 241 G4
st. Yarraville 367 D18
GLOMAR
ct. Dandenong S 536 A17
GLORIA
av. Dandenong N 501 L20
ct. Bundoora 285 B2
GLOUCESTER
av. Berwick 554 E10
ct. Eltham 287 K9
ct. Murrumbeena 457 B12
ct. Seaholme 409 H17
ct. Sydenham 274 K1
ct. Templestowe 331 F14
ct. Werribee 446 L12
dr. Heidelberg 329 E4
rd. Ashburton 417 J17
st. Grovedale 705 L12
st. Hadfield 281 A10
st. Mt Waverley 418 G12
st. Reservoir 282 G13
wy. Epping 197 K16
wy. Melton W 226 A14
GLOVER
cl. Mooroolbark 337 C11
ct. Berwick 554 A2
ct. Ferny Creek 466 B3
ct. Skye 601 H1
ct. Taylors Lakes 275 A1
ct. Toorak 415 A2
st. Heidelberg Ht 284 E19
st. Newcomb 704 A14
st. Oakleigh S 497 G3
st. S Melbourne 29 C10
st. S Melbourne 413 B5
GLUGSDEN
rd. Gruyere 298 L5
GLYN
ct. Cheltenham 496 L16
st. Belmont 706 D4
st. Jan Juc 711 E15
GLYNDA
st. Dandenong S 535 L13
st. Fawkner 281 G4
GLYNDEBOURNE
av. Toorak 415 H5
GLYNDON
av. Brighton 454 E12
av. Coburg N 281 E13
av. St Albans 320 H4
ct. Burwood E 419 F8
ct. Seaford 573 F13
rd. Camberwell 417 E6
GLYNELEA
cr. Skye 575 H16
GLYNNE
rd. Warranwood 334 H15
GLYNNS
rd. Eltham 289 D16
rd. N Warrandyte 289 D16
rd. Research 289 D16
GNARWIN
st. Mt Waverley 458 L4
GNARWYN
rd. Carnegie 456 K8
GNOORONG
st. Warneet 649 D13
GNOTUK
av. Aspendale 546 E8
GOA
ct. Keilor Dn 276 C14
GOATHLANDS
st. St Kilda E 414 L18
GOBLE
st. Laverton 407 C17
st. Niddrie 278 H19
GOBUR
ct. Meadow Ht 237 J6
GODALMIN
st. Eltham 287 D14
GODBEHEAR
ct. Ringwood 335 B18
GODBER
ct. Upwey 466 A16
rd. Diamond Ck 246 A16
GODDARD
ct. Mont Albert N 374 G10
GODFREY
av. St Kilda E 414 H15
av. Sunshine N 321 B12
av. Warrandyte 334 F1
cr. Dandenong 536 A3
ct. Surrey Hills 374 F19
la. Officer 557 C9
la. Pakenham 557 C9
st. Bentleigh 456 C19
st. Blairgowrie 679 L19
st. E Geelong 703 H14
st. Melbourne 23 G10
st. Thomson 703 H14
GODING
ct. Whittlesea 96 L8
GODINGS
rd. Moorooduc 658 K14
GODLEY
st. Reservoir 282 D4
GODWIN
av. Narre Warren 539 E16
cr. Cranbourne N 578 E8
st. Blairgowrie 696 A2
GOE
st. Caulfield S 455 K7
GOEGAN
st. Werribee 448 A16
GOFF
st. Beaconsfield 555 C16
st. Coburg 282 B20
GOGOLL
cr. Torquay 712 A6
GOLCONDA
av. Frankston 599 L18
cl. Hoppers Csg 405 D14
GOLD
st. Brunswick 325 C16
st. Cheltenham 496 L20
st. Clifton Hill 19 L9
st. Collingwood 19 K13
GOLDBOROUGH
ct. Frankston S 627 H13
GOLDEN
av. Bonbeach 547 A20
av. Chelsea 545 F11
av. Chelsea 547 A20
av. Werribee 447 D11
ct. Doncaster 331 E18
ct. Doveton 536 J6
ct. Frankston N 600 F9
gr. Glen Waverley 420 G19
gr. Mill Park 242 E4
gr. Ringwood 378 K5
gr. The Basin 425 G12
qd. Glen Iris 416 G12
wy. Bulleen 329 F12
wy. Hillside 231 L20
wy. Hillside 273 L1
GOLDEN ASH
ct. Meadow Ht 238 B1
gr. Hoppers Csg 405 C14
wk. Croydon N 335 L13
GOLDEN BEACH
wy. Torquay 712 G2
GOLDEN FLEECE
al. Melbourne 2 K11
al. Melbourne, off Coverlid Pl 24 F5
GOLDENFLEECE
pl. Hoppers Csg 448 A1
GOLDEN GLEN
rd. Forest Hill 420 B6
GOLDEN GROVE
ct. Keilor Lodge 275 L3
GOLDEN LEAF
av. Nar Warrn S 553 C20
GOLDEN RIDGE
dr. Croydon Hills 335 G17
GOLDEN SQUARE
cr. Hoppers Csg 447 K2
GOLDENTREE
dr. Chirnside Pk 336 H6
GOLDEN VIEW
ct. Wheelers Hill 460 K8
GOLDERS
st. Heidelberg 328 J5
GOLDERS GREEN
wk. Caroline Spr 317 L3
GOLDFIELD
ct. Wheelers Hill 461 C11
GOLDFINCH
ct. Carrum Downs 600 H2
pl. Rowville 503 D3
GOLDIE
pl. Melbourne 1 K10
pl. Melbourne 24 A6
GOLDING
av. Rowville 503 B7
av. Rowville 503 C7
ct. Dandenong N 502 B15
ct. Scoresby 462 J6
ct. Springvale S 499 G19
st. Canterbury 373 G19
st. Hawthorn 371 K17
GOLDLANG
st. Dandenong 535 E4
GOLDMANS
rd. Cottles Br 204 G1
rd. Panton Hill 204 G1
rd. St Andrews 204 G1
rd. Smiths Gly 204 G1
GOLD MEMORIAL
rd. Warrandyte 333 H4
rd. Warrandyte 334 A4
GOLD NUGGET
ri. Warrandyte 333 F4
GOLDSACK
cl. Cockatoo 471 G18
GOLDSBOROUGH
la. Melbourne 1 D11
la. Melbourne 23 K8
GOLDSMITH
av. Delahey 275 C13
av. Preston 283 A17
av. Ringwood N 378 E4
cl. Endeavour Hl 537 F7
gr. Northcote 326 D13
st. Elwood 454 D3
st. Elwood 454 E2
GOLDSWORTHY
ct. Kings Park 275 B18
la. Plenty 243 J9
GOLDTHORNS
av. Kew 372 H8
GOLEEN
st. Coburg N 281 G15
GOLF
av. Kingsbury 283 K9
av. Mt Waverley 418 K17
av. Rosanna 285 A19
la. Rye 697 H5
pde. Rye 697 D7
rd. Coburg N 281 K17
rd. Oakleigh S 457 J20
GOLF CLUB
rd. Cranbourne N 577 K3
rd. Hampton Pk 577 K3
GOLF COURSE
cir. Safety Bch 669 B20
la. Safety Bch 668 L18
la. Safety Bch 669 A18
GOLFERS
dr. Malvern East 417 E20
GOLF HILL
av. Doncaster 374 E1
GOLF LINKS
av. Oakleigh 457 K15
cr. Dingley Village 533 G9
ct. Doncaster 330 D20
ct. Doncaster 374 D1
dr. Mill Park 242 C4
dr. Sunbury 143 G16
dr. Yarrambat 201 B11
rd. Anglesea 713 D4
rd. Baxter 628 B13
rd. Berwick 553 G13
rd. Croydon 336 F16
rd. Frankston 627 H8
rd. Frankston S 627 H8
rd. Frankston S 628 B13
rd. Glenroy 280 C8
rd. Langwarrin S 645 A2
rd. Narre Warren 553 A12
GOLF VIEW
rd. Heatherton 497 J15
GOLFWOOD
cl. Dingley Village 533 B6
GOLIGHTLY
st. Pt Lonsdale 710 D5
GOMAN
rd. Moorooduc 658 C10
GOMI
ct. Frankston 600 H20

GOMMS
rd. Somerville 644 G13
GONA
ct. Ashburton 417 H17
st. Heidelberg W 327 L2
GONGFLERS
dr. Bend of Islands 292 A5
GOOCH
cl. Sydenham 274 L3
st. Prahran 414 L12
st. Thornbury 326 K9
GOODALL
ct. Berwick 554 E20
dr. Lilydale 338 K4
st. Hawthorn 372 C19
GOODE
ct. Sunshine W 365 B10
st. Gisborne 78 J13
st. Malvern East 457 B4
GOODENIA
cl. Meadow Ht 193 K20
pl. Hillside 274 E3
GOODENOUGH
ct. Heidelberg W 283 L19
GOOD GOVERNS
st. Mitcham 377 J16
GOODIN
gr. Glen Waverley 420 C20
GOODING
ct. Dandenong 536 D3
st. St Albans 320 C6
GOODJOHN
ct. Endeavour Hl 537 E4
GOODLET
pl. Eltham 288 F5
GOODMAN
dr. Noble Park 535 B5
st. Brunswick 325 D16
GOODRICH
ct. Craigieburn 194 E4
st. Bentleigh E 457 E16
GOODSON
st. Doncaster 331 A20
GOODWIN
cl. Hoppers Csg 448 B3
st. Blackburn 376 C14
st. Glen Iris 417 B9
st. Preston 326 B4
st. Richmond 26 G20
st. The Basin 424 L9
GOODWOOD
cr. Gladstone Pk 236 L19
cr. Gladstone Pk 237 A19
cr. Glen Waverley 460 G10
dr. Keilor Dn 275 L16
dr. Springvale 500 A18
st. Richmond 26 B11
st. Surrey Hills 418 C2
GOOLAGONG
rd. Blind Bight 650 G6
wy. St Albans 275 K18
GOOLD
st. Burwood 418 H11
GOOLGOWIE
st. Rosebud 700 K7
GOOLGUNG
gr. Greensborough 243 H18
GOONDAH
la. Healesville 214 C15
GOONYAH
ct. Greensborough 244 B18
GOORNA
ct. Rye 697 A9
GOOYONG
av. Chadstone 418 D20
GORAE
ct. Westmeadows 237 F12
GORDON
av. Elwood 454 E1
av. Frankston 599 J18
av. Geelong 702 K6
av. Geelong West 702 H6
av. Kew 372 A12
av. Laverton 406 K20
av. Montrose 381 L17
av. Oakleigh E 458 H13
av. Tecoma 466 C8
av.s, Altona Mdw 450 K1
bvd. Waurn Ponds 705 B11
cl. Nar Warrn S 552 F9
cr. Blackburn 375 K17
cr. Black Rock 529 E4
cr. Boronia 423 G15
cr. Kensington 33 J7
ct. Glenroy 280 B3
ct. Mooroolbark 381 G3
ct. Ringwood 422 D1
ct. View Bank 285 F20
ct. Woori Yallock 344 G15
gr. Malvern 415 J15
gr. Menzies Ck 467 L19
gr. Montmorency 287 C9
gr. Northcote 326 F16
gr. Preston 283 E20
gr. South Yarra 31 K4
gr. South Yarra 414 E2
pde. Yarraville 366 L18
pl. Carlton 18 H15
pl. Melbourne 24 J3
rd. Mt Waverley 419 C16
rd. Pakenham Up 559 J8
st. Balwyn 372 L10
st. Balwyn 373 A10
st. Beaumaris 530 G4
st. Bentleigh 495 L4
st. Brunswick W 325 A10
st. Bundoora 285 C2
st. Clifton Hill 20 D7
st. Coburg 281 B20
st. Coburg 325 A6
st. Cranbourne 604 F1
st. Cremorne 32 E2
st. Cremorne 414 H1
st. Croydon 380 E6
st. Elsternwick 454 K3
st. Elsternwick 454 K4
st. Essendon 324 G8
st. Fairfield 327 F17
st. Footscray 367 B8
st. Hampton 494 J5
st. Hawthorn E 372 F19
st. Lalor 241 E8
st. Malvern East 457 E4
st. Maribyrnong 323 C20
st. Maribyrnong 367 B4
st. Mont Albert 374 B16
st. Mornington 640 F12
st. Newport 410 E6
st. Noble Park 534 L4
st. Officer 555 K16
st. Rye 696 G1
st. Sunbury 142 F11
st. Toorak 32 L13
st. Toorak 414 L7
st. Toorak 415 A7
st. Tullamarine 278 G7
GORDONIA
cr. Narre Warren 539 C19
GORDON LUCK
av. Altona North 408 G4
GORDONS
rd. S Morang 198 L9
rd. S Morang 199 A9
rd. Templstw Lr 330 C8
GORE
pl. Geelong, off Corio St 703 B7
ri. Endeavour Hl 537 D5
st. Fitzroy 25 E2
GORENKOS
dr. Maidstone 322 H17
GORGE
rd. S Morang 199 H20
rd. S Morang 243 H1
GORHAM
av. Epping 197 H17
GORI
ct. Nar Warrn N 539 D12
GORMAN
al. Melbourne 24 H2
GOROKE
ct. Croydon S 380 A13
ct. Eltham 288 A6
GORONG
wk. Delahey 275 A11
GORRIE
ct. Wantirna S 462 D1
pl. Glenroy 279 H5
GORST
rd. Hurstbridge 202 E20
rd. Wattle Glen 202 E20
GORTON
ct. Sunbury 143 H3
GOSFIELD
rd. Hurstbridge 203 G11
rd. Hurstbridge 204 A11
rd. Panton Hill 204 A11
GOSFORD
cr. Broadmeadows 238 C15
cr. Pk Orchards 334 A19
ct. Pk Orchards 334 C20
GOSHAWK
ct. Carrum Downs 600 J2
GOSNEYS
la. Geelong, off Mercer St 702 K4
GOSS
tce. Williamstown 411 F13
GOSSAMER
st. Werribee 447 E11
GOSSE
ct. Sunbury 142 J11
GOTCH
la. E Melbourne 25 G4
GOTHA
st. Heidelberg Ht 328 D5
GOTHIC
ct. Sunshine W 364 B5
dr. Bacchus Msh 221 G16
rd. Aspendale 546 E6
rd. Rye 697 E9
GOTTARD
ct. Keilor Dn 276 D13
GOUDIESDALE
rd. Menzies Ck 467 F18
rd. Selby 467 F18
GOUGH
al. Melbourne 1 A7
al. Melbourne 23 H7
pl. Cremorne 25 K19
st. Cremorne 25 K20
st. Cremorne 31 L1
st. Elsternwick 455 B10
GOULBURN
av. Reservoir 283 E12
cct. Caroline Spr 318 C7
ct. Croydon Hills 335 K14
ct. St Albans 320 D13
ct. Werribee 447 D7
dr. Rowville 463 B17
pl. Clayton S 498 G8
st. Box Hill N 374 L10
st. Broadmeadows 238 F17
st. Cheltenham 496 K19
st. Yarraville 367 B15
wy. Taylors Lakes 233 F20
GOULD
cl. Wantirna S 462 F1
ct. Mt Waverley 459 G3
pl. Burnside 318 F8
pl. Mill Park 242 F8
pl. Mooroolbark 337 E11
st. Balwyn N 329 G19
st. Brighton 494 F2
st. Coburg N 281 G15
st. Deer Park 319 D9
st. Frankston 599 A18
wk. Truganina 405 G13
GOULDTHORP
av. Mentone 531 D7
GOURLAY
rd. Caroline Spr 274 B13
rd. Taylors Hill 274 B13
st. Balaclava 414 H19
GOUROCK
st. Reservoir 283 J3
GOVAN
ct. Footscray 366 L4
st. Footscray 366 L4
st. Langwarrin 629 D3
st. Langwarrin 629 D4
st. Seaford 599 E7
GOVE
st. Springvale 500 B9
GOVERNMENT
rd. Essendon 324 D5
rd. Frankston 627 F1
rd. Rye 697 K4
rd. The Basin 425 D14
rd. Tremont 425 D14
rd. Warrandyte 333 J2
rd. Wesburn 347 K13
GOVERNMENT HOUSE
dr. Melbourne 4 G17
dr. Melbourne 24 J18
GOVERNOR
rd. Braeside 532 F19
rd. Mordialloc 532 A20
GOVERNOR ARTHUR
dr. Patterson L 547 H20
GOVERNORS
rd. Coburg 281 J20
GOW
ct. Hallam 537 H13
GOWAN
rd. Mt Waverley 419 G18
GOWANBRAE
dr. Gowanbrae 279 C8
dr. Gowanbrae 279 D6
GOWAR
av. Camberwell 417 D4
GOWDIE
pl. Caroline Spr 318 D4
GOWER
st. Kensington 33 J11
st. Preston 326 K1
GOWRIE
av. Frankston S 626 L7
ct. Seabrook 451 A4
ct. Sunbury 143 F4
pl. Cranbourne W 577 G19
rd. Clematis 508 F3
st. Bentleigh E 457 E18
st. Glenroy 280 H2
GOWRIE PARK
dr. Melb Airport 235 K11
GOYA
ct. Gladstone Pk 279 A3
ct. Scoresby 462 C7
ct. Wheelers Hill 460 L13
GOYARRA
ct. Grovedale 706 D14
st. Rye 696 L8
st. Rye 697 A8
GRABAPPLE
rd. S Morang 199 J12
GRACE
av. Dandenong 536 D6
av. Mooroolbark 337 J16
cl. Wyndham Va 446 G15
ct. Frankston 600 G19
ct. Kew 371 H4
ct. Lalor 240 J5
ct. Mitcham 376 L16
ct. Mont Albert 374 E12
ct. Sunshine W 365 C11
ct. View Bank 285 L15
la. Fitzroy N 19 D7
st. Camberwell 416 J6
st. Cranbourne 578 E20
st. Essendon N 279 C20
st. Glen Waverley 460 A1
st. Laverton 407 E18
st. Malvern 416 A14
st. Melton S 268 E5
st. Mont Albert 374 D12
st. Moonee Pnd 323 L13
st. Rye 697 G2
st. St Albans 276 F20
st. Springvale 500 D8
st. Watsonia 285 D7
st. Yarraville 367 A13
st. Hawthorn, off Glenferrie Rd 371 L16
st.s, Altona Mdw 407 D20
GRACEBURN
av. Carnegie 456 H7
av. Healesville 214 E18
gr. St Albans 276 A17
rd. Healesville 214 C20
GRACEDALE
av. Eltham North 287 D1
av. Ringwood E 379 F13
ct. Strathmore 323 J1
GRACEFIELD
av. Dromana 686 B9
dr. Box Hill N 374 J8
GRACEHILL
av. Burwood 418 L11
GRACEMERE
dr. Pearcedale 646 H4
GRACE PARK
av. Springvale 499 L15
GRACIE
av. Chelsea 546 H15
av. Edithvale 546 H15
la. N Melbourne 17 F19
st. Northcote 326 F13
st. N Melbourne 34 F13
GRACILIS
ct. Endeavour Hl 536 J1
GRADUATE
cr. Wheelers Hill 460 D15
GRADY
cl. Mill Park 242 B5
ct. Frankston S 627 H9
la. Mornington 641 B11
GRAEME
av. Montmorency 286 H7
av. Ringwood 378 J4
cl. Doncaster 331 A15
st. Bulleen 329 H15
st. Dromana 686 E4
st. Frankston 600 B19
st. Vermont 421 H3
GRAF
rd. Somerville 644 H16
rd. Somerville 644 J19
GRAFTON
ct. Sunbury 142 L1
st. Coburg 325 D4
st. Elsternwick 455 B4
GRAGWEN
ct. Keysborough 533 H17
GRAHAM
av. Kilsyth 381 B9
av. McKinnon 456 C16
ct. Altona Mdw 451 G2
ct. Hampton Pk 551 J14
ct. Hoppers Csg 449 L1
ct. Keysborough 534 J8
ct. Macleod 285 C13
ct. Preston 282 G18
ct. Thomastown 241 G15
pl. Box Hill 375 A13
pl. Hawthorn E 372 G19
rd. Carrum 573 D8
rd. Clayton S 499 D14
rd. E Warburton 306 L18
rd. Highett 496 D16
rd. Kangaroo Grnd 247 F16
rd. Knoxfield 462 L6
rd. Silvan 385 A9
rd. View Bank 285 E20
rd. Wandin East 385 A9
st. Albert Park 29 A12
st. Albert Park 413 A7
st. Bacchus Msh 222 A19
st. Broadmeadows 237 L19
st. Fitzroy 19 B20
st. Glen Waverley 419 K19
st. Kensington 33 E9
st. Melton 269 A1
st. Newport 410 F6
st. Pascoe Vale S 324 K6
st. Port Melb 29 A12
st. Port Melb 412 G1
st. Sunshine 365 B4
st. Surrey Hills 374 A20
st. Surrey Hills 418 A2
st. W Footscray 366 K6
GRAHAM-MICHELE
cl. Keysborough 534 H13
GRAIL
ct. Glen Waverley 420 K15
GRAINGER
ct. Mulgrave 460 C16
st. Sunshine N 321 H13
GRAINGERS
rd. W Footscray 366 K10
GRAIN STORE
ct. Langwarrin 602 B17
GRAMAN
wy. Sydenham 274 J8
wy. Taylors Hill 274 J8
GRAMATAN
av. Beaumaris 529 L8
GRAMMAR
cl. Truganina 405 J13
st. Strathmore 280 B20
GRAMPIAN
st. Preston 282 D19
GRAMPIANS
ct. Taylors Lakes 276 B9
wy. Caroline Spr 317 K7
GRANARD
av. Pk Orchards 333 J17
GRANARY
la. Mentone 531 A7
GRANBY
cr. Highton 705 J8
cr. Highton 705 K8
ct. Endeavour Hl 537 C2
GRAND
bvd. Montmorency 287 A13
ct. Bangholme 549 J14
pde. Epping 241 F3
GRAND ARCH
dr. Berwick 553 H14
GRAND CANAL
bvd. Point Cook 450 K13
GRANDEUR
ct. Cranbourne 603 L5
GRANDIFLORA
ct. Dingley Village 533 E10
gr. Bundoora 242 G15
GRANDISON
gr. Oak Park 279 K10
st. Moonee Pnd 324 A10
GRAND PANORAMA
ct. Launching Pl 345 G13
GRAND VALLEY
ct. Lysterfield S 504 C16
tce. Ferntree Gly 464 C14
GRANDVALLEY
dr. Chirnside Pk 337 G6
GRANDVIEW
av. Beaumaris 529 L7
av. Croydon 336 A19
av. Dandenong 536 D7
av. Emerald 469 G13
av. Glen Iris 417 G10
av. Maribyrnong 323 C16
av. Mulgrave 499 K3
av. Pascoe Vale S 324 K3
av. Point Cook 450 D6
av. Ringwood E 379 C14
av. Rye 697 K5
av. Rye 697 L8
bvd. Craigieburn 150 E7
cr. Healesville 257 H1
cr. Hillside 232 B20

GREENVIEW
cl. Dingley Village 533 C7
cl. Lysterfield S 503 L15
ct. Bentleigh E 497 E7
ct. Epping 198 B19
ct. Greensborough 286 J2
ct. Rowville 463 G11
ct. Skye 601 G2
wy. Point Cook 450 L11
GREENVILLE
dr. Grovedale 706 D10
st. Mooroolbark 381 B2
GREENWALK
pl. Point Cook 450 F5
GREENWAY
ct. Wandana Ht 705 D4
dr. Mill Park 242 L5
dr. Mill Park 243 A6
GREENWAYS
ct. Parkdale 531 D11
rd. Glen Waverley 459 K3
GREENWELL
rd. Selby 466 L13
rd. Selby 467 A13
GREENWICH
cl. Wyndham Va 446 F8
cr. Caroline Spr 317 K4
ct. Glen Waverley 460 G11
pl. Campbellfield 239 H13
pl. View Bank 329 J3
GREENWOOD
av. Ringwood 378 E13
av. Sorrento 678 H6
dr. Bundoora 284 G6
dr. Carrum Downs 601 A6
dr. Launching Pl 345 E16
dr. Watsonia 285 A6
la. Forest Hill 420 K2
la. Mooroolbark 381 K2
st. Abbotsford 26 B1
st. Briar Hill 286 L5
st. Burwood 419 B9
st. Doncaster 330 F18
st. Newcomb 704 B16
st. Pascoe Vale S 281 A20
st. Wyndham Va 446 E11
GREENWOODS
cl. Dingley Village 533 C4
GREER
st. Footscray 367 J7
GREEVES
dr. Kilsyth 381 A9
st. Anglesea 713 E7
st. Fitzroy 19 A14
st. St Kilda 414 D17
GREG
ct. Narre Warren 538 G15
GREGG
ct. Hillside 274 G4
st. Diamond Ck 246 A11
GREG NORMAN
dr. Point Cook 451 A11
GREGORY
av. Frankston S 627 G10
av. Newtown 702 E14
cl. Endeavour Hl 538 A1
cr. Mulgrave 500 G3
ct. Carrum Downs 574 H16
ct. Cranbourne N 577 J9
ct. Doncaster 330 B20
ct. Pakenham 585 A3
ct. Sunbury 142 L14
ct. Sunbury 143 A14
ct. Werribee 447 E7
dr. Carrum Downs 574 L18
gr. Preston 283 C20
la. Kensington 33 E7
mw. Forest Hill 376 D20
pl. Melton W 225 L19
rd. Boronia 423 J14
st. Brunswick 325 D12
st. Mt Martha 656 B12
st. Oak Park 279 L14
st. Sunshine W 364 J5
GREIG
ct. Elwood 454 F2
pl. Werribee 447 B10
st. Albert Park 29 D12
st. Albert Park 413 B6
st. Reservoir 282 B1
st. Seddon 367 C12
st. Sunshine 321 G19
GREIGS
rd. Rockbank 270 G20
GREIGS-CAVALOT
rd. Bangholme 548 H14
GREIVE
st. Balwyn N 373 J6
GREMEL
rd. Reservoir 283 J13
GRENDA
ct. Dandenong S 535 H15
dr. Mill Park 242 B7
la. Dandenong, off George St 535 K10
GRENFELL
rd. Mt Waverley 418 G19
ri. Nar Warrn S 552 F7
wy. Rosebud 699 J4
GRENHILDA
rd. Rosanna 329 A2
GRENOBLE
ct. Highton 705 H5
GRENVILLE
ct. Berwick 554 A5
ct. Blackburn S 419 L2
gr. Rosebud W 698 K1
pl. Melton W 226 D18
st. Box Hill N 374 J10
st. Cockatoo 510 L6
st. Hampton 494 K7
st. Newtown 702 F13
tce. Roxburgh Pk 194 A9
GRESFORD
rd. Wantirna 422 G7
st. Sunshine N 321 D15
GRESHAM
ct. Endeavour Hl 537 J7
pl. Blackburn 375 K20
st. Melbourne 1 C11
st. Melbourne 23 J8
wy. Sunshine W 364 B9
wy. Sunshine W 364 C9
wy. Sunshine W 364 E9
GRESSWELL
rd. Bundoora 284 J9
rd. Macleod 284 J9
GRESSWELL PARK
dr. Macleod 285 C7
dr. Watsonia 285 C7
GRETA
av. Ferntree Gly 463 F7
ct. Broadmeadows 238 A9
ct. Highett 496 J15
ct. Templstw Lr 330 B12
st. Greensborough 285 J6
st. Oakleigh E 458 J16
GRETAL
ct. Taylors Lakes 275 J8
GRETANA
cr. Frankston 600 E18
st. Dandenong S 535 J15
GRETEL
ct. Croydon 336 J16
ct. Frankston 628 E10
ct. Hampton Pk 552 D16
ct. Scoresby 462 F8
gr. Melton 268 J2
pl. Berwick 554 K7
ps. Chirnside Pk 337 B4
GRETNA
cl. Westmeadows 236 F14
ct. Greenvale 193 D18
st. Mt Waverley 459 D7
GRETTON
ct. Highton 701 H17
GREVILLE
rd. Ferny Creek 466 C1
rd. Rosanna 329 C3
st. Essendon N 279 D20
st. Huntingdale 458 E13
st. Prahran 31 H17
st. Prahran 414 E9
GREVILLEA
av. Boronia 423 L11
cl. Eltham North 245 F16
cl. Hillside 274 B6
cr. Hoppers Csg 405 E16
ct. Forest Hill 420 K1
ct. Long Forest 224 G10
ct. Mornington 640 L17
ct. Mornington 641 A17
ct. Patterson L 573 H10
dr. Croydon N 335 L12
pl. Pakenham 584 K9
rd. Doncaster E 376 D6
rd. Kings Park 275 C17
rd. Langwarrin 601 K16
GREVILLIA
cr. Plenty 244 J11
ct. Altona Mdw 451 K1
ct. Frankston 599 K15
ct. Glen Waverley 460 D9
dr. Mill Park 243 A11
rd. Oak Park 280 D12
st. Doveton 536 G13
GREY
ct. Coburg 282 A19
ct. Sunbury 143 A16
ct. Wyndham Va 446 F7
st. Balwyn 372 L10
st. Belgrave 466 C16
st. Caulfield S 455 H11
st. Darley 221 F9
st. E Geelong 703 E13
st. E Melbourne 25 G4
st. Eltham 287 J10
st. Parkdale 531 L10
st. Ringwood E 379 B9
st. St Kilda 414 B14
st. South Yarra 32 D15
st. South Yarra 414 H8
st. Vermont 377 D20
GREYBOX
ct. Hillside 274 B1
GREYFERN
ct. Highton 701 L17
GREY GUM
ct. Tecoma 466 D8
ri. Diamond Ck 245 E12
GREYGUM
ct. Launching Pl 345 E12
tce. Croydon Hills 335 F14
GREYLEA
gr. Seabrook 450 L3
GREYSHARPS
rd. Hurstbridge 202 L15
rd. Hurstbridge 203 A14
GREYSTANES
cr. Endeavour Hl 502 L13
GREYSTOKE
ct. Berwick 554 A8
GREYTHORN
ct. Chirnside Pk 337 J4
rd. Balwyn N 374 A7
GREYTHORNE
ct. Narre Warren 538 J13
GRICE
al. Melbourne 1 E11
al. Melbourne 23 K8
av. Fitzroy N 20 A1
av. Mt Eliza 641 L5
cr. Essendon 324 A6
GRICES
rd. Berwick 580 B7
rd. Clyde North 580 B7
GRIEVE
pde. Altona 408 K20
pde. Altona North 409 A10
st. Bayswater 423 D8
st. Launching Pl 345 G16
st. Macleod 284 J15
GRIEVES
st. Newport 410 F7
st. Newport 410 F8
GRIFFIN
cl. Surrey Hills 418 C2
cr. Port Melb 412 H3
ct. Eltham 288 F4
ct. Lalor 241 L11
la. Melbourne 24 J2
st. Brighton East 495 C4
GRIFFITH
av. Bentleigh E 457 A15
pl. Carrum Downs 575 E15
st. Endeavour Hl 536 K3
st. Grovedale 706 B12
st. Knoxfield 463 C8
st. Maddingley 263 F2
st. Noble Park 534 K2
st. Werribee 447 K13
GRIFFITH PARK
rd. Eltham 287 H17
GRIFFITHS
ct. Dandenong N 501 L13
ct. Mt Waverley 459 A6
gr. Brighton East 455 F16
gr. Kew 372 J9
la. Warrandyte 332 K2
rd. Upwey 465 E15
st. Beaumaris 530 C9
st. Bellfield 328 B5
st. Caulfield S 455 L7
st. Reservoir 282 G9
st. Richmond 26 J10
GRIGG
av. Vermont 421 B2
GRIGGS
ct. Mornington 641 B14
GRIGORIEVA
ct. Burnside 318 E5
GRIMES
av. Taylors Lakes 275 L7
rd. Pt Lonsdale 707 G20
GRIMSBY
ct. Doncaster E 332 A17
GRIMSHAW
st. Bundoora 284 J2
st. Greensborough 285 C3
st. Greensborough 286 C4
st. Watsonia 285 C3
st. Watsonia N 285 C3
GRIMWADE
cr. Frankston 599 J16
ct. Caulfield N 415 B20
ct. Epping 242 C1
pl. Melton W 226 C17
st. Reservoir 282 K4
GRINDLAY
st. Newport 411 A8
GRINSTEAD
ct. Craigieburn 194 E2
GRINTER
st. Moolap 704 K19
GRIOTTE
st. Canterbury 373 F20
st. Canterbury 417 F1
GRIST
st. St Albans 319 J5
GROGAN
ct. Bayswater 423 C10
GRONG GRONG
ct. Toorak 415 H6
GRONN
pl. Brunswick W 324 J9
st. Reservoir 283 K4
GROOM
ct. Glen Waverley 420 F19
la. Fitzroy N 19 F6
st. Clifton Hill 20 E9
GROOME
ct. Altona Mdw 451 J11
GROSE
ct. Croydon Hills 335 D16
GROSS
ct. Grovedale 705 J13
ct. Mt Waverley 418 K15
GROSSMANS
rd. Torquay 711 A4
GROSVENOR
av. Mulgrave 500 G1
ct. Bundoora 284 J5
ct. Melton W 226 C12
ct. Portsea 678 A1
ct. Toorak 415 K7
dr. Wandana Ht 701 D17
dr. Wandana Ht 705 B1
pde. Balwyn 373 E10
pl. Carlton 18 F18
pl. Wantirna S 422 J14
pl. Werribee 447 B19
rd. Ferntree Gly 463 J12
rd. Glen Iris 416 G7
st. Abbotsford 371 A12
st. Balaclava 414 G20
st. Balaclava 414 H20
st. Blackburn N 376 A8
st. Brighton 454 F16
st. Doncaster 331 A19
st. Frankston S 626 H10
st. Moonee Pnd 324 A13
st. Niddrie 278 J20
st. South Yarra 32 B14
st. South Yarra 414 G7
wk. Lilydale 338 K1
wk. Lilydale 339 C5
GROUSE
ct. Werribee 448 C10
GROUT
st. Hampton 495 C7
st. Mentone 530 K8
GROVE
ct. Carrum Downs 574 J15
gdn. Berwick 554 C19
rd. Grovedale 706 C8
rd. Hawthorn 371 G13
rd. Marshall 706 G8
rd. Rosanna 329 A3
st. Eltham 287 J7
st. Vermont 421 D1
GROVEDALE
cl. Thomastown 240 F11
ct. Clayton 458 K18
rd. Surrey Hills 373 L14
GROVE END
rd. Endeavour Hl 537 D3
GROVE HALL
pl. Caroline Spr 317 L3
GROVELANDS
dr. Mulgrave 500 L5
GROVER
ct. Warranwood 334 K14
rd. Doncaster 331 E18
st. Pascoe Vale 280 E17
GROVES
st. Aspendale 546 D8
st. Keilor East 322 C4
GRUCHY
av. Chelsea Ht 547 F16
GRUMONT
rd. The Basin 425 H10
GRUNDY
st. Pascoe Vale S 324 J6
st. Westmeadows 236 L13
GRUNER
st. Sunbury 142 L10
st. Sunbury 143 A10
GRUYERE
cr. Ivanhoe East 328 L18
la. Ivanhoe East 328 K18
rd. Gruyere 297 C14
rd. Gruyere 341 C4
GRYLLS
st. Brunswick 325 H12
GRYPHON
wk. Kings Park 319 A2
GUAM
ct. Lalor 241 K8
GUAVA
cl. Sunshine W 364 A8
GUBBAH
ct. Ashwood 418 D18
GUELPH
st. Somerville 644 L13
st. Somerville 645 A13
GUERNSEY
av. Hampton E 496 A9
rd. Wandin East 340 K17
GUEST
av. Albanvale 319 B5
cl. Ringwood E 378 J10
rd. Oakleigh S 458 A16
rd. Pakenham 584 F3
st. Hawthorn 371 K17
st. Tootgarook 698 C5
GUESTS
la. Melbourne 1 D9
la. Melbourne 23 J7
GUIDEHOUSE
rd. Wesburn 348 B19
GUILA
ct. Epping 241 J3
GUILD
av. Noble Park 500 G13
GUILDFORD
av. Coolaroo 238 E7
av. Springvale 499 J18
cl. Frankston 627 K9
cr. Narre Warren 538 E19
ct. Keilor Dn 276 D13
dr. Doncaster E 332 G9
la. Melbourne 1 J5
la. Melbourne 23 L5
rd. Surrey Hills 373 J16
GUILFOYLE
av. Coburg N 281 C15
dr. Sassafras 426 H13
GUINANE
av. Hoppers Csg 448 G3
GUINEA
ct. Epping 198 E18
GUINESS
dr. Berwick 553 H13
GUINEVERE
pde. Glen Waverley 420 L17
GUINNESS
la. Kensington 33 F12
GULF
rd. Yarra Glen 209 A9
GULL
ct. Blind Bight 650 C9
ct. Patterson L 573 J10
ct. Rye 696 L14
wy. Nar Warrn S 552 F12
wy. Nar Warrn S 552 F13
GULLANE
dr. Sunbury 144 D12
GULLINE
cl. Bacchus Msh 221 K18
GULLQUIST
wy. Pakenham 584 C4
GULLS
wy. Frankston S 626 E8
wy. Sorrento 679 C17
GULLY
cr. Belgrave 466 G9
mw. Chirnside Pk 336 J8
tr. Lysterfield 505 D5
GULWA
av. Frankston 627 L6
GUM
cl. Broadmeadows 237 L12
cl. Hoppers Csg 405 F16
ct. Cranbourne N 578 B7
ct. Doveton 536 K8
ct. Knoxfield 463 D2
ct. Montrose 381 L8
ct. Werribee 448 H18
gld. Eltham 287 G4
gr. Bundoora 242 G14

rd. Kings Park 319 D3
st. Cockatoo 511 A8
st. Frankston N 600 C9
st. Sunshine W 364 H4
GUMBOW
cl. Bayswater N 380 J17
GUMBRAE
st. Reservoir 282 D11
GUMBUYA
cl. Eumemmerring 537 B14
GUM HILL
dr. Langwarrin 629 D13
GUMHILL
ct. Eltham 288 D7
GUMLEAF
ct. Deer Park 319 F10
la. Officer 582 G1
pl. Craigieburn 150 C13
GUMLEY
ct. Dingley Village 532 L5
GUM NUT
dr. Langwarrin 601 H16
GUMNUT
ct. Berwick 553 E4
la. Lynbrook 551 D18
ri. Bundoora 284 G8
GUM RIDGE
cl. Templestowe 332 A7
GUMS
av. Belgrave 466 D14
GUM TIP
ct. Mornington 656 J4
GUM TREE
rd. Research 288 F9
GUMTREE
cl. Croydon 380 C10
cl. St Albans 320 G10
cl. View Bank 285 L20
cl. Wheelers Hill 460 L13
ct. Campbellfield 239 F12
ct. Carrum Downs 575 F20
gr. Belgrave Ht 466 C19
gr. Hampton Pk 551 E12
pl. Moorooduc 643 L16
GUMVISTA
wk. Skye 575 G16
GUN BARREL
wy. Bangholme 548 L16
wy. Bangholme 549 A16
GUNBOWER
cl. Thomastown 240 E12
cr. Meadow Ht 194 D17
GUN CLUB
tr. Lysterfield 505 B13
GUNDARA
ct. Epping 241 K3
GUNDAROO
sq. Werribee 448 A20
GUNDOWRING
dr. Seabrook 451 A6
GUNDRY
gr. Watsonia N 243 D18
GUNGARLAN
dr. Keilor East 278 B19
GUNIDA
ct. St Andrews Bch 697 F20
GUNN
ct. Westmeadows 236 F13
st. Murrumbeena 457 B14
GUNNAWARRA
rd. Kurunjang 227 B12
GUNNEDAH
st. Albion 320 K19
GUNNII
nk. Mill Park 243 C10
GUNNS
rd. Hallam 537 H14
GUNSYND
cl. Thomastown 240 H16
ct. Bacchus Msh 221 F17
ct. Cranbourne W 577 G17
ct. Keilor Dn 275 K14
GUNTHER
av. Springvale 500 B16
ct. Mt Waverley 459 F8
GUNYAH
ct. Kurunjang 227 D14
mw. St Albans 320 L7
mw. St Albans 321 A7
rd. Blackburn N 376 C11
st. Rye 697 A5
GURLEY
ct. Grovedale 706 C10
GURNER
ct. Endeavour Hl 538 A8
la. Roxburgh Pk 194 A14
st. St Kilda 414 C15
GURNERS
la. Melbourne 1 F15
la. Melbourne 23 L10
la. Mt Martha 656 H8
la. Taylors Hill 274 F10
GURR
st. E Geelong 703 G11
GURRBORRA
wy. Bundoora 284 E3
GUSTAVIS
ct. Nar Warrn S 552 G17
GUTHRIE
st. Brunswick W 324 K16
GUY
ct. Fawkner 239 G20
ct. Montrose 382 D9
ct. Nar Warrn N 538 L11
ct. Sunshine W 364 G7
ct. Wantirna 422 D11
st. Upwey 465 E13
GUYMER
ct. Montmorency 287 A10
GUYRA
ct. Werribee 447 E11
GWALIA
ct. Rowville 463 H13
GWELO
st. W Footscray 366 D9
GWEN
ct. Taylors Lakes 275 G9
rd. Cranbourne W 577 C11
GWENDA
av. Blackburn 376 B16
av. Canterbury 373 B16
av. Moorabbin 496 C8
ct. Lower Plenty 286 J14
ct. Nar Warrn S 553 A20
st. Box Hill S 418 G2
st. Dandenong 535 K4
GWENDOLINE
av. Bentleigh 455 J18
GWENETH
av. Highton 701 J16
GWENMAY
ct. Ringwood N 378 F3
GWENNETH
cr. Sassafras 426 F16
GWENO
av. Frankston 626 K3
GWENT
st. Springvale S 533 K6
GWENTON
av. Cranbourne E 604 H5
GWILT
st. Westmeadows 237 E13
GWINGANA
cr. Glen Waverley 460 G5
GWYDIR
ct. Werribee 447 E7
GWYN
cr. Boronia 424 F14
ri. Vermont S 420 L8
ri. Vermont S 421 A8
GWYNNE
st. Cremorne 32 B2
st. Mt Waverley 419 C18
GWYTHER
rd. Highton 705 F3
GYLES
st. Pascoe Vale 280 G16
GYMEA
av. Rowville 502 C6
ct. Glen Waverley 420 D16
ct. Keysborough 534 G8
GYMKHANA
ct. Endeavour Hl 504 A18
pl. Keilor Park 277 H13
GYMPIE
la. Aspendale Gdn 547 A3
st. Bulleen 329 J14
GYPSY
ct. Mill Park 243 C12
GYRA
ct. Bundoora 285 A2
GYRO
ct. Gisborne 109 K7
GYTON
av. Glen Waverley 420 C15

H

HAAG
rd. Seville 341 G12
HACKETT
ct. Delahey 275 E10
st. Pascoe Vale S 324 F1
HACKETTS
la. Point Cook 449 F20
rd. Olinda 427 B18
rd. Yarrambat 201 F17
HACKWORTH
rd. Rye 696 D7
HADDINGTON
cr. Greenvale 237 A3
HADDON
ct. Meadow Ht 238 C5
ct. Mitcham 377 G12
HADFIELD
ct. Broadmeadows 238 D20
HADKINSON
st. Clayton S 499 A6
HADLEY
cl. Kealba 276 K19
ct. Glen Iris 416 F7
ct. Templestowe 332 A5
st. Seaford 599 G10
HADLOW
dr. Wantirna 422 G7
HAERING
rd. Boronia 423 J9
HAFEY
cr. Hoppers Csg 448 E4
HAFFENDEN
la. St Andrews 205 E1
HAGAN
ct. Belmont 702 J18
pl. Keysborough 534 C7
HAGEN
cl. Hoppers Csg 449 B2
ct. Diamond Ck 245 K13
dr. Berwick 553 L2
st. Lalor 240 H7
HAGGARDS
la. Woori Yallock 344 C13
HAIDEH
ct. Hoppers Csg 449 D2
pl. Wantirna S 462 A5
HAIG
av. Coburg 325 C7
av. Edithvale 546 J12
av. Healesville 257 G2
av. Monbulk 428 F18
ct. Doncaster E 376 B6
la. Southbank 23 K19
pl. Attwood 237 C12
rd. Mt Evelyn 339 B13
st. Balwyn 373 A10
st. Box Hill S 374 L20
st. Box Hill S 375 A20
st. Box Hill S 418 L2
st. Burwood 417 L13
st. Croydon 380 C2
st. Heidelberg Ht 328 D3
st. Mornington 640 G14
st. Reservoir 282 F15
st. Ringwood 378 D15
st. Southbank 23 J19
HAIGH
ct. Altona Mdw 451 G4
st. Oakleigh S 497 F4
HAILES
ct. Carrum Downs 574 L16
ct. Carrum Downs 574 L17
st. Greensborough 285 L2
st.e, Greensborough 286 B3
HAILEY
ct. Taylors Lakes 275 H2
ct. Templestowe 332 C10
HAILEYBURY
ct. Keysborough 534 E11
ct. Sunbury 144 G10
ct. Wantirna 422 J9
st. Brighton 494 H4
HAILSHAM
ct. Mulgrave 501 G3
HAINES
ct. Sunbury 143 F6
st. Cheltenham 530 L1
st. Hawthorn 372 B15
st. Mitcham 377 B12
st. N Melbourne 17 A13
st. N Melbourne 34 K14
HAINTHORPE
gr. Mulgrave 500 L5
gr. Mulgrave 501 A5
HAIR
ct. Beaconsfield 554 L16
HAITE
ct. Endeavour Hl 537 B4
pl. Roxburgh Pk 194 A15
HAKATERE
st. Northcote 327 B13
HAKEA
av. Rosebud W 699 B1
ct. Altona Mdw 407 L20
ct. Langwarrin 601 H20
ct. Mt Waverley 459 B2
ct. Thomastown 240 K12
ct. Werribee 447 K10
dr. Montrose 381 L17
dr. Mt Martha 656 E7
pl. Meadow Ht 193 J20
pl. Rowville 502 E5
rd. Keilor 276 F7
rd. Taylors Lakes 276 F7
st. Doveton 536 G12
st. Frankston 627 D5
st. Tecoma 466 B11
st. Templestowe 331 B7
st. Watsonia N 243 G20
st. Watsonia N 285 G1
HAKEA RIDGE
tr. Frankston N 600 F13
HAKEVILLE
av. Nunawading 376 H8
HALBERT
rd. Bayswater N 380 E14
HALCOT
cl. Mulgrave 501 D5
HALCYON
av. The Patch 467 J3
ct. Doncaster E 332 C15
dr. Wheelers Hill 460 J8
gr. Cockatoo 510 K10
wy. Nar Warrn S 552 H9
HALDANE
ct. Doncaster E 332 G8
rd. Eltham 287 G17
rd. Niddrie 278 J19
st. Beaumaris 530 C11
st. Bonbeach 573 B5
st. Keysborough 535 A11
HALE
ct. Burwood E 419 F7
st. Kew East 372 E4
HALES
cr. Jacana 237 K17
cr. Jacana 237 L18
ct. Keysborough 534 C9
ct. Mill Park 242 H9
ct. Northcote 326 H20
HALESWORTH
st. St Albans 320 G5
HALEY
ct. Noble Park 535 B6
st. Diamond Ck 245 K11
HALEYS GULLY
rd. Hurstbridge 202 C10
HALFMOON
pl. Pt Lonsdale 707 H18
HALFORD
la. Kensington 33 D8
st. Beaconsfld Up 542 F15
HALIDAY
ct. Greensborough 243 L20
ct. Greensborough 285 L1
HALIDON
cl. St Helena 245 A18
HALIFAX
av. Heidelberg 329 E2
cl. St Albans 275 J19
ct. Ashburton 417 K18
st. Brighton 454 K20
st. Brighton 455 A18
st. Dandenong 535 L1
st. Mont Albert N 374 E10
st. Mulgrave 500 D5
HALINKA
ct. Noble Park 534 D4
HALL
av. Altona Mdw 407 H18
av. Cockatoo 511 A5
ct. Berwick 554 F17
ct. Dandenong S 535 L13
ct. Meadow Ht 237 J2
ct. Thomastown 242 A13
rd. Carrum Downs 574 J19
rd. Cranbourne W 602 B1
rd. Gladstone Pk 237 D20
rd. Gladstone Pk 279 E1
rd. Healesville 214 H18
rd. Nar Warrn E 506 K18
rd. Ringwood N 334 E13
rd. Skye 575 G20
rd. Warrandyte S 334 E13
st. Braeside 532 G12
st. Brighton 454 L19
st. Brighton 455 A19
st. Brunswick 325 B11
st. Cheltenham 496 H20
st. Clifton Hill 20 H5
st. Coburg 325 E7
st. Epping 197 E17
st. Fairfield 327 F15
st. Hawthorn E 416 C7
st. Hoppers Csg 448 L4
st. McKinnon 456 E17
st. Moonee Pnd 324 B13
st. Mt Martha 669 B1
st. Newport 411 A5
st. Ormond 456 E16
st. Port Melb 368 E17
st. Spotswood 411 A5
st. Sunshine W 363 L4
st. Yarraville 367 E15
HALLAM
gr. Anglesea 713 H3
rd. Hallam 537 L20
rd. Hampton Pk 551 H18
rd. Lynbrook 551 H18
HALLAM NORTH
rd. Endeavour Hl 538 B3
rd. Lysterfield S 504 C17
rd. Nar Warrn N 504 C20
rd. Nar Warrn N 538 B9
HALLAM VALLEY
rd. Dandenong S 536 H20
rd. Dandenong S 551 A1
HALLCROFT
pl. Hawthorn E 372 H17
HALLETTS
wy. Bacchus Msh 221 G13
wy. Darley 221 F8
HALLEUR
rd. Harkaway 540 A10
HALLEY
av. Camberwell 417 B7
cr. Campbellfield 194 L20
ct. Bentleigh 496 F1
rd. Ferntree Gly 424 G19
rd. Panton Hill 204 H9
st. Blackburn 376 B20
HALLIDAY
ct. Hughesdale 457 E13
st. Mt Waverley 458 F3
HALLIFAX
ct. Doncaster E 332 H8
st. Seaford 573 E17
HALLINAN
ct. Cheltenham 531 B4
HALLIS
ct. Torquay 712 H2
HALLMARK
cl. Mill Park 242 L10
dr. Nar Warrn S 578 E3
pl. Keilor Dn 276 A12
rd. Mordialloc 532 C16
HALLOW
st. Bentleigh E 457 F16
HALLOWS
st. Glen Waverley 420 F14
HALLS
pde. Mitcham 377 E18
pde. Vermont 377 E18
tr. Kallista 467 B2
HALLSTON
ct. Meadow Ht 238 A4
HALPIN
st. Brunswick W 324 L14
HALSBURY
cl. Doncaster E 332 D13
ct. St Helena 245 D15
dr. Rowville 502 J3
pl. Skye 601 F2
st. Hadfield 280 J9
HALSEY
rd. Airport W 278 H12
st. Box Hill S 375 A20
st. Ferntree Gly 424 E19
st. Reservoir 282 C4
HALSHAM
ct. Greenvale 192 K18
HALSTEAD
ct. Cranbourne 578 B15
ct. Hillside 232 F20
pl. Geelong West 702 H6
st. Caulfield N 455 H1
st. Maidstone 366 E1
HALSTON
rd. Lalor 241 A5
HALTER
cr. Epping 198 E19
HALTON
rd. Dandenong N 501 D15
rd. Noble Park N 501 D15
HALWYN
cr. Preston 326 B5
HAM
pl. S Geelong 703 A14
rd. Ferny Creek 466 C4
HAMAL
st. Donvale 376 E3
HAMBLEDON
ct. Craigieburn 150 D20
rd. Hawthorn 415 J2
HAMBLETON
ct. Lysterfield 464 C17
st. Albert Park 29 K15

st. Albert Park 413 E8
st. Middle Park 29 K15
st. Middle Park 413 E8
HAMBLINGS
la. Geelong 703 B12
HAMEL
st. Albion 320 L20
st. Box Hill S 418 F4
st. Hampton 495 A6
HAMER
st. Brunswick E 325 L13
st. Moorabbin 496 D10
HAMERSLEY
ct. Mt Eliza 642 E2
ct. Reservoir 239 L20
HAMILTON
av. Blackburn 375 G12
cl. Endeavour Hl 537 E2
cl. Kilsyth 381 G10
cl. Malvern 415 L8
cr. Bacchus Msh 221 K13
cr. Doncaster E 375 K3
ct. Lalor 241 H7
ct. Pearcedale 647 J1
ct. Watsonia N 243 G19
dr. Cranbourne N 578 H9
dr. Ringwood N 378 H2
gr. Frankston S 627 B7
hwy. Fyansford 701 B5
hwy. Geelong West 702 D6
hwy. Herne Hill 702 D6
hwy. Manifold Ht 702 D6
pl. Mornington 640 H19
pl. Mt Waverley 419 A20
rd. Bayswater N 379 L19
rd. Bayswater N 423 L1
rd. Emerald 509 H5
rd. Malvern 415 L8
rd. New Gisborne 79 L1
rd. New Gisborne 80 H1
rd. N Warrandyte 290 E13
rd. Riddells Ck 80 H1
st. Alphington 327 G18
st. Balwyn 373 E11
st. Bentleigh 456 A18
st. Brighton 454 L10
st. Broadmeadows 237 L11
st. Brunswick W 325 A10
st. Craigieburn 150 H15
st. Deer Park 319 B17
st. Diggers Rest 141 L11
st. Elsternwick 455 A7
st. Gisborne 78 G12
st. Kew East 372 E6
st. Mont Albert 374 D16
st. Niddrie 279 A20
st. Niddrie 322 L2
st. Oakleigh 458 C14
st. Safety Bch 669 C14
st. Seddon 367 A13
st. Yarraville 367 A13
HAMISH
ct. Greensborough 244 B16
HAMLAN
pl. Newtown 702 G12
HAMLET
pl. Dingley Village 533 D3
st. Cheltenham 496 D17
HAMLYN
ct. Meadow Ht 237 K4
st. Aberfeldie 323 E9
HAMMEL
ct. Hallam 537 J18
HAMMENCE
st. Glen Waverley 420 F19
HAMMER
ct. Hoppers Csg 449 J2
HAMMERDALE
av. St Kilda E 414 H15
HAMMERSLEY
ct. Kilsyth 381 J6
ct. Lalor 240 H7
ct. Taylors Lakes 276 C9
pl. Caroline Spr 317 K8
HAMMERWOOD
grn. Officer 555 G20
HAMMOND
av. Airport W 279 B16
cct. Hopetoun Park 265 L6
cct. Hopetoun Park 266 A7
ct. Altona Mdw 451 C2
dr. Epping 197 G17
pl. Roxburgh Pk 194 E10
rd. Dandenong S 535 J20
rd. Dandenong S 549 G11
st. Altona 408 L15
st. Brighton 455 A19
st. Ringwood 378 C18
st. Sunshine N 321 C15
st. Thornbury 327 B11
HAMPDEN
av. Frankston 600 D18
ct. Rowville 463 H12
ct. Templestowe 331 F12
pl. Point Cook 450 A4
rd. Armadale 415 D13
rd. Kensington 33 K12
st. Braybrook 366 B3
st. Dallas 238 K10
st. Mornington 640 E17
HAMPSHIRE
cr. Sunshine 321 D20
ct. Bayswater N 380 F16
ct. Rowville 502 L6
ct. Rowville 503 A6
ct. Tarneit 405 C12
dr. Narr Warrn S 552 E18
rd. Doncaster 375 D4
rd. Forest Hill 420 J5
rd. Glen Waverley 459 H11
rd. Sunshine 365 C2
rd. Sunshine 365 C6
HAMPSON
pl. Caroline Spr 318 A4
HAMPSTEAD
cr. Glen Waverley 460 E12
ct. Thomastown 240 K11
dr. Hoppers Csg 448 H6
grn. Caroline Spr 317 L4
rd. Maidstone 322 G19
rd. Noble Park N 501 E17
HAMPTON
av. Sunshine 365 C7
cl. Narre Warren 539 F17
ct. Dandenong N 502 D13
ct. Glen Waverley 459 J8
ct. Hoppers Csg 405 B19
ct. Ivanhoe 328 D10
ct. Lilydale 338 K1
ct. Lilydale 339 C5
ct. Officer 555 J19
ct. Rosebud 684 F16
ct. Thomastown 241 K15
dr. Hampton Pk 551 F7
gr. Camberwell 417 F3
pde. W Footscray 366 E11
rd. Essendon W 322 K7
st. Brighton 455 B20
st. Brighton 495 A10
st. Hampton 494 L10
st. Newtown 702 F13
HAMS
rd. Waurn Ponds 705 A17
HAMSTEAD
ct. Endeavour Hl 503 C20
HAMSTERLEY
sq. Wantirna 422 F14
HANBURY
cl. Point Cook 450 H8
ct. Carrum Downs 575 E18
ct. Keysborough 534 B9
HANBY
st. Brighton 494 L3
HANCE
st. Yarraville 367 B17
HANCOCK
cl. St Helena 245 E16
cr. Braybrook 366 B1
dr. Berwick 553 J14
dr. Ferntree Gly 463 J7
st. Altona 409 A18
st. Southbank 3 A12
st. Southbank 23 L19
st. Vermont S 420 K8
HAND
st. Warburton 349 G1
HANDASYDE
av. Kilsyth S 425 A1
pl. Burwood, off Abrahams Ct 419 B7
HANDEL
ct. Blackburn 375 J19
ct. Bundoora 242 L20
HANDFIELD
st. Eltham 287 F8
HANDFORD
la. Officer 581 J6
HANDLEY
cr. Dandenong S 535 D11
ct. Blackburn N 376 B9
ct. Frankston S 626 L8
HANDS
rd. Kalorama 383 A11
HANDSCOMBE
ct. Croydon Hills 335 D14
HANDSWORTH
cr. Tullamarine 278 L3
HANI
ct. Torquay 712 G2
pl. Grovedale 706 F15
HANKE
pl. Sunbury 142 G7
rd. Doncaster 374 K3
HANLETH
av. Springvale 499 H17
HANLEY
ct. Pakenham 584 E3
st. Avondale Ht 321 L10
st. Narre Warren 553 F8
HANLON
cl. Mordialloc 532 E18
HANMER
st. Williamstown 411 H17
HANN
cl. Endeavour Hl 537 J5
st. Pearcedale 647 A6
HANNA
ct. Braybrook 366 C1
ct. Point Cook 450 F6
dr. Endeavour Hl 537 K3
la. S Melbourne 3 D20
la. S Melbourne 30 D2
st. Melbourne 31 B14
st. Melbourne 414 A7
st. Noble Park 535 B4
HANNAGAN
st. Aspendale Gdn 546 G2
HANNAH
av. Hillside 274 G5
cl. Glen Waverley 459 J9
cl. Melton W 225 L18
ct. Cranbourne 578 A11
st. Cheltenham 497 D16
st. Preston 283 H19
st. Seaford 599 G10
st. Southbank 3 A8
st. Southbank 23 L17
HANNAH PASCOE
dr. Gowanbrae 279 D7
HANNAM
ct. Roxburgh Pk 193 J13
HANNAN
st. Williamstown 411 B18
HANNASLEA
st. Box Hill 374 K18
HANNORA
cr. Croydon 335 E20
cr. Croydon 379 E1
HANNOVER
rd. Badger Creek 258 E8
HANOVER
ct. Avondale Ht 322 F8
ct. Endeavour Hl 536 L2
ct. Endeavour Hl 537 A2
rd. Vermont S 420 L10
rd. Vermont S 421 A9
st. Brunswick 325 C11
st. Fitzroy 18 L17
st. Oakleigh 457 L12
HANRAHAN
st. Thomastown 241 G20
HANS
av. Ringwood N 378 G1
ct. Mulgrave 500 B3
HANSA
wk. Heidelberg W 284 A20
HANSEN
cl. Burwood 419 B7
ct. Mt Martha 656 E8
ct. Narre Warren 539 A13
dr. Grovedale 706 G15
rd. Boronia 424 J15
rd. Kilsyth 381 E6
st. Altona North 410 D6
st. Brighton East 495 H1
st. Forest Hill 376 E20
st. Kew 371 L13
st. Mt Waverley 458 H3
st. W Footscray 366 H12
HANSFORD
cl. Kilsyth 381 G10
st. Narre Warren 553 C11
HANSLOPE
av. Alphington 327 F19
HANSLOW
wy. Taylors Lakes 275 F8
HANSON
ct. Taylors Lakes 233 C17
rd. Craigieburn 150 F15
st. Darley 222 D9
st. Niddrie 278 H18
HANSWORTH
st. Mulgrave 500 F4
st. Mulgrave 501 B6
HANWELL
ct. Croydon N 336 A14
ct. Glen Waverley 460 K6
HAPPY HOLLOW
dr. Greensborough 244 B13
dr. Plenty 244 B13
HAPPY VALLEY
av. Blairgowrie 696 C1
ct. Doncaster E 332 F11
ct. Rowville 502 L2
ct. Rowville 503 A2
ri. Diamond Ck 245 G10
HARBARD
st. Thomastown 240 G13
HARBER
ct. Glen Waverley 419 L15
HARBERTS
rd. Don Valley 346 B8
HARBINGER
ct. Wheelers Hill 460 H16
HARBISON
la. Gisborne 110 E8
HARBORNE
st. Macleod 285 F10
HARBOUR
dr. Patterson L 547 H20
dr. Patterson L 547 J20
esp. Docklands 23 A8
st. Beaconsfield 555 D13
st. Queenscliff 709 D16
wy. Blind Bight 650 E8
HARBURY
mw. Hampton Pk 551 F4
st. Reservoir 282 H10
HARCOMBE
dr. Sunbury 142 F9
HARCOURT
av. Caulfield 455 F3
av. Frankston S 626 K7
av. Mulgrave 500 A4
av. St Albans 320 K4
cl. Hampton Pk 551 K5
cl. Sunbury 142 H8
cr. Gladstone Pk 237 B20
cr. Gladstone Pk 279 C1
pde. Cremorne 25 K20
pde. Cremorne 31 L1
pl. Lower Plenty 286 H19
rd. Altona 407 H12
rd. Boronia 424 H11
sq. Wyndham Va 446 J9
st. Ashwood 418 E17
st. Blackburn N 375 L9
st. Doncaster 374 F2
st. Hawthorn E 372 E15
st. Newtown 702 B10
st. N Melbourne 17 E14
wy. Berwick 554 D2
HARDHAM
st. Belgrave 466 G18
HARDIDGE
ct. Doncaster 375 A4
st. Croydon 336 B19
HARDIE
rd. Brooklyn 366 B16
rd. Yarraville 366 B17
st. Hampton 494 J6
HARDIMAN
ct. Mill Park 242 A8
st. Bundoora 284 B8
st. Kensington 34 B11
HARDING
av. Bonbeach 545 E14
la. Bonbeach, off Harding Av 545 F14
rd. Macclesfield 471 C8
rd. Warrandyte 334 E3
st. Ascot Vale 324 D19
st. Bentleigh 495 L4
st. Coburg 326 A3
st. Highett 496 B12
st. Surrey Hills 374 D19
st. Thomastown 240 L15
st. Thomastown 241 A15
HARDINGE
st. Beaumaris 530 A10
HARDMAN
ct. Endeavour Hl 537 B5
HARDNER
rd. Mt Waverley 459 A8
HARDWARE
la. Taylors Hill 274 F8
st. Melbourne 1 K11
st. Melbourne 24 A5
HARDWICK
la. Kensington 33 F7
st. Coburg 325 J5
HARDWICKE
ct. Frankston 628 D11
st. Balwyn 373 B11
st. N Melbourne 17 B13
HARDWOOD
ct. Mitcham 376 L11
HARDY
av. Cannons Creek 649 G8
av. Craigieburn 150 G19
cl. Gladstone Pk 236 L16
cr. Heathmont 422 F2
ct. Bentleigh 455 H19
ct. Berwick 553 K6
ct. Oakleigh S 498 E2
gr. Beaumaris 530 E7
st. Brunswick 325 H11
st. Lilydale 338 E6
st. Mornington 641 B16
st. Preston 282 F18
st. Rye 696 G2
st. Selby 467 A13
st. South Yarra 31 L15
st. South Yarra 414 F8
tce. Ivanhoe East 328 F16
HARDYS
rd. Clyde North 580 A20
rd. Melton W 224 L12
rd. Melton W 225 A12
rd. Tooradin 652 D1
HARE
ct. Darley 221 K10
st. Fawkner 281 L6
HAREEBA
ct. Mornington 657 C5
HAREFIELD
cr. Kealba 320 L1
HARESTA
av. Dandenong S 535 J15
HAREWOOD
cl. Boronia 424 E6
st. Tooradin 651 K8
HAREWOOD MAINS
rd. Tooradin 652 B4
HAREWOOD PARK
rd. Gembrook 512 C16
HARFLEUR
av. Beaumaris 530 G10
HARGRAVE
cr. Wandana Ht 705 D2
ct. Cranbourne 603 L2
ct. Mill Park 242 J5
st. Airport W 279 D16
HARGREAVES
cr. Braybrook 365 L2
st. Cremorne 32 D3
st. Fitzroy 19 F15
st. Huntingdale 458 E15
st. Mornington 640 C16
HARICOT
ct. Keilor Dn 275 J11
ct. Seabrook 450 K6
HARKAWAY
dr. Cheltenham 497 H20
rd. Berwick 554 E1
rd. Harkaway 540 G8
rd. Nar Warrn N 540 G8
ri. Doncaster E 332 D14
HARKER
st. Alphington 327 J18
st. Burwood 418 C10
st. Healesville 257 G1
st. N Melbourne 17 C13
st. Sunbury 143 G14
HARKIN
av. Mentone 531 A10
HARKNESS
rd. Melton W 225 C17
HARLAND
sq. Wantirna 422 H12
HARLAW
ct. Wheelers Hill 460 H18
HARLEIAN
st. Blairgowrie 695 L1
HARLESTON
rd. Mt Eliza 626 D11
st. St Albans 320 G5
HARLEY
cr. Mooroolbark 381 A1
ct. Berwick 554 A4
ct. Keilor East 322 B3
ct. Thomastown 240 D15
pl. Wheelers Hill 460 H15
st. Dingley Village 533 F9
st. Knoxfield 462 L7
st. Knoxfield 463 A7
st. Sunshine N 321 E14
st.n, Knoxfield 462 L4
st.n, Knoxfield 463 A4
HARLINGFORD
ct. Wheelers Hill 461 D15
HARLINGTON
av. Eltham 287 K10
st. Clayton 498 G3
HARLOW
ct. Deer Park 319 B8
ct. Keysborough 535 B11
ct. Moorabbin 496 G11
HARMAN
av. Eltham 288 C4
cl. Doncaster E 332 H7

HARMER
rd. Hallam...537 F16
st. Reservoir...283 B3
HARMON
av. St Albans...320 J3
cl. Berwick...553 K16
HARMONY
cl. Lilydale...338 D14
ct. Springvale S...534 B3
dr. Tarneit...447 H1
HARMSWORTH
av. Wantirna...422 D10
st. Collingwood...19 L15
HARNESS
ct. Sydenham...274 L4
pl. Pakenham...585 F6
HARNETT
st. Boronia...424 J15
HAROLD
av. Glen Iris...416 G16
ct. Baxter...644 B3
ct. Whittlesea...96 G19
pl. Thornbury...326 J8
rd. Keysborough...533 K4
rd. Noble Park...533 K4
rd. Rye...696 E9
rd. Skye...602 C10
rd. Springvale S...533 K4
st. Ascot Vale...323 F16
st. Ashwood...418 A15
st. Blackburn...375 H13
st. Bonbeach...573 D1
st. Briar Hill...286 G3
st. Bulleen...330 A17
st. Cockatoo...471 F17
st. Glenroy...280 C6
st. Hawthorn E...372 G19
st. McKinnon...455 J15
st. Middle Park...29 L20
st. Middle Park...413 F10
st. Olinda...426 J9
st. Preston...327 A4
st. Sandringham...495 D18
st. Seaford...599 E1
st. Seddon...367 A11
st. Thornbury...326 D7
st. Wantirna...422 C9
HAROLD KEYS
dr. Nar Warrn S...552 F8
dr. Nar Warrn S...552 G6
HAROS
av. Nunawading...376 G18
HARP
rd. Kew...372 F7
rd. Kew East...372 F7
HARPER
av. Bentleigh E...496 H4
cl. Craigieburn...194 H2
ct. Port Melb...412 H5
la. Melbourne...1 G17
la. Melbourne...24 A11
pl. Mill Park...242 L5
pl. Mill Park...243 A5
st. Abbotsford...20 E17
st. Kensington...33 J8
st. Northcote...326 K19
st. Werribee...447 B13
HARPFIELD
rd. Beaconsfld Up...542 C12
HARPLEY
st. Cheltenham...531 C4
HARPTREE
cl. Rowville...503 C6
HARPUR
ct. Oakleigh E...458 H12
HARRA
ct. Oak Park...280 D12
HARRAP
ct. Diamond Ck...245 K5
rd. Mt Martha...656 H7
rd. Mt Martha...657 A8
HARRICKS
cr. Attwood...237 C12
rd. Keilor Park...277 G14
HARRIDGE
st. Rosebud...700 A1
HARRIER
cl. Blind Bight...650 C9
ct. Dingley Village...533 C10
ct. Mornington...640 L17
st. Werribee...448 C9
HARRIES
ct. Nar Warrn N...539 F12
HARRIET
st. Heathmont...379 D18
st. Seddon...367 B12
st. Werribee...448 E11
HARRIETT
cr. Mont Albert...374 F12

HARRINGTON
av. Balwyn N...373 K4
dr. Melton W...225 G18
pl. Doncaster E...332 H13
rd. Airport W...278 F14
st. Altona...408 J17
st. Diamond Ck...246 C14
HARRIS
av. Glen Iris...416 G9
av. Hoppers Csg...448 L2
cr. Glen Waverley...460 D7
ct. Clarinda...498 G10
ct. Pakenham...584 G6
gr. Bayswater...423 E4
pl. N Melbourne...17 D14
rd. Beaconsfld Up...542 H14
rd. Donvale...377 J3
rd. Wonga Park...335 L1
st. Altona North...365 E20
st. Blackburn N...375 K10
st. Brunswick...325 G13
st. Footscray...367 F13
st. N Melbourne...17 C14
st. St Albans...320 C7
st. Springvale...499 J10
HARRIS GULLY
rd. Warrandyte...333 E10
HARRISON
av. Burwood...418 A12
cr. Hawthorn...371 D13
ct. Altona Mdw...451 H2
ct. Carrum Downs...574 K19
ct. Highton...701 K18
ct. Mornington...640 L13
ct. Point Cook...450 E5
dr. Cranbourne...603 K3
pl. Fitzroy...19 A12
rd. Montrose...382 J4
st. Bellfield...327 L6
st. Box Hill N...375 B9
st. Brunswick E...326 B11
st. Deer Park...319 C15
st. Dromana...686 C4
st. Mitcham...377 C12
st. Ringwood...378 C10
st. The Basin...425 B12
HARRISONS
rd. Dromana...687 H11
rd. Red Hill...687 H11
rd. Werribee S...488 H1
HARROW
av. Somerville...644 K19
cl. Belmont...702 D20
ct. Doncaster...330 D20
ct. Sunbury...144 F10
gdn. Wantirna...422 F13
mw. Cheltenham...496 J13
pl. Endeavour Hl...537 E3
st. Blackburn S...419 E6
st. Box Hill...374 L16
st. Frankston...627 D5
st. Preston...327 E2
HARROWER
st. Roxburgh Pk...193 L9
HARROW HILL
ct. Frankston S...627 H18
HARRY
ct. Dingley Village...532 K6
ct. Frankston S...627 F12
ct. Mt Waverley...459 B4
st. Blackburn...375 G19
st. Brunswick W...324 J11
st. Cranbourne...604 B3
st. Doncaster E...376 C4
st. Hampton E...495 L8
st. Maidstone...322 H20
st. Maidstone...366 H1
st. Thornbury...327 D8
HARRY LACEY
la. Croydon...380 B3
HARRY NANCE
cl. Lysterfield...503 K1
HARSBURG
ct. Taylors Lakes...275 H9
HARSTON
st. Sandringham...495 B14
HART
av. Greensborough...286 C6
ct. Gladstone Pk...237 C16
pl. Taylors Lakes...233 C19
st. Airport W...279 A17
st. Caulfield N...455 H2
st. Hoppers Csg...448 K2
HARTIGAN
ct. Rosebud...700 A3
st. Blackburn...376 B12
HARTINGTON
dr. Wantirna...422 F15
st. Elsternwick...455 C8
st. Glenroy...279 L3
st. Kew...372 C8
st. Northcote...326 G15

HARTLAND
ct. Craigieburn...194 B1
rd. Vermont S...420 K12
wy. Eltham...288 A9
HARTLANDS
rd. Ivanhoe East...328 J15
HARTLEY
av. Caulfield...455 G3
av. W Footscray...366 E7
cr. Greenvale...193 C19
ct. Frankston...600 H17
ct. Mill Park...242 C6
ct. Noble Park N...501 E14
ct. Rosanna...284 L17
ct. Rosanna...285 A17
ct. Sorrento...679 B16
la. Newport...411 A11
lk. Endeavour Hl...537 G4
rd. Blackburn S...420 A5
rd. Croydon...336 D17
rd. Wonga Park...291 F17
st. Brighton...494 H4
st. Broadmeadows...238 D18
st. Southbank...368 K19
st. Northcote...327 A16
HARTNETT
cl. Mulgrave...499 J1
ct. Moonee Pnd...324 E10
dr. Seaford...599 H7
HARTPURY
av. Elwood...454 F1
HARTS
pde. Hawthorn E...416 D1
HARTSMERE
dr. Berwick...580 L1
HARTVILLE
ct. Thomastown...240 J11
HARTWELL
ct. Frankston...600 D19
ct. Mooroolbark...337 E18
ct. Werribee...446 L19
ct. Werribee...447 A19
pl. Cheltenham...496 L17
HARTWELL HILL
rd. Camberwell...417 E7
HARTWICK
ct. Grovedale...705 K13
HARTWOOD
ct. Chelsea Ht...547 F11
st. Kew East...372 G5
HARVARD
ct. Bundoora...284 K2
ct. Sunbury...144 D10
ct. Whittington...703 L19
HARVELL
ct. Doncaster...331 B13
ct. Highton...701 G15
HARVERSON
dr. Rosebud...699 L2
HARVEST
dr. Chirnside Pk...337 A4
HARVESTER
av. Sunshine N...321 D11
rd. Sunshine...321 B20
rd. Sunshine...365 B1
HARVEST HOME
rd. Epping...195 H6
rd. Epping...196 H7
rd. Epping...197 H9
rd. Wollert...195 H6
rd. Wollert...196 H7
rd. Wollert...197 A8
HARVEY
av. Herne Hill...701 J1
av. Templstw Lr...330 J11
cl. Altona Mdw...451 K2
cl. Epping...198 G16
ct. Cheltenham...497 A18
ct. Hampton Pk...552 B13
ct. Keilor East...322 C1
ct. Roxburgh Pk...194 B15
pl. Endeavour Hl...537 B5
st. Anglesea...713 A8
st. Belgrave Ht...506 F2
st. Brunswick...325 D16
st. Darley...221 K10
st. Malvern...415 L13
st. Mt Evelyn...339 D14
st. Prahran...415 B11
st. Richmond...26 H17
HARVIE
st. Glen Waverley...420 E19
HARWELL
ct. Westmeadows...236 L15
ct. Westmeadows...237 A15
rd. Ferntree Gly...463 H5
HARWICK
cl. Ringwood...378 L2
HARWOOD
cl. Mill Park...242 B4
cl. Sunshine W...363 L5

cl. Wheelers Hill...460 K13
ct. Berwick...554 B16
ct. Rowville...503 E3
pl. Melbourne...24 J4
pl. Roxburgh Pk...194 B12
rd. Bangholme...549 B19
st. Brighton...454 G8
HASKEN
ct. Berwick...554 B4
HASLAM
st. Seaford...600 A5
st. Williamstown...411 F13
HASLAMS
tr. Warrandyte...334 J5
tr. Warrandyte S...334 J5
HASLEMERE
st. Mitcham...377 B17
HASLUCK
cr. Lynbrook...551 E19
ct. Sunbury...143 H5
HASSED
rd. Bullengarook...77 A8
HASSETT
av. Canterbury...373 E20
av. Canterbury...417 E1
cr. Keilor East...322 A1
ct. Wantirna S...422 D20
st. Sunshine N...321 C16
HASTIE
ct. Altona Mdw...451 E4
HASTINGS
av. Beaumaris...530 F8
av. Blackburn S...419 D5
av. Boronia...424 E14
cr. Broadmeadows...237 G14
ct. Epping...198 A18
ct. Heidelberg...329 F2
rd. Frankston...627 E2
rd. Hawthorn E...416 F2
rd. Newport...411 C8
st. Bundoora...242 L20
st. Burwood...418 A10
st. Hampton...494 K7
st. McKinnon...455 J15
st. Pearcedale...646 L6
st. Pearcedale...647 A6
HATCH
st. Pearcedale...646 J4
HATFIELD
ct. Doncaster E...375 H5
ct. Keysborough...535 B11
ct. Vermont S...421 A10
ct. W Footscray...366 F12
dr. Berwick...554 A10
rd. Pakenham...557 K2
st. Balwyn N...372 L6
st. Balwyn N...373 A5
HATHAWAY
cl. Templestowe...332 C11
HATHERLEY
gr. Altona North...409 K9
rd. Chadstone...458 C5
HATHERLY
gr. Ferntree Gly...424 L20
HATTAH
ct. Taylors Lakes...276 A9
HATTEN
pl. Berwick...553 L18
HATTER
st. Oakleigh...457 J15
st. Pascoe Vale S...280 K20
HATTERAS
ct. Patterson L...573 J1
HATTON
ct. Sydenham...274 K3
gr. Coburg...325 H4
HATTY
ct. Campbellfield...239 J11
HAUGHTON
ct. Box Hill S...418 J3
ct. Hampton Pk...552 D9
pde. Rosanna...329 D2
rd. Clayton...458 G19
rd. Clayton...498 K2
rd. Clayton S...499 B4
rd. Oakleigh...457 K12
rd. Oakleigh S...458 D17
st. Cheltenham...531 C4
HAUL
rd. Melb Airport...235 J15
HAUNTED GULLY
rd. Officer...556 E9
HAVANA
cr. Frankston...600 G17
ct. Oakleigh S...497 G1
ri. Werribee...448 A12
HAVEAUX
st. Werribee...446 J17

HAVELOCK
av. Bundoora...284 G4
ct. Doncaster E...332 C14
ct. Lower Plenty...286 E13
pl. Berwick...554 K9
pl. Melbourne...24 B2
pl. Melton W...226 C16
pl. Wyndham Va...446 D12
rd. Bayswater...422 L4
rd. Hawthorn E...416 G2
st. Burwood...418 J9
st. Maidstone...366 J2
st. St Kilda...414 C17
HAVEN
av. Sorrento...679 B16
cl. Sunshine W...364 E6
ct. Aspendale Gdn...546 J4
ct. Cockatoo...511 D10
ct. Cranbourne...578 B16
ct. Mitcham...377 G18
ct. Mooroolbark...337 L19
ct. Narre Warren...552 K4
ct. Torquay...712 A4
ct. Werribee...447 L15
ct. Westmeadows...237 H11
HAVENSTOCK
ct. Wheelers Hill...460 H13
HAVERBRACK
av. Malvern...415 K11
dr. Mulgrave...501 G2
HAVERSHAM
av. Wheelers Hill...461 F15
HAVERSTOCK HILL
cl. Endeavour Hl...537 B1
HAVILAH
ct. View Bank...285 J16
HAVILLAND
dr. Roxburgh Pk...194 D9
HAWAII
ct. Rye...696 F1
HAWARD
wky. Rosanna...328 K3
HAWDON
dr. Cranbourne...578 B20
st. Dandenong N...501 K18
st. Eaglemont...328 K10
st. Heidelberg...328 K10
HAWEA
ct. Taylors Lakes...276 D9
HAWICK
ct. Greenvale...237 C1
HAWK
av. Pakenham...584 L2
ct. Werribee...448 A10
st. Doncaster E...375 K3
HAWKE
st. Parkdale...531 H8
st. W Melbourne...23 A3
HAWKER
av. Preston...283 B17
av. Roxburgh Pk...194 B10
gdn. Berwick...553 J9
st. Airport W...278 K13
st. Ivanhoe...327 K9
st. Ivanhoe...328 B9
st. Mt Martha...656 A10
HAWKES
dr. Mill Park...241 K6
dr. Mill Park...242 A8
la. Geelong, off Mercer St...702 L4
rd. N Warrandyte...289 L13
HAWKESBURY
av. Hillside...274 G1
ct. Thomastown...241 L16
rd. Werribee...447 E7
HAWKHURST
ct. Eltham North...245 L18
st. Yarraville...366 G17
HAWKING
av. Hampton Pk...551 G11
st. Preston...283 A18
HAWKINS
av. Mont Albert N...374 F10
ct. Keysborough...534 K10
pl. Melton...227 A16
rd. Baxter...644 E2
rd. Montrose...382 K4
HAWKSBURN
cl. South Yarra...32 K11
cl. South Yarra...414 L6
cr. Wantirna S...422 G19
rd. South Yarra...32 J13
rd. South Yarra...414 K7
HAWKSHEAD
ct. Croydon Hills...335 J11
HAWORTH
ct. Greenvale...192 K17
HAWSLEIGH
av. Balaclava...414 J19

HAWSON
av. Glen Huntly 456 B8

HAWTHORN
av. Belmont 702 H17
av. Caulfield N 415 G20
av. Sunshine N 321 D12
ct. Carrum Downs 575 D20
ct. Keilor East 321 J4
ct. Mill Park 242 E10
dr. Hoppers Csg 405 D19
gln. Hawthorn 415 K1
gr. Hawthorn 371 J14
gr. McKinnon 456 B15
gr. Montmorency 286 K7
gr. Taylors Hill 274 E8
la. Belgrave Ht 506 G1
rd. Blackburn S 419 K6
rd. Brighton East 455 F17
rd. Burwood E 420 A7
rd. Caulfield 455 G11
rd. Caulfield N 415 H20
rd. Caulfield S 455 G11
rd. Doveton 536 K12
rd. Forest Hill 420 A7
rd. Northcote 326 F14
rd. Vermont S 420 G8
rd. Vermont S 421 A7
st. Coburg 325 B7
st. Yarraville 367 B17

HAWTHORNE
wy. Croydon N 336 B17

HAWTHORY
rd. Kilsyth 381 B6
rd. Mooroolbark 381 B6

HAWTIN
st. Templestowe 331 C8

HAY
ct. Craigieburn 150 H18
ct. Doncaster E 332 G7
ct. Noble Park 500 J17
pl. Melbourne 1 A18
pl. Melbourne 23 J12
st. Box Hill S 375 B20
st. Preston 327 E6
st. Rye 696 J12

HAYBALE
pl. Melton W 226 A17

HAYBALL
ct. Brighton 454 H13

HAYDEN
av. Frankston 600 D17
cr. Albion 320 L20
cr. Albion 364 L1
cr. Albion 365 A1
ct. Bundoora 242 L20
ct. Knoxfield 463 C6
ct. Portsea 678 A4
rd. Clayton S 499 E16
st. Hoppers Csg 448 G4

HAYDENS
rd. Beaumaris 529 K10

HAYDN
pl. Nar Warrn S 552 H14
st. Blackburn 375 H19

HAYDON
ct. Craigieburn 194 G3
ct. Cranbourne 578 B18

HAYES
av. Rosebud 684 E20
av. Sorrento 678 J9
ct. Dandenong N 501 G7
ct. Highton 705 F7
ct. Kilsyth 381 G9
la. E Melbourne 25 L7
pde. Pascoe Vale 280 D18
pl. Alphington 327 E18
pl. Belgrave 466 G14
rd. Hampton Pk 551 D7
rd. Mernda 156 A15
rd. Strathmore 279 K20
rd. Strathmore 323 K1
st. Bentleigh 456 C19
st. Northcote 326 J12

HAYFIELD
ct. Sydenham 275 A6
rd. Mt Waverley 419 D13

HAYGARTH
ct. Wantirna S 462 B5

HAYLE
ct. Craigieburn 150 B15

HAYLES
mw. Baxter 644 B3
st. Boronia 424 E5

HAYLEY
ct. Mill Park 242 A7
dr. Somerville 644 G18

HAYLOCK
av. Cockatoo 511 D10

HAYMAN
av. Seaford 573 D18
tce. Mulgrave 500 K3

HAYMARKET
wk. Carlton 17 K15

HAYMER
ct. Braeside 532 E20

HAYNES
cr. Glen Iris 416 H10
ct. Aspendale Gdn 547 B6
ct. Melton 227 A17
st. Highett 495 L14
st. Silvan 384 F14

HAYRICK
la. Mooroolbark 337 E13

HAYRIDE
la. Chirnside Pk 337 F7

HAYS
pl. Geelong, off Corio St 703 C7

HAYSEYS
rd. Nar Warrn E 506 L18
rd. Nar Warrn E 507 A18

HAYSTACK
ct. Nar Warrn N 538 E11
pl. View Bank 285 L19

HAYWARD
ct. Vermont 421 E3
gr. Hampton 494 L6
gr. Hampton 495 A6
la. Melbourne 2 K7
la. Melbourne 24 E3
rd. Ferntree Gly 463 G1
st. Pascoe Vale S 280 H20

HAYWOOD
dr. Gisborne 79 H14
gr. Melton W 225 G20
st. Beaumaris 530 E6

HAZEL
av. Dandenong S 535 F11
av. Edithvale 546 J15
av. Highett 495 L11
av. Thomastown 240 J15
cr. Healesville 258 A4
ct. Ashwood 418 D12
ct. Hampton Pk 551 K14
dr. Templstw Lr 330 D14
gr. Frankston 627 G1
gr. Pascoe Vale 280 J17
gr. Tecoma 466 C9
st. Belmont 706 C1
st. Camberwell 416 L6
st. Camberwell 417 A6
st. Cockatoo 510 L6
st. Melton S 268 F7
st. Mt Evelyn 383 G5
st. Seaford 599 D2

HAZELDEAN
av. Brighton East 455 D17
ct. Hampton Pk 551 F5

HAZELDENE
ct. Berwick 554 F5
pl. Langwarrin 629 H4
st. Meadow Ht 237 L7

HAZELDINE
rd. Glen Iris 417 B12

HAZELDON
pl. South Yarra 32 E14
pl. South Yarra 414 H7

HAZELMERE
av. Cranbourne W 603 J2
av. Cranbourne W 603 J3

HAZEL ROSE
ct. Montmorency 286 H7

HAZEL VALE
rd. Tecoma 466 A18

HAZELWOOD
av. Cranbourne N 578 D9
cl. Dingley Village 533 B10
ct. Bundoora 242 F19
ct. Kings Park 275 D18
rd. Boronia 424 A16
rd. E Warburton 306 L14

HAZFORD
st. Healesville 212 K17

HAZLITT
ct. Cranbourne 578 A15

HEACHAM
rd. Eltham 287 A3

HEAD
ct. Vermont S 421 B9
la. Gisborne S 110 K18
rd. Wandin East 385 D10
st. Balwyn 372 K8
st. Blairgowrie 680 B19
st. Brighton 454 E8
st. Brighton 454 G8
st. Elwood 454 E8
st. Rosebud 684 A16
st. Strathmore 280 B20

HEADINGLEY
rd. Mt Waverley 419 D17

HEADINGLY
ct. Endeavour Hl 537 J7

HEADLAND WATERS
Mt Martha 669 B4

HEADLEY
st. Coburg N 281 G16

HEADLINE
ct. Heathmont 379 C19

HEADS
rd. Donvale 377 C5

HEALES
st. Dromana 685 L7

HEALESVILLE-KINGLAKE
rd. Chum Creek 213 B2
rd. Healesville 213 C18

HEALESVILLE-KOO WEE RUP
rd. Badger Creek 257 G8
rd. Healesville 257 H8
rd. Nangana 472 D1
rd. Woori Yallock 299 K14
rd. Woori Yallock 343 L19
rd. Yellingbo 387 G14
rd. Yellingbo 387 J7

HEALESVILLE-YARRA GLEN
rd. Healesville 212 D20
rd. Tarrawarra 210 G20
rd. Yarra Glen 253 F2
rd. Yarra Glen 254 A1

HEALEY
rd. Dandenong S 550 A7
st. Craigieburn 150 G19
st. Moorabbin 496 C7

HEALEYS
la. Melbourne 1 C7
la. Melbourne 23 H7

HEALS
rd. Mernda 156 A17

HEALY
dr. Epping 197 K15

HEANY
ct. Thomastown 240 G11
st. Mt Waverley 458 J3

HEANY PARK
rd. Rowville 503 A9

HEAPE
ct. Melbourne 2 A7
ct. Melbourne 24 A5
wy. Ringwood N 334 H20

HEARD
av. Diamond Ck 244 K9
av. Plenty 244 K9
av. Yarrambat 200 L20
cl. Berwick 553 K8
cr. Gisborne S 109 K15

HEARLE
av. Aspendale 546 A2

HEARN
rd. Mt Martha 669 B1
st. Altona North 410 B5
st. Dromana 685 E10

HEARNE
pde. E Geelong 703 H6

HEARSE
rd. Millgrove 348 E4

HEART
st. Dandenong S 535 L11

HEARTHSIDE
ct. Ringwood 378 A10

HEARTY
st. Blackburn S 419 K4

HEATH
av. Ferntree Gly 424 L16
av. Frankston 627 E1
av. Mt Evelyn 339 E16
av. Oakleigh 458 A12
cl. Altona Mdw 407 L19
cr. Hampton E 495 K8
ct. Darley 221 L9
ct. Doveton 536 H9
ct. Heathmont 379 B18
ct. Mornington 656 K4
ct. Noble Park N 501 D13
la. Arthurs Seat 686 G18
la. Red Hill 686 G18
mw. Langwarrin 601 K15
pl. E Geelong 703 E11
pl. Geelong 703 E11
pl. Meadow Ht 193 L18
rd. Belgrave Ht 506 C3
rd. Dromana 686 E7
rd. Mt Eliza 642 L4
st. Blackburn 375 J18
st. Glen Waverley 460 D10
st. Pascoe Vale 280 E17
st. Port Melb 29 A6
st. Port Melb 412 L4
st. Sandringham 495 E16
st. Templstw Lr 330 F9
st. Thomastown 241 C13

HEATHCOTE
ct. Endeavour Hl 537 L6
dr. Forest Hill 420 E3
gr. Lilydale 339 J3
st. Pascoe Vale 280 L13

HEATHDALE
cr. Nar Warrn N 538 C12
rd. Nar Warrn N 538 G12

HEATHER
av. Ashwood 418 F18
av. Brooklyn 365 J17
av. Emerald 510 E4
av. Hurstbridge 203 D20
av. Keilor East 322 E3
av. Pascoe Vale 281 A13
av. Sorrento 678 L13
av. Thomastown 240 K15
av. Wattle Glen 203 D20
ct. Anglesea 713 J3
ct. Glenroy 279 L2
ct. Hampton Pk 551 L13
ct. Hawthorn E 416 C4
ct. Hoppers Csg 405 B19
ct. Ringwood N 378 B2
gr. Belgrave S 506 G5
gr. Black Rock 529 G2
gr. Briar Hill 286 J4
gr. Cheltenham 496 G19
gr. Cranbourne E 579 F20
gr. Kew 372 J9
gr. Nunawading 376 G17
gr. Ringwood 378 B17
gr. Springvale 499 H16
gr. Templstw Lr 330 D8
rd. Caulfield S 455 E9
rd. Gisborne 78 B19
st. Balwyn N 373 F8
st. Bentleigh E 456 K20
st. S Melbourne 30 D4
st. S Melbourne 413 H3

HEATHERBRAE
av. Caulfield 456 A6
av. Ringwood 377 L12
cr. Sunbury 143 B4

HEATHERDALE
rd. Mitcham 377 K14
rd. Ringwood 377 K14
rd. Vermont 377 K20
rd. Vermont 421 K1

HEATHERDEW
cl. Endeavour Hl 537 G2

HEATHER GLADE
pl. Melton W 226 C19

HEATHERHILL
rd. Frankston 627 G5

HEATHERLEA
cr. Narre Warren 539 A19
ct. Blackburn N 376 A11
ct. Keilor East 321 J5
dr. Wheelers Hill 461 A10

HEATHERLEE
cl. Somerville 644 J18

HEATHERLEIGH
ct. Carrum Downs 601 B4
pl. Malvern East 456 L1

HEATHERMONT
av. Belgrave 466 H14

HEATHERTON
rd. Clayton S 498 H16
rd. Dandenong 501 E20
rd. Dandenong N 501 E20
rd. Endeavour Hl 537 A2
rd. Nar Warrn N 538 D4
rd. Noble Park 500 G19
rd. Springvale 499 B17
rd. Springvale S 499 B17

HEATHERWOOD
gr. Langwarrin 629 G4

HEATHFIELD
ct. Croydon 335 J19
ct. Newtown 701 L9
gr. Montrose 382 E10
rd. Brighton East 495 B4
ri. Box Hill N 375 D7

HEATHLAND
tr. Frankston N 600 G12
wy. Dingley Village 533 B10

HEATHLAND BOARDWALK
Frankston N 600 F11

HEATHMERE
cr. Endeavour Hl 537 G1

HEATHMONT
cl. Frankston 627 L7
rd. Heathmont 378 L19
rd. Heathmont 379 A20
rd. Ringwood 378 H14

HEATHS
ct. Mill Park 243 E3
la. Geelong, off Swanston St 703 E7
rd. Hoppers Csg 447 K3
rd. Hoppers Csg 449 A5
rd. Werribee 446 K9
rd. Werribee 447 A9
rd. Wyndham Va 446 K9

HEATHWOOD
cl. Craigieburn 150 E13
st. Ringwood E 379 D17

HEATHWREN
cl. Frankston S 628 B16

HEATON
av. Elwood 454 H4
av. Glen Iris 416 E15
cl. Sunshine W 364 A5
ct. Burwood E 419 H10

HEBB
st. Braybrook 321 L20

HEBDEN
st. Greensborough 244 F19

HEBE
ct. Frankston N 600 F9
pl. Sunshine W 364 A8

HECTOR
ct. Glen Waverley 420 L18
ct. Moorabbin 496 K9
st. Brighton 455 A17
st. Geelong West 702 D1

HEDDERWICK
rd. Dandenong S 550 J1
st. Balwyn N 374 A7
st. Essendon 323 E7

HEDDON
ct. Eltham 288 C4

HEDENPARK
dr. Hillside 232 G17

HEDGE END
rd. Mitcham 376 L9
rd. Nunawading 376 L9

HEDGELEY
av. Malvern East 416 J17
cl. Wantirna S 462 A1
dr. Berwick 554 C20
rd. Kealba 276 J18
rd. Keysborough 534 J11

HEDGELY
ct. Langwarrin 629 G4

HEDGEROW
ct. Albanvale 319 B5
ct. Keilor East 321 J5
ct. Nar Warrn S 553 C16

HEDGES
ct. Mt Martha 656 C12

HEDLAND
pl. Kings Park 275 B18

HEDLEY
ct. Narre Warren 538 K14
pl. Hampton Pk 551 L9
st. Anglesea 713 L4
st. Fawkner 239 E20
st. Hoppers Csg 449 C3

HEDLINE
pl. Macleod 285 H11

HEDWIG
dr. Mooroolbark 336 L11

HEFFERNAN
la. Melbourne 2 H10
la. Melbourne 24 E5
st. Laverton 407 B17

HEGGIES
la. Marcus Hill 707 A13

HEIDELBERG
ct. Badger Creek 258 F7
rd. Alphington 327 H19
rd. Clifton Hill 20 D2
rd. Clifton Hill 327 C20
rd. Fairfield 327 C20
rd. Ivanhoe 327 H19
rd. Northcote 326 K20

HEIDELBERG-KINGLAKE
rd. Cottles Br 203 E12
rd. Hurstbridge 202 L19
rd. Hurstbridge 203 E12
rd. St Andrews 205 D1
rd. Wattle Glen 246 J4

HEIDI
ct. Pakenham 585 F4

HEIN
rd. Pakenham 557 L4
rd. Pakenham Up 558 C1

HELD
st. Vermont 377 H20

HELDER
ct. Melton W 226 A19

HELEN
av. Croydon S..........380 C12
cl. Yarra Glen..........208 L20
cl. Yarra Glen..........209 A20
ct. Cheltenham........497 J20
ct. Diamond Ck........245 K8
ct. Lalor..................240 J7
ct. Melton W...........225 K20
ct. Narre Warren 539 B16
ct. Noble Park.........534 F1
rd. Chadstone..........458 C5
rd. Ferntree Gly 423 F17
rd. Ferny Creek........425 L14
rd. Mt Dandenong ...382 H18
st. E Geelong 703 E15
st. Frankston............626 K3
st. Heidelberg W 284 F18
st. Mt Dandenong ...382 H20
st. Mt Martha...........656 L8
st. Northcote............326 H16
st. St Albans 276 B17
vw. Glenroy..............280 G10
HELENA
av. Kallista...............467 D3
ct. Frankston............600 C18
ct. Rowville.............503 B3
ct. Rye.....................696 E2
rd. Lilydale 338 H6
st. Belmont..............701 K20
st. Clayton S 498 L6
st. Highton...............701 K20
st. Mt Martha...........656 A10
HELENE
ct. Boronia...............424 D18
st. Ardeer.................320 D19
st. Bulleen 329 G11
st. Eltham 287 J5
HELENS
wy. Langwarrin.........602 A19
HELENSLEA
rd. Caulfield N 455 C2
HELEUS
ct. Mt Waverley.......419 G14
HELIA
ct. Burwood E.........419 F8
HELIOPOLIS
st. Pascoe Vale S 324 G1
HELLENIC
ct. Carrum Downs...601 E5
HELLER
st. Brunswick..........325 B16
st. Brunswick W......325 A16
HELLIER
dr. Mill Park 242 K3
HELLION
ct. Keilor Dn............275 L11
HELLYER
st. Noble Park 534 J2
wy. Endeavour Hl 537 H5
HELM
ct. Carrum Downs...601 E4
ct. Epping...............197 A20
st. Aspendale..........546 C4
HELMER
cr. Thomson 703 K17
HELMICH
ct. Aspendale Gdn...546 H4
HELMS
st. Newcomb 704 E17
HELMSDALE
cr. Greenvale...........193 G17
ct. Cranbourne W....577 J16
rt. Templestowe 332 A9
HELMSLEY
av. Lysterfield..........464 D16
HELPMAN
cr. Epping...............197 G18
HELPMANN
st. Wantirna S.........462 B3
HELSAL
ct. Frankston...........628 E7
dr. Wantirna S.........422 B15
HELSTON
ct. Croydon Hills 335 G17
st. Balwyn N 329 K20
st. Balwyn N 373 K1
HELVETIA
ct. Frankston...........627 F7
HELWIG
av. Montmorency 286 K13
HEMAR
cr. Hillside..............232 E17
cr. Hillside..............232 F17
HEMBURROW
st. Preston..............282 F18
HEMEL
cl. Deer Park...........318 L9
ct. Vermont S 421 A11
HEMINGFORD
rd. Bentleigh E.........456 H18
HEMINGWAY
av. Templestowe 332 A10
HEMMING
st. Brighton East 495 L6
HEMMINGS
st. Dandenong 535 G7
HEMMINGWAY
la. Wyndham Va 446 F10
HEMPHILL
rd. Sunshine 365 G5
HEMPSTEAD
av. Vermont S 421 A11
HEMSTON
av. Portsea.............678 E3
av. Sorrento 678 E3
av. Sorrento 678 E6
HEMSWELL
ct. Highton..............705 J7
HEMSWORTH
ct. Roxburgh Pk......194 D9
HENBURY
wy. Taylors Lakes.....276 B10
HEND
st. Mt Waverley.......458 F4
HENDER
ct. Balwyn...............373 C8
st. Doncaster 374 D2
st. Mt Martha...........669 C2
st. Ringwood E 379 E13
HENDERS
st. Forest Hill 420 C2
HENDERSON
av. Malvern 415 L8
ct. Glen Waverley 420 F20
dr. Wandana Ht.......701 C18
dr. Wandana Ht.......701 C19
rd. Avonsleigh 471 A17
rd. Baxter................644 J5
rd. Clayton 459 H17
rd. Cockatoo 471 A17
rd. Keysborough 534 B6
rd. Knoxfield............463 A9
rd. Rowville..............462 J14
rd. Rowville..............462 L12
rd. Rowville..............463 A12
rd. Tullamarine........236 F20
rd. Yarra Glen..........209 B13
st. Brunswick W.......324 J11
st. Laverton 407 F11
st. Northcote............327 B19
st. N Melbourne........34 G13
st. Reservoir 282 J2
st. S Melbourne 29 C11
st. S Melbourne 413 B6
st. Sunshine N 321 G13
st. Upwey 465 J15
wy. Bundoora...........243 D13
HENDERSON HILL
rd. Silvan 384 C10
HENDERSONS
rd. Epping...............241 K2
rd. Seville................341 D14
rd. View Bank..........285 L18
rd. Wandin N...........341 D14
HENDON
ct. Carrum Downs...601 E1
ct. Clarinda 498 D10
HENDRA
ct. Elsternwick 455 D3
gr. Ringwood 378 K4
HENDREN
av. Altona North.......409 J6
HENDRICKS
cr. Jacana 237 H16
HENDRIKS
ct. Highton..............705 J4
HENDRY
st. Sunshine W 364 H3
HENHAM
st. Hawthorn E........416 E5
HENKEL
st. Brunswick...........325 D12
HENLET
av. Chirnside Pk.......292 H10
HENLEY
av. Mt Martha..........655 J14
av. Vermont S 420 H7
cl. Craigieburn 194 D4
cl. St Helena 245 B20
ct. Hoppers Csg.......405 A14
ct. Kealba................321 B1
ct. Moorabbin 496 H11
dr. Gladstone Pk......237 E18
dr. Wheelers Hill......460 H7
gdn. Sunshine N 321 A10
pl. Melton W...........225 K14
rd. Bend of Islands ..249 K19
rd. Kangaroo Grnd...248 F19
st. Balwyn...............373 D10
st. Pascoe Vale S 324 F6
HENLOW
ri. Hallam 538 B19
HENNESSEY
av. Herne Hill...........701 H1
HENNESSY
av. Elwood 414 E20
rd. Pakenham..........584 F3
st. Brunswick..........325 B15
st. Chadstone..........458 A5
wy. Dandenong N.....501 F12
HENRI
st. Warburton 305 H20
HENRICKS
ct. Mill Park 242 D9
HENRIETTA
st. Hampton E.........496 B8
st. Hawthorn...........371 L19
HENRY
av. Hallam 537 E14
cr. Seaford..............600 A4
ct. Caroline Spr 318 D10
ct. Epping 241 K1
dr. Altona Mdw........451 B4
rd. Croydon.............336 C19
rd. Dandenong S 535 F20
rd. Pakenham..........583 E10
rd. Wantirna S 422 J17
st. Abbotsford...........20 B20
st. Balwyn...............373 F12
st. Belmont..............706 A3
st. Blairgowrie..........679 F18
st. Boronia...............424 C11
st. Box Hill...............374 L16
st. Brighton East 455 G19
st. Brunswick...........325 E14
st. Carlton N 18 H6
st. Doncaster 330 L15
st. Eltham 287 H9
st. Fitzroy..................18 L12
st. Geelong 703 E10
st. Greensborough ..286 A6
st. Hawthorn...........372 C17
st. Healesville..........257 G5
st. Heatherton 497 K13
st. Highett...............496 D12
st. Keilor East..........322 C2
st. Kensington 33 J11
st. Kew...................371 G12
st. McCrae..............685 D11
st. Melton 226 J20
st. Montrose 382 C8
st. Noble Park 500 F20
st. Northcote............326 H16
st. Oakleigh.............458 D13
st. Pakenham..........584 K6
st. Queenscliff.........708 H19
st. Reservoir 282 K15
st. Ringwood 378 F15
st. St Albans 276 A20
st. Sandringham 495 B12
st. Seddon 367 B11
st. Somerville...........644 K15
st. Williamstown 411 B11
st. Windsor..............414 D11
st. Woori Yallock.....344 K17
st. Yarra Jctn 347 D20
HENRY CABLE
ct. Mill Park 242 D3
HENRY LAWSON
dr. Lynbrook 551 D17
HENRY SMITH
pl. Croydon Hills 335 F14
HENRYVILLE
st. St Kilda 414 F16
HENRY WILSON
dr. Rosebud W........699 F7
HENSHALL
rd. Strathmore.........279 L20
HENSHAW
ct. Greenvale...........192 K16
ct. Nar Warrn S.......552 K18
ct. Werribee 446 L20
ct. Werribee 447 A20
HENSLEY
ct. Endeavour Hl 538 A7
rd. Lalor..................240 L7
rd. Lalor..................241 A7
HENSLOW
ct. Brighton East 455 F15
HENTY
av. Altona................407 H15
av. Murrumbeena 457 B11
av. Fitzroy N, off
Rushall Cr..........326 F20
ct. Croydon.............380 F4
ct. Kew...................371 G11
ct. Keysborough 534 K12
ct. Mill Park 242 K5
ct. Mooroolbark 337 K15
ct. Sunbury 143 B12
ct. Taylors Lakes......275 F1
la. Melbourne 1 D14
la. Melbourne 23 K10
rd. Lower Plenty......286 B19
rd. View Bank..........285 L18
st. Brighton East 495 C1
st. Brunswick...........325 J10
st. Dandenong 535 L6
st. Melton S 268 F13
st. Pakenham..........584 H8
st. Reservoir 282 B11
st. Richmond 26 F9
st. Torquay 711 L6
wy. Pakenham..........584 F5
HENWOOD
st. Blackburn S 420 A3
st. Forest Hill 420 B3
HENZELL
rd. Research 288 H2
HEPBURN
av. Beaumaris..........529 K5
ct. Berwick..............553 K3
ct. Werribee 446 L16
ct. Werribee 447 A16
pl. Sydenham 274 H5
rd. Doncaster 375 B1
st. Dallas 238 H11
st. Hawthorn...........372 C18
wy. Caroline Spr 318 B5
wy. Caroline Spr 318 B6
HEPNER
rd. Dewhurst 510 E15
rd. Emerald 510 E15
HEPPNER
st. Blackburn N 375 J10
HERALD
ct. Glen Waverley 420 L18
ct. Narre Warren 553 C12
st. Cheltenham........497 D17
st. Cheltenham........497 D20
wk. Kings Park 274 L20
HERBERT
av. Hoppers Csg 448 K4
cr. Keilor East..........322 H3
cr. Sunbury..............142 K9
ct. Newcomb 704 A17
pl. Albert Park...........29 L14
pl. Kurunjang 227 H8
rd. Carrum Downs...575 B15
st. Albert Park...........29 K14
st. Albert Park 413 F7
st. Avondale Ht 322 A15
st. Beaumaris...........530 B9
st. Belmont..............702 J20
st. Blackburn S 419 H1
st. Boronia...............423 L10
st. Brunswick E 326 B13
st. Carlton N 18 H3
st. Croydon..............380 B9
st. Dallas 238 L11
st. Dandenong 535 K5
st. Footscray.............367 C7
st. Highett...............496 B12
st. Middle Park..........29 K14
st. Middle Park.........413 F7
st. Mornington.........640 J11
st. Mt Waverley........418 J15
st. Northcote...........326 G15
st. Parkdale.............531 F15
st. Pascoe Vale 280 B15
st. Preston...............326 J2
st. Ringwood 378 J8
st. St Kilda 414 D19
st. Watsonia 285 D9
st. Yarra Glen...........253 A2
st. Yarra Jctn 346 L16
HERBERTS
la. Diamond Ck 246 B7
HERCULES
st. Tullamarine........236 H19
HERD
rd. Belmont.............702 H20
HEREFORD
ct. Sydenham 232 H19
dr. Belmont..............706 C6
rd. Lilydale 338 J9
rd. Lilydale 339 A11
rd. Mt Evelyn...........338 J9
HERING
ct. Thomson 703 J18
HERIOT
cl. View Bank...........286 A15
ct. Wyndham Va 446 D7
HERITAGE
av. Chirnside Pk.......292 J12
av. Frankston S........627 G13
ct. Altona................409 A16
ct. Werribee 446 J11
ct. Wheelers Hill......460 J14
dr. Mill Park 242 B2
dr. Nar Warrn S.......579 C2
dr. Nar Warrn S.......579 G3
dr. Skye 601 F3
dr. Springvale..........499 F15
gdn. Sydenham 275 C9
la. Ivanhoe East 328 G14
st. Moonee Pnd 324 C10
wy. Gisborne...............78 L12
wy. Lysterfield..........464 C19
wy. Melton W...........226 C17
wy. Mickleham 149 K4
HERLIHYS
rd. Templstw Lr.......330 J9
HERMAN
cl. Taylors Lakes.....233 A20
ct. Rowville.............463 K18
rd. Lalor..................240 D10
st. Rosebud 700 F1
HERMANN
ct. Templestowe 331 E5
HERMES
ct. Keilor.................276 K12
HERMIONE
av. Oak Park............280 C11
HERMITAGE
cr. Bundoora...........242 J17
ct. Croydon.............335 E20
ct. Meadow Ht 238 B3
dr. Greenvale...........237 E3
rd. Newtown 702 G8
ri. Narre Warren 552 K5
st. Cheltenham........497 G19
st. Lilydale 338 G6
HERNE
cl. Moorabbin 496 F8
st. Manifold Ht........702 B1
HEROD
pl. Attwood.............237 D12
HEROES
av. Emerald 509 F3
av. Gembrook..........512 K10
HEROIC
ct. Mill Park 242 H10
HERON
av. Sunshine N 321 B12
cl. Baxter.................628 D20
cl. Blind Bight 650 D9
ct. Dingley Village ...532 L7
ct. Mornington........657 B2
ct. Pt Lonsdale........707 F19
ct. Ringwood N.......334 K20
ct. Rosebud W........698 J3
ct. Taylors Lakes.....275 J5
ct. Thomastown......240 J16
rd. St Albans 319 G9
ri. Craigieburn 149 G17
st. Mt Eliza..............641 J5
wy. Point Cook.........451 B14
HERRING
av. Yallambie...........285 G14
ct. Roxburgh Pk......194 A11
HERRINGTON
av. Carrum Downs...601 E3
trn. Caroline Spr 318 D5
HERRIOTTS
bvd. Glen Waverley....459 J9
HERTFORD
cr. Balwyn...............373 L12
cr. Wheelers Hill......460 L11
ct. Wantirna S.........422 J13
pl. Lalor..................241 J8
rd. Doncaster E 331 K17
rd. Sunshine 321 D20
rd. Sunshine 365 E1
st. Fitzroy..................19 D13
st. St Kilda E...........415 A16
HESKET
ct. Greenvale...........193 A19
HESLEDEN
st. Essendon...........324 B4
HESLOP
st. Parkdale.............531 F13
HESSE
ct. Westmeadows ...237 E11
la. Queenscliff.........709 A20
st. Queenscliff.........709 A20
HESSELL
rd. Berwick..............553 J4
rd. Harkaway...........539 J20
rd. Harkaway...........540 A16
HESSER
st. Albion 320 F18
HESTER
pl. Lysterfield..........464 E18
st. Blairgowrie.........679 E17
HESTON
st. Langwarrin.........601 G19
HESWALL
ct. Wantirna............422 E9
HETHERSETT
gr. Carnegie 457 A9
rd. Sassafras...........426 D16
HETREL
ct. Blackburn S 419 F6

HETTIE
ct. Torquay 712 D2
HETTY
ct. Rye 696 L14
HEVERSHAM
dr. Seaford 599 H4
gr. Greenvale 192 J16
HEWES
av. Chirnside Pk 336 K5
HEWISH
rd. Croydon 380 B4
HEWITT
ct. Strathmore 323 J1
st. Cheltenham 496 L13
st. Reservoir 283 B15
HEWITTS
rd. Carnegie 456 L6
HEWSON
ct. Wantirna S 422 D15
st. Melton 226 J18
HEX
st. W Footscray 366 D9
HEXHAM
ct. Craigieburn 194 H3
pl. Nar Warrn S 579 B4
st. Ardeer 320 B17
st. Warranwood 334 J16
HEYERS
rd. Grovedale 705 J15
HEYFIELD
ct. Narre Warren 538 H13
rd. Rye 696 H12
rd. Rye 697 A11
HEYGATE
ct. Mill Park 242 G9
HEYINGTON
av. Doncaster 374 F4
av. Thomastown 241 C15
bvd. Carrum Downs 601 A3
cir. Narre Warren 539 B20
cr. Noble Park N 501 E18
ct. Croydon 379 G7
ct. Somerville 645 C18
pl. Toorak 415 F6
HEYMOUNT
cl. Toorak 415 F5
HEYSEN
cl. Rowville 502 G4
ct. Mill Park 242 K7
ct. Mooroolbark 337 C10
dr. Skye 601 F4
dr. Sunbury 142 K9
gr. Doncaster E 332 F16
HEYSHAM
dr. Wheelers Hill 461 B8
pl. Keilor Dn 276 F12
wy. Templestowe 331 B6
HEYTESBURY
cr. Craigieburn 150 B20
st. Herne Hill 701 J3
HEYWOOD
cl. Dandenong N 502 D15
cr. Broadmeadows 237 J14
cr. Cranbourne N 578 F11
gr. Endeavour Hl 537 F1
st. Caulfield N 456 B1
st. Ringwood 378 C17
HIAH
cl. Greensborough 244 C17
HIBBERD
ct. Berwick 553 K3
st. Highett 496 J15
HIBBERTIA
rd. Springvale 500 K12
HIBBS
ct. Sunshine W 364 J8
HIBISCUS
av. Briar Hill 286 L6
av. Bundoora 242 H14
av. Cheltenham 531 G2
av. Frankston 600 C19
av. St Albans 320 G9
cl. Meadow Ht 193 J17
cr. Newcomb 704 C16
ct. Altona Mdw 407 K18
ct. Croydon 336 E16
ct. Doveton 536 L9
ct. Heidelberg W 328 B2
dr. Wheelers Hill 460 G14
gr. Rye 696 F2
rd. Blackburn N 375 G9
st. Wantirna 422 B3
wy. Keysborough 534 A15
HICK
st. Spotswood 410 J1
HICKEY
ct. Mill Park 243 B2
rd. Exford 267 A14
rd. Parwan 267 A14
st. Laverton 407 E17
st. Whittington 703 L19
HICKFORD
st. Brunswick E 325 K12
st. Reservoir 283 B3
HICKLING
av. Greensborough 286 C11
HICKMAN
av. Aspendale Gdn 546 K5
pl. Seville 341 H14
HICKORY
cr. Frankston N 600 A10
dr. Nar Warrn S 553 E20
st. Templstw Lr 330 L13
st. Werribee 447 E10
HICKORY DOWNS
pl. Hurstbridge 202 C17
HICKS
ct. Dandenong N 536 C1
ct. Rowville 463 F20
st. Parkdale 531 L10
HICKSON
rd. Officer 582 D3
HIDDLESTON
av. Box Hill S 418 J2
HIGGINS
av. Sunbury 143 F7
cl. Dingley Village 533 B2
ct. Bacchus Msh 221 J14
ct. Breakwater 703 J20
ct. Rye 696 L13
ct. Rye 697 A13
rd. Bentleigh 496 D1
st. Safety Bch 686 G2
HIGGS
av. Mill Park 242 K11
HIGH
ct. Maribyrnong 322 L12
pl. Dromana 686 C10
rd. Camberwell 416 H7
rd. Maribyrnong 323 C16
st. Armadale 415 C11
st. Ashburton 417 B14
st. Bayswater 423 G4
st. Beaumaris 530 B12
st. Belmont 706 A5
st. Berwick 554 D8
st. Coburg 325 D1
st. Cranbourne 604 E2
st. Dandenong 535 K5
st. Doncaster 374 C1
st. Epping 241 C7
st. Flemington 34 B1
st. Frankston 627 A1
st. Glen Iris 416 K13
st. Guys Hill 541 J17
st. Healesville 213 H20
st. Healesville 257 J1
st. Kew 371 J10
st. Kew 372 A9
st. Kew East 372 A9
st. Kew East 372 F6
st. Lalor 241 C7
st. Laverton 407 E18
st. Malvern 415 C11
st. Melton 226 F19
st. Melton W 225 E20
st. Mont Albert 374 D15
st. Moolap 704 G16
st. Mordialloc 531 H18
st. Newport 411 A5
st. Northcote 326 H20
st. N Melbourne 17 G15
st. Nunawading 376 E18
st. Prahran 31 F19
st. Prahran 414 C10
st. Preston 326 J5
st. Reservoir 283 A8
st. Seaholme 409 G19
st. Seville E 343 B13
st. Sorrento 678 J12
st. S Geelong 702 K15
st. Sunshine 365 G3
st. Templstw Lr 330 H8
st. Thomastown 241 B18
st. Thornbury 326 J11
st. Watsonia 285 E7
st. Werribee 447 G11
st. Windsor 31 F19
st. Windsor 414 C10
st. Yarraville 366 K15
st.s, Altona Mdw 407 E20
st.s, Kew 371 G13
tor, Mooroolbark 337 F9
HIGHAM
rd. Hawthorn E 372 F15
st. Cheltenham 530 J3
HIGHBROOK
ct. Diamond Ck 245 J8
HIGHBURY
av. Hampton E 496 A7
dr. Hillside 231 J17
gr. Kew 372 A10
gr. Prahran 415 B12
rd. Burwood 418 A10
rd. Glen Waverley 419 L13
rd. Mt Waverley 418 A10
rd. Mt Waverley 419 B12
rd. Rye 698 A6
rd. Rye 698 A7
rd. Tootgarook 698 A7
rd. Vermont S 420 F14
st. Balwyn N 373 C4
HIGHCLERE
av. Mt Waverley 459 C7
HIGHCLIFF
ct. Nar Warrn S 579 A3
rd. Upwey 465 E11
st. Moolap 704 J20
HIGHCLIFFE
cl. Gladstone Pk 237 A17
HIGHCOMBE
cr. St Albans 275 J18
HIGHETT
gr. Highett 496 D14
pl. Fitzroy 19 E14
rd. Hampton 495 E12
rd. Healesville 299 L5
rd. Highett 495 K12
rd. Highton 701 E10
rd. Melton 228 D17
st. Richmond 26 B7
st. Richmond 371 A14
HIGHFIELD
av. Blackburn S 419 F2
av. Mulgrave 499 K2
av. Warranwood 334 K13
dr. Grovedale 706 C15
dr. Langwarrin S 629 G20
dr. Langwarrin S 645 F2
gr. Kew 371 H11
rd. Camberwell 417 G8
rd. Canterbury 373 H20
rd. Canterbury 417 G8
rd. Chadstone 458 D5
rd. Doncaster E 376 D1
rd. Rosebud 684 J14
rd. Warburton 349 F3
HIGHFIELDE
av. Berwick 539 G19
HIGHGATE
ct. Frankston 599 K15
ct. Wyndham Va 446 F13
gr. Ashburton 417 E16
hill, Toorak 415 D2
pl. Narre Warren 538 F19
rt. Craigieburn 150 B13
st. Yarraville 366 J19
wy. Ferntree Gly 464 A12
HIGHGROVE
dr. Sunbury 144 G6
HIGHLAND
av. Balwyn 373 F9
av. Croydon 335 G19
av. Hampton Pk 551 G7
av. Highett 495 K15
av. Mitcham 377 G11
av. Oakleigh E 458 J14
bvd. Ringwood 379 C3
cl. Sunbury 143 J17
cr. Mooroolbark 381 A1
cr. Nar Warrn S 553 D18
ct. Dandenong 535 H5
ct. Eltham North 245 D18
dr. Frankston S 627 K17
dr. Pakenham 584 J1
rd. Keilor N 276 C3
st. Kingsbury 284 A10
wy. Highton 701 B16
HIGHLANDER
ct. Taylors Hill 274 E10
la. Melbourne 1 B19
la. Melbourne 23 K12
st. Torquay 711 L2
HIGHLANDS
av. Airport W 278 J14
ct. Sunbury 143 A10
rd. Thomastown 241 A13
HIGHLAWN
av. Airport W 278 K15
HIGHLEIGH
ct. Mooroolbark 337 D7
HIGHMONT
dr. Belmont 706 C6
dr. Vermont S 420 K14
HIGHMOORE
av. Bayswater 423 G4
HIGHMOUNT
dr. Hampton Pk 552 A15
HIGH POINT
av. Mooroolbark 337 C11
HIGHPOINT
cr. Eltham 287 E4
HIGHRIDGE
cr. Airport W 278 K16
HIGHRISE
ct. Highton 701 J12
ct. Hillside 231 K17
ct. Narre Warren 552 H1
HIGH STREET
rd. Ashburton 417 K16
rd. Ashwood 418 A16
rd. Glen Waverley 419 J18
rd. Mt Waverley 418 A16
rd. Wantirna S 421 A20
rd. Wantirna S 423 A18
HIGHTON
cl. Hampton Pk 551 D5
ct. Beaconsfield 555 D11
ct. Highton 701 H16
gr. Balwyn 373 A13
st. Ringwood E 379 D10
HIGHVALE
ct. Glen Waverley 420 E14
rd. Glen Waverley 420 D15
HIGH VIEW
cr. Gisborne 79 K13
ct. Wandana Ht 701 C18
HIGHVIEW
av. Cranbourne 578 C17
cr. Macleod 285 A11
ct. Lysterfield 503 K2
ct. Pakenham 585 A4
ct. Rye 697 G5
dr. Doncaster 375 B3
dr. Mooroolbark 337 A13
dr. S Morang 199 K18
gr. Burwood E 419 H10
pl. Craigieburn 150 F6
rd. Balwyn N 329 E19
rd. Bentleigh E 497 A4
rd. Ferny Creek 425 K19
rd. Frankston 627 L6
rd. Preston 283 E20
rd. Skye 602 B5
HIGH VISTA
ct. Nar Warrn N 538 C10
HIGHWOOD
dr. Hillside 232 C17
dr. Wheelers Hill 460 H10
HIGINBOTHAM
st. Brighton 454 F15
st. Coburg 281 E19
HIGSON
la. Melbourne 2 L18
la. Melbourne 24 H8
HILAIRE
pl. Whittlesea 96 E17
HILARY
av. McCrae 684 K13
av. Rye 696 F10
ct. Balwyn 373 J9
ct. Berwick 539 F18
ct. Noble Park 534 K4
gr. Bentleigh E 497 C4
gr. Glen Iris 416 F12
gr. Ringwood E 378 K13
st. Scoresby 462 C8
HILBERT
ct. Oakleigh 458 C9
rd. Airport W 278 F14
HILDA
av. Boronia 424 D3
cr. Hawthorn 371 J16
ct. Berwick 554 E20
ct. Mt Waverley 419 G16
mw. Aspendale Gdn 547 C7
pl. Whittlesea 96 E17
st. Balwyn 373 D9
st. Cheltenham 531 F4
st. Essendon 324 F8
st. Glenroy 280 E3
st. Malvern East 416 K20
HILDEBRAND
rd. Cottles Br 203 K1
HILDEGARD
ct. Kilsyth 381 H7
HILDEN
ct. Dandenong 536 F4
dr. Harkaway 541 C16
HILDERGARDE
ct. Brookfield 268 A10
HILGAY
st. Coolaroo 238 F7
HILL
ct. Dandenong N 501 J9
ct. Doncaster 330 L17
ct. Kangaroo Grnd 248 D13
ct. Keilor 276 K9
ct. Macleod 285 C17
ct. Rosebud 700 F5
ct. Warranwood 334 J12
gr. Preston 327 C1
gr. Sunbury 142 G10
rd. Balwyn N 373 F4
rd. Gruyere 298 F1
rd. Kallista 427 A20
rd. Kallista 467 A1
rd. Montrose 382 J4
rd. Warburton 349 G1
st. Altona North 409 F3
st. Belmont 706 B1
st. Bentleigh E 496 K2
st. Blackburn 375 H18
st. Box Hill S 374 K20
st. Box Hill S 418 K1
st. Cheltenham 496 K19
st. Cremorne 26 E19
st. Ferny Creek 425 E18
st. Flemington 34 B3
st. Frankston 627 H2
st. Gisborne 79 C14
st. Hawthorn 371 F15
st. Pakenham 585 E12
st. Pk Orchards 333 L8
st. Ringwood 378 J12
st. Ringwood E 378 J12
st. Rye 697 E7
st. Sorrento 678 L11
st. Sunshine 365 F5
st. Thornbury 326 C7
st. Toorak 415 C2
st. Tremont 425 E18
st. Whittlesea 96 K20
HILLANDALE
rd. The Patch 467 K1
ri. Berwick 539 H16
HILLARD
ct. Wheelers Hill 461 D19
st. Malvern East 457 A2
HILLARY
ct. Highton 701 F14
st. Braybrook 366 C5
HILLAS
ct. Mill Park 242 A3
HILLBORO
ct. Watsonia 285 E4
HILLBRICK
ct. Narre Warren 553 D7
HILLCREST
av. Berwick 539 F20
av. Brighton 455 A14
av. Caulfield S 455 L10
av. Chadstone 458 D6
av. Eltham 287 J17
av. Ferntree Gly 424 E20
av. Highett 496 A12
av. Kew 372 B10
av. Narre Warren 539 F20
av. Ringwood 377 L13
ct. Chadstone 458 D6
ct. Cockatoo 471 H20
ct. Donvale 332 K14
ct. Highton 701 D16
ct. Mill Park 242 F12
dr. Hillside 232 A17
dr. Langwarrin 630 A6
dr. Pt Lonsdale 710 E1
dr. Tootgarook 698 C6
dr. Westmeadows 236 F15
gr. Healesville 212 L15
gr. Springvale 500 A16
rd. Anglesea 713 E2
rd. Eltham North 245 E20
rd. Frankston 627 J5
rd. Glen Iris 417 C14
rd. Glenroy 280 C9
rd. Gruyere 298 F19
rd. Hurstbridge 203 A18
rd. Warrandyte S 335 A7
HILLCROFT
av. Hampton 495 F10
dr. Templestowe 331 C12
st. Reservoir 282 D12
HILLDALE
cl. Ringwood N 378 D5
HILL EDGE
ct. Lysterfield S 504 B15
HILLEDGE
la. Mooroolbark 337 E9
HILLFORD
st. Newcomb 703 L12
HILLGROVE
cl. Wheelers Hill 461 B19
HILLHOUSE
rd. Templestowe 332 A7
HILLIANA WATERS
Mill Park 243 C11
HILLINGDON
cr. Doncaster 330 C19
ct. Dingley Village 533 E7
dr. Diamond Ck 245 L6
pl. Prahran 32 D20
pl. Prahran 414 H10

HILLMAN
av. McCrae 684 H18
ct. Avondale Ht 322 C11
ct. Berwick 554 B17
st. Laverton 407 F12
HILLMARTIN
rd. Diamond Ck 245 C9
HILLPARK
dr. Mornington 641 D12
HILLRISE
cl. Nar Warrn S 579 D1
cr. Chirnside Pk 336 J7
ct. Mill Park 243 B6
ct. Mornington 641 E12
ct. Pakenham 584 K1
ct. Werribee 487 G1
HILLSIDE
av. Bentleigh 495 K1
av. Boronia 424 E6
av. Caulfield 455 F3
av. Dandenong N 536 B1
av. Dromana 686 A10
av. Glen Iris 416 E15
av. Northcote 327 C16
cr. Blackburn 375 E16
cr. Maribyrnong 323 C16
ct. Lilydale 338 G8
ct. Lysterfield S 503 J15
dr. Croydon 379 G9
gr. Airport W 278 G16
gr. Frankston S 626 L5
gr. Red Hill S 688 J20
gr. Upwey 466 A13
pde. Box Hill N 374 J10
pde. Glen Iris 416 L9
rd. Bulleen 329 L16
rd. Cockatoo 511 D9
rd. Mt Waverley 418 G15
rd. Rosanna 328 J3
st. Maddingley 263 G3
st. Springvale 500 E8
tce. Ascot Vale 323 F15
HILLSMEADE
dr. Melton W 225 H18
dr. Nar Warrn S 578 L1
HILLSTON
ct. Nar Warrn S 579 B2
rd. Moorabbin 496 D10
HILLSYDE
pde. Strathmore 280 C19
HILLTOP
av. Blairgowrie 695 K4
av. Clayton 459 A13
av. Glen Iris 417 D16
av. Macleod 285 D12
cl. Nar Warrn S 553 C17
cr. Burwood E 419 C10
cr. Ivanhoe East 328 G14
cr. Mt Evelyn 339 A20
ct. Croydon N 335 J10
ct. Sunbury 143 G19
ct. Yarra Jctn 346 L17
ct. Yarra Jctn 347 A17
mw. Frankston 628 E9
pl. Nar Warrn S 553 C18
rd. Hurstbridge 202 K10
rd. Up Fntree Gly 464 L5
ri. Launching Pl 345 C16
st. Herne Hill 702 A3
HILLVIEW
av. Mt Waverley 458 F3
av. Pascoe Vale S 324 K5
av. Rowville 462 F19
av. Rye 697 K8
ct. Bundoora 284 D1
ct. Croydon Hills 335 F11
ct. Hillside 232 A17
ct. Kangaroo Grnd 247 E13
ct. Keilor 276 H8
dr. Kilsyth 381 C9
dr.s, Carrum Downs 575 D18
dr.w, Carrum Downs 575 D17
pde. Templstw Lr 330 D10
pl. Berwick 554 A5
rd. Balwyn N 329 E20
rd. Greenvale 192 K12
rd. Greenvale 193 A13
ri. Gisborne S 110 G19
ri. Hampton Pk 552 B12
st. Dromana 686 F10
st. Yarra Jctn 347 D17
HILLVIEW QUARRY
rd. Dromana 686 C9
HILLWIN
st. Reservoir 282 C10
HILMA
st. Sunshine W 363 K5
HILSEA
ct. Mt Waverley 419 C13
HILSON
cl. Wantirna S 422 B19

HILTON
av. Springvale 499 H17
ct. Bentleigh E 497 C4
ct. Frankston 600 F19
ct. Mt Martha 656 A15
gr. Belgrave 466 G12
pl. Mooroolbark 337 K17
rd. Ferny Creek 426 A13
rd. Sassafras 426 C17
st. Beaumaris 529 K6
st. Clifton Hill 19 J7
st. Craigieburn 150 G17
st. Dandenong 536 E13
st. Glenroy 279 L3
st. Hadfield 280 C3
st. Mt Waverley 419 E17
wy. Melton W 226 B19
HILTONS
la. Box Hill 374 K14
HIMALAYA
ct. Eltham North 245 F15
rd. Ferntree Gly 425 A19
rd. Tremont 425 A20
HIMBECK
ct. Noble Park 501 A17
HINCHCLIFF
cr. Newcomb 704 A17
HINDLE
dr. Vermont 420 L5
dr. Vermont 421 A5
st. Grovedale 706 B10
HINDMARSH
ct. Cranbourne N 577 J7
dr. Wyndham Va 446 B5
dr. Wyndham Va 446 C7
st. Rowville 463 B17
wy. Taylors Hill 274 J14
HINDON
st. Blackburn 375 H15
HINE
ct. Darley 221 K7
HINKINS
st. Moonee Pnd 324 D14
HINKLER
av. Bentleigh E 496 G6
av. Macleod 285 C11
dr. Mill Park 242 H5
rd. Glen Waverley 460 D1
rd. Mordialloc 532 C11
rd.e, Glen Waverley 460 H2
st. Braybrook 365 K3
st. Mt Martha 656 A9
HINKLEY
av. Croydon 379 F2
HINRICHSEN
dr. Hallam 538 B19
dr. Hallam 538 D20
HINTON
cl. Gladstone Pk 236 L17
la. Prahran 32 A17
rd. Glen Huntly 456 D6
st. Rosebud 699 L2
HIRST
ct. Sunbury 143 A4
st. Blackburn 375 E19
HISCOCK
rd. Boneo 698 J6
rd. Boneo 699 A6
rd. Rosebud W 698 J6
rd. Rosebud W 699 A6
st. Chadstone 458 B4
HISKENS
st. Sorrento 678 K10
HISLOP
st. Doncaster E 375 G2
st. Keilor 277 B13
HISPANO
dr. Keilor Dn 276 A17
HI-TECH
pl. Rowville 462 L15
pl. Rowville 463 A14
pl. Seaford 599 H7
HIT OR MISS
rd. Healesville 212 J18
HOAD
ct. Mulgrave 500 J4
ct. Wantirna 422 E4
st. Sunshine N 321 C14
HOADLEY
av. Frankston S 626 K6
cr. Burwood E 420 E13
ct. Footscray 367 E5
HOBAN
av. Montmorency 286 G10
cl. Keilor Dn 276 G17
HOBART
pl. Wantirna S 422 K16
rd. Murrumbeena 457 B6
st. Bentleigh 496 E3
st. Ringwood 378 F8

HOBBS
cr. Reservoir 282 K6
ct. Endeavour Hl 537 E6
la. Geelong 703 D11
rd. Bullengarook 77 B8
rd. Gisborne 77 B8
rd. Wyndham Va 445 L1
st. Altona North 409 K7
st. Seddon 367 C11
HOBLER
pl. Darley 221 L7
HOBSON
cr. Mill Park 242 B3
ct. Sunbury 142 L16
ct. Sunbury 143 A16
st. Greensborough 285 J4
st. Newport 411 A6
st. Queenscliff 709 A17
st. Sandringham 495 D13
st. South Yarra 32 J16
st. South Yarra 414 K8
st. Thornbury 326 F8
HOBSONS
pl. Dingley Village 532 L9
rd. Kensington 33 B12
HOBSONS BAY
pde. Port Melb 412 G5
HOCKEY
dr. St Kilda 414 A12
HOCKING
ct. Mt Waverley 458 J2
st. Coburg N 281 C15
st. Footscray 367 A8
HOCKNELL
st. Canterbury 417 G1
HOCTOR
cl. Gladstone Pk 237 C18
HODDE
ct. Sydenham 274 L4
HODDER
st. Brighton East 455 G16
HODDLE
ct. Cranbourne 577 L15
ct. Melton W 225 H20
ct. Mill Park 242 K4
hwy. Cremorne 25 K18
hwy. E Melbourne 25 L8
hwy. Melbourne 25 K18
hwy. Richmond 25 L8
hwy. South Yarra 31 H14
hwy. South Yarra 31 K4
hwy. South Yarra 414 E4
hwy. Windsor 414 D12
pl. Diamond Ck 245 K13
st. Abbotsford 20 A20
st. Clifton Hill 20 C8
st. Collingwood 20 A20
st. E Melbourne 25 L9
st. Elsternwick 455 D7
st. Essendon 324 C9
st. Richmond 25 L9
st. Yarra Jctn 346 L16
st. Yarra Jctn 347 A16
st. Yarra Jctn 347 A17
wy. Altona Mdw 451 J8
HODGE
ct. Millgrove 348 F1
st. Werribee 447 F19
HODGES
cl. Rowville 463 D20
rd. Chum Creek 213 A7
st. Seaford 599 L6
HODGINS
cr. Frankston N 600 D9
ct. Brunswick W 324 D6
HODGKINSON
ct. Springvale 500 E10
st. Clifton Hill 19 H7
st. Dromana 685 L6
HODGSON
gr. Bentleigh E 497 D4
la. Kensington 33 D13
st. Brunswick 325 C17
st. Darley 221 L10
st. Fitzroy 19 F16
st. Geelong West 702 H1
st. Heidelberg 329 B5
st. Kew 371 D11
st. Mitcham 377 F17
st. Rosanna 329 B5
st. Templstw Lr 330 B12
tce. Richmond 26 F11
HODSON
rd. Warrandyte 333 H4
st. Preston 282 C19
HOEBERGIN
la. Hurstbridge 203 G19

HOFERT
la. Burnley, off Type St 371 B18
HOFFMAN
cct. Brunswick 325 B14
la. Brunswick 325 C14
st. Brunswick W 324 J13
st. Cheltenham 530 K2
tce. Williamstown 410 L17
HOFFMAN'S
rd. Essendon 323 B7
rd. Essendon W 323 B7
rd. Niddrie 323 B7
HOGAN
av. Warrandyte 334 F2
ct. Box Hill N 375 C6
ct. Darley 221 L4
ct. Wantirna S 422 D20
dr. Rye 696 H6
gr. Werribee 447 G13
pl. Mill Park 242 H9
rd. Glen Waverley 460 D2
st. Deer Park 319 A17
st. Fawkner 281 H1
st. Sunbury 143 G9
HOGANS
rd. Hoppers Csg 405 A18
HOHNES
rd. Eltham 287 D17
HOILES
rd. Wandin East 385 H2
HOKI
dr. Mornington 657 B6
HOLBEACH
st. Burwood E 420 A12
HOLBEIN
ct. Grovedale 705 K14
ct. Scoresby 462 C9
HOLBERG
st. Moonee Pnd 324 F15
HOLBERRY
st. Broadmeadows 238 E20
st. Nunawading 376 G19
HOLBOURNE
dr. Junction Vill 604 H12
HOLBROOK
cr. Brunswick W 324 J14
HOLBURN
wy. Epping 198 A16
HOLCOURT
rd. Laverton N 364 G17
HOLDEN
av. Avondale Ht 322 A10
ct. Fitzroy N, off Holden St 326 E19
rd. Kallista 427 G20
rd. Kallista 467 G1
rd. Olinda 427 G20
rd. Olinda 467 G1
rd. Plumpton 231 A7
rd. Rye 696 D5
rd. Seville 386 A13
rd. Silvan 386 A13
rd. Wandin East 386 A13
st. Fitzroy N 326 B18
HOLDER
pl. Berwick 554 G18
HOLDING
st. Beaumaris 530 A12
HOLDSWORTH
st. Ascot Vale 323 J16
HOLEHOUSE
st. Sunshine N 321 C16
HOLGATE
la. Kensington 33 G11
la. Kensington 368 D6
HOLLAND
av. Burwood 418 G8
av. Dingley Village 533 A9
ct. Flemington 34 C4
ct. Highton 705 J2
ct. Maidstone 366 F2
ct. Newport 411 D9
ct. Oakleigh 458 A11
dr. Melton 269 D1
gr. Caulfield N 415 J20
rd. Blackburn S 419 K2
rd. Burwood E 419 J8
rd. Ringwood E 379 A8
st. Healesville 213 L17
HOLLICK
st. Richmond 26 L4
HOLLINGSWORTH
av. Hawthorn 415 K1
HOLLINGTON
cr. Point Cook 450 C5
cr. Point Cook 450 D5
st. Berwick 580 L1

HOLLOWAY
cl. Sandringham 495 J17
cl. Sunbury 143 F4
ct. Noble Park 500 J17
dr. Bayswater 424 B8
rd. Brunswick 325 C12
rd. Croydon N 335 J9
rd. Sandringham 495 H17
st. Newport 410 G10
st. Ormond 456 E12
HOLLOWS
cr. Grovedale 706 G12
HOLLSMOOR
rd. Camberwell 417 K5
HOLLY
av. Dandenong N 501 H19
cl. Mill Park 242 E11
ct. Bayswater 423 C7
ct. Campbellfield 239 E13
ct. Mitcham 377 E14
dr. Dingley Village 532 J6
pl. Narre Warren 539 B15
st. Camberwell 372 J18
st. Preston 283 H18
HOLLYDALE
cl. Berwick 554 C15
ct. Melton W 225 H17
HOLLYDENE
ct. Narre Warren 538 G19
dr. Bangholme 549 J14
HOLLY GREEN
cl. Donvale 376 K6
cl. Rowville 503 D3
ct. Keilor East 321 K4
dr. Wheelers Hill 460 H12
HOLLYHOCK
ct. Cranbourne N 578 D8
HOLLYOAK
ct. Ferntree Gly 424 J18
ri. Eltham North 245 H19
HOLLYOAK HAVEN
Chirnside Pk 337 H1
HOLLYVIEW
ct. Rowville 463 K16
HOLLYWOOD
bvd. Pt Lonsdale 710 E2
cl. Templestowe 332 C7
HOLM
cl. Broadmeadows 238 A12
HOLMAN
rd. Emerald 469 F8
HOLMBURY
bvd. Mulgrave 501 G1
HOLMBY
rd. Cheltenham 530 K1
HOLME
rd. Ferntree Gly 463 H5
HOLMES
ct. Bayswater N 379 H17
rd. Moonee Pnd 323 J13
rd. Mooroolbark 381 D2
rd. Red Hill 687 C17
rd. Yarra Jctn 346 H16
st. Ardeer 364 B1
st. Brunswick 325 K10
st. Brunswick E 325 K10
st. Frankston 627 G4
st. Noble Park 535 B2
st. Northcote 326 L20
wy. Caroline Spr 318 B4
wy. Glen Waverley 459 L3
HOLMESDALE
cl. Werribee 446 L17
cl. Werribee 447 A17
HOLMHURST
ct. Brighton East 495 E5
HOLM PARK
rd. Beaconsfield 555 C10
HOLMWOOD
av. Anglesea 713 G5
av. Brighton 454 G14
brk. Dingley Village, off Albert Pl 532 K6
ct. Brighton 454 G14
pl. Carlton 18 D11
rd. Tottenham 366 B14
HOLOHAN
pl. Dandenong N 502 C19
HOLOWKO
ct. Taylors Lakes 276 E8
HOLROYD
av. St Kilda E 415 B16
ct. Blackburn S 419 H6
ct. St Kilda E 415 A16
dr. Epping 241 J4
st. Coburg 281 D19
st. Kew 371 G8
st. Seaford 599 K5
HOLSKAMP
st. Mt Waverley 419 A19

HOLSTEIN
ct. Rowville...502 C4
HOLSTEN
a.n, Kensington...33 C10
a.s, Kensington...33 C11
HOLSTOCK
ct. Jan Juc...711 E14
HOLT
ct. Mordialloc...532 A16
ct. Springvale S...499 D18
pde. Bundoora...283 L2
pde. Thomastown...283 G1
pde. Thomastown...283 J1
pl. Pakenham...584 L9
rd. E Geelong...703 J10
st. Ardeer...320 B18
st. Sunbury...143 D6
HOLTOM
st.e, Princes Hill...325 J19
st.w, Princes Hill...325 G19
HOLTON
ct. Hillside...232 F19
HOLTS
la. Darley...221 D11
HOLYHEAD
dr. Torquay...712 E4
HOLYROOD
av. Newtown...702 A13
av. Sorrento...679 B12
av. Strathmore...279 H20
cr. Ringwood...378 L2
cr. Ringwood...379 A2
ct. Watsonia N...243 D19
dr. Vermont...421 H4
st. Camberwell...417 F3
st. Hampton...494 J6
st. Highett...496 B12
HOLYWOOD
gr. Carnegie...456 F5
HOLZER
st. Sandringham...495 E12
HOLZGREFE
ct. Altona Mdw...451 E3
HOMAN
ct. Ringwood N...334 G12
HOME
rd. Newport...411 B7
st. Bayswater N...379 J15
st. Reservoir...283 D15
st. Sorrento...679 A11
HOMEBUSH
cr. Hawthorn E...372 H17
ct. Ringwood E...379 B16
la. N Melbourne...17 A12
rd. St Albans...319 G7
HOMELEIGH
rd. Keysborough...534 D19
HOMER
av. Croydon S...380 B13
ct. Ferntree Gly...463 F9
st. Moonee Pnd...324 C12
HOMESTEAD
cl. Croydon S...380 D14
cl. Melton W...226 A17
ct. Highton...705 E3
dr. Bangholme...548 D14
dr. Keilor Dn...276 H16
dr. Wheelers Hill...461 C11
pl. Mill Park...242 L7
rd. Berwick...553 G17
rd. Chirnside Pk...292 A18
rd. Eltham...287 C18
rd. Langwarrin...602 C17
rd. Templestowe...287 L19
rd. Wonga Park...335 J2
tr. Greenvale...191 E16
wy. Narre Warren...552 K4
wy. Sunbury...113 J15
HOMESTEAD RUN
Roxburgh Pk...193 L14
Seabrook...450 K7
HOMEWOOD
bvd. Hallam...538 B17
cl. Ferntree Gly...463 H9
ct. Meadow Ht...237 L4
ct. Rosanna...285 E20
la. Highton...705 K6
rd. Cranbourne S...630 G5
ri. Warrandyte...288 K20
st. Nunawading...376 F17
HONDA
dr. Mill Park...242 K2
HONE
av. Blackburn S...375 F20
av. Blackburn S...419 F1
ct. Mill Park...242 A2
HONEY
ct. Epping...241 K4
gr. St Albans...276 H20
HONEYEATER
cr. Craigieburn...149 F17
cr. Taylors Lakes...275 F2
pl. Carrum Downs...600 L5
tce. S Morang...243 J4
HONEY MYRTLE
ct. Langwarrin...601 K14
ri. Eltham North...245 E18
HONEYPOT
cl. Knoxfield...423 C19
HONEYSUCKLE
av. Hillside...274 E4
av. Wheelers Hill...460 F14
ct. Altona Mdw...407 K20
ct. Cranbourne N...578 E8
ct. Meadow Ht...238 C1
ct. Mill Park...242 C9
st. Frankston N...600 F10
wk. Croydon S...380 C13
wy. Chirnside Pk...293 J20
HONEYSUKLE
ct. Hoppers Csg...405 B15
HONNI
ct. Fawkner...239 G20
mw. Doncaster E...331 K16
HONOUR
av. Wyndham Va...446 F14
av. Hawthorn, off Wood...371 E16
ct. Mt Martha...657 B7
HONYBUN
ct. Donvale...377 D3
HOOD
cr. Caulfield N...455 C2
cr. Fawkner...281 L6
cr. Sunbury...143 B9
st. Berwick...553 K6
st. Airport W...279 A15
st. Balwyn N...373 B6
st. Belgrave Ht...466 B19
st. Collingwood...20 A18
st. Elwood...454 B1
st. Frankston...599 G13
st. Hampton...495 B8
st. Mont Albert...374 E14
st. Yarraville...367 B13
HOOK
ct. Craigieburn...150 A16
st. Altona Mdw...407 H20
st. St Albans...319 J4
HOOKER
av. Springvale...499 F17
rd. Ferntree Gly...423 E20
rd. Werribee...446 L13
rd. Werribee...447 A13
HOOKS
rd. Warburton...348 K4
HOOP
ct. Frankston N...600 B8
ct. Mill Park...242 B9
HOOPER
cr. Brunswick W...324 J15
dr. Skye...575 H14
gr. Mt Martha...669 E2
rd. Wonga Park...291 A20
st. Macleod...285 B10
st. Murrumbeena...457 E6
HOOP PINE
ct. Cranbourne N...578 B9
HOPBUSH
av. Sunbury...143 J4
HOPE
av. Donvale...377 B8
av. Montrose...382 A11
ct. Delahey...275 E14
ct. Doncaster E...332 D6
ct. Ferntree Gly...464 B11
ct. Frankston...599 E14
ct. Kew...371 H4
ct. Mill Park...242 G6
ct. Noble Park N...501 E13
pl. Seabrook...450 K4
st. Brighton East...455 C15
st. Brunswick...325 A11
st. Brunswick W...325 A11
st. Camberwell...416 L3
st. Camberwell...417 A3
st. Fitzroy N...326 B18
st. Geelong...703 D12
st. Geelong West...702 D4
st. Glen Iris...416 F15
st. Greensborough...244 H19
st. Preston...282 C20
st. Rosebud...683 H18
st. South Yarra...31 D7
st. South Yarra...414 B4
st. Spotswood...411 A2
st. Springvale...499 K7
st. W Footscray...366 G5
HOPES
ri. Frankston S...626 G5
HOPETOUN
av. Brunswick W...324 G7
av. Canterbury...373 D17
av. Mt Martha...656 A17
av. Reservoir...282 D15
cr. Coburg N...282 B13
cr. Point Cook...450 F4
cr. Point Cook...450 G3
ct. Bentleigh E...456 L17
ct. Westmeadows...236 J15
gr. Eaglemont...328 G13
gr. Ivanhoe East...328 G13
gr. South Yarra...32 G12
gr. South Yarra...414 J6
pde. Box Hill...374 H15
rd. Pk Orchards...333 L18
rd. Tooradin...651 G3
rd. Toorak...415 J9
st. Dandenong...535 H7
st. Elsternwick...455 C5
st. Kensington...33 J8
st. Mitcham...377 G16
st. Moonee Pnd...323 K13
st. Northcote...326 L14
HOPETOUN ACCESS
rd. Mt Martha...656 B19
HOPETOUN PARK
rd. Hopetoun Park...266 C4
rd. Hopetoun Park...266 C5
HOPETOWN
cr. Richmond...26 C5
pl. Fitzroy N...19 C2
HOPKINS
av. Heidelberg Ht...328 G4
av. Keilor...276 L11
av. Keilor...276 L12
av. Keilor...277 A12
cl. Rowville...462 H16
ct. Altona Mdw...451 J10
ct. Clayton S...498 G9
ct. Werribee...447 D7
rd. Rockbank...317 A9
rd. Truganina...317 A9
st. Dandenong...536 A3
st. Footscray...367 J8
st. Greensborough...286 C7
st. McKinnon...455 J16
st. S Geelong...702 K13
wy. Meadow Ht...194 B18
HOPMAN
cl. Wantirna S...462 F2
HOPPER
ct. Mill Park...243 C3
HOPPERS
la. Werribee...448 L8
la. Werribee...449 A8
la. Werribee S...449 A19
la. Werribee S...488 L3
HOPWOOD
ct. Nar Warrn S...552 H19
HORACE
st. Malvern...416 B15
HORATIO
cl. Rowville...503 E2
ct. Lilydale...338 J1
st. Noble Park...534 F4
HORDER
cr. Darley...221 K4
HORDERN
rd. Mt Evelyn...339 F19
HORFIELD
av. Box Hill N...374 H7
HORHAM
ct. St Albans...320 H5
HORIZON
bvd. Hampton Pk...551 J14
ct. Gisborne...78 H8
ct. Selby...507 B1
HORKINGS
st. Blackburn S...419 J2
HORNBUCKLE
cr. Melton...227 C16
ct. Ferntree Gly...463 H7
HORNBY
st. Beaumaris...529 J7
st. Brighton East...455 F18
st. Windsor...414 H13
HORNE
ct. Chelsea Ht...547 D14
ct. Langwarrin...629 C2
ct. Pakenham...584 H3
st. Brunswick...325 J16
st. Campbellfield...239 F14
st. Clifton Hill...20 F7
st. Elsternwick...454 K5
st. Frankston...599 C17
st. Hoppers Csg...405 J20
st. Sunbury...143 E14
st. Thomastown...240 J19
HORNEMAN
rd. Gisborne S...141 A5
HORNER
cl. Knoxfield...462 K4
st. Beaconsfield...555 C15
HORNERS
la. Rye...697 A2
rd. Warburton...349 L4
HORNSBY
av. Westmeadows...236 G15
ct. Greenvale...193 C18
dr. Langwarrin...629 J3
la. Kensington...33 D10
st. Malvern...416 B9
HORNSEA
ct. Noble Park N...501 E13
HORONDA
st. Greensborough...285 L4
HORSBURGH
gr. Armadale...415 G10
HORSCROFT
pl. Moorabbin...496 D7
HORSEMAN
ct. Nar Warrn S...552 J20
HORSESHOE
cr. Epping...198 D17
HORSESHOE BEND
rd. Keilor...277 E15
rd. Marshall...706 L19
rd. Torquay...712 G2
HORSFALL
st. Templstw Lr...330 H12
HORSFIELD
st. Cranbourne N...577 L5
HORSHAM
dr. Cranbourne E...578 J19
HORSLEY
st. Bentleigh...456 C19
HORSMUNDEN
rd. Moorabbin...496 F9
HORSWOOD
rd. Lysterfield...505 A19
rd. Nar Warrn N...505 A19
HORTENSE
st. Glen Iris...417 F12
st. Maribyrnong...323 C14
HORTON
cl. Brighton...454 G8
dr. Hampton Pk...551 G12
dr. Hampton Pk...551 G13
st. Reservoir...282 C13
HOSES
la. Grovedale...706 H14
HOSIE
st. Altona Mdw...451 J10
st. Bayswater N...380 B17
st. Richmond...26 J12
HOSIER
la. Melbourne...2 H19
la. Melbourne...24 G9
HOSKEN
st. Altona Mdw...451 G2
st. Balwyn N...373 H6
st. Balwyn N...373 J8
st. Reservoir...282 C15
st. Springvale S...500 C20
HOSKIN
st. Bayswater...423 D2
HOSKING
ct. Pakenham...584 G5
ct. Williamstown...410 K14
st. Williamstown...411 D13
HOSKINS
st. Tremont...465 J3
HOSSACK
st. Coburg N...281 D17
HOTCHKISS
wy. Keilor Dn...276 A15
HOTHAM
cl. Deer Park...319 A9
cr. Hoppers Csg...449 A3
ct. Diamond Ck...245 L12
ct. Lalor...240 G8
ct. Melton S...268 C13
ct. Mont Albert...374 E12
ct. Sunbury...143 H6
gr. Ripponlea...454 H3
pl. Cremorne...26 E20
pl. E Melbourne...25 G6
pl. N Melbourne...17 F15
pl. Geelong, off La Trobe Tce...702 K9
rd. Niddrie...278 H19
rd. Niddrie...279 A20
rd. Portsea...677 J5
rd. Sorrento...677 J5
rd. Sorrento...678 J7
rt. Burwood E...419 F11
st. Balaclava...414 J19
st. Balaclava...454 J3
st. Beaumaris...530 B7
st. Braybrook...365 J5
st. Collingwood...19 G11
st. Cranbourne...578 G20
st. E Melbourne...25 G7
st. Elsternwick...454 J3
st. Frankston S...626 H10
st. Hughesdale...457 F13
st. Mont Albert...374 E13
st. Moonee Pnd...323 K15
st. Preston...326 L6
st. Ripponlea...454 J3
st. St Kilda E...414 K19
st. Seddon...367 C12
st. S Melbourne...29 L4
st. Templstw Lr...330 E14
st. Williamstown...411 E12
HOTHLYN
dr. Craigieburn...194 D3
HOUDINI
dr. Diggers Rest...187 A9
HOUGHTON
rd. Warrandyte...333 E2
st. Balwyn N...373 D4
HOUGHTONS
la. Tarrawarra...211 D18
HOULDEN
ct. Narre Warren...539 F19
HOULDER
av. Junction Vill...604 H12
HOULIHAN
ct. Pakenham...584 G7
HOUNDSFORTH
st. Cranbourne E...578 J20
HOUNDSWOOD
cl. Doncaster E...332 C13
HOURIGAN
av. Clayton...458 L18
HOUSDEN
st. Broadmeadows...238 E20
HOUSMAN
cl. Burnside...318 G9
HOUSTON
av. Strathmore...279 L20
av. Strathmore...323 L1
ct. Box Hill S...419 B6
ct. Brooklyn...365 H19
ct. Reservoir...283 J17
st. Epping...197 E19
st. Mentone...531 L8
HOVE
pl. Craigieburn...150 C20
rd. Mt Martha...669 J2
rd. Rosebud...684 G20
rd. Rosebud...684 L20
HOVEA
ct. Boronia...424 K7
ct. Mill Park...243 C7
ct. Mt Waverley...419 D17
ct. Springvale S...534 B5
pl. Meadow Ht...237 J1
st. Mitcham...377 E10
st. Templestowe...331 B8
HOVELL
ct. Cranbourne...578 B18
st. Deer Park...319 C9
st. Grovedale...706 A12
HOWARD
av. Mt Waverley...458 H3
av. Ormond...455 J13
av. Ringwood E...379 A15
ct. Bayswater N...380 G20
ct. Clayton...459 C19
ct. Dandenong N...502 A16
ct. Doncaster...330 G16
ct. Glenroy...280 C1
la. N Melbourne...17 G19
pl. Berwick...553 L14
rd. Dingley Village...532 L9
rd. Olinda...427 B12
st. Altona Mdw...451 G5
st. Box Hill...374 J16
st. Brunswick...325 J11
st. Epping...197 G20
st. Glen Iris...416 K11
st. Greensborough...286 B5
st. Kew...371 G11
st. Maidstone...366 H3
st. Malvern East...456 G2
st. Mitcham...376 L16
st. N Melbourne...17 F20
st. Reservoir...283 A11
st. Richmond...32 F3
st. Richmond...414 J2
st. Seville...341 H12
st. South Yarra...32 B13
st. South Yarra...414 G7
st. W Melbourne...17 F20
HOWARD ROAD
trl. Braeside...532 L12
trl. Braeside...533 A12

HOWARDS
rd. Panton Hill 204 L11
rd. Panton Hill 205 A11
rd. Smiths Gly 204 L11
rd. Smiths Gly 205 A11
HOWARTH
st. Brunswick..........325 G13
HOWDEN
cr. Braybrook..........321 L20
ct. Mill Park 243 B3
st. Oakleigh E..........458 C10
HOWE
av. Dandenong N.....501 K11
cr. S Melbourne 29 L7
cr. S Melbourne 30 A9
cr. S Melbourne 413 F4
cr. S Melbourne 413 F5
ct. Geelong West.....702 G1
ct. Melton S...........268 C10
ct. Thomastown........240 G16
pde. Port Melb...........411 H3
pde. Port Melb...........412 C4
st. Fitzroy N 19 L3
st. Murrumbeena 457 D9
HOWELL
av. Beaumaris..........530 G6
av. Surrey Hills 374 D20
cl. Doncaster E 332 H13
ct. Research 288 H4
dr. Berwick..............554 J6
dr. Mt Waverley.......459 A6
pl. Braybrook..........365 J6
rd. Plenty 244 H8
st. Bentleigh...........496 A5
st. Brighton East 455 E16
st. Lalor...................241 A10
st. Rye....................696 J10
HOWES
st. Airport W 279 A10
HOWEY
pl. Melbourne 2 D14
pl. Melbourne 2 D15
pl. Melbourne 24 D8
rd. Mt Martha 655 H15
st. Gisborne..............78 H14
st. Pakenham..........584 F2
HOWGATE
ct. Eltham 287 L11
HOWIE
st. Glen Iris 417 C11
HOWITT
av. Hampton E.........495 H9
cr. Sunshine W 364 L9
cr. Sunshine W 365 A9
ct. Berwick..............553 H4
ct. Werribee............448 C19
dr. Templstw Lr.......330 E12
la. Melbourne 24 K7
la. Roxburgh Pk.......194 C11
pl. Burwood E 419 F12
rd. Caulfield N 455 E1
st. Dromana.............685 E10
st. Glen Iris..............416 H8
st. McCrae 685 E10
st. Northcote............327 C19
st. South Yarra..........32 J15
st. South Yarra........414 K8
HOWLETT
st. Kensington 33 E7
HOWLEYS
rd. Notting Hill.........459 E13
HOWQUA
ct. Epping 198 B20
ct. Glen Waverley 420 D15
ct. Vermont 421 A5
ct. Warranwood 334 J15
dr. Rosebud W.........698 L4
dr. Rosebud W.........699 A3
pl. Cranbourne........578 H16
wy. Taylors Hill.........274 K14
HOWSHIP
ct. Ringwood E 378 L11
HOWSON
cl. Endeavour Hl 537 B4
ct. Mont Albert........374 E12
pl. Roxburgh Pk......194 D15
st. Brunswick W......325 A15
HOY
ct. Delahey..............275 D11
HOYA
cr. Frankston N 600 F8
ct. Cranbourne N.....577 L6
HOYLAKE
av. Jan Juc..............711 G14
ct. Sunbury.............144 F15
gr. Mornington.........656 C2
HOYLE
ct. Clayton S 498 H5
ct. Cranbourne........578 F17

HOYSTED
av. Cranbourne N.....578 B9
cl. Mordialloc..........532 E18
HOYT
st. Hampton...........494 J6
HUB
arc. Melbourne 2 B13
HUBBARD
av. Mulgrave 500 K5
rd. Yarra Glen..........209 A15
HUBBLE
ct. Altona Mdw........451 K7
HUBERT
av. Glenroy.............280 F6
st. Mt Martha..........668 L7
st. Mt Martha..........669 A7
st. Preston.............282 L18
st. Upwey 466 A16
HUCKERBY
st. Cremorne 25 L18
HUCKSON
ri. Dandenong N.....502 B13
HUDDERSFIELD
rd. Deer Park..........319 A12
HUDSON
av. Frankston..........599 L16
cct. Meadow Ht 238 A2
ct. Ashburton..........417 K16
ct. Avondale Ht 322 D11
gr. Brunswick W......324 L16
pl. Carlton.................18 F19
pl. Melton 226 L17
pl. Rowville.............463 E19
rd. Spotswood 410 J1
st. Beaconsfield 554 L17
st. Caulfield N 455 K2
st. Coburg 325 F3
st. Cranbourne.........604 C4
st. Fawkner.............281 G3
st. Hampton............495 D9
st. McKinnon 456 G16
st. Moonee Pnd 323 J12
HUEGILL
dr. Burnside 318 E5
dr. Caroline Spr........318 E5
HUFF
st. Glen Waverley 459 J2
HUGGINS
ct. Altona Mdw........451 H3
rd. Donvale 377 F7
HUGH
al. Melbourne 2 H10
al. Melbourne 24 E6
st. Footscray............367 E7
st. Hawthorn E........416 F7
st. Knoxfield............463 D1
st. Ringwood 378 L4
HUGHENDEN
rd. St Kilda E...........415 B15
HUGHENDON
rd. Beaconsfield 556 E1
rd. Beaconsfld Up....556 F1
rd. Officer...............556 E1
HUGHES
av. Caroline Spr.......318 B4
av. Chelsea.............547 A12
av. Edithvale 547 A12
cl. Endeavour Hl 537 C3
cr. Dandenong N.....501 K20
ct. Campbellfield 239 B9
ct. Hampton Pk........551 E8
ct. Sunbury.............143 G8
ct. Wheelers Hill.......460 J12
ct. Woori Yallock.....344 H14
pde. Reservoir...........282 E1
pl. Hughesdale.........457 E12
rd. Blairgowrie.........679 C18
rd. Chirnside Pk.......292 F12
rd. Keilor East..........322 A2
rd. Sorrento 679 C18
rd. Up Fntree Gly 464 L5
st. Balwyn N 373 E8
st. Bentleigh E.........457 E18
st. Braybrook 365 L5
st. Brighton East 495 E1
st. Burwood............418 E10
st. Carlton N 325 J20
st. Hoppers Csg.......448 F1
st. Malvern East 456 H3
st. Montmorency 286 J7
st. Tremont..............465 H5
st. Upwey 465 H5
st. Upwey 465 H9
st. Wantirna S.........422 K17
st. Yarraville.............367 C18
HUGO
ct. Fawkner.............281 J1
ct. Narre Warren 539 E18
st. Beaumaris..........530 C8
st. Bulleen 329 G17

HUIA
cl. Altona Mdw........451 L4
HULETT
st. Albion 320 F17
HULL
ct. Greenvale...........193 C18
ct. Grovedale 706 A14
dr. Campbellfield 239 H13
rd. Croydon.............380 F3
rd. Lilydale 337 J14
rd. Mooroolbark 337 C19
rd. Mooroolbark 337 J14
rd. Mt Martha 669 J2
rd. Mt Martha 669 J4
st. Bentleigh E.........457 B20
st. Hawthorn...........372 B15
st. Richmond 26 E9
HULME
ct. Hillside..............274 G1
HUMBER
rd. Croydon N 336 C11
HUMBLE
st. E Geelong 703 J13
HUME
av. Melton S 268 D12
cl. Mill Park 242 J4
ct. Ashwood 418 F14
ct. Cranbourne N.....577 H8
ct. Frankston S........627 F10
dr. Delahey..............275 B9
dr. Lysterfield...........464 E17
dr. Sydenham 274 K9
dr. Taylors Hill.........274 C10
fwy. Craigieburn 150 G8
fwy. Mickleham 150 G8
hwy. Campbellfield 195 A15
hwy. Craigieburn 150 H11
hwy. Craigieburn 194 K6
hwy. Fawkner............281 E1
hwy. Somerton 195 A15
la. Mt Dandenong ...426 H1
rd. Caulfield N 455 D2
rd. Laverton N 408 B1
rd. Springvale S........499 J20
st. Armadale 415 F12
st. Beaumaris..........530 B7
st. Deer Park...........319 E16
st. Greensborough ..286 E3
st. Grovedale 706 A12
st. Huntingdale 458 E16
st. Kew...................371 E10
st. Mt Martha...........669 E4
st. Ringwood E 379 E14
st. Sunbury.............143 C12
st. Upwey 465 E14
HUMEVALE
ct. Meadow Ht 238 A4
HUMMELL
wy. Doncaster 331 B20
HUMMERSTONE
rd. Seaford.............599 G2
HUMMING BIRD
la. Kew...................372 C8
HUMOORE
av. Manifold Ht........702 B2
HUMPHREYS
av. Nunawading.......376 K13
wy. Rowville.............463 G19
HUMPHRIES
rd. Frankston S........626 F9
rd. Frankston S........643 D2
rd. Mt Eliza.............626 F9
HUNGERFORD
dr. Brookfield 268 B5
HUNSFORD
av. Notting Hill.........459 J14
HUNT
av. Rye...................697 G2
cr. Ascot Vale..........323 G16
cr. Clarinda 498 D11
ct. Hoppers Csg 405 A19
ct. Sunshine W 364 K8
ct. Wantirna S.........462 D5
dr. Seaford..............599 G3
rd. Herne Hill...........701 H3
rd. Macclesfield.......470 F8
st. Balwyn N 373 B7
st. Coburg 325 G4
st. Donvale 332 F20
HUNT CLUB
bvd. Cranbourne E 578 H20
rd. Nar Warrn S.......579 G2
HUNTER
av. Black Rock.........529 J5
av. Hoppers Csg 448 F1
av. Roxburgh Pk......193 K16
ct. Cranbourne N.....578 A10
ct. Frankston...........599 L18
ct. Pt Lonsdale........707 G20
ct. Ringwood E 379 F16
dr. Blackburn S 419 J2

rd. Camberwell........417 F3
rd. Healesville..........213 E20
rd. Healesville..........257 E1
rd. Kalorama 384 B9
rd. Mt Evelyn...........384 C8
rd. Silvan 384 C8
rd. Wandin East.......384 H4
ri. Endeavour Hl 537 E7
st. Abbotsford............20 F16
st. Brunswick W.......324 K12
st. Carnegie 456 J13
st. Croydon.............379 C2
st. Dandenong N 501 L8
st. Ferntree Gly 424 H16
st. Glen Waverley 419 K20
st. Hawthorn...........372 C20
st. Keilor.................277 D14
st. Kew...................372 F8
st. Malvern 416 A17
st. Melton S............268 H8
st. Monbulk 427 L19
st. Moolap 704 L17
st. Mornington.........640 G19
st. Northcote...........326 J12
st. Richmond 26 L13
st. Richmond 371 A17
HUNTERS
la. Geelong, off Brougham St......703 A5
rd. Mernda..............199 D4
HUNTER VALLEY
rd. Vermont S 421 C11
HUNTINGDALE
cl. Cranbourne........603 J4
ct. Craigieburn 150 D15
ct. Rowville.............502 E8
dr. Chirnside Pk.......337 E5
rd. Ashwood 418 F20
rd. Burwood............418 F20
rd. Chadstone..........418 F20
rd. Chadstone..........458 E9
rd. Huntingdale 458 D14
rd. Mt Waverley........418 F20
rd. Mt Waverley........458 E9
rd. Oakleigh............458 D14
rd. Oakleigh E..........458 D14
rd. Oakleigh S..........498 C2
HUNTINGDON
av. Bayswater N.......380 E18
dr. Wantirna S.........422 J19
rd. Bentleigh E.........456 H18
st. Newtown 702 F10
HUNTINGFIELD
ct. Carnegie 456 K14
ct. Eltham North.......246 A18
dr. Doncaster E 332 D14
dr. Hoppers Csg 448 E10
pl. Heidelberg Ht 328 E6
rd. Brighton.............454 J20
rd. Toorak...............415 F8
HUNTINGTON
ct. Pt Lonsdale........707 F19
ct. Werribee............447 E2
dr. Hampton Pk........551 K13
gr. Coburg 325 L5
tce. Burwood............418 B3
HUNTINGTOWER
cr. Langwarrin.........629 G3
cr. Mt Waverley........419 F20
cr. Mt Waverley........459 F1
rd. Armadale 415 H11
HUNTLEY
cl. Dingley Village ...533 D8
cl. Highton..............705 E1
ct. St Albans 320 K7
rd. Bentleigh............455 H17
st. Brighton.............454 J5
st. Watsonia N 285 G3
HUNTLY
av. Mooroolbark 337 G8
ct. Langwarrin..........601 H16
ct. Meadow Ht 237 K3
st. Footscray............367 D9
st. Glen Huntly 456 D6
st. Moonee Pnd 323 H14
HUNTSMAN
dr. Noble Park 534 L6
HUON
ct. Broadmeadows ..238 A12
ct. Bundoora...........284 B1
ct. Donvale 376 F3
ct. Frankston N 600 A8
ct. Keilor................276 K11
ct. Vermont S 420 J12
gr. Ashburton..........417 G18
gr. Bentleigh E.........497 D4
rd. Belgrave Ht 506 D2
HUON PARK
rd. Cranbourne N.....578 A7
HUON PINE
ct. Up Fntree Gly 464 K7

HURLESTONE
ct. Dandenong N.....501 F
HURLEY
ri. Roxburgh Pk......193 K1
st. Melton 226 F1
st. Reservoir ....282 F
st. Sorrento ....678 H
HURLINGHAM
st. Brighton East 455 E1
HURLSTONE
av. Preston..............327 A
cr. Mill Park ....242 L
cr. Mill Park ....243 A
pl. Mornington.........656 J
st. Brighton East 455 F1
HURON
cl. Rowville.............462 K1
HURREY
av. Mernda..............156 B1
HURRY
pl. Prahran................31 L1
pl. Prahran..............414 F
HURSLEY
ct. Craigieburn 150 A1
HURST
ct. Croydon N 336 C1
ct. Epping 197 J1
rd. Hurstbridge........202 K1
HURSTBRIDGE
rd. Diamond Ck.......246 A1
rd. Wattle Glen 246 A1
HURSTBRIDGE-ARTHURS CREEK
rd. Cottles Br...........202 J
rd. Hurstbridge........202 J
rd. Nutfield ....202 J
HURSTMON
st. Malvern East......416 K1
HURSTWOOD
rd. Sorrento ....678 F
HURTER
st. Blackburn S ....419 K
HURTLE
st. Ascot Vale..........323 G1
st. Lalor..................241 A1
HUSBAND
rd. Forest Hill ....420 G
HUSKEY
ct. Vermont S ....420 J
HUSKISSON
av. Lalor..................240 L
av. Lalor..................241 A
HUSSEYS
la. Pk Orchards ....334 A
la. Warrandyte ....334 A
la. Warrandyte ....334 D
HUSTLER
ct. Mt Waverley.......458 J
HUT
st. Whittlesea............96 K1
HUTCHESON
av. Highton..............705 K1
st. Moonee Pnd 324 C1
HUTCHINGS
ct. Chelsea.............547 B1
st. Cremorne 26 E1
HUTCHINS
av. Endeavour Hl ......537 F
cct. Bundoora...........242 D1
cl. Mordialloc..........532 C1
ct. Warranwood 334 L1
pl. Roxburgh Pk......194 A1
tce. Templestowe .....332 C
wy. Skye ....601 C
HUTCHINSON
av. Warrandyte 289 D2
dr. Kew...................371 G
dr. Lynbrook 551 D1
rd. Yarra Glen..........252 H
st. Albion ....364 J
st. Bentleigh............496 F
st. Brunswick E.......325 L1
st. Burwood E.........420 A
st. Coburg ....325 L
st. Lilydale ....338 C
HUTCHINS PARK
cl. Mornington.........656 H
HUTCHISON
av. Beaumaris..........530 F1
pl. Coburg 282 A2
st. Niddrie...............278 L2
HUTTON
av. Ferntree Gly 424 F1
pl. Kensington ....33 E
rd. Keysborough 533 J2
st. Dandenong ....535 K
st. Maidstone...........366 F
st. Thornbury...........326 D
HUTZUL
ct. Delahey..............275 B1

UXLEY
v. Dandenong N.....501 L11
v. Mulgrave..........500 J6
r. Endeavour Hl.....537 L6
t. Bayswater.........423 F11
t. Epping..............197 K16
t. Highton.............701 G13
UXTABLE
v. Altona North.......409 L2
d. Pakenham..........559 B3
d. Pakenham Up....559 B3
t. Mt Waverley.......419 G17
YACINTH
. Nar Warrn S.......553 F17
. Briar Hill............286 L6
YAM
l. Carlton................18 E16
l. Wantirna............422 A11
YATT
t. Grovedale..........705 K12
YBRID
t. Craigieburn........150 E14
YDE
t. Altona Mdw........451 G4
t. Dandenong S.....535 H15
t. Mulgrave...........500 D1
t. Deer Park..........319 D17
t. Diamond Ck........245 H10
t. Footscray...........367 G10
t. Hadfield.............281 A5
t. Seddon..............367 F13
t. Spotswood.........367 D20
t. Yarraville...........367 D20
t. Yarraville...........367 F12
YDEFIELD
r. Wyndham Va.....446 E8
YDEHILL
d. Harkaway...........540 H6
YDE PARK
k. Mooroolbark......337 D20
YDRA
t. Roxburgh Pk......194 F11
YDRANGEA
l. Burwood............418 A11
YDRIVE
l. Dandenong S.....550 G8
YDRO
t. Emerald.............510 C6
YETT
t. Sunshine W.......364 G8
YGEA
t. Altona Mdw........452 A3
YGEIA
v. Williamstn N......410 G13
t. Mornington........656 L5
r. Queenscliff.........709 C17
de. Ringwood N.......377 L8
t. Port Melb...........412 C5
t. Rye....................697 J4
YLAND
t. Anglesea...........713 D3
t. Berwick..............554 A3
t. Fyansford...........701 F4
t. Mordialloc...........532 E16
t. South Yarra..........31 K15
YLTON
r. Forest Hill..........420 H2
r. Rosanna............329 A3
YNE
t. Lilydale.............339 B5
YPERNO
t. Keilor Dn............275 K11
t. Kurunjang...........227 E9
y. Mt Martha...........656 H8
YSLOP
de. Malvern East......457 D4
t. Glen Iris.............417 L9
t. Hoppers Csg......448 H4
YSLOPS
d. Boneo...............700 L13
YSON
t. Carrum Downs...601 F1
YSSOP
r. Hallam...............538 D18
YTHE
l. Moorabbin.........496 G8
YTON
l. Westmeadows...236 F15
r. Croydon............335 K20
r. Kew..................371 D11

I

AIN
t. Kurunjang..........227 E9

IAN
av. Dandenong N.....502 A19
av. Ringwood E.......379 B6
cr. Airport W..........278 H16
cr. Mitcham...........377 D17
ct. Frankston S........627 B7
ct. Langwarrin.........629 C2
ct. Newcomb...........704 A15
ct. Rowville.............503 D5
gr. Burwood............418 J11
gr. Mt Waverley.......458 G8
pl. Croydon N..........335 K10
rd. Mt Martha..........668 J8
rd. Mt Martha..........669 A8
st. Balwyn...............373 F11
st. Noble Park.........500 J20
IANS
gr. Templstw Lr.......330 D8
IBBOTTSON
st. Watsonia...........285 F6
IBERA
ct. Eltham North......245 H18
IBERIA
ct. Burwood............418 B13
IBIS
ct. Baxter................644 D1
ct. Blind Bight.........650 C9
ct. Mickleham.........150 A3
ct. Mornington........657 B2
ct. Patterson L........573 J9
ct. Werribee............448 D10
ct. Wonga Park.......291 K19
gr. Rosebud W........698 J3
gr. St Albans...........319 G9
la. Yarra Jctn..........347 E12
st. Doncaster..........331 D20
wk. S Morang...........243 L3
wy. Cannons Creek...649 C6
wy. Portsea.............677 L4
IBSLEY
ct. St Albans...........275 J17
sq. Eltham...............288 D4
ICARUS
ct. Boronia..............423 H13
ct. Tootgarook........698 C7
IDA
ct. Donvale.............376 F3
ct. Langwarrin.........629 G7
ct. Reservoir...........282 E7
ct. Vermont.............421 H1
gr. Olinda...............427 D16
pl. Seabrook...........450 J3
st. Clayton S...........499 F9
st. Coburg N...........281 G16
st. Fitzroy N...........326 D17
st. Niddrie..............322 L4
st. Niddrie..............323 A4
IDEAL
av. Aspendale..........546 C5
ct. Rowville.............502 B5
IDINIA
ct. Doncaster..........330 J20
st. Kilsyth...............381 A4
IDON
av. Frankston S........627 A8
IDONIA
ct. Carrum Downs....601 B3
IDRIESS
ct. Mill Park............242 G5
IDWALL
ct. Highton..............705 K8
IENA
st. Dandenong S.....535 K15
IERINA
ct. Wantirna S.........422 A15
IEVERS
pl. Carlton................18 D19
st. Parkville.............325 E19
st. Upwey...............465 K13
tce. Carlton................18 D18
IFFLA
st. S Melbourne........29 D11
st. S Melbourne........29 E6
st. S Melbourne......413 B5
IFFLEY
ct. Ivanhoe.............328 B8
IGLOO
ct. Mornington........641 K18
pl. Keilor Dn...........275 G10
IKARA
cl. Kings Park.........319 E1
ct. Cheltenham........496 K16
ct. Frankston...........600 E17
st. Mornington.........656 J3
IKO
wy. Werribee...........446 H18
ILA
st. Glenroy..............280 G7
ILANA
ct. Nar Warrn S.......553 D19
ILANA VIEW
dr. Diamond Ck.......246 E9
ILANI
st. Epping...............198 A14
ILARI
ct. Mt Martha..........655 K20
ILFORD
ct. Craigieburn........194 E5
rd. Heathmont.........422 H1
ILIAS
ct. Bundoora...........242 G19
ILINGA
ct. Eltham North.....246 E20
ILIOS
cl. Forest Hill..........420 D6
ILLALONG
ct. Tootgarook........698 F6
ILLAROO
st. Rosebud............683 F20
st. Rosebud W........699 F1
ILLAWARA
cr. Bayswater N.......379 L14
ILLAWARRA
av. Rowville.............502 C7
cl. Chadstone..........458 E3
cl. Frankston...........628 D4
cr. Dandenong N.....501 G15
cr. Toorak...............415 F4
rd. Balwyn N...........373 F6
rd. Flemington...........33 G2
rd. Hawthorn...........372 B20
rd. Hawthorn...........416 B3
st. Glenroy..............280 A8
st. Williamstown.....411 F19
ILLAWONG
ct. Patterson L........573 L5
dr. Donvale.............332 K19
dr. Torquay.............711 H4
gr. Werribee............446 K15
mw. Langwarrin.........601 J15
tce. Burnside............318 H7
ILLIRA
av. Frankston...........600 H15
ILLONA
ct. Bulleen..............329 H14
ILLOUERA
av. Grovedale..........705 L14
ILLOURA
av. Ringwood E.......378 L12
cl. Noble Park N......501 D10
ct. Olinda...............426 J5
st. Watsonia...........285 G10
ILLOWA
cl. Frankston...........600 E17
st. Malvern East......416 K18
st. Mornington........640 L15
st. Mornington........641 A15
ILLOWRA
ct. Berwick.............553 H3
ILLUKA
cr. Mt Waverley.......459 G5
ILLUMINATE
ct. Kilsyth S............425 A1
ILMA
ct. Bulleen..............329 E12
ct. Parkdale............531 H14
ct. Seaford..............599 F2
gr. Bonbeach...........573 B6
gr. Northcote...........326 K15
ILORA
ct. Glen Waverley....460 A10
ILTON
av. Frankston...........599 H18
ILUKA
av. Aspendale..........546 F5
ct. Altona................408 J17
ct. Bundoora...........242 C19
ct. Ferntree Gly.......424 E20
ct. Jan Juc..............711 B18
ct. Sunshine W.......364 F6
dr. Werribee............446 J14
pl. Mornington........640 E17
pl. Ringwood N.......378 C4
rd. Rye....................697 K5
st. Black Rock.........529 J5
st. Safety Bch..........669 C13
st. Warneet.............649 E12
ILUKA ISLAND
Patterson L........573 J3
ILYUKA
ct. Portsea.............678 G3
IMAROO
st. Fawkner.............281 L11
IMBROS
st. Hampton............495 C5
IMES
st. Parkdale............531 H11
IMLACH
ct. Dingley Village...533 F7
IMMARNA
rd. Camberwell........417 D5
IMMERSET
dr. Chelsea Ht.........547 G18
IMPARA
ct. Scoresby...........462 D9
IMPERIAL
av. Bayswater..........423 D7
av. Caulfield S..........455 E6
av. Mt Waverley.......418 F20
av. Sunshine N.........321 E8
av. Wandin East.......340 L20
av. Wandin East.......341 A20
ct. Hillside...............231 H20
pl. Hoppers Csg......405 B13
IMPRESSA
cl. Langwarrin.........601 J19
IMRE
ct. Baxter................643 L2
ct. Clarinda............498 E11
INALA
ct. Burwood E.........419 F9
ct. Frankston...........600 G17
ct. Mulgrave............500 H3
ct. Yallambie...........286 C11
st. Rye....................696 L9
st. Rye....................697 A8
INCANA
cl. Hoppers Csg......405 C15
ct. Meadow Ht........193 K19
dr. Mill Park............243 D8
la. Mornington........656 F1
pl. Rowville.............502 D4
INCE
ct. Frankston...........600 C17
pl. Melton W...........226 D14
INCHCAPE
av. Wantirna............422 E5
pl. Melton W...........226 B15
INCINERATOR
rd. Melb Airport........235 B13
INDEPENDANCE
ri. Kilsyth S............381 A20
INDEPENDENCE
st. Moorabbin.........496 K11
INDIGO
ct. Broadmeadows..238 A10
ct. Frankston N.......600 E10
st. Wesburn............348 C20
wy. Bundoora...........242 E13
INDIGOFERA
wy. Langwarrin.........629 L4
INDRA
rd. Blackburn S.......419 E5
INDURA
st. Mt Martha..........656 E6
INDUSTRIAL
av. Hoppers Csg......405 K20
av. Notting Hill.........459 B13
av. Thomastown.......239 L19
dr. Braeside............532 F17
dr. Melton...............269 E2
dr. Somerville..........645 B13
dr. Sunshine W.......364 G13
INDUSTRY
cct. Kilsyth S............380 L15
ct. Lilydale.............338 E2
pl. Bayswater..........423 K4
INDUSTRY PARK
dr. Brooklyn............365 J15
INDWE
st. W Footscray.......366 D10
INEZ
av. Eltham...............287 E6
av. Ringwood..........378 B16
ct. Doncaster..........330 C15
ct. Melton...............268 J1
INGA
ct. Berwick.............554 J19
ct. Chadstone..........458 D2
ct. Chelsea.............547 C14
ct. Frankston...........628 C1
pde. Mt Martha..........656 B10
pde. Mt Martha..........656 E10
st. Burwood E.........419 E10
st. Oakleigh E.........458 H11
INGAMELLS
st. Cranbourne.......578 D18
INGARA
pl. Delahey.............275 A9
INGERSOLL
rd. Baxter...............645 G7
INGLEBRAE
ct. Essendon...........323 L10
ct. Noble Park N......501 D10
INGLENOOK
cr. Frankston...........600 H18
INGLES
st. Port Melb.............29 A3
st. Port Melb...........368 H18
INGLESBY
rd. Camberwell........416 H2
INGLESIDE
cr. Glen Waverley....459 H4
INGLETON
ct. Baxter................644 C2
ct. Narre Warren.....539 A15
INGLEWOOD
av. Forest Hill..........420 H5
av. Noble Park N......501 E17
cl. Doncaster E.......331 H15
cr. Rosebud............700 C3
ct. Gladstone Pk......237 A17
ct. Mill Park............243 E6
ct. Wheelers Hill......460 L8
dr. Thomastown......241 J18
INGLIS
av. Frankston...........599 C13
ct. Doncaster..........330 H18
ct. Glen Waverley....420 A17
rd. Beaconsfield.....554 H4
rd. Berwick.............554 H4
st. Box Hill N...........374 L8
st. Diamond Ck.......245 J9
st. Maddingley.........263 H1
st. Mornington........640 L12
st. Mornington........641 A12
st. Sunshine N........321 G18
st. Williamstn N......410 J13
INGLISBY
rd. Mont Albert........374 C13
INGOLDSBY
ct. Delahey.............275 B12
INGOT
rd. Diggers Rest......187 A9
INGRAM
av. Glen Waverley....460 D3
av. Sunshine W.......364 G7
cl. Narre Warren.....539 B15
rd. Anglesea............713 G3
rd. Coldstream........295 C16
rd. Gruyere.............296 F17
rd. Lilydale..............295 C16
st. Brunswick..........325 H17
INGRAMS
rd. Research...........288 H3
INGRID
ct. Herne Hill...........701 H2
st. Dandenong.........536 C3
st. Scoresby...........462 D7
INK
la. N Melbourne........34 E11
INKERMAN
gr. St Kilda, off
Inkerman St........414 D16
rd. Camberwell........416 J3
rd. Caulfield N.........415 C17
st. Balaclava...........414 D16
st. Maidstone..........366 K2
st. St Kilda.............414 D16
st. St Kilda E..........414 D16
INLET
pde. Tooradin...........651 K7
st. Aspendale..........546 D4
INMAN
st. Thornbury..........327 H8
INN
ct. Gladstone Pk......236 K16
INNELLAN
rd. Murrumbeena....457 B8
INNER
cr. Brighton.............454 J16
INNER HARBOUR
dr. Patterson L........573 H6
INNERLEVEN
ct. Frankston...........599 J16
INNES
ct. Berwick.............554 J18
ct. Taylors Lakes.....276 B9
ct. Tootgarook........698 E8
INNICHEN
cl. Frankston S........627 C15
INNIS
ct. Deer Park..........318 K12
INNISFALLEN
av. Templestowe.....331 J6
INNKEEPER
pl. Hoppers Csg......447 K1
pl. Sydenham.........274 L5
INNKEEPERS
wy. Attwood............236 L10
INNS
pl. Hoppers Csg......447 K1
INSIGNIA
cr. Berwick.............553 D3
INTERLAKEN
pde. Rosanna...........285 C18
INTERMAN
rd. Boronia.............424 F14

INTERNATIONAL
ct. Scoresby 462 C11
dr. Westmeadows 236 H18
sq. Tullamarine 278 E2
INTERVALE
dr. Avondale Ht 321 L7
dr. Wyndham Va 446 F12
INTREPID
st. Berwick 554 B10
INVERARY
ct. Portsea 678 D1
INVERAY
av. Jan Juc 711 D13
INVERBERVIE
ct. Wonga Park 291 G18
INVERELL
av. Mt Waverley 419 H19
INVERLEIGH
ct. Meadow Ht 237 L5
INVERLEITH
ct. St Kilda 414 A15
st. Hawthorn 372 C20
st. Hawthorn 416 C1
INVERLOCH
cr. Dallas 238 D10
st. Box Hill S 418 G5
st. Preston 327 C1
INVERLOCHY
st. Anglesea 713 L3
INVERMAY
ct. Frankston 628 D11
gr. Hawthorn E 416 D1
gr. Rosanna 328 J2
rd. Monbulk 427 K16
st. Reservoir 283 H5
INVERNESS
av. Armadale 415 G13
av. Armadale 415 H14
av. Blairgowrie 679 L18
av. Burwood 418 J6
av. The Basin 425 F14
cl. Pakenham 584 J2
ct. Croydon 379 G7
ct. Somerville 645 A20
dr. Kew East 372 K3
mw. Greenvale 192 L20
rd. Kalorama 383 C8
rd. Kalorama 383 D11
rd. Kalorama 383 E8
rd. Montrose 383 A4
rd. Mt Evelyn 383 A4
st. Brunswick E 325 L10
st. Clarinda 498 E5
st. Endeavour Hl 503 J19
st. Reservoir 283 H4
st. Seaford 599 H1
wy. Balwyn N 372 L3
wy. Balwyn N 373 A3
INVESTIGATOR
gr. Altona Mdw 452 A5
IOLANDA
st. Rye 696 K6
IOLANTHE
cl. Pk Orchards 334 C13
IONA
av. Belmont 705 L2
av. Brighton 455 A12
av. Highton 705 L2
av. Toorak 415 E9
ct. Frankston 600 F19
ct. Macleod 285 C10
ct. Mt Waverley 419 B15
ct. Wantirna S 423 A11
ct. Westmeadows 237 E10
st. Black Rock 529 F4
st. Clayton 459 B20
IPSWICH
ct. Wantirna 422 G9
pl. Craigieburn 150 D20
st. St Albans 320 G6
IPYDENE
ct. Chadstone 457 L2
IRAMOO
cct. Rockbank 270 B19
ct. Albanvale 318 L4
la. Yarraville 366 G18
st. Balwyn 373 G12
IRANDA
st. Frankston 628 A3
IREDALE
ct. Watsonia N 243 G19
IRELAND
av. Doncaster E 376 B3
av. Mitcham 377 D10
av. Narre Warren 553 A11
av. Wantirna S 422 K10
av. Wantirna S 423 A11
rd. Clayton S 499 D16
st. Burwood 418 D10
st. Ringwood 378 E16
st. Seaford 573 D15
st. W Melbourne 23 A2
st. W Melbourne 34 J20
st. W Melbourne 368 L11
IRENE
av. Up Fntree Gly 465 H8
cr. Mitcham 377 J11
ct. Chelsea 547 B15
ct. Cheltenham 497 D20
ct. Dandenong 536 F8
ct. Doncaster 330 E16
ct. Greensborough 244 J13
ct. Wheelers Hill 460 L13
gr. Selby 467 D18
pde. Cannons Creek 649 E9
pl. Prahran 32 L18
pl. Prahran 414 L9
pl. Prahran 415 A9
st. Coburg N 281 B15
st. Greensborough 244 K13
st. Millgrove 304 H19
st. Preston 326 L3
IRILBARRA
rd. Canterbury 373 B15
IRIS
av. Brooklyn 365 J17
cl. Cranbourne N 577 K4
cl. Keilor Dn 276 C14
cl. Mulgrave 501 E3
cl. Tootgarook 698 D7
cr. Boronia 424 B10
ct. Blackburn N 375 H10
ct. Cannons Creek 649 E8
ct. Doncaster E 332 F13
ct. Gowanbrae 279 C5
ct. Melton S 268 G9
ct. Mooroolbark 337 A11
rd. Glen Iris 416 H10
st. Bellfield 327 K6
st. Burwood 418 A7
st. Dromana 686 F8
wy. Bundoora 242 F13
IRISH
st. Bonbeach 573 E1
IRMA
gr. Pascoe Vale 280 L17
IRONBARK
cl. Eltham 288 C9
cl. Hampton Pk 552 B16
cl. Keysborough 534 A16
ct. Frankston N 599 K9
ct. Meadow Ht 193 K18
dr. Hoppers Csg 405 C14
dr. Templstw Lr 330 H14
rd. Bend of Islands 291 K7
rd. Diamond Ck 245 F1
rd. Maddingley 263 A4
rd. Yarrambat 201 A15
rd. Yarrambat 245 F1
st. St Albans 320 G11
st. View Bank 285 J19
IRONS
cl. Rowville 463 K10
ct. Epping 198 E17
IRONWORKERS
la. Maribyrnong 367 B2
IRREWARRA
ct. Seabrook 450 L3
IRRUKA
rd. Warburton 349 L8
IRVIN
ct. Fawkner 239 G20
IRVINE
av. Mt Martha 655 F19
cl. Endeavour Hl 503 K19
cr. Brunswick W 325 A7
cr. Frankston 600 F17
cr. Yarra Glen 209 B19
ct. Altona Mdw 451 E6
ct. Burwood 418 B4
ct. Westmeadows 236 J17
rd. Ivanhoe 328 E17
rd. Ivanhoe East 328 E17
st. Deer Park 319 C14
st. Glen Iris 417 D11
st. Mitcham 377 K15
st. Mt Evelyn 338 L16
st. Mt Evelyn 339 A16
st. Pascoe Vale 280 J19
st. Upwey 465 K12
IRVING
av. Box Hill 374 K13
av. Murrumbeena 457 B14
av. Prahran 415 A13
cl. Greenvale 192 J16
ct. Bundoora 243 E20
ct. Cheltenham 497 A14
ct. Maidstone 366 G2
ct. Rosebud W 699 C1
ct. Vermont 420 L6
pl. Point Cook 449 L6
pl. Footscray, off Albert St 367 E9
rd. Dandenong N 501 E18
rd. Melton 268 E1
rd. Pakenham 585 A3
rd. Toorak 415 F7
st. Footscray 367 F9
st. Malvern 415 K14
st. Mt Waverley 418 H20
st. Newport 411 B8
st. Niddrie 279 B19
IRVINGTON
st. Altona 409 F17
IRWELL
st. St Kilda 414 C17
IRWIN
av. Altona North 409 G2
ct. Whittington 704 D20
st. Clayton 459 D18
IRYMPLE
av. Glen Iris 416 F15
av. Kew East 372 H5
av. St Kilda 414 E18
ISA
gra. Kurunjang 226 K9
wy. Boronia 424 G2
ISAAC
ct. Cranbourne W 577 H19
ct. Endeavour Hl 537 L3
ct. Pakenham 585 C6
rd. Keysborough 534 J8
st. Cockatoo 471 F18
ISAAC EDEY
pl. Hampton Pk 551 L11
ISAACS
cl. Sunbury 143 H7
la. N Melbourne 17 C15
st. Laverton 407 D12
st. Preston 326 J3
ISAAC SMITH
cr. Cranbourne 603 K2
cr. Endeavour Hl 537 A4
ISABEL
av. Ringwood E 379 C13
cl. Caroline Spr 318 E11
cl. Mt Evelyn 339 J16
ISABELLA
cl. Chelsea Ht 547 D9
cr. Frankston 628 C12
ct. Doncaster 330 D19
gr. Hawthorn 371 E16
pl. Cranbourne N 578 H10
pl. Fitzroy N 19 C8
st. Geelong West 702 E1
st. Malvern 415 L15
st. Moorabbin 496 G10
st. Parkdale 531 H12
ISABELLA VINE
pl. Gowanbrae 279 E6
ISABELLE
ct. Mill Park 243 C12
ISING
st. Newcomb 703 L13
ISKANDAR
ct. Chadstone 458 E4
ISLA
av. Glenroy 280 E6
st. Sunshine N 321 D18
ISLAND
dr. Torquay 712 G1
pl. Mill Park 243 B6
rd. Keysborough 534 H18
ISLAY
ct. Mt Waverley 458 L5
ISLINGTON
pl. Caroline Spr 318 D9
st. Collingwood 25 L2
st. Sunshine 365 E2
ISMAILS
la. Launching Pl 345 H6
ISOBELLA
ct. Dandenong N 502 B18
ISON
ct. Altona Mdw 451 D4
ITALA
ct. Keilor Dn 276 A15
ITALIA
ct. Greensborough, off Oldstead Ct 244 H16
ITALLE
ct. Wheelers Hill 461 C17
ITHACA
ct. Chadstone 457 L2
rd. Frankston S 626 F9
ITKESTON
st. Herne Hill 701 J2
IVAN
av. Edithvale 546 K12
cr. Hampton Pk 551 G11
ct. Noble Park N 501 C11
ct. Portsea 678 A5
st. Doncaster 330 L17
st. Fitzroy N 326 E20
st. Strathmore 280 A15
IVANHOE
av. St Albans 320 G4
ct. Greenvale 237 C2
ct. Newcomb 703 L14
ct. Thomastown 241 G16
gr. Malvern East 457 G2
pde. Ivanhoe 328 C12
st. Glen Waverley 459 L8
st. Sorrento 679 A15
IVERNA
cl. Mulgrave 501 G5
IVES
rd. Altona North 409 A6
IVISON
wy. Hampton 495 C11
IVON
st. Bayswater N 379 J16
IVOR
pl. N Melbourne 17 H19
IVORY
ct. Sunshine W 364 K10
IVY
av. Kallista 467 B2
ct. Beaconsfield 555 C13
ct. Cranbourne N 578 B5
ct. Frankston N 600 E11
ct. Mill Park 242 E12
ct. Moorabbin 496 K8
ct. Mt Waverley 419 C14
la. Brunswick 325 E16
st. Bellfield 327 L5
st. Brunswick 325 E16
st. Burwood 419 A7
st. Cheltenham 531 D2
st. Cockatoo 511 C4
st. Hampton 495 F7
st. Newcomb 704 A12
st. Parkdale 531 J10
st. Prahran 32 G20
st. Prahran 414 J10
st. Preston 326 E4
st. St Albans 320 G9
IVY TOWER
ct. Taylors Lakes 275 H8
IXIA
cl. Hoppers Csg 405 C16
IZETT
st. Prahran 32 B18
st. Prahran 414 G9

J

JAANDA
ct. Blairgowrie 680 B19
JABIRU
ct. Werribee 447 J6
dr. Chelsea Ht 547 E16
pl. Hallam 538 D20
pl. Westmeadows 236 F12
wy. Whittlesea 96 C20
wy. Whittlesea 126 C1
JACANA
av. Broadmeadows 238 B18
av. Frankston 599 J18
av. Templstw Lr 330 B10
ct. Chadstone 458 C4
ct. Sunshine N 320 L11
dr. Carrum Downs 600 J1
rd. Forest Hill 420 E4
st. Chadstone 458 C4
st. Mornington 640 L16
st. Mornington 641 A16
st. Noble Park 535 A6
JACARANDA
av. Cheltenham 531 G2
av. Kilsyth 381 K6
cr. Mornington 641 A11
ct. Newcomb 704 C15
ct. Templstw Lr 330 K12
ct. Werribee 447 J9
dr. Baxter 644 D1
dr. Carrum Downs 574 L20
dr. Diamond Ck 245 D12
dr. Mill Park 242 F12
pl. Belmont 706 J5
pl. Craigieburn 150 A14
pl. View Bank 285 J20
rd. Wheelers Hill 460 F13
st. Doveton 536 J9
st. Oak Park 279 L10
JACINTA
ct. Aspendale Gdn 547 B6
ct. Doveton 536 L7
dr. Cranbourne W 577 F
wy. Kings Park 319 (
JACK
ct. Seaford 599
rd. Cheltenham 496 D
st. Carrum Downs 574 E
st. Mt Waverley 458
JACKA
bvd. St Kilda 413 L
rd. Avonsleigh 470 F
st. Balwyn N 373 H
st. Essendon 323
st. Ferny Creek 466 D
st. Launching Pl 345 J
st. Macleod 284 K
st. Preston 282 C
JACK HOLT
wy. Mordialloc 532 D
JACKIE
cl. Rowville 503 E
JACKMAN
cr. Keilor 276 K
ct. Wyndham Va 446 H1
rd. Newtown 701 K1
st. Preston 327 (
JACK ROBBIE
ct. Nar Warrn N 539 K
JACKS
av. Dingley Village 533 E
pl. Ringwood 335 B
rd. Oakleigh S 497
st. Newport 410
JACKSON
av. Mont Albert N 374
cct. Albanvale 319
ct. Doncaster E 375 H
dr. Langwarrin 629 C
pde. Coburg N 282 B
pl. Caroline Spr 318 A
rd. Highett 496 E1
rd. Wantirna S 422 H1
st. Anglesea 713
st. Croydon 380 C
st. Forest Hill 420 E
st. Maidstone 366 G
st. Mt Martha 669 D
st. Niddrie 323 A
st. Northcote 326 J1
st. Reservoir 282 L
st. St Kilda 414 A1
st. S Morang 243
st. Sunbury 143 H1
st. Toorak 415 E
st. Williamstown 411 G1
st. Burnley, off Tudor St 371 C1
wy. Dromana 686 E1
JACKSONS
rd. Chelsea 547 A1
rd. Mt Eliza 626 A1
rd. Mulgrave 501 D
rd. Narre Warren 539 A1
rd. Noble Park N 501 C1
JACKSONS CREEK
wy. Gisborne 79 C1
JACKSONS HILL
rd. Menzies Ck 467 L1
JACOB
ct. Thomastown 241 K1
dr. Rowville 463 H1
JACOBENA
pl. Templestowe 331 E
JACOBS
ct. Pakenham 584 H
dr. Clarinda 498 E1
st. Belmont 702 C1
JACOBUS
wk. Ferntree Gly 423 K1
JACOBY
ct. Mill Park 241 L
JACOBYS
la. N Melbourne 17 F1
JACOLYN
av. Rye 697 H
JACOV
gdn. Templestowe 331 G1
JACQUELINE
cl. Werribee 448 C1
ct. Berwick 554 C1
ct. Clarinda 498 C1
ct. Hillside 274 G
ct. Pakenham 584 J
ct. Pt Lonsdale 710 G
dr. Aspendale Gdn 546 J
pl. Pakenham 584 K
rd. Bundoora 285 B
rd. Mt Waverley 419 C1
tce. Nar Warrn S 579 H
JACQUES
rd. Nar Warrn N 538 H

ACYNTHE
t. Ringwood...378 J7
ADE
r. Bulla...190 B13
t. Aspendale Gdn...546 K4
t. Hampton Pk...551 C10
t. Narre Warren...539 D14
t. Wantirna S...421 L15
t. Yarra Glen...209 B20
t. Preston...327 F5
AFFA
t. Boronia...423 J9
AGGER
ct. Cranbourne E...604 H5
AGO
t. Werribee...448 B9
t. Burnley, off Bendigo St...371 C18
AGUAR
l. Nar Warrn N...538 D11
t. Epping...197 J15
r. Clayton...499 C4
AGUNGAL
t. Dromana...685 K8
AKE MICHAEL
r. Skye...575 H18
ALANA
t. Highton...705 G1
ALNA
l. Mulgrave...460 G20
l. Eltham...288 A16
ALTA
t. Keysborough...547 L2
AMBE
t. Hampton Pk...551 D6
AMBOREE
v. Frankston S...627 A5
l. Mornington...656 J2
a. Ashwood...418 C19
AMELA
t. Cranbourne...577 L11
AMES
v. Aspendale...546 B2
v. Highett...496 B14
v. Kew...372 A7
v. Mitcham...377 J13
v. Northcote...326 G16
v. Seaholme...409 J16
l. Sunbury...142 H4
r. Hampton...495 G10
t. Bacchus Msh...221 L12
t. Diamond Ck...244 K13
t. Hillside...231 K19
t. Mt Martha...655 K16
t. Narre Warren...539 B13
t. Tottenham...365 J8
a. Mordialloc...531 H17
a. S Melbourne...30 B6
de. Malvern East...457 J1
d. Croydon...336 D19
d. Ferntree Gly...423 E18
d. Glen Waverley...420 J20
t. Abbotsford...26 B2
t. Ascot Vale...323 G19
t. Baxter...644 E1
t. Bayswater...423 F3
t. Belmont...706 D3
st. Blackburn...375 H13
st. Box Hill...374 J17
st. Brighton...454 G12
st. Brunswick W...324 K12
st. Clayton S...498 K4
st. Clematis...508 K4
st. Dandenong...535 K5
st. Dromana...686 A7
st. Fawkner...281 K8
st. Fitzroy...19 A18
st. Frankston...599 F20
st. Glen Huntly...456 C8
st. Hawthorn...372 A18
st. Heidelberg Ht...328 F5
st. Laverton N...408 A3
st. Millgrove...304 G20
st. Montmorency...286 J12
st. Mordialloc...531 H17
st. Noble Park...500 F19
st. Northcote...326 H16
st. Pakenham...584 K5
st. Preston...326 C2
st. Richmond...26 G18
st. Ringwood...378 E13
st. Rye...696 G11
st. St Albans...319 H2
st. Seaford...573 E20
st. Seddon...367 B11
st. Selby...467 C15
st. Sorrento...678 L14
st. Strathmore...324 A1
st. Sunshine W...364 B2
st. Surrey Hills...373 L14
st. Templestowe...330 G7
st. Templestowe...330 L7

st. Templstw Lr...330 G7
st. Whittlesea...96 E19
st. Williamstown...411 G14
st. Windsor...414 G12
st. Geelong, off Ryrie St...703 A8
JAMES AUSTIN
pl. Hoppers Csg...447 K2
wy. Seabrook...450 K8
JAMES BATHE
wy. Nar Warrn S...578 J1
JAMESBRAD
ct. Mt Eliza...642 E1
JAMES COOK
dr. Cranbourne...603 L1
dr. Diamond Ck...245 L13
dr. Endeavour Hl...537 A5
dr. Endeavour Hl...537 G9
dr. Melton W...226 B17
dr. Wandana Ht...705 D3
JAMES KERR
wy. Croydon...380 B4
JAMES McFARLANE
wyn. Skye...575 H16
JAMES MILNE
dr. Croydon N...335 K15
JAMES MIRAMS
dr. Roxburgh Pk...194 A8
JAMES RUSE
ct. Mill Park...242 E4
JAMES SCULLIN
ct. Richmond...26 J15
JAMES SERVICE
pl. S Melbourne...29 L8
pl. S Melbourne...413 F4
JAMES WEST
st. Glen Waverley...459 K9
JAMES WYMAN
pl. Hampton Pk...552 B12
JAMIE
cl. Cranbourne...578 F17
ct. Pakenham...559 G20
mw. Berwick...554 K18
JAMIESON
av. Footscray...367 J7
av. Rowville...463 C17
cl. Roxburgh Pk...194 C12
ct. Epping...242 B1
ct. Greensborough...244 K13
ct. Langwarrin...629 H10
ct. Pakenham...584 K9
ct. Werribee...446 L9
ct. Werribee...447 A9
rd. Wonga Park...335 E3
st. Cheltenham...496 J18
st. Coburg...325 B4
st. Dromana...686 F11
st. Fitzroy N...19 F7
st. Northcote...326 K18
st. St Albans...319 H3
st. Thomson...703 J18
tce. Taylors Hill...274 L12
tce. Taylors Hill...274 L13
wy. Point Cook...450 F12
JAMIL
ct. Endeavour Hl...538 A4
JAMISON
av. Endeavour Hl...537 E10
st. Laverton...407 E18
st.s, Altona Mdw...407 E20
JAN
ct. Greensborough...286 B9
ct. Lalor...240 H4
ct. Mt Eliza...626 J19
JANCOL
ct. Berwick...554 H12
JANDA
ct. Box Hill N...374 J6
JANDEN
cl. Knoxfield...463 B7
JANDO
ct. Rowville...463 J15
JANE
av. St Albans...275 K19
ct. Boronia...424 D2
ct. Dingley Village...533 B7
ct. Kilsyth S...381 C14
ct. Langwarrin...629 C7
ct. Meadow Ht...238 D3
ct. Mernda...156 A16
st. Bentleigh E...496 L6
st. Berwick...554 B9
JANEFIELD
dr. Bundoora...243 A14
JANELAINE
ct. Springvale S...499 E19
JANE-MAREE
pl. Cranbourne...578 A14
JANESDELL
av. Ferny Creek...425 G17

JANET
cr. Bundoora...242 J18
ct. Hampton Pk...552 A13
ct. Heathmont...422 H2
ct. Narre Warren...539 A15
ct. Newcomb...704 B15
ct. Portsea...677 H5
ct. Yallambie...286 C12
st. Blackburn...375 E18
st. Boronia...424 G7
st. Brighton East...495 J5
st. Dandenong N...501 K18
st. Keilor East...322 F5
st. Templstw Lr...330 B12
JANETTE
ct. Carrum Downs...575 E14
JANFOURD
ct. Mt Waverley...459 C5
JANG
pl. Kurunjang...227 C13
JANICE
av. Cheltenham...497 F18
ct. Campbellfield...239 F19
gr. Dandenong...535 G2
pl. Ringwood N...334 G16
rd. Glen Waverley...459 J8
st. Macleod...285 H11
JANIESLEIGH
rd. Tremont...465 E6
rd. Up Fntree Gly...465 E6
JANINA
ct. Vermont S...420 J11
ct. Wheelers Hill...461 B17
JANINE
ct. Doncaster E...332 D8
ct. Newcomb...704 E13
ct. Somerville...645 A18
rd. Nar Warrn N...538 H11
rd. Springvale S...500 B20
st. Scoresby...462 F10
JANKE
ct. Carrum Downs...575 F14
JANMARA
ct. Dandenong N...501 H13
ct. Endeavour Hl...504 A19
JAN MAREE
ct. Pakenham...584 G2
JANNALI
dr. Dingley Village...533 E9
JANOS
cl. Narre Warren...538 H15
JANSON
cl. Nar Warrn S...552 G12
ct. Croydon N...335 J9
st. Maidstone...366 F2
JANUS
st. Tullamarine...278 F3
JANVILLE
st. Boronia...423 J12
JAPADDY
st. Mordialloc...532 E10
JAPONICA
ct. Newcomb...704 D14
ct. St Albans...319 E8
dr. Yarra Glen...209 C11
gr. Frankston S...627 D8
st. Bundoora...242 K16
JAQUES
gr. Forest Hill...420 E5
st. Hawthorn E...372 G15
JARDIER
tce. S Morang...198 L12
JARDINE
cr. Sunbury...143 G15
ct. Nar Warrn S...578 L2
rd. Macclesfield...471 F8
JARED
wy. Altona Mdw...451 C5
JARMA
cov. Doncaster E...331 K17
rd. Heathmont...378 F18
JARMAN
ct. Hoppers Csg...405 A16
ct. Sorrento...679 A15
dr. Langwarrin...602 A20
st. Mordialloc...532 E16
JARRAH
ct. Boronia...424 K6
ct. Delahey...275 C10
ct. Frankston N...599 L9
ct. Glen Waverley...460 B10
ct. Greensborough...243 J18
ct. Hoppers Csg...405 D18
ct. Montrose...382 E6
ct. Narre Warren...553 C8
ct. Templstw Lr...330 J13
dr. Braeside...532 G17
dr. Carrum Downs...575 D18
pl. Belmont...706 G6
pl. Point Cook...449 L5

pl. Waurn Ponds...705 D16
ps. Deer Park...319 B9
JARRAHDALE
st. Cheltenham...497 C20
JARRETT
ct. Rowville...463 E19
JARROD
pl. Croydon N...335 L9
JARROT
ct. Meadow Ht...238 B2
JARRYD
cr. Berwick...554 K18
JARVIE
st. Brunswick E...325 K15
JARVIS
av. Croydon...380 H5
cr. Dandenong N...536 C1
rd. Waurn Ponds...705 A12
JASERFOLD
st. Balwyn N...373 F3
JASMIN
cl. Mt Martha...656 B9
ct. Narre Warren...539 B15
ct. Waurn Ponds...705 E14
JASMINE
cl. Hoppers Csg...405 B14
ct. Bayswater N...380 K16
ct. Blackburn S...419 G4
ct. Cranbourne N...578 C8
ct. Dingley Village...532 K4
ct. Eltham North...245 D18
ct. Frankston...600 B17
ct. Meadow Ht...238 C1
ct. Point Cook...449 K6
ct. Rowville...463 J16
dr. Mill Park...242 C11
pl. Melton W...226 C14
rd. Bayswater N...379 J14
st. Caulfield S...455 H8
JASON
cl. Berwick...554 B18
cl. Balwyn N...329 G20
ct. Donvale...332 J16
ct. Noble Park...500 J17
ct. View Bank...285 J19
pl. Frankston...600 G20
pl. Hampton Pk...551 D12
pl. Melton W...225 L15
rd. Carrum Downs...575 E14
st. Oakleigh S...458 E19
JASPER
ct. Hampton Pk...551 C9
ct. Mt Martha...655 E20
pl. Point Cook...449 K6
rd. Bentleigh...496 C6
rd. Kalorama...382 L11
rd. Kalorama...383 A11
rd. McKinnon...456 C20
rd. Ormond...456 C20
st. Noble Park...500 H18
tce. Frankston...627 A5
tce. Frankston S...627 A5
JASSA
st. Bentleigh E...457 E16
JAY
ct. Werribee...447 L8
ri. Berwick...554 K19
JAYBREE
ct. Grovedale...706 A9
JAYCEE
cr. Carrum Downs...574 H16
JAYCO
ct. Mulgrave...500 E5
JAYDEE
ct. Rowville...502 B2
JAYE
pl. Cranbourne W...577 G18
JAYNE
ct. Dandenong S...551 A9
st. Frankston...600 A20
JAYSON
av. Eltham...287 D18
st. Burwood E...420 B7
JEAN
av. Clayton...498 L3
ct. Keysborough...534 L12
ct. Mooroolbark...337 B10
pl. Grovedale...705 H14
st. Aberfeldie...323 C11
st. Cheltenham...496 G18
st. Forest Hill...376 D20
st. Lalor...241 G11
st. McKinnon...455 L16
st. Nar Warrn S...579 G1
st. Reservoir...282 H7
st. Templstw Lr...330 G10
st. Up Fntree Gly...464 L5
JEANBART
ct. Wantirna S...422 B19

JEANETTE
cl. St Helena...244 L17
ct. Mulgrave...501 H7
ct. Ringwood E...379 C11
st. Bayswater...423 D10
st. Clayton S...498 G4
st. Woori Yallock...344 E15
JEANETTE MAREE
ct. Kilsyth...381 D16
JEANINE
cr. Fawkner...281 E2
JEANNE
st. Cockatoo...510 L9
JEANNINE
ct. Mt Martha...656 C7
JEAVONS
ct. Altona Mdw...451 G5
JEDAN
ct. Rowville...503 G2
JEDBURGH
pl. Greenvale...236 L2
JEDDA
ct. Cheltenham...497 A20
st. Rye...696 L11
JEDEM
cl. View Bank...286 B16
JEEVES
av. Kalorama...383 C13
JEFF
ct. Oakleigh S...498 A10
ct. Sunshine N...320 L11
ct. Sunshine N...321 A11
JEFFCOTT
pl. W Melbourne...23 E5
st. W Melbourne...1 A2
st. W Melbourne...23 D6
JEFFERS
st. Noble Park...501 B18
JEFFERSON
gr. Doncaster E...332 H12
rd. Croydon S...379 G12
st. St Albans...319 G5
JEFFERY
av. Noble Park...534 E3
ct. Greensborough...286 D8
st. Blackburn...375 L19
JEFFREY
av. Altona North...410 D3
cl. St Albans...320 E13
ct. Clayton S...499 D15
ct. Epping...241 L4
dr. Ringwood...378 K5
dr. Yarrambat...201 B11
gr. Bayswater...423 B6
st. Bentleigh...496 F1
st. Campbellfield...239 E18
st. Dandenong N...536 A1
st. Hampton Pk...551 D10
st. Keilor East...322 C4
st. Mt Waverley...459 E6
st. Northcote...327 B20
st. Reservoir...283 A16
st. Templstw Lr...330 C12
JEFFREYS
ct. Bacchus Msh...221 J14
JEFFRIES
pde. Melbourne...4 G5
pde. Melbourne...24 H12
JEFFS
ct. Endeavour Hl...537 B6
JEJANA
tce. Rowville...503 B8
JELBART
ct. Eltham...288 A9
ct. Rosebud...699 L2
JELF
ct. Fawkner...281 J11
JELIMAR
ct. Sunbury...142 J8
JELLICO
dr. Scoresby...462 A8
JELLICOE
av. Monbulk...428 G17
ct. Werribee...447 L13
st. Box Hill S...375 A20
st. Cheltenham...496 K18
st. Ivanhoe...327 L8
st. Noble Park...535 B2
st. Werribee...447 K14
JELLINDALE
ct. Highton...702 A16
JELLS
rd. Cheltenham...531 G1
rd. Mulgrave...461 A19
rd. Wheelers Hill...461 B11
JEM
cl. Brunswick E...326 C14
JEMA
cl. Nar Warrn S...552 E11
ct. Boronia...424 B9

JENELLE
ct. Baxter 644 C1
JENHILL
ct. Rowville 463 J18
JENKEI
ct. Rye 697 D9
JENKENS
st. Frankston N 600 C11
JENKIN
st. Brunswick E 325 L16
st. Reservoir 282 C13
JENKINS
cl. Ringwood N 377 L4
ct. Kealba 276 K20
ct. Wantirna 422 G12
dr. Templestowe 332 A10
st. Caulfield S 455 H10
st. Mordialloc 532 D18
st. Noble Park 500 J16
st. Northcote 327 A12
JENNA
cl. Greensborough 285 L8
ct. Ferntree Gly 464 B12
JENNER
cl. Mornington 656 L6
cl. Mornington 657 A6
ct. Hampton Pk 551 B8
st. Blackburn S 419 D5
JENNI
ct. Hoppers Csg 447 L3
JENNIFER
av. Parkdale 532 A10
cr. Bayswater N 380 D17
cr. Pt Lonsdale 710 F1
ct. Avondale Ht 322 B16
ct. Grovedale 706 E12
ct. Keilor 276 L11
ct. Keilor 277 A11
ct. Langwarrin 601 L16
ct. Macleod 285 H11
ct. Mt Waverley 459 E4
ct. Narre Warren 539 F18
ct. Ringwood 378 L6
ct. Vermont S 420 K7
ct. Warrandyte 333 A5
ct. Whittlesea 96 L18
rd. Lilydale 338 H6
st. Cheltenham 497 B19
st. Fawkner 281 H2
st. Junction Vill 604 K14
st. Noble Park N 501 D15
JENNINGS
ct. Rosebud W 699 F6
rd. Bayswater N 380 H19
rd. Monbulk 468 E2
st. Laverton 407 E14
st. Moonee Pnd 323 K11
st. Noble Park 500 E20
st. Sandringham 495 D18
JENNISON
ct. Chelsea Ht 547 F16
JENNY
ct. Cranbourne N 578 G11
ct. Ferny Creek 465 L3
ct. Hillside 274 G5
ct. Mooroolbark 336 L12
ct. Scoresby 462 C6
JENOLA
pde. Wantirna S 422 B19
JENOLAN
av. Grovedale 706 B11
JENSEN
ct. Wheelers Hill 460 J16
rd. Broadmeadows 238 C17
rd. Preston 283 G20
rd. Up Fntree Gly 465 E7
st. Hadfield 280 H9
JEPHSON
st. Blairgowrie 696 B2
JEPSON
st. Yarraville 366 F14
JEREMIC
ct. Croydon N 336 E14
JEREMY
ct. Mornington 640 J20
JERICHO
ct. Berwick 553 F5
JERILDERIE
dr. Berwick 539 H20
JEROME
ct. Frankston 628 B11
JERRIBRY
pl. Blackburn 376 B20
JERROLD
st. Footscray 367 B5
JERSEY
cl. Endeavour Hl 537 G4
ct. Belmont 706 C5
pde. Carnegie 456 K6
rd. Bayswater 424 A6
st. Balwyn 373 D13
st. Coburg 281 C19
JERULA
av. Mt Eliza 626 C10
JERVIS
st. Camberwell 417 J7
JERVOIS
st. St Kilda E 414 H16
JESICA
rd. Campbellfield 239 C5
JESMOND
rd. Croydon 380 B11
JESS
ct. Ringwood E 379 E14
st. Reservoir 282 J5
JESSAMBER
ct. Diamond Ck 246 D11
JESSAMINE
av. Prahran 414 L13
JESSE
ct. Nar Warrn N 539 G9
st. Glen Iris 417 K11
JESSICA
cl. Wantirna S 421 K14
dr. Hampton Pk 552 D15
mw. Berwick 554 K6
pl. Delahey 275 D11
JESSICAS
la. Eltham 287 H3
JESSIE
st. Blackburn N 376 D9
st. Coburg 325 E7
st. Cranbourne N 578 H11
st. Cremorne 26 A18
st. Noble Park 534 L6
st. Northcote 326 K19
st. Oak Park 280 B10
st. Preston 326 G2
st. Sunshine 365 G5
JESSON
cr. Dandenong 536 F6
JESSOP
ct. Gladstone Pk 279 A2
st. Greensborough 285 L4
JESSUP
cl. Mulgrave 501 F1
JESTER
ct. Kings Park 274 L19
JETSKE
ct. Dingley Village 532 K6
JETTI
la. Torquay 711 J2
JETTY
rd. Boneo 700 F6
rd. Dromana 686 C8
rd. Rosebud 700 D4
rd. Rosebud 700 F6
rd. Sandringham 494 K12
JEUNE
gr. Berwick 553 J14
JEWELL
cr. Brunswick W 324 H14
st. Yarraville 366 J17
JEZABEEL
ct. Flemington 33 J2
JICKELL
av. Glen Iris 417 E9
JIKA
ct. Werribee 446 K15
pl. Richmond 26 A7
st. Coburg 281 K20
st. Heidelberg 329 B8
JILBA
ct. Tootgarook 698 C7
JILL
ct. Ringwood 378 J6
pl. Gisborne S 110 E17
JILLARD
wk. Hoppers Csg 448 A1
JILLIAN
av. Highett 495 H13
dr. Rye 697 C13
st. Cranbourne 604 A3
st. Dandenong N 501 J18
st. Mooroolbark 337 H16
st. Tullamarine 278 F4
wy. Mt Martha 657 D9
JILMAX
ct. Forest Hill 376 E19
JILPANGER
rd. Donvale 332 G19
JIM
ct. Millgrove 304 J19
JIMBA
ct. View Bank 286 C16
JINCHILLA
av. Frankston S 627 G17
JINDA
pl. Melton W 225 J18
JINDABYNE
av. Chadstone 418 C20
av. Dandenong N 502 B17
ct. Ferntree Gly 464 B16
JINDALEE
av. Yallambie 286 B14
cl. Rowville 462 L18
ct. Bulleen 329 H12
ct. Frankston 628 D6
ct. Nar Warrn S 553 B18
gdn. Cranbourne W 603 F1
JINDARA
ct. Gladstone Pk 279 C2
JINDIVICK
st. Maribyrnong 322 J15
JINGAI
ct. Frankston 600 H16
JINGELLA
av. Ashwood 418 A19
JINGHI
rd. Reservoir 283 B5
JINJELLA
rd. Highton 701 K14
JINKANA
gr. Eltham 288 C6
JIRRAH
ct. Aspendale 546 H7
JISING
ct. Doncaster E 375 F2
JITSU
rd. Mt Evelyn 339 E12
J J TULLY
dr. Doncaster 331 C20
JOAMI
st. Cheltenham 497 C17
JOAN
av. Dromana 686 D3
av. Ferntree Gly 424 K16
cr. Burwood E 420 A8
ct. Campbellfield 239 H12
ct. Heathmont 378 E19
ct. Mulgrave 501 E2
ct. Noble Park N 501 D19
ct. Reservoir 239 K20
ct. St Albans 276 G18
ct. Werribee 448 A16
ct. Woori Yallock 344 H14
st. Melton 226 G20
st. Moorabbin 496 G10
st. Sunshine W 363 L4
st. Sunshine W 364 A4
st. Sunshine W 364 C4
JOANNA
ct. Mt Waverley 459 B4
ct. Torquay 712 F2
st. Nunawading 376 J20
JO-ANNE
pl. Kings Park 319 E2
JOANNE
av. Chirnside Pk 336 K6
ct. Bayswater N 380 E17
ct. Epping 197 H14
JOBERT
ct. Blackburn S 419 J3
st. Springvale 500 A16
JOBSON
st. Williamstown 411 D14
JOCELYN
av. Balwyn N 374 D4
ct. Doncaster E 331 J19
ct. Forest Hill 376 H20
ct. Nunawading 420 H1
st. Lalor 240 J7
st. Surrey Hills 373 K16
JODI
av. Wheelers Hill 460 K18
pl. Hampton Pk 552 D14
st. Cheltenham 531 H1
JODIE
cl. Doveton 536 L7
ct. Campbellfield 239 H12
ct. Greensborough 244 L14
pl. Kilsyth S 381 A20
JOEL
av. Altona North 409 G7
ct. Bayswater 423 B6
ct. Heathmont 378 F19
ct. Moorabbin 497 C9
pl. Gladstone Pk 279 A3
wy. Hampton Pk 551 L7
JOELLE
ct. Aspendale Gdn 546 L6
JOFFRE
av. Edithvale 546 H12
pde. Cockatoo 511 C2
rd. Pascoe Vale 280 H12
rd. Silvan 384 K11
st. Broadmeadows 238 E17
st. Camberwell 417 K6
st. Croydon 380 B2
st. Healesville 257 H2
st. Noble Park 535 B1
st. Reservoir 283 B16
JOHANN
av. Scoresby 462 H8
JOHANNA
ct. Dingley Village 532 K5
ct. Pakenham 585 L3
JOHANSEN
pl. Darley 221 L7
JOHANSONS
rd. Warrandyte 334 G3
rd. Warrandyte S 334 G3
JOHN
ct. Bundoora 243 B20
ct. St Albans 320 C12
ct. Somerville 645 A15
pl. Newtown 702 G12
pl. Geelong, off Little Malop St 703 D8
st. Altona North 409 E2
st. Balwyn 373 E12
st. Bayswater 423 G6
st. Beaumaris 530 B10
st. Bentleigh E 456 J20
st. Blackburn 375 J12
st. Box Hill 374 L16
st. Brunswick E 326 A16
st. Clifton Hill 20 D5
st. Collingwood 19 J17
st. Dandenong S 536 B14
st. Eltham 287 G11
st. Elwood 454 E3
st. Emerald 469 E15
st. Fitzroy 19 A15
st. Flemington 33 J1
st. Frankston 599 G18
st. Geelong West 702 E2
st. Glenroy 280 H1
st. Glen Waverley 419 K20
st. Hawthorn 372 B17
st. Ivanhoe 328 C14
st. Kew 372 F12
st. Lalor 240 J4
st. Langwarrin 629 B6
st. Lilydale 338 A6
st. Malvern East 416 B20
st. Mordialloc 531 H17
st. Oakleigh 458 C13
st. Oak Park 279 K13
st. Pakenham 584 K7
st. Pascoe Vale 280 K18
st. Ringwood N 378 E6
st. St Albans 319 H2
st. Sandringham 495 E12
st. Seddon 367 B10
st. S Melbourne 30 A4
st. Sunbury 143 K11
st. Templstw Lr 330 G13
st. Tootgarook 698 C4
st. Wandin N 340 H14
st. Werribee 448 D16
st. Williamstown 411 D12
st. Geelong, off Little Malop St 703 A7
JOHN AUGUST
wk. Seabrook 450 L6
JOHN BALL
pl. Werribee 447 B7
JOHN BARR
ct. Berwick, off Keith Taylor Dr 554 D9
JOHN BATMAN
dr. Melton W 225 H20
JOHN BERTRAM
dr. Sorrento 679 C17
JOHN COOKE
tce. Seabrook 450 L7
JOHN EDGCUMBE
wy. Endeavour Hl 537 E7
JOHN FAWKNER
dr. Endeavour Hl 537 H8
JOHN FISHER
dr. Berwick 554 F13
JOHN HOLLAND
ct. Blackburn 375 K11
JOHN HUNTER
ct. Mill Park 242 D4
dr. Endeavour Hl 537 G11
JOHN JOSEPH
ct. Nar Warrn N 539 H11
JOHN LECKY
rd. Seabrook 450 L8
JOHN LISTON
dr. Newport 411 A11
la. Newport 411 A11
JOHN MONASH
dr. Skye 575 G15
JOHN PAUL
dr. Hillside 274 E2
JOHN PHELPS
ct. Seabrook 451 A
JOHN ROWELL
la. Mornington 640 K1
JOHN RYAN
dr. S Morang 243 H
JOHNS
cr. Mt Evelyn 338 K1
dr. Rye 696 I
gr. Doncaster E 332 D
la. Smiths Gly 205 D1
rd. Mornington 640 B2
rd. Selby 467 D1
st. Up Fntree Gly 465 C
JOHNSON
av. Carrum 573 A
av. Hoppers Csg 448 C
av. Rye 680 G2
bl. Meadow Ht 237 J
ct. Rosebud W 683 F1
ct. Roxburgh Pk 194 D1
dr. Ferntree Gly 423 F1
dr. Glen Waverley 460 E
la. Albert Park 29 H1
pl. Endeavour Hl 537 C
st. Avondale Ht 322 B1
st. Avonsleigh 470 F1
st. Belmont 706 E
st. Footscray 367 D
st. Hawthorn 372 A1
st. Moonee Pnd 324 H1
st. Noble Park 534 L
st. Northcote 326 H1
st. Oakleigh 457 J1
st. Pascoe Vale S 324 E
st. Reservoir 283 A
st. Richmond 26 L
st. Richmond 371 A1
st. Rosebud W 683 E1
st. St Kilda E 414 K1
st. S Melbourne 29 A
st. Sunshine N 321 F1
st. Thomastown 240 L1
st. Thomastown 241 A1
st. Thornbury 326 H1
JOHNSONS
rd. Mernda 156 A1
JOHNSTON
av. Eumemmerring 536 L1
av. Eumemmerring 537 A1
av. Newcomb 704 A1
ct. Dandenong S 536 B1
pde. Ferny Creek 465 H
st. Abbotsford 20 D1
st. Ashburton 417 D1
st. Burwood 419 E
st. Collingwood 19 A1
st. Fitzroy 19 A1
st. Mentone 531 C
st. Newport 410 H
st. Port Melb 29 A1
st. Port Melb 412 L
st. Wandin East 340 K1
JOHNSTONE
st. Broadmeadows 237 H1
st. Jacana 237 H1
st. Malvern 416 A1
st. Pt Lonsdale 707 J2
st. Seaford 599 E
st. Westmeadows 237 D1
JOHN WEDGE
pl. Seabrook 450 K
wyn. Skye 575 H1
JOINER
st. Williamstown 410 J1
JOLEN
ct. Donvale 332 K1
JOLIE
gr. Box Hill 375 B1
JOLIE VUE
rd. Balwyn N 329 E1
JOLIMONT
av. Mulgrave 501 D
la. E Melbourne 25 C1
pl. Dingley Village 499 B2
pl. Narre Warren 539 F1
rd. E Melbourne 25 C1
rd. Forest Hill 420 H
rd. Vermont 420 H
rd. Vermont 421 A
st. E Melbourne 25 C1
tce. E Melbourne 25 E1
JOLLEY
st. Brunswick W 324 L
JOLLIFFE
cr. Rosanna 328 L
cr. Rosanna 329 A
JOLLY
ct. Roxburgh Pk 193 L
pl. Sydenham 274 K
st. Dandenong 535 F

Frankston...599 G19
S Morang...243 H3

MARY

Berwick...554 G10

N

Keysborough...534 D9
Laverton N...408 A4

NAS

Richmond...26 B4

NATHAN

Burwood E...419 J8
Bayswater N...380 H17
Eumemmerring...537 B15
Noble Park...534 K4
Pakenham...559 F19
Gisborne...78 L20

NATHON

Mornington...656 J1
Taylors Lakes...275 G5
Wantirna S...422 E17
Darley...221 L10

NES

Up Fntree Gly...465 G7
Rosanna...285 C19
Smiths Gly...206 E6
Aspendale Gdn...547 A6
Bundoora...242 H20
Darley...221 L8
Endeavour Hl...537 A6
Laverton...407 F12
Mt Waverley...458 F9
Sunshine W...364 H10
Melbourne...2 L8
Melbourne...24 G3
N Melbourne...17 E17
Roxburgh Pk...194 C14
Caroline Spr...318 E9
Geelong...703 B11
Richmond...371 C16
W Melbourne...23 B1
Brooklyn...365 C17
Dandenong...535 G6
Kangaroo Grnd...247 G11
Somerville...644 K20
Wattle Glen...247 G11
Brunswick...325 G10
Lilydale...338 E4
Thornbury...327 F8

NQUIL

Diamond Ck...245 J6
Doncaster E...332 E13

NSON

Melton W...225 J19

RDAN

Boronia...423 G15
Endeavour Hl...537 C3
Glen Waverley...460 E7
Roxburgh Pk...194 C15
Monbulk...428 C17
Pt Lonsdale...710 F2
Ashwood...418 C18
Brunswick W...324 K15
Clayton S...498 J4
Malvern...416 B15
Somerville...645 C15

ROMA

Wonga Park...336 D8

SEF

Bundoora...242 G16

SEPH

New Gisborne...79 G6
Pk Orchards...334 D19
Wantirna S...462 A4
Hillside...274 F3
Pakenham...585 B6
Footscray...367 K7
Blackburn N...375 G6
Broadmeadows...238 B17
Bundoora...284 G2
Ringwood E...379 C6
Templstw Lr...330 G14

SEPH BANKS

Cranbourne...603 K2
Endeavour Hl...537 B4

SEPHINA

Carrum Downs...601 E4

SEPHINE

Cranbourne N...578 G10
Mt Waverley...419 F17
Narre Warren...538 H16
Ferntree Gly...464 A13
Melton W...225 L13
Plenty...244 J11
Preston...283 C18
Langwarrin...601 H19
Oak Park...279 K11

SHUA

Springvale S...499 G18
Bundoora...242 G20
Kings Park...319 C2
Narre Warren...539 A14

JOSIE

ct. Lilydale...338 G14
ct. Pk Orchards...377 H1

JOSLYN

dr. Research...289 D8

JOULES

ct. Deer Park...319 C9
ct. Macleod...285 F11

JOUSTING

pl. Glen Waverley...420 K16

JOVIC

rd. Epping...241 D3

JOWETT

av. Sunshine W...364 J9

JOY

av. Mt Evelyn...383 E1
cl. Werribee...447 F3
ct. Lilydale...338 E12
ct. Narre Warren...539 E18
mw. Pakenham...584 F2
pde. Noble Park...500 F19
st. Balwyn N...329 K19
st. Bentleigh E...456 H18
st. Braybrook...365 L4
st. Donvale...376 G4
st. Frankston...599 E20
st. Melton S...268 E5
st. Mt Waverley...419 J14
st. South Yarra...32 J15

JOYCE

av. Frankston...599 F18
av. Glen Waverley...460 E7
av. Greensborough...286 D3
av. Oakleigh S...497 K1
cl. St Albans...320 E12
ct. Bayswater N...380 K15
ct. Doncaster...330 C15
pde. Herne Hill...701 J1
rd. Seville E...342 L13
st. Boronia...423 K10
st. Carrum...573 B8
st. Cheltenham...531 G1
st. Cranbourne W...603 G1
st. Elwood...454 F7
st. Melton...226 G20
st. Nunawading...376 E18
st. Prahran...414 L11
st. Prahran...415 A11
st. Springvale...499 K6

JOYCES

rd. Smiths Gly...206 E6

JOYHILL

av. Box Hill S...419 B6

JOYNER

st. Moorabbin...497 C10

JOYNT

st. Balwyn N...373 H4
st. Macleod...284 J14

JOYOUS GARD

ct. Murrumbeena...457 C6

JUAN

ct. Dingley Village...533 C1

JUANE PARK

dr. Diamond Ck...245 E12

JUBA

ct. Mulgrave...500 J2

JUBILATION

ct. Frankston S...626 J11

JUBILEE

av. Seaford...599 G11
cr. Mill Park...243 D12
pl. Richmond...26 K5
rd. Montrose...381 L19
rd. Mt Dandenong...381 L19
st. Blackburn...376 C13
st. Mt Waverley...418 L14
st. Newport...410 G9
st. Nunawading...376 C13
st. Windsor...414 G12

JUDAS

ct. Doveton...536 K9

JUDD

ct. Rockbank...270 C3
pde. Cheltenham...531 E4
st. Camberwell...416 L3
st. Camberwell...417 A3
st. Carnegie...456 J11
st. Richmond...26 D10

JUDE

ct. Aspendale Gdn...547 A6

JUDGE

pl. Roxburgh Pk...194 C14
ri. Endeavour Hl...537 H10
st. Portsea...678 C3
st. Sunshine...365 F9

JUDGES

ct. Reservoir...283 K6

JUDI

cl. Eltham...288 B7

JUDITH

av. Boronia...424 F7
av. Warrandyte...333 E1
cl. Narre Warren...539 B18
ct. Aspendale Gdn...546 F2
ct. Croydon...336 H15
ct. Doncaster...331 A17
ct. Lalor...240 J6
ct. Mt Waverley...459 E5
ct. Springvale S...499 F18
ct. Vermont S...420 J10
st. Bundoora...285 B2
st. Burwood...418 E9
st. Carnegie...456 H12
st. Dandenong N...502 C20
st. Dromana...686 C6
st. Keilor East...322 H4

JUDKINS

av. Belgrave...466 H18
av. Hoppers Csg...405 A19

JUDY

ct. Melton...268 K1
ct. Vermont...421 A2
st. Noble Park...534 E4
st. Tullamarine...278 F5

JUEL

cr. Healesville...213 G18

JUKES

rd. Boronia...423 D13
rd. Fawkner...281 E4

JULES

ct. Yarra Glen...208 L20
ct. Yarra Glen...252 L1

JULIA

ct. Cranbourne N...578 J9
ct. Croydon N...336 A12
ct. Doncaster...330 E17
gr. Sorrento...678 K14
st. Bayswater...423 B6
wy. Keilor Park...277 K13

JULIAN

av. Scoresby...462 C6
ct. Bundoora...284 L5
ct. Dromana...686 C6
pl. Melton W...226 C15
st. Newtown...702 G11
st. Werribee...447 F10
st. Yarraville...366 G14

JULIANA

cl. Frankston...628 D12
ct. Croydon...379 E3
dr. Carrum Downs...601 B3
st. Bentleigh E...456 K18

JULIAN ASTON

pl. Diamond Ck...244 L12
pl. Diamond Ck...245 A12

JULIE

cl. Wantirna S...422 B19
ct. Ashwood...418 A16
ct. Dingley Village...533 B7
ct. Greensborough...244 L15
ct. Langwarrin...601 L19
ct. Sunshine N...321 A11
ct. Upwey...465 L8
rd. Croydon...379 K7
st. Blackburn N...376 D11
st. Bundoora...284 F1

JULIENNE

ct. Doncaster E...332 G7

JULIET

av. Healesville...258 J7
cr. Healesville...214 E16
ct. Dandenong N...501 H15
st. Moonee Pnd...324 G11

JULINDA

ct. Greensborough...286 D5

JULIS

st. Bentleigh E...457 F16

JULIUS

cr. Noble Park N...501 D12
ct. Berwick...553 L6
ct. Diamond Ck...246 A13
st. Coburg N...282 A18

JULL

pde. Ringwood N...378 H1

JUMBUCK

ct. Berwick...553 G6
ct. Plenty...244 G10

JUMBUNNA

ct. Greensborough...286 H1

JUMJUM

cl. Croydon Hills...335 G15

JUMPING CREEK

rd. Warrandyte...290 H19
rd. Wonga Park...291 G16

JUNCTION

cl. Junction Vill...604 K15
rd. Blackburn N...376 B9
rd. Dingley Village...498 H20
rd. Merricks N...688 L8

rd. Mt Evelyn...339 G18
rd. Nunawading...376 F10
rd. Surrey Hills...373 J17
st. Newport...410 J4
st. Preston...326 K4
st. Ringwood...378 G10
st. Seddon...367 E11
st. Yarra Jctn...347 F18

JUNE

av. Balwyn N...373 K7
av. Dromana...686 K4
cl. Wheelers Hill...461 E13
cr. Glen Iris...416 L15
cr. Templestowe...331 B9
ct. Bayswater...422 L9
ct. Keysborough...535 A7
pl. Aspendale Gdn...546 J6
sq. Ringwood N...377 L5
st. Fawkner...281 K3
st. Highett...495 H12
st. Moolap...704 L17
st. Sunbury...142 H13

JUNIPER

av. Glen Waverley...460 B6
cr. Thomastown...240 K14
ct. Frankston N...600 D10
ct. Keysborough...534 E11
ct. Narre Warren...553 E9
ct. Taylors Lakes...275 C2
la. Sunbury...143 E15
rd. Wantirna...422 C3

JUPITER

ct. Carrum Downs...575 B15
st. Caulfield S...455 D9

JURA

av. Pk Orchards...333 G20
ct. Pk Orchards...333 G20
ct. Pk Orchards...377 G1

JURANG

ct. Skye...601 H2
st. Balwyn...373 G11

JURAT

rd. Lilydale...339 F9

JURGA

ct. Seaholme...409 J16

JURY

ct. Keilor Dn...275 J12
st. Beaconsfld Up...541 F7
st. Wheelers Hill...461 C20

JUSTICE

tr. Warburton...349 A15
tr. Warburton...349 C20

JUSTIN

av. Glenroy...280 F6
cct. Hampton Pk...551 K6
ct. Cheltenham...531 G3
ct. Croydon N...335 L9
ct. Frankston...628 D8
ct. Narre Warren...538 G15
ct. Wantirna S...422 L20
dr. Noble Park N...501 B12
pl. Pakenham...584 H1
rd. Tottenham...365 K10

JUSTINA

cl. Vermont S...420 G8
st. Blackburn...376 C13

JUTHER

ct. Springvale S...499 F19

JUTLAND

ct. Grovedale...706 E11

J V SMITH

st. Bundoora...284 E5

K

K

av. Werribee S...488 D9
rd. Werribee S...488 B10

KAARUMBA

gr. Balwyn...373 L12

KACATICA

pl. Brookfield...268 C5

KADANA

st. Glenroy...279 G9

KADINA

cl. Frankston...600 H20
ct. Mooroolbark...337 E12

KADIR

st. Bentleigh E...457 F16

KAHLE

ct. Thomson...703 K18

KAIKOURA

av. Hawthorn E...416 D8

KAISMAN

sq. Wantirna...422 G12

KALAMUNDA

tce. Healesville...212 H19

KALANG

ct. Patterson L...573 K7
rd. Camberwell...417 E6
rd. Glenroy...280 B8
st. Blackburn...375 F19

KALARA

cl. Lalor...240 K8
pl. Vermont S...420 K14

KALASTAIRE

gr. Berwick...553 J15

KALAWAR

av. Bayswater N...380 F18

KALBAR

ct. Scoresby...462 A6
rd. Eltham North...246 D20
rd. Eltham North...246 E20
rd. Eltham North...288 E2

KALBARRI

ct. Taylors Lakes...276 C9

KALDOR

ct. Glen Waverley...419 L16

KALENO

vw. Balwyn...373 F8

KALERA

ct. Wheelers Hill...460 J18

KALGOORLIE

ct. Campbellfield...239 E18

KALGURLI

ct. Balwyn...373 J10

KALIMNA

av. Mulgrave...499 K2
av. Noble Park...534 J5
cr. Coolaroo...238 C7
cr. Doncaster...331 C20
cr. Rye...697 F9
ct. Rowville...503 A8
dr. Mornington...640 K9
st. Balwyn...373 E11
st. Bentleigh E...496 K4
st. Carrum...573 B10
st. Essendon...324 C6
st. Mooroolbark...337 A16
st. Preston...282 H17
st. Vermont...420 L6

KALINA

ct. Kilsyth...380 L4

KALINDA

rd. Croydon...379 C1
rd. Ringwood...335 C19
rd. Ringwood...379 C1

KALINGER

ct. Donvale...332 G19

KALINGRA

rd. Tottenham...365 K12

KALINYA

dr. Wantirna...422 B13

KALISTA

av. Hillside...274 E6
cr. Watsonia N...243 H19
ct. Burwood E...419 L12

KALKA

st. Balwyn N...329 H19
st. Blackburn...375 J19

KALLAMONDAH

rd. Ferny Creek...465 L4

KALLARA

cr. Narre Warren...539 E19
gr. Maribyrnong...367 B2
rd. Warneet...649 F13

KALLARROO

ct. N Warrandyte...290 E10

KALLAY

ct. View Bank...285 E18
st. Clayton S...498 F7
st. Croydon...379 D2
st. Dandenong N...501 K18
st. Mt Waverley...419 B12

KALLIS

dr. Glenroy...280 G10

KALLISTA

ct. Cheltenham...531 H1
ct. Preston...327 F1
pl. Melton W...226 D16
rd. Springvale...499 H16

KALLISTA-EMERALD

rd. Emerald...468 J10
rd. Kallista...467 C3
rd. The Patch...467 H3
rd. The Patch...469 A13

KALMAINE

ct. Diamond Ck...245 J7

KALMAN

dr. Boronia...424 G1
dr. Boronia...424 G2
rd. Epping...198 E20
rd. Epping...242 E1

KALMIA

av. Mt Waverley...419 B15
ct. Narre Warren...539 D20
st. Frankston...627 L7

KALONGA
ct. Glen Waverley 460 D8
rd. Balwyn N 374 B8
KALORAMA
pl. Thomastown 240 F12
tce. Kalorama 382 L12
KALPARRIN
av. Greensborough 286 B2
KALTARA
cl. Vermont S 421 F7
KALULU
rd. Belgrave 466 E12
KALYMNA
gr. Chadstone 458 D6
gr. St Kilda E 415 A17
KALYNA
ct. Delahey 275 B15
KALYPTOS
wk. Cranbourne 578 A20
KAMAROOKA
dr. Diamond Ck 246 F8
dr. Wattle Glen 246 G9
st. Albion 320 K20
KAMBALDA
cct. Kings Park 275 C19
KAMBAR
ct. Kurunjang 226 L12
KAMBARA
dr. Mulgrave 500 H4
KAMBEA
cr. View Bank 285 E18
gr. Caulfield N 415 B20
KAMBORA
ct. Mooroolbark 336 K13
KAMBROOK
rd. Caulfield 455 L6
rd. Caulfield N 455 L6
KAMEEL
ct. Cranbourne N 577 J4
dr. Yarra Glen 209 B18
KAMERUKA
ct. Werribee 447 C12
KAMIL
st. Melton S 268 E4
KAMMICH
ct. Berwick 540 A18
ct. Endeavour Hl 538 A3
KAMO
ct. Taylors Lakes 276 A7
KAMONA
ct. Altona Mdw 452 A4
KAMPMAN
st. Bulleen 329 G17
KANA
st. Grovedale 706 C14
KANANDAH
ct. Research 288 J3
KANANOOK
av. Seaford 599 C10
KANANOOK CREEK
bvd. Frankston 599 A18
KANARU
ct. Nar Warrn N 538 C4
KANBURRA
st. Rye 697 B8
KANDANGA
gr. Bulleen 329 J13
KANDRA
st. Dandenong N 501 G17
st. Ringwood E 379 F17
KANDY
ct. Frankston 628 A3
KANE
ct. Yarra Glen 209 B18
dr. Kings Park 319 D2
st. Preston 282 E20
KANEIRA
av. Croydon 380 D10
KANEVAROO
pl. Nar Warrn S 552 G9
KANGAN
dr. Berwick 554 D12
KANGAROO
rd. Chelsea 546 J15
rd. Hughesdale 457 A10
rd. Hughesdale 457 G11
rd. Murrumbeena 457 A10
tce. S Morang 243 H2
KANGAROO GROUND-ST ANDREWS
rd. Kangaroo Grnd 247 L14
rd. Panton Hill 204 E20
rd. St Andrews 205 A8
rd. Smiths Gly 204 K11
KANGAROO GROUND-WARRANDYTE
rd. Kangaroo Grnd 248 A20
rd. N Warrandyte 290 B16
rd. Warrandyte 290 B16
KANGAROO GROUND-WATTLE GLEN
rd. Kangaroo Grnd 247 A9
rd. Wattle Glen 246 K8
KANGERONG
av. Dromana 686 D3
rd. Box Hill 375 A14
KANIMBLA
ct. Heidelberg W 284 D18
ct. Rye 697 F5
dr. Lalor 240 L5
dr. Lalor 241 A5
KANIVA
ct. Bentleigh E 497 B1
st. Dallas 238 F9
KANMORE
cr. Hillside 232 G18
cr. Hillside 232 H19
KANNAN
bvd. Braybrook 321 L18
KANO
ct. Keysborough 534 K14
KANOOKA
av. Ashwood 418 D13
av. Templstw Lr 330 G12
ct. Keilor Dn 276 G17
gr. Clayton 499 A2
gr. Doveton 536 H13
gr. Meadow Ht 193 H18
rd. Boronia 423 B11
rd. Wantirna S 423 B11
KANOWINDRA
cr. Greensborough 285 K9
KANOWNA
st. Hampton 495 C11
st. Williamstown 411 K18
KANTIKA
dr. Epping 241 K3
KANUMBRA
ct. Hallam 538 B20
KANYA
ct. Frankston 599 L20
rd. Mt Eliza 625 H19
KAOLA
st. Belgrave 466 B17
KAOLIN
cl. Epping 197 J18
ct. Blackburn N 375 H10
KAPILI
wy. Eltham 288 B14
KARA
ct. Blairgowrie 696 D2
ct. Montrose 382 E8
ct. Pakenham 585 F1
ct. Wantirna 422 C14
gr. Aspendale 546 B4
st. Doncaster E 375 K3
st. Frankston S 627 K18
wk. Cranbourne 578 A19
wk. Vermont S 421 E7
KARABEAL
ct. Montrose 382 B13
KARABEC
pl. Lilydale 338 K12
KARABIL
cl. Scoresby 462 D9
KARADOC
av. Pascoe Vale 280 L12
ct. Bonbeach 573 B5
st. Dromana 686 F3
KARALEE
ct. Bayswater 423 C8
KARAMOOKA
av. Chum Creek 213 A8
KARAN
ct. Noble Park 500 E18
KARANA
av. Grovedale 706 C15
ct. Croydon 336 F20
pl. Glen Iris 416 J15
KARATOGA
ct. Tootgarook 698 D9
KARAWA
cl. Rosebud W 699 F2
KARBAROOK
av. Prahran 415 B13
KARDELLA
cl. Mill Park 242 E9
la. Mt Eliza 641 J4
la. Seville E 343 D12
st. Malvern East 416 F17
KARDINIA
cr. Warranwood 334 L14
cr. Warranwood 335 A14
dr. Albanvale 319 C4
dr. Yallambie 286 C15
pl. S Geelong 702 J13
rd. Glen Iris 417 B14
st. Belmont 702 H17
st. Watsonia 285 J8
KARDINIAN
av. Cheltenham 531 G1
KAREE
ct. Greensborough 285 L9
KAREELA
dr. Tootgarook 698 E7
rd. Frankston 628 A1
st. Mordialloc 532 B19
KARELLA
cr. Mornington 640 F18
KAREN
cl. Langwarrin 630 A5
cl. Nar Warrn S 552 E11
ct. Avondale Ht 322 F10
ct. Blairgowrie 680 C20
ct. Doncaster E 375 H2
ct. Heathmont 422 J2
ct. Mill Park 242 K8
ct. Montrose 382 K4
ct. Mt Waverley 458 G9
ct. Vermont S 420 H10
ct. Wantirna 422 H5
ct. Warrandyte 333 D2
pl. Melton W 226 A14
pl. St Albans 320 G14
st. Box Hill N 375 D8
st. Cheltenham 496 H17
st. Highett 496 H17
st. Selby 467 F16
KARIBOO
gr. Greensborough 243 L18
KARIMA
ct. Ringwood N 378 D2
KARIN
cr. Glenroy 279 J1
ct. Mooroolbark 337 A10
pl. Berwick 553 K14
KARINA
cl. Croydon Hills 335 H16
ct. Keilor 276 G7
la. Vermont S 421 C7
st. Frankston S 626 L14
st. Mornington 656 H5
KARINGAL
cr. Aspendale 546 F7
dr. Briar Hill 286 J3
dr. Eltham 287 A4
dr. Frankston 600 B17
dr. Greensborough 286 J3
dr. Montmorency 287 A4
dr. Rosebud W 699 F1
st. Altona 408 J17
st. Croydon N 336 F12
wy. Thomastown 240 F12
KARINYA
cl. Werribee 447 H3
ct. Sunbury 113 H17
KARISTA
av. Heathmont 379 C20
KARITA
ct. Lilydale 338 L4
KARJEN
pl. Wheelers Hill 460 J10
KARKALA
pl. Hampton Pk 552 C16
KARKAROOK
rd. Rye 697 K5
KARLA
ct. Notting Hill 459 H13
KARLEEN
ct. Mornington 656 F2
KARLOO
cl. Epping 241 L3
la. Seville 386 H14
KARMA
av. Malvern East 456 L4
ct. Craigieburn 150 B17
ct. Frankston 600 C19
KARNAK
cl. Croydon 336 G12
cr. Coolaroo 238 E4
ct. Glen Waverley 460 K4
rd. Ashburton 417 C20
KARO
ct. Doveton 537 A11
ct. Melton 268 E2
KAROBRAN
dr. Vermont S 420 K10
KAROL
ct. Hampton Pk 551 C6
KAROO
rd. Ferntree Gly 463 H12
rd. Rowville 463 C15
KAROOLA
ct. Hoppers Csg 448 F8
st. Hampton 495 B11
KAROOMBA
av. Herne Hill 701 K3
KAROONDA
ct. Meadow Ht 194 B20
st. Rosebud W 699 E1
wy. Hampton Pk 551 K16
KAROU
ct. Glen Waverley 420 J14
ct. Vermont S 420 K8
KARRAKATTA
st. Black Rock 529 F4
KARRALLA
ct. Chirnside Pk 337 J7
KARRI
cr. Hoppers Csg 405 D17
ct. Boronia 424 L7
ct. Frankston N 599 K9
gr. Epping 241 L2
KARRIN
cl. Yallambie 286 C11
ct. Ashwood 418 C19
KARRUM KARRUM
ct. Nar Warrn S 578 K1
KARS
st. Frankston 626 L5
st. Frankston S 626 K9
KARTHINA
pl. Kurunjang 227 B14
KARU
ct. Bundoora 243 A20
ct. Keilor Dn 275 K12
KARWIN
cl. Berwick 553 G6
KARWITHA
st. Vermont 421 C3
KASEM
dr. Werribee 447 E6
KASHMIR
cr. Frankston 600 A18
pl. Melton W 226 C14
KASHMIRA
st. Bentleigh E 457 G17
KASOUKA
rd. Camberwell 372 L20
rd. Camberwell 373 A20
rd. Camberwell 416 L1
rd. Camberwell 417 A1
st. Maribyrnong 322 J17
KASSAN
gdn. Endeavour Hl 537 K2
KATANDRA
cr. Broadmeadows 238 A11
ct. Bayswater 423 C10
ct. Mt Waverley 459 G4
rd. Ormond 456 C12
st. Mt Eliza 626 C20
KATARINA
pl. Whittington 703 L20
KATAWA
gr. Brunswick 325 J12
KATE
ct. Langwarrin 601 G20
ct. Pakenham 559 F20
pl. Ferntree Gly 463 F7
pl. Sunshine W 364 D9
st. St Albans 319 L4
KATE CHARLESWORTH
pl. Croydon Hills 335 G13
KATERINA
la. Macclesfield 470 H1
KATHERINE
ct. Hampton Pk 551 L13
pl. Melbourne 23 J13
pl. Mt Evelyn 339 K15
KATHLEEN
av. Mt Waverley 419 A14
cl. Bayswater N 379 G17
cr. Hoppers Csg 447 K3
ct. Beaconsfield 555 C13
ct. Bundoora 284 F1
ct. Hampton Pk 551 E10
ct. Montmorency 286 L9
ct. Sunshine 321 F19
gr. Bulleen 329 L14
st. Blackburn N 376 E9
st. Nunawading 376 D9
st. Pascoe Vale S 324 J5
st. Preston 283 F20
st. Rosanna 329 B3
st. W Footscray 366 G11
KATHRIN
av. Dingley Village 533 E6
KATHRYN
av. Lalor 240 J5
cl. Pakenham 559 F19
ct. Bundoora 285 C1
ct. Clayton S 499 E15
ct. Sunbury 142
rd. Knoxfield 463
st. Campbellfield 239 E
st. Doveton 536
KATHY
ct. Mooroolbark 336 L
KATHYS
la. Attwood 237 A
KATJUSHA
ct. Pakenham 584
KATLYN
pl. Frankston S 643
KATNOOK
ct. Meadow Ht 238
KATOOMBA
ct. Heidelberg W 283 L
ct. Keysborough 534 E
dr. Mulgrave 501
st. Hadfield 280
st. Hampton E 496
KATRINA
av. Murrumbeena 457 C
cl. Hallam 537 K
ct. Carrum Downs 575 E
ct. Mooroolbark 337 A
ct. Noble Park N 501 C
ct. Thomastown 240 H
dr. Gladstone Pk 279
dr. Gladstone Pk 279
pl. Melton W 226 C
st. Blackburn N 375
st. Doncaster 374
KATTA
ct. Ashwood 418 D
KATUNGA
cr. Broadmeadows 237 K
KATUPNA
ct. Vermont S 421
KAULA
ct. Wheelers Hill 460 L
KAUMPLE
st. Pascoe Vale 280 K
KAURI
ct. Croydon 380
ct. Doncaster E 375
ct. Hampton Pk 552
ct. Mitcham 376 L
ct. Werribee 447
gr. Glen Waverley 459
pl. Whittlesea 96 C
KAVANAGH
ct. Rowville 463 F
st. Southbank 3 D
st. Southbank 4
st. Southbank 24 B
st. Southbank 24 E
KAVEL
ct. Sunbury 143 A
KAWANA
cr. Glen Waverley 460
KAWARREN
st. Balwyn N 329 K
st. Balwyn N 373
KAY
av. Lalor 240
ct. Boronia 424
ct. Box Hill N 374
ct. Broadmeadows 237 L
ct. Oakleigh S 458 G
ct. Sunshine W 364 H
ct. Vermont 421
ct. Yallambie 285 E
rd. Chum Creek 213
st. Blairgowrie 679 E
st. Carlton 18 H
st. Carrum Downs 575 D
st. Mt Waverley 419 B
st. Springvale 499 G
KAYBROOK
ct. Oakleigh S 498
KAYDEN
st. Cheltenham 497 C
KAYE
cr. Laverton 407 D
ct. Coburg 281 G
ct. Dandenong N 501 L
rd. Upwey 466 A
KAYES
la. Dandenong, off Foster St 535 L
KAYLA
ct. Epping 198 E
KAYLENE
ct. Mt Martha 657
KAYS
av. Hallam 537 D
KEA
ct. Werribee 448 C
KEADY
st. Coburg N 281 G

EAKI
t. Niddrie 322 K1
EAL
d. Springvale S 533 L5
EAM
t. Essendon N 323 E1
t. Ivanhoe East 328 L14
t. Ivanhoe East 329 A13
EAMY
v. Cheltenham 496 K16
EAN
t. Caulfield S 455 L7
t. Ringwood 377 L11
EANE
t. Coburg N 281 J16
EARNEY
v. Altona 408 L15
r. Aspendale Gdn 546 F3
a. Templestowe 288 E19
a. Templestowe 332 F1
t. Bayswater 423 K5
EARSLEY
t. Altona North 409 A7
EAST
t. Frankston S 626 K4
EATING
v. Sorrento 679 B16
r. Dandenong S 535 G14
r. Dandenong S 535 G15
t. Highton 705 G5
t. Lower Plenty 286 H15
t. Beaumaris 529 J8
t. Black Rock 529 J8
EATON
y. Aspendale Gdn 546 L5
EATS
v. Kingsbury 283 K10
l. Templestowe 332 B11
t. Ashwood 418 C14
t. Boronia 424 J4
t. Bundoora 284 J1
t. Rye 696 G3
t. Truganina 405 F13
d. Dromana 685 L10
d. Mooroolbark 337 G19
t. Burwood E 419 H9
t. Canterbury 373 D17
t. Elwood 454 E3
t. Heidelberg Ht 328 F2
t. St Albans 319 G2
t. Sandringham 495 E16
EBUN
t. Pk Orchards 333 J18
EDA
l. Greensborough 244 C15
EDLESTON
d. Herne Hill 701 K2
y. Rowville 463 F18
EECH
l. Noble Park N 501 E8
EEFER
t. Mordialloc 532 B10
EELAH
t. Woori Yallock 344 J14
EELE
t. Collingwood 19 H11
EELER
v. Bayswater 423 G7
EELEY
a. Princes Hill 325 J20
EELEYS
a. Kallista 467 J8
EELING
t. Patterson L 573 G11
EELY
t. Reservoir 282 J2
EEN
v. Warrandyte 333 H1
t. Glen Iris 416 J9
EENAN
t. Dandenong N 501 J16
EEP
v. Fitzroy N 20 A1
EER
r. Aspendale Gdn 546 J5
EERA
st. Geelong 702 J1
st. Geelong West 702 J1
KEEROK
av. Seaford 599 L3
KEERON
st. Caulfield S 455 F8
KEESHAN
ct. Altona 408 K15
KEETS
ct. Springvale 500 B17
KEFFORD
av. Lalor 240 H6
ct. Mont Albert N 374 F9

KEILLER
av. Parkdale 531 L9
st. Hampton E 496 A7
KEILOR
av. Reservoir 283 G11
rd. Essendon 323 C1
rd. Essendon N 323 C1
rd. Keilor East 278 F17
rd. Niddrie 278 F17
KEILOR PARK
dr. Keilor East 277 K18
dr. Keilor Park 277 J14
dr. Tullamarine 278 A11
KEILY
rd. Gisborne 79 B16
KEIPHA
rd. Cranbourne S 602 L18
rd. Cranbourne S 603 A18
KEIR
av. Doncaster E 331 H19
KEITH
av. Edithvale 546 G11
av. Epping 197 J19
av. Sunbury 142 F11
cr. Broadmeadows 238 C20
ct. Brighton 454 F19
ct. Keysborough 534 D10
ct. Nunawading 376 F10
ct. Research 288 J7
ct. Wandin N 340 L13
gr. Keilor East 322 F1
gr. Ringwood 378 B15
pde. Beaconsfield 555 K8
st. Alphington 327 J15
st. Beaumaris 530 H4
st. Coburg 325 L2
st. Hampton E 495 L9
st. Maidstone 322 G20
st. Oakleigh E 458 H16
st. Parkdale 531 J12
st. Tootgarook 698 E5
st. Yarra Jctn 347 K16
KEITH CAMPBELL
ct. Scoresby 462 F10
KEITH TAYLOR
dr. Berwick 554 D9
KEIWA
pl. Rowville 463 D17
pl. Taylors Hill 274 J15
KELBA
st. Balwyn N 373 F8
KELBOURNE
gr. Sunbury 143 A5
KELBOW
cl. St Helena 245 B16
KELBURN
rd. Berwick 553 L16
st. Caulfield N 415 D16
KELDALE
ct. Noble Park 500 H17
KELL
ct. Greensborough 286 A7
pl. Templestowe 332 D5
st. Greensborough 286 A7
KELLAND
av. Hillside 232 E19
KELLAWAY
av. Moonee Pnd 324 C12
cr. Mill Park 242 G5
ct. Wantirna 422 F8
st. Maribyrnong 322 L20
st. Maribyrnong 323 A20
st. Maribyrnong 366 L1
st. Mt Waverley 419 F14
KELLBOURNE
dr. Rowville 463 G14
KEL LEMON
ct. Mt Martha 656 C15
KELLER
cl. Greenvale 237 C4
ct. Hampton Pk 551 K12
KELLERHER
st. Lalor 241 E9
KELLET
wy. Roxburgh Pk 194 A12
KELLETT
gr. Kew 372 A3
st. Cranbourne N 577 L4
st. Northcote 327 A13
st. Reservoir 283 D15
KELLETTS
rd. Ferntree Gly 463 L16
rd. Lysterfield 463 L16
rd. Rowville 462 J15
rd. Rowville 463 A15
KELLEY
gr. Preston 326 C5
KELLIE
ct. Hampton Pk 551 C9

KELLS
av. Herne Hill 702 A4
KELLY
av. Hampton E 495 J6
cl. Rye 697 K9
ct. Broadmeadows 238 A20
ct. Pakenham 559 F20
ct. Somerville 645 C17
ct. Warranwood 335 B14
dr. Langwarrin 629 L1
mw. Berwick 554 L18
pl. Mill Park 243 A6
rd. Cranbourne S 603 K20
st. Bayswater 423 B3
st. Chadstone 457 L4
st. Diamond Ck 246 B12
st. Doncaster 330 L17
st. Sunbury 143 D12
st. Werribee 447 K14
KELLYBROOK
cl. Delahey, off Ryland Cct 275 C11
KELLYS
av. Burnside 318 F9
la. Sandringham 495 B14
rd. Warburton 349 L2
KELMAN
ct. Westmeadows 237 D15
st. Frankston 599 H20
KELMAR
st. Albanvale 318 L3
st. Cheltenham 497 A18
KELMSCOTT
ct. Armadale 415 G11
KELRINDA
cl. Oakleigh S 498 A7
KELSALL
ct. Hampton E 495 L10
KELSBY
st. Reservoir 282 H9
KELSEY
ct. Craigieburn 194 D1
ct. Pt Lonsdale 710 D3
KELSO
ct. Wheelers Hill 461 D15
pl. Berwick 554 D15
pl. Wantirna 422 J7
st. Coldstream 295 E14
st. Cremorne 25 L19
st. Frankston 599 E19
st. Mentone 530 K9
wy. Point Cook 450 G6
KELSON
st. Coburg 325 C2
KELSTERN
ct. Highton 705 J9
KELTIE
ri. Endeavour Hl 537 G10
st. Glen Iris 417 J12
KELVAN
gr. Doncaster E 332 E6
KELVERNE
st. Reservoir 282 B9
KELVIN
av. Montmorency 286 H7
av. Seaford 599 D2
cl. Niddrie 322 L4
ct. Prahran 415 B12
ct. Ringwood N 378 F2
dr. Ferntree Gly 463 K1
gr. Ashburton 417 F14
gr. Chelsea 546 J17
gr. Langwarrin 602 E16
gr. Prahran 415 B12
gr. Preston 282 L20
gr. S Morang 199 H20
gr. S Morang 243 H1
gr. Springvale 500 A12
gr. Thornbury 326 K11
gr. Werribee 447 A13
pl. Carlton 18 C18
rd. Alphington 327 J17
rd. Bayswater N 380 F14
st. Ascot Vale 324 A17
KELVINSIDE
dr. Templestowe 330 L9
rd. Noble Park 500 G15
st. Balwyn N 329 K19
st. Hughesdale 457 E11
KELWAY
cr. Eltham 287 B4
KELWIN
ct. Hoppers Csg 449 E1
KEMBLA
st. Cheltenham 531 H4
st. Hawthorn 416 B2
KEMERTON
cl. Point Cook 450 H10

KEMP
av. Mt Evelyn 339 E15
av. Mt Waverley 459 A3
av. Thomastown 240 H15
ct. Rowville 463 J19
pl. Sunbury 142 H9
rd. Portsea 678 G3
rd. Sorrento 678 G3
st. Burwood 418 B6
st. Carrum 573 E11
st. Northcote 326 G10
st. Springvale 500 A7
st. Thornbury 326 G10
st. Upwey 465 G8
KEMPS
st. Ringwood E 378 L7
st. Ringwood E 379 A7
KEMPSON
ct. Keysborough 535 A14
wk. Berwick 554 E8
KEMPSTON
ct. Croydon N 335 K10
ct. Rowville 502 J3
st. Greensborough 285 J2
KEMPTON
ct. Epping 198 A16
ct. Seabrook 450 L4
KEMSLEY
ct. Hawthorn E 372 E14
KENARRA
ct. Hurstbridge 203 G13
KENAUD
av. Mt Eliza 626 B18
KENBRY
rd. Heathmont 422 L1
KENDAL
ct. Croydon Hills 335 K13
KENDALE
ct. Bayswater N 380 J20
st. Airport W 278 K18
KENDALL
av. Parkville 17 H1
cl. Templestowe 331 L10
ct. Oakleigh E 458 J12
ct. Rosebud 699 K3
ct. Sunbury 142 L9
dr. Narre Warren 538 L14
rd. Ringwood N 334 E12
rd. Warrandyte S 334 E12
rd. Yallambie 285 J13
st. Canterbury 373 E18
st. Coburg 325 E3
st. Elwood 454 G3
st. Essendon 324 F9
st. Hampton 495 H7
st. Mt Waverley 419 J14
st. Nunawading 376 E10
st. Preston 326 B4
st. Ringwood 378 E13
KENDALLS
la. Hurstbridge 202 F13
KENDARI
av. Balwyn N 373 B7
ct. Hampton Pk 552 B9
KENDON
cl. Wheelers Hill 460 L7
KENDRA
pl. Keysborough 534 J11
KENILWORTH
av. Beaconsfield 555 A16
av. Frankston 627 K4
av. Officer 581 G1
av. Wonga Park 335 G4
cr. Glen Waverley 419 K13
gr. Glen Iris 416 F10
pde. Ivanhoe 327 L13
st. Balwyn 374 A9
st. Reservoir 282 K9
KENJI
st. Mornington 640 K18
KENJULIE
dr. Bentleigh E 497 A5
KENLEIGH
gr. Prahran 414 L13
gr. Prahran 415 A13
KENLEY
ct. Burwood E 419 H11
ct. Frankston 628 G4
ct. Meadow Ht 237 K7
ct. Toorak 415 G8
KENLON
st. Bentleigh E 497 C7
KENMAN
cl. Templestowe 331 F8
KENMARE
av. Croydon 379 J2
st. Mont Albert 374 C11
st. Mont Albert N 374 C11
st. Watsonia 285 D8

KENMORE
ct. Frankston 628 C7
KENNA
dr. Lalor 241 F6
st. Macleod 284 J15
st. Moonee Pnd 324 D12
KENNARD
pl. Burwood E 420 C12
KENNAUGH
st. Oakleigh E 458 K16
KENNEALY
st. Surrey Hills 373 J20
KENNEDIA
av. Springvale 500 K12
KENNEDY
av. Chelsea Ht 547 G17
av. Nar Warrn N 539 J5
av. Ringwood 378 E8
ct. Cranbourne N 577 J9
gr. Highton 705 J1
pde. Roxburgh Pk 194 B9
rd. Avonsleigh 470 L11
rd. Pakenham 559 C19
rd. St Andrews 206 D1
st. Bentleigh E 457 E20
st. Blairgowrie 696 C1
st. Fairfield 327 G15
st. Glenroy 279 J9
st. Glen Waverley 420 E20
st. Keilor 277 C13
st. Reservoir 282 D13
st. Richmond 26 L6
st. Sunshine 365 D2
KENNETH
av. Emerald 469 G17
av. Sassafras 426 G16
cl. Hoppers Csg 405 E18
ct. Pearcedale 646 L3
ct. Pearcedale 647 A3
ct. Thomastown 240 K18
rd. Bayswater 423 J8
st. Anglesea 713 J1
st. Belmont 702 D18
st. Braybrook 365 L1
st. Bulleen 329 K17
st. Noble Park 534 K6
st. Preston 327 E1
st. Rosanna 329 B1
st. Sandringham 495 G12
KENNETT
st. Ashwood 417 L16
KENNEY
st. Sunshine W 364 H7
KENNINGTON
rd. Rosebud 684 F17
KENNINGTON PARK
dr. Endeavour Hl 503 A20
KENNON
st. Doncaster E 331 L20
KENNY
la. Monbulk 428 G20
pl. Geelong 703 C12
st. Attwood 237 A12
st. Attwood 237 C13
st. Balwyn N 373 J7
st. Richmond 26 F8
st. Westmeadows 237 A12
st. Westmeadows 237 C13
KENROSS
cl. Point Cook 450 G7
ct. Braybrook 365 H5
ct. Wantirna 422 G6
dr. Wheelers Hill 461 D18
KENSEI
gdn. Cranbourne W 577 F16
KENSINGTON
av. Frankston S 628 C16
cr. Altona Mdw 451 D5
ct. Greenvale 237 F6
ct. Hampton Pk 551 H4
ct. Mulgrave 500 D2
ct. Thomastown 241 J15
ct. Ferntree Gly, off Soverign Crest Bvd 464 A13
gdn. Vermont S 420 G6
pl. Narre Warren 539 B14
pl. Wantirna S 422 F18
rd. Kensington 33 A16
rd. Kensington 368 A8
rd. South Yarra 32 J9
rd. South Yarra 414 K5
rd. W Melbourne 33 A16
rd. W Melbourne 368 A8
KENSLEY
st. Up Fntree Gly 465 G7
KENSWICK
dr. Hillside 232 G20
dr. Hillside 232 H20

KENT
av. Brighton 454 F10
av. Croydon 335 K20
cl. Blackburn N 376 B7
ct. Avondale Ht 322 F8
ct. Belmont 706 E2
ct. Bulleen 329 G12
ct. Bundoora 284 L6
ct. Craigieburn 194 D3
ct. Cranbourne N 577 J5
ct. Deer Park 318 K8
ct. Doncaster E 332 E7
ct. Eltham 287 K9
ct. Glen Waverley 420 F16
ct. Heidelberg 329 F3
ct. Keysborough 534 L9
ct. Toorak 415 F9
ct. Werribee 446 J11
gr. Caulfield N 415 D19
gr. Frankston 627 L4
la. Hawthorn 372 A17
la. Prahran 414 L11
mw. Cranbourne N 577 J5
pl. Somerville 644 H17
pl. S Melbourne 29 J2
rd. Box Hill 374 J17
rd. Lalor 241 L11
rd. Launching Pl 345 E17
rd. Narre Warren 553 C7
rd. Pascoe Vale 280 H12
rd. Rye 697 F7
rd. Surrey Hills 373 J19
st. Ascot Vale 324 D19
st. Braybrook 365 J5
st. Clifton Hill 19 J7
st. Dromana 686 D9
st. Fitzroy 19 C16
st. Glen Iris 416 E12
st. Hawthorn 372 A17
st. Kew 372 B10
st. Knoxfield 463 C3
st. Mornington 640 F17
st. Richmond 26 H7
st. Richmond 371 A14
st. Seddon 367 D11
st. Warburton 305 B18
st. Windsor 31 K20
st. Windsor 414 E10
st. Yarraville 367 D17
wy. Tullamarine 278 H2

KENT-HILL
cl. Wandana Ht 701 D20

KENT-HUGHES
rd. Eltham 287 L15

KENTHURST
ct. Lilydale 338 J10
ct. Mill Park 242 E2

KENTIA
ct. Aspendale Gdn 547 A4

KENTISH
pl. Chirnside Pk 336 J7

KENTMERE
ct. Greenvale 193 A17

KENTON
pl. Gladstone Pk 237 B16
pl. Kealba 276 L19
wk. Nar Warrn S 578 F1

KENTUCKY
cl. Narre Warren 539 F17
ct. Notting Hill 459 J12
rd. Red Hill S 688 L15

KENTWOOD
rd. Macleod 285 J11

KENVARRA
cr. Jan Juc 711 D14

KENWAY
st. Sunbury 113 G20
st. Sunbury 143 G1

KENWITH
gr. Newtown 702 F8

KENWOOD
cr. Ringwood 379 B2
ct. Preston 326 H5
la. Hawthorn 371 L19

KENWORTH
ct. Rowville 463 B13

KENWORTHY
ri. Mornington 657 A3

KENWYN
ct. Ferntree Gly 464 D6
ct. Greensborough 244 D15

KEOGH
ct. Box Hill S 419 B5
ct. Meadow Ht 238 A3
ct. Pascoe Vale 280 K16
st. Burwood 418 F12
st. Rosebud 684 D18

KEOL
st. Clayton S 499 C4

KEON
cr. Sunshine W 364 J3
ct. Balwyn N 329 L20
pde. Reservoir 283 B1
pde. Thomastown 241 B20
st. Thornbury 326 C6

KEOWN
ct. Campbellfield 239 G14
pl. Geelong, off McKillop St 702 K9

KEPPEL
dr. Hallam 551 L1
st. Carlton 18 D10
st. Carlton 18 E11

KEPPLER
cct. Seaford 574 A18

KERABOITE
ct. Mt Eliza 626 F14

KERAM
cr. Highton 701 H19

KERANG
av. Reservoir 283 G12
ct. Broadmeadows 238 E15
ct. Taylors Lakes 276 E8
pl. Thomastown 240 C12

KERBY
st. Eltham 287 C14

KEREFORD
pl. Sunbury 143 G6

KERFERD
av. Point Cook 450 A4
av. Sorrento 678 J10
cl. Melton S 268 C13
la. Albert Park 29 K13
pl. Albert Park 29 K12
pl. Albert Park 413 E6
rd. Albert Park 29 F18
rd. Albert Park 413 C9
rd. Glen Iris 416 J12
rd. Glen Iris 416 K12
rd. Glen Waverley 460 C12
rd. Hampton 495 C10
st. Coburg 281 C19
st. Essendon N 279 F20
st. Malvern East 416 C17

KERGER
ct. Grovedale 705 J13

KERGO
pl. Wantirna S 462 K2

KERLEY
st. Geelong, off Mercer St 702 L5

KERMEEN
st. Sunshine W 364 F8

KERMODE
st. W Melbourne 368 D14

KERN
pl. Donvale 332 L17

KERNAN
av. Pascoe Vale 280 E19
st. Moonee Pnd 324 B9
st. Strathmore 279 K20

KERNOT
av. Mulgrave 460 D17
cr. Noble Park N 501 C15
ct. Westmeadows 237 G13
rd. Parkville 17 L14
st. E Geelong 703 G11
st. S Kingsville 410 G3
st. Spotswood 410 G3

KERR
av. Oak Park 279 J10
cr. Camberwell 416 H6
cr. Montrose 382 D10
la. Box Hill N 374 H8
st. Bacchus Msh 221 K14
st. Beaumaris 530 F5
st. Blackburn 375 F11
st. Fitzroy 19 A11
st. Kingsville 366 G13
st. Lilydale 337 K3
st. Preston 327 F7
st. S Melbourne 29 F1
st. S Melbourne 413 C1

KERRI
ct. Sunbury 143 B8
st. Bundoora 284 G1

KERRIBEE
ct. Clayton S 498 H9

KERRIE
cr. Eltham 287 D6
ct. Grovedale 706 E12
ct. Springvale S 533 K2
rd. Glen Waverley 420 H20

KERRIE ANNE
ct. Skye 575 G18

KERRILEA
ct. Kilsyth S 424 L3

KERRIMUIR
st. Box Hill N 375 D9

KERRINS
ct. Highton 705 F5
la. Templestowe 331 K3

KERRISDALE
pl. Sunbury 142 L8

KERRISON
av. Noble Park 500 E18
av. St Albans 275 J18
dr. Hampton Pk 551 D9

KERRS
la. Lysterfield 505 J18
la. Nar Warrn E 505 J18
la. N Melbourne 34 L13
rd. Maddingley 263 B8
rd. St Andrews 205 C1

KERRY
av. Mt Martha 656 F5
cl. Berwick 554 K6
cl. Doncaster E 331 G19
cl. View Bank 285 F20
ct. St Albans 320 D12
pde. Balwyn 374 C10
pde. Mont Albert N 374 C10
rd. Warranwood 335 E12
st. Langwarrin 601 F19
st. Seaford 599 H4

KERRY ANNE
cr. Wonga Park 336 D6

KERRYLIN
ct. Blackburn 376 D13

KERSEY
pl. Doncaster 331 C13

KERSHAW
dr. Nar Warrn S 552 E20
dr. Nar Warrn S 578 E1
st. Mordialloc 531 L14
st. Oakleigh S 497 F4
st. Parkdale 531 L14

KERTA
cl. Greensborough 243 K18
cl. Hoppers Csg 405 A18

KERYN
cl. Templestowe 331 L9

KESTREL
cl. Blind Bight 650 B9
cl. Chelsea Ht 547 C9
ct. Baxter 644 D1
ct. Carrum Downs 575 A20
ct. Carrum Downs 601 A1
ct. Mornington 640 K16
ct. Taylors Lakes 275 G2
pl. Werribee 447 K4
wy. Craigieburn 149 F16

KESWICK
av. Belgrave Ht 506 E1
cr. Bayswater N 380 F20
ct. Delahey 275 B14
ct. Nar Warrn S 579 A4
gln. Greensborough 244 F20
ri. Eltham 287 L6
st. Bentleigh E 457 B16

KETNOR
st. Cranbourne 604 B5

KETT
pl. Kensington 33 H6
st. Blackburn N 376 D8
st. Lower Plenty 286 H12
st. Nunawading 376 F9

KETWICK
ct. Ferntree Gly 424 A17
ct. Sydenham 274 J3

KEVERELL
rd. Caulfield N 455 G1

KEVIN
av. Blackburn 375 G11
av. Ferntree Gly 464 A4
cl. Beaconsfield 554 L17
ct. Cheltenham 497 D20
ct. Donvale 376 K6
ct. Kilsyth 381 B9
ct. Melton S 268 G4
ct. Somerville 645 B15
gr. Kew 371 D10
st. Bundoora 284 G1
st. Mt Waverley 458 F9
st. Pascoe Vale 280 K18
st. Sunshine 365 F4
st. Tootgarook 698 E2

KEVINGTON
st. Werribee 448 B18

KEVLAR
cl. Braeside 532 K12
ct. Wonga Park 291 L18

KEW
ct. Donvale 376 K7
ct. Narre Warren 553 B10
pl. Wantirna 421 L12

KEY
la. Pakenham 583 L17

KEYES
ct. Wantirna S 462 L1
ct. Wantirna S 463 A1
pl. Gladstone Pk 237 E16
st. Ashburton 417 C16

KEYNES
ct. Deer Park 319 A9

KEYS
av. Brighton East 455 D15
ct. Narre Warren 553 C6
rd. Cheltenham 496 L12
rd. Keysborough 547 H4
rd. Moorabbin 496 L12
st. Beaumaris 530 D12
st. Dandenong 535 K8
st. Frankston 599 B18

KEYSBOROUGH
av. Keysborough 533 J10
st. Craigieburn 150 D15

KEYSTONE
cr. Kew East 372 K1
ct. Lynbrook 551 F16

KHALIL
av. Dandenong N 536 E1

KHARTOUM
ct. Frankston 628 C11
st. Burnley 371 C18
st. Caulfield N 415 G17
st. W Footscray 366 J5

KHASSA
pde. Ringwood 378 F11

KIA
ct. Preston 327 K2
ri. Frankston S 627 H15

KIAH
mw. Eltham 288 D7
st. Glen Waverley 420 C16

KIAKA
la. Rowville 462 K18

KIALLA
av. Glen Iris 416 H14
ct. Noble Park N 501 C14
pl. Langwarrin 629 B8

KIALOA
ct. Narre Warren 539 B17
ct. Taylors Lakes 275 K10

KIAMA
cl. Montmorency 286 G11
cl. Scoresby 462 C6
cl. Vermont S 420 L11
ct. Mooroolbark 336 J13
ct. Oakleigh E 458 K11
ct. Rye 697 C5
dr. Lalor 241 B6
rd. Flemington 33 H2
rd. Werribee 447 G20
st. Glenroy 280 A9
st. Moorabbin 496 J9

KIANDRA
cl. Aspendale 546 B4
cl. Greensborough 244 J19
cl. Noble Park 534 K5
ct. Doncaster E 331 J18
ct. Frankston 627 K4
mw. Hampton Pk 552 B11
st. Mornington 656 H5
wy. Wyndham Va 446 H14

KIA ORA
av. Mt Martha 656 C11
av. Upwey 465 L12
pde. Ferntree Gly 464 K3

KIA-ORA
rd. Reservoir 282 D12

KIATA
ct. Coolaroo 238 E5
ct. Mt Eliza 641 K3
ct. Seabrook 451 A5

KIBO
ct. Cranbourne N 578 B4

KIDDERMINSTER
dr. Wantirna 422 E8

KIDDLE
st. Fawkner 281 J10

KIDDS
rd. Doveton 536 G9

KIDGELL
st. Lilydale 337 L3

KIDMAN
av. Belmont 706 D4
st. Yarraville 366 D14
wy. Nar Warrn S 579 B1

KIELY
av. Werribee 447 L20

KIERAN
ct. Carrum Downs 575 A15

KIERENS
wy. Chadstone 458 D4

KIERNAN
av. Ivanhoe 328 B
cl. Mill Park 242
rd. Macclesfield 471 H

KIERS
av. Mt Waverley 419 H
ct. Caulfield N 415 E
ct. View Bank 285 F

KIEV
wk. Delahey 275 B

KIEWA
cl. Croydon Hills 335 K
cr. Dallas 238 E
cr. Keilor 276 L
ct. Aspendale 546 H
ct. Dandenong N 501
ct. Werribee 448 B1
st. Ashwood 418 F1
st. Clifton Hill 20 G
st. Clifton Hill 20 G
st. Doncaster 375 E

KILA
st. Heidelberg W 284 A

KILANDER
ct. Ferntree Gly 464 E

KILANI
ct. Eltham North 288 F

KILARA
ct. Croydon 379 H
pl. Clarinda 498 E
rd. Mentone 531 A1

KILBERRY
av. Springvale S 533 K
bvd. Hampton Pk 552 C1
cr. Hallam 537 H1

KILBIRNIE
cl. Mt Eliza 641 K

KILBORN
ct. Kilsyth 381 G
ct. Mill Park 242 F

KILBRIDE
st. Keysborough 535 A1

KILBURN
cr. Frankston 628 E
ct. Keysborough 534 D
ct. Wheelers Hill 461 D1
gr. Mt Martha 655 G1
st. Strathmore 280 B1

KILBY
cl. Epping 241 H
ct. Campbellfield 239 A
ct. Noble Park 534 L
rd. Kew East 372 C

KILCATTEN
ri. Rowville 503 B

KILCUNDA
dr. Rowville 463 J1

KILDARE
ct. Frankston 628 A
st. Burwood 418 E
st. Geelong West 702 E
st. Hawthorn E 372 F1

KILDRUMMIE
ct. Sorrento 678 H

KILEE
pl. Avondale Ht 322 E

KILEEN
av. Brighton East 495 B

KILFERA
ct. Narre Warren 539 G1

KILGERRON
ct. Nar Warrn S 553 A1

KILGOUR
ct. Geelong, off La Trobe Tce 702 K1
st. E Geelong 703 E1
st. Geelong 702 K1
st. S Geelong 702 K1

KILLARA
ct. Belmont 702 A2
ct. Noble Park 534 G
ct. Rosebud 684 F1
ct. Werribee 487 A
mw. Bulleen 329 E1
rd. Campbellfield 239 F
rd. Coldstream 295 E1
rd. Gruyere 296 B1
rd. Gruyere 342 L
st. Box Hill N 375 B
st. Lalor 240 C
st. Reservoir 283 A1
st. Sunshine W 364 K

KILLARNEY
ct. Berwick 554 J
rd. Templstw Lr 330 B1
st. Rye 680 E2

KILLARRA
av. Camberwell 417 D

KIRCALDY
ct. Greenvale..........193 D20
KIREEP
rd. Balwyn..............373 J12
KIRK
ct. Tullamarine........278 F6
pl. Geelong, off Little Malop St...703 C8
rd. Cockatoo 471 H10
rd. Pt Lonsdale........710 D4
st. Ascot Vale..........323 J19
st. Kensington 33 C12
st. Noble Park.........534 J1
st. Ringwood 378 C15
KIRKBRIDE
wy. Craigieburn 194 F1
KIRKBY
st. Coburg 326 A7
KIRKDALE
st. Brunswick E.......326 B14
KIRKFELL
ct. Berwick.............554 A7
KIRKFORD
dr. Mooroolbark......337 C7
KIRKHAM
ct. Berwick.............554 J5
dr. Greenvale...........193 D20
dr. Greenvale...........193 G17
rd. Belgrave S..........506 B11
rd. Dandenong S.....535 G14
rd. Murrumbeena....457 C12
rd.w,Keysborough....535 A13
KIRKMORE
av. Jan Juc.............711 D14
KIRKPATRICKS
rd. Macclesfield.......470 H1
KIRKS
la. Melbourne 1 K11
la. Melbourne 24 A7
KIRKSTONE
rd. Point Cook.........450 H10
rd. Point Cook.........450 H12
KIRKTON
dr. Kurunjang..........227 E11
KIRKWALL
ct. Glen Waverley....460 F11
ct. Greenvale...........193 H17
KIRKWELL
ct. Greenvale...........237 E3
KIRKWOOD
av. Sandringham 495 E17
av. Seaford.............599 E10
cr. Hampton Pk.......552 C10
ct. Montrose...........381 K12
dr. Camberwell.........417 C5
st. Beaumaris...........530 D3
KIRRA
cl. Nar Warrn S.......552 F13
ct. Croydon.............379 F6
ct. Kurunjang..........227 E14
ct. Pakenham...........584 H7
ct. Springvale S.......499 G20
KIRRAWEE
av. Wantirna S.........422 L12
av. Wantirna S.........423 A12
ct. Noble Park.........534 H7
KIRRI
st. Rye...................697 C7
KIRRIBILLI
av. Keysborough 534 F9
cl. Langwarrin.........602 C18
KIRRILEE
ct. Berwick.............553 L17
KIRRUM
cl. Wantirna S.........422 K20
KIRSTEN
ct. Mooroolbark......337 B12
KIRSTIN
cl. Oakleigh S..........497 H7
KIRSTINA
rd. Glen Waverley....460 D6
KIRTAIN
dr. Croydon.............335 H19
KIRTON
ct. Doncaster 331 B18
KIRWAN
av. Lalor.................241 J11
av. Roxburgh Pk......194 B12
KIRWANA
gr. Montmorency 287 B13
KIRWIN
av. Eltham North......288 A1
KIRWOOD
st. Blairgowrie.........695 H2
KISMET
cl. Ringwood..........379 A3
rd. Sunbury.............143 C1
KITARA
ct. Frankston..........628 C4

KITCHEN
rd. Beaconsfld Up....542 L17
rd. Dandenong S.....550 D7
KITCHENER
gr. Preston.............283 C20
pde. Cockatoo 511 D3
rd. Croydon.............380 B1
rd. Pascoe Vale 280 H12
rd. Silvan 384 K10
rd. Tecoma..............466 E12
st. Balwyn...............372 K11
st. Balwyn...............373 A11
st. Box Hill S............375 A20
st. Box Hill S............419 A2
st. Broadmeadows..238 B16
st. Brunswick W......324 J9
st. Kew East............372 E5
st. Mentone 530 L10
KITE
av. Bayswater N.......380 D18
ct. Werribee 447 L9
KITEROA
st. Belmont 702 C20
KITMONT
st. Murrumbeena....457 E8
KITSON
cr. Airport W...........278 J16
cr. Templstw Lr.......330 G9
ct. Altona Mdw........451 C3
ct. Rowville.............503 J1
rd. Clayton S 498 H8
st. Frankston............599 C14
st. Ringwood 378 H16
KITTY
st. Clematis.............508 G4
KITTYHAWK
st. Airport W 278 D16
KITZ
la. Melbourne 1 F13
la. Melbourne 23 L9
KIUNA
rd. Keilor N..............276 E1
KIWI
ct. Chelsea Ht..........547 E12
ct. Mill Park 242 H10
ct. New Gisborne 79 C3
pl. Cranbourne W....577 G17
rt. Keilor Dn............275 H12
KLAUER
st. Frankston...........599 D15
st. Seaford 599 J8
KLEAD
ct. Ringwood N.......378 E5
KLEIN
cr. Roxburgh Pk......194 A10
KLEINE
st. Noble Park 534 F2
KLEINERT
rd. Boronia..............423 D15
KLEMKE
ct. Grovedale 706 A12
KLIM
pl. Burnside 318 D6
KLINE
ct. Brookfield 268 A5
KNAITH
rd. Ringwood E 378 L12
rd. Ringwood E 379 A12
KNAPP
st. Altona North.......409 E1
st. Preston..............282 E20
KNAPTON
av. Beaconsfld Up....541 J11
KNEALE
dr. Box Hill N...........375 A9
KNEE
la. Croydon N 335 K12
KNEEN
st. Fitzroy N 326 E20
KNEES
rd. Pk Orchards.......333 L13
rd. Pk Orchards.......334 A15
rd. Warrandyte 333 L13
KNELL
st. Mulgrave 500 F4
KNIGHT
av. Herne Hill............701 L4
av. Sunshine N 321 D9
cr. Roxburgh Pk......193 L15
ct. Donvale 333 B10
ct. Endeavour Hl 537 F9
ct. Ferntree Gly 463 F7
ct. Hillside...............231 J19
ct. Meadow Ht 238 B3
la. Geelong, off Malop St..........703 F8
mw. Williamstown 411 A15
pl. Dandenong N.....501 G12
pl. Rye...................697 E9
st. Aberfeldie...........323 E8
st. Blairgowrie.........696 A3
st. Clayton S 498 H5
st. Coburg N 281 G16
st. Elwood 454 F3
st. Watsonia 285 G5
st. Williamstown 411 B16
KNIGHTON
av. Airport W 278 D16
pl. Mornington........656 J3
KNIGHTS
dr. Glen Waverley 421 A17
rd. Gembrook..........512 K11
rd. Mannerim 707 A1
rd. Pt Lonsdale.........707 G4
wy. Kings Park 274 L18
KNIGHTSBRIDGE
av. Altona Mdw........451 E5
av. Nunawading.......376 K12
ct. Glen Waverley....420 B16
ct. Narre Warren 539 A14
ct. Somerville..........645 B18
KNOLE
st. Hadfield 281 A10
KNOLLBROOK
cl. Highton..............701 F20
KNOTT
st. Langwarrin.........629 D3
st. Safety Bch..........669 C13
KNOWING
ct. Cranbourne W....577 H18
KNOWLE
gr. Hurstbridge........202 K15
KNOWLES
rd. Dandenong S 550 K7
rd. Dandenong S 551 A7
st. Northcote...........326 J19
KNOWSLEY
ct. Wantirna............422 B12
KNOX
ct. Altona Mdw........451 C4
ct. Kurunjang 227 F8
ct. Sunbury..............143 G9
la. Melbourne 2 D6
la. Melbourne 24 C4
pl. Knoxfield............463 B7
pl. Melbourne 2 E5
pl. Melbourne 24 C4
rd. Blairgowrie.........695 L5
st. Canterbury 372 L15
st. Canterbury 373 A15
st. Carrum Downs....574 K16
st. Malvern East 416 F17
st. Noble Park 534 G3
st. Reservoir 282 D14
st. Yarraville............367 D15
KNUTSFORD
st. Balwyn...............373 D14
KOALA
av. Badger Creek 258 F13
av. Nunawading.......376 K18
cr. Westmeadows ...236 G13
ct. Chelsea..............547 B15
ct. Doncaster E 375 G2
ct. Frankston S........627 E9
ct. Keysborough 534 E7
ct. Somerville..........645 D17
rd. Seville................385 G1
rd. Wandin East.......385 G1
wk. S Morang...........243 K4
KODRE
st. St Albans 319 J4
KOEL
ct. Carrum Downs...600 J3
pl. Werribee............447 L5
KOETONG
ct. Mulgrave 500 J3
pde. Mt Eliza.............625 K19
KOGARAH
ct. Keysborough 534 G9
KOGIA
st. Mt Eliza..............641 J3
KOHURAU
ct. Taylors Lakes.....276 D10
KOITAKI
ct. Heidelberg W.....284 B20
KOKARIBB
rd. Carnegie 456 J7
KOKODA
ct. Boronia..............424 D3
ct. Lalor..................241 F6
rd. Williamstown 411 A15
st. Heidelberg W 328 C3
st. Sorrento 679 D16
KOLAN
ct. Werribee 447 G7
KOLINDA
cr. Rosebud W........683 E20
KOLIVAS
ct. Hillside..............274 E2

KOLONGA
ct. Greensborough ..285 L10
ct. Vermont S 420 F11
KOLOR
wy. Templestowe 331 E14
KOLORA
cr. Mt Eliza.............641 L3
rd. Heidelberg W 284 C17
KOMBI
rd. Clayton S 499 E6
KONAC
ct. Berwick..............553 G2
KONAGADERRA
rd. Oaklands Jctn 191 E1
KONG
ct. Hampton Pk.......551 L8
KONRAD
ct. Ferntree Gly 463 E6
st. Bentleigh E.........497 A3
KONRADS
cr. Highton..............705 H4
cr. Mill Park 242 D9
ct. Truganina 405 G14
KONTEK
wy. Sydenham 274 J4
KOOKABURRA
av. Tecoma..............466 D10
av. Werribee............448 B10
la. Mt Evelyn...........339 D11
la. Yellingbo.............387 J18
st. Altona 408 F20
st. Frankston............599 D14
wk. S Morang...........243 K3
KOOKABURRA DELL
Upwey 465 K10
KOOLENA
cl. Clayton S 499 F11
KOOLKUNA
av. Doncaster 374 G2
la. Hampton............494 L8
KOOLUNA
ct. Frankston...........600 F15
KOOLYA
ct. Rye...................697 A7
ct. Yallambie...........286 C12
KOOMALOO
ct. Carrum Downs...574 K18
KOOMBA
rd. Wantirna............421 L9
KOOMBAHLA
ct. Rowville.............503 A6
ct. Werribee............448 G18
KOOMBOOLOOMBA
ct. Lilydale 337 L2
KOONALDA
av. Glen Waverley....460 B9
gr. Dandenong N.....501 G20
rd. Gladstone Pk.......279 A1
KOONAWARRA
st. Clayton 458 L16
wy. Diamond Ck........245 G8
KOONUNG
ct. Doncaster 330 B19
rd. Blackburn N 375 K10
st. Balwyn N 374 A1
st. Dandenong N.....501 F14
KOONYA
av. Blairgowrie.........679 D19
KOORA
ct. Yallambie...........286 C11
KOORALI
cl. Noble Park 534 D5
st. Keilor................276 F9
KOORANG
pl. Berwick..............553 G6
KOORINGA
cr. Wheelers Hill......460 H16
ct. Rosebud 684 F18
pl. Torquay 711 K6
rd. Carnegie 456 F11
KOORINGAL
gr. Brighton.............454 L9
rd. Blairgowrie.........680 C20
rd. Upwey 465 E14
KOORNALLA
cr. Mt Eliza..............625 G17
KOORNANG
rd. Carnegie 456 H13
rd. Ormond 456 H13
rd. Scoresby 462 E10
KOORNONG
cr. N Warrandyte.....290 F13
KOORONG
av. Bayswater N.......380 J19
av. Rosebud 683 K20
ct. Highton..............705 G4
KOOROORA
ct. Vermont 421 A6

KOOS
rd. Panton Hill ....248 D
KOO WEE RUP
rd. Pakenham...........585 B1
KOO WEE RUP NORTH-NAR NAR GOON
rd. Nr Nr Goon 586 L1
KOOYONG
cl. Hampton Pk.......551 J1
cl. Hawthorn E, off Kaikoura Av........416 D
pl. Highton..............701 E
rd. Armadale 415 F1
rd. Caulfield.............455 D1
rd. Caulfield N 415 E2
rd. Caulfield S...........455 D1
rd. Elsternwick 455 D1
rd. Gardenvale..........455 D1
rd. Geelong ....702 K
rd. Toorak 415 F1
KOOYONGA
gr. Mornington........656 D
KOOYONGKOOT
rd. Hawthorn............372 B2
rd. Hawthorn............416 A
KORIELLA
dr. Sunbury.............143 C1
KORINA
ct. Langwarrin.........629 C
KOROIT
av. Dallas 238 D1
pl. Geelong 703 D1
pl. Taylors Lakes.....276 B
st. Nunawading.......376 D1
KORONG
ct. Broadmeadows..238 C1
ct. Mornington........640 L1
ct. Mornington........641 A1
rd. Heidelberg W 284 D1
KORONIS
rd. Keilor.................276 K
KOROROIT
app. Caroline Spr.......318 B
ct. Kurunjang 227 G1
st. Albion ....364 L
st. Albion ....365 A
st. W Footscray........366 D1
KOROROIT CREEK
rd. Altona ....407 L
rd. Altona 409 C1
rd. Williamstown 410 A1
rd. Williamstn N 410 A1
KOROWA
st. Rye...................697 C
st. Sunshine W ....364 J
KORRA
ct. Blairgowrie.........696 B
KOSCIUSKO
ct. Lalor.................240 H
ct. Wheelers Hill......460 K
rd. Balwyn N 329 G1
KOSKY
st. Sunshine W ....364 K
KOSSECKS
pl. Belmont.............706 J
KOTOR
cl. Mt Martha..........656 B1
KOVAL
ct. Springvale S.......533 K
KOWA
ct. Greensborough ..244 B1
KOWHAI
cl. Altona Mdw........452 A
KRAFT
ct. Pakenham..........584 G
KRAMBRUK
st. Sunshine W ....364 J
KRAMER
dr. Berwick..............554 D
st. Werribee............448 A
KRIEGEL
wy. Dandenong N.....502 C1
KRIS
ct. Doncaster E ....332 G
ct. Melton W...........226 A1
KRISHNA
ct. Noble Park ....535 B
KRISTEN
cl. Frankston S........627 D2
cl. Frankston S........643 D1
cl. Glen Waverley....421 A2
ct. Boronia..............423 K1
KRISTIAN
ct. Mt Martha..........656 H
KRISTINA
ct. Pakenham..........584 H1
KRISTINE
ct. Cheltenham........497 G2

RISTY
. Jan Juc 711 C15
RITHIA
. Coburg N 281 G12
RONA
Keilor Lodge 276 B3
RONE
. Mordialloc 531 L16
ROWERA
. Mooroolbark 337 A14
RUSES
l. N Warrandyte 290 D11
RYSTAL
t. Mooroolbark 336 K12
RYSTEL GLENN
dn. Boronia 424 G14
UALA
. St Albans 275 J19
UBBA
l. Ringwood N 377 L6
UBIS
v. Aspendale 546 D4
r. Dingley Village 533 A6
r. Ringwood N 377 L5
UBURA
l. St Albans 321 A6
UEBLER
t. Glen Waverley 420 B18
ULANDA
t. Patterson L 573 L6
ULIN
l. Cranbourne 578 C19
ULNINE
v. Mitcham 377 J17
ULPA
t. Kurunjang 227 E13
ULSI
t. Croydon Hills 335 G13
UMALA
r. Somerville 644 E19
d. Bayswater 423 C8
UMALI
t. Noble Park 534 K5
UMARA
l. Clayton 459 A18
UMBADA
v. Upwey 466 A12
UMBARI
t. New Gisborne 79 F8
UNAT
t. Deer Park 318 J16
UNDY
l. Greensborough 244 C19
UNYUNG
d. Mt Eliza 625 G17
UNZEA
l. Meadow Ht 193 K19
t. Mt Waverley 419 C20
URANDA
r. Berwick 553 K3
r. Oakleigh E 458 K11
t. Wattle Glen 246 G9
st. Lalor 240 F10
st. Langwarrin 629 D9
URANGA
ct. Mornington 640 B20
rd. View Bank 285 K17
KURDIAN
ct. Yallambie 286 D12
URINGAI
rd. Tootgarook 698 D7
URINGGAI
cr. Noble Park 534 F6
URNAI
av. Reservoir 282 C12
URNETH
pl. South Yarra 31 G4
pl. South Yarra 414 D2
URONG
av. Frankston 628 A1
KURRAJONG
av. Croydon 380 J3
av. Glen Waverley 460 A7
av. St Kilda E 414 L16
av. St Kilda E 415 A16
cl. View Bank 285 K19
cr. Melton S 268 F7
cr. Watsonia N 285 G2
ct. Cranbourne N 578 B4
ct. Frankston S 627 H12
ct. Grovedale 706 F9
dr. Altona Mdw 407 K20
rd. Delahey 275 C10
rd. Narre Warren 539 D20
st. Bentleigh E 457 F17
vw. Mill Park 243 E10
wy. Blackburn N 375 G10

KURRAK
rd. Plenty 200 C20
rd. Plenty 244 C1
rd. Yarrambat 200 C20
KURRAWA
cr. Patterson L 573 K10
KURRUP
st. Mt Martha 655 L16
KURT
pl. Cranbourne 603 K3
pl. Noble Park 534 K6
KURUNG
ct. Gisborne 78 J20
dr. Kings Park 275 A18
KURUNJANG
dr. Kurunjang 227 A15
KUTCHER
ct. Sunshine W 364 B8
KUYURA
rd. Mt Evelyn 383 D3
KWINANA
av. Glen Waverley 420 A18
ct. Campbellfield 239 F18
ct. Ivanhoe 328 B8
st. Glen Waverley 419 L17
KYA
cl. Ferntree Gly 423 K19
KYABRAM
st. Coolaroo 238 F4
KYAK COURSE
Delahey 275 F12
KYA-LAMI
ri. Mooroolbark 337 L18
KYAMBA
ct. Bayswater N 379 K14
KYARRA
rd. Glen Iris 416 H11
st. Hampton 495 C11
KYBERD
ct. Chelsea 547 B19
KYBROLYDE
ct. Research 289 B4
KYEAMBA
gr. Toorak 415 H6
KYEEMA
av. Highton 701 C16
av. Highton 701 E16
KYILLA
ct. Frankston S 627 B5
KYLE
av. Belmont 702 F17
la. Hopetoun Park 224 D19
pl. Croydon N 335 L11
rd. Altona North 410 A2
wy. Bacchus Msh 221 J12
KYLIE
cl. Mooroolbark 337 K18
cl. Mornington 641 D16
ct. Hallam 537 K13
ct. Hampton Pk 551 K12
ct. Pakenham 585 B3
la. Seville E 343 A5
pl. Cheltenham 496 L13
pl. Gladstone Pk 279 A3
pl. Montmorency 287 A9
KYLTA
rd. Heidelberg W 284 C17
KYM
pl. Melton 269 A2
KYME
pl. Port Melb 412 L5
KYMME
ct. Glen Waverley 421 A20
KYNE
pl. Eltham 288 F4
KYNETON
av. Reservoir 283 F11
cct. Caroline Spr 318 C8
la. Caroline Spr 318 C8
KYNOCH
la. Maribyrnong 322 J16
st. Deer Park 319 C14
KYNUNA
ct. Nar Warrn S 578 L2
KYORA
ct. Melton 268 G2
dr. Kew East 372 K2
pde. Balwyn N 372 L1
pde. Balwyn N 373 A1
KYOTO
ct. Rowville 463 B14
KYRA
cl. Lilydale 338 J13
KYRELI
cl. Donvale 333 C11
KYRENIA
ct. Warrandyte 333 B6
KYRIE
ct. Carrum Downs 601 B3

KYUP
st. Mt Eliza 625 K20

L

LAANE
av. Rosanna 329 B2
LAANECOORIE
dr. Ferntree Gly 464 A16
LABASSA
ct. Narre Warren 539 E15
gr. Caulfield N 415 C18
wy. Seabrook 451 A4
LABILLIERE
st. Maddingley 263 G1
LABRENT
ct. Mt Martha 655 E20
LABUAN
pl. Wantirna 422 D12
st. Sorrento 679 E16
LABURNUM
ct. Brighton 455 A19
gr. Doveton 537 B10
pl. Hillside 273 J7
pl. Rockbank 273 J7
st. Blackburn 375 G15
st. Brighton 455 A20
st. Parkdale 531 H13
LACE
st. Eumemmerring 536 J15
LACEBARK
ct. Oakleigh S 498 A9
rd. Delahey 275 B10
st. Doveton 536 K8
LACENET
av. Frankston N 600 D11
LACEY
pl. Melbourne 2 L10
pl. Melbourne 24 G4
st. Croydon 380 B3
st. Lalor 241 J11
LACEYS
rd. Hurstbridge 203 J10
rd. Panton Hill 203 J10
LACHAN
pl. Keysborough 534 C7
LACHLAN
cl. Cranbourne N 577 L7
cr. Roxburgh Pk 194 C7
ct. Keilor Park 278 A13
ct. Pakenham 558 K20
ct. Sunbury 143 B5
ct. Werribee 447 F8
dr. Endeavour Hl 537 G1
gra. Bulleen 329 H9
la. Taylors Hill 274 K12
la. Whittlesea 96 L7
rd. Boronia 424 K13
rd. Melton S 268 D10
rd. Sunshine W 364 F5
st. Bundoora 284 E2
st. Mentone 531 F5
LACKENHEATH
ct. Dingley Village 533 C4
dr. Tullamarine 278 K1
LACY
st. Avondale Ht 322 C16
st. Braybrook 322 B19
st. Selby 467 D16
LADBROKE
st. Epping 197 L16
LADD
ct. Bacchus Msh 221 K13
rd. Emerald 510 D11
rd. New Gisborne 79 D2
sq. Emerald 510 E13
st. Bundoora 285 C7
st. Watsonia 285 C7
LADDS
la. N Melbourne 17 K18
LADE
av. Kilsyth 381 C12
ct. Ringwood 378 G7
ct. Rowville 463 E20
LADNER
ct. Chadstone 458 E4
LADONGA
pl. Rowville 462 K17
LADY BARLOW
ct. Patterson L 547 H19
LADY BETTY
pde. View Bank 285 G18
LADY BEVERLEY
cct. Somerville 644 E17
LADY BRASSEYS
dr. Kew 372 J8

LADYKIRK
cl. Berwick 554 L5
LADY LOCHS
dr. Kew 372 H8
LADY NELSON
cr. Altona Mdw 451 L3
dr. Sorrento 679 A14
wk. Patterson L 547 G20
wy. Taylors Lakes 275 F8
LADY PENRHYN
av. Mill Park 242 E3
ct. Cranbourne W 603 H1
LADY ROSE
cr. Sydenham 275 C7
LADYS
wk. Ferntree Gly 464 K3
wk. Tremont 464 K3
LADY WELLINGTON
ct. Patterson L 547 H19
LAE
ct. Ashburton 417 H17
ct. Herne Hill 702 A2
st. Heidelberg W 327 L3
st. W Footscray 366 E13
LAEMMLE
st. Dandenong N 501 G17
LAFFAN
ct. Broadmeadows 238 D19
LAFITTE
ct. Lalor 240 F10
LAFRANK
st. Burwood 419 A10
LAGARNA
dr. Kurunjang 226 G13
dr. Kurunjang 226 G14
LAGEN
ct. Bundoora 283 L1
LAGGAN
ct. Endeavour Hl 503 H17
LAGNICOURT
st. Hampton 495 C6
LAGO
cl. Keilor Dn 276 A14
LAGOON
la. Port Melb 29 A9
pl. Patterson L 573 G11
LAGOONA
ct. Blackburn 376 B20
LAGUNA
cl. Keilor Lodge 276 C4
pl. Grovedale 706 E8
LAHA
cr. Preston 283 G18
LAHINCH
st. Broadmeadows 238 B19
st. Broadmeadows 280 B1
st. Preston 327 D3
LAHONA
av. Bentleigh E 496 G3
LAHY
st. St Albans 319 G5
LAIDLAW
ct. Keysborough 534 C7
ct. Vermont 377 J20
LAING
ct. Forest Hill 420 E6
pl. Macleod 285 B11
st. Mont Albert 374 E13
LAINIE
av. Keysborough 534 C12
ct. Wantirna S 422 B17
LAIRA
st. Geelong West 702 F6
LAIRD
cl. Aspendale Gdn 546 H5
ct. Heidelberg 328 L7
dr. Altona Mdw 451 K2
pl. Narre Warren 539 A15
st. Croydon 336 J19
LAITY
st. Richmond 26 H6
LAKALA
cl. Hampton Pk 552 D9
rd. Seville 342 B15
LAKE
av. Mitcham 377 F14
av. Pascoe Vale 280 G11
dr. Dingley Village 532 H6
dr. Waurn Ponds 705 D9
gr. Coburg N 281 H18
rd. Blackburn 376 A17
rd. Forest Hill 376 C19
rd. Nunawading 376 C19
st. Avondale Ht 322 A9
st. Carnegie 456 E7

st. Reservoir 282 E10
st. Geelong, off Park St 703 F9
tr. Lysterfield 504 J13
tr. Lysterfield 504 L18
LAKE BOGA
av. Deer Park 318 K16
LAKE EYRE
pl. Caroline Spr 317 K7
LAKEFIELD
wy. Deer Park 319 F11
LAKE KING
cir. Braeside 547 E1
LAKELAND
ct. Dingley Village 533 B1
ct. Pt Lonsdale 707 F19
LAKE PARK
ct. Lysterfield S 504 B15
LAKER
dr. Pt Lonsdale 710 D7
LAKES
dr. Craigieburn 193 K3
dr. Sunbury 144 D13
dr. Taylors Lakes 275 J4
LAKES ENTRANCE
dr. Pt Lonsdale 707 G18
LAKESFIELD
dr. Ferntree Gly 464 A17
LAKESIDE
av. Reservoir 282 D8
bvd. Pakenham 583 L3
bvd. Rowville 462 K16
cr. Croydon Hills 335 F13
ct. Safety Bch 669 C19
dr. Albert Park 30 J9
dr. Broadmeadows 239 A18
dr. Burwood E 420 D11
dr. Emerald 469 H18
dr. Lower Plenty 286 E19
dr. Melbourne 30 H9
dr. Melbourne 31 A17
dr. Melbourne 413 K5
dr. Point Cook 450 J12
dr. Roxburgh Pk 194 E12
dr. Roxburgh Pk 194 F11
dr. St Kilda 414 B10
dr. S Melbourne 413 K5
pl. Williamstown 410 H16
LAKE VIEW
ct. Emerald 470 A20
dr. Nar Warrn S 552 F11
dr. Nar Warrn S 552 F13
dr. Safety Bch 668 L19
dr. Safety Bch 669 A19
la. Safety Bch 668 L20
la. Safety Bch 669 A20
LAKEVIEW
av. Rowville 462 E18
dr. Lilydale 338 B14
dr. Mickleham 149 F3
dr. Scoresby 462 C12
gr. Wyndham Va 446 C8
tce. Beaconsfield 555 B11
tce. Melton W 225 J18
tce. Templstw Lr 330 B13
tce.n, Beaconsfield 555 C11
LAKEWAY
cl. Caroline Spr 318 B8
LAKEWOOD
bvd. Braeside 532 J16
bvd. Deer Park 319 G13
dr. Knoxfield 463 C1
LALA
av. Warburton 349 J3
LALANI
tce. Templestowe 331 L11
LALBERT
cr. Prahran 415 C12
ct. Ferntree Gly 463 L15
LALEHAM
ct. Eltham 288 A9
ct. Frankston 599 K16
LALINA
cl. Frankston 600 F14
LALLA
ct. Kew 372 F9
st. Kew 372 E8
LALOMA
ct. Templstw Lr 330 K11
LALOR
cl. Mulgrave 501 F2
ct. Caroline Spr 318 E10
ct. Springvale S 499 D18
ct. Sunbury 142 L17
ct. Sunbury 143 A17
ct. Williamstown 410 H14
st. Dallas 238 C10
st. Port Melb 412 L4
LALORS
la. Healesville 257 J2
rd. Healesville 257 H3

LALUMA
st. Essendon 323 G6
LALWA
st. Blackburn 375 J20
LALWINYA
st. Delahey 275 B10
LA MAMA
la. Carlton 18 F14
pl. Carlton 18 F14
LAMANA
st. Mordialloc 532 C18
LAMAR
ct. Dandenong N 502 C18
LAMARK
ct. Greenvale 236 K3
LAMART
st. Strathmore 279 G12
LAMAT
ct. Frankston 628 H2
LAMB
ct. Bundoora 242 K20
st. Cranbourne 604 D4
st. Moonee Pnd 324 D14
LAMBASSA
gr. Reservoir 283 D2
LAMBECK
dr. Melb Airport 277 K6
dr. Tullamarine 277 K6
dr. Tullamarine 277 K8
LAMBERT
av. Newtown 702 E13
av. Sunbury 142 L11
ct. Blairgowrie 680 D20
ct. Endeavour Hl 537 H10
ct. Rosebud 699 K2
gr. St Kilda E 414 K16
pl. Doncaster E 332 F14
pl. Roxburgh Pk 193 J16
rd. Caulfield N 415 E17
rd. Pearcedale 630 J15
rd. Toorak 415 C8
st. Diamond Ck 245 F10
st. Frankston N 600 C9
st. Richmond 26 J7
LAMBERTS
tr. Lysterfield 504 E11
LAMBETH
av. Armadale 415 H13
ct. Epping 197 K18
ct. Keysborough 534 B8
pl. St Kilda 414 E15
st. Kensington 34 C8
st. Kings Park 319 A1
wk. Balwyn, off
Barnsbury Rd 372 L12
LAMBHILL
cr. Highton 701 G16
LAMBOLE
ct. St Albans 275 G19
LAMBOURNE
av. Rowville 463 J15
rd. Watsonia 285 D8
st. Surrey Hills 374 F20
st. Surrey Hills 418 F1
LAMBRUK
ct. Yallambie 286 C13
LAMELLAH
st. Caulfield 455 G5
LAMIN
la. Toorak 415 B6
LAMINA
av. Mill Park 242 C2
LAMING
rd. Deer Park 319 C11
LAMMAS
ct. Mulgrave 501 E5
LAMOND
ct. Greenvale 237 D3
LAMONT
av. The Patch 467 J3
cr. Cranbourne 577 L19
ct. Wantirna S 421 L18
LAMORNA
ct. Eltham 287 K9
LAMPLIGHT
wy. Attwood 237 A10
LAMPLIGHTER
ct. Whittlesea 96 F16
LAN
av. Altona Mdw 451 C3
LANA
ct. Airport W 278 E16
pl. Narre Warren 538 L15
st. Blackburn S 419 F6
wy. Maribyrnong 367 B2
LANAGHAN
av. Caroline Spr 318 C5

LANARK
ct. Glen Waverley 420 L19
st. Brunswick 325 L9
st. Brunswick E 325 L9
st. Clayton S 498 H6
st. Epping 197 K15
wy. Gowanbrae 279 D6
LANCASHIRE
la. N Melbourne 17 D17
LANCASTER
av. Avondale Ht 322 A13
av. Narre Warren 553 B6
av. Newcomb 704 B18
av. Newtown 701 L6
ct. Greenvale 192 L18
ct. Greenvale 193 A18
ct. Keysborough 534 A8
ct. Officer 555 F20
ct. Somerville 644 G16
dr. Point Cook 450 C4
pl. Chirnside Pk 337 E1
rd. Mooroolbark 337 J18
st. Ashburton 417 J17
st. Bentleigh E 456 H17
st. Sunshine N 321 G14
wy. Melton W 226 E15
LANCE
cl. Aspendale Gdn 547 A6
rd. Bayswater 423 G8
rd. Diggers Rest 187 H13
rd. Sunshine N 321 F11
LANCEFIELD
ct. Endeavour Hl 537 F3
LANCELOT
cl. Wantirna S 462 L2
cr. Glen Waverley 420 L16
ct. Hillside 231 J17
ct. Kings Park 275 A18
LANCEWOOD
av. Heidelberg W 328 A1
LANCIA
ct. Epping 197 K14
ct. Ferntree Gly 464 C6
dr. Keilor Dn 276 A13
dr. Tootgarook 698 E8
LANCING
ct. Wheelers Hill 460 J18
LANCOM
ri. Rowville 503 J1
LANDALE
av. Croydon 380 D4
rd. Toorak 415 A5
st. Box Hill 374 K19
LANDARA
ct. Mooroolbark 337 F15
LANDAU
ct. Cranbourne N 578 H11
ct. Taylors Lakes 275 J2
dr. Warranwood 334 J13
pl. Avondale Ht 322 D11
pl. Melton W 226 B15
LANDBURY
rd. Bundoora 242 C20
LANDCOX
st. Brighton East 455 D15
LANDELL
ct. Ringwood E 379 D14
LANDELLS
rd. Pascoe Vale 280 K16
LANDEN
av. Balwyn N 374 B6
av. Glen Waverley 460 L1
pl. Toorak 415 F3
LANDERS
ct. Caroline Spr 318 A4
LANDEX
ct. Diamond Ck 246 A7
LANDHILL
ct. Hallam 538 B16
LANDLES
ri. Roxburgh Pk 193 L12
st. McKinnon 456 E17
LANDO
pl. Springvale S 533 J6
LANDON
pl. Carrum Downs 601 F2
LANDOR
cl. Hoppers Csg 405 A18
ct. Narre Warren 539 D15
LANDRA
av. Reservoir 283 C2
ct. Berwick 554 H20
ct. Grovedale 705 L16
pl. Greensborough 243 L19
st. Rye 696 G8
LANDRIDGE
st. Glen Waverley 420 E18
LANDSBOROUGH
av. Rowville 463 E13
av. Taylors Lakes 275 D1
av. Wheelers Hill 460 H19

cl. Endeavour Hl 537 F6
dr. Sunbury 142 L12
LANDSCAPE
ct. Eltham North 245 L18
ct. Wheelers Hill 461 F15
dr. Boronia 424 D5
dr. Doncaster E 332 E14
dr. Hillside 231 K18
dr. Mooroolbark 337 G11
LANDSDALE
cr. Wantirna S 422 H18
LANDSDOWNE
ct. Frankston 628 C13
st. Blairgowrie 680 A20
LANDSIDE
rd. Melb Airport 235 J14
LANDSTEAD
ct. Carrum Downs 601 B3
LANDSTROM
qd. Kilsyth 380 K8
LANDY
av. Highton 705 H3
cl. Mill Park 242 F9
ct. Burnside 318 H11
ct. Kilsyth 381 F11
ct. Pt Lonsdale 707 H19
ct. Wantirna S 462 E3
ct. Wheelers Hill 460 L9
rd. Jacana 237 K19
st. Reservoir 282 E8
LANE
cr. Reservoir 283 C10
ct. Darley 221 L4
rd. Ferntree Gly 424 F19
st. Blackburn N 376 D10
wy. Cranbourne 578 D17
LANENA
ct. Frankston 600 H14
LANE NO 5
Geelong 702 L11
LANE NO 10
Geelong, off
Moorabool St 703 A10
LANE NO 11
Geelong 703 A11
LANE NO 20
Geelong, off
Maud St 702 K10
LANE NO 25
Geelong, off
Little Ryrie St 703 C9
LANE NO 28
Geelong, off
Yarra St 703 C7
LANE NO 29
Geelong, off
Fenwick St 702 L8
LANES
tr. Lysterfield 505 H4
LANG
ct. Malvern East 457 D2
rd. Langwarrin 629 E4
rd. Melton S 268 G3
rd. Mt Waverley 458 G4
st. Beaumaris 529 L11
st. Clifton Hill 20 A8
st. Princes Hill 325 G18
st. South Yarra 31 J11
st. South Yarra 414 E6
LANGBOURNE
dr. Nar Warrn S 552 D18
LANGDALE
dr. Croydon Hills 335 J13
LANGDON
av. Blairgowrie 679 F16
cr. Craigieburn 194 E1
rd. Caulfield N 455 G2
LANGEWAN
rd. Langwarrin 629 K6
LANGFORD
av. Mitcham 377 F19
cr. Donvale 377 A7
ct. Tecoma 466 B11
rd. Sorrento 678 G4
st. N Melbourne 34 E11
st. Surrey Hills 374 A14
st. Williamstown 411 E17
LANGFORDS
la. N Melbourne 34 L9
LANGHAM
ct. Grovedale 706 D9
pl. Hawthorn E 372 H18
st. Avondale Ht 322 A16
LANGHORNE
st. Altona Mdw 451 K5
st. Dandenong 536 B9
LANGLEY
cr. Dandenong S 535 H14
pl. Roxburgh Pk 194 A10
pl. S Morang 243 G1
rd. Cranbourne S 630 G3

st. Ardeer 320 C19
st. Ringwood E 379 B12
LANGLI
av. Warranwood 334 K12
LANGMORE
dr. Hillside 232 E17
la. Berwick 554 D8
LANGOLD
ct. Noble Park 535 D1
LANGON
st. Lalor 240 D10
LANGRIDGE
pl. Skye 601 G2
st. Abbotsford 25 L1
st. Collingwood 19 G20
st. Fairfield 327 F17
st. Hoppers Csg 448 K2
st. Middle Park 413 H12
LANGRIGG
av. Edithvale 546 G10
av. Mt Martha 655 H15
LANGS
la. Melbourne 23 H9
rd. Ascot Vale 323 J20
rd. Flemington 323 J20
rd. Ivanhoe 327 L12
LANGSHAW
st. Altona North 365 J20
LANGSLOW
rd. Aspendale Gdn 546 G3
st. Bentleigh E 456 L19
LANGSTON
st. Northcote 327 A19
LANGTON
st. Glenroy 279 K2
st. Glenroy 279 K4
st. Jacana 237 K20
wy. Greenvale 192 L18
LANGTREE
av. Pascoe Vale S 324 H5
ct. Blackburn 376 B11
LANGVALE
ct. Mill Park 242 E2
LANGVILLE
st. Malvern East 456 H4
LANGWARRIN
cr. Langwarrin 601 H20
LANGWELLS
pde. Northcote 326 J13
LANGWITH
av. Boronia 424 A12
LANHAM
st. Oakleigh E 458 H16
LANIER
cr. Croydon N 335 K9
LANIGAN
st. Fawkner 281 K4
LANKESTER
st. Templestowe 330 K7
LANNING
cr. Seville 342 B15
LANOMA
ct. Wheelers Hill 460 J19
pl. Sorrento 679 C16
LANSBURY
cr. Highton 701 F15
LANSDOWN
st. Balwyn N 373 E5
st. Brighton East 455 D13
st. Hampton 495 D11
LANSDOWNE
ct. Grovedale 706 J13
pl. Carlton 18 A19
rd. Endeavour Hl 503 B14
rd. St Kilda E 415 A16
st. E Melbourne 25 B7
st. Pascoe Vale S 281 A20
LANSELL
av. Highett 495 H15
av. Safety Bch 669 C15
av. Safety Bch 669 C17
cl. Nar Warrn S 553 A16
cl. Ringwood N 378 D4
cr. Camberwell 417 A3
ct. Carrum Downs 600 L3
ct. Carrum Downs 601 A3
ct. Rowville 463 F18
ct. Thomastown 241 F15
ct. Toorak 415 D5
dr. Cranbourne N 578 G11
dr. Doncaster 331 A18
dr. Highton 701 F20
pl. Melton W 226 D16
pl. Mt Martha 656 E7
rd. Glen Waverley 460 H5
rd. Mooroolbark 337 F14
rd. Toorak 415 D5
rd. Toorak 415 E2
rd. Wyndham Va 446 D10

LANSOR
st. Springvale S 533
LANSVALE
ct. Frankston 627
LANTANA
av. Hoppers Csg 448
av. Thomastown 240 K
cl. Greensborough 244 J
ct. Dandenong N 501 H
ct. Frankston 600 C
ct. St Albans 320 G
ct. Wantirna 422
dr. Narre Warren 553 G
dr. Wonga Park 291 H
rd. Gardenvale 455 C1
st. Blackburn N 375
st. Clayton 459 B
st. Doncaster E 332 D
st. Ivanhoe 328
LANTERN
cl. Epping 198 C1
ct. St Albans 319
pl. Lilydale 294 B1
LANVOS
dr. Diamond Ck 245
LANYON
ct. Lysterfield 464 B1
st. Dandenong S 550
LA PEROUSE
cl. Sunbury 144 C1
LAPSTONE
cr. Yallambie 285 L1
LAPWING
ct. Langwarrin 629
LARA
cl. Thomastown 240 E1
ct. Deer Park 319
ct. Doncaster 374
ct. Frankston 599 L
ct. Hallam 537 G1
ct. Mt Evelyn 338 L1
ct. St Helena 244 L
ct. St Helena 245 A1
pl. Melton W 226 B2
pl. Patterson L 573
st. Malvern 416
st. South Yarra 32 B1
wy. Campbellfield 239
LARADO
pl. Clayton S 499 E1
LARAINE
ct. Bonbeach 573 D
pl. Melton W 226 C1
LARAMIE
rd. Nar Warrn S 552 L2
LARBERT
av. Balwyn N 329 H1
rd. Mooroolbark 337 J1
rd. Noble Park 500 H1
LARCH
cr. Diamond Ck 245 A1
cr. Mt Waverley 419 G1
la. Dingley Village 532 H
st. Blackburn 376 A1
st. Caulfield S 455 G
st. Langwarrin 628 K
st. Thomastown 241 E1
LARCOM
ct. Greensborough 244 D1
LARCOMBE
st. Highton 705 J
LARDNER
rd. Frankston 627 G
LARGE
st. Springvale 499 G1
LARGS
ct. Greenvale 193 B2
st. Seaford 573 D1
LARISSA
av. Ringwood 378 G1
av. Tullamarine 278 F
ct. Croydon 380 G
rd. St Albans 320 H
st. Heidelberg W 328 A
LARK
rd. Exford 267 C1
st. Altona 408 F2
LARKIN
av. Airport W 279 C1
cl. Mt Martha 656 J
ct. Bundoora 242 H1
ct. Doncaster E 332 H
dr. Croydon 335 G2
pde. Queenscliff 709 D1
pl. Hoppers Csg 449 H
LARK RISE
ct. Narre Warren 538 H1
LARKSONG
ct. Springvale S 534 A

ARKSPUR
av. Doncaster..........375 B4
cl. Epping..........198 G20
dr. St Albans..........320 E8
ARKWOOD
la. Craigieburn..........193 L2
ARLAC
st. Hadfield..........280 J5
ARMAN
st. Bentleigh E..........456 L20
ARMOUR
rd. Pakenham..........557 G15
ARNACA
ct. Templestowe..........331 L13
ARNACH
rd. Baxter..........645 G3
rd. Langwarrin S..........645 G3
rd. Pearcedale..........645 G3
rd. Pearcedale..........640 D4
ARNARK
ct. Chelsea Ht..........547 F11
ARNE
av. Bayswater..........423 B4
av. Donvale..........376 L3
cl. Berwick..........553 H13
gr. Preston..........326 L6
ARNOO
av. Brunswick W..........325 A12
dr. Doncaster E..........332 H7
ARNOOK
cl. Greensborough..........244 A20
cr. Aspendale..........546 E4
cr. Mooroolbark..........337 B16
st. Prahran..........415 B12
A ROCHELLE
bvd. Point Cook..........450 F12
AROOL
av. St Helena..........244 K17
cl. Doncaster E..........331 K15
cr. Seaford..........573 D13
cr. Sunshine W..........364 F6
A ROSE
st. Brunswick..........325 E10
AROSE
pl. Werribee..........447 L14
ARPENT
st. Glen Waverley..........420 E17
ARRA
ct. Seabrook..........450 L4
ARRY
ct. Noble Park..........500 D19
ARSON
rd. Diamond Ck..........202 A17
ARTER
ct. Bundoora..........242 G18
ct. Hoppers Csg..........449 D1
ct. Kurunjang..........227 D10
ct. Mt Martha..........656 L10
ct. Mt Martha..........657 A10
ct. Wantirna S..........462 B4
ARWOOD
cl. Avondale Ht..........322 F16
ASCELLE
dr. Vermont S..........421 B13
ASCELLES
av. Toorak..........415 C5
av. View Bank..........285 H18
ct. Frankston..........628 C12
dr. Lalor..........240 J8
pl. Highton..........701 F19
sq. Kensington..........33 B10
st. Carnegie..........456 J11
st. Coburg..........325 B4
st. Springvale..........500 A10
ASER
ct. Taylors Lakes..........275 J5
dr. Rowville..........462 L15
dr. Rowville..........463 A14
ASIANDRA
av. Forest Hill..........376 K20
av. Nunawading..........376 K20
cct. Narre Warren..........553 D2
ASSA
ct. Dandenong N..........501 F10
ASSITER
ct. Nar Warrn S..........552 G6
st. Sunbury..........143 A13
ASSWADE
ct. Brighton..........494 G3
ATHAM
cl. Mill Park..........243 C6
cr. Dandenong N..........501 K19
ct. Doncaster E..........331 J18
ct. Forest Hill..........376 J20
ct. Glen Waverley..........419 K18
dr. Portsea..........677 H6
st. Bentleigh E..........457 A17
st. Ivanhoe..........328 B15
st. Mornington..........641 B19
st. Northcote..........326 G13
st. Tarneit..........447 F6
st. Werribee..........447 F6
LATHAMS
rd. Carrum Downs..........574 B19
rd. Seaford..........574 B19
LATIMER
pl. Gladstone Pk..........236 K19
st. Noble Park..........534 G3
LATINA
ct. Nar Warrn N..........538 C10
LATONA
av. Knoxfield..........462 K6
av. Preston..........326 E3
st. Mentone..........530 K9
LA TROBE
bvd. Newtown..........702 J14
bvd. S Geelong..........702 J14
ct. Sunbury..........143 H6
pl. Melbourne..........2 G11
pl. Melbourne..........24 E5
st. Melbourne..........1 A4
st. Melbourne..........2 C4
st. Melbourne..........23 A8
st. W Melbourne..........1 A4
tce. Belmont..........702 K19
tce. Geelong..........702 K19
tce. Geelong West..........702 K19
tce. Newtown..........702 K19
tce. S Geelong..........702 K19
LATROBE
av. Alphington..........327 H20
av. Alphington..........371 H1
av. Bundoora..........284 C1
av. Portsea..........677 J4
ct. Caulfield S..........455 L8
ct. Craigieburn..........150 G15
ct. Croydon Hills..........335 J14
ct. Rowville..........463 B19
ct. Werribee..........447 G8
ct. Wheelers Hill..........461 B10
dr. Mt Martha..........655 L15
pde. Dromana..........685 F8
rd. Yarrambat..........200 G18
st. Box Hill S..........374 L20
st. Brunswick..........325 K10
st. Bulleen..........329 J10
st. Bulleen..........329 L10
st. Caulfield S..........455 L7
st. Cheltenham..........530 J4
st. Cranbourne..........578 E19
st. Footscray..........367 B7
st. Hughesdale..........457 H13
st. Mentone..........530 J4
st. Mentone..........531 A4
st. Moonee Pnd..........323 K15
st. Newport..........411 B9
st. Windsor..........31 L20
st. Windsor..........414 F11
tce. Taylors Hill..........274 G9
LATROSE
st. Keilor Park..........278 C14
LATS
av. Carrum Downs..........575 E20
LATURNS
ct. Vermont S..........420 L14
ct. Vermont S..........421 A14
LAUBES
rd. Ferny Creek..........465 L1
LAUDER
ct. Gowanbrae..........279 D4
dr. Bundoora..........242 E20
pl. Berwick..........554 F15
LAUDERDALE
rd. Narre Warren..........553 B4
LAUER
st. Doncaster..........331 E20
LAUFFRE
wk. Caroline Spr..........318 B3
LAUGHING WATERS
rd. Eltham..........288 F14
LAUGHLIN
av. Nunawading..........376 F16
LAUGHTON
ct. Altona Mdw..........451 K3
LAUNCHING
wy. Carrum..........573 C7
LAUNDER
st. Hawthorn..........372 A18
LAUNDERS
av. Wonga Park..........291 G18
LAURA
av. Belmont..........705 L1
ct. Bayswater N..........380 G20
ct. Box Hill N..........375 B7
ct. Greensborough..........285 J2
ct. Sunshine N..........321 B10
ct. Whittlesea..........96 E17
dr. Hampton Pk..........552 D11
gr. Avondale Ht..........322 C15
gr. Mt Waverley..........419 G16
la. Mooroolbark..........381 J1
pl. Fitzroy N..........19 A7
rd. Knoxfield..........462 J7
rd. Knoxfield..........463 A6
rd. Wantirna S..........462 J7
st. Aspendale..........546 B3
st. Brunswick..........325 G14
st. Caulfield S..........456 A8
st. Clayton S..........499 A6
st. Fitzroy N..........19 B7
st. Moonee Pnd..........323 L14
st. Tootgarook..........698 B2
LAURAVILLE
av. Werribee..........448 B19
LAUREATE
cl. Sunbury..........143 D4
LAUREL
av. Boronia..........423 K11
av. Doveton..........536 L10
av. Doveton..........537 A10
cr. Campbellfield..........239 F12
cr. Carrum Downs..........574 J20
cr. Carrum Downs..........574 K20
cr. Carrum Downs..........600 J1
ct. Frankston N..........599 K10
ct. Glen Waverley..........460 E11
ct. Hawthorn E..........372 E15
ct. Heidelberg Ht..........284 G19
ct. Maidstone..........366 J3
ct. Olinda..........427 G17
ct. Sunbury..........144 F12
gr. Belgrave..........466 L16
gr.n, Blackburn..........375 H18
gr.s, Blackburn..........375 G20
st. Ashburton..........417 F17
st. Bentleigh E..........456 K20
st. Preston..........283 H17
st. Rye..........696 E6
st. St Albans..........320 H8
st. St Albans..........320 J9
st. Whittlesea..........96 E20
LAUREL BANK
pde. Newtown..........702 H9
LAUREL HILL
dr. Eltham North..........245 H19
LAUREN
cl. Dingley Village..........532 J5
ct. Epping..........198 D15
ct. Frankston S..........627 L15
dr. Hampton Pk..........551 L8
LAURENCE
av. Airport W..........278 J17
gr. Ringwood E..........379 A12
LAURENCIA
ct. Mont Albert..........374 F16
LAURENS
st. N Melbourne..........34 H19
st. Rosebud..........684 H14
st. W Melbourne..........34 H19
st. W Melbourne..........368 K10
LAURENTEN
ct. Langwarrin..........629 B8
LAURI ANN
st. Templstw Lr..........330 D14
LAURICELLA
av. Keilor East..........322 B4
pl. Caroline Spr..........318 A3
LAURIE
av. Sunshine N..........320 L14
av. Sunshine N..........321 A14
av. Tecoma..........466 C13
rd. Doncaster E..........332 D11
rd. Wandin N..........340 D12
st. Doreen..........201 B7
st. Newport..........410 G8
st. Reservoir..........283 H6
st. Yarrambat..........201 B7
LAURINA
cr. Frankston N..........600 C6
ct. Doveton..........536 H8
ct. Hillside..........274 B5
trn. Mill Park..........243 D11
LAURISON
rd. Eltham..........287 D3
LAURISTON
av. Selby..........467 E19
ct. Cheltenham..........496 K17
ct. Mulgrave..........500 B3
ct. Ringwood..........378 F7
dr. Coldstream..........295 E16
dr. Endeavour Hl..........537 L7
wk.n, Sunbury, off Belleview Dr..........143 F16
wk.s, Sunbury, off Belleview Dr..........143 F16
wy. Sunbury..........143 F15
LAURUS
ct. Dandenong N..........501 G17
ct. Narre Warren..........539 D20
LAUTOKA
dr. Wonga Park..........291 J19
LAUTREC
av. Wheelers Hill..........460 K14
ct. Doncaster E..........331 K15
st. Frankston..........628 D9
LAVARACK
st. Melton S..........268 J10
LAVELLE
st. Blackburn S..........420 A1
LAVENDER
ct. Bayswater..........423 C6
ct. Mill Park..........242 D11
ct. Newcomb..........704 C15
la. Carrum Downs..........574 L19
pl. Berwick..........539 H19
pl. Hoppers Csg..........405 C15
st. Ringwood..........378 G14
LAVENDER FARM
rd. Emerald..........509 B9
LAVENDER PARK
rd. Eltham..........287 G17
LAVER
cl. Mulgrave..........500 J4
ct. Mill Park..........242 J4
ct. Wantirna S..........422 D20
st. Kew..........371 C11
LAVEROCK
ct. Taylors Lakes..........275 K7
LAVERTON
st. Williamstown..........411 C16
LAVERY
cl. Mornington..........641 C14
pl. Attwood..........237 C12
LAVIAH
ct. Templestowe..........332 D5
LAVIDGE
rd. Ashwood..........418 E15
st. Hawthorn..........371 H17
LAVINGTON
ct. Craigieburn..........150 B20
LAW
ct. Rowville..........502 K1
ct. S Morang..........243 H2
ct. Sunshine W..........364 H12
st. Blairgowrie..........696 B4
st. Briar Hill..........286 G3
st. Heidelberg Ht..........328 D3
st. S Melbourne..........30 E4
LAWANNA
dr. Templestowe..........331 C12
st. Noble Park N..........501 D15
LAWBOROUGH
av. Parkdale..........531 L10
LAWERENCE
pl. Geelong, off Little Ryrie St..........703 A8
LAWES
st. Hawthorn..........371 F14
LAWFORD
st. Box Hill N..........374 L7
st. Doncaster..........330 J20
LAWLER
la. Coldstream..........295 A9
LAWLESS
dr. Cranbourne N..........578 A7
LAWLEY
st. Reservoir..........282 E2
LAWN
cr. Braybrook..........322 C20
cr. Braybrook..........366 B1
ct. Craigieburn..........150 L20
ct. Frankston..........599 J16
rd. Noble Park..........500 D19
LAWNCLIFFE
ct. Rowville..........503 G1
LAWNHILL
rd. Malvern..........416 A8
LAWRANCE
gr. Portsea..........678 B5
st. Murrumbeena..........457 E6
LAWRENCE
av. Aspendale..........546 E7
av. Sunbury..........142 K4
cr. Noble Park N..........501 E16
ct. Altona North..........409 H3
ct. Bayswater..........423 D2
ct. Bundoora..........242 H20
ct. Cranbourne N..........577 K6
ct. N Warrandyte..........290 A11
ct. The Patch..........467 J4
dr. Berwick..........554 B2
rd. Mt Waverley..........459 F2
rd. Panton Hill..........204 L20
rd. Panton Hill..........205 A20
rd. Pt Lonsdale..........707 G20
st. Ardeer..........320 C20
st. Ardeer..........364 C1
st. Blackburn S..........419 H2
st. Brighton..........454 K18
st. Brunswick..........325 J12
st. Doncaster E..........375 H3
st. Eaglemont..........328 L11
st. Hadfield..........280 K8
st. Kew East..........372 K6
st. Seddon..........367 A11
st. Somerville..........645 B15
LAWRENNY
ct. Toorak..........415 F2
LAWREY
rd. Diamond Ck..........245 L1
st. Frankston..........599 E20
LAWRY
ct. Keilor East..........322 C1
pl. Meadow Ht..........237 K7
st. Northcote..........326 J14
LAWSON
av. Frankston S..........627 E10
cl. Cranbourne..........603 K1
cr. Rosebud..........684 D17
cr. Thomastown..........240 D19
ct. Croydon N..........336 A12
ct. Grovedale..........706 G12
ct. Mornington..........656 G1
ct. Mulgrave..........460 D17
ct. Taylors Lakes..........275 J1
ct. Watsonia N..........243 H20
gr. South Yarra..........32 A4
pde. Heidelberg Ht..........328 F2
pde. Highett..........495 H15
pl. Footscray..........367 F10
rd. Gisborne..........78 F1
rd. Melton S..........268 F11
rd. Merrimu..........222 H11
rd. Mooroolbark..........381 F3
st. Albion..........320 K18
st. Balwyn N..........373 A7
st. Bentleigh..........496 F1
st. Blackburn..........376 A13
st. Brighton East..........495 G3
st. Elwood..........454 B2
st. Essendon..........324 F11
st. Footscray..........367 F10
st. Hampton..........495 G6
st. Hawthorn E..........416 E7
st. Moonee Pnd..........324 F11
st. Oakleigh E..........458 H13
st. Reservoir..........283 C11
st. Sunbury..........143 B14
wy. Endeavour Hl..........537 H4
wy. Endeavour Hl..........537 J4
LAWSONS
ct. Templestowe..........332 B8
rd. Emerald..........469 L20
LAWTON
av. Geelong West..........702 G3
st. Braybrook..........365 H5
LAXDALE
rd. Camberwell..........417 H7
LAYARD
st. Dromana..........685 H7
LAYER
la. Cannons Creek..........648 E8
la. Pearcedale..........648 E8
LAYFIELD
st. Croydon Hills..........335 K12
st. S Melbourne..........30 A5
LAYTON
av. Greensborough..........286 K2
cr. Mt Martha..........656 J8
cr. Newtown..........702 A8
ct. Glen Waverley..........420 F16
pl. Mill Park..........242 E10
LEA
cr. Bundoora..........285 A6
rd. Mulgrave..........500 F3
st. Ferntree Gly..........464 B4
st. Mt Martha..........656 B9
wy. Rosebud..........684 B18
LEABURN
av. Caulfield N..........415 E19
LEACH
av. Box Hill N..........375 C12
st. Briar Hill..........286 H2
st. Briar Hill..........286 H4
LEADER
st. Campbellfield..........194 J18
LEAFIELD
st. Watsonia..........285 C8
LEAGH
ct. Scoresby..........462 J8
LEAH
av. Upwey..........465 L15
ct. Rowville..........503 B3
ct. Rye..........697 K9
ct. Werribee..........448 B14
gr. Carrum Downs..........574 D19
LEAHE
wy. Chirnside Pk..........336 G7
LEAHY
st. Maddingley..........263 C7

LEAKE
ct. Altona Mdw........451 H9
st. Essendon..........323 J4
LEAKES
rd. Laverton N.........407 A7
rd. Plumpton...........228 L17
rd. Rockbank...........270 L14
rd. Tarneit..............405 A5
rd. Truganina..........405 G6
LEAMINGTON
cr. Caulfield E.........456 E4
cr. Glen Waverley....460 J2
st. Reservoir...........282 F8
LEAN
av. Herne Hill...........701 J3
LEANDER
st. Footscray...........366 L7
LEANE
dr. Eltham North......246 B20
dr. Eltham North......288 A2
LEANNA
ct. Cranbourne W....577 K19
LEANNE
cr. Keysborough.....534 C8
ct. Cranbourne.......578 C16
ct. Doncaster E.......332 G6
LEAR
ct. Greensborough..244 B16
LEARMONTH
cr. Sunshine W.......365 B9
ct. Caroline Spr.......318 B7
rd. Carrum Downs...574 B8
rd. Patterson L........574 B8
st. Heidelberg.........328 J4
st. Moonee Pnd......324 A13
st. Queenscliff.........709 A18
st. Sunbury.............142 F12
st. Tullamarine........278 G4
LEARMOUTH
st. Belmont.............706 C4
LEASON
st. Kew East............372 H3
LEATHERS
ct. Altona Mdw........451 H6
LEATHERWOOD
cl. Rowville.............502 D4
cr. Wheelers Hill......460 H14
dr. Hoppers Csg......405 A11
gr. Meadow Ht........193 K17
st. Frankston S........627 K16
LEAVESDON
av. Kealba...............276 L20
LEAWARRA
cr. Doncaster E.......331 K15
dr. Heathmont.........378 K17
pde. Frankston..........627 L3
st. Rye....................697 A5
LEBANON
cr. Mulgrave...........500 B4
st. Dandenong.........536 E8
st. Strathmore.........279 J15
st. Strathmore.........280 B16
LEBER
st. Warrandyte........333 E4
LEBUNYA
cl. Mooroolbark......337 E15
ct. Greensborough..244 C19
LE CATEAU
st. Pascoe Vale S....324 H3
LECHLADE
av. South Yarra..........32 K8
av. South Yarra........414 L4
LECHTE
rd. Mt Waverley.......419 C17
LECKIE
dr. Albanvale...........319 B4
pl. Geelong West.....702 G5
st. Bentleigh............496 F1
LECKY
rd. Officer...............582 E10
rd. Officer S............582 E10
st. Cranbourne........604 G2
LEDBURY
cr. Bundoora...........285 A5
ct. Toorak...............415 K8
LEDDY
st. Forest Hill..........420 J3
LEDGER
av. Fawkner.............281 H7
LEDUC
tce. Narr Warrn S.......552 H6
LEE
av. Mt Waverley.......419 H19
av. Springvale..........500 F6
ct. Heathmont.........378 E18
pde. Mitcham............377 E13
st. Altona North.......365 H20
st. Arthurs Seat.......686 A15
st. Brunswick E........326 C12
st. Carlton N.............18 G6
st. Craigieburn........150 D17
st. Deer Park...........318 J16
st. Fawkner.............281 F10
st. Flemington...........33 L1
st. Frankston...........628 A4
st. Noble Park.........535 C3
st. St Albans...........319 F2
LEE ANDY
ct. Ferntree Gly.......463 G5
LEE-ANDY
ct. Dingley Village...533 B6
LEE ANN
cr. Croydon.............336 G13
LEE-ANN
st. Blackburn S.......420 A5
st. Forest Hill..........420 A5
LEE ANNE
cr. Bundoora...........284 H5
LEECH
ct. Jacana...............237 G16
ct. Nar Warrn N.......538 L10
LEED
st. Dandenong........536 D2
LEEDS
ct. Greenvale...........193 B17
dr. Kilsyth S............381 C14
pl. Campbellfield.....239 H13
rd. Mt Waverley.......419 E17
st. Canterbury.........373 G20
st. Doncaster E........375 J5
st. Footscray...........367 F8
st. Richmond............26 D7
LEEK
st. Yarraville............367 E16
LEEMAK
cr. Berwick..............540 A18
LEENA
ct. Warranwood......335 B16
LEES
ct. Epping...............241 J5
ct. Rosanna.............285 E20
pl. Melbourne............24 H5
rd. Lower Plenty......286 E13
st. McKinnon...........456 A16
st. Northcote...........327 A18
LEESIDE
st. Dandenong N.....501 G19
LEESON
gr. Lalor..................240 H6
pl. Keysborough.....534 C7
LEEWARRA
dr. Glen Waverley....420 G14
LEFERN
ct. Carrum Downs...601 F3
LE FEVRE
st. Sandringham.....495 E17
LEFEVRE
ct. Frankston...........628 C11
st. Spotswood.........366 J20
LE FEY
ct. Glen Waverley....420 L15
LEFLAN
cl. Ringwood N.......378 E4
LEGACY
dr. Mt Martha..........655 H19
LE GALLIENNE
cr. Mulgrave...........460 C16
LEGANA
ct. Endeavour Hl.....537 K5
ct. Patterson L........573 K3
ct. Werribee............446 K13
st. Mt Waverley.......459 C7
st. St Albans...........320 H9
LEGEND
av. Glen Waverley....420 K17
ct. Hallam...............538 B16
ct. Rowville.............503 B8
LEGERWOOD
rd. Nar Warrn N.......538 K10
LEGG
ct. Endeavour Hl.....537 C7
rd. Emerald.............509 E5
rd. Macclesfield.......470 D4
LEGGATT
cr. Mt Martha..........655 E18
st. Melton S............268 H9
LEGGETT
dr. Mt Evelyn...........339 K19
wy. Sorrento............679 F13
LEGGO
pl. Richmond............26 E10
LEGH
st. Reservoir...........282 C4
LEGON
rd. Oakleigh S.........458 E19
st. Port Melb...........412 L6
LE GRAND
cl. Mt Eliza.............642 C1
ct. Wheelers Hill......461 C17
mw. Mt Eliza.............642 D2
LEHEM
av. Oakleigh S.........497 H3
LEHHONG
cl. Rowville.............502 H1
LEHMANN
av. Grovedale..........705 H16
cr. Frankston N.......600 A9
pl. Croydon Hills.....335 J17
LEHMANNS
rd. Wollert...............197 J2
LEICESTER
av. Glen Waverley....459 H5
av. Mt Eliza.............626 B19
cr. Melton...............227 A16
ct. Somerville..........645 C19
ct. Wantirna S.........422 J14
mw. Kensington..........33 E12
pl. Carlton.................18 A17
pl. Wyndham Va.....446 E9
sq. Malvern.............415 K7
sq. Seaholme...........409 H17
sq. Tullamarine........279 A8
st. Balwyn N...........374 B2
st. Carlton.................17 L20
st. Fitzroy..................19 A10
st. Heidelberg Ht.....328 G4
st. Preston..............326 E2
LEICHARDT
cl. Taylors Lakes.....275 K1
cr. Reservoir............282 L2
ct. Mill Park............242 J6
dr. Wyndham Va.....446 F6
st. McCrae..............684 K16
st. Sunbury..............142 L13
LEIGH
cl. Lilydale..............338 K10
ct. Craigieburn........149 L15
ct. Dallas.................238 E12
ct. Doveton..............536 L6
ct. Eltham North......245 G16
ct. Macleod.............285 G11
dr. Pakenham..........559 E20
pl. Richmond............26 C10
rd. Croydon.............380 C7
rd. Highton..............701 D15
st. Footscray...........366 L5
st. Huntingdale........458 E13
st. Mt Waverley.......418 H20
st. Oakleigh S.........497 F5
st. Werribee............447 D10
LEIGHTON
av. Emerald.............509 B4
cr. Deer Park...........318 L11
cr. Fawkner.............239 F20
ct. Frankston...........600 A15
ct. Toorak...............415 C7
rd. Bayswater N.......380 G16
LEILA
cl. St Albans...........320 K7
ct. Bacchus Msh.....222 B12
ct. Endeavour Hl.....537 J3
ct. Thomastown......241 J13
rd. Carnegie............456 D11
rd. Carnegie............456 J12
rd. Murrumbeena....456 J12
rd. Ormond.............456 D11
rd. Warburton.........349 J5
st. Deer Park...........318 K16
st. Essendon...........324 G9
st. Mt Waverley.......418 J20
st. Prahran................32 G18
st. Prahran..............414 J9
LEILANI
ct. Cranbourne W....577 F17
ct. Highton..............701 E10
ct. Keilor Dn............275 L16
ct. Mornington.........641 J17
gr. Thomastown.......240 G17
LEINDAN
ct. Mt Eliza.............626 J18
LEINSTER
gr. Brunswick E.......325 K15
gr. Northcote..........326 D11
gr. Thornbury..........326 D10
st. Ormond.............456 E14
LEISCHA
ct. Greensborough..244 B16
st. Langwarrin.........602 E12
LEISHA
ct. Wonga Park.......291 G14
LEISURE
wy.n,Rosebud...........700 E3
wy.s,Rosebud...........700 E4
LEISURELAND
dr. Langwarrin.........630 B11
LEITCH
st. Ferntree Gly.......464 G3
LEITH
av. Sunshine............365 B5
cr. Hampton E..........495 K11
cr. Port Melb...........412 D4
ct. Endeavour Hl.....503 H18
ct. Frankston...........599 H17
ct. Rye....................697 B14
ct. Sunbury..............144 F11
rd. Macleod.............285 A14
rd. Montrose............382 C9
wk. Macleod.............285 B14
LEITHEAD
st. Brunswick..........325 J10
LE JOHN
st. Rowville.............503 B2
LELAND
st. Altona................408 J18
st. Blairgowrie.........696 D1
LEMAIR
av. Glen Waverley....420 A18
LEMAL
av. Boronia..............423 D13
LEMAN
cr. Noble Park.........500 L20
LEMANA
cr. Mt Waverley.......459 G5
ct. Mornington.........641 C16
LE MANS
ct. Doncaster...........330 D15
LEMCO
wk. Delahey..............275 C15
LEMINS
rd. Waurn Ponds.....705 A16
LEMMING
pl. N Melbourne........17 B10
LEMMON
av. Keilor East..........278 B17
st. Williamstn N......411 A13
LEMNIAN
ct. Langwarrin..........629 F8
LEMNOS
av. Pascoe Vale S....324 H3
st. Croydon.............379 L5
LEMON
gr. Bayswater..........423 D5
gr. Mt Waverley.......459 H4
gr. Nunawading.......376 K10
rd. Balwyn N...........374 B3
LEMONGROVE
cr. Croydon Hills.....335 E17
LEMONGUM
rd. Yellingbo............387 K20
LEMONT
av. Mt Waverley.......459 F7
st. Endeavour Hl.....537 J11
LEMPRIERE
av. Mt Martha..........655 E18
av. St Kilda E..........414 L19
av. St Kilda E..........415 A19
cl. Templestowe.....331 D3
ct. Altona Mdw........451 G6
LENA
ct. Berwick..............554 D20
ct. Hoppers Csg......447 L3
ct. Thomastown......240 K15
gr. Kilsyth...............380 L9
gr. Ringwood..........378 J14
pl. Carrum Downs...601 F4
st. View Bank..........285 H20
LENARO
st. Dandenong S.....535 J14
LENDOR
ct. Cheltenham........497 H20
LENHAM
cl. Ferntree Gly.......463 G3
LENKUNYA
ct. Eltham North......245 E18
LENNA
ct. Chadstone..........458 D2
st. Burwood E..........419 D10
LENNE
ct. Camberwell........417 F4
rd. Beaconsfld Up....542 F11
LENNON
av. Flemington.........323 K20
cct. Nar Warrn S.......578 J3
st. W Melbourne.......33 L16
st. W Melbourne.....368 F8
LENNOX
av. Glen Waverley....421 A19
cr. Bundoora...........242 E19
ct. Scoresby............462 C9
gr. Sassafras...........426 G13
st. Hawthorn...........371 G16
st. Moonee Pnd......323 J15
st. Moorabbin.........497 B10
st. Northcote...........326 K15
st. Richmond............26 C16
st. Yarraville............367 D15
LENOAK
st. Gladstone Pk......279 C
LENOLA
st. Macleod.............285 F1
st. Watsonia............285 F1
LENORE
cr. Williamstown.....411 E1
st. Springvale..........500 A
LENS
st. Coburg N...........281 B1
LENTARA
cr. Wyndham Va.....446 H1
ct. Cheltenham........496 A1
LENTELL
av. Sorrento............678 H
LEN THOMAS
pl. Narre Warren.....552 G
LENTINI
pl. Keilor Lodge.......275 L
st. Hoppers Csg......449 K
LENTON
rd. Keysborough.....534 G1
LEO
cl. Wantirna S.........423 A1
pl. Aspendale Gdn...546 E
st. Bentleigh E.........496 L
st. Fawkner.............281 F
LEO FINK
ct. St Kilda E...........414 K1
LEON
av. Rosanna............329 A
av. Rosebud.............684 E1
ct. Donvale.............376 E
ct. Ferntree Gly.......464 D
st. Cheltenham........496 L1
st. Wheelers Hill......461 D1
LEONARD
av. Aspendale..........546 F
av. Berwick..............553 F
av. Glenroy..............280 E
av. Noble Park.........534 J
av. St Albans...........320 G
cl. Clarinda.............498 E
cr. Ascot Vale...........367 H
cr. Bundoora...........243 C2
cr. Eltham...............287 F1
cr. Flemington.........367 H
ct. Doncaster...........330 K1
ct. Pakenham..........585 A
ct. Sorrento............678 J
ct. Vermont S.........420 L
ct. Wandana Ht.......701 C2
dr. Langwarrin.........601 L1
dr. Somerville..........644 K1
rd. Kilsyth...............381 A
rd. Lilydale..............339 G
st. Ashwood............418 F1
st. Balwyn...............373 A1
st. Bayswater..........422 L
st. Bayswater..........423 A
st. Belmont.............702 B1
st. Burwood............418 K1
st. Dandenong.........536 D
st. Fawkner.............281 L
st. Frankston...........599 J1
st. Hampton E.........495 L
st. Heidelberg Ht.....328 F
st. Northcote...........327 C1
st. Parkville...............17 J
st. Preston..............282 H1
st. Ringwood...........378 J
st. Sunshine............321 D2
st. Tootgarook........698 B
st. Upwey...............465 E1
st. Werribee............447 C1
LEONE
pl. Hillside...............232 D1
LEONI
av. Heathmont.........378 J1
LEONIE
av. Bentleigh E.........497 A
av. Mt Waverley.......458 K
ct. Brighton.............455 B1
ct. Narre Warren.....539 D1
LEONINA
ct. Somerville..........644 H1
LEONIS
av. Balwyn N...........329 D1
LEONNE
ct. Hampton Pk.......551 J
LEONOR
ct. Reservoir...........283 J
LEONS
ct. Blackburn..........376 C2
rd. Springvale S.......533 L
LEOPOLD
av. Springvale S.......534 A
cr. Hampton Pk.......551 K1
cr. Mont Albert........374 C1
st. Burwood............418 A1
st. Caulfield S..........456 A1

t. Glen Iris 416 C13
t. Maribyrnong 323 F14
t. Melbourne 31 A11
t. Melbourne 414 A6
t. Preston 282 H18
t. South Yarra 31 F7
t. South Yarra 414 C4
E PAGE
t. Moorabbin 496 C10
EPPITT
d. Beaconsfld Up 557 E3
d. Pakenham 557 E3
EPROSA
l. Endeavour Hl 502 L19
a. Tecoma 466 E8
ERDERDERG
t. Bacchus Msh 222 B16
ERDERDERG GORGE
d. Darley 222 B1
ERDERDERG PARK
d. Merrimu 222 G8
d. Merrimu 223 A10
ERINA
l. Wheelers Hill 461 G16
t. Oakleigh E 458 H16
ERNES
t. Forest Hill 420 J2
EROUX
t. Oakleigh 458 D9
EROY
l. Doncaster E 331 K16
ERWICK
t. Frankston 628 B7
ESA
t. Mt Martha 657 A10
ESAY
t. Mt Waverley 458 H7
t. Rowville 502 K3
r. St Helena 245 E15
ESDEN
t. Bentleigh E 496 H7
ESDON
av. Cranbourne 578 A13
ESLEIGH
st. Fawkner 281 K11
ESLEY
dr. Hampton Pk 552 D13
gr. Noble Park 500 F18
st. Camberwell 417 L7
ESLIE
av. Boronia 424 J14
av. Coburg N 281 B16
ct. Burwood 418 G13
ct. Clayton S 498 G5
ct. Hillside 274 F2
ct. Lower Plenty 286 E12
gr. Brighton 494 G3
gr. Ringwood N 378 F3
rd. Clarinda 498 G12
rd. Essendon 323 L10
rd. Gisborne 80 D11
rd. Laverton N 364 J17
st. Belgrave 466 G11
st. Brunswick 325 E13
st. Bulleen 329 L16
st. Croydon 336 G17
st. Dandenong S 535 F11
st. Donvale 332 G18
st. Elsternwick 455 C4
st. Frankston S 626 K8
st. Hawthorn 372 C20
st. Newport 410 F6
st. Newtown 702 C9
st. Richmond 371 A13
st. St Albans 320 E1
st. St Kilda E 414 J16
st. Thomastown 241 L15
st. Woori Yallock 344 G14
ESNEY
st. Richmond 26 G18
ESPRAY
av. Bentleigh E 496 H3
ESS
la. Coburg 326 A8
ESTER
av. Ringwood E 379 E14
av. St Albans 320 F4
st. Moolap 704 H18
st. Woori Yallock 344 K18
LESTWICK
ri. Wantirna S 421 L15
LETCHWORTH
av. Brighton East 495 H5
pl. Epping 197 K20
pl. Wheelers Hill 461 A7
LETHBRIDGE
st. Moonee Pnd 324 D9
LEUMEAR
st. Oakleigh E 458 J14
LEUNIG
pl. Footscray 367 J7
LEURA
av. Rosanna 285 D19
cr. Rosebud 700 F1
ct. Gladstone Pk 237 E20
ct. Werribee 448 B18
gr. Hawthorn E 416 E3
st. Doncaster E 332 A20
st. Murrumbeena 457 C12
st. Surrey Hills 373 H19
LEVANSWELL
rd. Moorabbin 497 A11
LEVANTO
st. Mentone 531 E7
LEVENDALE
av. Mooroolbark 381 H4
ct. Vermont 421 B6
LEVENIA
st. St Albans 320 B10
LEVER
av. Blairgowrie 679 H20
st. Coburg 325 A5
st. Oakleigh 458 B9
LEVESON
st. N Melbourne 17 D19
LEVIEN
st. Essendon 323 J9
LEVIN
st. Springvale S 534 B1
LEVUKA
st. Seaford 599 E5
LEWANA
st. Rye 697 B6
LEWELLIN
gr. Carrum 573 C9
gr. Rosanna 285 D17
LEWES
dr. Malvern East 456 L1
LEWIN
ct. Altona Mdw 451 G2
st. Carrum Downs 600 L1
st. Deer Park 318 J16
st. Sunbury 143 A15
LEWIS
av. Burnside 318 F10
cl. Mill Park 242 J9
ct. Anglesea 713 D3
ct. Delahey 275 D15
ct. Grovedale 706 F11
ct. Nunawading 376 F17
ct. Richmond 26 F4
ct. Sunshine W 364 J8
gr. Mt Waverley 458 G7
pl. Hoppers Csg 449 B4
rd. Beaconsfld Up 542 L3
rd. Emerald 542 L3
rd. Healesville 258 D5
rd. Montrose 382 G10
rd. N Warrandyte 290 C17
rd. Silvan 384 H5
rd. Wandin East 384 H5
rd. Wantirna S 423 A17
st. Brighton 454 G13
st. Camberwell 417 L6
st. Coburg N 281 F18
st. Darley 221 H7
st. Flemington 33 L3
st. Frankston 599 D18
st. Glenroy 280 A7
st. Kingsville 366 H13
st. Mordialloc 531 K17
st. Mt Waverley 418 K14
st. Ormond 456 D15
st. Pearcedale 646 L4
st. Pearcedale 647 A4
st. Springvale 499 K9
st. Thornbury 326 D8
LEWISHAM
cl. Hampton Pk 552 C8
rd. Windsor 414 J12
rd.n,Prahran 32 H20
rd.n,Prahran 414 K10
LEWIS SPENCER
pl. Croydon Hills 335 G14
LEWISTON
gr. Greenvale 237 G2
LEWTON
rd. Mt Waverley 458 J6
LEX
gr. Oak Park 280 C12
LEXCEN
cl. Berwick 553 K5
cl. Melton 268 H2
LEXHAM
sq. Eltham 288 B8
LEXIA
pl. Mulgrave 459 L16
pl. Waurn Ponds 705 F14
st. Ashburton 417 E16
LEXINGTON
cl. Ferntree Gly 463 L12
ct. Werribee 446 J20
pl. Carrum 573 E11
st. Vermont 420 K5
LEXON
wy. Taylors Lakes 275 F6
LEXTON
av. Dandenong 535 F4
ct. Ringwood N 334 K19
ct. Seaford 573 F14
ct. Vermont S 420 J12
dr. Langwarrin 601 H17
gr. Prahran 415 B13
rd. Box Hill N 375 C11
st. Balwyn N 372 L7
st. Balwyn N 373 A7
st. Coolaroo 238 H6
st. Nar Warrn S 579 G3
LEY
ct. Frankston 600 B16
LEYDEN
av. Portsea 677 L3
st. Brunswick E 325 K16
LEYLAND
rd. Ferntree Gly 463 K5
rd. Mt Waverley 418 H12
st. Croydon 335 H19
LEYTE
cl. Doncaster 331 A16
pde. Heidelberg W 284 C19
LEYTON
ct. St Albans 275 H18
LIA
ct. Yarra Glen 208 L19
ct. Yarra Glen 209 A19
LIAM
cl. Hillside 232 A19
st. Clayton S 499 C4
LIAN
cl. Wheelers Hill 461 C15
LIAPIS
cct. Ravenhall 317 H10
LIARDET
cr. Frankston 628 F2
st. Port Melb 29 A10
st. Port Melb 412 K4
LIAT
wy. Greensborough 285 K8
LIBBETT
av. Clayton S 499 E14
LIBELLA
ct. Carrum Downs 601 C6
LIBERATOR
st. Ashburton 417 J16
LIBERE
ct. Doncaster 331 F20
LIBERTY
av. Rowville 502 J6
ct. Dingley Village 532 L7
ct. St Helena 245 E16
dr. Mill Park 243 E4
pde. Bellfield 327 K7
pde. Heidelberg W 327 L4
pde. Ivanhoe 327 J10
pl. Thomastown 240 E18
LIBNA
st. Carnegie 456 H13
LIBORIA
st. Balwyn 373 H10
LIBRA
cl. Lilydale 338 L7
ct. Templestowe 331 C8
ct. Wantirna S 422 L19
ct. Wantirna S 423 A19
pl. St Albans 275 H18
st. Balwyn N 373 A1
LICENCE
rd. Belgrave Ht 506 F3
rd. Belgrave S 506 F3
LICENSE
rd. Diggers Rest 187 A12
LICHEN
gr. Highton 701 K17
LICHFIELD
av. Jacana 237 J18
LICOLA
ct. Broadmeadows 238 A12
ct. Brookfield 268 D4
ct. Dandenong S 549 D9
st. Vermont S 420 H14
st. Yarrambat 200 E18
LIDDAMORE
cl. Berwick 554 L5
ct. Rowville 503 G1
LIDDELL
ct. Mt Waverley 458 F9
LIDDESDALE
av. Frankston S 626 J4
gr. Eltham North 245 D19
LIDDIARD
st. Hawthorn 372 A15
LIDDICOAT
ct. Taylors Lakes 275 F7
LIDDLE
wy. Vermont 377 L20
wy. Vermont 421 K1
LIDDY
st. Kensington 33 H6
wk. Kensington 33 H6
LIDGATE
av. Rowville 462 F19
LIDGERWOOD
cl. Hoppers Csg 405 E17
LIDGETT
st. Bacchus Msh 221 K16
LIDO
ct. Epping 197 L15
ct. Oakleigh S 497 K8
LIEBER
gr. Carrum Downs 574 E20
LIEGE
av. Noble Park 535 C4
st. Selby 467 D13
LIESBET
cl. Torquay 712 G3
LIESMA
st. Rye 696 L6
LIGAR
st. Dromana 685 K7
st. Sunbury 143 E11
LIGHT
ct. Sunbury 142 L13
ct. Sunbury 143 A13
LIGHT FOOT
st. Burnley 371 C17
LIGHTFOOT
pl. Bundoora 284 E4
st. Mont Albert 374 C12
LIGHTHORSE
cr. Nar Warrn S 578 F1
LIGHTWOOD
cl. Hillside 274 B1
cr. Meadow Ht 193 J20
ct. Berwick 554 K5
ct. S Morang 243 L3
dr. Ferntree Gly 423 G19
dr. Sunbury 143 J6
la. Plenty 244 G12
rd. Noble Park 500 A14
rd. Springvale 500 A14
wk. Yallambie 286 A11
LIGNUM
ct. Templstw Lr 330 L14
LILAC
av. Brooklyn 365 H17
av. Dandenong N 501 G18
cr. Berwick 539 H17
cr. Brighton East 455 E18
ct. Blackburn N 375 H8
ct. Frankston S 627 K5
ct. Mill Park 242 G12
ct. Mt Waverley 419 D14
mw. Gowanbrae 279 C5
ri. Lilydale 338 D14
st. Bayswater 423 C6
st. Bentleigh E 456 J20
LILARDIA
av. Maribyrnong 367 C2
LILEURA
av. Beaumaris 530 F10
LILEY
la. Newport 411 A11
st. Newport 411 A11
LILI
st. Epping 198 B15
LILIAN
ct. Beaumaris 530 H5
ct. Greensborough 244 L14
pde. Eltham 287 K8
pde. Ringwood 379 B3
st. Bulleen 329 L14
st. Glen Waverley 459 K4
st. Upwey 465 K15
LILICUR
rd. Montmorency 286 L7
LILLE
st. Surrey Hills 417 L1
LILLEE
cl. Wantirna S 462 D4
cr. Tullamarine 277 J7
LILLIAN
av. Rye 696 F10
cl. Bayswater N 380 G16
cl. Hampton Pk 551 D10
ct. View Bank 329 J1
st. Brunswick 325 G10
st. Clayton 458 J20
st. Cranbourne 577 K17
st. Glen Iris 417 K12
st. Nunawading 376 D18
st. Pascoe Vale 280 K13
LILLIAS
cr. Nar Warrn S 579 F1
LILLIMUR
av. Heidelberg W 284 C16
rd. Ormond 456 C13
LILLIPUT
la. Edithvale 546 G14
st. Broadmeadows 238 B11
LILLIS
ct. Millgrove 304 F19
ct. Ringwood E 379 C13
ct. Sunshine W 364 F9
LILLY
st. Clifton Hill 20 E5
LILLY PILLY
av. Bundoora 242 F15
av. Doveton 536 L11
av. Doveton 537 A11
LILLYPILLY
cr. Kings Park 275 D17
la. Kilsyth S 425 B3
la. Plenty 244 H11
LILY
av. Mt Evelyn 384 B1
av. Selby 467 E19
dr. Sydenham 275 B7
rd. Lilydale 339 D6
st. Bentleigh 455 J19
st. Braybrook 365 J1
st. Coburg N 281 B14
st. Essendon W 322 K8
st. Fairfield 327 G16
st. Glen Waverley 419 K19
st. Seddon 367 B9
LILYDALE
ct. Thomastown 240 C13
gr. Hawthorn E 372 E17
LILY VALE
cl. Berwick 554 B14
LIM
ct. Mulgrave 501 K6
ct. New Gisborne 79 B1
LIMA
ct. Frankston 600 B18
ct. Westmeadows 237 E12
st. St Albans 320 C10
LIMASSOL
ct. Donvale 332 L10
LIME
av. Balwyn N 374 B4
ct. Bellfield 328 B7
st. Altona 408 K13
st. Whittlesea 96 F19
LIMEBURNERS
rd. E Geelong 703 K10
wy. Portsea 678 C3
LIMERICK
pl. Geelong, off Corio St 703 B7
LIMERWICK
ct. Frankston 628 A5
LIMESTONE
rd. Boneo 699 B20
rd. Fingal 698 D20
rd. Fingal 699 B20
LIMOSA
cl. Frankston 600 E17
ct. Mornington 640 L16
ct. Mornington 641 A16
LIMPOPA
sq. Roxburgh Pk 194 G5
LINACRE
cr. Gladstone Pk 237 E20
cr. Gladstone Pk 279 D1
rd. Hampton 495 A10
st. Watsonia 285 C7
LINCKENS
cr. Balwyn 373 H10
LINCOLN
av. Bayswater 422 J5
av. Coburg N 281 C13
av. Glen Waverley 460 B3
av. Mont Albert N 374 E5
av. Oakleigh 458 B11
av. Point Cook 450 D6
av. Sorrento 678 D8
ct. Ivanhoe 328 D9
ct. Noble Park 534 C2
dr. Bulleen 329 K15
dr. Cheltenham 531 F1
dr. Keilor East 322 D2
dr. Lower Plenty 286 H14
dr. Thomastown 240 K16
mw. Kensington 33 F12
pde. Aspendale 546 E7
pl. Carlton 18 B18
pl. Windsor 414 H11
rd. Croydon 336 C18
rd. Essendon 323 H7

LITTLE LITHGOW
st. Abbotsford...26 F3
LITTLE LONSDALE
st. Melbourne...1 A6
st. Melbourne...2 C6
st. Melbourne...23 F7
LITTLE LOTHIAN
st.n, N Melbourne...17 A16
st.s, N Melbourne...34 L18
LITTLE LYELL
st. S Melbourne...29 D7
LITTLE MALOP
st. Geelong...702 K7
LITTLE MARION
st. Fitzroy...18 L18
LITTLE MARY
st. Spotswood...366 L20
LITTLE MAUD
st. Geelong...703 B11
LITTLE MERCER
st. Geelong, off Mercer St...702 K4
LITTLE MERTON
st. Albert Park...29 H12
LITTLE MILLER
st. Brunswick E...326 A17
LITTLE MORAY
pl. S Melbourne...3 A19
pl. S Melbourne...30 B2
LITTLE MOUNTAIN
st. S Melbourne...29 D8
LITTLE MYERS
st. Geelong...702 K9
LITTLE NAPIER
st. Fitzroy...19 C20
LITTLE NELSON
pl. Williamstown...411 H16
LITTLE NICHOLSON
st. Abbotsford...26 E3
LITTLE O'GRADY
st. Albert Park...29 G13
LITTLE OPIE
st. Ferntree Gly...424 K19
LITTLE OSBORNE
st. Williamstown...411 C17
LITTLE OXFORD
st. Collingwood...19 G19
LITTLE PAGE
st. Albert Park...29 E15
st. Middle Park...29 K18
LITTLE PALMERSTON
st. Carlton...18 F11
LITTLE PARK
st. South Yarra...31 E7
LITTLE PARKER
st. Williamstown...411 G16
LITTLE PELHAM
st. Carlton, off Leicester St...18 A16
LITTLE PESCOTT
st. Newtown...702 F7
LITTLE PRINCES
st. Flemington...34 E1
st. Travancore...324 H20
LITTLE PROVOST
st. N Melbourne...17 A17
LITTLE QUEEN
st. Melbourne...1 G11
st. Melbourne...23 L8
LITTLE QUEENSBERRY
st. Carlton...18 C19
LITTLER
ct. Altona Mdw...451 J3
LITTLE RICHMOND
st. Geelong...703 E12
LITTLE RIVER
st. Whittlesea...96 J19
LITTLE ROSE
st. Richmond...26 G19
LITTLE RUBY
st. Preston...327 C2
LITTLE RYRIE
st. Geelong...702 K8
LITTLE ST VINCENT
st. Albert Park...29 C12
LITTLE SMITH
st. Fitzroy...25 E1
st. Kensington...34 A8
st. Yarraville...367 B13
LITTLE SMYTHE
st. Geelong, off Brougham St...703 A5
LITTLE SWALLOW
st. Port Melb...412 G6
LITTLE TRIBE
st. S Melbourne...29 D9
LITTLE TURNER
st. Abbotsford...20 D14
LITTLE UNION
st. Brighton East...455 C15
LITTLE VALLEY
rd. Templestowe...331 C9
LITTLE VICTORIA
st. Fitzroy...25 C1
LITTLE WALKER
la. Clifton Hill...20 H3
LITTLE WEBB
st. N Melbourne...17 D19
LITTLE WELLINGTON
st. Collingwood...19 H15
LITTLE WILLIAM
st. Melbourne...1 F11
st. Melbourne...23 K8
LITTLE WITHERS
st. Albert Park...29 F13
LITTLEWOOD
st. Hampton...495 A7
LITTLE YARRA
rd. Yarra Jctn...347 D19
LITTLE YORK
st. S Melbourne...29 L2
LITTON
ct. Craigieburn...150 G20
LIVERMORE
cl. Vermont S...421 G7
LIVERPOOL
dr. Keysborough...534 A10
rd. Boronia...425 B6
rd. Kilsyth...381 C7
rd. Kilsyth...381 D14
rd. Kilsyth...425 B6
rd. Kilsyth S...381 D14
rd. The Basin...425 B6
st. Bentleigh E...457 C20
st. Coburg...325 C4
st. Fitzroy N...326 A19
st. Footscray...366 K7
st. Melbourne...24 J4
LIVIANA
dr. Rowville...502 L6
dr. Rowville...503 A6
LIVINGSTON
st. Deer Park...318 K10
st. Highett...496 C12
LIVINGSTONE
cl. Burwood...418 E5
ct. Mt Eliza...626 J16
dr. Greenvale...191 K15
pde. Preston...327 A3
rd. Eltham...287 J6
rd. Malvern East...456 K2
rd. Vermont S...420 J10
sq. Point Cook...450 F9
st. Coburg N...282 A14
st. Ivanhoe...327 K12
LIVONIA
pl. Dandenong N...501 J11
LIVORNO
la. Point Cook...450 E8
LIZA
ct. Glenroy...280 G10
L L
rd. Officer...555 L12
LLANEAST
st. Armadale...415 H14
LLANOS
av. Malvern East...457 K1
LLEWELLYN
av. Aspendale Gdn...547 B6
ct. Cranbourne N...577 L7
ct. Noble Park...535 B4
pl. Eumemmerring...537 A15
st. Beaumaris...530 H4
LLOYD
av. Epping...197 G19
av. Narre Warren...553 D7
av. Reservoir...283 B2
ct. Blackburn S...419 L5
ct. Brookfield...268 B4
ct. Templestowe...332 B14
rd. Research...289 A9
st. Balwyn N...373 E6
st. Belmont...706 G1
st. Deer Park...319 C18
st. Heidelberg Ht...328 D2
st. Kensington...33 L17
st. Knoxfield...463 C5
st. Langwarrin...629 B4
st. Malvern East...416 H19
st. Mont Albert N...374 G11
st. Newport...410 E10
st. Northcote...327 C17
st. Rye...696 J7
st. Strathmore...279 K19
st. W Melbourne...33 L17
st. W Melbourne...368 F8
st.n, Knoxfield...463 C4
LLOYDS
av. Caulfield E...456 D5
pl. Attwood...237 A12
LLOYD WEBBER
dr. Carrum Downs...575 D15
LOATTA
st. Rye...697 B7
LOBATOR
st. Frankston N...600 D8
LOBB
st. Brunswick...325 G13
st. Coburg...325 G1
LOBELIA
ct. Blackburn N...375 H8
ct. Cranbourne N...578 A6
ct. Dingley Village...532 K5
ct. S Morang...243 K1
st. Reservoir...282 B10
LOBOSCO
ct. Kilsyth...425 E1
LOCAN
ct. Altona Mdw...451 F2
LOCARNO
av. Kallista...467 G5
ct. Mulgrave...501 B6
LOCH
av. Monbulk...468 J2
av. St Kilda E...414 L20
av. St Kilda E...415 A20
av. St Kilda E...454 L1
cr. Strathmore...280 A17
ct. Bentleigh E...497 D2
ct. Glen Waverley...460 F11
rd. Dandenong N...502 A15
st. Camberwell...372 K18
st. Coburg...325 F5
st. Cranbourne...578 E19
st. E Geelong...703 F13
st. Ferntree Gly...463 F1
st. Hawthorn E...372 E20
st. Kew...372 B6
st. Kilsyth...381 A5
st. Pt Lonsdale...710 G4
st. St Kilda W...413 L13
st. Surrey Hills...374 E18
st. Yarraville...366 L14
LOCHABAR
ct. Ivanhoe...328 F9
LOCHABER
av. Frankston...628 B7
LOCHALSH
ct. Endeavour Hl...503 H19
LOCH ARD
dr. Williamstn N...410 G12
LOCHARD
dr. Torquay...712 D3
LOCHARN
cr. Keysborough...534 J12
ct. Kealba...276 J17
LOCHER
av. Reservoir...283 F2
LOCH FYNE
ct. Sorrento...679 B14
LOCHGOIN
mw. Highton...701 E11
LOCHIEL
av. Edithvale...546 F10
av. Mt Martha...655 H15
ct. Greenvale...237 C2
LOCHINVAR
rd. Glen Waverley...460 B9
st. Pascoe Vale S...324 L5
LOCHMABEN
ct. Clarinda...498 E8
ct. Greenvale...237 D2
LOCHNORRIES
gr. Reservoir...283 A16
LOCH RAE
ct. Hawthorn...371 J19
LOCHTON
ct. Greenvale...193 B18
LOCINDA
st. Highett...495 L12
LOCK
av. Werribee...447 J19
ct. Sunbury...143 J3
rd. Gisborne S...110 A18
st. Airport W...278 J17
st. Fawkner...281 H8
LOCKE
st. Brighton East...455 D18
st. Essendon...323 K10
st. Rye...696 H4
LOCKENS
av. Glen Waverley...459 K9
LOCKERBIE
ct. Greenvale...193 C20
ct. St Kilda E...415 B18
LOCKEY
av. Arthurs Seat...685 J14
LOCKHART
av. Attwood...237 B11
ct. Hoppers Csg...448 F9
ct. Kilsyth...381 E9
dr. Rosebud...699 K4
rd. Ringwood N...378 D4
st. Camberwell...417 J3
st. Caulfield...455 G4
st. Kensington...33 E10
LOCKHEED
st. Strathmr Ht...279 D10
LOCKIE
pl. Taylors Hill...274 H15
LOCKINGTON
cr. Dandenong...535 H1
cr. Pt Lonsdale...710 B5
LOCKLEY
cl. Endeavour Hl...537 L9
st. Hadfield...280 J5
LOCKS
wy. Belgrave S...506 L5
wy. Belgrave S...507 A5
LOCKSLEY
av. Kew...372 H9
av. Reservoir...282 G13
ch. Vermont...421 C4
cl. Bayswater...423 A9
cl. Dingley Village...533 D10
cl. Heathmont...379 D19
rd. Eaglemont...328 E14
rd. Ivanhoe...328 E14
rd. Ivanhoe...328 E15
rd. Rye...697 H4
LOCKTON
av. Reservoir...282 B1
LOCKWOOD
av. Brighton East...455 D12
dr. Roxburgh Pk...194 B8
gr. Thomastown...240 C12
rd. Belgrave Ht...506 D1
rd. Belgrave Ht...506 F1
rd. Belgrave S...506 E3
st. Bentleigh...496 C5
st. Pt Lonsdale...710 E3
LOCKWOODS
rd. Boronia...424 F6
LOCUM
ct. Wheelers Hill...460 K19
LODDEN
st. Sunshine N...321 D16
LODDON
av. Keilor...276 K13
av. Reservoir...283 G12
cl. Caroline Spr...318 B5
cl. Rowville...463 C17
ct. Clayton S...498 F8
ct. Croydon Hills...335 J15
ct. Thomastown...241 K16
ct. Werribee...447 G8
dr. Taylors Hill...274 J12
st. Box Hill N...375 B10
LODE
ct. Diggers Rest...187 D13
LODERS
rd. Moorooduc...658 G11
LODGE
cl. Rowville...502 H3
cr. Berwick...553 L7
ct. View Bank...285 K19
rd. Camberwell...417 E7
st. Greensborough...286 D9
st. Maddingley...221 K20
st. Noble Park...501 A18
LOEMAN
ct. Burwood E...419 H10
st. Essendon...324 D9
st. Strathmore...280 B19
st. Strathmore...280 C19
LOEMANS
rd. Bulla...189 J19
rd. Bulla...232 L8
rd. Bulla...233 C7
LOFTS
av. Kew...372 B13
LOFTUS
ct. Keysborough...534 D8
st. E Geelong...703 G14
LOFTY
av. Camberwell...417 F5
LOGAN
av. Altona...409 A15
av. Kalorama...382 L15
av. Kalorama...383 A14
av. Ormond...456 G14
av. Pk Orchards...333 L9
av. Warrandyte...333 L9
ct. Mentone...531 F6
ct. Noble Park...535 C3
ct. Sunbury...143 A18
pl. Berwick...553 L1
st. Canterbury...373 E20
st. Frankston...599 J20
st. Glenroy...280 C6
LOGANBERRY
cl. Cranbourne N...577 K4
LOGAN PARK
tr. Lysterfield...504 L20
tr. Nar Warrn N...504 L20
LOGIE
ct. Oakleigh...457 L9
st. Oakleigh...457 J8
LOG SCHOOL
rd. Doncaster...374 G4
LOHSE
st. Laverton...407 D17
LOIS
ct. Bentleigh E...497 D2
ct. Langwarrin...602 A19
ct. Thomastown...240 L15
pl. Mt Eliza...626 B12
st. Ringwood E...379 B11
st. St Albans...276 F19
LOJOSA
ct. Ferntree Gly...423 J19
LOLA
st. Mulgrave...500 H4
LOLLER
st. Brighton...454 L18
st. Springvale...499 L7
LOLLIPOP
dr. Wyndham Va...446 C9
LOLOMA
ct. Glen Iris...417 K11
LOMA
ct. Tootgarook...698 C8
st. Noble Park...500 D19
st. Ringwood E...379 C12
LOMA LINDA
gr. Balwyn N...373 L8
LOMANDRA
ct. Bundoora...242 E14
wy. St Albans...319 F8
LOMAR
ct. Frankston...628 F1
LOMATIA
cl. Frankston S...628 A16
ct. N Warrandyte...289 L18
LOMBARD
ct. Nar Warrn N...538 D7
rd. Vermont...377 J20
wy. Seaford...600 A6
LOMBARDY
av. Dromana...686 G7
LOMIC
ct. Templestowe...332 B4
LOMOND
av. Kilsyth...381 A5
ct. Endeavour Hl...537 L6
ct. Lalor...240 G8
ct. Warrandyte...332 K4
ct. Werribee...446 K13
dr. Glen Waverley...420 J18
st. Glen Iris...416 K9
tce. E Geelong...703 G14
tce. Malvern East...417 F20
tce. Thomson...703 G14
LONDON
cr. Narre Warren...539 B12
cr. Narre Warren...539 B13
ct. Blackburn N...376 A9
ct. Craigieburn...150 B15
ct. Dandenong N...501 G14
ct. Greensborough...286 B10
ct. Hoppers Csg...405 E19
ct. Kurunjang...227 D10
dr. Bayswater...424 A5
la. Mooroolbark...337 L17
rd. Broadmeadows...238 C17
st. Bentleigh...496 D2
LONDON BRIDGE
rd. Portsea...677 D4
LONDREW
av. Springvale S...499 F18
ct. Maribyrnong...323 A12
ct. Tullamarine...278 J1
LONG
dr. Sunbury...142 J3
pl. Hughesdale...457 F15
st. Elsternwick...455 A2
st. Frankston...627 H3
st. Langwarrin...629 C2
st. Mentone...531 F9
st. Reservoir...240 G20
st. Williamstown...411 A15
LONGACRES
rd. Yallambie...285 G16

LONG BEACH
cr. Mt Waverley.......458 K8
LONGBEACH
cl. Aspendale..........546 E3
LONGBOURNE
av. Notting Hill.........459 K13
LONGBRAE
av. Forest Hill..........420 K4
ct. Forest Hill..........420 J6
LONG CRESCENT NORTH
Langwarrin.........628 L11
LONG CRESCENT SOUTH
Langwarrin.........628 L12
LONGFELLOW
av. Mooroolbark......381 G2
dr. Delahey.............275 D16
LONGFIELD
ct. Watsonia N........243 D19
st. Burnley.............371 C17
LONGFORD
cl. Hampton Pk.......551 E4
cr. Coolaroo............238 C6
ct. Kealba................320 L1
ct. Kealba................321 A1
ct. Springvale..........499 J4
LONGFOREST
rd. Long Forest........224 D17
LONG GULLY
rd. Healesville..........212 C17
rd. Panton Hill.........204 J14
rd. Panton Hill.........249 B4
LONGHURST
cr. Hillside..............274 D1
LONG ISLAND POINT
Patterson L.........573 H7
LONGLAND
rd. Mitcham...........377 J14
LONGLEAF
st. Frankston N.......600 B10
LONGMORE
st. St Kilda W..........413 K12
LONGMUIR
rd. Watsonia...........285 G7
LONG POCKITT
la. Belgrave............467 B16
la. Selby.................467 B16
LONGS
rd. Lower Plenty......286 D13
rd. Yellingbo...........388 C5
LONGSTAFF
ct. Doncaster E.......332 E15
ct. Vermont............421 J4
rd. Bayswater..........424 C1
st. Carnegie............456 K13
st. Ivanhoe East......328 L15
st. Kew East............372 G3
wy. Sunbury.............142 G6
LONGTOWN
ct. Craigieburn........194 G3
LONGUEVILLE
la. Grovedale..........706 F12
LONG VALLEY
wy. Doncaster E.......332 G12
wy. Eltham North......288 A1
LONG VIEW
rd. Croydon S..........379 F10
LONGVIEW
av. Bentleigh E.........456 L20
av. Manifold Ht.........702 B5
ct. Thomastown........242 B18
pde. Rosanna............284 J17
rd. Balwyn N............373 D3
rd. Mt Evelyn...........339 J18
st. Pascoe Vale........280 F14
LONGWOOD
av. St Albans...........319 G8
ct. Meadow Ht..........238 C3
dr. Epping...............198 E15
dr. Epping...............198 G17
LONHILL
ct. Endeavour Hl......537 K10
LONIE
st. N Melbourne........34 H6
LONSDALE
av. Hampton E.........495 K7
av. Rowville.............463 E18
cct. Hoppers Csg......449 B4
cr. Cranbourne N.....577 K10
la. Melbourne............1 G7
la. Melbourne...........23 K6
pl. Sunbury.............142 L18
pl. Sunbury.............143 A18
st. Bulleen..............329 L11
st. Caulfield S..........456 A7
st. Coburg...............281 C20
st. Dandenong.........536 A8
st. Geelong.............703 B12
st. McCrae..............684 J13
st. Melbourne.............1 A8
st. Melbourne.............2 C8
st. Melbourne...........23 F8
st. Pt Lonsdale........710 F7
st. Rosebud............684 J13
st. S Geelong..........703 A12
LONSDALE PARK
la. Launching Pl......344 J4
LOOKER
rd. Montmorency....286 K13
st. Murrumbeena....457 C6
LOOKOUT
rd. Kalorama...........383 D8
rd. Red Hill..............687 D16
LOOKOVER
rd. Donvale............377 H4
LOOMAI
cl. Greensborough..244 D20
LOONGANA
av. Glenroy.............279 G7
st. Rye....................697 B7
LOOP
rd. Werribee...........487 J1
LOOREA
ct. Greensborough..244 C15
LORAC
av. Brighton............454 G13
ct. Sydenham.........274 K3
LORACK
cl. Mulgrave...........500 J2
LORAINE
av. Box Hill N...........374 H7
LORAM
ct. Blackburn S.......419 L5
ct. Glen Waverley....420 G19
LORANNE
st. Bentleigh...........496 A1
LORD
av. Dingley Village...533 B7
pl. Braybrook..........365 L3
pl. Braybrook..........366 A4
pl. Richmond............26 L13
rd. Gruyere.............342 K6
st. Bacchus Msh.....222 C18
st. Brunswick E.......325 L15
st. Caulfield E.........456 D4
st. Doncaster E.......375 H2
st. Fawkner.............281 E2
st. McKinnon..........456 G16
st. Richmond............26 K17
st. Richmond...........371 A16
LORDING
st. Ferntree Gly.......424 G18
LORD RODNEY
dr. Patterson L........547 H19
wy. Patterson L........547 G19
LORDS
ri. Berwick..............554 D19
LORD SOMERS
rd. Ferny Creek.......425 E18
rd. Tremont.............425 E18
LORD WEAVER
gr. Bonbeach..........545 E14
LOREEN
st. Oakleigh S..........457 J16
LORENA
cl. Hoppers Csg......447 L3
LORENSEN
av. Coburg N...........281 E13
LORENZ
st. Sunshine...........321 F20
LORENZO
wy. Aspendale Gdn...547 A5
LORETTA
av. Wheelers Hill.....461 E13
ct. Seabrook...........450 J5
pl. Sunshine W........364 B9
st. Carrum Downs...601 D5
LORETTAS
wy. Anglesea............713 G4
LORETTO
av. Ferntree Gly.......423 G17
st. Cremorne............26 A17
LORGROVE
ct. Avondale Ht.......322 E11
LORICA
av. Broadmeadows..238 A19
LORIENNE
st. Heathmont.........378 E18
LORIKEET
cr. Whittlesea............96 B20
cr. Whittlesea..........126 B1
ct. Boronia..............424 A11
ct. Diamond Ck........245 D12
ct. Frankston...........628 C5
ct. Mornington.........640 K16
ct. Werribee............447 K6
st. Nunawading.......376 J18
LORIMER
rd. Kangaroo Grnd...246 H15
rd. Wattle Glen........247 B10
st. Greensborough..285 K3
st. Melton...............268 G2
st. Port Melb...........367 H19
st. Port Melb...........411 G4
st. Southbank...........23 A17
st. Southbank..........368 F17
LORINDA
cl. Sydenham.........274 J5
LORIS
dr. Grovedale..........706 E14
st. Blackburn..........375 G20
st. Silvan................384 E13
st. Springvale S.......533 L2
LORMER
st. Yarraville...........367 C18
LORNA
av. Northcote...........327 C14
cr. Sunshine W.......364 B3
ct. Aspendale Gdn...546 K6
ct. Mooroolbark.......337 H16
ct. Templstw Lr.......330 J10
ct. The Basin...........425 A10
pl. Melton W...........225 L17
st. Bacchus Msh.....222 A13
st. Cheltenham.......497 C20
st. Clematis............508 K4
st. Cranbourne........604 C3
st. Seaford.............599 H9
LORNE
gr. Camberwell........372 L19
pde. Mont Albert.......374 C16
rd. Hawthorn E........372 F17
rd. Prahran..............415 A10
st. Caulfield E.........456 E3
st. Fawkner.............281 G10
st. Lalor..................241 G11
st. Melbourne...........31 D19
st. Melbourne..........414 B10
st. Moonee Pnd......324 A15
st. Yarraville...........366 L18
LORRAINE
av. Langwarrin.........601 C20
av. Warrandyte........333 F3
cr. Jacana..............237 G16
ct. Hampton.............494 J6
ct. Hampton Pk.......551 E10
ct. Pakenham..........585 D7
ct. Sunshine...........364 K2
ct. Warranwood......334 H13
ct. Wheelers Hill......460 K17
dr. Briar Hill............286 K6
dr. Burwood E.........419 G8
pde. View Bank........285 G20
pl. Bacchus Msh.....222 B14
st. Boronia.............424 G8
st. Cheltenham.......531 B4
st. Dandenong........535 F5
st. Essendon..........323 K9
st. Frankston...........599 F16
st. Hampton.............494 J6
LORRAINE LEE
wy. Sydenham.........275 B8
LORREAN
av. Brighton East.....455 G13
LORRIMORE
ct. Mt Eliza..............642 J1
LOS ANGELES
ct. Ripponlea..........414 G20
LOSSI
ct. Keilor Lodge.......276 B3
LOTHAIR
st. Pascoe Vale S....324 H6
LOTHIAN
st. N Melbourne........34 L20
st. W Melbourne.......34 L20
LOTIS
ct. Keilor Dn...........276 B16
LOTRIEL
ct. Mt Martha...........655 J13
LOTUS
cr. Deer Park...........319 G10
cr. Mulgrave............500 H4
cr. St Albans...........319 G10
ct. Cheltenham.........531 F2
ct. Diamond Ck........245 L6
ct. Epping...............197 K15
ct. Meadow Ht.........237 J1
ct. Wantirna............422 F6
LOUDEN
pl. Melbourne.............2 E10
pl. Melbourne...........24 D6
LOUDON
rd. Burwood............418 A8
LOUGHIES
tr. Ringwood N.......378 A4
LOUGHNAN
rd. Ringwood..........377 L10
rd. Ringwood N.......377 L10
st. Richmond............26 A13
LOUIS
av. Dandenong........536 D2
av. Warburton.........305 L19
ct. Newtown............701 L8
st. Airport W...........279 A12
st. Doveton.............537 A8
st. Glen Iris.............416 E15
st. Greensborough..286 B7
st. Heathmont.........379 D19
st. Reservoir...........282 J7
wy. Sunbury.............143 H6
LOUISA
ct. Narre Warren.....539 B16
ct. Oakleigh S..........497 G7
pl. Templestowe.......331 L8
st. Brunswick..........325 G12
st. Coburg..............325 G3
st. Croydon.............380 J5
st. Kilsyth...............380 J5
st. Mt Evelyn...........339 C17
LOUIS BUVELOT
wyn.Diamond Ck.......245 A13
LOUISE
av. Mont Albert........374 D17
ct. Doncaster...........330 B20
ct. Glen Waverley....419 L17
ct. Hallam...............538 B14
ct. Rowville.............463 L17
ct. Seaford.............599 K2
ct. Skye.................575 G18
ct. Springvale S.......499 F20
st. Brighton East.....455 F13
st. Clifton Hill...........20 H7
st. Heidelberg.........329 C5
st. Lalor..................241 G9
st. Melbourne...........31 B13
st. Melbourne..........414 A7
st. Rye...................696 H6
LOUISE BAILLE
av. Nar Warrn S.......553 G20
LOUISE MACK
wk. Lynbrook...........551 E19
LOUISVILLE
av. Pascoe Vale S....324 H6
LOUPIE
st. Mooroolbark......381 H3
LOURIE
ct. Ringwood..........377 L10
LOUVAIN
st. Coburg N...........281 B17
LOVAT
ct. Coolaroo............238 E3
pl. Melton...............268 L2
LOVE
cl. Maddingley.........264 C3
st. Black Rock.........529 E1
st. Camberwell.........417 D7
st. Yarraville...........366 J18
LOVELACE
st. Preston.............327 D2
LOVELL
cl. Rowville.............463 J15
ct. Whittington........704 C20
dr. St Albans...........320 E13
st. Hawthorn E........416 E6
LOVELY
st. Fawkner.............281 E3
LOVERIDGE
wk. Berwick.............554 E7
LOVETT
dr. Avondale Ht.......322 G8
LOVITT
cl. Diamond Ck.......246 E9
LOWALDE
dr. Epping...............197 L19
LOWAN
av. Templstw Lr.......329 L8
av. Yallambie...........286 D11
ct. Dallas................238 D12
ct. Ferntree Gly.......463 G10
ct. Frankston...........600 D16
ct. Werribee............446 K15
st. Brunswick E.......326 C15
LOWANA
cr. Forest Hill..........420 E6
LOWDEN
ct. Nar Warrn S.......552 H19
LOWE
av. Altona...............408 L15
cr. Sunshine...........365 H3
ct. Bayswater N......379 G16
ct. Doncaster E.......375 H2
st. Ivanhoe.............328 B12
st. Mt Eliza..............642 K1
LOWELL
av. Kingsbury..........283 J11
LOWEN
av. Heathmont.........378 J20
rd. Cockatoo...........510 K9
rd. Glen Waverley....419 L16
LOWENPARK
dr. Hoppers Csg......449 G2
LOWER
cr. Mt Eliza..............642 F6
ct. Nunawading.......376 L19
ct. Nunawading.......377 A19
dr. Kew...................371 H5
esp. St Kilda............414 A17
la. Melbourne...........25 B20
rd. Eltham North......287 H1
rd. Wattle Glen........246 J4
LOWER DANDENONG
rd. Braeside............531 H8
rd. Dingley Village...531 H8
rd. Mentone............531 H8
rd. Moorabbin Aprt..531 H8
rd. Mordialloc..........531 H8
rd. Parkdale............531 H8
LOWER GRIEVE
rd. Avonsleigh.........470 F20
LOWER HEIDELBERG
rd. Eaglemont..........328 J14
rd. Ivanhoe.............328 C14
rd. Ivanhoe East......328 C14
rd. Ivanhoe East......328 J14
st. Heidelberg.........328 J14
LOWER HOMESTEAD
rd. Chirnside Pk.......292 B15
rd. Chirnside Pk.......292 D14
rd. Wonga Park.......292 B15
rd. Wonga Park.......292 D14
LOWER PAPER MILLS
rd. Fyansford...........701 D6
LOWER PLENTY
rd. Heidelberg.........328 H3
rd. Rosanna............328 H3
rd. View Bank..........285 J15
LOWER SOMERVILLE
rd. Baxter................645 E6
rd. Somerville..........645 H14
LOWER TERRACE
cr. Noble Park N......501 C13
LOWER VIEW
rd. Montrose...........382 B15
rd. Mt Dandenong...382 B15
LOWES
rd. Chum Creek.......213 D8
rd. Healesville..........213 D8
rd. Yarra Jctn..........347 D14
LOWESS
la. Point Cook.........451 B7
LOWRY
ct. Nar Warrn N.......539 C11
LOWSON
st. Fawkner.............281 F2
LOWTHER
ct. Cranbourne N.....578 D10
st. Alphington.........327 H18
LOXFORD
ct. Nar Warrn S.......552 H18
LOXLEY
bvd. Nar Warrn S.......553 D15
ct. Doncaster E.......331 H15
ct. Hoppers Csg......405 A17
LOXTON
av. Wantirna S.........462 C2
st. Kew...................372 J14
tce. Epping...............198 H16
tce. S Morang...........198 H16
LOXWOOD
av. Keysborough.....534 B10
LOYOLA
av. Brunswick..........325 J15
ct. Watsonia...........285 E4
gr. Burnley..............371 C20
rd. Werribee............448 A19
LUAIN
av. Oakleigh S..........497 H2
LUANA
la. Sunbury.............143 F16
LUANDA
st. Keysborough.....534 J13
LUBBROOK
cl. Ferntree Gly.......463 G8
LUBECK
ct. Meadow Ht.........238 A6
LUBEL
st. Anglesea............713 K1
LUBRANO
st. Brighton East.....455 F14
LUBY
ct. Melton...............268 G2
LUCALBYN
ct. Wandana Ht.......701 D18

LUCAN
ct. Sunbury 143 A2
st. Caulfield N 415 C15
LUCANIA
cl. Ringwood E 379 F17
LUCAS
av. Kilsyth 381 B12
cl. Boronia 424 E7
cr. Seaford 599 K1
ct. Nar Warrn S 552 G14
ct. Noble Park 500 L16
ct. Sunshine W 364 F8
pl. Tullamarine 278 K3
st. Brighton East 495 B2
st. Caulfield S 455 E11
st. Newcomb 704 C14
st. Reservoir 282 E15
LUCERNE
av. Mornington 640 K14
cr. Alphington 371 K1
cr. Frankston 628 G1
ct. Narre Warren 538 L20
rd. Ferntree Gly 463 F8
st. Ashburton 417 E18
st. Campbellfield 239 F14
st. Mentone 531 C10
st. Mt Waverley 419 J13
st. Vermont 421 E4
LUCETTA
wy. Sydenham 275 C7
LUCIA
ct. Carrum Downs 601 D3
st. Blackburn S 419 G5
LUCIAN
av. Springvale 500 A9
LUCIEER
ct. Templestowe 331 H9
LUCIELLA
ct. Dandenong N 502 C18
LUCIEN
rd. Rye 696 L3
LUCIFER
st. Balwyn N 373 G1
LUCILIA
pl. Bundoora 242 K15
LUCILLE
av. Croydon S 379 G11
av. Reservoir 283 E3
LUCINDA
cl. Heathmont 379 D18
ct. Warranwood 335 C14
LUCK
st. Eltham 287 H7
LUCKIE
st. Nunawading 376 D13
LUCKINS
rd. Bentleigh 496 E5
LUCKNOW
ct. Mitcham 377 A17
st. Mitcham 377 A17
st. Travancore 324 G18
LUCY
cl. Rowville 463 H15
ct. Bundoora 242 F20
ct. Narre Warren 539 B13
pl. Ringwood N 334 H20
st. Gardenvale 455 B10
wy. E Geelong 703 K5
LUCY HILL
ri. Rowville 503 D4
LUDBROOK
av. Caulfield S 455 D11
LUDEMAN
ct. Reservoir 282 H2
LUDLOW
ct. Officer 555 J19
LUDSTONE
st. Hampton 495 B6
LUDWELL
cr. Bentleigh E 497 D2
LUDWIG
st. Springvale S 534 A1
LUENA
rd. Balwyn N 374 B8
LUGANO
av. Dromana 686 H5
st. Lalor 240 D9
LUGARNO
ct. Keysborough 534 E7
LUGG
st. Altona 408 L13
LUGO
ct. Tullamarine 278 E5
LUGTON
st. Alphington 371 H1
LUISA
av. Dandenong S 549 H11
ct. Brookfield 268 C4
ct. Montmorency 286 L9
LUKE
av. Blackburn 376 D13
ct. Frankston S 627 K12
ct. Hampton Pk 551 D11
ct. Keysborough 534 B7
ct. Mill Park 243 A3
pl. Guys Hill 541 H20
st. Clayton 459 B20
st. Reservoir 282 E7
LUKIN
ct. Mill Park 242 B8
LULIE
st. Abbotsford 20 C14
LULWORTH
pl. Frankston 600 H17
st. Blackburn N 376 B10
LULY
st. Altona North 409 J6
LUM
rd. Wheelers Hill 460 J16
rd. Wheelers Hill 460 J19
rd. Wheelers Hill 460 K11
LUME
ct. Noble Park 535 A3
LUMEA
pl. Melton W 225 L15
LUMEAH
av. Olinda 426 J10
cr. Ferntree Gly 463 G7
ct. Dingley Village 533 A2
rd. Caulfield N 455 D2
LUMLEAH
ct. Greensborough 286 D10
LUMLEY
ct. Prahran 414 L12
LUNAN
pl. Frankston S 627 G12
LUNAR
cr. Vermont 421 D4
LUND
ct. Highton 705 J3
LUNE
ct. Torquay 712 B3
LUNETTE
av. Preston 282 L17
LUNIK
ct. Whittington 704 B20
LUNN
ct. Altona Mdw 406 L20
ct. Narre Warren 539 B18
LUNTAR
rd. Oakleigh S 497 H4
LUPIN
ct. Cranbourne N 578 A4
ct. St Albans 320 G8
st. Blackburn N 375 J8
st. Dromana 686 F8
LUPTON
st. Geelong West 702 F6
LURG
av. Sunshine N 320 L13
LURLINE
st. Bundoora 284 E4
st. Cranbourne 604 B3
LURNEA
rd. Glen Iris 417 B14
LUSATIA PARK
rd. Woori Yallock 345 A19
LUSCANDER
ct. Hillside 232 E19
LUSCOMBE
av. Carrum Downs 574 L16
ct. Kilsyth 381 C9
st. Brunswick 325 J17
LUSH
ct. Altona Mdw 451 C1
la. Melbourne 2 H17
la. Melbourne 24 G8
LUSHER
rd. Croydon 379 L9
LUSK
dr. Vermont 421 F3
LUTANA
ct. Frankston 628 C4
ct. Mooroolbark 381 J4
ct. Mt Martha 656 E5
ct. Wheelers Hill 461 C18
st. Rosebud W 699 E2
LUTEA
ct. Mill Park 243 D7
LUTHER
av. Grovedale 706 G11
pl. Frankston 600 J18
st. Box Hill N 375 D7
LUTON
av. Red Hill 687 F10
cl. Epping 198 A18
ct. Croydon 335 G18
ct. Darley 222 C10
ct. Doncaster E 332 E8
ct. Kealba 276 L20
ct. Keysborough 534 D8
ct. Rowville 462 F20
la. Hawthorn 371 L17
pl. Clayton S 499 E10
wy. Bundoora 284 K1
LUXFORD
ct. Springvale 499 K15
st. St Albans 276 G20
LUXMOORE
st. Cheltenham 496 E18
LUXTON
rd. South Yarra 32 J14
rd. South Yarra 414 K7
tce. Seaford 573 D18
LUZON
ct. Lalor 241 H6
LYALA
ct. Endeavour Hl 504 C20
LYALL
cl. Dandenong N 501 F12
dr. Werribee 446 L19
dr. Werribee 447 A19
rd. Berwick 554 E7
st. Cranbourne 604 E3
st. Hawthorn 372 B19
st. St Albans 320 D5
st. Tooradin 651 H9
LYDD
ct. Craigieburn 194 D1
LYDFORD
ct. Diamond Ck 245 L8
ct. Werribee 446 K13
rd. Ferntree Gly 463 K3
LYDGATE
st. Blairgowrie 696 B2
LYDHURST
ct. Hoppers Csg 405 A17
LYDIA
av. Campbellfield 239 A10
ct. Balwyn 373 B12
ct. Forest Hill 420 A6
ct. Torquay 712 D4
ct. Wantirna S 422 E19
st. Bentleigh 456 F20
st. Brunswick 325 G15
LYDIA MARY
dr. Berwick 553 K5
LYDSON
st. Murrumbeena 457 D9
LYELL
av. Lalor 241 L10
pde. Greensborough 285 L6
pl. Taylors Lakes 275 E1
rd. Boronia 423 E13
st. Gisborne 78 J12
st. St Kilda 414 D16
st. S Melbourne 29 E7
st. S Melbourne 413 C4
st. Yarraville 367 F17
wk. Forest Hill 420 D2
LYGON
la. Carlton 18 E15
st. Brunswick E 325 K16
st. Carlton 2 K1
st. Carlton 24 D1
st. Carlton N 18 F10
st. Caulfield S 455 H11
st. Coburg 325 K8
tce. Carlton 18 E15
LYKING
st. Pascoe Vale 281 A17
LYLE
av. Beaconsfield 555 C15
gr. Aspendale 546 C4
rd. Sassafras 426 J13
st. Bacchus Msh 221 K15
st. Brunswick 325 D12
st. Noble Park 500 H18
LYME
ct. Rosebud W 698 L4
LYN
ct. Ringwood N 378 A5
ct. Somerville 645 C15
st. Greensborough 286 A11
st. Yallambie 286 A11
LYNBIE
ct. Rosebud W 699 E6
LYNBROOK
bvd. Lynbrook 551 D18
bvd. Lynbrook 551 F17
LYNCH
cl. Epping 197 J19
cr. Brighton 494 K1
ct. Altona Mdw 451 C3
ct. Balwyn 373 C8
ct. Mt Martha 656 C15
pl. Melbourne 2 D10
pl. Melbourne 24 C6
pl. Roxburgh Pk 194 D12
rd. Brooklyn 365 F19
rd. Fawkner 281 F8
st. Brighton 494 K3
st. Footscray 367 F6
st. Hawthorn 371 J16
st. Sunshine 321 D20
LYNDA
cl. Cheltenham 496 J13
ct. Aspendale Gdn 546 H4
ct. Doncaster E 332 H7
LYNDAL
cl. Doncaster E 332 G7
ct. Berwick 553 K16
LYNDALE
ct. Dandenong N 501 F14
ct. Ferntree Gly 464 F6
ct. Oakleigh S 498 B6
LYNDALL
cl. Hoppers Csg 448 G5
rd. Belgrave S 506 K4
LYNDEN
gr. Mt Waverley 418 G14
st. Camberwell 417 G6
LYNDFORD
ct. St Albans 275 H20
LYNDHURST
cr. Box Hill N 375 B5
cr. Brunswick E 326 A10
cr. Hawthorn 372 C15
ct. Langwarrin 629 B8
rd. Gladstone Pk 236 L16
rd. Gladstone Pk 237 A16
st. Richmond 26 H13
LYNDOCH
st. Box Hill S 418 H3
LYNDON
dr. Rosebud 699 K2
rd. Boronia 424 J8
st. Lalor 241 A8
st. Ripponlea 454 J2
LYNE
gr. Brunswick W 324 J7
st. Tooradin 651 F6
LYNEDOCH
av. St Kilda E 415 A17
LYNES
rd. Tooradin 650 K1
rd. Tooradin 651 D1
LYNETTE
av. Beaumaris 529 L8
av. Warrandyte 333 D2
cr. Lalor 240 K4
cr. Watsonia 285 C9
ct. Berwick 554 J20
ct. Mulgrave 500 G4
ct. Noble Park 535 A3
st. Boronia 424 H8
st. Nunawading 376 F10
LYNIAN
ct. Clarinda 498 C6
ct. Ferntree Gly 463 H6
LYNN
dr. Ferntree Gly 463 L4
mw. Sunbury 142 H4
st. Coburg 281 J20
st. Coburg 325 K1
st. Mt Waverley 418 H11
st. St Albans 320 F5
st. Sassafras 426 J15
st. Seaford 573 E17
st. Warrandyte 290 D16
LYNNBRAE
av. Hurstbridge 202 L18
av. Hurstbridge 203 A18
LYNNE
av. Wantirna S 422 J17
ct. Balwyn N 373 L2
ct. Hallam 537 H15
ct. Langwarrin 601 K18
ct. Nunawading 376 G11
ct. Taylors Lakes 275 F6
st. Chelsea Ht 547 H16
st. Donvale 376 E4
st. Lalor 241 J11
LYNNWOOD
pde. Templstw Lr 330 J12
LYNOTT
st. St Kilda 414 F17
LYNTON
ct. Balwyn N 374 C4
st. Scoresby 462 F9
LYNWAY
ct. Bayswater 423 D8
LYNWOOD
av. Olinda 427 G19
av. Ringwood E 379 C14
cr. Lower Plenty 286 J15
LYNX
av. Roxburgh Pk 194 F9
LYON
rd. View Bank 285 F19
st. Coburg N 281 C15
st. Essendon 323 G7
st. Rosebud 684 G16
LYONES
pde. Up Fntree Gly 465 A6
LYONS
av. Frankston S 627 A6
ct. Dandenong N 501 K19
ct. Mentone 531 F7
ct. Sunbury 143 G3
dr. Selby 467 B15
pl. Doncaster E 332 K12
rd. Croydon N 336 D11
ri. Eltham 288 F4
st. Bentleigh E 457 E18
st. Carnegie 456 E9
st. Cranbourne 604 E1
st. Footscray 367 F12
st. Glenroy 280 H3
st. Maidstone 366 K3
st. Mt Waverley 419 G18
st. Port Melb 29 A8
st. Port Melb 412 L5
st. Rye 697 F4
st. Seddon 367 F12
st. Westmeadows 237 F15
st. Williamstown 411 E15
LYONSVILLE
av. Preston 283 E20
LYPPARDS
rd. Langwarrin 602 E15
LYRE
ct. Gladstone Pk 279 C3
LYREBIRD
ct. Boronia 424 B10
ct. Taylors Lakes 275 H3
ct. Vermont S 420 G13
ct. Werribee 448 B6
dr. Carrum Downs 600 J4
gdn. Berwick 539 H19
wk. Whittlesea 126 D1
LYRIC
ct. Glen Waverley 460 C10
ct. The Basin 425 B8
ct. Warranwood 335 C16
gr. Camberwell 417 A4
LYSANDER
ct. Chelsea Ht 547 F12
st. Brighton East 495 E1
LYSBETH
st. McKinnon 455 K16
LYSTER
cl. Seaford 599 E11
tr. Lysterfield 504 J8
LYSTERFIELD
rd. Ferntree Gly 464 G6
rd. Ferntree Gly 464 H10
rd. Lysterfield 464 J16
rd. Up Fntree Gly 464 H10
LYSTERFIELD HILLS
tr. Lysterfield 503 J10
LYSTERVILLE
av. Malvern 416 B16
LYTHAM
ct. Frankston 599 J16
ct. Greenvale 192 J16
ct. Langwarrin 629 H1
ct. Sunbury 144 E13
LYTTLE
av. Essendon 324 D4
LYTTON
st. Burwood 418 E11
st. Carlton 18 D9
st. Elwood 454 B2
st. Glenroy 279 H7
st. Kew 372 E12

M

MABEL
st. Camberwell 417 J3
st. Ivanhoe 327 J10
MABEN
pl. Armadale 415 G14
MABERLEY
cr. Frankston S 627 F17
MAC
cr. Parkdale 531 J14
McADAM
sq. Croydon 335 H18
McAFEE
ct. Dandenong N 501 J9
MACALISTER
ct. Keilor 276 L12
ct. Meadow Ht 194 A18
ct. Werribee 447 F7

McALISTER
st. Frankston...599 F18
McALLISTER
mw. Kensington...33 D9
rd. Monbulk...428 F17
rd. Monbulk...428 H15
McALPIN
st. Tootgarook...698 G2
McALPINE
ct. Altona...408 L16
ct. Dandenong...536 C1
la. Kew...372 A8
MACAO
ct. Cheltenham...497 E20
McARDLE
st. Dingley Village...533 C10
McAREE
ct. Altona Mdw...451 G5
MACARTHUR
ct. Mill Park...242 L6
ct. Mill Park...243 A6
dr. Cranbourne...603 K1
pl.n, Carlton...18 H13
pl.s, Carlton...18 H13
rd. Parkville...17 F4
st. E Melbourne...24 L5
McARTHUR
av. St Albans...320 F4
av. Fitzroy N, off Rushall Cr...326 G20
rd. Beaconsfld Up...542 L9
rd. Ivanhoe East...328 J15
rd. Vermont...421 A3
st. Bentleigh...495 K3
st. Dromana...685 J7
st. Malvern...416 B12
st. W Footscray...366 F10
McARTHURS
rd. Altona North...409 F4
rd. S Morang...199 G8
MACARTNEY
av. Kew...372 F13
st. Reservoir...283 A9
MACASSAR
st. Balwyn N...373 B7
MACAULAY
ct. Eltham...287 G10
la. S Geelong...702 J13
rd. Kensington...33 K10
rd. N Melbourne...34 G11
st. Williamstn N...410 C10
MACAULEY
pl. Bayswater...423 H4
McAULEY
dr. Rosanna...285 D20
McBAIN
st. Altona...409 B20
MACBEAN
ct. Greenvale...236 K5
McBEAN
st. Clayton...498 F1
MACBETH
st. Braeside...532 H16
McBRIDE
cr. Seaford...599 L1
rd. Beaconsfld Up...542 E16
st. Bacchus Msh...221 K17
st. Cockatoo...511 A4
McBRYDE
st. Fawkner...281 L2
McBURNIE
dr. Kurunjang...226 G12
McCABE
pl. Epping...198 H17
pl. N Melbourne...34 J6
pl. S Morang...198 H17
McCAFFERY
ri. Pakenham...584 J2
McCALLUM
ct. Greenvale...237 B2
rd. Doncaster...331 C16
rd. Keilor...277 B14
st. Brighton...454 G15
McCANN
pl. Geelong, off Corio St...703 D7
McCARDLE
ct. Endeavour Hl...537 G3
McCARRON
pde. Essendon...323 G8
McCARTEN
st. Reservoir...283 B14
McCARTHY
gr. Montmorency...286 K13
rd. Olinda...427 L13
rd. Silvan...428 B11
st. Hampton...494 L6
McCARTNEY
dr. Nar Warrn S...578 J3
McCARTY
av. Epping...197 H19
McCASKER
av. Reservoir...282 K4
McCAULEY
av. Point Cook...450 E4
McCAW
av. Flemington...323 K20
McCLARES
rd. Vermont...420 L5
rd. Vermont...421 A5
McCLELLAND
brk. Langwarrin...628 G13
dr. Frankston N...600 L16
dr. Langwarrin...601 A12
dr. Langwarrin...628 J3
dr. Langwarrin S...628 F16
dr. Mill Park...242 H4
dr. Skye...600 L16
MACCLESFIELD
rd. Avonsleigh...470 D17
rd. Emerald...470 E17
rd. Monbulk...428 K12
McCLURE
rd. Dingley Village...533 B1
st. Thornbury...327 H12
McCOLL
ct. Brunswick W...324 H8
rd. Mont Albert N...374 E7
st. Montmorency...286 G12
st. Preston...283 D18
st. Reservoir...283 D16
st. Sunshine N...321 H13
McCOLLS
wy. Portsea...678 E1
McCOMAS
gr. Burwood...418 F10
st. Reservoir...283 E15
McCOMB
bvd. Frankston S...626 F8
cr. Bayswater...423 J8
st. Lilydale...338 A3
st. Sunbury...142 H13
McCOMBE
st. Rosebud...683 J17
McCOMBIE
st. Elsternwick...454 K4
McCONCHIE
av. Kew East...372 C5
McCONNELL
cl. Anglesea...713 F2
cr. Roxburgh Pk...194 F13
st. Kensington...33 K7
McCORMACK
av. Epping...197 G19
cr. Hoppers Csg...448 G2
ct. Darley...222 A11
rd. Maddingley...263 A4
st. Port Melb...29 B9
McCORMICK
ct. Oakleigh S...498 B7
McCORMICKS
rd. Carrum Downs...575 G13
rd. Carrum Downs...575 G19
rd. Carrum Downs...601 F6
rd. Skye...575 G19
rd. Skye...601 F6
McCOUBRIE
av. Sunshine W...364 L10
av. Sunshine W...365 A10
McCOY
st. Coburg N...281 G14
McCRACKEN
av. Blackburn S...419 H3
av. Flemington...323 L20
av. Northcote...326 F14
av. Pascoe Vale...280 D16
st. Essendon...323 G6
st. Kensington...33 K7
st. Sunshine...365 F1
McCRACKENS
la. Melbourne...1 C15
la. Melbourne...23 K10
McCRAE
cl. Scoresby...462 H8
mw. Richmond...25 L11
mw. Richmond...26 A10
rd. Rosanna...329 D1
st. Dandenong...536 B9
st. Elwood...454 F2
st. Maddingley...263 J1
st. Reservoir...283 A6
McCREDDEN
ct. Box Hill S...418 J2
McCRORY
st. Coburg...325 H3
McCUBBIN
cl. Mill Park...243 A7
ct. Sunbury...142 H10
dr. Taylors Lakes...233 A19
st. Burwood...419 A10
st. Footscray...367 A4
st. Ivanhoe East...328 L13
st. Ivanhoe East...329 A13
st. Kew East...372 J1
tce. Doncaster E...332 E16
wy. Berwick...554 H19
McCULLOCH
av. Seaford...599 D9
st. Dromana...685 L7
st. Essendon N...323 F2
st. Nunawading...376 J14
st. Warrandyte...333 J1
McCULLY
st. Ascot Vale...324 B17
McCURDY
rd. Herne Hill...701 H2
McCURE
ct. Ringwood E...379 F17
McCUTCHEON
cl. Mt Eliza...626 E15
st. Northcote...326 J13
wy. Collingwood...19 L17
MACDAVID
ct. Melton W...226 B14
McDERMOTT
av. Mooroolbark...337 B16
MACDHUI
av. Eltham North...245 B18
MACDONALD
av. Altona North...410 B5
gr. Mornington...640 H16
pl. Sunbury...143 A5
st. Glen Iris...416 G8
McDONALD
av. Ivanhoe...327 L14
av. Templestowe...331 J7
cr. Boronia...424 J9
ct. Bacchus Msh...221 K19
ct. Nar Warrn S...552 J14
la. Carlton...18 E20
la. Roxburgh Pk...194 A10
la. Sunshine...365 C2
pl. Glenroy...279 J4
rd. Brooklyn...365 J15
rd. Queenscliff...707 L16
rd. Rye...697 H5
st. Beaumaris...530 B4
st. Belmont...702 G18
st. Coburg N...281 F18
st. E Geelong...703 E14
st. Melton S...268 H7
st. Mordialloc...531 K17
st. Northcote...327 B19
st. Preston...282 F20
st. Werribee...447 H17
st. Williamstown, off Madigan Ct...410 L16
McDONALDS
la. Mulgrave...460 A15
rd. Epping...197 J18
rd. Mill Park...199 B20
rd. Mill Park...243 D1
rd. S Morang...199 B20
rd. S Morang...243 E1
McDONALDS DRAIN
rd. Pakenham...585 K19
MACDONNELL
ct. Kilsyth...381 J6
ct. Taylors Lakes...275 K1
McDONNELL
rd. Coburg N...281 H15
McDONOUGH
la. Vermont...421 L2
MACDOUGAL
st. Blairgowrie...679 G17
McDOUGALL
rd. Sunbury...143 C16
st. Anglesea...713 K2
st. Brunswick...325 F17
st. Fawkner...281 F5
st. Geelong West...702 D3
McDOWALL
rd. Hampton Pk...551 D12
st. Mitcham...377 C12
McDOWELL
st. Greensborough...285 K6
st. Rosebud...684 C15
MACE
ct. Mt Evelyn...339 A20
ri. Hallam...538 C18
MACEDON
av. Balwyn N...373 B3
av. Dallas...238 J10
av. Dromana...686 D7
cl. Caroline Spr...317 J7
cl. New Gisborne...80 C6
ct. Nunawading...376 K9
ct. Templstw Lr...330 G8
rd. Templstw Lr...330 F14
st. Hoppers Csg...449 A1
st. Keilor...277 D13
st. Maribyrnong...322 L19
st. Maribyrnong...323 A19
st. Sunbury...143 J11
McELROY
st. Sunshine W...364 K8
McEVOY
st. Kew...371 C10
McEWAN
rd. Heidelberg Ht...328 F1
rd. Heidelberg W...284 F20
rd. Pk Orchards...334 D17
McEWEN
dr. Sunbury...143 G4
MACEY
av. Avondale Ht...322 D12
gr. Ringwood N...378 E5
st. Cranbourne...578 G20
st. Croydon S...380 A12
McFADZEAN
av. Reservoir...282 G3
av. Reservoir...282 G8
st. Coldstream...295 F14
MACFARLAN
av. Blairgowrie...679 F17
la. South Yarra...31 L10
la. South Yarra...414 F5
st. South Yarra...31 K10
st. South Yarra...414 E5
MACFARLAND
st. Brunswick...325 E10
McFARLAND
st. Bacchus Msh...222 B15
McFARLANE
cr. Dandenong...536 A7
cr. Epping...197 L19
ct. Ferntree Gly...464 A17
ct. Highett...496 F13
la. Albert Park...29 F13
st. Keilor East...322 D4
st. Montmorency...286 K10
st. Northcote...326 J13
McFEES
rd. Dandenong N...501 J18
McGAHY
ct. Templestowe...332 A14
st. Templstw Lr...330 G14
McGEORGE
ct. Sunbury...142 G8
rd. Gisborne...109 E14
rd. Gisborne S...109 E14
McGHEE
av. Mitcham...377 D14
McGILL
ct. Pakenham...558 L20
ct. Sunbury...144 D11
McGINESS
av. Roxburgh Pk...194 D10
McGIVERN
ct. Bayswater N...424 H1
McGLONE
st. Mitcham...377 A14
McGLYNN
av. S Morang...243 G2
McGOUN
st. Richmond...26 D9
MACGOWAN
av. Glen Huntly...456 B9
McGOWAN
av. Preston...282 C19
ct. Altona Mdw...451 H7
st. Southbank...3 E12
st. Southbank...24 C18
McGOWANS
la. Burwood...418 L7
pl. Carlton...18 D13
rd. Donvale...376 J4
McGOWN
rd. Mt Eliza...626 E16
McGRATH
cl. Kealba...276 L20
ct. Richmond...26 G15
rd. Werribee...446 G19
rd. Wyndham Va...446 G19
rd. Wyndham Va...446 H10
st. Bacchus Msh...222 C19
st. Bellfield...328 B5
st. Caulfield...455 J6
st. Sunshine...365 G3
McGRATHS
la. Melbourne...24 J6
MACGREGOR
av. Portsea...678 B2
ct. Rowville...463 E12
st. Malvern East...456 H3
st. Parkdale...531 J11
McGREGOR
av. Beaumaris...529 J8
av. Brunswick W...324 K7
av. Healesville...214 A15
av. Mt Martha...669 C3
av.e, Healesville...214 E15
ct. Bacchus Msh...221 K19
ct. Dingley Village...533 C6
ct. Mt Evelyn...339 D15
ct. Sunshine W...364 A7
rd. Gisborne...79 J19
rd. Pakenham...584 E20
st. Canterbury...373 G19
st. Clayton...498 J1
st. Fairfield...327 F14
st. Middle Park...30 E20
st. Middle Park...413 H11
st. Pascoe Vale...281 A12
McGRETTONS
rd. Healesville...257 D1
McGUIGAN
dr. Cranbourne W...603 F1
gr. Ferntree Gly...464 H8
McGUINNESS
rd. Bentleigh E...497 E3
McGUIRE
cr. Williamstown...410 J14
st. Cheltenham...497 E15
st. Greenvale...237 C1
McHALE
ct. Essendon...323 J6
McHENRY
st. St Kilda E...414 K20
MACHINERY
dr. Point Cook...450 A3
McILRAITH
ct. Croydon...380 L2
McILROYS
rd. Red Hill...687 K13
McILWRAITH
pl. Melbourne...24 J5
st. Princes Hill...18 F1
st. Princes Hill...325 J20
McILWRICK
st. Windsor...414 G12
McINDOE
pde. Parkdale...531 F16
McINNES
cl. Sunbury...143 A9
ct. Pakenham...584 J1
McINTOSH
av. Hoppers Csg...448 G4
ct. Aspendale Gdn...546 K4
pl. Monbulk...428 F16
rd. Altona North...409 K8
st. Airport W...278 K13
st. Northcote...326 G16
st. Oakleigh...458 B15
st. Sunshine...364 J2
MACINTYRE
la. Yering...252 C18
McINTYRE
al. Melbourne...2 D6
al. Melbourne...24 C4
av. Roxburgh Pk...194 D11
cl. Ferntree Gly...463 L7
ct. Point Cook...450 D6
dr. Altona...409 A14
rd. Kealba...321 D5
rd. Sunshine N...321 B17
st. Burwood...418 C9
st. E Geelong...703 J12
McINTYRES
rd. Pk Orchards...333 D17
McIVER
pl. Kensington...33 J5
st. Brunswick...325 G14
st. Ferntree Gly...464 D7
McIVOR
ct. Melton W...225 H19
rd. St Albans...320 C3
st. Cheltenham...496 K19
st. Dallas...238 F12
st. Reservoir...283 C14
wy. Attwood...237 B12
MACK
cr. Clarinda...498 G10
ct. Belmont...706 H3
rd. Nar Warrn S...552 K14
st. Reservoir...283 B4
MACKA
av. Greensborough...287 A1
MACKAY
av. Glen Huntly...456 D10
av. Mooroolbark, off Reay Rd...337 C20
rd. Yallambie...285 G14
st. Essendon...323 L6
st. Greenvale...236 L5
st. Prahran...32 H18
st. Prahran...414 K9
st. Springvale S...533 K3
st. Yarraville...367 C12
wk. Roxburgh Pk...193 K15

McKAY
av. Black Rock 529 G1
cl. Berwick 554 J11
ct. Dandenong N 502 C19
ct. Ringwood 378 D19
pl. Attwood 237 A11
rd. Rowville 462 L20
rd. Rowville 463 A20
st. Alphington 327 J13
st. Brunswick 325 D17
st. Coburg 325 G1
st. Mordialloc 531 L13
st. Parkdale 531 L13
st. Richmond 26 K4
st. Sunshine 365 E4
McKAYS
rd. Langwarrin 602 A18
McKEAN
st. Box Hill N 375 C12
st. Fitzroy N 20 A2
McKECHNIE
st. St Albans 320 B5
MACKEITH
ct. Mt Eliza 626 D20
McKELL
av. Sunbury 143 E6
MACKELLAR
av. Wheelers Hill 460 E16
cl. Nar Warrn N 538 B11
dr. Roxburgh Pk 194 A9
McKELLAR
st. Bayswater 423 A7
st. Watsonia 285 E4
MACKELROY
rd. Plenty 244 D10
McKELVIE
ct. Glen Waverley 459 J9
McKENDRICK
la. W Melbourne 23 C3
McKENNA
rd. Forest Hill 420 E3
rd. Glen Waverley 459 J11
st. Avondale Ht 322 D14
MACKENNEL
st. Ivanhoe East 328 L14
McKENRY
pl. Dandenong N 501 K14
MACKENZIE
cl. Taylors Lakes 233 H20
ct. Croydon S 379 J11
rd. W Melbourne 367 J16
st. Brunswick 325 E11
st. Cheltenham 530 H3
st. Cockatoo 511 B9
st. Melbourne 2 K2
st. Melbourne 24 E1
st. Reservoir 282 C5
McKENZIE
av. Healesville 214 J16
cr. Hoppers Csg 448 B3
cr. Roxburgh Pk 194 B10
cr. Roxburgh Pk 194 C10
ct. Greensborough 286 B8
ct. Merrimu 222 H7
ct. Oakleigh E 458 G12
gr. Montrose 382 D13
gr. Mt Dandenong 382 D13
la. Nar Warrn N 539 A9
rd. Beaconsfld Up 542 L17
st. Belmont 702 E17
st. Doncaster E 332 D18
st. Geelong 703 B11
st. Melton 226 J20
st. Richmond 26 K8
st. Seaford 599 E1
wy. Langwarrin 629 C1
McKENZIE-KING
dr. Millgrove 348 F2
McKEON
av. Pascoe Vale S 324 J5
cct. Dandenong N 502 B13
rd. Donvale 377 D9
rd. Mitcham 377 D9
McKERCHAR
st. Glenroy 281 B5
McKERRAL
pl. Croydon N 335 K11
MACKERRAS
ct. Wheelers Hill 460 G18
MACKEY
st. Lalor 241 E9
MACKIA
ct. Niddrie 322 K2
MACKIE
ct. Blairgowrie 680 A18
ct. Kew 371 F10
gr. Brighton East 455 G15
rd. Bentleigh E 457 D19
rd. Mulgrave 500 B2

McKILLOP
la. Fitzroy N 326 E19
pl. Endeavour Hl 537 K4
pl. Geelong, off
McKillop St 702 K9
rd. Mt Evelyn 383 J3
rd. Mt Evelyn 384 E1
rd. Wandin East 384 E1
st. E Geelong 703 G12
st. Geelong 702 K9
st. Melbourne 1 K13
st. Melbourne 24 B8
st. South Yarra 32 J16
McKIMMIES
rd. Bundoora 242 C12
rd. Lalor 241 K12
rd. Mill Park 242 C12
McKINLEY
av. Malvern 415 K16
ct. Dandenong N 501 H8
dr. Roxburgh Pk 194 E15
MACKINNON
ct. Attwood 237 E11
ct. Keysborough 534 D9
gr. Glenroy 280 B9
McKINNON
ct. Melton W 226 B19
rd. Bentleigh E 456 A16
rd. McKinnon 455 J16
st. Blackburn 375 L18
st. Thomastown 240 J14
tce. Christmas Hills 207 H18
MACKINTOSH
rd. Wheelers Hill 460 H8
McKIRDY
st. Springvale 499 F16
McKITTRICK
rd. Bentleigh 496 D4
MACKLIN
wy. Caroline Spr 318 C4
MACKS
la. Geelong, off
Brougham St 703 B6
pl. Hoppers Csg 447 L1
MACLACHLAN
ct. Greenvale 193 E20
McLACHLAN
st. Northcote 326 G19
st. Templestowe 330 L7
MACLAGAN
cr. Reservoir 282 K6
MACLAINE
ct. Nar Warrn N 538 E7
MACLAREN
ct. Greenvale 193 F20
ct. Greenvale 237 F1
McLAREN
av. Cranbourne 604 D2
ct. Rosebud 685 A20
pl. Mornington 640 F13
st. Mt Waverley 458 G3
st. Tullamarine 278 F6
st. Upwey 465 L13
McLARTY
la. S Melbourne 29 D9
pl. Geelong, off
Little Malop St 703 A7
McLAUGHLAN
av. Eumemmerring 537 B15
McLAUGHLANS
la. Greensborough 244 F12
la. Plenty 244 D12
la. Plenty 244 F12
McLAUGHLIN
av. Sandringham 495 F16
cr. Mill Park 242 K5
st. Ardeer 320 B20
st. Ardeer 364 C1
McLAURIN
av. Roxburgh Pk 194 D12
rd. Carnegie 456 K8
MACLEAN
ct. Seaford 573 E19
st. Williamstown 411 F14
McLEAN
al. Melbourne 1 K6
al. Melbourne 23 L5
av. Bentleigh 455 H18
cr. Dandenong N 501 L20
ct. Frankston S 627 F20
ct. Sunbury 143 G3
ct. Wantirna S 422 L20
ct. Wantirna S 423 A20
ct. Wantirna S 463 A1
st. Albion 364 J1
st. Brunswick W 324 J8
McLEANS
rd. Bundoora 242 C20
McLEAR
rd. Arthurs Seat 685 K14

McLEISH
tce. Pakenham 558 J20
McLELLAN
st. Bayswater 424 C7
McLELLAND
wy. Burwood E 420 D12
McLENNAN
st. Braybrook 365 J1
st. Eumemmerring 536 L15
McLENNANS
rd. Plenty 244 E7
McLENNON
av. Maddingley 263 E4
MACLEOD
pde. Macleod 284 K15
wy. Lynbrook 551 C16
McLEOD
dr. Darley 221 K8
pl. Mt Waverley 418 K19
rd. Carrum 573 B9
rd. Mt Martha 669 C1
rd. Patterson L 573 H6
rd. St Albans 319 F1
st. Doncaster 374 D3
st. Rye 680 E20
st. Springvale 499 J9
st. Sunshine N 321 C15
st. Thomastown 241 A16
McLEODS
rd. Diggers Rest 232 C1
McLISTER
st. Spotswood 411 A2
McLOCHLAN
st. Mt Waverley 458 F1
McLOUGHLIN
ct. Pascoe Vale 281 A11
McMAHEN
st. Keysborough 535 A9
McMAHENS
rd. Bangholme 548 B18
McMAHON
av. Anglesea 713 A6
ct. Darley 222 A10
ct. Ringwood N 378 H2
ct. Sunbury 143 G3
rd. Reservoir 283 C7
st. Blairgowrie 679 D19
McMAHONS
rd. Coburg N 281 H16
rd. Ferntree Gly 423 J20
rd. Frankston 599 G18
rd. Frankston 627 F2
rd. Launching Pl 344 H3
McMASTER
ct. Pakenham 584 D4
ct. Toorak 415 D4
MACMEIKAN
st. Whittlesea 96 D19
McMEIKAN
st. Kensington 33 K8
McMEIKANS
rd. Yering 253 E16
McMICKEN
la. Prahran 415 B11
MACMILLAN
av. Greenvale 237 D3
st. Mooroolbark 381 B2
McMILLAN
av. Geelong 702 J1
ct. Cranbourne N 577 J8
pl. Geelong, off
Little Ryrie St 703 C9
st. Anglesea 713 E7
st. Clayton S 498 L5
st. Elsternwick 454 L6
McMULLEN
rd. Officer 556 K20
McMURRAY
st. Nunawading 376 E12
McMURTRY
wy. Frankston 627 J9
McNAB
av. Footscray 367 F9
ct. Dandenong 535 J2
wy. Greenvale 236 L1
McNABB
av. Geelong West 702 G1
st. Berwick 554 D7
McNABS
rd. Keilor 276 H2
rd. Melb Airport 234 L14
rd. Melb Airport 235 A16
McNAE
st. Moonee Pnd 324 E14
McNAIR
la. Brunswick W 324 K14
McNALLY
st. Mt Waverley 459 A4

MACNAMARA
st. Ferny Creek 466 D3
McNAMARA
av. Airport W 278 J17
av. Roxburgh Pk 194 E9
ct. Pakenham 584 E5
mw. Kensington 33 C11
rd. Avonsleigh 470 G19
rd. Laverton 407 D13
st. Beaumaris 530 G4
st. Macleod 284 L15
st. Macleod 285 A15
st. Preston 282 C16
st. Richmond 26 H16
McNAMARAS
rd. Millgrove 303 G19
rd. Wesburn 303 E20
McNAUGHT
st. Beaumaris 530 B7
McNAUGHTON
rd. Clayton 499 E3
MACNEIL
dr. Altona Mdw 451 C2
McNEIL
av. Lilydale 339 H7
st. Bellfield 328 B6
McNEILAGE
st. Spotswood 411 A3
McNEILL
av. E Geelong 703 H14
ct. E Geelong 703 H14
McNICHOLL
wy. Delahey 275 F11
McNICOL
cl. Meadow Ht 238 A1
rd. Belgrave 466 B17
rd. Tecoma 466 B16
rd. Tecoma 466 B17
st. Geelong West 702 J7
McNICOLL
ct. Bacchus Msh 221 L13
MACORNA
st. Frankston 627 F5
st. Watsonia N 285 F3
McOWAN
cr. Yarra Jctn 347 D15
McPHAIL
st. Essendon 323 K8
McPHEE
ct. Thomastown 240 J14
McPHEES
rd. Whittlesea 96 H17
MACPHERSON
st. Carlton N 18 C1
st. Dandenong 536 D9
st. Footscray 367 B6
st. Princes Hill 18 C1
McPHERSON
av. Carnegie 456 F4
bvd. Roxburgh Pk 193 K16
pl. Werribee 447 D19
st. Brunswick 325 K9
st. Coburg 325 E4
st. Essendon 324 E12
st. Keilor East 322 C6
st. Maddingley 263 G3
st. Moonee Pnd 324 E12
st. Reservoir 282 J16
st. Warrandyte 290 D19
McQUADE
ct. Noble Park N 501 D11
la. Dandenong 535 L8
MACQUARIE
cir. Braeside 547 F3
ct. Cranbourne N 577 K6
dr. Thomastown 241 H19
dr. Wyndham Va 446 F7
pl. Boronia 424 E1
pl. Williamstown 411 D17
rd. Toorak 415 H7
st. Melton S 268 F11
st. Prahran 32 B20
st. Prahran 414 G10
st. Williamstown 411 E13
McQUIES
rd. Seville E 387 F4
McQUILLAN
wy. Burnside 318 C8
wy. Caroline Spr 318 C8
MACRAE
bvd. Keilor Dn 276 H13
McRAE
av. St Albans 319 G1
mw. Endeavour Hl 537 H5
st. Seaford 599 D1
MACRINA
st. Oakleigh E 458 G13
MACRO
ct. Rowville 462 L14
ct. Rowville 463 A14

McROBERT
st. Newport 410 L5
MACROBERTSON
la. Fitzroy 19 F12
st. Templstw Lr 330 G8
wy. Hoppers Csg 405 D20
MACROBERTSONS
la. Kew 372 G12
McRORIE
st. Anglesea 713 J1
MACROSTY
ct. Frankston 628 C7
McSHANE
dr. Kealba 276 K18
st. Balwyn N 373 J5
st. Reservoir 282 H4
McSWAIN
st. Parkdale 531 K11
McTAGGART
st. Kensington 33 E8
MACULATA
cl. St Albans 320 J7
dr. Cranbourne W 577 K19
gr. Bundoora 242 F14
wk. Vermont S 420 L11
wk. Vermont S 421 A11
MACULOSA
ct. Endeavour Hl 536 K1
McVEAN
st. Brunswick 325 B17
McVEIGH
pl. Hoppers Csg 448 A3
McWHAE
av. St Kilda E 454 L1
McWILLIAM
st. Springvale 500 E7
MADA
cl. Greensborough 243 L20
MADANG
av. Balwyn 374 C10
MADDEN
av. Carnegie 456 F8
av. Geelong West 702 J3
dr. Bacchus Msh 221 K18
gr. Burnley 371 A20
gr. Burnley 371 D20
gr. Kew 371 E11
gr. Richmond 26 J18
rd. Heatherton 498 B18
rd. Nar Warrn S 578 J2
rt. Berwick 553 K9
st. Albert Park 29 K11
st. Albert Park 413 E6
st. Balwyn N 373 H5
st. Essendon N 323 H2
st. Maidstone 366 H3
st. Ringwood 377 L14
st. Seaford 599 L7
MADDENS
la. Gruyere 298 A1
MADDINGLEY
bvd. Bacchus Msh 222 A18
MADDOCK
st. Footscray 367 A3
st. Prahran, off
Chapel St 414 G12
MADDOX
rd. Newport 410 F9
rd. Williamstown 410 F14
rd. Williamstn N 410 F12
MADDY
ct. Rowville 503 B7
MADEIRA
ct. Doncaster 330 K19
ct. Frankston 600 C18
ct. Roxburgh Pk 194 E7
MADEL
av. Strathmore 324 B2
MADELEINE
cr. Somerville 644 F15
ct. Emerald 510 H17
pl. Melton W 225 L14
rd. Clayton 458 K20
st. Blairgowrie 680 D20
st. Doncaster 330 E15
MADELEY
dr. Wesburn 348 C16
MADELINE
ct. Avondale Ht 322 D7
st. Glen Iris 417 H12
st. Glen Waverley 420 B18
st. Preston 283 D17
st. Warburton 349 F3
MADELYN
ct. Cranbourne S 603 G20
MADERA
dr. Thomastown 240 E17
MADIGAN
cr. Mill Park 242 G9
ct. Highton 705 J4

ct. Roxburgh Pk 193 J15
ct. Williamstown 410 L16
dr. Glen Waverley 461 A4
MADINA
pl. Torquay 712 D2
MADINE
wy. Eltham 288 B7
MADISON
av. Dandenong N 501 G8
av. Narre Warren 538 K15
av. Point Cook 450 F4
cl. Taylors Lakes 275 H2
ct. Bundoora 284 A1
ct. Cheltenham 497 F20
ct. Mt Waverley 458 H1
dr. Hoppers Csg 448 J7
MADOLINE
st. Pascoe Vale 280 L16
MADONNA
ct. Vermont 421 H5
MADRAS
la. Caroline Spr 318 E9
wk. Keilor Dn 276 F12
MADURA
ct. Wheelers Hill 460 H17
st. Rosebud 684 G14
st. Travancore 324 F18
MAFFRA
ct. Dandenong N 502 A9
ct. Pt Lonsdale 710 C6
st. Coolaroo 238 H4
MAGARRA
cr. Berwick 553 J2
MAGDALA
av. Strathmore 279 K20
av. Strathmore 323 K1
MAGDALEN
st. Pascoe Vale S 280 F19
MAGDALENA
pl. Berwick 553 F3
pl. Rowville 502 L4
pl. Rowville 503 A4
MAGDALENE
ct. Sunbury 144 G11
MAGENTA
ct. Mill Park 242 D12
ct. Mt Waverley 419 G13
ct. Sunshine W 364 C8
pl. Carlton 18 E18
MAGGIE
mw. Safety Bch 669 C15
st. Yarraville 367 D15
MAGGINS
la. Wesburn 348 A9
MAGGS
st. Croydon 379 D2
st. Doncaster E 376 B3
MAGHULL
st. Brunswick E 326 A14
MAGID
av. Wheelers Hill 460 C13
dr. Narre Warren 539 B20
dr. Narre Warren 552 K3
MAGNA
ct. Mt Waverley 419 C12
MAGNET
la. New Gisborne 79 D6
MAGNOLIA
av. Kings Park 275 D18
av. Oakleigh S 497 F1
bvd. Meadow Ht 193 K20
cl. Yarra Glen 209 A10
ct. Glen Waverley 459 J6
ct. Lalor 240 K10
ct. Rye 696 F2
ct. Templstw Lr 330 L14
ct. Werribee 447 J8
dr. Templstw Lr 330 K14
gr. Montrose 381 K10
rd. Gardenvale 455 C11
rd. Ivanhoe 328 E9
st. Doveton 536 J12
st. Mordialloc 532 B12
st. Oak Park 280 C12
st. St Albans 320 K8
st. Wantirna 422 B3
MAGNUS
st. St Albans 320 C9
MAGPIE
ct. Carrum Downs 600 L3
ct. Meadow Ht 238 C2
ct. Werribee 448 B10
la. Warrandyte 290 B19
rd. Clematis 508 B1
rd. Menzies Ck 508 B1
wk. S Morang 243 K4
MAGRA
pl. Endeavour Hl 537 E5
pl. Roxburgh Pk 194 C13
MAGUIRE
dr. Sunbury 143 K10
MAHALA
ct. Blackburn S 419 H4
ct. Clayton S 499 E17
ct. Keysborough 535 A8
st. Pt Lonsdale 710 D2
MAHER
ct. Werribee 447 F20
rd. Laverton 407 A18
st. Brighton 494 J2
st. Fawkner 281 F5
st. Highett 496 H15
MAHLAN
cl. Hillside 232 G19
MAHOGANY
av. Berwick 553 H4
av. Frankston N 599 L8
cl. Grovedale 706 E8
ct. Greensborough 286 K2
ct. Mt Martha 657 B10
ct. Pakenham 585 G1
tr. Lysterfield 504 K16
MAHON
av. Altona North 409 K2
av. Beaconsfield 555 D14
cl. Mornington 640 H20
cr. Narre Warren 553 E9
ct. Taylors Lakes 276 E7
MAHONEY
cr. Seaford 599 D5
st. Bacchus Msh 222 C17
st. Fitzroy 19 A14
st. Templestowe 330 J7
st. Templstw Lr 330 J7
MAHONEYS
ct. Warrandyte 333 B4
rd. Burwood E 420 C10
rd. Campbellfield 239 F19
rd. Fawkner 239 F19
rd. Forest Hill 420 C10
rd. Reservoir 239 F19
rd. Thomastown 239 F19
rd. Thomastown 241 A20
MAHONGA
dr. Rowville 462 G17
MAHONIA
ct. Ferntree Gly 423 H19
MAHONY
st. Upwey 465 K12
MAHY
ct. Coldstream 295 F11
MAIDA
av. Bayswater 423 E2
av. Sunshine N 321 D9
ct. Lower Plenty 286 D12
MAIDEN
ct. Epping 198 D18
MAIDENHAIR
mw. Aspendale Gdn 547 B4
MAIDIE
st. Highton 701 G9
MAIDSTONE
av. Burwood E 420 B11
pl. Ferntree Gly 463 E2
st. Altona 408 G14
st. Ringwood 378 C15
MAILEY
st. Sunshine W 364 F5
MAILLARD
st. Cockatoo 511 B8
MAILRUN
ct. Hoppers Csg 447 L1
MAIN
dr. Bundoora 284 C9
dr. Kew 371 G6
dr. Macleod 284 G9
dr. Springvale 500 H12
rd. Broadmeadows 238 L16
rd. Clayton S 499 A9
rd. Eltham 287 E15
rd. Eltham North 287 L3
rd. Gembrook 512 J11
rd. Hurstbridge 203 A14
rd. Lower Plenty 286 D15
rd. Monbulk 428 C17
rd. Montmorency 287 A15
rd. Research 288 G3
rd. Research 289 A1
rd.e, St Albans 320 D4
rd.e, St Albans 321 A5
rd.w, Albanvale 319 A3
rd.w, Kings Park 318 L3
rd.w, Kings Park 319 A3
rd.w, St Albans 319 G3
st. Bacchus Msh 221 L17
st. Belgrave 466 G14
st. Blackburn 375 H20
st. Coburg 281 F20
st. Croydon 380 A4
st. Diamond Ck 245 F11
st. Elsternwick 455 D3
st. Emerald 509 F2
st. Greensborough 286 C3
st. Lilydale 338 K4
st. Lilydale 339 B2
st. Mordialloc 531 J17
st. Mordialloc 531 K18
st. Mornington 640 E13
st. Nar Warrn N 539 E5
st. Northcote 327 D15
st. Oak Park 280 B15
st. Pakenham 584 J5
st. Pascoe Vale 280 B15
st. Thomastown 240 C13
st. Thomastown 241 A14
st. Upwey 465 J11
MAIN CREEK
rd. Red Hill 686 G18
MAINE
st. Tootgarook 698 C2
MAINEHEY
cr. Springvale 499 L15
MAIN STREET
ml. Box Hill 374 K15
MAIN WHITTLESEA
rd. Mernda 155 L15
MAIR
st. Brighton 494 H5
MAIS
st. Reservoir 283 G6
MAISEY
rd. Gembrook 512 H17
MAISIE
la. Port Melb 29 B7
rd. Emerald 509 C6
MAITLAND
av. Kew 372 J8
cl. Mulgrave 501 H3
cl. Rowville 463 E13
cl. Thomastown 240 D17
pl. Caroline Spr 318 E10
st. Geelong West 702 J3
st. Glen Iris 416 C12
st. Narre Warren 553 E7
MAIVARY
la. Northcote 327 B16
MAIYA
ct. Cheltenham 530 E3
MAIZE
pl. Narre Warren 553 C1
MAJDAL
st. Bentleigh E 457 F15
MAJELLA
ct. Kew 372 H9
MAJESTIC
dr. Emerald 510 D3
dr. Somerville 645 B15
MAJOR
cr. Lysterfield 463 L20
rd. Fawkner 281 F6
rd. Panton Hill 204 E11
st. Doncaster E 331 K20
st. Highett 496 C13
st. Northcote 326 J17
st. Ringwood 378 L3
MAJORCA
st. St Albans 320 H11
MAJORE
st. Hawthorn 371 F17
MAJTLIS
st. Blackburn N 375 F9
MAKEHAM
av. Rowville 503 D7
MALA
ct. Grovedale 706 E8
MALABAR
cl. Sunshine W 364 E6
cr. Eltham 288 A10
ct. Keysborough 534 F10
ct. Wheelers Hill 460 J19
pl. Sorrento 679 C15
rd. Blackburn 375 E14
MALACCA
rd. Canterbury 373 B16
st. Heidelberg W 284 D20
st. McKinnon 456 D15
MALAHANG
pde. Heidelberg W 328 C2
MALAKOFF
st. Caulfield N 415 H17
st. St Kilda E 414 J16
MALANDA
ct. Berwick 554 B14
MALANE
st. Bentleigh E 456 H20
st. Ormond 456 B12
MALANIE
cl. Nar Warrn N 538 C7
MALASET
pl. Vermont 421 C4
MALATA
wy. Lysterfield 463 K20
MALBAR
st. Chum Creek 213 A12
MALCOLM
cr. Doncaster 374 J4
cr. Keysborough 535 B9
ct. Croydon N 336 E11
ct. Frankston 599 K18
ct. Kealba 320 L2
ct. Mooroolbark 337 B10
ct. Mt Waverley 458 G1
ct. Narre Warren 553 A6
ct. Pakenham 584 J2
ct. Ringwood E 379 C14
ct. St Albans 321 A2
dr. Chelsea 547 B19
pl. Campbellfield 239 H11
rd. Braeside 532 G15
rd. Croydon N 336 E11
rd. Langwarrin 629 D2
st. Bacchus Msh 222 C17
st. Blackburn 375 G20
st. Boronia 424 C8
st. McKinnon 456 E17
st. Oak Park 280 D11
st. Preston 282 C17
st. South Yarra 32 F7
st. South Yarra 414 J4
MALDEN
st. Footscray 367 E7
MALDON
cr. Doncaster E 332 A17
ct. Narre Warren 538 K15
ct. Sunshine N 320 L11
ct. Wheelers Hill 461 E15
pl. Wattle Glen 246 G9
st. Broadmeadows 238 F14
tce. Forest Hill 420 E3
MALE
st. Brighton 454 J19
MALEELA
av. Balwyn 373 C13
gr. Rosanna 285 D19
MALEI
ct. Templestowe 331 L11
MALES
rd. Moorooduc 657 J10
MALFORD
wy. Mulgrave 500 L6
wy. Mulgrave 501 A6
MALIBU
gr. Keilor Lodge 276 C5
mw. Chadstone 458 E3
pl. Torquay 711 G12
MALIN
st. Kew 372 D14
MALINDA
wy. Croydon S 379 K13
MALING
rd. Canterbury 373 D20
MALL
ct. Blackburn N 375 F10
MALLACOOTA
ct. Taylors Lakes 275 L8
MALLANA
ct. Croydon 380 C9
MALLARD
cl. Hillside 232 D18
ct. Chelsea Ht 547 F17
MALLAWA
ct. Burwood E 419 G12
st. Clayton S 498 L6
MALLEE
ct. Berwick 553 J3
ct. Kings Park 275 F17
ct. Mulgrave 501 E1
st. Frankston N 600 B9
MALLEEHEN
st. Werribee 448 D8
MALLESON
st. Richmond 26 H14
MALLINSON
ct. Airport W 278 F16
MALLORY
ct. Bayswater N 380 G13
ct. Cranbourne 578 A19
MALLUM
av. Frankston 600 B16
MALMO
ct. Keysborough 534 J13
MALMSBURY
cr. Rowville 463 F19
dr. Ashwood 418 C16
dr. Meadow Ht 237 K6
pl. Caroline Spr 318 D8
st. Hawthorn 372 C16
st. Kew 371 K8
MALO
cl. Epping 197 L18
MALONE
st. Geelong 702 L4
MALONEY
la. W Melbourne 23 E4
st. Kensington 33 K5
st. Sunshine W 364 G8
MALONGA
ct. Caulfield N 415 F15
MALOP
st. Geelong 703 A7
MALPAS
st. Preston 283 C18
MALSEED
st. Croydon 336 F18
MALSTER
ct. Keilor Dn 275 J11
MALTA
st. Ivanhoe 327 J9
MALTARRA
st. Clayton S 498 H4
MALTBY
bps. Cocoroc 487 E5
bps. Werribee S 448 H18
ct. Berwick 580 K1
wk. Burwood 419 B7
MALTHOUSE
la. Melbourne 24 J8
MALTON
ct. Altona 408 D15
MALTRAVERS
cr. Cranbourne N 578 G8
rd. Eaglemont 328 E13
rd. Ivanhoe 328 E13
rd. Ivanhoe East 328 E13
MALTREVERS
pl. Wyndham Va 446 D6
MALUA
cr. Mill Park 242 J12
rd. Ferntree Gly 423 G17
st. Ormond 455 L14
st. Reservoir 282 B11
MALURA
pl. Frankston 628 E5
MALVEN
cl. Werribee 446 K10
MALVERN
av. Glen Iris 417 A9
av. Tullamarine 279 A8
gr. Caulfield N 415 K18
gr. Manifold Ht 702 B4
pl. Narre Warren 553 C10
rd. Armadale 415 A9
rd. Glen Iris 416 J14
rd. Malvern 415 A9
rd. Malvern East 416 J14
rd. Mont Albert 374 E12
rd. Mont Albert N 374 E12
rd. Prahran 414 K8
rd. South Yarra 32 F16
rd. South Yarra 414 K8
rd. Toorak 415 A9
st. Bayswater 423 J4
st. Vermont 377 D20
MALVINA
ct. Rowville 502 J3
pl. Carlton 18 A15
st. Burwood 419 A11
MALVOLIO
st. Glen Huntly 456 C8
MAMBOURIN
st. Werribee 447 D15
MANALLACK
st. Brunswick 325 E16
MANATEE
av. Mt Eliza 625 G18
MANATOKA
cr. Hampton Pk 552 C15
MANATUNGA
cct. Greensborough 244 C20
cct. Greensborough 286 C1
st. Clayton 459 A18
MANCHELLE
cl. Frankston S 627 B14
MANCHESTER
ct. Epping 198 B15
dr. Skye 601 F2
dr. Sydenham 232 J19
gr. Glen Huntly 456 C6
la. Melbourne 2 D17
la. Melbourne 24 E9
rd. Mooroolbark 337 A18
st. Hawthorn 372 B20
MANCIPLE
st. Rye 696 E5
MANDALA
ct. Mulgrave 500 H5
ct. Wantirna S 462 F5
MANDALL
av. Ivanhoe 327 K14

MARGOT
av. Doncaster..........331 A14
ct. Cranbourne N.....578 H10
st. Chadstone..........458 A2
st. Ferntree Gly.......464 D3
st. W Footscray.......366 G12
MARGRAVE
st. St Albans...........319 K1
MARGTMARY
av. Preston.............282 F19
MARGUERITA
av. Mt Martha..........655 D20
MARHAM
pl. Tullamarine........278 K2
MARI
cl. Greensborough..244 B20
tce. Croydon Hills.....335 H13
MARIA
av. Nunawading.......376 J12
cr. Pakenham..........585 B5
ct. Cranbourne N.....578 F9
ct. Hadfield............280 K6
dr. Langwarrin.........601 J18
st. Laverton N.........407 H6
MARIAN
ct. Blackburn..........375 E19
ct. Eltham North.......245 F16
st. Hawthorn...........372 A20
MARIANA
av. Croydon S..........379 G11
MARIANNE
av. Rye...................696 D8
wy. Doncaster..........330 E16
wy. Mt Waverley.......419 C16
MARIBYRNONG
bvd. Footscray..........367 G4
ct. Werribee............447 F8
rd. Ascot Vale..........323 J15
rd. Moonee Pnd.......323 J15
st. Footscray...........367 H12
st. Footscray...........367 J8
MARIDA
ct. Berwick.............554 B16
MARIE
av. Heidelberg Ht.....284 E20
av. Springvale..........500 F6
cl. Tullamarine........278 F4
ct. Bundoora...........285 B5
ct. Mt Eliza.............626 F20
ct. Mt Waverley.......458 G9
st. Boronia.............424 E14
st. Doveton.............536 L9
st. Doveton.............537 A9
st. Oak Park............279 L11
st. Vermont.............377 H20
MARIE DALLEY
dr. Kew, off Coombs Av........371 E10
MARIEMONT
av. Beaumaris..........530 F8
av. Wantirna............422 H10
MARIE WALLACE
wy. Bayswater, off Valma St..........423 E8
MARIGOLD
av. Altona North.......365 K20
cr. Gowanbrae.........279 E4
st. S Morang............199 J13
MARIGOLDS
rd. Yallambie...........285 G15
MARILLA
ct. Mt Eliza.............641 L9
MARILLAC
ct. Frankston...........628 C11
MARILYN
cr. Ringwood..........379 B3
ct. Blackburn N........376 D9
ct. Watsonia...........285 C8
st. Doncaster...........330 C16
MARIN
la. Braybrook..........321 L17
la. Maribyrnong......322 J15
MARINA
av. Frankston..........628 A3
av. McCrae.............684 L18
cl. Gladstone Pk......279 B3
ct. Notting Hill.........459 K15
dr. Melton..............226 K18
gr. Bonbeach...........545 F15
rd. Mentone............530 J9
st. Vermont............421 E4
st. Werribee...........447 F5
MARINDA
dr. Skye.................601 D8
MARINE
av. Mornington........640 D16
av. St Kilda.............414 B20
dr. Mt Martha..........668 L10
dr. Mt Martha..........669 A10
dr. Roxburgh Pk......194 G6
dr. Safety Bch.........686 F1
pde. Abbotsford..........20 F17
pde. Elwood.............454 B2
pde. St Kilda............414 B19
MARINER
cl. Cranbourne N.....578 E9
ct. Taylors Lakes.....275 J7
st. Williamstown.....411 G12
vw. Patterson L........573 H6
MARINERS ISLAND
Patterson L........573 H4
MARINGA
cl. Wantirna S.........422 B17
ct. Keilor Dn...........276 G16
st. Bulleen.............329 H10
MARINIQUE
dr. Aspendale Gdn...547 A4
MARINO
ct. Mornington........657 C3
la. Caroline Spr.......318 C3
wy. Greensborough..244 L15
MARION
av. Balwyn..............373 E10
av. Brunswick W......324 K11
av. Cockatoo...........511 A4
av. Kilsyth..............380 L2
av. Mooroolbark.......380 L2
ct. Craigieburn........150 B16
ct. Keysborough......534 C11
la. Fitzroy.................18 L19
rd. Rosebud............700 K3
st. Altona North.......409 K4
st. Altona North.......410 C4
st. Bentleigh............456 F20
st. Brighton.............454 L15
st. Brighton.............455 A15
st. Coburg N...........281 B17
st. Dandenong.........535 H7
st. Fitzroy.................19 A19
st. Footscray...........367 A5
st. Pt Lonsdale........710 G2
st. Seaford.............599 G4
wk. Hoppers Csg......447 L3
wy. Eltham North......246 A20
MARIPOSA
ct. Wantirna S.........422 C15
pl. Port Melb...........412 E5
MARISA
cr. Berwick.............554 H19
cr. Berwick.............580 H1
ct. Carrum Downs...601 D4
MARISSA
cr. Greensborough..244 K15
ct. Langwarrin.........601 K17
MARITA
ct. Cheltenham.......497 A16
MARITANA
av. Reservoir...........282 H16
cr. Thomastown.......240 H17
ct. Balwyn..............373 J10
MARJORAM
cl. Hallam..............538 C16
MARJORIE
av. Belmont.............706 A4
av. Dingley Village...533 D7
av. Sunbury.............142 F12
cl. Bulleen.............330 A17
ct. McCrae.............684 K16
st. Preston.............327 E1
MARJORY
pl. Tullamarine........278 F6
st. Fawkner............281 K5
st. Thomastown......241 E15
st. Yarraville...........367 A16
MARK
ct. Chadstone..........458 D4
ct. Dandenong N.....501 K10
ct. Diggers Rest......187 G15
ct. Epping...............241 G4
ct. Hampton Pk........551 C7
ct. Noble Park.........500 D20
ct. Seabrook...........450 J6
ct. Wollert..............153 F14
dr. Hillside.............274 G6
pl. Melton W...........225 K17
pl. Nunawading.......376 F12
st. Bayswater..........423 D2
st. Fitzroy N.............19 G1
st. Fitzroy N............326 D20
st. Keilor East.........278 E19
st. Mooroolbark.......337 F17
st. Mt Martha..........656 B12
st. N Melbourne........34 E9
st. N Melbourne........34 H9
st. Rosebud............684 D16
st. St Albans............319 F3
st. Sunshine W........363 L2
st. View Bank...........285 L17
st. Warrandyte.........290 G20
MARK ANTHONY
dr. Dandenong S.....549 E11
MARKER
rd. Melb Airport.......235 L8
MARKET
ct. Reservoir...........283 B5
ct. Skye.................575 G17
la. Melbourne.............2 L11
la. Melbourne...........24 G5
la. N Melbourne........17 E15
pl. Braybrook...........321 J19
pl. Camberwell.........372 J20
pl. Port Melb............412 K5
pl. S Melbourne........29 K2
rd. Brooklyn............365 E11
rd. Sunshine............365 E11
rd. Werribee............447 F11
st. Boronia..............424 F7
st. Dandenong.........536 A7
st. Essendon............323 C2
st. Essendon............323 F3
st. Geelong, off Myers St..........703 A9
st. Keilor Park.........277 L13
st. Kensington..........33 H7
st. Lilydale..............338 E5
st. Melbourne.............1 G18
st. Melbourne...........24 A10
st. Montmorency....413 E1
st. Newport.............410 H10
st. Nunawading.......376 H15
st. Ringwood.........378 C12
st. Rye....................696 J3
st. St Kilda.............414 D17
st. Southbank............3 A16
st. Southbank..........29 J2
st. S Melbourne..........3 A16
st. S Melbourne........29 J2
st. S Melbourne......413 E1
st. South Yarra..........32 C15
st. South Yarra........414 G8
st. W Footscray.......366 J7
tce. Taylors Hill........274 E8
MARKET STREET
ml. Box Hill.............374 K15
MARKEY
ct. Altona Mdw........451 K6
MARKHAM
av. Ashburton..........417 F18
cl. Altona Mdw.........451 C6
ct. Keysborough.....534 B8
rd. Gisborne..............80 K4
wy. Altona Mdw........451 D6
MARKHILL
pl. Heathmont.........422 H1
pl. Knoxfield............423 D20
MARKLIN
st. Cranbourne.........578 F20
MARKS
av. Heidelberg Ht.....284 E18
av. Rosebud............683 G18
ct. Harkaway...........540 F17
la. Emerald.............510 G16
la. Footscray...........367 K6
st. Brunswick...........325 J13
st. Coburg..............325 D5
st. Pascoe Vale.......280 B15
st. Strathmore.........279 K19
MARKSTONE
ct. Sunshine...........321 F19
MARLA
ct. Frankston..........600 E19
MARLAND
rd. Boronia.............424 G10
MARLBOROUGH
av. Camberwell.......417 B3
cr. Hoppers Csg.......448 E9
ct. Noble Park.........534 J5
rd. Bayswater.........423 C2
rd. Heathmont.........378 E20
rd. Heathmont.........422 E1
st. Balaclava...........414 G18
st. Bentleigh E.........457 B19
st. Caulfield N.........415 D16
st. Fawkner.............281 G11
st. Glenroy..............280 A5
st. Herne Hill...........701 J3
st. Mont Albert........374 C14
st. Sydenham..........274 K1
wy. Sydenham.........274 L1
MARLEE
ct. Grovedale.........706 C11
MARLEIGH
st. Vermont............420 K5
MARLENE
cl. Doncaster E.......332 F7
ct. Cheltenham........497 F20
ct. Ferntree Gly.......464 A17
ct. Hampton Pk........551 E9
ct. Springvale..........500 E7
MARLESFORD
av. Wantirna............422 F14
cr. Berwick.............554 D18
MARLEY
cl. Rowville.............463 F20
mw. Cranbourne E.....604 H5
MARLEYBOURNE
ct. Greenvale..........237 F4
MARLIN
tce. Seabrook..........450 J7
MARLIN BAY
Patterson L........573 G8
MARLINO
av. Warburton.........349 E1
MARLO
ct. Broadmeadows..238 B15
ct. S Morang...........199 K16
dr. Melton W...........225 L13
gr. Beaumaris..........530 E5
gr. Mt Eliza.............641 L5
pl. Frankston...........600 H17
pl. Hallam..............537 E17
sq. Wyndham Va.....446 J9
st. Wantirna............422 E11
MARLOCK
cl. Thomastown......240 J12
st. Frankston N.......600 F9
wy. Delahey.............275 C10
MARLOO
ct. Croydon Hills.....335 F15
MARLOW
pl. Eltham..............288 B8
st. Mooroolbark......337 B16
MARLOWE
st. Canterbury.........373 D18
MARLTON
cr. St Kilda.............414 F13
MARLYN
ct. Highton.............701 K17
MARMA
ct. Grovedale.........706 C16
rd. Murrumbeena....457 B12
MARMAL
ct. Tullamarine........236 E19
MARMARA
dr. Elsternwick........454 L8
dr. Elsternwick........455 A8
MARMION
st. Rye...................696 G10
MARMONT
pl. Ferntree Gly.......464 A14
MARNA
ct. Noble Park.........535 C1
st. Dromana............686 D5
st. Healesville.........257 G4
MARNE
av. Wyndham Va.....446 D15
ct. Bundoora...........284 F6
rd. Mt Evelyn..........382 J1
st. St Kilda E..........415 A17
st. South Yarra..........31 G8
st. South Yarra........414 D4
st. Surrey Hills........417 L2
MARNEBECK
ct. Cranbourne.........578 B19
MARNEY
ct. Brookfield..........268 C5
MARNGO
ct. Kurunjang..........227 C13
MARNI
st. Dandenong S.....549 H7
MARNIE
dr. Cranbourne W....577 F20
pl. Hallam..............538 D14
MARNOCK
rd. Newtown...........702 C15
MARNOO
ct. Tootgarook........698 B7
st. Braybrook..........365 H4
MAROCK
pl. Balwyn..............373 D14
MARON
cl. Seabrook...........450 K7
MARONEY
ct. Doncaster E.......332 H14
MARONG
ct. Boronia.............424 L4
ct. Broadmeadows..238 D15
ct. Greensborough..244 J19
gr. Balwyn..............373 L13
tce. Forest Hill.........420 D1
MAROO
st. Hughesdale........457 F7
MAROOCHY
pl. Burnside............318 H6
MAROONA
rd. Brighton............455 A12
rd. Carnegie............456 E6
rd. Highett..............496 A11
MAROONDAH
ct. St Albans...........320 F13
hwy. Blackburn.........375 C15
hwy. Box Hill.............374 C13
hwy. Chirnside Pk......337 A8
hwy. Coldstream........295 A19
hwy. Croydon.............379 B5
hwy. Croydon N.........335 J20
hwy. Gruyere............254 F20
hwy. Healesville.........257 B10
hwy. Lilydale............295 A19
hwy. Lilydale............337 A8
hwy. Lilydale............339 A3
hwy. Mitcham...........376 G14
hwy. Mont Albert........374 C13
hwy. Mooroolbark......337 A8
hwy. Nunawading.......376 G14
hwy. Ringwood..........379 B5
hwy. Ringwood E.......379 B5
hwy. Ringwood N.......379 B5
hwy. Surrey Hills........374 B13
pde. Healesville.........214 E13
rd. Ashwood............418 F15
tce. Bundoora...........242 C19
MAROONG
dr. Eltham North......288 G1
dr. Research...........246 G20
dr. Research...........288 G2
MAROORA
st. Malvern East......456 J3
MAROUANDS
rd. Truganina..........405 K10
MAROUBRA
av. Noble Park.........534 G7
MARQUET
ct. Hillside..............274 F1
MARQUIS
av. Mornington........657 A5
rd. Bentleigh...........496 E5
st. Ashburton..........417 E14
MARRA
ct. Endeavour Hl.....537 D7
MARRAKAI
ct. Eltham..............287 C3
MARRAROO
cl. Bayswater N.......380 J16
MARRBRIDGE
rd. Moorabbin.........496 K9
MARRIAGE
rd. Brighton East.....455 B20
MARRIOT
rd. Bentleigh...........496 C5
rd. Keilor Dn...........275 L11
MARRIOTT
cr. Skye.................575 H15
pde. Glen Waverley....460 C3
st. Caulfield............455 J3
st. Oakleigh............458 A8
st. Parkdale............531 H10
st. St Kilda.............414 E16
MARRITA
ct. Pt Lonsdale.......710 D3
MARROO
st. Doncaster..........374 H3
MARRSON
pl. Glenroy.............279 H3
MARS
ct. Newcomb..........704 D13
st. Caulfield S.........455 E9
MARSDEN
av. Pascoe Vale S....324 G6
cr. Doncaster E.......331 J17
cr. St Albans...........320 A4
ct. Cranbourne N.....578 A9
ct. Kilsyth S............424 L1
ct. Mill Park............242 E1
wk. Roxburgh Pk......194 C12
MARSEILLES
wy. Point Cook.........450 F11
MARSH
cr. Sunbury.............142 J14
ct. Wantirna S.........462 D5
st. Altona North.......409 F3
st. Maidstone..........322 K20
MARSHALL
av. Clayton.............459 A16
av. Doncaster..........375 C2
av. Highett..............495 K15
av. Kew..................372 D10
av. Montmorency....286 L13
av. St Albans...........320 L3
av. St Albans...........321 A4
cl. Carrum Downs....600 J1
cl. Sunbury.............143 D2
ct. Hampton Pk........551 C6
dr. Mill Park............242 G6
dr. Reservoir...........283 G3
pl. Clifton Hill............20 F4
pl. Hallam..............537 F14
pl. Newtown...........702 H12
rd. Airport W...........278 J11
rd. Box Hill N...........375 D8
st. Flemington..........33 G3
st. Ivanhoe.............328 D16

st. Moonee Pnd 324 A12
st. Mt Evelyn 339 G19
st. Newtown 702 G12
st. Noble Park 501 C20
st. Rye 698 A2
st. S Melbourne 29 L4
st. Sunshine N 321 F13
st. Tootgarook 698 A2
st. Wheelers Hill 461 D20
tce. Montrose 382 D14
tce. Mt Dandenong 382 D14

MARSHALLS
rd. Christmas Hills 207 D1
rd. St Andrews 207 D1

MARSHALLTOWN
rd. Grovedale 706 G9
rd. Marshall 706 G9

MARSHAM
rd. Mt Waverley 419 C14
st. Noble Park N 501 F16

MARSON
cr. Hallam 538 B16
ct. Pakenham 584 E6

MARSTON
st. Bentleigh 496 D2

MARTELL
st. Broadmeadows 238 B17

MARTENS
ct. Sunbury 142 G9
ct. Taylors Lakes 275 B1
pl. Dingley Village 532 L3

MARTHA
ct. Craigieburn 150 H17
st. Donvale 376 F5
st. Seaford 599 F5

MARTI
ct. Sunshine W 364 E7

MARTIN
cl. S Morang 199 E11
cr. Glen Iris 416 E14
ct. Bentleigh E 497 C7
ct. Berwick 554 C17
ct. Doncaster 331 B15
ct. Fairfield 327 G18
ct. Forest Hill 420 G4
ct. Montrose 382 B13
ct. Seaholme 409 J16
ct. Toorak 415 C6
pl. Bayswater 423 C5
pl. Cranbourne 578 A16
pl. Glen Waverley 420 C16
pl. Pakenham 585 A1
rd. Glen Iris 416 J10
st. Beaumaris 530 C12
st. Belgrave 466 C17
st. Box Hill N 375 C7
st. Brighton 454 F10
st. E Geelong 703 E15
st. Heathmont 379 C20
st. Heidelberg 328 J7
st. Mt Martha 669 A2
st. Notting Hill 459 G14
st. Pascoe Vale 280 L13
st. Preston 327 B1
st. Rosebud 684 G16
st. St Kilda 414 E17
st. Seaford 599 F5
st. S Melbourne 29 L8
st. S Melbourne 413 F4
st. Springvale S 534 B3
st. Sunshine 365 D3
st. Thomson 703 E15
st. Thornbury 326 J10

MARTINDALE
pl. Templestowe 331 L7

MARTINE
ct. Hoppers Csg 447 K3

MARTINGALE
ct. Epping 198 F17
pl. Pakenham 585 E5

MARTINS
la. Portsea 677 K3
la. View Bank 285 G16

MARTYR
rd. Warburton 349 D2

MARVIL
av. Narre Warren 539 E13

MARVILLE
ct. Boronia 423 H13

MARVIN
av. Rye 697 C3

MARWAL
av. Balwyn N 373 B4

MARWARRA
st. Ringwood E 378 J13

MARWEN
dr. Derrimut 363 G14

MARWICK
st. Flemington 324 F20

MARY
av. Edithvale 546 J10
av. Heidelberg Ht 328 E4
av. Highett 496 B16
av. Werribee 447 K17
av. Wheelers Hill 461 D12
cl. Woori Yallock 344 B13
ct. Berwick 554 L8
ct. Croydon N 336 A12
ct. Epping 241 C1
ct. Mornington 640 H16
ct. Noble Park 535 C7
ct. St Albans 320 B11
ct. Somerville 645 B15
pl. Wattle Glen 246 K1
st. Balwyn N 374 B6
st. Beaumaris 529 L5
st. Blackburn 375 L15
st. Box Hill N 375 C13
st. Brighton 454 J17
st. Carlton 18 D16
st. Carlton N 325 K19
st. Clayton 498 K1
st. Coburg 325 G2
st. Dromana 686 E8
st. Emerald 469 J20
st. Essendon 323 B5
st. Ferny Creek 426 B15
st. Footscray 367 D6
st. Frankston 599 A16
st. Hampton Pk 551 B6
st. Hawthorn 371 J15
st. Kew 372 A10
st. Malvern 416 A8
st. Melton S 268 G5
st. N Melbourne 17 E14
st. Officer 582 L7
st. Officer 583 A7
st. Pakenham 558 B20
st. Preston 282 K20
st. Preston 326 K2
st. Richmond 32 H3
st. Richmond 414 K2
st. Ringwood 377 K13
st. Safety Bch 668 K20
st. St Kilda W 413 L14
st. Spotswood 366 J20
st. Springvale 500 A10
st. Upwey 465 C10
st. Wandin East 340 L18
st. Wandin East 341 A18
st. Windsor 414 J11

MARYBOROUGH
av. Kingsbury 283 L10
rd. Boronia 423 K15

MARY BRYANT
ct. Mill Park 242 E5

MARYGATE
pl. Berwick 554 G8

MARYKIRK
dr. Wheelers Hill 461 C16

MARYLAND
cl. Thomastown 240 E15
st. Caulfield S 455 K8

MARYLEBONE
st. Sunbury 144 E8

MARYLIN
ct. Bentleigh E 496 H6

MARYLOU
ct. Delahey 275 D10

MARYLYN
pl. Cranbourne 578 A12

MARYN
cl. Berwick 553 L6

MARY ROSE
st. Blairgowrie 679 J19

MARYROSE
cr. Endeavour Hl 537 L1

MARYSTON
st. Yarraville 366 J14

MARYVALE
st. Sunshine 365 E2

MARYVILLE
st. Ripponlea 454 H1

MARY WALSH
st. Maribyrnong 367 C2

MASARYK
ct. Vermont 421 A3

MASCHES HILL
rd. Monbulk 427 L20
rd. Monbulk 467 L1

MASCOMA
st. Ascot Vale 324 F17
st. Strathmr Ht 279 C9

MASCOT
av. Bonbeach 573 A7

MASEFIELD
av. Mooroolbark 381 F1
av. Sandringham 495 C17
ct. Delahey 275 E15

MASERATI
dr. Epping 197 J14

MASHIE
ct. Rosebud 700 B9

MASHOOBRA
st. Coburg N 281 C13

MASKED OWL
rd. S Morang 199 H13

MASKELL
cr. Lower Plenty 286 F14
st. Brighton 454 L16
st. Selby 467 B17

MASKELLS HILL
rd. Selby 467 A19

MASLEN
cl. Frankston 599 H18

MASON
av. Elwood 454 F1
av. Safety Bch 686 G1
ct. Bayswater N 379 H19
ct. Highett 496 G13
ct. Highton 705 J3
ct. Melton 268 J1
ct. Mt Waverley 458 H9
ct. Queenscliff 707 K18
ct. Templstw Lr 330 G10
dr. Braeside 532 G15
gr. Sassafras 426 G11
la. Mont Albert 374 D15
pl. South Yarra 31 E7
st. Altona North 409 K5
st. Campbellfield 239 G12
st. Collingwood 25 F1
st. Dandenong 535 L9
st. Ferntree Gly 464 G7
st. Hawthorn 371 E14
st. Mt Eliza 642 E5
st. Newport 410 H6
st. Northcote 326 K18
st. Reservoir 282 L15
st. South Yarra 31 E7
st. Whittlesea 96 L19
wy. Berwick 553 L8

MASONIC
av. Warrandyte 290 D20

MASONS
la. Abbotsford 20 F15
la. Bacchus Msh 221 K13
la. Melbourne 2 E13
la. Melbourne 24 D7
la. Mernda 154 D10
la. Mernda 155 A11
la. Mernda 156 A12
la. Werribee S 488 C18
la. Wollert 153 J10
la. Wollert 154 D10
rd. Blackburn 376 A20

MASSEY
av. Reservoir 282 E3
st. Box Hill S 419 A5

MASSON
rd. Parkville 18 B13

MASTERS
cct. Roxburgh Pk 194 A9
st. Caulfield 455 H6
st. Dandenong 536 D10

MASTERTON
pl. Cranbourne E 578 H19

MAST GULLY
rd. Ferny Creek 466 B5
rd. Upwey 465 J10

MATEO
cl. Dandenong N 502 B11

MATER
st. Collingwood 19 H10

MATHER
cl. Croydon 380 C1
rd. Mt Eliza 642 G2
rd. Noble Park 534 K3

MATHERS
av. Kew East 372 C4
av. Launching Pl 345 E16

MATHESON
ct. Berwick 554 D2
ct. Wheelers Hill 460 L18
rd. Forest Hill 420 F6

MATHEW
ct. Langwarrin 629 F4
pl. Mt Evelyn, off Camric Ct 339 E18

MATHEWS
ct. Reservoir 283 K16
st. Melton S 268 F11

MATHIAS
rd. Olinda 427 A3

MATHIESON
pl. Burwood 418 E5
st. Coburg N 281 G12

MATHILDE
rd. Surrey Hills 374 B20

MATHIS
av. Keilor Dn 276 B13
av. Tootgarook 698 B7

MATHOURA
cl. Noble Park N 501 C11
rd. Toorak 415 A8

MATILDA
av. Wantirna S 422 B15
ct. Belmont 706 H3
ct. Eltham 287 C4
rd. Moorabbin 496 K10

MATIPO
st. Doveton 536 H12

MATISI
st. Thornbury 327 H7

MATISSE
dr. Templestowe 332 C9

MATLOCK
av. Mulgrave 500 F1
cl. Jan Juc 711 B16
ct. Bangholme 549 H13
ct. Caulfield N 415 G16
ct. Thomastown 240 E12
rd. Boronia 423 B11
rd. Wantirna S 423 B11
st. Canterbury 373 C19
st. Hoppers Csg 449 D1
st. Preston 326 C3

MATONG
rd. Mt Eliza 625 H18

MATSON
dr. Upwey 465 L16

MATTEA
ct. Lilydale 338 F3
ct. Reservoir 283 K17

MATTERS
rd. Pakenham Up 511 E20

MATTHEW
cl. Hoppers Csg 448 A3
cl. Keysborough 534 G13
ct. Hampton Pk 551 F10
ct. Taylors Lakes 275 F5
rt. Endeavour Hl 537 K3
st. Carnegie 456 F7
st. Glen Waverley 419 J19
st. McCrae 685 B15
st. Mt Martha 656 B12
st. Tooradin 651 G6

MATTHEW FLINDERS
av. Endeavour Hl 537 E8

MATTHEWS
av. Airport W 279 A18
cr. Roxburgh Pk 194 B15
ct. Brighton East 455 E16
ct. Ferntree Gly 464 H4
ct. Launching Pl 345 F17
ct. Mill Park 242 F7
ct. Pakenham 584 D3
ct. Sunshine W 363 L7
ct. Toorak 415 C2
la. S Melbourne 30 H4
mw. Kensington 33 D11
pl. Dandenong N 501 L13
rd. Bentleigh E 497 D4
st. Sunshine 365 F6

MATTHIESON
st. Highett 496 G15

MATTINGLEY
cr. Brunswick W 325 A8

MATTINGLY
la. N Melbourne 17 C17

MAUCHLINE
ct. Noble Park N 501 E11

MAUD
rd. Dromana 685 K9
st. Balwyn N 372 L4
st. Balwyn N 373 A4
st. Geelong 702 K10
st. Ivanhoe 327 L13
st. Ormond 455 L13

MAUDE
av. Doncaster E 376 C3
av. Glenroy 280 G6
ct. Narre Warren 538 F15
st. Box Hill N 375 A9
st. Chadstone 418 E19
st. Cheltenham 496 J20
st. Mt Martha 655 L13
st. Murrumbeena 457 D12

MAUGHAN
pde. Balwyn N 373 L6
rd. Mt Eliza 642 C9

MAUGIE
pl. Abbotsford 20 D11
st. Abbotsford 20 C11
st. Abbotsford 20 D11

MAUREEN
cl. Cranbourne W 603 E2
cr. Noble Park 534 G4
ct. Dandenong N 501 G19
ct. Heatherton 497 H15
ct. Melton W 225 L19
ct. Narre Warren 538 F15
st. Mt Waverley 419 A13

MAUREVA
ct. Bundoora 285 C2

MAURICE
av. Ringwood 378 B15
av. Somerton 194 H11
ct. Keilor East 278 G20
ct. Nar Warrn N 538 H10
ct. Wantirna S 422 J17
rd. Gruyere 340 L4
rd. Gruyere 341 A4
st. Cockatoo 510 L9
st. Dandenong 535 E2
st. Hawthorn E 372 E14

MAURINE
ct. Ringwood N 378 G1

MAURY
la. Chelsea 546 K20
rd. Chelsea 546 K20

MAUS
st. Highton 701 K20

MAVERICK
cl. Doncaster 331 A15
st. Sorrento 679 B12

MAVERSTON
st. Glen Iris 417 E10

MAVHO
st. Bentleigh 456 A20

MAVIS
av. Beaconsfield 555 J9
av. Brighton East 455 D14
cr. Kings Park 275 E20
ct. Broadmeadows 238 E19
ct. Yallambie 285 E16
st. Coburg 325 D5
st. Footscray 367 A4

MAVISTA
av. Glen Waverley 420 C15

MAVRON
st. Ashwood 418 D17

MAWARRA
av. Rosebud W 699 E2
cr. Chadstone 458 D1
ct. Highton 701 K15

MAWBY
rd. Bentleigh E 496 G4

MAWSON
av. Anglesea 713 G4
av. Deer Park 319 C10
cl. Mill Park 243 A6
cl. Taylors Lakes 275 H4
cl. Wantirna S 462 C3
cl. Wyndham Va 446 E7
ct. Cranbourne N 577 L10
ct. Mulgrave 460 C17
ct. Sunbury 143 B13
ct. Vermont 421 F4
st. Kew 372 H13
st. Melton 226 G18

MAX
cl. Rowville 463 H15
ct. Noble Park 500 D19

MAXFLO
ct. Highett 495 L15

MAXIA
rd. Doncaster E 375 L5

MAXINE
ct. Mentone 531 G5
ct. Mt Waverley 458 F4
ct. Noble Park 535 D1
dr. St Helena 245 A16

MAXWELD
st. Ardeer 320 B20

MAXWELL
av. Altona North 410 D6
av. Belmont 706 K1
ct. Attwood 237 C10
ct. Blackburn S 419 G1
ct. Langwarrin 629 D9
ct. Millgrove 348 F1
ct. Moorabbin 496 F11
ct. Noble Park 535 B4
ct. Seaford 599 L1
ct. Toorak 415 E3
gr. Caulfield 455 K4
gr. Glen Waverley 420 A18
gr. Point Cook 450 A6
st. Ashburton 417 B17
st. Blairgowrie 679 K19
st. Dandenong S 536 C15
st. Kew 372 D11
st. Lalor 241 F10
st. Mornington 656 F4
st. Mornington 656 H1
st. Northcote 327 C15
st. Springvale S 534 C4

MAY
av. Altona Mdw 451 D4
av. Rye 697 E3
ct. Bundoora 284 F2
ct. Dandenong 536 C2
ct. Ferntree Gly 463 F6
ct. Glen Waverley 459 K9
ct. Grovedale 706 B10
ct. Mitcham 377 J11
gr. South Yarra 32 H11
gr. South Yarra 414 K6
gr. Sunbury 142 H10
pl. Port Melb 412 J3
pl. Red Hill 688 C7
rd. Beaconsfield 555 H17
rd. Junction Vill 604 H12
rd. Lalor 241 C11
rd. Mooroolbark 337 J17
rd. Officer 555 H17
rd. Toorak 32 L16
rd. Toorak 414 L8
rd. Toorak 415 A8
st. Aberfeldie 323 B11
st. Altona North 409 K3
st. Balwyn 373 B11
st. Bentleigh E 456 G19
st. Brighton 454 K10
st. Bundoora 284 E2
st. Cannons Creek 649 G9
st. Cheltenham 496 H18
st. Coburg 281 F19
st. Doncaster E 332 B19
st. Elsternwick 454 L4
st. Elwood 454 G2
st. Fitzroy N 326 C17
st. Footscray 366 L3
st. Frankston S 626 K4
st. Glenroy 280 K4
st. Hampton 495 D8
st. Kew 372 C13
st. Macleod 285 A14
st. Mornington 640 E14
st. Newport 410 E4
st. Northcote 327 C19
st. Preston 282 F17
st. Silvan 384 F14
st. Sunshine 365 G3
st. Tullamarine 278 G4

MAYBURY
ct. Berwick 554 L20
ct. Rowville 463 J20
dr. Mill Park 242 F10

MAYEGLEN
ct. Cockatoo 511 C7

MAYFAIR
Mont Albert N, off Scarborough Sq 374 E7
av. Point Cook 449 L4
av. Templstw Lr 330 G11
cl. Gladstone Pk 237 B18
cl. Narre Warren 539 B14
cr. Narre Warren 539 C14
ct. Chirnside Pk 336 J6
ct. Croydon 335 K20
ct. Frankston 600 C17
ct. Keysborough 534 K8
ct. Mulgrave 500 L4
dr. Ferntree Gly 464 C6
dr. Newtown 701 K10
st. Wyndham Va 446 E9

MAYFIELD
av. Brunswick 325 B16
av. Camberwell 417 F4
av. Malvern 415 K7
ct. Croydon 335 H19
ct. Grovedale 706 H14
ct. Montrose 381 K11
dr. Mill Park 242 L11
dr. Mt Waverley 458 H5
gr. Altona Mdw 450 J1
gr. Caulfield N 415 K18
pl. Ferntree Gly 463 L13
rd. Cranbourne E 579 D20
rd. Cranbourne E 604 L6
st. Abbotsford 26 G1
st. Coburg 325 F3
st. Greensborough 285 K2
st. St Kilda E 414 K20

MAYFIN
ct. Sunbury 143 C4

MAYFLOWER
ct. Brighton East 455 C18

MAY GIBBS
cr. Lynbrook 551 C18

MAYGRAND
pl. Kilsyth S 425 A1

MAYGROVE
wy. Mulgrave 501 E4

MAYLANDS
av. Balwyn N 372 L6
av. Balwyn N 373 A6
cr. Glen Waverley 460 G12
st. Albion 320 J19

MAYLING
ct. Watsonia 285 F9

MAYNARD
pl. Kings Park 319 B2
st. Preston 327 B2

MAYNE
st. Cheltenham 497 B15
st. Sunshine W 364 K5
st. Sunshine W 365 A5

MAYO
cl. Templestowe 332 A5
ct. Chelsea Ht 547 G16
ct. Wandin N 340 L13
ct. Wandin N 341 A13
st. Sunshine 364 L8
st. Sunshine 365 A8

MAYONA
rd. Montmorency 286 G7
rd.e, Montmorency 286 K9

MAY PARK
av. Ashwood 417 L16

MAYRAH
ct. Grovedale 706 C14

MAYROSE
cr. Brighton East 495 B3

MAYRUCK
ri. Hampton Pk 551 K12

MAYS
rd. Eltham 288 A13

MAYSBURY
av. Brighton 494 G2
av. Elsternwick 455 A4
av. Rosebud 683 J17

MAYSIA
st. Canterbury 417 D1

MAYSTON
st. Hawthorn E 372 G19

MAYSWOOD
ct. Moorabbin 496 K8

MAYTON
ct. Grovedale 706 E9

MAYUNE
ct. Cranbourne 578 B18

MAYVIEW
dr. Monbulk 468 K2

MAYWOOD
dr. Epping 241 L1
rd. Cranbourne S 630 L10

MAZDA
ct. Southbank 23 D18
ct. S Melbourne 23 D18

MAZEEPA
st. Healesville 257 J4

MAZZEI
wy. Sydenham 274 J4

MEABY
st. Jan Juc 711 F13

MEAD
ct. Oakleigh 457 L14
ct. Wantirna S 462 B4

MEADE
wy. Sydenham 274 H4

MEADEN
st. Ashburton 417 E17
st. Southbank 23 G20
st. Southbank 29 H1
st. Southbank 413 D1

MEADER
st. Doncaster 330 K20

MEADOW
av. Rye 698 A5
cr. Badger Creek 258 F12
cr. Montmorency 286 L8
cr. Mt Waverley 459 G4
ct. Blackburn S 419 J6
ct. Dingley Village 533 C9
ct. Nar Warrn S 553 C17
ct. View Bank 285 K19
ct. Wandin N 340 K16
gr. Balwyn 372 L11
gr. Balwyn 373 A11
la. Ferntree Gly 463 F6
la. Mt Eliza 626 G14
pl. Templestowe 331 K9
rd. Croydon N 336 D15
st. St Kilda E 415 A20

MEADOWBANK
av. Chirnside Pk 336 G8
av. Doncaster 375 B4
cl. Lysterfield S 504 A15
ct. Craigieburn 194 A3
ct. Kings Park 275 D18
dr. Sunshine N 320 L11
st. Glenroy 281 B4

MEADOWBROOK
dr. Wheelers Hill 460 G15
pl. Keysborough 534 B10

MEADOW CROFT
ct. Cranbourne E 578 H20

MEADOW FAIR
wy. Chirnside Pk 293 F20

MEADOWGATE
dr. Chirnside Pk 337 D6

MEADOW GLEN
dr. Epping 198 D19
dr. Melton W 225 G17
dr. Melton W 225 H17

MEADOWLARK
la. Mooroolbark 337 D13

MEADOWS
ct. Chadstone 458 B6
st. Coburg 282 A20

MEADOWVALE
dr. Grovedale 705 G13
pl. Lilydale 338 D13

MEADOW VIEW
pl. Mornington 656 K5
rd. Somerville 644 D19

MEADOWVIEW
ct. Ferntree Gly 464 A8
la. Emerald 469 F15

MEADOW WOOD
wk. Narre Warren 552 K4

MEADS
ct. St Albans 275 G18

MEAGAN
cl. Thomastown 240 J11
ct. Aspendale Gdn 546 H2

MEAGER
st. Deer Park 319 B17

MEAGHAN
ct. Rowville 463 J19

MEAGHER
ct. Maidstone 322 H17
rd. Ferntree Gly 423 L20
st. Watsonia 285 G5

MEAKA
ct. Warrandyte 332 L6
ct. Warrandyte 333 A6

MEAKER
av. Brunswick W 324 L16
av. Oak Park 280 B11

MEAKIN
st. E Geelong 703 H12
st. Watsonia N 285 F3

MEANDER
rd. Hurstbridge 202 J15

MEANEY
st. Elsternwick 455 D4

MEASHAM
pl. Hawthorn 372 A15

MEDA
ct. Grovedale 706 C16

MEDBURY
av. Greensborough 285 J8
av. Watsonia 285 J8

MEDDINGS
ct. Altona North 365 E20
ct. Thomson 703 J17

MEDEO
ct. Delahey, off Albertine Cr 275 F9

MEDFIELD
av. Avondale Ht 322 D13

MEDFORD
st. Altona 408 J16

MEDHURST
ct. Greensborough 244 A18
rd. Gruyere 296 L11
st. Burwood E 419 E8
st. Sandringham 495 G16

MEDICAL
rd. Parkville 17 K13

MEDICI
ct. Keilor Lodge 276 B5

MEDINA
rd. Glen Waverley 419 L18
rd. Keilor Dn 276 E15

MEDINAH
cl. Sunbury 144 F12
ri. Hampton Pk 552 D9

MEDLAR
ct. Mill Park 243 A9
st. Pearcedale 646 G2

MEDLEY
cl. Harkaway 540 B14
pl. South Yarra 32 C12
st. South Yarra 32 C13
st. South Yarra 414 G6

MEDLOW
la. Somerville 644 E20

MEDORA
av. Bundoora 242 F19

MEDORO
gr. Mulgrave 500 C1

MEDSTEAD
ct. Craigieburn 194 C1

MEDWAY
av. Cheltenham 497 G19
cr. Boronia 423 K9
cr. Darley 221 H2
rd. Craigieburn 150 C15
rd. Keilor East 322 G7
st. Box Hill N 374 K11
st. Seddon 367 D11

MEEHAN
ct. Endeavour Hl 537 E6
ct. Keilor 277 A13
st. St Albans 319 F7

MEEK
rd. Oaklands Jctn 191 D10
st. Brighton 454 G12
st. Werribee 447 G11

MEEKING
dr. Pakenham 584 C6

MEEKS
la. N Melbourne 17 J18

MEERLU
av. Frankston 600 C20

MEERUT
st. Mitcham 377 B15

MEGAN
cl. Cranbourne W 577 E19

MEHEGAN
av. Coburg N 282 B18

MEIKLE
st. Maddingley 221 K20

MEIN
pl. Mt Eliza 642 J1
st. Springvale 500 C9

MEKONG
cl. Werribee 447 G6
pl. Roxburgh Pk 194 F6

MELALEUCA
av. Doncaster 330 H15
av. Rosebud W 683 C20
av. Templstw Lr 330 H15
cl. Hillside 274 A2
cr. Langwarrin 629 K3
ct. Berwick 553 H3
ct. Frankston 627 L8
ct. Rowville 463 J17
dr. Carrum 573 C7
dr. Clarinda 498 E4
dr. Glen Waverley 460 A7
dr. Meadow Ht 193 K20
dr. Thomastown 240 J12
dr. Upwey 465 G17
rd. Mt Martha 656 F6
wy. Box Hill S, off Peppermint Gr 375 B20

MELANDA
ct. Frankston 628 E5

MELANEE
ct. Lalor 240 H10

MELANIE
cl. Keysborough 534 K11
ct. Wantirna S 462 L2
cl. Wantirna S 463 A2
ct. Langwarrin 601 K20
ct. Mt Waverley 458 G9
dr. Werribee 447 G20

MELANIE BLAIR
pl. Skye 575 H18

MELBA
av. Lilydale 338 B8
av. Sunbury 142 F9
ct. Balwyn 373 J10
ct. Burwood E 419 G9
ct. Mulgrave 500 F1
hwy. Coldstream 295 C9
hwy. Dixons Ck 210 A10
hwy. Yarra Glen 209 B19
hwy. Yarra Glen 253 C6
hwy. Yering 253 C6
hwy. Yering 295 C9
pde. Anglesea 713 E8
pl. Chirnside Pk 337 E1
st. Epping 197 G17
st. Nar Warrn S 553 G20
wy. Croydon Hills 335 H16

MELBALL
st. Bentleigh E 496 H5

MELBE
cr. Dandenong 536 A6

MELBOURNE
av. Glenroy 280 A5
dr. Melb Airport 235 K12
pl. Melbourne 2 K13
pl. Melbourne 24 G6
rd. Blairgowrie 679 E17
rd. Gisborne 79 B13
rd. Newport 411 A9
rd. Rye 696 H6
rd. Rye 697 A5
rd. Sorrento 678 H10
rd. Spotswood 410 L3
rd. Williamstown 411 E15
st. Murrumbeena 457 B6
st. Wantirna S 422 K17
st.n, Wantirna S 422 K16
st.s, Ringwood 378 E12

MELBOURNE HILL
rd. Warrandyte 333 E4

MELBOURNE-LANCEFIELD
rd. Bulla 144 H3
rd. Sunbury 114 H2

MELBY
av. St Kilda E 414 K19

MELCOMBE
rd. Ivanhoe 328 E10

MELDAN
st. Burwood 418 D7

MELDRETH
st. Surrey Hills 373 K14

MELDRUM
av. Mill Park 242 K8
cl. Taylors Lakes 233 A20
ct. Doncaster E 332 F16
ct. Nar Warrn S 552 G18
ct. Sunbury 142 J10
st. Kew East 372 F3

MELFIN
dr. Hillside 232 D18

MELFORT
av. Essendon 324 D3

MELIA
ct. Mill Park 243 B10
ct. Werribee 447 J8
la. Maribyrnong 322 H16
st. Doveton 536 H13

MELIBEE
st. Blairgowrie 696 B4

MELINA
ct. Endeavour Hl 537 D2

MELINGA
cr. Chadstone 458 E1
cr. Mornington 640 L17
cr. Mornington 641 A17

MELISSA
cl. Hurstbridge 203 C13
ct. Bayswater N 379 H16
ct. Eltham North 245 D19
ct. Hampton Pk 551 L14
ct. Mooroolbark 336 L12
ct. Narre Warren 539 B15
ct. View Bank 286 A16
gr. Vermont S 421 B9
nk. Deer Park 319 E9
st. Donvale 332 G20
st. Mt Waverley 458 G9
st. Strathmore 280 A17

MELITA
av. Werribee 447 F19

MELL
st. Toorak 415 A8

MELLIODORA
ct. Endeavour Hl 502 K20
pl. Yallambie 286 B11

MELLON
ct. Sunbury 142 H13

MELLOR
ri. Roxburgh Pk 193 K14
st. Sunshine 321 E20

MELLOWOOD
ct. Carrum Downs 601 B4
ct. Ferntree Gly 423 H17

MELODY
cl. Lilydale 338 F13
ct. Mooroolbark 337 C13

MELODY HILL
ct. Dandenong N 501 K9

MELON
st. Braybrook 366 A4

MELOSA
av. Brighton East 495 G1
av. Clayton S 498 H8

MELRICH
rd. Bayswater 424 B6

MELROSE
av. Coldstream 295 E13
av. Highton 701 J15
av. Macleod 285 B12
av. Malvern East 457 A1
ct. Berwick 554 D15
ct. Boronia 424 K7
ct. Glen Waverley 421 A19
dr. Melb Airport 236 A15
dr. Mt Martha 655 H18
dr. Strathmr Ht 279 A8
dr. Tullamarine 236 A15
dr. Tullamarine 278 H3
dr. Tullamarine 278 K6
dr. Tullamarine 279 A8
la. N Melbourne 34 J11
pl. Mill Park 242 H12
pl. Werribee 448 D17

st. Braybrook 365 L3
st. Cremorne 25 L19
st. Mont Albert N 374 F11
st. Moonee Pnd 323 H14
st. Mordialloc 531 J14
st. Newport 410 H9
st. N Melbourne 34 J11
st. Parkdale 531 J14
st. Sandringham 495 A14
tce. Somerville 645 B16

MELS
pl. Lysterfield 463 K20

MELSETTA
ct. Carrum Downs 575 B17

MELTON
av. Camberwell 417 L9
av. Carnegie 456 F11
av. Sunshine N 320 L14
cl. Werribee 447 J7
cr. Lalor 241 B6
ct. Dallas 238 D12
gr. Croydon 335 F18
hwy. Hillside 231 G20
hwy. Hillside 274 D1
hwy. Keilor Lodge 275 J4
hwy. Melton 269 H3
hwy. Plumpton 228 A18
hwy. Plumpton 231 B20
hwy. Rockbank 228 A18
hwy. Sydenham 275 A2
hwy. Taylors Lakes 275 A2

MELTON-GISBORNE
rd. Kurunjang 227 E15
rd. Melton 227 E17

MELTON VALLEY
dr. Melton 227 D19

MELVA
ct. Frankston 627 G4
ct. Sydenham 274 H3
st. Bentleigh E 457 D16

MELVERTON
dr. Hallam 538 A18

MELVIEW
dr. Ringwood N 378 D3
dr. Springvale S 499 E19
dr. Wyndham Va 446 C12

MELVILLE
av. Frankston 626 L3
av. Newtown 702 A8
cl. Keilor 276 K10
ct. Mt Waverley 459 D4
dr. Greensborough 286 K2
rd. Brunswick W 324 L13
rd. Pascoe Vale S 324 L2
st. Fitzroy N 326 D18
st. Hawthorn 371 G14
st. Port Melb 412 H4
st. Tootgarook 698 C2

MELVILLE PARK
dr. Berwick 554 E11

MELVIN
st. Frankston 599 D20

MELWOOD
ct. Meadow Ht 238 A5

MEMBERS
dr. Flemington 367 L1

MEMBREY
cl. Werribee 446 J14
st. Northcote 326 J17

MEMORIAL
av. Emerald 509 E3
av. Epping 197 E18
dr. Nar Warrn N 539 D8
dr. Noble Park 500 G16
dr. Plenty 244 G8

MEMORY
ct. Kilsyth S 424 L3
la. Rowville 503 B8

MENA
av. Cheltenham 531 C2
av. Croydon 379 L4
ct. Wheelers Hill 461 B17
st. Frankston 599 K20

MENANA
rd. Glenroy 279 G8

MENARRA
st. Doncaster 330 D19
st. Strathmore 279 H13

MENCK
st. Nunawading 376 F13

MENDES
pde. Sorrento 679 B11

MENDIP
rd. Reservoir 283 C13

MENDORA
cr. Wantirna S 422 F19

MENIN
rd. Forest Hill 376 H20
rd. Monbulk 428 B17
rd. Nunawading 376 H20

MENINDEE
ct. Lilydale 338 C2

MENLO
av. Tecoma 466 E9

MENSA
ct. Roxburgh Pk 194 G10

MENTHA
st. Sunshine W 364 E2

MENTMORE
cl. Sunshine W 364 C6

MENTON
ct. Avondale Ht 322 E9

MENTONE
pde. Mentone 531 B8

MENTOR
ct. Epping 198 C20

MENZIE
gr. Eaglemont 328 G13

MENZIES
av. Brighton 494 G3
av. Dandenong N 501 J19
cl. Frankston S 626 H5
cr. Ringwood N 378 B4
ct. Brunswick W 324 J7
dr. Sunbury 143 F6
dr. Bundoora, off College Dr 284 F12
pde. Lalor 241 J10
pl. Keilor East 321 K5
rd. Kangaroo Grnd 248 F20
rd. Menzies Ck 468 E18
st. Box Hill 375 A19
st. Braybrook 365 L1
st. Rye 696 H9

MEPHAN
st. Footscray 367 A2
st. Maribyrnong 367 A2

MEPPEL
dr. Clayton S 498 K5

MERA
cl. Deer Park 318 K13

MERBEIN
st. Pascoe Vale 281 A11

MERBOW
st. Oakleigh 458 B11

MERCANTILE
pde. Kensington 33 D11
pl. Melbourne 1 A18
pl. Melbourne 23 J12

MERCEDES
ct. Rosanna 329 D1
dr. Thomastown 242 A17
st. Keilor 277 B11

MERCER
ct. Coldstream 295 F12
ct. Dandenong N 502 B9
ct. Delahey 275 B12
pde. Newtown 702 F9
pl. Point Cook 449 L6
pl. Geelong, off Mercer St 702 L4
rd. Armadale 415 H12
st. Geelong 702 L4
st. Oakleigh E 458 D10
st. Queenscliff 708 L19

MERCHANT
av. Thomastown 242 A19
st. Rye 696 E4

MERCHANTS
ct. Werribee 447 J20

MERCHISTON
gr. Strathmore 323 K2

MERCIA
av. The Basin 425 A13

MERCIER
st. Coburg N 281 D18

MERCIL
rd. Alphington 327 H17
st. Alphington 327 H17

MERCURY
cr. Newcomb 704 E13
st. Caulfield S 455 E9

MERCY
ct. Nar Warrn S 579 F3

MERDON
pl. Kurunjang 227 B13

MERE
ct. Sunbury 144 G14

MEREDITH
av. Templestowe 332 A11
cl. Nar Warrn S 552 J16
cr. Hampton Pk 552 B13
pl. Portsea 677 H4
st. Broadmeadows 238 C19
st. Elwood 454 B2
st. Kings Park 319 E2
st. Malvern 416 B10
st. Mt Waverley 458 J3
st. Noble Park N 501 D15
st. Sandringham 495 J19

MEREWEATHER
av. Frankston 599 C15

MERIBAH
cl. Mornington 656 G4
ct. Frankston 627 K5
ct. Noble Park 534 E6
ct. Parkdale 531 J9

MERIBEL
wy. Lynbrook 551 G15

MERIBIL
cl. Mt Eliza 626 J19

MERIDIAN
ct. Langwarrin 601 F18
ct. Mooroolbark 337 B13
pde. Wantirna S 422 D19

MERILYN
wy. Frankston S 627 E20
wy. Rosebud 700 A1

MERIMBULA
ct. Taylors Lakes 276 B7
rd. Ferny Creek 425 K20

MERINDA
ct. Frankston 628 C3
ct. Grovedale 706 D15

MERINGER
ct. Nunawading 376 K11

MERINO
av. Dallas 238 D10
ct. Highton 701 G16
mw. Kensington 33 B10
st. Laverton N 364 G19
st. Reservoir 283 J6

MERION
ct. Rowville 462 C20
ct. Sunbury 144 H13

MERITON
pl. Clayton S 498 K6

MERIVALE
dr. Wantirna 422 F9

MERLE
st. Blackburn N 375 K10

MERLEWOOD
ct. Bundoora 242 E18

MERLIN
al. Melbourne 1 H10
al. Melbourne 23 L7
cr. Ferntree Gly 463 G7
ct. Frankston 600 B18
ct. Notting Hill 459 J15
st. Chum Creek 213 A13
st. Doncaster 374 L2
st. Healesville 213 A13

MERLINS
tr. Warrandyte 334 D1

MERLOW
st. Albion 320 G20
st. Altona 408 H16

MERLYN
av. Clayton S 498 J7
st. Coburg N 281 E12
st. Maribyrnong 367 A1

MERMAID
ct. Patterson L 573 K11

MERNA
dr. Templestowe 331 F7

MERNDA
av. Ashburton 417 K14
av. Bonbeach 573 A6
av. Burwood 417 K14
av. Carnegie 456 F8
av. Cheltenham 496 E17
av. Glen Iris 417 K14
pde. Belmont 706 F3
rd. Kooyong 415 L6
rd. Olinda 427 F17
st. Rye 696 G10
st. Sunshine W 364 L3
st. Sunshine W 365 A3

MEROLA
wy. Campbellfield 239 C2

MERON
ct. Greensborough 286 B9

MERRAFIELDS
ct. Taylors Lakes 276 F8

MERRALYN
st. Belmont 706 K2

MERRAN
ct. Wheelers Hill 461 E18

MERRANG
ct. Wheelers Hill 460 H12

MERRANS
rd. Healesville 214 J15

MERRETT
av. Flemington 323 L20
av. Hoppers Csg 448 G2
dr. Williamstown 410 K14

MERRETTS
pl. Melbourne 1 B10
pl. Melbourne 23 H8

rd. Avonsleigh 471 B8
rd. Macclesfield 471 B8

MERRI
dr. Braeside 547 F2
dr. Campbellfield 239 H9
pde. Northcote 326 E17
st. Brunswick 325 F15
st. Templstw Lr 330 F9

MERRIBELL
av. Coburg 326 A3
dr. Waurn Ponds 705 F15
dr. Waurn Ponds 705 F16

MERRICK
cr. Glen Waverley 460 B9
ct. Highton 705 H4
st. Keysborough 534 L11

MERRICKS
cl. Ferntree Gly 464 D6
st. Broadmeadows 237 H15

MERRIFIELD
st. Brunswick 325 F13

MERRIGAL
ct. Frankston S 626 J13

MERRIGAN
ct. Roxburgh Pk 194 A13

MERRIGUM
cr. Clarinda 498 D8
ct. Doncaster 331 F18
ct. Highton 701 E11
la. Belgrave 466 C16
la. Launching Pl 345 E17

MERRIJIG
av. Cranbourne 578 G16

MERRILANDS
rd. Reservoir 282 K1

MERRILL
cr. Croydon Hills 335 D12
cr. Warranwood 335 D12
ct. Mooroolbark 337 A11
dr. Epping 198 C18
st. Mulgrave 500 F4

MERRILONG
st. Ringwood E 379 A13

MERRIMAN
la. Melbourne 23 G7

MERRIMU
ct. St Albans 320 E12
la. Sherbrooke 466 H2
st. Murrumbeena 457 E6

MERRINDALE
dr. Croydon S 380 E11
dr. Kilsyth 380 E11

MERRION
gr. Kew, off Merrion Pl 371 H11
pl. Kew 371 H11

MERRITS
rd. Panton Hill 204 H15

MERRITT
ct. Altona 408 K14

MERRIVALE
av. Sunshine W 364 A5
pl. Roxburgh Pk 194 A7
wy. Bundoora 284 G8

MERRIWEE
cr. Toorak 415 J6

MERRIWOOLA
st. St Kilda E 455 A1

MERRY
st. Ringwood E 378 L12

MERRYLANDS
av. Portsea 678 G3

MERRYN
cl. Bundoora 242 G15
cl. Endeavour Hl 537 G5
ct. Templestowe 331 H7
gr. Wantirna S 422 B16

MERSEY
cl. Rowville 463 E18
cr. Seaford 573 E15
ct. Werribee 447 H7
rd. Kilsyth 381 C13
st. Box Hill N 375 B12
st. Bundoora 284 B1
st. Ringwood N 378 D7

MERTHER
rd. Ivanhoe 327 L8

MERTHYR
pl. Aspendale Gdn 547 B7

MERTON
av. Brighton 454 G10
cl. Cheltenham 531 D2
cl. Mt Waverley 419 H16
cl. Sunbury 143 B11
ct. Coldstream 295 F16
ct. Endeavour Hl 503 C20
gr. Healesville 213 G17
gr. Manifold Ht 702 C4
pl. Albert Park 29 H15
pl. Albert Park 413 D7

st. Albert Park 29 G11
st. Albert Park 413 D6
st. Altona 407 G16
st. Altona Mdw 451 F6
st. Box Hill 374 L17
st. Camberwell 417 G7
st. Caulfield N 455 B1
st. Ivanhoe 328 B16
st. St Albans 320 D7
st. S Melbourne 29 F8
st. S Melbourne 413 C5
st. Springvale 500 B13

MERTZ
ct. Point Cook 450 F5

MERUKA
dr. Eltham 287 C8

MERVILLE
av. Malvern East 457 A4

MERVIN
st. Bentleigh E 496 H5

MERVYN
cr. Ivanhoe 328 D15
rd. Belgrave S 506 A11
st. Doncaster 374 J3
st. Newtown 702 F11

MERYL
st. Armadale 415 G13
st. Doncaster E 375 J5

MERZ
pl. Roxburgh Pk 194 C8

MESETA
st. Mooroolbark 337 D9

MESKILL
cr. View Bank 286 A15

MESSINA
cr. Keilor Lodge 276 A4
ct. Kurunjang 227 C11

MESSMATE
ct. Berwick 553 G4
ct. Emerald 470 A17
ct. Mt Martha 656 F7
rd. Ferntree Gly 423 F19
rd. Torquay 711 D3
ri. Eltham North 245 F18
st. Frankston N 599 L11
st. Lalor 241 C11

MET
rd. Melb Airport 235 B9

METCALF
cr. Rowville 463 D18
pl. Epping 197 K19

METELMAN
ct. Broadmeadows 238 F19

METEOR
ri. Kealba 321 A2
st. Mt Waverley 419 A12

METERY
rd. Eltham 287 H13

METHERALL
st. Sunshine N 320 K13
st. Sunshine N 321 A13

METHVEN
st. Brunswick E 325 K15
st. Coburg 325 G4

METROPOLITAN
av. Craigieburn 150 C14
av. Nunawading 376 D15
ct. Burwood 418 B4
ct. Keilor 276 H8

METTERS
st. Maribyrnong 367 B2

METUNG
ct. Dingley Village 532 L8
st. Balwyn 373 B10

METYLENE
av. Springvale 499 F13

METZ
pl. Keilor Dn 276 A15

MEW
ct. Mill Park 242 A3

MEYER
cl. Blackburn 375 L11
ct. Brighton East 455 C13
rd. Burwood 418 A11
st. Cockatoo 511 B8

MEYERS
pl. Melbourne 24 J5

MEYRICK
cr. View Bank 285 G19

MEYTAN
wy. Albanvale 319 B4

MIA
ct. Reservoir 282 A3
ct. Sunshine W 364 J7
ct. Werribee 448 D16
pl. Meadow Ht 194 A17
st. Clarinda 498 G11

MIAMI
ct. Oakleigh S 497 G1
st. Hawthorn E 416 D2

MICA
ct. Kings Park 275 B18
ct. Narre Warren 539 D13
MICHAEL
av. Glen Waverley 460 F3
av. St Albans 276 G18
ct. Altona North 365 L20
ct. Berwick 554 K6
ct. Eltham North 245 G17
ct. Forest Hill 420 J5
ct. Hillside 274 F2
ct. Niddrie 322 K3
ct. Noble Park 535 B6
ct. Seaford 599 G3
ct. Springvale 500 G7
ct. Woori Yallock 344 F14
la. Melbourne 1 H12
la. Melbourne 24 A8
la. Mt Evelyn 339 K15
pl. Ringwood N 378 J1
st. Beaumaris 530 F6
st. Brunswick 325 E15
st. Dromana 685 L10
st. Fitzroy N 326 E20
st. Lalor 241 J8
st. Pakenham 558 B20
st. Rye 696 J3
st. Scoresby 462 D8
st. Templstw Lr 330 E13
wy. Somerville 644 J15
MICHEALA
ct. Langwarrin 601 L19
MICHELE
ct. Rye 696 K1
dr. Scoresby 462 E5
MICHELINE
st. Tullamarine 278 G4
MICHELLAN
ct. Bayswater 422 K4
ct. Donvale 332 H18
MICHELLE
av. Watsonia N 243 G20
cl. Thomastown 240 G17
ct. Cranbourne W 577 J19
ct. Hoppers Csg 405 F18
ct. Noble Park 534 D6
ct. Oakleigh S 498 A6
ct. Rosanna 285 D20
dr. Berwick 554 A19
dr. Hampton Pk 551 L14
pl. Melton W 226 C18
pl. Wheelers Hill 460 J10
MICHELTON
gr. Point Cook 450 G10
MICHIGAN
pl. Rowville 462 L16
tce. Broadmeadows 238 K12
tce. Thomastown 240 G11
MICKLE
st. Dandenong S 549 H8
st. Tooradin 651 G9
MICKLEHAM
rd. Attwood 236 J18
rd. Craigieburn 149 A16
rd. Craigieburn 192 J1
rd. Gladstone Pk 236 J18
rd. Greenvale 192 H20
rd. Tullamarine 278 J3
rd. Westmeadows 236 J18
rd. Yuroke 192 J1
MIDAS
ct. Meadow Ht 237 K5
MIDDLE
cr. Brighton 454 J15
ct. Thomastown 242 A16
rd. Camberwell 416 H6
rd. Derrimut 363 A8
rd. Malvern East 457 J5
rd. Maribyrnong 323 B13
rd. Pearcedale 630 H10
rd. Pearcedale 646 F7
st. Ascot Vale 324 D18
st. Hadfield 280 H7
wy. Yellingbo 387 J9
MIDDLEBOROUGH
rd. Blackburn 375 D17
rd. Blackburn N 375 E11
rd. Blackburn S 419 C11
rd. Box Hill 375 D17
rd. Box Hill N 375 E11
rd. Box Hill S 419 C11
rd. Burwood 419 C11
rd. Burwood E 419 C11
MIDDLEBROOK
dr. Ringwood N 334 H19
dr.n,Ringwood N 334 H18
MIDDLEFIELD
dr. Blackburn N 375 K7
MIDDLEHAM
cl. Cranbourne W 577 H16
cl. Lysterfield 464 D17
MIDDLEHUT
rd. Doreen 201 L1
rd. Nutfield 201 L1
MIDDLESEX
rd. Surrey Hills 373 J20
rd. Surrey Hills 417 J2
st. Sunshine N 321 G16
MIDDLETON
ct. Greenvale 193 D18
dr. Woori Yallock 344 G13
la. Southbank 4 B20
la. Southbank 30 H1
la. S Melbourne 30 H1
pl. W Melbourne 23 D4
st. Black Rock 529 E1
st. Braybrook 366 C2
st. Highett 496 C16
st. Lalor 241 D9
st. Watsonia N 285 F3
MIDHOLM
ct. Thomastown 240 L11
MIDHURST
ct. Craigieburn 149 L14
rd. Croydon 335 J18
MIDLAND
wy. Taylors Lakes 233 E20
MIDLOTHIAN
ct. Point Cook 450 G6
pl. Glen Waverley 460 F8
st. Malvern East 457 G4
MIDVALE
av. Balwyn N 373 H1
MIDWAY
cl. Gladstone Pk 279 D1
cr. Lalor 241 G5
ct. Keilor Park 278 A12
st. Heidelberg W 328 A1
st. Mt Waverley 418 J15
MIGA
cl. Greensborough 244 B20
MIGHTY APOLLO
la. W Melbourne 23 A2
MIHAN
ct. Pakenham 559 J17
st. Noble Park 501 A18
MIHIL
st. Preston 327 C5
MIKADO
rd. Mt Evelyn 339 E12
st. Hadfield 280 H6
MIKKELL
ct. Pakenham 585 A3
MILAN
ct. Bonbeach 573 B5
ct. Dandenong N 502 A15
ct. Sunbury 142 L4
st. Doncaster E 376 A3
st. Mentone 530 L9
st. Wantirna 422 F6
MILANO
ct. Bundoora 242 H18
pl. Cranbourne N 578 J10
MILAS
ct. Keilor Dn 276 C15
MILBORNE
cr. Eltham 288 D4
MILBREY
cl. Wantirna S 422 A20
MILBURN
cct. Caroline Spr 318 A4
ct. Endeavour Hl 538 A4
gr. St Kilda E 415 A20
pl. Craigieburn 150 H20
rd. Keilor 277 C7
st. Keilor 277 A12
MILDARA
st. Vermont S 421 D9
MILDENHALL
ct. Altona Mdw 451 J2
MILDURA
av. Sandringham 494 L13
av. Warburton 348 K3
cr. Dallas 238 F8
cr. Endeavour Hl 537 D2
MILE
la. Parkville 17 J5
la. Parkville 325 E20
MILE END
rd. Carnegie 456 G5
MILES
av. Ringwood 378 D11
cl. Mill Park 243 B4
ct. Bacchus Msh 221 J18
ct. Cranbourne 577 L19
gr. Seaford 599 E5
pl. Roxburgh Pk 194 D14
rd. Parwan 265 C17
st. Bentleigh 495 K1
st. Deer Park 319 C16
st. Ivanhoe 327 L13
st. Mulgrave 499 K1
st. Newtown 702 F10
st. Richmond 26 B12
st. Southbank 3 F16
st. Southbank 24 D19
MILEWA
ct. Mornington 656 G3
MILFAY
av. Kew 371 F9
av. Moonee Pnd 324 B13
ct. Balwyn N 374 A2
MILFORD
av. Burwood 418 H8
av. Wheelers Hill 461 A9
cl. Albanvale 318 L6
cr. Frankston 600 F18
ct. Kings Park 319 A1
ct. Meadow Ht 237 K2
gr. Rosanna 285 B20
pl. Belmont 706 A7
pl. Bundoora 284 L1
st. Bentleigh E 496 J5
st. Kilsyth 381 G6
st. Moolap 704 K20
st. Newport 410 J9
st. Thomastown 242 A12
MILFUL
cl. Rowville 463 J18
MILFULL
ct. Narre Warren 539 H16
MILGATE
ct. Forest Hill 376 J20
ct. Mooroolbark 337 G11
ct. Nunawading 420 J1
st. Oakleigh S 458 F17
tce. Sunbury 142 H2
wy. Avondale Ht 322 C12
MILINA
ct. Frankston 600 H17
MILITARY
rd. Avondale Ht 322 B8
rd. Avondale Ht 322 C11
tr. Langwarrin 628 G13
MILKWORT
tr. Frankston N 600 G10
MILKY
la. Whittlesea 96 D6
MILL
av. Forest Hill 420 E4
av. Yarraville 366 G18
ct. View Bank 285 K17
ct. Wesburn 348 A12
ct. Wheelers Hill 461 C19
la. Williamstown 411 D18
pl. Melbourne 1 L18
rd. Gisborne 79 C11
rd. Oakleigh 457 J11
rd. Yarra Glen 208 L17
st. Aspendale 546 B1
st. Pakenham 584 D1
MILLAH
rd. Balwyn 373 E14
MILLAN
ct. Glen Waverley 460 B11
MILLAR
rd. Tullamarine 278 G1
MILLARD
st. Bentleigh E 497 A3
st. Frankston 627 F3
st. Templstw Lr 329 L8
MILLAWA
av. St Albans 320 D4
MILLBANK
dr. Deer Park 319 A12
dr. Mt Eliza 626 G20
pl. Cranbourne 578 H17
st. Bacchus Msh 221 L17
MILLEARA
rd. Avondale Ht 322 C8
rd. Keilor East 278 D19
st. The Basin 425 H8
MILLENNIUM
ct. Knoxfield 462 J10
mw. Richmond 371 A15
wy. Torquay 711 H12
MILLER
cl. Eltham 287 H3
cr. Mt Waverley 418 K19
ct. Bundoora 284 L1
ct. Cranbourne 577 L10
ct. Dandenong N 536 D1
ct. Hoppers Csg 405 C18
gr. Kew 371 F12
gr. Ringwood E 379 B9
la. S Melbourne 30 H4
la. S Melbourne 413 K3
pl. Doncaster 331 D17
pl. W Melbourne 17 A20
rd. Healesville 300 B15
rd. Heathmont 379 E19
rd. Macclesfield 471 H1
rd. The Basin 424 J8
st. Alphington 327 J18
st. Berwick 554 G6
st. Blairgowrie 696 A3
st. Box Hill 375 B15
st. Brighton 454 E13
st. Brunswick E 326 A17
st. Carnegie 456 E10
st. Coburg 325 J5
st. Elsternwick 454 J4
st. Epping 241 D1
st. Essendon 323 J7
st. Fawkner 281 J6
st. Fitzroy N 326 A17
st. Healesville 213 L20
st. Heidelberg Ht 328 E5
st. Highett 495 L14
st. Newcomb 704 B13
st. Prahran 32 J17
st. Prahran 414 L9
st. Preston 326 D5
st. Preston 326 J6
st. Richmond 26 A13
st. Sandringham 495 H16
st. Sunbury 143 D12
st. Thornbury 326 D5
st. W Melbourne 34 L20
MILLERS
rd. Altona 409 F20
rd. Altona North 409 J8
rd. Brooklyn 365 K18
rd. Seaholme 409 F20
rd. Wattle Glen 247 E11
MILLETT
rd. Gisborne S 141 A1
MILLEWA
av. Malvern East 457 D4
cr. Dallas 238 D12
wy. Wyndham Va 446 F13
MILLGATE
dr. Mornington 641 C20
MILLGROVE
av. Thomastown 240 E11
st. Scoresby 462 B6
wy. Berwick 554 C20
MILLIARA
gr. Brighton East 455 E16
st. Mt Waverley 419 G17
MILLICENT
av. Balwyn N 329 G20
av. Bulleen 329 L17
av. Toorak 415 D8
ct. Mornington 640 L8
st. Burwood 418 C9
st. Carrum 573 D8
st. Rosanna 329 A1
MILLIE
ct. Rowville 503 D3
MILLIGAN
pde. Sydenham 274 K3
MILLIS
av. Bentleigh E 497 A4
MILLOO
cr. Mt Waverley 419 D13
MILL PARK
dr. Mill Park 242 J10
MILLPERRA
ct. Frankston 600 H14
MILLPORT
ct. Endeavour Hl 503 K17
ri. Greenvale 237 G2
MILLS
av. Sassafras 426 J12
av. Somerton 194 G17
cl. Footscray 367 F5
la. Geelong, off Bellerine St 703 C10
rd. Belgrave Ht 466 H20
rd. Braeside 532 G12
rd. Dandenong 535 E10
rd. Hurstbridge 203 G14
st. Albert Park 29 J19
st. Albert Park 413 D10
st. Altona North 410 A8
st. Cheltenham 497 E16
st. Glen Iris 417 G10
st. Hampton 495 A7
st. Middle Park 29 H19
st. Middle Park 413 D10
st. Sunshine N 321 F15
MILLSON
cl. Bundoora 242 G16
ct. Pascoe Vale 281 A14
MILLSTREAM
av. Point Cook 450 B4
cct. St Albans 319 F6
MILLSWYN
av. Hampton Pk 551 G5
pl. South Yarra 31 E5
st. South Yarra 31 D7
st. South Yarra 414 B4
MILLWARD
st. Brunswick 325 B17
MILLWOOD
av. Berwick 554 B8
ct. Templestowe 331 G13
MILNE
av. Seaford 599 D8
ct. Delahey 275 D15
ct. Langwarrin 629 D7
ct. Pt Lonsdale 710 C6
pl. Eltham North 245 C17
pl. Ringwood N 378 G3
rd. Mont Albert N 374 F7
rd. Pk Orchards 334 D18
st. Mitcham 376 L13
st. Templestowe 330 L8
st. Thomastown 241 D18
MILNER
av. Anglesea 713 G6
cl. Templestowe 331 F7
ct. Cranbourne 577 L14
MILNERS
rd. Yarra Jctn 347 C20
MILOJEVIC
ct. Cranbourne 578 E17
MILONE
ct. Werribee 447 F19
MILORA
ct. Pt Lonsdale 710 C5
MILPA
ct. Rye 697 G9
MILPARINKA
st. Safety Bch 669 D11
wy. Berwick 554 F11
MILPERA
cr. Wantirna 422 A13
MILPORT
ct. Point Cook 450 G7
MILROY
cr. Seaford 573 F14
ct. Wheelers Hill 461 F17
st. Brighton East 455 C14
MILSOM
av. Templstw Lr 330 F10
pl. S Melbourne 29 D3
MILTHORPE
rd. Yarrambat 201 K19
MILTON
av. Clayton S 499 C8
av. St Albans 320 J2
cl. Warrandyte 333 G4
cr. Box Hill S 418 G2
cr. Heidelberg Ht 328 D2
cr. Mulgrave 500 G5
cr. Preston 326 K5
ct. Aspendale Gdn 546 H3
ct. Mooroolbark 381 F2
dr. Wyndham Va 446 D14
pde. Bundoora 242 J20
pde. Glen Iris 416 D10
pde. Malvern 416 B7
pl. Cremorne 26 F17
pl. Gladstone Pk 279 E1
pl. Nar Warrn S 552 J15
rd. Rye 696 G3
st. Ascot Vale 324 C16
st. Bentleigh 455 J19
st. Canterbury 373 E20
st. Carnegie 456 F6
st. Elwood 414 E20
st. Elwood 454 C1
st. Ferntree Gly 464 F4
st. Glenroy 280 B9
st. Heathmont 379 A18
st. Macleod 285 C12
st. Nunawading 376 D18
st. Pascoe Vale S 280 J20
st. W Footscray 366 K7
st. W Melbourne 23 G1
wy. Hurstbridge 203 D14
MILVERTON
ct. Grovedale 706 H13
st. Camberwell 417 G8
st. Melton 226 J16
st. Moonee Pnd 323 L14
MIMI
ct. Somerville 644 E16
MIMOSA
av. Campbellfield 239 F12
av. Emerald 510 E4
av. Kilsyth 381 C8
av. Mt Evelyn 383 B1
av. Oakleigh S 458 B17
ct. Croydon S 379 E12
ct. Doncaster E 332 F18
ct. Frankston 628 F7
rd. Carnegie 456 G8
rd. Carnegie 456 H5
rd. Mill Park 242 F11

rd. Selby 467 C15
st. Doveton 536 L8
st. Glen Waverley 420 K20
st. Newcomb 704 A15
MINAK
rd. Selby 467 C14
MINAKI
av. Doncaster E 332 C20
MINATO
pl. Taylors Lakes 275 H3
MINCHA
av. Templstw Lr 329 L9
st. Brunswick W 324 K16
st. Frankston 627 E6
MINCHINBURY
dr. Vermont S 421 E9
MINDAH
ct. Vermont S 421 C8
MINDANAO
ct. Armadale 415 G11
MINDARA
av. Rowville 502 E7
ct. Diamond Ck 245 K6
ct. Hoppers Csg 448 G8
MINDORO
cr. Lalor 241 J6
MINE
rd. Cottles Br 202 H1
rd. Nutfield 202 H1
st. Greensborough 244 G19
MINER
ct. Werribee 447 K10
MINERS
ct. Diggers Rest 187 A12
ct. Mulgrave 501 F3
MINERVA
av. Balwyn N 373 G1
cr. Keilor Dn 276 B11
cr. Vermont S 420 H12
ct. Wheelers Hill 460 D14
dr. Williamstn N 410 F12
rd. Herne Hill 702 A5
rd. Manifold Ht 702 A5
rd. Newtown 702 A5
rd. Newtown 702 A6
MINES
rd. Ringwood E 378 K9
MINE SHAFT
rd. Christmas Hills 206 F11
rd. Macclesfield 470 K1
rd. Smiths Gly 206 F11
MINETT
ct. Narre Warren 552 F2
MINETTE
ct. Ormond 455 J13
MINGANA
rd. Wantirna S 422 L11
rd. Wantirna S 423 A11
MINGETA
av. Blackburn S 419 K6
MINIATA
wk. Vermont S 420 L10
wk. Vermont S 421 A10
MINIFIE
av. Anglesea 713 G6
MINIMBAH
ct. Frankston S 626 K12
MINJAH
ct. Dingley Village 533 D6
MINKA
pl. Skye 601 D7
MINKARA
ct. Croydon 380 G7
MINKELL
ct. Wantirna 422 A9
MINLYA
av. Mt Waverley 459 D4
MINNA
st. Blackburn 375 E15
MINNIE
st. Brunswick 325 J15
st. Sandringham 495 D12
st. Yarraville 367 F17
MINNIMURRA
rd. Rye 697 B3
MINNO
ct. Frankston 600 J19
MINNS
la. Geelong, off Little Malop St 703 A7
pl. Geelong, off Little Malop St 703 A8
rd. Kurunjang 226 H5
rd. Melton W 226 B4
MINOGUE
cr. Hoppers Csg 448 F3
st. Kew East 372 G2
MINONA
st. Fawkner 281 J4
st. Hawthorn 372 C18
MINT
ct. Chelsea Ht 547 H18
st. Wantirna 422 C3
MINTARO
ct. Templestowe 331 E14
wy. Seabrook 450 L4
MINTBUSH
cl. Keysborough 534 A16
rd. Wesburn 348 D16
MINTER
ct. Pk Orchards 333 H10
st. Belgrave 466 E14
MINTO
st. Kew East 372 E4
MINTON
cl. Boronia 424 J4
dr. Frankston 599 J17
wk. Nar Warrn S 579 F2
MINYA
ct. Rowville 463 F13
MIOWERA
grn. Greensborough 244 D14
MIRA
st. Blackburn S 419 G6
MIRABEL
av. Ringwood E 379 C8
MIRABELLA
cl. Werribee 447 J3
cr. Box Hill S 419 C4
ct. Warrandyte 333 C7
dr. Tullamarine 278 L5
dr. Tullamarine 279 A5
MIRAGE
wk. Point Cook 450 D5
MIRAM
ct. Westmeadows 237 H12
MIRAMAH
cl. Rowville 502 J2
MIRAMAR
ct. Donvale 332 G16
MIRAMS
st. Ascot Vale 323 K17
MIRANDA
cl. Clayton S 499 E11
cl. Torquay 712 E4
ct. Mitcham 377 C13
ct. Noble Park 534 H6
gdn. Hampton Pk 552 D10
pl. Frankston 627 K10
rd. Reservoir 283 D6
st. Sorrento 678 F9
MIRANG
av. Croydon 380 E9
av. Mt Martha 655 H14
ct. Frankston 599 K16
MIRBELIA
cr. Mill Park 243 B8
MIRBOO
ct. Brookfield 268 C6
ct. Dallas 238 C12
st. Dandenong N 501 F13
MIRCELLA
pl. Melton W 226 D19
MIRIAM
cl. Narre Warren 538 L15
cl. Wantirna S 421 L15
cl. Wheelers Hill 461 B20
ct. Airport W 278 G16
ct. Bundoora 285 C2
ct. Somerville 644 F16
ct. Templestowe 331 G8
dr. Yarra Glen 208 L19
st. Caulfield 456 A5
st. Rosanna 329 D2
st. Thomastown 241 L12
MIRINO
st. Blairgowrie 696 B7
MIRKA
la. St Kilda 414 D16
MIRLS
st. Newport 410 K8
MIRM
la. Sydenham 274 K7
MIRNONG
ct. Croydon N 336 D12
MIRRA
ct. Bundoora 284 L4
MIRRABOOK
ct. Berwick 553 H1
MIRRAM
ct. Epping 241 K2
MIRRAMS
la. Brighton East 495 C4
MIRRIAM
av. Rosebud W 683 E18
MIRRIM
pl. Gowanbrae 279 E6
MIRROR
ct. Taylors Lakes 275 K6
MIRSTAN
ct. Hillside 232 E20
MISSEN
ct. Altona Mdw 451 G3
MISSENS
rd. Cranbourne W 577 C12
MISSION
pl. Carlton 18 E19
st. Sorrento 679 B16
MISSISSIPPI
cl. Rowville 462 J17
pl. Werribee 447 J4
MISSOURI
av. Brighton 454 L9
pl. Werribee 447 H6
MISTEN
av. Altona North 409 F2
MISTLETOE
cl. Knoxfield 463 B2
MISTY
cl. Frankston 600 G18
st. Campbellfield 239 H15
wk. Bundoora 284 F7
MITA
cl. Narre Warren 538 G16
MITARM
cl. Mt Evelyn 339 J15
MITCHAM
rd. Donvale 376 G2
rd. Mitcham 377 A7
rd. Vermont 421 C1
MITCHELL
av. Altona North 410 C5
av. Ashwood 418 E18
av. Boronia 424 H7
av. Montmorency 287 A13
av. Warrandyte 290 A18
cr. Meadow Ht 238 D1
cr. Port Melb, off Nott St 412 J7
ct. Attwood 237 B10
ct. Berwick 555 A20
ct. Cranbourne N 577 J8
ct. Croydon N 335 L14
ct. Darley 222 A9
ct. Diamond Ck 245 L13
ct. Glenroy 280 A2
ct. Noble Park 500 J17
ct. Taylors Lakes 275 G7
ct. Werribee 447 F7
gr. Taylors Hill 274 H13
pde. Pascoe Vale S 324 G1
pl. Rowville 503 D2
rd. Caulfield N 455 G2
rd. Lilydale 338 L12
rd. Lilydale 339 A11
rd. Lilydale 339 A12
rd. Melton S 268 F12
rd. Mont Albert N 374 F8
st. Ashburton 417 K17
st. Belmont 702 J19
st. Bentleigh 496 B3
st. Blackburn N 375 K9
st. Brunswick 325 G9
st. Brunswick E 325 G9
st. Burnley 371 B18
st. Doncaster E 375 H2
st. Fairfield 327 A15
st. Glenroy 279 L2
st. Maidstone 322 E20
st. Maidstone 366 J1
st. Maribyrnong 367 A1
st. Mentone 531 C8
st. Mornington 640 D20
st. Northcote 326 J15
st. Preston 326 E5
st. Rosebud 684 E14
st. St Albans 320 A4
st. St Kilda 414 D18
st. Seaford 599 E3
MITCHELLS
la. Sunbury 142 G14
MITCHELTON
ct. Vermont S 421 D10
MITCHEM
st. Maddingley 264 A3
MITFORD
cr. Craigieburn 194 G2
cr. Craigieburn 194 G3
pde. W Footscray 366 C14
pl. St Kilda 414 C20
st. Elwood 454 D1
st. St Kilda 414 C19
MITIC
ct. Frankston S 626 J10
MITRE
cr. Bayswater 423 H7
cr. Berwick 553 G5
cr. Frankston N 600 D6
ct. Broadmeadows 237 J13
la. Melbourne 1 G15
la. Melbourne 24 A9
MITTA
cl. Rowville 463 F16
ct. Croydon Hills 335 K16
ct. Keilor 276 L12
ct. Keilor 277 A12
ct. Werribee 448 C19
pl. Taylors Hill 274 L14
st. Box Hill N 374 K9
MITTAGONG
ct. Berwick 539 J20
MITTA MITTA
wy. Meadow Ht 194 C18
MIZMAZE
rd. Sherbrooke 426 J19
MLADEN
ct. Coolaroo 238 E4
MOAMA
cr. Pascoe Vale S 324 F5
pl. Rowville 463 F12
rd. Malvern East 456 F1
st. Braybrook 365 J4
MOANA
dr. Mooroolbark 336 J13
pl. Donvale 332 K18
MOASCAR
st. Pascoe Vale S 324 H2
MOAT
dr. Bundoora 284 D13
MOATA
ct. Grovedale 705 J13
MOATE
st. Healesville 214 J16
st. Langwarrin 629 B2
MOCHRIE
gr. St Albans 319 F7
MOCK
st. Forest Hill 420 E6
st. Sandringham 495 C14
MOCKERIDGE
dr. Mill Park 242 E6
MOCKRIDGE
av. Burnside 318 D8
av. Caroline Spr 318 C8
st. Wantirna S 462 F3
MOE
ct. Dallas 238 F10
MOFFAT
cl. Endeavour Hl 503 G17
ct. Greenvale 193 D20
st. Brighton 494 J4
st. St Albans 319 G1
st. South Yarra 31 J14
st. South Yarra 414 E7
MOFFATT
cr. Hoppers Csg 448 K4
st. Avondale Ht 322 A16
MOHILLA
st. Mt Eliza 641 H2
MOHR
st. Tullamarine 278 C9
MOINA
ct. Patterson L 573 K6
MOIR
dr. Roxburgh Pk 194 F8
st. Hawthorn 372 B14
MOIRA
av. Carnegie 456 G10
av. Ferntree Gly 423 H17
av. Highett 495 H14
av. Reservoir 282 A1
gr. Glen Waverley 420 F17
rd. Kilsyth 381 D7
st. Malvern East 416 K17
st. Sunshine 364 L7
st. Sunshine 365 A7
MOKHTAR
dr. Hoppers Csg 449 D2
MOKOAN
cl. Caroline Spr 317 L7
MOLAN
st. Ringwood 377 K14
MOLBRAY
st. Box Hill N 375 C8
MOLDEN
ct. Kings Park 275 A20
st. Bentleigh E 456 H14
MOLESWORTH
ct. Highton 705 J7
ct. W Footscray 366 H6
st. Canterbury 373 G20
st. Coburg 281 E19
st. Hawthorn E 372 D15
st. Kew 371 G7
st. N Melbourne 17 B12
st. Prahran 415 C9
st. Seaford 599 L5
MOLGA
cl. Kurunjang 227 B15
MOLINEUX
wy. Roxburgh Pk 194 C16
MOLLAND
ct. Craigieburn 194 D1
MOLLER
st. Oakleigh 458 C15
MOLLETON
st. Blackburn 375 H19
MOLLIS
cl. Narre Warren 553 G11
MOLLISON
st. Abbotsford 20 D20
st. Dandenong N 501 D18
st. Noble Park N 501 D18
MOLLISONS
hill, Hampton Pk 551 K12
MOLLOY
ct. Werribee 446 K17
rd. Yallambie 285 J13
st. Rye 696 L2
MOLOGA
rd. Heidelberg W 284 D17
MOLONEY
cl. Mordialloc 532 D19
ct. Berwick 554 B18
la. Maribyrnong 367 C2
MOLONG
av. Highett 495 K11
MOLVIG
ri. Sunbury 142 G6
MOMBA
cl. Kurunjang 227 B13
MONA
pl. South Yarra 31 J7
pl. South Yarra 414 E4
st. Seaford 573 E19
wk. Oakleigh 457 J12
MONACO
av. Bonbeach 573 B4
cr. Beaumaris 530 F4
ct. Westmeadows 236 J15
pde. Dromana 686 G8
pl. Avondale Ht 322 C7
st. Doncaster 330 E17
st. Parkdale 531 E14
MONAGHAN
pl. Melbourne 2 E17
pl. Melbourne 24 E9
rd. New Gisborne 79 E7
MONAHAN
la. Carlton 18 C18
MONAHANS
la. Caroline Spr 273 J18
la. Plumpton 273 J18
rd. Cranbourne 577 K16
rd. Cranbourne W 603 J3
MONAK
pl. Yallambie 286 B13
MONAMIE
av. Highett 496 B12
MONAMORE
st. Fairfield 327 G17
MONARCH
wy. Craigieburn 150 D7
MONARO
cl. Kealba 277 A20
cl. Kooyong 415 L6
cl. Wantirna S 423 B10
cr. Narre Warren 538 K20
ct. Mooroolbark 336 H13
ct. Vermont S 420 H8
rd. Kooyong 415 L5
MONASH
av. Balwyn 373 B10
av. Olinda 426 K8
av. Templstw Lr 330 F10
av. Thornbury 326 K11
cr. Clayton S 499 D10
ct. Whittington 703 L19
dr. Mulgrave 460 C15
fwy. Burnley 32 C3
fwy. Burnley 415 E1
fwy. Chadstone 457 B1
fwy. Cremorne 32 B3
fwy. Cremorne 414 G2
fwy. Dandenong N 500 J1
fwy. Dandenong N 501 A3
fwy. Doveton 536 J3
fwy. Endeavour Hl 536 J3
fwy. Glen Iris 416 C8
fwy. Glen Waverley 459 B7
fwy. Hawthorn 415 E1
fwy. Kooyong 416 C8
fwy. Malvern 416 C8
fwy. Malvern East 416 C8
fwy. Malvern East 417 B20

MT COTTRELL
rd. Melton 270 C6
rd. Melton S 270 A20
rd. Rockbank 228 C20
rd. Rockbank 270 A20
MT DANDENONG
rd. Croydon 379 G6
rd. Kilsyth 380 D5
rd. Montrose 381 A6
rd. Montrose 381 L10
rd. Ringwood E 378 H11
MT DANDENONG TOURIST
rd. Ferny Creek 465 J3
rd. Kalorama 382 H19
rd. Kalorama 383 A12
rd. Montrose 382 C10
rd. Montrose 383 A9
rd. Mt Dandenong 382 H19
rd. Olinda 426 G2
rd. Olinda 427 A11
rd. Sherbrooke 426 B19
rd. Tremont 465 D5
MT DERRIMUT
rd. Deer Park 319 D20
rd. Derrimut 363 C13
MT DONNA BUANG SUMMIT
rd. Warburton 305 A4
MT EAGLE
rd. Ivanhoe East 328 L13
wy. Wyndham Va 446 C12
MT EIRENE
rd. Gembrook 512 L20
MT ELIZA
wy. Mt Eliza 626 A17
wy. Mt Eliza 626 A18
MT ERIN
cr. Frankston S 627 H10
rd. Ferny Creek 425 F18
MOUNTFIELD
av. Malvern East 457 J1
rd. Kilsyth 381 E4
rd. Mitcham 376 L10
st. Brunswick 325 H11
st. Canterbury 372 K14
MOUNTFORD
dr. Springvale 500 K8
MT GISBORNE
rd. Gisborne 78 K20
rd. Gisborne 109 A11
MT GRAND VIEW
rd. Pearcedale 630 F17
MT HILDA
rd. Pearcedale 630 E14
MT IDA
av. Hawthorn E 416 E4
av. Rosanna 328 J2
MT KOROIT
rd. Plumpton 228 L6
rd. Rockbank 270 L14
MT KOROROIT
rd. Melton 228 B4
rd. Toolern Va 228 B4
MT LEBANON
rd. Chum Creek 213 A11
MOUNTLEIGH
ct. Glen Waverley 460 L3
MT MARTHA
rd. Mt Martha 669 A10
MT MORTON
rd. Belgrave 466 C18
rd. Belgrave Ht 466 B19
rd. Belgrave Ht 506 B3
rd. Belgrave S 506 F4
MT PLEASANT
dr. Mt Waverley 459 C4
gr. Armadale 415 D11
rd. Belmont 702 B17
rd. Belmont 702 C17
rd. Eltham 287 G14
rd. Eltham 288 G12
rd. Forest Hill 376 J20
rd. Highton 701 F16
rd. Monbulk 428 D17
rd. Nunawading 376 H17
rd. Preston 326 B3
rd. Research 288 G12
rd. Research 289 A11
MT RIDDELL
rd. Healesville 257 C8
rd. Healesville 257 H6
rd. Healesville 258 C2
MT RIDLEY
rd. Craigieburn 149 A3
rd. Mickleham 149 A3
MT SHAMROCK
rd. Pakenham 558 K10
MOUNT VIEW
ct. Burwood 418 A9
MOUNTVIEW
av. Parkdale 531 J13
ct. Frankston 627 D4
rd. Highett 496 J15
rd. Malvern 415 L9
st. Aspendale 546 B1
MT VIEW
av. Hallam 537 K14
gr. Balwyn N 372 L1
gr. Balwyn N 373 A1
pde. Croydon 336 G19
pde. Mooroolbark 337 A19
rd. Boronia 424 H10
rd. Ferny Creek 425 G18
rd. Rosebud 684 G17
rd. Templestowe 331 E10
rd. Thomastown 240 L13
rd. Thomastown 241 A13
rd. Up Fntree Gly 464 L7
st. Croydon 380 A4
MOUNT VUE
rd. Healesville 212 J18
MT WISE
rd. Yarra Glen 208 E15
MOURELL
st. Sunshine W 364 G10
MOURIK
ct. Wantirna 422 C11
MOUSHALL
av. Niddrie 323 B3
MOWAT
st. Geelong West 702 E2
MOWBRAY
cr. Kurunjang 226 L13
ct. Carrum Downs 601 E2
ct. Doncaster E 332 B18
ct. Noble Park N 501 A7
ct. Sunbury 143 H4
dr. Wantirna S 462 C1
st. Hawthorn E 416 F6
MOXHAMS
rd. Monbulk 468 E1
rd. Monbulk 468 E2
MOYA
cl. Endeavour Hl 537 L5
cr. Noble Park 500 F18
ct. Yallambie 285 F16
MOYANGUL
dr. Keilor East 278 B18
MOYLAN
la. Kensington 33 D10
rd. Glen Waverley 420 B18
st. Bentleigh E 456 H17
MOYLANS
la. Melbourne 1 H17
la. Melbourne 24 A10
MOYNE
cr. Coolaroo 238 D4
MOYSEYS RUN
Beaumaris 530 A9
MOYSTON
cl. Vermont S 421 E9
ct. Meadow Ht 237 L5
la. Waurn Ponds 705 B17
MOZART
cir. Donvale 332 G20
ct. Bundoora 242 E17
st. St Kilda 414 E18
MUCHELL
gr. Coburg 326 A6
MUDDY CREEK
rd. Nar Warrn E 507 E13
MUDDY GATES
la. Tooradin 651 D1
MUDFORD
st. Sunshine W 364 H8
MUDGEE
ct. Chadstone 458 D2
st. Burwood E 419 E11
MUDIE
av. Sunbury 142 L9
MUDLARK
ct. Carrum Downs 600 L3
ct. Berwick, off Allardice Pde 539 H19
rd. Whittlesea 126 C1
MUDO
ct. Rowville 503 B6
MUELLER
ct. Endeavour Hl 537 J5
MUES
st. Keilor East 322 C5
MUGAVIN
rd. Mt Evelyn 339 L11
MUGG
la. N Melbourne 34 L10
MUHALLS
rd. Emerald 470 A1
rd. Macclesfield 470 A1
MUIR
ct. Chelsea Ht 547 G17
ct. Ringwood 378 D20
ct. Rosebud W 683 D20
la. Hawthorn 371 D14
rd. Christmas Hills 251 C3
st. Bacchus Msh 221 K17
st. Frankston 626 L2
st. Hawthorn 371 D14
st. Highett 496 B12
st. Mt Waverley 419 E17
st. Richmond 26 A8
st. Spotswood 366 H20
MUIRFIELD
av. Jan Juc 711 F14
cl. Heatherton 497 J15
ct. Burwood 418 B4
ct. Frankston 599 J17
ct. Rowville 462 C19
dr. Sunbury 144 F13
mw. Chirnside Pk 292 H10
MUIRHEAD
cr. Werribee 447 F13
ct. Greenvale 237 F2
MUIRKIRK
cl. Endeavour Hl 537 H1
MUIRS
ct. Taylors Lakes 233 F20
MUIR SMYTH
pl. Mt Evelyn 339 F14
MULAWA
st. Croydon N 336 A16
MULBERRY
cr. Frankston N 600 D6
ct. Cranbourne N 578 D8
ct. Eltham 287 K10
pde. Heidelberg W 328 A2
ps. Craigieburn 150 A13
st. Richmond 26 B11
MULCAHY
ct. Altona Mdw 451 H7
rd. Pakenham 557 L18
MULDOWNEY
st. Aberfeldie 323 D10
MULDURI
cr. Croydon S 379 L14
MULGA
pl. Carrum Downs 575 F18
ri. Narre Warren 553 F11
st. Altona 408 J19
st. Thomastown 241 E13
MULGOA
av. Dandenong N 501 H19
ct. Keysborough 534 E10
st. Brighton 454 E13
MULGOWRIE
ct. Greensborough 244 J20
ct. Greensborough 286 J1
MULGRA
st. Frankston S 626 L14
MULGRAVE
st. Ashwood 418 C17
st. Elsternwick 455 B2
st. Glen Waverley 420 C17
st. Kensington 34 A7
st. Reservoir 283 F10
wy. Croydon N 335 L15
MULGUTHRIE
ct. Hallam 537 L16
MULHALL
dr. St Albans 320 G10
MULHOLLAND
cr. Grovedale 705 J17
MULKARRA
dr. Chelsea 547 B16
MULLANE
rd. Pakenham 559 F16
MULLENGER
rd. Braybrook 321 K17
MULLENS
rd. Vermont S 420 F9
rd. Warrandyte 290 C19
MULLER
rd. Heathmont 422 L1
MULLIN
ct. Cranbourne 577 L18
MULLINS
ct. Williamstown 411 A17
mw. Williamstown 411 A18
MULLOCK
rd. Diggers Rest 187 C12
MULLUM
ct. Springvale S 534 B6
dr. Donvale 332 K17
pl. Doncaster E 332 J10
MULLUM MULLUM
rd. Ringwood 378 F8
MULQUINEY
cr. Highton 705 F6
MULSANE
wy. Mornington 656 F2
MULSANNE
wy. Donvale 376 J5
wy. Warranwood 334 J14
MULWALA
ct. Wyndham Va 446 B5
gdn. St Albans 321 B6
MUMMERY
st. Mt Waverley 459 B3
MUNCH
pl. Sunbury 142 H6
MUNDARA
ct. Glen Waverley 460 J1
dr. Ringwood 334 L19
dr. Ringwood 335 A19
MUNDARING
dr. Cranbourne 604 D2
MUNDAY
ct. Skye 575 G20
st. Torquay 712 A12
MUNDOORA
ct. Mornington 641 C15
MUNDY
rd. Sunbury 110 K15
rd. Sunbury 111 A14
st. Geelong 703 A12
st. Mentone 530 J9
st. Watsonia 285 D6
MUNGALA
cr. Blairgowrie 696 B7
MUNGANA
ct. Taylors Lakes 276 A9
MUNGARI
st. Dingley Village 533 D5
MUNICA
ct. Frankston 627 F6
MUNICH
dr. Keilor Dn 276 F16
MUNJONG
pl. Delahey 275 B11
MUNRO
av. Ashburton 417 D18
av. Carnegie 456 F8
av. Cheltenham 496 E17
av. Edithvale 546 J12
av. Lilydale 338 L11
av. Mt Waverley 419 G20
av. Sunshine N 321 C10
cl. Hampton Pk 551 J4
ct. Altona Mdw 451 H9
ct. Bacchus Msh 221 H14
ct. Meadow Ht 237 K3
sq. Footscray 367 H6
st. Armadale 415 F11
st. Ascot Vale 323 K17
st. Black Rock 529 G2
st. Blairgowrie 695 L4
st. Brighton 454 H19
st. Brunswick 325 B15
st. Coburg 325 A2
st. Cremorne 32 B2
st. Cremorne 414 G1
st. Hawthorn E 372 E20
st. Kew East 372 K3
st. Lalor 241 E11
st. Macleod 285 C16
st. Mitcham 377 G18
st. Northcote 327 A14
st. Port Melb 29 A2
st. Port Melb 413 A1
st. Ringwood 378 B10
st. Southbank 23 B20
st. Southbank 413 A1
st. S Melbourne 29 A2
st. S Melbourne 413 A1
MUNROS
la. N Melbourne 17 E15
MUNSTER
av. Carnegie 456 F4
ct. Endeavour Hl 537 B2
tce. N Melbourne 34 J18
MUNTZ
av. Glenroy 279 J3
st. Caulfield N 415 F16
MURA
cl. Greensborough 244 A19
ct. Grovedale 706 C15
MURAWA
dr. Rosebud 700 K5
st. Frankston 627 F5
MURCH
cr. Anglesea 713 J3
MURCHISON
av. Taylors Lakes 275 E1
av. Vermont S 421 E8
cr. Clayton S 499 E11
ct. Herne Hill 702 A3
ct. Werribee 447 G7
dr. Roxburgh Pk 194 F15
st. Carlton 18 K14
st. St Kilda E 414 L15
st. St Kilda E 415 A15
wy. Thomastown 241 L17
MURDO
rd. Clayton 459 F19
MURDOCH
av. Mulgrave 460 C17
av. Narre Warren 539 D16
ct. Altona North 365 F20
ct. Ferntree Gly 463 H7
ct. Keilor East 322 B1
ct. Sunbury 144 G10
st. Camberwell 417 C5
MURDOCK
av. Point Cook 450 E6
ct. Maddingley 263 G4
st. Brunswick 325 E9
st. Clayton S 498 K6
MURENE
ct. Boronia 423 J9
MURIEL
ct. Coburg N 282 B18
ct. Epping 197 H19
ct. Reservoir 283 H3
st. Glen Iris 417 J10
st. Niddrie 322 L3
st. Niddrie 323 A3
st. Northcote 327 C17
MURIEL REIDY
st. Maribyrnong, off Eveline Av 367 C2
MURILLO
ct. Doncaster 331 B14
ct. Wheelers Hill 460 L15
MURNDAL
ct. Berwick 554 B14
ct. Frankston S 627 G13
dr. Donvale 376 L5
MURNONG
st. Maribyrnong 322 J17
MURPHY
gr. Preston 283 D20
pl. Roxburgh Pk 194 C9
rd. Doncaster E 331 G20
rd. Pakenham 559 E20
rd. Woodstock 125 A8
st. Altona North 409 H4
st. Brighton 454 J11
st. Chadstone 457 L3
st. Clarinda 498 H10
st. Deer Park 319 B11
st. Kew 371 D11
st. N Melbourne 17 E13
st. Oak Park 279 L11
st. Preston 282 C16
st. Richmond 26 L10
st. Richmond 371 A15
st. South Yarra 32 A8
st. South Yarra 32 B6
st. South Yarra 414 F4
MURPHYS
ct. Maidstone 322 H17
rd. Exford 267 A19
rd. Parwan 266 F18
wy. Emerald 509 F3
MURRA
ct. Ashwood 418 C18
st. Bentleigh E 456 L14
st. Burwood 419 A8
MURRABIT
gr. Taylors Lakes 276 D7
MURRAC
st. Coldstream 295 C12
MURRAGONG
av. Bundoora 284 L4
MURRAJONG
ct. Sunshine 321 K6
MURRALINGA
pl. Mt Eliza 642 B8
MURRAY
cl. Frankston 628 F5
cl. Noble Park 534 K
cr. Rowville 463 A19
ct. Carrum 573 D10
ct. Cranbourne 578 B17
ct. Greenvale 237 A4
ct. Tootgarook 698 B
ct. Vermont S 420 H6
ct. Werribee 447 C10
dr. Burwood 418 B7
dr. Wattle Glen 246 J7
la. Caulfield 455 F5
la. Seville E 343 C12
pl. Ringwood 378 C13
rd. Coburg 281 K19
rd. Croydon 379 F2
rd. Dandenong N 501 L10
rd. Diamond Ck 245 G
rd. Eden Park 95 D17
rd. Gisborne 80 K13
rd. Heidelberg W 327 G
rd. McKinnon 455 J14

N

st. Somerville 644 L16
st. Somerville 645 A16
st. S Kingsville 410 E3
st. Surrey Hills 374 C20
st. Torquay 712 B6
NEWARK
cl. Werribee 446 J12
ct. Albanvale 319 A7
ct. Glen Waverley 460 G10
NEWBAY
cr. Brighton 454 G14
NEWBERRY
av. Bonbeach 545 E13
ct. Hampton Pk 552 D10
NEWBIGIN
ct. Burwood 419 B10
NEWBOLD
av. Craigieburn 150 G19
NEWBRIDGE
cl. Dingley Village 533 A2
NEWBURGH
ct. Point Cook 450 H6
pl. Hawthorn E 372 D17
NEWBURN
ct. Nunawading 376 G16
NEWBURY
cl. Templstw Lr 330 E8
ct. Ashwood 418 F14
ct. Carrum Downs 601 D3
ct. Wantirna S 422 K18
dr. Berwick 580 L1
st. Deer Park 319 C8
st. Kew East 372 J2
st. Mitcham 376 L9
st. Werribee 448 A9
NEWCASTLE
ct. Greenvale 193 D18
rd. Bayswater 424 B5
st. Newport 410 J6
st. Newtown 702 C13
st. Preston 327 B8
st. Thornbury 327 B8
st. Yarraville 367 C17
NEWCOMBE
ct. Clarinda 498 E8
ct. Mill Park 242 H3
ct. Wantirna S 462 E4
dr. St Albans 275 K19
dr. St Albans 275 K20
NEWCOMEN
rd. Springvale 499 H9
NEWELL
cl. Taylors Lakes 233 J20
cl. Wantirna 422 C11
st. Bayswater N 379 G17
st. Footscray 367 F7
NEW ENGLAND
wy. Narre Warren 539 F17
NEW FARM
rd. Werribee 487 B1
NEWGROVE
rd. Healesville 257 K1
rd. Healesville 258 A2
NEWHALL
st. Moonee Pnd 324 A14
NEWHAM
cr. Dallas 238 D12
gr. Ormond 456 B13
wy. Altona Mdw 451 D2
NEWHAVEN
ct. Lilydale 294 B19
ct. Mill Park 242 L10
ct. Mill Park 243 A10
dr. Berwick 539 H17
rd. Burwood E 420 A12
rd. Craigieburn 194 F4
st. Thomastown 240 D11
wy. St Albans 319 G6
NEW HOLLAND
dr. Cranbourne E 604 H3
NEWINGTON
av. Rosebud W 699 G6
gr. Caulfield N 455 L1
la. Chelsea 546 K20
pde. Chelsea 545 D11
pde. Chelsea 546 K20
NEWLAND
st. Altona Mdw 407 F19
st. Newcomb 704 D14
NEWLANDS
cr. Doncaster E 332 J13
ct. Box Hill S 418 H4
ct. Clarinda 498 E10
ct. Wantirna 422 J9
la. Beaumaris 529 K6
rd. Coburg N 281 K17
rd. Reservoir 281 K15
st. Richmond 26 H8
NEWLYN
cl. Templestowe 331 E13
ct. Ferntree Gly 464 A15

dr. Craigieburn 194 B2
st. Caulfield 455 J4
NEWMAN
av. Carnegie 456 G12
av. Noble Park 534 K6
cr. Niddrie 322 K1
ct. Berwick 554 G10
rd. Mooroolbark 336 K18
rd. Nunawading 376 F12
rd. Wantirna S 422 K10
st. Brunswick 325 A10
st. Brunswick W 325 A10
st. Kensington 33 D12
st. Niddrie 278 K20
st. Preston 326 G5
st. Ringwood 377 L15
st. Sunshine 321 H20
st. Sunshine 365 H1
st. Thornbury 326 C8
NEWMANS
rd. Templestowe 331 J5
NEWMARKET
rd. Altona 407 H13
st. Flemington 33 H2
st. Flemington 33 J4
st. Northcote 326 L17
wy. Flemington 33 J2
NEWMILL
cl. Endeavour Hl 537 K2
NEWMINISTER
wy. Point Cook 450 J9
NEW MORNING
wy. Mornington 656 H1
NEWNHAM
ct. Glen Waverley 460 B9
NEWPORT
cr. Hawthorn E 372 G18
rd. Clayton S 498 H5
st. Nunawading 376 K9
NEWRY
cl. Wantirna S 462 J2
la. Windsor 414 K11
st. Carlton N 18 H5
st. Cheltenham 496 L17
st. Fitzroy N 19 A6
st. Richmond 26 L16
st. Richmond 371 A18
st. Windsor 414 K12
NEWSOM
ct. Berwick 554 B4
st. Ascot Vale 323 G17
NEWSON
st. Keysborough 534 G14
NEWSTEAD
ct. Doncaster E 332 E6
st. Caulfield 455 G4
st. Maribyrnong 323 D14
wy. Wantirna S 422 H19
NEWTON
av. Langwarrin S 629 C20
av. Mt Evelyn 339 E15
av. Sorrento 678 L10
cr. Lalor 241 D8
ct. Keysborough 534 D9
ct. St Kilda 414 B15
ct. Seaholme 409 J15
ct. Watsonia N 243 E20
ct. Watsonia N 285 E1
gr. Glen Waverley 420 J20
la. Dandenong 535 L7
pde. Moonee Pnd 324 D15
st. Chadstone 457 L6
st. Cremorne 32 E2
st. Cremorne 414 H1
st. Ferntree Gly 464 E4
st. Glenroy 280 G9
st. Kensington 33 E12
st. Mt Martha 656 A12
st. Reservoir 283 E16
st. Seaford 573 E16
st. Surrey Hills 374 E20
st. Thomastown 241 A16
NEWTOWN
rd. Macleod 285 D17
NEYLAND
ct. Altona Mdw 451 H6
NEYLON
st. Yarraville 366 F14
NGARVENO
st. Moonee Pnd 324 E15
NGUMBY
ct. Vermont S 421 B8
NHILL
ct. Dallas 238 D11
NIAGARA
la. Melbourne 1 L10
la. Melbourne 24 A6
rd. Donvale 377 C8
wy. Werribee 447 J4
NIBLETT
ct. Grovedale 705 K15

NIBLICK
st. Anglesea 713 A5
st. Kingsbury 283 L10
st. Rye 696 J4
NICE
pl. Point Cook 450 F11
NICHOL
st. Preston 327 C2
st. Sunbury 142 B11
NICHOLAS
av. Glen Waverley 420 J15
ct. Carrum Downs 575 E15
ct. Ferntree Gly 464 A17
ct. Keilor East 322 J5
ct. Narre Warren 539 E16
ct. Pakenham 585 F5
ct. Pt Lonsdale 710 G4
ct. Ringwood N 377 L6
ct. Rosebud 700 G3
dr. Dandenong S 549 H11
gr. Heatherton 497 K15
la. Kangaroo Grnd 248 J19
pl. Brookfield 268 A4
st. Ashburton 417 D20
st. Blairgowrie 695 L3
st. Broadmeadows 238 B15
st. Epping 197 G16
st. Keysborough 534 D9
st. Lilydale 338 A7
st. Newtown 702 D11
st. Wandin East 340 L18
st. Wandin East 341 A18
NICHOLI
wk. Vermont S 421 A10
NICHOLLS
ct. Mordialloc 532 E11
ct. Plenty 244 D3
rd. Ormond 456 E13
st. Macleod 285 B10
st. Malvern 415 K15
NICHOLS
dr. Mornington 656 J1
la. Kensington 33 D13
rd. Chum Creek 213 B12
NICHOLSDALE
rd. Camberwell 417 K3
NICHOLSON
av. Mt Waverley 418 J13
av. Reservoir 283 G12
cl. Endeavour Hl 537 B3
cl. Research 288 G4
cl. Werribee 446 L10
cr. Jan Juc 711 E14
cr. Lilydale 338 J13
cr. Meadow Ht 194 A19
cr. Mt Evelyn 338 J13
ct. Belmont 702 A19
ct. Clayton 498 K2
ct. Greenvale 193 F20
ct. Greenvale 237 F1
la. Chelsea, off Showers Av 546 J18
pde. Sunshine W 364 E9
pl. Melbourne 1 A6
pl. Melbourne 23 G6
st. Abbotsford 26 D3
st. Altona Mdw 407 G20
st. Balwyn N 372 L6
st. Bentleigh 456 B19
st. Brunswick E 326 A15
st. Carlton 18 K19
st. Carlton N 19 A8
st. Carlton N 326 A20
st. Coburg 325 L7
st. E Melbourne 24 K3
st. Essendon 324 B8
st. Fitzroy 24 K3
st. Fitzroy N 19 A8
st. Fitzroy N 326 A20
st. Footscray 367 F6
st. Footscray 367 F10
st. Hawthorn E 372 G18
st. McKinnon 456 B17
st. Nunawading 376 H14
st. Olinda 426 H9
st. Ringwood E 378 K12
st. Seaford 599 C7
st. Seddon 367 E13
st. South Yarra 31 J12
st. South Yarra 414 E6
st. Yarraville 367 E13
tce. Taylors Hill 274 J14
NICKLAUS
dr. Hoppers Csg 405 B18
pl. Chirnside Pk 292 H10
NICKOLS
ct. Boronia 423 D12
NICKSON
cl. Dingley Village 533 B2
ct. Ringwood N 334 J17
ct. Seaford 600 B1
st. Bundoora 284 E1

NICOL
dr. Waurn Ponds 705 A10
dr.n, Waurn Ponds 705 B9
dr.s, Waurn Ponds 705 B12
st. Hampton 495 E10
st. Highett 495 K14
NICOLA
ct. Keilor East 278 F20
ct. Pakenham 559 G19
NICOLE
av. Dandenong N 536 A1
av. Springvale S 499 G18
cl. Endeavour Hl 537 L3
cr. Diamond Ck 245 F13
ct. Bayswater N 380 C15
ct. Clarinda 498 D8
ct. Gisborne 78 L20
ct. Mooroolbark 337 A11
ct. Rowville 503 D5
ct. Skye 601 F3
ct. Werribee 448 B16
st. Mt Waverley 459 D6
wy. Dandenong S 550 B2
NICOLL
st. Blackburn N 376 D11
st. Nunawading 376 D11
NICOSIA
ct. Williamstn N 410 G12
NIDDRIE
arc. Niddrie 279 B20
NIEL
st. Croydon 380 D1
NIELSEN
av. Nunawading 376 G10
ct. Altona Mdw 451 H4
NIEWAND
av. Burnside 318 E7
av. Caroline Spr 318 E7
NIGEL
cr. Gladstone Pk 237 D16
ct. Badger Creek 258 D9
ct. Ringwood 378 K2
ct. Scoresby 462 E8
NIGHTINGALE
cl. Donvale 332 H20
dr. Werribee 448 A9
st. Balaclava 414 G19
wk. Williamstown 411 F12
NIGHTJAR
ct. Werribee 447 K5
NIGRA
st. Doveton 536 K10
NIGRETTA
ct. Mt Waverley 419 F19
ct. Pt Lonsdale 707 J19
NIKE
ct. Carrum Downs 601 B3
NIKI
cl. Albanvale 318 L6
ct. Bentleigh E 497 E8
ct. Frankston 628 E10
NIKKI
pl. Berwick 554 J20
NILAND
ri. Templestowe 331 E6
NILE
ct. Werribee 447 J5
NILLUMBIK
sq. Diamond Ck 246 F9
NILMA
ct. Frankston 599 L20
NIMARY
ct. Eltham North 245 C16
NIMBIN
ct. Noble Park N 500 L7
NIMBLEFOOT
wy. Lilydale 294 C19
NIMBUS
ct. Hampton Pk 551 L15
ct. Whittington 704 B20
NIMMO
cr. Kurunjang 227 A14
ct. Mulgrave 501 F2
rd. Diamond Ck 246 C3
st. Essendon 323 D7
st. Middle Park 30 B20
st. Middle Park 413 F11
NIMO
ct. Sunbury 142 L3
ct. Sunbury 143 A3
NIMROD
ri. Chelsea Ht 547 D9
NINA
ct. Bentleigh E 497 E8
ct. Ringwood 378 J8
ct. Watsonia 285 C4
pl. Wantirna 422 C12
st. Sunshine W 364 B4

NINALEE
ct. Springvale 499 L17
ct. Wantirna 422 B9
wy. Somerville 644 F18
NINDA
ct. Westmeadows 237 H10
NINETEENTH
av. Eden Park 95 D17
NINEVAH
cr. Wheelers Hill 460 H17
NINION
ct. Greensborough 243 K20
ct. Greensborough 285 K1
NINNIS
ct. Roxburgh Pk 193 J16
NINTH
av. Anglesea 713 D12
av. Chelsea Ht 547 E15
av. Rosebud 684 B18
av.s, Rosebud 684 B20
NIOBE
ct. Templstw Lr 330 K16
NIOKA
cl. Cockatoo 471 G18
ct. Eltham 287 D8
ct. Endeavour Hl 537 L4
ct. Greensborough 243 J18
ct. Pk Orchards 333 K14
pl. Rowville 462 K20
st. Chadstone 458 B1
NIREEDA
ct. Wandana Ht 701 D20
NIRRINGA
av. Aspendale 546 F5
ct. Mt Martha 656 E6
NIRVANA
av. Malvern East 456 L4
cl. Langwarrin S 629 G17
cr. Bulleen 329 K12
ct. Frankston 628 F8
dr. S Morang 199 J20
pl. Melton W 225 L15
NISBETT
st. Reservoir 283 J15
NISSAN
dr. Dandenong S 550 C4
NISSEN
ct. Seaholme 409 J15
NITA
st. Hadfield 280 K9
NITH
ct. Glen Waverley 420 J19
NITHSDALE
rd. Noble Park 500 H16
NIVEA
tce. S Morang 198 K13
NIVES
ct. Burwood E 419 G9
NIXON
ct. Bentleigh E 497 B3
ct. Maddingley 263 D5
ct. Roxburgh Pk 194 A11
pl. Port Melb 29 H5
rd. Lysterfield 465 G19
rd. Upwey 465 G19
st. Balwyn N 373 G6
st. Melton 227 A20
st. Rosebud 700 F1
st. Sunshine 365 G3
NIZAM
ct. Wantirna 422 G8
NOACK
rd. Harkaway 540 G11
NOAH
cl. Mornington 641 D17
NOAKI
st. Pearcedale 647 K1
NOBEL
cl. Greensborough 244 D15
st. View Bank 285 J19
NOBELIUS
av. Narre Warren 552 L5
ct. Mill Park 243 C5
st. Emerald 469 G10
NOBILITY
st. Moolap 704 J16
NOBLE
av. Strathmore 324 A2
ct. Keilor East 322 B1
ct. Sunshine W 363 L7
dr. Epping 241 G4
pl. Wandana Ht 701 C19
pl. Werribee 448 A11
st. Anglesea 713 C8
st. Mulgrave 460 C18
st. Newtown 701 L9
st. Noble Park 500 D20
st. Noble Park 534 C2
wy. Sunbury 142 F14

NOBLE BANKS
dr. St Albans 319 J10
NOBLES
la. Sherbrooke 426 H19
NOCKOLDS
cr. Noble Park 500 H15
NOCTON
st. Reservoir 282 C14
NODDING
av. Frankston N 600 C9
NODOSA
tr. Lysterfield 505 B12
NOEL
ct. Dromana...........686 C6
ct. Moorabbin 496 F11
ct. Noble Park N......501 C10
ct. Thomastown 241 J14
rd. Langwarrin.........629 L1
rd. Moolap 704 G15
st. Brighton East 455 E14
st. Brunswick E.......326 B16
st. Dromana...........686 B5
st. Ivanhoe............328 D13
st. Rye..................697 B4
NOELHURST
ct. Werribee...........446 J20
NOELLE
st. Bulleen 329 F10
NOGA
av. Keilor East.........322 D2
NOILA
st. Grovedale 706 B14
NOKES
ct. Montmorency 286 H11
NOKUNA
ct. Greensborough ..243 J18
NOLA
ct. Bundoora...........285 B6
ct. Croydon............336 K16
ct. Hampton Pk.......551 C9
ct. Scoresby 462 D5
ct. Toorak 415 E9
st. Coburg N...........281 K18
st. Doncaster 330 C18
NOLA-ANNE
av. Reservoir 282 J13
NOLAN
av. Brooklyn 365 H18
av. Kew....................371 C9
av. Mooroolbark 337 J17
cl. Doncaster E 332 D16
cl. Nar Warrn N.......539 J11
cl. Vermont S 421 A7
ct. Ashwood 418 B14
ct. S Melbourne 30 B8
ct. Sunbury.............142 L10
dr. Epping 197 G17
pl. Taylors Lakes.....233 B19
rd. Emerald 509 D6
st. Frankston............627 A1
st. Niddrie...............322 L2
st. Niddrie...............323 A2
NOMA
ct. Queenscliff.........707 K18
NOMAD
la. Highton..............701 E11
rd. Airport W...........279 C16
NONDA
av. Doncaster E 332 C18
NONNA
st. Oakleigh E..........458 H11
NOOJEE
ct. Dandenong N.....501 F13
ct. Yallambie...........286 C15
NOOLA
cl. Noble Park 534 D6
NOON
st. Dandenong S 535 H13
NOONAN
ct. Altona Mdw........451 K5
rd. Hoppers Csg 448 E7
NOONE
st. Clifton Hill............19 K8
NOORA
av. Oakleigh S..........497 F1
ct. Aspendale 546 H6
ct. Croydon.............336 A19
NOORABIL
ct. Greensborough ..244 F18
NOORDENNE
av. Seaholme...........409 H15
NOORILIM
cl. Templestowe 331 E15
wy. Pearcedale 646 J4
NOORONG
av. Bundoora...........284 J4
NORA
ct. Narre Warren 539 A20
ct. Warranwood......334 J15
NORAL
ct. Templestowe 331 K14
NORBERT
st. Balwyn..............373 C12
NORBROKE
ct. Mill Park 242 G10
NORBURY
la. Caroline Spr.......317 L4
rd. Beaconsfld Up....542 L17
NORCAL
rd. Nunawading......376 J15
NORCOTT
rd. Marshall............706 L6
NORDIC
av. Keilor Lodge.......276 A4
av. Taylors Lakes.....275 K2
rd. Dandenong N.....501 J14
NORFOLK
av. Grovedale 706 A12
av. Oakleigh.............458 C11
av. Ringwood 378 C18
av. Wantirna S.........422 L10
av. Wantirna S.........423 A10
bvd. Torquay 712 G1
cct. Doncaster 375 D4
cl. Berwick..............539 J18
cl. Hillside...............273 J3
cl. Somerville............644 G16
cr. Bundoora...........284 F6
cr. Frankston N 600 A7
ct. Coburg N............282 A13
ct. Fawkner.............281 J2
ct. Werribee.............446 L12
ct. Werribee.............447 A12
dr. Narre Warren 553 B9
dr. Portsea 666 L20
gr. Sunbury.............144 E8
pl. Aspendale Gdn....547 B4
rd. Lysterfield..........505 C19
rd. Mt Martha...........669 L1
rd. Surrey Hills.........373 L19
st. Blackburn N........376 B10
st. Glen Waverley....459 H11
st. Maidstone..........366 H3
st. Moonee Pnd 323 J12
st. Yarraville...........367 C17
NORFORD
cr. Cranbourne N.....578 F9
gr. Kooyong.............416 A6
NORGE
st. Sunshine 321 H20
NORHAM
ct. Berwick..............554 D14
NORISHA
ct. Dandenong N.....536 E1
NORLAND
st. Cheltenham........531 C2
NORLANE
ct. Thomastown......240 F12
st. Keysborough 534 F11
NORLING
mw. Sunbury............142 J6
NORMA
av. Cheltenham........531 E3
av. Oakleigh S..........497 K1
av. Rye..................696 J1
cl. Nar Warrn S.......552 F17
cr. Knoxfield............463 D3
cr.s, Knoxfield.........463 D5
ct. Avondale Ht 322 E14
ct. View Bank..........285 J17
rd. Forest Hill 420 D5
st. Diamond Ck 245 K12
st. Doncaster 375 D2
st. Melton 226 G20
st. Sunshine 365 G5
NORMAN
av. Chelsea Ht.........547 D14
av. Frankston S........626 G8
av. South Yarra.........32 J11
av. South Yarra........414 K6
av. Sunbury.............143 G16
av. Watsonia N 243 G20
cr. Pt Lonsdale.........710 C2
ct. Box Hill S............418 H2
ct. Dandenong S 535 K15
ct. Highton..............701 J19
ct. Mt Waverley........418 L17
ct. Ringwood............378 G6
gr. Thomastown......241 A14
la. South Yarra.........32 J10
pl. Narre Warren 553 F13
rd. Croydon..............336 B20
rd. Mt Martha..........656 D11
rd. Research 288 H7
st. Camberwell.........417 L4
st. Coburg 325 G6
st. Doncaster E 331 H20
st. Ferntree Gly 464 F8
st. Ivanhoe..............328 C13
st. McKinnon 455 J14
st. Mitcham 377 D17
st. St Albans 276 G20
st. Sunshine 365 G9
st. The Basin...........425 A10
NORMAN BERRY
dr. Seville................341 H15
NORMANBY
av. Caulfield N 415 K18
av. Sunshine W 364 H14
av. Thornbury...........326 B8
ct. Heidelberg W 284 A18
dr. Greenvale...........237 C3
pl. Richmond............26 B10
pl. Windsor, off Newry St...........414 K11
rd. Bentleigh E.........497 B4
rd. Caulfield E..........456 B1
rd. Caulfield N 415 L18
rd. Clayton 459 D13
rd. Kew 372 G11
rd. Kew East............372 G11
rd. Notting Hill.........459 D13
rd. Port Melb............29 A2
rd. Sorrento 678 E10
rd. Southbank 29 A2
rd. Southbank 413 A1
rd. S Melbourne 29 A2
rd. S Melbourne 413 A1
st. Brighton.............454 F17
st. Cranbourne.........578 F19
st. E Geelong 703 F12
st. Hughesdale........457 H13
st. Moonee Pnd 323 L15
st. S Melbourne 29 D6
st. S Melbourne 413 B3
st. Sydenham 274 L2
st. Windsor.............414 K11
tce. Mt Martha..........655 G17
NORMANDY
rd. Elwood 454 C5
st. Ashburton..........417 E17
NORMANTON
pl. Berwick..............554 F12
NORM CLARK
wk. Rosebud, off Wannaeue Pl......684 B15
NORMDALE
rd. Bentleigh E.........497 B5
NORMLEITH
gr. Boronia.............424 H10
NORRAY
av. Mt Waverley.......419 C15
NORRIS
cr. Bundoora...........284 A1
cr. Healesville..........258 B8
cr. Thomastown......284 A1
ct. Blackburn 375 L19
ct. Noble Park N......501 G15
dr. Lilydale 338 H7
la. N Melbourne 34 L12
rd. Pakenham..........560 C13
rd. Rowville.............463 A20
st. Coburg N 281 F14
st. Noble Park 534 L3
st. Surrey Hills.........373 H15
NORTH
av. Altona Mdw.........407 F18
av. Belmont.............706 J2
av. Bentleigh............496 A2
av. Bentleigh............496 A5
av. Bulleen 329 J9
av. Mt Evelyn...........339 C20
av. Mt Evelyn...........339 D20
av. Strathmore..........324 D2
cnc. Beaumaris..........530 A9
cr. Heidelberg W 284 C20
ct. Forest Hill 420 E3
ct. Highett...............496 G12
ct. Surrey Hills 418 A2
dr. Melb Airport.........235 K11
dr. Springvale...........500 J10
gwy. Langwarrin 629 H2
gwy. Wyndham Va 446 C11
lk. Chirnside Pk........337 D5
rd. Airport W............278 G12
rd. Avondale Ht 321 K10
rd. Bentleigh E..........456 B13
rd. Brighton.............454 F11
rd. Brighton.............454 G11
rd. Carnegie 456 B13
rd. Caulfield S...........455 C12
rd. Clayton 457 G15
rd. Cranbourne S.....630 F9
rd. Gardenvale.........455 C12
rd. Hughesdale.........457 G15
rd. Huntingdale 457 G15
rd. Kilsyth 381 D6
rd. Langwarrin..........628 J6
rd. Lilydale 338 H5
rd. Lilydale 339 A6
rd. Menzies Ck 467 L15
rd. Murrumbeena 456 B13
rd. Newport.............411 A8
rd. Oakleigh S..........457 G15
rd. Ormond 456 A13
rd. Reservoir 283 B13
rd. Werribee............448 F12
st. Ardeer...............364 E1
st. Ascot Vale...........324 C17
st. Brunswick...........325 K10
st. Hadfield 280 H5
st. Preston..............282 C18
st. Richmond...........371 B14
st. Seddon 367 D11
tce. Clifton Hill 20 A5
NORTHAM
av. Highton..............705 K4
ct. Mill Park 242 D9
rd. Bentleigh E..........497 A1
rd. Wantirna 422 H5
st. Glen Waverley.....461 B6
NORTHAMPTON
cr. Caroline Spr.......318 D8
cr. Caroline Spr.......318 E8
pl. South Yarra..........31 K7
NORTH BOUNDARY
tr. Lysterfield S.......503 A10
NORTHBOURNE
rd. Campbellfield 195 B20
NORTH BOX
ct. Hadfield 281 A5
NORTHBROOK
av. Malvern 415 L12
NORTH CIRCULAR
rd. Gladstone Pk.......237 A17
NORTHCLIFFE
rd. Edithvale............546 J14
NORTH CLUSTER
Pakenham..........584 K2
NORTHCORP
bvd. Broadmeadows ..238 J14
bvd. Broadmeadows ..238 L17
bvd. Broadmeadows ..239 A18
NORTHCOTE
av. Balwyn...............373 H15
av. Caulfield N 455 J2
rd. Armadale 415 E10
st. Northcote............327 A16
st. Richmond............26 F20
st. Richmond............32 F1
st. Seaford...............573 F17
tce. Mornington........640 D13
NORTHCOTT
av. Croydon..............336 G18
st. Melton S 268 H10
NORTHERN
av. Brighton East 455 E12
av. Moorabbin Aprt..531 K3
cr. Craigieburn 150 G15
rd. Heidelberg Ht 284 C15
rd. Heidelberg W 284 C15
NORTHERNHAY
st. Reservoir............283 A14
NORTHERN RING
rd. Bundoora...........242 C17
rd. Campbellfield 239 F19
rd. Fawkner.............239 F19
rd. Greensborough ..243 B16
rd. Thomastown......239 F19
rd. Thomastown......240 J17
rd. Thomastown......241 A17
rd. Watsonia N 243 B16
NORTHEY
cl. Thomastown......240 H11
cr. Hoppers Csg 405 A19
NORTHGATE
dr. Springvale S.......533 K7
dr. Thomastown......241 H18
dr. Thomastown......242 A19
st. Pascoe Vale 280 F18
st. Pascoe Vale S 280 E19
NORTH GATEWAY
Coldstream 295 C13
NORTH GLIDE
rd. Melb Airport.......235 B6
NORTHLEIGH
av. Craigieburn 194 D1
NORTH OATLANDS
rd. Yarrambat..........200 F16
NORTHROCK
ct. Craigieburn 149 L17
NORTHROP
ct. Strathmr Ht........279 C9
NORTHUMBERLAND
dr. Epping 197 L16
rd. Pascoe Vale 280 F17
rd. Sunshine N.........321 F18
st. Collingwood..........25 J1
st. S Melbourne 29 J2
NORTH VALLEY
rd. Highton..............701 J17
rd. Pk Orchards 333 J14
NORTH WEALD
wy. Fawkner.............281 F1
NORTH WHARF
rd. Docklands............23 A1
rd. Docklands..........368 L1
NORTHWOOD
dr. View Bank..........285 K1
dr. Whittlesea...........96 E1
st. Ringwood E 379 B1
NORTON
cl. Carrum Downs...574 L1
dr. Melton ....269 E
pl. Roxburgh Pk......194 A1
rd. Croydon.............380 C
rd. Kallista..............467 C
rd. Parwan 265 J2
st. Pascoe Vale 280 G1
st. Sunshine W ....364 D
NORTONS
la. Wantirna S.........461 F
NORVAL
cl. Williamstown 411 H1
cr. Coolaroo............238 D
cr. Wheelers Hill......460 G1
tce. Altona Mdw........451 L
NORVEL
rd. Ferntree Gly 423 J1
st. Blackburn 375 J2
NORVILLE
st. Bentleigh E.........497 B
NORWAY
av. Blackburn 375 G1
NORWEENA
st. Doncaster 330 C1
NORWEGIAN
ct. Mt Martha..........656 L
wy. Nar Warrn S.......578 H
NORWICH
av. Thomastown......240 G1
cl. Chirnside Pk.......336 G
cr. Campbellfield 239 G1
pl. Templestowe 331 H1
st. Boronia.............423 L1
st. St Albans ....320 F
st. Werribee............447 H1
NORWOOD
av. Brighton.............494 G
cr. Moonee Pnd 324 A1
ct. Bundoora...........284 H
ct. Cranbourne........577 L1
ct. Wheelers Hill.......460 H1
dr. Keilor East..........321 K
pl. Flemington...........33 L
rd. Caulfield N 415 C1
rd. Mill Park 242 E1
st. Albion 320 G2
st. Flemington...........33 L
st. Glen Iris.............417 F1
st. Herne Hill............701 K
st. Oakleigh S..........497 J
st. Sandringham 495 D1
NOSKE
st. Newtown ....702 A
NOTLEN
st. Ringwood ....378 D
NOTRE DAME
dr. Sunbury.............144 D1
NOTT
av. Frankston...........627 D
st. Balwyn..............373 D1
st. Belmont.............706 D
st. Malvern East 416 E1
st. Nunawading.......376 L1
st. Port Melb.............29 A
st. Port Melb............412 J
NOTTAGE
st. St Kilda E 415 B1
NOTTINGHAM
av. Somerville..........644 G1
ct. View Bank..........329 J
sq. Wantirna............422 G1
st. Glen Waverley.....419 L1
st. Kensington ....34 B
st. Prahran...............31 L1
st. Prahran..............414 E
st. Sunshine N.........321 H1
wy. Sydenham 232 H1
NOTTINGWOOD
st. Doncaster E 331 L1
NOUMEA
ct. Mulgrave ....500 C
NOURELL
ct. Meadow Ht ....238 A
NOUVELLE
gr. S Morang...........198 L1
NOVA
av. Deer Park...........319 A
cr. Craigieburn 150 K1
ct. Safety Bch..........669 D1
ct. Wheelers Hill......461 E1
dr. Dandenong ....536 E
st. Oakleigh S..........458 E2

NOVARA
pde. St Albans ...320 H7
NOVELLO
ct. Eltham ...287 L10
NOVIAN
st. Coburg N ...281 E12
NOWA
ct. Frankston ...628 C1
ct. Werribee S ...488 D10
NOWELL
ct. Endeavour Hl ...537 E8
ct. Roxburgh Pk ...194 C15
NOWIE
cl. Kurunjang ...227 B11
NOWINGI
ct. Vermont ...421 A6
NOWRA
ct. Mornington ...656 G3
st. Moorabbin ...496 H7
NOYES
st. Highett ...495 J15
NUGENT
ct. Endeavour Hl ...537 D1
st. Monbulk ...428 D18
st. Preston ...283 B19
NUGONG
pl. Lynbrook ...551 G17
NUKARA
ct. Frankston ...600 A18
NULGARRAH
cr. Greensborough ...244 J20
NULLAWARRE
av. Rosebud ...700 L5
NULLAWIL
st. Springvale ...500 D6
NULLICA
ct. Berwick ...553 H4
NUMERALLA
st. Mooroolbark ...337 A14
NUMERING
ct. Kurunjang ...226 L13
NUMINBAH
ct. Taylors Lakes ...276 A9
NUMIRA
pl. St Albans ...321 B7
NUNAN
pl. Reservoir ...283 H15
st. Brunswick E ...326 B10
NUNANA
ct. Ferntree Gly ...464 D9
NUNDAH
dr. Eltham ...288 D6
NUNGA
ct. Mt Eliza ...626 H15
NUNGERNER
st. Balwyn ...373 B10
NUNGEROO
ct. Eltham ...286 L3
NUNKERI
st. Vermont ...421 B4
NUNN
av. Truganina ...405 G14
cl. Mill Park ...242 B7
ct. Whittington ...704 B18
NUNNEY
ct. Craigieburn ...150 A14
NUNNIONG
st. Werribee ...448 B20
NUNNS
rd. Mornington ...640 B18
NURAGI
ct. Werribee ...447 C12
NURAYLIA
av. Croydon ...380 K2
NURLA
ct. Frankston ...628 D6
ct. Sunshine W ...364 J7
pl. St Helena ...244 L17
NURLENDI
rd. Vermont ...421 B6
NURSERY
av. Frankston ...627 J1
av. Frankston ...628 A2
ct. Dingley Village ...533 E10
la. Blind Bight ...650 G1
rd. Croydon ...335 G20
wy. Burwood ...418 A12
NURTEN
pde. Aspendale Gdn ...546 K6
NUSPAN
ct. Kurunjang ...227 F6
NUTALL
la. Mont Albert ...374 C16
NUTTALL
ct. Sunshine W ...365 B10
NUTWOOD
st. Reservoir ...283 J7

NYADALE
dr. Scoresby ...462 B10
NYAH
ct. Dallas ...238 G8
pl. Cranbourne W ...577 E18
st. Keilor East ...278 E20
NYALA
ct. Keysborough ...534 J13
NYANDA
cl. Keilor Dn ...276 H17
ct. Croydon ...380 F10
NYE
rd. Swan Bay ...708 C5
NYLAND
ct. Portsea ...678 G2
NYM
ct. Greensborough ...243 K18
NYMPH
st. Mitcham ...377 J16
NYON
pl. Berwick ...554 D4
NYORA
av. Boronia ...424 L13
av. Tremont ...424 L15
cl. Endeavour Hl ...537 G5
cl. Frankston ...600 H19
cl. Taylors Lakes ...275 J2
ct. Westmeadows ...237 G11
gr. Caulfield N ...455 B1
la. Mt Eliza ...626 A20
rd. Eltham ...288 C10
rd. Glen Iris ...417 D14
st. Malvern East ...416 F17
NYORIE
ct. Ivanhoe ...328 C18
NYRANG
st. Chadstone ...458 E3

O

OAK
av. Boronia ...424 D11
av. Cheltenham ...531 B4
av. Doveton ...536 K13
av. Elsternwick ...454 L7
av. Emerald ...469 J14
av. Mentone ...531 B4
av. Warburton ...348 K3
cr. Caulfield N ...455 L3
cr. Templstw Lr ...330 H13
ct. Altona North ...410 C7
ct. Box Hill S ...375 B20
ct. Braybrook ...365 L3
ct. Gowanbrae ...279 D5
ct. Heidelberg W ...328 B1
ct. Kew ...371 G6
ct. Lalor ...240 G8
ct. Mt Waverley ...419 B15
ct. Somerville ...645 D19
gr. Balaclava ...454 J1
gr. Brighton ...454 K12
gr. Langwarrin ...628 L2
gr. Malvern East ...456 J1
gr. Mt Eliza ...626 A13
gr. Mt Evelyn ...383 B4
gr. Mt Martha ...669 G1
gr. Ripponlea ...454 J1
gr. Springvale ...500 A15
la. Croydon S ...379 H13
pl. Melton W ...226 D14
pl. South Yarra ...32 E14
pl. South Yarra ...414 J7
st. Airport W ...278 K17
st. Beaumaris ...530 D11
st. Bentleigh ...456 A19
st. Canterbury ...372 J14
st. Dingley Village ...532 G7
st. Flemington ...33 J1
st. Hawthorn ...371 E13
st. Herne Hill ...701 H2
st. Parkville ...34 H1
st. Parkville ...324 K20
st. Pascoe Vale ...280 C13
st. Preston ...283 H18
st. Surrey Hills ...418 E2
st. Whittlesea ...96 F16
OAKBANK
av. Highton ...701 H12
av. Mill Park ...242 H11
bvd. Whittlesea ...96 F16
ct. Mooroolbark ...337 H10
ct. Roxburgh Pk ...194 B8
ct. St Helena ...245 C20
ct. Wheelers Hill ...461 G15
gr. Pascoe Vale ...280 K17
pl. Somerville ...644 H13
rd. Keilor N ...276 C2
rd. Melton S ...268 F14

rd. Mornington ...641 D11
rd. Mt Eliza ...641 D11
st. Newport ...411 C9
OAKDALE
av. Balwyn ...373 B14
ct. Springvale ...499 K8
pl. Thomastown ...240 F15
rd. Upwey ...465 C11
OAKDEN
dr. Bundoora ...284 D4
pl. Cranbourne W ...603 J2
st. Pearcedale ...646 L3
OAKDENE
cr. Carnegie ...456 L6
ct. Mt Waverley ...459 C2
ct. Noble Park N ...501 E11
ct. Rowville ...463 E13
gr. Laverton ...406 L19
gr.s, Altona Mdw ...450 K1
pl. Ivanhoe East ...328 J14
OAKERN
st. Mt Waverley ...458 H4
OAKES
av. Clayton S ...499 B6
ct. Altona Mdw ...451 F2
ct. Sunshine W ...364 G10
pl. Carrum Downs ...601 D4
st. Alphington ...327 K20
OAKFIELD
ct. Bayswater ...423 F9
ct. Frankston S ...627 F8
ct. Melton S ...268 H6
OAKGROVE
dr. Nar Warrn S ...552 J17
dr. Nar Warrn S ...552 K19
OAKHAM
av. Burwood E ...419 F8
OAK HILL
rd.e, Pearcedale ...630 K13
rd.w, Pearcedale ...630 E12
OAKHILL
av. Reservoir ...283 C16
ct. Berwick ...554 A7
rd. Mt Waverley ...418 K13
OAKHURST
av. Heidelberg ...328 K4
ct. Frankston ...599 K15
ct. Gladstone Pk ...237 A18
OAKLAND
av. Upwey ...466 A8
dr. Warrandyte ...332 L3
dr. Warrandyte ...333 A1
st. Maribyrnong ...323 D15
st. Mornington ...640 F20
OAKLANDS
av. Ferntree Gly ...464 A2
cr. Frankston ...599 H17
ct. Highett ...496 D13
rd. Bulla ...191 B19
rd. Oaklands Jctn ...191 C12
wy. Pakenham ...583 L5
OAKLEAF
ct. Ringwood ...334 L19
ct. Ringwood ...335 A19
pl. Nar Warrn S ...552 H8
OAKLEIGH
cr. Ormond ...456 D14
rd. Carnegie ...456 D10
rd. Glen Huntly ...456 D10
rd. Ormond ...456 D10
st. Oakleigh E ...458 E10
OAKLEY
ct. Gisborne ...79 A14
dr. Avondale Ht ...322 G10
st. Beaumaris ...530 F5
st. Mt Dandenong ...426 H5
OAKMAN
wy. Hampton Pk ...552 B15
OAKMONT
cl. Rowville ...502 E8
ct. Hillside ...231 L17
ct. Sunbury ...144 B10
OAKOVER
rd. Preston ...326 C4
OAK PARK
ct. Oak Park ...279 L12
OAKPARK
dr. Chadstone ...458 B7
OAK POST
pl. Cranbourne E ...604 J1
OAKRIDGE
cl. Delahey ...275 C11
cl. Lysterfield S ...504 A15
OAKS
ct. Dandenong ...536 F5
ct. Lysterfield S ...504 D17
st. Lilydale ...338 K5
OAKTON
cl. Wheelers Hill ...460 J14

OAK TREE
ri. Wantirna ...422 C6
OAKTREE
av. Wyndham Va ...446 D9
cl. Mooroolbark ...337 H19
cl. View Bank ...285 K18
dr. Hampton Pk ...551 C5
dr. Kallista ...469 C7
dr. Pakenham ...585 G5
rd. Croydon N ...336 B17
ri. Lysterfield ...464 A20
OAKVIEW
ct. Highton ...705 G8
OAKWOOD
av. Brighton ...455 A13
av. Dandenong N ...501 D17
av. Noble Park N ...501 D17
cr. Waurn Ponds ...705 D16
ct. Hillside ...232 A20
ct. Narre Warren ...538 G20
ct. Templestowe ...331 L14
dr. Carrum Downs ...575 D18
dr. Keysborough ...534 C12
la. Tecoma ...466 D13
rd. Albanvale ...319 B7
OAMARU
st. Northcote ...327 A13
OARSOME
dr. Delahey ...275 E11
OASIS
cl. Ferntree Gly ...463 E1
ct. Patterson L ...573 L9
OAT
cl. Delahey ...275 B13
OATES
ct. Cranbourne N ...578 J8
ct. Taylors Lakes ...275 G7
st. Frankston ...599 D19
OATLAND
rd. Plenty ...244 C11
OATLANDS
rd. Nar Warrn N ...538 J11
OBAN
ct. Endeavour Hl ...537 H2
ct. Greenvale ...193 D19
pl. South Yarra ...32 K14
pl. South Yarra ...414 L7
rd. Donvale ...377 H3
rd. Mt Martha ...669 B11
rd. Ringwood ...378 H3
rd. Ringwood N ...377 K2
rd. Ringwood N ...378 H3
st. Burwood E ...419 C11
st. Frankston ...627 D3
st. South Yarra ...32 K13
st. South Yarra ...414 L7
OBAN WOODS
Ringwood N ...378 A4
OBAR
cr. S Morang ...243 F1
OBEID
dr. Sunbury ...187 B4
OBERON
av. Ferny Creek ...465 J2
av. Hawthorn E ...372 G18
av. Oakleigh E ...458 H13
av. St Albans ...320 E4
bvd. Campbellfield ...239 G14
ct. Wantirna S ...462 F2
dr. Belmont ...706 D6
dr. Carrum Downs ...575 A15
dr. Carrum Downs ...575 B16
st. Coburg ...325 D3
st. Dandenong N ...502 B17
st. Forest Hill ...420 G5
wy. Newport ...411 A12
OBERWYL
cl. Rowville ...463 G19
rd. Camberwell ...417 H8
OBOE
cl. Mornington ...641 D12
O'BRIEN
cl. Dingley Village ...533 A9
cl. Glen Waverley ...461 B5
cl. Kew ...371 F4
cr. Blackburn S ...419 F6
ct. Altona Mdw ...451 K2
dr. St Albans ...320 F9
pl. Carlton ...18 J9
st. Newcomb ...704 A12
st. Sunbury ...143 H15
O'BRIENS
la. Templestowe ...331 H5
OBSERVATION
dr. Rye ...697 J5
OBSERVATORY
rd. Mt Dandenong ...382 F18
OCCOLD
ct. St Albans ...320 H6
OCEAN
bvd. Jan Juc ...711 A18
ct. Altona Mdw ...451 K5

gr. Mt Eliza ...626 D11
gr. Seabrook ...450 J6
mw. Torquay ...712 H1
out. Torquay ...711 G12
rd. Blairgowrie ...679 H19
rd. Pt Lonsdale ...710 C7
st. Dromana ...686 G9
st. Hampton ...495 A8
st. Ormond ...455 L13
st. Rosebud ...684 C20
OCEAN BEACH
rd. Sorrento ...678 F11
OCEANIC
dr. Patterson L ...547 H20
OCEAN REEF
dr. Patterson L ...573 J10
OCEAN VIEW
cr. Torquay ...711 G12
cr.e, Kallista ...468 F14
cr.w, Kallista ...468 E14
OCHRE
pl. Mt Waverley ...419 F13
pl. Sunbury ...143 E17
O'CONNELL
ct. Williamstown ...410 K16
la. Carlton ...18 F16
pl. Geelong, off Corio St ...703 C7
rd. Merrimu ...222 H8
rd. Merrimu ...223 A8
st. Burnley, off Tudor St ...371 C16
st. Geelong West ...702 J3
st. Kingsbury ...284 B9
st. Moorabbin ...496 K11
st. N Melbourne ...17 J17
O'CONNOR
av. Mt Evelyn ...339 G14
cr. Hampton E ...495 J10
ct. Altona Mdw ...451 H5
ct. Reservoir ...282 G7
rd. Knoxfield ...462 J5
rd. Knoxfield ...462 K6
st. Black Rock ...529 F1
st. Brunswick E ...325 K16
st. Reservoir ...282 J7
O'CONNORS
rd. The Patch ...467 H3
OCTAGONAL
wy. Mt Martha ...657 C10
OCTAN
la. Roxburgh Pk ...194 F8
OCTANTIS
st. Doncaster E ...332 C17
OCTAVIA
cr. St Kilda ...414 D13
ct. Burwood ...418 B13
st. Mornington ...640 E13
st. St Kilda ...414 E13
OCTAVIUS
av. Caulfield N ...455 L1
cl. Frankston S ...627 J10
ODDYS
la. Cremorne ...32 C3
O'DELL
ct. Lilydale ...338 F2
ODELL
cl. Deer Park ...318 K13
pl. Carrum Downs ...600 F3
ODENPA
ct. Greensborough ...244 B19
ODENWALD
rd. Eaglemont ...328 H10
ODESSA
av. Keilor Dn ...276 C11
ct. Mulgrave ...501 G4
st. St Kilda ...414 F15
ODETTE
ct. Ringwood E ...378 J12
pl. Melton W ...226 B18
ODIN
st. Strathmore ...280 A15
O'DONNELL
cl. Aspendale Gdn ...547 C8
dr. Caroline Spr ...318 B3
st. Reservoir ...282 G6
st. View Bank ...285 H19
O'DONOGHUE
st. Mill Park ...242 H1
O'DONOHUE
rd. Anglesea ...713 B12
st. Dromana ...686 B4
O'DOWD
st. Reservoir ...283 C11
O'DRISCOL
ct. Highton ...705 G6
O'DWYER
st. Mordialloc ...532 D17

O'FARRELL
pl. Geelong, off Little Ryrie St.....703 A8
st. Yarraville..........367 A12
OFFICER
ct. Sunbury..........142 J4
st. Meadow Ht..........238 D2
OFFICER SOUTH
rd. Officer..........582 C17
rd. Officer S..........582 C17
OFFICER-UPPER BEACONSFIELD
rd. Officer..........556 J14
rd. Officer..........557 A11
rd. Pakenham..........557 A11
OGDEN
st. Glenroy..........281 A4
OGILVIE
st. Essendon..........323 C7
OGILVY
av. Greenvale..........237 E1
rd. Clematis..........509 A2
OGLE
cl. Mill Park..........242 B4
O'GRADY
av. Frankston..........599 C16
bvd. Lynbrook..........551 D19
pl. Burnside..........318 C6
pl. Carlton..........18 D20
rd. Hallam..........551 C2
rd. Hampton Pk..........551 C2
st. Albert Park..........29 G13
st. Albert Park..........413 D6
st. Brunswick..........325 B15
st. Burwood E..........420 A8
st. Carlton N..........18 J6
st. Clifton Hill..........20 E3
O'GRADYS
rd. Carrum Downs..........600 H2
O'HAGAN
pl. Bacchus Msh..........221 J16
O'HARA
st. Blackburn..........375 H13
OHARA
ct. Taylors Lakes..........275 E1
O'HEA
st. Coburg..........281 E20
st. Pascoe Vale..........281 A19
st. Pascoe Vale S..........280 E18
O'HERNS
rd. Epping..........195 G13
rd. Epping..........197 A14
rd. Somerton..........195 A12
OHIO
cr. Narre Warren..........552 F1
OKE
st. Ringwood E..........379 B8
O'KEEFE
cr. Bacchus Msh..........222 C13
st. Bellfield..........328 B6
st. Preston..........327 C3
OKUNDA
pl. Eltham..........287 A4
OLA COHN
pl. E Melbourne..........25 K6
OLANDA
ct. Vermont..........421 D6
OLD
rd. Olinda..........427 D13
OLD AQUEDUCT
rd. Diamond Ck..........244 L12
OLD AUGHTIE
dr. Albert Park..........30 B11
OLD BAKER
rd. Wandin East..........385 G5
OLD BAKERY
la. Mentone..........531 A8
OLD BAYSWATER-SASSAFRAS
rd. Sassafras..........425 L11
OLD BEACONSFIELD
rd. Emerald..........509 F6
OLD BEENAK
rd. Yellingbo..........387 J16
OLD BELGRAVE
rd. Up Fntree Gly..........465 C7
rd. Upwey..........465 F9
OLD BURKE
rd. Kew East..........372 K1
OLD BURWOOD
rd. Burwood E..........419 E9
OLDBURY
av. Sunbury..........144 E6
OLD CALDER
hwy. Keilor..........276 J8
hwy. Keilor East..........276 J8
hwy. Taylors Lakes..........276 D6
OLD CAPE SCHANCK
rd. Boneo..........700 A13
rd. Boneo..........700 A20
rd. Rosebud..........700 A13
rd. Rosebud..........700 D4
OLD COACH
rd. Berwick..........554 E1
rd. Kalorama..........382 F13
rd. Montrose..........382 E11
rd. Mt Dandenong..........382 H20
rd. Sassafras..........425 H10
rd. The Basin..........425 H10
OLD COONARA
rd. Olinda..........427 D15
OLD CORDITE
av. Maribyrnong..........322 G14
OLD DALRY
rd. Don Valley..........346 B6
OLD DANDENONG
rd. Dingley Village..........532 H1
rd. Heatherton..........497 H6
rd. Oakleigh S..........497 H6
OLD DIAMOND CREEK
rd. Diamond Ck..........245 C11
OLD DON
rd. Badger Creek..........258 K15
rd. Don Valley..........346 C6
OLD EASTERN
ct. Oakleigh S..........458 B17
OLD ELTHAM
rd. Lower Plenty..........286 F14
OLD EMERALD
rd. Monbulk..........428 G12
rd. Monbulk..........469 C1
OLDERSHAW
rd. Melton..........226 G18
OLD FERNSHAW
rd. Healesville..........214 B17
OLDFIELD
gr. Gladstone Pk..........237 D17
pl. Epping..........198 G16
st. Sunshine W..........364 J5
OLDFIELDS
pl. Geelong, off Little Myers St.....703 B10
OLD FLOUR MILL
rd. Highton..........701 D11
OLD FOOTSCRAY
rd. Docklands..........23 C11
rd. Docklands..........369 B16
OLD FOREST
rd. Ferntree Gly..........424 G16
rd. The Basin..........425 A12
OLD GEELONG
rd. Brooklyn..........365 C17
rd. Hoppers Csg..........449 C5
rd. Laverton..........407 B12
rd. Laverton N..........407 B12
rd. Pt Lonsdale..........707 H18
rd. Werribee..........448 L7
rd. Werribee..........449 A7
OLD GEMBROOK
rd. Cockatoo..........511 E7
rd. Emerald..........469 H20
rd. Emerald..........509 H1
rd. Pakenham Up..........559 C5
OLD GIPPSLAND
rd. Lilydale..........338 G8
rd. Mt Evelyn..........339 D9
OLD GUNNS
ct. Hallam..........537 L12
OLD HALL
dr. Caroline Spr..........317 J2
OLDHAM
la. Dandenong..........535 L9
OLD HEALESVILLE
rd. Dixons Ck..........210 C15
rd. Dixons Ck..........211 A12
rd. Healesville..........211 H14
rd. Tarrawarra..........210 C15
rd. Tarrawarra..........211 H14
rd. Yarra Glen..........209 K16
rd. Yarra Glen..........210 C15
OLD HEIDELBERG
rd. Alphington..........327 L18
OLD HEREFORD
rd. Mt Evelyn..........339 E11
OLDHOME
ct. Nar Warrn S..........552 J20
OLD HURSTBRIDGE
rd. Wattle Glen..........246 J6
OLDIS
av. Northcote..........326 J16
OLD KENT
rd. Mooroolbark..........337 B12
OLD LILYDALE
rd. Healesville..........213 F20
rd. Ringwood E..........379 C8
OLD LOWER PLENTY
rd. View Bank..........286 B15
OLD MAIN
rd. Ferny Creek..........466 A2
OLD MAIN CREEK
rd. Arthurs Seat..........686 F18
OLDMEADOW
st. Dandenong N..........536 B1
OLD MELBOURNE
rd. Chirnside Pk..........336 K9
OLD MENZIES CREEK
rd. Menzies Ck..........467 H20
rd. Menzies Ck..........507 G4
rd. Selby..........467 H20
rd. Selby..........507 G4
OLD MILL
pl. Chirnside Pk..........337 H7
OLD MONBULK
rd. Belgrave..........466 H13
OLD MOOROODUC
rd. Dromana..........670 D13
rd. Moorooduc..........657 G16
rd. Tuerong..........657 G16
rd. Tuerong..........657 G20
rd. Tuerong..........670 D12
OLD MORNINGTON
rd. Mt Eliza..........626 B15
OLD MORNINGTON-FLINDERS
rd. Dromana..........687 F9
OLD MOUNTAIN
rd. Kalorama..........382 H13
OLD ORCHARD
dr. Wantirna S..........422 D17
wy. Doncaster..........331 E18
OLD PARA
ct. Montmorency..........286 F8
OLD PLENTY
rd. Mernda..........155 K18
rd. Mernda..........156 A6
rd. S Morang..........199 H19
rd. Yan Yean..........156 A6
OLD POST OFFICE
la. Carrum..........573 A9
OLD PRINCES
hwy. Beaconsfield..........555 B13
OLD RESERVOIR
rd. Belgrave..........466 G17
OLD RIDDELL
rd. Sunbury..........142 F1
OLD SNEYDES
rd. Werribee..........449 A8
OLD SOLDIER
rd. Cockatoo..........472 H15
rd. Gembrook..........472 H15
OLDSTEAD
ct. Greensborough..........244 H16
rd. Greensborough..........244 H16
OLD STUD
rd. Wantirna S..........422 G16
OLD TARRANGO
rd. Yarra Jctn..........347 K18
OLDTRACK
pl. Hoppers Csg..........447 L2
OLD TRAFFORD
ct. Berwick..........554 C19
OLD VINEYARD
rd. Sunbury..........187 A7
OLD WARBURTON
rd. Seville..........341 L12
rd. Seville E..........343 B13
rd. Warburton..........348 G12
rd. Warburton..........349 A10
rd. Wesburn..........348 B12
OLD WARRANDYTE
rd. Donvale..........376 G2
rd. Ringwood N..........334 F14
rd. Ringwood N..........334 G20
OLD YARRA
rd. Wonga Park..........291 G18
OLEA
ct. Mill Park..........243 B8
OLEANDA
cr. Nunawading..........376 K19
OLEANDER
dr. St Albans..........320 E7
st. Doveton..........536 J13
st. Glen Waverley..........460 C10
st. Rye..........698 A5
OLEARIA
cl. Endeavour Hl..........502 L20
cr. Langwarrin..........601 K20
OLEOSA
ct. Frankston..........628 H1
OLGA
ct. Ringwood E..........379 C5
pl. Mt Martha..........656 H9
st. Coburg..........325 D5
st. Scoresby..........462 H7
OLIN
ct. Wheelers Hill..........461 C17
OLINDA
av. Beaumaris..........529 K9
av. Olinda..........426 H9
av. Springvale..........499 H17
cl. Thomastown..........240 E12
cr. Olinda..........426 K10
cr. Vermont..........421 F5
ct. Broadmeadows..........237 H14
ct. Cheltenham..........497 H20
gr. Oakleigh S..........458 F19
pl. Frankston..........628 E4
rd. Mt Evelyn..........339 A20
st. Caulfield S..........455 J10
st. Glen Waverley..........460 F6
OLINDA CREEK
rd. Kalorama..........383 A14
rd. Olinda..........383 H18
OLINDA-MONBULK
rd. Monbulk..........427 E17
rd. Olinda..........426 L10
rd. Olinda..........427 A9
OLIPHANT
ct. Mulgrave..........460 C17
st. W Melbourne..........367 K15
wy. Seaford..........573 L18
OLIVE
av. Harkaway..........540 D14
av. Mt Waverley..........458 F4
ct. Campbellfield..........239 E12
ct. Chelsea Ht..........547 G17
ct. Epping..........198 B17
gr. Airport W..........278 G15
gr. Boronia..........424 E9
gr. Frankston..........599 D19
gr. Heidelberg..........328 K5
gr. Keysborough..........534 L14
gr. Keysborough..........535 A14
gr. Lilydale..........382 H2
gr. Mentone..........531 G9
gr. Parkdale..........531 G9
gr. Pascoe Vale..........280 J16
gr. Ringwood..........378 B14
gr. Sunbury..........142 J8
gr. Tecoma..........466 C9
la. Ringwood E..........379 B11
pl. Melton W..........226 E15
rd. Eumemmerring..........537 A15
rd. Eumemmerring..........537 B12
rd. Hampton Pk..........551 E15
rd. Lynbrook..........551 E15
st. Blairgowrie..........679 J17
st. Caulfield S..........455 F6
st. Clayton S..........498 K4
st. Dandenong..........536 B6
st. Hampton..........495 G7
st. Malvern East..........416 K20
st. Mornington..........640 D20
st. Reservoir..........282 K11
wy. Wyndham Va..........446 E14
OLIVEBANK
rd. Ferntree Gly..........424 J18
OLIVER
av. Blackburn..........376 C16
ct. Campbellfield..........239 E19
ct. Ferntree Gly..........463 L7
ct. Greensborough..........286 A7
ct. Kilsyth S..........380 K19
ct. Mulgrave..........501 L6
ct. Nar Warrn S..........552 J16
rd. Templestowe..........331 K8
st. Ashburton..........417 C16
st. Manifold Ht..........702 D2
st. Ringwood..........378 G8
st. Yarra Glen..........252 K3
OLIVERS
la. Melbourne..........2 K19
la. Melbourne..........24 H9
rd. Mickleham..........149 A10
OLIVETREE
cl. Werribee..........447 C9
OLIVETTE
av. Up Fntree Gly..........465 H7
OLIVIA
ct. Gisborne..........79 C11
ct. Rowville..........462 F17
OLLEY
wy. Mornington..........657 A6
OLNEY
av. Thomson..........703 J18
ct. Knoxfield..........462 K2
O'LOUGHLAN
st. Ormond..........455 L14
O'LOUGHLIN
pl. S Morang..........199 K18
OLRON
ri. Doncaster E..........331 L17
OLSEN
cl. Mooroolbark..........337 H12
ct. Werribee..........448 D8
pl. Broadmeadows..........238 D19
st. Frankston..........599 B18
OLSON
pl. Sunbury..........142 H9
OLSTEAD
dr. Baxter..........644 B2
OLTON
ps. Caroline Spr..........317 J4
OLVER
st. Preston..........282 K18
OLWEN
av. Belmont..........706 D
st. Nunawading..........376 H9
OLYMPIA
ct. Ormond..........455 J13
pl. Melton W..........226 E16
st. Tottenham..........366 A9
OLYMPIAD
cr. Box Hill N..........374 J9
OLYMPIAN
av. Mt Waverley..........458 G1
OLYMPIC
av. Cheltenham..........496 E18
av. Frankston..........627 L3
av. Montmorency..........287 A1
av. Springvale S..........534 A1
ct. Forest Hill..........420 C3
ct. Glen Waverley..........420 G18
ct. Montmorency..........286 L12
pde. Dromana..........686 H8
st. Bundoora..........284 J3
wy. Wyndham Va..........446 E10
OLYMPUS
dr. Croydon S..........380 B13
dr. Templstw Lr..........330 J16
OLYVE
ct. Surrey Hills..........418 B2
O'MALLEY
cr. Dandenong N..........501 J19
ct. Sunbury..........143 G8
OMAMA
rd. Murrumbeena..........457 C6
OMANIA
dr. Badger Creek..........258 K15
OMAR
st. Caulfield S..........455 F7
st. Maidstone..........366 F1
st. Rye..........696 F9
st. Templstw Lr..........330 G7
O'MARA
st. Fawkner..........281 J7
OMAROO
rd. Frankston..........600 A19
OMARU
ri. Greensborough..........244 C19
OMEGA
ct. Mitcham..........377 F11
ct. Thomastown..........241 L14
st. Sunshine..........321 D19
OMEO
ct. Bentleigh E..........496 K1
ct. Blackburn S..........419 F1
ct. Mulgrave..........500 J4
pde. Warranwood..........334 L13
pde. Warranwood..........335 A13
st. Dallas..........238 C11
st. Noble Park N..........501 D9
OMUNA
ct. Safety Bch..........669 C11
ONCIDIUM
gdn. Keilor Dn..........275 J13
ONDEAN
ct. Frankston..........628 E10
ONDELLA
wy. Delahey..........275 E9
ONDINE
ct. Keysborough..........534 L10
dr. Wheelers Hill..........460 H18
ONE CHAIN
rd. Somerville..........645 A16
O'NEIL
rd. Beaconsfield..........542 C20
rd. Beaconsfield..........555 F16
rd. Beaconsfield..........556 C1
rd. Officer..........555 F16
rd. Officer..........556 A11
rd. Officer..........556 D4
O'NEILL
av. Elsternwick..........454 L8
av. Elsternwick..........455 A8
av. Hoppers Csg..........448 L1
av. Hoppers Csg..........449 A1
wy. Warranwood..........335 C11
ONEILL
pl. Sunbury..........142 H14
O'NEILLS
rd. Melton..........226 H17

ONE TREE
hill, Donvale...332 L18
ONE TREE HILL
rd. Christmas Hills...206 H9
rd. Ferny Creek...425 G19
rd. Smiths Gly...206 C6
ONKARA
ct. Eltham...288 D6
st. Frankston...600 G16
ONSLOW
av. Campbellfield...239 F18
ct. Noble Park...534 E3
ONTARIO
pl. Rowville...462 L15
pl. Rowville...463 A15
st. Caulfield N...415 D18
ONYX
ct. Narre Warren...539 D13
OONAH
cl. Eltham...287 A3
st. Cockatoo...471 H19
OORINDI
cl. Kurunjang...227 C12
OPAL
ct. Bayswater...423 G7
ct. Bentleigh E...497 C2
ct. Dromana...685 J10
ct. Eltham...287 C3
ct. Lilydale...338 L10
ct. Meadow Ht...238 D2
ct. Mulgrave...500 G1
ct. Narre Warren...539 E14
ct. Skye...601 G3
pl. St Albans...320 K9
st. Forest Hill...420 H3
st. Preston...327 D2
OPALA
ct. Donvale...332 L19
ct. Kings Park...319 E1
ct. Wyndham Va...446 H15
OPAWA
st. Brighton...454 G14
OPERATIONS
rd. Melb Airport...235 B10
OPHELIA
st. Ferntree Gly...463 F1
OPHIR
rd. Mt Waverley...459 F2
st. Broadmeadows...238 F20
st. Moonee Pnd...324 A10
OPIE
rd. Albanvale...318 K5
rd. Deer Park...318 J9
st. Ferntree Gly...424 K20
OPLOO
ct. Dingley Village...532 J5
OPOSSUM
ri. Warrandyte...333 F6
OPPY
cr. Hoppers Csg...448 G3
ORA
ct. Rye...696 L7
ct. Rye...697 A7
st. Hampton Pk...551 F9
ORAMA
av. Carrum Downs...575 D14
ct. Templestowe...332 B13
dr. Carrum Downs...575 E15
st. Deer Park...318 L15
ORAN
cl. Keilor Dn...276 D15
ct. Doncaster E...332 D7
ORANA
cr. Chelsea...547 A15
cr. Rosebud W...699 G1
ct. Belgrave S...506 G3
ct. Bundoora...284 L3
ct. Frankston...628 C1
ct. Moorabbin...496 C8
ct. Sunshine W...364 H7
dr. Mt Martha...655 J19
dr. Watsonia...285 H8
pl. Chelsea Ht...547 D11
pl. Epping...197 E17
pl. Melton W...226 D16
rd. Highton...701 A11
st. Blackburn...375 F19
st. Wyndham Va...446 C11
ORANGE
av. Reservoir...283 B8
ct. Bellfield...328 C7
ct. Doveton...536 J9
gr. Balaclava...414 J18
gr. Bayswater...423 D6
gr. Camberwell...417 A6
gr. Essendon N...323 G1
st. Bentleigh E...457 F19
st. Braybrook...365 L1
st. Williamstn N...410 E12
ORANNA
ct. Glen Waverley...420 C15
ORARI
av. Brunswick E...326 A12
ORAVEL
av. Malvern East...457 C2
st. Balwyn N...329 L20
st. Balwyn N...373 L1
ORBEL
ct. Eltham...288 B6
ORBIT
dr. Whittington...704 C19
ORBITAL
dr. Kealba...321 A2
ORBOST
ct. Vermont...421 K3
ORCA
st. Mt Eliza...641 J2
ORCADES
av. Rye...696 E2
mw. Port Melb...412 G6
pl. Eltham North...245 F15
ORCHARD
av. Eltham North...287 E2
cr. Mont Albert N...374 C6
ct. Gladstone Pk...237 E20
ct. Gladstone Pk...279 E1
ct. Somerville...645 D14
dr. Croydon...379 G9
gr. Blackburn S...375 H20
gr. Blackburn S...419 H4
gr. Emerald...469 F19
gr. Heathmont...422 K1
gr. Warrandyte...332 J4
la. Avonsleigh...470 J9
la. Mt Eliza...626 B10
rd. Bayswater...423 D3
rd. Doreen...201 A3
rd. Gembrook...512 C12
ri. Pk Orchards...334 D20
st. Armadale...415 G13
st. Brighton...454 H12
st. E Geelong...703 G11
st. Frankston S...626 G5
st. Glen Waverley...419 K18
st. Kilsyth...381 A10
wy.n,Rowville...503 C4
wy.s,Rowville...503 C4
ORCHID
av. Boronia...424 B12
av. Dandenong N...501 F18
av. Mornington...640 E18
av. Rosebud W...699 B2
ct. Hoppers Csg...405 G17
ct. Lalor...240 K9
ct. Pk Orchards...333 L15
rd. Belgrave S...506 D8
sq. Sydenham...274 L8
st. Heathmont...422 L1
st. Heathmont...423 A1
st. Launching Pl...346 C16
st. Nar Warrn S...579 C1
ORD
ct. Mentone...531 F5
ct. Werribee...447 H9
pl. Rowville...462 H16
ORDISH
rd. Dandenong S...549 D6
ORDNANCE
res. Maribyrnong...322 K15
ORDUNA
pl. Wheelers Hill...460 K18
OREGAN
cl. Wheelers Hill...460 J13
OREGON
cl. Cheltenham...496 J13
cl. Frankston S...627 L15
ct. Cranbourne N...578 C9
ct. Nar Warrn S...552 E14
dr. Doncaster E...376 E3
dr. Donvale...376 F3
pl. Mill Park...243 B5
ORFORD
av. Kew...372 F13
rd. Ashburton...417 L14
st. Moonee Pnd...323 G14
st. St Albans...320 F6
ORGAN PIPES
rd. Keilor N...232 K12
ORGILL
st. Dandenong...536 D11
ORIANA
ct. Flemington...324 F20
wy. Sydenham...275 B7
ORIEL
rd. Bellfield...327 L12
rd. Heidelberg W...328 B4
rd. Ivanhoe...327 L12
ORIENT
av. Mitcham...377 D18
gr. Brunswick...325 E11
gr. Preston...326 E3
pl. Heidelberg...328 K8
ORIFLAMME
ct. Aspendale Gdn...546 G3
ORIOLE
ct. Carrum Downs...575 A20
dr. Werribee...447 L5
ORION
av. St Albans...275 G17
cl. Ferntree Gly...424 C19
cl. Taylors Lakes...275 G1
ct. Eltham North...245 J17
ct. Lilydale...338 H1
ct. Mulgrave...460 D20
ct. Springvale S...499 H19
mw. Port Melb...412 G5
pl. Doncaster E...332 C18
st. Balwyn N...329 A20
st. Hoppers Csg...448 H6
st. Vermont...377 D20
wy. Roxburgh Pk...194 F10
ORKNEY
cl. Endeavour Hl...503 J18
ORLANDA
ct. Mornington...640 L17
ct. Mornington...641 L13
ORLANDO
cl. Wantirna S...421 K18
st. Hampton...494 K7
ORLEANS
rd. Avondale Ht...322 B9
ORLI
ct. Wheelers Hill...461 A18
ORLIT
cl. Cranbourne N...577 J5
ct. Epping...198 F16
ORLOFF
cl. Clayton S...499 D17
ct. Burwood E...419 C11
ct. Sunshine N...320 L10
st. Bentleigh E...497 A6
st. Keysborough...535 A8
ORME
rd. Diamond Ck...246 A15
rd. Diamond Ck...246 G16
rd. Kangaroo Grnd...246 G16
st. Diamond Ck...246 F16
st. Kangaroo Grnd...246 F16
ORMEAU
rd. Mt Evelyn...383 H3
ORMEROD
ct. Gisborne...78 K7
ORMISTON
cl. Wantirna...422 G14
st. Mt Waverley...419 G14
ORMOND
av. Mitcham...376 L11
av. Sunshine...365 D7
esp. Elwood...454 C6
pl. Carlton...18 E17
pl. Kilsyth S...380 K17
rd. Ascot Vale...324 E16
rd. Clayton...498 G3
rd. Eaglemont...328 H13
rd. E Geelong...703 F11
rd. Elwood...454 D4
rd. Hampton Pk...551 J15
rd. Lynbrook...551 C14
rd. Moonee Pnd...324 E16
rd. Nar Warrn S...552 E16
rd. Nar Warrn S...578 G1
rd. Ormond...456 E13
rd. W Footscray...366 G12
ri. Roxburgh Pk...193 L12
st. Brunswick...325 D10
st. Healesville...257 K1
st. Kensington...33 J14
st. Mordialloc...531 L17
st. Pascoe Vale...280 J15
ORMONDE
ct. Eltham North...245 H16
rd. Ferntree Gly...464 B7
rd. Ferntree Gly...464 D8
ORMSBY
cl. Carrum Downs...575 E18
cl. Gladstone Pk...237 E20
gr. Toorak...415 B6
ORMSKIRK
st. Newtown...702 A11
ORNA
st. Ferntree Gly...463 J1
ORNATA
rd. Mt Dandenong...426 D1
ORONSAY
cr. Eltham North...245 G15
ORR
ct. Laverton...407 E13
la. Montmorency...286 L14
pl. Roxburgh Pk...194 E15
st. Carlton...18 D20
st. Heidelberg Ht...284 G16
st. Heidelberg W...284 G16
st. Manifold Ht...702 C1
st. Strathmore...279 J20
st. Strathmore...323 K1
ORRELL
ct. Mt Waverley...458 J4
ORRONG
av. Frankston...599 A17
av. Reservoir...283 A9
cr. Camberwell...417 B5
cr. Caulfield N...415 C16
ct. Mornington...656 J1
gr. Caulfield N...415 D17
gr. Mt Eliza...642 F8
rd. Armadale...415 C13
rd. Caulfield N...415 B20
rd. Elsternwick...455 A3
rd. Elsternwick...455 A7
rd. Mooroolbark...337 E14
rd. St Kilda E...415 B20
rd. Toorak...415 D5
ORSETT
ct. Carrum Downs...601 F1
ct. Mill Park...242 F11
ORSINO
st. Springvale...500 A9
ORSON
st. Scoresby...462 E7
ORSOVA
cl. Eltham North...245 H17
ct. Bundoora...284 G6
ORTHLA
av. Heidelberg W...284 C17
ORTOLAN
av. Broadmeadows...238 A17
ORTON
pl. Roxburgh Pk...194 B16
ri. Endeavour Hl...537 H8
ORUNGAL
ct. Torquay...712 D4
ORVIETO
st. Coburg N...281 D12
ORVILLE
st. Altona Mdw...407 G20
st. Coolaroo...238 F7
st. Malvern East...456 K1
ORWIL
st. Frankston...599 E16
OSBERT
st. Sunshine...321 F20
OSBORN
gr. Pakenham...559 C19
OSBORNE
av. Belgrave Ht...466 C20
av. Bentleigh...456 F19
av. Clayton S...498 J10
av. Clayton S...499 D11
av. Gladstone Pk...236 L16
av. Glen Iris...416 E13
av. McKinnon...456 F19
av. Mt Waverley...458 G8
av. Springvale...499 G11
cl. Brighton...454 K11
cl. Deer Park...318 K11
cl. Williamstown...411 G18
ct. Hawthorn...371 D14
dr. Mt Martha...655 L12
gr. Preston...326 L4
rd. Christmas Hills...207 G17
rd. N Warrandyte...290 F14
st. Brunswick...325 E11
st. Dandenong...535 J4
st. Maddingley...263 G8
st. Northcote...326 E14
st. Safety Bch...669 B14
st. South Yarra...32 A15
st. South Yarra...414 F7
st. Williamstown...411 B16
tce. Roxburgh Pk...194 B12
OSBURN
av. Balwyn N...373 C4
OSCAR
ct. Berwick...553 G4
st. Seddon...367 A12
O'SHANASSY
st. N Melbourne...17 A15
st. Sunbury...143 G14
O'SHANNASSY
st. Essendon N...323 F1
O'SHANNESSY
ct. Altona Mdw...451 J7
st. Nunawading...376 H14
st. Pakenham...584 G3
O'SHAUGHNESSY
st. Kew...371 H12
O'SHEA
rd. Berwick...580 C1
O'SHEAS
rd. Christmas Hills...206 J15
OSIER
pl. Cockatoo...471 H20
OSLAND
ct. Whittlesea...96 E16
OSLO
wy. Keilor Dn...276 E17
OSMENT
st. Armadale...415 E11
OSMOND
pl. Caroline Spr...317 J7
OSNEY
av. Ivanhoe...328 A9
OSPREY
av. Mt Eliza...625 G18
ct. Carrum Downs...601 B1
ct. Torquay...712 C4
st. Vermont...421 J2
st. Werribee...447 L8
OSRIC
ct. Ashburton...417 F13
OSSETT
st. Sorrento...678 F10
OSTEND
cr. Clayton S...498 K5
OSTERLEY
st. Werribee...447 H19
OSTIA
ct. Thomastown...240 C13
O'SULLIVAN
ct. Fawkner...281 F6
rd. Glen Waverley...420 B20
rd. Woodstock...125 A17
st. Pakenham...585 D12
O'SULLIVANS
rd. Lilydale...339 F5
OSWALD
st. Cheltenham...497 D16
st. Dandenong...536 B3
st. Elsternwick...455 C10
OSWAY
st. Broadmeadows...237 L20
OSWIN
ct. Kilsyth...381 E4
st. Kew East...372 H5
OTARIA
st. Mt Eliza...641 H2
OTFORD
cl. Moorabbin...496 G7
OTIRA
rd. Caulfield N...415 C20
rd. Knoxfield...462 K6
OTIS
ct. Mulgrave...501 A5
pl. Eltham...288 C5
O'TOOLES
rd. Cranbourne...604 A5
OTTAWA
av. Blackburn...376 C20
rd. Toorak...415 F8
OTTER
st. Collingwood...19 G15
OTTERBURN
dr. Berwick...553 L3
OTTERINGTON
gr. Ivanhoe East...328 G16
wy. Lilydale...338 K2
wy. Lilydale...339 C5
OTTERY
ct. Craigieburn...150 B20
OTWAY
ct. Doncaster E...331 J17
ct. Lalor...240 J7
ct. Werribee...447 H9
grn. Caroline Spr...317 J6
pl. Keilor...276 K11
st. Knoxfield...463 B7
OULTON
cr. Reservoir...283 H15
st. Caulfield N...415 F20
st. Fawkner...281 J2
OUTER
cr. Brighton...454 H15
OUTHWAITE
av. Doncaster...330 B19
rd. Heidelberg Ht...284 C20
rd. Heidelberg W...284 C20
OUTLOOK
av. Yarra Jctn...347 B16
cr. Briar Hill...287 A6
ct. Chadstone...458 C6
ct. Ferntree Gly...464 B8
ct. Keilor East...322 H5
dr. Berwick...554 D5
dr. Camberwell...417 K8
dr. Dandenong N...501 L8
dr. Doncaster...375 C2
dr. Eaglemont...328 J13
dr. Glenroy...279 E7
dr. Hampton Pk...551 G8
dr. Kalorama...383 B17
dr. Nunawading...376 J9

dr. Werribee 447 B10
la. Gisborne 80 A18
rd. Coburg N 281 L18
rd. Emerald 509 F7
rd. Frankston 627 K6
rd. McCrae 685 D11
rd. Mt Waverley 418 G15
rd. Tremont 425 C17
ri. Bundoora 284 E2
wy. Sunbury 143 F18

OUTLOOK RIDE
Kurunjang 227 A12

OUYEN
ct. Dallas 238 G8

OVAL
wy. Nunawading 376 G15

OVANDO
st. Preston 327 D3

OVATA
cl. Yallambie 286 A11
ct. Frankston S 627 L16
dr. Tullamarine 278 C8

OVENS
ct. Broadmeadows 238 A9
ct. Clayton S 498 G8
ct. Croydon Hills 335 J16
ct. Dandenong N 502 A9
ct. Keilor 276 L12
ct. Mentone 531 G5
ct. Sunbury 142 L13
ct. Sunshine W 364 H14
ct. Werribee 448 B19
pl. Rowville 463 A19
st. Box Hill N 374 L10
st. Brunswick 325 F12
st. Moonee Pnd 324 D14
st. Yarraville 367 B16

OVERALL
dr. Skye 575 H14

OVERBANK
rd. Eltham 288 H13
rd. Eltham 289 A14
rd. Research 289 A14

OVERBAY
av. Dromana 686 D9

OVEREND
cl. Hampton E 495 H10
st. Brunswick 325 K12

OVERLAND
dr. Narre Warren 552 L3
dr. Vermont S 420 L14
dr. Vermont S 421 A14
pl. Keilor East 321 L3

OVERLEA
av. Rosebud 684 H15

OVERMAN
ct. Essendon 324 C8

OVERNEWTON
cl. Keilor 276 J7
rd. Keilor 276 J7

OVERPORT
rd. Frankston S 627 A17

OVERS
ct. Hoppers Csg 405 H20
st. Airport W 278 K18

OVERSEAS
dr. Noble Park N 501 A15

OVERTON
cl. Ferntree Gly 463 L14
cl. Greenvale 192 K18
rd. Frankston 599 D12
rd. Seaford 599 D12

OVERTON LEA
bvd. Sydenham 274 L6
bvd. Sydenham 275 A3
bvd. Sydenham 275 A8

OVINGTON
ct. Mill Park 243 C5
pl. Altona Mdw 451 E6

OWARRA
st. Rye 697 B9

OWEN
cl. Frankston 600 C20
cl. Keilor Dn 276 B12
ct. Pakenham 584 E5
ct. Rye 696 J2
ct. Somerville 645 C15
ct. Thomastown 241 K14
ct. Werribee 448 D7
st. Boronia 424 G13
st. Brunswick W 324 J13
st. Carlton 18 K15
st. Footscray 367 C3
st. Kallista 466 L2
st. Kallista 467 A2
st. Kew 372 G7
st. Maribyrnong 367 C3
st. Mitcham 377 A17
st. Mordialloc 531 J19

OWENS
av. Glen Waverley 460 B7
ct. Hampton Pk 551 G12
rd. Woori Yallock 345 A20
rd. Woori Yallock 388 K12
st. Doncaster E 331 H16

OWERS
pl. Cockatoo 471 H13

OXENFORD
ri. Nar Warrn S 552 K19

OXFORD
cl. Croydon Hills 335 D16
cl. Sunbury 144 E9
cl. Templestowe 332 A2
ct. Dandenong N 502 C13
ct. Ivanhoe 328 D10
ct. Mt Martha 669 K1
dr. Bundoora 284 K2
dr. Thomastown 241 J15
gr. Vermont S 420 G6
la. South Yarra 32 F11
rd. Laverton N 363 L17
rd. Sorrento 678 D7
st. Belmont 706 D1
st. Box Hill 374 J16
st. Brighton East 455 C13
st. Camberwell 417 K6
st. Collingwood 25 G1
st. Frankston 627 E5
st. Hadfield 280 L5
st. Kew East 372 K5
st. Malvern 415 L14
st. Mt Waverley 459 E3
st. Newport 410 J6
st. Northcote 327 A17
st. N Melbourne 17 G15
st. Nunawading 376 K8
st. Oakleigh 457 L12
st. South Yarra 32 D10
st. South Yarra 414 H5
st. Sunshine N 321 G15
st. W Footscray 366 H5
st. Whittington 703 L19
wy. Wyndham Va 446 C13

OXFORD DOWNS
rd. Macclesfield 470 B1

OXLEY
av. Bundoora 242 H18
cl. Glen Waverley 460 F11
ct. Broadmeadows 238 A16
ct. Chirnside Pk 336 J8
ct. Cranbourne N 577 J8
ct. Langwarrin 601 G16
ct. Melton S 268 E12
ct. Wyndham Va 446 H8
pl. Keilor 276 J10
rd. Bend of Islands 291 F2
rd. Hawthorn 372 A18
st. Sunbury 143 A13
wy. Endeavour Hl 537 E7

OZAN
cr. Jan Juc 711 C14

OZONE
av. Aspendale 546 C5
av. Beaumaris 530 D6
av. Emerald 510 A9
av. Mt Martha 656 B10
av. Seaford 599 C8
av. Sorrento 678 E10
rd. Bayswater 423 F8
st. Hampton 495 F8
st. Port Melb 412 B5
st. Rye 697 H4

OZZIMO
dr. Hillside 274 F5

P

PAAS
pl. Williamstown 410 J14

PACE
cr. Chelsea 547 B14

PACH
rd. Wantirna S 422 L10

PACIFIC
av. Sorrento 679 C17
bvd. Beaumaris 529 L10
cl. Wantirna 422 C12
dr. Aspendale Gdn 547 A4
dr. Heidelberg W 284 A19
dr. Mooroolbark 337 L17
pl. Taylors Lakes 275 E2
tce. Mt Martha 668 L4
tce. Mt Martha 669 A4
wy. Forest Hill 420 C2

PACKARD
st. Keilor Dn 276 C16

PACKARD COURSE
Mill Park 242 J3

PACKER
st. Murrumbeena 457 E7

PACKHAM
cr. Glen Waverley 419 K16
ct. Darley 222 B10
pl. Wonga Park 335 J10
st. Box Hill N 375 C10

PACKINGTON
pl. Prahran 414 L12
pl. Prahran 415 A12
st. Prahran 414 L12
st. Prahran 415 A12

PADDINGTON
av. Carrum Downs 600 G3
rd. Hughesdale 457 H9

PADDLEWHEELER
pkt. Croydon N 336 A13

PADDOCK
ct. Ferntree Gly 463 F6
st. Whittlesea 96 L18

PADDYS
la. Nar Warrn N 538 H12
la. Pk Orchards 377 F1

PADGHAM
ct. Box Hill N 375 A5

PADLEY
st. Pearcedale 646 L4
st. Pearcedale 647 A4

PADSTOWE
ct. Craigieburn 194 G4

PADSTUM
av. Lalor 240 D9

PADUA
ct. Gladstone Pk 279 C2
ct. Glen Waverley 420 B13
ct. Vermont 421 H4
dr. Mornington 641 D12

PADULA
ct. Hillside 274 G7

PAGE
av. Kew East 372 D3
av. Port Melb 412 E4
cl. Noble Park 500 H18
ct. Dandenong N 501 L20
ct. Lalor 242 A11
ct. Mulgrave 501 E2
ct. Wonga Park 291 H17
pl. Sunbury 143 H7
st. Albert Park 29 F15
st. Albert Park 413 C8
st. Balwyn N 373 E8
st. Beaumaris 529 K8
st. Cheltenham 530 L2
st. Clifton Hill 19 K7
st. Coburg 325 H3
st. Middle Park 29 K18
st. Middle Park 413 C8
st. Mitcham 376 L12

PAGEANT
wk. Kings Park 274 L19

PAGET
av. Glenroy 280 C5
st. Hughesdale 457 F8

PAGETT
rd. Carrum Downs 574 J14

PAGNOCCOLO
st. Werribee 447 G19

PAGODA
ct. Doncaster 330 L16

PAIGE
st. Nar Warrn S 553 G20

PAINE
st. Blairgowrie 680 B20
st. Newport 411 B10

PAINSDALE
pl. Carlton 18 D11

PAISLEY
av. Boronia 424 H11
cl. Templestowe 332 A9
ct. Gowanbrae 279 C6
ct. Mulgrave 500 H1
ct. Werribee 448 D17
dr. Frankston 599 L20
st. Balwyn 372 L8
st. Balwyn 373 A8
st. Box Hill N 374 K9
st. Coolaroo 238 D5
st. Footscray 367 D8

PAJO
ct. Doncaster E 332 F19

PAKENHAM
rd. Cockatoo 511 B3
rd. Cockatoo 511 B6
rd. Mt Burnett 511 B6
rd. Pakenham 584 E2
st. Blackburn 375 E20

PAKINGTON
st. Geelong West 702 H6
st. Kew 371 L9
st. Newtown 702 G14
st. St Kilda 414 E16

PALACE
ct. Kings Park 275 A18

PALAGIA
ct. Strathmr Ht 279 C8

PALAMINO
ct. Belmont 706 B6
ct. Highton 701 D15
ct. Lower Plenty 330 G1

PALAMINO VALLEY
ct. Greenvale 237 B6

PALANA
ct. Springvale S 534 C3
st. Glenroy 279 G8

PALARA
ct. Montmorency 286 F11
st. Delahey 275 A10

PALAZZO
ct. Greenvale 237 D3

PALERMO
st. Mentone 531 B11
st. South Yarra 32 E11
st. South Yarra 414 H6

PALFREYMAN
st. South Yarra 32 F14
st. South Yarra 414 J7

PALINGA
st. Greensborough 244 K20

PALJAN
ct. Cheltenham 497 H19

PALKANA
st. Frankston 600 G16

PALL
ml. Mt Waverley 418 L20

PALLANT
av. Reservoir 282 E2

PALLETT
st. Coburg N 281 D16

PALLIDUS
wy. Narre Warren 553 C2

PALL MALL
ct. Wandana Ht 701 E18

PALM
av. Caulfield N 415 D15
av. Reservoir 283 B8
cl. Hillside 274 D3
cl. St Albans 320 G8
ct. Campbellfield 239 F13
ct. Ferntree Gly 464 B14
ct. Frankston 599 A16
ct. Mt Waverley 419 A17
ct. St Kilda E 414 J14
ct. Templstw Lr 330 A9
gr. Balwyn 372 L13
gr. Balwyn 373 A13
gr. Dromana 686 F4
gr. Kilsyth 381 D7
plz. Dandenong 536 A8
st. Deer Park 318 L17
st. Fairfield 327 F14
st. Hoppers Csg 405 F17
st. Thomastown 241 F13
wy. Nar Warrn S 552 G13

PALMA
ct. Frankston S 627 L18

PALM BEACH
cr. Mt Waverley 458 K10
dr. Patterson L 573 F11

PALMER
av. Balwyn 373 A9
av. Brighton East 455 E17
av. Croydon N 336 C14
cl. Darley 221 F1
cl. Rowville 462 E20
ct. Hoppers Csg 405 C17
ct. Mt Waverley 459 A8
ct. Roxburgh Pk 194 A9
la. Dandenong N 501 H18
pde. Cremorne 32 B3
pde. Cremorne 32 C2
pde. Cremorne 414 G1
pl. Hawthorn 371 D16
rd. Sunbury 112 B1
st. Braybrook 365 H5
st. Collingwood 19 L16
st. E Melbourne 25 D10
st. Fawkner 239 E20
st. Fitzroy 18 L18
st. Footscray 367 H7
st. Northcote 327 A17
st. Oakleigh 457 K9
st. Richmond 26 K10
st. Richmond 371 A15
st. S Melbourne 30 C5
st. S Melbourne 413 G3
st. Upwey 465 K16

PALMERS
rd. Truganina 406 E13

PALMERSTON
av. Dromana 686 B7
av. Templstw Lr 330 J16
cr. Frankston S 626 H8
cr. S Melbourne 30 F6
cr. S Melbourne 413 K2
cr. Taylors Lakes 233 F18
ct. Greensborough 285 K4
ct. Wheelers Hill 461 E14
gr. Oakleigh 457 K10
pl. Carlton 18 D11
pl. Highton 701 F15
pl. S Melbourne 30 H5
rd. Ferntree Gly 464 A14
rd.e, Ringwood 378 A17
rd.w, Ringwood 377 L17
st. Berwick 554 H8
st. Camberwell 373 A20
st. Camberwell 417 A1
st. Carlton 18 E11
st. Melton 268 L1
st. W Footscray 366 E6

PALM GROVE
bvd. Aspendale Gdn 546 K3

PALM ISLAND
ct. Patterson L 573 J10

PALM TREE
ct. Safety Bch 669 A18
dr. Safety Bch 669 A18

PALMTREE
pl. Aspendale Gdn 547 B5

PALM VISTA
dr. Safety Bch 669 C18

PALMWOOD
ct. Jan Juc 711 C19

PALMYRA
ct. Greensborough 244 G18

PALOMA
ct. Boronia 424 L5
ct. Hoppers Csg 448 E5
pl. Melton W 226 E15
st. Bentleigh E 457 E18

PALOMINO
dr. Sunbury 143 K17

PALPERA
tce. Greensborough 244 B15

PALTARA
ct. Eltham 288 D7
ct. Meadow Ht 194 E20

PALTARRA
ct. Croydon 380 H7
ct. Doncaster E 332 F7

PAM
av. Balwyn N 374 B5
ct. Bentleigh E 456 J19
ct. Kilsyth S 381 C14
ct. Mooroolbark 337 D17

PAMAY
rd. Mt Waverley 419 H13

PAMBARA
ct. Donvale 333 C12

PAMBURRA
ct. Greensborough 244 C20

PAMELA
av. Keilor East 322 J3
av. Rye 696 J2
ct. Blackburn S 419 K6
ct. Bundoora 243 C20
ct. Clarinda 498 C12
ct. Darley 221 G1
ct. Frankston S 626 L10
ct. Melton W 225 L18
ct. Millgrove 348 G1
ct. Narre Warren 539 A16
ct. Scoresby 462 F7
ct. Somerville 644 F14
ct. Springvale S 499 K20
ct. Thomastown 240 F15
ct. Warrandyte 332 J2
ct. Werribee 447 A10
gr. Templstw Lr 330 D8
pl. Langwarrin 629 B1
pl. Mornington 656 E2
pl. Ringwood N 378 B4
st. Mt Waverley 458 J6
st. Noble Park 535 B3

PAMIR
st. Dandenong N 502 A16

PAMPAS
st. N Melbourne 34 H10

PAMPERO
ct. Mooroolbark 337 C9

PANAMA
st. Williamstown 411 G16

PANAMUNA
av. Taylors Lakes 275 K7

PANDAN
pl. Aspendale Gdn 547 B5

PANDANUS
ct. Heidelberg W 328 C2

PANDORA
av. Thomastown 240 C16
cr. Croydon S 380 A11
ct. Whittington 704 A18

PANEL
st. Mitcham 377 K18
PANFIELD
av. Ringwood 378 H4
PANGBOURNE
av. Melton W 226 B13
PANKINA
ct. Dingley Village 533 F10
PANMURE
st. Frankston 599 J14
PANNAM
dr. Hoppers Csg 405 A20
PANNELL
ct. Grovedale 705 J13
PANORAMA
av. Highett 496 A12
av. Lower Plenty 286 J15
av. Officer 555 J19
av. Ringwood N 378 C8
cl. Bundoora 284 D2
ct. Bulleen 329 F13
ct. Glenroy 279 F7
ct. Lysterfield S 503 J14
dr. Chelsea Ht 547 F18
dr. Croydon N 335 J10
dr. Forest Hill 420 D8
dr. Gisborne 79 L15
dr. Hillside 274 C3
dr. Mt Martha 669 E3
dr. Tootgarook 698 E6
rd. Herne Hill 702 A2
rd. Kalorama 382 K16
ri. Lilydale 338 L6
ri. Lilydale 339 A6
st. Clayton 459 B20
tr. Frankston N 600 F11
wy. Point Cook 451 A13
PANORAMIC
av. Dromana 686 D8
dr. Langwarrin 601 L20
gr. Glen Waverley 460 E3
rd. Balwyn N 373 E4
PANTE
pl. Werribee 447 E3
PANTEG
rd. Sassafras 426 D17
PANTHER
pl. Eltham 287 G9
pl. Fairfield 327 C20
pl. Fairfield 371 C1
pl. Northcote 327 D20
PANTON
dr. Melb Airport 234 J11
PANTONS SPUR
rd. Healesville 212 G19
PAOA
pl. Templestowe 331 K11
PAOLA
cct. Point Cook 450 E8
PAPAS
la. Wattle Glen 247 B5
PAPEIRA
ct. Mill Park 242 A4
PAPERBARK
av. Sunbury 143 E17
dr. Mt Martha 656 K8
dr. Mt Martha 657 A9
pl. Knoxfield 463 C2
pl. Plenty 244 H12
st. Doveton 536 L12
tr. Langwarrin 628 K14
PAPHOS
ct. Greensborough 244 F13
PAPROTH
gr. Altona North 409 K8
PAPUA
st. Watsonia 285 G7
PAPWORTH
ct. Meadow Ht 237 L2
PAR
ct. Darley 221 G1
pl. Mornington 641 C10
st. Anglesea 713 B6
PARA
ct. Doncaster 330 K19
ct. Wheelers Hill 460 L19
ct. Wheelers Hill 461 A19
rd. Briar Hill 286 C4
rd. Greensborough 286 C4
rd. Lower Plenty 286 E13
rd. Montmorency 286 E13
st. Balwyn 373 A8
PARABURDOO
la. Kings Park 275 A17
PARADE
ct. Sunbury 144 E10
sq. Maribyrnong 322 K16
PARADISE
av. Clematis 508 J4
gr. Emerald 509 D2
PARAGRENE
ct. Montmorency 286 E12
PARAM
st. Grovedale 706 D9
PARAMOUNT
av. Blackburn S 419 H6
av. Kilsyth 381 C11
cr. Mt Martha 669 C9
ct. Tullamarine 278 K4
rd. Tottenham 366 C12
rd. W Footscray 366 C12
wy. Pakenham 585 E5
PARAN
cl. Endeavour Hl 537 L9
pl. Glen Iris 416 J13
PARANA
ct. Roxburgh Pk 194 G6
st. Aspendale 531 K20
PARANDA
ct. Vermont 421 J2
PARAS
dr. Carrum Downs 601 D6
PARATEA
av. Frankston S 627 D19
ct. Greensborough 244 L20
dr. Rowville 502 H1
PARATTAH
ct. Rosebud 700 G2
PARAWEENA
ct. Greensborough 244 H19
pl. Epping 198 C17
PARDALOTE
av. Carrum Downs 601 B2
cl. Queenscliff 707 L18
cl. Werribee 447 K4
PARDELLA
pl. Mt Martha 657 B7
PARDELOTE
ct. Mornington 640 K16
PARDIN
ct. Bayswater N 380 J18
PARDON
pl. Geelong, off Maud St 702 K10
PARDONER
rd. Rye 696 E6
PARDY
st. Pascoe Vale 280 E18
PAREORA
av. Brunswick E 326 A12
PARER
rd. Airport W 278 E14
st. Burwood 418 C9
st. Frankston 599 H19
st. Mt Martha 656 A9
st. Oakleigh 458 B15
st. Reservoir 282 B7
wy. Roxburgh Pk 194 C9
PARFAIT
ct. Wantirna S 462 C2
PARFREY
av. Lalor 240 G10
PARGETER
ct. Pakenham 584 D4
PARHAM
ct. Altona Mdw 451 K4
PARHNAM
ct. Carrum Downs 601 D2
PARINGA
bvd. Meadow Ht 238 A1
cr. Anglesea 713 E4
ct. Chadstone 418 B19
ct. Frankston 628 B3
dr. St Albans 321 A7
rd. Altona North 365 H20
rd. Portsea 677 J6
wy. Burnside 318 H8
PARIS
av. Croydon S 380 C12
cl. Carrum Downs 575 D14
ct. Mooroolbark 337 L17
rd. Broadmeadows 238 D17
PARK
av. Alphington 327 J19
av. Burnley 371 D17
av. Burwood 418 A11
av. Doncaster 330 B19
av. Glen Huntly 456 D9
av. Preston 282 G20
av. Rosebud W 683 C19
av. Sandringham 495 G17
av. Wattle Glen 246 L7
bvd. Ferntree Gly 423 G16
cl. Vermont 421 B2
cr. Aberfeldie 323 F11
cr. Bentleigh 495 L1
cr. Boronia 424 C14
cr. Caulfield N 415 L19
cr. Fairfield 327 D20
cr. Kew 372 A6
cr. Moonee Pnd 323 F11
cr. S Geelong 702 J13
cr. Williamstn N 410 J12
dr. Belgrave 466 H18
dr. Bundoora 284 G14
dr. Clifton Hill 20 K4
dr. Dandenong S 550 C9
dr. Keilor East 321 L5
dr. Maribyrnong 322 L12
dr. Maribyrnong 323 A12
dr. Parkville 17 F12
dr. Sunshine N 320 L11
dr. Sunshine N 321 A11
dr. Vermont 421 B1
gr. Burnley 371 C19
gr. Dromana 685 H8
gr. Parkville 17 E11
gr. Tarneit 405 D12
la. Aspendale 546 F9
la. Craigieburn 194 A2
la. Croydon 379 K9
la. Heidelberg 329 A8
la. Kew 372 D14
la. Montmorency 286 F10
la. Mt Waverley 458 L4
la. Noble Park 500 J18
la. Pakenham 584 K2
la. Point Cook 450 H9
la. St Kilda W 413 L13
la. Somerville 644 L17
la. Somerville 645 A17
la. South Yarra 31 H13
la. Sunbury 143 G16
la. Torquay 712 B12
pde. Altona 408 G16
pde. Fitzroy N 19 J2
pl. Fawkner 281 F2
pl. Fitzroy N 19 H3
pl. Hoppers Csg 405 C14
pl. S Melbourne 30 A6
pl. South Yarra 31 J9
pl. South Yarra 414 D5
rd. Aspendale 546 E9
rd. Chadstone 458 A8
rd. Cheltenham 496 G20
rd. Dandenong N 501 J13
rd. Donvale 377 B7
rd. Eltham 287 L4
rd. Glen Iris 416 H10
rd. Hillside 232 B18
rd. Lysterfield 463 K20
rd. Middle Park 413 H11
rd. Montrose 382 H4
rd. Mt Martha 669 A3
rd. Mt Waverley 418 L17
rd. Noble Park 534 C2
rd. Oakleigh 458 A8
rd. Pk Orchards 333 F20
rd. Prahran 415 A11
rd. Ringwood N 378 D6
rd. Sorrento 678 G12
rd. Surrey Hills 418 D2
rd. Warburton 349 J3
rd. Yarra Jctn 347 A15
sq. Nar Warrn S 553 C19
sq. Port Melb 412 H6
st. Abbotsford 26 C2
st. Altona North 410 C4
st. Belmont 706 K3
st. Blackburn 375 E16
st. Brighton 454 E17
st. Broadmeadows 238 K18
st. Brunswick 325 A17
st. Brunswick W 324 K17
st. Burnley 371 C18
st. Carlton N 325 F18
st. Coburg 325 H3
st. Elsternwick 455 D4
st. Epping 197 E16
st. Fitzroy N 326 C19
st. Footscray 367 B4
st. Frankston 627 C1
st. Geelong 703 E8
st. Glen Waverley 460 D3
st. Hawthorn 372 A16
st. Maddingley 264 B2
st. Malvern 416 A12
st. Melbourne 1 C6
st. Melbourne 23 H6
st. Moonee Pnd 323 G10
st. Mordialloc 531 L19
st. Northcote 326 F17
st. Parkville 324 K17
st. Pascoe Vale 280 C13
st. Princes Hill 325 F18
st. St Kilda W 413 J12
st. Seaford 599 E1
st. S Melbourne 29 G8
st. S Melbourne 413 D4
st. S Melbourne 413 E4
st. South Yarra 31 F7
st. South Yarra 414 C4
st. Wandin East 340 L17
st. Wandin East 341 A17
wy. Braeside 532 L15
PARK CITY
dr. Lynbrook 551 F15
PARKDALE
av. Balwyn 373 J10
av. Eltham North 287 D2
dr. Carrum Downs 575 C20
PARKER
av. Boronia 424 E15
ct. Endeavour Hl 537 C3
ct. Manifold Ht 702 B1
ct. Roxburgh Pk 194 B14
la. The Patch 468 B2
mw. Williamstown 411 A15
rd. Hurstbridge 203 A15
rd. Silvan 385 A19
rd. Wandin East 385 G14
st. Anglesea 713 D8
st. Brighton East 455 F20
st. Clayton 459 C18
st. Footscray 367 G11
st. Ormond 456 F13
st. Pascoe Vale 280 D17
st. Preston 282 J17
st. Richmond 26 H15
st. Springvale S 534 A3
st. Templestowe 330 K7
st. Templstw Lr 330 H7
st. Torquay 711 L11
st. Werribee 447 C14
st. Williamstown 411 F17
PARKERS
rd. New Gisborne 79 E2
rd. Parkdale 531 F15
PARKES
ct. Sunbury 143 F7
st. McCrae 685 D13
wy. Hampton Pk 551 E12
PARKGATE
dr. Ringwood 335 B19
la. Grovedale 706 H14
PARKHAVEN
av. Kingsbury 283 H9
cl. Healesville 258 C4
dr. Heathmont 422 H1
wy. Knoxfield 423 C19
wy. Mill Park 243 D5
PARK HILL
dr. Kew 372 F9
rd. Kew 372 B9
PARKHILL
cr. Mill Park 243 C6
ct. Donvale 377 B7
ct. Wantirna S 422 E16
ct. Westmeadows 236 G15
dr. Ashwood 418 E14
dr. Berwick 553 G4
dr. Berwick 553 H5
dr. Ringwood N 378 C5
pl. Cheltenham, off Hall St 496 H20
PARKHURST
dr. Knoxfield 423 B17
st. Mornington 656 F2
PARKIN
av. Caroline Spr 318 C5
av. Caroline Spr 318 D4
av. Cheltenham 497 A18
st. Glen Iris 416 F8
PARKINS
la. Cremorne 25 L19
PARKINSON
st. Mt Waverley 458 F9
wy. Roxburgh Pk 194 C17
PARKLA
br. Chirnside Pk 337 G4
PARKLAND
av. Hampton Pk 551 F9
cl. Frankston S 626 J12
ct. Highton 705 E2
ct. Keysborough 534 E11
dr. Chelsea 547 B20
gr. Kingsbury 283 H10
pl. Forest Hill 420 D6
PARKLANDS
av. Alphington 327 J16
av. Briar Hill 286 J4
av. Chirnside Pk 336 L5
cl Donvale 332 K12
cl. Ferntree Gly 463 L8
cr. Brighton East 455 G18
ct. Narre Warren 538 H20
dr. Thomastown 241 H16
gr. Mt Eliza 642 C7
gr. Werribee 447 D8
PARKLANE
wy. Ferntree Gly 463 J12
PARKLEA
av. Deer Park 319 E13
cl. Narre Warren 539 A18
ct. Mill Park 242 G12
ct. Templestowe 331 H13
PARKLEIGH
ct. Langwarrin 629 D2
ct. Vermont S 420 H11
PARKLINK
pl. Ringwood N 378 A3
PARKMORE
rd. Bentleigh E 456 L18
rd. Forest Hill 420 G4
rd. Keysborough 535 A11
rd. Rosebud 684 H14
PARKSIDE
av. Balwyn 373 A13
av. Box Hill 374 J19
av. Keilor East 321 L3
av. Oakleigh 458 B14
bvd. Carrum 573 E10
bvd. Lysterfield S 503 K16
bvd. Pascoe Vale S 324 D6
cl. Lilydale 339 A9
cr. Mornington 656 K2
cr. Mornington 656 K3
cr. Seaholme 409 H17
cr. Torquay 711 L5
dr. Keilor East 322 A4
gr. Frankston S 626 K8
la. N Melbourne 17 F14
mw. Cranbourne W 577 K16
ri. Craigieburn 150 C5
st. Beaumaris 530 G4
st. Blackburn 376 A16
st. Elsternwick 455 C8
st. Malvern 415 L13
st. Sorrento 678 H13
wk. Laverton 407 D12
PARKSTONE
av. Pascoe Vale S 324 F4
av. Pascoe Vale S 324 H4
dr. Bayswater N 380 G19
PARKVALLEY
dr. Chirnside Pk 337 F4
PARK VIEW
cr. Hampton E 495 K9
ct. Forest Hill 420 B6
dr. Aspendale 546 D5
PARKVIEW
av. Brunswick E 326 B11
av. Greensborough 285 K5
cl. Coburg 325 L1
cl. Dandenong 536 F4
cl. Hoppers Csg 405 D15
cr. Bundoora 284 C4
ct. Grovedale 706 G14
ct. Lalor 240 E9
ct. Ringwood N 334 L18
ct. Torquay 711 G11
dr. Carnegie 456 K13
dr. Ferntree Gly 464 D6
dr. Frankston 628 D4
dr. Sunbury 143 F16
pl. Doncaster 330 B19
rd. Alphington 371 J1
rd. Brighton East 455 D17
st. Airport W 278 H15
tce. Chirnside Pk 336 K7
tce. Lysterfield S 503 K15
tce. Sydenham 275 C8
PARKVILLE
pl. Donvale 332 H19
st. Burnley 371 B20
tce. Taylors Hill 274 H8
PARKWAY
Melton W 225 H18
cl. Scoresby 462 E9
PARK WEST
dr. Derrimut 364 D15
rd. Eltham 287 K4
PARKWOOD
cl. Craigieburn 194 A3
dr. Highton 705 G8
pl. Melton W 226 E15
pl. Templestowe 331 B5
ri. Ringwood N 334 H19
PARLIAMENT
pl. E Melbourne 24 L5
st. Brighton 454 J14
PARLINGTON
st. Canterbury 372 K16
PARMA
ct. Balwyn N 374 C5
PARMAN
av. Pakenham 584 G1
av. Pakenham 584 G2
PARMELIA
dr. Taylors Lakes 275 H7
PARNELL
cr. Gladstone Pk 237 B20
ct. Roxburgh Pk 194 D11
st. Cheltenham 496 L15
st. Elsternwick 455 C9
PAROO
av. Roxburgh Pk 194 D8

PAROOK
ct. Diamond Ck.......245 G8
PARR
ct. Avondale Ht.......322 C8
ct. Taylors Lakes.....233 A19
PARRAKEET
ct. Taylors Lakes.....275 G4
rd. Werribee...........448 C9
PARRAMATTA
cr. Noble Park.........534 F6
ct. Caroline Spr.......318 E10
rd. Keilor.................276 J10
rd. Werribee...........447 E8
st. Williamstown.....411 G15
PARRING
rd. Balwyn..............373 J12
PARROT
ct. Carrum Downs...600 K5
rd. Launching Pl......300 L20
PARRS
rd. Croydon............380 G7
PARRY
ct. Mornington........641 C11
dr. Mooroolbark......337 D14
rd. Eltham North......245 F17
st. Croydon............380 D8
st. Moonee Pnd......324 A11
PARSLOW
cl. Lynbrook...........551 G18
st. Clifton Hill............20 C8
st. Malvern.............416 B10
PARSLOWS
rd. Seville...............387 F9
rd. Seville E.............387 F9
rd. Yellingbo............387 F9
PARSON
st. Rye....................696 E3
PARSONS
av. Glen Waverley....420 H16
av. Springvale..........499 K11
la. Olinda...............426 K9
rd. Eltham North......246 D20
rd. Eltham North......288 D1
st. Clayton S...........498 K4
st. Croydon.............336 F17
st. Kensington..........34 A6
st. Mordialloc..........532 A18
st. Northcote...........326 L18
st. Sunshine...........365 E5
PARTON
ct. Carnegie............456 E7
pl. Craigieburn........194 H3
PARTRIDGE
cr. Carrum Downs...601 B1
cr. Frankston...........628 C12
st. Lalor..................241 D6
wy. Mooroolbark......337 C8
PARVA
av. Frankston...........627 C6
PARVIN
ct. Vermont S.........420 G10
PARWAN
cr. Mornington........641 D13
ct. Caroline Spr.......318 C7
ct. Frankston...........600 G16
ct. Meadow Ht.........237 K6
rd. Maddingley........264 A3
PARWAN-EXFORD
rd. Maddingley........264 K10
rd. Parwan..............265 A10
PARWAN SOUTH
rd. Parwan..............265 B20
PARWOOD
av. Nar Warrn S.......553 F18
PASADENA
av. Beaumaris..........529 L9
cr. Bentleigh E.........497 D4
st. Rye....................696 H10
PASCAL
rd. Seaford.............573 K19
PASCALL
st. Mt Waverley.......419 F13
PASCHAL
st. Bentleigh...........496 E4
PASCHKE
cr. Lalor..................241 D8
PASCO
st. Williamstown.....411 E16
PASCOE
av. Bentleigh...........455 H16
av. Croydon.............380 H3
av. Kilsyth..............380 H4
av. Springvale..........500 C17
av. Strathmore.........324 E2
ct. Melton W............225 J19
ct. Mooroolbark......337 K15
rd. Boronia..............424 E15
st. Glen Iris............417 H13
st. Pascoe Vale.......280 G11
st. Westmeadows...237 B15

PASCOE VALE
rd. Broadmeadows..237 K20
rd. Coolaroo............238 B7
rd. Essendon............324 D5
rd. Glenroy..............279 L3
rd. Jacana...............237 K20
rd. Meadow Ht.........238 B7
rd. Moonee Pnd......324 D5
rd. Oak Park............280 A10
rd. Pascoe Vale.......280 A10
rd. Strathmore.........280 D19
PASCUZZI
wy. Hampton Pk.......552 A8
PASK
st. Oakleigh E..........458 D10
PASLEY
st. Dromana.............685 J8
st. South Yarra..........31 H12
st. Sunbury.............143 D14
st.n, South Yarra.........31 H11
st.s, South Yarra.......414 D6
PASSCHENDAELE
st. Hampton............495 B6
PASSFIELD
st. Brunswick W......324 J13
PASTONS
gr. Mt Martha..........669 E4
PASTORAL
pl. Sydenham..........274 L6
st. Frankston S........626 K9
PATCHELL
rd. Dandenong S.....535 H14
PATCHING
av. Noble Park.........534 E4
PATEMAN
st. Watsonia...........285 D6
PATER
cl. Narre Warren.....538 H16
PATERN
st. Highton..............701 K19
PATERNOSTER
la. Berwick..............554 E7
rd. Cockatoo............510 H8
rd. Emerald.............510 D10
rd. Mt Burnett..........511 B12
PATERSON
av. Langwarrin.........629 C2
cr. Greensborough..286 D6
ct. Brookfield...........268 B3
dr. Lynbrook............551 C16
dr. Lynbrook............551 D18
rd. Officer S.............582 D19
rd. Officer S.............583 C20
rd. Springvale S.......533 K5
st. Abbotsford............20 H16
st. Croydon N.........336 E13
st. Hawthorn............372 B18
st. Princes Hill.........325 H20
st. Rosebud............684 E14
PATERSONS
la. N Melbourne........17 E19
PATEY
ct. Grovedale...........706 B14
PATHO
ct. Westmeadows...237 E10
PATIENCE
st. Hadfield.............280 J6
PATIO
ct. Narre Warren.....538 H20
ct. Vermont S.........420 F12
PATKIN
ct. Burwood............419 A8
PATMORE
ct. Mill Park............241 L3
PATO
pl. Noble Park N......501 B13
PATON
cr. Boronia..............423 J13
ct. Greensborough..286 A10
rd. Emerald.............469 K3
rd. Macclesfield........469 K3
st. Anglesea............713 L1
st. Frankston...........628 B1
st. Montmorency.....286 J11
PATONGA
cr. Grovedale...........706 C15
ct. Noble Park.........534 F6
dr. Delahey..............275 B16
pl. Greensborough..287 A1
PATRICIA
av. Blairgowrie.........679 D19
av. Bundoora............285 B3
av. Montrose............382 D11
cl. Werribee.............448 C16
ct. Berwick..............554 C8
ct. Hampton Pk.......551 K13
ct. Yallambie............285 G16
dr. Fawkner..............281 E2
pl. Melton W............226 C15
rd. Blackburn...........375 E13

st. Box Hill..............374 L18
st. Keilor East..........322 G4
st. Millgrove............304 G19
st. Oakleigh S..........497 E2
PATRICK
av. Croydon N.........336 C14
cl. Greensborough..244 L15
ct. Airport W...........278 F14
ct. Boronia..............423 J15
ct. Melton W............226 A14
ct. Mitcham.............377 J15
ct. Seaford..............599 F7
ct. Wheelers Hill......461 A10
st. Box Hill N...........375 D13
st. Campbellfield.....239 J10
st. Glenroy..............280 B9
st. Millgrove............304 G20
st. Oakleigh E..........458 K15
st. St Albans...........275 K19
st. Thomastown.......241 J13
st. Whittington.........703 L20
st. Woori Yallock.....344 C13
PATRICK NORTHEAST
dr. Narre Warren.....552 K2
PATRONA
st. Dandenong.........536 E14
st. Thomastown.......240 F11
PATTANGA
ct. Mornington........641 A17
PATTEN
ct. Newtown............701 K6
ct. Sunshine W........364 H9
PATTERDALE
ct. Croydon Hills.....335 H11
PATTERSON
av. Burwood............418 D5
av. Hoppers Csg......448 F4
av. Keilor.................276 K12
av. Sunshine............365 D8
cl. Caroline Spr.......318 B4
ct. Endeavour Hl.....537 H8
pl. S Melbourne.........29 G5
pl. S Melbourne......413 D3
rd. Bentleigh............495 K2
st. Bacchus Msh.....221 L15
st. Bayswater..........423 B8
st. Bonbeach...........573 A5
st. Brunswick...........325 C9
st. Carnegie............456 K13
st. Coburg...............325 K5
st. E Geelong..........703 K12
st. Middle Park........413 H12
st. Mill Park............242 H5
st. Nunawading.......376 D17
st. Preston..............327 A3
st. Ringwood E........378 K12
st. Ringwood E........379 B10
st. Safety Bch..........669 C15
PATTERSONS
rd. Clyde North........579 K20
PATTISON
st. Moonee Pnd......324 G15
st. St Kilda..............414 C13
PATTON
cr. Hoppers Csg......449 B4
ct. Altona Mdw.........451 G7
ri. Mt Martha...........669 F5
PATTULOS
la. Craigieburn........194 J8
PATTY
st. Mentone.............530 J5
st. Mentone.............531 A6
PATULLOS
la. Somerton............194 J8
rd. Cottles Br...........203 B6
PATYAH
st. Diamond Ck.......245 L12
PAU
st. Coburg N............281 F16
st. Noble Park.........500 K20
PAUL
av. Box Hill N...........374 J5
av. Keilor East..........322 D1
av. Wantirna S.........422 K14
cl. Mt Evelyn...........339 K15
cr. Epping...............197 H14
ct. Bundoora............285 B1
ct. Dandenong.........535 G9
ct. Endeavour Hl.....537 G9
ct. Frankston S........627 G14
ct. Hampton Pk.......551 F10
ct. Melton W............225 L17
gr. Beaconsfld Up....542 F13
pl. Langwarrin..........629 C1
rd. Forest Hill...........420 D4
st. Cheltenham........496 F20
st. Croydon.............380 L1
st. Doncaster...........374 C1
st. Malvern East......457 C3
st. Rye....................697 A12

PAULA
cl. Sunshine W........364 B9
cr. Doncaster E........376 E6
ct. Langwarrin..........629 E7
ct. Oakleigh S..........458 F19
tce. Endeavour Hl.....537 F1
wy. Chirnside Pk......336 F7
PAULETTE
cl. St Helena...........244 L20
ct. Blackburn S.......419 H3
ct. Scoresby...........462 A6
PAULINE
av. Dingley Village....533 D8
av. Tecoma..............466 C10
ct. Hallam................552 C2
ct. Hampton Pk.......552 C14
ct. Mt Martha..........656 C5
PAULKA
ct. Epping...............198 D15
PAULS
ct. Ringwood N........378 E5
la. Dixons Ck...........211 D11
PAULSON
rd. Campbellfield.....239 E14
PAVEY
ct. Macleod.............285 J11
pl. Vermont S.........420 J10
PAVIOUR
ct. Dandenong N.....502 C17
PAVITT
la. Kilsyth...............425 E5
la. The Basin...........425 E5
PAVO
st. Balwyn N...........329 C20
st. Balwyn N...........373 C1
st. Belmont.............705 L2
PAW PAW
rd. Brooklyn............365 D18
PAX
ct. Noble Park N......501 D15
st. Frankston...........599 E19
PAXCROFT
av. Kalorama...........383 B12
PAXTON
cl. Berwick..............580 L1
dr. Glen Waverley....460 K5
st. Malvern East......416 F18
st. Ringwood...........378 F7
st. S Kingsville........410 F3
PAY
dr. Werribee............487 J2
PAYDON
ct. Dandenong N.....502 B12
wy. Hampton Pk.......552 B8
PAYNE
ct. Berwick..............553 K6
rd. Beaconsfield......555 G6
rd. New Gisborne......79 H2
rd. Officer...............556 C9
st. Brunswick...........325 H9
st. Caulfield N.........455 L2
st. Gladstone Pk......236 K18
st. Glen Iris.............416 F14
st. Surrey Hills........373 H19
st. Torquay.............712 A10
PAYNES
la. Box Hill, off
Watts St............374 L14
pl. Melbourne.............2 L10
pl. Melbourne...........24 G5
rd. Chirnside Pk.......292 E15
rd. Mt Waverley.......458 J4
rd. Seville...............341 K16
rd. Wonga Park.......292 E15
PAYNTERS
rd. Wonga Park.......291 K15
PAYWIT
ct. Pt Lonsdale........707 H19
st. Preston..............282 G18
PEACE
ct. Doveton.............536 H12
st. Box Hill S...........374 L20
st. Glen Iris.............416 L15
st. Highett...............496 G14
st. Springvale..........499 L6
PEACEDALE
gr. Blackburn..........376 D13
gr. Nunawading.......376 D13
PEACH
ct. Doveton.............536 J8
st. Pearcedale.........646 H2
wy. Templestowe.....332 C13
PEACH BLOSSOM
ct. Nar Warrn S.......553 C20
PEACHEY
ct. Pascoe Vale.......280 H10
PEACHWOOD
pl. Croydon Hills.....335 F17
ri. Doncaster E.......332 F12

PEACOCK
cl. Mill Park............242 L5
st. Brighton.............495 A1
st. Brunswick W......324 J8
st. Burwood............418 H11
st. Hoppers Csg......448 F9
PEAK
ct. Blackburn..........376 C20
dr. Harkaway...........540 B15
pl. Werribee............447 G15
st. Malvern East......457 J2
PEAR
ct. Burwood E.........419 K8
ct. Wonga Park.......335 H11
PEARCE
ct. Altona Mdw........451 J2
ct. Niddrie...............322 L4
ct. Noble Park N......501 D12
ct. Pearcedale.........647 A4
la. Dandenong.........535 L9
st. Bacchus Msh.....222 E17
st. Burwood............419 A11
st. Caulfield S..........455 J7
st. Laverton............407 F13
st. Yarraville............366 L17
PEARCEDALE
pde. Broadmeadows..237 K16
rd. Cranbourne S.....630 L5
rd. Pearcedale.........646 J11
PEARCEY
gr. Pascoe Vale.......280 L16
PEARL
ct. Cranbourne W....577 J20
ct. Mill Park............242 G5
ct. Mt Evelyn...........339 J17
ct. Noble Park.........534 D4
ct. Tootgarook........698 C8
pl. Ferntree Gly.......423 L20
pl. Ferntree Gly.......463 L1
st. Brooklyn............365 D19
st. Essendon W.......323 A6
st. Glenroy..............280 D8
st. Niddrie...............323 A6
st. Northcote...........326 H18
st. N Melbourne........34 H9
st. Torquay.............712 B10
PEARSE
rd. Blairgowrie.........696 A6
st. Bellfield..............328 C6
PEARSON
cr. Coolaroo............238 E5
ct. Rosebud............699 J3
gr. Caulfield N.........415 C18
pl. N Melbourne........17 E17
st. Brighton.............455 A15
st. Brunswick W......325 A14
st. Cremorne.............26 E18
st. Dandenong N.....501 L18
st. Mornington........640 G14
st. Rosebud W........683 A20
st. Williamstown.....411 G13
PEART
ct. Brookfield...........268 B3
PEARTREE
ct. Doncaster E.......332 D11
pl. Knoxfield............423 A20
wy. Glen Waverley....420 C15
PEARWOOD
st. Ringwood...........378 G15
PEARY
st. Belmont.............702 F19
PEATE
av. Glen Iris.............416 K9
PEAVEY
rd. New Gisborne......79 E8
PEBBLE BEACH
ct. Sunbury.............144 G13
PECAN
ct. Epping...............241 L2
ct. Frankston N.......600 F7
ct. Lysterfield...........503 J1
ct. Oakleigh S..........498 A7
ct. Templstw Lr.......330 J14
PECHAM
st. Glenroy..............279 J2
PECK
av. Strathmore.........279 L16
av. Strathmore.........280 C17
rd. Pakenham..........557 D15
st. Bayswater..........423 B5
st. Flemington.........323 L19
st. Vermont S.........420 L7
st. Vermont S.........421 A7
PECKOVER
ct. Endeavour Hl.....537 E5
PECKS
rd. Sydenham..........275 A8
PECKVILLE
st. Clifton Hill............20 A8
st. N Melbourne........34 K11
st. Port Melb...........412 H3

PECOS
pl. Roxburgh Pk......194 F7
PEDDER
ct. Dandenong N.....502 C14
PEDEN
st. Chirnside Pk.......337 J4
PEDERSEN
av. Reservoir...........283 J2
wy. Montmorency....287 C11
PEDLEY
wy. Lynbrook...........551 E19
PEEBLES
st. Endeavour Hl.....503 J20
PEEL
ct. Gladstone Pk......237 B15
gr. Mt Martha..........656 B11
pl. S Melbourne........29 H4
st. Berwick..............554 F7
st. Collingwood.........19 G19
st. Eltham...............287 D11
st. Kew...................371 K9
st. Melbourne...........23 H3
st. Mitcham.............377 A13
st. Newport.............411 C8
st. Northcote...........327 C17
st. N Melbourne........17 H20
st. The Patch...........467 L4
st. W Melbourne.......23 H3
st. Windsor.............414 D12
PEELMANS
la. Maddingley........222 A20
PEERLESS
ct. Avondale Ht.......322 F10
PEERS
st. Brunswick E.......326 B15
st. Richmond............26 B6
PEET
st. Pakenham..........585 C12
PEGASUS
ct. Roxburgh Pk......194 F10
PEGGIE
ct. Narre Warren.....539 C18
PEGGY
st. Sunbury.............142 G12
PEJARO
ct. Knoxfield............463 A6
pl. Endeavour Hl.....537 K6
PEKINA
ct. Carrum Downs...600 F5
pl. Wheelers Hill......460 H19
sq. Sorrento............679 D16
PELHAM
cr. Wyndham Va.....446 E7
ct. Armadale...........415 F15
ct. Epping...............198 F19
ct. Pt Lonsdale........710 G1
dr. Vermont S.........420 L10
pl. Balwyn..............372 L14
pl. Carlton................18 C17
st. Carlton................17 K16
st. Carlton................18 C17
PELICAN
ct. Chelsea Ht..........547 C9
ct. Nar Warrn S.......552 F13
pl. Mt Eliza.............625 L11
pl. Werribee............448 C9
st. Westmeadows....236 J14
wk. Whittlesea.........126 B1
PELICAN POINT
rd. Point Cook.........451 B15
PELL
st. Bentleigh E.........457 F16
PELLA
ct. Coolaroo............238 D5
PELLATT
st. Beaumaris..........530 E8
PELLET
st. Greensborough..286 B7
PELLEW
st. Reservoir...........282 H14
st. Sandringham.....495 E15
st. Sunshine W.......364 H5
PELLEY
pl. Geelong............703 A9
PELLING
rd. Murrumbeena....457 D11
PELLITA
wy. Langwarrin.........629 L2
PELLONG
ct. Bayswater N.......380 J18
PELMET
cr. Thomastown......240 L18
PELSON
ct. Dandenong S.....550 H7
PELUSO
pl. Richmond............26 E11
PEMBERLEY
dr. Notting Hill.........459 K14
PEMBERTON
dr. Narre Warren.....538 F20
PEMBROKE
av. Frankston...........628 G1
cl. Taylors Lakes.....233 H20
cr. Cheltenham........497 B17
cr. Craigieburn........194 B1
ct. Berwick..............553 L2
ct. Ringwood...........378 B9
dr. Somerville..........644 G14
la. Wyndham Va.....446 F9
pl. Portsea.............678 C7
rd. Balwyn..............373 E14
rd. Mooroolbark.......381 G4
st. Epping...............197 L16
st. Greensborough..244 F20
st. Surrey Hills........374 E20
PEMBROOKE
rd. Portsea, off Hotham Rd.........678 C6
PEMBURY
ct. Nar Warrn S.......579 E1
PENALGA
rd. Mooroolbark......381 H4
PENANG
pl. Geelong, off Alexandra Av......703 E7
st. McKinnon..........456 D16
PENARTH
ct. Craigieburn........150 B14
PENDA
cl. Doncaster..........331 C14
PENDER
al. Melbourne...........23 G8
av. Mornington........656 D2
pl. Melbourne.............2 L10
pl. Melbourne...........24 G4
st. Preston.............282 L19
st. Thornbury..........326 L7
PENDEREL
ct. Wonga Park.......292 A16
wy. Bulleen.............329 K10
PENDLE
cl. Gladstone Pk......279 B1
cl. Nar Warrn S.......579 B5
ct. Jan Juc.............711 C16
pl. Kilsyth..............381 G8
st. Box Hill.............375 D14
PENDLETON
pl. Lysterfield..........464 A19
PENDULA
ct. Narre Warren.....553 G11
PENELOPE
ct. Gisborne.............79 D10
PENFOLD
pl. Albanvale...........318 K4
pl. Melbourne.............1 J13
pl. Melbourne...........24 B8
PENGANA
av. Glenroy.............279 G8
st. Rosebud............684 G14
PENGELLY
ct. Sunshine...........365 E1
st. Werribee............447 D18
PENGHANA
pl. Kings Park.........275 C18
PENGUIN
cl. Blind Bight.........650 C8
st. Melton...............226 F16
PENHURST
ct. Glen Waverley....460 K5
st. Narre Warren.....538 H14
st. Nar Warrn N.......538 J14
PENHYRN
av. Croydon............379 H3
PENINA
ct. Sunbury............144 E11
PENINGTON
st. Glen Waverley....460 L6
PENINSULA
av. Rye...................696 L5
av. Rye...................697 A5
bvd. Seaford.............599 H6
cr. Langwarrin.........629 G2
pl. Mt Eliza, off Nepean Hwy.......641 L4
PENLEIGH
cr. Mt Martha..........655 L18
ct. Moonee Pnd......323 L11
ct. Mt Waverley......418 K14
ct. St Kilda E..........415 A14
PENLOW
ct. Hillside..............274 D1
PENLYNNE
av. Vermont............421 G4
PENMAN
st. Blairgowrie.........696 B5
PENN
cl. Werribee............448 B15
ct. Rowville.............463 L18
ct. Tootgarook........698 C8
pl. Dingley Village...533 F10
st. Balwyn N...........373 F2
st. Clayton.............498 F2
st. Fawkner.............281 G4
PENNA
av. Sunshine N........321 F10
ct. Ferntree Gly.......423 E20
PENNELL
av. St Albans...........319 L5
ct. Rowville.............502 K4
st. Eltham...............287 C5
PENNINGTON
cl. Mt Eliza.............626 E20
ct. Baxter...............644 C2
dr. Mt Martha..........657 B12
st. Keilor East..........322 D4
PENNY
la. Berwick..............539 G19
la. McCrae..............685 B10
la. Moonee Pnd......324 C14
la. Mt Eliza.............626 A15
la. South Yarra..........32 D10
la. South Yarra........414 H5
la. Mont Albert N, off Scarborough Sq...374 E7
wk. Mont Albert N, off Sewell St...........374 E7
PENNYCROSS
ct. Rowville.............503 F2
PENNYGREEN
dr. Gisborne.............78 J14
PENNYROYAL
cr. Kurunjang..........227 A15
PENOLA
cl. St Albans...........320 L8
cl. St Albans...........321 A8
ct. Noble Park N......501 D10
dr. Seville...............341 J15
pl. Wheelers Hill......460 J17
st. Preston.............326 G4
st. Torquay.............712 F3
PENOLE
wy. Wyndham Va.....446 C14
PENRHYN
av. Glen Iris............417 L12
ct. Keilor Lodge.......275 L2
PENRITH
cl. Bayswater N.......380 D19
cr. Bundoora...........242 D18
ct. Berwick..............554 A8
ct. Eltham...............287 L6
st. Boronia..............423 L11
PENROSE
ct. Croydon N.........336 E11
ct. Mill Park...........243 E5
st. Box Hill S...........419 B5
PENRYN
pl. Craigieburn........150 F20
PENSBURY
av. Mill Park...........242 G11
PENSBY
ct. Ringwood..........335 C18
PENSHURST
ct. Hillside..............274 E4
pl. Warranwood......335 B12
PENTAL
rd. Caulfield N.........415 G17
PENTATHLON
st. Bundoora...........284 J3
PENTECOST
rd. Mornington........640 J17
PENTLAND
ct. Glen Waverley....460 K4
dr. Epping...............198 A16
dr. Narre Warren.....553 B12
pde. Seddon............367 C14
pde. Yarraville...........367 C14
rd. Pt Lonsdale........710 E3
st. Ascot Vale..........323 G16
st. Williamstown.....411 C13
PENTLAND HILLS
rd. Pentland Hl.......221 A14
PENTLOWE
av. Templstw Lr.......330 C7
rd. Wantirna S........423 A13
st. Hoppers Csg......448 E10
PENTON
ct. Diamond Ck.......245 L7
ct. Somerville..........644 K18
PENZA
ct. Keilor Dn...........276 F15
PENZANCE
pl. Sydenham.........232 J18
rd. Pascoe Vale......280 H13
PEONY
ct. Nar Warrn S.......579 C2
PEPE
ct. Frankston...........628 H2
PEPPER
ct. Templestowe.....332 B14
ct. Wattle Glen.......246 G8
PEPPERCORN
ct. Avondale Ht.......322 E11
ct. Cranbourne N.....578 B9
ct. Hillside..............274 F5
la. S Melbourne.........30 F5
la. Sunbury.............143 G20
pde. Epping..............241 K1
pl. Surrey Hills, off Canterbury Rd....374 A18
st. Point Cook.........451 B7
tce. Pascoe Vale S....324 E5
PEPPERDINE
wy. Highton.............705 E2
PEPPERELL
av. Glen Waverley....459 K2
PEPPERMINT
ct. Altona Mdw.......407 K19
ct. Ashwood...........418 C16
ct. Doncaster E.......332 B15
ct. Emerald.............509 D4
ct. Hampton Pk.......551 J5
gr. Box Hill S...........375 B20
gr. Eltham...............288 C9
gr. Knoxfield............463 C1
gr. Langwarrin.........601 J14
gr. Meadow Ht.........194 A18
pl. Croydon Hills.....335 E13
pl. Somerville..........644 E14
st. Doveton.............536 G11
wk. S Morang...........243 K3
PEPPERTREE
wy. Lilydale.............338 B13
PEPPIN
st. Camberwell........416 L2
PERADON
wy. Hillside..............232 G20
PERCEVAL
cr. Taylors Lakes.....233 A20
ct. Lysterfield..........464 D18
st. Sunbury.............143 C9
wy. Doncaster E.......332 G15
wy. Mill Park...........242 K9
PERCIVAL
st. Bayswater..........423 K8
st. Brighton East.....495 H1
st. Oak Park............279 J10
st. Preston..............282 L17
st. Rosebud W........683 E18
PERCIVALE
av. Glen Waverley....420 L17
PERCY
pl. Prahran................32 A19
pl. Prahran..............414 F10
st. Balwyn..............373 C12
st. Black Rock.........495 E19
st. Brunswick..........325 E13
st. Croydon S..........379 K11
st. Fawkner.............281 K8
st. Fitzroy N.............19 B6
st. Hawthorn...........372 B14
st. Heidelberg W.....284 E16
st. Kensington..........33 H7
st. Mitcham.............377 C14
st. Mordialloc..........532 B19
st. Newport.............410 F3
st. Newtown...........702 F12
st. Noble Park.........534 E1
st. Prahran................32 A19
st. Prahran..............414 F10
st. Rye....................696 J7
st. St Albans...........320 C6
PERCY JONES
ct. Highton.............705 G5
PEREGRINE
pl. Carrum Downs...601 B1
PERENNIAL
ri. Grovedale..........705 H13
PERICLES
ct. Sorrento............679 A13
PERICOE
st. Frankston...........627 K5
PERIMETER
rd. Melb Airport.......234 E8
rd. Melb Airport.......234 G6
rd. Melb Airport.......235 A9
rd. Melb Airport.......235 K15
rd. Melb Airport.......236 A18
PERITON
pl. Vermont............421 C5
PERKIN
av. Pascoe Vale.......280 E11
ct. Dandenong........535 H3
PERKINS
av. Bellfield.............327 L7
av. Bellfield.............328 A7
cl. Delahey.............275 F11
dr. Carrum Downs...575 E15
gr. Burnside...........318 F9
pl. Torquay.............711 J7
st. Mornington........640 E17
PERMIEN
st. Dromana............685 K6
PERON
ct. Boronia..............424 K4
ct. Narre Warren.....538 F19
PERONNE
st. Pascoe Vale S....324 H1
PEROVIL
pl. Chelsea Ht..........547 D15
PERPY
cl. Croydon S..........380 B12
PERRA
st. Ferntree Gly.......424 K19
PERRET
wk. Sydenham.........274 K7
PERRETT
av. St Albans...........320 G1
st. Brunswick W......325 B8
st. Grovedale..........706 F14
PERRINS
st. S Melbourne........30 A6
st. S Melbourne......413 F3
PERRINS CREEK
rd. Olinda...............427 A12
rd. Olinda...............427 B16
PERRI RASO
ri. Rowville.............503 B8
PERROMBA
av. Eaglemont..........328 J9
PERRON
cl. Craigieburn........150 C19
PERRONE
wk. Yallambie...........286 A14
PERROTT
ct. Mill Park...........242 K5
PERRUMBA
st. Greensborough..286 L1
PERRY
cl. Breakwater.........703 H19
cl. Melton...............226 F18
ct. Brighton East.....455 G17
ct. Herne Hill...........702 A3
ct. Kew...................372 J10
ct. Roxburgh Pk......194 B16
ct. Tullamarine........278 K3
rd. Bangholme.........549 A6
rd. Dandenong S......549 A6
rd. Keysborough.....534 G19
st. Alphington.........327 F20
st. Collingwood.........19 G14
st. Fairfield.............327 G17
st. Moorabbin.........496 C8
st. St Albans...........320 D5
st. Seddon.............367 C12
st. South Yarra..........32 B14
st. South Yarra........414 G7
st. Williamstown.....411 D15
PERSHING
st. Reservoir...........282 F14
PERSHORE
ct. Westmeadows...236 K15
PERSICA
pl. Niddrie..............322 K2
PERSIMMON
ct. Doncaster..........331 E19
PERTAKA
cl. Montmorency....286 G11
PERTH
av. Albion...............320 H19
ct. Frankston...........599 H16
ct. Gowanbrae........279 D4
ct. Wantirna S.........422 L16
st. Belmont.............706 H1
st. Blackburn S.......419 D1
st. Heidelberg W.....284 B18
st. Murrumbeena.....457 B5
st. Prahran...............31 K19
st. Prahran..............414 E10
PERU
ct. Mt Waverley.......459 F3
PERVERSI
av. Diamond Ck.......246 D10
PERYMAN
st. Pearcedale.........646 J5
PESCARA
pl. Donvale.............376 J2
pl. Wantirna............422 A9
PESCOTT
st. Newtown...........702 F8
PETA
ct. Blairgowrie.........679 D18
PETAIN
rd. Silvan...............384 J11
PETALNINA
cr. Wantirna............422 A9

PETER
av. Anglesea 713 F6
av. Blackburn N 375 L11
av. Parkdale 531 H14
ct. Dandenong 536 C2
ct. Lalor 240 K6
ct. Langwarrin 601 K18
ct. Mooroolbark 337 A10
ct. Narre Warren 538 L14
ct. Pakenham 585 B4
ct. St Albans 276 A18
ct. Seaford 600 A3
dr. Ferntree Gly 424 D19
dr. Sunshine W 364 C8
pl. Melton W 226 D16
st. Box Hill N 374 J6
st. Croydon S 379 K11
st. Doncaster E 375 G4
st. Dromana 686 B5
st. Eltham 287 E7
st. Footscray 367 E6
st. Grovedale 706 C13
st. Oakleigh S 458 D19
st. Preston 326 H3
st. Rye 696 J7
st. South Yarra 31 L12
st. Springvale 500 B18
PETERBOROUGH
cr. Deer Park 318 J9
PETER BUDGE
av. Templestowe 331 H13
PETER CHANEL
ct. Deer Park 319 B14
PETERHO
bvd. Pt Lonsdale 707 E19
PETERHOUSE
ct. Sunbury 144 G11
PETER KENT
dr. Somerville 645 D18
PETER LALOR
ml. Lalor 241 C11
PETERLEE
ct. Craigieburn 194 F1
PETERLEIGH
gr. Essendon 324 B6
PETER PAN
pl. Bacchus Msh 221 F16
PETERS
av. Mulgrave 459 L20
cl. Maddingley 263 D4
dr. Cheltenham 497 F19
la. Abbotsford 20 B15
rd. Belgrave 466 F9
rd. Gisborne 80 G14
rd. Seville E 343 B14
st. Airport W 278 J17
st. Cannons Creek 649 C8
st. Watsonia 285 G4
PETERSFIELD
ct. Boronia 424 J5
PETERSON
av. Coburg N 282 A18
rd. Officer 556 K11
rd. Officer 557 A9
st. Highett 495 J12
st. Seaford 599 J1
PETHAJOHN
pde. Grovedale 705 G14
PETHYBRIDGE
cl. Dingley Village 533 E8
PETINA
wy. Sunshine W 364 C9
PETLEY
ct. Carrum Downs 601 E3
PETRA
ct. Epping 241 G3
PETRE
av. Altona Mdw 451 F2
ct. Roxburgh Pk 194 D10
PETREL
av. Sorrento 679 D15
cl. Mt Eliza 641 K5
cl. Torquay 712 C2
ct. Carrum Downs 601 B2
ct. Werribee 448 A10
st. Geelong West 702 G2
PETRIANA
ct. Torquay 712 E3
PETRIE
st. Frankston 599 E18
PETRIK
dr. Taylors Lakes 276 E7
PETRONELLA
av. Wheelers Hill 461 C11
PETT
ct. Heathmont 423 B1
PETTER
st. Glen Waverley 460 B3
PETTYS
la. Doncaster 374 F2

PEUGEOT PURSUIT
Mill Park 242 J2
PEVENSEY
cr. Geelong 703 E9
la. Geelong, off Alexandra Av 703 F8
st. Geelong 703 F8
PEVERIL
cl. Kings Park 319 A2
cr. Cranbourne N 578 F9
ct. Narre Warren 538 K13
st. Brunswick 325 F8
st. Glen Waverley 459 K7
PEVERILL
st. Balwyn 372 K13
st. Malvern East 457 J2
PEYTON
dr. Mill Park 242 K3
PEZZIMENTZ
pl. Chirnside Pk 336 E7
PHAIR
ct. Altona 408 H17
PHALARIS
ct. Delahey 275 A14
PHAR LAP
cl. Kurunjang 227 E6
PHARLAP
cl. Mill Park 242 J11
mw. Cranbourne W 577 F16
PHEASANT
pde. Warburton 350 C3
st. Burwood 418 L10
PHELAN
ct. Kurunjang 226 J11
ct. Tullamarine 278 H3
dr. Cranbourne N 577 J4
pl. Narre Warren 539 F16
st. Preston 283 B19
PHILIP
av. Doncaster 330 E15
ct. Pakenham 584 L4
ct. Thomastown 241 H13
rd. Hallam 537 D16
st. Altona Mdw 451 H7
st. Cheltenham 496 D17
st. Dandenong N 502 A20
st. Heathmont 378 E18
st. Lower Plenty 286 K14
st. Manifold Ht 702 D1
st. Mornington 640 F13
st. Vermont 421 D5
PHILIPPA
ct. View Bank 285 H16
rd. Boronia 424 K14
PHILIPSON
st. Albert Park 29 E17
st. Albert Park 413 C9
PHILLIP
av. Box Hill N 375 C11
av. Springvale 500 G8
ct. Cranbourne N 578 A10
ct. Greensborough 286 C7
dr. Sunbury 142 H4
dr. Wonga Park 336 D5
rd. Avonsleigh 470 G18
rd. Keilor East 322 E6
rd. Knoxfield 462 L3
rd. Knoxfield 463 A3
rd. Woori Yallock 344 H17
st. Bentleigh 496 A2
st. Dallas 238 C11
st. Frankston 599 G12
st. Melton S 268 J3
st. Mentone 530 L5
st. Mentone 531 A5
st. Reservoir 239 K20
st. Rosebud 684 H14
PHILLIPA
st. Blairgowrie 696 C3
PHILLIPDALE
ct. Ferntree Gly 463 F7
PHILLIPPS
rd. W Melbourne 368 B13
PHILLIPS
av. Carnegie 456 K8
cr. Rosanna 285 A18
ct. Northcote 326 G20
la. Geelong, off Little Ryrie St 703 A8
st. Alphington 327 K20
st. Coburg 325 C5
st. St Kilda E 414 G15
PHILLIS
st. Elwood 454 G7
PHILPOTT
st. E Geelong 703 J11
PHIPPS
av. Boronia 424 H5
cr. Diamond Ck 246 B12
PHLOX
st. Dromana 686 G5

PHOEBE
ct. St Helena 244 K17
PHOENIX
av. Hoppers Csg 405 A13
ct. Braeside 532 L14
ct. Doncaster E 332 C17
ct. Roxburgh Pk 194 G9
dr. Wheelers Hill 460 K15
la. W Melbourne 1 A4
la. W Melbourne 23 F6
la. St Kilda, off St Kilda Rd 414 D13
st. Brunswick 325 D14
st. South Yarra 32 B13
st. South Yarra 414 G7
st. Sunshine N 321 C18
PHOTINIA
ct. Upwey 465 G17
st. Doveton 536 H11
PHYLLIS
av. Boronia 424 C16
ct. Vermont 421 H2
pde. Deer Park 319 A9
pde. Rye 696 G2
st. Bayswater 422 L7
st. Bayswater 423 A7
PHYSICS
dr. Bundoora, off Science Dr 284 C12
PIA
ct. Taylors Lakes 276 C9
dr. Rowville 503 B5
dr. Rowville 503 C5
dr. Rowville 503 C6
PIANGAL
pl. Taylors Lakes 276 C7
PICADILLY
cl. Greensborough 286 C8
pl. Sydenham 275 D8
pl. Wheelers Hill 461 B9
st. Oakleigh S 457 J17
PICASSO
ct. Wheelers Hill 460 K14
PICCADILLY
av. Wantirna S 422 J14
cr. Keysborough 534 B8
ct. Greenvale 237 F4
ct. Kilsyth 381 E4
ct. Nar Warrn S 553 E15
la. Wyndham Va, off Bromley St 446 E9
pl. Bulleen 329 G12
PICCOLOTTO
dr. Melton W 225 K18
PICKEN
ct. Springvale 500 C9
PICKERING
cl. Hoppers Csg 449 A4
pl. Doncaster E 332 H11
pl. Kallista 467 E2
rd. Mulgrave 459 L15
PICKERSGILL
av. Sunshine W 364 K9
cr. Roxburgh Pk 193 K16
ct. Endeavour Hl 537 C6
PICKETT
cr. Belmont 706 D5
st. Dandenong 535 J9
st. Footscray 367 D9
st. Reservoir 283 B5
PICKFORD
st. Burwood E 420 A8
st. Prahran 415 A12
PICKINGS
la. Dromana 669 G18
rd. Safety Bch 668 L17
rd. Safety Bch 669 A17
PICKLES
st. Albert Park 29 A14
st. Port Melb 29 A14
st. Port Melb 412 L7
PICK'N'PAN
wy. Warrandyte 333 F4
PICKWICK
pl. Chelsea Ht 547 D9
PICKWOOD
cl. Montrose 382 E6
ri. Research 288 J2
PICKWORTH
av. Mill Park 242 B5
cr. Rowville 502 L6
ct. Rosanna 284 L18
ct. Rosanna 285 A19
dr. Anglesea 713 A7
dr. Dingley Village 533 A6
PICNIC
st. Frankston S 626 G10
PICO
av. Pt Lonsdale 707 E20

PICOLA
ct. Dingley Village 533 E5
ct. Meadow Ht 238 A4
PICOLO
cl. Vermont S 420 K13
ct. Frankston 599 L16
PICTON
st. Geelong West 702 J3
PICTOR
ct. Donvale 376 H5
PIDGEON
ct. Sunbury 142 H7
PIEBALD
ct. Endeavour Hl 503 L19
PIEDMONT
av. Warburton, off Younga Rd 306 A19
cl. Endeavour Hl 536 L4
cl. Endeavour Hl 537 A4
ct. Croydon N 335 K16
st. Box Hill S 374 G20
PIER
rd. Mordialloc 531 J20
rd. St Kilda 413 K14
rd. St Kilda W 413 K14
st. Altona 409 C20
st. Dromana 686 B4
st. Port Melb 412 E5
st. Rye 697 D7
PIERA
st. Brunswick E 325 K16
PIERCE
rd. New Gisborne 79 K5
PIERRE
ct. Millgrove 304 H20
st. Woori Yallock 344 C14
PIERSON
dr. Croydon 380 A4
PIES
la. N Melbourne 34 J7
PIETRO
rd. Heatherton 497 L18
PIGALLE
dr. Mornington 657 B6
PIGDON
st. Carlton N 325 G19
st. Princes Hill 325 G19
PIGDONS
rd. Highton 705 D10
rd. Waurn Ponds 705 D10
PIGEON
st. Werribee 447 K9
PIGEON BANK
la. Kangaroo Grnd 290 D8
la. N Warrandyte 290 D8
PIGOTT
st. Docklands 23 A12
st. Docklands 368 K17
PIGTAIL
rd. Warrandyte 334 E1
tr. Warrandyte 334 D4
PIKE
cl. Nar Warrn S 552 F13
ct. Noble Park 534 E4
pl. Bacchus Msh 221 G15
st. Cheltenham 497 A16
PILAIN
cr. Keilor Dn 276 A12
PILBARA
av. Burnside 318 G6
ct. Belmont 706 B5
ct. Kings Park 275 B17
PILDRA
ct. Seaford 600 B5
PILGRIM
ct. Ringwood 377 L19
ct. Rosanna 285 E20
dr. Hillside 231 J18
st. Seddon 367 A10
PILITA
st. Forest Hill 420 F2
PILKINGTON
st. Fitzroy N 326 D18
PILLARS
rd. Bangholme 547 G5
rd. Keysborough 548 F8
rd. Keysborough 549 A9
PILLEY
st. St Kilda E 414 K14
PILMER
rd. Healesville 258 D1
st. Bacchus Msh 222 A19
PILOSA
pl. Endeavour Hl 502 L20
PILRIG
av. Newtown 702 D11
PIMBA
pl. Nar Warrn S 579 C2

PIMBIT
ct. Kurunjang 227 C13
PIMELEA
wy. Hillside 274 E5
PIMELIA
ct. Frankston 627 L8
ct. Rowville 502 K4
PIMENTO
cl. Nar Warrn S 579 E1
PIMM
ct. Glen Waverley 419 J19
PIMMYS
ct. Skye 601 D7
PIMPALA
av. Seaford 600 A6
ct. Wantirna 422 B13
PINAROO
av. Sunshine W 364 G6
cct. Meadow Ht 194 D19
ct. Wyndham Va 446 H14
st. Newtown 702 J10
PINCOTT
st. Newtown 702 H12
PINDAN
ct. Mt Waverley 419 F13
PINDARA
cl. Gisborne 78 J20
rd. Arthurs Seat 685 J15
PINDARI
av. Epping 198 D20
av. Mill Park 242 D2
av. Taylors Lakes 275 L7
ct. Grovedale 706 A16
dr. Bayswater 423 B10
dr. St Helena 244 H17
st. Glen Waverley 420 C18
st. Mt Martha 655 K18
st. Noble Park N 501 E15
PINE
av. Badger Creek 257 L20
av. Briar Hill 286 K5
av. Camberwell 416 H5
av. Elwood 454 F7
av. Mornington 640 C19
av. Pk Orchards 334 A16
av. Werribee 447 J16
cl. Broadmeadows 238 A12
cr. Aspendale 546 A1
cr. Boronia 424 C15
cr. Panton Hill 204 F15
cr. Ringwood N 378 B7
ct. Aspendale 546 B1
ct. Croydon 379 F7
ct. Kew 371 G6
ct. Kings Park 275 E18
ct. Waurn Ponds 705 E16
dr. Altona Mdw 407 K19
gr. Langwarrin 628 L2
gr. Malvern 415 K14
gr. Mickleham 150 B3
gr. Windsor 414 J12
la. Heatherton 498 B16
pl. Melton S 268 G6
rd. Bayswater 423 G6
rd. Mooroolbark 381 H1
rdg. Donvale 376 G2
st. Brighton 455 A20
st. Brighton East 455 A20
st. Cheltenham 496 K19
st. Dromana 686 F6
st. Frankston N 599 J10
st. Hawthorn 371 F13
st. Ivanhoe 328 D15
st. Lilydale 338 F6
st. Parkdale 531 H13
st. Reservoir 282 H12
st. St Albans 320 H8
st. Surrey Hills 418 D2
st. Thomastown 241 F13
wy. Doncaster E 376 B1
PINECONE
ct. Werribee 447 E5
PINECREST
dr. Highton 705 K5
PINEDA
ct. Glen Waverley 420 C14
PINE HILL
dr. Doncaster E 332 G12
PINEHILL
ct. Cranbourne N 578 D11
ct. Highton 705 F4
dr. Frankston 628 A6
dr. Pakenham 585 J9
dr. Rowville 503 F2
PINEHILLS
dr. Greensborough 243 L20
dr. Greensborough 285 K1
PINEHURST
pl. Chirnside Pk 292 J10
PINELANDS
ct. Narre Warren 538 G20

PINELEA
- gr. Gisborne 78 K17

PINE LODGE
- ct. Templestowe 332 A9

PINENEEDLE
- ct. Albanvale 318 L5

PINES
- gr. Oak Park 279 L10
- wy. Craigieburn 150 E15

PINETREE
- av. Glen Waverley 420 B14
- cl. Croydon 380 B10
- cr. Lalor 240 G8
- ct. Belmont 706 A8
- ct. Ringwood N 334 H20

PINE VALE
- ct. Epping 197 E20

PINEVALE
- ct. Boronia 424 G15

PINE VALLEY
- wy. Templestowe 331 A10

PINE VIEW
- ct. Lysterfield 464 A20

PINEVIEW
- cl. Wheelers Hill 461 F15
- ct. Mt Martha 656 H5
- ct. Nar Warrn S 553 F19
- ct. Werribee 447 E6

PINEVILLE
- av. Geelong West 702 G6

PINEWOOD
- av. Dandenong N 501 G18
- av. Ringwood E 379 C16
- cl. St Albans 319 E9
- cr. Berwick 553 G2
- cr. St Albans 319 E9
- cr. Wonga Park 336 B3
- dr. Carrum Downs 575 C18
- dr. Mt Waverley 459 F5
- dr. Templestowe 331 D8
- dr. Thomastown 240 G15
- dr. Wantirna S 422 H15
- mw. Cheltenham 496 K13

PINEY
- rdg. Endeavour Hl 537 H4

PINIOS
- pl. Roxburgh Pk 194 G6

PINJARA
- ct. Hillside 274 F4
- la. Bundoora 284 F6

PINJARRA
- ct. Eltham North 245 G15
- ct. Narre Warren 538 F19

PINK
- al. Melbourne 2 L14
- al. Melbourne 24 H6

PINKERTON
- st. Melton 227 B17

PINKNEY
- st. Northcote 326 L18

PINNACLE
- av. Ferntree Gly 423 L19
- cl. Highton 701 J11
- cr. Brookfield 268 A3
- cr. Bulleen 329 J13
- ct. Lalor 240 G9
- pl. Berwick 553 E3
- rd. Altona North 408 J6
- ri. Lilydale 338 E13
- wy. Hampton Pk 551 K15

PINNAROO
- cl. Hurstbridge 203 F14
- cr. Burnside 318 F6
- ct. Greensborough 286 H1

PINNATA
- pl. Narre Warren 539 E20

PINNOCK
- av. Roxburgh Pk 193 L12

PINNOCKS
- rd. Emerald 469 B20

PIN OAK
- cr. Flemington 33 K1
- cr. Flemington 324 E19
- ct. Narre Warren 538 H18
- ct. Vermont S 420 F12

PINOAK
- av. Point Cook 449 K5
- cl. Burwood 418 A11
- ct. Highton 705 J5
- st. St Albans 320 H9

PINOT
- pl. Mt Martha 657 B8

PINTAIL
- cl. Bundoora 284 E3
- cr. Taylors Lakes 275 J4

PINTO
- cl. Endeavour Hl 504 B20
- wy. Highton 701 C15
- wy. Sunbury 143 K16

PINUS
- pl. Meadow Ht 193 K19

PIONEER
- av. Upwey 465 K10
- cl. Vermont S 421 C13
- cl. Werribee 447 K7
- ct. Berwick 554 B17
- ct. Rowville 463 A16
- ct. Thomastown 240 L13
- ct. Thomastown 241 A13
- ct. Wheelers Hill 461 C12
- dr. Templestowe 331 H12
- pl. Hampton Pk 551 L12
- rd. Belmont 705 K11
- rd. Diamond Ck 245 B1
- rd. Grovedale 705 K10
- rd. Sunbury 143 G6
- rd. Yarrambat 245 B1
- wy. Kilsyth S 381 A20

PIPE
- ct. Blackburn N 375 G10
- rd. Laverton N 364 C20

PIPER
- cr. Eltham North 288 C2
- cr. Frankston S 626 K12
- dr. Chelsea Ht 547 D8
- la. Torquay 711 H2
- rd. Ferntree Gly 464 A1
- st. Fawkner 281 G8

PIPERITA
- rd. Ferntree Gly 423 F18

PIPING
- la. Mordialloc 532 C16
- la. Mt Martha 656 H8

PIPIT
- ct. Carrum Downs 600 E4

PIPPARD
- st. Box Hill 374 L15

PIPPIN
- av. Burwood E 419 J9
- av. Glen Waverley 419 J16
- ct. Darley 222 A10
- ct. The Basin 424 L8
- ct. Wonga Park 335 H11

PIRI
- gr. Altona Mdw 451 L5

PIRITA
- pl. Cranbourne W 577 G19

PIRRA
- pl. Narre Warren 539 D14

PISA
- ct. Doveton 536 J4

PISANI
- ct. Mill Park 241 L6

PISCES
- ct. Donvale 377 J7
- ct. Lilydale 338 L8
- ct. Lilydale 339 A8

PITCAIRN
- pl. Patterson L 573 F11

PITCHES
- st. Moonee Pnd 324 A9

PITFIELD
- cr. Rowville 463 D20

PITMAN
- ct. Hampton Pk 551 D9
- st. Craigieburn 150 C14
- st. Dandenong N 501 L17
- st. Newcomb 703 L17

PITT
- rd. Kilsyth 380 K9
- st. Ashburton 417 B18
- st. Brunswick 325 K15
- st. Carlton 18 H11
- st. Docklands 368 E16
- st. Eltham 287 G11
- st. Fawkner 281 J8
- st. Flemington 34 D1
- st. Mornington 640 D18
- st. Oakleigh S 497 H1
- st. Reservoir 282 D10
- st. Ringwood 378 F12
- st. W Footscray 366 D5

PITTA
- cl. Werribee 447 K7
- pl. Carrum Downs 575 B20

PITTOSPORUM
- gr. Doveton 536 J10

PITURA
- pl. Eltham North 287 K1

PIVATO
- ct. Cannons Creek 649 F6

PIVOT
- ct. Doncaster 375 E4
- ct. Keilor Dn 276 A12
- pl. Mill Park 242 J2

PIZER
- st. Geelong West 702 G6

PIZZEY
- st. Sunshine 365 F4

PLAIN
- st. Tootgarook 698 D2

PLAISTED
- st. Coburg N 281 F13

PLAISTOW
- ct. Cranbourne N 578 C10

PLANE
- ct. Altona North 410 C7
- ct. Campbellfield 239 F13
- ct. Templestowe 331 L14
- la. Melb Airport 234 F9
- st. Lalor 241 F13
- st. Thomastown 241 F13

PLANET
- ct. Whittington 704 D19

PLANE TREE
- av. Dingley Village 532 H4

PLANT
- rd. Melb Airport 235 A11
- st. Malvern 415 L10
- st. Northcote 326 J18

PLANTATION
- av. Brighton East 495 B1
- av. Frankston N 599 J10
- dr. Rosebud 700 G6
- la. Briar Hill 286 F7
- st. Maribyrnong 323 D13

PLANTE
- ct. Sunbury 143 C14

PLATANI
- gr. Roxburgh Pk 194 F6

PLATEAU
- cr. Hampton Pk 551 J15
- rd. Reservoir 282 C9

PLATH
- cl. Delahey 275 F13

PLATINA
- pl. Chelsea Ht 547 F12

PLATO
- cr. Wheelers Hill 460 C14
- cr. Thomastown 240 J16

PLATYPUS
- al. Melbourne 1 K10
- al. Melbourne 24 B7
- ct. Maribyrnong 322 H15
- pl. S Morang 243 K2

PLAYER
- cl. Hoppers Csg 405 C18
- cl. Wantirna S 462 D4

PLAYFIELD
- gr. Mornington 656 L3

PLAYFORD
- ct. Berwick 554 H18

PLAYNE
- st. Frankston 599 B20

PLAZA
- cr. Dingley Village 532 L8
- ct. Lilydale 338 B1
- ct. Wantirna S 422 F18

PLEASANCE
- st. Bentleigh 455 J20
- st. Fitzroy N 326 C16

PLEASANT
- av. Doncaster 375 D1
- av. Kew 372 H9
- cl. Mill Park 242 D12
- dr. Heathmont 379 C19
- pl. Wyndham Va 446 D12
- rd. Bulleen 329 K12
- rd. Ferntree Gly 464 K1
- rd. Hawthorn E 416 E2
- rd. Templstw Lr 329 K12
- rd. Thomastown 241 A13
- ri. Croydon S 379 F11
- st. Kilsyth 381 B8
- st. Newtown 702 G10
- st. Pascoe Vale 280 G15

PLEASANT VIEW
- av. Preston 283 E19
- cr. Wheelers Hill 460 J7
- ct. Mt Martha 655 D17

PLEDGER
- cl. Diamond Ck 245 K12
- cl. Nar Warrn S 552 G18

PLENTY
- cl. Caroline Spr 318 C5
- cl. Taylors Lakes 233 F18
- ct. Altona Mdw 451 C2
- la. Greensborough 286 B8
- rd. Bundoora 283 K12
- rd. Bundoora 284 E7
- rd. Kingsbury 283 E15
- rd. Mernda 155 J19
- rd. Mill Park 242 J19
- rd. Mill Park 243 B5
- rd. Preston 326 K5
- rd. Reservoir 283 E15
- rd. S Morang 243 D3
- rd. Whittlesea 126 C10
- rd. Yan Yean 156 A9

PLENTY RIVER
- dr. Greensborough 244 A19

PLEONE
- ct. Werribee 446 K18

PLESSEY
- la. N Melbourne 34 G6

PLIMSOLL
- gr. Fairfield 327 F16

PLOUGH
- ri. Nar Warrn S 552 H20

PLOVER
- cl. Frankston 600 G20
- ct. Endeavour Hl 537 A3
- ct. Mt Eliza 641 K6
- ct. Patterson L 573 H10
- pl. Carrum Downs 600 L5
- pl. Craigieburn 149 F17
- st. Melton 226 F16

PLOW
- st. Thornbury 326 J8

PLOWMAN
- ct. Epping 242 A1
- pl. Frankston 627 A1
- st. Olinda 427 C13

PLUM
- ct. Gembrook 512 C12
- st. Doveton 536 K7

PLUMBS
- *la. Geelong, off McKillop St 703 C10*

PLUME
- ct. Glen Waverley 421 A17

PLUMER
- st. Croydon 380 D2

PLUMLEY
- st. Mont Albert 374 D12

PLUMMER
- av. Flemington 323 K20
- av. Frankston S 626 H4
- ct. Mentone 530 K9
- rd. Laverton N 364 G16
- rd. Mentone 530 K10
- st. New Gisborne 79 C3
- st. Port Melb 412 C3

PLUMPTON
- av. Craigieburn 150 F18
- av. Glenroy 280 B8
- ct. Endeavour Hl 537 L8
- rd. Diggers Rest 187 A12
- rd. Diggers Rest 231 A6
- rd. Plumpton 231 A19
- rd. Plumpton 273 A13

PLUMTREE
- ct. Eltham 287 K11
- ri. Croydon Hills 335 E17

PLUNKET
- st. Brighton East 495 E1

PLUNKETT
- av. Carnegie 456 E11
- rd. Dandenong 536 D14
- st. Bellfield 328 B7
- st. Cheltenham 497 A20
- st. Geelong West 702 G6

PLUTO
- ct. Newcomb 704 E14
- pl. Hoppers Csg 405 D13

PLYM
- st. Bentleigh 496 B5

PLYMOUTH
- cl. Sunshine N 321 B8
- ct. Craigieburn 150 B16
- ct. Dandenong N 502 B12
- ct. Epping 197 J17
- ct. Nunawading 376 J12
- dr. Nunawading 376 J12
- rd. Croydon Hills 335 D17
- rd. Ringwood 335 A17
- rd. Ringwood 335 D17
- rd. Warranwood 335 A17
- st. Bentleigh E 457 B20
- st. Geelong West 702 G4
- st. Glen Waverley 420 G15
- st. Heidelberg 329 F5
- st. Pascoe Vale 280 J13

POA
- ct. Delahey 275 A14

POATH
- rd. Hughesdale 457 D14
- rd. Oakleigh 457 D14

POCKETT
- la. Healesville 257 K2
- rd. Healesville 257 K1

PODBURY
- cr. E Geelong 703 G7

PODMORE
- st. Dandenong S 536 A13

POET
- ct. Keilor Dn 275 L10
- rd. Bentleigh E 457 D16

POETS
- ct. Glen Waverley 421 A19
- gr. Elwood 454 F3
- la. Sherbrooke 426 J20
- la. Truganina 405 F13

POHLMAN
- av. Fitzroy N 20 B1
- *la. Prahran, off Grandview Gr 415 B9*

POINCIANA
- ct. Werribee 447 K9
- st. Frankston S 627 D8

POINT
- av. Beaumaris 529 L11

POINT COOK HOMESTEAD
- rd. Point Cook 451 A20

POINT HENRY
- rd. Moolap 704 L13

POINT KING
- rd. Portsea 678 G3
- rd. Sorrento 678 G3

POINT LONSDALE
- rd. Pt Lonsdale 707 J20

POINT NEPEAN
- rd. Blairgowrie 679 J17
- rd. Dromana 685 A11
- rd. McCrae 685 A11
- rd. Portsea 666 H20
- rd. Rosebud 683 J16
- rd. Rosebud W 683 C18
- rd. Rye 696 K1
- rd. Rye 697 B1
- rd. Sorrento 678 H5
- rd. Tootgarook 698 A2

POINT ORMOND
- av. Elwood 454 B4

POINT SIDE
- ct. Glen Waverley 460 G2

POINTSIDE
- av. Bayswater N 380 A19

POKOLBIN
- ct. Bangholme 549 H13

POLARIS
- ct. Carrum Downs 575 B14
- dr. Doncaster E 332 D17
- wy. Chirnside Pk 337 F1

POLAT
- ct. Mt Evelyn 339 K16

POLE
- st. Seddon 367 E11

POLICE
- rd. Dandenong N 502 C8
- rd. Endeavour Hl 502 G8
- rd. Mulgrave 500 B5
- rd. Mulgrave 501 C7
- rd. Mulgrave 501 L8
- rd. Noble Park N 501 C7
- rd. Rowville 502 C8
- rd. Springvale 500 B5

POLK
- ct. Dandenong N 501 G9

POLLARD
- ct. Altona 409 F17
- pde. Healesville 213 H16
- pl. Sunbury 143 H8

POLLEY
- ct. Grovedale 705 K13

POLLINA
- cl. Hampton Pk 551 E5
- st. Bentleigh E 496 G3

POLLINGTON
- st. St Kilda 413 L16

POLLOCK
- ct. Delahey 275 A11
- dr. Mill Park 242 J1
- pl. Roxburgh Pk 193 L15

POLLY KELLY
- pl. Frankston S 627 J10

POLLY WOODSIDE
- dr. Altona Mdw 452 A4

POLO
- pde. Caulfield N 455 E1

POLTAVA
- wk. Delahey 275 B15

POLWARTH
- cr. Belmont 706 B7

POLYDOR
- ct. Epping 197 L16
- pl. Blackburn N 375 J9

POMMEL
- cr. Epping 198 F17
- st. Pakenham 585 F4
- st. Pakenham 585 F5

POMORA
- av. Torquay 712 E2

PONDEROSA
- pl. Dromana 686 J3

PONSFORD
av. Wantirna S....422 E20
av. Wantirna S....462 E1
pl. S Morang....198 H17
pl. Sunbury....142 H14
PONT
ct. Keysborough....533 L8
PONTFORD
ct. Wheelers Hill....461 E16
PONTIN
ct. Burwood E....419 H12
PONTING
st. Williamstown....410 B13
PONTO
ct. Endeavour Hl....537 G8
PONYARA
rd. Mt Martha....668 L4
rd. Mt Martha....669 A4
POOL
st. Port Melb....412 L4
POOLE
av. Hampton....495 F10
ct. Endeavour Hl....537 J4
st. Burwood....419 A7
st. Deer Park....319 A17
st. McCrae....685 C14
POOLEY BRIDGE
rd. Mordialloc....532 D17
POOLMAN
st. Port Melb....412 F3
POORINDA
ri. Narre Warren....553 G10
POPE
av. Boronia....424 H5
ct. Mooroolbark....337 E19
pl. Greensborough....286 D3
rd. Blackburn....375 K13
POPES
rd. Keysborough....535 A7
POPLAR
av. Ashwood....418 D14
av. Hawthorn....372 A18
cl. Rowville....463 J16
cr. Bellfield....327 K5
cr. Emerald....469 H13
ct. Belmont....706 H6
ct. St Albans....320 J8
dr. Rosebud....700 G2
gr. Carnegie....456 L5
gr. Langwarrin....629 A2
rd. Parkville....324 L18
st. Box Hill....374 H14
st. Campbellfield....239 F13
st. Caulfield S....455 F7
st. Frankston N....600 B9
st. Newcomb....704 A14
st. Thomastown....241 F13
POPPY
pl. Carrum Downs....574 L19
POPPYS
ct. Warrandyte....333 C4
PORENA
ct. Ferntree Gly....423 L20
POROSA
ct. Langwarrin....629 L3
PORSCHE
ct. Epping....197 J14
PORT
la. Plenty....244 A9
st. Highett....496 J15
st. Newport....410 E10
PORTAL
pl. Patterson L....547 J20
st. Ascot Vale....324 A19
PORTARLINGTON
rd. Moolap....704 A11
rd. Newcomb....704 A11
PORTARLINGTON-QUEENSCLIFF
rd. Pt Lonsdale....707 G12
rd. Swan Bay....707 G12
PORTCHESTER
bvd. Officer....555 G19
PORTEOUS
rd. Melton W....225 G1
rd. Toolern Va....225 G1
PORTER
av. Highton....705 J2
av. Roxburgh Pk....194 E15
ct. Deer Park....319 D11
ct. Mill Park....242 G8
la. Kensington....33 J6
rd. Balwyn....373 K10
rd. Bentleigh....496 D6
rd. Carnegie....456 J9
rd. Heidelberg Ht....328 G2
st. Briar Hill....286 J6
st. Eltham....287 D16
st. Fitzroy N....326 C19
st. Hampton....495 G10
st. Hawthorn E....372 H20
st. Melton S....268 H9
st. Prahran....32 A19
st. Prahran....414 F10
st. Templestowe....330 L5
st. Templestowe....331 D5
st. Templestowe....332 A6
PORTERS
rd. Wesburn....348 A11
PORTLAND
la. Melbourne....2 J13
la. Melbourne....24 F7
pde. Seaford....573 E19
pl. Endeavour Hl....537 F2
pl. South Yarra....32 B12
pl. South Yarra....414 G6
pl. Thomastown....240 F11
st. Carnegie....456 H13
st. Coburg....325 B4
st. Mulgrave....501 G7
st. Richmond....26 D13
PORTMAN
rd. The Patch....468 C7
st. Oakleigh....457 K11
PORTMANS
la. Point Cook....450 G10
PORT MARNOCK
ct. Sunbury....144 H11
PORTMARNOCK
pl. Chirnside Pk....292 J9
PORTO
ct. Cranbourne N....578 G9
PORTOBELLO
pl. Wheelers Hill....461 D14
PORTOFINO
dr. Cranbourne N....578 J10
PORT PHILLIP
arc. Melbourne....2 D19
cr. Williamstown, off Anchorage Av....411 D17
dr. Mornington....656 H1
vw. Frankston S....627 G11
PORTREE
pl. Nar Warrn S....578 L2
st. Macleod....285 A11
PORTRUSH
av. Mornington....656 D2
PORTSEA
pl. Narre Warren....539 F20
PORTSMOUTH
cr. Grovedale....706 B13
pl. Epping....241 H5
st. Heathmont....422 F1
st. Mt Waverley....419 D19
POSEIDON
cl. Mill Park....242 J10
POSITARNO
wy. Point Cook....450 E8
POSSUM
la. Heathmont....422 L2
pl. Berwick....553 K15
pl. S Morang....243 K2
POST OFFICE
pl. Carlton....18 F14
pl. Glenroy....279 L5
pl. Port Melb....412 K7
pl. Malvern East, off Dandenong Rd....416 C20
pl. St Kilda, off Inkerman St....414 E16
POTOMAC
cl. Werribee....447 G5
POTTENGER
wy. St Albans....320 B11
POTTER
ct. Northcote....326 F15
ct. Templstw Lr....330 C9
st. Armadale....415 D11
st. Black Rock....495 E20
st. Craigieburn....194 J1
st. Dandenong....535 J7
st. Geelong West....702 F7
POTTERY
ct. Brunswick....325 C14
dr. Blackburn N....375 G10
POTTON
av. Rosebud....684 D20
POTTS
rd. Langwarrin....601 J11
rd. Skye....601 H10
st. Parkdale....531 D8
POULSON
st. Carrum....573 C9
POULTER
av. Greensborough....286 C3
cr. Clarinda....498 C11
st. Ashburton....417 J15
POULTON
cl. Heathmont....379 E18
POUND
rd. Clyde North....580 B8
rd. Cranbourne N....579 F6
rd. Dandenong S....550 K6
rd. Hampton Pk....551 C6
rd. Nar Warrn S....552 E9
rd. Warrandyte....333 C3
POUND BEND
rd. Warrandyte....289 E18
POUTAKIDIS
la. Wattle Glen....247 B4
POVOLO
mw. Eltham....288 A9
POWDERHAM
rd. Caulfield N....415 G20
POWELL
cr. Maidstone....366 E1
ct. Dandenong S....535 H14
ct. Montrose....382 E9
dr. Hoppers Csg....448 H8
dr. Hoppers Csg....449 A5
pl. Geelong, off Little Malop St....703 C8
st. Croydon....336 J18
st. E Geelong....703 G13
st. Reservoir....282 H15
st. South Yarra....31 L11
st. South Yarra....414 F6
st. Yarraville....366 L18
st. Yarraville....367 A18
POWELLS
rd. Lysterfield....504 J4
tr. Lysterfield....504 H11
POWER
av. Ashwood....417 L19
av. Chadstone....418 C20
av. Hawthorn....371 H18
av. Toorak....415 J6
cl. Gladstone Pk....237 B19
pl. Taylors Lakes....233 C16
rd. Bayswater....423 J5
rd. Boronia....423 K6
rd. Doveton....536 H14
rd. Endeavour Hl....502 L18
rd. Endeavour Hl....503 A18
rd. Melb Airport....235 A11
st. Balwyn....373 E12
st. Croydon N....335 K11
st. Dandenong....536 C11
st. Hawthorn....371 H19
st. Newport....411 B11
st. Pascoe Vale S....280 G19
st. Preston....327 E5
st. St Albans....276 A18
st. Southbank....3 D6
st. Southbank....24 B15
st. Toorak....415 K5
st. Williamstown....411 B11
POWERS
st. Donvale....332 H15
POWIS
ct. Noble Park N....501 E16
POWLETT
mw. E Melbourne....25 G8
st. Altona Mdw....407 G20
st. E Melbourne....25 H8
st. Heidelberg....328 H6
st. Maddingley....263 J1
st. Moorabbin....497 E12
st. Mordialloc....531 K17
st. Sunbury....143 L14
POWLEY
pde. Macleod....285 D10
pde. Watsonia....285 D10
POWRIE
ct. Ringwood N....378 G2
POWYS
dr. Beaumaris....530 F9
POYNER
av. Lilydale....338 B2
POYNTON
av. Ringwood....377 L11
POZIERES
av. Elwood....454 B1
PRAHN
ct. Brookfield....267 L5
PRAHRAN
gr. Elsternwick....455 B2
PRAIRIE
ct. Narre Warren....552 H1
PRANJIC
pl. Rowville....503 B6
PRASINO
ct. Carrum Downs....601 E5
PRATICO
ct. Forest Hill....420 F1
PRATT
av. Frankston S....627 A7
cl. Taylors Lakes....233 C17
ct. Epping....198 E15
ct. Fitzroy N....20 A1
ct. Melton....227 D16
ct. Werribee....448 A9
st. Moonee Pnd....324 C13
st. Reservoir....283 A8
st. Ringwood....378 F11
st. Tootgarook....698 D2
PREAD
wk. Roxburgh Pk....194 B10
PRECIOUS
rd. Diggers Rest....187 A10
PREFECT
st. Strathmore....280 B20
PREMIER
av. Mitcham....377 D19
ct. Highton....701 E17
PRENDERGAST
av. Keilor East....278 B17
rd. Sunbury....143 F5
st. Pascoe Vale S....324 J6
PRENTICE
av. Rye....697 E6
ct. Roxburgh Pk....194 C12
st. Altona North....410 D7
st. Brunswick....325 E13
st. Elsternwick....455 C4
st. St Kilda E....414 J16
st. Yarraville....366 K14
PRENTON
ct. Wantirna....422 E9
PRESCOTT
av. Mt Martha....655 F17
av. Safety Bch....668 K19
pl. Avondale Ht....322 C11
st. Sunshine W....364 J10
PRESENTATION
pl. Brighton....454 J10
PRESGRAVE
pl. Melbourne....2 D14
pl. Melbourne....24 E8
PRESIDENT
rd. Albanvale....319 C6
rd. Nar Warrn S....552 F20
PRESIDENTS
ct. Werribee....446 K9
PRESSWELL
cl. Altona Mdw....452 A6
PRESTBURY
dr. Vermont S....420 G7
PRESTIGE
dr. Clayton S....498 L10
PRESTON
av. Endeavour Hl....537 G10
av. Roxburgh Pk....193 L16
ct. Werribee....448 A15
pl. Taylors Lakes....275 A1
rd. Hughesdale....457 F10
st. Bentleigh E....456 H16
st. Coburg....325 C4
st. Fawkner....281 G3
st. Geelong West....702 J4
st. Preston....326 K1
st. Rye....696 G6
st. Sunbury....142 J11
PRESTWICK
av. Jan Juc....711 F14
ct. Frankston....599 K17
pl. Chirnside Pk....292 J9
PRETORIA
st. Balwyn....372 L11
st. Balwyn....373 A11
st. Caulfield....455 F5
PRETTY HILL
la. Wattle Glen....247 C11
PRICE
av. Montmorency....286 J8
av. Mt Waverley....419 G20
ct. Diamond Ck....245 F13
rd. Kalorama....382 L17
rd. Kalorama....383 A17
st. Essendon....323 C7
st. Mitcham....377 F15
st. Newtown....702 F13
st. Oakleigh S....458 G18
st. Reservoir....282 J15
st. Torquay....711 L11
PRICES
rd. Millgrove....348 E3
rd. Monbulk....428 E14
PRIDE
av. Bundoora....242 E13
ct. Hampton Pk....551 G12
st. Torquay....712 A12
PRIDHAM
ct. Endeavour Hl....537 K8
st. Kensington....34 A5
st. Maribyrnong....322 L20
st. Maribyrnong....323 A20
st. Prahran....32 L20
st. Prahran....414 L10
st. Prahran....415 A10
PRIESTLEY
av. Hoppers Csg....405 A20
cr. Mt Evelyn....383 K6
PRIMA
ct. Tullamarine....278 E8
PRIMARY
pl. Maribyrnong....323 B15
PRIME
ct. Berwick....553 L14
PRIMO
ct. Greensborough....244 H14
PRIMROSE
cr. Brighton East....455 D18
ct. Cranbourne N....578 A5
ct. Gowanbrae....279 D5
la. Sorrento....678 H11
pl. Epping....198 F20
rd. Croydon N....336 E14
st. Blackburn N....375 H10
st. Brunswick E....326 C13
st. Essendon....324 D10
st. Moonee Pnd....324 D10
st. Windsor....414 H12
PRIMROSE HILL
cl. Endeavour Hl....537 A1
PRIMULA
av. Brooklyn....365 G19
bvd. Gowanbrae....279 D6
cl. Bundoora....242 L15
ct. Rowville....463 J20
st. Blackburn N....375 F8
wy. Nar Warrn S....579 E1
PRINCE
cr. Seaford....600 A4
st. Belgrave....466 E17
st. Blairgowrie....679 F18
st. Box Hill S....419 A1
st. Clayton....458 L18
st. Emerald....469 D18
st. Essendon N....279 E20
st. Ferntree Gly....424 D19
st. Gisborne....78 K14
st. Hampton....495 E6
st. Hampton E....495 L6
st. Healesville....213 K20
st. Healesville....257 K1
st. Maribyrnong....367 A1
st. Mornington....640 C20
st. Sassafras....426 F13
st. Springvale....500 A11
st. Sunshine N....321 F14
PRINCE ALBERT
cr. Taylors Lakes....275 H6
mw. Patterson L....547 J18
PRINCE ANDREW
av. Lalor....241 E9
PRINCE CHARLES
st. Clayton....498 H3
PRINCE EDWARD
av. McKinnon....456 C16
av. Mitcham....377 K12
PRINCELY
tce. Templestowe....331 H7
PRINCE OF WALES
av. Mill Park....242 B3
PRINCE PATRICK
st. Richmond....32 F3
st. Richmond....414 J2
PRINCES
av. Caulfield E....456 D1
cl. Prahran....32 D18
cl. Prahran....414 H9
cl. Prahran....414 J9
ct. Blackburn S....419 G2
ct. Werribee....448 A13
fwy. Altona....407 C20
fwy. Altona Mdw....407 C20
fwy. Altona North....407 L7
fwy. Beaconsfield....554 G15
fwy. Berwick....553 H8
fwy. Cocoroc....487 A6
fwy. Laverton....406 F20
fwy. Laverton....407 C20
fwy. Laverton N....407 L7
fwy. Narre Warren....553 H8
fwy. Point Cook....449 G4
fwy. Werribee S....449 A16
hwy. Beaconsfield....554 J10
hwy. Beaconsfield....555 C20
hwy. Belmont....706 B6
hwy. Berwick....553 K7
hwy. Brooklyn....365 B18
hwy. Carnegie....456 K4
hwy. Caulfield N....415 K17
hwy. Clayton....458 E11
hwy. Dandenong....535 F1
hwy. Dandenong S....536 B12
hwy. Dandenong S....537 A16
hwy. Doveton....536 B12
hwy. Eumemmerring....537 A16
hwy. Flemington....33 A10
hwy. Flemington....368 A5
hwy. Flemington....368 D2

hwy.Footscray 367 B8
hwy.Geelong 702 J12
hwy.Geelong West 702 J12
hwy.Grovedale 705 A13
hwy.Hallam 537 J17
hwy.Highton 706 B6
hwy.Hughesdale 457 K8
hwy.Huntingdale 458 E11
hwy.Kensington 33 A10
hwy.Kensington 368 A5
hwy.Kensington 368 D2
hwy.Kingsville 366 J11
hwy.Laverton N 365 B18
hwy.Malvern 415 J17
hwy.Malvern East 456 K4
hwy.Mulgrave 499 F1
hwy.Murrumbeena 456 K4
hwy.Nr Nr Goon 586 H1
hwy.Nr Nr Goon N 586 H1
hwy.Narre Warren 552 H2
hwy.Newtown 702 J12
hwy.Noble Park 500 G11
hwy.Noble Park N 500 G11
hwy.N Melbourne 33 H4
hwy.Oakleigh 457 K8
hwy.Oakleigh 458 E11
hwy.Oakleigh E 458 E11
hwy.Officer 555 J18
hwy.Pakenham 584 A1
hwy.S Geelong 702 J12
hwy.Springvale 500 G11
hwy.Tottenham 365 L15
hwy.Waurn Ponds 705 A13
hwy.Werribee 447 L15
hwy.Werribee 487 A2
hwy.W Footscray 366 J11
hwy.Yarraville 365 L15
pl. Port Melb 412 J5
st. Abbotsford 26 G2
st. Carlton 18 G8
st. Caulfield N 415 C17
st. Fitzroy 19 A20
st. Fitzroy 24 K1
st. Flemington 34 B4
st. Port Melb 29 A5
st. Port Melb 412 H6
st. St Kilda 414 C14
st. Watsonia 285 D5
st. Williamstown 411 D11
tce. Jan Juc 711 D17
tce. Pascoe Vale S 324 J3
wk. Melbourne 24 J11

PRINCES DOMAIN
dr. Hallam 537 H16

PRINCES PARK
dr. Carlton N 18 A6

PRINCESS
av. Emerald 509 H2
av. Highett 496 E16
av. Springvale 499 H15
ct. Mooroolbark 338 A17
la. N Melbourne 17 J19
pl. Melton W 226 E16
st. Bayswater 422 L8
st. Bayswater 423 A8
st. Coburg N 281 G12
st. Fawkner 281 G11
st. Kew 371 J10
st. Kew 371 K3
st. N Melbourne 17 J19
st. Oakleigh 457 L13
st. Pascoe Vale 280 J11
st. Richmond 26 J13
st. St Albans 320 C5
st. Seddon 367 E13
st. Yarraville 367 E13

PRINCESS JULIANA
pl. Carrum Downs 575 A14

PRINCESS MARIA
pl. Hampton Pk 551 H11

PRINCETON
pl. Broadmeadows 238 J12
pl. Templestowe 332 B6

PRINCETOWN
av. Craigieburn 194 D2
dr. Braeside 547 F2
rd. Mt Waverley 459 A2

PRINCE WILLIAM ALEXANDER
ct. Carrum Downs, off Princess Juliana Pl 575 A14

PRINGLE
pl. Altona Mdw 451 L5

PRINTERS
la. Geelong, off Corio St 703 A7

PRION
cl. Blind Bight 650 D8
rd. Mt Dandenong 426 E2

PRIOR
av. Gladstone Pk 236 L19
av. Gladstone Pk 237 A19
ct. Brookfield 268 B3
ct. Delahey 275 D13
ct. Rowville 463 J18
rd. Malvern East 457 J3
rd. Noble Park 534 D2

PRIORS
rd. Monbulk 468 C2
rd. Monbulk 468 C6
rd. The Patch 468 C6

PRIORSWOOD
cl. Dingley Village 533 B9
wy. Sunbury 143 K15

PRISCILLA
cl. Wheelers Hill 461 E13
ct. Melton W 226 A13
ct. Wantirna 422 D11

PRISMALL
st. Altona North 410 D7

PRITCHARD
av. Braybrook 365 J6

PRIVET
ct. Doveton 536 J6

PROBUS
st. Ivanhoe 328 A11

PROCTOR
cr. Keilor Dn 275 G10
st. Williamstown 410 J14

PRODUCTION
rd. Melton 269 E2

PROFESSORS
la. Kangaroo Grnd 289 J12
wk. Parkville 17 L12

PROFITA
av. Sydenham 275 B7

PROGRESS
av. Carrum 573 A11
ct. Laverton N 364 L16
rd. Eltham 287 A2
rd. Eltham North 287 A2
rd. Silvan 384 K12
st. Ascot Vale 323 H19
st. Dandenong S 536 J17
st. Mornington 641 A20
st. Strathmore 280 D20

PROHASKY
st. Port Melb 412 B3

PROMENADE
Belmont 702 E15

PROSE
st. Balwyn N 329 G19

PROSPECT
av. Belmont 702 F20
av. Warburton 349 L4
ct. Ringwood 378 H9
ct. Sunbury 143 B11
dr. Keilor East 321 K4
gr. Black Rock 529 G5
gr. Northcote 326 J15
la. Geelong, off Corio St 703 D7
rd. Bulleen 329 L15
rd. Newtown 702 F9
rd. Rosanna 328 K3
rd. Wandin N 340 L15
rd. Wandin N 341 A15
st. Box Hill 374 H14
st. Essendon W 322 L8
st. Glenroy 279 J8
st. Mt Waverley 418 J13
st. Pascoe Vale 280 G16
wk. Hughesdale 457 G7

PROSPECT HILL
cr. Dandenong N 502 C15
cr. Hurstbridge 202 J9
dr. Bundoora 284 D3
rd. Camberwell 372 K20
rd. Camberwell 373 A20
rd. Canterbury 372 K20
rd. Croydon 380 C10
rd. McCrae 685 C10
rd. Narre Warren 538 H18
rd. Surrey Hills 373 H20
rd. Surrey Hills 417 H1

PROSPECTOR
ct. Wheelers Hill 461 C12
dr. St Albans 319 H7

PROSPER
pde. Glen Iris 417 G13

PROSPERITY
rd. Lower Plenty 286 F14

PROSSORS
la. Red Hill 687 J20

PROTEA
cr. St Albans 320 F8
ct. Langwarrin 601 L16
ct. Mill Park 242 C10
ct. Newcomb 704 C16
st. Carrum Downs 575 B18

PROTON
ct. Whittington 704 C20

PROUDFOOT
st. Mont Albert 374 E16

PROUSE
pl. Werribee 447 E12

PROVAN
dr. Wyndham Va 446 F15

PROVIDENCE
rd. Greenvale 191 L14

PROVIS
cl. Burnside 318 D6

PROVOST
st. N Melbourne 17 A16

PROWSE
av. Balwyn 373 D13
la. Bundoora 284 E4
st. Brunswick 325 F9

PRUDENCE
cr. Carrum Downs 574 L17
ct. Lilydale 338 D14

PRUE
ct. Fawkner 281 G9
ct. Warranwood 334 H15

PRUNELLA
cl. Doncaster 330 J18

PRUNUS
ct. Bellfield 327 L6
gr. Doveton 536 K13

PRYDE
ct. Wheelers Hill 460 J12

PRYOR
st. Eltham 287 H8

PRYTON
ct. Balwyn 374 B10

PUCKLE
la. Moonee Pnd 324 C13
st. Moonee Pnd 324 B13

PUEBLA
st. Torquay 711 L7

PUERTA
st. Burwood 418 C6

PUFFIN
cl. Chelsea Ht 547 G19
ct. Endeavour Hl 537 A4

PUFFING BILLY
pl. Emerald 509 E3

PUKAKI
ct. Taylors Lakes 276 E10

PULFORD
cr. Mill Park 242 K3
ct. Melton W 225 K17

PULI
st. Werribee 447 F18

PULLAR
st. Maidstone 366 G1

PULLEN
ct. Springvale 500 A8
dr. Wattle Glen 246 L1
dr. Wattle Glen 247 A1

PULLMAN
ct. St Kilda E 455 B1

PULLYN
st. Clayton 498 L3

PULSAR
pl. Kealba 321 B1

PULTNEY
st. Dandenong 536 B10

PUMMEROY
la. St Kilda, off St Kilda Rd 414 E15

PUMP
st. Heathmont 379 A17

PUMPKIN
la. St Kilda, off Blessington St 414 C19

PUMPS
la. Wantirna S 421 F17
rd. Wantirna S 421 H17

PUNARI
ct. Seaford 600 B5
mw. Eltham 287 C7

PUNCH
la. Melbourne 24 H4

PUNJEL
dr. Diggers Rest 187 F13

PUNKERRI
cct. Greensborough 244 C14

PUNT
la. W Footscray 366 F6
rd. Cremorne 25 K19
rd. E Melbourne 25 K19
rd. Melbourne 25 K19
rd. St Kilda 414 D11
rd. South Yarra 31 H12
rd. South Yarra 414 D7
rd. Windsor 414 D11

PURCELL
cr. Roxburgh Pk 194 A14
ct. Bundoora 243 A20
ct. Werribee 447 F18
st. N Melbourne 17 C17

PURCHAS
st. Werribee 447 D6

PURCHES
av. Pascoe Vale S 324 J4
st. Mitcham 377 H18
st. Vermont 377 H20

PURDY
av. Dandenong 535 H7

PURINUAN
rd. Reservoir 283 B6

PURLEY
ct. Hillside 232 E16
dr. Dandenong N 501 L14

PURNELL
st. Altona 408 F19
st. Anglesea 713 L3

PURRI
cl. Greensborough 244 B20

PURRUMBETE
av. Manifold Ht 702 B1

PURSE
st. Mt Waverley 418 L14

PURSELL
av. Blackburn S 419 L2

PURSER
av. Ringwood E 378 L9
av. Ringwood E 379 A9

PURTEL
st. Mordialloc 532 E16

PURTELL
st. Bentleigh E 496 G3

PURTON
rd. Pakenham 584 C1

PURVES
rd. Arthurs Seat 685 J16

PUSHKIN
ct. Doncaster E 331 L16

PUSKAS
rd. Keysborough 533 J15

PUTNEY
cl. Endeavour Hl 537 L7
cl. Wantirna 422 E8
la. Frankston 627 K9

PUTT
gr. Keysborough 534 C9

PYALONG
av. Rosanna 285 A19
cr. Broadmeadows 238 H12
cr. Dallas 238 H12

PYCNANTHA
ct. Endeavour Hl 502 L19

PYE
st. Port Melb 412 B4

PYGMALION
ri. Warrandyte 333 A2

PYINGERRA
cr. Cheltenham 530 E2

PYKE
ct. Mulgrave 500 H1
dr. Gladstone Pk 237 E19
st. Dandenong 535 E3
st. Werribee 447 G18

PYMM
av. Eltham North 287 C1

PYNE
st. Caulfield 455 G5

PYRAMUS
pl. Altona Mdw 451 K5

PYRUS
ct. Doveton 536 J7
pl. Donvale 377 C1

PYTCHLEY
rd. Croydon 380 F1

PYTHIAS
ct. Millgrove 348 E4

Q

QUADRAT
cl. Berwick 553 E2

QUAIL
cl. Chelsea Ht 547 G18
cr. Melton 226 F15
ct. Carrum Downs 600 H3
ct. Nar Warrn S 552 F14
ct. Werribee 448 D9
pl. Craigieburn 149 F16
wy. Rowville 503 D3
wy. Rowville 503 D4

QUAILLE
ct. Darley 221 K5

QUAINTANCE
st. Mt Waverley 418 K15

QUALITY
dr. Dandenong S 549 J6
st. Frankston 599 D19

QUAMBY
av. Frankston 628 E6
av. Guys Hill 555 L2
av. South Yarra 32 L12
av. South Yarra 414 L6
ct. View Bank 285 L18
ct. Werribee 446 J15
pl. Donvale 332 K19
rd. Guys Hill 555 K2
rd. Ringwood N 334 H17

QUANDOLAN
cl. Ivanhoe East 328 L17

QUANDONG
ct. Frankston 628 B4
st. Thomastown 241 C12

QUANTOCK
st. Canterbury 373 E20
st. Canterbury 417 E1

QUANTUM
cl. Dandenong S 550 K7

QU'APPELLE
st. Pt Lonsdale 710 E6

QUARBING
st. Werribee 447 C12

QUARRION
dr. Carrum Downs 600 J3

QUARRY
cir. Coburg 281 K19
cl. Belmont 702 G16
rd. Ferntree Gly 464 J5
rd. Langwarrin 601 B12
rd. Lilydale 338 H1
rd. Melb Airport 235 L11
rd. Mitcham 377 C10
rd. Mitcham 377 F8
rd. Narre Warren 539 G16
rd. Tottenham 365 L9
rd. Up Fntree Gly 464 J5
tr. Lysterfield 504 A6

QUARRY HILLS
dr. Berwick 553 L6

QUARTOK
av. Werribee 447 C12

QUARTZ
pl. Narre Warren 539 F13
st. Bulla 190 B14
st. Delahey 275 A15

QUAT QUATTA
av. Ripponlea 454 J2

QUAYLE
rd. Seville 341 D19
rd. Wandin East 341 D19

QUEEN
ct. Yarra Glen 252 D10
rd. Lilydale 338 H6
st. Altona 452 D2
st. Altona Mdw 451 H1
st. Belmont 706 D1
st. Blackburn 375 J15
st. Brunswick E 325 K12
st. Burnley 371 C19
st. Coburg 325 A7
st. Dandenong 535 F2
st. Essendon 323 H3
st. Fitzroy N 326 C17
st. Footscray 367 C8
st. Frankston 599 F18
st. Kew 371 K11
st. Lalor 241 G8
st. Melbourne 1 J18
st. Melbourne 23 K2
st. Melbourne 23 K3
st. Mornington 640 D14
st. Nunawading 376 K14
st. Ormond 456 A14
st. Parkdale 531 D9
st. Queenscliff 708 H18
st. Reservoir 283 A15
st. St Kilda E 414 G16
st. Seaholme 409 G20
st. S Melbourne 29 H6
st. Surrey Hills 417 H2
st. Williamstown 411 D12
st. Yarra Jctn 347 E17

QUEEN BEATRIX
dr. Carrum Downs 575 A14

QUEENS
av. Ascot Vale 324 D18
av. Caulfield E 456 D5
av. Doncaster 375 C1
av. Hawthorn 372 C17
av. Mont Albert 374 F13
av. Oakleigh 457 J13
av. Springvale 499 H10
av. Springvale 499 K12
cr. Bacchus Msh 221 K17
ct. Berwick 554 C6
ct. Jan Juc 711 D15
ct. Rye 697 E8
ct. Werribee 448 B12
la. Melbourne 30 L6
la. Melbourne 31 A6

la. Melbourne 31 C16
la. Melbourne 413 L3
la. Melbourne 414 B8
pde. Ashwood 418 A17
pde. Clifton Hill 19 D8
pde. Fawkner 281 G11
pde. Fitzroy N 19 D8
pde. Glen Iris 417 K11
pde. Hillside 232 B19
rd. Albert Park 31 C16
rd. Melbourne 30 L6
rd. Melbourne 30 L8
rd. Melbourne 31 A9
rd. Melbourne 31 C16
rd. Melbourne 413 L3
rd. Melbourne 413 L4
rd. Newtown 702 A9
rd. Pearcedale 646 E8
rd. Seville 385 G4
rd. Silvan 384 F13
rd. Sorrento 678 G11
rd. Wandin East 384 F13
rd. Wandin East 385 G4
rd. Wandin N 385 A9
sq. Sandringham 495 B12
wy. St Kilda 414 E12
wy. Windsor 414 E12

QUEENSBERRY
ct. Hillside 231 J19
pl. Carlton 18 C19
pl. N Melbourne 17 C17
st. Carlton 17 L18
st. Keilor Park 278 A14
st. N Melbourne 17 A17
st. N Melbourne 34 J17

QUEENS BRIDGE
sq. Southbank 3 F3
sq. Southbank 24 B13

QUEENSBRIDGE
st. Southbank 3 B8
st. Southbank 24 A16

QUEENSBURY
wy. Werribee 446 K10

QUEENSCLIFF
rd. Moolap 704 E18
rd. Newcomb 704 E18
rd. Thomastown 240 E11

QUEENSFERRY
pl. Greenvale 236 K1

QUEENS PARK
rd. Highton 701 H8
rd. Newtown 701 H8

QUEENSPOINT
cr. Queenscliff 707 J18

QUEENSTOWN
rd. Boronia 423 E15

QUEENSVILLE
st. Kingsville 366 L13

QUEENS WHARF
rd. Melbourne 1 B20
rd. Melbourne 23 K13

QUEEN VICTORIA
cr. Taylors Lakes 275 J6

QUELLTALER
pl. Vermont S 421 D11

QUENGO
ct. Seaford 573 E19

QUENTIN
rd. Malvern East 457 G3
st. Forest Hill 420 F5
st. Scoresby 462 F7
wy. Eltham 288 C6

QUERCUS
ct. Camberwell 417 J8
ct. Mt Waverley 419 B20

QUEST
ct. Craigieburn 150 L20
ct. Glen Waverley 420 L17
ct. Mooroolbark 337 J10

QUICK
st. Pascoe Vale 280 E13

QUICKSILVER
dr. Torquay 711 J8

QUIET
dr. Bangholme 549 J14

QUILAN
ct. Caroline Spr 318 B5

QUILL
ct. Mt Martha 656 E6

QUINELLA
cl. Keilor Park 278 A12

QUINLAN
ct. Werribee 447 B9

QUINN
cr. Mt Evelyn 338 K20
cr. Mt Evelyn 338 L19
cr. Mt Evelyn 339 A19
cr. Mt Evelyn 339 A20
cr. Mt Evelyn 383 A1
ct. Altona Mdw 451 D2
ct. Rowville 463 L17
gr. Keilor East 322 D6
st. Dandenong 536 D13
st. Deer Park 318 J17
st. Heidelberg 329 B6
st. Preston 327 J4
st. Seaford 599 G9
wy. Montmorency 287 A15

QUINNS
pde. Mt Eliza 642 D7
rd. Bentleigh E 456 K20

QUINTON
ct. Mt Eliza 626 E14
ct. Mt Waverley 419 E13
rd. Camberwell 417 K3

QUIRK
ct. Endeavour Hl 537 K1

QUIST
ct. Dandenong S 550 A4
ct. Mill Park 242 H3

QUIXLEY
gr. Wantirna 422 B11

R

RAAF
st. Whittington 703 L18

RABAUL
ct. Boronia 424 E4

RACECOURSE
dr. Springvale 500 C14
rd. Altona 409 L13
rd. Flemington 33 F4
rd. Flemington 34 C5
rd. Kensington 33 F4
rd. Mornington 641 E19
rd. Mt Martha 656 K12
rd. Mt Martha 657 A9
rd. Noble Park 500 G13
rd. N Melbourne 34 C5
rd. Pakenham 585 D8
rd. Sunbury 143 G9
rd. Werribee 446 L17
rd. Werribee 447 A17
rd.n, Pakenham 585 D4

RACHAEL
ct. Pakenham 585 B2
ct. Seabrook 450 K3
dr. Mooroolbark 381 H4

RACHAL
cl. Mt Evelyn 339 K17

RACHEL
ct. Sydenham 275 C7
dr. Cranbourne N 577 J5
st. Dandenong N 501 K17

RACHELLE
dr. Wantirna 422 E6
rd. Keilor East 322 F6

RACING CLUB
la. Melbourne 1 L11

RADCLIFF
av. Cheltenham 496 K18

RADCLIFFE
st. W Melbourne 34 B18
st. W Melbourne 368 G9

RADFORD
ct. Brookfield 268 B4
rd. Reservoir 282 B7
st. Williamstown 411 A16

RADIANT
cr. Forest Hill 420 E5

RADIATA
cl. Ringwood N 334 H20
ct. Mill Park 242 A9
ct. Narre Warren 539 E20
rd. Gisborne 78 L8
st. Frankston N 600 A8

RADIO
st. Maidstone 322 E19

RADLEIGH
dr. Wheelers Hill 460 K16

RADLEY
st. Mornington 640 G17

RADNOR
ct. Mt Dandenong 426 F5
st. Camberwell 416 K7
st. Heidelberg 328 K4

RADOVIC
ct. Cranbourne N 577 J5

RADSTOCK
pl. Craigieburn 194 D2

RADUETT
ct. Endeavour Hl 503 D20

RAE
av. Edithvale 546 G11
ct. Bundoora 285 C2
ct. Darley 221 K4
ct. Melton S 268 H3
ct. Pakenham 584 E3
ct. Prahran 414 L12
st. Bentleigh E 497 C7
st. Chadstone 457 K5
st. Fitzroy N 19 B8
st. Hawthorn 372 C14
st. Mt Waverley 419 H13
st. Rosebud W 683 E19
st. Templstw Lr 330 B10

RAEBURN
ct. Newcomb 704 A15
st. Pascoe Vale 280 K16

RAEMUR
ct. Hoppers Csg 449 C4

RAES
rd. Sunbury 114 E20

RAEWYN
ct. Langwarrin 601 K17
ct. Springvale S 534 A5

RAFFINDALE
cr. Cranbourne W 577 G16
ct. Mill Park 242 H10

RAFTER
dr. St Albans 275 K19

RAGLAN
ct. Kurunjang 227 A14
ct. Maidstone 366 H1
ct. Research 288 H3
pl. Craigieburn 150 A20
pl. S Melbourne 30 C8
pl. S Melbourne 413 H4
rd. Research 288 H4
st. Avondale Ht 322 C15
st. Caulfield N 415 F18
st. Darley 222 B8
st. Diggers Rest 142 A13
st. Maidstone 366 H1
st. Newtown 702 J8
st. N Melbourne 17 D19
st. Port Melb 29 A5
st. Port Melb 412 L2
st. Preston 326 L5
st. Queenscliff 708 K19
st. St Kilda E 414 H16
st. S Melbourne 30 A8
st. S Melbourne 413 F4

RAGLIN
cl. Somerville 644 G14

RAHEEN
av. Wantirna 422 D14
ct. Vermont S 421 A13
dr. Kew 371 E9
pl. Melton W 226 E15

RAHNSTON
ct. Vermont 421 K1

RAILTON
ct. Gisborne 79 C16
gr. Preston 327 A5

RAILWAY
arc. Hawthorn 372 A17
av. Armadale 415 H16
av. Ashwood 418 E17
av. Beaconsfield 555 B16
av. Brighton 454 H20
av. Laverton 407 A19
av. Oakleigh 458 C15
av. Pakenham 585 A8
av. Ringwood E 378 K12
av. Up Fntree Gly 465 A6
av. Werribee 447 K13
cr. Bentleigh 496 B3
cr. Broadmeadows 238 B15
cr. Croydon 380 B2
cr. Dallas 238 B12
cr. Hampton 494 L9
cr. Moonee Pnd 324 A11
cr. Williamstown 411 C15
gr. Croydon 380 A3
gr. Mornington 640 E12
la. Fitzroy N 326 A19
pde. Bayswater 423 G3
pde. Camberwell 372 J19
pde. Dandenong 535 C4
pde. Deer Park 319 B19
pde. Eltham 287 G5
pde. Healesville 213 E20
pde. Highett 496 C12
pde. Menzies Ck 468 C18
pde. Murrumbeena 457 B7
pde. Newport 410 F10
pde. Noble Park 535 C4
pde. Pascoe Vale 280 C14
pde. Seaford 573 C13
pde. Wandin N 340 K14
pde. Wandin N 341 A14
pde.n, Glen Waverley 460 C1
pde.s, Chadstone 418 C19
pde.s, Deer Park 319 A18
pde.w, Northcote 326 H12
pl. Balaclava 414 H19
pl. Belgrave 466 H14
pl. Brunswick 325 E16
pl. Coburg 325 F4
pl. Cremorne 26 D17
pl. Fairfield 327 D18
pl. Footscray 367 H7
pl. Preston 326 H5
pl. Ringwood 378 D13
pl. Southbank 29 H1
pl. South Yarra 32 G13
pl. South Yarra 414 J7
pl. W Melbourne 23 A4
pl. W Melbourne 34 A17
pl. W Melbourne 34 J20
pl. W Melbourne 368 F9
pl. W Melbourne 368 K11
pl. Williamstown 411 C15
pl. Fitzroy N, off Byrne St 326 D19
pl. Hawthorn, off Evansdale Rd 371 G17
pl.e, Ascot Vale 324 D18
pl.e, Preston 326 J6
pl.n, Williamstown 411 G17
pl.w, Flemington 324 D19
rd. Baxter 644 C3
rd. Blackburn 375 H15
rd. Blackburn 375 L14
rd. Briar Hill 286 E5
rd. Carnegie 456 H7
rd. Cheltenham 530 J1
rd. Eltham 287 H4
rd. Emerald 509 F4
rd. Epping 241 E3
rd. Ferntree Gly 464 H4
rd. Mt Evelyn 339 B20
rd. Mt Evelyn 382 L2
rd. Mt Evelyn 383 A2
rd. Seville 342 A10
rd. Sunshine N 321 E6
rd. Wesburn 347 E12
rd. Yarra Jctn 347 E12
st. Fitzroy N 326 C19
st. Northcote 326 G17
st. Yarra Jctn 347 C15
st.n, Altona 408 L18
st.s, Altona 408 L18
tce. Geelong 702 L6
tce. Williamstown 411 J18
wk. Cheltenham 496 J20
wk.s, Hampton 494 L9
wk.s, Hampton 495 A9

RAIMENO
st. Lalor 241 G9

RAIN
ct. Doveton 536 L8

RAINBIRD
cl. Cranbourne W 577 F16
ct. Epping 198 C20
ct. Keilor Dn 275 L16

RAINBOW
al. Melbourne 2 F13
al. Melbourne 24 E7
ct. Mt Waverley 418 J17
ct. Pearcedale 646 K3
ct. Rye 696 E3
ct. Sunbury 143 H15
ct. Taylors Lakes 275 H6

RAINBOW VALLEY
rd. Pk Orchards 333 C15

RAINE
ct. Delahey 275 E12

RAINER
st. Pascoe Vale S 324 H5

RAINHAM
cl. Greensborough 244 D20
cl. Greensborough 286 D1

RAINIER
av. Dromana 686 H9

RAINONE
pl. Tarneit 447 J1

RAINSFORD
ct. Dingley Village 532 L5
dr. Noble Park N 501 E9
pl. View Bank 286 A17
st. Elwood 454 G2
st. Werribee 447 F19
tce. Campbellfield 239 G12

RAINTREE
rd. Templestowe 332 D5

RAINY HILL
rd. Cockatoo 471 E14

RAISELL
rd. Cranbourne W 577 H20

RAITERI
ct. Croydon 335 D20
ct. Croydon 379 E1

RAITH
av. Sandringham 495 C17
ct. St Kilda E 414 K15
tce. Newtown 701 K5

RALEIGH
ct. Werribee 446 L11
dr. Nar Warrn S 552 G19
gr. Essendon N 323 G1
rd. Maribyrnong 322 L14
rd. Maribyrnong 323 A15
st. Blackburn S 420 A3
st. Clarinda 498 F5
st. Essendon 324 B7
st. Footscray 367 D9
st. Forest Hill 420 A3
st. Malvern 415 L17
st. Melbourne 31 F20
st. Melbourne 414 D10
st. Seville 341 J14
st. Spotswood 411 B2
st. Thornbury 326 J9
st. Westmeadows 237 B13
st. Windsor 31 F20
st. Windsor 414 D10

RALEIGHS
rd. Melton 227 A17

RALEON
av. Frankston S 627 K11

RALPH
av. St Albans 320 L4
av. St Albans 321 A4
cr. Hampton Pk 552 C11
ct. Altona Mdw 451 G8
ct. Ferntree Gly 463 L5
ct. Mt Waverley 418 K12
st. Blackburn S 419 J1
st. Bulleen 330 A15
st. Hampton 495 D11
st. Reservoir 282 K9
st. Sunshine W 364 B6

RALPHS
av. Sorrento 678 L13

RALRON
ct. Pakenham 584 L1

RALSTON
av. Sunshine N 321 D10
st. South Yarra 31 J10
st. South Yarra 414 E5

RALTON
av. Glen Waverley 460 F5

RALUND
rd. Doncaster 330 D17

RAMADA
ct. Lilydale 338 K3

RAMAGE
ct. Kings Park 275 B20
la. Gembrook 512 L15
rd. Mt Dandenong 426 E3
st. Bayswater 424 B4

RAMBLE
cr. Croydon 379 F3

RAMLEH
rd. Reservoir 283 H6

RAMLER
mw. Portsea 677 J3

RAMONA
av. Malvern East 457 E1
ct. Boronia 424 L4
pl. Melton W 226 C16

RAMPART
av. Glen Waverley 420 L14

RAMPTONS
rd. Eltham 287 B5

RAMSAY
av. Kew East 372 D5
cl. Doncaster E 332 D15
cr. Darley 221 G6
ct. Cheltenham 497 C20
ct. Endeavour Hl 537 C4
ct. Mt Martha 655 H17
ct. Sunbury 142 H8
la. Melbourne 1 C11
la. Melbourne 23 J8
st. Aberfeldie 323 B9
st. Anglesea 714 A4
st. Bayswater N 379 L19
st. Brighton 454 G20
st. Spotswood 411 B3

RAMSBURY
st. Craigieburn 194 B2

RAMSDEN
st. Clifton Hill 20 D5

RAMSEY
cl. Gladstone Pk 237 D16
ct. Mulgrave 500 H2
st. Burwood E 419 E8

RAMSON
ct. Altona Mdw 451 D3

RAMU
av. Tremont 425 D19
gr. Ashburton 417 H18
pde. Heidelberg W 284 A20

RANCEBY
cl. Rowville 463 H12

RANCH
ct. Mornington 656 F4
ct. Narre Warren 552 H1

RANCHER
- dr. Mornington 657 B6

RAND
- st. Greensborough 286 E4

RANDALL
- av. Chelsea 547 A12
- av. Edithvale 547 A12
- ct. Mt Waverley 418 J16
- pl. South Yarra 31 E6
- st. Maribyrnong 323 A13

RANDELL
- cr. Hampton E 495 J6
- ct. Doncaster E 331 K16
- ct. Mill Park 242 E2
- st. Parkdale 531 H15

RANDLE
- ct. Nar Warrn N 539 C7

RANDO
- ct. Frankston S 627 A6

RANDOLF
- ct. Templstw Lr 330 E8

RANDOLPH
- st. Hawthorn 371 F14

RANDOM
- st. Frankston 627 J3

RANDWICK
- av. Bacchus Msh 221 D14
- ct. Epping 197 J17
- ct. Noble Park N 501 B9
- dr. Keilor Park 278 A13

RANEEN
- dr. Langwarrin 602 B16
- pl. Berwick 554 B19

RANELAGH
- ct. Glen Iris 417 H9
- dr. Mt Eliza 626 A18

RANFURLIE
- cr. Glen Iris 416 G14
- ct. Forest Hill 420 J4
- dr. Glen Waverley 460 D8
- pl. Point Cook 450 A7
- rd. Forest Hill 420 G4

RANGE
- rd. Burwood E 419 L9
- rd. Mt Martha 670 D2
- rd. Olinda 426 E9
- rd. Sassafras 426 G10
- rd. Tuerong 670 L4
- st. Camberwell 416 L7
- st. Camberwell 417 A7

RANGER
- ct. Seaford 573 F13

RANGE VIEW
- ct. Croydon 380 F2
- tce. Bulleen 329 K11

RANGEVIEW
- av. Malvern East 457 F4
- ct. Glen Waverley 460 H3
- ct. View Bank 285 J16
- dr. Skye 575 G20
- gr. Balwyn N 373 B5
- rd. Boronia 424 E11
- rd. Diamond Ck 245 L9
- rd. Donvale 377 E8
- rd. Lower Plenty 286 K16
- rd. Mt Evelyn 339 F17
- st. Deer Park 319 G11

RANGOON
- ct. Mulgrave 500 C2

RANKIN
- av. Sunshine N 321 G10
- la. Albert Park 29 H14
- rd. Boronia 423 J16
- rd. Ferntree Gly 423 J16
- rd. Herne Hill 702 A4
- st. Altona 408 J19
- st. Panton Hill 204 F18

RANKINS
- la. Melbourne 1 L11
- la. Melbourne 24 B7
- rd. Kensington 34 A9
- rd. Monbulk 468 J2
- rd. Monbulk 468 K5

RANLEIGH
- ct. Moorabbin 496 K10
- ri. Sunbury 143 B4
- ri. Templstw Lr 330 G13

RANMORE
- gr. Caroline Spr 317 K2

RANNOCH
- av. Mt Eliza 625 J13

RANSOM
- av. Altona 409 A15

RAOUL
- ct. Yarrambat 201 B12

RAPALLO
- wy. Cranbourne N 578 H11

RAPANEA
- av. Templstw Lr 330 H14
- ct. Endeavour Hl 536 K1

RAPHAEL
- cr. Frankston 628 B10
- ct. Grovedale 705 J15
- ct. Scoresby 462 C7
- dr. Wheelers Hill 460 K14
- st. Abbotsford 26 C1
- st. Caulfield N 415 E18
- st. Hallam 538 D19

RAQUEL
- cl. Carrum Downs 601 C5

RASHEDA
- st. Watsonia 285 F9

RASHU
- ct. Clarinda 498 G11

RASMAY
- ct. The Patch 467 L4

RASMUSSEN
- ct. Coburg 282 A19
- dr. Templestowe 331 C11

RASON
- ct. Keilor Dn 276 E14

RASSAY
- ct. Frankston 600 J16

RATA
- st. Wheelers Hill 461 B19

RATCLIFFE
- cl. Mill Park 242 D5
- ct. Keysborough 535 A10

RATHCOWN
- rd. Reservoir 283 C7

RATHDOWN
- st. Coburg 281 A20

RATHDOWNE
- cct. Melton W 226 D15
- pl. Carlton 18 H14
- st. Brunswick E 325 K20
- st. Carlton 18 G20
- st. Carlton N 18 H7

RATHGAEL
- av. Mt Martha 655 J14

RATHGAR
- rd. Ferntree Gly 464 C13

RATHMINES
- gr. Hawthorn E 372 E15
- rd. Hawthorn E 372 E16
- rd. Toorak 415 A4
- st. Fairfield 327 D17
- st. Fairfield 327 D19
- st. Newtown 702 F13
- st. Thornbury 327 E10

RATHMULLEN
- qd. Doncaster 330 H19
- rd. Boronia 423 E15

RATHO
- av. Brighton East 495 A4

RATTEN
- av. Kew East 372 A5

RATTRAY
- ct. Altona Mdw 451 G5
- rd. Montmorency 286 G10

RAU
- ct. Broadmeadows 238 B9
- ct. Grovedale 706 A11

RAUTMAN
- cr. Sunshine W 365 A10

RAVA
- ct. Aspendale Gdn 546 H2

RAVELL
- mw. Langwarrin 629 G3

RAVEN
- cl. Carrum Downs 600 L2
- cl. Carrum Downs 601 A1
- cr. Narre Warren 552 H1
- ct. Blackburn S 419 H7
- ct. Oakleigh S 457 L17
- gr. Werribee 447 H18
- st. Doncaster E 375 K3
- st. Geelong West 702 F1
- st. Kew 371 C10
- st. Noble Park 535 B3

RAVENGLASS
- ct. Croydon Hills 335 J12

RAVENHALL
- st. Braybrook 365 J3

RAVENHILL
- bvd. Roxburgh Pk 193 L14
- bvd. Roxburgh Pk 194 A16
- cr. Endeavour Hl 537 D9
- wy. Wantirna S 422 K19

RAVENNA
- st. St Albans 320 H5

RAVENS
- ct. Carrum Downs 601 D2
- gr. St Kilda E 414 J15

RAVENSCOURT
- cl. Rowville 463 G20
- cr. Mt Eliza 625 J14
- pl. Alphington 327 G18
- rd. Tottenham 365 K11

RAVENSLEA
- cr. Deer Park 318 L13

RAVENSTHORPE
- cr. Narre Warren 553 F10

RAVENSWOOD
- av. Ivanhoe East 328 G14
- ct. Doncaster E 332 D13
- ct. Glen Waverley 420 E16
- ct. Montrose 382 D7
- ct. Nunawading 376 F17
- ct. Seabrook 451 B3

RAWDON
- ct. Boronia 424 K5
- ct. Mill Park 242 K11
- st. Bulla 190 C17

RAWDON HILL
- dr. Dandenong N 501 H13

RAWHITI
- rd. Emerald 509 F8

RAWLINGS
- av. Ferntree Gly 424 A18
- st. Surrey Hills 374 B19

RAWLINSON
- st. Croydon 380 D2

RAWSON
- av. Sunshine 321 E20
- ct. Ringwood E 379 B16

RAY
- ct. Scoresby 462 H9
- ct. Werribee 446 K17
- dr. Balwyn N 374 A3
- dr. Balwyn N 374 A4
- rd. Burwood E 419 K11
- st. Beaumaris 530 E11
- st. Croydon 380 J3
- st. Dandenong 535 E3
- st. Malvern 416 A14
- st. Pascoe Vale 280 K19
- st. Safety Bch 686 G2
- st. Seville E 343 C11

RAYDON
- ct. Deer Park 318 J12
- ct. Grovedale 706 D13

RAYERN
- ct. Bentleigh E 496 J6

RAYFIELD
- av. Craigieburn 150 F18

RAYHUR
- st. Clayton S 499 C4

RAYLEIGH
- av. Queenscliff 708 A19

RAYMENT
- st. Alphington 327 F15
- st. Fairfield 327 F15
- st. Thornbury 326 H10

RAYMOND
- av. Frankston 599 E15
- av. Langwarrin 629 B1
- ct. Brighton East 495 K5
- ct. Oakleigh 458 D7
- ct. Ringwood E 379 F15
- dr. Dromana 685 L10
- gr. Caulfield S 455 F11
- rd. Laverton N 364 E16
- rd. Rowville 503 B1
- rd. Rye 696 D9
- rd. Seaford 599 F4
- st. Ashwood 418 F16
- st. Beaumaris 530 G4
- st. Blackburn N 375 L8
- st. Dandenong S 535 K13
- st. Lalor 240 L8
- st. Lalor 241 A8
- st. Melton S 268 K4
- st. Mt Martha 669 A3
- st. Noble Park 534 G2
- st. Preston 326 B1
- st. Somerville 644 J12
- st. Sunshine W 364 F4
- st. Tootgarook 698 C4

RAYMOND ELLIOT
- ct. Pk Orchards 333 B15

RAYMOND McMAHON
- bvd. Endeavour Hl 537 F5

RAYNER
- cl. Rowville 463 H18
- ct. Preston 282 G17
- la. Kensington 33 E13
- st. Altona 408 L20
- st. Footscray 367 B5

RAYNES
- st. Balwyn 373 H9
- st. Caulfield S 455 F10

RAYNES PARK
- rd. Hampton 495 D8

RAYSUN
- ct. Mornington 657 B5

RAYVILLE
- av. Torquay 712 C3

RAYWOOD
- ct. Thomastown 240 E16
- la. Emerald 469 E18

REABURN
- av. St Albans 320 H2
- cr. Brunswick W 324 J15

REACH
- st. Campbellfield 239 E4

READ
- st. Newtown 701 K5
- st. Seville 341 K16
- st. Templestowe 331 F5

READE
- pl. Gladstone Pk 236 K16

READING
- av. Balwyn N 373 K7
- cl. Roxburgh Pk 194 D16

REARDEN
- cl. Endeavour Hl 537 B3
- cr. Roxburgh Pk 194 A14

REARK
- av. Noble Park 500 G13
- ct. Templestowe 331 B5

REAY
- rd. Mooroolbark 337 B20

REBECCA
- cl. Chelsea Ht 547 E10
- cl. Fawkner 281 E2
- cl. Frankston 628 E8
- cl. Lilydale 338 F17
- cl. Templestowe 331 J13
- cl. Wheelers Hill 461 C13
- cr. Altona Mdw 451 K4
- ct. Cranbourne N 577 J6
- ct. Hillside 274 F4
- ct. Oakleigh S 497 G1
- ct. Sorrento 678 F9
- ct. Wantirna S 462 B1
- pl. Niddrie 322 K3
- rd. Malvern East 457 H3
- st. Doveton 537 A7

REBOUND
- ct. Narre Warren 553 A6

RECKLESS
- la. Mordialloc 532 C16

RECREATION
- rd. Rye 697 C2
- rd. Yan Yean 156 G4

RED
- rd. Gembrook 512 L19

REDAN
- cl. Hoppers Csg 405 B13
- ct. Westmeadows 237 G13
- rd. Caulfield N 415 L20
- rd. Caulfield N 456 A1
- st. St Kilda 414 F14

REDBANK
- ct. Kings Park 319 D3

RED BLUFF
- st. Black Rock 495 E19

REDBOURNE
- av. Mt Eliza 642 A1

RED BOX
- cl. Eltham North 245 F18
- ct. Long Forest 224 G11

RED BRICK
- la. Diamond Ck 246 G12

RED CHERRY
- wk. Croydon Hills 335 E17

REDCLIFFS
- av. Warburton 348 K4

REDCOURT
- av. Armadale 415 C14

REDCRAZE
- cl. Cranbourne W 577 H16
- ri. Mill Park 242 K10

REDDAN
- ct. Doncaster 330 E20
- ct. Sunbury 143 G16

REDDINGTON
- tce. Doncaster E 332 F14

REDDITCH
- cr. Deer Park 318 K9

REDDROP
- ct. Altona Mdw 451 E4
- st. Maddingley 264 B2

REDESDALE
- rd. Ivanhoe 328 B18
- st. Meadow Ht 238 B3

REDFERN
- cl. Thomastown 240 D14
- cr. Eumemmerring 536 L14
- cr. Eumemmerring 537 A14
- cr. Mulgrave 500 D2
- ct. Boronia 423 K15
- rd. Hawthorn E 372 G20

REDFIELD
- ct. Mill Park 242 J12
- ct. Wheelers Hill 461 D19

REDGDON
- av. Frankston 599 H19

RED GUM
- dr. Dandenong S 549 F6
- trl. Braeside 533 D14
- wy. Yallambie 285 J15

REDGUM
- av. Carrum Downs 575 F20
- cl. Keysborough 534 A16
- cl. Werribee 447 B7
- ct. Mill Park 243 B7
- ct. Rowville 463 J16
- pl. Bundoora 284 E3
- pl. Narre Warren 553 D12
- st. Maribyrnong 322 J15

RED HILL
- rd. Beaconsfld Up 542 B4
- rd. Emerald 542 B4
- rd. Red Hill S 688 H20
- rd. Springvale 499 K18

REDHILL
- av. Burwood E 420 A10
- ct. Craigieburn 149 L16
- ct. Endeavour Hl 537 C1
- rd. Monbulk 427 K17

REDHOLME
- st. Moorabbin 496 B7

REDINGTON
- dr. Noble Park N 501 D13

REDLAND
- dr. Mitcham 377 B19

REDLEAF
- wy. Wheelers Hill 460 L11

REDLEAP
- av. Mill Park 242 J8
- ct. Endeavour Hl 503 L19

REDMAN
- cl. Narre Warren 538 L18

REDMILL
- ct. Lilydale 338 H2

REDMOND
- ct. Mt Waverley 419 F15
- ct. Rosebud 699 J2
- st. Kew 371 F7

REDMORE
- ct. Berwick 554 L20

RED OAKS
- wy. S Morang 199 H10

REDPATH
- cl. Epping 198 G17
- cl. Oakleigh S 498 E2
- cr. Springvale 500 C6
- ct. Sunbury 142 G15
- ct. Werribee 448 D8

RED PLUM
- pl. Doncaster E 332 F12

RED SHIRT GULLY
- rd. Cottles Br 204 C6
- rd. Panton Hill 204 F10

REDSTART
- st. Doveton 536 J5

REDSTONE
- ct. Whittington 704 E20

REDSTONE HILL
- rd. Sunbury 144 E20

REDVERS
- st. Surrey Hills 373 H18

REDWOOD
- av. Hampton Pk 551 L17
- cl. Gladstone Pk 279 D1
- cl. Meadow Ht 193 K17
- ct. Junction Vill 604 J13
- ct. Lysterfield 464 A20
- ct. Mill Park 242 E12
- ct. Narre Warren 553 B8
- dr. Dingley Village 532 H8
- dr. Notting Hill 459 C13
- rd. Gembrook 512 L12
- st. Heidelberg W 328 A3

REECE
- ct. Lilydale 338 D11
- ct. Rowville 503 B6
- ct. S Morang 199 L16

REED
- av. Beaconsfld Up 542 H19
- cr. Taylors Lakes 275 G5
- ct. Endeavour Hl 537 K1
- ct. Plumpton 273 A18
- la. Albert Park 29 A14
- st. Albert Park 29 A15
- st. Albert Park 413 A7
- st. Spotswood 410 J2

REEDPOLLOCK
- dr. Warrandyte 332 K10

REEDWOOD
- av. Burwood E 419 D10

REEDY
- ct. Hallam 538 C14
- wk. Taylors Hill 274 L13

REEF
ct. Aspendale Gdn...546 L3
ct. Aspendale Gdn...547 A3
REEMA
bvd. Endeavour Hl...537 L2
REES
ct. Mt Waverley...458 K8
rd. Melton S...268 C16
rd. Sunbury...142 K5
rd. Sunbury...143 A5
st. Burwood...419 B11
REEVE
ct. Cheltenham...496 K18
ct. Gisborne...79 A20
ct. Keilor...276 L9
dr. Keilor...276 L10
pl. Rowville...463 D18
st. Mt Martha...655 K15
REEVES
cl. Gladstone Pk...237 E17
cr. Richmond...26 L13
ct. Hampton Pk...551 F12
ct. Kew...371 C11
rd. Christmas Hills...207 G18
st. Blairgowrie...696 B4
st. Clifton Hill...19 H8
st. Watsonia...285 F5
REFUGE
cl. Doncaster E...332 C15
REGAL
av. Doncaster E...376 D1
av. Hallam...537 K16
av. Thomastown...241 L13
ct. Carrum Downs...575 D19
ct. Glen Waverley...460 J2
ct. Melton S...268 F15
ct. Montmorency...286 L8
ct. Vermont S...420 J9
dr. Springvale...499 K11
rd. Jan Juc...711 C18
ri. Craigieburn...150 F6
REGAN
ct. Bundoora...242 K16
st. Box Hill N...375 C13
st. St Albans...275 L17
REGANS
rd. Hampton Pk...551 D9
REGATTA
ct. Aspendale Gdn...546 K3
REG CHALKE
cr. Deer Park...319 G11
REGENCY
cl. Wandana Ht...701 D19
dr. Narre Warren...553 C5
gr. Kew...372 J10
pl. Doncaster E...331 K18
pl. Glen Waverley...460 F11
pl. Melton W...226 E15
ri. Chirnside Pk...336 F7
st. Dandenong N...501 F19
tce. Lysterfield...463 K19
REGENT
av. Springvale...499 H15
cl. Berwick...539 G18
ct. Blackburn N...376 A10
ct. Frankston...600 C18
ct. Sandringham...495 K18
ct. Wantirna S...422 K14
pde. Cheltenham...497 A17
pl. Bundoora...284 L1
st. Ascot Vale...324 D16
st. Belmont...702 E18
st. Brighton East...495 B2
st. Camberwell...417 K6
st. Diggers Rest...142 A12
st. Elsternwick...454 L4
st. Fitzroy...18 L20
st. Hadfield...280 K5
st. Hoppers Csg...448 J5
st. Jan Juc...711 E16
st. Keilor East...322 B3
st. Mernda...154 K20
st. Mernda...155 A20
st. Mt Waverley...459 E4
st. Oakleigh...457 L13
st. Prahran...32 E20
st. Prahran...414 H10
st. Preston...282 F16
st. Reservoir...282 F16
st. Richmond...26 A5
st. Sunbury...142 B11
st. Whittington...703 L18
st. Yarraville...367 B14
REGENTS PARK
ct. Ferntree Gly...463 H13
REGEZIA
ct. Mill Park...243 D8
REGHON
dr. Sunbury...142 H12
REGINA
ct. Eltham North...246 A20
ct. Hillside...231 J20
st. Kilsyth...381 H7
st. Ringwood...378 E16
st. Rosanna...284 K17
st. Springvale S...533 L4
st. Wheelers Hill...460 F15
tce. Doncaster E...332 E5
REGINALD
cl. Berwick...554 K6
ct. Broadmeadows...238 D19
ct. Cranbourne W...577 F19
st. Springvale S...534 A1
wy. Mt Martha...656 K11
REGIS
cl. Werribee...446 K12
ct. Watsonia...285 E4
REGISTRY
la. Carlton...18 G15
REGNAN
rd. Kallista...467 F5
REGNANS
av. Endeavour Hl...502 K20
REGWORTH
ct. Highett...495 H13
REICHELT
av. Montmorency...286 L11
av. Montmorency...287 B14
REID
ct. Dandenong N...535 K1
ct. Mornington...641 B14
mw. Berwick...554 G18
st. Ardeer...320 D17
st. Ashwood...417 L17
st. Balwyn...373 C13
st. Bayswater...424 B7
st. Beaumaris...530 A12
st. Box Hill N...374 L7
st. Fitzroy N...19 B1
st. Frankston...627 E4
st. Heidelberg...329 B5
st. Murrumbeena...457 D14
st. Northcote...326 K12
st. Oakleigh S...457 J16
st. Parkdale...531 L9
st. Sorrento...679 C13
st. S Morang...243 G2
st. Wesburn...347 L14
REIDFORD
av. Preston...282 G20
REIDS
la. Warranwood...334 L11
la. Warranwood...335 A11
REIGATE
rd. Highton...701 F16
REILLY
ct. Croydon S...380 C12
la. S Melbourne...29 H7
st. Ringwood...378 E17
st. Springvale...500 B7
REIS
st. St Albans...320 B2
REISLING
st. Doncaster...330 J19
REITA
av. Wantirna S...462 J1
RELOWE
cr. Balwyn...374 C9
cr. Mont Albert N...374 C9
RELPH
av. Portsea...666 G20
REMANY
cl. Hillside...232 F20
REMBRANDT
ct. Bundoora...242 K17
dr. Wheelers Hill...460 K14
REMER
ct. Cheltenham...531 F3
REMINGTON
ct. Ringwood N...378 D8
dr. Dandenong S...550 F9
dr. Glen Waverley...460 J4
wy. S Morang...198 J15
REMO
cl. Yarra Glen...208 L20
pl. Tullamarine...278 F6
st. Mentone...530 L9
st. Mentone...531 A9
REMON
av. Camberwell...417 F2
REMONT
ct. Cheltenham...497 E18
REMONY
av. Highton...701 G20
REMUERA
st. Caulfield S...455 J12
REMUS
wy. Taylors Lakes...275 G7
REMY
ct. Donvale...376 H7
ct. Vermont S...420 J14
la. Fitzroy N...19 F6
RENA
ct. Mulgrave...500 E5
RENAE
wy. Sydenham...275 B9
RENBOLD
pl. Mulgrave...501 G5
RENDA
ct. Nar Warrn N...539 E12
RENDCOMB
st. Kilsyth S...424 L1
RENDELL
ct. Hughesdale...457 F7
pl. Hampton Pk...551 H12
RENDLE
av. Greensborough...243 L20
RENDLESHAM
av. Mt Eliza...625 J14
RENE
cl. Mill Park...242 F6
ct. Montrose...381 L8
st. Beaumaris...530 F5
st. Preston...283 C17
RENEE
av. Endeavour Hl...537 L3
cl. Mulgrave...501 E3
ct. Cranbourne W...577 J19
RENFEW
ct. Greenvale...237 F2
RENFREE
st. Dandenong S...535 J14
RENFREW
st. Blackburn N...376 C8
RENMARK
ct. Berwick...554 C20
ct. Vermont S...421 C9
RENMUIR
ct. Frankston...628 F4
RENNAT
ct. Berwick...540 A18
RENNICK
st. Preston...327 H5
RENNIE
st. Coburg...325 G6
st. Frankston S...626 L7
st. Seddon...367 C11
st. Thornbury...326 C6
st. Williamstown...411 E13
RENNISON
ct. Wheelers Hill...460 J12
st. Beaumaris...530 C13
st. Braybrook...366 C2
st. Parkdale...531 G16
RENO
rd. Sandringham...495 G17
RENOIR
av. Templestowe...332 C8
ct. Wheelers Hill...460 K16
RENOU
rd. Wantirna S...422 A15
RENOUF
ct. Mt Evelyn...383 H1
RENOWDEN
st. Cheltenham...497 J20
RENOWN
st. Balwyn N...373 K7
st. Bentleigh...496 E1
st. Burwood...418 K10
st. Coburg N...281 F17
st. Essendon N...323 E1
st. Ferntree Gly...424 E18
st. Maidstone...322 E20
RENSHAW
dr. Eltham...287 L5
st. Doncaster E...375 F3
RENTAL
tce. Carlton...18 F20
RENTON
ct. Sunbury...143 B7
ct. Sunbury, off Stewarts La...143 C7
RENVER
rd. Clayton...499 G1
RENWARL
cl. Berwick...554 G10
RENWICK
cl. Craigieburn...194 G3
rd. Ferntree Gly...463 H2
st. Glen Iris...417 B10
st. Glen Iris...417 C10
REO
cr. Campbellfield...194 G20
ct. Glen Waverley...460 K5
REPTON
rd. Malvern East...456 G3
RESCHKE
ct. Laverton...407 E18
RESCORLA
av. Croydon...380 C10
RESEARCH
av. Bundoora...284 G14
av. Research...246 J20
av. Research...288 J1
dr. Croydon S...380 E13
dr. Mill Park...243 B6
RESEARCH-WARRANDYTE
rd. N Warrandyte...289 F8
rd. Research...288 J4
rd. Research...289 A6
RESERVE
av. Campbellfield...239 D13
av. Carnegie...456 G8
av. Mitcham...377 E15
cct. Diamond Ck...245 J10
ct. Glenroy...279 H4
pl. Port Melb...412 K4
rd. Beaumaris...530 A12
rd. Belgrave...466 D16
rd. Black Rock...530 B5
rd. Box Hill...375 D17
rd. Camberwell...416 H2
rd. Cheltenham...530 B5
rd. Gisborne...78 H13
rd. Grovedale...706 G13
rd. Hawthorn...416 A3
rd. Hoppers Csg...405 B20
rd. Marshall...706 G13
rd. Melton...227 C20
rd. N Warrandyte...289 G14
rd. Ringwood...378 G9
rd. Seaford...573 B13
rd. Wonga Park...292 B15
rd.w, Melton...268 L1
st. Berwick...554 D10
st. Carlton N...18 G5
st. Preston...327 G7
st. Springvale...500 A9
RESERVES
rd. Mt Evelyn...383 G2
RESERVOIR
cr. Rowville...503 B9
rd. Coolaroo...194 E18
rd. Frankston...627 H1
rd. Monbulk...428 G10
rd. Nar Warrn N...538 J4
rd. Silvan...428 H10
rd. Sunbury...141 F3
rd. Sunbury...142 H8
rd. Sunbury...143 A8
rd. Yan Yean...126 C19
st. Reservoir...282 K13
tr. Langwarrin...628 K10
RESIDENCE
rd. Waurn Ponds...705 B11
REST
ct. Westmeadows...237 H10
RESTON
ct. Deer Park...318 L8
ct. Highton...705 K5
RETFORD
cl. Bayswater N...380 E19
ct. Doncaster E...332 A17
RETHEL
cl. Keilor Dn...276 E15
RETLAND
dr. Whittlesea...126 D5
RETREAT
av. Aspendale...546 C4
cct. Beaconsfield...555 C12
pl. Port Melb...412 K5
pl. Werribee...447 E13
rd. Belgrave S...505 L9
rd. Hampton...495 D9
rd. Newtown...702 F8
REUBEN
ct. Blackburn S...419 K6
st. Cheltenham...496 L18
st. Ferntree Gly...464 C1
REUMAH
ct. Balwyn...373 C14
ct. Heathmont...378 G18
ct. Noble Park...534 E6
pl. Aspendale Gdn...546 L4
REVE
st. Boronia...424 D15
REVELL
cr. St Albans...275 H18
st. Blairgowrie...680 A20
st. Blairgowrie...695 K2
st. Blairgowrie...695 L1
REVENUE
pl. Lilydale...294 A19
REVILO
ct. Mulgrave...501 L7
REVO
st. Newport...410 F10
REX
av. Alphington...371 G1
av. Rye...697 C3
ct. Noble Park...534 H4
ct. Ringwood E...379 D13
ct. Somerville...644 F16
ct. Wantirna...422 G12
pl. Dingley Village...533 A4
pl. Hadfield...280 K6
rd. Campbellfield...195 E19
st. Frankston...599 E19
st. Kings Park...275 D18
st. Preston...327 H5
REYNARD
ct. Langwarrin...601 L16
st. Coburg...325 A4
st. Epping...197 G11
st. Pascoe Vale S...324 F3
REYNELLA
cl. Vermont S...421 E10
REYNOLDS
av. Ringwood...378 D10
av. Wheelers Hill...460 L15
ct. Endeavour Hl...537 J9
ct. Roxburgh Pk...193 L15
ct. Werribee...447 C10
la. Belgrave...466 F13
la. Kensington...33 B11
pde. Pascoe Vale S...324 J3
pl. Melton S...268 F4
rd. Belmont...706 A5
rd. Diamond Ck...246 H15
rd. Doncaster E...332 F10
rd. Donvale...332 G10
rd. Eltham...288 E15
rd. Kangaroo Grnd...246 H15
rd. Pakenham...559 B7
rd. Research...288 F12
rd. Templestowe...331 G9
rd. Warrandyte...332 G10
rd. Wattle Glen...246 H10
st. Hampton E...496 A7
st. N Melbourne...34 F12
REYS
cl. Mordialloc...532 D17
REZES
st. Wantirna S...422 K17
RHEANVA
st. Berwick...554 C6
RHINE
dr. Roxburgh Pk...194 E6
st. Werribee...447 H6
RHODA
st. Dingley Village...533 B8
RHODE ISLAND
Patterson L...573 H7
ct. Taylors Lakes...275 J7
RHODEN
ct. Dandenong N...501 K14
gr. Eumemmerring...537 A14
RHODES
ct. Vermont...421 D5
dr. Glen Waverley...460 H4
pde. Glenroy...280 D10
st. St Albans...320 D8
st. Springvale...500 B11
RHONDA
cl. Endeavour Hl...537 F1
ct. Bayswater...423 E9
ct. Bundoora...243 D20
ct. Frankston...600 E16
ct. Moorabbin...496 F10
ct. Ringwood N...378 B3
rd. Silvan...384 C11
st. Avondale Ht...322 A16
st. Doncaster...330 C18
st. Mt Waverley...459 D5
st. Rosanna...329 D3
RHONDELLA
ct. Pt Lonsdale...710 B6
RHUBANE
ct. Blackburn...376 C13
RHUR
st. Dandenong S...535 K18
RHUS
cl. Endeavour Hl...536 J1
ct. Werribee...447 K8
RHYL
cl. Endeavour Hl...537 B2
RHYLL
ct. Westmeadows...237 E11
RIALTO
av. Cranbourne N...578 E9
gr. Dromana...686 H8
st. Albanvale...319 D3
RIALTON
av. Blackburn N...376 A9
RIATTA
av. Grovedale...706 D16
ct. Rye...697 A5
RIBBLESDALE
av. Wyndham Va...446 C13
RIBBON
ct. Aspendale Gdn...547 B5
ct. Frankston N...600 C10
ct. Mill Park...242 D10

RIX
rd. Officer 581 F2
st. Glen Iris 416 F8
ROACH
av. Aberfeldie 323 D9
dr. Altona Mdw 451 G6
pl. Roxburgh Pk 194 E14
rd. Lilydale 339 B8
ROANOKE
ct. Epping 197 L17
ct. Sorrento 679 B14
ROB
cl. Hoppers Csg 448 A3
ct. Berwick 554 F1
ct. Boronia 424 F8
ROBB
cl. Bulleen 329 E12
ct. Hampton Pk 551 H10
st. Essendon 323 J10
st. Reservoir 283 D16
st. Spotswood 411 B2
ROBBIE
cl. Rowville 463 J20
ROBBIES
rd. Yarrambat 201 K10
ROBBINS
ct. Bundoora 242 L20
st. Ivanhoe 328 B10
st. Keilor 277 B14
wy. Hampton Pk 551 H11
ROBBS
la. Geelong, off Bayley St 703 A6
pde. Northcote 326 J13
rd. W Footscray 366 J10
ROBDON
ct. Donvale 377 C5
ROBE
ct. Glen Waverley 460 K2
st. St Kilda 414 A17
ROBERN
pde. View Bank 285 G19
ROBERNA
ct. Langwarrin 601 G20
st. Moorabbin 497 B12
ROBERT
ct. Croydon 336 G13
ct. Gisborne 79 C15
ct. Hampton Pk 551 L13
ct. Kurunjang 226 G13
ct. View Bank 285 H16
la. E Melbourne 25 K8
st. Balwyn N 373 K6
st. Bentleigh 496 C2
st. Bulleen 329 G10
st. Burwood E 419 L7
st. Chadstone 458 D3
st. Collingwood 19 J19
st. Dandenong 536 C6
st. Elwood 454 G2
st. Lalor 240 K9
st. Lilydale 338 A7
st. Montmorency 286 L10
st. Parkdale 531 H9
st. Sassafras 426 C17
st. Somerville 644 L18
st. Somerville 645 A18
st. Spotswood 411 A2
ROBERTA
ct. Bundoora 285 C1
gr. Frankston 599 F18
st. Dandenong 535 L2
ROBERT LYALL
pl. Hoppers Csg 447 K1
ROBERT MOLYNEUX
av. Endeavour Hl 537 G10
ROBERTS
av. Airport W 279 C16
av. Box Hill S 418 L5
av. Hoppers Csg 405 A20
av. Hoppers Csg 448 L1
av. Hoppers Csg 449 A1
av. Mulgrave 499 J2
cr. Sunshine W 364 H9
ct. Brighton East 495 K4
ct. Endeavour Hl 537 J11
ct. Sunbury 142 L9
rd. Airport W 278 D16
rd. Belmont 702 B19
rd. Christmas Hills 207 B13
rd. Cranbourne 577 L16
rd. Cranbourne 577 L17
rd.n, Mornington 641 H17
rd.s, Mornington 657 G2
st. Brunswick E 326 B13
st. Essendon 323 E7
st. Ferntree Gly 464 D7
st. Frankston 627 H5
st. Glen Waverley 460 D6
st. Keilor East 322 D6
st. Noble Park 500 J20
st. Northcote 326 J17
st. Rye 697 D5
st. W Footscray 366 F12
st. Yarraville 366 F16
wy. Doncaster E 332 G17
ROBERTSON
av. St Kilda 414 E13
cr. Boronia 424 D4
cr. Laverton 407 F11
ct. Pt Lonsdale 707 H20
dr. Mornington 640 L15
dr. Mornington 641 A15
pde. Aspendale 546 E6
st. Gisborne 78 J11
st. Kensington 34 B9
st. Preston 283 A19
st. Thomson 703 J17
st. Toorak 415 C4
st. Williamstown 410 L16
ROBERTSONS
rd. Darley 221 J2
rd. Taylors Lakes 275 B2
ROBERTSWOOD
cl. Doncaster E 332 D12
ROBESON
st. Preston 326 D5
ROBHILL
ri. Templestowe 331 E9
ROBIN
cl. Doveton 536 J4
ct. Doncaster 331 A15
ct. Keysborough 534 C9
ct. Pakenham 584 L3
ct. Wantirna 422 D4
dr. Carrum Downs 574 K18
gr. Mt Waverley 419 G19
pde. Healesville 213 H15
pde. Rye 696 D6
pl. Craigieburn 149 F17
pl. S Morang 243 J3
st. Altona 408 F19
st. Hoppers Csg 448 G6
st. Melton 226 H16
ROBINA
ct. Dingley Village 533 C9
ct. Rowville 502 L3
rd. Eaglemont 328 G10
rd. Monbulk 428 D20
rd. Sydenham 275 A9
ROBIN HILL
dr. Mornington 656 L5
ROBIN HOOD
ct. Doncaster E 332 A17
rd. Ivanhoe East 328 H16
ROBINIA
cl. Hillside 274 B5
cl. Nar Warrn S 579 C1
gr. Werribee 446 L9
st. Frankston 627 K7
ROBINLEE
av. Burwood E 420 A9
ROBINS
av. Reservoir 283 G3
cl. Mt Martha 656 D16
ROBINSON
cr. Hampton Pk 551 G9
ct. Bayswater N 424 H1
ct. Delahey 275 F10
ct. Donvale 376 L6
dr. Burwood E 420 D12
gr. Bulleen 329 J15
pl. Portsea 677 J4
rd. Carrum Downs 574 A12
rd. Footscray 367 E4
rd. Harkaway 539 L13
rd. Hawthorn 372 C20
rd. Hawthorn 416 B4
rd. Nar Warrn N 539 E6
rd. Reservoir 282 K15
rd. Surrey Hills 373 K17
st. Brighton East 455 F20
st. Clayton 458 F19
st. Croydon 379 D3
st. Dandenong 535 K9
st. Jacana 237 J17
st. Malvern 415 L8
st. Moonee Pnd 324 B9
st. Mt Martha 669 D4
st. Prahran 32 L17
st. Prahran 414 L9
st. Prahran 415 A9
st. Sunshine 365 E5
ROBINSONS
brk. Langwarrin 628 J14
rd. Deer Park 318 H15
rd. Deer Park 318 H20
rd. Derrimut 363 A14
rd. Frankston 627 J12
rd. Frankston S 627 J12
rd. Langwarrin 628 G14
rd. Langwarrin S 628 G14
rd. Langwarrin S 629 D15
rd. Langwarrin S 630 A16
rd. Pearcedale 630 A16
rd. Pearcedale 647 D1
rd. Ravenhall 318 H20
rd. Seaford 599 E3
rd. Truganina 363 A14
ROBINSWOOD
pde. Nar Warrn S 579 A4
ROBINVALE
av. Thomastown 240 D11
ct. Endeavour Hl 503 F20
ROBJANT
st. Hampton Pk 551 B8
ROBLYN
cr. Tootgarook 698 C6
ROBOROUGH
av. Mt Eliza 626 A19
ROBROSS
st. Cheltenham 497 C19
ROB ROY
rd. Christmas Hills 206 A11
rd. Malvern East 457 F2
rd. Smiths Gly 206 A11
st. Glen Waverley 459 J6
ROBSON
av. Avondale Ht 322 A13
st. Sunshine N 321 G14
ROBUSTA
av. Bundoora 242 D14
ROBY
ct. Greensborough 244 D16
ROBYN
av. Albanvale 319 D4
ct. Carrum 573 E11
ct. Dandenong N 501 K11
ct. Hampton Pk 551 D10
ct. Mooroolbark 337 A13
ct. Oakleigh S 497 G7
ct. Rye 696 K5
dr. Nunawading 376 E10
st. Doncaster 331 B19
ROCCO
dr. Scoresby 462 A8
ROCHDALE
dr. Burwood E 419 F7
sq. Lalor 241 E8
ROCHE
ct. Chelsea Ht 547 G16
ct. Epping 198 A19
ct. Oakleigh S 497 J7
st. Hawthorn 371 H17
st. St Albans 275 K19
ROCHELL
ct. Clarinda 498 D11
ROCHELLE
ct. Aspendale Gdn 547 C7
ct. Doncaster E 332 J13
ct. Nar Warrn S 552 E14
ct. Wantirna S 462 H1
ct. Wheelers Hill 460 H10
ROCHE'S
tce. Williamstown 411 E13
ROCHESTER
dr. Thomastown 241 H16
rd. Balwyn 373 F14
rd. Canterbury 373 F17
rd. Somerville 644 G15
st. Braybrook 365 L5
st. Fitzroy 19 D13
st. Kew 371 C11
vst. Officer 555 G19
ROCHFORD
pl. Nar Warrn S 552 F7
st. Bentleigh E 456 J15
ROCHUSSEN
ct. Mt Eliza 641 L7
ROCK
ct. Pakenham 558 K7
gdn. Dromana 686 B10
st. Craigieburn 150 D17
st. Werribee 447 F12
ROCKAWAY
dr. View Bank 285 K16
ROCKBANK
ct. Meadow Ht 237 L5
rd. Ardeer 320 B19
ROCKBANK MIDDLE
rd. Burnside 317 J5
rd. Caroline Spr 317 J5
ROCKBEARE
ct. Clayton 458 K17
gr. Ivanhoe 327 L16
ROCKBROOK
rd. St Kilda E 414 K20
ROCKCLIFF
ct. Mornington 640 C14
ROCKCLIFFE
st. Eltham 287 K13
ROCKE
st. Ivanhoe 328 A15
ROCKFORD
ct. Noble Park 534 L4
ROCKINGHAM
cl. Kew 371 E12
st. Kew 371 E12
ROCKLANDS
rd. Ashwood 418 F15
ri. Meadow Ht 194 A20
ROCKLEA
cr. Skye 575 H16
ct. Port Melb 412 C2
dr. Torquay 711 J9
rd. Bulleen 329 F13
ROCKLEIGH
dr. Mt Martha 669 C4
ROCKLEIGH PARK
rd. Nar Warrn N 538 E4
ROCKLEY
cl. Diamond Ck 245 J7
rd. South Yarra 32 G9
rd. South Yarra 414 J5
ROCK LODGE
ct. Frankston S 627 A13
ROCKMAN
ct. Nar Warrn N 538 H11
ROCK O'CASHEL
la. Geelong, off Little Malop St 703 B8
ROCKSLEIGH
av. Tecoma 466 D13
ROCKWALL
cl. Sydenham 275 A7
ROCKWOOD
pl. Hillside 232 D17
st. Ardeer 320 B18
ROCKY
la. South Yarra 32 D12
ROCKYS
wy. Lilydale 338 D11
wy. Lilydale 338 E11
ROD
st. Herne Hill 701 J1
RODD
rd. Airport W 279 A10
st. Dandenong 535 K8
RODDA
ct. Gladstone Pk 237 D18
pde. Eltham 287 F16
st. Coburg 325 J2
RODDICK
gr. Queenscliff 708 A19
RODEN
ct. Doncaster E 331 K17
st. W Melbourne 23 A3
RODEO
ct. Endeavour Hl 504 A19
RODERICK
cl. View Bank 285 L17
dr. Kurunjang 227 E12
st. Doncaster E 375 K1
RODGER
ct. Bundoora 284 D1
rd. Panton Hill 204 H17
rd. Wandin N 340 G10
RODGERSON
st. Box Hill 374 H12
RODINGS
st. Hadfield 281 B7
RODLEIGH
st. Croydon 336 G14
RODMAN
st. Reservoir 282 L3
RODMAR
cl. Hillside 274 F1
ct. Sorrento 679 B14
RODNEY
av. Coburg N 281 C13
cl. Blackburn S 419 H4
cl. Wheelers Hill 461 D12
ct. Broadmeadows 238 E15
ct. Frankston 599 D16
ct. Hoppers Csg 405 C20
ct. Mornington 640 B17
ct. Skye 575 G17
ct. Springvale S 500 C19
ct. View Bank 285 H16
dr. Keilor Dn 276 A16
dr. Knoxfield 462 J3
pl. Carlton 18 F17
st. Bayswater 423 B6
st. Gisborne 79 B14
st. Moorabbin 496 G10
st. Rye 696 F7
RODWELL
pl. Gladstone Pk 236 L16
pl. Gladstone Pk 237 A16
ROE
ct. Mt Waverley 419 C17
wy. Mill Park 242 G1
ROEBOURNE
cr. Campbellfield 239 F18
ROEBUCK
st. Newtown 702 H8
ROEHAMPTON
av. Wantirna 422 H11
cr. Mt Eliza 625 K15
ROEMER
cr. Alphington 371 J1
ROESZLER
la. Melbourne 1 G14
la. Melbourne, off Bank Pl 24 A9
ROFF
ct. Altona Mdw 451 C3
st. Reservoir 283 G2
ROGAN
ct. Langwarrin 601 K18
la. Kensington 33 F8
ROGER
ct. Nunawading 376 F10
ct. Rowville 502 J2
st. Belmont 702 C20
st. Doncaster E 376 A3
ROGERS
av. Brighton East 455 F16
av. Carrum Downs 574 H16
cl. Burnside 318 F9
rd. Bentleigh 496 D5
st. Coburg 281 G19
st. Dandenong 535 K2
st. Eumemmerring 536 L15
st. Eumemmerring 537 A15
st. Mentone 531 C9
st. Pakenham 584 H7
st. Port Melb 368 J18
st. Richmond 26 B13
ROGERSON
ct. Balwyn 373 H10
st. Avondale Ht 322 A12
ROHAN
ct. Fawkner 281 K1
ct. Hampton Pk 551 K7
st. View Bank 285 J20
ROJIM
ct. Wattle Glen 246 G8
ROKEBY
cl. Hallam 538 B18
cr. Craigieburn 150 A17
st. Collingwood 25 J2
ROKEWOOD
cr. Meadow Ht 237 H5
ct. Endeavour Hl 537 E2
ROLA
cl. Endeavour Hl 538 A1
ROLAIN
av. S Morang 198 L13
av. S Morang 198 L14
ROLAINE
cl. Lilydale 338 J9
ROLAND
av. Mt Evelyn 339 J18
av. Strathmore 279 K18
st. Mt Waverley 418 H13
ROLEX
ct. Noble Park 535 D5
ROLLAND
ct. Brookfield 268 C4
ct. Endeavour Hl 537 H7
ct. Montmorency 287 A11
st. Coburg 281 E20
ROLLAWAY
ri. Chirnside Pk 337 D1
ROLLING HILLS
rd. Chirnside Pk 337 E1
ROLLING MEADOWS
dr. Sunbury 144 C8
ROLLINGS
cl. Rosebud 700 J4
rd. Up Fntree Gly 465 B8
ROLLINGTON
dr. Ringwood 378 L4
ROLLO
st. Coburg N 281 B13
ROLLS
ct. Glen Waverley 460 G1
ct. Rye 696 L13
st. Coburg 325 H5
ROLORAN
av. Croydon 336 J19
ROLSTONE
ct. Narre Warren 553 E7
ROMA
av. Badger Creek 258 J14
av. Cranbourne 578 A16
ct. Eumemmerring 537 C13
ct. Springvale S 534 A6
ct. Templstw Lr 330 E13
ct. Thomastown 240 C14
ct. Tullamarine 278 F5

pde. Upwey 465 G12
st. Bentleigh 496 D3
st. Hoppers Csg 448 H5
st. Scoresby 462 F6

ROMALYN
ct. Werribee 447 L16

ROMANO
av. Mill Park 242 E1

ROMAWI
st. Altona 409 A19

ROME
ct. Glen Waverley 419 K17
tce. Mooroolbark 337 L17

ROME BEAUTY
av. The Basin 424 K9

ROMEO
ct. Mill Park 242 L3
ct. Mill Park 243 A3
ct. Torquay 712 E4
rd. Healesville 258 K7

ROMERIL
ct. Altona Mdw 451 K6

ROMFORD
ct. Doncaster E 331 L18

ROMILLY
av. Templstw Lr 330 L12
cr. Mulgrave 501 A6

ROMINA
wy. S Morang 199 L16

ROMME
ct. Frankston 628 B10

ROMNEY
av. Tootgarook 698 D2
cl. Moorabbin 496 F9
ct. Mt Waverley 458 F9

ROMOLY
dr. Forest Hill 420 C6

ROMSEY
av. Sunshine N 320 L13
av. Sunshine N 321 A13
cr. Dallas 238 F12
pl. Langwarrin 601 H15
ri. Doncaster E 331 G18
st. Noble Park 500 F20
st. Reservoir 283 D1

ROMY
ct. Altona Mdw 451 D5

RONA
av. Yarraville 367 F16
ct. Baxter 643 L2
st. Ferntree Gly 424 J19
st. Reservoir 282 H15

RONALD
av. Altona North 409 K8
av. Bulleen 329 J11
av. Frankston S 626 G8
av. Noble Park 500 G14
av. Selby 467 B18
av. Sorrento 678 H12
av. S Morang 243 G3
cl. Gladstone Pk 279 C3
cr. Boronia 424 H10
ct. Pakenham 584 G5
ct. Somerville 644 J15
ct. Sunbury 142 L11
ct. Sunbury 143 A11
ct. Watsonia N 285 E2
gr. Keilor East 322 D1
gr. Millgrove 348 G2
rd. Croydon 379 J9
rd. Emerald 470 B17
st. Box Hill N 375 A7
st. Clematis 508 K3
st. Coburg N 282 A16
st. Dandenong 536 D9
st. Essendon N 279 D20
st. Mitcham 377 B18
st. Moorabbin 496 E7
st. Ringwood 378 K5
st. Tootgarook 698 G3

RONALDSAY
pl. Point Cook 450 H8

RONCLIFFE
rd. Highton 701 H17

RONDE
ct. Healesville 257 F2

RONDELL
av. W Footscray 366 F7

RONDOR
cl. Westmeadows 236 H15

RONDU
pl. Eltham 288 A7

RONLEY
st. Blackburn 375 J20

RONLYN
st. Rosebud W 683 F19

RONSTON
ct. Wheelers Hill 461 C16

ROODING
st. Brighton 454 K13

ROOKE
ct. Sunshine W 364 F9

ROOKERY
rd. Point Cook 450 H9

ROOKS
rd. Mitcham 376 L15
rd. Nunawading 376 L15
rd. Vermont 376 L19
rd. Vermont 377 A19
rd. Vermont 420 L1
rd. Vermont 421 A1

ROOKWOOD
st. Balwyn N 373 F3

ROONEY
st. Maidstone 366 F1
st. Richmond 26 K20
st. Templstw Lr 330 E13

ROONEYS
la. Richmond 26 B13

ROOSEVELT
ct. Brighton East 495 E4
ct. Dingley Village 532 L7
st. Coburg N 281 C17

ROPE
wk. Brunswick, off La Rose St 325 E9

ROPER
ct. Gladstone Pk 237 C19
ct. Taylors Lakes 275 K2
pl. Doncaster E 332 E15
st. Moorabbin 496 J11

ROPLEY
av. Balwyn 372 L10
av. Balwyn 373 A10
gra. Frankston 599 F12
gra. Upwey 465 E10

RORY
ct. Lilydale 338 D12
ct. Werribee 446 L10
ct. Werribee 447 A10

ROSA
av. Springvale 500 C17
st. Scoresby 462 G7
st. Templstw Lr 330 F14

ROSALA
av. Altona North 409 G2

ROSALEEN
ct. Narre Warren 539 D19

ROSALIE
av. Cranbourne 578 A17
av. Dromana 686 G4
ct. Hampton Pk 551 K8
ct. Pakenham 584 H8
ct. Wantirna S 422 C17
rd. Mornington 657 B3
st. Springvale 500 A10

ROSALIND
cr. Blackburn 376 A19
st. Queenscliff 707 K19

ROSALINE
av. Mt Waverley 419 B18

ROSAMOND
cr. Doncaster E 332 C20
rd. Footscray 366 L2
rd. Maidstone 322 L20
rd. Maidstone 323 A20
rd. Maribyrnong 322 L20
rd. Maribyrnong 323 A20
rd. Maribyrnong 366 L2
st. Balaclava 414 G18

ROSAMUNDE
st. Rye 696 E4

ROSANNA
ct. Badger Creek 258 E8
ct. Carnegie 456 K11
ct. Craigieburn 150 E15
rd. Heidelberg 329 A7
rd. Rosanna 329 A7
st. Carnegie 456 J10

ROSAPENNA
cl. Sunbury 144 F12

ROSCIUS
pl. Sorrento 679 B13

ROSCO
dr. Templestowe 332 A6

ROSCOE
ct. Noble Park N 501 E12

ROSCOMMON
pl. Herne Hill 702 A4

ROSCREA
ct. Werribee 447 C13
rd. Melton 226 J16

ROSE
al. Melbourne 23 G8
av. Boronia 423 K12
av. Bulleen 330 A13
av. Croydon 380 C2
av. Dandenong N 501 G18
av. Glen Waverley 420 A20
av. Hurstbridge 202 L16
av. Hurstbridge 203 A16
av. Niddrie 322 K5
av. Rosebud 683 J17
av. Surrey Hills 374 A20
av. Surrey Hills 418 A1
av. Templstw Lr 330 A13
ct. Brighton 454 G20
ct. Croydon 379 K1
ct. Delahey 275 E9
ct. Gowanbrae 279 D5
ct. Greenvale 237 C3
ct. Jacana 237 G16
ct. Lilydale 338 L9
ct. McCrae 684 K13
ct. Newcomb 703 L15
ct. Reservoir 282 H13
ct. Somerville 644 F13
ct. Thomastown 240 J16
dr. Doveton 536 G11
la. Cranbourne 578 C14
st. Altona 408 K20
st. Armadale 415 D10
st. Bentleigh 455 L19
st. Box Hill 375 A17
st. Braybrook 365 K1
st. Brighton 455 A11
st. Brunswick 325 B9
st. Burnley 26 K19
st. Burnside 318 G9
st. Clayton 498 L1
st. Clifton Hill 20 E3
st. Coburg 324 L4
st. Doncaster 374 J2
st. Essendon 323 L7
st. Fitzroy 19 A10
st. Frankston S 626 H7
st. Hawthorn E 372 F20
st. Highett 496 A14
st. Ivanhoe 328 B15
st. McKinnon 455 L17
st. Pascoe Vale 280 K10
st. Richmond 26 G19
st. Richmond 26 J19
st. Rosebud W 683 A19
st. Sandringham 495 F17
st. Sorrento 679 A11
st. Tecoma 466 E12
st. Up Fntree Gly 465 B7

ROSEBANK
av. Clayton S 499 B8
av. Ringwood N 378 E5
av. Strathmore 324 C2
ct. Ferntree Gly 463 L14
dr. Cranbourne N 578 E10
dr. Cranbourne N 578 F8
dr. Point Cook 451 B7
tce. Templstw Lr 330 B14

ROSEBERRY
av. Brighton East 455 C16
av. Chelsea 546 H16
av. Keilor Dn 275 K14
av. Preston 282 L20
gr. Glen Huntly 456 B6
st. Ascot Vale 323 K17
st. Hawthorn E 372 E19

ROSEBERY
st. Altona Mdw 451 H1

ROSEBROOK
st. Rosebud 683 J18

ROSEBUD
av. Moorabbin 496 F9
av. Rosebud 700 H4
cr. Broadmeadows 237 G15
pde. Rosebud 684 C20
pde. View Bank 285 G19

ROSEBUD-FLINDERS
rd. Boneo 699 H10
rd. Boneo 699 H17
rd. Rosebud 699 H10
rd. Rosebud W 699 H10

ROSEBURN
ct. Lower Plenty 286 E18

ROSEDALE
av. Glen Huntly 456 D7
cr. Dallas 238 F9
cr. Ringwood E 378 K11
ct. Endeavour Hl 537 F2
dr. Lalor 240 K10
gr. Frankston S 627 D20
gr. Frankston S 627 G16
gr. Frankston S 643 C1
gr. Ivanhoe 328 A11
pl. Wyndham Va 446 H11
rd. Glen Iris 417 B12

ROSE GARDENS
pl. Hoppers Csg 448 A1

ROSE HEDGE
dr. Sydenham 275 C9

ROSEHILL
av. Caulfield N 455 G2
ct. Mill Park 242 K10
ct. Narre Warren 539 G14
ct. Noble Park N 501 B7
dr. Bacchus Msh 221 E13
rd. Essendon W 322 H5
rd. Essendon W 323 A5
rd. Keilor East 322 H5
rd. Lower Plenty 286 F18
rd. Lower Plenty 286 H18
rd. Niddrie 322 H5
rd. Niddrie 323 A5
st. Scoresby 462 H6

ROSELAND
cr. Hoppers Csg 448 E8
gr. Doncaster 331 B17
gr. Ivanhoe 328 D9

ROSELANDS
ct. Langwarrin 629 H3
gr. Bundoora 243 C13

ROSELEA
ct. Sunshine 321 E19
st. Box Hill N 375 C7
st. Caulfield S 455 H7

ROSELEIGH
bvd. Sydenham 275 B8

ROSELLA
av. Boronia 424 D11
av. Clarinda 498 C10
av. Werribee 447 L8
av. Werribee 448 A9
cr. Healesville 257 L1
ct. Blackburn S 419 K6
ct. Pearcedale 646 K4
ct. Westmeadows 236 J14
rd. Parkdale 531 G17
rd. Wesburn 347 D4
ri. Eltham 287 B3
st. Doncaster E 375 K4
st. Frankston 599 C13
st. Murrumbeena 457 C8
tr. Frankston N 600 E11
wk. S Morang 243 K2

ROSELYN
cr. Bentleigh E 456 J18
cr. Boronia 423 C14

ROSEMAN
rd. Chirnside Pk 337 J3

ROSEMAR
cct. View Bank 285 J19

ROSEMARY
av. Croydon Hills 335 G16
av. Springvale 499 L16
cl. Hoppers Csg 447 K3
cr. Frankston N 600 B10
ct. Campbellfield 239 E11
ct. Carrum Downs 601 C5
ct. Mulgrave 460 A13
ct. View Bank 285 K16
dr. Lalor 240 H5
gr. Glen Iris 417 L10
rd. Beaumaris 530 C7
st. Chadstone 458 D4
st. Templstw Lr 330 H8

ROSEMONT
av. Caulfield N 455 F1
cr. Kalorama 382 L16
ct. Dandenong N 501 F19
dr. Bulleen 329 J8
dr. Narre Warren 553 D11
rd. Lilydale 295 B20
st. Surrey Hills 374 D18

ROSEMORE
st. Rosebud 684 G14

ROSEN
st. Blackburn S 419 K3

ROSENE
ct. Keysborough 534 G13

ROSENEATH
pl. S Melbourne 29 K2
st. Clifton Hill 20 E7

ROSENTHAL
cr. Reservoir 282 J3

ROSER
dr. Altona Mdw 451 D3

ROSETTA
av. Sorrento 679 D14

ROSETTI
la. Elwood 454 C3

ROSEVILLE
av. Blairgowrie 695 H1
av. Doncaster 331 A19

ROSEWALL
ct. Wantirna S 462 D5
pl. Clarinda 498 E7
st. Sunshine N 321 D14

ROSEWARNE
av. Cheltenham 496 L17

ROSEWIN
ct. Berwick 539 J17
ct. Carrum Downs 575 E14

ROSEWOOD
bvd. Lysterfield 464 C19
ct. Frankston 627 J9
ct. Grovedale 705 L15
ct. Mulgrave 500 J2
ct. Nar Warrn S 579 C2
la. St Albans 319 E7
pl. Chirnside Pk 336 G8
pl. Craigieburn 150 D14

ROSHERVILLE
pl. S Melbourne 29 F2

ROSICA
ct. Roxburgh Pk 194 C6

ROSIE
ct. Aspendale Gdn 547 C8

ROSINA
dr. Melton 268 E1
st. Bentleigh 496 E6
st. Rye 696 F9

ROSINE
ct. Doncaster 330 F17

ROSINGS
ct. Notting Hill 459 K12

ROSLYN
av. Rye 696 G1
ct. Dandenong N 502 A10
ct. Donvale 376 K3
ct. Eltham 287 C4
rd. Belmont 701 F18
rd. Cranbourne S 602 J15
rd. Highton 701 F18
st. Brighton 454 L20
st. Brighton 455 A20
st. Brighton 494 L4
st. Brighton 495 A4
st. Burwood 418 C8
st. Montrose 381 J10
st. Mt Martha 655 J19
st. Newport 410 K9
st. Rye 697 B15
st. Somerville 645 B15
st. Strathmore 279 L16
wy. Whittlesea 96 E17

ROSNEY
pl. Torquay 712 D4
st. Hawthorn, off Evansdale Rd 371 G17

ROSNY
pl. Mooroolbark 381 H3
pl. Williamstown 411 D14
st. Port Melb 412 D4

ROSS
av. The Basin 425 E11
cr. Heathmont 378 F19
cr. Skye 575 J17
ct. Brookfield 268 C3
ct. Mill Park 242 D4
ct. Mt Waverley 459 F8
ct. Niddrie 279 B19
ct. Springvale 500 C17
ct. Sunbury 143 D8
ct. Yallambie 286 D11
pl. S Melbourne 29 L2
rd. Altona North 409 G9
rd. Croydon 379 F5
rd. Gruyere 341 J4
st. Alphington 327 H15
st. Aspendale 546 E8
st. Belgrave 466 E16
st. Bentleigh 456 D19
st. Coburg 281 G19
st. Dandenong 536 E8
st. Doncaster E 375 G2
st. Elsternwick 454 K5
st. Ferntree Gly 463 G3
st. Heatherton 532 E2
st. Huntingdale 458 E14
st. Kew 372 H14
st. Mitcham 377 A17
st. Mornington 640 E12
st. Newport 410 K5
st. Niddrie 279 B20
st. Northcote 326 J20
st. Port Melb 412 H4
st. Port Melb 412 J4
st. Reservoir 282 D1
st. St Albans 320 D6
st. S Melbourne 3 A17
st. S Melbourne 30 A1
st. S Melbourne 413 F1
st. Surrey Hills 373 K14
st. Tecoma 466 D11
st. Toorak 415 B6

ROSSACK
dr. Grovedale 705 G12
dr. Waurn Ponds 705 G12

ROSSCOMMON
pl. Seabrook 450 L4

ROSSDALE
ct. Glen Waverley 420 F15
st. Craigieburn 150 H16
st. Oakleigh E 458 L15

ROSSEAU
st. Williamstown 411 G15

ROSSER
st. Brunswick 325 F13

ROSSERDALE
cr. Mt Eliza 625 J13
ROSSETTI
ct. Pakenham 584 D4
ROSSFIELD
av. Kew 372 B13
ROSS GREGORY
dr. Albert Park 414 A11
dr. St Kilda 414 A11
ROSSHIRE
rd. Newport 410 E10
ROSSI
st. Ivanhoe 328 B11
ROSSITER
av. Endeavour Hl 537 G9
av. Roxburgh Pk 194 C13
av. Roxburgh Pk 194 C16
ct. Ferntree Gly 464 B11
ct. Seaford 573 H20
rd. Carrum Downs 574 F11
ROSSLARE
ct. Hoppers Csg 405 E18
pde. St Albans 320 H7
ROSSLYN
av. Seaford 599 D10
ct. Seaford 599 D11
st. Blackburn S 419 K1
st. Hawthorn E 416 D3
st. W Melbourne 23 A4
ROSSMITH
av. Beaumaris 530 G6
ROSSMOYNE
st. Thornbury 326 K8
ROSS PINCOTT
dr. Mooroolbark 337 B14
ROSS SMITH
av. Frankston 599 B18
ROSSTOWN
rd. Carnegie 456 G4
ROSSTREVOR
cr. Mitcham 377 A19
ROSS WAIT
rd. Gisborne 78 F1
ROSTELLA
av. Wheelers Hill 460 H11
cr. Keilor East 321 K3
ROSTILL
ct. Toorak 415 G4
ROSTO
ct. Tullamarine 236 J20
ROSTRATA
vw. Mill Park 243 D10
ROSTREVOR
pde. Mont Albert 374 D12
pde. Mont Albert N 374 D12
ROSTRON
wy. Roxburgh Pk 193 L13
ROSWELL
st. Glen Waverley 460 L3
ROSYTH
rd. Rye 697 E4
ROTARY
ct. Box Hill S 418 J4
dr. Keilor East 322 B5
ROTHAN
av. Boronia 424 D6
ROTHBURY
ct. Wantirna 422 F14
ROTHERHAM
st. Belmont 702 B20
ROTHERWOOD
av. Mitcham 377 C9
av. Ringwood E 379 D16
cl. Wantirna 422 E12
dr. Malvern East 457 H1
pl. Lilydale 338 K10
rd. Ivanhoe East 328 E14
st. Richmond 26 A12
ROTHESAY
av. Brighton 454 G12
av. Elwood 454 F3
av. Malvern East 416 H19
av. Mornington 640 K10
ct. Noble Park N 501 B12
ct. Templestowe 332 C12
pl. Greenvale 193 A19
pl. Melton W 226 A15
ROTHRAY
av. Sunshine N 321 C11
ROTHSAY
av. Burwood 418 J6
la. Melbourne 2 B18
la. Melbourne 24 D10
ROTHSBY
wy. Greenvale 193 G17
ROTHSCHILD
st. Caulfield S 456 A7
st. Glen Huntly 456 A7

ROTHWELL
ct. Epping 197 H16
ct. Mitcham 377 H11
st. Ascot Vale 324 B18
ROTOROA
ct. Taylors Lakes 276 E10
ROTORUA
st. Caulfield S 455 J11
ROUEN
rd. Cockatoo 511 B5
st. Hampton 495 A5
ROUGET
rd. Wandin East 341 B17
ROUKE
st. Lilydale 337 K4
ROULSTON
ct. Noble Park N 501 C11
ROUNDHAY
ct. Berwick 554 F6
ROUND TOWER
rd. Dandenong S 550 H1
ROURKE
st. Bayswater 423 K9
ROUSE
st. Cranbourne 577 L15
st. Port Melb 412 J6
ROUSSAC
st. Sunshine N 321 B9
ROUT
st. Cremorne 25 L17
ROVER
ct. Keilor Dn 276 C12
ct. Tuerong 670 L3
st. Sunbury 142 F11
ROW
ct. Portsea 677 K1
ROWALLAN
av. Harkaway 540 H10
av. Harkaway 541 A9
ct. Balwyn N 374 B4
ct. Doncaster E 332 D20
ROWAN
av. Bentleigh E 496 H4
av. Boronia 424 J11
av. Brooklyn 365 F18
av. The Basin 424 J11
ct. Belmont 706 D7
ct. Carrum Downs 600 K1
ct. Frankston N 600 F9
ct. Mt Waverley 459 G4
dr. Doveton 536 H8
dr. Kealba 276 K17
dr. Kealba 276 L18
dr. Kealba 277 A18
pl. Bayswater 423 E5
rd. Dingley Village 533 G7
rd. Springvale S 533 H6
st. Croydon 380 C8
st. Doncaster E 331 J17
st. Elsternwick 455 A6
st. Glenroy 279 L3
st. Preston 326 D4
st. Vermont 421 J2
ROWANS
la. Port Melb, off Lalor St 412 L4
rd. Highett 496 F13
rd. Moorabbin 496 G11
ROWAN TREE
ct. View Bank 285 L18
ROWE
ct. Avondale Ht 322 F9
st. Alphington 327 K18
st. Fitzroy N 19 H3
st. Maribyrnong 323 A20
st. Montrose 381 L19
ROWELL
av. Camberwell 416 J7
ct. Melton S 268 H11
pl. Taylors Lakes 233 A18
st. Rosanna 285 C20
ROWELLYN
av. Carrum Downs 601 E1
ROWEN
ct. Cranbourne N 578 G9
st. Glen Iris 417 H12
st. Thomastown 242 A14
ROWENA
ct. Keysborough 534 F10
pde. Richmond 26 A12
rd. Malvern East 457 H4
ri. Wantirna S 422 C20
st. Caulfield N 415 J20
ROWERN
ct. Box Hill N 375 E12
ROWES
rd. Werribee 446 K9
rd. Werribee 447 A11
ROWITTA
dr. Glen Waverley 420 C16

ROWLAND
av. Ivanhoe East 328 F16
ct. Hampton Pk 551 E4
ct. Ferntree Gly 464 B7
ct. Glen Waverley 419 L16
ct. Wonga Park 336 C8
pl. Point Cook 450 E4
st. Bentleigh E 496 K7
st. Kew 372 F12
st. Mont Albert 374 F16
ROWLANDERSON
wy. Taylors Lakes 233 C17
ROWLANDS
av. Noble Park 534 D3
st. Blairgowrie 679 E18
ROWSLEY
rd. Mt Eliza 625 H19
ROWSLEY STATION
rd. Maddingley 263 A13
ROWSON
ct. Altona Mdw 451 G5
gr. Clarinda 498 H12
rd. Chum Creek 212 G6
st. Boronia 423 L11
ROXANNE
cl. Scoresby 462 G8
pl. Newcomb 704 D18
ROXBURGH
ct. Epping 197 L17
rd. Wantirna 422 J8
st. Ascot Vale 324 A17
st. Preston 326 K6
ROXBURGH PARK
dr. Roxburgh Pk 193 L13
ROXBY
cl. Eltham 287 L10
ct. Berwick 553 L2
st. Epping 241 D3
st. Manifold Ht 702 C3
ROXLEY
pl. Mulgrave 501 G3
ROXY
cl. Berwick 554 K20
mw. Deer Park 318 K13
ROY
cl. Nar Warrn N 539 B12
ct. Boronia 423 D12
ct. Keysborough 534 L11
ct. Mt Eliza 626 A16
rd. Olinda 427 E17
st. Donvale 376 E5
st. Geelong 702 K5
st. Geelong 702 L5
st. Glenroy 280 E2
st. Melbourne 31 C15
st. Melbourne 414 B8
st. Oakleigh E 458 J16
ROYA
ct. Hoppers Csg 449 D2
ct. Mt Martha 656 L10
ROYADIE
rd. Blairgowrie 695 L5
ROYAL
arc. Melbourne 2 B13
arc. Melbourne 24 C8
av. Bonbeach 573 C2
av. Essendon N 279 G20
av. Glen Huntly 456 C9
av. Heathmont 378 L16
av. Heathmont 379 A16
av. Mooroolbark 337 F18
av. Portsea 678 A2
av. Sandringham 495 D17
av. Springvale 499 J15
av. Wandin East 341 A19
cr. Armadale 415 F11
cr. Camberwell 372 K19
cr. Hillside 232 A19
cr. Hillside 232 A20
cr. Officer 555 F19
ct. Ivanhoe 328 A9
ct. Jan Juc 711 D17
ct. Mt Waverley 418 H14
ct. Seabrook 450 L3
dr. Bangholme 549 K14
la. Fitzroy 18 L19
la. Melbourne 2 G13
la. Melbourne 24 E6
la. Surrey Hills 374 C20
pde. Carlton 17 J15
pde. Carlton N 17 K7
pde. Caulfield S 455 E6
pde. Emerald 469 L20
pde. Emerald 509 L1
pde. Parkdale 531 G15
pde. Parkville 17 J15
pde. Pascoe Vale S 324 L4
pde. Reservoir 283 A9
pl. Cremorne 26 E17
pl. S Morang 198 L13
rd. Bonbeach 573 C2
rd. Croydon S 379 J12

st. Mornington 640 D13
st. Up Fntree Gly 465 F9
tce. Highett 496 E12
ROYAL CHARLOTTE
dr. Patterson L, off Harbour Dr 547 H19
ROYALDEN
cl. Boronia 424 J8
ROYAL MELBOURNE
bvd. Burwood 418 B4
ROYAL PALMS
Aspendale Gdn 547 A4
ROYAL PINES
pl. Burwood 418 B4
ROYAL TROON
av. Heatherton 497 H16
pl. Heatherton 497 H16
ROYALTY
av. Highett 496 E16
st. Clayton 458 L18
ROYAN
mw. Point Cook 450 F11
ROYCLIFF
ct. Box Hill N 374 H9
ROYCROFT
av. Aspendale 546 D8
av. Burnside 318 E8
av. Highton 705 K3
av. Mill Park 242 E8
av. Wantirna S 422 D20
cl. Glen Waverley 461 A5
ct. Endeavour Hl 503 L20
ROYDEN
rd. Warrandyte 334 E6
ROYD GRANGE
ct. Belmont 702 E17
ROYDON
st. Hampton E 495 J7
ROYENA
ct. Warranwood 334 K12
rd. Moorabbin 496 J9
ROYLE
av. Kallista 467 C2
st. Frankston 599 H19
ROYLSTON
ri. Hurstbridge 203 D14
ROYMAR
ct. Wonga Park 336 D8
ROYSTON
av. Berwick 554 D2
av. Malvern East 416 C16
cl. Mill Park 242 F10
ct. Boronia 423 H14
ct. Brookfield 268 B6
ct. Carrum Downs 601 F1
ct. Kew 372 H9
ct. Mt Eliza 641 D4
pl. Caroline Spr 318 C5
pl. Gladstone Pk 237 C19
pl. Melbourne 2 D18
pl. Melbourne 24 E10
st. Diamond Ck 246 B13
st. View Bank 285 J20
ROYTON
st. Burwood E 419 G7
ROZELLE
av. Ringwood E 379 F14
ROZZY
pde. Narre Warren 539 D16
RUA
ct. Oakleigh 458 C7
RUABON
rd. Toorak 415 B8
RUARI
ct. Kurunjang 226 G14
RUBBER
la. Carrum Downs 574 J14
RUBEN
dr. Sydenham 274 J7
RUBENS
ct. Grovedale 705 J15
ct. Scoresby 462 C8
ct. Wheelers Hill 461 A15
gr. Canterbury 372 L16
gr. Canterbury 373 A16
pl. Templestowe 332 B9
RUBEO
dr. Altona Mdw 451 F3
RUBICON
av. Taylors Hill 274 K13
cr. Doncaster 375 E2
ct. Hallam 538 B20
ct. Sunbury 143 C11
pl. Epping 198 A20
pl. Werribee 448 C20
st. Dallas 238 C10
st. Reservoir 283 D14
RUBICON VALLEY
Montrose 381 L18

RUBIDA
ct. Boronia 424 E14
ct. Endeavour Hl 536 J1
dr. Langwarrin 629 K4
pl. St Albans 320 L8
RUBINA
ct. Noble Park N 501 D17
RUBITON
ct. Gisborne 79 G8
RUBUS
ct. Meadow Ht 193 J20
RUBY
cl. Rowville 503 B7
ct. Lalor 240 H6
ct. Meadow Ht 237 J5
pl. Berwick 554 J6
pl. Dingley Village 533 A4
pl. Werribee 447 H9
rd. Montrose 381 K14
st. Balwyn 373 D9
st. Burwood E 420 A9
st. Donvale 376 K5
st. Essendon W 322 L7
st. Hawthorn 371 K16
st. Ormond 455 L14
st. Preston 327 D3
RUCKER
st. Northcote 326 F19
RUDA
st. Doncaster 374 D2
RUDD
av. Torquay 711 L11
RUDDUCK
la. Coldstream 295 A7
st. Dromana 685 E11
st. McCrae 685 E11
RUDLOE
pl. Hampton Pk 551 F4
RUDOLF
ct. Dingley Village 533 A6
ct. Ringwood N 378 A5
RUDOLPH
st. Hoppers Csg 448 L3
st. Hoppers Csg 449 A3
RUDSTONE
bnd. Greenvale 192 J18
RUDYARD
ct. Lilydale 338 G13
st. Oakleigh S 497 F3
RUE DE GARE
Wandin N 340 K15
RUFFEY
st. Templestowe 330 H7
st. Templstw Lr 330 H7
RUFFINS
la. Geelong West 702 J6
RUFFLES
cl. Nar Warrn S 552 G15
ct. Cranbourne W 577 F17
RUFFORD
st. Sunshine N 321 D15
RUFFY
dr. Cranbourne 578 B18
RUFUS
ct. Narre Warren 539 D20
st. Epping 197 E20
RUGBY
ct. Doncaster E 332 B17
ct. Mt Eliza 625 L20
rd. Hughesdale 457 H8
st. Belmont 706 D1
RUHBANK
av. Balwyn 373 C13
RULE
cl. Mill Park 243 B4
st. Richmond 26 F7
RULLA
ct. Ferntree Gly 464 A7
RUMANN
av. Scoresby 462 H7
RUMBRIAH
rt. St Albans 321 B6
RUMPF
av. Balwyn N 374 A3
RUNCORN
cr. Deer Park 319 B13
RUNDELL
wy. Pakenham 584 D2
RUNDLE
dr. Carrum Downs 575 E14
dr. Carrum Downs 575 E15
RUNNYMEDE
la. Gisborne 109 A5
rd. Belgrave 466 E18
st. Doncaster E 331 L17
st. Mt Waverley 419 A13
RUNYAN
ct. Ringwood N 378 D2

RUPERT
ct. Broadmeadows 238 C20
ct. Thomastown 241 J14
dr. Mulgrave 500 J4
rd. E Warburton 306 L19
st. Brunswick E 326 B15
st. Collingwood 25 K2
st. Doncaster E 376 B2
st. Elsternwick 455 D10
st. Highett 496 B13
st. Mitcham 377 E15
st. Newport 411 C8
st. Parkdale 531 H12
st. Ringwood 378 H9
st. W Footscray 366 D7
RUPERTSDALE
rd. Sunbury 144 F6
RUPERTSWOOD
dr. Brookfield 267 J7
ri. Nar Warrn S 578 J1
RUPICOLA
ct. Hillside 274 B2
ct. Rowville 502 D5
RUSDEN
st. Brighton 454 J6
st. Elsternwick 454 J6
RUSH
ct. Altona 408 L15
pl. Carlton 18 D18
pl. Warrandyte 333 A1
RUSHALL
cr. Fitzroy N 326 F20
st. Fairfield 327 F17
RUSHCLIFFE
ct. Frankston 599 J15
RUSHDALE
ct. Kings Park 319 B1
ct. Mill Park 243 E7
st. Knoxfield 463 D7
RUSHFORD
la. Werribee 447 J15
RUSHMEAD
st. Malvern 415 L17
RUSHWOOD
dr. Craigieburn 194 L4
RUSHWORTH
st. Watsonia 285 F5
RUSKIN
av. Croydon 380 G5
cl. Templestowe 332 A12
ct. Bundoora 242 H17
ct. Eltham 288 A10
ct. Glen Iris 417 C8
rd. Glen Iris 417 C9
st. Elwood 454 C3
RUSS
ct. Wantirna S 423 A11
RUSSDANN
ct. Springvale S 533 L1
RUSSEL
st. Sunshine 365 C2
RUSSELL
av. Anglesea 713 D3
av. Berwick 554 E6
av. Mooroolbark 337 G18
cr. Boronia 423 D14
cr. Doncaster E 376 D4
cr. Mt Waverley 459 B5
cr. Sorrento 678 K12
ct. Altona Mdw 451 H5
ct. Brookfield 268 A7
ct. Dandenong S 536 C15
ct. Melbourne 24 H10
ct. Mentone 530 J6
ct. Woori Yallock 344 H13
la. Newcomb 704 B15
pl. Melbourne 2 H13
pl. Melbourne 24 F6
pl. Williamstown 411 D12
rd. Hawthorn E 372 G20
rd. Seville 341 H15
rd. Warrandyte 290 D20
st. Abbotsford 20 B20
st. Brunswick 325 E13
st. Bulleen 329 L9
st. Camberwell 372 L18
st. Campbellfield 239 A9
st. Caulfield S 455 H12
st. Coburg 325 H3
st. Cranbourne 604 F4
st. Darley 222 B9
st. Emerald 509 D4
st. Essendon 324 A9
st. Greensborough 286 A10
st. Ivanhoe 328 C16
st. McCrae 684 L15
st. Melbourne 2 J17
st. Melbourne 2 J20
st. Melbourne 4 J1
st. Melbourne 24 E2
st. Mt Evelyn 339 H16
st. Newtown 702 H11
st. Northcote 327 C17
st. Nunawading 376 E14
st. Prahran 414 L11
st. Preston 282 J18
st. Springvale 500 D8
st. Surrey Hills 374 B20
st. Toorak 415 J8
st. Tootgarook 698 B3
st. Werribee 447 H19
st. W Footscray 366 H8
RUSSELLS
pl. Hawthorn E 372 E18
RUSSELTON
st. Keilor Park 278 B14
RUSSET
ct. Keysborough 534 K11
ct. Lalor 241 A5
rd. Ringwood E 379 A12
RUSSETT
ct. Frankston 628 C8
RUSSLIE
ct. Glen Waverley 460 G11
RUSSO
pl. Kilsyth 381 B6
RUSTIC
ct. Thomastown 240 F17
dr. Bangholme 549 K14
dr. Boronia 424 E7
ri. Croydon N 336 A17
ri. Nar Warrn N 538 D10
RUTH
av. Sorrento 678 K8
ct. Bayswater 422 L8
ct. Glen Waverley 460 K5
ct. Melton S 268 J4
ct. Newcomb 704 E14
ct. Springvale S 499 F18
rd. Mornington 656 E3
st. Balwyn N 373 H1
st. Donvale 376 E5
st. Lalor 241 H10
st. St Albans 319 J2
st. Sunshine N 321 D16
RUTHERFORD
pde. Warneet 649 D15
pde. Warneet 649 G11
rd. Seaford 573 L19
rd. Tecoma 466 A11
rd. View Bank 285 H20
st. Maddingley 263 C7
wy. Roxburgh Pk 194 A13
RUTHERGLEN
cr. Gowanbrae 279 C4
rd. Vermont S 421 E9
st. Noble Park 534 G5
wy. Taylors Lakes 276 C7
RUTHVEN
cl. Hillside 232 G18
cr. Lalor 241 G7
st. Launching Pl 345 H17
st. Macleod 284 J16
st. Newtown 702 B7
st. Rosanna 284 J16
st. Sunbury 143 F8
wy. Ringwood E 379 E7
RUTLAND
av. Mt Eliza 625 J15
av. Templestowe 331 F7
ct. Altona Mdw 451 D5
ct. Keysborough 534 A8
rd. Berwick 554 F7
rd. Box Hill 374 L15
st. Braybrook 366 B4
st. Clifton Hill 20 D9
st. Newtown 702 G13
st. Niddrie 278 J20
RUTLEDGE
la. Melbourne 2 H18
la. Melbourne 24 G9
RUTMAN
cl. Werribee 447 L6
RUTTER
av. Healesville 213 K18
RUVINA
st. Aspendale 546 B2
RUYTON
ct. Sunbury 144 F10
dr. Rosebud W 698 L4
dr. Rosebud W 699 A4
st. Burwood 417 G6
st. Camberwell 417 G6
RYALL
ct. Doncaster 331 F18
RYAN
cl. Hoppers Csg 448 C2
ct. Bacchus Msh 221 L13
ct. Berwick 554 H12
ct. Ferntree Gly 463 K7
ct. Melton 268 K1
ct. Sunshine N 321 F18
gr. Blackburn S 419 K4
la. Caroline Spr 318 B5
la. Toolern Va 228 A3
mw. Dingley Village 533 C2
pl. Geelong, off
Myers St 703 A9
rd. Delahey 275 D11
rd. Seville E 343 C10
st. Brunswick E 326 B13
st. Coburg 281 F19
st. Diamond Ck 245 J8
st. Footscray 367 F7
st. Northcote 326 E15
st. Reservoir 282 H3
st. Seaford 600 A1
RYANS
la. Altona 409 A18
la. N Melbourne 17 E17
rd. Belgrave Ht 505 K3
rd. Belgrave S 505 J11
rd. Clayton S 498 J13
rd. Diamond Ck 245 E17
rd. Eltham 287 D8
rd. Eltham North 245 E17
rd. Eltham North 287 D2
rd. Healesville 213 C14
rd. Lysterfield 505 J11
rd. Melton 227 L17
rd. Pakenham 585 K12
rd. St Helena 245 E17
RYBURNE
av. Ashburton 417 C20
RYDAL
pl. Wheelers Hill 460 J16
RYDALDENE
wy. Berwick 554 E4
RYDE
av. Mt Eliza 625 K17
st. Preston 326 C5
RYDEN
cl. Greensborough 244 E16
RYDER
ct. Doncaster E 332 H10
ct. Frankston 628 F5
ct. Mt Waverley 458 L9
pl. Sunshine 365 E4
st. Lalor 241 B9
st. Niddrie 279 A20
st. Niddrie 322 L2
st. Niddrie 323 A2
st. Noble Park 501 D20
st. Sunshine W 364 K4
RYE
ct. Delahey 275 A13
ct. Glen Waverley 420 F15
st. Box Hill N 375 B6
st. Dallas 238 C9
st. Mitcham 377 D10
RYEBURNE
av. Hawthorn E 372 H16
RYECROFT
ct. Noble Park N 501 B12
ct. Vermont 421 B5
st. Brunswick W 324 J11
RYEFIELD
ct. Diamond Ck 246 A7
RYELANDS
dr. Berwick 553 D1
dr. Narre Warren 539 C20
dr. Narre Warren 553 D1
RYE OCEAN BEACH
rd. Rye 697 C15
RYLAND
av. Croydon 379 G1
cct. Delahey 275 C11
pl. Thomastown 240 G11
st. Ashburton 417 F14
st. Coburg N 281 F15
RYLANDES
dr. Gladstone Pk 236 K17
RYLANDS
pl. Wantirna 422 H8
rd. Dandenong 535 G4
RYLETT
ct. Frankston S 627 H16
RYLIE
la. Maribyrnong 322 J15
RYLSTON
ct. Mt Eliza 642 G1
RYLSTONE
st. Ferntree Gly 424 J19
RYMER
av. Safety Bch 669 D17
RYMILL
ct. Altona North 409 G3
RYONG
st. Grovedale 706 E15
RYRIE
ct. Lilydale 338 J8
ct. Montmorency 286 K11
la. Melbourne 1 J17
la. Melbourne 24 B10
pl. Vermont S 420 L13
pl. Wheelers Hill 461 G18
st. E Geelong 702 K7
st. Geelong 702 K7
st. Geelong 703 A8
st. Healesville 257 G1
RYTHDALE
dr. Glen Waverley 460 L4

S

SABASON
ct. Doncaster E 332 F20
SABATO
st. Croydon 380 J1
st. Rye 696 J10
SABINE
av. Dandenong N 501 H14
SABO
pl. Mt Martha 657 B9
SABOT
ct. Taylors Lakes 275 H7
SABRE
ct. Ferntree Gly 463 G7
ct. Narre Warren 553 C12
ct. Point Cook 450 E4
ct. Tullamarine 236 H20
SACHIKO
pl. Berwick 553 K17
SACKVILLE
rd. Mernda 198 L1
st. Collingwood 19 G13
st. Heidelberg Ht 328 D4
st. Kew 372 E12
st. Montmorency 286 L14
st. Safety Bch 668 L18
SACRAS
ct. Sydenham 275 A4
SADDLEBACK
rdg. Chirnside Pk 337 H6
SADDLERS
ct. Epping 198 D18
la. Geelong, off
Mercer St 702 K3
SADIE
ct. Noble Park 535 D1
st. Glenroy 280 J4
st. Mt Waverley 458 J6
SADLER
ct. Dingley Village 533 A3
st. Williamstown 410 L14
SAFFRON
ct. Burwood E 420 B10
dr. Hallam 538 C16
dr. Narre Warren 538 C16
dr. Narre Warren 538 G17
st. Newtown 702 H10
SAGAMORE
ct. Caulfield N 415 D17
SAGAN
ct. Glen Waverley 420 A15
SAGE
av. St Albans 321 A5
cl. Hillside 231 K18
ct. Langwarrin 601 J16
dr. Frankston S 627 B10
pl. Rowville 502 H4
st. Oakleigh E 458 G12
st. Pascoe Vale 280 L11
SAGES
rd. Baxter 643 G2
rd. Frankston S 643 G2
rd. Glenroy 281 D4
SAGOE
la. Box Hill 375 C15
SAGRAMORE
ct. Glen Waverley 420 L16
SAHARA
ct. Portsea 678 B4
SAHRA
ct. Epping 198 A15
SAILSBURY
st. Thomastown 241 J15
SAINSBURY
av. Greensborough 285 L7
av. Hillside 274 D3
ct. Greenvale 237 C6
ST AGNES
cl. Craigieburn 194 A2
ct. Avondale Ht 322 D9
ct. Carrum Downs 601 C4
ct. Glenroy 280 C5
ST ALBANS
rd. Breakwater 703 F13
rd. E Geelong 703 F13
rd. Kealba 276 K16
rd. Keilor 277 A11
rd. St Albans 320 D7
rd. Sunshine N 320 G12
rd. Thomson 703 F13
st. Mt Waverley 419 B19
ST AMBROSE
gr. Lilydale 338 K2
gr. Lilydale 339 C5
ST ANDREW
st. Sunshine W 364 J4
ST ANDREWS
av. Rosanna 285 A19
av. Rosebud 700 L2
cl. Carrum Downs 575 C15
cl. Croydon 380 J7
cr. Bulleen 329 F12
ct. Black Rock 529 G1
ct. Burwood 418 B4
ct. Chirnside Pk 292 H9
ct. Eltham North 245 D20
ct. Mt Waverley 458 J10
ct. Nar Warrn S 552 E20
ct. Rowville 502 B1
ct. Sunbury 144 E14
dr. Chirnside Pk 337 H5
dr. Craigieburn 193 L2
dr. Heatherton 497 H16
dr. Jan Juc 711 F13
dr. Rye 696 H5
dr. Sunshine N 321 H16
dr. Werribee 446 J17
pl. E Melbourne 25 A5
rd. Bayswater 423 D10
rd. Panton Hill 248 A8
st. Brighton 454 H17
st. N Melbourne 17 F19
st. Queenscliff 709 A19
wy. Darley 221 H1
ST ANDRIES
st. Camberwell 417 B7
ST ANNS
ct. Hoppers Csg 405 C19
ST ANTHONY
ct. Seabrook 450 H5
ST ANTHONYS
pl. Kew 371 L11
ST AUBIN
st. Beaumaris 530 G9
ST AUBINS
av. Caulfield N 415 B20
wy. Sorrento 678 J6
ST AUSTELL
ct. Craigieburn 194 H4
ct. Croydon Hills 335 G16
rd. Belgrave S 506 G5
ST BERNARDS
cr. Lynbrook 551 G18
ct. Wantirna S 422 L19
ct. Wantirna S 423 A19
dr. Keilor East 322 H5
rd. Alphington 327 L19
ST BOSWELLS
av. Berwick 554 C19
ST BRIDGETS
ri. Balwyn N 374 C5
ST CATHERINES
ct. Mornington 657 A2
dr. Highton 701 F20
la. Toorak 415 F4
ST CLAIR
bvd. Roxburgh Pk 194 A13
cr. Mt Waverley 419 H19
rd. Wantirna S 422 L10
rd. Wantirna S 423 A10
ST CLAIRE
av. S Morang 198 K15
wk. Doncaster E 332 B18
ST CLEMS
rd. Doncaster E 376 C6
st. Eltham North 245 C20
st. St Helena 245 B19
ST CLERE
ct. Frankston 628 F2
ST CLOUD
ct. Highton 701 H9
ct. Mt Waverley 458 J9
ST COLUMBS
st. Hawthorn 372 B18
ST CRISPIN
st. Richmond 26 G17
ST CUTHBERTS
av. Dingley Village 533 D9
ST DAVID
st. Fitzroy 19 C15
st. Northcote 326 L12
st. Thornbury 326 L12
st. Thornbury 326 L9
ST DAVIDS
dr. Wantirna 422 F5
ST DENYS
cr. Wonga Park 291 J18

ST DUTHUS
st. Preston 282 F19
ST EDMONDS
gr. Glen Iris 416 F10
rd. Prahran 32 B20
rd. Prahran 414 G10
ST ELMO
av. Ferntree Gly 424 F17
cr. Highton 701 F18
rd. Ivanhoe 328 D11
ST ELMOS
cl. Rosebud W 699 C5
ST FAITHS
rd. Montmorency 286 K8
ST FILLANS
ct. Frankston 628 B7
ST FINBARS
cr. Brighton East 455 E19
ST FORT
ct. Harkaway 540 G15
ST GABRIEL
pl. Highton 701 E16
ST GEORGE
av. Montrose 382 G9
ct. Frankston 600 B19
ST GEORGES
av. Bentleigh E 456 K20
av. Caroline Spr 317 K3
av. Caroline Spr 317 K4
av. Mont Albert 374 D17
av. Templestowe 331 A11
av. Templstw Lr 331 A11
cr. Ashburton 417 B18
cr. Croydon 380 F4
ct. Brighton East 455 C20
ct. Glen Waverley 461 A5
ct. Greensborough 244 G16
ct. Highton 701 F19
ct. Hoppers Csg 448 E9
ct. Parkdale 531 H9
ct. Toorak 415 E5
ct. Fitzroy N, off St Georges Rd 326 D19
gr. Parkville 34 J4
rd. Armadale 415 F14
rd. Beaconsfld Up 541 K9
rd. Elsternwick 454 L4
rd. Elsternwick 455 A4
rd. Fitzroy N 19 D2
rd. Fitzroy N 326 C20
rd. Northcote 326 E15
rd. Preston 326 H3
rd. Thornbury 326 H3
rd. Toorak 415 C1
rd. Whittlesea 96 H2
rd.s, Fitzroy N 19 A6
ST GOTHARDS
rd. Alphington 327 L20
ST HELENA
pl. Ferntree Gly 464 B12
rd. Briar Hill 286 D2
rd. Eltham North 245 B17
rd. Greensborough 244 K20
rd. Greensborough 286 D2
rd. St Helena 244 K20
rd. St Helena 245 B17
ST HELENS
cr. Nar Warrn N 538 D12
ct. Vermont 421 D4
rd. Hawthorn E 416 E3
ST HELIERS
st. Abbotsford 20 J15
ST HELLIER
st. Heidelberg Ht 328 D4
ST HUBERT
rd. Ivanhoe East 328 K15
ST HUBERTS
rd. Carnegie 456 F7
rd. Yering 253 E17
ST IVES
av. Frankston S 627 D17
ct. Croydon Hills 335 G17
ct. The Basin 425 A8
gr. Mt Martha 656 A17
pl. Melton W 226 B15
rd. Bentleigh E 456 H19
ST JAMES
av. Bentleigh 456 F18
av. Kallista 467 C1
av. Mont Albert 374 E17
av. Montrose 382 F9
av. Springvale 499 H14
cl. Brighton 454 J11
cr. Mt Eliza 641 H4
ct. Blackburn S 419 G2
ct. Doncaster E 332 D10
ct. Narre Warren 553 D10
ct. Wantirna S 422 K14
ct. Watsonia 285 G9
la. Melbourne 1 C15
la. Melbourne 23 K10
mw. Brighton 454 J12
pde. Elsternwick 455 A9
pl. Kew 371 H12
pl. Toorak 415 F8
rd. Armadale 415 F13
rd. Heidelberg 328 J3
rd. Heidelberg 329 A3
rd. Rosanna 329 A3
rd. Rosanna 329 C3
st. Geelong West 702 F6
st. Hadfield 281 B6
st. Moonee Pnd 324 A10
tce. Hawthorn, off Isabella Gr 371 E17
wk. Caroline Spr 317 K3
ST JAMES PARK
dr. Brighton 454 J13
ST JAMES WOOD
dr. Tarneit 405 D12
ST JOHN
cir. Chirnside Pk 292 G10
pl. Melton W 226 E17
pl. Rowville 462 L17
pl. Rowville 463 A17
st. Windsor 32 A20
st. Windsor 414 F10
ST JOHNS
av. Camberwell 416 K2
av. Croydon 380 F4
av. Frankston 627 G5
av. Mont Albert 374 E17
av. Springvale 499 J16
ct. Narre Warren 553 D9
ct. Reservoir 283 G2
la. Melbourne 1 H10
la. Melbourne 23 L7
la. Mt Eliza 626 C15
la. Toorak 415 A9
pde. Kew 372 A11
pl. N Melbourne 17 F17
rd. Bulla 190 H8
rd. Oaklands Jctn 190 H8
rd. Warburton 349 E2
rd. Wonga Park 335 G4
wy. Mulgrave 500 C5
ST JOHNS WOOD
Skye 575 G16
rd. Blairgowrie 695 H3
rd. Mt Waverley 418 K17
tce. Berwick 554 C19
ST KILDA
av. Upwey 465 J9
rd. Melbourne 2 E20
rd. Melbourne 4 D19
rd. Melbourne 24 G13
rd. Melbourne 31 B8
rd. Melbourne 413 L1
rd. Prahran 414 C10
rd. St Kilda 414 C10
st. Baxter 644 L3
st. Brighton 454 F15
st. Elwood 454 F15
st. Mt Eliza 642 C8
ST KILIAN
st. Hampton 494 L5
ST KINNORD
st. Aberfeldie 323 F10
ST KYRILLOS
pl. Hallam 538 E17
ST LAWRANCE
wy. Rowville 463 E16
ST LAWRENCE
cl. Werribee 447 G6
ST LEGER
pl. Epping 198 E18
ri. Bundoora 284 E4
ST LEONARDS
av. St Kilda 414 A16
av. Yarraville 366 H18
av. Yarraville 366 J18
cl. Noble Park 534 C3
cl. South Yarra 31 H1
cl. South Yarra 370 D20
cl. South Yarra 414 D1
pl. St Kilda, off St Leonards Av 414 B15
rd. Ascot Vale 323 J16
rd. Healesville 213 L17
rd. Selby 467 E16
ST LOUIS
pl. Thomastown 240 E13
pl. Burnley, off Cherrill St 371 B20
ST LUKE
st. S Melbourne 30 B3
ST MALO
av. Doncaster 330 D17
st. Prahran 32 K20
st. Prahran 414 L10
ST MARGARETS
pl. Berwick 554 G10
rd. Healesville 258 E4
ST MARK
av. Montrose 382 H7
ST MARKS
cl. Dingley Village 533 E7
ST MARTINS
cl. Kooyong 415 L5
ct. Wantirna S 462 C5
la. South Yarra 31 E6
pl. S Morang 198 K13
pl. South Yarra 31 E5
ST MARYS
pl. Dromana 686 B9
ST MATTHEWS
la. Geelong, off Walls St 703 D12
ST MICHAEL
st. Tarneit 405 D12
ST MICHAELS
wk. Melbourne 2 L15
wk. Melbourne 24 G7
ST MICHEL
cl. Avondale Ht 322 C7
ST MITCHELL
cct. Mornington 641 D16
ST MUIR
dr. Warrandyte 332 K4
ST NEOTS
av. Northcote 326 J16
ST NINIANS
ct. Brighton 454 E14
rd. Brighton 454 E13
ST PATRICKS
al. Melbourne 1 H11
al. Melbourne, off Little Bourke St 23 L7
pl. Lilydale 338 K2
pl. Lilydale 339 C5
ST PAULS
rd. Sorrento 678 H14
ST PETERS
cl. Carrum Downs 575 D14
ct. Bentleigh E 497 A2
ST PHILLIP
st. Brunswick E 325 K17
ST PHILLIPS
pl. Box Hill N 374 L7
st. Abbotsford 20 D19
ST RAFAEL
pl. Whittlesea 96 F16
ST RAPHAEL
st. Avondale Ht 322 B9
ST REMO
pl. Dromana 686 H8
ST RONANS
ct. Eltham 287 C6
ct. Sunbury 144 F1
rd. Glen Waverley 460 G9
SAINTSBURY
cr. Dandenong N 501 J13
ST SHENOUDA
ct. Hallam 538 E16
ct. Hallam 538 F16
ST THOMAS
av. Wantirna 422 E5
ST VIGEONS
rd. Reservoir 283 D5
ST VINCENT
pl. Albert Park 29 G10
pl.n, Albert Park 29 G9
pl.s, Albert Park 29 G10
pl.s, Albert Park 413 D5
st. Albert Park 29 C11
st. Albert Park 413 B6
st. Caulfield E 456 E5
ST WARDEN
ct. Keilor Dn 275 L13
SALADIN
av. Glen Waverley 459 K7
SALAMANDER
av. Thomastown 240 H16
dr. Taylors Lakes 275 G1
SALCOMBE
ct. Craigieburn 194 D2
SALDANNA
wy. Sorrento 679 B15
SALE
ct. Dallas 238 H8
SALEM
av. Oakleigh S 497 H2
ct. Vermont S 420 J7
SALERNO
wy. Rowville 502 H5
SALFORD
av. Balwyn 373 E14
ct. Grovedale 706 F9
ct. Mulgrave 500 H1
mw. Caroline Spr 317 K2
SALI
ct. Oakleigh S 497 K8
SALIBA
ct. Sunshine W 364 H8
SALICINA
ct. Endeavour Hl 502 K19
SALICKI
av. Epping 241 E4
SALIGNA
ct. Langwarrin 629 K1
dr. Tullamarine 278 C9
wk. Vermont S 420 L11
wk. Vermont S 421 A11
SALIGNUS
ct. Narre Warren 539 C20
SALINA
wk. Caroline Spr 318 B3
SALISBURY
av. Blackburn 375 E17
av. Cockatoo 511 D11
av. Ivanhoe 328 A16
av. Mont Albert 374 D16
av. Warburton 306 A20
bnd. Lilydale 338 K2
bnd. Lilydale 339 C5
cr. Fitzroy N 19 B2
ct. Glen Waverley 459 H10
ct. Heathmont 378 L19
ct. Heathmont 379 A19
ct. Hillside 231 J18
ct. Sydenham 274 J2
ct. Wantirna 422 G15
gr. Hawthorn 372 A14
gr. Northcote 326 K12
rd. Ashwood 418 C18
rd. Beaconsfld Up 542 G16
st. Balwyn 373 C14
st. Brighton 454 J6
st. Caulfield N 415 G18
st. Coburg 325 K3
st. Essendon N 279 F20
st. Glenroy 280 A4
st. Moonee Pnd 324 E10
st. Newport 410 H9
st. Richmond 26 G6
st. Sandringham 495 F13
st. Sunshine N 321 G13
st. Up Fntree Gly 465 D7
st. Werribee 447 K15
st. Yarraville 366 L18
SALLY
cl. Wantirna S 422 C17
ct. Mt Eliza 642 A9
ct. Newcomb 704 E13
ct. Warranwood 334 J14
ct. Woori Yallock 344 G13
SALLY FRANCIS
ct. Scoresby 462 C9
SALMON
av. Essendon 323 L3
rd. Boronia 423 F15
st. Mentone 530 L6
st. Mentone 531 A6
st. Port Melb 368 C18
SALMON BAY
Patterson L 573 G8
SALMOND
st. Deer Park 319 A12
SALONIKA
st. Sorrento 679 A12
SALSBURG
ct. Vermont S 421 C14
SALTA
dr. Altona North 408 J10
SALTAIR
ct. Berwick 554 H20
st. Hampton E 495 J10
SALTAIRE
la. Mornington 640 G20
SALTAU
st. Keilor East 322 C5
SALTBUSH
ct. Rowville 502 L2
ct. Sunshine W 364 D8
gld. Frankston 600 A16
st. Point Cook 450 K11
SALTER
st. Essendon 324 A5
SALTERS RUSH
rd. Smiths Gly 206 B5
SALTLEY
st. S Kingsville 410 E3
SALTMARSH
pl. St Albans 319 F6
SALTRAM
ct. Carrum Downs 575 D20
SALTWATER
cr. Maribyrnong 322 G16
SALUATORE
ct. Sunshine W 364 B8
SALURN
ct. Vermont S 420 L13
ct. Vermont S 421 A13
SALVANA
av. Mitcham 376 L10
ct. Taylors Lakes 233 B19
SALVIA
ct. Rosebud 700 G2
ct. Warranwood 334 H14
st. St Albans 320 G8
SALWEEN
cr. Roxburgh Pk 194 D7
SAM
cl. Endeavour Hl 537 J2
SAMADA
st. Frankston 627 G4
st. Notting Hill 459 H13
SAMAHER
ct. Endeavour Hl 537 L1
SAMANTHA
cl. Wheelers Hill 461 C13
cr. Cranbourne N 578 H8
ct. Frankston 628 D9
ct. Gisborne 79 D11
ct. Knoxfield 463 C10
ct. Templestowe 331 J13
dr. Mornington 641 C17
pl. Yallambie 286 A12
SAMARA
gr. Gladstone Pk 279 A2
SAMARI
cl. Keilor 276 K13
SAMARIA
st. Dandenong N 501 H14
SAMARINDA
av. Ashburton 417 G16
SAMBELA
st. Kensington 33 E11
SAMBELL
rd. Sunbury 113 D20
SAMBETH
wk. Kensington 33 E12
SAMBUCO
ct. Sydenham 274 J3
SAMOS
ct. Whittington 704 D19
SAMPSON
dr. Mt Waverley 459 C7
la. Melbourne 1 H6
la. Melbourne 23 K5
SAMS
wy. Toorak 32 L16
SAMSON
st. Hadfield 281 A7
SAMUEL
cl. Berwick 539 H19
cl. Mt Martha 656 C9
cl. Wheelers Hill 461 E12
ct. Bentleigh E 497 C2
ct. Bundoora 242 F19
ct. Werribee 447 K7
dr. Campbellfield 239 J12
la. Melbourne 1 H17
la. Melbourne 24 B10
rd. Blackburn S 419 G7
st. Blairgowrie 679 D18
st. Brunswick 325 K14
st. Croydon 336 A20
st. Ringwood 378 G10
SAMUEL BEAVIS
pl. Croydon Hills 335 G15
SAMUEL EVANS
ct. Seabrook 450 L8
SAN ANGELO
rd. Research 289 E11
SAN ANTONIO
ct. Mentone 531 C13
SAN CARLOS
wk. Croydon, off Main St 380 B4
SANCTUARY
cl. Balwyn 373 H11
cl. Werribee 447 D18
ct. Lilydale 338 C13
dr. Bundoora 284 F8
pl. Aspendale Gdn 546 F2
pl. Templestowe 332 F2
ri. Mickleham 150 B1
ri. Narre Warren 538 G15
wy. Beaconsfield 555 B12
wy. Beaconsfield 555 D13
SANCTUARY LAKES
bvd. Point Cook 450 K12
SANCTUARY LAKES SOUTH
bvd. Point Cook 451 A13
SANCTUARY PARK
dr. Rosebud W 699 C4
SANDALA
ct. Dandenong N 502 A18
SANDALONG
ct. Bonbeach 573 C5

SANDALWOOD
av. Hillside 232 E19
dr. Narre Warren 553 C2
dr. Oakleigh S 498 A8
rt. Frankston S 628 A17
SANDARA
ct. Mt Eliza 625 K12
SANDAY
st. Glen Waverley 460 G4
SAND DUNE
ri. Torquay 712 G1
SANDELLS
rd. Tecoma 466 C12
SANDEMAN
pl. Fitzroy 19 E17
SANDERLING
cr. Mornington 640 L16
ct. Rosebud W 699 F4
st. Werribee 448 A10
SANDERS
av. Sunshine W 364 K6
av. Sunshine W 365 A5
ct. Narre Warren 553 B11
pl. Richmond 26 F19
rd. Box Hill 375 C17
rd. Doncaster E 332 F19
rd. Frankston S 627 F11
rd. Frankston S 627 G11
SANDERSON
st. Yarraville 366 E15
SANDFIELD
dr. Carrum Downs 601 B2
SANDFORD
av. Sunshine N 320 L13
av. Sunshine N 321 A13
cl. Rowville 503 D7
ct. Meadow Ht 237 K5
gr. Yarraville 367 D16
st. Highett 496 F13
SANDGATE
av. Croydon 335 G18
av. Frankston 627 J7
av. Glen Waverley 459 H7
bvd. Ferntree Gly 463 E4
pl. Berwick 554 J8
rd. Blackburn S 419 H3
SANDHAM
st. Elsternwick 455 B4
rd. Westmeadows 236 F14
st. Elsternwick 455 A4
SANDHURST
cr. Bundoora 284 K1
cr. Jan Juc 711 B19
ct. Eltham North 245 K19
ct. Wheelers Hill 461 B7
gr. Warranwood 335 A13
mw. Hampton Pk 552 B11
rd. Wantirna 422 G13
st. Doncaster E 331 H18
SANDILANDS
ct. Narre Warren 539 H15
st. S Melbourne 30 G7
st. S Melbourne 413 J4
SANDLEFORD
ct. Sunbury 142 F10
?. Dingley Village 533 B10
SANDLEWOOD
ct. Grovedale 706 C8
ct. Kings Park 275 D17
la. Point Cook 450 L10
SANDON
ct. Forest Hill 420 D2
SANDOVER
dr. Roxburgh Pk 194 C5
dr. Roxburgh Pk 194 D5
wy. Taylors Lakes 233 G19
SANDOWEN
av. Burwood E 419 L11
SANDOWN
?. Mill Park 242 L13
ct. Somerville 644 H14
rd. Ascot Vale 33 C1
rd. Ascot Vale 324 A20
rd. Springvale 500 A13
rd. Brighton 454 E15
SANDPIPER
cl. Blind Bight 650 E8
cl. Chelsea Ht 547 F19
ct. Boronia 424 A11
ct. Rosebud W 699 E4
dr. Taylors Lakes 275 H3
gr. Maribyrnong 322 H15
pl. Frankston 628 B2
pl. Williamstown 410 K17
st. St Albans 319 G9
st. Werribee 448 D10
wy. Mt Eliza 641 K5
wy. S Morang 199 J13
SANDRA
av. Eltham 287 D7
av. Fawkner 281 E1
av. Noble Park 534 E2
ct. Croydon 336 H14
ct. Donvale 332 K17
ct. Knoxfield 462 K5
ct. Langwarrin 601 L19
ct. Rye 696 L4
ct. Somerville 645 B14
ct. Wheelers Hill 460 E15
gr. Bentleigh 496 E6
st. Balwyn N 329 J19
st. Bulleen 329 F17
st. Doveton 537 B8
st. Forest Hill 420 B4
st. Kings Park 275 E19
st. Melton 268 G1
SANDRIDGE
av. Port Melb 412 B5
ct. Patterson L 573 K10
SANDRINGHAM
pde. Newtown 701 L13
rd. Sandringham 495 B14
st. Wantirna 422 C5
SANDSTONE
av. Seabrook 450 K7
ct. Delahey 275 A15
SANDTOFT
ct. Highton 705 K8
SANDVYK
ct. Scoresby 462 B8
SANDWELL
ct. Caroline Spr 317 J3
SANDWICH
av. Jan Juc 711 G15
SANDY
ct. Cannons Creek 649 D8
ct. Dandenong N 501 F18
ct. Noble Park 534 C6
ct. Portsea 678 D3
ct. Taylors Lakes 275 K7
pl. Maribyrnong 323 A13
rd. St Andrews Bch 697 F20
st. Nunawading 376 D12
wyn. Kilsyth S 381 A20
SANDY POINT
rd. Point Cook 450 J13
SANG
ct. Ringwood 378 J4
SANGLEN
tce. Belmont 701 K20
SANICKI
ct. Bentleigh E 497 F8
SANIKY
st. Notting Hill 459 H12
SAN LEANDRO
dr. Reservoir 283 F2
SAN MARCO
la. W Melbourne 17 G20
SAN MARTIN
dr. Croydon N 335 K16
SAN REMO
dr. Avondale Ht 322 E9
dr. Werribee 447 C8
rd. Ringwood N 378 D6
SANSOM
ct. Taylors Lakes 233 D17
st. Gisborne 79 D16
SANTA BARBARA
dr. Frankston 600 C16
SANTA CRUZ
bvd. Roxburgh Pk 194 D7
SANTA MONICA
bvd. Pt Lonsdale 710 D1
dr. Keilor Lodge 276 C4
SANTARAM
st. Bentleigh E 457 G17
SANTA ROSA
bvd. Doncaster E 332 G11
SANTED
ct. Rowville 462 E20
SANTIAGO
st. Doncaster 374 F2
st. St Albans 320 H10
SANTLEY
cl. Mill Park 242 G10
SANTOLIN
ct. Hillside 274 F3
SANTON
st. Greensborough 285 J5
SANTOS
ct. Keilor Dn 276 F17
SAPLING
tce. St Albans 319 G6
SAPPHIRE
av. Boronia 424 K11
cl. Point Cook 451 B13
ct. Glen Waverley 420 G17
ct. Lower Plenty 286 H14
ct. Narre Warren 539 G13
ct. Werribee 446 L15
ct. Werribee 447 A15
dr. Hampton Pk 551 C10
st. Essendon W 323 A6
st. Forest Hill 420 H3
st. Niddrie 323 A6
st. Preston 327 D1
SARA
av. Brighton East 495 F1
ct. Bayswater N 380 F20
ct. Fawkner 239 G20
ct. Noble Park 534 C6
dr. Wheelers Hill 461 C17
gr. Tottenham 365 K9
pl. Aspendale Gdn 546 F2
rd. Scoresby 462 G9
st. Pt Lonsdale 707 H20
st. Rye 696 G9
SARABANDE
cr. Torquay 711 J8
SARAH
cl. Clayton S 499 D15
cr. Templestowe 331 F9
ct. Eltham North 245 G18
ct. Kurunjang 226 H13
ct. Montrose 381 L10
ct. Nar Warrn S 552 L14
ct. Pakenham 559 E19
ct. Vermont 420 L4
ct. Vermont 421 A4
ct. Wantirna S 462 A4
pl. Frankston S 627 J10
pl. Hampton Pk 551 L9
st. Black Rock 529 F1
st. Campbellfield 239 H10
SARATOGA
cr. Keilor Dn 275 J12
SARAZEN
st. Rye 696 J3
SARDINE
st. Port Melb 411 G2
SARGASSO
av. Keysborough 534 G16
SARGENT
st. Doncaster 374 J5
st. Geelong West 702 F2
SARGON
gr. Brighton 454 L9
gr. Brighton 455 A9
SARGOOD
ct. Endeavour Hl 537 K8
st. Altona 409 C19
st. Coburg 325 G4
st. Hampton 495 D11
st. Toorak 415 D8
SARI
la. Hampton E 496 A6
SARIC
ct. Plumpton 273 D14
SARNIA
ct. Narre Warren 539 D15
SARNO
ct. Cranbourne 603 K2
SARONA
st. Dandenong 536 E8
SARONG
st. Watsonia 285 F10
SARONVALE
cr. Hillside 274 F1
SAROSE
ct. Dingley Village 532 L5
SARSHAS
wy. Mt Martha 657 B7
SARTON
rd. Clayton 499 G1
SARTORI
st. Burwood E 419 G8
SARTRE
ct. Glen Waverley 420 A14
SARZANA
st. Mentone 531 E5
SASH
cl. Carrum Downs 601 E4
SASHA
ct. Hallam 538 D20
ct. Langwarrin 629 K5
ct. Tullamarine 278 H1
ct. Werribee 446 L10
pl. Noble Park N 501 B10
SASKIA
ct. Greensborough 243 L20
SASSAFRAS
ct. Boronia 424 H16
dr. Frankston 600 J19
dr. Sunbury 143 D17
dr. Templstw Lr 330 H13
SASSAFRAS CREEK
rd. Olinda 426 H14
rd. Olinda 427 A18
rd. Sassafras 426 H14
rd. Sherbrooke 426 H14
rd. Sherbrooke 427 A18
SASSELLA
st. Deer Park 319 C13
st. Oakleigh S 497 E3
SASSES
av. Bayswater 423 D10
SATELBERG
ct. Heidelberg W 328 A2
SATIN
st. Bundoora 242 D15
SATORI
ct. Ferntree Gly 464 A7
SATTERLEY
cl. Endeavour Hl 537 B5
SATTERLY
wy. Roxburgh Pk 194 B14
SATURN
ct. Wheelers Hill 460 L19
st. Balwyn N 373 F2
st. Caulfield S 455 E10
st. Newcomb 704 D15
tce. Doncaster E 332 E17
SAUER
rd. New Gisborne 79 F2
SAUL
ct. Greensborough 285 J10
SAUNDERS
cl. Rowville 463 K18
ct. Roxburgh Pk 193 L14
rd. New Gisborne 79 C4
st. Clayton S 499 F9
st. Coburg 325 B7
SAUVAGE
cr. Burnside 318 E4
wy. S Morang 198 J13
SAVAGE
ct. Nunawading 376 K10
ct. Werribee 446 J18
st. Belmont 701 L20
st. Pakenham 584 J9
SAVANNA
ct. Berwick 554 C3
dr. Mooroolbark 337 C10
SAVANNAH
cr. Epping 197 L19
ct. Frankston 599 K15
pl. Chadstone 458 E4
SAVARIS
ct. Donvale 377 B6
SAVERNAKE
ct. Doncaster E 332 D7
SAVIGE
av. Mt Waverley 459 H2
rd. Yallambie 285 G13
st. Ascot Vale 324 B19
st. Newport 410 F6
SAVILLE
ct. Ferntree Gly 463 L12
ct. Rye 697 G3
ct. Tarneit 405 C12
ct. Templestowe 330 L9
pl. S Morang 198 K14
st. Ferny Creek 466 B1
SAVIO
st. Chadstone 458 C3
SAVONA
st. Mentone 531 D7
SAWLEY
gr. Wyndham Va 446 E13
SAWREY
pl. Mill Park 242 L9
pl. Mill Park 243 A9
SAXBY
ct. Burnside 318 D6
ct. Wantirna S 422 K13
rd. Glen Iris 416 L15
SAXIL
ct. Seaford 599 K1
gr. Healesville 212 H14
SAXON
av. Wantirna 422 F12
ct. Oakleigh 458 D8
dr. Mooroolbark 337 J18
st. Brunswick 325 F15
st. Burwood E 419 H12
st. Doncaster 331 A18
st. Rye 696 D7
SAXON WOOD
dr. Vermont S 420 F7
SAXONWOOD
ct. Ferntree Gly 424 J17
ct. Frankston 628 C12
dr. Doncaster E 331 K17
dr. Narre Warren 553 B8
SAXONY
ct. Mulgrave 500 J2
SAXTON
st. Box Hill N 374 J9
SAYERS
la. Brighton 454 H19
rd. Ferny Creek 465 K5
rd. Hoppers Csg 405 A12
rd. Laverton 406 D13
rd. Laverton N 406 D13
rd. Tarneit 405 A12
rd. Truganina 405 G12
rd. Upwey 465 K5
SAYLE
st. Yarra Glen 252 L3
SAYVON
ct. Dromana 686 C9
SCAMMEL
st. Campbellfield 194 J20
SCAMMELL
cl. Mt Waverley 459 F4
cr. Torquay 712 D3
SCAMPTON
cr. Tullamarine 278 J2
ct. Highton 705 J7
SCANLAN
st. Bentleigh E 497 C7
st. Berwick 554 G8
SCARBOROUGH
av. Craigieburn 149 K17
av. Cranbourne W 603 G3
av. Cranbourne W 603 H1
cl. Pt Lonsdale 707 H18
dr. Hampton E 495 H10
dr. Heidelberg 329 G2
dr. Nar Warrn S 552 G18
dr. Patterson L 573 G6
gr. Beaumaris 530 G7
pl. Kensington 34 C7
rd. Epping 197 K18
rd. Vermont S 420 H8
sq. Mont Albert N 374 E7
wy. Kings Park 319 C2
SCARLET
dr. Bundoora 242 D13
dr. Doveton 536 H6
st. Mordialloc 532 A11
SCARLET ASH
ct. Eltham 288 C10
dr. Templstw Lr 330 G14
SCARLET OAK
ct. Blackburn S 420 B6
SCARLETT
av. Carrum Downs 575 G14
st. Geelong West 702 F3
SCENIC
av. Ringwood E 379 B14
cr. Eltham 287 E4
cr. Kalorama 383 C10
ct. Croydon N 335 K14
ct. Dandenong N 501 K11
ct. Ferntree Gly 463 G6
ct. Gisborne 79 C10
dr. Ashwood 418 C15
dr. Beaconsfield 555 C11
dr. Launching Pl 345 G14
dr. Point Cook 451 A8
pl. Arthurs Seat 685 L13
pl. Kealba 276 L19
pl. Kealba 277 A19
pl. Maribyrnong 323 A12
rd. Highton 701 E18
rd. Wandana Ht 701 E18
ri. Doncaster 330 L16
ri. Eltham North 245 E16
tce. Craigieburn 150 E7
SCENIC VIEW
dr. Mt Martha 669 F2
SCENTBARK
ct. Launching Pl 345 F14
SCEPTRE
ct. Taylors Lakes 275 J8
SCHAEFFER
rd. Hurstbridge 203 F16
SCHAFTER
dr. Doncaster E 332 G9
SCHANCK
pl. Endeavour Hl 537 D5
SCHEELE
st. Surrey Hills 374 A14
SCHERMAN
dr. Altona Mdw 451 K6
SCHILD
st. Yarraville 367 D16
SCHMIDT
ct. Seaford 600 A1
SCHNAPPER POINT
dr. Mornington 640 C11
SCHNEIDER
cr. Clarinda 498 C8
st. Ferntree Gly 424 K20
SCHOFIELD
st. Essendon 323 L4
st. Moorabbin 496 D9
SCHOLTZ
rd. Christmas Hills 206 G19

SCHONING
ct. Croydon N 335 L10
SCHOOL
ct. Glenroy 280 C10
ct. Nar Warrn S 552 F17
la. Brunswick W 324 L12
la. Bulla 189 L16
la. Christmas Hills 250 L1
la. Diggers Rest 187 E14
la. Ferny Creek 466 A3
la. Maddingley 264 G10
la. Tarrawarra 211 G18
la. Yarra Jctn 346 J14
rd. Ferny Creek 465 J1
rd. Menzies Ck 467 L15
rd. Olinda 426 L9
rd. Olinda 427 A9
rd. Seville 342 A12
rd. Silvan 384 J16
rd. Tremont 465 C6
rd. Up Fntree Gly 465 C6
st. Blackburn S 375 E20
st. Blackburn S 419 E1
st. Geelong 703 A11
wk. Croydon S 380 C13
SCHOOLHALL
st. Oakleigh 457 J14
SCHOOL HOUSE
rd. Woori Yallock 344 B19
rd. Woori Yallock 345 A20
SCHOOLHOUSE
la. Sunbury 143 G19
SCHOONER BAY
dr. Frankston 628 E7
dr. Patterson L 573 G8
SCHOTTERS
rd. Mernda 155 L18
SCHULER
ct. Narre Warren 552 G2
SCHULZ
st. Bentleigh E 496 K6
SCHUTT
ct. Williamstown 410 L15
dr. Rye 696 K14
st. Newport 410 K7
SCIENCE
dr. Bundoora 284 C12
SCOBLE
ct. Vermont 420 L3
pl. Narre Warren 539 E19
st. Frankston S 626 L8
SCONE
cl. Eltham North 245 C18
SCORESBY
rd. Bayswater 423 H12
rd. Ferntree Gly 463 E1
SCOTCH
cct. Hawthorn 416 C3
ct. Sunbury 144 F11
pde. Bonbeach 547 B17
pde. Bonbeach 573 D1
pde. Chelsea 547 B17
SCOTCHMANS CREEK
rd. Warburton 349 D4
SCOTCHMER
st. Fitzroy N 326 B20
SCOTIA
cr. Keysborough 534 C7
gr. South Yarra 32 C13
gr. South Yarra 414 G7
st. Moonee Pnd 323 H14
st. N Melbourne 17 C16
st. Preston 326 E4
SCOTLAND
av. Greensborough 285 L3
st. Braybrook 366 B5
SCOTSBURN
av. Clayton 498 F2
av. Oakleigh S 498 F2
cl. Mulgrave 501 E6
ct. Grovedale 706 G15
ct. Mornington 657 C2
gr. Toorak 415 G6
gr. Werribee 447 H13
st. Hawthorn 415 J1
wy. Endeavour Hl 537 G2
SCOTSGATE
wy. Berwick 554 K9
SCOTSMORE
rd. Springvale S 534 A5
SCOTT
al. Melbourne 2 D18
al. Melbourne, off Flinders La 24 E10
av. Clayton S 499 E12
av. St Albans 319 L5
cl. Hallam 537 K14
cl. Templestowe 332 C12
ct. Altona Mdw 451 K4
ct. Patterson L 547 G20
ct. Wantirna S 422 L20
ct. Wantirna S 423 A20
gr. Burwood 418 A10
gr. Glen Iris 416 F13
gr. Kingsbury 283 H10
gr. Somerville 644 L13
rd. Cranbourne S 603 C20
rd. Cranbourne S 630 L5
rd. Laverton N 407 L3
rd. Yarra Glen 208 K10
st. Anglesea 713 L3
st. Beaumaris 530 C11
st. Belmont 702 E19
st. Blairgowrie 696 A2
st. Canterbury 373 E20
st. Caulfield S 455 K12
st. Cranbourne 604 C4
st. Dandenong 535 J8
st. Dromana 686 B10
st. Elwood 454 F3
st. Essendon 323 H11
st. Hampton E 496 B11
st. Hawthorn 416 C2
st. Heathmont 422 E3
st. Keilor 276 L10
st. Kew 372 C12
st. Melton 226 H15
st. Mitcham 377 F20
st. Moonee Pnd 323 H11
st. Mornington 640 G19
st. Northcote 326 G13
st. Seaford 599 E3
st. Seddon 367 A10
st. Sunbury 143 A12
st. Thomastown 241 C12
st. Vermont 377 F20
st. Werribee 447 L12
wyn. Blairgowrie 679 J18
SCOTTS
pde. Ivanhoe 328 D16
pl. Carlton 18 B16
st. Bentleigh 456 E20
SCOTTS ANGLE
rd. Wattle Glen 246 K3
SCOTTSDALE
st. Surrey Hills 374 B20
SCOVELL
cr. Maidstone 366 J1
SCREEN
rd. Diggers Rest 187 B11
st. Frankston 627 H5
SCULLIN
ct. Mill Park 242 L4
ct. Mill Park 243 A4
ct. Sunbury 143 G3
st. Altona 409 E17
st. Dandenong N 501 L19
st. Maidstone 366 F3
SCURRAH
ct. Keilor East 322 J4
SEA
ct. Craigieburn 150 G18
pde. Mentone 530 H9
tce. Mentone 530 J9
SEABIRD
cct. Torquay 712 C4
wy. Portsea 678 A5
SEA BREEZE
la. Williamstown 410 H16
SEABREEZE
av. Ferny Creek 425 G18
SEABROOK
av. Rosebud 700 J3
bvd. Seabrook 450 L2
wy. Seaford 573 E13
SEABY
av. Up Fntree Gly 465 A6
SEACH
st. Caulfield S 455 F12
SEACOMBE
gr. Brighton 454 E14
pl. Cranbourne 578 H17
st. Dromana 686 E3
st. Fawkner 281 H8
st. Fitzroy N 19 D1
st. Fitzroy N 326 B20
SEACREST
av. Seaford 599 K3
SEA EAGLE
av. Point Cook 450 D4
SEAFARER
ct. Patterson L 573 G10
SEAFOAM
st. Hampton E 496 A9
SEAFORD
rd. Seaford 599 F4
rd. Seaford 599 H4
SEAFORTH
rd. Wantirna S 423 A10
SEAGULL
av. Altona 408 G19
cl. Blind Bight 650 E9
la. Maribyrnong 322 J15
SEA HAZE
ct. Mt Eliza 641 L7
SEAHAZE
st. Arthurs Seat 686 A14
SEAHOLME
av. Seaholme 409 H17
SEAL
st. Rosebud 684 C18
SEAL ROCK
av. Arthurs Seat 685 H14
SEAMER
rd. Monbulk 428 J15
SEAMISTS
dr. Arthurs Seat 685 F19
SEAMONS
ct. Endeavour Hl 537 K10
SEAN
cl. Wheelers Hill 461 D13
ct. Kurunjang 226 H14
SEAQUESTA
ct. Frankston 628 E10
SEAQUINN
cl. Dromana 686 D3
SEARCH
rd. Diggers Rest 187 C11
SEARES
dr. Ringwood E 379 B6
pl. S Morang 198 L12
SEARLE
ct. Dandenong N 501 L14
ct. Werribee 447 D18
st. Geelong West 702 E6
SEASCAPE
cl. Ferntree Gly 424 K18
cl. Ferntree Gly 424 L17
pl. Safety Bch 669 B16
st. Clayton 459 B18
SEASIDE
cl. Seabrook 450 J6
pde. Mt Martha 668 L5
pde. Mt Martha 669 A5
SEATHORPE
st. Bentleigh E 496 J4
SEATON
ct. Mt Waverley 459 H3
ct. Somerville 644 L13
dr. Dingley Village 533 D5
pl. Rowville 463 F19
rd. Highett 496 A11
rd. Mornington 656 C2
ri. Hallam 552 B1
st. Glen Iris 417 B16
SEATTLE
ct. Knoxfield 463 D6
sq. Narre Warren 539 F16
st. Balwyn N 329 H19
SEAVER
gr. Reservoir 282 E9
SEA VIEW
av. Ferny Creek 466 C1
pde. Belmont 702 G17
SEAVIEW
av. Bentleigh 456 D18
av. Brighton 494 H5
av. Mornington 640 G19
av. Safety Bch 669 A17
cl. Rosebud 700 K5
cr. Black Rock 529 E3
cr. Mulgrave 500 A3
cr. Seaholme 409 G19
ct. Dandenong N 501 J14
pde. Dromana 686 B8
pde. Williamstown 410 A13
rd. Cockatoo 510 K8
rd. Frankston S 626 K11
st. Blairgowrie 679 F16
st. Caulfield S 455 F9
st. Dromana 686 F10
st. Emerald 510 A9
st. Mt Waverley 418 J13
SEAWIND
la. Arthurs Seat 685 J14
SEBAN
ct. Wantirna S 462 F5
SEBASTIAN
st. Epping 197 G16
SEBASTOPOL
st. Caulfield N 415 F18
st. St Kilda E 414 J16
SEBIRE
av. Wandin N 341 A15
SEBROFF
st. Frankston 627 C5
SEC
brk. Langwarrin 628 J8
SECCULL
dr. Chelsea Ht 547 G16
SECOMB
ct. Glen Waverley 420 A17
pl.n, Footscray 367 J7
pl.s, Footscray 367 J7
SECOND
av. Altona North 409 L7
av. Anglesea 713 C9
av. Aspendale 546 F9
av. Box Hill N 375 E7
av. Brunswick 325 D8
av. Chelsea Ht 547 E14
av. Cockatoo 510 H4
av. Craigieburn 150 G17
av. Dandenong N 501 J15
av. Eden Park 95 A15
av. Eden Park 95 F16
av. Hadfield 281 C11
av. Hoppers Csg 448 K6
av. Kew 372 J8
av. Melton S 268 G6
av. Moorabbin Aprt 531 K5
av. Murrumbeena 457 B11
av. Pakenham 584 K3
av. Rosebud 683 L19
av. Rowville 462 E18
av. Springvale 500 H10
av. Sunshine 365 E8
cr. Hadfield 281 D10
ct. Cranbourne 603 J6
ct. Preston 282 C18
dr. Springvale 500 G11
rd. Springvale 500 J10
st. Black Rock 529 G6
st. Clayton S 499 D5
st. Geelong West 702 G3
st. Moorabbin Aprt 531 L4
st. Parkdale 531 D9
st. Warrandyte 333 F1
SECRETS
wy. Mt Martha 657 C8
SECTION
rd. Greenvale 192 E20
SEDDON
st. Ivanhoe 328 C13
st. Olinda 427 B17
st. Seddon 367 A12
SEDGEFIELD
pl. Craigieburn 194 G3
tce. St Albans 319 G7
SEDGMAN
ct. Mill Park 242 H4
st. Brunswick E 325 K14
SEDGWICK
rd. Boronia 423 E14
SEEBECK
dr. Nar Warrn S 552 F17
dr. Nar Warrn S 552 H17
rd. Rowville 502 C5
SEEBREEZE
dr. Aspendale 546 D4
SEFTON
ct. Mt Waverley 419 F15
la. Caroline Spr 317 K3
pl. Camberwell 373 A18
st. Bulleen 329 K17
st. Pascoe Vale 280 D14
SEGARTA
cct. Ferntree Gly 464 A6
SEGTOUNE
st. Kew 372 F7
SEINE
cl. Werribee 447 H6
SEISMAN
st. Port Melb 412 L5
SEISMIC
ct. Rowville 462 L13
ct. Rowville 463 A13
SELBORNE
cl. Wantirna 422 H9
rd. Toorak 415 C7
SELBOURNE
av. Werribee 447 J2
pl. Hampton Pk 551 L16
rd. Kew 372 A12
st. Ascot Vale 324 A16
st. Coburg 325 C6
st. Hawthorn 372 C16
wy. Mulgrave 501 E6
SELBY
av. Noble Park 500 G14
ct. Berwick 554 D20
ct. Croydon N 336 E10
ct. Hopetoun Park 265 K6
pl. Craigieburn 150 G20
rd. Woori Yallock 344 C16
st. Dallas 238 D8
st. Mt Waverley 458 G7
st. Preston 283 D18
SELBY-AURA
rd. Menzies Ck 467 K19
rd. Selby 467 D16
SELET
st. Mt Evelyn 383 K7
SELINA
av. Mooroolbark 337 F15
ct. Frankston 628 F4
st. Footscray 367 H8
SELKIRK
av. McKinnon 456 F1
av. Wantirna 422 E
ct. Berwick 554 D1
rd. Woodstock 125 A1
SELL
st. Doncaster E 376 A
st. Keilor Park 278 C1
SELLARS
rd. Emerald 509 L
st. Watsonia N 285 H
SELLERS
st. Glen Waverley 420 B1
SELLICK
dr. Croydon 380 E1
SELLWOOD
rt. Cheltenham 496 J1
SELMAN
av. Ferntree Gly 464 G
SELOLA
ct. Fawkner 281 G
SELSDON
ct. Greensborough 244 E1
tce. Donvale 376 K
SELSEY
ct. St Albans 275 J2
st. Seaford 573 D1
SELWOOD
ct. Berwick 554 B
ct. Mill Park 243 E
ct. Mornington 640 L1
ct. Mornington 641 A1
ct. Rowville 462 H2
ct. Watsonia N 243 D1
pl. Altona Mdw 451 F
st. Hawthorn E 416 G
SELWORTHY
av. Oakleigh S 457 H1
SELWYN
av. Craigieburn 150 D1
av. Elwood 454 D
ct. Mulgrave 500 G
ct. Templestowe 330 L
ct. Toorak 415 G
la. Mt Dandenong 426 F
st. Albion 320 G2
st. Blackburn 375 F1
st. Brighton 454 G1
st. Canterbury 373 G2
st. Elsternwick 454 K
SENAR
st. Kilsyth 381 H
SENBIN
ct. Greensborough 243 J1
SENGA
st. Noble Park 534 D
SENIOR
cl. Mill Park 242 C
ct. Watsonia N 243 G2
SENNA
ct. Thomastown 240 J1
SENNITTS
rd. The Patch 468 C
SENTRY
pl. Aspendale Gdn 547 E
pl. Maribyrnong 322 K1
rd. Coburg 281 J2
SEPARATION
st. Alphington 327 H1
st. Fairfield 327 A1
st. Mornington 640 F1
st. Northcote 326 J1
SEPIK
va. Mt Evelyn 339 E1
SEPPELT
av. Mt Martha 656 B1
SEPTEMBER
st. Moolap 704 L1
SEPTIMUS
cl. Mill Park 242 K
SEQUOIA
ct. Nar Warrn S 553 C1
SERAFINI
ct. Eltham 287 C
SERCOMBE
gr. Hawthorn 372 A1
SERENDIP
ct. Narre Warren 539 D1
SERENITY
wy. Pt Lonsdale 707 G1
wy. S Morang 199 J2
SERGEANT
st. Blackburn 375 F1
SERICA
ct. Grovedale 706 A1
ct. Keilor Dn 276 G1
pl. Wheelers Hill 460 H1
SERJEANT
ct. Seaford 573 J1

SERONG
st. Kensington 33 G5
SERPELLS
la. Hawthorn 372 A17
rd. Doncaster E 332 F12
rd. Templestowe 331 A9
tce. Donvale 332 H15
SERPENS
ct. Roxburgh Pk 194 F8
SERPENTINE
ct. Lalor 240 H9
ct. Werribee 447 H8
rd. Keysborough 533 L8
st. Mont Albert 374 F15
SERRATA
ct. Hillside 274 G7
SERRELL
st. Malvern East 456 K4
SERVANTE
st. Sunshine 365 E3
SERVICE
rd. Blackburn 375 F14
rd. Melb Airport 235 H12
rd. Watsonia 285 F9
st. Caulfield N 415 K20
st. Coburg 281 F20
st. Essendon N 323 H2
st. Hampton 495 B9
st. Sunshine 365 D1
SESAME
st. Mt Waverley 419 H15
SESTON
st. Reservoir 283 K17
SETANI
cr. Heidelberg W 284 B19
SETH
pl. Mt Evelyn 339 L16
SETON
cl. Greenvale 193 B20
SETTE
ct. Greensborough 244 J16
SETTLEMENT
rd. Belmont 706 E3
rd. Bundoora 284 D1
rd. Sunbury 112 C4
rd. Sunbury 113 A2
rd. Thomastown 241 C17
rd. Wesburn 347 E12
rd. Yarra Jctn 346 J12
rd. Yarra Jctn 347 A12
rd.w,Sunbury 111 E3
SETTLER
ct. Glen Waverley 459 L6
ct. Werribee 447 K8
SETTLERS
ct. Rowville 463 J15
ct. Vermont S 420 L12
ct. Vermont S 421 A12
wy. Frankston S 627 J11
wy. Mt Martha 656 J6
wy. St Albans 319 G8
wy. St Helena 245 B20
wy. Sunbury 113 G12
SETTLERS HILL
cr. Croydon Hills 335 G15
cl. Nar Warrn N 538 F12
ri. Pakenham 584 H1
SEVENOAKS
av. Croydon 335 J18
av. Heidelberg 329 F2
rd. Burwood E 420 A12
st. Balwyn 373 C10
SEVENTH
av. Altona North 409 J7
av. Anglesea 713 C13
av. Chelsea Ht 547 D14
av. Dandenong 535 H5
av. Eden Park 95 A16
av. Eden Park 95 A7
av. Hadfield 281 D5
av. Rosebud 684 A19
rd. Springvale 500 L11
rd. Springvale 501 A11
st. Parkdale 531 E11
SEVERINO
pl. Sunbury 142 J12
SEVERN
cr. Rowville 463 E17
ct. Dandenong N 501 G14
ct. Mt Waverley 418 H15
ct. Roxburgh Pk 194 G6
st. Balwyn N 373 A6
st. Box Hill N 374 H12
st. Epping 198 B18
st. Moonee Pnd 323 J11
st. Newport 410 G9
st. Yarraville 366 K17
SEVES
st. Altona 409 F20
SEVILLE
cl. Thomastown 240 E15
ct. Cheltenham 497 H20
ct. Kings Park 275 C19
ct. Meadow Ht 238 C4
gr. Scoresby 462 B7
st. Camberwell 417 A6
SEWART
cl. Vermont S 421 C13
SEWELL
ct. Frankston S 627 J11
dr. Harkaway 541 E17
ri. Bundoora 284 E4
st. Mont Albert N 374 E6
SEXTON
ct. Altona Mdw 451 E2
ct. Endeavour Hl 537 L7
st. Airport W 278 J12
SEYMOUR
av. Armadale 415 H13
av. Carnegie 456 F6
av. Mt Eliza 626 A16
cl. Grovedale 706 H14
cl. Wantirna 422 J10
dr. Diamond Ck 245 A3
dr. Plenty 245 A3
gr. Brighton 494 J4
gr. Camberwell 416 J3
rd. Elsternwick 455 B3
rd. Nr Nr Goon N 560 G14
rd. View Bank 286 B17
st. Belgrave 466 E14
st. Broadmeadows 238 B16
st. Preston 326 K4
st. Ringwood 378 B13
st. Seville 341 J11
SHABA
ct. Meadow Ht 194 B17
SHACKELL
st. Coburg 325 B2
st. Kingsville 366 K11
SHACKLETON
st. Belmont 702 C18
SHADA
dr. Cranbourne W 577 G15
SHADFORTH
st. Westmeadows 237 C14
SHADI
ct. Cranbourne W 577 H20
ri. Yarra Glen 209 B18
SHADOWPLAY
rd. Mooroolbark 337 C13
SHADWELL
ct. Whittington 704 A18
st. Cheltenham 497 B20
SHADY
gr. Forest Hill 420 H1
gr. Rowville 463 F17
pl. Noble Park 534 C5
wy. Croydon S 380 A14
SHAE
ct. Kings Park 319 D2
SHAFER
ct. Endeavour Hl 537 G5
rd. Blackburn N 375 G9
SHAFT
ct. Hoppers Csg 449 J2
SHAFTESBURY
av. Malvern 416 B11
av. St Andrews 205 H1
ct. Keysborough 534 B7
dr. Berwick 539 L20
pde. Thornbury 326 E9
st. Coburg 325 C7
st. Essendon 324 C6
st. Frankston 627 H4
SHAFTON
st. Huntingdale 458 E16
SHAFTSBURY
av. Berwick 553 J14
bvd. Point Cook 450 G8
dr. Mulgrave 460 E20
SHAH
ct. Torquay 712 H2
SHAKESPEARE
av. Mooroolbark 337 G20
av. Mooroolbark 381 G1
av. Preston 283 A17
dr. Bundoora 242 G17
dr. Delahey 275 D16
dr. Templestowe 332 A11
gr. Hawthorn 371 E17
gr. Heidelberg Ht 284 G19
gr. Northcote 326 E13
gr. St Kilda 414 B18
pl. Cremorne 26 E17
st. Carlton N 18 G4
SHALBURY
av. Eltham 287 L5
SHALE
ct. Delahey 274 L16
SHALIMAR
cr. Boronia 424 J7
cr. Dandenong N 501 L15
ct. Sorrento 679 A13
ct. Vermont S 420 H11
pl. Melton W 225 L15
SHALLESS
dr. Camberwell 417 C3
SHALLOT
cl. Glen Waverley 420 K16
SHAMROCK
cl. Nar Warrn S 553 D18
dr. Mill Park 243 F5
pl. Melton W 225 A16
pl. S Melbourne 29 F2
st. Abbotsford 371 A12
st. Brunswick W 325 B9
st. Essendon 323 L7
st. Richmond 26 F18
SHANAHAN
cr. McKinnon 456 G17
SHAND
ct. Berwick 553 K4
rd. Reservoir 283 D13
st. Safety Bch 669 A15
SHANDEAU
av. Clayton 458 K19
SHANDEEN
ct. Meadow Ht 237 L4
SHANDFORD
av. Brighton 454 E13
SHANDON
st. Mornington 640 J13
st. Mornington 641 A13
SHANDS
la. N Melbourne 34 K11
st. Beaumaris 530 H4
SHANE
av. Seabrook 450 H5
cl. Lilydale 338 L12
cr. Croydon S 379 E10
ct. Avondale Ht 322 G10
ct. Carrum Downs 601 D3
ct. Gladstone Pk 279 D2
SHANHUNS
rd. Cottles Br 204 C8
rd. Panton Hill 204 C8
SHANKLAND
bvd. Meadow Ht 193 L20
SHANKLIN
st. Box Hill N 375 A6
st. Hurstbridge 202 L13
SHANLEY
st. Pascoe Vale 280 J12
SHANNON
av. Ferntree Gly 424 E19
av. Geelong West 702 C6
av. Manifold Ht 702 C6
av. Newtown 702 B14
cl. Werribee 447 H6
cr. Watsonia 285 H10
ct. Clarinda 498 E8
ct. Dingley Village 532 L4
ct. Mooroolbark 336 K11
ct. St Albans 275 G19
dr. Mill Park 243 D4
gr. Roxburgh Pk 194 D7
pl. Langwarrin 601 L19
pl. Mill Park 242 L12
st. Box Hill N 374 H10
st. Frankston 599 B19
wy. Berwick 554 J7
wy. Sydenham 275 B8
SHANNS
av. Mt Martha 656 B7
SHAPIRO
ct. Reservoir 283 J2
SHARA
ct. Belmont 706 H5
ct. Narre Warren 539 A17
SHARAN
av. Mentone 531 K8
SHAREN
ct. Rosebud 684 H16
SHARLAND
cl. Mt Evelyn 338 J19
SHARMAN
ct. Bentleigh 496 G1
ct. Bundoora 242 G16
SHARNA
ct. Ferntree Gly 463 J7
SHARNALEE
ct. Lilydale 338 D12
SHARNE
ct. Cranbourne N 578 G11
ct. Doncaster E 375 J2
SHARON
ct. Mooroolbark 336 L12
ct. Taylors Lakes 275 E5
rd. Springvale S 500 C20
st. Doncaster 331 E19
SHARP
gr. Coburg N 281 E13
st. Bulla 190 E17
st. Hoppers Csg 448 F3
st. Newtown 702 H12
st. Northcote 326 L16
SHARPE
ct. Berwick 553 L19
st. Cranbourne 578 C17
st. Reservoir 282 J14
SHARPES
rd. Watsonia N 285 D3
SHARPLEY
av. Safety Bch 669 B12
SHARPS
ct. Heathmont 378 L18
ct. Heathmont 379 A18
rd. Melb Airport 278 C7
rd. Tullamarine 278 C7
SHARRA
ct. Clarinda 498 C10
SHARROCK
av. Cheltenham 531 G1
cl. Caroline Spr 318 C5
dr. Dingley Village 533 B7
SHARROW
rd. Mitcham 377 G11
SHARYN
st. Cranbourne W 577 H17
SHASTA
av. Brighton East 455 B19
av. Ringwood E 378 L13
av. Ringwood E 379 A13
wy. Portsea 677 J3
SHAUN
av. Blackburn S 419 K7
ct. Croydon N 336 A12
ct. Springvale 499 K17
ct. Templestowe 331 D7
SHAW
cl. Dandenong N 501 F12
ct. Altona Mdw 451 K8
ct. Coburg N 281 B12
ct. Delahey 275 C14
ct. Sunbury 143 C9
rd. Junction Vill 604 H13
st. Ashwood 417 L17
st. Dromana 686 F3
st. Fawkner 281 F1
st. Ivanhoe 327 L13
st. Niddrie 322 L1
st. Niddrie 323 A2
st. Richmond 26 H13
st. Springvale S 534 B4
SHAWLANDS
av. Blackburn S 419 J2
rd. Tullamarine 278 J3
SHAWNEE
ct. Narre Warren 552 F1
SHAWS
rd. Werribee 447 C9
SHAXTON
cir. Frankston 628 D11
SHAYLOR
ct. Greensborough 285 L7
SHEA
st. Bacchus Msh 221 J15
st. Newport 410 K11
SHEAHAN
cr. Hoppers Csg 448 L1
cr. Hoppers Csg 449 A1
SHEAHANS
rd. Bulleen 329 K10
rd. Templstw Lr 329 K10
SHEALES
st. Dandenong 536 A3
SHEARER
cl. Hoppers Csg 405 B18
cl. Sydenham 275 A8
ct. Frankston S 627 H9
ct. Mill Park 242 B5
ct. Mornington 641 E12
ct. Narre Warren 553 F13
dr. Rowville 502 K6
pl. Roxburgh Pk 194 B11
SHEARERS
ct. Vermont S 420 L12
ct. Vermont S 421 A12
SHEARGOLD
ct. Reservoir 239 L20
SHEARMAN
cr. Mentone 530 K6
ct. Keysborough 535 A9
SHEARSON
cr. Mentone 531 H5
SHEARWATER
ct. Mornington 640 K17
ct. Pt Lonsdale 707 G18
dr. Carrum Downs 600 H2
dr. Pakenham 583 L4
pl. Craigieburn 194 A4
pl. Rosebud W 698 L3
pl. Rosebud W 699 A3
SHEBLER
pl. Melton 226 L17
SHEDDEN
st. Pascoe Vale 281 A18
SHEEDY
rd. Gisborne 79 D15
rd. Hoppers Csg 448 E4
st. Richmond 26 J12
SHEEHAN
ct. Dandenong N 502 B20
rd. Heidelberg W 284 B17
SHEEHANS
rd. Blackburn 375 G20
rd. Red Hill 687 E19
SHEEPFOLD
ct. Melton W 226 A18
SHEEPRUN
pl. Hoppers Csg 447 L1
SHEEPSTATION CREEK
rd. Hoddles Ck 388 E14
rd. Yellingbo 388 C6
SHEFFIELD
cl. Pakenham 584 H2
ct. Thomastown 240 L15
ct. Thomastown 241 A15
rd. Kilsyth 425 G5
rd. Montrose 425 G5
rd. The Basin 425 F9
rd.n,Montrose 382 F11
rd.s,Montrose 381 K18
st. Bentleigh E 457 C20
st. Brunswick W 325 B10
st. Caulfield S 455 G10
st. Coburg 325 H4
st. Eltham 287 K5
st. Nar Warrn S 553 E15
st. Preston 282 F17
SHEFFIELDS
la. Heidelberg 328 L7
SHEILA
ct. Thomastown 240 G17
st. Preston 283 G20
st. Rye 697 L4
SHEILDS
ct. Bacchus Msh 221 L19
SHELAGH
ct. Warrandyte 333 B5
SHELBOURNE
ct. Meadow Ht 238 C5
ct. Mornington 640 G12
SHELBURY
pl. Frankston S 627 G17
SHELDON
av. Darley 221 L8
av. Mooroolbark 337 F20
ct. Gladstone Pk 237 D19
pl. Clayton S 499 D10
pl. Sunshine W 364 D6
pl. Wheelers Hill 461 A7
SHELDRAKE
cl. Frankston 628 D3
st. Keysborough 534 G15
SHELDUCK
pl. Craigieburn 149 G17
SHELFORD
cr. Kallista 468 F12
ct. Cheltenham 531 D1
ct. Ferntree Gly 424 A17
gr. Dingley Village 533 B7
SHELL
ct. Patterson L 573 K11
SHELLARD
st. Newport 410 E5
SHELLEY
av. Bundoora 242 K20
av. Kilsyth 380 K6
av. Newtown 702 A6
cl. Grovedale 706 A10
cl. Torquay 711 G11
ct. Ashwood 418 B15
ct. Hampton Pk 551 D10
ct. Kilsyth 380 K7
ct. Templestowe 332 C11
pl. Truganina 405 F13
st. Elwood 454 C3
st. Heidelberg Ht 328 E2
st. Keilor East 322 D3
st. Mornington 640 D15
st. Richmond 26 C5
SHELLY
av. Boronia 424 D3
ct. Bacchus Msh 221 L19
st. Footscray 367 G8
st. Noble Park 534 D4
SHELTER
tr. Lysterfield S 503 C13
SHELTON
cr. Noble Park N 501 D8

SHENFIELD
av. Bonbeach 545 E12
av. Chelsea 545 E12
la. Bonbeach, off Shenfield Av 545 E12
SHEOAK
av. Rosebud W 699 C1
ct. Highton 705 F4
ct. Hoppers Csg 405 F17
ct. Meadow Ht 238 C2
gr. Mt Martha 668 L8
gr. Mt Martha 669 A7
gr. St Albans 319 F10
la. Maribyrnong 322 H16
mw. Cheltenham 496 J14
rd. Frankston S 627 J16
st. Doveton 537 B9
st. Plenty 244 G11
tr. Frankston N 600 F11
SHEOKE
gr. Sorrento 679 C18
SHEPHERD
av. Roxburgh Pk 194 E10
ct. Dingley Village 533 E6
ct. Williamstn N 411 A13
rd. Glen Waverley 460 K3
st. Braybrook 365 L1
st. Footscray 367 B6
st. Glenroy 279 J4
st. Surrey Hills 374 D20
st. Surrey Hills 418 D1
SHEPHERDS
gr. Kings Park 274 L20
la. Sunbury 188 H7
SHEPHERDS FLAT
la. Cottles Br 204 E5
SHEPHERDS HUT
la. Langwarrin S 629 J18
SHEPPARD
ct. Altona Mdw 451 L6
dr. Scoresby 462 E7
st. Coburg N 281 E14
st. Moorabbin 496 E7
st. Thornbury 327 H8
SHEPPARDS
la. Chirnside Pk 337 D6
SHEPPARSON
av. Carnegie 456 J8
SHEPPERD
wy. Deer Park 319 H11
SHEPRETH
av. Noble Park 534 K3
st. Surrey Hills 373 K13
SHERATON
cl. Burwood E 420 B12
cr. Ferntree Gly 463 H8
SHERBOURNE
av. Bayswater N 380 E18
dr. Carrum Downs 575 C14
rd. Briar Hill 286 G7
rd. Eltham 287 A7
rd. Gladstone Pk 279 B1
rd. Montmorency 286 G7
st. Essendon 323 L10
tce. Newtown 701 L5
SHERBROOK
av. Ringwood 378 A13
tce. Lilydale 338 K2
tce. Lilydale 339 C5
SHERBROOKE
av. Elsternwick 454 L6
av. Oakleigh S 497 G8
cr. Taylors Lakes 276 B10
ct. Doncaster E 376 C6
ct. Nar Warrn S 553 E16
rd. Kallista 466 K1
rd. Sassafras 426 D19
rd. Sherbrooke 426 D19
rd. Sherbrooke 467 A2
st. Eltham 287 F3
SHERBROOKE LODGE
rd. Sherbrooke 466 H2
SHERDLEY
grn. Caroline Spr 317 L4
SHERGOLDS
la. Dromana 687 C9
SHERIDAN
av. Frankston 599 C15
av. Mooroolbark 337 A12
av. Rowville 503 D5
cl. Kilsyth S 380 K18
ct. Brighton 454 J13
ct. Dingley Village 532 K5
ct. Endeavour Hl 537 L7
ct. Heathmont 379 D20
gr. Caulfield S 455 D11
rd. Rosebud 684 H15
wy. Roxburgh Pk 194 B11
SHERIE
ct. Keysborough 534 E11
SHERINGA
cr. Grovedale 705 K15
ct. Mornington 641 C16
SHERINGHAM
dr. Werribee 448 A16
dr. Wheelers Hill 460 K11
SHERLOCK
dr. Mornington 657 B4
rd. Croydon 336 H19
rd. Mooroolbark 336 L18
SHERLOWE
cr. View Bank 285 L16
ct. Bentleigh E 497 D2
SHERMAN
ct. Berwick 554 F12
dr. Bayswater N 380 H19
st. Forest Hill 420 J3
SHERRIFF
cl. Millgrove 348 B1
rd. Emerald 509 H1
ri. Pakenham 585 C6
SHERRIN
ct. Werribee 448 C7
SHERRY
ct. Bacchus Msh 221 G16
SHERWIN
cl. Mt Martha 656 F9
ct. Melton 227 G18
pl. Roxburgh Pk 194 F15
st. Kensington 33 E9
st. Whittlesea 96 K18
SHERWOOD
av. Chelsea 546 L19
av. Ringwood E 378 K13
av. Rosebud 700 G6
av. Warburton 350 C1
cl. Albanvale 319 A4
cr. Dandenong N 502 C14
cr. Mt Martha 656 A20
ct. Croydon 379 F7
ct. Doncaster E 331 L18
ct. Highton 705 G3
ct. Langwarrin S 628 G15
ct. Sunbury 143 J10
ct. Wantirna S 423 A16
dr. Thomastown 240 D15
rd. Eaglemont 328 E12
rd. Ivanhoe 328 E12
rd. Junction Vill 604 J15
rd. Mt Waverley 458 L1
rd. Nar Warrn S 578 E1
rd. Nar Warrn S 578 E2
rd. Rye 697 H7
rd. Surrey Hills 418 C1
rd. Tooradin 651 F1
ri. Vermont S 420 G13
st. Glen Iris 417 C16
st. Hadfield 281 B9
st. Ormond 455 J13
st. Richmond 26 A11
wy. Lysterfield 464 E19
wy. Lysterfield 464 F18
SHERWOOD FOREST
dr. Rye 696 J8
SHETLAND
av. Brunswick W 324 L8
cl. Highton 701 C16
cl. Vermont S 420 G7
ct. Belmont 706 C6
ct. Pakenham 558 L19
dr. Wantirna 422 K7
st. Endeavour Hl 503 G19
wy. Sunbury 143 K16
SHEVLINS
la. Woori Yallock 344 E17
SHIBOR
dr. Vermont 421 K2
SHIEL
st. N Melbourne 34 J12
SHIELA
st. Blackburn N 376 A8
SHIELD
ct. Glen Waverley 421 A18
ct. Kilsyth 381 A5
rd. Yellingbo 386 K17
SHIELDS
ct. Altona Mdw 451 F4
ct. Blackburn S 419 G1
ct. Sydenham 274 J7
st. Flemington 34 B4
st. Sunbury 143 F15
st. Sunbury 143 H16
SHIELS
la. Carlton 18 J14
SHIERLAW
av. Canterbury 373 G17
SHIERS
st. Alphington 327 J16
st. Reservoir 240 B20
SHILO
ct. Thomastown 240 F16
SHINE
ct. Narre Warren 539 C15
SHINNERS
av. Berwick 539 E19
av. Narre Warren 539 E19
SHINYRUBY
ct. Vermont S 420 G6
SHIPLEY
ct. Sunshine N 320 L11
st. Box Hill 374 J14
st. South Yarra 31 K6
st. South Yarra 414 E3
SHIPMAN
st. Blairgowrie 696 C5
SHIPSTON
rd. Cheltenham 531 C3
SHIPTON
ct. Campbellfield 239 G15
ct. Noble Park N 501 D14
SHIRALEE
ct. Wheelers Hill 461 C15
SHIRAZ
cl. Mt Martha 657 B9
cr. Narre Warren 539 A18
ct. Bundoora 242 J17
ct. Noble Park N 501 E9
dr. Waurn Ponds 705 G13
SHIRE
ct. Highton 701 D16
rd. Dromana 685 G9
SHIRLEY
av. Glen Waverley 419 J20
av. Seaford 573 F18
av. Sorrento 678 H12
cr. Woori Yallock 344 G13
ct. Boronia 424 F16
ct. Brighton East 455 E15
ct. Croydon 380 B9
ct. Doncaster E 375 G4
ct. Mitcham 377 A12
gr. Heidelberg 328 J4
gr. St Kilda E 414 L14
gr. St Kilda E 415 A14
rd. Warburton 305 G20
st. Altona Mdw 451 J1
st. Fawkner 281 E4
st. Mooroolbark 337 A15
st. Noble Park 500 E18
st. St Albans 319 J2
SHIRLIAN
st. Cheltenham 531 F1
SHIRLOW
av. Rye 697 L4
SHIRRA
pl. Attwood 237 E12
SHIRVINGTON
pl. Donvale 376 H3
SHOAL
ct. Dingley Village 532 K9
SHOALHAVEN
st. Bundoora 284 E3
st. Werribee 447 G8
SHOEMAKER
st. Attwood 237 A11
SHOEMARK
rd. Cranbourne W 577 D10
SHOLDEN
ct. Wandana Ht 705 B1
SHOOBRA
rd. Elsternwick 455 B7
SHOPPERS
la. Taylors Lakes 276 B6
SHORE
gr. Coburg N 281 J17
nk. Doncaster E 332 G14
SHORING
rd. Diggers Rest 187 A11
SHORT
av. Oak Park 279 K10
cr. The Basin 425 C13
cr. Tremont 425 C13
la. Pakenham 558 A12
rd. Eltham North 287 H2
rd. Gisborne 109 B10
rd. Hampton Pk 551 G14
st. Airport W 279 C13
st. Altona North 410 A8
st. Belmont 702 B18
st. Boronia 424 C10
st. Box Hill 375 C15
st. Camberwell 416 J6
st. Canterbury 373 G19
st. Dandenong 535 G9
st. Doncaster 375 A1
st. Footscray 367 E9
st. Glen Waverley 460 B3
st. Hampton E 495 J8
st. Keilor East 322 G4
st. Macleod 285 A10
st. Maidstone 366 H2
st. Malvern East 417 A20
st. Murrumbeena 457 D7
st. Northcote 326 J20
st. Ringwood E 379 C10
st. Springvale 500 C12
st. Torquay 711 L7
st. Vermont 421 B2
SHORT CUT
rd. Eltham 287 G15
wk. Lysterfield 504 H13
SHORTHORN
wk. Nar Warrn S 578 H1
SHORTLANDS
rd. Ringwood 422 A1
SHORTRIDGE
cct. Roxburgh Pk 194 B9
SHORTS
pl. Geelong, off Little Malop St 703 A8
rd. Coburg N 281 C13
rd. Eltham 289 A11
rd. Research 289 A11
SHOTTON
rd. Mt Eliza 641 F10
SHOUBRA
ct. Highton 701 G20
dr. Highton 701 H20
SHOWERS
av. Chelsea 546 J18
st. Braybrook 365 K5
st. Preston 326 H4
SHOWGROUNDS
rd. Whittlesea 96 K17
SHOW JUMP
cr. Endeavour Hl 503 L19
SHREWSBURY
ct. Frankston 628 D12
rd. Nunawading 376 K8
st. Bentleigh E 456 J17
st. Malvern East 457 J2
SHRIDAN
pl. Richmond 26 E11
SHRIMPTON
ct. Balwyn 374 B11
SHRIVES
rd. Hampton Pk 552 D7
rd. Narre Warren 552 D7
rd. Nar Warrn S 552 D7
SHROPSHIRE
st. Heidelberg 329 E4
SHRUBBY
wk. Croydon S 380 A14
SHUTE
av. Berwick 554 D5
cl. Templestowe 332 A11
SHUTER
st. Moonee Pnd 324 B14
SIANDRA
pl. Berwick 554 G13
SIBELIUS
ct. Langwarrin 629 J6
SIBELLA
ct. Greensborough 243 L20
SIBERIA
la. Kensington 33 H7
SIBLEY
st. Werribee 448 B9
SIBTHORPE
st. Mordialloc 532 D9
SIBYL
av. Frankston S 627 B20
SICA
ct. Sydenham 274 J7
SIDDELEY
ct. Dingley Village 532 L5
st. Docklands 23 F15
SIDDONS
wy. Hallam 537 D19
SIDING
rd. Parwan 266 H18
SIDNEY
ct. Narre Warren 539 B13
pl. Caroline Spr 318 C9
st. Cranbourne 577 L15
st. Warrandyte 334 E1
SIDWELL
av. St Kilda E 415 A18
ct. Lower Plenty 286 H20
ct. St Kilda E 415 A18
SIEBEN
cl. Mill Park 242 C9
ct. Truganina 405 G13
SIEDE
ct. Cheltenham 496 F17
SIENNA
cr. Endeavour Hl 537 K7
ct. Rowville 463 G16
pl. Point Cook 450 H12
SIERRA
ct. Hoppers Csg 448 F
pl. Chirnside Pk 337 J
pl. Doncaster E 331 K2
SIGVARD
bvd. Hallam 538 B1
SILAS
av. Frankston 599 G1
SILBER
ct. Melton W 225 L1
SILFLAY
ct. Warranwood 335 C1
SILICON
pl. Tullamarine 278 F1
SILK
av. Manifold Ht 702 B
ct. Dandenong N 502 D2
ct. Epping 198 F1
ct. Werribee 447 F1
la. Wesburn 347 L
pl. W Melbourne 34 K1
st. Rosanna 285 C1
SILKHORN
cr. Mt Martha 656 C1
SILKWOOD
av. Berwick 539 F1
la. Craigieburn 150 E1
wy. Rowville 503 C
SILKY OAK
dr. Bundoora 242 D1
gr. Sunbury 143 F1
SILVAN
av. Springvale 499 H1
ct. Emerald 510 E
ct. Rowville 463 B1
ct. St Albans 320 D1
ct. Taylors Hill 274 K1
ct. Werribee 448 A1
gr. Hampton Pk 551 J
gr. Mornington 640 K1
rd. Monbulk 428 D1
rd. Mt Evelyn 383 J
rd. Olinda 383 L2
rd. Olinda 427 G1
rd. Silvan 384 C1
rd. Silvan 385 A1
rd. Silvan 428 H
rd. Wattle Glen 246 L
rd. Wattle Glen 247 A
st. Oakleigh S 497 J
wy. Hillside 274 F
SILVANA
ct. Doncaster E 332 F
ct. Wheelers Hill 460 H1
SILVAN VIEW
st. Kalorama 382 J1
SILVER
av. Frankston N 600 D
gr. Nunawading 376 G1
st. Cheltenham 497 A2
st. Collingwood 19 J2
st. Eltham 287 D
st. Malvern 416 A
st. Newcomb 704 A1
st. Werribee 447 F1
SILVER ASH
av. Ashwood 418 D1
SILVER BIRCH
av. Dingley Village 532 H
cl. Croydon N 335 L1
ct. Nar Warrn S 553 C2
SILVERBIRCH
ri. Mill Park 242 L
SILVER CREEK
dr. Lynbrook 551 F1
SILVERDALE
cl. Rowville 503 A
ct. Doncaster E 331 H1
ct. Springvale S 534 C
rd. Eaglemont 328 F1
ri. Bundoora 284 F
SILVERDENE
av. Sydenham 275 B
SILVERENE
ct. Vermont S 421 C1
SILVEREYE
cr. Werribee 448 B
pl. S Morang 243 J
SILVER LEAF
ct. Forest Hill 376 D2
SILVERLEAVES
bvd. Berwick 539 H1
SILVERLEY
rd. Croydon 380 G
SILVER RIDGE
rd. Pt Lonsdale 707 F1
SILVERTHORN
ct. Mill Park 242 E

SILVERTON
cl. Laverton N 364 L16
dr. Ferntree Gly 463 K4
dr. Noble Park N 501 D12
pl. Craigieburn 150 A16
st. Malvern East 456 J2
SILVERTOP
cl. Lynbrook 551 G16
cr. Frankston N 600 A11
ct. Mill Park 243 B6
st. Frankston N 599 L11
SILVERTREE
av. Delahey 274 L13
av. Delahey 275 A14
av. Taylors Hill 274 L13
SILVER WATTLE
cl. Rosebud W 699 B4
st. Yallambie 285 K14
SILVERWATTLE
rd. Launching Pl 346 A13
SILVERWOOD
ct. Hillside 231 L20
wy. Glen Waverley 420 K20
SILVESTER
cr. St Albans 320 A1
pde. Roxburgh Pk 193 L12
SIM
ct. Box Hill S 418 J4
ct. Glenroy 279 L9
st. Mitcham 377 D15
st. Mt Waverley 419 F14
SIMCOCK
av. Spotswood 411 B1
st. Somerville 644 L13
st. Somerville 645 A13
SIMETO
wy. Roxburgh Pk 194 G6
SIMLA
cl. View Bank 329 F1
st. Heathmont 378 K20
st. Mitcham 377 B15
SIMMIE
st. Sunshine W 364 J5
SIMMINGTON
cct. Greenvale 192 L18
cct. Greenvale 193 A18
SIMMONDS
ct. Bentleigh E 457 A19
ct. Wantirna S 422 E16
pl. Endeavour Hl 537 B5
pl. Roxburgh Pk 194 C14
ct. Hughesdale 457 F14
SIMMONS
cl. Cockatoo 471 H19
ct. Anglesea 713 L3
ct. Greensborough 286 F3
ct. South Yarra 32 F15
ct. South Yarra 414 J8
dr. Seaholme 409 J16
la. Belgrave S 506 K3
st. Box Hill N 374 K10
st. South Yarra 32 E14
st. South Yarra 414 H7
st. Tecoma 466 B7
SIMMS
rd. Greensborough 286 E7
SIMON
av. Noble Park 534 D4
av. Rowville 462 K20
ct. Brookfield 268 B4
ct. Darley 221 L10
ct. Epping 197 G15
ct. Hampton Pk 552 A14
ct. Rosanna 329 E1
ct. Werribee 448 F17
ct. Wheelers Hill 460 E15
dr. Pakenham 585 C6
st. Blackburn N 375 L8
st. Clayton S 498 H6
SIMONE
cr. Doncaster E 332 F5
ct. Hallam 538 C14
rd. Bacchus Msh 221 L13
SIMPSON
av. Sunbury 142 K14
av. Yallambie 285 F11
ct. Hallam 537 J13
ct. Meadow Ht 237 J7
ct. Werribee 446 J17
dr. Dandenong N 536 B1
dr. Mt Waverley 419 C15
la. Kensington 33 B11
pl. Hawthorn 371 F15
pl. Keilor East 322 B1
rd. Ferntree Gly 424 B20
st. Bacchus Msh 222 C18
st. E Melbourne 25 K9
st. Kew 372 F8
st. Mitcham 377 C16
st. Moorabbin 497 E12
st. Noble Park 500 E20
st. Northcote 326 L19
st. Pt Lonsdale 710 F7
st. Sunshine N 321 F14
st. Thomastown 240 H14
st. Yarraville 367 B16
wy. Seabrook 450 K8
SIMPSONS
ct. Heathmont 422 G3
rd. Box Hill 375 C14
rd. Christmas Hills 206 B19
rd. Christmas Hills 250 B1
rd. Clayton S 498 K15
rd. The Basin 425 J8
SIMS
ct. Carrum Downs 575 D15
sq. Kensington 33 E7
st. Braybrook 365 L6
st. Pascoe Vale 280 J14
st. Reservoir 282 L3
st. Sandringham 495 B15
st. W Melbourne 367 J10
SINATRA
wy. Cranbourne E 604 J5
SINCLAIR
av. Edithvale 546 F12
av. Glen Iris 416 F9
av. Rye 697 E3
av. Templstw Lr 330 J10
cr. Macleod 285 D11
ct. Attwood 237 D10
ct. Hampton Pk 551 D6
ct. Mill Park 242 C3
ct. Mt Martha 655 J16
la. Edithvale, off Sinclair Av 546 F12
rd. Bayswater 423 J8
rd. Dandenong 535 E10
rd. Hurstbridge 204 A13
rd. Panton Hill 204 A13
st. Blairgowrie 695 J2
st. Cheltenham 496 H19
st. Elsternwick 454 K4
st. Oakleigh S 458 E20
st. Somerville 644 K16
SINCLAIRS
rd. Plumpton 273 A20
rd. Rockbank 317 A5
SINGER
av. Glen Waverley 420 H16
av. Keilor Dn 276 B12
SINGERS
la. Melbourne 1 F4
la. Melbourne 23 J4
SINGLETON
dr. Endeavour Hl 537 K6
dr. Mulgrave 500 G5
pl. Noble Park N 501 F16
rd. Balwyn N 329 J20
st. Collingwood 19 J18
tce. Kalorama 382 E14
tce. Montrose 382 E14
tce. Mt Dandenong 382 B18
tce. Mt Dandenong 382 E14
SINNOTT
st. Burwood 418 F11
st. Preston 327 B2
SINNS
av. Werribee 447 L15
SION
cl. Eltham 288 A11
SIRDAR
st. Melton 226 K16
SIRENS
pl. Hallam 538 E15
SIRET
ct. Roxburgh Pk 194 D5
SIR GARNET
rd. Surrey Hills 373 H16
SIR HAROLD
cl. Endeavour Hl 537 H4
SIRI
ct. Kings Park 319 E3
SIRIUS
ct. Keilor Dn 275 J13
ct. Mill Park 242 K12
ct. Yallambie 285 G16
pl. Nar Warrn S 552 H11
SIR JOHN MONASH
dr. Caulfield E 456 C1
SIR LAURENCE
dr. Seaford 599 J6
SIROCCO
la. Newport 411 A12
SIR WILLIAM
st. Kew 371 H9
SISKA
ct. Frankston 628 F7
SITAR
ct. Burwood E 419 J11
SITELLA
ct. Carrum Downs 600 J3
SITTELLA
ct. Werribee 447 K4
SIXTH
av. Altona North 409 K4
av. Altona North 409 K7
av. Anglesea 713 C11
av. Aspendale 546 F8
av. Burwood 418 B12
av. Chelsea Ht 547 F13
av. Cockatoo 510 H6
av. Dandenong 535 H6
av. Eden Park 95 A12
av. Eden Park 125 A5
av. Hadfield 281 C7
av. Rosebud 684 A20
av. Springvale 500 H10
av. Springvale 500 K10
av. Springvale 501 A10
st. Parkdale 531 E11
SIYAN
ri. Diamond Ck 246 A13
SKARDONS
rd. Cottles Br 204 G1
rd. St Andrews 204 G1
SKEFFINGTON
st. Bellfield 328 A6
SKEHAN
bvd. Altona Mdw 451 C1
SKELTON
pl. Sorrento 678 K9
rd. Craigieburn 194 G2
SKENE
ct. Greenvale 237 D2
pl. Fitzroy N 19 C2
st. Burwood E 419 C12
st. Flemington 367 L1
st. Newtown 702 D7
SKEWES
st. Avondale Ht 322 A9
st. Braybrook 365 K2
SKINNER
ct. Grovedale 705 K16
SKIPTON
cl. Keilor Dn 275 K13
ct. Mill Park 242 J11
ct. Wantirna 422 D11
pl. Endeavour Hl 504 A20
rd. Hughesdale 457 F10
rd. Olinda 427 G19
st. Box Hill 375 D13
st. St Albans 320 K6
SKUA
ct. Blind Bight 650 E8
SKUSE
ct. Greenvale 237 F1
SKY
ct. Jan Juc 711 B16
ct. Werribee 447 A10
la. Ashburton 417 G17
vw. Wonga Park 291 J16
SKYE
cr. Endeavour Hl 503 H19
ct. Chelsea Ht 547 G18
ct. Glen Waverley 460 J6
ct. Sunbury 143 B4
pl. Doncaster E 331 H16
rd. Frankston 599 H13
rd. Gruyere 298 F1
rd. Langwarrin 600 C16
rd. Wantirna 422 J8
st. Macleod 285 B10
SKYLINE
dr. Gisborne 78 G8
dr. Keilor 277 C14
dr. Maribyrnong 367 D2
rd. Bend of Islands 250 C20
rd. Bend of Islands 251 A15
rd. Christmas Hills 251 H7
rd. Yarra Glen 208 B20
rd. Yarra Glen 208 F7
rd. Yarra Glen 251 H7
rd.n, Christmas Hills 208 B19
rd.n, St Andrews 208 E5
rd.n, Steels Ck 208 E5
rd.n, Yarra Glen 208 B19
ri. Craigieburn 150 D8
SLADE
ct. Bundoora 285 C1
SLADEN
cl. Thomastown 240 D16
st. Cranbourne 603 K3
SLATER
av. Blackburn N 376 B9
ct. Narre Warren 553 D11
ct. Seaford 599 K1
pde. Keilor East 321 K1
pl. Burwood, off Livingstone Cl 418 E6
st. Melbourne 31 B9
st. Melbourne 414 B5
st. Northcote 327 C16
SLATTERY
cr. Gisborne 79 A7
ct. Maddingley 263 D5
st. Werribee 448 A15
SLEDGE
cl. Braybrook 321 L17
SLEETH
av. Dandenong 536 C8
ct. Melton W 225 L18
SLESSOR
av. Lynbrook 551 D16
dr. Delahey 275 E13
SLEVIN
st. Lilydale 338 A4
SLIM
ct. Sunbury 143 E2
SLINGSBY
av. Beaconsfield 554 K16
SLOAN
ct. Sunbury 141 L8
SLOANE
ct. Altona Mdw 451 D6
ct. Keysborough 533 L8
st. Maribyrnong 322 L17
SLOANS
rd. N Warrandyte 290 A10
rd. Warrandyte 290 A19
SLOSS
rd. Healesville 258 B2
SLOUGH
rd. Altona 408 E15
st. Deer Park 319 C14
SLYM
ct. Springvale S 533 L5
SMALE
ct. Noble Park N 501 C17
ct. Seaford 599 K1
SMALL
ct. Mill Park 241 L4
rd. Bentleigh 496 C5
st. Hampton 494 L9
SMART
ct. Delahey 275 D12
ct. Grovedale 705 K15
st. Sunshine W 364 H2
st. Hawthorn, off Elgin St 371 H14
SMEATON
av. Dallas 238 C10
av. Hoppers Csg 448 H2
ct. Craigieburn 150 D19
ct. Frankston S 627 H13
SMEDLEY
la. Yarra Glen 209 H10
rd. Pk Orchards 377 K2
rd. Pk Orchards 378 A1
rd. Ringwood N 378 A1
SMEED
st. Black Rock 529 E1
SMETHURST
av. Pakenham 584 E6
st. Cranbourne 604 F1
SMETHWICK
grn. Caroline Spr 317 J3
SMIKE
st. Yallambie 285 H15
SMILEY
cr. Essendon W 323 A9
rd. Broadmeadows 238 F19
SMITH
av. Croydon 336 F19
av. Thomastown 241 H14
av. Williamstown 411 A16
cr. Footscray 367 E4
ct. Nar Warrn S 552 H13
ct. Sunbury 142 H2
rd. Camberwell 417 B7
rd. Springvale 500 E8
st. Albert Park 29 E11
st. Albert Park 413 C6
st. Alphington 327 J14
st. Bentleigh 456 D19
st. Brooklyn 365 E19
st. Brunswick W 324 K13
st. Burwood E 419 C11
st. Carrum 573 C8
st. Caulfield E 456 B1
st. Caulfield N 456 B1
st. Clifton Hill 19 F14
st. Coburg N 281 F16
st. Collingwood 25 F2
st. Fitzroy 19 F20
st. Fitzroy N 19 F14
st. Grovedale 706 G11
st. Hampton 495 H7
st. Healesville 257 F1
st. Kensington 34 A7
st. Maddingley 263 G3
st. Maidstone 322 J19
st. Marshall 706 L12
st. Melton 226 L18
st. Moonee Pnd 324 A11
st. Mt Martha 656 B9
st. Noble Park 501 B19
st. Port Melb 412 C3
st. Queenscliff 708 G19
st. Reservoir 283 B4
st. Richmond 26 C5
st. St Kilda 414 C18
st. S Melbourne 29 E10
st. S Melbourne 29 E5
st. S Melbourne 413 C3
st. S Melbourne 413 C5
st. Thornbury 326 C8
st. Williamstown 411 H19
SMITHACRES
rd. Montrose 381 K9
SMITHDENE
av. Ringwood E 379 D11
SMITHFIELD
ct. Keysborough 534 D12
rd. Flemington 33 B9
rd. Flemington 368 B4
rd. Kensington 33 B9
sq. Wantirna 422 K9
wk. Vermont 421 K1
SMITHS
la. Clyde North 581 F20
la. Pearcedale 647 F5
la. Smiths Gly 205 L3
rd. Parwan 263 J16
rd. Parwan 264 D16
rd. Templestowe 331 J11
rd. Yellingbo 387 K20
SMITHS GULLY
rd. Christmas Hills 206 B5
rd. St Andrews 205 E6
rd. Smiths Gly 205 E6
rd. Smiths Gly 206 B5
SMITHSON
ct. Dandenong S 535 G14
SMOKEY
ct. Somerville 644 E17
SMOLIC
ct. Tullamarine 236 E18
SMORGAN
ct. Kew 371 H5
SMORGON
sq. Kensington 33 E8
SMOULT
dr. Kurunjang 226 J14
SMYTH
pl. Geelong, off Little Ryrie St 703 B9
st. Chelsea Ht 547 H17
st. Frankston 599 D19
st. Mt Waverley 458 K6
st. Toorak 32 L14
st. Toorak 414 L7
st. Toorak 415 A7
SMYTHE
av. Balwyn 374 B13
la. Melbourne 24 G4
st. Geelong 703 A5
SNAEFELL
cr. Gladstone Pk 236 K16
SNAKE GULLY
dr. Bundoora 284 D3
dr. Bundoora 284 E5
SNAPPER POINT
dr. Patterson L 573 G7
SNEAD
cl. Hoppers Csg 405 B18
ct. Dingley Village 533 A6
ct. Mt Waverley 458 J8
SNEDDON
ct. Mulgrave 501 E2
dr. Glen Waverley 420 D20
dr. Nar Warrn S 552 H15
SNELL
gr. Oak Park 280 B11
gr. Oak Park 280 D11
gr. Pascoe Vale 280 D11
SNEYDES
rd. Point Cook 449 H12
rd. Werribee 448 C13
rd. Werribee S 449 A14
rd. Werribee S 449 C14
SNIDERS
la. Melbourne 2 D7
la. Melbourne 24 C5
SNIPE
cl. Chelsea Ht 547 F18
ct. Werribee 448 B10
tr. Nar Warrn N 538 H1
SNODGRASS
st. Pakenham 584 J5
SNOOKS
ct. Brighton 454 J14

SNOW
ct. Darley 222 B10
ct. The Basin 424 L8
st. Keilor Park 278 B14
SNOWBALL
av. Mt Evelyn 339 C18
rd. Eltham 287 B3
SNOWBERRY
pl. Nar Warrn S 579 D1
SNOWDEN
cl. Keilor Dn 276 D11
dr. Glen Waverley 460 J2
pl. Canterbury 373 D17
pl. Vermont 420 L5
pl. Vermont 421 A5
pl. Wantirna S 422 J15
st. Laverton 407 D14
st. Sunshine 321 E19
SNOWDON
av. Caulfield 455 H4
dr. Cheltenham 531 G4
SNOW GUM
pl. Somerville 644 D13
rd. Doncaster E 332 E19
SNOWGUM
cl. Rowville 463 J16
ct. Keysborough 534 A9
ct. Mulgrave 501 E1
ct. Nar Warrn S 553 D20
wk. Mornington 656 K2
SNOWVIEW
dr. Yarra Jctn 346 K17
SNOWY
ct. Clayton S 498 F8
ct. Werribee 447 H8
st. Dandenong N 501 L8
SOAME
st. Deer Park 319 D10
SOANES
dr. Mooroolbark 336 K10
SOBAR
ct. Keilor Dn 275 L11
SOCIETY
ct. Kilsyth 380 L8
SODEN
rd. Bangholme 547 E6
SODERLUND
dr. Doncaster 330 G16
SOFIA
ct. Sunshine N 321 E16
SOKLENG
cl. Rowville 502 H1
SOLAIRE
wy. S Morang 198 L12
SOLANDER
ct. Roxburgh Pk 194 A15
st. Dromana 686 D4
SOLAR
ct. Glen Waverley 460 L3
ct. Nunawading 376 J9
dr. Whittington 704 B19
SOLDIERS
rd. Berwick 554 J20
rd. Berwick 580 J5
rd. Clyde North 580 J5
SOLENT
cr. Taylors Lakes 275 G8
SOLFERINO
pl. Mt Waverley 419 G13
wy. Carrum Downs 575 G15
SOLITACE
wk. Glen Waverley 459 K1
SOLLEY
ct. Carrum Downs 600 F4
SOLLY
av. Princes Hill 325 H18
SOLLYA
ct. Narre Warren 553 E11
SOLOMON
ct. Sunbury 142 K3
dr. Deer Park 319 E10
dr. Keilor 277 A14
la. Truganina 405 J14
st. Mt Waverley 458 F5
SOLOMONS
tce. Mt Martha 656 C15
SOLSON
ct. Springvale S 533 K7
pl. Donvale 376 J5
SOLWAY
cl. Ferntree Gly 463 J8
cl. Patterson L 547 H18
ct. Epping 197 L18
ct. St Helena 245 A18
dr. Glen Waverley 420 F15
gdn. Werribee 446 K9
st. Ashburton 417 C20
SOLWOOD
la. Blackburn 375 K15

SOMALI
cl. Eltham North 245 H16
st. Pascoe Vale S 324 H2
SOMERLAYTON
cr. Fawkner 281 J1
SOMERLEIGH
cr. Greensborough 244 E20
cr. Greensborough 286 E1
rd. Laverton N 364 H16
SOMERS
av. McCrae 684 L17
av. Macleod 285 A13
av. Malvern 415 K9
av. Mt Martha 655 G20
cl. McCrae 685 A17
cl. Mill Park 242 B5
ct. Avondale Ht 322 F9
ct. Glen Waverley 459 J1
pde. Altona 408 G20
rd. N Warrandyte 289 L16
st. Balaclava 414 G20
st. Bentleigh 455 H18
st. Burwood 418 B9
st. Mitcham 377 G16
st. Newtown 702 G9
st. Noble Park 500 D17
st. Sunshine N 321 G12
SOMERSET
cl. Werribee 446 L11
cr. Croydon 379 L1
ct. Blackburn S 419 H6
ct. Mulgrave 500 K4
ct. Nar Warrn S 579 A4
ct. Rowville 503 D6
dr. Dandenong N 502 B11
dr. Dromana 686 D10
dr. Keysborough 534 L9
dr. Mt Martha 669 K3
dr. Portsea 678 F2
dr. Sunshine N 321 A9
dr. View Bank 329 H3
pl. Melbourne 2 A11
pl. Melbourne 24 B7
pl. Safety Bch 669 C16
pl. Windsor 414 H12
rd. Campbellfield 239 D14
rd. Frankston S 627 B15
rd. Glen Iris 417 D9
st. Avondale Ht 322 B11
st. Box Hill N 375 B6
st. Elsternwick 455 B3
st. Epping 197 L17
st. Pascoe Vale 280 D17
st. Richmond 26 H8
st. Richmond 371 A14
st. St Kilda 414 E15
st. Wantirna S 422 K12
st. Wantirna S 423 A13
SOMERTON
cr. St Albans 275 G19
ct. Darley 222 B11
rd. Bulla 190 E12
rd. Bulla 190 H12
rd. Greenvale 192 B14
rd. Greenvale 193 B15
rd. Greenvale 193 G16
rd. Oaklands Jctn 190 H12
rd. Oaklands Jctn 191 B13
rd. Roxburgh Pk 193 G16
SOMERTON PARK
dr. Campbellfield 194 K20
SOMERVILLE
cr. Somerville 645 D15
rd. Brooklyn 365 B11
rd. Hampton Pk 551 D8
rd. Kingsville 366 J13
rd. Sunshine W 364 J11
rd. Sunshine W 364 K11
rd. Sunshine W 365 B11
rd. Tottenham 366 A13
rd. W Footscray 366 A13
rd. Yarraville 366 H13
st. Coburg 325 E5
st. Doncaster 330 G17
SOMES
st. Wantirna S 462 A4
SOMME
av. Frankston 626 J3
pde. Edithvale 546 G14
SOMMERS
dr. Altona Mdw 451 H10
pl. Geelong 703 E9
st. Belmont 702 H16
SOMMERSBY
ct. Lysterfield 464 B20
rd. Point Cook 450 F10
rd. Point Cook 450 F11
SOMMEVILLE
dr. Roxburgh Pk 194 E14
SONG
st. Narre Warren 539 C20

SONGBIRD
av. Chirnside Pk 337 A3
SONGLARK
cr. Werribee 447 K4
SONIA
cl. Lilydale 338 C15
ct. Cranbourne W 577 F14
ct. Werribee 446 L11
ct. Werribee 447 A11
st. Carrum Downs 574 E18
st. Dandenong S 549 K8
st. Donvale 376 E4
st. Ringwood 378 H7
SONJA
ct. Narre Warren 553 B12
SONLEY
st. Maidstone 366 G3
SOPHI
ct. Mulgrave 500 E4
SOPHIA
av. Aspendale 546 C6
ct. Campbellfield 239 H12
ct. Carrum Downs 601 D4
gr. Parkdale 531 E13
gr. Tecoma 466 B12
pl. Melton W 226 B17
SOPHIE
ct. Hallam 537 H14
ct. Mornington 641 C20
st. Kilsyth 381 F8
SOPHORA
ct. Templstw Lr 330 K14
SORBONNE
dr. Sunbury 144 E10
SORBUS
cl. Endeavour Hl 536 L2
SORELL
ct. Keilor Dn 276 F13
SORGHUM
wy. Delahey 275 A13
SORREL
cr. Warranwood 334 J12
SORRELL
ct. Altona Mdw 451 J5
SORRENT
ct. Gisborne 78 K18
SORRENTO
av. Berwick 539 J17
pl. Epping 197 E17
st. Broadmeadows 237 H15
wy. Point Cook 450 E8
SORRETT
av. Malvern 415 K11
SOTTILE
dr. Cranbourne 603 K5
SOUDAN
rd. W Footscray 366 J5
st. Coburg 325 A1
st. Malvern 415 K16
SOUHAIL
ct. Berwick 554 B19
ct. Cranbourne W 577 J19
SOUTER
st. Beaconsfield 555 B16
st. Eltham 287 D16
st. Springvale 499 G13
SOUTH
av. Altona Mdw 451 F6
av. Bentleigh 496 A5
av. Mt Evelyn 383 C2
brk. Lysterfield 504 F17
cnc. Beaumaris 530 A10
cr. Heidelberg W 328 C1
cr. Northcote 326 J19
ct. Highett 496 G13
ct. Surrey Hills 418 A2
dr. Werribee S 488 A9
gwy. Langwarrin 629 H1
lk. Chirnside Pk 337 D6
pde. Blackburn 375 H15
rd. Airport W 278 H14
rd. Bentleigh 496 B6
rd. Bentleigh E 497 A7
rd. Braybrook 365 J4
rd. Brighton 494 H4
rd. Brighton East 495 B5
rd. Hampton E 495 B5
rd. McCrae 684 J13
rd. Menzies Ck 467 L16
rd. Moorabbin 496 B6
rd. Rosebud 684 F15
rd. Werribee 448 F16
st. Ascot Vale 324 D18
st. Belmont 702 B19
st. Hadfield 280 H9
st. Hawthorn 415 L1
st. Preston 327 A3
st. Seddon 367 D11
tce. Avondale Ht 322 A6
tce. Clifton Hill 20 A7
tce. Seabrook 451 B6

SOUTHAM
ct. Bulleen 329 H15
st. Brunswick W 324 F7
SOUTHAMPTON
cr. Abbotsford 26 L2
cr. Abbotsford 371 A11
st. Footscray 367 A7
SOUTH ANDERSON
ct. Cranbourne 577 L11
SOUTH AUDLEY
st. Abbotsford 26 K3
st. Brunswick 325 J13
SOUTHBANK
bvd. Southbank 3 H5
bvd. Southbank 24 C14
prm. Southbank 24 C13
wk. Taylors Hill 274 G8
SOUTH BOUNDARY
rd.e, Pearcedale 646 D7
rd.e, Somerville 646 D7
rd.w, Pearcedale 645 K4
SOUTHBOURNE
av. Dandenong S 535 J13
SOUTH BOX
ct. Hadfield 281 A6
SOUTH CAROLINE
st. South Yarra 31 K10
st. South Yarra 414 E5
SOUTH CENTRE
rd. Melb Airport 235 L20
SOUTH CHARLES
ct. Cranbourne 577 L12
SOUTH CIRCULAR
rd. Gladstone Pk 236 L19
rd. Gladstone Pk 237 A20
SOUTH CORPORATE
av. Rowville 502 A1
SOUTH DALY
st. Brunswick W 324 K15
SOUTHDEAN
Melton W 225 G19
st. Dandenong 535 L2
SOUTHDOWN
av. Glen Waverley 460 B3
cr. Belmont 706 C7
SOUTHDOWNE
cl. Springvale 500 B14
SOUTHERN
cr. Craigieburn 150 E16
ct. Forest Hill 420 E3
dr. Dingley Village 533 F9
rd. Heidelberg Ht 328 A1
rd. Heidelberg W 328 A1
rd. Mentone 531 K8
rd. Moorabbin Aprt 531 K8
SOUTHERN CROSS
dr. Roxburgh Pk 194 F10
st. Chirnside Pk 337 G1
SOUTHERNHAY
st. Reservoir 283 A14
SOUTHEY
ct. Elwood 454 E1
gr. Elwood 454 E1
rd. Boronia 424 G4
st. Blackburn N 375 K10
st. Brighton 455 A15
st. Elwood 454 D1
st. Kensington 34 A13
st. Sandringham 495 C16
st. Williamstn N 410 D12
SOUTHFORK
dr. Kilsyth S 381 B15
SOUTHGATE
av. Southbank 3 L5
av. Southbank 4 D4
av. Southbank 24 D13
av. Southbank 24 F13
st. Parkville 34 J5
SOUTH GATEWAY
Avondale Ht 321 K9
Coldstream 295 C14
SOUTH GIPPSLAND
fwy. Dandenong S 551 B7
fwy. Doveton 537 C19
fwy. Eumemmerring 537 C19
fwy. Hallam 537 C19
fwy. Hampton Pk 551 B7
hwy. Cranbourne 578 C11
hwy. Cranbourne E 604 E5
hwy. Cranbourne N 577 H1
hwy. Dandenong S 536 F16
hwy. Dandenong S 550 H1
hwy. Hampton Pk 551 D12
hwy. Hampton Pk 577 H1
hwy. Junction Vill 604 E5
hwy. Lynbrook 551 D12
hwy. Lynbrook 577 H1
hwy. Tooradin 650 J1
hwy. Tooradin 651 A3

SOUTH HILL
tr. Warrandyte 334 D5
SOUTHLAND
st. Glen Iris 417 A12
SOUTH LOCALISER
rd. Melb Airport 235 E19
SOUTH MADDINGLEY
rd. Maddingley 263 J13
SOUTH PARK
cl. Keysborough 533 J9
st. Northcote 326 F18
SOUTH RING
rd. Werribee 487 L1
SOUTH SHORE
av. Point Cook 450 L14
SOUTH VALLEY
rd. Highton 705 H7
rd. Pk Orchards 333 J15
SOUTHWARD
av. Port Melb 412 H3
SOUTHWELL
cl. Endeavour Hl 537 G10
SOUTH WHARF
rd. Montmorency, off Lorimer St 23 E17
SOUTHWICK
bvd. Altona Mdw 451 E
SOUTHWOLD
st. St Albans 320 F6
SOUTHWOOD
cl. Wantirna 421 L1
SOVEREIGH
ct. Templestowe, off Oakwood Ct 331 L14
SOVEREIGN
cl. Patterson L 547 G1
ct. Epping 198 A1
ct. Mornington 641 F1
pl. Wantirna S 422 F1
ri. Diamond Ck 245 J
rt. Hoppers Csg 448 D
wy. Avondale Ht 322 B1
wy. Hillside 231 J2
SOVEREIGN POINT
ct. Doncaster 330 K1
SOVERIGN CREST
bvd. Ferntree Gly 464 A1
SOWTER
ct. Donvale 376 K
SPAIN
ct. Northcote 326 F1
SPALDING
av. Sunshine N 321 E
ct. Rowville 502 J
SPANIEL
ct. Mill Park 242 K
SPANISH GULLY
rd. Smiths Gly 205 K
SPARK
ct. Vermont S 420 L
gr. Preston 327 C
la. Melbourne 24 K
st. Murrumbeena 457 C1
SPARKFORD
rd. Craigieburn 150 B1
st. Ivanhoe 327 K1
SPARKS
av. Burwood 418 L1
av. Fairfield 327 F1
av. Thornbury 327 G1
st. Beaumaris 530 C1
SPARROW
av. Anglesea 713 D
SPAVIN
dr. Sunbury 143 B
SPEAKMEN
st. Kensington 33 B1
SPEAN
ct. Endeavour Hl 503 H1
SPEAR
ct. Altona 408 K1
ct. Bulleen 329 G1
ct. Glen Waverley 420 L1
SPEARFELL
ct. St Albans 319 F
SPEARWATER
wy. Burwood 418 B
SPEEDIE
st. Coburg N 281 J1
SPEEDWAY
dr. Calder Park 232 K1
SPEEDWELL
st. Somerville 645 B1
SPEERS
ct. Warrandyte 332 G
SPEIGHT
st. Newport 410 H
st. Thornbury 327 A1

SPELLMAN
av. Sydenham 274 K5
SPENCE
st. Burwood 418 E10
st. Keilor Park 277 K13
SPENCER
av. Avonsleigh 470 C17
av. Dromana 686 F2
av. Roxburgh Pk 194 B9
ct. Berwick 554 F17
ct. Melton S 268 C12
dr. Carrum Downs 575 E15
pl. Richmond 26 H12
rd. Camberwell 373 B20
rd. Camberwell 373 C19
rd. Olinda 427 G15
rd. Parkville 18 B12
st. Blairgowrie 680 B20
st. Docklands 23 E5
st. Essendon 323 C4
st. Essendon 323 F4
st. Hawthorn 371 G15
st. Heidelberg Ht 284 F20
st. Melbourne 23 E5
st. Mentone 531 A6
st. Mt Martha 669 D3
st. Northcote 326 H11
st. Nunawading 376 H9
st. Preston 282 K18
st. Sunshine W 364 G15
st. Thomastown 241 G16
st. Thornbury 326 H11
st. W Melbourne 34 L20
ENSER
t. St Kilda 414 B18
PENSLEY
t. Clifton Hill 20 E4
t. Rosebud 684 G14
PERO
v. Mt Eliza 626 C19
PERRY
r. Tullamarine 278 G2
PICE
. Hallam 538 C18
PICER
vd. Altona Mdw 451 B4
t. Aspendale Gdn 546 J5
t. Beaumaris 530 G6
PILLERS
d. Macclesfield 471 F1
PINDRIFT
t. Carrum Downs 600 L5
y. Point Cook 450 H7
PINEBILL
t. Healesville 258 A1
PINIFEX
t. St Albans 319 F8
PINK
t. Brighton 455 A11
PINNAKER
t. Aspendale Gdn 546 L3
. Mornington 656 H1
PINNINGDALE
. Seabrook 450 K6
PINOSA
. Endeavour Hl 536 L1
PLENDENS
k. Narre Warren 553 C2
PLIT ROCK
d. Beaconsfld Up 542 L17
POLETO
. Keilor Lodge 275 L4
POONBILL
t. Carrum Downs 601 A1
PORING
. Roxburgh Pk 194 D14
t. Endeavour Hl 537 K10
PORTSGIRL
rc. Melbourne 24 E8
t. Melbourne 24 E8
PORTSMANS
r. Pakenham 584 A2
POTTED GUM
r. Bundoora 242 F13
PRATLING
t. Reservoir 282 G11
PRAY
v. Mordialloc 532 D20
t. Elwood 454 E4
t. Frankston 599 F15
t. Mornington 640 H16
t. Parkdale 531 F14
t. Rosebud 684 B20
PRAY POINT
d. Blairgowrie 679 D20
PRING
ct. Caroline Spr 318 B6
ct. Pakenham 583 L4
. Ringwood 335 C18
r. Hoppers Csg 448 J2
dr. Hoppers Csg 449 A2
la. Coldstream 254 J19
la. Gruyere 254 J19
la. Gruyere 298 F1
rd. Belgrave S 505 L11
rd. Caulfield S 455 K12
rd. Dingley Village 533 D2
rd. Hampton E 495 L12
rd. Highett 495 L12
rd. Junction Vill 604 G12
rd. Malvern 415 L12
rd. Monbulk 428 J20
rd. Monbulk 468 J1
rd. Silvan 428 K3
rd. Springvale S 533 D2
ri. Glen Waverley 459 L2
sq. Hallam 537 J16
st. Belmont 706 H2
st. Box Hill 374 H13
st. Bulleen 329 L9
st. Coburg 282 A19
st. Doveton 536 J7
st. E Melbourne 24 J2
st. Ferntree Gly 464 G4
st. Fitzroy 18 L12
st. Frankston 627 B2
st. Geelong West 702 H6
st. Greensborough 244 F19
st. Melbourne 24 J2
st. Mt Evelyn 339 G17
st. Niddrie 278 G18
st. Prahran 32 L19
st. Prahran 414 L10
st. Prahran 415 A10
st. Preston 282 H18
st. Reservoir 282 J14
st. Rye 696 J2
st. Sandringham 495 G18
st. Thomastown 240 J15
st. Thomastown 241 A15
st. Torquay 711 L8
st. Tullamarine 278 G5
st.e, Port Melb 413 B4
st.n, Port Melb 29 A6
st.s, Port Melb 29 A7
st.w, Port Melb 412 L3
SPRINGBANK
ct. Bulleen 329 G14
ct. Point Cook 450 K12
pl. View Bank 329 G1
ri. Nar Warrn N 538 D3
st. Tullamarine 236 E18
wy. Brookfield 267 L9
SPRINGFIELD
av. Camberwell 417 F5
av. Clayton S 498 H4
av. Croydon 380 D4
av. St Kilda E 414 L19
av. St Kilda E 415 A19
av. Toorak 415 C7
cl. Caroline Spr 318 E4
cr. Hampton Pk 551 K12
ct. Mill Park 242 K6
ct. Noble Park N 501 E18
dr. Narre Warren 552 F1
rd. Blackburn 376 B11
rd. Blackburn N 375 D10
rd. Boronia 423 L15
rd. Box Hill N 375 D10
rd. Gruyere 297 C2
rd. Gruyere 297 H3
rd. Mitcham 376 J11
rd. Nunawading 376 J11
rd. Springvale S 499 G19
st. Briar Hill 286 H4
SPRING GARDENS
st. South Yarra 31 H13
SPRINGHALL
pde. Pascoe Vale S 324 K3
SPRING HILL
ct. Queenscliff 707 K19
SPRINGHILL
rd. Hurstbridge 202 G14
SPRINGHURST
cr. Grovedale 705 L17
SPRINGLAKE
av. Caroline Spr 317 K7
av. Caroline Spr 317 L8
av. Caroline Spr 318 A8
SPRINGS
rd. Clarinda 498 F9
rd. Clayton S 498 F9
st. Cockatoo 510 L6
SPRINGSIDE
cr. Keysborough 535 B9
dr. Grovedale 706 E10
SPRINGSONG
ps. Chirnside Pk 337 G1
SPRINGVALE
rd. Aspendale Gdn 547 D7
rd. Bangholme 547 D7
rd. Braeside 533 G20
rd. Braeside 547 D7
rd. Burwood E 420 E11
rd. Chelsea Ht 547 D7
rd. Dingley Village 533 J10
rd. Donvale 376 H3
rd. Forest Hill 376 F20
rd. Forest Hill 420 E11
rd. Glen Waverley 460 C7
rd. Keysborough 547 D7
rd. Mulgrave 500 A8
rd. Nunawading 376 F20
rd. Springvale 499 K19
rd. Springvale S 533 H10
rd. Vermont S 420 E11
rd. Wheelers Hill 460 B20
SPRING VALLEY
av. Craigieburn 150 G16
dr. Clayton S 499 E12
dr. Templestowe 331 L6
dr. Torquay 711 H12
SPRINGVALLEY
cr. Keysborough 534 B11
wy. Nar Warrn S 552 E14
SPRINGWATER
sq. Point Cook 450 K12
SPRINGWOOD
av. Narre Warren 552 J4
cl. Donvale 332 K15
vw. Bundoora 284 G7
SPRINGYBARK
tr. Langwarrin 629 B11
SPRINT
st. Keilor Park 278 B15
SPROUL
st. Sunshine N 321 B9
SPRUCE
ct. Frankston N 600 E7
ct. Gladstone Pk 237 D19
ct. Narre Warren 538 J19
dr. Rowville 463 H18
SPRUZEN
av. Kew East 372 A4
SPRY
st. Coburg N 281 F14
SPRYS
la. Hurstbridge 203 C17
SPUNNER
ct. Sorrento 678 F8
SPUR
la. Carlton 18 J15
SPURGEON
cl. Rye 697 C14
SPURLING
cl. S Geelong 702 L13
cl. S Geelong 703 A13
st. Maidstone 366 H1
SPURR
st. Craigieburn 150 F17
SPURWAY
la. Brunswick 325 D17
SPYGLASS
ct. Sunbury 144 B10
SQUATTER
ct. Werribee 447 J7
SQUIRE
ct. Glen Waverley 420 L18
st. Blairgowrie 696 A3
SQUIRES
ct. Caroline Spr 318 C5
SREDNA
st. W Footscray 366 C9
STABLE
ct. Endeavour Hl 504 A20
gr. Skye 575 G17
STABLEFORD
av. Glen Waverley 459 J4
ct. Rowville 463 H20
STABLES
pl. Sydenham 274 L5
STACEY
ct. Endeavour Hl 538 B2
st. Junction Vill 604 G12
STACKPOLE
cr. Sunbury 142 H14
STACKPOOLE
st. Noble Park 534 L6
STADAM
pl. Hillside 232 F18
STADIUM
dr. Keilor Park 277 J10
dr. Tullamarine 277 J10
STAFF
st. Seddon 367 C10
STAFFORD
ct. Bayswater N 380 E19
ct. Doncaster E 332 B18
ct. Ivanhoe East 328 G14
pl. Chirnside Pk 336 G6
pl. Narre Warren 539 B16
pl. Williamstown 411 J16
st. Abbotsford 20 B15
st. Blackburn S 419 E2
st. Footscray 366 L7
st. Herne Hill 701 K3
st. Hoppers Csg 405 D14
st. Huntingdale 458 D15
st. Melton S 268 G10
st. Northcote 327 D17
st. Preston 326 C3
st. Richmond 371 A17
STAG
la. Yarra Glen 210 B15
STAGECOACH
bvd. S Morang 199 K16
cl. Hoppers Csg 447 L1
cr. Sydenham 274 L6
STAINSBY
cl. Endeavour Hl 537 C4
cr. Roxburgh Pk 194 D16
STAKE
rd. Diggers Rest 187 B10
STALEY
st. Brunswick 325 G13
STALLARD
ct. Watsonia N 243 D18
STALLION
ct. Nar Warrn S 578 K1
STAMFORD
cl. Bacchus Msh 221 L16
cr. Rowville 462 G19
ct. Broadmeadows 238 J12
ct. Eltham 288 D4
ct. Ringwood N 334 L19
gr. Caroline Spr 317 J4
rd. Oakleigh 458 C9
STANBURY
ct. Sunshine W 364 B5
STANDALE
ct. Highton 701 L16
STANDARD
av. Box Hill 374 G17
STANDEN
ct. Warranwood 335 B13
STANDFIELD
st. Bacchus Msh 222 A19
STANDRING
ct. Donvale 332 G18
STANE BRAE
ct. Wonga Park 291 C15
STANFIELD
ct. Glen Waverley 420 D18
dr. Wandana Ht 705 C1
STANFORD
cl. Fawkner 281 F1
cl. Werribee 446 K11
ct. Frankston 600 C17
ct. Sunbury 144 E10
ct. Whittington 704 A19
st. Ascot Vale 323 G18
st. Sunshine 365 D6
STANGER
st. Yarraville 366 D16
STANHILL
dr. Cranbourne S 602 L12
STANHOPE
ct. Ringwood 378 C18
ct. South Yarra 32 J10
ct. South Yarra 414 K5
gr. Camberwell 372 L19
gr. Camberwell 373 A19
st. Armadale 415 J13
st. Black Rock 529 G2
st. Broadmeadows 238 E17
st. Dandenong S 535 H13
st. Eltham 287 E8
st. Geelong West 702 D6
st. Malvern 415 K13
st. Mont Albert 374 D16
st. Upwey 465 K14
st. W Footscray 366 D6
STANILAND
av. Malvern 415 L16
gr. Elsternwick 454 L4
gr. Elsternwick 455 A5
STANIS
st. Eumemmerring 536 L15
st. Eumemmerring 537 A15
STANLAKE
ri. Templstw Lr 330 E8
st. Footscray 366 L5
st. Reservoir 282 K13
STANLEY
av. Cheltenham 530 J1
av. Eltham 287 J5
av. Hawthorn E 372 F17
av. Mt Waverley 458 H9
av. Ringwood E 379 B11
cr. Brookfield 268 A4
cr. Mt Martha 668 K6
cr. Mt Martha 669 A6
ct. Deer Park 318 L11
ct. Hoppers Csg 405 C18
ct. Thomastown 241 K14
dr. Doncaster 331 A14
dr. Somerton 194 H11
gr. Blackburn 375 F12
gr. Canterbury 372 L16
gr. Canterbury 373 A16
pde. Caulfield N 415 G19
pl. Hawthorn E 372 H20
rd. Healesville 258 D5
rd. Keysborough 534 F18
rd. Laverton N 364 E18
rd. Monbulk 428 D20
rd. Vermont S 420 H10
st. Altona 408 H19
st. Belgrave 466 H12
st. Black Rock 529 G4
st. Box Hill S 374 J19
st. Brighton 455 A18
st. Brunswick 325 K12
st. Bulleen 329 G16
st. Carrum 573 B8
st. Chirnside Pk 336 H5
st. Collingwood 19 G16
st. Cranbourne 578 A17
st. Dandenong 535 H8
st. Don Valley 346 E6
st. Elsternwick 454 L5
st. Elsternwick 455 A5
st. Essendon 323 L9
st. Frankston 599 E18
st. Glenroy 279 K9
st. Hampton Pk 551 F10
st. Ivanhoe 327 K10
st. Kew 371 L12
st. Malvern East 416 J16
st. Newtown 702 E12
st. Northcote 327 B19
st. Olinda 426 J4
st. Pascoe Vale 280 K19
st. Richmond 26 D16
st. Somerville 645 D15
st. Somerville 645 D16
st. South Yarra 32 H10
st. South Yarra 414 K5
st. The Basin 425 A9
st. W Footscray 366 G5
st. W Melbourne 23 A4
st. Williamstown 411 F12
tce. Surrey Hills 373 H18
STANLEY GROSE
dr. Malvern East 417 A18
STANLEY JONES
dr. S Morang 243 J2
STANSELL
st. Kew 372 C13
STANSFIELD
ct. Frankston S 628 D16
STANTON
cl. Mt Martha 656 K10
cl. Nar Warrn S 552 G13
cr. Rosanna 285 A16
ct. Darley 222 C11
ct. Gisborne S 110 E18
ct. Glen Waverley 461 B3
ct. Seabrook 450 K3
ct. Westmeadows 236 L15
ct. Westmeadows 237 A15
dr. Diamond Ck 245 K13
gr. Lilydale 339 L5
pl. Mill Park 242 E5
st. Abbotsford 20 B18
st. Doncaster 374 E3
st. Highett 496 J15
STANWORTH
ct. Preston 282 J19
STAPLES
st. Hadfield 281 B6
wy. Seabrook 450 L8
STAPLEY
cr. Altona North 410 D5
cr. Chadstone 458 A6
STAR
al. Melbourne 2 F11
al. Melbourne 24 E6
cr. Hallam 551 H1
ct. Fawkner 281 F6
gr. Bundoora 242 D15
st. Geelong, off Myers St 703 A8
STARBOARD
la. Patterson L 547 H20
STARCHENKO
ct. Carrum Downs 575 E16
STARCROSS
av. Croydon 379 K5
STARKIE
rd. Sunbury 110 L16
rd. Sunbury 111 A16
STARLING
rd. Diamond Ck 245 D8
rd. Officer 556 H20

STONEMASONS
tr. Lysterfield S...503 G11
STONEWALL
cl. Deer Park...319 G11
STONEY
rd. Belgrave...466 H13
STONEY CREEK
rd. Beaconsfld Up...542 J8
STONINGTON
pl. Ringwood...378 L1
pl. Ringwood...379 A1
STONNINGTON
ct. Lysterfield...464 A19
dr. Watsonia N...243 F20
pl. Toorak...415 H9
STONY
ri. Maribyrnong...322 G16
STONY CREEK
rd. Kangaroo Grnd...289 J12
rd. N Warrandyte...289 J12
STONYFORD
rd. Silvan...384 B15
STOOKE
st. Yarraville...366 D16
STORE
st. Melb Airport...235 B11
STOREN
cl. Ferntree Gly...424 G18
STORER
dr. Dromana...685 K10
STOREY
av. Hampton...495 D9
av. Research...288 H2
ct. Tootgarook...698 E8
rd. Reservoir...283 B13
st. Yarraville...367 B14
STORK
av. Belmont...706 F2
STORNOWAY
dr. Baxter...644 C1
gln. View Bank...286 B16
pl. Camberwell...417 H7
rd. Camberwell...417 H6
STORRER
st. Geelong...703 D10
STORRINGTON
av. Hoppers Csg...405 B20
STORTFORD
av. Ivanhoe...327 K10
STORY
rd. Warburton...349 H6
st. Parkville...17 F11
STOTT
st. Box Hill S...418 F5
st. Northcote...326 H12
st. Preston...326 G4
st. Thornbury...326 H9
STOTTS
la. Frankston S...628 A20
STOW
cl. Epping...198 E19
STOWE
av. Greensborough...286 B6
STOWHEAD
la. Caroline Spr...317 L3
STRABANE
av. Balwyn...374 C9
av. Mont Albert N...374 C9
STRACHAN
av. Manifold Ht...702 B2
cl. Taylors Lakes...233 A19
la. Melbourne...24 J7
pl. Melton S...268 G13
st. Oak Park...280 A11
STRACHANS
rd. Mornington...640 B18
STRACHEN
ct. Sunbury...142 K4
STRADA
cr. Wheelers Hill...460 E13
cr. Wheelers Hill...460 F16
STRADBROKE
av. Brighton East...455 E17
av. Frankston S...627 B8
av. Heidelberg...328 J7
av. Toorak...415 D7
cl. Berwick...539 G19
cr. Mulgrave...500 D1
ct. Noble Park N...501 B7
dr. St Albans...320 E7
rd. Boronia...424 B15
rd. Montrose...382 A10
st. Oakleigh S...458 D17
st. W Footscray...366 J9
wy. Wyndham Va...446 F11
STRADBROOK
ct. Carrum Downs...601 D1

STRADELLA
av. Vermont S...420 H13
cl. Mill Park...242 G11
ct. Mt Eliza...642 J1
STRADISHALL
wy. Tullamarine...278 K2
STRADLING
av. Geelong...702 K2
STRADMORE
av. Templestowe...331 C7
STRAFFORD
av. Cranbourne...577 L13
STRAHAN
ct. Boronia...423 E14
ct. Keilor Dn...276 E13
STRAKER
st. N Melbourne...34 E12
STRAND
cl. Glen Waverley...460 L4
ct. Templestowe...332 A14
STRANG
st. Hoppers Csg...448 K2
STRANGER
st. Brunswick...325 G18
STRANKS
av. Brunswick W...325 A10
STRANRAER
cl. Greenvale...193 G17
STRASBOURG
rd. Rosanna...328 L3
rd. Rosanna...329 A3
STRATFORD
av. Bentleigh E...457 A19
av. Kew...371 J11
cl. Somerville...644 J20
ct. Grovedale...706 E14
ct. Mulgrave...460 E20
pl. Bundoora...284 L2
rd. Rye...696 L12
rd. Rye...697 A12
sq. Wantirna...422 C9
st. Hadfield...281 B7
wy. Point Cook...450 G8
STRATHAIRD
cl. Eltham North...245 F16
dr. Nar Warrn S...578 E1
st. Strathmore...279 G13
STRATHALBYN
st. Kew East...372 F6
STRATHALLAN
la. Brighton, off
Male St...454 L18
rd. Macleod...285 B13
STRATHALLYN
rd. Ringwood...378 F7
STRATHAVAN
dr. Berwick...554 G16
STRATHAVEN
pl. Lilydale...338 K2
pl. Lilydale...339 C5
STRATHBOGIE
ct. Kilsyth...381 J8
wk. Blackburn S, off
Feathertop Ch...419 F12
STRATHCAIRN
av. Jan Juc...711 D13
STRATHCONNAN
pl. Wheelers Hill...461 B12
STRATHCONNON
sq. Tullamarine...236 E18
STRATHDON
pl. Point Cook...450 H7
STRATHEARN
av. Coburg...325 D7
av. Murrumbeena...457 B14
ct. Carrum Downs...601 D1
dr. Sunbury...143 B6
STRATHEDEN
ct. Rye...696 E1
ct. Sydenham...274 K2
pl. Mooroolbark...337 J20
STRATHFIELD
pde. Croydon...335 D20
pde. Croydon...379 D1
STRATHFORD
ct. Werribee...446 K10
st. Epping...198 B16
STRATHMERTON
st. Reservoir...283 C8
STRATHMIGLO
ct. Bayswater N...380 G19
STRATHMORE
cr. Hoppers Csg...448 F6
dr. Jan Juc...711 A14
st. Bentleigh...456 D18
st. Rye...697 F5
STRATHNAVER
av. Strathmore...279 G12

STRATHWYN
pl. Kew East...372 F6
STRATTON
cl. Kings Park...319 A1
ct. Bayswater...423 B8
STRATUS
ct. Hampton Pk...551 L15
STRAUGHAN
st. Glen Iris...417 E9
STRAVANE
wy. Hampton Pk...551 H12
STRAW
st. Brunswick W...325 A11
STRAWBENT
ri. Narre Warren...552 J4
STRAWBERRY
cl. Grovedale...705 H13
STREAM
wk. Hallam...538 E16
STREETLY
cl. Tullamarine...278 J3
STREETON
cct. Mill Park...242 L9
cct. Mill Park...243 A8
cr. Ivanhoe East...328 L14
cr. Ivanhoe East...329 A14
ct. Burwood E...419 G7
ct. Mont Albert...374 F17
ct. Rowville...502 G4
ct. Skye...601 H4
ct. Sunbury...142 K5
ct. Taylors Lakes...275 A1
la. Doncaster E...332 D16
rd. Bayswater...424 C1
wy. Berwick...554 G18
STRELDEN
av. Oakleigh E...458 K13
STRELDON
av. Strathmore...279 J14
STRETTLE
st. Kensington...33 E8
st. Thornbury...326 C7
STRETTON
ct. Mt Waverley...458 G6
pl. Wyndham Va...446 D6
STREZLECKI
av. Sunshine W...364 L13
av. Sunshine W...365 A12
gr. Laverton...406 K19
gr.s, Altona Mdw...450 K1
STRICKLAND
av. Highton...705 J3
av. Hoppers Csg...449 C2
av. Mill Park...242 E7
cr. Burnside...318 E6
ct. Blackburn N...376 A10
ct. Greensborough...286 F4
dr. Wheelers Hill...460 L8
STRICTA
ct. Frankston N...600 C6
STRINGER
ct. Sunbury...113 H7
rd. Blairgowrie...679 F18
STRINGERS
pl. Geelong...703 C12
ri. Donvale...332 L18
STRINGY BARK
pl. S Morang...243 L4
ri. Croydon N...336 B12
STRINGYBARK
bvd.n, Mt Evelyn...339 K17
bvd.s, Mt Evelyn...339 J17
cl. Forest Hill...376 D20
cl. Nunawading...420 D1
cr. Frankston N...599 K9
ct. Berwick...553 H5
ct. Hillside...274 F4
ct. Ringwood N...334 J20
la. Seville E...343 D11
pl. Meadow Ht...193 L17
rd. Cockatoo...511 A8
rd. Eltham...288 B13
STRODE
pl. Richmond...26 A11
st. Richmond...26 A11
STROMA
av. Balwyn N...329 H20
STRONER
av. Keilor East...322 F6
STRONG
av. Thomastown...240 J19
dr. Hampton Pk...551 L9
st. Breakwater...703 F16
st. S Geelong...703 A11
st. S Geelong...703 C14
st. S Geelong...703 E16
st. Spotswood...366 F19
STROUD
ct. Kilsyth S...424 L2
st. Balwyn...373 D8

STRUAN
av. Endeavour Hl...503 K18
av. Mooroolbark...337 E16
st. Toorak...415 C3
STRZELECKI
ct. Cranbourne N...577 K9
ct. Kilsyth...381 H7
ct. Taylors Lakes...275 K3
STUART
av. Cheltenham...496 E18
av. Hampton Pk...551 H9
av. Jan Juc...711 D17
cl. Bayswater N...380 G18
cl. Frankston...626 L3
cr. Nunawading...376 H11
ct. Balwyn N...374 C4
ct. Keilor...276 K10
rd. Lilydale...337 K6
rd. Seville E...343 A13
st. Armadale...415 H13
st. Bayswater N...380 G17
st. Dandenong...536 B8
st. Greensborough...245 B20
st. Moonee Pnd...324 F16
st. Noble Park...534 J2
st. St Helena...245 B20
st. Sorrento...678 K9
st. The Basin...425 A10
st. Balaclava, off
William St...414 H18
STUBB
st. Somerton...195 D18
STUBBS
av. Mt Evelyn...339 A15
st. Kensington...34 D10
STUBER
rd. Altona North...408 K6
STUBLEY
ct. Greensborough...286 B4
STUD
ct. Lower Plenty...330 H1
ct. Skye...575 G19
rd. Bayswater...422 K8
rd. Dandenong...536 C8
rd. Dandenong N...536 C8
rd. Knoxfield...462 H11
rd. Rowville...462 G20
rd. Scoresby...462 G1
rd. Wantirna...422 K8
rd. Wantirna S...462 G1
STUDD
rd. Pakenham...558 C19
STUDLEY
av. Kew...371 G10
ct. Doncaster...330 G17
ct. Laverton...407 C17
ct. Mill Park...242 K13
pl. Mt Martha...656 D7
rd. Brighton East...495 H5
rd. Eaglemont...328 G10
rd. Heidelberg...328 G10
rd. Ivanhoe...328 E11
st. Abbotsford...20 B15
st. Craigieburn...150 B17
st. Doncaster...330 F18
st. Maidstone...366 J4
st. Mulgrave...500 C5
STUDLEY PARK
rd. Kew...20 L15
rd. Kew...371 B9
STUMBLERS
la. Tooradin...651 F7
STUMPY GULLY
rd. Moorooduc...643 F20
rd. Moorooduc...658 L6
STURDEE
rd. Black Rock...495 G20
rd. Donvale...377 D8
st. Ascot Vale...324 C19
st. Box Hill...375 A19
st. Chelsea...547 C18
st. Coburg N...281 F16
st. Reservoir...283 A4
st. Seaford...600 B3
STURIO
pde. Mt Eliza...625 G18
STURIS
ct. Westmeadows...237 D15
STURNS
la. Geelong...703 C12
STURROCK
ct. Altona Mdw...451 H10
ct. Berwick...553 K6
ct. Mill Park...198 F20
ct. Mill Park...242 F1
st. Brunswick...325 L9
STURT
ct. Cranbourne N...577 K7
ct. Grovedale...706 A13
ct. Taylors Lakes...233 J20
pl. Diamond Ck...246 A13
pl. Frankston S...627 F10
rd. Melton S...268 E12
st. Collingwood...19 L18
st. Essendon...323 K5
st. Flemington...33 H1
st. Flemington...324 D20
st. Southbank...3 F19
st. Southbank...30 D1
st. Sunbury...143 C12
st. Sunshine...321 G20
st. Yarraville...366 J14
st.n, Croydon...380 D3
st.s, Croydon...380 C4
STUTT
av. Doncaster...374 D1
STUTZ
cl. Keilor Dn...276 A10
STYLES
ct. Wonga Park...291 K14
STYMIE
st. Kingsbury...283 H9
STYNES
wy. Cranbourne W...577 F14
SUAAD
ct. Cranbourne W...577 H19
pl. Langwarrin...602 B16
SUBIACO
ct. Glen Waverley...419 L17
SUBZERO
cl. Kurunjang...227 E8
cl. Rowville...503 A2
SUDA
av. Ringwood...378 F10
ct. Avondale Ht...322 F7
SUE
ct. Hampton Pk...551 L8
pl. Berwick...554 K18
pl. Carrum Downs...600 K4
SUEMAR
st. Mulgrave...500 E4
SUERULLA
ct. Rowville...503 C8
SUFFERN
av. Bayswater...423 B3
SUFFOLK
av. Coburg...325 D1
av. Cockatoo...511 D5
cr. Mt Martha...669 L2
ct. Grovedale...706 A14
pl. Campbellfield...239 H14
rd. Dandenong N...502 C11
rd. Sunshine N...321 C16
rd. Surrey Hills...373 K20
st. Blackburn...375 H12
st. Maidstone...366 E4
st. Nunawading...376 K8
st. Reservoir...283 A6
st. Wantirna S...422 L14
st. W Footscray...366 E4
SUGAR BUSH
dr. Lynbrook...551 G15
SUGAR GUM
ct. Nar Warrn S...552 F12
ct. Up Fntree Gly...464 K6
dr. Bundoora...284 E3
dr. Hillside...273 L5
dr. Hillside...274 A3
SUGARGUM
ct. Nunawading...376 F16
ct. View Bank...285 L18
dr. Altona...409 B17
dr. Mulgrave...501 E2
gr. Deer Park...319 G11
wk.n, Point Cook...450 C4
wk.s, Point Cook...450 C4
wy. Sunbury...143 G17
SUGARLOAF
av. Lynbrook...551 G16
bnd. Brookfield...267 J7
cl. Burwood E...419 F11
dr. Chirnside Pk...337 B6
la. Berwick...554 J17
rd. Beaconsfld Up...542 K16
tr. Christmas Hills...249 K10
SUGDEN
pl. Melbourne...2 D13
pl. Melbourne...24 D7
SULBY
pl. Gladstone Pk...237 C15
SULKY
ct. Endeavour Hl...538 B1
SULLIVAN
av. Rowville...463 K18
ct. Belmont...706 B1
ct. Wantirna...422 H5
dr. Somerville...645 C14
pl. Footscray...367 E9
rd. St Albans...319 F7
st. Bellfield...328 C6
st. Moorabbin...497 A8
st. Preston...327 H5

st. Rye 697 G3
st. Sorrento 678 G12
st. Springvale 499 L7

SULLIVANS
rd. Sunbury 113 D1

SULVA
rd. Warrandyte S 334 J5

SUMAK
rd. Mt Martha 656 H9

SUMERS
st. Laverton 407 C16

SUMERSETT
av. Oakleigh S 457 J18

SUMMER
la. Ringwood 378 A16
pl. Mooroolbark 337 J9
st. E Geelong 703 G10

SUMMERFIELD
dr. Mornington 657 C6

SUMMERHILL
av. Malvern East 416 H19
av. Wheelers Hill 461 F14
cl. Ferntree Gly 463 F5
cr. Mt Eliza 642 D6
ct. Hillside 231 L17
rd. Beaumaris 529 K5
rd. Brighton East 455 D20
rd. Craigieburn 150 H6
rd. Footscray 366 K5
rd. Glen Iris 417 D14
rd. Maidstone 366 K5
rd. Montrose 382 B13
rd. Reservoir 283 G14
rd. Templestowe 331 D2
rd. Tootgarook 698 D7
rd. W Footscray 366 K5
rd. Wollert 153 A8
ri. Bundoora 284 F6
tce. Highton 705 E3

SUMMERHILL PARK
dr. Mooroolbark 337 K16

SUMMERLAKE
cl. Point Cook 451 B14

SUMMERLEA
gr. Hawthorn 371 K20
rd. Mt Dandenong 426 G2
rd. Narre Warren 538 L19

SUMMERS
st. Deer Park 319 B17
st. Prahran 32 H17
st. Prahran 414 J9

SUMMIT
av. Belmont 706 A3
av. Emerald 510 B9
av. Hampton E 495 J9
av. Oak Park 279 K10
cr. Glen Waverley 460 G5
cr. Ringwood N 378 A7
ct. Boronia 424 F5
ct. Bundoora 284 D4
ct. Hampton Pk 551 J14
ct. Lalor 240 J10
ct. Mooroolbark 336 L20
ct. St Helena 245 E15
dr. Bulleen 329 G12
dr. Eaglemont 328 K12
dr. Mickleham 150 B4
mw. Hillside 232 A18
rd. Burwood 418 K7
rd. Frankston 627 C5
rd. Lilydale 338 J7
rd. Lysterfield 503 J3
rd. Noble Park N 501 A12
ri. Maribyrnong 322 G17

SUMMONER
st. Blairgowrie 695 J3

SUMNER
av. Northcote 326 D15
av. Fitzroy N, off Rushall Cr 326 F20
ct. Berwick 554 J11
pl. Point Cook 449 L5
rd. Baxter 643 C6
st. Brunswick E 326 B15

SUN
av. Spotswood 411 C5
cr. Sunshine 365 B2
ri. Ashburton 417 G17
ri. Patterson L 573 L8
st. Moolap 704 L16

SUNBEAM
av. Ringwood E 379 A9
ct. Nar Warrn S 553 C18
st. Glenroy 280 H2
st. Pascoe Vale 281 A12

SUNBIRD
cr. Carrum Downs 600 K5
cr. Hoppers Csg 405 E20
gdn. Epping 241 J1

SUNBURST
av. Balwyn N 373 D3
ct. Mooroolbark 337 G9
st. Oakleigh E 458 J12

SUNBURY
cr. Surrey Hills 373 L17
dr. Melb Airport 235 K10
rd. Bulla 144 C14
rd. Bulla 190 B15
rd. Melb Airport 191 A19
rd. Melb Airport 235 E1
rd. Sunbury 144 C14

SUNCREST
pl. Sunshine 365 A3

SUNDANCE
ct. Point Cook 450 L13

SUNDERLAND
av. Ashburton 417 J17
av. Sunbury 113 A20
av. Sunbury 142 L1
av. Sunbury 143 A1
rd. Wandana Ht 701 C20
rd. Wandana Ht 705 B1
ri. Greensborough 286 J3

SUN DEW
av. Boronia 424 C11

SUNDEW
av. Long Forest 224 F11
av. Rosebud W 699 B2
cl. Hillside 274 D2
ct. Aspendale Gdn 546 L4
ct. Aspendale Gdn 547 A4
ct. Knoxfield 423 C20
pde. Launching Pl 346 A13
st. Bundoora 242 D13

SUNDOWN
ct. Narre Warren 552 G1
wk. Frankston S 627 K17

SUNDOWNER
av. Clarinda 498 E10
ct. Wheelers Hill 461 C11

SUNHILL
av. Burwood 418 L11
av. Ringwood 378 J4
av. Rosebud 684 J15
ct. Ardeer 320 C18
ct. Beaconsfield 555 C12
ct. St Kilda E 414 L16
rd. Glen Iris 416 J10
rd. Mt Waverley 419 A17
rd. Templstw Lr 330 C11

SUNISH
ct. Sunbury 143 E4

SUNLIGHT
cr. Brighton East 495 H4

SUNLINE
av. Noble Park N 501 C18

SUNLIT
ct. Hampton E 496 A11

SUNMORE
cl. Heatherton 497 H12

SUNNINGDALE
av. Jan Juc 711 F13
av. Mornington 656 D4
av. Sunbury 144 F11
ct. Rowville 462 D19
rd. Rosebud 684 H19
wy. Heatherton 497 J16

SUNNINGHILL
ct. Mitcham 377 E9

SUNNY
ct. Seaford 600 B3
ct. Selby 467 A13
ri. Templestowe 332 B3

SUNNYBANK
cl. Lysterfield S 504 A16
rd. Langwarrin 629 F10

SUNNYBROOK
ct. Craigieburn 193 L3
dr. Wheelers Hill 460 L10

SUNNYHILL
rd. Belgrave 466 C17

SUNNY HOLLOW
la. Pentland Hl 221 A14

SUNNY PARK
cl. Gisborne 79 D10

SUNNYRIDGE
ct. Chirnside Pk 336 L8

SUNNYSIDE
av. Brighton East 455 D15
av. Camberwell 416 H3
av. Dandenong 536 D7
av. Kallista 427 B19
av. Nunawading 376 K11
cr. Wattle Glen 246 H8
dr. Berwick 553 F2
gr. Bentleigh 455 K20
rd. Gruyere 342 K13
rd. Mt Eliza 641 D5
rd. Mt Waverley 458 J10
rd. Seville 342 K13
rd. Seville E 342 K13
tce. Emerald 469 G12

SUNNYSLOPES
rd. Kallista 467 E1

SUNNYVALE
cr. Keysborough 534 E13
ct. Hampton Pk 551 G7

SUNRAE
ct. Seaford 573 C12

SUNRAY
av. Cheltenham 496 L19
ct. Croydon 380 G6
ct. Donvale 376 H7
ct. Eltham 288 D7

SUNRISE
cl. Safety Bch 669 B15
cr. Templstw Lr 330 D14
ct. Epping 241 K1
ct. Gisborne 78 H8
ct. Hampton Pk 551 K14
ct. Lysterfield 503 K1
dr. Greensborough 244 H14
dr. Mulgrave 500 H3
pl. Wyndham Va 446 G12

SUNRISE HILL
rd. Montrose 382 C13

SUNSET
av. Beaumaris 529 L7
av. Olinda 426 H6
av. Templestowe 331 L6
bvd. Jacana 237 H19
cr. Mt Eliza 626 E18
ct. Craigieburn 194 A2
ct. Highton 705 F3
ct. Hoppers Csg 448 J8
ct. Keysborough 534 B11
ct. Mitcham 377 D10
dr. Heathmont 378 H20
dr. Kilsyth S 381 B15
gr. Dandenong S 535 H12
pl. Hampton Pk 551 K15
tce. Ferntree Gly 464 D14
tr. Lysterfield 505 E2
wy. Dromana 686 A8

SUNSET STRIP
Jan Juc 711 A18
Silvan 385 A19
Sorrento 679 B13

SUNSHINE
av. Kealba 276 H18
av. Kealba 320 K1
av. Keilor Lodge 276 B5
av. Mitcham 377 D16
av. St Albans 276 H18
av. Taylors Lakes 276 B7
cl. Greensborough 244 H16
dr. Mt Martha 669 C1
gr. Rye 697 J6
rd. Braybrook 365 H7
rd. Sunshine 365 H7
rd. Tottenham 365 H7
rd. W Footscray 365 H7
st. Campbellfield 239 C16
st. Oakleigh E 458 J14
st. Pascoe Vale 281 A12
st. Rowville 502 G5

SUN VALLEY
bvd. Lynbrook 551 G16

SUNVIEW
ct. Dingley Village 533 C10

SUPERIOR
av. Rowville 462 J16
dr. Dandenong S 549 H9
tce. Narre Warren, off Kentucky Cl 539 F17

SUPPLY
dr. Epping 241 F4

SUPREME
pl. Doncaster E, off Jising Ct 375 G2

SURACE
ct. Dandenong N 502 C18

SURAT
pl. Rowville 463 G15

SURF
av. Beaumaris 529 J9
rd. Rye 697 C18
rd. St Andrews Bch 697 C18
st. Parkdale 531 F15
st. Seaholme 409 G20

SURF BEACH
dr. Torquay 711 L14

SURFCOAST
hwy. Belmont 706 G8
hwy. Grovedale 706 E18
hwy. Torquay 711 K7

SURFVIEW
tce. Jan Juc 711 D15

SURMAN
av. E Warburton 306 L18
ct. Sunshine N 321 B9

SURREY
av. Surrey Hills 373 L16
cl. Hallam 537 G16
cr. Oakleigh E 458 H15
ct. Bayswater 423 G10
ct. Carrum Downs 600 G3
ct. Craigieburn 194 B1
ct. Ivanhoe 328 D9
ct. Somerville 644 H15
dr. Box Hill 374 G19
dr. Box Hill 374 J17
dr. Keilor East 322 H7
rd. Blackburn 375 L13
rd. Blackburn N 375 L13
rd. Cranbourne S 603 A16
rd. Dandenong N 502 D14
rd. Mt Waverley 418 J17
rd. South Yarra 32 G16
rd. South Yarra 414 J8
rd. Warburton 349 A3
rd.e, Croydon 380 E1
rd.n, South Yarra 32 G11
rd.n, South Yarra 414 J6
rd.w, Croydon 380 B1
st. Bentleigh E 496 G4
st. Box Hill S 418 K1
st. Hadfield 281 A9
st. Mornington 640 G17
st. Pascoe Vale 281 A15
st. Ringwood 378 C16
st. Rosebud 684 H16
st. Sunshine N 321 J14

SURVEY
st. Burnley 371 C19

SURVEYORS
pl. Southbank 23 G20

SUSAN
cl. Narre Warren 538 F16
ct. Campbellfield 239 H12
ct. Cheltenham 496 L14
ct. Cranbourne 603 L2
ct. Hampton Pk 551 F11
ct. Keilor East 278 F18
ct. Mt Waverley 418 L15
ct. Seaford 600 A3
ct. Templstw Lr 330 G12
ct. Vermont S 420 J10
pl. Rye 697 L9
st. Albion 320 G19
st. Bayswater 423 B7
st. Dromana 686 C6
st. Eltham 287 E12
st. Mordialloc 532 B9
st. Sandringham 495 B13

SUSANNE
av. Nunawading 376 E10

SUSANS
ct. Croydon N 336 D14

SUSI
ct. Noble Park 534 C6

SUSMAN
st. Newport 411 A8

SUSMANN
ct. Altona Mdw 451 H2

SUSPENSION
st. Ardeer 364 B1

SUSSEX
av. Mornington 640 C20
cr. Seaford 600 B4
ct. Glen Waverley 460 J3
ct. Grovedale 706 D12
ct. Mill Park 242 J12
ct. Somerville 644 F17
ct. Sunbury 143 D15
ct. Tarneit 405 D12
pl. Heidelberg 329 F2
rd. Caulfield S 455 H12
rd. Frankston S 626 L9
rd. Rye 697 F7
st. Blackburn N 376 B11
st. Blairgowrie 680 D19
st. Box Hill N 375 E9
st. Brighton 454 G18
st. Bundoora 243 D20
st. Moonee Pnd 323 J12
st. Noble Park 534 J7
st. Pascoe Vale 281 A20
st. Pascoe Vale 281 B11
st. Pascoe Vale 281 B16
st. Pascoe Vale S 281 A20
st. Preston 327 B6
st. Ringwood 378 D18
st. Seaholme 409 G17
st. Sunshine N 321 G16
st. Warburton 305 B18
st. Yarraville 367 C17

SUTCH
st. Northcote 326 D14

SUTCLIFFE
ct. Highton 705 H3

SUTHERLAND
av. Aspendale Gdn 546 J3
av. Kew East 372 C5
av. Melton S 268 J7
ct. Altona Mdw 451 J3
ct. Endeavour Hl 537 C4
ct. Epping 197 G18
ct. Mulgrave 460 D17
pl. Armadale 415 E14
pl. Burwood 419 C7
rd. Armadale 415 E13
rd. Beaconsfld Up 542 F12
rd. Dandenong 535 G4
rd. Diamond Ck 244 L10
st. Albanvale 319 C4
st. Bacchus Msh 222 A14
st. Brunswick 325 C11
st. Coburg 281 E20
st. Hadfield 280 L6
st. Malvern East 457 C3
st. Melbourne 1 L6
st. Melbourne 24 A4
st. Geelong, off Maud St 703 B10
wy. Roxburgh Pk 194 C14

SUTTON
av. Altona North 410 B4
av. Boronia 424 C17
cl. Gladstone Pk 236 K20
cl. Hoppers Csg 448 B2
ct. Bundoora 284 L5
ct. Burwood E 420 D13
ct. Glen Waverley 459 H8
gr. Richmond 26 A14
pde. Mont Albert N 374 D10
pl. Carlton 18 H12
st. Balwyn N 373 E4
st. Carlton N 18 J4
st. Chelsea Ht 547 G16
st. Kooyong 416 A6
st. Mornington 640 F12
st. N Melbourne 34 F8
st. Reservoir 283 A8
st. S Kingsville 410 J3

SUTTONS
la. Geelong, off Kilgour St 703 A11

SUVA
st. Mulgrave 500 C3

SUVLA
gr. Coburg N 281 G13

SUZANA
pl. Rowville 503 C5

SUZANNE
ct. Briar Hill 286 H3
ct. Noble Park 500 J16
ct. Pakenham 585 B4
ct. Ringwood N 378 D7
ct. The Basin 425 B10
st. Dandenong 536 A2

SWABY
sq. Footscray 367 H7

SWAIN
ct. Heathmont 379 C18
st. Greenvale 236 G2

SWAITH
ct. Westmeadows 237 A15

SWALES
ct. Mt Martha 656 H6

SWALLOW
cl. Mornington 657 A5
ct. Patterson L 573 J8
st. Port Melb 412 G6
st. Preston 327 A1
st. S Morang 199 H14
st. Werribee 448 C8

SWAMP GUM
pl. Somerville 644 D14

SWAMPRAT
tr. Frankston N 600 H10

SWAN
av. Westmeadows 236 H14
ct. Carrum Downs 600 G3
ct. Glen Waverley 420 J19
ct. Mornington 657 B1
ct. Nar Warrn S 552 F14
ct. Newport 411 D9
ct. Thomastown 241 K16
ct. Wantirna 422 D4
pl. Dingley Village 533 A9
rd. Murrumbeena 457 C12
st. Blackburn S 419 E4
st. Burnley 371 A19
st. Cremorne 26 A16
st. Eltham 287 D9
st. Footscray 367 A7
st. Keilor Park 277 K14
st. Melbourne 25 E15
st. Melton 226 H17
st. Richmond 26 A16
st. Tooradin 651 J8
st. Werribee 447 G7
wk. Chelsea 546 K17

SWAN BAY
rd. Swan Bay 708 C1

SWANHURST
grn. Caroline Spr 317 K4

SWANLEY
av. Bayswater N 380 A19

SWANN
dr. Derrimut 363 F11
SWANPOOL
av. Chelsea 546 J16
SWANS
rd. Darley 221 A1
wy. Rosebud W 698 J3
wy. Rosebud W 699 A2
SWANSEA
ct. Belgrave 466 E13
ct. Craigieburn 194 A2
gr. Mornington 640 D19
pde. St Albans 320 J5
rd. Chelsea 546 J20
rd. Lilydale 338 H9
rd. Montrose 382 C9
rd. Mt Evelyn 338 H9
rd. Mt Evelyn 382 E8
SWANSFIELD
ct. Warrandyte 332 L3
ct. Warrandyte 333 A3
SWANSON
cr. Chadstone 458 B6
SWANSTON
ct. Taylors Hill 274 E9
pl. Geelong, off Little Malop St 703 D8
st. Bulleen 330 A12
st. Carlton 18 B20
st. Geelong 703 D8
st. Heidelberg Ht 284 F19
st. Melbourne 2 E15
st. Melbourne 2 E3
st. Melbourne 24 B1
st. Mentone 531 B7
st. Parkville 18 B20
st. Preston 327 K4
st. Queenscliff 708 J19
st. S Geelong 703 B15
st. Templstw Lr 330 A9
st. Williamstown 411 B14
SWANTON
st. Port Melb 411 J5
SWARAN
ct. Oakleigh S 498 A6
wy. Werribee 447 L6
SWAYFIELD
rd. Mt Waverley 419 A14
SWEENEY
dr. Narre Warren 553 B7
SWEENEYS
la. Eltham 288 A18
SWEENY
ct. Highton 705 F8
SWEETFERN DELL
Frankston S 626 J6
SWEET GUM
av. Narre Warren 538 J20
SWEETLAND
rd. Box Hill 375 C17
rd. Mooroolbark 337 B17
SWEETWATER
dr. Frankston S 627 C9
SWEET WATTLE
pl. Somerville 645 C17
SWEYN
st. Balwyn N 374 A5
st. Balwyn N 374 D3
SWIFT
ct. Carrum Downs 601 C2
ct. Keilor Dn 276 A11
dr. Glen Waverley 460 G11
st. Frankston 599 G16
st. Hoppers Csg 448 L4
st. Hoppers Csg 449 A4
st. Northcote 327 D13
st. Preston 327 A2
st. Thornbury 327 D13
wy. Dandenong S 549 H10
SWILK
st. Templestowe 330 K7
SWINBORNE
st. Box Hill S 418 L6
SWINBURNE
av. Hawthorn 372 A18
av. Mooroolbark 381 E1
st. Gisborne 78 J7
wk. Hawthorn, off Railway Arc 327 A17
SWINDEN
av. Cheltenham 531 A3
SWINDON
av. Glen Waverley 460 L3
cr. Keilor Dn 276 D12
ct. Lalor 241 J6
gr. McKinnon 456 D16
mw. Westmeadows 237 H12
rd. Hughesdale 457 H10
rd. St Albans 320 K7

SWINTON
av. Kew 371 E11
ct. Baxter 644 C3
wy. Greenvale 237 A5
SWISS
ct. Endeavour Hl 503 B20
SWISS CHALET
rd. Badger Creek 258 G10
SWITCHBACK
rd. Chirnside Pk 293 D20
SWORD
wk. Kings Park 274 L19
SWORDS
st. Dandenong 535 K9
SWORD SEDGE
tr. Frankston N 600 H12
SWYER
st. Hampton 495 G12
SYBIL
ct. Keilor Dn 275 J10
st. Hampton E 496 B9
SYCAMORE
av. Emerald 469 K14
av. Mentone 531 H7
av. Tullamarine 278 J5
cr. Boronia 424 E17
cr. Campbellfield 239 E12
ct. Nar Warrn S 553 E20
gr. Balaclava 454 J1
gr. Mt Evelyn 383 C5
rd. Frankston S 627 D9
st. Box Hill S 418 L3
st. Camberwell 417 H4
st. Caulfield S 455 E7
st. Langwarrin 628 L1
st. Malvern East 457 B3
st. Mill Park 242 B9
SYDARE
av. Malvern East 457 D4
SYDENHAM
av. Manifold Ht 702 B5
la. Surrey Hills, off Balmoral Cr 374 C18
rd. Delahey 275 G11
rd. Sydenham 275 C5
st. Highett 495 J15
st. Moonee Pnd 324 A13
st. Seddon 367 A10
wy. Surrey Hills, off Beatrice Av 374 B18
SYDNEY
av. Emerald 469 D18
av. Geelong 703 D10
av. Mt Evelyn 383 G3
cr. Lalor 241 E8
ct. Geelong, off Admiral Pl 703 D9
pde. Geelong 703 D9
pl. Port Melb 412 L3
rd. Bayswater 423 A7
rd. Brunswick 325 F17
rd. Campbellfield 239 C11
rd. Coburg 325 G3
rd. Coburg N 281 G18
rd. Fawkner 239 C11
rd. Fawkner 281 F9
rd. Hadfield 281 F9
st. Albion 364 K1
st. Ascot Vale 324 E16
st. Avondale Ht 322 B15
st. Bacchus Msh 222 A19
st. Cheltenham 530 H3
st. Clayton S 498 J4
st. Collingwood 20 A14
st. Footscray 367 A7
st. Macleod 285 D13
st. Murrumbeena 457 B6
st. Nar Warrn S 579 G3
st. Newport 410 F10
st. Prahran 415 C10
st. Rye 697 B15
st. Somerville 644 K16
SYDNEY NOLAN
pl. Diamond Ck 245 B13
SYDNEY PARKINSON
av. Endeavour Hl 537 G8
SYDNEY WILSON
ct. Bundoora 284 D5
SYKES
av. Ferntree Gly 423 L18
ct. Pakenham 584 H5
la. N Melbourne 17 D13
SYLEHAM
st. St Albans 320 G6
SYLPHIDE
wy. Wantirna S 462 C1
SYLVAN
av. Keysborough 534 G16
av. Warburton 349 K6
cr. Ashwood 418 F16
cr. Kew 371 E10
ct. Dandenong N 502 F14
ct. Forest Hill 420 K3
ct. Ivanhoe 328 A19
ct. Newtown 701 K10
dr. Rosebud 700 F5
gr. Pascoe Vale 280 J17
st. Balwyn N 373 E6
st. Montmorency 286 J12
wy. Campbellfield 239 H11
SYLVANA
st. Wantirna S 421 L17
SYLVANDALE
ct. Yarrambat 201 C10
SYLVANDER
st. Balwyn N 373 K2
st. Clayton S 498 H8
SYLVANWOOD
cr. Narre Warren 538 H17
SYLVERLY
gr. Caulfield 455 G3
SYLVESTER
cr. Malvern East 457 B1
gr. Preston 283 C19
st. Oak Park 279 K13
SYLVIA
cl. Hillside 274 F6
cr. Black Rock 529 F4
ct. Thomastown 241 L12
ct. Whittington 703 L20
gr. Ringwood 378 B17
la. Narre Warren 553 A6
rd. Beaconsfield 555 C14
st. Blackburn S 419 G6
st. Dandenong N 501 J17
st. Ferntree Gly 464 B2
st. Templstw Lr 330 B12
st. View Bank 285 F18
SYME
ct. Sunbury 142 K11
rd. Healesville 300 A16
rd. Pakenham 558 E19
rd. Woori Yallock 300 A16
rd. Woori Yallock 344 B14
st. Brunswick 325 C14
st. St Albans 319 G1
st. Williamstown 411 H16
SYMES
st. Lower Plenty 286 K15
SYMINGTON
rd. Long Forest 224 F1
SYMON
cr. Greensborough 244 K15
cr. Thomastown 240 L16
cr. Thomastown 241 A16
SYMOND
st. Yarra Glen 208 L17
st. Yarra Glen 209 A18
SYMONDS
st. Hawthorn E 372 F20
st. Queenscliff 709 A16
SYMONS
rd. Avonsleigh 470 E20
rd. Avonsleigh 510 E1
st. Healesville 213 H20
st. Preston 282 D16
SYNDAL
st. Fawkner 281 K9
SYNNOT
st. Werribee 447 F18
SYON
cl. Deer Park 318 K12
SYPHON
wk. Lysterfield S 503 F14
SYTHNEY
ct. Surrey Hills 374 A19
SZER
wy. Carrum Downs 600 J2

T

TABBITA
st. Moorabbin 496 L11
TABILK
ct. Wantirna 422 G6
st. Fawkner 281 F10
TABOR
ct. Sunbury 144 D10
mw. Frankston 628 E4
TABULAM
ct. Grovedale 705 L13
TACABERRY
av. Nar Warrn N 539 H5
TACOMA
st. Pk Orchards 333 E19
TAD
ct. Cranbourne N 578 A5
TADDOR
dr. Cranbourne 578 F17
TADEDOR
ct. Forest Hill 420 F5
TADEMA
cr. Eltham 288 B6
ct. Noble Park N 501 D11
TADJI
cl. Croydon N 335 L15
ct. Mornington 641 D15
st. Sorrento 679 E15
TADSTAN
ct. Clayton S 499 D16
dr. Hampton Pk 551 C8
dr. Tullamarine 278 H2
pl. Donvale 376 J2
TAEGTOW
wy. Altona Mdw 451 G8
TAFT
cl. Dandenong N 501 H8
TAGELL
rd. Heathmont 378 K15
TAGGART
la. Elwood 454 C4
TAGGERTY
cr. Meadow Ht 238 A6
ct. Keilor 276 L12
TAHARA
ct. Thomastown 240 J12
ct. Werribee 447 E2
rd. Toorak 415 E4
TAHBILK
ct. Vermont S 421 F9
TAHITI
ct. Mulgrave 500 C3
ct. Rye 696 F2
TAHLEE
pl. Montmorency 287 B8
pl. Vermont S 421 C7
TAINTON
rd. Burwood E 420 A8
st. Wandin N 340 K13
st. Wandin N 341 A13
TAISHO
ct. Werribee 446 H18
TAIT
ct. Bundoora 242 K17
ct. Oakleigh S 498 A6
la. W Melbourne 23 A2
st. Fitzroy N 326 D20
st. Footscray 367 E4
st. Newport 411 A7
st. Ringwood N 378 E7
TAITS
la. Geelong, off Mundy St 703 B12
TAKAPUNA
st. Caulfield S 455 J11
TAKETA
cr. Frankston 628 H1
TALAB
ct. Chelsea Ht 547 H17
TALARA
ct. Cranbourne 578 G17
ct. Frankston 628 B1
TALARNO
av. Vermont S 421 D7
TALASKIA
rd. Up Fntree Gly 465 C9
TALBA
ct. Carrum Downs 601 A6
TALBETT
st. Burwood 418 J10
TALBOT
av. Balwyn 373 G15
av. Belgrave 466 C14
av. Bentleigh 495 K1
av. Oakleigh S 458 D20
av. Oakleigh S 498 D2
av. St Kilda E 414 K20
av. Thomastown 241 H14
cl. Keilor Dn 276 A16
cr. Kooyong 416 A5
ct. Frankston 600 G20
ct. Hampton Pk 551 D10
ct. Noble Park 534 K7
gr. McCrae 684 J17
pl. Sunbury 143 H5
rd. Mt Waverley 458 L6
rd. Strathmore 324 E2
st. Altona Mdw 451 J1
st. Brunswick 325 D12
st. Footscray 367 G9
st. Greensborough 286 D7
st. Hadfield 281 A9
st. Hampton 494 L7
st. Keilor East 322 G5
st. Mitcham 377 H14
st. Newtown 702 E10
st. Sunshine N 321 F14
st. Templstw Lr 330 D14

TALDRA
cr. Seaford 600 A3
ct. Belmont 706 F6
dr. Ferntree Gly 463 K8
dr. Ferntree Gly 463 L6
st. Box Hill N 375 C9
TALFORD
st. Doncaster E 376 C2
TALGARNO
cl. Taylors Lakes 276 D8
st. Broadmeadows 237 L13
TALIA
ct. Melton S 268 E5
ct. Rowville 462 L18
ct. Werribee 447 D11
TALI-KARNG
cl. Rowville 462 K15
TALINA
cl. Hoppers Csg 447 K2
TALINGA
ct. Berwick 554 H20
ct. Mornington 641 C14
rd. Cheltenham 495 L18
rd. Sandringham 495 L18
TALISMAN
pl. Lysterfield 464 C19
ri. Glen Waverley 460 F7
TALLANGATTA
pl. Berwick, off Tallara Sq 553 F2
TALLANT
av. Sorrento 679 D14
TALLARA
sq. Berwick 553 E2
TALLAROOK
ct. Croydon Hills 335 F15
st. Blairgowrie 680 B19
TALLAROON
ct. Greensborough 286 L2
TALLAWARRA
ri. Donvale 377 G4
TALLENT
st. Croydon 380 A2
TALLERK
cl. Greensborough 244 B18
ct. Kings Park 319 A2
TALLINTYRE
rd. Sunshine W 364 F9
TALLIS
cl. Camberwell 372 J19
dr. Mornington 640 L10
dr. Mornington 641 A10
TALLOW WOOD
dr. Greensborough 244 L20
dr. Greensborough 286 K1
TALLOWWOOD
st. Frankston N 599 K10
TALLY
ct. Berwick 539 H20
TALLY HO
ct. Burwood 420 B13
TALMA
cl. Eltham 287 K10
pl. Cranbourne W 577 F18
TALMAGE
st. Albion 321 A19
st. Albion 365 A1
TALMARA
ct. Mt Martha 657 D8
TALOFA
av. Brighton East 455 C18
av. Ringwood E 378 L12
av. Ringwood E 379 A12
TAL TALS
cr. Mt Martha 656 C16
TALWONG
ct. Research 246 G20
ct. Research 288 G1
TALWOOD
cl. Wantirna S 422 A16
ct. Burwood E 420 B13
TAMA
ct. Grovedale 705 J14
TAMALA
av. Marshall 706 L10
av. Notting Hill 459 J14
TAMAR
cl. Gisborne 78 J15
ct. Keilor 276 L13
ct. Mentone 531 G7
ct. Narre Warren 539 H15
dr. Deer Park 318 K10
dr. Melton S 268 K5
gr. Oakleigh 458 A10
rd. Springvale S 534 B5
st. Aberfeldie 323 E10
st. Bayswater 422 L8
st. Bayswater 423 A8
st. Bundoora 284 B2
st. Ringwood N 378 E7

TAMARA
cl. Berwick...540 C18
ct. Bundoora...242 F16
ct. Thomastown...240 D17
st. Albanvale...319 D4
st. Wantirna S...462 C1
TAMARIND
cr. Werribee...447 K8
TAMARISK
av. Glen Waverley...460 D11
dr. Frankston N...600 E5
rd. Narre Warren...553 E11
TAMBET
st. Bentleigh E...457 C19
TAMBO
av. Reservoir...283 D13
cl. Clayton S...498 F9
cl. Croydon Hills...335 H16
cr. Taylors Hill...274 K14
ct. Dandenong N...501 K9
ct. Dingley Village...533 A8
ct. Glen Waverley...419 J17
ct. Keilor...276 L13
ct. Keilor...277 A13
ct. Langwarrin...601 G16
ct. Mentone...531 E5
ct. Werribee...448 A20
wy. Berwick...539 J20
TAMBOON
ct. Meadow Ht...194 D20
dr. Greensborough...245 A20
dr. Rowville...463 A16
dr. St Helena...244 L20
dr. St Helena...245 A20
TAMBOR
ct. Lalor...240 J9
TAMBORINE
wy. Caroline Spr...317 H6
TAMBORITHA
pl. Hoppers Csg...449 C3
TAME
st. Diggers Rest...187 D13
TAMLIN
pl. Chirnside Pk...336 H7
TAMLYN
cl. Sunshine W...364 C9
st. Thomson...703 G15
TAMMANY
dr. Clarinda...498 C10
TAMORA
wy. Sydenham...275 B7
TAMPE
rd. Rowville...462 J13
TAMROY
ct. Kurunjang...227 D10
TAMUK
st. Maribyrnong...322 H16
TAMWORTH
ct. Cranbourne...577 J10
rd. Kilsyth...381 F7
TAN
ct. Keilor...277 A15
TANAMI
ct. Bulleen...329 H8
ct. Nar Warrn S...579 A2
TANBRIDGE
wy. Warranwood...335 B12
TANDARA
av. Doncaster...375 E2
ct. Bangholme...549 J14
ct. Black Rock...529 J6
ct. Chadstone...418 B20
ct. Montrose...382 A12
ct. Mt Martha...656 D8
TANDAROOK
cr. Donvale...377 F6
TANDARRA
cr. Lalor...241 B7
ct. Carrum Downs...601 C2
dr. Ringwood...335 B18
TANDDERWEN
ct. Nar Warrn N...539 C5
TANDERRA
cr. Wantirna...422 B13
st. Rye...697 C7
TANDERUM
dr. Coburg...281 K20
TANDRAGEE
cl. Wantirna S...421 L19
TANGARA
la. Nar Warrn E...541 E2
TANGARI
ct. Greensborough...244 A19
TANGEMERE
av. Tullamarine...278 J3
TANGENONG
ri. Frankston S...626 J11
TANGERINE
ct. Mt Martha...656 L9
ct. Mt Martha...657 A9
dr. Nar Warrn S...578 G3
dr. Nar Warrn S...578 H4
TANGERMERE
pl. Lilydale...338 E13
TANGLEWOOD
rd. Rowville...502 E8
st. Kings Park...275 C18
TANGYES
st. Pascoe Vale...280 K15
TANIA
ct. Carrum Downs...601 E4
ct. Dandenong...536 F9
ct. Pakenham...584 H8
ct. Ringwood...378 G8
dr. Highton...701 G20
pl. Melton W...226 A14
pl. Ringwood N...378 D2
st. Sunshine N...321 B10
TANIKKA
ct. Lilydale...338 D12
TANILBA
st. Werribee...446 L14
TANITA
cl. Hillside...232 F19
TANIYHA
pl. Sunshine N...321 G17
TANJIL
ct. Dandenong N...501 L9
ct. Keilor...276 L13
ct. Keilor...277 A13
ct. Mt Waverley...419 C19
ct. Thomastown...240 J12
ct. Werribee...447 L20
TANKARD
st. Kensington...33 D12
TANNAROO
cr. Delahey...275 B16
TANNER
av. Kew East...372 B5
gr. Northcote...327 B15
pl. Sunbury...142 F9
st. Glen Waverley...420 J15
st. Oakleigh E...458 C10
st. Richmond...26 A14
TANNOCK
st. Balwyn N...373 L2
TANTALLION
bvd. Officer...555 H20
TANTALLON
bvd. Officer...555 H20
TANTANI
st. Frankston...600 G16
TANTI
av. Mornington...640 F11
st. Cheltenham...497 D20
TANTRAM
av. St Kilda E...455 A1
TANUNDA
cl. Narre Warren...553 G10
cl. Scoresby...462 A6
gr. Belmont...706 F6
mw. St Albans...321 B6
st. Vermont S...421 E10
TANYA
ct. Clarinda...498 G11
ct. Croydon Hills...335 F15
ct. Lilydale...338 F14
ct. Rowville...462 K19
ct. Somerville...644 E15
pl. Wheelers Hill...461 E18
st. Rye...696 K7
wy. Eltham...287 E9
TANYALEE
ct. Mt Martha...656 G9
TAPAROO
rd. Templestowe...332 A14
TAPLIN
pl. Carlton N...19 A3
st. Fitzroy N...326 C20
wy. Roxburgh Pk...194 E10
TARA
av. Blackburn...375 E13
av. Kew...371 G11
cl. Croydon...380 D10
cl. Rowville...503 C5
ct. Doncaster...374 E1
ct. Hallam...537 L16
ct. Mornington...656 F3
ct. Rye...696 K12
ct. Torquay...711 K9
ct. Wantirna...422 E6
ct. Yallambie...285 L14
dr. Frankston...627 C6
gr. Carnegie...456 H13
pl. Noble Park N...501 E9
st. Hawthorn E...372 G18
TARADALE
ct. Meadow Ht...238 C3
TARAGO
cr. Clayton S...498 F9
ct. Ferntree Gly...464 C16
tce. Taylors Hill...274 H16
TARAGRIN
dr. Carrum Downs...574 D19
TARAKAN
av. Ashburton...417 G16
st. Boronia...424 E4
st. Heidelberg W...328 C4
st. Sorrento...679 D16
TARANA
av. Glenroy...279 G8
av. Up Fntree Gly...464 J9
cr. Kings Park...319 E1
pl. Chelsea Ht...547 E11
TARANAKI
av. Brunswick E...326 A12
TARANNA
st. Mornington...640 L15
st. Mornington...641 A15
TARANTO
ct. Boronia...424 E14
dr. Noble Park...534 F1
TARAS
av. Altona North...408 K9
TARATA
ct. Bundoora...242 L15
dr. Doveton...536 K14
TARA VALLEY
la. Highton...701 E10
TARBET
ct. Endeavour Hl...503 H16
TARCOOLA
av. Meadow Ht...194 B20
cl. Epping...198 D20
dr. Burnside...318 F7
dr. Greensborough...286 C13
dr. Narre Warren...539 A16
dr. Yallambie...286 C13
TAREE
cl. Pakenham...584 H2
ct. Hoppers Csg...448 F7
pl. Mill Park...243 E4
pl. Yallambie...286 C14
st. Kings Park...319 D1
TARELLA
dr. Keilor Dn...276 G16
dr. Mt Waverley...419 B13
rd. Chelsea...546 J15
rd. Clayton...459 A20
st. Hampton Pk...551 L7
TARENE
st. Dandenong S...535 H14
TARGET
rd. Templestowe...332 G3
rd. Warrandyte...288 G20
rd. Warrandyte...332 G3
TARHILLA
dr. Launching Pl...345 C15
TARIFF
dr. Werribee...487 H2
TARLEE
ct. Aspendale...546 E7
dr. Albanvale...318 K5
TARLETON
rd. Plumpton...273 A7
TARLO
cct. Cranbourne W...577 F18
TARMAC
dr. Tullamarine...278 E1
TARMAROO
ct. Croydon Hills...335 F15
TARNAGULLA
rd. Croydon S...379 H12
TARNARD
dr. Braeside...532 G10
TARNEIT
rd. Hoppers Csg...447 H10
rd. Tarneit...447 H10
rd. Werribee...447 J11
st. Werribee...447 H11
TARNOOK
ct. Dingley Village...533 D6
st. Vermont S...421 F8
TARO
pl. Noble Park N...501 B13
TARONGA
cr. Croydon...380 H2
ct. Campbellfield...239 H15
ct. Noble Park...534 H7
ct. Nunawading...376 E9
TARONGO
dr. Aspendale...546 G5
TAROOK
av. Rye...697 A2
ct. Frankston...627 F6
wy. Mornington...640 E17
TAROONA
av. Mt Waverley...459 F2
av. Warrandyte...333 G1
cl. Mt Eliza...626 D19
pl. Port Melb...412 F5
TARQUIN
pl. Hillside...232 D19
TARRA
pl. Dallas...238 F8
pl. St Andrews...206 D1
TARRALEAH
pl. Boronia...423 E13
TARRAN
st. Laverton...407 F10
TARRANGO
rd. Wesburn...347 K18
rd. Yarra Jctn...347 K18
TARRAN GOWER
pl. Berwick...553 G2
TARRANGOWER
av. Mitcham...377 J12
TARRANNA
gr. Chum Creek...213 A9
TARRANT
ct. Keilor Dn...276 B11
TARRAWARRA
rd. Coldstream...254 H12
rd. Tarrawarra...210 G19
TARRAWILL
st. Rye...697 B8
TARRENGOWER
st. Yarraville...367 B16
TARRING
ct. Highton...701 H18
TARUNA
ri. Montrose...382 A16
TARVER
st. Port Melb...412 C3
TARWARRI
av. Rosebud W...699 F2
ct. Greensborough...244 C20
pl. Burwood E...419 G11
TARWIN
av. Hampton E...495 J9
ct. Brookfield...268 D5
ct. Dandenong N...501 K9
ct. Keilor...276 L14
ct. Keilor...277 A14
ct. Langwarrin...601 H15
ct. Rowville...463 B17
dr. Croydon Hills...335 J15
pl. Meadow Ht...194 B19
pl. Mornington...657 B4
pl. Wyndham Va...446 H10
TASHINNY
rd. Toorak...32 L13
rd. Toorak...414 L7
rd. Toorak...415 A7
TASKER
st. Templstw Lr...330 B13
TASMA
la. Mornington...640 D12
pl. Noble Park...534 D6
st. Ascot Vale...324 F17
TASMAN
av. Belmont...706 E2
av. Deer Park...319 B10
av. Nunawading...376 F9
av. Strathmr Ht...279 C10
av. Upwey...465 G14
cl. Wantirna S...462 C1
cr. Taylors Lakes...275 D1
ct. Carrum Downs...575 F15
ct. Montrose...382 A7
ct. Patterson L...547 G19
ct. Sunbury...142 L12
ct. Sunbury...143 A12
dr. Bundoora...242 H18
dr. Rye...696 D9
pl. Endeavour Hl...537 D6
pl. Hoppers Csg...405 D19
pl. Wyndham Va...446 G8
rd. Bentleigh E...497 D3
st. Preston...326 D2
TASSEL
rd. Safety Bch...668 L20
rd. Safety Bch...669 A20
TASSELL
st. Hadfield...280 H9
TATE
av. Wantirna S...422 J12
ct. Hallam...537 K13
ct. Noble Park N...501 B13
st. Ivanhoe...328 A12
st. Pascoe Vale...280 D18
st. Thomson...703 H16
TATES
pl. S Melbourne...29 F2
TATHRA
ct. Boronia...424 K6
ct. Grovedale...706 A13
ct. Jan Juc...711 D15
pl. St Helena...244 H17
TATIANA
st. Wantirna S...462 C2
TATIARA
av. Clarinda...498 C
av. Croydon N...336 B1
TATLOW
dr. Epping...197 K1
TATMAN
dr. Altona Mdw...451 K
TATONG
ct. Broadmeadows...238 B1
rd. Brighton East...495 J
TATRA
cl. Clarinda...498 C1
ct. Thomastown...240 D1
TATTENHAM
st. Caulfield E...456 E
TATTERSALLS
la. Melbourne...2 F1
la. Melbourne...24 D
TATTERSON
ct. Templestowe...331 L1
rd. Dandenong S...535 K2
st. Hampton Pk...551 H
TATTLAR
pl. Rowville...463 F1
TATTLER
st. Carrum Downs...601 C
TATURA
cr. Broadmeadows...238 A1
ct. Frankston...600 E1
st. Cheltenham...531 G
TATYOON
cl. Aspendale Gdn...546 G
TAUNTON
av. Oakleigh S...457 J1
av. Preston...282 J1
cr. Scoresby...462 B
dr. Bundoora...242 J1
dr. Cheltenham...531 H
pl. Craigieburn...194 A
pl. Gladstone Pk...237 A1
st. Doncaster E...331 L1
st. Sunshine...365 F
TAUPO
cr. Rowville...463 C1
TAURIMA
ct. Burnside...318 E
TAURUS
av. Dandenong N...502 B1
ct. Lilydale...338 L
ct. Lilydale...339 A
rd. Doncaster E...332 E1
st. Balwyn N...329 B2
st. Balwyn N...373 B1
TAVERNER
ct. Scoresby...462 A7
sq. Frankston...628 A1
st. Maddingley...264 A1
st. Moorabbin...496 D
TAVISTOCK
ct. Craigieburn...194 D2
ct. Croydon Hills...335 G1
pl. Melbourne...1 H1
pl. Melbourne...24 B1
rd. Frankston S...627 F
rd. Monbulk...428 B17
TAWONGA
ct. Glen Waverley...419 K1
st. Broadmeadows...238 A
TAYLER
st. Geelong West...702 J4
TAYLOR
av. Aspendale...546 D7
av. Burwood E...419 C10
av. Maribyrnong...367 C2
av. Reservoir...282 H13
cl. Prahran...415 A12
cr. Mt Martha...655 K13
ct. Dandenong N...501 K14
ct. Endeavour Hl...537 C7
ct. Highton...701 L18
ct. Malvern East...417 A20
ct. Mt Waverley...459 C6
dr. Darley...221 L11
dr. Gladstone Pk...236 L19
dr. Gladstone Pk...237 A19
mw. Kensington...33 C12
pl. Roxburgh Pk...194 B17
rd. Dixons Ck...211 F8
rd. Hurstbridge...203 B15
rd. Mooroolbark...337 E18
rd. Mt Burnett...511 G15
st. Ashburton...417 C19
st. Brighton East...455 F13
st. Cranbourne...604 A3
st. Eltham...287 H9
st. Fitzroy N...326 B17
st. Lilydale...338 A7
st. Moonee Pnd...324 B12
st. Moorabbin...496 C7
st. Oakleigh...457 K9
st. Parkdale...531 G10

st. Thornbury 326 D7
st. Yarraville 367 E17
TAYLORS
ct. Caroline Spr 318 E8
la. Rowville 462 L19
la. Rowville 463 A19
rd. Burnside 274 B15
rd. Caroline Spr 273 H14
rd. Croydon 380 B8
rd. Dandenong S 550 F14
rd. Kings Park 275 A16
rd. Lyndhurst 550 F14
rd. Plumpton 273 A13
rd. St Albans 275 G17
rd. Skye 576 B20
rd. Skye 602 A7
rd. Taylors Hill 274 B15
TAYLORS HILL
bvd. Taylors Hill 274 E8
TAYPORT
gdn. Endeavour Hl 503 H17
TEA
ct. Greenvale 192 K20
TEA GARDENS
dr. Avondale Ht 322 E11
TEAGUE
av. Brunswick W 324 L15
av. Mentone 531 A6
cl. Nunawading 376 G16
st. Niddrie 322 L3
st. Niddrie 323 A3
TEAK
av. Ringwood E 379 F16
ct. Boronia 424 D17
ct. Coolaroo 238 D3
ct. Doncaster 375 C4
ct. Thomastown 240 K14
st. Caulfield S 455 G8
TEAL
cr. Lalor 241 B6
ct. Blind Bight 650 B10
ct. Dandenong N 502 C17
ct. Forest Hill 420 K6
ct. Keysborough 534 K10
ct. Melton 226 G17
ct. Mornington 640 L17
ct. Nar Warrn S 552 G13
ct. St Albans 319 G9
ct. Sunbury 144 D12
ct. Williamstown 410 H14
la. Briar Hill 287 A5
pl. Baxter 628 D20
st. Hoppers Csg 448 F5
st. Rosebud W 698 J3
TEALA
ct. Gladstone Pk 279 B3
TE-ARAI
av. St Kilda E 415 B15
TEASDALE
ct. Highton 701 H13
ct. Sunshine W 364 K7
TEA TREE
pl. Rosebud 683 L19
pl. Somerville 644 E15
ri. Portsea 678 C8
TEA-TREE
tr. Langwarrin 628 H10
TEATREE
pl. Keysborough 534 A16
pl. Seabrook 450 J7
pl. S Morang 243 K1
TEBBUTT
ct. Mill Park 242 H4
TECHNICAL
dr. Craigieburn 194 L5
TECHNO PARK
dr. Williamstown 410 C13
TECK
st. Ashwood 418 E17
TECOMA
ct. Gladstone Pk 279 B3
ct. Mill Park 242 C9
ct. Oakleigh S 497 G5
st. Ferntree Gly 424 J20
st. Frankston N 600 F9
TEDBURN
ct. Craigieburn 194 C1
TEDDINGTON
rd. Hampton 495 E7
wy. Wantirna 422 J11
TEDDY
cr. Springvale S 533 L7
TEDSTONE
cr. Balwyn 373 D12
TEE
ct. Frankston 599 J17
st. Kingsbury 283 K8
TEEDA
ct. Melton S 268 F5
TEENA
ct. Wonga Park 336 D7
TEESIDE
ct. Point Cook 450 L10
TEEWAH
ct. Bangholme 549 H13
TEGWEN
st. Belmont 706 K3
TEHONGI
ct. Beaumaris 529 K9
TEKAPO
cr. Taylors Lakes 276 D9
TE-KOI
av. Belgrave 466 G12
TELEGRAPH
rd. Beaconsfield 556 A1
rd. Guys Hill 556 A1
TELEPHONE
rd. Exford 267 A20
rd. Parwan 267 A20
TELFER
ct. Rowville 463 G20
TELFORD
cl. Deer Park 318 L8
cl. Mornington 657 C2
ct. Hampton Pk 551 D4
ct. Meadow Ht 237 L4
ct. Sunshine N 321 A9
ct. Wantirna 422 G11
dr. Berwick 553 J3
st. Highett 495 K12
TELOPEA
av. Doncaster E 332 F18
cr. Mill Park 243 A8
ct. Frankston N 600 E8
ct. Oakleigh S 498 A9
pl. Burwood E 419 L7
pl. Hillside 273 J5
rd. Emerald 469 B20
st. Wantirna S 422 L12
st. Wantirna S 423 A12
TELSTAR
ct. Whittington 704 B20
TELSTRA
tr. Langwarrin 628 H9
TEMBY
cl. Endeavour Hl 537 J10
st. Watsonia 285 H6
TEMORA
ri. Berwick 553 L3
st. Mordialloc 532 B9
TEMPANY
st. Fitzroy N 19 B3
TEMPERANCE HALL
la. N Melbourne 17 E17
TEMPLE
ct. Mt Martha 656 H8
ct. Noble Park 534 D1
ct. Templstw Lr 330 H9
dr. Thomastown 241 C18
la. Dandenong 536 A7
rd. Belgrave S 506 K3
rd. Selby 467 A20
rd. Selby 467 B19
rd. Selby 507 A1
st. Ashwood 417 L18
st. Brunswick W 324 K13
st. Hawthorn E 372 H16
TEMPLE COURT
pl. Melbourne 1 F14
pl. Melbourne 23 L9
TEMPLEMAN
ct. Aspendale Gdn 546 L4
TEMPLEMORE
dr. Templestowe 332 C5
TEMPLER
av. Hampton Pk 552 A8
TEMPLESTOWE
rd. Bulleen 329 H8
rd. Templstw Lr 329 H8
TEMPLETON
cr. Pakenham 584 E3
ct. Werribee 447 B10
dr. Mill Park 243 E5
la. Windsor, off Erica St 414 K12
st. Wantirna 422 D14
TEMPLEWOOD
av. Noble Park N 501 D13
cr. Avondale Ht 322 C10
cr. Avondale Ht 322 C11
ct. Berwick 539 L19
TEMPY
ct. Broadmeadows 238 H12
TEMUKA
av. Brunswick E 325 L12
TENANDRA
ct. Berwick 553 H3
TENBY
ct. Craigieburn 150 C14
TENCH
ct. Mill Park 242 C3
ri. Endeavour Hl 537 D4
TENERIFFE
cl. Epping 241 H4
TENHAM
gr. Cheltenham 531 C2
TENNANT
st. Sunshine N 321 C9
TENNENT
st. Dromana 686 C8
TENNIS
ct. Mornington 657 A6
gr. Caulfield N 415 E16
TENNYSON
av. Caulfield N 455 J2
av. Clayton S 499 B7
av. Kilsyth 380 K7
av. Preston 283 A17
ct. Melton S 268 C12
ct. Mulgrave 460 D19
ct. Sunbury 143 E2
ct. Templestowe 331 L11
dr. Delahey 275 E15
dr. Truganina 405 F13
st. Brighton 494 G2
st. Burwood 419 B9
st. Carrum 573 C7
st. Elwood 414 E19
st. Elwood 454 G2
st. Essendon 324 E9
st. Highett 496 H15
st. Kensington 33 J15
st. Kew 372 A6
st. Malvern East 456 F1
st. Mitcham 377 H14
st. Moonee Pnd 324 E11
st. Richmond 26 B15
st. St Kilda 414 E19
st. Sandringham 495 B15
st. Seddon 367 B11
st. Watsonia 285 E6
st. Williamstn N 410 C12
TENTERDEN
pl. Mill Park 242 D10
st. Yarraville 366 H18
TENTH
av. Anglesea 713 C12
av. Springvale 500 K8
av. Springvale 501 A8
TENYA
ct. Mornington 640 L15
TEOFILO
dr. Lysterfield 503 J1
TEPPO
ct. Diggers Rest 141 L12
TERALBA
cl. Dingley Village 533 G8
cl. Mill Park 242 A2
TERAMA
cr. Bayswater 423 C8
ct. Glen Waverley 420 C18
TERANG
av. Burwood E 419 F10
pl. Frankston 600 F17
st. Dallas 238 H11
TERARA
ct. Endeavour Hl 537 J6
st. Cockatoo 471 F18
TEREDDAN
dr. Kilsyth S 381 B18
TERENCE
ct. Doncaster 330 J17
dr. Cranbourne N 577 K5
st. Sunbury 143 J13
TERESA
ct. Altona Mdw 451 F6
ct. Chelsea Ht 547 F16
ct. Epping 241 G3
ct. Reservoir 283 J3
ct. Rye 698 A6
ct. Templstw Lr 330 K10
pl. Melton W 226 B18
st. Greensborough 285 H5
TEREVA
cr. Wheelers Hill 460 F15
TEREX
dr. Laverton N 408 G2
TERI
st. Frankston 600 C19
TERINGA
ct. Doncaster E 332 G9
pl. Toorak 415 F5
TERMINUS
la. Geelong, off Roy St 702 L5
TERN
av. Rosebud W 698 K4
cl. Blind Bight 650 D8
cl. Chelsea Ht 547 F18
ct. Carrum Downs 600 G3
ct. Endeavour Hl 537 A3
ct. Melton 226 F16
ct. Werribee 448 C9
gr. Mt Eliza 641 K6
TERNES
rd. Upwey 465 E12
TERRABULLA
ct. Werribee 447 C12
TERRACE
gdn. Nar Warrn S 579 E1
pl. Truganina 405 L14
row. Whittlesea 96 E15
TERRA COTTA
dr. Blackburn 376 C15
dr. Nunawading 376 C16
TERRANA
st. Cockatoo 471 H18
TERRAPIN
dr. Nar Warrn S 552 E15
TERRARA
ct. Montmorency 286 G11
pl. Ringwood N 378 D4
rd. Vermont 421 A8
rd. Vermont S 421 B10
TERRA ROSSA
ct. Mooroolbark 337 D9
TERRELL
cl. Endeavour Hl 537 B4
ct. Roxburgh Pk 194 D17
TERRENS
cl. Hampton E 495 K9
TERRIGAL
av. Oakleigh S 457 L20
av. Oakleigh S 497 L1
cl. Ringwood N 378 C4
cr. Kilsyth 381 A4
ct. Bayswater 423 C9
ct. Werribee 446 L14
dr. Noble Park N 501 D9
dr. Patterson L 573 K10
pl. Greensborough 287 A1
st. Chadstone 457 L1
st. Mornington 641 D15
TERRONT
ct. Deer Park 318 L13
TERROR
st. Keilor Park 278 C16
TERRUNG
ct. Croydon N 336 E11
TERRY
av. Sorrento 679 B11
cl. Narre Warren 538 L16
ct. Hampton Pk 551 J13
ct. Springvale S 533 L4
st. Balwyn 373 B11
st. Heidelberg Ht 284 F20
st. Noble Park 501 B19
st. Pearcedale 646 J6
st. Rosebud W 683 A20
TERRYE
ct. Hillside 274 G4
TERRYS
av. Belgrave 466 E8
av. Sherbrooke 466 D7
av. Tecoma 466 D7
TERTULLIAN
ct. Frankston 628 D7
TESRON
ct. Werribee 447 G20
TESSELAAR
av. Maddingley 263 K2
TESSIE
pl. Rowville 503 B7
TESTAR
gr. Caulfield N 415 D19
TETBURY
rd. Arthurs Seat 686 E18
TETILA
av. Grovedale 705 H14
TETLOW
tce. Lysterfield 503 K1
TETON
ct. Highett 496 H13
TETOORA
cl. Rowville 463 G11
TETRAGONA
qd. Rowville 502 E6
wy. Frankston S 627 F19
wy. Greensborough 245 B14
TETTENHALL
rdg. Belmont 705 L8
THACKERAY
ct. Croydon 380 G3
qd. Avondale Ht 322 C10
rd. Reservoir 283 A12
st. Elwood 454 B1
THACKERS
la. Geelong 703 F8
THACKRAY
rd. Port Melb 412 E1
st. Balwyn N 373 D4
THAI
ct. Mt Waverley 459 E3
THALIA
ct. Meadow Ht 238 C4
THAMER
st. Rosebud W 699 G7
THAMES
av. Springvale 499 F14
bvd. Werribee 447 G2
bvd. Werribee 447 G3
ct. Cranbourne E 578 J17
ct. Deer Park 318 L11
ct. Mulgrave 460 E20
pl. Mt Martha 669 J3
pl. Newport 411 A12
prm. Bangholme 547 D16
prm. Chelsea 546 K17
prm. Chelsea Ht 547 D16
st. Box Hill 375 A12
st. Box Hill N 374 H12
st. Dandenong N 502 C12
st. Frankston S 626 J5
st. Hadfield 280 L5
st. Heidelberg Ht 328 F6
st. Northcote 327 A15
st. Surrey Hills 373 K20
st. Surrey Hills 417 K1
wy. Roxburgh Pk 194 E6
THANA
st. Bentleigh E 457 H18
THANE
ct. Seaford 599 K2
THANET
ct. Ringwood 378 C14
st. Malvern 416 A15
THANOS
ct. Boronia 423 D12
ct. Hallam 537 H14
ct. Hampton Pk 551 J10
THARLE
st. Dandenong 535 F10
THARRATT
st. Thornbury 327 A7
THATCHER
ct. Whittington 704 A19
rd. Wantirna 421 L6
THAXTED
ct. Watsonia N 285 G3
pde. Wantirna 422 G7
rd. Murrumbeena 457 B11
THEA
av. Balwyn N 374 A5
ct. Keilor Park 278 A13
gr. Doncaster E 375 J5
THEAR
st. E Geelong 703 E12
THE ARCADE
Junction Vill 604 J13
THE ARCHES
Sunbury 143 F20
THEATRE
pl. Canterbury 373 F18
THE AVENUE
Balaclava 414 H19
Belmont 702 C17
Blackburn 375 G16
Chelsea 546 J19
Coburg 325 G6
Ferntree Gly 464 E4
Glenroy 279 H9
Hampton 494 L6
Hampton 495 A6
McCrae 684 K12
Malvern East 416 H20
Montrose 382 G7
Nar Warrn S 553 E20
Nar Warrn S 579 E1
Niddrie 278 H20
Oakleigh 457 L10
Pakenham 584 J3
Parkville 17 J1
Parkville 325 D20
Point Cook 450 H7
Rosebud W 698 J2
Spotswood 366 F20
Sunbury 143 G17
Sunshine W 363 K7
Surrey Hills 374 A19
Upwey 465 K9
Windsor 414 J12
THE AVENUE OF HONOUR
Bacchus Msh 222 H19
Bacchus Msh 265 C2
THE BEACHWAY
Chelsea 546 J18
THE BELLEVUE
Hillside 274 B1

THE BEND
Port Melb 412 B5
THE BIRCHES
Doveton 536 K13
THE BLOCK
arc. Melbourne 2 C15
THE BOULEVARD
Aberfeldie 323 B11
Aberfeldie 323 E12
Balwyn N 372 L1
Eaglemont 329 B10
Glen Waverley 420 D16
Hawthorn 372 A19
Heathmont 379 A19
Ivanhoe 328 A17
Ivanhoe 328 E15
Ivanhoe East 328 D16
Ivanhoe East 328 E15
Ivanhoe East 328 L18
Ivanhoe East 329 A17
McCrae 685 D12
Malvern East 417 H19
Montrose 382 F7
Nar Warrn S 553 B20
N Warrandyte 289 F13
Pascoe Vale S 324 E4
Pascoe Vale S 324 H4
Patterson L 573 E6
Point Cook 450 B4
Port Melb 412 B5
Thomastown 241 C13
Yarraville 366 J19
THE BOULEVARDE
Doncaster 331 B16
Gisborne 79 B10
Warrandyte 289 G14
THE BREAKWATER
Point Cook 449 L4
THE BRENTWOODS
Chirnside Pk 337 G1
THE BRIARS
Lysterfield 503 H2
Mooroolbark 337 H8
ct. Seabrook 451 A2
THE BROADWAY
Altona North 410 C3
THE CAUSEWAY
Melbourne 2 C13
Melbourne 24 C7
Taylors Hill 274 F9
THE CENTREWAY
Preston 282 J20
Ringwood 378 F9
THE CHANCERY
Lilydale 338 K2
Lilydale 339 C6
THE CIRCLE
Altona North 410 D5
THE CIRCUIT
Gladstone Pk 279 A4
Greensborough 286 A4
Lilydale 338 C14
THE CLOSE
Beaumaris 530 F10
Frankston S 626 L6
Hampton Pk 551 E12
Hoppers Csg 448 K5
Langwarrin 629 J2
Mt Waverley 418 K17
Scoresby 462 G8
Somerville 645 A19
Thomastown 240 F16
THE COMMON
Croydon S 380 C14
Nar Warrn S 578 E1
THE CONCORD
Bundoora 284 L4
THE CONDER
Ivanhoe East 328 L14
Ivanhoe East 329 A14
THE CORSO
Parkdale 531 D12
THE COTSWOLDS
Sunbury 144 C8
THE COURT
Hoppers Csg 448 E2
THE COVE
Port Melb 412 E5
THE CRESCENT
Ascot Vale 324 B16
Belgrave Ht 466 D19
Footscray 367 D5
Highett 496 F12
Kensington 33 C10
Kew 371 J5
Mt Evelyn 339 H19
Nar Warrn S 579 C1
Point Cook 450 G9
Port Melb 412 F5
Rosebud 683 J19
Sandringham 494 L13
Sandringham 495 A13
Sassafras 426 F16
Springvale 499 K15
Wesburn 348 B7
Waurn Ponds, off
Nicol Dr 705 A9
THE CRESENT
Ferntree Gly 464 E2
THE CREST
Attwood 236 L12
Attwood 237 A12
Bulleen 329 J16
Frankston S 627 A6
Highton 701 H12
Langwarrin 629 K2
Watsonia N 285 G2
Wonga Park 291 J19
Yarra Glen 208 H5
THE CROFT
Croydon N 336 A10
Lysterfield 503 H2
Ringwood N 378 A4
THE CROFTS
Richmond 25 L12
THE CROSS
wy. Keilor East 322 A5
wy.s, Avondale Ht 321 L7
THE CROSSOVER
Carnegie 456 J8
THE CROSSWAY
Strathmore 324 C2
THE CUTTING
Portsea 666 J20
THE DELL
Croydon N 336 A9
Nar Warrn N 538 D10
THE DEVIATION
Wheelers Hill 461 A14
THE DRIVE
Rosebud 683 H18
THE ELMS
Donvale 332 H15
Hillside 273 K4
THE ENTRANCE
Mt Evelyn 339 J17
THE ESPLANADE
Clifton Hill 20 J1
Clifton Hill 371 A1
Edithvale 546 F12
Fairfield 327 E20
Geelong 702 K1
Maribyrnong 323 C13
Nar Warrn S 579 H1
Research 288 J1
St Kilda 413 L16
St Kilda 414 A17
Sydenham 274 L2
Torquay 712 B12
la. Edithvale, off
The Esplanade 546 G12
s. Geelong 702 K2
THE ESTUARY
pl. Hallam 538 E15
THE EYRIE
Eaglemont 328 G11
Eltham North 245 K20
Hampton Pk 551 E12
Lilydale 338 F5
McCrae 685 C10
THE FAIRWAY
Bonbeach 573 C5
Hampton Pk 551 F9
Kingsbury 283 H8
Rowville 462 D20
THE FRED HOLLOWS
wy. Mill Park 242 H1
THE GABLES
Albion 321 A20
THE GALLEY
Rosebud W 683 B20
THE GATEWAY
Berwick 553 E3
Croydon S 380 B14
Lilydale 294 A20
THE GEORGIAN
rd. Olinda 427 A8
THE GLADE
Bonbeach 545 F15
Dandenong 536 E11
Ferntree Gly 464 J2
Hampton Pk 551 E14
Langwarrin 629 K2
Lysterfield 503 H2
Lysterfield 503 J1
Mitcham 377 E10
Mooroolbark 337 G18
Ringwood N 378 A8
Sunbury 113 J12
View Bank 286 A17
Wheelers Hill 461 B7
THE GLADES
Doncaster 331 A18
Hoppers Csg 448 D2
THE GLEN
Carrum Downs 575 B17
Donvale 376 J6
Ferntree Gly 464 H2
Frankston 599 J18
Hurstbridge 202 L18
Hurstbridge 203 A18
Rye 698 A3
THE GLENN
Hoppers Csg 448 D2
THE GOATS
la. Eaglemont 328 K11
THE GRANGE
Hampton Pk 551 J5
Malvern East 416 G20
Ringwood N 334 K20
Templestowe 331 F13
Wantirna 422 A13
Yallambie 286 A13
THE GREEN
Endeavour Hl 537 B2
Mill Park 243 E4
Somerville 645 A19
THE GREENWAY
Heathmont 423 B1
THE GROVE
Boronia 424 F9
Camberwell 416 H7
Caroline Spr 318 A3
Coburg 325 G6
Dromana 685 L9
Frankston S 626 G6
Glen Waverley 459 K1
Greensborough 244 F13
Hillside 273 J4
Langwarrin 629 J2
Mt Dandenong 426 H1
Reservoir 283 B2
THE GUMS
S Morang 199 L18
THE HAVEN
Bayswater 423 F11
THE HEATH
Croydon N 336 A10
THE HEIGHTS
Frankston S 627 A5
Hillside 232 A18
Somerville 644 K19
Sorrento 678 G4
Sunbury 143 F19
THE HELM
Frankston S 627 C14
Rosebud W 699 B1
THE HIGHWAY
Bentleigh 456 E20
Mt Waverley 459 B1
Upwey 465 K9
THEILE
ct. Truganina 405 G13
THE KNOLL
Ferntree Gly 463 G6
Langwarrin 629 K2
Mt Eliza 626 G14
Somerville 645 F15
THE LAIRIDGE
Kensington 33 G6
THE LAKES
bvd. S Morang 198 K13
bvd. S Morang 198 K15
bvd. S Morang 199 H12
THE LANE
Ferny Creek 466 A3
Pascoe Vale S 324 F1
Toorak 415 E4
Yarra Glen 209 C17
THE LINK
Keilor Park 277 L12
Mill Park 243 C4
Rosebud 684 B18
THELMA
av. Boronia 424 F15
av. Essendon N 279 C20
ct. Werribee 447 L18
ri. Hampton Pk 552 D12
st. Beaconsfield 555 C13
st. Carrum 573 D10
st. Noble Park 535 B6
st. Nunawading 376 F11
THE LOCH
Croydon Hills 335 F13
THE LODGE
Langwarrin 602 B18
THE LOOP
Blairgowrie 679 K17
Hadfield 280 K6
THE MALL
Croydon S 379 J10
Frankston 627 C6
Point Cook 450 G10
Templstw Lr 330 F14
Wantirna 422 F7
THE MEARS
Epping 198 D15
THEMEDA
ct. Delahey 275 A14
ct. Meadow Ht 193 L18
wyn. Sydenham 275 A8
THE MEWS
Frankston 628 A7
Hampton Pk 552 A14
Hawthorn 371 J19
Highton 705 E1
Hoppers Csg 448 D2
Somerville 645 B14
Sunshine W 364 E6
Torquay 711 G12
Vermont 421 J3
View Bank 285 J17
Wantirna 421 L12
THE MIDWAY
Lilydale 338 C14
THE MOOR
Balwyn N 373 C2
THE MOUNT
Croydon S 379 F10
THE NOOK
Balwyn N 373 C2
Bayswater N 379 L18
Doncaster E 332 F12
Ferntree Gly 464 C8
Langwarrin 629 D1
View Bank 285 J19
Watsonia N 285 H3
THE OAKS
Croydon 380 H6
Hillside 273 J4
Ivanhoe East 328 F14
Narre Warren 553 D1
Sunbury 144 B8
THEOBALD
st. Thornbury 327 H8
THEODORE
av. Noble Park 534 F3
ct. Toorak 415 G3
st. St Albans 320 A2
st. Surrey Hills 374 F18
tce. Berwick 553 F4
THE OLD FORD
Werribee 447 B8
THE OLD STOCK RUN
Sunbury 144 D7
THE OUTLOOK
Glen Waverley 460 F4
Heathmont 422 L1
Heathmont 423 A1
Lysterfield 503 J2
Lysterfield S 503 L14
Somerville 644 L19
THE OVAL
Berwick 554 D19
THE PANORAMA
Eaglemont 328 K11
Mickleham 150 F5
THE PARADE
Ascot Vale 323 J15
Clarinda 498 C4
Northcote 326 J20
THE PARK WAY
Chirnside Pk 337 C4
Diamond Ck 246 C10
THE PARKWAY
Caroline Spr 317 J6
Hampton Pk 552 A17
Patterson L 547 H20
Sunbury 113 E15
Templestowe 332 D3
THE PASS
Croydon 379 F9
Rosebud 684 B17
THE PATCH
rd. The Patch 467 J5
THE PEAK
Hillside 231 K17
THE PENINSULA
Caroline Spr 317 L6
THE PINES
Doveton 536 H13
Kew 372 F14
out. Doncaster E 332 D7
THE PLACE
Croydon S 380 A15
Toorak, off
Toorak Rd 415 B5
THE POINT
S Morang 198 K15
THE PORTAL
Lilydale 338 F14
THE PRIORY
Templestowe 331 L1
THE PROMENADE
Nar Warrn S 553 D2
Nar Warrn S 579 B
Nar Warrn S 579 B
Point Cook 450 C
S Morang 198 K1
THE QUADRANGLE
Glen Waverley 460 A1
THE QUADRANT
Nar Warrn S 553 F2
THE QUARTERDECK
Portsea 678 D
THE QUAYS
Nar Warrn S 579 G
THE RAMEO
Bundoora 285 A
THE RANGE
Frankston S 627 A
THE REGENCY
Hillside 231 J1
Hillside 231 J2
THERESA
av. Langwarrin 629 B
gdn. Endeavour Hl 537 K
st. Bentleigh 496 F
st. Richmond 26 K1
st. Sunshine N 321 D1
st. Tullamarine 278 H
THERESE
av. Mt Waverley 458 H
THE RETREAT
Hampton Pk 551 E1
THE RIALTO
Malvern East 457 D
w. Malvern East 457 C
THE RIDGE
Blackburn 376 A1
Canterbury 372 L1
Frankston S 626 L
Glen Waverley 420 D1
Hampton Pk 552 C1
Highton 701 F1
Knoxfield 463 C
Lilydale 338 E1
Mt Eliza 642 D
Roxburgh Pk 193 L1
Somerville 644 K1
Templestowe 288 F2
Templestowe 332 F
THE RIDGEWAY
Ivanhoe 328 C1
Kensington 33 G1
Pakenham 585 A
THE RIDGE WEST
Knoxfield 463 B
THE RIGHI
Dromana 686 H
Eaglemont 328 G1
Eaglemont 328 H1
South Yarra 31 J
South Yarra 414 E
Wyndham Va 446 C1
THE RISE
Diamond Ck 246 D
Frankston 628 A
Glen Waverley 459 L
Narre Warren 539 G1
Somerville 644 L1
Somerville 645 A1
Wantirna 422 A1
Warrandyte 332 L
Warrandyte 333 A
THE ROBBINS
Seabrook 450 K
THERRY
st. Coldstream 295 F1
st. Melbourne 23 K
THE SANDS
Aspendale Gdn 546 K
THE SEEKERS
cr. Mill Park 242 H
THE SERPENTINE
Tecoma 466 D
THE SILO
View Bank 329 K
THE SKYLINE
Sunbury 144 B
THE SPINNEY
Belmont 706 A
THE SPUR
Frankston S 626 L
Frankston S 627 A
Hampton Pk 551 L1
THE STRAND
Belgrave S 506 A1
Chelsea 546 J1
Keilor East 321 L
Lysterfield 503 J

Melton 268 L2
Moonee Pnd 324 C11
Nar Warrn S 578 L4
Nar Warrn S 578 L5
Newport 411 E8
Newport 411 E9
Point Cook 450 C5
Preston 282 J20
Wandana Ht 701 C18
Williamstown 411 F11

THE SUMMIT
Ringwood N 378 A3

THE TERRACE
Armadale 415 G14
Blackburn 375 F15
Croydon 379 L3
Lysterfield 503 H2
Melton 268 L2
Nar Warrn S 553 E20
Seabrook 451 B6
Somerville 644 L19

THE TROSSACHS
Frankston 628 B7

THE TRUMP
cl. Sunbury 143 E5

THE VAUCLUSE
Richmond 26 E13
South Yarra 32 H12

THE VIEW
Rosebud 700 J5

THE VILLAGE
grn. Sunbury 144 E7

THE VINE
Chirnside Pk 336 K5

THE VINEYARD
Waurn Ponds 705 E16

THE WALK
Melbourne 24 C7
Taylors Hill 274 F9

THE WALLABY RUN
Chirnside Pk 337 D3

THE WELKIN
trl. Kurunjang 226 G10

THE WILLOWS
Gisborne 78 H18

THEWLIS
rd. Pakenham 557 J19

THE WOODLAND
Wheelers Hill 460 K12

THE WRIDGEWAY
Mt Evelyn 384 A5

THEXTONS
rd. Yellingbo 387 J8

THEYER
st. Eumemmerring 536 K15

THICKINS
st. Pascoe Vale 280 F14

THIELE
ct. Blackburn 375 E15
st. Doncaster 331 C20

THIRD
av. Altona North 409 L5
av. Altona North 409 L7
av. Anglesea 713 C9
av. Aspendale 546 F9
av. Box Hill N 375 E6
av. Brunswick 325 D8
av. Chelsea Ht 547 E14
av. Cockatoo 510 H5
av. Dandenong N 501 J15
av. Eden Park 95 A8
av. Hadfield 281 B11
av. Hadfield 281 D10
av. Hoppers Csg 448 K5
av. Pakenham 584 K2
av. Rosebud 683 L19
av. Rowville 462 E18
av. Springvale 500 H10
av. Sunshine 365 E8
cr. Hadfield 281 C10
ct. Cranbourne 603 J6
dr. Springvale 500 H11
rd. Springvale 500 K10
st. Black Rock 529 G7
st. Clayton S 499 D5
st. Moorabbin Aprt 531 K4
st. Parkdale 531 D10
st. Warrandyte 289 E20

THIRLMERE
ct. Berwick 554 A8

THISTLE
cl. Hoppers Csg 405 B15
ct. Delahey 275 A16
ct. Meadow Ht 194 B18
gr. Highett 496 D14
st. Brunswick 325 B9
st. Essendon 323 K6
st. Pascoe Vale S 324 G1
st. Surrey Hills 418 A1

THISTLE BROOK
ct. Gowanbrae 279 F6

THISTLEDOWN
wk. St Albans 319 H8

THISTLETHWAITE
st. S Melbourne 29 D4
st. S Melbourne 413 B2

THISTLEWOOD
la. Cranbourne E 604 J1

THOM
st. New Gisborne 79 B3

THOMAS
av. Hampton E 495 L7
av. Melton S 268 G4
av. Warburton 349 F2
cr. Cranbourne 603 L2
cr. Lilydale 382 F2
ct. Doncaster 375 A3
ct. Eaglemont 328 H10
ct. Glen Waverley 460 C9
ct. Hallam 537 K13
ct. Parkdale 531 H14
dr. Mt Martha 657 C9
pl. Pakenham 584 K10
pl. Prahran 32 A16
pl. Prahran 414 F8
rd. Healesville 214 B20
rd. Healesville 258 C1
rd. Laverton N 364 E18
rd. Red Hill S 688 F20
rd.n, Emerald 469 F8
rd.s, Emerald 469 F10
st. Airport W 278 H13
st. Baxter 644 D1
st. Belmont 706 J1
st. Box Hill S 418 J4
st. Brighton East 455 H20
st. Brunswick 325 H14
st. Camberwell 417 L5
st. Clayton 498 K3
st. Croydon S 379 J11
st. Dandenong 535 L8
st. Doncaster E 376 C4
st. Dromana 686 A7
st. Eltham 288 B5
st. Ferntree Gly 464 C3
st. Geelong West 702 F6
st. Hampton 495 A9
st. Hawthorn 371 J17
st. Kew 372 E12
st. Laverton 407 D17
st. Malvern East 457 C4
st. Mitcham 377 E12
st. Moonee Pnd 324 D12
st. Mordialloc 531 L17
st. Mornington 640 L14
st. Mornington 641 A14
st. Noble Park 534 J3
st. Officer 581 F1
st. Pakenham 584 L9
st. Preston 283 B18
st. Richmond 26 E9
st. Ringwood 378 F15
st. Rosebud 683 K18
st. Roxburgh Pk 193 K15
st. St Albans 319 J1
st. Selby 467 D17
st. S Morang 243 H2
st. Thomastown 240 L12
st. Thomastown 241 A12
st. Williamstown 411 E11
st. Yarraville 366 L19
st. Port Melb, off Ross St 412 H4
st.n, Windsor 32 B20
st.s, Windsor 414 F11

THOMAS ARNOLD
av. Glen Waverley 459 K10

THOMAS BREW
la. Croydon 380 B3

THOMAS BRUNTON
pde. Roxburgh Pk 194 D13
pde. Roxburgh Pk 194 F16

THOMAS CARR
dr. Tarneit 405 A11

THOMAS HARDY
dr. Templestowe 332 C11

THOMASINA
st. Bentleigh E 456 J16

THOMAS LAWFORD
pl. Croydon Hills 335 G14

THOMAS MITCHELL
dr. Endeavour Hl 537 K7

THOMPSON
cct. Mill Park 242 F5
cr. Research 288 G6
cr. Roxburgh Pk 194 B10
ct. Altona Mdw 451 K9
ct. Endeavour Hl 537 D9
ct. Werribee 448 E11
dr. Wantirna 422 A8
rd. Bangholme 574 G5
rd. Carrum Downs 574 G5
rd. Patterson L 573 H6
rd. Upwey 465 J14
st. Abbotsford 26 K3
st. Avondale Ht 321 L10
st. Campbellfield 239 C16
st. Clayton 458 H19
st. Frankston 599 B19
st. Glen Waverley 420 F16
st. Kensington 33 F6
st. Kensington 34 C9
st. Ormond 455 K14
st. Sunshine 365 G2
st. Watsonia 285 H6
st. Williamstown 411 G19
tr. Lysterfield 504 L13

THOMPSONS
ct. Balwyn N 329 F18
rd. Balwyn N 329 E17
rd. Bulleen 329 E17
rd. Carrum Downs 575 F7
rd. Clyde North 580 A13
rd. Cranbourne 578 D11
rd. Cranbourne E 578 D11
rd. Cranbourne E 579 A12
rd. Cranbourne N 578 D11
rd. Cranbourne W 577 A9
rd. Diggers Rest 232 B6
rd. Kalorama 382 H12
rd. Kalorama 383 A11
rd. Keilor N 232 B6
rd. Lyndhurst 575 F7
rd. Montrose 382 H12
rd. Skye 575 F7
rd. Templstw Lr 330 B12

THOMSON
av. Laverton 407 E12
av. Murrumbeena 457 A10
av. Olinda 427 H17
ct. Rowville 462 L16
ct. Rowville 463 A16
dr. Rosanna 285 A16
rd. Beaconsfld Up 542 F9
ri. Parkdale 531 G16
st. Belmont 702 F19
st. Brighton 454 K11
st. Essendon 323 F7
st. Maidstone 366 H4
st. Melbourne 1 F10
st. Melbourne 23 L8
st. Northcote 327 A18
st. Pt Lonsdale 710 G2
st. Seddon 367 C12
st. S Melbourne 30 B9
st. S Melbourne 413 G5
tce. Dromana 686 K5
tce. Rye 696 J5
wy. Taylors Hill 274 K14

THOMSON PARK
dr. Whittlesea 126 C3

THOONA
gr. Greensborough 286 D6

THOONEN
ct. Keysborough 534 D13

THOR
ct. Bundoora 284 L5
ct. Keilor East 277 K17
st. Strathmore 280 A15

THORBURN
rd. Hampton 495 G10

THORESBY
gr. Ivanhoe 328 E12

THORN
st. Camberwell 372 J18
st. Essendon 323 J6

THORNBILL
cl. Healesville 214 A20
dr. Carrum Downs 600 L4
dr. Werribee 447 L10
pl. Craigieburn 149 G17

THORNBURY
cr. Malvern East 417 A20
la. Highton 701 J15

THORNCOMBE
wk. Doncaster E 332 D14

THORNDON
dr. St Albans 320 D7

THORNE
pl. Geelong, off Swanston St 703 D9
st. E Geelong 703 G10

THORNHILL
dr. Forest Hill 420 F2
dr. Keilor Dn 276 B15
rd. Highton 705 F4

THORNLEIGH
cl. Templestowe 331 G14
pl. Westmeadows 236 F14

THORNLEY
cl. Ferntree Gly 463 E4
ct. Greenvale 193 A16
dr. Berwick 554 F19

THORNS
rd. Wattle Glen 247 C7

THORNTON
av. Bundoora 284 L5
av. Sunbury 143 B10
av. Surrey Hills 373 J14
cl. Hallam 538 B19
cr. Mitcham 376 L15
ct. Dandenong N 502 A12
ct. Mooroolbark 337 J8
ct. The Basin 425 B9
rd. Mt Eliza 626 G11
st. Eltham 287 C15
st. Kew 371 F11
st. Lalor 240 H6
st. Macleod 284 L10
st. Macleod 285 A10
st. Oakleigh S 497 F4

THORNYCROFT
st. Campbellfield 194 J20

THOROGOOD
ct. Grovedale 706 F10
ct. Taylors Lakes 275 F7

THOROUGHBRED
av. Werribee 446 J19
dr. Highton 701 C17

THORPDALE
av. Coolaroo 238 E4

THORPE
av. Hoppers Csg 448 L4
av. Hoppers Csg 449 A4
ct. Altona Mdw 451 G4
pl. Burnside 318 E6
st. Lilydale 338 D16
st. Newport 410 E9
st. Sunshine 365 C5

THREADBOW
cr. Wheelers Hill 460 J12

THREADNEEDLE
st. Balwyn 374 A12

THREDBO
ct. Dandenong N 502 C16
ct. Epping 198 A20

THRICE
la. Kurunjang 226 J12

THROSBY
cr. Deer Park 319 C10
ct. Endeavour Hl 537 H6

THROSSELL
la. Melbourne 24 L8

THROUGH
rd. Camberwell 417 H8
rd. Noble Park 500 J15
rd. Ringwood N 378 E6
st. Hawthorn 371 J19

THROWER
st. Reservoir 282 D8

THRUSH
ct. Werribee 448 D8

THULE
ct. Brighton 454 H10

THURBRO
dr. Keysborough 535 A9

THURLEIGH
av. Croydon S 379 J13

THURLING
st. Mentone 530 K9

THURLOO
dr. Safety Bch 669 C12
st. Chadstone 457 L1

THURMAID
ct. Roxburgh Pk 194 D15

THURMOND
ct. Endeavour Hl 537 E4

THURRA
ct. Dandenong N 502 B10

THURSO
ct. Endeavour Hl 503 K19
st. Malvern East 417 F20

THURSTON
st. Box Hill 374 J16

THURZA
ct. Wheelers Hill 461 C15

THWAITES
rd. Pakenham 559 B20
rd. Pakenham 585 A1
st. Albion 320 F18

THYER
rd. Ivanhoe 328 B17

THYME
ct. Croydon Hills 335 H16
rd. Campbellfield 239 E12

THYRA
st. Sunshine 365 A6

TIAMO
ri. Sydenham 275 C8

TIBARI
ct. Croydon 380 C9

TIBARRI
ct. Mooroolbark 337 D12

TIBBLES
st. Beaumaris 530 B3

TIBER
cl. Werribee 447 H4

TIBIR
st. Blairgowrie 696 B6

TIBROCKNEY
st. Highett 496 A15

TICHBORNE
pl. S Melbourne 3 C19
pl. S Melbourne 30 C1

TIDAL
pl. Torquay 712 H1

TIDCOMBE
cr. Doncaster E 332 E7

TIDE
st. Elwood 454 F5

TIE
st. Mont Albert N 374 E5

TIEMEN
rd. Yarrambat 201 A18

TIERNAN
st. Footscray 367 E5
st. Glen Waverley 460 L4
st. Preston 327 D5

TIERNEY
ct. Werribee 447 G4

TIFFANY
av. Cheltenham 531 G3
cr. Roxburgh Pk 194 B7
ct. Doncaster 330 L18
ct. Keilor 277 B14
ct. Montrose 382 J4
gr. S Morang 198 K13
gr. Templestowe 331 J8
pl. Sydenham 275 C8

TIGRIS
cl. Werribee 447 F5
ct. Roxburgh Pk 194 E5

TIKALARA
pl. Templestowe 332 F1

TIKANTI
ct. Chelsea Ht 547 D11

TIKI
ct. Wheelers Hill 461 B20

TILBA
ct. Berwick 553 H6
pl. Wantirna S 423 B12
st. Aberfeldie 323 D11

TILBURN
rd. Deer Park 319 F20

TILBURY
ct. Cranbourne E 578 J17
ct. Kings Park 319 C2
st. Thomastown 240 G15

TILIA
ct. Frankston N 600 E10

TILLBROOK
ct. Noble Park N 501 C12

TILLBUSH
cl. Hoppers Csg 405 A17

TILLER
la. Patterson L 547 H20
st. Burwood E 419 G10

TILLEY
rd. Maddingley 263 C5
st. Cheltenham 531 D2
st. Coburg N 282 B15
wk. Roxburgh Pk 194 D11

TILLEYS
rd. Maddingley 264 B6

TILLOTSON
tce. Armadale, off Orrong Rd 415 C9

TILLS
dr. Warrandyte 290 D16

TILLY
ct. Newcomb 704 B16

TILMOUTH
pl. Nar Warrn S 578 L3

TILNEY
cl. Mulgrave 500 L5

TILSON
dr. Vermont 421 C2

TIM
ct. Hampton 494 K6

TIMARA
ct. McCrae 685 E12

TIMARRON
ct. Langwarrin 630 A7

TIMARU
av. Brunswick E 325 L12
cl. Sorrento 679 D15
ct. Wheelers Hill 460 H18

TIMBARRA
ct. Grovedale 706 D11

TIMBER
la. Glen Waverley....459 L1
rdg. Doncaster..........330 C16
TIMBERGLADE
dr. Noble Park N......501 C12
TIMBERGLADES
Pk Orchards.......333 L20
dr. Bundoora...........284 G7
rd. Montrose...........382 B12
TIMBERLINE
rd. Launching Pl......344 F5
rd. Woori Yallock.....344 G5
TIMBERSIDE
dr. Beaconsfield......555 E13
TIMBERTOP
ct. Frankston N.......600 A12
ct. Mooroolbark......337 F7
dr. Rowville............502 C4
dr. Vermont............421 A5
rd. Ringwood N.......377 L10
rd. Sunbury............144 D11
rdg. Warrandyte........333 E5
TIMBERVIEW
tce. Croydon Hills.....335 F12
TIMBOON
cr. Broadmeadows..237 H14
TIMCHRIS
ct. Melton W...........226 B14
TIME
ct. Torquay............712 E3
la. South Yarra..........32 G9
TIMES
st. Cheltenham........497 D17
TIMEWELL
cr. Boronia.............424 J10
TIMINS
st. Sunbury............143 F14
TIMMINGS
st. Chadstone..........457 L4
TIMMINS
cr. Rye....................697 D5
ct. Mill Park............242 C4
ct. Wheelers Hill......460 J11
st. Northcote...........326 H18
TIMMIS
av. Cheltenham........530 D2
TIMMOTHY
cl. Pakenham..........559 E19
dr. Wantirna S.........422 D17
TIMMS
av. Croydon.............380 H3
av. Kilsyth..............380 K3
cr. Dingley Village...533 A7
ct. Kilsyth..............380 K3
ct. Sunbury.............142 L10
pl. Doncaster E.......332 D6
st. Nar Warrn S.......552 H20
TIMOK
la. Roxburgh Pk......194 D6
TIMOR
cl. Burwood............418 D6
ct. Boronia.............424 D4
ct. Coolaroo............238 F7
pde. Heidelberg W.....328 C1
TIMOTHY
ct. Hallam...............537 H14
ct. Kings Park..........319 D2
ct. Templestowe.....331 K2
la. Melbourne.............1 L7
la. Melbourne...........24 A5
TIN
al. Parkville..............17 L11
TINA
cl. Carrum Downs...601 E3
cl. Fawkner............239 G20
ct. Clarinda............498 D10
ct. Mulgrave...........500 H4
TINAGEL
wy. Mornington........656 L4
TINAPHER
dr. Rye....................696 K5
TINARA
ct. Cranbourne N.....578 D9
TINAROO
gr. Lilydale.............337 L3
TINARRA
ct. Kilsyth..............381 C12
ct. Wantirna S.........422 A17
TINDAL
ct. Frankston S.......627 G16
ct. Greensborough..244 C16
TINDALE
ct. Attwood............237 E10
TINDALS
rd. Donvale............333 B15
rd. Pk Orchards.......333 B15
rd. Warrandyte........333 D4
TINGARA
ct. Patterson L........573 K4
TINGLE
cl. Narre Warren.....553 B8
TINKS
rd. Narre Warren.....538 G20
TINNING
st. Brunswick..........325 C9
TINONEE
ct. Yallambie...........285 L11
TINTAGEL
ct. Mt Eliza.............626 A9
TINTALDRA
dr. Taylors Lakes.....276 E9
TINTERN
av. Bayswater N.......379 G14
av. Preston..............282 D19
av. Ringwood E.......379 G14
av. Toorak..............414 L6
av. Toorak..............415 A6
cr. Wantirna S.........462 C4
ct. Frankston S.......627 J15
ct. Seabrook...........450 L5
dr. Springvale S.......499 H19
gr. Cheltenham........496 K15
gr. St Albans...........275 J19
mw. Cheltenham........496 L14
ri. Glen Waverley....460 K3
TINTINARA
cr. Belmont.............706 E6
TINTO
cl. Deer Park...........318 K12
ct. Mt Waverley.......418 J14
gr. Tecoma.............466 C10
TINWORTH
pl. Ringwood N.......378 J2
TIPPET
st. Clayton S...........499 D5
TIRANA
st. Mitcham............377 A10
TIRHATUAN
dr. Rowville.............502 J2
TIRO
ct. Bundoora...........285 A5
ct. Hawthorn E........372 D14
TIRRAY
cl. Greensborough..243 K18
TISDALL
dr. Langwarrin........629 K5
st. E Geelong..........703 G14
TITAN
dr. Carrum Downs...574 G20
st. Whittington........704 B20
TITANIA
cr. Ferny Creek........425 F19
cr. Ferny Creek........465 G1
cr. Tremont.............425 F19
tce. Ferny Creek........465 H2
tce. Tremont.............465 J2
TITCH
st. Footscray...........367 C3
TITCHER
rd. Noble Park N......501 D16
TITIAN
ct. Grovedale..........705 J14
TI TREE
av. Bayswater..........422 J4
ct. View Bank..........285 L18
dr. Doveton.............536 K10
TI-TREE
av. Blairgowrie........695 G1
av. Bonbeach...........545 F15
cr. Seaford.............600 C4
ct. Kilsyth..............381 L7
gr. Mornington........656 C1
gr. Parkdale............531 E13
gr. Seaford.............573 C16
gr.e, Parkdale...........531 E14
la. Mt Eliza.............626 C13
TITUS
av. Hoppers Csg......448 L2
ct. Reservoir...........283 G3
TIUNA
ct. Glen Waverley....460 L5
gr. Elwood..............454 C5
TIVENDALE
rd. Officer...............556 F20
TIVERTON
ct. Bayswater N.......380 F20
dr. Mulgrave...........500 H1
st. Belmont.............702 A18
TIVEY
pde. Balwyn..............373 B9
st. Reservoir...........282 J5
TIVOLI
arc. Melbourne.............2 F13
ct. Eumemmerring..537 C13
ct. Keilor Lodge.......275 L4
gdn. Rowville.............503 B8
pl. Point Cook..........449 L5
pl. South Yarra...........31 J6
pl. South Yarra.........414 E3
rd. South Yarra...........32 G9
rd. South Yarra.........414 J5
TOAGARA
st. Rye...................697 B6
TOBIAS
av. Glen Waverley....460 E6
ct. Carrum Downs...575 E14
la. Mont Albert........374 C13
TOBIN
av. Northcote...........326 J17
dr. Queenscliff.........709 B18
TOBRUK
av. Heidelberg W.....328 A4
av. Tremont.............425 D15
cr. Williamstown.....411 A16
ct. Lalor.................241 G7
rd. Ashburton..........417 J16
st. Bulleen..............330 B18
TODD
ct. Cranbourne W....603 E2
ct. Croydon.............380 K1
ct. Darley................221 K8
ct. Mentone.............531 F5
gr. Somerville..........645 D14
rd. Port Melb...........367 K19
rd. Port Melb...........411 L1
st. Bentleigh............495 J1
TODMAN
cl. Bacchus Msh.....221 E17
cl. Mill Park............242 L9
ct. Melton W...........226 C14
st. Watsonia............285 F8
TOINETTE
ct. Doncaster E.......331 L19
TOIRRAM
cr. Cranbourne........577 K11
rd. Mt Waverley.......458 K3
TOKOL
ct. Kurunjang..........227 C13
TOLEDO
rd. St Albans...........320 K6
TOLGA
cl. Carrum Downs...575 C14
ct. Bayswater..........423 C8
TOLHURST
av. Boronia.............424 K4
pl. Mt Martha..........656 D7
TOLLHOUSE
rd. Kings Park.........275 C20
TOLLINGTON
av. Malvern East......416 G17
TOLLKEEPERS
pde. Attwood............236 L11
pde. Attwood............237 A11
TOLLS
av. Mentone............531 C6
TOLMIE
av. Gruyere.............342 J8
av. Werribee............447 L19
ct. Broadmeadows..237 L9
pl. Geelong, off Gheringhap St....703 A7
ri. Hallam...............538 B18
wy. Glen Waverley....420 E15
wy. Mt Martha..........656 H6
TOLSON
ct. Roxburgh Pk......194 A12
TOLSTOY
ct. Doncaster E.......331 L15
TOM
st. Anglesea............714 A3
TOMAH
ct. Grovedale..........706 C10
TOMAR
cl. Croydon.............379 F8
ct. Cheltenham........497 C19
TOMASETTI
cr. Narre Warren.....538 F18
TOMASINA
ct. Langwarrin.........601 B20
TOM BEGG
ct. Wheelers Hill......460 K9
TOMBOLO
ct. Mooroolbark......337 C9
TOM GEARON
ct. Nar Warrn N.......539 J11
TOM HILLS
ct. Port Melb, off Webb Rd..........412 H5
TOMINTOUL
ct. Clarinda............498 D8
TOM JONES
ct. Nar Warrn N.......539 D5
TOMKIN
ct. Altona Mdw........451 D1
TOM MAW MEMORIAL
dr. Rosebud............699 J5
TOM RIGG
st. Deer Park...........319 H11
TOM ROBERTS
cr. Yallambie...........285 J15
gld. Diamond Ck.......245 B13
rd. Kallista..............467 B3
TONBRIDGE
st. Carrum..............573 B9
TONELLI
cr. Mill Park............242 D8
pl. Burnside............318 F8
TONGE
st. Anglesea............713 J6
TONGIO
ct. Broadmeadows..238 A11
TONGOLA
ct. Cranbourne........578 B18
TONGUE
st. Yarraville...........367 C14
TONI
ct. Wantirna............422 C4
st. Campbellfield.....239 G9
st. Doncaster..........331 B18
TONKIN
av. Balwyn..............373 H9
av. Coburg N...........281 B12
st. Safety Bch..........668 L16
st. Safety Bch..........669 A16
TONKINS
la. Richmond............26 A12
TONMAR
ct. Forest Hill..........420 G6
TONNANT
ct. Lilydale.............294 J20
TONY
pl. Mooroolbark......337 K18
st. Warrandyte........333 E4
TONYL
ct. Greensborough..286 D9
TOOAN
ct. Westmeadows...237 J11
TOOGOOD
ct. Pakenham Up....560 B5
TOOGOODS
ri. Box Hill N...........375 D7
TOOHEY
cl. Hampton Pk.......551 E14
ct. Bellfield.............328 A5
st. Bellfield.............328 A6
st. Footscray...........367 H9
TOOLAMBOOL
rd. Carnegie............456 H5
TOOLANG
ct. Mt Waverley.......459 G6
rd. Selby.................467 C13
TOOLANGI
gr. Preston..............327 E6
rd. Alphington.........327 J17
TOOLEBEWONG
rd. Badger Creek.....257 L16
TOOLERN
av. Dromana.............686 F9
st. Melton S............268 H9
TOOLIM
wk. Sydenham.........274 K7
TOOLIMERIN
av. Bayswater N.......380 H20
TOOLOOMBA
ct. Frankston...........600 F16
TOOMAH
st. Nar Warrn S.......578 K1
TOOMBAH
st. Mt Waverley.......459 F7
TOOMBAK
wk. Sydenham.........274 L7
TOOMBARRA
pl. Greensborough..287 A1
TOOMEY
st. Vermont............377 J19
TOOMUC VALLEY
rd. Pakenham..........558 C4
rd. Pakenham..........558 D13
rd. Pakenham Up....558 D3
TOON
ct. Dandenong N.....501 K13
TOONGABBIE
ct. Keysborough.....534 H8
ct. Werribee............447 C12
TOORA
cr. Badger Creek.....258 D7
ct. St Albans...........320 G13
dr. Westmeadows...237 E11
st. Ivanhoe..............328 D13
TOORAC
dr. Briar Hill............286 K6
rd. Upwey...............465 L18
TOORADIN
av. Dallas................238 C8
TOORADIN STATION
rd. Tooradin............651 H6
TOORAK
av. Baxter...............644 L2
av. Croydon.............379 L2
av. The Basin...........425 E12
av. Toorak...............415 J5
ct. Greensborough..244 J15
dr. Dingley Village...533 D6
pde. Geelong.............702 K2
rd. Camberwell........417 C8
rd. Hawthorn E........416 A7
rd. Kooyong............416 A7
rd. Malvern.............415 B5
rd. Melbourne..........414 B4
rd. Mt Dandenong....426 F2
rd. South Yarra..........31 C7
rd. South Yarra..........32 A9
rd. South Yarra........414 B4
rd. Toorak...............415 B5
st. Tootgarook........698 F6
TOORANG
av. Balwyn N...........373 D1
TOORONGA
ct. Ashwood...........418 F18
rd. Glen Iris.............416 C10
rd. Hawthorn E........416 C10
rd. Malvern East......416 B18
rd. Ringwood E.......378 K13
st. Dandenong N.....502 B19
TOOROURRONG
rd. Upwey...............466 B6
TOOTAL
rd. Dingley Village...532 L3
rd. Springvale S.......499 B20
TOOTH
ct. Mill Park............241 K7
TOOTLES
ct. Hoppers Csg......405 D20
TOOYAL
st. Frankston...........599 D14
TOPAROA
la. Mt Martha..........656 J7
TOPAZ
av. Wyndham Va.....446 E14
ct. Mulgrave...........500 F1
ct. Wantirna S.........421 L16
dr. Hillside..............231 J18
pl. Narre Warren.....539 D14
pl. St Albans...........320 J9
st. Blairgowrie.........696 A4
wy. Hampton Pk.......551 C9
TOPE
st. S Melbourne..........3 B20
st. S Melbourne........24 C20
st. S Melbourne........30 C1
st. S Melbourne......413 G1
TOPPINGS
rd. Wonga Park.......291 J18
TOPTANI
dr. Nar Warrn S.......579 E2
TOR
rd. Belgrave Ht........506 C2
TORANA
ct. Doveton.............537 B10
ct. Hoppers Csg......448 E6
TORBAY
ct. Werribee............446 K13
st. Macleod.............285 B12
TORBRECK
cl. Hoppers Csg......449 C2
st. Glen Waverley....460 A9
TORI
pl. Patterson L........547 J20
TORINA
ct. Mt Eliza.............626 C20
TORINO
st. St Albans...........320 K5
TORLEY
rd. Emerald.............509 F9
TORMEY
st. Balwyn N...........373 J4
st. Reservoir...........282 G1
TORMORE
rd. Boronia.............424 A12
TORMORVEY
av. Hillside..............232 E20
TOROA
rd. Mt Dandenong...426 E3
TORONTO
av. Doncaster..........374 F3
TORORO
ct. Croydon N.........336 D11
TOROWATTA
pl. Burnside............318 H9
TORQUATA
ct. Hoppers Csg......405 D16
TORQUAY
av. Chadstone.........458 E4
av. Seaford.............573 D17
bvd. Jan Juc.............711 D16
cl. Dingley Village...532 K7

st. Brunswick..........325 D16
wy. S Morang...........198 J13
TRIPOLI
ct. Hallam...............537 G14
TRIPOVICH
st. Brunswick..........325 F13
TRISH
wk. Werribee............448 F18
TRISHA
dr. Rowville.............503 A5
TRIST
st. Watsonia N.........285 G3
TRISTAN
ct. Eltham North......245 G18
ct. Hadfield.............281 B9
TRISTANA
hts. S Morang...........198 J14
TRISTANIA
st. Doncaster E.......375 G3
st. Doveton.............536 L12
st. Frankston S........627 D9
TRISTRAM
ct. Glen Waverley....420 K16
dr. Cranbourne W....577 G16
TRISTRON
ct. Melton W...........226 C13
TRITON
ct. Gladstone Pk......279 C3
ct. Ringwood...........335 B20
dr. Keysborough.....534 F10
TRIUMPH
cl. Glen Waverley....460 A3
ct. Highton..............701 E16
TROEDEL
st. Pearcedale.........646 L6
st. Pearcedale.........647 A6
TROLLABY
cl. Gladstone Pk......236 L16
TROODOS
ri. Eltham North......288 G2
ri. Research...........288 G2
TROON
av. Jan Juc..............711 F15
av. Mornington........656 D3
cr. Sunshine N.........321 H16
ct. Endeavour Hl.....537 H1
ct. Rowville.............462 D19
ct. Sunbury.............144 F13
pl. Frankston...........600 F18
rd. McCrae..............684 K19
rd. Rosebud............684 K19
TROOPER
ct. Wheelers Hill......461 B13
TROTT
pl. Keilor East..........278 A20
TROTTING
pl. Epping..............198 D16
TROUP
ct. Werribee............447 G12
TROVE PARK
dr. Vermont............421 B4
TROY
cl. Sunshine W.......364 C6
ct. Forest Hill.........420 C4
ct. Werribee............447 L8
st. Bonbeach...........573 C1
st. Glen Waverley....420 H15
tce. Lysterfield..........463 K20
TRUCK CITY
dr. Campbellfield.....194 L20
TRUDGEON
av. Reservoir...........282 K16
TRUDI
ct. Donvale.............377 A2
TRUDY
pl. Mt Evelyn...........339 J20
TRUE
av. Carrum..............573 D7
TRUEMANS
rd. Boneo................698 G11
rd. Boneo................698 J15
rd. Fingal.................698 G11
rd. Fingal.................698 L20
rd. Fingal.................699 A18
rd. Rosebud W.........698 G11
rd. Tootgarook.........698 G11
TRUGANINA
av. Seabrook...........450 K8
wy. Truganina..........405 J14
TRUGANINI
rd. Carnegie............456 H8
TRUGO
la. Footscray...........367 F9
TRUMAN
ct. Altona Mdw........451 F4
st. S Kingsville........410 F3
TRUMPER
pl. Epping...............198 G15
st. Camberwell........416 K4
TRUMPINGTON
gr. Kallista...............468 C16
gr. Menzies Ck........468 C16
TRUNCATA
ct. Mill Park............243 D8
TRURO
cr. Keilor Lodge.......275 K4
st. Abbotsford...........20 C12
TRUSCOTT
av. Roxburgh Pk......194 C8
ct. Mill Park............243 A5
ct. Wheelers Hill......460 F16
st. Brunswick E.......325 L18
st. Glenroy..............280 G8
st. Whittington........703 L18
TRUSLOVE
ct. Endeavour Hl.....537 L9
TRYTHALL
ct. Altona Mdw........451 G3
st. Beaconsfield......555 A15
TSCHAMPIONS
rd. Macclesfield.......470 G2
TUANS
tr. Yarra Glen..........208 F6
TUBE
st. Sunshine N........321 F11
TUCK
ct. Narre Warren.....539 B15
st. Cheltenham.........530 K3
st. Moorabbin.........496 B7
wk. Fawkner.............281 F1
TUCKER
av. Brighton.............455 A17
av. Port Melb...........412 G4
rd. Bentleigh............456 G20
rd. Bentleigh............496 F6
rd. McKinnon..........456 G20
rd. Ormond.............456 G20
rd. Vermont............421 E5
st. Bundoora...........242 K20
st. Cranbourne........578 C20
st. Fawkner.............281 H8
st. W Footscray.......366 J4
TUCKERS
rd. Templestowe.....331 K14
TUCKETT
st. Alphington.........327 G19
st. Murrumbeena....457 C7
TUCKEY
st. Sorrento............679 C13
TUCKFIELD
ct. Macleod.............285 D11
TUDAWALI
cr. Wheelers Hill......460 G18
TUDBALL
ct. Bacchus Msh.....221 L14
TUDOR
cr. Noble Park N......501 D17
ct. Balwyn N...........374 A2
ct. Blackburn S.......419 J6
ct. Craigieburn........150 B18
ct. Edithvale............546 K9
ct. Frankston...........600 A17
ct. Glen Waverley....459 H10
ct. Heathmont.........378 K15
ct. Hoppers Csg......405 B20
ct. Ivanhoe.............328 D9
ct. Keilor East..........322 H6
ct. Narre Warren.....539 E13
ct. Wantirna............422 F12
dr. Mooroolbark......338 A16
pl. Melton W...........226 E15
rd. Doncaster..........330 E18
rd. Rosebud............700 K3
rd. Sunshine N........321 C14
st. Bentleigh E.........457 E19
st. Burnley..............371 C17
st. Burwood............418 E10
st. Glenroy..............280 A7
TUDOR COURT
rd. Yellingbo............387 H9
TUDOR ROSE
cr. Sydenham.........275 D9
TUDOR VILLAGE
dr. Lilydale.............338 L5
dr. Lilydale.............339 A5
TUERONG
rd. Moorooduc........657 H16
rd. Tuerong.............657 G17
rd. Tuerong.............657 H16
st. Rye....................697 B5
TUFFS
gr. Grovedale..........705 K12
TUFNEL
ct. Endeavour Hl.....537 A1
TUGAN
pl. Ringwood N.......334 K19
TUGUN
rd. Lilydale.............338 H8
TUHAN
st. Chadstone..........457 K3
TUHANS
rd. Mt Waverley.......458 G4
TULAR
av. Oakleigh S..........497 H3
TULIP
cl. Hoppers Csg......405 B16
cr. Boronia..............424 C15
ct. Doncaster E.......332 F13
ct. Hillside..............274 D4
ct. Lalor.................240 L9
ct. Notting Hill.........459 J14
ct. Warranwood......334 J15
gr. Cheltenham........496 F20
st. Black Rock.........495 G19
st. Cheltenham........495 G19
st. Silvan................428 L5
TULKARA
gr. Vermont............421 K2
TULLAMARINA
av. Tullamarine........278 K7
TULLAMARINE
fwy. Airport W...........279 B17
fwy. Essendon N........279 C19
fwy. Gladstone Pk......236 E15
fwy. Gladstone Pk......278 L2
fwy. Gladstone Pk......279 A4
fwy. Gowanbrae........279 A4
fwy. Melb Airport.......236 E15
fwy. Niddrie..............279 C19
fwy. Strathmore.........279 C19
fwy. Tullamarine........236 E15
fwy. Westmeadows.....236 E15
TULLAMARINE PARK
rd. Tullamarine........278 B10
TULLAMORE
av. Doncaster..........330 D20
TULLAROOP
ct. Ferntree Gly.......464 A14
ct. St Albans...........320 E13
TULLIDGE
st. Melton...............269 B1
TULLIMBAR
cct. Vermont S.........420 F11
TULLIUS
av. Oakleigh E..........458 K12
TULLO
pl. Richmond............26 G11
TULLOCH
av. Kurunjang..........227 C15
cl. Cranbourne W....577 G17
ct. Bacchus Msh.....221 F15
ct. Keilor Dn............275 K10
ct. Mill Park............242 J11
st. Deer Park...........319 C17
st. Millgrove............348 D1
wy. Roxburgh Pk......194 A11
wy. Roxburgh Pk......194 B12
TULLOCK
gr. Glen Waverley....459 K10
TULLUS
ct. Kings Park.........274 L17
TULLY
ct. Doncaster..........330 L18
ct. Ivanhoe.............327 L8
ct. Werribee............447 H9
rd. Clarinda.............498 G11
st. E Geelong..........703 E13
TULLYVALLIN
cr. Sorrento............679 B16
TULONG
cl. Mooroolbark......337 E16
st. Hurstbridge........203 F13
TULSA
dr. Sunbury.............144 E11
TULSK
ct. Hampton Pk.......551 G13
TULUM
ct. Frankston...........599 F17
TUMBLE TREE
ct. Highton..............705 F3
TUMUT
cl. Epping...............198 A19
ct. Berwick..............554 C20
ct. Keilor.................276 L13
ct. Patterson L........573 K3
ct. Wantirna S.........422 D16
ct. Werribee............447 H8
TUNA
la. Pt Lonsdale........707 F14
TUNALEY
pde. Reservoir...........283 F1
TUNBERRY
ct. Rowville.............462 C19
TUNBRIDGE
cr. Lalor.................241 J8
mw. Westmeadows...237 H13
st. Flemington.........324 D19
wy. Ferntree Gly.......463 F4
TUNBURY
av. Ringwood...........378 L3
av. Ringwood...........379 A3
cl. Ringwood...........378 L3
ct. Highton..............701 F15
TUNLEY
cl. Endeavour Hl.....537 F8
pl. Roxburgh Pk......194 C15
TUNNECLIFFE
ct. Keilor East..........277 L16
TUNNEL
st. Warrandyte........334 B2
TUNSTALL
av. Boronia..............424 B9
av. Nunawading.......376 H13
rd. Donvale.............376 E7
sq. Doncaster E.......376 E2
TUPPAL
pl. Keilor East..........278 C18
TUPPEN
st. Yarraville............366 J15
TURAKINA
av. Edithvale............546 G13
TURANA
st. Doncaster..........331 B19
TURANGA
pl. Hallam...............537 L15
rd. Gisborne..............78 H12
TURANO
la. Roxburgh Pk......194 D6
TURBO
dr. Bayswater N.......379 L17
TURELLA
ct. Lalor.................240 D9
ct. Mooroolbark......337 D13
TURFAN
cl. Keilor Dn............276 E16
TURIA
gr. Roxburgh Pk......194 E6
TURIN
pl. Keilor Lodge.......276 B5
TURKEITH
av. Herne Hill...........702 A1
cr. Croydon N.........336 D11
TURNBERRY
av. Nar Warrn S.......578 L2
ct. Frankston...........628 B6
ct. Heatherton.........497 G15
dr. Sunbury.............144 G12
rd. Sunshine N........321 H14
TURNBULL
al. Melbourne............24 J4
av. Oakleigh E..........458 K12
av. Toorak...............415 H4
ct. Brunswick W.......324 G10
ct. Carrum Downs....601 B6
ct. Ringwood...........378 F9
dr. Pascoe Vale S....324 G4
gr. Northcote...........326 H14
la. Melbourne............23 J8
st. Clifton Hill............20 B4
st. Mornington.........640 E16
TURNER
al. Melbourne..............2 E11
al. Melbourne............24 D6
av. Glen Huntly........456 B9
cl. Springvale...........500 C6
cr. Braybrook..........365 K5
ct. Dandenong........536 E3
ct. Glen Waverley....459 J3
ct. S Morang...........243 H1
ct. Sunbury.............143 F6
pl. S Geelong..........703 A13
rd. Boronia..............424 D13
rd. Highett...............496 G14
rd. Langwarrin..........629 B2
st. Abbotsford...........20 C13
st. Abbotsford...........20 D13
st. Armadale............415 E10
st. Bacchus Msh.....221 L18
st. Berwick..............554 J10
st. Briar Hill...............286 H4
st. Croydon.............380 C5
st. Glen Iris..............416 H8
st. Malvern East......416 D20
st. Moonee Pnd......324 H11
st. Pascoe Vale S....280 L20
st. Port Melb...........368 C18
st. Thornbury...........327 H10
st. Westmeadows....236 L14
TURNERS
la. Healesville..........211 K8
la. Officer..................557 A4
TURNHAM
av. Rosanna............328 L1
TURNLEY
st. Balwyn N...........329 H20
st. Balwyn N...........373 H1
TURNSTONE
ct. Carrum Downs...600 E4
st. Doncaster E.......376 A4
TURQUOISE
cl. St Albans...........320 K9
TURRAMURRA
dr. Keysborough.....534 F9
dr. Rowville.............502 H1
TURRANA
st. Rye....................697 A5
TURTUR
cl. Mill Park............242 B7
TURVILLE
pl. Port Melb...........412 J5
TUSANNE
pl. Doncaster E.......331 K18
TUSCAN
ct. Thomastown......240 K17
ct. Waurn Ponds.....705 B16
TUSCANY
ri. Templestowe.....331 G5
TUSKAR
pl. Carrum Downs...601 E3
TUSSOCK
cr. Sydenham.........274 K8
ct. Frankston...........599 L15
gr. Deer Park...........319 E12
st. Narre Warren.....553 F10
TUTA
cl. Croydon Hills.....335 G15
ct. Greensborough..244 A18
TUTTAWATTA
rd. Selby.................467 B14
TUXEN
av. Carrum Downs...574 K17
ct. Brighton East.....495 K4
ct. Highton..............701 H9
st. Balwyn N...........373 G6
st. Balwyn N...........373 H4
TWAKURRA
st. Rye....................697 F8
TWEED
ct. Glen Waverley....420 K18
ct. Langwarrin.........629 B5
ct. Werribee............447 H5
pl. Hawthorn, off
Tweed St............371 J17
st. Hawthorn...........371 J17
st. Highett...............495 K12
st. Ringwood E.......378 L13
st. Vermont............421 J1
TWEEDIE
ct. Box Hill N...........375 B6
pl. Richmond............26 F7
TWEEDLE
rd. Gisborne S.........109 B19
TWEEDSIDE
st. Essendon...........323 G8
TWELFTH
av. Anglesea............713 D13
TWENTIETH
av. Eden Park............95 E16
TWENTYMAN
ct. Seaholme...........409 J15
TWENTYSECOND
av. Eden Park............95 C5
av. Whittlesea............95 C5
TWICKENHAM
cr. Burnley..............415 C1
TWILIGHT
pl. Safety Bch..........669 B16
TWIN
ct. Ferntree Gly.......423 L17
TWINING
av. Bundoora...........242 D13
TWISDEN
rd. Bentleigh............495 L2
TWITT
st. Moolap...............704 H18
TWO BAYS
cr. Mt Martha..........655 D18
cr. Selby.................467 E16
rd. Mt Eliza..............642 J7
TWOFOLD
cl. Dingley Village...532 K8
TWOHIG
ct. Dandenong N.....501 J17
TWYFORD
cl. Doncaster E.......332 J13
cl. Hillside..............232 E18
st. Box Hill N...........375 C9
st. Fawkner.............281 K2
st. Williamstown.....411 F18
TYABB
ct. Broadmeadows..237 G15
ct. Frankston...........600 F17
gr. Aspendale..........546 G6
TYALLA
cl. Lower Plenty......286 H14
cr. Toorak...............415 G4
ct. Hampton Pk.......551 G10

ct. Mulgrave 500 F2
gr. Mornington 640 F17
TYAS
pl. Carrum Downs 601 E3
TYBURN
cl. Werribee 446 J13
TYE
av. Selby 467 B16
TYERS
cr. Rowville 463 B18
ct. Dallas 238 D10
ct. Frankston 628 C1
la. Keysborough 534 D18
TYLDEN
ct. Grovedale 706 D11
ct. Mentone 531 J7
pl. Westmeadows 236 L14
TYLER
ct. Epping 197 K19
dr. Carrum Downs 575 E17
st. Preston 282 L16
st. Reservoir 283 A16
st. Sunshine 365 E3
TYLOID
sq. Wantirna 422 E14
TYMON
rd. Cockatoo 511 F10
TYNAN
st. Preston 282 E19
TYNDALL
st. Surrey Hills 373 H20
wy. Mill Park 243 D5
TYNE
cl. Deer Park 318 L12
cl. Nunawading 376 G16
ct. Frankston 599 J18
ct. Mt Waverley 418 H15
st. Box Hill N 374 K11
st. Camberwell 417 G7
st. Carlton 18 E13
TYNEFIELD
ct. Brighton 454 G9
TYNEHEAD
pl. Geelong, off Maud St 702 L10
TYNER
rd. Wantirna S 422 J19
TYNHAM
cl. Ferntree Gly 463 F2
ct. Mornington 656 K3
TYNONG
st. Box Hill N 375 C9
st. Croydon 335 L19
TYNTYNDER
cl. Berwick 554 C16
dr. Carrum Downs 601 C4
TYPE
st. Burnley 371 B17
TYQUIN
st. Laverton 407 F14
TYREE
av. Springvale 499 L16
pl. Dandenong S 550 A6
TYRELL
ct. Altona Mdw 451 H3
ct. Keilor 276 L12
ct. Keilor 277 A12
ct. Meadow Ht 194 C18
ct. Rowville 463 D18
TYRES
ct. Sunshine N 321 C9
TYRO
ct. Montrose 382 F9
TYROL
ct. Doncaster E 331 G16
ct. Epping 197 L18
st. Dandenong N 502 D17
TYRONE
av. Macleod 285 C12
av. Rye 680 G20
ct. Avondale Ht 322 F7
ct. St Helena 245 B16
ct. Wheelers Hill 460 L19
dr. Eltham North 288 F1
st. Camberwell 417 C6
st. Langwarrin 629 C6
st. N Melbourne 17 G16
st. Ormond 456 E14
st. Seaford 599 H4
st. South Yarra 31 K14
st. South Yarra 414 E7
st. Werribee 448 B12
TYRRELL
av. Blackburn 375 H13
cr. Fawkner 281 J9
pl. Wyndham Va 446 A6
st. Mont Albert N 374 F9
tce. Braeside 547 F1
TYSON
ct. Darley 221 L10
ct. Lalor 240 H9
ct. Ringwood 378 L3
ct. Ringwood 379 A3
ct. Wantirna S 422 F20
ct. Wantirna S 462 E1
st. Fawkner 281 J4
st. Richmond 26 A14
wy. Sydenham 274 H5
TYSSEN
ct. Doncaster E 331 G15

U

UGANDA
st. Burwood 418 D6
ULAH
ct. Scoresby 462 B6
ULLARA
ct. Frankston 600 G14
ULM
cl. Mill Park 243 A6
st. Coburg N 281 C14
st. Laverton 407 C15
ULMARA
pl. Greensborough 244 A20
pl. Greensborough 286 A1
pl. Keilor Dn 276 G16
ULMER
rd. Emerald 510 C7
ULRIC
ct. Frankston 628 F5
ULRICH
ct. View Bank 285 E19
ULSTER
ct. Hoppers Csg 448 E8
la. Melbourne 24 K6
ULTIMO
pl. Toorak 415 E3
ULUPNA
rd. Ormond 456 D13
ULYSSES
av. Croydon S 380 D12
UNA
st. Mt Waverley 419 F19
st. Sunshine 365 G1
st. Tootgarook 698 E2
st. Watsonia N 285 G2
UNAVALE
cr. Boronia 423 H11
UNDERA
ct. Fawkner 281 K9
UNDERBANK
bvd. Bacchus Msh 221 E17
UNDERHILL
ct. Sunbury 142 F10
UNDERWOOD
cl. Mill Park 242 F3
dr. Donvale 376 G5
la. Lilydale 338 K8
rd. Boronia 424 D14
rd. Ferntree Gly 464 G1
UNGARA
cl. Eltham North 245 E17
UNGARIE
ct. Hampton Pk 551 F12
UNIACKE
ct. Melbourne 1 A10
ct. Melbourne 23 H8
UNICORN
wy. Kings Park 275 A18
UNION
av. Pakenham 558 K20
dr. Bundoora, off College Dr 284 E13
gr. Springvale 499 L14
la. Melbourne 2 D13
la. Melbourne 24 D7
pl. Carlton 18 D12
pl. Newtown 702 H11
pl. S Melbourne 30 C4
rd. Ascot Vale 323 L19
rd. Balwyn 374 A17
rd. Balwyn 374 A20
rd. Dandenong S 535 F18
rd. Langwarrin 629 G2
rd. Lilydale 338 K7
rd. Parkville 18 A12
rd. Somerton 194 J17
rd. Surrey Hills 374 A17
rd. Surrey Hills 417 L2
rd. Wandin N 340 L16
st. Armadale 415 G13
st. Belmont 702 E20
st. Brighton East 455 C15
st. Brunswick 325 A15
st. Brunswick W 324 J16
st. Kew 371 L10
st. Melbourne 414 C11
st. Melbourne 414 D11
st. Northcote 326 F18
st. N Melbourne 17 A18
st. Port Melb 412 J3
st. Preston 282 D16
st. Reservoir 282 D16
st. Richmond 26 C11
st. S Melbourne 29 L3
st. Sunshine 365 G4
st. Templstw Lr 330 F7
st. Williamstown 411 E12
st. Windsor 414 D11
st. Geelong, off Ryrie St 703 B8
UNION LOOP
rd. Clayton 459 D15
UNITING
la. Bulla 190 L18
la. Bulla 191 A18
UNITT
ct. Broadmeadows 237 L12
st. Melton 226 J18
UNITY
ct. Warburton 349 K6
wy. Kilsyth 381 A7
UNIVERSE
ct. Whittington 704 D19
UNIVERSITY
dr. Mill Park 243 C4
dr. Taylors Hill 274 D9
pl. Carlton 18 G14
pl. Clayton 459 H16
rd. Bayswater 422 L3
rd. Bayswater 423 A3
st. Carlton 18 F14
UNLEY
ct. Vermont 420 K6
gr. Ascot Vale 324 C16
UNO
st. Belmont 702 B19
UNSWORTH
rd. Ringwood N 378 E6
UNTHANK
ct. Somerville 644 F18
UNWIN
st. Templestowe 330 K5
UONGA
rd. Bentleigh 496 C4
UPALONG
rd. Mt Dandenong 382 G20
UPLAND
ct. Eltham North 287 B2
rd. Strathmore 324 B1
UPLANDS
ct. Meadow Ht 237 K7
ct. Narre Warren 538 H19
pl. Thomastown 240 D12
rd. Balwyn N 372 L7
rd. Chirnside Pk 336 E5
rd. Yarra Glen 208 G5
UPMINSTER
ct. Frankston 599 K17
UPPER
ct. Nunawading 376 L19
ct. Nunawading 377 A19
rd. Wattle Glen 246 J4
UPPER COONARA
rd. Kallista 427 C19
rd. Olinda 427 C19
rd. Olinda 427 G20
UPPER CRESCENT
rd. Yarra Jctn 346 H15
UPPER GRIEVE
rd. Avonsleigh 470 G19
UPPER HEIDELBERG
rd. Heidelberg 328 G8
rd. Heidelberg Ht 328 F8
rd. Ivanhoe 328 B14
UPPER PAPER MILLS
rd. Fyansford 701 B6
UPPER SKENE
st. Newtown 702 A7
UPSNDOWNS
rd. Dromana 670 C14
UPTON
cl. Diamond Ck 245 L6
cr. Narre Warren 553 D8
ct. Burwood E 419 H11
ct. Mulgrave 501 G2
ct. Ringwood 335 B19
ct. Werribee 448 D7
ct. Wonga Park 291 F17
dr. Hillside 232 B17
pl. Prahran 414 L11
pl. Prahran 415 A11
rd. Emerald 509 E5
rd. Windsor 31 L20
rd. Windsor 414 E12
st. Altona 409 A18
st. Altona 409 A19
UPTONS
la. Geelong, off Maud St 703 B10
UPWEY
av. Springvale 499 J17
URAL
ct. Dandenong N 502 D17
URALLA
ct. Mooroolbark 337 A13
pl. Yallambie 286 B13
rd. Mt Martha 656 B15
st. Vermont 421 G3
URANA
av. Sunshine N 320 L14
av. Sunshine N 321 A14
dr. Keilor East 278 B19
st. Kilsyth 381 C10
st. Newtown 702 J12
st. Newtown 702 J13
URANDALINE
gr. Caulfield 455 K3
URBAN
pl. Albanvale 319 C7
st. Braeside 532 H14
URE
rd. Cockatoo 472 L13
rd. Gembrook 512 G8
rd. Nangana 472 K1
URE CREEK
rd. Launching Pl 300 J20
UREN
ct. Altona Mdw 451 K3
ct. Thomastown 241 J14
ct. Williamstown 410 K15
rd. Emerald 469 H8
URQUHART
ct. Darley 221 K7
ct. Greenvale 193 D20
ct. Hampton Pk 551 K6
st. Coburg 325 L1
st. Hawthorn 372 A19
st. Northcote 20 E1
URSA
st. Balwyn N 329 C20
st. Balwyn N 373 C1
st. Belmont 706 C3
URSULA
cl. Wheelers Hill 461 D13
st. Box Hill N 375 B7
URWIN
st. Yarraville 366 D16
USHER
ct. Dandenong S 535 H15
UTAH
ct. Dandenong N 501 L9
rd. Glen Waverley 419 J17
UTOPIA
pl. Burnley 371 B20
UTRECHT
ct. Donvale 377 B3
UTRILLO
cl. Scoresby 462 A7
UVADALE
gr. Kew 372 D10
UXBRIDGE
av. Doncaster 330 C20

V

VABIRO
ct. Greensborough 243 K18
VADLURE
av. St Kilda E 414 L19
VAIL
pl. Cranbourne S 603 J11
st. Prahran 415 B13
VAIN
cl. Mill Park 242 J10
VAINA
st. Werribee 447 D10
VAL
ct. Dandenong 536 E6
VALADERO
ct. Mill Park 242 H11
VALANNE
st. Brighton East 455 G13
VALDA
av. Mont Albert N 374 G6
av. Ringwood E 379 D8
cl. Berwick 554 K8
ct. Cranbourne 577 K11
gr. Brighton 454 K17
st. Anglesea 713 K1
st. Watsonia 285 C7
VALDALE
ct. Heathmont 379 D18
VALDEMAR
ct. Brighton East 495 J4
VALDOONE
ct. Oak Park 279 H10
VALE
rd. Belgrave Ht 506 E2
st. Albanvale 319 C5
st. Bentleigh 496 C3
st. E Melbourne 25 K11
st. Glen Iris 417 C16
st. Heathmont 378 E19
st. Mornington 640 F15
st. N Melbourne 17 F15
st. Pascoe Vale 280 C15
st. Reservoir 282 D15
st. Rosebud W 698 K2
st. St Kilda 414 C17
VALENCIA
ct. Kings Park 275 C19
rd. Lilydale 338 L10
rd. Lilydale 339 A10
st. Aberfeldie 323 E11
st. Glenroy 280 G6
tce. Templestowe 331 L8
VALENCY
ct. Mitcham 377 F19
rd. Glen Iris 416 G12
VALENTE
st. Altona Mdw 407 K18
VALENTINE
av. Kew 371 K11
av. Thomastown 241 J13
cr. Sunshine W 364 G10
ct. Glen Waverley 459 J1
gr. Armadale 415 H16
rd. Langwarrin 601 C19
st. Bayswater 423 G3
st. Bulleen 330 A16
st. Ivanhoe 327 J10
st. Rye 696 F5
VALENTINO
dr. Croydon 379 F6
VALEPARK
cl. Noble Park N 501 C11
cr. Cranbourne 603 L2
dr. Donvale 332 H17
dr. Donvale 332 J16
VALERIAN
av. Altona North 409 K2
st. Hampton 495 G12
VALERIE
ct. Hampton Pk 551 E10
ct. Heathmont 378 F18
ct. Melton S 268 J5
ct. Seaford 599 G3
ct. Vermont S 420 G8
dr. Cranbourne 603 L3
dr. Wonga Park 335 J3
st. Bentleigh E 496 G7
st. Boronia 423 H14
st. Kew East 372 E6
st. Lalor 241 H9
st. Millgrove 304 H19
st. Noble Park 534 K4
st. Pascoe Vale 280 H13
st. Templstw Lr 330 D10
VALERO
pl. Thomastown 240 K16
VALETTA
cr. Knoxfield 463 B3
st. Carrum 573 B8
st. Malvern 415 K13
VALEWOOD
ct. Narre Warren 538 G19
dr. Kealba 276 L19
dr. Kealba 277 A19
dr. Launching Pl 345 F16
dr. Mulgrave 500 E1
dr. Wyndham Va 446 G11
VALIANT
ct. Glen Waverley 421 A16
sq. S Morang 198 K12
st. Abbotsford 20 F15
VALIAS
st. N Warrandyte 289 G12
VALKSTONE
st. Bentleigh E 456 H17
VALKYRIE
cr. Ringwood 335 C20
VALLENCE
rd. Maddingley 264 E2
rd. Maddingley 264 E5
VALLEY
cr. Glenroy 279 G4
ct. Craigieburn 150 C16
ct. Croydon S 380 A15
ct. Dandenong N 502 B11
ct. Diamond Ck 245 G11
ct. Mt Eliza 641 H4

dr. Rye 697 G7
mw. Wyndham Va 446 D9
pde. Glen Iris 416 J10
rd. Bundoora 284 A1
rd. Frankston 627 L6
rd. Langwarrin 601 E10
rd. Mt Waverley 459 C1
rd. Research 288 H3
rd. Seville 341 L12
rd. Skye 601 E10
rd. Wattle Glen 246 L7
rd. Wattle Glen 247 A6
rd. Wonga Park 336 B5
rd. Yarra Glen 208 H5
st. Oakleigh S 458 D19
wy. Warrandyte 333 H5

VALLEY FAIR
dr. Narre Warren 552 J4

VALLEY FARM
rd. Healesville 213 J9

VALLEY HO
rd. Chirnside Pk 337 J3

VALLEY PARK
gr. Eltham 287 D15

VALLEY VIEW
cr. Berwick 553 H2
cr. Sunbury 113 H7
ct. Bulleen 330 G14
ct. Glen Waverley 460 H3
ct. Lilydale 338 D14
ct. Niddrie 322 L3
ct. S Morang 199 L18
rd. Glen Iris 416 H16
rd. Hurstbridge 202 G13
ri. Hampton Pk 552 A12
tr. Lysterfield 504 B10

VALLEYVIEW
dr. Rowville 463 B13

VALLOTA
cr. Noble Park 534 D5

VALMA
av. Cranbourne 577 L15
ct. Forest Hill 376 H20
ct. Nunawading 420 H1
st. Bayswater 423 E8

VALMONT
av. Beaumaris 530 G9

VALNERE
st. Maribyrnong 367 A1

VALONIA
av. Surrey Hills 374 C18
ct. Craigieburn 150 B17
dr. Eltham 288 B6

VAN
ct. Gladstone Pk 237 D16
ct. Melton W 226 A20
ct. Narre Warren 539 A16

VANBERG
rd. Essendon 324 E7

VANBROOK
st. Forest Hill 420 G3

VANCE
ct. Darley 222 D11
ct. Keysborough 534 C9
ct. Narre Warren 538 L12
st. Lilydale 338 K5

VANCOUVER
st. Mornington 640 D12

VAN DER HAAR
av. Berwick 553 K7

VANDEVEN
ct. Ferntree Gly 423 L17

VAN DIEMAN
av. Nunawading 376 F9

VANESSA
av. Highton 705 H1
av. Keysborough 534 K8
av. Lalor 241 A6
cr. Wheelers Hill 460 L18
ct. Frankston 600 A17
ct. Oakleigh S 498 A9
ct. St Helena 244 L19
ct. Somerville 645 B16
ct. Warranwood 334 L12
dr. Hampton Pk 551 C7
rd. Campbellfield 239 C4
wy. Delahey 275 D11

VAN HAASTER
ct. Rowville 502 B6
gr. Skye 575 G19

VANILLA
st. Bundoora 242 F15

VANITY
ct. Dandenong 535 L9

VANNAM
dr. Ashwood 418 C16

VAN NESS
av. Glen Iris 417 A9
av. Maribyrnong 323 C17
av. Mornington 656 E1

VAN UNEN
ct. Doncaster E 332 G9

VAN WYK
ct. Springvale S 534 A2

VARCOE
cl. Burwood 418 E6
ct. Frankston 628 F6

VARDON
av. Beaumaris 530 D4
st. Springvale 500 A17

VARGA
cl. Mill Park 242 F1
rd. Smiths Gly 205 C5

VARLEY
ct. Ferntree Gly 464 D6

VARMAN
ct. Nunawading 376 F15

VARNA
ct. Hillside 274 E3
pl. Keilor Dn 276 E14

VARSITY
ct. Albanvale 319 A7

VARYDALE
av. Torquay 712 A6

VARZIN
av. Surrey Hills 374 A20

VASA
pl. Keilor Lodge 276 A3

VASEY
av. Lalor 241 D8
av. Mt Waverley 459 G2
cl. Mt Martha 656 C15
cnc. Croydon 379 E6
cnc. Croydon 379 F8
cnc. Ringwood E 379 E6
ct. Melton S 268 H11
gr. Donvale 377 E8
ri. Endeavour Hl 537 G4
st. Ascot Vale 324 A19
st. Bentleigh E 497 A6
st. Ivanhoe East 328 H17

VAUCLUSE
av. Gladstone Pk 279 C2
ct. Wheelers Hill 460 H14
ri. Highton 701 E15
st. Brighton 454 H13

VAUGHAN
av. Canterbury 373 G17
cr. Kew 371 G4
rd. Ferntree Gly 424 F17
st. Airport W 279 C14
st. Richmond 371 B15
st. Sunbury 143 K14
tce. N Melbourne 34 H11

VAUTIER
pl. S Morang 198 K15
st. Elwood 454 E6

VAUX
st. Pascoe Vale S 324 H2

VAUXHALL
rd. Balwyn 373 F14
rd. Northcote 327 B17

VAYNOR
st. Niddrie 322 L4
st. Niddrie 323 A4

VEAR
st. Heidelberg W 284 G17

VEARINGS
rd. Epping 196 B13

VEARS
rd. Ashburton 417 J15
rd. Burwood 417 J15
rd. Glen Iris 417 J15

VEDA
av. Mt Martha 656 H9
ct. Templestowe 331 E14

VEEMA
av. Croydon 379 K5

VEGA
cl. Lilydale 338 L6
cl. Noble Park 534 D5
ct. Newcomb 704 D14
st. Balwyn N 329 C20
st. Balwyn N 373 C1

VEGAS
ct. Narre Warren 553 D12

VEITCH
pl. Geelong, off Corio St 703 D7
st. Ivanhoe East 328 J16

VELA
pl. Roxburgh Pk 194 F8

VELDEN
av. Ferntree Gly 464 B2

VELLA
ct. Ferntree Gly 464 F2
ct. Springvale S 499 F20
dr. Sunshine W 365 A11

VELLVUE
ct. Tootgarook 698 D5

VELMA
gr. Ringwood E 379 D8

VELRA
av. Murrumbeena 457 D14

VELVET
av. Bundoora 242 E13

VENABLES
ct. Berwick 554 B17

VENETIAN
ct. Croydon 380 G6

VENICE
av. Mitcham 377 A10
ct. Avondale Ht 322 E8
ct. Frankston 600 F19
ct. Glen Waverley 420 B14
gdn. Endeavour Hl 537 J2
st. Box Hill S 374 G20
st. Box Hill S 418 G1
st. Mentone 530 L9
st. Mentone 531 A9
st. Mornington 640 C17

VENN
mw. Templstw Lr 330 D10

VENTICH
st. Glen Iris 417 J11

VENTNOR
cr. Coolaroo 238 E3
pl. Keilor Dn 276 C12
st. Balwyn N 329 K19
st. Chadstone 458 B6
st. Mitcham 377 B18
st. Preston 326 C5

VENTOR
ct. Craigieburn 194 D3

VENTURA
ct. Keilor Lodge 276 B4
pl. Point Cook 450 D5
st. Ashburton 417 K16
st. Blackburn N 376 A7

VENTURE
dr. Berwick 554 B10
wy. Braeside 532 J15

VENUE
cl. Eltham 288 B9

VENUS
ct. Dingley Village 533 A9
ct. Hillside 232 B18
ct. Newcomb 704 D13
ct. Thomastown 240 G14
st. Caulfield S 455 D10

VERA
cr. Rye 696 L8
cr. Rye 697 A8
ct. Dandenong 535 H2
ct. Millgrove 304 F19
st. Bulleen 330 B16
st. Frankston 627 F4
st. Murrumbeena 457 D13
st. Oakleigh S 497 G2
st. Werribee 448 C12
st. Williamstown 411 C17

VERBENA
av. The Basin 425 A11
cr. Noble Park 534 D6
ct. Frankston S 627 G12
rd. Springvale 500 J12
st. Blackburn N 375 J7
st. Mordialloc 532 B12
st. Templestowe 331 B7

VERDAL
ct. Grovedale 706 C10

VERDALE
cl. Mitcham 377 H18

VERDANT
av. Ardeer 320 C18
av. Toorak 415 A3
ct. Glen Waverley 460 K1
dr. Keysborough 534 G17
pl. Dingley Village 533 C3

VERDEN
pl. Keilor Dn 276 E13

VERDI
ct. Bundoora 242 L20
ct. Templestowe 332 C9

VERDON
st. Dromana 685 K7
st. Williamstown 411 D15

VERDUN
dr. Narre Warren 553 C5
dr. Narre Warren 553 E6
gr. Reservoir 282 J15
st. Maidstone 322 K20
st. Surrey Hills 417 L2

VERE
ct. Plumpton 273 A13
st. Abbotsford 20 B16
st. Collingwood 19 J16
st. Richmond 26 E6

VERENE
av. Templstw Lr 330 G12

VERES
la. Geelong West 702 J4

VEREY
ct. Dandenong 535 G9

VERGESS
ct. Ringwood 378 H15

VERINA
wy. Lilydale 338 G14

VERITY
ct. Altona Mdw 451 E3
st. Richmond 26 B11

VERMAY
av. Frankston 599 L19

VERMEER
ct. Grovedale 705 K14

VERMILION
pl. Mt Waverley 419 G13

VERMONT
av. Bundoora 242 D19
av. Sunshine N 321 G10
ct. Blackburn S 420 A5
pde. Greensborough 285 L5
st. Blackburn S 420 A6
st. Glen Waverley 460 B8

VERNA
pl. St Albans 320 E12

VERNAL
av. Mitcham 377 D18
rd. Oakleigh S 497 H4

VERNDA
dr. Melton W 226 B13

VERNE
cl. Delahey 275 E15
ct. Templestowe 332 A10

VERNER
av. Frankston 627 E6
st. E Geelong 703 C13
st. Geelong 703 C13
st. S Geelong 703 A12

VERNIER
st. Spotswood 366 J20

VERNON
av. Heidelberg W 284 E17
cl. Jan Juc 711 C16
cr. Sunshine W 364 B3
ct. Epping 241 J4
ct. Hoppers Csg 449 C1
ct. Noble Park 534 D2
rd. Beaconsfield 555 K9
st. Blackburn S 420 A2
st. Blairgowrie 696 C7
st. Brighton East 495 G1
st. Croydon 379 K7
st. Donvale 377 D1
st. Glen Iris 417 C15
st. Huntingdale 458 E13
st. S Kingsville 410 G3
st. Spotswood 366 G20
st. Strathmore 280 B18
st. Up Fntree Gly 465 G8

VERONA
ct. Bayswater 423 A9
dr. Hampton Pk 551 E5
dr. Keilor Lodge 275 L4
st. Belgrave S 506 H1
st. Box Hill S 374 G20
st. Box Hill S 418 G1
st. Dromana 686 H8
st. Vermont S 421 E7

VERONICA
av. Chirnside Pk 337 B3
av. Newcomb 704 C16
cr. Mill Park 243 A10
ct. Noble Park 534 D5
ct. Werribee 447 G13
pl. Sunshine W 363 L8
st. Ferntree Gly 424 G20
st. Langwarrin 629 A3
st. Northcote 326 D11
st. Oakleigh S 497 E2

VERSAILLES
pl. Narre Warren 539 F16

VERT
st. Keilor 277 B11

VERVALE
av. Fawkner 281 K9

VERWOOD
ct. Craigieburn 194 G4

VESPER
dr. Narre Warren 552 H3
st. Burnley, off Tudor St 371 C17

VESTA
la. Newport 411 A12

VIADUCT
rd. Sunbury 143 D20

VIALLS
av. Parkdale 531 J12

VIA MEDIA
Box Hill 375 C17

VICARAGE
wy. Watsonia N 243 D19

VICARS
st. Balwyn N 373 H2
st. Hawthorn 372 A15

VIC BOLT
av. Kilsyth 381 F12

VICKERS
av. Strathmr Ht 279 D9
dr. Richmond 371 C13
la. Roxburgh Pk 194 D10
st. Reservoir 282 B8

VICKERY
st. Bentleigh 456 C18
st. Bentleigh 456 C19
st. Malvern East 416 F20

VICKI
ct. Doncaster E 375 H4
pl. Langwarrin 629 L1
st. Blackburn S 420 A4
st. Croydon 336 H14
st. Forest Hill 420 A4

VICKIE
ct. Rosebud 684 H17

VICTOR
av. Cheltenham 530 F3
av. Dandenong N 501 K15
av. Guys Hill 541 H20
av. Kew 372 J9
av. Rye 697 J8
av. Seaford 573 C20
cr. Forest Hill 420 D5
cr. Narre Warren 553 C3
ct. Hampton Pk 552 A9
ct. Hoppers Csg 448 F5
ct. Lalor 240 L9
ct. Melton S 268 G5
pl. Attwood 237 D11
rd. Bentleigh 455 H20
rd. Brighton East 455 H20
rd. Clematis 508 J2
rd. Glen Iris 417 A15
rd. Oakleigh S 497 F5
st. Beaumaris 530 B9
st. Pt Lonsdale 710 D6
st. Sunshine N 321 G19

VICTORIA
av. Albert Park 29 D17
av. Albert Park 413 B8
av. Canterbury 373 D16
av. Cremorne 26 A20
av. Glen Waverley 460 E4
av. Mitcham 377 A12
av. Monbulk 428 F19
av. Ripponlea 454 H1
av. Rosanna 284 K18
av. Springvale 499 J14
cl. Carlton 18 F15
cl. Eltham North 246 B20
cl. Eltham North 288 B1
cr. Abbotsford 20 F20
cr. Mont Albert 374 C14
cr. Mont Albert 374 D13
cr. Mt Martha 655 J13
cr. Safety Bch 668 J20
cr. St Albans 320 B3
ct. Dandenong N 501 J17
ct. N Melbourne 17 D19
ct. Springvale 499 J15
dr. Thomastown 240 E12
dr. Tottenham 366 A12
gr. Brunswick 325 J11
gr. Ferny Creek 466 B4
gr. Hawthorn E 372 E17
gr. Roxburgh Pk 194 C6
la. Albert Park 29 G13
pde. Carlton 24 K2
pde. Carlton 25 A2
pde. Collingwood 24 L2
pde. Collingwood 25 A2
pde. E Melbourne 24 L2
pde. E Melbourne 25 A2
pde. Fitzroy 24 K2
pde. Fitzroy 25 A2
pde. Frankston 627 D4
pde. Melbourne 24 L2
pde. Melbourne 25 A2
pl. Carlton 18 J8
pl. Richmond 26 H4
rd. Bayswater 423 F9
rd. Camberwell 372 J17
rd. Chirnside Pk 293 L19
rd. Chirnside Pk 337 J7
rd. Gruyere 341 A10
rd. Hawthorn E 372 E17
rd. Langwarrin S 629 L20
rd. Lilydale 293 L19
rd. Lilydale 337 J7
rd. Narre Warren 538 J18
rd. Northcote 327 B19
rd. Seville 341 E10

rd. Sydenham 232 K19
rd. Thornbury....327 B11
rd. Wandin N....340 F10
rd. Wandin N....341 A10
rd. Yering....252 B20
rd. Yering....293 L19
rd.n,Malvern 416 B18
rd.s,Malvern 416 B19
sq. St Albans 320 B3
st. Abbotsford....26 B3
st. Altona Mdw....451 F8
st. Box Hill....375 B17
st. Brighton....454 F18
st. Brunswick....325 G13
st. Brunswick E....325 K13
st. Brunswick W....324 K12
st. Bulleen 329 L10
st. Carlton....2 J1
st. Carlton....17 K20
st. Coburg 325 D2
st. Darley....222 C7
st. Diamond Ck....246 A12
st. Doncaster 331 F20
st. Doncaster E 331 F20
st. Elsternwick 455 C6
st. Ferntree Gly 464 G2
st. Fitzroy....19 A13
st. Flemington....34 C4
st. Footscray....367 C10
st. Glenroy....279 J9
st. Greensborough ..286 C10
st. Hurstbridge....202 K10
st. Launching Pl....346 G16
st. Melbourne 2 J1
st. Melbourne 17 K20
st. Melbourne 24 B1
st. Melb Airport....236 D13
st. Moonee Pnd 323 L11
st. N Melbourne....34 L19
st. Parkdale....531 J11
st. Preston....327 D6
st. Richmond....26 B3
st. Ringwood E 379 C11
st. Safety Bch....669 A15
st. St Kilda....413 L16
st. Sandringham 495 E16
st. Seddon....367 C10
st. S Geelong....703 A14
st. S Melbourne 30 E3
st. Sunshine 365 E4
st. Templestowe 331 F20
st. Up Fntree Gly 465 B10
st. Wandin N....340 B13
st. Westmeadows 236 D13
st. W Melbourne 34 J19
st. Williamstown 411 B18
st. Windsor....414 H11
st. Yarra Jctn 346 H14
tce. Belmont....702 C16
tce. South Yarra....32 G6
tce. South Yarra....414 J3
wy. Caroline Spr....317 L7
wy. Caroline Spr....318 A7

VICTORIA HOTEL
la. N Melbourne....17 H20

VICTORIA KNOX
av. Ferntree Gly 463 K12

VICTORY
av. Wandin East....340 L17
bvd. Ashburton....417 G18
ct. Brighton East 455 H17
ct. Narre Warren 538 L17
pde. Ascot Vale....323 J19
pl. Mt Eliza....642 F8
pl. S Geelong....703 A14
rd. Airport W....278 J11
rd. Clarinda....498 F14
rd. Langwarrin....630 A15
st. Croydon....336 D17
st. Fawkner....281 K6
st. Keilor Park 277 K15
st. Mitcham 377 G14
st. Murrumbeena 457 A12
st. Sandringham 495 D15
wy. Carrum Downs 575 D14
wy. Highton....701 E15

VIDA
ct. Wantirna S....462 C4
st. Aberfeldie....323 E12

VIDOTTO
ct. Pearcedale 647 G1

VIENNESE
wy. Mooroolbark 337 L18

VIEW
cr. Montrose....382 E10
ct. Brighton....494 G3
ct. Dandenong N....502 B10
ct. Gisborne....80 D15
ct. Heathmont....379 E19
ct. Hillside....232 B17
pt. Kew....371 L4
rd. Bayswater....423 F3
rd. Belgrave....466 E10
rd. Epping....197 D17
rd. Glen Waverley 420 E17
rd. Lower Plenty 286 L17
rd. Rye....697 B3
rd. Springvale....500 B18
rd. Tecoma....466 E10
rd. The Basin....425 C11
rd. The Patch....467 G2
rd. Vermont 421 F2
rd. Yarra Jctn 346 H16
st. Alphington 371 J1
st. Avonsleigh....470 E17
st. Belmont....702 G16
st. Canterbury 373 D16
st. Clayton 498 F1
st. Coburg N....281 J15
st. Croydon....380 H3
st. Essendon W....322 L8
st. Glenroy....280 A1
st. Hampton Pk....551 E9
st. Hawthorn....372 D15
st. Healesville....213 J20
st. Highett....496 E14
st. Mentone 530 J8
st. Mornington....640 C16
st. Mt Evelyn....339 D20
st. Pascoe Vale 280 D15
st. Reservoir 282 E11
st. St Albans 320 C4
st. Surrey Hills 374 E18
st. Upwey 465 J12
st. Wandin East....340 L17
st. Warburton 350 C2
st. Werribee....447 E4
st. W Footscray....366 G5
st. Woori Yallock....344 B14
tce. Sunbury....142 D7

VIEWBANK
ct. Aspendale....546 E5
ct. Point Cook....451 C7
dr. Keilor East....322 H5
pl. Mill Park 243 C7
rd. Glen Iris....416 G13
rd. Mt Waverley....458 J10
ri. Beaconsfield 555 D11

VIEW GRAND
rd. Maribyrnong 322 L13

VIEWGRAND
wy. Greensborough ..244 H15

VIEW HILL
cr. Eltham 287 L12
rd. Cockatoo 511 A11

VIEWHILL
rd. Balwyn N 373 H3

VIEWMONT
ct. Croydon N 335 L14
ct. Doncaster E 332 H9

VIEW MOUNT
ct. Eltham 288 E8
rd. Glen Waverley 460 G12
rd. Wheelers Hill....460 G12

VIEWMOUNT
ct. Nar Warrn S....553 F18

VIEW POINT
rd. McCrae....685 B10

VIEWPOINT
av. Glen Waverley 460 F5
av. Mt Eliza....626 B16
dr. Chirnside Pk....337 B5
rd. Balwyn N 329 F18

VIEWTECH
pl. Rowville....502 C3

VIGANO
ct. Mooroolbark 337 G12

VIGGERS
pde. Glen Waverley 460 F10

VIGIL
av. Glen Waverley 420 J16

VIGILANT
av. Nunawading....376 E12

VIGO
st. Seddon....367 C11

VIGOR
ct. Darley....221 G4

VIKA
av. Monbulk 428 J19

VIKING
ct. Carrum Downs ...575 B15
ct. Cheltenham....497 B14
ct. Epping 198 A17

VILA
ct. Mt Waverley....458 F6

VILLA
rd. Springvale....499 F12
st. Heidelberg 329 A8
wk. Werribee....447 C8

VILLAGE
av. Doncaster 330 D18
av. Taylors Lakes....276 A5
cl. Carrum Downs ...575 B17
cl. Mt Martha....656 A16
cl. Westmeadows ...237 H12
cr. Chelsea....547 A14
ct. Mulgrave 460 B13
ct. Rowville....502 H5
dr. Dingley Village ...532 K5
dr. Hampton Pk....551 J7
dr. Pakenham....584 K3
dr. Reservoir 283 J14
grn. Chirnside Pk....336 L4
la. Carrum 573 B8
la. Mt Eliza....626 A16
wk. Box Hill....374 J16
wk. Mooroolbark....381 K4
wk. Vermont S 421 D7
wk. Toorak, off
Toorak Rd 415 B5
wy. Maribyrnong 322 J15
wy. Toorak, off
Toorak Rd 415 B5

VILLAGE GREEN
dr. St Kilda....414 A12

VILLAMANTA
pl. Geelong West....702 H6
st. Geelong West....702 H7

VILLANOVA
ct. Pk Orchards....334 D12

VILLAWOOD
cl. Berwick....539 J18
ct. Highton....705 G4

VILLEA
av. Grovedale 705 K16
ct. Bundoora....284 L6

VILLEROY
st. Hampton....495 A5

VILLERS
sq. Malvern East....456 L4

VILLIERS
st. Elsternwick 454 L3
st. Elsternwick 455 A3
st. Frankston S....626 H11
st. N Melbourne....17 E15

VILLOSA
cl. Langwarrin....629 J3
ct. Mill Park 243 D8

VIM
st. Melton....268 J2

VIMINALIS
ct. Endeavour Hl 536 K1

VIMY
ct. Pascoe Vale S 324 H3
rdg. Healesville....257 H1
st. Reservoir 282 C7

VINCENT
av. Geelong 702 K1
av. St Albans 320 E4
cr. Noble Park 500 K17
cr. Werribee....447 F10
ct. Cranbourne N....578 E9
ct. Greensborough ..243 J20
ct. Whittington....704 A19
mw. Chirnside Pk....336 G7
pl. Kensington 33 D9
rd. Pk Orchards 334 E15
st. Bayswater....423 C3
st. Brighton East 495 J3
st. Brunswick....325 C16
st. Coburg 325 D2
st. Cockatoo 511 C8
st. Deer Park....319 B18
st. Edithvale....546 H12
st. Glen Iris....416 D15
st. Macleod....285 A11
st. Mulgrave 500 D4
st. Oak Park 279 H11
st. Sandringham 495 C13
st. Surrey Hills 374 A16
st. Tootgarook 698 F5

VINCE STELLA
cl. St Albans 319 F8

VINCT
cl. Keilor Dn....276 C11

VINE
cr. Wonga Park....291 G17
ct. Braybrook....366 A1
ct. Doncaster....330 K18
ct. Glen Waverley 460 K3
ct. Hillside....274 C5
ct. Narre Warren 553 G9
gr. Carnegie 456 E8
st. Blackburn 375 H15
st. Braybrook....366 A1
st. Eltham 287 E6
st. Heidelberg 329 B8
st. Moonee Pnd 324 E14
st. Ringwood 378 C16
st. W Footscray....366 D6
st. Windsor....414 G13

VINEN
rd. Scoresby 462 B6

VINES
ct. Mill Park 242 B6

VINEY
st. Clarinda 498 D9

VINEYARD
rd. Sunbury....187 A5

VINNY
ct. Langwarrin....629 C3

VINTAGE
ct. Kilsyth S 381 A20
gr. Chirnside Pk....336 K4

VINTER
av. Croydon....379 K8

VIOLA
av. Brooklyn 365 F18
av. Mt Dandenong 426 F5
av. Olinda....426 F5
cr. Highett....496 D12
ct. Frankston....600 G17
ct. Keysborough 534 A16
ct. Mill Park 243 A11
st. Reservoir 282 K11

VIOLEN
st. Bayswater....423 E4

VIOLET
cr. Brighton East 455 E18
ct. Blackburn S 419 L4
ct. Doncaster 330 G16
ct. Noble Park 534 D5
ct. Wonga Park 292 B14
gr. Hawthorn....372 B20
gr. Kew East....372 H7
st. Belmont....701 L20
st. Essendon....323 K8
st. Frankston S....626 J4
st. Glen Iris....416 H10
st. Rosebud W....698 L1
st. Williamstn N 410 H11

VIPONT
st. Footscray....367 H7

VIRGILIA
ct. Rowville....502 L2
st. Doveton....536 H13

VIRGILLIA
st. Blackburn N 375 J8

VIRGINIA
cr. Bundoora....242 B19
ct. Bulleen 329 K11
ct. Caulfield S....455 K8
ct. Mentone 532 A7
ct. Montmorency 287 C10
gr. Malvern East 457 H4
st. Cranbourne....578 A17
st. Mornington....640 J18
st. Mt Waverley....458 K1
st. Newtown 702 H8
st. Pascoe Vale 280 K10
st. Springvale....500 A11
wy. Ferntree Gly 423 J16

VIRGO
pl. Wantirna S....422 L19

VIRIDIS
pl. Endeavour Hl 502 K20

VISCOUNT
dr. Doncaster 331 A14
wy. Forest Hill 420 D8

VISION
av. Sorrento 679 E14
ct. Wyndham Va 446 D11
dr. Burwood E....420 E12
st. Chadstone....458 A1
st. Strathmore....279 H13

VISTA
av. Kew....372 H10
av. Mt Waverley....418 G14
av. Ringwood E 379 B14
cl. Gisborne....79 C9
cr. Rowville....463 C20
cr. Rowville....503 C1
ct. Berwick....553 L6
ct. Box Hill N....375 E7
ct. Forest Hill 420 F2
ct. Frankston S....626 L8
ct. Ringwood E 379 B15
ct. Yarrambat....200 K15
dr. Chirnside Pk....337 A5
dr. Emerald 510 C1
dr. Keilor East....322 B5
dr. Melton 226 G19
gr. Sherbrooke 426 J18
gr. Toorak 415 A3
pl. Beaconsfield 555 B13
rd. Belgrave Ht 506 B3
rd. Hampton....494 K5
rd. Newtown 702 B11
st. Bulleen 330 A17
st. Doncaster 330 A17
st. Olinda....426 K12
st. St Albans 320 D6
wy. Wyndham Va 446 D13

VISTAWAY
ct. Donvale 332 H18

VISTULA
ct. Springvale S....533 K6

VITIS
av. Noble Park....534 C6
dr. Bundoora....242 F14

VIVA
st. Glen Iris....416 C14

VIVALDI
ct. Templestowe 332 C9

VIVIAN
ct. Doncaster 374 F3
ct. Oakleigh S....458 G19
gr. Hawthorn....371 H18
st. Belmont....702 C17
st. Blackburn N 375 G7
st. Ivanhoe....327 J10
st. Mt Waverley....418 H20
wy. Mt Martha....656 J7

VIVIANI
cr. Heathmont....378 G20

VIVIANNE
av. Mont Albert N....374 F6

VIVIANNES
wy. Melton 268 K3

VIVIEN
st. Bentleigh E....496 K3
st. Dandenong S 535 K16

VIVIENNE
av. Boronia....423 L14
ct. Doncaster E 332 H7
ct. Healesville....212 J13
st. Seaford....599 J9
wy. Berwick....554 F18

VIZARD
st. Dandenong 536 A2

VOCE
ct. Belmont....706 F4

VOCKLER
st. Yarraville....367 D18

VOGELZANG
ct. Skye 601 D9

VOGUE
av. Vermont S 420 H9

VOLANT
rd. Rockbank....270 C9

VOLANTIS
cr. Roxburgh Pk....194 G9

VOLGA
st. Hadfield 280 J7

VOLITANS
av. Mt Eliza....641 J5

VOLK
rd. Cranbourne W....577 D12

VOLTRI
st. Cheltenham....531 E4
st. Mentone 531 E4
st. Mentone 531 H5

VOLUM
st. Manifold Ht....702 B3

VONADAWN
av. Ringwood E 379 A14

VON NIDA
cr. Rosanna 284 L19
cr. Rosanna 285 A19
ct. Dingley Village ...533 A6
ct. Mill Park 242 D5
ct. Rowville....502 L6
dr. Hoppers Csg....405 C19

VOSGES
st. Selby 467 D13

VOSTOK
ct. Whittington....704 E19

VOUMARD
st. Oakleigh S....458 A17

VOWELL
dr. Pearcedale 648 A8

VUE
ct. Rowville....503 H1
rd. Mt Eliza....626 E12

VULCAN
gr. Williamstown 411 D16

VULE
st. St Albans 319 J5

VUNABERE
av. Bentleigh....495 J2

W

WACHTER
ct. Noble Park....501 B20

WACKETT
st. Laverton 407 C12

WADDELL
ct. Altona Mdw....451 H5
st. Bacchus Msh 222 A18

WADDINGTON
cr. Springvale S...533 K5
ct. Highton...705 J6
WADE
ct. Cheltenham...497 F19
ct. Langwarrin...601 K20
WADESON
rd. Hurstbridge...202 D17
WADEY
st. Southbank...4 C15
st. Southbank...24 H18
WADHAM
ct. Endeavour Hl...503 A20
pde. Mt Waverley...419 A18
rd. Ivanhoe...328 A8
st. Pascoe Vale S...324 F6
WADHURST
dr. Boronia...423 C15
WADI
st. Boronia...424 B16
WADSLEY
av. Pakenham...584 J7
rd. Carrum Downs...574 A8
rd. Patterson L...574 A8
WAGGA
ct. Keysborough...534 E6
rd. Reservoir...283 C3
WAGNER
st. Blackburn S...419 K5
WAGON
rd. Templestowe...332 A8
WAGSTAFF
ct. Brighton...454 J14
dr. Mill Park...243 D6
la. Dandenong...536 A10
st. Mt Waverley...459 B5
st. Rye...696 E7
WAGTAIL
wy. Whittlesea...126 C1
WAHGOO
rd. Carnegie...456 L9
WAHGUNYAH
cr. Langwarrin...629 D9
dr. St Albans...320 L6
dr. St Albans...321 A6
WAHINE
ct. Templestowe...331 L10
WAHRONGA
av. Highton...701 H16
WAHROONGA
av. Keysborough...534 G8
cr. Greensborough...244 K19
cr. Murrumbeena...457 D6
ct. Glen Iris...416 L13
ct. Rowville...463 H13
rd. Murrumbeena...457 C6
WAIHI
av. Brunswick E...326 A12
WAIMARIE
dr. Mt Waverley...459 C1
WAIMEA
gr. Selby...466 L14
WAINEWRIGHT
av. Mooroolbark...337 E11
ct. Sunbury...142 F10
WAINTREE
ct. Endeavour Hl...537 H6
WAINUI
av. Heathmont...378 K18
WAIORA
av. Beaumaris...529 L6
cl. Wantirna S...422 D19
ct. Pt Lonsdale...707 J20
pde. W Footscray...366 E10
rd. Caulfield N...415 D15
rd. Heidelberg Ht...328 H3
rd. Macleod...284 J15
rd. Rosanna...328 H2
WAIROA
av. Brighton East...455 D13
WAIROU
st. Taylors Lakes...276 D10
WAITARA
av. Keysborough...534 E8
ct. Lalor...240 E9
ct. Wheelers Hill...460 K17
WAITE
ct. Mill Park...242 L3
ct. Sunshine W...364 H8
WAITES
ct. Brooklyn...365 H19
ct. Templestowe...331 E8
WAKANUI
st. Northcote...327 A13
WAKATIPU
ct. Taylors Lakes...276 C10
WAKE
ct. Lalor...241 H6
WAKEFIELD
av. Frankston S...627 B8
cl. Eltham...287 C4
ct. Cranbourne N...577 L9
ct. Point Cook...450 C4
la. Sherbrooke...466 J2
pl. Templestowe...331 E6
ri. Endeavour Hl...537 G7
st. Blackburn N...376 D10
st. Hawthorn...372 A16
st. Kensington...33 E12
st. Nunawading...376 D10
WAKEFIELDS
gr. Camberwell...417 J6
WAKEFUL
pl. Mill Park...242 L9
pl. Mill Park...243 A9
WAKELIN
cr. Taylors Lakes...275 A1
WAKEMAN
ct. Dingley Village...533 A3
WAKENSHAW
cr. Pakenham...584 G7
WAKLEY
cr. Wantirna S...421 L17
WAKOOL
av. Deer Park...319 B18
av. Mentone...530 H8
av. Rosebud...700 J7
cl. Frankston...628 E6
WALA
pl. Greensborough...244 B18
WALARA
dr. Mt Martha...655 J19
WALBROOK
dr. Vermont S...420 J6
rd. Rye...696 F6
st. Watsonia N...285 G1
WALBUNDRY
av. Balwyn N...372 L3
av. Balwyn N...373 A3
av. Ferntree Gly...464 L1
av. Frankston...599 G12
dr. Kew East...372 K3
WALCHA
ct. Chadstone...458 B2
WALCOTT
pl. Nar Warrn S...578 L2
WALDAU
ct. Doncaster...331 F17
WALDEMAR
rd. Eaglemont...328 G10
WALDEN
av. Wheelers Hill...460 L8
ct. Bundoora...284 L2
ct. Springvale S...499 H19
gr. Carnegie...456 J11
pl. Lalor...241 J7
rd. Mentone...530 L10
rd. Mentone...531 A10
st. W Footscray...366 G6
WALDHEIM
rd. Bayswater...423 A4
WALDORF
ct. Bentleigh E...497 D5
WALDRON
pl. Geelong...703 E12
WALER
ct. Highton...701 C15
WALERNA
rd. Glen Iris...417 A12
WALES
ct. Hallam...537 H15
ct. Hillside...231 J17
st. Brunswick W...324 K9
st. Hampton...495 E12
st. Kingsville...366 K13
st. Northcote...327 A12
st. Springvale...500 B11
st. Thornbury...327 A11
WALHALLA
ct. Mooroolbark...337 F16
dr. Ringwood E...379 D14
st. Pascoe Vale S...324 K6
WALKER
av. Hampton...495 G8
av. Mitcham...377 D19
av. Preston...327 B2
cl. Altona North...409 J3
ct. St Albans...320 F12
ct. Sunbury...142 H4
ct. View Bank...329 H2
gr. Cheltenham...531 A1
pl. Braybrook...366 A1
rd. Montrose...382 B9
rd. Mt Waverley...419 E14
rd. Seville...342 B12
rd. Wonga Park...335 E2
st. Anglesea...713 J3
st. Balwyn...373 D11
st. Belmont...706 K3
st. Braeside...532 F14
st. Brunswick W...324 K13
st. Clifton Hill...20 H3
st. Coburg...325 G3
st. Dandenong...535 L9
st. Doncaster...375 A3
st. Healesville...213 K20
st. Healesville...257 K1
st. Moonee Pnd...324 D13
st. Murrumbeena...457 C9
st. Newport...410 L6
st. Northcote...326 G20
st. Parkville...17 J1
st. Prahran...32 D17
st. Prahran...414 G9
st. Southbank...3 A7
st. Southbank...23 L16
st. The Basin...425 E11
st. Torquay...712 B9
WALKERS
la. Healesville...213 K17
rd. Carrum...573 B10
rd. Mt Eliza...626 E20
rd. Nunawading...376 H15
WALL
ct. Chadstone...457 L3
pl. Richmond...26 J14
st. Beaumaris...530 F6
st. Noble Park...534 G1
st. Richmond...26 J14
WALLABAH
st. Mt Waverley...459 F6
WALLABY
av. Sassafras...426 F13
tr. Lysterfield...504 A8
wk. S Morang...243 J1
wy. Badger Creek...258 F13
WALLACE
av. Bayswater...423 F7
av. Dandenong...535 E4
av. Donvale...332 J16
av. Frankston...627 K4
av. Murrumbeena...457 A13
av. Oakleigh S...458 D19
av. Point Cook...450 C2
av. Toorak...415 A5
cr. Beaumaris...530 G5
cr. Strathmore...324 E2
dr. Greenvale...237 D1
gr. Brighton...494 J1
la. Bundoora...284 D4
pde. Healesville...258 E2
pl. Caroline Spr...318 A8
pl. Mill Park...242 G4
pl. Mt Martha...656 D8
rd. Burwood...418 A7
rd. Christmas Hills...207 K12
rd. Cranbourne...603 K1
rd. Seville...341 F15
rd. Wantirna S...422 J20
rd. Wantirna S...423 A20
rd. Wantirna S...463 A1
sq. Melton...226 L18
st. Balwyn...373 E10
st. Beaconsfield...555 C14
st. Bentleigh E...496 H2
st. Brunswick W...324 L11
st. Delahey...275 A12
st. Ivanhoe...328 A13
st. Maidstone...366 H3
st. Newtown...702 E10
st. Preston...326 E2
st. S Geelong...703 A13
wy. Mooroolbark...336 L14
WALLACES
rd. Dromana...669 J19
WALLAN
ct. Dallas...238 C8
rd. Whittlesea...95 K2
WALLARA
cl. Doncaster E...332 H10
cr. Bundoora...284 K4
cr. Croydon...380 B10
dr. Kings Park...275 D20
rd. Aspendale...546 G7
rd. Werribee...446 J16
WALLARANO
dr. Noble Park...534 F5
WALLAROO
av. Narre Warren...538 J20
sq. Werribee...447 L19
WALLEN
rd. Hawthorn...371 G19
rd. Ormond...456 G13
st. Brighton East...455 E19
WALLER
ct. Ascot Vale...324 C20
ct. Cheltenham...530 K4
ct. Mooroolbark...337 E10
ct. Sunbury...143 D8
pl. McCrae...685 B12
WALLINGFORD
st. Cheltenham...531 A2
WALLIS
av. Glen Iris...417 B11
av. Ivanhoe East...328 G16
ct. Heathmont...422 J1
ml. Niddrie...279 B20
st. Anglesea...713 G7
WALLMAH
cl. Templestowe...330 J7
WALLOWA
cr. Frankston N...600 D7
cr. Narre Warren...538 J18
rd. Eltham North...245 D16
rd. St Helena...245 D16
WALLS
rd. Werribee...446 K18
st. Geelong...703 D11
WALLUM
rd. Edithvale...546 H15
WALLY
ct. Altona North...365 L20
WALMER
av. St Albans...320 D4
st. Abbotsford...371 B12
st. Kew...371 B11
st. Ringwood...378 D17
WALNUI
gr. Beaconsfield...542 D20
gr. Beaconsfld Up...542 D20
WALNUT
av. Emerald...509 D2
cr. Noble Park...534 D6
ct. Cranbourne N...578 C8
ct. Kings Park...275 F19
ct. Mulgrave...500 D1
dr. Kilsyth...381 K7
rd. Balwyn N...373 J3
rd. Greensborough...286 K2
st. Carnegie...456 L5
st. Cremorne...26 D20
st. Cremorne...32 D2
st. Malvern...416 A9
st. Ormond...456 F15
st. Whittlesea...96 D18
wy. Hoppers Csg...405 E16
WALNUT TREE
ct. View Bank...285 L17
WALPA
ct. Westmeadows...237 E12
WALPOLE
av. Belmont...706 C5
av. Rosebud...683 G19
av. Rosebud W...683 G19
ct. Watsonia...285 C9
st. Kew...371 K10
st. Mt Martha...656 C11
WALSAL
av. Reservoir...283 C16
WALSH
av. Moorabbin...496 G11
av. Scoresby...462 B6
av. Thornbury...327 F8
ct. Mill Park...243 A5
ct. Pakenham...584 G5
rd. Bullengarook...77 A8
rt. Berwick...553 J8
st. Balwyn...372 L13
st. Balwyn...373 A13
st. Broadmeadows...238 B20
st. Coburg...325 H4
st. Eltham...287 C16
st. Kew...372 H14
st. Noble Park...500 F19
st. Ormond...456 D12
st. Preston...327 D4
st. South Yarra...31 H8
st. South Yarra...414 D4
st. Sunshine N...321 E16
st. W Melbourne...23 F2
WALSHAM
ct. Wheelers Hill...461 B8
rd. Blackburn...375 K19
WALSHE
ct. Altona Mdw...451 C4
WALSINGHAM
cr. Kurunjang...227 C14
WALSTAB
st. Brighton East...495 B1
WALTER
st. Ascot Vale...323 H15
st. Bulleen...330 A14
st. Cranbourne...578 C19
st. E Geelong...703 K12
st. Glen Waverley...420 D17
st. Hadfield...280 H8
st. Mitcham...377 G14
st. Moorabbin...497 A9
st. Noble Park...534 L4
st. Port Melb...412 G3
st. Preston...282 L18
st. Safety Bch...686 H2
st. St Albans...320 D1
st. Seddon...367 D10
st. South Yarra...32 K11
st. South Yarra...414 L6
st. Sunshine...365 G5
st. Tecoma...466 D12
st. Williamstn N...410 H12
wy. Whittlesea...96 E17
WALTER LYNCH
wy. Chirnside Pk...336 G6
WALTERS
av. Airport W...278 L18
ct. Altona Mdw...451 D2
ct. Rowville...503 D1
la. Dixons Ck...211 B8
st. Brunswick...325 D10
st. Craigieburn...150 H18
WALTER WITHERS
ct. View Bank...329 K1
WALTHAM
dr. Mornington...657 A3
pl. Avondale Ht...322 E12
pl. Richmond...26 F12
rd. Newport...411 B8
st. Flemington...33 K1
st. Richmond...26 E12
st. Sandringham...495 A13
WALTON
av. Preston...327 B4
cl. Craigieburn...194 F1
ct. Bacchus Msh...221 J16
ct. Narre Warren...553 E7
st. Airport W...279 B11
st. Brunswick...325 G16
st. Kew...371 K9
st. Melton S...268 G14
WALTON HEATH
cr. Mt Waverley...458 J8
ct. Sunbury...144 G12
WALWA
pl. Werribee...448 A20
st. Mitcham...377 K16
WALWORTH
av. Caulfield N...455 G2
ct. Keysborough...534 C8
WAMBA
av. Rye...697 J6
rd. Bentleigh E...496 H6
rd. Ivanhoe East...328 F15
WANAKA
cl. Rowville...462 L16
cl. Rowville...463 A16
dr. Taylors Lakes...276 D10
WANALTA
rd. Carnegie...456 E6
WANAWONG
cr. Camberwell...417 D6
WANBANNA
av. Greensborough...243 K17
WANBROW
av. Balwyn N...373 K8
WANDA
av. Wandin N...340 F12
cl. Portsea...678 A5
ct. Aspendale...546 G6
ct. Greensborough...243 J17
ct. Hallam...537 J13
rd. Caulfield N...415 F17
rd. Cranbourne S...602 L19
rd. Cranbourne S...603 A17
st. Mulgrave...500 E5
WANDANA
cr. Mooroolbark...336 K13
ct. Frankston S...627 B12
dr. Wandana Ht...705 B4
st. Mooroolbark...336 K14
WANDARRA
wy. Warranwood...335 C15
WANDARRI
ct. Cheltenham...496 A19
WANDEEN
rd. Glen Iris...416 H13
st. Balwyn N...330 A20
WANDELLA
ct. Albanvale...319 C6
rd. Frankston...627 J5
rd. Mornington...656 G3
WANDERER
ct. Berwick...539 H19
ct. Werribee...448 B5
WANDIN
ct. Forest Hill...420 H4
ct. Meadow Ht...238 D3
ct. Werribee...448 A19
rd. Camberwell...373 B20
rd. Camberwell...417 B1
WANDIN CREEK
rd. Seville...386 A6
rd. Wandin East...386 A6

WANDIN EAST
rd. Wandin East.......385 E5
rd. Wandin East.......385 E6
WANDO
gr. St Kilda E...........415 B14
WANDOO
av. Clarinda.............498 E4
cl. Hurstbridge........203 H17
ct. Wheelers Hill......460 F13
WANDSWORTH
av. Deer Park...........319 B13
rd. Surrey Hills........373 K15
WANG
ct. Cranbourne........578 C20
WANGANUI
ct. Taylors Lakes.....276 D9
WANGARA
rd. Cheltenham........495 K17
rd. Sandringham.....495 K17
WANGARATTA
st. Richmond............26 B16
WANGARRA
rd. Frankston...........600 A19
WANKE
cr. Dandenong........535 J1
WANNAEUE
pl. Rosebud............684 C15
WANNAN
ct. Clayton S...........498 G9
ct. Kilsyth...............381 C7
st. Highett...............496 H13
WANNAWONG
rd. Sassafras...........426 D14
WANNON
ct. Brookfield..........268 D6
ct. Keysborough.....534 G10
ct. Rowville.............463 D16
ct. Toorak...............415 G4
pl. Taylors Hill.........274 J13
st. Gladstone Pk......279 A2
WANRUA
st. Cheltenham........496 C17
WANTIRNA
rd. Ringwood..........378 D14
rd. Wantirna............422 D5
WANTIRNA-SASSAFRAS
rd. Bayswater..........423 K2
rd. Boronia..............424 H4
rd. Ferny Creek........426 A12
rd. Sassafras...........426 A12
rd. The Basin...........425 D10
rd. Wantirna............422 C8
WAPITI
st. Maribyrnong......322 J15
WARA
cl. Noble Park N......501 B12
WARADGERY
dr. Rowville.............462 C19
dr. Rowville.............462 D20
WARAIN
ct. Werribee............446 J14
WARANA
ct. Glenroy..............279 H6
dr. Hampton Pk........551 L8
wy. Mt Eliza.............642 B1
WARANGA
cr. Broadmeadows..238 D15
cr. St Albans...........320 C12
rd. Bayswater..........423 H8
st. Box Hill N..........375 B8
st. Dandenong N.....501 L9
wy. Taylors Hill.........274 K15
WARATAH
av. Bayswater N.......379 L20
av. Beaumaris..........529 L6
av. Belgrave.............466 J17
av. Belgrave.............467 A17
av. Burwood.............418 A6
av. Glen Huntly........456 D8
av. Mordialloc...........532 B12
av. Mornington.........640 L9
av. Point Cook..........450 A5
av. Selby..................466 J17
av. The Basin...........424 L11
av. Tullamarine........278 J5
cr. Blackburn...........375 G18
ct. Langwarrin.........629 E9
ct. Lilydale..............338 A13
dr. Altona Mdw.........451 C6
dr. Dandenong N.....501 H16
dr. Templstw Lr.........330 F9
la. Taylors Hill.........274 L13
mw. Keysborough.....534 A16
pl. Grovedale...........706 F9
pl. Melbourne.............2 J10
pl. Melbourne...........24 F5
st. Ascot Vale..........324 E16
st. Bentleigh E.........457 E16
st. Campbellfield.....239 F12
st. Doveton.............536 L8
st. Geelong West......702 D2
st. Glen Waverley....420 J20
st. Melton S.............268 E7
st. Pascoe Vale........281 A18
st. Rye....................697 K4
st. Seaholme...........409 G18
st. Thomastown......241 E13
st. W Footscray.......366 F13
wy. Cockatoo...........511 H1
WARBLA
st. Dandenong N.....501 G20
WARBLER
cl. Werribee............447 K6
ct. Boronia..............424 B11
ct. Carrum Downs...600 L4
wk. S Morang...........243 J3
WARBURTON
al. Melbourne.............1 L10
al. Melbourne...........24 B6
ct. Endeavour Hl......537 F6
ct. Mill Park............242 J6
hwy.Launching Pl......346 C13
hwy.Lilydale.............339 C3
hwy.Millgrove...........348 C4
hwy.Seville...............341 G15
hwy.Seville E............343 A13
hwy.Wandin East......341 B16
hwy.Wandin N...........340 A9
hwy.Wandin N...........341 B16
hwy.Warburton.........348 C4
hwy.Wesburn............347 L13
hwy.Woori Yallock.....344 H16
hwy.Woori Yallock.....345 A18
hwy.Yarra Jctn.........347 E15
la. Melbourne.............1 L11
la. Melbourne...........24 B7
rd. Camberwell.........373 C18
rd. Canterbury.........373 C18
st. Brunswick..........325 J16
WARD
av. Caulfield N.........455 K2
av. Oakleigh S..........457 H17
ct. Altona Mdw.........451 J10
ct. Wonga Park........292 A17
dr. Mill Park............243 D4
gr. Heidelberg.........328 K4
gr. Pascoe Vale S....324 J5
rd. Berwick..............553 H18
rd. Kallista...............467 J8
rd. Queenscliff.........707 L20
rd. The Patch...........467 J8
rd. The Patch...........468 A8
st. Ashburton...........417 F16
st. Beaumaris...........530 B12
st. Bentleigh............456 B18
st. Brighton East......455 E19
st. Cheltenham.........531 C3
st. Diamond Ck.........246 D11
st. Glenroy..............280 K2
st. Preston..............326 B2
st. S Melbourne........29 K4
st. S Melbourne........413 E2
WARDALE
rd. Springvale S......534 A1
WARDE
st. Footscray...........367 J8
WARDENS
wk. Coburg..............281 J19
WARDLE
cl. Blackburn S.......419 F2
WARDLOW
ct. Croydon Hills.....335 E14
WARDROP
gr. Northcote...........326 K15
WARDS
gr. Bentleigh E.........496 L3
rd. Monbulk.............469 D1
rd. Monbulk.............469 G1
WARE
cr. Ringwood E.........379 C8
WAREE
st. Lilydale..............338 L4
WAREHAM
ct. Hillside...............232 E19
st. Springvale...........500 A8
WARES
rd. Wesburn............347 J10
WARGUNDY
av. Rye....................697 F9
WARIANNA
ct. Kurunjang..........227 C12
WARIBA
la. Mornington.........640 C15
WARIDA
av. Malvern East......457 A2
WARILDA
ct. Mornington.........656 H3
WARINA
rd. Carnegie............456 K10
WARLAND
rd. Hampton E.........496 A8
WARLEIGH
gr. Brighton.............454 L14
gr. Brighton.............455 A14
rd. Footscray...........366 J8
rd. W Footscray.......366 J8
WARLEY
rd. Malvern East......456 F2
WARMINGTON
rd. Sunshine W.......364 K9
rd. Sunshine W.......365 A9
WARNCLIFFE
rd. Ivanhoe East......328 H17
WARNE
gr. Epping...............198 G16
pl. Berwick..............554 J9
st. Brunswick..........325 E10
st. Coolaroo............238 G7
st. Eaglemont..........328 K12
WARNEET
rd. Blind Bight.........650 F7
rd. Warneet.............649 G12
WARNER
av. Ashburton..........417 H17
av. Mornington.........640 L13
av. Mornington.........641 A13
ct. Donvale.............377 H7
la. Melbourne...........23 G7
pl. Geelong, off Little Ryrie St......703 A8
rd. Nr Nr Goon N.....560 L13
st. Coburg N...........281 C15
st. Essendon...........323 K4
st. Malvern.............416 B10
st. Oakleigh.............458 D15
WARNES
rd. Mitcham............377 J13
WARNGAR
cl. Carrum Downs...575 E13
WARNOCK
st. Broadmeadows..238 F18
WARNOO
ct. Frankston S........627 B5
WAROONA
ct. Pakenham..........585 A4
WARRA
ct. Thomastown......240 D11
rd. Upwey...............465 L18
st. Toorak...............415 J5
WARRABEL
rd. Ferntree Gly.......464 D2
WARRABURRA
av. Rosebud............683 J20
WARRADALE
ct. Noble Park N......501 D11
WARRAGAMBA
ct. Keysborough.....534 E10
WARRAGUL
st. Dallas................238 F10
WARRAH
ct. Gladstone Pk......279 B1
st. Mornington.........640 L15
WARRAIN
av. Mornington.........640 K8
av. Rosebud............700 K6
st. Frankston...........627 E5
WARRALONG
av. Greensborough..285 K10
ct. Langwarrin.........629 D8
WARRAMUNGA
rd. Bundoora...........284 E2
WARRANDYTE
brk. Langwarrin.........629 C14
rd. Doncaster E........331 L5
rd. Langwarrin.........629 D9
rd. Langwarrin S.......645 B2
rd. Pk Orchards.......378 F5
rd. Ringwood..........378 E8
rd. Ringwood N........378 F5
rd. Templestowe......331 K5
rd. Warrandyte........289 J20
rd. Warrandyte........332 H3
rd. Warrandyte........333 A3
WARRANDYTE-RINGWOOD
rd. Pk Orchards.......334 E13
rd. Ringwood N........334 E13
rd. Warrandyte........290 D18
rd. Warrandyte S.....334 E13
WARRANILLA
av. Rosebud............683 J18
WARRANWOOD
rd. Warranwood.......335 B16
WARRAWEE
av. Beaconsfield......555 K8
av. Noble Park.........534 F7
cct. Frankston.........600 E15
dr. Bundoora...........285 A2
rd. Mt Evelyn...........383 C6
rd. Wantirna S.........422 L11
WARRAWEE CIRCUIT
wk. Frankston N.......600 F13
WARRAWEENA
rd. Clayton S...........498 H9
rd. Sorrento............678 G5
WARRAWITUR
ct. Bonbeach...........573 C5
WARRAWONG
dr. Berwick.............553 H1
WARREENA
gr. Chum Creek.......213 A8
WARREGO
ct. Thomastown......241 L15
pl. Taylors Lakes.....233 F20
WARREN
av. Yarrambat..........201 C10
cl. Mill Park............242 A8
cl. Narre Warren.....553 C8
ct. Altona Mdw.........451 F3
ct. Dandenong N.....502 D19
ct. Keilor East.........322 C2
ct. Mooroolbark.......337 F17
ct. Mt Waverley.......418 L15
ct. Thomson...........703 G16
la. Yarra Jctn..........346 L16
la. Yarra Jctn..........347 A16
pl. Gladstone Pk......279 D1
rd. Cheltenham.........497 C15
rd. Mordialloc..........531 L15
rd. Parkdale.............531 L15
rd. View Bank...........285 F19
st. Bonbeach...........573 A4
st. Burwood.............418 B8
st. Doncaster...........374 F3
st. Pascoe Vale S....324 H5
st. Thomson...........703 G16
WARREN PARK
pl. Nar Warrn S.......552 J10
WARRENWOOD
av. Hoppers Csg......448 K7
cl. Ferntree Gly.......464 J3
pl. Bundoora...........283 L1
pl. Narre Warren.....553 F12
WARRICK
ct. Avondale Ht.......322 H8
dr. Bangholme.........549 K13
gr. Templestowe......331 L8
st. Ascot Vale..........324 F17
WARRIEN
ct. Bayswater..........423 H8
rd. Croydon N.........336 B17
WARRIGAL
ct. Keysborough.....534 E9
hwy.Bentleigh E........497 F14
hwy.Cheltenham.......497 F14
hwy.Heatherton........497 F14
hwy.Moorabbin.........497 F14
hwy.Oakleigh S.........497 F14
rd. Ashburton..........417 K20
rd. Ashwood............417 K20
rd. Bentleigh E.........457 H20
rd. Bentleigh E.........497 G7
rd. Burwood............417 K20
rd. Burwood............418 A7
rd. Camberwell.........418 A7
rd. Chadstone..........457 J6
rd. Cheltenham.........497 E20
rd. Cheltenham.........531 D6
rd. Glen Iris.............417 K20
rd. Heatherton.........497 E20
rd. Hughesdale.........457 H13
rd. Mentone............531 C11
rd. Moorabbin.........497 E20
rd. Oakleigh.............457 H13
rd. Oakleigh S..........457 H20
rd. Oakleigh S..........497 G7
rd. Parkdale.............531 C11
rd. Surrey Hills.........374 A20
rd. Surrey Hills.........418 A7
WARRIN
ri. Langwarrin.........629 E4
WARRINA
ct. Burwood E.........419 F11
dle. Greensborough..244 D19
st. Chadstone..........418 D19
WARRINDALE
cl. Langwarrin.........629 C7
WARRINER
ct. Oakleigh E..........458 G12
WARRINGA
cr. Hoppers Csg......448 F6
rd. Frankston...........626 J3
rd. Frankston S........626 J3
WARRINGAH
cr. Eltham...............287 B5
rd. Chum Creek.......213 F5
WARRINGAL
pl. Heidelberg.........328 G8
st. Bulleen..............329 H9
WARRINGTON
av. Vermont S.........421 B11
cl. Narre Warren.....538 H19
cr. Deer Park...........318 K11
cr. Wattle Glen........246 H7
WARRIPARRI
cr. Greensborough..244 A20
WARRISS
ct. Gladstone Pk......237 C18
WARRISTON
st. Brighton.............455 B15
WARROCK
av. Donvale.............376 L5
ct. Berwick..............554 B15
ct. Frankston S........627 H12
WARROOL
ct. Greensborough..244 B17
WARRS
rd. Maribyrnong......323 C15
rd. Maribyrnong......323 C17
st. Preston..............326 J5
WARRUGA
av. Bayswater..........423 B8
ct. Croydon.............336 K16
pl. Greensborough..285 K8
WARSAW
ct. Clarinda.............498 H11
WARTOOK
wy. Rowville.............463 B16
WARUKA
cl. Endeavour Hl......537 K6
ct. Mornington.........641 B16
WARWICK
av. Springvale..........499 L13
av. Surrey Hills.........374 A20
cl. Wantirna............422 F8
ct. Berwick..............554 E19
ct. Dandenong N.....502 C12
ct. Glen Waverley....460 G11
ct. Rye....................697 A14
ct. Surrey Hills.........374 A20
ct. Thomastown......241 K13
ct. Vermont S.........421 B11
pl. Croydon N.........335 J11
pl. Tullamarine........278 L7
pl. Tullamarine........279 A7
rd. Greensborough..286 B5
rd. Kalorama...........382 L18
rd. Kalorama...........383 A18
rd. Montrose............382 A11
rd. Olinda................426 L16
rd. Olinda................427 A17
rd. Pascoe Vale........280 J14
rd. Sunshine N.........321 C15
st. Bentleigh E.........457 B20
st. Box Hill N...........375 E9
st. Newtown............701 L6
st. N Melbourne........17 F18
WARWICK FARM
rd. Olinda................426 L17
WARWICK HILL
dr. Pt Lonsdale........710 D3
WARWICKSHIRE
ct. Narre Warren.....539 F17
WASHINGTON
av. Malvern East......456 K3
av. Point Cook.........450 D3
dr. Frankston...........600 D17
dr. Oakleigh S..........497 H7
la. Malvern East......456 K3
st. Dallas................238 J9
st. Essendon...........323 J8
st. St Albans...........319 J5
st. Toorak...............415 A4
WASHUSEN
rd. Heathmont.........422 J1
WASLEY
st. Albion.................320 F19
WASTELL
st. Northcote...........327 A18
WATCHET
ct. Craigieburn........150 B14
WATCHTOWER
rd. Coburg..............281 K20
WATER
rd. Officer................555 E20
rd. Preston..............327 J2
st. Camberwell.........417 D7
wy. Frankston S........627 F11
WATERBURY
trn. Craigieburn........193 L4
WATERDALE
cl. Melton W...........225 J19
dr. Cranbourne S.....603 C20
dr. Cranbourne S.....630 L5
pl. Aspendale Gdn....546 J4
rd. Bellfield..............328 C12
rd. Bundoora...........284 D20
rd. Heidelberg Ht.....328 D5
rd. Heidelberg W.....284 D20
rd. Heidelberg W.....328 D5

rd. Ivanhoe 328 B18
rd. Ivanhoe 328 C12
ri. Craigieburn 193 K4

WATERFALL GULLY
rd. Arthurs Seat 685 K20
rd. Rosebud 700 E4

WATERFIELD
rd. Kallista 468 H8
rd. Monbulk 468 H8
rd. The Patch 468 H8
st. Coburg 325 G2

WATERFORD
av. Craigieburn 194 A3
av. Maribyrnong 322 J16
cl. Caroline Spr 317 L7
cl. Nar Warrn N 504 D19
ct. Point Cook 451 B14
ri. Pakenham 583 L2
wy. Melton W 225 H18

WATERFRONT
bvd. Werribee 447 E4

WATERHOUSE
ct. Greenvale 193 D17

WATERLILY
la. Lilydale 338 J11

WATERLOO
av. Warburton 349 E2
cr. St Kilda 414 D15
ct. Keysborough 534 B7
pl. Ferntree Gly 464 A12
pl. Mornington 640 E13
pl. Richmond 26 G12
pl. S Melbourne 29 K3
rd. Collingwood 19 J20
rd. Glenroy 280 A7
rd. Northcote 326 K16
rd. Oak Park 280 A7
st. Belmont 702 G19
st. Brighton 454 L18
st. Camberwell 372 K20
st. Camberwell 416 K1
st. Carlton 18 E10
st. Geelong West 702 J2
st. Heathmont 378 G20
st. Williamstown 411 F12

WATERLOOFLAT
rd. Bullengarook 77 A8

WATERMAN
dr. Wantirna 422 C9
pl. Frankston 627 B4

WATERMANS
ct. Pt Lonsdale 707 F20

WATERMARK
wy. Point Cook 450 B4

WATERMILL
ct. Mill Park 242 H9

WATERMOOR
av. Kilsyth S 424 L2

WATER RESERVE
rd. Rockbank 270 K8

WATERS
av. Up Fntree Gly 464 H9
ct. Clarinda 498 H11
dr. Seaholme 409 J14
edg. Williamstown 411 A17
gr. Heathmont 422 F3
wy. Bundoora 284 A7

WATERSEDGE
cl. Knoxfield 463 B2
tce. Highton 701 J9

WATERSIDE
cl. Hoppers Csg 405 E15
dr. Braeside 547 E2
dr. Cranbourne E 578 J20

WATERSUN
ct. Point Cook 450 L14
rd. Jan Juc 711 B19

WATERVALE
bvd. Taylors Hill 274 J14

WATERVIEW
cl. Dandenong S 550 L3
cl. Dandenong S 551 A3
cl. Queenscliff 707 L18
ct. Croydon Hills 335 F12
dr. Deer Park 319 F12
dr. Deer Park 319 G12
la. Deer Park 319 G12
tce. Lilydale 338 H9

WATERWAYS
bvd. Braeside 547 F2

WATERY GULLY
rd. Kangaroo Grnd 247 B8
rd. Wattle Glen 247 B8

WATFORD
cr. Craigieburn 149 L16
ct. Epping 197 K17
ct. Somerville 644 K19
rd. St Albans 320 F6

WATKINS
cr. Mt Evelyn 383 H2
ct. Ferntree Gly 463 G10
ct. Springvale 500 D10
la. Gembrook 512 L14
pl. Langwarrin 601 L17
st. Aspendale 545 L1
st. Diamond Ck 245 H12
st. Fawkner 281 L3
st. Fitzroy N 19 C3
wy. Kensington 33 E8

WATLING
tce. Doncaster E 332 F15

WATSON
av. Belmont 706 C1
av. Dromana 686 F3
av. Mont Albert N 374 F6
cl. Rowville 462 E19
ct. Altona 409 E17
ct. Clarinda 498 C8
ct. Lalor 242 B10
ct. Melton 226 H17
gdn. Berwick 553 K9
gr. Braybrook 365 J1
gr. Glen Huntly 456 D6
pl. Melbourne 2 G17
pl. Melbourne 24 F9
pl. S Geelong 702 K14
rd. Gisborne 109 C9
rd. Mt Martha 655 H14
rd. Noble Park N 501 C10
rd. Officer S 583 C20
rd. Sorrento 678 J11
ri. Keilor 277 B13
st. Armadale 415 D9
st. Bacchus Msh 221 K17
st. Brunswick 325 E17
st. Dandenong N 501 J20
st. Frankston S 627 G8
st. Glen Iris 417 D11
st. Macleod 285 F11
st. Malvern East 416 J18
st. Preston 327 C3
st. S Kingsville 366 F20
st. Watsonia 285 F11

WATSONIA
rd. Watsonia 285 E8
st. Oakleigh 458 A15

WATSONS
gr. Werribee 447 D19
rd. Diggers Rest 187 B7
rd. Glen Waverley 460 E12
rd. Newcomb 703 L14
rd. Sunbury 187 B7
wk. Kensington 33 G7

WATT
av. Oak Park 280 D13
ct. Bacchus Msh 221 G15
rd. Mornington 640 J18
rd. Mornington 641 A18
st. Airport W 278 J18
st. Bentleigh E 457 C15
st. Gisborne 79 B13
st. S Kingsville 410 H3
st. Spotswood 410 H3
st. Springvale 499 L10
st. Sunshine 365 B4
st. Thornbury 326 G7

WATTAMOLLA
av. Werribee 447 D12
rdg. Donvale 377 G3

WATTERS
rd. Officer 556 J6

WATTIES
rd. Templestowe 287 L20

WATTLE
av. Balwyn N 372 L3
av. Balwyn N 373 A3
av. Beaumaris 529 L8
av. Belgrave 466 E12
av. Bundoora 284 G9
av. Emerald 509 B5
av. Glen Huntly 456 D9
av. Kings Park 275 E18
av. Macleod 284 G9
av. Maidstone 366 E3
av. Montmorency 286 J8
av. Mt Evelyn 339 C20
av. Mt Martha 655 J14
av. Ringwood 378 F9
av. Werribee 448 A14
av. Werribee 448 D15
cl. Meadow Ht 193 J17
cl. Rowville 463 J17
ct. Emerald 510 D2
ct. Forest Hill 376 E19
ct. Jan Juc 711 B17
ct. Long Forest 224 G11
ct. Templstw Lr 330 A8
dr. Bundoora 243 B15
dr. Doveton 536 G13
dr. Frankston 628 A7
dr. Sunbury 143 J5
dr. Watsonia 285 C9
dr. Watsonia 285 D10
gr. Coburg 325 D6
gr. Eltham 288 A12
gr. Hawthorn 371 J18
gr. McKinnon 456 A16
gr. Malvern East 456 K2
gr. Mulgrave 500 B5
gr. Nar Warrn S 579 C2
gr. Point Cook 450 B4
gr. Portsea 678 A3
gr. Portsea 678 A4
gr. Reservoir 282 F13
gr. Seaholme 409 G18
pl. McCrae 684 J13
pl. Melton S 268 D7
pl. Somerville 644 J13
rd. Bayswater N 379 G16
rd. Hawthorn 371 H18
rd. Kew East 372 D2
rd. Maidstone 322 J18
rd. Rosebud 684 J15
st. Box Hill N 374 J11
st. Prahran 32 C16
st. Prahran 414 G8
st. Springvale 500 B13
st. Thomastown 241 G13
st. W Footscray 366 G11

WATTLE BIRD
pl. Knoxfield 423 B19
wy. Langwarrin 601 K16

WATTLEBIRD
ct. Burwood 418 B6
ct. Dingley Village 533 C10
ct. Werribee 447 L6
wk. S Morang 243 H4
wy. Healesville 258 A1

WATTLE-BLOSSOM
rd. Warrandyte 290 D19

WATTLEBRAE
st. Reservoir 282 E11

WATTLEGLADE
ct. Wheelers Hill 461 A10

WATTLEGLEN
st. Craigieburn 150 C17

WATTLE GLEN-KANGAROO GROUND
rd. Kangaroo Grnd 247 G12

WATTLE GULLY
cl. Somerville 645 B20

WATTLEPARK
av. Moolap 704 H16

WATTLES
ct. Healesville 214 A16

WATTLE TREE
la. Croydon N 336 A13
la. Frankston 628 C4
rd. Boronia 424 A20
rd. Ferntree Gly 424 A18

WATTLETREE
av. Wonga Park 291 L19
cl. Lysterfield S 503 L16
ct. Glen Waverley 460 H1
rd. Armadale 415 E14
rd. Eltham 287 H1
rd. Eltham North 245 F18
rd. Hurstbridge 202 G9
rd. Malvern 415 F14
rd. Malvern East 416 A15
rd. Warburton 306 B20
wk. S Morang 243 L3

WATTLE VALLEY
dr. Hillside 231 L19
rd. Belgrave 466 D18
rd. Brunswick W 324 K14
rd. Camberwell 417 F5
rd. Canterbury 417 F5
rd. Mitcham 377 G10
rd. Mt Evelyn 339 H14

WATTLE VALLEY RD EXTENSION
Burwood 417 F8
Camberwell 417 F8

WATTLEVIEW
ri. Scoresby 462 J5

WATTON
cl. Clayton S 499 D15
st. Werribee 447 F17

WATTS
cr. Mt Eliza 625 L13
ct. Melton W 226 A16
pde. Mt Eliza 625 L12
rd. Doreen 156 D16
rd. Healesville 257 C1
rd. Sorrento 678 K8
rd. Yan Yean 156 G6
st. Box Hill 374 L13
st. Box Hill N 374 L14
st. Laverton 407 F16

WAU
st. Heidelberg W 328 A3

WAUCHOPE
av. Narre Warren 553 D6
la. Dandenong 535 G10

WAURN PARK
ct. Belmont 705 L9

WAURNVALE
dr. Belmont 705 L8

WAVE
av. Mt Waverley 459 A6
st. Elwood 454 F5
st. Frankston 599 F14
st. Hampton 495 A9

WAVELL
av. Kilsyth 380 K5
st. Bentleigh 456 D18
st. Box Hill 375 A19

WAVENEY
rd. Mt Eliza 626 D9
st. St Albans 320 F5

WAVENHOE
av. St Kilda E 414 L15

WAVERLEY
av. Ivanhoe 328 A14
av. Kew 372 C9
cl. Narre Warren 553 C10
ct. Craigieburn 150 C15
ct. Gladstone Pk 237 C18
pde. Pascoe Vale S 324 J3
rd. Glen Waverley 460 E6
rd. Malvern East 456 E1
rd. Malvern East 457 C2
rd. Mt Waverley 458 F3
rd. Wheelers Hill 460 E6
st. Aberfeldie 323 H12
st. Brighton East 495 B1
st. Broadmeadows 237 L20
st. Essendon 323 H12
st. Moonee Pnd 323 H12
st. Richmond 26 E16
st. Upwey 465 K14

WAVERLEY PARK
dr. Cranbourne N 577 K5

WAVERLY
st. Sandringham 495 F16
st. Sorrento 678 K14

WAVERTREE
av. Caroline Spr 317 J3

WAVISH
ct. Werribee 448 A6

WAXMAN
pde. Brunswick W 324 G9

WAY
dr. Bangholme 549 J13

WAYAMBA
pl. Templestowe 331 H12

WAYCOTT
wy. Mt Evelyn 339 G14

WAYGARA
st. Eumemmerring 537 B14

WAYLAND
ct. Diamond Ck 245 J6

WAYLETT
ct. Deer Park 318 K12

WAYNE
av. Boronia 423 G15
ct. Aspendale 546 A1
ct. Clarinda 498 E6
ct. Dandenong 535 E10
ct. Heathmont 379 E19
ct. Rye 696 L15
ct. Rye 697 A15
ct. Wheelers Hill 460 E15
rd. Wonga Park 292 D7

WAYSIDE
ct. Hampton Pk 551 E7
dr. Bangholme 549 K13

WEABRA
ct. Chadstone 458 C2

WEAFGREEN
ct. Camberwell 417 K3

WEALD
ct. Frankston 628 E5

WEALTHILAND
dr. Mill Park 243 E2

WEATHERALL
rd. Cheltenham 530 C3

WEATHERLAKE
st. Watsonia 285 F4

WEATHERLY
ct. Rye 696 L4
ct. Rye 697 A4
gr. Brighton 454 L19
gr. Brighton 455 A19
st. Melton 268 K2

WEATHERSTON
st. Seaford 599 E4

WEAVER
ct. Altona Mdw 451 H2
tce. St Albans 319 F7

WEBB
av. Springvale 500 B7
cl. Meadow Ht 237 L7
cl. Warrandyte 334 C3
cr. New Gisborne 78 L4
ct. Bellfield 327 K6
ct. Hopetoun Park 265 L5
ct. Rowville 463 K10
ct. Sunbury 113 H19
ct. Vermont 421 C2
la. E Melbourne 25 L11
pl. Doncaster E 376 C1
rd. Airport W 279 A11
rd. Port Melb 412 H5
st. Altona 408 L20
st. Anglesea 714 A1
st. Brighton 454 F17
st. Burwood 418 D11
st. Caulfield 455 H4
st. Coburg 281 D19
st. Fitzroy 19 D18
st. Glen Iris 417 A9
st. Kingsville 366 K12
st. Mornington 640 B17
st. Narre Warren 552 L6
st. Seaford 599 K7
st. Warburton 305 G20
st. Warrandyte 290 A18

WEBBER
pde. Keilor East 277 L20

WEBBS
rd. Ferny Creek 465 L4

WEBER
cr. Burwood E 419 E11
ct. Altona Mdw 451 K5
dr. Mornington 656 E2
st. Brighton East 455 G13

WEBSTER
av. Croydon 379 H4
cr. Watsonia 285 G10
ct. Bayswater 423 C3
ct. Highton 705 G5
rd. Armadale, off Fulton St 415 D11
st. Camberwell 417 L3
st. Dandenong 535 L12
st. Dandenong S 535 L12
st. Malvern East 457 J6
st. Seddon 367 A12
st. Sorrento 678 L12

WEBSTERS
rd. Templestowe 331 J3

WEDD
st. Cheltenham 530 L1

WEDDERBURN
cr. Mt Evelyn 339 B18

WEDDING
ct. Broadmeadows 238 D19

WEDGE
cr. Rowville 463 C15
ct. Darley 221 L9
ct. Glen Waverley 459 J3
ct. Seaford 573 J18
rd. Carrum Downs 575 B13
rd. Skye 575 B13
rd. Skye 576 D15
st. Dandenong 536 C12
st. Epping 241 D1
st. Kingsbury 283 J8
st. Werribee 447 F14
st. Werribee 447 G16

WEDGEWOOD
av. Belgrave 466 G9
dr. Rosebud 700 B7
rd. Hallam 537 E19

WEDMORE
rd. Boronia 424 D2

WEEBILL
ct. Werribee 448 A5
pl. Carrum Downs 600 L5

WEEDEN
cr. Hallam 538 C17
dr. Vermont S 420 H12
dr. Vermont S 421 A13
dr. Werribee 447 A9
st. Keysborough 534 B18

WEEDON
ps. Caroline Spr 318 D5

WEEKES
dr. Burnside 318 E4

WEEKS
cl. Rowville 463 H19
pl. Geelong 703 C11

WEEMALA
ct. Bayswater 422 L9
ct. Bayswater 423 A9
ct. Greensborough 244 C17
ct. Meadow Ht 194 B20

fwy. Southbank 23 A18
fwy. Southbank 368 E20
fwy. S Melbourne 23 A18
fwy. S Melbourne 368 E20
fwy. Spotswood 366 A19
fwy. Yarraville 366 A19

WESTGATE
av. Albion 320 G19
dr. Altona North 408 K3
dr. Laverton N 407 G7
st. Oakleigh 457 J15
st. Pascoe Vale S 280 H20

WEST GATEWAY
Keilor East 321 L4

WESTGREEN
ct. Essendon 324 C5

WESTHAM
cr. Bayswater 423 D3
ct. Bundoora 284 K5

WEST HAVEN
ct. Chirnside Pk 337 C4

WEST HILL
dr. Mt Evelyn 338 L18
dr. Mt Evelyn 339 A18

WESTLAKE
dr. Melton W 225 G18

WESTLANDS
rd. Emerald 509 D3
rd. Glen Waverley 420 J19

WESTLEIGH
cr. Narre Warren 538 J20
ct. Mill Park 242 B2
dr. Werribee 446 K20
dr. Werribee 447 A19
pl. Keilor East 321 L3

WESTLEY
av. Brighton 454 L11
av. Ivanhoe 328 C13
pl. Brookfield 267 L10
rd. Millgrove 348 D2
st. Carrum 573 D7
st. Ferntree Gly 464 B1
st. Hawthorn E 372 H15
st. Oakleigh 458 A9

WEST MEADOWS
la. Truganina 405 F8

WEST MELTON
dr. Melton W 225 L16

WESTMERE
cr. Coolaroo 238 E8
dr. Boronia 424 F15
pl. View Bank 285 L15

WESTMILL
dr. Hoppers Csg 448 A1

WESTMINSTER
av. Dandenong N 502 B12
cl. Blackburn S 419 E6
ct. Hampton Pk 551 L11
ct. Somerville 645 C18
dr. Avondale Ht 322 B12
dr. Rowville 502 K3
dr. Rowville 503 A3
dr. Werribee 446 K12
gr. Sorrento 678 D9
st. Balwyn 374 A13
st. Bulleen 329 G12
st. Grovedale 706 E12
st. Oakleigh 458 A13

WESTMORE
av. Sorrento 679 D14
dr. Heathmont 378 E19

WESTMORELAND
rd. Sunshine N 321 D18

WESTMOUNT
rd. Healesville 214 A16

WESTON
pl. Geelong, off Corio Pl 703 F8
st. Balwyn 373 D12
st. Brunswick 325 F16
st. Brunswick E 325 F16

WESTPOOL
dr. Hallam 537 H20

WESTS
rd. Maribyrnong 322 K17

WESTSIDE
av. Port Melb 368 B18
dr. Laverton N 364 K17
dr. Laverton N 365 A17

WESTVIEW
ct. Springvale S 533 L6

WESTVILLE
ct. Thomastown 240 H11

WEST VISTA
pl. Nar Warrn N 538 B10

WESTWARD HO
dr. Sunbury 144 B10

WESTWOOD
dr. Bayswater N 380 H20
dr. Bulleen 330 A17
dr. Burnside 318 F6
dr. Doncaster 330 A17
dr. Mill Park 243 D5
dr. Ravenhall 318 G14
pl. Melbourne 24 J6
ps. Chirnside Pk 337 E4
wy. Albion 320 G18

WETHERBY
ct. Hillside 231 K19
ct. Rowville 503 H2
rd. Doncaster 375 F3
rd. Doncaster E 375 F3

WETHERSDANE
dr. Hampton Pk 552 E7

WETLAND
tr. Frankston N 600 G9
wk. Mt Martha 656 H15

WETLANDS
trl. Braeside 533 C18

WETTENHALL
rd. Frankston 627 K8

WETZELL
st. Box Hill N 375 A6

WEVLIN
cl. Endeavour Hl 537 J4

WEWAK
pde. Heidelberg W 328 C2
rd. Ashburton 417 G18

WEXFORD
ct. Keilor Dn 276 E13

WEYBRIDGE
st. Surrey Hills 373 J14

WEYBURN
ct. Heidelberg 328 L6
pl. Avondale Ht 322 E10
rd. Boronia 424 E2

WEYMAR
cr. Wandin N 340 K13
st. Cheltenham 496 L19

WEYMOUTH
ct. Craigieburn 194 G4
dr. Dromana 686 A10

WHALLEY
ct. Doncaster E 375 G4
dr. Wheelers Hill 461 B18
dr. Wheelers Hill 461 D19
st. Northcote 326 L15

WHARF
rd. Port Melb 411 H1
st. Queenscliff 709 B16

WHARTON
av. Broadmeadows 238 K13
st. Surrey Hills 373 J14

WHATLEY
st. Carrum 573 D10

WHEAT
wk. Delahey 275 B13

WHEATGRASS
ct. Hillside 232 A16

WHEATLAND
cr. Dingley Village 533 C1
rd. Malvern 416 A16

WHEATLEY
av. Roxburgh Pk 194 A11
rd. Bentleigh 455 L19
rd. McKinnon 456 A16
rd. Ormond 456 A16

WHEATSHEAF
ct. Nar Warrn N 538 F12
rd. Glenroy 280 B7

WHEELER
ct. Sunbury 142 J7
ct. Wheelers Hill 460 J11
pl. Essendon 324 C9
pl. Geelong, off Malop St 703 E8
st. Berwick 554 F7
st. Coldstream 295 D12
st. Ormond 456 C14
st. Pascoe Vale S 324 G2

WHEELERS
ct. Maribyrnong 322 K15

WHELAN
ct. Darley 221 F3

WHELANS
la. Parwan 265 F8
rd. Healesville 212 A3
rd. Parwan 265 C10
rd. Parwan 265 D8

WHERNSIDE
av. Toorak 415 H8
ct. Mill Park 242 K12
ct. Mooroolbark 338 B16

WHICKSON
ct. Doncaster E 332 G11

WHILTSHIRE
pl. Chirnside Pk 336 G6

WHIMBREL
cr. Carrum Downs 600 H3
cr. Rosebud W 699 E5
ct. Werribee 447 K5

WHINWELL
st. Millgrove 348 B2

WHIPBIRD
cl. Werribee 447 L5
ct. Rowville 503 E2
dr. Carrum Downs 600 K3

WHIPSTICK GULLY
rd. Warrandyte 289 L19

WHISTLER
dr. Point Cook 450 E7
rd. Launching Pl 345 G4
wk. S Morang 243 K3

WHISTLEWOOD
cl. Doncaster E 332 D12

WHITBURN
st. Clayton 458 L18

WHITBY
st. Brunswick W 324 K12
st. Mornington 640 H12
st. Reservoir 282 J8
wy. Seaford 573 E17

WHITE
av. Bacchus Msh 221 J19
av. Bayswater N 379 L20
av. Bayswater N 423 L1
av. Kew East 372 B4
ct. Meadow Ht 237 J3
ct. Mill Park 242 F5
ct. Nunawading 376 L7
la. Beaconsfld Up 557 G2
la. Pakenham 557 G2
rd. Bullengarook 77 A17
rd. Bullengarook 77 A8
rd. Wantirna S 422 H17
st. Avondale Ht 322 B16
st. Beaumaris 530 A11
st. Belmont 705 L1
st. Bentleigh E 457 G16
st. Coburg 325 E5
st. Cremorne 26 C18
st. Fairfield 327 G16
st. Fitzroy N 326 B17
st. Footscray 367 D6
st. Frankston 599 B19
st. Glen Iris 416 C15
st. Healesville 214 B15
st. Maribyrnong 322 L16
st. Maribyrnong 323 A16
st. Mordialloc 531 K15
st. Mt Waverley 419 C18
st. Oakleigh E 458 K16
st. Parkdale 531 H15
st. Parkdale 531 K15
st. Reservoir 283 A7
st. Silvan 384 H15
st. S Melbourne 23 A20
st. Williamstown 411 C11
st. Windsor 414 H12
wy. Bulleen 329 H14

WHITE ASH
ct. Narre Warren 538 J19
ct. Vermont S 420 F13

WHITECLIFFE
av. Frankston S 626 F5
dr. Rowville 503 A8

WHITE CLIFFS
rd. Rye 696 L3
rd. Rye 697 A3

WHITEFIELD
ct. Mill Park 242 D7

WHITEFRIARS
ri. Lilydale 338 K2
ri. Lilydale 339 C6
wy. Donvale 377 E5

WHITEGUM
wy. Bundoora 284 E3

WHITEHALL
cr. Werribee 446 J12
ct. Caulfield N 415 C16
ct. Nar Warrn S 553 E15
ct. Templestowe 332 A13
pl. Lalor 241 L11
st. Footscray 367 G13
st. Yarraville 367 G13

WHITEHART
la. Melbourne 2 A10
la. Melbourne 24 B6

WHITEHAVEN
cl. Craigieburn 150 G20
cr. Mulgrave 500 H3
cr. Noble Park N 501 D9
st. Wantirna 422 K8
st. Wyndham Va 446 F12

WHITEHEAD
ct. Altona Mdw 451 D1
gr. Rosebud 683 G20
gr. Rosebud W 683 G20
st. Blairgowrie 679 K19

WHITE HILL
rd. Dromana 687 F9
rd. Red Hill 687 G11

WHITEHILL
av. Sunshine N 321 D8

WHITEHORSE
rd. Balwyn 372 L11
rd. Blackburn 375 H14
rd. Box Hill 374 F14
rd. Croydon 336 C17
rd. Croydon 379 E2
rd. Croydon N 336 C17
rd. Mitcham 377 F13
rd. Mont Albert 374 F14
rd. Nunawading 377 F13
rd. Ringwood 378 K9
rd. Ringwood N 378 K8
rd. Surrey Hills 372 L11

WHITELAW
ct. Eaglemont 328 J11
st. Reservoir 283 B10

WHITELEY
pde. Taylors Lakes 233 B20

WHITE LODGE
ct. Donvale 377 B4
ct. Kew 371 G7

WHITELY
pde. W Footscray 366 D13

WHITEMAN
st. Southbank 3 A6
st. Southbank 29 H1

WHITES
la. Craigieburn 149 A15
la. Glen Waverley 460 D9
la. Mickleham 149 A15
la. Rye 697 C2
la. Wheelers Hill 460 H10
pl. Richmond 371 B16
rd. Arthurs Seat 685 L20
rd. Mt Duneed 705 C20
rd. Mt Duneed 706 F20
rd. Werribee S 488 J17
wy. Sorrento 678 F8

WHITESIDE
rd. Clayton S 498 K8
rd. Officer 555 K18
st. Springvale 500 A6

WHITESIDES
av. Sunshine W 363 L2
av. Sunshine W 364 D2

WHITESTONE
ct. Endeavour Hl 537 J1

WHITEWOOD
st. Frankston N 600 E9

WHITFIELD
st. Truganina 405 G15
wk. Truganina 405 G15

WHITFORD
wy. Frankston 628 E4

WHITING
ct. Skye 575 J14
ct. Wantirna S 422 K20

WHITLEY
cr. Craigieburn 194 F2

WHITMORE
pl. Hillside 232 E19
pl. Wyndham Va 446 C7

WHITMORR
ct. Noble Park 501 B19

WHITMUIR
rd. Bentleigh 455 K19
rd. McKinnon 455 K19

WHITNEY
wy. Epping 198 H16

WHITNEYS
rd. Somerville 646 L20

WHITON
gr. Wyndham Va 446 G10
st. Mt Waverley 458 E9

WHITTACKER
ct. Williamstown 411 A15

WHITTAKER
av. Laverton 407 D11
st. Maidstone 366 E1

WHITTEN
ct. Highton 705 G6

WHITTENOOM
st. Doncaster E 376 B4

WHITTENS
la. Doncaster 375 A4

WHITTIER
st. Kingsbury 283 J11

WHITTON
ct. Black Rock 529 H1
ct. Rowville 502 J5
pde. Coburg N 282 A17

WHITTY
st. Sunshine 365 D

WHITWORTH
av. Springvale 499 J

WHYALLA
pl. Burnside 318 H

WHYTE
ct. Newtown 702 A
gr. Mont Albert 374 D1
st. Brighton 494 K
st. Rosebud W 683 E2

WIAKTUN
cr. Mt Waverley 459 D

WIARANDO
ct. Doncaster E 332 E1

WICHILL
cl. Greenvale 192 K1

WICK
cl. Craigieburn 194 D

WICKHAM
av. Forest Hill 376 G2
ct. Chirnside Pk 336 J
ct. Greenvale 193 B1
ct. Mill Park 242 E
gr. Strathmore 324 C
rd. Croydon 336 H1
rd. Hampton E 495 J1
rd. Moorabbin 496 E1
st. Melton S 268 F1

WICKHAMS
rd. Launching Pl 345 D1

WICKING
ct. Blackburn S 419 K

WICKLOW
av. Croydon 379 L
la. Melbourne 1 D
la. Melbourne 23 J
st. Ormond 456 E1
st. Pascoe Vale 280 J1
st. Seaford 599 K

WICKS
ct. Oakleigh S 498 B
rd. The Basin 425 E1

WIDDOP
av. Rosebud 700 B
cr. Hampton E 495 J1

WIDDY
ct. Sunshine W 365 C1

WIDFORD
st. Broadmeadows 238 C2
st. Glenroy 280 C4
st. Hawthorn E 416 F5

WIDNES
ct. Deer Park 319 B12

WIGAN
rd. Bayswater 424 B6

WIGGENS
pl. Doncaster E 332 F11

WIGGS
rd. Moolap 704 L19

WIGHT
st. Kensington 33 K9

WIGHTMAN
st. Footscray 367 H8

WIGSTONE
st. Noble Park 534 L1

WIGTON
st. Ascot Vale 324 E19

WILAM
ct. Cranbourne 578 B18

WILANA
st. Ringwood 378 F13

WILBERTON
dr. Springvale 499 G13

WILBRAHAM
ct. Frankston 628 F1

WILBUR
cr. Hughesdale 457 G8

WILBURTON
pde. Balwyn N 329 L19

WILBY
ct. Broadmeadows 237 L10
ct. St Albans 320 E6
st. Sorrento 678 E10

WILCOX
ct. Noble Park 500 D19
st. Preston 282 L19

WILD
cr. Roxburgh Pk 193 K13
ct. Endeavour Hl 537 E6
st. Parkdale 531 J11
st. Reservoir 282 K15

WILDBERRY
cl. Croydon Hills 335 F16
ct. Knoxfield 463 C1

WILD CHERRY
dr. Eltham 288 C15
la. Yarrambat 201 E19
rd. Montrose 382 C12

d. Ormond 456 F13
t. Maribyrnong 322 J16
WILDCOAST
v. Blairgowrie 696 B6
WILDCROFT
t. Carrum Downs 601 A4
WILD DUCK
l. Blind Bight 650 B10
y. Whittlesea 96 A16
WILDE
t. Mooroolbark 337 F19
WILDFIRE
t. Mill Park 243 C12
WILDFLOWER
r. Hoppers Csg 405 B16
t. Hillside 274 E5
t. Warrandyte 333 D5
WILD-LIFE
de. Balwyn N 373 L6
WILDOER
r. Aspendale Gdn 547 C7
WILDWOOD
v. Vermont S 420 F13
cl. Knoxfield 423 B19
t. Albanvale 319 A5
t. Cranbourne N 578 A6
gr. Ringwood 378 C10
pl. Mulgrave 501 F6
rd. Bulla 190 G16
rd. Whittlesea 96 B6
rd. Whittlesea 96 L17
rd.s, Bulla 190 B2
wk. Croydon S 380 B14
WILELA
ct. Noble Park 535 B2
WILEMAN
rd. Sunbury 142 A9
WILFRED
ct. Glen Waverley 460 B9
rd. Ivanhoe East 328 G16
st. Rosebud 684 H13
WILGA
av. Altona 452 H1
av. Selby 467 D18
ct. Meadow Ht 193 K17
ct. Narre Warren 538 E19
ct. Noble Park N 501 F15
ct. Wantirna S 423 B12
st. Mt Waverley 459 C6
WILGAH
rd. Rosebud 684 H20
st. St Kilda E 414 L17
st. St Kilda E 415 A17
st. Thomastown 241 D13
WILGRA
av. Ashburton 417 J14
cr. Caulfield 456 A4
WILGUL
wy. Mornington 640 F17
WILHELMA
av. Bayswater 423 G11
WILHELMINA
ct. Croydon 379 E3
WILKENS
la. Silvan 428 L3
WILKES
ct. Mernda 154 H8
pl. Blackburn S 419 D4
st. Ferntree Gly 464 C2
st. Narre Warren 552 H2
WILKILLA
rd. Mt Evelyn 383 E7
WILKIN
ct. Endeavour Hl 537 A1
WILKINS
av. Beaumaris 530 H6
st. Anglesea 713 J1
st. Newport 411 C9
st. Yarraville 366 G16
WILKINSON
cr. Bellfield 327 L5
ct. Roxburgh Pk 194 B14
pl. Glen Waverley 459 L9
rd. Sunshine 365 F1
st. Brunswick 325 F13
st. Burwood E 420 A8
st. Hoppers Csg 448 F2
st. Macleod 285 G11
st. Reservoir 283 D14
st. Tootgarook 698 G1
wy. Endeavour Hl 537 D6
wy. Pk Orchards 334 D20
WILKS
av. Malvern 415 L9
la. Caulfield N, off Wilks St 415 D15
rd. Officer 557 A8
st. Caulfield N 415 D15
WILL
st. Forest Hill 420 H1
WILLA
av. View Bank 285 F17
WILLANDRA
av. Canterbury 373 G18
ct. Taylors Lakes 275 L10
ct. Werribee 448 C15
WILLANJIE
ct. Bundoora 284 E1
WILLANSBY
av. Brighton 455 A15
WILLARD
ct. Lalor 241 A6
wy. Chirnside Pk 337 B5
WILLATON
st. St Albans 320 D8
WILLAURA
cr. Broadmeadows 237 K15
pl. Yallambie 286 A13
WILLCYRUS
st. Surrey Hills 374 E18
WILLEN
st. Cheltenham 497 D15
WILLESDEN
dr. Waurn Ponds 705 E15
rd. Hughesdale 457 F9
WILLETT
av. Oak Park 279 K10
WILLEY
st. Sunshine N 321 D16
WILLGILSON
ct. Oakleigh 457 L13
WILLIAM
av. Dandenong S 535 L14
av. Hallam 537 E15
cct. Caroline Spr 318 C9
cr. Millgrove 348 G1
cr. Rosebud W 683 D20
ct. Werribee 448 G9
pl. Balaclava, off William St 414 H19
rd. Berwick 553 L5
rd. Blairgowrie 695 L2
rd. Bullengarook 77 B7
rd. Carrum Downs 574 K18
rd. Carrum Downs 575 A18
rd. Croydon 336 C20
rd. Lilydale 338 F17
rd. Red Hill 686 K18
rd. The Patch 468 A9
st. Abbotsford 26 E3
st. Armadale 415 G12
st. Bacchus Msh 222 A15
st. Balaclava 414 H19
st. Belmont 706 A1
st. Boronia 424 C11
st. Box Hill 375 A17
st. Brighton 454 L15
st. Brighton 455 A17
st. Brunswick 325 F10
st. Bulleen 329 L12
st. Clifton Hill 20 H7
st. Cranbourne 578 C20
st. Cremorne 26 E19
st. Donvale 376 K7
st. Emerald 510 A4
st. Essendon 323 F3
st. Fawkner 281 G6
st. Ferntree Gly 464 B3
st. Glenroy 279 H6
st. Greensborough 285 K3
st. Hawthorn 372 B17
st. Kalorama 383 C10
st. Keilor Park 277 K13
st. Lalor 241 E11
st. McCrae 684 L13
st. Melbourne 1 E18
st. Melbourne 23 H4
st. Melton 227 C20
st. Mernda 154 L19
st. Mernda 155 A19
st. Mitcham 377 C11
st. Moorabbin 496 E11
st. Mt Waverley 458 K2
st. Murrumbeena 457 E8
st. Newcomb 704 A16
st. Newport 410 K6
st. Newtown 702 D7
st. Northcote 327 C18
st. Oakleigh 458 D13
st. Preston 282 J19
st. Ringwood 378 B9
st. St Albans 276 A20
st. Seddon 367 B11
st. Somerton 194 H16
st. South Yarra 32 C11
st. South Yarra 414 G5
st. Sunshine 365 F9
st. Up Fntree Gly 465 B7
st. W Melbourne 1 E18
st. W Melbourne 17 G20
st. W Melbourne 23 H4
st.e, Lilydale 338 B6
st.w, Lilydale 338 B6
WILLIAM ANGLISS
dr. Laverton N 363 F19
dr. Laverton N 363 G17
WILLIAM BUCKLEY
ct. Seabrook, off Cotterell Wy 450 L6
wy. Sorrento 679 A16
WILLIAM CLARKE
wyn. Nar Warrn S 578 H1
WILLIAM COOPER
st. Maribyrnong 367 C2
WILLIAM GILL
pl. Croydon Hills 335 G14
WILLIAM GOODE
ct. Sorrento 679 A12
WILLIAM HOVELL
dr. Endeavour Hl 537 F6
WILLIAM HUNTER
ct. Rosebud 700 G3
WILLIAM LEAKE
av. Seabrook 450 L7
WILLIAM LEONARD
ct. Nar Warrn S 579 F2
WILLIAM McPHERSON
cr. Seabrook 450 L8
WILLIAM PERRY
cl. Endeavour Hl 537 D7
WILLIAMS
av. Keilor East 278 A18
cl. Dingley Village 533 E10
cr. Woori Yallock 344 G16
ct. Richmond 26 F4
gr. Bonbeach 545 E13
la. Ferntree Gly 464 F1
pl. S Melbourne 29 F3
rd. Blackburn 375 J13
rd. Briar Hill 286 F6
rd. Coburg N 281 E18
rd. Dandenong S 550 D1
rd. Don Valley 346 D7
rd. Laverton 407 F16
rd. Mooroolbark 337 F18
rd. Mornington 640 C16
rd. Mt Eliza 625 L11
rd. Olinda 426 L6
rd. Olinda 427 A7
rd. Pk Orchards 378 D1
rd. Pt Lonsdale 710 F2
rd. Prahran 32 K20
rd. Prahran 414 K13
rd. Ringwood N 378 D1
rd. South Yarra 32 K20
rd. South Yarra 414 L8
rd. South Yarra 415 A6
rd. Toorak 32 K20
rd. Toorak 414 L8
rd. Toorak 415 A6
rd. Windsor 414 K13
rd.n, South Yarra 414 L2
rd.n, South Yarra 415 A2
rd.n, Toorak 414 L2
rd.n, Toorak 415 A2
ri. Sunbury 113 G7
st. Dromana 686 E3
st. Frankston 626 L2
st. Mentone 531 B6
st. S Melbourne 29 F3
WILLIAM SALTHOUSE
wy. Patterson L 547 H19
WILLIAMS BAY
gr. Williamstown 410 H16
WILLIAMSBROOK
tce. Bundoora 243 C14
WILLIAMSON
av. Strathmore 323 L1
rd. Ferntree Gly 424 F19
rd. Gembrook 512 L16
rd. Maidstone 322 J17
rd. Maribyrnong 322 J17
rd. Mont Albert N 374 E6
st. Berwick 554 H9
st. Mordialloc 532 E17
st. Tootgarook 698 B3
WILLIAMSONS
rd. Doncaster 330 L16
rd. S Morang 199 E17
rd. Sunbury 114 E10
rd. Templestowe 331 B12
rd. Templstw Lr 330 L16
WILLIAMSTOWN
jnc. Newport 411 A12
rd. Kingsville 366 K18
rd. Port Melb 411 G6
rd. Seddon 366 K18
rd. Yarraville 366 K18
WILLIAM WRIGHT
wyn. Hoppers Csg 447 L1
WILLIS
cl. Hampton Pk 551 B7
ct. Altona Mdw 451 F5
ct. Darley 221 J9
ct. Vermont 421 B1
la. Hampton 494 L8
la. Hampton 495 A8
pl. Delahey 275 D10
pl. S Geelong 702 L14
rd. Kallista 469 A6
rd. Menzies Ck 468 H18
rd. Monbulk 469 A6
st. Armadale 415 J12
st. Balwyn N 373 F4
st. Frankston 599 E19
st. Greensborough 286 F1
st. Hampton 494 L8
st. Heatherton 497 L15
st. Kensington 33 C9
st. Prahran 415 A12
st. Richmond 26 F20
st. Richmond 32 F1
st. St Albans 320 C8
st. Yarraville 367 C15
WILLISON
st. Bayswater 423 G8
WILLJOHN
dr. Mt Martha 657 A10
WILLMETTE
ct. Lilydale 338 B2
WILLMOTT
dr. Craigieburn 150 B13
dr. Hoppers Csg 448 E8
st. Aspendale 546 B2
WILLOBY
av. Glen Iris 416 G16
st. Junction Vill 604 G11
WILLONGA
st. Rye 697 C4
st. Strathmore 279 L15
WILLORA
cr. Cranbourne W 577 F20
ct. Frankston S 626 L15
WILLORNA
ct. Doncaster E 332 E8
WILLOUGHBY
av. Caroline Spr 318 C3
st. Reservoir 282 G11
WILLOW
av. Cheltenham 531 G2
av. Glen Waverley 419 L15
av. Mitcham 377 G15
av. St Albans 320 F8
bnd. Bulleen 330 A18
bnd. Doncaster 330 A18
ct. Bellfield 327 K6
ct. Keysborough 534 E13
ct. Kilsyth 381 L6
ct. Narre Warren 552 L7
ct. Whittington 704 A19
ct. Whittlesea 96 D16
dr. Avondale Ht 321 K7
dr. Hampton Pk 551 G4
dr. Rowville 463 H16
gr. Canterbury 417 C1
gr. Coburg 325 D5
gr. Kew East 372 D2
la. Carlton 18 H12
la. Richmond 32 F2
rd. Bangholme 549 H13
rd. Frankston 628 D4
rd. Up Fntree Gly 464 J9
st. Box Hill N 374 H10
st. Dingley Village 532 H7
st. Elsternwick 454 K2
st. Essendon 324 A8
st. Malvern 416 B9
st. Preston 326 B3
st. Werribee 447 E11
wy. Craigieburn 150 B12
WILLOW BANK
gr. Ivanhoe 327 L17
WILLOWBANK
ct. Glen Waverley 420 E18
ct. Templestowe 331 K10
rd. Fitzroy N 326 C16
rd. Gisborne 78 J17
wy. Attwood 237 A11
WILLOWDENE
cl. Somerville 645 D20
WILLOWFIELD
ct. Highton 701 F9
WILLOW-GLEN
ct. Dingley Village 533 A10
WILLOWGREEN
wy. Point Cook 450 G7
WILLOW TREE
wy. Chirnside Pk 337 H6
WILLOWTREE
cr. Niddrie 322 K2
dr. Werribee 448 C15
WILLS
av. Mt Waverley 459 E1
ct. Cranbourne N 577 J7
ct. Endeavour Hl 537 J8
ct. Grovedale 706 B12
ct. Mooroolbark 337 L16
ct. Taylors Lakes 275 K1
rd. Dixons Ck 209 L2
rd. Melton S 268 D12
rd. Whittlesea 96 A19
st. Balwyn 372 K10
st. Boronia 423 H10
st. Glen Iris 416 G11
st. Hawthorn E 416 H1
st. Kew 371 G6
st. Melbourne 1 G4
st. Melbourne 23 J4
st. Mornington 640 E20
st. Pascoe Vale S 280 J20
st. Sunbury 143 A12
st. Westmeadows 237 B15
WILLSLIE
cr. Berwick 554 C18
WILLSMERE
rd. Kew 371 K6
WILLSMORE
st. Williamstn N 410 E12
WILLUNGA
ct. Berwick 554 A16
wy. Bundoora 242 F13
WILLURAH
st. Forest Hill 420 J3
WILLY
ct. Dingley Village 533 C5
WILLYS
av. Keilor Dn 275 K12
WILMA
av. Dandenong 535 G6
av. Mulgrave 499 L3
av. Seville E 343 C13
ct. Beaconsfield 555 D14
ct. Doncaster 375 D3
st. Bentleigh 496 D3
WILMOT
dr. Delahey 275 F14
st. Macleod 285 D17
st. Malvern East 456 G3
WILMOTH
av. Carnegie 456 L12
st. Northcote 327 D13
st. Thornbury 327 D13
WILMOTT
ct. Berwick 553 L19
WILNA
st. Pascoe Vale 280 H17
WILONA
wy. Berwick 554 G14
WILONG
cl. Kurunjang 227 A12
WILPENA
ct. St Albans 321 A6
pl. Vermont S 420 L9
pl. Vermont S 421 A9
WILRAY
st. Grovedale 706 H9
WILSHIRE
ct. Endeavour Hl 537 K9
WILSON
av. Brunswick 325 E16
av. Montmorency 286 H10
av. Parkville 18 A14
av. Werribee 448 E13
bvd. Reservoir 282 F3
cnc. Croydon N 336 C14
cr. Dromana 686 B6
ct. Cranbourne 578 A17
dr. Carrum Downs 574 L17
gr. Aspendale 546 C5
gr. Camberwell 417 C7
gr. Seaford 573 F16
pl. Bacchus Msh 221 J17
pl. Geelong, off Fitzroy St 703 E10
rd. Blairgowrie 679 L19
rd. Diamond Ck 246 D1
rd. Glen Waverley 460 E4
rd. Melton S 268 D10
rd. Wattle Glen 246 D1
st. Bentleigh 455 H19
st. Berwick 554 E7
st. Braybrook 365 K4
st. Brighton 454 K16
st. Brighton 455 A18
st. Brunswick 325 D16
st. Cheltenham 496 L17
st. Cheltenham 496 L20
st. Coburg 325 G1
st. Dandenong 536 B11
st. Fawkner 281 K11
st. Ferntree Gly 424 C20
st. Glen Iris 416 C14
st. Greensborough 244 J14
st. Healesville 213 K18
st. Highett 495 J14

st. Macleod 285 C14
st. Mont Albert 374 B16
st. Moonee Pnd 324 D11
st. Murrumbeena 457 D5
st. Oakleigh 457 L15
st. Princes Hill 18 D1
st. Princes Hill 325 H20
st. Ringwood E 378 K10
st. Rosebud 684 E15
st. S Melbourne 30 C5
st. South Yarra 32 E13
st. South Yarra 414 H7
st. Surrey Hills 374 B16
st. Yarraville 367 B17

WILSONS
la. Lilydale 337 K5
la. Sunbury 142 E13
rd. Doncaster 374 E3
rd. Mornington 640 D16
rd. Newcomb 704 B20

WILTON
av. Newcomb 703 L15
cl. Chelsea Ht 547 F17
cl. Croydon N 335 L10
cl. Wyndham Va 446 C13
cr. Wheelers Hill 461 B7
ct. S Morang 243 G3
dr. Greensborough 244 E14
gr. Elwood 454 C4
gr. Sassafras 426 G16
grn. Officer 555 H20
pl. Attwood 237 D12
st. Blackburn N 375 K9
wy. Doncaster 375 E4

WILTON VALE
cr. Malvern East 416 K17

WILTONVALE
av. Hoppers Csg 448 H6
rd. S Morang 199 L8

WILTSHIRE
av. Bayswater 423 G8
ct. Altona Mdw 451 G7
dr. Kew 371 F4
dr. Roxburgh Pk 193 K14
dr. Somerville 644 F15
pl. Wyndham Va 446 F9
rd. Gladstone Pk 237 B18
st. Richmond 26 G17
st. Sunshine N 321 G17

WILUNA
ct. Briar Hill 286 G4
ct. Scoresby 462 C7

WILY
ct. Lilydale 338 E12

WIMBA
av. Kew 372 F11
ct. Coolaroo 238 D7

WIMBLE
st. Northcote 326 J16
st. Parkville 17 H10

WIMBLEDON
av. Elwood 414 E20
av. Mt Eliza 625 K15
ct. Doncaster E 332 D10
ct. Mooroolbark 337 K16
ct. Portsea 678 B4
ct. St Kilda E 414 L17
ct. St Kilda E 415 A17
gr. Eaglemont 328 H10

WIMBORNE
av. Chelsea 545 E11
av. Mt Eliza 625 J16
ct. Bayswater N 380 H20
la. Chelsea, off Wimborne Av 545 E12

WIMMERA
av. Manifold Ht 702 B4
av. Reservoir 283 E13
cr. Keilor Dn 276 F16
ct. Berwick 553 F5
ct. Werribee 447 F8
pl. St Kilda 414 A16
st. Belmont 702 E20
st. Box Hill N 375 A9
st. Moorabbin 496 G11
st. Ormond 456 G12

WIMPOLE
cr. Bellfield 327 K5

WIMPORT
st. Heidelberg 328 J6

WIN
pl. Hallam 537 E13

WINALLA
av. Rowville 502 E7

WINAMURRA
cr. Thomastown 240 G12

WINBIRRA
pde. Ashwood 418 B19

WINBOURNE
ct. Wantirna 422 G13
rd. Mt Waverley 458 K1

WINBROOK
ct. Doncaster 330 L18
wy. Avondale Ht 322 D11

WINBY
ct. The Basin 425 A9

WINCANTON
ct. Noble Park N 501 C8

WINCH
rd. Diggers Rest 187 B11

WINCHESTER
av. Epping 198 A18
ct. Kings Park 275 A18
dr. Bayswater N 380 F17
pl. Geelong, off Little Myers St 703 A9
rd. Nunawading 376 L8
st. Moonee Pnd 324 A14
wy. Broadmeadows 238 K12

WINCOTT
pl. Vermont 421 C6

WINDALE
st. Dandenong 536 E13

WINDARRA
ct. Mornington 641 B15
ct. Sunbury 142 G10
gr. Jan Juc 711 C15

WINDBREAK
ct. Albanvale 319 B5

WINDEATT
cl. Mill Park 242 B7

WINDELLA
av. Kew East 372 F5
av. Rosebud 683 K19
cr. Glen Waverley 459 L10
qd. Doncaster 375 C4

WINDEMERE
st. Berwick 554 A9

WINDERMERE
av. Doncaster E 332 A18
cr. Brighton 494 J1
cr. Gladstone Pk 279 C2
cr. Mulgrave 501 E6
ct. Blackburn 375 K20
dr. Ferntree Gly 463 G7
dr. Ferntree Gly 463 G9

WINDING
wy. N Warrandyte 290 C13

WINDLE
av. Truganina 405 F14
ct. Truganina 405 G16
tce. Burnside 318 E7

WINDMILL
ct. Wheelers Hill 461 C20
ri. Diamond Ck 245 F14
st. Bundoora 242 D15
st. Newtown 701 L10

WINDOO
st. Frankston N 599 L8

WINDOURAN
dr. Mitcham 377 C16

WINDSONG
ps. Chirnside Pk 337 F5

WINDSOR
av. Bentleigh 456 F19
av. McKinnon 456 F19
av. Mt Waverley 418 G19
av. Oakleigh S 458 B17
av. Oakleigh S 498 A2
av. Springvale 499 F13
av. Strathmore 279 H20
av. Wyndham Va 446 H9
cl. Boronia 424 J5
cr. Altona North 409 L8
cr. Bundoora 284 L2
cr. Mont Albert 374 A17
cr. Surrey Hills 374 A17
ct. Frankston 600 A17
dr. Avondale Ht 322 E8
dr. Lysterfield 464 C17
dr. Officer 555 G18
gdn. Caroline Spr 318 C8
la. Surrey Hills 374 A18
pl. Melbourne 24 K5
pl. Melton W 225 L14
pl. Windsor 414 G12
rd. Croydon 380 C3
rd. Newtown 702 A14
rd. Templstw Lr 330 F13
st. Braybrook 365 L6
st. Burwood E 420 A10
st. Footscray 367 C9
st. Hallam 537 H15
st. Kew 372 F7
st. Macleod 285 D14
st. Pascoe Vale 280 K14
st. Seddon 367 C11
tce. Williamstown 411 K17

WINDSOR PARK
ri. Mooroolbark 337 D20

WINDWARD
ct. Arthurs Seat 685 L14

WINFIELD
dr. Kurunjang 226 F14
rd. Balwyn N 374 C2
rd. Balwyn N 374 C7
rd. Mont Albert N 374 C7

WINGA
pl. St Helena 244 J17

WINGALA
av. Keysborough 534 F10

WINGAN
av. Camberwell 417 H3
ct. Sunshine W 363 K8

WINGARA
av. Keilor East 278 D19
ct. Bangholme 549 H14
ct. Rosebud W 699 G4
dr. Rosebud W 699 G3
pl. Mt Evelyn 339 G17

WINGARRA
dr. Grovedale 706 A15

WINGATE
av. Ascot Vale 324 A18
av. Mt Waverley 459 G2
av. Ringwood E 379 F14
cl. Knoxfield 463 A5
ct. Endeavour Hl 537 K8
st. Bentleigh E 496 K7
st. Tootgarook 698 C4

WINGED FOOT
ct. Sunbury 144 F14
dr. Sunshine N 321 H15

WINGFIELD
st. Footscray 367 H8

WINGHAM
ct. Frankston 600 A18
st. Dandenong N 502 A10

WINGROVE
pl. Ringwood 378 J8
st. Alphington 327 H18
st. Cheltenham 496 L14
st. Fairfield 327 D18
st. Forest Hill 420 J5

WINGS
wy. Attwood 237 A12

WINGSPAN
av. S Morang 199 J13

WINIFRED
cr. Glen Iris 417 A16
cr. Toorak 415 B3
ct. S Morang 243 H2
ct. Templestowe 331 E4
gr. Blairgowrie 679 H19
rd. Mooroolbark 337 H17
st. Essendon 323 K4
st. Frankston 627 F4
st. Northcote 326 D14
st. Nunawading 376 E9
st. Oakleigh 458 C9
st. Oak Park 279 J11
st. Pascoe Vale S 324 H5
st. Preston 282 L16
st. St Albans 320 A1
st. Seville 341 K16
st. Williamstown 411 B15

WINILBA
rd. Sunbury 113 E20
rd. Sunbury 143 E1

WINJALLOCK
cr. Vermont S 421 F8

WINKLER
dr. Taylors Lakes 233 D18

WINMALEE
dr. Glen Waverley 460 A9
rd. Balwyn 373 G10

WINMARLEIGH
cl. Brighton 494 G3

WINN
gr. Fawkner 281 G8
gr. Lalor 242 A11
st. Millgrove 304 G20

WINNEKE
ct. Ferntree Gly 464 A14

WINNERS
cir. Aspendale Gdn 546 F1
cir. Aspendale Gdn 546 F2

WINNETKA
dr. Lilydale 338 C3

WINNETTE
ct. Ringwood 378 L4
ct. Ringwood 379 A4

WINNIE
ct. Narre Warren 539 D18

WINNIFRED
cr. Knoxfield 462 L7

WINNIMA
av. Hampton Pk 551 E7

WINNINGTON
st. Deer Park 319 C12

WINNIPEG
st. Rowville 462 K15

WINONA
gr. Pascoe Vale S 324 G6
rd. Mt Eliza 642 H5

WINSCOMBE
av. Tecoma 466 D13

WINSHAM
ct. Craigieburn 150 B15

WINSLOW
av. Lalor 241 B7
cr. Deer Park 318 J12
ct. Gladstone Pk 278 L2
ct. Gladstone Pk 279 A2
ct. Keysborough 534 L10
gr. Vermont S 420 F6

WINSOME
st. Mentone 531 A5

WINSON GREEN
rd. Canterbury 373 G15

WINSTANLEY
rd. Thomson 703 J17

WINSTER
ct. Greenvale 237 D3

WINSTON
ct. Blackburn S 420 A5
ct. Grovedale 706 F15
ct. Moorabbin 497 C9
ct. Mt Martha 655 J18
ct. Noble Park 535 E5
dr. Caulfield S 455 H10
dr. Doncaster 330 L17
rd. View Bank 285 J17
st. Glen Waverley 420 H17
st. Lalor 241 L10
st. Maidstone 366 D2
wy. Murrumbeena 456 L13
wy. Wyndham Va 446 H9

WINSWOOD
cl. Vermont S 421 F7

WINTER
cr. Kingsbury 283 G10
cr. Reservoir 283 G10
ct. Mill Park 242 F9
st. Belmont 706 G6
st. E Geelong 703 G10
st. Malvern 415 K14
wy. Glen Waverley 419 L20
wy. Glen Waverley 459 L1
wy. Point Cook 451 B7

WINTERHILL
lk. Bundoora 284 G7

WINTERLEY
rd. Pt Lonsdale 710 E7

WINTERS
la. Nar Warrn N 539 D5
wy. Doncaster 330 C17

WINTERSET
cl. Mordialloc 532 D17

WINTERSUN
ct. Roxburgh Pk 194 C8
dr. Albanvale 318 L5
rd. Berwick 539 H17

WINTERTON
cl. Epping 241 J1
ct. Hallam 538 B15
ct. Wantirna 422 E12
dr. Wheelers Hill 460 L8
rd. Clayton 499 D1

WINTLE
cl. Roxburgh Pk 194 B11
rd. Emerald 509 E8

WINTON
av. Frankston 627 E7
cl. Epping 198 A17
ct. Broadmeadows 238 A11
ct. Craigieburn 150 H20
ct. Keilor Dn 276 B11
ct. Montrose 381 L8
rd. Ashburton 417 A19
rd. Ashburton 417 D19
rd. Malvern East 417 A19
st. Burwood 419 A11
st. Kew 372 F7

WINWOOD
dr. Ferntree Gly 464 D3

WINYARD
dr. Mooroolbark 337 B18

WINYARRA
ct. Wantirna 422 B13

WIPPA
ct. Ashwood 418 B19

WIRILDA
cl. Belgrave S 506 K4
cl. Thomastown 240 G12
cr. Frankston N 600 E8
ct. Doveton 536 J9
ct. Langwarrin 601 J20
ct. Long Forest 224 G1
ct. Meadow Ht 193 J20
ct. Springvale S 533 L4
ct. Sunbury 143 J5

pl. Keilor Dn 276 H16
wy. Maidstone 366 F3

WIRINGA
av. Camberwell 417 F4
cr. Mt Eliza 641 L5
ct. Sunshine W 364 B8

WIRKSWORTH
st. Herne Hill 701 L1

WIRRABARA
ct. Yallambie 286 B15

WIRRABARRA
pl. Berwick 553 F2

WIRRAWAY
cr. Thomastown 240 F17
ct. Ashburton 417 J17
dr. Port Melb 367 K19
rd. Airport W 279 D14
rd. Strathmore 279 D14

WIRREANDA
ct. Blackburn 375 L20

WIRRUNA
rd. Dromana 685 K9

WIRTH
ct. Newcomb 704 C16
rd. Pk Orchards 334 D14
st. Mt Waverley 419 A19

WISE
av. Seaford 599 F5
cl. Windsor, off McIlwrick St 414 J12
wy. Roxburgh Pk 193 K15

WISEMAN
ct. Essendon 324 D7
rd. Monbulk 428 K8
rd. Silvan 428 K8
st. Hawthorn E 416 D3

WISEWOULD
av. Seaford 599 D12
st. Flemington 33 C2

WISHART
st. Hampton E 495 J8
st. Kew 372 E8

WISLA
cct. Roxburgh Pk 194 C6

WISTARIA
wy. Hoppers Csg 405 D15

WISTERIA
ct. Clarinda 498 B10
ct. Cranbourne N 578 C8
dr. Bundoora 242 F13
la. Mt Dandenong 426 K1

WITCHWOOD
cl. Albanvale 319 A6
cl. South Yarra 31 J4
cl. South Yarra 414 E2
cr. Burwood E 419 H10

WITHAM
dr. Coldstream 295 E13

WITHERS
av. Mulgrave 500 H6
cl. Sunbury 142 L9
cl. Sunbury 143 A9
rd. Bayswater 424 C2
st. Albert Park 29 C16
st. Albert Park 413 B8
st. Ivanhoe East 328 K14
st. Sunshine 365 D3
wy. Eltham 287 D12

WITKEN
av. Wantirna S 462 K2

WITNEY
ct. Darley 222 D10
wy. Bundoora 284 L3

WITNISH
st. Yarra Jctn 346 H14

WITT
ct. Box Hill N 375 D6
st. Mitcham 377 H14

WITTENBERG
ct. Narre Warren 552 F2

WITTERNBERG
av. Frankston 628 E11

WITTICK
st. Darley 221 G8

WITTIG
st. Doncaster 374 J3

WITTON
ct. Greenvale 192 J18
st. Deer Park 319 D17

WOBURN
cl. Kealba 276 L20
st. Heidelberg 328 J4

WODALLA
ct. Mill Park 242 L10
ct. Mill Park 243 A10
gr. New Gisborne 79 C1

WODONGA
cr. Thomastown 240 D13
st. Broadmeadows 238 F17

WOFF
st. Beaumaris 530 B5
WOKING
st. Craigieburn 194 C4
WOLAI
av. Bentleigh E 457 F20
WOLANGI
ct. Greensborough 244 D19
WOLBERS
rd. Dingley Village 533 D5
WOLF
ct. Endeavour Hl 537 D9
st. Wantirna S 422 G19
WOLFDENE
ct. Mornington 640 D16
WOLFE
rd. Melton 227 B16
WOLLAHRA
pl. Heathmont 379 C17
ri. Wyndham Va 446 D3
WOLLERT
st. Rye 697 B7
WOLLOMBI
rd. Exford 267 G19
WOLMAN
dr. Frankston 628 D11
WOLSELEY
av. Glen Waverley 460 G1
cl. Mont Albert 374 C15
cr. Balwyn 372 L10
cr. Blackburn 375 K17
gr. Brighton 494 J3
pde. Kensington 33 K12
pl. Rowville 502 H3
st. Coburg 325 G7
st. Hawthorn E 372 D18
st. Highett 496 C12
st. S Melbourne 29 G2
WOLSELY
cl. Werribee 447 G2
WOLSLEY
av. Frankston 600 G19
st. Bentleigh 495 L3
WOLVERHAMPTON
st. Footscray 367 C7
WOLVERTON
dr. Gladstone Pk 237 B19
WOLVISTON
av. Hillside 232 E19
av. Hillside 232 G17
WOMBALANA
rd. Selby 467 B15
WOMBALANO
rd. Mt Evelyn 383 E5
WOMBAT
cr. Emerald 510 C3
ct. Eltham North 246 C18
ct. Greensborough 286 B10
ct. Westmeadows 236 J13
dr. Eltham North 246 A19
pl. S Morang 243 J1
rd. Mt Dandenong 382 H16
WOMBELANO
st. Menzies Ck 468 J18
WONDALEA
cr. Wantirna 422 A11
cr. Wantirna 422 A12
WONDALGA
st. Dandenong N 502 B17
WONDAREE
st. Rye 697 A9
WONDERLAND
tce. Mt Martha 668 L4
tce. Mt Martha 669 A4
WONDOORA
av. Ferny Creek 465 K3
WONGA
av. Pascoe Vale 280 L12
ct. Bentleigh E 457 B15
gr. McCrae 685 D10
la. McCrae 685 D10
pl. Gowanbrae 279 F5
rd. Millgrove 348 F1
rd. Ringwood 334 L19
rd. Ringwood 335 A19
rd. Ringwood 378 G5
rd. Ringwood 378 K2
rd. Ringwood N 334 L19
rd. Ringwood N 378 G5
rd. Ringwood N 378 K2
rd. Warranwood 334 J11
rd. Warranwood 335 A14
WONGALA
wy. Mooroolbark 337 C16
WONGANELLA
dr. Keilor East 278 C19
WONGELLA
ct. Aspendale 546 F7

WONG HEE
rd. Emerald 509 F10
rd.w,Emerald 509 E10
WONTHULONG
dr. Bayswater N 380 H18
WONUKA
ct. Croydon Hills 335 H16
ct. Doncaster E 331 J15
WOOD
cr. Burnside 318 F8
ct. Cranbourne 577 L19
rd. Nar Warrn S 553 E16
st. Avondale Ht 322 A14
st. Beaconsfield 555 B15
st. Beaumaris 530 B5
st. Bentleigh 496 E2
st. Deer Park 319 C18
st. Fitzroy 19 D16
st. Hawthorn 371 E16
st. Mornington 640 H19
st. N Melbourne 17 A12
st. Nunawading 376 H16
st. Preston 282 L18
st. Ringwood E 379 A14
st. Rosebud 684 B16
st. Sandringham 495 D13
st. S Geelong 703 C18
st. Springvale 500 B10
st. Strathmore 323 J2
st. Templestowe 330 J6
st. Templstw Lr 330 G6
st. Thomastown 241 G19
WOODALL
st. Black Rock 529 J5
WOODBINE
ct. Wantirna 423 B16
gr. Chelsea 546 L19
rd. Cranbourne N 578 C10
WOODBRIDGE
pl. Burnside 318 D6
WOODBURN
av. Berwick 539 G18
cr. Meadow Ht 237 J5
pl. Craigieburn 194 H1
rd. Hawthorn 416 C3
WOODBURY
ct. Avondale Ht 321 L15
ct. Nar Warrn S 552 F12
WOODBYNE
cr. Mornington 641 D19
WOOD-CHURCH
cl. Ringwood 335 C19
WOODCOCK
cl. Flemington 33 D3
ct. Cranbourne W 577 G16
ct. Dandenong N 536 C1
wk. Aspendale Gdn 546 G2
WOODCREST
rd. Vermont 420 L4
WOODDALE
gr. Donvale 377 B9
gr. Mitcham 377 B9
WOODED
wy. Montmorency 286 K12
WOODFERN
ct. Highton 705 K5
WOODFIELD
pl. Sunbury 143 B10
WOODFORD
av. Kew, off
Princess St 371 J10
cl. Ringwood E 379 F8
WOODFULL
ct. Keilor East 322 B1
rd. Lower Plenty 286 J17
st. Prahran 415 B10
wy. Epping 198 H17
wy. S Morang 198 H17
WOODGATE
st. Southbank 29 B2
st. Southbank 413 A1
st. S Melbourne 29 B2
st. S Melbourne 413 A1
WOODHALL
wyn.Donvale 376 K4
WOODHEAD
st. Fitzroy N 326 D20
WOODHENGE
dr. Cranbourne E 578 J20
WOODHILL
cl. Research 288 K6
pl. Mill Park 243 C6
WOODHOUSE
gr. Box Hill N 374 J8
rd. Doncaster E 332 C19
rd. Donvale 332 G20
WOODHURST
gr. Kalorama 383 E14
WOODINGTON
dr. Wheelers Hill 461 B18

WOODLAKE
pl. Wyndham Va 446 D8
WOODLAND
av. Croydon 379 H3
av. Mt Eliza 626 B12
cl. Blairgowrie 696 A5
ct. Dingley Village 533 E6
dr. Albanvale 319 A5
dr. Cheltenham 496 K16
gr. Briar Hill 286 K4
gr. Montmorency 286 L8
gr. Selby 467 C17
pl. Point Cook 450 E5
st. Doncaster 330 F18
st. Essendon 323 K2
st. Essendon 324 E3
st. Strathmore 323 K2
st. Strathmore 324 E3
wk. Lysterfield S 503 J11
wy. Gruyere 341 L5
WOODLAND PARK
ri. Croydon S 379 L13
WOODLANDS
av. Camberwell 417 C2
av. Clematis 509 B4
av. Cockatoo 511 D2
av. Emerald 509 B4
av. Kew East 372 H6
av. Pascoe Vale S 324 J5
av. Sassafras 426 G14
cr. Narre Warren 553 G9
ct. Craigieburn 150 D16
ct. Mordialloc 532 A15
dr. Braeside 532 K10
dr. Braeside 532 K15
dr. Greenvale 191 C18
dr. Somerville 644 D14
edg. Templestowe 332 B7
gr. Bundoora 284 G7
gr. Frankston 627 A4
gr. Frankston S 628 A4
gr. Malvern East 457 H7
gr. Safety Bch 686 H1
pl. Lalor 240 F9
rd. Cranbourne S 602 K13
rd. Cranbourne S 603 A14
rd. Heathmont 378 G18
ri. Macleod 285 K11
st. Clematis 508 L3
WOODLAWN
st. Richmond 26 A14
WOODLEA
cr. Craigieburn 150 D13
ct. Frankston 599 H14
dr. Glen Waverley 460 A11
pl. Ferntree Gly 463 F9
pl. Langwarrin 629 B10
st. Doncaster E 331 H15
WOODLEE
ri. Lilydale 338 J11
st. Dandenong 535 L4
WOODLEIGH
av. Upwey 466 B7
cr. Vermont S 420 L10
cr. Vermont S 421 A10
ct. Launching Pl 345 F16
pl. Gladstone Pk 237 B16
st. Thomastown 240 F14
WOODLEY
ct. Highton 701 H17
st. Narre Warren 553 F7
WOODLOT
la. Tooradin 652 E10
WOODLYN
cl. Mt Eliza 626 C18
mw. Mt Eliza 626 D17
WOODMASON
av. Somerville 645 C19
rd. Boronia 424 A8
st. Malvern 415 K10
WOODPECKER
ps. Chirnside Pk 337 G6
WOODRIDGE
cl. Montrose 381 J11
ct. Eltham 288 C7
WOODROW
ct. Cockatoo 511 B10
ct. Narre Warren 553 F12
WOODRUFF
ct. Hillside 231 L18
ct. Point Cook 451 B8
st. Kensington 33 F8
st. Port Melb 412 K1
WOODS
av. Mordialloc 532 A17
cl. Meadow Ht 194 D20
la. Ferny Creek 426 B16
pl. Rowville 463 K10
pl. Roxburgh Pk 193 L12
rd. Pearcedale 645 K6
rd. Truganina 405 G6
rd. Yan Yean 156 H6
st. Ascot Vale 323 F16
st. Balwyn 373 H9
st. Laverton 407 D17
st. Newport 410 E8
st. St Albans 276 F20
st. Yarraville 367 C15
WOODSIDE
av. Clayton 458 L15
av. Frankston S 627 J15
av. Ringwood 378 E10
cl. Hampton Pk 551 L16
cl. Somerville 645 B15
cr. Toorak 32 L12
cr. Toorak 414 L6
cr. Toorak 415 A6
ct. Werribee 447 J2
dr. Rowville 503 E1
mw. Roxburgh Pk 194 A8
rd. Seville 342 C12
st. Fitzroy N 19 K1
st. Fitzroy N 326 F20
WOODS POINT
rd. E Warburton 306 C20
rd. E Warburton 306 K20
rd. Warburton 350 B2
WOODSTOCK
cl. Sunbury 143 C6
ct. Doncaster E 332 A18
dr. Gladstone Pk 236 K20
pl. Springvale S 534 B2
rd. Mt Waverley 458 K1
st. Balaclava 414 G19
st. Canterbury 372 J15
st. Newtown 702 H13
WOODTHORPE
av. Rosebud W 683 C19
WOODVALE
cl. Essendon 324 B3
ct. Mill Park 242 E11
dr. Carrum Downs 601 C2
gr. Essendon 324 B3
gr. Rosebud 684 H16
rd. Boronia 423 L15
rd. Wesburn 348 A7
WOODVIEW
ct. Dandenong N 501 K11
ct. Wheelers Hill 461 B18
pl. Knoxfield 423 C20
WOODVILLE
av. Ormond 456 B10
rd. Mooroolbark 337 C17
st. Balwyn N 373 K2
WOODVILLE PARK
dr. Hoppers Csg 448 G6
WOODWARD
la. Dandenong 535 G6
st. Springvale 500 B17
WOODWORTH
cl. Endeavour Hl 537 E9
ct. Roxburgh Pk 194 B15
st. New Gisborne 79 B3
WOODY
lk. Croydon S 380 B13
WOODYARD
ct. Altona Mdw 451 H4
WOOLACOTT
st. Coburg 325 G5
WOOLART
st. Strathmore 279 H12
WOOLBOARD
rd. Port Melb 412 D1
WOOLCOCK
av. Kew East 372 D5
WOOLERT
st. Ashwood 418 C18
WOOLERTON
ct. Donvale 377 H7
WOOLHOUSE
st. Northcote 326 D13
WOOLLAHRA
av. Keysborough 534 E7
WOOLLEY
st. Essendon 323 F6
WOOLMER
ct. Croydon Hills 335 D16
ct. Frankston S 628 D15
WOOLNOUGH
dr. Epping 242 A2
dr. Mill Park 242 A5
WOOLPACK
rd. Bacchus Msh 264 J6
rd. Maddingley 264 J6
st. Hoppers Csg 447 L1
WOOLRICH
rd. Olinda 427 D11
WOOLSCOUR
la. Marshall 706 L5
WOOLSHED
av. St Albans 319 H10

WOOLSTON
dr. Frankston S 627 A8
WOOLSTONE
cl. Kealba 320 L1
cl. Kealba 321 A1
WOOLTANA
rd. Keysborough 535 A10
WOOLTON
av. Thornbury 326 E10
WOOLVET
av. Belmont 706 J4
WOOLWICH
dr. Mulgrave 500 D1
WOOMBI
av. Rosebud 683 K19
WOOMERA
av. Keysborough 535 B8
st. Rye 696 L7
st. Rye 697 A7
st. View Bank 285 H18
WOONA
ct. Yallambie 286 B14
pl. Keilor Dn 276 H14
WOONAH
st. Chadstone 418 A20
WOONGARRA
ct. Eltham North 246 D19
WOONSOCKET
ct. St Kilda 414 C13
WOONTON
cr. Rosebud 684 E19
st. Rosebud 684 G17
WOORABINDA
cl. Ringwood N 378 D3
WOORAL
ct. Notting Hill 459 H13
WOORALLA
dr. Mornington 642 C11
dr. Mt Eliza 642 B2
WOORARA
ct. Chirnside Pk 292 J13
WOORARRA
av. Doncaster E 332 C19
WOORAYL
st. Carnegie 456 J5
WOORIGOLEEN
dr. Keilor East 278 B20
rd. Toorak 415 E6
WOORILL
ct. Vermont 421 B3
WOORILLA
ct. Frankston 599 L19
WOORITE
pl. Keilor East 278 D17
pl. Wyndham Va 446 F13
WOORI YALLOCK
rd. Avonsleigh 471 C20
rd. Cockatoo 471 C20
rd. Cockatoo 471 J9
rd. Nangana 471 J9
WOORNACK
rd. Carnegie 456 J10
WOOTEN
cl. Frankston 599 H18
WOOTTEN
cr. Langwarrin 629 C1
WOOTTON
ct. Melton S 268 J11
gr. Caulfield N 415 D19
WORCESTER
rd. Gisborne 79 A15
st. Huntingdale 458 E12
st. Lilydale 338 E16
WORDEL
pl. Kurunjang 226 L13
WORDEN
ct. Whittington 704 C20
WORDSWORTH
av. Clayton S 499 C7
av. Heidelberg Ht 284 E20
cl. Delahey 275 C16
ct. Bundoora 242 G17
st. Moonee Pnd 324 E15
st. Mooroolbark 337 E19
st. St Kilda 414 B20
WORGAN
cl. Mill Park 242 E4
WORKS
la. Wantirna S 461 F2
WORNS
la. Yarrambat 200 F18
WORONORA
ct. Noble Park 534 H7
WORRALL
st. Burwood 419 B8
st. Croydon 380 F3

WORRELL
st. Dandenong N 502 D20
st. Nunawading 376 H8
WORROWING
ct. Kurunjang 227 D15
WORSLEY
av. Clayton S 499 E10
ct. Epping 197 J16
rd. Bangholme 574 L5
rd. Bangholme 575 A5
rd. Carrum Downs 574 K12
WORTHING
av. Burwood E 419 K12
av. Doncaster E 331 J18
ct. Mulgrave 500 H2
rd. Devon Mdw 604 J20
rd. Highett 496 C12
rd. Moorabbin 496 C12
WORTLEY
av. Mt Waverley 418 K12
WOTAMA
ct. Noble Park N 501 F16
WOTAN
cl. Keilor Dn 275 L14
dr. Epping 198 D20
WOYNA
av. Rosebud W 683 A20
WRAITH
st. Brunswick 325 G10
WRAP
ct. Nar Warrn S 578 L1
WRAY
cov. Sunshine W 364 C5
cr. Mt Evelyn 339 D18
st. Anglesea 713 H2
WRECK
st. Jan Juc 711 A20
WRECKYN
pl. N Melbourne 17 G15
st. N Melbourne 17 F15
WREDE
ct. Altona Mdw 451 H9
pl. Richmond 26 A6
WREFORD
rd. Blackburn S 419 H1
WREN
cl. Nunawading 376 G19
ct. Templstw Lr 329 L9
ct. Werribee 448 B9
ct. Whittlesea 96 B20
ct. Whittlesea 126 B1
dr. Noble Park N 501 B10
pl. Melton 226 G16
rd. Moorabbin 497 E9
st. Altona 408 H18
st. Hampton Pk 551 G9
WRENDALE
dr. Donvale 376 L7
WREXHAM
ct. Deer Park 318 K9
rd. Ferntree Gly 423 K20
rd. Windsor 414 K12
WRIDGWAY
av. Burwood 418 K10
WRIGHT
av. Donvale 376 H5
av. Upwey 465 J8
ct. Mill Park 242 H6
ct. Sunbury 142 H9
pl. Geelong, off Little Ryrie St 703 A8
rd. Avonsleigh 510 E1
rd. Emerald 470 E20
rd. Emerald 510 E1
rd. Keilor Park 277 H12
st. Bentleigh 455 K19
st. Blackburn 375 F12
st. Brighton 454 G13
st. Carrum 573 C9
st. Clayton 499 A1
st. Clifton Hill 20 H4
st. Essendon 324 A4
st. Hawthorn 372 C14
st. Hoppers Csg 448 L5
st. Kew East 372 G6
st. Laverton 407 D16
st. McKinnon 455 K17
st. Middle Park 29 K20
st. Middle Park 413 E10
st. Mt Evelyn 339 H16
st. Reservoir 282 J12
st. Richmond 26 F18
st. Seaford 599 H8
st. Sunshine 365 B7
st. Sunshine W 364 G6
st. The Basin 425 A12
st. Westmeadows 236 F14
WRIGHTS
ct. Ringwood 378 D19
tce. Prahran 32 L19
tce. Prahran 414 L10
tce. Prahran 415 A10
WRIGLEY
cr. Roxburgh Pk 194 D9
WRIXON
av. Brighton East 455 H16
st. Kew 372 D14
WROXHAM
ct. Fawkner 281 J2
gdn. Greensborough 286 K2
WUGGA
ct. Ashwood 418 C17
WUNALLA
rd. Seaford 573 E13
WUNDA
ct. St Andrews Bch 697 E19
st. Dromana 685 J10
WUNGAN
st. Macleod 284 L13
st. Macleod 285 A13
WUNGAROO
ct. Greensborough 244 K19
WUNNAMURRA
dr. Keilor East 278 B19
WURRINDI
ct. Frankston 628 B5
WURRUK
av. Preston 282 L17
st. Fawkner 281 H9
WURRUNJERRI
pl. View Bank 329 K1
WURUNDJERI
la. Smiths Gly 206 B7
wy. Docklands 23 A6
WUSTEMENN
pl. Richmond 26 D11
WYALL
st. Brunswick W 324 H9
WYALONG
st. Albion 320 J19
WYANDRA
wy. Rowville 463 F15
WYANGALA
ct. Ferntree Gly 464 A16
WYATT
ct. Glen Waverley 460 L5
pl. Melton W 226 C15
st. Seaford 573 C17
WYCLIFFE
cr. Eltham 288 A7
WYCOMBE
ri. Hampton Pk 551 D6
wy. Werribee 446 L18
WYDELL
cl. Bundoora 242 F19
WYE
ct. Ferntree Gly 463 E4
st. Lalor 240 H10
WYENA
st. Rye 697 B6
wy. Templestowe 332 A15
WYETT
ct. Bayswater N 380 J19
WYKEHAM
ct. Frankston 599 E14
WYLDWOOD
cl. Somerville 645 C19
WYLIE
st. Wesburn 348 B9
WYLIES
la. N Melbourne 17 C16
WYLYE
cl. Gladstone Pk 237 C18
WYMBIR
av. Preston 327 D1
WYMLET
st. Fawkner 281 G9
WYNDARA
ct. Ringwood 334 L20
ct. Ringwood 335 A20
WYNDARRA
cr. Dingley Village 533 A2
WYNDEN
dr. Frankston 628 B2
WYNDHAM
dr. Lynbrook 551 H15
pl. Rowville 502 K7
st. Werribee 447 H11
WYNEN
ct. Narre Warren 538 F17
WYNETTE
av. Balwyn 373 A10
av. Up Fntree Gly 465 D10
cl. Hampton Pk 551 J11
WYNFIELD
dr. Highton 701 H12
WYNNE
ct. Vermont S 421 D7
st. Rosebud W 698 K2
WYNNETTE
ct. Epping 198 D20
WYNNEWOOD
ct. Templestowe 331 K7
WYNNSTAY
rd. Mt Eliza 642 C7
rd. Prahran 415 C11
rd. Seaford 573 F17
WYNSTAY
gr. Ivanhoe 327 L14
WYNTON
ct. Eltham 288 B6
WYNTOUR
st. Whittlesea 96 D18
WYNVALE
ct. Eltham North 246 E20
ct. Eltham North 288 E1
WYNYARD
cr. Balwyn N 373 K8
st. Glen Waverley 420 F16
st. S Melbourne 30 B5
WYNYEH
st. Malvern East 416 L18
WYOLA
ct. Rowville 463 F15
WYONG
ct. Grovedale 706 E10
ct. Patterson L 573 K8
st. Keilor East 278 D19
WYPERFELD
av. Taylors Lakes 276 B9
cct. Caroline Spr 317 J7
WYRALLA
cr. Gisborne 78 H20
WYRUNGA
st. Ringwood E 379 C6
WYTON
cl. Westmeadows 237 B15
ct. Springvale S 533 K4
WYUNA
av. Hawthorn 371 F17
cl. Greensborough 244 A20
ct. Bentleigh 496 B5
ct. Frankston 628 B4
ct. Mt Martha 669 C9
ct. Portsea 677 K6
ct. Wheelers Hill 461 E17
dr. Noble Park 500 K15
la. Aspendale 546 B5
pde. Belmont 702 H18
rd. Caulfield N 455 L1
rd. Kangaroo Grnd 289 J3
rd. Research 289 J3
st. Brunswick W 324 J16
st. Fawkner 281 G10
st. Ferntree Gly 464 G2
st. Rosebud W 699 F1
wk. Mooroolbark 337 D15
WYVERN
wk. Kings Park 319 A1

X

XAVIER
av. Hawthorn 371 L14
ct. Sunbury 144 E10
dr. Wheelers Hill 460 L18
dr. Wheelers Hill 461 A18
gr. Reservoir 283 C15
st. Oak Park 280 A11

Y

Y
st. Ashburton 417 F15
YACHT
ct. Mornington 640 B17
ct. Taylors Lakes 275 G9
YACKATOON
av. Aspendale 546 G7
YAGOONA
av. Noble Park 534 F6
YALAMBEE
av. Aspendale 546 F6
YALDARA
cl. Mt Waverley 419 A18
dr. Berwick 553 K3
YALE
ct. Meadow Ht 238 C2
ct. Sunbury 144 D10
ct. Whittington 704 A19
dr. Epping 197 A20
pl. Bundoora 284 J2
st. Melton S 268 J5
wk. Kings Park 275 A20
YALITA
rd. Vermont S 420 L8
YALLAMBA
pl. Heathmont 379 B19
YALLAMBEE
ct. Dandenong N 501 F12
pl. Burnside 318 F7
wy. Croydon 380 H1
wy. Olinda 427 E6
YALLAMBIE
rd. Macleod 285 F11
rd. Yallambie 285 F11
YALLAROO
ct. Doncaster E 331 H17
YALLEON
dr. Kurunjang 226 K7
dr. Kurunjang 226 L8
YALLOP
ct. Keilor East 321 L1
YALLOURN
pde. Ringwood 377 L15
st. Ardeer 320 D20
st. Ardeer 364 D1
YALONGA
av. Werribee 448 B19
YALTA
cl. Greensborough 244 E18
ct. Clayton S 499 E15
YALTARA
av. Bundoora 284 K4
cl. Cranbourne W 577 E20
dr. Wyndham Va 446 H15
YALUMBA
ct. Berwick 554 E20
ct. Vermont S 421 E10
wy. Roxburgh Pk 194 B7
YAMALA
dr. Frankston S 626 E8
YAMBIE
la. Chadstone 458 E4
YAMBILL
av. Rosebud 700 L8
YAMBLA
st. Clifton Hill 20 H8
YAMBUK
ct. Vermont S 421 G8
YANAKIE
cr. Caulfield N 455 E1
YANCHEP
ct. Taylors Lakes 276 C10
YANDELL
cl. Greensborough 286 E1
cl. Vermont S 420 K13
YANDIAH
ct. Frankston 600 G14
YANDILLA
ct. Berwick 553 E4
st. Balwyn 374 A10
YANDO
pl. Wyndham Va 446 E13
st. Greensborough 285 K1
YANDOIT
ct. Meadow Ht 237 L6
YANDRA
ct. Ferntree Gly 464 E1
YANGA
la. Taylors Hill 274 K11
YANGOORA
ct. Mt Waverley 459 F5
pl. Greensborough 286 L2
YANIGAN
dr. Glen Waverley 420 D18
YANINA
ct. Croydon 336 G20
ct. Glen Waverley 460 H5
YANKOS
dr. Werribee 448 E18
YANN
st. Preston 326 K4
YANNATHAN
st. Tooradin 651 J7
YANNUGA
st. Rye 697 C8
YAN YEAN
pl. St Albans 320 D13
rd. Diamond Ck 244 K11
rd. Doreen 156 L19
rd. Doreen 156 L5
rd. Doreen 201 B7
rd. Plenty 244 K11
rd. Yarrambat 200 H20
rd. Yarrambat 201 A16
YARALLA
cr. St Helena 244 K18
cr. Sunshine W 364 F7
ct. Keysborough 534 E10
ct. Meadow Ht 194 D20
rd. Oakleigh S 497 F1
rd. Panton Hill 204 A20
rd. Panton Hill 247 L2
YARANA
rd. Alphington 327 J17
st. Ferntree Gly 463 E1
YARANG
ct. Heathmont 378 E19
YARCK
ct. Sunbury 143 C11
ct. Westmeadows 237 H11
YARCOMBE
cr. Craigieburn 194 B4
YARDIE
ct. Lower Plenty 287 B17
YARDLEY
ct. Berwick 554 F20
ct. Forest Hill 420 J4
ct. Frankston 600 J16
ct. Maidstone 366 F4
dr. Wheelers Hill 460 L20
dr. Wheelers Hill 461 A20
st. Maidstone 366 E3
YARILLA
rd. Sassafras 426 D14
YARINGA
ct. Rye 698 A5
YARLA
ct. Frankston 628 H1
YARMOUTH
av. St Albans 320 G6
st. Ringwood 378 C17
YAR-ORRONG
rd. Toorak 415 G7
YARRA
av. Reservoir 283 D11
bvd. Burnley 371 D16
bvd. Burnley 415 D1
bvd. Burnley 415 H2
bvd. Kew 20 H19
bvd. Kew 20 K13
bvd. Kew 371 B8
ct. Dandenong N 502 A10
ct. Keilor 276 L12
ct. Mentone 531 G7
ct. Oakleigh S 497 H6
ct. Templstw Lr 330 A7
ct. Yarra Glen 208 L20
ct. Yarra Glen 209 A20
gr. Hawthorn 371 F18
la. Hawthorn 371 K20
la. Caroline Spr, off Brookside Ct 318 B6
pl. Craigieburn 150 G16
pl. S Melbourne 30 A2
rd. Croydon 335 K18
rd. Croydon Hills 335 J11
rd. Croydon N 335 J11
rd. Wonga Park 335 H1
st. Abbotsford 20 B16
st. Geelong 703 A11
st. Hawthorn 371 F18
st. Heidelberg 328 K8
st. Heidelberg 329 A8
st. Kew 371 G9
st. Richmond 32 F2
st. Richmond 414 J1
st. S Geelong 702 L14
st. S Melbourne 30 A2
st. South Yarra 32 C8
st. South Yarra 414 G4
st. Warrandyte 289 H20
st. Werribee 447 E7
st. Williamstown 411 C10
st. Yarra Glen 208 L20
st. Yarra Glen 209 A20
st. Yarra Jctn 346 L16
st. Yarra Jctn 347 A16
wy. Taylors Hill 274 H14
YARRA BANK
ct. Abbotsford 20 F19
ct. Abbotsford 370 J10
hwy. Melbourne 4 J7
hwy. Melbourne 24 J13
hwy. Melbourne 25 E17
YARRABEE
ct. Frankston 628 B4
ct. Mt Waverley 418 K19
dr. Hoppers Csg 448 F5
rd. Mt Dandenong 426 F2
ri. Pk Orchards 333 K14
YARRA BEND
rd. Fairfield 371 B1
YARRABIN
dr. Mt Martha 656 D8
st. Brunswick W 324 H9
YARRA BRAE
cl. Wonga Park 291 J11
YARRA BRAES
rd. Eltham 288 B15

YARRABURN
- cl. Bentleigh E 497 D3
- gr. Scoresby 462 B6

YARRADALE
- ct. Watsonia N 243 F19
- rd. Toorak 415 E2

YARRADUCT
- pl.n, Croydon 379 H8
- pl.s, Croydon 379 H8

YARRAFORD
- av. Alphington 327 F20

YARRA GLEN
- dr. Yarra Glen 253 B1
- rd. Coldstream 295 D7
- rd. Yering 253 C6
- rd. Yering 295 D7

YARRA HILL
- cl. Lower Plenty 287 B20
- la. Chirnside Pk 336 F7

YARRA JUNCTION-NOOJEE
- rd. Yarra Jctn 347 B16

YARRALEA
- st. Alphington 327 K20

YARRALEEN
- pl. Bulleen 329 F13

YARRA LINKS
- wy. Bentleigh E 497 D7

YARRALOCH
- wy. Gruyere 298 G6
- wy. Gruyere 298 L20

YARRALUMLA
- dr. Langwarrin 602 C17

YARRAM
- cr. Clayton 498 H2
- ct. Frankston 600 G15
- ct. Kings Park 275 D20

YARRAMAN
- rd. Noble Park 534 J4

YARRAM CREEK
- la. Pt Lonsdale 707 G13
- la. Swan Bay 707 G13

YARRAN
- ct. Hampton Pk 551 E13
- gr. Bayswater 423 D7

YARRARIDGE
- dr. Chirnside Pk 336 K7

YARRA RIVER
- ct. N Warrandyte 290 F9

YARRAVALE
- rd. Kew 371 G8

YARRA VALLEY
- bvd. Bulleen 329 H8
- bvd. Chirnside Pk 336 K6

YARRA VIEW
- ct. N Warrandyte 289 K15
- rd. Yarra Glen 251 J6
- rd. Yarra Glen 252 K2

YARRAVIEW
- pde. Rosanna 284 K17
- rd. Chirnside Pk 292 H13

YARRAWATERS
- rd. S Morang 198 K17

YARRAWONGA
- wy. Burwood 418 B5

YARRAYNE
- st. Rye 697 B8

YARRBAT
- av. Balwyn 373 G11

YARRINUP
- av. Chadstone 418 D20

YARROW
- ct. Berwick 554 D17

YARROWEE
- st. Ferntree Gly 464 H8

YARTO
- ct. Meadow Ht 238 B2

YASMIN
- ct. Hampton Pk 551 H13
- ct. Rosebud W 699 H3

YASS
- ct. Patterson L 573 L9

YATALA
- ct. Sorrento 679 D15

YATAMA
- ct. Greensborough 244 D20
- ct. Hoppers Csg 448 J6
- ct. Mt Waverley 418 K18

YATE
- mw. Berwick 553 G6

YATES
- ct. Mooroolbark 381 E2
- ct. The Basin 424 K9
- pl. Mill Park 243 D4
- rd. Wattle Glen 246 L1
- wyn. Doncaster E 332 H11

YATTON
- pl. Craigieburn 194 D3

YAWLA
- st. Bentleigh 455 H17

YEA
- ct. Croydon Hills 335 J16
- ct. Forest Hill 376 E19
- rd. Whittlesea 96 J18
- st. Dallas 238 G12

YEADON
- ct. Epping 197 L17

YEAMAN
- rd. Montrose 382 A11

YEATS
- dr. Delahey 275 E14

YELLOW BOX
- tce. Heidelberg 329 E5

YELLOWBOX
- av. S Morang 199 J12

YELLOW GUM
- rd. Delahey 275 C11
- ri. Greensborough 244 H15

YELLOWGUM
- bvd. Sunbury 143 J7

YELLOWSTONE
- cl. Rowville 462 J17

YELTA
- ct. Coolaroo 238 F7

YEMAYA
- ct. Watsonia 285 C4

YENDA
- ct. Hoppers Csg 448 E8

YENDON
- cl. Mitcham 377 G11
- rd. Carnegie 456 F7

YENEDA
- st. Balwyn N 374 A7

YENNO
- dr. Derrimut 363 G11

YENNORA
- ct. Keysborough 534 E9

YEO
- ct. Meadow Ht 237 K3

YEOMAN
- ct. Pk Orchards 334 B13

YEOMANS
- ct. Box Hill S 418 H3
- rd. Kangaroo Grnd 290 C5
- st. Northcote 326 J18

YEOVIL
- ct. Craigieburn 150 C18
- ct. Wheelers Hill 460 L18
- ct. Wheelers Hill 461 A17
- rd. Glen Iris 417 H10

YERAMBA
- ct. Beaconsfld Up 542 K12
- rt. Berwick 553 J2

YERING
- ct. Bayswater 423 G7
- pl. Chirnside Pk 336 K7
- st. Coolaroo 238 F7

YERLATA
- ct. Portsea 678 B6

YERONGA
- av. Upwey 465 J12

YERRAWA
- dr. Watsonia 285 H8

YERRIM
- *la. Sydenham, off Themeda Wyn 274 L8*

YERRIN
- st. Balwyn 373 G12

YERTCHUK
- av. Ashwood 418 E14

YETTA
- ct. Keilor East 321 K6

YEW
- ct. Cranbourne N 577 K5

YEWERS
- av. Mt Eliza 641 J6
- st. Footscray 367 H9
- st. Sunshine 365 G3

YIANNIS
- ct. Springvale 499 G5

YILEEN
- ct. Ashwood 418 C17
- ct. Donvale 333 A18

YILLEEN
- cl. Thomastown 240 D15
- cl. Yallambie 286 C13

YIMBALA
- cr. Greensborough 286 L2

YINNAR
- st. Dallas 238 D8

YIOTA
- ct. Berwick 553 L17
- pl. Sydenham 274 K7

YOLANDE
- ct. Templestowe 331 E7

YOLANTA
- ct. Seabrook 450 J5
- pl. Sunshine W 364 C9

YOLLAND
- st. Tootgarook 698 G2

YONDE
- ct. Greensborough 243 L18

YONGA
- rd. Balwyn 373 L11

YONGALA
- ct. Clayton S 498 J8
- ct. Grovedale 705 L15
- st. Balwyn 373 E9

YONI
- ct. Hallam 552 C1

YOORALA
- rd. Rye 697 J6

YOORALLA
- st. Ashwood 418 D17

YOOTHA
- ct. Rye 697 C6

YORK
- av. Ivanhoe East 328 F14
- av. Oakleigh 458 C11
- cl. Altona Mdw 451 L2
- ct. Frankston 600 D17
- ct. Heathmont 422 F2
- ct. Keysborough 534 L9
- ct. Wantirna S 422 L11
- ct. Wantirna S 423 A11
- ct. Warranwood 334 K14
- la. Surrey Hills 373 L20
- la. Surrey Hills 417 L1
- pl. Bundoora 284 L1
- pl. Carlton 18 F15
- pl. Fitzroy N 19 A7
- pl. Prahran 32 G19
- pl. Prahran 414 J10
- pl. S Melbourne 29 K3
- rd. Berwick 554 C7
- rd. Glen Iris 416 H12
- rd. Montrose 382 K3
- rd. Mt Evelyn 382 K3
- rd. Mt Evelyn 383 A3
- st. Airport W 279 A15
- st. Albion 320 J18
- st. Bentleigh E 457 B20
- st. Blackburn S 419 E5
- st. Bonbeach 545 F13
- st. Bonbeach 573 A2
- st. Brighton 454 L16
- st. Brighton 455 A16
- st. Bulleen 329 H12
- st. Caulfield S 455 E8
- st. Collingwood 19 K14
- st. Eltham 287 G10
- st. Fitzroy N 19 A7
- st. Geelong 702 K2
- st. Glenroy 279 H6
- st. Glen Waverley 420 G16
- st. Hawthorn 372 B14
- st. Mont Albert 374 B15
- st. Moonee Pnd 323 K13
- st. Mornington 640 E17
- st. Pascoe Vale S 280 J20
- st. Prahran 32 G20
- st. Prahran 414 J10
- st. Reservoir 282 D15
- st. Richmond 26 A6
- st. Rosebud 700 F3
- st. St Kilda W 413 K12
- st. Sorrento 678 F10
- st. S Melbourne 3 A18
- st. S Melbourne 29 F4
- st. S Melbourne 413 D2
- st. Strathmore 279 K19
- st. Surrey Hills 374 B15
- st. Warburton 305 B19
- st. Yarraville 367 E16

YORKMINSTER
- av. Wantirna 422 F9

YORKSHIRE
- ct. Epping 198 B16
- st. Blackburn N 376 B11
- st. Pascoe Vale 280 L15
- st. Richmond 32 F2
- st. Richmond 414 J1

YORSTON
- ct. Elsternwick 455 B5

YOSE
- st. Ferntree Gly 464 B2

YOUELL
- st. Footscray 367 G12

YOULDEN
- st. Kensington 33 H6

YOUNG
- ct. Delahey 275 D14
- rd. Hallam 538 A15
- st. Albert Park 29 L14
- st. Albert Park 413 F7
- st. Ashburton 417 F14
- st. Bacchus Msh 222 C17
- st. Beaconsfld Up 542 H12
- st. Box Hill 374 H14
- st. Brighton 454 F15
- st. Coburg 325 E3
- st. Donvale 377 D7
- st. Epping 197 E17
- st. Fitzroy 19 C16
- st. Fitzroy 25 B1
- st. Frankston 627 B1
- st. Glen Iris 416 C14
- st. Ivanhoe 328 C14
- st. Kew 371 B11
- st. Moonee Pnd 324 C14
- st. Oakleigh 458 A15
- st. Preston 327 A4
- st. St Kilda E 414 H16
- st. Seddon 367 C10
- st. Springvale 500 A6
- st. Sunshine W 364 G3

YOUNGA
- rd. Warburton 306 A18

YOUNGER
- av. Caulfield S 455 E12
- av. Rye 696 J1
- ct. Kew 371 F11
- st. Coburg 325 L3

YOUNGMAN
- st. Preston 283 A19

YOUNGS
- la. N Melbourne 17 B12
- rd. St Andrews 204 K1
- rd. St Andrews 205 A2
- rd. Smiths Gly 205 A2
- rd. Yarrambat 201 B13

YOUTH
- rd. Eltham 287 G8

YOU YANGS
- av. Dromana 686 D8

YOW YOW RISING
- . St Andrews 207 C1

YUILE
- ct. Cranbourne 603 K5
- st. Ashburton 417 D13

YUILLE
- st. Brighton 494 K4
- st. Frankston 627 E5
- st. Frankston S 627 A8
- st. Geelong West 702 F5
- st. Melton 227 B18

YUILLES
- rd. Mornington 640 H19

YUKON
- ct. Rowville 462 J17

YULONG
- ct. Greensborough 286 D11

YULUMA
- ct. Frankston 600 G16

YUNGERA
- st. Fawkner 281 G9

YUNKI
- ct. Ashwood 418 B18

YUNUPINGU
- ct. Mill Park 198 H20
- ct. Mill Park 242 H1

YUONGA
- ct. Lalor 240 J9

YURANA
- ct. St Helena 244 J18

YURNGA
- av. Olinda 427 E14
- rd. Menzies Ck 467 L12

YUROKE
- rd. Greenvale 193 A13
- st. Fawkner 281 G9

YURUGA
- ct. Mooroolbark 337 A14
- dr. Macclesfield 470 J2

YVETTE
- ct. Aspendale Gdn 547 B7
- ct. Epping 198 H20
- dr. Rowville 503 A2
- pl. Mt Waverley 459 E1

YVONNE
- av. Croydon S 379 J11
- cl. Mill Park 242 L8
- ct. Heatherton 497 G15
- ct. Rowville 502 J2
- ct. Wheelers Hill 460 H6
- pl. Melton W 226 C18
- rd. Mt Dandenong 426 G4
- st. Belmont 706 D4

Z

ZACHARY HICKS
- cr. Endeavour Hl 537 B7

ZADOC
- ct. Blackburn S 419 D4

ZAGREB
- ct. Keilor Park 277 K15

ZAMMIT
- ct. Frankston 628 D3

ZANDER
- av. Nunawading 376 D11
- ct. Doncaster 331 D20

ZARA
- ct. Albanvale 318 L5
- ct. Frankston 600 C20

ZARRO
- st. Scoresby 462 E6

ZEAL
- st. Brunswick W 324 K9
- st. New Gisborne 79 B1

ZEALANDIA
- rd.e, Croydon N 336 C16
- rd.w, Croydon N 336 C16

ZEALLY BAY
- rd. Torquay 711 L8

ZEBRAFINCH
- ct. Carrum Downs 600 H5

ZEBRINA
- cl. Hillside 273 J2

ZEDEL
- ct. Keilor Dn 276 A11

ZEEHAN
- rd. Boronia 423 F13

ZEISING
- ct. Boronia 423 L12

ZELKOVA
- tce. Bundoora 242 D14

ZENA
- dr. S Morang 199 L16
- pl. Berwick 553 K2

ZENITH
- rd. Dandenong S 550 B3
- st. Pascoe Vale 280 G15

ZENNOR
- ct. Craigieburn 194 G4

ZEPLIN
- pl. W Melbourne 23 G1

ZERBE
- av. Doncaster E 332 C14

ZERFAS
- st. Scoresby 462 G6

ZETLAND
- rd. Mont Albert 374 E14
- st. Abbotsford 26 G1

ZEUS
- ct. Chelsea Ht 547 H18
- ct. Templstw Lr 330 K17

ZEVENBOOM
- la. Melbourne 2 A6
- la. Melbourne 24 A4

ZIEMA
- ct. Thomastown 240 G16
- ct. Werribee 446 H18

ZIG ZAG
- rd. Belgrave Ht 466 G20
- rd. Belgrave S 506 H1
- rd. Eltham North 245 L20
- rd. Eltham North 287 L3
- rd. Hurstbridge 202 L14
- rd.n, Eltham North 246 A19

ZILLA
- ct. Dandenong S 535 K20

ZIMMER
- ct. Campbellfield 239 B9
- ct. Epping 241 L1

ZINA
- gr. Mooroolbark 381 H4

ZINNEA
- ct. Mill Park 243 B11

ZINNIA
- st. Reservoir 282 B10

ZIRCON
- cl. Narre Warren 539 E14
- st. Wyndham Va 446 E14

ZITA
- st. Mulgrave 500 G3

ZODIAC
- st. Burwood 418 B13

ZOE
- ct. Northcote 326 D13

ZOLA
- ct. Berwick 554 E20
- ct. Glen Waverley 420 A14

ZSI ZSI
- ct. Somerville 644 E14

ZULU
- rt. Keilor Dn 275 J12

ZURZOLO
- tce. Epping 198 E19

AIRPORTS / AIRFIELDS

BAYS, BEACHES, ETC

Stony Creek
North Warrandyte.............289 K11
Tottenham.........................365 J9
Stony Creek Backwash.........367 E19
Strathbaan Creek.................349 D7
Stringybark Creek................340 E16
Sugarloaf Reservoir.............250 F7
Sullivan Bay.........................679 E12
Sunnyside Beach.................641 B4
Surf Beach...........................710 C8
Sutton Lake..........................462 J16
Swan Bay.............................708 H7
Sweetwater Creek................626 J6
Tanti Creek...........................640 G11
Tassells Creek......................669 C12
Taylors Creek.......................276 J14
Taylors Lake.........................275 K5
Thompsons Gully..................334 D2
Ti-tree Creek.........................468 H11
Toolern Creek.......................227 D17
Toomuc Creek.......................558 E17
Tootgarook Beach................698 D1
Troup Creek.........................538 D20
Troup Creek East Branch......539 D18
Tugwell Creek.......................348 L18
Tyrone Foreshore Reserve....680 H20
Walsdorf Creek.....................540 G17
Wandin Yallock Creek...........341 K11
Waterfall Creek.....................700 J1
Watery Gully.........................246 L8
Watkins Bay.........................530 A14
Watsons Creek
Kangaroo Ground.............291 D2
Panton Hill.......................206 A19
Wattle Creek
Cockatoo..........................510 B1
Seville East.......................343 C19
Waurn Ponds Creek.............706 F6
Weeroona Bay......................666 J19
Werribee River
Bacchus Marsh.................221 B19
Werribee...........................447 C11
Wild Cattle Creek..................341 C15
Williamstown Beach.............411 C18
Woori Yallock Creek.............469 A6
Wylies Creek........................603 L16
Yankee Jims Creek...............347 H7
Yan Yean Reservoir..............126 K18
Yarra Creek............................96 D11
Yarraman Creek....................535 D2
Yarra River
Christmas Hills..................251 D17
Fairfield............................371 C7
Ivanhoe............................328 B19
Southbank..........................23 D16
Yuroke Creek........................193 E17
Zeally Bay............................712 E9

CARAVAN, TOURIST & MOBILE HOME PARKS

ALTONA NORTH
Half Moon
cnr Geelong & Millers Rds...365 K16
ANGLESEA
Driftwood
45 Murray St......................713 F5
Family
Cameron Rd......................713 K6
Narambi
11 Camp Rd......................713 H2
ARDEER
West City
610 Ballarat Rd..................320 D16
ASPENDALE
Seabreeze
151 Nepean Hwy...............546 D8
ATTWOOD
Melbourne Airport
Caravan Village
360 Mickleham Rd............236 L12
BACCHUS MARSH
Cherry Inn
Bacchus Marsh Rd............221 H15
BANGHOLME
Willow Lodge
418 Frankston-
Dandenong Rd.................549 G13
BELMONT
Barwon
Barrabool Rd.....................702 J16
Billabong
59 Barrabool Rd...............702 E16
Riverglen
Barrabool Rd.....................702 E16
Sherwood Forest
70 Bailey St.......................706 J5
Southside
87 Barrabool Rd...............702 E16
BLAIRGOWRIE
William Rd........................680 B20
BONBEACH
Chelsea Gardens
100 Broadway...................547 E20
Patterson River
473 Station St..................573 A7
BRAYBROOK
Ashley Gardens
Holiday Village
Ashley St..........................366 D1
CAMPBELLFIELD
Northside
cnr Hume Hwy &
Cooper St..........................195 B19
Sylvan
1780 Hume Hwy...............239 D10
CARRUM DOWNS
Caravan Gardens
Frankston-Dandenong Rd..600 H1
Kingston Lodge
51 Frankston-
Dandenong Rd.................574 L16
CHELSEA HEIGHTS
Blue Gum Park
Wells Rd...........................547 E9
COBURG NORTH
Melbourne
265 Elizabeth St................282 C13
CRAIGIEBURN
Apollo Gardens
Hume Hwy........................194 L7
DANDENONG SOUTH
Shawlands
South Gippsland Hwy........536 F17
Twin Bridge
370 Frankston-
Dandenong Rd.................549 K12
DINGLEY VILLAGE
Five Ways
597 Lower Dandenong Rd..533 G10
DONCASTER EAST
Crystal Brook
Warrandyte Rd..................332 H4
DROMANA
8 Nepean Hwy...................687 A2
Kangerong
105 Point Nepean Rd........686 D3
Ponderosa
10 Ponderosa Pl...............686 J3
Waihola Lodge
8 William St......................686 E3
FRANKSTON SOUTH
Holiday Village
cnr Robinsons &
Frankston-Flinders Rds......627 J12
HEALESVILLE
Ashgrove
Don Rd.............................258 G8
Badger Creek
Don Rd.............................258 K12
HIGHTON
Geelong
Colac Rd...........................705 H10
JAN JUC
Sunset Strip......................711 A17
LANGWARRIN
Log Cabin
cnr Skye Rd &
McClelland Dr...................600 K19
LAVERTON NORTH
Honey Hush
6 Leakes Rd......................407 G8
LILYDALE
Pine Hill
Warburton Hwy.................339 H6
MCCRAE
Bendemeer
701 Point Nepean Rd.........684 L12
MONBULK
Baynes Park
Baynes Park Rd.................428 A18
MORNINGTON
98 Bungower Rd...............641 E15
NARRE WARREN
Fullard Rd.........................553 A7
OFFICER
Blue Gum Eastside
Brunt Rd...........................555 J19
PAKENHAM
cnr Princes Hwy &
Racecourse Rd..................585 C5
POINT LONSDALE
Beacon Resort
78 Bellarine Hwy...............707 K19
Four Winds
40 Bellarine Hwy...............708 A20
Golightly
Bowen Rd.........................710 J1
Royal
Point Lonsdale Rd............710 H2
Spring Hill
84 Bellarine Hwy...............707 K19
Springs
54 Bellarine Hwy...............707 L20
PORTSEA
70 Back Beach Rd.............677 J3
QUEENSCLIFF
Recreation Reserve............708 L20
Victoria Park.....................708 L19
ROSEBUD
Amberlee
306 Jetty Rd......................700 E6
Carrington
110 Elizabeth Dr...............700 H3
Heather Lodge
1219 Point Nepean Rd......683 L16
Kenray
138 Eastbourne Rd...........684 E20
McRose
753 Point Nepean Rd........684 H13
Romany
765 Point Nepean Rd........684 G13
Rosebud Model
1057 Point Nepean Rd......683 G17
Siesta
759 Point Nepean Rd........684 G13
Sunrise
27 Rosebud Pde................684 C16
Tudor
1 Old Cape Schanck Rd....700 D7
ROSEBUD WEST
Navarac
1553 Point Nepean Rd.......683 F18
Sundowner Willows
349 Eastbourne Rd...........683 D20
ROWVILLE
Stud Rd............................502 G5
RYE
Foreshore Reserve
Point Nepean Rd...............697 C1
Glenvue
Glenvue Rd.......................697 C10
Kanasta Karavan Kamp
9 Sinclair Av......................697 E4
SAFETY BEACH
Halcyon
107 Marine Dr...................668 L17
Miami
82 Marine Dr.....................668 K18
Robin Park
90 Marine Dr.....................668 K18
Valley Holiday Park
154 Marine Dr...................669 A14
SEAFORD
Beach
257 Nepean Hwy...............599 C9
Gladeswood
200 Nepean Hwy...............599 C6
The Shade
260 Nepean Hwy...............599 C9
SORRENTO
Foreshore Reserve
Point Nepean Rd...............679 G16
Midway
86 St Pauls Rd.................678 J13
Nautilus
Point Nepean Rd...............678 L10
Rose
791 Melbourne Rd............678 H11
SPRINGVALE
Sundowner
870 Princes Hwy...............500 C6
SPRINGVALE SOUTH
Caravan Court
641 Springvale Rd.............533 K5
SUNSHINE
Sunshine
252 Sunshine Rd...............365 F7
TOORADIN
Tooradin Station Rd...........651 G7
TORQUAY
Bell St...............................712 A13
Bernell
Surfcoast Hwy..................711 K8
Zeally Bay
cnr Darian Rd &
The Esplanade..................712 D5
WANTIRNA
Wantirna Park
203 Mountain Hwy............422 B8
WARBURTON
Woods Point Rd................350 B2
WILLIAMSTOWN NORTH
Hobsons Bay
158 Kororoit Creek Rd.......410 G13
YARRA JUNCTION
Doon Reserve
Doon Rd...........................346 K11
Jacyallock
Tarrango Rd......................348 A20
YARRAVILLE
Footscray
163 Somerville Rd.............366 L14

CLUBS

ALTONA RSL
31 Sargood St...................409 C19
ANGLESEA RSL
Murray St..........................713 G5
ASPENDALE/EDITHVALE RSL
111 Kinross Av
Edithvale...........................546 K10

BACCHUS MARSH RSL
201 Main St 222 C17
BAYSWATER RSL
626 Mountain Hwy 423 D4
BEAUMARIS RSL
489 Balcombe Rd 529 L6
BENTLEIGH RSL
538 Centre Rd 456 D20
BERWICK RSL
17 Langmore La 554 E8
BORONIA RSL
198 Dorset Rd 424 D14
BOX HILL RSL
26 Nelson Rd 374 J13
CAMBERWELL CITY RSL
403 Camberwell Rd 416 K3
CARLTON RSL
60 Arness St
Carlton North 18 K2
CAULFIELD RSL
4 St Georges Rd
Elsternwick 454 L5
CHELSEA RSL
4 Thames Prm 546 K18
CHELTENHAM/
MOORABBIN RSL
293 Centre Dandenong Rd ..531 K2
CLAYTON RSL
163 Carinish Rd 498 L2
COBURG RSL
323 Sydney Rd 325 G4
CRANBOURNE RSL
South Gippsland Hwy 604 F6
DONCASTER EAST RSL
cnr Doncaster Rd &
Leeds St 375 K1
DROMANA/RED HILL RSL
cnr Gibson & Noel Sts 686 B5
EAST MALVERN RSL
9 Ellison St 417 A19
ELTHAM RSL
804 Main Rd 287 G11
ELWOOD RSL
2 Pine Av 454 F6
EMERALD RSL
Memorial Av 509 E4
EPPING RSL
Harvest Home Rd 197 C8
ESSENDON AFL
cnr Napier & Brewster Sts ..324 B6
FAIRFIELD RSL
7 Railway Pl 327 D18
FAWKNER RSL
135 Lorne St 281 F10
FITZROY AFL
2 Charles St
Northcote 326 F17
FLEMINGTON/
KENSINGTON RSL
25 Rankins Rd
Kensington 34 B6
FOOTSCRAY RSL
48 Geelong Rd 367 D7
FRANKSTON RSL
183 Cranbourne Rd 627 L2
GEELONG RSL
50 Barwon Heads Rd
Belmont 702 K19
GEMBROOK RSL
Main Rd 512 K11
GLENROY RSL
186 Glenroy Rd 280 A6
GREENSBOROUGH RSL
111 Main St 286 C3
HAMPTON RSL
25 Holyrood St 494 J6
HAWTHORN AFL
37 Linda Cr 371 K16
HAWTHORN RSL
Glenferrie Rd 371 L18
HEALESVILLE RSL
275 Maroondah Hwy 213 K18
HEIDELBERG RSL
87 Mount St 328 J8
HEIDELBERG WEST RSL
180 Bell St 328 E6
HIGHETT RSL
1 Station St 496 E13
KEILOR EAST RSL
16 Hoffmans Rd
Essendon 323 B7
KEW RSL
63 Cotham Rd 371 L10
LILYDALE RSL
52 Anderson St 338 F6
MARIBYRNONG/
MAIDSTONE RSL
56 Raleigh Rd
Maribyrnong 323 D14
MELBOURNE AFL
26 Jolimont Tce 25 E10
MELTON RSL
12 McKenzie St 227 A19
MENTONE RSL
9 Palermo St 531 B11
MIDDLE PARK RSL
Canterbury Rd 30 G20
MITCHAM RSL
26 McDowall St 377 C12
MONTMORENCY RSL
Petrie Park,
Mountain View Rd 286 K10
NEWPORT RSL
cnr Market & Derwent Sts ..410 L8
NOBLE PARK RSL
1128 Heatherton Rd 500 J19
NORTH BALWYN RSL
Centre Wy, Trentwood Estate
Balwyn North 373 L2
NORTHCOTE RSL
496 High St 326 J12
NORTH MELBOURNE AFL
Fogarty St 34 H14
NORTH & WEST
MELBOURNE RSL
25 Rankins Rd
Kensington 34 B6
OAKLEIGH RSL
95 Drummond St 457 K9
PAKENHAM RSL
James St 584 K5
PASCOE VALE RSL
40 Cumberland Rd 280 H18
PRAHRAN RSL
301 High St 414 J11
PRESTON RSL
Kelvin Gr 326 L1
QUEENSCLIFF RSL
9 King St 709 A19
RESERVOIR RSL
251 Spring St 282 L10
RETURNED NURSES
Anzac House,
4 Collins St
Melbourne 24 K6
RETURNED SERVICEWOMEN
Anzac House, 4 Collins St
Melbourne 24 K6
RICHMOND AFL
Punt Rd 25 J14
RICHMOND RSL
401 Church St 26 F16
RINGWOOD RSL
16 Station St 378 E13
ROSEBUD RSL
117 Eastbourne Rd 684 C20
RYE RSL
5 Nelson St 697 F3
ST KILDA AFL
Linton St
Moorabbin 496 D8
ST KILDA RSL
88 Acland St 414 B17
SEAFORD RSL
Station St 599 D1
SOMERVILLE
SENIOR CITIZENS
Somerville 644 J17
SORRENTO-
PORTSEA BEACH RSL
1 Hurley St 678 J8
SOUTH MELBOURNE RSL
Ferrars Pl 29 L8
SPOTSWOOD/
KINGSVILLE RSL
16 Mary St 366 K20
SPRINGVALE RSL
cnr Osborne &
Princess Avs 499 J11
SUNBURY RSL
Barkly St 143 J11
SUNSHINE RSL
99 Dickson St 365 E3
TEMPLESTOWE RSL
156 Parker St 331 A8
TOORAK RSL
72 Clendon Rd 415 E6
TRAMWAYS/
EAST MELBOURNE RSL
391 Gore St
Fitzroy 19 F12
UPPER BEACONSFIELD RSL
Halford St
Beaconsfield Upper 542 F15
UPPER YARRA RSL
Settlement Rd
Yarra Junction 347 E13
UPWEY/BELGRAVE RSL
1 Mast Gully Rd 465 J10
WARBURTON RSL
Main Rd 349 D3
WARRANDYTE RSL
113 Brackenbury St 290 B18
WATSONIA RSL
6 Morwell Av 285 E6
WAVERLEY RSL
Coleman Pde
Glen Waverley 460 C2
WEST ST KILDA RSL
23 Loch St
St Kilda West 413 L13
WILLIAMSTOWN RSL
128 Ferguson St 411 D14
YARRA GLEN RSL
45 Bell St 253 A1

GOLF COURSES & DRIVING RANGES

Albert Park Driving Range 30 D15
Altona Lakes 410 C8
Amstel 603 H4
Anglesea 713 C4
Ascot Vale Driving Range 323 E17
Bacchus Marsh 221 H1
Bacchus Marsh West 263 B6
Balyang (Par 3) 702 C14
Barwon Valley 702 L19
Beaconhills Country Club 542 H6
Bembridge 9 Hole 646 L15
Berwick-Beaconsfield
Driving Range 555 G3
Box Hill 418 K4
Brighton Municipal 495 F2
Broadmeadows Pitch & Putt ..237 G14
Bulleen Driving Range 329 J7
Bundoora Park 284 A5
Camberwell 329 C18
Capital 532 C1
Centenary Park 600 K14
Chelsea 547 A11
Cheltenham 530 F2
Chirnside Park Country Club ..337 E2
Churchill Park 503 F16
Coburg North Driving Range ..281 K17
Commonwealth 497 J4
Craigieburn 149 L19
Craigieburn 150 A19
Cranbourne 578 D5
Croydon 336 F17
Dandenong Workers 536 F11
Devil Bend 658 K16
Dorset 380 H8
Dromana (Par 3) 687 B2
Eagle Ridge 699 B14
Eastern 330 G20
Eastwood 381 C20
Edgars Driving Range 240 J18
Elsternwick Park 454 J5
Emerald Resort 470 A15
Epping Driving Range 197 B14
Essendon Municipal 323 F18
Frankston 627 L10
Gisborne 78 F16
Golf Park Driving Range 497 G9
Goonawarra 144 D14
Green Acres 372 D1
Heathmont Golf Park (Par 3) ..379 F20
Heidelberg 286 E16
Huntingdale 458 B19
Ivanhoe 328 F18
Keilor 233 K18
Kew 372 E2
Keysborough 533 K20
Keysborough
Pitch & Putt (Par 3) 547 L1
Kingsbury Driving Range 283 L12
Kingston Heath 497 J16
Kingston Links 462 B19
Kingswood 533 B5
Kooringal 452 D2
Lalor 239 L7
Latrobe 328 A20
Long Island Country Club 599 H11
Lonsdale 710 D4
Malvern Valley 417 F20
Medway 322 F17
Melton Golf Range 269 G6
Melton Valley 227 D18
Metropolitan 457 K16
Montuna 555 H1
Moorabbin Driving Range 532 G7
Morack 421 H8
Mornington Country 641 B9
Morrabbin Municipal 532 G7
Mt Martha Municipal 670 A4
Mt Martha Valley
Country Club 687 A1
Northcote Municipal 326 C9
Northern 280 E7
Oakleigh Municipal 458 A7
Olinda 427 C8
Pakenham & District 585 J2
Patterson River
Country Club 573 D5
Peninsula Country Club 600 C13
Portsea 677 H1
Queenscliff 709 D11
Queens Park 701 J8
RACV Country Club 213 D18
Richmond 371 C20
Ringwood 422 C1
Riversdale 418 H18
Rosanna 330 C2
Rosebud 700 H9
Rosebud Country Club 700 A5
Rosebud Park 700 L2
Rossdale 546 F8
Royal Melbourne 529 L3
Royal Park 325 C19
Sandringham Driving Range ..495 L18
Sandringham Municipal 529 L1
Seaford Driving Range 599 K7
Skye 601 L6
Sorrento 678 G4
Southern 533 G11
Spring Park 533 H9
Spring Valley 499 D14
Strathallan 284 H7
Sunshine 363 K6

HOTELS & MOTELS

INFORMATION

Hotel	Page	Grid
Phoenix Hotel Melbourne	24	J9
Portsea Village Resort Portsea	677	L1
Princes Park Motor Inn Brunswick	325	F17
Pugg Mahones Irish Pub Melbourne	1	L7
Queensbridge Hotel Southbank	3	F3
Queenscliff Hotel Queenscliff	709	B17
Quest Flemington-A Quest Inn Flemington	33	E5
Quest Kew-A Quest Inn Kew	371	K9
Quest On Bourke Hotel Melbourne	2	K12
Quest On Flinders Lane Melbourne	2	H18
Quest On Lygon Carlton	18	F6
Quest On St Kilda Rd St Kilda	414	D13
Quest On William Melbourne	1	E11
Quest Williamstown-A Quest Inn Williamstown	411	H16
Radisson President Melbourne	31	D19
Railway Hotel/Motel Maddingley	263	L1
Ramada Inn Parkville	325	E18
Redan Quest Lodging St Kilda	414	F14
Red Ant Hotel Melbourne	2	J13
Red Bluff Hotel Sandringham	495	C17
Regency Hotel Melbourne	24	J3
Richmond Quest Lodging Cremorne	25	L19
Ringwood Lake Motor Inn Ringwood	378	H10
Ringwood Regent Motor Inn Ringwood	378	L8
Riverside Inn Melbourne	1	B19
Rose Garden Motor Inn Belmont	702	J20
Rydges Melbourne Melbourne	24	J4
Rydges Riverwalk Richmond	371	D16
Rye Motel Rye	698	F1
St Georges Motor Inn Thornbury	326	G9
St Kilda Quest Inn St Kilda	414	A15
Saltair Motel Sorrento	678	J11
Sandown Regency Noble Park	500	K15
Saville On Russell Melbourne	2	K9
Saville Park Suites Hotel Melbourne	24	F2
Savoy Park Plaza International Melbourne Melbourne	23	G10
Shannon Motor Inn Newtown	702	C7
Sheraton Towers Southgate Southbank	4	A4
Shoan Heights City Apartment Hotel Melbourne	24	J4
Skyways International Hotel/Motel Airport West	279	A9
Southern Comfort Motor Inn Belmont	706	B5
South Melbourne Quest Lodging South Melbourne	30	H4
South Yarra Mews-A Quest Lodging South Yarra	31	H14
Stamford Plaza Melbourne Melbourne	2	L14
Star Bar Southbank	29	L1
Sunshine Motor Inn Ardeer	320	D17
Surf City Motel Torquay	712	B10
Surfcoast Resort Motel Anglesea	713	H4
The Canterbury Hotel/Motel Forest Hill	420	F2
The Chifley Hotel Melbourne	2	L9
The Chifley On Flemington North Melbourne	17	H16
The Intrepid Fox Hotel South Melbourne	29	L2
The Radisson On Flagstaff Gardens Melbourne	1	F2
The Ranch Motel Mornington	656	E4
The Sebel Melbourne Melbourne	1	H15
The Sebel Suites-St Kilda Rd Melbourne	30	J2
The Townhouse Carlton	18	C16
The Yarra Glen Grand Yarra Glen	253	A2
Toorak Manor Toorak	32	L14
Torquay Hotel/Motel Torquay	711	L12
Torquay Tropicana Motel Torquay	711	K5
Travel Inn Hotel Carlton	18	G15
Treasury Motor Lodge East Melbourne	25	H4
Tullamarine Airport Motor Inn Westmeadows	236	K16
Victoria Vista Melbourne	2	G14
Vue Grand Private Hotel Queenscliff	709	A18
Waltzing Matilda Hotel/Motel Springvale	499	K18
Waterside Hotel Melbourne	1	A19
Werribee Motor Lodge Werribee	447	K15
Werribee Park Motor Inn Werribee	448	A17
Windsor Quest Inn Windsor	31	G19
York On Lilydale Resort Mt Evelyn	382	H3
Young & Jacksons Hotel Melbourne	2	E19

LIBRARIES

Library	Page	Grid
Abbotsford	20	B18
Albert Park	29	J11
Altona	409	C19
Ascot Vale	323	L16
Ashburton	417	E15
Association for The Blind Braille & Talking Book South Yarra	31	K15
Bacchus Marsh	222	C17
Balwyn	373	G13
Beaumaris	530	A8
Belmont	702	G19
Bentleigh	456	C20
Blackburn	375	K15
Boronia	424	C14
Box Hill	375	A15
Brighton	454	K16
Brighton East	495	E2
Brunswick	325	F15
Brunswick West	324	L8
Bulleen	329	J11
Camberwell	416	J2
Carlton North	18	H5
Carnegie	456	J6
Carrum Downs	575	C20
Caulfield South Caulfield	455	G3
Chelsea	546	K19
Cheltenham	530	K1
Chilwell	702	H12
Clayton	498	K3
Clayton South Clarinda	498	F10
Coburg	325	G2
Craigieburn	150	F18
Cranbourne	604	K5
Croydon	380	B6
Deer Park Albanvale	319	E8
Doncaster	330	L19
Doncaster East	332	D9
Doveton	536	K12
East Melbourne	25	J8
Elsternwick	455	A4
Eltham	287	G9
Endeavour Hills	537	F5
Fairfield	327	E16
Fawkner	281	H4
Ferntree Gully	464	F5
Fitzroy	19	D16
Fitzroy North	326	D19
Flemington	33	L5
Footscray	367	E8
Footscray West West Footscray	366	J7
Gisborne	79	A12
Gladstone Park	237	B19
Glenroy	279	L6
Glen Waverley	460	D3
Greensborough	244	D18
Grovedale	706	C14
Hampton	495	A9
Hawthorn	371	L18
Healesville	213	J19
Highett	496	E13
Highton	701	K19
Ivanhoe	328	D12
Keilor	277	C13
Keilor East	322	B6
Kew	371	L10
Kingston Clarinda	498	D9
Lalor	241	D11
Lilydale	338	E7
McKinnon	456	B16
Malvern	415	K12
Malvern East	457	E3
Maribyrnong	323	A16
Melton	226	K20
Middle Park	30	C19
Montrose	382	C10
Moonee Ponds	324	D12
Mooroolbark	337	B19
Mordialloc	531	G13
Mornington	640	E12
Mt Evelyn	339	D18
Mt Waverley	419	A19
Narre Warren	552	L3
Newcomb	704	B17
Newport	410	L7
Newtown	702	C9
Niddrie	279	A19
Northcote	326	J14
North Melbourne	17	D18
Nunawading	376	K14
Oakleigh	457	K10
Oakleigh South	497	G3
Pakenham	584	L7
Port Melbourne	412	L5
Prahran-Windsor	32	C19
Preston	326	L1
Queenscliff	709	B18
Reservoir	282	K10
Richmond	26	F16
Ringwood	378	E12
Rosanna	328	L1
Rosebud	684	C15
Rowville	462	H19
Royal Victorian Institute for The Blind Windsor	31	L20
St Albans	320	B3
St Kilda	414	F18
Sandringham	495	A13
Somerville	645	A15
South Melbourne	29	L5
South Yarra	32	H10
Spotswood Yarraville	366	H17
Springvale	499	L16
State Library of Victoria Melbourne	2	G5
Sunbury	143	K12
Sunshine	365	F1
Thomastown	240	L14
Torquay	711	L9
Tullamarine	278	G5
Vermont South	420	K10
Watsonia	285	F7
Werribee	447	H15
Werribee	448	E4
Wheelers Hill	461	B14
Williamstown	411	E14
Yarra Junction	346	L16

LOOKOUTS

Lookout	Page	Grid
Arthurs Seat	685	H14
Barwon Valley	701	K6
Brownhill Heights	701	B19
Burkes	426	D1
Coppins	678	D11
Eltham War Memorial Park	248	B16
Hardies	710	D8
Monbulk Creek Lookout	505	B4
Montpellier	701	H14
Mt Dandenong	382	D17
Murrays	685	G13
Red Bluff	495	D20
Rip View	710	H7
Southern	250	G11

PLACES OF INTEREST

Place	Page	Grid
Albert Park Adventure Playground (Parks Victoria) Middle Park	30	E17
Albert Park Lake Albert Park	30	G13
Alpine Toboggan Park Plenty Rd Whittlesea	126	B2
Anzac House 4 Collins St Melbourne	24	K6
Arthurs Seat Chair Lift	685	H12

Place	Page	Ref
Tabaret Rialto Plaza Melbourne	1	B16
Tasmanian Ferry Terminal Port Melbourne	412	G7
The Beach House Cafe 63a Ormond Esp St Kilda	454	D6
The Bluestone Cottage Bell St Coburg	325	J2
The Briars Homestead Nepean Hwy Mornington	656	G16
The Heights Homestead 140 Aphrasia St Newtown	702	B8
The Janet Lady Clarke Memorial In Queen Victoria Gardens	4	J9
The University of Melbourne	17	L14
The Willows Historical Homestead Melton	227	A20
Tommy Finns Trout Farm Warburton	348	J2
Trades Hall	2	L1
TV Pop Movie Museum Mornington	641	C12
Victorian Arts Centre	4	D7
Victoria's Open Range Zoo	487	J4
Vodafone Arena	25	E14
Werribee Park Mansion & Gardens	488	A8
West Gate Bridge	411	E2
Woodlands Historic Homestead Greenvale	191	F16
World Trade Centre cnr Flinders & Spencer Sts	23	G15
Yarra Valley Tourist Railway Coldstream	295	A12
Healesville	213	A20
Yarra Glen	253	G3

RACECOURSE & TROTTING TRACKS

Place	Page	Ref
CAULFIELD Station St Caulfield East	456	C3
CRANBOURNE South Gippsland Hwy	604	E5
FLEMINGTON Epsom Rd	367	K4
GEELONG St Albans Rd Breakwater	703	G19
MOONEY VALLEY McPherson St	324	F12
MORNINGTON Racecourse Rd	641	G18
PAKENHAM Racecourse Rd	585	B8
SANDOWN Racecourse Rd Springvale	500	E13
SANDOWN PARK GREYHOUND TRACK Lightwood Rd Springvale	500	C16
WERRIBEE Bulban Rd	447	C16
YARRA GLEN Armstrong Gr	209	E20

SHOPPING COMPLEXES - MAJOR

Place	Page	Ref
Altona Gate	409	J1
Arndale Civic	380	B5
Australia On Collins	2	C15
Barkly Square	325	G17
Bayswater Village	423	G4
Beaumaris Concourse	530	A10
Berwick Country Craft	555	A7
Berwick Marketplace	554	E7
Boronia	424	D12
Box Hill Central	374	K15
Brandon Park	460	C13
Brentford Square	420	L2
Brimbank Central	319	D7
Broadmeadows Shopping Square	238	A15
Bulleen Plaza	329	J12
Bunnings	1	L13
Camberwell	416	J1
Canterbury Gardens	380	J15
Caribbean Gardens	462	C13
Caulfield Plaza	456	D1
Central Square	451	F1
Centrepoint Mall	2	D13
Chadstone	457	G5
Chapel Plaza	32	D14
Chirnside Park	337	A6
Civic Plaza	244	C16
Clarinda	498	D9
Coburg	325	G3
Coburg Trash & Treasure	281	J13
Coburns	226	E20
Collins Place	24	K7
Como Centre	32	E9
Cranbourne Park	604	D3
Croydon	379	L2
Daimaru	2	C5
Devon Plaza	375	L1
Diamond Creek Plaza	245	L10
Diamond Village	285	J8
Direct Factory Outlets	531	K2
Dromana Hub	686	B4
Eastland	378	D11
Endeavour Hills	537	G5
Epping Plaza	241	C2
Footscray Market	367	G8
Footscray Plaza	367	F9
Forest Hill Chase	420	C2
Fountain Gate	552	L2
Galleria Shopping Plaza	2	A13
Gisborne Village	78	K12
Gladstone Park	236	K19
Greensborough	286	A3
Greenvale	192	J17
Hampton Park	551	J9
Healesville Walk Shopping Centre	213	K19
Highpoint City	323	B17
Highton	701	K19
Hoppers Crossing	449	B6
Ivanhoe Plaza	328	B13
Jam Factory	32	E12
Karingal Hub	628	G3
Keilor Downs Plaza	276	E16
Kilsyth	381	A6
Knox City	422	J16
Knox Tower Point	422	L16
Lakeside Village	276	A5
Lakeview	573	J5
Lalor Plaza	241	K11
Laverton Market	407	F8
Lilydale Marketplace	338	C7
Lygon Court	18	F13
Macedon Square	330	F15
Malvern Central	415	J15
Meadow Heights	238	B2
Melbourne Central	2	C5
Melbourne Westend Market	321	A16
Melbourne Wholesale Fish	368	F12
Melbourne Wholesale Fruit And Vegetable	368	E11
Midtown Plaza	2	F11
Milleara Mall	322	B6
Mill Park Lakes	242	K1
Mill Park Stables	242	H8
Mitcham	377	B13
Moonee Ponds Central	324	C12
Mordialloc Plaza	531	J19
Mornington Central	640	F13
Mornington Village	640	F15
Mountain Gate	464	A2
Mt Waverley	419	A20
Newcomb	704	B17
North Blackburn Square	375	K11
Northcote Central	326	J13
Northcote Plaza	326	K13
Northland	283	J20
Oakleigh Central	457	K12
Olive Tree	338	C6
Pakenham	584	K8
Parkdale Plaza	531	J14
Parkmore	534	G11
Pinewood	459	G7
Pipeworks Fun Market	239	J18
Plenty Hill Shopping Centre	284	H1
Port Phillip Plaza	683	J17
Prahran Market	32	B15
Pran Central	32	D16
Preston Market	282	K20
Preston South	326	K5
Queen Victoria	23	J1
Richmond Plaza	26	F10
Ringwood	378	C12
Ringwood Square	378	C13
Rosebud Village	684	C15
Roxburgh Park Shopping Centre	194	E17
St Albans	320	B5
St Helena Market Square	245	B15
Scoresby Village	462	F9
Somerville Plaza	644	J15
Southgate	4	B3
South Melbourne Market	29	J3
Sportsgirl Centre	2	D15
Springvale Plaza	499	H18
Stud Park	462	J19
Sunbury Square	143	H11
Sunshine Centre Plaza	365	D1
Target	283	H14
The Downs, Carrum Downs Regional	575	B20
The Gateway	629	G2
The Glen	420	D20
The Mall	328	B4
The Pines	332	E9
Thompson Parkway	578	B10
Tooronga Village	416	D8
Town & Country	705	J10
Tunstall Square	376	F2
Vermont South	420	K10
Village City Centre	2	H11
Wantirna Trash & Treasure Market	422	C7
Warringal Village	329	A7
Watergardens	275	D4
Waverley Gardens	501	C6
Werribee Plaza	448	D4
Westfield Shoppingtown Airport West	278	L10
Doncaster	330	L20
Southland	496	J17
Wheelers Hill	461	B15
Whitehorse Plaza	374	J14
Woodgrove Shopping Centre	226	D20
Woodville Park	448	G7
Wyndham Vale	446	E12
Yarra Valley	338	F6

SPORTING VENUES

Place	Page	Ref
Bob Jane Stadium South Melbourne	30	E10
Broadmeadows Motor Cycle Park	239	G17
Brunswick Velodrome	326	B10
Calder Park Raceway	232	H15
Camberwell Sportsground	416	K3
Canterbury Sportsground Surrey Hills	373	H16
Carey Grammar Sportsground Bulleen	329	C16
Carlton Cricket Ground Carlton North	325	F20
Caulfield Cricket Ground	415	L19
Coburg Velodrome	281	C16
Cockatoo Sports Area	511	B6
Collingwood Football Ground Abbotsford	20	D13
Colonial Stadium West Melbourne	23	C9
Dandenong Police Paddocks Reserve Endeavour Hills	502	J11
Essendon Cricket Ground	324	B7
Frank Holohan Soccer Complex Endeavour Hills	502	K16
Gembrook Sportsground	512	F9
George Knott Athletic Field Clifton Hill	326	K20
Glenferrie Sportsground Hawthorn	371	K16
Greenvale Equestrian Centre	192	D18
Hanks Baseball Park Yarraville	366	G18
Hartwell Sportsground	417	H11
Healesville Amateur Racing Club	213	B18
Healesville Sporting Complex	258	E5
Heidelberg Cricket Ground	329	B6
J A Monahan Sporting Complex Queenscliff	708	L20
Kardinia Park	702	K11
Kevin Bartlett Sporting & Recreation Complex Burnley	415	G1
Knox Regional Netball Complex Ferntree Gully	464	A5
Kooyong Lawn Tennis Club Toorak	415	K4
Ladies Athletic Club Oval Parkville	325	D19
McPherson Baseball Field Parkville	325	B19
Melbourne Cricket Ground (MCG)	25	G11
Melbourne Indoor Sports & Entertainment Centre (The Glasshouse)	25	D15
Melbourne Park	25	B12
Melbourne Sports & Aquatic Centre	30	B13
Mentone Grammar Sportsground Braeside	533	G14
Moorabbin Reserve	496	E8
National League Soccer Stadium Epping	197	E9
National Water Sports Centre	547	L19
Newport Football Ground	410	K8
Northcote Velodrome	327	F11
Northern Region Sports Complex Coburg North	281	K17
North Melbourne Cricket Ground	34	H14

Olympic Park.........................25 E16
Pakenham Indoor
Pakenham.........................584 B2
Port Melbourne
Cricket Ground..................412 L1
Princes Park..........................18 A3
Richmond Cricket Ground......25 K13
Rod Laver Arena....................25 C14
St Kilda Cricket Ground
Junction Oval....................414 C12
St Kilda Football Club Ground
Moorabbin........................496 D8
Sandown
Motor Racing Circuit..........500 E13
Sandringham Cricket Ground..494 L11
Shell Stadium......................702 L12
Sir D Nicholls
Sporting Complex
Thornbury.........................326 G6
State Equestrian Centre
Werribee South.................488 C5
State Hockey Centre..............17 B2
State Netball Centre...............34 L2
Sydney Pargeter
Recreation Reserve............503 A18
Trinity Grammar
Sporting Complex
Bulleen............................329 E14
Victorian Baseball &
Softball Centre..................407 H16
Victoria Park..........................20 D12
Vodafone Arena.....................25 E14
Waverley Football Ground.....460 C6
Waverley Park.....................501 B2
Waverley Womens
Sports Centre
Wheelers Hill.....................461 C7
Werribee Recreation Centre..447 A14
Whitten Oval
Footscray..........................367 A8
Williamstown Cricket Ground..411 H20

TENPIN BOWLING

Box Hill Bowl.......................374 J14
Box Hill
Squash Bowl & Swim........374 E10
Chadstone Bowl...................457 F5
Dandenong Bowl
Dandenong South..............536 J15
Ed Fleming Lanes
Mooroolbark.....................337 A20
Essendon Bowl....................324 B8
Footscray Bowl....................367 G9
Frankston Bowl....................628 C2
Geelong Bowling Lanes
Belmont............................705 L6
Keon Park..........................241 C20
Knox
Wantirna South.................422 L16
Melton Bowling Centre.........226 J19
Mentone Tenpin Bowl..........531 D8
Moorabbin Bowl..................496 B8
Northcote Bowl....................327 B14
Ringwood Olympic Bowl......378 C13
Riverside Super Bowl
Werribee..........................447 H20
Rosebud Tenpin Bowl
Rosebud West...................699 G5
Sunshine Super Bowl..........321 A19

TERTIARY & OTHER INSTITUTIONS

AUSTRALIAN CATHOLIC
UNIVERSITY
Mercy Campus
Ascot Vale........................324 F18
BARTON INSTITUTE OF TAFE
Richmond Campus
70 Gwynne St....................26 B20
Richmond Campus
Cremorne St......................26 A19
BOX HILL
INSTITUTE OF TAFE
Doncaster Campus............332 H6
Elgar Rd Campus..............374 G12
Mitcham Campus..............377 A14
Nelson Campus.................374 J14
Whitehorse Campus.........374 L15
CENTRAL GIPPSLAND
INSTITUTE OF TAFE
Chadstone Campus...........457 L4
CHISHOLM INSTITUTE
Berwick Campus...............554 D13
Bonbeach Campus............573 B5
Cranbourne Campus.........604 H4
Dandenong Campus.........536 B3
Moorabbin Campus..........496 G7
Noble Park Campus..........534 K1
Rosebud Campus.............699 H7
DEAKIN UNIVERSITY
Geelong Campus...............705 B10
Melbourne Campus...........418 G7
Rusden Campus...............459 G13
Toorak Campus................415 K9
EASTERN INSTITUTE OF TAFE
Lilydale
Open Learning Centre........338 B6
ENGLISH LANGUAGE CENTRE
Blackburn
120 Eley Rd.......................419 H8
Broadmeadow
Blair St............................238 D15
Brunswick
406 Victoria St.................325 D13
Collingwood
Cambridge St....................25 G1
Debney Meadows
Victoria St
Flemington........................34 D3
Footscray
Primary School, Hyde St...367 F11
Holmes
185 Spring St
Melbourne........................24 J4
Maribyrnong
River St...........................323 B18
Spastic Society of Victoria,
South St
Braybrook........................366 A5
Travancore
Flemington St..................324 G19
GORDON INSTITUTE OF TAFE
Manufacturing Industry
Training Centre.................703 K19
HOLMESGLEN
INSTITUTE OF TAFE
Chadstone Campus...........417 K20
Waverley Campus.............459 L4
JOHN BATMAN
INSTITUTE OF TAFE
Coburg North Campus.......281 E17
Fitzroy Campus.................19 J1
Heathmont Campus..........378 H16
Watsonia Campus.............285 H6
KANGAN INSTITUTE OF TAFE
Avondale-Brimbank
Campus...........................322 B13
Broadmeadows Campus...237 K14
Mooney Valley Campus....324 C9
Moreland Campus............325 H6
LA TROBE UNIVERSITY
Bundoora Campus.............284 D11
Carlton Campus.................18 B18
Melbourne...........................1 H2
MAHARISHI VEDIC
Bungay St
Watsonia..........................285 D3
MELBOURNE COLLEGE
OF TEXTILES
Brunswick Campus...........325 E15
Pascoe Vale Campus........280 H19
MONASH MT ELIZA
BUSINESS COLLEGE
Kunyung Rd
Mt Eliza............................625 H19
MONASH UNIVERSITY
Berwick Campus...............554 B12
Caulfield Campus.............456 E1
Clayton Campus...............459 C16
Victorian College of
Pharmacy Campus............17 K1
NORTHERN MELBOURNE
INSTITUTE OF TAFE
Collingwood Campus...........19 H14
Epping Campus................241 H2
Greensborough................244 E17
Heidelberg Campus
Heidelberg West..............328 C4
Parkville Campus.............324 K19
Preston Campus..............326 H2
OUTER EASTERN
COLLEGE OF TAFE
Healesville Campus
1 Badger Creek Rd............213 L19
PALLOTTI COLLEGE
McNamaras Rd
Millgrove...........................303 H19
ROYAL MELBOURNE
INSTITUTE OF TECHNOLOGY
Bundoora Campus.............242 H14
Bundoora East Campus....243 B12
City Campus........................2 F1
TAFE Sector.......................18 D20
ST LEOS INTERNATIONAL
Hay St
Box Hill South..................375 B20
ST PAULS MISSIONARY
Nortons La
Wantirna South................461 E3
SWINBURNE UNIVERSITY OF
TECHNOLOGY
Hawthorn Campus............372 A17
Lilydale Campus..............338 C9
Prahran Campus..............414 G11
SWINBURNE UNIVERSITY OF
TECHNOLOGY-TAFE
Croydon Campus..............380 C6
Hawthorn Campus............372 A17
Healesville Campus...........213 J18
Lilydale Campus..............338 C9
Prahran Campus..............414 G11
Wantirna Campus
Wantirna South................422 G18
THEOLOGICAL COLLEGE
Salvation Army Training,
Eastern Victoria
cnr Canterbury & Elgar Rds
Box Hill South..................374 G19
Tabor
222 Oban Rd
Ringwood North..............378 C2
Whitley
271 Royal Pde
Parkville............................17 K4
THE UNIVERSITY
OF MELBOURNE
Facility of Agriculture,
Forestry & Horticulture
Werribee..........................448 E15
Institute of Early
Childhood Development....371 E11
Parkville............................17 L14
School of
Agriculture & Forestry
Derrimut..........................363 E6
Veterinary Science
Clinical Centre
Werribee..........................448 J9
Victorian College of
Agriculture & Horticulture
Burnley Campus...............371 F19
Victorian College of
Agriculture & Horticulture
Gilbert Chandler Campus
Werribee..........................448 E15
Victorian College of The Arts..4 D11
Whitley College
Parkville............................17 K4
VICTORIA COLLEGE OF
AGRICULTURE &
HORTICULTURE
Gilbert Chandler Campus
Werribee..........................448 E15
VICTORIA UNIVERSITY
City Campus........................2 A18
City Flinders Campus...........1 L19
City King Campus.................1 A9
City South Melbourne
Campus..............................3 C10
Footscray Park Campus....367 E5
Melton Campus................268 D10
Newport Campus.............410 K10
Nicholson Campus...........367 F10
St Albans Campus...........320 B9
Sunbury Campus.............143 H18
Sunshine Campus............321 D18
Werribee Campus.............448 L10
Yarraville Campus...........367 E14
VICTORIA UNIVERSITY -
TAFE DIVISION
Footscray Park Campus.....367 F5
Melton Campus................268 E10
St Albans Campus...........320 B9
Sunbury Campus.............143 H18
Werribee Campus.............448 L10
WESTALL ARTS &
LANGUAGE CENTRE
Rosebank Av
Clayton............................499 E9
WILLIAM ANGLISS
INSTITUTE OF TAFE............23 F6

THEATRES, CINEMAS & DRIVE-IN THEATRES

AIRPORT WEST
Airport West, Village 8
Westfield Shoppingtown....278 L10
ALBERT PARK
Gasworks (Anthill)
21 Graham St.....................29 B14
BALWYN
Balwyn
233 Whitehorse Rd............373 D12

THEATRES

BELGRAVE
Cameo Belgrave
550 Monbulk Rd ... 466 F14
BOX HILL
Oxford Childrens
cnr Oxford & Station Sts ... 374 K16
BRIGHTON
Brighton Bay Twin
294 Bay St ... 454 L14
Dendy Brighton Twin
26 Church St ... 454 H17
BURWOOD
Phoenix
Deakin University ... 418 G8
CARLTON
Comedy Club
380 Lygon St ... 18 F13
Courthouse
349 Drummond St ... 18 G12
Dancehouse
Community Centre,
150 Princes St ... 18 H8
IMAX
Rathdowne St ... 18 H17
La Mama
205 Faraday St ... 18 F14
Movie House
235 Faraday St ... 18 E13
Nova
Lygon Court, 380 Lygon St .. 18 F13
CAULFIELD
Caulfield Arts Complex
cnr Glen Eira &
Hawthorn Rds ... 455 G3
CHELTENHAM
Southland, Village 8
1239 Nepean Hwy ... 496 H17
CLIFTON HILL
Organ Factory
6 Page St ... 19 K7
COBURG
Progress
236 Reynard St ... 325 B4
COBURG NORTH
Coburg Twin
Newlands Rd ... 281 J13
COLLINGWOOD
Collingwood College Theatre
Vere St ... 19 L16
Last Laugh
64 Smith St ... 19 F20
CRANBOURNE
Cranbourne, Century 4
Cranbourne Park
Shopping Centre ... 604 D3
CROYDON
Croydon
3 Hewish Rd ... 380 B4
DONCASTER
Doncaster Village Twin
Westfield Shoppingtown,
Doncaster Rd ... 330 L20
Playhouse Theatre
Doncaster Rd ... 331 A20
DROMANA
Dromana Twin
Nepean Hwy ... 687 B2
EAST MELBOURNE
Dallas Brooks Hall
300 Victoria Rd ... 25 E3
State Film Theatre
1 Macarthur St ... 24 L6
State Film Theatre
St Andrews Pl ... 25 A5
ELSTERNWICK
Classic Cinema
9 Gordon St ... 454 K4
FAIRFIELD
Northcote Amphitheatre
Fairfield Park ... 371 C1
FITZROY
Universal
19 Victoria St ... 19 A13
FOOTSCRAY
Footscray Community
Arts Centre
45 Moreland Rd ... 367 J9
FOREST HILL
Forest Hill, Hoyts 10
Forest Hill Chase ... 420 D2
GEELONG WEST
Pix
23 Elizabeth St ... 702 E4
GLEN WAVERLEY
Century City Walk
285 Springvale Rd ... 460 D2
HAWTHORN EAST
Village
200 Camberwell Rd ... 372 G20
HEIDELBERG
Banyule Theatre
Buckingham Dr ... 329 E5
LILYDALE
Athenaeum
Castella St ... 338 E5
MALVERN EAST
Chadstone , Hoyts 8
Chadstone
Shopping Centre ... 457 G5
Malvern Community
Arts Centre
29a Burke Rd ... 416 F20
Malvern Theatre
Burke Rd ... 416 F20
MARIBYRNONG
Highpoint, Hoyts 10
Highpoint City
Shopping Centre ... 323 B17
MELBOURNE
Athenaeum
188 Collins St ... 2 G15
Capitol Cinema
113 Swanston St ... 2 E14
Chinatown
200 Bourke St ... 2 H11
Comedy
240 Exhibition St ... 24 J4
Forum
The Old State Theatre
154 Flinders St ... 2 J18
George Fairfax Studio,
Victorian Arts Centre
100 St Kilda Rd ... 4 D7
Glasshouse Theatre
RMIT, 360 Swanston St ... 2 F3
Her Majestys
219 Exhibition St ... 24 G4
Hoyts Cinema Centre
140 Bourke St ... 2 L11
Kino
Collins Place, 45 Collins St .. 24 J7
Lumiere
108 Lonsdale St ... 24 J3
Melbourne Concert Hall
Victorian Arts Centre,
100 St Kilda Rd ... 4 D4
Playhouse,
Victoria Arts Centre
100 St Kilda Rd ... 4 D7
Princess
163 Spring St ... 24 J4
Regent
186 Flinders La ... 2 G17
Rialto
24/525 Collins St ... 1 B17
Russell, Greater Union
131 Russell St ... 2 J13
Russell Street
(Melbourne Theatre Co)
19 Russell St ... 2 J18
Shaft
264 Swanston St ... 2 F9
Sidney Myer Music Bowl
Alexandra Av ... 24 L15
State, Victorian Arts Centre
100 St Kilda Rd ... 4 E6
Village City Centre
206 Bourke St ... 2 H11
MELTON
Melton Twin
cnr McKenzie &
Alexandra Sts ... 226 K20
MOONEE PONDS
Incinerator
180 Holmes Rd ... 323 G12
MORDIALLOC
Shirley Burke
Parkers Rd ... 531 F13
MORNINGTON
Mornington
1 Main St ... 640 D12
MT WAVERLEY
Waverley, Pinewood
Pinewood Dr ... 459 G7
MULGRAVE
Waverley Gardens Twin
Waverley Gardens
Shopping Centre ... 501 C6
NORTHCOTE
Valhalla Cinema
89 High St ... 326 H18
NUNAWADING
Nunawading Arts &
Entertainment Centre
379 Whitehorse Rd ... 376 K13
PRESTON
Northland, Hoyts 8
Northland Shopping Centre .. 283 J20
RESEARCH
Eltham Little
Eltham
Performing Arts Centre
Main Rd ... 288 K2
RESERVOIR
Cinema North
911 High St ... 282 L9
RINGWOOD EAST
Karralika
Mines Rd ... 378 K9
ROSANNA
Heidelberg Theatre Company
37 Turnham Av ... 328 L2
ROSEBUD
Rosebud Twin
3 Rosebud Pde ... 684 C15
ST KILDA
Astor Theatre
cnr Chapel St &
Dandenong Rd ... 414 G13
National
cnr Barkly & Carlisle Sts ... 414 C17
Palais
Lower Esplanade ... 414 A17
SORRENTO
Athenaeum
Ocean Beach Rd ... 678 J8
SOUTHBANK
Grant Street
Grant St ... 4 D13
Malthouse (Playbox)
113 Sturt St ... 3 K15
Village Megaplex
Crown Casino,
Clarendon St ... 23 K15
SOUTH MELBOURNE
Napier Street (Arena)
199 Napier St ... 30 B7
SOUTH YARRA
Longford
59 Toorak Rd ... 31 L8
Polyglot
27a Cromwell Rd ... 32 H14
St Martins
44 St Martins La ... 31 E5
THE BASIN
The Basin
Doongalla Rd ... 425 J8
TOORAK
Trak
445 Toorak Rd ... 415 B5
UPPER FERNTREE GULLY
1812 Theatre
Rose St ... 465 B7
WANTIRNA SOUTH
Knox, Village 10
Tower Point, Burwood Hwy .. 422 L16
WEST MELBOURNE
Festival Hall
Dudley St ... 23 A5

WINERIES

Winery	Map	Ref
Barak Estate	658	C8
Bianchet	294	A9
Coldstream Hills	298	A9
Craiglee	144	A14
Darling Park Vineyards	688	K19
De Bortoli	210	E1
Domaine Chandon	254	L11
Dromana Estate	687	J5
Dromana Valley Wines	669	J18
Ermes Estate	658	L13
Fergussons	210	A1
Goonawarra	144	B13
Halcyon Daze	336	G1
Hickinbotham of Dromana	669	K17
Karina Vineyard	687	J6
Long Gully	212	D14
Lovegrove of Cottles Bridge	204	E4
Loveys Estate	210	D1
McWilliams Lilydale	342	L19
Main Ridge Estate	686	K20
Massoni Main Creek Vineyard	687	B20
Moorooduc Estate	658	F12
Mornington Star Estate	641	E7
Mornington Vineyards Estate	670	K7
Mt Eliza Estate	641	F8
Mt Martha Vineyard	670	J3
Paternoster	510	E9
Port Philip Estate	688	L17
Prince Albert Winery (off Map)	705	A16
St Huberts	254	E18
Seville Estate	342	E19
Tallarida	699	L13
The Briars	656	G16
Vermont	421	C11
Vintina Estate	641	H7
Wantirna Estate	421	F19
Warramatre	298	A7
Wildwood	190	K4
Yarra Burn	347	H13
Yarra Edge	293	E8
Yarra Ridge Vineyard	252	E3
Yarra Track	211	F14
Yarra Valley Hills	334	K10
Yering Station	253	D8

PUBLISHING DATES

1st Edition ... 1991
2nd Edition ... 1993
3rd Edition ... 1997
4th Edition ... 1999
5th Edition ... 2001

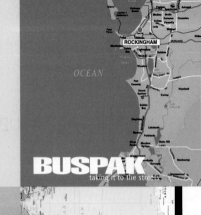

MAP SYMBOLS

CltyLink Tollway with electronic toll	CITYLINK Toll 5 TOLLWAY
Freeway or Motorway	CALDER FREEWAY
Proposed Freeway	Proposed Freeway
Primary Arterial Road	MELTON HIGHWAY
Secondary Arterial / Collector Road	SUNSHINE AV
Local Access Road	VERONA DR
Lane with One-way Traffic Route	MILLER LA
Un-trafficable / Proposed Road	SHEOAK CL
Railway Line with Station (distance from Flinders St Stn)	Somerville 55
Tramway	
Roundabouts	
Traffic Lights and Level Crossing	
Road and Rail Bridges & Bridge Clearance Heights	4.5m
Distance by road from GPO	22
Victorian Route Numbers	M1 A420 B420 C777
National / Alternative / State & Metropolitan Route Shields	1 1 180 10
Suburb Name	BURNSIDE
Locality Name	Jolimont
Ferry Route	
Walking Track, Cycleway	
Park, Reserve, Golf Course, etc (with Oval)	
School or Hospital	
Caravan Park, Cemetery, Shopping Centre, etc	
Mall, Plaza	
Swamp, Land Subject to Inundation	

- Caravan Park
- Car Park
- College - Private
- - State
- Golf Course
- Hospital
- Hotel
- Library
- Lookout
- Motel
- Picnic Area
- Place of Worship
- Police Station
- Post Office
- School - Private
- - Public
- Shopping Centre
- Swimming Pool
- Wineries

STREET MAPS overlap on each page to help in re-locating position on an adjoining page.

ADJOINING MAP NUMBERS are shown in the borders and corners of the street maps.

REFERENCE NUMBERS AND LETTERS within the borders of the street maps are the reference co-ordinates given in the indexes, see "How To Find A Street" - inside front cover.

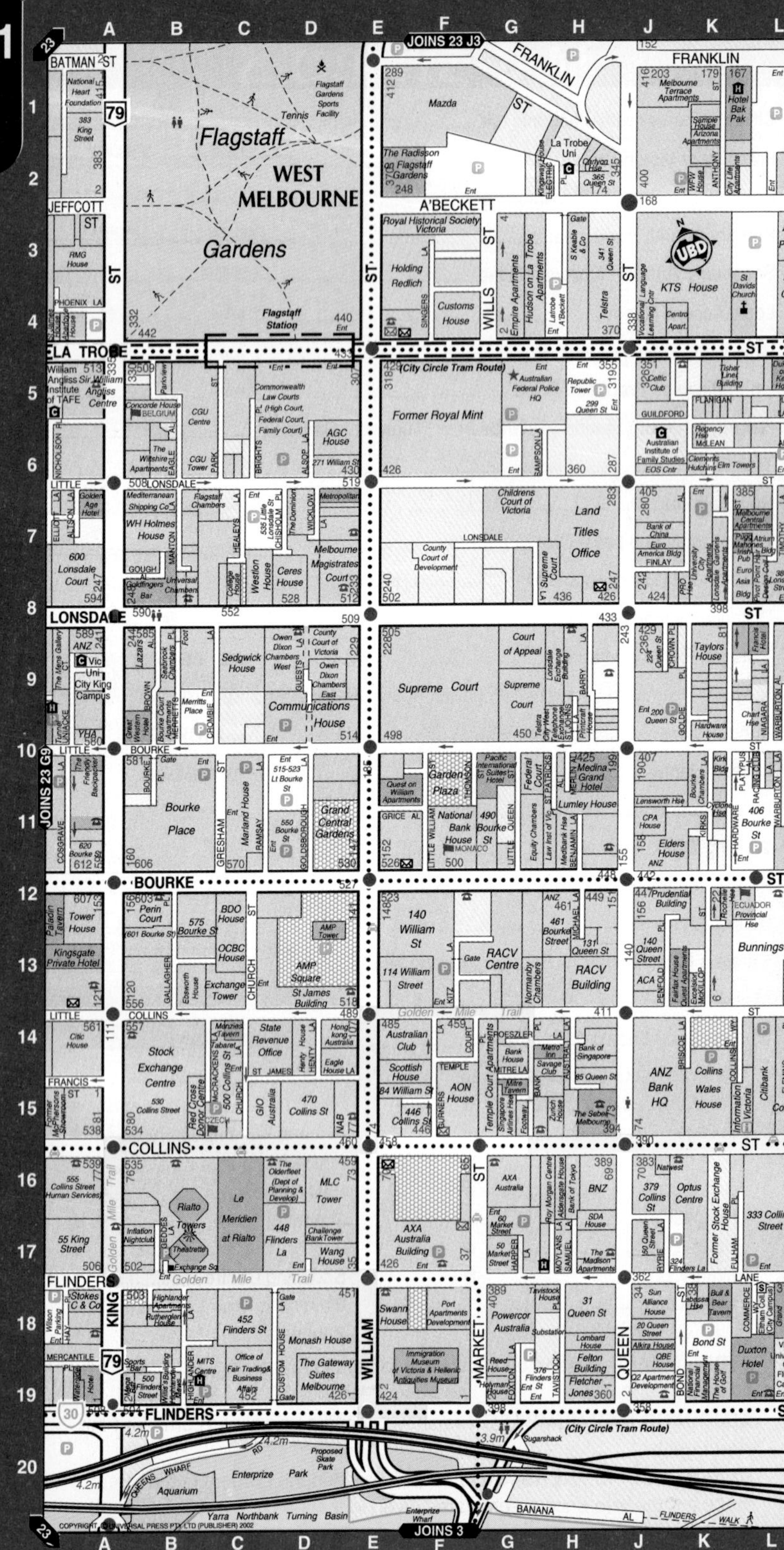
A B C D E F G H J K L
JOINS 23 J3
FRANKLIN
BATMAN ST
National Heart Foundation
383 King Street
Flagstaff Gardens Sports Facility
Tennis
Flagstaff
WEST MELBOURNE
Gardens
Flagstaff Station
Mazda
FRANKLIN ST
La Trobe Uni
The Radisson on Flagstaff Gardens
Melbourne Terrace Apartments
Hotel Bak Pak
JEFFCOTT ST
RMG House
PHOENIX LA
A'BECKETT
Royal Historical Society Victoria
Holding Redlich
Customs House
WILLS ST
Empire Apartments
Hudson on La Trobe Apartments
Telstra
KTS House
St Davids Church
LA TROBE ST
William Angliss Institute of TAFE
Sir William Angliss Centre
(City Circle Tram Route)
Commonwealth Law Courts (High Court, Federal Court, Family Court)
AGC House
Former Royal Mint
Australian Federal Police HQ
Republic Tower
Australian Institute of Family Studies
GUILDFORD
FLANIGAN
CGU Centre
CGU Tower
The Wiltshire Apartments
LITTLE LONSDALE
Mediterranean Shipping Co
Flagstaff Chambers
WH Holmes House
Melbourne Magistrates Court
Childrens Court of Victoria
County Court of Development
Land Titles Office
600 Lonsdale Court
Westion House
Ceres House
LONSDALE
LONSDALE ST
Sedgwick House
Owen Dixon Chambers West
County Court of Victoria
Owen Dixon Chambers East
Communications House
Supreme Court
Court of Appeal
Vic Uni City King Campus
Taylors House
Merritts Place
LITTLE BOURKE
Bourke Place
Marland House
Grand Central Gardens
Garden Plaza
Quest on William Apartments
National Bank House
Federal Court
Medina Grand Hotel
Lumley House
Elders House
406 Bourke St
BOURKE
BOURKE ST
Tower House
Kingsgate Private Hotel
Perin Court
575 Bourke St
BDO House
OCBC House
Exchange Tower
AMP Square
AMP Tower
St James Building
140 William St
114 William Street
RACV Centre
RACV Building
Prudential Building
140 Queen Street
Bunnings
LITTLE COLLINS
Golden Mile Trail
Citic House
Stock Exchange Centre
State Revenue Office
Hongkong Australia
Australian Club
Scottish House
AON House
Bank of Singapore
ANZ Bank HQ
Collins Wales House
Citibank
FRANCIS ST
530 Collins Street
Red Cross Donor Centre
500 Collins St
GIO Australia
470 Collins St
446 Collins St
84 William St
Temple Court Apartments
COLLINS
COLLINS ST
555 Collins Street
Le Meridien at Rialto
Rialto Towers
MLC Tower
448 Flinders La
Challenge Bank Tower
Wang House
AXA Australia Building
AXA Australia
BNZ
SDA House
379 Collins St
Optus Centre
Former Stock Exchange House
333 Collins Street
55 King Street
FLINDERS
LANE
452 Flinders St
Monash House
The Gateway Suites Melbourne
Swann House
Port Apartments Development
Immigration Museum of Victoria & Hellenic Antiquities Museum
Powercor Australia
31 Queen St
Felton Building
Fletcher Jones
Bond St
Duxton Hotel
KING
WILLIAM
MARKET
QUEEN
FLINDERS
(City Circle Tram Route)
Sugarshack
Enterprize Park
Proposed Skate Park
Aquarium
QUEENS WHARF RD
Yarra Northbank Turning Basin
Enterprize Wharf
BANANA AL
FLINDERS WALK
JOINS 3
JOINS 23 G9

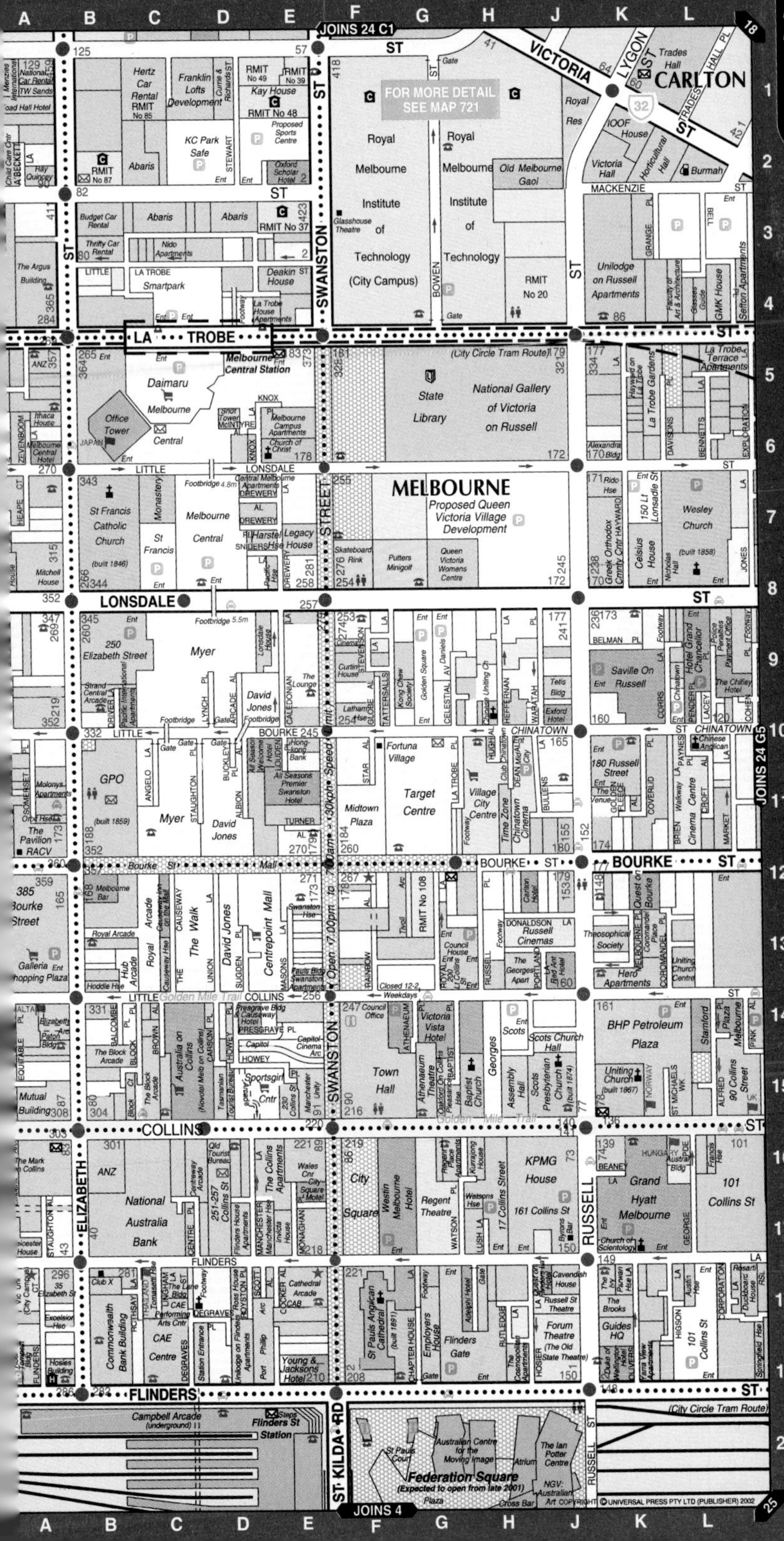

A B C D E F G H J K L

JOINS 24 C1

18

VICTORIA ST

LYGON ST

Trades Hall

CARLTON

TRADES HALL PL

Menzies
129 National Car Rental
TW Sands
Road Hall Hotel

Hertz Car Rental
RMIT No 85
Franklin Lofts Development
Currie & Richards ST
RMIT No 49
RMIT No 39
Kay House
RMIT No 48
Proposed Sports Centre
KC Park Safe
STEWART
Abaris
RMIT No 87
Ray Quincey
Oxford Scholar Hotel
Child Care Cntr
A'BECKETT

FOR MORE DETAIL SEE MAP 721

Royal Melbourne Institute of Technology (City Campus)

Glasshouse Theatre

Royal Melbourne Institute of Technology

BOWEN

Old Melbourne Gaol

Royal Res

IOOF House

Victoria Hall

Horticultural Hall

Burmah

MACKENZIE ST

BELL

Budget Car Rental
Abaris
Abaris
RMIT No 37
Thrifty Car Rental
Nido Apartments
The Argus Building
LITTLE LA TROBE
Smartpark
Deakin House
La Trobe House Apartments

SWANSTON ST

RMIT No 20

GRANGE PL

Unilodge on Russell Apartments

Faculty of Art & Architecture

Glasses Guide

GMK House

Sefton Apartments

LA TROBE ST

Melbourne Central Station

(City Circle Tram Route)

ANZ

Daimaru Melbourne

Office Tower

Central

JAPAN

Ithaca House

Melbourne Central Hotel

ZEVENBOOM

Shot Tower

McINTYRE

KNOX

Melbourne Campus Apartments

Church of Christ

State Library

National Gallery of Victoria on Russell

Hayward on La Trobe

La Trobe Gardens

La Trobe Terrace Apartments

DAVISONS

BENNETTS

EXPLORATION

Alexandra Bldg

LITTLE LONSDALE ST

Footbridge 4.8m

Central Melbourne Apartments

DREWERY

St Francis Catholic Church (built 1846)

Monastery

St Francis

Melbourne Central

Harstel Hse

Legacy House

SNIDERS

HEAPE CT

Mitchell House

MELBOURNE

Proposed Queen Victoria Village Development

Skateboard Rink

Putters Minigolf

Queen Victoria Womens Centre

Rido Hse

150 Lt Lonsdale St

Greek Orthodox Cmnty Cntr

HAYWARD

Celsius House

Wesley Church (built 1858)

Nicholas Hall

JONES

LONSDALE ST

Footbridge 5.5m

250 Elizabeth Street

Myer

Lonsdale House

Strand Central Arcade

Pacific International Apartments

DRIVER LA

LYNCH

ARCADE AL

David Jones

Footbridge

Gate

CALEDONIAN

The Lounge

Cinema

STEVENSON

Curtin House

Latham Hse

GLOBE

TATTERSALLS

Kong Chew Society

Golden Square

Daniels

CELESTIAL AV

Chinese Uniting Ch

HEFFERNAN

WARATAH

Tetis Bldg

Exford Hotel

BELMAN PL

Saville On Russell

Chinatown

CORRS

Hotel Grand Chancellor

PENDER PL

Police Penalties Payment Office

The Chifley Hotel

LACEY

COHEN

LITTLE BOURKE

GPO (built 1859)

ANGELO

STAUGHTON

BUCKLEY

All Seasons Welcome Hotel

LOUDEN

Hong-kong Bank

All Seasons Premier Swanston Hotel

TURNER

ALBION

Myer

David Jones

Molonys Apartments

SOMERSET

Orbit Hse

The Pavilion

RACV

Speed Limit 30kph 7.00am to 7.00pm Open

Fortuna Village

Target Centre

STAR

Midtown Plaza

LA TROBE

HUGHES AL

Club Chinatown

Village City Centre

DEAN MidAL

Time Zone

Chinatown Cinema

BULLENS

CHINATOWN

180 Russell Street

The Venue

GOLDEN FLEECE

COVERLID

Chinese Anglican

Walkway

PAYNES

Cinema Centre

BRIEN

CROFT

MARKET

JOINS 24 G5

BOURKE ST MALL

BOURKE ST

385 Bourke Street

Melbourne Bar

Royal Arcade

Causeway Inn on the Mall

CAUSEWAY

The Walk

David Jones

Centrepoint Mall

Swanston Hse

Galleria Shopping Plaza

Hub Arcade

Hoddle Hse

Causeway Hse

THE

UNION

SUGDEN

MASONS

Fauls Bldg

Swanston Apartments

RAINBOW

Tivoli

Arc

RMIT No 108

Council House

Closed 12-2 Weekdays

ROYAL LA

LT Collins St

RUSSELL

Footway

Carlton Hotel

DONALDSON LA

Russell Cinemas

The Georges Apart

PORTLAND

Red Ant Hotel

Theosophical Society

Quest on Bourke

MELBOURNE PL

Coromandel Place

COROMANDEL

Uniting Church Centre

Hero Apartments

LITTLE COLLINS

Golden Mile Trail

ALTA

Elizabeth Arc

Paton Bldg

EQUITABLE

BALCOMBE

The Block Arcade

BLOCK

BROWN

Australia on Collins

(Novotel Melb on Collins)

CARSON

Presgrave Bldg & Causeway Hotel

PRESGRAVE PL

HOWEY

Capitol

Capitol Cinema Arc

Sportsgirl Cntr

Tasmanian Tourist Bureau

230 Collins St

Manchester Unity

Mutual Building

The Block Arcade

Block Ct

Council Office

ATHENAEUM

Victoria Vista Hotel

Town Hall

Athenaeum Theatre

Oakford on Collins Pleasant Apart

BAPTIST

Baptist Church

Georges

Scots

Scots Church Hall

Assembly Hall

Scots Presbyterian Church (built 1874)

BHP Petroleum Plaza

Uniting Church (built 1867)

NORWAY

ST MICHAELS WK

Stamford Plaza

ALFRED

90 Collins Street

Melbourne

PINK

UK

COLLINS ST

Golden Mile Trail

The Mark on Collins

ANZ

National Australia Bank

ELIZABETH

STAUGHTON AL

Leicester House

Centreway Arcade

CENTRE PL

Old Tourist Bureau

251-257 Collins St

Flinders House Apartments

MANCHESTER

Manchester Apartments

The Collins Apartments

Invicta House

Wales Cnr

City Square Motel

MONAGHAN

City Square

Westin Melbourne Hotel

Regent Place Apartments

Regent Theatre

Kurrajong House

WATSON

Watsons Hse

LUSH LA

17 Collins Street

KPMG House

161 Collins St

Byrons Wine Bar

HUNGARY

BEANEY

Grand Hyatt Melbourne

Church of Scientology

Austral Bldg

Francis Hse

GEORGE

101 Collins St

RUSSELL

FLINDERS LA

Vic Uni (City Campus)

35 Elizabeth St

Excelsior Hse

Hosies Building

Club X

HAYLAND

Townsend Hse

LINGHAM

The Lane Bldg

CAE Performing Arts Cntr

Footway

Ross House

ROYSTON PL

SCOTT AL

DEGRAVES

CAE Centre

Commonwealth Bank Building

ROTHSAY

DEGRAVES

Station Entrance

Unilodge on Flinders Apartments

Phillip

Port

Arc

COCKER AL

Cathedral Arcade

CAB

Young & Jacksons Hotel

St Pauls Anglican Cathedral (built 1891)

CHAPTER HOUSE

Employers House

Footway

Adelphi Hotel

Flinders Gate

Gate

RUTLEDGE

The Cosmopolitan Apartments

Quest on Flinders Lane

Cavendish House

Russell St Theatre

Forum Theatre (The Old State Theatre)

HOSIER

The Flinders Hse

The Brooks

Guides HQ

Duke of Wellington Hotel

OLIVERS

Yarra View Apartments

HIGSON

101 Collins St

Austin Hse

CORPORATION

Duckboard House

Rosarti Hse

RSL

Springfield Hse

FLINDERS ST

Campbell Arcade (underground)

Steps

Flinders St Station

ST. KILDA RD

St Pauls Court

Australian Centre for the Moving Image

Atrium

The Ian Potter Centre

NGV: Australian Art

Federation Square (Expected to open from late 2001)

Plaza

Cross Bar

RUSSELL ST

(City Circle Tram Route)

JOINS 4

25

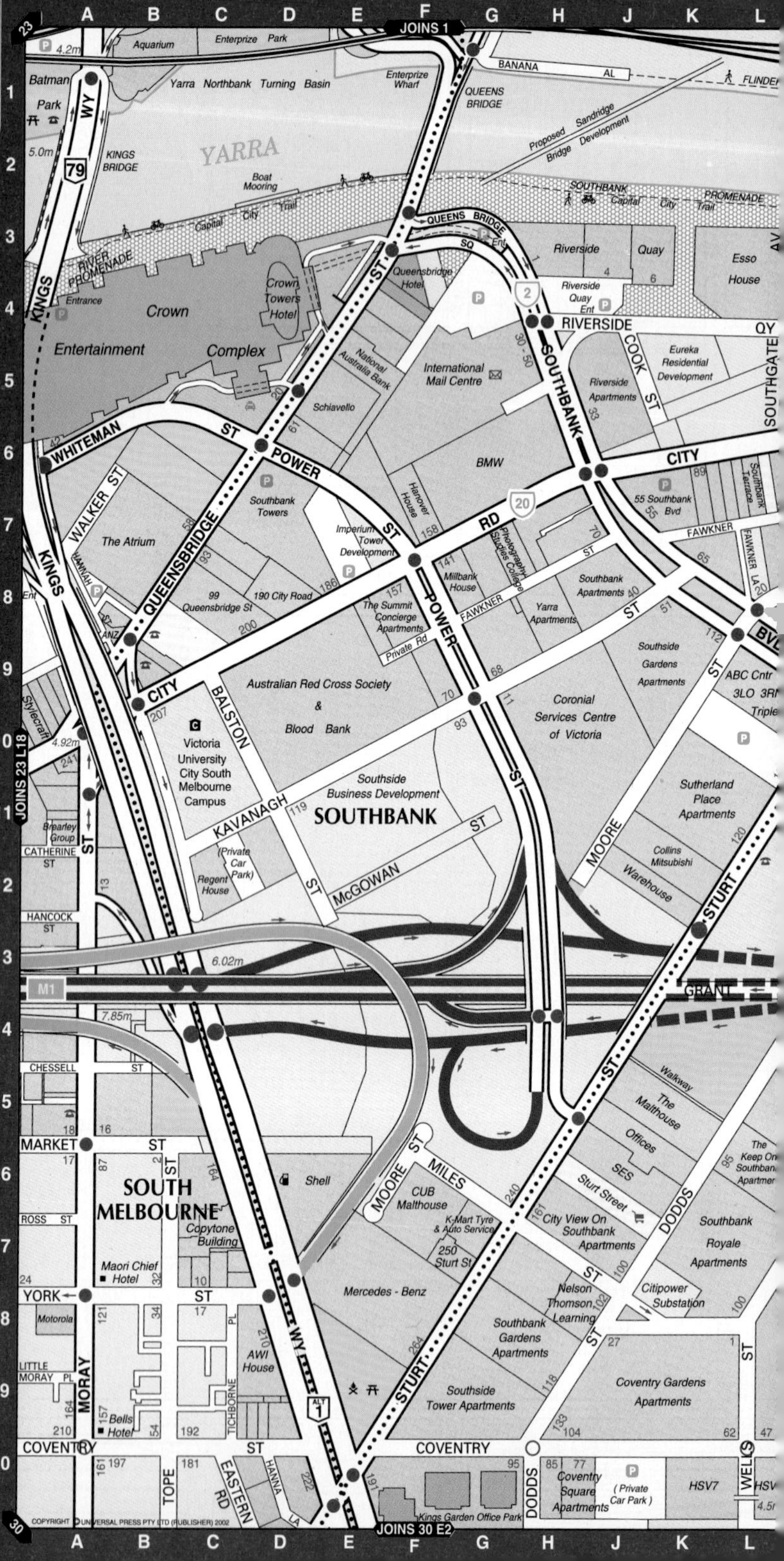

Aquarium
Enterprize Park
Batman Park
Yarra Northbank Turning Basin
Enterprize Wharf
BANANA AL
FLINDERS
QUEENS BRIDGE
KINGS BRIDGE
KINGS WY
79
YARRA
Proposed Sandridge Bridge Development
Boat Mooring
Capital City Trail
RIVER PROMENADE
SOUTHBANK PROMENADE
QUEENS BRIDGE SQ
Riverside Quay
Esso House
Riverside Quay Ent
Crown Towers Hotel
Queensbridge Hotel
Entrance
Crown Entertainment Complex
National Australia Bank
International Mail Centre
RIVERSIDE QY
COOK ST
Eureka Residential Development
SOUTHGATE AV
Riverside Apartments
Schiavello
SOUTHBANK BVD
WHITEMAN ST
QUEENSBRIDGE ST
POWER ST
BMW
CITY RD
Hanover House
Southbank Towers
Imperium Tower Development
55 Southbank Bvd
Southbank Terrace
FAWKNER ST
FAWKNER LA
WALKER ST
The Atrium
HANNAH ST
Photographic Studies College
Millbank House
Southbank Apartments
Yarra Apartments
99 Queensbridge St
190 City Road
The Summit Concierge Apartments
Private Rd
Southside Gardens Apartments
ABC Cntr 3LO 3RN Triple J
Australian Red Cross Society & Blood Bank
Coronial Services Centre of Victoria
Stylecraft
BALSTON ST
Victoria University City South Melbourne Campus
Southside Business Development
SOUTHBANK
Sutherland Place Apartments
KAVANAGH ST
Brearley Group
CATHERINE ST
(Private Car Park)
Regent House
MOORE ST
Collins Mitsubishi
Warehouse
McGOWAN ST
HANCOCK ST
STURT ST
M1
GRANT ST
CHESSELL ST
Walkway
The Malthouse Offices
SES
MARKET ST
Shell
MOORE ST
MILES ST
CUB Malthouse
The Keep On Southbank Apartments
SOUTH MELBOURNE
Sturt Street
DODDS ST
ROSS ST
Copytone Building
K-Mart Tyre & Auto Service
City View On Southbank Apartments
Southbank Royale Apartments
Maori Chief Hotel
250 Sturt St
YORK ST
Mercedes - Benz
Nelson Thomson Learning
Citipower Substation
Motorola
AWI House
Southbank Gardens Apartments
LITTLE MORAY PL
MORAY ST
TICHBORNE PL
Coventry Gardens Apartments
Southside Tower Apartments
Bells Hotel
ALT 1
COVENTRY ST
TOPE ST
EASTERN RD
HANNA LA
Kings Garden Office Park
DODDS ST
Coventry Square Apartments
(Private Car Park)
HSV7
WELLS ST

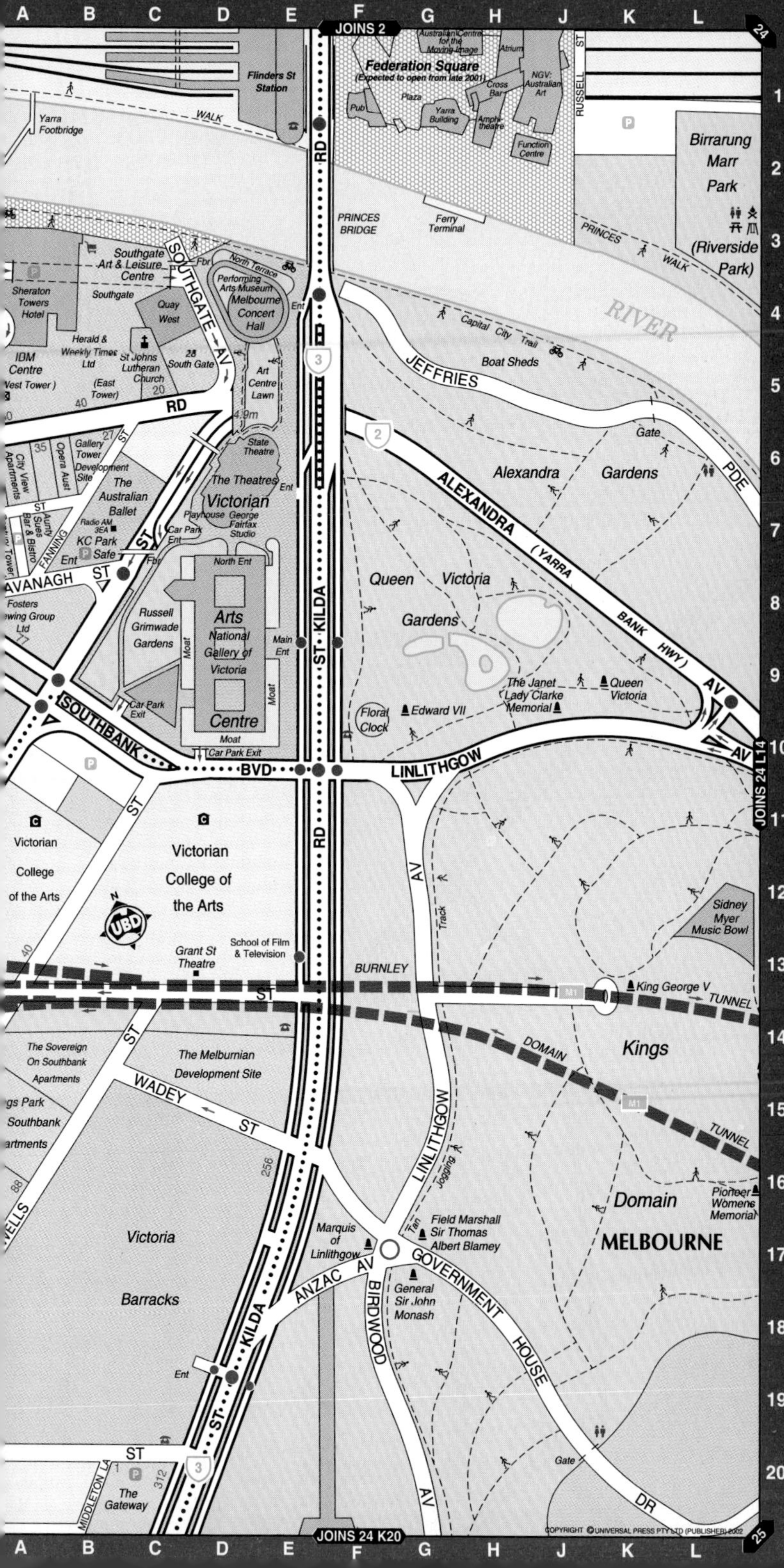

A B C D E F G H J K L

JOINS 2

Australian Centre for the Moving Image
Atrium
Federation Square
(Expected to open from late 2001)
Plaza
Pub
Cross Bar
NGV: Australian Art
Yarra Building
Amphitheatre
Function Centre
Flinders St Station
Yarra Footbridge
WALK
RUSSELL ST
Birrarung Marr Park (Riverside Park)
PRINCES BRIDGE
Ferry Terminal
PRINCES WALK
RIVER
Southgate Art & Leisure Centre
SOUTHGATE AV
North Terrace
Performing Arts Museum
Melbourne Concert Hall
Sheraton Towers Hotel
Southgate
Quay West
Herald & Weekly Times Ltd
St Johns Lutheran Church
28 South Gate
IDM Centre
(East Tower)
West Tower)
Art Centre Lawn
Capital City Trail
Boat Sheds
JEFFRIES
RD
4.9m
State Theatre
The Theatres
Victorian
Playhouse
George Fairfax Studio
Gallery Tower Development Site
City View Apartments
Opera Aust
The Australian Ballet
Radio AM 3EA
KC Park Safe
Aunty Sues Bar & Bistro
FANNING ST
Car Park Ent
CAVANAGH ST
Fosters Brewing Group Ltd
North Ent
Russell Grimwade Gardens
Arts
National Gallery of Victoria
Centre
Moat
Main Ent
Car Park Exit
Car Park Exit
ST KILDA RD
SOUTHBANK BVD
Alexandra Gardens
ALEXANDRA (YARRA BANK HWY) AV
Gate
PDE
Queen Victoria Gardens
The Janet Lady Clarke Memorial
Queen Victoria
Floral Clock
Edward VII
LINLITHGOW AV
Victorian College of the Arts
Victorian College of the Arts
School of Film & Television
Grant St Theatre
BURNLEY ST
Track
Sidney Myer Music Bowl
King George V
TUNNEL
M1
DOMAIN TUNNEL
Kings Domain
The Sovereign On Southbank Apartments
The Melburnian Development Site
WADEY ST
Kings Park Southbank Apartments
WELLS
Victoria Barracks
Jogging
Tan
Field Marshall Sir Thomas Albert Blamey
Marquis of Linlithgow
ANZAC AV
BIRDWOOD AV
GOVERNMENT HOUSE DR
General Sir John Monash
Pioneer Womens Memorial
MELBOURNE
Ent
ST
MIDDLETON LA
The Gateway
Gate
JOINS 24 L14
JOINS 24 K20

MAP 17 FOLLOWS

PREVIOUS MAP 4

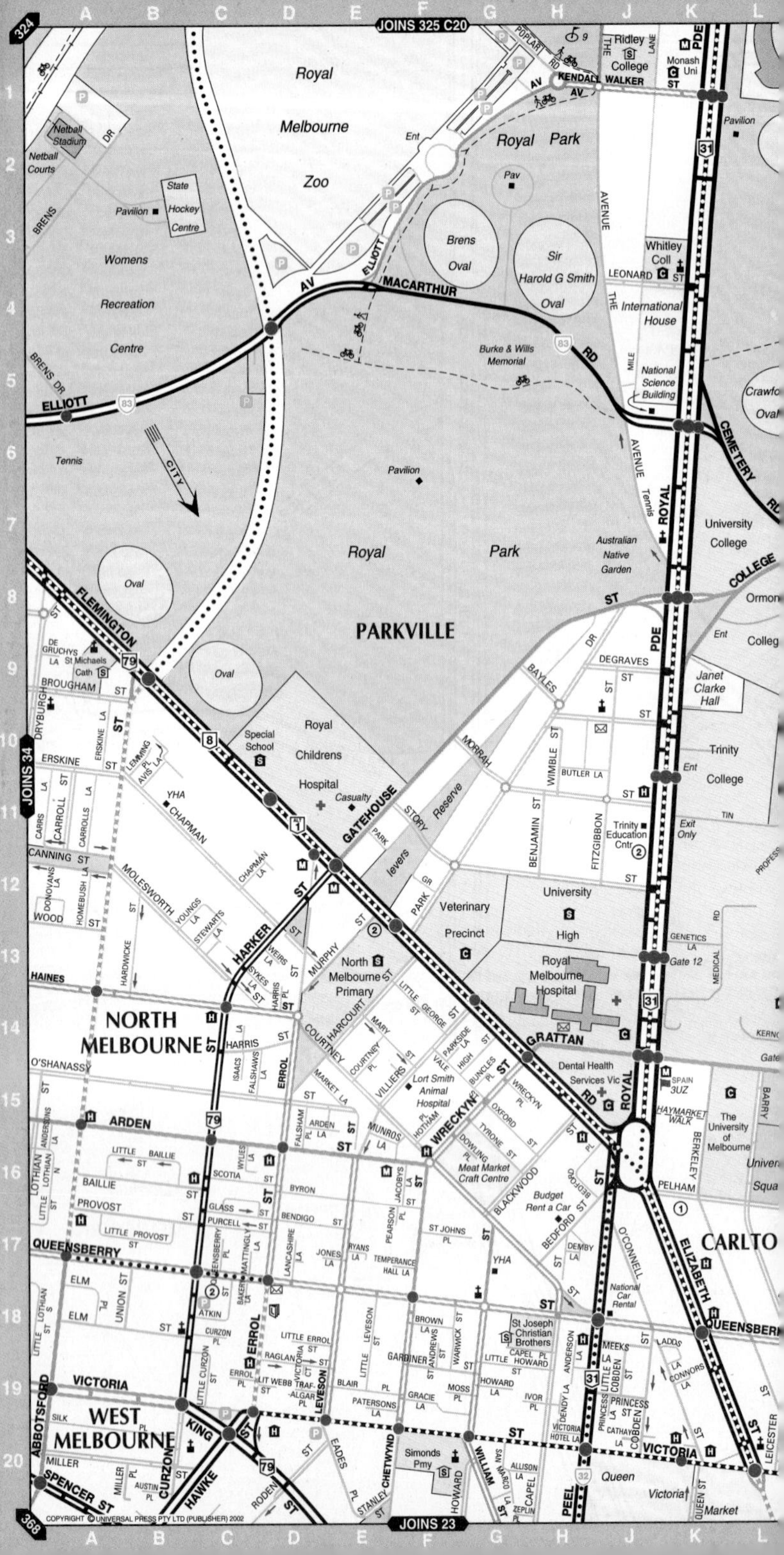
A B C D E F G H J K L
JOINS 325 C20
324
Royal Melbourne Zoo
Netball Stadium
Netball Courts
State Hockey Centre
Pavilion
Womens Recreation Centre
BRENS DR
ELLIOTT AV
MACARTHUR RD
POPLAR RD
KENDALL
WALKER ST
Ridley College
Monash Uni
Royal Park
Brens Oval
Sir Harold G Smith Oval
Whitley Coll
LEONARD ST
International House
Burke & Wills Memorial
National Science Building
THE AVENUE
Crawford Oval
CEMETERY RD
Tennis
CITY
Pavilion
Royal Park
Australian Native Garden
University College
COLLEGE
Ormond College
Oval
FLEMINGTON RD
PARKVILLE
DE GRUCHYS LA
St Michaels Cath
BROUGHAM ST
DRYBURGH
Oval
DEGRAVES ST
Janet Clarke Hall
BAYLES
Special School
Royal Childrens Hospital
Casualty
ERSKINE ST
LEMMING PL
AVIS LA
YHA
CHAPMAN ST
MORRAH ST
WIMBLE ST
BUTLER LA
Trinity College
CARRS
CARROLL ST
CARROLLS LA
GATEHOUSE ST
STORY ST
Ievers Reserve
BENJAMIN ST
FITZGIBBON
Trinity Education Cntr
Exit Only
TIN
CANNING ST
MOLESWORTH ST
DONOVANS LA
HOMEBUSH LA
WOOD ST
HARKER ST
PARK GR
Veterinary Precinct
University High
GENETICS LA
Gate 12
MEDICAL
HARDWICKE
YOUNGS LA
STEWARTS LA
WEIRS LA
SYKES LA
HARRIS PL
MURPHY ST
North Melbourne Primary
LITTLE GEORGE ST
Royal Melbourne Hospital
HAINES
NORTH MELBOURNE
HARRIS ST
HARCOURT ST
MARY
PARKSIDE
GRATTAN ST
KERNOT
O'SHANASSY ST
ISAACS
FALSHAWS LA
ERROL
COURTNEY ST
VILLIERS
Lort Smith Animal Hospital
VALE
HIGH
BUNCLES PL
WRECKYN ST
Dental Health Services Vic
SPAIN 3UZ
HAYMARKET WALK
The University of Melbourne
BARRY
ARDEN ST
FALSHAM
MARKET LA
MUNROS LA
HOTHAM
OXFORD
TYRONE ST
ROYAL PDE
BERKELEY
LOTHIAN
LITTLE BAILLIE ST
BAILLIE
SCOTIA
WYLIES
BYRON
JACOBYS
Meat Market Craft Centre
DOWLING
BLACKWOOD
BEDFORD ST
PELHAM
Budget Rent a Car
University Square
PROVOST
GLASS
PURCELL
BENDIGO
PEARSON
LITTLE PROVOST ST
QUEENSBERRY
MATTINGLY LA
LANCASHIRE
JONES LA
RYANS LA
TEMPERANCE HALL LA
ST JOHNS PL
YHA
DEMBY
O'CONNELL
ELIZABETH
CARLTON
ELM
UNION ST
ATKIN
BAKER
National Car Rental
QUEENSBERRY
CURZON PL
LITTLE ERROL
LEVESON ST
BROWN LA
ST ANDREWS
WARWICK ST
St Joseph Christian Brothers
CAPEL PL
LITTLE HOWARD
ANDERSON
MEEKS LA
LADDS LA
CONNORS LA
RAGLAN ST
GARDINER
VICTORIA
ERROL PL
LITTLE CURZON
LIT WEBB
TRAF-ALGAR PL
BLAIR
PATERSONS LA
GRACIE LA
MOSS PL
HOWARD LA
IVOR PL
DENDY LA
LITTLE COBDEN
PRINCESS ST
CATHAY LA
COBDEN
VICTORIA ST
ABBOTSFORD
SILK PL
WEST MELBOURNE
KING ST
CHETWYND
VICTORIA HOTEL LA
MILLER
HAWKE
EADES
Simonds Pmy
SAN MARCO
ALLISON
CAPEL
PEEL
Queen Victoria Market
QUEEN ST
LEICESTER
SPENCER ST
AUSTIN PL
RODEN ST
STANLEY ST
HOWARD
WILLIAM ST
ZEPLIN
JOINS 34
JOINS 23
368
79 83 8 1 31 32 2

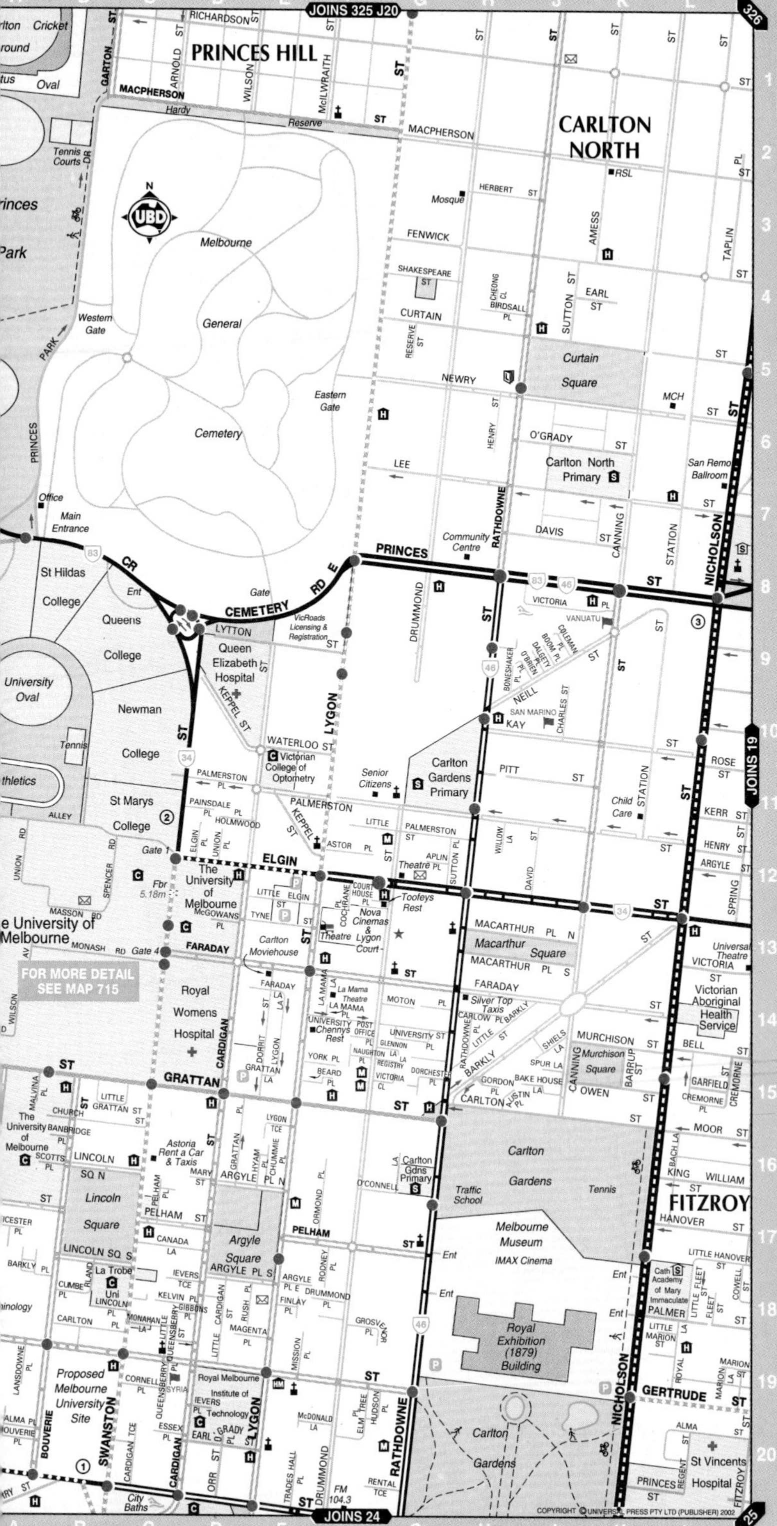
JOINS 325 J20
PRINCES HILL
CARLTON NORTH
Melbourne
General
Cemetery
Princes Park
Western Gate
Eastern Gate
Main Entrance
St Hildas College
Queens College
Newman College
St Marys College
University Oval
Queen Elizabeth Hospital
Victorian College of Optometry
The University of Melbourne
FOR MORE DETAIL SEE MAP 715
Royal Womens Hospital
Carlton Gardens Primary
Curtain Square
Carlton North Primary
Macarthur Square
Murchison Square
Argyle Square
Lincoln Square
Carlton Gardens
Melbourne Museum
IMAX Cinema
Royal Exhibition (1879) Building
Traffic School
FITZROY
St Vincents Hospital
Victorian Aboriginal Health Service
Proposed Melbourne University Site
Royal Melbourne Institute of Technology
PRINCES
CEMETERY RD E
ELGIN
GRATTAN
RATHDOWNE
NICHOLSON
LYGON
SWANSTON
CARDIGAN
GERTRUDE
MACPHERSON
JOINS 19
JOINS 24
326
25

JOINS 326 C20
JOINS 18
JOINS 25
325
24
FITZROY NORTH
FITZROY
COLLINGWOOD
Edinburgh Gardens
Tennis
William Peterson Community Oval
John Batman Institute of TAFE Fitzroy Campus
St Johns Catholic Pmy
Croation Cath Centre
Organ Factory Theatre
Clifton Hill Primary
Child Care
Council Depot (Recycling)
Kinetik Energy
Senior Citizens Club
St Brigids Pmy
Harold McCracken Nursing Home
San Remo Ballroom
Fitzroy North Pmy
MCH
Gary Owen Park
Stationers Supplies
RSL
Youth Centre Child Care
Tenants Union
Universal Theatre
3RRR FM Radio
Victorian Aboriginal Health Service
Min. of Educ.
Fitzroy Primary
Northern Melbourne Institute of TAFE Collingwood Campus
TAFE
St Josephs Cath Pmy
Whitlam Place
Fitzroy Legal Service
Sacred Heart Pmy
St Marys House of Welcome
Nursery
Atherton Gardens Reserve
Youth Centre
Collingwood Alternative School
Theatre
Collingwood College
Indoor Tennis
Community Health Centre
Mosque
Brotherhood of St Laurence
St Vincents Hosp
Collingwood English Language
NICHOLSON ST
BRUNSWICK ST
ST GEORGES RD
QUEENS PDE
ALEXANDRA PDE
(EASTERN HWY)
GEORGE ST
SMITH ST
WELLINGTON ST
JOHNSTON ST
GERTRUDE ST
LANGRIDGE ST
HODDLE ST
FITZROY ST
NAPIER ST
GORE ST
OXFORD ST
CAMBRIDGE ST
ALFRED CR
GRANT ST
McKEAN ST
RICHARDSON ST
REID ST
SKENE PL
SALISBURY CR
ANNAND ST
WATKINS ST
MACPHERSON ST
BROOKES CR
TEMPANY ST
BOSTON PL
FENWICK ST
CHURCH ST
CURTAIN ST
FREEMAN ST
NEWRY ST
PERCY ST
LAURA PL
YORK ST
COLEMAN ST
GRACE LA
CECIL ST
WESTGARTH ST
LEICESTER ST
ROSE ST
KERR ST
HENRY ST
ARGYLE ST
HARRISON PL
VICTORIA ST
GREEVES ST
BELL ST
GARFIELD ST
CREMORNE PL
MOOR ST
KING WILLIAM ST
HANOVER ST
LITTLE HANOVER ST
PALMER ST
MARION LA
ALMA ST
PRINCES ST
GRAHAM ST
DUKE ST
ST DAVID ST
EXHIBITION ST
CHAPEL ST
HODGSON ST
STANLEY ST
CONDELL ST
CHARLES ST
WEBB ST
PEEL ST
DERBY ST
MATER ST
HOTHAM ST
KEELE ST
EASEY ST
SACKVILLE ST
PERRY ST
OTTER ST
LITTLE WELLINGTON ST
NAPOLEON ST
VERE ST
SINGLETON ST
GIPPS ST
GLASSHOUSE RD
ROBERT ST
WATERLOO RD
GLASGOW ST
MONTAGUE ST
YORK ST
McCUTCHEON WAY
COUNCIL ST
NOONE ST
HODGKINSON ST
PAGE ST
ROWE ST
PARK PDE
PARK PL
WOODSIDE ST
MICHAEL ST
DELBRIDGE ST
FALCONER ST
ABBOT ST
COPPER LA
BALLARAT ST
CHARLOTTE ST
EMERALD ST
PALMER ST
CAMPBELL ST
STURT ST
RUPERT ST
CROMWELL ST
COPYRIGHT © UNIVERSAL PRESS PTY LTD (PUBLISHER) 2002

JOINS 326 J20

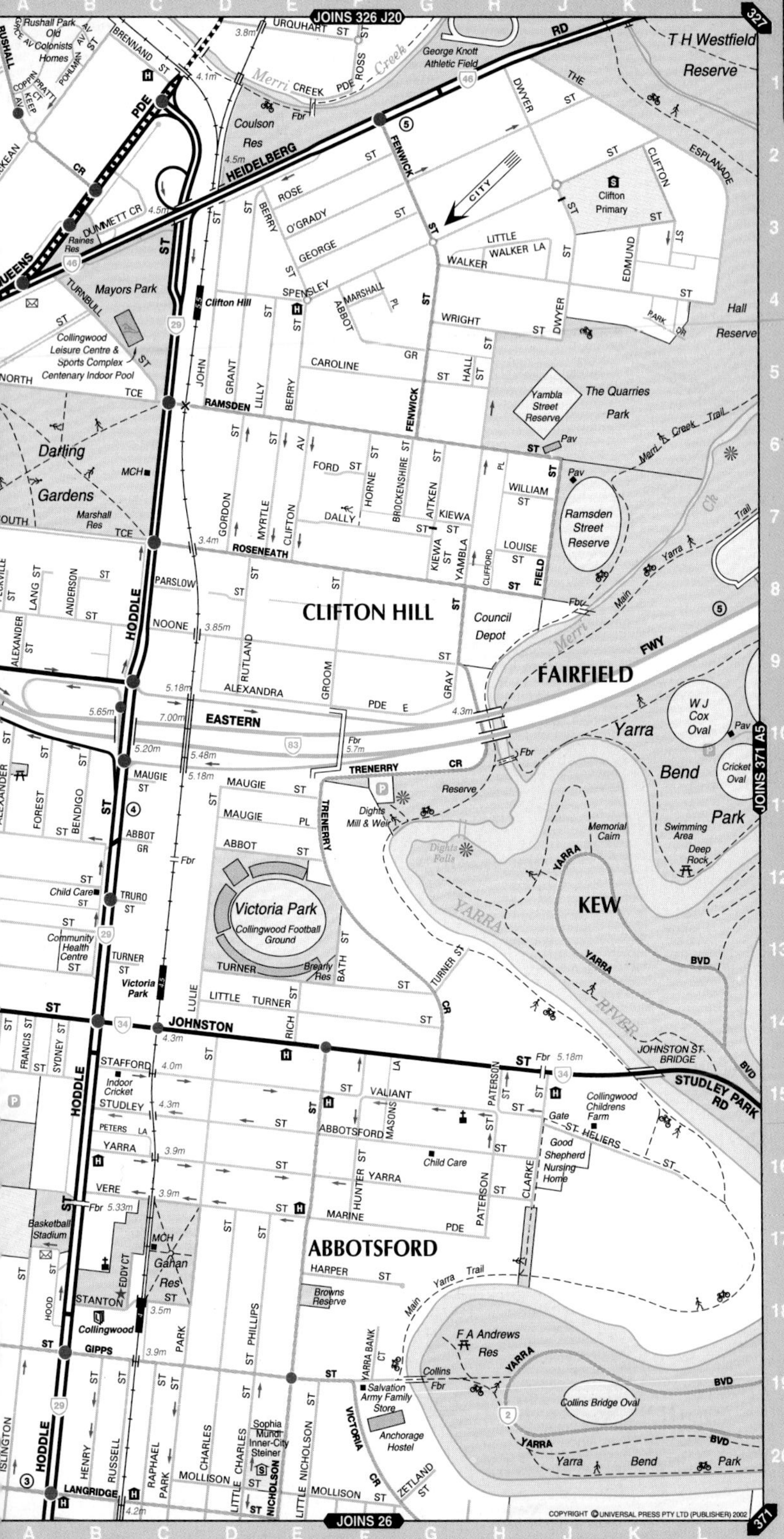

MAP 23 FOLLOWS

JOINS 371 A5

JOINS 26

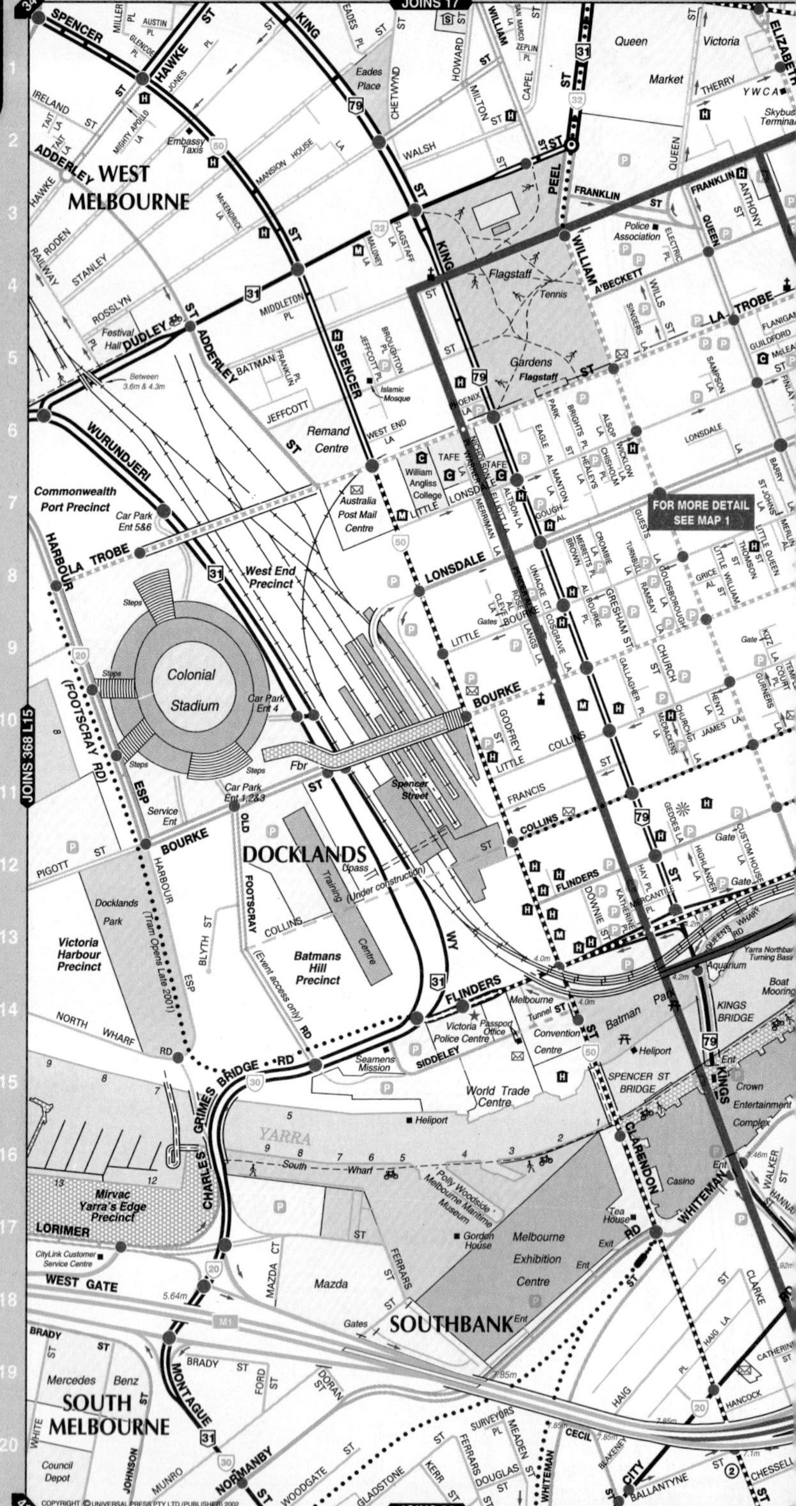
JOINS 17
JOINS 29
JOINS 368 L15
PREVIOUS MAP 20
34
412
WEST MELBOURNE
DOCKLANDS
SOUTHBANK
SOUTH MELBOURNE
Queen Victoria Market
Flagstaff Gardens
Colonial Stadium
Commonwealth Port Precinct
West End Precinct
Remand Centre
Australia Post Mail Centre
William Angliss College
Spencer Street
Victoria Harbour Precinct
Docklands Park
Batmans Hill Precinct
Mirvac Yarra's Edge Precinct
World Trade Centre
Melbourne Exhibition Centre
Crown Entertainment Complex
Casino
Polly Woodside Melbourne Maritime Museum
Batman Park
Aquarium
Victoria Police Centre
Seamens Mission
Mazda
Mercedes Benz
Council Depot
FOR MORE DETAIL SEE MAP 1
YARRA
SPENCER
HAWKE ST
KING
WILLIAM
ELIZABETH
LA TROBE
LONSDALE
BOURKE
COLLINS
FLINDERS
DUDLEY
WURUNDJERI
HARBOUR ESP
CLARENDON
WHITEMAN
NORMANBY
MONTAGUE
CITY RD
WEST GATE
LORIMER
CHARLES GRIMES BRIDGE RD
COPYRIGHT © UNIVERSAL PRESS PTY LTD (PUBLISHER) 2002

JOINS 18
JOINS 25
JOINS 30
19
31
A
B
C
D
E
F
G
H
J
K
L
1
2
3
4
5
6
7
8
9
10
11
12
13
14
15
16
17
18
19
20
MELBOURNE
FITZROY
FOR MORE DETAIL SEE MAP 2
FOR MORE DETAIL SEE MAP 3
FOR MORE DETAIL SEE MAP 4
VICTORIA
SWANSTON
LYGON
RATHDOWNE
Carlton
Gardens
St Vincents Hospital
VICTORIA PDE
City Baths
Avis Rent a Car
Ansett
Hertz Rent a Car
Old Melbourne Gaol
Royal Melbourne Institute of Technology (City Campus)
RUSSELL
EXHIBITION
SPRING
NICHOLSON
ALBERT
EVELYN
Synag
Fire Museum
MFB HQ
Parliament Gardens
GISBORNE
LA TROBE
Melbourne Central
Thrifty Car Rental
LONSDALE
LITTLE LONSDALE
Comedy Theatre
Her Majestys Theatre
Cinema
Parliament Houses of Parliament
State Government Offices
Treasury Gardens
MACARTHUR
Gordon Res
BOURKE
BOURKE STREET MALL
GPO
COLLINS
LITTLE COLLINS
Town Hall
Kino Cinema
City Square
ELIZABETH
QUEEN
WILLIAM
FLINDERS
FLINDERS ST
Flinders Street
Federation Square
WELLINGTON PDE S
BATMAN AVENUE BRIDGE
BATMAN AV
Birrarung Marr Park
PRINCES WALK
RIVER
Ferry Terminal
PRINCES BRIDGE
(Riverside Park)
Capital City Trail
Boat Sheds
JEFFRIES
Alexandra Gardens
ALEXANDRA (YARRA BANK HWY) AV
Concert Hall
Tunnel
Southgate
Sheraton Towers
Esso House
Riverside Quay
QUEENS BRIDGE
QUEENS BRIDGE SQ
SOUTHBANK
SOUTHGATE AV
CITY RD
IBM
Aust Ballet
Victorian Arts Centre
ST KILDA RD
Queen Victoria Gardens
Floral Clock
LINLITHGOW
Sidney Myer Music Bowl
Kings Domain
BURNLEY TUNNEL
DOMAIN TUNNEL
Childrens Court
Radio 3TT
POWER ST
ABC RADIO 3LO,3RN,JJJ
BVD
Victorian College of the Arts
Coronial Services Cntr of Victoria
Red Cross Blood Bank
School of Art
Grant Street Theatre
WADEY ST
GOVERNMENT HOUSE
Domain
Victorian Uni of Technology
KAVANAGH
McGOWAN
MORAY
FWY
WY
Fire Station
Playbox Theatre Centre Malthouse
Police Hospital
Victoria Barracks
SES
MILES
Army Workshop
STURT
DODDS
Substation
WELLS
COVENTRY
HSV-7
MIDDLETON
ANZAC AV
BIRDWOOD
QUEENSBRIDGE
MOORE

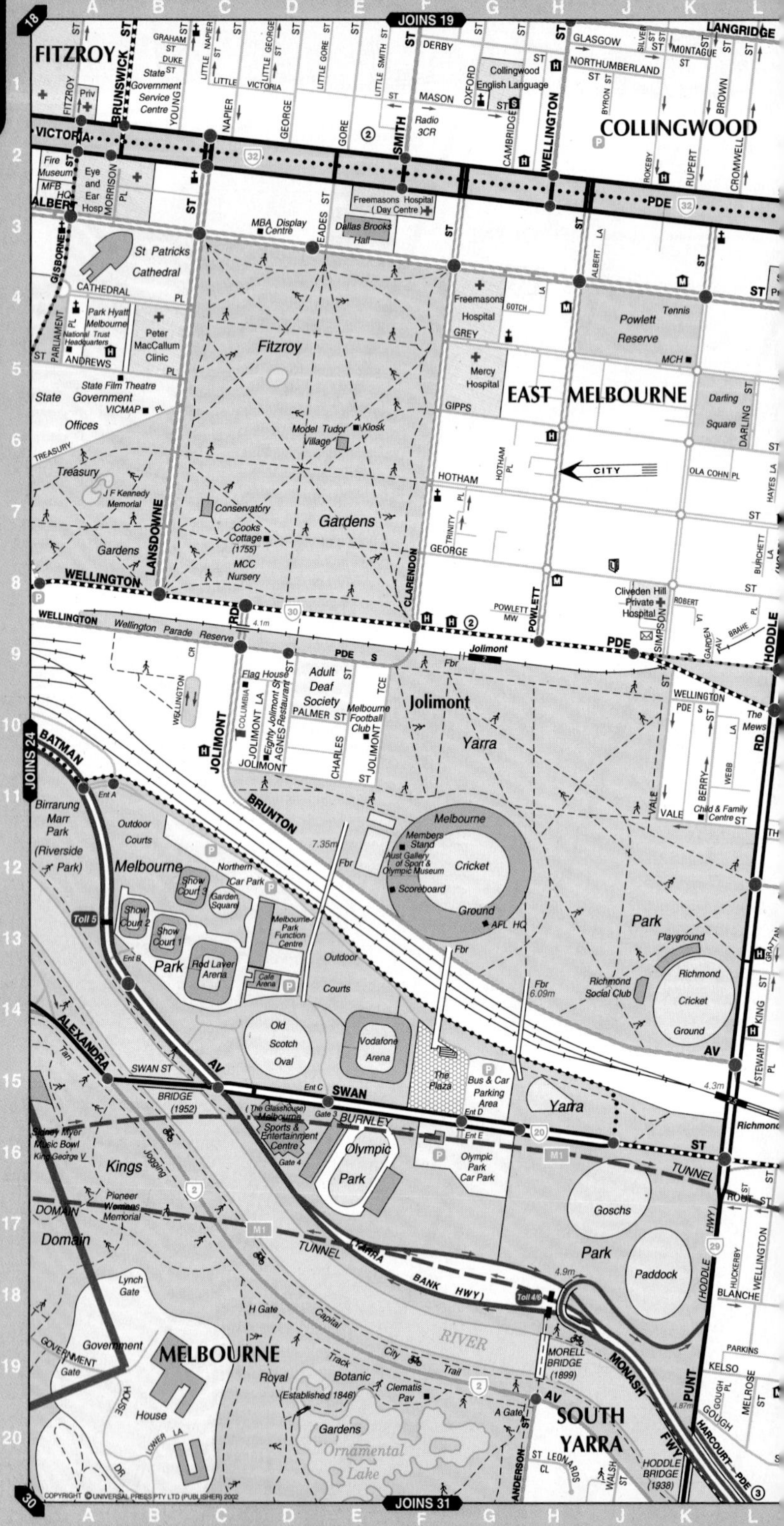

JOINS 19
FITZROY
COLLINGWOOD
EAST MELBOURNE
Fitzroy Gardens
Jolimont
Yarra Park
Melbourne Cricket Ground
Melbourne Park
Olympic Park
Goschs Paddock
Kings Domain
Royal Botanic Gardens
MELBOURNE
SOUTH YARRA
Birrarung Marr Park (Riverside Park)
St Patricks Cathedral
Treasury Gardens
VICTORIA PDE
WELLINGTON PDE
BATMAN AV
BRUNTON AV
SWAN ST
ALEXANDRA AV
MONASH FWY
PUNT RD
HODDLE ST
JOINS 24
JOINS 31
COPYRIGHT © UNIVERSAL PRESS PTY LTD (PUBLISHER) 2002

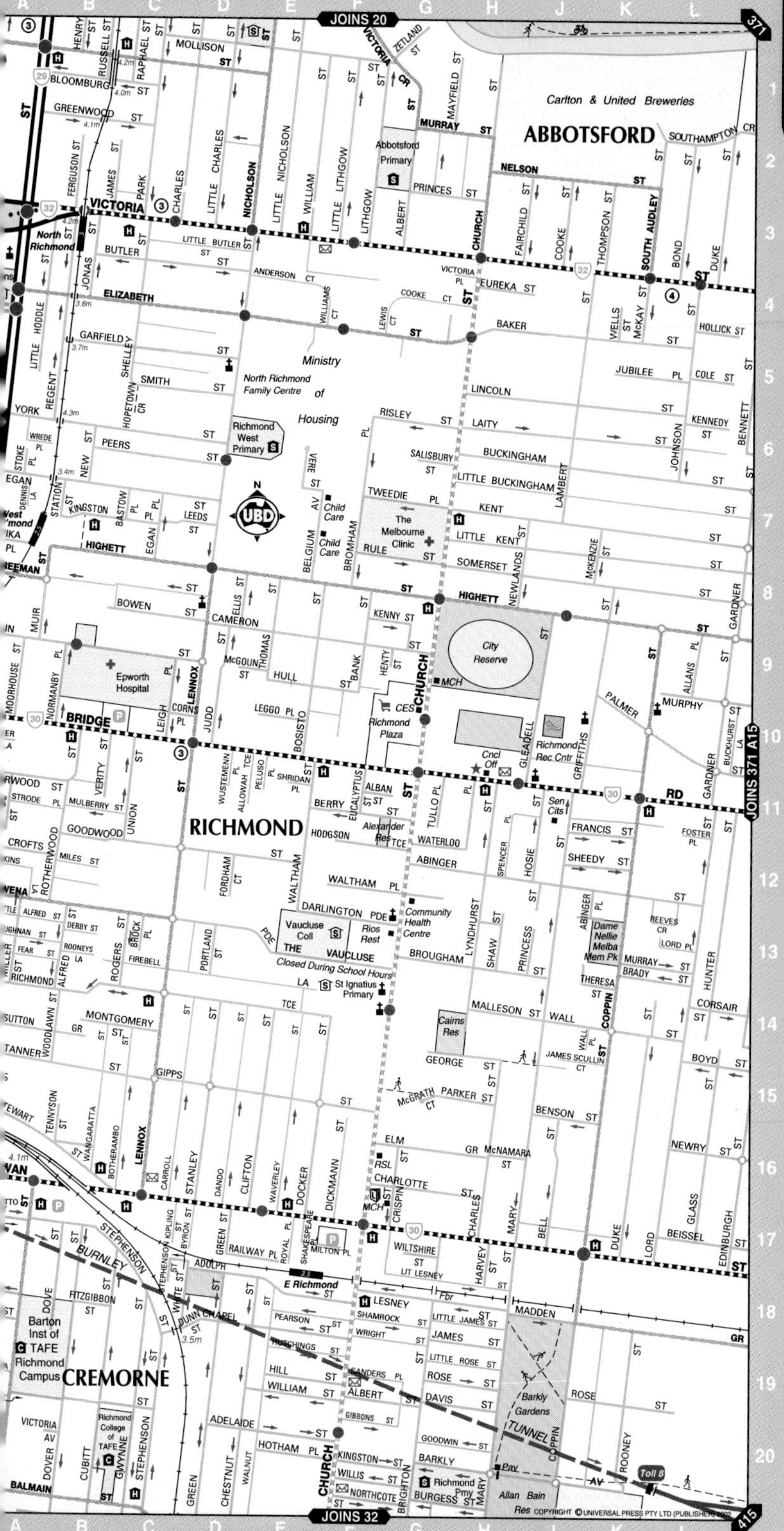

MAP 29 FOLLOWS

368
JOINS 23
PREVIOUS MAP 26

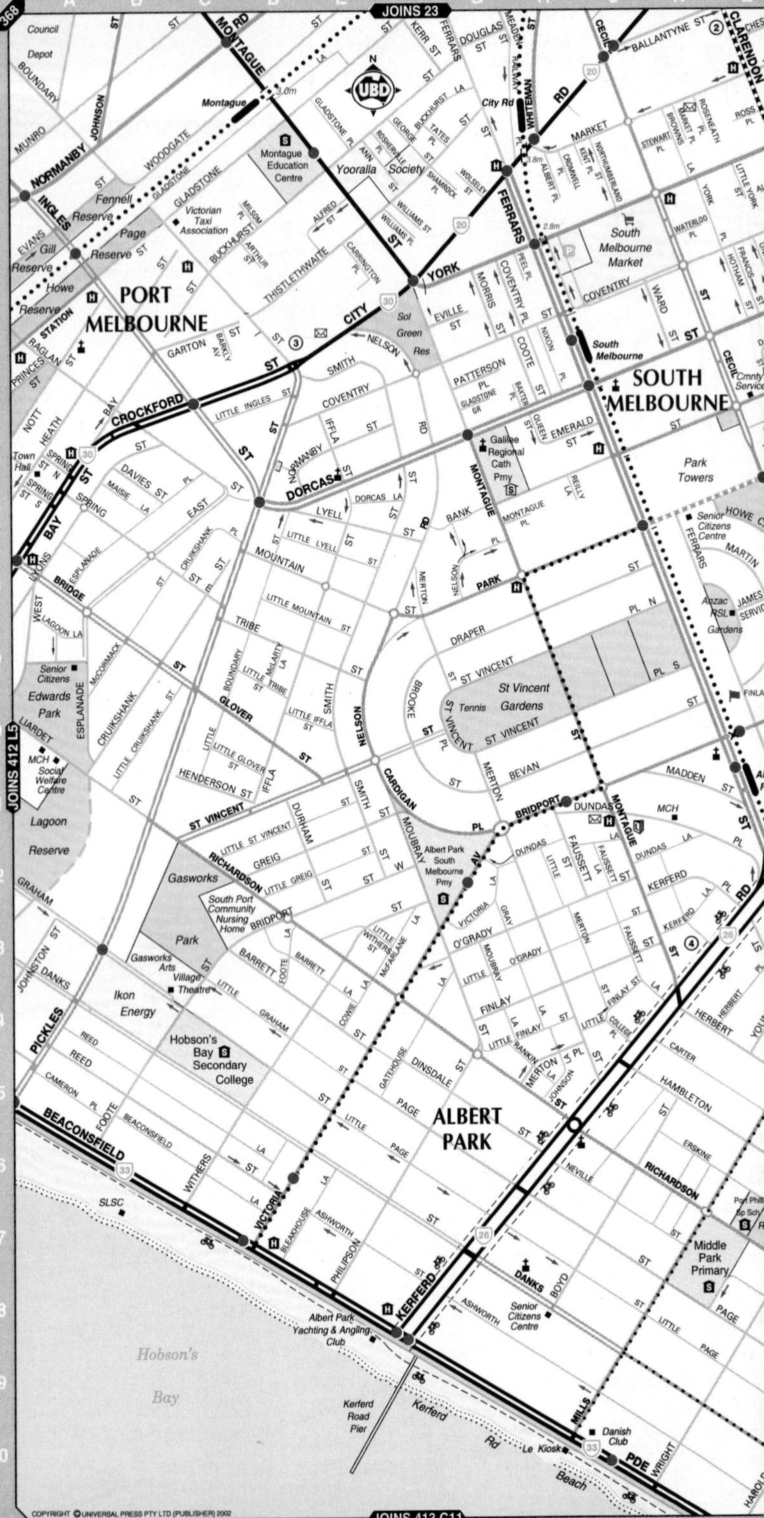

JOINS 412 L5
JOINS 413 C11

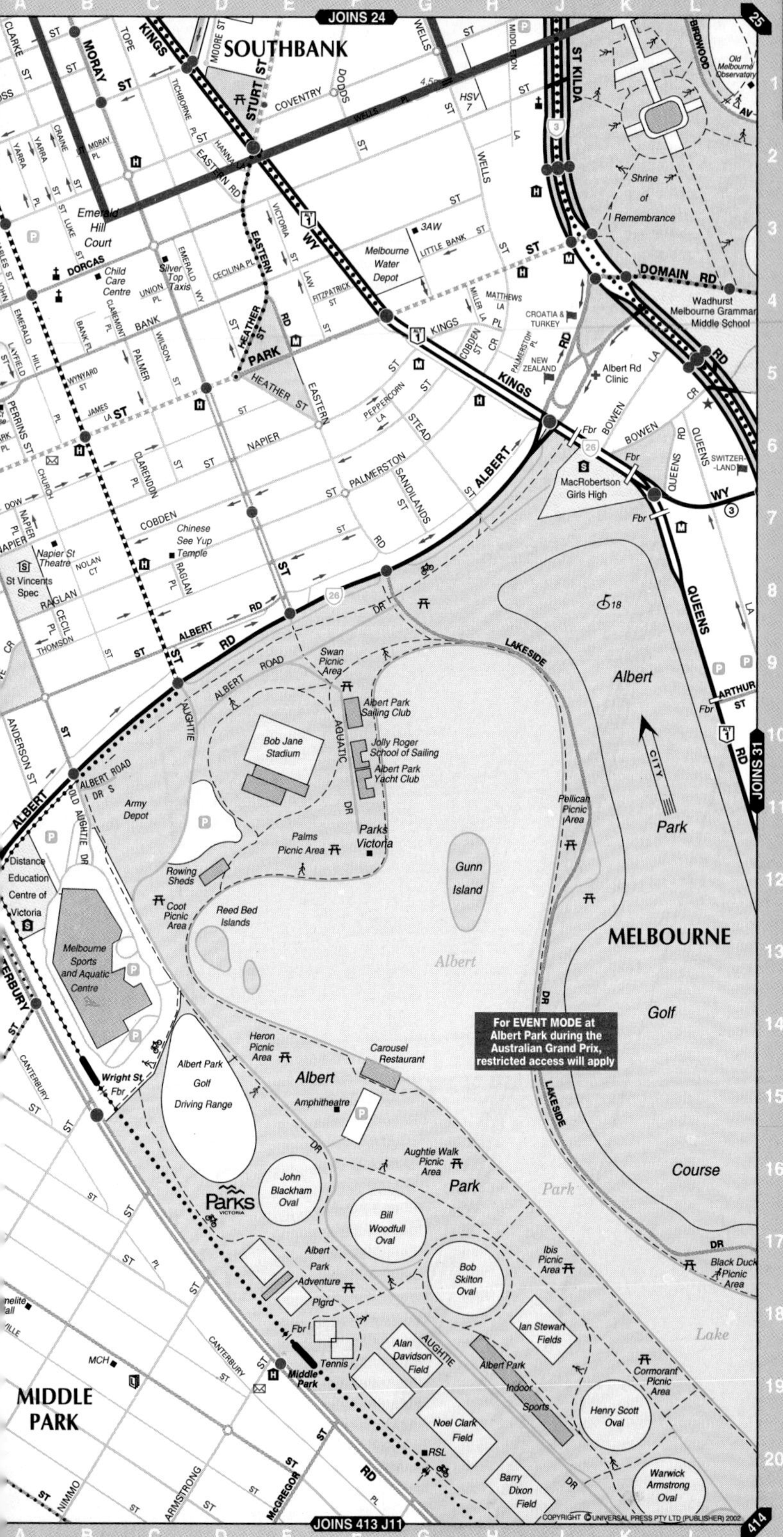
JOINS 24
SOUTHBANK
Shrine of Remembrance
Old Melbourne Observatory
Melbourne Water Depot
Wadhurst Melbourne Grammar Middle School
Albert Rd Clinic
MacRobertson Girls High
Emerald Hill Court
Child Care Centre
Silver Top Taxis
Chinese See Yup Temple
Napier St Theatre
St Vincents Spec
Swan Picnic Area
Albert Park Sailing Club
Jolly Roger School of Sailing
Albert Park Yacht Club
Bob Jane Stadium
Army Depot
Parks Victoria
Palms Picnic Area
Pelican Picnic Area
Gunn Island
Rowing Sheds
Coot Picnic Area
Reed Bed Islands
Distance Education Centre of Victoria
Melbourne Sports and Aquatic Centre
Albert Park
MELBOURNE
Albert Park Golf Course
For EVENT MODE at Albert Park during the Australian Grand Prix, restricted access will apply
Heron Picnic Area
Carousel Restaurant
Amphitheatre
Albert Park Golf Driving Range
John Blackham Oval
Bill Woodfull Oval
Bob Skilton Oval
Aughtie Walk Picnic Area
Ibis Picnic Area
Black Duck Picnic Area
Albert Park Adventure Plgrd
Ian Stewart Fields
Albert Park Lake
Alan Davidson Field
Albert Park Indoor Sports
Cormorant Picnic Area
Henry Scott Oval
Noel Clark Field
Barry Dixon Field
Warwick Armstrong Oval
Wright St
Middle Park
MIDDLE PARK
JOINS 31
JOINS 413 J11
COPYRIGHT © UNIVERSAL PRESS PTY LTD (PUBLISHER) 2002

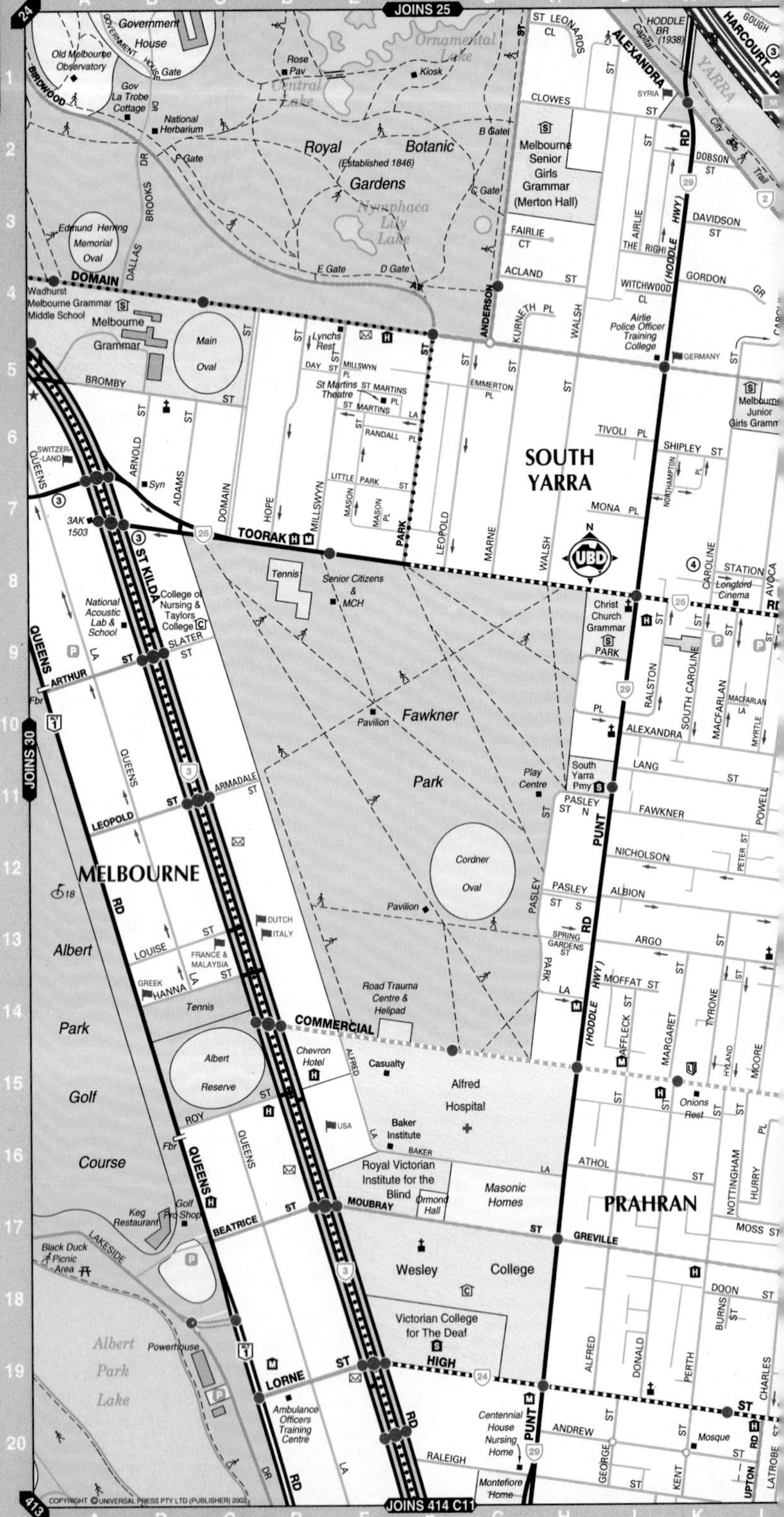
JOINS 25
Government House
Old Melbourne Observatory
Gov La Trobe Cottage
National Herbarium
Royal Botanic Gardens
(Established 1846)
Ornamental Lake
Central Lake
Nymphaea Lily Lake
Rose Pav
Kiosk
Edmund Herring Memorial Oval
DOMAIN
Wadhurst Melbourne Grammar Middle School
Melbourne Grammar
Main Oval
BROMBY
ST LEONARDS CL
CLOWES
Melbourne Senior Girls Grammar (Merton Hall)
FAIRLIE CT
ACLAND ST
ANDERSON
KURNETH PL
WALSH
ALEXANDRA
HODDLE BR (1938)
HARCOURT
YARRA
Capital City Trail
SYRIA
DOBSON ST
DAVIDSON ST
GORDON GR
WITCHWOOD CL
Airlie Police Officer Training College
GERMANY
Melbourne Junior Girls Grammar
St Martins Theatre
Lynchs Rest
MILLSWYN
ST MARTINS LA
RANDALL PL
LITTLE PARK ST
EMMERTON PL
TIVOLI PL
SHIPLEY ST
SOUTH YARRA
MONA PL
TOORAK
SWITZERLAND
3AK 1503
ST KILDA
College of Nursing & Taylors College
Tennis
Senior Citizens & MCH
National Acoustic Lab & School
SLATER ST
ARTHUR
Christ Church Grammar
STATION
Longford Cinema
Fawkner Park
Pavilion
Play Centre
Cordner Oval
ALEXANDRA
LANG ST
FAWKNER
NICHOLSON
ALBION
PASLEY ST
ARGO
SPRING GARDENS ST
MOFFAT ST
South Yarra Pmy
PUNT RD
(HODDLE HWY)
JOINS 30
ARMADALE ST
LEOPOLD ST
MELBOURNE
Albert Golf Course
Albert Park
LOUISE ST
FRANCE & MALAYSIA
DUTCH
ITALY
GREEK
HANNA
Tennis
Albert Reserve
Road Trauma Centre & Helipad
COMMERCIAL
Chevron Hotel
Casualty
Alfred Hospital
Baker Institute
BAKER
ROY ST
QUEENS RD
Royal Victorian Institute for the Blind
Ormond Hall
Masonic Homes
MOUBRAY ST
GREVILLE ST
PRAHRAN
ATHOL ST
Keg Restaurant
Golf Pro Shop
BEATRICE
LAKESIDE
Black Duck Picnic Area
Wesley College
Victorian College for The Deaf
HIGH ST
Albert Park Lake
Powerhouse
LORNE ST
Ambulance Officers Training Centre
Centennial House Nursing Home
Montefiore Home
ANDREW
RALEIGH
DOON ST
Mosque
MOSS ST
NOTTINGHAM
Onions Rest
COPYRIGHT © UNIVERSAL PRESS PTY LTD (PUBLISHER) 2002
JOINS 414 C11

JOINS 26
371
CREMORNE
RICHMOND
Richmond TAFE
BALMAIN
WILLIS ST
NORTHCOTE ST
Richmond Pmy
BURGESS ST
BARKLY
Allan Bain Reserve
COPPIN ST
ROONEY ST
Toll 8
Toll 7
FWY
COTTER ST
BENT ST
GWYNNE
PDE
CHESTNUT
GORDON ST
AMSTERDAM
Citipower Terminal
WILLOW
YORKSHIRE
NEWTON ST
YARRA ST
DOVER
CUBITT
MUNRO ST
PALMER
GREEN
ELECTRIC ST
DALE ST
PRINCE PATRICK ST
Charles Evans Res
PALMER PDE
ODDYS LA
HARGREAVES ST
HOWARD ST
BRIGHTON
DURHAM
MARY
McConchie Res
Ped Upass
MONASH
CHURCH
(CITYLINK
TWY)
RIVER
Herring Island
Quarry Reserve
Herring Reserve
Boat Sheds
Thomas Oval
Como Park North
Como Reserve
Jetty
Como Landing
ALEXANDRA
Capital City Trail
Darling Gardens
AV
Melbourne High
CLAREMONT ST
COPELEN ST
VICTORIA TCE
MALCOLM ST
FORREST HILL
DALY ST
ALMEIDA CR
ATV Channel 10
Pavilion
Como Park
CITY
Como House
Ent
LECHLADE AV
MURPHY ST
DARLING
South Yarra
YARRA
CLAREMONT
TOORAK
Fun Factory
Como Centre
RIVER
TIVOLI
TIME LA
Rockley Gardens
ROCKLEY
KENSINGTON
COMO
FULHAM
RD
JOINS 415
PENNY LA
OXFORD
BOND ST
CHAMBERS
Reserve
WILLIAM
CHAPEL
FORSTER
CUNNINGHAM
CLARA
PALERMO
OXFORD
SURREY
DRAIN RESERVE
CROMWELL
STANLEY ST
STANHOPE
NORMAN AV
Tennis
BUNALBO AV
CULLAH AV
WALTER ST
HAWKSBURN CL
MAY GR
QUAMBY AV
DAVIS
ARTHUR PL
FITZGERALD
Sen Cits
PORTLAND
St Josephs
MEDLEY
ROCKY LA
DAVISON
Jam Factory
Stonnington City Council Depot & Rubbish Baler
Hawksburn
HOPETOUN GR
THE VAUCLUSE
WILLIAMS
WOODSIDE CR
CLIFF
GARDEN
WILSON
CASSELL
HAWKSBURN
OBAN
GORDON ST
PHOENIX
HOWARD
Grosvenor Res
SCOTIA GR
ELLIS
RAILWAY PL
TASHINNY RD
SMYTH
GROSVENOR
LARA
BARRY
SIMMONS
HAZELDON
OAK
PALFREYMAN
Polyglot Theatre
LUXTON
ASHE GR
PERRY ST
ELIZABETH
BALMORAL PL
GREY ST
MOTHERWELL
BROWNING WK
SIMMONS
BARNSBURY
EVELINA RD
OSBORNE
BALMORAL
Prahran Market
MARKET
BRAY
SURREY
CAVENDISH PL
CROMWELL PL
CROMWELL
JOY
HOWITT
McKILLOP
HOBSON
MAY RD
SAMS WY
MALVERN
RD
Pran Central
Rec Centre
Victoria House Private Hospital
Court House
WATTLE
CARLTON
HINTON
Grattan Gardens
WALKER ST
Tennis
SUMMERS ST
CLARKE
DIXON ST
FRANCIS
MILLER
ROBINSON ST
CATO
BRENCHLEY PL
GRATTAN
IZETT
CHATHAM ST
PRINCES
LITTLE
Child Care
Princes Gardens
BELLA ST
ESSEX
BENDIGO
CL
LEILA
MACKAY
IRENE PL
ERROL
WESTBOURNE
CONTINENTAL WY
Town Hall
KING
MURRAY
SPRING ST
PORTER
PERCY PL
PERCY
CECIL PL
CES
ANCHOR PL
YORK PL
WRIGHTS TCE
ST MALO ST
PRIDHAM
HIGH
ST EDMONDS
MACQUARIE
MAPLES LA
HILLINGDON PL
CLIFTON
MOUNT
REGENT
BANGS
BENDIGO
YORK
IVY
LEWISHAM
Victoria Gardens
TRINIAN
WILLIAMS
BAYVIEW
Aberdeen Res
ABERDEEN
THOMAS
Swinburne University of Technology
VICTORIA
JOINS 414 J11
415

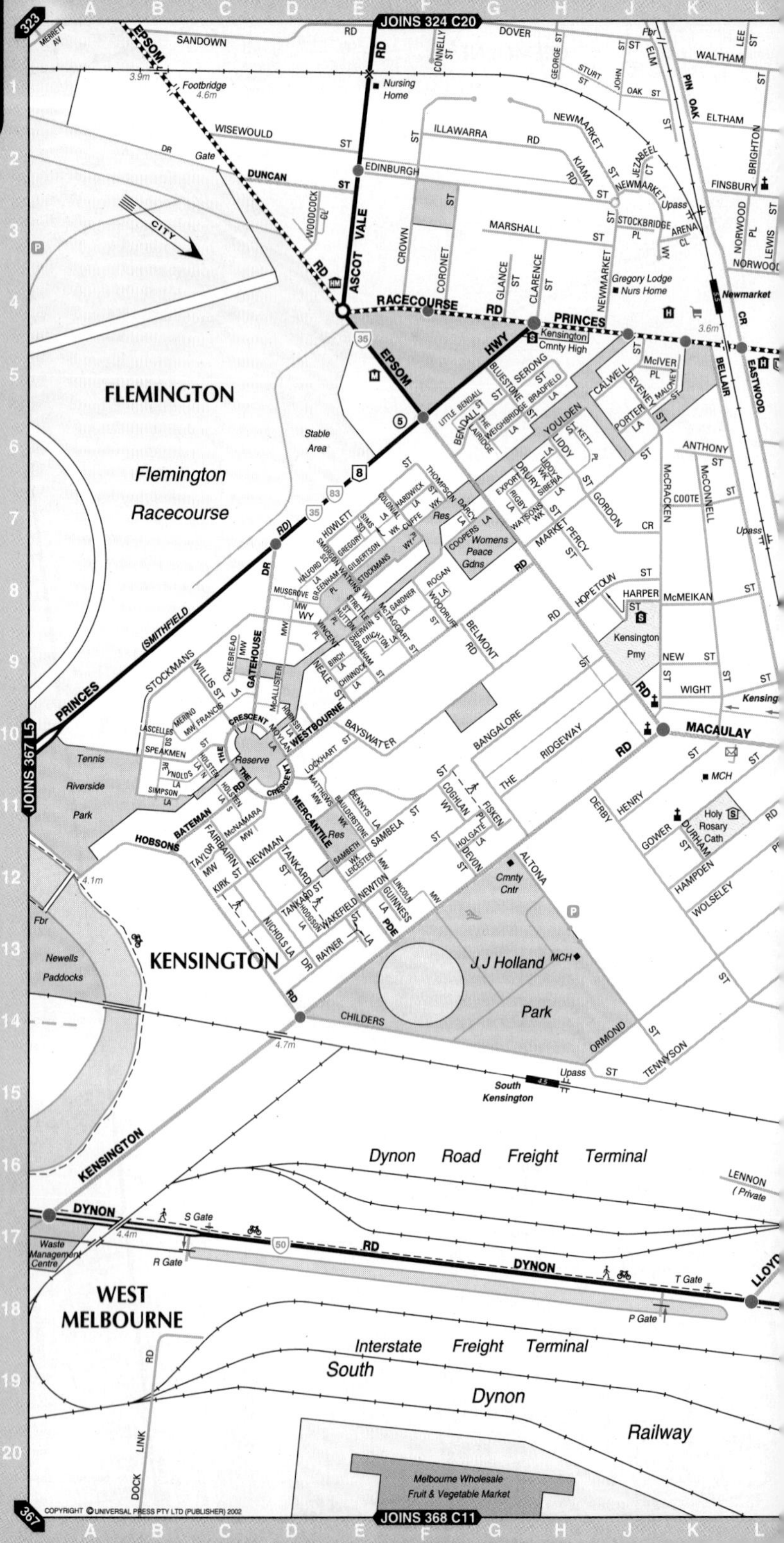

JOINS 324 C20
JOINS 368 C11
JOINS 367 L5
323
367
A B C D E F G H J K L
1 2 3 4 5 6 7 8 9 10 11 12 13 14 15 16 17 18 19 20
FLEMINGTON
Flemington
Racecourse
KENSINGTON
WEST
MELBOURNE
EPSOM
SANDOWN
MERRETT AV
DOVER
ASCOT VALE RD
Nursing Home
Footbridge
WISEWOULD
DUNCAN ST
EDINBURGH
ILLAWARRA RD
NEWMARKET
KIAMA RD
MARSHALL ST
STOCKBRIDGE PL
ARENA CL
CROWN
CORONET
GLANCE ST
CLARENCE ST
Gregory Lodge
Nurs Home
RACECOURSE RD
PRINCES HWY
Kensington Cmnty High
Newmarket
WALTHAM
ELTHAM
BRIGHTON
FINSBURY
NORWOOD
NORWOOD PL
LEWIS ST
PIN OAK
BELLAIR
EASTWOOD
McIVER PL
CALWELL
DEVENEY
MALONEY
PORTER LA
YOULDEN
SERONG
BRADFIELD
BLUESTONE
WEIGHBRIDGE
LITTLE BENDALL
BENDALL
LIDDY
KETT
ANTHONY ST
McCRACKEN
McCONNELL
COOTE
GORDON
CR
Upass
Stable Area
SMITHFIELD
DR
Womens Peace Gdns
COOPERS
DARCY
THOMPSON
HARDWICK
COLONIAL
CUFFE
HOWLETT
GREGORY
GILBERTSON
STOCKMANS
HALFORD
GREENHAM
WATKINS
STRETTLE
MUSGROVE
VINCENT
HUTTON
SHERWIN
GRAHAM
CRICHTON
McTAGGART
GARDNER
ROGAN
WOODRUFF
BELMONT RD
EXPORT
DRURY
RIGBY
WATSONS WK
MARKET
PERCY
HOPETOUN
HARPER
McMEIKAN
Kensington Pmy
NEW ST
WIGHT
MACAULAY RD
Kensing
CAKEBREAD MW
GATEHOUSE
McALLISTER
NEALE
BIRCH
CHINNOCK
WESTBOURNE
BAYSWATER
BANGALORE
THE RIDGEWAY
STOCKMANS
WILLIS ST
MERINO
FRANCIS
LASCELLES
SPEAKMEN
SIMPSON
HOLSTEN
THE CRESCENT
Reserve
MOYLAN
HORNSBY
Tennis
Riverside
Park
LOCKHART
MATTHEWS
DENNYS
BAULDERSTONE
MERCANTILE
Res
SAMBELA
COGHLAN
FISKEN
HOLGATE
DEVON
ALTONA
Cmnty Cntr
DERBY
HENRY
GOWER
DURHAM
Holy Rosary Cath
MCH
HAMPDEN
WOLSELEY
BATEMAN
HOBSONS
TAYLOR
FAIRBAIRN
McNAMARA
KIRK
NEWMAN
TANKARD
HODGSON
WAKEFIELD
NEWTON
GUINNESS
LINCOLN
NICHOLS LA
RAYNER
SAMBETH
LEICESTER
J J Holland
Park
CHILDERS
ORMOND
TENNYSON
Fbr
Newells
Paddocks
South
Kensington
KENSINGTON
Dynon Road Freight Terminal
LENNON
(Private
DYNON RD
Waste Management Centre
S Gate
R Gate
T Gate
P Gate
LLOYD
Interstate Freight Terminal
South Dynon Railway
DOCK LINK RD
Melbourne Wholesale Fruit & Vegetable Market

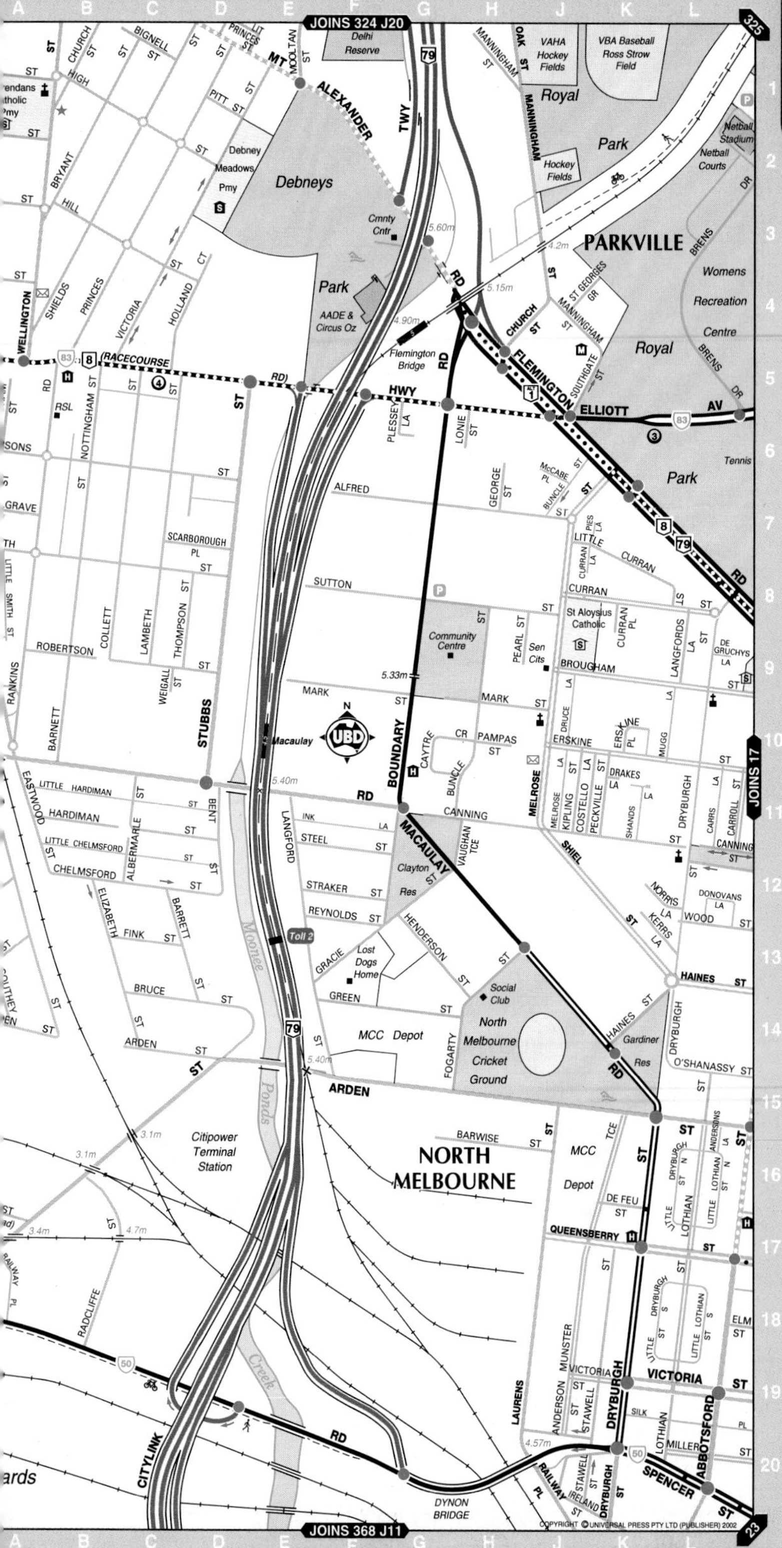

MAP 77 FOLLOWS

JOINS 17

PREVIOUS MAP 34

LIMIT OF MAPS

A B C D E F G H J K L

LIMIT OF MAPS

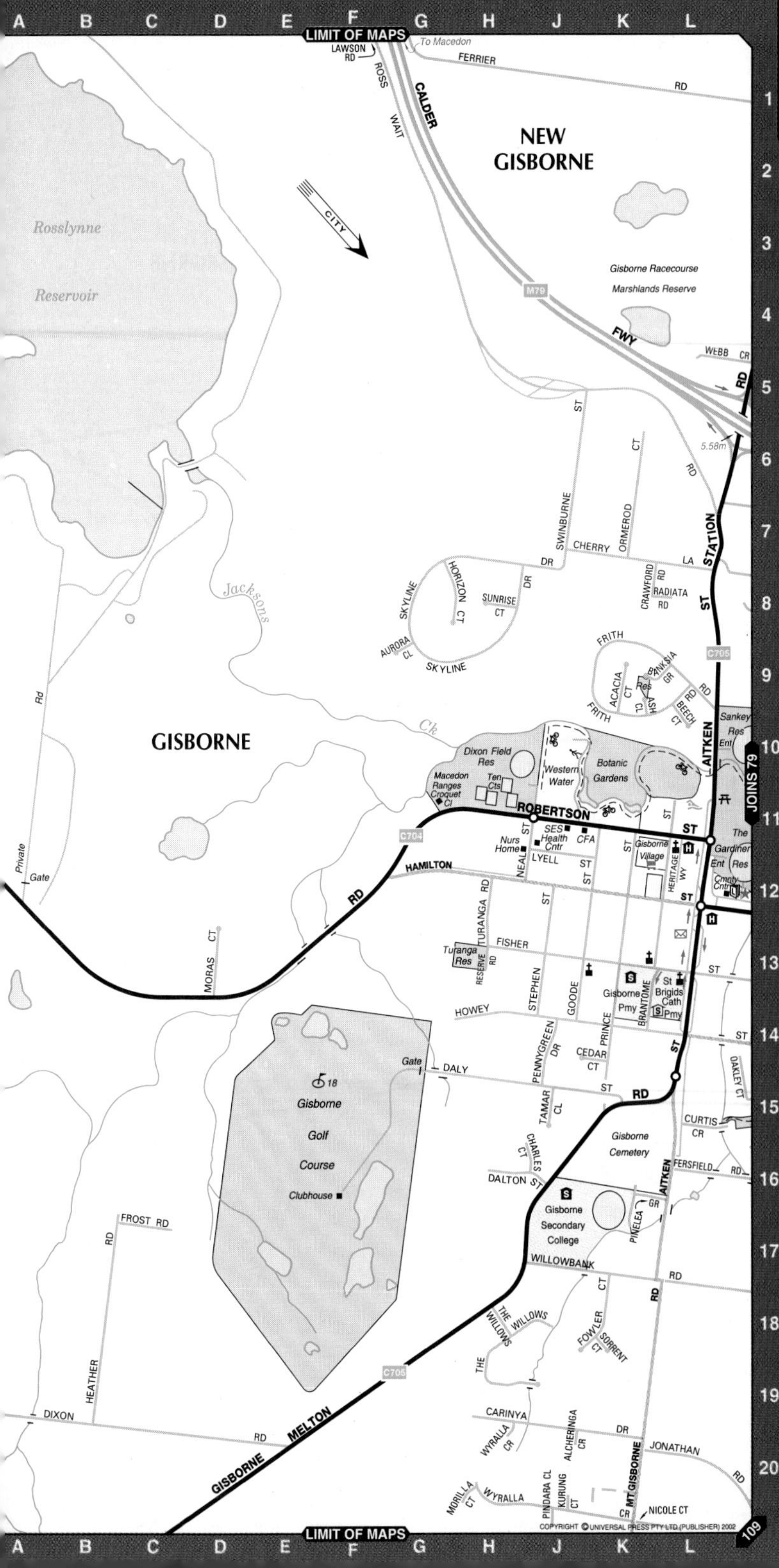

LIMIT OF MAPS

To Macedon

NEW GISBORNE

GISBORNE

Rosslynne Reservoir

Gisborne Racecourse Marshlands Reserve

Dixon Field Res

Macedon Ranges Croquet Cl

Western Water

Botanic Gardens

Sankey Res

The Gardiner Res

Cmnty Cntr

Gisborne Village

Turanga Res

Gisborne Pmy

St Brigids Cath Pmy

Gisborne Golf Course

Clubhouse

Gisborne Cemetery

Gisborne Secondary College

LAWSON RD, ROSS WAIT, CALDER FWY, FERRIER RD, WEBB CR, STATION RD, SWINBURNE ST, ORMEROD CT, CHERRY LA, CRAWFORD RD, RADIATA RD, SKYLINE DR, HORIZON CT, SUNRISE CT, AURORA CL, FRITH, ACACIA CT, BANKSIA GR, ASH CT, BEECH CT, AITKEN ST, ROBERTSON RD, HAMILTON ST, LYELL ST, NEAL ST, HERITAGE WY, TURANGA RD, FISHER ST, RESERVE RD, STEPHEN ST, GOODE ST, PRINCE ST, BRANTOME ST, HOWEY, PENNYGREEN DR, CEDAR CT, DALY ST, TAMAR CL, CHARLES CT, DALTON ST, CURTIS CR, OAKLEY CT, FERSFIELD RD, PINELEA GR, WILLOWBANK RD, THE WILLOWS, FOWLER CT, SORRENT, MORAS CT, FROST RD, HEATHER RD, DIXON RD, GISBORNE MELTON RD, CARINYA DR, WYRALLA CR, ALCHERINGA CR, JONATHAN RD, MT GISBORNE RD, MORILLA CT, PINDARA CL, KURUNG CT, NICOLE CT, Private Rd

Jacksons Ck

SES, Health Cntr, CFA, Nurs Home, Ten Cts

M79, C704, C705

Gate

5.58m

JOINS 79

CITY

A B C D E F G H J K L

LIMIT OF MAPS

NEW GISBORNE

BARRINGO RD, FERRIER RD, New Gisborne Prmy, ZEAL ST, ARGYLE ST, Res, COMIC CT, GALILEE CT, ARWON CT, WODALLA GR, LIM CT, CARBINE CT, GALLIVAN RD, CHESSY PARK, PARKERS RD, PAYNE RD, Ross Watt Res Tennis, DALRAY CR, KIWI CT, LADD RD, SAUER RD, Macedon Ranges Maintenance & Works Depot, WOODWORTH ST, THOM ST, FARRELL ST, PLUMMER ST, SAUNDERS, BARRY LA, HAMILTON RD, C708, WEBB CR, 5.58m, MAGNET, STATION, MORROW RD, CALDER, MORROW RD E, MONAGHAN RD, JOSEPH AV, BEATRICE CT, JOSEPH AV, KUMBARI CT, PEAVEY RD, RD, PIERCE RD, KILMORE, SLATTERY CR, CHERRY RD, M79, AITKEN, C705, RUBITON CT, Sankey Ent, Reserve, The, Gardiner Ent, Reserve, Court House, MOUNTAIN, VISTA CL, SUNNY PARK CL, VIEW, SCENIC CT, THE BOULEVARDE, PENELOPE CT, WY, JACKSONS CREEK WY, SAMANTHA CT, OLIVIA CT, MILL RD, ERINVALE CL, KILMORE, 5.86m, CITY, Ck, Western Water Waste - Water Purification Plant, Private Rd, Gate, HIGH VIEW, HAYWOOD DR, Cmnty Cntr, ST, MELBOURNE, Jacksons, WATT ST, RIDDELL ST, HILL ST, C791, FISHER ST, CALTHORPE ST, RODNEY ST, HOWEY ST, OAKLEY CT, WORCESTER, GRANT, BRUCE CT, RD, SHEEDY, RD, 5.33m, EMMELINE DR, ROBERT CT, CURTIS CR, Reserve, BEATTIE CT, AV, GARDINER ST, Res, RAILTON CT, CAROLL CT, Res, KEILY, SANSOM ST, CARNEGIE CT, RD, FERSFIELD RD, RD, GREENVALE, PANORAMA DR, WILLOWBANK RD, BLOOMFIELD RD, M79, RD, FWY, McGREGOR, BENNETT RD, JONATHAN REEVE CT, RD, BRADY

JOINS 78

JOINS 109

A B C D E F G H J K L

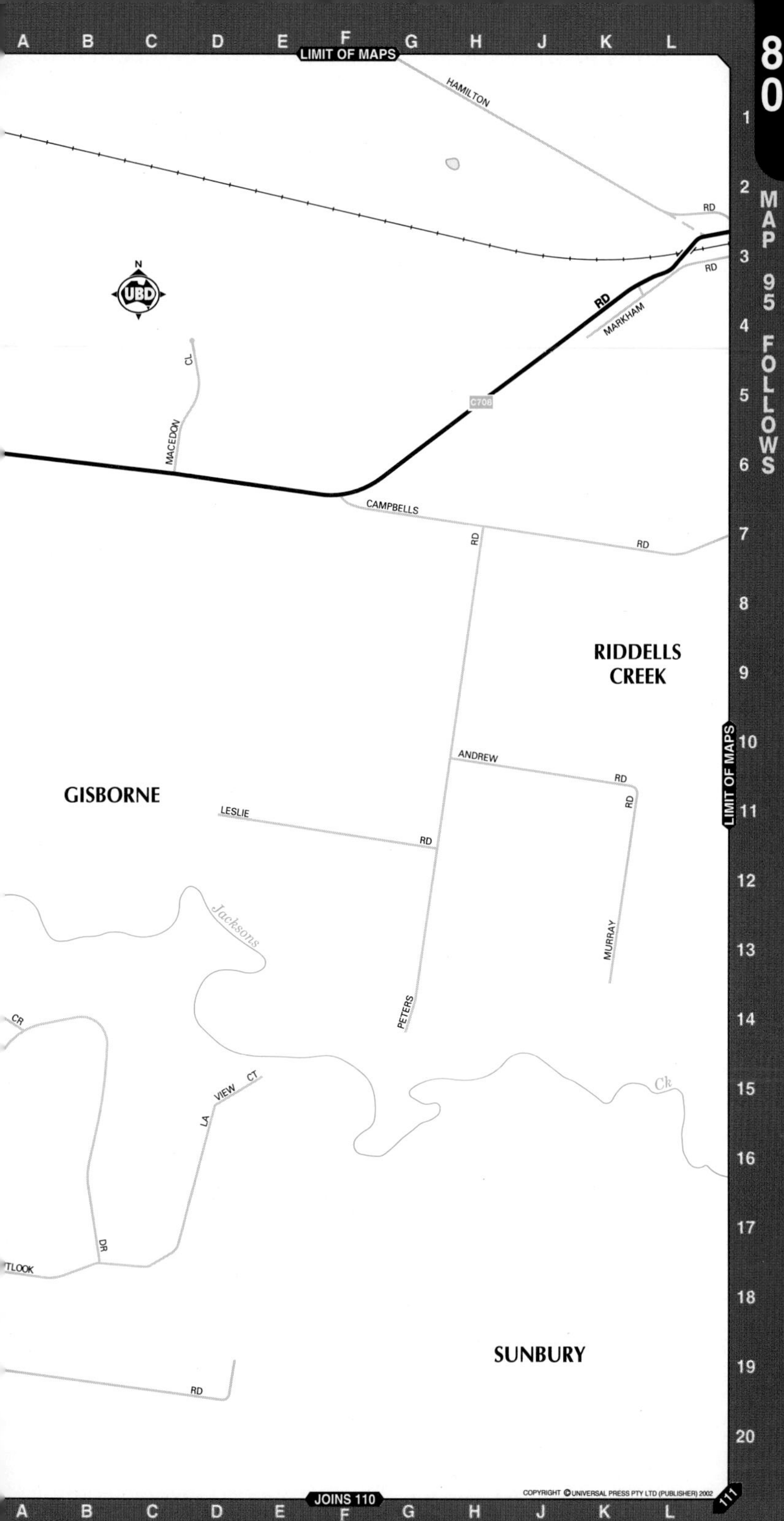

MAP 95 FOLLOWS
LIMIT OF MAPS
JOINS 110
111

PREVIOUS MAP 80

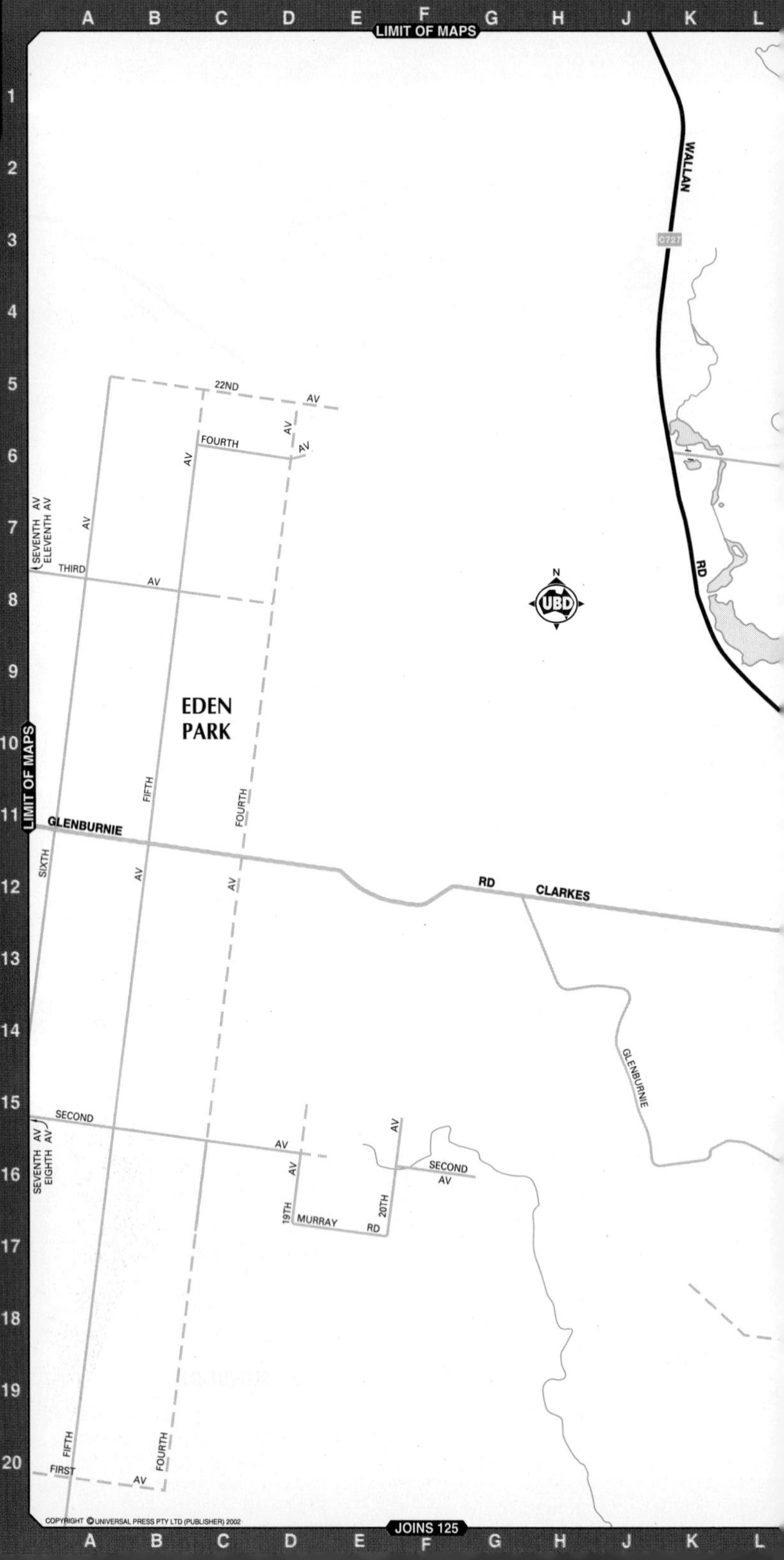
A B C D E F G H J K L
1 2 3 4 5 6 7 8 9 10 11 12 13 14 15 16 17 18 19 20
LIMIT OF MAPS
LIMIT OF MAPS
WALLAN
RD
C727
N
UBD
22ND
AV
FOURTH
AV
AV
AV
SEVENTH AV
ELEVENTH AV
AV
THIRD
AV
EDEN
PARK
FIFTH
FOURTH
GLENBURNIE
SIXTH
AV
AV
RD
CLARKES
GLENBURNIE
SECOND
SEVENTH AV
EIGHTH AV
AV
AV
AV
SECOND
AV
19TH
MURRAY
RD
20TH
FIFTH
FIRST
AV
FOURTH

JOINS 125

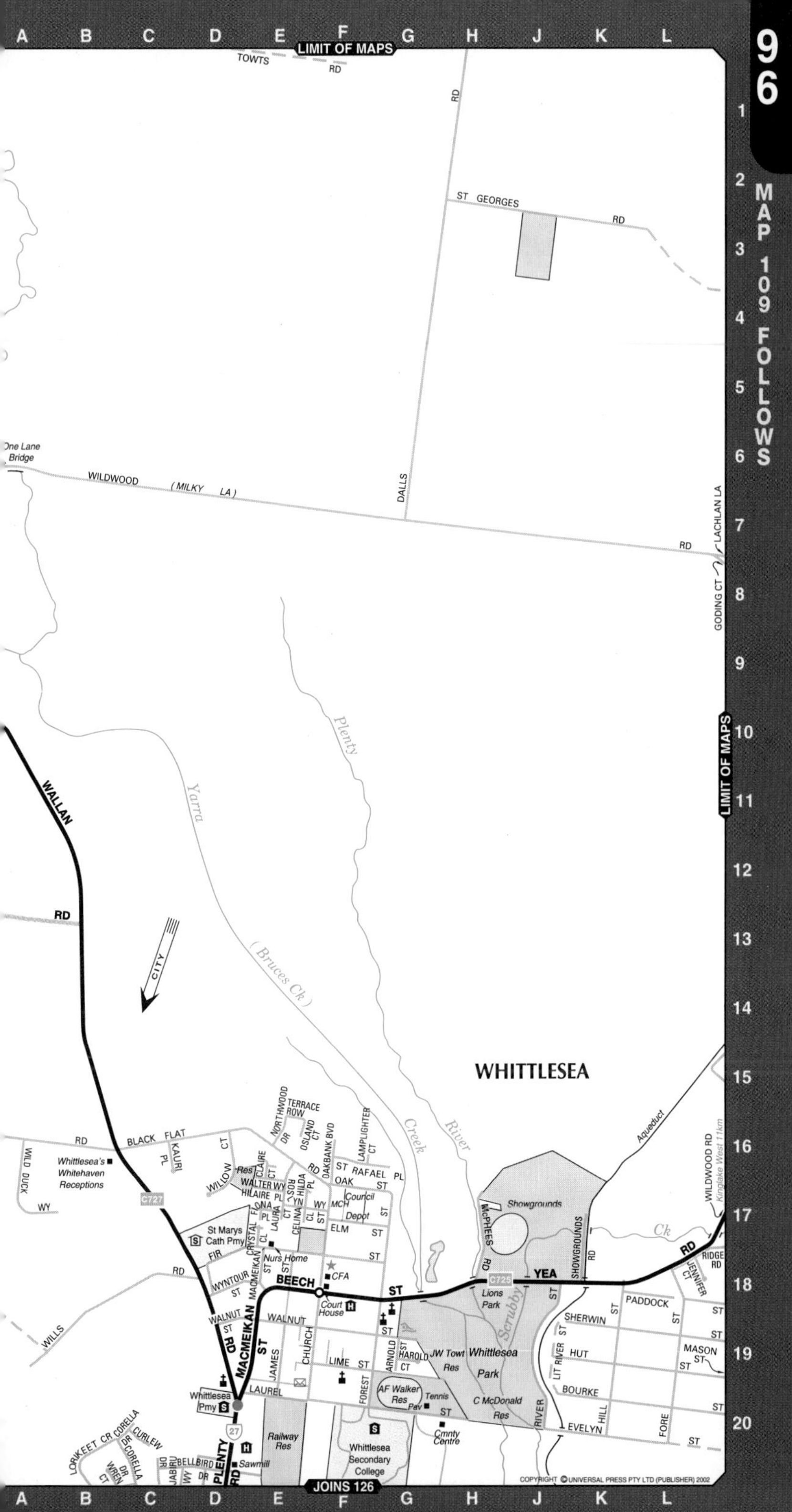
LIMIT OF MAPS
MAP 109 FOLLOWS
JOINS 126
WHITTLESEA
TOWTS RD
ST GEORGES RD
DALLS RD
WILDWOOD (MILKY LA) RD
One Lane Bridge
LACHLAN LA
GODING CT
WALLAN RD
CITY
Yarra (Bruces Ck)
Plenty River
Creek
Aqueduct
BLACK FLAT RD
WILD DUCK WY
Whittlesea's Whitehaven Receptions
KAURI PL
WILLOW CT
NORTHWOOD DR
TERRACE ROW
OSLAND CT
OAKBANK BVD
LAMPLIGHTER CT
ST RAFAEL PL
OAK ST
Council Depot
ELM ST
Showgrounds
McPHEES RD
SHOWGROUNDS RD
YEA RD
C727
C725
St Marys Cath Pmy
FIR
WYNTOUR ST
BEECH ST
CFA
Nurs Home
Court House
Lions Park
Scrubby
WALNUT ST
MACMEIKAN ST
PLENTY RD
CHURCH ST
JAMES ST
LIME ST
ARNOLD ST
HAROLD CT
JW Towt Res
Whittlesea Park
AF Walker Res
Tennis Pav
C McDonald Res
LAUREL ST
FOREST ST
Railway Res
Whittlesea Secondary College
Cmnty Centre
Whittlesea Pmy
Sawmill
WILLS
LORIKEET CR
CORELLA DR
CURLEW
WREN CT
JABIRU WY
BELLBIRD DR
PADDOCK ST
SHERWIN ST
HUT ST
LIT RIVER ST
BOURKE ST
EVELYN ST
HILL ST
FORE ST
MASON ST
RIDGE RD
JENNIFER CT
RIVER ST
WILDWOOD RD Kinglake West 11km
Ck

PREVIOUS MAP 96

JOINS 79

78

LIMIT OF MAPS

LIMIT OF MAPS

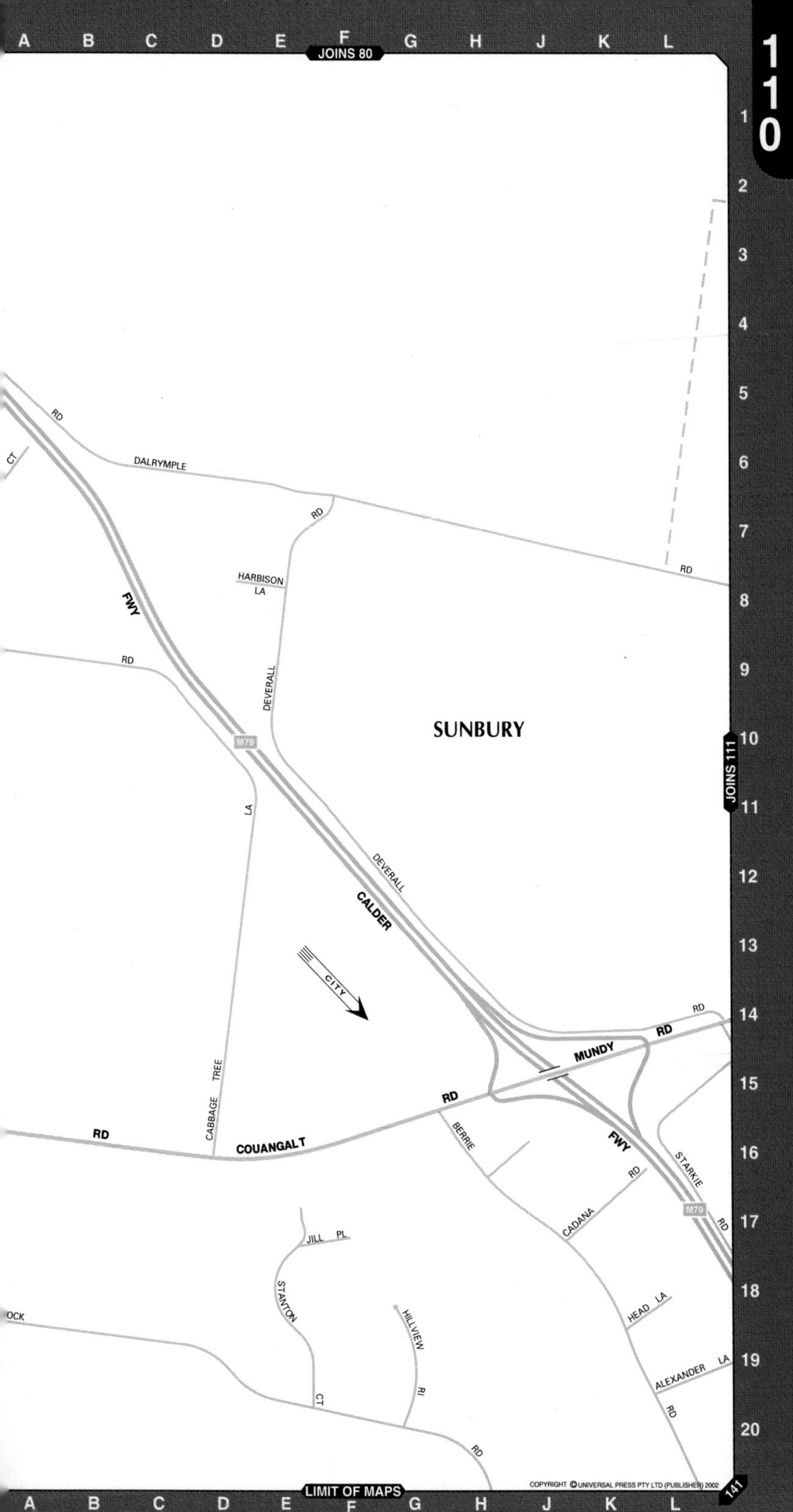
A B C D E F G H J K L
JOINS 80
1 2 3 4 5 6 7 8 9 10 11 12 13 14 15 16 17 18 19 20
JOINS 111
SUNBURY
DALRYMPLE
RD
CT
HARBISON LA
DEVERALL
CALDER FWY
M79
CABBAGE TREE LA
DEVERALL
CITY
MUNDY RD
COUANGALT RD
BERRIE
STARKIE RD
CADANA RD
JILL PL
STANTON CT
HILLVIEW RI
HEAD LA
ALEXANDER LA
OCK
LIMIT OF MAPS
141

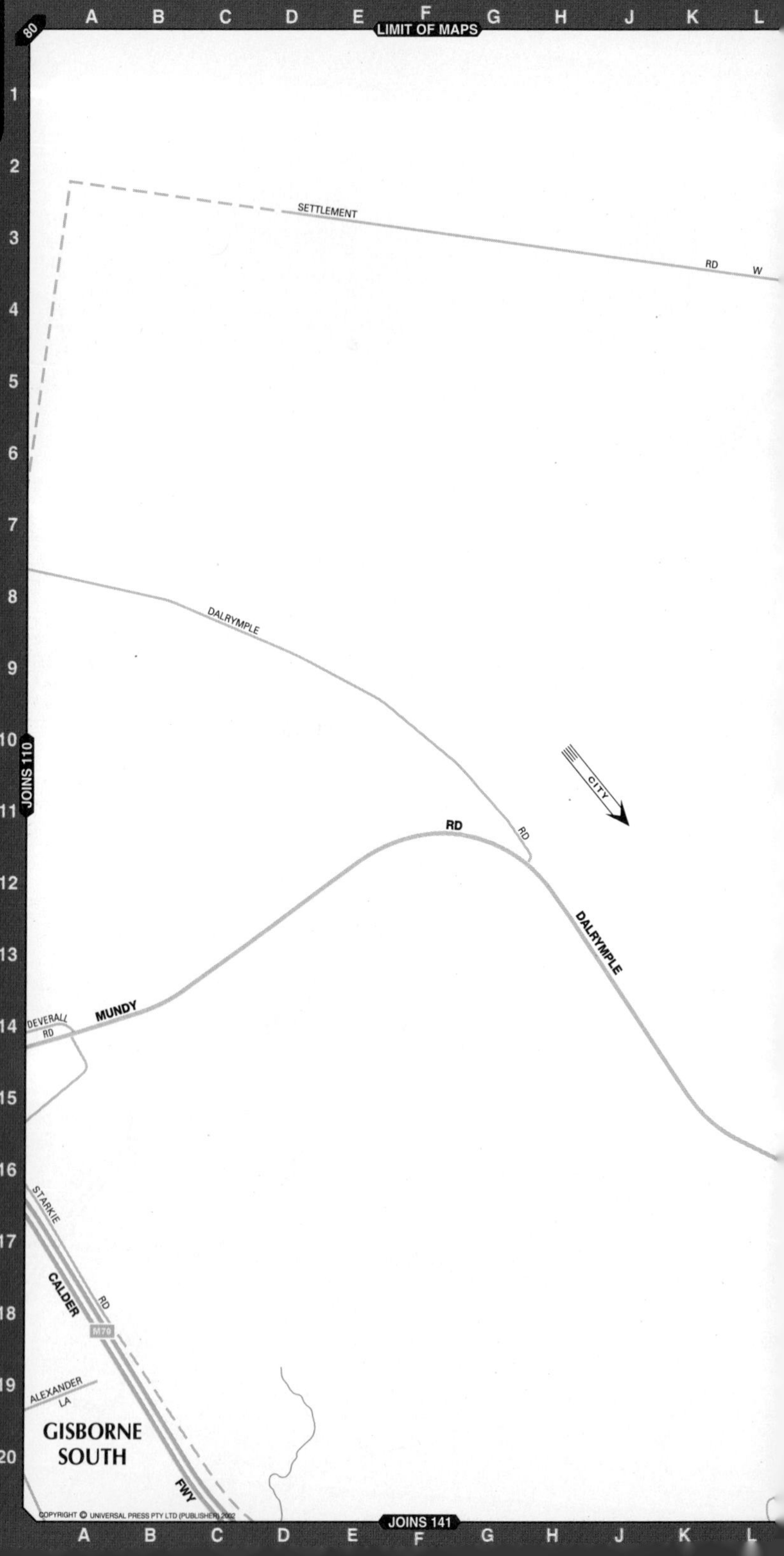

A B C D E F G H J K L

80

LIMIT OF MAPS

SETTLEMENT RD W

DALRYMPLE RD

CITY

MUNDY RD

DALRYMPLE

DEVERALL RD

STARKIE RD

CALDER FWY

M79

ALEXANDER LA

GISBORNE SOUTH

JOINS 110

JOINS 141

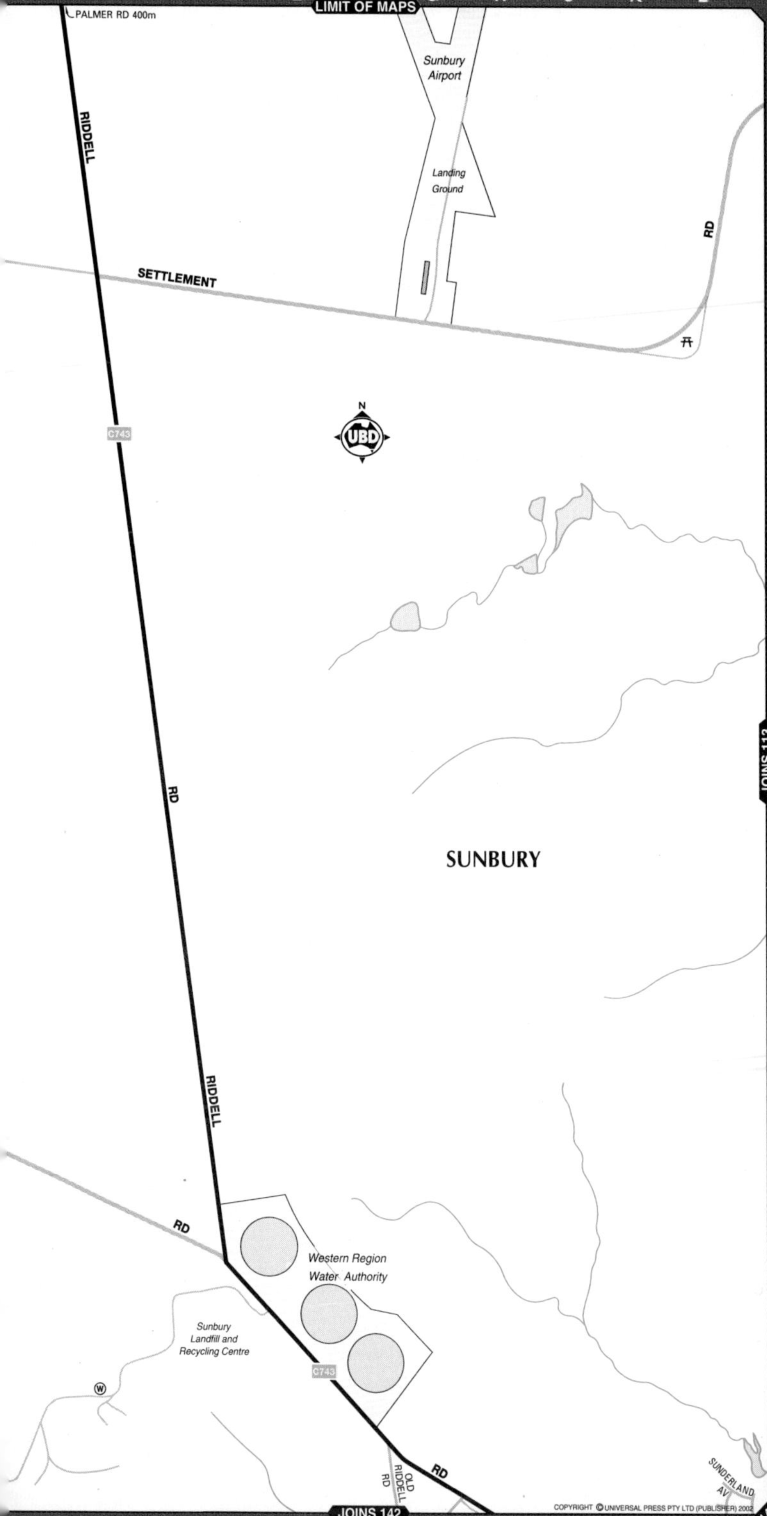

A B C D E F G H J K L

LIMIT OF MAPS

PALMER RD 400m

Sunbury Airport

Landing Ground

RIDDELL RD

SETTLEMENT RD

C743

SUNBURY

Western Region Water Authority

Sunbury Landfill and Recycling Centre

OLD RIDDELL RD

SUNDERLAND AV

RD

JOINS 113

JOINS 142

143

1 2 3 4 5 6 7 8 9 10 11 12 13 14 15 16 17 18 19 20

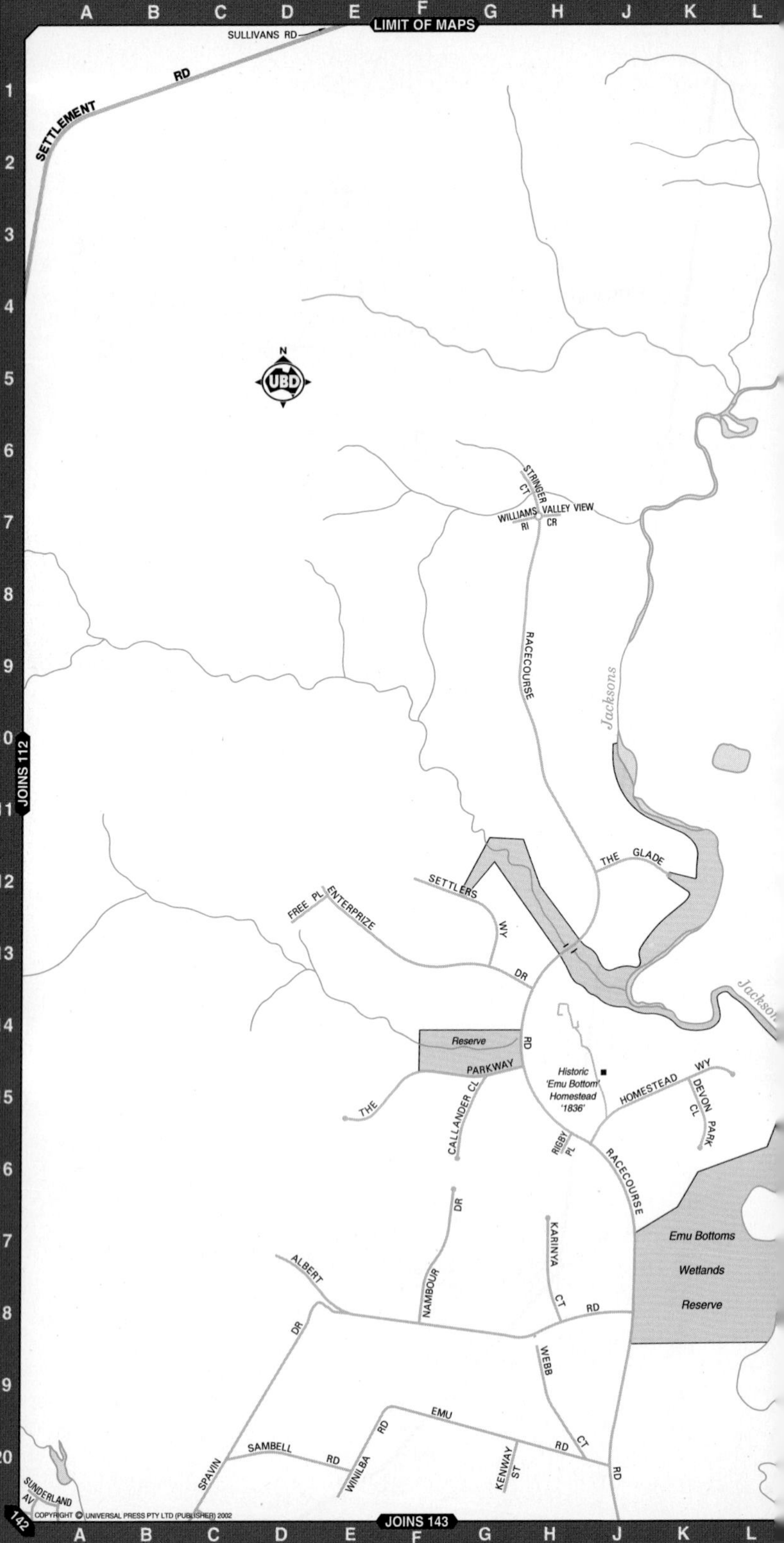

JOINS 112

JOINS 143

142

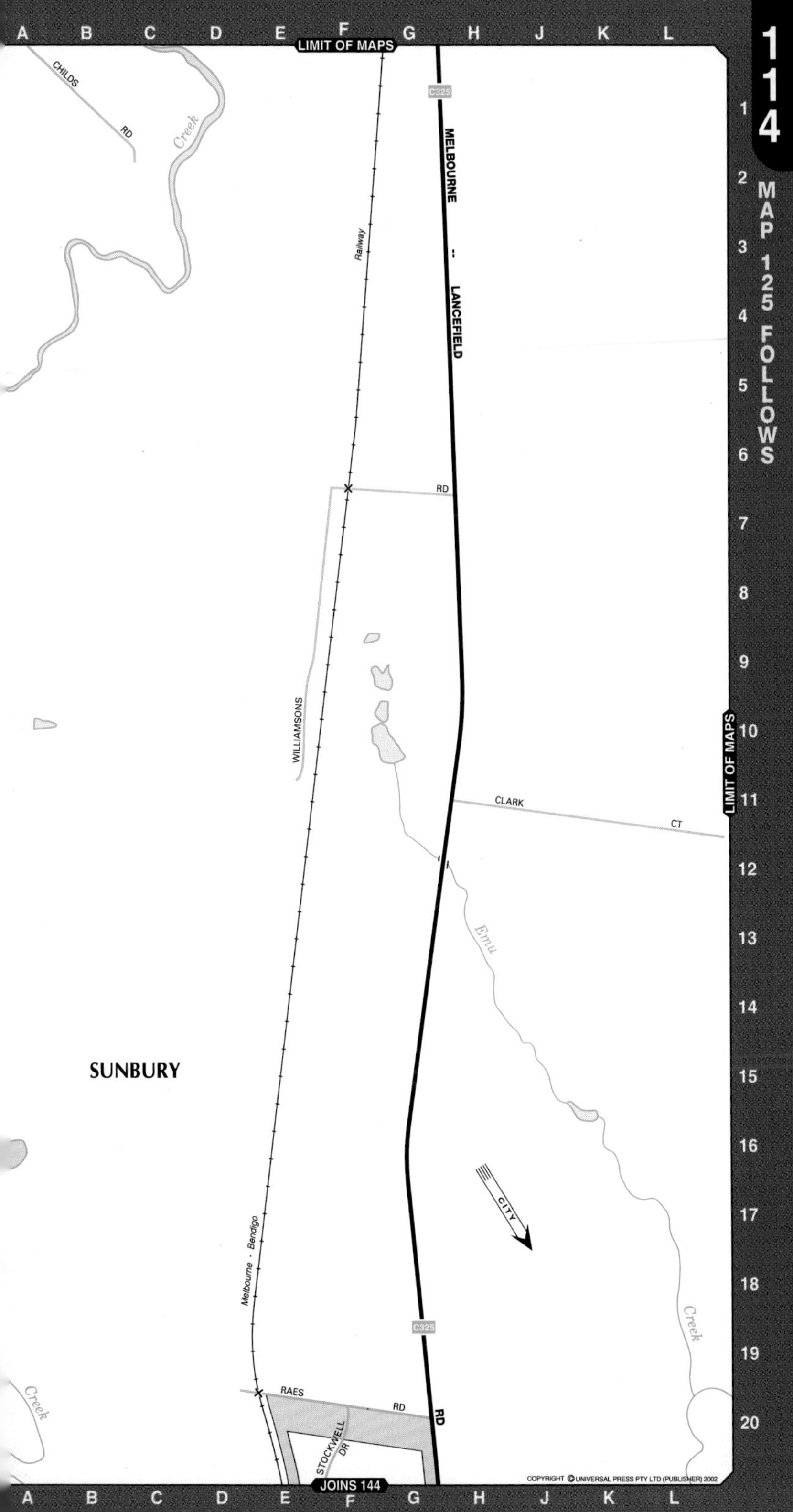
LIMIT OF MAPS
CHILDS RD
Creek
C325
MELBOURNE - LANCEFIELD RD
Railway
RD
WILLIAMSONS
CLARK CT
Emu Creek
SUNBURY
CITY
Melbourne - Bendigo
RAES RD
STOCKWELL DR
Creek
JOINS 144
MAP 125 FOLLOWS
LIMIT OF MAPS

PREVIOUS MAP 114

JOINS 95

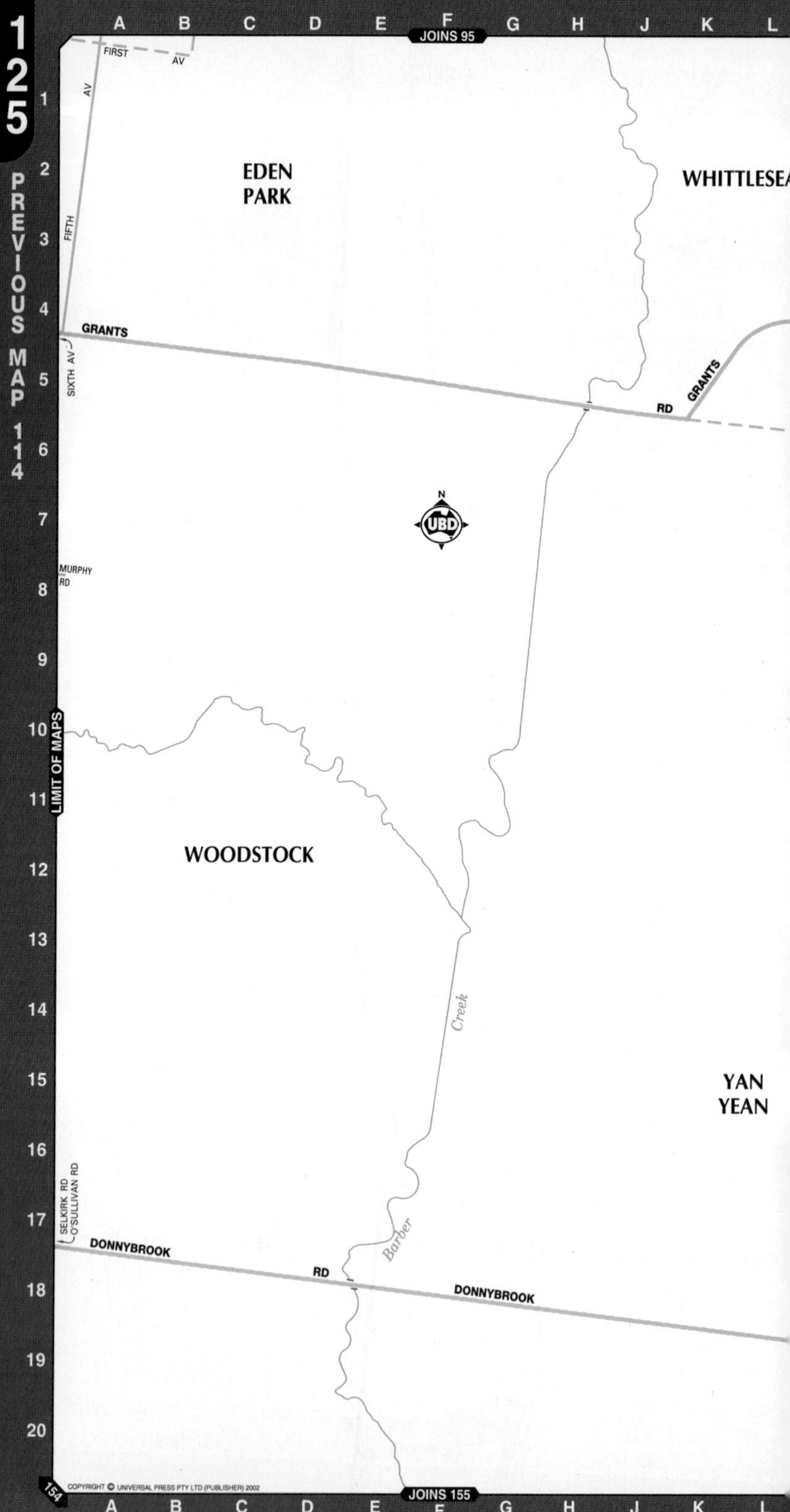

154

JOINS 155

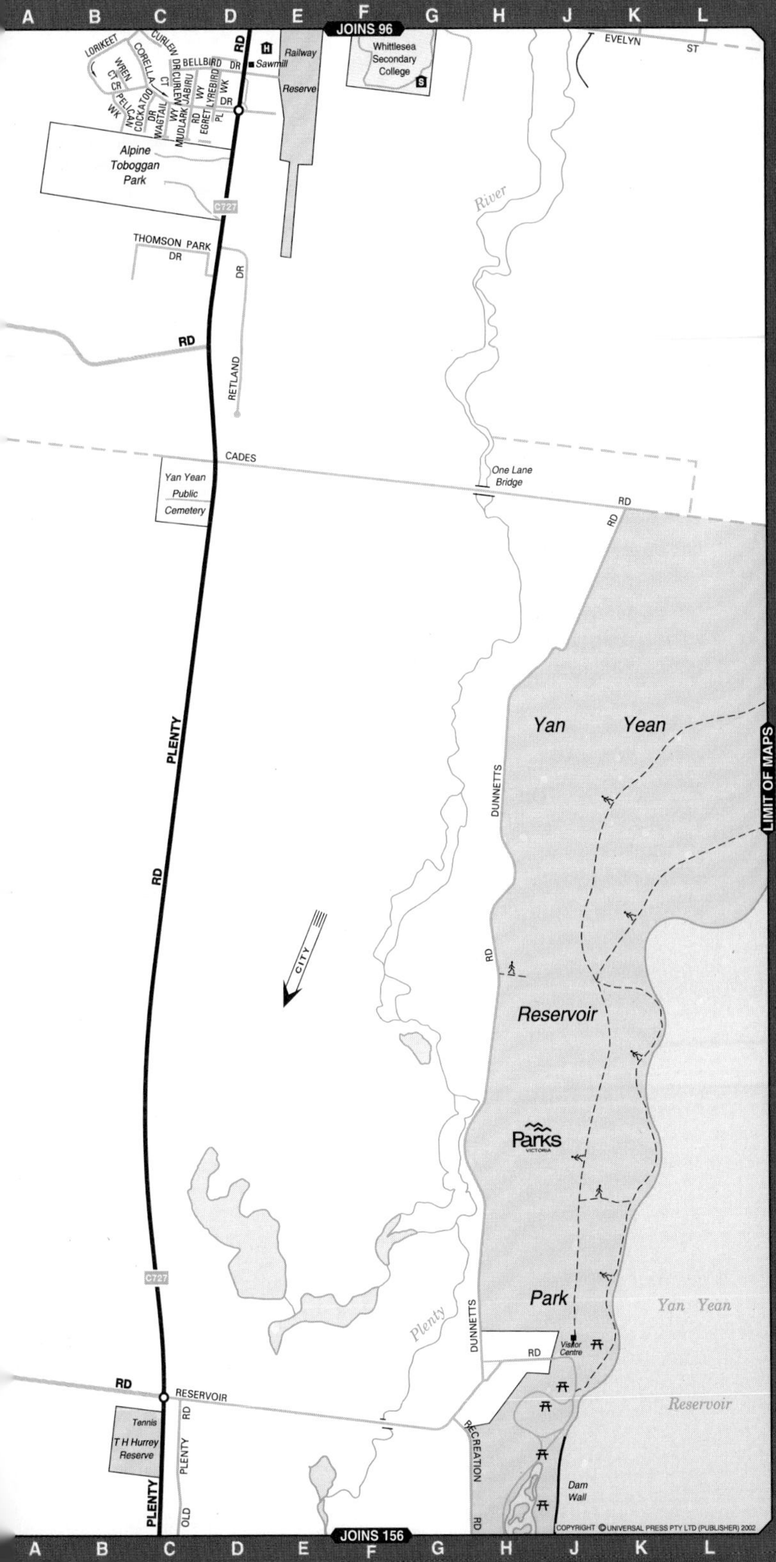

JOINS 96

A B C D E F G H J K L

LORIKEET CURLEW CORELLA WREN CT CR PELICAN WK COCKATOO DR WAGTAIL CT DR CURLEW WY MUDLARK JABIRU RD EGRET WY LYREBIRD PL WK BELLBIRD DR DR RD

Sawmill

Railway Reserve

Whittlesea Secondary College

EVELYN ST

Alpine Toboggan Park

C727

THOMSON PARK DR

DR

RD

RETLAND

River

CADES

Yan Yean Public Cemetery

One Lane Bridge

RD

RD

Yan Yean Reservoir Park

Parks VICTORIA

DUNNETTS

RD

CITY

PLENTY RD

C727

Plenty

DUNNETTS RD

Visitor Centre

Yan Yean Reservoir

RD RESERVOIR

Tennis T H Hurrey Reserve

RD PLENTY OLD

PLENTY

RECREATION RD

Dam Wall

LIMIT OF MAPS

MAP 141 FOLLOWS

1 2 3 4 5 6 7 8 9 10 11 12 13 14 15 16 17 18 19 20

JOINS 156

A B C D E F G H J K L

PREVIOUS MAP 126

JOINS 111

110

A B C D E F G H J K L

1 2 3 4 5 6 7 8 9 10 11 12 13 14 15 16 17 18 19 20

LIMIT OF MAPS

LIMIT OF MAPS

A B C D E F G H J K L

A B C D E F G H J K L

JOINS 112

113

OLD RIDDELL RD
RIDDELL RD
C743
Blind Creek
SUNDERLAND AV
GRAFTON CT
CLEVELAND RI
CANTERBURY
ALBEMARLE DR
BUNDANOON AV
BEDFORD CT
DR
SMITH CT
MILGATE
GREENHILL CT
RD
AV
DOUTNEY CT
LONG DR
FULLBROOK DR
BATES CL
SOLOMON CT
WESTALL CL
Reserve
TCE
LYNN MW
ABBOTT CT
LONG DR
LAWRENCE
PHILLIP AV
MILAN CT
RD
STEWARTS
NIMO CT
LISTER CR
WALKER CT
BANNON
JAMES CL
STRACHEN CT
PHILLIP
OFFICER CT
DR
DADSWELL CT
COATES CT
REES
LA
Reserve
Killara Primary
REES
STREETON CT
BRIERLY CT
ALLEN CT
RD
MUNCH PL
LONGSTAFF WY
MOLVIG RI
DR
NORLING MW
DR
The Common
Reserve
DALKEITH CT
BALMORAL CCT
HANKE PL
WHEELER CT
DAWN CT
GR
Creek
CASSAB MW
FULLWOOD
PIDGEON CT
JELIMAR CT
TRACIE CT
CT
KATHRYN
KERRISDALE
PL
RESERVOIR RD
CITY VW
VIEW TCE
MOUNT DR
CARLA VW
RD
Jeh Wit
BAKER RI
FULLWOOD
OLIVE
ANTHONY ST
RESERVOIR RD
LA
ATKINSON CL
McGEORGE CT
CONDOR PL
Heysen
RAMSAY CT
HARCOURT CL
BUSH PL
RICHARDSON AV
BLYTON
CR
ROBERTS CT
DARGIE CT
CT
MELBA CL
CRAWFORD WY
BLACKMAN
GIBSON CT
TANNER PL
KEMP
Drive
WRIGHT
Reserve
HEYSEN
MUDIE AV
WITHERS CL
MARTENS CT
OLSON PL
MELBA
HERBERT CR
AV
GRUNER ST
HARCOMBE DR
DYSON
BARADINE
MAY
GR
ASHTON CT
KENDALL CT
BUCKMASTER ST
WILEMAN
UNDERHILL CT
SANDLEFORD
WINDARRA CT
FELTON
AV
MELDRUM CT
ANNOIS
TIMMS CT
WAINEWRIGHT CT
McCUBBIN CT
Res
HILL GR
DRYSDALE ST
LINDSAY
COUNIHAN
ST
DUNDAS
NOLAN CT
AV
DR
ABELIA CT
DR
DOBELL
GAP RD
C707
Sunbury Riding Centre
PRESTON ST
MCH
RONALD CT
NICHOL
REGENT ST
GORDON ST
ROVER ST
BOWEN ST
DOWLING CT
ST
FREMANTLE RD
GOSSE CT
CR
SYME CT
LANDSBOROUGH DR
TORRES CT
DR
DARWIN ST
KEITH
MARJORIE AV
AV
BENNETT CT
SEVERINO PL
COWPER
DUFFY CT
FORREST ST
CHARTER RD
W
CHARTER
CHARTER RD
RD
AUSTIN CT
E
TASMAN CT
REGENT ST
M79
FITZROY ST
LEARMONTH
PEGGY ST
REGHON DR
Sunbury Heights Primary
OVENS CT
ST
CALDER
ST
RAGLAN ST
WILSONS
Pav
Eric Boardman Memorial Reserve
Pav
Pav
Basketball Stadium
ST
JUNE ST
McCOMB
DOLAN CT
DR
LEICHARDT ST
LIGHT RD
CT
MITCHELLS LA
ST
COLLINS
GIBBONS ST
MELLON CT
TOWER CT
REGHON
Sunbury Downs Sec Coll
SIMPSON AV
ELIZABETH DR
BURKE CT
MOORE
BARRINGTON
MITCHELLS DR
PONSFORD PL
ONEILL PL
MARSH CR
LA
GREGORY CT
DEAKIN ST
RD
NOBLE CT
CHAPPELL CT
BRADMAN
ARCHER AV
ALDERMAN CL
CR
STACKPOLE
BORDER
BVD
Pavilion
Soccer & Hockey Gnds
Langama Park
WY
BENAUD PL
BRADMAN DR
LA
REDPATH CT
MANNING CT
HOBSON CT
DR
DAVENPORT CT
ANGAS CT
LALOR CT
BACKHAUS AV
LONSDALE PL
FWY
M79
RD

1 2 3 4 5 6 7 8 9 10 11 12 13 14 15 16 17 18 19 20

JOINS 143

LIMIT OF MAPS

187

A B C D E F G H J K L

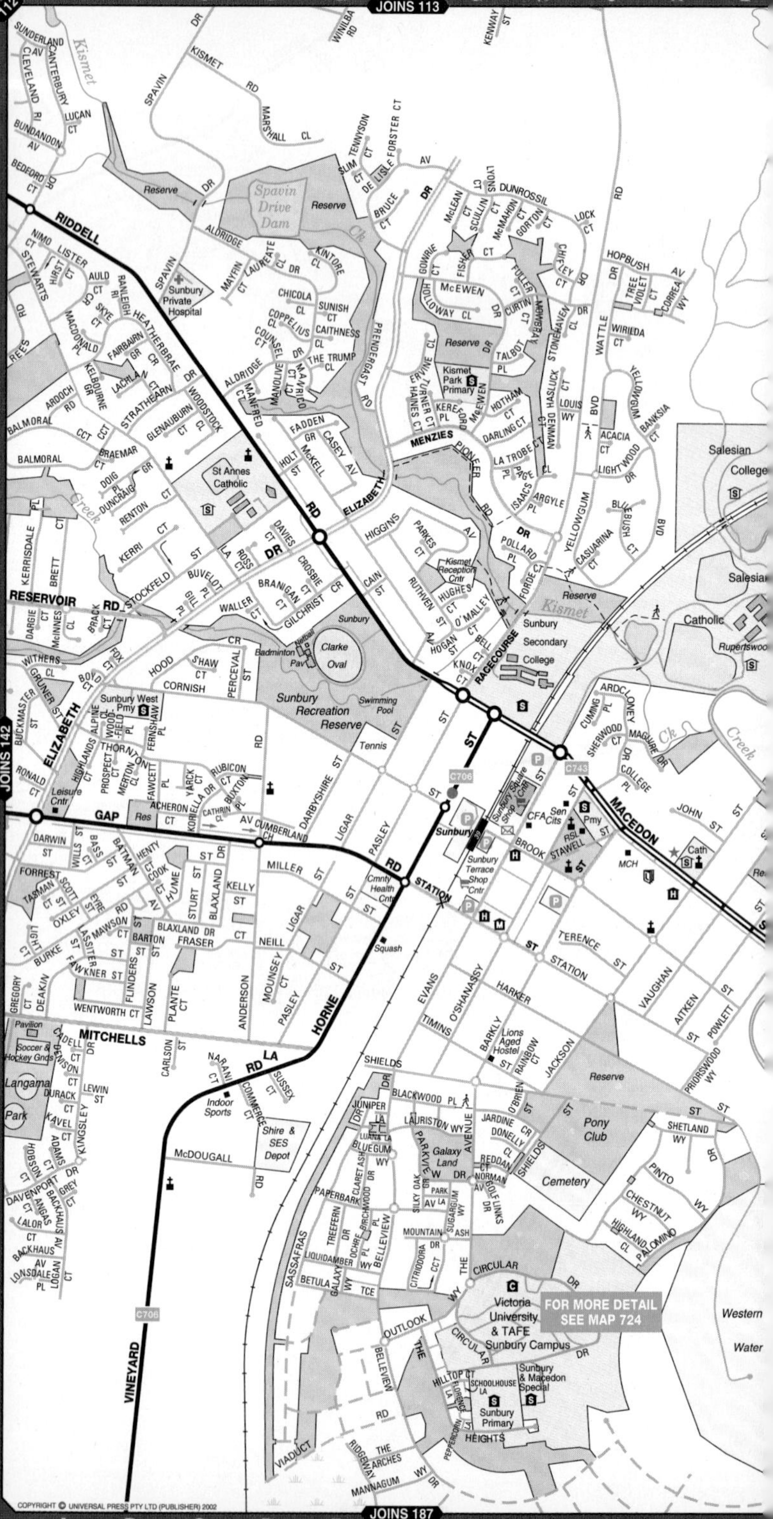

112
JOINS 113
JOINS 142
JOINS 187
FOR MORE DETAIL SEE MAP 724

A B C D E F G H J K L

1 2 3 4 5 6 7 8 9 10 11 12 13 14 15 16 17 18 19 20

SUNDERLAND AV
CANTERBURY
CLEVELAND RI
LUCAN CT
BUNDANOON AV
BEDFORD CT
DR
Kismet
SPAVIN
KISMET
RD
MARSHALL CL
WINILBA RD
KENWAY ST
TENNYSON CT
FORSTER CT
SLIM CT
DE LISLE CT
AV
Reserve
Spavin Drive Dam
Reserve
BRUCE CT
DR
LYONS CT
DUNROSSIL
McLEAN CT
SCULLIN CT
McMAHON CT
GORTON CT
LOCK CT
RD
RIDDELL
NIMO
LISTER
STEWARTS
HIRST CT
AULD CT
RANLEIGH RI
ALDRIDGE
Ck
MAYFIN CT
LAUREATE CL
DR
KINTORE CL
GOWRIE CT
FISHER CT
CT
CHIFLEY DR
HOPBUSH AV
SPAVIN DR
Sunbury Private Hospital
CHICOLA CL
SUNISH CT
HOLLOWAY CL
McEWEN
FULLER CT
MOWBRAY
TREE VIOLET CT
CORREA WY
DR
SKYE CT
HEATHERBRAE
COPPELIUS CL
CAITHNESS CL
CURTIN CT
STONEHAVEN CL
DR
WATTLE
WIRILDA CT
RD
MACDONALD
CR
COUNSEL CT
PRENDERGAST
Reserve
DR
REES
FAIRBAIRN GR
CR
THE TRUMP CL
TALBOT PL
LACHLAN CT
DR
MANRICO CT
Kismet Park Primary
HASLUCK CT
YELLOWGUM
KELBOURNE GR
WOODSTOCK
ALDRIDGE
MANOLIVE
ERVINE CL
TURNER CT
HAINES CT
KEREFORD PL
McEWEN
HOTHAM CT
DENMAN CT
LOUIS WY
BVD
BANKSIA
ARDOCH RD
STRATHEARN
MANFRED
FADDEN GR
CASEY AV
MENZIES
PIONEER
DARLING CT
ACACIA CT
Salesian College
BALMORAL
CCT CCT
GLENAUBURN CT CL
HOLT ST
McKELL
LA TROBE CT
PAGE CL
LIGHTWOOD DR
BALMORAL
BRAEMAR CT
GR
St Annes Catholic
DOIG PL
DUNCRAIG
ELIZABETH
ISAACS PL
ARGYLE
BLUEBUSH CT
BVD
Creek
RENTON CT
RD
HIGGINS
PARKES CT
DR
YELLOWGUM
KERRISDALE PL
BRETT CT
KERRI CT
ST
LA
ROSS CT
DAVIES CT
DR
AV
POLLARD PL
CASUARINA CT
BUVELOT PL
CROSBIE CT
CAIN ST
Kismet Reception Cntr
FORDE CT
Salesian
STOCKFELD
GILL PL
BRANIGAN CT
CR
RUTHVEN
HUGHES CT
Reserve
RESERVOIR RD
WALLER CT
GILCHRIST
Sunbury
O'MALLEY
Kismet
Sunbury Secondary College
Catholic
DARGIE CT
McINNES CT
CL
BRACK CT
CR
Netball
Clarke Oval
HOGAN ST
BELL CT
RACECOURSE
Rupertswood
WITHERS CL
FOX CT
HOOD
SHAW CT
PERCEVAL
Badminton
Pav
KNOX CT
GRUNER ST
BOYD CT
CORNISH
ARDCLONEY PL
BUCKMASTER ST
ELIZABETH
Sunbury West Pmy
FERNSHAW PL
Sunbury Recreation Reserve
Swimming Pool
ST
ST
CUMING PL
SHERWOOD CT
MAGUIRE DR
Ck
Creek
ALPINE CT
WOODFIELD
RD
DR
HIGHLANDS
THORNTON
Tennis
COLLEGE DR
RONALD CT
PROSPECT CT
MERTON CL
FAWCETT PL
YARCK CT
RUBICON CT
BUXTON PL
DARBYSHIRE ST
C706
ST
Sunbury Square Shop Cntr
ST
C743
Leisure Cntr
KORELLA DR
CATHRIN CL
Sunbury
CFA
Sen Cits
Pmy
MACEDON
JOHN ST
ST
GAP
Res
ACHERON CT
AV
CUMBERLAND CH
LIGAR
PASLEY
BROOK
RSL
STAWELL ST
DARWIN ST
WILLS ST
BASS ST
BATMAN
HENTY CT
ST DR
Sunbury Terrace Shop Cntr
MCH
Cath
FORREST
COOK
HUME
MILLER ST
RD
SCOTT ST
TASMAN CT
ST
CT
ST
KELLY ST
Cmnty Health Cntr
STATION
EYRE ST
STURT ST
BLAXLAND
OXLEY
MAWSON CT
ST
BARTON ST
BLAXLAND DR
LIGAR
Squash
TERENCE ST
LIGHT CT
BURKE ST
LASSITER ST
FAWKNER ST
FLINDERS ST
FRASER
CT
NEILL ST
ST
STATION
VAUGHAN
AITKEN
ST
EVANS
O'SHANASSY
HARKER
GREGORY CT
DEAKIN CT
WENTWORTH CT
LAWSON
PLANTE CT
ANDERSON
MOUNSEY CT
PASLEY
HORNE
POWLETT
TIMINS
BARKLY
Lions Aged Hostel
RAINBOW CT
JACKSON
ST
Pavilion
MITCHELLS
CARLSON ST
Soccer & Hockey Gnds
CADELL DR
DENISON CT
NARANI CT
RD
LA
SUSSEX CT
SHIELDS
Reserve
PRIORSWOOD WY
Langama Park
DURACK CT
LEWIN ST
Indoor Sports
COMMERCE CT
BLACKWOOD PL
KAVEL CT
KINGSLEY
JUNIPER
LAURISTON WY
AVENUE
JARDINE CR
O'BRIEN ST
ST
Pony Club
SHETLAND WY
Shire & SES Depot
DONELLY CL
ADAMS CT
McDOUGALL
BLUEGUM WY
Galaxy Land
PARKVIEW DR
REDDAN CT
SHIELDS
DR
HOBSON CT
DAVENPORT DR
GREY CT
RD
CLARET ASH
SILKY OAK
NORMAN AV
GOLF LINKS DR
Cemetery
PINTO WY
BACKHAUS
PAPERBARK
BIRCHWOOD
PARK AV
SUGARGUM WY
CHESTNUT WY
ANGAS CT
LALOR CT
TREEFERN DR
OCHRE PL
BELLEVIEW
MOUNTAIN ASH
HIGHLAND CL
PALOMINO
BACKHAUS AV
LOGAN CT
LONSDALE PL
SASSAFRAS
LIQUIDAMBER WY
CITRIODORA
CCT DR
THE
CIRCULAR
DR
C706
BETULA
GALAXY WY
TCE
WY
Victoria University & TAFE Sunbury Campus
Western Water
VINEYARD
OUTLOOK
BELLEVIEW
THE
CIRCULAR
DR
HILLTOP CT
SCHOOLHOUSE LA
Sunbury & Macedon Special
RD
FLORENCE LA
Sunbury Primary
VIADUCT
RIDGEWAY
THE ARCHES
PEPPERCORN
HEIGHTS
MANNAGUM WY
DR

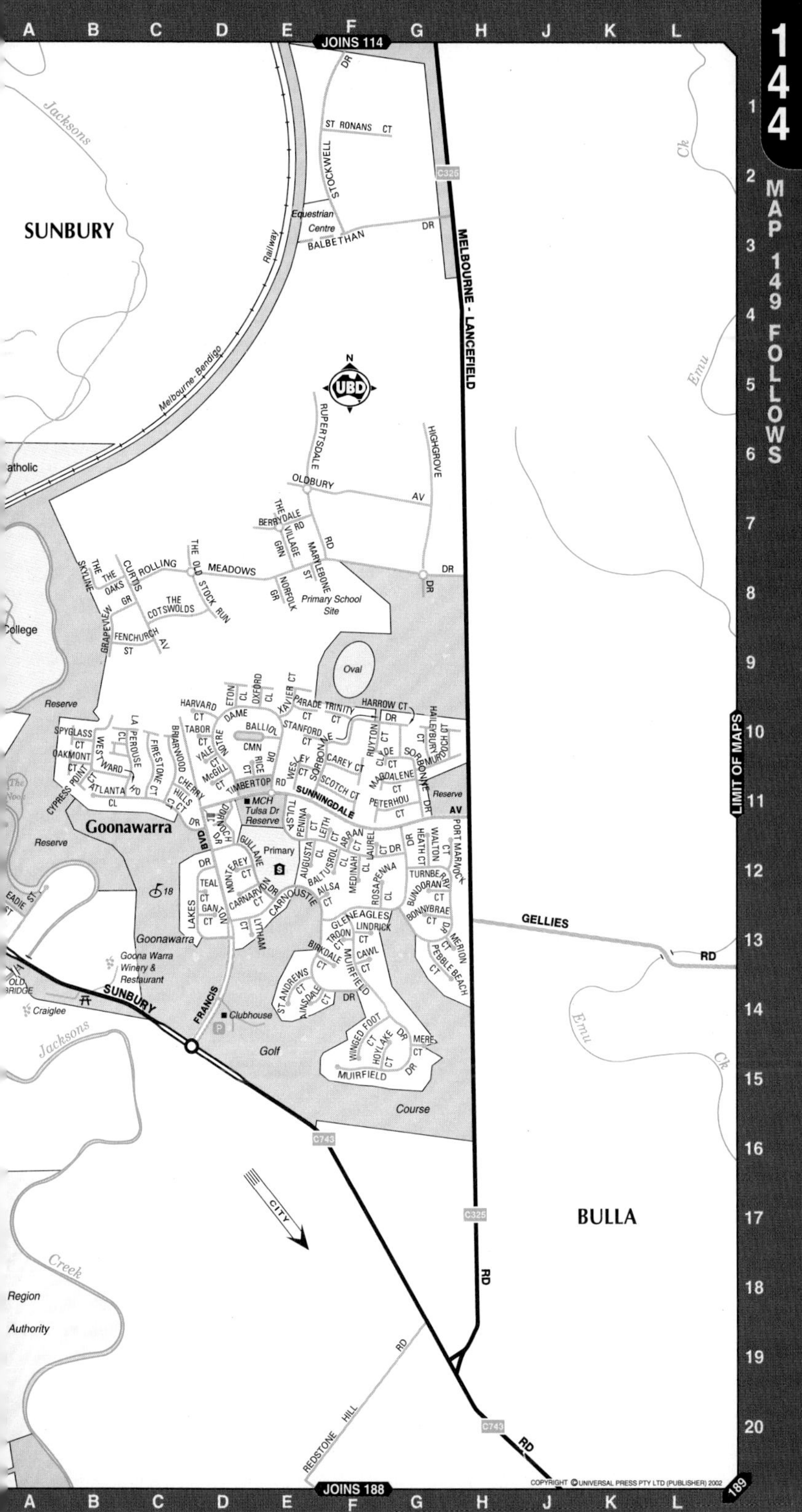

JOINS 114
SUNBURY
Goonawarra
BULLA
MELBOURNE - LANCEFIELD RD
SUNBURY RD
GELLIES RD
Melbourne-Bendigo Railway
Equestrian Centre
BALBETHAN DR
ST RONANS CT
STOCKWELL DR
RUPERTSDALE
OLDBURY AV
HIGHGROVE DR
ROLLING MEADOWS
THE OLD STOCK RUN
THE COTSWOLDS
Primary School Site
Oval
Reserve
MCH
Tulsa Dr Reserve
SUNNINGDALE AV
Primary
Goonawarra
Goona Warra Winery & Restaurant
Craiglee
Clubhouse
Golf Course
MUIRFIELD DR
REDSTONE HILL RD
Jacksons Creek
Emu Ck
Region Authority
College
CITY
MAP 149 FOLLOWS
LIMIT OF MAPS
JOINS 188

PREVIOUS MAP 144

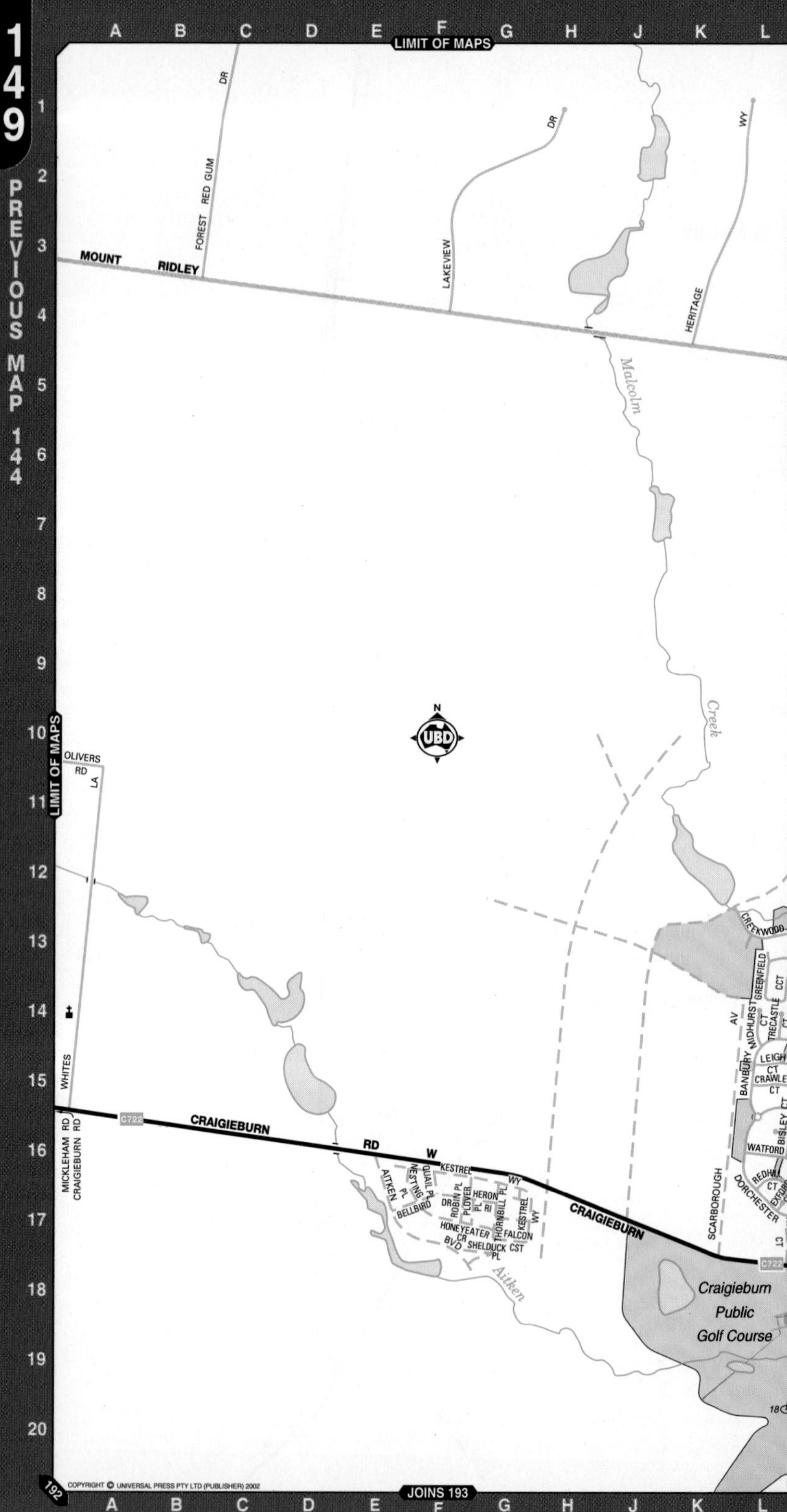

192

JOINS 193

MAP 153 FOLLOWS

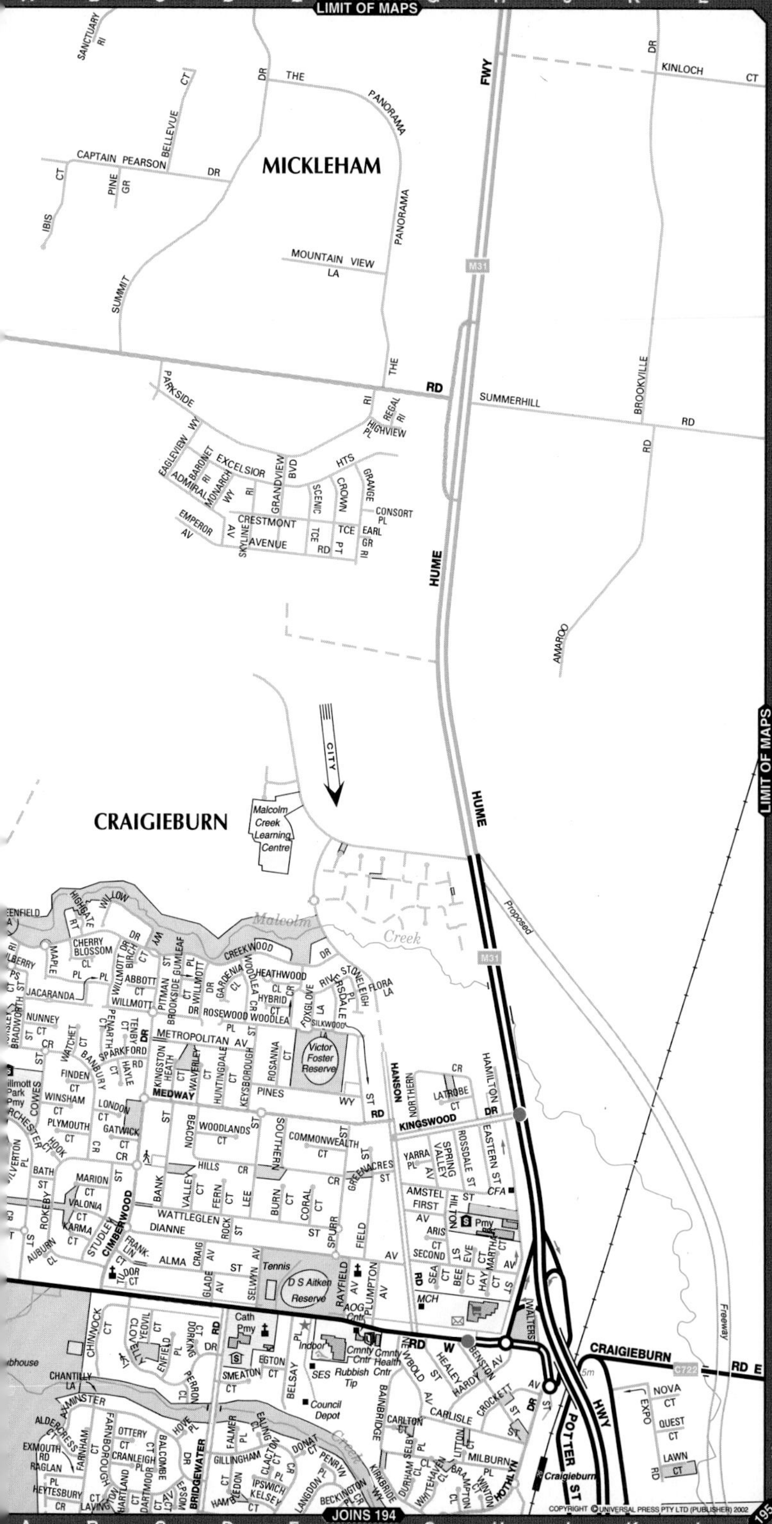

LIMIT OF MAPS

MICKLEHAM

CRAIGIEBURN

Malcolm Creek Learning Centre

Victor Foster Reserve

D S Aitken Reserve

HUME FWY

HUME HWY

CRAIGIEBURN RD E

SUMMERHILL RD

JOINS 194

195

PREVIOUS MAP 150

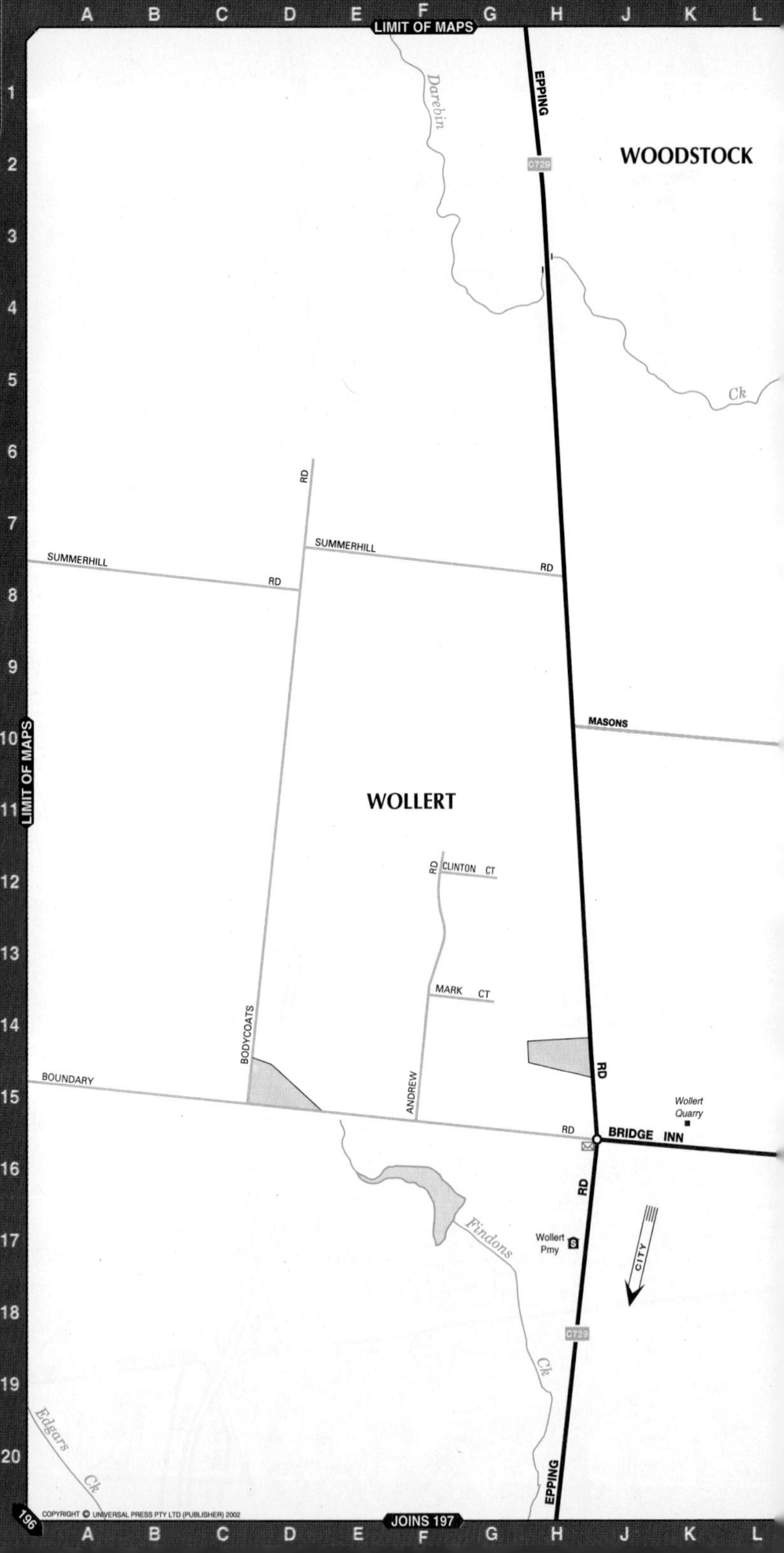

LIMIT OF MAPS

WOODSTOCK

WOLLERT

EPPING RD

C729

Darebin

Ck

SUMMERHILL RD

MASONS

BODYCOATS RD

CLINTON CT

MARK CT

ANDREW RD

BOUNDARY RD

BRIDGE INN

Wollert Quarry

Wollert Pmy

Findons Ck

CITY

Edgars Ck

196

JOINS 197

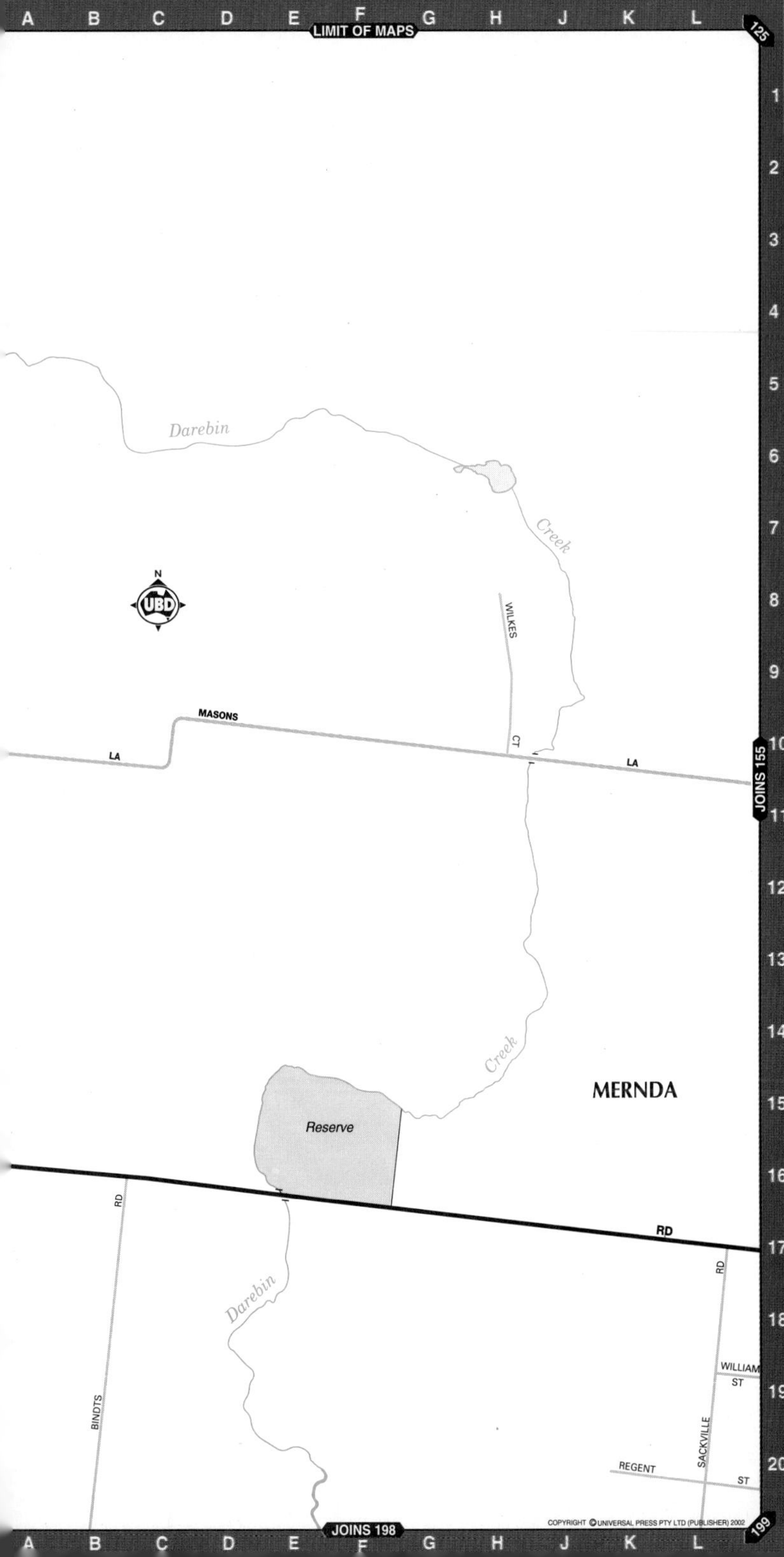

LIMIT OF MAPS
125
JOINS 155
JOINS 198
199

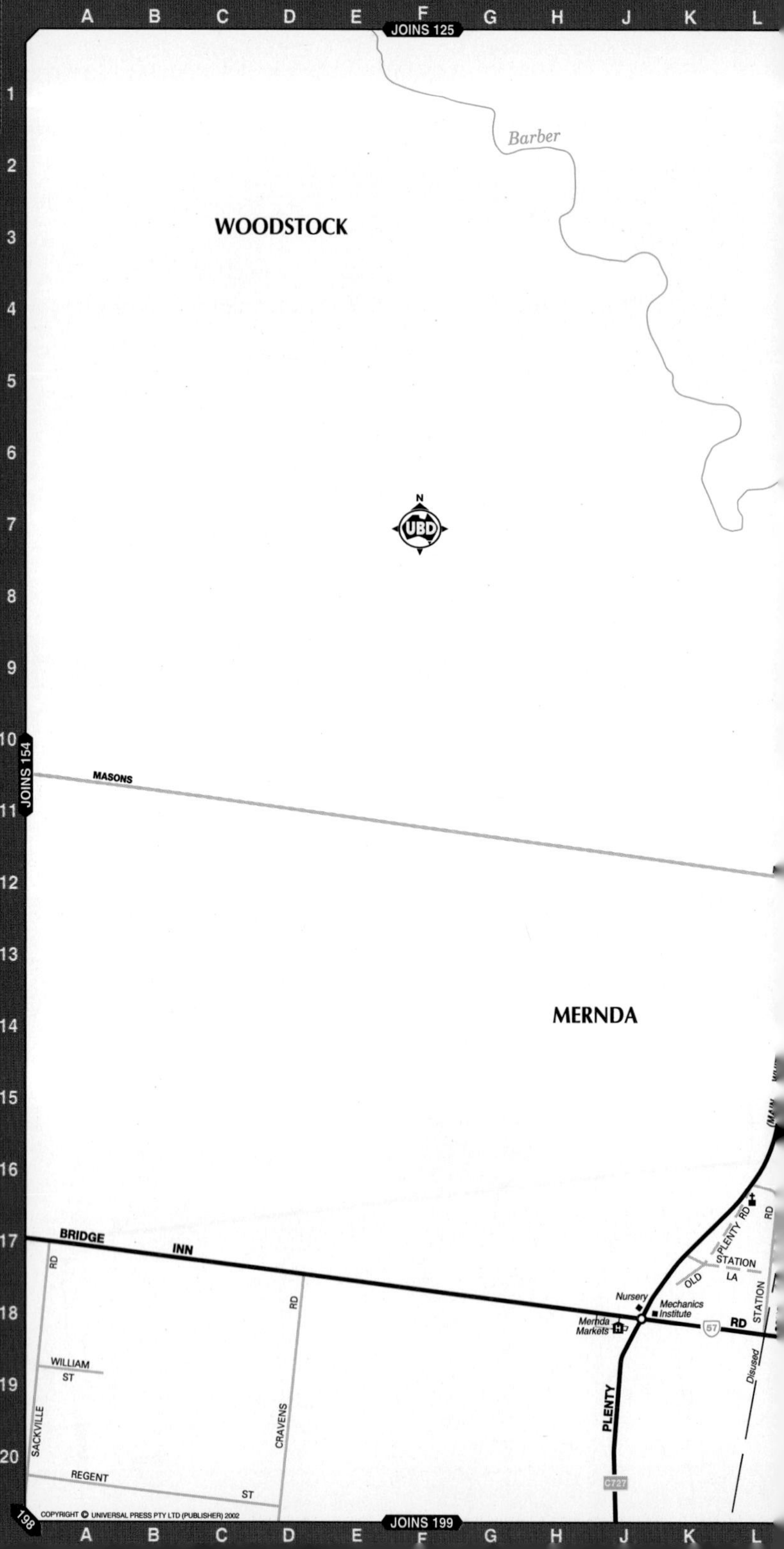

JOINS 125

198

JOINS 199

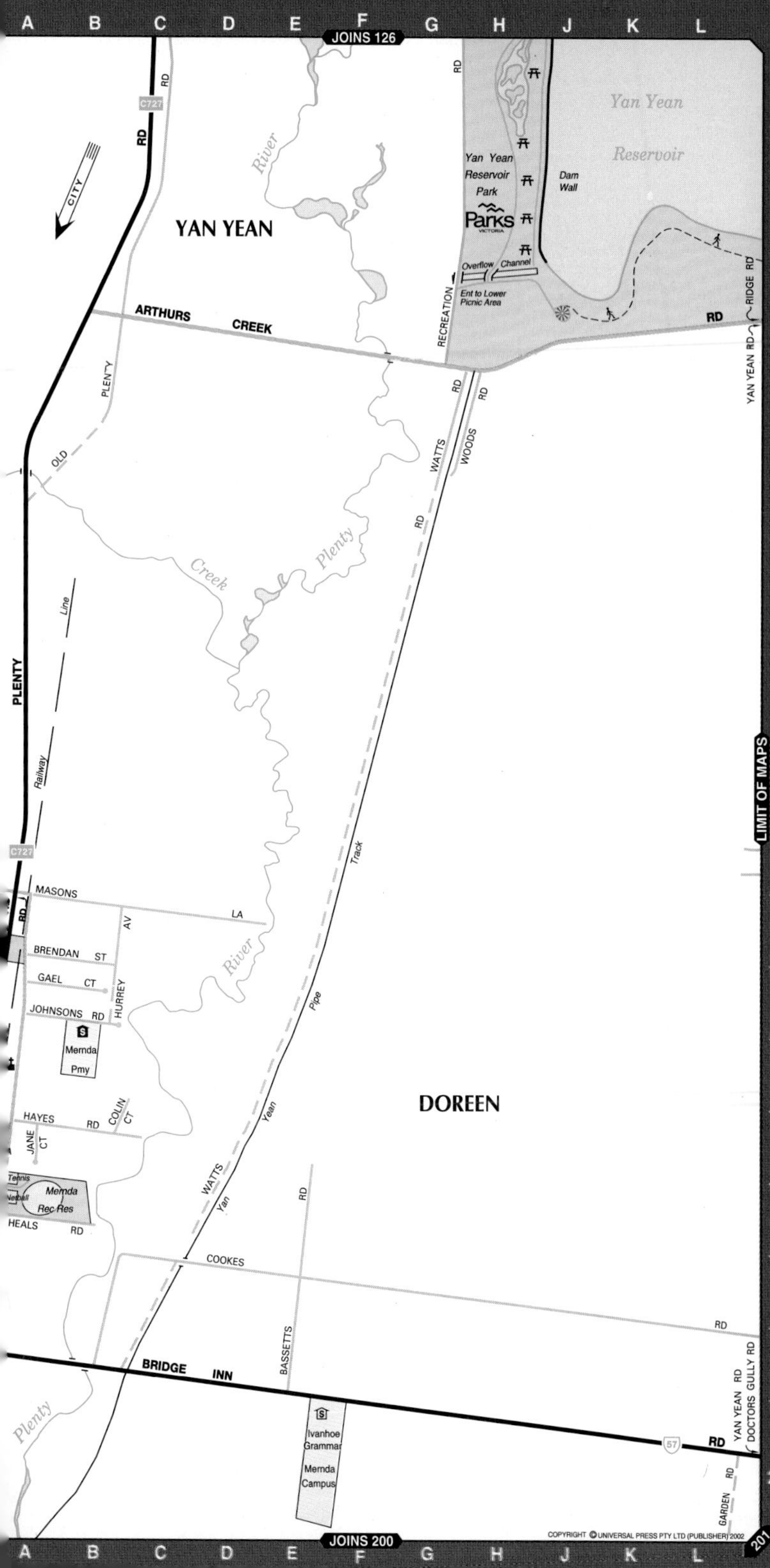

YAN YEAN
CITY
C727
RD
ARTHURS CREEK RD
Yan Yean Reservoir
Yan Yean Reservoir Park
Parks VICTORIA
Dam Wall
Overflow Channel
Ent to Lower Picnic Area
RECREATION RD
RIDGE RD
YAN YEAN RD
WATTS RD
WOODS RD
OLD PLEN'Y RD
River
Plenty River
Creek
Railway Line
PLENTY RD
LIMIT OF MAPS
MASONS LA
BRENDAN ST
GAEL CT
JOHNSONS RD
HURREY AV
Mernda Pmy
HAYES RD
COLIN CT
JANE CT
Tennis
Netball
Mernda Rec Res
HEALS RD
Yan Yean Pipe Track
WATTS
DOREEN
COOKES RD
BASSETTS RD
BRIDGE INN RD
57
Ivanhoe Grammar Mernda Campus
DOCTORS GULLY RD
GARDEN RD
Plenty

PREVIOUS MAP 156

JOINS 143

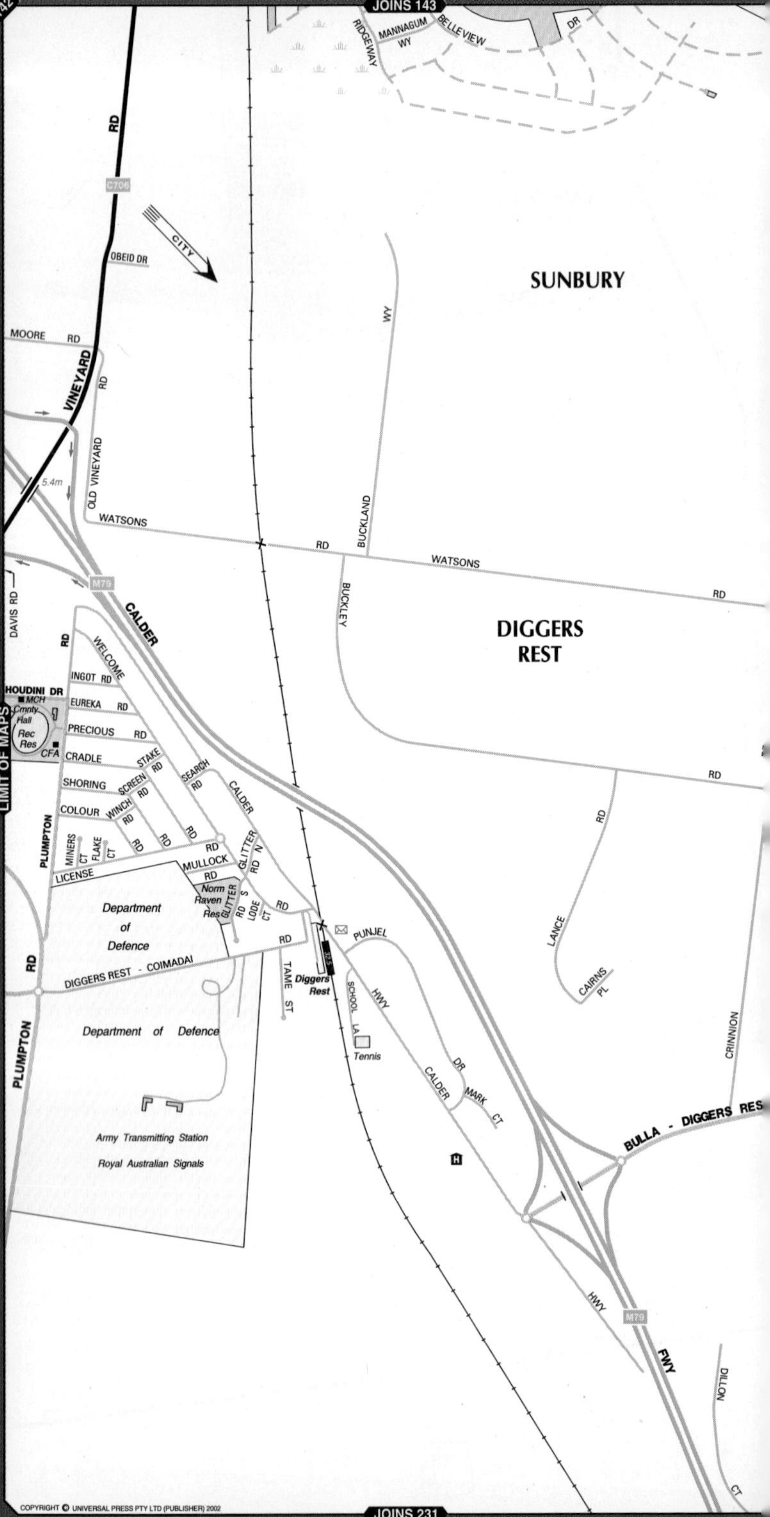
142
SUNBURY
DIGGERS REST
RIDGEWAY
MANNAGUM WY
BELLEVIEW
DR
RD
C706
CITY
OBEID DR
WY
MOORE RD
VINEYARD
RD
OLD VINEYARD
5.4m
WATSONS
RD
BUCKLAND
WATSONS
RD
M79
DAVIS RD
CALDER
BUCKLEY
RD
WELCOME
INGOT RD
HOUDINI DR
MCH
Cmnty Hall
Rec Res
CFA
EUREKA RD
PRECIOUS RD
CRADLE
STAKE RD
SHORING
SCREEN RD
SEARCH RD
CALDER
COLOUR
WINCH RD
RD
RD
RD
PLUMPTON
MINERS CT
FLAKE CT
RD
MULLOCK RD
GLITTER RD N
LICENSE
Norm Raven Res
GLITTER RD S
LODE CT
RD
Department of Defence
RD
PUNJEL
RD
TAME ST
Diggers Rest
SCHOOL LA
HWY
DIGGERS REST - COIMADAI
RD
Department of Defence
Tennis
LANCE
CAIRNS PL
CRINNION
PLUMPTON
DR
CALDER
MARK CT
Army Transmitting Station
Royal Australian Signals
BULLA - DIGGERS RES
HWY
M79
FWY
DILLON
CT
LIMIT OF MAPS

JOINS 231

A B C D E F G H J K L
JOINS 144
BULLA
SUNBURY RD
C743
REDSTONE HILL RD
Jacksons Creek
SHEPHERDS LA
N
UBD
Holden Flora & Fauna Reserve
LA
GLENCOE DR
DUNCANS LA
DUNCANS
RD
MOREFIELD CT
MANINGA PARK CT
JOINS 189
JOINS 232
233
1 2 3 4 5 6 7 8 9 10 11 12 13 14 15 16 17 18 19 20

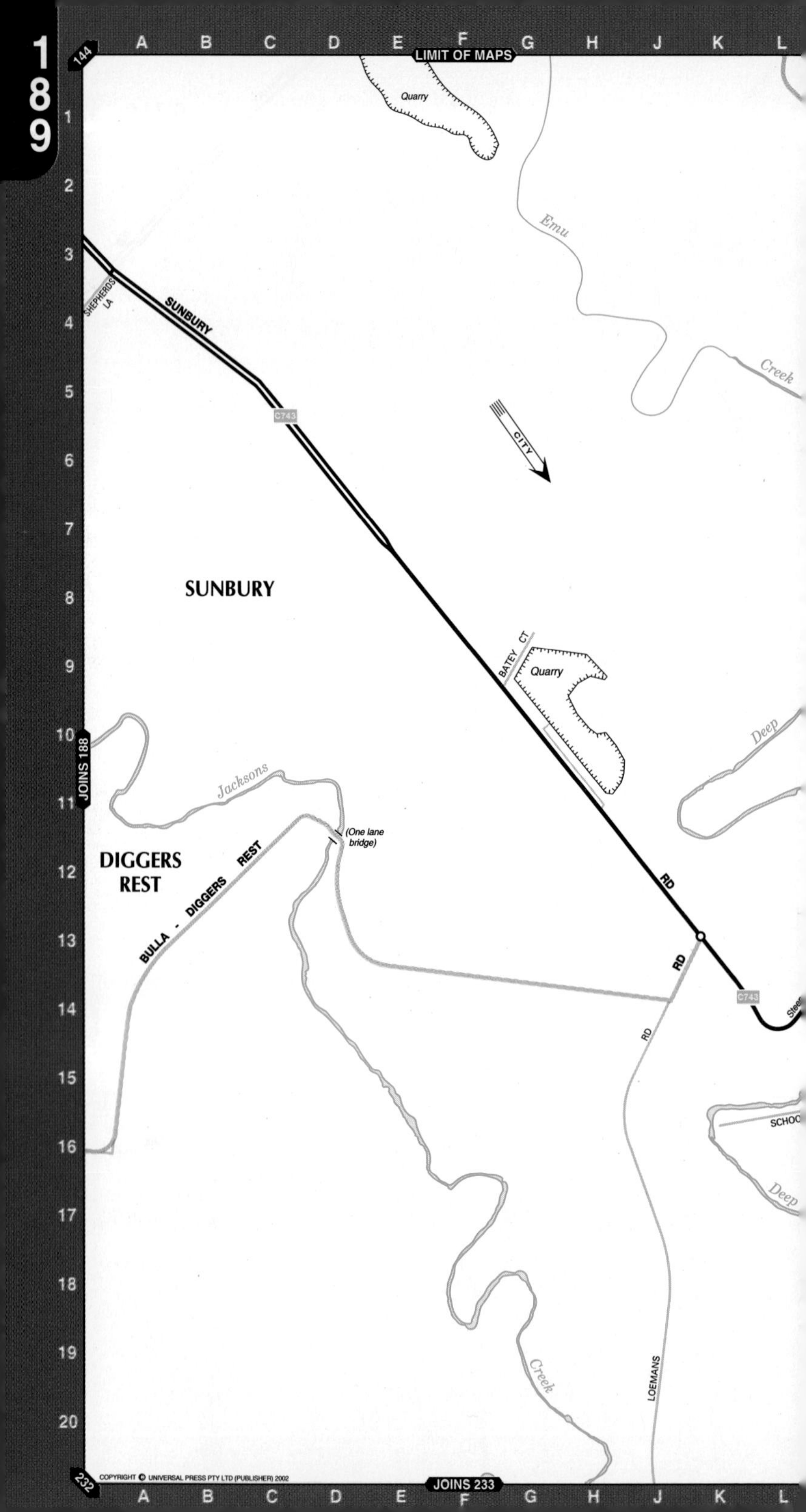

144

LIMIT OF MAPS

A B C D E F G H J K L

1 2 3 4 5 6 7 8 9 10 11 12 13 14 15 16 17 18 19 20

Quarry

Emu Creek

SHEPHERDS LA

SUNBURY RD

C743

CITY

SUNBURY

BATEY CT

Quarry

Deep Creek

Jacksons Creek

(One lane bridge)

DIGGERS REST

BULLA - DIGGERS REST RD

LOEMANS RD

Steele

SCHOO

JOINS 188

232

JOINS 233

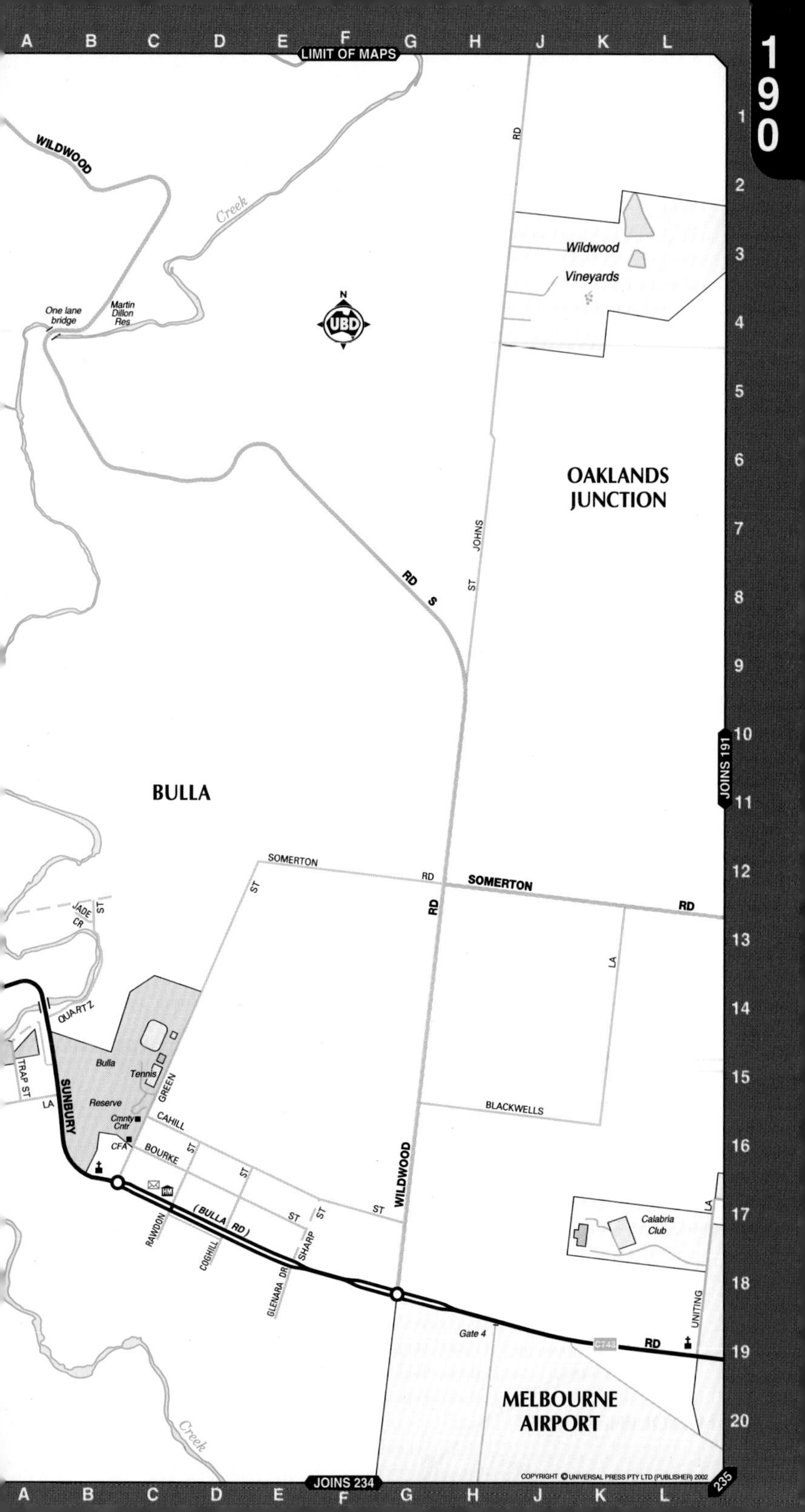

LIMIT OF MAPS

WILDWOOD

Creek

One lane bridge

Martin Dillon Res

Wildwood Vineyards

OAKLANDS JUNCTION

JOHNS ST RD

RD S

BULLA

SOMERTON RD

SOMERTON ST

SOMERTON RD

JADE CR

ST

QUARTZ

LA

Bulla Reserve

Tennis

GREEN

TRAP ST

LA

SUNBURY

Cmnty Cntr

CFA

CAHILL

BOURKE ST

ST

BLACKWELLS

WILDWOOD RD

(BULLA RD)

RAWDON

COGHILL

GLENARA DR

SHARP ST

ST

Calabria Club

LA

UNITING

Gate 4

C743

RD

MELBOURNE AIRPORT

Creek

JOINS 191

JOINS 234

235

JOINS 190
JOINS 235
234

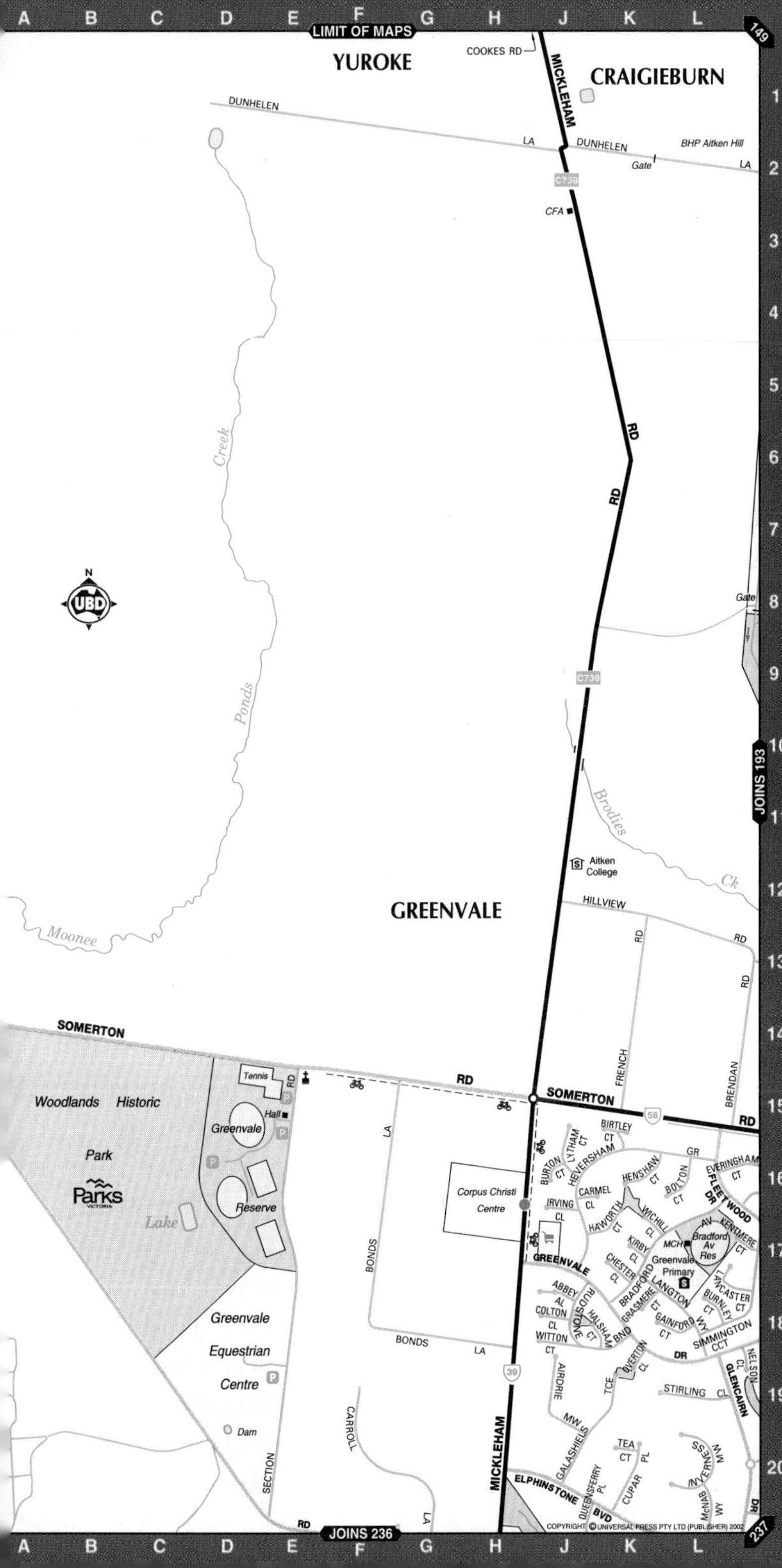

LIMIT OF MAPS

YUROKE

CRAIGIEBURN

GREENVALE

COOKES RD
MICKLEHAM RD
DUNHELEN LA
BHP Aitken Hill
Gate
C739
CFA
Creek
Ponds
Moonee
Brodies Ck
Aitken College
HILLVIEW RD
FRENCH
BRENDAN RD
SOMERTON RD
58
Woodlands Historic Park
Parks Victoria
Lake
Tennis
Hall
Greenvale Reserve
RD
LA
BONDS LA
Corpus Christi Centre
BIRTLEY CT
LYTHAM CT
BURTON CT
HEVERSHAM GR
HENSHAW CT
BOLTON CT
EVERINGHAM CT
FLEETWOOD DR
KENTMERE CT
CARMEL CL
IRVING CL
HAWORTH CT
WICHILL CL
KIRBY CL
MCH
Bradford Av Res
Greenvale Primary
GREENVALE DR
CHESTER CL
BRADFORD AV
LANGTON WY
LANCASTER CT
BURNLEY CT
ABBEY AL
COLTON CL
RUDSTONE BND
HALSHAM CT
GRASMERE CT
GAINFORD CT
SIMMINGTON CCT
WITTON CT
OVERTON CL
NELSON CL
GLENCAIRN
STIRLING CL
AIRDRIE MW
TCE
GALASHIELS
TEA CT
CUPAR PL
INVERNESS MW
McNAB WY
ELPHINSTONE BVD
QUEENSFERRY PL
Greenvale Equestrian Centre
Dam
SECTION RD
CARROLL
MICKLEHAM
39

149
JOINS 193
JOINS 236
237

JOINS 149

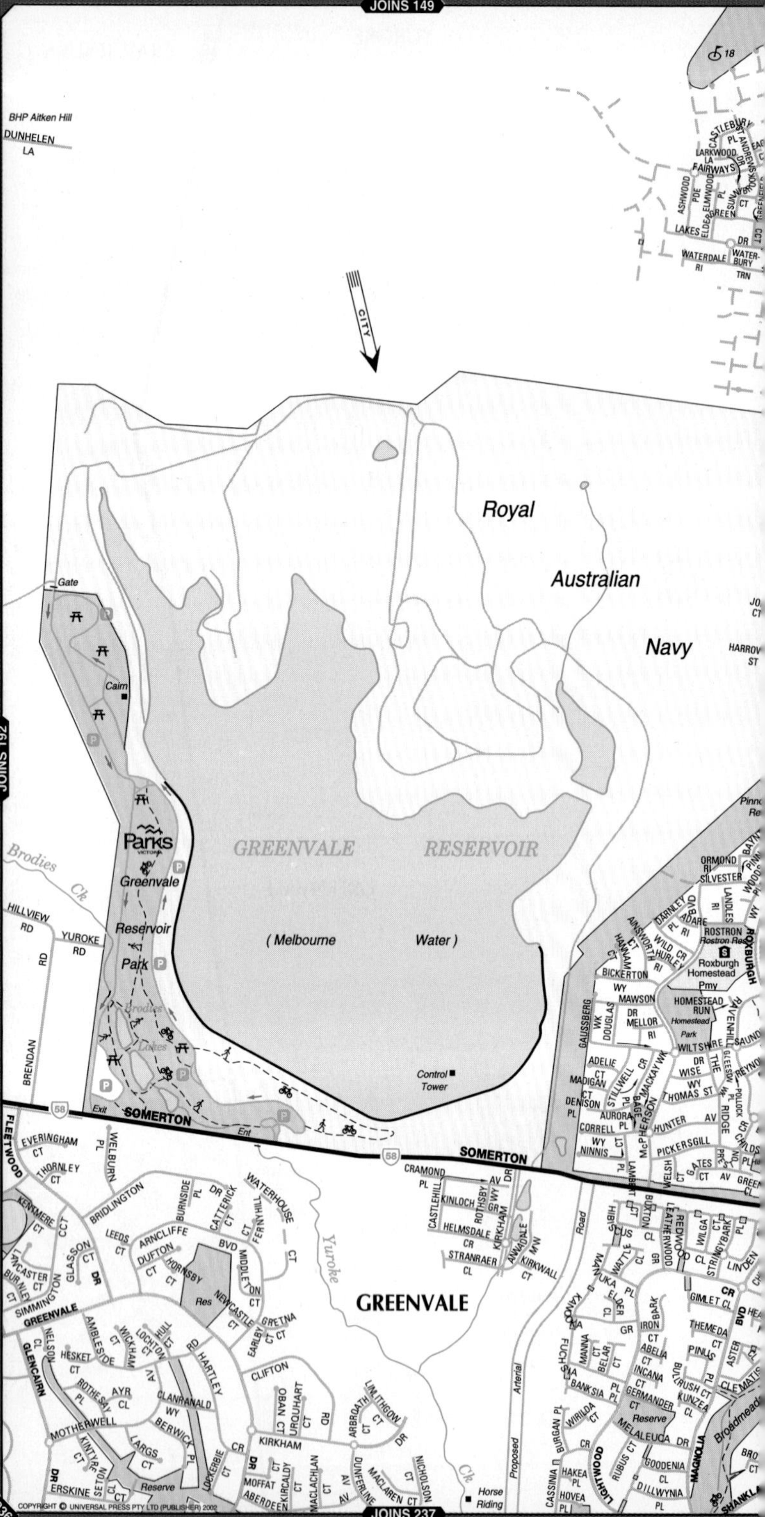

A B C D E F G H J K L

BHP Aitken Hill
DUNHELEN LA
CASTLEBURY PL
ST ANDREWS DR
LARKWOOD LA
FAIRWAYS
ASHWOOD PDE
ELMWOOD PL
SUNNYBROOK CT
ELDERGREEN
LAKES
DR
WATERDALE RI
WATERBURY TRN
CITY
Royal
Australian
Navy
HARROW ST
Gate
Cairn
GREENVALE RESERVOIR
(Melbourne Water)
Parks VICTORIA
Greenvale Reservoir Park
Brodies Ck
Brodies Lakes
HILLVIEW RD
YUROKE RD
BRENDAN RD
Control Tower
Exit
Ent
SOMERTON
58
Pinnacle Re
ORMOND RI
SILVESTER
DARNLEY BVD
ADARE PL
LANDLES RI
ROSTRON
Rostron Res
ROXBURGH
Roxburgh Homestead Pmy
AINSWORTH CT
HANNAM CT
WILD CR
HURLEY RI
BICKERTON WY
MAWSON DR
GAUSSBERG WK
DOUGLAS
MELLOR RI
HOMESTEAD RUN
Homestead Park
RAVENHILL
WILTSHIRE
ADELIE CT
STILLWELL CR
MACKAY WK
DR WISE WY
THE RIDGE
GLEESON
MADIGAN CT
DENISON PL
THOMAS ST
POLLOCK
AURORA PL
McPHERSON
BAGE
CORRELL PL
HUNTER AV
WY NINNIS
LAMBERT
WELSH
PICKERSGILL
GATES
CT AV
CHILDS
EVERINGHAM CT
FLEETWOOD
WELBURN PL
THORNLEY CT
KENTMERE
BRIDLINGTON
BURNSIDE PL
CATTERICK DR
WATERHOUSE CT
FERNHILL CT
CRAMOND PL
CASTLEHILL CT
KINLOCH GR
ROTHSBY WY
HELMSDALE CR
KIRKHAM DR
STRANRAER CL
AVONDALE MW
KIRKWALL CT
Road
HIBIS CT
CUS CL
BUXTON
LEATHERWOOD
REDWOOD CL
WILGA
STRINGYBARK
LINDEN
GLASSON DR
LEEDS CT
ARNCLIFFE
DUFTON CT
HORNSBY CT
BVD
MIDDLETON
Res
NEWCASTLE CT
Yuroke Ck
GREENVALE
LANCASTER CT
BURNLEY CT
SIMMINGTON
GREENVALE
GLENCAIRN
NELSON CL
AMBLESIDE CT
WICKHAM
LOCHTON CT
HULL CT
HARTLEY RD
EARLBY CT
GRETNA CT
MANUKA
WATTLE CT
ELDER CL
KANOONA
BARK
IRON
GR
GIMLET CL
CR
THEMEDA CT
PINUS
ASTER
ABELIA
INCANA CT
BULRUSH CT
KUNZEA CL
CLEMATIS
FUCHSIA
MANNA CT
BELAR CT
BANKSIA PL
GERMANDER
Reserve
Broadmeadows
HESKET CT
ROTHESAY PL
AYR CL
CLANRANALD WY
CLIFTON
OBAN CT
URQUHART CT
RD
ARBROATH CT
LINLITHGOW CT
DR
MOTHERWELL
BERWICK PL
KINTYRE CT
LARGS CT
KIRKHAM
CR
DR
LOCKERBIE CT
MOFFAT CT
KIRKCALDY CT
MACLACHLAN CT
AV
DUNFERLINE AV
MACLAREN CT
NICHOLSON CT
Proposed Arterial
BURGAN PL
WIRILDA CT
CR
MELALEUCA DR
MAGNOLIA
BRO CT
SHANKLAND
ERSKINE
SETON CT
CL
DR
Reserve
ABERDEEN
Horse Riding
CASSINIA
HAKEA PL
HOVEA PL
LIGHTWOOD
RUBUS CT
GOODENIA CL
DILLWYNIA PL

JOINS 192

236

JOINS 237

A B C D E F G H J K L

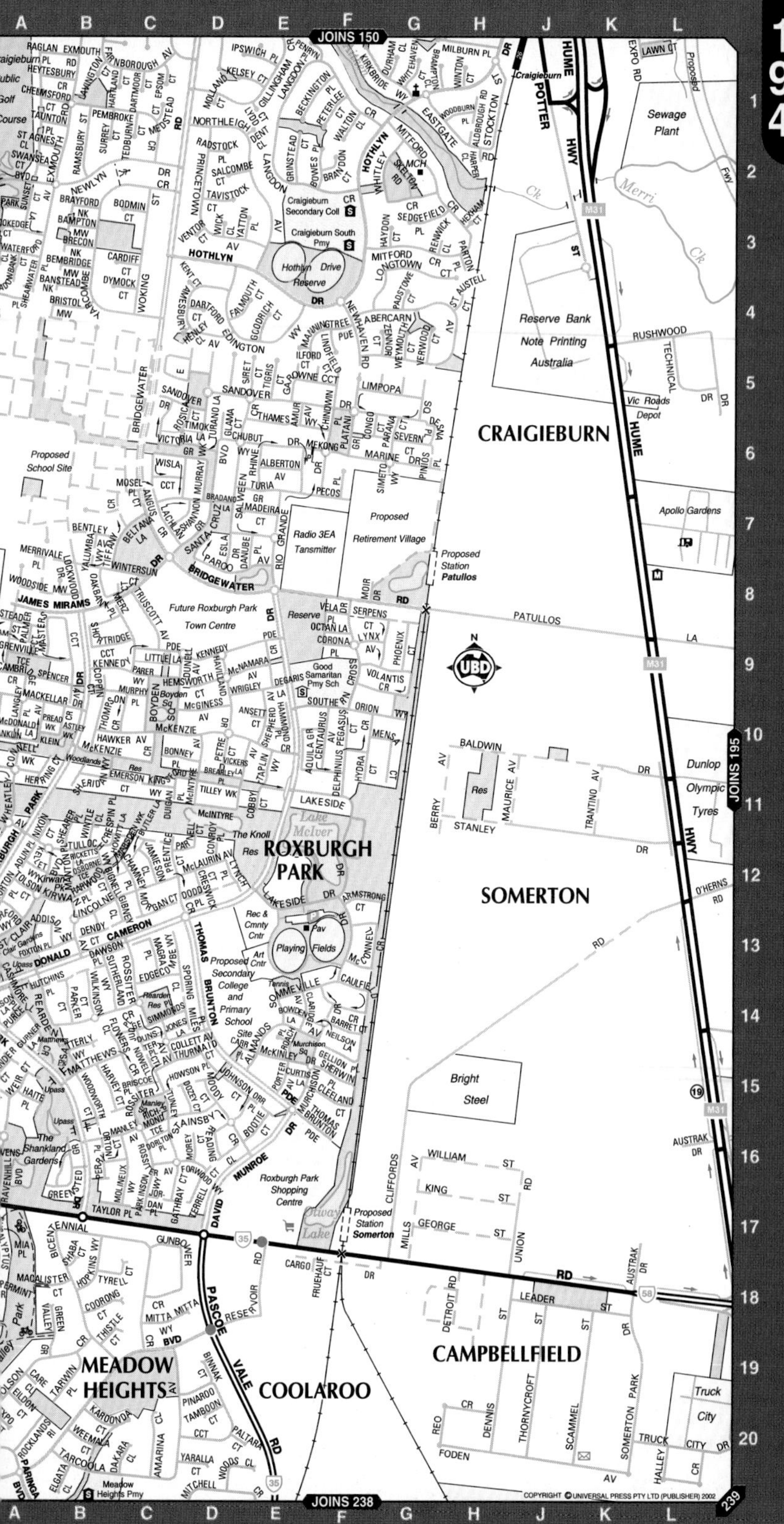
A B C D E F G H J K L
JOINS 150
JOINS 195
JOINS 238
239
1 2 3 4 5 6 7 8 9 10 11 12 13 14 15 16 17 18 19 20
CRAIGIEBURN
ROXBURGH PARK
SOMERTON
CAMPBELLFIELD
MEADOW HEIGHTS
COOLAROO
Craigieburn Public Golf Course
Sewage Plant
Merri Ck
Craigieburn Secondary Coll
Craigieburn South Pmy
Hothlyn Drive Reserve
Reserve Bank Note Printing Australia
Vic Roads Depot
Apollo Gardens
Proposed School Site
Radio 3EA Tansmitter
Proposed Retirement Village
Proposed Station Patullos
Future Roxburgh Park Town Centre
Good Samaritan Pmy Sch
Dunlop Olympic Tyres
Lake McIver
The Knoll Res
Rec & Cmnty Cntr
Playing Fields
Art Cntr
Proposed Secondary College and Primary School Site
Bright Steel
The Shankland Gardens
Roxburgh Park Shopping Centre
Otway Lake
Proposed Station Somerton
Truck City
Meadow Heights Pmy
HUME HWY
POTTER ST
M31
PATULLOS LA
SOMERTON RD
PASCOE VALE RD
BRIDGEWATER RD
HOTHLYN DR
THOMAS BRUNTON PDE
DAVID MUNROE DR
O'HERNS RD
AUSTRAK DR
BALDWIN DR
COPYRIGHT © UNIVERSAL PRESS PTY LTD (PUBLISHER) 2002

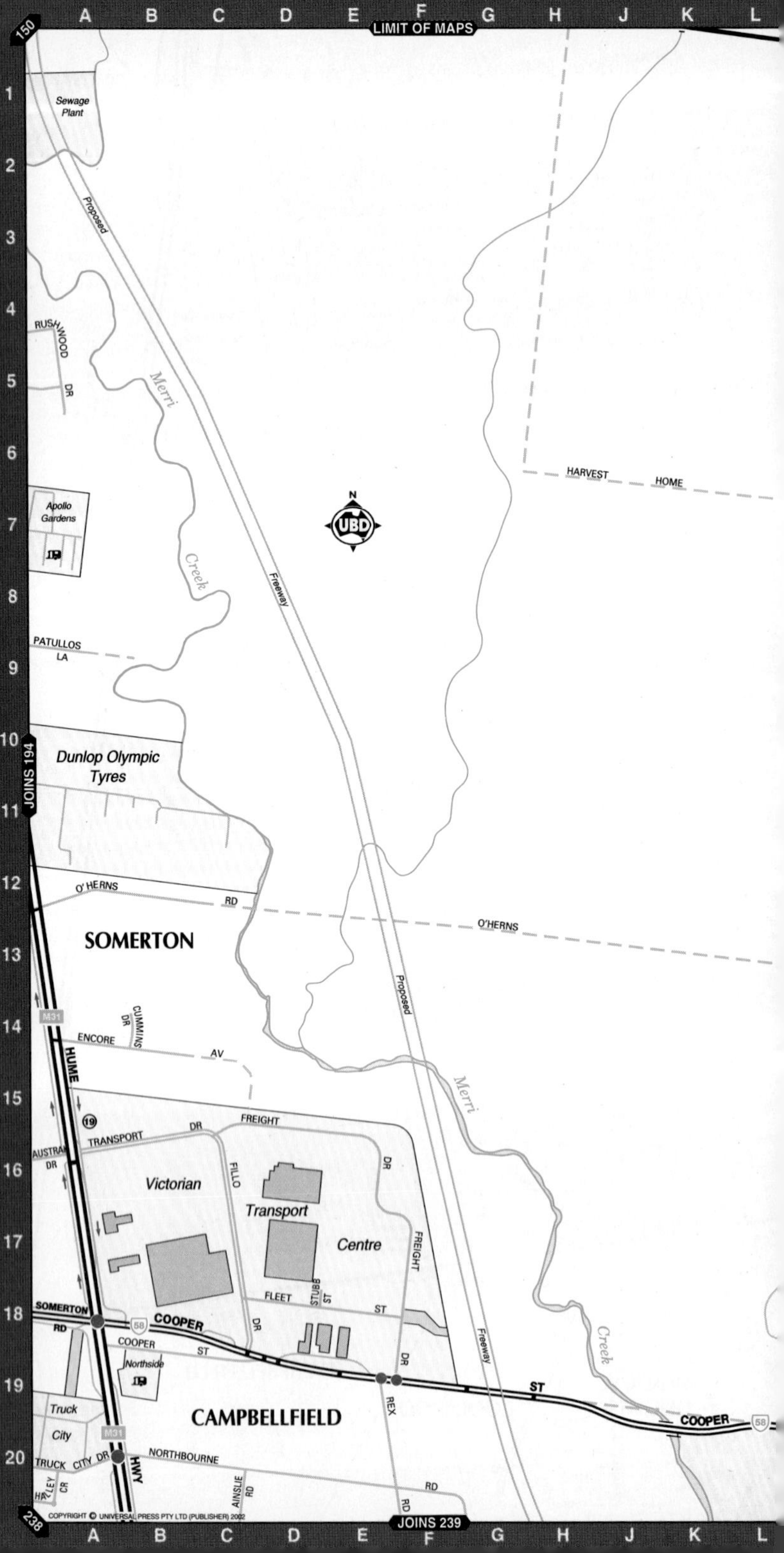

238

JOINS 239

JOINS 197

JOINS 240

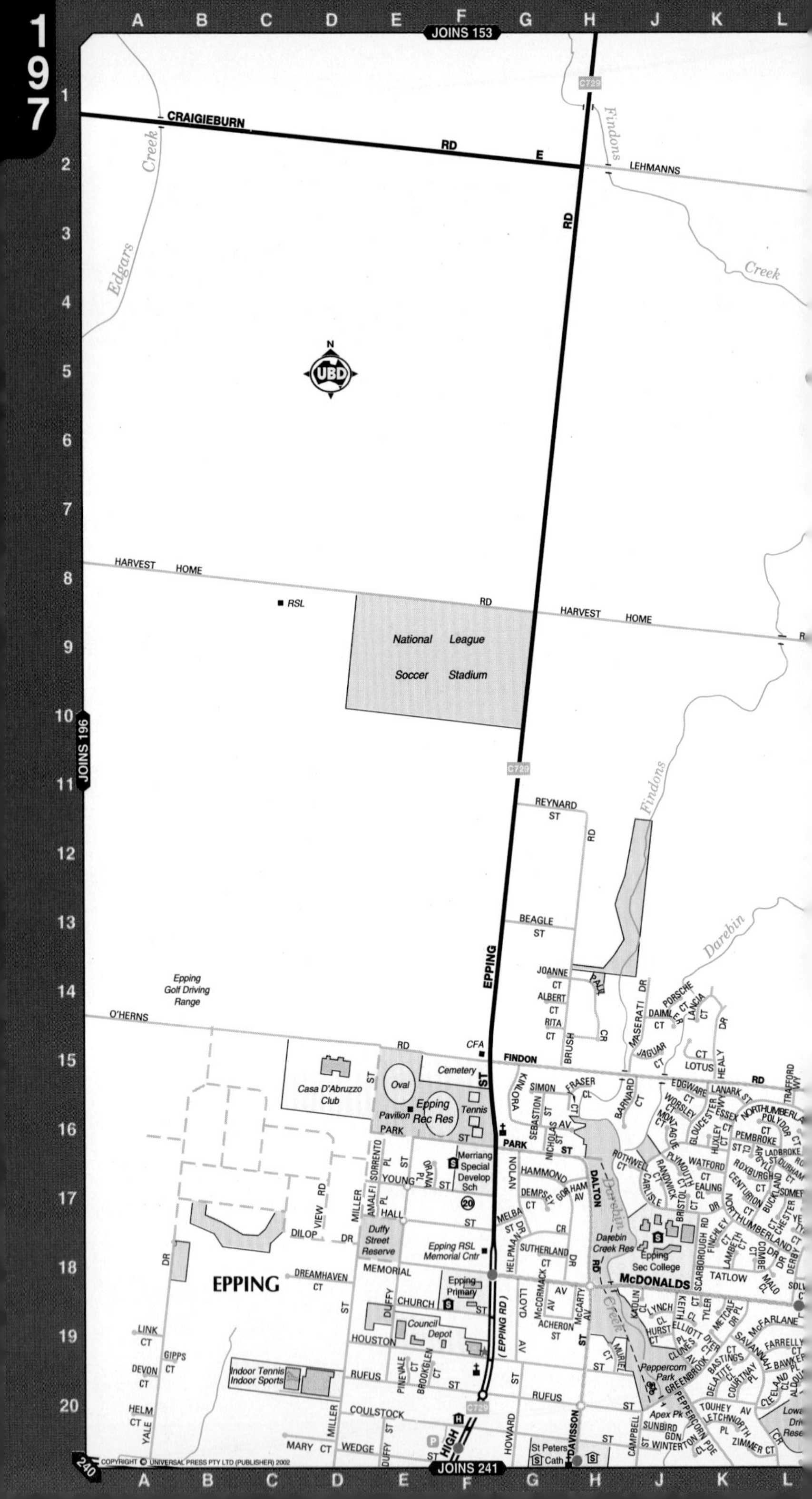
JOINS 153
C729
CRAIGIEBURN
RD
E
LEHMANNS
Findons
Creek
Edgars
RD
N
UBD
HARVEST
HOME
RSL
RD
HARVEST
HOME
National League
Soccer Stadium
JOINS 196
C729
REYNARD
ST
RD
BEAGLE
ST
EPPING
Darebin
JOANNE
CT
ALBERT
CT
RITA
CT
PAUL
CR
BRUSH
MASERATI DR
PORSCHE
CT
LANCIA
CT
DAIMLER
CT
JAGUAR
CT
LOTUS
CT
HEALY
DR
Epping
Golf Driving
Range
O'HERNS
RD
CFA
FINDON
RD
Cemetery
ST
Casa D'Abruzzo
Club
Oval
Epping
Rec Res
Pavilion
Tennis
PARK
ST
PARK
ST
KINLORA
SIMON
FRASER
CL
SEBASTION
NICHOLAS
AV
BARNARD
CT
EDGWARE
LANARK ST
TRAFFORD
WORSLEY
MONTAGUE
GLOUCESTER
ESSEX
NORTHUMBERLAND
POLYDOR
PEMBROKE
HUXLEY
ROTHWELL
PLYMOUTH
WATFORD
EALING
ROXBURGH
DURHAM
LADBROKE
SORRENTO
PL
ST
ORANA
PL
YOUNG
ST
Merriang
Special
Develop
Sch
20
NOLAN
HAMMOND
DALTON
HAM
AV
CARLISLE
RANDWICK
BRISTOL
CENTURION
BUCKLAND
SOMERS
MILLER
AMALFI
PL
HALL
ST
DEMPSEY
GOR
CT
DILOP
VIEW
RD
DR
Duffy
Street
Reserve
MELBA
ST
DR
HELPMAN
CR
SUTHERLAND
DR
Darebin
Creek Res
Epping
Sec College
SCARBOROUGH
FINCHLEY
LAMBETH
NORTHUMBERLAND
CHESTER
COMBE
DERBY
Epping RSL
Memorial Cntr
MEMORIAL
DR
EPPING
DREAMHAVEN
CT
McDONALDS
TATLOW
MALO
CL
Epping
Primary
CHURCH
ST
DUFFY
(EPPING RD)
LLOYD
McCORMACK
AV
McCARTY
AV
ACHERON
ST
KATLIN
LYNCH
CL
HURST
CT
ELLIOTT
KEITH
TYLER
METCALF
DR PL
McFARLANE
SAVANNAH
FARRELLY
LINK
CT
GIPPS
CT
DEVON
CT
Council
Depot
HOUSTON
AV
ST
MURIEL
CLUNES
DYER
BASTINGS
DELATITE
COURTNAY
BAWKER
CLELAND
Indoor Tennis
Indoor Sports
RUFUS
PINEVALE
CT
BROOKGLEN
CT
ST
ST
RUFUS
Peppercorn
Park
GREENBROOK
HELM
CT
YALE
COULSTOCK
ST
MILLER
C729
HOWARD
DAVISSON
ST
Apex Pk
PEPPERCORN PDE
TOUHEY
AV
LETCHWORTH
PL
ZIMMER CT
SUNBIRD
GDN
WINTERTON CL
CAMPBELL
MARY
CT
WEDGE
DUFFY
ST
HIGH
St Peters
Cath
JOINS 241
240

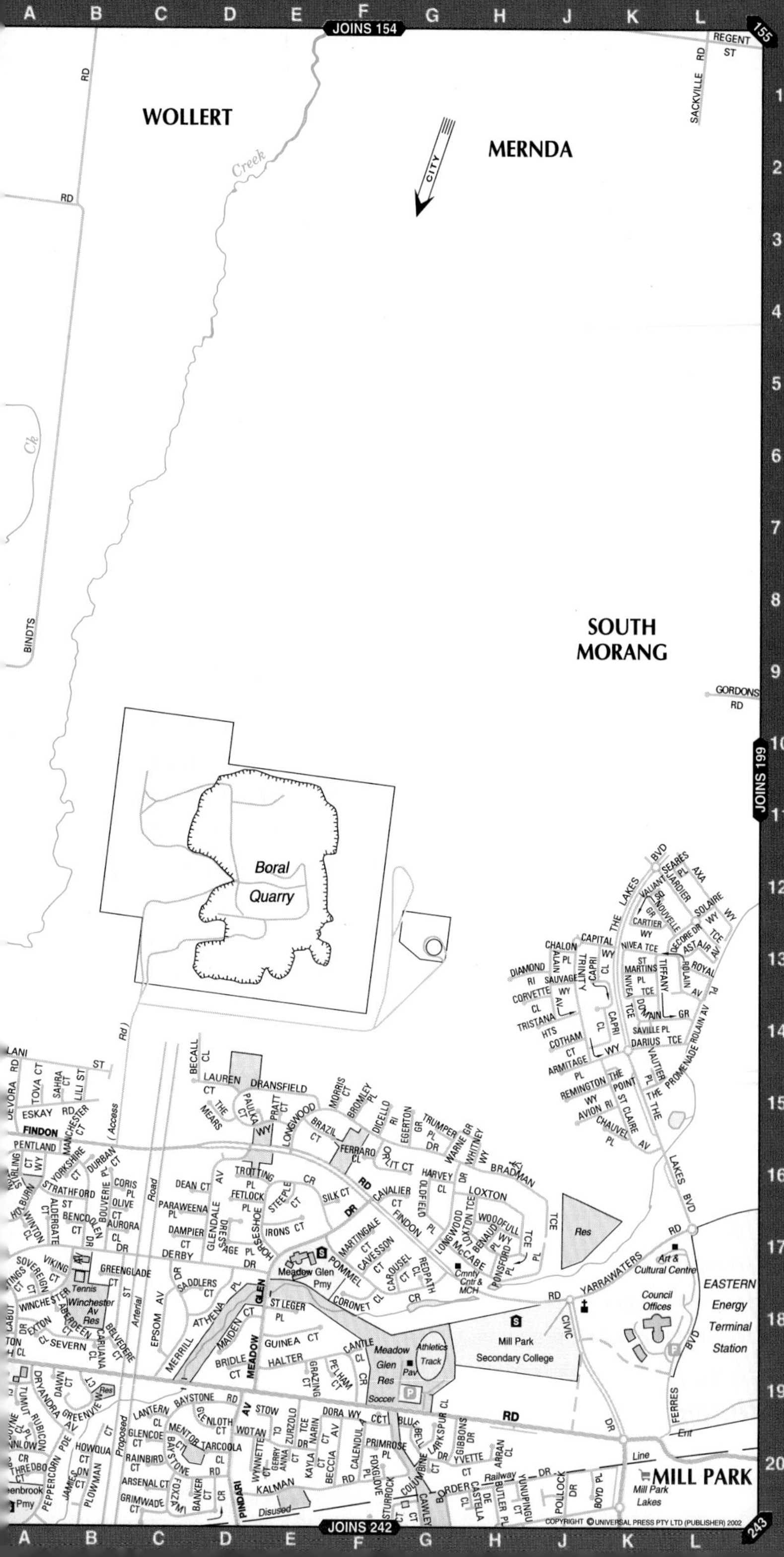

1 2 3 4 5 6 7 8 9 10 11 12 13 14 15 16 17 18 19 20

WOLLERT

MERNDA

SOUTH MORANG

MILL PARK

CITY

Creek
Ck

REGENT ST
SACKVILLE RD
RD
RD
BINDTS
GORDONS RD

Boral Quarry

JOINS 199

LANI
DEVORA RD
TOVA CT
SAHRA CT
LILLI ST
ST
ESKAY RD
MANCHESTER CT
FINDON
PENTLAND
STIRLING CT
WY
YORKSHIRE CT
DURBAN PL
CORIS PL
OLIVE CT
AURORA CL
HOLBURN
STRATHFORD ST
BOUVERIE
BENCOOLEN DR
ALDERGATE CT
WINTON CL
SOVEREIGN CT
VIKING CT
WINCHESTER
ABERDEEN CT
Tennis
Winchester Av Res
GREENGLADE CT
ST
BELVEDERE CT
CARUANA CL
SEVERN
EXTON CL
CABOT
DR
TON CL
(Access
Rd)
Road
Arterial
Proposed
EPSOM AV
MERRILL
BECALL CL
LAUREN CT
DRANSFIELD
THE MEARS
PAULKA CT
PRATT CT
WY
LONGWOOD
MORRIS CT
BROMLEY CT
DICELLO RI
EGERTON GR
TRUMPER PL
WARNE GR
WHITNEY WY
DR
BRAZIL CT
FERRARO CL
ORLIT CT
HARVEY CL
BRADMAN
TROTTING PL
FETLOCK PL
STEEPLE CT
CR
SILK CT
CAVALIER CT
OLDFIELD PL
LOXTON TCE
LONGWOOD
WOODFULL WY
BENAUD PL
McCABE
PONSFORD PL
TCE
PL
Res
DEAN CT
PARAWEENA PL
DAMPIER CT
DERBY
GLENDALE AV
DRESSAGE PL
HORSESHOE
IRONS CT
DR
FINDON
MARTINGALE CT
CAVESSON CT
CAROUSEL CT
REDPATH CL
Cmnty Cntr & MCH
POMMEL
Meadow Glen Pmy
CORONET CL
CR
SADDLERS CT
DR
ATHENA PL
MAIDEN CT
GLEN
MEADOW
ST LEGER PL
GUINEA CT
HALTER
BRIDLE CT
CANTLE CL
GRAZING CT
PELHAM CT
CR
Meadow Glen Res
Athletics Track
Pav
Soccer
Mill Park Secondary College
YARRAWATERS
RD
Art & Cultural Centre
Council Offices
CIVIC
EASTERN Energy Terminal Station
LAKES BVD
BVD
FERRES
RD
DR
Ent
Line
THE LAKES BVD
SEARES PL
AXA
JARDIER
VALIANT SQ
GR
NOUVELLE
CARTIER WY
SOLAIRE WY
WY
DECORE DR
TCE
ASTAIR AV
CAPITAL WY
CHALON PL
ALAIN
TRINITY
CAPRI CL
NIVEA TCE
ST MARTINS PL
NIVEA TCE
TIFFANY
ROLAIN AV
ROYAL PL
DIAMOND RI
SAUVAGE
CORVETTE WY
CL
AV
TRISTANA HTS
CAPRI CL
DOMAIN GR
SAVILLE PL
ROLAIN AV
COTHAM CT
ARMITAGE PL
WY
DARIUS TCE
THE PROMENADE
REMINGTON WY
THE POINT
VAUTIER PL
AVION RI
ST CLAIRE
THE
CHAUVEL PL
AV
DRYANDRA AV
TUMUT PL
RUBICON
DAWN CT
GREENVIEW CT
Res
BAYSTONE RD
LANTERN CL
GLENCOE CT
GLENLOTH CT
MENTOR CT
TARCOOLA CL
BAYSTONE
STOW
WOTAN
WYNNETTE CT
GERRY ANNA CT
ZURZOLO TCE
KAYLA CT
NARIN DR
BECCIA CT
AV
DORA WY
CALENDULA
PRIMROSE PL
FOXGLOVE
CCT
BLUEBELL
LARKSPUR CL
GIBBONS DR
YVETTE CT
ARRAN CL
RD
Railway
DR
YUNUPINGU
POLLOCK
DR
BOYD PL
HOWQUA CT
RAINBIRD CT
ARSENAL CT
GRIMWADE CT
FOXZAN
BANKER CT
CR
RD
PINDARI
KALMAN
Disused
STURROCK
COLUMBINE
CAWLEY
BORDER
CASTELLA
BUTLER PL
PEPPERCORN PDE
JAMES CT
PLOWMAN
Greenbrook Pmy
Mill Park Lakes

154
JOINS 155

A B C D E F G H J K L

REGENT ST
CRAVENS RD
HUNTERS RD
PLENTY
Line
Railway
Disused
C727

MERNDA

SOUTH MORANG

N
UBD

McARTHURS RD
WILTONVALE
RD

GORDONS RD
GIRVAN PL
MARTIN CL
FITZGERALD CT
RED OAKS
GRABAPPLE RD
THE LAKES
YELLOWBOX AV
BVD
WY
FLOWERING AV
GUM GR
MASKED OWL RD
SANDPIPER TCE
WINGSPAN
PLENTY
MARIGOLD DR
ST
FLYING FOX
FEATHERPARK
SWALLOW ST
TCE
EVERGREEN
GORDONS RD

Hawkstowe Park
Parks Victoria
Red Gum Picnic Area
P
Ent
Park Office
Exit

AXA WY
JARDIER TCE

JOINS 198

San Carlo Nursing Home
DAMON CL
MARLO CT
REECE CT
BUSHMANS
STAGECOACH
ROMINA WY
ZENA DR
BLUESTONE
BLACKSMITH AV
23
BELLOWS ST
ANVIL CT
BVD
COACHMAN DR
HIGHVIEW
COBBLESTONE
VALLEY VIEW CT
STAGECOACH BVD
HIGHVIEW
O'LOUGHLIN PL

EASTERN Energy Terminal Station
WILLIAMSONS RD
CFA
Railway
Disused
Line
OLD PLENTY RD
C727
Emmaus Village Ret Homes
BETHANY CT
AMBER CT
SERENITY WY
DR
ALLAMANDA CR
Tennis
South Morang Rec Res
PLENTY RD

MILL PARK
McDONALDS RD
GORGE RD
KELVIN GR
NIRVANA

242
JOINS 243

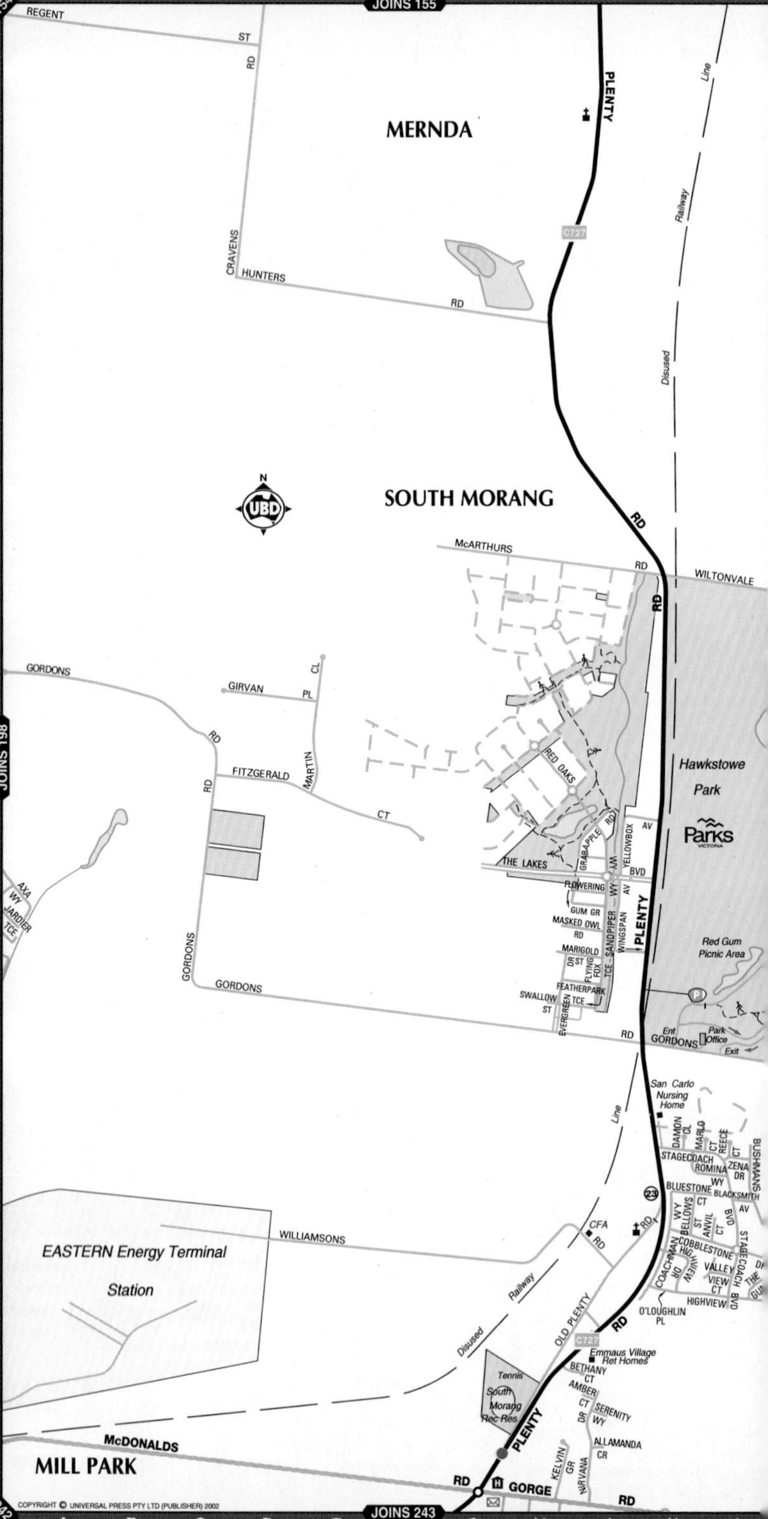

JOINS 156

JOINS 201

JOINS 244

245

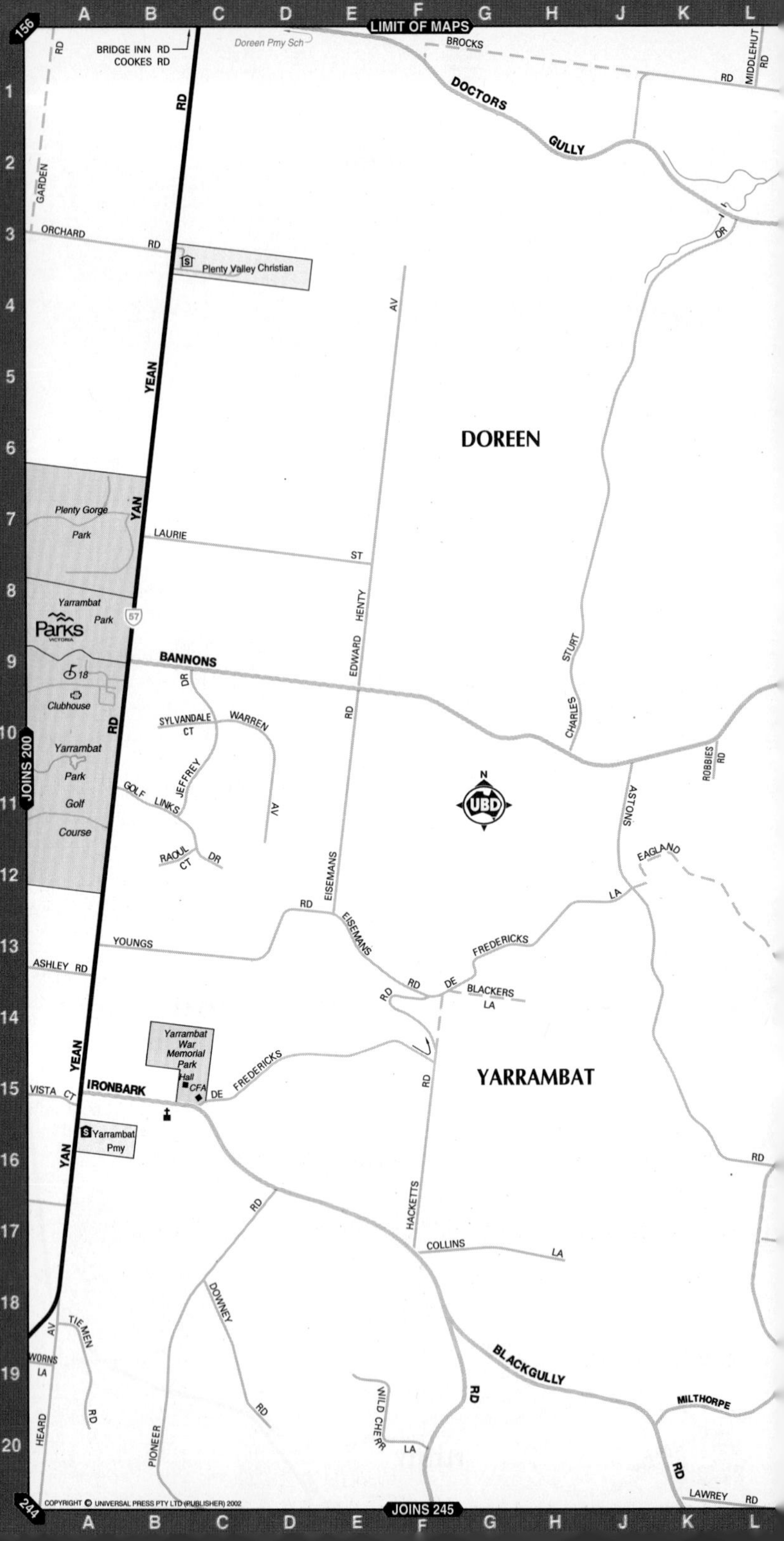

A B C D E F G H J K L
LIMIT OF MAPS
156
BRIDGE INN RD
COOKES RD
Doreen Pmy Sch
BROCKS
DOCTORS
GULLY
MIDDLEHUT RD
RD
GARDEN
ORCHARD RD
Plenty Valley Christian
AV
YEAN RD
DR
DOREEN
Plenty Gorge Park
YAN
LAURIE ST
Yarrambat Park
Parks VICTORIA
57
BANNONS
EDWARD HENTY RD
STURT
CHARLES
DR
SYLVANDALE CT
WARREN AV
JEFFREY
Clubhouse
Yarrambat Park Golf Course
RD
JOINS 200
GOLF LINKS
RAOUL CT
DR
ROBBIES RD
ASTONS
UBD
N
EAGLAND
EISEMANS RD
LA
YOUNGS
ASHLEY RD
FREDERICKS
DE
BLACKERS LA
RD
Yarrambat War Memorial Park
Hall
CFA
FREDERICKS DE
YEAN
VISTA CT
IRONBARK
YARRAMBAT
Yarrambat Pmy
YAN
HACKETTS RD
RD
COLLINS LA
DOWNEY RD
TIEMEN RD
AV
WORNS LA
BLACKGULLY RD
MILTHORPE
WILD CHERRY LA
HEARD
PIONEER
RD
LAWREY RD
1 2 3 4 5 6 7 8 9 10 11 12 13 14 15 16 17 18 19 20
244
JOINS 245

A B C D E F G H J K L
LIMIT OF MAPS
NUTFIELD
COTTLES BRIDGE
HURSTBRIDGE
DIAMOND CREEK
WATTLE GLEN
CHAPEL LA
FLORENCE RD
BROCKS
DOCTORS GULLY RD
MINE RD
LINTONS BRIDGE
HURSTBRIDGE ARTHURS CREEK RD
WY
RD
CREEK
LA N
CITY
Arthur's
BOYDS RD
BOYDS RD
WATTLETREE RD
BURKES BRIDGE RD
Ck
CREIGHTON
CEDUNA CT
BANNONS LA
PROSPECT HILL CR
WATTLETREE RD
MOUNTAIN VIEW RD
BINGLEY AV
HILLTOP RD
VICTORIA ST
WATTLETREE
ACACIA RD
HALEYS GULLY RD
BROAD GULLY RD
LA
FAWKNER
LINNET AV
VALLEY VIEW RD
CR
BATMAN AV
KENDALLS LA
KENDALLS
SPRINGHILL RD
HURST
MEANDER RD
SHANKLIN ST
STEWART ST
ZIG ZAG RD
MONASH BR
Fbr
KNOWLE GR
Ben Frilay Oval
GREYSHARPS RD
Hurstbridge
Diamond Valley Secondary College
MEANDER
Ck
Diamond
ROSE AV
AV
C746
KINGLAKE
HICKORY DOWNS PL
WADESON RD
LARSON RD
RD
RD
GLENHAVEN RD
THE GLEN
LYNNBRAE
Scrubby
Creek
HEIDELBERG
Temple Ridge Reserve
PULLEN DR
GORST
BEAN RD
DR
JOINS 203
JOINS 246
247
1 2 3 4 5 6 7 8 9 10 11 12 13 14 15 16 17 18 19 20

LIMIT OF MAPS
A B C D E F G H J K L
1 2 3 4 5 6 7 8 9 10 11 12 13 14 15 16 17 18 19 20
COTTLES BRIDGE
HURSTBRIDGE
WATTLE GLEN
HILDEBRAND RD
COTTLES BRIDGE - STRATHEWEN RD
DUNMOOCHIN RD
BARREENONG
Steep
PATULLOS RD
THURSTBRIDGE
BURKES BRIDGE
ARTHURS CREEK RD
Arthurs Ck
CHRISTIAN
Diamond Creek
LACEYS
Learning Co-op Pmy
KINGLAKE
HEIDELBERG
(MAIN RD)
C746
GOSFIELD RD
CAROLINE CR
Emergency Access
Fergusons Paddock
Fbr
Tennis
CFA
Pmy
Cmnty Cntr
MONASH BR
MCH
MELISSA CL
CARLYLE CL
DUNSTAN DR
MILTON WY
ROYLSTON AV
RI
BAMBARA
TULONG ST
KENARRA CT
COOLAROO RD
CHERRY TREE AV
PINNAROO CL
RD
Council Depot
MILLS
MANUKA
ANZAC
GREYSHARPS RD
Hurstbridge
CURTAIN
STEVEN ST
FAIRDELL CR
PARKER RD
TAYLOR
CURTAIN RD
FLATROCK
SCHAEFFER
DAPHNE CR
ROSE AV
AV
WANDOO CL
SPRYS LA
THE GLEN
LYNNBRAE
HILLCREST
Reservoir
DEWAR DR
HOEBERGIN
LA
Temple Ridge Reserve
BAILEY GULLY (Private) Rd
HEATHER
PULLEN DR
SILVAN RD
COCHRANES
JOINS 202
JOINS 247
246

JOINS 205

1
2
3
4
5
6
7
8
9
10
11
12
13
14
15
16
17
18
19
20

JOINS 248

249

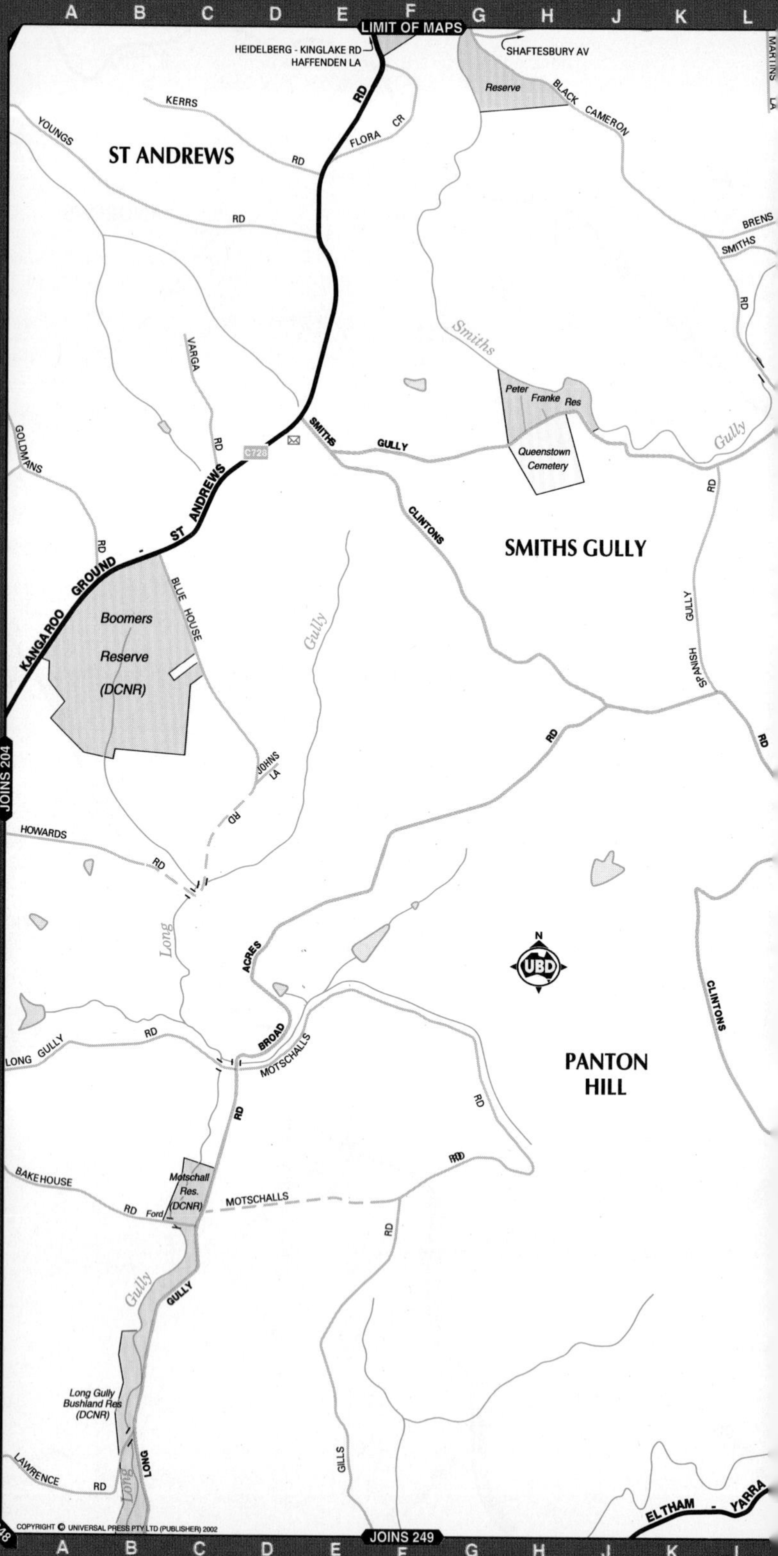

248
JOINS 249

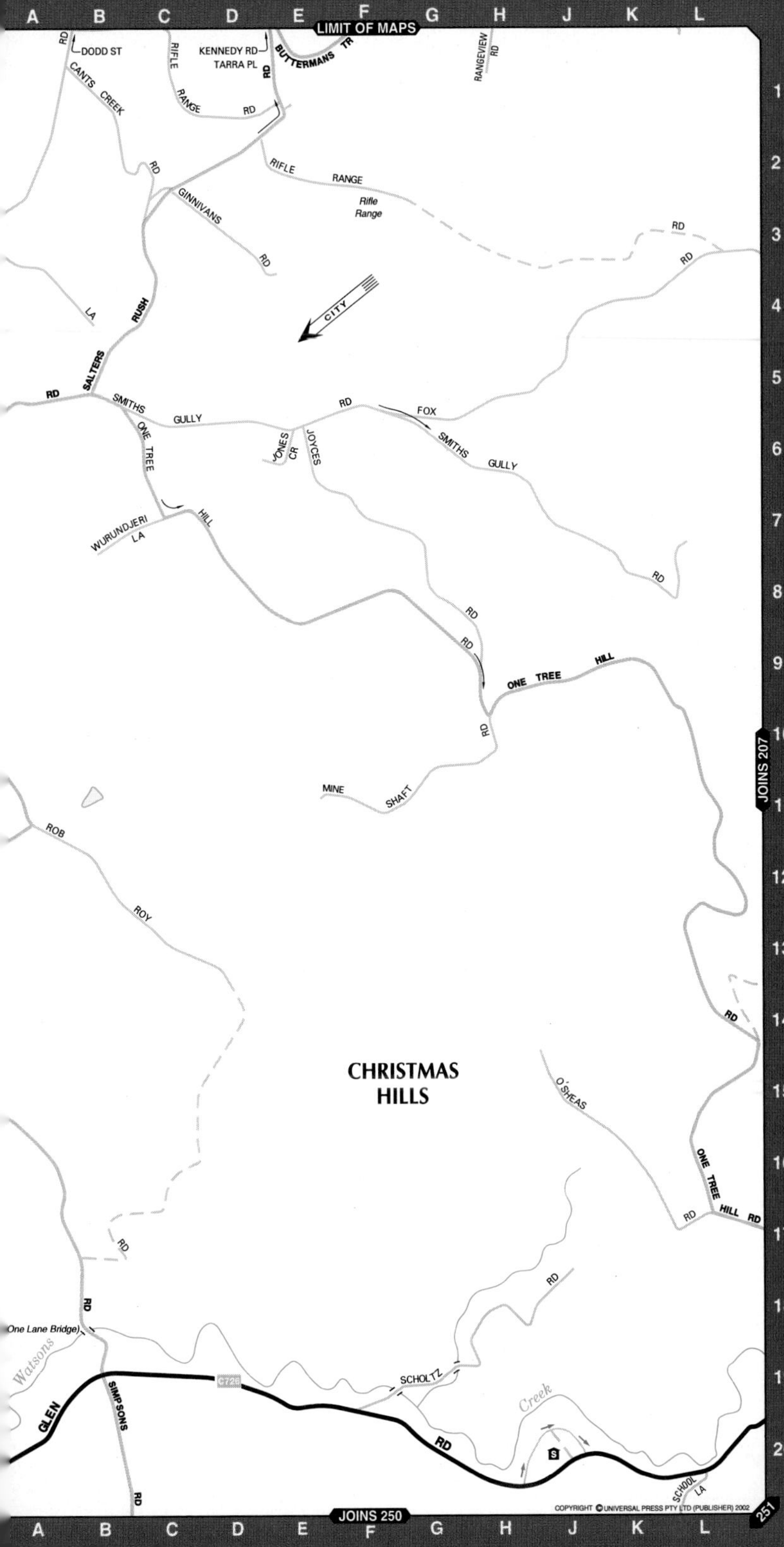

A B C D E F G H J K L

LIMIT OF MAPS

DODD ST
RD
CANTS CREEK RD
RIFLE RANGE RD
KENNEDY RD
TARRA PL
RD
BUTTERMANS TR
RANGEVIEW RD
RIFLE RANGE RD
Rifle Range
GINNIVANS RD
RD
RD
LA
RUSH
SALTERS
RD
CITY
SMITHS GULLY RD
FOX
SMITHS GULLY
JONES CR
JOYCES RD
ONE TREE
HILL
WURUNDJERI LA
RD
RD
RD
ONE TREE HILL
RD
MINE SHAFT
ROB ROY
RD
CHRISTMAS HILLS
O'SHEAS
RD
ONE TREE HILL RD
RD
RD
RD
One Lane Bridge
Watsons
GLEN
SIMPSONS RD
C726
SCHOLTZ
Creek
RD
SCHOOL LA

JOINS 207

JOINS 250

251

1 2 3 4 5 6 7 8 9 10 11 12 13 14 15 16 17 18 19 20

A B C D E F G H J K L

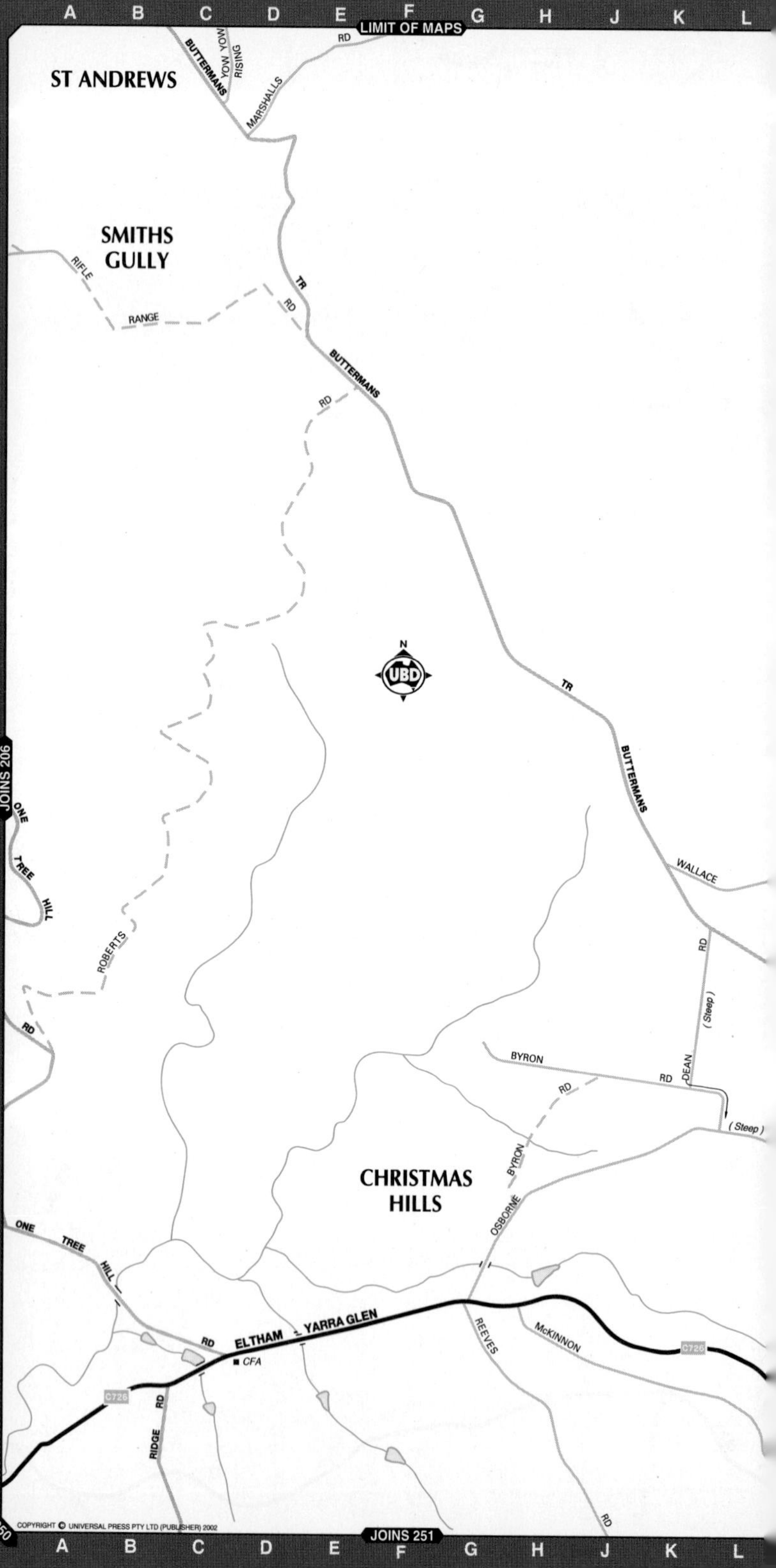

A B C D E F G H J K L
1 2 3 4 5 6 7 8 9 10 11 12 13 14 15 16 17 18 19 20
LIMIT OF MAPS
ST ANDREWS
SMITHS GULLY
CHRISTMAS HILLS
BUTTERMANS
YOW YOW
RISING
MARSHALLS
RD
RIFLE
RANGE
TR
RD
BUTTERMANS
RD
TR
BUTTERMANS
WALLACE
RD
(Steep)
DEAN
BYRON
RD
RD
(Steep)
BYRON
OSBORNE
ROBERTS
RD
ONE TREE HILL
ONE TREE HILL
RD
ELTHAM
YARRA GLEN
CFA
REEVES
McKINNON
C726
C726
RIDGE
RD
RD
UBD
N
JOINS 206
JOINS 251
250

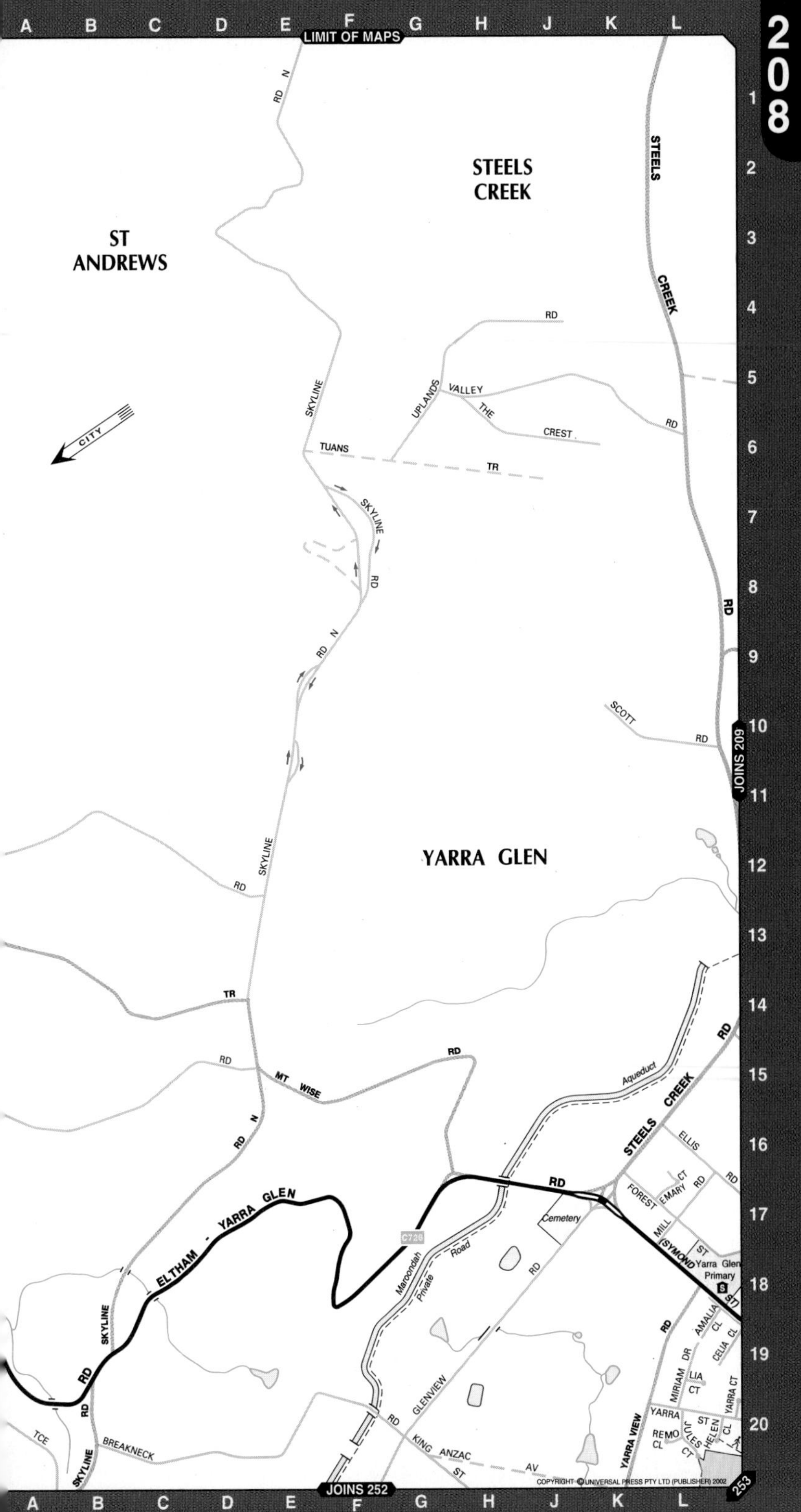

208
A B C D E F G H J K L
LIMIT OF MAPS
1 2 3 4 5 6 7 8 9 10 11 12 13 14 15 16 17 18 19 20
STEELS CREEK
ST ANDREWS
YARRA GLEN
CITY
STEELS CREEK RD
SKYLINE RD N
SKYLINE RD
UPLANDS
VALLEY RD
THE CREST
RD
TUANS TR
SCOTT RD
JOINS 209
TR
MT WISE RD
RD
Aqueduct
ELTHAM - YARRA GLEN RD
C726
Maroondah Private Road
Cemetery
FOREST
EMARY CT
MILL RD
ELLIS RD
(SYMOND ST)
Yarra Glen Primary
AMALIA CL
CELIA CL
MIRIAM DR
LIA CT
YARRA CT
YARRA ST
HELEN CL
JULES CT
REMO CL
YARRA VIEW RD
GLENVIEW RD
KING ST
ANZAC AV
TCE
BREAKNECK RD
SKYLINE RD
JOINS 252
253
COPYRIGHT © UNIVERSAL PRESS PTY LTD (PUBLISHER) 2002

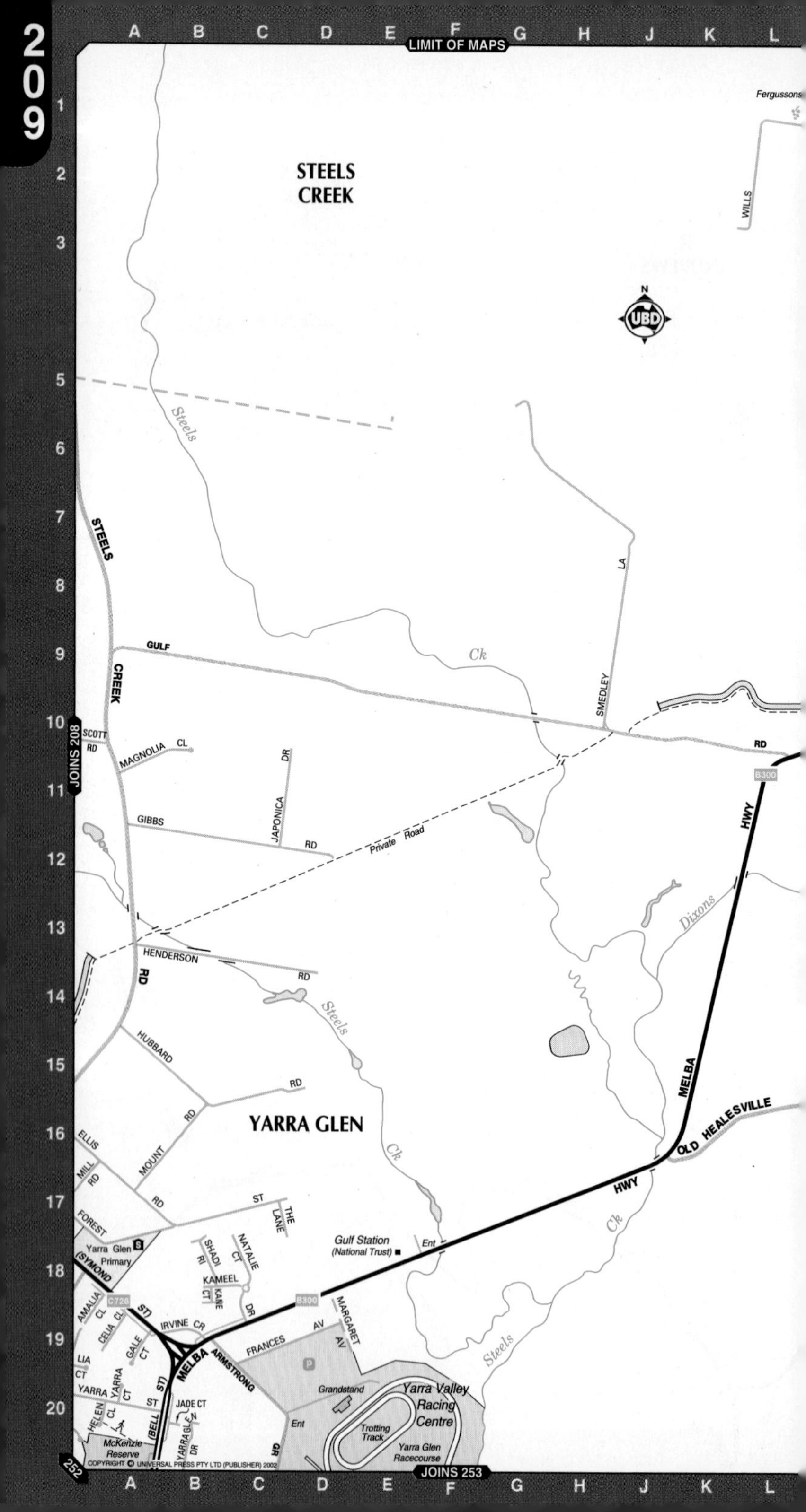

A B C D E F G H J K L

LIMIT OF MAPS

JOINS 208

252

JOINS 253

A B C D E F G H J K L

LIMIT OF MAPS

JOINS 211
JOINS 254

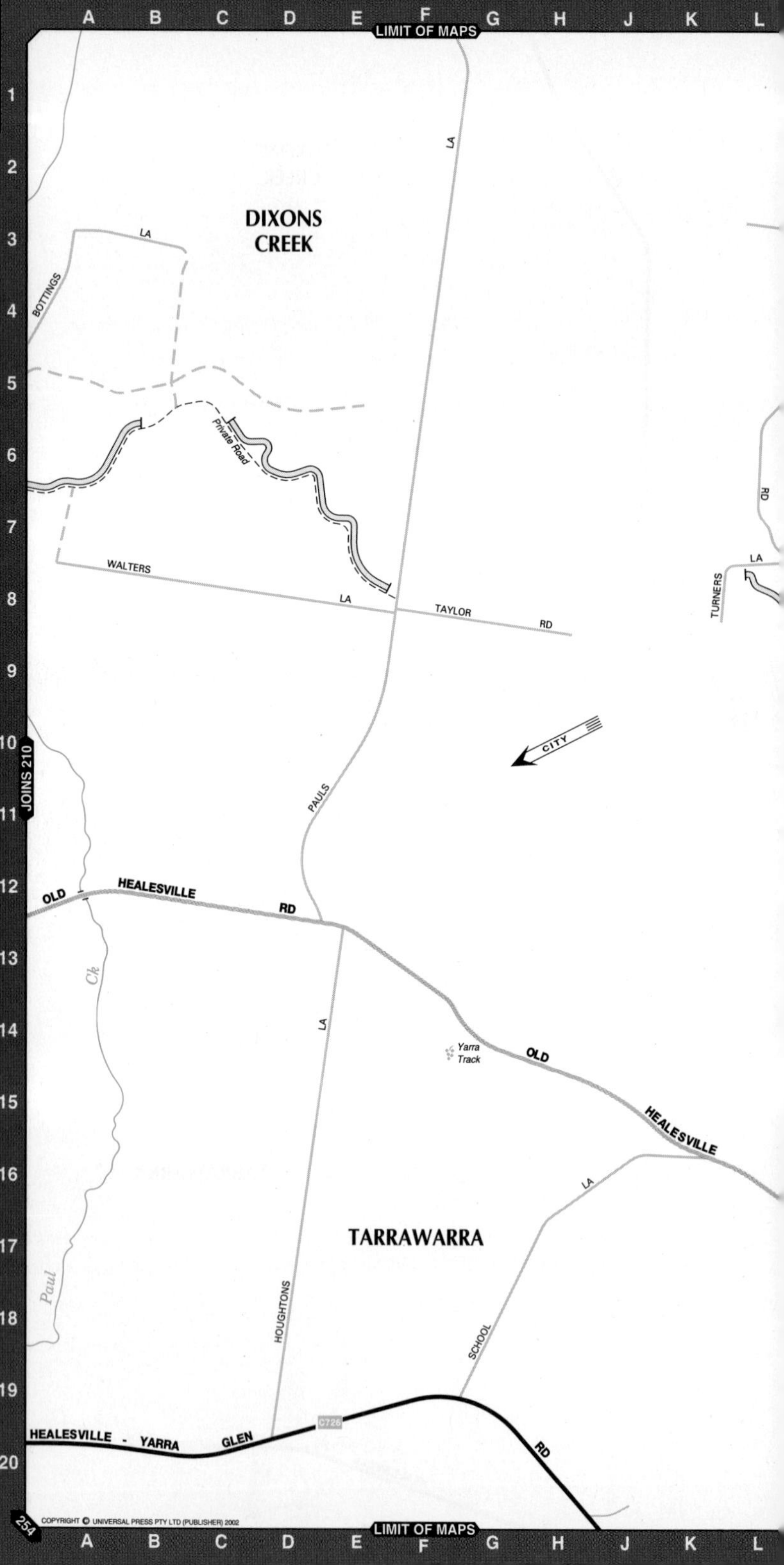

LIMIT OF MAPS

A B C D E F G H J K L

DIXONS CREEK

TARRAWARRA

BOTTINGS LA

Private Road

WALTERS LA

TAYLOR RD

TURNERS LA

RD

LA

CITY

PAULS LA

OLD HEALESVILLE RD

Ck

Paul

Yarra Track

HOUGHTONS LA

SCHOOL LA

HEALESVILLE - YARRA GLEN RD

C726

1 2 3 4 5 6 7 8 9 10 11 12 13 14 15 16 17 18 19 20

JOINS 210

254

LIMIT OF MAPS

A B C D E F G H J K L

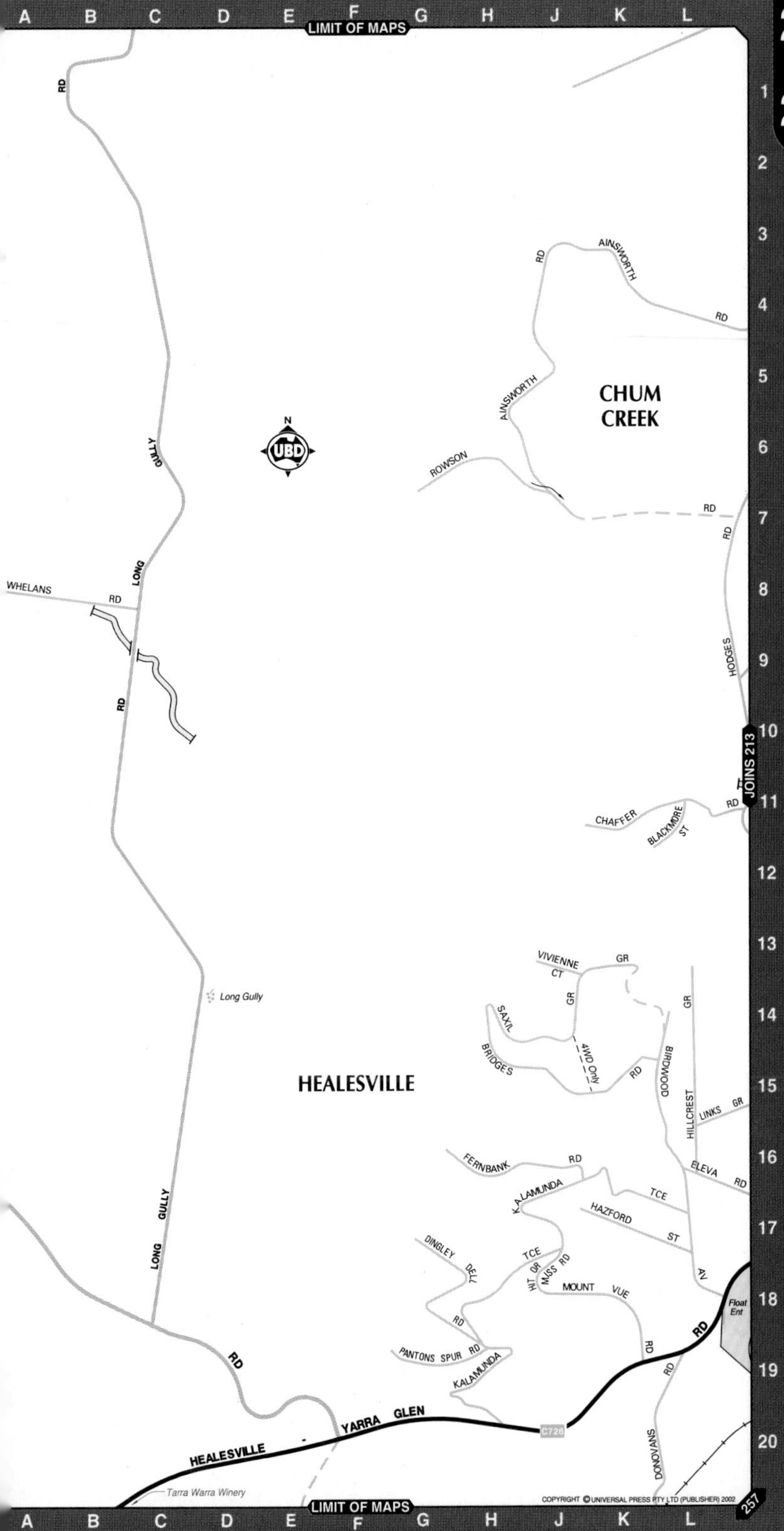

CHUM CREEK

HEALESVILLE

AINSWORTH RD
ROWSON
RD
HODGES
LONG GULLY RD
WHELANS RD
Long Gully
CHAFFER
BLACKMORE ST
RD
VIVIENNE CT
GR
SAXIL
BRIDGES RD
4WD Only
BIRDWOOD AV
HILLCREST GR
LINKS GR
FERNBANK RD
ELEVA RD
KALAMUNDA TCE
HAZFORD ST
DINGLEY DELL
HIT OR MISS RD
MOUNT VUE RD
PANTONS SPUR RD
KALAMUNDA
DONOVANS RD
Float Ent
HEALESVILLE - YARRA GLEN RD
C726
Tarra Warra Winery

JOINS 213

257

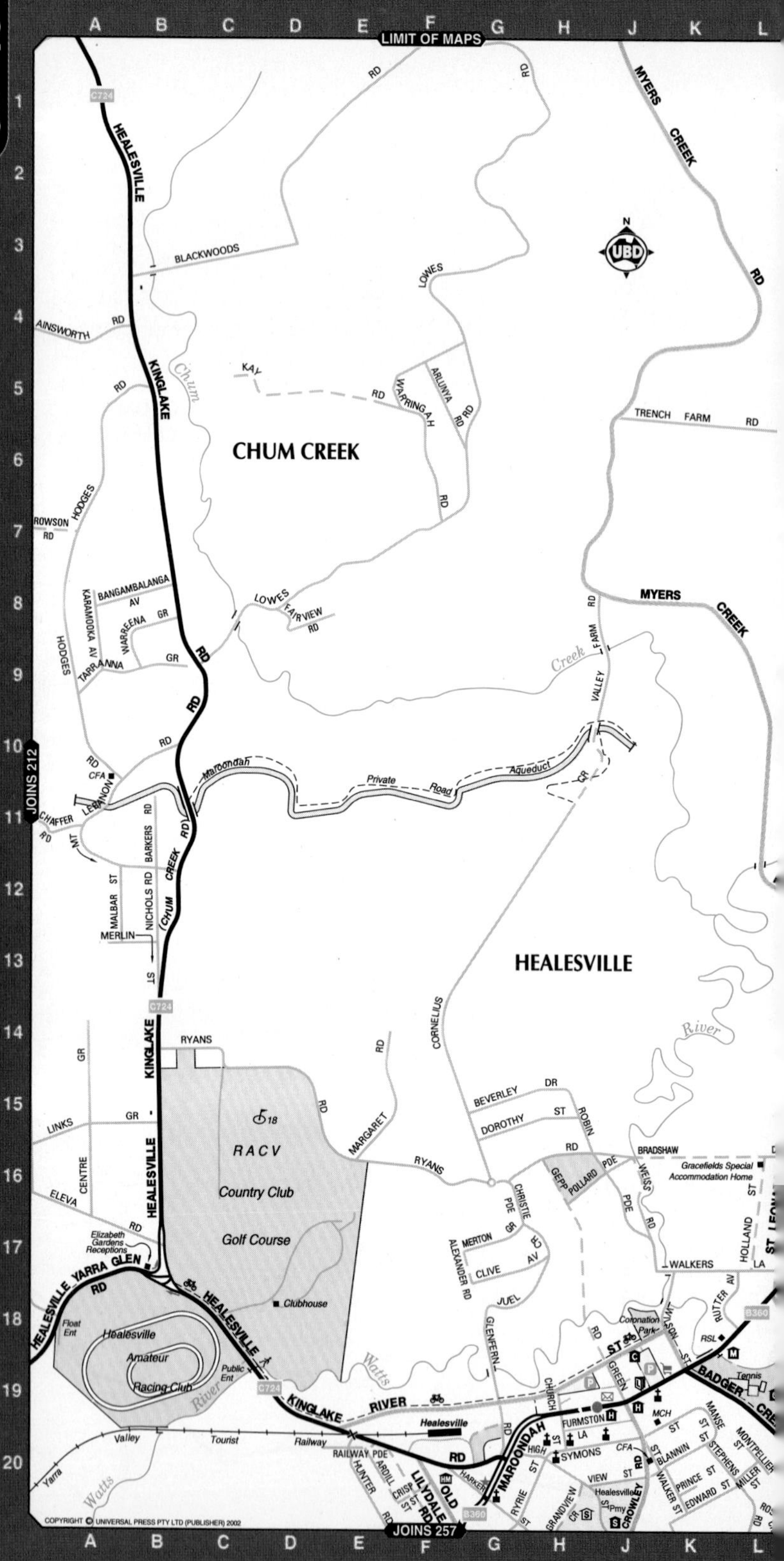

A B C D E F G H J K L

LIMIT OF MAPS

CHUM CREEK

HEALESVILLE

HEALESVILLE KINGLAKE RD
BLACKWOODS
AINSWORTH RD
LOWES
KAY
WARRINGAH RD
ARLUNYA RD
TRENCH FARM RD
MYERS CREEK RD
HODGES
ROWSON RD
BANGAMBALANGA AV
KARAMOOKA AV
WARREENA GR
TARRANNA GR
LOWES
FAIRVIEW RD
FARM
VALLEY
Creek
Chum
Maroondah Private Road Aqueduct
CR
CFA
LEBANON
CHAFFER RD
MT
BARKERS RD
NICHOLS RD
MALBAR ST
MERLIN
ST
CHUM CREEK RD
C724
RYANS
GR
LINKS
CENTRE
ELEVA
RD
RACV
Country Club
Golf Course
Clubhouse
MARGARET
RD
RYANS
CORNELIUS
River
BEVERLEY DR
DOROTHY ST
ROBIN
RD
BRADSHAW
GEPP
POLLARD
PDE
WEISS RD
Gracefields Special Accommodation Home
ST
HOLLAND
ST LEONARDS
WALKERS LA
RUTTER AV
CHRISTIE
PDE
GR
MERTON
ALEXANDER RD
CLIVE AV
CR
JUEL
GLENFERN
RD
Coronation Park
RSL
B360
Elizabeth Gardens Receptions
HEALESVILLE YARRA GLEN RD
HEALESVILLE KINGLAKE RD
Float Ent
Healesville Amateur Racing Club
Public Ent
River
Watts
KINGLAKE RIVER
GREEN
ST
MASON ST
BADGER CREEK
Tennis
CHURCH
FURMSTON
MCH
MANSE
MONTPELLIER
Valley Tourist Railway
Healesville
RAILWAY PDE
HUNTER RD
ARDILL
CRISP ST
LILYDALE RD
OLD
RD
HARKER
MAROONDAH
RYRIE ST
HIGH ST
LA
SYMONS
CFA
RD
BLANNIN ST
STEPHENS ST
PRINCE ST
EDWARD ST
MILLER ST
WALKER ST
VIEW ST
GRANDVIEW CR
Healesville Pmy
CROWLEY
ROSE
Yarra
Watts

JOINS 212

JOINS 257

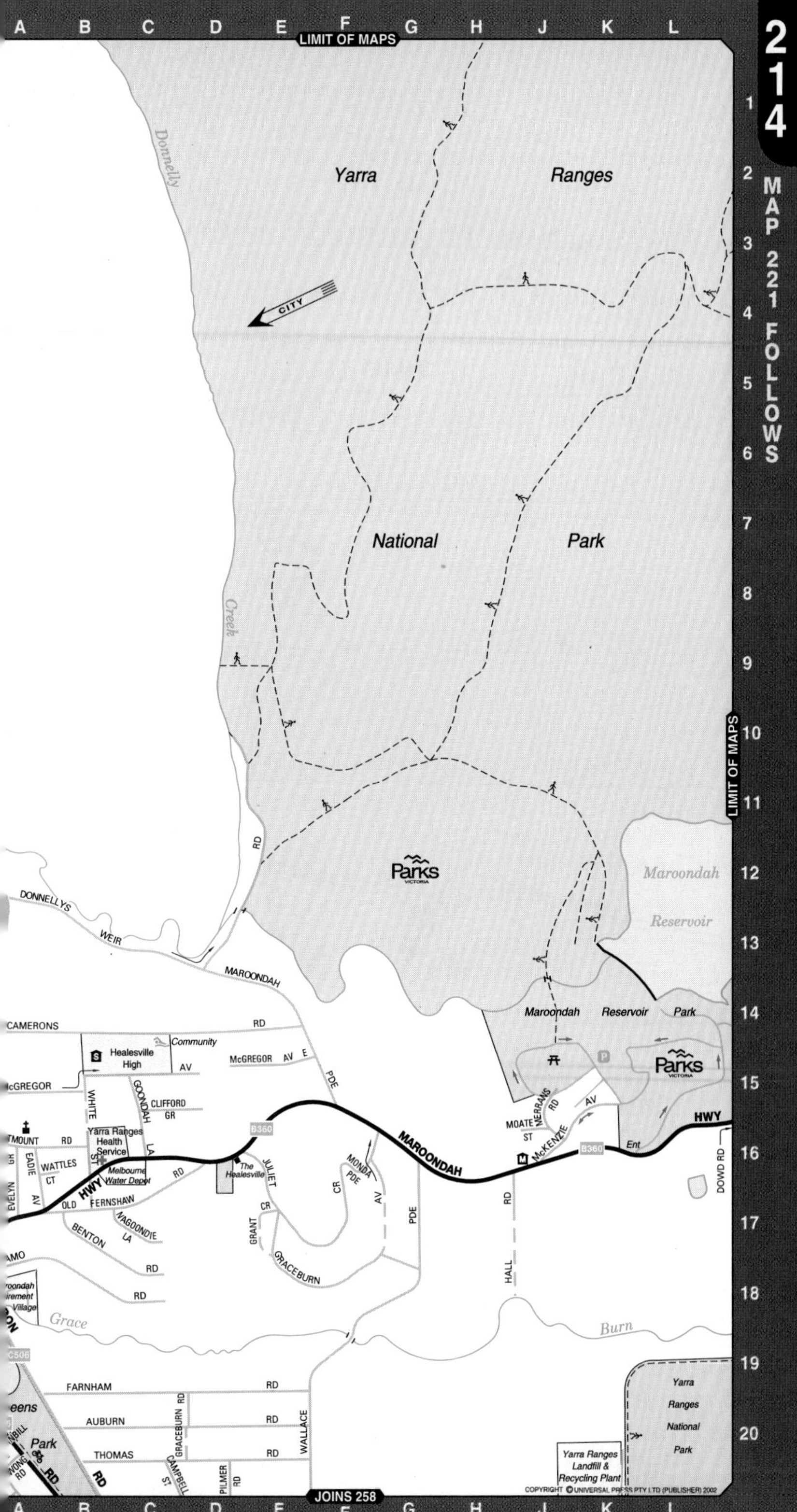
LIMIT OF MAPS
Yarra Ranges
National Park
CITY
Donnelly Creek
Parks VICTORIA
Maroondah Reservoir
Maroondah Reservoir Park
DONNELLYS WEIR RD
MAROONDAH HWY
CAMERONS RD
Healesville High
Community
McGREGOR AV E
McGREGOR
PDE
WHITE ST
GOONDAH LA
CLIFFORD GR
Yarra Ranges Health Service
Melbourne Water Depot
The Healesville
JULIET
MONDA PDE
CR
AV
MOATE ST
MERRANS RD
McKENZIE AV
B360
Ent
DOWD RD
WATTLES CT
EADIE AV
EVELYN
OLD FERNSHAW RD
BENTON
WAGOONDIE LA
GRANT CR
GRACEBURN
HALL RD
Grace Burn
FARNHAM RD
AUBURN RD
THOMAS RD
GRACEBURN RD
WALLACE
CAMPBELL ST
PILMER RD
C506
Park
Yarra Ranges National Park
Yarra Ranges Landfill & Recycling Plant
JOINS 258
MAP 221 FOLLOWS

PREVIOUS MAP 214

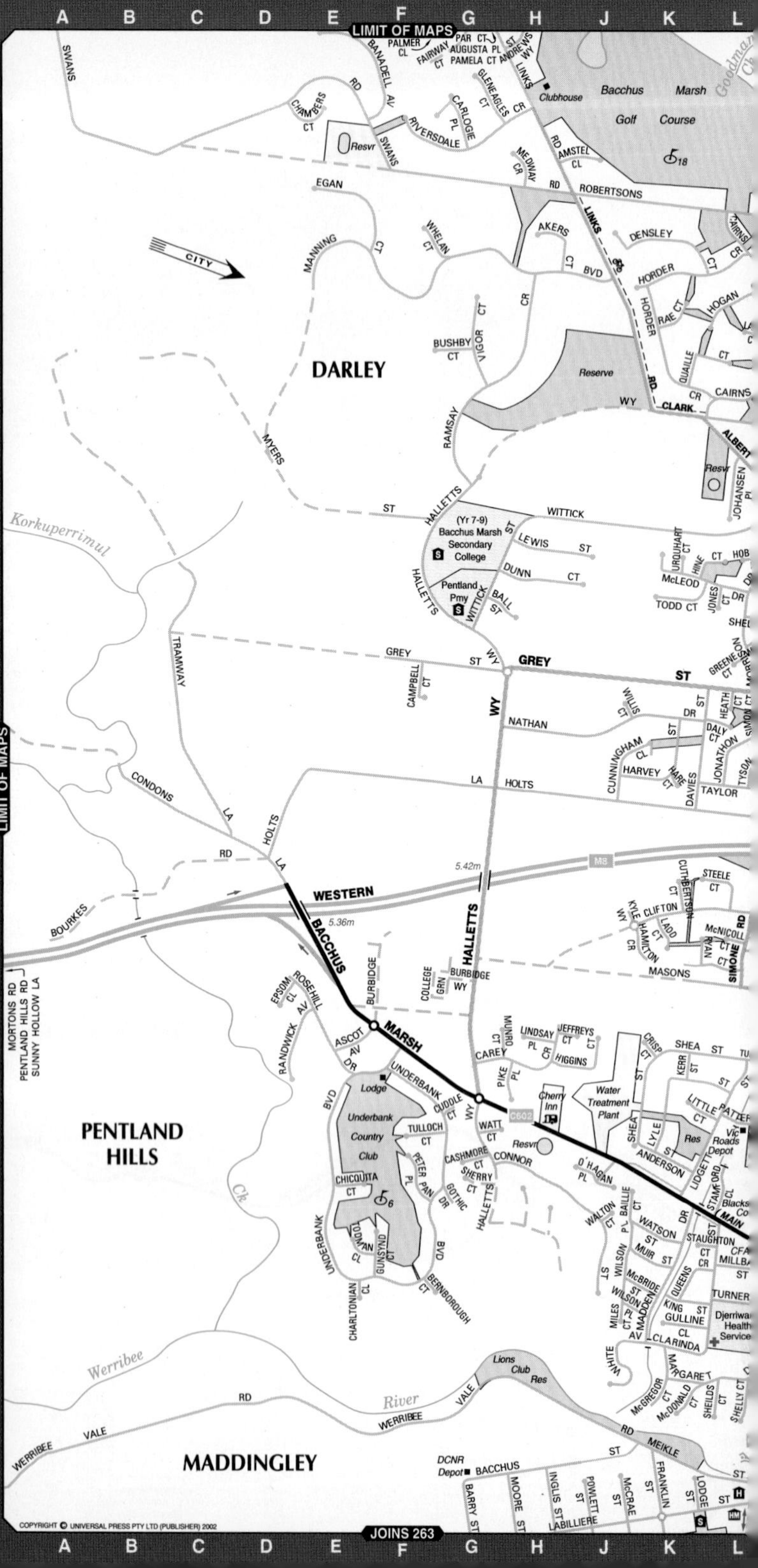

LIMIT OF MAPS

A B C D E F G H J K L

DARLEY

PENTLAND HILLS

MADDINGLEY

Bacchus Marsh Golf Course

Clubhouse

(Yr 7-9) Bacchus Marsh Secondary College

Pentland Pmy

Underbank Country Club

Lodge

Water Treatment Plant

Cherry Inn

Lions Club Res

Reserve

Resvr

Vic Roads Depot

Djerriwarrh Health Service

DCNR Depot

WESTERN FWY

BACCHUS MARSH RD

HALLETTS WY

GREY ST

HOLTS LA

WERRIBEE VALE RD

Werribee River

Korkuperrimul Ck

MORTONS RD, PENTLAND HILLS RD, SUNNY HOLLOW LA

5.42m

5.36m

CITY

JOINS 263

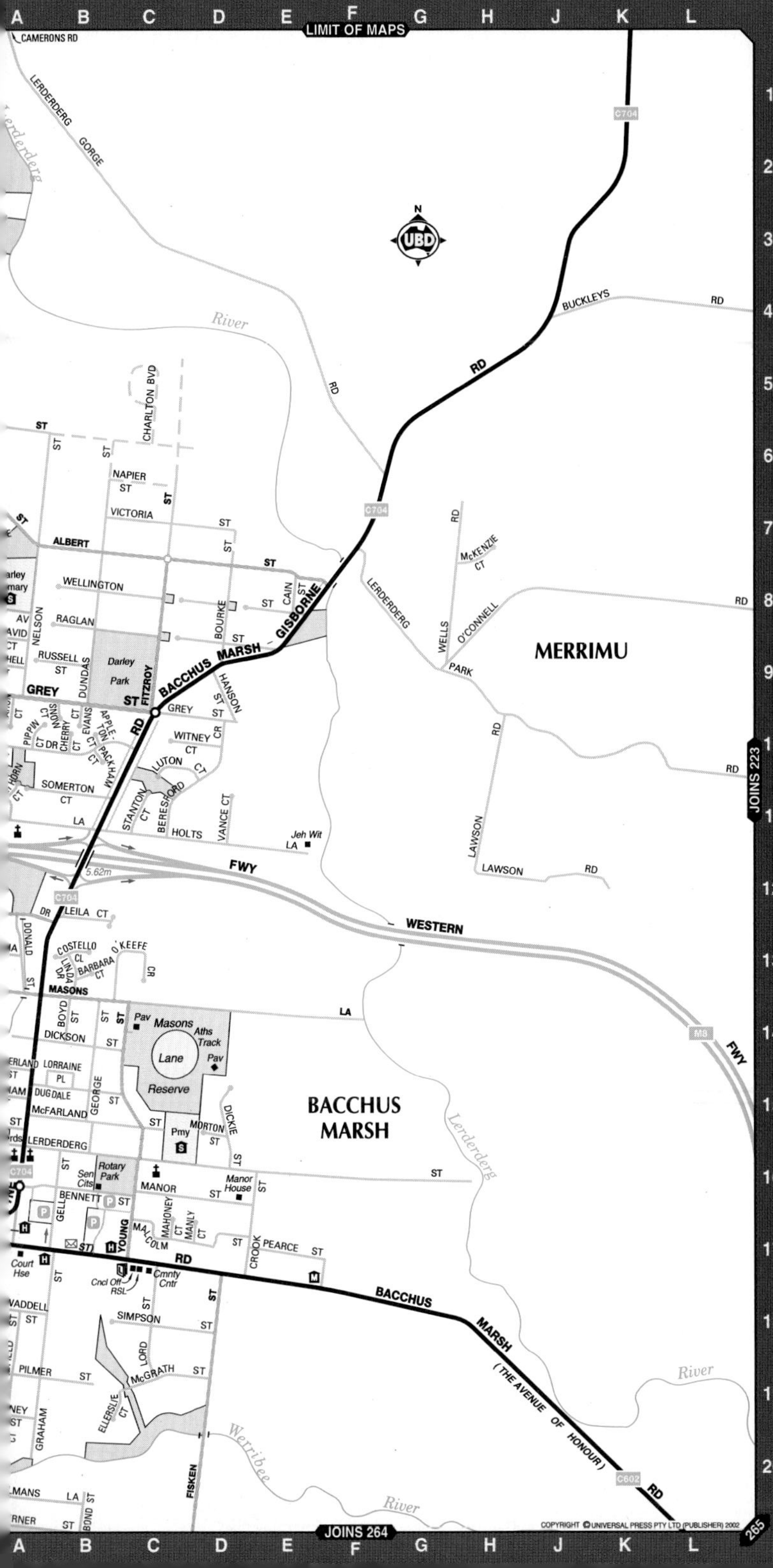

JOINS 223

JOINS 264

265

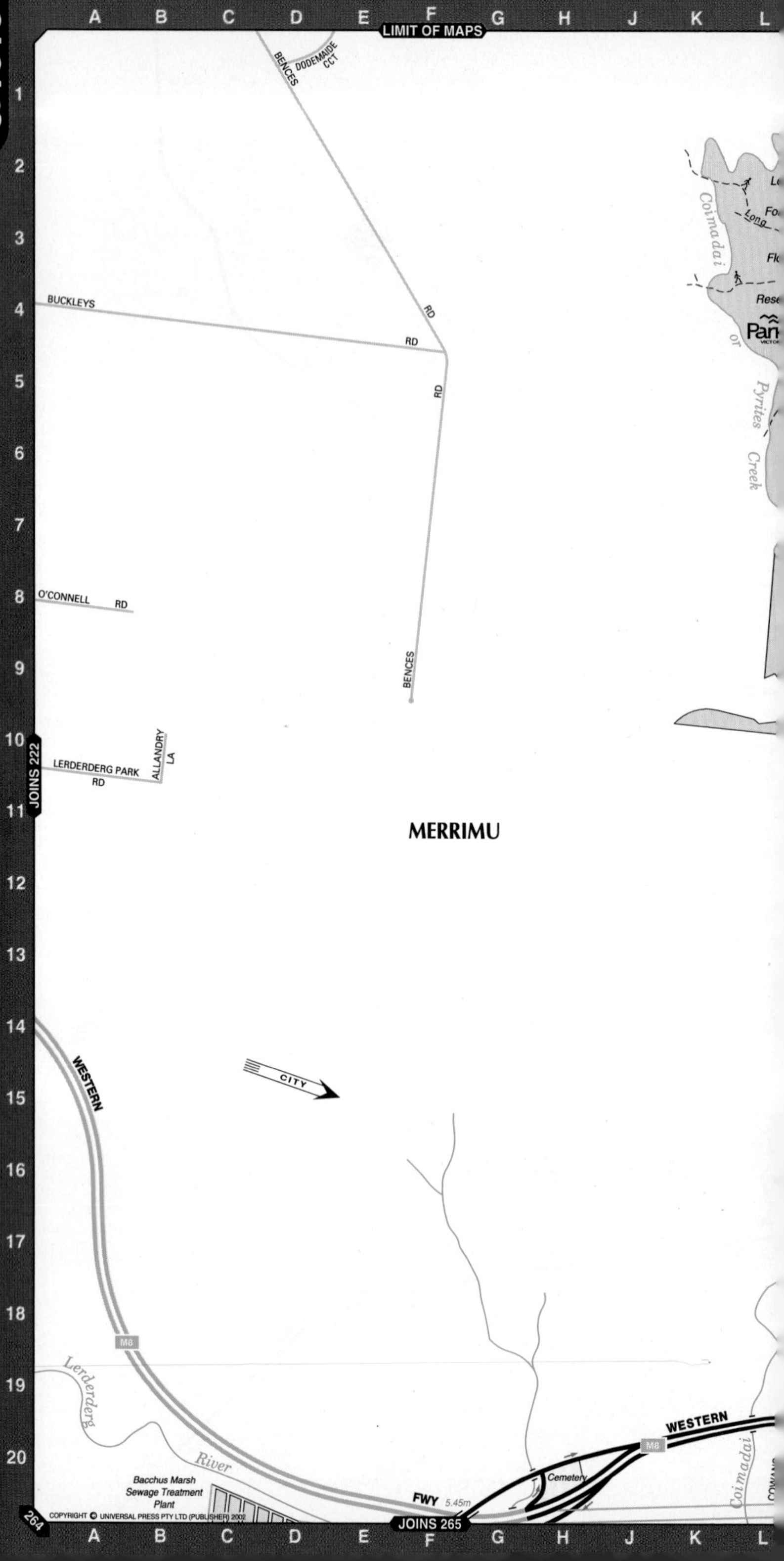

JOINS 222

JOINS 265

264

JOINS 225

JOINS 266

267

A B C D E F G H J K L
LIMIT OF MAPS
TOOLERN VALE
PORTEOUS RD
GIBLIN LA
CITY
MELTON WEST
HARKNESS RD
HARDYS RD
SHAMROCK PL
BULLOCK TR
BULMANS RD
WEST MELTON
Res
Melton Catholic Regional College
St Catherines Cath Pmy
PICCOLOTTO DR
PULFORD CT
PAUL CT
HANNAH CL
BECKER CL
MARK PL
SILBER CT
TRETHOWAN CL
ERNEST PL
GREGORY CT
MAUREEN
HELEN CT
BULMANS
HIGH
ENDEAVOUR PL
PASCOE CT
BATMAN DR
JOHN ST
HODDLE CT
FLEETWOOD
McIVOR CT
GLENEAGLES DR
HAYWOOD GR
RIDGEWAY
SOUTHDEAN
HARRINGTON DR
MEADOW GLEN
BLUEBELL CT
HOLLYDALE AV CT DR
TRENTWOOD
STIRLING TCE
WATERFORD WY
HILLSMEADE
WESTLAKE GARDEN TCE
PARKWAY DR
LAKEVIEW TCE
JINDA PL
JONSON AV
WATERDALE CL DR
ELIANA CT
JOSEPHINE CT
CENTENARY
DURHAM PL
ARGYLL
WINDSOR
GAINSBOROUGH
HENLEY PL
JASON PL
BALFOUR PL
LUMEA PL
CAMBRIAN
MORROW ST
Arnolds Creek
JOINS 224
JOINS 267

LIMIT OF MAPS

TOOLERN VALE

KURUNJANG

MELTON

Navan Park

Mowbray College

Kurunjang Secondary College

Melton Specialist School

Melton Secondary College

Melton Aquatic Centre

Melton Indoor Rec Cntr

Woodgrove Shopping Centre

Retarding Basin

McPherson Park Recreation Reserve

Jeh Wit

MINNS RD

COBURNS RD

HIGH ST

CENTENARY AV

STATION RD

O'NEILLS RD

PALMERSTON ST

Arnolds Creek

Eastern Branch

JOINS 227

JOINS 268

269

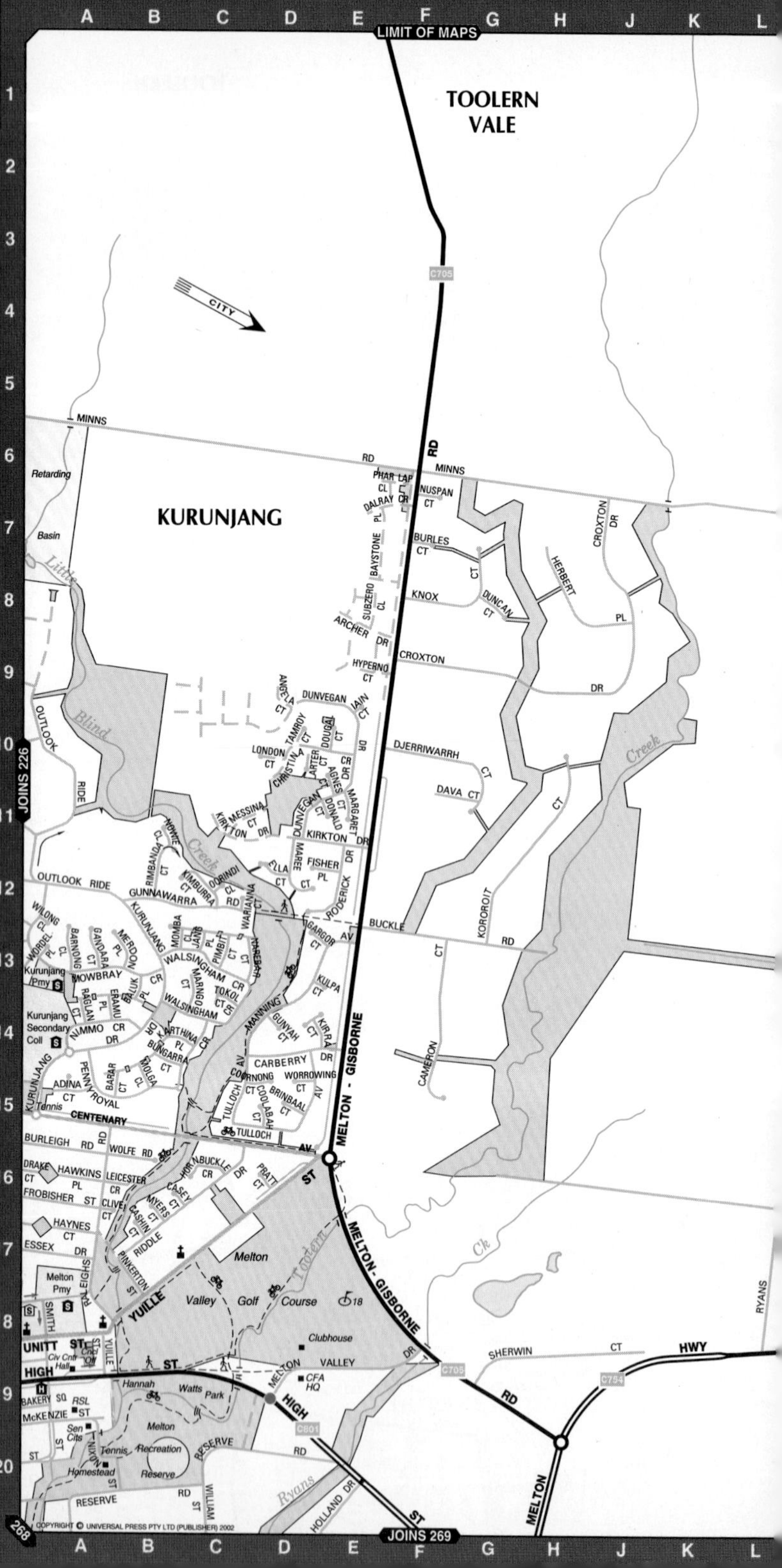

LIMIT OF MAPS
TOOLERN VALE
KURUNJANG
CITY
MINNS RD
Retarding Basin
Little Blind Creek
OUTLOOK RIDE
JOINS 226
PHAR LAP CL
DALRAY PL
NUSPAN CT
BURLES CT
BAYSTONE CR
SUBZERO CL
KNOX
DUNCAN CT
HERBERT
CROXTON DR
ARCHER DR
HYPERNO CT
DUNVEGAN
IAIN CT
ANGELA CT
TAMROY CT
DOUGAL CT
LONDON CT
CHRISTINA CT
CARTER CT
AGNES CT
DJERRIWARRH CT
DAVA CT
MESSINA CT
KIRKTON DR
DONALD CT
MARGARET DR
FISHER PL
ELLA CT
MAREE CT
RODERICK DR
BUCKLE AV
KOROROIT CT
RD
Creek
GUNNAWARRA RD
RIMBANDA CL
HOWIE CT
KIMBURRA CT
DORINDI CL
WARIANNA
WILONG CL
WORDELL CT
BARNONG CT
GANDARA PL
MERDON PL
KURUNJANG
MOMBA CL
JANIS PL
PIMBITI CT
GARGOR CT
KULPA CT
MOWBRAY
WALSINGHAM CR
MARINGO CT
TOKOL CT
Kurunjang Pmy
BALUK PL
ERAMU CT
RAGLAN CT
MANNING
GUNYAH CT
KIRRA CT
Kurunjang Secondary Coll
NIMMO CR DR
KARTHINA PL
BUNGARRA
CARBERRY DR
CAMERON
ADINA CT
PENNY ROYAL
BARAR CT
MOLGA CL
CORRONG CT
WORROWING AV
BRINBAAL CT
COOLABAH CT
TULLOCH CT
Tennis
CENTENARY
BURLEIGH RD
WOLFE RD
MELTON - GISBORNE RD
DRAKE CT
HAWKINS PL
LEICESTER CR
HORNBUCKLE CR
PRATT CT
FROBISHER ST
CLIVE CT
CASEY CT
MYERS CT
CASHIN CT
HAYNES CT
RIDDLE
ESSEX DR
PINKERTON ST
Melton Valley Golf Course 18
Melton Pmy
RALEIGHS
YUILLE ST
SMITH
Clubhouse
UNITT ST
Civ Cntr Hall
HIGH ST
MELTON VALLEY DR
CFA HQ
SHERWIN CT
HWY
RYANS
C705
C754
C801
Ck
BAKERY SQ
RSL
McKENZIE ST
Hannah Watts Park
Sen Cits
Melton Recreation Reserve
Tennis
Homestead
NIXON
RESERVE RD
WILLIAM ST
Ryans
HOLLAND DR
MELTON
JOINS 269
268

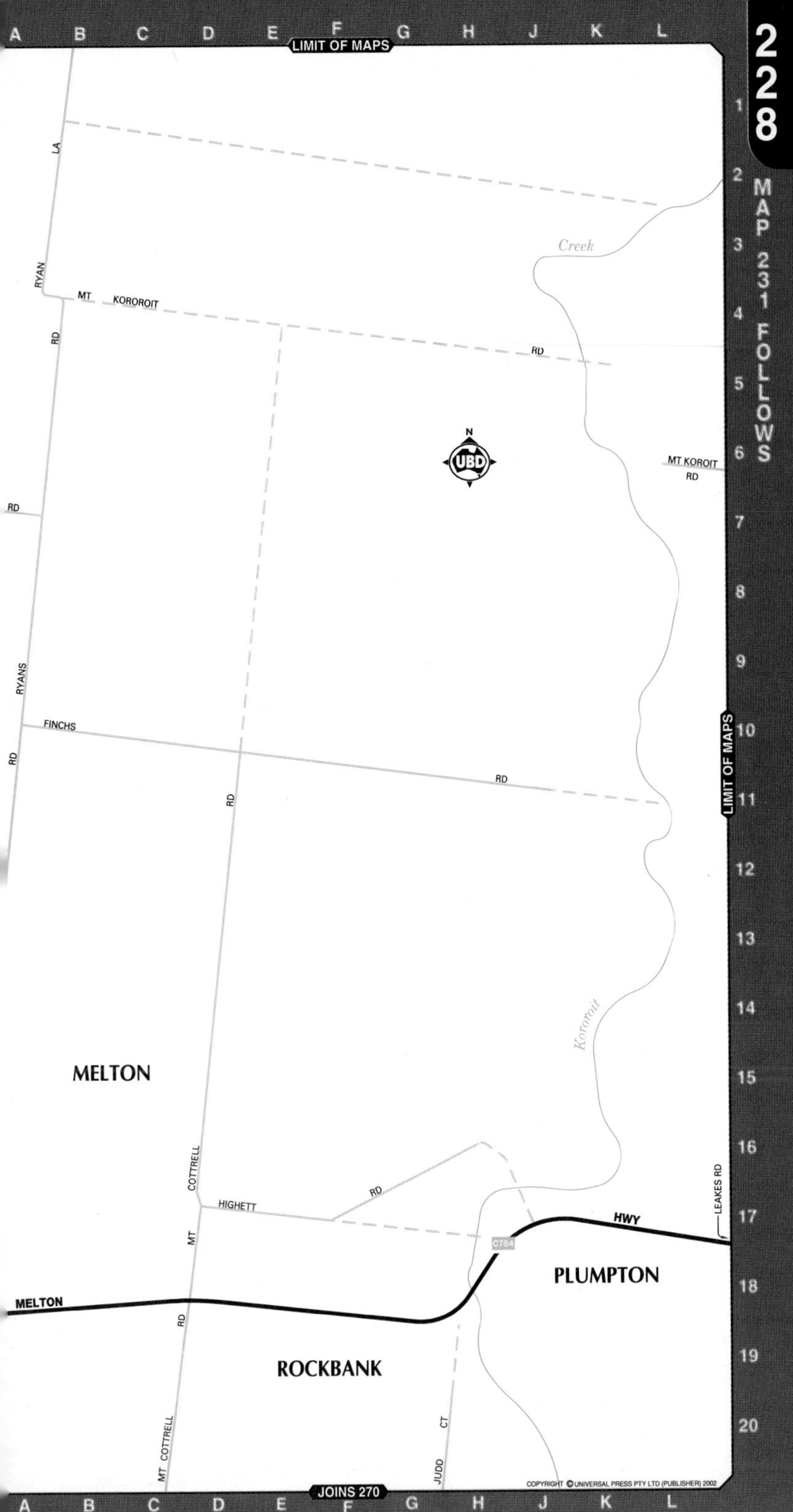
LIMIT OF MAPS
MAP 231 FOLLOWS
RYAN LA
MT KOROROIT RD
Creek
MT KOROIT RD
RD
RYANS RD
FINCHS RD
RD
LIMIT OF MAPS
Kororoit
MELTON
COTTRELL
HIGHETT RD
MT RD
HWY
C754
LEAKES RD
PLUMPTON
MELTON
ROCKBANK
MT COTTRELL
JUDD CT
JOINS 270

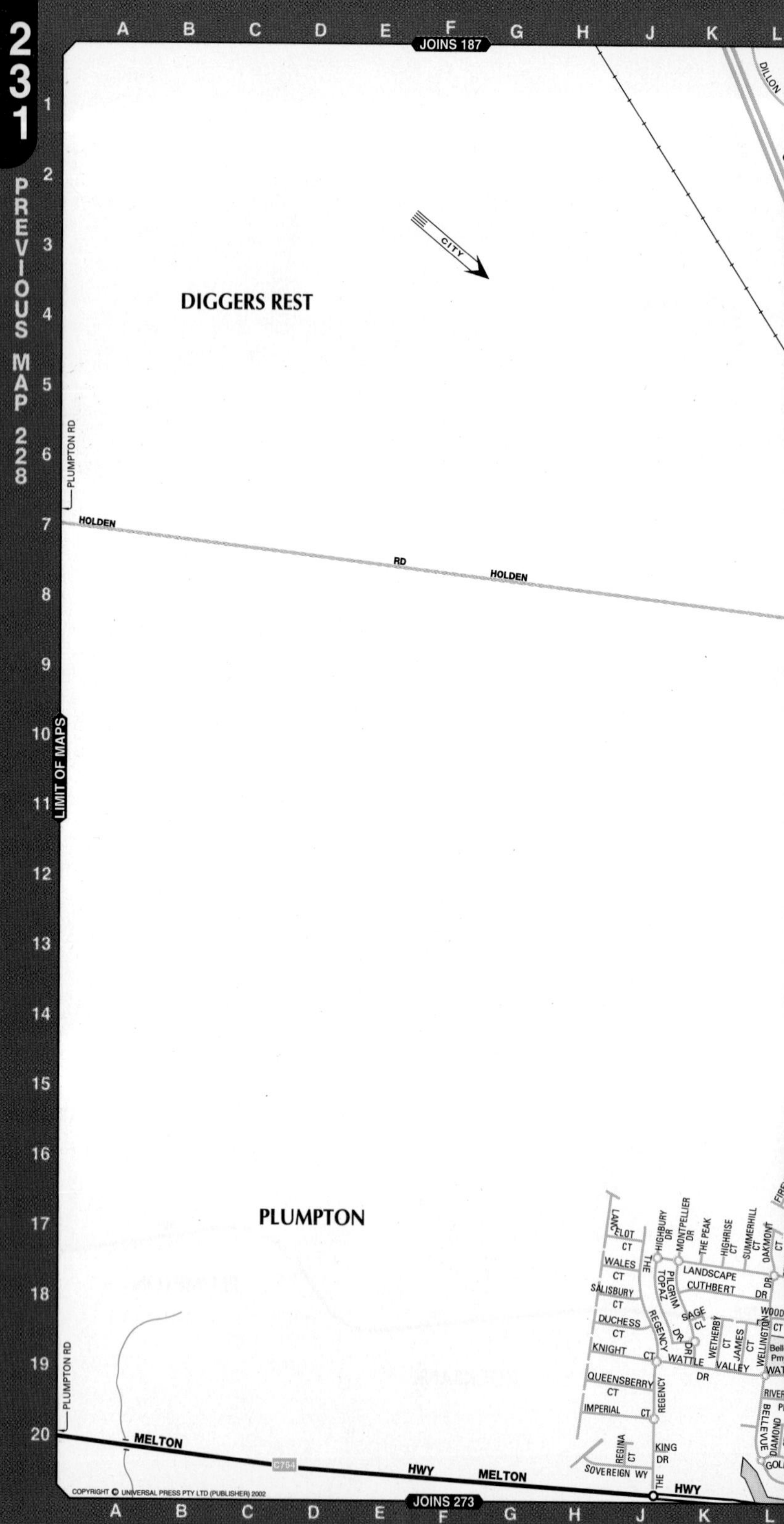
A B C D E F G H J K L
JOINS 187
PREVIOUS MAP 228
LIMIT OF MAPS
DILLON
CITY
DIGGERS REST
PLUMPTON RD
HOLDEN
RD
HOLDEN
PLUMPTON
LANCELOT CT
WALES CT
SALISBURY CT
DUCHESS CT
KNIGHT CT
QUEENSBERRY CT
IMPERIAL CT
THE REGENCY
HIGHBURY DR
MONTPELLIER DR
THE PEAK
HIGHRISE CT
SUMMERHILL CT
OAKMONT
LANDSCAPE DR
CUTHBERT DR
PILGRIM TOPAZ
SAGE CL
WETHERBY CT
JAMES CT
WELLINGTON
WATTLE VALLEY DR
REGENCY CT
REGINA CT
KING DR
SOVEREIGN WY
THE
BELLEVUE
DIAMOND
MELTON
C754
HWY
MELTON
HWY
JOINS 273

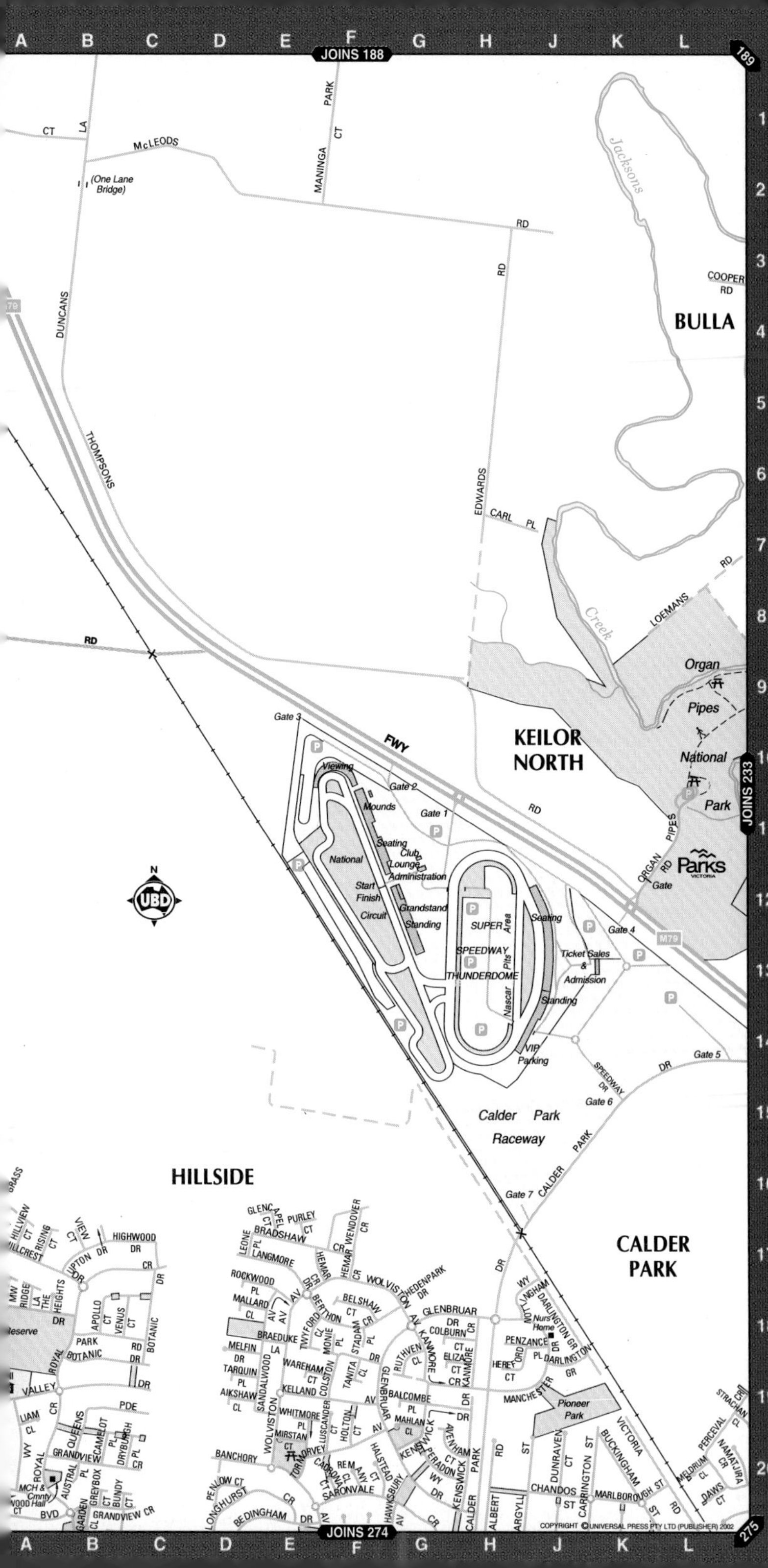

BULLA

KEILOR NORTH

HILLSIDE

CALDER PARK

Calder Park Raceway

Organ Pipes National Park

Parks Victoria

National Start Finish Circuit

SUPER SPEEDWAY THUNDERDOME

Grandstand Standing

Ticket Sales & Admission

VIP Parking

Pioneer Park

Jacksons Creek

McLEODS RD
DUNCANS LA
THOMPSONS RD
EDWARDS RD
MANINGA PARK CT
CARL PL
LOEMANS RD
COOPER RD
ORGAN PIPES RD
CALDER FWY
SPEEDWAY DR
CALDER PARK DR
(One Lane Bridge)

JOINS 233

JOINS 189
JOINS 232
JOINS 275
188
274

A B C D E F G H J K L

1 2 3 4 5 6 7 8 9 10 11 12 13 14 15 16 17 18 19 20

BULLA

Jacksons Creek

COOPER RD

LOEMANS RD

Organ Pipes National Park

Parks Victoria

CITY

CALDER FWY

M79

Gate 5

CALDER PARK DR

CALDER PARK

TAYLORS LAKES

Keilor & District Model Aircraft Society

Sydenham

Golf Driving Range

Clubhouse

Keilor Public Golf Course

Overnewton Anglican Cmnty College

Keilor Lodge Campus

Reserve

Soccer Fields

School Site

ROWLAND POWER PL, HANSON CT, ANDERSON WY, CHALMERS PL, CAMBRIDGE CR, SANSOM CT, TRINDALL PL, FITZGERALD CT, PRATT CL, STEDMAN CT, CAMBRIDGE CR, WINKLER CR, MORETTI AV, GLENELG DR, COLEMAN CT, FORREST PL, PALMERSTON RD, BALONNE CL, PLENTY CL, CARNARVON CL, CAPRICORN CT, BRUCE WY, ROWELL PL, KINNARD CT, SALVANA CT, PARR CT, BLACKMAN CR, LINDSAY CT, HART PL, McCUBBIN CR, NOLAN PL, COLLIER CT, POE, STRACHAN CL, PERCEVAL CR, RIGBY CT, MELDRUM CL, NAMATJIRA CR, BLACKMAN CR, WHITELEY, DAWS CT, PERCEVAL, HERMAN CL, MARTENS CT, DR, MOONIE CL, MUIRS CT, BRUSELL CL, SANDOVER WY, WARREGO PL, GOULBURN WY, BRUNNER CT, ROBERTSONS RD, TASMAN, MIDLAND WY, DERWENT CR, LANDSBOROUGH AV, LYELL PL, KINGS, SALAMANDER DR, WELLESLEY CR, BUCHANAN CT, MACKENZIE CL, NEPEAN CT, STURT CT, PEMBROKE CL, ARCADIA CL, NEWELL DR, LAWSON CT, LEICHARDT CL, RD

22

18

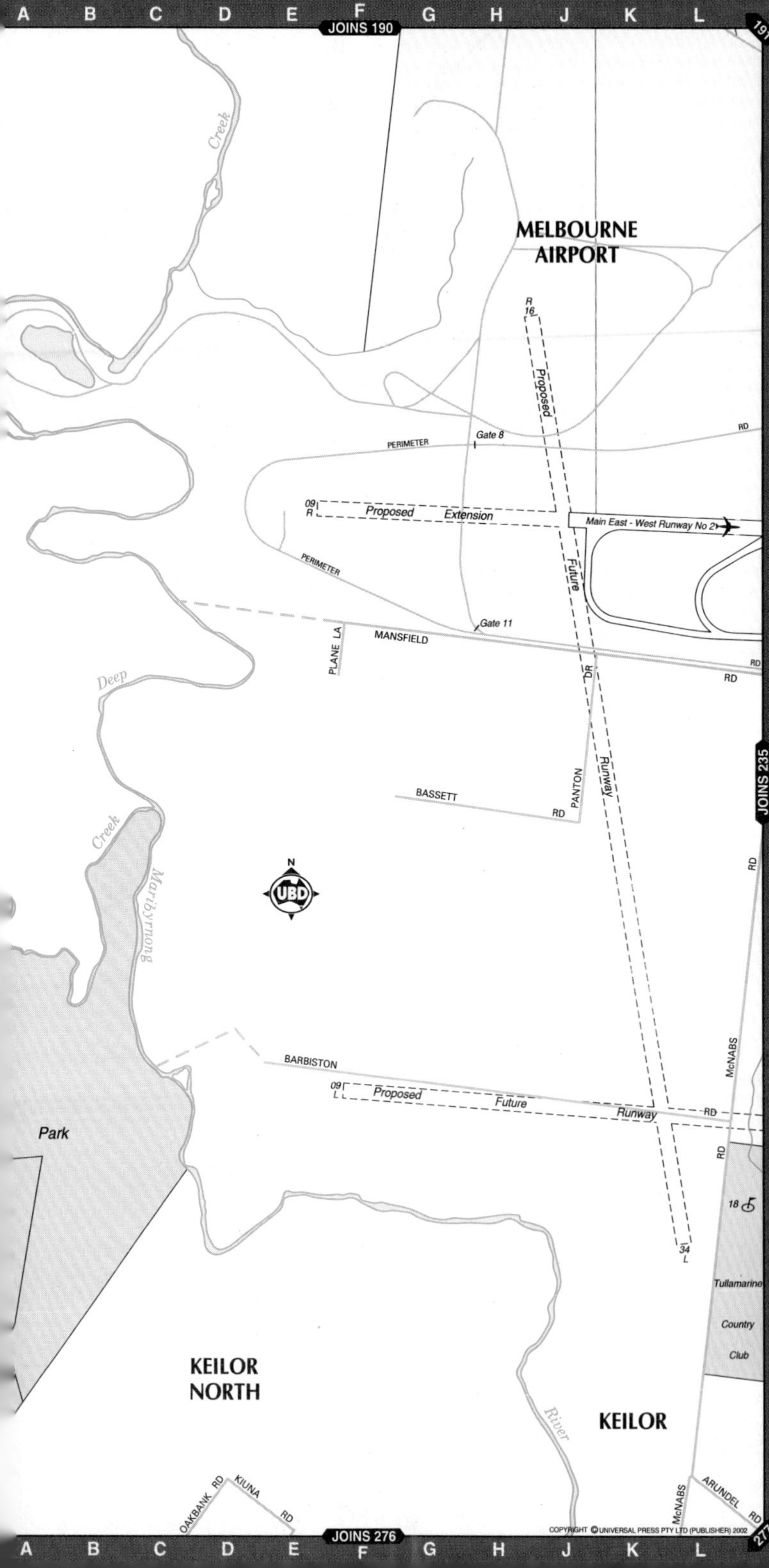

MELBOURNE AIRPORT
Creek
R 16
Proposed
PERIMETER
Gate 8
RD
09 R
Proposed Extension
Main East - West Runway No 2
PERIMETER
Future
Gate 11
MANSFIELD
PLANE LA
DR
RD
RD
Deep
Runway
BASSETT
RD
PANTON
JOINS 235
Creek
Maribyrnong
RD
N
UBD
McNABS
BARBISTON
09 L
Proposed Future Runway
RD
Park
RD
18
34 L
Tullamarine Country Club
KEILOR NORTH
River
KEILOR
OAKBANK RD
KIUNA RD
McNABS
ARUNDEL RD

JOINS 191
190
JOINS 234
JOINS 277
276

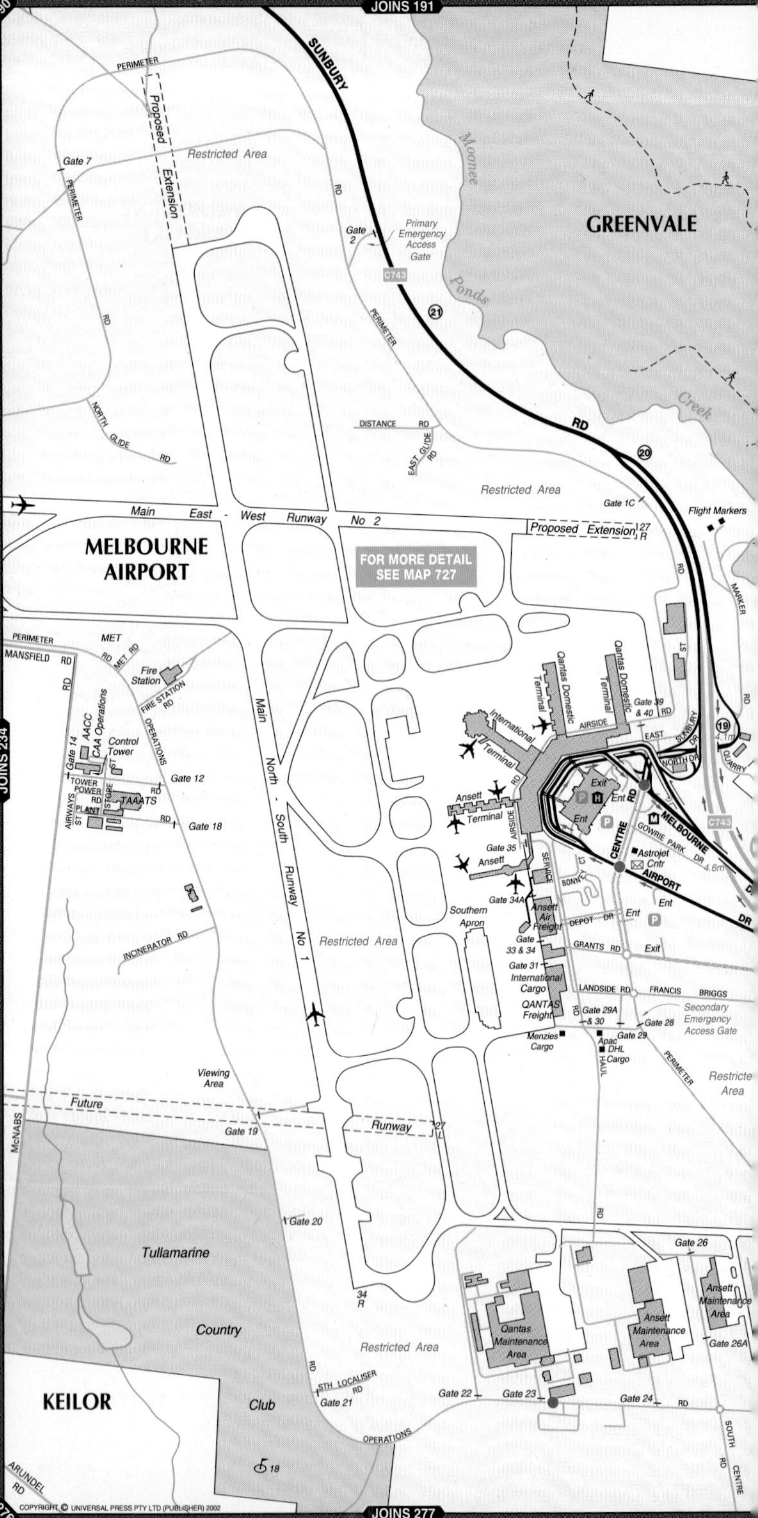

A B C D E F G H J K L

1 2 3 4 5 6 7 8 9 10 11 12 13 14 15 16 17 18 19 20

GREENVALE

MELBOURNE AIRPORT

KEILOR

Tullamarine

Country

Club

Moonee Ponds Creek

SUNBURY RD

PERIMETER RD

Proposed Extension

Restricted Area

Gate 7

Gate 2

Primary Emergency Access Gate

C743

21

20

19

DISTANCE RD

EAST GLIDE RD

NORTH GLIDE RD

Main East - West Runway No 2

Proposed Extension

27 R

Gate 1C

Flight Markers

MARKER RD

FOR MORE DETAIL SEE MAP 727

PERIMETER RD

MET RD

MET

MANSFIELD RD

Fire Station

FIRE STATION RD

OPERATIONS RD

AACC

CAA Operations

Control Tower

Gate 14

Gate 12

TOWER RD

POWER RD

PLANT

STORE ST

TAAATS

AIRWAYS ST

Gate 18

Main North - South Runway No 1

Qantas Domestic Terminal

Qantas Domestic Terminal

International Terminal

AIRSIDE

Gate 39 & 40

EAST RD

SUNBURY RD

NORTH DR

QUARRY

4.1m

Ansett Terminal

Gate 35

Ansett

AIRSIDE

Exit

Ent

MELBOURNE

CENTRE RD

GOWRIE PARK DR

Astrojet Cntr

AIRPORT DR

4.6m

SERVICE RD

BONNEY CT

Gate 34A

Southern Apron

Ansett Air Freight

DEPOT DR

Gate 33 & 34

GRANTS RD

Exit

Gate 31

International Cargo

LANDSIDE RD

FRANCIS BRIGGS

QANTAS Freight

Gate 29A & 30

Gate 28

Secondary Emergency Access Gate

Menzies Cargo

Apac

Gate 29

DHL Cargo

HAUL RD

INCINERATOR RD

Restricted Area

Viewing Area

Future Runway

27 L

Gate 19

McNABS RD

Gate 20

Gate 26

Ansett Maintenance Area

34 R

Qantas Maintenance Area

Ansett Maintenance Area

Gate 26A

Restricted Area

STH LOCALISER RD

Gate 21

Gate 22

Gate 23

Gate 24

RD

SOUTH CENTRE RD

OPERATIONS

ARUNDEL RD

18

Woodlands Historic Park
Parks VICTORIA
Gellibrand Hill 204m
Gate
SWAIN ST
PROVIDENCE RD
SECTION RD
CARROLL LA
MICKLEHAM RD
ELPHINSTONE
CUPAR PL
INVERNESS
McNAB WY
MW
DR
BVD
TCE
DUMFRIES
QUEENSFERRY PL
Attwood
BUCHANAN PL
JEDBURGH PL
GLENCAIRN
RD
DUNBAR CT
LAMARK CT
DUNDEE CT
DRUMMOND
Res
BARRYMORE
GREENOCK CT
ST
Ck
MACBEAN CT
MACKAY ST
MONTROSE CT
Motor Driving School
Victoria Police
Dept of Agriculture Research Station
Stud Farm
Dog Kennels
ATTWOOD
CITY
Moonee Ponds Ck
Fbr
bourne rport e Park
CHANDOS PL
INNKEEPERS WY
ALANBRAE TCE
COACH HOUSE DR
BLACKSMITH DR
ARDLIE
TOLLKEEPERS PDE
THE CREST
Melbourne Airport Caravan Village
Ten Cts
Westmeadows Res
Cmnty Cntr
GRUNDY
ST
Willowbrook Reserve
WESTMEADOWS
JABIRU PL
Cleanaway
VICTORIA ST
WESTERN AV
GUNN CT
BARON CT
THORNLEIGH PL
WEIR
BAMFORD
COPELAND RD
ASHFORD
KOALA CR
GRANGE PL
BEECROFT DR
SWANS
WOMBAT CT
ROSELLA CT
BROLGA ST
PELICAN ST
BENT ST
COOPERS HILL DR
FAWKNER ST
TURNER ST
FORMAN
TYLDEN PL
ARDLIE ST
HARWELL CT
STANTON CT
SANDHAM
GARDENVIEW GR
FIELDERS WK
PARK HILL CT
HORNSBY
DENHAM CT
AV
DOUGLAS CT
GLENCAIRN
HOPETOUN
MONACO CT
BRAMCOTE DR
WRIGHT
GRETNA CL
HYTON CL
HILLCREST
ARNSIDE CR
EVITA TCE
ARJAY CT
RONDOR CL
DUNCAN CT
AVION PL
PERSHORE
BROADMEADOWS RD
RD
CR
BAY CT
DUNDEE CL
LYNDHURST
RODWELL CT
SNAEFELL CL
HARDY
READE
OSBORNE
CHISHOLM CL
COSTAIN AV
INN
DUGGAN
BYFIELD CT
MOOAR
TROLLABY
BRAEMAR CL
GALWAY
GLOBAL DR
IRVINE CT
RYLANDES
GLADSTONE PARK
BOOTH
Tullamarine Business Centre
DOLPHIN CT
HINTON CL
Gladstone Park Res
Cmnty Cntr
PAYNE ST
Nurs Home
CIRCULAR RD
Gladstone Park Primary
TAYLOR DR
Gladstone Park
SOUTH
INTERNATIONAL DR
MICKLEHAM
DUDLEY
BELMONT CT
LATIMER PL
GLADSTONE PARK DR
GOODWOOD CR
PRIOR
BARTON CT
AYLESBURY RD
CIRCULAR AV
FLEETWOOD
STOCK
SUTTON CL
BRIAR CT
BOWER
AITKEN PL
GREENACRE GR
ELMHURST RD
MOSSFIELD MW
18
C743
MELROSE
TULLAMARINE FWY
GREENHILL
Gate
ST
SMOLIC CT
SPRINGBANK
STRATHCONNON SQ
MARMAL CT
DR
HENDERSON RD
DERBY
TULLAMARINE
Restricted Area
PERIMETER RD
Gate 27
e 27A
Melbourne Airport Club
LINK
RD
GARDEN
CATALINA
HERCULES ST
DAKOTA CT
SABRE CT
BMX
Tullamarine Reserve
DERBY ST
Ten Cts
FREIGHT RD
BOYSE CT
CUSTOM
ROSTO CT
DR
MILLAR RD
SASHA CT
5.0m
48
39
UBD

JOINS 193

JOINS 236

JOINS 279

192

278

A B C D E F G H J K L

1 2 3 4 5 6 7 8 9 10 11 12 13 14 15 16 17 18 19 20

GREENVALE

MEADOW HEIGHTS

ATTWOOD

WESTMEADOWS

GLADSTONE PARK

JACANA

Broadmeadows Valley Park

400 Acres Reserve

Yuroke Ck

Moonee Ponds

Horse Riding

St Carlo Borromeo

Cmnty Cntr

Westmeadows Hts Pmy

Erinbank Secondary College

Westmeadows Primary

Kangan Institute of TAFE Hume Campus

Spec Dev Sch

Broadmeadows West Pmy

Hillcrest Secondary

Basketball Stadium

Leisure Centre

Pitch & Putt Golf

Jacana Reserve

Johnstone St Reserve

Mc Lellan Nurs Home

Jacana Pmy

Jack Ginifer Reserve

Gladstone Views Pmy

Gladstone Park Primary

Gladstone Park Sec Coll

Gladstone Park Res

Broadmeadows Club

Proposed Golf Club

Law Court

Vic Roads

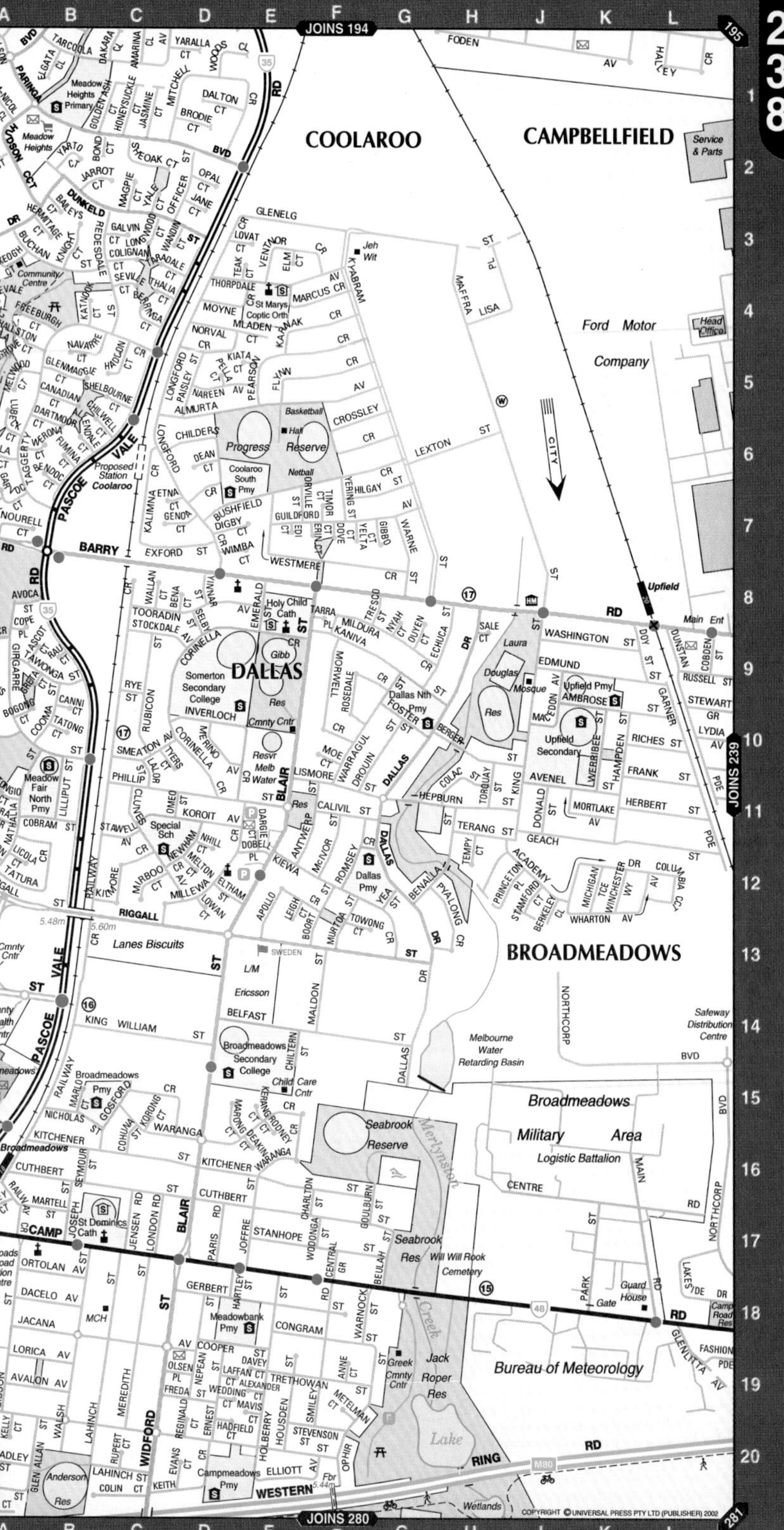
JOINS 194
195
COOLAROO
CAMPBELLFIELD
DALLAS
BROADMEADOWS
Ford Motor Company
Progress Reserve
Meadow Heights Primary
Meadow Heights
Community Centre
St Marys Coptic Orth
Coolaroo South Pmy
Proposed Station Coolaroo
Holy Child Cath
Somerton Secondary College
Gibb Res
Cmnty Cntr
Resvr Melb Water
Dallas Nth Pmy
Laura Douglas Res
Mosque
Upfield Pmy
Upfield Secondary
Meadow Fair North Pmy
Special Sch
Dallas Pmy
Lanes Biscuits
L/M Ericsson
Broadmeadows Secondary College
Child Care Cntr
Broadmeadows Pmy
Seabrook Reserve
Merlynston Creek
Melbourne Water Retarding Basin
Broadmeadows Military Area
Logistic Battalion
Safeway Distribution Centre
St Dominics Cath
Seabrook Res
Will Will Rook Cemetery
Meadowbank Pmy
Guard House
Bureau of Meteorology
Greek Cmnty Cntr
Jack Roper Res
Lake
Anderson Res
Campmeadows Pmy
Wetlands
Service & Parts
Head Office
Upfield
PASCOE VALE RD
BARRY RD
CAMP RD
RING RD
WESTERN RING RD
KING WILLIAM ST
RIGGALL ST
BLAIR ST
DALLAS DR
JOINS 239
JOINS 280
281
COPYRIGHT © UNIVERSAL PRESS PTY LTD (PUBLISHER) 2002

JOINS 195

JOINS 238

JOINS 281

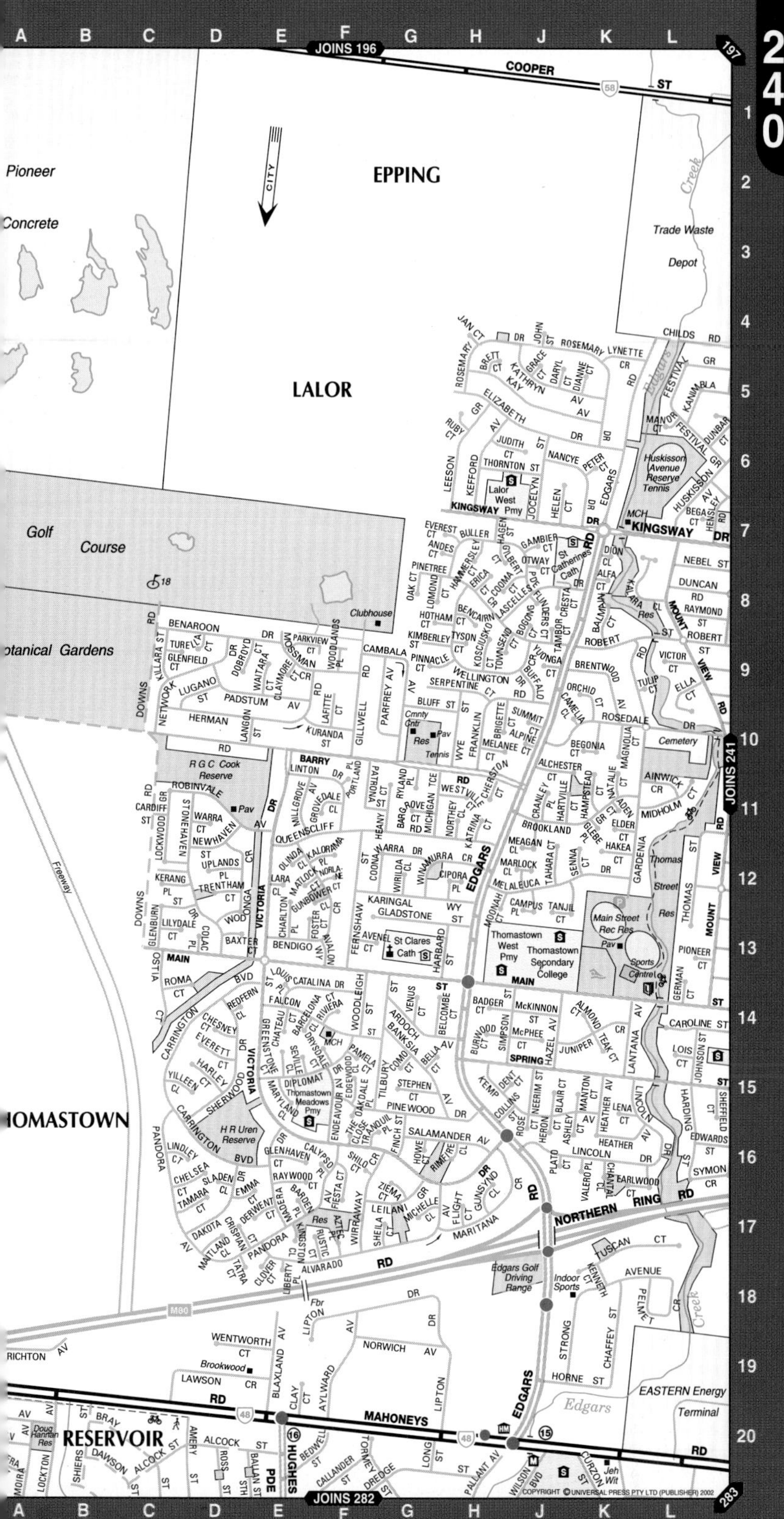
JOINS 196
EPPING
LALOR
THOMASTOWN
RESERVOIR
Golf Course
Botanical Gardens
Pioneer Concrete
Trade Waste Depot
COOPER ST
EDGARS RD
KINGSWAY
MAIN ST
NORTHERN RING RD
MAHONEYS RD
JOINS 241
JOINS 282
EASTERN Energy Terminal
COPYRIGHT © UNIVERSAL PRESS PTY LTD (PUBLISHER) 2002

A B C D E F G H J K L

JOINS 197

JOINS 240

JOINS 283

EPPING

LALOR

THOMASTOWN

The Northern Hospital

Epping Plaza Shopping Complex

Trade Waste Depot

St Peters Cath

St Monicas Cath Coll Sen

Northern Melb Institute of TAFE Epping Campus

PTC Epping Depot

Epping

St Monicas Catholic Coll Junior South Campus

Gloria Twins Receptions

Top Kart Racing

Lalor North Secondary College

V R Michael Reserve

Partridge Street Reserve

Soccer

Lalor Park Pmy

Lalor Nth Pmy

Lalor

Lalor Reserve

Pav

Tennis

Peter Lalor Secondary College

Queens Lodge Ret Vill

W A Smith Reserve

Lalor Pmy

Res

Lalor Secondary College

St Lukes Cath

Peter Lalor ML

Lalor Plaza

Lalor East Pmy

Thomastown East Pmy

Alexander Res

Little Aths

Thomastown Mosque

Thomastown Pmy

Nurs Home

Goodyear Tyres

UBD

EASTERN Energy Terminal

Keon Park

Tenpin Bowling

Kinetik Energy

Market

Lowalde Drive Res

COOPER ST, MARY CT, WEDGE ST, MILLER ST, DUFFY ST, HIGH ST, COULSTOCK ST, HOWARD ST, DAVISSON ST, CAMPBELL ST, SUNBIRD GDN, WINTERTON CL, LETCHWORTH PL, PEPPERCORN CT, ZIMMER CT, SAVANNAH CR, HENRY CT, SUNRISE CT, MAYWOOD DR, PECAN CL, DELMONT CL, HENDERSONS RD, MIRRAM CT, KARRI DR, KANTIKA GR, GUNDARA ST, ARANDA PL, KARLOO CL, NARINA WY, JEFFREY CT, BEST CL, HONEY CT

JOVIC RD, ROXBY ST, RAILWAY RD, GRAND SUPPLY DR, TERESA CT, PETRA CT, MONICA CT, PDE, BUCH DR, MARK CT, GLOBE PL, NOBLE CL, TENERIFFE CL, AYERS CT, SUPPLY DR, ELAINE CL, PORTSMOUTH PL, SALICKI AV, GUILA CT, VERNON ST, KILBY CL, BROOME CT, HOLROYD CT, LEES PL, GILLESPIE RD, CHILDS RD, LIONHEART CT, BOWMAN ST, CARBON CT

BELLARINE DR, HALSTON RD, RUSSET CT, CURRAWONG AV, COLUMBIA RD, KANIMBLA, DUNBAR CT, FESTIVAL GR, MELTON AV, TEAL, KIAMA DR, HUSKISSON, WILLARD CT, VANESSA, BEGA CT, LINOAK, TANDARRA CR, WINSLOW AV, AVONDALE RD, EPPING RD, MONASH ST, GIBSON ST, CHIFLEY ST, KINGSFORD ST, BALLARAT ST, KENNA DR, KOKODA CT, CORAL ST, MIDWAY CR, LUZON CT, WAKE CT, BATAAN CT, DERNA CR, MANUS ST, TOBRUK CT, BALI PL, MINDORO CR, CROMWELL CT, SWINDON, ASHDOWN CT, WALDEN CR, BEAUMONT, HAWKES DR, PISANI CT, TOOTH CT, FENECK, FLINTOFF CT, GAZE CT, MONEGHETTI

KINGSWAY DR, NEBEL ST, DUNCAN, FRANK ST, RAYMOND ST, LYNDON, ROBERT, PARTRIDGE ST, ANDERSON ST, CURTIN AV, CUTLER CT, STATION ST, PASCHKE CR, ROCHDALE SQ, GORDON, EDMONDSON AV, CHERRY CT, RUTHVEN CR, HAMILTON CT, BURTON AV, QUEEN ST, TUNBRIDGE CR, HERTFORD PL, GUAM CT, DAREBIN DR, MICHAEL, VASEY AV, NEWTON, SYDNEY ST, KELLERHER, PRINCE ANDREW AV, ETHEL AV, KING ST, RAIMENO ST, LOUISE ST, DELMARE ST, VALERIE ST, CLIFTON, DONALD ST

DICKENS ST, MOUNT VIEW RD, RICHARDS ST, RYDER ST, HOWELL ST, GRATWICK ST, MACKEY ST, MIDDLETON ST, DERRICK ST, CHOWNE ST, WEST CT, EAST CT, EVANS ST, MAXWELL, RUTH ST, BUNTING CT, FISHER GR, CASEY DR, BOND CT, LYELL AV, DEBRA CT, MENZIES PDE, DENNIS ST, BOSTON, DEAKIN, BRUCE AV, BLACKBURN ST, TRAMOO, DAVID ST, HURTLE ST, ARNDELL ST, TRAVERS ST, WILLIAM ST, MUNRO ST, JEAN ST, LORNE ST, DALTON RD, KIRWAN AV, CYPRUS ST, MESSMATE ST, SCOTT ST, (ROW), LACEY ST, LYNNE, McKIMMIES RD, BLACKWOOD ST, MAPLE, WHITEHALL ST, GRIFFIN CT

WESTALL ST, CHAPPELL ST, THOMAS, PLEASANT RD, CENTRAL AV, PIONEER CT, HIGHLANDS RD, MCH, MAIN ST, QUANDONG ST, CURRAJONG ST, HEATH, FIR ST, FRENCH ST, WILGAH ST, MULGA ST, LARCH ST, PLANE ST, PINE ST, PALM ST, ASH ST, ELM ST, THE BOULEVARD, WATTLE ST, POPLAR ST, CLEVELAND ST, LEILA CT, WARWICK DR, JACOB CT, BENO CT, MIRIAM ST, REGAL AV, VALENTINE, BARBARA CT, STELLA CT, PATRICK ST, PHILIP CT, TALBOT AV, ALFRED AV, NOEL CT, STANLEY CT, DELTA CT, BATES, WARATAH ST, MYRTLE ST, THE CEDAR, BEECH ST, BELAH ST, ACACIA, BORONIA, BUCKINGHAM CT, SMITH AV, RUPERT CT, UREN CT, BICKLEY, OWEN CT, LESLIE ST, CHAPMAN AV

CAROLINE ST, NORMAN GR, STEWART ST, ALEXANDER ST, DOROTHY AV, GEOFFREY ST, CHARLES ST, MARCIA ST, FREDERICK ST, EDNA ST, MARJORY ST, LANSELL CT, KINGSLEY CT, DOUGLAS CT, GRAHAM CT, JOHNSON ST, SPRING ST, HEYINGTON, OXFORD ST, WEMBLEY CT, KENSINGTON CT, SALISBURY ST, LIONEL ST, CAMBRIDGE CT, HAMPTON, RICHARDSON, WARREGO, HAWKESBURY, BRIDGEWATER, MURCHISON, HARDING ST, SHEFFIELD CT, McLEOD ST, EDWARDS ST, CLARKE ST, ALISON ST, SPENCER ST, IVANHOE CT, ROCHESTER, ASCOT CT, CUMBERLAND, PARKLANDS, LODDON CT, SWAN CT, SYMON CR, NEWTON ST, NORTHERN RING RD, M80

AUSTARC AV, SETTLEMENT RD, CLIVEDEN CT, BROCK, NORTHGATE DR, INGLEWOOD DR, ENTERPRISE PL, ABRUZZO CR, MILNE ST, CHARNFIELD CT, TEMPLE DR, MACQUARIE DR, BRAND, GREEN, WOOD ST, BOSTOCK CT, HANRAHAN ST, CENTOFAN PL, NEVIN DR, APEX CT, MAHONEYS ROAD, KEON PDE, DUNSTANS, DALTON

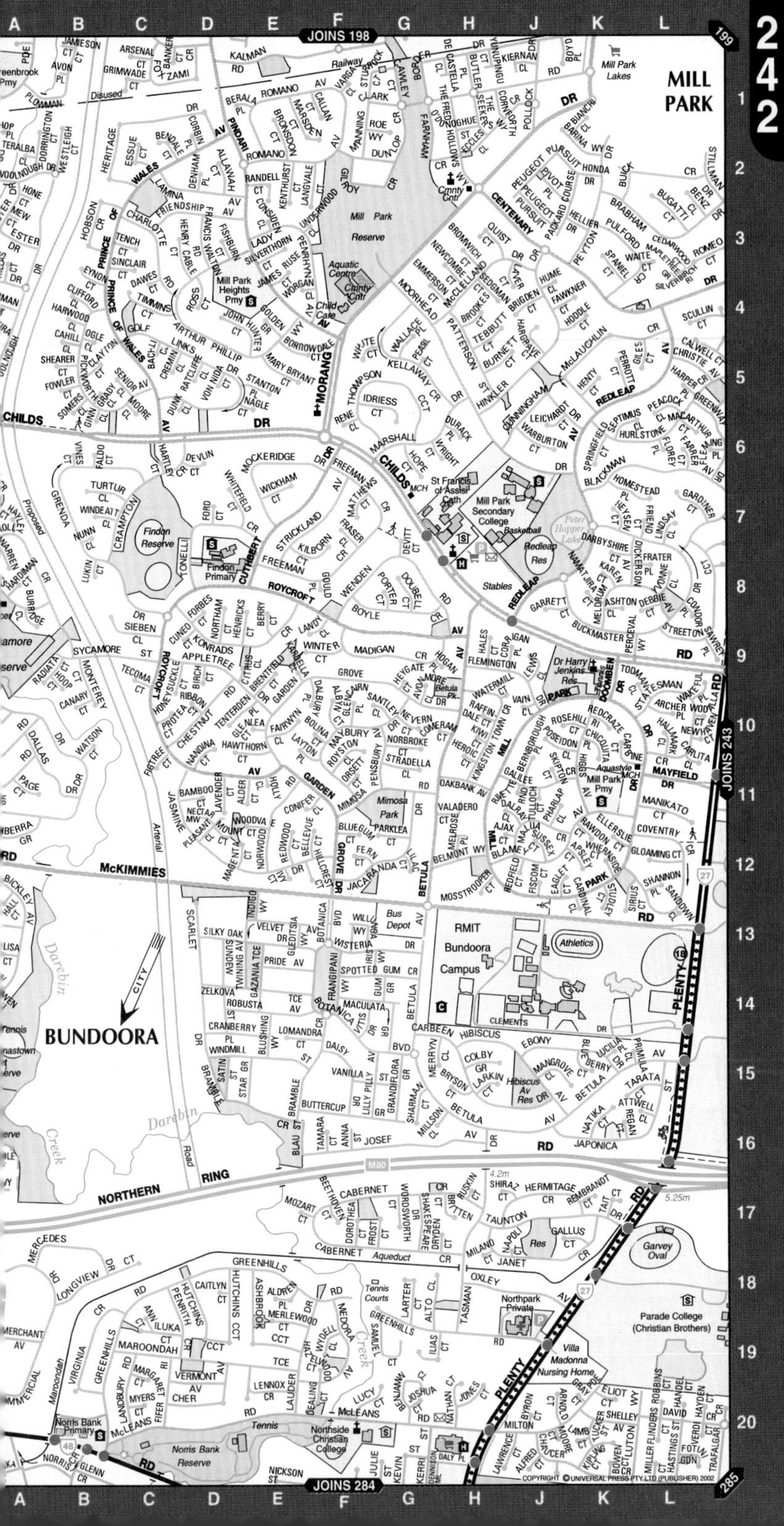

MILL PARK
BUNDOORA
JOINS 198
JOINS 243
JOINS 284
199
285
Mill Park Lakes
Mill Park Reserve
Aquatic Centre
Cmnty Cntr
Child Care
Mill Park Heights Pmy
St Francis of Assisi Cath
Mill Park Secondary College
Basketball
Peter Hopper Lake
Redleap Res
Stables
Findon Reserve
Findon Primary
Dr Harry Jenkins Res
Betula Pk
Aquastyle
Mill Park Pmy
Mimosa Park
Bus Depot
RMIT Bundoora Campus
Athletics
Hibiscus Av Res
Darebin Creek
CITY
Arterial
Proposed
Railway
Disused
NORTHERN RING ROAD
M80
McKIMMIES RD
CHILDS RD
PLENTY RD
CENTENARY DR
MORANG DR
Garvey Oval
Northpark Private
Villa Madonna Nursing Home
Parade College (Christian Brothers)
Norris Bank Primary
Norris Bank Reserve
Northside Christian College
Tennis
Tennis Courts
Aqueduct
Res
4.2m
5.25m
COPYRIGHT © UNIVERSAL PRESS PTY LTD (PUBLISHER) 2002

198
JOINS 199
JOINS 242
JOINS 285
284

A B C D E F G H J K L

1 2 3 4 5 6 7 8 9 10 11 12 13 14 15 16 17 18 19 20

MILL PARK

SOUTH MORANG

BUNDOORA

WATSONIA NORTH

McDONALDS RD

PLENTY RD

GORGE RD

CENTENARY DR

UNIVERSITY DR

DEVELOPMENT BVD

BLOSSOM PARK DR

NORTHERN RING RD

GREENSBOROUGH BPS

GREENSBOROUGH

MEMORIAL AV

RIVER AV

GOLDSWORTHY

HONEYEATER

Morang South Primary

Nurs Home

Telopea Park Tennis

Proposed Pmy School

Kelynack Pav Reserve

Yellow Gum Park

Parks Victoria

Plenty River

RMIT Bundoora East Campus

Janefield Training Centre

Kiosk

Special School

Administration

Edmund Rice College

Parade College (Christian Brothers)

Admin

Dr J M Wright Oval

Binnak Park

Res

Fbr

6.0m

M80

UBD

N

ALLWYN, STALLMAN, BEAN, BENTLEY, BENZ, BRABHAM, ROMEO, LUKE, HOWDEN, HICKEY, BRADLEY, BREMNER, ATLANTA, HOPPER, MILES, CREAN, RULE, HURLSTONE, EVATT, SCULLIN, WALSH, CALWELL, CHRISTIE, TRUSCOTT, HARPER, GREENWAY, CHISHOLM, MACARTHUR, MANSON, FARRER, FLEMING, KELLY, BLACKMAN, GARDINER, McCUBBIN, BUVELOT, STREETON, CONDOR, SAWREY, WEALTHLAND, SHANNON, HEATHS, YATES, TAREE, LIBERTY, WARD, THE GREEN, TRENTHAM, TYNDALL, SHAMROCK, DEAKIN, NOBELIUS, MONTANA, WESTWOOD, NARELLE, EMILY, PARK, HAVEN, RILEY, PENROSE, TEMPLETON, ADAM, SELWOOD, STOCKDALE, INGLEWOOD, RUSHDALE, BOTTLEBRUSH, BUNDY, OVINGTON, OREGON, RESEARCH, SILVERTOP, WOODHILL, AUSTRALIS, LATHAM, RIVERGUM, EUCALYPT, PARKHILL, WAGSTAFF, MANHATTAN, VIEWBANK, HILLRISE, REDGUM, DIOSMA, GARDENVIEW, MIRBELIA, HOVEA, LUTEA, INCANA, REGEZIA, TRUNCATA, ACMENA, ALBA, VILLOSA, TELOPEA, OLEA, MEDLAR, MANUKA, BLOSSOM, CASSIA, MELIA, DAPHNE, VERONICA, WAKEFUL, NEWHAVEN, CARLITA, AZALEA, AGONIS, GUNNII, MANNA, KURRAJONG, ROSTRATA, VIOLA, ZINNEA, CALLISTEMON, CANANGA, LAURINA, ASTER, GREVILLIA, RICCANA, HILLIANA, WATERS, ISABELLE, WILDFIRE, GYPSY, JUBILEE, CASTLE HILL, BENDEMERE, GRASSMERE, ROSELANDS, HENDERSON, WILLIAMSBROOK, RIVERS, JANEFIELD, RICHARDS, WATTLE

KELVIN, N'RVANA, BRIAR, LANGLEY, OBAR, JACKSON, GEORGE, McGLYNN, REID, ALLAN, RONALD, GARRY, WILTON, KIPPING, CECIL, JOLLY, BUSSELL, TURNER, WINIFRED, DOREEN, THOMAS, KANGAROO, ANGELA, LAW, GRANT, WALLABY, WOMBAT, ROGEN, JONES, STANLEY, ROBIN, WARBLER, KINGFISHER, WATTLEBIRD, SILVEREYE, RIVERSIDE, GLIDER, LOBELIA, TEATREE, POSSUM, PLATYPUS, JOHN, KOOKABURRA, BURRA, WHISTLER, ROSELLA, RYAN, IBIS, LIGHT, WATTLE, MANNA, GUM, PEPPERMINT, FANTAIL, BROLGA, KOALA, MAGPIE, STRINGY BARK, RIVER, REDGUM

COLLENDINA, EASTGATE, MOORA, KINKA, DWYER, GOOLGUNG, JARRAH, BRINAWA, WANDA, WANBANNA, KARIBOO, NOKUNA, TIRRAY, BOOYAN, NIOKA, EVERAH, SENBIN, VAIRO, KERTA, YONDE, CHAPPELL, SELWOOD, RICE, STALLARD, NAUGHTIN, EDMUND, GUNDRY, VICARAGE, LONGFIELD, BINNAK, GLENDALOUGH, DUNRAVEN, HOLYROOD, DORRINGTON, YARRADALE, BERKERLEY, STONEHAVEN, STONINGTON, MACORNA, HAMILTON, ALMA, EIDA, ELTON, IREDALE, FERNLEA, BALFOUR, GILLINGHAM, BYRNE, DAMIEN, KALISTA, GERRARD, MICHELLE, ATKINS, NORMAN, BAWDEN, LAWSON, SELLARS, SENIOR, HAKEA, CHEADLE, ANDERSON, CURTIN, IRVING, CARSON, BENTLEY, NEWTON, GRANT, SUSSEX, RHONDA, BOSTON, COLE, PAMELA, LEONARD, JACQUELINE, PAUL, BERRINGA, KARU, JOHN, STEVEN, CANUNGRA, BALANDA, PURCELL, HAYDEN, DAVID, VERDI, FOTINI, TRAFALGAR, LANDRA, AINTREE, RENDLE, ARMSTRONG, VINCENT, GILMOUR, NINION, BLANCHARD, PINEHILLS, SIBELLA, SASK, HALIDAY, ALBERT

A B C D E F G H J K L

JOINS 200
201
JOINS 245
JOINS 286
287

1 2 3 4 5 6 7 8 9 10 11 12 13 14 15 16 17 18 19 20

PLENTY

DIAMOND CREEK

GREENSBOROUGH

ST HELENA

Middle Gorge Park

Parks Victoria

Municipal Depot

(Tip Closed)

KURRAK RD

ARMSTRONG RD

CHARLESVILLE RD

NICHOLLS CT

WESTGARTH ST

BROWNS LA

FANECO RD

SEYMOUR DR

HEARD AV

YAN YEAN RD

BELLA VISTA CT

NAMATJIRA AV

RIVER AV

CITY

RIVER AV

McLENNANS RD

MEMORIAL DR

HOWELL RD

CFA

Plenty Park

Tennis

Hockey

Pony Club

SUTHERLAND RD

BECK RD

JUMBUCK CT

CRAIG RD

BUTLERS RD

MACKELROY RD

OATLAND RD

McLAUGHLANS LA

COMELY BANK RD

McLAUGHLANS DR

HAPPY HOLLOW

GELLIBRAND PL

Dry Ck

PAPHOS CT

THE GROVE

SHEOAK ST

MANNA MW

LILLYPILLY LA

CAMPHORA CT

DAVIESIA DR

LIGHTWOOD LA

TREETOP

PAPERBARK PL

GREVILLIA TCE

JOSEPHINE CT

CR

Jeh Wit

Ministry of Education Complex

Sutherland Homes

Ent

DIAMOND CREEK RD

AQUEDUCT RD

JAMES CT

JAMIESON CT

IRENE CT

IRENE ST

MORA PL

WILSON

DAVID HOCKNEY DR

JULIAN PL

ASTON PL

OLD AQUEDUCT RD

COOGEE CT

MONOMEATH AV

JODIE WY

LILIAN CT

EZIO CT

St Thomas the Apostle

PRIMO CT

CARMEL CL

SUNRISE

YELLOW GUM RI

COSHAM CT

MARISSA CR

MARINO DR

JULIE CT

PATRICK CL

VIEWGRAND WY

TOORAK CT

SYMON

BILLABONG CT

CARLO CT

BILLY TEA CT

PLENTY RIVER DR

MIONERA GRN

WILTON DR

ACWORTH CT

MUSGROVE DR

NOBEL CL

NAIRNE TCE

BAYONNE CL

Diamond Hills Estate Reserve

OLDSTEAD RD

OLDSTEAD CT

SUNSHINE RD

SETTE CT

ST GEORGES CT

Arterial Road

Proposed

PALPERA TCE

PUNKERRI CR

LOOREA CT

KEDA PL

TRACEY PL

HAMISH CT

LEAR CT

LEISCHA CT

LARCOM CT

GLENWOOD

KENWYN CT

SELSDON CT

TRENT CL

CRANA CL

TINDAL CT

GAMBIA CT

ROBY CT

Civic Plaza

Apollo Parkways Primary

BRENTWICK DR

Diamond Valley Sp Dev Sch

Northern Melb Institute of TAFE Greensborough Campus

DIAMOND HILLS DR

HIAH CT

CIVIC DR

Civic Centre

Sports Centre

BERYL

DOOWI CT

COROWA

KOWA CT

WARROOL CL

AKIMA

NANDALY CT

WEEMALA CT

BULLANOO CT

HURST

TALLERK CT

GOONYAH CT

WALA PL

TUTA CL

HWY

St John of God Services Victoria Churinga

Greenhills Prmy

GREEN GULLY CT

TATHRA PL

BALOO CT

BEALES ST

ELAROO CT

PINDARI DR

ALLUMBA

NATASHA CT

PHOEBE CT

LAROOL CL

JEANETTE CL

"Leith Park" Luscombe House Old Colonists Home

WINGA CT

YARALLA

MARDI CT

ADORI CL

DELLA CR

NURLA PL

MOORINA CT

ALGONA

LARA DR

Anthony Beale Res

St Katherines Anglican (Hist)

YURANA

MARONG CT

MCH

WAHROONGA CR

MURUMBA

DOUGLAS CT

COVALA CT

PARAWEENA CT

ALBION ST

NOORABIL CT

PALMYRA CT

GREENHILL RD

BUNYARRA CL

YALTA CL

CARBORA CL

DLE CR

DELPURA GLN

ERANG

SPRING ST

HEBDEN

PEMBROKE ST

MINE ST

HOPE ST

FOREST ST

CREST ST

KIANDRA CL

BALLANDRY CT

CANARA

WUNGAROO

PALINGA ST

VANESSA DR

CHANTELLE

BAMBARA CT

CONARGO CT

NULGARRAH CR

MANOOKA

LANTANA CR

GOWRIE CT

ST HELENA RD

PAULETTE CL

TAMBOON

PARATEA RI

BEECH DR

TALLOW WOOD

KESWICK GLN

CAIRNS ST

CARNON

BRUCE ST

ANABA CT

ALBION

SOMERLEIGH CR

RAINHAM CL

LOOMA CL

OMARU RI

BARKALA

DARLY GLN

ODENPA CT

KUNDY CT

MURA CL

TANGARI CT

BIRRAKAY CT

MIGA

MARI CL

PAMBURRA CL

LEBUNYA

WARRINA CL

GEEWAN CT

WOLANGI

GIRRALONG

NAROO CL

YATAMA

AVANDINA

MANATUNGA CT

MANATUNGA CCT

TARWARRI

RIVER

WARRIPARRI

LARNOOK CL

GILWAY CT

PURRI

Ped Und

BEELA

WYUNA

ULMARA PL

CR

RI

DIAMOND CREEK

5.6m

8.00m

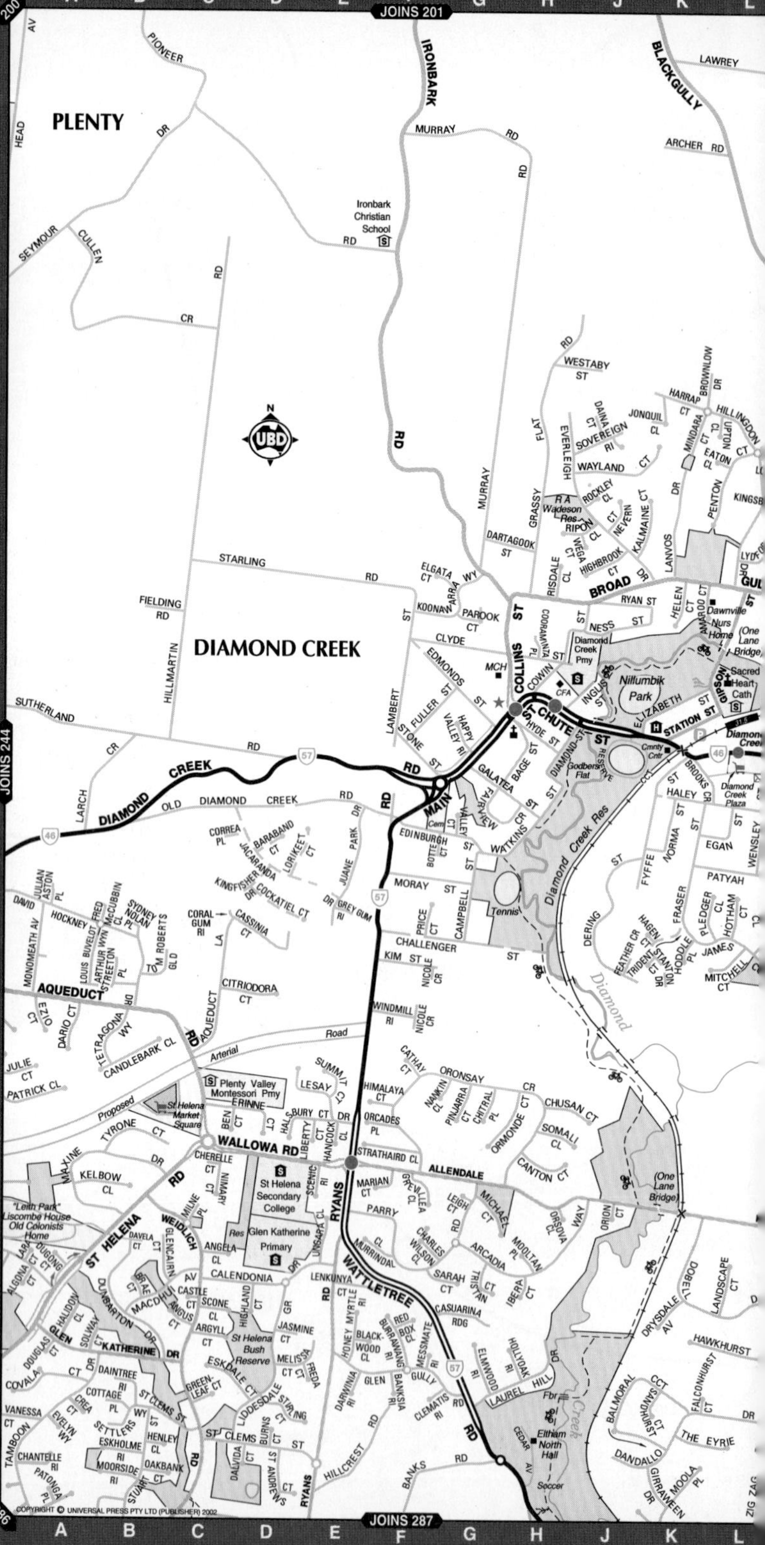

JOINS 201
JOINS 244
JOINS 287
200
286

A B C D E F G H J K L

1 2 3 4 5 6 7 8 9 10 11 12 13 14 15 16 17 18 19 20

PLENTY

DIAMOND CREEK

UBD

Ironbark Christian School

Plenty Valley Montessori Pmy

St Helena Market Square

St Helena Secondary College

Glen Katherine Primary

"Leith Park" Liscombe House Old Colonists Home

St Helena Bush Reserve

Eltham North Hall

Soccer

Fbr

Diamond Creek Pmy

Diamond Creek Plaza

Cmnty Cntr

Godbers Flat

Nillumbik Park

Dawnville Nurs Home

Sacred Heart Cath

(One Lane Bridge)

R A Wadeson Res

Diamond Creek Res

Diamond Creek

Diamond Creek (station)

Tennis

MCH

CFA

Cem

Res

Proposed Arterial Road

PIONEER DR, HEAD AV, SEYMOUR RD, CULLEN CR, IRONBARK RD, MURRAY RD, BLACKGULLY RD, LAWREY, ARCHER RD, STARLING RD, FIELDING RD, HILLMARTIN RD, SUTHERLAND RD, LARCH CR, DIAMOND CREEK RD, OLD DIAMOND CREEK RD, WESTABY ST, HARRAP CT, BROWNLOW DR, HILLINGDON, JONQUIL CL, DAINA CT, SOVEREIGN RI, MINDARA CT, UPTON CL, EATON CT, WAYLAND CT, EVERLEIGH DR, FLAT, GRASSY, ROCKLEY CL, NEVERN CT, KALMAINE CT, PENTON, KINGSB..., RIPON CL, WEGA CT, HIGHBROOK CT, LANVOS DR, DARTAGOOK ST, RISDALE CL, BROAD, LYD..., GU..., ELGATA CT, ARRA WY, KOONAN ST, PAROOK CT, COLLINS ST, COORAMINTA PL, RYAN ST, NESS ST, HELEN CT, AMAROO CT, CLYDE, EDMONDS ST, COWIN ST, INGLIS ST, ELIZABETH ST, GIPSON ST, STATION ST, CHUTE ST, HYDE ST, DIAMOND ST, BROOKS CR, HALEY ST, NORMA ST, EGAN, WENSLEY ST, FYFFE ST, PATYAH, FULLER ST, HAPPY VALLEY RI, LAMBERT, STONE ST, GALATEA ST, BAGE ST, FAIRVIEW CR, MAIN, VALLEY CT, WATKINS, EDINBURGH ST, BOTTE CT, MORAY ST, CAMPBELL, PRICE CT, CHALLENGER ST, KIM ST, NICOLE CR, WINDMILL RI, DERING, FRASER, HAGEN CT, FEATHER CR, TRIDENT CT, STANTON DR, HODDLE PL, PLEDGER CL, HOTHAM CT, JAMES, MITCHELL CT, CORREA PL, BARABAND CT, JACARANDA, LORIKEET CT, JUANE PARK DR, KINGFISHER DR, COCKATIEL CT, GREY GUM RI, CORAL GUM RI, CASSINIA CT, LA, CITRIODORA CT, JULIAN ASTON PL, DAVID, HOCKNEY, FRED McCUBBIN CL, SYDNEY NOLAN PL, MONOMEATH AV, LOUIS BUVELOT, ARTHUR WYN, STREETON PL, TOM ROBERTS GLD, AQUEDUCT RD, EZIO CT, DARIO CT, TETRAGONA WY, CANDLEBARK CL, JULIE CT, PATRICK CL, SUMMIT CT, LESAY CT, ERINNE, BEN CT, HALSBURY CT, LIBERTY CT, HANCOCK CT, HIMALAYA CT, ORCADES PL, CATHAY CT, ORONSAY CR, NANKIN CL, PINJARRA CT, CHITRAL PL, ORMONDE CT, CHUSAN CT, SOMALI CL, CANTON CT, TYRONE CT, WALLOWA RD, CHERELLE CT, NIMARY CT, SCENIC RI, RYANS RD, STRATHAIRD CL, ALLENDALE, MARIAN CT, GREVILLEA CL, PARRY, LEIGH CT, MICHAEL CT, ORSOVA CT, WAY, ORION CT, MAXINE, KELBOW CL, ST HELENA RD, WEIDLICH RD, MILNE PL, DAVELA CT, GLENCAIRN AV, ANGELA CL, UNSARA CL, CHARLES WILSON CL, ARCADIA, MOOLTAN PL, MURRINDAL CL, SARAH CT, TRISTAN CT, IBERA CT, WATTLETREE RD, LARA CT, DUGONG CT, ALGONA CT, HALIDON CT, DUNBARTON DR, BRAE CT, MACDHUI, CASTLE CT, ANGUS CT, SCONE CL, CALENDONIA, LENKUNYA, HIGHLAND CT, GR, ARGYLL CT, JASMINE CT, HONEY MYRTLE RI, RED BOX CL, BURRAWANG, MESSMATE CT, CASUARINA RDG, GLEN KATHERINE DR, SOLWAY, DOUGLAS CT, BLACKWOOD CL, ESKDALE CT, MELISSA CT, FREDA CT, ELMWOOD RI, HOLLYOAK RI, LAUREL HILL DR, COVALA CT, DAINTREE RI, COTTAGE PL, CREA CT, ST CLEMS ST, GREENLEAF CT, LIDDESDALE CT, STIRLING, DARWINIA RI, GLEN, BANKSIA RI, GULLY, CLEMATIS RI, CEDAR AV, VANESSA CT, EVELYN WY, SETTLERS, HENLEY CL, ESKHOLME RI, MOORSIDE RI, OAKBANK CT, STUART, TAMBOON, CHANTELLE RI, PATONGA PL, CLEMS ST, DALVIDA CT, BURNS CT, ST ANDREWS CT, HILLCREST RD, BANKS RD, DRYSDALE AV, DOBELL, LANDSCAPE CT, HAWKHURST, FALCONHURST, BALMORAL CCT, SANDHURST CT, THE EYRIE, DANDALLO DR, GIRRAWEEN, MOOLA PL, ZIG ZAG

46, 57

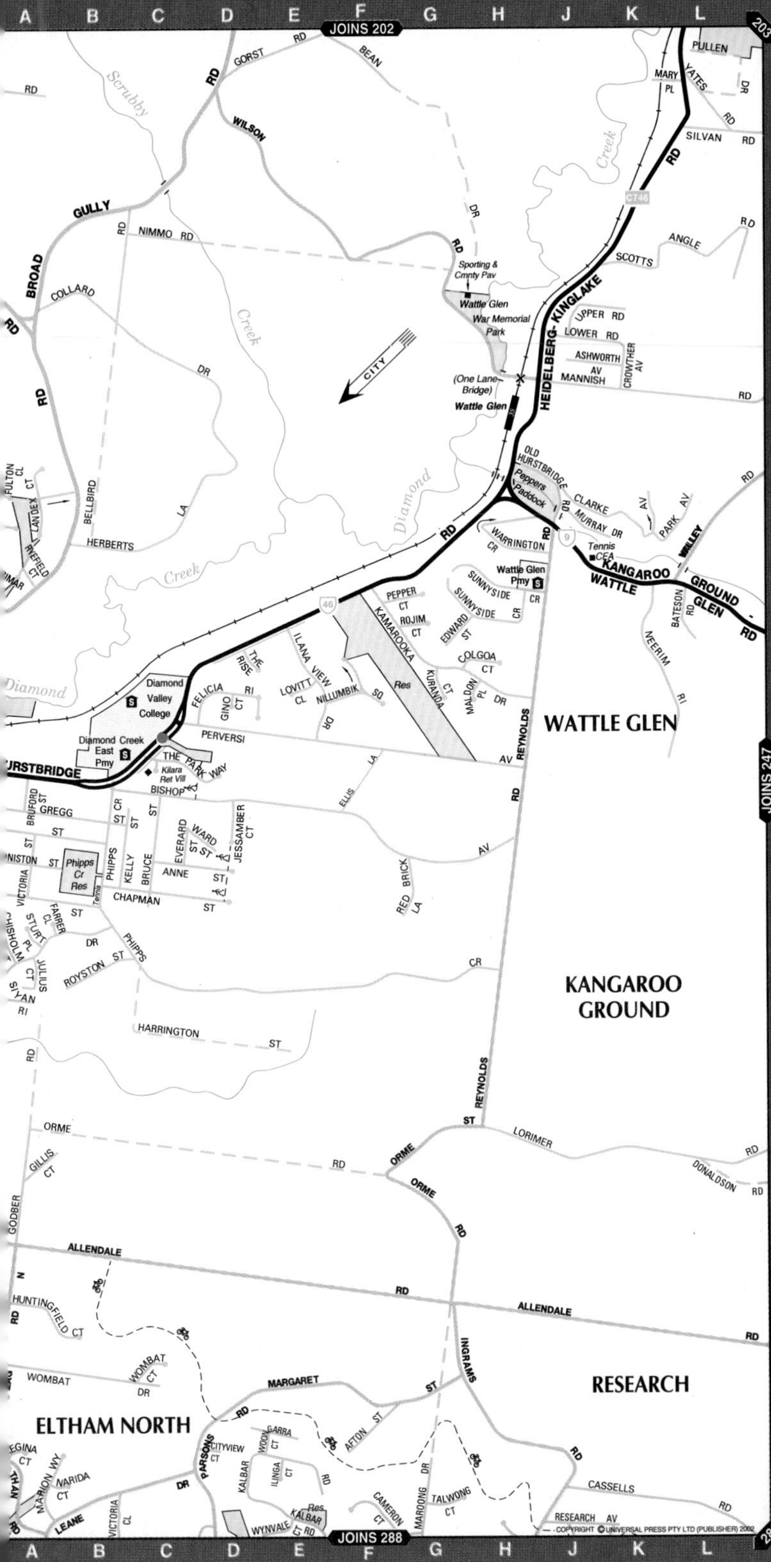

JOINS 202
203

WATTLE GLEN

KANGAROO GROUND

RESEARCH

ELTHAM NORTH

HEIDELBERG-KINGLAKE RD
KANGAROO GROUND - WATTLE GLEN RD
HURSTBRIDGE
BROAD GULLY RD
REYNOLDS RD
ALLENDALE RD
ORME RD
INGRAMS RD
MARGARET ST
PERVERSI AV

Sporting & Cmnty Pav
Wattle Glen War Memorial Park
(One Lane Bridge)
Wattle Glen
Peppers Paddock
Wattle Glen Pmy
Tennis CFA
Diamond Valley College
Diamond Creek East Pmy
Kilara Ret Vill
Phipps Cr Res
Res

JOINS 247

JOINS 288
289

JOINS 203

A B C D E F G H J K L

1 2 3 4 5 6 7 8 9 10 11 12 13 14 15 16 17 18 19 20

WATTLE GLEN

PANTON HILL

KANGAROO GROUND

RESEARCH

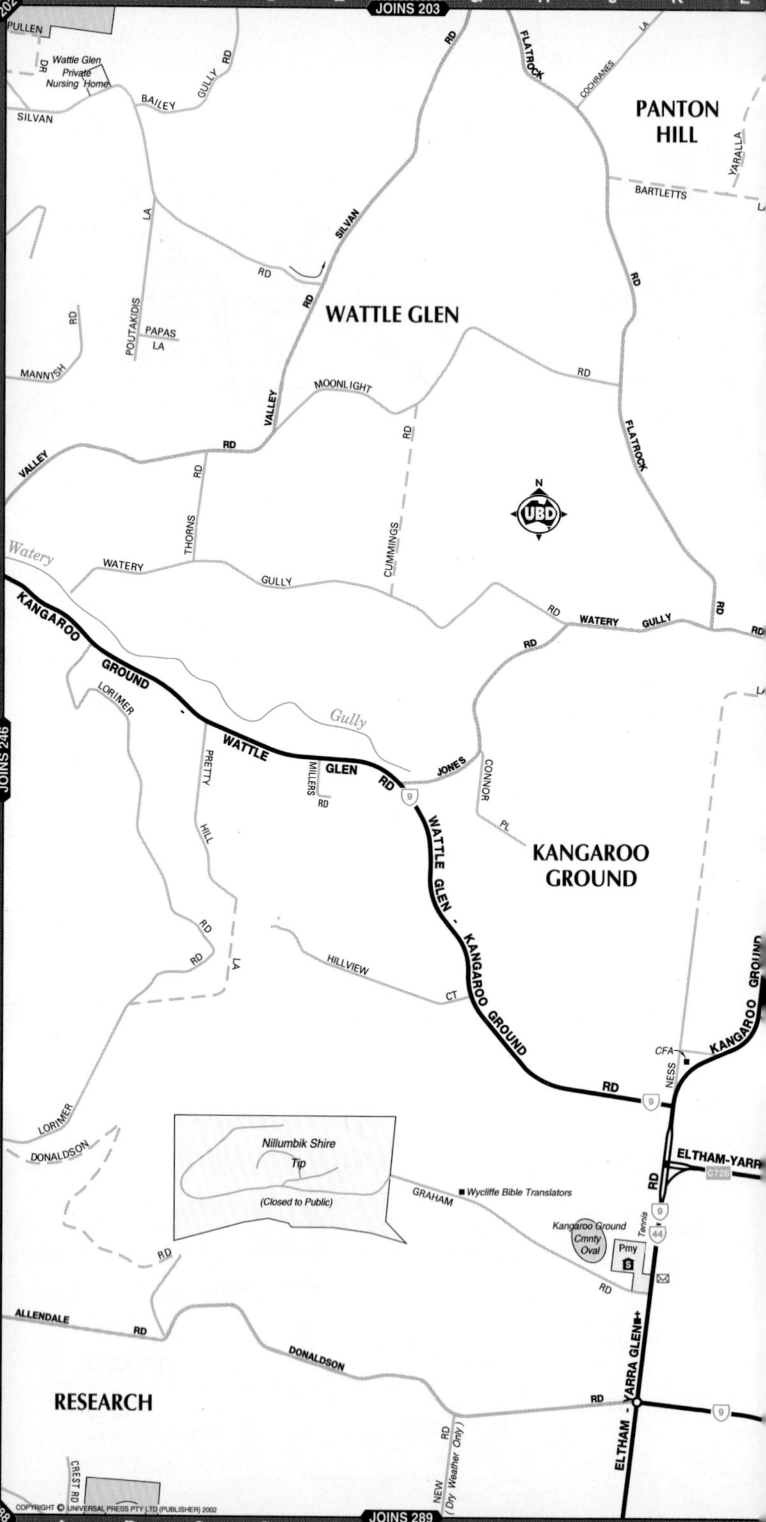

PULLEN DR

Wattle Glen Private Nursing Home

SILVAN

BAILEY GULLY RD

FLATROCK RD

COCHRANES LA

YARALLA

BARTLETTS

SILVAN RD

POUTAKIDIS LA

PAPAS LA

MANNISH RD

MOONLIGHT RD

VALLEY RD

THORNS RD

CUMMINGS RD

WATERY GULLY RD

Watery Gully

KANGAROO GROUND - WATTLE GLEN RD

WATTLE GLEN - KANGAROO GROUND RD

LORIMER RD

PRETTY HILL RD

MILLERS RD

JONES RD

CONNOR PL

HILLVIEW CT

LA

NESS

CFA

KANGAROO GROUND

ELTHAM-YARR

C726

Nillumbik Shire Tip (Closed to Public)

GRAHAM RD

Wycliffe Bible Translators

Kangaroo Ground Cmnty Oval

Tennis

Pmy

DONALDSON

ALLENDALE RD

DONALDSON RD

NEW RD (Dry Weather Only)

ELTHAM - YARRA GLEN RD

CREST RD

JOINS 246

202

288

JOINS 289

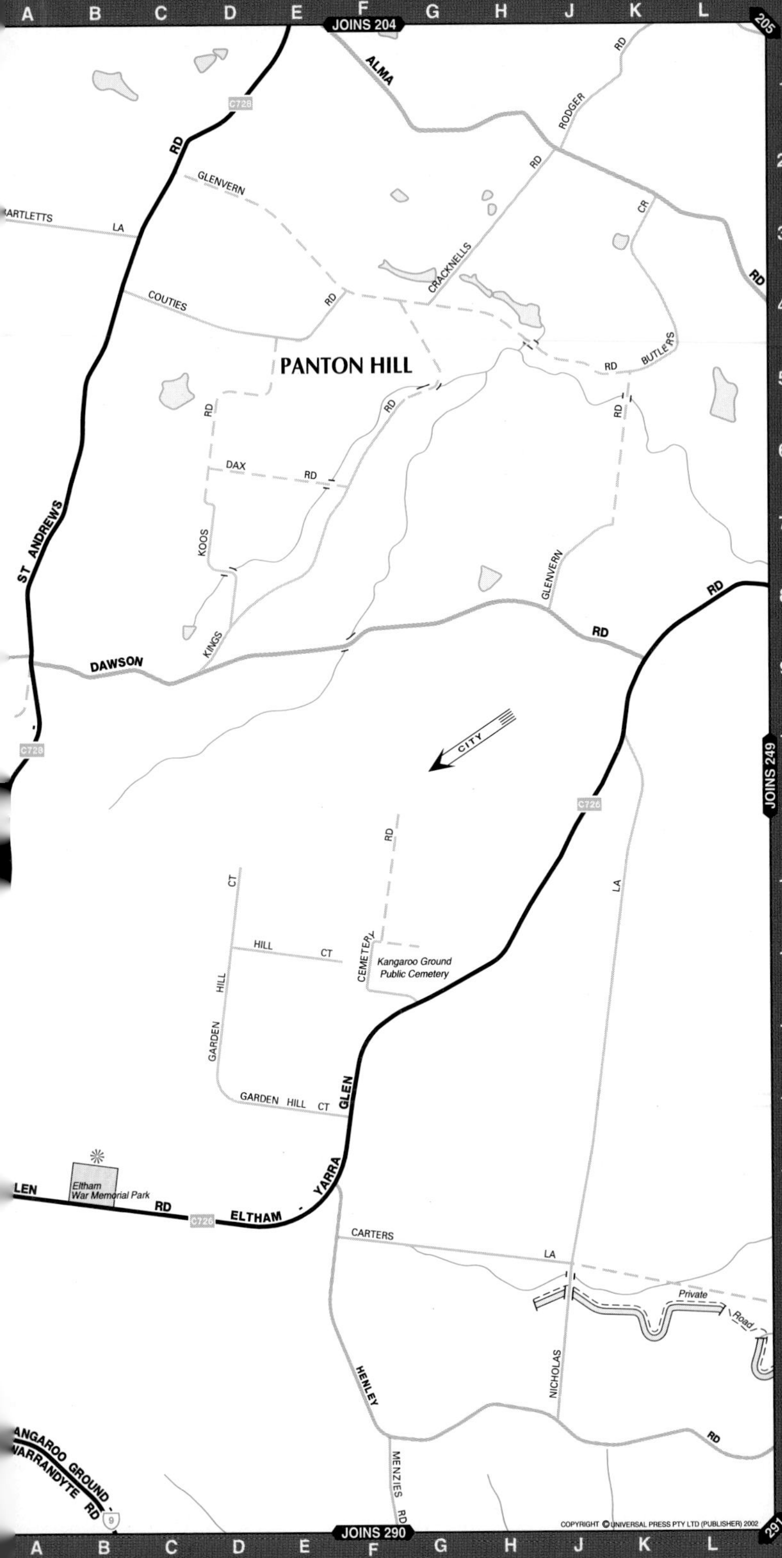

A B C D E F G H J K L

JOINS 204

205

PANTON HILL

ALMA RD
RODGER RD
ST ANDREWS RD
C728
GLENVERN RD
BARTLETTS LA
COUTIES RD
CRACKNELLS RD
CR
BUTLERS RD
KOOS RD
DAX RD
KINGS RD
GLENVERN RD
DAWSON RD
RD
CITY
JOINS 249
C726
CT
HILL CT
CEMETERY RD
Kangaroo Ground Public Cemetery
GARDEN HILL
GARDEN HILL CT
LA
GLEN
ELTHAM - YARRA
GLEN RD
Eltham War Memorial Park
CARTERS LA
Private Road
NICHOLAS
HENLEY RD
MENZIES RD
KANGAROO GROUND - WARRANDYTE RD
9

1 2 3 4 5 6 7 8 9 10 11 12 13 14 15 16 17 18 19 20

JOINS 290

291

A B C D E F G H J K L

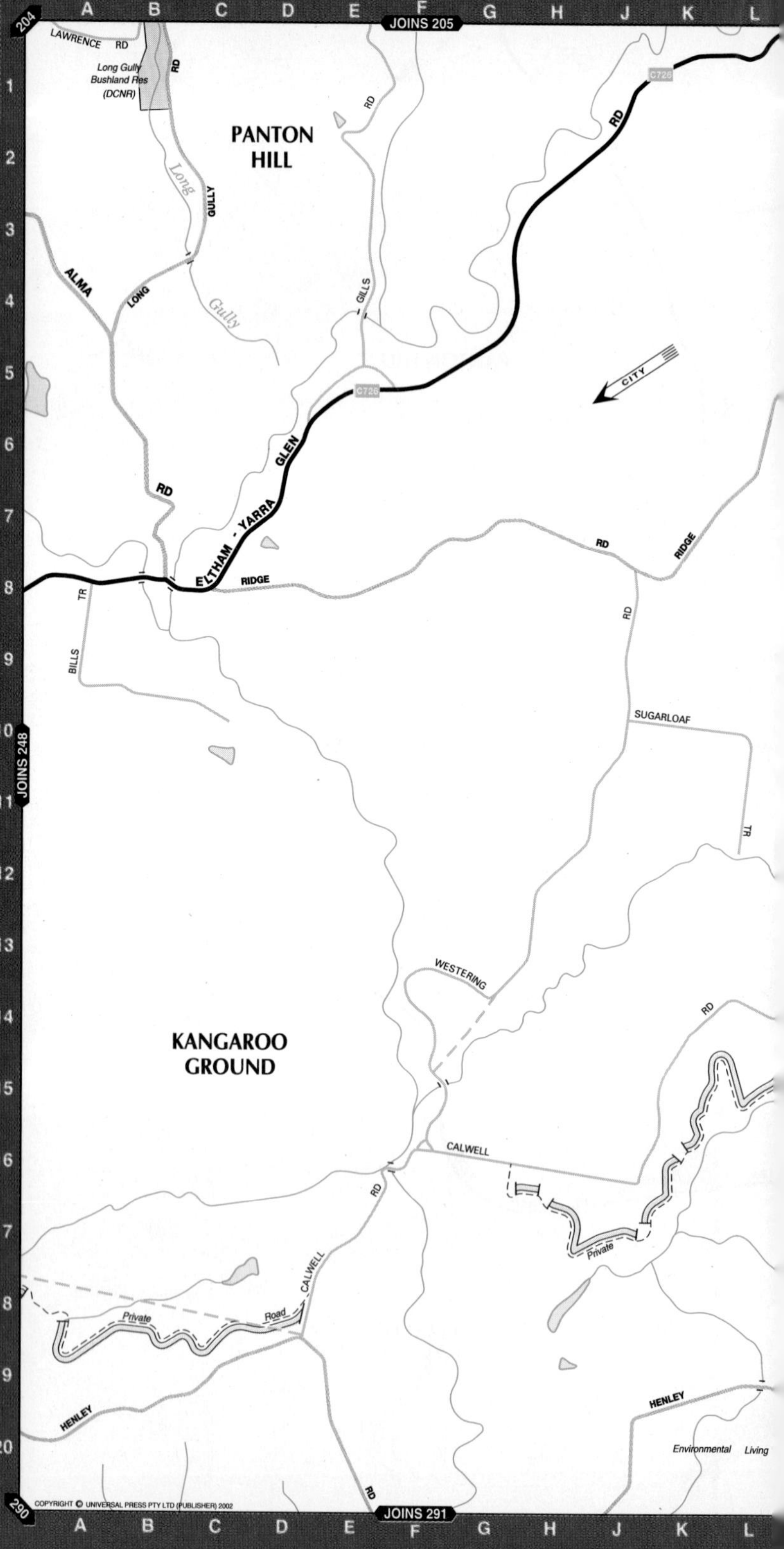
JOINS 205
204
LAWRENCE RD
Long Gully Bushland Res (DCNR)
RD
PANTON HILL
Long
GULLY
RD
C726
RD
ALMA
LONG
Gully
GILLS
CITY
C726
GLEN
RD
ELTHAM - YARRA
RD
RIDGE
TR
RIDGE
RD
BILLS
SUGARLOAF
JOINS 248
TR
WESTERING
RD
KANGAROO GROUND
CALWELL
RD
Private
CALWELL
Private
Road
HENLEY
HENLEY
Environmental Living
RD
290
JOINS 291

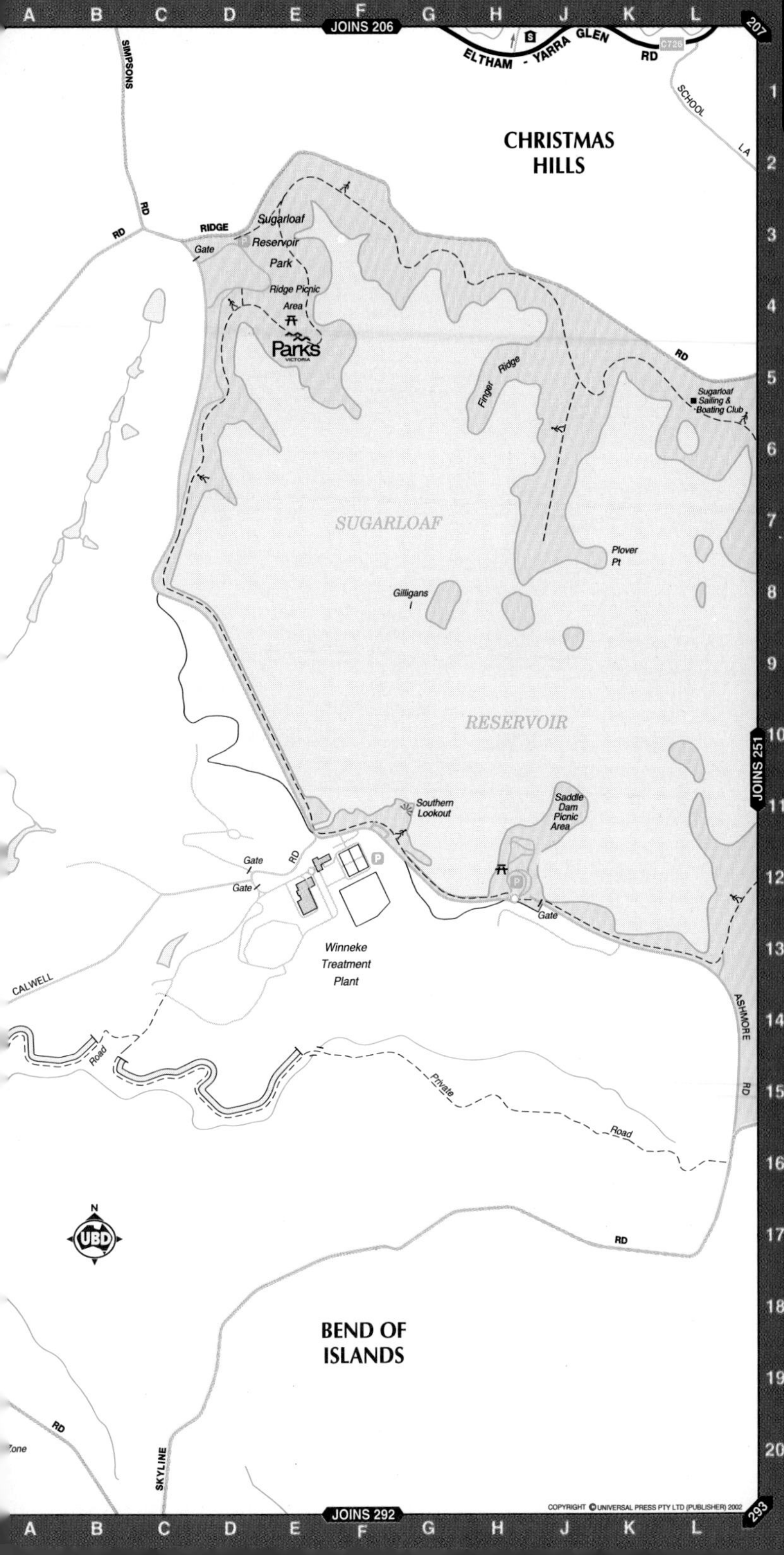

ELTHAM - YARRA GLEN RD
C726
SCHOOL LA
SIMPSONS RD
RIDGE RD
CHRISTMAS HILLS
Gate
Sugarloaf Reservoir Park
Ridge Picnic Area
Parks VICTORIA
Finger Ridge
RD
Sugarloaf Sailing & Boating Club
SUGARLOAF RESERVOIR
Plover Pt
Gilligans I
Southern Lookout
Saddle Dam Picnic Area
Gate
RD
Gate
Gate
Winneke Treatment Plant
CALWELL
Road
Private Road
ASHMORE RD
RD
N
UBD
BEND OF ISLANDS
RD
Zone
SKYLINE

206
JOINS 207

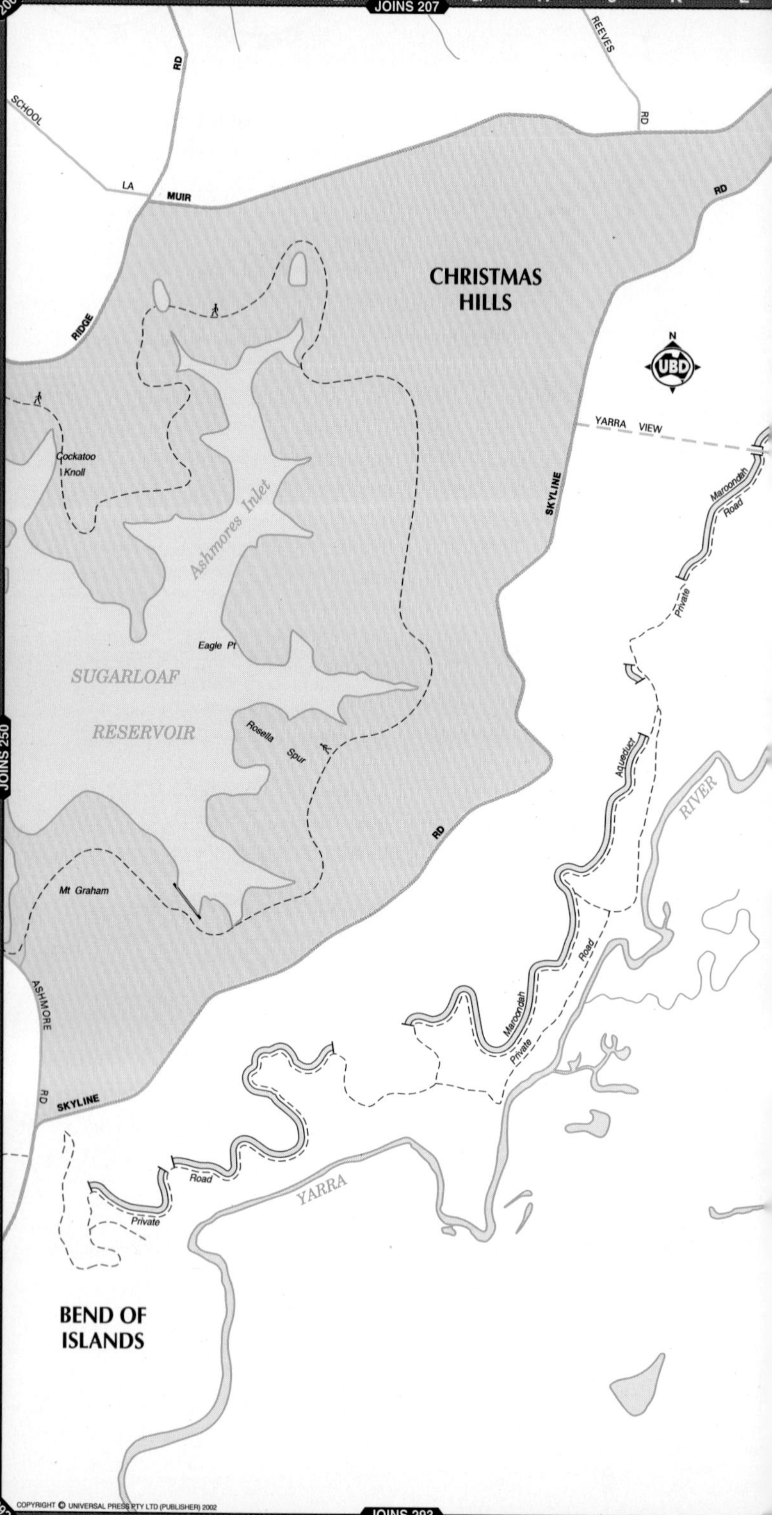

A B C D E F G H J K L

SCHOOL LA
RD
MUIR RD
REEVES RD
RIDGE

CHRISTMAS HILLS

N UBD

YARRA VIEW
SKYLINE
Maroondah Road
Private

Cockatoo Knoll
Ashmores Inlet
Eagle Pt
SUGARLOAF RESERVOIR
Rosella Spur
Aqueduct
RIVER
RD
Mt Graham
Maroondah Private Road
ASHMORE RD
SKYLINE
Road
Private
YARRA

BEND OF ISLANDS

1 2 3 4 5 6 7 8 9 10 11 12 13 14 15 16 17 18 19 20

JOINS 250

292
JOINS 293

A B C D E F G H J K L

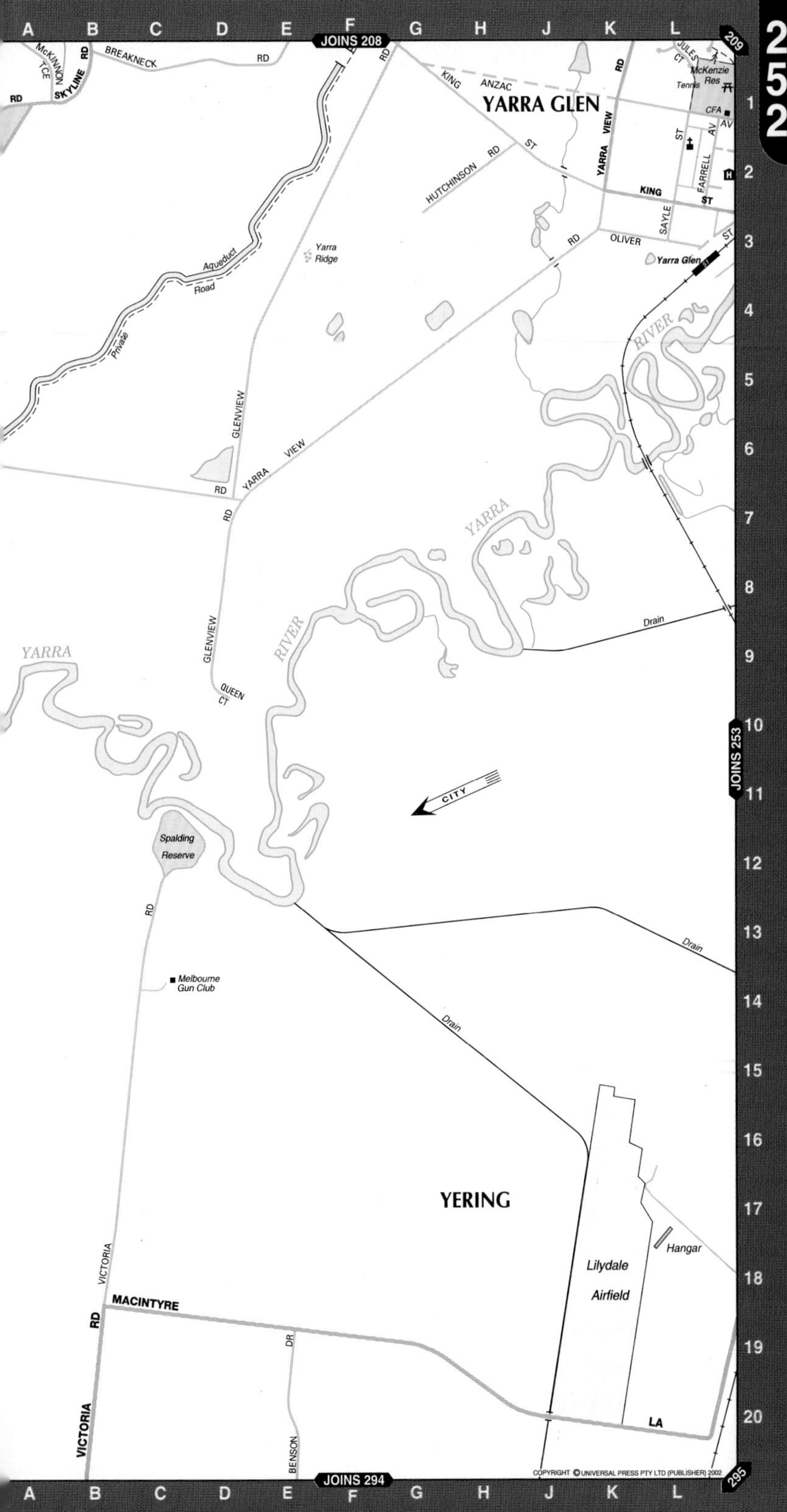
A B C D E F G H J K L
JOINS 208
209
BREAKNECK RD
McKINNON TCE
SKYLINE RD
KING ANZAC
YARRA GLEN
YARRA VIEW RD
JULES CT
McKenzie Res
Tennis
CFA
AV
ST
FARRELL
HUTCHINSON RD
KING ST
SAYLE
OLIVER
RD
Yarra Glen
Aqueduct Road
Private
Yarra Ridge
GLENVIEW
YARRA VIEW RD
RIVER
YARRA
Drain
YARRA
RIVER
GLENVIEW
QUEEN CT
CITY
Spalding Reserve
RD
Melbourne Gun Club
Drain
Drain
YERING
Hangar
Lilydale Airfield
VICTORIA RD
MACINTYRE
DR
LA
BENSON
VICTORIA
JOINS 253
JOINS 294
295
1 2 3 4 5 6 7 8 9 10 11 12 13 14 15 16 17 18 19 20

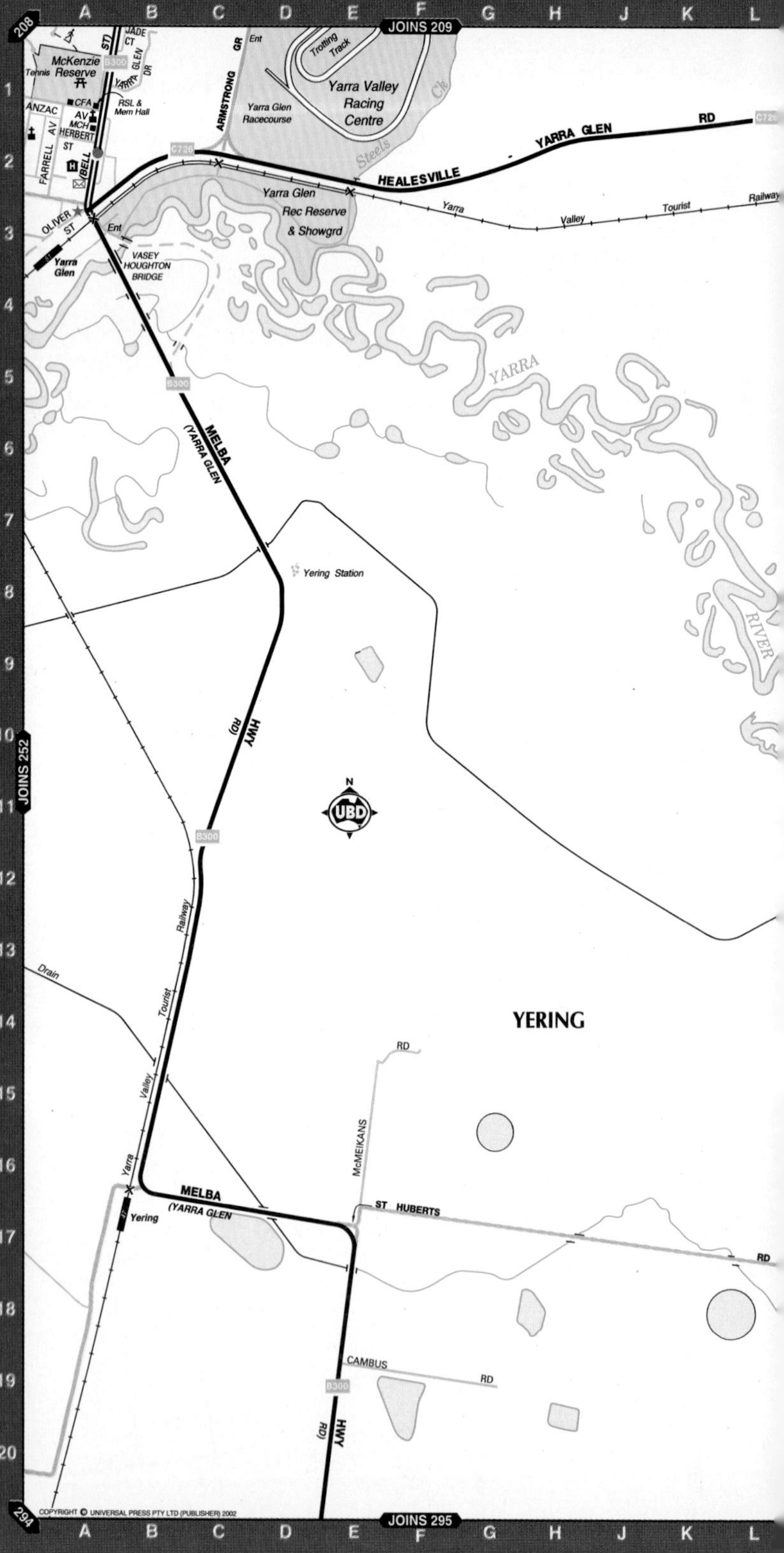

JOINS 209
JOINS 252
JOINS 295
208
294
McKenzie Reserve
Tennis
JADE CT
GLEN DR
YARRA GLEN
BELL ST
ANZAC AV
FARRELL AV
HERBERT ST
OLIVER ST
CFA
MCH
RSL & Mem Hall
ARMSTRONG GR
Ent
Trotting Track
Yarra Valley Racing Centre
Yarra Glen Racecourse
Steels Ck
HEALESVILLE - YARRA GLEN RD
Yarra Glen Rec Reserve & Showgrd
Yarra Valley Tourist Railway
Yarra Glen
VASEY HOUGHTON BRIDGE
YARRA RIVER
MELBA (YARRA GLEN RD) HWY
Yering Station
YERING
Drain
McMEIKANS RD
ST HUBERTS RD
Yering
CAMBUS RD
B300
C726

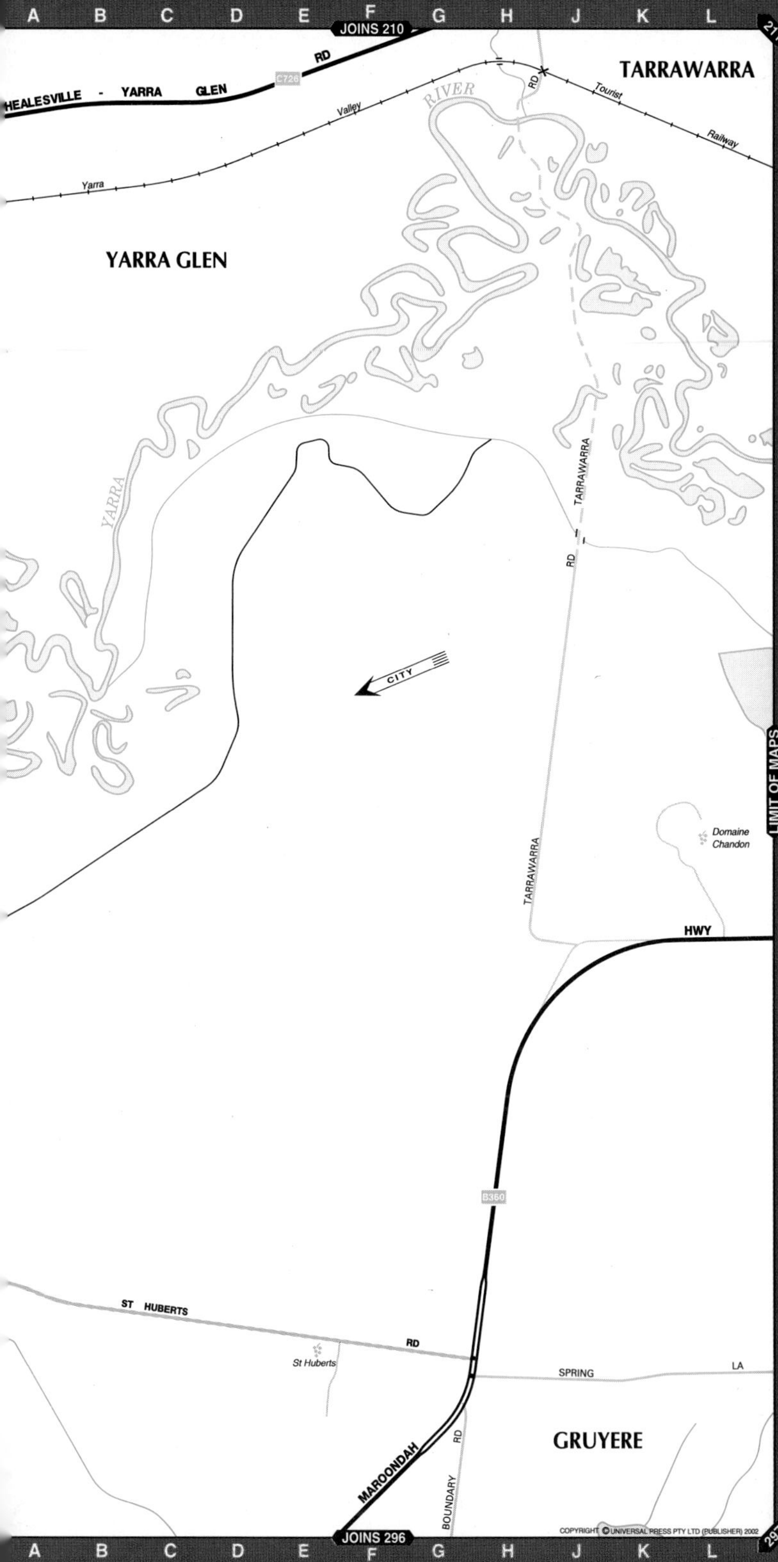

TARRAWARRA

HEALESVILLE - YARRA GLEN RD

C726

Yarra Valley Tourist Railway

RIVER

RD

YARRA GLEN

YARRA

TARRAWARRA RD

CITY

LIMIT OF MAPS

Domaine Chandon

TARRAWARRA

HWY

B360

ST HUBERTS RD

St Huberts

SPRING LA

GRUYERE

MAROONDAH

BOUNDARY RD

A B C D E F G H J K L
1 2 3 4 5 6 7 8 9 10 11 12 13 14 15 16 17 18 19 20
212
Watts R
WATTS RD
McGRETTONS
HUNTER ST
ARDILL ST
CRISP ST
RD
SMITH RD
RONDE CT
CONSTANCE CT
BONA AV
ST
RD
RYRIE ST
HARKER ST
B360
MAROONDAH HWY
GRANDVIEW CR
HIGH ST
Healesville Pmy
St Brigids
Cath Pmy
RD
HAIG AV
VIMY RDG
JOFFRE ST
CROWLEY RD
WALKER ST
PRINCE ST
EDWARD ST
STEPHENS RD
ROSELL CR
ORMOND ST
NEWGROVE
LALORS LA
POCKETT RD
POCKETT LA
GEORGE RD
Nurs Home
LALORS RD
BRUMFIELD RD
MARNA ST
Jeh Wit
AYRES
STEEL ST
HENRY ST
MAZEEPA ST
Yarra Valley Water Purification Plant
ARGOON RD
SES Depot
Vic Roads Depot
MT RIDDELL
AIRLIE RD
AIRLIE
HWY
MT RIDDELL RD
HEALESVILLE
HEALESVILLE - KOO WEE RUP
MAROONDAH
B360
LIMIT OF MAPS
ALBERT
LA
(DALRY RD)
Coranderrk Bushland
(Reserve fo
Worowa College
BARAK
YARRA
C411
Badger
TOOLEBEWONG
RIVER
GRUYERE
RD
PIN

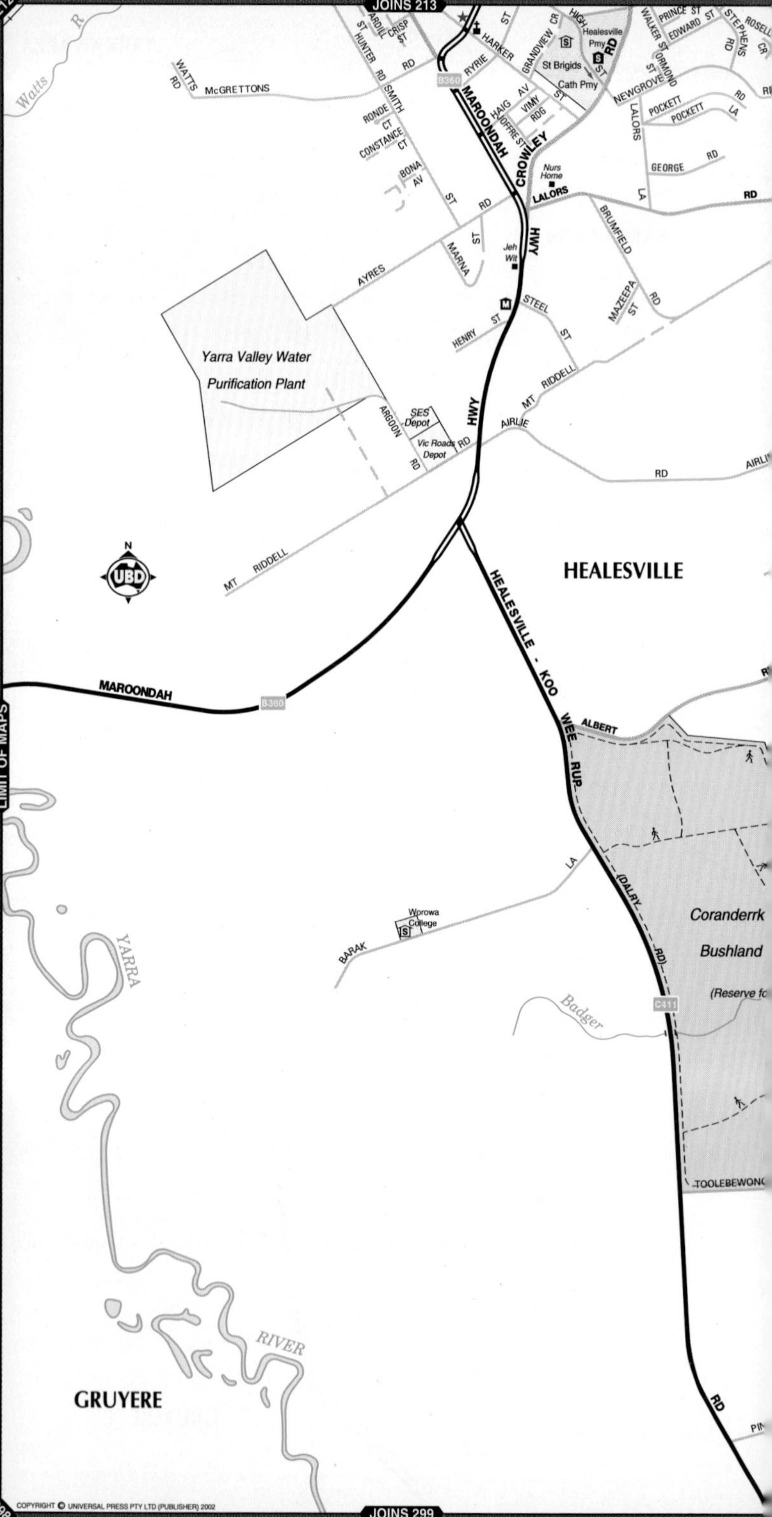

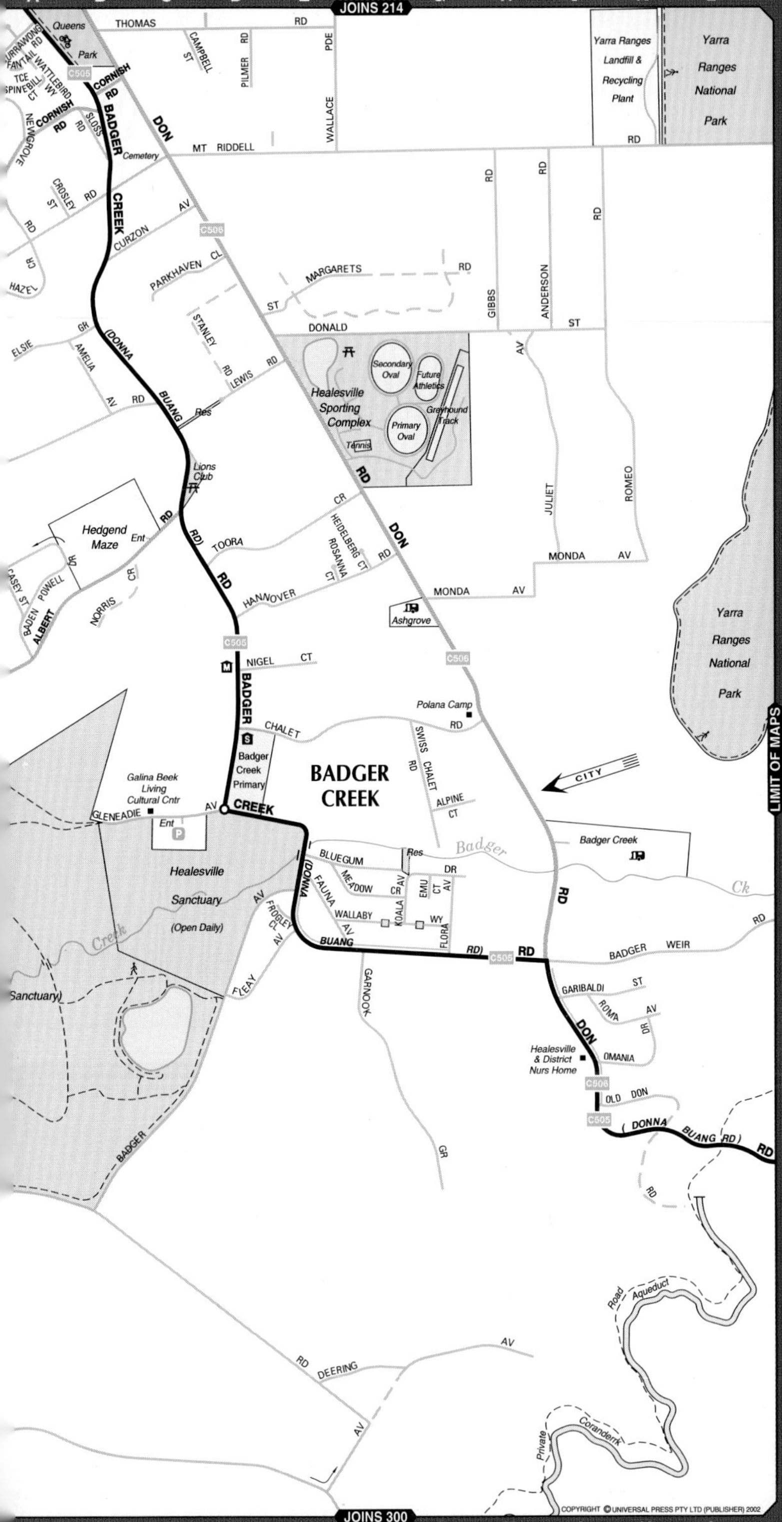

JOINS 214

MAP 263 FOLLOWS

JOINS 300

JOINS 221

PREVIOUS MAP 258

LIMIT OF MAPS

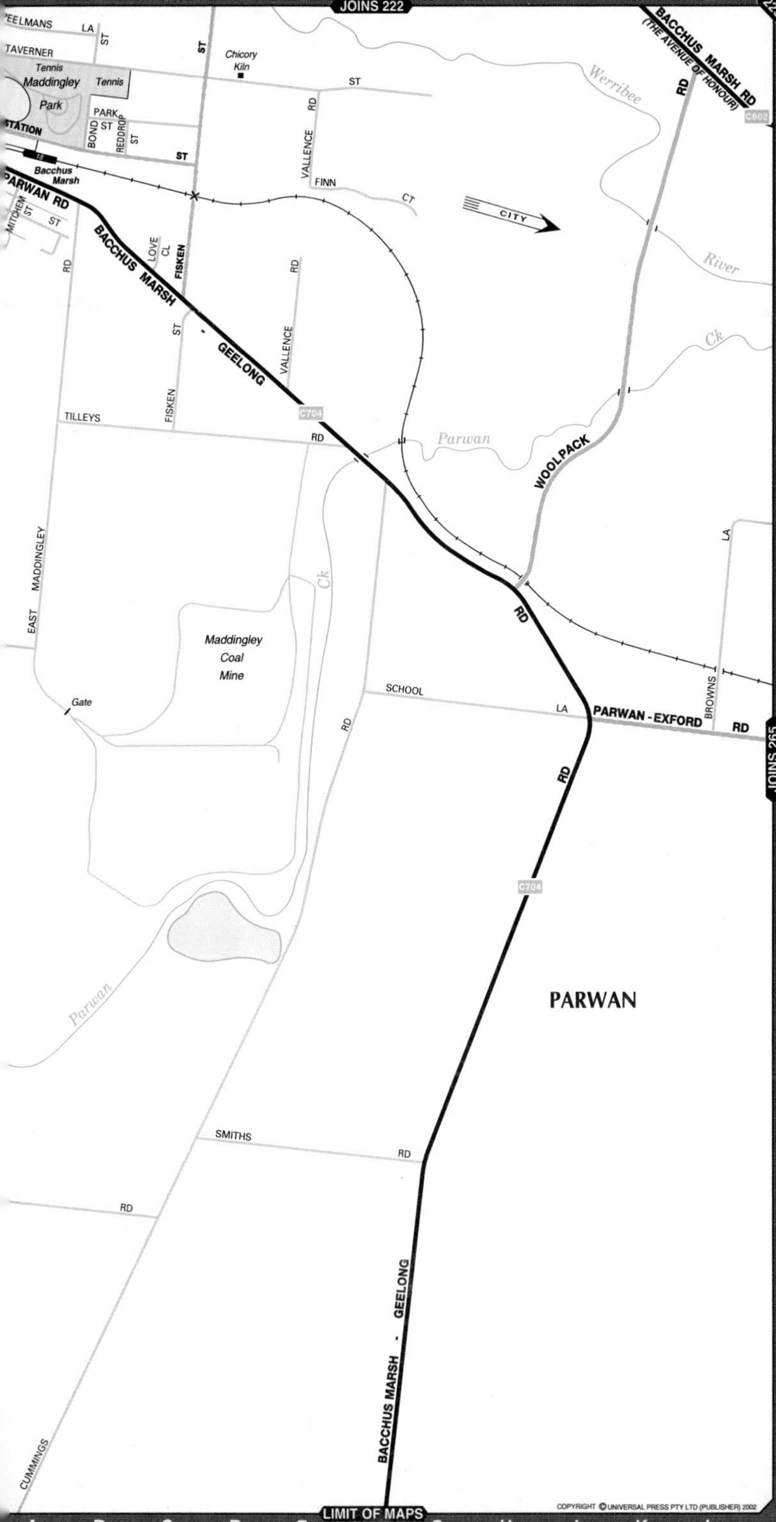

JOINS 222
223

PEELMANS LA
TAVERNER ST
Tennis
Maddingley Park
Tennis
PARK ST
BOND ST
REDDROP ST
STATION ST
Bacchus Marsh
PARWAN RD
MITCHEM ST
FISKEN ST
Chicory Kiln
ST
VALLENCE RD
FINN CT
CITY
Werribee River
BACCHUS MARSH RD (THE AVENUE OF HONOUR)
C602
RD
Ck
LOVE CL
BACCHUS MARSH - GEELONG RD
VALLENCE RD
TILLEYS RD
C704
Parwan
WOOLPACK RD
EAST MADDINGLEY RD
Ck
Maddingley Coal Mine
Gate
SCHOOL LA
RD
PARWAN - EXFORD RD
BROWNS LA
JOINS 265
C704
Parwan
PARWAN
SMITHS RD
RD
BACCHUS MARSH - GEELONG
CUMMINGS

LIMIT OF MAPS

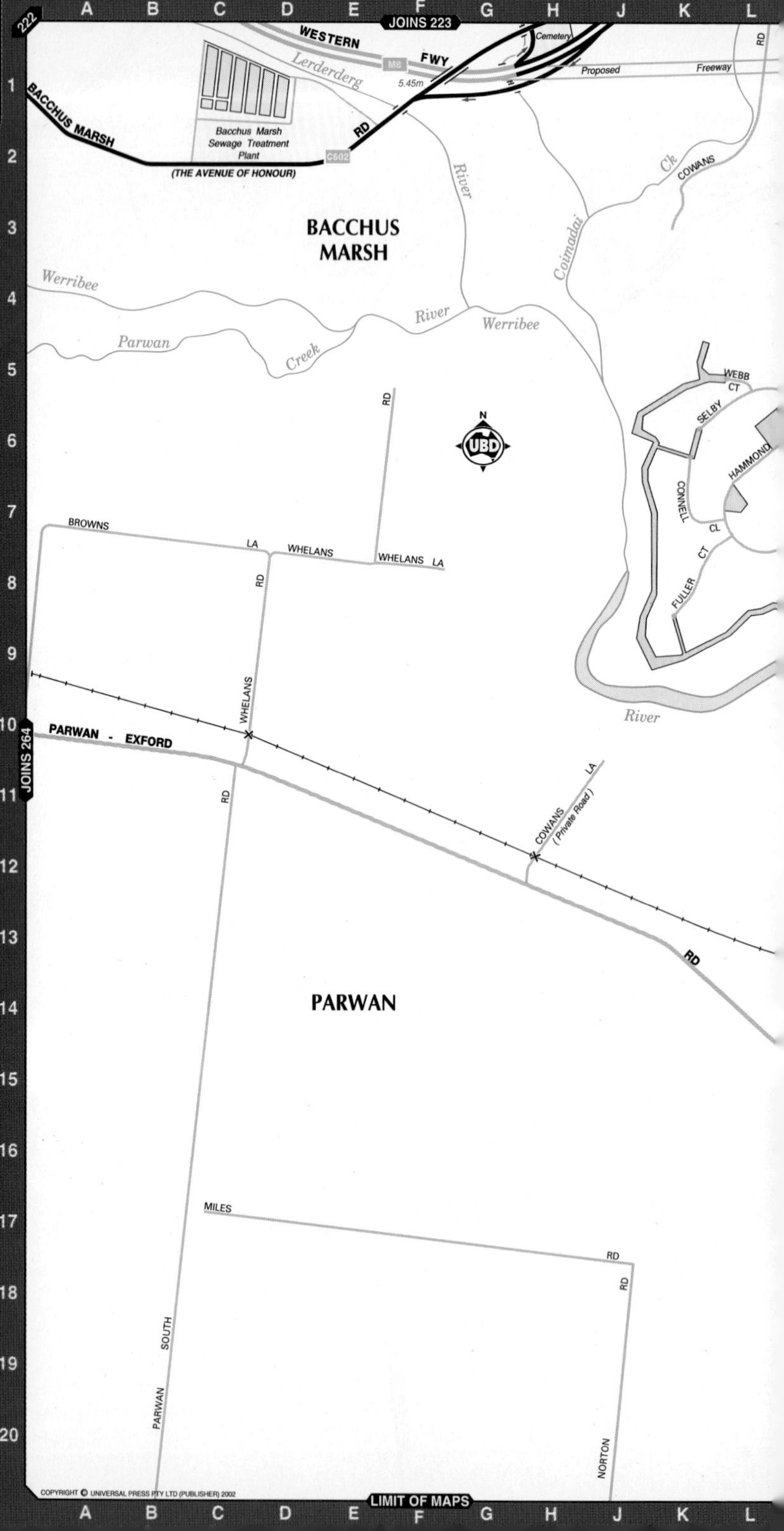

222
JOINS 223

A B C D E F G H J K L

1 2 3 4 5 6 7 8 9 10 11 12 13 14 15 16 17 18 19 20

WESTERN FWY
M8
5.45m
Cemetery
Proposed Freeway
RD
Lerderderg
River
BACCHUS MARSH RD
(THE AVENUE OF HONOUR)
C602
Bacchus Marsh Sewage Treatment Plant
Ck
COWANS
Coimadai
BACCHUS MARSH
Werribee
Parwan
Creek
River
Werribee
WEBB CT
SELBY
HAMMOND
CONNELL CL
FULLER CT
RD
N
UBD
BROWNS LA
WHELANS
WHELANS LA
RD
WHELANS
River
PARWAN - EXFORD RD
COWANS LA (Private Road)
RD
PARWAN
MILES RD
RD
PARWAN SOUTH
NORTON

JOINS 264

LIMIT OF MAPS

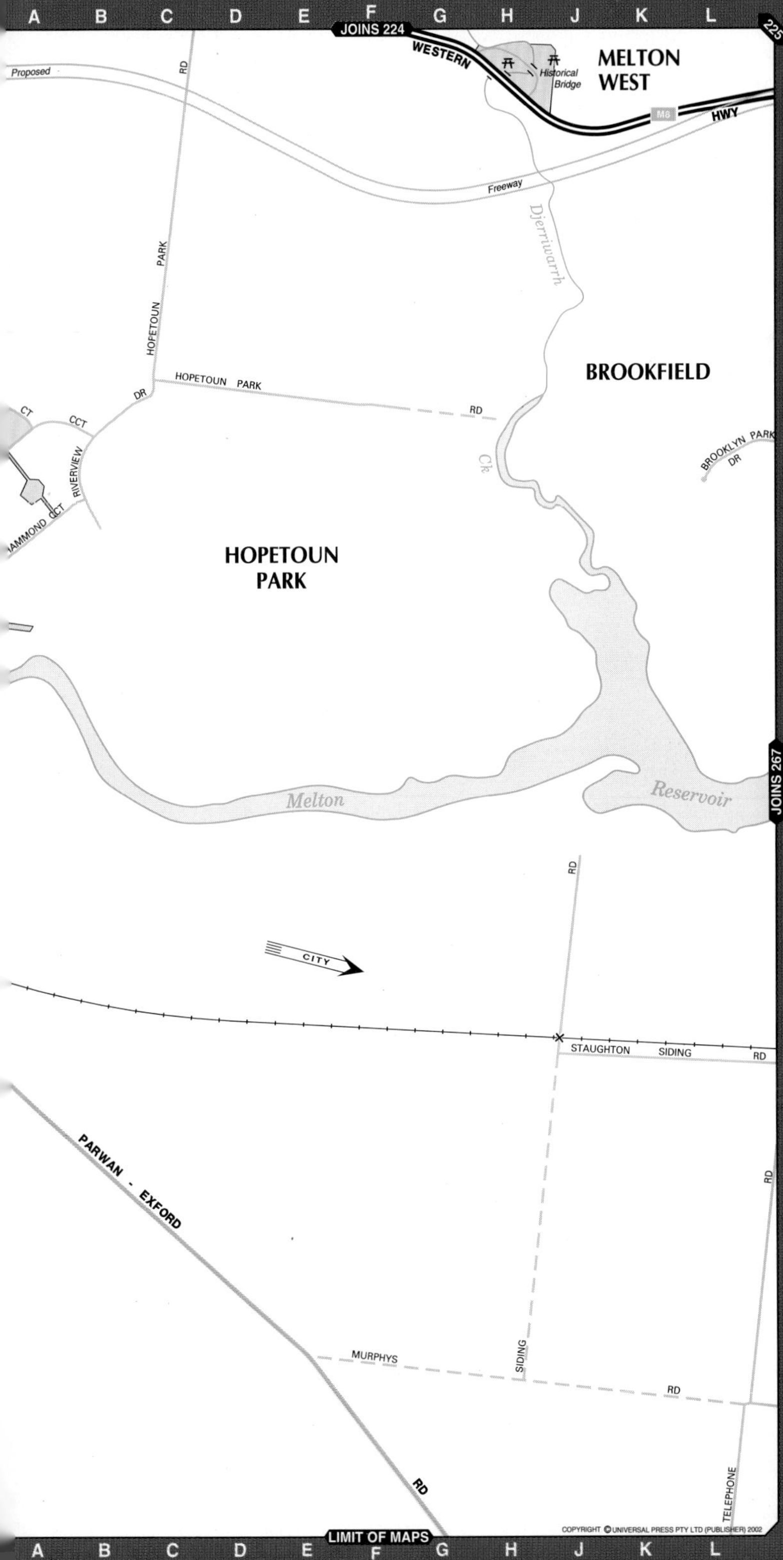
JOINS 224
225
WESTERN
HWY
M8
Historical Bridge
MELTON WEST
Proposed
Freeway
RD
HOPETOUN PARK
HOPETOUN PARK RD
DR
CT
CCT
RIVERVIEW
HAMMOND CCT
Djerriwarrh Ck
BROOKFIELD
BROOKLYN PARK DR
HOPETOUN PARK
Melton Reservoir
JOINS 267
RD
CITY
STAUGHTON SIDING RD
PARWAN - EXFORD RD
MURPHYS RD
SIDING
TELEPHONE
RD
LIMIT OF MAPS
A B C D E F G H J K L
1 2 3 4 5 6 7 8 9 10 11 12 13 14 15 16 17 18 19 20

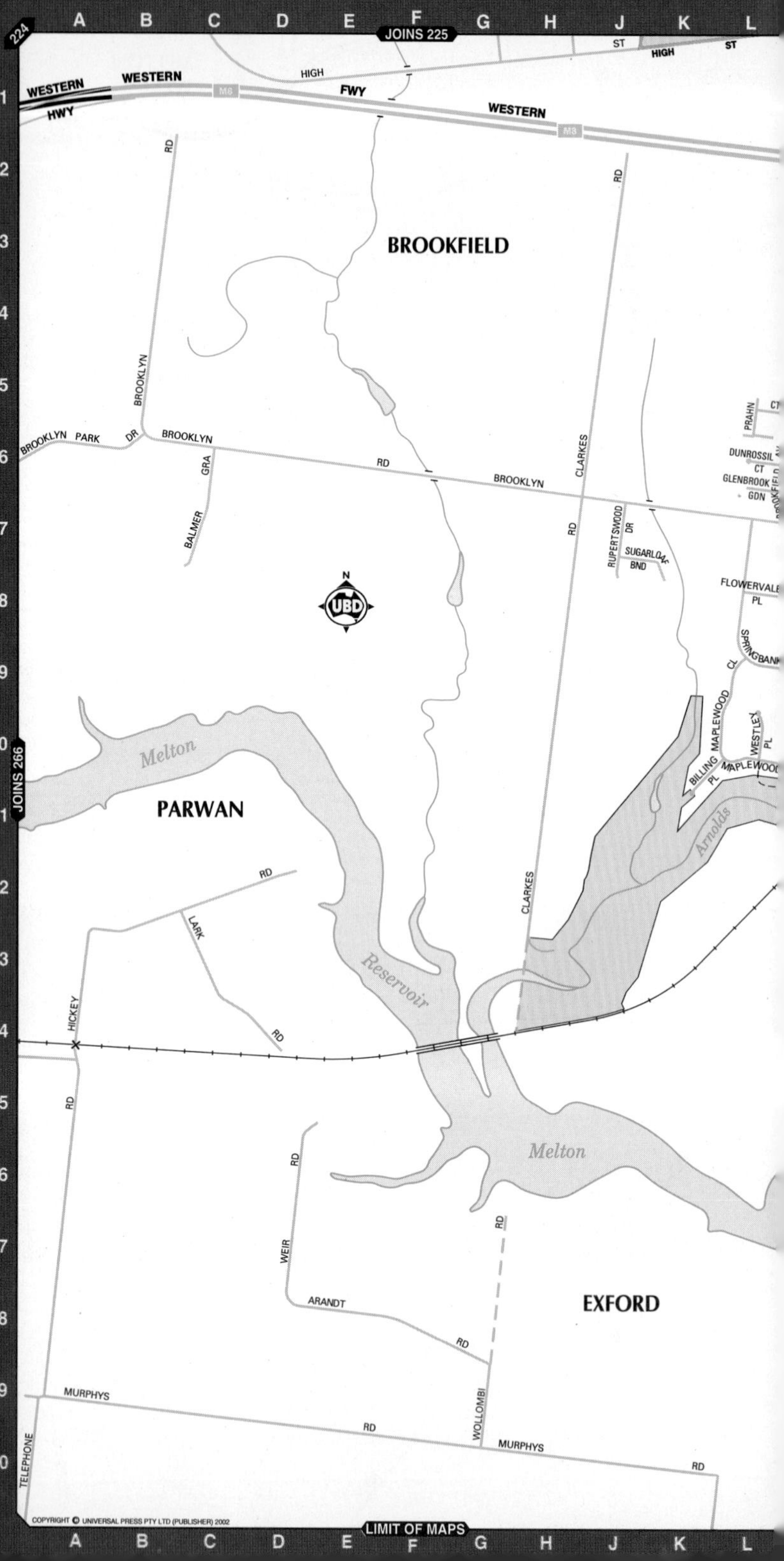

JOINS 225

JOINS 266

LIMIT OF MAPS

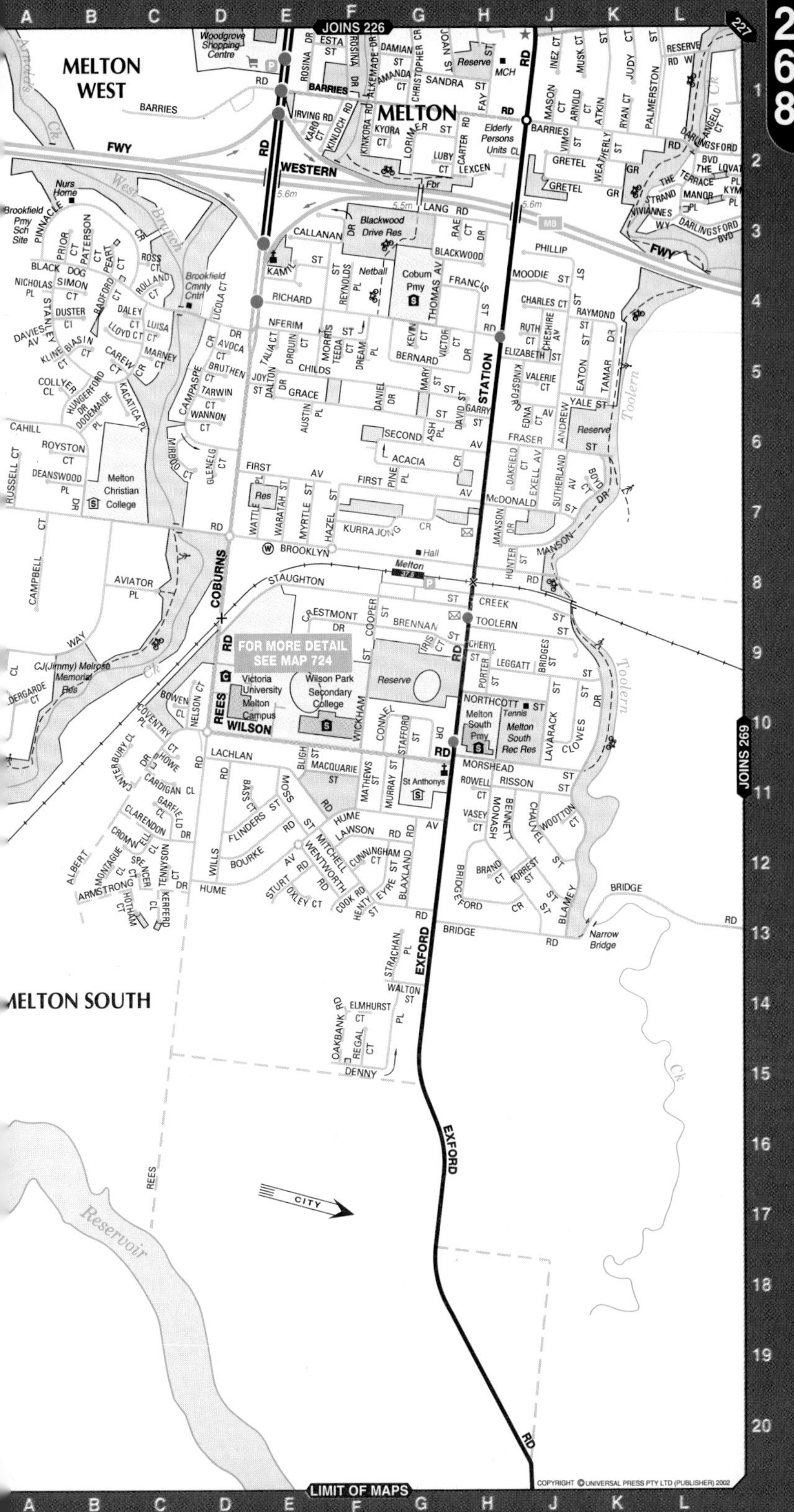
A B C D E F G H J K L
JOINS 226
227
MELTON WEST
MELTON
MELTON SOUTH
Woodgrove Shopping Centre
WESTERN FWY
COBURNS RD
STATION RD
EXFORD RD
REES RD
FOR MORE DETAIL SEE MAP 724
Victoria University Melton Campus
Wilson Park Secondary College
Melton Christian College
Cobum Pmy
Melton South Pmy
Melton South Rec Res
Blackwood Drive Res
CJ(Jimmy) Melrose Memorial Res
Brookfield Pmy Sch Site
Brookfield Cmnty Cntr
Elderly Persons Units
St Anthonys
Narrow Bridge
Toolern Ck
Reservoir
CITY
JOINS 269
LIMIT OF MAPS
1 2 3 4 5 6 7 8 9 10 11 12 13 14 15 16 17 18 19 20

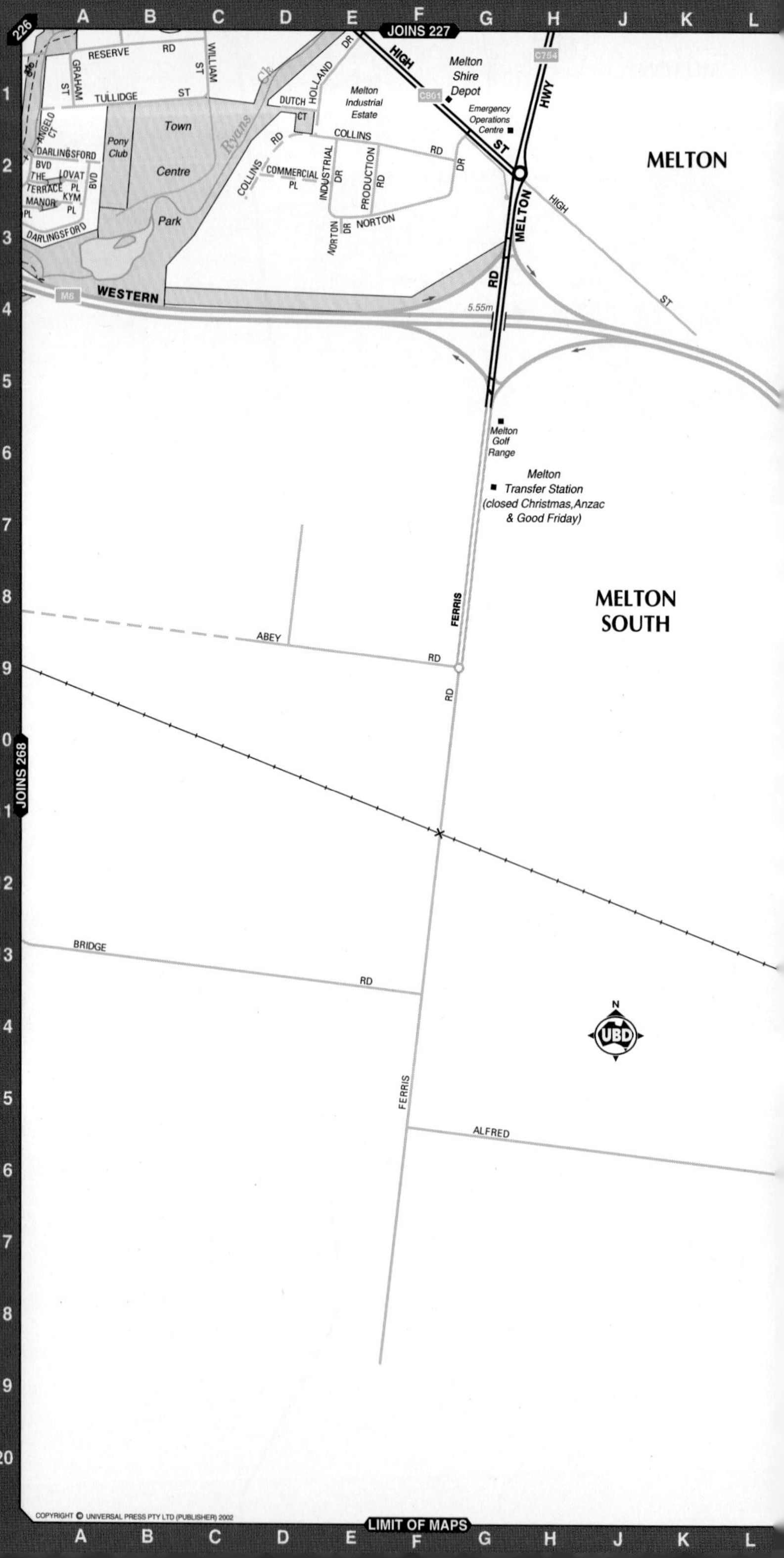

226
JOINS 227
JOINS 268
LIMIT OF MAPS

A B C D E F G H J K L

MELTON

MELTON SOUTH

Melton Shire Depot

Emergency Operations Centre

Melton Industrial Estate

Town Centre Park

Pony Club

Melton Golf Range

Melton Transfer Station (closed Christmas, Anzac & Good Friday)

RESERVE RD
GRAHAM ST
WILLIAM ST
TULLIDGE ST
ANGELO CT
DARLINGSFORD BVD
THE TERRACE
LOVAT PL
KYM PL
MANOR PL
DARLINGSFORD
BVD
Ryans Ck
DUTCH CT
HOLLAND DR
COLLINS RD
COLLINS RD
COMMERCIAL PL
INDUSTRIAL DR
PRODUCTION RD
NORTON DR
NORTON
DR
HIGH ST
HWY
C801
C754
M8
WESTERN
MELTON RD
HIGH ST
5.55m
FERRIS RD
ABEY RD
BRIDGE RD
FERRIS
ALFRED

N
UBD

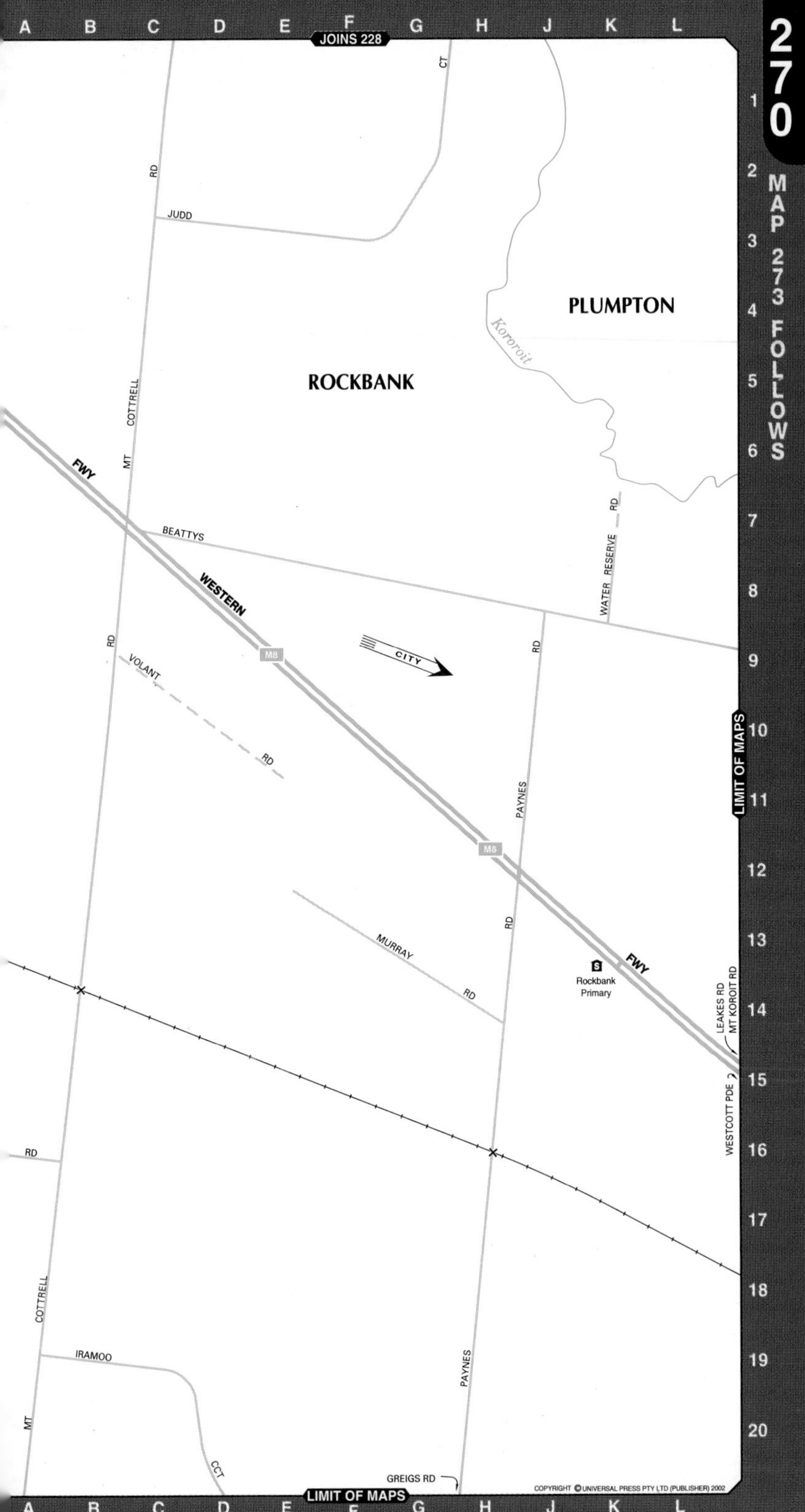
A B C D E F G H J K L
JOINS 228
1 2 3 4 5 6 7 8 9 10 11 12 13 14 15 16 17 18 19 20
MAP 273 FOLLOWS
CT
MT COTTRELL RD
JUDD
PLUMPTON
Kororoit
ROCKBANK
WESTERN FWY
M8
BEATTYS
WATER RESERVE RD
CITY
VOLANT RD
PAYNES RD
LIMIT OF MAPS
MURRAY RD
Rockbank Primary
LEAKES RD
MT KOROIT RD
WESTCOTT PDE
RD
MT COTTRELL
IRAMOO
CCT
GREIGS RD
LIMIT OF MAPS

PREVIOUS MAP 270

JOINS 231

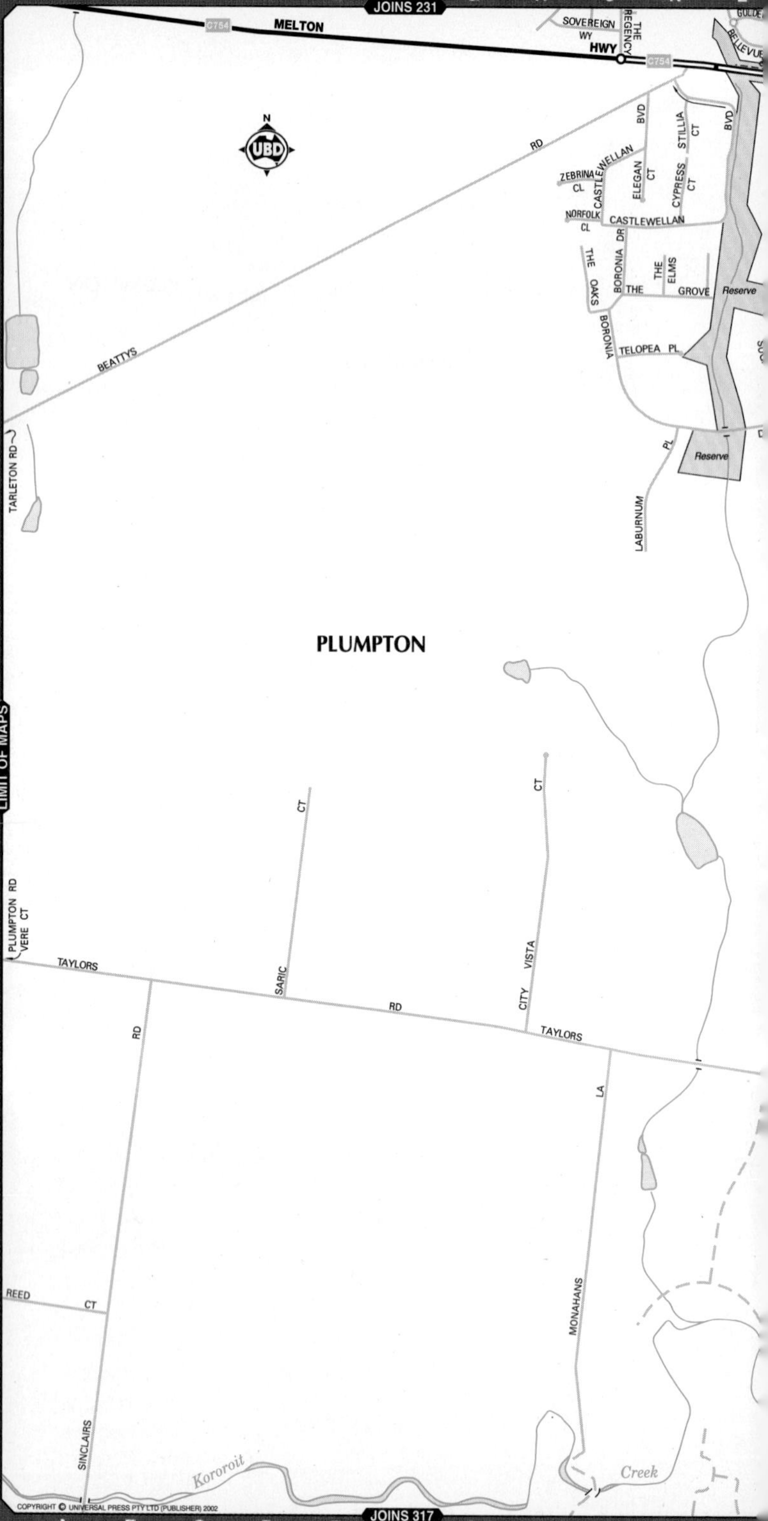

JOINS 317

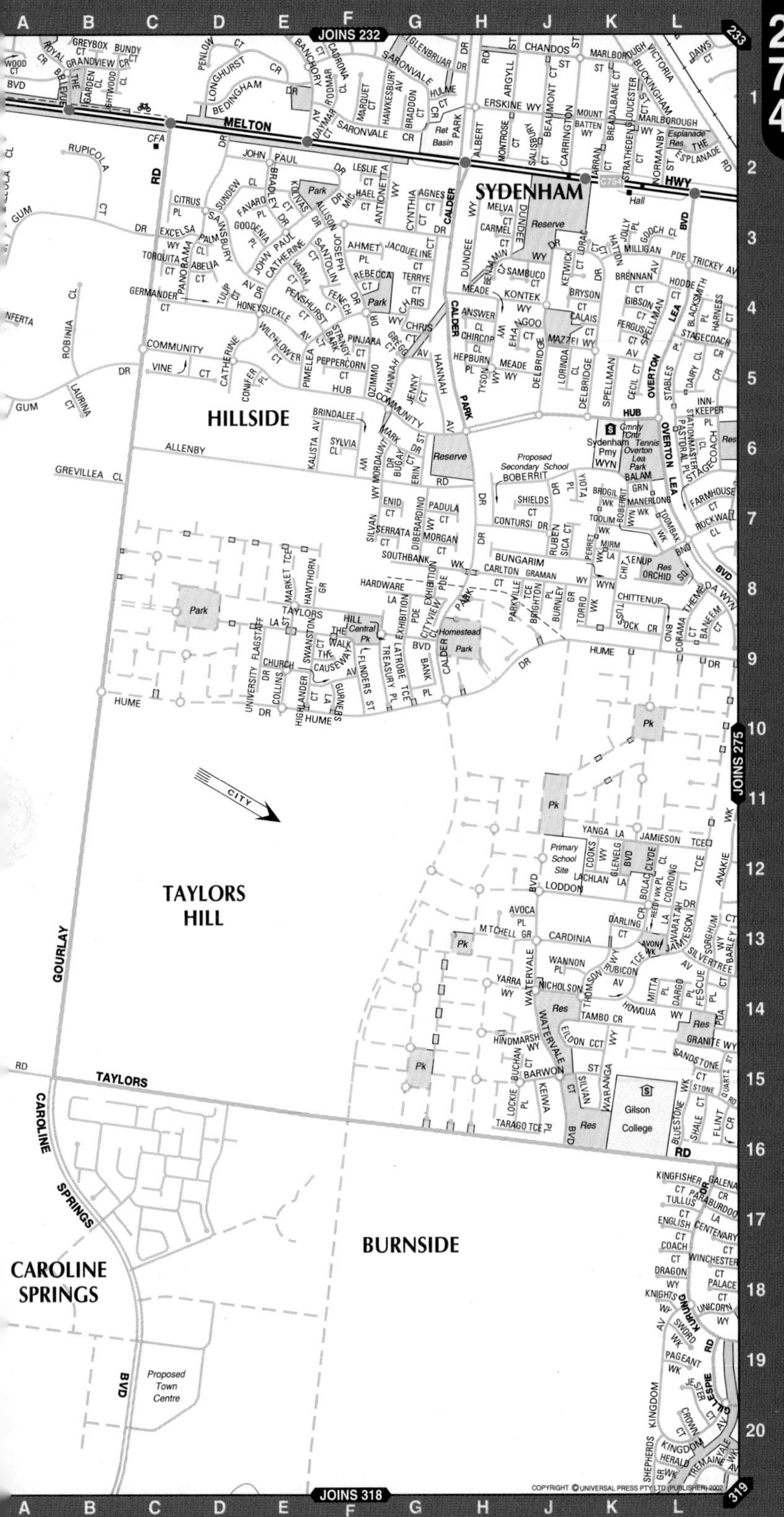
JOINS 232
233
SYDENHAM
HILLSIDE
TAYLORS HILL
BURNSIDE
CAROLINE SPRINGS
MELTON HWY
CALDER PARK DR
GOURLAY RD
TAYLORS RD
CAROLINE SPRINGS BVD
HUME DR
OVERTON LEA BVD
Proposed Secondary School
Primary School Site
Proposed Town Centre
Gilson College
Sydenham Pmy
Cmnty Cntr
Homestead Park
Central Pk
Reserve
CITY
JOINS 275
JOINS 318
319

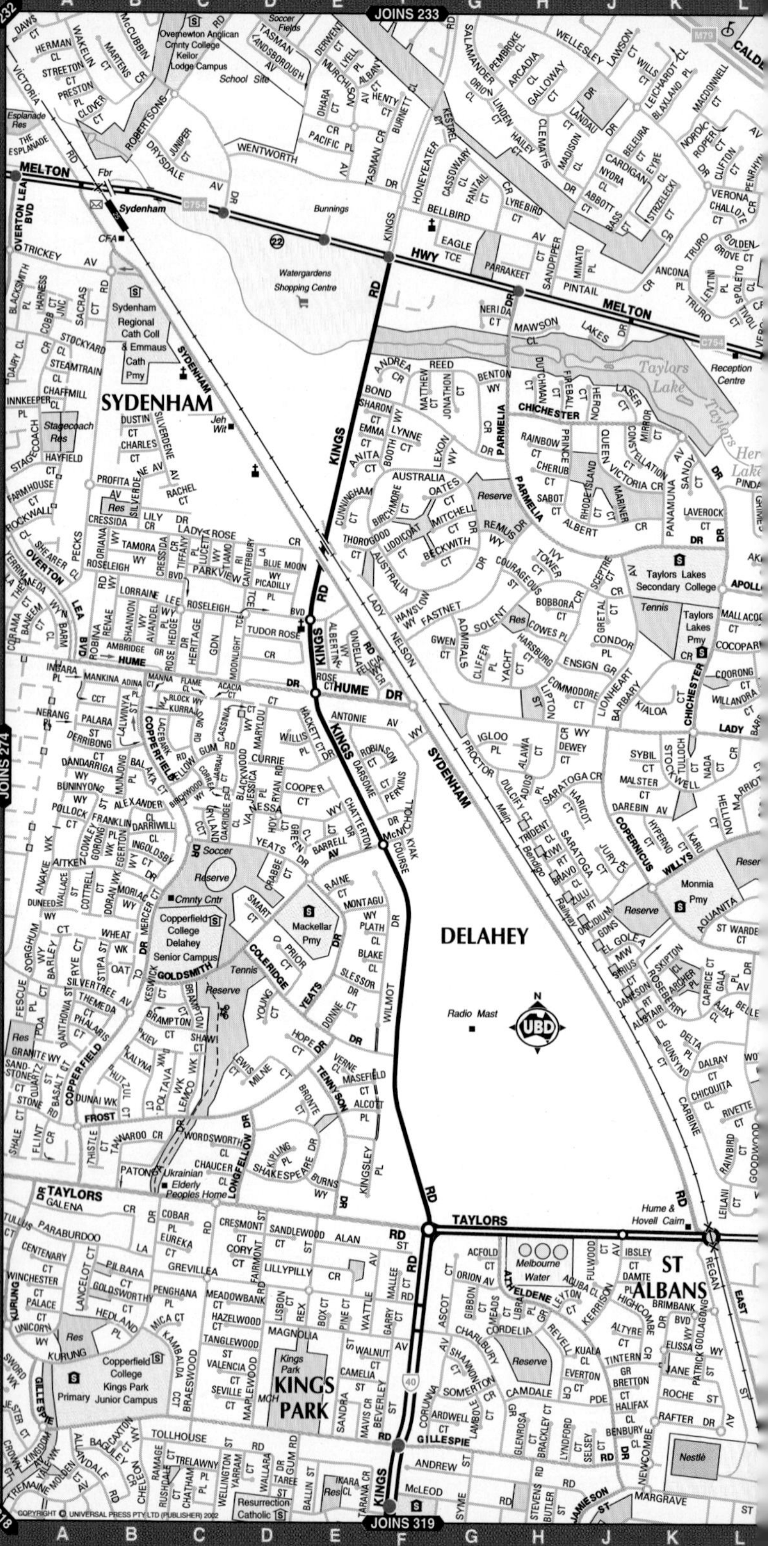

JOINS 233
JOINS 274
JOINS 319
232
318

A B C D E F G H J K L

SYDENHAM

DELAHEY

KINGS PARK

ST ALBANS

MELTON HWY

KINGS RD

SYDENHAM RD

HUME DR

TAYLORS RD

GILLESPIE RD

Watergardens Shopping Centre

Bunnings

Sydenham Regional Cath Coll & Emmaus Cath Pmy

Overnewton Anglican Cmnty College Keilor Lodge Campus

Taylors Lakes Secondary College

Taylors Lakes Pmy

Taylors Lake

Reception Centre

Copperfield College Delahey Senior Campus

Mackellar Pmy

Monmia Pmy

Copperfield College Kings Park Junior Campus

Resurrection Catholic

Ukrainian Elderly Peoples Home

Hume & Hovell Cairn

Melbourne Water

Nestlé

Radio Mast

Cmnty Cntr

Soccer Reserve

Stagecoach Res

Esplanade Res

JOINS 234

235

A B C D E F G H J K L

1 2 3 4 5 6 7 8 9 10 11 12 13 14 15 16 17 18 19 20

CITY

KEILOR NORTH

KEILOR LODGE

KEILOR

TAYLORS LAKES

KEILOR DOWNS

KEALBA

St Albans East

Maribyrnong River

CALDER FWY M79

SUNSHINE AV

CALDER HWY

OLD CALDER HWY

GREEN GULLY RD

ST ALBANS RD

SUNSHINE HWY

AGONIS DR

KIUNA RD

OAKBANK

HIGHLAND

McNABS

ARUNDEL RD

Keilor North Cath Regional College

Lakeside Village

Leisure Centre

Tennis

Keilor Retirement Village

Child Care Cntr

Kingfisher Lake

Spoonbill Lake

Overnewton Receptions

Lowther Hall

Keilor Grammar

Anglican Grammar Sports Complex

Overnewton Anglican Community College

St Augustines Cath

Mary Mackillop Pmy

Retirement Home

Keilor Downs Secondary College

Keilor Downs Pmy

Calder Rise Neighbourhood Park

Green Gully Reserve

Taylors Creek

Rugby

Pavilion

Soccer

Tennis

Basketball

Traffic Safety Cntr

Clubhouse

MACRAE BVD

Nurs Home

St Albans Leisure Pool Centre

Keilor Downs Plaza

Res

MCH

St Albans North Pmy

Churchill Reserve

Kealba Secondary College

St Pauls Kealba Pmy

5.5m

5.7m

JOINS 277

JOINS 320

321

JOINS 235

A B C D E F G H J K L

MELBOURNE AIRPORT

KEILOR

KEILOR PARK

KEALBA

Tullamarine Country Club

Quarry

Radio Mast

International Basketball Centre

Council Depot

Keilor Engineering Services Centre

Athletics Club

Keilor Park Recreation Reserve

Keilor Primary

Keilor Res

Caroline Chisholm Park

Lagoon Res

Calder Rise Pmy

Bonfield Reserve

Gumms Corner

Visitors Centre

Purification Plant

Brimbank Park

Maribyrnong Valley Parklands

Horseshoe Bend Farm

Field Centre

Prop Cem Extension

Keilor Cemetery

Solaris Power Terminal Station

ARUNDEL RD

BROWNS RD

ANNANDALE RD

MILBURN RD

CALDER FWY

OLD CALDER HWY

KEILOR PARK DR

FULLARTON RD

WESTERN RING RD

MACEDON ST

GREEN GULLY RD

ST ALBANS RD

JOINS 276

JOINS 321

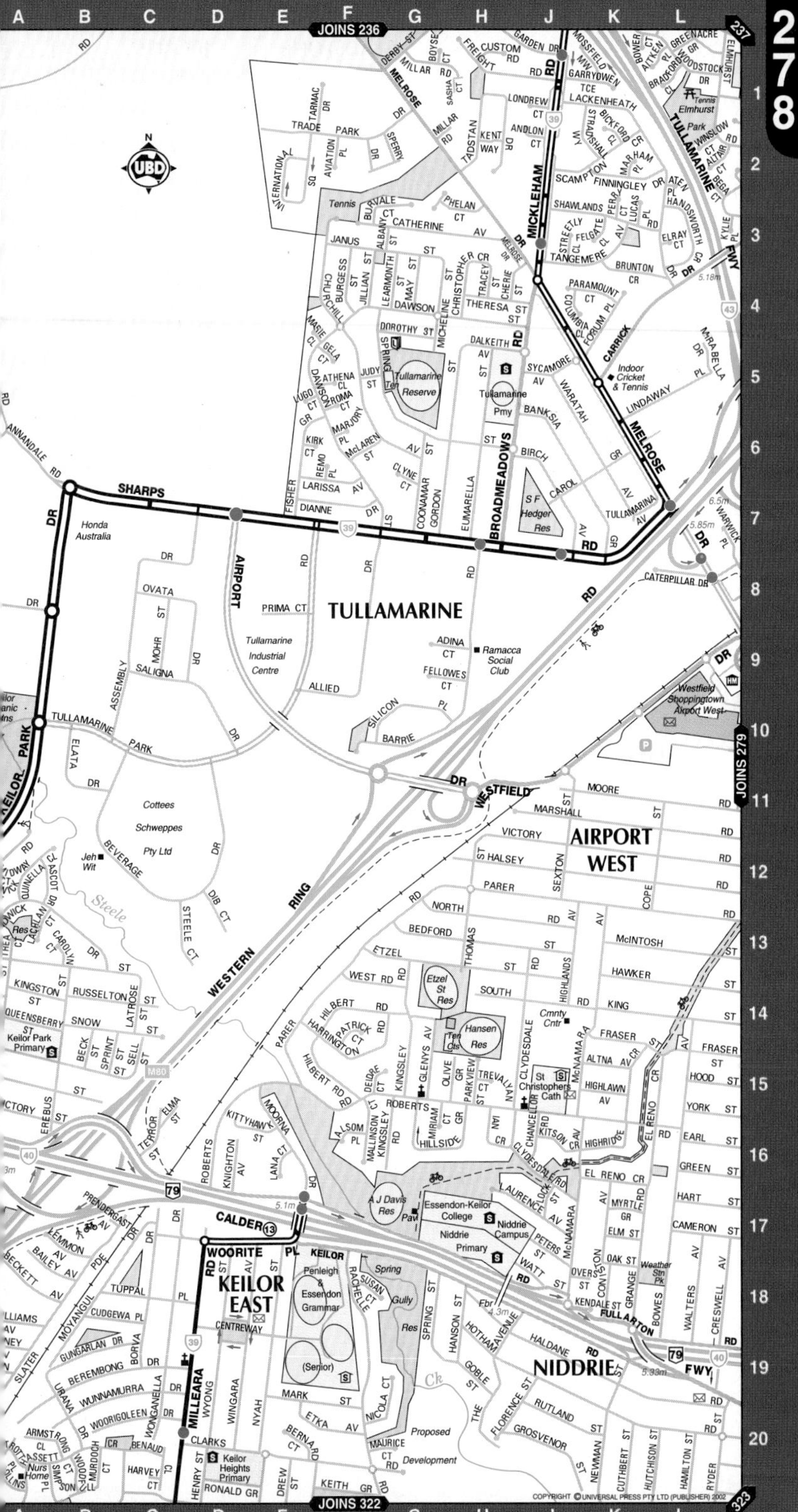
A B C D E F G H J K L
JOINS 236
237
JOINS 279
JOINS 322
323
1 2 3 4 5 6 7 8 9 10 11 12 13 14 15 16 17 18 19 20
UBD
N
TULLAMARINE
AIRPORT WEST
KEILOR EAST
NIDDRIE
SHARPS RD
AIRPORT DR
MICKLEHAM RD
MELROSE DR
BROADMEADOWS RD
WESTERN RING RD
TULLAMARINE FWY
CALDER FWY
FULLARTON RD
MILLEARA RD
KEILOR PARK DR
TULLAMARINE PARK DR
WESTFIELD DR
CATERPILLAR DR
ANNANDALE RD
GARDEN DR
CUSTOM RD
FREIGHT RD
DERBY ST
BOYSE CT
MILLAR RD
SASHA CT
LONDREW CT
ANDLON CT
TADSTAN DR
KENT WAY
TARMAC DR
TRADE PARK DR
AVIATION PL
SPERRY DR
INTERNATIONAL SQ
MOSSFIELD MW
GARRYOWEN TCE
LACKENHEATH
BICKFORD CL
STRADSHALL WY
MARHAM PL
SCAMPTON
FINNINGLEY DR
SHAWLANDS
PERRY CT
LUCAS PL
STREETLY ST
FELGATE CL
TANGEMERE CL
BRUNTON CR
ELRAY CT
HANDSWORTH CR
ATEN PL
BOWER CT
AITKEN PL
GREENACRE
WOODSTOCK DR
BRADFORD CL
ELMHURST
Tennis
Elmhurst Park
WINSLOW RD
ALTAIR CT
BEGA CT
KYLIE PL
BURVALE CT
PHELAN CT
CATHERINE AV
JANUS ST
ALBANY CT
CHURCHILL
BURGESS ST
JILLIAN ST
LEARMONTH ST
MAY ST
DAWSON ST
CHRISTOPHER CR
TRACEY ST
CHERIE ST
THERESA ST
MICHELINE ST
DOROTHY ST
DALKEITH AV
PARAMOUNT CT
COLUMBIA CL
FORUM PL
CARRICK
Indoor Cricket & Tennis
MIRABELLA DR
LINDAWAY
SYCAMORE AV
WARATAH
BANKSIA
BIRCH
CAROL GR
TULLAMARINA AV
MARIE CL
GELA CT
ATHENA CL
ROMA CT
JUDY ST
SPRING ST
Tullamarine Reserve
Tullamarine Pmy
LUGO CT
MARJORY PL
McLAREN ST
KIRK CT
REMO PL
LARISSA AV
CLYNE CT
DIANNE
FISHER
COONAMAR
GORDON
EUMARELLA
S F Hedger Res
WARWICK DR
Honda Australia
PRIMA CT
Tullamarine Industrial Centre
OVATA
MOHR ST
SALIGNA
ASSEMBLY
ALLIED
ADINA CT
FELLOWES CT
Ramacca Social Club
SILICON PL
BARRIE
Westfield Shoppingtown Airport West
ELATA
Cottees Schweppes Pty Ltd
BEVERAGE
Jeh Wit
DIB CT
STEELE CT
Steele
MOORE
MARSHALL
VICTORY
HALSEY
SEXTON
PARER
NORTH
COPE
BEDFORD
McINTOSH
ETZEL
HAWKER
WEST RD
SOUTH
KING
THOMAS
HIGHLANDS
Etzel St Res
Hansen Res
Cmnty Cntr
FRASER
ALTNA CR
McNAMARA
HILBERT RD
HARRINGTON
PATRICK CT
GLENYS AV
KINGSLEY
DEIDRE CT
OLIVE GR
PARKVIEW
TREVALYAN
CLYDESDALE
St Christophers Cath
HIGHLAWN AV
HOOD
YORK
EL RENO CR
HIGHRIDGE
ROBERTS
MIRIAM CT
HILLSIDE
IAN CR
CHANCELLOR RD
KITSON CR
EARL
GREEN
HART
CAMERON
MALLINSON CT
ALSOM PL
KITTYHAWK ST
MOORNA
KNIGHTON AV
LANA CT
A J Davis Res
Essendon-Keilor College
Niddrie Campus
Niddrie Primary
LAURENCE AV
PETERS
WATT
LOCK ST
MYRTLE RD
ELM ST
OAK ST
CONISTON
GRANGE
BOWES
WALTERS
CRESWELL
Weather Stn Pk
OVERS ST
KENDALE ST
HALDANE RD
HOTHAM AVENUE
HANSON ST
GOBLE ST
FLORENCE ST
RUTLAND
GROSVENOR
NEWMAN
CUTHBERT ST
HUTCHISON ST
HAMILTON ST
RYDER
KINGSTON
RUSSELTON
QUEENSBERRY
SNOW
LATROSE
Keilor Park Primary
BECK ST
SPRINT ST
SELL ST
EREBUS
TERROR ST
ELMA
PRENDERGAST AV
LEMMON AV
BAILEY AV
BECKETT
TUPPAL
MOYANGUL PDE
CUDGEWA PL
GUNGARLAN DR
BEREMBONG DR
WUNNAMURRA DR
WOORIGOLEEN DR
WONGANELLA
BORVA
URANA DR
SLATER
ARMSTRONG
WOODS
MURDOCH CT
BENAUD
HARVEY CT
CROTTA
SSETT
Nurs Home
SIMPSON
WOORITE PL
KEILOR
Penleigh & Essendon Grammar
(Senior)
Spring Gully Res
SUSAN CT
RACHELLE
CENTREWAY
WYONG
WINGARA
NYAH
MARK ST
ETKA AV
BERNARD CT
NICOLA CT
MAURICE CT
Proposed Development
CLARKS
HENRY ST
Keilor Heights Primary
RONALD GR
DREW ST
KEITH GR
Ck
QUINELLA
ASCOT DR
LACHLAN
CAROLYN
Res
5.1m
4.3m
5.33m
5.18m
6.5m
5.85m
Fbr
39
40
43
79
M80
13

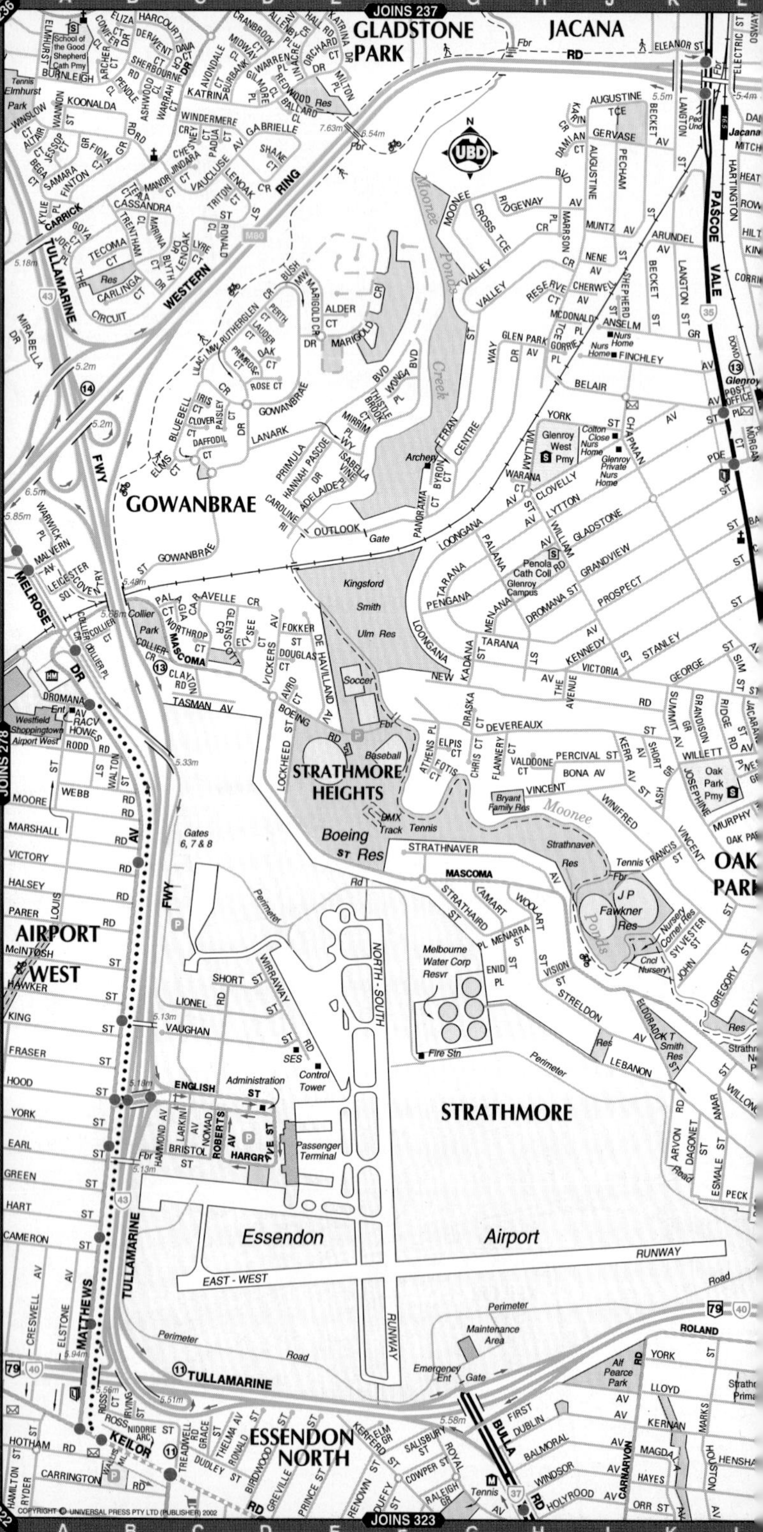

A B C D E F G H J K L

236

JOINS 237

GLADSTONE PARK

JACANA

GOWANBRAE

STRATHMORE HEIGHTS

AIRPORT WEST

STRATHMORE

ESSENDON NORTH

OAK PARK

Glenroy

Elmhurst Park
School of the Good Shepherd Cath Pmy
Redwood Res
Jacana
Moonee Ponds Creek
Archery
Glenroy West Pmy
Colton Close Nurs Home
Glenroy Private Nurs Home
Nurs Home
Glenroy Post Office
Penola Cath Coll Glenroy Campus
Kingsford Smith Ulm Res
Collier Park
Soccer
Baseball
BMX Track
Tennis
Boeing St Res
Bryant Family Res
Strathnaver Res
J P Fawkner Res
Nursery Corner Res
Cncl Nursery
Oak Park Pmy
Melbourne Water Corp Resvr
Fire Stn
K T Smith Res
Westfield Shoppingtown Airport West
RACV
Gates 6, 7 & 8
SES
Control Tower
Administration
Passenger Terminal
Essendon Airport
Maintenance Area
Emergency Ent
Gate
Alf Pearce Park
WESTERN RING
TULLAMARINE FWY
M80
DROMANA AV
MATTHEWS AV
KEILOR RD
BULLA RD
PASCOE VALE RD
MELROSE DR
ROLAND
RUNWAY
EAST - WEST
NORTH - SOUTH
Perimeter Road

1 2 3 4 5 6 7 8 9 10 11 12 13 14 15 16 17 18 19 20

JOINS 278

322

JOINS 323

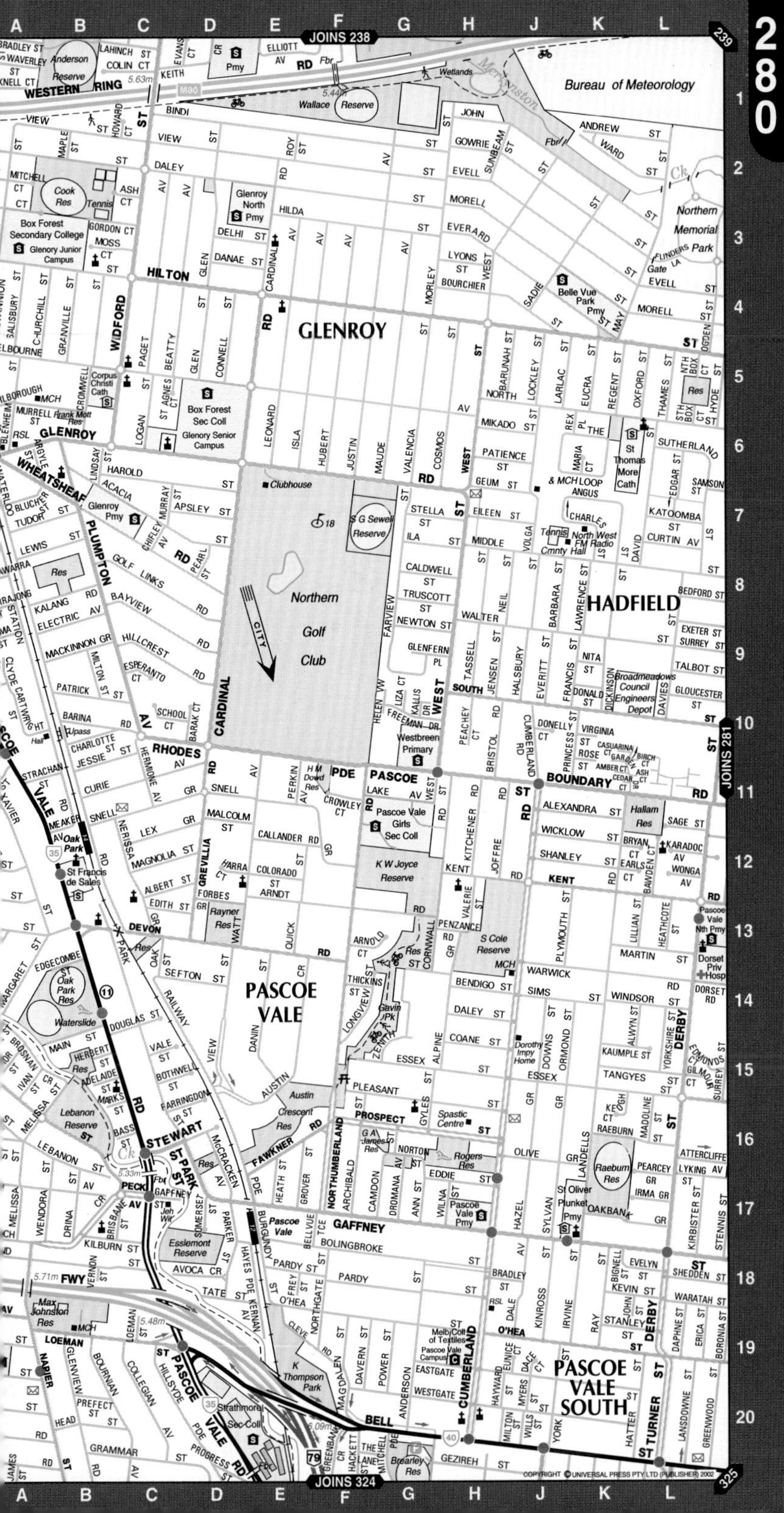
JOINS 238
239
Bureau of Meteorology
GLENROY
HADFIELD
Northern Golf Club
PASCOE VALE
PASCOE VALE SOUTH
Northern Memorial Park
Box Forest Secondary College
Glenroy Junior Campus
Box Forest Sec Coll
Glenroy Senior Campus
Pascoe Vale Girls Sec Coll
K W Joyce Reserve
S Cole Reserve
Raeburn Res
Esslemont Reserve
Strathmore Sec Coll
Westbreen Primary
Broadmeadows Council Engineers Depot
JOINS 281
JOINS 324
325
COPYRIGHT © UNIVERSAL PRESS PTY LTD (PUBLISHER) 2002

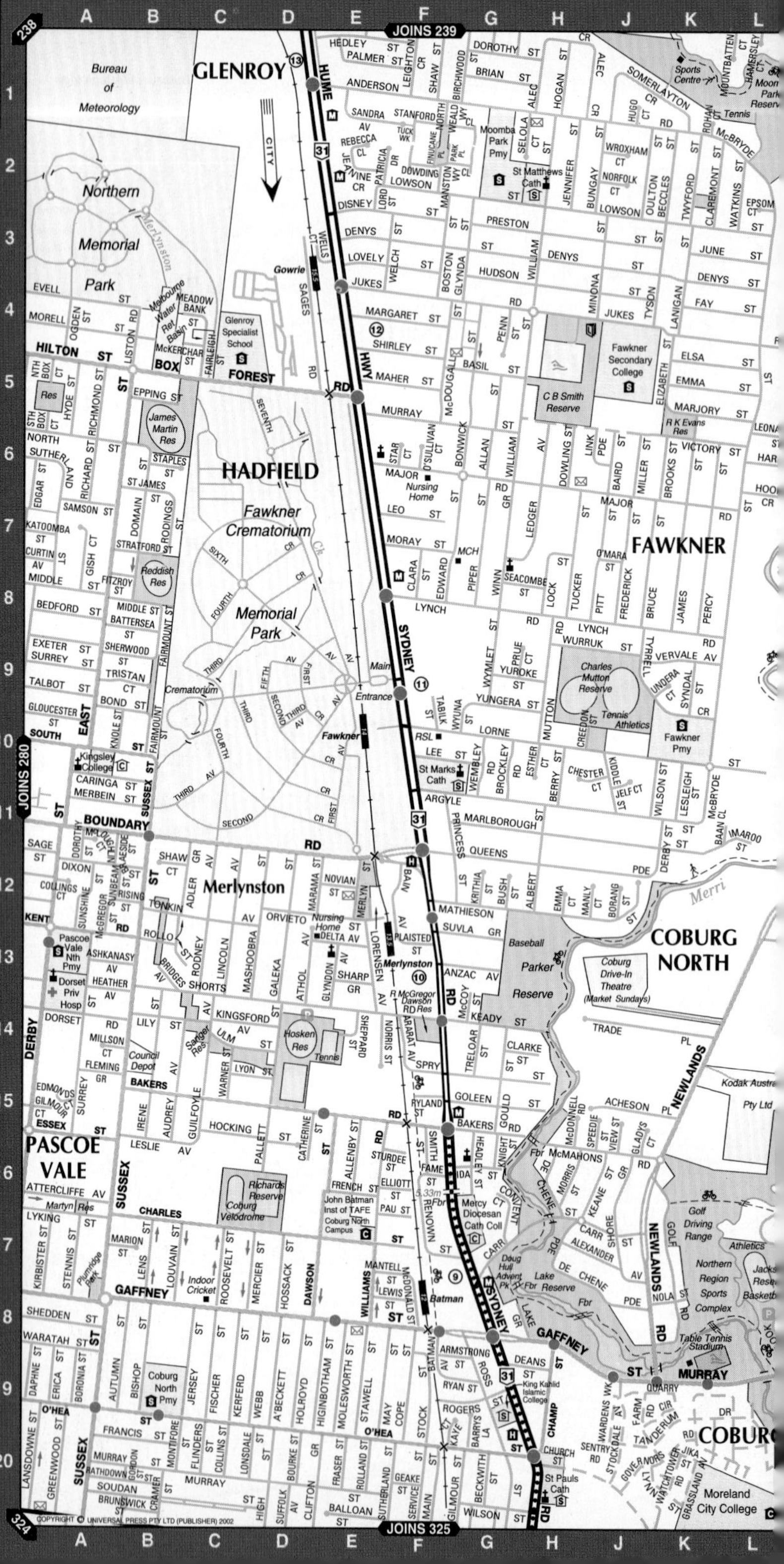

A B C D E F G H J K L

238
JOINS 239

GLENROY

Bureau of Meteorology

Northern Memorial Park

Glenroy Specialist School

HADFIELD

Fawkner Crematorium

Memorial Park

Main Entrance

FAWKNER

Fawkner Secondary College

C B Smith Reserve

Charles Mutton Reserve

Fawkner Pmy

Moomba Park Pmy

St Matthews Cath

St Marks Cath

Kingsley College

James Martin Res

Reddish Res

Merlynston

COBURG NORTH

Coburg Drive-In Theatre (Market Sundays)

Baseball Parker Reserve

Hosken Res

Pascoe Vale Nth Pmy

Dorset Priv Hosp

Council Depot

PASCOE VALE

Richards Reserve Coburg Velodrome

John Batman Inst of TAFE Coburg North Campus

Mercy Diocesan Cath Coll

Doug Hull Advent Pk

Lake Reserve

Golf Driving Range

Northern Region Sports Complex

Table Tennis Stadium

Kodak Australia Pty Ltd

Coburg North Pmy

King Kahlid Islamic College

St Pauls Cath

Moreland City College

COBURG

Indoor Cricket

Martyn Res

JOINS 280

1 2 3 4 5 6 7 8 9 10 11 12 13 14 15 16 17 18 19 20

324
JOINS 325

A B C D E F G H J K L

A B C D E F G H J K L
JOINS 240
241
MAHONEYS RD
Merrilands Secondary College
L E Cotchin Reserve
Pavilion
HUGHES PDE
MASSEY AV
DAVIDSON
BARTROP
Radford Nursing Home
HALSEY
LEGH
MACKENZIE ST
GLASGOW
B T Connor Reserve
Soccer
BROADHURST AV
Macedonian Social Club
St Joseph The Worker Catholic
Ruthven Pmy
Tennis Res
BOTHA
McFADZEAN AV
GELLIBRAND
MACLAGAN
Ruthven
RESERVOIR
LEAMINGTON
Tennis
Edwardes Park
Preston Yacht Club
Edwardes Lake
Athletics
EDWARDES ST
BANBURY RD
J E Moore Park
Pav
Reservoir Private Hosp
HENTY ST
Cinema Centre North
St Gabriel Cath
RSL
Reservoir
JOINS 283
HIGH ST
Open 7 days Waste Transfer Section
Exit
Melbourne C'van Park
Reservoir West Pmy
Crispe Park
Park WRIGHT
Melbourne
No 1
Reservoirs No 2 Water
Cash Reserve
Reserve
GE Robinson Park Tennis
Nursing Home
F G Pike Res
Kodak Australia Pty Ltd
Newlands Pmy
GILBERT RD
REGENT ST
J S Grey Res
W K Larkins Res Tennis
L W Williams Res
SPRING ST
PRESTON
Nursing Home
Cath
F G Cox Res
Regent
Res
MURRAY RD
Preston West Pmy
Sen Cit
Sen Cits
Preston
Preston Market
Court House
CRAMER
JOINS 326
327
COPYRIGHT © UNIVERSAL PRESS PTY LTD (PUBLISHER) 2002

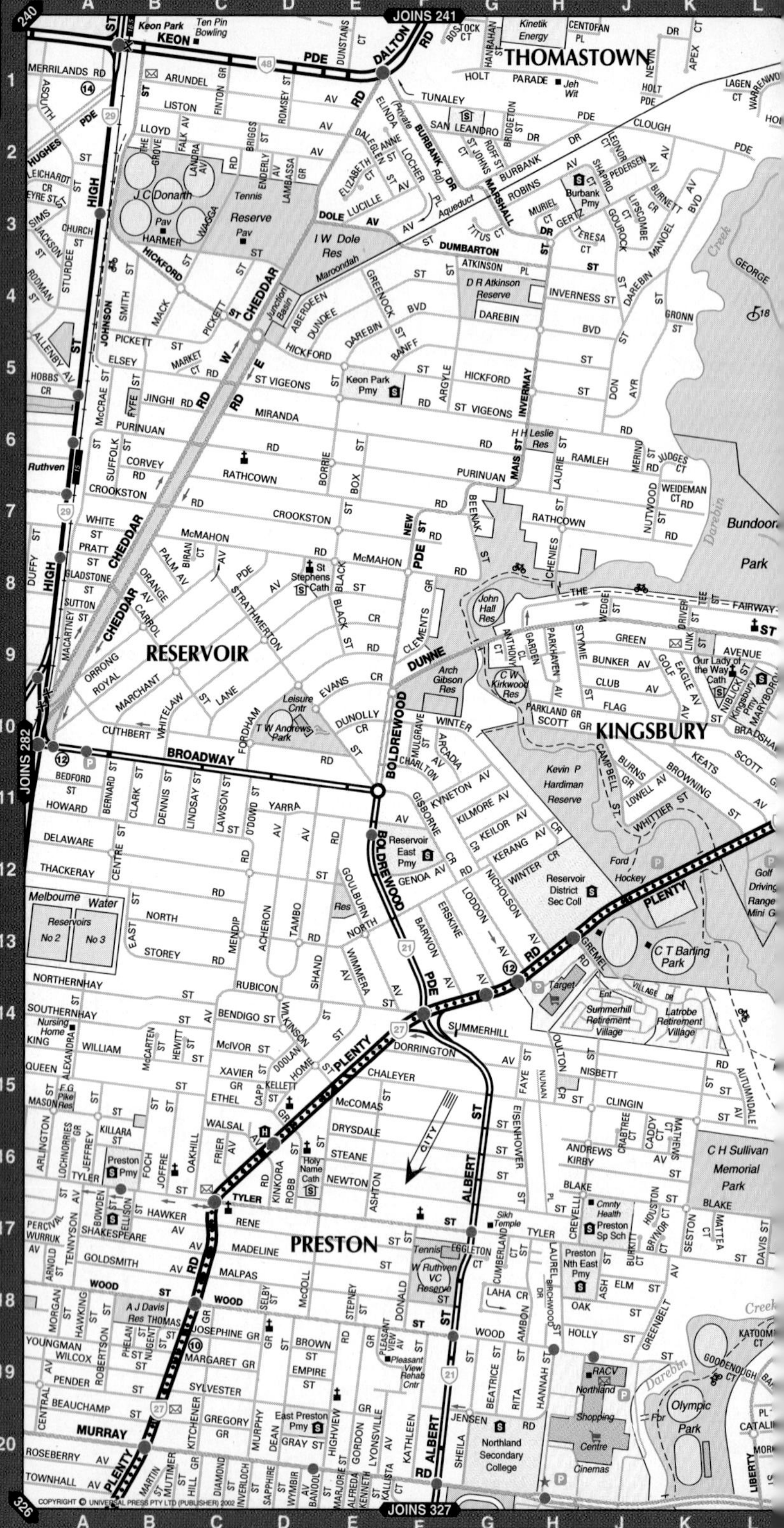

240

JOINS 241

A B C D E F G H J K L

1 2 3 4 5 6 7 8 9 10 11 12 13 14 15 16 17 18 19 20

THOMASTOWN

RESERVOIR

KINGSBURY

PRESTON

Bundoora Park

Keon Park

J C Donath Reserve

I W Dole Res

D R Atkinson Reserve

Keon Park Pmy

H H Leslie Res

John Hall Res

Arch Gibson Res

C W Kirkwood Res

Kevin P Hardiman Reserve

Leisure Cntr

T W Andrews Park

Reservoir East Pmy

Reservoir District Sec Coll

C T Barling Park

Summerhill Retirement Village

Latrobe Retirement Village

C H Sullivan Memorial Park

Melbourne Water Reservoirs No 2 No 3

Preston Pmy

A J Davis Res

Ruthven VC Reserve

Preston Nth East Pmy

Preston Sp Sch

East Preston Pmy

Northland Secondary College

Northland Shopping Centre

Olympic Park

HIGH ST

CHEDDAR RD

BROADWAY

BOLDREWOOD PDE

PLENTY RD

ALBERT ST

MURRAY RD

DALTON RD

KEON PDE

JOINS 282

326

JOINS 327

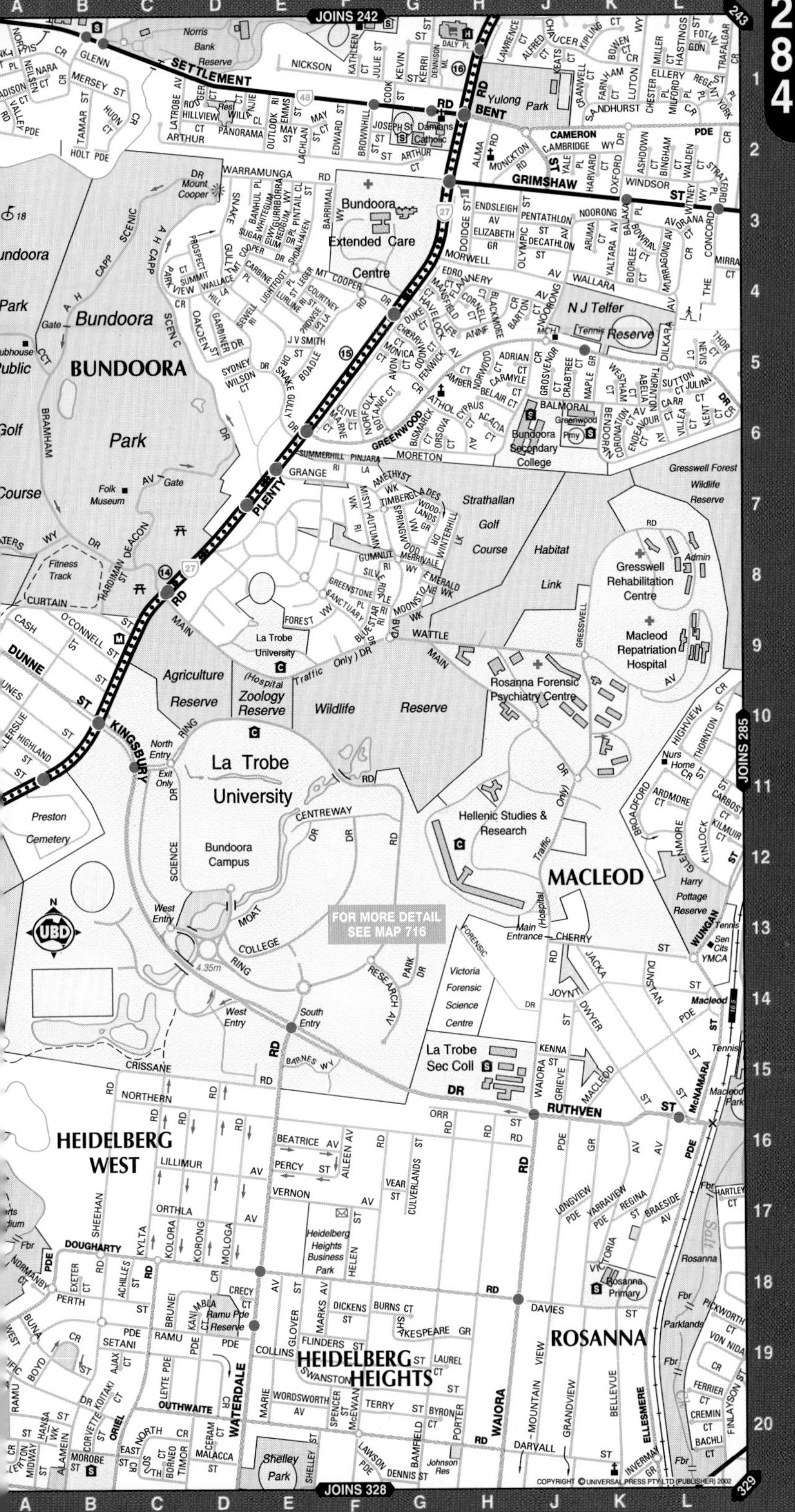
JOINS 242
JOINS 243
JOINS 285
JOINS 328
JOINS 329
SETTLEMENT RD
BENT ST
GRIMSHAW ST
PLENTY RD
KINGSBURY DR
RUTHVEN ST
WATERDALE RD
WAIORA RD
BUNDOORA
Bundoora Park
Bundoora Extended Care Centre
Yulong Park
N J Telfer Reserve
Bundoora Secondary College
Strathallan Golf Course
Habitat Link
Gresswell Forest Wildlife Reserve
Gresswell Rehabilitation Centre
Macleod Repatriation Hospital
Rosanna Forensic Psychiatry Centre
Agriculture Reserve
Zoology Reserve
Wildlife Reserve
La Trobe University
Bundoora Campus
Hellenic Studies & Research
FOR MORE DETAIL SEE MAP 716
MACLEOD
Harry Pottage Reserve
Victoria Forensic Science Centre
La Trobe Sec Coll
Preston Cemetery
Folk Museum
Fitness Track
HEIDELBERG WEST
HEIDELBERG HEIGHTS
Heidelberg Heights Business Park
Ramu Pde Reserve
Shelley Park
ROSANNA
Rosanna Primary
Rosanna Parklands
Macleod Park
Norris Bank Reserve
St Damians Catholic
COPYRIGHT © UNIVERSAL PRESS PTY LTD (PUBLISHER) 2002

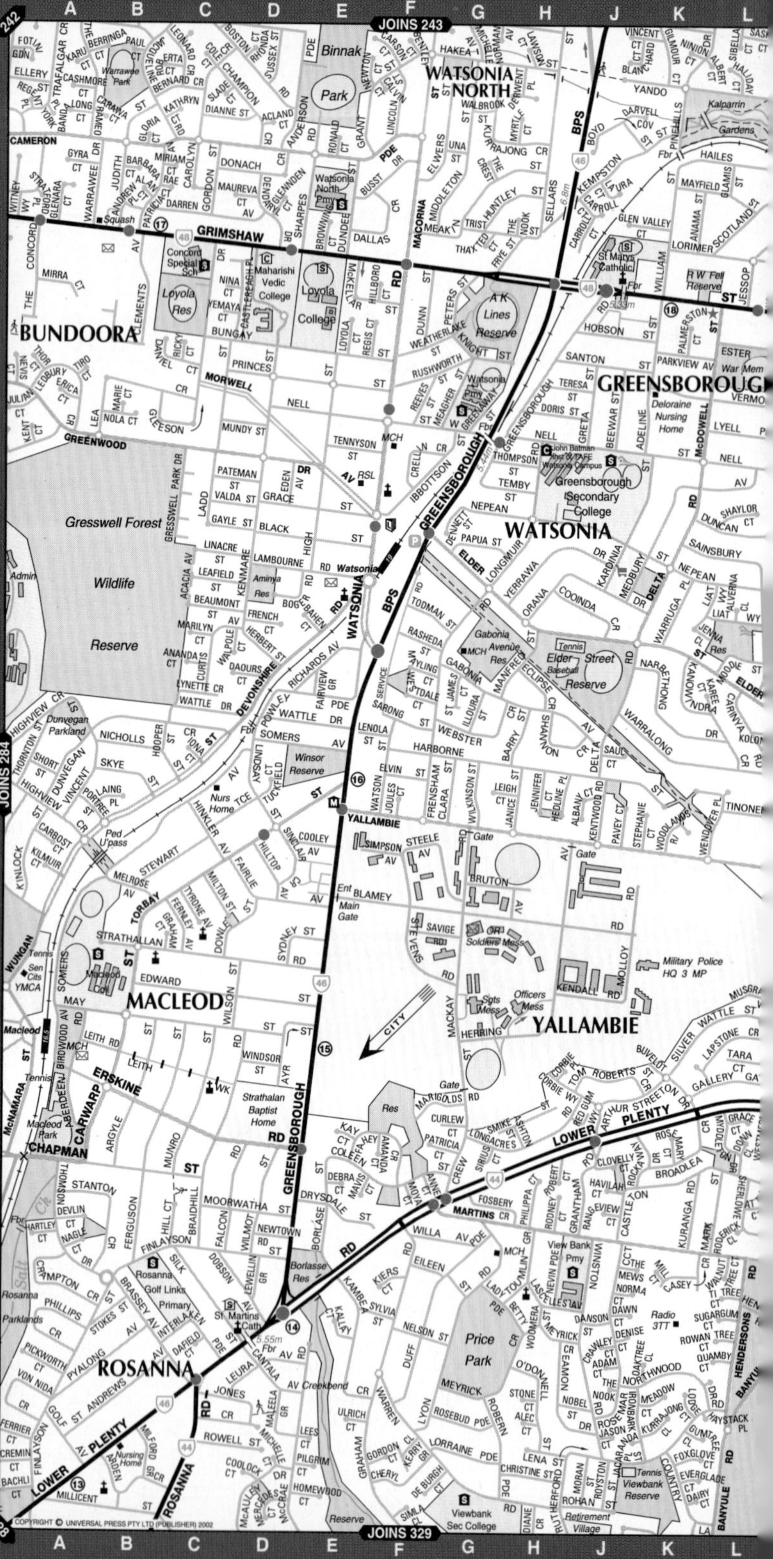

JOINS 243

242

A B C D E F G H J K L

1 2 3 4 5 6 7 8 9 10 11 12 13 14 15 16 17 18 19 20

WATSONIA NORTH

BUNDOORA

GREENSBOROUGH

WATSONIA

MACLEOD

YALLAMBIE

ROSANNA

Binnak Park

Kalparrin Gardens

Warrawee Park

Concord Special Sch

Loyola Res

Maharishi Vedic College

Loyola College

Watsonia North Pmy

St Marys Catholic

R W Fell Reserve

A K Lines Reserve

Watsonia Pmy

Deloraine Nursing Home

John Batman Inst of TAFE Watsonia Campus

Greensborough Secondary College

Gresswell Forest Wildlife Reserve

Aminya Res

Gabonia Avenue Res

Elder Street Reserve

Dunvegan Parkland

Winsor Reserve

Nurs Home

Ped U'pass

Macleod Coll

Military Police HQ 3 MP

Officers Mess

Sgts Mess

OR Soldiers Mess

Strathalan Baptist Home

Macleod Park

Rosanna Parklands

Rosanna Golf Links Primary

St Martins Cath

Borlasse Res

View Bank Pmy

Radio 3TT

Price Park

Viewbank Reserve

Viewbank Sec College

Retirement Village

Nursing Home

JOINS 284

328

JOINS 329

A B C D E F G H J K L

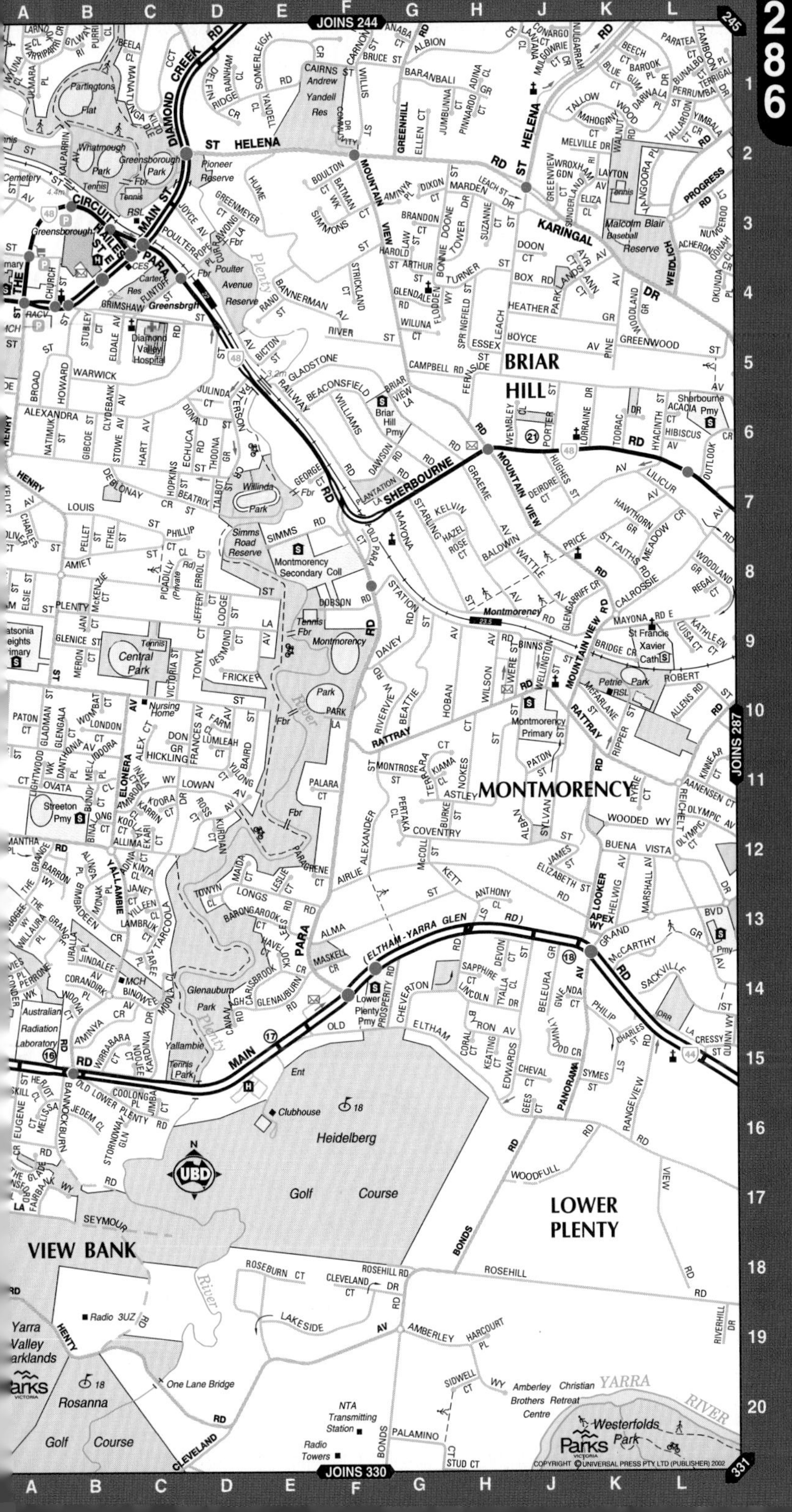

JOINS 244
245
JOINS 287
JOINS 330
331
BRIAR HILL
MONTMORENCY
LOWER PLENTY
VIEW BANK
Greensborough
Partingtons Flat
Whatmough Park
Greensborough Park
Pioneer Reserve
Cairns Andrew Yandell Res
Diamond Valley Hospital
Poulter Avenue Reserve
Carter Res
Greensbrgh
Briar Hill Pmy
Malcolm Blair Baseball Reserve
Sherbourne Pmy
Willinda Park
Simms Road Reserve
Montmorency Secondary Coll
Montmorency
Central Park
Nursing Home
Streeton Pmy
St Francis Xavier Cath
Petrie Park
Montmorency Primary
Australian Radiation Laboratory
Yallambie
Glenauburn Park
Tennis Park
Clubhouse
Heidelberg Golf Course
Lower Plenty Pmy
Radio 3UZ
Yarra Valley Parklands
Rosanna Golf Course
One Lane Bridge
NTA Transmitting Station
Radio Towers
Amberley Christian Brothers Retreat Centre
Westerfolds Park
YARRA RIVER
Plenty River
ST HELENA RD
DIAMOND CREEK RD
MAIN ST
MOUNTAIN VIEW RD
KARINGAL DR
SHERBOURNE RD
RATTRAY RD
ELTHAM-YARRA GLEN RD
MAIN RD
LOWER PLENTY RD
ROSEHILL RD
BONDS RD
COPYRIGHT © UNIVERSAL PRESS PTY LTD (PUBLISHER) 2002

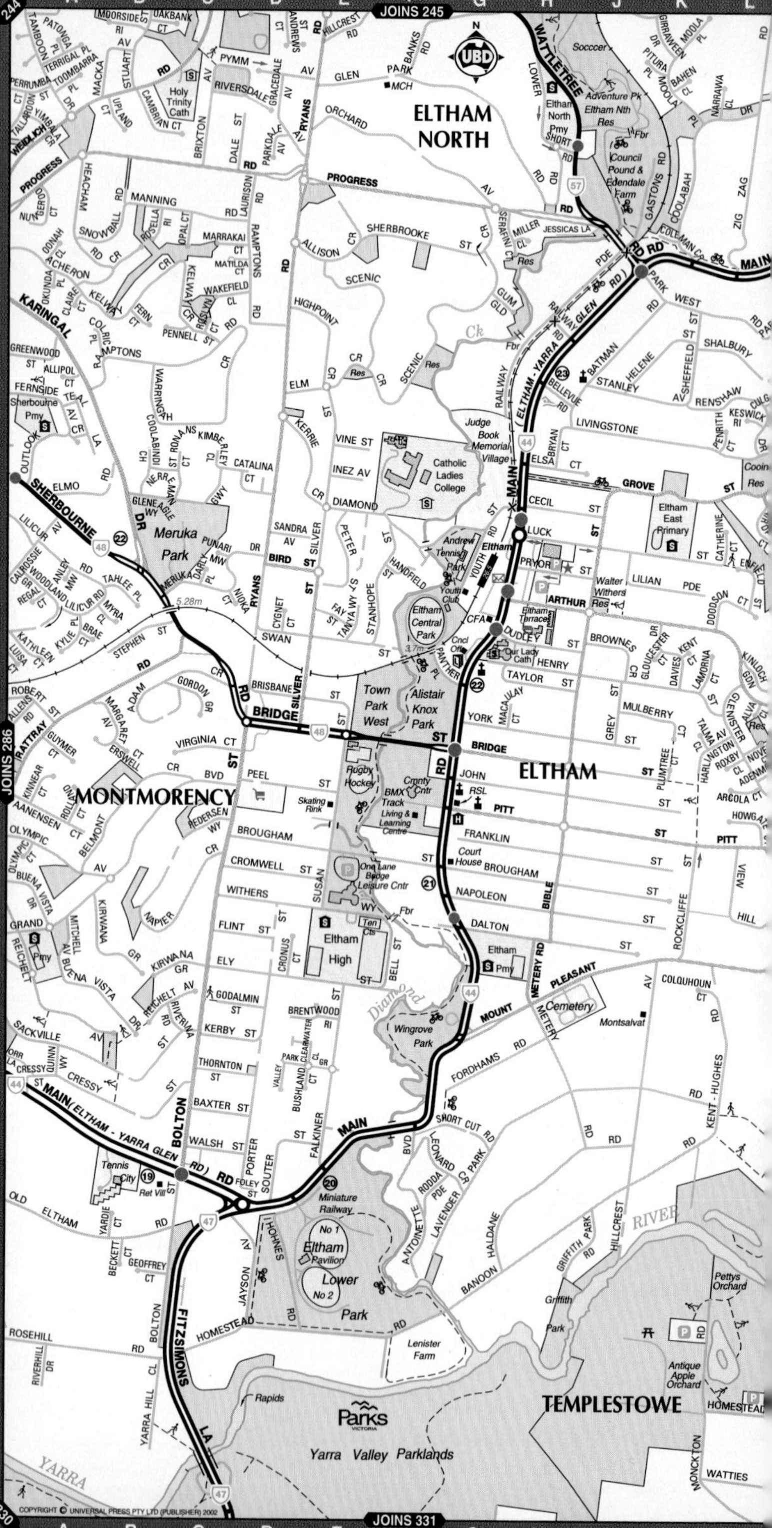

244

A B C D E F G H J K L

JOINS 245

ELTHAM NORTH

ELTHAM

MONTMORENCY

TEMPLESTOWE

Meruka Park

Town Park West

Alistair Knox Park

Eltham Central Park

Catholic Ladies College

Judge Book Memorial Village

Eltham High

Eltham Lower Park

Wingrove Park

Yarra Valley Parklands

Parks Victoria

Lenister Farm

Montsalvat

Cemetery

JOINS 286

330

JOINS 331

A B C D E F G H J K L

RESEARCH

WARRANDYTE

CASSELLS RD, RESEARCH AV, CUDGEE CT, AMBASSADOR RI, THE ESPLANADE, CANDLEBARK CT, CONTOUR CL, PICKWOOD RI, Performing Arts Centre, STOREY AV, HENZELL RD, VALLEY RD, INGRAMS RD, MCH, Research Primary, LINDON STRIKE CT, RAGLAN CT, KANANDAH CT, CFA, BRONWYN CT, MARCONI CT, FLEMING CT, BONDS CT, RESEARCH WARRANDYTE RD

TALWONG CT, CAMERON CT, TYRONE DR, CALTOWIE CT, MAROONG DR, KILANI CT, ECHIDNA RD, TROODOS RI, MAROONG DR, ENGLEWOOD PL, Research Tennis Park, Ballara Receptions, MAIN RD, NICHOLSON ST, THOMPSON CT, HOWELL CL, BELDOE ST, FINNIGAN ST, MORELLE ST, EVA ST, AV, RD, Yarramie Park, CR, THOMPSON RD, CROWE CT, GOOD-LET PL, BRINKKOTTER, BOOTH CT, KYNE PL, GRIFFIN CT, LYONS RI, DUKE RT, NORMAN CR, ASHLEY CT, KEITH CT, BELINDA RD, BRENDA RD, WOODHILL CL

NATHAN RD, MARION WY, VICTORIA CL, KIRWIN AV, VALLEY ST, FIONA CT, WY, ARTISTS HILL, PIPER CR, CLEARVIEW CT, RIDGEVIEW, CLOUD CT, PARSONS RD, WYNVALE CT, Res, DARKAN CT, NATALIE MW, KALBAR RD, BROOKE CT, Alan Marshall Res, Child Care, BAYFIELD DR, MILBORNE PL, MORDEN PL, CROFTON MW, CROFTON CT, HEDDON CT, FLORISTON, STAMFORD CT, MILBORNE, IBSLEY SQ, ASHDALE GR, FRANK ST, APREY PL, ACACIA CT, FOSTER RD, GLADWYN AV, ABERSHAM CT, HARMAN, THOMAS ST, ANDREWS, BEARD ST, AV, FRANK, DE MUIR, WY, OTIS CT, Res, ELDUERA ST, NUNDAH DR, CT, JINKANA GR, EURAH PL, AMAROO, ALLAMBIE DR, ONKARA, EURABBIE CT, ARUNTA, GOROKE CT, VALONIA, WYNTON CT, ORBEL CT, QUENTIN, TADEMA CR, BARINGA PL, ANKA CL, PALTARA CT, KIAH MW, BAINBRIDGE, CHRISTINE AV, MADINE WY, JUDI CL, Res, WOODRIDGE CT, SUNRAY CT, GUMHILL CT, Res, RD, VIEW MOUNT CT, WYCLIFFE, LEXHAM SQ, DR, EUCALYPTUS, DIOSMA, Res, BARRIEDALE CT, WY, MARLOW PL, CR RD, DECROFT CT, Linear Park, MONCLAIRE, HARTLAND CT, POLOLO MW, PEPPERMINT GR, STOKES PL, IRONBARK CT, SCARLET ASH, NYORA, Pauline Toner Butterfly Res, AVENUE CL, ST, AVARN CT, RUSKIN CR, Eltham Christian School, MALABAR, WATTLE GR, EUCALYPTUS RD, Arthur Bird Res, MOUNT PLEASANT RD, KING ST, STRINGYBARK RD, MAYS RD, KAPILI WY

REYNOLDS RD, GUM TREE RD (Very Steep 4 Wheel Drive Only), MT PLEASANT RD, CITY, MOUNT PLEASANT, RD, LAUGHING WATERS RD, OVERBANK RD, RIVER, YARRA, YARRA BRAES RD, WILD CHERRY DR, HILL, Proposed Yarra Valley Parklands, Parks VICTORIA, Longridge Park, RD, Longridge Pk (Entry by appointment Phone 131 963 - Parks Victoria), Sweeneys Flats, SWEENEYS, Parks VICTORIA, Tikalara Park, Parks VICTORIA, Mullum Mullum Ck, Fbr, KEARNEY LA, (Priv Rds), ARLUNYA PL, THE RIDGE, TARGET RD, ALEXANDER RD, HOMEWOOD RI, RIVULET PL, RD

JOINS 289

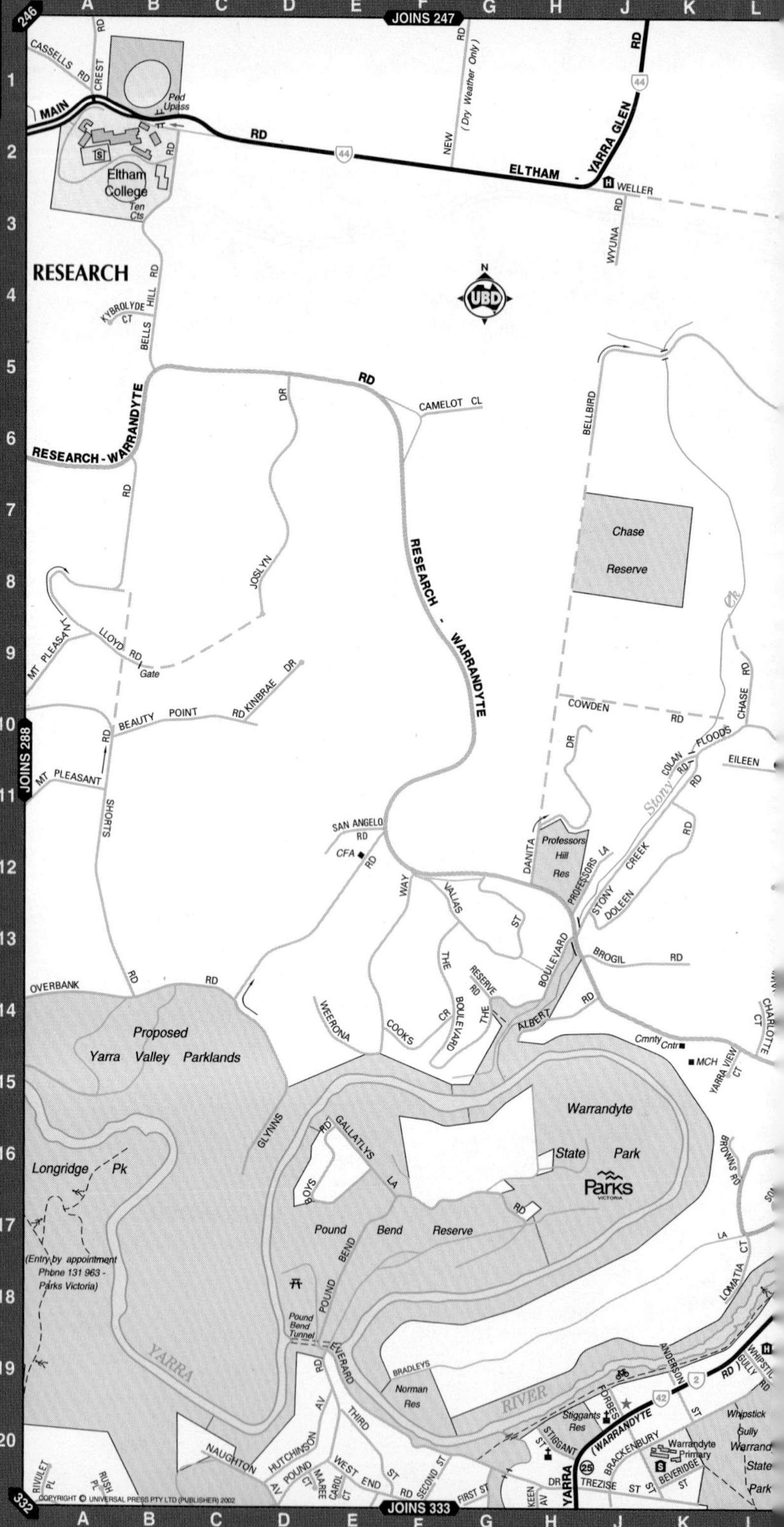

246 JOINS 247 JOINS 288 332 JOINS 333

A B C D E F G H J K L

CASSELLS RD CREST RD MAIN RD Ped Upass Eltham College Ten Cts ELTHAM - YARRA GLEN RD NEW RD (Dry Weather Only) WELLER WYUNA RD

RESEARCH

KYBROLYDE CT HILL RD BELLS RD RESEARCH - WARRANDYTE RD CAMELOT CL BELLBIRD JOSLYN DR

Chase Reserve

LLOYD RD Gate MT PLEASANT LA KINBRAE DR BEAUTY POINT RD COWDEN RD CHASE RD FLOODS RD EILEEN COLAN RD MT PLEASANT RD SHORTS RD Stony Creek

SAN ANGELO RD CFA RD DANITA DR Professors Hill Res PROFESSORS LA STONY CREEK RD DOLEEN WAY VALIAS ST BOULEVARD BROGIL RD

OVERBANK RD WEERONA COOKS CR THE BOULEVARD THE RESERVE RD ALBERT RD CHARLOTTE CT Cmnty Cntr MCH YARRA VIEW CT

Proposed Yarra Valley Parklands

Warrandyte State Park

Parks Victoria

GLYNNS BOYS RD GALLATLYS LA RD BROWNS RD

Longridge Pk

Pound Bend Reserve

(Entry by appointment Phone 131 963 - Parks Victoria)

POUND BEND LA LOMATIA CT

Pound Bend Tunnel EVERARD YARRA RIVER BRADLEYS Norman Res ANDERSON ST RD GULLY WHIPSTICK RD

Whipstick Gully Warrandyte State Park

RD HUTCHINSON AV THIRD NAUGHTON AV POUND CT MAREE CT CAROL CT WEST END RD SECOND ST FIRST ST KEEN AV STIGGANT ST Stiggants Res FORBES (WARRANDYTE) YARRA DR TREZISE ST BRACKENBURY ST BEVERIDGE ST Warrandyte Primary

RIVULET PL RUSH PL

JOINS 248
249
JOINS 291
JOINS 334
335

A B C D E F G H J K L

1 2 3 4 5 6 7 8 9 10 11 12 13 14 15 16 17 18 19 20

KANGAROO GROUND

NORTH WARRANDYTE

WARRANDYTE

WONGA PARK

KANGAROO GROUND - WARRANDYTE RD

MENZIES RD

BOURCHIERS RD

YEOMANS RD (Private Road)

CITY

CHASE VIEW CT

PIGEON BANK LA

Pigeon Bank Gully

YARRA RIVER CT

MORILLA PL

MARBERT CT

KALLARROO CT

SLOANS RD

LAWRENCE CT

KRUSES RD

ALOOLA

BOYD

WINDING WY

KOORNONG CR

HAMILTON

KOORNONG

DINGLEY DELL

DINGLEY CL

ATON ST

BLOOMS

BANNING RD

OSBORNE RD

RIVER

Stanebrae Res

Blue Tongue Bend

Warrandyte State Park

Jumping Creek Reserve

YARRA

LYNN ST

TILLS

LEWIS RD

CASTLE RD

Black Flat Reserve

Parks VICTORIA

The Island

Tennis

RSL

BRACKENBURY

MITCHELL

WEBB

LA

AV

DR

ST

WARRANDYTE - RINGWOOD RD

MAGPIE ST

MULLENS

McPHERSON ST

RUSSELL

WATTLE BLOSSOM RD

MASONIC AV

DAVID RD

State Park

PIGTAIL RD

NELSON DR

MARK ST

JUMPING CREEK RD

Jumping Ck

Warrandyte State Park The Common

248
JOINS 249
JOINS 290
JOINS 335
334

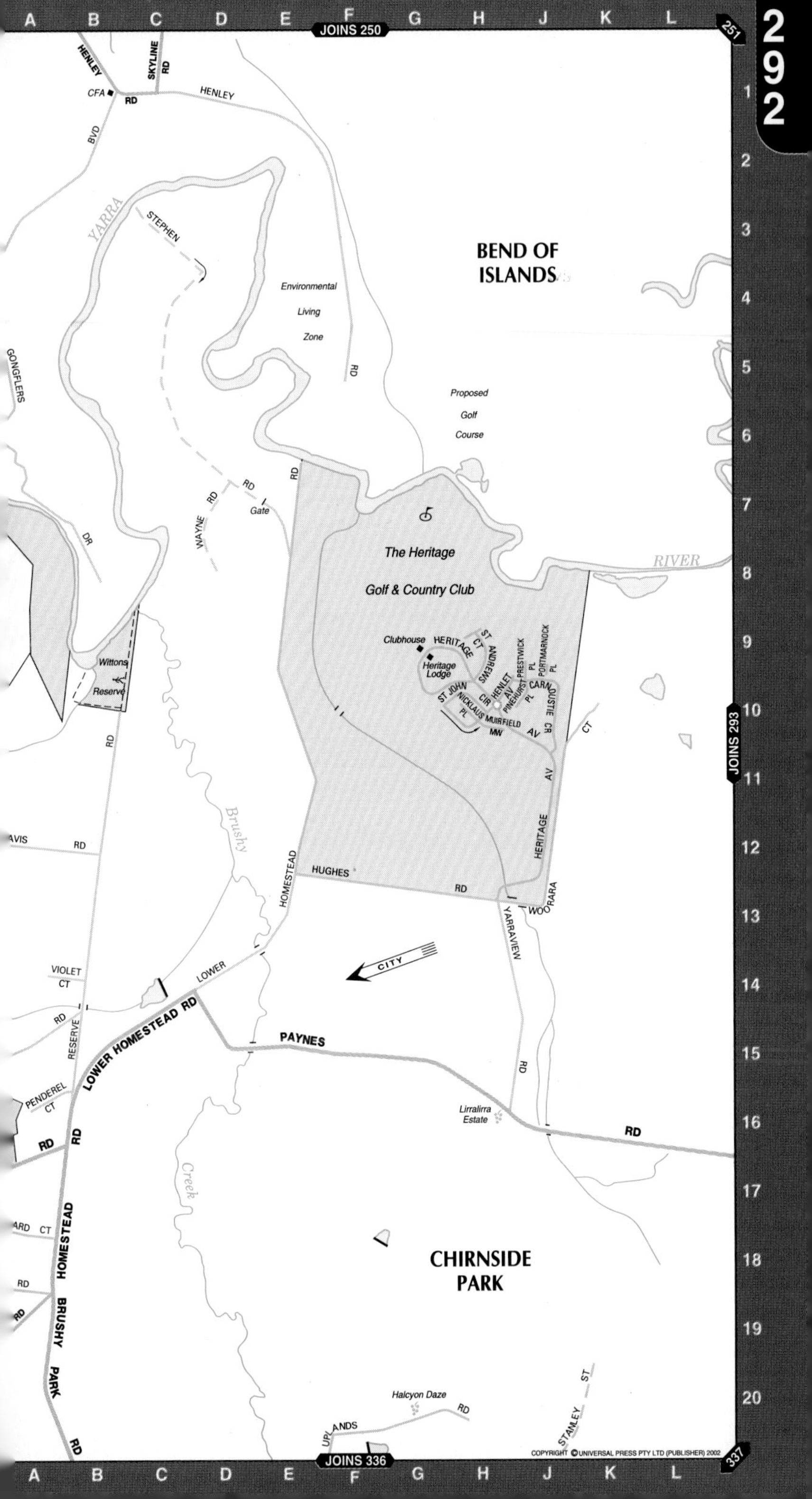

BEND OF ISLANDS

Environmental Living Zone

Proposed Golf Course

The Heritage Golf & Country Club

Clubhouse
Heritage Lodge

CHIRNSIDE PARK

HENLEY RD
SKYLINE RD
HENLEY BVD
CFA
YARRA RIVER
STEPHEN RD
WAYNE RD
Gate
GONGFLERS DR
Wittons Reserve
HERITAGE CT
ST ANDREWS CIR
PRESTWICK PL
PORTMARNOCK PL
HENLEY AV
PINEHURST PL
CARNOUSTIE CR
ST JOHN
NICKLAUS PL
MUIRFIELD MW
HERITAGE AV
CT
AVIS RD
Brushy Creek
HOMESTEAD RD
HUGHES RD
YARRAVIEW RD
WOORARA
CITY
VIOLET CT
LOWER HOMESTEAD RD
RESERVE RD
PAYNES RD
PENDEREL CT
Lirralirra Estate
ARD CT
BRUSHY PARK RD
Halcyon Daze
UPLANDS RD
STANLEY ST

JOINS 293

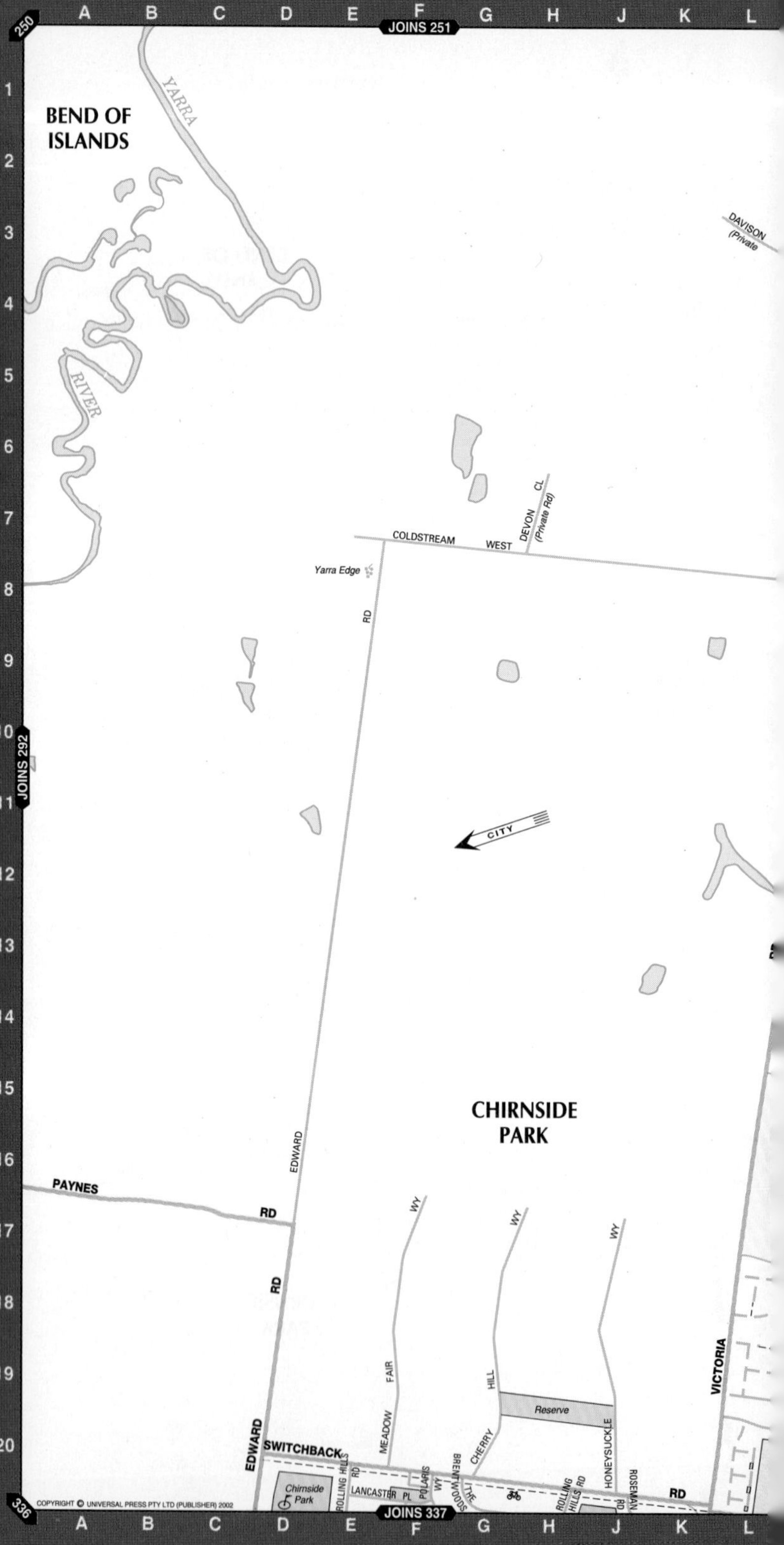

250
JOINS 251
JOINS 292
JOINS 337
336

A B C D E F G H J K L

BEND OF ISLANDS

YARRA RIVER

DAVISON (Private

COLDSTREAM WEST
DEVON CL (Private Rd)
Yarra Edge
RD
CITY

CHIRNSIDE PARK

PAYNES RD
EDWARD RD
EDWARD RD
WY
WY
WY
MEADOW FAIR
HILL
CHERRY
Reserve
HONEYSUCKLE RD
ROSEMAN
VICTORIA
SWITCHBACK RD
ROLLING HILLS RD
LANCASTER PL
POLARIS WY
BRENTWOODS
THE
ROLLING HILLS RD
Chirnside Park

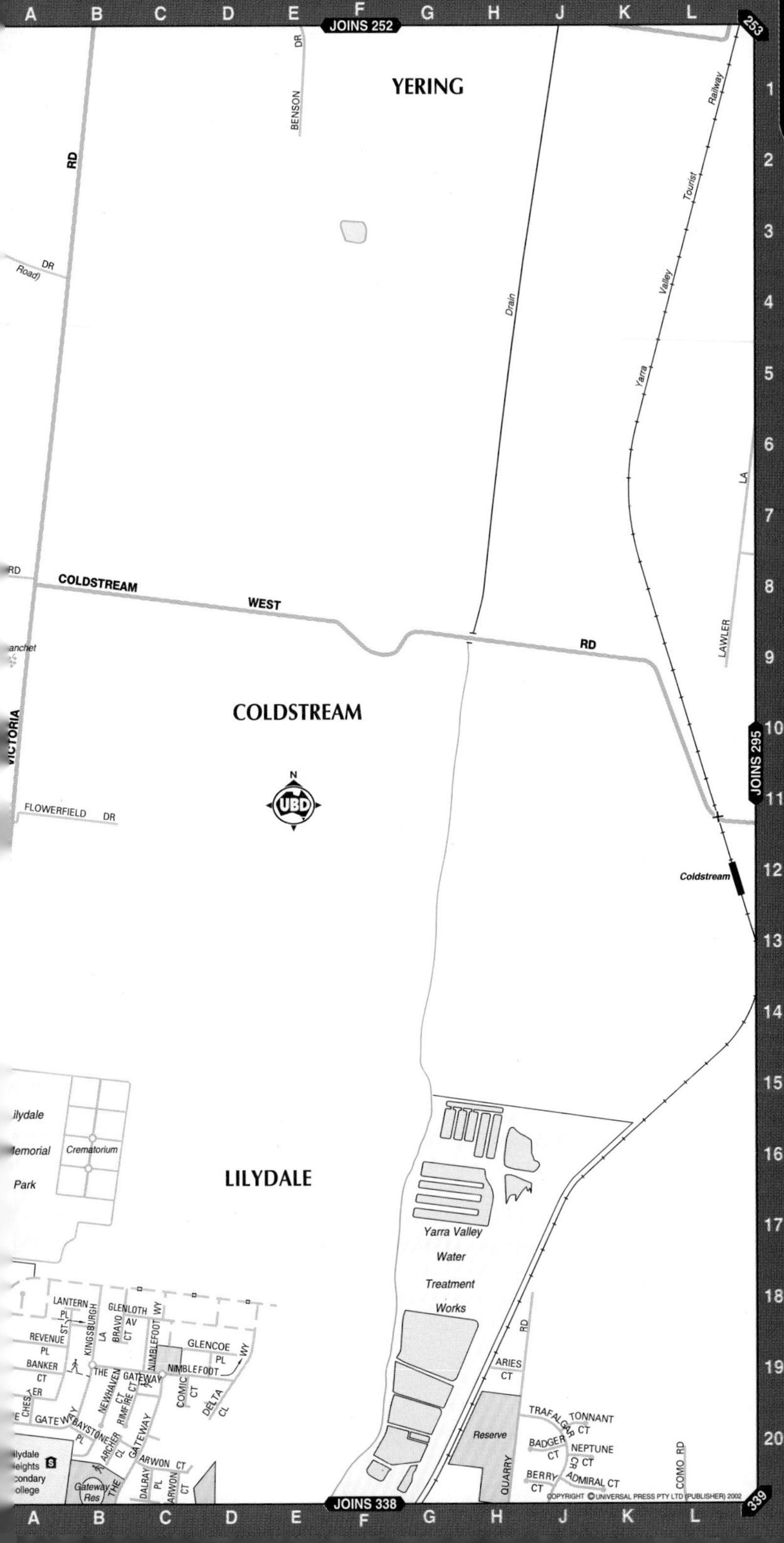

A B C D E F G H J K L
JOINS 252
253
YERING
BENSON DR
RD
DR
Road)
Drain
Yarra Valley Tourist Railway
LA
LAWLER
RD
COLDSTREAM WEST RD
anchet
COLDSTREAM
VICTORIA
FLOWERFIELD DR
JOINS 295
Coldstream
UBD
Lilydale Memorial Park
Crematorium
LILYDALE
Yarra Valley Water Treatment Works
LANTERN PL
GLENLOTH WY
ST
KINGSBURGH
LA
BRAVO AV
CT
NIMBLEFOOT
REVENUE PL
GLENCOE PL
WY
BANKER CT
THE GATEWAY
NIMBLEFOOT
CHESTER
GATEWAY
NEWHAVEN CT
RIMFIRE CT
COMIC CT
DELTA CL
BAYSTONE PL
ARCHER CL
GATEWAY
ARWON CT
DALRAY PL
ARWON CT
Lilydale Heights Secondary College
Gateway Res
THE
RD
ARIES CT
Reserve
QUARRY
TRAFALGAR CR
TONNANT CT
BADGER CT
NEPTUNE CT
BERRY CT
ADMIRAL CT
COMO RD
JOINS 338
339

252
JOINS 253

JOINS 294
338
JOINS 339

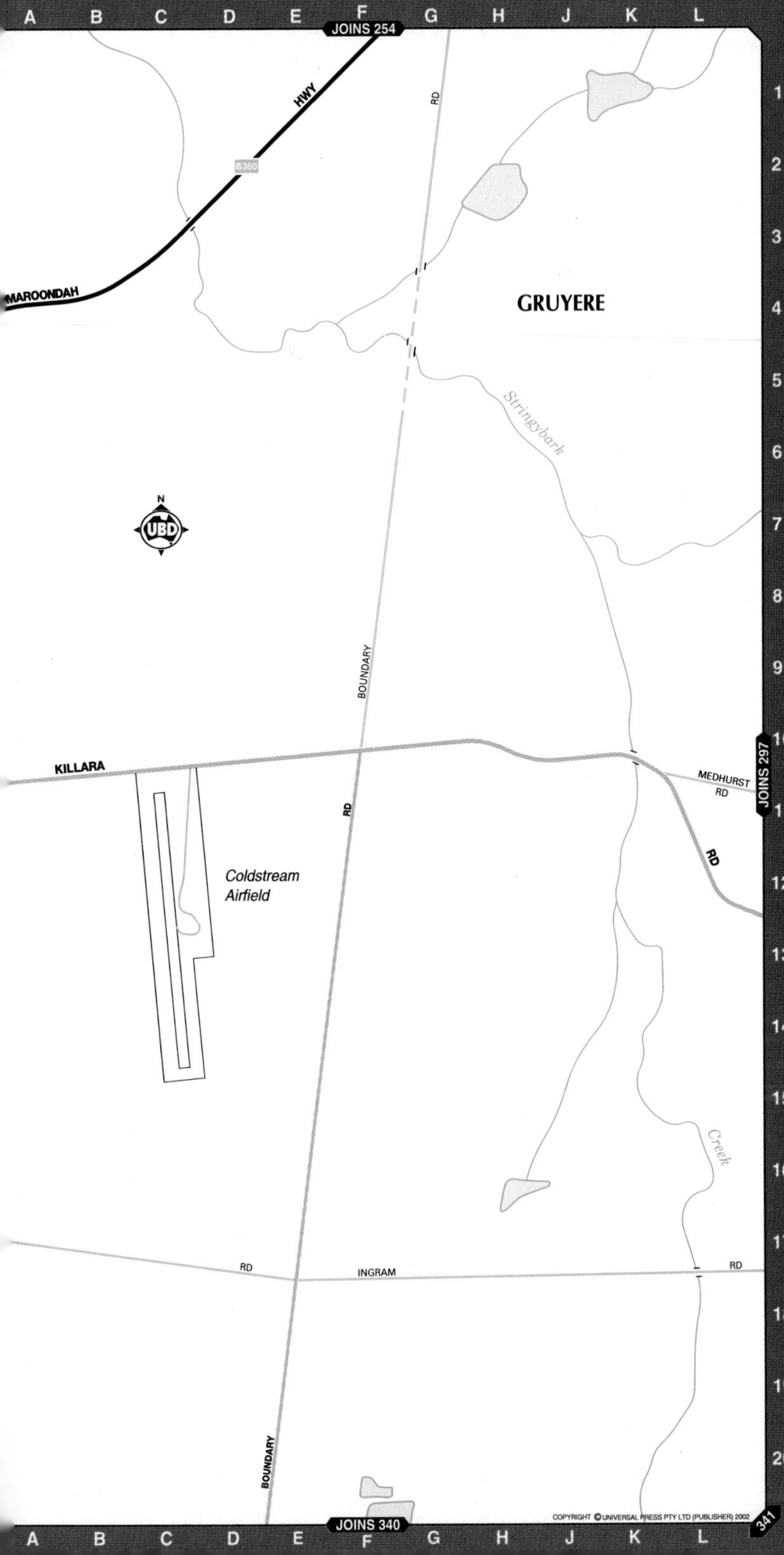

JOINS 254

GRUYERE

MAROONDAH HWY

B360

BOUNDARY RD

Stringybark Creek

KILLARA RD

MEDHURST RD

Coldstream Airfield

INGRAM RD

JOINS 297

JOINS 340

341

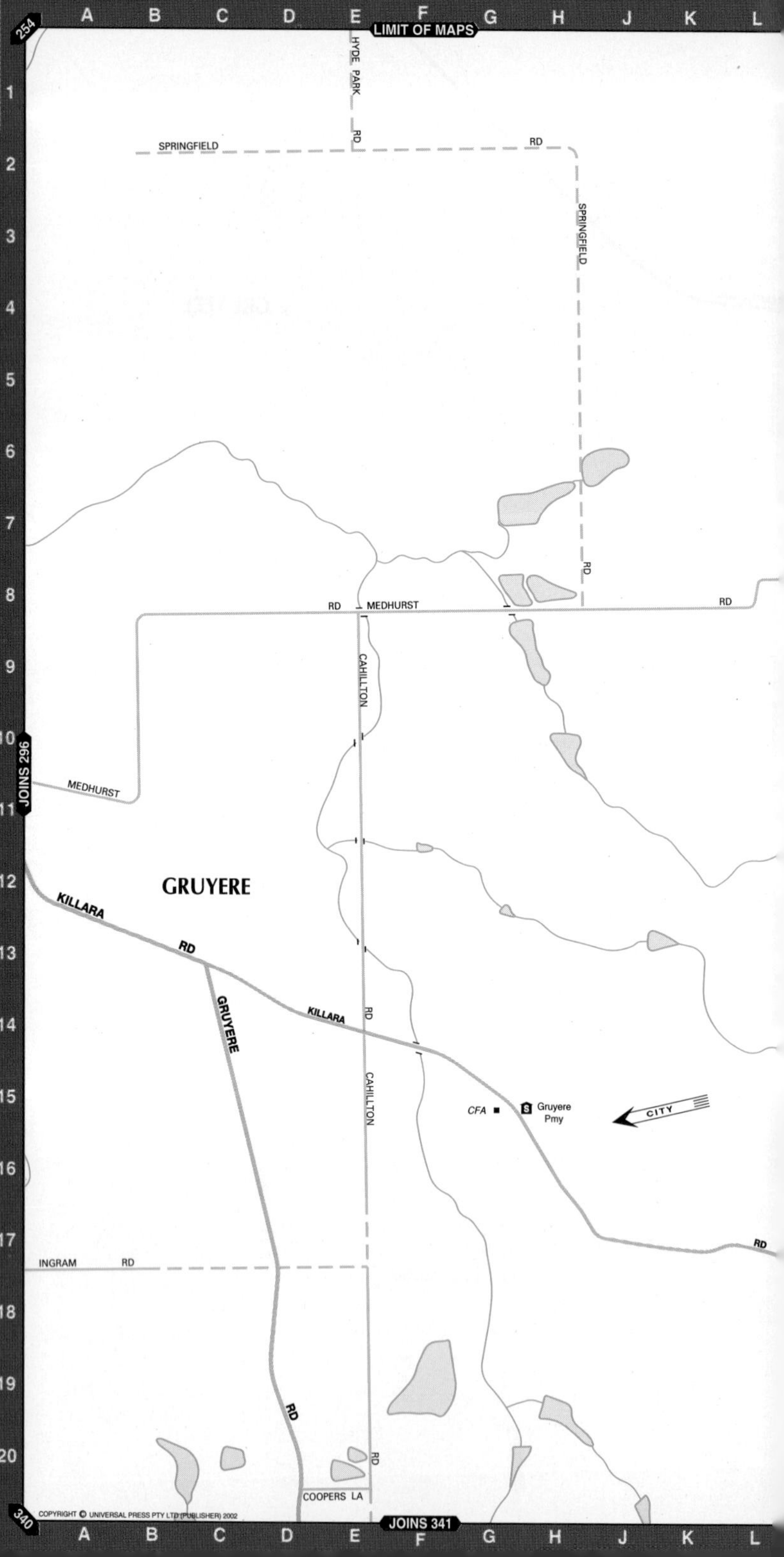

254
LIMIT OF MAPS

A B C D E F G H J K L

HYDE PARK RD
SPRINGFIELD RD
SPRINGFIELD RD
MEDHURST RD
MEDHURST RD
CAHILLTON RD
MEDHURST
JOINS 296
GRUYERE
KILLARA RD
KILLARA RD
GRUYERE RD
CAHILLTON RD
CFA
Gruyere Pmy
CITY
RD
INGRAM RD
COOPERS LA

340
JOINS 341

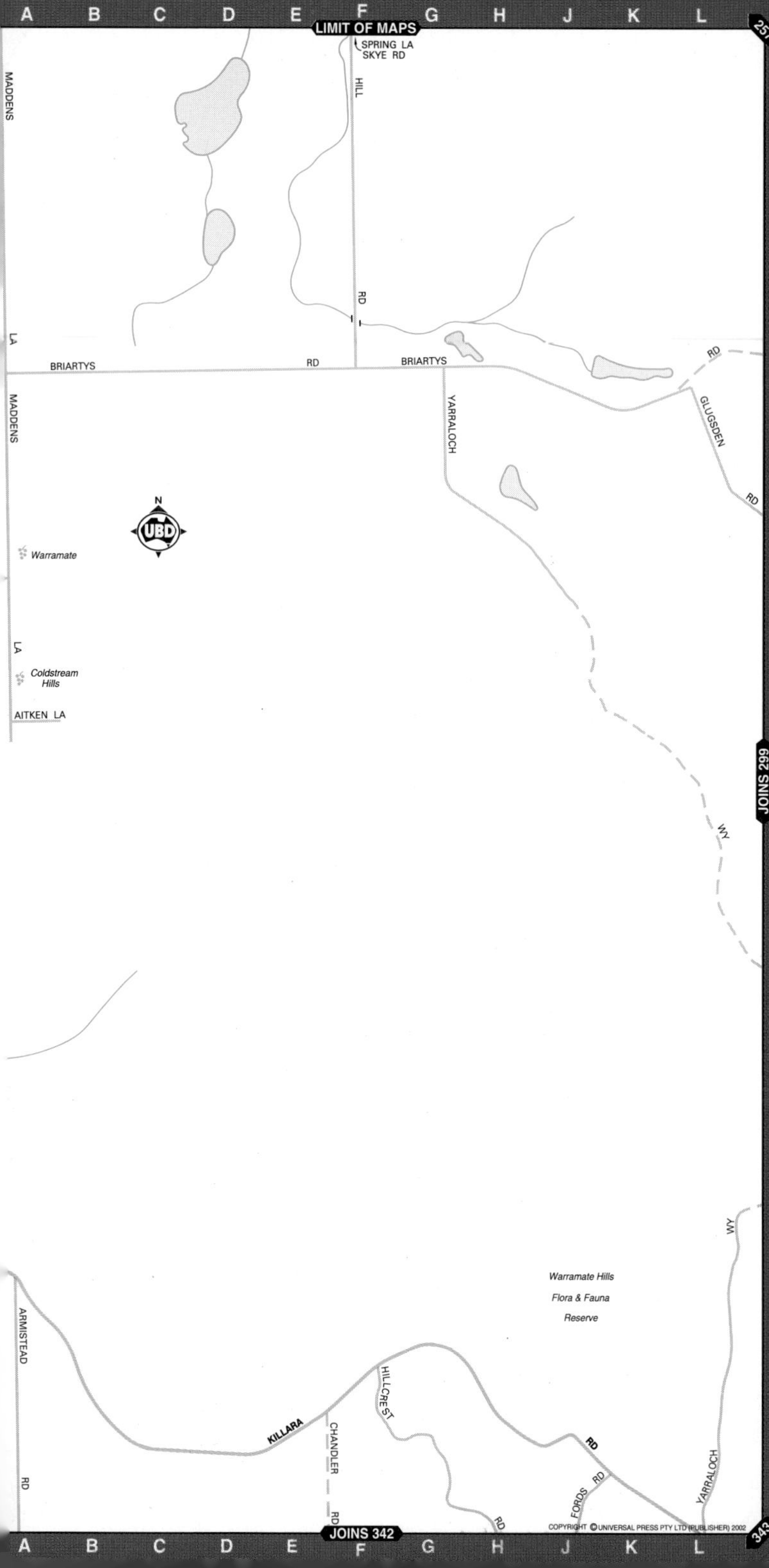

A B C D E F G H J K L

LIMIT OF MAPS
257

SPRING LA
SKYE RD
HILL RD
MADDENS LA
BRIARTYS RD
BRIARTYS RD
YARRALOCH WY
GLUGSDEN RD
MADDENS LA
N
UBD
Warramate
Coldstream Hills
AITKEN LA

JOINS 299

Warramate Hills Flora & Fauna Reserve

ARMISTEAD RD
KILLARA RD
HILLCREST RD
CHANDLER RD
FORDS RD
YARRALOCH WY

JOINS 342
343

1 2 3 4 5 6 7 8 9 10 11 12 13 14 15 16 17 18 19 20

A B C D E F G H J K L

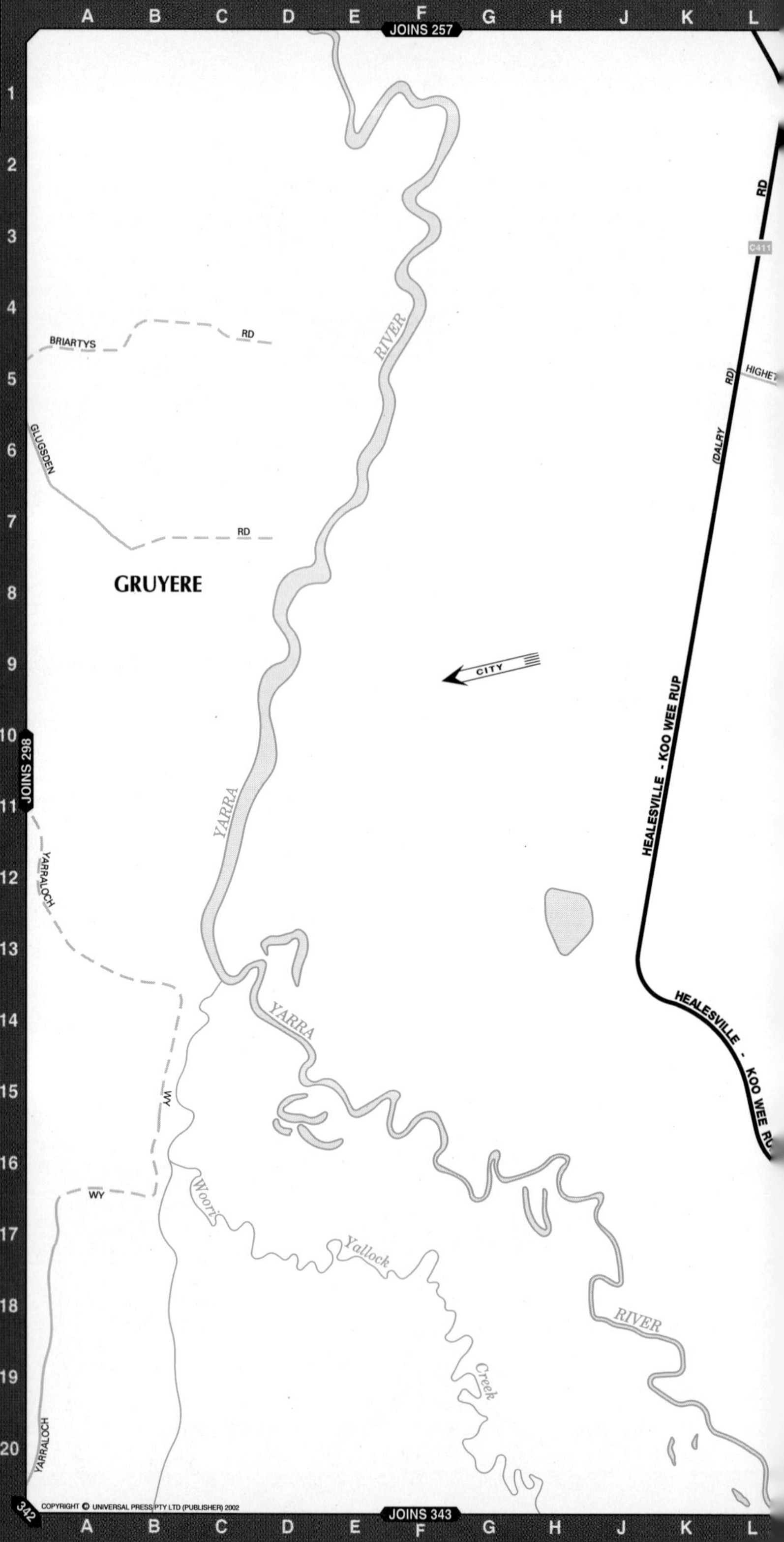
A B C D E F G H J K L
1 2 3 4 5 6 7 8 9 10 11 12 13 14 15 16 17 18 19 20
BRIARTYS
RD
GLUGSDEN
RD
GRUYERE
RIVER
YARRA
CITY
RD
C411
HIGHET
RD
(DALRY
HEALESVILLE - KOO WEE RUP
HEALESVILLE - KOO WEE RU
YARRALOCH
WY
WY
YARRA
Woori
Yallock
Creek
RIVER
YARRALOCH

JOINS 257
JOINS 298
JOINS 343
342

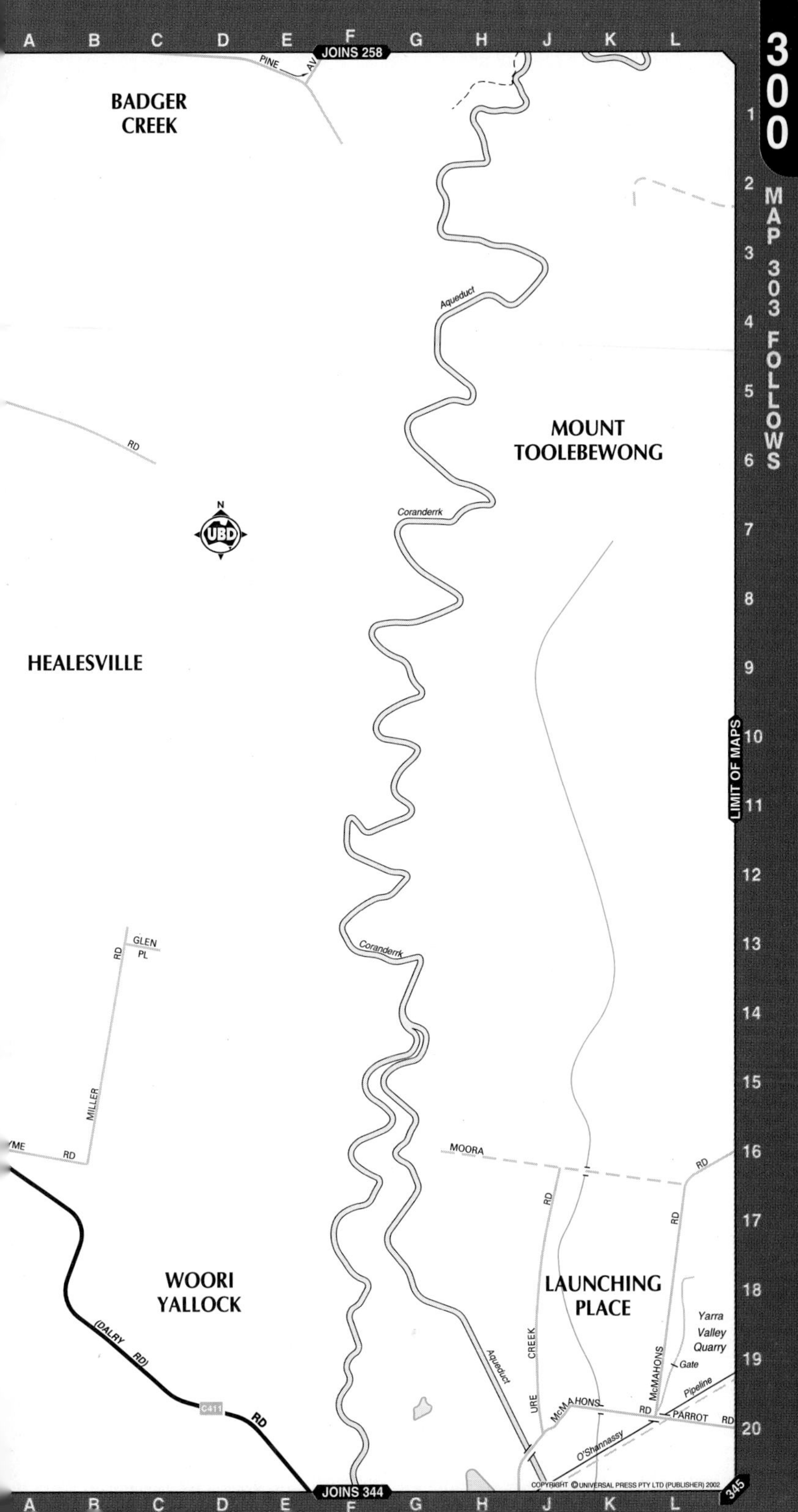
A B C D E F G H J K L
JOINS 258
PINE AV
BADGER CREEK
Aqueduct
RD
MOUNT TOOLEBEWONG
Coranderrk
HEALESVILLE
GLEN PL
RD
Coranderrk
MILLER
YME RD
MOORA
RD
RD
RD
WOORI YALLOCK
LAUNCHING PLACE
Yarra Valley Quarry
(DALRY RD)
Aqueduct
CREEK
URE
McMAHONS
McMAHONS
Gate
Pipeline
RD
PARROT
RD
O'Shannassy
C411
RD
JOINS 344
MAP 303 FOLLOWS
LIMIT OF MAPS
1 2 3 4 5 6 7 8 9 10 11 12 13 14 15 16 17 18 19 20

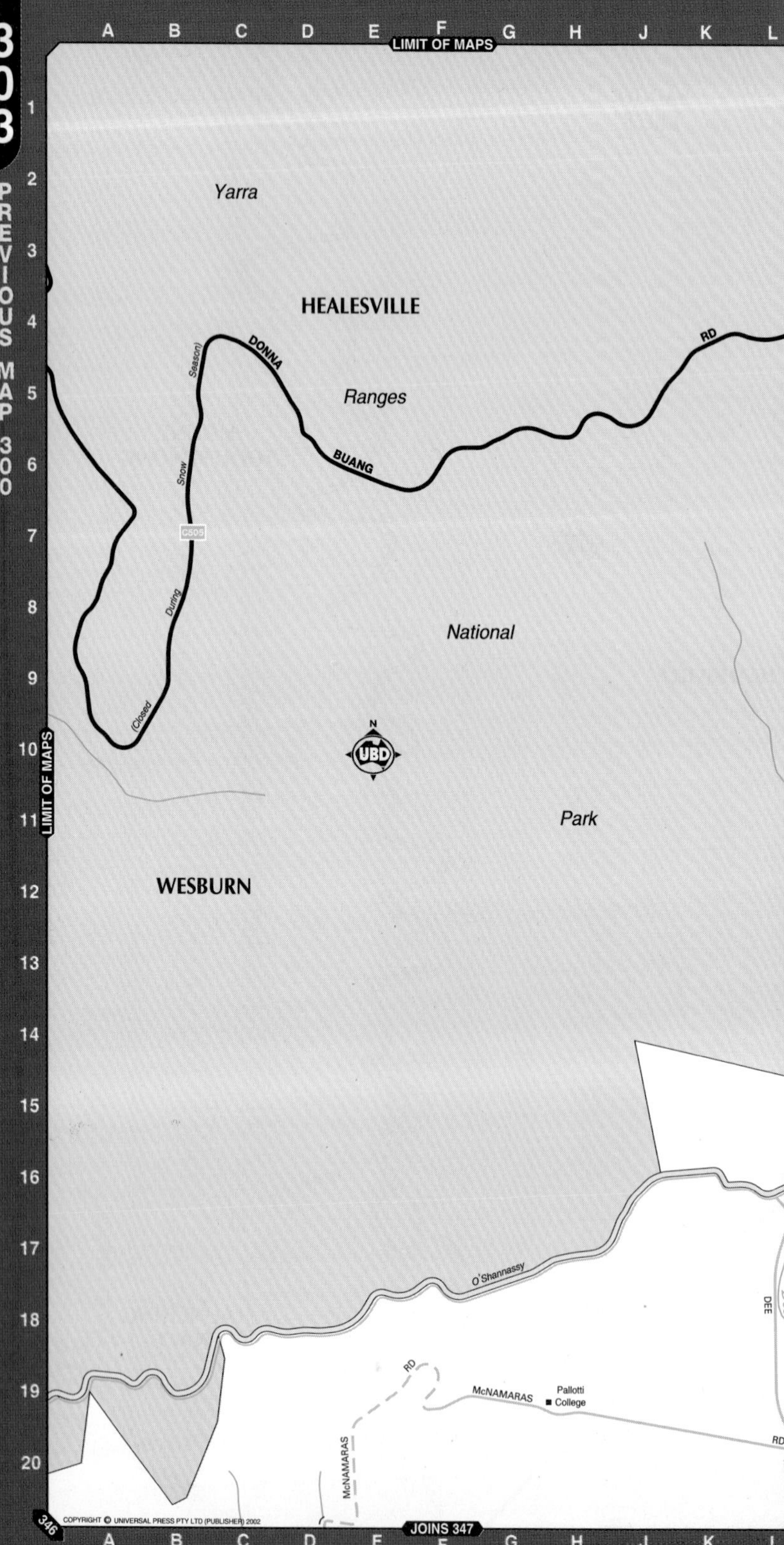
A B C D E F G H J K L
LIMIT OF MAPS
1 2 3 4 5 6 7 8 9 10 11 12 13 14 15 16 17 18 19 20
PREVIOUS MAP 300
Yarra
HEALESVILLE
DONNA
RD
Ranges
BUANG
(Closed
During
Snow
Season)
C505
National
Park
LIMIT OF MAPS
WESBURN
O'Shannassy
DEE
Dee
RD
McNAMARAS
Pallotti
College
McNAMARAS
RD
RD
346
JOINS 347

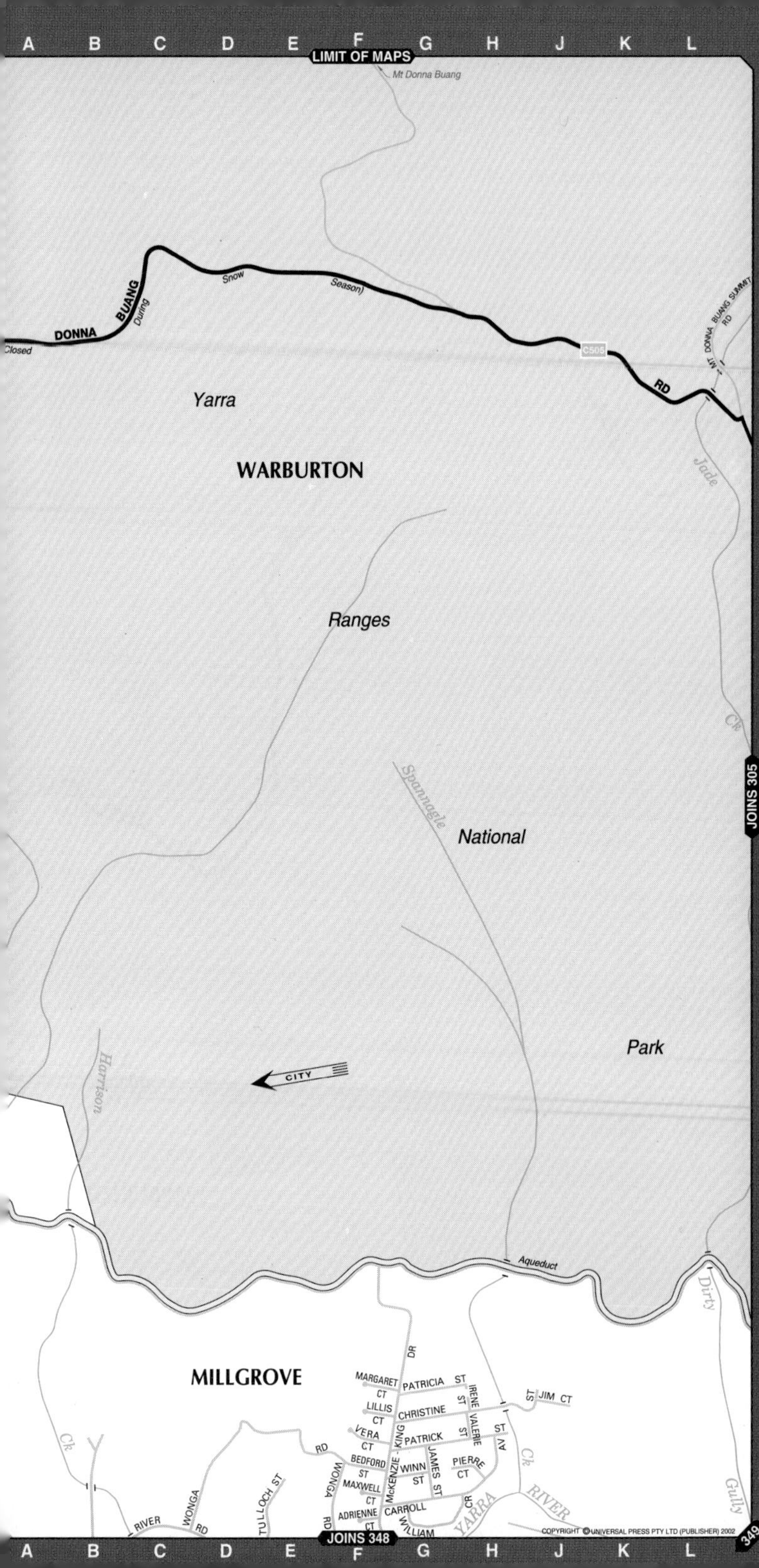
LIMIT OF MAPS
Mt Donna Buang
DONNA BUANG RD
Closed During Snow Season)
C505
MT DONNA BUANG SUMMIT RD
Yarra
WARBURTON
Ranges
National
Park
Jade Ck
Spannagle
Harrison
CITY
Aqueduct
Dirty Gully
MILLGROVE
DR
MARGARET CT
PATRICIA ST
LILLIS CT
CHRISTINE ST
IRENE ST
VALERIE ST
JIM CT
ST
VERA CT
PATRICK ST
AV
BEDFORD ST
McKENZIE - KING
WINN ST
JAMES ST
PIERRE CT
MAXWELL CT
WONGA RD
ADRIENNE CT
CARROLL CR
WILLIAM
YARRA RIVER
Ck
RIVER
TULLOCH ST
JOINS 305
JOINS 348
349
COPYRIGHT © UNIVERSAL PRESS PTY LTD (PUBLISHER) 2002

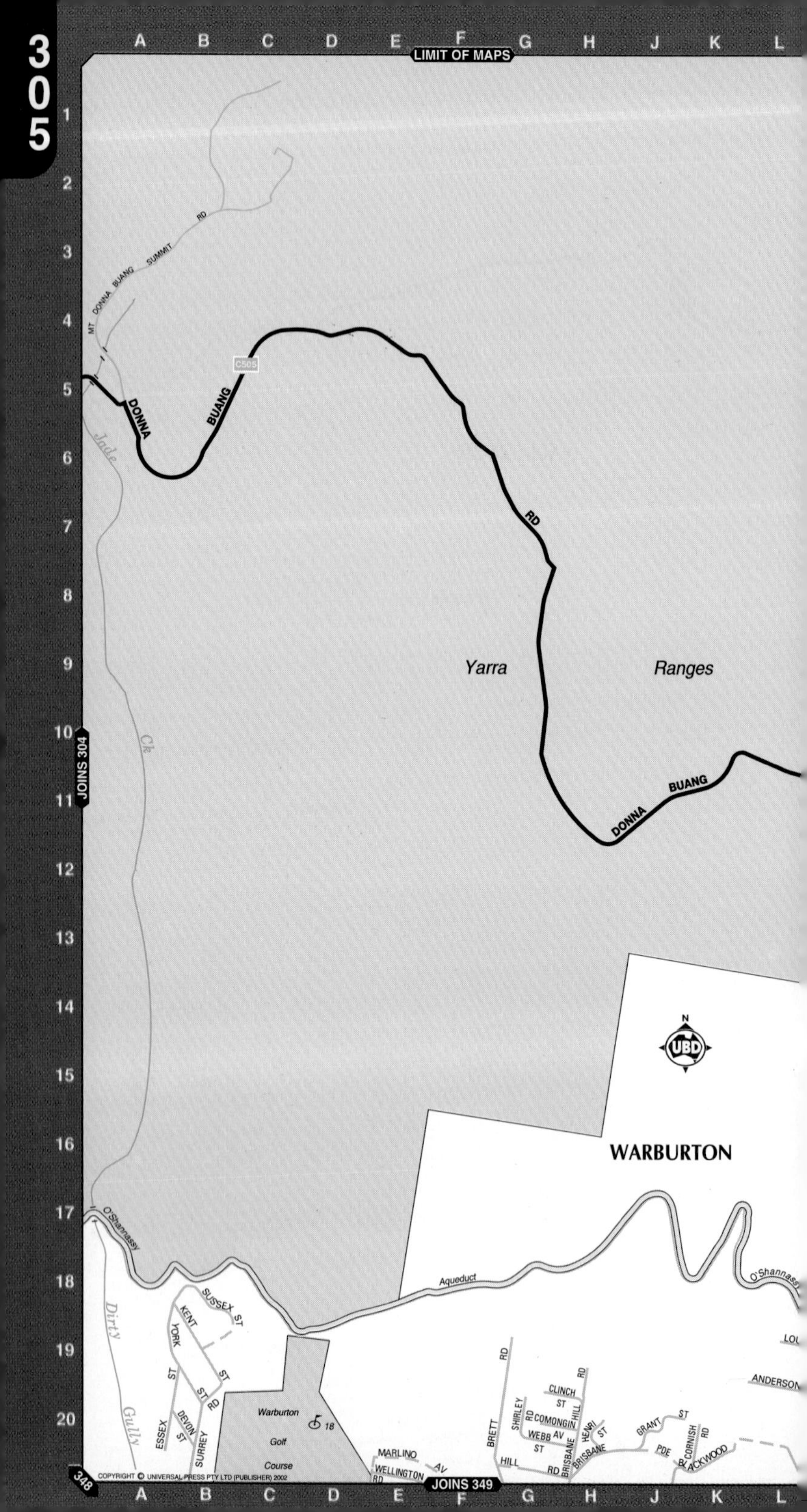

A B C D E F G H J K L

LIMIT OF MAPS

JOINS 304

348

JOINS 349

A B C D E F G H J K L

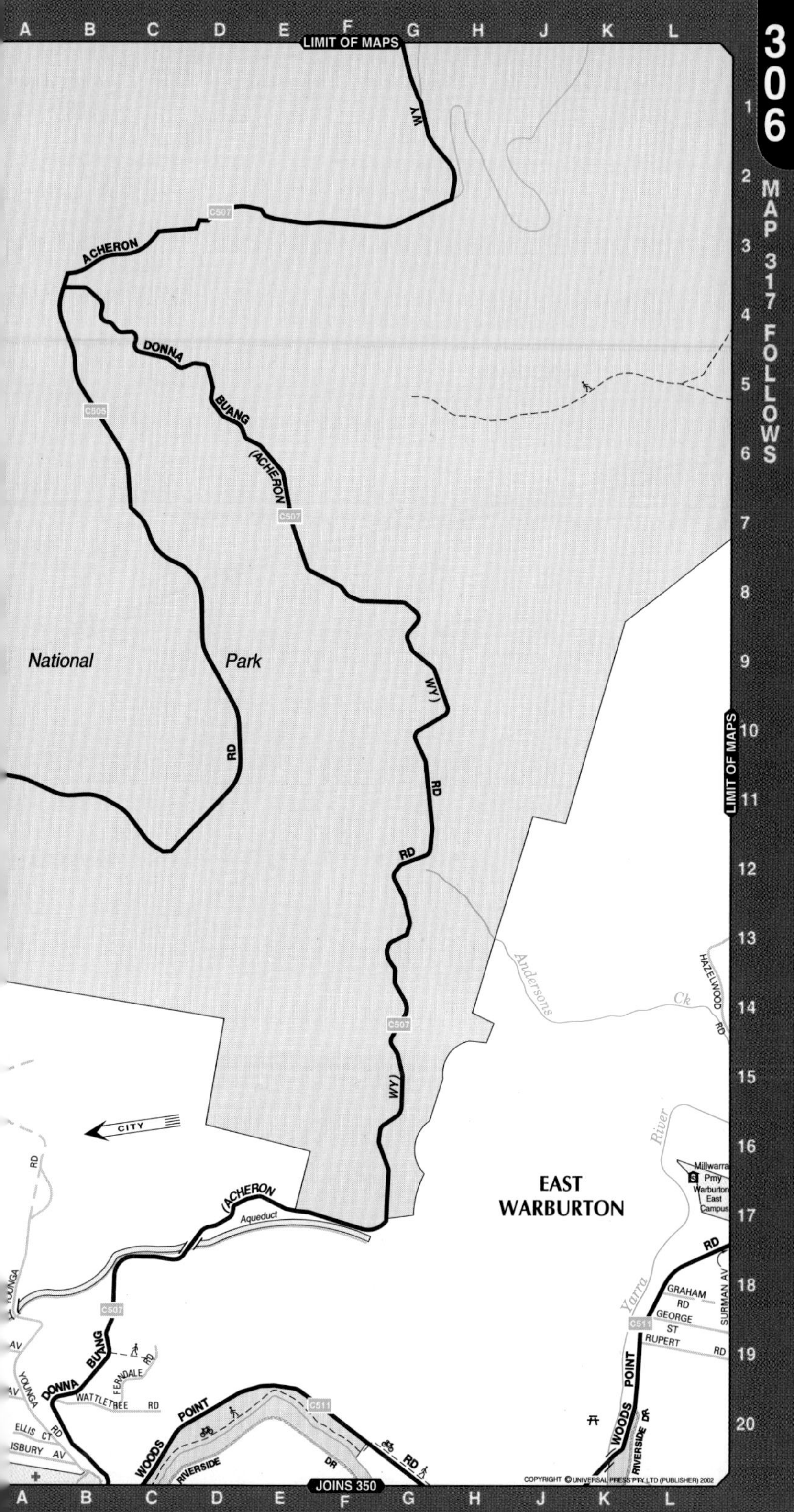
A B C D E F G H J K L
LIMIT OF MAPS
MAP 317 FOLLOWS
WY
C507
ACHERON
DONNA
BUANG
(ACHERON
C505
C507
National
Park
WY)
RD
RD
RD
LIMIT OF MAPS
Andersons
Ck
HAZELWOOD
RD
C507
WY)
CITY
RD
(ACHERON
Aqueduct
EAST
WARBURTON
River
Millwarra
Pmy
Warburton
East
Campus
RD
GRAHAM
RD
GEORGE
ST
RUPERT
RD
SURMAN AV
Yarra
C511
C507
YOUNGA
AV
BUANG
DONNA
FERNDALE
RD
WATTLETREE
RD
YOUNGA
RD
ELLIS CT
ISBURY AV
POINT
C511
WOODS
RIVERSIDE
DR
RD
WOODS
POINT
RIVERSIDE DR
JOINS 350
1 2 3 4 5 6 7 8 9 10 11 12 13 14 15 16 17 18 19 20

PREVIOUS MAP 306
JOINS 273
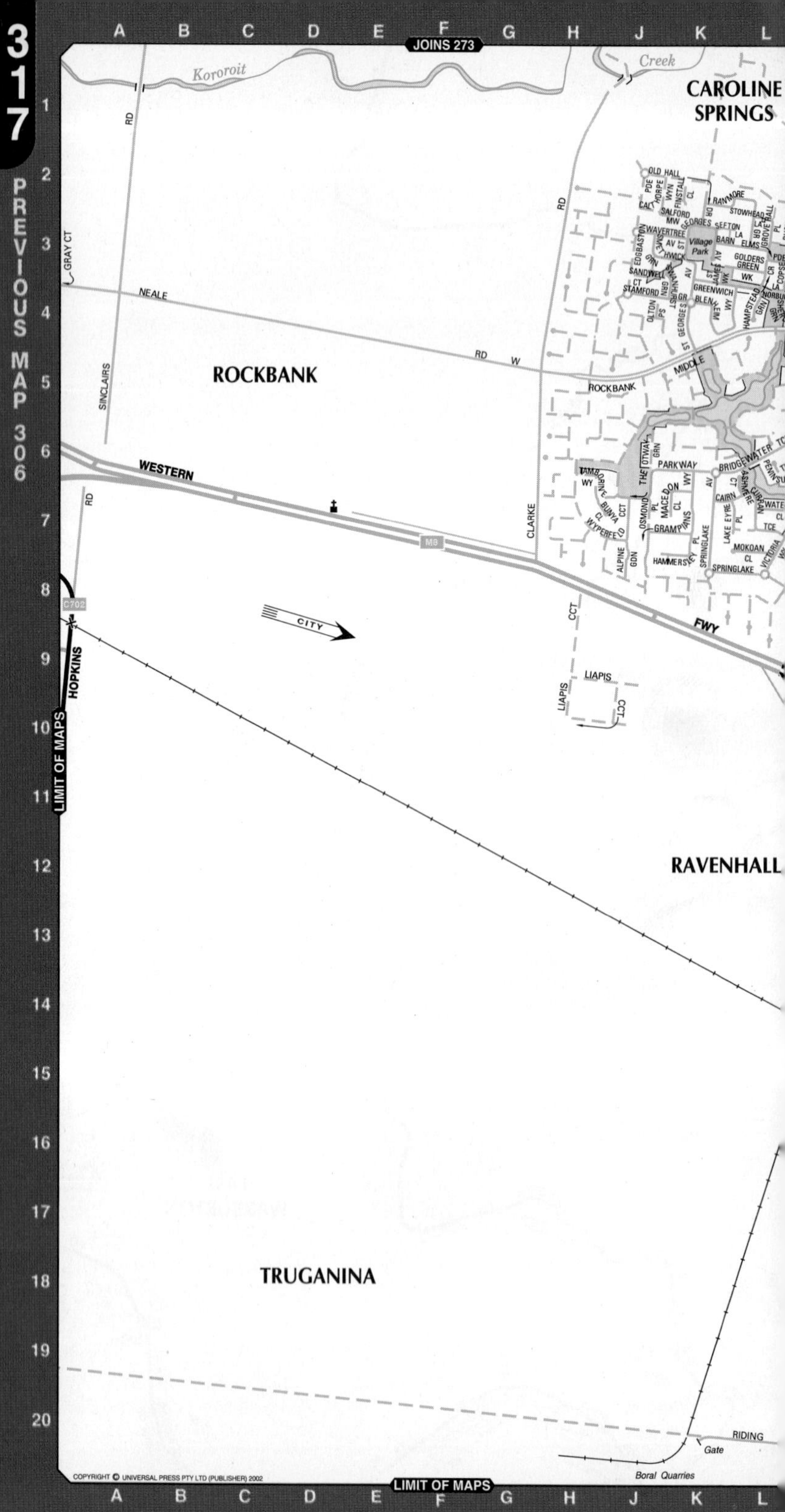

LIMIT OF MAPS

JOINS 274
275
BURNSIDE
ALBANVALE
DEER PARK
CAROLINE SPRINGS BVD
WESTWOOD DR
WESTERN (BALLARAT RD) HWY
M8
ROBINSONS RD
JOINS 319
Kororoit Ck
Isabella Williams Memorial Reserve
Aboriginal Reserve
Tamar Reserve
Deer Park Secondary College
Evergreen Res
Future Retirement Village
Future Shopping Plaza
Proposed Commercial Development
Future Hotel
Linear Park
Lake
Tennis
Playing Field
Brookside Pmy
Mowbray Coll
Cmnty Cntr
Cath
CFA
Fbr Billingham Res
Rotary Pk
Deer Park West Pmy
Bon Thomas Reserve
Metropolitan Womens Correctional Centre
Proposed Fwy
Railway
Disused
FOLEYS RD
EGAN ST
DEER ST
QUINN ST
BAYLISS RD
CAMPBELL AV
LIMIT OF MAPS
363
COPYRIGHT © UNIVERSAL PRESS PTY LTD (PUBLISHER) 2002

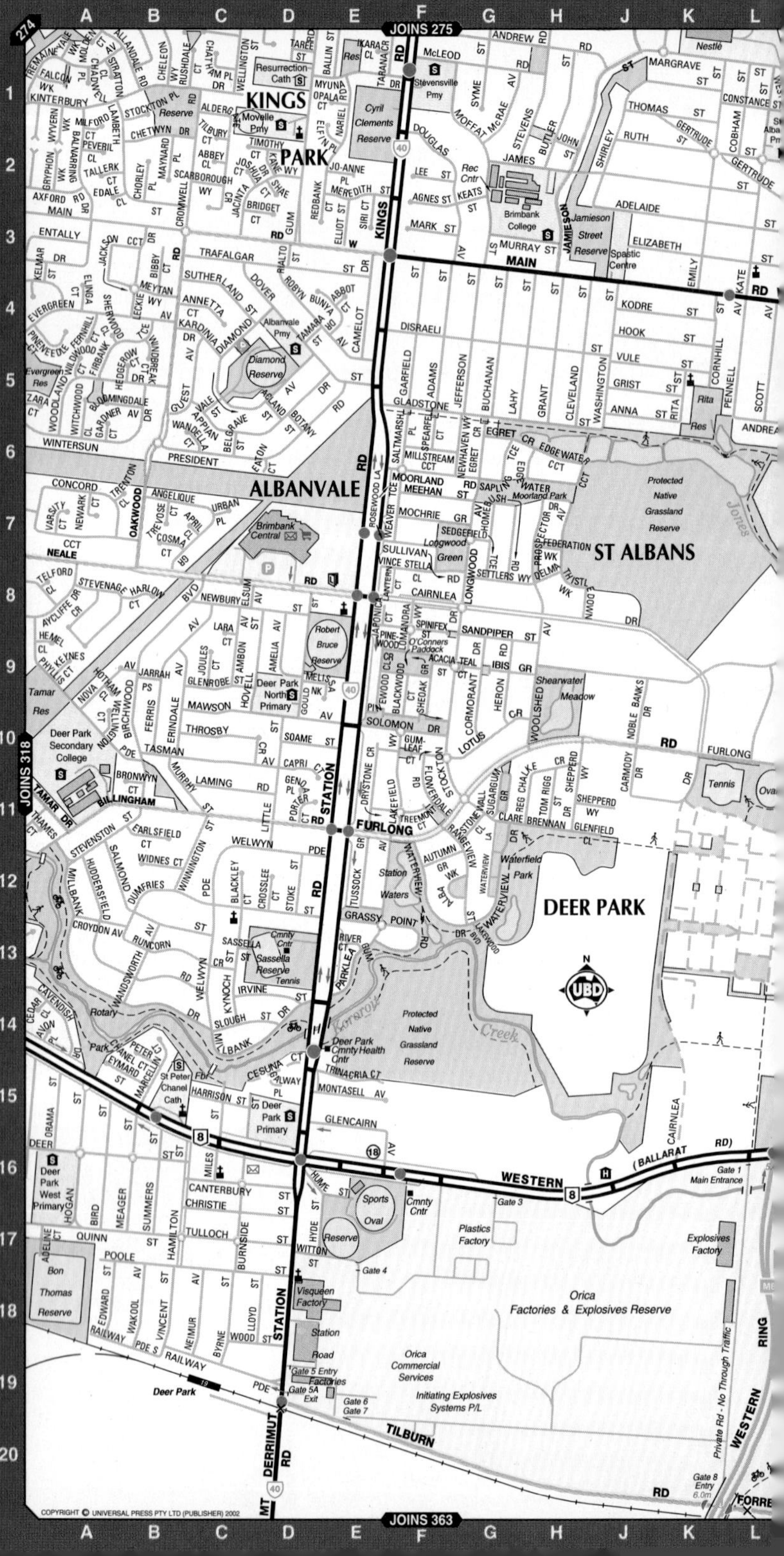

A B C D E F G H J K L

274
JOINS 275
JOINS 318
JOINS 363

1 2 3 4 5 6 7 8 9 10 11 12 13 14 15 16 17 18 19 20

KINGS PARK

ALBANVALE

ST ALBANS

DEER PARK

KINGS RD

MAIN RD

STATION RD

FURLONG RD

WESTERN (BALLARAT RD)

MT DERRIMUT RD

TILBURN RD

WESTERN RING RD

Resurrection Cath

Stevensville Pmy

Cyril Clements Reserve

Movelle Pmy

Rec Cntr

Brimbank College

Jamieson Street Reserve

Spastic Centre

Albanvale Pmy

Diamond Reserve

Evergreen Res

Rita Res

Protected Native Grassland Reserve

Brimbank Central

Longwood Green

Moorland Park

Robert Bruce Reserve

Deer Park North Primary

Shearwater Meadow

Tamar Res

Deer Park Secondary College

Tennis

Station Waters

Waterfield Park

Cmnty Cntr

Sassella Reserve

Kororoit Creek

Rotary Park

Deer Park Cmnty Health Cntr

St Peter Chanel Cath

Deer Park Primary

Deer Park West Primary

Sports Oval

Reserve

Plastics Factory

Explosives Factory

Bon Thomas Reserve

Visqueen Factory

Orica Factories & Explosives Reserve

Orica Commercial Services

Initiating Explosives Systems P/L

Gate 1 Main Entrance

Gate 3

Gate 4

Gate 5 Entry Factories

Gate 5A Exit

Gate 6

Gate 7

Gate 8 Entry 6.0m

Private Rd - No Through Traffic

Deer Park

Nestlé

UBD

A B C D E F G H J K L

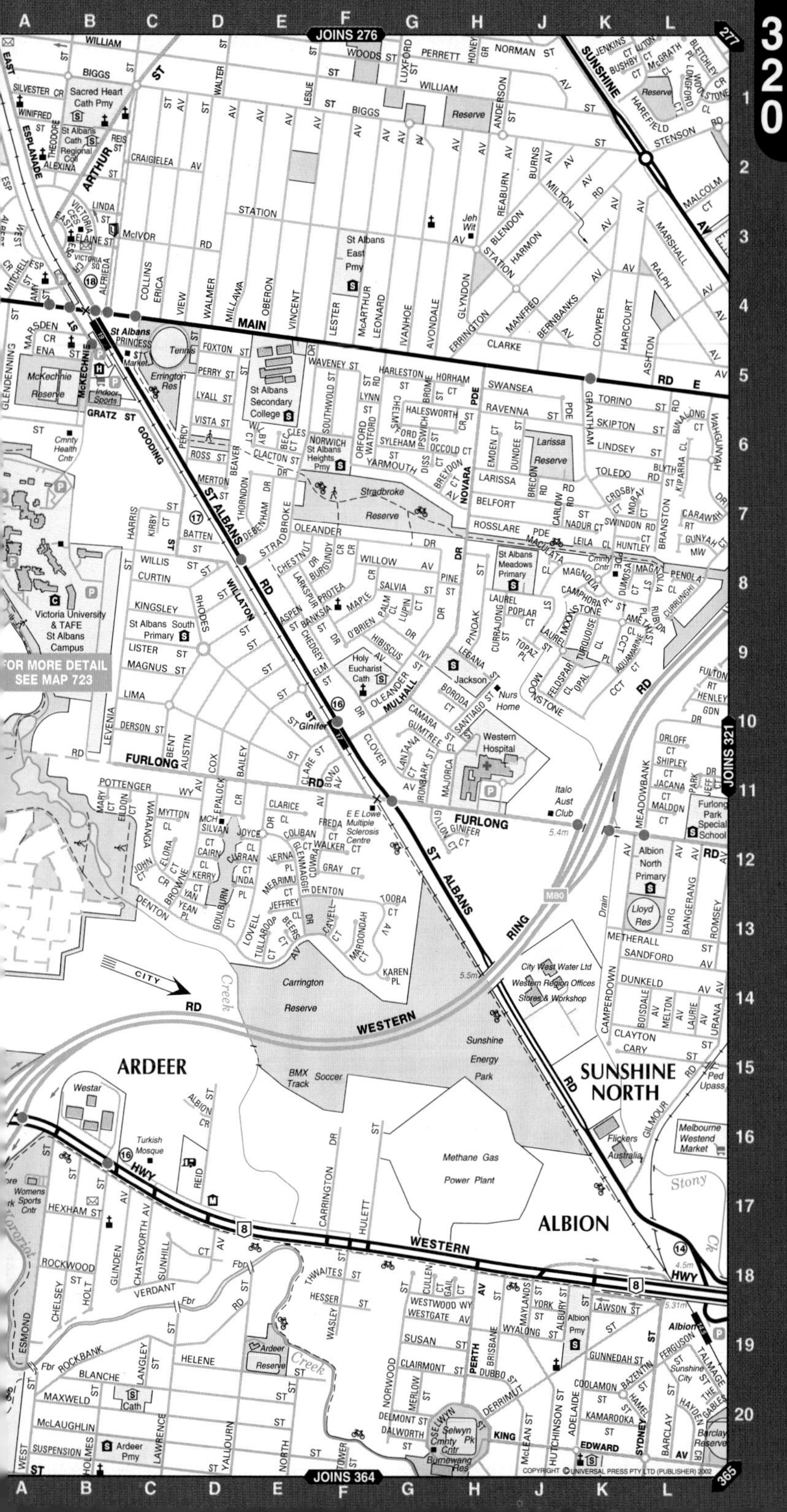
JOINS 276
JOINS 277
JOINS 321
JOINS 364
365
FOR MORE DETAIL SEE MAP 723
ARDEER
SUNSHINE NORTH
ALBION
ST ALBANS RD
MAIN RD
MAIN RD E
FURLONG RD
WESTERN RING RD
WESTERN HWY
CITY RD
SUNSHINE AV
St Albans
St Albans East Pmy
St Albans Secondary College
St Albans Heights Pmy
St Albans Meadows Primary
St Albans South Primary
Victoria University & TAFE St Albans Campus
McKechnie Reserve
Indoor Sports
Errington Res
Tennis
Stradbroke Reserve
Larissa Reserve
Holy Eucharist Cath
Jackson
Nurs Home
Western Hospital
Italo Aust Club
E E Lowe Multiple Sclerosis Centre
Carrington Reserve
Sunshine Energy Park
BMX Track
Soccer
Methane Gas Power Plant
City West Water Ltd Western Region Offices Stores & Workshop
Albion North Primary
Lloyd Res
Furlong Park Special School
Flickers Australia
Melbourne Westend Market
Westar
Turkish Mosque
Womens Sports Cntr
Ardeer Reserve
Ardeer Pmy
Albion Pmy
Selwyn Pk
Cmnty Cntr
Burnewang Res
Sunshine City
Barclay Reserve
Sacred Heart Cath Pmy
St Albans Cath
Regional Coll
Cmnty Health Cntr
Cmnty Cntr
Jeh Wit
Reserve
Stony Ck
Creek
Kororoit Ck
Ped Upass
M80
COPYRIGHT © UNIVERSAL PRESS PTY LTD (PUBLISHER) 2002

KEALBA

KEILOR EAST

ST ALBANS

SUNSHINE NORTH

SUNSHINE

Brimbank Park

Solaris Power Terminal Station

Quarry

E J WHITTEN BRIDGE

TRESTLE BRIDGE

Sterling Drive Res

Thompson Street Reserve

Furlong Park Special School

Melbourne Westend Market

Dempster Park

Victoria University Sunshine Campus

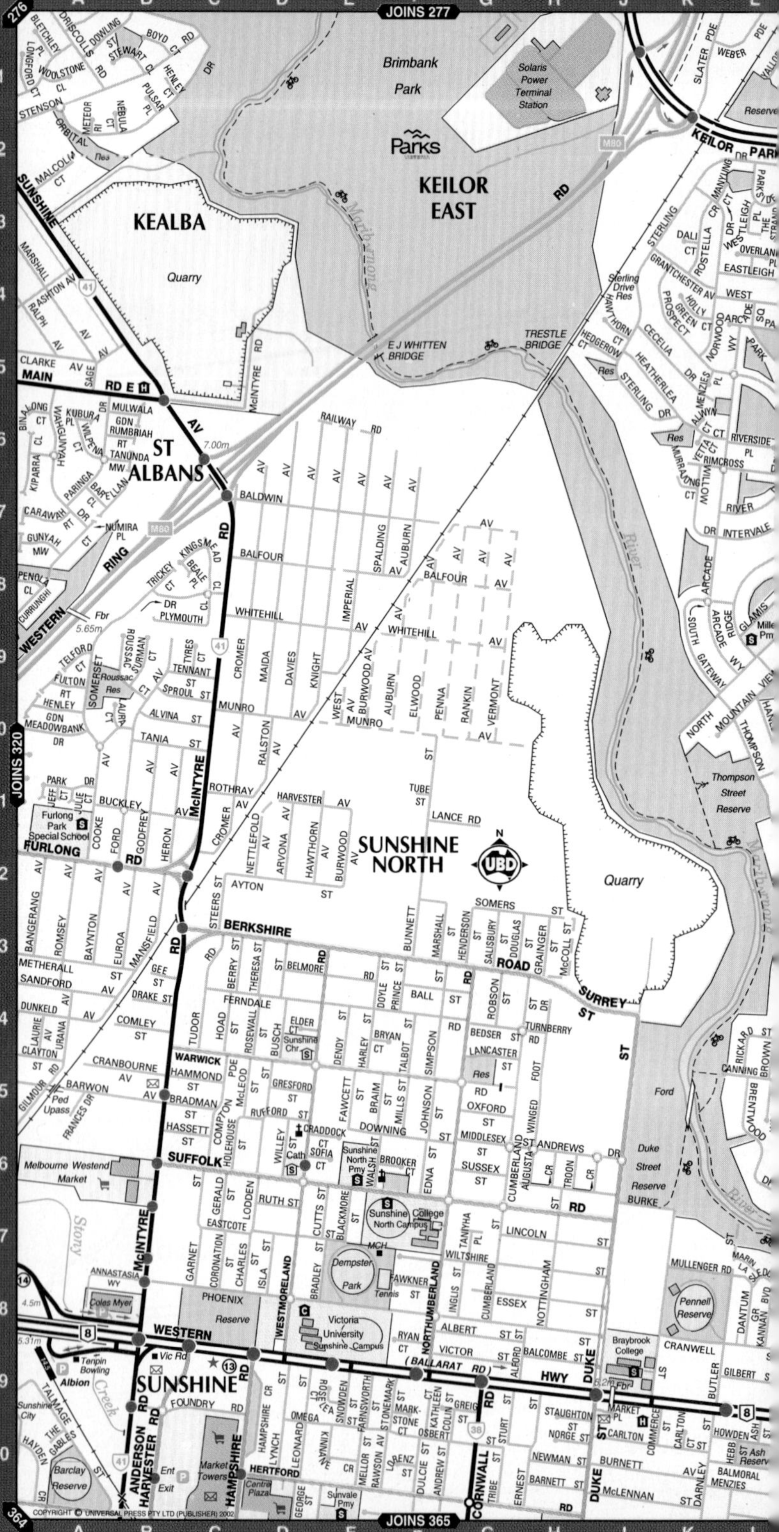

Sunshine College North Campus

Phoenix Reserve

Duke Street Reserve

Pennell Reserve

Braybrook College

Barclay Reserve

Market Towers

Centre Plaza

JOINS 320

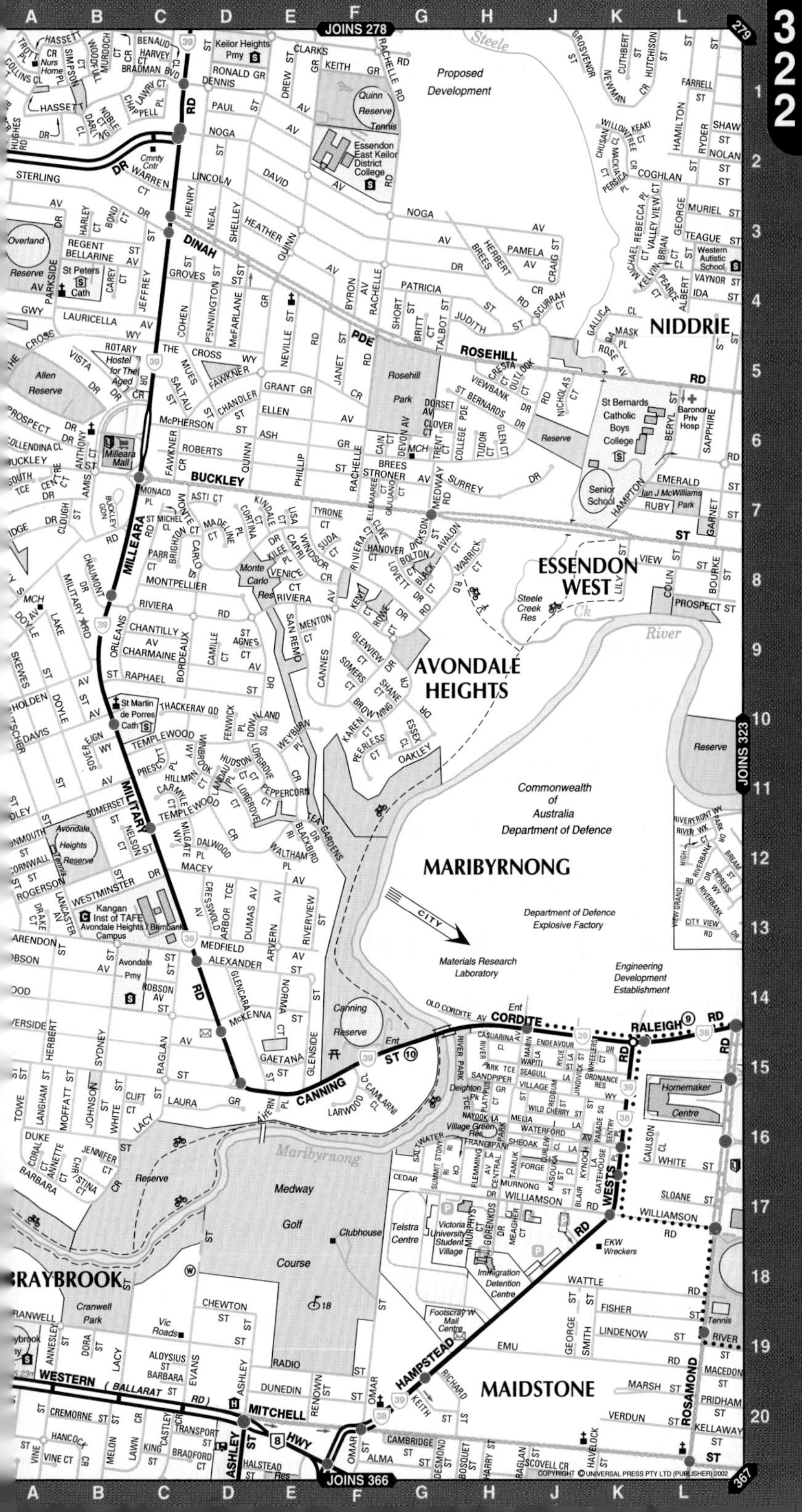
JOINS 278
279
JOINS 323
JOINS 366
367
NIDDRIE
ESSENDON WEST
AVONDALE HEIGHTS
MARIBYRNONG
BRAYBROOK
MAIDSTONE
Proposed Development
Keilor Heights Pmy
Quinn Reserve
Essendon East Keilor District College
Overland Reserve
St Peters Cath
Allen Reserve
Rotary Hostel for The Aged
Milleara Mall
Rosehill Park
St Bernards Catholic Boys College
Senior School
Ian J McWilliams Park
Baronor Priv Hosp
Western Autistic School
Monte Carlo Res
Steele Creek Res
Steele Ck
Maribyrnong River
St Martin de Porres Cath
Avondale Heights Reserve
Kangan Inst of TAFE Avondale Heights / Brimbank Campus
Avondale Pmy
Commonwealth of Australia Department of Defence
Department of Defence Explosive Factory
Materials Research Laboratory
Engineering Development Establishment
Canning Reserve
Homemaker Centre
Medway Golf Course
Clubhouse
Cranwell Park
Vic Roads
Telstra Centre
Victoria University Student Village
Immigration Detention Centre
Footscray W Mail Centre
EKW Wreckers
CITY
MILLEARA RD
MILITARY RD
BUCKLEY ST
ROSEHILL RD
CORDITE AV
RALEIGH RD
CANNING ST
WESTS RD
HAMPSTEAD RD
WESTERN (BALLARAT RD)
MITCHELL ST
ASHLEY ST
ROSAMOND RD
WILLIAMSON RD
RIVER ST
COPYRIGHT © UNIVERSAL PRESS PTY LTD (PUBLISHER) 2002

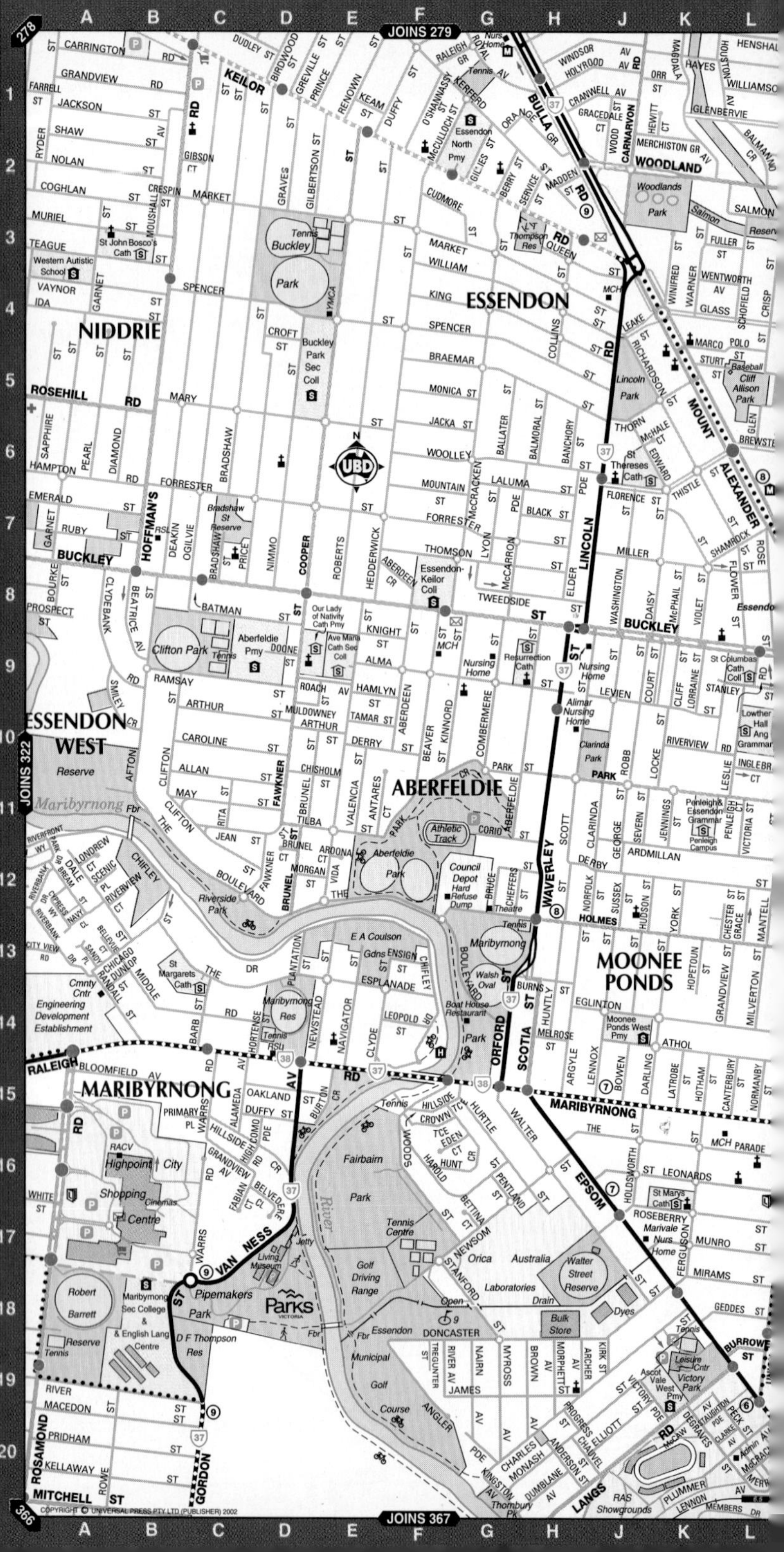

278

JOINS 279

A B C D E F G H J K L

1 2 3 4 5 6 7 8 9 10 11 12 13 14 15 16 17 18 19 20

NIDDRIE

ESSENDON

ESSENDON WEST

ABERFELDIE

MOONEE PONDS

MARIBYRNONG

Buckley Park

Clifton Park

Lincoln Park

Woodlands Park

Aberfeldie Park

Riverside Park

Fairbairn Park

Pipemakers Park

Highpoint City Shopping Centre

Robert Barrett Reserve

D F Thompson Res

Essendon Municipal Golf Course

Golf Driving Range

Orica Australia Laboratories

Walter Street Reserve

RAS Showgrounds

Maribyrnong River

Engineering Development Establishment

JOINS 322

366

JOINS 367

A B C D E F G H J K L

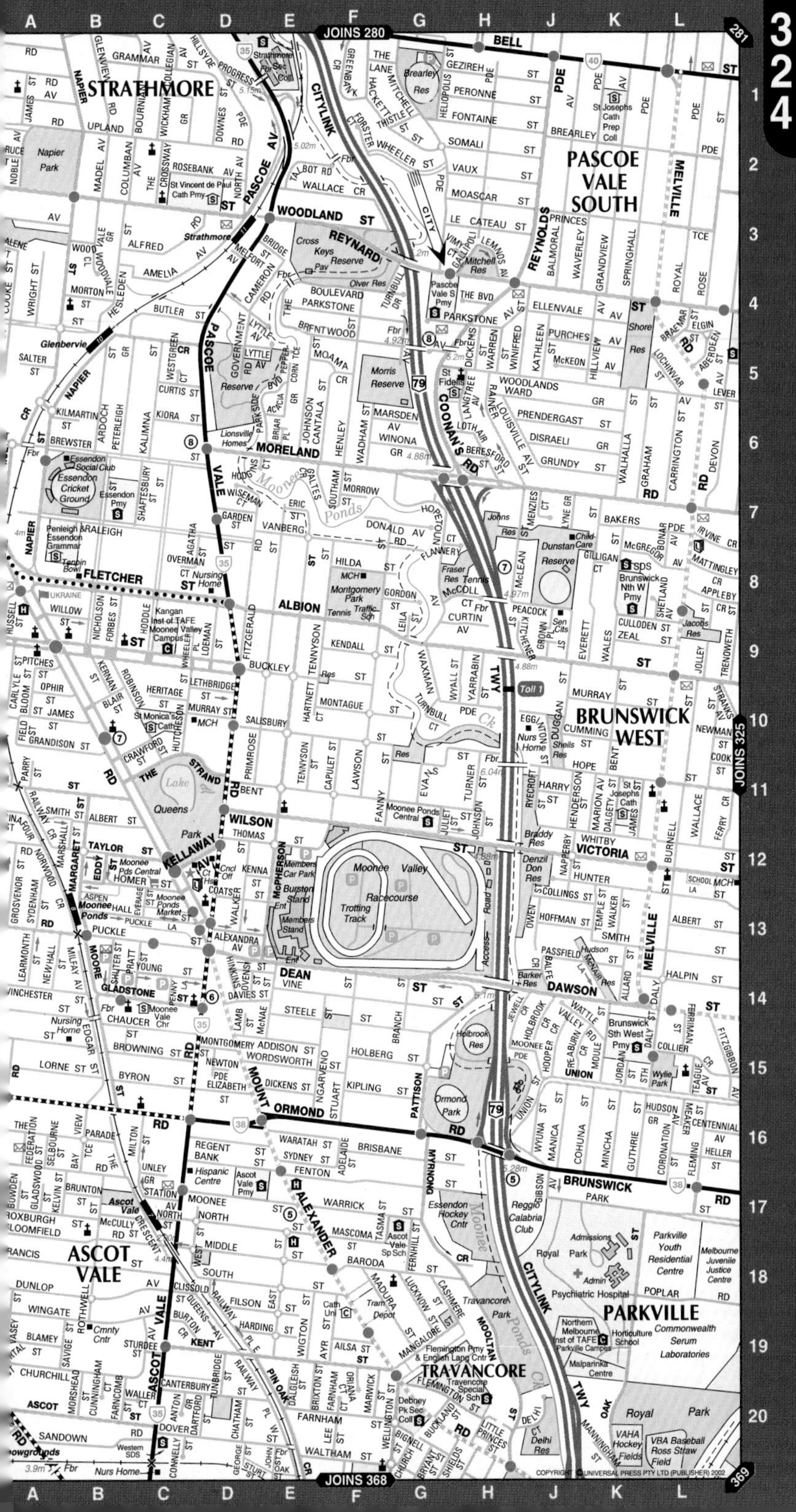
JOINS 280
281
STRATHMORE
PASCOE VALE SOUTH
BRUNSWICK WEST
ASCOT VALE
TRAVANCORE
PARKVILLE
CITYLINK
PASCOE VALE RD
MORELAND
ALBION
BUCKLEY
WOODLAND ST
BELL ST
Moonee Valley Racecourse
Queens Park
Royal Park
Royal Park Psychiatric Hospital
Parkville Youth Residential Centre
Melbourne Juvenile Justice Centre
Commonwealth Serum Laboratories
Essendon Cricket Ground
Morris Reserve
Cross Keys Reserve
Government Reserve
Dunstan Reserve
Montgomery Park
Ormond Park
Holbrook Res
Mitchell Res
Brearley Res
MT ALEXANDER RD
MOONEE PONDS
ORMOND RD
BRUNSWICK RD
MELVILLE
JOINS 325
JOINS 368
369
COPYRIGHT © UNIVERSAL PRESS PTY LTD (PUBLISHER) 2002

JOINS 281
JOINS 324
JOINS 369
280
368
COBURG
Coburg East
BRUNSWICK WEST
BRUNSWICK
BRUNSWICK EAST
PARKVILLE
PRINCES HILL
CARLTON NORTH
Moreland City College
Royal Park
Royal Melbourne Zoo
Princes Park
Optus Oval Carlton Cricket Ground
Gilpin Park
Clifton Tennis Park
Brunswick Sec Coll
Barkly Square Shopping Centre
Melbourne Juvenile Justice Centre
North West Hosp (Mt Royal)
Commonwealth Serum Laboratories
Vaucluse Hospital
John Fawkner Hospital
Bridges City Oval Reserve
Alex.G.Gillion Oval
Council Depot
Princes Hill Pmy
Anderson Res
Reaburn Res
Bush Reserve
A B C D E F G H J K L
1 2 3 4 5 6 7 8 9 10 11 12 13 14 15 16 17 18 19 20

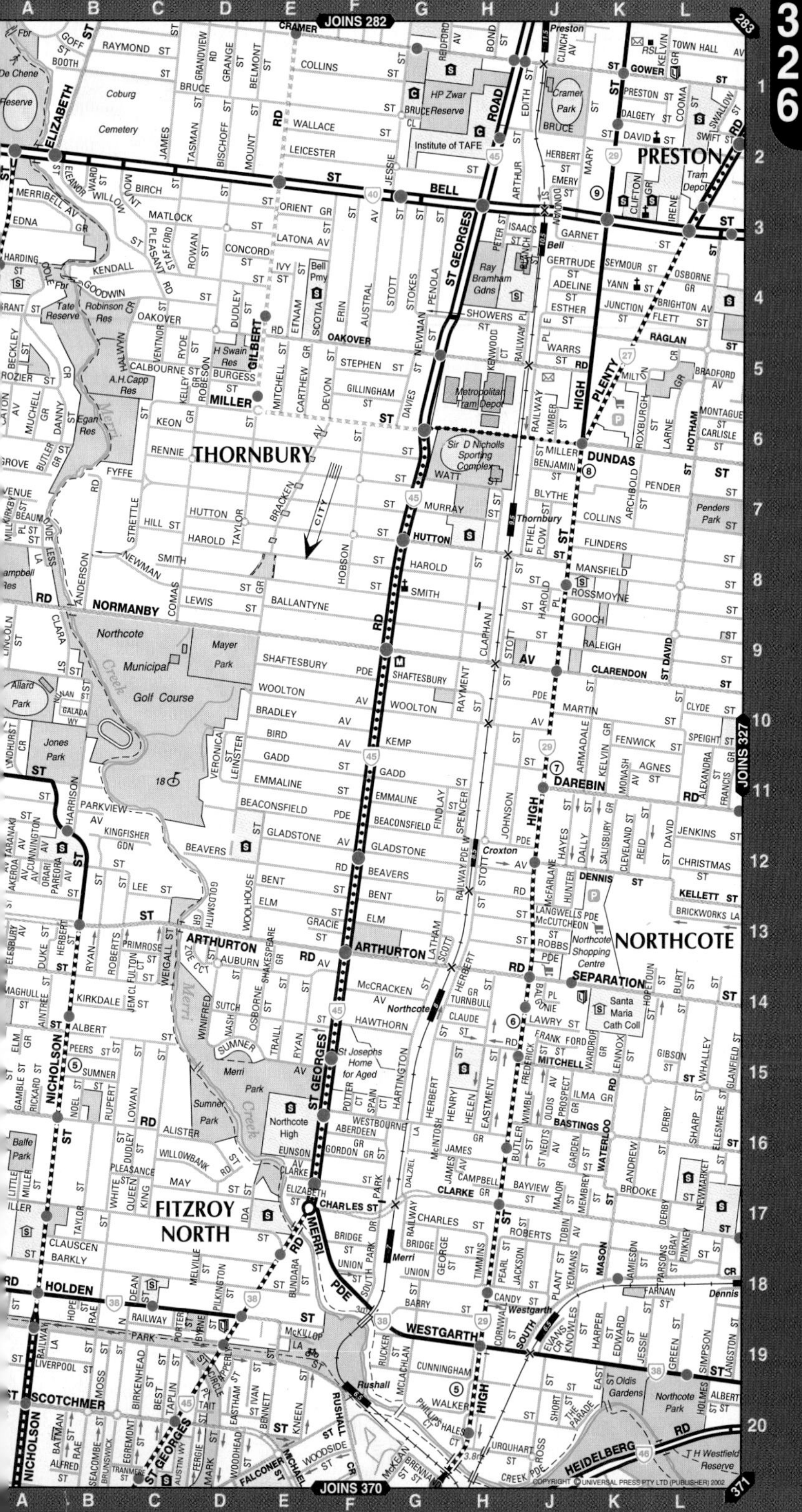
JOINS 282
283
PRESTON
THORNBURY
NORTHCOTE
FITZROY NORTH
JOINS 327
JOINS 370
371
Coburg Cemetery
HP Zwar Reserve
Institute of TAFE
Cramer Park
Ray Bramham Gdns
Metropolitan Tram Depot
Sir D Nicholls Sporting Complex
Penders Park
Northcote Municipal Golf Course
Mayer Park
Allard Park
Jones Park
A.H.Capp Res
Tate Reserve
Robinson Res
Egan Res
H Swain Res
Merri Creek
Merri Park
Sumner Park
Northcote High
St Josephs Home for Aged
Northcote Shopping Centre
Santa Maria Cath Coll
Balfe Park
Northcote Park
Oldis Gardens
T H Westfield Reserve
ST GEORGES RD
HIGH ST
BELL ST
NORMANBY AV
SEPARATION ST
WESTGARTH ST
HEIDELBERG RD
MERRI PDE
NICHOLSON ST
PLENTY RD
DUNDAS ST
ARTHURTON RD
CLARENDON ST
DAREBIN RD
HOLDEN ST
SCOTCHMER ST
Croxton
Thornbury
Northcote
Merri
Westgarth
Rushall
Bell
Preston
COPYRIGHT © UNIVERSAL PRESS PTY LTD (PUBLISHER) 2002

A B C D E F G H J K L
1 2 3 4 5 6 7 8 9 10 11 12 13 14 15 16 17 18 19 20
JOINS 283
282
JOINS 326
JOINS 371
370
PRESTON
THORNBURY
NORTHCOTE
FAIRFIELD
ALPHINGTON
Northland Shopping Centre
Northland Home Centre
T W Blake Park
Commonwealth Industrial Gases Limited
H L T Culton Park
T A Cochrane Res
Penders Park
Penders Grove Pmy
Hayes Park
Thornbury-Darebin Secondary College
John Cain Memorial Park
Wales St Pmy
Pottery
Aquatic Centre
McDonnell Park
R Thompson Reserve
Johnson Park
Westgarth Pmy
Fairfield Pmy
Pitcher Park
Parklands
Rockbeare Park
Darebin Creek Forest Park
C Cummins Reserve
Cartledge Reserve
Seddon Reserve
Rossi Pk
Alphington Park
Australian Paper
T H Westfield Reserve
Fairfield Park
Coate Park
Alphington
Fairfield
Darebin
Creek
CITY
Fbr 5.53m
MURRAY RD
GOWER ST
BELL ST
ALBERT ST
STATION ST
CHIFLEY DR
PLENTY RD
DAREBIN RD
VICTORIA RD
SEPARATION ST
GRANGE RD
HEIDELBERG RD
CHANDLER HWY
LIVINGSTONE ST
LIBERTY PDE
WESTGARTH ST
HIGH ST
COPYRIGHT © UNIVERSAL PRESS PTY LTD (PUBLISHER) 2002

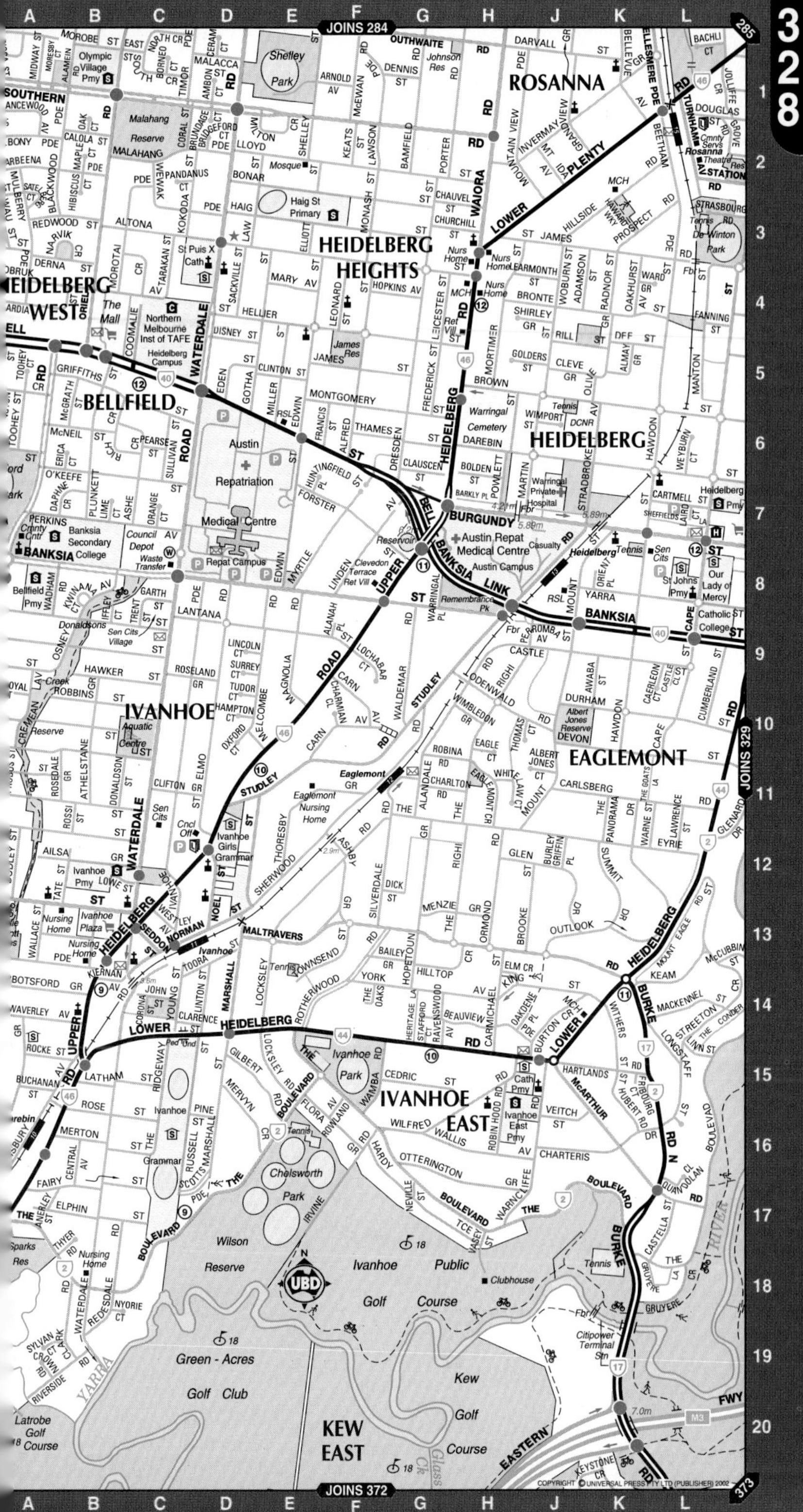
A B C D E F G H J K L
JOINS 284
285
1 2 3 4 5 6 7 8 9 10 11 12 13 14 15 16 17 18 19 20
ROSANNA
HEIDELBERG HEIGHTS
HEIDELBERG WEST
BELLFIELD
HEIDELBERG
IVANHOE
EAGLEMONT
IVANHOE EAST
KEW EAST
Olympic Village Pmy
Shelley Park
Malahang Reserve
Johnson Res
Haig St Primary
St Puis X Cath
The Mall
Northern Melbourne Inst of TAFE Heidelberg Campus
James Res
Warringal Cemetery
Austin Repatriation Medical Centre
Repat Campus
Austin Repat Medical Centre
Austin Campus
Remembrance Pk
Warringal Private Hospital
Banksia Secondary College
Council Depot
Waste Transfer
Bellfield Pmy
Donaldsons
Sen Cits Village
Aquatic Centre
Eaglemont Nursing Home
Ivanhoe Girls Grammar
Ivanhoe Pmy
Ivanhoe Plaza
Ivanhoe Park
Ivanhoe Grammar
Chelsworth Park
Wilson Reserve
Ivanhoe Public Golf Course
Clubhouse
Green - Acres Golf Club
Kew Golf Course
Latrobe Golf Course
Citipower Terminal Stn
Albert Jones Reserve
St Johns Pmy
Our Lady of Mercy
Catholic College
Heidelberg Pmy
Rosanna Station
De Winton Park
Sparks Res
YARRA
RIVER
EASTERN FWY
LOWER PLENTY RD
UPPER HEIDELBERG RD
LOWER HEIDELBERG RD
BANKSIA ST
WATERDALE RD
BURKE RD
STUDLEY RD
JOINS 329
JOINS 372
373

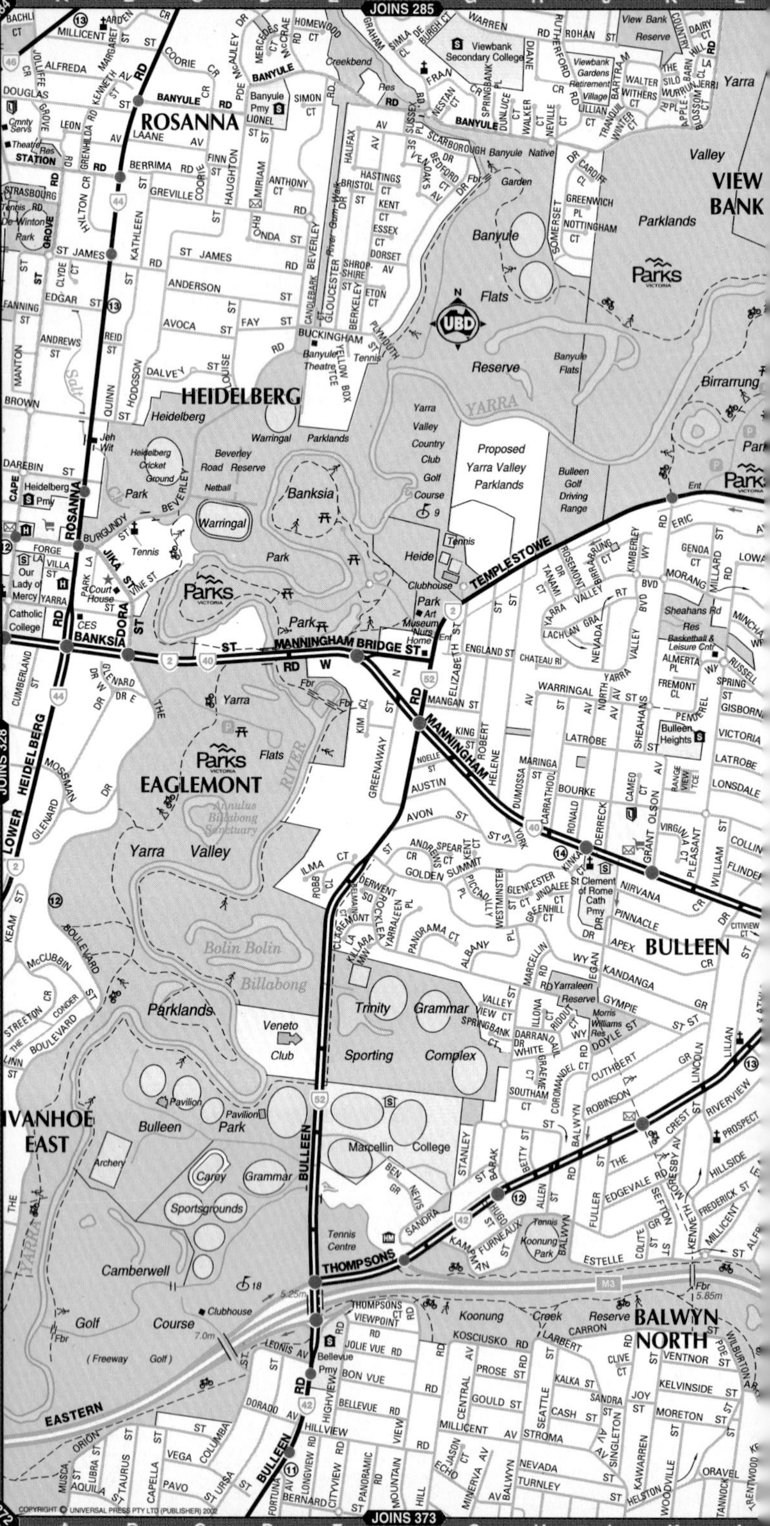

A B C D E F G H J K L

JOINS 285

284

ROSANNA

HEIDELBERG

VIEW BANK

EAGLEMONT

BULLEEN

IVANHOE EAST

BALWYN NORTH

Viewbank Secondary College

Banyule Pmy

Banyule Native Garden

Banyule Flats Reserve

Parks Victoria

Yarra Valley Parklands

Birrarung

Heidelberg Cricket Ground

Beverley Road Reserve

Warringal Parklands

Banksia Park

Heide Park

Art Museum

Yarra Valley Country Club Golf Course

Proposed Yarra Valley Parklands

Bulleen Golf Driving Range

Heidelberg Pmy

Our Lady of Mercy Catholic College

Court House

Yarra Flats

Annulus Billabong Sanctuary

Bolin Bolin Billabong

Yarra Valley Parklands

Veneto Club

Trinity Grammar Sporting Complex

Bulleen Park

Marcellin College

Carey Grammar Sportsgrounds

Camberwell Golf Course

(Freeway Golf)

Tennis Centre

Koonung Creek Reserve

Koonung Park

Bellevue Pmy

St Clement of Rome Cath Pmy

Bulleen Heights

Yarraleen Reserve

Morris Williams Res

Sheahans Rd Res Basketball & Leisure Cntr

MANNINGHAM BRIDGE ST

BANKSIA ST

ROSANNA RD

LOWER HEIDELBERG RD

BULLEEN RD

MANNINGHAM RD

TEMPLESTOWE RD

THOMPSONS RD

EASTERN FWY

BANYULE RD

YARRA RIVER

JOINS 328

1 2 3 4 5 6 7 8 9 10 11 12 13 14 15 16 17 18 19 20

372

JOINS 373

A B C D E F G H J K L

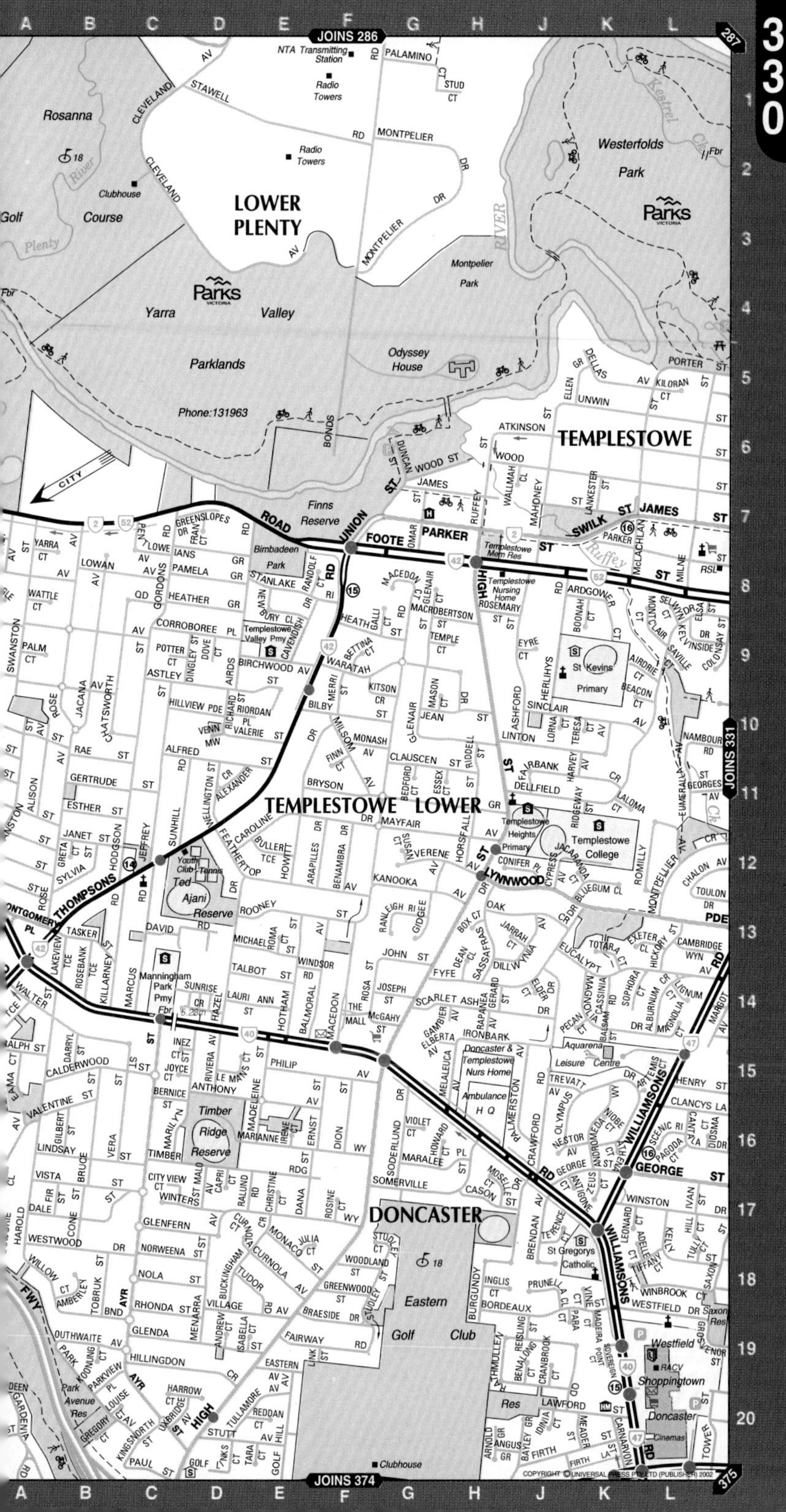
JOINS 286
LOWER PLENTY
Yarra Valley Parklands
Phone:131963
Westerfolds Park
Rosanna Golf Course
Montpelier Park
Odyssey House
Finns Reserve
TEMPLESTOWE
TEMPLESTOWE LOWER
Ted Ajani Reserve
Timber Ridge Reserve
Manningham Park Pmy
St Kevins Primary
Templestowe College
Templestowe Heights Primary
Aquarena Leisure Centre
DONCASTER
Eastern Golf Club
St Gregorys Catholic
Westfield Shoppingtown
JOINS 331
JOINS 374
COPYRIGHT © UNIVERSAL PRESS PTY LTD (PUBLISHER) 2002

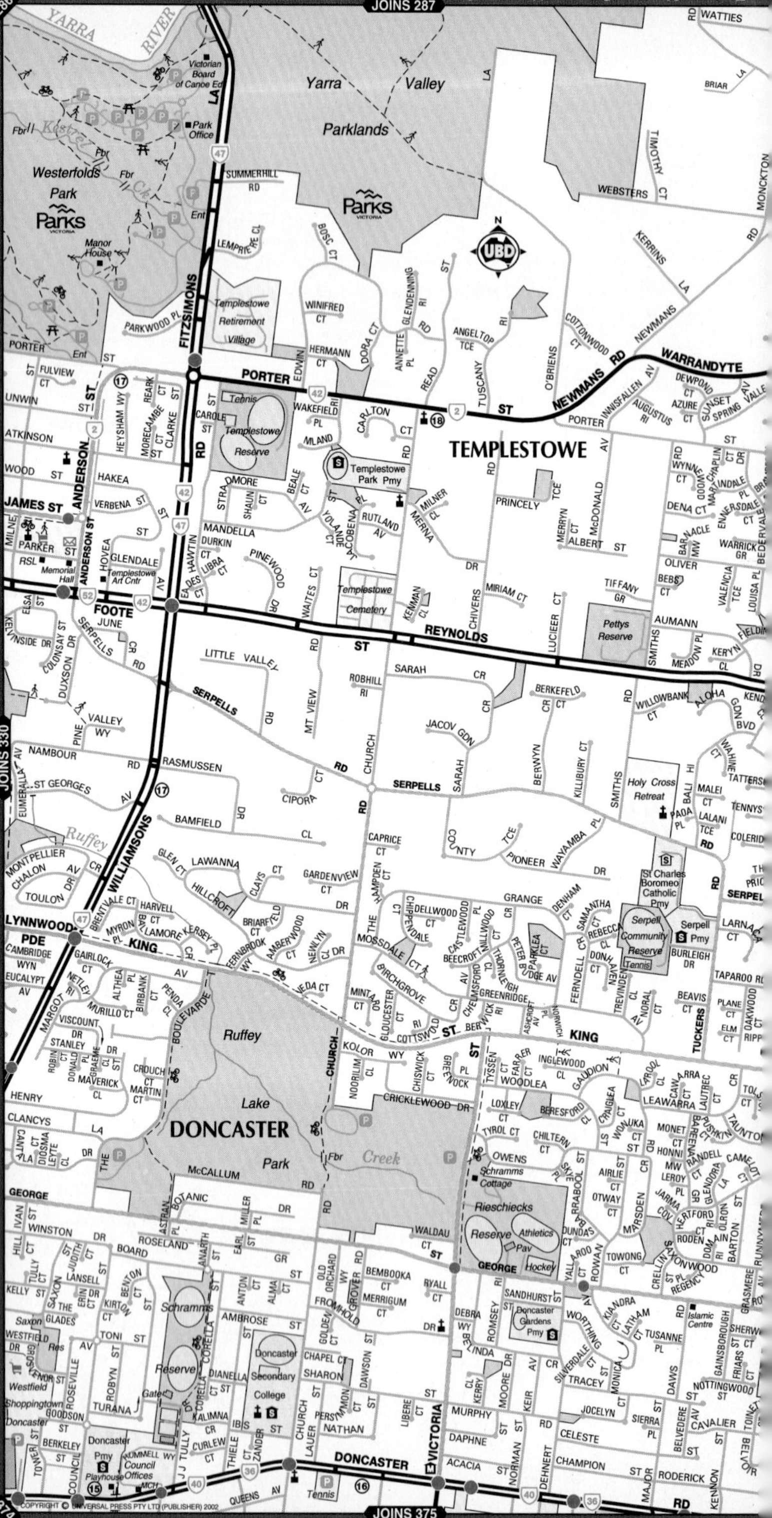

Yarra River
Victorian Board of Canoe Ed
Yarra Valley Parklands
WATTIES RD
BRIAR LA
Park Office
Kestrel Ck
Fbr
Westerfolds Park
Parks Victoria
TIMOTHY CT
SUMMERHILL RD
WEBSTERS
MONCKTON RD
Ent
Manor House
LEMPRIERE CL
BOSC CT
KERRINS LA
Templestowe Retirement Village
WINIFRED CT
GLENDENNING RI
ST
PARKWOOD PL
RD
ANGELTOP TCE
RI
COTTONWOOD CT
NEWMANS RD
PORTER
Ent
HERMANN CT
EDWIN
DORA CT
ANNETTE PL
READ
TUSCANY
O'BRIENS
WARRANDYTE
FULVIEW CT
PORTER ST
ST
NEWMANS
INNISFALLEN AV
DEWPOND CT
AZURE CT
SUNSET AV
SPRING VALLEY
UNWIN ST
ANDERSON ST
HEYSHAM WY
MORECAMBE ST
REARK CT
CLARKE ST
FITZSIMONS LA
CAROLE ST
Tennis
Templestowe Reserve
WAKEFIELD RI
PL
CARLTON CT
AUGUSTUS RI
ST
ATKINSON
MLAND
TEMPLESTOWE
WOOD ST
HAKEA
Templestowe Park Pmy
STRADMORE
BEALE AV
YOLANDE CT
JACOBENA PL
MILNER CL
PRINCELY TCE
McDONALD AV
WYNNE CT
DENA CT
JAMES ST
VERBENA ST
ST
SHAUN CT
RUTLAND AV
MERNA
MERRYN CT
ALBERT ST
BARNACLE MW
WARRICK GR
MILNE
PARKER ST
RSL Memorial Hall
HOVEA
GLENDALE
Templestowe Art Cntr
MANDELLA
DURKIN CT
LIBRA CT
PINEWOOD DR
WAITES CT
Templestowe Cemetery
KENMAN CL
CHIVERS
MIRIAM CT
DR
TIFFANY GR
OLIVER
BEBS CT
VALENCIA TCE
LOUISA PL
FOOTE
EADES CT
HAWTIN
ELSA
JUNE
KELVINSIDE DR
COLONSAY ST
SERPELLS CR
REYNOLDS
LUCIEER CT
Pettys Reserve
SMITHS
AUMANN
MEADOW PL
KERYN CL
FIELDING
DUXSON
LITTLE VALLEY RD
ST
ROBHILL RI
SARAH CR
BERKEFELD CR CT
WILLOWBANK CT
ALOHA
KENDALL
BVD
PINE VALLEY WY
SERPELLS
JACOV GDN
MT VIEW
RD
CHURCH
BERWYN
KILLIBURY CT
NAMBOUR
RD
RASMUSSEN
RD
CIPORA CT
SERPELLS
SARAH
SMITHS
Holy Cross Retreat
BALI HI
MALEI CT
LALANI TCE
PADA PL
TATTERSALL
TENNYSON
COLERIDGE
EUMERALLA ST
ST GEORGES AV
BAMFIELD
DR
CL
WILLIAMSONS
COUNTY TCE
WAYAMBA PL
PIONEER
DR
RD
Ruffey
MONTPELLIER
CHALON AV
TOULON DR
CR
GLEN CT
LAWANNA
HILLCROFT
CLAYS CT
GARDENVIEW CT
DR
CAPRICE CT
THE HAMPDEN CT
GRANGE
DENHAM CT
St Charles Boromeo Catholic Pmy
SERPELLS
LYNNWOOD PDE
BRENTVALE CT
HARVELL CT
MYRON PL
BALLAMORE
KERSEY PL
CR
BRIARFIELD CT
AMBERWOOD CT
NEWLYN CL
DR
FERNBROOK WY
CHIPPENDALE
DELLWOOD CT
CASTLEWOOD PL
MILLWOOD CT
PETER BUDGE AV
PARKLEA CT
SAMANTHA CT
REBECCA CT
Serpell Community Reserve
Tennis
Serpell Pmy
LARNACA CT
CAMBRIDGE
WYN
EUCALYPT AV
KING
GAIRLOCK CT
AV
MOSSDALE CT
BIRCHGROVE
BEECROFT CL
THORNLEIGH
GREENRIDGE
FERNDELL CR
DONHAVEN CT
TREVINDEN CL
NORAL AV
BURLEIGH DR
TAPAROO RD
MARGOT
NETLEY RI
ALTHEA PL
BIRBANK CT
PENDA CL
BOULEVARDE
VEDA CT
MINTARO CT
GLOUCESTER CT
RI
CHELMSFORD
ASHCROFT PL
NORWICH
BEAVIS CT
PLANE CT
ELM CT
OAKWOOD CT
RIPPON
VISCOUNT DR
MURILLO CT
STANLEY DR
ROBIN CT
DONALD PL
GRAEME PL
Ruffey
COTTSWOLD
ST
BERWICK
KING
TUCKERS
MAVERICK CL
CRUDGE CT
MARTIN CT
KOLOR WY
NOORILIM CL
CHISWICK CT
GREENOCK
PL
ST
TYSSEN CT
FARRER CT
INGLEWOOD CL
GAUDION
WOODLEA
LAPOOL CT
ARRA CT
LEAWARRA
LAUTREC CT
TOLSTOY
HENRY CL
Lake
CRICKLEWOOD DR
LOXLEY
BERESFORD
CRAIGLEA
WONUKA
MONET CT
BARENA
PUSHKIN
TAUNTON
CLANCYS LA
DONCASTER
TYROL CT
CHILTERN CT
ST
HONNI CT
CANTALA
DIOSMA
LEYTE CL
DR
THE
Park
Fbr
Creek
OWENS
Schramms Cottage
SKYE
BARRABOOL
AIRLIE CT
OTWAY CT
MW
LEROY
RANDELL CT
CAMELOT
McCALLUM
RD
GEORGE
BOTANIC
MILLER PL
DR
RD
Rieschiecks Reserve
Athletics
Pav
MARSDEN
JARMA
COV
GLENDORA
GR
HERTFORD
IVAN
ST
HILL CT
WINSTON
DR
ASTRAN
EARL
ST
GR
WALDAU CT
ST
DUNDAS
Hockey
GEORGE
RODEN CT
DOMAIN
BARTON
RUNNYMEDE
TULLY CT
JUDITH CT
LANSELL
ROSELAND
BOARD
ANARTH
OLD ORCHARD WY
GROVER
BEMBOOKA CT
RYALL CT
ROWAN
TOWONG CT
CRELLIN
SAXONWOOD
REGENCY
KELLY ST
SAXON
THE GLADES
ERIN
KIRTON
BENTON
Schramms
ANTON CT
ALMA CT
ST
FROMHOLD
MERRIGUM CT
RI
SANDHURST
YALLAROO
KIANDRA CT
LATHAM
GRASMERE
Saxon
WESTFIELD DR
Res
AV
TONI ST
AMBROSE
Doncaster Secondary College
GOLDEN CT
DR
DEBRA WY
ROMSEY
Doncaster Gardens Pmy
WORTHING
TUSANNE PL
Islamic Centre
GAINSBOROUGH
SHERWOOD
FRIARS CT
GROSVENOR ST
ROSEVILLE
ROBYN
Reserve
DIANELLA CT
CORELLA
CHAPEL CT
SHARON
DAWSON
BELINDA
MOORE DR
AV
CR
SILVERDALE CT
MONICA CT
TRACEY
DAWS
NOTTINGWOOD
Westfield Shoppingtown Doncaster
GOODSON
TURANA
Gate
KALIMNA
CR
IBIS
ST
CHURCH
PERSIMMON CT
NATHAN
LIBERE CT
KERRY CL
KEIR
MURPHY
JOCELYN
SIERRA PL
CAVALIER
TOINETTE
BERKELEY
TOWER
COUNCIL
Doncaster Pmy
Playhouse
RUMMELL WY
Council Offices
MCH
JJ TULLY
CURLEW CT
THIELE
ZANDER
LAUER
DONCASTER
VICTORIA
DAPHNE
ACACIA
ST
NORMAN
DEHNERT
CELESTE
CHAMPION
ST
MAJOR
RODERICK
KENNON
BELVEDERE
BELVOIR
QUEENS AV
Tennis
RD

JOINS 330
JOINS 375
374

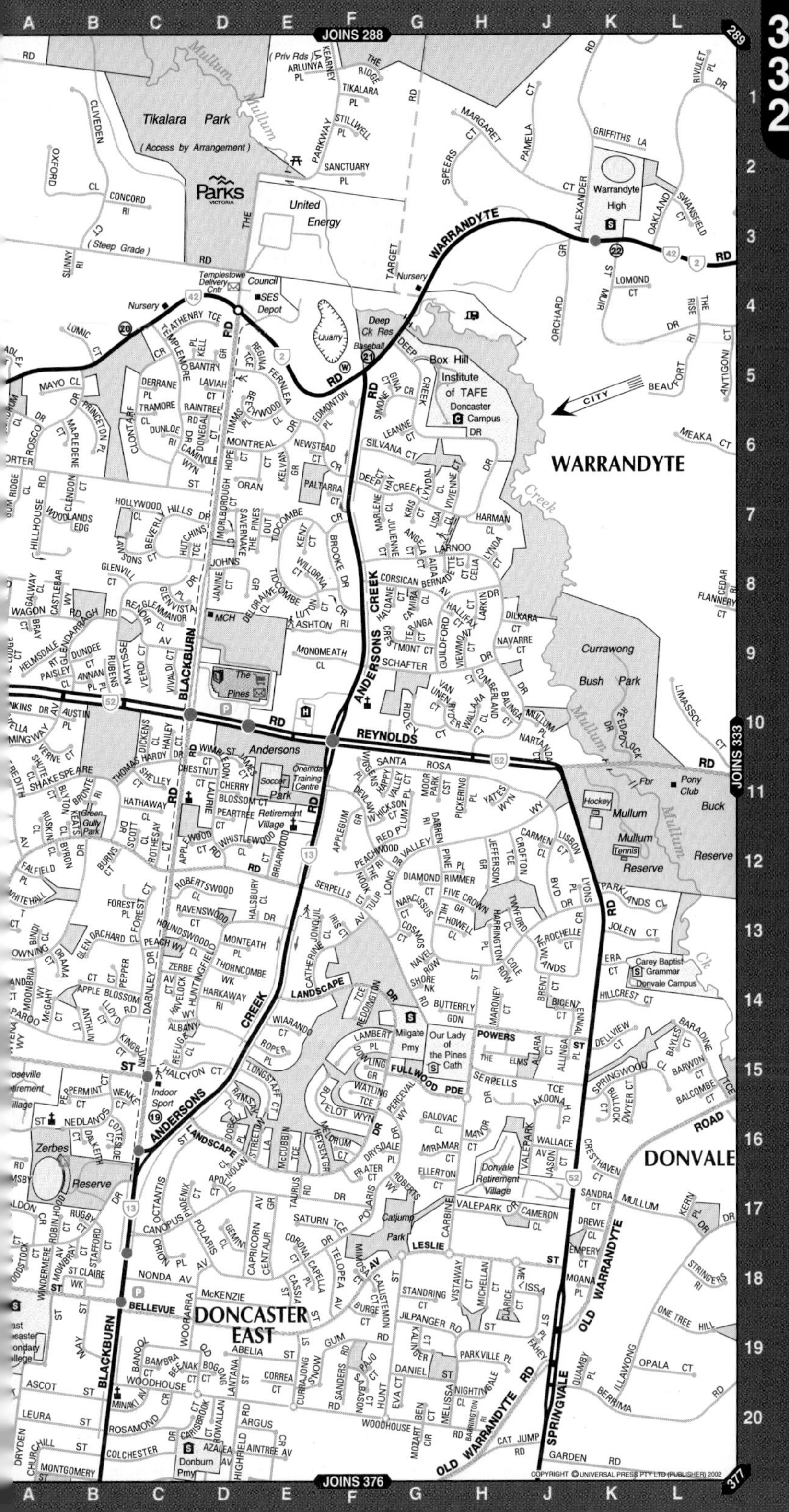
JOINS 288
289
Tikalara Park
(Access by Arrangement)
Parks VICTORIA
United Energy
WARRANDYTE RD
Warrandyte High
Templestowe Delivery Cntr
Council
SES Depot
Nursery
Quarry
Deep Ck Res
Baseball
Box Hill Institute of TAFE Doncaster Campus
CITY
WARRANDYTE
Creek
Currawong Bush Park
MCH
The Pines
REYNOLDS RD
Andersons Park
Onemda Training Centre
Soccer
Retirement Village
JOINS 333
Pony Club
Hockey
Mullum Mullum Reserve
Buck Reserve
Tennis
Carey Baptist Grammar Donvale Campus
Milgate Pmy
Our Lady of the Pines Cath
Indoor Sport
Zerbes Reserve
Green Gully Park
Donvale Retirement Village
Catjump Park
DONVALE
DONCASTER EAST
Donburn Pmy
BLACKBURN RD
ANDERSONS CREEK RD
OLD WARRANDYTE RD
SPRINGVALE RD
JOINS 376
377
COPYRIGHT © UNIVERSAL PRESS PTY LTD (PUBLISHER) 2002

JOINS 289

288

JOINS 332

376

JOINS 377

JOINS 290
291
JOINS 335
JOINS 378
379

WARRANDYTE SOUTH

WARRANWOOD

RINGWOOD NORTH

Warrandyte State Park

The Common

The 100 Acres

Colman Park

Quambee Reserve

Monterey Bush Park

Yarra Valley Hills

Reach Out Christian Cntr

Youth Dimension Education Centre

Alfreds Homestead Restaurant

Potters Cottage

Warranwood Pmy

Rudolph Steiner

The Michael Centre

Parkwood Sec Coll

WARRANDYTE - RINGWOOD RD

CROYDON RD

WONGA RD

JUMPING CREEK RD

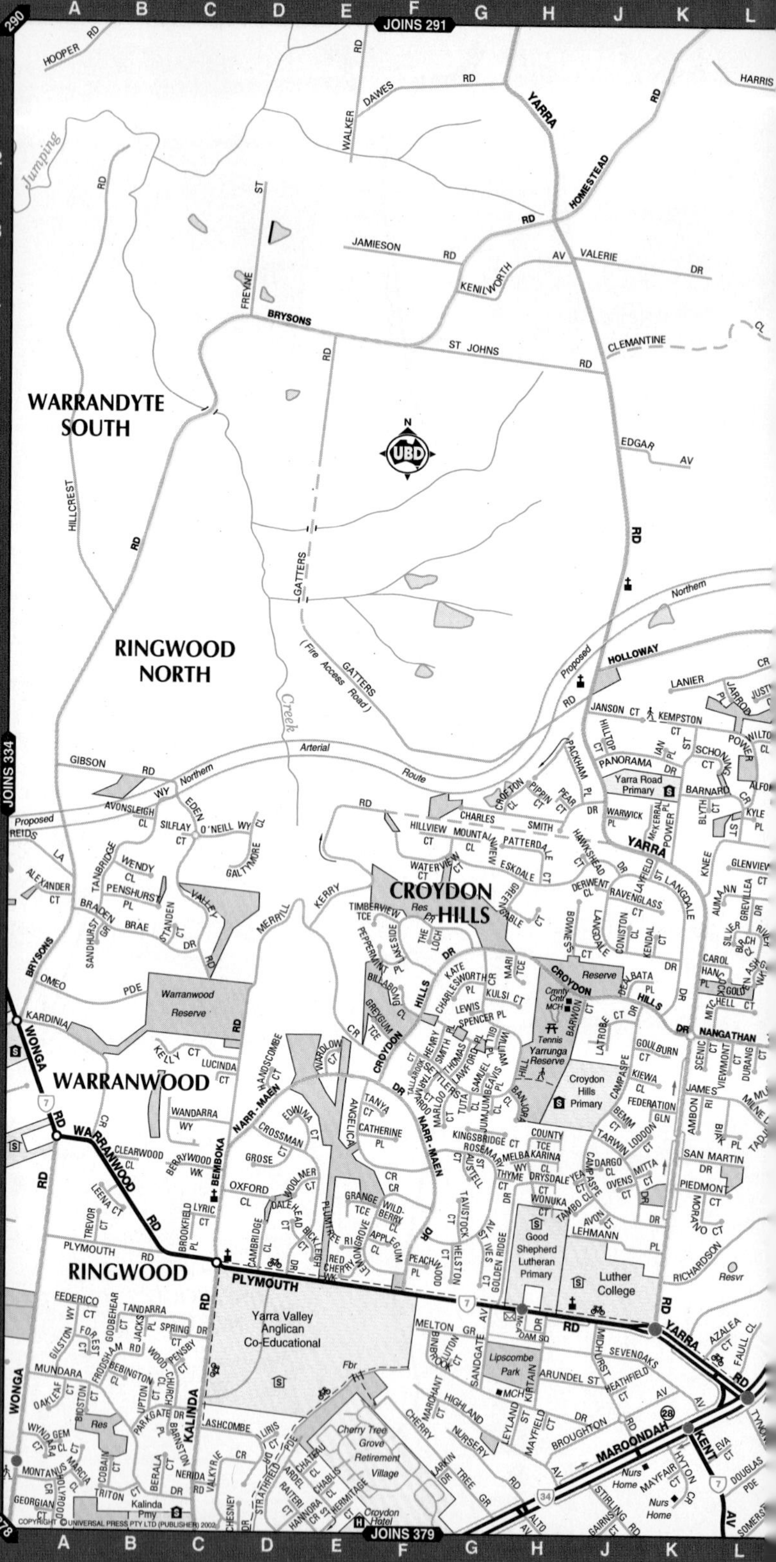

A B C D E F G H J K L

290
JOINS 291
JOINS 334
378
JOINS 379

1 2 3 4 5 6 7 8 9 10 11 12 13 14 15 16 17 18 19 20

WARRANDYTE SOUTH

RINGWOOD NORTH

CROYDON HILLS

WARRANWOOD

RINGWOOD

HOOPER RD
DAWES RD
WALKER RD
YARRA RD
HOMESTEAD RD
HARRIS
Jumping Creek
FREYNE ST
JAMIESON RD
KENILWORTH AV
VALERIE DR
BRYSONS RD
ST JOHNS RD
CLEMANTINE CL
EDGAR AV
HILLCREST RD
GATTERS RD
(Fire Access Road)
Northern Arterial Route
Proposed
HOLLOWAY RD
LANIER CR
JANSON CT
KEMPSTON
HILLTOP CT
PANORAMA DR
IAN PL
SCHONING ST
POWER
Yarra Road Primary
BARNARD
GIBSON RD
WY
EDEN
AVONSLEIGH CL
SILFLAY CT
O'NEILL WY CL
GALTYMORE CL
REIDS LA
ALEXANDER CT
TANBRIDGE
WENDY CL
PENSHURST PL
VALLEY RD
BRADEN GR
BRAE
STANDEN CT DR
SANDHURST
MERRILL
KERRY
CROFTON CL
PIPPIN CT
PEAR CT
PACKHAM PL
CHARLES SMITH DR
HILLVIEW CT
MOUNTAINVIEW CL
PATTERDALE CT
HAWKSHEAD
WARWICK PL
McKERRAL PL
BLYTH CT
KYLE PL
WATERVIEW CT
ESKDALE CT
GREENGABLE CT
DERWENT CL
RAVENGLASS CT
LAYFIELD ST
LANGDALE
KNEE
GLENVIEW CT
AUMANN
GREVILLEA DR
TIMBERVIEW TCE
Res
PEPPERMINT PL
LAKESIDE
THE LOCH
HILLS DR
BOWNESS
CONISTON CL
KENDAL CT
SILVER BIRCH CT
RIVER
CAROL PL
HANCOCK CT
OMEO PDE
Warranwood Reserve
KARDINIA
WONGA RD
KELLY CT
LUCINDA CT
BILLABONG CL
GREYGUM CT
CROYDON CR
KATE CHARLESWORTH PL
MARI TCE
KULSI CT
LEWIS SPENCER PL
CROYDON HILLS DR
Reserve
DEALBATA PL
Cmnty Cntr MCH
BARWON CT
LATROBE CT DR
GOULBURN CT
SCENIC CT
VIEWMONT CT
DURANG CT
NANGATHAN
MITCHELL CT
HANDSCOMBE CT
WARDLOW CT
NARR-MAEN DR
HENRY SMITH
THOMAS
SETTLERS
TALLAROOK
MARLOO
TUTA CL
LAWFORD
SAMUEL PL
JUMJUMBEAVIS
Tennis Yarrunga Reserve
BANJORA
Croydon Hills Primary
CAMPASPE
KIEWA CL
FEDERATION GLN
JAMES
AMBON
MILNE
WANDARRA WY
TANYA CT
EDWINA CT
ANGELICA
CROSSMAN CT
CATHERINE PL
KINGSBRIDGE CT
COUNTY TCE
ROSEMARY
MELBA
KARINA CL
BEMM CT
TARWIN
LODDON
SAN MARTIN DR
CLEARWOOD CL
BERRYWOOD WK
BEMBOKA RD
GROSE CT
OXFORD CL
WOOLMER CT
DALEHEAD CT
CAMBRIDGE CL
GRANGE TCE
WILDBERRY CL
AUSTELL
THYME WY
DRYSDALE CT
YEA
DARGO CL
OVENS CT
MITTA CT
PIEDMONT CT
MORANO CT
LEENA CT
TREVOR CT
BROOKFIELD PL
LYRIC CT
PLUMTREE RI
BICKLEIGH
LEMONGROVE
APPLEGUM CL
CHERRY WK
RED
TAVISTOCK CT
HELSTON CT
ST IVES AV
GOLDEN RIDGE
WONUKA CT
TAMBO CL
AVON CT
LEHMANN PL
RICHARDSON
Resvr
PLYMOUTH RD
PEACHWOOD CT
Good Shepherd Lutheran Primary
Luther College
FEDERICO CT
GODBEHEAR
TANDARRA CT
JACKS PL
SPRING DR
GILSTON WY
FOREST CT
FRODSHAM
PENSBY CT
WOODCHURCH
BEBINGTON CL
Yarra Valley Anglican Co-Educational
MELTON GR
BINBROOK
SANDGATE AV
Lipscombe Park
ARUNDEL ST
KIRTAIN
MCH
ADAMS SQ
MIDHURST
SEVENOAKS
AZALEA CT
FAULL CL
HEATHFIELD CT AV
MUNDARA
OAKLEAF CT
BIDSTON
UPTON CL
PARKGATE DR
BARNSTON
Res
KALINDA RD
ASHCOMBE
LIRIS CT
Fbr
MARCHANT CT
HIGHLAND
CHERRY
NURSERY
LEYLAND ST
MAYFIELD
BROUGHTON DR
MAROONDAH
KENT AV
EVA CT
TYNON
WYNDARA CT
GEM CL
MONTANUS CR
MARCIA CL
COBAIN CT
BERALA CT
NERIDA
VALKYRIE
CR
STRATHFIELD PDE
ARDEL
CHATEAU CL
CHABLIS CL
Cherry Tree Grove Retirement Village
LARKIN DR
TREE GR
Nurs Home
MAYFAIR CT
HYTON CR
DOUGLAS PDE
GEORGIAN CT
HOLYROOD
TRITON CT
Kalinda Pmy
CHESNEY DR
RAITERI CT
HANNORA CR
HERMITAGE
Croydon Hotel
ALTO AV
GAIRNS CT
STIRLING RD
Nurs Home
SOMERSET
28
7
34

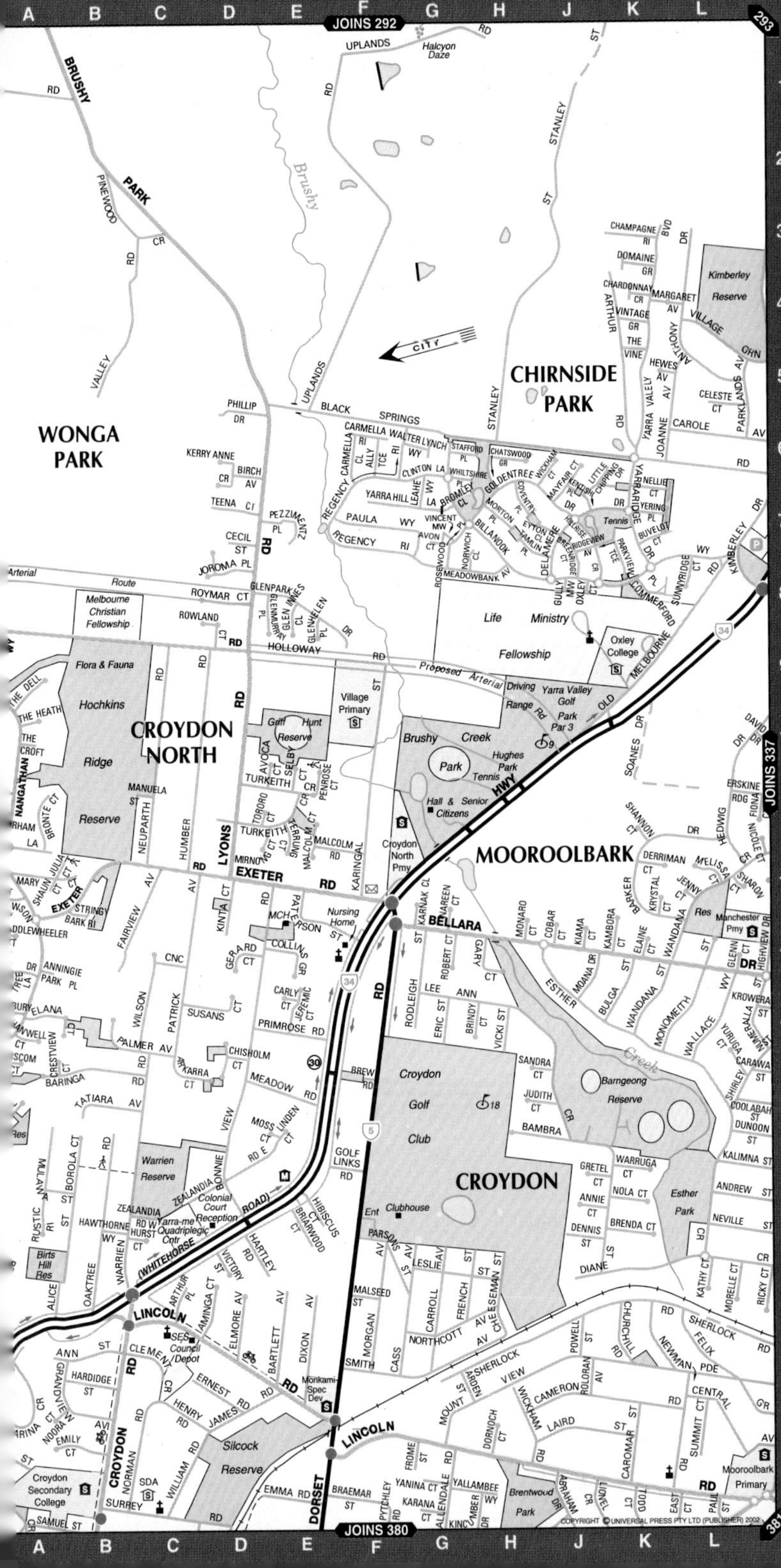

JOINS 292
293
WONGA PARK
CHIRNSIDE PARK
CROYDON NORTH
MOOROOLBARK
CROYDON
Kimberley Reserve
Hochkins Ridge Reserve
Flora & Fauna
Melbourne Christian Fellowship
Life Ministry Fellowship
Oxley College
Yarra Valley Golf Park Par 3
Brushy Creek Park
Hughes Park
Village Primary
Croydon North Pmy
Croydon Golf Club
Barngeong Reserve
Esther Park
Warrien Reserve
Silcock Reserve
Brentwood Park
Croydon Secondary College
Mooroolbark Primary
Manchester Pmy
Birts Hill Res
Colonial Court Reception
Yarra-me Quadriplegic Cntr
Monkami Spec Dev
Nursing Home
Hall & Senior Citizens
SES Council Depot
Halcyon Daze
MAROONDAH HWY
WHITEHORSE ROAD
EXETER RD
LYONS RD
DORSET RD
LINCOLN RD
BELLARA DR
BLACK SPRINGS RD
HOLLOWAY RD
Proposed Arterial Route
JOINS 337
JOINS 380
381
COPYRIGHT © UNIVERSAL PRESS PTY LTD (PUBLISHER) 2002

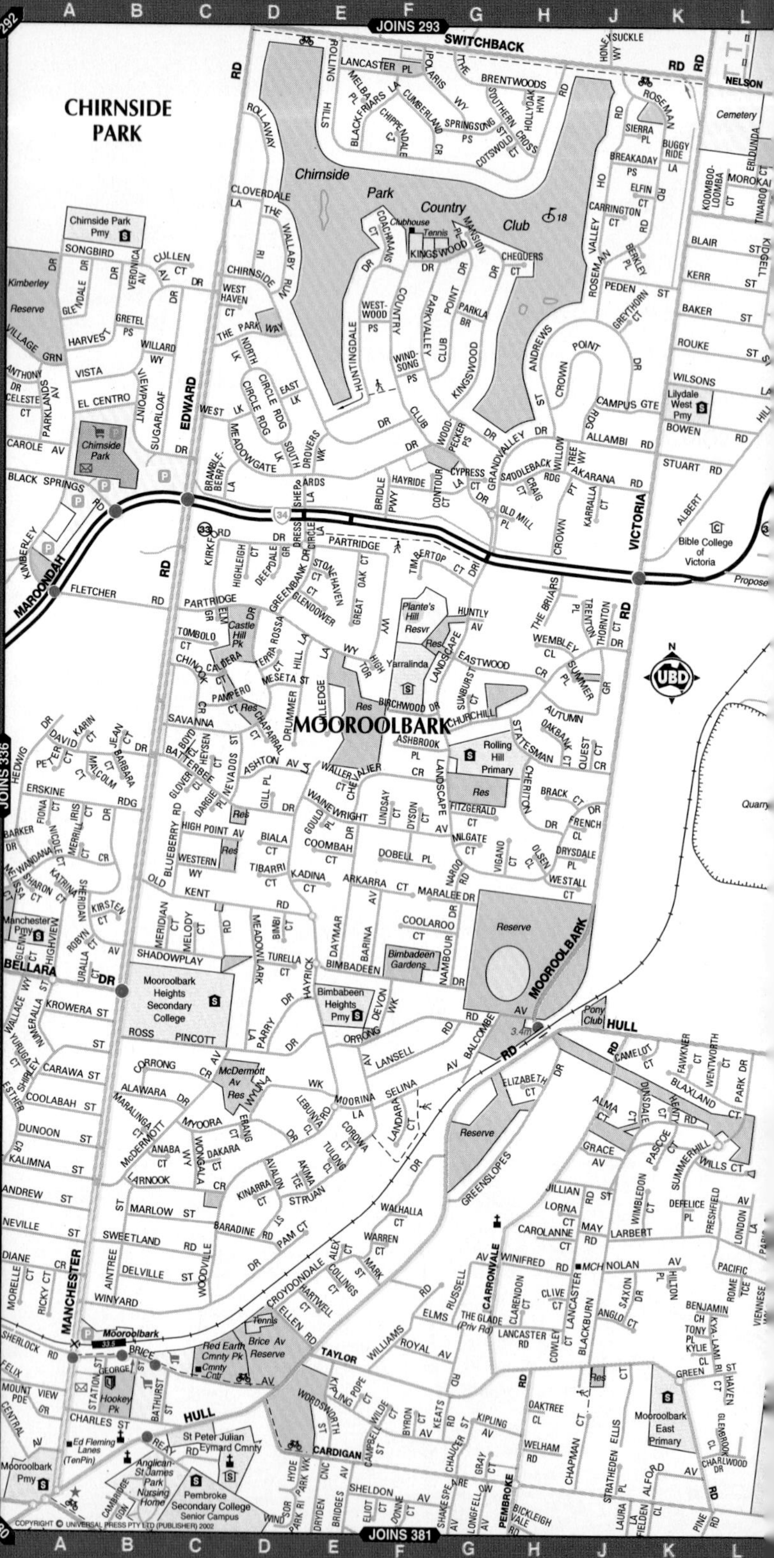

292
JOINS 293
JOINS 336

A B C D E F G H J K L

CHIRNSIDE PARK

MOOROOLBARK

Chirnside Park Country Club

Chirnside Park Pmy

Chirnside Park

Kimberley Reserve

Lilydale West Pmy

Bible College of Victoria

Cemetery

Plante's Hill Resvr

Yarralinda

Rolling Hill Primary

Castle Hill Pk

Quarry

Manchester Pmy

Mooroolbark Heights Secondary College

Bimbabeen Heights Pmy

Bimbadeen Gardens

McDermott Av Res

Reserve

Pony Club

Red Earth Cmnty Pk

Brice Av Reserve

Hookey Pk

Ed Fleming Lanes (TenPin)

Anglican-St James Park Nursing Home

St Peter Julian Eymard Cmnty

Pembroke Secondary College Senior Campus

Mooroolbark Pmy

Mooroolbark East Primary

Mooroolbark

SWITCHBACK RD

EDWARD RD

MAROONDAH

VICTORIA RD

MANCHESTER RD

MOOROOLBARK RD

HULL RD

380
JOINS 381

A B C D E F G H J K L

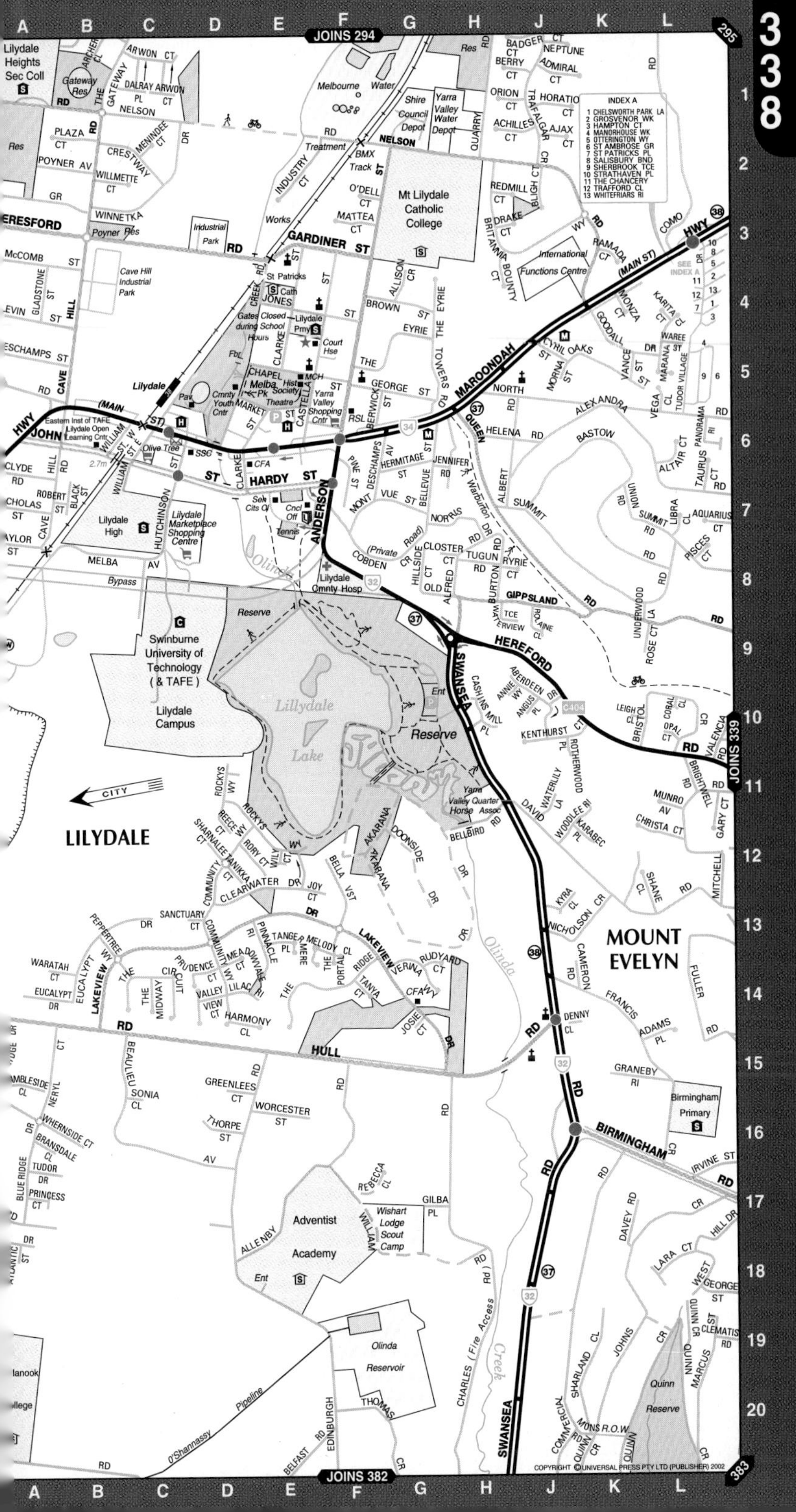
JOINS 294
295
A B C D E F G H J K L
1 2 3 4 5 6 7 8 9 10 11 12 13 14 15 16 17 18 19 20
Lilydale Heights Sec Coll
Gateway Res
Melbourne Water Treatment Works
Shire Council Depot
Yarra Valley Water Depot
INDEX A
1 CHELSWORTH PARK LA
2 GROSVENOR WK
3 HAMPTON CT
4 MANORHOUSE WK
5 OTTERINGTON WY
6 ST AMBROSE GR
7 ST PATRICKS PL
8 SALISBURY BND
9 SHERBROOK TCE
10 STRATHAVEN PL
11 THE CHANCERY
12 TRAFFORD CL
13 WHITEFRIARS RI
BMX Track
Mt Lilydale Catholic College
Industrial Park
Cave Hill Industrial Park
International Functions Centre
St Patricks Cath
Lilydale Pmy
Court Hse
Melba Pk
Cmnty Youth Cntr
Hist Society
Theatre
Yarra Valley Shopping Cntr
RSL
Lilydale
Eastern Inst of TAFE Lilydale Open Learning Cntr
Olive Tree
SSC
CFA
Sen Cits Cl
Cncl Off
Tennis
Lilydale High
Lilydale Marketplace Shopping Centre
Lilydale Cmnty Hosp
Swinburne University of Technology (& TAFE) Lilydale Campus
Reserve
Lillydale Lake
Reserve
Yarra Valley Quarter Horse Assoc
CITY
LILYDALE
MOUNT EVELYN
MAROONDAH HWY
HEREFORD RD
SWANSEA RD
GIPPSLAND RD
BIRMINGHAM RD
HULL RD
Birmingham Primary
Adventist Academy
Wishart Lodge Scout Camp
Olinda Reservoir
Quinn Reserve
O'Shannassy Pipeline
JOINS 339
JOINS 382
383
COPYRIGHT © UNIVERSAL PRESS PTY LTD (PUBLISHER) 2002

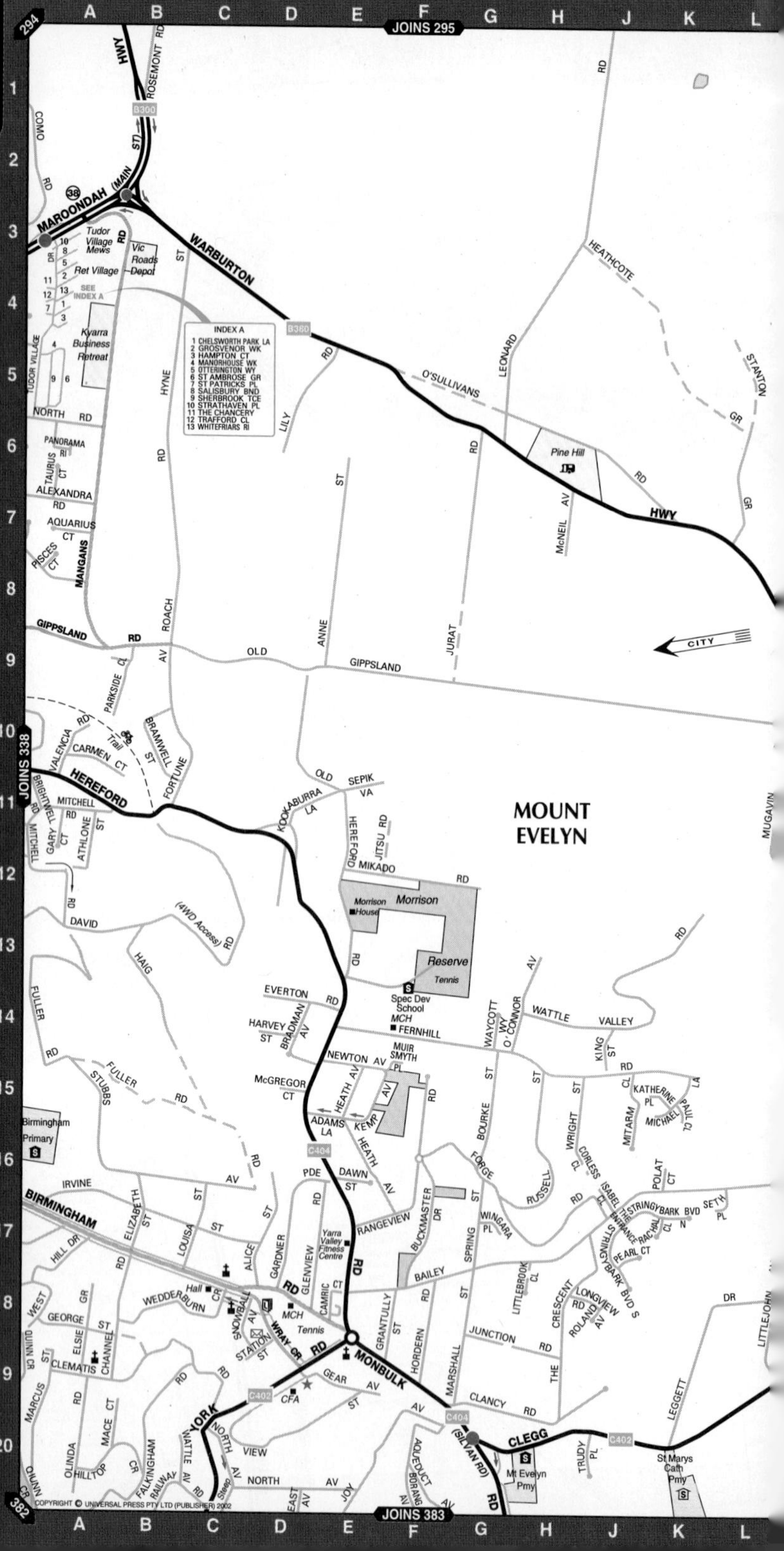

294
JOINS 295
JOINS 338
JOINS 383
382

A B C D E F G H J K L

MOUNT EVELYN

INDEX A

SEE INDEX A

MAROONDAH HWY (MAIN ST)
B360
ROSEMONT RD
COMO RD
WARBURTON HWY
Tudor Village Mews
Ret Village
Vic Roads Depot
Kyarra Business Retreat
TUDOR VILLAGE DR
NORTH RD
PANORAMA RI
TAURUS CT
ALEXANDRA RD
AQUARIUS CT
PISCES CT
MANGANS RD
GIPPSLAND RD
HYNE ST
ROACH AV
LILY RD
ANNE ST
O'SULLIVANS
LEONARD
JURAT RD
Pine Hill
McNEIL AV
HEATHCOTE RD
STANTON GR
OLD GIPPSLAND RD
CITY
PARKSIDE CL
VALENCIA RD
CARMEN CT
Trail
BRAMWELL ST
FORTUNE
HEREFORD RD
BRIGHTWELL RD
MITCHELL
GARY CT
ATHLONE ST
OLD SEPIK VA
KOOKABURRA LA
HEREFORD RD
JITSU RD
MIKADO RD
Morrison House
Morrison Reserve
Tennis
Spec Dev School
MUGAVIN
DAVID RD
(4WD Access) RD
HAIG
FULLER RD
STUBBS
EVERTON RD
HARVEY ST
BRADMAN AV
MCH
FERNHILL
NEWTON AV
MUIR SMYTH PL
McGREGOR CT
HEATH AV
ADAMS LA
KEMP
WAYCOTT WY
O'CONNOR AV
WATTLE VALLEY RD
KING ST
BOURKE ST
FORGE
RUSSELL
WRIGHT ST
CORLESS CL
ISABEL CL
MITARM CL
KATHERINE PL
PAUL CL
MICHAEL LA
POLAT CT
Birmingham Primary
IRVINE AV
BIRMINGHAM RD
ELIZABETH ST
LOUISA ST
ALICE ST
GARDNER RD
PDE
DAWN ST
C404
RANGEVIEW
BUCKMASTER DR
SPRING ST
WINGARA PL
THE ENTRANCE
STRINGYBARK BVD N
STRINGYBARK BVD S
SETH PL
RACHAL CL
PEARL CT
HILL DR
WEST
GEORGE ST
ELSIE GR
CHANNEL
CLEMATIS ST
QUINN CR
WEDDERBURN
Hall
CR
SNOWBALL AV
STATION ST
WRAY CR
MCH
Tennis
GLENVIEW
CAMRIC CT
Yarra Valley Fitness Centre
BAILEY RD
GRANTULLY ST
HORDERN
LITTLEBROOK CL
CRESCENT
THE
LONGVIEW AV
ROLAND RD
JUNCTION RD
LITTLEJOHN DR
MONBULK RD
GEAR AV
CFA
C402
YORK RD
NORTH AV
VIEW
MARCUS
OLINDA
HILLTOP
MACE CT
FALKINGHAM
RAILWAY
WATTLE AV
Steep
NORTH AV
EAST AV
JOY
AQUEDUCT
BORANG AV
(SILVAN RD)
CLANCY RD
MARSHALL
CLEGG RD
Mt Evelyn Pmy
TRUDY PL
LEGGETT
St Marys Cath Pmy

1 2 3 4 5 6 7 8 9 10 11 12 13 14 15 16 17 18 19 20

A B C D E F G H J K L
COLDSTREAM
LILYDALE
GRUYERE
WANDIN NORTH
WANDIN EAST
Picnic Hill Bushland Reserve
Wandin North Pmy
Graham Colling Reserve
Wandin North Rec Res
Cmnty Hall
Hall
Tennis
WARBURTON HWY
B380
VICTORIA RD
BOUNDARY RD
RODGER RD
MAURICE RD
CORMILIO DR
WELLINGTON RD
DARINDA AV
WANDA AV
STEWART AV
LAURIE RD
EVANS GR
BAILEY RD
CLEGG RD
C402
FOREST RD
McKILLOP
DOVAVALLEY RD
JOHN ST
ALFRED
EDMOND CR
GEORGE ST
MEADOW CT
GREENGLADES CT
GUERNSEY RD
UNION RD
JOHNSTON ST
VIEW ST
VICTORY AV
PARK RD
NICHOLAS ST
MARY ST
DELANCEY
FALK RD
ELSIE ST
IMPERIAL AV
PROSPECT RD
RUE DE GARE
RAILWAY PDE
CONNERS FLAT
STEPHEN RD
TAINTON ST
WEYMAR
MORRIS CT
KEITH CT
FARRAR WY
MAYO CT
Creek
Stringybark
1 2 3 4 5 6 7 8 9 10 11 12 13 14 15 16 17 18 19 20

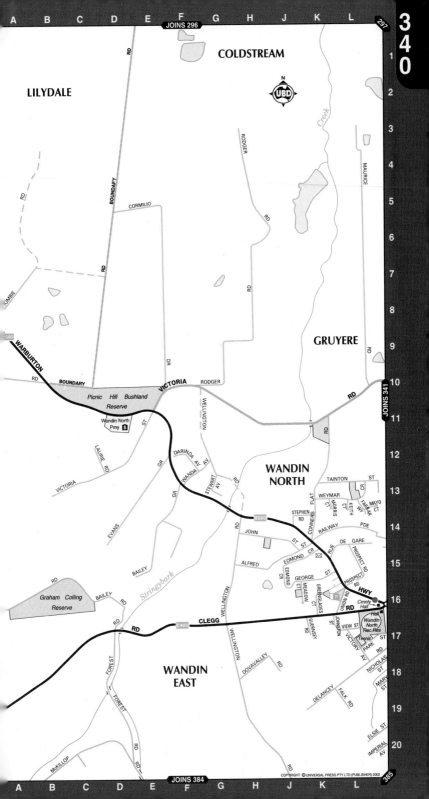

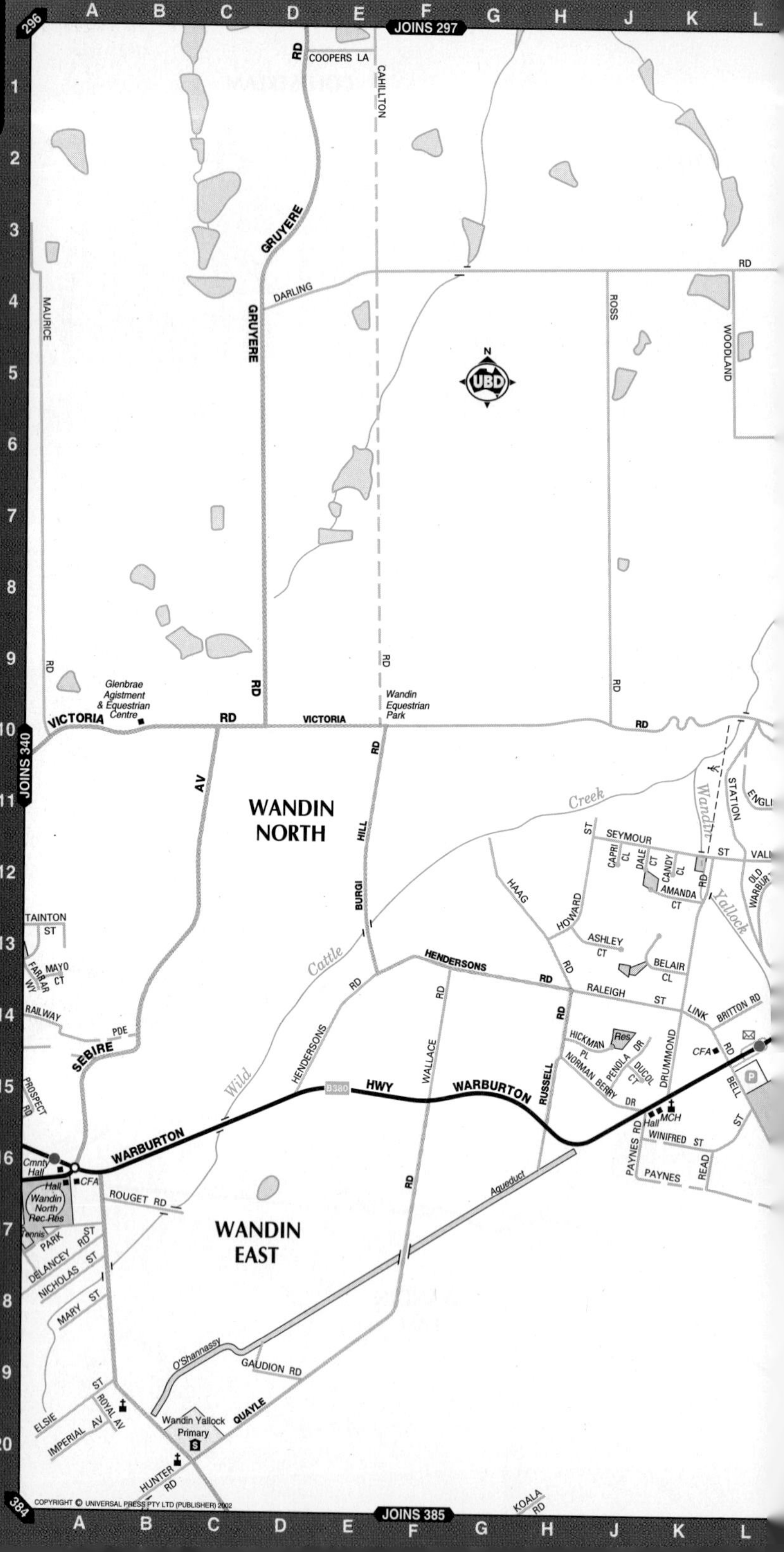

296
JOINS 297
JOINS 340
JOINS 385
384

A B C D E F G H J K L

WANDIN NORTH

WANDIN EAST

COOPERS LA
CAHILLTON RD
GRUYERE RD
DARLING RD
MAURICE RD
ROSS RD
WOODLAND RD
VICTORIA RD
Glenbrae Agistment & Equestrian Centre
Wandin Equestrian Park
AV
BURGI HILL RD
Cattle Creek
Wild
Wandin Yallock
STATION
ENGLI
SEYMOUR ST
VALI
CAPRI CL
DALE CT
CANDY CL
AMANDA CT
OLD WARBUR
HAAG RD
HOWARD
ASHLEY CT
BELAIR CL
HENDERSONS RD
RALEIGH ST
LINK
BRITTON RD
WALLACE RD
RUSSELL
HICKMAN PL
Res
PENOLA DR
DUCOL CT
NORMAN BERRY DR
DRUMMOND
CFA
BELL RD
ST
TAINTON ST
MAYO CT
FARRAR WY
RAILWAY PDE
SEBIRE
PROSPECT RD
B380
WARBURTON HWY
MCH
Hall
PAYNES RD
WINIFRED ST
PAYNES
READ
Cmnty Hall
Hall
CFA
Wandin North Rec Res
Tennis
ROUGET RD
PARK RD
ST
DELANCEY ST
NICHOLAS ST
MARY ST
Aqueduct
O'Shannassy
GAUDION RD
ELSIE ST
ROYAL AV
IMPERIAL AV
Wandin Yallock Primary
QUAYLE
HUNTER RD
KOALA RD

A B C D E F G H J K L

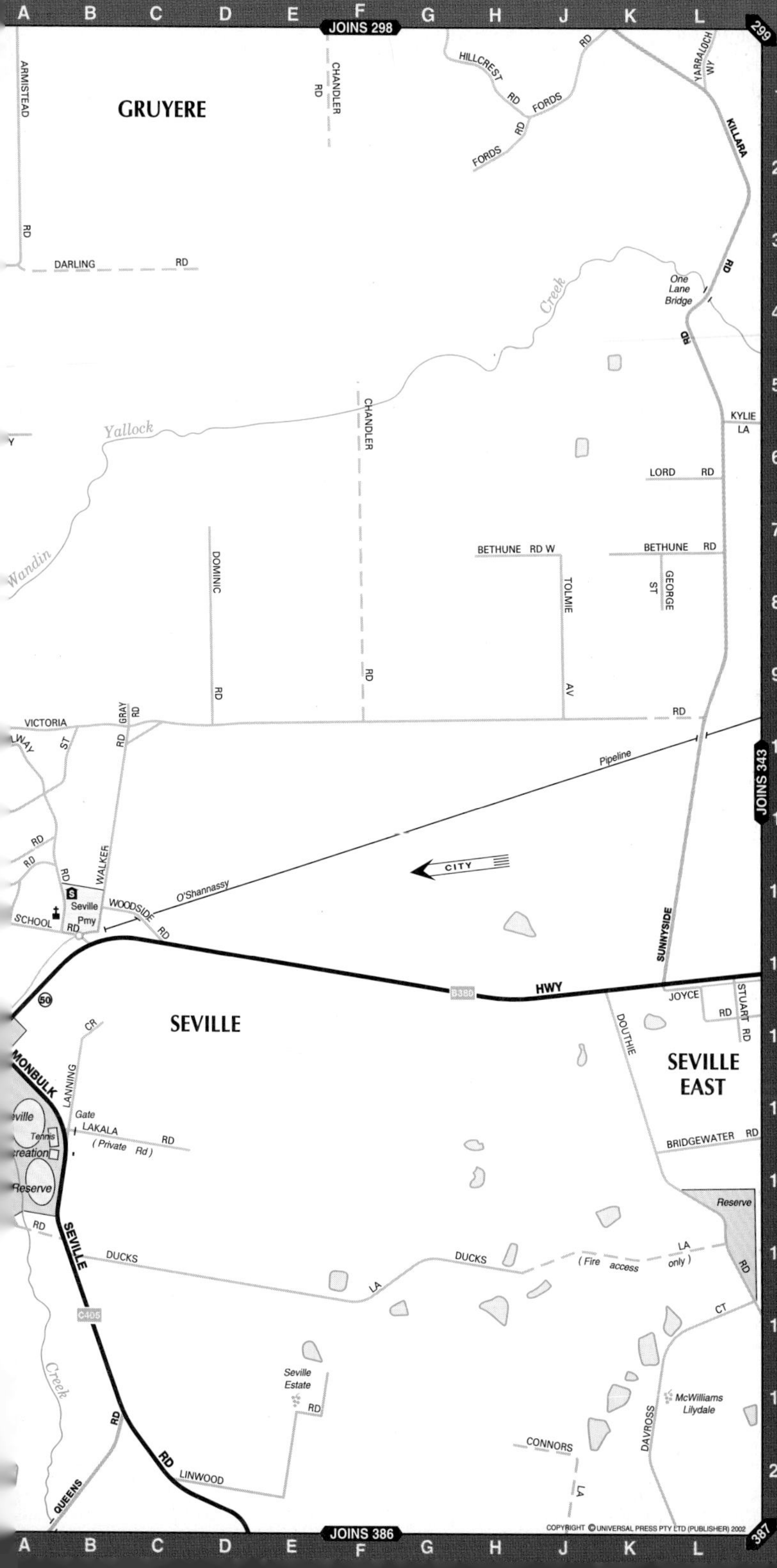

JOINS 298
299
JOINS 343
JOINS 386
387

A B C D E F G H J K L

1 2 3 4 5 6 7 8 9 10 11 12 13 14 15 16 17 18 19 20

GRUYERE

SEVILLE

SEVILLE EAST

ARMISTEAD RD
CHANDLER RD
HILLCREST RD
FORDS RD
FORDS
RD
YARRALOCH WY
KILLARA RD
DARLING RD
Creek
One Lane Bridge
Yallock
KYLIE LA
LORD RD
Wandin
DOMINIC RD
BETHUNE RD W
TOLMIE AV
BETHUNE RD
GEORGE ST
VICTORIA ST
GRAY RD
RD
Pipeline
WALKER RD
CITY
O'Shannassy
Seville Pmy
SCHOOL RD
WOODSIDE RD
SUNNYSIDE
B380 HWY
JOYCE RD
STUART RD
50
CR
MONBULK
LANNING
DOUTHIE
Seville Recreation Reserve
Tennis
Gate
LAKALA (Private Rd) RD
BRIDGEWATER RD
Reserve
SEVILLE RD
DUCKS LA
DUCKS
(Fire access only) LA
RD
C405
CT
Creek
Seville Estate
RD
McWilliams Lilydale
DAVROSS
CONNORS LA
LINWOOD RD
QUEENS RD

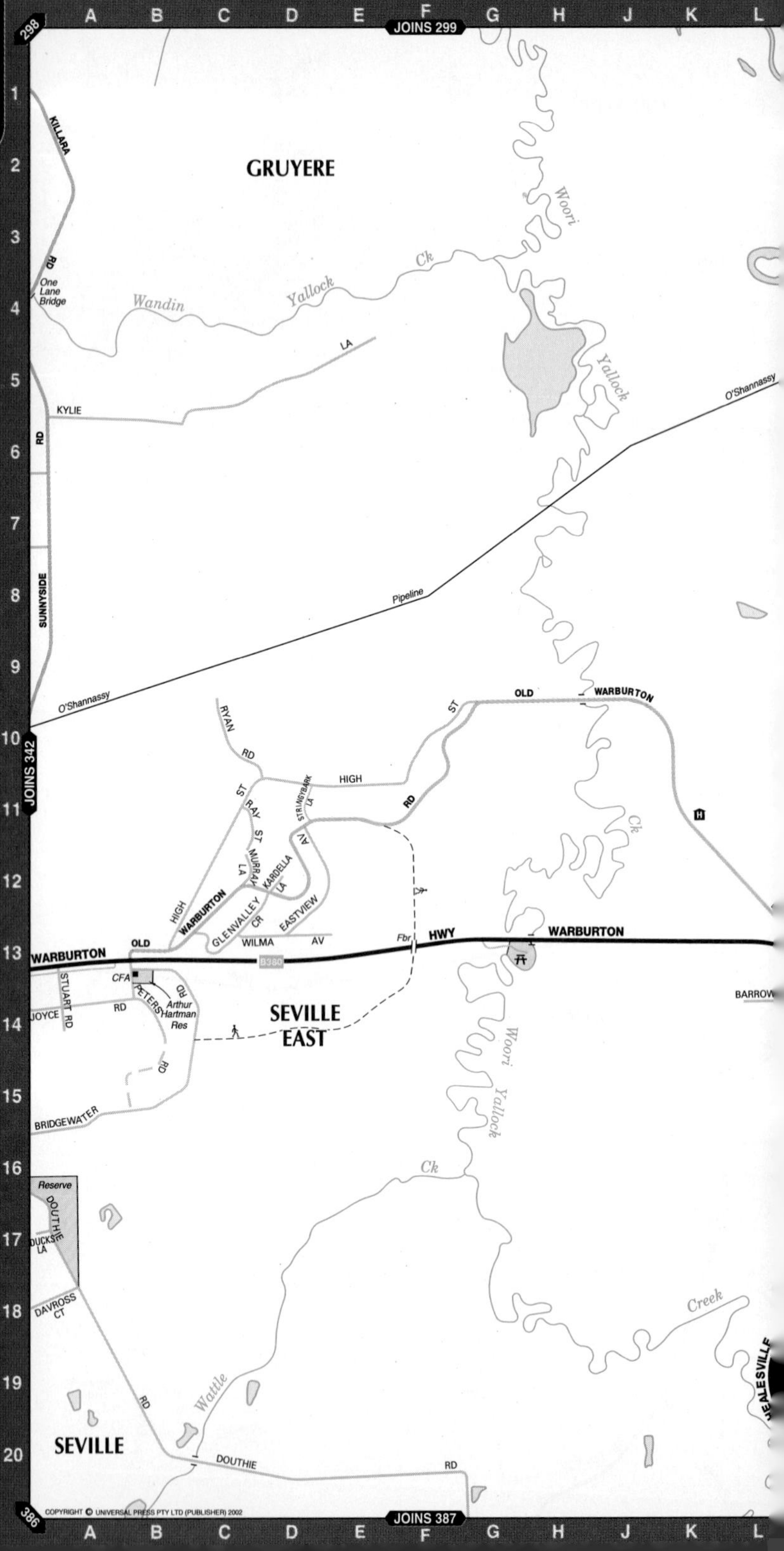

298
JOINS 299

A B C D E F G H J K L

1 2 3 4 5 6 7 8 9 10 11 12 13 14 15 16 17 18 19 20

JOINS 342

386
JOINS 387

JOINS 300

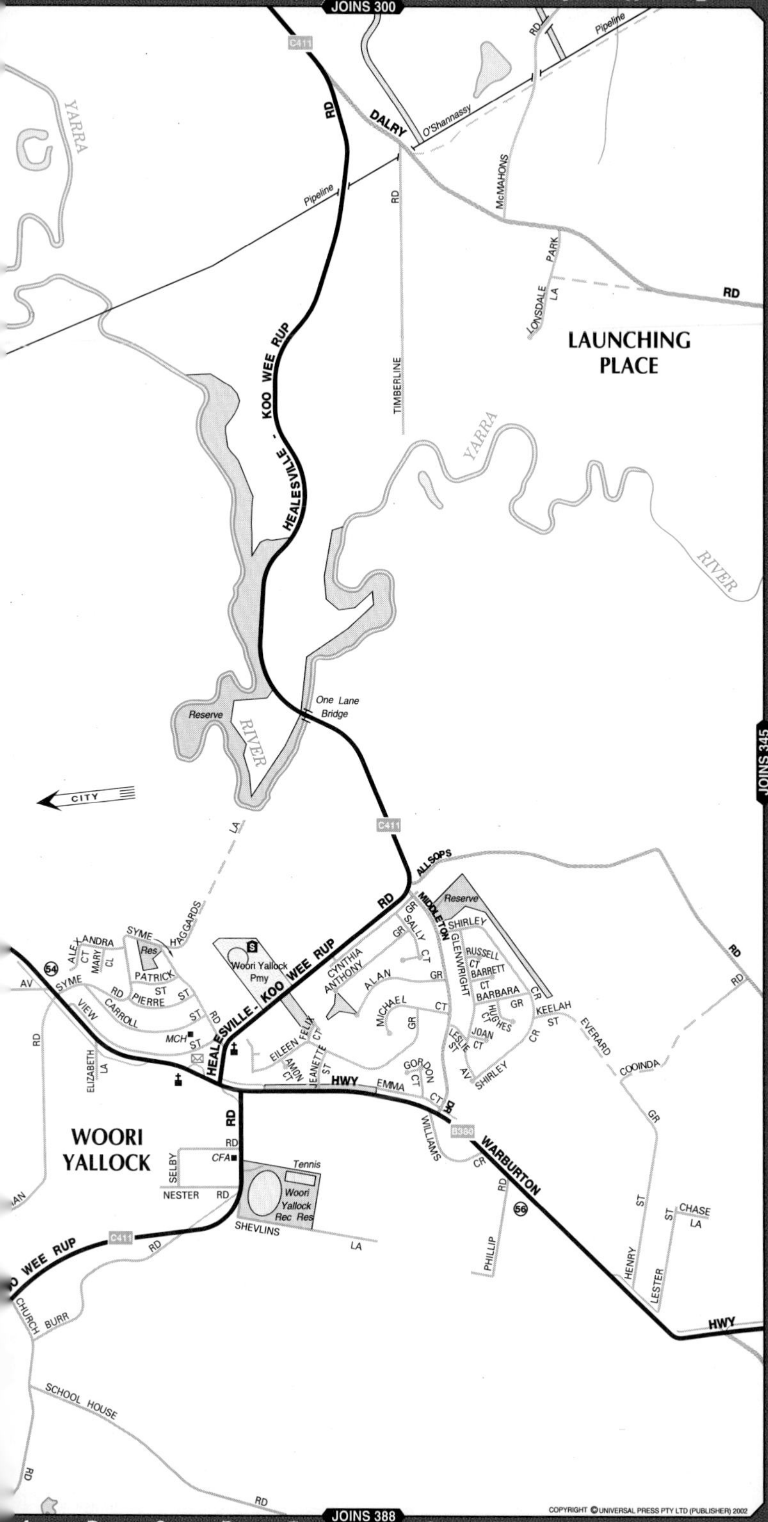

JOINS 345

JOINS 388

A B C D E F G H J K L

1 2 3 4 5 6 7 8 9 10 11 12 13 14 15 16 17 18 19 20

LAUNCHING PLACE

WOORI YALLOCK

HEALESVILLE - KOO WEE RUP RD

C411

DALRY RD

O'Shannassy Pipeline

TIMBERLINE RD

McMAHONS RD

LONSDALE LA

PARK

YARRA RIVER

Reserve

One Lane Bridge

CITY

HAGGARDS LA

ALLSOPS RD

MIDDLETON DR

Reserve

SHIRLEY

GLENWRIGHT

RUSSELL CT

BARRETT CT

BARBARA GR

HUGHES CT

JOAN CT

LESLIE ST

SHIRLEY AV

SHIRLEY CR

KEELAH ST

EVERARD

COOINDA GR

SALLY CT

CYNTHIA GR

ANTHONY

ALAN GR

MICHAEL CT

GR

FELIX CT

EILEEN

AMON CT

JEANETTE ST

GORDON CT

EMMA CT

HWY

WARBURTON HWY

B380

56

WILLIAMS CR

PHILLIP RD

HENRY ST

LESTER ST

CHASE LA

ALEXANDRA CT

MARY CL

SYME

Res

PATRICK ST

PIERRE ST

SYME RD

AV

54

CARROLL ST

VIEW ST

MCH

Woori Yallock Pmy

ELIZABETH LA

RD

CFA

SELBY RD

NESTER RD

Tennis

Woori Yallock Rec Res

SHEVLINS LA

KOO WEE RUP RD

CHURCH

BURR

SCHOOL HOUSE RD

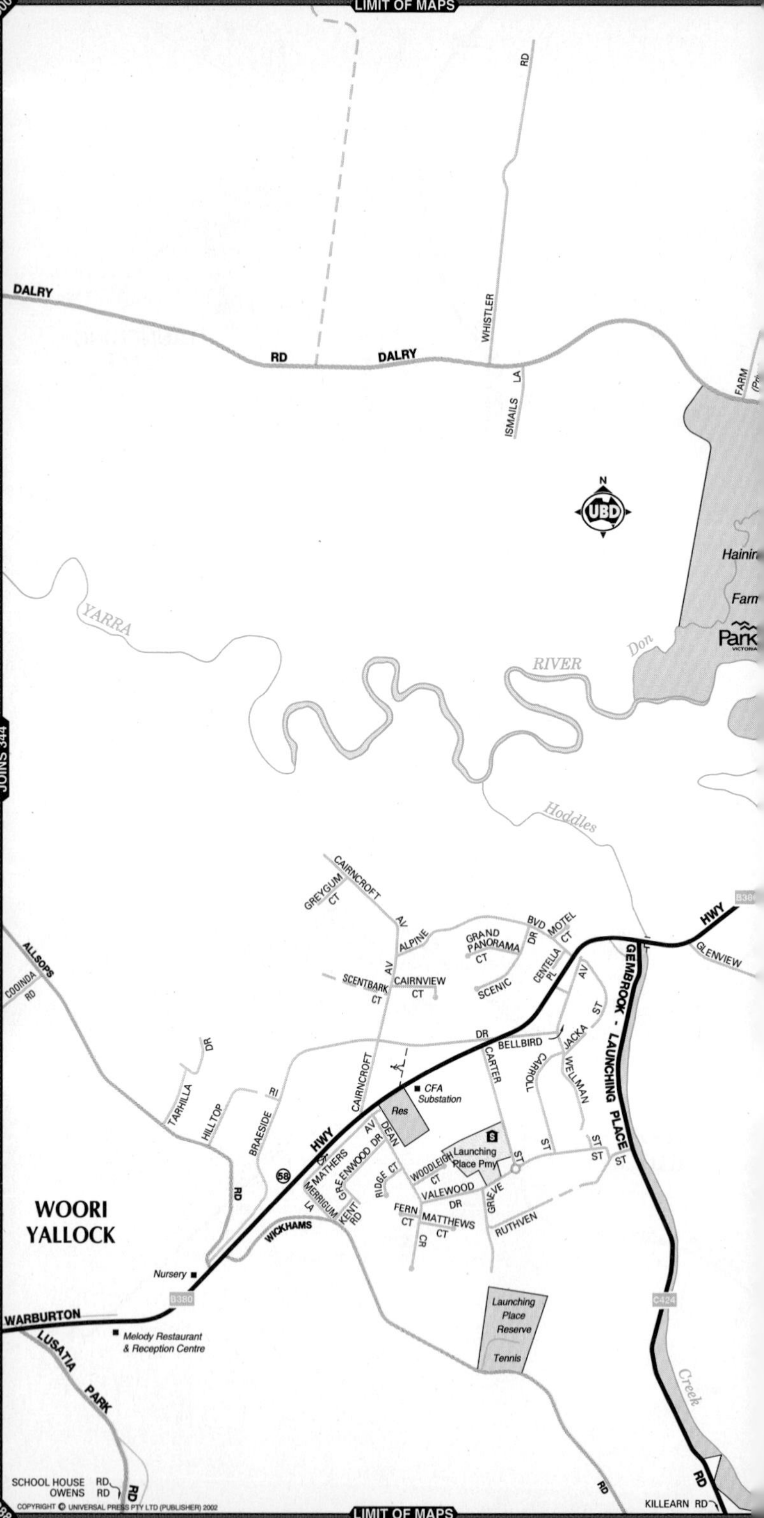

LIMIT OF MAPS
DALRY RD
WHISTLER RD
ISMAILS LA
FARM
YARRA RIVER
Don
Haining Farm
Parks Victoria
Hoddles
CAIRNCROFT AV
GREYGUM CT
ALPINE AV
GRAND PANORAMA CT
BVD DR
MOTEL CT
CENTELLA PL
SCENTBARK CT
CAIRNVIEW CT
SCENIC
HWY
GLENVIEW
GEMBROOK - LAUNCHING PLACE RD
ALLSOPS
COOINDA RD
TARHILLA DR
HILLTOP
BRAESIDE RI
BELLBIRD DR
CARTER ST
CARROLL ST
JACKA ST
WELLMAN ST
CFA Substation
Res
Launching Place Pmy
MATHERS AV
GREENWOOD DR
DEAN
RIDGE CT
WOODLEIGH CT
VALEWOOD DR
GRIEVE ST
MERRIGUM LA
KENT RD
FERN CT
MATTHEWS CR
RUTHVEN
WICKHAMS RD
WOORI YALLOCK
Nursery
B380
WARBURTON HWY
Melody Restaurant & Reception Centre
LUSATIA PARK RD
Launching Place Reserve
Tennis
C424
Creek
SCHOOL HOUSE RD
OWENS RD
KILLEARN RD
JOINS 344
300
388

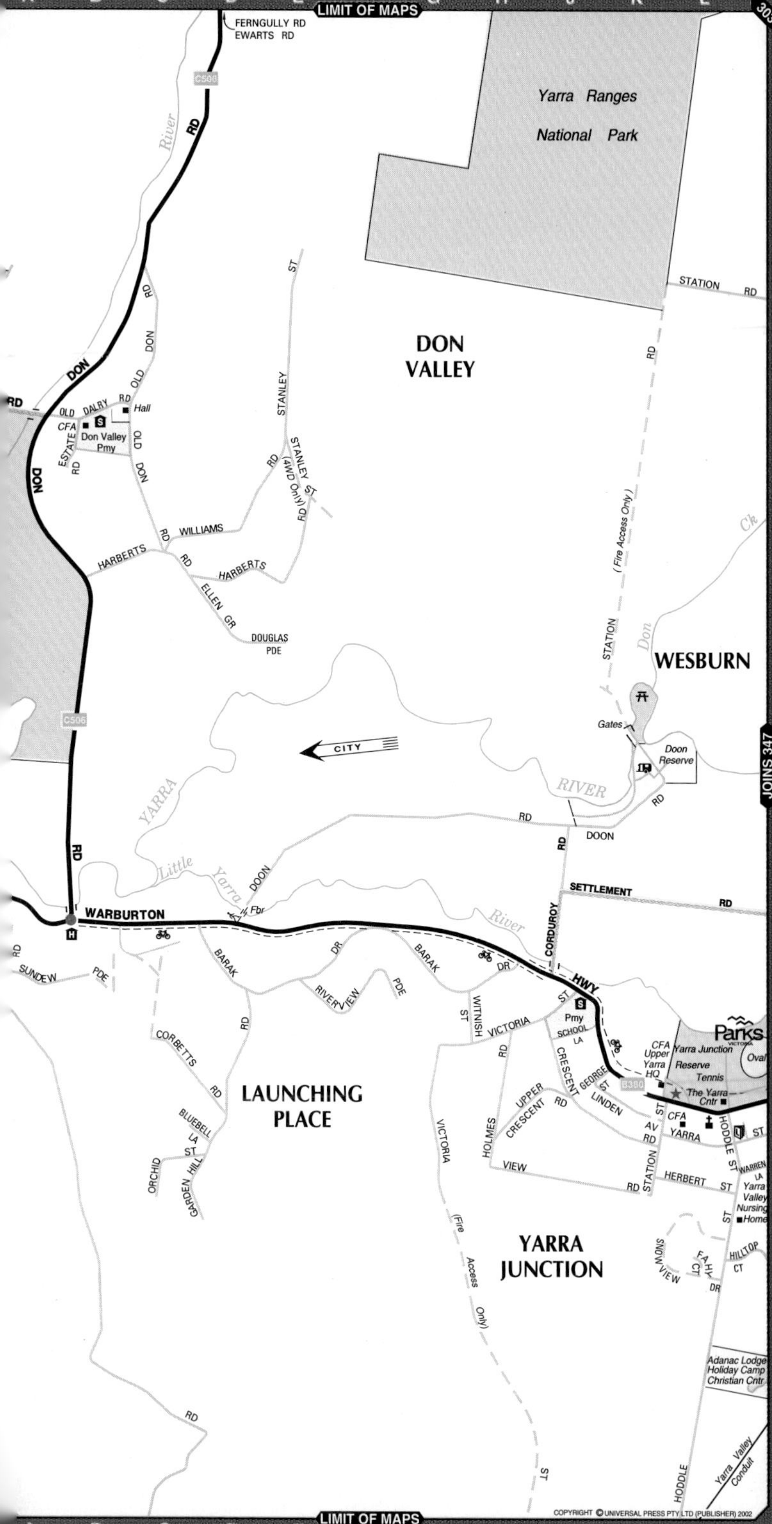

LIMIT OF MAPS

303

FERNGULLY RD
EWARTS RD

Yarra Ranges National Park

DON VALLEY

WESBURN

LAUNCHING PLACE

YARRA JUNCTION

DON RD
OLD DON RD
OLD DALRY RD
ESTATE RD
Hall
CFA
Don Valley Pmy
STANLEY ST
STANLEY ST (4WD Only) RD
WILLIAMS RD
HARBERTS RD
ELLEN GR
DOUGLAS PDE
STATION RD
STATION RD (Fire Access Only)
Don Ck
Gates
Doon Reserve
YARRA RIVER
Little Yarra River
CITY
DOON RD
CORDUROY RD
SETTLEMENT RD
WARBURTON HWY
Fbr
SUNDEW PDE
BARAK DR
RIVERVIEW PDE
WITNISH ST
VICTORIA RD
CORBETTS RD
BLUEBELL LA
ORCHID ST
GARDEN HILL
Pmy
SCHOOL LA
CRESCENT
GEORGE ST
LINDEN AV
UPPER CRESCENT RD
HOLMES
VIEW RD
STATION ST
HERBERT ST
CFA
YARRA ST
HODDLE ST
WARREN LA
Parks Victoria
CFA Upper Yarra HQ
Yarra Junction Reserve
Tennis
Oval
The Yarra Cntr
Yarra Valley Nursing Home
MONS VIEW
FAHY CT
HILLTOP CT
DR
VICTORIA (Fire Access Only) ST
Adanac Lodge Holiday Camp Christian Cntr
Yarra Valley Conduit
HODDLE

JOINS 347

LIMIT OF MAPS

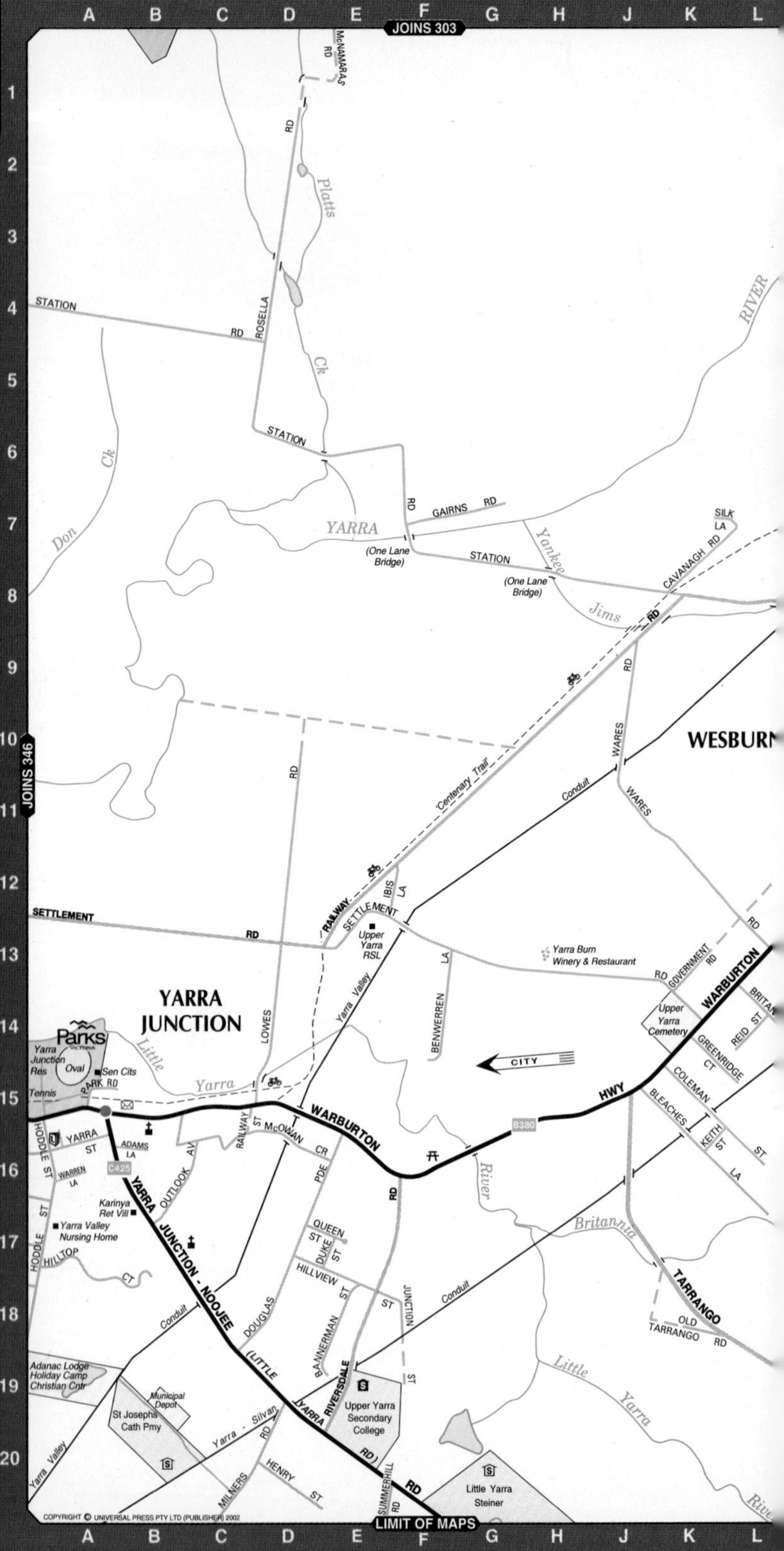

JOINS 303
JOINS 346

LIMIT OF MAPS

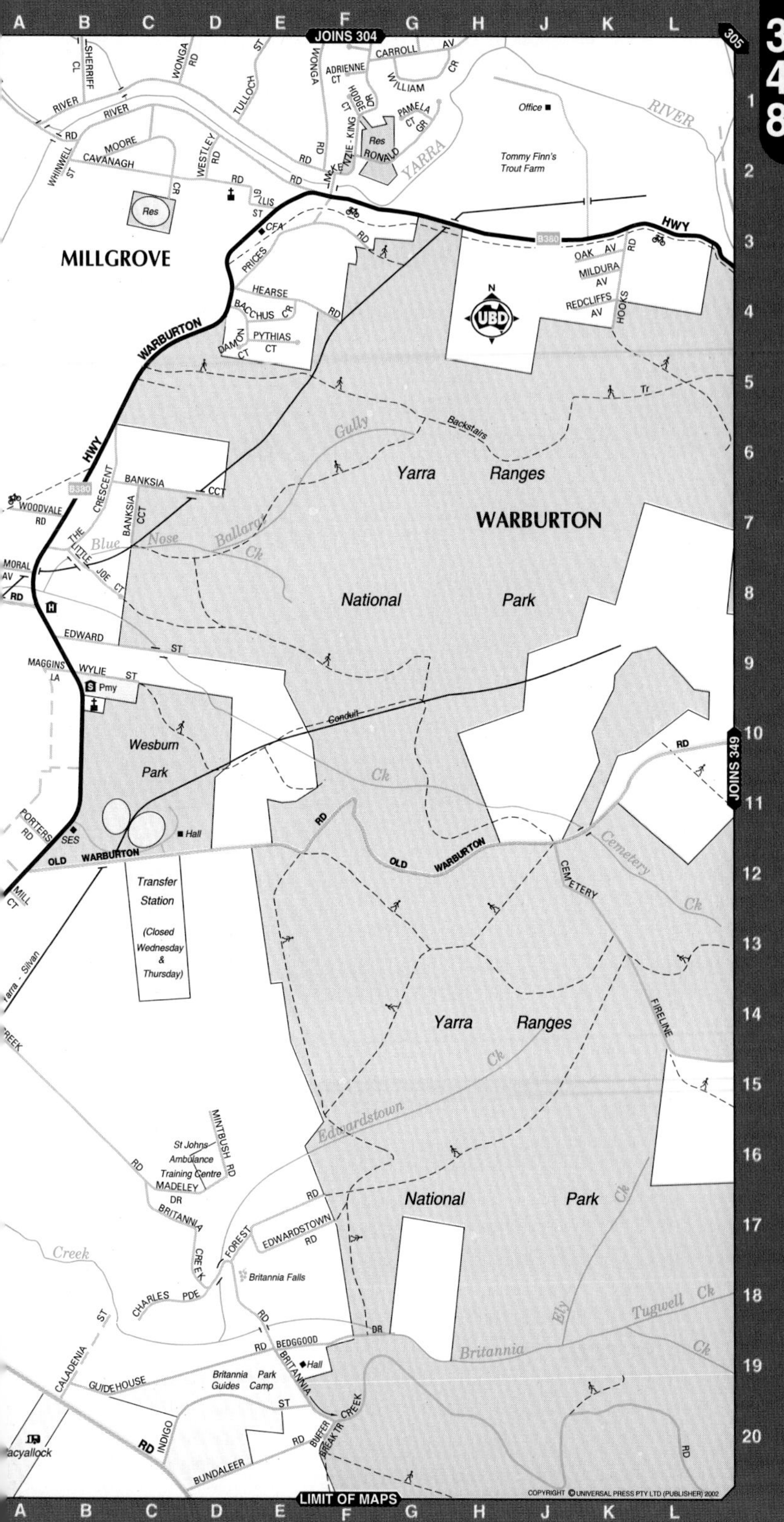
JOINS 304
MILLGROVE
WARBURTON
Yarra Ranges
National Park
Wesburn Park
Transfer Station (Closed Wednesday & Thursday)
Tommy Finn's Trout Farm
Britannia Falls
Britannia Guides Park Camp
St Johns Ambulance Training Centre
JOINS 349
LIMIT OF MAPS
WARBURTON HWY
OLD WARBURTON RD
CEMETERY RD
FIRELINE
EDWARDSTOWN RD
BRITANNIA CREEK RD
FOREST RD
COPYRIGHT © UNIVERSAL PRESS PTY LTD (PUBLISHER) 2002

JOINS 305
304
JOINS 348
LIMIT OF MAPS

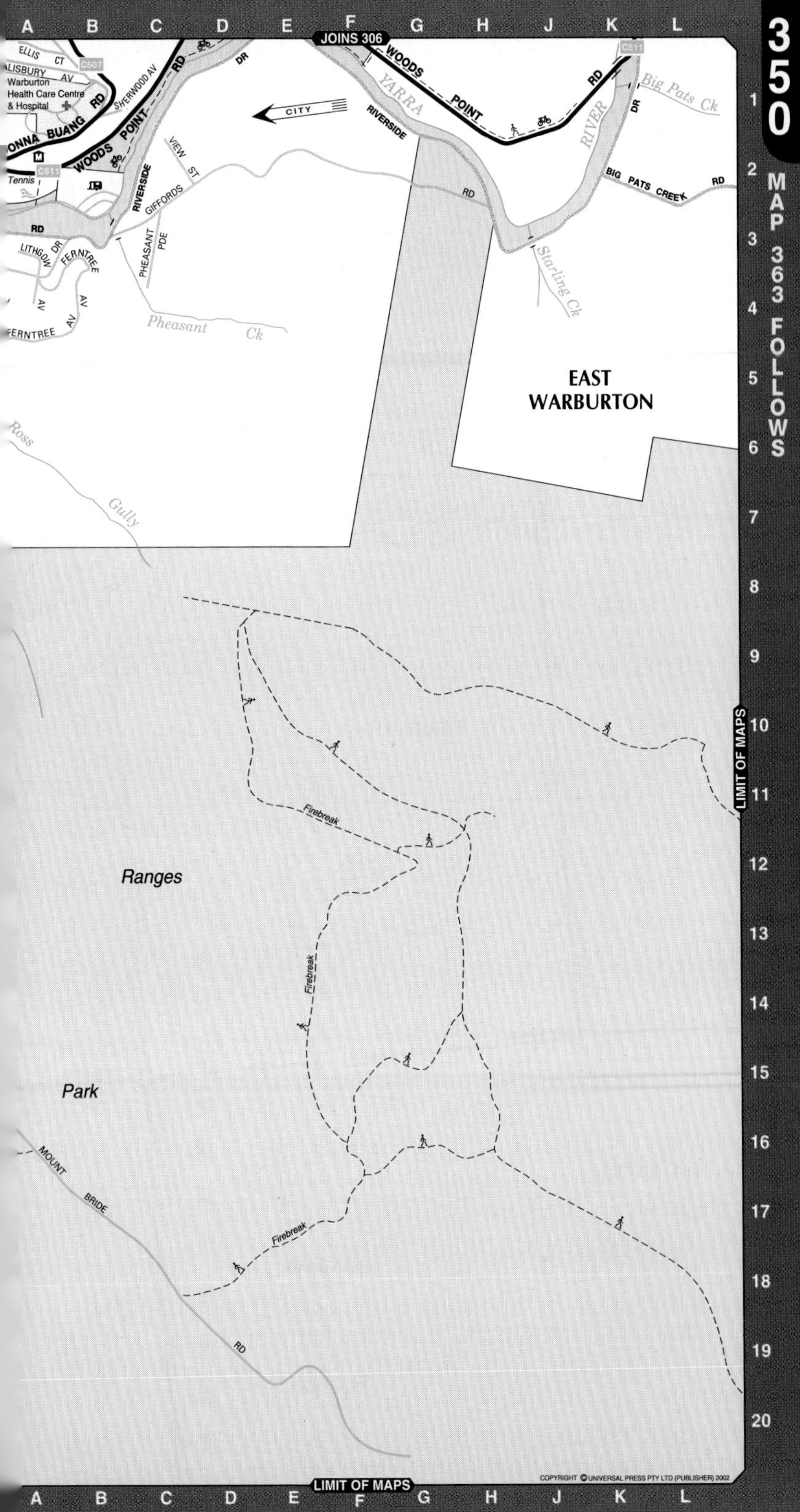

A B C D E F G H J K L
JOINS 306
ELLIS CT
SALISBURY AV
C507
Warburton Health Care Centre & Hospital
DONNA BUANG RD
SHERWOOD AV
WOODS POINT RD
DR
CITY
C511
Tennis
RD
RIVERSIDE
VIEW ST
GIFFORDS
PHEASANT PDE
LITHGOW DR
FERNTREE AV
FERNTREE AV
Pheasant Ck
YARRA
RIVERSIDE
RD
WOODS POINT RD
RIVER
DR
Big Pats Ck
BIG PATS CREEK RD
Starling Ck
EAST WARBURTON
Ross Gully
Firebreak
Firebreak
Firebreak
Ranges
Park
MOUNT BRIDE RD
LIMIT OF MAPS
1 2 3 4 5 6 7 8 9 10 11 12 13 14 15 16 17 18 19 20
MAP 363 FOLLOWS
LIMIT OF MAPS

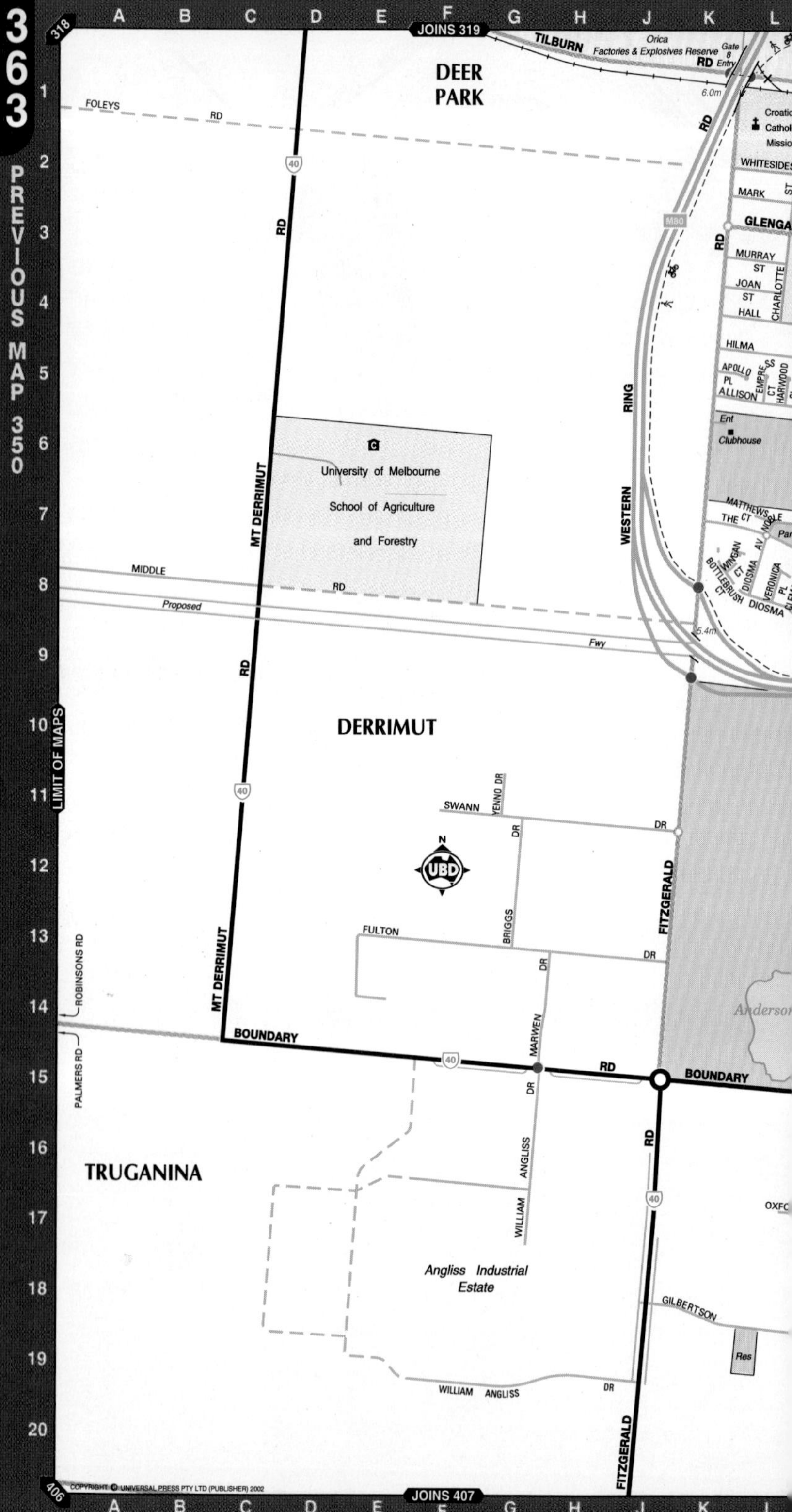

JOINS 319
DEER PARK
TILBURN RD
Orica Factories & Explosives Reserve
Gate 8 Entry
FOLEYS RD
Croation Catholic Mission
WHITESIDES
MARK ST
GLENGAL
MURRAY ST
JOAN ST
HALL
CHARLOTTE
HILMA
APOLLO PL
ALLISON
EMPRESS
HARWOOD CT
M80
WESTERN RING RD
Clubhouse
University of Melbourne School of Agriculture and Forestry
MT DERRIMUT RD
MIDDLE RD
Proposed Fwy
MATTHEWS CT
THE NOBLE
Park
WINGAN CT
BOTTLEBRUSH CT
DIOSMA AV
VERONICA PL
DIOSMA
DERRIMUT
SWANN DR
YENNO DR
BRIGGS DR
FITZGERALD RD
FULTON DR
MARWEN DR
BOUNDARY RD
ROBINSONS RD
PALMERS RD
TRUGANINA
ANGLISS DR
WILLIAM
Angliss Industrial Estate
GILBERTSON
OXFO
Res
WILLIAM ANGLISS DR
Anderson
PREVIOUS MAP 350
LIMIT OF MAPS
318
406
JOINS 407

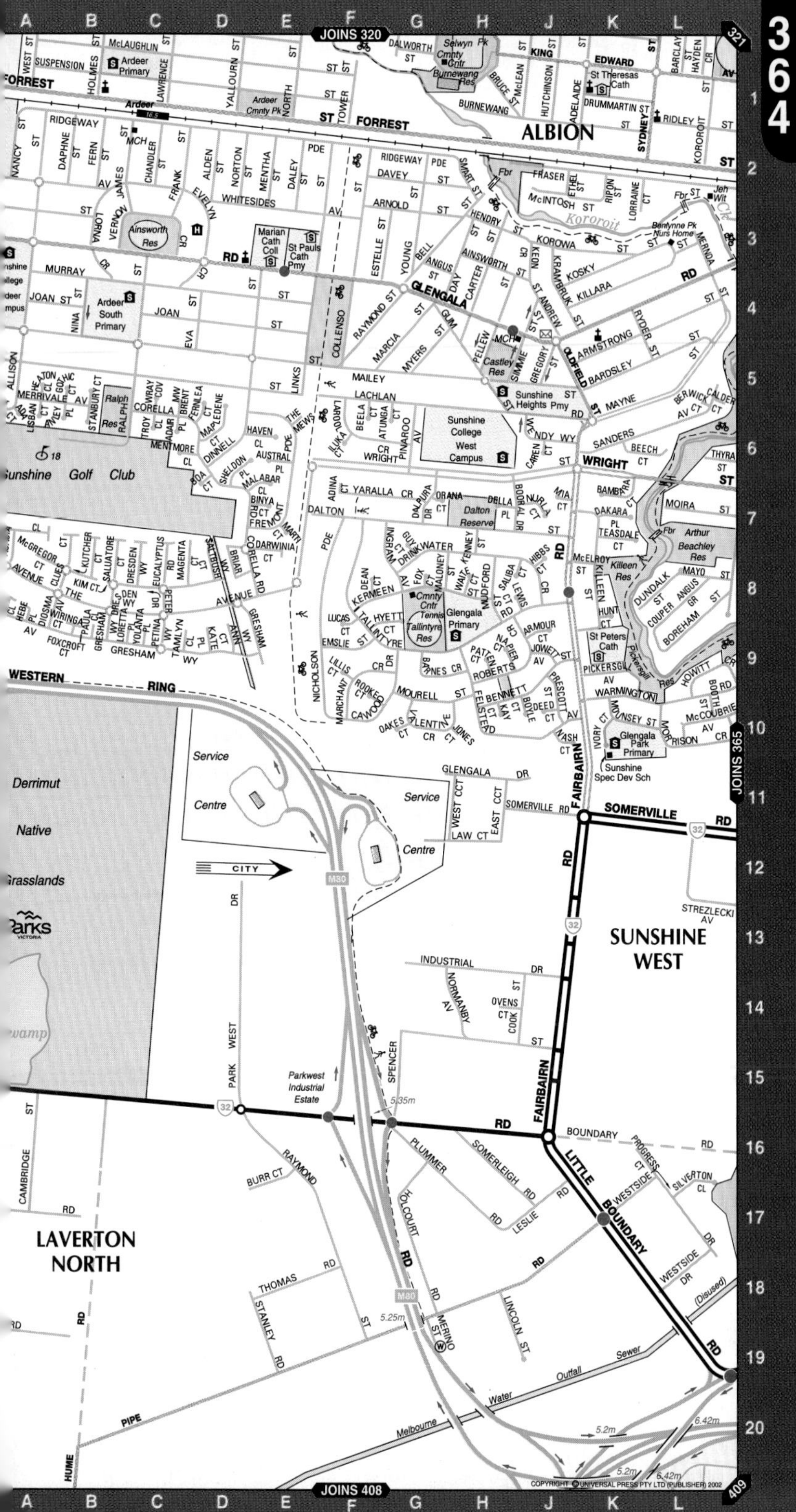
JOINS 320
321
A B C D E F G H J K L
FORREST
SUSPENSION
Ardeer Primary
McLAUGHLIN ST
HOLMES ST
LAWRENCE ST
WEST ST
YALLOURN ST
Ardeer Cmnty Pk
NORTH
TOWER
FORREST ST
DALWORTH ST
Selwyn Pk Cmnty Cntr
Burnewang Res
BURNEWANG
BRUCE ST
McLEAN ST
HUTCHINSON ST
KING ST
EDWARD ST
St Theresas Cath
ADELAIDE ST
DRUMMARTIN ST
SYDNEY
RIDLEY ST
BARCLAY ST
HAYDEN CR
KORORROIT
ALBION
Ardeer
RIDGEWAY
NANCY ST
DAPHNE ST
FERN ST
MCH
CHANDLER ST
ALDEN ST
NORTON ST
MENTHA ST
DALEY ST
PDE
RIDGEWAY PDE
DAVEY ST
SMART ST
Fbr
FRASER
ETHEL ST
RIPON ST
LORRAINE CT
Jeh Wit
McINTOSH ST
Kororoit
Benlynne Pk Nurs Home
MERNDA
JAMES AV
FRANK
EVELYN
WHITESIDES
AV
ARNOLD ST
HENDRY
LORNA ST
VERNON
Ainsworth Res
CR
Marian Cath Coll
St Pauls Cath Pmy
ESTELLE ST
YOUNG ST
BELL
AINSWORTH
KOROWA ST
KEON CR
KRAMBRUK
KOSKY
RD
Sunshine College Ardeer Campus
MURRAY
RD
JOAN ST
Ardeer South Primary
JOAN
EVA
NINA
GLENGALA
ANGUS ST
DAY
CARTER
RAYMOND ST
COLLENSO
MARCIA
MYERS
GUM
MCH
ST ANDREW
KILLARA
ARMSTRONG
RYDER ST
BARDSLEY
PELLEW
Castley Res
SIMMIE
GREGORY ST
OLDFIELD ST
ALLISON
HEATON
GOTHIC
MERRIVALE
STANBURY CT
Ralph Res
RALPH
WRAY CT
COV
LISBAN
TROY
CORELLA
MENTMORE
BRENT PL
FERNLEA
MAPLEDENE
LINKS
MAILEY
LACHLAN
THE MEWS
LAROOL
ILUKA
BEELA
ATUNGA
PINAROO AV
WRIGHT
Sunshine College West Campus
Sunshine Heights Pmy
MAYNE
BERWICK
CALDER
WENDY WY
CAREN CT
SANDERS
BEECH CT
WRIGHT ST
THYRA ST
HAVEN CL
AUSTRAL PL
DINNELL CT
SHELDON
MALABAR
BINYA
FREMONT
18
Sunshine Golf Club
ADINA CT
YARALLA CR
DALPURA
ORANA
DELLA
BOORAL DR
NURLA CT
MIA CT
BAMBARA
DAKARA
TEASDALE
MOIRA
Arthur Beachley Res
DALTON
Dalton Reserve
PL
PDE
INGRAM
GUY CT
DRINKWATER
KENNEY ST
HIBBS CT
McELROY
Killeen Res
DUNDALK ST
ANGUS GR
MAYO ST
McGREGOR CT
KUTCHER CT
SALUATORE
DRESDEN WY
EUCALYPTUS RD
MAGENTA CT
SALTBUSH WY
BRIAR
CORELLA RD
DARWINIA CT
MARTI CT
AVENUE
THE AVENUE
KIM CT
CLUES
DEN WY
PETER
DEAN
KERMEEN
FOX CT
MALONEY
WAITE
MUDFORD
SALIBA ST
LEWIS CR
Cmnty Cntr
Tennis
Tallintyre Res
Glengala Primary
KILLEEN
HUNT CT
COUPER
BOREHAM
HEBE
DIOSMA
WIRINGA CT
PAULA
GRESHAM
LORETTA
YOLANTA
PETINA
TAMLYN
KATE
ANN
GRESHAM
LUCAS CT
HYETT
TALLINTYRE
EMSLIE
ARMOUR CT
JOWETT AV
St Peters Cath
PICKERSGILL AV
Pickersgill Res
HOWITT
BOOTH RD
FOXCROFT CT
GRESHAM WY
WESTERN RING
NICHOLSON
LILLIS CT
MARCHANT
ROOKE CT
CAWOOD
BARNES CR
PATTEN CT
NAPIER CT
ROBERTS
BENNETT
KAY
BOYLE
FELSTEAD
DEED CT
PRESCOTT AV
MOURELL ST
OAKES CT
VALENTINE CR
JONES CT
NASH CT
WARMINGTON
MUNSEY ST
MORRISON
McCOUBRIE AV
Glengala Park Primary
Sunshine Spec Dev Sch
IVORY CT
FAIRBAIRN
Service Centre
Derrimut Native Grasslands
Parks VICTORIA
GLENGALA DR
Service Centre
WEST CCT
EAST CCT
LAW CT
SOMERVILLE RD
SOMERVILLE RD
32
CITY
M80
SUNSHINE WEST
STREZLECKI AV
DR
INDUSTRIAL DR
NORMANBY AV
OVENS CT
COOK ST
Swamp
PARK WEST
Parkwest Industrial Estate
SPENCER
5.35m
FAIRBAIRN
BOUNDARY RD
PROGRESS CT
LITTLE BOUNDARY
WESTSIDE
SILVERTON CL
CAMBRIDGE ST
RD
BURR CT
RAYMOND
PLUMMER
SOMERLEIGH RD
LESLIE RD
HOLCOURT RD
LAVERTON NORTH
THOMAS RD
STANLEY RD
M80
MERINO ST
LINCOLN ST
WESTSIDE DR
(Disused)
5.25m
RD
HUME
PIPE
Melbourne Water Outfall Sewer
5.2m
6.42m
COPYRIGHT © UNIVERSAL PRESS PTY LTD (PUBLISHER) 2002
JOINS 408
409
JOINS 365
1 2 3 4 5 6 7 8 9 10 11 12 13 14 15 16 17 18 19 20

JOINS 321
320
JOINS 364
JOINS 409
408

A B C D E F G H J K L

1 2 3 4 5 6 7 8 9 10 11 12 13 14 15 16 17 18 19 20

SUNSHINE

SUNSHINE WEST

BROOKLYN

Barclay Res
K G Chaplin Reserve
Market Towers
Centre
Plaza
Sunshine Swim & Leisure Cntr
Sunvale Primary
Cnci Off
Cmnty Cntr
Kevin Wheelahan Gardens
Sunshine East Primary
Sports Cntr
MCH Kinder Smith Res
Caroline Chisholm Cath Coll
Cmnty Health Cntr
Jeh Wit St
Cath
Sunshine
Sunshine Primary
Sunshine College
Parsons Res
Tennis
Croquet
O'Brien Park
Hill Reserve
Ret Vill
Tennis
English Lang Centre
Dept of Admin Services Transport & Storage Group
Arthur Beachley Res
Buckingham Reserve
Kororoit Ck
Stony
Dalgety and Elders Wool Handling Centre
Simsmetal
Brooklyn Landfill & Waste Recycling
Jupps Motor Auctions
Half Moon
Brooklyn Industrial Estate
Melb Water Depot
DN Duanne Reserve
Brooklyn Res
Pmy
Cath
Ten
The Memorial Park Crematorium and Floral Lawn Cemetery
Urban Forest Res
Tennis W L J Crofts Res
A W Bond Res

HAYDEN CR, TALMAGE ST, KING EDWARD AV, KORORIOT, RIDLEY ST, FORREST ST, FRASER ST, SUN CREST PL, MERINDA, GLENGALA RD, ANDERSON RD, DURHAM RD, HARVESTER RD, HAMPSHIRE RD, RUSSELL ST, BENNETT PL, DEVONSHIRE RD, SUN CR, CITY PL, DERBY, WATT ST, CORIO ST, GRAHAM, LEITH AV, THORPE ST, MORRIS ST, BENJAMIN ST, CHAPMAN ST, THYRA ST, COUCH ST, WRIGHT ST, MAYNE ST, SANDERS, CALDER CT, STANFORD ST

HERTFORD ST, DAWSON ST, GEORGE ST, NEIL ST, SERVICE ST, MANN PL, McDONALD PL, CLARKE ST, WITHERS ST, CENTRE ST, DICKSON ST, RSL PL, STATION PL, RITCHIE ST, MARTIN ST, WHITTY ST, TYLER ST, SERVANTE ST, PIZZEY ST, RYDER PL, VICTORIA ST, ROBINSON ST, DRAYTON ST, PARSONS ST, HILL ST, McKAY ST, DONALD ST, KINGAROY ST, CORNWALL RD, MONASH ST, KEVIN ST, PENGELLY CT, ALEXANDRA AV, KENNEDY ST, MARYVALE ST, ISLINGTON ST, McCRACKEN ST, WILKINSON ST, BRISLINGTON ST, GERTRUDE ST, DULCIE ST, TAUNTON ST, ANDREW ST, CAMERON ST, BARNARD CT, COOPER ST, MATTHEWS ST, JESSIE ST, HEMPHILL RD

NEWMAN ST, TRIBE ST, BARNETT ST, ERNEST ST, DOROTHY AV, UNA ST, THOMPSON ST, ALICE ST, APPLEBY CT, McGRATH ST, YEWERS ST, BAKER ST, LOWE CR, MAY ST, NIXON ST, HIGH ST, UNION ST, COBREY ST, DUKE ST, MONICA ST, NORMA ST, ALFRED ST, WALTER ST, McLENNAN ST, LILY ST, TRELOAR, DEDERICK ST, GR WATSON GR, DOBSON CR, RAVENHALL ST, MYALLA ST, MARNOO ST, MYAMYN ST, MOAMA ST, DARNLEY ST, SOUTH RD, LAWTON AV, PALMER ST, KENROSS CT, HOWELL PL, PRITCHARD AV, CRICK ST, KENT AV, HOTHAM AV, STEWART ST, TURNER ST, BEACHLEY CT, BURNETT AV, BALMORAL AV, MENZIES ST, ORANGE ST, SHEPHERD ST, KENNETH ST, ROSE ST, SKEWES ST, HARGREAVES ST, HINKLER ST, MELROSE ST, JOY ST, OAK, WILSON ST, ARTHUR ST, KINGSFORD ST, GARDEN, USA ST, HUGHES ST, SHOWERS ST, ENDERBY CT, SIMS ST, WINDSOR ST

MOIRA ST, FREEMAN ST, MAYO ST, ARDOYNE ST, DUNBAR AV, CANNON ST, BOREHAM ST, HOWITT CR, BUCKINGHAM CR, WARMINGTON RD, BOOTH ST, McCOUBRIE AV, GOODE CT, RAUTMAN CT, NUTTALL CR, BICKLEY CT, WIDDY CT, LEARMONTH CR, MORRISON CR, HAMPTON AV, BOLITHO ST, ORMOND AV, PATTERSON AV, WESTERN AV, CENTRAL AV, FIRST AV, SECOND AV, THIRD AV, FOURTH AV, MARKET RD, GREEN ST, LINDA ST, JUDGE ST, NORMAN ST, WILLIAM ST, SUNSHINE RD, JAMES CT, SARA GR, QUARRY RD, FREDERICK ST, JUSTIN RD, AMANDA RD, ALICK RD, RAVENSCOURT RD, KALINGRA RD

GRACE CT, VELLA DR, SOMERVILLE RD, STREZLECKI AV, DIAMOND DR, BUNTING RD, McDONALD RD, INDUSTRY DR, PARK TRADE PL, PRINCES HWY, IRIS AV, LILAC AV, CORRIGAN AV, HEATHER AV, STENHOUSE AV, CYPRESS AV, EAMES AV, NOLAN AV, MILLERS RD, CONIFER AV, VIOLA AV, ALMOND AV, AZALEA AV, ROWAN AV, BRACK AV, PRIMULA AV, PAW PAW ST, CLELLAND RD, PEARL ST, BURGESS ST, SMITH ST, LYNCH RD, BUCHANAN RD, CARLSSON CT, RICHARDS CT, HOUSTON CT, WAITES CT, BOUNDARY RD, SILVERTON CL, WESTSIDE DR, JONES RD, OLD GEELONG RD, Melbourne Water Outfall Sewer (Disused), GRIEVE PDE, WEST GATE FWY, MANGAN CT, MEDDINGS CT, MURDOCH CT, FREEMANS CT, MISTEN AV, ROSALA AV, IRWIN AV, CHAMBERS RD, PARINGA RD, LEE ST, BOND ST, LANGSHAW ST, DUOSA RD, BEEVERS ST, CLEMATIS, WALLY CT, MICHAEL ST, MARIGOLD, KNAPP ST, HARRIS ST, GADSDEN ST, GLADE

6.09m, 6.42m, 5.35m, 5.03m, 5.53m

JOINS 322
JOINS 367
JOINS 410
323
411
BRAYBROOK
MAIDSTONE
WEST FOOTSCRAY
KINGSVILLE
TOTTENHAM
YARRAVILLE
West Base Industrial Park
Tottenham
Go Karts
Ashley Gardens Holiday Village
Costella Res
Dobson Res
Scovell Res
Rogers Res
Johnson Res
Kevin Shorten Res
Hansen Reserve
Cycle Track
Dunlop Olympic Tyres
Footscray Cemetery
Bradmill Textiles
McIvor Reserve
Hanks Baseball Park
Angliss Res
CJ Cruickshank Park
Bassett Res
McDonald Res
Yarraville Oval
Donald McLean Reserve
Spotswood Oval
Edwards Res
Melbourne Water Pumping Stn
Kingsville Primary
Wembley Pmy
Footscray West Pmy
Footscray North Pmy
Corpus Christi Cath
Templeton Lodge Nurs Home
Gaudion Res
PUNT Neighbhd Hse
Lions Pk
Eleanor Cntr
Em Shephead Gdns
Martin Res
Rosamond Sp Sch
Inner Western SSC
Dinjerra Pmy Sch
Solaris Power
CITY
MITCHELL
WESTERN
BALLARAT RD
CHURCHILL AV
ASHLEY ST
ESSEX
BARKLY
GEELONG RD
PRINCES HWY
SOMERVILLE RD
FRANCIS ST
DOCKLANDS HWY
WEST GATE FWY
WILLIAMSTOWN RD
ROSAMOND RD
DEMPSTER ST
PARAMOUNT RD
ROBERTS ST
SUMMERHILL RD
COPYRIGHT © UNIVERSAL PRESS PTY LTD (PUBLISHER) 2002

JOINS 323

MARIBYRNONG

FOOTSCRAY

FLEMINGTON

SEDDON

YARRAVILLE

SPOTSWOOD

FOR MORE DETAIL SEE MAP 723

KELLAWAY ST, MITCHELL ST, VALNERE ST, MERLYN ST, PRINCE ST, ROWE ST, MONASH ST, BIRDWOOD, MEPHAN ST, KALLARA ST, METTERS ST, LANA ST, FERGUSON ST, EDGEWATER BVD, WILLIAM COOPER ST, MARY ST, WALSH ST, SKYLINE DR, EXAMINER ST, MOLONEY LA, EVELINE AV, LILARDIA AV, FOUNDRY LA, IRONWORKERS ST, TAYLOR ST, OWEN ST, AV, GORDON ST, TITCH ST, EMPIRE ST, R, ELDRIDGE ST, Heatley Res, MCH, KINNEAR ST

Nurs Home, Inner Western SSC, MAY ST, MADDOCK ST, STEET ST, PARK ST, MAVIS ST, McCUBBIN ST, ARTHUR ST, WESTERN, COHAN, Eleanor Cntr, Emerg Ent, Western Hospital, Main Ent, MARION ST, Cncl Depot, Child Care Cntr, RAYNER ST, NAISMITH ST, JERROLD ST, HWY, CHATHAM ST, ST

Footscray Res, Henry Turner Memorial Res, FARNSWORTH AV, Footscray City Coll, ROBINSON ST, RIPPON ST, SMITH ST, RD, TAIT ST, DAWSON ST, FERN TCE, Youth Cl, CT, Ten, HOADLEY, Vic Uni & TAFE, Footscray Park Campus, Vic Uni, TIERNAN ST, DROOP ST, PETER ST, DAVID ST, MILLS CL, MYERS RD, FISHER

MONASH ST, DUMBLANE AV, KINGSTON AV, LANGS RD, PDE, LEONARD CR, RAS Showgrounds, PLUMMER AV, LENNON, Showgrounds, MEMBER, Gate, Flemington Racecourse, Flemington Racecourse, MARIBYRNONG BVD, Footscray Park

WESTERN (BALLARAT RD) HWY, STIRLING ST, LYNCH ST, NEWELL ST, BEEVERS ST, MUNRO SQ, SECOMB PL N, SECOMB PL S, PALMER ST, SWABY ST, VIPONT ST, GREER ST, MARKS LA, JAMIESON AV, LEUNIG PL, Newells Paddock, JOSEPH RD, RAILWAY PL, NEILSON PL, WARDE ST, MARIBYRNONG ST, HOPETOUN BRIDGE, HOPKINS ST, DYNON, WIGHTMAN, SELINA, WINGFIELD ST, LT JOHN, YEWERS ST, SIMS ST, Channel

SHEPHERD ST, WHITE ST, THE CRESCENT, Nurs Home, JOHNSON ST, CATHERINE ST, MARY ST, CENTRAL AV, RSL, Gate, HERBERT ST, LEANDER ST, ESSEX ST, ELEANOR, EVERARD, SOUTHAMPTON, SWAN, ADELAIDE, SYDNEY, MACPHERSON, LATROBE ST, CRESWICK, WOLVERHAMPTON, COMMERCIAL, Footscray Pmy, Gilmore Coll for Girls, COWARD ST, GALLANT ST, LINDA CT, FORD ST, FITZROY ST, HUGH ST, MALDEN ST, CROWN ST, DONALD, BLACKSTON ST, DENNIS ST, RYAN ST, BYRON ST, NICHOLSON ST, LEEDS ST, DALMAHOY ST, MOORE ST, SHELLY ST, COWPER ST

BARKLY ST, David Spurling Res, Tennis, Whitten Oval, HOCKING ST, CROSS ST, GORDON ST, BATMAN ST, PRINCES HWY, QUEEN ST, DARLING ST, BUCKINGHAM ST, ERROL ST, ANN ST, WINDSOR ST, PAISLEY ST, Nurs Home, PICKETT ST, HUNTLY ST, DEVON PL, SULLIVAN PL, FRENCH ST, IRVING ST, CHAMBERS ST, Footscray Market, TRUGO LA, McNAB AV, Footscray, TALBOT ST, TOOHEY ST, BUNBURY ST, HYDE ST, West Footscray, Middle Footscray, RALEIGH ST, Sen Cits Cntr, SHORT ST, Railway Res

BUCKLEY ST, LILY ST, ALEXANDER ST, SCOTT ST, SYDENHAM ST, MARGARET ST, EMMA ST, PILGRIM ST, West Suburban Taxis, WERNER ST, STAFF ST, ADMIRAL ST, BILSTON ST, BUTE ST, ARRAN ST, Victoria University Nicholson Campus, LAWSON ST, COWPER ST, NAPIER ST, MORELAND ST, Schintler Res, FOOTSCRAY RD

WILLIAMSTOWN RD, CHARLES ST, ALFRED ST, EDWARD ST, HENRY ST, JOHN ST, JAMES ST, WILLIAM ST, CUTHBERT ST, YOUNG ST, GLEDHILL ST, WINDSOR ST, VIGO ST, VICTORIA ST, WALTER ST, PILGRIM ST, AUSTIN ST, BOURKE ST, COLLINS ST, NORTH ST, SOUTH ST, KENT ST, MEDWAY ST, JUNCTION ST, ALBERT ST, Footscray Pmy, PARKER ST, STATION ST, RD ST, HAROLD ST, LAWRENCE ST, TENNYSON ST, RENNIE ST, HOBBS ST, POLE ST, BRISTOW ST, EASTWOOD ST, OSCAR ST, SEDDON ST, ACTON ST, THOMSON ST, PERRY ST, Seddon, LYONS ST, DOCKLANDS HWY, Wharves, MARIBYRNONG ST, DAHLENBURG ST, COODE RD, FLORENCE ST, WEBSTER ST, BROWNING ST, GREIG ST, HOTHAM ST, BELL ST, Mappin Res, YOUELL ST, O'FARRELL ST, CHAPMAN ST, HARRIET ST, MACKAY ST, DANE ST, PRINCESS ST, WHITEHALL ST, MORELAND ST

BURNS ST, GRACE ST, HAMILTON ST, STEWART ST, FIELDING ST, LITTLE SMITH ST, MCH, MONTAGUE ST, HOOD ST, REGENT ST, AGNES ST, BAYVIEW ST, SOMERVILLE RD, BROOK ST, STOREY ST, GAMON ST, TONGUE ST, BARNET ST, PENTLAND ST, BELLAIRS AV, FAIRLIE ST, STEPHEN ST, Western Suburbs Nurs Home, BERRY ST, LIT BERRY ST, Victoria University Yarraville Campus, NICHOLSON ST, Ten HARRIS, Hammer Res, Yarraville Gardens, SOMERVILLE RD, Mobil, CUMMINS ST, BP Australia, GIBBONS ST, Conaust Victoria Pty Ltd, OLIPHANT ST, MACKENZIE ST, No 4 West, No 3 West, No 2 West, No 1 West, SWANSON DOCK, Container Ship Dock

FORREST ST, AVOCA ST, Cath Pmy, ALICE ST, CASTLEMAINE ST, GEORGE ST, BLANCHE ST, GOULBURN ST, Yarraville Oval, Yarraville W Tennis, Pmy, CUMING ST, MURRAY ST, CANTERBURY ST, BIRMINGHAM ST, WOODS ST, LENNOX ST, KNOX ST, HALL ST, Yarraville, ANDERSON ST, SIMPSON ST, Sen Cits, Beaton Res, TARRENGOWER ST, WILLIS ST, MAGGIE ST, DUCKER ST, SCHILD ST, LEEK ST, BLACKWOOD ST, OVENS ST, SANDFORD GR, YORK ST, RONA AV, CSR, Spec Dev Sch, MARJORY ST, GLADSTONE ST, WILSON ST, GRAY ST, EARSDON ST, ASTON ST, DICKENS ST, PEARCE ST, POWELL ST, BEATRICE ST, HAWTHORN ST, SUSSEX ST, FREDERICK ST, CLARENDON ST, FEHON ST, KENT ST, LIT ST, MINNIE ST, LYELL ST, NORFOLK ST, MCH, HANCE ST, BUNBURY ST, NEWCASTLE ST, HYDE ST, TAYLOR ST, Yarraville Wharves, No 1 Berth

FRANCIS ST, MORVEN ST, Anderson Reserve, BALLARAT ST, BANOOL AV, HUGHES ST, LORIMER ST, BEVERLEY ST, Cmnty Cntr, FRASER ST, GLOBE ST, VOCKLER ST, CAMPBELL ST, Orica Australia, FRANCIS ST, Holden Swinging Basin, Mobil Oil Terminal, Holden Oil Dock, YARRA, POWELL ST, EVANS ST, GORDON PDE, Westgate Golf Course, THOMAS ST, WEST GATE FWY, Res, Stoney Creek Backwash, LORIMER ST, Boat Storage, Ent, Hawker de Havilland, WIRRAWAY DR, Helipad, TODD RD, Dept of Defence Aeronautical Research Laboratory, SEC

Spotswood Oval, Clubhouse, CREEK ST, HALL ST, Esso, STEPHEN ST, BRIDGE ST, AV, THE AVENUE, SIMCOCK AV, RMIT & ASTA Aerospace Technologies, WHARF RD, Herald & Weekly Times

JOINS 366

JOINS 411

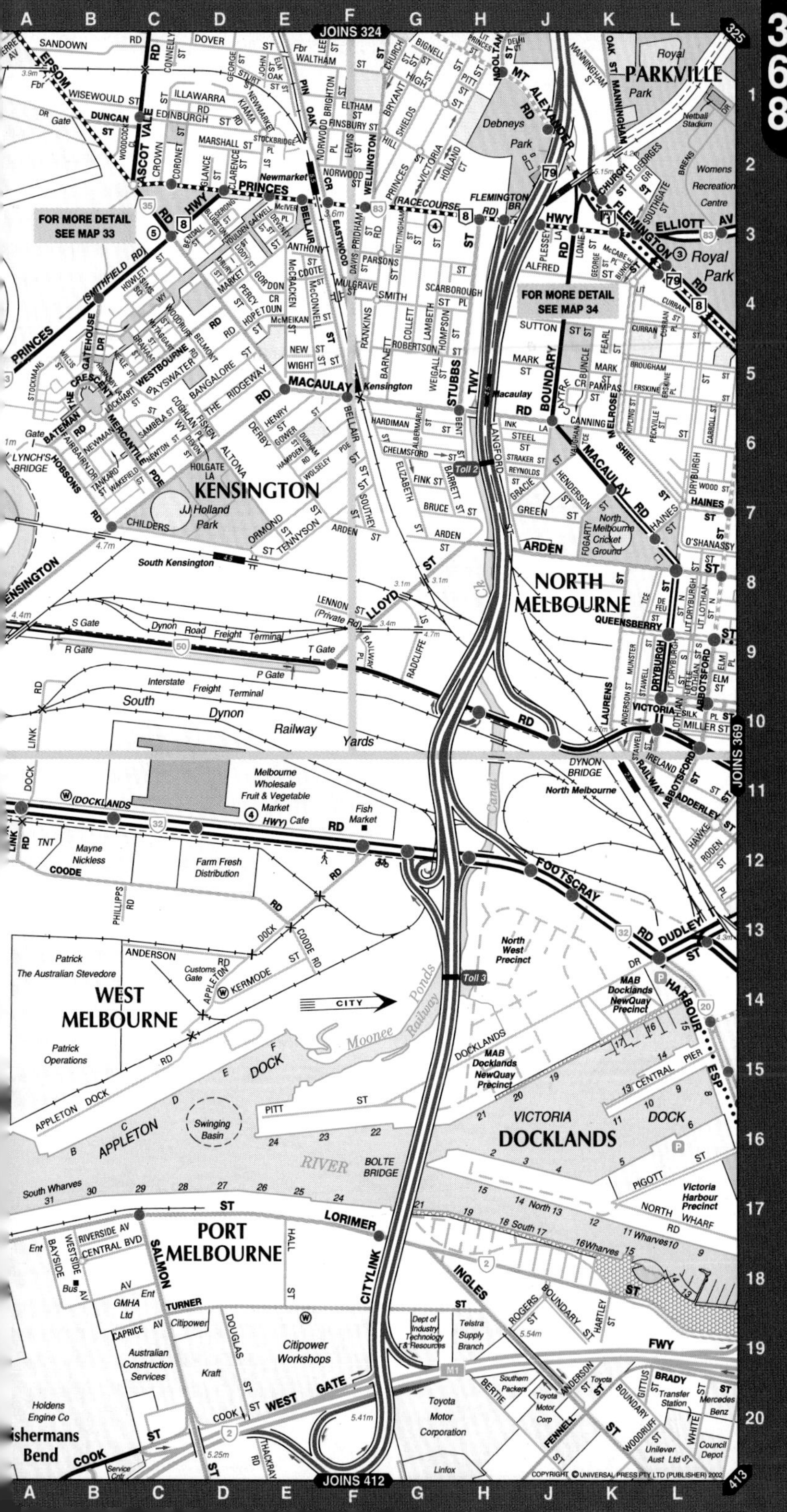

368
JOINS 324
JOINS 369
JOINS 412
325
413
A B C D E F G H J K L
1 2 3 4 5 6 7 8 9 10 11 12 13 14 15 16 17 18 19 20
PARKVILLE
Royal Park
Netball Stadium
Womens Recreation Centre
Debneys Park
Royal Park
FOR MORE DETAIL SEE MAP 33
FOR MORE DETAIL SEE MAP 34
KENSINGTON
JJ Holland Park
NORTH MELBOURNE
North Melbourne Cricket Ground
South Kensington
Kensington
Macaulay
North Melbourne
Dynon Road Freight Terminal
South Dynon Railway Yards
Interstate Freight Terminal
Melbourne Wholesale Fruit & Vegetable Market
Fish Market
Cafe
Mayne Nickless
Farm Fresh Distribution
TNT
Patrick The Australian Stevedore
Patrick Operations
WEST MELBOURNE
Customs Gate
North West Precinct
MAB Docklands NewQuay Precinct
CITY
Moonee Ponds
Swinging Basin
APPLETON DOCK
VICTORIA DOCK
DOCKLANDS
Victoria Harbour Precinct
RIVER
BOLTE BRIDGE
South Wharves
North Wharves
PORT MELBOURNE
GMHA Ltd
Citipower
Citipower Workshops
Australian Construction Services
Kraft
Holdens Engine Co
Fishermans Bend
Dept of Industry Technology & Resources
Telstra Supply Branch
Toyota Motor Corporation
Southern Packers
Toyota Motor Corp
Transfer Station
Mercedes Benz
Unilever Aust Ltd
Council Depot
Linfox
EPSOM RD
SANDOWN RD
DOVER ST
WISEWOULD ST
DUNCAN ST
ASCOT VALE RD
PRINCES HWY
SMITHFIELD RD
MT ALEXANDER RD
FLEMINGTON RD
RACECOURSE RD
ELLIOTT AV
MACAULAY RD
BELLAIR ST
STUBBS ST
BOUNDARY RD
ARDEN ST
LLOYD ST
DYNON RD
DOCKLANDS HWY
FOOTSCRAY RD
DUDLEY ST
HARBOUR ESP
CITYLINK
LORIMER ST
WEST GATE FWY
SALMON ST
TURNER ST
INGLES ST
COOK ST
DRYBURGH ST
QUEENSBERRY ST
VICTORIA ST
LAURENS ST
HAINES ST
COPYRIGHT © UNIVERSAL PRESS PTY LTD (PUBLISHER) 2002

A B C D E F G H J K L

324
JOINS 325
JOINS 368

1 2 3 4 5 6 7 8 9 10 11 12 13 14 15 16 17 18 19 20

CARLTON NORTH

PARKVILLE

CARLTON

NORTH MELBOURNE

WEST MELBOURNE

MELBOURNE

DOCKLANDS

SOUTHBANK

Royal Melbourne Zoo

Royal Park

Princes Park

Optus Oval Carlton Cricket Ground

Golf Course

Netball Stadium

State Hockey Centre

Womens Recreation Centre

Melbourne General Cemetery

Royal Childrens Hospital

Vet Precinct

University High

Royal Melbourne Hospital

The University of Melbourne

Uni of Melb

Royal Womens Hospital

Carlton Gardens

Royal Exhibition Building

Queen Victoria Market

Flagstaff Gardens

Flagstaff

Melbourne Central

State Houses of Parliament

Parliament

GPO

Town Hall

City Square

Federation Square

Flinders Street

Spencer Street

Birrarung Marr Park

(Riverside Park)

Alexandra Gardens

Queen Victoria Gardens

Kings Domain

Colonial Stadium

Victoria Harbour Precinct

World Trade Centre

Crown Entertainment Complex

Casino

Melbourne Exhibition Centre

Southgate

Sheraton Towers

Arts Centre

College of the Arts

Victoria Barracks

Police Hospital

Coronial Services Cntr

Red Cross

Council Depot

Curtain Square

Nth Carlton Pmy

Carlton Pmy

PRINCES BRIDGE

SPENCER ST BRIDGE

YARRA

FOR MORE DETAIL SEE MAP 17

FOR MORE DETAIL SEE MAP 18

FOR MORE DETAIL SEE MAP 24

FOR MORE DETAIL SEE MAP 23

ELLIOTT AV, MACARTHUR RD, FLEMINGTON RD, GATEHOUSE ST, ROYAL PDE, CEMETERY RD WEST, CEMETERY RD EAST, COLLEGE CRESCENT, PRINCES ST, ELGIN ST, GRATTAN ST, VICTORIA ST, KING ST, SPENCER ST, PEEL ST, ELIZABETH ST, SWANSTON ST, LYGON ST, RATHDOWNE ST, NICHOLSON ST, LA TROBE ST, LONSDALE ST, BOURKE ST, COLLINS ST, FLINDERS ST, WILLIAM ST, QUEEN ST, EXHIBITION ST, SPRING ST, RUSSELL ST, HARBOUR ESP, WURUNDJERI WAY, DUDLEY ST, CLARENDON ST, KINGS WAY, QUEENSBRIDGE ST, SOUTHBANK BVD, ST KILDA RD, ALEXANDRA AV, LINLITHGOW AV, CITY RD, MORAY ST, WEST GATE FWY, MONTAGUE ST, NORMANBY RD

412
JOINS 413

A B C D E F G H J K L

JOINS 326
327
FITZROY NORTH
CLIFTON HILL
COLLINGWOOD
ABBOTSFORD
KEW
FITZROY
EAST MELBOURNE
RICHMOND
CREMORNE
Jolimont
Edinburgh Gardens
John Batman College of TAFE
Darling Gardens
The Quarries Park
Victoria Park
Fitzroy Gardens
Powlett Reserve
City Reserve
Yarra Park
Melbourne Cricket Ground
Richmond Cricket Ground
Melbourne Park
Old Scotch Oval
Olympic Park
Former Army Depot
Gosch's Paddock
Royal Botanic Gardens
Government House
Yarra Bend Park
Carlton & United Breweries
Epworth Hospital
Clifton Hill
Victoria Park
Collingwood
North Richmond
West Richmond
Richmond
East Richmond
Jolimont
FOR MORE DETAIL SEE MAP 19
FOR MORE DETAIL SEE MAP 20
FOR MORE DETAIL SEE MAP 25
FOR MORE DETAIL SEE MAP 26
JOINS 371
JOINS 414
415
COPYRIGHT © UNIVERSAL PRESS PTY LTD (PUBLISHER) 2003

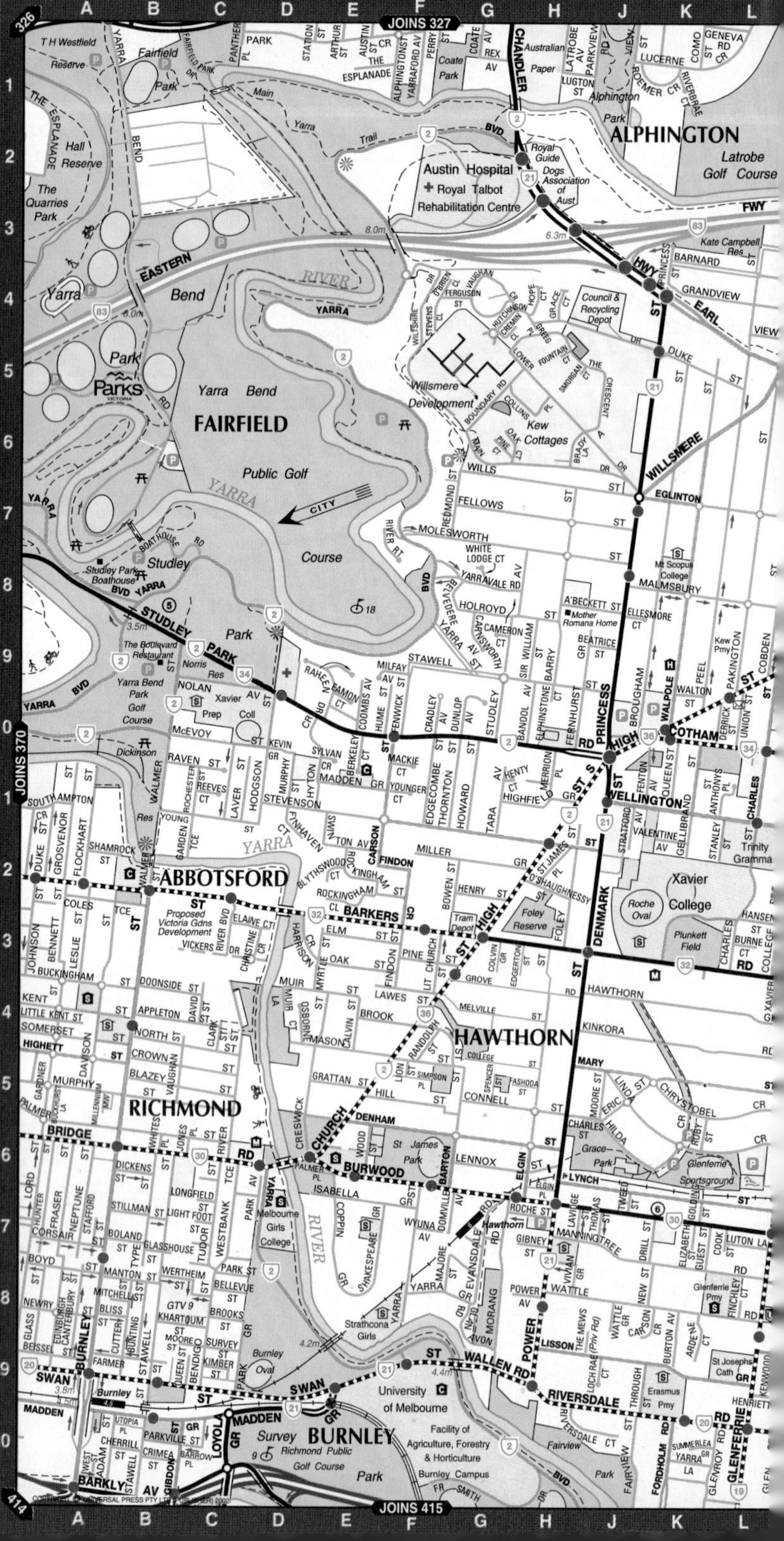

326 | JOINS 327 | JOINS 370 | 414 | JOINS 415

A B C D E F G H J K L

1 2 3 4 5 6 7 8 9 10 11 12 13 14 15 16 17 18 19 20

ALPHINGTON

FAIRFIELD

ABBOTSFORD

HAWTHORN

RICHMOND

BURNLEY

T H Westfield Reserve

Fairfield Park

Hall Reserve

The Quarries Park

Yarra Bend Park

Parks Victoria

Yarra Bend Public Golf Course

Studley Park

Studley Park Boathouse

The Boulevard Restaurant

Norris Res

Yarra Bend Park Golf Course

Dickinson Res

Xavier Prep Coll

Main Yarra Trail

Austin Hospital

Royal Talbot Rehabilitation Centre

Royal Guide Dogs Association of Aust

Australian Paper

Alphington Park

Latrobe Golf Course

Kate Campbell Res

Council & Recycling Depot

Willsmere Development

Kew Cottages

Mt Scopus College

Mother Romana Home

Kew Pmy

Trinity Grammar

Xavier College

Roche Oval

Plunkett Field

Foley Reserve

Tram Depot

Proposed Victoria Gdns Development

Melbourne Girls College

St James Park

Grace Park

Glenferrie Sportsground

Hawthorn

Glenferrie Pmy

St Josephs Cath

Strathcona Girls

Burnley Oval

University of Melbourne

Facility of Agriculture, Forestry & Horticulture

Burnley Campus

Survey Richmond Public Golf Course

Burnley Park

Fairview Park

Erasmus Pmy

GTV 9

EASTERN FWY

CHANDLER HWY

PRINCESS ST

HIGH ST

STUDLEY PARK RD

BARKERS RD

BURWOOD RD

BRIDGE RD

SWAN ST

RIVERSDALE RD

WALLEN RD

CHURCH ST

BURNLEY ST

DENMARK ST

POWER ST

GLENFERRIE RD

YARRA RIVER

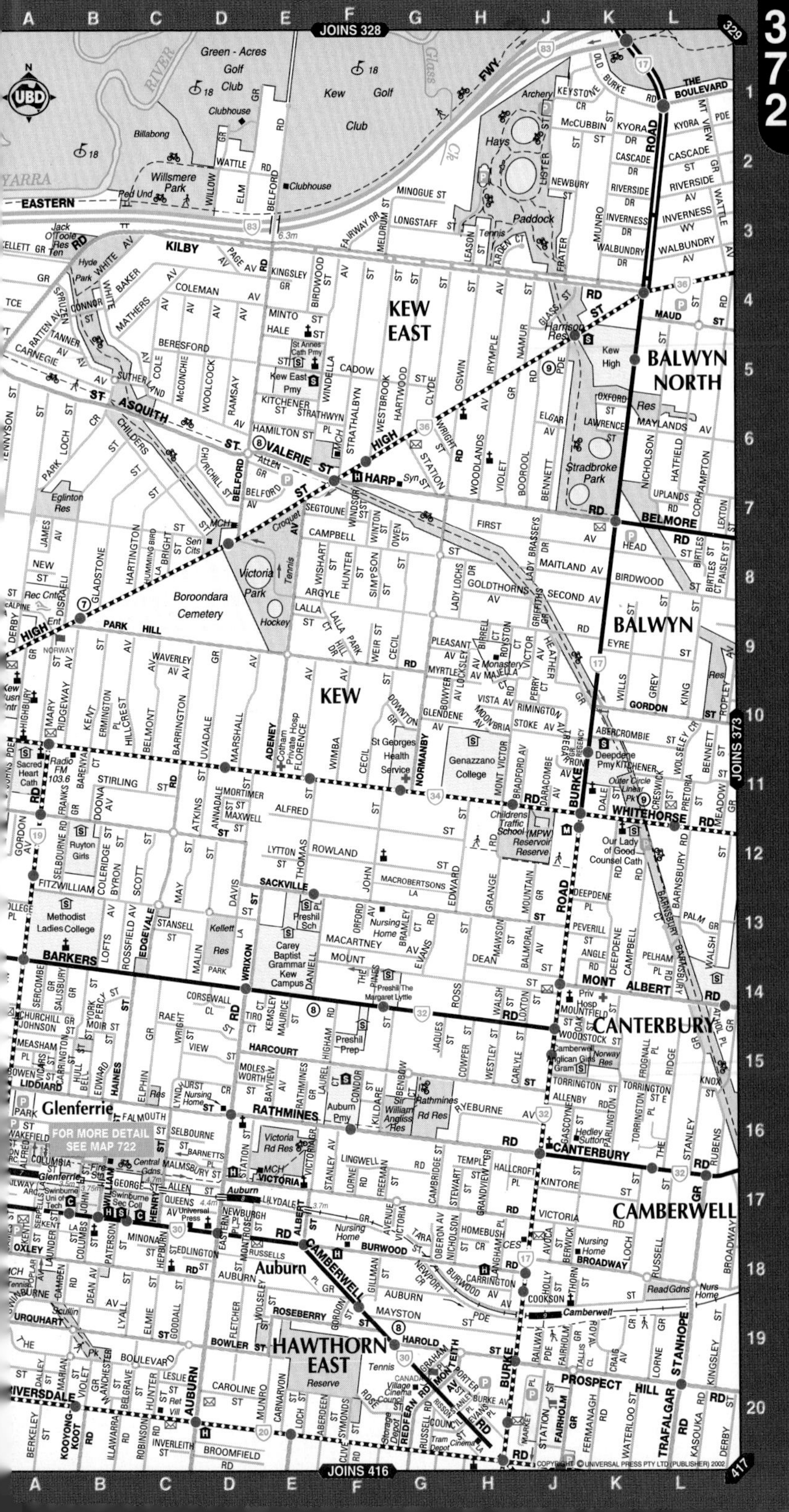
A B C D E F G H J K L
JOINS 328
329
UBD
Green - Acres Golf Club
Clubhouse
Billabong
Willsmere Park
Kew Golf Club
Clubhouse
YARRA
RIVER
EASTERN FWY
Glass Ck
Hays Paddock
Archery
Tennis
KEW EAST
BALWYN NORTH
BALWYN
KEW
CANTERBURY
CAMBERWELL
Glenferrie
Auburn
HAWTHORN EAST
Hyde Park
Eglinton Res
Boroondara Cemetery
Victoria Park
Hockey
Croquet
Harrison Res
Kew High
Stradbroke Park
Res
St Annes Cath Pmy
Kew East Pmy
St Georges Health Service
Genazzano College
Childrens Traffic School
(MPW) Reservoir Reserve
Sacred Heart Cath
Radio FM 103.6
Ruyton Girls
Methodist Ladies College
Kellett Res
Carey Baptist Grammar Kew Campus
Preshil Sch
Preshil Prep
Nursing Home
Deepdene Pmy
Our Lady of Good Counsel Cath
Outer Circle Linear Pk
Camberwell Anglican Girls Gram
Norway Res
Priv Hosp
Hedley Sutton
Auburn Pmy
Sir William Angliss Res
Rathmines Rd Res
Victoria Rd Res
Swinburne Univ of Tech
Swinburne Sec Coll
FOR MORE DETAIL SEE MAP 722
Central Gdns
Universal Press
Read Gdns
Nurs Home
Tennis
Village Cinema Council
Tram Depot
Storage Depot
Reserve
HIGH ST
VALERIE ST
HARP
ASQUITH
BELFORD RD
KILBY RD
PARK HILL RD
COTHAM RD
WHITEHORSE RD
BURKE RD
BARKERS RD
MONT ALBERT RD
RATHMINES RD
CANTERBURY RD
BURWOOD RD
CAMBERWELL RD
RIVERSDALE RD
PROSPECT HILL RD
BELMORE RD
HARCOURT
SACKVILLE
WRIXON
GLENFERRIE RD
AUBURN RD
VICTORIA
TRAFALGAR
STANHOPE
JOINS 373
JOINS 416
417
1 2 3 4 5 6 7 8 9 10 11 12 13 14 15 16 17 18 19 20
COPYRIGHT © UNIVERSAL PRESS PTY LTD (PUBLISHER) 2002

A B C D E F G H J K L

328

JOINS 329

1 2 3 4 5 6 7 8 9 10 11 12 13 14 15 16 17 18 19 20

BALWYN NORTH

BALWYN

Deepdene

CANTERBURY

East Camberwell

Riversdale

SURREY HILLS

JOINS 372

416

JOINS 417

A B C D E F G H J K L

JOINS 330
JOINS 331
JOINS 375
JOINS 418
JOINS 419

A B C D E F G H J K L

DONCASTER

MONT ALBERT NORTH

BOX HILL NORTH

MONT ALBERT

BOX HILL

BOX HILL SOUTH

Eastern Golf Club
Clubhouse
Westfield Shoppingtown Doncaster
Koonung Creek Reserve
Wilson Rd Res
Birralee Pmy
St Bridgets Cath Pmy
Koonung Ck
Bushy Ck
Elgar Park
Miniature Railway
Frank Sedgman Res
Box Hill North Pmy
Koonung Secondary College
Memorial Park
Gawler Chain
Mont Albert Reserve
Box Hill Senior Sec Coll
Hagenauer Reserve
Mont Albert Pk
Mont Albert Pmy
Box Hill Institute of TAFE
Kingsley Gardens
Box Hill Hospital & Surgi Cntr
Box Hill Gardens
Lynwood Nursing Home
Holy Redeemer Cath
Surrey Hills Pmy
Surrey Park
Landfill
Brickworks
Box Hill Indoor Rec Cntr
Telstra Tower
Hayville Retirement Village
Kingswood College
Surrey Hills Nurs Home

EASTERN FWY
DONCASTER RD
ELGAR RD
STATION ST
WHITEHORSE RD
MAROONDAH HWY
CANTERBURY RD
BELMORE RD
WARRIGAL RD
UNION RD
MIDDLEBOROUGH RD

1 2 3 4 5 6 7 8 9 10 11 12 13 14 15 16 17 18 19 20

330
JOINS 331
JOINS 374
JOINS 419
418

A B C D E F G H J K L

1 2 3 4 5 6 7 8 9 10 11 12 13 14 15 16 17 18 19 20

DONCASTER

DONCASTER EAST

BLACKBURN NORTH

BOX HILL NORTH

BOX HILL

BLACKBURN

BOX HILL SOUTH

DONCASTER RD

WETHERBY RD

EASTERN FWY

TRAM RD

STATION ST

MIDDLEBOROUGH RD

SPRINGFIELD RD

WHITEHORSE RD

MAROONDAH HWY

CANTERBURY RD

BLACKBURN RD

Koonung Creek

Eram Park

Tram Road Reserve

Eastern Reserve

Boronia Grove Res

Koonung Reserve

Springfield Park

Bolton Park

Box Hill Oval

Box Hill Cemetery

Blacks Walk Reserve

Sparks Reserve

Kalang Park

Furness Park

Wandinong Sanctuary

Morton Park

Doncaster Playhouse

Council Offices

National Bus Company

Doncaster Community Centre

Doncaster Reserve Indoor Sports

Blackburn High

North Blackburn Square

St Vincent De Paul Nursing Home

Blackburn Nursing Home

St Leos International College

Box Hill High

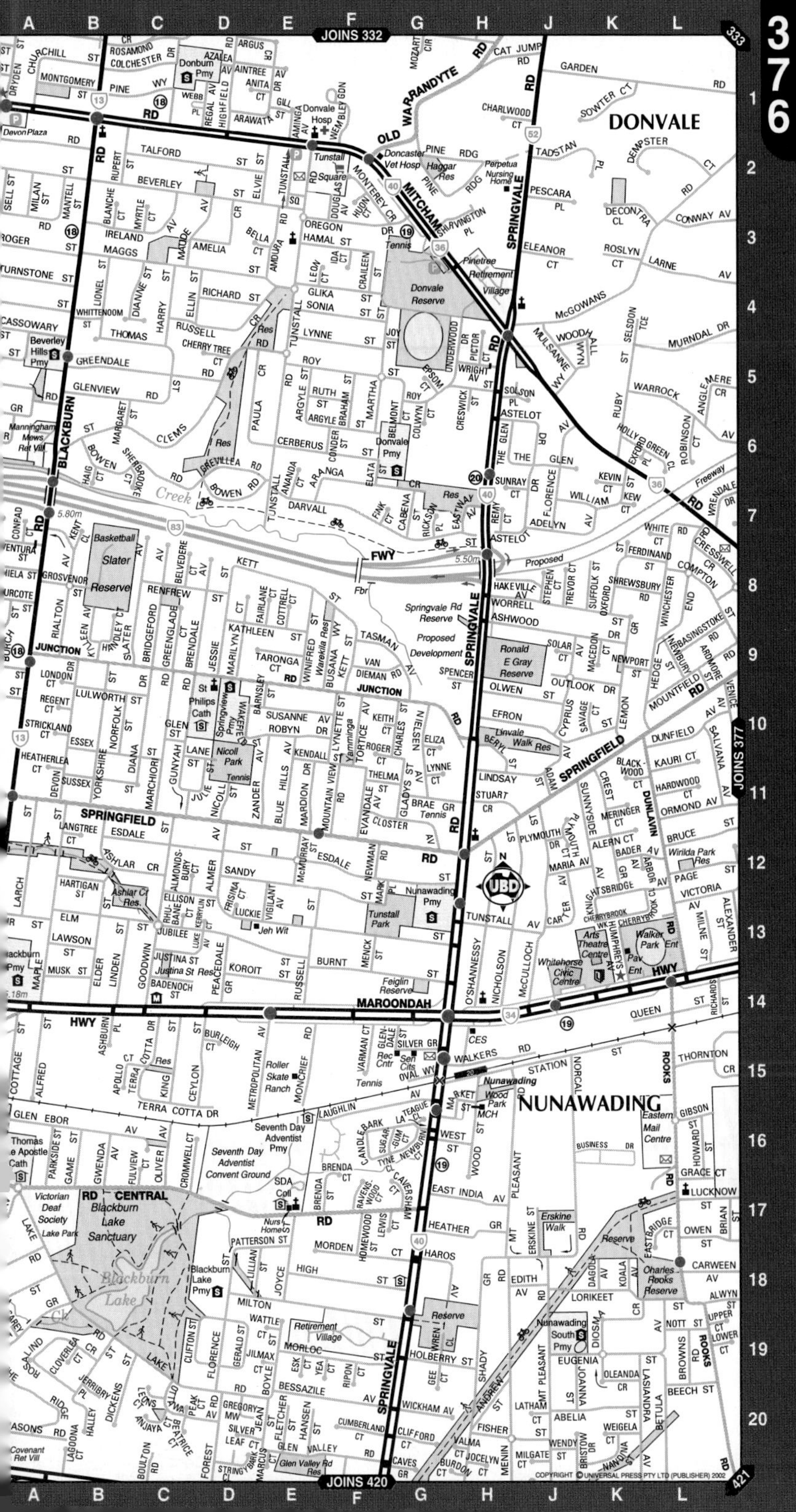
JOINS 332
JOINS 377
JOINS 420
333
421
A B C D E F G H J K L
1 2 3 4 5 6 7 8 9 10 11 12 13 14 15 16 17 18 19 20
DONVALE
NUNAWADING
OLD WARRANDYTE RD
MITCHAM RD
SPRINGVALE RD
BLACKBURN RD
JUNCTION RD
SPRINGFIELD RD
MAROONDAH HWY
CENTRAL RD
FWY
Freeway
Proposed
Donvale Hosp
Doncaster Vet Hosp
Haggar Res
Perpetua Nursing Home
Tunstall Square
Donvale Reserve
Pinetree Retirement Village
Beverley Hills Pmy
Manningham Mews Ret Vill
Donvale Pmy
Slater Reserve
Basketball
Springvale Rd Reserve
Proposed Development
Ronald E Gray Reserve
Warekila Res
St Philips Cath
Springview Pmy
Nicoll Park
Tennis
Linvale Walk Res
Ashlar Ct Res.
Jeh Wit
Tunstall Park
Nunawading Pmy
Feiglin Reserve
Arts Theatre Centre
Whitehorse Civic Centre
Walker Park
Blackburn Pmy
Justina St Res
Roller Skate Ranch
Rec Cntr
Sen Cits
CES
Nunawading Wood Park
MCH
Eastern Mail Centre
Seventh Day Adventist Pmy
Seventh Day Adventist Convent Ground
SDA Coll
Nurs Homes
Thomas e Apostle Cath
Victorian Deaf Society
Lake Park
Blackburn Lake Sanctuary
Blackburn Lake
Blackburn Lake Pmy
Retirement Village
Reserve
Erskine Walk
Charles Rooks Reserve
Nunawading South Pmy
Glen Valley Rd Res
Covenant Ret Vill
Devon Plaza
Creek
5.80m
5.50m
5.18m
COPYRIGHT © UNIVERSAL PRESS PTY LTD (PUBLISHER) 2002

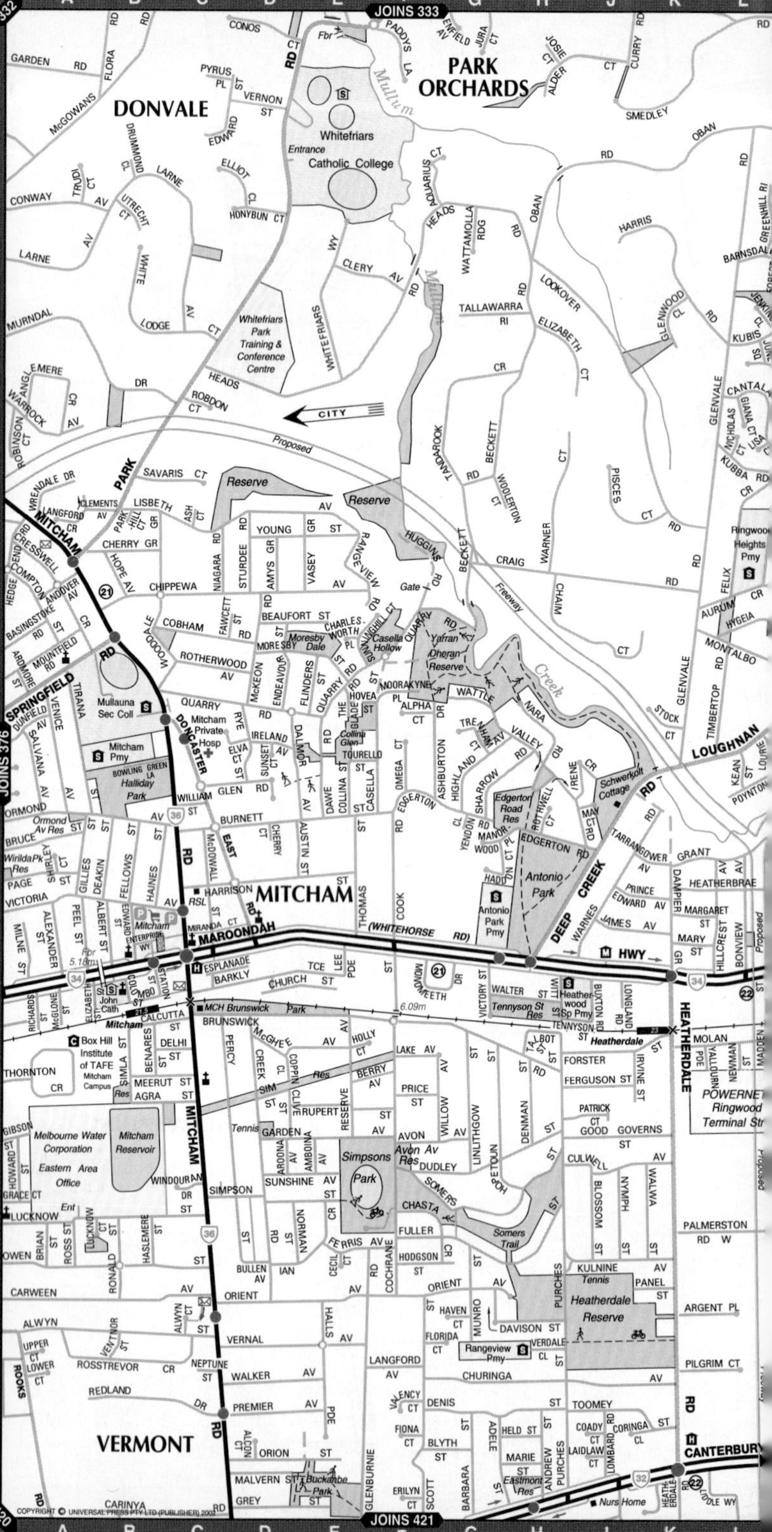

A B C D E F G H J K L

332 JOINS 333

DONVALE

PARK ORCHARDS

MITCHAM

VERMONT

Whitefriars Catholic College

Whitefriars Park Training & Conference Centre

Mullum Mullum Creek

Mullauna Sec Coll

Mitcham Private Hosp

Mitcham Pmy

Halliday Park

Yafran Dheran Reserve

Casella Hollow

Moresby Dale

Colling Glen

Edgerton Road Res

Antonio Park

Antonio Park Pmy

Schwerkolt Cottage

Ringwood Heights Pmy

Box Hill Institute of TAFE Mitcham Campus

Melbourne Water Corporation Eastern Area Office

Mitcham Reservoir

Simpsons Park

Avon Av Res

Somers Trail

Heatherdale Reserve

Rangeview Pmy

Heatherwood Sp Pmy

Tennyson St Res

POWERNET Ringwood Terminal Str

Buckanbe Park

Eastmont Res

MAROONDAH HWY (WHITEHORSE RD)

MITCHAM RD

DONCASTER EAST RD

SPRINGFIELD RD

PARK RD

HEATHERDALE RD

DEEP CREEK RD

LOUGHNAN RD

CANTERBURY RD

Mitcham

Heatherdale

Proposed Freeway

CITY

JOINS 376

420 JOINS 421

A B C D E F G H J K L

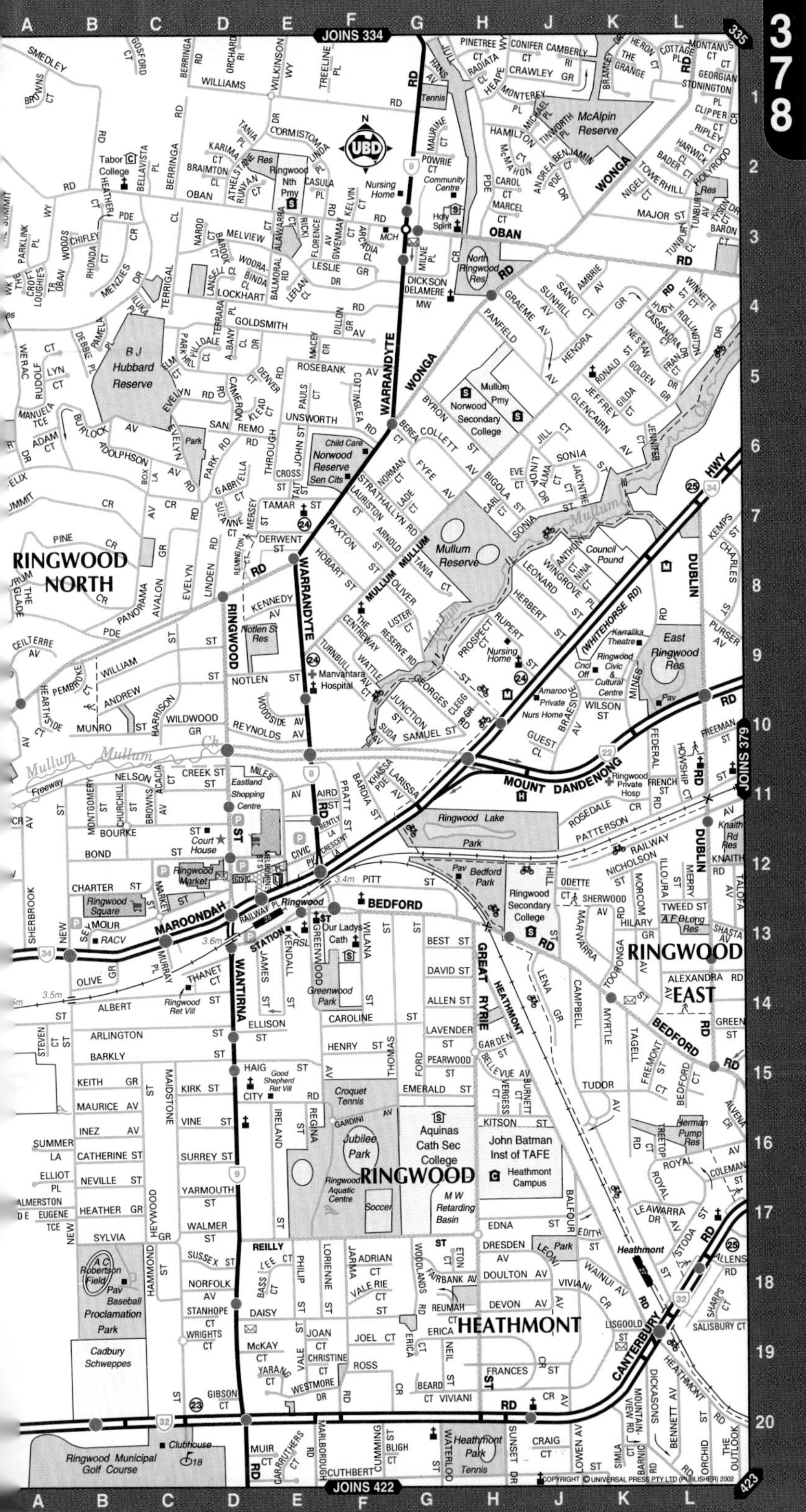

JOINS 334
JOINS 379
JOINS 422
335
423
RINGWOOD NORTH
RINGWOOD
RINGWOOD EAST
HEATHMONT
WARRANDYTE RD
WONGA RD
OBAN RD
RINGWOOD RD
MAROONDAH HWY
(WHITEHORSE RD)
MOUNT DANDENONG RD
WANTIRNA RD
GREAT RYRIE ST
CANTERBURY RD
BEDFORD RD
DUBLIN RD
McAlpin Reserve
B J Hubbard Reserve
Norwood Reserve
Mullum Reserve
East Ringwood Res
Ringwood Lake Park
Bedford Park
Jubilee Park
Greenwood Park
A C Robertson Field
Proclamation Park
Heathmont Park
Ringwood Municipal Golf Course
Eastland Shopping Centre
Ringwood Market
Ringwood Square
Aquinas Cath Sec College
John Batman Inst of TAFE Heathmont Campus
Ringwood Secondary College
Norwood Secondary College
Tabor College
Manvantara Hospital
Ringwood Private Hosp
Cadbury Schweppes
COPYRIGHT © UNIVERSAL PRESS PTY LTD (PUBLISHER) 2002

A B C D E F G H J K L

JOINS 335

334

1 2 3 4 5 6 7 8 9 10 11 12 13 14 15 16 17 18 19 20

MONTANUS CT
TRITON CT
MUNDARA DR
NERIDA RD
VALKYRIE CR
STRATHFIELD ST
ARDEL CT
STRAITER CL
CHABLIS CL
HERMITAGE CT
ARDEL CT
CHANNORA ST
Cherry Tree Grove Retirement Village
CHERRY TREE GR
NURSERY RD
HWY
ALTO
STIRLING
GAIRNS CT
Nurs Home
HYTON CR
ROSE CT
SOMERSET
NELSON
KEN
GEORGIAN CT
STONINGTON PL
CLIPPER CT
RIPLEY CT
AVIS CT
Kalinda Urban Forest
Kalinda Primary
KALINDA
BEGA CT
CHESNEY CT
Douglas Maggs Res
Croydon Hotel
GLADYS
RYLAND
MONTEITH ST
Res
KENMARE AV
AV
RD
TOORAK
GLEN
CARMEN CT
EPACRIS CT
ASHTON CT
CR RD
BVD
MARCUS
COREEN CT
ALEC ST
CR PDE
HOLYROOD
BERKLEY
ADELE
KENWOOD CT
DUNCAN CT
HUNTER
MAGGS ST
KALLAY CT
(WHITEHORSE RD)
MURRAY
GR
WOODLAND
AV
Res
TUNBURY AV
TYSON
BARON CT
FIONA CT
LILIAN
MARILYN
ROBINSON ST
ST
HINKLEY AV
Croydon West Pmy
EDEN ST
AV
PENHYRN
Grandfill Res
ALTO
THE TERRACE
ELLESMERE
OBAN
FREDERIC
ABBEY
KISMET
PDE
HIGHLAND
AILSA CT
Fbr
GRAYLING CR
RD
BRENTNALL RD
RAMBLE
JULIANA CT
WILHELMINA
Res
Cmnty Cntr
AINSLIE
ANTHONY ST
COLUMBIA AV
WEBSTER
FOREST CT
AV
BANOOL CT
GLENORA
Croydon
WINNETTE
FLORA CT
KINTA
Peter Vergers Res
Tennis
Mullum Mullum
Maroondah Secondary College
Ainslie Park
BEAUFORT
CUTTS AV
AV
RICHARDS AV
MURRAY
WEBSTER
CROYDON
WICKLOW
RINGWOOD
RD
MAROONDAH
OLGA CT
BRONHILL
DARIN CT
CLAIRE CT
EDITH
BEAUFORT
ROSS
CLEGG
Sacred Heart Monastery
VEEMA AV
GALLIPOLI PDE
ANZAC
LEMNOS
RIDGWAY
Mullum
CARCOOLA
CARAMUT GR
CALOLA CT
Don-Wood Nursing Home
DIANA
AV
Mingarra Ret Vill
Ent
STARCROSS AV
4.62m
ELIZABETH CT
SEARES
IAN AV
DR
WYRUNGA
DYNES ST
Res
RD
MOUNT 27
BALCOMBE CT
DANDENONG
CURRONG GR
PDE
RD
ST
WESLEY CT
ALAN ST
EVERARD
JOSEPH ST
26
VASEY
KIRRA CT
VALENTINO DR
INVERNESS CT
KILARA CT
GLENWOOD
MORALLA
RD
VERNON
KEMPS
LILYDALE
RD
EVON
AV
RUTHVEN AV
PINE CT
CECIL CCT
HEYINGTON CT
JULIE RD
CHARLES
KING ST
OLD
VALDA AV
MIRABEL AV
CNC
SHERWOOD CT
MONTANA
CROYDON WY
O'Shannassy
VINTER
DUBLIN
HOLLAND
WARE
VELMA
ANGUS
VASEY
CNC
YARRADUCT PL N
YARRADUCT PL S
FORTUNA
ST
OKE ST
SUNBEAM
Maroondah Hospital
DAVEY DR
CR
WY
TOMAR CL
WOODFORD CL
DR
FIELD ST
PARK LA
AV
PURSER
AV
GREY
CHEONG
HILLSIDE
BAYSWATER
RONALD
LUSHER
EASTFIELD
DUNN
ST
ORCHARD
Cheong Park
Netball
MORRIS
Fbr
MOUNT DANDENONG
BONA
MILLER
FAIRVIEW
SHORT ST
Cheong Sanc
THE LONG PASS
RD
Pony Club
MCH
Trotting Track
FREEMAN ST
ST
GR
AV
RICHARD CT
HIGHTON AV
MORINDA
SHANE CR
THE MOUNT
VIEW
PLEASANT RI
MARIANA
CLARE ST
THE MALL
EASTFIELD
JOINS 378
Ringwood East
PATTERSON
SMITHDENE
ANDREW
SHANE CR
LUCILLE AV
YVONNE AV
MACKENZIE
PERCY ST
PETER ST
RD ST
RD
DUBLIN
RAILWAY
Knaith Rd Res
LAURENCE GR
STANLEY AV
WENWOOD
OLIVE
LOIS
VICTORIA LA
JEANETTE CT
BRUCE CT
LOMA
CAMELIA CT
ACACIA CT
CR
MIMOSA CT
ANDREW CR
ARSCOTT CL
BLUE MIST DR
THOMAS
ST
KNAITH
ST RD
ST
ST
BANKSIA
BRIDGE CT
TARNAGULLA RD
BELMONT
ROYAL
CROYDON SOUTH
KING RD
TALOFA AV
RUSSET RD
NORTHWOOD
LANGLEY
BONDI
Tintern Anglican Girls Grammar
JEFFERSON RD
FARADAY
BLAZEY
SHASTA
MERRILONG
Eastwood Pmy
ALEXANDRA
LILLIS
ISABEL
BYWAYS
REX CT
OAK LA
THURLEIGH AV
MULDURI
ALEXANDRA RD
WOOD
SCENIC AV
VISTA
GRANDVIEW
MALCOLM
CLELAND ST
BURONGA
HENDER
GRACEDALE
Tinternvale Pmy
TINTERN
RD
GARDENIA ST
BORONIA AV
MALINDA WY
WOODLAND PARK RI
BLUEGUM
MULDURI CR
VONADAWN AV
COOLOOLI CT
WALHALLA
JESS CT
LESTER DR
WINGATE
AV
DUNLOP
CENTRAL
JASMINE RD
KYAMBA CT
GREEN ST
ST
LYNWOOD
LANDELL CT
HUME
AV
Irabina Special Development School
RD
ILLAWARA
RD
HOWARD AV
CHEEVERS CT
VISTA
MAPLE CT
FLORA ST
RAYMOND
ROZELLE CT
WENDOVER AV
FAIR LA
HOME ST
TOWER CT
ADINA CL
RINGWOOD EAST
BRAEWOOD
AV
BYRNE RD
CONSIDINE CT
BEDFORD
Wombolano Park
ROTHERWOOD AV
Tennis
Gracedale Park
Jeh Wit
BERRY RD
BAKER RD
BRANCH
Herman Pump Res
ALVENA
HOMEBUSH
RAWSON
PINEWOOD
FERNWOOD AV
HEATHWOOD
FITZGERALD ST
TEAK AV
LOWE CT
IVON ST
ROYAL AV
COLEMAN ST
HUNTER CT
WATTLE RD
MELISSA CT
RD W
Fbr
BAYFIELD
CR
RD
CANTERBURY
FINLAYSON ST
KANDRA ST
KATHLEEN CL
GAYNE CT
HOLMES CT
CITY
STODA
PUMP
ARINGA CT
WOLLAHRA PL
GRAY ST
LUCANIA CL
NEWELL ST
TURBO
AUMANN ST
BANKSIA CT
CULVERLANDS
VALDALE CT
LUCINDA CL
COVEN CT
POULTON CT
McCURE CT
GREENHILL
NATALIE CT
BAYSWATER
ALLENS
25
DAWSONS GLN
SWAIN CT
BARBARA CT
HARRIET ST
Dupont Australia
THE NOOK
SHARPS CT
MILTON
HEATH CT
MONT CT
ST
PLEASANT DR
HEATHMONT
ST W
ALOAH ST E
SALISBURY CT
LOUIS
ST
VIEW CT
ATUNGA CT
ALOAH
MASON CT
THE BOULEVARD
WENDY CT
Heathmont East Pmy
ALKIRA CT
CANTERBURY
HAMILTON
BEVERLEY CT
HEADLINE CT
WAYNE CT
MILLER CT
RAMSAY ST
Tennis
YALLAMBA PL
LOCKSLEY
DANIELLE
WARATAH AV
RD
BROMLEY CL
KARISTA AV
ARMSTRONG
SHERIDAN CT
RD
32
BRONALDI
HEATHMONT
THE BOULEVARD
ANNE CT
MARTIN
ST
Heathmont Golf Park Par 3
BUNGALOOK RD
CANTERBURY CT
27
WHITE
ORCHID
THE OUTLOOK
THE GREENWAY
RD
H E Parker Reserve
BUNGALOOK
CR
BELLBIRD DR
BUNGALOOK
RD Fbr
PARK
GLEN Cmnty Cntr
Glen Park
ELMHURST RD

422

JOINS 423

A B C D E F G H J K L

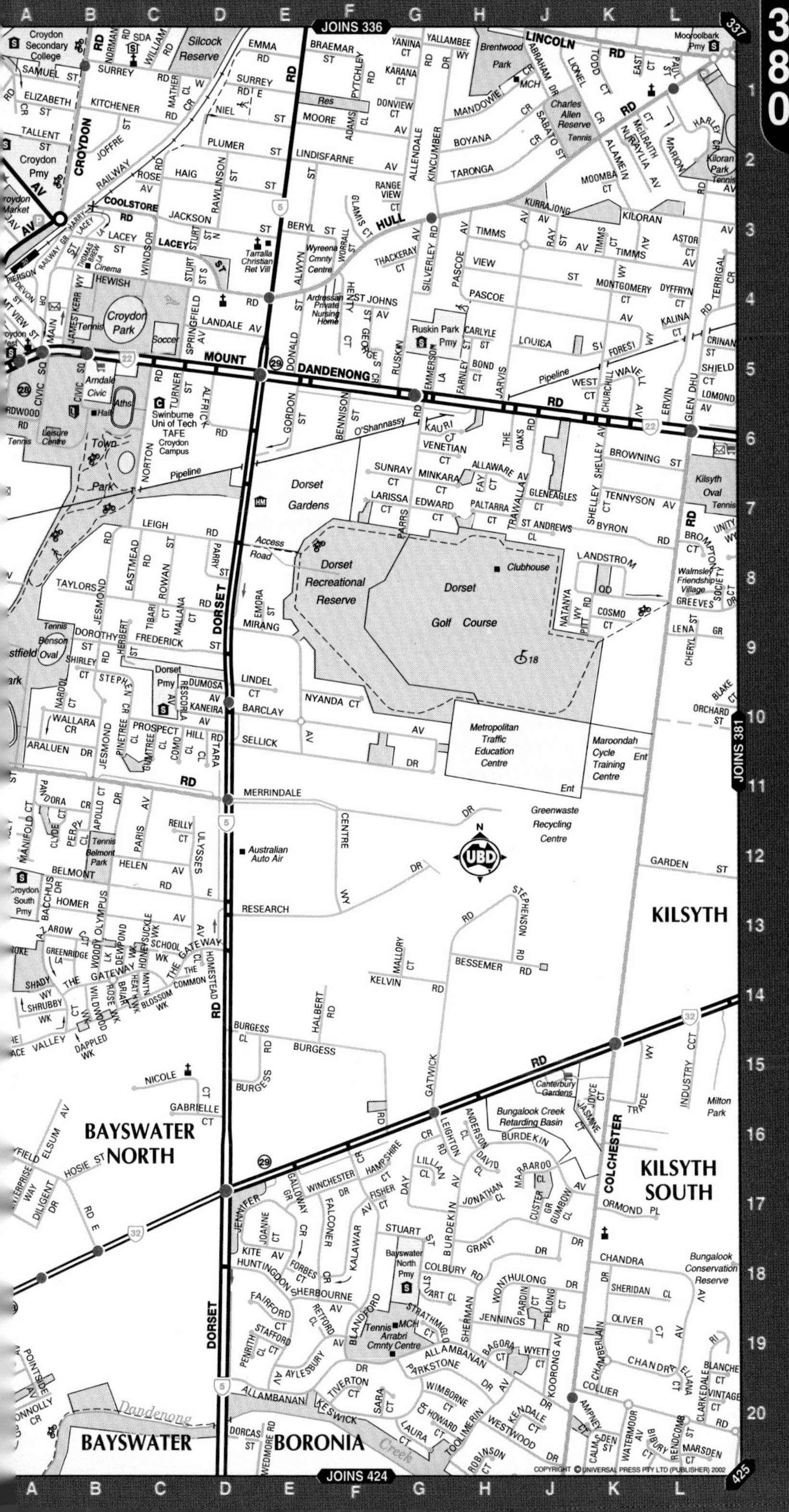
JOINS 336
337
JOINS 381
JOINS 424
425
A B C D E F G H J K L
1 2 3 4 5 6 7 8 9 10 11 12 13 14 15 16 17 18 19 20
CROYDON
KILSYTH
KILSYTH SOUTH
BAYSWATER NORTH
BAYSWATER
BORONIA
Croydon Secondary College
Silcock Reserve
Brentwood Park
Charles Allen Reserve
Kiloran Park
Mooroolbark Pmy
Croydon Pmy
Croydon Market
Tarralla Christian Ret Vill
Wyreena Cmnty Centre
Ardrossan Private Nursing Home
Ruskin Park Pmy
Croydon Park
Soccer
Arndale Civic
Leisure Centre
Town Park
Swinburne Uni of Tech TAFE Croydon Campus
Dorset Gardens
Dorset Recreational Reserve
Dorset Golf Course
Clubhouse
Kilsyth Oval
Walmsley Friendship Village
Benson Oval
Dorset Pmy
Metropolitan Traffic Education Centre
Maroondah Cycle Training Centre
Greenwaste Recycling Centre
Australian Auto Air
Belmont Park
Croydon South Pmy
Canterbury Gardens
Bungalook Creek Retarding Basin
Milton Park
Bungalook Conservation Reserve
Bayswater North Pmy
Tennis MCH Arrabri Cmnty Centre
Dandenong Creek
MOUNT DANDENONG RD
DORSET RD
COLCHESTER RD
LINCOLN RD
HULL RD
CROYDON RD
MAROONDAH HWY
Pipeline
UBD
COPYRIGHT © UNIVERSAL PRESS PTY LTD (PUBLISHER) 2002

A B C D E F G H J K L

336
JOINS 337

Nursing Home
CAMBRIDGE GDN
Pembroke Secondary College Senior Campus
WINDSOR PARK
RI CNC
BRIDGES AV
SHELDON AV
ELIOT CT
DONNE CT
CT
BROOKES CT
SHAKESPEARE AV
AV
CARDIGAN RD
CARDIGAN
CAMBRIDGE
HIGHLAND
HARLEY CR
MACMILLAN ST
GREENVILLE ST
CR
RD
DRYDEN CR
SWINBURNE
MASEFIELD AV
AV
Mooroolbark Heights Reserve
LONGFELLOW
RD
BICKLEIGH - VALE RD
EDNA
WALLING LA
LAURA LA
FIELDEN CL
RD
PINE
PINE RD
Kiloran Tennis Park
Centenary
HOLMES RD
DRYDEN
DENNIS CT
YATES CT
CT
MILTON CNC
GORDON CT
O'Shannassy
GREENWOOD LA
DR
MOUNTAIN
MARION AV
KILORAN AV
BALLANTYNE
DUNROSSIL DR
CR
LAWSON RD
ZINA
GR
DYSART PL
FERN
LEIGH
VILLAGE WK
COTTAGE CL
ASTOR CT
CR
CRADLEY CT
ALASTAIR CT
Pipeline
RD
Pembroke Pmy
LOUPIE ST
ROSNY PL
DR CT
DELMONT
TERRIGAL
IDINIA ST
RD
BAINBRIDGE CT
OSWIN CT
AV
RD
Pembroke Secondary College Cambridge Campus
PEMBROKE
RACHAEL
LUTANA CT
DR
O'Shannassy
ST
PICCADILLY CT
COLEBROOK RD
MORRISON CR
LEVENDALE
PENALGA RD
Res
ERVIN
CRINAN ST
BIRKENHEAD
DALLAS CT
FLORENCE ST
MOUNTFIELD
FERGUSON DR
ZINA
AV
AMELIA CT
MARGARET CT
HAWTHORY
CAROLINE ST
ST
BEATRICE
CAMBRIDGE
SHIELD CT
LOCH ST
LOMOND
CATHERINE CT
Elizabeth Bridge Res
RD
GLEN DHU
CAMERON CT
Kilsyth Primary
ANITA
DURHAM
Senior Citizen Club
ST
ER
ERICA
CR
ST
WY
MACDONNELL CT
AV
MAPLE CT
WILLOW CT
MOUNT DANDENONG
RUSSO PL
COLLINS PL
CHARLES ST
EOTHEN
RD
NORTH
HANSEN LA
Hansen Park
TOWER ST
RD
BRISTOL
CT
HAMMERSLEY CT
JACARANDA
ACACIA
AV
Kilsyth Oval
Tennis
31
LIVERPOOL
MOIRA
RD
WY
RD
BELVOIR CT
RD
MILFORD
ST
SENAR
ST
STRZELECKI CT
Res
AMBER CT
TI-TREE CT
ST
BEECH ST
UNITY WY
DR
MOUNTAIN
CHURCH ST
CT
WANNAN
PALM
GLENDALE
ASHBY
DERBY
DENMAN ST
TAMWORTH
BALMORAL
CARINA CT
TREETOP DR
HILDEGARD CT
REGINA
WALNUT
BROMPTON CT
FRIENDLY CT
LEONARD RD
PLEASANT ST
MCH GR AV
CHERYLNNE
St Richards Cath Pmy
22
32
EDENHOPE
PENDLE PL
EDEN
WY
ST
ATHERTON CT
STRATHBOGIE
FIR CT
Mt Waverley
CHESTNUT
Walmsley Friendship Village
SOCIETY
GR
FELLOWSHIP
KILSYTH
MIMOSA AV
CT
DR
Wirraminna Reserve
CORNELIA
CL
ALPINE
STIRLING CT
WY
Montrose Reservoir
DOREE
GREEVES CT
LENA GR
CHERYL ST
AARON PL
RD
HILLVIEW
DEBORAH ST
SOPHIE ST
DR
FLINDERS CT
BRETBY
WINTON CT
BANKSIA
RD
GR
KEVIN CT
LUSCOMBE CT
GRAHAM AV
GEOFFREY
KILSYTH
ARNOLD ST
HAYES CT
KILBORN CT
DR
RD
CLAIRE CT
SMITHACRES
MAGNOLIA
SARAH
ST
ORCHARD
ST
URANA
ST
LOCKHART CT
GLADESVILLE
DONALD CL
DAVID CL
HAMILTON CR
HANSFORD CL
Kirkbrae Presbyterian Ret Vill
Hazelmere Nursing Home
33
MT
FERNBANK CT
Gladesville Pmy
Kilsyth Sports Centre
Pinks Reserve
BUTTLER ST
CR
CHERYLNNE
LANDY CT
BELINDA CL
EVA CT
PARAMOUNT AV
BELINDA CL
TINARRA CT
AV
ARLIE CR
WOODRIDGE
ROSLYN ST
33
KIRKWOOD
CRESTVIEW
ACTOAL
MAYFIELD CT
RD
GRATTEN
ASH
GARDEN
LUCAS
LADE AV
VIC BOLT AV
CL
DR
ST
RD
FUSSELL
GR
CT
MERSEY RD
32
Chaucer Park
Quarry
Quarry
RUBY
CANTERBURY
31
DR
Eastwood Plaza
JANE CT
PAM CT
LEEDS
DR
LIVERPOOL
INDUSTRY CT
SOUTHFORK
EAST SPUR CT
RD
BRIGHT
SUNSET DR
Milton Park
JEANETTE
MAREE CT
CLOVERLEA DR
Bilanoo Pmy
CITY
GLASGOW
HAKEA DR

KILSYTH SOUTH

Bungalook Conservation Reserve
TEREDDAN DR
Ghilgai
RUBICON
VALLEY
ROWE ST
JUBILEE
SHEFFIELD
RD
GLASGOW
EUNICE CT
RI
WY
CLARKEDALE
BLANCHE CT
CHLOE CL
VINTAGE CT
JODIE PL
PIONEER
SANDY WYN
18
Eastwood Golf Course
RD
COLLIER RD
INDEPENDANCE RI
MARSDEN CT
SHEFFIELD
LOBOSCO CT

424
JOINS 425
JOINS 380

1 2 3 4 5 6 7 8 9 10 11 12 13 14 15 16 17 18 19 20

A B C D E F G H J K L

A B C D E F G H J K L

JOINS 338
339

1 2 3 4 5 6 7 8 9 10 11 12 13 14 15 16 17 18 19 20

LILYDALE

MOUNT EVELYN

MOOROOLBARK

MONTROSE

KALORAMA

MOUNT DANDENONG

Billanook College

Pipeline RD

EDINBURGH RD

THOMAS CR

CHARLES RD

OLIVE GR

Olinda

York on Lilydale

Yarra View Nursery

YORK RD

C402

C401

MARNE

COMMERCIAL RD

QUINN

DUNS R.O.W.

BLUE WREN CT

Quinn Reserve

RAILWAY RD

MARCUS ST

CARDIGAN RD

BELFAST RD

PARK RD

HILL RD

TIFFANY CT

KAREN

HARRISON RD

HAWKINS RD

Mt Evelyn Christian

Gumnut Village

MOUNTAIN AV

MOORE

Keith Hume Fraser Reserve

Soccer

Tennis

Montrose Parks VICTORIA

PICKWOOD

JARRAH CT

CL

MONTROSE

Ent

Montrose Brickworks Flora Reserve

EMERY LA

SWANSEA RD

LEITH RD

AVENUE

ST MARK AV

THE AVENUE

THE BOULEVARD

CASCADE ST

DORCHESTER AV

BELVEDERE DR

ST JAMES

ST GEORGE AV

RAVENSWOOD CT

BEAUMONT CT

GREENHILLS AV

BELL ST

HENRY ST

BURLEY

TASMAN CT

FOULDS CT

ANNE CT

TREVALLYN RD

WALKER RD

Montrose Pmy

Hall

MCH

Cmnty Cntr

CFA

C415

DANDENONG RD

RICHARDS

KARA CT

KING ST

BOND CT

POWELL CT

TYRO CT

Reserve

RD N

UBD

Reserve

CR

COPELAND DR

GUY CT

TOWNSEND CT

GR

HEATHFIELD GR

LEWIS RD

BROWNS RD

VIEW CR

HEATHFIELD

FIELD CT

KERR CR

SHEFFIELD

GIBBS RD

MOUNT DANDENONG TOURIST RD

36

34

35

Tennis

DEVENISH AV

STRADBROKE RD

YEAMAN

Montrose Community Reserve

Netball

AILEEN AV

WICK RD

WARWICK

FRANCES AV

PATRICIA AV

STEPHEN RD

TIMBERGLADES

WILD CHERRY RD

SUMMERHILL RD

SUNRISE HILL RD

CURRAWONG

KARABEAL CT

MARTIN CT

BOXTREE RD

TANDARA CT

Fbr

RD S

OLD COACH RD

BROWNS

THOMPSONS

JASPER RD

BAYVIEW TCE

KALORAMA TCE

McKENZIE

TCE

OLD MOUNTAIN TCE

Reserve

RICKETTS CT

BONZA VIEW

BARBERS

Forest Reserve

SINGLETON

MARSHALL

LOWER VIEW RD

Track

Dandenong Ranges National Park

Parks VICTORIA

Jennings Reserve

Gate

CFA

C403

SILVAN VIEW ST

CRAIG AV

FALLS RD

TOSARI RD

LOGAN AV

ROSEMONT CR

DUNBAR AV

PRICE RD

Mt Dandenong 633m

3.35m

Restaurant

Fbr

Musk Park

GTV9 Tower

OBSERVATORY RD

WOMBAT RD

41

PANORAMA RD

MOUNT RD

DCNR Arboretum

Mechanics Res

MCH

FARNDONS RD

Mt Dandenong Pmy

COACH RD

EILEEN AV

CAROLINE CR

WARWICK

BEN CT

RUNA

RI

BRACKEN AV

GORDON AV

SINGLETON RD

Fireline

Fire Access Only

(Doongalla Forest)

Decite

Glasgow Track

Kyeema Memorial Cairn

RIDGE RD

William Ricketts Sanctuary

Parks VICTORIA

Gallery

Display Cntr

Ent

42

HELEN RD

OLD BLYTHES

Kyeema

ABV2 Tower

HSV7 Tower

Gate

EYRE RD

Singleton Reserve

YARRABEE RD

UPALONG RD

HELEN ST

OLD ST

HUME LA

WISTERIA LA

JOINS 383

JOINS 426
427

A B C D E F G H J K L

338
JOINS 339
JOINS 382
426
JOINS 427

A B C D E F G H J K L

MOUNT EVELYN

MONTROSE

KALORAMA

OLINDA

MARCUS ST
OLINDA RD
HILLTOP
CR
RD
WATTLE AV
NORTH AV
AV
AQUEDUCT
Mt Evelyn Pmy
TRUDY PL
St Marys Cath Primary
QUINN CR
FALKINGHAM
RAILWAY
RAILWAY RD
MIMOSA AV
RD
Steep (Priv Rd)
CENTRE AV
EAST AV
LIQUIDAMBAR LA
JOY
BORANG
BANDOL AV
RENOUF CT
Melba Centre
FALLS RD
SOUTH
GLEN HOLME
MONBULK
WATKINS
RESERVES RD
Olinda
AV
CR
ORMEAU
Mt Evelyn Reserve RD
TRAMWAY
Creek
C402
YORK
KUYURA RD
SYDNEY
FCYA Oasis Youth Camp
(SILVAN RD)
McKILLOP ST
Mt Evelyn Recreation Camp
INVERNESS
CURRAJONG
OAK GR
MURRUMBUNG RD
RD
AV
CURRAJONG AV
(Fire access only)
WOMBALANO RD
AV
RD
HAZEL AV
C404
MARGARET RD
DOROTHY
Melbourne Water
SYCAMORE GR
CR
WARRAWEE
PRIESTLEY CR
NEKLA ST
SELET ST
Melbourne Water
Reserve
CITY
BLAKISTON RD
WILKILLA RD
MOUNTAIN
INVERNESS RD
LOOKOUT RD
INVERNESS
FERNGULLY GR
Dandenong Ranges National Park
Parks Victoria
Reserve
Creek
MT DANDENONG TOURIST RD
Reserve
C415
37
CR RD
GR
BRIDGE GR
SCENIC
WILLIAM ST
INVERNESS
FERNGULLY
MOUNTAIN VIEW RD
THOMPSONS RD
RD
JASPER RD
HANDS
ALMA LA
GRANGE
CHILDS RD
RD
ERITH
RD
Karwarra Native Gardens
Kalorama Memorial Res
GR
PAXCROFT AV
FARRINGDON
MT DANDENONG TOURIST RD
39
JEEVES AV
RD
Forest Reserve
Kalorama Park
CREEK
WOODHURST
OLINDA
LOGAN
Reserve
Parks Victoria
Melbourne Water Reserve
OLINDA CREEK
BARBERS
AV
LINK RD
RD
DUNBAR AV
PRICE
BARBERS
OUTLOOK
ERNEST
MYRA CT
DR
RD
RD
Creek
OLINDA CREEK
Gate
RD
OLINDA CREEK
Gate
RD
RD
WARWICK
BEN CT
RD
DOUGHTYS
Olinda Falls Reserve
Olinda
Dandenong Ranges National Park
Parks Victoria
Lyrebird Gully
CENTRE
SILVAN
FALLS RD
BARTLETT
GEORGES
EAGLENEST
SILVAN RD
RD
Olinda Falls

1 2 3 4 5 6 7 8 9 10 11 12 13 14 15 16 17 18 19 20

WANDIN EAST

SILVAN

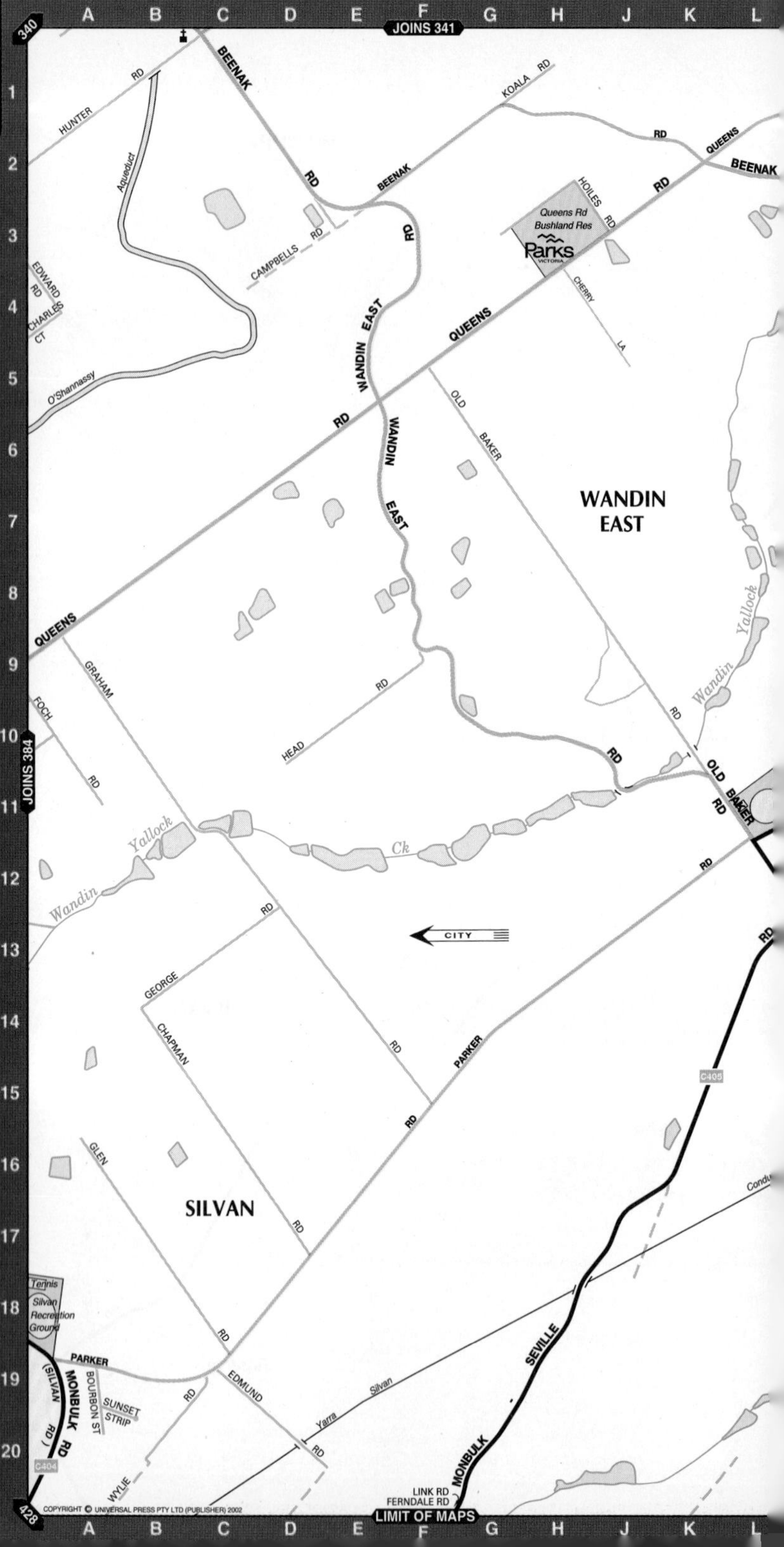

JOINS 341

JOINS 384

LIMIT OF MAPS

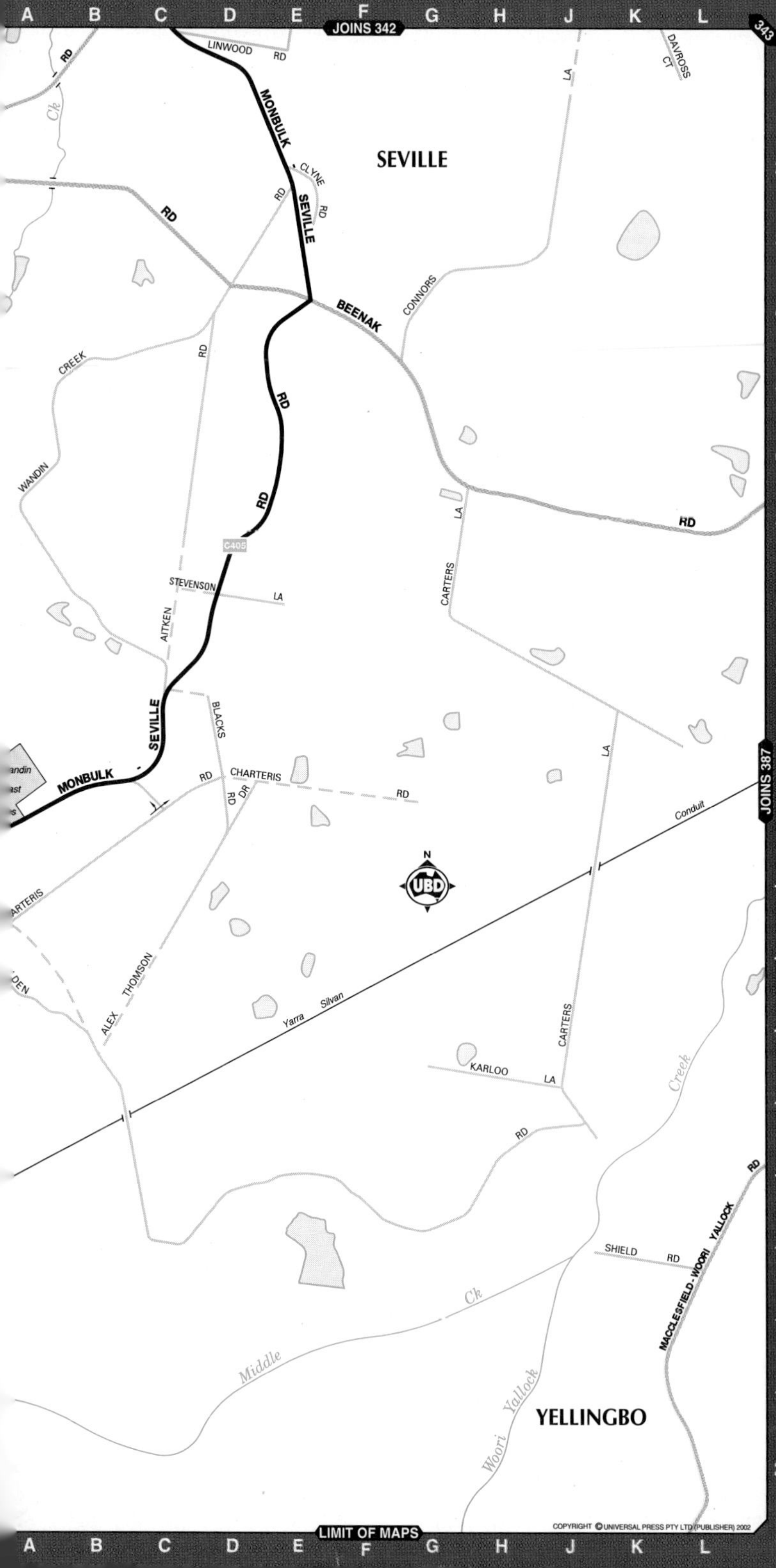

JOINS 342
343
JOINS 387
LIMIT OF MAPS

A B C D E F G H J K L

SEVILLE

YELLINGBO

LINWOOD RD
MONBULK SEVILLE RD
CLYNE RD
DAVROSS CT
LA
RD
BEENAK RD
CONNORS
CREEK
WANDIN
C405
STEVENSON LA
AITKEN
CARTERS LA
BLACKS RD
CHARTERIS RD
DR
MONBULK
andin
ast
CHARTERIS
ALEX THOMSON
DEN
Yarra Silvan Conduit
KARLOO LA
CARTERS LA
RD
Creek
SHIELD RD
MACCLESFIELD - WOORI YALLOCK RD
Middle Ck
Woori Yallock
Ck

1 2 3 4 5 6 7 8 9 10 11 12 13 14 15 16 17 18 19 20

342
JOINS 343
JOINS 386

A B C D E F G H J K L

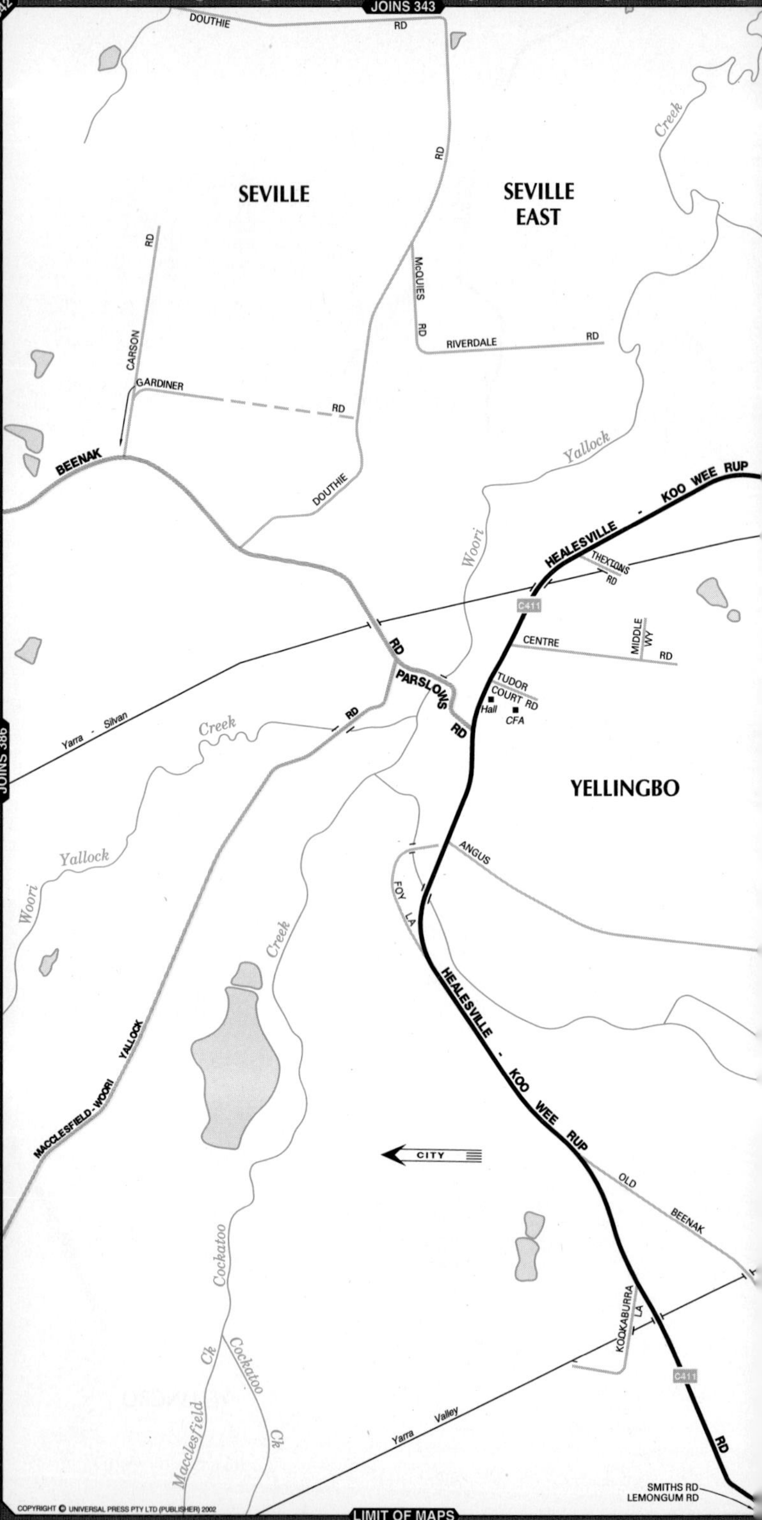

1 2 3 4 5 6 7 8 9 10 11 12 13 14 15 16 17 18 19 20

SEVILLE

SEVILLE EAST

YELLINGBO

DOUTHIE RD

McQUIES RD

RIVERDALE RD

CARSON RD

GARDINER RD

BEENAK RD

DOUTHIE

PARSLOWS RD

HEALESVILLE - KOO WEE RUP RD

THEXTONS RD

C411

CENTRE RD

MIDDLE WY

TUDOR COURT RD

Hall

CFA

ANGUS

FOY LA

OLD BEENAK

KOOKABURRA LA

SMITHS RD

LEMONGUM RD

Yarra - Silvan

Yarra Valley

MACCLESFIELD-WOORI YALLOCK

Woori Yallock Creek

Yallock

Woori

Creek

Cockatoo Creek

Cockatoo Ck

Macclesfield Ck

CITY

LIMIT OF MAPS

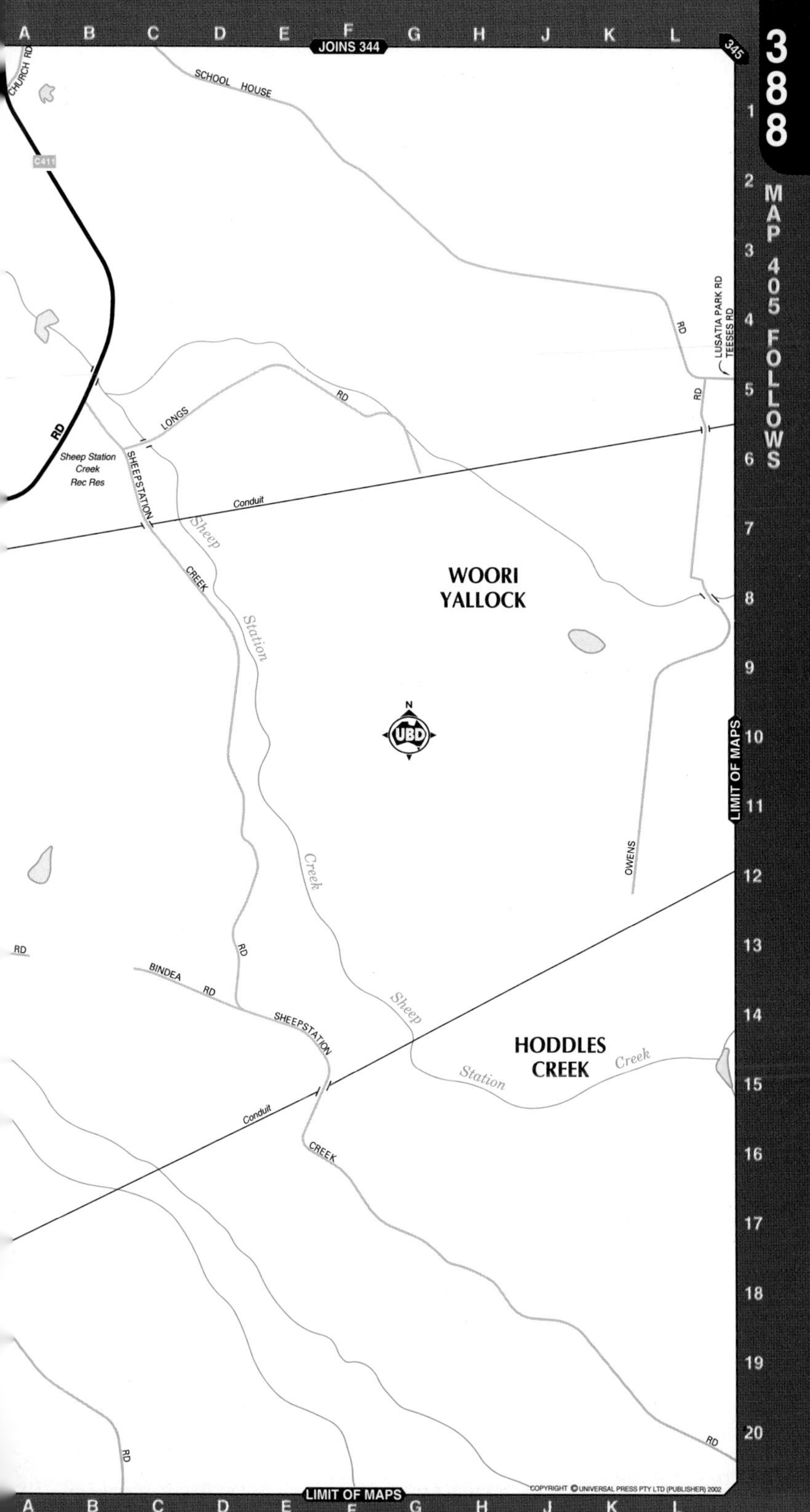

JOINS 344
345
CHURCH RD
C411
SCHOOL HOUSE
RD
LUSATIA PARK RD
TEESES RD
RD
LONGS
RD
RD
Sheep Station Creek Rec Res
SHEEPSTATION
Conduit
Sheep
CREEK
WOORI YALLOCK
Station
UBD
N
Creek
OWENS
RD
RD
BINDEA
RD
SHEEPSTATION
Sheep
HODDLES CREEK
Station
Creek
Conduit
CREEK
RD
RD
LIMIT OF MAPS
MAP 405 FOLLOWS

PREVIOUS MAP 388

LIMIT OF MAPS

448

JOINS 449

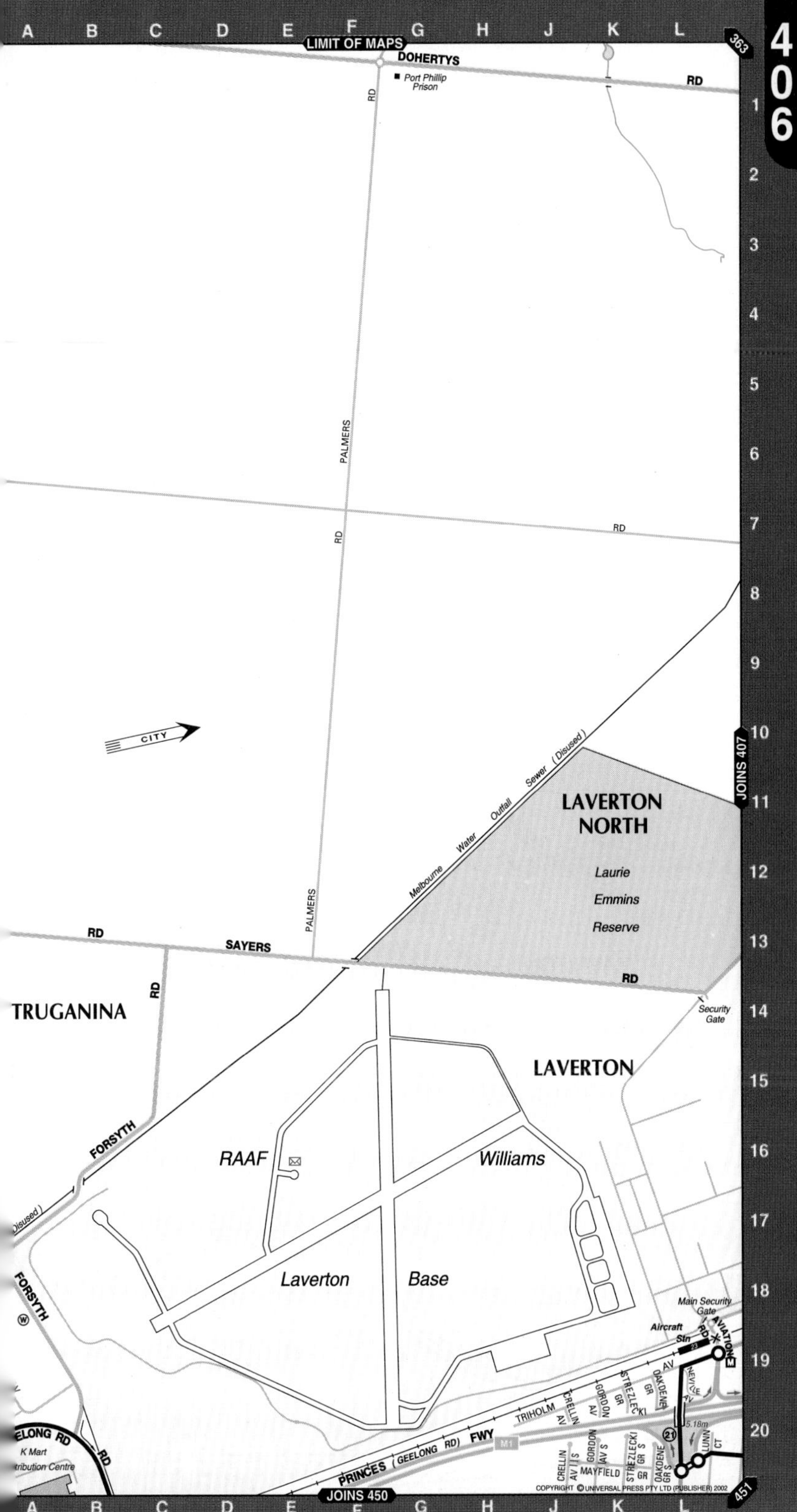
LIMIT OF MAPS
363
DOHERTYS
RD
Port Phillip Prison
PALMERS
RD
RD
CITY
JOINS 407
Melbourne Water Outfall Sewer (Disused)
LAVERTON NORTH
Laurie Emmins Reserve
SAYERS
RD
RD
PALMERS
RD
TRUGANINA
RD
Security Gate
LAVERTON
FORSYTH
RAAF
Williams
Laverton
Base
Disused
FORSYTH
Main Security Gate
Aircraft Stn
AVIATION RD
AV
TRIHOLM
CRELLIN
GORDON
STREZLECKI
OAKDENE
NEVILLE AV
LUNN CT
CRELLIN AV
GORDON AV S
STREZLECKI GR S
OAKDENE GR S
MAYFIELD
GR
PRINCES (GEELONG RD) FWY
M1
GEELONG RD
K Mart
Distribution Centre
RD
JOINS 450
451
COPYRIGHT © UNIVERSAL PRESS PTY LTD (PUBLISHER) 2002

A B C D E F G H J K L
JOINS 363
1 2 3 4 5 6 7 8 9 10 11 12 13 14 15 16 17 18 19 20
DOHERTYS RD
TRUGANINA
LAVERTON NORTH
Smorgon Steel Mill
SCOTT
Melbourne
Melbourne Water Outfall Sewer (Disused)
FITZGERALD RD
MARIA
EVERAISE CT
WESTGATE DR
Kayes
CHERRY
PRINCES
LEAKES RD
Rubble & Riches Laverton Market
Honey Hush
Orica Aust Ltd
FLEET ST
RMIT Industrial Technology Centre
KOROROIT
5.18m
Laverton
CITY
JOINS 406
GEELONG RD
OLD
Laurie Emmins Reserve
Mini Bike Track
LAVERTON
Security Gate
RAAF Williams Laverton Base
CLIFF CR
CROPLEY ST
ROBERTSON
TARRAN ST
HENDERSON CR
CHIRNSIDE
Laverton Plains Primary
WHITTAKER
THOMSON AV
BLADIN ST
KAYE CR
WACKETT
BUTCHER CR
PARKSIDE WK
ISAACS ST
JONES CT
HILLMAN ST
BURNLEY ST
BRIGGS ST
MCH
COLE
EATON PDE
BARWISE
BELLIN ST
PEARCE ST
St Martin de Porres
CAMPBELL ST
McNAMARA RD
SNOWDEN ST
ORR CT
CRESWICK
EVANS CR
EADES ST
TYQUIN
JENNINGS ST
CHAVE CT
Laverton Secondary College
McCormack Park
FWY
HARCOURT RD
BURNS RD
NEWMARKET RD
DUNKLEY RD
CORA
HENTY
ALBURY
MANSFIELD
DANGLOW
Victorian Baseball & Softball Centre
MERTON ST
Low Bridge 2.6 Metres
Ck
ULM
COBBY ST
DE BRUN CT
KINGSFORD ST
SUMERS ST
BADGE CT
CARTLEDGE ST
Frank Gibson Res
CHARLESWORTH
ARMSTRONG ST
WILLIAMS RD
WRIGHT
Woods St Res
BURTON AV
WATTS
ALLEN
BURKE CT
STUDLEY CT
HEFFERNAN ST
GOBLE ST
THOMAS
WOODS ST
LOHSE ST
HICKEY
Laverton
MAHER RD
Fbr
4.44m
(GEELONG RD)
M1
Little Athletics
Soccer
Softball
Laverton Park
AB Shaw Reserve
HALL
HIBISCUS CT
VALENTE ST
JJ Stewart Res
CLOVER CT
PINE DR
PEPPERMINT CT
HEATH CT
EUCALYPT CT
KURRAJONG
HAKEA CT
Sewage Treatment Works
HONEYSUCKLE CT
GREVILLIA CT
Main Security Gate
MAHER
AVIATION RD
RAILWAY AV
NEVILLE AV
AILSA ST
ASCOT ST
BALMORAL ST
BRUCE ST
Cmnty Cntr
Civic Cntr
CROWN ST
MCH
DONALD ST
EPSOM ST
Laverton Primary
FITZROY ST
GRACE ST
HIGH ST
RESCHKE CT
JAMISON ST
NORTH AV
NEWLAND ST
Altona Meadows Pmy
ALTONA MEADOWS
5.48m
CAMERON
ALMA AV
PRINCES
Chr Cmnty Cntr
NICHOLSON
ORVILLE
POWLETT
HOOK
ROSEBERY
SHIRLEY
TALBOT
VICTORIA
KIORA
LINDEN
MERTON
LUNN CT
CENTRAL AV
JOINS 451
450

JOINS 364
365
The Memorial Park Crematorium and Floral Lawn Cemetery
DOHERTYS RD
FWY
Coles-Myer Distribution Warehouse
Fowles Auction Centre
Bunge Bio Products
Westgate Transport
Calleja Transport
ALTONA NORTH
Native Grassland Reserve
Dow Irrigated Tree Plantation
Target Distribution Centre
CREEK RD
Hoechst Chemicals
Geon Australia
Dow Chemicals
BASF
Powercor
Kemcor Elastomers
Kemcor Olefins
CIG
Nippondenso
GRIEVE PDE
JOINS 409
MAIDSTONE ST
Kemcor Plastics
ALTONA
F Rush Reserve
A H Ford Reserve
Altona West Pmy
Altona Sec Coll
CIVIC PDE
St Joseph Cath Girls
Westona
Altona Primary
Port Phillip Ret Vill
Pondage
QUEEN ESPLANADE
JOINS 452

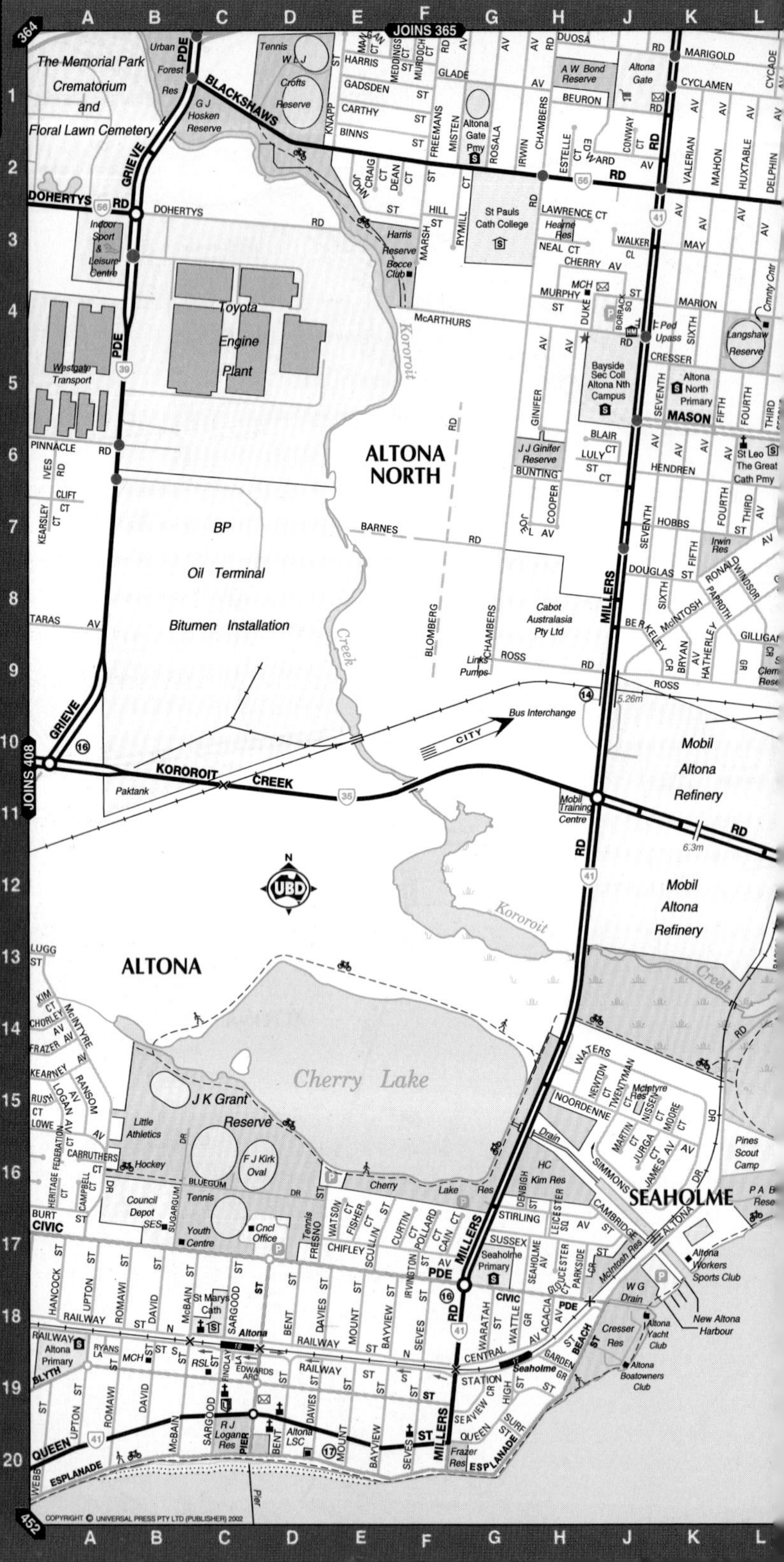

JOINS 365
364
JOINS 408
452

ALTONA NORTH

ALTONA

SEAHOLME

The Memorial Park Crematorium and Floral Lawn Cemetery

Toyota Engine Plant

BP Oil Terminal Bitumen Installation

Mobil Altona Refinery

Cherry Lake

J K Grant Reserve

Kororoit Creek

Altona Gate

Cabot Australasia Pty Ltd

St Pauls Cath College

Bayside Sec Coll Altona Nth Campus

Altona North Primary

New Altona Harbour

Altona Workers Sports Club

JOINS 366
367
SOUTH KINGSVILLE
SPOTSWOOD
NEWPORT
WILLIAMSTOWN NORTH
WILLIAMSTOWN
BLACKSHAWS RD
MELBOURNE RD
MASON ST
CHAMPION RD
MADDOX RD
KOROROIT CREEK RD
Newport Lakes Reserve
Paisley Park
Altona Lakes Golf Course
Newport Railway Workshops
Williamstown Cemetery
Mobil Altona Refinery
J T Gray Reserve
Altona Coastal Park (Western Wetlands)
Altona Bay
Caltex Oil Terminal
Victoria University Newport Campus
Newport Football Ground
Bayside Sec Coll Paisley Campus
Hobsons Bay Primary
Spotswood Pmy
Newport Lakes Pmy
Altona East Pmy
JOINS 411
INDEX A
1 LAKESIDE PL
2 SEA BREEZE LA
3 STONEHENGE MW
4 WILLIAMS BAY GR
INDEX B
1 FARRELL LA
3 FARRELL MW
2 MULLINS MW
INDEX C
1 BURGOYNE CT
2 KNIGHT MW
3 PARKER MW
4 WHITTACKER CT

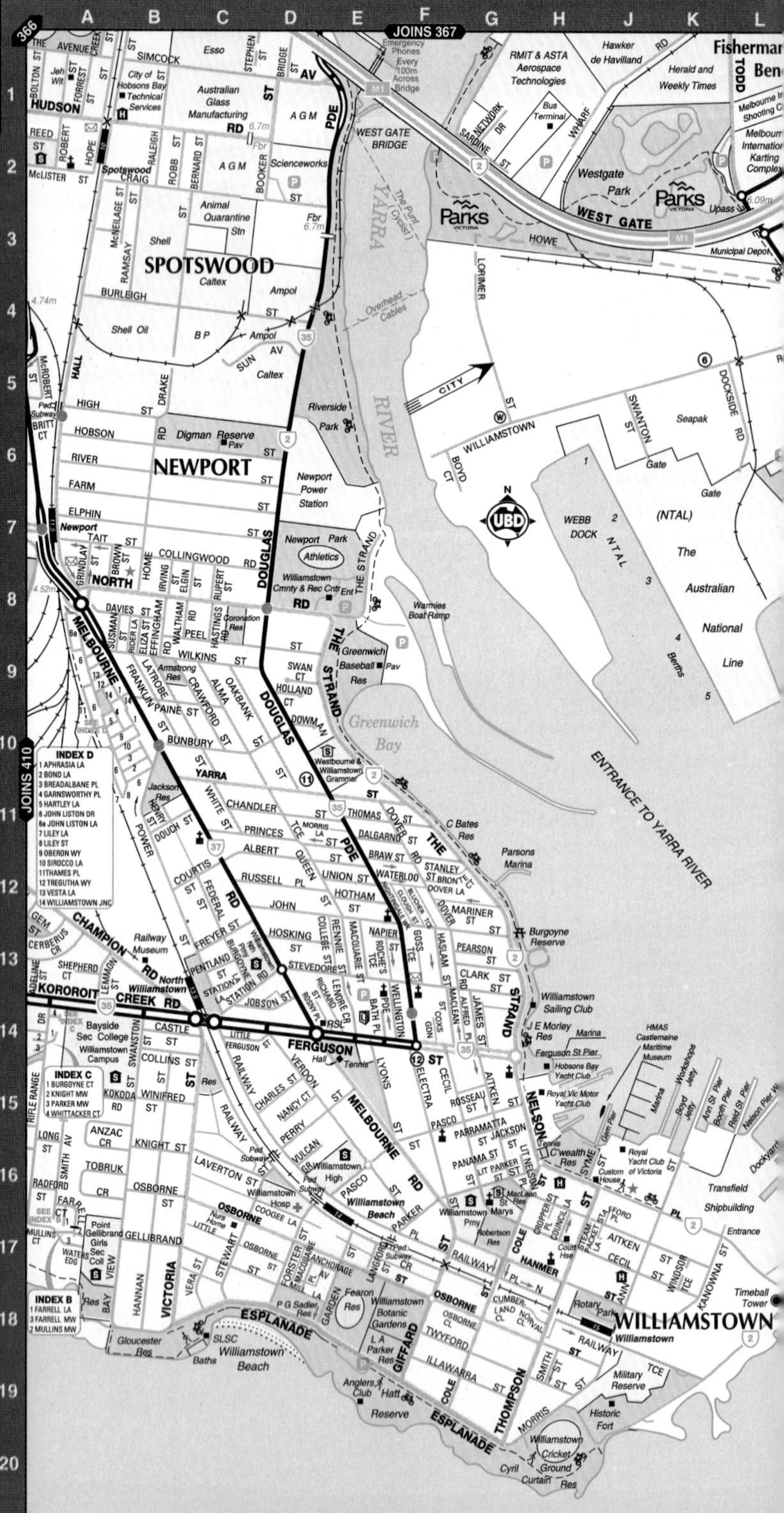

JOINS 367

JOINS 410

366

SPOTSWOOD

NEWPORT

WILLIAMSTOWN

INDEX D
1 APHRASIA LA
2 BOND LA
3 BREADALBANE PL
4 GARNSWORTHY PL
5 HARTLEY LA
6 JOHN LISTON DR
6a JOHN LISTON LA
7 LILEY LA
8 LILEY ST
9 OBERON WY
10 SIROCCO LA
11 THAMES PL
12 TREGUTHA WY
13 VESTA LA
14 WILLIAMSTOWN JNC

INDEX C
1 BURGOYNE CT
2 KNIGHT MW
3 PARKER MW
4 WHITTACKER CT

INDEX B
1 FARRELL LA
3 FARRELL MW
2 MULLINS MW

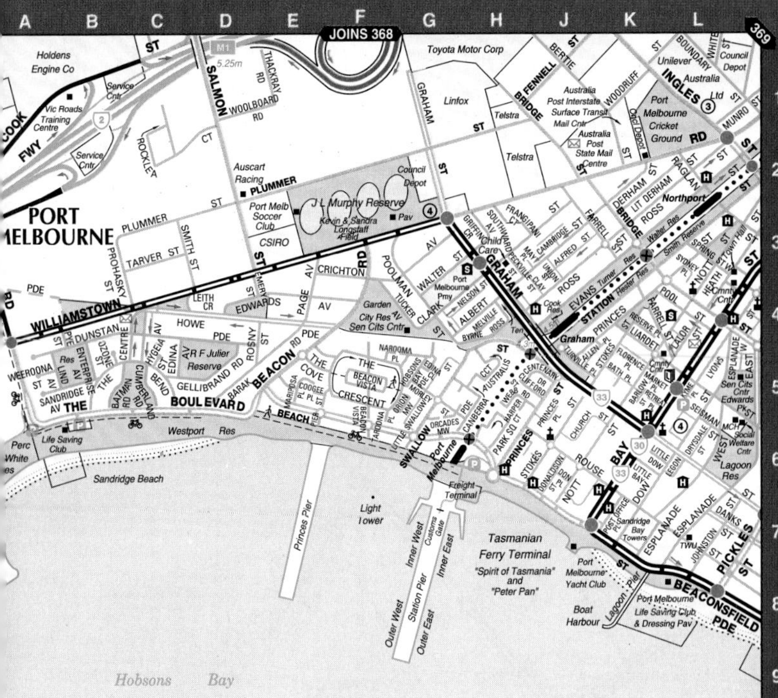

Hobsons Bay

Graving Dock

Gellibrand Pier

Mobil Tanks

Breakwater Pier

PORT PHILLIP

JOINS 413

A B C D E F G H J K L

368

JOINS 369

SOUTH MELBOURNE

PORT MELBOURNE

ALBERT PARK

MIDDLE PARK

MELBOURNE

ST KILDA WEST

PORT PHILLIP

FOR MORE DETAIL SEE MAP 29

FOR MORE DETAIL SEE MAP 30

JOINS 412

WHITE ST, JOHNSON ST, NORMANBY RD, MONTAGUE ST, MUNRO ST, BOUNDARY ST, WOODGATE ST, GLADSTONE ST, INGLES ST, EVANS ST, BUCKHURST ST, THISTLETHWAITE ST, YORK ST, CITY RD, Montague, 3.0m, Yooralla Society, Northport, STATION ST, RAGLAN ST, BAY ST, BARTON ST, SMITH ST, COVENTRY ST, CROCKFORD ST, NOTT ST, SPRING ST W, HEATH ST, NORMANBY PL, DORCAS ST, LYELL ST, NELSON RD, MOUNTAIN ST, BRIDGE ST, EAST ST, SPRING ST E, TRIBE ST, LYONS ST, ESPLANADE, DOW ST, LIARDET ST, CRUIKSHANK ST, GLOVER ST, HENDERSON ST, IFFLA ST, ST VINCENT ST, Lagoon Res, ESPLANADE E, RICHARDSON ST, GREIG ST, DURHAM ST, Gasworks Pk, BRIDPORT ST, BARRETT ST, GRAHAM ST, JOHNSTON ST, DANKS ST, REED ST, CAMERON PL, FOOTE ST, PICKLES ST, WITHERS ST, VICTORIA AV, BEACONSFIELD PDE, PHILIPSON ST, KERFERD RD

KERR ST, DOUGLAS ST, MEADE ST, CITY Rd, WHITEMAN ST, CECIL ST, BALLANTYNE ST, MARKET ST, FERRARS ST, 3.8m, South Melb Market, WARD ST, South Melbourne, PATTERSON PL, COOTE ST, EVILLE ST, EMERALD ST, BANK ST, PARK ST, MONTAGUE ST, DRAPER ST, MERTON ST, St Vincent Gardens, ST VINCENT PL N, ST VINCENT PL S, BROOKE ST, CARDIGAN PL, BEVAN ST, MADDEN ST, DUNDAS PL, MOUBRAY ST, FAUSSETT ST, KERFERD PL, O'GRADY ST, FINLAY ST, HERBERT ST, DINSDALE ST, MERTON PL, HAMBLETON ST, PAGE ST, BOYD ST, DANKS ST, MILLS ST, WRIGHT ST, HAROLD ST, NIMMO ST, YOUNG ST, HOWE CR, MARTIN ST, JAMES SERVICE PL, NAPIER ST, PERRINS ST, Albert Park, ALBERT RD, CANTERBURY RD, ST 3.7m

ROSS ST, CLARKE ST, CLARENDON ST, TOPE ST, MORAY ST, PALMER ST, COBDEN ST, RAGLAN ST, CECIL PL, THOMSON ST, MOORE ST, STURT ST, MILES ST, DODDS ST, COVENTRY ST, DORCAS ST, EASTERN RD, KINGS WAY, WELLS ST, HEATHER ST, BANK ST, KINGS PL, MILLER ST, STEAD ST, PALMERSTON CR, SANDILANDS ST, ALBERT RD, ST KILDA RD, Shrine of Remembrance, DOMAIN RD, BOWEN LA, QUEENS WY, MacRobertson Girls High, LAKESIDE DR, AQUATIC DR, Albert, Gunn Island, Reed Bed Islands, CITY, Melbourne Sports and Aquatic Centre, Wright St, AUGHTIE DR, Golf Driving Range, Albert Park Golf Course, Park, Middle Park, Parks Victoria

ARMSTRONG ST, McGREGOR ST, PATTERSON ST, PARK ST, LANGRIDGE ST, FRASER ST, YORK ST, LONGMORE ST, COWDEROY ST, DEAKIN ST, Kerferd Rd Beach, Cummins Res, PIER RD, MARY ST, St Kilda Harbour, St Kilda Breakwater, St Kilda Pier, 5.25m, Catani Gardens, JACKA BVD, St Kilda

JOINS 453

A B C D E F G H J K L

JOINS 370
371
JOINS 415
JOINS 454
455

CREMORNE
RICHMOND
SOUTH YARRA
Hawksburn
PRAHRAN
WINDSOR
ST KILDA
ST KILDA EAST
BALACLAVA
ELWOOD

Royal Botanic Gardens
Melbourne Grammar
Main Oval
Melbourne Senior Girls Grammar (Merton Hall)
Darling Gdn
Melbourne Boys High
Herring Island (Parks Victoria)
Como Park Nth
Como Park
Fawkner Park
Cordner Oval
Road Trauma Centre & Helipad
Albert Cricket Gnd
Alfred Hospital
Royal Vic Inst for the Blind
Lake
Princes Gardens
Victoria Gardens
St Kilda Cricket Ground Junction Oval
Christ Brothers College
St Michaels CEGGS
Alma Park West
Alma Park East
Peanut Farm Res
St Kilda Botanical Gardens
St Kilda Marina
McConchie Res

FOR MORE DETAIL SEE MAP 31
FOR MORE DETAIL SEE MAP 32

South Yarra
Hawksburn
Prahran
Windsor
Balaclava

HODDLE BRIDGE
ALEXANDRA AV
MONASH FWY
PUNT RD
HODDLE HWY
TOORAK RD
COMMERCIAL RD
HIGH ST
ST KILDA RD
QUEENS WY
DANDENONG RD
CHAPEL ST
CHURCH ST
WILLIAMS RD
MALVERN RD
GREVILLE ST
UNION ST
INKERMAN ST
CARLISLE ST
BALACLAVA RD
BRIGHTON RD
HOTHAM ST
ALMA RD
FITZROY ST
GREY ST
BARKLY ST
MARINE PDE
PRINCES ST
WELLINGTON ST
LORNE ST
MOUBRAY ST
DOMAIN RD
DAVIDSON ST
MOTHERWELL ST
COMMERCIAL RD
PRINCES ST
HIGH ST
KING ST
PRAHRAN
CHATHAM ST
WALKER ST
VICTORIA ST
EASTBOURNE ST
DUKE ST
PEEL ST
ALBERT ST
JOHNSON ST
GROSVENOR ST
MAYFIELD
McHENRY ST
MILTON ST

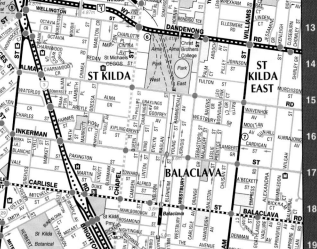

370
JOINS 371
JOINS 414
JOINS 455
454

A B C D E F G H J K L

1 2 3 4 5 6 7 8 9 10 11 12 13 14 15 16 17 18 19 20

BURNLEY

TOORAK

PRAHRAN

ARMADALE

ST KILDA EAST

CAULFIELD NORTH

Survey Park
Burnley Sporting & Recreation Complex
Bastow Oval
Loughnan Oval
Fletcher Oval
Fairview Park
Loys Paddock Res
Como Park Nth
Como Park
Scotch College
Senior School
Junior School
H A Smith Reserve
St Kevins Cath College
Kooyong Lawn Tennis Club
Vision Australia Foundation
St Catherines Girls
Toorak Pmy
Brookville Gdns
Loreto
Orrong Park
Toorak Park
Victory Sq
Rural Water
Deakin Uni Toorak Campus
Lauriston Girls
Kids Hospice
Malvern Recreation Reserve
St Josephs Cath Pmy
De La Salle Cath Coll
Tram Depot
St Francis Xavier Gabrini Hosp
King David
Labassa House
Melb Grammar Grimwade Hse
Ripponlea Pmy
Caulfield Park
Caulfield Cricket Ground

Heyington
Toorak
Armadale
Malvern
Malvern Central
Kooyong

TWICKENHAM CR
MONASH FWY
YARRA BVD
ALEXANDRA AV
WILLIAMS RD
ORRONG RD
GRANGE RD
TOORAK RD
MALVERN RD
HIGH ST
DANDENONG RD
WATTLETREE RD
ALMA RD
INKERMAN RD
BALACLAVA RD
KOOYONG RD
GLENFERRIE RD
HAWTHORN RD
PRINCES HWY
NORMANBY RD
BAMBRA RD

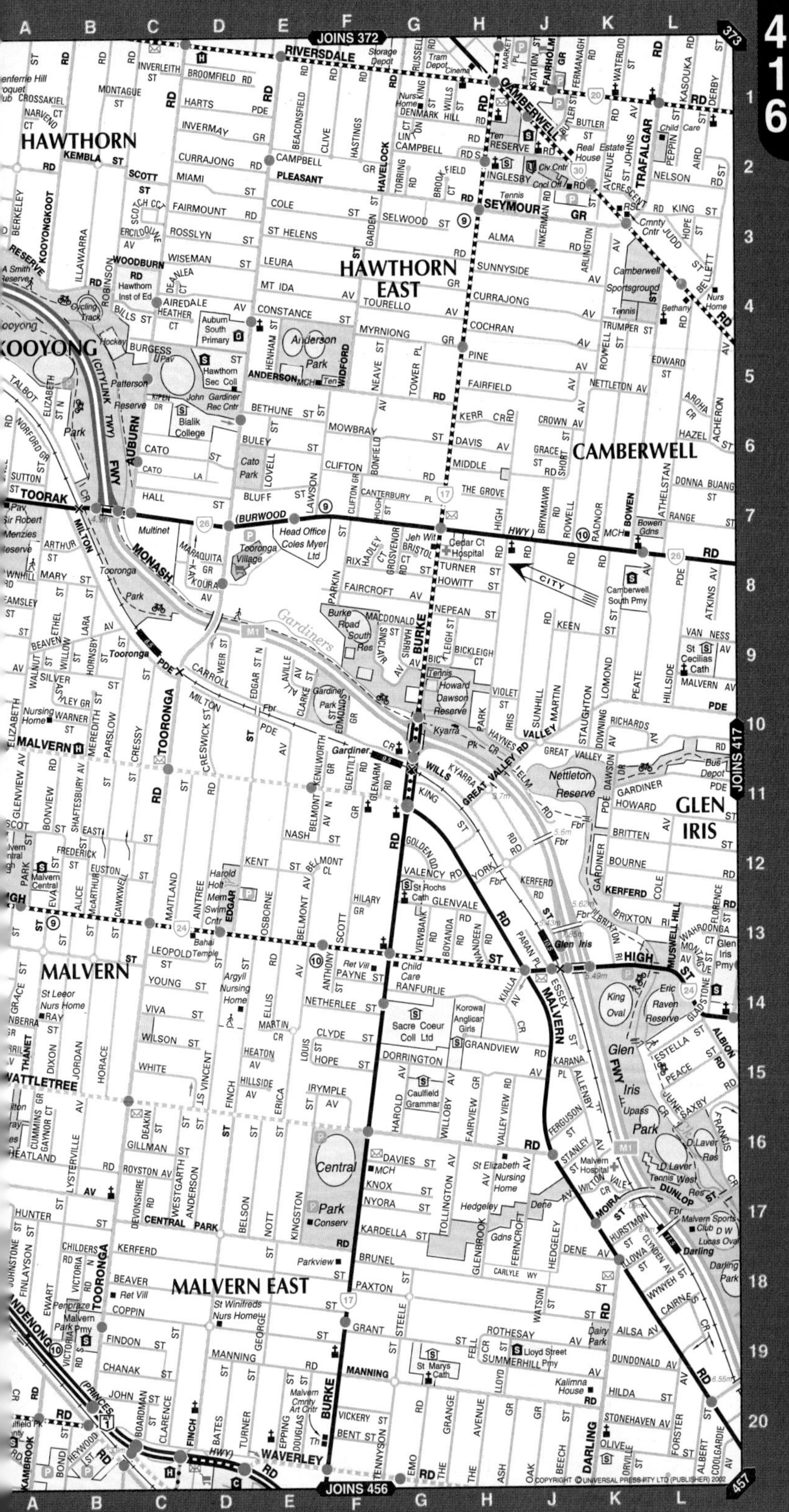
A B C D E F G H J K L
JOINS 372
373
HAWTHORN
HAWTHORN EAST
CAMBERWELL
KOOYONG
GLEN IRIS
MALVERN
MALVERN EAST
RIVERSDALE RD
CAMBERWELL RD
BURKE RD
(BURWOOD HWY)
TOORAK RD
MONASH FWY
(CITYLINK TWY)
AUBURN RD
GLENFERRIE RD
TOORONGA RD
WARRIGAL RD
HIGH ST
MALVERN RD
WAVERLEY RD
(PRINCES HWY)
DANDENONG RD
GARDINERS CK
GREAT VALLEY RD
SEYMOUR GR
TRAFALGAR RD
CAMPBELL GR
CITY
Anderson Park
Cato Park
Tooronga Village
Burke Road South Res
Howard Dawson Reserve
Gardiner Park
Nettleton Reserve
King Oval
Eric Raven Reserve
Glen Iris Park
Central Park
Hedgeley Dene Gdns
Camberwell Sportsground
Hawthorn Sec Coll
Bialik College
Auburn South Primary
Camberwell South Pmy
Sacre Coeur Coll Ltd
Caulfield Grammar
Harold Holt Mem Swim Cntr
Cedar Ct Hospital
Malvern Hospital
Head Office Coles Myer Ltd
JOINS 417
JOINS 456
457
COPYRIGHT © UNIVERSAL PRESS PTY LTD (PUBLISHER) 2002

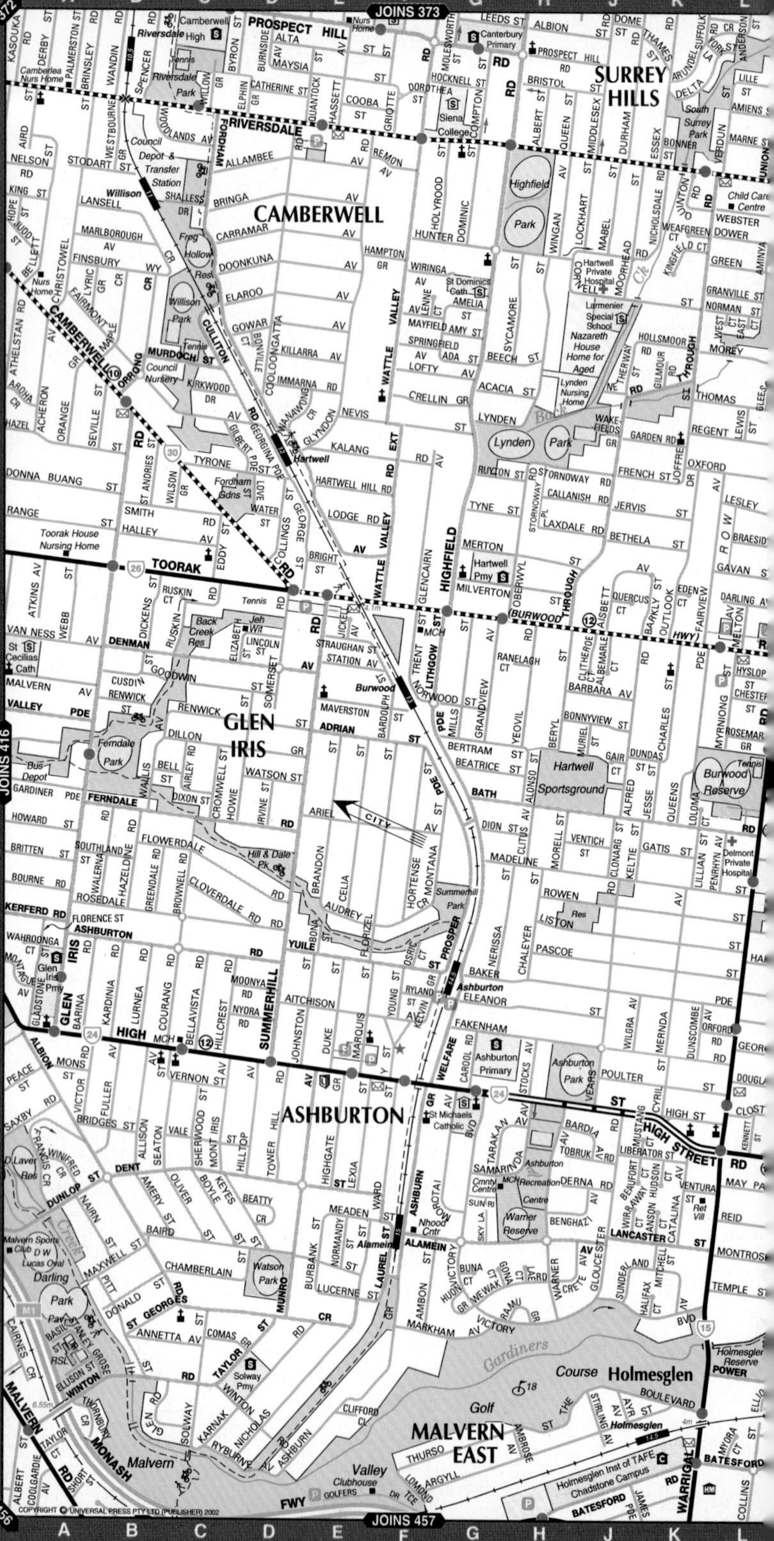

A B C D E F G H J K L

JOINS 373

372

CAMBERWELL

SURREY HILLS

GLEN IRIS

ASHBURTON

MALVERN EAST

Holmesglen

PROSPECT HILL
RIVERSDALE RD
CAMBERWELL RD
TOORAK RD
BURWOOD HWY
HIGH ST
HIGH STREET RD
WARRIGAL RD
MONASH FWY
MALVERN RD
DUNLOP ST
GLEN IRIS RD
SUMMERHILL RD
HIGHFIELD RD
WATTLE VALLEY RD
FORDHAM AV
CULLITON RD
ORRONG RD
TRAFALGAR RD
PROSPER PDE
WELFARE PDE
ASHBURN GR
ALAMEIN AV
LANCASTER ST
BATESFORD RD
HOLMESGLEN BOULEVARD
GARDINER PDE
FERNDALE RD
DENMAN AV
TOORONGA RD
BURKE RD
WAVERLEY RD
THROUGH RD
UNION RD
STORNOWAY RD

Camberwell High
Canterbury Primary
Riversdale Park
Council Depot & Transfer Station
Willison
Riversdale
Frog Hollow Res
Willison Park
Council Nursery
Siena College
St Dominics Cath
Hartwell Private Hospital
Larmenier Special School
Nazareth House Home for Aged
Lynden Nursing Home
Highfield Park
Lynden Park
Back Creek
South Surrey Park
Child Care Centre
Fordham Gdns
Hartwell
Hartwell Pmy
Hartwell Sportsground
Burwood Reserve
Burwood
Back Creek Res
St Cecilias Cath
Toorak House Nursing Home
Ferndale Park
Bus Depot
Hill & Dale Pk
Summerhill Park
Glen Iris Pmy
Ashburton
Ashburton Primary
Ashburton Park
St Michaels Catholic
Ashburton Recreation Centre
Cmnty Centre
Warner Reserve
Nhood Cntr
Alamein
Watson Park
Solway Pmy
D Laver Res
Malvern Sports Club
Lucas Oval
Darling Park
Malvern
Valley Clubhouse
Golf Course
Gardiners Creek
Holmesglen Inst of TAFE Chadstone Campus
Holmesglen Reserve
Delmont Private Hospital
Ret Vill
CITY
Res

JOINS 416

1 2 3 4 5 6 7 8 9 10 11 12 13 14 15 16 17 18 19 20

456

JOINS 457

A B C D E F G H J K L

A B C D E F G H J K L
JOINS 374
375
BOX HILL SOUTH
Kingswood College
INDEX A
1 CARLOGIE CT
2 EAGLE RIDGE RI
3 GLEN EAGLES CT
4 HUNTINGTON TCE
5 IRVINE CT
6 METROPOLITAN CT
7 MUIRFIELD CT
8 ROYAL MELB BVD
9 ROYAL PINES PL
10 ST ANDREWS CT
11 SPEARWATER WY
12 YARRAWONGA WY
Wattle Park
Chalet
Parks Victoria
Public Golf Course
RIVERSDALE RD
ELGAR RD
WARRIGAL RD
Roberts McCubbin Pmy
Box Hill Golf Course
Wattle Park Primary
Princess Elizabeth Junior Sch for Deaf Children
Gardiners Creek Reserve
Deakin University Melbourne Campus
FOR MORE DETAIL SEE MAP 718
Mt Scopus Memorial College
Presbyterian Ladies College
Fountain Court Retirement Village
Greenwood Office Park
Royal Victorian Inst for the Blind
BURWOOD HWY
Electricity Supply Corporation
Bennettswood Tennis Club
Burwood Cemetery
Cath Pmy
BURWOOD
HIGHBURY RD
JOINS 419
Lundgren Reserve
STATION ST
Gordon & Gotch Ltd
Gardiners Ck Reserve
Ashwood Spec Sch
Federal Tennis Reserve
Essex Heights Reserve
Essex Heights Pmy
Parkhill Pmy
Hillside Spec Sch
Ashwood Secondary College
Damper Creek Reserve
HIGH STREET RD
Hebrew Mem Hosp
MOUNT WAVERLEY
ASHWOOD
Ashwood Reserve
Hockey
Electra Reserve
Hall
Riversdale Golf Course
Clubhouse
Tennis
Jingella Reserve
Abbeyfeild House
Reserve
Jordanville
HUNTINGDALE RD
GLADSTONE
Batesford Pav Reserve
Jordan Reserve
JOINS 458
459
COPYRIGHT © UNIVERSAL PRESS PTY LTD (PUBLISHER) 2002
1 2 3 4 5 6 7 8 9 10 11 12 13 14 15 16 17 18 19 20

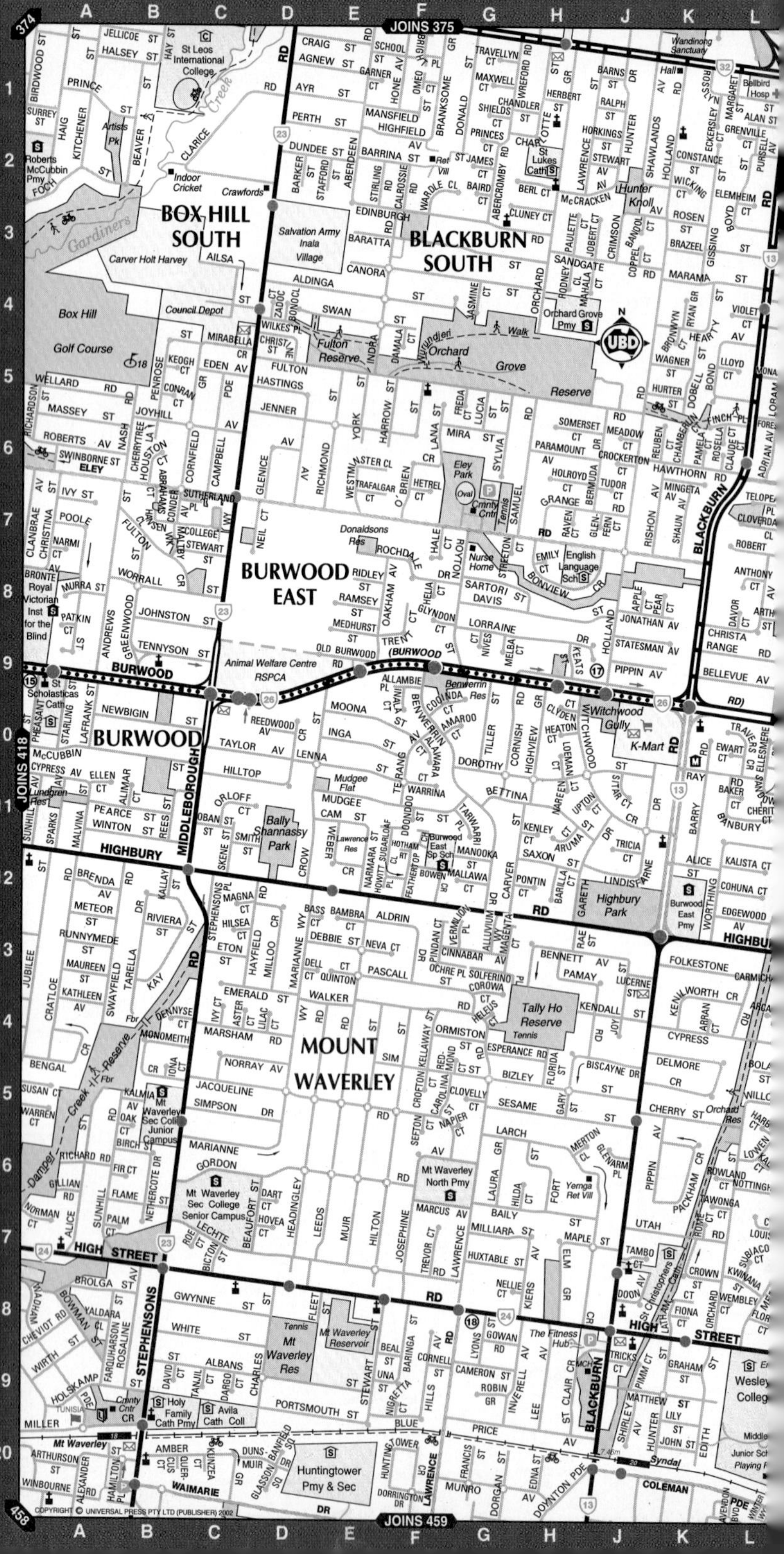

A B C D E F G H J K L

374
JOINS 375

BOX HILL SOUTH

BLACKBURN SOUTH

BURWOOD EAST

BURWOOD

MOUNT WAVERLEY

St Leos International College
Roberts McCubbin Pmy
Artists Pk
Indoor Cricket
Crawfords
Gardiners Creek
Carver Holt Harvey
Box Hill Golf Course
Council Depot
Salvation Army Inala Village
Fulton Reserve
Orchard Grove Reserve
Wurundjeri Walk
Orchard Grove Pmy
St Lukes Cath
Hunter Knoll
Ret Vill
Wandinong Sanctuary
Bellbird Hosp
Eley Park
Cmnty Cntr
Nurse Home
English Language Sch
Donaldsons Res
Royal Victorian Inst for the Blind
Animal Welfare Centre RSPCA
St Scholasticas Cath
Benwerrin Res
Witchwood Gully
K-Mart
Lundgren Res
Mudgee Flat
Bally Shannassy Park
Lawrence Res
Burwood East Sp Sch
Highbury Park
Burwood East Pmy
Tally Ho Reserve
Mt Waverley Sec Coll Junior Campus
Damper Creek Reserve
Mt Waverley Sec College Senior Campus
Mt Waverley North Pmy
Yemga Ret Vill
Orchard Res
Wesley College
Mt Waverley Res
Mt Waverley Reservoir
The Fitness Hub
St Christophers Cath
Holy Family Cath Pmy
Avila Cath Coll
Cmnty Cntr
Huntingtower Pmy & Sec
Middle Junior Sch Playing Fd

BURWOOD HWY
HIGHBURY RD
MIDDLEBOROUGH RD
HIGH STREET RD
STEPHENSONS RD
BLACKBURN RD
WAIMARIE DR
COLEMAN PDE
Mt Waverley
Syndal

1 2 3 4 5 6 7 8 9 10 11 12 13 14 15 16 17 18 19 20

JOINS 418
458
JOINS 459

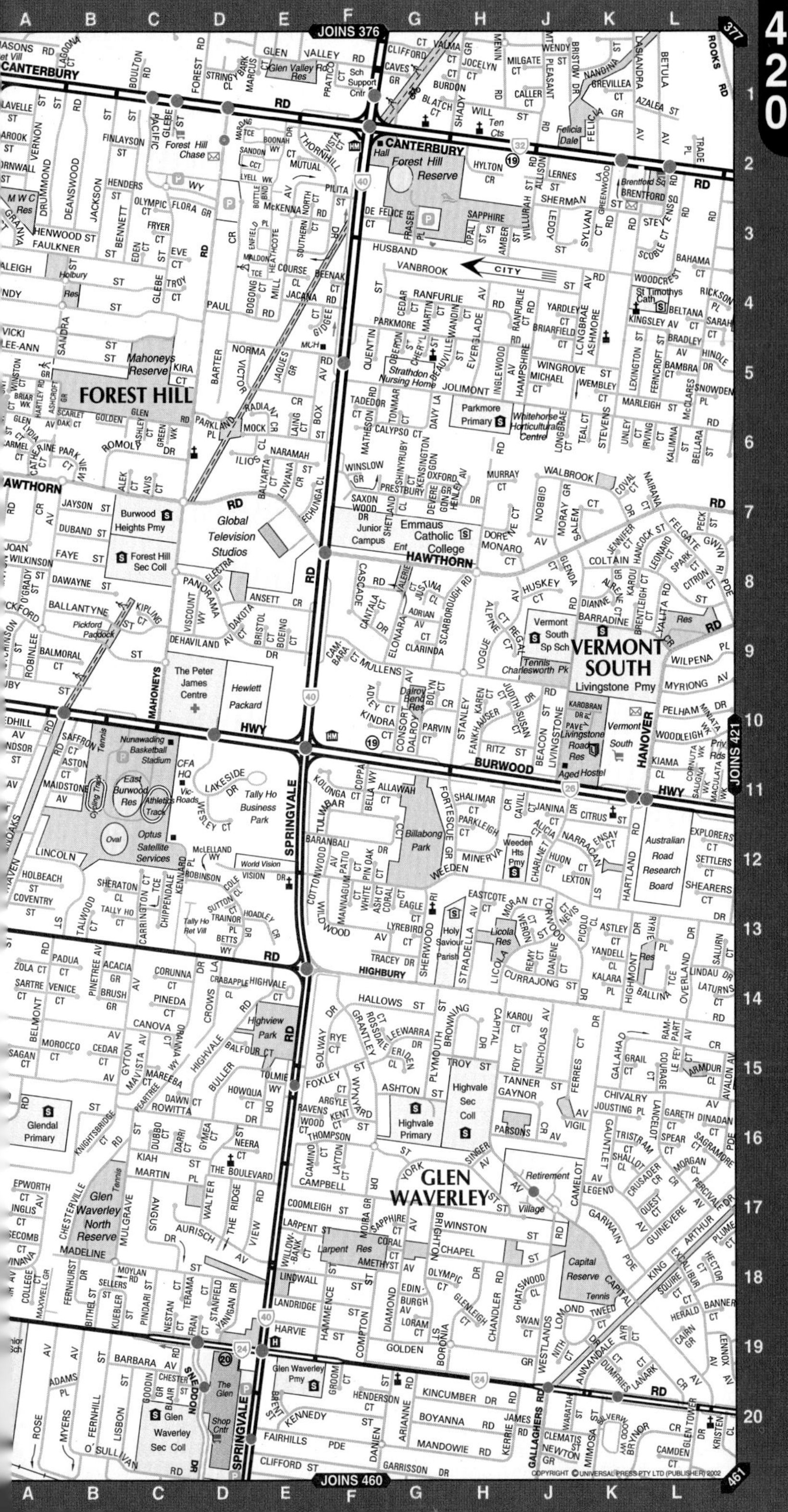
A B C D E F G H J K L
JOINS 376
377
CANTERBURY RD
FOREST HILL
Forest Hill Chase
Forest Hill Reserve
Glen Valley Res
Mahoneys Reserve
Holbury Res
Felicia Dale
Brentford Sq
St Timothys Cath
Strathdon Nursing Home
Parkmore Primary
Whitehorse Horticultural Centre
HAWTHORN RD
Burwood Heights Pmy
Forest Hill Sec Coll
Global Television Studios
Emmaus Catholic College
Junior Campus
Pickford Paddock
The Peter James Centre
Hewlett Packard
VERMONT SOUTH
Vermont South Sp Sch
Tennis Charlesworth Pk
Livingstone Pmy
Dalroy Bend Res
Livingstone Road Res
Vermont South
Aged Hostel
BURWOOD HWY
SPRINGVALE RD
Nunawading Basketball Stadium
CFA HQ
Vic-Roads
East Burwood Res
Cycling Track
Athletics Track
Oval
Optus Satellite Services
Tally Ho Business Park
World Vision
Tally Ho Ret Vill
Billabong Park
Weeden Hts Pmy
Australian Road Research Board
Holy Saviour Parish
Licola Res
HIGHBURY RD
Highview Park
Highvale Sec Coll
Highvale Primary
Glendal Primary
GLEN WAVERLEY
Retirement Village
Glen Waverley North Reserve
Larpent Res
Capital Reserve
Tennis
Glen Waverley Pmy
Glen Waverley Sec Coll
The Glen Shop Cntr
JOINS 421
JOINS 460
461
COPYRIGHT © UNIVERSAL PRESS PTY LTD (PUBLISHER) 2002
1 2 3 4 5 6 7 8 9 10 11 12 13 14 15 16 17 18 19 20

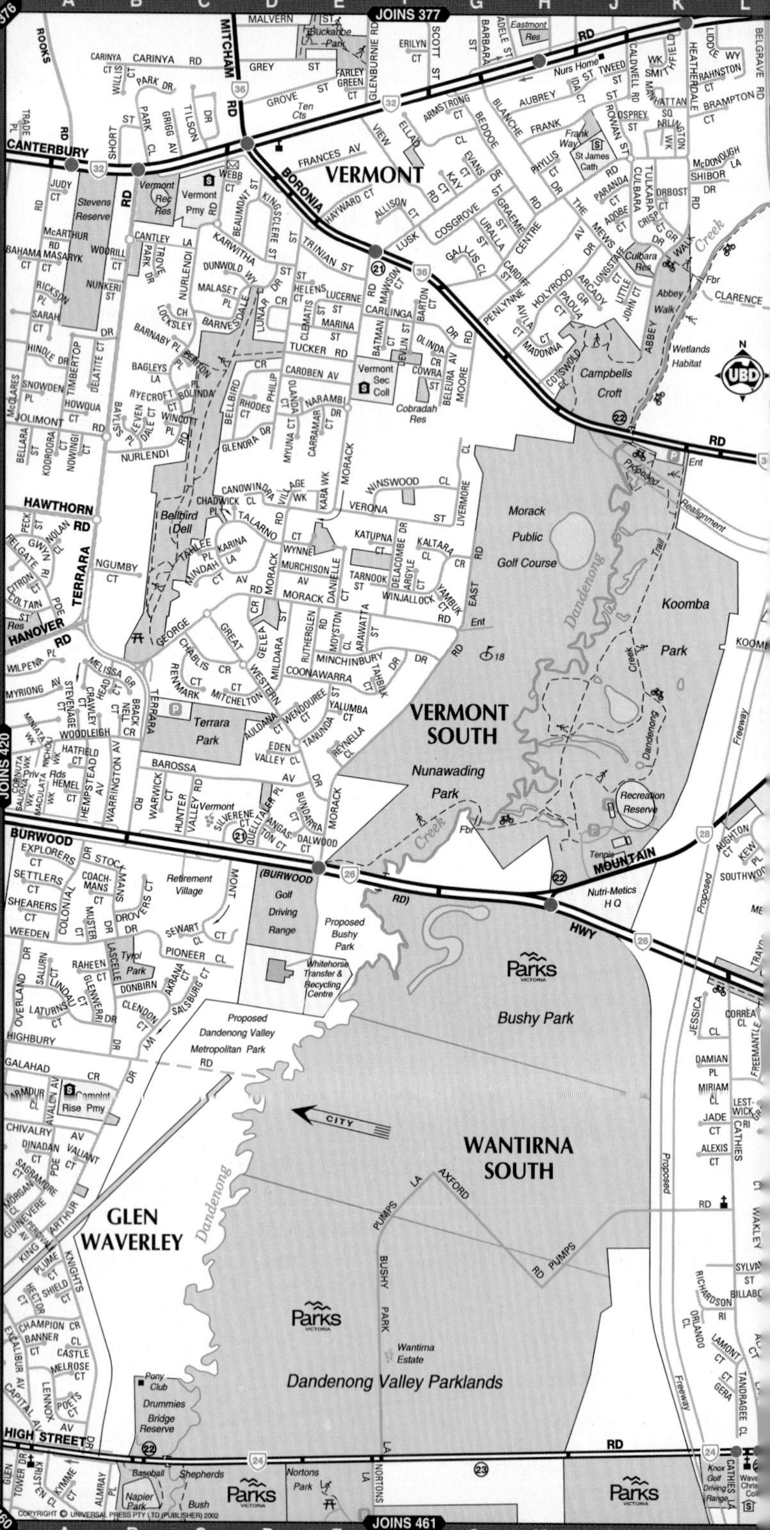

A B C D E F G H J K L

JOINS 377

376

VERMONT

VERMONT SOUTH

WANTIRNA SOUTH

GLEN WAVERLEY

CANTERBURY RD

BORONIA RD

MITCHAM RD

HAWTHORN RD

HANOVER RD

TERRARA RD

BURWOOD HWY

MOUNTAIN HWY

HIGH STREET RD

EAST RD

MORACK RD

Stevens Reserve

Vermont Rec Res

Vermont Pmy

Vermont Sec Coll

Cobradah Res

Bellbird Dell

Terrara Park

Morack Public Golf Course

Koomba Park

Nunawading Park

Recreation Reserve

Campbells Croft

Wetlands Habitat

Abbey Walk

Culbara Res

St James Cath

Buckanbe Park

Eastmont Res

Nurs Home

Retirement Village

Golf Driving Range

Proposed Bushy Park

Whitehorse Transfer & Recycling Centre

Tyrol Park

Proposed Dandenong Valley Metropolitan Park

Camelot Rise Pmy

Bushy Park

Nutri-Metics HQ

Dandenong Valley Parklands

Wantirna Estate

Pony Club

Drummies Bridge Reserve

Baseball

Shepherds Bush

Napier Park

Nortons Park

Knox Golf Driving Range

Waverley Christian Coll

Dandenong Creek

Proposed Realignment

Parks Victoria

CITY

JOINS 420

1 2 3 4 5 6 7 8 9 10 11 12 13 14 15 16 17 18 19 20

460

JOINS 461

A B C D E F G H J K L

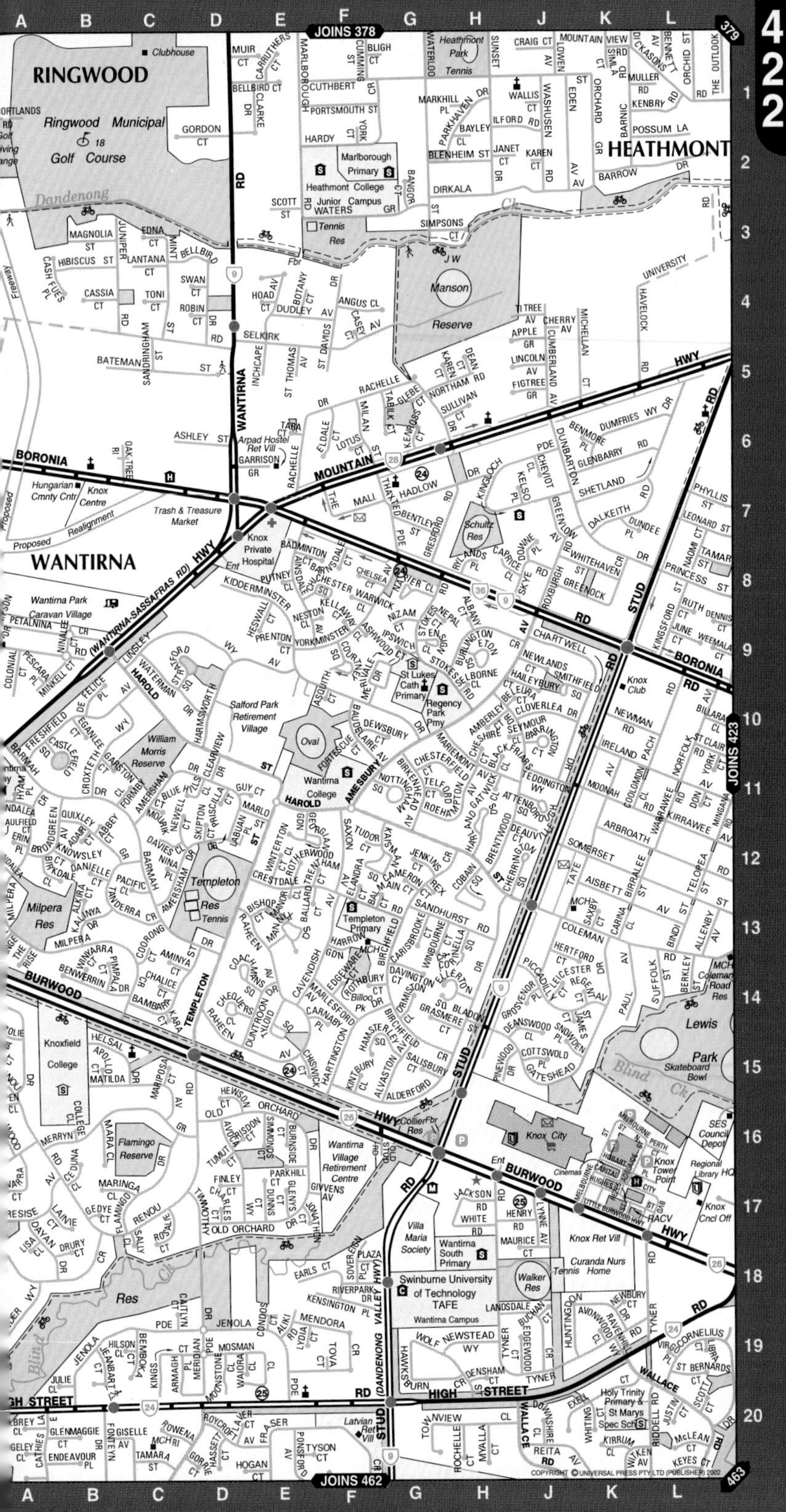
JOINS 378
379
RINGWOOD
Clubhouse
Ringwood Municipal Golf Course
HEATHMONT
Heathmont Park Tennis
Marlborough Primary
Heathmont College Junior Campus
Tennis Res
Dandenong
Ck
Manson Reserve
UNIVERSITY
WANTIRNA RD
MOUNTAIN HWY
BORONIA RD
Hungarian Cmnty Cntr
Knox Centre
Trash & Treasure Market
Proposed Realignment
WANTIRNA
Knox Private Hospital
Arpad Hostel Ret Vill
Wantirna Park Caravan Village
(WANTIRNA-SASSAFRAS RD) HWY
Schultz Res
St Lukes Cath Primary
Regency Park Pmy
Salford Park Retirement Village
William Morris Reserve
Oval
Wantirna College
HAROLD ST
STUD RD
Knox Club
JOINS 423
Templeton Res Tennis
Templeton Primary
Milpera Res
Billoo Pk
BURWOOD HWY
Knoxfield College
Flamingo Reserve
Wantirna Village Retirement Centre
Knox City
Cinemas
Knox Towers Point
SES Council Depot
Regional Library HQ
Knox Cncl Off
RACV
Lewis Park
Skateboard Bowl
Blind Ck
Villa Maria Society
Wantirna South Primary
Knox Ret Vill
Curanda Nurs Home
Walker Res
Swinburne University of Technology TAFE
Wantirna Campus
Res
HIGH STREET RD
STUD RD (DANDENONG VALLEY HWY)
Holy Trinity Primary & St Marys Spec Sch
Latvian Ret Vill
JOINS 462
463
COPYRIGHT © UNIVERSAL PRESS PTY LTD (PUBLISHER) 2002

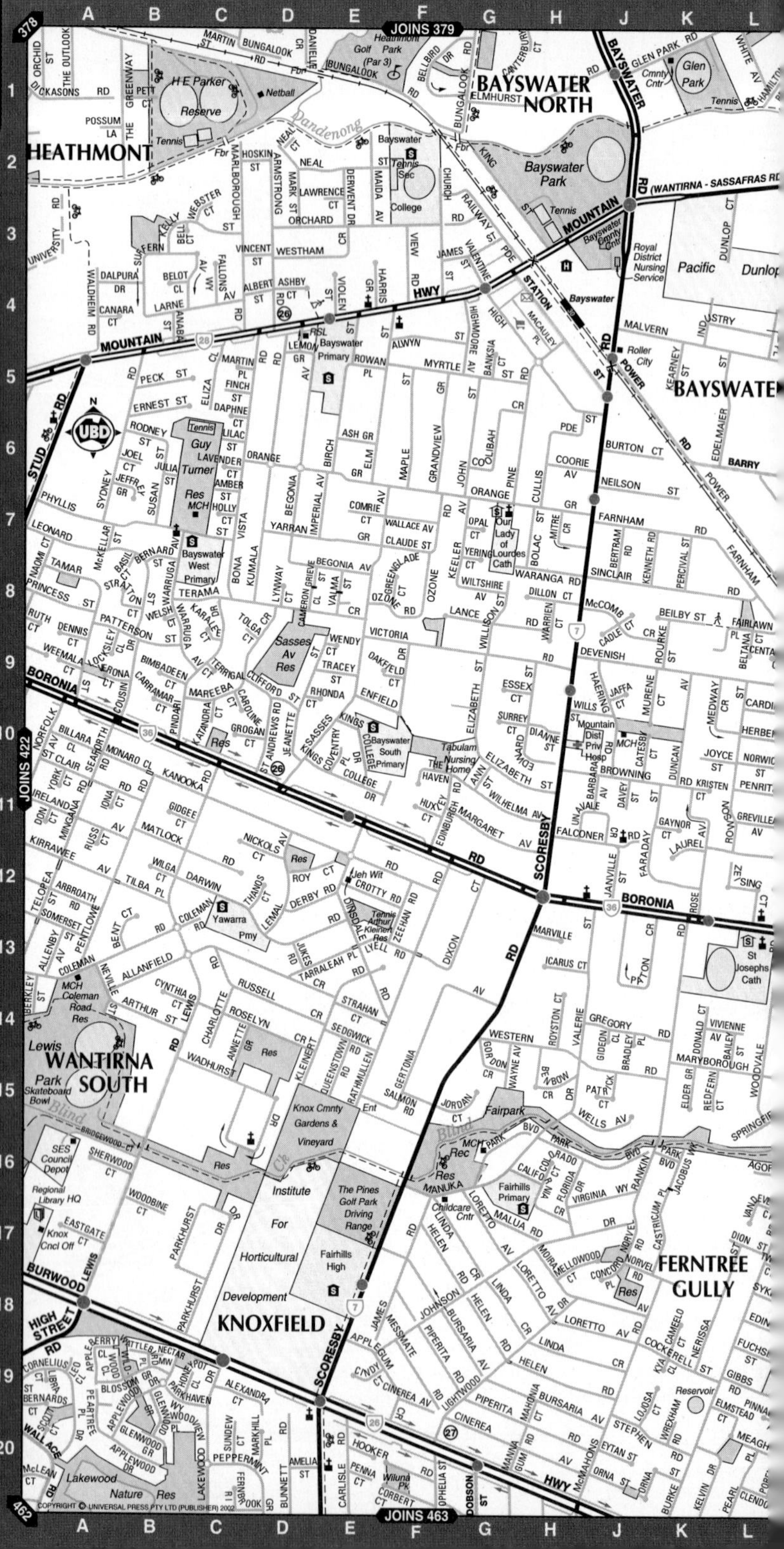

378
JOINS 379
JOINS 422
JOINS 463
462

A B C D E F G H J K L

1 2 3 4 5 6 7 8 9 10 11 12 13 14 15 16 17 18 19 20

HEATHMONT

BAYSWATER NORTH

BAYSWATER

WANTIRNA SOUTH

KNOXFIELD

FERNTREE GULLY

H E Parker Reserve
Heathmont Golf Park (Par 3)
Glen Park
Bayswater Park
Bayswater Tennis Sec College
Bayswater Cmnty Cntr
Royal District Nursing Service
Pacific
Dunlop
Bayswater Primary
Guy Turner Res
Bayswater West Primary
Our Lady of Lourdes Cath
Sasses Av Res
Bayswater South Primary
Tabulam Nursing Home
Mountain Dist Priv Hosp
Yawarra Pmy
Tennis Arthur Kleinert Res
St Josephs Cath
MCH Coleman Road Res
Lewis Park Skateboard Bowl
Knox Cmnty Gardens & Vineyard
Institute For Horticultural Development
The Pines Golf Park Driving Range
Fairhills High
Fairpark
MCH Rec Res
Fairhills Primary
Childcare Cntr
SES Council Depot
Regional Library HQ
Knox Cncl Off
Lakewood Nature Res
Reservoir
Wiluna Pk
Roller City

MOUNTAIN HWY
MOUNTAIN RD (WANTIRNA - SASSAFRAS RD)
BAYSWATER RD
STUD RD
BORONIA RD
SCORESBY RD
BURWOOD HWY
HIGH STREET RD
POWER RD
Dandenong Ck
Blind Ck

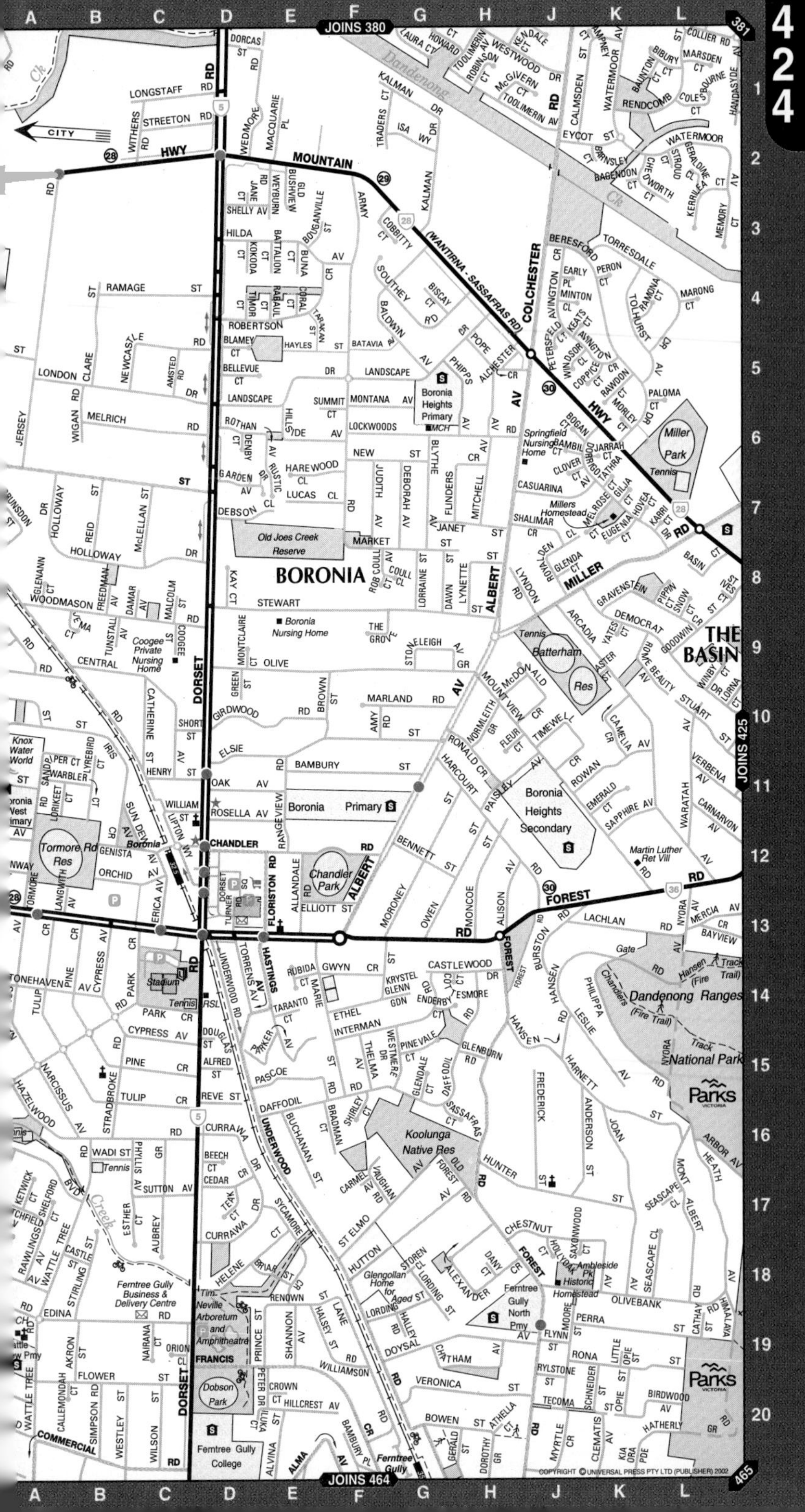

424
JOINS 380
381
JOINS 425
JOINS 464
465
A B C D E F G H J K L
1 2 3 4 5 6 7 8 9 10 11 12 13 14 15 16 17 18 19 20
CITY
BORONIA
THE BASIN
MOUNTAIN HWY
(WANTIRNA - SASSAFRAS RD)
DORSET RD
COLCHESTER RD
FOREST RD
BORONIA RD
MILLER RD
ALBERT AV
UNDERWOOD RD
Dandenong Ck
Old Joes Creek Reserve
Boronia Heights Primary
Boronia Nursing Home
Coogee Private Nursing Home
Knox Water World
Tormore Rd Res
Stadium
Boronia Primary
Chandler Park
Batterham Res
Boronia Heights Secondary
Miller Park
Springfield Nursing Home
Millers Homestead
Martin Luther Ret Vill
Dandenong Ranges National Park
Chandlers (Fire Trail)
Hansen Track (Fire Trail)
Parks VICTORIA
Koolunga Native Res
Glengollan Home for Aged
Ferntree Gully North Pmy
Ambleside Pk Historic Homestead
Ferntree Gully Business & Delivery Centre
Tim Neville Arboretum and Amphitheatre
Dobson Park
Ferntree Gully College
Ferntree Gully
COPYRIGHT © UNIVERSAL PRESS PTY LTD (PUBLISHER) 2002

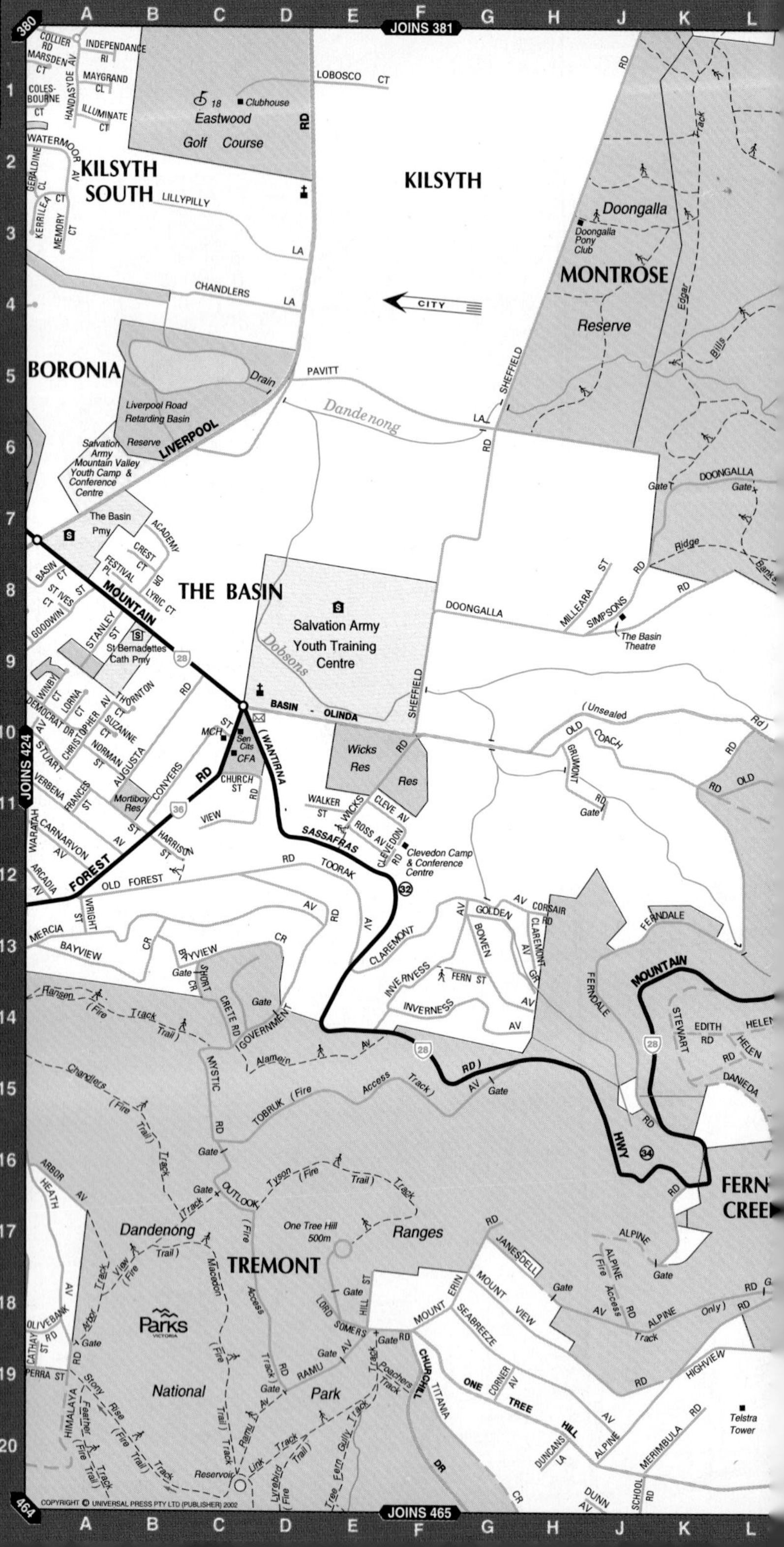

380
JOINS 381
JOINS 424
JOINS 465
464

KILSYTH SOUTH

KILSYTH

BORONIA

MONTROSE

THE BASIN

TREMONT

FERN CREEK

Eastwood Golf Course

18 Clubhouse

Doongalla Reserve

Doongalla Pony Club

Liverpool Road Retarding Basin Reserve

Salvation Army Mountain Valley Youth Camp & Conference Centre

The Basin Pmy

Salvation Army Youth Training Centre

St Bernadettes Cath Pmy

The Basin Theatre

Wicks Res

Mortiboy Res

Clevedon Camp & Conference Centre

One Tree Hill 500m

Dandenong Ranges National Park

Telstra Tower

JOINS 382
383
JOINS 427
JOINS 466
467

A B C D E F G H J K L

1 2 3 4 5 6 7 8 9 10 11 12 13 14 15 16 17 18 19 20

MOUNT DANDENONG

OLINDA

SASSAFRAS

SHERBROOKE

(Doongalla Forest)

Dandenong Ranges National Park

Dandenong Ranges National Park

(Sherbrooke Forest)

Parks VICTORIA

ABV2 Tower
HSV7 Tower
Gate
Burkes
630m
ATV10 Tower
Singleton Reserve
RIDGE RD
BONNIE VIEW RD
EYRE RD
ORNATA RD
Kyeema Track
PRION
RAMAGE RD
TOROA
UPALONG RD
OLD COACH RD
HELEN ST
HUME
GROVE THE
ANN CT
FERNGLEN AV
WISTERIA LA
BLYTHES RD
Ck
FALLS
DINGLEY LA
SELWYN LA
YARRABEE
TOORAK RD
C403
MOUNT DANDENONG TOURIST RD
C415
FENTON ST
SUMMERLEA AV
CAMBRIDGE
CLAVERTON AV
CAMPBELL
GLADYS CT
YVONNE RD
RADNOR CT
EDITH CT
VIOLA AV
OAKLEY ST
FAIRHAVEN RD
FORDYCE
STANLEY ST
DICKENS
ILLOURA CT
DULCIE DOMUM RD
WILLIAMS
Olinda
Gate
Edward Henty Cottage
SUNSET AV
Res
Rankin Track
Dacite Track
Camelia Track
Channel Ten
Track
Stables
Dandenong Creek
Track Gate RD
Gate
Dodds Track
Gate
Dandenong Creek
BASIN OLINDA (Dirt Gravel Road) RD
RANGE (Fire Access) RD
Track
Bradley Track
Gate
Gate
RANGE
GEORGE ST
DODDS
DANDENONG
GAYNERS RD
OLINDA AV
HAROLD ST
NICHOLSON ST
Resvr
MONASH AV
CARDS LA
FALLS
CHARLEMONT
National Rhododendron Garden
Reservoir
SCHOOL RD
PARSONS LA
Olinda Pmy
OLINDA-MONBULK RD
Res
CFA
EVEREST
OLINDA
LUMEAH AV
BEAUMONT ST
BELLA VISTA CR
VISTA
AURORA RI
MASON GR
Sassafras Pmy
CHUDLEIGH CR
DRIFFIELD CR
MILLS AV
Kenloch Function Centre
PERRINS CREEK RD
Reserve
BAYSWATER-SASSAFRAS RD
KILSYTH... ANTIRNA-SASSAFRAS
HILTON RD
Gate
Dog Track
Fire Access Rd
School Track
HWY 28
Hall
PRINCE ST
WALLABY AV
LENNOX GR
GUILFOYLE DR
COLEHURST
LYLE RD
WANNAWONG ST
YARILLA RD
CODLOONGATTA RD
GRANDVIEW GR
WOODLANDS AV
Sassafras Creek
SASSAFRAS CREEK
LYNN ST
COLEHURST CR
ALLISON AV
CLARKE (Fire Access Track)
TRACEY CT
BREEN
MARY ST
Sherbrooke Community
FLORENCE AV
GWENNETH CR
KENNETH AV
WILTON GR
THE CRESCENT
WOODS LA
ALICE
HETHERSETT RD
ROBERT ST
ELLIS AV
PANTEG RD
WARWICK FARM RD
WARWICK RD
MYRTLE RD
TCE
TOURIST
HILTON
Ferny Ck Horticultural Society
Alfred Nicholas Memorial Gardens
Burnham Beeches Estate
Dandenong Ranges Gardens Regional Off
Ent
COLSTON AV
VISTA GR
CLARKMONT
Ferny Creek Reserve
CFA
SHERBROOKE RD
Ferny Creek Picnic Ground
MIZMAZE RD
NOBLES LA
Creek
RD
AV
BRAE CT
BRAESIDE
Monument Track
Hacket Track
Moore
Wattle Track
Gate
Main Ent
POETS LA
George Tindale Memorial Gardens
SAVILLE ST
GREVILLE RD
OLD MAIN RD
Break

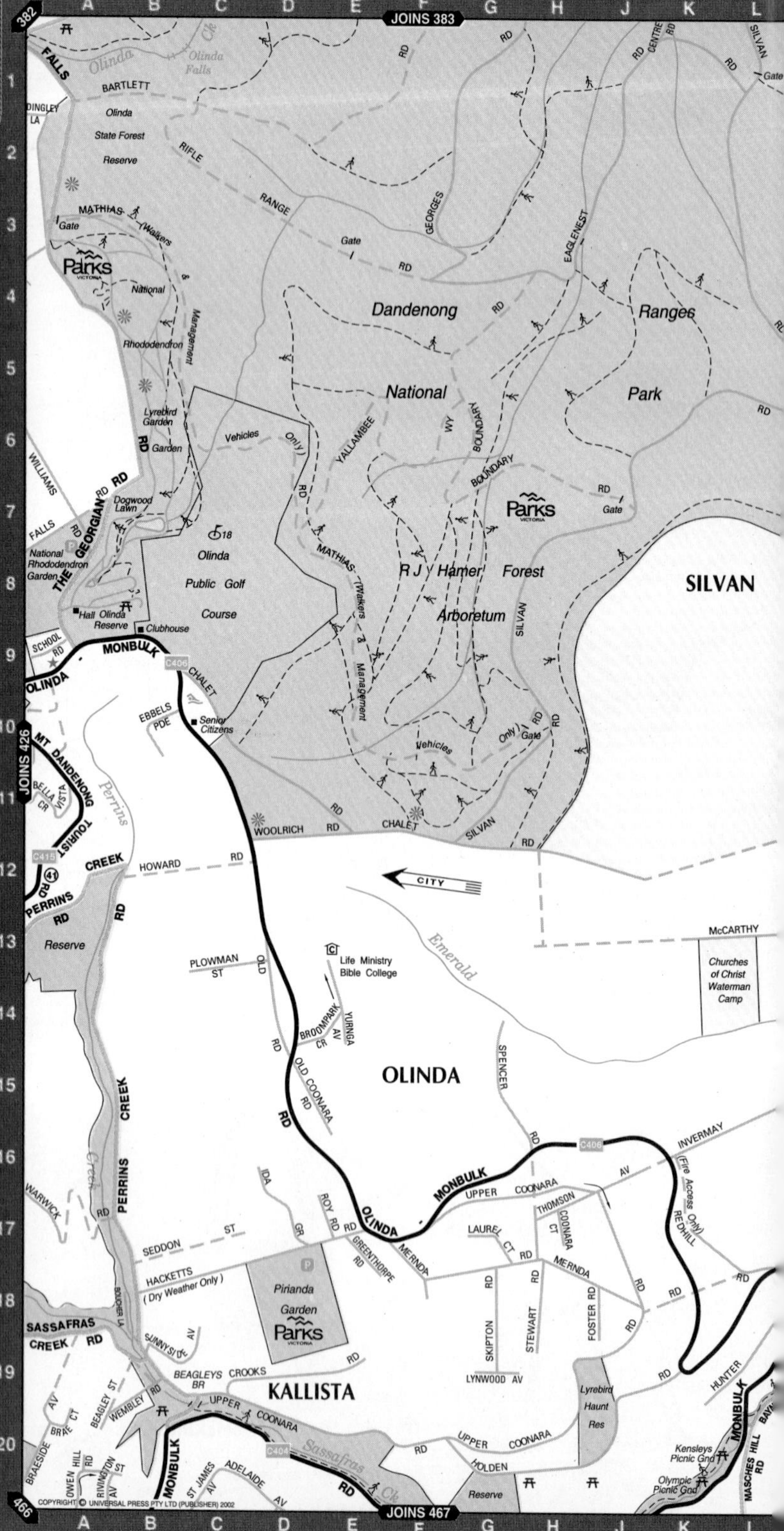

382
JOINS 383
JOINS 426
JOINS 467
466

A B C D E F G H J K L

1 2 3 4 5 6 7 8 9 10 11 12 13 14 15 16 17 18 19 20

Dandenong National Park

Olinda State Forest Reserve

National Rhododendron Garden

Olinda Public Golf Course

R J Hamer Forest Arboretum

SILVAN

OLINDA

KALLISTA

Life Ministry Bible College

Churches of Christ Waterman Camp

Pirianda Garden

Lyrebird Haunt Res

Kensleys Picnic Gnd

Olympic Picnic Gnd

Reserve

Dogwood Lawn

Lyrebird Garden

Hall Olinda Reserve

Clubhouse

Senior Citizens

MONBULK RD
MT DANDENONG TOURIST RD
THE GEORGIAN RD
PERRINS CREEK RD
SASSAFRAS CREEK RD
HACKETTS RD (Dry Weather Only)
OLD COONARA RD
UPPER COONARA RD
MATHIAS (Walkers & Management Vehicles Only) RD
SILVAN RD
CHALET RD
WOOLRICH RD
HOWARD RD
SEDDON ST
McCARTHY
INVERMAY AV
REDHILL RD (Fire Access Only)
MERNDA RD
SPENCER RD
BOUNDARY RD

COPYRIGHT © UNIVERSAL PRESS PTY LTD (PUBLISHER) 2002

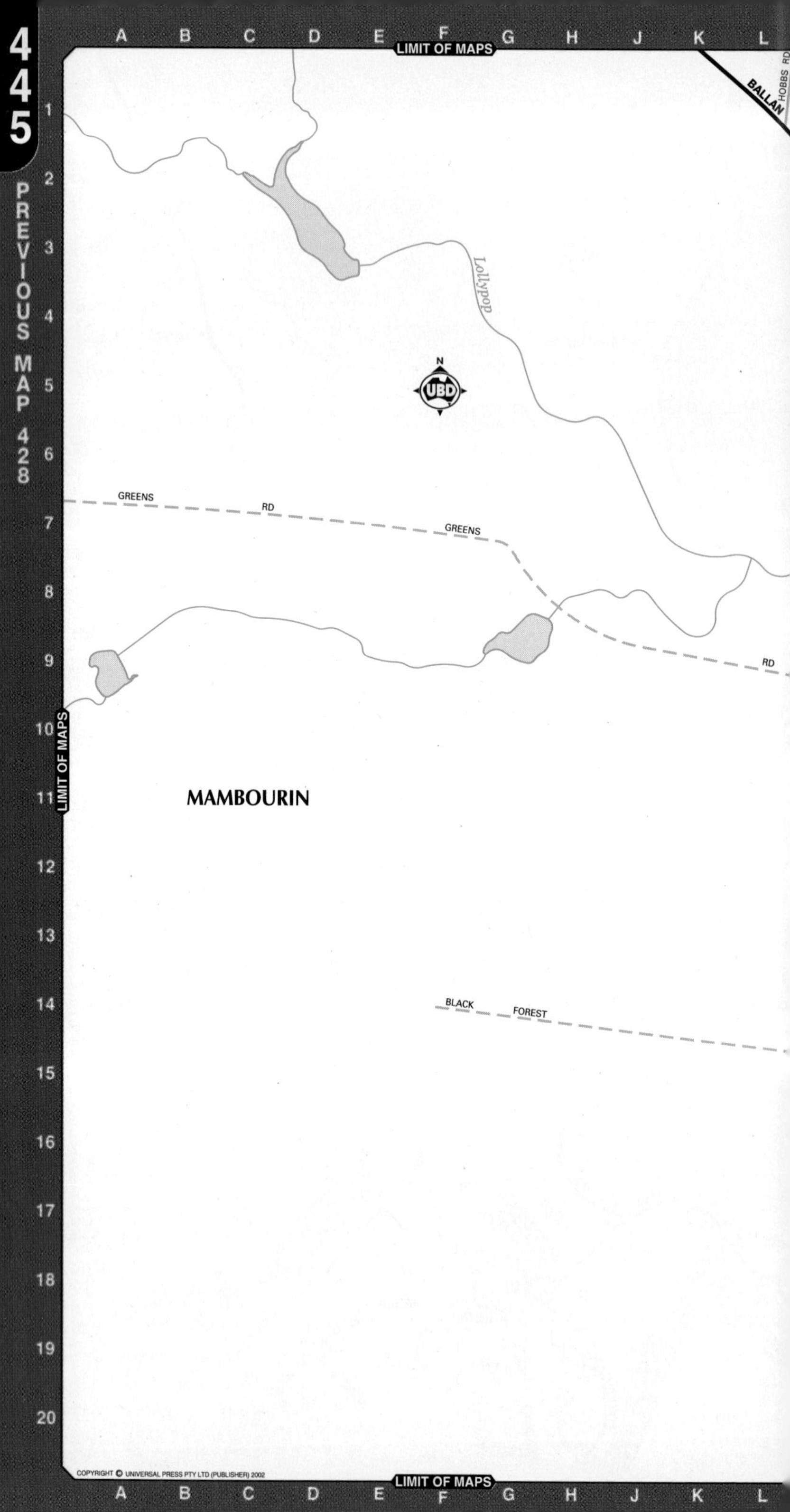

A B C D E F G H J K L
LIMIT OF MAPS
BALLAN
HOBBS RD
PREVIOUS MAP 428
Lollypop
N
UBD
GREENS
RD
GREENS
RD
LIMIT OF MAPS
MAMBOURIN
BLACK
FOREST
LIMIT OF MAPS

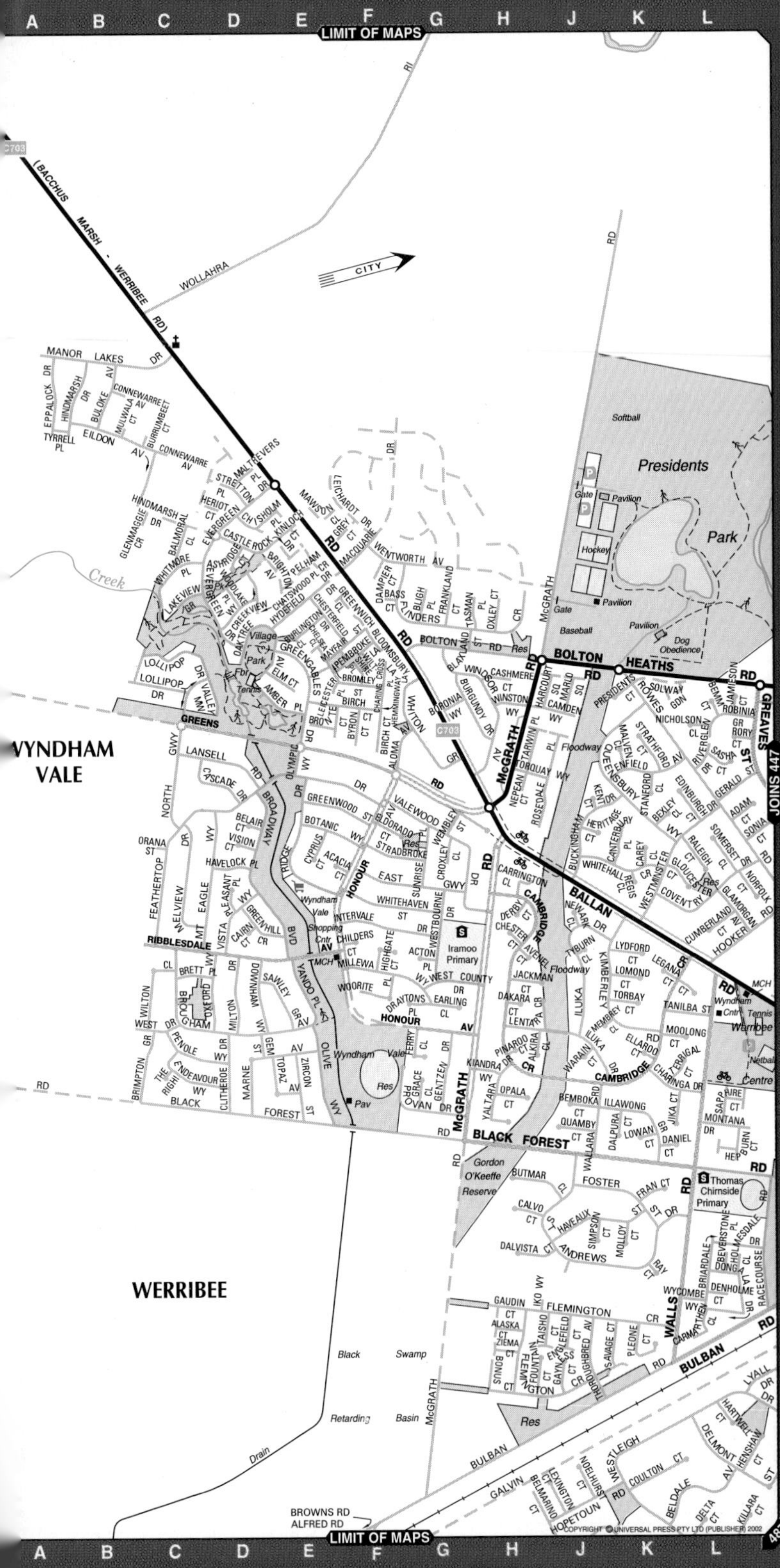

LIMIT OF MAPS

WYNDHAM VALE

WERRIBEE

(BACCHUS MARSH - WERRIBEE RD)

C703

CITY

WOLLAHRA

Presidents Park

Softball

Hockey

Baseball

Pavilion

Gate

Dog Obedience

Village Park

Wyndham Vale Shopping Cntr

Iramoo Primary

Gordon O'Keeffe Reserve

Thomas Chirnside Primary

Wyndham Cntr

Tennis

Werribee

Netball

Centre

Wyndham Vale

Res

Pav

Black Swamp Retarding Basin

Drain

Creek

Floodway

MANOR LAKES DR, EPPALOCK DR, HINDMARSH DR, BULOKE AV, CONNEWARRE AV, MULWALA CT, BURRUMBEET CT, TYRRELL PL, EILDON AV, CONNEWARRE AV, HINDMARSH DR, GLENMAGGIE CR, BALMORAL CL, MALTREVERS PL, STRETTON DR, HERIOT CT, CHISHOLM, EVERGREEN CL, CASTLEROCK, KINLOCH CT, ASHRIDGE CT, BRIGHTON, PELHAM, WHITMORE, LAKEVIEW GR, WOODLAKE, CREEKVIEW, CHATSWOOD PL, HYDEFIELD, OAKTREE DR, BURLINGTON, CHESTERFIELD, GREENWICH, BLOOMSBURY, MAYFAIR, PEMBROKE, GREENGABLES, LEICESTER, BROMLEY, CHARING CROSS, BIRCH CT, BYRON CT, HEMINGWAY, ALOMA AV, WHITTON, LOLLIPOP DR, VALLEY WY, ELM CT, AMBER PL, OLYMPIC DR, GREENS RD, LANSELL, CASCADE DR, BROADWAY, RIDGE, GREENWOOD ST, BOTANIC WY, CYPRUS, ACACIA, EL DORADO PL, VALEWOOD DR, WEMBLEY, STRADBROKE, HONOUR AV, EAST, SUNRISE, CROXLEY CL, GWY, WHITEHAVEN ST, INTERVALE DR, WESTBOURNE, CHILDERS CR, HIGHGATE CT, ACTON PL, MILLEWA, WOORITE, DRAYTONS, EARLING CL, WEST COUNTY DR, NORTH, ORANA ST, BELAIR, VISION, HAVELOCK PL, PLEASANT, EAGLE, FEATHERTOP, MELVIEW, MT VISTA, GREENHILL, CAIRN, RIBBLESDALE AV, BRETT PL, BROUGHAM, OXFORD, MILTON, DOWNHAM WY, SAWLEY GR, YANDO PL, WILTON, WEST DR, PENOLE, ENDEAVOUR, MARNE, GEM, TOPAZ AV, ZIRCON ST, OLIVE WY, BRIMPTON GR, THE RIGHI, BLACK, CLITHEROE, FOREST, FERRY, GRACE, PROVAN, GENTZEN DR, MAWSON, LEICHARDT DR, GREY, MACQUARIE, WENTWORTH AV, DAMPIER, BASS, FLINDERS, BLIGH PL, FRANKLAND, TASMAN, OXLEY CT, BOLTON RD, BLAYLAND, WINDSOR, CASHMERE, BURGUNDY, BORONIA, WINSTON, HARCOURT, MARLO SQ, CAMDEN, McGRATH RD, STARWIN PL, NEPEAN CT, TORQUAY WY, ROSEDALE, BUCKINGHAM, HEATHS RD, PRESIDENTS, ROWES, SOLWAY GDN, NICHOLSON CL, BENNY, JAMIESON, ROBINIA, RORY, SASHA, GREAVES ST, MALVERN, QUEENSBURY, STRATHFORD, ENFIELD, STANFORD, EDINBURGH DR, BEXLEY, RIVERGLEN, GERALD, ADAM, SONIA, KENT, HERITAGE, CANTERBURY, CAREY, RALEIGH, SOMERSET DR, NORFOLK, WHITEHALL, REGIS, WESTMINSTER, GLOUCESTER, COVENTRY, GLAMORGAN, CUMBERLAND AV, HOOKER, CARRINGTON CL, CAMBRIDGE CR, BALLAN RD, DERBY, CHESTER, AVENEL, NEWARK DR, TYBURN, LYDFORD, LOMOND, KIMBERLEY, LEGANA, TORBAY, TANILBA ST, JACKMAN, DAKARA, LENTARA, ILUKA, MEMBREY, ELLAROO, MOOLONG, TERRIGAL, CHARINGA DR, PINAROO, ALKIRA, KIANDRA, WARAIN, CAMBRIDGE, OPALA, YALTARA, BEMBOKA, ILLAWONG, JIKA CT, QUAMBY, DALPURA, LOWAN, DANIEL, WALLARA, SAPPHIRE, MONTANA, HEPBURN, BLACK FOREST RD, BUTMAR, FOSTER, FRAN CT, CALVO, HAVEAUX, SIMPSON, MOLLOY, DALVISTA, ANDREWS, RAY, WALLS RD, BEVERSTONE, HOLMESDALE, BRIARDALE, DONGA, DENHOLME, RACECOURSE, WYCOMBE, CARMARTHEN, GAUDIN, IKO WY, FLEMINGTON, ALASKA, ZIEMA, TAISHO, ENGLEFIELD, BONUS, FOUNTAIN, GAYNESS, THOROUGHBRED AV, SAVAGE, PLEONE, BULBAN RD, LYALL DR, HARTWELL, HENSHAW, DELMONT AV, WESTLEIGH, NOELHURST, COULTON CT, BELDALE, DELTA CT, KILLARA, GALVIN, BELMARINO, LEXINGTON, HOPETOUN, BROWNS RD, ALFRED RD

JOINS 447

487

LIMIT OF MAPS

A B C D E F G H J K L

LIMIT OF MAPS

TARNEIT

WYNDHAM VALE

Werribee River

Presidents Park

Riverband Historical Park

Italian Social & Soccer Club

Galvin Park

Soccer

Pav

Tennis

Galvin Park Secondary College

Westgrove Primary

Bethany Cath Pmy

MCH

Golden Square Reserve

Wilson Reserve

Glen Devon Pmy

Manorvale Pmy

Nurs Home

Werribee Basketball

Netball

Werribee Rec Centre

Werribee Racecourse

Grandstand

Werribee Racecourse (Disused)

Thomas Chirnside Pmy

St Andrews Cath

Wyndham Park

Chirnside Park

Heated

Werribee District Hosp

Werribee Primary

Corpus Christi Primary

Soldiers Reserve

Werribee Secondary College

MacKillop Catholic Regional College

VicRoads

Indoor Sport Centre

Melbourne Water Farm

Werribee

HEATHS RD

SHAWS RD

TARNEIT RD

BALLAN RD

PRINCES HWY

BULBAN RD

DUNCANS RD

CHERRY ST

WATTON ST

SYNNOT ST

WERRIBEE ST

RAILWAY AV

Water Channel

C703

C109

C108

32

30

JOINS 446

JOINS 487

A B C D E F G H J K L

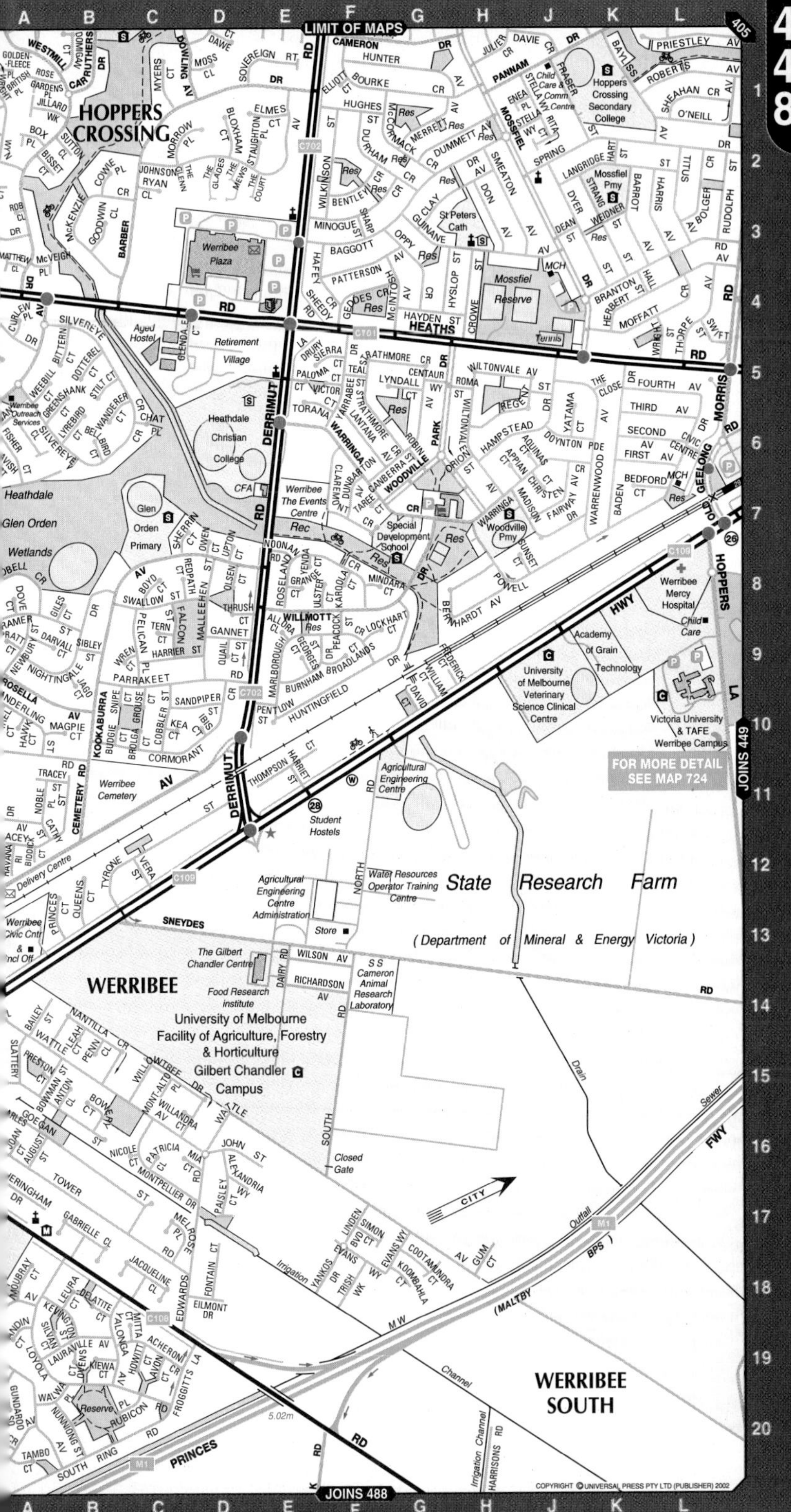
LIMIT OF MAPS
405
HOPPERS CROSSING
Hoppers Crossing Secondary College
Werribee Plaza
St Peters Cath
Mossfiel Reserve
Mossfiel Pmy
Child Care & Comm Centre
Aged Hostel
Retirement Village
Heathdale Christian College
Heathdale
Glen Orden
Wetlands
Glen Orden Primary
Werribee Outreach Services
Werribee The Events Centre
Special Development School
Woodville Pmy
Werribee Mercy Hospital
Child Care
Academy of Grain Technology
University of Melbourne Veterinary Science Clinical Centre
Victoria University & TAFE Werribee Campus
FOR MORE DETAIL SEE MAP 724
JOINS 449
Werribee Cemetery
Student Hostels
Agricultural Engineering Centre
Agricultural Engineering Centre Administration
Water Resources Operator Training Centre
State Research Farm
(Department of Mineral & Energy Victoria)
Store
The Gilbert Chandler Centre
S S Cameron Animal Research Laboratory
Food Research institute
WERRIBEE
University of Melbourne Facility of Agriculture, Forestry & Horticulture
Gilbert Chandler Campus
Werribee Civic Cntr & Incl Off
Delivery Centre
Closed Gate
CITY
Drain
Sewer
Outfall
Irrigation
Channel
Irrigation Channel
(MALTBY
BPS
FWY
M W
PRINCES
WERRIBEE SOUTH
5.02m
JOINS 488
DERRIMUT RD
HEATHS RD
GEELONG RD
PRINCES HWY
SNEYDES RD
HOPPERS LA
MORRIS RD
C702
C701
C109
C108
M1
COPYRIGHT © UNIVERSAL PRESS PTY LTD (PUBLISHER) 2002

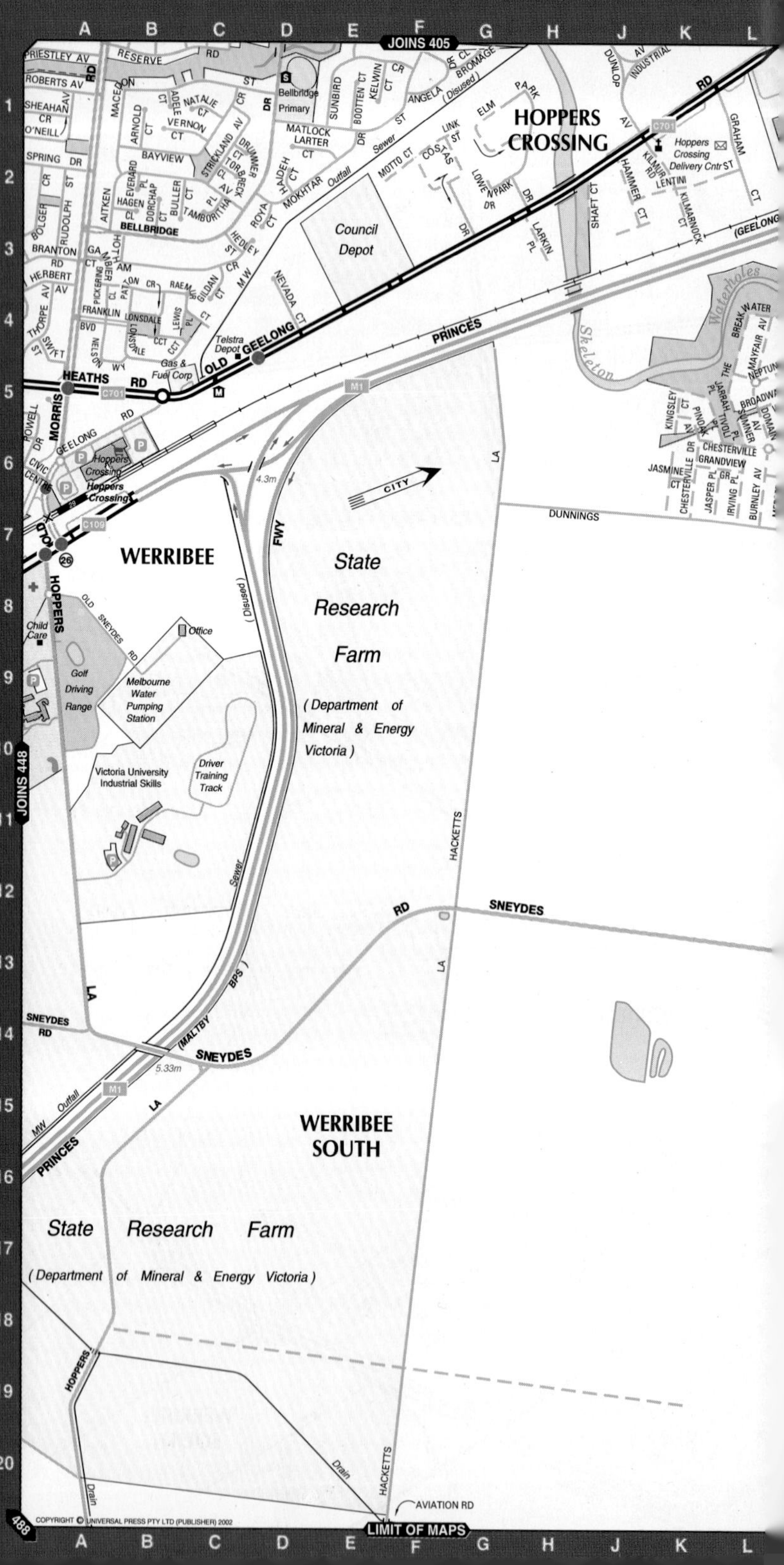
A B C D E F G H J K L
1 2 3 4 5 6 7 8 9 10 11 12 13 14 15 16 17 18 19 20
JOINS 405
JOINS 448
488
LIMIT OF MAPS
HOPPERS CROSSING
WERRIBEE
WERRIBEE SOUTH
BELLBRIDGE
State Research Farm
(Department of Mineral & Energy Victoria)
State Research Farm
(Department of Mineral & Energy Victoria)
Council Depot
Bellbridge Primary
Telstra Depot
Gas & Fuel Corp
Hoppers Crossing
Hoppers Crossing Delivery Cntr
Office
Melbourne Water Pumping Station
Golf Driving Range
Child Care
Victoria University Industrial Skills
Driver Training Track
CITY
4.3m
5.33m
PRINCES FWY
OLD GEELONG RD
HEATHS RD
SNEYDES RD
OLD SNEYDES RD
HACKETTS LA
HOPPERS LA
DUNNINGS RD
AVIATION RD
MORRIS RD
(MALTBY BPS)
MW Outfall Sewer
(Disused)
Skeleton
Waterholes
Drain
C701
C109
M1
26
29
PRIESTLEY AV
RESERVE RD
ROBERTS AV
SHEAHAN CR
O'NEILL
SPRING DR
BOLGER CR
RUDOLPH ST
BRANTON RD
HERBERT AV
THORPE AV
SWIFT ST
FRANKLIN BVD
NELSON WY
MACEDON ST
ARNOLD CT
ADELE CT
NATALIE CT
VERNON CT
BAYVIEW
STRICKLAND AV
DRUMMER CT
TOR BRECK
AITKEN
EVERARD PL
HAGEN CL
DORCHAP CT
BULLER CT
TAMBORITHA PL
HOTHAM
PICKERING
PATTON CR
RAEMUR CT
GILDAN CT
LONSDALE CCT
LEWIS PL
ROYA CT
HEDLEY ST
HAIDEH CT
MOKHTAR DR
MATLOCK CT
LARTER CT
SUNBIRD
BOOTTEN CT
KELWIN CT
ANGELA ST
BROMAGE DR
NEVADA CT
MOTTO CT
COSTAS
LINK ST
ELM PARK
LOWE PARK DR
LARKIN PL
DUNLOP AV
INDUSTRIAL AV
SHAFT CT
HAMMER CT
KILMUIR RD
LENTINI
KILMARNOCK CT
GRAHAM ST
BREAKWATER
MAYFAIR AV
NEPTUNE
THE
JARRAH PL
TIVOLI
PINOAK AV
KINGSLEY CT
BROADWAY
SUMNER AV
DOMAIN
CHESTERVILLE DR
GRANDVIEW GR
JASMINE CT
JASPER PL
IRVING PL
BURNLEY AV
CIVIC CENTRE
GEELONG RD
COPYRIGHT © UNIVERSAL PRESS PTY LTD (PUBLISHER) 2002

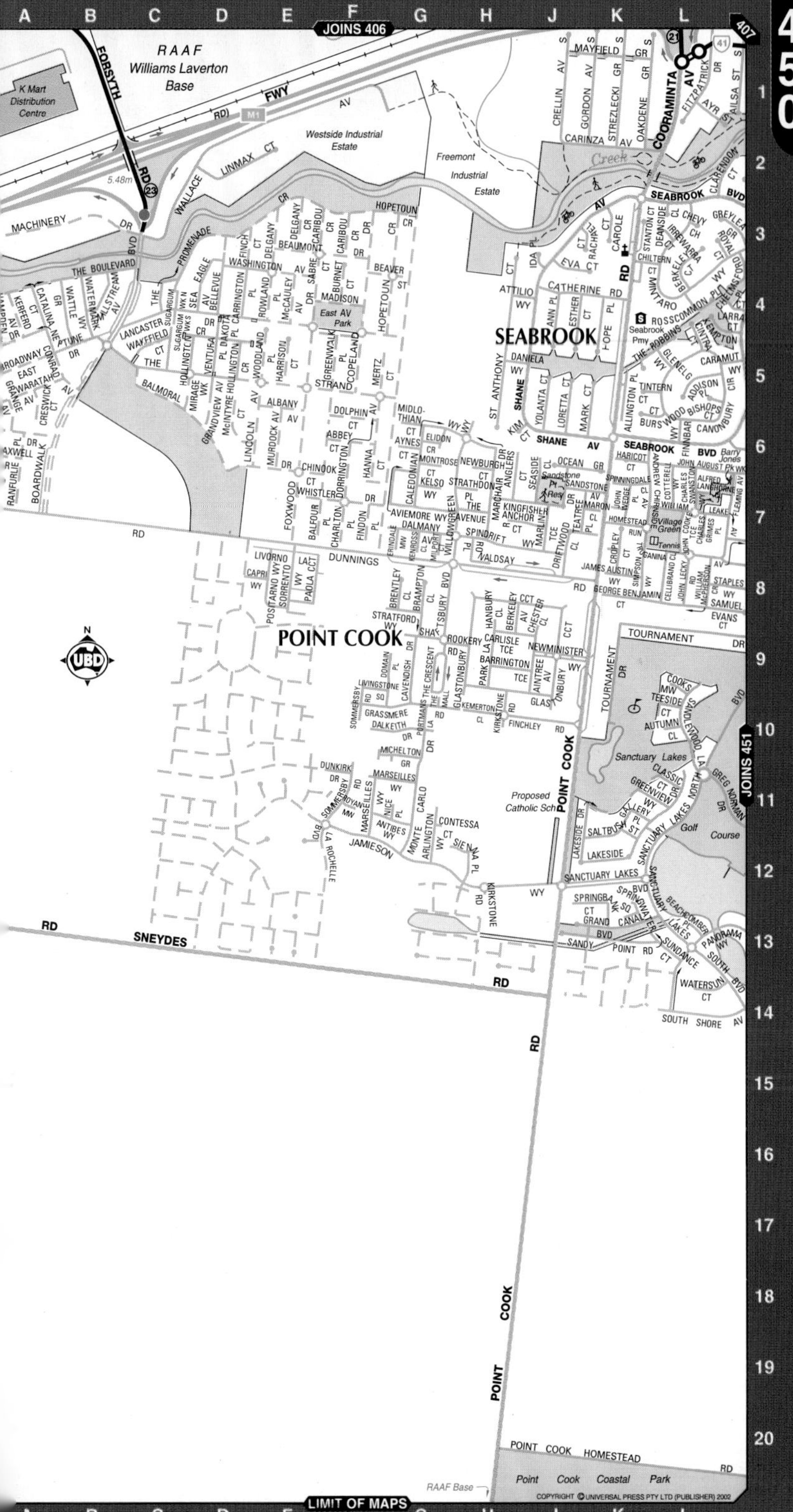

JOINS 406
407
RAAF Williams Laverton Base
K Mart Distribution Centre
FORSYTH RD
FWY
Westside Industrial Estate
Freemont Industrial Estate
SEABROOK
POINT COOK
Seabrook Pmy
East AV Park
Sanctuary Lakes
Golf Course
Proposed Catholic Sch
DUNNINGS RD
SNEYDES RD
POINT COOK RD
POINT COOK HOMESTEAD RD
Point Cook Coastal Park
RAAF Base
JOINS 451
LIMIT OF MAPS
COPYRIGHT © UNIVERSAL PRESS PTY LTD (PUBLISHER) 2002

A B C D E F G H J K L

406

JOINS 407

CENTRAL AV

QUEEN ST

SEABROOK

ALTONA MEADOWS

Altona Green Primary

Sanctuary Lakes Golf Course

Sanctuary Lakes

Skeleton Waterholes

JOINS 450

POINT COOK

POINT COOK HOMESTEAD RD

LIMIT OF MAPS

A B C D E F G H J K L

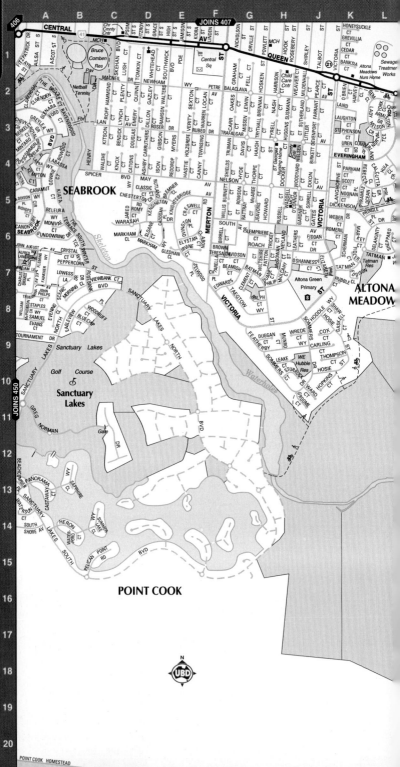

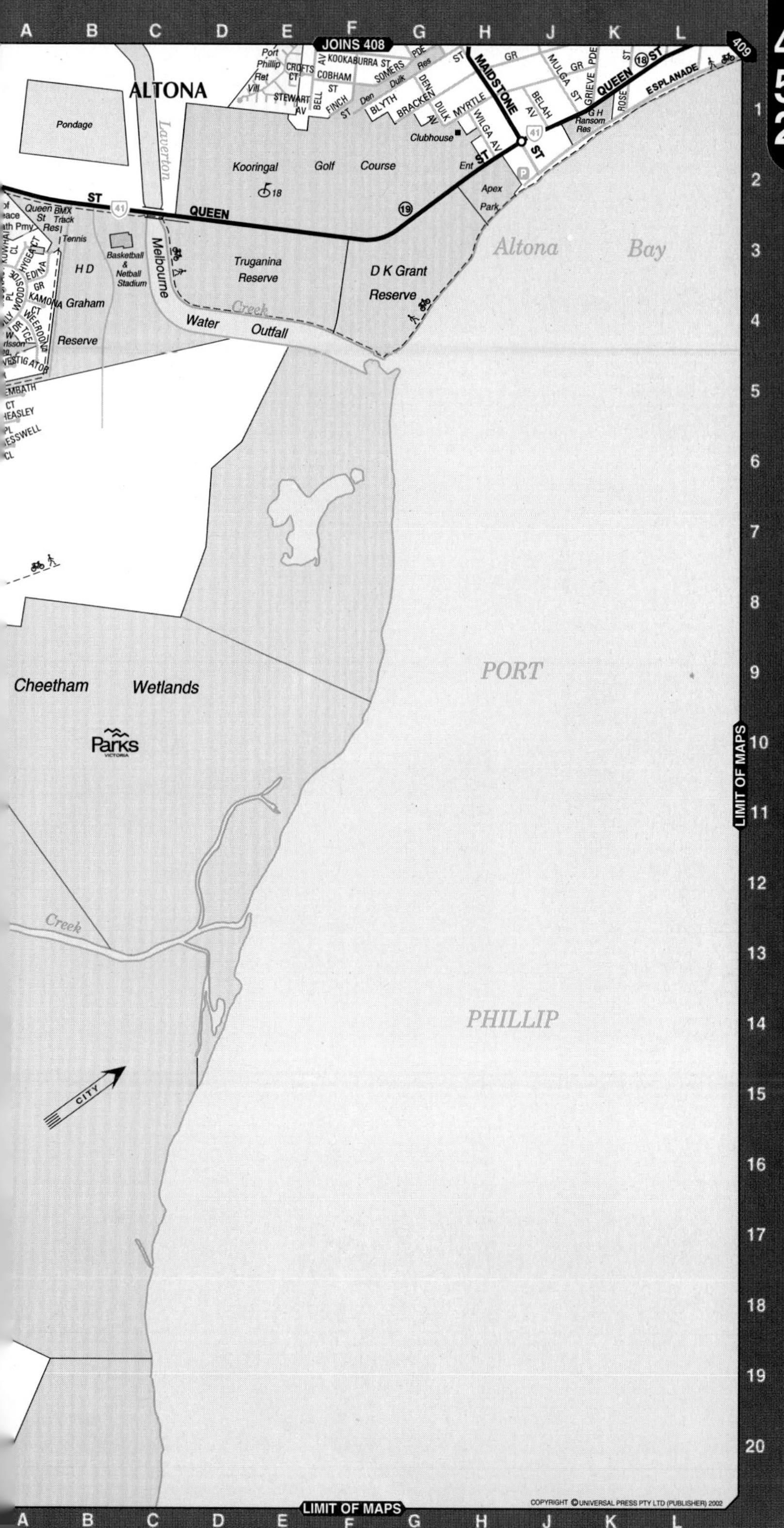
JOINS 408
ALTONA
Pondage
Laverton
Kooringal Golf Course
Clubhouse
QUEEN ST
MAIDSTONE ST
ESPLANADE
Apex Park
Altona Bay
Truganina Reserve
D K Grant Reserve
H D Graham Reserve
Basketball & Netball Stadium
Melbourne Water Outfall
Creek
Cheetham Wetlands
Parks Victoria
CITY
PORT
PHILLIP
LIMIT OF MAPS
409

412

A B C D E F G H J K L

JOINS 413

ST KILDA

1
2
3
4
5
6 PORT
7
8
9
10 PHILLIP

11
12
13
14
15
16
17
18
19
20

JOINS 493

A B C D E F G H J K L

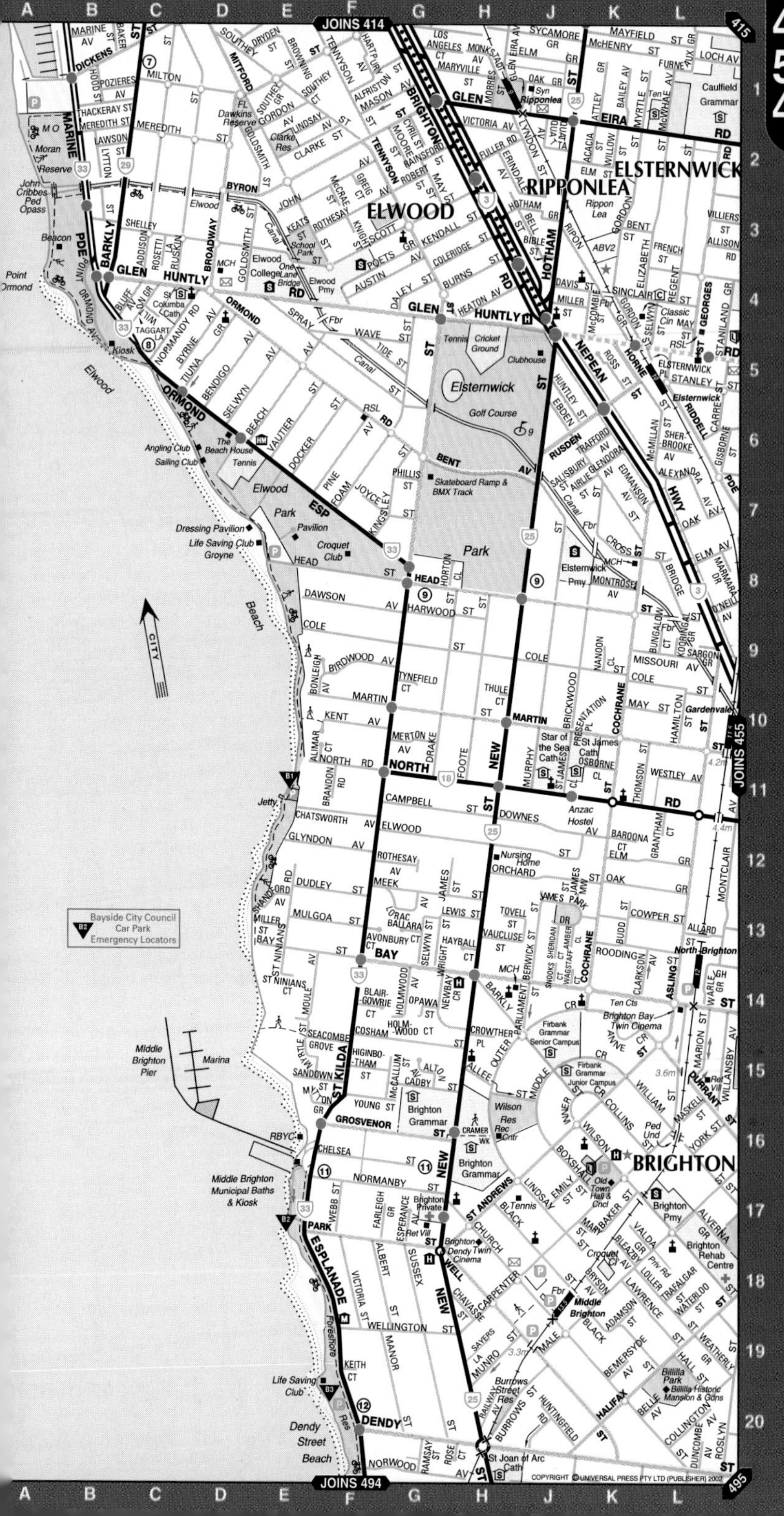
A B C D E F G H J K L
JOINS 414
415
ELSTERNWICK
RIPPONLEA
ELWOOD
BRIGHTON
Elsternwick Golf Course
Elsternwick Park
Elwood Park
Point Ormond
Elwood Beach
CITY
Bayside City Council Car Park Emergency Locators
Middle Brighton Pier
Marina
Middle Brighton Municipal Baths & Kiosk
Dendy Street Beach
Caulfield Grammar
Brighton Grammar
Firbank Grammar Senior Campus
Firbank Grammar Junior Campus
Wilson Res Rec Cntr
Billilla Park
Billilla Historic Mansion & Gdns
Brighton Rehab Centre
Old Town Hall & Cncl
Middle Brighton
North Brighton
Gardenvale
Elsternwick
Ripponlea
JOINS 455
JOINS 494
495
MARINE PDE
GLEN HUNTLY RD
ORMOND ESP
BRIGHTON RD
HOTHAM ST
NEPEAN HWY
NEW ST
ST KILDA ST
NORTH RD
BAY ST
ESPLANADE
DENDY ST
GROSVENOR ST
GLEN EIRA RD
BARKLY ST
COPYRIGHT © UNIVERSAL PRESS PTY LTD (PUBLISHER) 2002
1 2 3 4 5 6 7 8 9 10 11 12 13 14 15 16 17 18 19 20

414

JOINS 415

A B C D E F G H J K L

1 2 3 4 5 6 7 8 9 10 11 12 13 14 15 16 17 18 19 20

CAULFIELD NORTH

CAULFIELD

CAULFIELD SOUTH

ELSTERNWICK

GARDENVALE

BRIGHTON EAST

McKINNON

BRIGHTON

BENTLEIGH

JOINS 454

494

JOINS 495

A B C D E F G H J K L

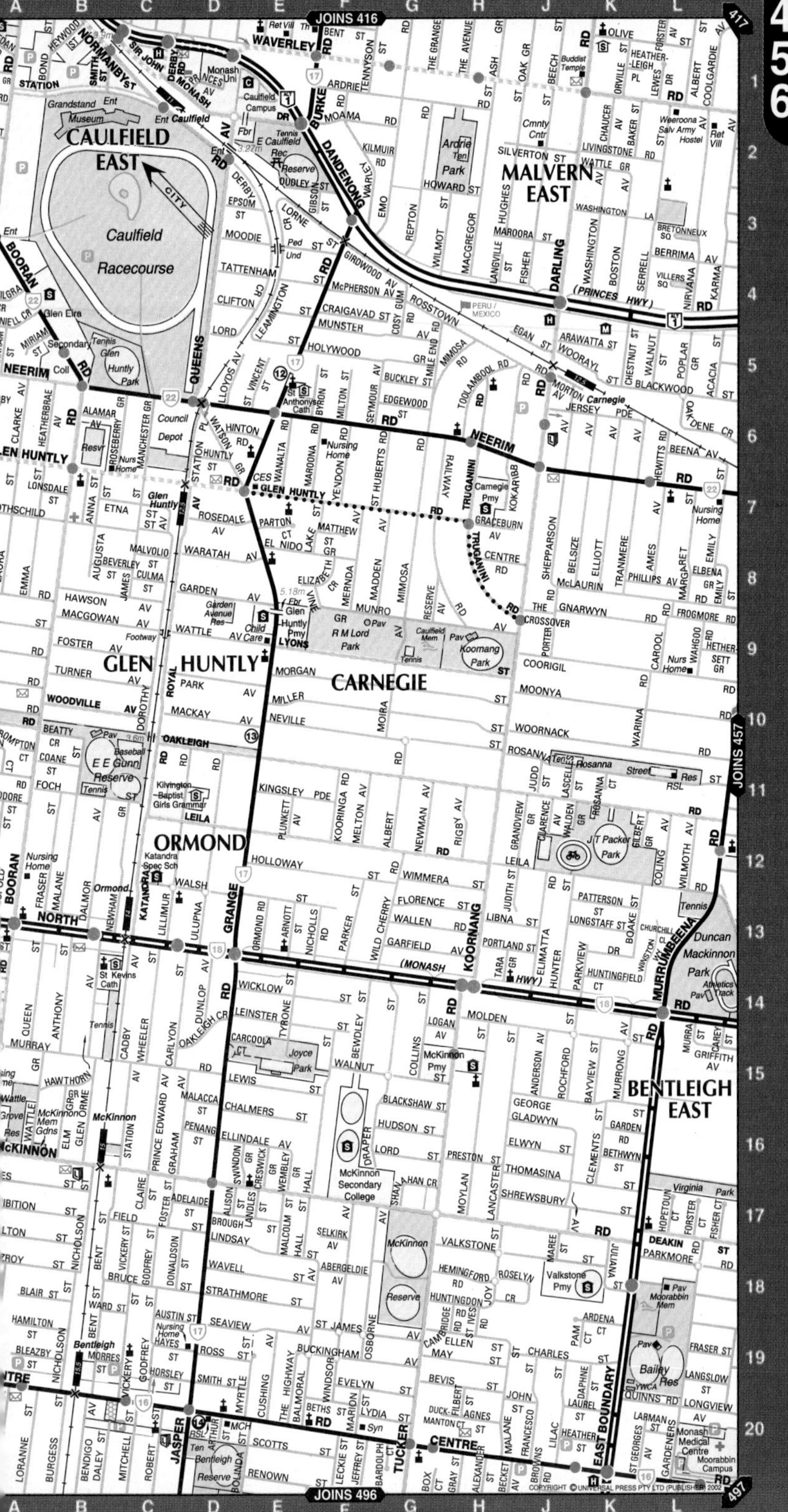
A B C D E F G H J K L
JOINS 416
417
CAULFIELD EAST
Caulfield Racecourse
CITY
Monash Uni
Caulfield Campus
WAVERLEY RD
DANDENONG RD
BURKE RD
MALVERN EAST
Ardrie Ten Park
DARLING RD
(PRINCES HWY)
PERU / MEXICO
ROSSTOWN RD
NEERIM RD
Carnegie
GLEN HUNTLY RD
Glen Huntly
GLEN HUNTLY
CARNEGIE
R M Lord Park
Koornang Park
Caulfield Mem
KOORNANG RD
ROSANNA ST
Rosanna
J T Packer Park
ORMOND
Ormond
NORTH RD
(MONASH HWY)
GRANGE RD
Joyce Park
E E Gunn Reserve
Kilvington Baptist Girls Grammar
Katandra Spec Sch
St Kevins Cath
BENTLEIGH EAST
Duncan Mackinnon Park
MURRUMBEENA RD
McKinnon Secondary College
McKinnon Reserve
McKinnon
McKinnon Pmy
Valkstone Pmy
Moorabbin Mem
Bailey Res
EAST BOUNDARY RD
Bentleigh
Bentleigh Reserve
CENTRE RD
Monash Medical Centre Moorabbin Campus
JOINS 457
JOINS 496
497
1 2 3 4 5 6 7 8 9 10 11 12 13 14 15 16 17 18 19 20

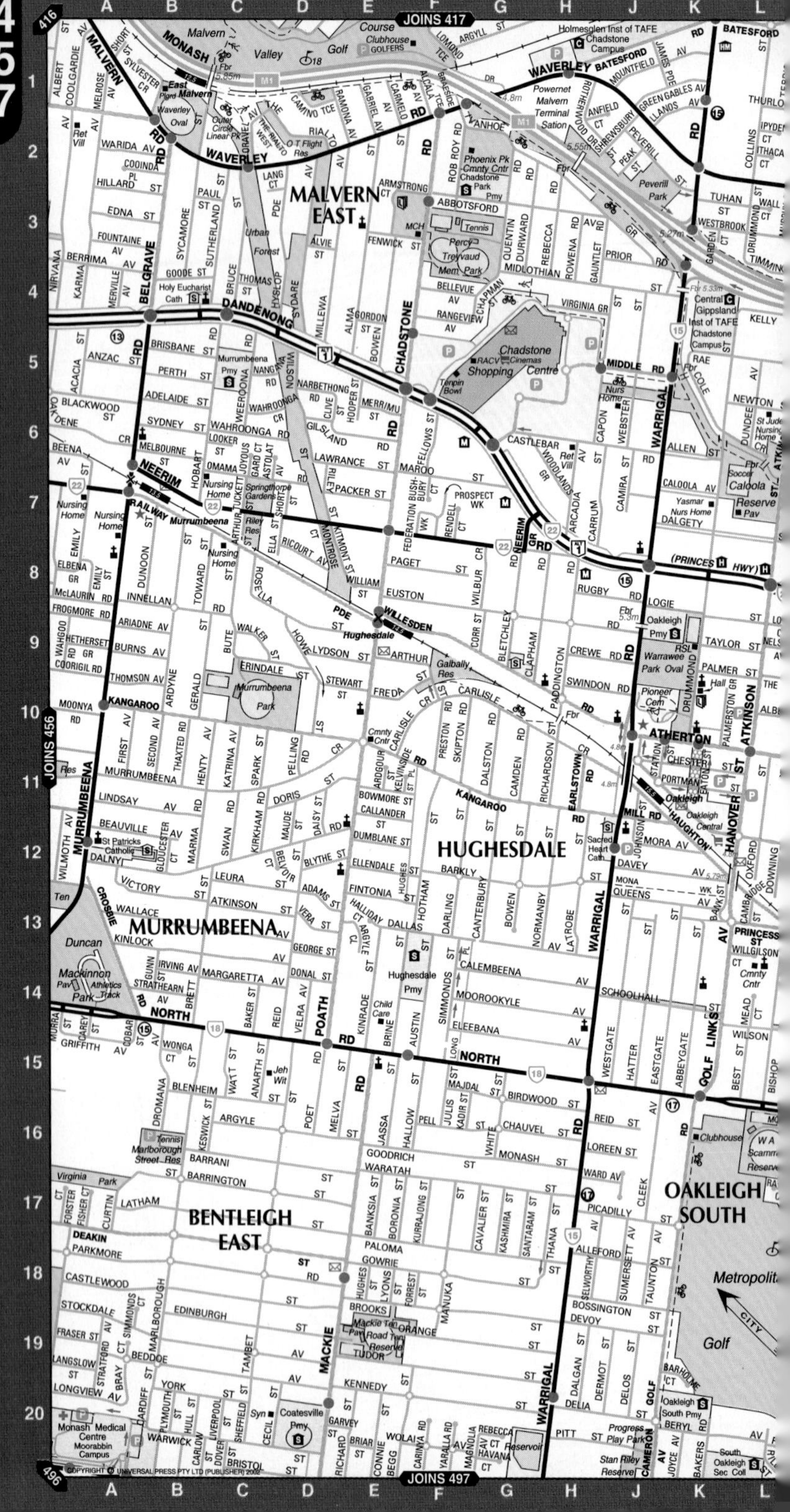
JOINS 417
JOINS 456
JOINS 497
416
496
MALVERN EAST
HUGHESDALE
MURRUMBEENA
BENTLEIGH EAST
OAKLEIGH SOUTH
Malvern Valley Golf Course
Holmesglen Inst of TAFE Chadstone Campus
Powernet Malvern Terminal Sation
Chadstone Shopping Centre
Central Gippsland Inst of TAFE Chadstone Campus
Percy Treyvaud Mem Park
Phoenix Pk Cmnty Cntr
Murrumbeena Park
Duncan Mackinnon Park
Caloola Reserve
Warrawee Park Oval
Pioneer Cem
Mackie Rd Ten Reserve
Monash Medical Centre Moorabbin Campus
Metropolitan Golf
Stan Riley Reserve
WAVERLEY RD
DANDENONG RD
NEERIM RD
NORTH RD
WARRIGAL RD
CHADSTONE RD
POATH RD
MURRUMBEENA RD
BELGRAVE RD
KANGAROO RD
ATHERTON RD
MIDDLE RD
(PRINCES HWY)
GOLF LINKS
HANOVER ST
ATKINSON ST
MACKIE RD
MONASH
COPYRIGHT © UNIVERSAL PRESS PTY LTD (PUBLISHER) 2002

JOINS 418
419
MOUNT WAVERLEY
CHADSTONE
OAKLEIGH
OAKLEIGH EAST
HUNTINGDALE
CLAYTON
Salesian Catholic College
Salesian College Playing Fields
Jordan Reserve
Mayfield Park
Sussex Hts Pmy
Municipal Golf Course
Scotchmans Run Reserve
Amsleigh Park Pmy
Reg Harris Reserve
Hunt Reserve
Princes Highway Reserve
Jack Edwards Res
Huntingdale Golf Course
Army Oakleigh Barracks
Davies Reserve
Clayton West Pmy
Clayton North Primary
Monash Medical Centre
Carlson Avenue Res
Bayview Conference Centre
Mount Waverley Pmy
WAVERLEY RD
PRINCES HWY
(DANDENONG RD)
(MONASH HWY)
FERNTREE GULLY RD
HUNTINGDALE RD
STEPHENSONS RD
CLAYTON RD
FWY
JOINS 459
JOINS 498
499
COPYRIGHT © UNIVERSAL PRESS PTY LTD (PUBLISHER) 2002

A B C D E F G H J K L

JOINS 419

418

MOUNT WAVERLEY

NOTTING HILL

CLAYTON

Industrial Estate

Huntingtower Pmy & Secondary
Valley Reserve
Syndal South Pmy
Melbourne Water Retarding Basin
Waverley Priv Hosp
Holmesglen Inst of TAFE Waverley Campus
CSIRO Petroleum
Pinewood Reserve
Pinewood Pmy
Pinewood Cinema
Tunnel Fairway Reserve
Skateboard Ramp
Bus & Del Centre
England Rd Res
Herriotts Glen Res
Hardwarehouse
Waste Transfer Station
Council Depot
Melbourne Water Notting Hill Service Reservoir
Carlson Avenue Res
Bayview Conference Centre
CSIRO
Deakin University Rusden Campus
Monash Pmy
Monash University Clayton Campus
Sports Area
Marshall Res
Monash Secondary College
Bus Terminal
Main Entrance
FOR MORE DETAIL SEE MAPS 719-720
Monash Sp Dev Sch
Youth Cl
Fregon Reserve
Monash Medical Centre

WAIMARIE DR, VALLEY RD, SHERWOOD RD, WILLIAM, PRINCETOWN RD, KEMP, CHARLTON, ALBERT, WAVERLEY RD, HAMILTON PL, ALEXANDER ST, VIRGINIA, THE HIGHWAY, BRUCE ST, MUMMERY, HAKEA CT, OAKDENE CT, BISHOP CT, COOINDA CT, WAIKTUN CR, BRINE ST, NAGARA CT, MINLYA AV, AMBER GR, GLASSON SQ, DORRINGTON DR, YVETTE PL, CLARKE CT, HUNTINGTOWER RD, WILLS AV, BOND ST, OPHIR RD, LAWRENCE ST, REGENT ST, THAI CT, FLAVIA CT, PERU CT, OXFORD ST, MELVILLE CT, JENNIFER CT, DEVON CT, SCAMMELL CL, KATANDRA CT, MEADOW CT, MUNRO ST, DORGAN ST, FRANCIS ST, MORSHEAD ST, MONTGOMERY AV, TAROONA AV, VASEY AV, WINGATE, SAVIGE AV, DEAN ST, MORRISON CT, GENOA CT, GOULD CT, DOYNTON PDE, SEATON CT, ROWAN CT, LEMON GR, EDNA ST, SOMERS CT, VALENTINE CT, FIANDER AV, MOTT CT, FALCONER, TURNER CT, WEDGE, STABLEFORD, INGLESIDE, FRANKLIN, LILIAN ST, COTSWOLD CT, CROSBY DR, COLEMAN AV, DUNSCOMBE, HUFF ST, PEPPERELL AV, MARBRAY DR, GREENWAYS, THE GROVE, SOUTHACE WK, WINTER WY, THE RISE, AVENDON BVD, TIMBER, SPRING RI, AUTUMN CT, BUNKER CR, HOLMES WY

McNALLY ST, MORLEY ST, ALISON ST, TALBOT, ERICA ST, WAVE, HOWELL AV, HARRY ST, JOANNA CT, WAGSTAFF, RUSSELL CR, GREENHAM CT, CARINYA CT, FRENCH ST, JANFOURD CT, RHONDA ST, BETTY CT, JUDITH CT, JEFFREY ST, ANTHONY ST, BIRDIE, FAIRWAY ST, GRIFFITHS CT, WILGA ST, BYRD CT, TAYLOR CR, NICOLE CT, LEGANA CR, SAMPSON DR, APSLEY CT, GRETNA CT, HIGHCLERE AV, TORRO CT, DUN CT, WALLABAH ST, PINEWOOD DR, YANGOORA CT, COOLARN ST, ILLUKA CR, LEMANA CR, TOOLANG CT, TOOMBAH ST, CENTREWAY, LEMONT AV, GUNTHER CT, DEBORAH CT, ROSS CT, LEICESTER, CHIARA CT, ROB ROY ST, MARGATE ST, BLOSSOM CT, MAGNOLIA CT, GERRARD CT, MARCELLA CT, CAMBRIDGE, PEVERIL CR, DURWARD, SANDGATE, ASCOT CT, BRISTOL CT, CARDIFF CT, SALADIN DR, VANHOE, SETTLER CT, SUTTON CT, HAMPTON CT, FOREST CT, JANICE CT, ABBOT CT, CHIVERS AV, ENGLAND RD, McKELVIE CT, HERRIOTTS, BAKER AV, MAY CT, JAMES CT, COLLEY GR, CALLAGHAN, IVANHOE, HANNAH CL, LOCKENS AV, WEST ST, COPTFIELD CT, WILKINS PL, TULLOCK, THOMAS ARNOLD, MARGARET CT, RAY CL, BVD, WINDELLA

THERESE AV, NAGLE AV, PALMER CT, EXPO CT, HARDNER RD, RICKETTS RD, STEPHENSONS RD, KINGSWOOD, KINGSLEY GR, FORSTER RD, Ilford, LIONEL, AVONHURST, SALISBURY CT, TUDOR CT, BALMORAL CT, NORFOLK, DORSET, McKENNA, AVON CT, BLACKBURN RD, FERNTREE GULLY RD, GILBY, HAMPSHIRE RD, FWY, CITY

CLAYTON RD, BUSINESS PARK DR, COMMERCIAL RD, INDUSTRIAL AV, REDWOOD DR, HILLTOP AV, CARLSON AV, FLORENCE AV, BAYVIEW AV, NORMANBY RD, HOWLEYS RD, ELWOOD CT, FINCH, DARCY CT, TRENT CT, SANIKY, CASSIA ST, SAMADA ST, CAPRI ST, BINGLEY CT, KENTUCKY CT, GRANGE ST, ROSINGS CT, LONGBOURNE AV, WOORAL AV, KARLA CT, DALPURA AV, TAMALA AV, PEMBERLEY DR, AKUNA, WESTERFIELD DR, BERRYDALE CT, TULIP CT, RISDON CT, CHANDOR CT, MERLIN CT, HUNSFORD CT, MARINA, ERAWAN AV, GEDDES, DUNLOP RD

GARDINER, RING RD N, OUTER RING RD W, INNER RING RD W, ENGINEERING RD, UNION LOOP RD, RD N, RING RD S, MARTIN ST, DUERDIN ST, WOODSIDE AV, GLENBROOK, KOONAWARRA, STOCKDALE, MARSHALL, BEDDOE, UNIVERSITY PL, COB PL, HENDERSON RD, NANTILLA, LEXIA, PICKERING

PRINCES HWY, WELLINGTON RD, (MONASH HWY), (DANDENONG HWY), BELEURA GR, ROYALTY ST, PRINCE ST, MYRIONG ST, KUMARA, MANATUNGA, BROWNS CT, SEASCAPE ST, ATLANTIC ST, HOWARD, CANTALA ST, FORTUNA ST, LANTANA ST, TARELLA RD, COBAIN ST, PARKER ST, IRWIN ST, ARNOTT ST, MORTON ST, DENNIS ST, BETTINA ST, CONNAM AV, MURDO RD, HOURIGAN AV, FREGON, KANOOKA GR, BROWNS, IONA, LUKE ST, PANORAMA, EVELYN ST, ADALEIGH CT, TREFOREST DR, DOOGA CT, WINTERTON, WRIGHT ST, CAMBRO, RENVER, SARTON, Proposed Arterial Road, GARDEN, MILES, ANZED CT, PETERS

5.7m, 5.5m, 5.48m, Fbr 5.2m

JOINS 458

498

JOINS 499

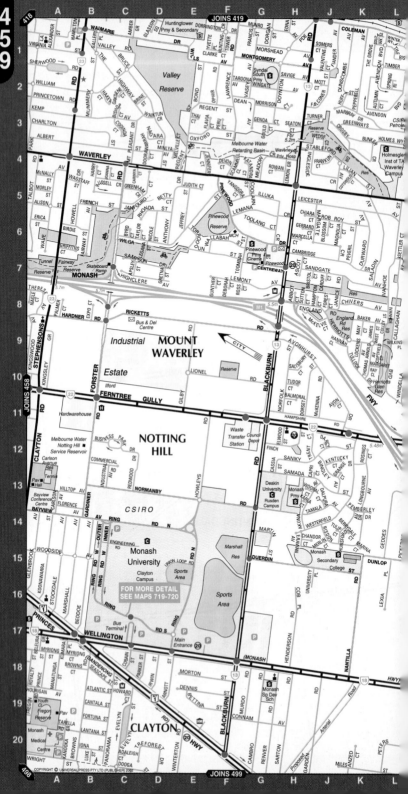

JOINS 420
JOINS 461
JOINS 500
421
501
A B C D E F G H J K L
1 2 3 4 5 6 7 8 9 10 11 12 13 14 15 16 17 18 19
GLEN WAVERLEY
WHEELERS HILL
MULGRAVE
SPRINGVALE RD
WAVERLEY RD
FERNTREE GULLY RD
WELLINGTON RD
MONASH FWY
BRANDON PARK DR
GALLAGHERS RD
WHITES RD
WHITES LA
BLACKBURN
STRADA CR
WATSONS RD
Mount View Primary
Glen Waverley Primary
Glen Waverley South Primary
Brentwood Secondary College
Glen Waverley Sec Coll
Glenallen Spec Sch
St Leonards Cath
Carronbank Sch for the Deaf & Blind
Central Res
Glen Waverley Res
Waverley Football Ground
Athletics Track
Melbourne Water Corporation Resvr
Victoria Police Training Academy
Oak Tree Hill Retirement Village
The Victorian Rehabilitation Centre
Berengarra Spec School
Brandon Office Park
Brandon Park Res
Brentwood Reserve
Wheelers Hill Pmy
Wheelers Hill Secondary College
Brandon Park Secondary College
Good Shepherd Cath
Brandon Park Primary
Lum Reserve
Waverley Meadows Primary
Columbia Park
Mazenod Catholic College
Monash Gardens Units & Hostel
Freeway Reserve
Cmnty Cntr & Sen Cits
Jennings Industrial Estate
Ensign Lab
Bayer Aust Ltd
Renold Aust
Safeway Stores
Civic Cntr Cncl Off
Cmnty Health Cntr
Australian Unity Nursing Home
Glen Waverley
BOGONG
COPYRIGHT © UNIVERSAL PRESS PTY LTD (PUBLISHER) 2002
UBD

420 · JOINS 421 · JOINS 460 · 500 · JOINS 501

A B C D E F G H J K L

1 2 3 4 5 6 7 8 9 10 11 12 13 14 15 16 17 18 19 20

Baseball
Shepherds Bush
Parks Victoria
Nortons Park
NORTONS Ent
Dandenong Valley Parklands
Driving Range
CATHIES Proposed
Wave Chris Colle
Napier Park
WORKS LA
St Pauls Missionary College
LA
Knox City Council Refuse Transfer Station
Shepherds Bush
Parks Victoria
Tennis
18
Waverley Municipal Golf Course
Clubhouse
GLEN WAVERLEY
WANTIRNA SOUTH
Dandenong Ck
Blind Ck
LA
Freeway
WAVERLEY RD
Waverley Womens Sports Centre
Jells East Picnic Area
Pines Picnic Area
Elms Picnic Area
Jells Park
WHEELERS HILL
Jells Lake
Caulfield Grammar
Jells Park Primary
Woolshed Farm Shows
Chesterfield Farm
Farm Ent
Original Homestead
Jells Park South
FERNTREE GULLY RD
Gallery Reserve
Wheelers Hill
Columbia Park
St Justins Catholic Primary
Res
Cumberland View Ret Village
Mulgrave Reserve
Ent
Waverley Pitch & Putt Golf Course
Mini Golf
Dandenong Ck
Dandenong Valley Parklands
Corhanwarrabul Ck
Freeway
WELLINGTON RD
(MONASH HWY)
Gate 1 Gate 2 Gate 3 Gate 4 Gate 5
C D E F G H

KYMME CT, ALMRAY PL, KRISTEN CT, TORWOOD CL, GLEN TOWER DR, GLENVILLE, ALTON CT, CALGARY CT, CRESWICK ST, APPLETREE, LISA CT, LINKS AV, SOLAR CT, WELL ST, CONNAUGHT AV, DR, STANTON PL, ROSS CT, SHEPHERD RD, ATHELDENE, TIERNAN, NARA PL, DR, STRAND CL, MADIGAN CT, GEORGES CT, ASTON HEATH, ST GEORGES, KAWANA CR, CHAPMAN, O'BRIEN CL, WYATT CT, COWRIE, ALLURE CT, MADIGAN, FENTON CT, ROYCROFT, DEVITT CT, NORTHAM DOUBELL, BLVD, PENINGTON, DOMINION, CURRIE, TCE, WENDEN CT, ST, EALING CT, CAMBRIAN, LETCHWORTH, WILTON, THE GLADE, GARRYCK, WALDEN AV, SHELDON, ENFIELD, WALSHAM, SANDHURST CT, CR, DR, STRICKLAND AV, BURBANK, BEAUMONT, DRAPER, FREEMAN ST, HEYSHAM, CLARKE, AVERY CT, BUXTON CT, MORECOMBE DR, MILFORD, KINGS, LYNN PL, PICCADILLY, SUNNYBROOK DR, DARLINGTON AV, HEATHERLEA DR, Tennis, GREENBRIAR AV, WATTLEGLADE CT, PATRICK CT, LATROBE CT, AQUILA CT, REDLEAF WY, BLUEGUM, HERTFORD CR, TRACEY CT, JELLS RD, STRATHCONNAN PL, AJAX DR, HOMESTEAD, GOLDFIELD CT, SUNDOWNER, PETRONELLA, PIONEER, MARY, COLONIAL, PROSPECTOR, ADAM, RODNEY, LEON, DANIELLE, GEORGINA, SAMUEL, ALEX, ADELE, BASIL, PRISCILLA, CHRISTINA, JUNE, AMELIA AV, TROOPER, STOCKADE, SAMANTHA, REBECCA, URSULA, SEAN, LORETTA, IRENE CT, DONALD, BELINDA, AZTEC CT, GUMTREE CL, THE DEVIATION, REMBRANDT, COUNTY CL, REYNOLDS AV, DALI CT, MURILLO, RAPHAEL, RUBENS, FALCON, CREST, PORTOBELLO, BRAEMAR, KINLOCH, KILBURN, PALMERSTON, EATON, CALVIN, DUVAL, SUMMERHILL, OAKBANK, CALDERWOOD, BRUFORD AV, DENE CT, PHOENIX, LIAN, CHIRALEE, THURZA, WENDY, ERSKINE, CHIPPING, KELSO, MALDON, SANDSCAPE, FERNLY, PINEVIEW, ELLSTEAD, GARNETT, FREE, HARLINGFORD, WELLWOOD, HILL, NOVA, DARVELL, LERINA, CRONIA, BRAMLEY, MARYKIRK, RONSTON, CRAIG, PONTFORD, BLADEN, GRANDVIEW RD, JANINA CT, DIANNA, ITALLE, COPE, FEATHERTOP, WYUNA, MENA, SARY, BRONWYN, LE GRAND, NELSE, CANTALA, OLIN, NARRABRI, BELLARA WY, KIM, MILROY, HAVERSHAM, RYRIE, NADIA, GRANTCHESTER, MERRAN, FAYETTE, TANYA, COLUMBIA, YEOVIL CT, ORLI, XAVIER, AVIVA, WOODVIEW, WHALLEY, KENROSS, WESLEY, GALWAY, WOODINGTON, MILL, LUTANA, REDFERN, GERALDINE, CRYSTAL, PARA, GLENCROFT, HILLGROVE, BRACKEN, HILLARD, NERITA, TOURMALINE, MOONSTONE, RATA, MIRIAM, TIKI, WINDMILL, JURY, GRAY, MARSHALL, BATTY, YARDLEY

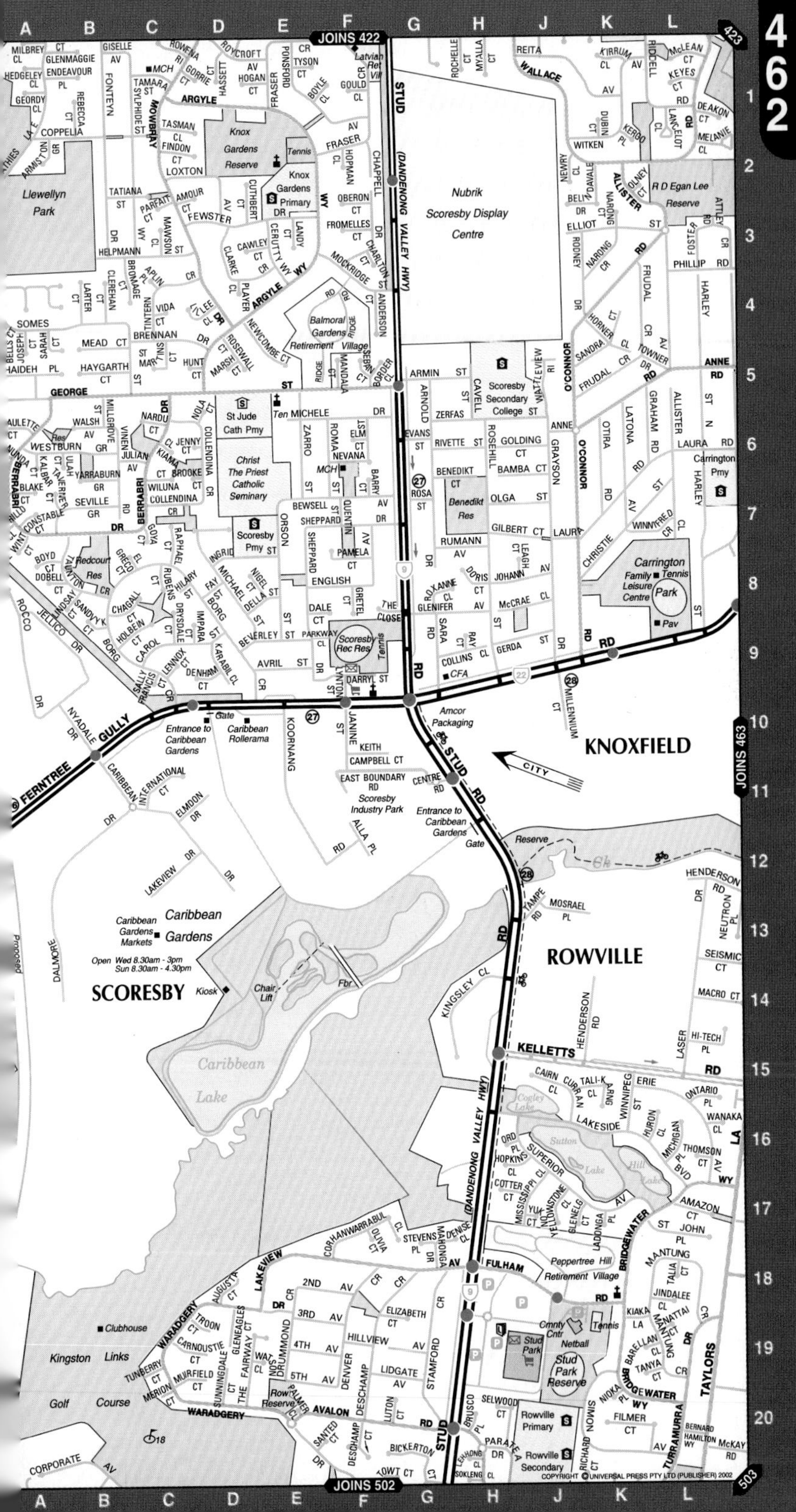
A B C D E F G H J K L
JOINS 422
423
JOINS 463
JOINS 502
503
1 2 3 4 5 6 7 8 9 10 11 12 13 14 15 16 17 18 19 20
Llewellyn Park
Knox Gardens Reserve
Tennis
Knox Gardens Primary
Nubrik Scoresby Display Centre
R D Egan Lee Reserve
Balmoral Gardens Retirement Village
STUD (DANDENONG VALLEY HWY)
ARGYLE
GEORGE
MCH
Latvian Ret Vill
St Jude Cath Pmy
Christ The Priest Catholic Seminary
Scoresby Pmy
Scoresby Secondary College
Benedikt Res
Carrington Pmy
Carrington Family Leisure Centre
Park
Tennis
Pav
Redcourt Res
Scoresby Rec Res
CFA
Amcor Packaging
KNOXFIELD
CITY
Entrance to Caribbean Gardens
Gate
Caribbean Rollerama
Scoresby Industry Park
FERNTREE GULLY RD
STUD RD
Reserve
ROWVILLE
SCORESBY
Caribbean Gardens
Caribbean Gardens Markets
Open Wed 8.30am - 3pm
Sun 8.30am - 4.30pm
Kiosk
Chair Lift
Fbr
Caribbean Lake
KELLETTS RD
Cogley Lake
Sutton Lake
Hill Lake
LAKESIDE
FULHAM
Peppertree Hill Retirement Village
Cmnty Cntr
Tennis
Netball
Stud Park
Stud Park Reserve
Rowville Primary
Rowville Secondary
Clubhouse
Kingston Links Golf Course
Row Reserve
WARADGERY
AVALON
LAKEVIEW
BRIDGEWATER
TAYLORS
TURRAMURRA
CORPORATE AV
COPYRIGHT © UNIVERSAL PRESS PTY LTD (PUBLISHER) 2002

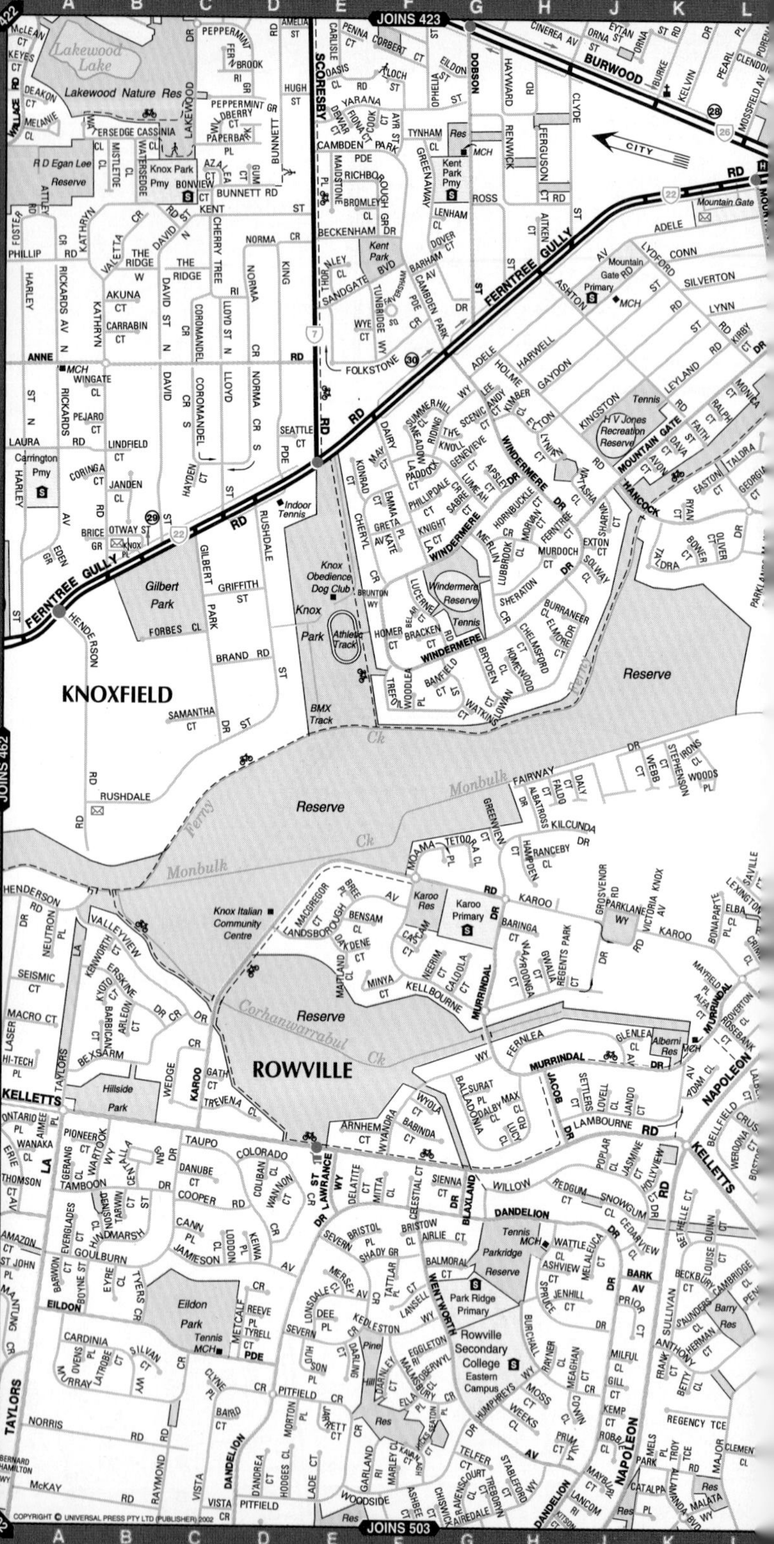

JOINS 423

422

JOINS 462

KNOXFIELD

ROWVILLE

Lakewood Lake

Lakewood Nature Res

R D Egan Lee Reserve

Knox Park Pmy

Kent Park Pmy

Mountain Gate Primary

H V Jones Recreation Reserve

Carrington Pmy

Gilbert Park

Knox Obedience Dog Club

Knox Park

Athletic Track

BMX Track

Windermere Reserve

Reserve

Monbulk Ck

Ferny Ck

Knox Italian Community Centre

Karoo Res

Karoo Primary

Corhanwarrabul Ck

Hillside Park

Albemi Res

Eildon Park

Parkridge Reserve

Park Ridge Primary

Rowville Secondary College Eastern Campus

Barry Res

Pine Hill Res

CITY

SCORESBY RD

FERNTREE GULLY RD

BURWOOD HWY

MOUNTAIN GATE DR

KELLETTS RD

NAPOLEON RD

WINDERMERE DR

MURRINDAL DR

DANDELION DR

WENTWORTH AV

STUD RD

502

JOINS 503

JOINS 424
425
JOINS 465
JOINS 504
505

FERNTREE GULLY

UPPER FERNTREE GULLY

TREMONT

LYSTERFIELD

Ferntree Gully College

Dr Bluett Memorial Plgrd

Ferntree Gully Pmy

Knox Regional Netball Complex

Glenfern Park

Ferntree Gully Recreation Reserve

St Josephs Catholic College

St Johns Cath

Kings Park

Coonara Cmnty Sch

Lakesfield Reserve

Parks Victoria

Burwood Hwy

Lysterfield Rd

Glenfern Rd

Dorset Rd

Blackwood Park Rd

Forest Rd

Ferny Ck

Monbulk Ck

The Boulevard (Fire Trail)

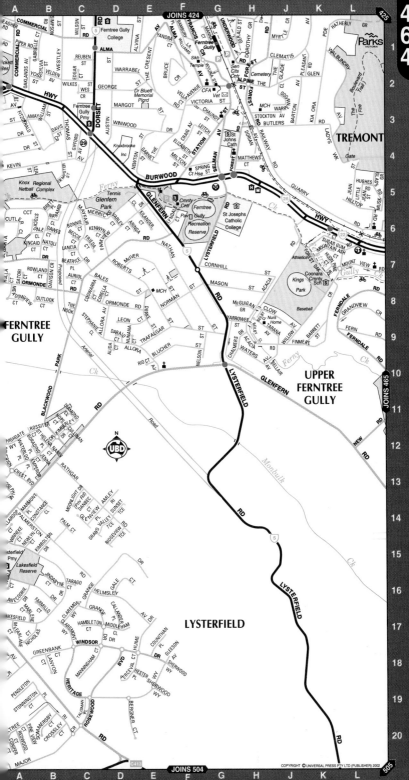

JOINS 425

JOINS 464

JOINS 505

424

504

A B C D E F G H J K L

1 2 3 4 5 6 7 8 9 10 11 12 13 14 15 16 17 18 19 20

FERNY CREEK

Dandenong Ranges National Park (Parks Victoria)

TREMONT

UPPER FERNTREE GULLY

UPWEY

LYSTERFIELD

Acacia Picnic Ground

Janesleigh Dell Picnic Area

Ferntree Gully

Devil's Elbow

Reserve

Upper Ferntree Gully Pmy

Talaskia Res Tennis

Angliss Health Service

Chandler House

Gilmour Park

Archery Club

Belmont Tower

Roma Reserve

Upwey Primary

Upwey High

Upwey South Pmy

Upwey South Reserve

Monbulk Creek Retarding Basin

Lysterfield Lake Park

BURWOOD HWY

MOUNT DANDENONG TOURIST RD

MOUNT DANDENONG RD

MORRIS RD

GLENFERN RD

Sherbrooke Forest
Hackett Break
Moore Break
Monument Track
Wattle Track
Sherbrooke Track
Edgebrooke Tk
O' Donohue Track
Main Ent
POETS LA
SHERBROOKE RD
George Tindale Mem Gardens
BRAESIDE AV
O'Donohue Picnic Ground
LODGE RD
GEORGES RD
BACK RD
Gate
Parks Victoria
OWEN ST
WAKEFIELD LA
MERRIMU LA
Falls Picnic Ground
Falls
Adele Gully
Dandenong Ranges National Park
SHERBROOKE
Tree Fern Tk
Ridge Track
Woodfull Track
Hillclimb Track
Pound Creek
Pound Creek Picnic Ground
Clematis Creek
Tregellas Track
Micawber Park Picnic Ground
A'vard Track
Pole Track
Lipscombe Break
Coles Ridge
Welch Track

SAVILLE ST
GREVILLE RD
SEA VIEW AV
OLD MAIN RD
C415
FERN GR
TOURIST RD
FERNBROOK
FERN AV
BELGRAVE - FERNY CREEK RD
JACKA ST
MACNAMARA ST
HAM RD
GLOVER CT
VICTORIA GR
MAST GULLY RD
ELLIOTT AV
TOORURRONG RD
WOODLEIGH AV
GULLY
FLORENCE AV
OAK AV
LAND AV
SIMMONS ST
CECIL CT
MYRTLE GR
GORDON AV
ANDERSON ST
TERRYS AV
GREY GUM CT
BAY
KINROSS RD
LEPROSA LA
CARRINGTON CT
BLACKWOOD AV
GRANDVIEW CR
HAZEL GR
MENLO AV
MORVEN AV
SANDELLS RD
DURANG RD
ALEXANDER AV
DOUGLAS ST
ACACIA
BRENDA GR
OLIVE GR
THE SERPENTINE
KOOKABURRA AV
PETERS RD
WEDGEWOOD ST
GALLAGHER ST
GULLY CR
GLEN HARROW RD
COLE AV
FOREST RD
KAYE
ALPINE
TINTO GR
PAULINE AV
CLAIR GR
AUSTRAL AV
VIEW RD
Violet Larsen Res
BENNETT AV
ERIC AV
GLEN HARRON
LANGFORD CT
ALEC ST
ROSS ST
FRAME AV
CURRIE AV
KITCHENER
LESLIE ST
C404
BELGRAVE
HAKEA
SOPHIA
NEVADA AV
RUTHERFORD
COLLIER AV
TECOMA
TE-KOI AV
KALULU RD
HILTON
FERGUSON
STANLEY ST
MONBULK RD
CAPORN AV
Reserve
BURWOOD HWY
WALTER ST
FRANCIS ST
ROSE ST
WATTLE AV
ENA
Puffing Billy Station Belgrave
CAMPBELL ST
Tecoma Pmy
WINSCOMBE AV
ROCKSLEIGH AV
DICKINSON
SWANSEA CT
St Thomas More Cath
OLD
STONEY
NATION RD
4.5m
GREENWELL
C412
CLIFFORD GR
Tecoma
LAURIE GR
OAKWOOD LA
ALLANDALE
BAYVIEW
CFA
GEMBROOK RD
COLOMBO
WAIMEA GR
Selby Pmy
MORLEY RD
CFA
HILLSIDE GR
CATHERINE AV
WY
Jeh Wit
SEYMOUR ST
Cameo Cinema & Citizens Advice Bureau
MAIN ST
Belgrave
HAYES PL
MCH
RAILWAY PL
HEATHERMONT AV
Mater Christi College
Puffing Billy ST
GLENFERN CL
DELL
TALBOT ST
GUMS CT
MINTER AV
BENSON
BELGRAVE
DALKEITH CR
CLEMATIS ST
CARRAMAR CR
FAIRY
BURNHAM RD
STATION
EDWARD ST
Tennis Borthwick Pk
FARQUHARSON AV
COLIN AV
CREEK RD
BELGRAVE AV
GEORGE ST
GREY
BEST ST
ROSS ST
AVONDALE
BLAIR
LAUREL GR
PARK DR
MERRIGUM LA
VALE
McNICOL
HAZEL
Belgrave Recreation Reserve
RESERVE RD
MARTIN
KAOLA ST
Belgrave Lake Park
Ent
DR
ARBOR AV
BELGRAVE-HALLAM RD
Dandenong Reservoir
WARATAH
SUNNYHILL RD
APSLEY RD
BROADWAY
PRINCE ST
OLD RESERVOIR RD
FULLER ST
MAPLE AV
BORONIA AV
CEDAR GR
CURRAJONG
BEECH AV
Gate
MT MORTON RD
WATTLE VALLEY RD
Primary
RUNNYMEDE
BELLBIRD ST
HARDHAM ST
JUDKINS
PARK
Monbulk Creek
GLEN
THE CRESCENT
COLBY DR
MANUKA AV
Bush Reserve
Birds Land
BELGRAVE HEIGHTS
HOOD ST
MOUNT
GUMTREE GR
MARAMA RD
LOCKWOOD RD
CRESCENT
Reserve
MILLS
ROW
OSBORNE AV
KESWICK
ZAG
ZIG
ELGIN
VERONA ST
SELBY
MORTON
AVONSIDE
Belgrave Heights Convention Centre
Central Park

JOINS 427

JOINS 466

426

506

JOINS 507

JOINS 428

JOINS 469

JOINS 508
509

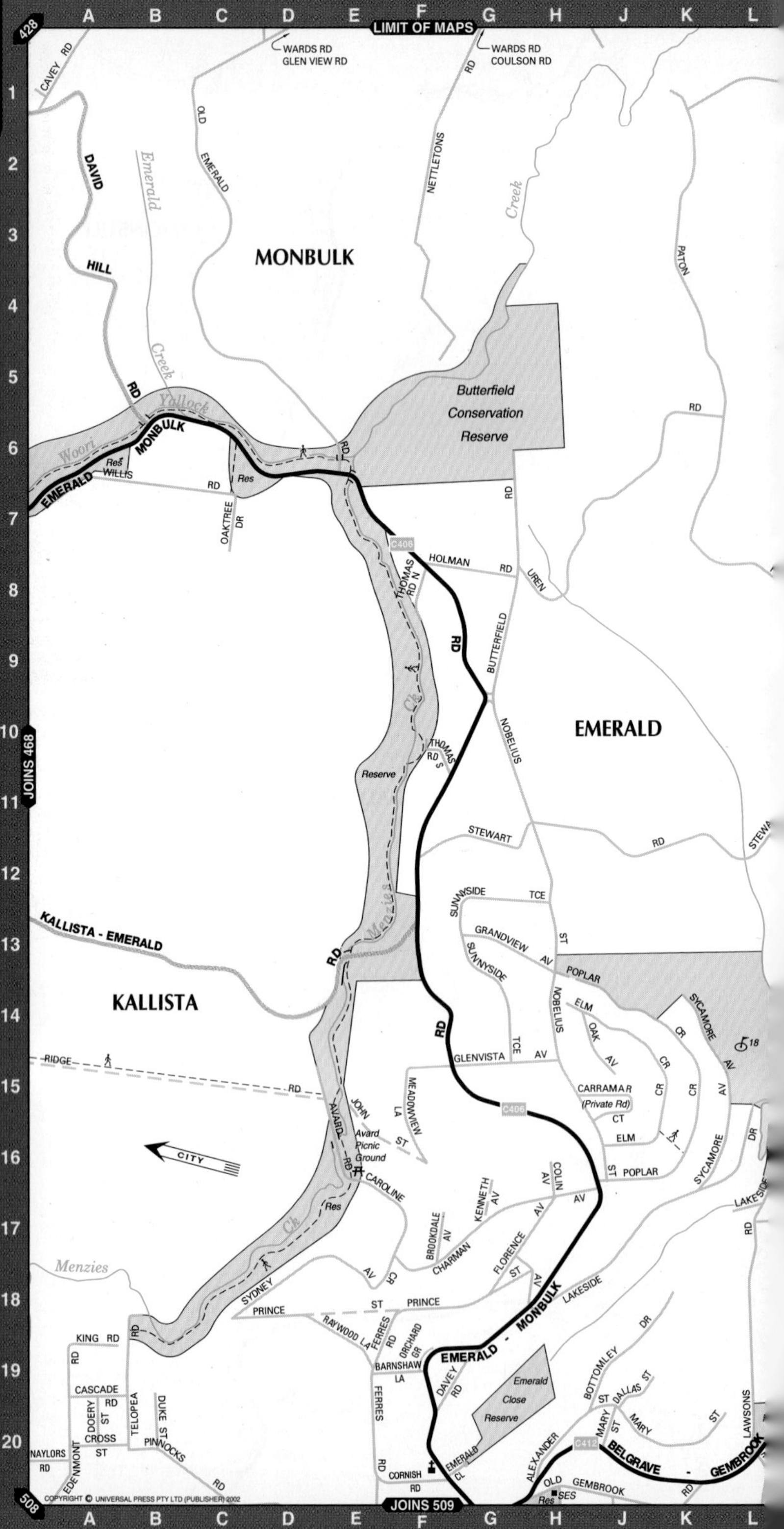

428

LIMIT OF MAPS

JOINS 468

508

JOINS 509

JOINS 471
JOINS 510
511

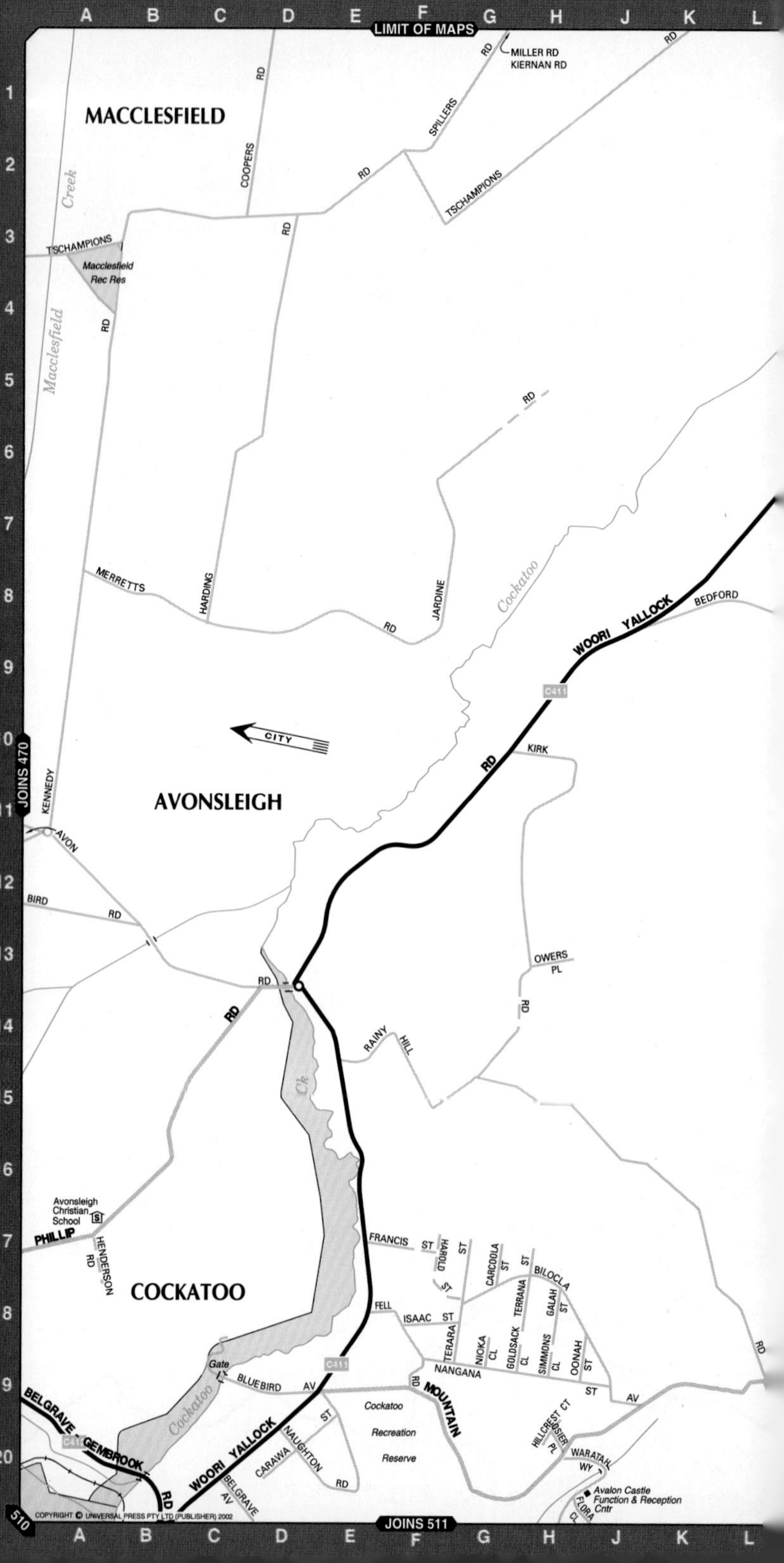

A B C D E F G H J K L

LIMIT OF MAPS

1 2 3 4 5 6 7 8 9 10 11 12 13 14 15 16 17 18 19 20

MACCLESFIELD

AVONSLEIGH

COCKATOO

MILLER RD
KIERNAN RD
SPILLERS RD
COOPERS RD
TSCHAMPIONS RD
Macclesfield Creek
Macclesfield Rec Res
MERRETTS RD
HARDING RD
JARDINE RD
Cockatoo Ck
WOORI YALLOCK RD
C411
BEDFORD
KIRK
CITY
KENNEDY
AVON
BIRD RD
OWERS PL
RAINY HILL RD
Avonsleigh Christian School
PHILLIP
HENDERSON RD
FRANCIS ST
HAROLD ST
CARCOOLA ST
BILOCLA
TERRANA ST
GALAH ST
FELL
ISAAC ST
TERARA
NIOKA CL
GOLDSACK CL
SIMMONS CL
OONAH ST
NANGANA ST
AV
Gate
BLUEBIRD AV
MOUNTAIN RD
Cockatoo Recreation Reserve
BELGRAVE GEMBROOK RD
NAUGHTON ST
CARAWA RD
BELGRAVE AV
HILLCREST CT
OSIER PL
WARATAH WY
Avalon Castle Function & Reception Cntr
FLORA CL

JOINS 470
JOINS 511
510

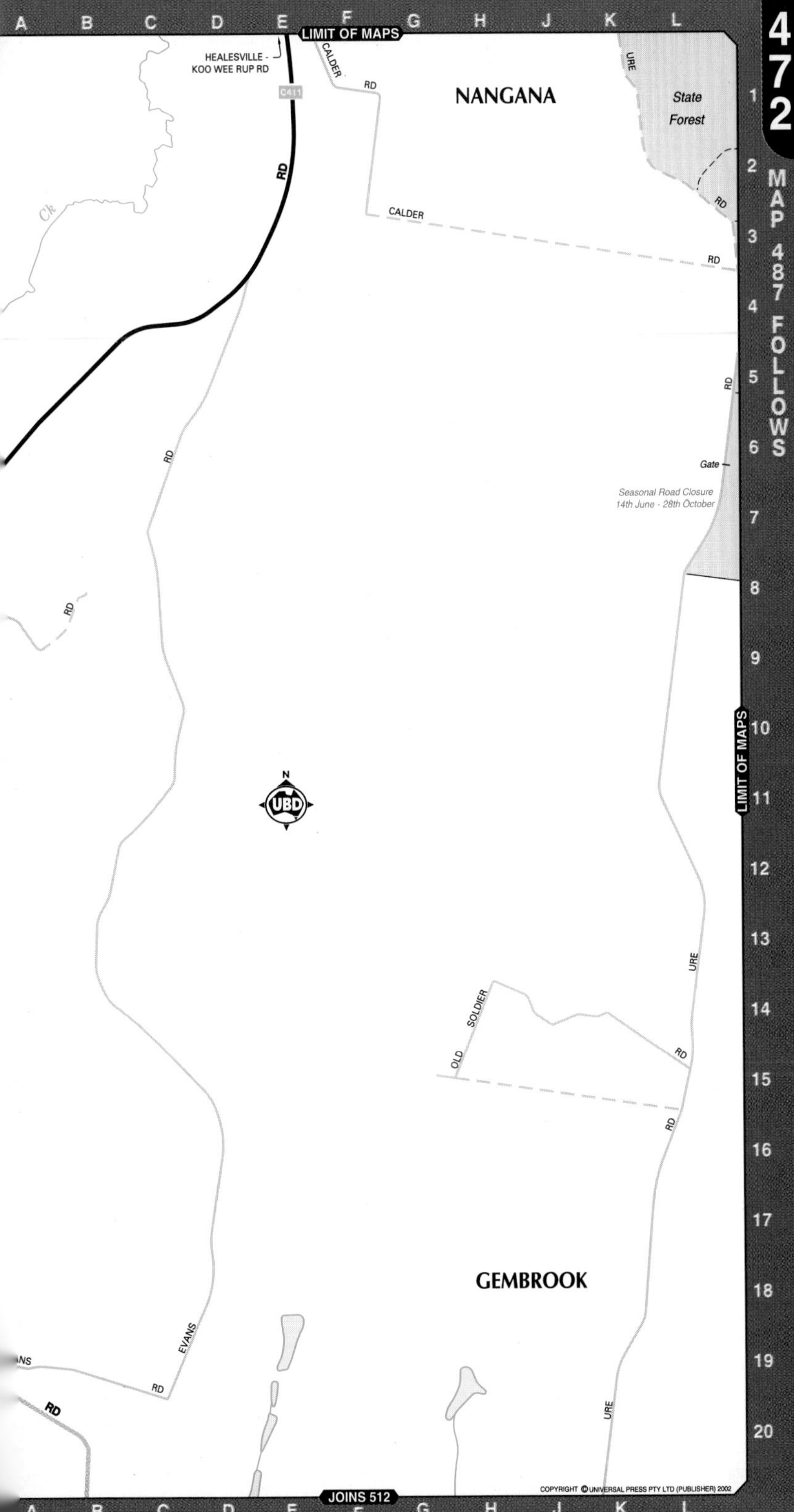

MAP 487 FOLLOWS

PREVIOUS MAP 472

JOINS 447

446

LIMIT OF MAPS

LIMIT OF MAPS

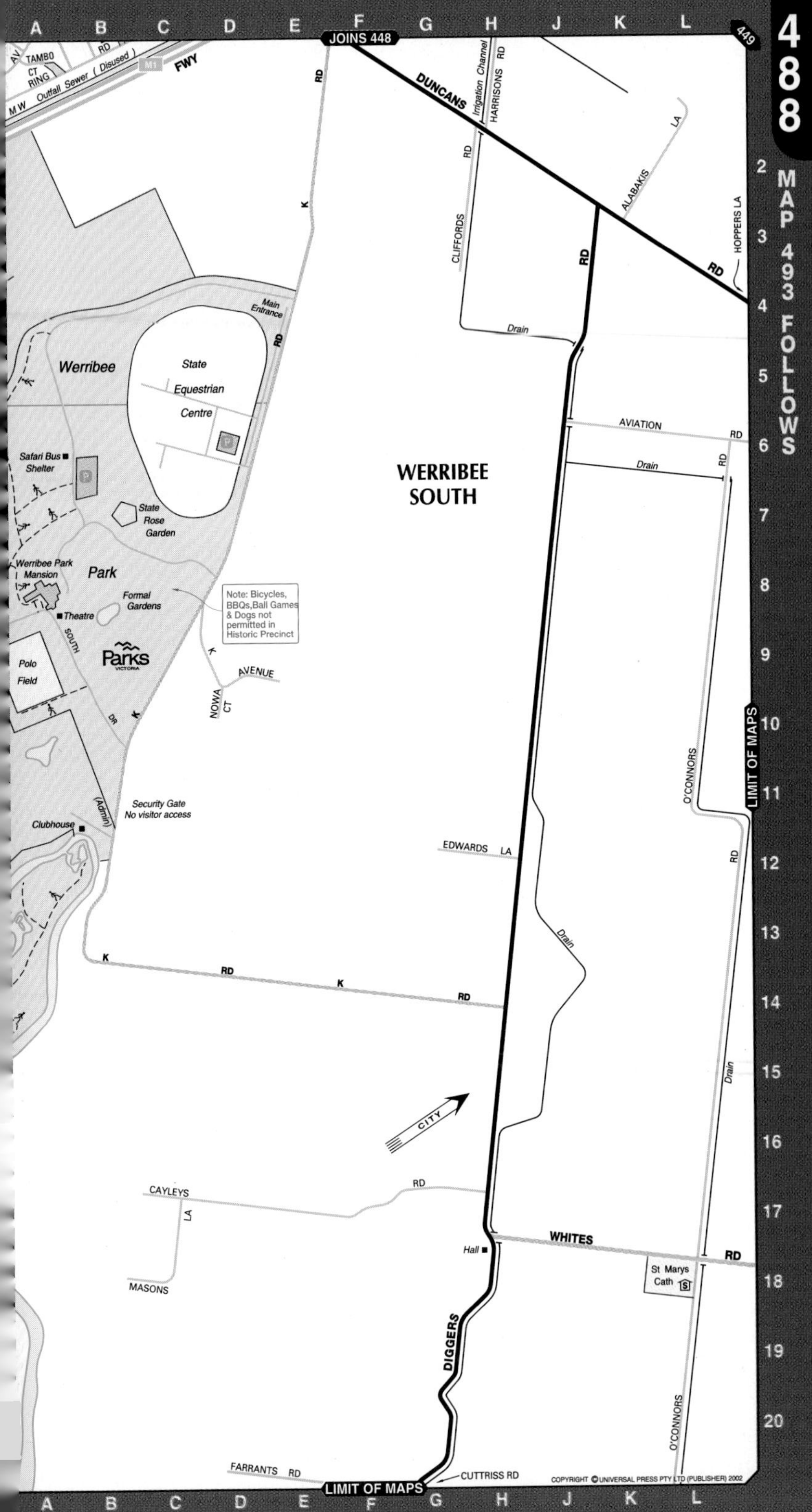
JOINS 448
449
MAP 493 FOLLOWS
LIMIT OF MAPS
DUNCANS RD
HARRISONS RD
Irrigation Channel
CLIFFORDS RD
ALABAKIS LA
HOPPERS LA
TAMBO CT
RING
M W Outfall Sewer (Disused)
M1 FWY
Werribee Park
State Equestrian Centre
Main Entrance
Safari Bus Shelter
State Rose Garden
Werribee Park Mansion
Formal Gardens
Theatre
Note: Bicycles, BBQs,Ball Games & Dogs not permitted in Historic Precinct
Polo Field
Parks VICTORIA
SOUTH DR
(Admin)
Security Gate
No visitor access
Clubhouse
NOWA CT
AVENUE
WERRIBEE SOUTH
AVIATION RD
Drain
EDWARDS LA
K RD
CITY
CAYLEYS RD
LA
MASONS
WHITES RD
Hall
St Marys Cath
O'CONNORS RD
DIGGERS
FARRANTS RD
CUTTRISS RD

PREVIOUS MAP 488

JOINS 453

PORT

PHILLIP

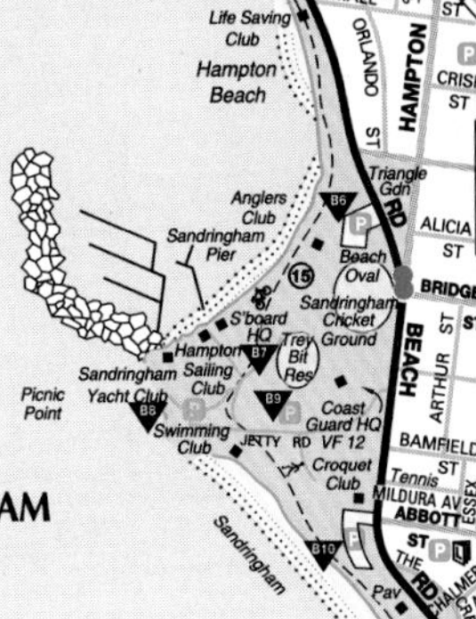

SANDRINGHAM

CITY

THE RD
CHALMERS AV
CRESCENT
Pav
Life Saving Club
Beach

JOINS 495

Bayside City Council Car Park Emergency Locators

A B C D E F G H J K L

JOINS 455

454

1 2 3 4 5 6 7 8 9 10 11 12 13 14 15 16 17 18 19 20

BRIGHTON EAST

Brighton Municipal Golf Course

Brighton Secondary College

Dendy Park

Athletics Track

Victory Park

Bentleigh West Primary

St Leonards Coll

Haileybury Prep College Castlefield

Castlefield Res

Lucas St Reserve

Hanby St Res

HAMPTON

Hampton Primary

R J Sillitoe Reserve

Wishart Reserve

W L Simpson Reserve

Immac Heart of Mary Cath

HAMPTON EAST

Berendale Sp Sch

Glamis Av Res

All Weather Athletic Track

Jack Brockhoff Sports Cntr

Basketball & Netball

Thomas St Res

David St Reserve

Widdop Cr Reserve

G L Basterfield Park

Linacre Private Hospital

Peterson St Reserve

A J Steel Res

R G Chisholm Reserve

Sandringham Pmy

SANDRINGHAM

Sandringham Secondary College

Allambee Park

Sacred Heart Cath

Child Care

Life Saving Club

Sandringham Beach Park

John Batman Gardens

Ten Cts

Sandringham East Pmy

Bay Rd Reserve - Heathland Sanctuary

Firbank Grammar (Co-Ed Junior Campus)

Skate Bowl

Cncl Off

Civic Centre

S'Ham & District Memorial Hospital

Spring St Reserve

Tulip St Reserve

George St Reserve

Sandringham Golf Driving Range

Merindah Park

BLACK ROCK

Red Bluff

Sandringham Municipal Golf Course

Royal Melbourne Golf Course

PORT PHILLIP

HAMPTON ST, BEACH RD, BLUFF RD, CUMMINS RD, NEPEAN HWY, SOUTH RD, DENDY ST, BAY RD, HIGHETT RD, LINACRE RD, BRIDGE ST, WICKHAM RD, ABBOTT ST, TULIP ST, RED BLUFF ST

JOINS 494

JOINS 529

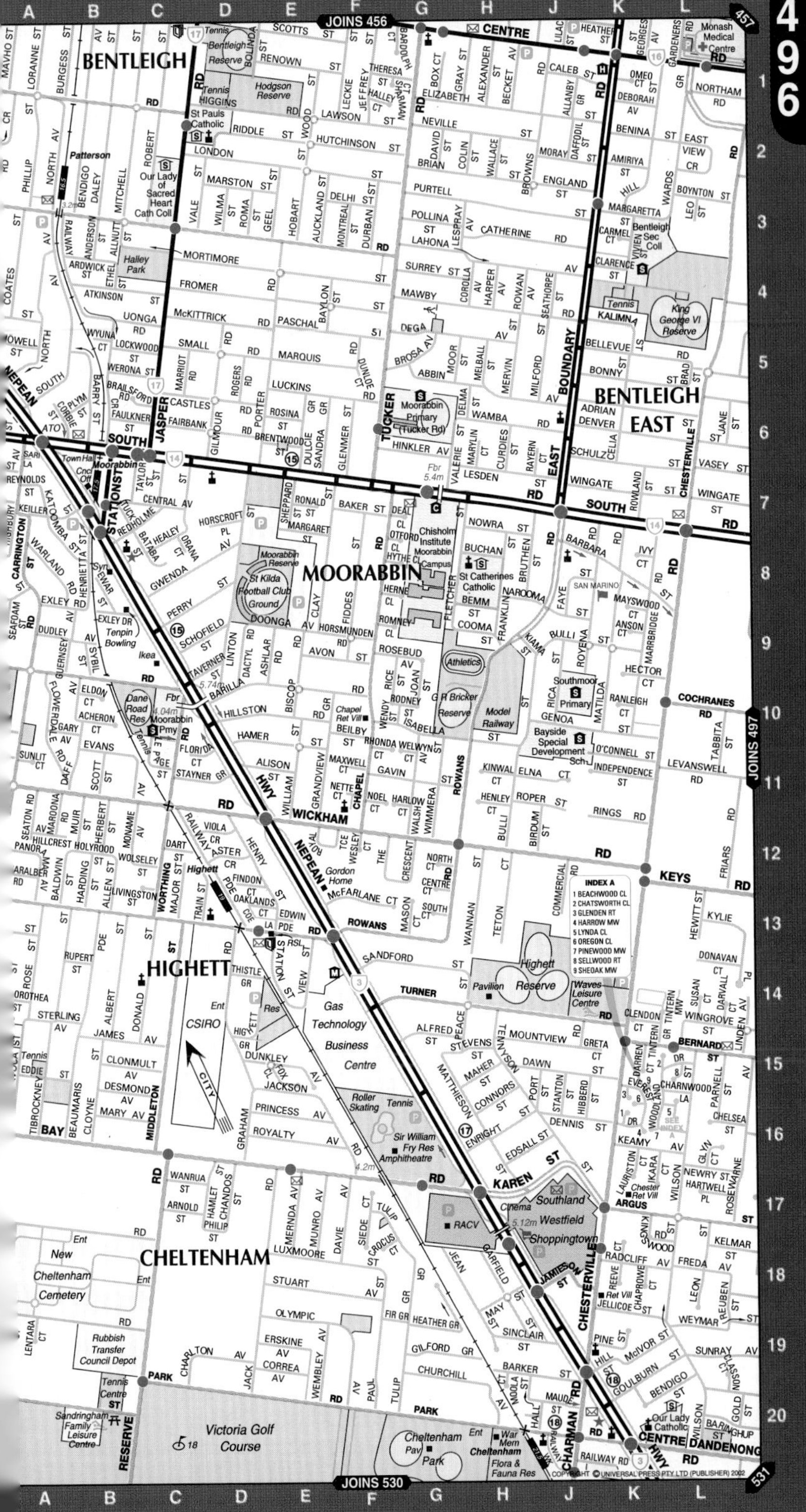

JOINS 456
JOINS 497
JOINS 530
457
531
A B C D E F G H J K L
1 2 3 4 5 6 7 8 9 10 11 12 13 14 15 16 17 18 19 20
BENTLEIGH
BENTLEIGH EAST
MOORABBIN
HIGHETT
CHELTENHAM
CENTRE RD
SOUTH RD
NEPEAN HWY
JASPER RD
BOUNDARY RD
EAST BOUNDARY RD
CHESTERVILLE RD
WICKHAM RD
KEYS RD
BERNARD ST
COCHRANES RD
TUCKER RD
CHARMAN RD
PARK RD
RESERVE RD
BAY RD
KAREN ST
DANDENONG RD
Monash Medical Centre
Bentleigh Reserve
Hodgson Reserve
St Pauls Catholic
Our Lady of Sacred Heart Cath Coll
Halley Park
Patterson
Bentleigh Sec Coll
King George VI Reserve
Moorabbin Primary (Tucker Rd)
Chisholm Institute Moorabbin Campus
St Catherines Catholic
Moorabbin Reserve
St Kilda Football Club Ground
Exley Dr Tenpin Bowling
Ikea
Dane Road Res
Moorabbin Pmy
Athletics
G R Bricker Reserve
Model Railway
Southmoor Primary
Bayside Special Development Sch.
SAN MARINO
Chapel Ret Vill
Gordon Home
Highett Reserve
Pavilion
Waves Leisure Centre
CSIRO
CITY
Gas Technology Business Centre
Roller Skating
Tennis
Sir William Fry Res Amphitheatre
RACV
Southland Westfield Shoppingtown
Cinema
Chester Ret Vill
New Cheltenham Cemetery
Rubbish Transfer Council Depot
Sandringham Family Leisure Centre
Victoria Golf Course
Cheltenham Pav Park
War Mem Cheltenham
Flora & Fauna Res
Our Lady Catholic
Reeve Ret Vill
INDEX A
1 BEACHWOOD CL
2 CHATSWORTH CL
3 GLENDEN RT
4 HARROW MW
5 LYNDA CL
6 OREGON CL
7 PINEWOOD MW
8 SELLWOOD RT
9 SHEOAK MW
SEE INDEX A
COPYRIGHT © UNIVERSAL PRESS PTY LTD (PUBLISHER) 2002

JOINS 457
JOINS 496
JOINS 531
456
530
A B C D E F G H J K L
1 2 3 4 5 6 7 8 9 10 11 12 13 14 15 16 17 18 19 20
BENTLEIGH EAST
MOORABBIN
HEATHERTON
CHELTENHAM
CENTRE RD
SOUTH RD
WARRIGAL RD
WARRIGAL HWY
KINGSTON RD
OLD DANDENONG RD
CENTRE DANDENONG RD
BOURKE
COCHRANES
KEYS RD
Monash Medical Centre Moorabbin Campus
Centenary Park
St James Catholic College
Warrawee Nursing Home
St Peters Catholic
Oakmoor Nursing Home
Stan Riley Reserve BMX Track
South Oakleigh Secondary College
Vic Roads
Commonwealth Golf Course
Yarra Yarra Golf Course
Dales Park
Moorabbin Heights Primary
Proposed Golf Park Driving Range
Retarding Basin
Heatherton Terminal Station
Karkarook Park
Parks Victoria
Riding Area For Disabled
Trotting
Barkers St Reserve
Bus Depot
Keys Road Reserve
South East Water & UNITED Energy Customer Service Centres
RACV Accident Repairs
Cavendish Mews Ret Vill
Cheltenham Secondary College
Kingston Centre & Rehabilitation
Kingston Heath Golf Course
Le Page Park
Le Page Pmy
Kingston Heath Retirement Village
Melbourne Water Retarding Basin
Kingston Heath Primary
Cheltenham East Primary
Kingston Heath Hockey
Ron Brownless Pavilion Reserve
Retirement Village
COPYRIGHT © UNIVERSAL PRESS PTY LTD (PUBLISHER) 2002

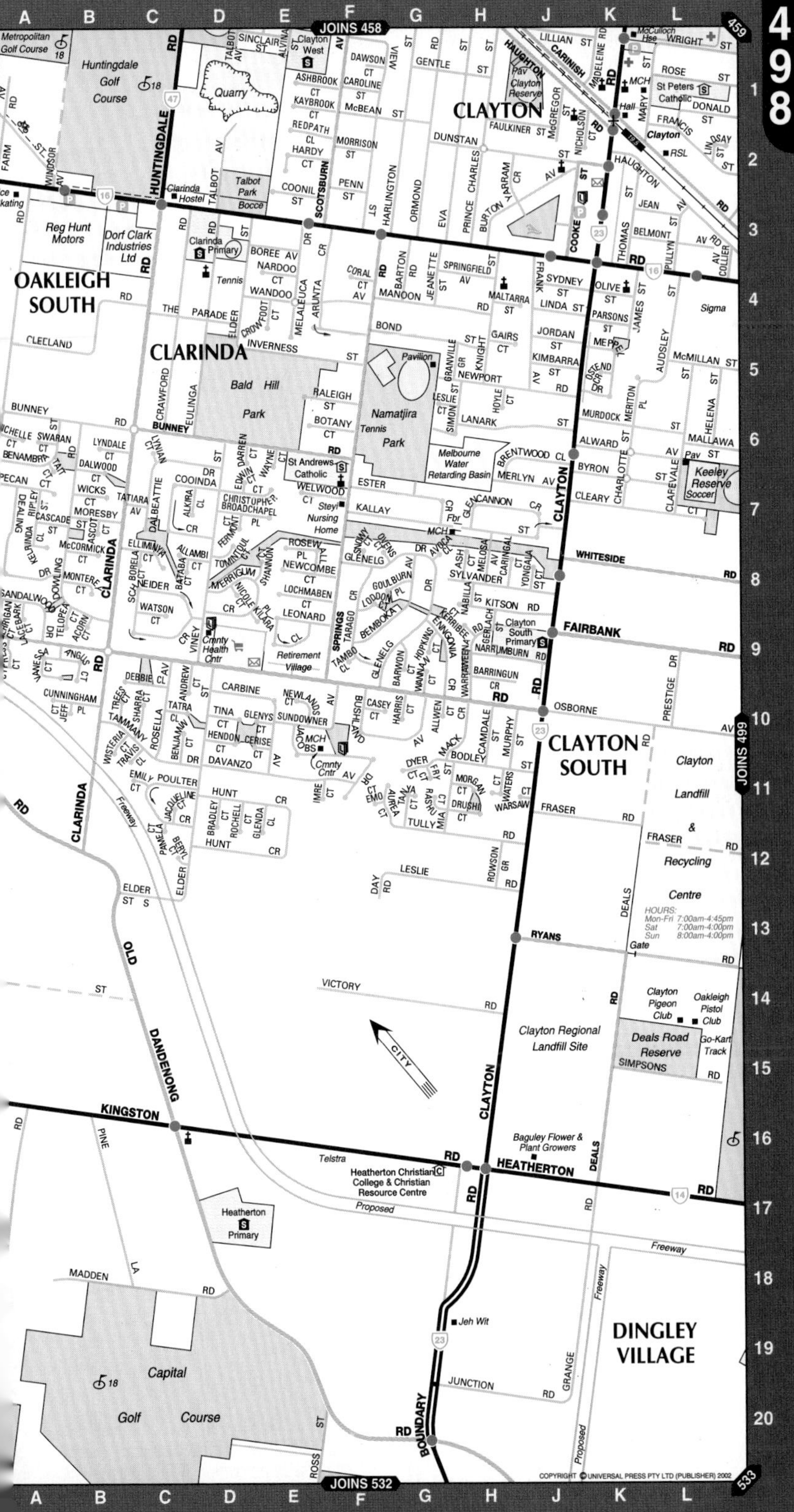
JOINS 458
JOINS 499
JOINS 532
459
533
CLAYTON
OAKLEIGH SOUTH
CLARINDA
CLAYTON SOUTH
DINGLEY VILLAGE
Huntingdale Golf Course
Metropolitan Golf Course
Bald Hill Park
Namatjira Park
Clayton Landfill & Recycling Centre
Clayton Regional Landfill Site
Deals Road Reserve
Capital Golf Course
Keeley Reserve Soccer
Heatherton Christian College & Christian Resource Centre
Heatherton Primary
Baguley Flower & Plant Growers
KINGSTON RD
HEATHERTON RD
CLAYTON RD
OLD DANDENONG RD
CLARINDA RD
HUNTINGDALE RD
BOUNDARY RD
WHITESIDE RD
FAIRBANK RD
OSBORNE AV
RYANS RD
DEALS RD
CENTRE RD

A B C D E F G H J K L

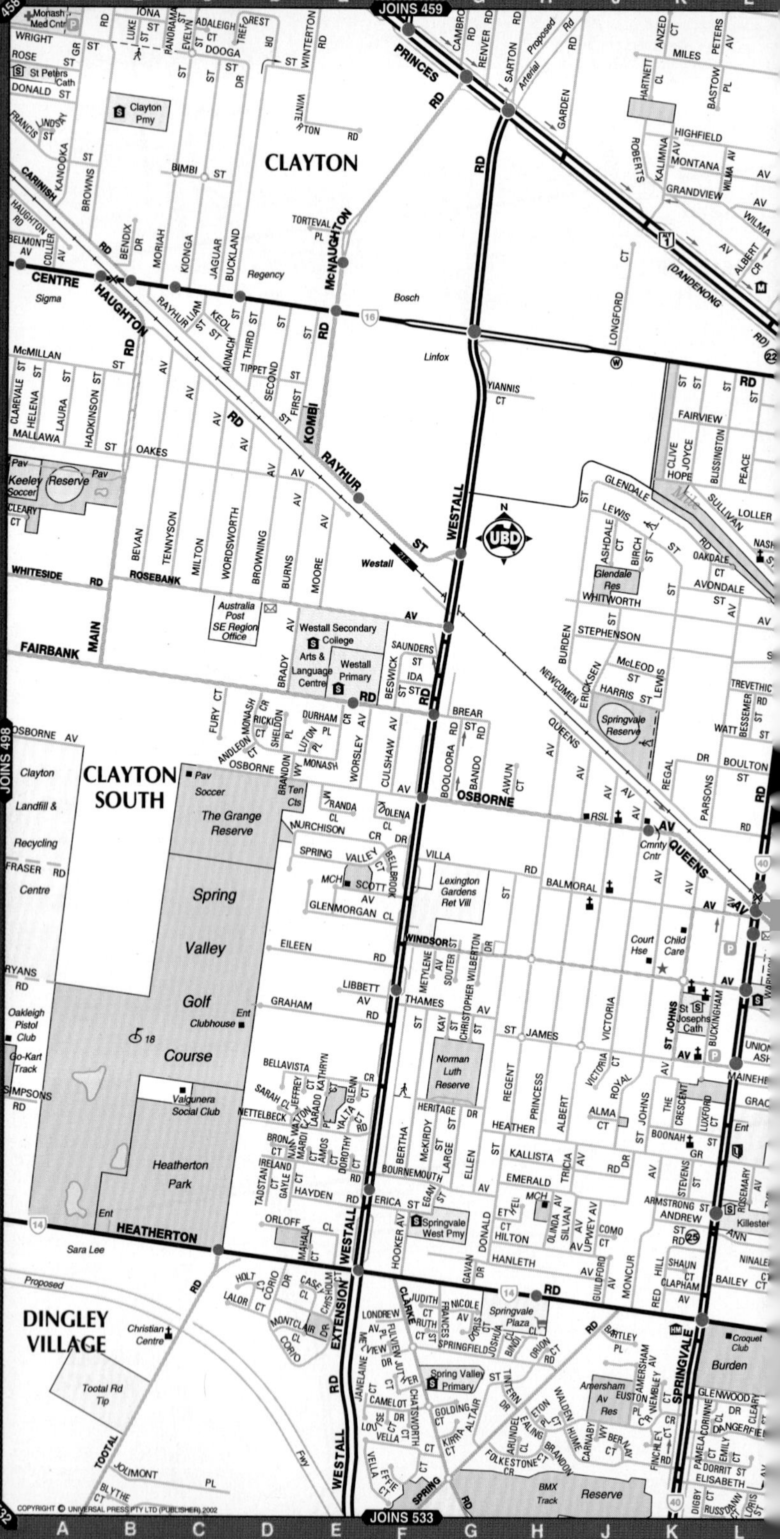

JOINS 459

458

CLAYTON

CLAYTON SOUTH

DINGLEY VILLAGE

Monash Med Cntr
St Peters Cath
Clayton Pmy
Regency
Bosch
Sigma
Linfox
Westall
Keeley Reserve
Soccer
Pav
Australia Post SE Region Office
Westall Secondary College
Arts & Language Centre
Westall Primary
Clayton Landfill & Recycling Centre
The Grange Reserve
Soccer
Ten Cts
Spring Valley Golf Course
Clubhouse
Ent
Oakleigh Pistol Club
Go-Kart Track
Valgunera Social Club
Heatherton Park
Sara Lee
Christian Centre
Tootal Rd Tip
Lexington Gardens Ret Vill
Norman Luth Reserve
Springvale West Pmy
Springvale Plaza
Spring Valley Primary
Glendale Res
Springvale Reserve
RSL
Cmnty Cntr
Court Hse
Child Care
St Josephs Cath
Amersham Av Res
Croquet Club
Burden
BMX Track
Reserve
Killester

PRINCES RD
CENTRE RD
HAUGHTON RD
RAYHUR ST
KOMBI RD
McNAUGHTON RD
WESTALL RD
WESTALL RD EXTENSION
FAIRBANK RD
WHITESIDE RD
MAIN RD
OSBORNE AV
HEATHERTON RD
SPRINGVALE RD
QUEENS AV
DANDENONG RD
TOOTAL RD
CLARKE RD
WINDSOR AV
THAMES AV
LIBBETT AV
GRAHAM RD
EILEEN RD
BALMORAL AV
ST JOHNS AV
GLENDALE RD
CLAYTON RD
LONGFORD CT
MOORE AV
BURNS AV
BROWNING AV
WORDSWORTH AV
MILTON AV
TENNYSON AV
BEVAN AV
ROSEBANK AV
OAKES AV
FRASER RD
RYANS RD
SIMPSONS RD
JOLIMONT PL
BLYTHE CT

JOINS 498

JOINS 533

532

1 2 3 4 5 6 7 8 9 10 11 12 13 14 15 16 17 18 19 20

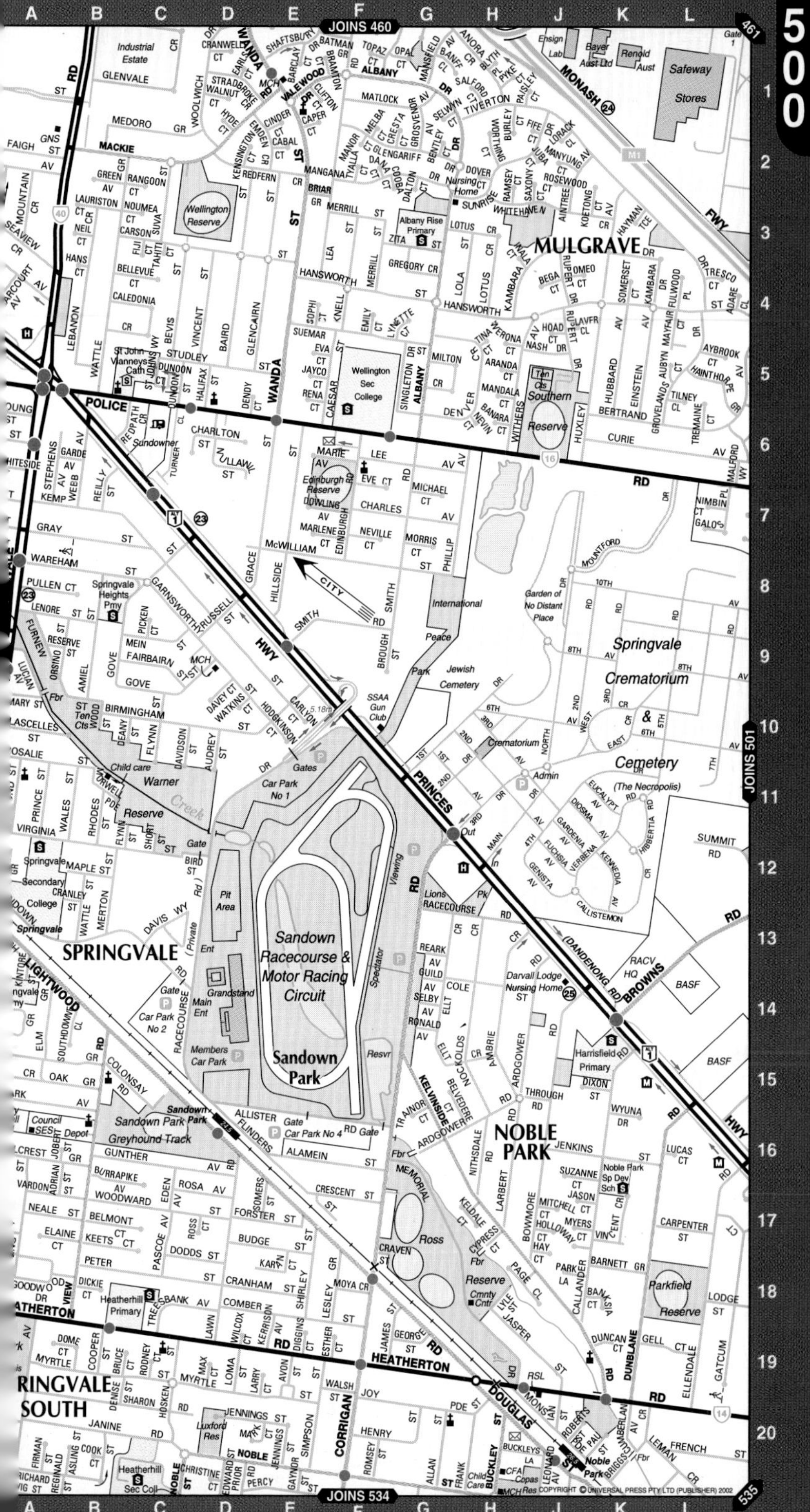
JOINS 460
461
MULGRAVE
SPRINGVALE
NOBLE PARK
SPRINGVALE SOUTH
Sandown Racecourse & Motor Racing Circuit
Sandown Park
Springvale Crematorium & Cemetery (The Necropolis)
Garden of No Distant Place
International Peace Park
Jewish Cemetery
Wellington Sec College
Wellington Reserve
Southern Reserve
Edinburgh Reserve
Warner Reserve
Sandown Park Greyhound Track
Ross Reserve
Parkfield Reserve
Safeway Stores
PRINCES HWY
POLICE RD
HEATHERTON RD
MONASH FWY
DANDENONG RD
BROWNS RD
JOINS 501
JOINS 534
535

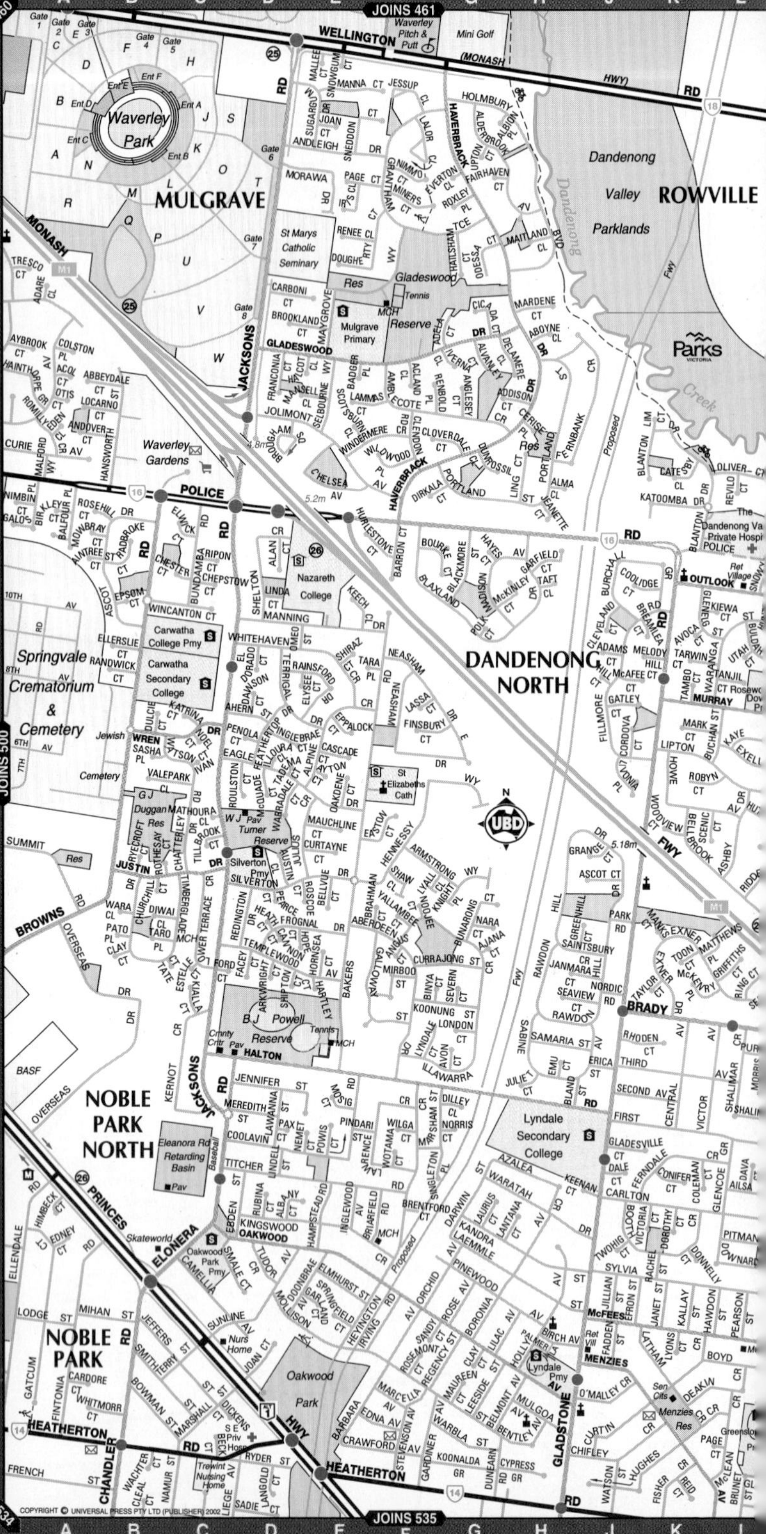

460
JOINS 461
JOINS 500
JOINS 535
534

A B C D E F G H J K L

1 2 3 4 5 6 7 8 9 10 11 12 13 14 15 16 17 18 19 20

MULGRAVE

ROWVILLE

DANDENONG NORTH

NOBLE PARK NORTH

NOBLE PARK

Waverley Park

Waverley Gardens

Waverley Pitch & Putt

Mini Golf

Dandenong Valley Parklands

Parks Victoria

Dandenong Creek

St Marys Catholic Seminary

Gladeswood Reserve

Mulgrave Primary

Nazareth College

Carwatha College Pmy

Carwatha Secondary College

Springvale Crematorium & Cemetery

Jewish Cemetery

St Elizabeths Cath

G J Duggan Res

W J Turner Reserve

Silverton Pmy

B J Powell Reserve

Cmnty Cntr

Eleanora Rd Retarding Basin

BASF

Lyndale Secondary College

Lyndale Pmy

Oakwood Park Pmy

Oakwood Park

Skateworld

Nurs Home

Trewint Nursing Home

S E Priv Hosp

Menzies Res

Sen Cits

The Dandenong Valley Private Hospital

Ret Village

WELLINGTON RD (MONASH HWY)

MONASH FWY M1

POLICE RD

JACKSONS RD

HAVERBRACK AV

GLADESWOOD DR

MURRAY RD

BRADY RD

PRINCES HWY

HEATHERTON RD

GLADSTONE RD

CHANDLER RD

BROWNS RD

ELONERA RD

HALTON RD

MENZIES AV

McFEES RD

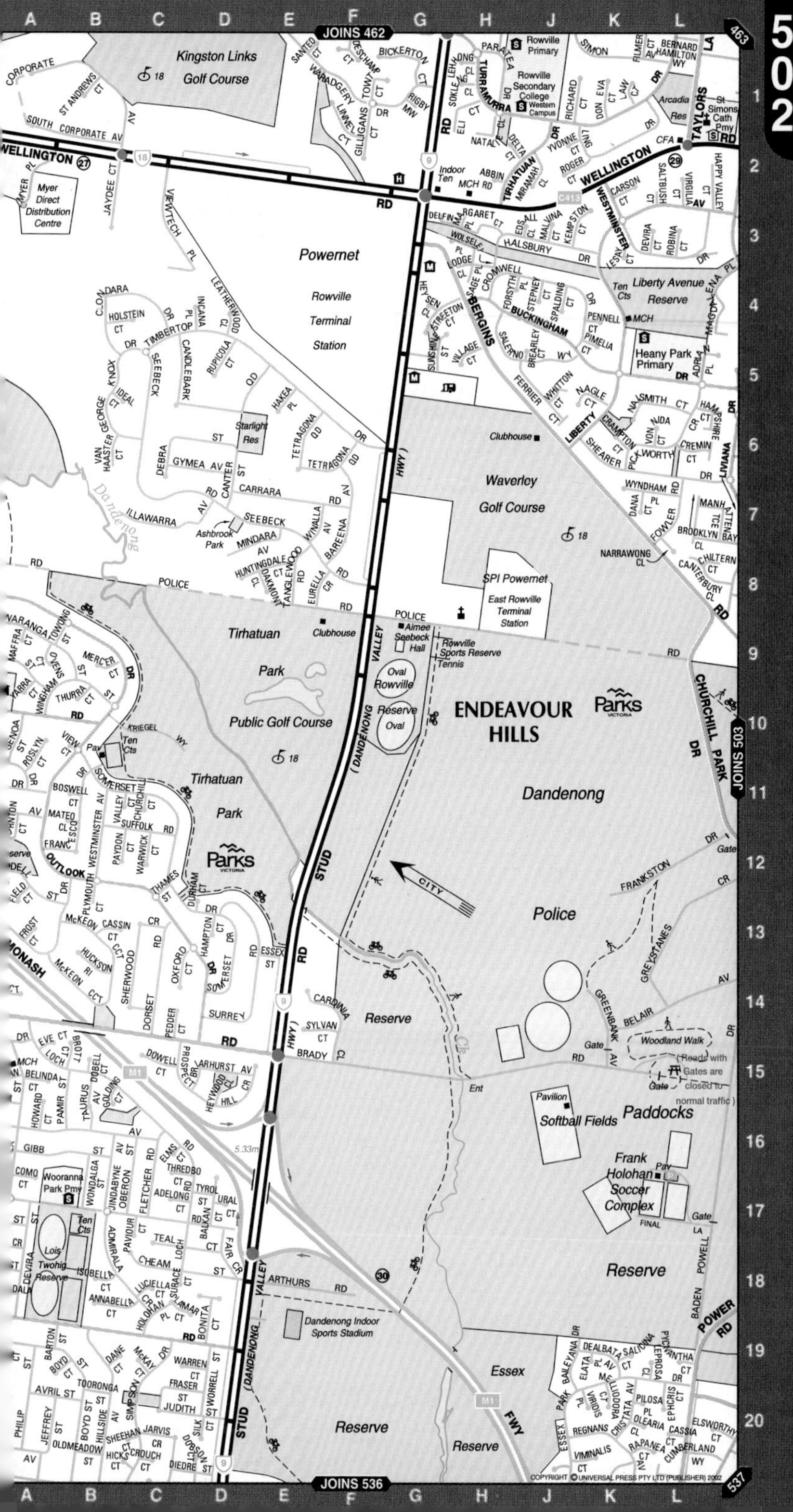

JOINS 462
JOINS 463
JOINS 503
JOINS 536
JOINS 537
Kingston Links Golf Course
WELLINGTON RD
Myer Direct Distribution Centre
Powernet Rowville Terminal Station
Rowville Primary
Rowville Secondary College Western Campus
Indoor Ten
Arcadia Res
St Simons Cath Pmy
Liberty Avenue Reserve
Heany Park Primary
Starlight Res
Ashbrook Park
Dandenong
Waverley Golf Course
SPI Powernet East Rowville Terminal Station
Clubhouse
POLICE RD
Tirhatuan Park
Public Golf Course
Aimee Seebeck Hall
Rowville Sports Reserve
Tennis
Oval Rowville Reserve Oval
ENDEAVOUR HILLS
Parks VICTORIA
Dandenong Police Paddocks Reserve
(DANDENONG VALLEY HWY)
STUD RD
CITY
CHURCHILL PARK DR
Woodland Walk
(Roads with Gates are closed to normal traffic)
Pavilion Softball Fields
Frank Holohan Soccer Complex
Wooranna Park Pmy
Lois Twohig Reserve
Dandenong Indoor Sports Stadium
Essex Reserve
M1 FWY
MONASH
POWER RD
5.33m
COPYRIGHT © UNIVERSAL PRESS PTY LTD (PUBLISHER) 2002
A B C D E F G H J K L
1 2 3 4 5 6 7 8 9 10 11 12 13 14 15 16 17 18 19 20

JOINS 463

JOINS 502

ROWVILLE

LYSTERFIELD SOUTH

ENDEAVOUR HILLS

Churchill National Park

Churchill Park Golf Course

Heany Park Knox District Scout & Guide Camp

Lysterfield Hills Lookout

John Strover Res

Albert E Temple Reserve

Sydney Pargeter Rec Res

Police Paddocks

Quarry

(Roads with Gates are closed to normal traffic)

WELLINGTON RD

NAPOLEON RD

CHURCHILL PARK DR

KENNINGTON PARK

GLENEAGLES

MOSSGIEL PARK DR

POWER RD

HEANY PARK RD

JOINS 537

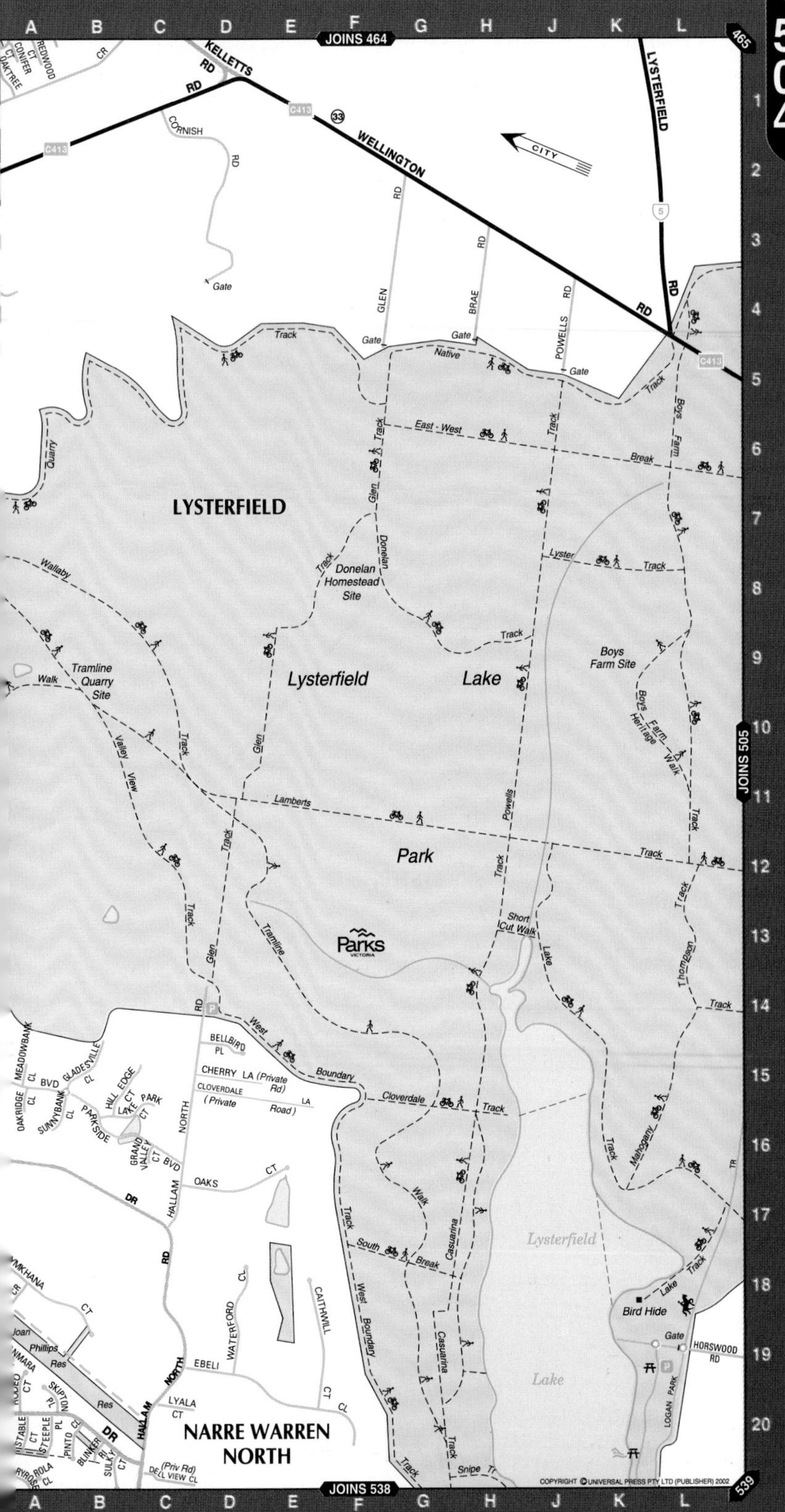
JOINS 464
JOINS 505
JOINS 538
465
539
LYSTERFIELD
Lysterfield Lake Park
NARRE WARREN NORTH
KELLETTS RD
WELLINGTON RD
LYSTERFIELD RD
CORNISH RD
GLEN RD
BRAE RD
POWELLS RD
CITY
Gate
Native Track
East - West Break
Glen Track
Donelan Track
Donelan Homestead Site
Lyster Track
Boys Farm Track
Boys Farm Site
Boys Farm Heritage Walk
Wallaby Walk
Quarry
Tramline Quarry Site
Valley View Track
Lamberts Track
Powells Track
Short Cut Walk
Lake Track
Tramline
Parks Victoria
West Boundary
Cloverdale Track
Thompson Track
Mahogany Track
Casuarina Track
South Break
Walk
Snipe Tr
Lysterfield Lake
Bird Hide
HORSWOOD RD
LOGAN PARK
BELLBIRD PL
CHERRY LA (Private Rd)
CLOVERDALE LA (Private Road)
NORTH HALLAM RD
OAKS CT
MEADOWBANK CL
GLADESVILLE BVD
OAKRIDGE CL
SUNNYBANK CL
HILL EDGE CT
LAKE PARK CT
PARKSIDE
GRAND VALLEY BVD
DR
WATERFORD CL
CAITHWILL CT
EBELI
LYALA CT
HALLAM DR
(Priv Rd) DELL VIEW CL
COPYRIGHT © UNIVERSAL PRESS PTY LTD (PUBLISHER) 2002

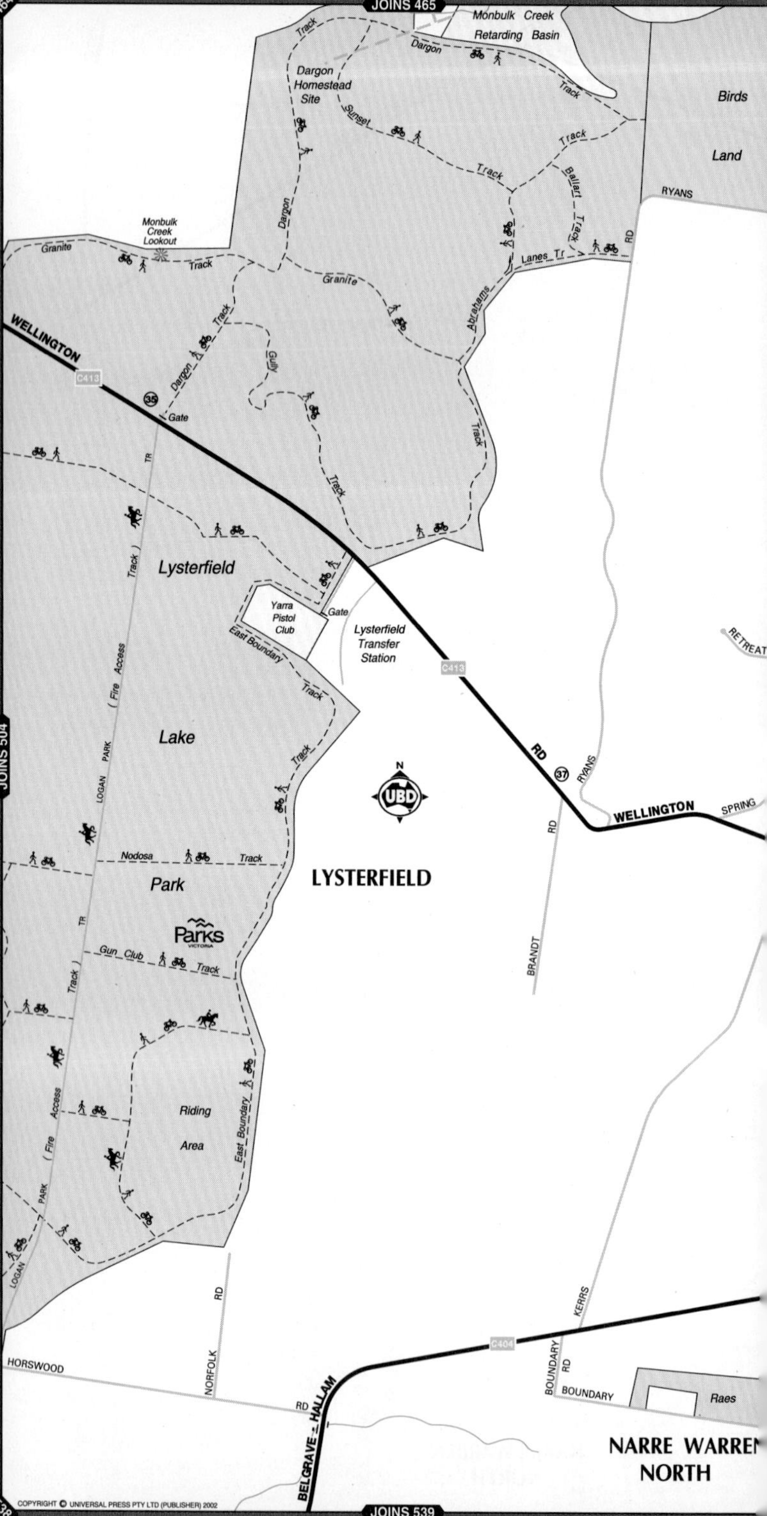

464
JOINS 465
JOINS 504
538
JOINS 539

A B C D E F G H J K L

Monbulk Creek Retarding Basin
Dargon Track
Dargon Homestead Site
Sunset Track
Birds Land
Ballart Track
RYANS RD
Monbulk Creek Lookout
Granite Track
Lanes Tr
Abrahams Track
WELLINGTON
C413
Dargon Track
Gully Track
Gate
35
LOGAN PARK TR
Lysterfield Lake Park
Yarra Pistol Club
Gate
Lysterfield Transfer Station
East Boundary Track
RETREAT
RD
37
RYANS
WELLINGTON
SPRING
(Fire Access Track)
Nodosa Track
LYSTERFIELD
BRANDT RD
Parks VICTORIA
Gun Club Track
Riding Area
East Boundary
NORFOLK RD
KERRS
HORSWOOD RD
C404
BOUNDARY RD
BOUNDARY
Raes
BELGRAVE – HALLAM
NARRE WARREN NORTH

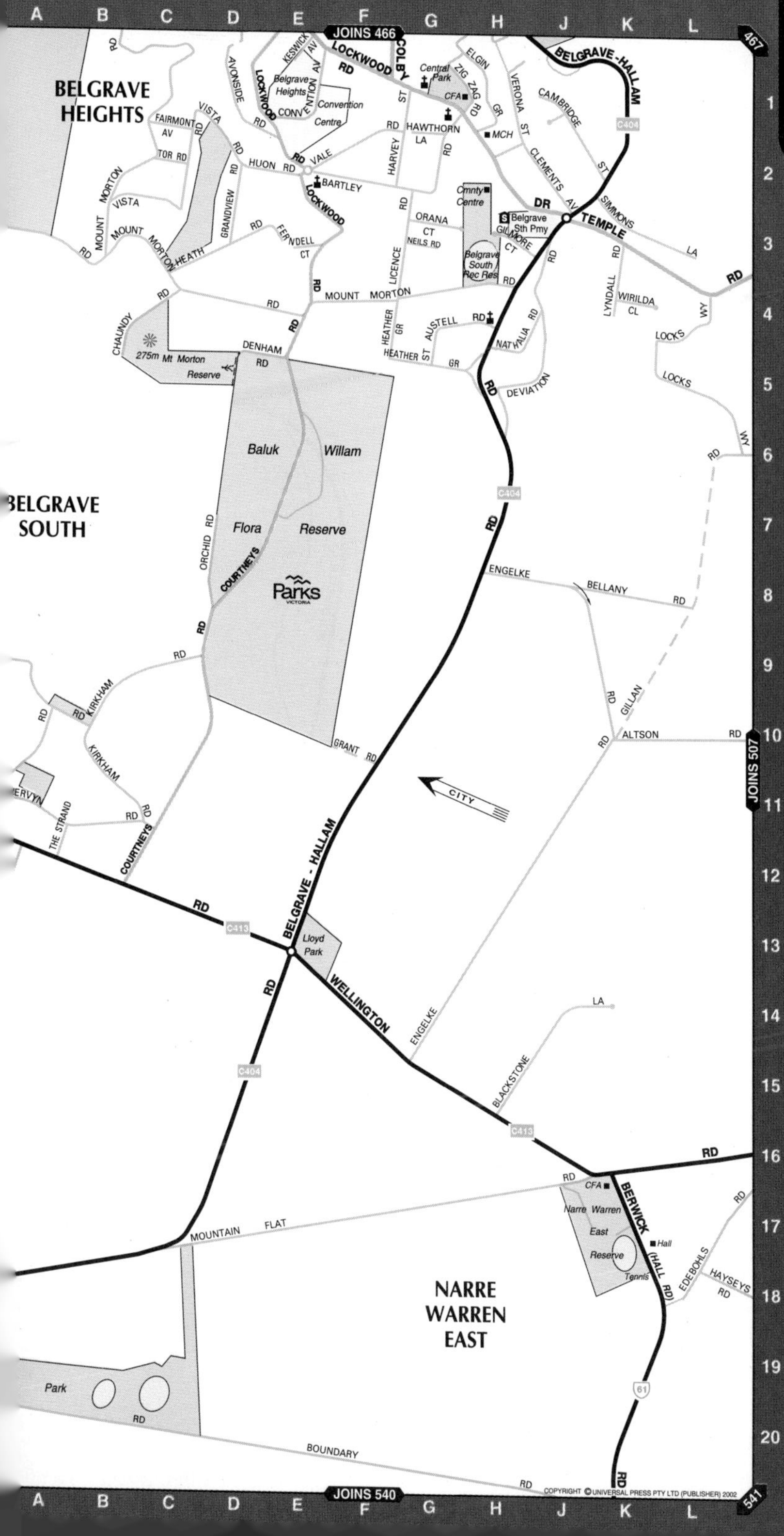

BELGRAVE HEIGHTS
BELGRAVE SOUTH
NARRE WARREN EAST
LOCKWOOD RD
COLBY
Central Park
CFA
ZIG ZAG RD
ELGIN
VERONA ST
CAMBRIDGE ST
BELGRAVE-HALLAM
C404
Belgrave Heights
Convention Centre
CONVENTION AV
KESWICK
AVONSIDE RD
FAIRMONT AV
VISTA RD
TOR RD
HUON RD
VALE RD
BARTLEY
HARVEY ST
HAWTHORN LA
MCH
CLEMENTS AV
SIMMONS ST
TEMPLE RD
DR
Cmnty Centre
Belgrave Sth Pmy
GILMORE CT
Belgrave South Rec Res
ORANA CT
NEILS RD
LICENCE
LA
LYNDALL RD
WIRILDA CL
MOUNT MORTON RD
MOUNT VISTA
GRANDVIEW
HEATH
FERNDELL CT
CHAUNDY
275m Mt Morton Reserve
DENHAM RD
HEATHER GR
AUSTELL ST
NATHALIA RD
DEVIATION
LOCKS WY
Baluk Willam Flora Reserve
Parks Victoria
ORCHID RD
COURTNEYS RD
ENGELKE
BELLANY RD
GILLAN RD
ALTSON RD
GRANT RD
KIRKHAM RD
MERVYN
THE STRAND
CITY
C413
Lloyd Park
WELLINGTON
BLACKSTONE
Narre Warren East Reserve
Tennis
Hall
BERWICK (HALL RD)
EDEBOHLS
HAYSEYS RD
MOUNTAIN FLAT RD
Park
BOUNDARY RD
61

JOINS 467

JOINS 506

JOINS 541

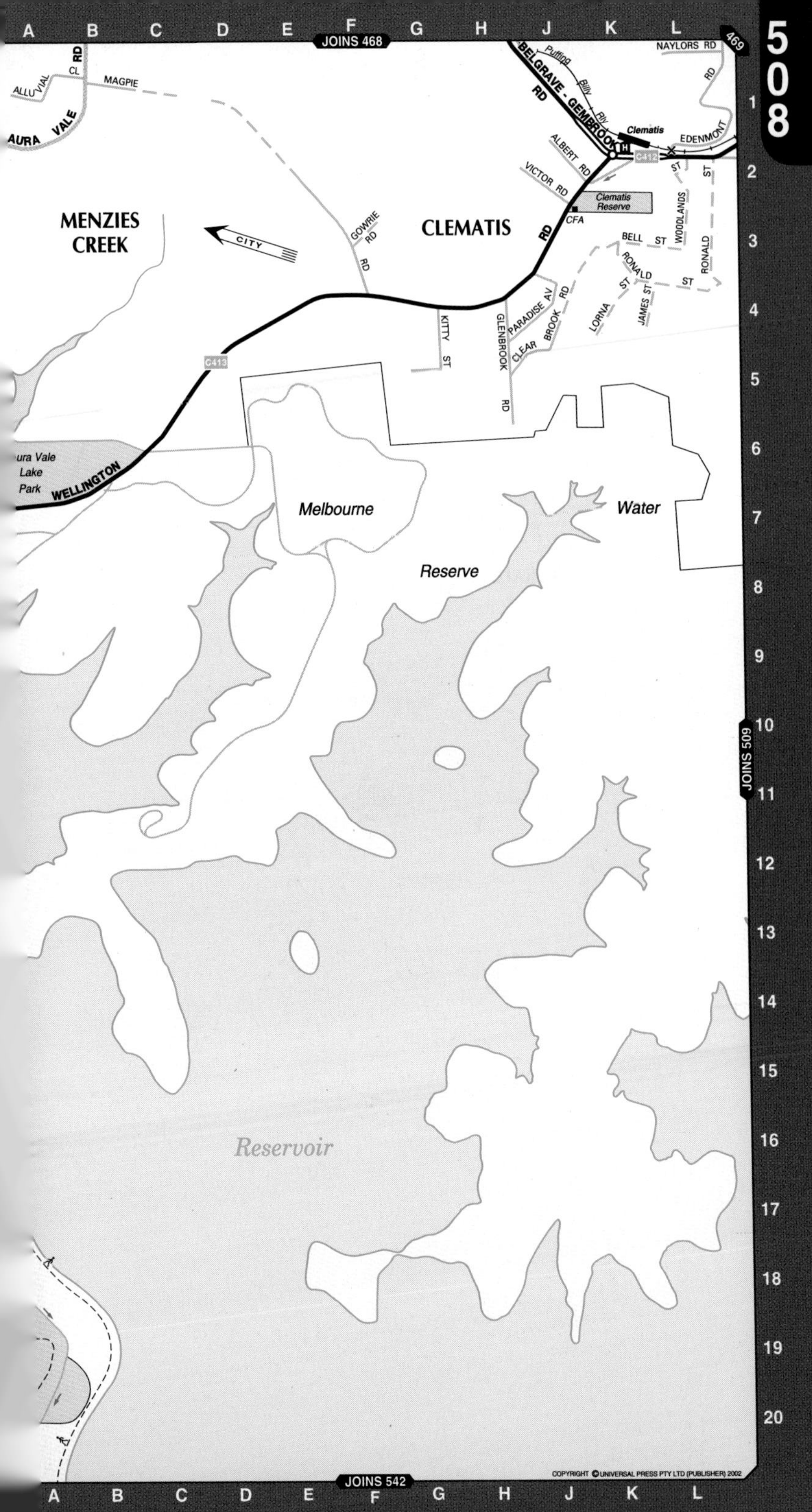

JOINS 468
469
NAYLORS RD
RD
ALLUVIAL
CL
RD
MAGPIE
AURA VALE
Puffing Billy Rly
BELGRAVE - GEMBROOK RD
Clematis
EDENMONT
ALBERT RD
C412
VICTOR RD
Clematis Reserve
CFA
ST
ST
MENZIES CREEK
CITY
GOWRIE RD
RD
CLEMATIS
RD
BELL ST
WOODLANDS
RONALD
RONALD ST
RONALD
LORNA ST
JAMES ST
PARADISE AV
BROOK RD
GLENBROOK RD
CLEAR
KITTY ST
C413
Aura Vale Lake Park
WELLINGTON
Melbourne
Water
Reserve
Reservoir
JOINS 509

JOINS 469
468
JOINS 508
542

A B C D E F G H J K L

1 2 3 4 5 6 7 8 9 10 11 12 13 14 15 16 17 18 19 20

CLEMATIS

EMERALD

Melbourne Water Reserve

Reservoir

PINNOCKS RD
RD
EDENMONT
BELGRAVE - GEMBROOK RD
OGILVY RD
ST
CLEMATIS PARK RD
Railway
C412
ANNE
PINNOCKS RD
WALNUT AV
PARADISE GR
BERRYS RD
COMO ST
FERRES
CORNISH RD
RD
EMERALD - MONBULK RD
EMERALD CL
ALEXANDER ST
BELGRAVE - GEMBROOK RD
OLD GEMBROOK RD
SES
Pav
Tennis
Emerald Reserve
SHERRIFF RD
DURBAN
RD
EMERALD LAKE RD
ROYAL PDE
CFA
EMERALD
LAKE RD
Hall
PRINCESS AV
Nobelius Heritage Park
Emerald Lake Park
(MAIN ST)
Cmnty Centre
KINGS RD
Nursing Home
AV
BEACONSFIELD - EMERALD RD
CRICHTON RD
Emerald Museum
Puffing Billy
ALBERT
Clematis Park Reserve
CHURCH ST
RONALD
MEMORIAL
KILVINGTON DR
MURPHYS WY
HEROES
Emerald
PUFFING BILLY PL
WESTLANDS RD
RSL
AV
S Emerald Pmy
RAILWAY RD
WOODLANDS AV
LEIGHTON AV
BAYVIEW RD
RUSSELL ST
PEPPERMINT CT
BENSON ST
Hogan Park
Nobelius
Railway
STATION
AMBROSE ST
SELLARS
RD
BOUNDARY RD W
BOUNDARY RD E
UPTON RD
LEGG RD
DR
RD
HAMILTON
CLOVERLEIGH AV
WATTLE AV
BIRCH AV
CURTIS RD
MAISIE RD
NOLAN RD
OLD BEACONSFIELD
OUTLOOK RD
STEEL RD
KILVINGTON
DEWHURST RD
C406
WESTLANDS
RAWHITI RD
WINTLE RD
DIXON RD
TORLEY RD
RD
LAVENDER FARM RD
WONG HEE RD W
DR
WONG HEE Steep RD
DEERY
N
UBD

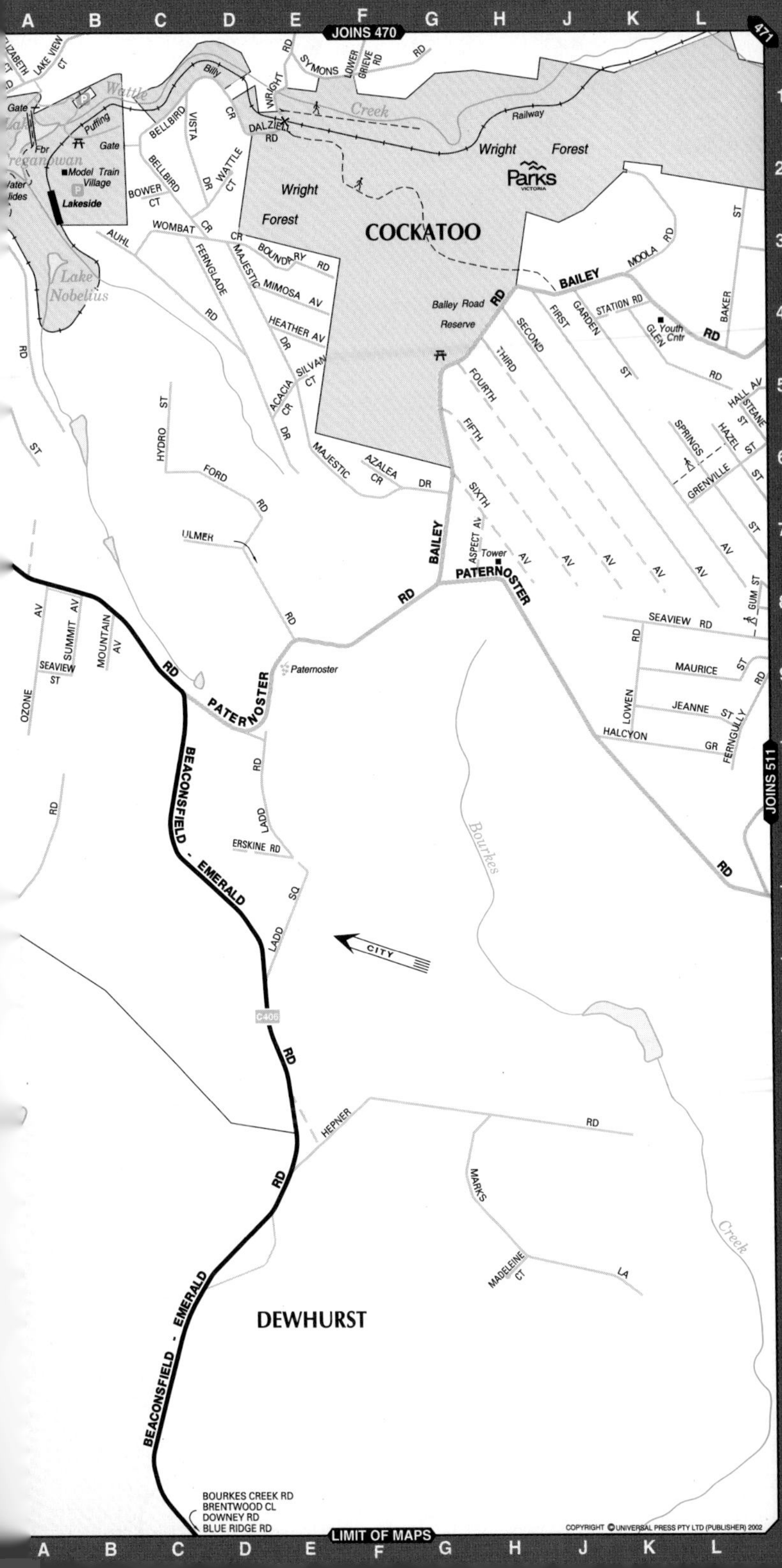

COCKATOO

DEWHURST

Wright Forest

Parks VICTORIA

Balley Road Reserve

Lakeside

Model Train Village

Lake Nobelius

Paternoster

Tower

Youth Cntr

CITY

C406

BOURKES CREEK RD
BRENTWOOD CL
DOWNEY RD
BLUE RIDGE RD

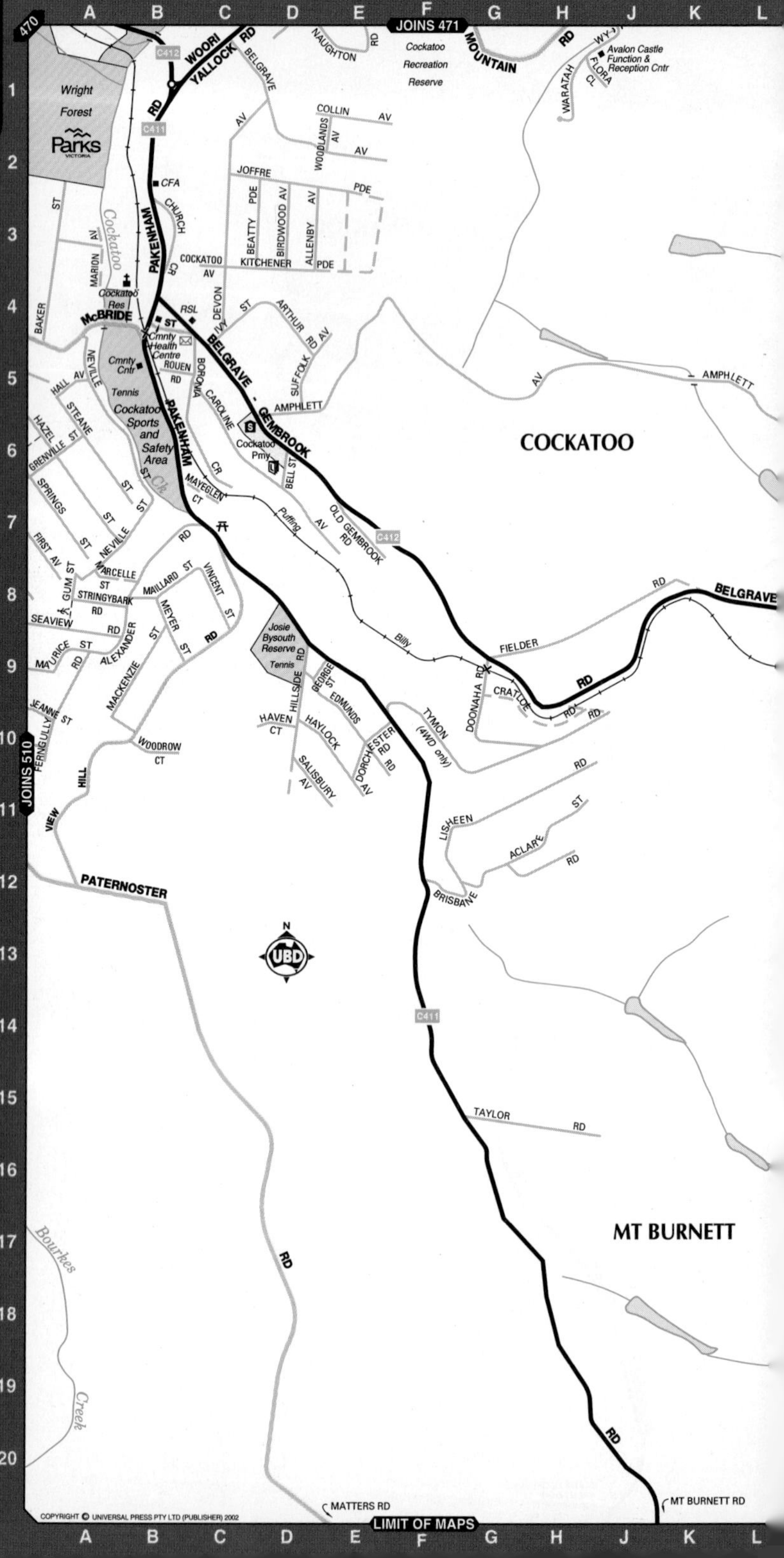

A B C D E F G H J K L
JOINS 471
470
Wright Forest
Parks Victoria
Cockatoo Recreation Reserve
WOORI YALLOCK RD
MOUNTAIN RD
NAUGHTON RD
BELGRAVE AV
Avalon Castle Function & Reception Cntr
WARATAH
FLORA CL
COLLIN AV
WOODLANDS AV
JOFFRE PDE
CFA
CHURCH CR
PAKENHAM RD
BEATTY PDE
BIRDWOOD AV
ALLENBY AV
KITCHENER PDE
COCKATOO AV
Cockatoo Res
MARION AV
BAKER ST
McBRIDE ST
RSL
DEVON
IVY ST
ARTHUR RD
AV
Cmnty Health Centre
ROUEN RD
BORONIA
Cmnty Cntr
NEVILLE
HALL AV
STEANE ST
Tennis
Cockatoo Sports and Safety Area
BELGRAVE - GEMBROOK
SUFFOLK AV
AMPHLETT
CAROLINE CR
Cockatoo Pmy
BELL ST
COCKATOO
AMPHLETT
HAZEL
GRENVILLE ST
SPRINGS ST
MAYEGLEN CT
Ck
FIRST AV
NEVILLE ST
OLD GEMBROOK RD
Puffing Billy
C412
GUM ST
MARCELLE ST
STRINGYBARK RD
MAILLARD ST
VINCENT ST
MEYER ST
SEAVIEW RD
MAURICE ST
RD
ALEXANDER
MACKENZIE
Josie Bysouth Reserve
Tennis
HILLSIDE RD
GEORGE ST
EDMUNDS
FIELDER RD
BELGRAVE RD
DOONAHA RD
CRATLOE RD
JEANNE ST
FERNGULLY
HAVEN CT
HAYLOCK
TYMON (4WD only)
DORCHESTER RD
WOODROW CT
SALISBURY AV
JOINS 510
HILL VIEW
LISHEEN RD
ACLARE ST
RD
PATERNOSTER RD
BRISBANE
UBD
C411
TAYLOR RD
MT BURNETT
Bourkes Creek
MATTERS RD
MT BURNETT RD
LIMIT OF MAPS

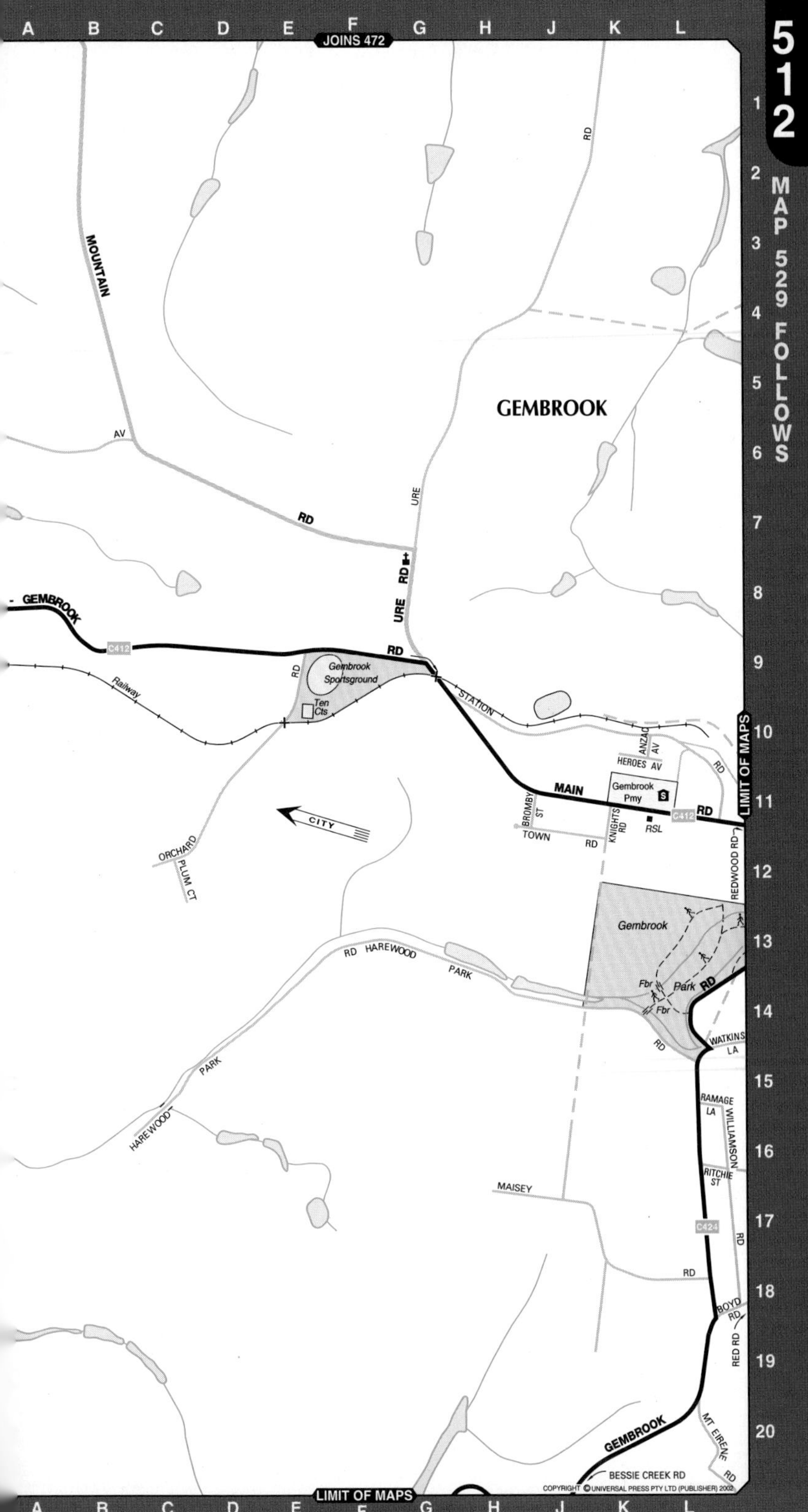
A B C D E F G H J K L
JOINS 472
MAP 529 FOLLOWS
1 2 3 4 5 6 7 8 9 10 11 12 13 14 15 16 17 18 19 20
GEMBROOK
MOUNTAIN
AV
RD
RD
URE
URE RD
RD
GEMBROOK
C412
Railway
RD
Gembrook Sportsground
Ten Cts
STATION
ANZAC AV
HEROES AV
RD
Gembrook Pmy
MAIN
RD
C412
BROMBY ST
TOWN RD
KNIGHTS RD
RSL
CITY
ORCHARD
PLUM CT
LIMIT OF MAPS
REDWOOD RD
Gembrook Park
RD
Fbr
Fbr
RD HAREWOOD PARK
RD
WATKINS LA
PARK
HAREWOOD
RAMAGE LA
WILLAMSON RD
RITCHIE ST
MAISEY RD
C424
BOYD RD
RED RD
GEMBROOK
MT EIRENE RD
BESSIE CREEK RD
LIMIT OF MAPS

PREVIOUS MAP 512

494

JOINS 495

A B C D E F G H J K L

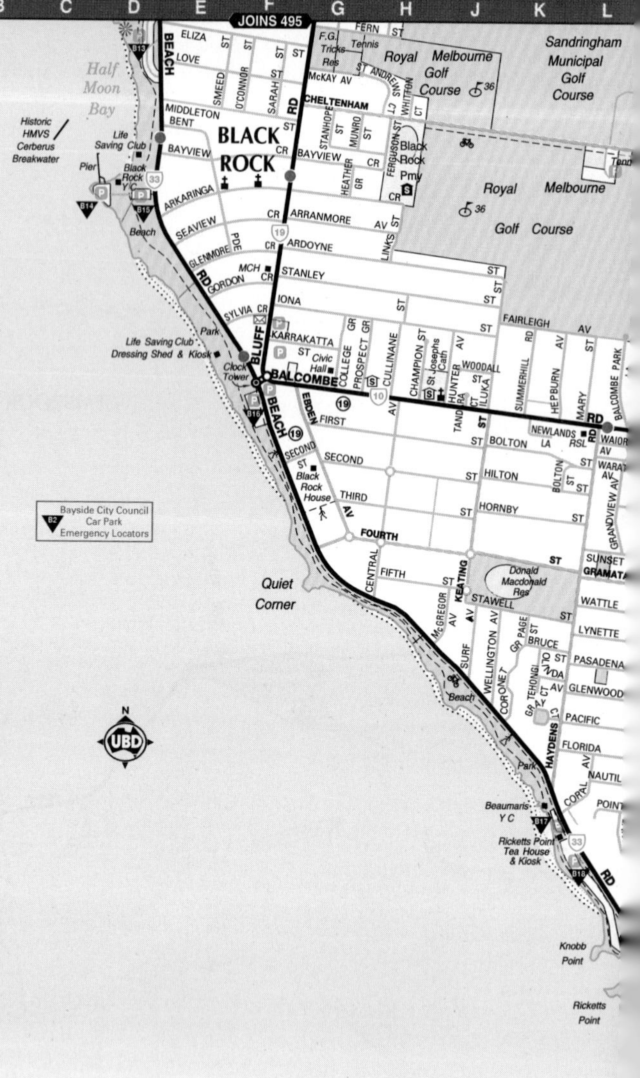

A B C D E F G H J K L

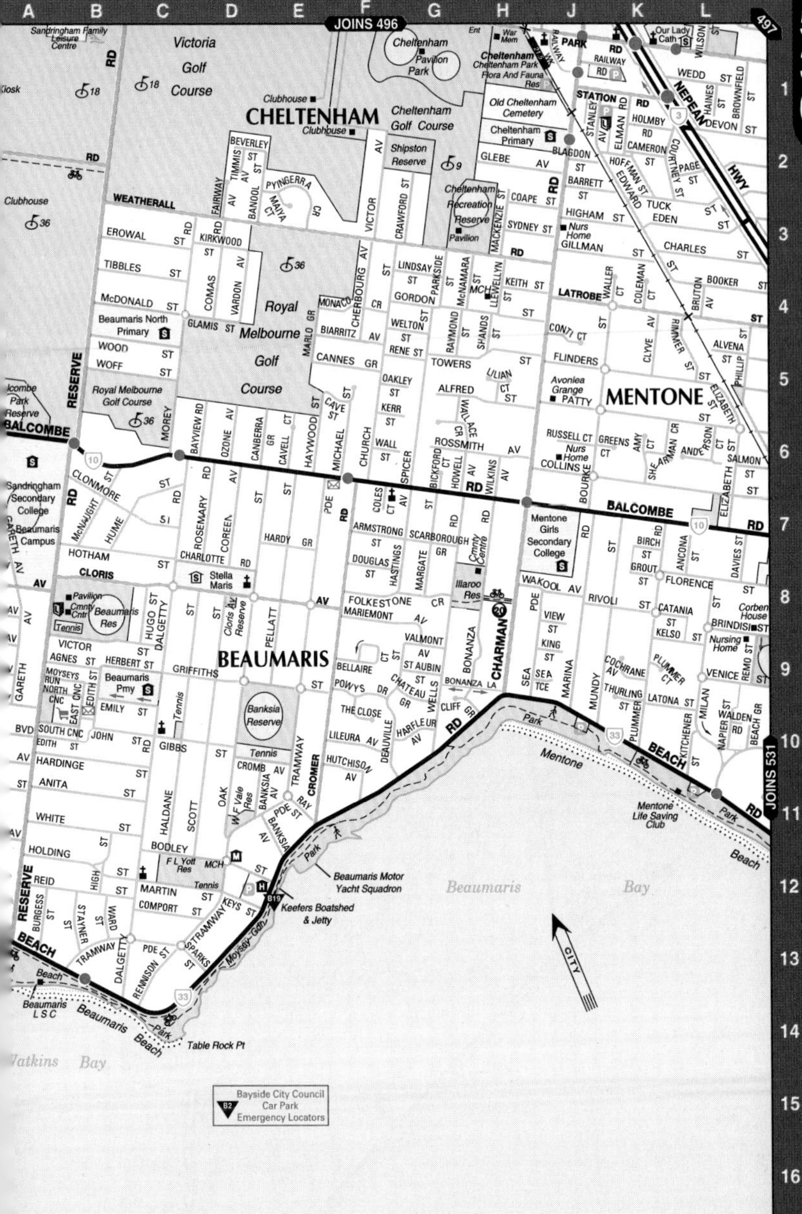
JOINS 496
JOINS 531
497
545
CHELTENHAM
BEAUMARIS
MENTONE
Victoria Golf Course
Cheltenham Golf Course
Royal Melbourne Golf Course
Cheltenham Pavilion Park
Old Cheltenham Cemetery
Cheltenham Primary
Shipston Reserve
Cheltenham Recreation Reserve
Beaumaris North Primary
Royal Melbourne Golf Course
Sandringham Secondary College Beaumaris Campus
Stella Maris
Beaumaris Pmy
Banksia Reserve
Mentone Girls Secondary College
Illaroo Res
Beaumaris Motor Yacht Squadron
Keefers Boatshed & Jetty
Mentone Life Saving Club
Table Rock Pt
Beaumaris Bay
Watkins Bay
PHILLIP
CITY
Bayside City Council Car Park Emergency Locators

496
JOINS 497
JOINS 530
JOINS 545

A B C D E F G H J K L

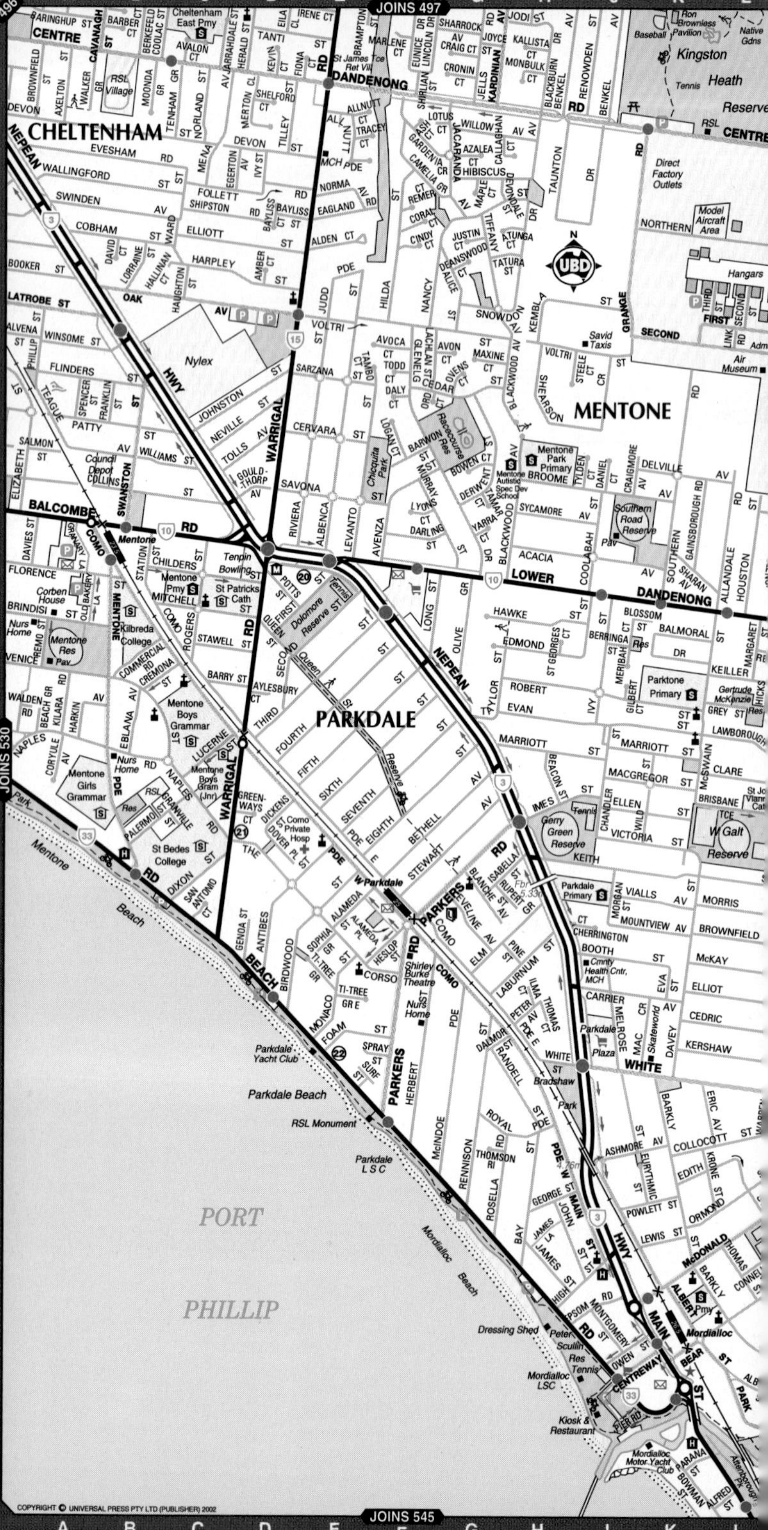

CHELTENHAM

MENTONE

PARKDALE

PORT PHILLIP

Kingston Heath Reserve

Cheltenham East Pmy
RSL Village
Nylex
Council Depot
Mentone Pmy
St Patricks Cath
Tenpin Bowling
Dolomore Reserve
Kilbreda College
Mentone Res
Mentone Boys Grammar
Mentone Boys Gram (Jnr)
Mentone Girls Grammar
St Bedes College
Como Private Hosp
Chiquita Park
Racecourse Res
Mentone Park Primary
Mentone Autistic Spec Dev School
Southern Road Reserve
Parktone Primary
Gerry Green Reserve
Parkdale Primary
W Galt Reserve
Cmnty Health Cntr, MCH
Parkdale Plaza
Skateworld
Shirley Burke Theatre
Direct Factory Outlets
Model Aircraft Area
Hangars
Air Museum
Savid Taxis
Ron Brownless Pavilion
Native Gdns
Parkdale Yacht Club
Parkdale Beach
RSL Monument
Parkdale LSC
Mentone Beach
Mordialloc Beach
Dressing Shed
Peter Scullin Res
Mordialloc LSC
Kiosk & Restaurant
Mordialloc Motor Yacht Club
Mordialloc

NEPEAN HWY
WARRIGAL RD
BALCOMBE RD
LOWER DANDENONG RD
DANDENONG RD
CENTRE DANDENONG RD
BEACH RD
PARKERS RD
MAIN ST
CENTREWAY

1 2 3 4 5 6 7 8 9 10 11 12 13 14 15 16 17 18 19 20

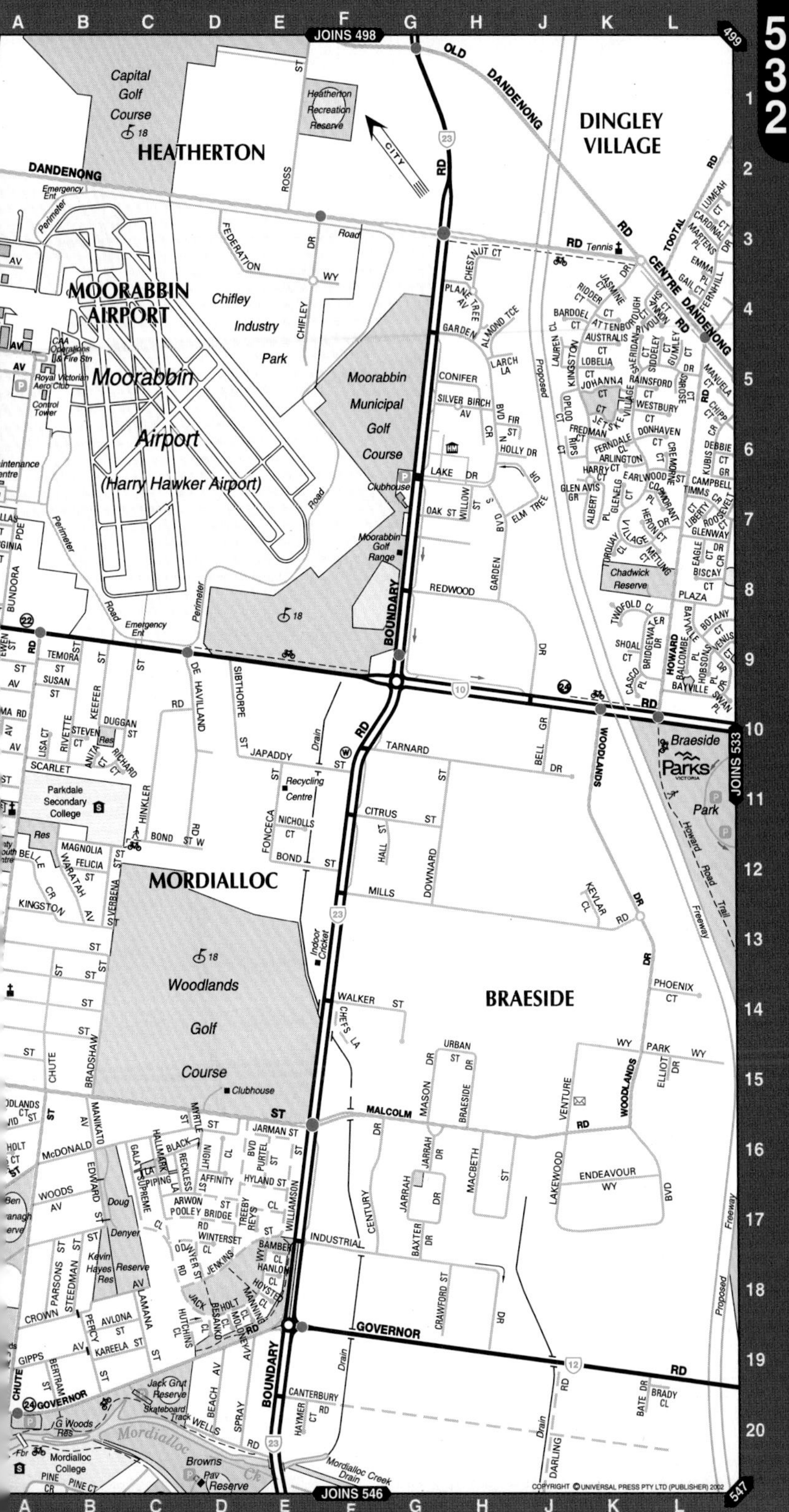
JOINS 498
499
Capital Golf Course
HEATHERTON
Heatherton Recreation Reserve
CITY
DINGLEY VILLAGE
DANDENONG
OLD DANDENONG RD
MOORABBIN AIRPORT
Chifley Industry Park
Moorabbin Airport
(Harry Hawker Airport)
Moorabbin Municipal Golf Course
Clubhouse
Moorabbin Golf Range
Chadwick Reserve
BOUNDARY RD
CENTRE DANDENONG RD
Parkdale Secondary College
MORDIALLOC
Woodlands Golf Course
Clubhouse
BRAESIDE
Braeside Park
Parks Victoria
JOINS 533
Howard Road Trail
Freeway
Proposed
Recycling Centre
Indoor Cricket
MALCOLM
INDUSTRIAL
GOVERNOR RD
Kevin Hayes Reserve
Doug Denyer Reserve
Jack Grut Reserve
Skateboard Track
G Woods Res
Mordialloc College
Browns Reserve
Mordialloc Ck
Mordialloc Creek Drain
JOINS 546
547

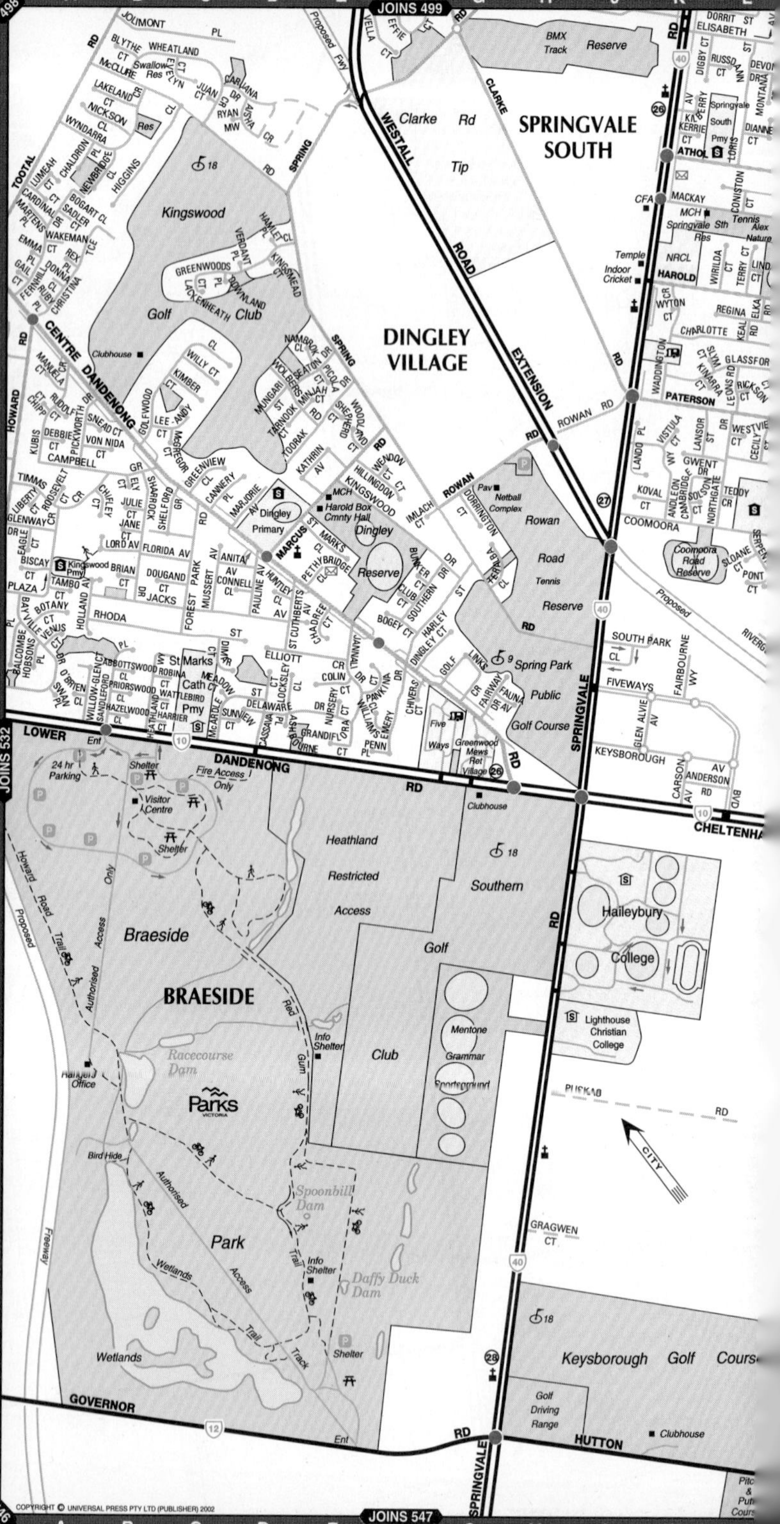

JOINS 499

JOINS 532

JOINS 547

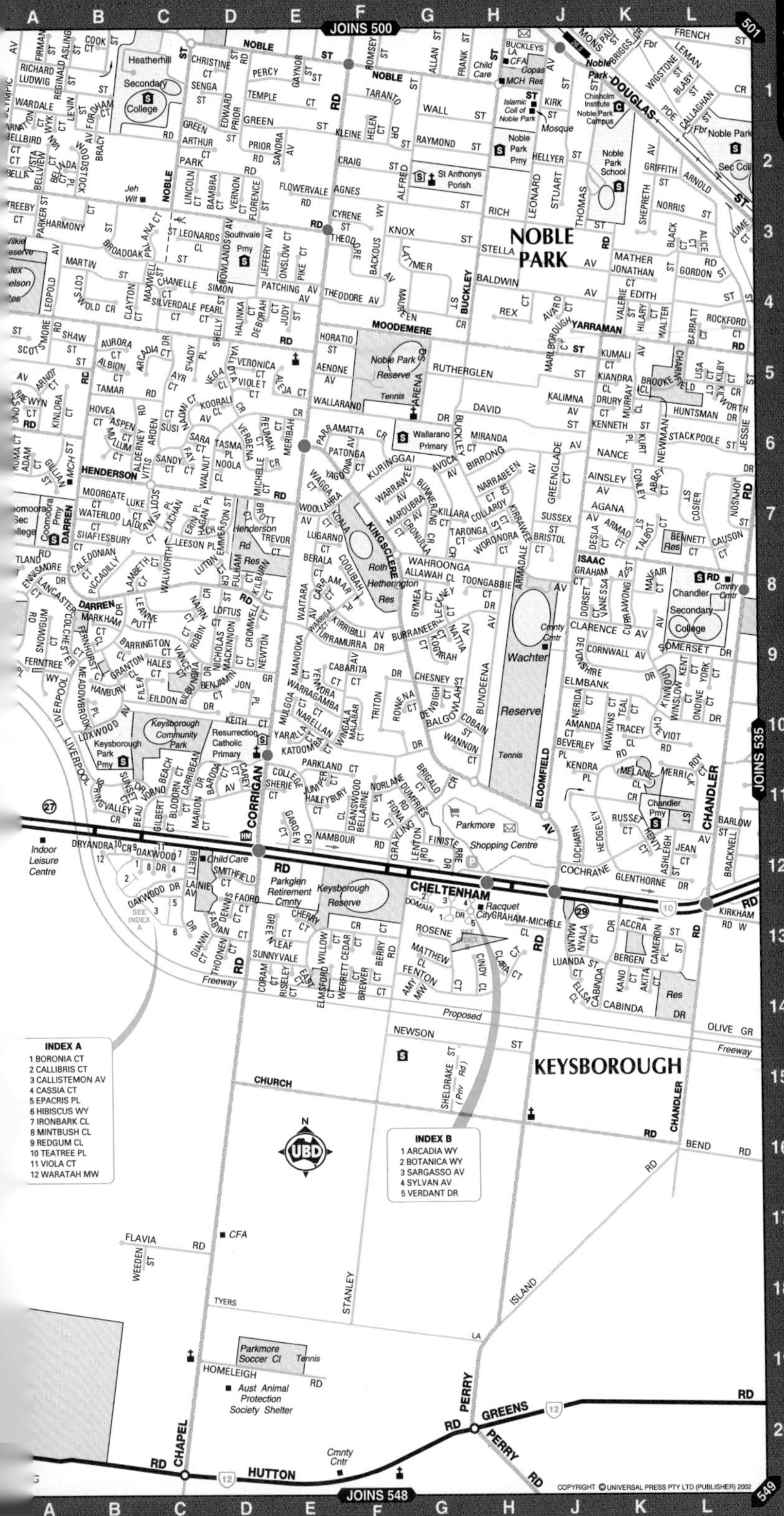

JOINS 500

501

NOBLE PARK

KEYSBOROUGH

INDEX A

1 BORONIA CT
2 CALLIBRIS CT
3 CALLISTEMON AV
4 CASSIA CT
5 EPACRIS PL
6 HIBISCUS WY
7 IRONBARK CL
8 MINTBUSH CL
9 REDGUM CL
10 TEATREE PL
11 VIOLA CT
12 WARATAH MW

INDEX B

1 ARCADIA WY
2 BOTANICA WY
3 SARGASSO AV
4 SYLVAN AV
5 VERDANT DR

JOINS 535

JOINS 548

549

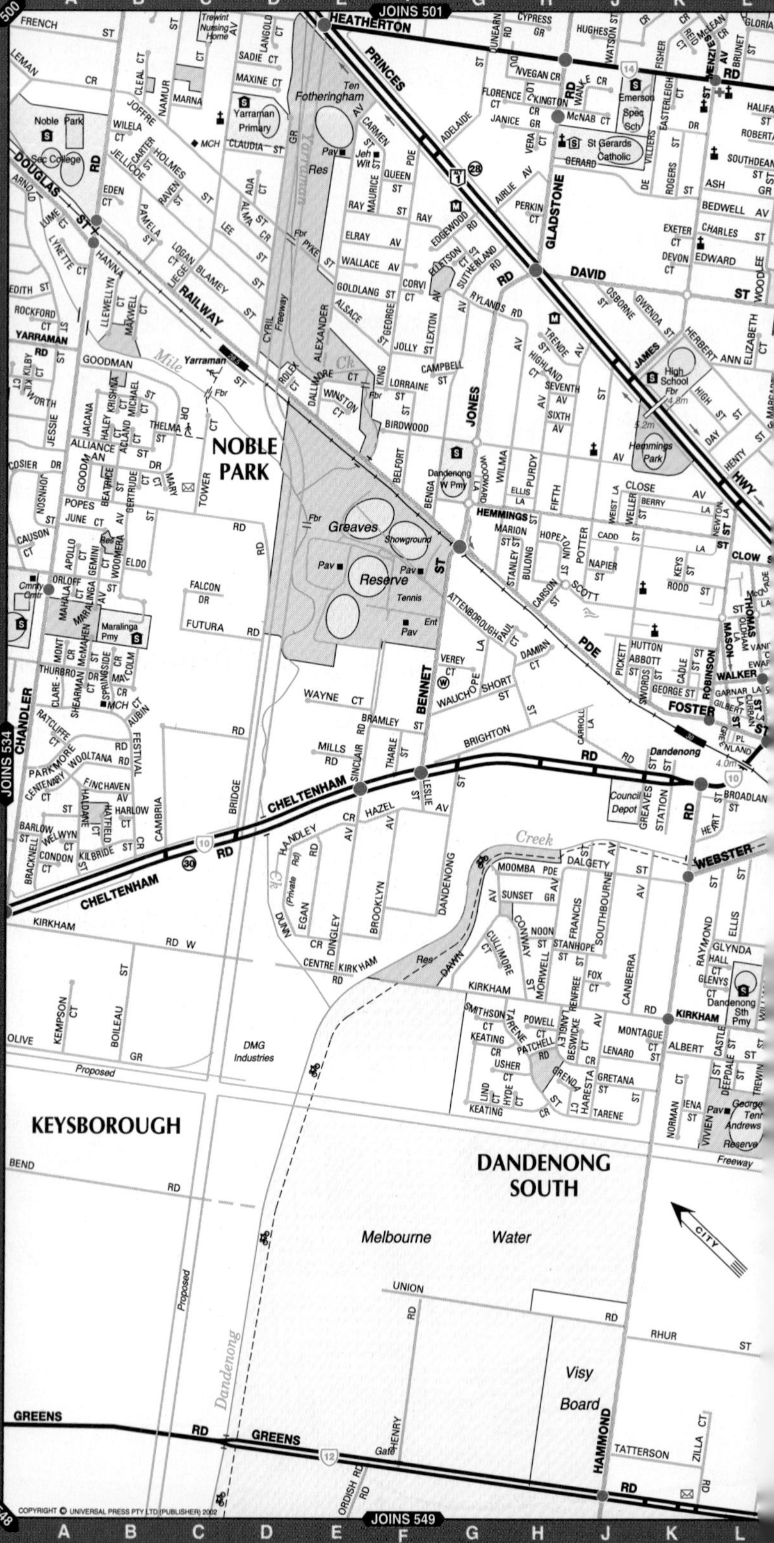

JOINS 501

A B C D E F G H J K L

NOBLE PARK

KEYSBOROUGH

DANDENONG SOUTH

Greaves Reserve

Melbourne Water

Visy Board

DMG Industries

JOINS 534

JOINS 549

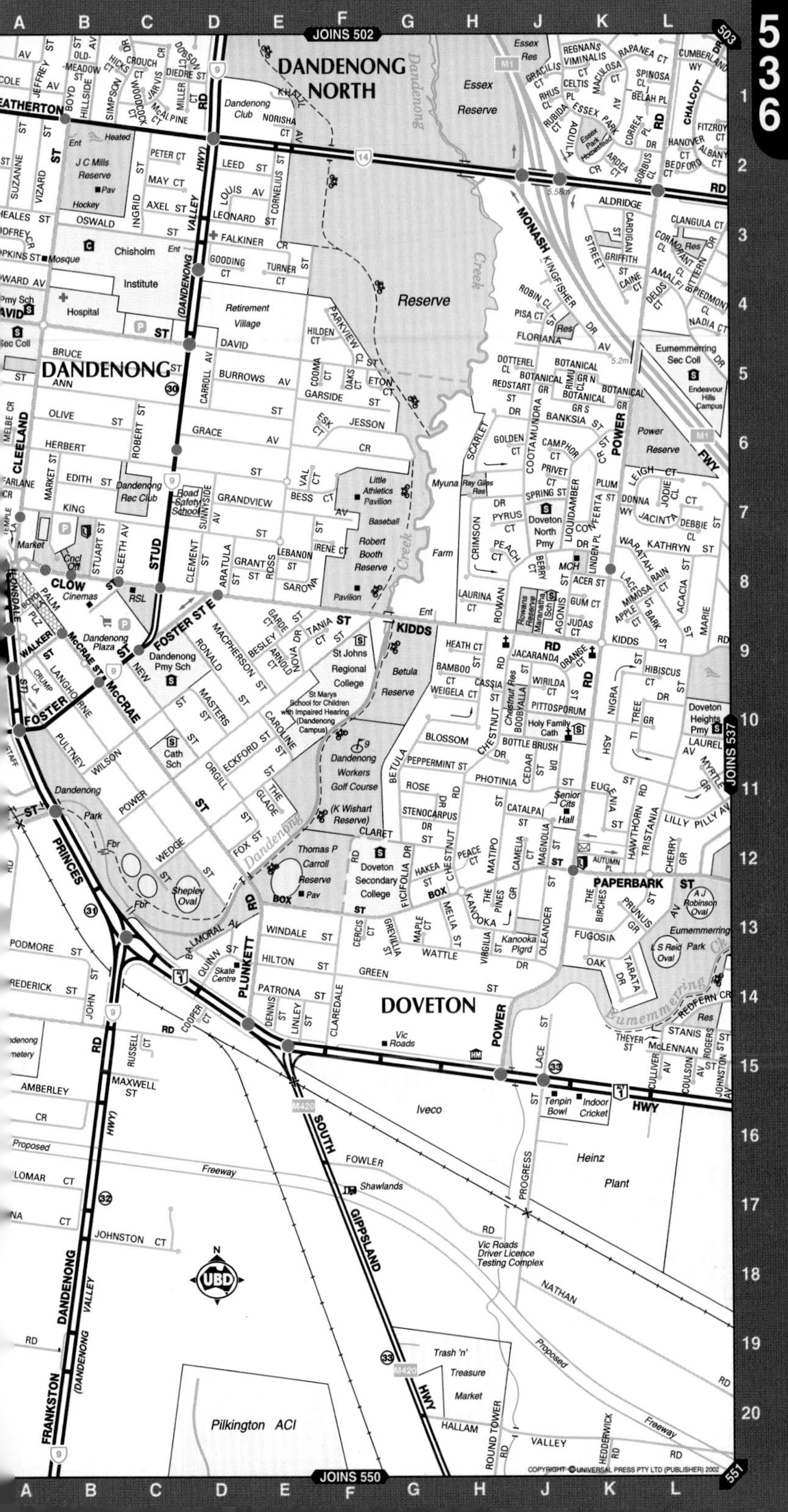
536
JOINS 502
JOINS 537
JOINS 550
503
551
DANDENONG NORTH
DANDENONG
DOVETON
Essex Res
Essex Reserve
Dandenong Club
Dandenong Creek
Reserve
J C Mills Reserve
Chisholm Institute
Hospital
Retirement Village
Little Athletics Pavilion
Baseball
Robert Booth Reserve
Myuna Farm
Ray Giles Res
Doveton North Pmy
Eumemmerring Sec Coll
Endeavour Hills Campus
Power Reserve
Dandenong Rec Club
Road Safety School
Cinemas
Dandenong Plaza
Dandenong Pmy Sch
St Johns Regional College
St Marys School for Children with Impaired Hearing (Dandenong Campus)
Betula Reserve
Dandenong Workers Golf Course (K Wishart Reserve)
Cath Sch
Dandenong Park
Shepley Oval
Thomas P Carroll Reserve
Doveton Secondary College
Holy Family Cath
Doveton Heights Pmy
Senior Cits Hall
Kanooka Plgrd
A J Robinson Oval
L S Reid Oval
Eumemmerring Park
Eumemmerring Ck
Skate Centre
Vic Roads
Iveco
Tenpin Bowl
Indoor Cricket
Heinz Plant
Shawlands
Vic Roads Driver Licence Testing Complex
Trash 'n' Treasure Market
Pilkington ACI
PRINCES HWY
SOUTH GIPPSLAND HWY
DANDENONG VALLEY HWY
FRANKSTON DANDENONG RD
MONASH FWY
HEATHERTON RD
POWER RD
KIDDS RD
PAPERBARK ST
FOSTER ST E
McCRAE ST
CLOW ST
STUD RD
PROGRESS ST
NATHAN RD
HALLAM VALLEY RD
Proposed Freeway
COPYRIGHT © UNIVERSAL PRESS PTY LTD (PUBLISHER) 2002

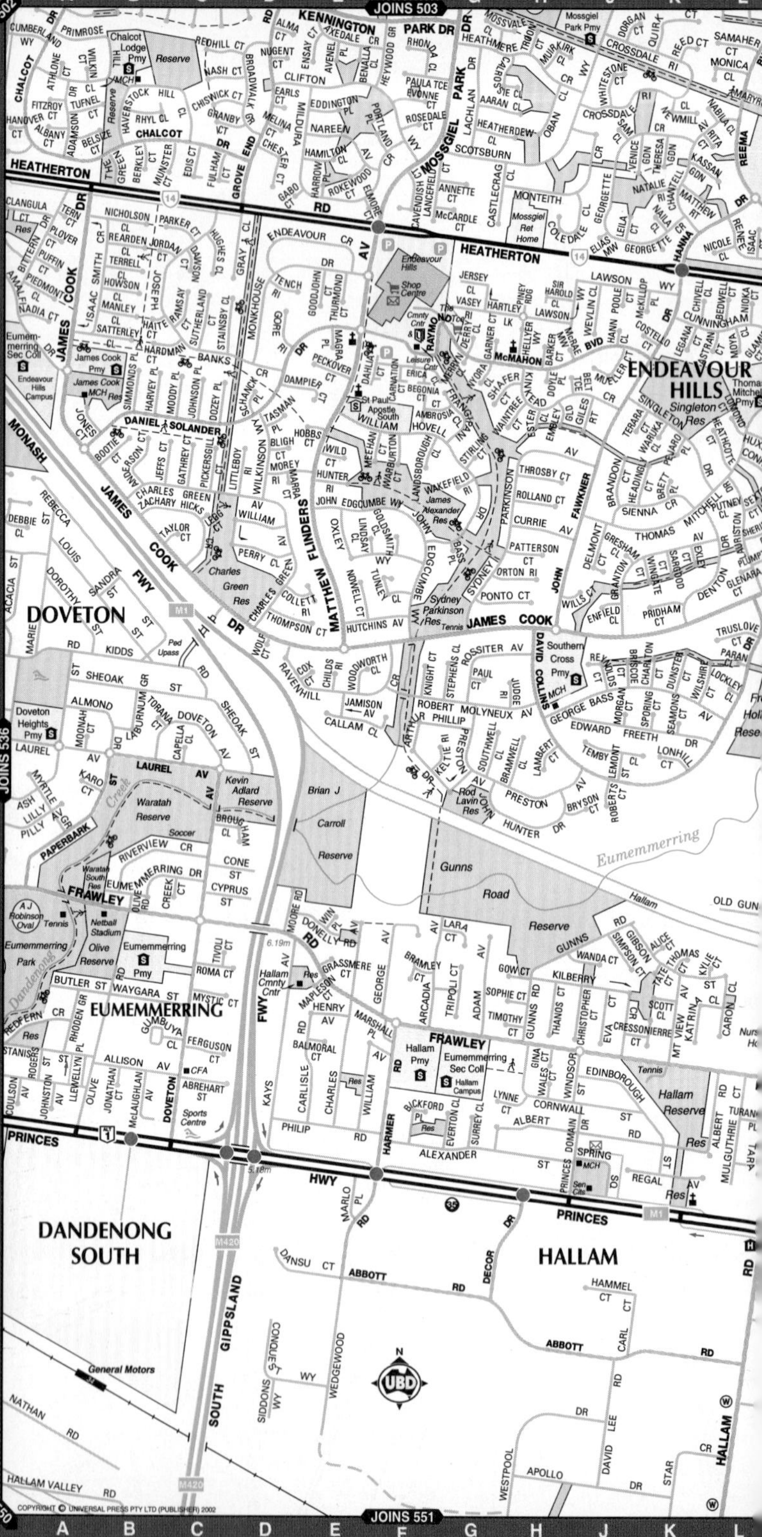

JOINS 503

JOINS 536

JOINS 551

502

550

A B C D E F G H J K L

1 2 3 4 5 6 7 8 9 10 11 12 13 14 15 16 17 18 19 20

ENDEAVOUR HILLS

DOVETON

EUMEMMERRING

DANDENONG SOUTH

HALLAM

HEATHERTON RD

JAMES COOK DR

MATTHEW FLINDERS AV

MOSSGIEL PARK DR

KENNINGTON PARK DR

MONASH FWY

SOUTH GIPPSLAND FWY

PRINCES HWY

FRAWLEY RD

GUNNS RD

ABBOTT RD

HALLAM RD

HALLAM VALLEY RD

NATHAN RD

General Motors

Endeavour Hills Shop Centre

Endeavour Hills Sec Coll

Eumemmerring Sec Coll

Doveton Heights Pmy

Hallam Pmy

Southern Cross Pmy

Gunns Road Reserve

Brian J Carroll Reserve

Waratah Reserve

Kevin Adlard Reserve

Charles Green Res

Sydney Parkinson Res

Eumemmerring Creek

JOINS 504

NARRE WARREN NORTH

Lysterfield Lake

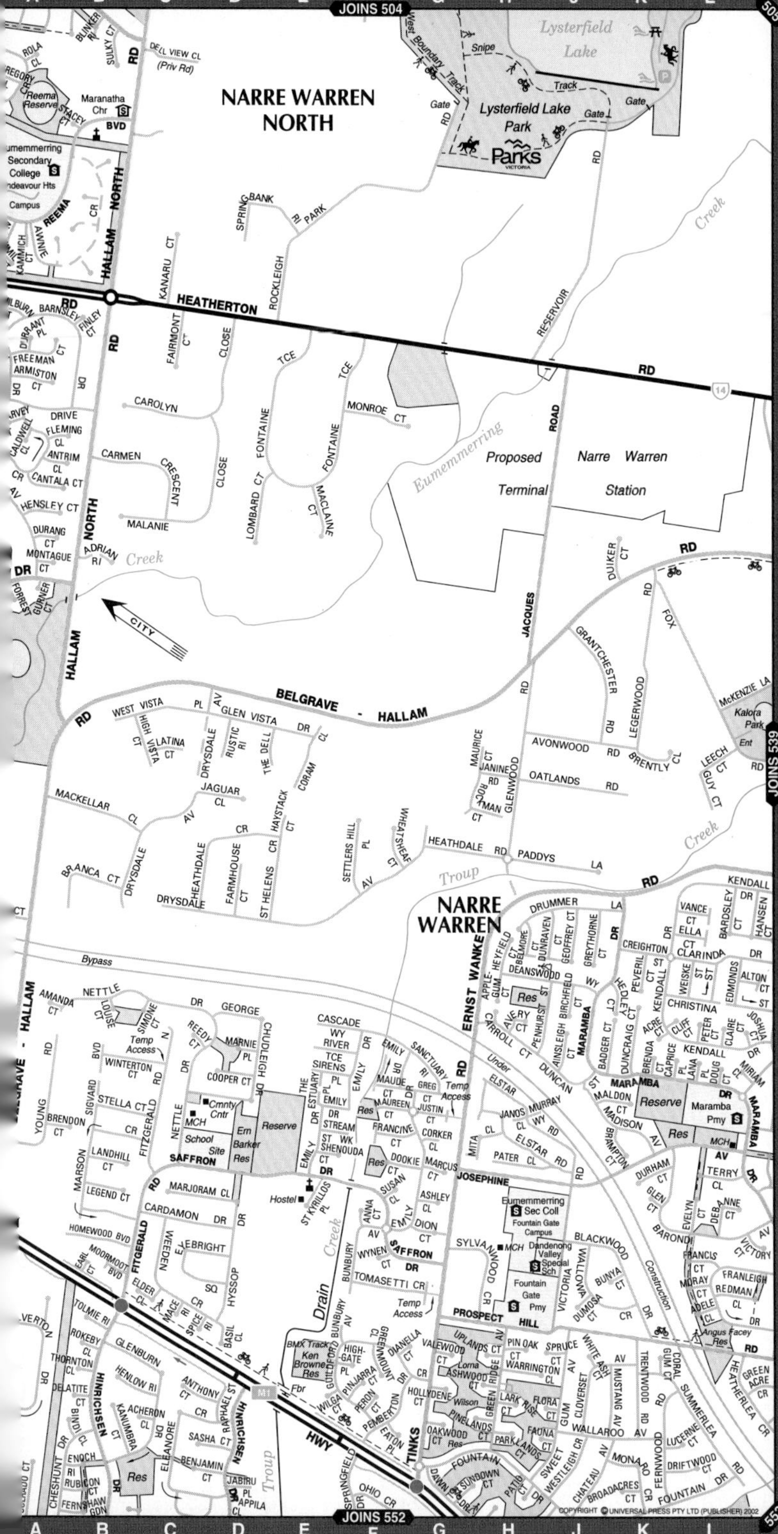

Lysterfield Lake Park

Parks Victoria

Proposed Terminal

Narre Warren Station

NARRE WARREN

JOINS 539

JOINS 552

505

553

JOINS 505
504
JOINS 538

A B C D E F G H J K L

1 2 3 4 5 6 7 8 9 10 11 12 13 14 15 16 17 18 19 20

NARRE WARREN NORTH

NARRE WARREN

Eumemmerring Ck
Campbelltown Miniature Rly Park
C404
HALLAM RD
BELGRAVE - HALLAM RD
HEATHERTON RD
ROBINSON RD
A'BECKETT ST
Narre Warren Nth Pmy
Tennis Hall
Res
WINTERS LA
MAIN ST
Claire Robinson Park
TOM JONES CT
TANDDERWEN CT
AURISCH DR
BAILEY
TACABERRY AV
KENNEDY AV
CITY
CRANSTON CL
CASDAR CT
RANDLE
Narre Warren North Road Retarding Basin
BETHEL CL
MEMORIAL DR
NORTH RD
Troup Creek
ASCOT CT
BELLAIRE CT
AUTUMNDALE CT
BON CT
JESSE CT
ANGELA CT
ARANMORE CR
CRAWLEY
CFA
Pony Club
Iven's Reserve
McKENZIE LA
BOB ST
Kalora Park
Ent
FOX
ARNOTT PL
DOUGLAS LA
MARGARET CT
CANTWELL RD
STEPHANIE CT
CLEVELAND CL
JOSEPH CT
JOHN
TOM GEARON CT
NOLAN CL
JACK ROBBIE CT
BRUNDRETT RD
Rose Farm
CHARL CL
ALFRED CL
LOWRY CT
ROY CL
Jack Thomas Reserve
Soccer
Mary McKillop Cath Pmy
BMX Track
HARRIES CT
HARRIES CT
Kurll Park
ERNST WANKE RD
KENDALL DR
LONDON CR
BARDSLEY CT
HANSEN CT
BARUNAH CT
LUCY CT
SIDNEY CT
JAMES CT
Jeh Wit
CELESTINE PL
TUDOR CT
GORI CT
RENDA CT
AMBER CR
ONYX CT
MICA CT
MARVIL AV
LEONIE CT
DIAMOND CT
SAPPHIRE CT
ARTZ CT
THE RISE
MONTBRAE CT
CLARINDA DR
EDMONDS CT
ALTON CT
JACKSONS
LONDON CR
KNIGHTSBRIDGE
KENSINGTON
MAYFAIR CL
CHARING CROSS PL
EMERALD CT
TOPAZ PL
ZIRCON
OPAL CT
FELDSPAR CT
GARNET CR
JADE CT
BERYL CT
PIRRA PL
SARNIA CT
Reserve
ELLENVALE DR
ROSEHILL CT
TAMAR CT
SANDILANDS CCT
JOSHUA CT
CLAIRE CT
GARRETT CT
JANETFREDA CT
DANIEL CT
DAVID CT
MIRIAM CL
ANACONDA CT
TUCK CT
JASMIN CT
MELISSA CT
SHINE CT
KURRAJONG
SERENDIP
LABASSA RD
JOLIMONT PL
ESTELLA CT
KILFERA
MARAMBA
Maramba Pmy
ESKDALE CT
INGLETON CT
LAIRD PL
HOLLY CT
INGRAM CL
DON DR
LANDOR CT
ARISTOTLE CT
CARMELA CL
ANTONIETTA CT
BROWTOP PL
PHELAN CT
FORDE CT
QUARRY RD
MILFULL CT
TARCOOLA
STAFFORD PL
JUAN CT
NICHOLAS CT
GODWIN CT
VERSAILLES PL
PAMELA CT
HELEN CT
LOUISA CT
CLASSIC CT
HILLANDALE
BRIGHTON RT
TERRY
DEBANNE CT
VAN
SHARA CT
BOSCO CL
ANDENE DR
MURDOCH
ROZZY PDE
TREWIN CT
Res
CONSTANCE
BUCKINGHAM CL
WARWICKSHIRE
SEATTLE SQ
NEW ENGLAND WY
BROWTOP
SILVERLEAVES
WINTERSUN
MORNINGTON
CARRUM
SORRENTO
East Ck
BARONDI AV
VICTORY
DELTA CT
KIALOA CT
ANACONDA CT
WARREN
ANDREW CT
DENISE
Prospect Hill
Oatlands Primary
DENVER
CLARRISA
DALBURY
HAMPTON
KENTUCKY
MANHATTAN MW
BOSTON CT
BLUEBELL BVD
LILAC CT
NEWHAVEN DR
WINTERSUN CT
ROSEWIN CT
CHELSEA CR
FRANLEIGH DR
REDMAN CL
PARKLEA
LUNN CL
JUDITH CL
Troup
Retarding Basin
ELSA PL
JOY CL
HUGO CT
VENNIFER CT
BROOKFIELD AV
GLENSIDE WK
NESTLE
COLUMBIA DR
SHIRAZ CT
ABERDEEN CR
FACEY
ARCHIBALD CL
BENSON CT
OAKWOOD
REGENT
WOODBURN AV
JERILDERIE
GARDEN CT
NORFOLK
VILLAWOOD
NATRENE
FINCH ST
CULLEN RT
PROSPECT HILL
NARRE
WINNIE CT
PEGGIE CT
ELIZABETH
ROSALEEN CT
SHINNERS
SCOBLE PL
HOULDEN CT
HILARY
PENNY
HIGHFIELDE AV
DYLAN CT
BASANO
ALLARDICE CT
SAMUEL
CALEDONIA
WANDERER
GREENACRE CR
MURRELL CT
GARRYOWEN CR
CATHIE CT
Harry Oakes Res
ABELIA
KIM CL
Reserve
STRADBROKE CL
LAVENDER PL
ALLARDICE PDE
CROWN
DEVONSHIRE CT
HEATHERLEA
GORDONIA
SONG CT
CORNUS CT
KALLARA
LAURUS CT
RADIATA CT
FAIRVIEW AV
PORTSEA PL
LYREBIRD GDN
TAMBO WY
EUROA
ALLUNGA
HESSELL
LITHGOW CT
MAGID
HEYINGTON
RYELANDS DR
DIOSMA CT
KALMIA CT
TORWOOD CL
DAINTREE GR
HILLCREST AV
BEDALE CT
TALLY
MITTAGONG CT
SHAFTES
FIRA CT
NORA CT
CIR
SALIGNUS CT
CASUARINA CT
RUFUS CT
PINNATA CL
COACHWOOD
CHERRY TREE
PARK HILL DR
MIRRABOOK CT
WARRAWONG DR
Hallam Bypass Under Construction

552
JOINS 553

JOINS 506

JOINS 541

507

555

JOINS 554

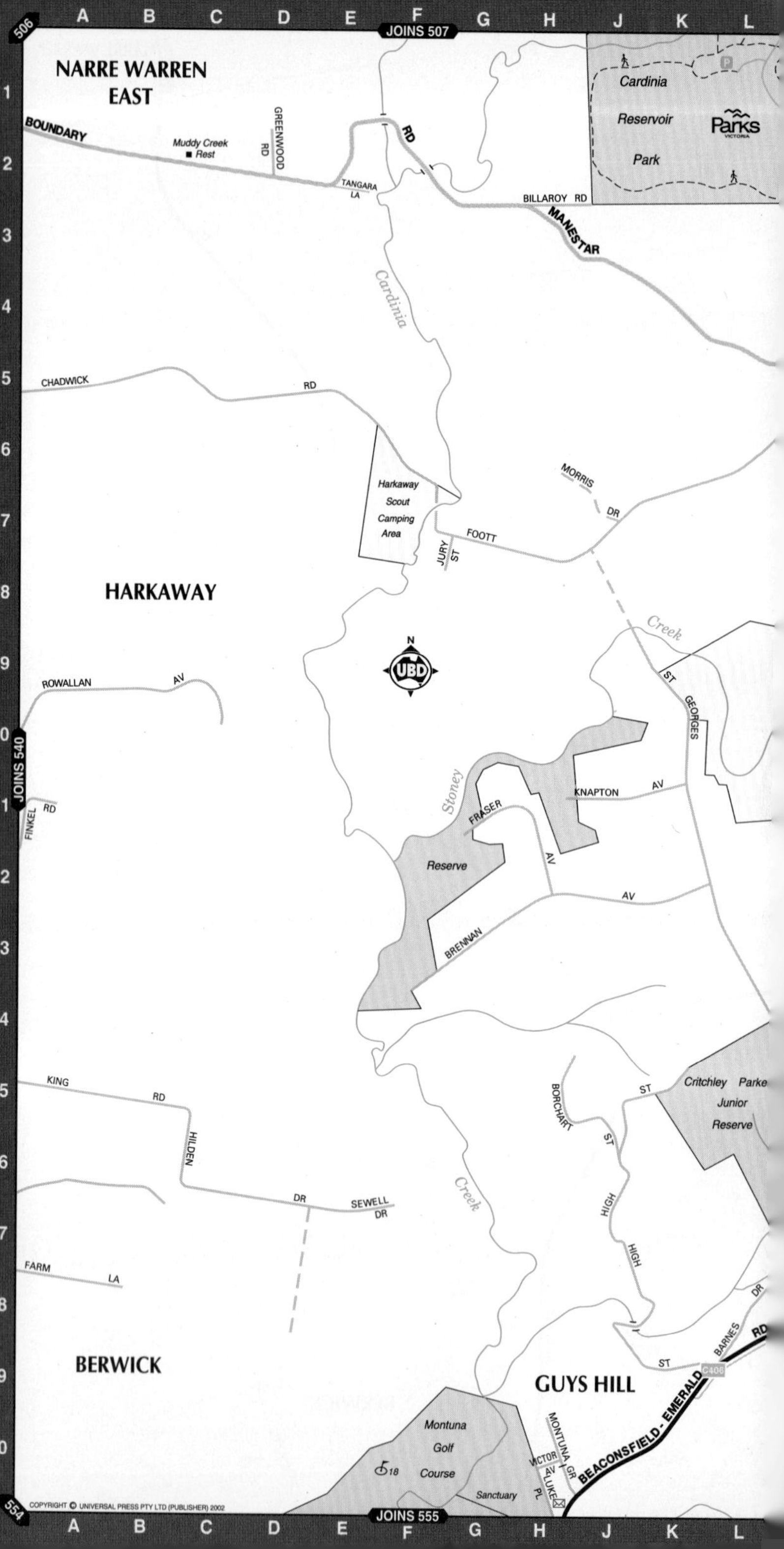

A B C D E F G H J K L
506
JOINS 507
NARRE WARREN EAST
BOUNDARY RD
Muddy Creek Rest
GREENWOOD RD
TANGARA LA
BILLAROY RD
MANESTAR
Cardinia Reservoir Park
Parks VICTORIA
Cardinia
CHADWICK RD
Harkaway Scout Camping Area
MORRIS DR
FOOTT
JURY ST
HARKAWAY
Creek
ROWALLAN AV
ST GEORGES
JOINS 540
FINKEL RD
Stoney
FRASER AV
KNAPTON AV
Reserve
AV
BRENNAN
KING RD
HILDEN
BORCHART ST
ST
Critchley Parker Junior Reserve
Creek
DR
SEWELL DR
HIGH
HIGH
FARM LA
DR
BARNES ST
RD
C406
BERWICK
GUYS HILL
BEACONSFIELD - EMERALD
Montuna Golf Course
18
Sanctuary
MONTUNA GR
VICTOR AV
LUKE PL
554
JOINS 555
A B C D E F G H J K L
1 2 3 4 5 6 7 8 9 10 11 12 13 14 15 16 17 18 19 20

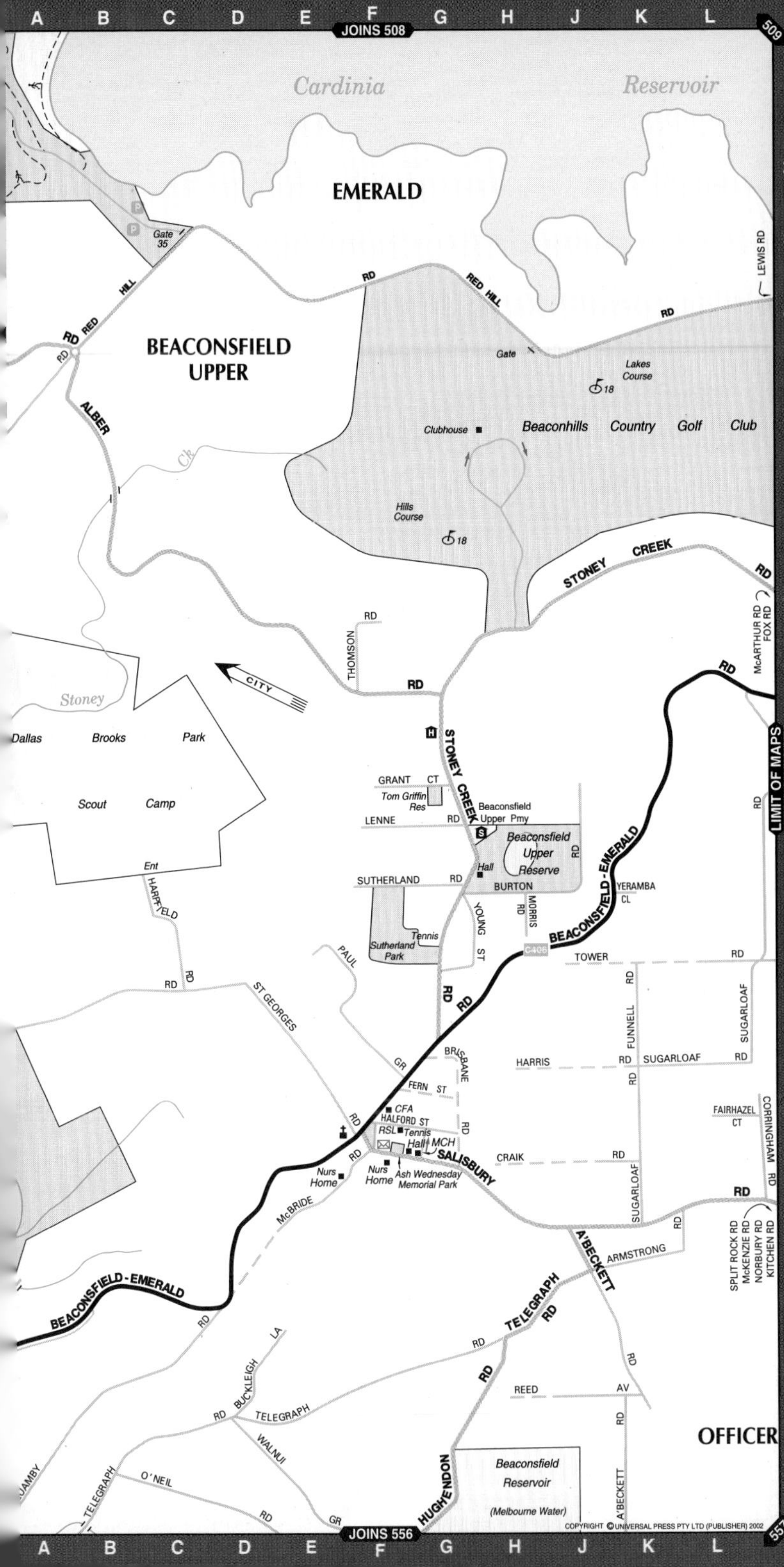
A B C D E F G H J K L
JOINS 508
509
1 2 3 4 5 6 7 8 9 10 11 12 13 14 15 16 17 18 19 20
Cardinia Reservoir
EMERALD
BEACONSFIELD UPPER
Gate 35
RED HILL RD
LEWIS RD
ALBER RD
Gate
Lakes Course
18
Clubhouse
Beaconhills Country Golf Club
Hills Course
18
Ck
STONEY CREEK RD
McARTHUR RD
FOX RD
THOMSON RD
CITY
Stoney
Dallas Brooks Park
Scout Camp
Ent
HARPFIELD RD
LIMIT OF MAPS
STONEY CREEK RD
GRANT CT
Tom Griffin Res
Beaconsfield Upper Pmy
LENNE RD
Beaconsfield Upper Reserve
Hall
SUTHERLAND RD
BURTON RD
Tennis
Sutherland Park
YOUNG ST
MORRIS RD
BEACONSFIELD-EMERALD RD
YERAMBA CL
C406
TOWER RD
PAUL
ST GEORGES RD
FUNNELL RD
SUGARLOAF RD
HARRIS RD
BRISBANE RD
GR
FERN ST
CFA
HALFORD ST
RSL
Tennis
Hall
MCH
SALISBURY RD
Nurs Home
Nurs Home
Ash Wednesday Memorial Park
CRAIK RD
FAIRHAZEL CT
CORRINGHAM RD
McBRIDE RD
A'BECKETT RD
ARMSTRONG RD
SPLIT ROCK RD
McKENZIE RD
NORBURY RD
KITCHEN RD
BEACONSFIELD-EMERALD RD
TELEGRAPH RD
BUCKLEIGH LA
REED AV
OFFICER
TELEGRAPH RD
WALNUI GR
HUGHENDON RD
Beaconsfield Reservoir (Melbourne Water)
O'NEIL RD
QUAMBY
A'BECKETT RD
JOINS 556
557

PREVIOUS MAP 542

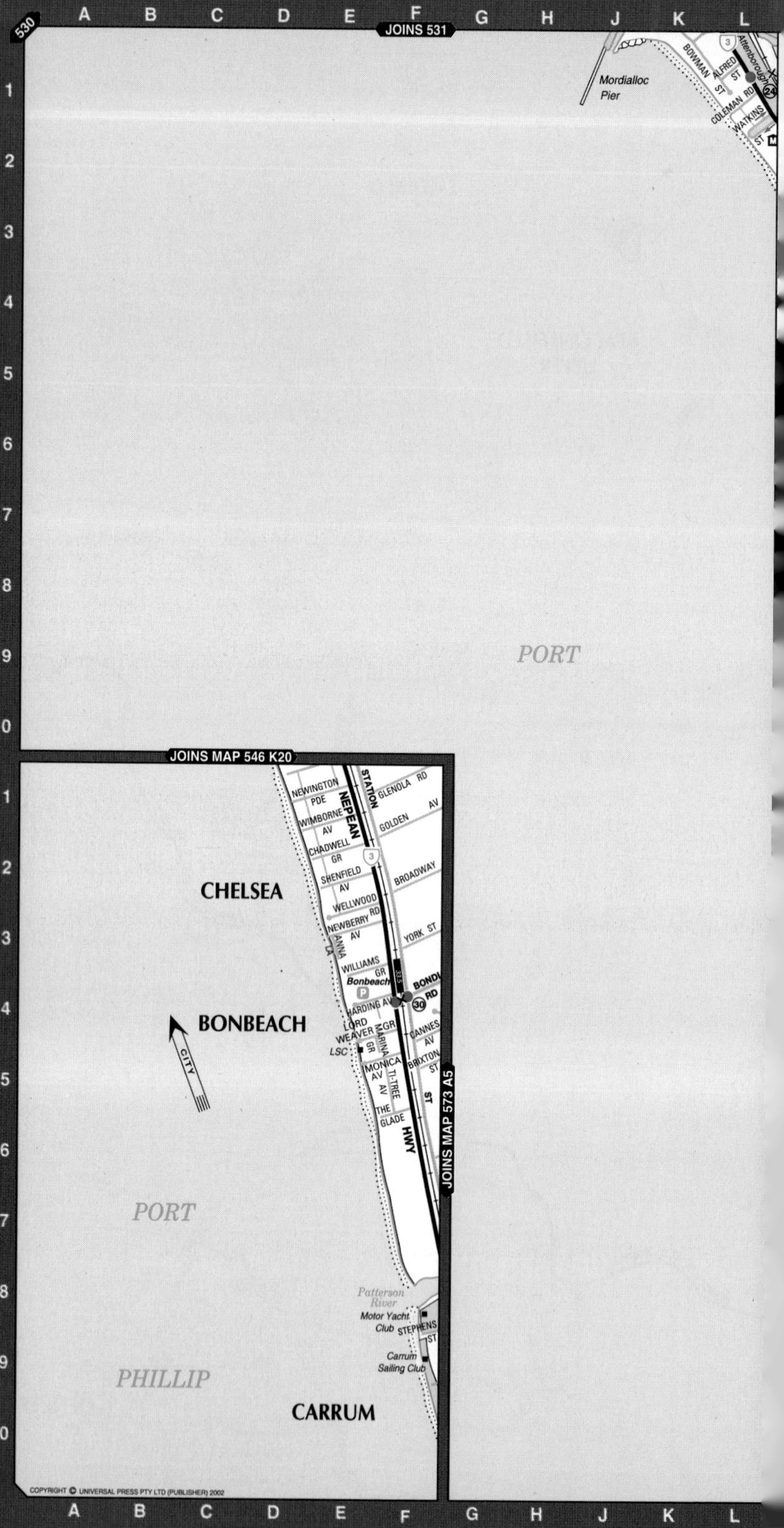

530

JOINS 531

A B C D E F G H J K L

1 2 3 4 5 6 7 8 9 10 11 12 13 14 15 16 17 18 19 20

Mordialloc Pier

BOWMAN ST
ALFRED ST
Attenborough
COLEMAN RD
WATKINS ST

PORT

JOINS MAP 546 K20

NEWINGTON PDE
WIMBORNE AV
CHADWELL GR
SHENFIELD AV
WELLWOOD RD
NEWBERRY AV
ANNA LA
WILLIAMS GR
Bonbeach
HARDING AV
LORD GR
WEAVER GR
MARINA GR
MONICA AV
TI-TREE AV
THE GLADE
NEPEAN HWY
STATION ST
GLENOLA RD
GOLDEN AV
BROADWAY
YORK ST
BONDI RD
CANNES AV
BRIXTON ST
LSC

CHELSEA

BONBEACH

CITY

JOINS MAP 573 A5

PORT

PHILLIP

Patterson River

Motor Yacht Club

STEPHENS ST

Carrum Sailing Club

CARRUM

A B C D E F G H J K L

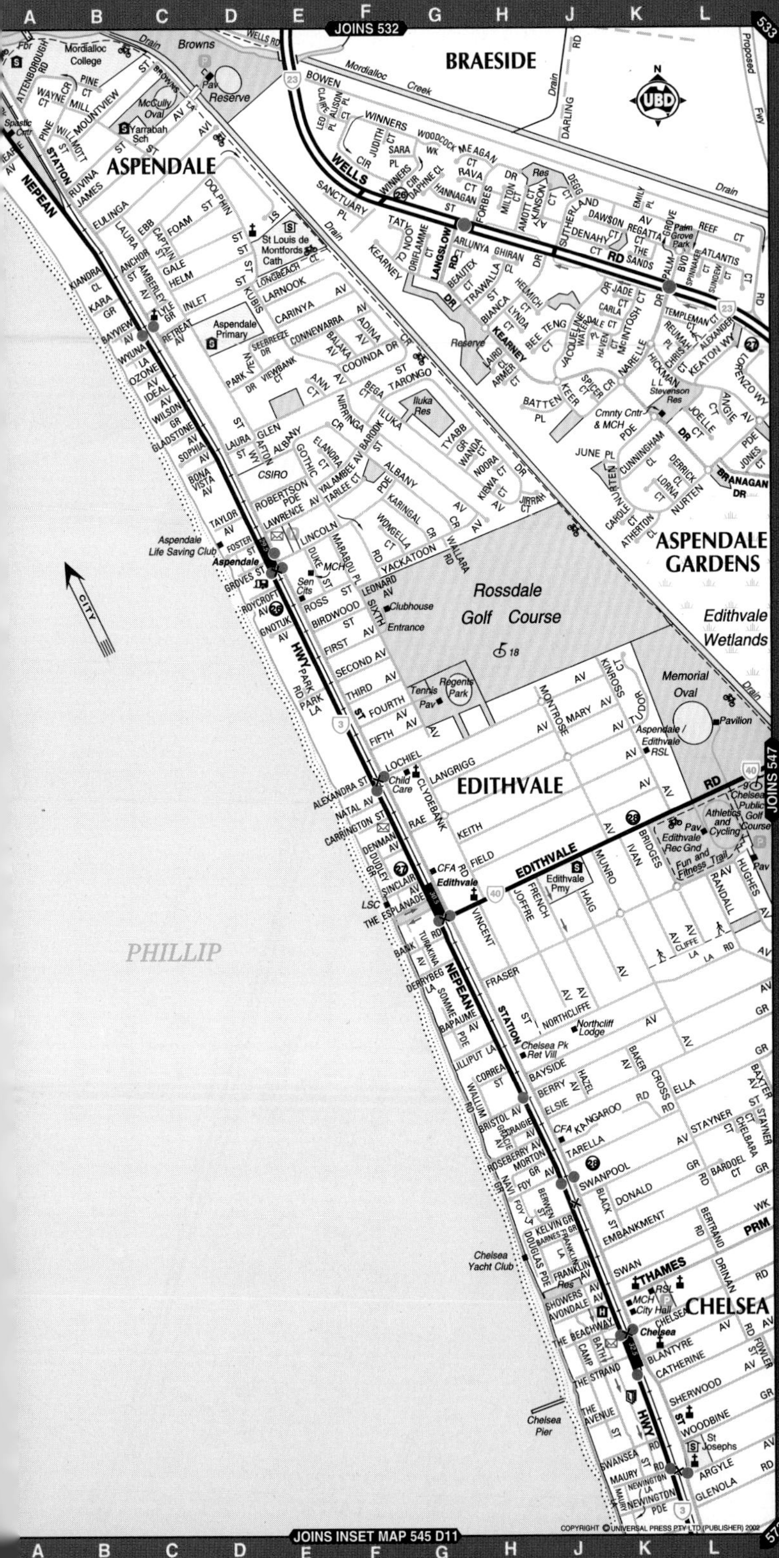

JOINS 532

A B C D E F G H J K L

BRAESIDE

ASPENDALE

ASPENDALE GARDENS

EDITHVALE

CHELSEA

PHILLIP

Mordialloc College

Browns Reserve

McCully Oval

Yarrabah Sch

St Louis de Montfords Cath

Aspendale Primary

Iluka Res

Rossdale Golf Course

Clubhouse

Entrance

Regents Park

Tennis Pav

Edithvale Wetlands

Memorial Oval

Pavilion

Aspendale / Edithvale RSL

Chelsea Public Golf Course

Athletics and Cycling

Edithvale Rec Gnd

Fun and Fitness Trail

Edithvale Pmy

Aspendale Life Saving Club

Stevenson Res

Cmnty Cntr & MCH

Palm Grove Park

Northcliff Lodge

Chelsea Pk Ret Vill

Chelsea Yacht Club

Chelsea Pier

City Hall

St Josephs

NEPEAN HWY

WELLS RD

EDITHVALE RD

STATION ST

THAMES PRM

JOINS 547

JOINS INSET MAP 545 D11

A B C D E F G H J K L

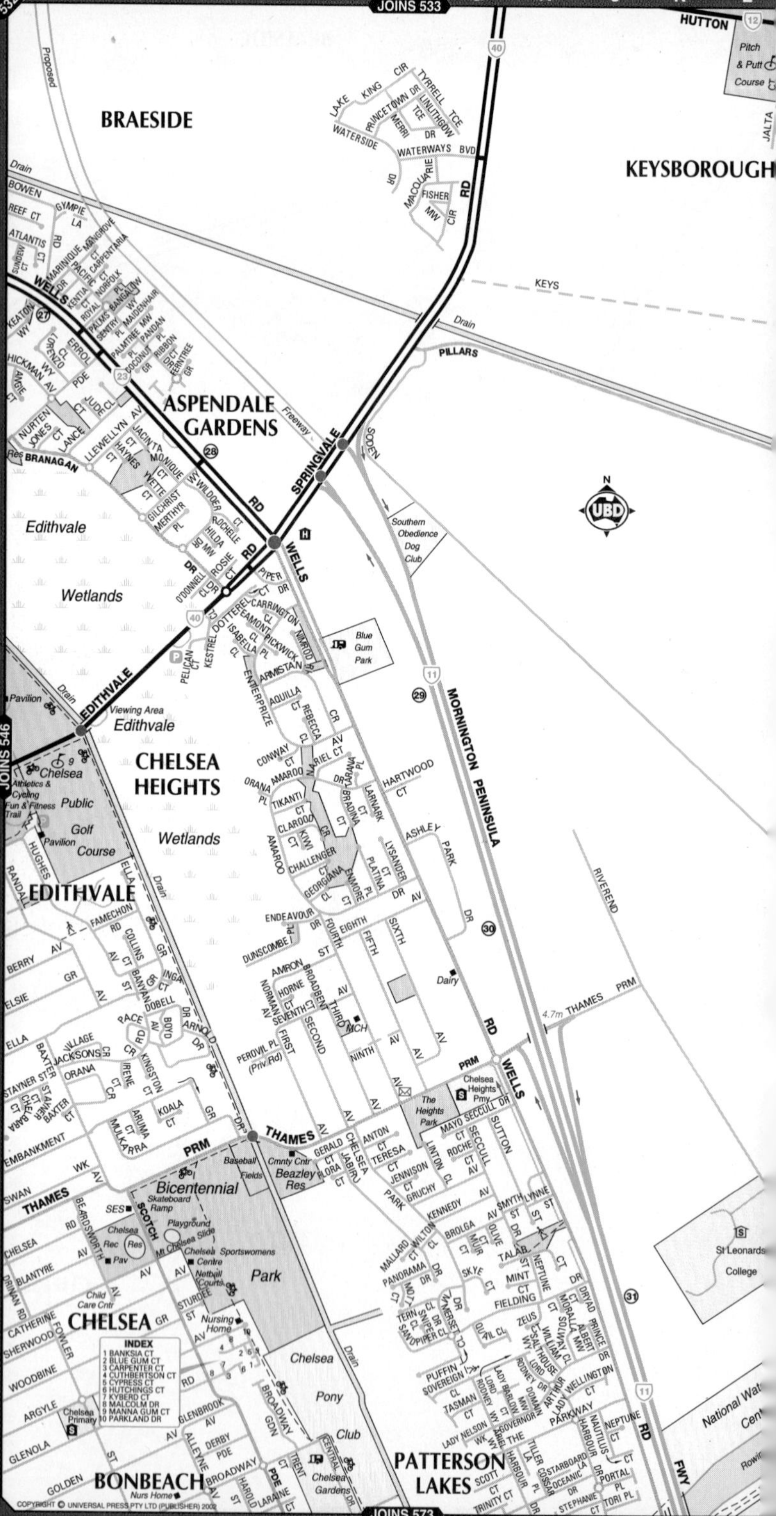
JOINS 533
JOINS 573
JOINS 546
532
BRAESIDE
KEYSBOROUGH
ASPENDALE GARDENS
Edithvale Wetlands
CHELSEA HEIGHTS
Wetlands
EDITHVALE
CHELSEA
BONBEACH
PATTERSON LAKES
WELLS RD
SPRINGVALE RD
EDITHVALE RD
MORNINGTON PENINSULA FWY
THAMES PRM
KEYS
PILLARS
HUTTON
BOWEN
Pitch & Putt Course
Southern Obedience Dog Club
Blue Gum Park
Chelsea Public Golf Course
Viewing Area
Bicentennial Park
Chelsea Pony Club
St Leonards College
The Heights Park
Chelsea Heights Pmy
Beazley Res
Chelsea Primary
Nurs Home
Nursing Home
Chelsea Gardens
Dairy
INDEX
1 BANKSIA CT
2 BLUE GUM CT
3 CARPENTER CT
4 CUTHBERTSON CT
5 CYPRESS CT
6 HUTCHINGS CT
7 KYBERD CT
8 MALCOLM DR
9 MANNA GUM CT
10 PARKLAND DR

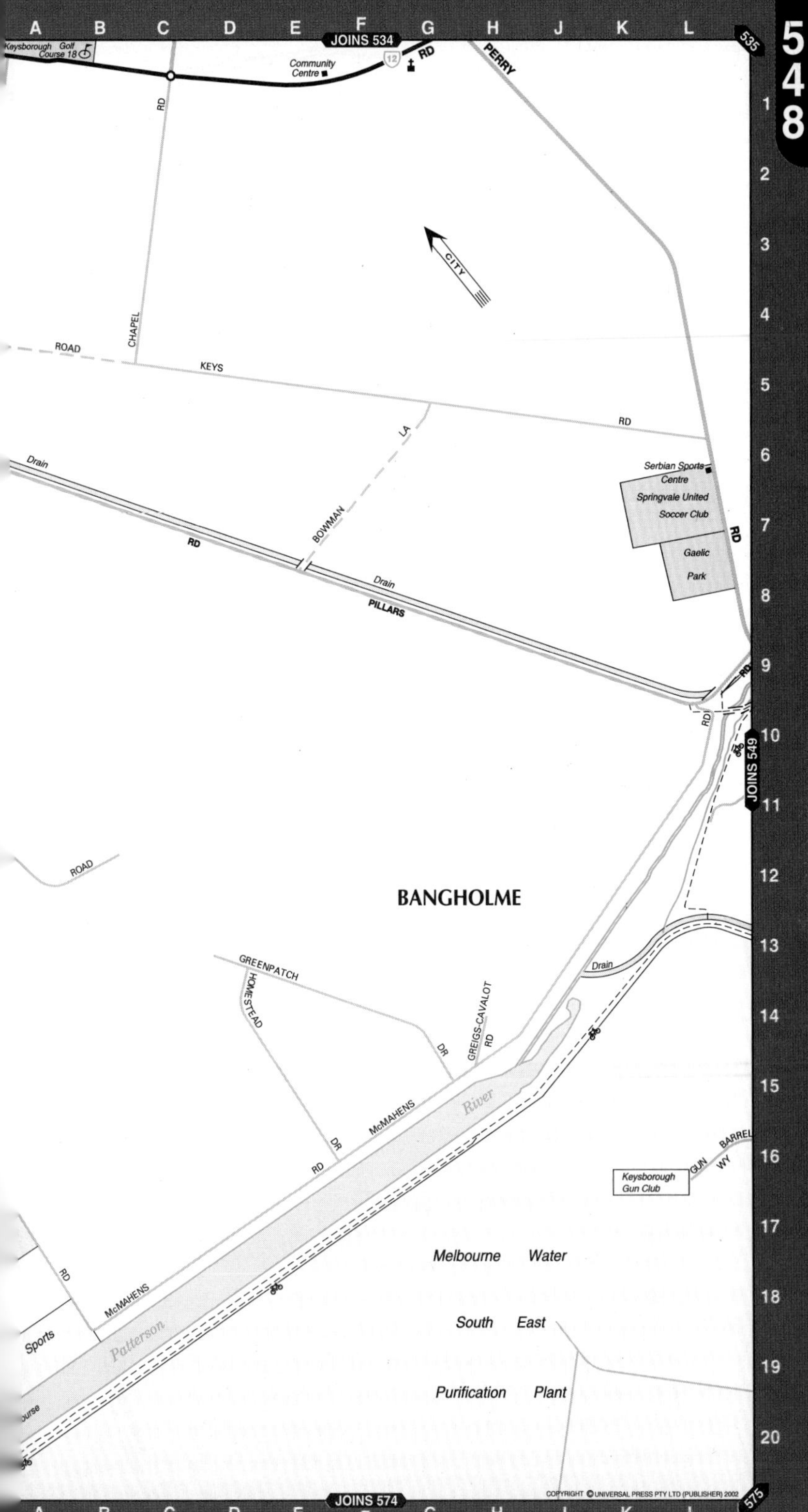

A B C D E F G H J K L
JOINS 534
535
Keysborough Golf Course 18
Community Centre
RD
PERRY
12
RD
CITY
CHAPEL
ROAD
KEYS
RD
LA
Drain
BOWMAN
RD
Drain
PILLARS
Serbian Sports Centre
Springvale United Soccer Club
RD
Gaelic Park
RD
RD
JOINS 549
ROAD
BANGHOLME
Drain
GREENPATCH
HOMESTEAD
GREIGS-CAVALOT
RD
DR
River
McMAHENS
DR
RD
GUN
BARREL
WY
Keysborough Gun Club
RD
McMAHENS
Melbourne Water
South East
Purification Plant
Sports
Patterson
JOINS 574
575
1 2 3 4 5 6 7 8 9 10 11 12 13 14 15 16 17 18 19 20

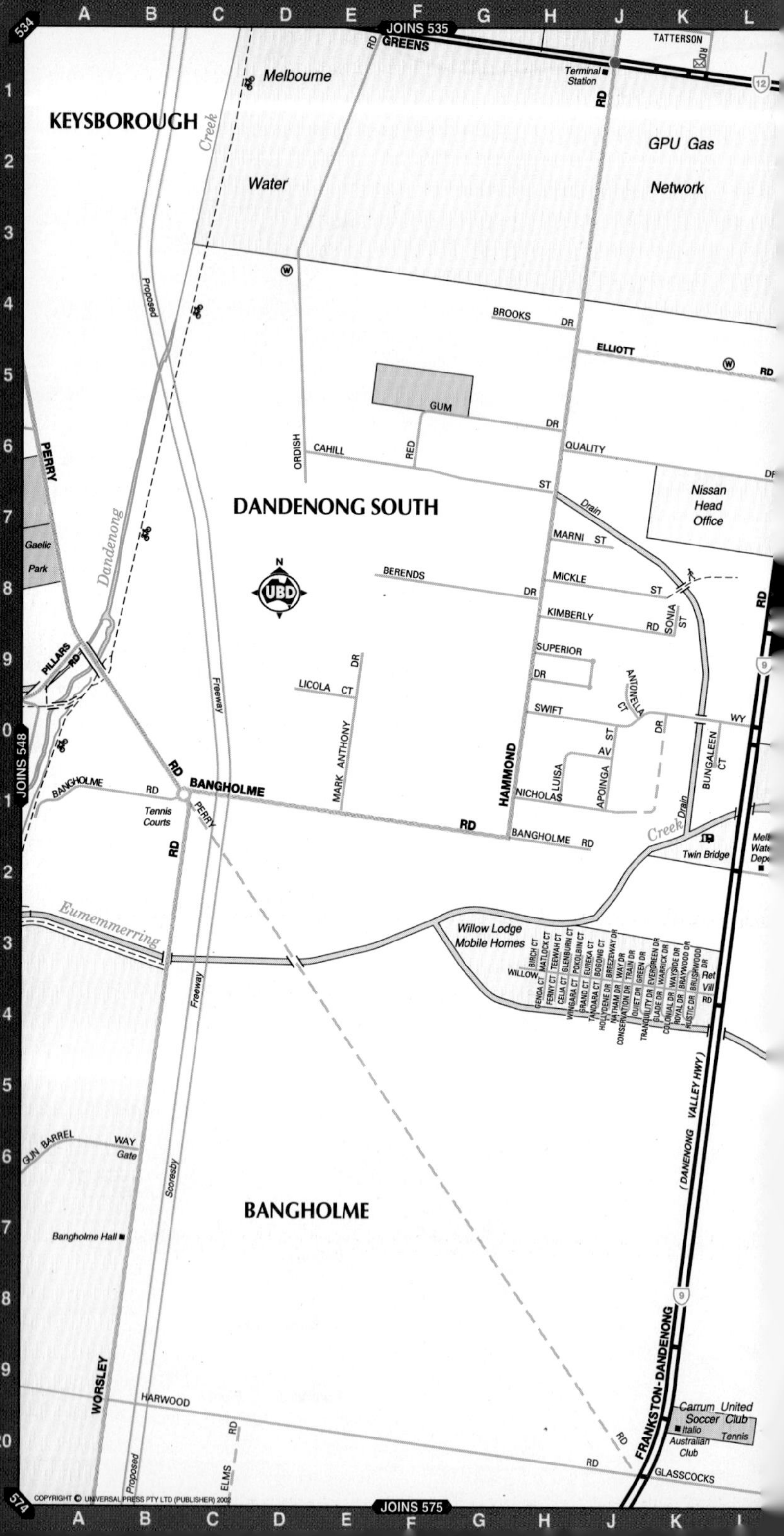

JOINS 535
534
KEYSBOROUGH
Melbourne
Water
Creek
GREENS RD
TATTERSON RD
Terminal Station
GPU Gas
Network
Proposed
BROOKS DR
ELLIOTT RD
GUM DR
RED
ORDISH
CAHILL ST
QUALITY DR
Nissan
Head
Office
DANDENONG SOUTH
Drain
PERRY
Gaelic
Park
Dandenong
MARNI ST
BERENDS DR
MICKLE ST
KIMBERLY RD
SONIA ST
SUPERIOR DR
ANTONELLA CT
SWIFT WY
PILLARS RD
LICOLA CT
MARK ANTHONY DR
Freeway
BANGHOLME RD
Tennis Courts
PERRY RD
HAMMOND RD
LUISA ST
APOINGA AV
NICHOLAS
DR
BUNGALEEN CT
Creek
Drain
Twin Bridge
JOINS 548
Eumemmerring
Willow Lodge
Mobile Homes
WILLOW
BIRCH CT
MATLOCK CT
TEEWAH CT
GLENBURN CT
POKOLBIN CT
EUREKA CT
BOGONG CT
BREEZEWAY DR
GENOA CT
FERNY CT
CELIA CT
WINGARA CT
GRAND CT
TANDARA CT
HOLLYDENE DR
NATHAM DR
WAY DR
TRAIN DR
CONSERVATION DR
QUIET DR
GREEN DR
TRANQUILITY DR
GLADE DR
EVERGREEN DR
COLONIAL DR
WARRICK DR
WAYSIDE DR
ROYAL DR
BRAYWOOD DR
RUSTIC DR
BRUSHWOOD DR
Ret Vill
RD
(DANDENONG VALLEY HWY)
GUN BARREL WAY
Gate
Scoresby
BANGHOLME
Bangholme Hall
FRANKSTON-DANDENONG RD
WORSLEY
HARWOOD RD
ELMS RD
Proposed
Carrum United
Soccer Club
Italio Australian Club
Tennis
GLASSCOCKS RD
574
JOINS 575

GREENS RD
Pilkington ACI
WILLIAMS RD
NICOLE WY
ST
CAPITAL DR
RD
SOUTH GIPPSLAND HWY
ROUND TOWER RD
HALLAM VALLEY RD
HEDDERWICK
Proposed Freeway
Drain
Reserve
WATERVIEW CL
M420
Coles Distribution Centre
Ent
CARTER WY
Creek
ZENITH
LANYON
RD
ADVANTAGE DR
DR
NISSAN DR
DANDENONG VALLEY HWY
MONTEREY RD
CITY
TYREE PL
COMMERCIAL
HEALEY
POUND RD
PELCON CT
KNOWLES RD
HEALEY RD
KITCHEN RD
HEALEY DR
QUANTUM CL
HYDRIVE CL
ENGLAND ST
PARK
GALLI CT
GAINE RD
ABBOTTS RD
REMINGTON
Eumemmerring
AUSCO PL
Retarding Basin
COLEMANS RD
Pacific Waste Management
LYNDHURST
TAYLORS RD
BAYLISS RD
Drain
RD

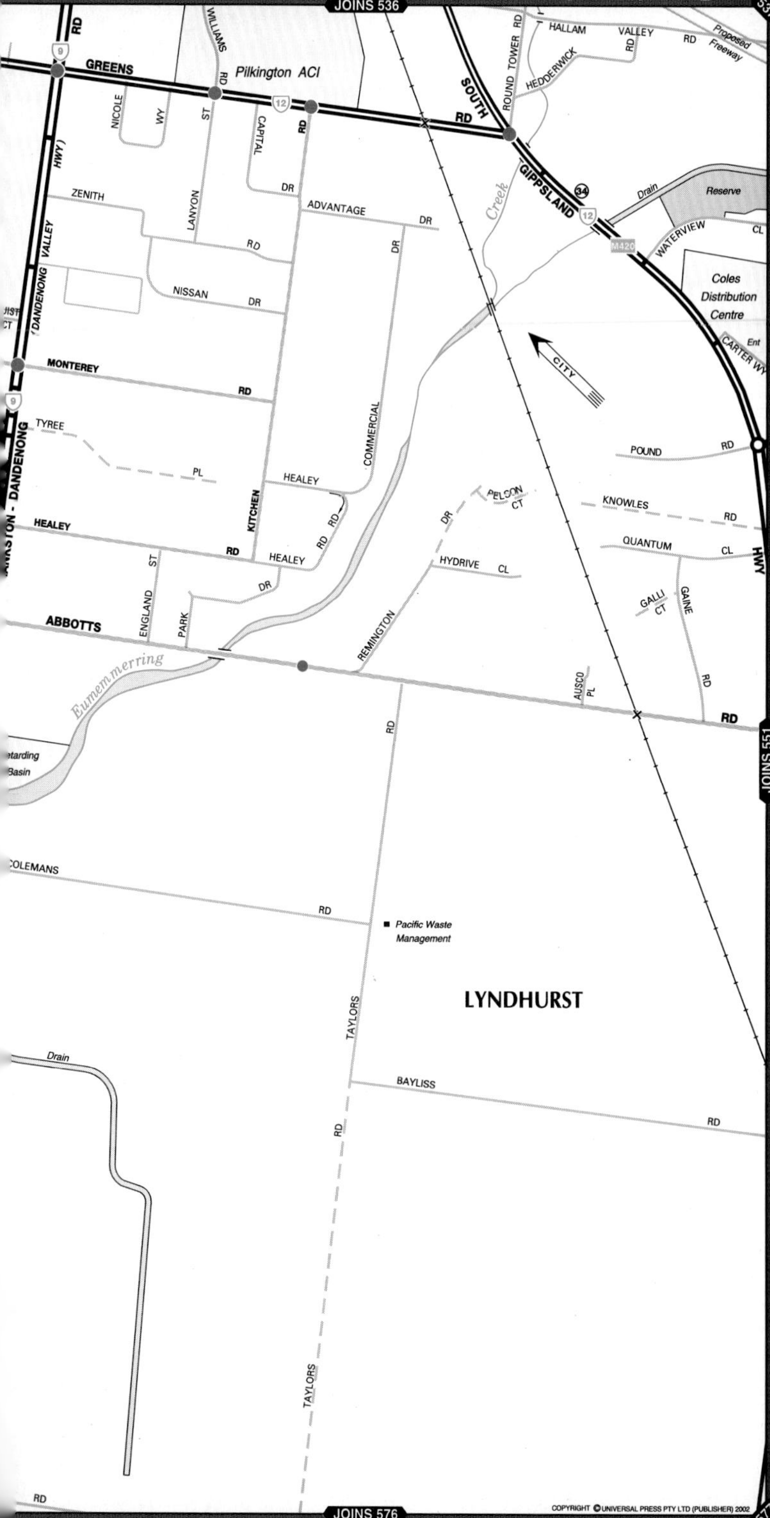

536 · JOINS 537

A B C D E F G H J K L

1 2 3 4 5 6 7 8 9 10 11 12 13 14 15 16 17 18 19 20

HALLAM

LYNBROOK

Proposed HALLAM VALLEY Freeway RD
O'GRADY
APOLLO DR · WESTPOOL DR · STAR CR · EMPIRE WY · KEPPEL · RD
Hallam · BANNON CT · RD
Reserve · WATERVIEW CL
K M Reedy Reserve · Hockey · Football-Cricket Pav · Soccer · Hockey & Soccer · Tennis
Coles Distribution Centre
CARTER WY · Ent
SOUTH GIPPSLAND FWY
M420 · 12 · 5.38m · 6.3m · 5.45m
Drain · WILLOW DRIVE
POUND RD
AFFRA PL · TELFORD CT · BRUNEL CT · LONGFORD CL · ROWLAND CL · CONIFER CL · RUDLOE PL · DR · HARBURY MW · ADLEY PL · DULNAIN CT · EDGERTON CT · CHANNELLE CL · KENSINGTON CT · GARFIELD CT · MUNRO CT · DARLING CL · CAROLINE PL
OAKTREE DR · FULHAM CL · CHISWICK CT · ASHFORD CL · EDSALL CL · VERONA CT · DALVANA CT · HAZELDEAN CT · NARELLAN CR · MILLSWYN DR · ELLASWOOD CT · BARNSBURY CL · AVOCA CL · PEPPERMINT CT · Res · THE HARCOURT CL · BLACKWOOD
CASUARINA CT · BARRINGTON PL · HIGHTON CL · WYCOMBE CT · RIMINGTON CT · POLLINA CT · ASHDALE CL · BECKINGTON DR · AV · MANNING CL · TRAVALLA CT · COTHAM SQ · GRANGE DR · COPPIN CL · URQUHART · JUSTIN FAYE PL · BUNYA PL · GABRIELLE CL · CCT · CANDLE · JOEL WY · JUSTIN
MARY KAROL CT · ST · GARNET CT · WILLIS CL · Res · VANESSA · MARSHALL CT · SINCLAIR CT · JAMBE CT · RD · WAYSIDE CT · AV · Sen Cits · HAMPTON CL · ANDERSON DR · HIGHLAND · GREEN VALLEY · SUNNYVALE CT · BROOK CT · VILLAGE DR
George Knowles Res · MARK CT · BELVEDERE CT · HAYES RD · Res · GLEN CT · WINNIMA · BRIDE · Hampton Park Rec Res · Tennis · BELLVUE CT · COTTAGE AV CT · DEANSWOOD · SILVAN CR · Reserve · LEONNE CT · DELACOMBE CT · ROHAN CT · BRADLEY CT · TARELLA ST · ROSALIE CT · LAUREN DR · WARANA
KNOWLES RD · SOMERVILLE · ROBJANT · JENNER CT · RD · ST · ALMA · Hampton Park Pmy · MCH · RD · HUGHES CT · BRENTNALL CT · DR · ST · FAIRWAY · CFA · AV · ST · OUTLOOK DR · HALLAM RD
TADSTAN DR · Marjorie Eastick Res · REGANS RD · FOX CL · KERRISON DR · CODY AV · MARLENE CT · NOLA CT · PITMAN CT · CLIVE · KELLIE CT · JAYNE CT · THE VIEW · PARKLAND ORA · WREN · ROBINSON · DORTAD CR · Hampton Park · CRAIGIE CT · STRONG DR · SUE · HEDLEY PL
JASPER CT · FORDHOLM · River Gum Pmy · TATTERSON ST · Cmnty Hall · COMMERCE DR · ENTERPRISE AV · STUART · ROBB CT
TOPAZ WY · CLIVE · LILLIAN CT · EMERALD CT · JEFFREY · TALBOT · GEORGE CT · KATHLEEN · Res · LORRAINE · MATTHEW CT · ANDREW · Hampton Park Secondary College · DR · TYALLA CT · KING DAVID CT · DR · CORAL · Reserve
ABBOTTS RD · JADE CT · SAPPHIRE DR · AQUAMARINE ST · MARGARET CT · ROBYN · SHELLEY · DAVID CT · VALERIE CT · STANLEY ST · PAUL CT · EVELYN · SUSAN CT · GENERAL CT · JOSHUA · THANOS CT · PRINCESS CT · KOOYONG CL · ROAD · Retirement Village · CLAUDE · LINDA · AV
CAIRNS · FEENEY CT · Res · ST RD · DOROTHY CT · CAMPBELL · IVAN · MARIA PL · CRESCENT · EDEYS · ISAAC PL · WESTMINSTER
BRANTON DR · MOSIG CT · LUKE CT · JASON RD · ALASTER CT · BERRIDALE · ALPINE WK · THE CLOSE · CT · PARKES WY · LA · MARIE CT · REEVES · Reserve · CAIRNS · CHESTER DR · HAWKING CL · PRIDE CT · CASH CL · CLIVE · RILEY PL · ROBBINS AV · WY · WYNETTE CL · CONWAY CT · DENVER · RD · St Kevins Cath Pmy · MOLLISONS · HILL · MAYRUCK · RISE · EDEY · RU
BRANTON DR · McDOWALL · ELANORA WK · GREENLEA · THE EYRIE GR · GUMTREE · OWENS CT · HORTON DR · STRAVANE · BAEZ WY · RENDELL PL · KYLIE CT · SPRINGFIELD · CR · PIONEER PL · KELLER CT · CHERYL · KATHERINE CT · HEATHER
CENTRAL · THE RETREAT · YARRAN CT · BATEMAN GR · BRUTUS ST · CENTRAL · FARSKIENE · CUSH PL · PL · TULSK CT · DONEGAL WY · YASMIN CT · WY · HUNTINGTON · DR · RD
HORTON RD · WENDY CT · TERRY CT · PATRICIA CT · HAZEL CT · ROBERT CR · MICHELLE · MELIS
ORMOND · THE GLADE · TOOHEY CL · BATEMAN · SHORT · RD · SUMMIT CT · GRAHAM CT · LEOPOLD · Res · HORIZON CT · SUNRISE · BVD
RD · HWY) · RD · THE SPUR · CIRRU · STRAT · NIMBL · RIDGE CT · SUNSET PL · PINNACLE · DEWPOINT · ALPHA CT · PLATEAU CR · AV
DUTTON · GILMORE CL · Mackellar Park · DOBSON · BUCKLEY · TRANTER · OLIVE · SILVER CREEK DR · GLENSHEE · PARK CITY WY · MERIBEL · SUGAR BUSH DR · WYNDHAM DR · ARGYLE PL · ORMOND · STELLATO PL · ELPARA WY · KAROONDA · WOODSIDE CL · SELBOURNE PL · RED
Lyndhurst BAYLISS RD · PORT · DURACK PL · HUTCHINSON · FORBES CR · DAV · BRADY CL · DR · BVD · PATERSON DR · MACLEOD AV · WY · SLESSOR AV · DYSON · LINDSAY CR · LAWSON · HENRY · CHAUNCY WY · DR · KEYSTONE CT · SUN VALLEY BVD · DERBY · BROOME · BVD · LYNBROOK · TOWERHILL · SUGARLOAF AV · SILVERTOP CL · (WESTERN
Commercial Sands (Private Waste Disposal) · A780 · MAY GIBBS · CR · GUMNUT LA · PATERSON · LYNBROOK DR · BLUE RANGE CR · BVD · CAVERSHAM TCE · NUGONG CL · PARSLOW · ST BERNARDS CR · COBBLER GRA · HALLAM
AMY MACK WK · ELDERSHAW DR · HASLUCK CR · PEDLEY WY · LOUISE MACK WK · Proposed Lynbrook Station
DARCY LA · CULOTTA LA · NILAND CR · O'GRADY BVD · DANDENONG - HASTINGS · HWY
AYLMER RD

JOINS 550 · 576 · JOINS 577

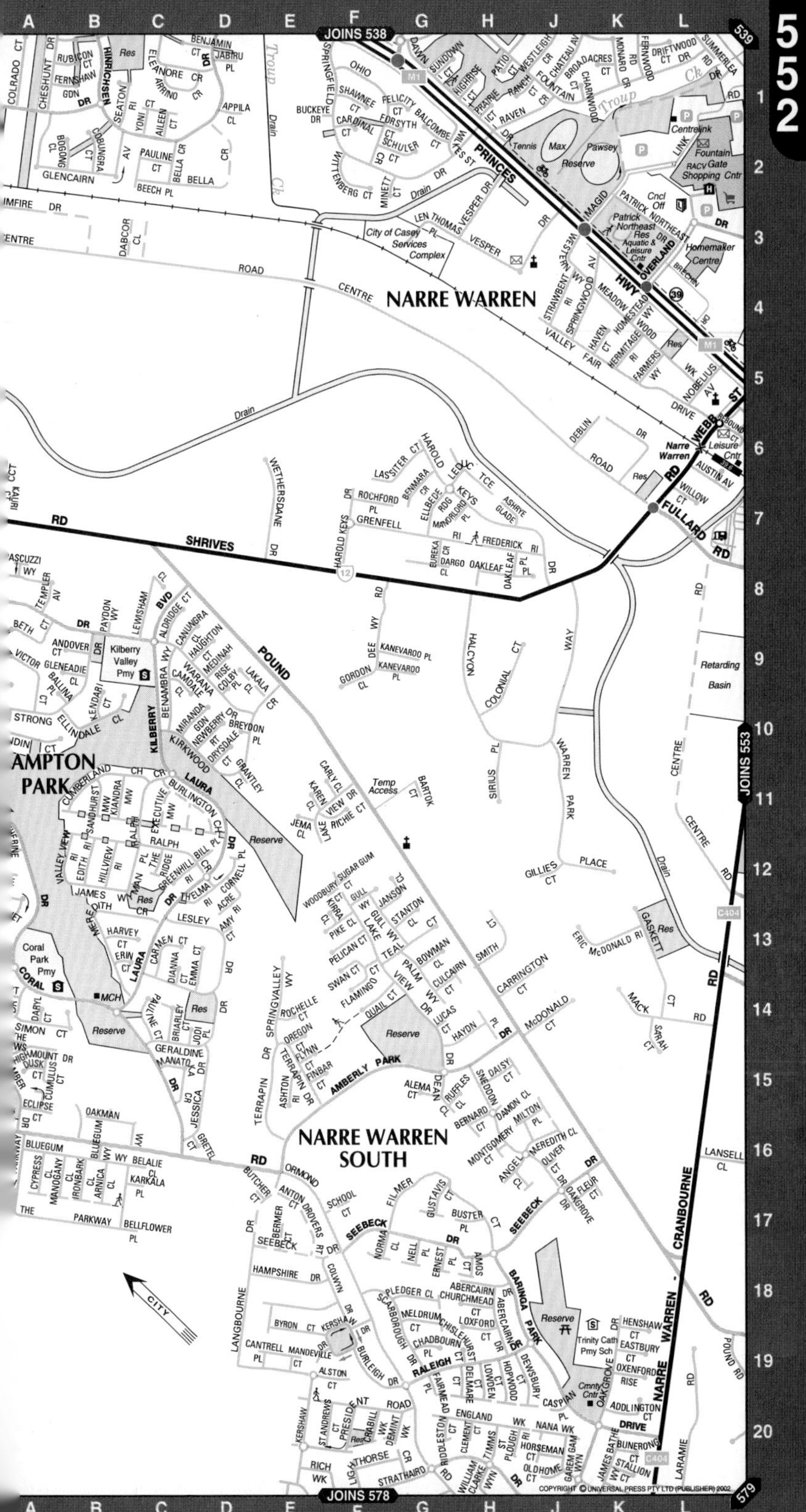

JOINS 538
NARRE WARREN
NARRE WARREN SOUTH
HAMPTON PARK
PRINCES HWY
SHRIVES RD
POUND RD
CENTRE ROAD
NARRE WARREN - CRANBOURNE RD
JOINS 553
JOINS 578
COPYRIGHT © UNIVERSAL PRESS PTY LTD (PUBLISHER) 2002

A B C D E F G H J K L

538 · JOINS 539

UBD

NARRE WARREN

NARRE WARREN SOUTH

NORA CT · HEYNGTON · SALIGNUS CT · DIOSMA CT · CASUARINA CT · RUFUS CT · COACHWOOD CR · HILLCREST AVN · BELDALE CT · PARKHILL DR · MIRRA CT · ATTUNGA CT · GINGHAM PL · ERNST WANKE · CITRINUS CR · CALLISTEMON CR · ALBENS PL · MAIZE PL · RYELANDS · CHERRY TREE LA · Timbarra Pmy Sch · ABOOK CT · COOMA CT · Hessells Road Retarding Basin · LOGAN PL · ROXBURGH · CAMIRA CT · WARRAWONG CT · MAGARRA CR · WEMBLY DR · CIVIC PL · PEMBROKE CT

Fountain Gate Shopping Centre · LINK · Hallam · C404 · NARRE WARREN NORTH RD · CALLISTEMON CR · PALLIDUS WY · SANDALWOOD · THE OAKS · COACHWOOD CR · WIRRAB PL · ARRA · CULMARA · TARRAN · GOWER PL · Reserve · ADELONG CT · TELFORD · GENA · HAGEN CT

SPLENDENS WK · Bypass · ASIANDRA CCT · FARRER PL · TALLARA SQ · SUNNY SIDE · PINEWOOD · KONAC CT · VALLEY VIEW · BUDERIM CT · YERAMBA RT · MALLEE CT · EMERSON CT · HIBBERD CT · DALPURA CT · FARNSWORTH CT · Reserve

OVERLAND DR · VICTOR · Homemaker Centre · FLORET PL · INSIGNIA CR · FESTIVAL CT · QUADRAT CL · AMAROO CT · TCE · THE · MAGDALENA · DULKARA · LEONARD DR · AVA CT · NANGWARRY · ILLOWRA CT · GLENDALE · YALDARA · OTTERBURN

GATEWAY · ADELAIDE CT · TENANDRA CT · MELALEUCA CT · BAYLISS · HEPBURN · KURANDA · PINNACLE PL · EMMA CT · THEODORE CT · BANGALAY CT · COOLABAH · GR · TELFORD DR · CHARTER CL · YANDILLA CT · COOLONG · GUMNUT CT · COOWARRA · OSCAR CT · MAHOGANY CT · BOWEN CT · HESSELL · Kirsty Lottkowitz Reserve · SHAND CT · CONFAIT · GLENBRAE

BRECHIN · Under · NERANG CT · BOREE AV · MESSMATE CT · CAMDEN WAY · NULLICA CT · HOWITT CT · AV · AVEBURY DR · FLORENCE AV · LEXCEN CL · BERTRAND CT · CARRINGTON PL · WILLIAM · SSC · M1 · WEBB ST · LAUDERDALE · VERDUN DR · Percy Trewin Reserve · WIMMERA CT · JERICHO CT · MITRE CT · PARKHILL DR · MCH · Cmnty Ctr · Hugh Hodson Reserve · LYDIA MARY · CELESTE CT

NOBELIUS AV · Tennis · REGENCY DR · COVENTRY RD · CR · Don Bosco Cath Pmy · DON BOSCO DR · VERDUN DR · Construction · CURRINGA CL · KARWIN CL · JUMBUCK CT · YATE MW · STRINGYBARK CT · ARGYLE CT · GRANT CT · Berwick Priv Nursing Home · MORINDA · PAYNE CT · HARDY CT · STURROCK CT · MARYN CL · QUA

PRINCES HWY · Narre Warren · MALCOLM · SYLVIA · REDBOUND · Child Care Ctr · Cmnty Ctr · Leisure Ctr · Nick Dredge Res · LANCASTER AV · KEYS CT · WAUCHOPE AV · LLOYD · WOODLEY ST · KOORANG · TILBA CT · M1 · PRINCES · 41 · 5.4m · HOOD CT

AUSTIN AV · MORAN ST · STEWART · KENT · RD · MAITLAND ST · WALTON CT · ST · Res · SWEENEY · ANGUS CT · CROWLEY AV · HILLBRICK CT · DUNKINSON · RICHARDSON · ROLSTONE CT · HANLEY CT · TRALEE CT · TEE CT · Cyril Molyneux Reserve · VAN DER HAAR AV · LODGE · EZARD CT · DUNNELL RI · FOULDS CT · DUCKWORTH

Narre Warren · Ent · Narre Warren Stn Pmy · BRADLEY · SAXONWOOD · FULLARD RD · CFA · Berwick Lodge Pmy · CLARK CT · HEARD CL · UPTON CR · FIONA · DR · FERMOY WY · MANSFIELD · CR · WY

REDWOOD · TINGLE CT · CL · JARRAH CT · WARREN CL · TCE · DRIVE · DARLING · BEVERLY CT · CAMEO CT · BRIAR CT · CL · WOODLANDS · COLLINS · WALSH RT · HAWKER GDN · NEAGLE GDN · WATSON MW · MADDEN GDN · Ray Bastin Reserve · C404 · CAULFIELD CT · CAMBERWELL · WESLEY · DR · MAHON CR · VINE CT · BIRCH CT · CR · CRAIG DR · CL · DANIHER

CENTRE · Retarding Basin · CRANBOURNE · NORFOLK · ST JOHNS CT · ST JAMES CT · FUCHSIA CT · JUNIPER CT · RAVENSTHORPE · TANUNDA CL · WAY · Sweeney Reserve · LANTANA · BURWOOD CT · KEW CT · ARMADALE · DR · COTTON WOOD CT · TUSSOCK CT · POORINDA RI · WAY

JOINS 552 · WAVERLEY CT · MALVERN PL · BALWYN CT · MONT DR · Res · MONTEREY CT · RD · PENDULA CT · IRELAND · FAIRLEIGH CT · SANDERS CT · WESLEY · COONARA CT · HANSFORD CT · GREENDALE CT · ROSEMONT CT · SLATER CT · SOLLYA CT · AZALEA · DR · MULGA CR · SR · DRIVE · CORONATA · MOLLIS · M1 · RIPLEY CT · TAMARISK CT · MCH

NARRE WARREN · FLEETWOOD · DR · FLEETWOOD DR · Hallam Valley Primary · DARLING · FORMOSA CT · John Byron Reserve · ARGUS CT · DELPHIN CT · HERALD CT · SABRE CT · COTSWOLD · REDGUM PL · MANNA GUM CT · AUREA CT · NANDINA · Drain

CENTRE RD · SONJA CT · PENTLAND DR · ADA CT · VEGAS AV · WOODROW CT · WARRENWOOD · DELL ST · COSTATA CT · RD · Reserve · GOLF LINKS · SHEARER CT · DR · BLUE GUM CT · NORMAN PL · RD · GOLF · LINKS · ALBERTA WY · GUINESS DR · LARNE CL · LISBURN WY · CADELL PL · GLENISLA WY · PRIME CT · Ent

CENTRE · Drain · DINGLE CT · KINSALE · BEXLEY WY · EGLINTON CT · JEUNE GR · HANCOCK · BELLEVUE · DAHLEN PL · EUSTON KARIN PL · PRIME · Temp Access · GRAND ARCH DR · SHAFTSBURY AV · DANEHILL GR · POSSUM CT · AMI CT · Rese

C404 · KILGERRON CT · BVD · WHITEHALL CT · SHEFFIELD ST · LOXLEY CT · PICCADILLY CT · LOXLEY BVD · SHERBROOKE CT · CENTRE · KALASTAIRE GR · BILBY · BEND · LYNDAL CT · School Site

LANSELL CL · WY · COBBLESTONE · RD · WOOD · HOMESTEAD · SACHIKO CT · CARABOTT PL · GLEN · ERIN WY · HARMON CT · BELLEVUE DR · FEDERATION · HEDGEROW CT · CRYSTAL BROOK · FERN · Reserve · APPLEWOOD PL · FERNY CT · BLOOMFIELD · YIOTA CT · KIRRILEE · CLAREMONT GLN

EVE CL · GR · MEADOW CT · BIRCHWOOD · HYACINTH RI · HILLTOP · SHAMROCK CR · ACORN CT · DIANTHUS · Drain · WARD · CT · BREE CT · Fac · HILLTOP PL · SUNBEAM CT · CL · HIGHLAND CL · PARWOOD · VIEWMOUNT CT · BELLEVUE · DOMAIN · DR

POUND RD · EDEN · GARDEN CT · JINDALEE · MOONBEAN · DEWDROP PL · HIGHLAND · CR · ILANA CT · AV · CL · TREETOP · PINEVIEW · WY · APSLEY TCE · FARNBOROUGH · HATTEN PL · STEPHANIE · SH · DOMAIN DR · GREAVES

RD · POUND · CYPRESS HILL DR · SEQUOIA CT · GRANDVIEW TCE · AVENUE · RD · DR · BOUNTY WY · BOUNTY · RD · CLOCKT · BOULEVARD · SILVER BIRCH · PARK SQ · EASTERN PARK SQ · CONIFER · THE · HICKORY · EVERGOLD CL · ARDBLAIR · LOUISE · BAILE · EDWIN ST

LARAMIE · GWENDA CT · PEACH BLOSSOM · ELM CT · APPLE BLOSSOM · THE PROMENADE · SNOWGUM TERRACE · THE QUADRANT · SYCAMORE · MELBA · PAIGE ST · FEDERATION · NADEEN · KIPPENROSS · ELIZABETH · JACQUELINE · TCE AV · BERWICK SPRINGS PRM · Drain

RD · THE · GOLDEN LEAF AV · HILLRISE · GARDENIA · CL · THE · KIPPENROSS DR · BEGONIA WY · CT

578 · JOINS 579

A B C D E F G H J K L

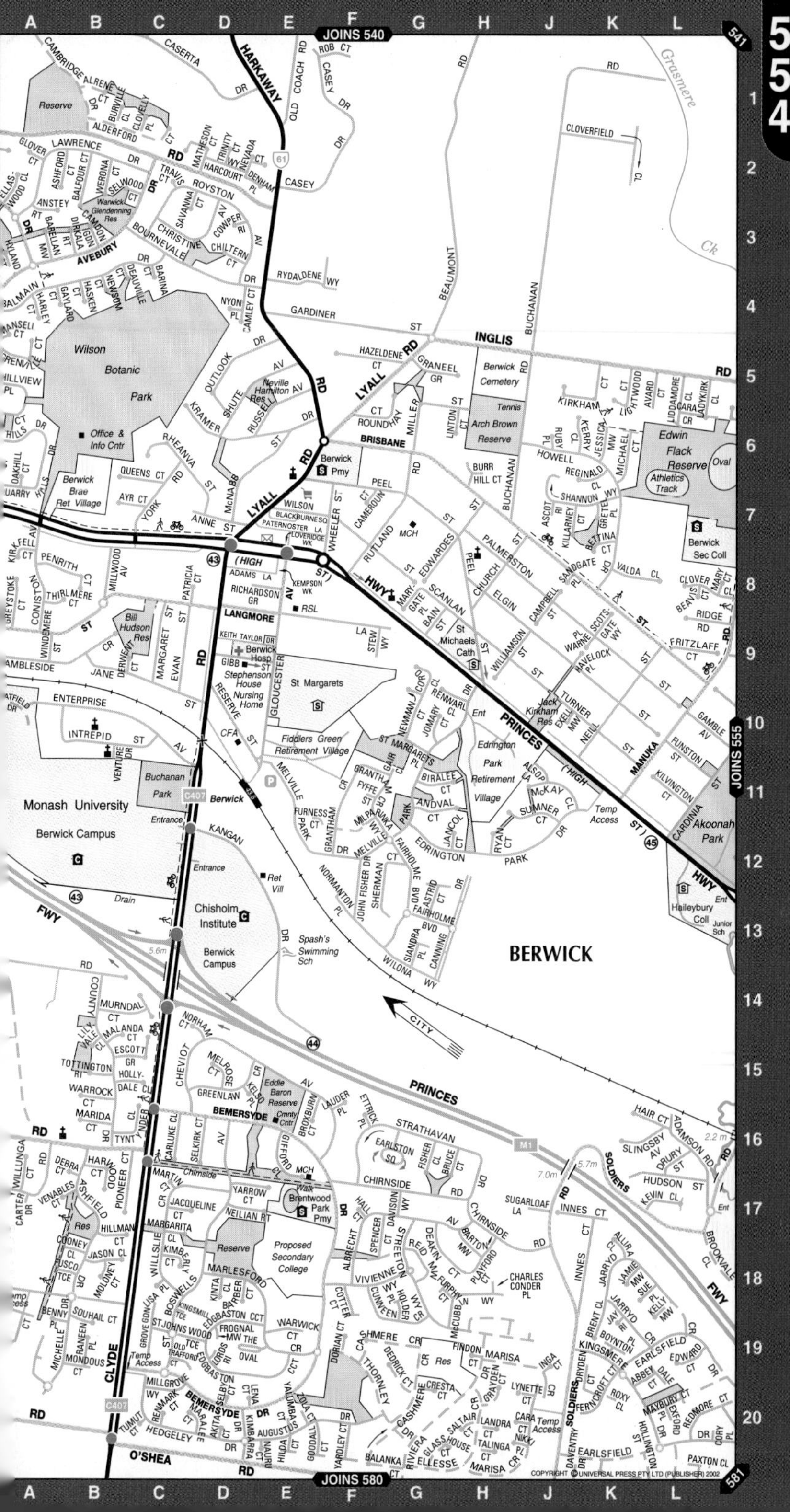
A B C D E F G H J K L
JOINS 540
JOINS 555
JOINS 580
541
581
1 2 3 4 5 6 7 8 9 10 11 12 13 14 15 16 17 18 19 20
BERWICK
Wilson Botanic Park
Office & Info Cntr
Berwick Brae Ret Village
Monash University
Berwick Campus
Chisholm Institute
Berwick Campus
Buchanan Park
Berwick
Entrance
Drain
Spash's Swimming Sch
Ret Vill
Bill Hudson Res
Berwick Hosp
Stephenson House Nursing Home
St Margarets
Fiddlers Green Retirement Village
Edrington Park Retirement Village
St Michaels Cath
Jack Kirkham Res
Berwick Cemetery
Arch Brown Reserve
Tennis
Edwin Flack Reserve
Oval
Athletics Track
Berwick Sec Coll
Akoonah Park
Haileybury Coll
Junior Sch
Temp Access
Neville Hamilton Res
Berwick Pmy
Eddie Baron Reserve
Cmnty Cntr
Brentwood Park Pmy
Proposed Secondary College
Reserve
Res
MCH
RSL
CFA
HARKAWAY RD
CASEY DR
CLOVERFIELD CL
Grasmere Ck
GARDINER ST
INGLIS RD
BEAUMONT RD
BUCHANAN RD
LYALL RD
BRISBANE ST
PEEL ST
PALMERSTON ST
PRINCES HWY (HIGH ST)
PRINCES FWY
CLYDE RD
O'SHEA RD
SOLDIERS RD
LAWRENCE RD
LANGMORE LA
ENTERPRISE AV
KANGAN DR
BEMERSYDE DR
CHIRNSIDE AV
MANUKA RD
CITY
CASERTA DR
OLD COACH RD
ROYSTON RD
AVEBURY DR
WILSON ST
ANNE ST
CLOVER CT
FRITZLAFF CT
STRATHAVAN DR
MARLESFORD RT
CASHMERE CR
EARLSFIELD DR
SUGARLOAF LA
INNES CT
HUDSON ST
FINDON DR
MARISA CT
NORMANTON PL
WILONA WY
COPYRIGHT © UNIVERSAL PRESS PTY LTD (PUBLISHER) 2002

JOINS 541

JOINS 554

JOINS 581

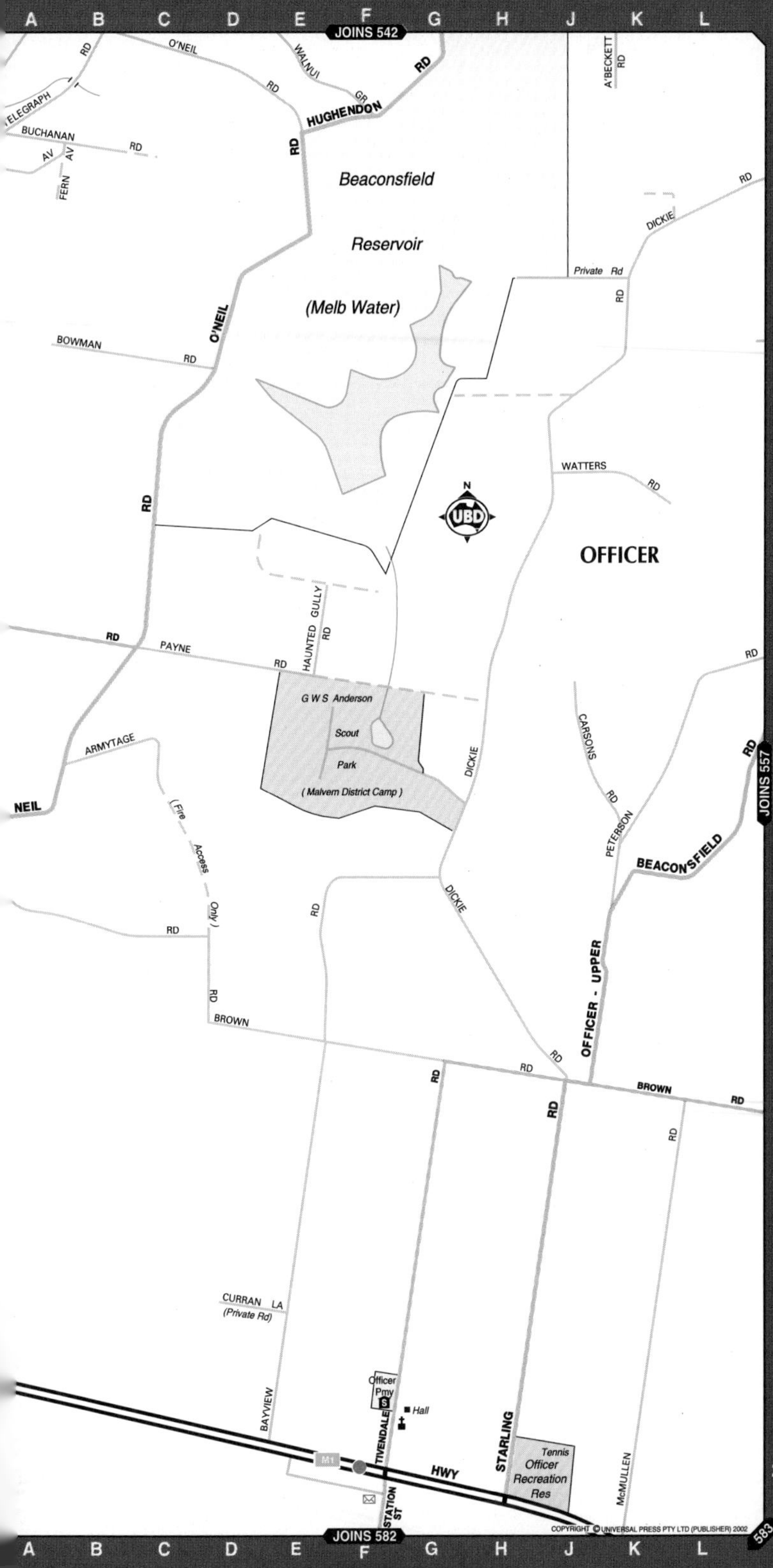

JOINS 542

JOINS 557

JOINS 582

583

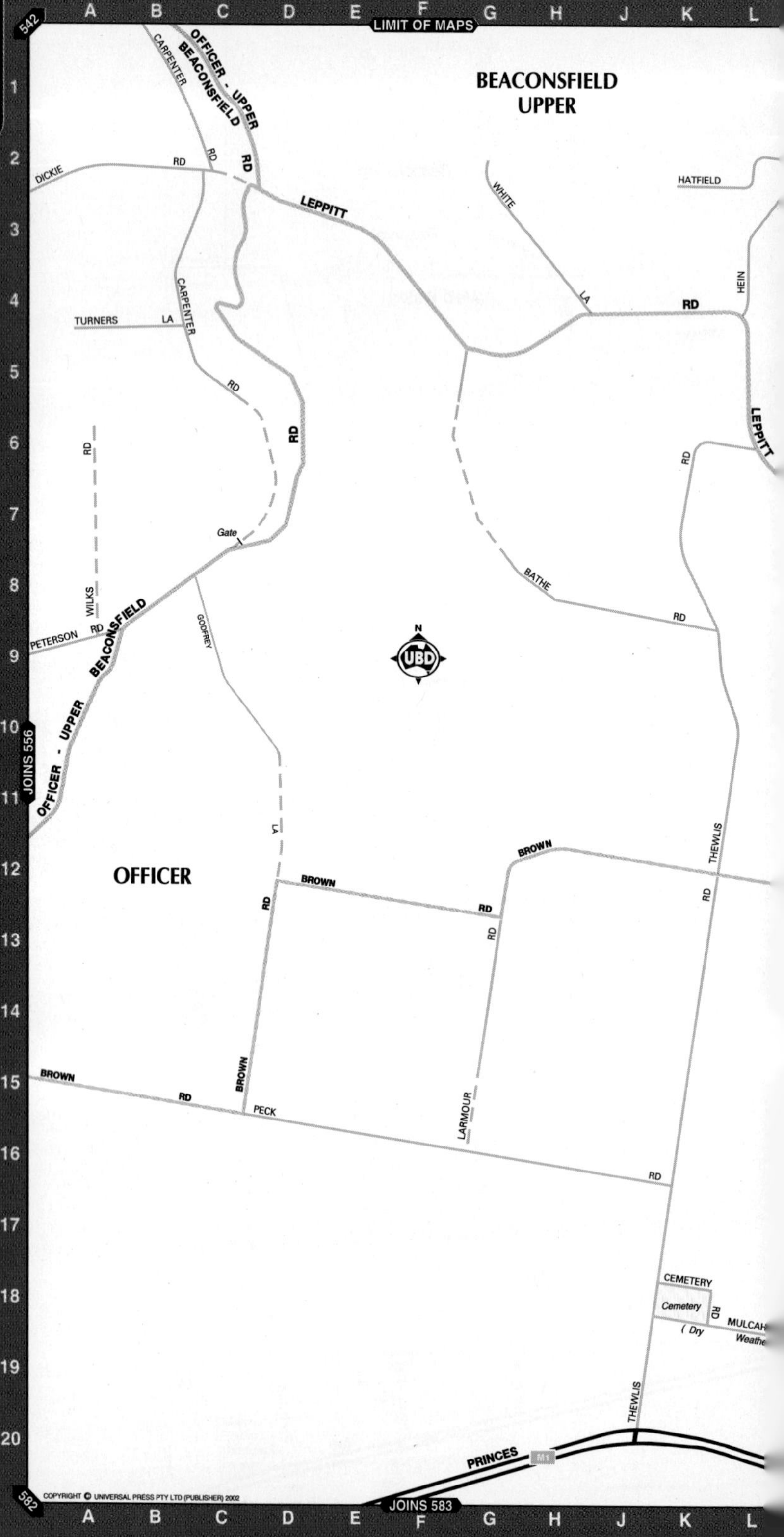

A B C D E F G H J K L

LIMIT OF MAPS

542

BEACONSFIELD UPPER

OFFICER

OFFICER - UPPER BEACONSFIELD RD
CARPENTER RD
DICKIE RD
LEPPITT RD
WHITE LA
HATFIELD
HEIN
TURNERS LA
WILKS RD
Gate
PETERSON RD
GODFREY LA
BATHE RD
BROWN RD
THEWLIS RD
LARMOUR RD
PECK RD
CEMETERY RD
Cemetery
MULCAH(Y)
(Dry Weathe(r)
PRINCES
M1

JOINS 556
JOINS 583
582

A B C D E F G H J K L
LIMIT OF MAPS
CARNE RD
PAKENHAM UPPER
BERGLUND RD
HEIN RD
TOOMUC VALLEY RD
Toomuc Ck
CSR Readymix
PBM Quarries Pakenham
CITY
ROCK CT
MT SHAMROCK RD
Creek
(GEMBROOK RD)
C411
JOINS 559
SHORT LA
CFA
PAKENHAM
Toomuc
Pakenham
STUDD RD
(Private Rd)
Only)
SYME RD
MICHAEL ST
MARY ST
DOHERTY ST
PURTON RD
SES Cardinia Shire Depot
Beacon Hills Christian College
Minibah Handicapped Childrens Centre
PAKENHAM
BALMORAL
BENOR CT
WY
JUSTIN PL
McLEISH HIGHLAND TCE
GLEANMOR TCE
DR
EDDIE BARRON TCE
LINDLEY TCE
FLEMING TCE
SHETLAND CT
UNION
LACHLAN CT
McGILL CT
AV
BRUCE CT
ABERDEEN HTS
AYR CT
EAGLE DR
ANGUS CT
AHERN RD
BREYLEIGH DR
HWAY
1 2 3 4 5 6 7 8 9 10 11 12 13 14 15 16 17 18 19 20

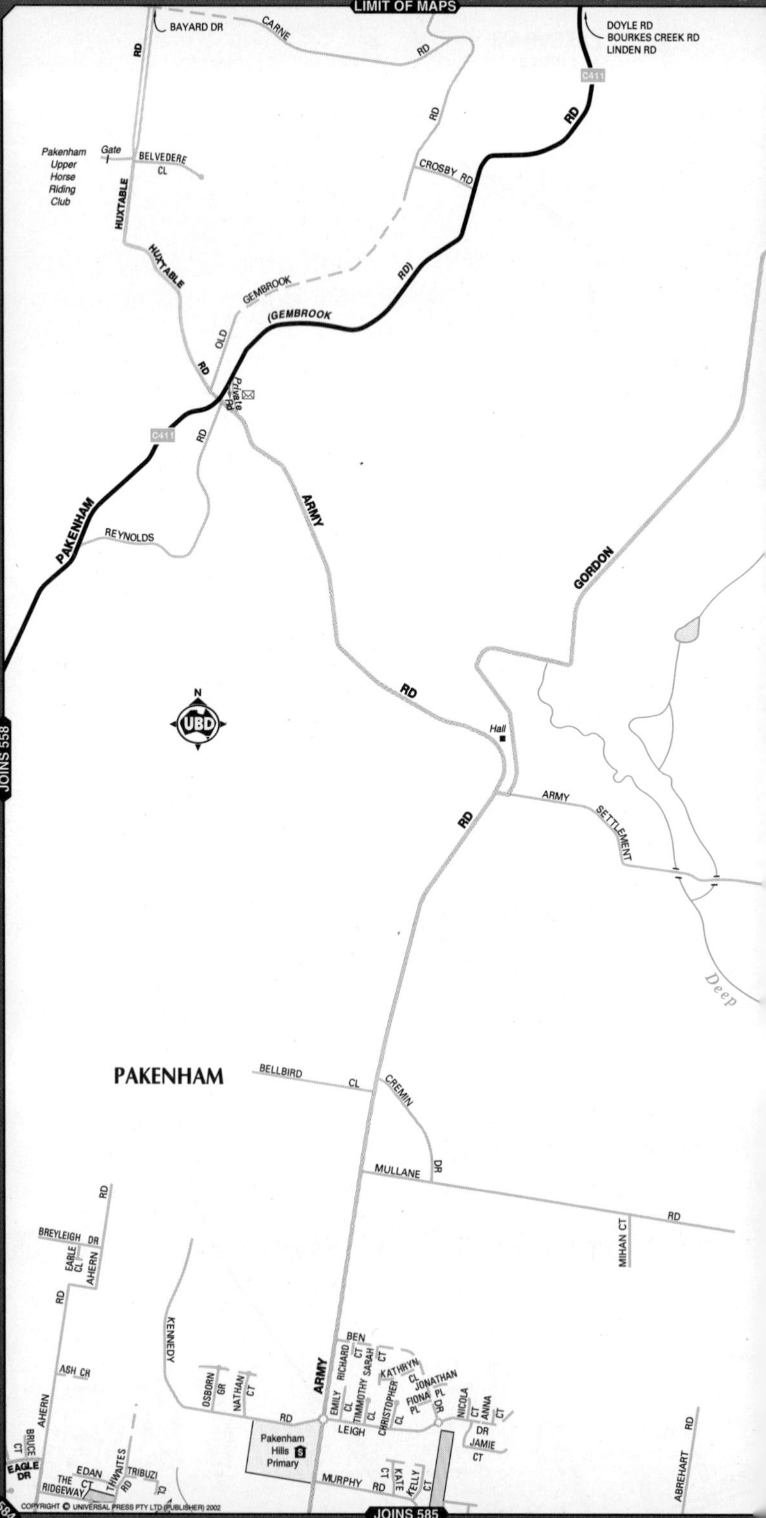

A B C D E F G H J K L

LIMIT OF MAPS

BAYARD DR
CARNE RD
DOYLE RD
BOURKES CREEK RD
LINDEN RD
C411
RD
Pakenham Upper Horse Riding Club
Gate
BELVEDERE CL
CROSBY RD
HUXTABLE
HUXTABLE RD
GEMBROOK
OLD GEMBROOK RD
(GEMBROOK RD)
Private Rd
C411
PAKENHAM
REYNOLDS
ARMY RD
GORDON
Hall
ARMY SETTLEMENT
Deep

JOINS 558

PAKENHAM

BELLBIRD CL
CREMIN DR
MULLANE RD
MIHAN CT
BREYLEIGH DR
EARLE CL
AHERN RD
ASH CR
KENNEDY
OSBORN GR
NATHAN CT
ARMY
BEN CT
RICHARD CT
SARAH CT
TIMMOTHY CL
EMILY CL
KATHRYN CL
JONATHAN PL
CHRISTOPHER CL
FIONA PL
DR
NICOLA CT
ANNA CT
LEIGH DR
JAMIE CT
Pakenham Hills Primary
BRUCE CT
EAGLE DR
EDAN CT
THWAITES RD
TRIBUZI CL
THE RIDGEWAY
MURPHY RD
KATE CT
KELLY CT
ABREHART RD

584
JOINS 585

1 2 3 4 5 6 7 8 9 10 11 12 13 14 15 16 17 18 19 20

LIMIT OF MAPS

MAP 573 FOLLOWS

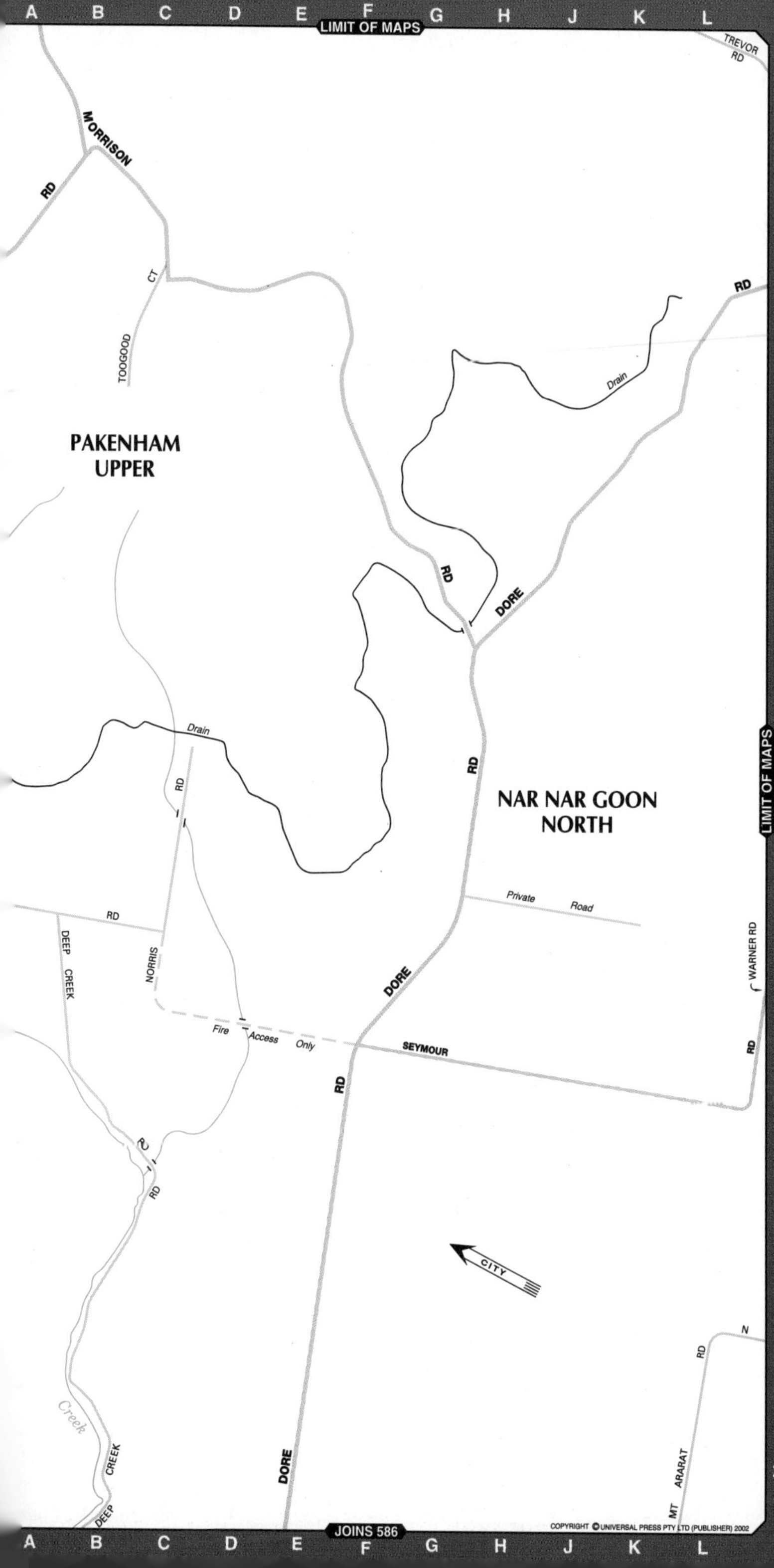

A B C D E F G H J K L

1 2 3 4 5 6 7 8 9 10 11 12 13 14 15 16 17 18 19 20

TREVOR RD

MORRISON RD

TOOGOOD CT

RD

Drain

PAKENHAM UPPER

DORE RD

Drain

NAR NAR GOON NORTH

NORRIS RD

Private Road

RD

DEEP CREEK

WARNER RD

Fire Access Only

SEYMOUR RD

DORE RD

CITY

N RD

Creek

DEEP CREEK RD

MT ARARAT RD

LIMIT OF MAPS

JOINS 586

PREVIOUS MAP 560

JOINS 547

546

JOINS INSET MAP 545 F15

JOINS 599

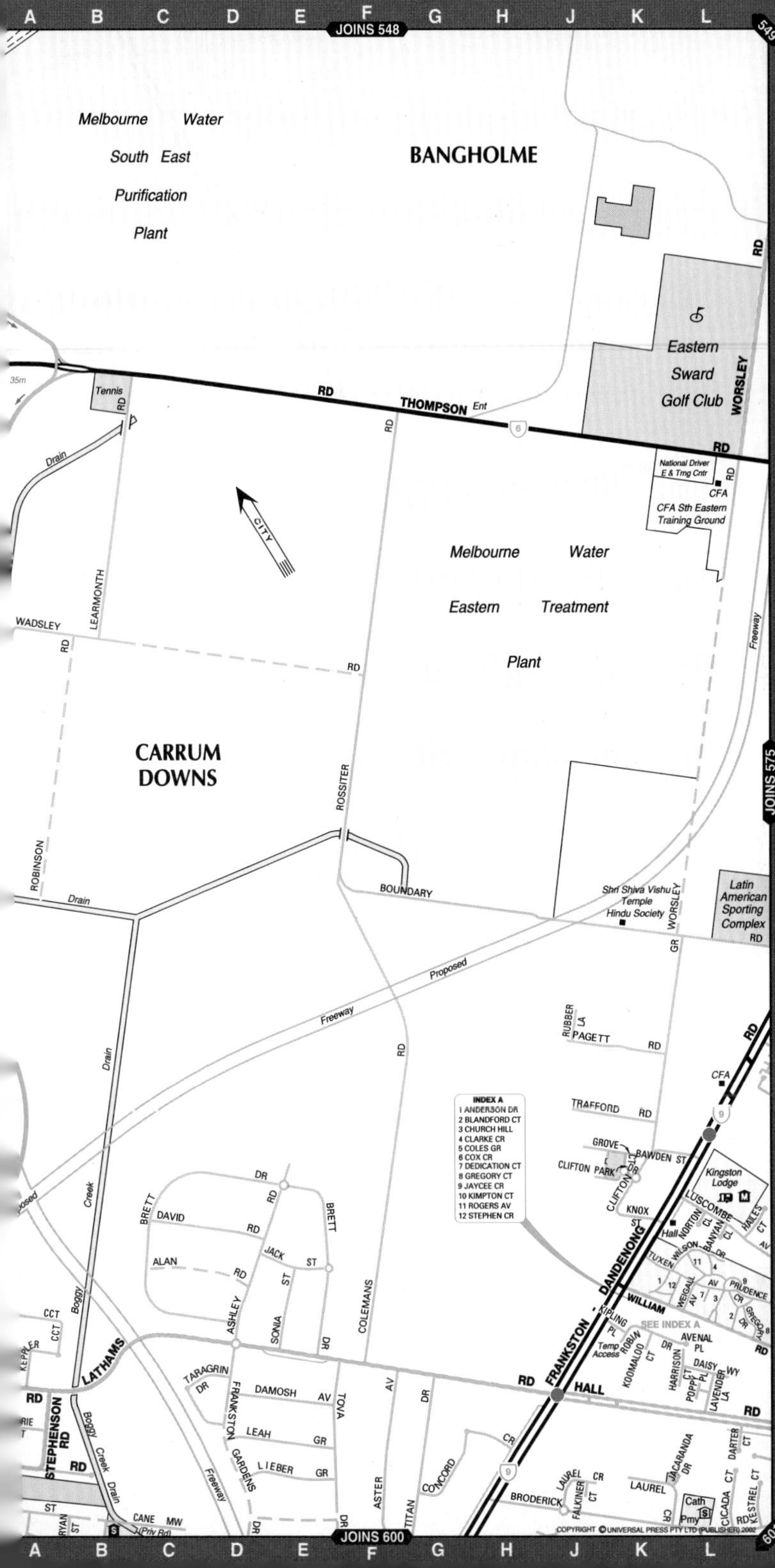
JOINS 548
549
BANGHOLME
Melbourne Water South East Purification Plant
Eastern Sward Golf Club
WORSLEY RD
THOMPSON RD
Tennis
National Driver E & Trng Cntr
CFA
CFA Sth Eastern Training Ground
Melbourne Water Eastern Treatment Plant
CITY
LEARMONTH RD
WADSLEY RD
ROSSITER RD
CARRUM DOWNS
ROBINSON RD
Drain
BOUNDARY RD
Shri Shiva Vishu Temple Hindu Society
Latin American Sporting Complex
Freeway Proposed
JOINS 575
RUBBER LA
PAGETT RD
TRAFFORD RD
INDEX A
1 ANDERSON DR
2 BLANDFORD CT
3 CHURCH HILL
4 CLARKE CR
5 COLES GR
6 COX CR
7 DEDICATION CT
8 GREGORY CT
9 JAYCEE CR
10 KIMPTON CT
11 ROGERS AV
12 STEPHEN CR
GROVE
BAWDEN ST
CLIFTON PARK
Kingston Lodge
LUSCOMBE
KNOX ST
Hall
FRANKSTON - DANDENONG RD
WILLIAM
SEE INDEX A
HALL RD
Boggy Creek Drain
BRETT DR
DAVID RD
ALAN RD
JACK ST
SONIA ST
ASHLEY
COLEMANS
LATHAMS RD
STEPHENSON RD
TARAGRIN DR
DAMOSH AV
TOVA
FRANKSTON GARDENS DR
LEAH GR
LIEBER GR
ASTER AV
TITAN DR
CONCORD CR
BRODERICK
LAUREL CR
JACARANDA DR
Cath Pmy
JOINS 600
601
COPYRIGHT © UNIVERSAL PRESS PTY LTD (PUBLISHER) 2002

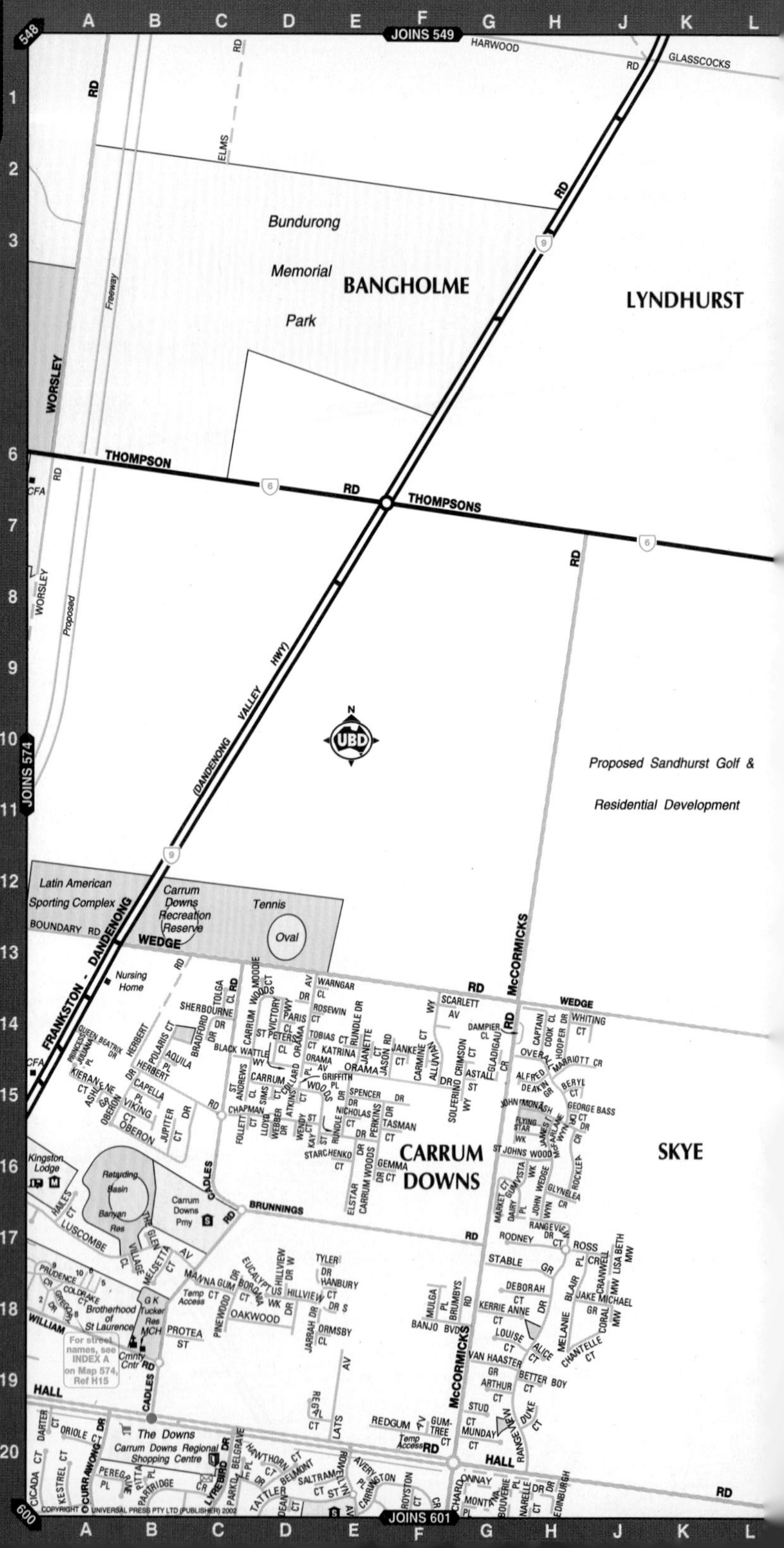
548
JOINS 549
HARWOOD
GLASSCOCKS
RD
ELMS
RD
Bundurong
Memorial
Park
BANGHOLME
LYNDHURST
WORSLEY
Freeway
THOMPSON
RD
THOMPSONS
CFA
WORSLEY
Proposed
(DANDENONG VALLEY HWY)
JOINS 574
Proposed Sandhurst Golf &
Residential Development
Latin American
Sporting Complex
Carrum
Downs
Recreation
Reserve
Tennis
Oval
BOUNDARY RD
WEDGE
FRANKSTON - DANDENONG
Nursing
Home
McCORMICKS
RD
WEDGE
CARRUM
DOWNS
SKYE
Kingston
Lodge
Retarding
Basin
Banyan
Res
Carrum
Downs
Pmy
CADLES
BRUNNINGS
RD
Brotherhood
of
St Laurence
Temp
Access
For street
names, see
INDEX A
on Map 574,
Ref H15
Cmnty
Cntr
HALL
The Downs
Carrum Downs Regional
Shopping Centre
HALL
RD
Temp
Access
COPYRIGHT © UNIVERSAL PRESS PTY LTD (PUBLISHER) 2002
600
JOINS 601

A B C D E F G H J K L
JOINS 550
551
1 2 3 4 5 6 7 8 9 10 11 12 13 14 15 16 17 18 19 20
GLASSCOCKS
RD
RD
RD
RD
CITY
Proposed Lyndhurst
EASTERN Energy
Terminal Station
TAYLORS
RD
DANDENONG -HASTINGS
RD
6
A780
Horse
Hospital
RD
JOINS 577
(WESTERN PORT HWY)
TAYLORS
RD
WEDGE
RD
RD
Kennel Control
Council
Park
Dam
Meeting
Room
Judging
Rings
Canine
Sporting Complex
DANDENONG - HASTINGS
CRANBOURNE
WEST
TAYLORS
JOINS 602
603

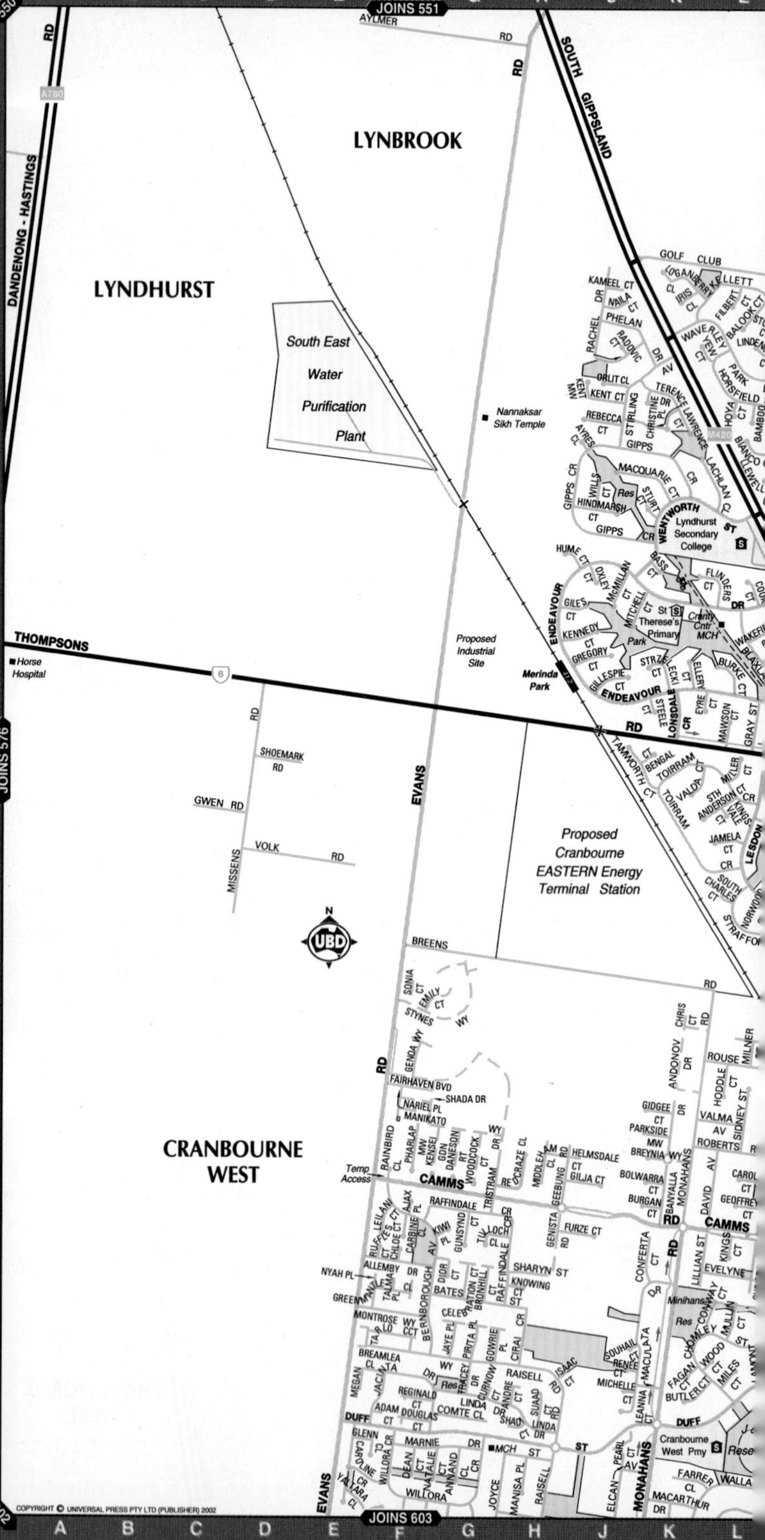

JOINS 551
JOINS 576
JOINS 603
550
602
LYNBROOK
LYNDHURST
CRANBOURNE WEST
DANDENONG - HASTINGS RD
SOUTH GIPPSLAND
THOMPSONS RD
EVANS RD
South East Water Purification Plant
Nannaksar Sikh Temple
Horse Hospital
Proposed Industrial Site
Merinda Park
Proposed Cranbourne EASTERN Energy Terminal Station
Lyndhurst Secondary College
St Therese's Primary
Cranbourne West Pmy
AYLMER RD
SHOEMARK RD
GWEN RD
VOLK RD
MISSENS
BREENS RD
CAMMS RD
MONAHANS RD
DUFF ST
ENDEAVOUR DR
Temp Access

JOINS 552

553

JOINS 579

JOINS 604

A B C D E F G H J K L

1 2 3 4 5 6 7 8 9 10 11 12 13 14 15 16 17 18 19 20

HAMPTON PARK

NARRE WARREN SOUTH

CRANBOURNE NORTH

CRANBOURNE

CRANBOURNE EAST

Cranbourne Golf Course

Clubhouse

Municipal Reserve

Courtenay Gardens Pmy

Lawson Poole Reserve

Rangebank Pmy

Donnelly Recreation Reserve

Cranbourne Park Pmy

Cranbourne

Res

MCH

CITY

Proposed Bypass

RICH
LIGHTHORSE
STRATHAIRD
KENTON WK
KERSHAW
SHERWOOD RD
EXETER PL
THE COMMON
CHESTERFIELD DR
KINGSTON AV
FEEHAN AV
COMMUNITY PDE
HALLMARK ST
EARLWOOD DR
CHATSWOOD DR
ARTISTS WK
CRAFT WK
BARONET CR
ORMOND DR
TIMMS
PLOUGH ST
HORSEMAN CT
OLDHOME CT
GARAM DR
WILLIAM CLARKE WYN
STRATHAIRD
SHORTHORN WK
FORRESTER WK
RUPERTSWOOD RI
JAMES CL
CLIVEDEN CT
BOOMERANG CT
TOUMAH ST
KARRUM CT
BATHE WY
BUNERONG CT
STALLION CT
KARRUM
LARAMIE RD
HILLSMEADE DR
WRAP CT
GALLOWAY
WALCOTT PL
PORTREE PL
TURNBERRY
DELHUNTLY
AVRIL DR
JARDINE
MADDEN RD
ABBEY RD
KYNUNA CT
TILMOUTH PL
DUNMERA CR
BUNGALOW LA
MARGIE SQ
NORWEGIAN WY
RIGBY CT
TANGERINE DR
LENNON CCT
McCARTNEY DR
CHAIN CT
BLUE JAY CT
LITTLECROFT AV
HIGHCLIFF CT
SOMERSET CT
STRAND
ROBINSWOOD PDE
THE CT
ALDERLEY
CROMFORD CR

FLAX CT
KIBO CT RD
LUPIN CT
KURRAJONG
Res DR
FIG CT
FOXGLOVE CT
LAWLESS CT
TAD
BALSAM CT
PRIMROSE CT
IVY CT
FLORA CT
WAVERLEY PARK
LOBELIA
CUMQUAT CT
WILDWOOD CT
EVERGREEN GUM CT
HUON PARK
ELIZABETH
CAITLYN CT
DIOSMA CT
CHESHUNT
HOYSTED
COURTENAY
JASMINE CT
WALNUT CT
CHERRYPLUM CT
HOLLYHOCK
HONEYSUCKLE CT
ROSEBANK
FORSYTH CT
NESBIT
MONASH WY
MALTRAVERS
FRASER CT
GODWIN
HOOP PINE CT
WISTERIA CT
MULBERRY CT
ARNOTT ST
HAZELWOOD
CYPRESS
RIALTO AV
MARINER
PEVERIL CR
NORFORD CR
GLENLEIGH CT
FOSTERS
HAMILTON
SAMANT HA
DAPHNE WY
OATES CT
JULIA CT
HAMILTON DR
OREGON CT
PEPPERCORN CT
BLUEBERRY CL
FERNCROFT CT
BALLANEE GR
TINARA CT
CRAIGTON CT
COURTENAY AV
VINCENT CT
BARTOLO
MARIA CT
CONWAY CT
PORTO CT
ROWEN CT
ANDREA
DIANNE CT
BROOMIE CR
MARSDEN CT
PHILLIP CT
HUNTER CT
CANDYTUFT CT
WOODBINE RD
HOYSTED
FRANKS WY
BRENTWOOD DR
FRANCES
DENHAM CR
JOSEPHINE
ISABELLA PL
MILANO PL
PORTOFINO DR
PLAISTOW CT
LOWTHER CT
CORIYULE CT
PINEHILL CT
ROSEBANK
FILOMENA CT
GABRIELLA CT
ELDA CT
HEYWOOD
LANSELL CR
CAREY ST
SHARNE CT
JENNY CT
RAPALLO WY
MARGOT CT
JESSIE CT
BRAD CT
ALAMANDA LANDAU CT

THOMPSONS RD
SOUTH GIPPSLAND HWY
NARRE WARREN - CRANBOURNE RD
C404
M420

MARYLYN PL
GORDON AV
BLANCHE CL
MAREE PL
JANE
DONNELLY CT
FENFIELD
CLAIRMONT
DE MONT CT
CURTIS CT
BRUMBY ST
HALSTEAD CT
DUMAS CT
GLENWOOD CT
AVERNE AV
ROSE LA
HAVEN CT
CIRCLE
BELMAR
LEANNE CT
AINSLEIGH CT
ARDMORE ST
HIGHVIEW DR S
LANE AV
DR N WY
MILOJEVIC CT
TADDOR
JAMIE CL
HOYLE CT
ARLEON CR
Res
MERRIJIG CT
ASHTON
DUNMORE AV
EMU CT
HOWQUA PL
BELLARINE DR
TALARA CT
SEACOMBE PL
MILLBANK PL
TILBURY
BUTTERWICK DR
BATWICK TCE
CAM BRIDGE CL
BRINDALEE PL
BRINDALEE CT
CORNWELL CR
ESSEX CT
THAMES CT
TRAFALGAR WY
ROSALIE AV
VIRGINIA
DAMIAN CT
MURRAY
STANLEY ST
CRANBOURNE PL
INGAMELLS ST
CAMMS RD
SHARPE ST
WILAM
TONGOLA CT
RUFFY CT
HAYDON CT
LAMONT
BOURKE
HOWELL CT
MAYUNE CT
GEORGE ST
STATION ST
BOWEN ST
CANTERBURY
NORMANBY
BARKLY
LOCH
LATROBE
FAIRFIELD ST
DUFF
HAMPTON
MARNEBECK AV
KULIN CL
WANG CT
KARA WK
KALYPTOS WK
BUNURONG PL
DUNBAR
BARILLA CT
CLARENDON DR
TAYLOR ST
JILLIAN ST
HARRY ST
TUCKER ST
WALTER ST
WILLIAM ST
ALEXANDER ST
ARUNDEL ST
GRACE ST
SMETHURST ST
GORDON ST
HIGH ST
MARKLIN
MACEY ST
HOTHAM
ARNOLD ST
MASTERTON PL
HORSHAM DR
HUNT CLUB
WATERSIDE DR
WOODHENGE DR
HOUNDSFORTH ST
BVD
MEADOW CROFT CT
BRIARCREST DR
OAK POST PL

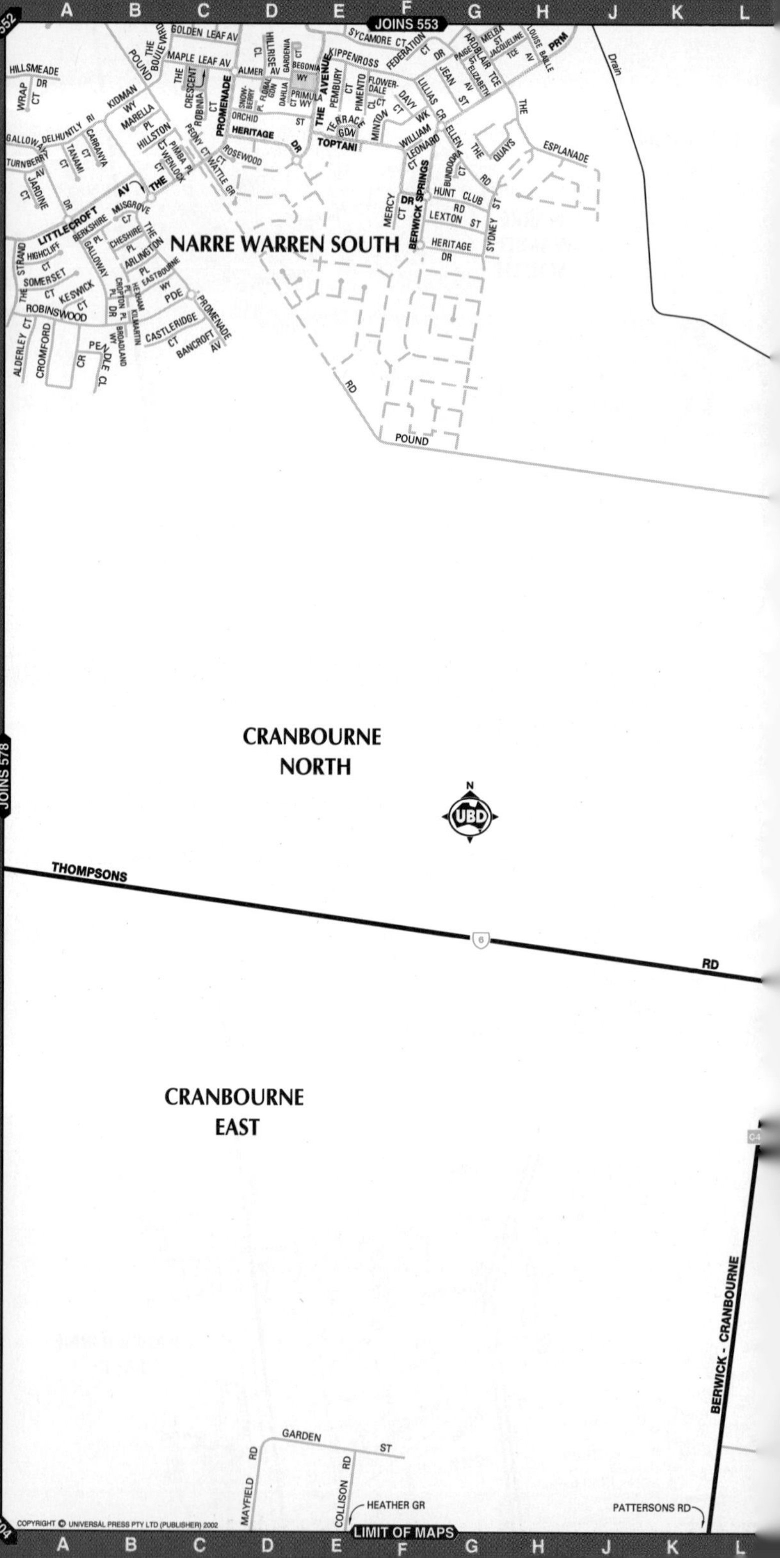
JOINS 553
JOINS 578
LIMIT OF MAPS
552
604
NARRE WARREN SOUTH
CRANBOURNE NORTH
CRANBOURNE EAST
THOMPSONS
RD
BERWICK - CRANBOURNE
POUND
RD
GARDEN
ST
MAYFIELD
RD
COLLISON
RD
HEATHER GR
PATTERSONS RD
Drain
HILLSMEADE
DR
WRAP
CT
GOLDEN LEAF AV
MAPLE LEAF AV
THE BOULEVARD
POUND
KIDMAN
WY
MARELLA
PL
HILLSTON
CT
DELHUNTLY RI
CARRANYA
TANAMI
CT
GALLOWAY
TURNBERRY
AV
JARDINE
CT
DR
LITTLECROFT
AV
THE
BERKSHIRE
PL
MUSGROVE
CT
CHESHIRE
PL
ARLINGTON
PL
EASTBOURNE
WY
PDE
PROMENADE
AV
THE STRAND
HIGHCLIFF
CT
SOMERSET
CT
KESWICK
CT
ROBINSWOOD
ALDERLEY
CT
CROMFORD
CR
PENDLE CL
CROFTON PL
BROADLAND WY
HEXHAM PL
KILMARTIN
CASTLERIDGE
CT
BANCROFT
GALLOWAY
PL
THE CRESCENT
ROBINIA
CT
PROMENADE
PIMBA PL
PEONY CT
WENLOCK
WATTLE GR
ROSEWOOD
ALMER
AV
HILLRISE CL
GARDENIA CT
BEGONIA
WY
SNOWBERRY PL
FLORAL GDN
DAHLIA CT
PRIMULA WY
ORCHID
ST
HERITAGE
DR
THE AVENUE
TERRACE GDN
TOPTANI
KIPPENROSS
PEMBURY
CT
PIMENTO
FLOWERDALE
CL
CT
MINTON
CT
SYCAMORE CT
FEDERATION
CT
DAVY
WK
WILLIAM
LEONARD
CT
LILLIAS
CR
JEAN
AV
ST
DR
PAIGE
ARDBLAIR
TCE
ELIZABETH
MELBA
ST
JACQUELINE
TCE
AV
LOUISE
BAILLE
PRM
THE
QUAYS
ELLEN
CT
BUNDOORA
RD
ESPLANADE
THE
MERCY
CT
BERWICK SPRINGS
DR
HUNT CLUB
RD
LEXTON ST
SYDNEY ST
HERITAGE
DR
N
UBD
6

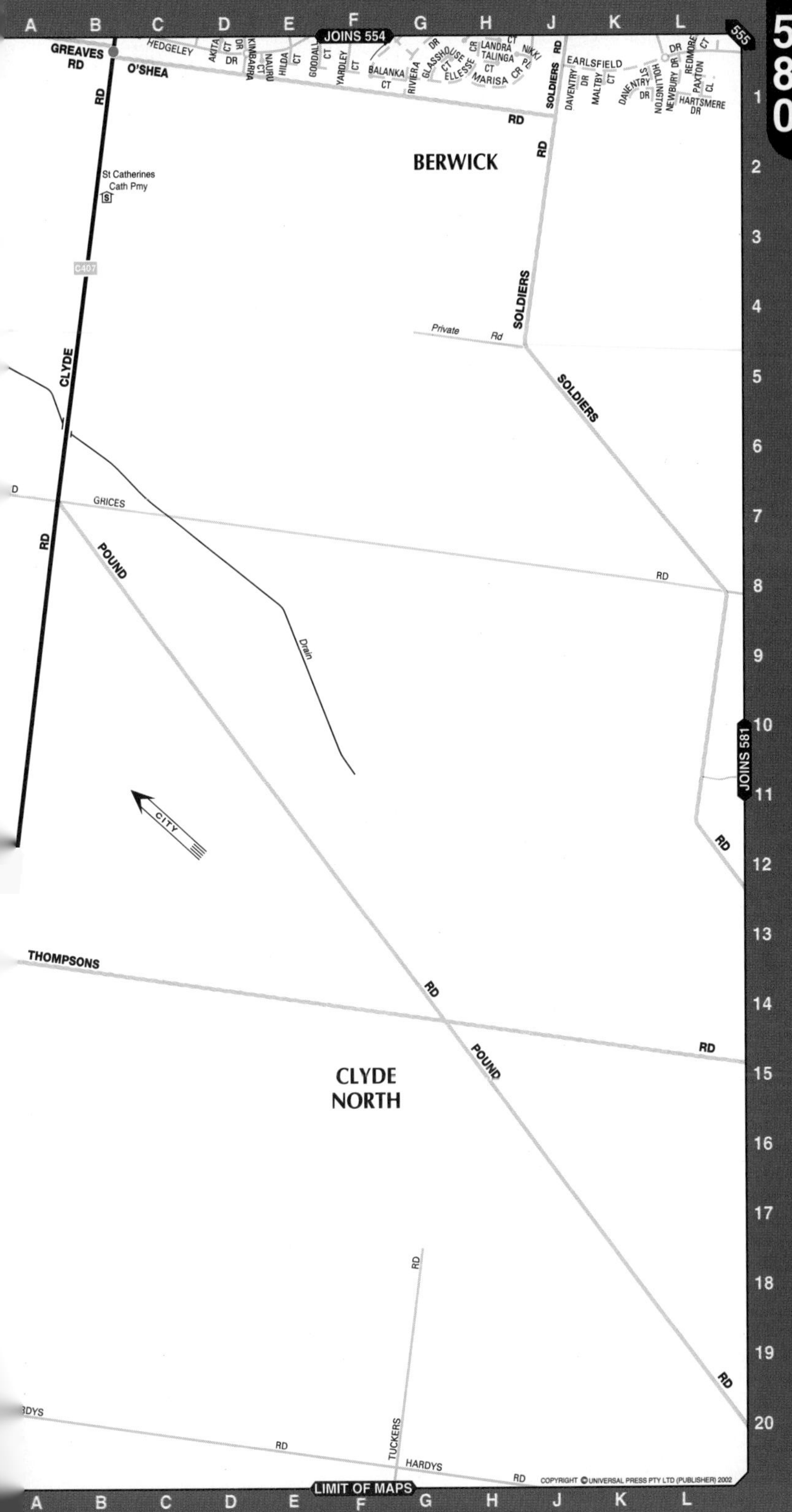
JOINS 554
555
GREAVES RD
CLYDE RD
O'SHEA RD
HEDGELEY
AKITA CT
DR
KIMBARRA
NAURU CT
HILDA CT
GOODALL CT
YARDLEY CT
BALANKA CT
RIVIERA DR
GLASSHOUSE CT
ELLESSE
LANDRA CR
TALINGA CT
MARISA CR
NIKKI PL
CT
SOLDIERS RD
EARLSFIELD
DAVENTRY DR
MALTBY CT
DAVENTRY DR
HOLLINGTON ST
NEWBURY DR
REDMORE CT
PAXTON CL
HARTSMERE DR
DR
BERWICK
St Catherines Cath Pmy
C407
Private Rd
SOLDIERS
GRICES RD
POUND RD
Drain
CITY
JOINS 581
THOMPSONS RD
CLYDE NORTH
TUCKERS RD
HARDYS RD
LIMIT OF MAPS

554
JOINS 555
JOINS 580
LIMIT OF MAPS

A B C D E F G H J K L

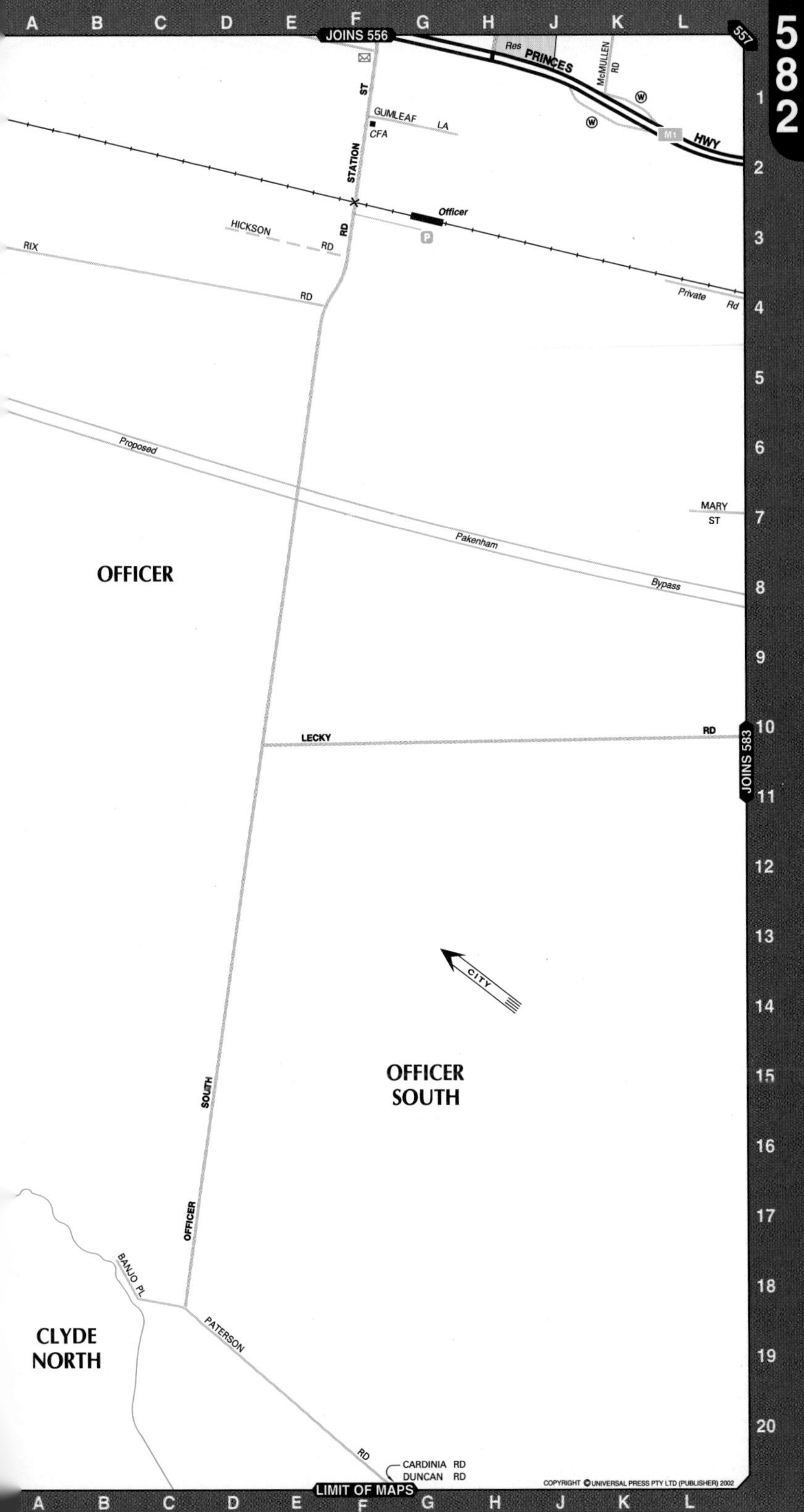
JOINS 556
557
Res
PRINCES
HWY
M1
McMULLEN RD
STATION ST
GUMLEAF LA
CFA
Officer
HICKSON RD
RIX RD
RD
Private Rd
Proposed Pakenham Bypass
MARY ST
OFFICER
LECKY RD
JOINS 583
CITY
OFFICER SOUTH
OFFICER SOUTH RD
BANJO PL
CLYDE NORTH
PATERSON RD
CARDINIA RD
DUNCAN RD
LIMIT OF MAPS

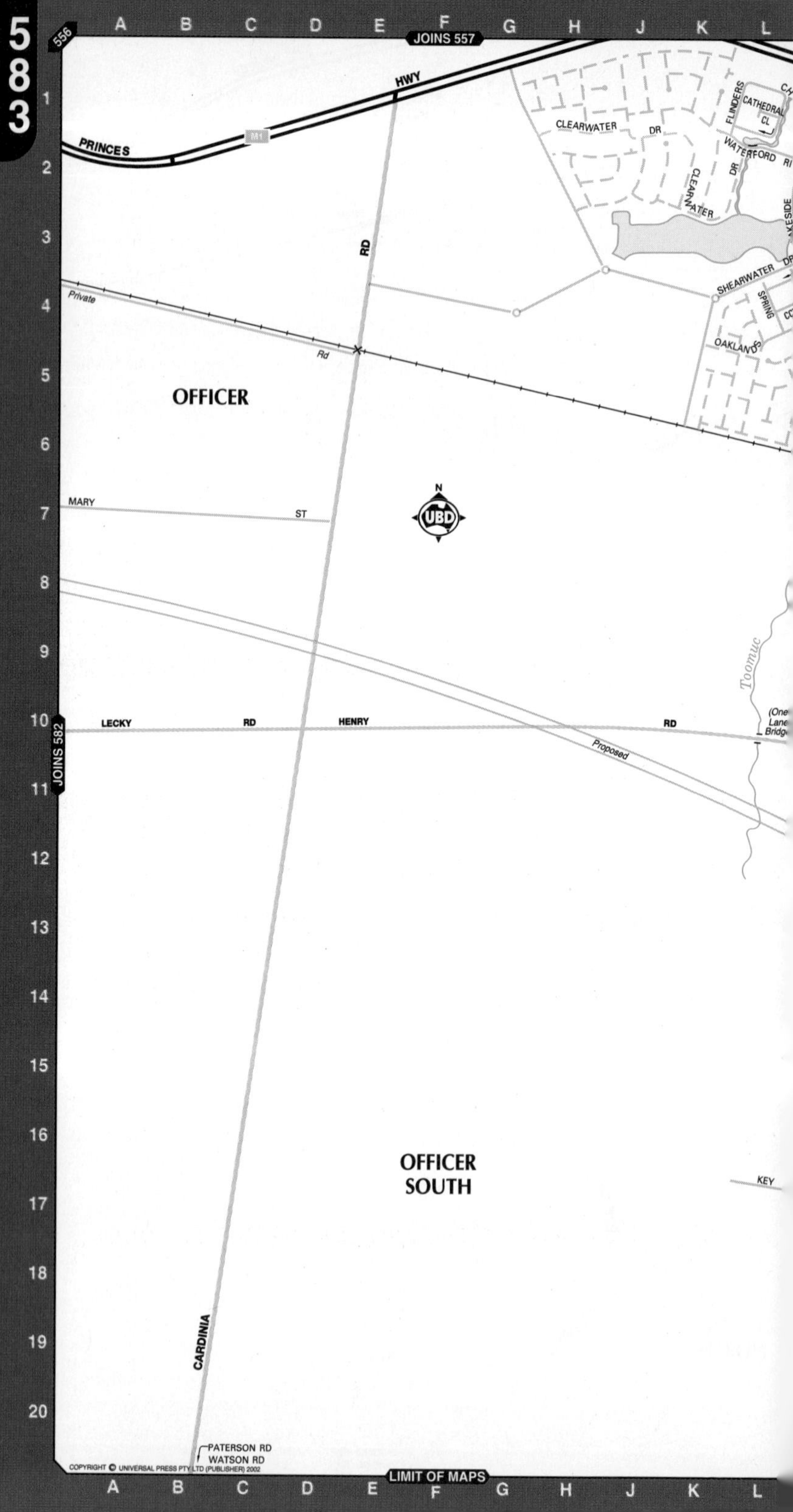
A B C D E F G H J K L
556
JOINS 557
PRINCES
HWY
M1
RD
CLEARWATER
DR
FLINDERS
CATHEDRAL
CL
WATERFORD
DR
CLEARWATER
LAKESIDE
SHEARWATER
SPRING
OAKLANDS
Private
Rd
OFFICER
MARY
ST
N
UBD
Toomuc
LECKY
RD
HENRY
RD
(One Lane Bridge)
Proposed
JOINS 582
OFFICER SOUTH
KEY
CARDINIA
PATERSON RD
WATSON RD
LIMIT OF MAPS
1 2 3 4 5 6 7 8 9 10 11 12 13 14 15 16 17 18 19 20

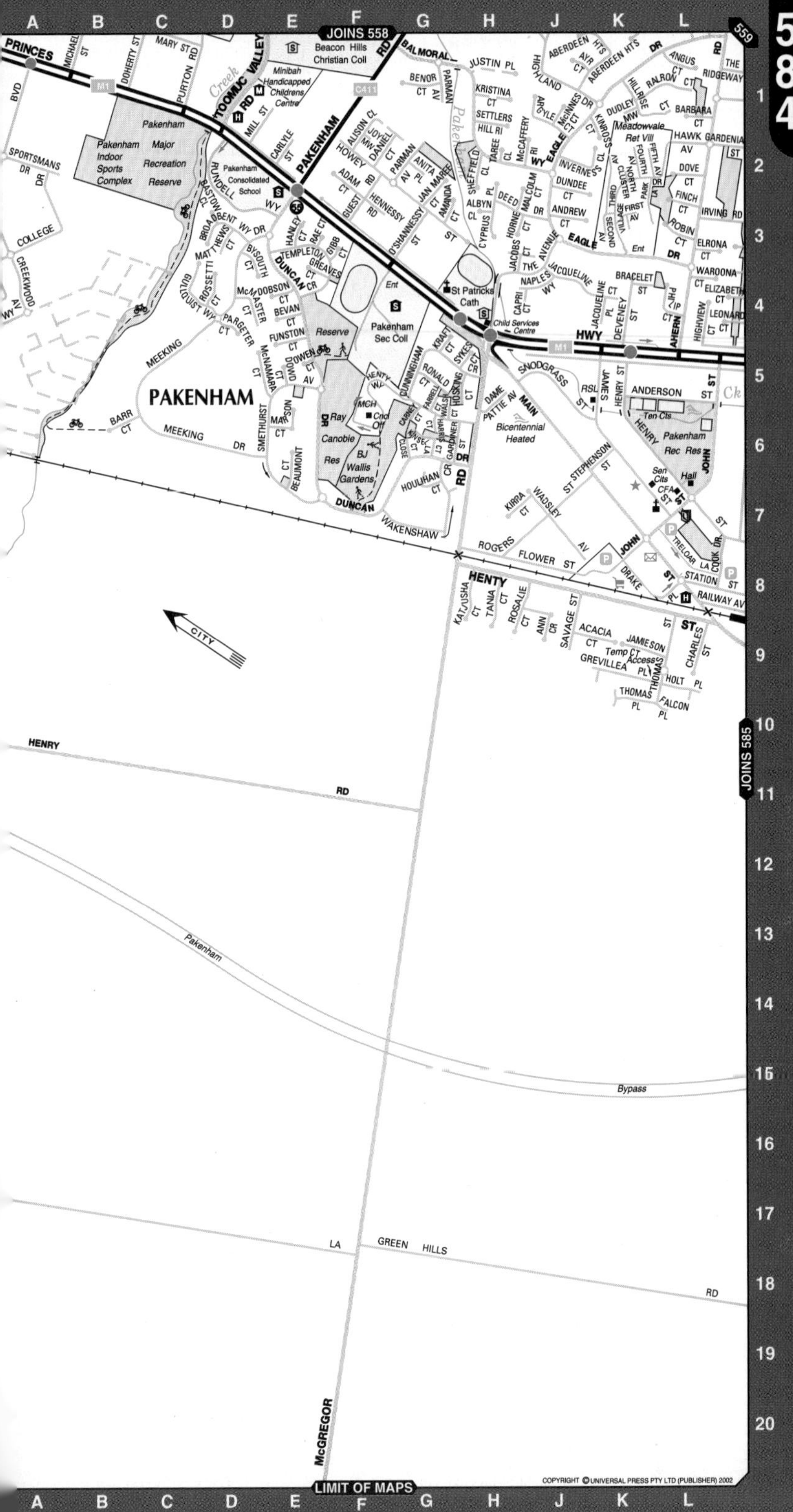
A B C D E F G H J K L
JOINS 558
559
PRINCES
BVD
MICHAEL ST
DOHERTY ST
MARY ST
PURTON RD
Creek
TOOMUC VALLEY RD
Beacon Hills Christian Coll
Minibah Handicapped Childrens Centre
MILL ST
C411
M1
BALMORAL
BENOR CT
PARMAN AV
JUSTIN PL
HIGHLAND
ABERDEEN HTS
AYR CT
ABERDEEN HTS
DR
ANGUS CT
THE RIDGEWAY
RALRON CT
HILLRISE
BARBARA CT
DUDLEY MW
KINROSS CL
Meadowvale Ret Vill
HAWK
GARDENIA
KRISTINA CT
SETTLERS HILL RI
ARGYLE
McINNES CT
EAGLE WY
Pakenham Major Recreation Reserve
Pakenham Indoor Sports Complex
SPORTSMANS DR
PAKENHAM
CARLYLE ST
ALISON CL
JOYCE MW
DANIEL CT
HOWEY
ADAM CT
GUEST RD
HENNESSY
ANITA PL
JAN MAREE
AMANDA CT
SHEFFIELD CL
TAREE CL
McCAFFERY RI
INVERNESS CL
DUNDEE CT
ANDREW CT
THIRD AV
SECOND AV
NORTH AV
CLUSTER
FOURTH AV
FIFTH AV
PARK DR
FIRST AV
DOVE CT
FINCH CT
IRVING RD
ROBIN CT
Pakenham Consolidated School
RUNDELL
BASTOW CL
BROADBENT WY
DR
COLLEGE
CREEKWOOD AV
WY
MATTHEWS CT
ROSSETTI CT
GUILDQUIST WY
BYSOUTH CT
HANLEY CT
RAE CT
TEMPLETON CT
GIBB CT
GREAVES CT
DUNCAN CR
O'SHANNESSY ST
ST
ALBYN CL
CYPRUS CL
DEED DR
MALCOLM CT
HORNE CT
JACOBS CT
THE AVENUE
EAGLE DR
Ent
ELRONA CT
WAROONA CT
ELIZABETH CT
McMASTER
DOBSON CT
BEVAN CT
PARGETER CT
FUNSTON CT
Ent
Pakenham Sec Coll
St Patricks Cath
NAPLES WY
JACQUELINE
JACQUELINE PL
DEVENEY ST
BRACELET CT
PHILIP CT
HIGHVIEW CT
LEONARD CT
CAPRI CT
Child Services Centre
HWY
AHERN
MEEKING
Reserve
OWEN CT
DOWD AV
McNAMARA CT
CUNNINGHAM
KRAFT CT
SYKES CR
RONALD CT
HENTY WAY
HOSKING CT
SNODGRASS
RSL
JAMES ST
HENRY ST
ANDERSON ST
Ck
PAKENHAM
SMETHURST
MARSON CT
Ray Canobie Res
DR
MCH
Cncl Off
DAME PATTIE AV
MAIN
Ten Cts
Pakenham Rec Res
HENRY
JOHN
Bicentennial Heated
Hall
BARR CT
MEEKING DR
BEAUMONT CT
BJ Wallis Gardens
HOULIHAN CT
GARDINER ST
RD DR
STEPHENSON ST
Sen Cits
CFA
DUNCAN
KIRRA CT
WADSLEY
WAKENSHAW
ROGERS
FLOWER ST
AV
JOHN
TRELOAR LA
COOK DR
ST
HENTY
DRAKE
STATION ST
RAILWAY AV
KATRUSHA CT
TANIA CT
ROSALIE CT
ANN CR
SAVAGE ST
ACACIA CT
JAMIESON
Temp Access
GREVILLEA PL
THOMAS
HOLT PL
CHARLES ST
THOMAS PL
FALCON PL
CITY
HENRY RD
JOINS 585
Pakenham
Bypass
LA GREEN HILLS RD
McGREGOR
LIMIT OF MAPS
1 2 3 4 5 6 7 8 9 10 11 12 13 14 15 16 17 18 19 20

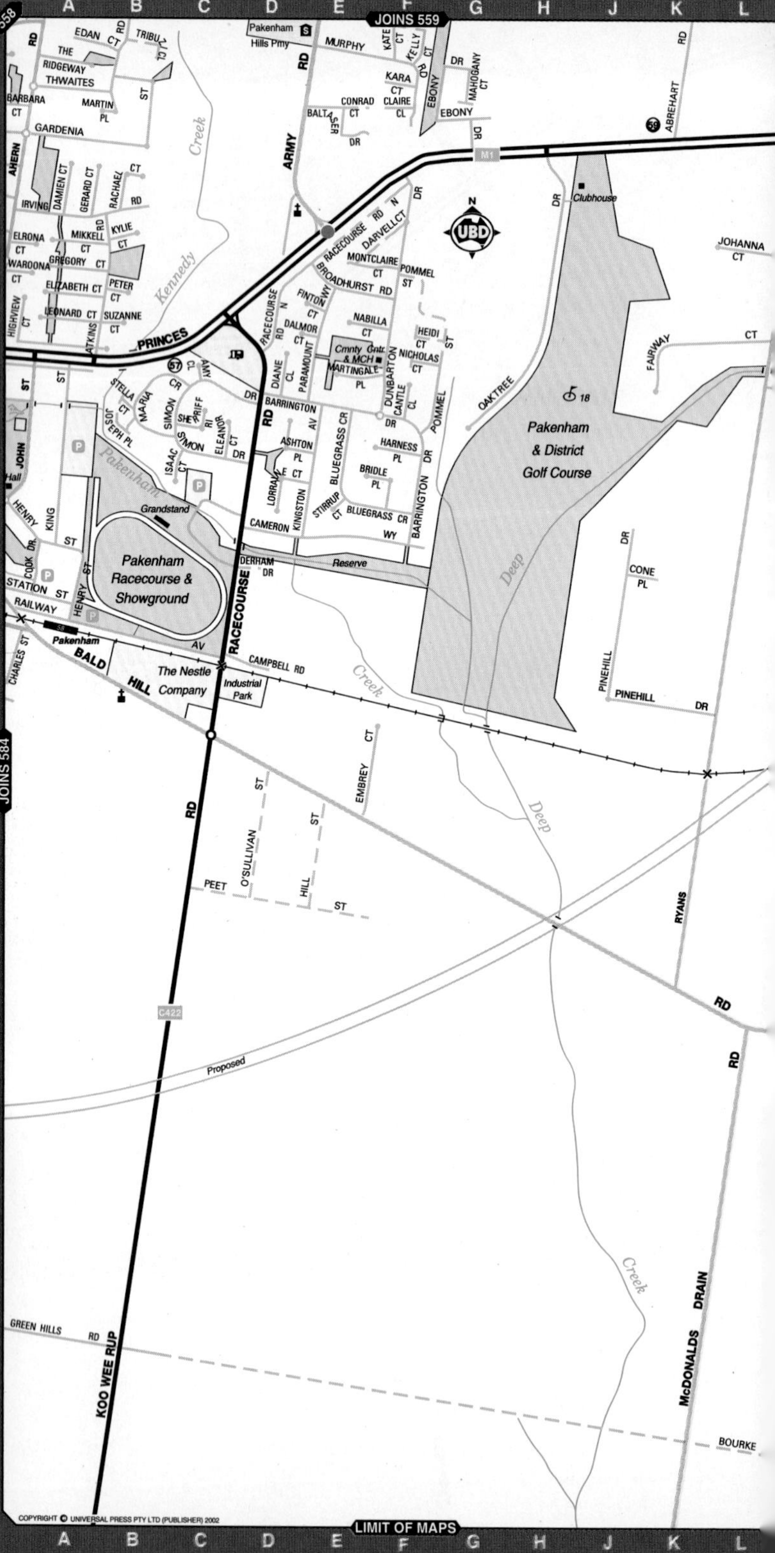

JOINS 559

JOINS 584

558

A B C D E F G H J K L

1 2 3 4 5 6 7 8 9 10 11 12 13 14 15 16 17 18 19 20

EDAN CT
TRIBU
THE RIDGEWAY
THWAITES
BARBARA CT
MARTIN PL
GARDENIA
AHERN RD
DAMIEN CT
GERARD CT
RACHAEL CT
IRVING
ELRONA CT
MIKKELL CT
KYLIE CT
WAROONA CT
GREGORY CT
ELIZABETH CT
PETER CT
LEONARD CT
SUZANNE CT
HIGHVIEW CT
ATKINS ST
PRINCES
Kennedy Creek
Pakenham Hills Pmy
MURPHY
KATE CT
KELLY CT
KARA CT
CONRAD CT
CLAIRE CL
BALTASER DR
EBONY
EBONY DR
MAHOGANY CT
ARMY RD
M1
RACECOURSE RD N
DARVELL CT
MONTCLAIRE CT
POMMEL ST
BROADHURST RD
FINTON WY
NABILLA CT
DALMOR CT
HEIDI CT
NICHOLAS CT
Cmnty Cntr & MCH
MARTINGALE PL
DIANE CL
PARAMOUNT AV
DUNBARTON DR
CANTLE CL
POMMEL DR
BARRINGTON DR
OAKTREE
Clubhouse
ABREHART RD
JOHANNA CT
FAIRWAY CT
Pakenham & District Golf Course
18
57
STELLA CT
MARIA CR
AMY CL
JOSEPH PL
SIMON CR
SHE PRIFF RI
ELEANOR CT
SIMON
ISAAC CT
ASHTON PL
LORRAINE CT
BLUEGRASS CR
HARNESS PL
BRIDLE PL
KINGSTON
STIRRUP CT
BLUEGRASS CR WY
CAMERON
BARRINGTON DR
JOHN ST
Hall
HENRY ST
KING ST
COOK DR
STATION ST
RAILWAY
HENRY ST
Pakenham
Grandstand
Pakenham Racecourse & Showground
DERHAM DR
Reserve
Deep Creek
AV
Pakenham
CHARLES ST
BALD HILL RD
The Nestle Company
Industrial Park
CAMPBELL RD
RACECOURSE RD
CONE PL
PINEHILL DR
EMBREY CT
O'SULLIVAN ST
HILL ST
PEET ST
C422
Proposed
RYANS RD
GREEN HILLS RD
KOO WEE RUP RD
McDONALDS DRAIN
BOURKE

LIMIT OF MAPS

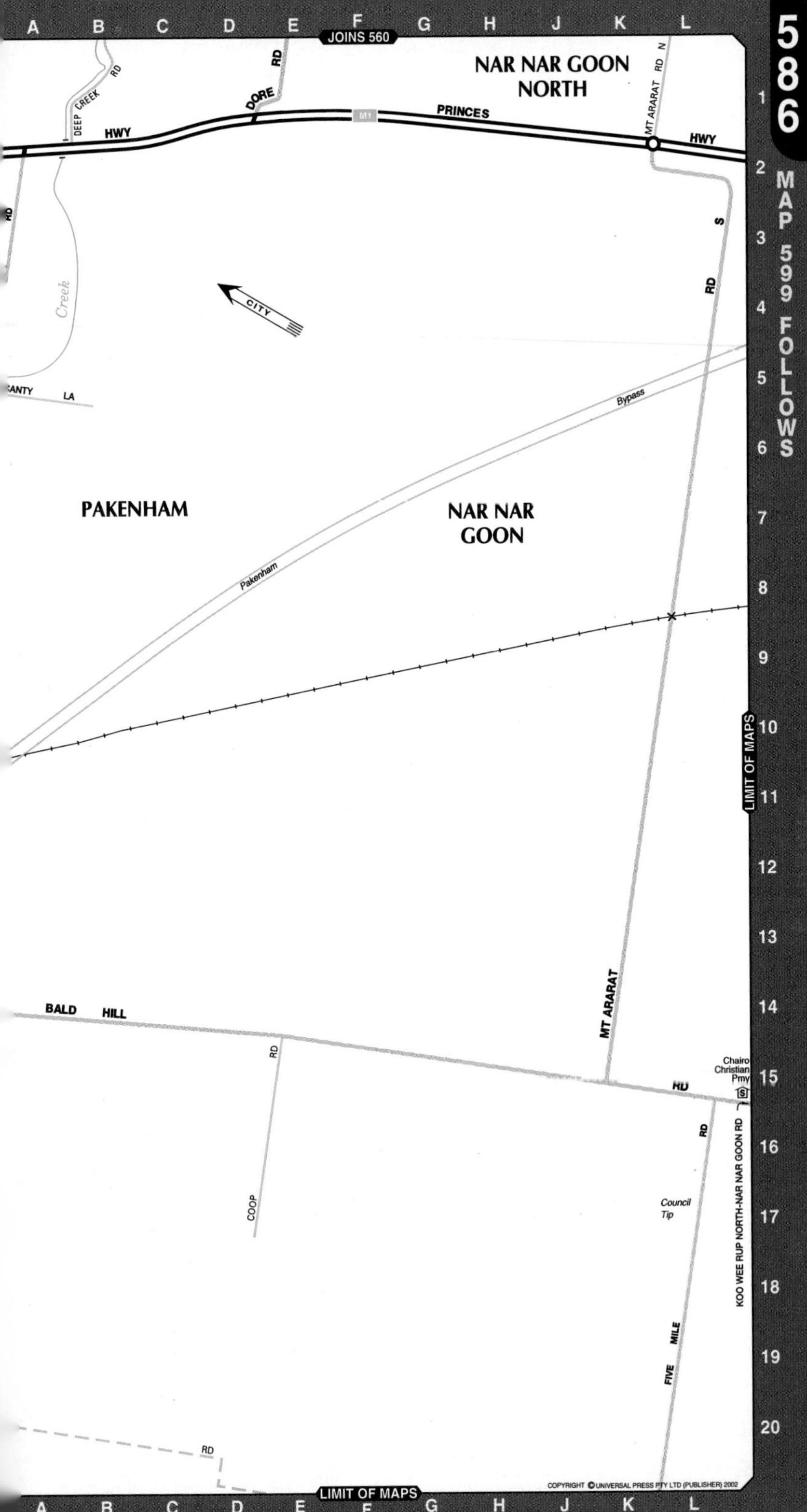
JOINS 560
NAR NAR GOON NORTH
DEEP CREEK RD
DORE RD
PRINCES HWY
M1
MT ARARAT RD N
MT ARARAT RD S
CITY
Creek
CANTY LA
PAKENHAM
Pakenham Bypass
NAR NAR GOON
BALD HILL RD
COOP RD
MT ARARAT
Chairo Christian Pmy
KOO WEE RUP NORTH-NAR NAR GOON RD
Council Tip
FIVE MILE RD
RD
MAP 599 FOLLOWS
LIMIT OF MAPS

PREVIOUS MAP 586

JOINS 573

A B C D E F G H J K L

1 2 3 4 5 6 7 8 9 10 11 12 13 14 15 16 17 18 19 20

LIMIT OF MAPS

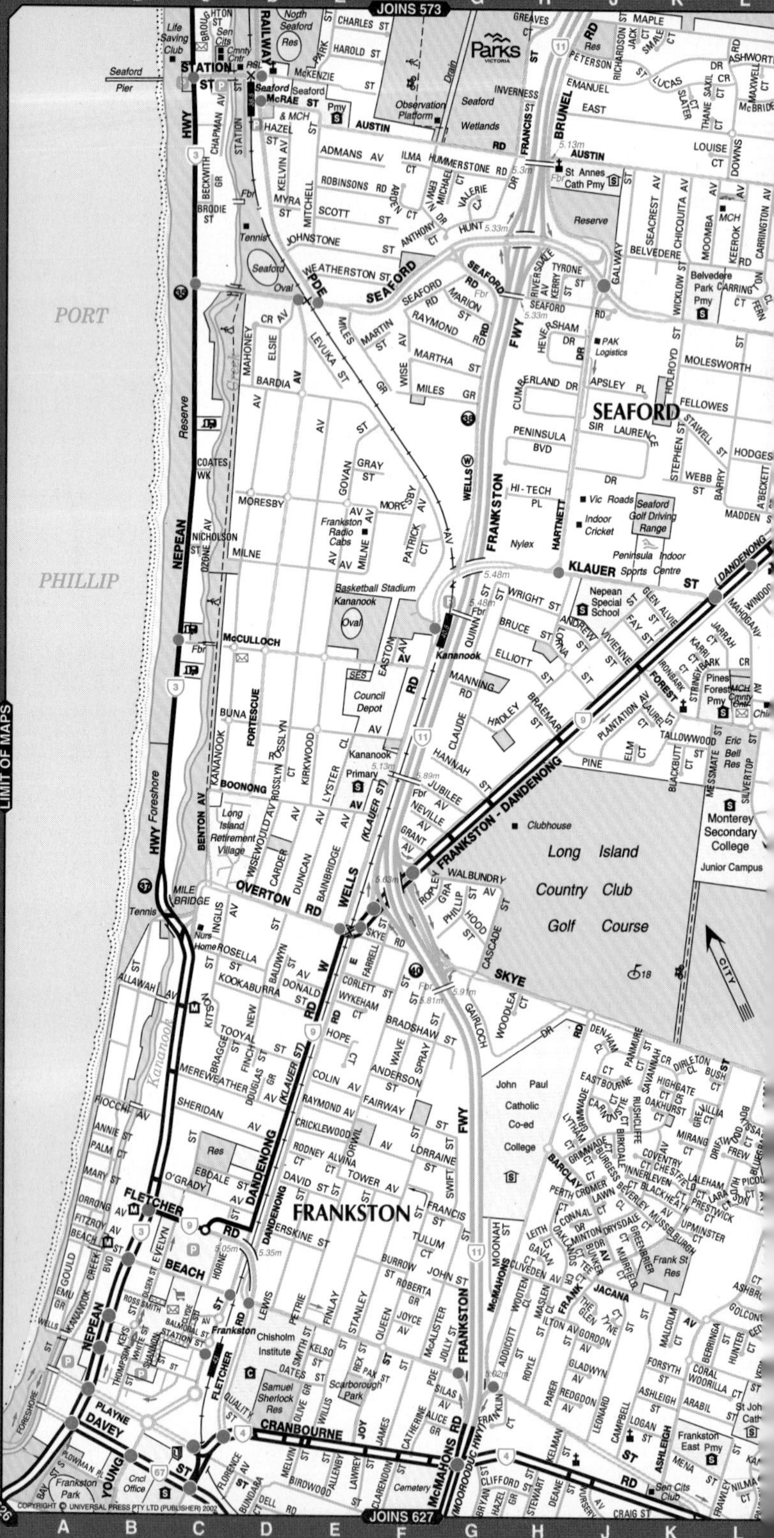

PORT PHILLIP

Seaford Pier
Life Saving Club
STATION ST
BROUGHTON ST
Sen Cits
Cmnty Cntr
RSL
RAILWAY
North Seaford Res
CHARLES ST
HAROLD ST
McKENZIE
Seaford
McRAE ST
& MCH
Pmy
AUSTIN
HAZEL ST
Parks VICTORIA
Observation Platform
Seaford Wetlands
Drain
GREAVES
MAPLE
ASHWORTH
PETERSON
RICHARDSON ST
JACK CT
SMALE CT
LUCAS
EMANUEL
EAST
INVERNESS
BRUNEL RD
FRANCIS ST
McBRIDE
LOUISE CT
DOWNS
AUSTIN
St Annes Cath Pmy
HWY
CHAPMAN AV
BECKWITH GR
BRODIE ST
ADMANS AV
ILMA CT
HUMMERSTONE RD
ROBINSONS RD
ARDEN CT
ERWIN
MICHAEL
VALERIE CT
KELVIN AV
MYRA ST
MITCHELL
SCOTT ST
ANTHONY CT
HUNT
Reserve
SEACREST AV
CHICQUITA AV
MOOMBA AV
KEEROK RD
CARRINGTON AV
MCH
Tennis
JOHNSTONE ST
BELVEDERE
Seaford Oval
WEATHERSTON ST
SEAFORD RD
SEAFORD
RIVERSDALE
KERRY
TYRONE ST
GALWAY
Belvedere Park Pmy
CARRINGTON
WICKLOW ST
FERN
PDE
MILES
MARION ST
RAYMOND RD
HEVERSHAM DR
SEAFORD
PAK Logistics
CR AV
MAHONEY
ELSIE
LEVUKA ST
MARTIN ST
WISE AV
MARTHA ST
FWY
HOLROYD ST
MOLESWORTH
BARDIA AV
MILES GR
CUMBERLAND DR
APSLEY PL
FELLOWES
SEAFORD
Reserve
SIR LAURENCE
STAWELL ST
PENINSULA BVD
HODGES
WELLS
COATES WK
GRAY ST
GOVAN
DR
STEPHEN ST
WEBB ST
BARRY
A'BECKETT
HI-TECH PL
MORESBY
MORESBY AV
Vic Roads
Seaford Golf Driving Range
MADDEN
NEPEAN
NICHOLSON ST
OZONE
Frankston Radio Cabs
PATRICK CT
Indoor Cricket
Nylex
HARTNETT
MILNE
MILNE AV
Peninsula Indoor Sports Centre
KLAUER ST
DANDENONG
Basketball Stadium
Kananook Oval
WRIGHT ST
Nepean Special School
GLEN ALVIE
WINDOO
MAHOGANY
McCULLOCH
Kananook
BRUCE ST
ANDREW
LORNA
VIVIENNE ST
FAY ST
JARRAH CT
KARRI CT
IRONBARK
STRINGYBARK
CR
EASTON
AV
QUINN
ELLIOTT ST
MANNING RD
Pines Forest Pmy
MCH Cmnty Cntr
SES
Council Depot
FORTESCUE
RD
HADLEY
BRAEMAR ST
FOREST
PLANTATION AV
LAUREL CT
BUNA
ROSSLYN
KIRKWOOD
CLAUDE
TALLOWWOOD
ELM CT
BLACKBUTT CT
Eric Bell Res
KANANOOK
Kananook Primary
HANNAH ST
PINE
MESSMATE ST
SILVERTOP
BOONONG
ROSSLYN CT
LYSTER CL
JUBILEE
NEVILLE
GRANT
FRANKSTON - DANDENONG
Monterey Secondary College
Junior Campus
Foreshore
BENTON AV
Long Island Retirement Village
WISEWOULD AV
CARDER
DUNCAN
BAINBRIDGE
WELLS (KLAUER ST)
Clubhouse
Long Island Country Club Golf Course
OVERTON RD
MILE BRIDGE
Tennis
INGLIS
ROPLEY
WALBUNDRY
GRA
PHILLIP
HOOD ST
CASCADE
SKYE RD
CITY
Nurs Home
ROSELLA
BALDWYN
FARRELL
KOOKABURRA
DONALD
CORLETT ST
WYKEHAM
SKYE
WOODLEA CT
ALLAWAH AV
KITSON
NEW
BRADSHAW ST
GAIRLOCH
DR
DENHAM
PANMURE
SAVANNAH CR
DIRLETON CL
BUSH CT
TOOYAL ST
BRAGGE ST
FINCH ST
HOPE
WAVE
SPRAY
Kananook Creek
MEREWEATHER AV
DOUGLAS ST
COLIN AV
ANDERSON ST
EASTBOURNE CT
CARNOUSTIE
HIGHGATE
OAKHURST
FIOCCHI AV
SHERIDAN
RAYMOND AV
FAIRWAY
John Paul Catholic Co-ed College
LYTHAM
GRIMWADE
RUSHCLIFFE
ELLIA
MIRANG
ANNIE ST
PALM CT
CRICKLEWOOD
LORRAINE ST
FWY
BARCLAY
BURGESS
BIRKDALE
COVENTRY
CHESTERFIELD
INNERLEVEN
FREW
DRIFTWOOD
MARY ST
Res
RODNEY ALVINA
SWIFT
PERTH
CROMER
LAWN
BEVERLEY
BLACKHEATH
LALEHAM
PRESTWICK
ORRONG
O'GRADY
EBDALE ST
DAVID ST
TOWER AV
LARA
PICOLA
FITZROY AV
FLETCHER
DANDENONG
FRANKSTON
FRANCIS ST
CONNAL
OAKLANDS
MINTON
DRYSDALE
GREENBRIER
MUSSELBURGH
UPMINSTER
BEACH ST
ERSKINE ST
TULUM CT
MOONAH ST
LEITH
GAVAN
BUNKER
MUIRFIELD
Frank St Res
GOULD
EVELYN
BEACH
HORNE
BURROW ST
JOHN ST
CLIVEDEN
Frank
ASHBROOK
EMU GR
KANANOOK CREEK BVD
WELLS
NEPEAN
OLSEN ST
ROSS SMITH AV
CLYDE
BALMORAL ST
STATION ST
Frankston
LEWIS
PETRIE
FINLAY
STANLEY
QUEEN
ROBERTA GR
JOYCE AV
McALISTER
JOLLY ST
FRANKSTON
McMAHONS
WOOTEN
MASLEN
ILTON AV
GORDON AV
THE GLEN
TYNE
JACANA
MALCOLM AV
BERRINGA
HUNTER
GOLCONDA
KEYS
WHITE ST
SHANNON AV
THOMPSON
Chisholm Institute
SMYTH ST
KELSO
OATES ST
REX ST
PAX
ADDICOTT
ROYLE
GLADWYN
FORSYTH
CORAL
WOORILLA
St John Cath
FLETCHER
Samuel Sherlock Res
OLIVE GR
WILLIS
Scarborough Park
PDE
SILAS AV
PARER
REDGDON AV
ASHLEIGH ST
ARABIL
FORESHORE
PLAYNE
DAVEY
QUALITY
CRANBOURNE
JOY
JAMES
CATHERINE
ALICE GR
FRANKLIN CT
McMAHONS RD
KELMAN
LEONARD
CAMPBELL
LOGAN ST
ASHLEIGH
Frankston East Pmy
YOUNG
ST
FLORENCE AV
MELVIN ST
ALLENBY ST
LAWREY
CLARENDON
(MOOROODUC HWY)
CLIFFORD
HAZEL GR
STEWART
DEANE
NURSERY
MENA ST
NILMA
PLOWMAN PL
Frankston Park
BAY ST
Cncl Office
BUNDARA
BIRDWOOD
DELL
RD
Cemetery
BRYAN ST
CRAIG ST
Sen Cits Club
FRAWLEY

626

JOINS 627

A B C D E F G H J K L

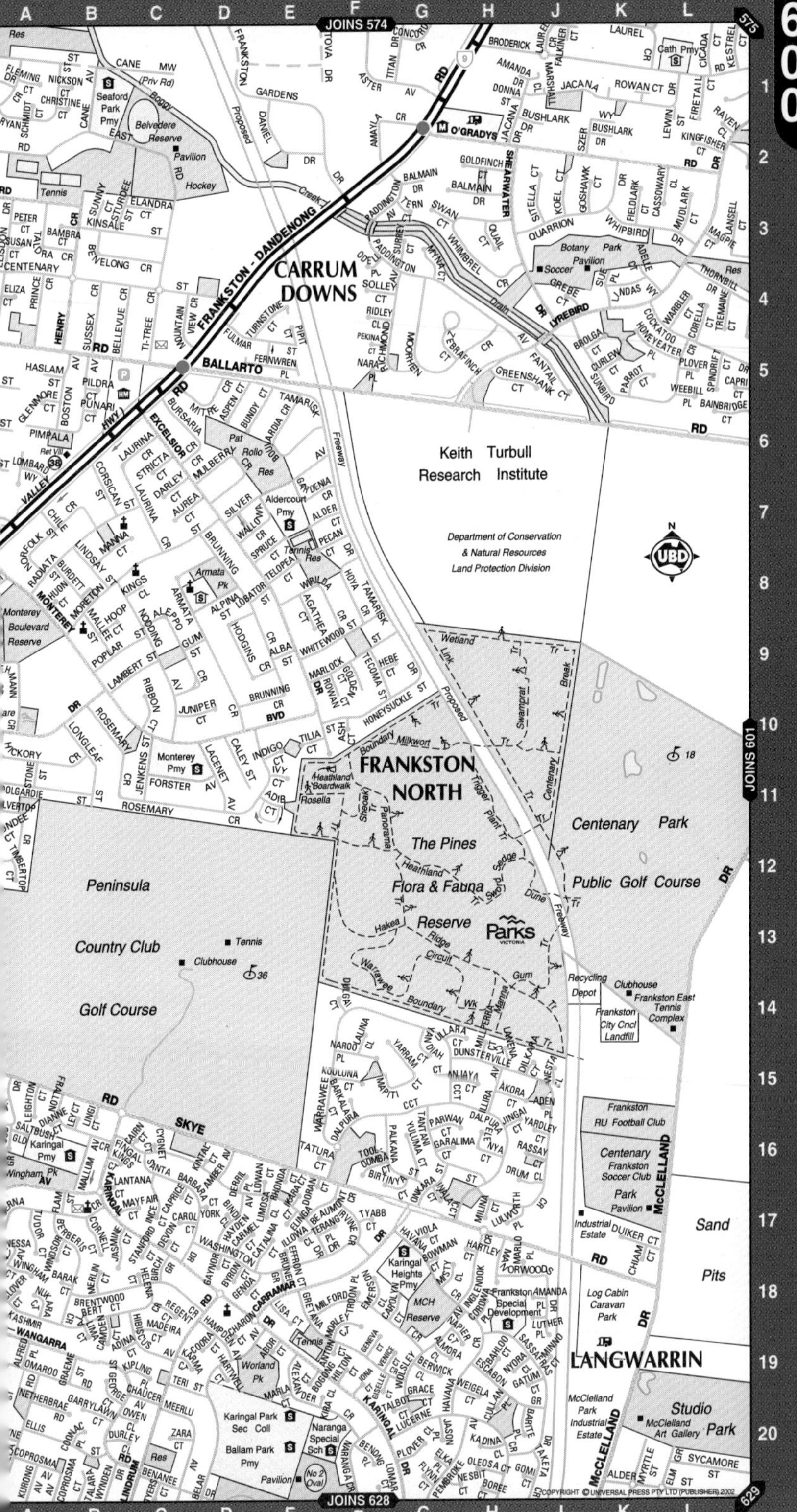
JOINS 574
575
CARRUM DOWNS
FRANKSTON - DANDENONG RD
BALLARTO RD
Keith Turbull Research Institute
Department of Conservation & Natural Resources Land Protection Division
FRANKSTON NORTH
The Pines Flora & Fauna Reserve
Centenary Park Public Golf Course
Peninsula Country Club Golf Course
Frankston RU Football Club
Centenary Frankston Soccer Club Park
Sand Pits
Log Cabin Caravan Park
LANGWARRIN
McClelland Park Industrial Estate
Studio Park
McClelland Art Gallery
Karingal Park Sec Coll
Ballam Park Pmy
Naranga Special Sch
Worland Pk
Monterey Pmy
Aldercourt Pmy
Seaford Park Pmy
Belvedere Reserve
Botany Park
Recycling Depot
Frankston City Cncl Landfill
Frankston East Tennis Complex
Karingal Heights Pmy
MCH Reserve
Frankston Special Development
Monterey Boulevard Reserve
Armata Pk
Pat Rollo Res
SKYE RD
McCLELLAND DR
JOINS 601
JOINS 628
629
COPYRIGHT © UNIVERSAL PRESS PTY LTD (PUBLISHER) 2002

A B C D E F G H J K L

JOINS 575

574

1 2 3 4 5 6 7 8 9 10 11 12 13 14 15 16 17 18 19 20

HALL RD

CICADA CT, KESTREL CT, FIRETAIL CT, SPOONBILL CT, RAVEN CL, BOWERBIRD PL, LYREBIRD, MAGPIE CT, CURRAWONG DR, PEREGRINE PL, FALCON CT, PARTRIDGE CT, PITTA PL, OSPREY CT, CR, AVOCET CT, PETREL CT, PARDALOTE CT, SWIFT CT, SANDFIELD, TATTLER AV, HAWTHORN CT, BELMONT CT, PARKDALE DR, DEAN CT, MAPLEWOOD CT, STRADBROOK, STRATHEARN CT, EXFORD CT, TANDARRA CT, RAVENS CT, SALTRAM CT ST, ROWELLYN AV, Rowellyn Park Pmy, MCH, Reserve, MOWBRAY DR, TREHERNE CT, PARYNAM, SHANE CT, NEWBURY CT, EARNSHAW, PETLEY CT, TYAS CT, TUSKAR PL, HERRINGTON, ALLIED WY, AVERY PL, CARRINGTON, HYSON CT, ROYSTON CT, HENDON, ORSETT CT, BURBERRY CT, LANDON PL, LEFERN CT, TINA CL, CATERINA AV, McCORMICKS RD

CHARDONNAY, MONTANA PL, BOUVERIE PL, NARELLE CT, DELATITE CT, GLOVER CT, EDINBURGH PK, HERITAGE DR, BALINGA, HALSBURY, GREENVIEW PL, BARRINE CT, JURANG CL, MANCHESTER WY, DELPURA CT, LANGRIDGE PL, MONTANA, ASHFIELD DR, OPAL CT, CARAWA PL, HERITAGE DR, NICOLE CT, DAINA CT, HEYSEN DR, STREETON CT, ARLENE, GAMBLE RD

KYRIE CT, NIKE CT, JULIANA, LANSELL CT, CLENDON CT, LANDSTEAD, IDONIA CT, HEYINGTON BVD, Reserve, THORNBILL, HEATHERLEIGH, MELLOWOOD, TYNTYNDER, LINDEN CT, GRATLEA, FAIRHAVEN RD, CHARLEVILLE CT, DUNROBIN, LUCIA CT, SOPHIA, MARCELLA, TANIA CT, JOSEPHINA CT, HELM CT, LENA CT, ST AGNES CT, MARISA, ALLIED, LORETTA, OAKES CT, CARMELA, SASH CL, GAMBLE, CORELLA CT, TREMAINE CT, WILD CROFT, EDENBRIDGE, COCKATOO DR, SPINDRIFT, DRAKE CT, DORCHESTER CT, DERBY, CAPRI CT, BAINBRIDGE CT, GREENWOOD, DEVAS CT, TALBA CT, CARRUM CT, BELLA, TURNBULL CT, LIBELLA CT, ROSEMARY CT, DION, RAQUEL CL, ARCADIA DR, GREENSLOPES, BURLORN CL, DENIS CT, PRASINO CT, HELLENIC CT, DRIFTWOOD MW, CLOVER PL, PARAS, ATHENIUM CT, BALLARTO RD

BLUE WREN RI, PARK WY, FLORA, ELPARA PL, MINKA PL, HUTCHINS WY, DR, CT, AUG, USTA, MARINDA DR, Jehovahs Witness, McCLELLAND DR, VOGELZANG CT, CALWELL CT, ALTER CT, DARNLEY, VALLEY RD, Skye Pmy, CFA, POTTS RD

Skye Golf Course

CARRUM DOWNS

JOINS 600

18

McCLELLAND DR

QUARRY RD

POTTS RD

VALLEY RD

CANDWINDARA CT, BOTTLEBRUSH CT, PEPPERMINT GR, HONEY MYRTLE, CORIANDER CT, BLUE GUM MW, Woodlands Pmy, ILLAWONG MW, ROMSEY PL, TARWIN CT, GUM NUT, COTONEASTER, SAGE CT, MANUKA MW, FERN MW, HEATH MW, BIRD WATTLE, GREVILLEA, OXLEY CT, TAMBO CT, LEXTON, HUNTLY CT, Reserve, STEVENS, BIRGITA CT, MARISSA RD, RAEWYN CT, EUCALYPT CT, PROTEA CT, REYNARD, BRYSON CT, APOLLO, GRANITE CT, EILEEN CT, ROGAN CT, PETER CT, BEACON CT, LYNNE CT, ALLINGTON, WATKIN PL

Sand Pits

LANGWARRIN

ANTHONY CT, WEISE CT, MERIDIAN, CHANDOS PL, COLWYN ST, KERRY, FIRBANK CL, ROBERNA ST, PRESTON, KATE CT, CATHERINE CT, ANTHONY ST, JOSEPHINE ST, MARIA DR, CRANBOURNE–FRANKSTON RD, IMPRESSA CL, WADE, OLEARIA, MELANIE CT, BURGESS, CLAIRE CT, MICHEALA CT, NORTH, JULIE, PANORAMIC, HAKEA CT, WIRILDA, ACACIA WYN, CUNEATA, CLEMATIS, BEVERLEY CT, LANGWARRIN, LYTHAM, JACKSON, BOWER, EVERGREEN WY, NOEL GWY, AIRLIE, SHANA, DENISE

Studio Park

TOMASINA CT, CHATSWOOD, AV, DUNRAVEN CT, LORRAINE, LONG ST, VALENTINE RD, AV, PATERSON AV, Sports Club, Lloyd Park, SYCAMORE, POPLAR, GR, ASH GR, TURNER, ST

628

JOINS 629

A B C D E F G H J K L

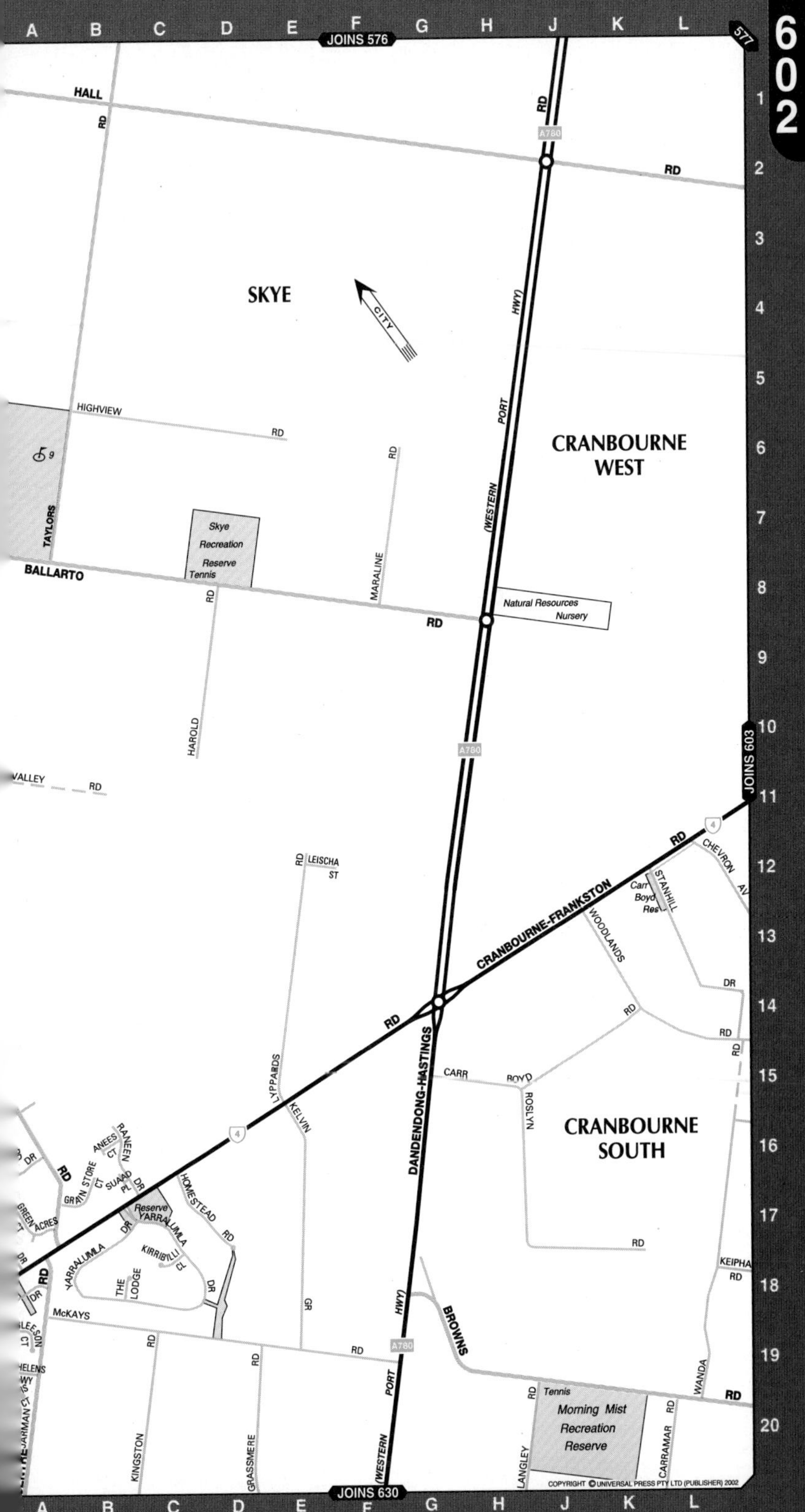
JOINS 576
577
HALL
RD
RD
A780
RD
SKYE
CITY
HWY
PORT
(WESTERN
CRANBOURNE
WEST
HIGHVIEW
RD
RD
MARALINE
TAYLORS
Skye
Recreation
Reserve
Tennis
BALLARTO
RD
RD
Natural Resources
Nursery
HAROLD
A780
JOINS 603
VALLEY
RD
RD
LEISCHA
ST
CRANBOURNE-FRANKSTON
RD
CHEVRON
AV
STANHILL
Carr Boyd Res
WOODLANDS
DR
RD
RD
RD
RD
DANDENDONG-HASTINGS
LYPPARDS
KELVIN
CARR
BOYD
ROSLYN
CRANBOURNE
SOUTH
RANEEN
ANEES
CT
SUAAD
PL
DR
GRAIN STORE
CT
GREEN ACRES
Reserve
YARRALUMLA
DR
HOMESTEAD
RD
KIRRIBILLI
CL
YARRALUMLA
THE LODGE
DR
RD
KEIPHA
RD
McKAYS
GR
HWY
BROWNS
A780
RD
RD
RD
PORT
WANDA
RD
Tennis
Morning Mist
Recreation
Reserve
RD
KINGSTON
GRASSMERE
(WESTERN
LANGLEY
CARRAMAR
JOINS 630
COPYRIGHT © UNIVERSAL PRESS PTY LTD (PUBLISHER) 2002

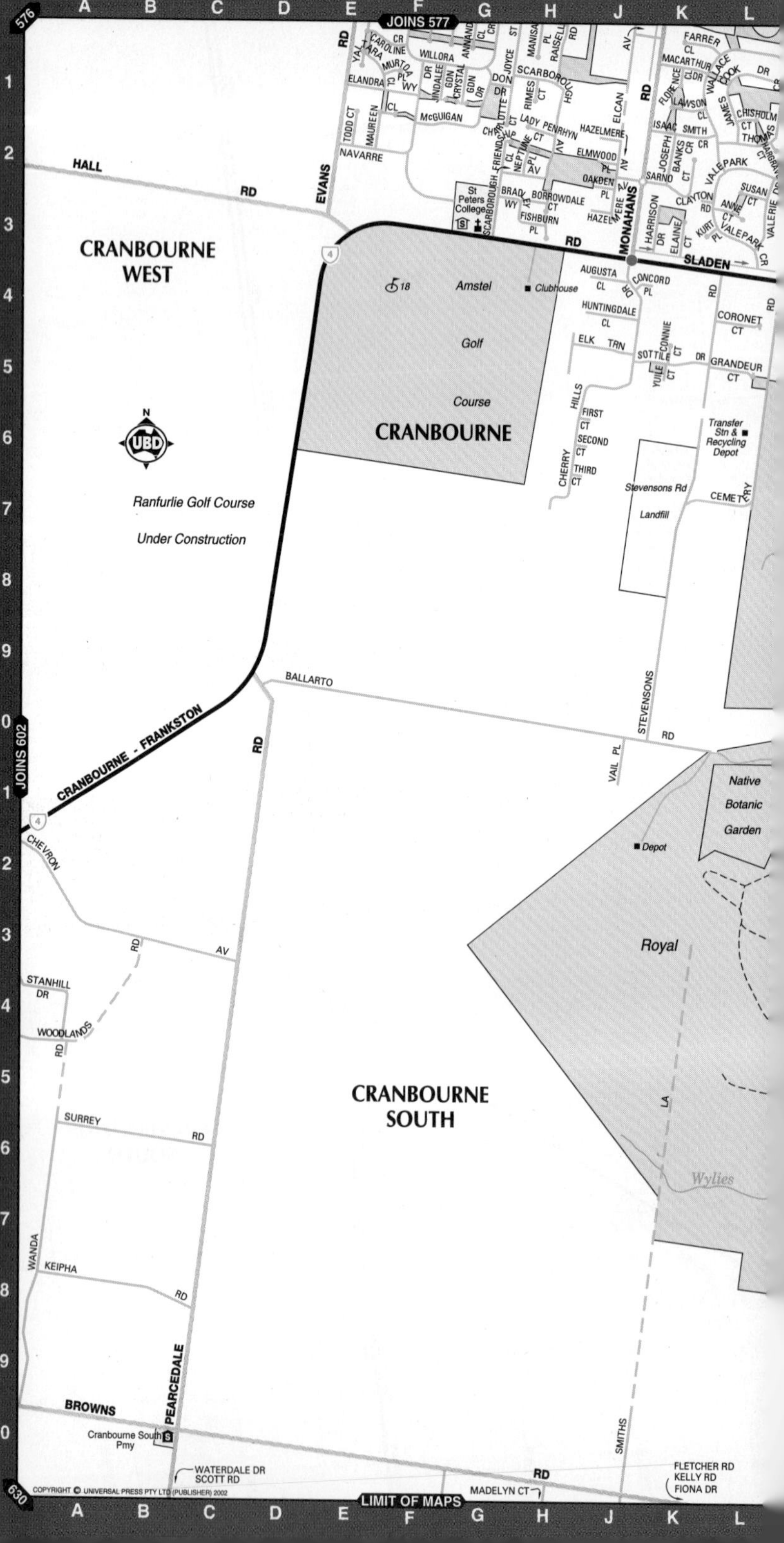

576
JOINS 577

A B C D E F G H J K L

FARRER CL
MACARTHUR CL
WALLACE
COOK DR
CAROLINE CR
WILLORA
ANNAND
YALTARA
MURTOA PL
ELANDRA CL
WY
JINDALEE DR
CRYSTAL GDN
GDN DR
JOYCE ST
MANISA
RAISELL PL
RD
DON DR
SCARBOROUGH
RIMES CT
ELCAN
AV
RD
FLORENCE CL
LAWSON CL
ISAAC
SMITH
JAMES
CHISHOLM CT
THOMAS
HARGRAVE CT
McGUIGAN
TODD CT
MAUREEN
LADY PENRHYN
HAZELMERE
NEPTUNE
ELMWOOD AV
JOSEPH
BANKS CT
CR
SARNO
VALEPARK
SUSAN CT
NAVARRE
HALL
RD
EVANS
RD
St Peters College
SCARBOROUGH
FRIENDSHIP
BRADLEY WY
BORROWDALE CT
FISHBURN PL
OAKDEN PL
HAZEL
MERE AV
MONAHANS
HARRISON DR
ELAINE CT
CLAYTON RD
ANNE CT
KURT PL
VALEPARK CR
VALERIE
RD
SLADEN

CRANBOURNE WEST

4

18
Amstel Golf Course
Clubhouse

AUGUSTA CL
CONCORD PL
DR
HUNTINGDALE CL
RD
CORONET CT
ELK TRN
SOTTILE DR
CONNIE CT
YUILE CT
GRANDEUR CT
HILLS
FIRST CT
SECOND CT
THIRD CT
CHERRY

CRANBOURNE

Transfer Stn & Recycling Depot
Stevensons Rd Landfill
CEMETERY

N
UBD

Ranfurlie Golf Course
Under Construction

BALLARTO
RD
STEVENSONS
RD
VAIL PL

JOINS 602

CRANBOURNE - FRANKSTON
4

Native Botanic Garden
Depot
CHEVRON
RD
AV
Royal
STANHILL DR
WOODLANDS
RD
LA
CRANBOURNE SOUTH
SURREY
RD
Wylies
WANDA
KEIPHA
RD
PEARCEDALE
BROWNS
Cranbourne South Pmy
SMITHS
WATERDALE DR
SCOTT RD
RD
MADELYN CT
FLETCHER RD
KELLY RD
FIONA DR

630
LIMIT OF MAPS

A B C D E F G H J K L

1 2 3 4 5 6 7 8 9 10 11 12 13 14 15 16 17 18 19 20

CRANBOURNE EAST

JUNCTION VILLAGE

DEVON MEADOWS

Cranbourne Recreation Reserve

Botanic Gardens

Cranbourne Secondary College

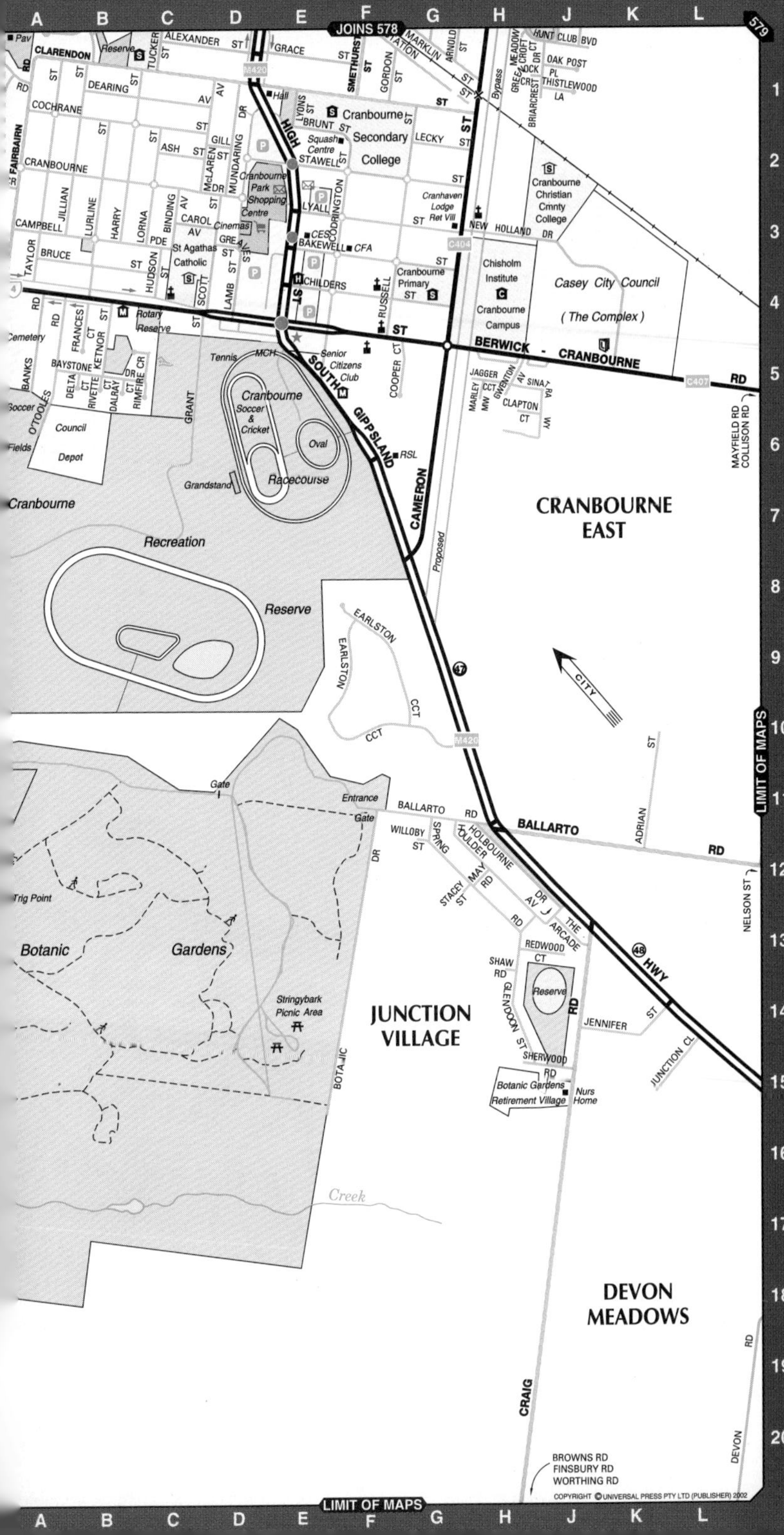

Cranbourne Christian Cmnty College

Casey City Council (The Complex)

Chisholm Institute Cranbourne Campus

Cranbourne Park Shopping Centre

Cranbourne Soccer & Cricket

Racecourse

Botanic Gardens Retirement Village

Stringybark Picnic Area

BERWICK - CRANBOURNE RD

SOUTH GIPPSLAND HWY

BALLARTO RD

CAMERON

CRAIG RD

HIGH ST

BROWNS RD
FINSBURY RD
WORTHING RD

PREVIOUS MAP 604

A B C D E F G H J K L

1 2 3 4 5 6 7 8 9 10 11 12 13 14 15 16 17 18 19 20

PORT

PHILLIP

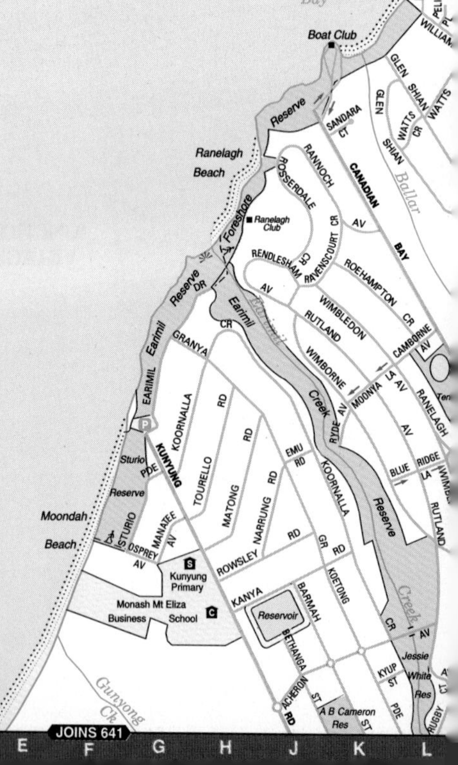

640

JOINS 641

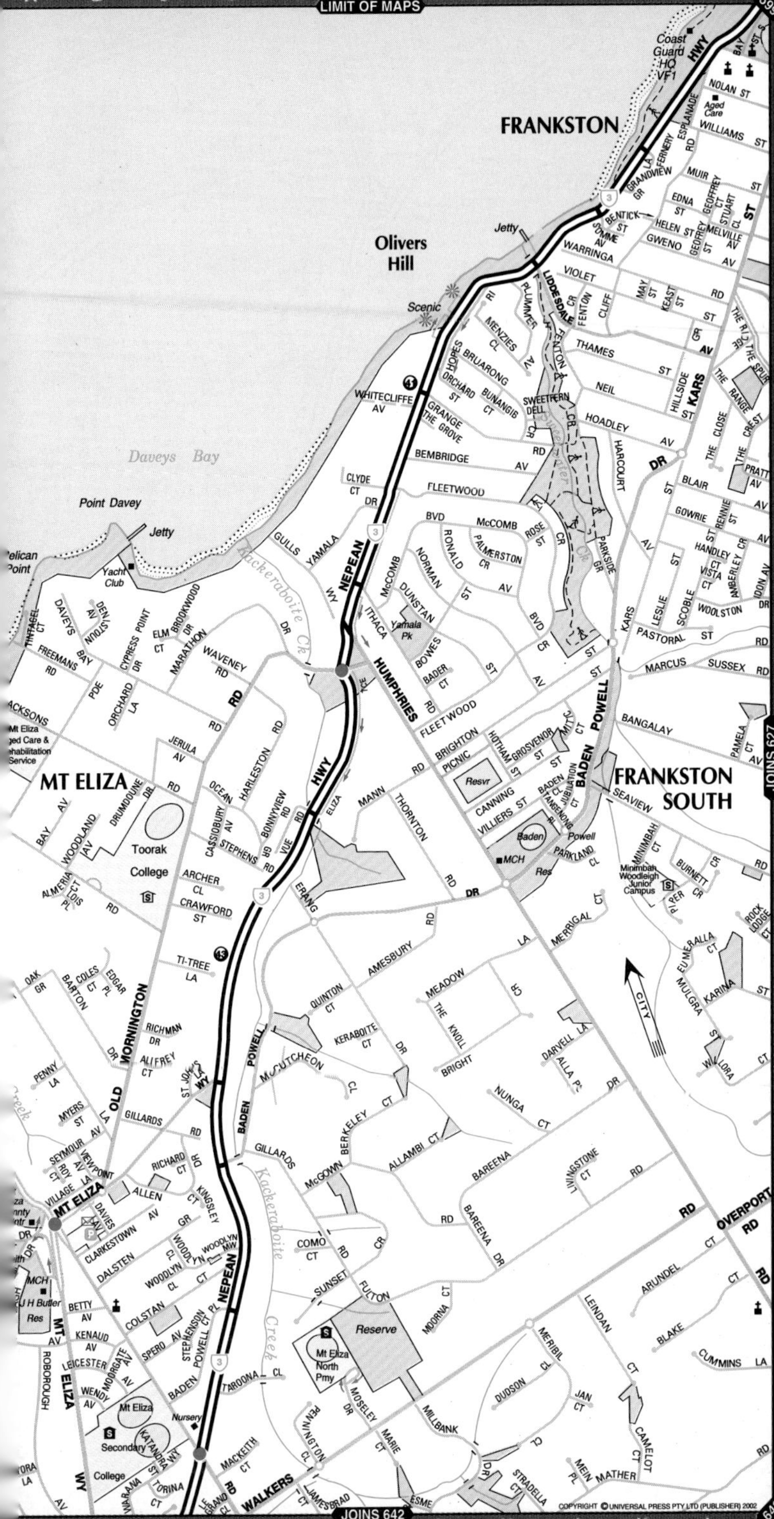

FRANKSTON

Olivers Hill

Daveys Bay

Point Davey

Pelican Point

MT ELIZA

FRANKSTON SOUTH

Coast Guard HQ VF1
Jetty
Scenic
Yacht Club
Aged Care
Mt Eliza Aged Care & Rehabilitation Service
Toorak College
Resvr
Baden Powell Res
MCH
Minimbah Woodleigh Junior Campus
Yamala Pk
Reserve
Mt Eliza North Pmy
Mt Eliza Secondary College
Nursery
J H Butler Res
CITY

NEPEAN HWY
BAY ST
NOLAN ST
WILLIAMS ST
ESPLANADE
FERNERY RD
GRANDVIEW GR
MUIR ST
EDNA ST
GEOFFREY CT
STUART CL
BENTICK ST
SOMME AV
HELEN ST
MELVILLE AV
GWENO AV
WARRINGA RD
VIOLET
LIDDESDALE
FENTON CR
CLIFF
MAY ST
KEAST ST
THAMES ST
NEIL
HILLSIDE ST
KARS ST
HOADLEY AV
HARCOURT
THE RISE
THE SPUR
THE RANGE
THE CLOSE
THE CREST
PRATT AV
BLAIR
GOWRIE
RENNIE ST
HANDLEY CR
VISTA CT
AMBERLEY
LESLIE
SCOBLE
WOOLSTON DR
PASTORAL ST
MARCUS
SUSSEX RD
BANGALAY
PAMELA CT AV
SEAVIEW
BADEN POWELL DR
WHITECLIFFE AV
HOPES RI
PLUMMER AV
MENZIES CL
BRUARONG
ORCHARD ST
BUNANGIB CT
SWEETFERN DELL
GRANGE THE GROVE
BEMBRIDGE AV
CLYDE CT
FLEETWOOD DR
BVD
McCOMB BVD
RONALD
PALMERSTON CR
ROSE ST
NORMAN AV
DUNSTAN ST
ITHACA
BOWES
BADER CT
HUMPHRIES RD
FLEETWOOD
BRIGHTON PICNIC
HOTHAM ST
GROSVENOR ST
CANNING ST
VILLIERS ST
JUBILATION CT
TANGENONG
PARKLAND CL
PARKSIDE GR
MANN RD
THORNTON RD
GULLS WY
YAMALA DR
TINTAGEL CT
DAVEYS BAY
DENISTOUN AV
FREEMANS RD
PDE
CYPRESS POINT DR
ELM CT
BROOKWOOD DR
MARATHON
WAVENEY RD
ORCHARD LA
JACKSONS
JERULA AV
HARLESTON RD
OCEAN
CASSIOBURY AV
STEPHENS
BONNYVIEW GR
VUE RD
ELIZA
DRUMDOUNE DR
WOODLAND AV
BAY AV
ALMERIA CT
LOIS PL
ARCHER CL
CRAWFORD ST
TI-TREE LA
ERANG
AMESBURY
QUINTON CT
KERABOITE CT
MEADOW CR
THE KNOLL
BRIGHT
MERRIGAL CT
MINIMBAH CT
BURNETT CR
PIPER CR
ROCK LODGE
EUMERALLA CT
MULGRA ST
KARINA ST
WILLORA CT
DARVELL LA
ALLA PL
NUNGA CT
OAK GR
COLES CT
EDGAR PL
BARTON
OLD MORNINGTON RD
RICHMAN DR
ALLFREY CT
ST JOHNS LA
PENNY LA
MYERS ST
GILLARDS RD
POWELL
BADEN
McCUTCHEON CL
BERKELEY CT
ALLAMBI CT
BAREENA
LIVINGSTONE CT
GILLARDS
McGOWN
SEYMOUR AV
VIEWPOINT
VILLAGE
RICHARD CT
ALLEN
KINGSLEY
DAVIES
CLARKESTOWN AV
DALSTEN GR
WOODLYN CL
WOODLYN MW
COMO CT
RD
SUNSET
FULTON
MOORNA CT
OVERPORT RD
ARUNDEL CT
LEINDAN
BLAKE
CUMMINS LA
MERIBIL
DUDSON CL
JAN CT
CAMELOT
MATHER
MEIN PL
STRADELLA CT
ESME
MILLBANK
MARIE
MOSELEY DR
PENNINGTON CL
JAMES BRAD CT
WALKERS RD
MACKEITH CT
LE GRAND CL
BETTY AV
KENAUD AV
COLSTAN
STEPHENSON CT
SPERO AV
LEICESTER
MOORGATE
WENDY AV
ROBOROUGH
MT ELIZA WY
KATANDRA WY
TORINA CT
WARANA
TAROONA CL
Kackeraboite Ck
Sweetwater Ck

JOINS 627

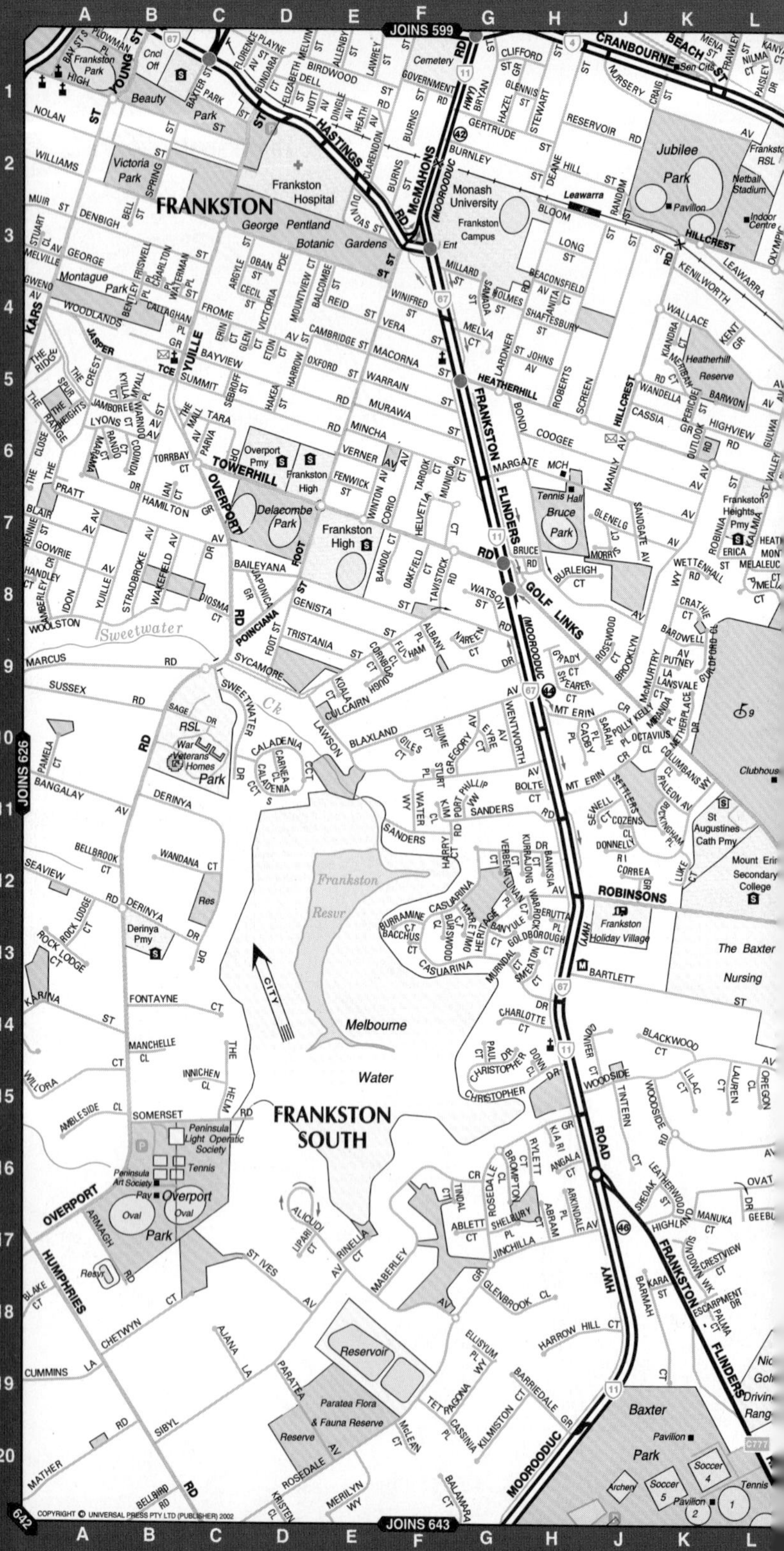

A B C D E F G H J K L

JOINS 599

FRANKSTON

Frankston Park
Beauty Park
Victoria Park
Frankston Hospital
George Pentland Botanic Gardens
Monash University Frankston Campus
Jubilee Park
Frankston RSL
Netball Stadium
Indoor Centre
Leawarra
Montague Park
Heatherhill Reserve
Overport Pmy
Frankston High
Delacombe Park
Bruce Park
Frankston Heights Pmy
RSL War Veterans Homes Park
St Augustines Cath Pmy
Mount Erin Secondary College
Frankston Holiday Village
The Baxter Nursing
Derinya Pmy
Frankston Resvr
Melbourne Water

FRANKSTON SOUTH

Peninsula Light Operatic Society
Peninsula Art Society
Overport Park
Reservoir
Paratea Flora & Fauna Reserve
Baxter Park

FRANKSTON - FLINDERS RD
McMAHONS RD (MOOROODUC HWY)
MOOROODUC HWY
CRANBOURNE RD
BEACH ST
HASTINGS RD

1 2 3 4 5 6 7 8 9 10 11 12 13 14 15 16 17 18 19 20

JOINS 626

JOINS 643

642

A B C D E F G H J K L

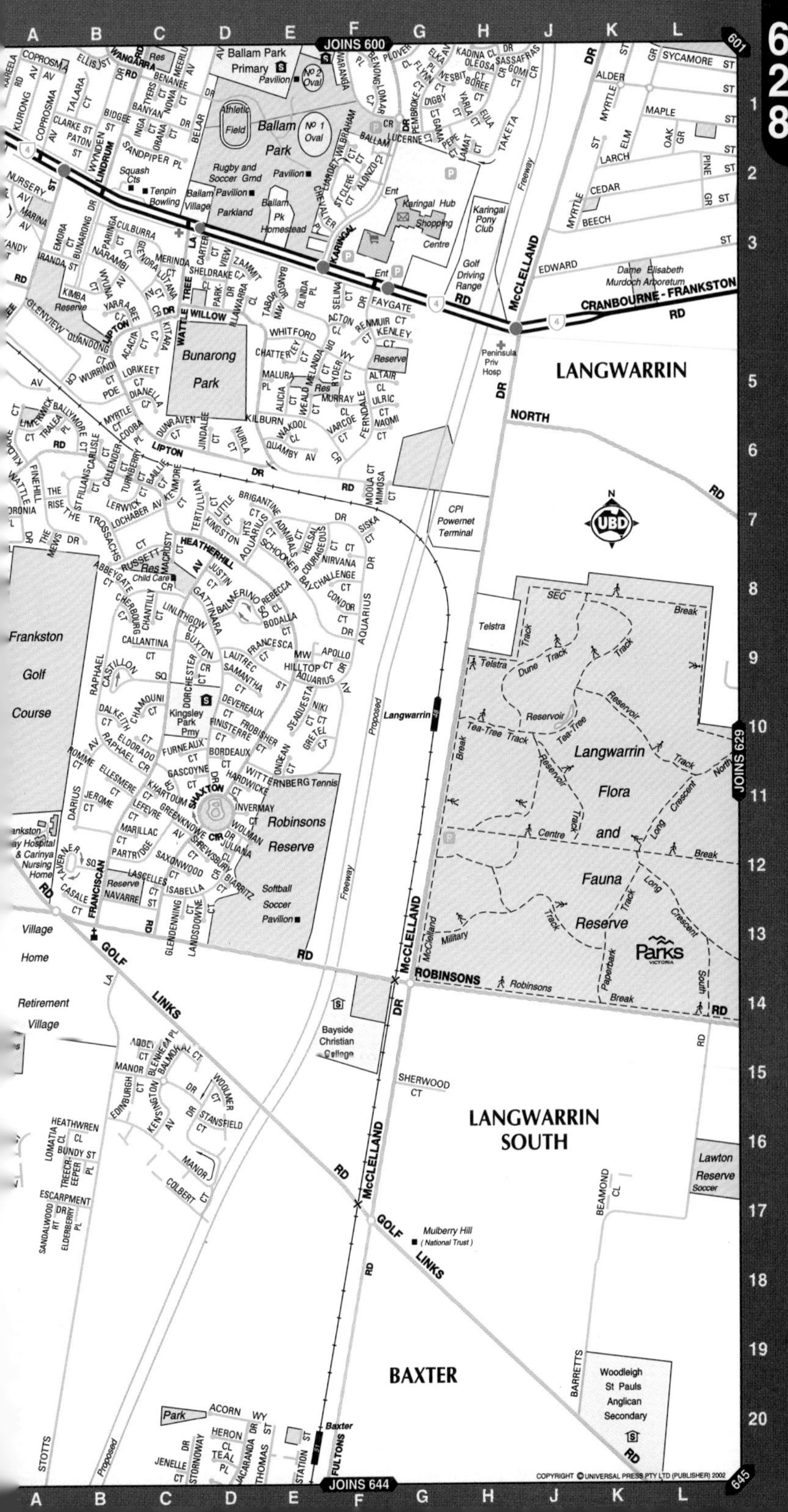
JOINS 600
JOINS 629
JOINS 644
601
645
LANGWARRIN
LANGWARRIN SOUTH
BAXTER
Langwarrin Flora and Fauna Reserve
Frankston Golf Course
Robinsons Reserve
Bunarong Park
Ballam Park
CRANBOURNE - FRANKSTON RD
McCLELLAND DR
GOLF LINKS RD
ROBINSONS RD
NORTH RD
Karingal Hub Shopping Centre
Dame Elisabeth Murdoch Arboretum
Woodleigh St Pauls Anglican Secondary
Bayside Christian College
Mulberry Hill (National Trust)
Village Home Retirement Village
Lawton Reserve Soccer
CPI Powernet Terminal
Peninsula Priv Hosp
Karingal Pony Club
Golf Driving Range

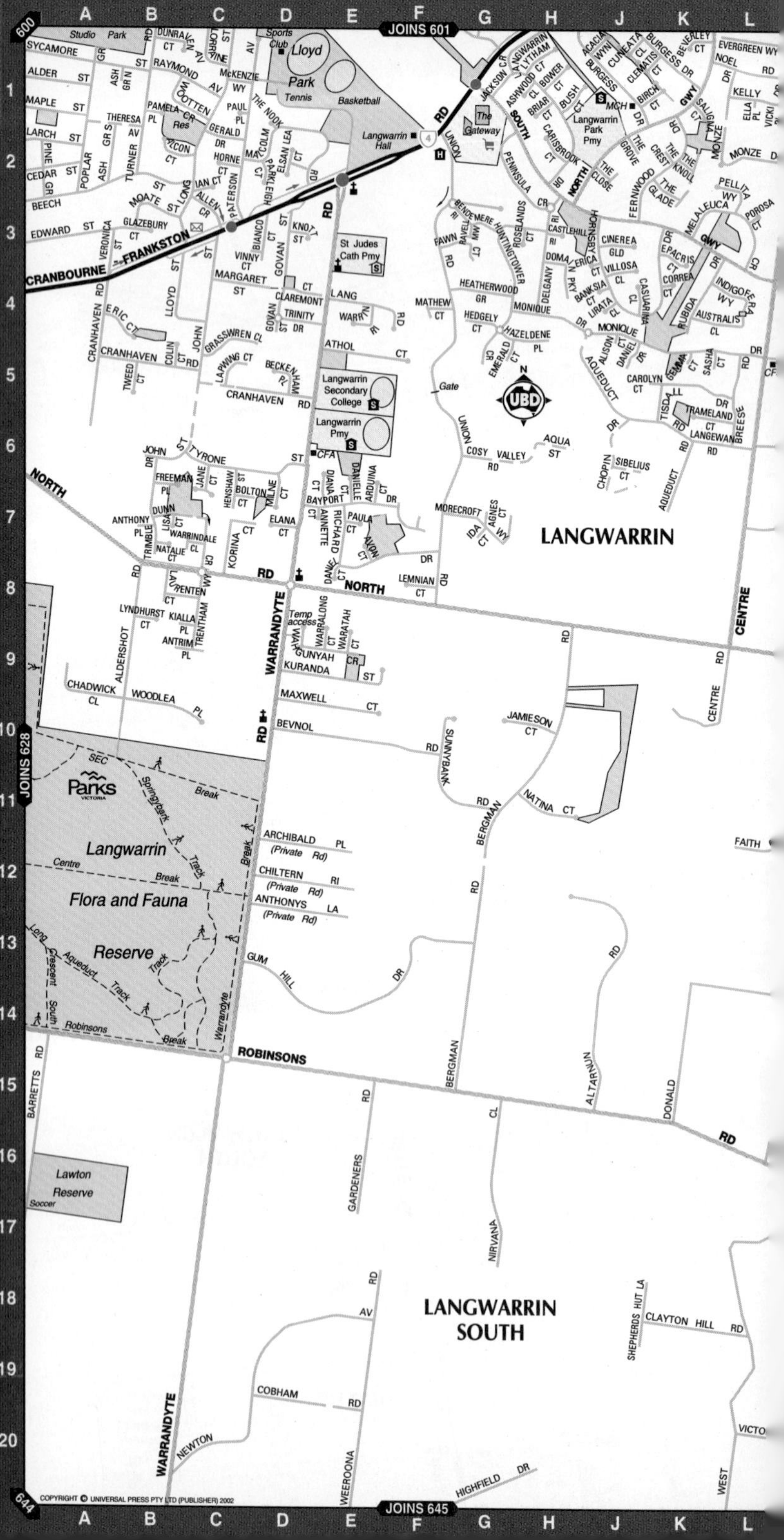

A B C D E F G H J K L

600

JOINS 601

Studio Park
SYCAMORE GR
ALDER ST
MAPLE ST
LARCH ST
PINE GR
CEDAR ST
POPLAR AV
ASH GR
BEECH ST
EDWARD ST
VERONICA ST
CRANBOURNE – FRANKSTON RD
DUNRAVEN AV
LORRAINE ST
RAYMOND ST
ASH GR N
ASH GR S
THERESA AV
TURNER ST
PAMELA PL
WOOTTEN CR
Res
ALCON CT
McKENZIE AV
PAUL PL
GERALD DR
HORNE ST
MOATE ST
LONG ST
ALLEN CR
IAN CT
PATERSON ST
GLAZEBURY CT
Sports Club
Lloyd Park
Tennis
Basketball
THE NOOK
MALCOLM CT
PARKLEIGH CT
ELSAN LEA
Langwarrin Hall
BIANCO CT
GOVAN ST
KNOTT ST
VINNY CT
MARGARET ST
CLAREMONT CT
TRINITY DR
LANG CT
WARREN RI
St Judes Cath Pmy
JACKSON CR
LANGWARRIN LYTHAM
ASHWOOD CT
BRIAR CT
BOWER CT
BUSH CT
CARISBROOK DR
SOUTH
The Gateway
UNION RD
PENINSULA
ACACIA WYN
CUNEATA CL
CLEMATIS CT
BURGESS DR
BEVERLEY CT
EVERGREEN WY
NOEL DR
KELLY
ELLA PL
VICKI
MCH
BIRCH CT
Langwarrin Park Pmy
GROVE
THE CREST
THE KNOLL
THE GLADE
THE CLOSE
SALIGNA CT
MONZE
MONZE DR
GWY
NORTH
FERNWOOD
PELLITA WY
MELALEUCA
POROSA CT
BENDEMERE RI
RAVEN MW
HUNTINGTOWER
ROSELANDS CT
CASTLEHILL RI
HORNSBY
CINEREA GLD
VILLOSA CL
EPACRIS CT
CORREA CT
INDIGOFERA WY
AUSTRALIS CL
FAWN CT
DOMAIN PKY
ERICA CT
BANKSIA CT
LIRATA CL
CASUARINA
RUBIDA
DELGANY
HEATHERWOOD GR
MATHEW CT
HEDGELY CT
MONIQUE DR
HAZELDENE PL
EMERALD CR
ALISON CT
DANIEL CT
AQUEDUCT
CAROLYN CT
GEMMA CT
SASHA CT
CF
ERIC CT
CRANHAVEN RD
LLOYD ST
JOHN ST
COLIN CT
GRASSWREN CL
LAPWING CT
BECKENHAM PL
ATHOL CT
TWEED CT
Langwarrin Secondary College
Langwarrin Pmy
Gate
UBD
TISDALL DR
TRAMELAND RD
LANGEWAN
BREESE
COSY VALLEY RD
AQUA ST
CHOPIN
SIBELIUS CT
JOHN DR
TYRONE ST
CFA
FREEMAN PL
JANE CT
HENSHAW ST
BOLTON CT
MILNE CT
DIANA CT
DANIELLE CT
ARDUINA CT
BAYPORT DR
NORTH
DUNN CT
ANTHONY PL
LISA CT
WARRINDALE CL
TRIMBLE CT
NATALIE CR
KORINA CT
ELANA CT
PAULA CT
ANNETTE CT
RICHARD CT
ALVON CT
MORECROFT CT
IDA CT
AGNES WY
LANGWARRIN
DANE CT
LEMNIAN CT
NORTH RD
WARRANDYTE RD
LAURENTEN CT
LYNDHURST CT
KIALLA PL
TRENTHAM WY
ANTRIM PL
ALDERSHOT
Temp access
WARRALONG CT
WARATAH CT
WAHGUNYAH CR
KURANDA ST
CENTRE RD
CHADWICK CL
WOODLEA PL
MAXWELL CT
BEVNOL RD
JAMIESON CT
SUNNYBANK RD
NATINA CT
BERGMAN RD
SEC Break
Springybank Track
Parks Victoria
Langwarrin Flora and Fauna Reserve
Centre Break
Long Crescent South
Aqueduct Track
Robinsons Break
Warrandyte
ARCHIBALD PL (Private Rd)
CHILTERN RI (Private Rd)
ANTHONYS LA (Private Rd)
GUM HILL DR
FAITH
ALTARNUN
ROBINSONS RD
BARRETTS RD
GARDENERS RD
NIRVANA CL
DONALD
Lawton Reserve
Soccer
LANGWARRIN SOUTH
AV
SHEPHERDS HUT LA
CLAYTON HILL RD
COBHAM RD
VICTO
NEWTON
WARRANDYTE
WEEROONA
HIGHFIELD DR
WEST

JOINS 628

644

JOINS 645

A B C D E F G H J K L

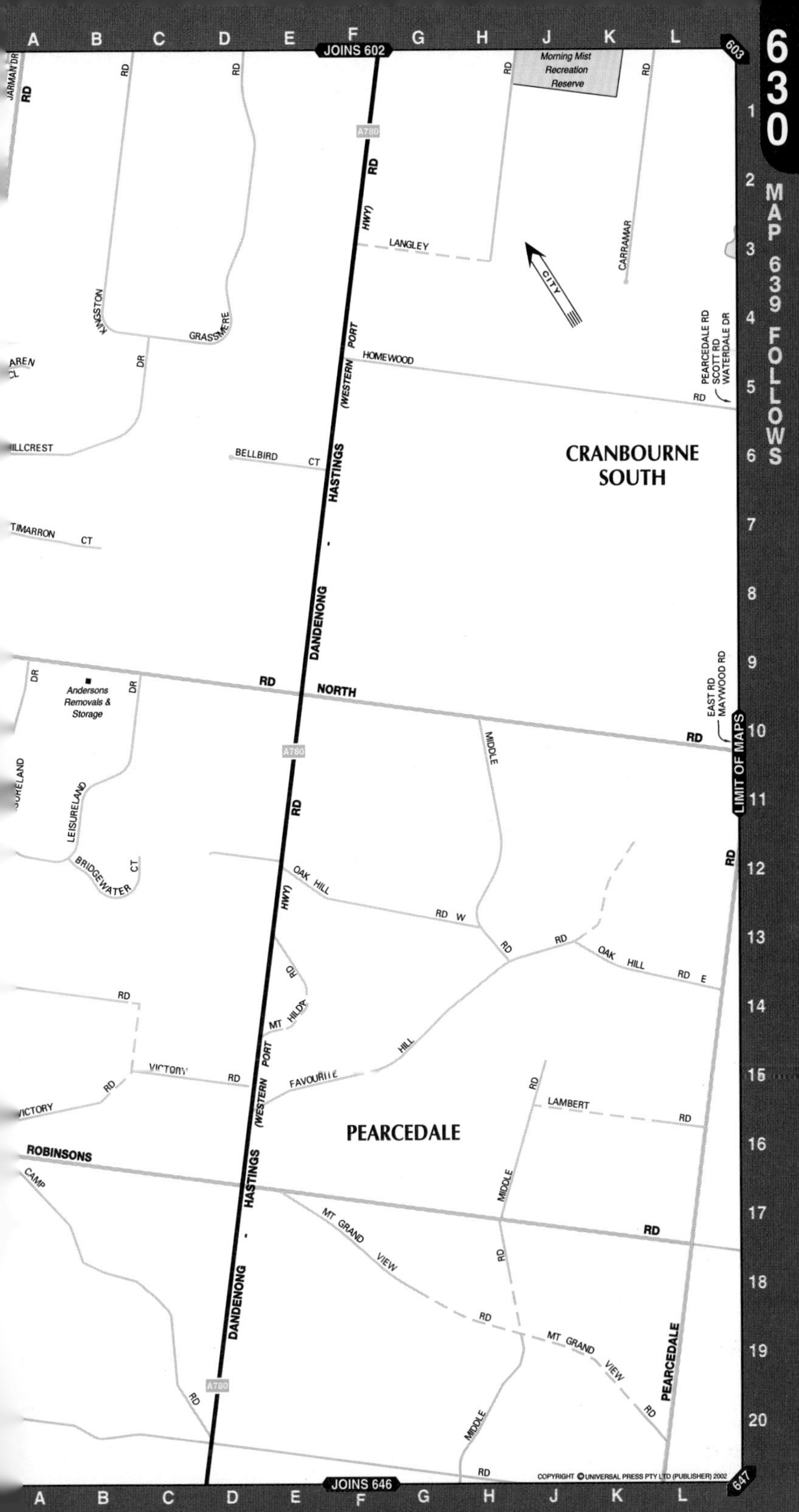
JOINS 602
603
Morning Mist
Recreation
Reserve
A780
DANDENONG - HASTINGS RD (WESTERN PORT HWY)
LANGLEY
CITY
CARRAMAR
KINGSTON
GRASSMERE
HOMEWOOD
PEARCEDALE RD
SCOTT RD
WATERDALE DR
CRANBOURNE
SOUTH
HILLCREST
BELLBIRD CT
TIMARRON CT
NORTH RD
Andersons
Removals &
Storage
EAST RD
MAYWOOD RD
MIDDLE
LIMIT OF MAPS
LEISURELAND
BRIDGEWATER CT
OAK HILL RD W
OAK HILL RD E
MT HILDA RD
VICTORY RD
FAVOURITE HILL RD
LAMBERT RD
PEARCEDALE
ROBINSONS RD
CAMP RD
MT GRAND VIEW RD
MIDDLE RD
PEARCEDALE RD
COPYRIGHT © UNIVERSAL PRESS PTY LTD (PUBLISHER) 2002
JOINS 646
647
MAP 639 FOLLOWS

PREVIOUS MAP 630

628

A B C D E F G H J K L

PORT

Linle
Poin

JOINS 655

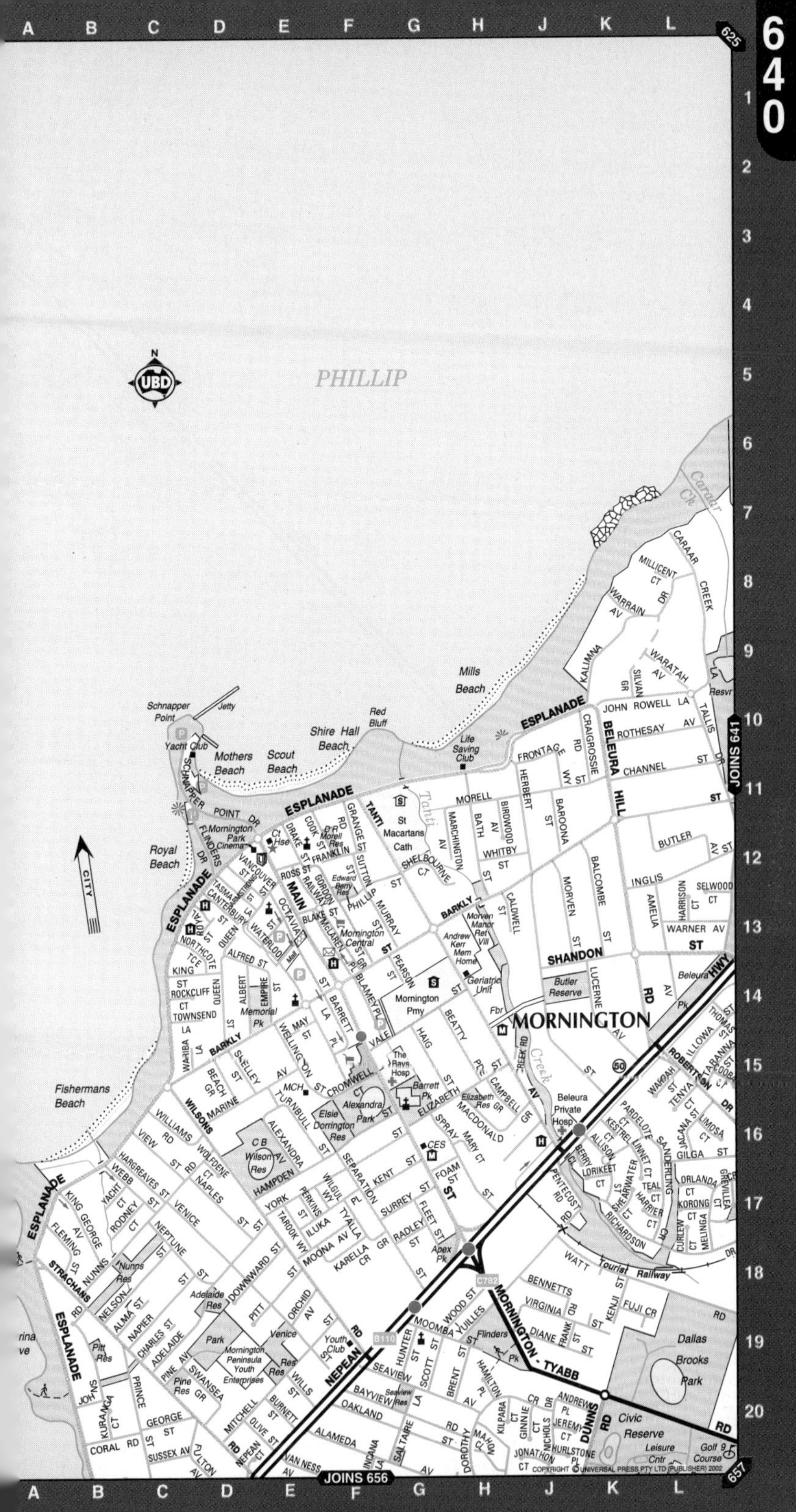

PHILLIP
MORNINGTON
Mills Beach
Red Bluff
Shire Hall Beach
Scout Beach
Mothers Beach
Schnapper Point
Jetty
Yacht Club
Royal Beach
Fishermans Beach
ESPLANADE
MAIN ST
BARKLY ST
TANTI AV
WILSONS RD
NEPEAN HWY
MORNINGTON - TYABB RD
BELEURA HILL RD
St Macartans Cath
Mornington Park Cinema
Mornington Central
Mornington Pmy
Butler Reserve
Alexandra Park
Barrett Pk
Elsie Dorrington Res
C B Wilson Res
Beleura Private Hosp
Dallas Brooks Park
Civic Reserve
Leisure Cntr
Golf 9 Course
Tourist Railway
Apex Pk
Flinders Pk
Nunns Res
Pitt Res
Pine Res
Adelaide Res
Youth Club
Mornington Peninsula Youth Enterprises
Andrew Kerr Mem Home
Geriatric Unit
Morven Manor Ret Vill
Life Saving Club
Caraar Ck
Tanti Ck
CITY
JOINS 641
JOINS 656
625
657
COPYRIGHT © UNIVERSAL PRESS PTY LTD (PUBLISHER) 2002

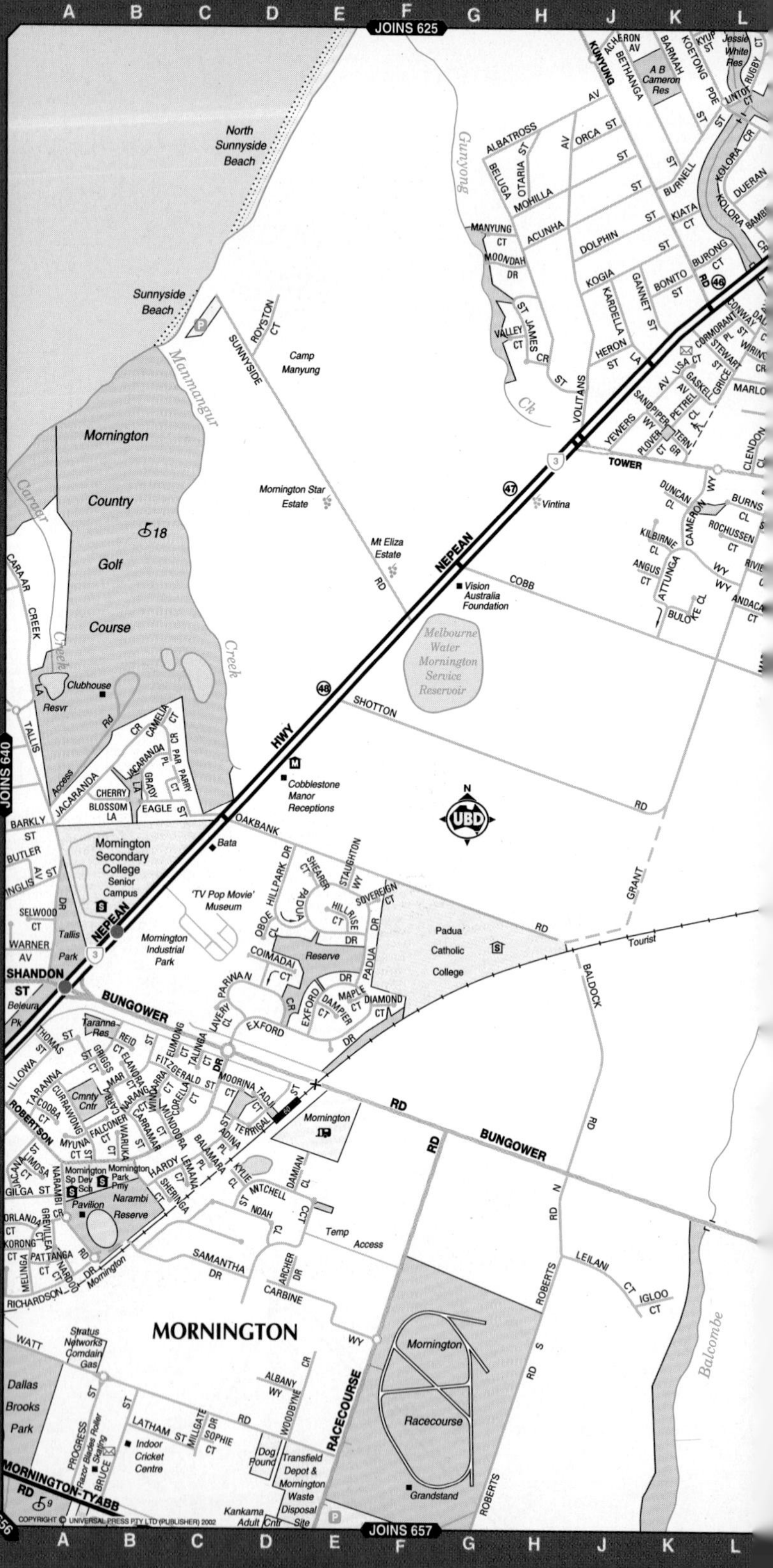
A B C D E F G H J K L
1 2 3 4 5 6 7 8 9 10 11 12 13 14 15 16 17 18 19 20
JOINS 625
JOINS 640
JOINS 657
656
North Sunnyside Beach
Sunnyside Beach
Mornington Country Golf Course
Clubhouse
Resvr
Camp Manyung
Mornington Star Estate
Mt Eliza Estate
Vintina
Vision Australia Foundation
Melbourne Water Mornington Service Reservoir
Cobblestone Manor Receptions
Bata
'TV Pop Movie' Museum
Mornington Secondary College Senior Campus
Tallis Park
Mornington Industrial Park
Padua Catholic College
Reserve
Beleura Pk
Taranna Res
Cmnty Cntr
Mornington Sp Dev Sch
Mornington Park Pmy Sch
Pavilion
Narambi Reserve
Mornington
Temp Access
MORNINGTON
Stratus Networks Comdain Gas
Dallas Brooks Park
Indoor Cricket Centre
Razor Blades Roller Skating
Dog Pound
Transfield Depot & Mornington Waste Disposal Site
Kankama Adult Cntr
Mornington Racecourse
Grandstand
A B Cameron Res
Jessie White Res
Gunyong
Manmangur Creek
Caraar Creek
Balcombe
Tourist
NEPEAN HWY
BUNGOWER RD
RACECOURSE RD
MORNINGTON-TYABB RD
SHANDON ST
COBB RD
SHOTTON RD
OAKBANK RD
TOWER RD
GRANT RD
BALDOCK RD
ROBERTS RD N
ROBERTS RD S
SUNNYSIDE RD
ROYSTON CT
WATT RD
LATHAM ST
PROGRESS ST
BRUCE ST
MILLGATE DR
SOPHIE CT
ALBANY WY
WOODBYNE CR
SAMANTHA DR
CARBINE WY
ARCHER DR
LEILANI CT
IGLOO CT
KUNYUNG RD
ALBATROSS AV
ORCA ST
BELUGA ST
OTARIA ST
MOHILLA ST
ACUNHA ST
DOLPHIN ST
KOGIA ST
KARDELLA ST
GANNET ST
BONITO ST
HERON LA
VOLITANS AV
MANYUNG CT
MOONDAH DR
VALLEY CT
ST JAMES CR
ACHERON AV
BETHANGA ST
BARMAH ST
KOETONG PDE
KYUP ST
BURNELL ST
KIATA CT
BURONG CT
LINTOF CT
KOLORA CR
DUERAN
CORMORANT PL
CONWAY
STEWART ST
GASKELL AV
GRICE
MARLO
USA CT
SANDPIPER WY
PETREL CL
TERN GR
PLOVER CT
YEWERS
CLENDON
DUNCAN CL
CAMERON WY
BURNS CL
KILBIRNIE CL
ROCHUSSEN CT
ANGUS CT
ATTUNGA WY
BULOKE CL
ANDACA CT
CARAAR CREEK LA
TALLIS DR
JACARANDA AV
CAMELIA CR
JACARANDA PL
GRADY LA
PAR PARRY CT
CHERRY
BLOSSOM LA
EAGLE CT
BARKLY ST
BUTLER AV
INGLIS ST
SELWOOD CT
WARNER AV
STAUGHTON WY
SHEARER CT
HILLPARK DR
PADUA DR
HILLRISE CT
SOVEREIGN CT
OBOE CL
COIMADAI CT
EXFORD DR
DAMPIER CT
MAPLE CT
DIAMOND CT
LAVERY CL
PARWAN CR
TALINGA CT
EUMONG CT
REID ST
THOMAS ST
GRIGGS ST
ELANORA CT
FITZGERALD ST
MOORINA CT
TADJI ST
ILLOWA ST
TARANNA ST
COOBA CT
CURRAWONG CT
MAR CT
NARANG CT
WINDARRA CT
CORELLA CT
MUNDOORA CT
CARRAMAR ST
WARUKA CT
FALCONER CT
MYUNA CT
ROBERTSON ST
TERRIGAL CT
ADINA ST
BALAMARA PL
HARDY CT
LEMANA ST
SHERINGA CT
KYLIE CL
MITCHELL CT
NOAH CT
DAMIAN CL
JACANA CT
LIMOSA CT
NARAMBI CR
GILGA ST
ORLANDA CT
GREVILLEA CT
KORONG CT
PATTANGA CT
NARDOO RD
MELINGA CT
RICHARDSON DR
Mornington
COPYRIGHT © UNIVERSAL PRESS PTY LTD (PUBLISHER) 2002

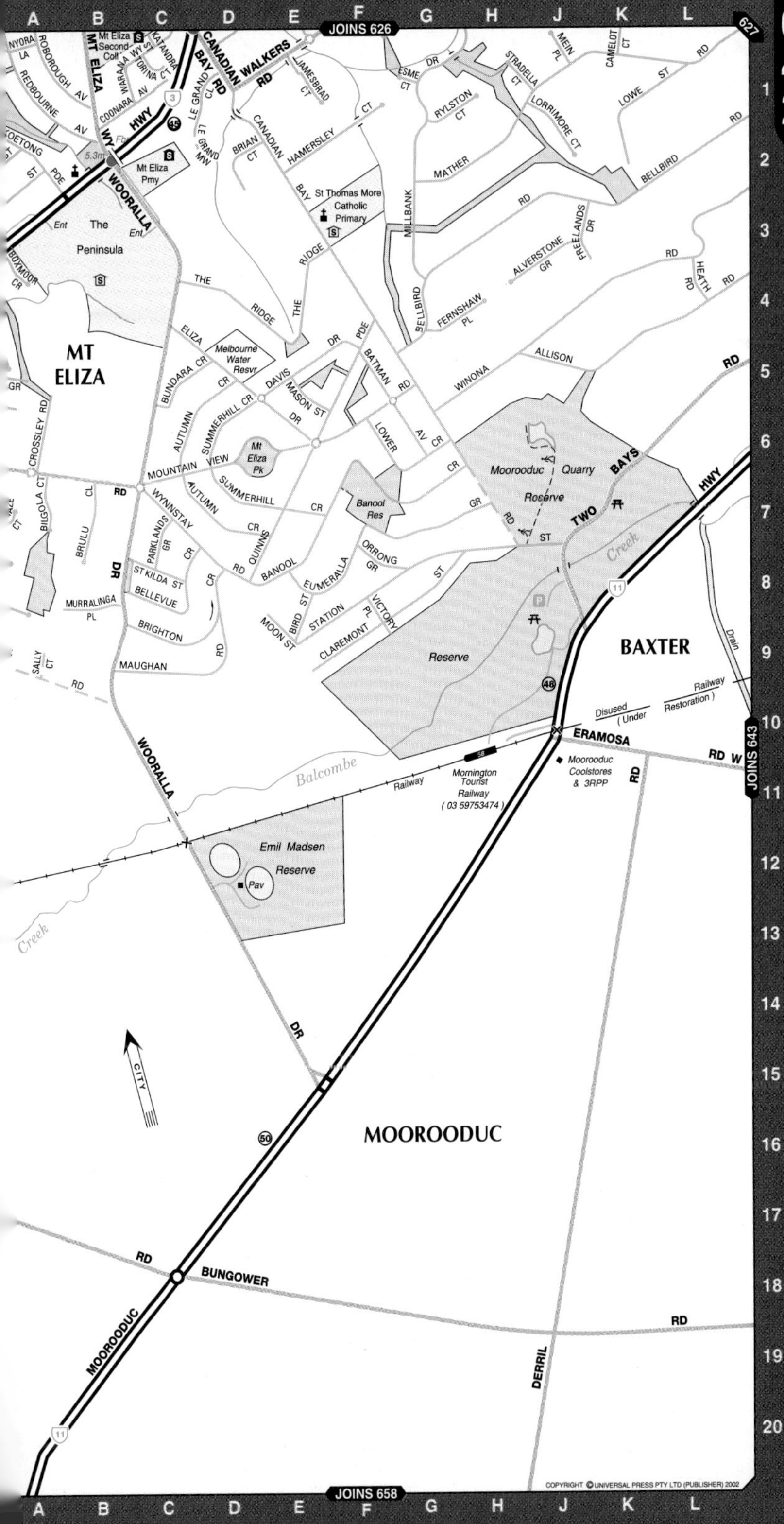

A B C D E F G H J K L

JOINS 626

627

1 2 3 4 5 6 7 8 9 10 11 12 13 14 15 16 17 18 19 20

MT ELIZA

BAXTER

MOOROODUC

NYORA LA
ROBOROUGH AV
REDBOURNE AV
MT ELIZA WY
Mt Eliza Second Coll
WARANA WY
KATANDRA ST
TORINA CT
COONARA AV
OETONG
ST
PDE
5.3m
Mt Eliza Pmy
WOORALLA DR
CANADIAN BAY RD
WALKERS RD
LE GRAND CL
LE GRAND MW
JAMESBRAD CT
BRIAN CT
CANADIAN BAY RD
HAMERSLEY CT
St Thomas More Catholic Primary
ESME CT
DR
RYLSTON CT
STRADELLA CT
LORRIMORE CT
MEIN PL
CAMELOT CT
LOWE ST
RD
MATHER
BELLBIRD RD
MILLBANK
FREELANDS DR
ALVERSTONE GR
HEATH RD
FERNSHAW PL
BELLBIRD
The Peninsula
Ent
BOXMOOR CR
THE RIDGE
Melbourne Water Resvr
ELIZA CR
BUNDARA CR
DAVIS DR
PDE
BATMAN RD
MASON ST
LOWER
AV
CR
WINONA
ALLISON RD
SUMMERHILL CR
AUTUMN
MOUNTAIN VIEW RD
Mt Eliza Pk
SUMMERHILL CR
WYNNSTAY
Mooroduc Quarry Reserve
TWO BAYS RD
HWY
Banool Res
GR
RD
ST
CROSSLEY RD
GR
BIGOLA CT
CL
BRULU
PARKLANDS GR
QUINNS
BANOOL RD
ORRONG GR
ST KILDA ST
BELLEVUE
EUMERALLA ST
ST
Creek
MURRALINGA PL
BIRD ST
STATION
VICTORY
PL
CLAREMONT
MOON ST
BRIGHTON RD
Reserve
MAUGHAN
SALLY CT
RD
Drain
Railway
Disused (Under Restoration)
ERAMOSA RD W
Mooroduc Coolstores & 3RPP
RD
Balcombe
Railway
Mornington Tourist Railway (03 59753474)
Emil Madsen Reserve
Pav
Creek
CITY
DR
BUNGOWER RD
MOOROODUC
DERRIL

JOINS 643

JOINS 658

A B C D E F G H J K L

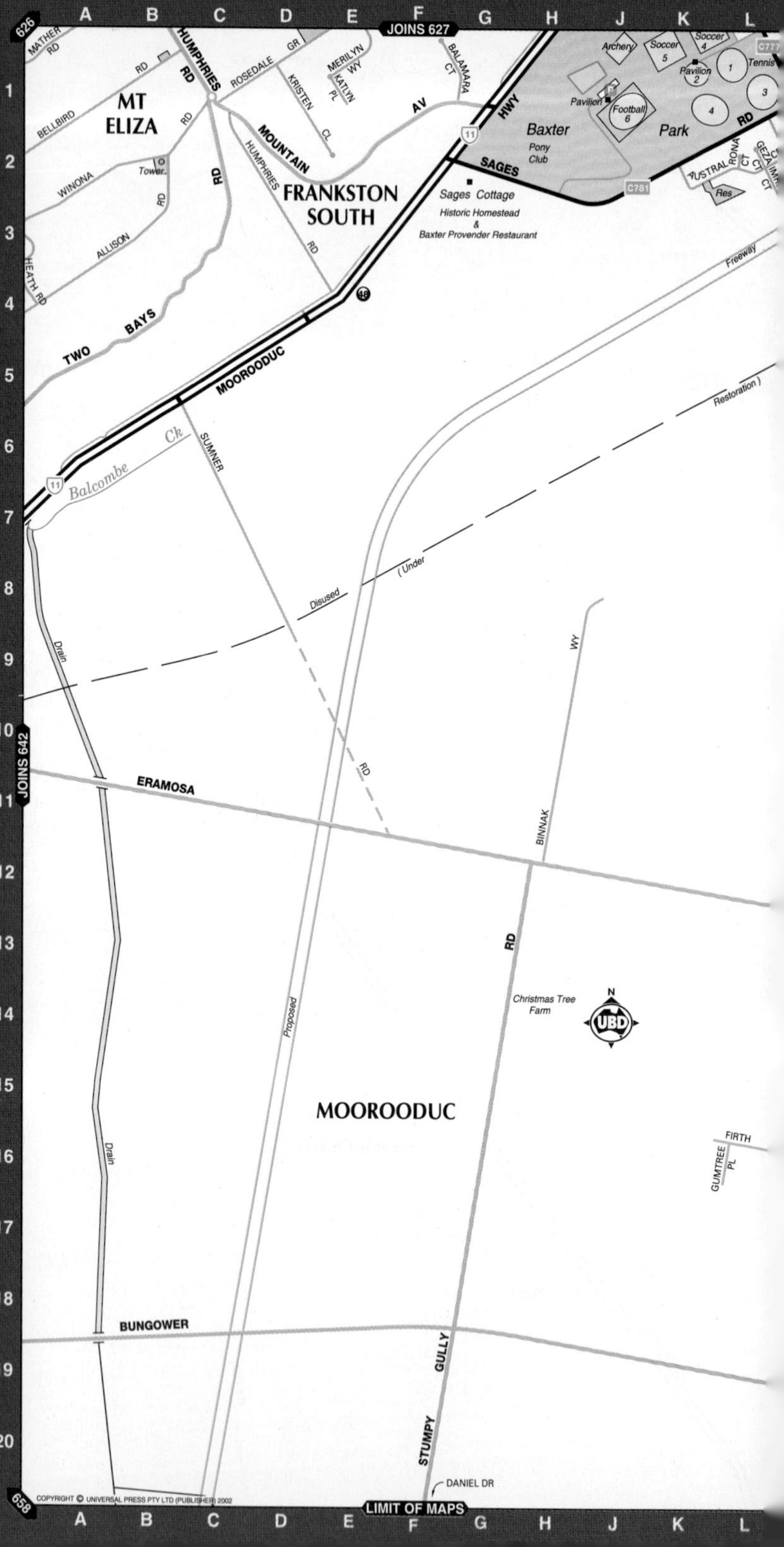

JOINS 627
626

MT ELIZA

FRANKSTON SOUTH

MOOROODUC

MATHER RD
RD
HUMPHRIES RD
ROSEDALE GR
MERILYN WY
KATLYN PL
KRISTEN CL
BALAMARA CT
AV
HWY
BELLBIRD
RD
MOUNTAIN
HUMPHRIES RD
WINONA RD
Tower
RD
ALLISON
HEATH RD
TWO BAYS
MOOROODUC
SAGES RD
Baxter Park
Pony Club
Archery
Soccer 5
Soccer 4
Pavilion 2
Pavilion
Football 6
Tennis
C777
C781
AUSTRAL
RONA CT
GEZA CT
Res
Sages Cottage
Historic Homestead & Baxter Provender Restaurant
Freeway
Restoration)
(Under
Disused
Balcombe Ck
SUMNER RD
Drain
Proposed
ERAMOSA
BINNAK RD
WY
Christmas Tree Farm
UBD
N
FIRTH
GUMTREE PL
BUNGOWER
STUMPY GULLY
DANIEL DR

JOINS 642

658
LIMIT OF MAPS

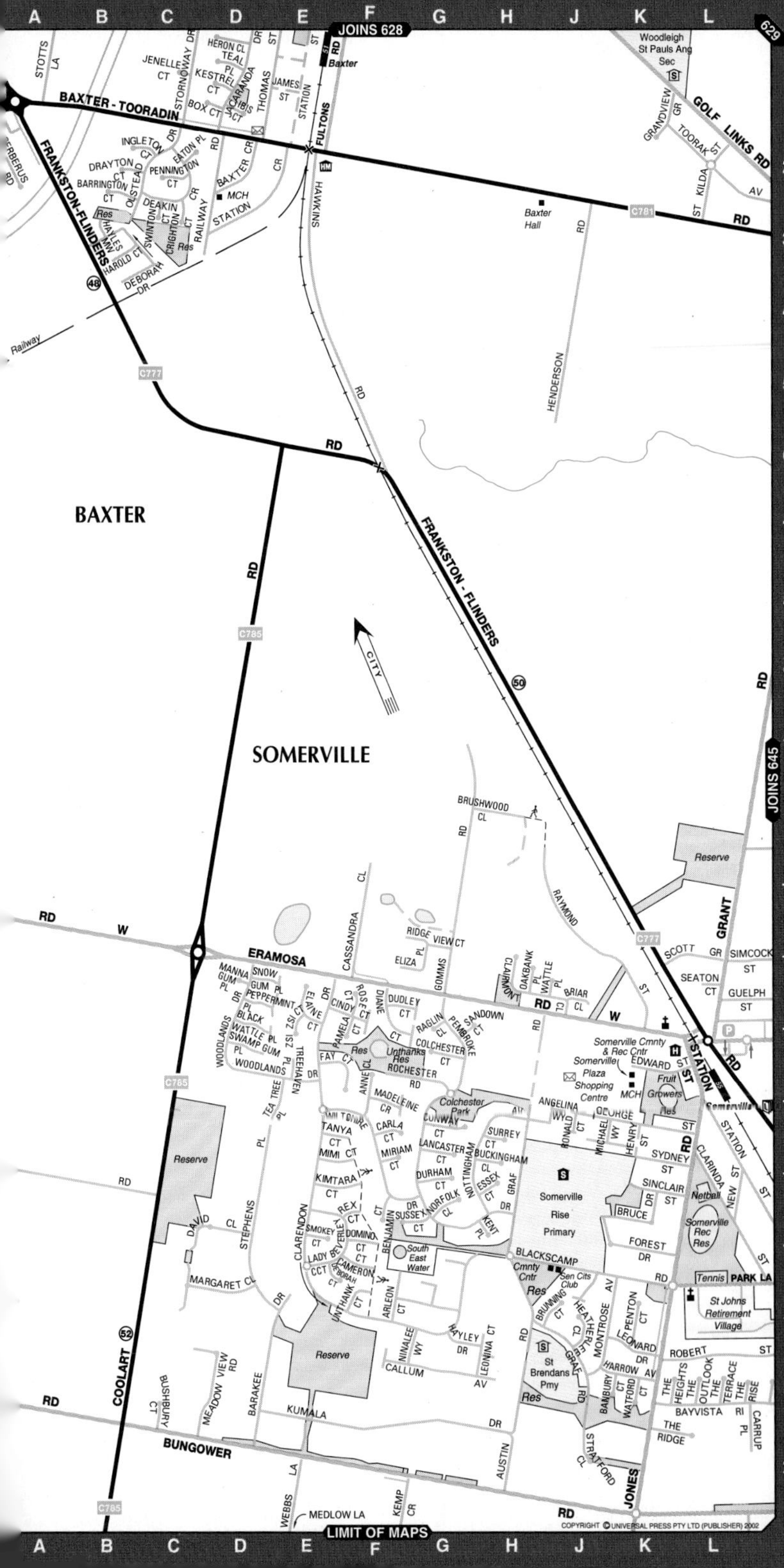

JOINS 628
629
JOINS 645
LIMIT OF MAPS

BAXTER

SOMERVILLE

BAXTER - TOORADIN RD
FRANKSTON-FLINDERS RD
FRANKSTON - FLINDERS RD
ERAMOSA RD W
BUNGOWER RD
COOLART RD
GOLF LINKS RD
HAWKINS RD
HENDERSON RD
STATION ST
JONES RD
GRANT RD
Woodleigh St Pauls Ang Sec
Baxter Hall
Baxter
Somerville
Somerville Cmnty & Rec Cntr
Somerville Plaza Shopping Centre
Fruit Growers Res
Colchester Park
Somerville Rise Primary
South East Water
Cmnty Cntr
Sen Cits Club
St Brendans Pmy
St Johns Retirement Village
Somerville Rec Res
Netball
Tennis
Reserve
CITY

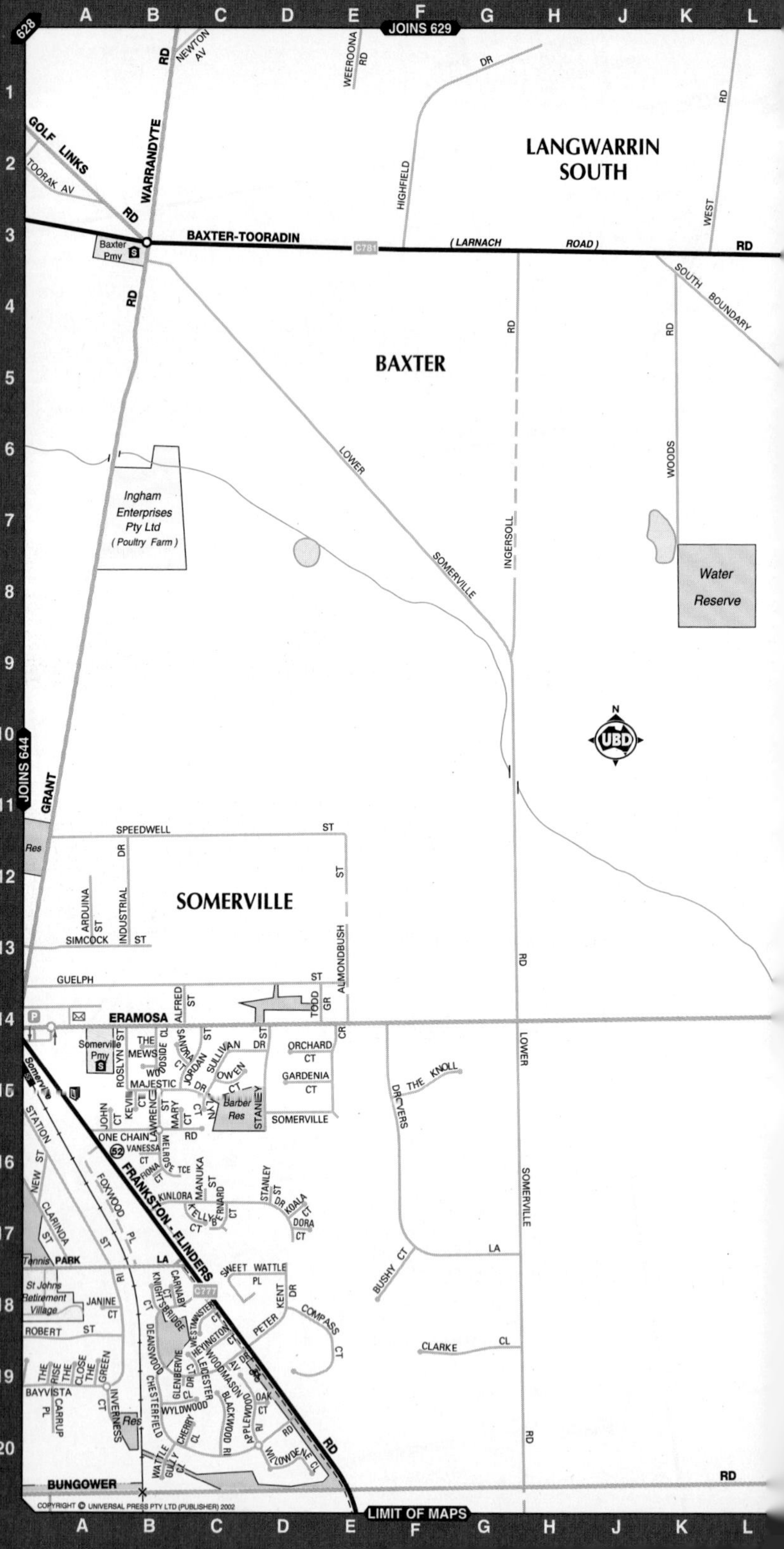
JOINS 629
628
JOINS 644
LIMIT OF MAPS
LANGWARRIN SOUTH
BAXTER
SOMERVILLE
BAXTER-TOORADIN RD
(LARNACH ROAD)
C781
WARRANDYTE RD
GOLF LINKS RD
TOORAK AV
NEWTON AV
WEEROONA RD
HIGHFIELD DR
WEST RD
SOUTH BOUNDARY RD
WOODS RD
INGERSOLL RD
LOWER SOMERVILLE RD
Baxter Pmy
Ingham Enterprises Pty Ltd (Poultry Farm)
Water Reserve
UBD
GRANT RD
Res
SPEEDWELL ST
INDUSTRIAL DR
ARDUINA ST
SIMCOCK ST
ALMONDBUSH ST
GUELPH ST
TODD GR
ALFRED ST
ERAMOSA RD
Somerville Pmy
Somerville
ROSLYN ST
THE MEWS
WOODSIDE CL
SANDRA CT
JORDAN DR
SULLIVAN DR
OWEN CT
MAJESTIC DR
ORCHARD CT
GARDENIA CT
Barber Res
STANLEY CR
SOMERVILLE RD
JOHN CT
KEVILL CT
LAWRENCE ST
MARY CT
STATION ST
ONE CHAIN RD
VANESSA CT
MELROSE TCE
FIONA CT
MANUKA ST
KINLORA CT
KELLY CT
BERNARD CT
STANLEY ST
KOALA DR
DORA CT
DROVERS
THE KNOLL
NEW ST
CLARINDA ST
FOXWOOD PL
FRANKSTON - FLINDERS RD
52
LA
Tennis PARK
SWEET WATTLE PL
KENT DR
BUSHY CT
C777
St Johns Retirement Village
JANINE CT
ROBERT ST
KNIGHTSBRIDGE CT
CARNABY CT
PETER
COMPASS CT
CLARKE CL
DEANSWOOD
WESTMINSTER
HEYINGTON
THE RISE
THE CLOSE
THE GREEN
GLENBERVIE DR
LEICESTER
WOODMASON
BAYVISTA
CARRUP PL
INVERNESS CT
CHESTERFIELD
WYLDWOOD
BLACKWOOD RI
APPLEWOOD RI
OAK CT
WILLOWDENE CL
CHERRY CL
GULLY CL
WATTLE
BUNGOWER RD

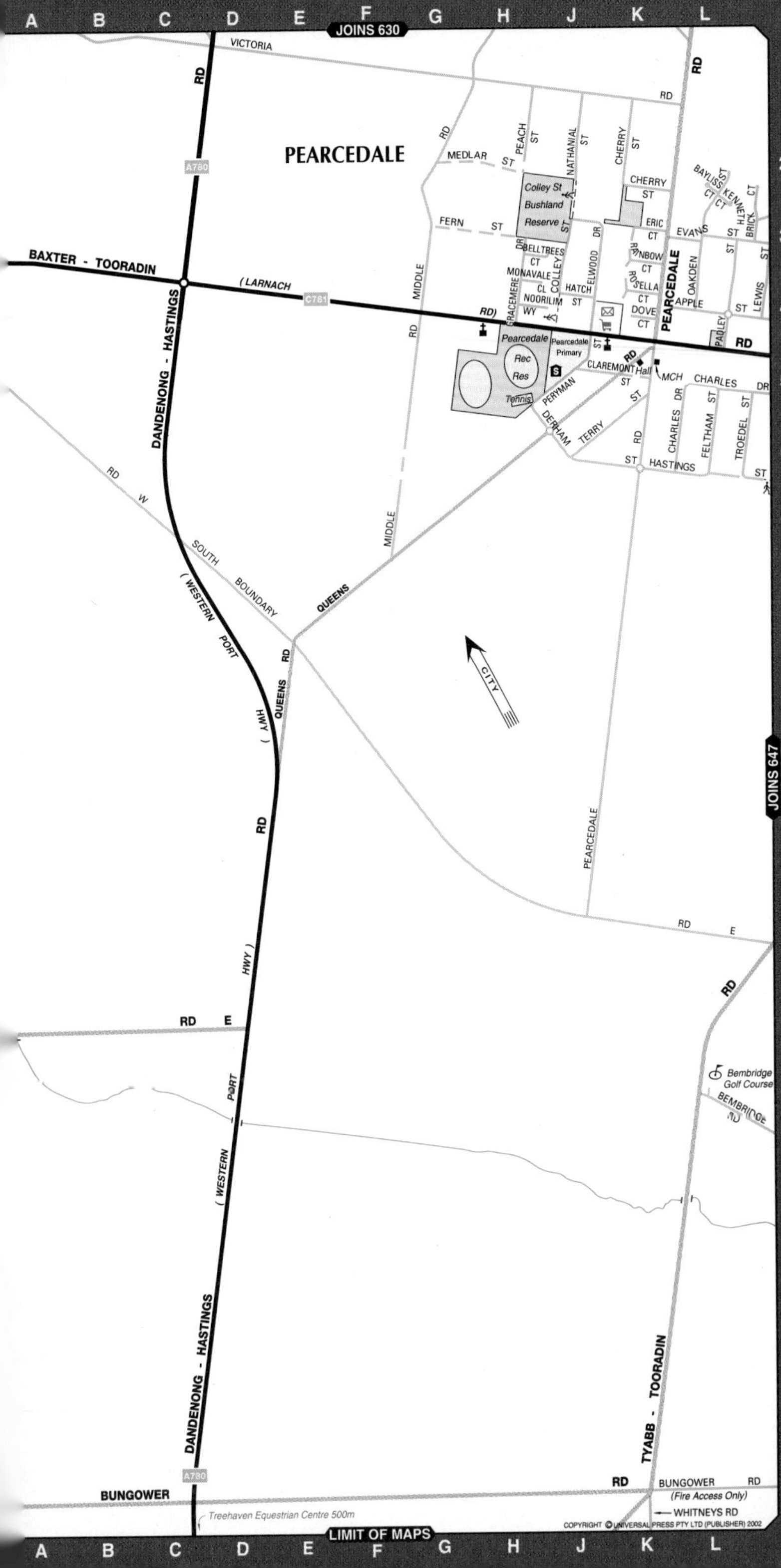

A B C D E F G H J K L

JOINS 630

PEARCEDALE

VICTORIA RD
DANDENONG - HASTINGS RD
A780
BAXTER - TOORADIN (LARNACH RD)
C781
MIDDLE RD
MEDLAR ST
PEACH ST
NATHANIAL ST
CHERRY ST
CHERRY ST
BAYLISS CT
KENNETH ST
BRICK CT
Colley St Bushland Reserve
FERN ST
ERIC CT
EVANS ST
BELLTREES CT
RAINBOW CT
ROSELLA CT
DOVE CT
MONAVALE CL
NOORILIM WY
GRACEMERE DR
COLLEY ST
HATCH ST
ELWOOD DR
PEARCEDALE RD
OAKDEN ST
APPLE ST
LEWIS ST
PADLEY
Pearcedale Rec Res
Tennis
Pearcedale Primary
CLAREMONT RD
Hall
MCH
CHARLES DR
PERYMAN ST
DERHAM ST
TERRY ST
CHARLES DR
FELTHAM ST
TROEDEL ST
HASTINGS ST
SOUTH BOUNDARY RD W
QUEENS RD
(WESTERN PORT HWY)
CITY
PEARCEDALE RD E
RD E
Bembridge Golf Course
BEMBRIDGE RD
TYABB - TOORADIN RD
BUNGOWER RD
(Fire Access Only)
WHITNEYS RD
Treehaven Equestrian Centre 500m

JOINS 647

1 2 3 4 5 6 7 8 9 10 11 12 13 14 15 16 17 18 19 20

LIMIT OF MAPS

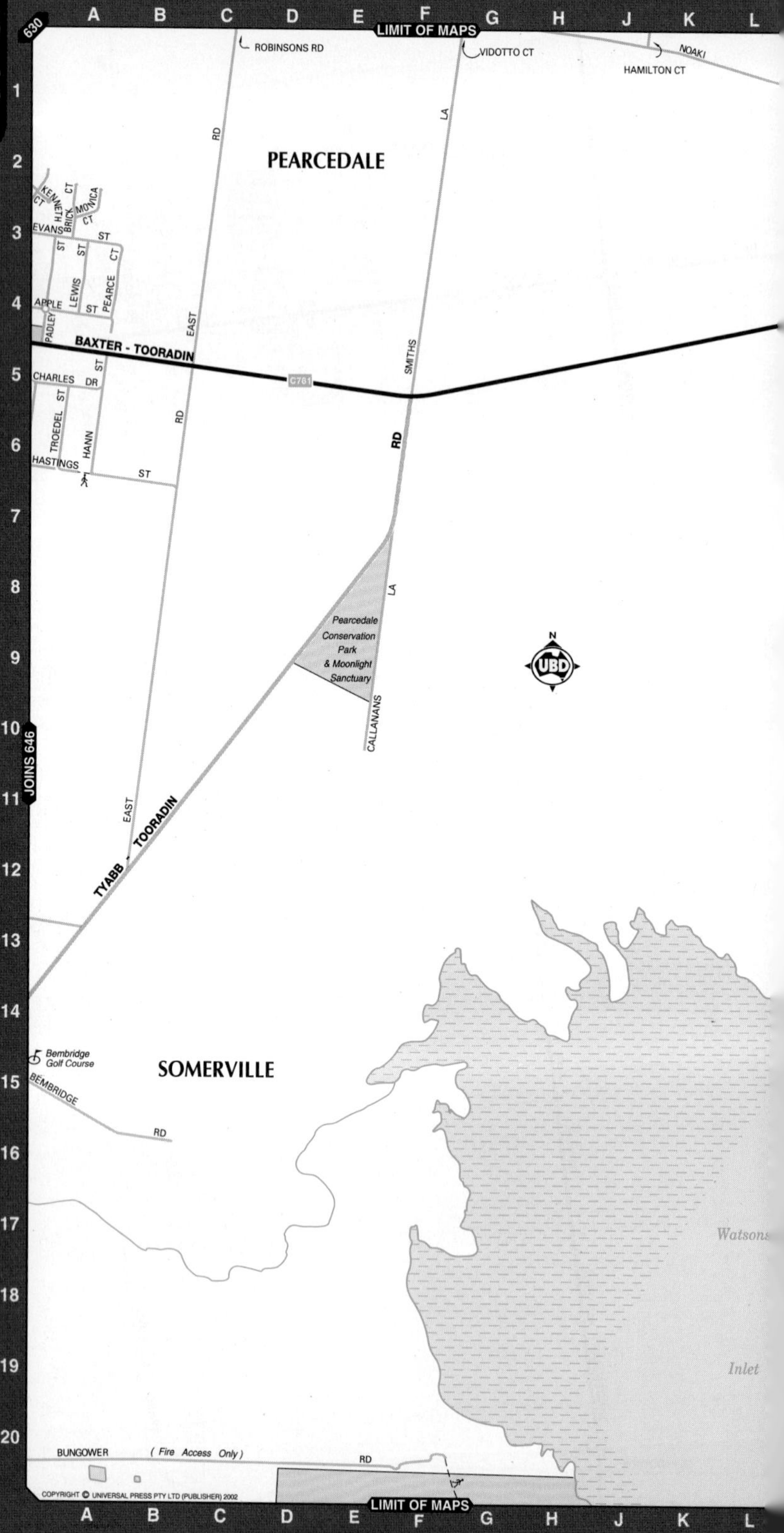

630

A B C D E F G H J K L

LIMIT OF MAPS

ROBINSONS RD

VIDOTTO CT

NOAKI

HAMILTON CT

PEARCEDALE

KENNETH CT
BRICK CT
MONICA CT
EVANS ST
ST
ST
CT
LEWIS
PEARCE
APPLE
ST
PADLEY
BAXTER - TOORADIN
C781
ST
CHARLES DR
ST
TROEDEL
HANN
HASTINGS
ST
EAST RD
SMITHS RD
LA

Pearcedale Conservation Park & Moonlight Sanctuary

CALLANANS LA

JOINS 646

EAST

TYABB - TOORADIN

SOMERVILLE

Bembridge Golf Course

BEMBRIDGE RD

Watsons Inlet

BUNGOWER (Fire Access Only) RD

LIMIT OF MAPS

A B C D E F G H J K L

1 2 3 4 5 6 7 8 9 10 11 12 13 14 15 16 17 18 19 20

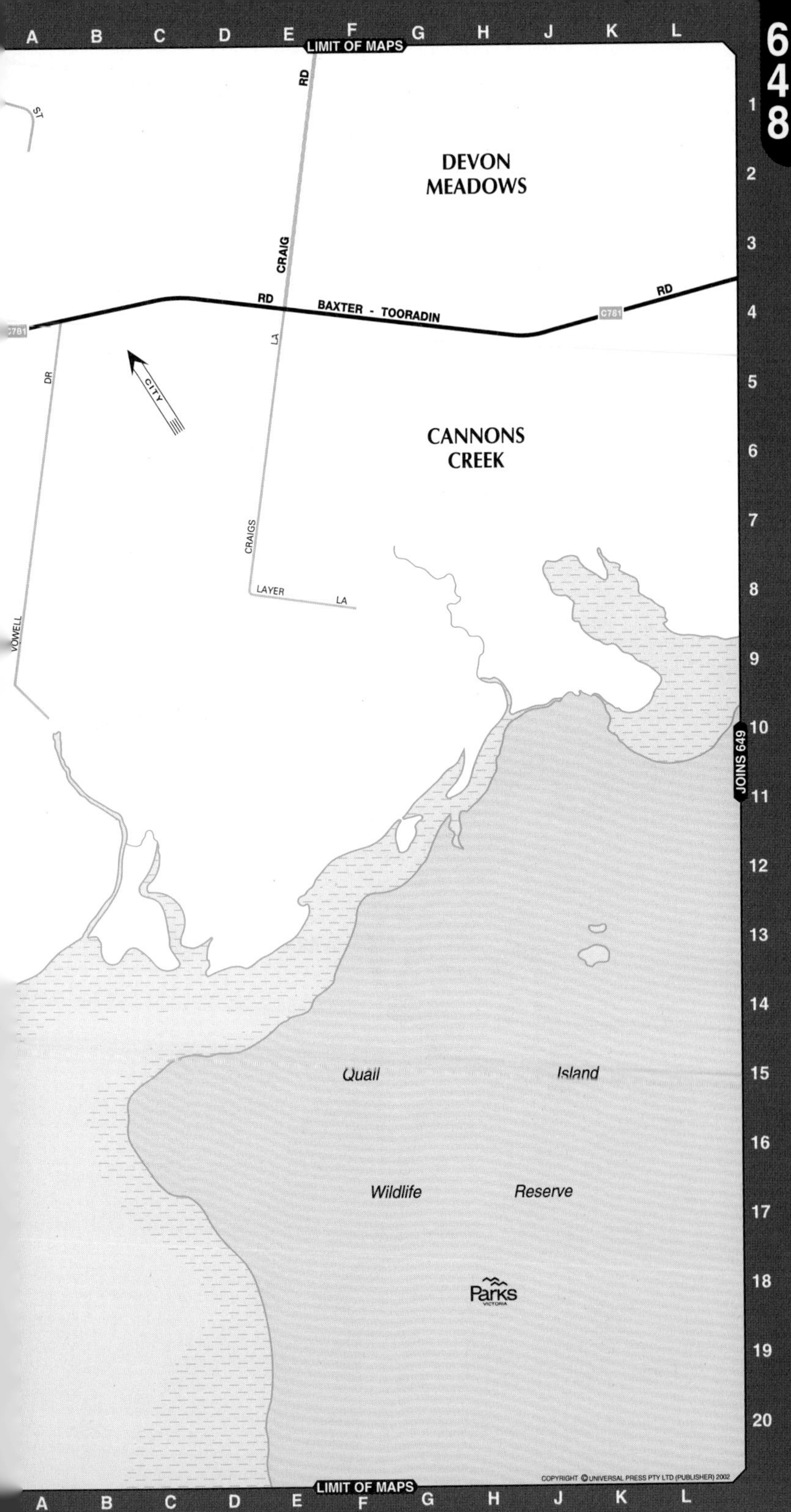
LIMIT OF MAPS
DEVON
MEADOWS
CRAIG
RD
BAXTER - TOORADIN
RD
C781
CITY
DR
LA
CANNONS
CREEK
CRAIGS
LAYER
LA
VOWELL
ST
JOINS 649
Quail
Island
Wildlife
Reserve
Parks
VICTORIA
LIMIT OF MAPS

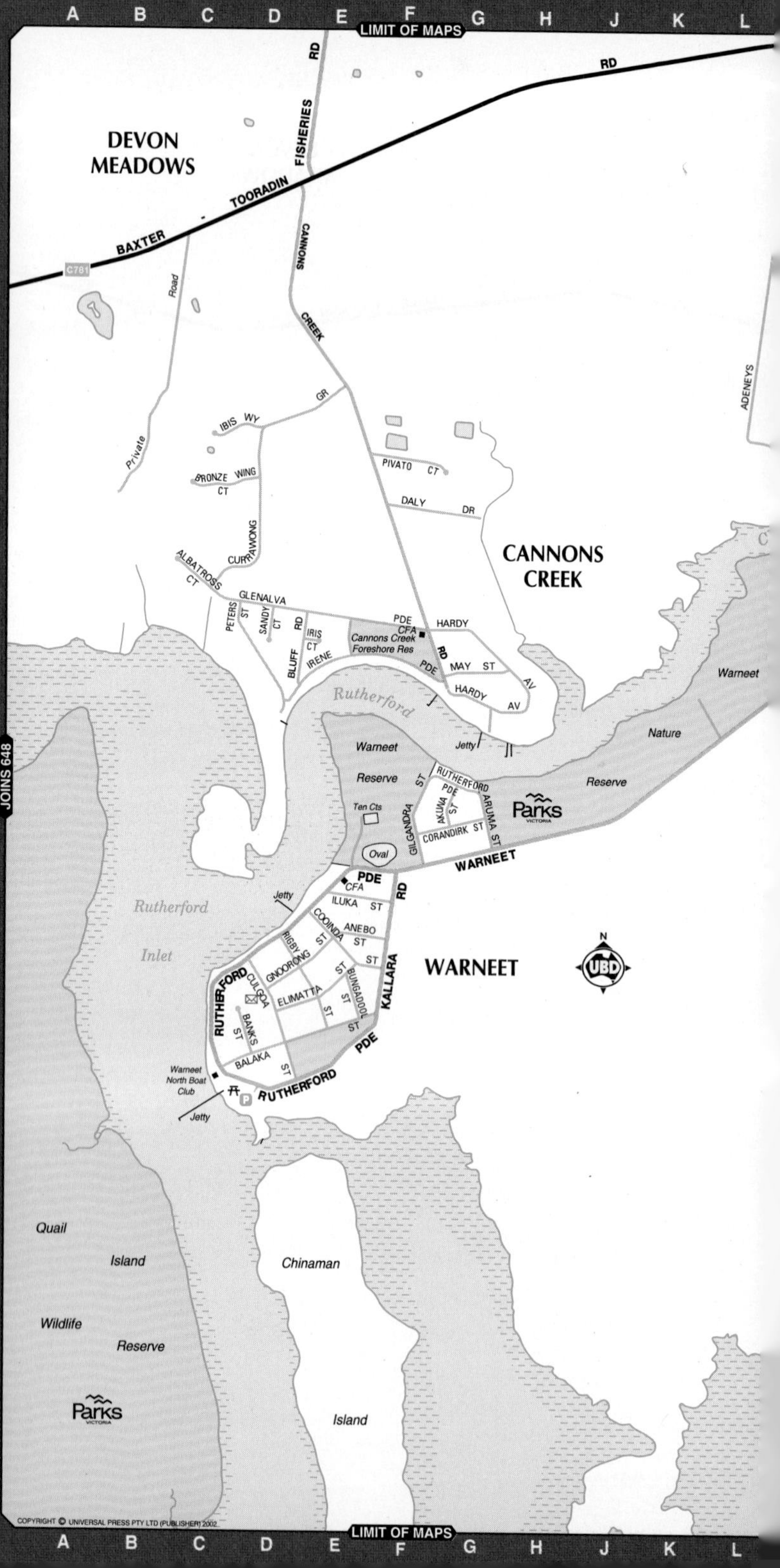

A B C D E F G H J K L

LIMIT OF MAPS

DEVON MEADOWS

CANNONS CREEK

WARNEET

BAXTER - TOORADIN RD

C781

FISHERIES RD

CANNONS CREEK RD

Private Road

ADENEYS

IBIS WY

GR

BRONZE WING CT

PIVATO CT

DALY DR

CURRAWONG

ALBATROSS CT

GLENALVA

PETERS ST

SANDY CT

BLUFF RD

IRIS CT

IRENE

PDE

CFA

HARDY

Cannons Creek Foreshore Res

MAY ST

HARDY AV

AV

Rutherford

Jetty

Warneet Reserve

Warneet Nature Reserve

ST

RUTHERFORD PDE

AKUNA ST

ARUMA ST

Ten Cts

Parks VICTORIA

GILGANDRA

CORANDIRK ST

Oval

WARNEET RD

PDE

CFA

ILUKA ST

Jetty

COOINDA ST

ANEBO ST

ST

RIGBY

GNOORONG

Rutherford Inlet

RUTHERFORD

CULGOA

ELIMATTA ST

BUNGADOOL ST

KALLARA

BANKS ST

BALAKA ST

PDE

Warneet North Boat Club

RUTHERFORD

P

Jetty

N

UBD

Quail Island Wildlife Reserve

Chinaman Island

Parks VICTORIA

JOINS 648

LIMIT OF MAPS

A B C D E F G H J K L

A B C D E F G H J K L

LIMIT OF MAPS

BAXTER - TOORADIN RD
C781
EDWARDS LA
NURSERY LA
LYNES RD
SOUTH GIPPSLAND HWY
M420
Western Contour Drain
CITY

BLIND BIGHT

TOORADIN

WARNEET RD
GOOLAGONG RD
DILKHOOSA AV
Creek
BLIND BIGHT RD
SKUA CT
CORMORANT CL
PRION CL
FISHERMANS DR
EGRET CT
SANDPIPER CL
TERN CL
GANNET CR
PENGUIN CL
CHANNEL CL
DOTTEREL CL
GULL CT
IBIS CT
HARBOUR WY
SEAGULL CL
HERON CL
ALBATROSS CL
KESTREL CL
GENTLE
HARRIER CL
TEAL CT
ANNIE CL
FALCON DR
EAGLE CT
WILD DUCK
ANCHORAGE DR
Jetty

Blind Bight

WESTERN PORT

1 2 3 4 5 6 7 8 9 10 11 12 13 14 15 16 17 18 19 20

JOINS 651

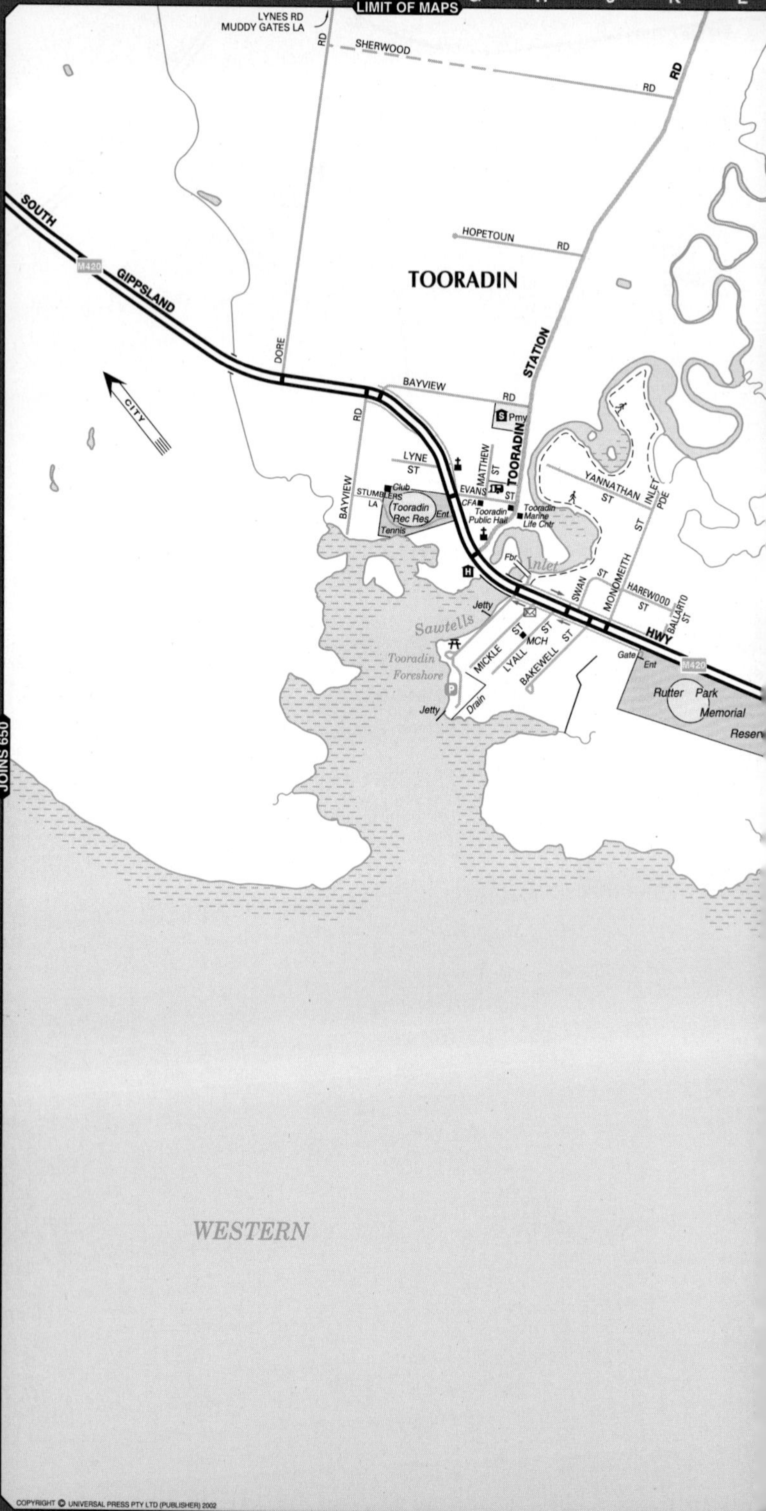

A B C D E F G H J K L

LIMIT OF MAPS

LYNES RD
MUDDY GATES LA
SHERWOOD RD
RD
HOPETOUN RD
TOORADIN
SOUTH GIPPSLAND HWY
M420
DORE RD
BAYVIEW RD
CITY
STATION RD
TOORADIN
Pmy
LYNE ST
MATTHEW ST
EVANS ST
BAYVIEW
STUMBLERS LA
Club
Tooradin Rec Res
Tennis
Ent
CFA
Tooradin Public Hall
Tooradin Marine Life Cntr
YANNATHAN ST
INLET PDE
Fbr
Inlet
SWAN ST
MONOMEITH ST
HAREWOOD ST
BALLARTO ST
Jetty
Sawtells
MICKLE ST
LYALL ST
MCH
BAKEWELL ST
Tooradin Foreshore
Jetty
Drain
Gate
Ent
Rutter Park Memorial Reserve
WESTERN

JOINS 650

1 2 3 4 5 6 7 8 9 10 11 12 13 14 15 16 17 18 19 20

A B C D E F G H J K L

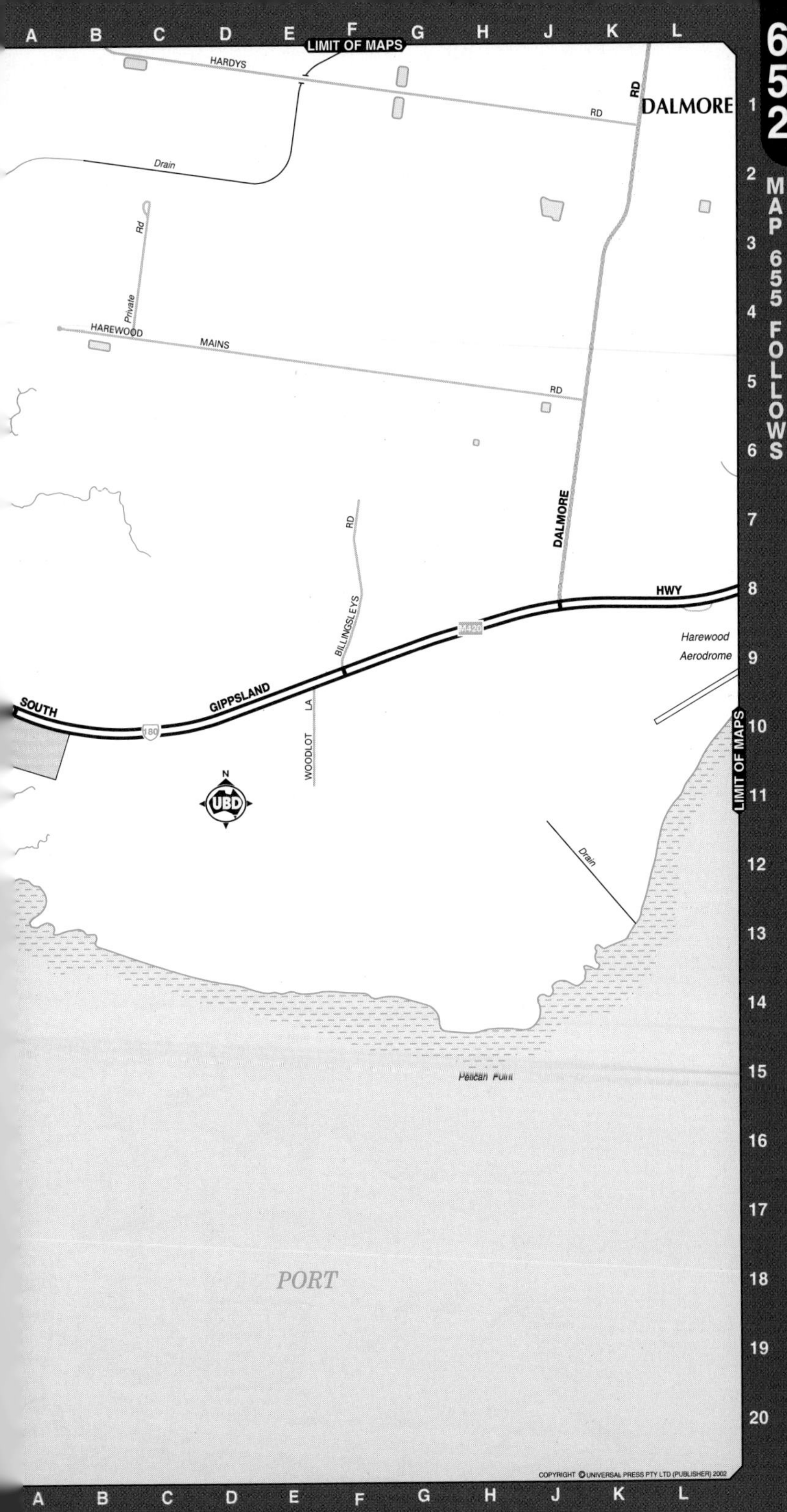

MAP 655 FOLLOWS

PREVIOUS MAP 652

JOINS 639

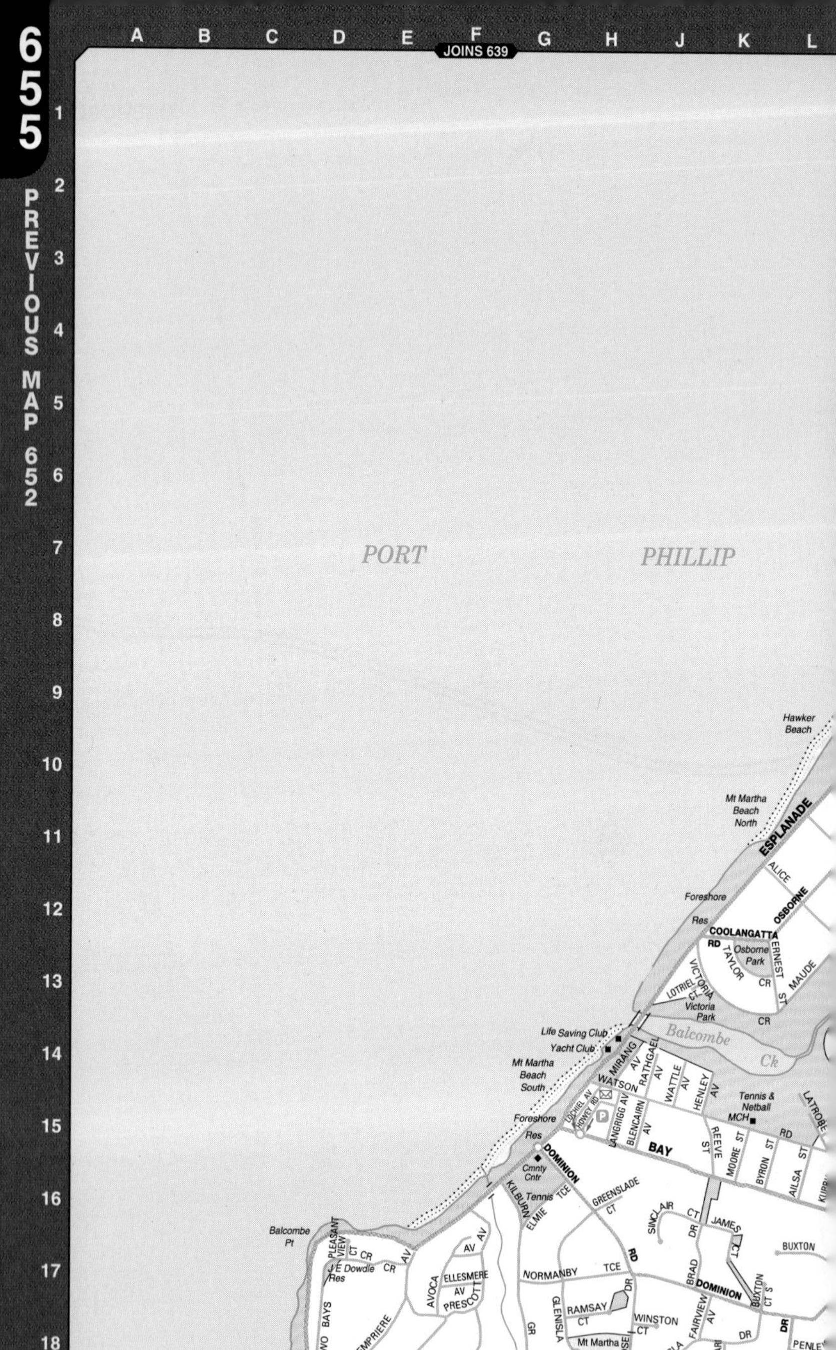

668

JOINS 669

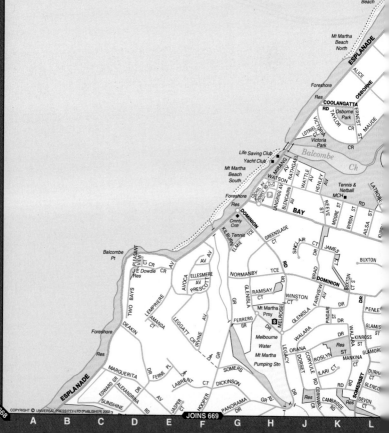

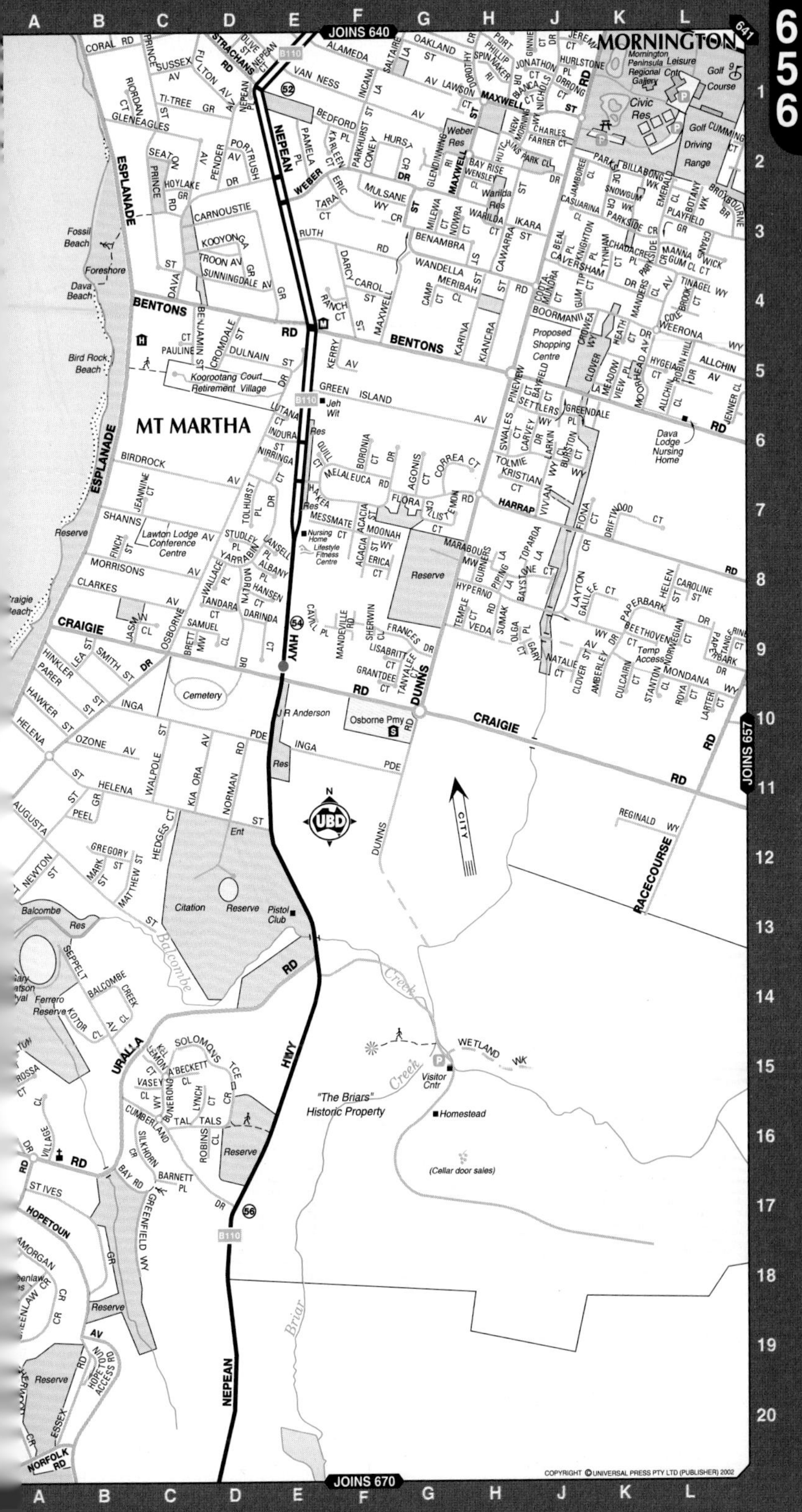

656
JOINS 640
641
MORNINGTON
Mornington Peninsula Regional Gallery
Leisure Cntr
Golf Course
Civic Res
Golf Driving Range
MT MARTHA
Fossil Beach
Foreshore
Dava Beach
Bird Rock Beach
Kooroorang Court Retirement Village
Proposed Shopping Centre
Dava Lodge Nursing Home
Lawton Lodge Conference Centre
Nursing Home
Lifestyle Fitness Centre
Reserve
Cemetery
J R Anderson
Osborne Pmy
Citation Reserve
Pistol Club
Balcombe Res
Ferrero Reserve
"The Briars" Historic Property
Visitor Cntr
Homestead
(Cellar door sales)
WETLAND WK
CITY
ESPLANADE
BENTONS RD
NEPEAN HWY
CRAIGIE RD
DUNNS RD
RACECOURSE RD
GREEN ISLAND AV
HARRAP RD
BALCOMBE CREEK
Briar
JOINS 657
JOINS 670
COPYRIGHT © UNIVERSAL PRESS PTY LTD (PUBLISHER) 2002

640
JOINS 641
JOINS 656
670
LIMIT OF MAPS

A B C D E F G H J K L

1 2 3 4 5 6 7 8 9 10 11 12 13 14 15 16 17 18 19 20

MORNINGTON

MT MARTHA

TUERONG

Transfield & Mornington Waste Disposal Centre
Kankama Adult Centre
Mornington Racecourse
Grandstand
Trainers Floats & Jockeys Ent
Kirton Reserve
Electricity Substation
Golf Course
Golf Driving Range
Swim School
The Mornington Retirement Village

MORNINGTON - TYABB RD
C782
HWY
11
BENTONS RD
CRAIGIE RD
MOOROODUC HWY
MORNINGTON PENINSULA FWY
OLD MOOROODUC RD
C784
TUERONG RD
RACECOURSE RD
BENTON GRANGE DR
BARAK
MALES
HARRAP RD
ROBERTS RD
BRUCE ST
WENSLEYDALE DR
BALCOMBE CT
Balcombe Creek
Devil Bend Creek
Creek

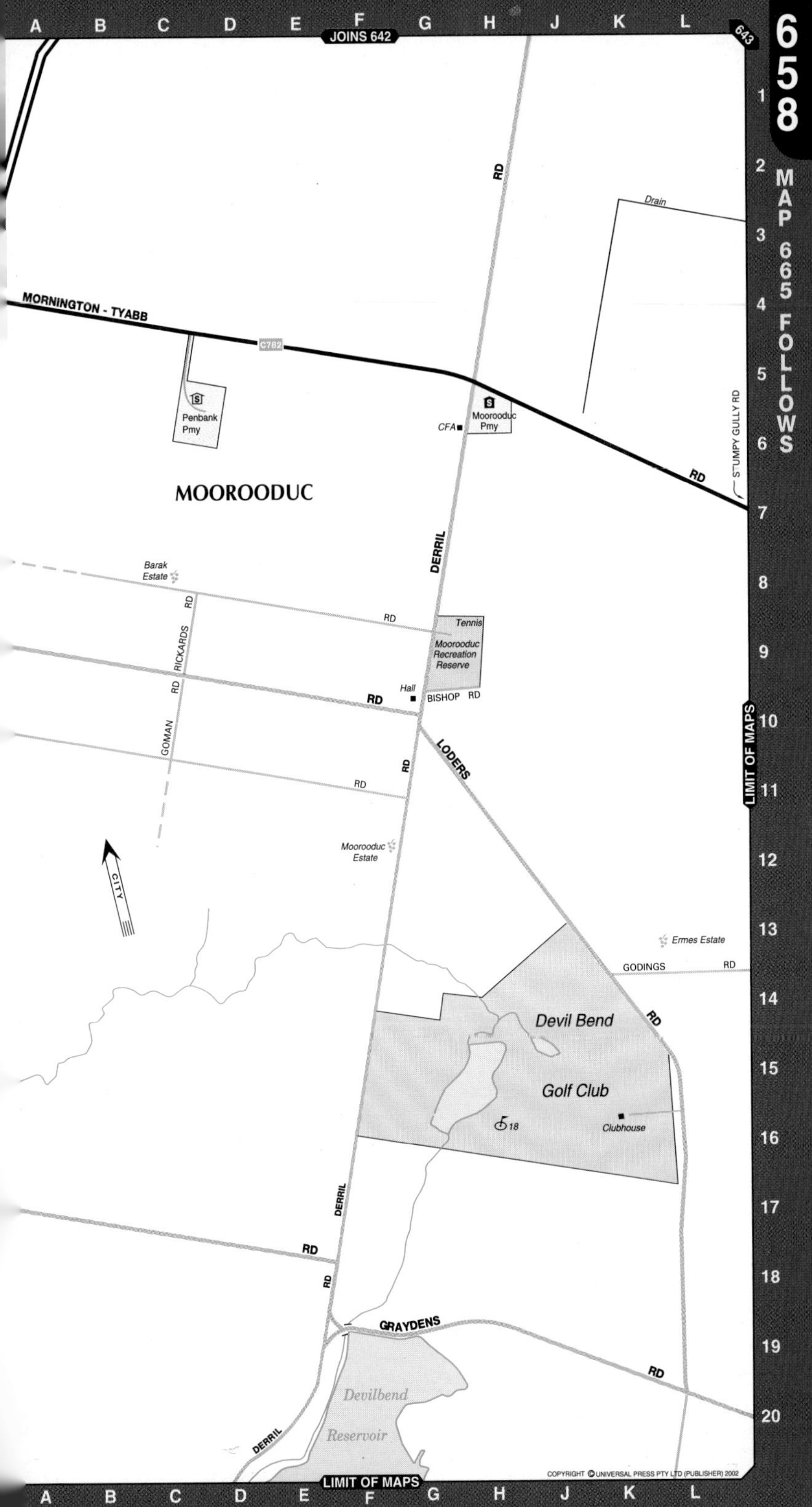
JOINS 642
643
MORNINGTON - TYABB
C782
RD
Penbank
Pmy
Mooroodu
Pmy
CFA
MOOROODUC
DERRIL
RD
Drain
STUMPY GULLY RD
Barak
Estate
RD
RICKARDS
RD
GOMAN
RD
Tennis
Mooroodu
Recreation
Reserve
Hall
BISHOP RD
LODERS
RD
RD
Mooroodu
Estate
CITY
Ermes Estate
GODINGS RD
RD
Devil Bend
Golf Club
18
Clubhouse
DERRIL
RD
RD
GRAYDENS
RD
Devilbend
Reservoir
DERRIL
LIMIT OF MAPS
A B C D E F G H J K L
1 2 3 4 5 6 7 8 9 10 11 12 13 14 15 16 17 18 19 20

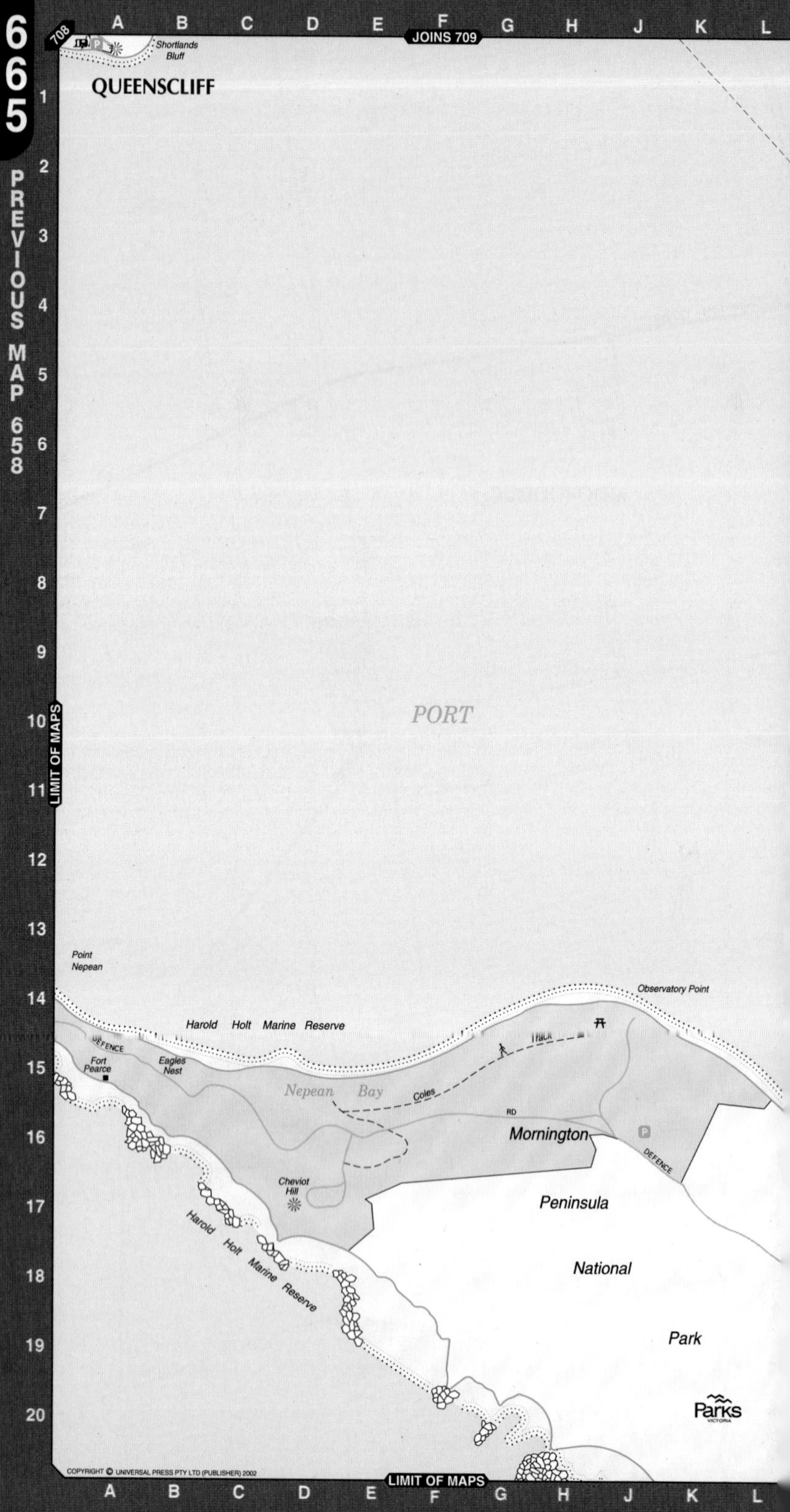

A B C D E F G H J K L
JOINS 709
708
Shortlands Bluff
QUEENSCLIFF
PREVIOUS MAP 658
LIMIT OF MAPS
PORT
Point Nepean
Observatory Point
Harold Holt Marine Reserve
DEFENCE
Fort Pearce
Eagles Nest
Nepean Bay
Coles
TRACK
RD
Mornington
DEFENCE
Cheviot Hill
Peninsula
National
Park
Harold Holt Marine Reserve
Parks VICTORIA
LIMIT OF MAPS

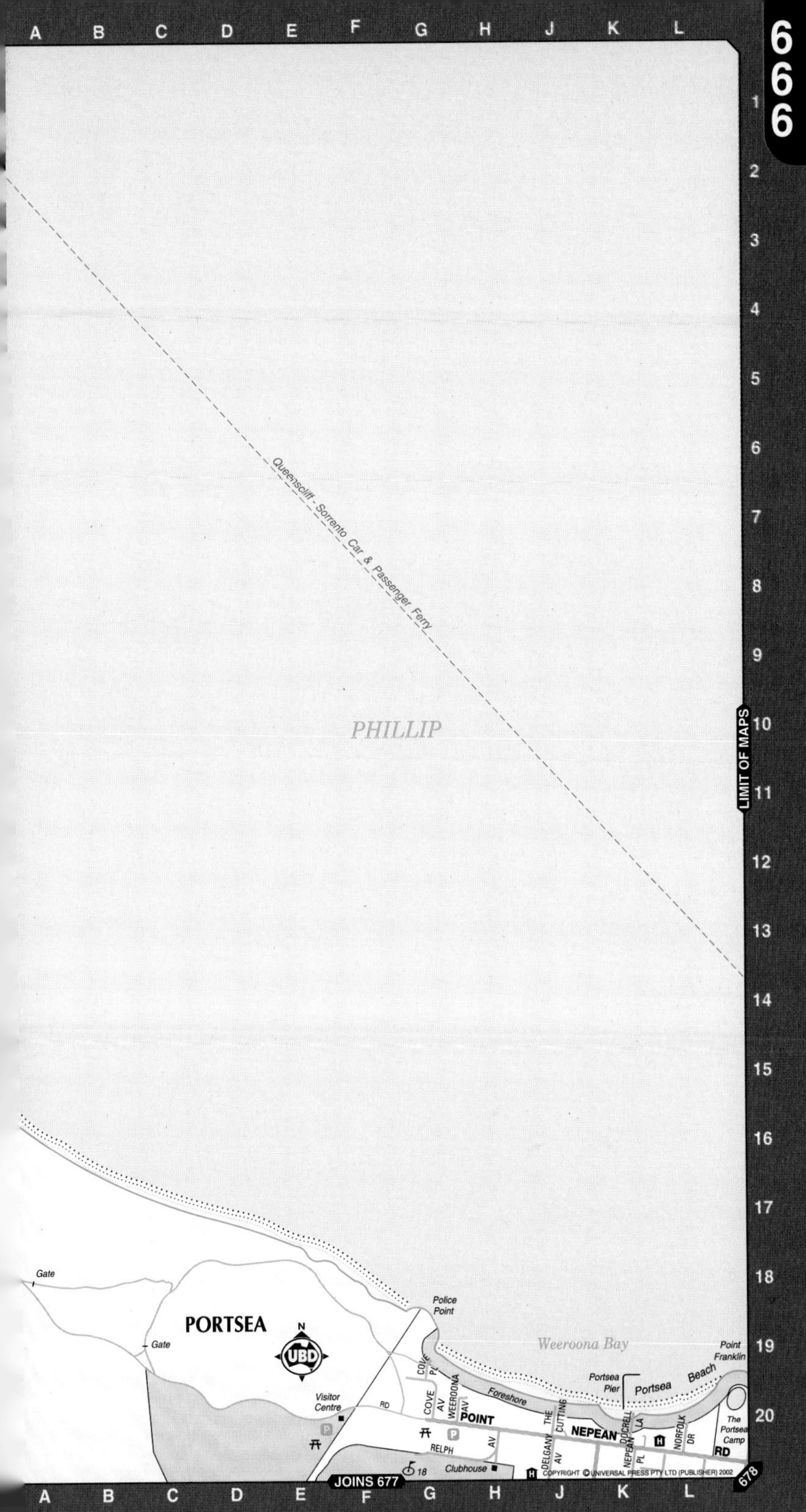
A B C D E F G H J K L
1 2 3 4 5 6 7 8 9 10 11 12 13 14 15 16 17 18 19 20
Queenscliff - Sorrento Car & Passenger Ferry
PHILLIP
LIMIT OF MAPS
Gate
Gate
PORTSEA
Police Point
Weeroona Bay
Point Franklin
Portsea Pier
Portsea Beach
Foreshore
Visitor Centre
RD
COVE PL
COVE AV
WEEROONA AV
POINT
NEPEAN
RD
THE CUTTING
DELGANY AV
OCRELL LA
NEPEAN PL
NORFOLK DR
The Portsea Camp
RELPH AV
18
Clubhouse
JOINS 677
678

PORT

JOINS 685

A B C D E F G H J K L
1 2 3 4 5 6 7 8 9 10 11 12 13 14 15 16 17 18 19 20
655
UBD
MT MARTHA
ESPLANADE
Foreshore
Reserve
SEASIDE
PONYARA RD
BURDOO WY
WONDERLAND TCE
PACIFIC TCE
DR
PDE
STANLEY
CAPRI
FAIRBAIRN
HUBERT ST
CR
AV
IAN RD
SHEOAK GR
Martha Point
BRADFORD RD
ASQUITH AV
ESPLANADE
ELLERINA RD W
MARINE DR
JOINS 669
PHILLIP
Dromana
Bay
CITY
Beach
Coast Guard VF7
CR
TONKIN PDE
ST
DROMANA
Halcyon
PICKINGS RD
LINK DR
COUTTS ST
ST
RD
GOLF COURSE
Robin Park
SACKVILLE ST
FARRELL ST
Miami
PRESCOTT
Dunns
MORGAN AV
PDE
BRIAN
DALE AV
AV
LAKE VIEW
LA
DR
CLYDE
RD
TASSEL
LAKE
SAFETY BEACH
Safety
BALMORAL
DROMANA AV
ST
FAIRWAY
Don Bosco Camp
MARINE
MASON AV
WOODLANDS GR
VICTORIA CR
MARY
FAIRWAY
LA
JOINS 686
687

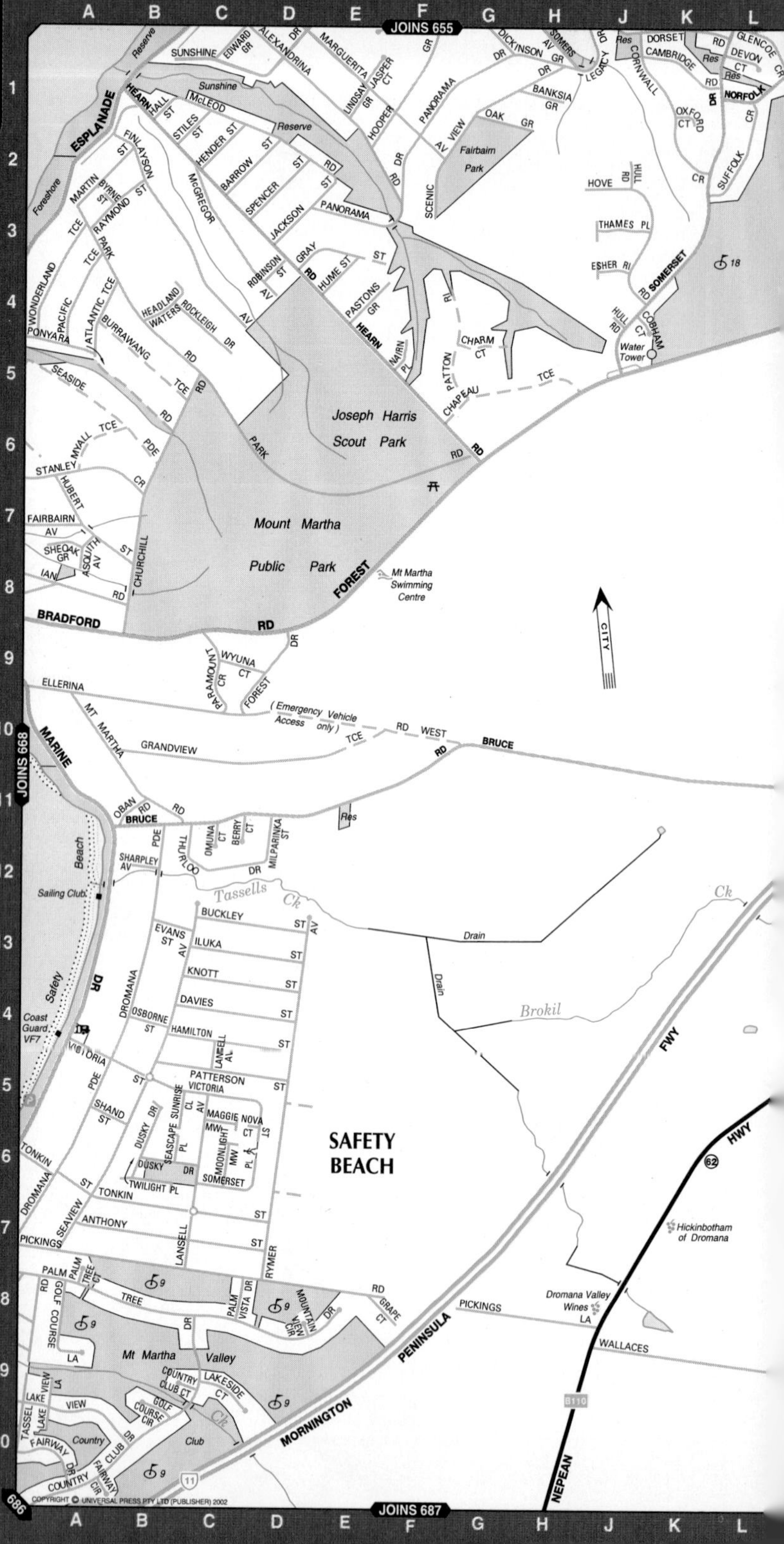

JOINS 655

JOINS 668

Esplanade, Foreshore, Reserve, Sunshine St, Sunshine Reserve, Edward Gr, Alexandrina Dr, Marguerita Gr, Lindsay Gr, Jasper Ct, Hooper Dr, Panorama Rd, View Av, Scenic Rd, Fairbairn Park, Oak Gr, Dickinson Gr, Somers Av, Legacy Dr, Banksia Gr, Cornwall Dr, Dorset Rd, Cambridge Rd, Glencoe Cr, Devon Ct, Norfolk Cr, Oxford Ct, Suffolk Cr, Hove Rd, Hull Rd, Thames Pl, Esher Rl, Somerset Rd, Cobham Ct, Water Tower

Hearn Rd, Hall St, McLeod St, Stiles St, Hender St, Barrow St, Spencer St, Jackson St, Panorama Rd, Finlayson St, Martin Tce, Byrne St, Raymond St, Park Tce, McGregor Av, Robinson Av, Gray St, Hume St, Pastons Gr, Nairn Pl, Patton Rl, Charm Ct, Chapeau Tce

Wonderland Tce, Pacific Tce, Atlantic Tce, Ponyara, Burrawang Rd, Headland Waters, Rockleigh Dr, Seaside Pde, Myall Tce, Stanley Cr, Hubert St, Fairbairn Av, Sheoak Gr, Asquith Av, Ian, Churchill Rd, Bradford Rd, Forest Rd

Joseph Harris Scout Park

Mount Martha Public Park

Mt Martha Swimming Centre

CITY

Paramount Cr, Wyuna Ct, Forest Dr, Ellerina Rd, Mt Martha Rd, Grandview Tce, (Emergency Vehicle Access only), Bruce Rd West, Bruce Rd, Marine Dr, Oban Rd, Res

Beach, Sailing Club, Sharpley Av, Pde, Thurloo Dr, Omuna Ct, Berry Ct, Milparinka St, Tassells Ck, Drain, Brokil Ck

Safety Beach, Coast Guard VF7, Buckley St, Evans St, Iluka St, Knott St, Davies St, Dromana Av, Osborne St, Hamilton St, Lansell Al, Victoria Pde, Patterson St, Victoria St, Shand St, Dusky Dr, Seascape Pl, Sunrise Cl, Maggie Av, Nova Ct, Moonlight Mw, Twilight Pl, Somerset St, Tonkin St, Dromana, Seaview, Anthony St, Pickings St, Lansell, Rymer Av

SAFETY BEACH

Mornington Peninsula Fwy, Nepean Hwy 62, Hickinbotham of Dromana, Dromana Valley Wines, Pickings La, Wallaces, B110, 11

Palm Tree Ct, Palm Vista Dr, Grape Ct, Mountain View Cir, Golf Course Rd, Mt Martha Valley Country Club, Lakeside Ct, Country Club Ct, Golf Course Cir, Lake View La, Tassel, Fairway Dr, Country Club Cir, Ck

JOINS 687

686

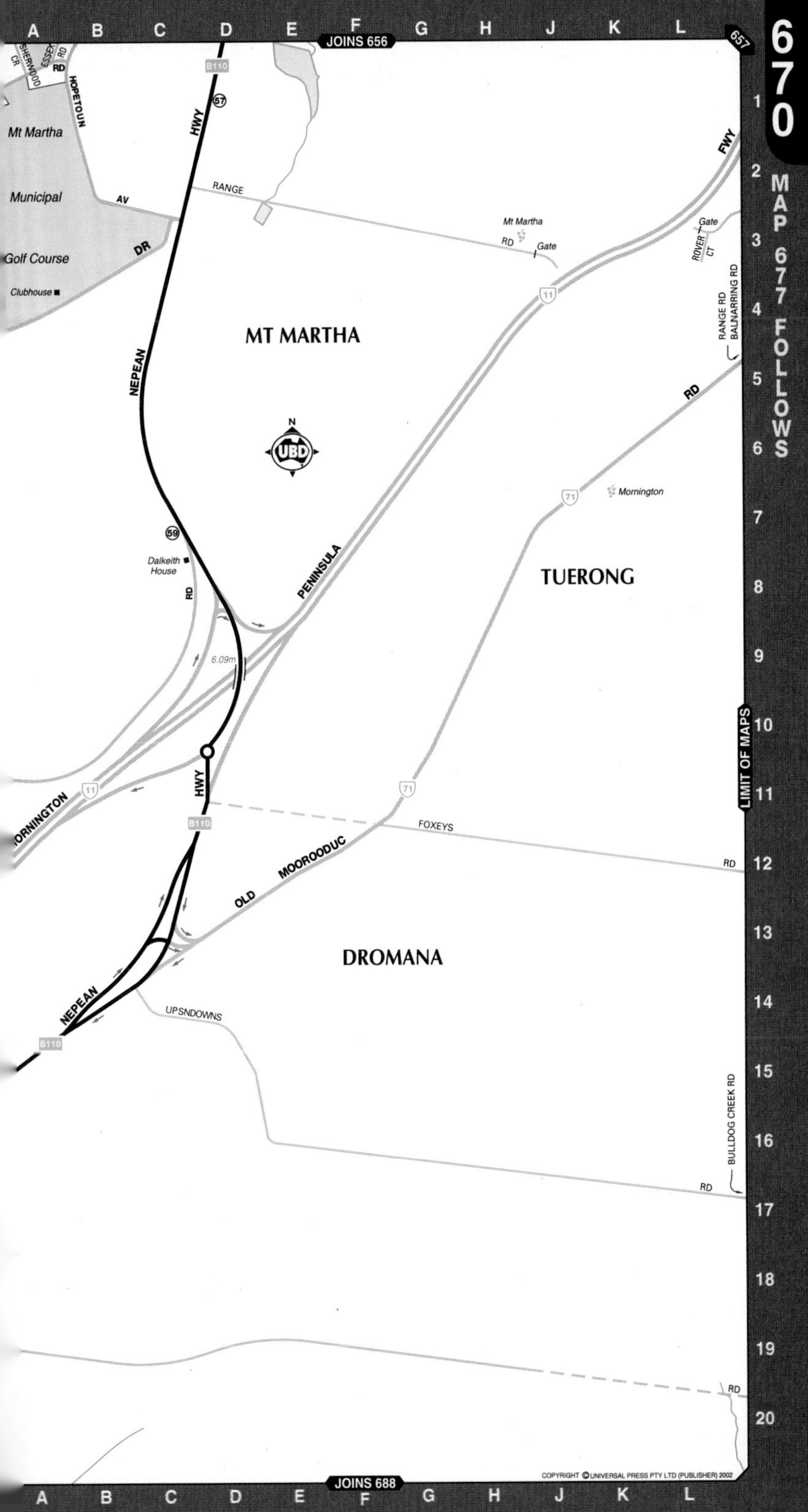
A B C D E F G H J K L
JOINS 656
657
SHERWOOD CR
ESSEX RD
RD
HOPETOUN
Mt Martha
Municipal
Golf Course
Clubhouse
AV
DR
RANGE
HWY
NEPEAN
B110
57
Mt Martha
RD
Gate
FWY
Gate
ROVER CT
RANGE RD
BALNARRING RD
11
MT MARTHA
RD
N
UBD
71
Mornington
59
Dalkeith House
RD
PENINSULA
TUERONG
6.09m
HWY
11
MORNINGTON
71
FOXEYS
RD
OLD
MOOROODUC
DROMANA
NEPEAN
B110
UPSNDOWNS
BULLDOG CREEK RD
RD
RD
LIMIT OF MAPS
1 2 3 4 5 6 7 8 9 10 11 12 13 14 15 16 17 18 19 20
MAP 677 FOLLOWS
JOINS 688

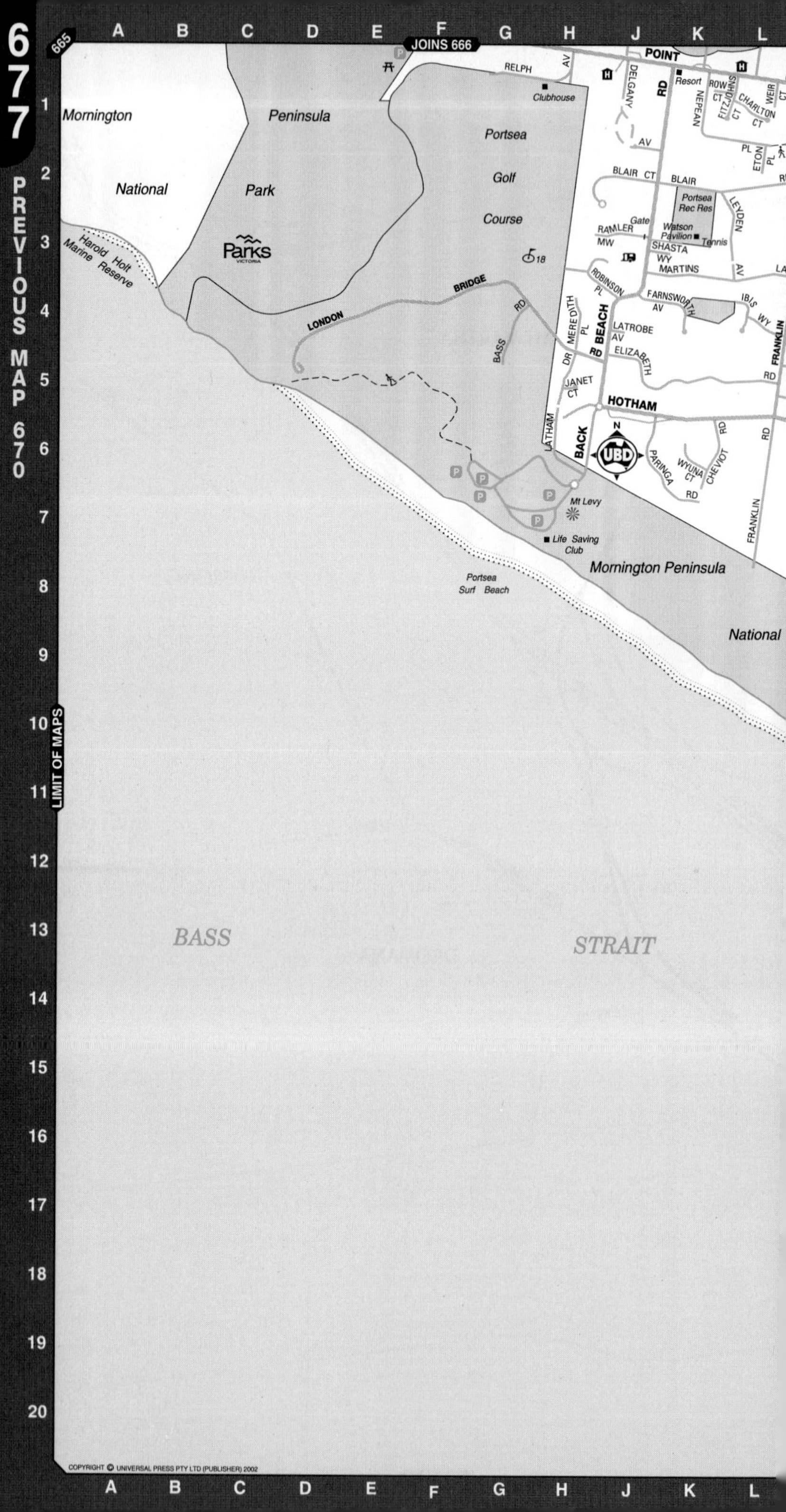

A B C D E F G H J K L
JOINS 666
665
PREVIOUS MAP 670
LIMIT OF MAPS
Mornington
Peninsula
National
Park
Parks VICTORIA
Harold Holt Marine Reserve
Portsea
Golf
Course
Clubhouse
RELPH
AV
POINT
RD
DELGANY
Resort
ROW
FITZJOHNS CT
NEPEAN
CHARLTON CT
WEIR CT
ETON PL
PL
AV
BLAIR CT
BLAIR
RD
Portsea Rec Res
LEYDEN
RAMLER MW
Gate
Watson Pavilion
Tennis
SHASTA WY
MARTINS
AV
LA
ROBINSON PL
FARNSWORTH AV
IBIS WY
FRANKLIN
LONDON
BRIDGE
RD
BASS
MEREDITH PL
BEACH RD
LATROBE AV
ELIZABETH
DR
JANET CT
HOTHAM
RD
LATHAM
BACK
UBD
PARINGA
WYUNA CT
CHEVIOT
RD
RD
FRANKLIN
Mt Levy
Life Saving Club
Mornington Peninsula
National
Portsea Surf Beach
BASS
STRAIT
1 2 3 4 5 6 7 8 9 10 11 12 13 14 15 16 17 18 19 20

A B C D E F G H J K L

LIMIT OF MAPS

The Portsea Camp
NEPEAN RD
Pier
Collins Bay
Foreshore Reserve
Shelly Beach
Point McArthur
Point King
PORT PHILLIP
Queenscliff - Sorrento Car & Passenger Ferry
NAIRANA CT
GROSVENOR CT
GR
94
AV
B110
THE NAMARONG ST
INVERARY CT
MORETON ST
DICKSON LA
MCCOLLS WY
ST
AV
SOMERSET DR
NYLAND CT
MERRYLANDS AV
ILYUKA CT
POINT KING RD
James Ford Res
ROYAL AV
MACGREGOR
THE QUARTERDECK
LIMEBURNERS WY
DRIVER
Res
HEMSTON
CARTER CT
WATTLE
CYPRESS CT
WELBECK AV
KEMP RD
Scenic Walk
JUDGE ST
SANDY CT
TRANQUILITY CT
GAVAN ST
DURCELL GR
AV
SAHARA CT
THE HEIGHTS
HAYDEN CT
WATTLE
ELGAR GR
WIMBLEDON CT
DUFFY ST
Sorrento Golf Course
Clubhouse
LANGFORD RD
LFNTELL AV
NETLEY AV
FRIMMELL
IVAN CT
GR
WY
WARRAWEENA RD
POINT RD
92
SEABIRD WY
LAWRANCE
KINDRA CL
ERNEST CT
CAMPBELLS
SORRENTO
18
KILDRUMMIE CT
WANDA CL
YERLATA CT
CROAD ST
HURSTWOOD RD
GREENWOOD AV
LEONARD CT
ROBINS WY
Aquarium
HEMSTON AV
BOSTON CT
RD
PEMBROKE PL
PORTSEA
OXFORD RD
BOROONDARA RD
NEPEAN
Sorrento Park
Sorrento Pier
Helipad
HOTHAM RD
Searoad Ferry Terminal
CITY
CANTERBURY ST
CLOVELLY CL
DONALDA AV
Pav
HOTHAM
AUSTIN AV
ESPLANADE
Policemans Point
TEA TREE RI
CUTTERS
LINCOLN AV
WHITES WY
David MacFarlane Reserve
HURLEY ST
GEORGE ST
COOPER GR
RUTH AV
MORGAN ST
STONE
CAMBRIDGE WYN
SPUNNER CT
WELLAND DR
Tennis
RSL
Cinema
WATTS RD
STUART ST
GRANGE RD
Sorrento Front Beach
DURHAM PL
WESTMINSTER GR
REBECCA CT
MIRANDA ST
OCEAN BEACH RD
HAYES AV
HILL
CONSTITUTION RD
SKELTON PL
EXETER CL
WILBY ST
Hist Soc Mus
MELBOURNE
DARLING
MCH
Hall
KERFERD
Cath
RD
ALBANY CT
NEWTON
RD
B110
Park
Parks VICTORIA
Cemetery
NORMANBY
OZONE AV
YORK ST
Sen Cits Cntr
Pioneer Mem Gdn
RD
Pmy
PDE
HISKENS
Nautilus
AV
RD
Refuse Hopper
OSSETT
OCEAN BEACH
QUEENS
RD
COPPIN RD
DARK
WATSON RD
AV
ST
RICHARD ST
CECIL
Sphinx Rock
Coppins
PRIMROSE LA
CAPRI GR
AV
BOWEN
ST PAULS
HILL
ST
SALONIKA
CLARK CR
CORSAIR GR
PARK
SULLIVAN ST
SHIRLEY
AV
HIGH
WEBSTER
ST CR
Amphitheatre
Mornington Peninsula
RONALD
ST
RUSSELL
AV
Sorrento Back Beach
PARKSIDE
RD
RALPHS AV
HEATHER
National
ST
GR
RD
ST
ST PAULS
KING
JULIA
ARNOTT
RD
Park
WAVERLY
JAMES
BAY
St Pauls Beach
DIAMOND
ABBOTSFORD
ST
ST
Jubilee Point
Diamond Bay
IVANHOE CT
STEVENS ST
The Dog's Head

JOINS 679

1 2 3 4 5 6 7 8 9 10 11 12 13 14 15 16 17 18 19 20

695

A B C D E F G H J K L

A B C D E F G H J K L

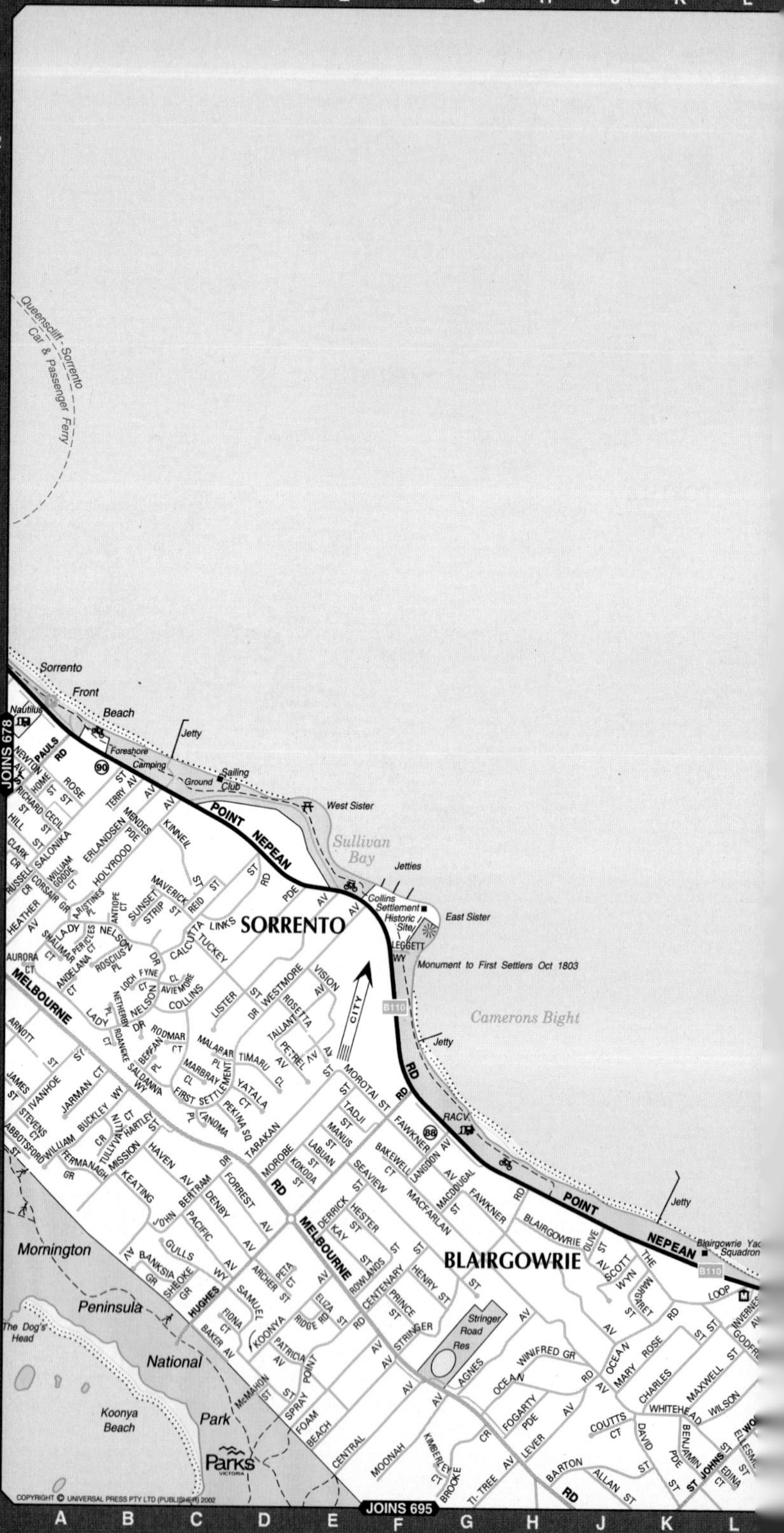

Queenscliff - Sorrento Car & Passenger Ferry

Sorrento Front Beach

Nautilus

JOINS 678

Foreshore Camping Ground

Jetty

Sailing Club

West Sister

Sullivan Bay

Jetties

Collins Settlement Historic Site

East Sister

Monument to First Settlers Oct 1803

Camerons Bight

Jetty

RACV

Jetty

Blairgowrie Yacht Squadron

SORRENTO

BLAIRGOWRIE

POINT NEPEAN RD

MELBOURNE RD

B110

CITY

Stringer Road Res

Mornington Peninsula National Park

The Dog's Head

Koonya Beach

Parks Victoria

JOINS 695

A B C D E F G H J K L

MAP 683 FOLLOWS

PREVIOUS MAP 680

A B C D E F G H J K L

PORT

LIMIT OF MAPS

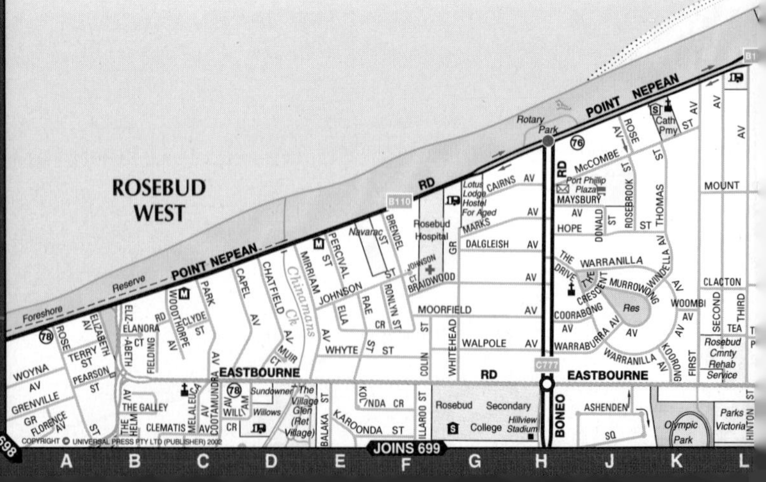

698

JOINS 699

A B C D E F G H J K L

PHILLIP
CITY
Rosebud Pier
Rosebud Jetty
Rosebud Beach
Tom Salt Park
Eastern Lighthouse
George Kilburn Park
Ray Baker Park
McCRAE
ROSEBUD
POINT NEPEAN RD
LONSDALE ST
MORNINGTON PENINSULA FWY
JETTY RD
Lawson Park
Rosebud Park Public Golf Course
Rosebud Retirement Village
Rosebud Pmy
Cinema
Sunrise
Kenray
Romany
McRose
Siesta
Bendemeer
MCH
Cmnty Cntr
Tennis
Rec Res
Res
JOINS 685
JOINS 700
667
COPYRIGHT © UNIVERSAL PRESS PTY LTD (PUBLISHER) 2002

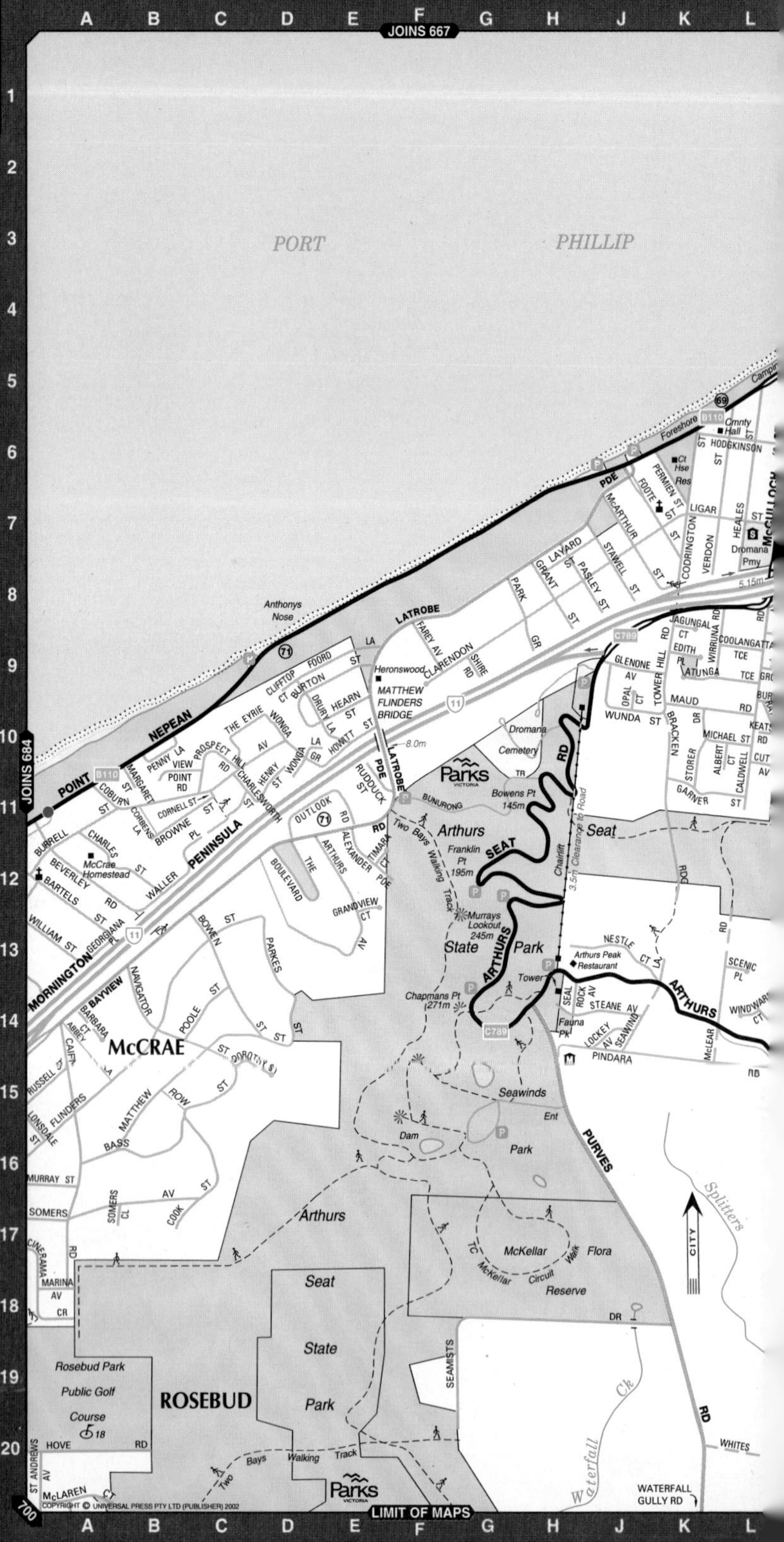
A B C D E F G H J K L
JOINS 667
JOINS 684
LIMIT OF MAPS
700
1 2 3 4 5 6 7 8 9 10 11 12 13 14 15 16 17 18 19 20
PORT
PHILLIP
Anthonys Nose
POINT
NEPEAN
LATROBE
PDE
Foreshore
Campi
Cmnty Hall
HODGKINSON
Ct Hse Res
PERMIEN ST
FOOTE ST
McARTHUR
LIGAR
CODRINGTON
VERDON
HEALES
Dromana Pmy
McCULLOCH
LAYARD
GRANT
PASLEY ST
STAWELL ST
PARK GR
5.15m
JAGUNGAL CT
EDITH PL
WIRRUNA RD
COOLANGATTA TCE
ATUNGA
GLENONE AV
TOWER HILL RD
OPAL CT
MAUD RD
WUNDA ST
BRACKEN DR
MICHAEL ST
KEATS RD
STORER
ALBERT CT
CALDWELL
CUT AV
GARNER ST
FAREY AV
CLARENDON RD
SHIRE
Heronswood
MATTHEW FLINDERS BRIDGE
FOORD ST
CLIFFTOP CT
BURTON
HEARN ST
DRURY LA
THE EYRIE
WONGA
AV
HOWITT ST
PENNY LA
VIEW
POINT RD
PROSPECT HILL RD
CHARLESWORTH ST
HENRY ST
WONGA GR
MARGARET ST
COBURN
CORNELL ST
BROWNE PL
CORBENS LA
RUDDUCK ST
OUTLOOK RD
TIMARA CT
PENINSULA
BURRELL
CHARLES ST
McCrae Homestead
BEVERLEY RD
BARTELS ST
WALLER
WILLIAM ST
GEORGIANA PL
MORNINGTON
BOULEVARD
THE ARTHURS
ALEXANDER PDE
GRANDVIEW CT AV
BOWEN ST
PARKES ST
8.0m
Dromana Cemetery
TR
BUNURONG
Parks VICTORIA
Bowens Pt 145m
Arthurs
Seat
Franklin Pt 195m
SEAT
Two Bays Walking Track
Murrays Lookout 245m
Chairlift 3.5m Clearance to Road
ARTHURS
State
Park
Tower
Chapmans Pt 271m
Arthurs Peak Restaurant
NESTLE CT LA
SCENIC PL
SEAL ROCK AV
STEANE AV
LOCKEY AV
SEAWIND
WINDWARD CT
Fauna Pk
PINDARA RD
McLEAR RD
BAYVIEW
NAVIGATOR
POOLE ST
BARBARA CT
ABBEY
CAIFA
McCRAE
DOROTHY ST
RUSSELL
FLINDERS
MATTHEW
ROW ST
BASS
LONSDALE ST
MURRAY ST
SOMERS
SOMERS CL
AV
COOK ST
Dam
Seawinds
Ent
PURVES RD
CITY
Splitters
McKellar
Flora
McKellar Circuit Walk
Reserve
DR
CINERAMA
MARINA AV
CR
Seat
State
Park
SEAMISTS
Rosebud Park Public Golf Course 18
ROSEBUD
HOVE RD
ST ANDREWS AV
McLAREN CT
Two Bays Walking Track
Waterfall Ck
WHITES
WATERFALL GULLY RD
B110
C789
69
71
11

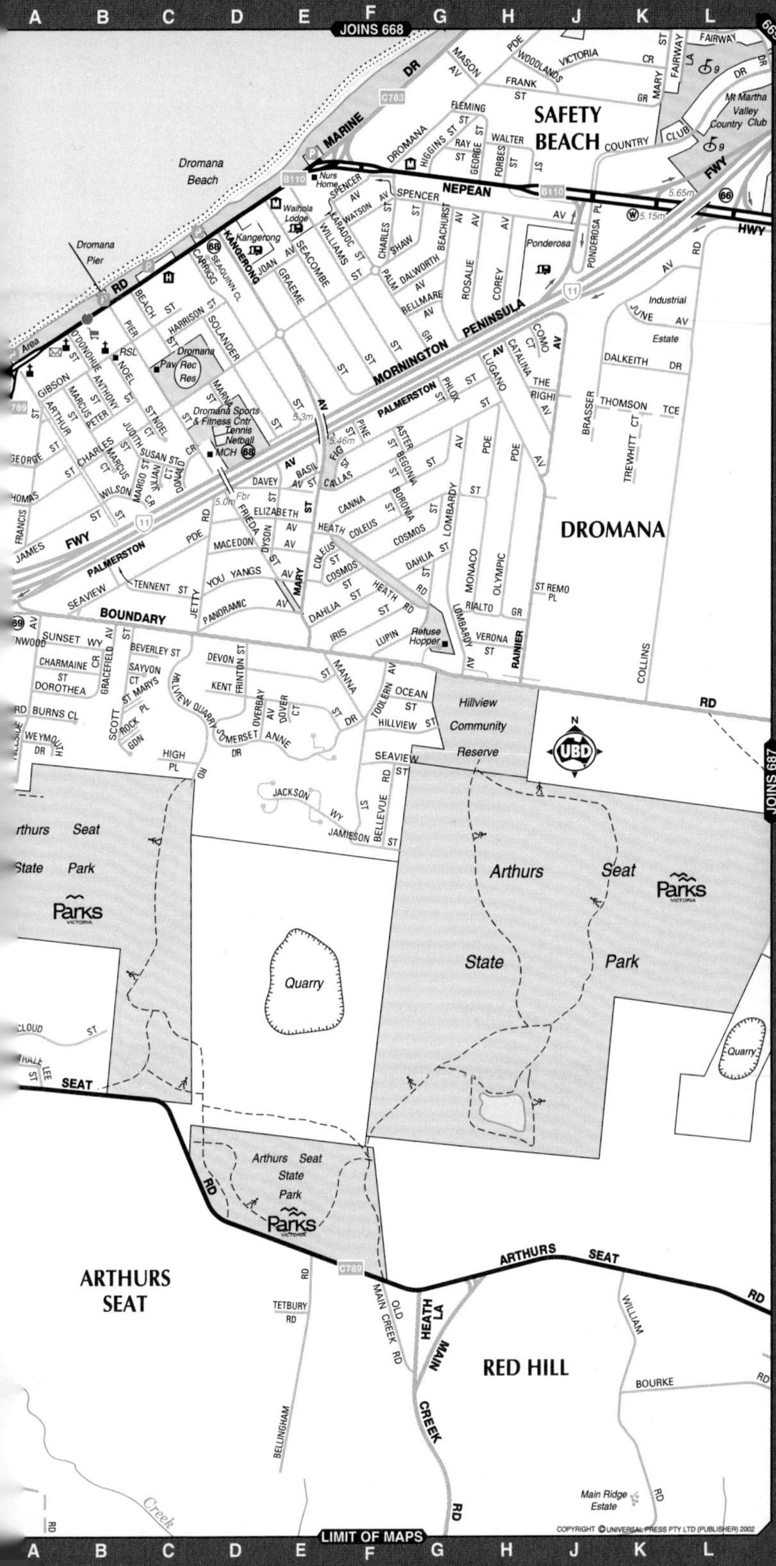

JOINS 668
669
JOINS 687
LIMIT OF MAPS

A B C D E F G H J K L

1 2 3 4 5 6 7 8 9 10 11 12 13 14 15 16 17 18 19 20

SAFETY BEACH

DROMANA

ARTHURS SEAT

RED HILL

Dromana Beach

Dromana Pier

Mt Martha Valley Country Club

Industrial Estate

Ponderosa

Hillview Community Reserve

Arthurs Seat State Park

Parks VICTORIA

Quarry

Main Ridge Estate

Dromana Pav Rec Res

Dromana Sports & Fitness Cntr

Tennis Netball

MCH

RSL

Waihola Lodge

Nurs Home

Kangerong

Refuse Hopper

MARINE DR

NEPEAN HWY

MORNINGTON PENINSULA FWY

PALMERSTON AV

BOUNDARY RD

ARTHURS SEAT RD

MAIN CREEK RD

OLD MAIN CREEK RD

HEATH LA

KANGERONG

POINT NEPEAN RD

C783 B110 C789 11 66 68 69

5.65m 5.15m 5.3m 5.46m 5.0m Fbr

MASON AV, WOODLANDS, VICTORIA CR, FAIRWAY, FRANK ST, FLEMING, MARY ST, FAIRWAY LA, GR, DR, COUNTRY CLUB DR, DROMANA, HIGGINS ST, RAY ST, GEORGE, WALTER, FORBES ST, ST, SPENCER ST, SPENCER AV, WATSON, KARADOC ST, WILLIAMS ST, CHARLES ST, SHAW, BEACHURST AV, PALM, DALWORTH AV, BELLMARE AV, ROSALIE, COREY, PONDEROSA PL, GR, SEACOMBE, GRAEME, JOAN AV, SEAGUINN CL, CARRIGG, BEACH ST, HARRISON ST, SOLANDER, PIER ST, O'DONOHUE ST, NOEL, GIBSON, MARCUS ST, ANTHONY ST, PETER, ARTHUR, JUDITH, ST NOEL CT, SUSAN ST, MARINA ST, GEORGE ST, CHARLES CT, MARCUS ST, MARGO ST, JULIAN CT, DONALD CR, WILSON CR, THOMAS, FRANCIS, JAMES, FWY, PALMERSTON PDE, TENNENT ST, SEAVIEW, JETTY, YOU YANGS AV, PANORAMIC AV, MACEDON, DYSON ST, FRIEDA, DAVEY ST, ELIZABETH AV, BASIL AV, MARY ST, FIG ST, CALLAS, PINE, ASTER ST, BEGONIA ST, BORONIA ST, CANNA, COLEUS ST, HEATH, COSMOS ST, DAHLIA ST, COLEUS ST, HEATH RD, IRIS, LUPIN, DAHLIA ST, PHLOX ST, LUGANO AV, CATALINA, COMO CT, THE RIGHI AV, LOMBARDY AV, MONACO PDE, OLYMPIC PDE, RIALTO GR, VERONA ST, RAINIER, ST REMO PL, JUNE AV, DALKEITH DR, THOMSON TCE, BRASSER, TREWHITT CT, COLLINS, RD, SUNSET WY, SHERWOOD AV, BEVERLEY ST, CHARMAINE CR, DOROTHEA ST, GRACEFIELD AV, SAYVON CT, ST MARYS PL, BURNS CL, SCOTT, ROCK GDN, WEYMOUTH DR, HILLSIDE, HIGH PL, HILLVIEW QUARRY RD, DEVON ST, FRINTON ST, KENT, OVERBAY AV, DOVER CT, SOMERSET DR, ANNE, MANNA ST, DR, TOOLERN AV, OCEAN ST, HILLVIEW ST, SEAVIEW ST, BELLEVUE RD, JACKSON WY, JAMIESON ST, CLOUD ST, HAZEL LEE ST, SEAT, TETBURY RD, BELLINGHAM, WILLIAM RD, BOURKE RD, Creek

A B C D E F G H J K L

JOINS 669

668

SAFETY BEACH

FAIRWAY DR
COUNTRY CLUB DR
FAIRWAY CIR
Mt Martha Valley Country Club
MORNINGTON PENINSULA FWY
Dromana Golf Course
Dromana
Dromana Twin Drive-in Theatre
NEPEAN HWY
B110
COLLINS RD
Dunns
Bald Hill
Drain
Moats Corner
BITTERN - DROMANA (DUNNS CREEK RD) RD
C788
C787
Creek
Drain
Dromana Estate
Karina
LA
RD
WHITE HILL (MORNINGTON - FLINDERS RD)
Recreation Reserve
CITY
Wildlife Sanctuary
Dromana Secondary College
Peninsula Special Dev
OLD MORNINGTON - FLINDERS RD
Dromana Reservoir
SHERGOLDS
BOUNDARY RD
Gate
Road
JOINS 686
EATONS CUTTING
(Fire
LUTON AV
HARRISONS
Bald Hill Creek
Private
Marion Rosetzky Gallery
McILROYS
RD
Access
Tracks)
Quarry
Arthurs Seat State Park
Circuit
CUTTING
EATONS RD
LOOKOUT RD
Parks VICTORIA
Gate
HOLMES RD
Arthurs Seat State Park
ARTHURS SEAT RD
C789
COLLINS ST
BOURKE RD
ELIZABETH RD
EATONS CUTTING
Red Hill Consolidated Pmy
ARTHURS SEAT
SHEEHANS
Red Hill Recreation Reserve
Showground & Market
Tennis
ARKWELLS
MCH
Massoni Main Creek
ANDREWS
PROSSORS LA

1 2 3 4 5 6 7 8 9 10 11 12 13 14 15 16 17 18 19 20

LIMIT OF MAPS

A B C D E F G H J K L

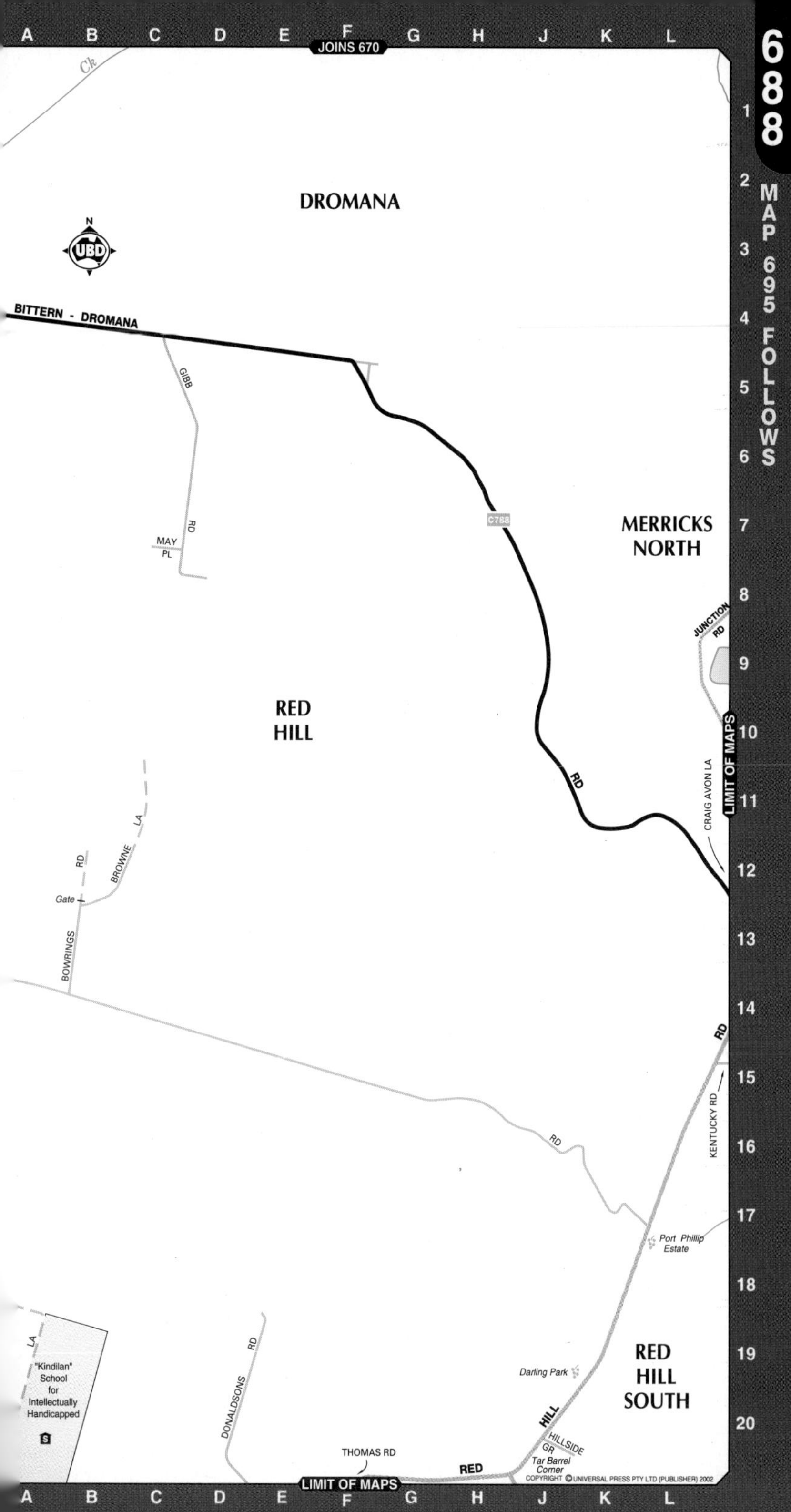

A B C D E F G H J K L
JOINS 670
1 2 3 4 5 6 7 8 9 10 11 12 13 14 15 16 17 18 19 20
MAP 695 FOLLOWS
Ck
DROMANA
BITTERN - DROMANA
GIBB
RD
MAY
PL
C788
MERRICKS
NORTH
JUNCTION
RD
RED
HILL
RD
CRAIG AVON LA
LIMIT OF MAPS
BROWNE
LA
RD
Gate
BOWRINGS
RD
KENTUCKY RD
Port Phillip
Estate
LA
"Kindilan"
School
for
Intellectually
Handicapped
DONALDSONS
RD
RED
HILL
SOUTH
Darling Park
HILL
HILLSIDE
GR
Tar Barrel
Corner
THOMAS RD
RED
LIMIT OF MAPS

PREVIOUS MAP 688

678

JOINS 679

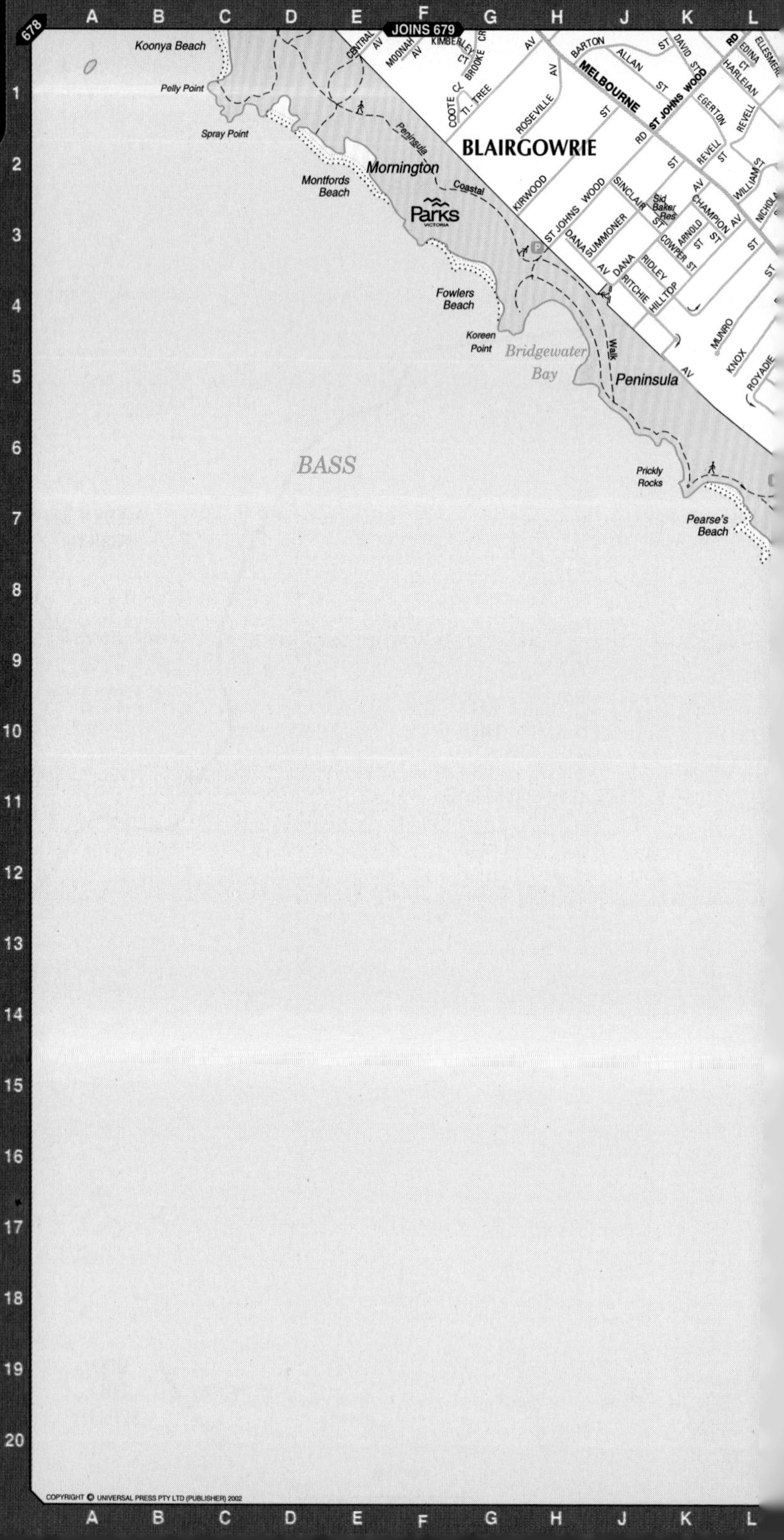

A B C D E F G H J K L

BLAIRGOWRIE

Koonya Beach
Pelly Point
Spray Point
Montfords Beach
Mornington Peninsula Coastal Walk
Parks Victoria
Fowlers Beach
Koreen Point
Bridgewater Bay
Prickly Rocks
Pearse's Beach
BASS

CENTRAL AV
MOONAH AV
KIMBERLEY CT
BROOKE CR
COOTE CL
TI-TREE
ROSEVILLE AV
KIRWOOD
BARTON
ALLAN ST
DAVID ST
MELBOURNE RD
ST JOHNS WOOD RD
EGERTON
HARLEIAN
EDINA CT
ELLESMERE
REVELL ST
WILLIAM ST
NICHOLAS
SINCLAIR ST
Sid Baker Res
CHAMPION AV
ARNOLD ST
COWPER ST
SUMMONER
DANA AV
RITCHIE
RIDLEY
HILLTOP
MUNRO
KNOX
ROYADIE

1 2 3 4 5 6 7 8 9 10 11 12 13 14 15 16 17 18 19 20

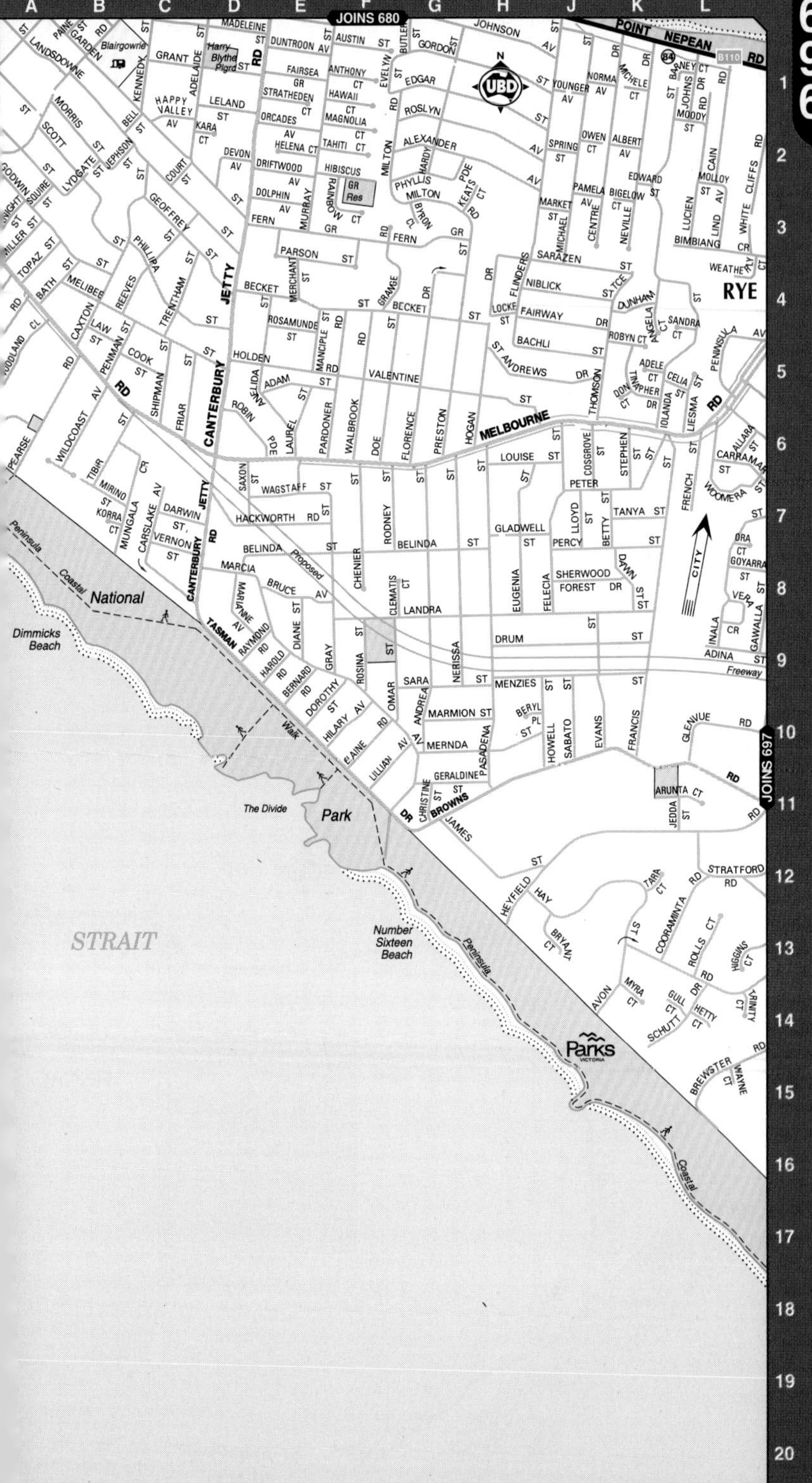
JOINS 680
JOINS 697
A B C D E F G H J K L
1 2 3 4 5 6 7 8 9 10 11 12 13 14 15 16 17 18 19 20
UBD
N
POINT NEPEAN RD
B110
84
RYE
Blairgowrie
Harry Blythe Plgrd
GR Res
JOHNSON AV
MADELEINE ST
DUNTROON AV
AUSTIN ST
BUTLER ST
GORDON ST
GRANT ST
ADELAIDE ST
FAIRSEA GR
ANTHONY CT
EVELYN CT
EDGAR
STRATHEDEN CT
HAWAII CT
ROSLYN ST
YOUNGER AV
NORMA AV
MICHELE CT
BARNEY CT
JOHNS DR
MOODY ST
LELAND ST
HAPPY VALLEY AV
KARA CT
ORCADES AV
MAGNOLIA CT
HELENA CT
TAHITI CT
MILTON RD
ALEXANDER AV
SPRING ST
OWEN CT
ALBERT AV
CAIN ST
CLIFFS RD
DEVON AV
DRIFTWOOD AV
HIBISCUS
RAINBOW CT
HARDY
PHYLLIS
MILTON
BYRON CL
KEATS CT
PDE RD
EDWARD ST
MOLLOY ST
LIND AV
PAMELA AV
BIGELOW CT
MARKET ST
DOLPHIN AV
MURRAY ST
FERN GR
FERN GR
CENTRE
NEVILLE
MICHAEL
LUCIEN
WHITE
BIMBIANG CR
PARSON ST
SARAZEN ST
WEATHERLY CT
BECKET ST
MERCHANT ST
GRANGE ST
BECKET DR
FLINDERS DR
NIBLICK ST
TCE
DUNHAM
LOCKE ST
FAIRWAY DR
ANGELA CT
SANDRA CT
ROSAMUNDE ST
MANCIPLE RD
BACHLI ST
ROBYN CT
PENINSULA AV
HOLDEN RD
ST ANDREWS DR
THOMSON
ADELE CT
CELIA ST
VALENTINE ST
DON CT
TWAPHER DR
IOLANDA ST
LIESMA ST
ADAM ST
ANGELIDA
ROBIN PDE
LAUREL ST
PARDONER ST
WALBROOK ST
DOE ST
FLORENCE ST
PRESTON ST
HOGAN ST
MELBOURNE RD
COSGROVE ST
STEPHEN ST
FRENCH ST
ALLARA ST
CARRAMAR ST
WOOMERA ST
LOUISE ST
PETER
SAXON ST
WAGSTAFF ST
RODNEY ST
HACKWORTH RD
LLOYD ST
BETTY ST
TANYA ST
GLADWELL ST
PERCY ST
BELINDA ST
BELINDA ST
Proposed
DAWN ST
SHERWOOD FOREST DR
CHENIER CT
EUGENIA
FELECIA
CITY
ORA CT
GOYARRA ST
VERA
MARCIA
BRUCE AV
CLEMATIS CT
LANDRA
DIANE ST
MARIANNE AV
RAYMOND RD
DRUM ST
INALA CR
GAWALLA
ADINA ST
Freeway
HAROLD RD
BERNARD RD
GRAY ST
ROSINA ST
NERISSA
SARA ST
MENZIES ST
DOROTHY ST
HILARY AV
OMAR RD
ANDREA AV
MARMION ST
BERYL PL ST
GLENVUE RD
HOWELL ST
SABATO ST
EVANS
FRANCIS
ELAINE
LILLIAN AV
MERNDA
PASADENA
GERALDINE ST
CHRISTINE ST
BROWNS DR
JAMES
ARUNTA CT
JEDDA ST
STRATFORD RD
HEYFIELD ST
HAY
TARA CT
COORAMINTA
ROLLS CT
BRYANT CT
HIGGINS CT
AVON
MYRA CT
GULL CT
HETTY CT
SCHUTT CT
TRINITY CT
BREWSTER CT
WAYNE CT
LANDSDOWNE
PAINE ST
GARDEN RD
KENNEDY
BELL ST
MORRIS ST
SCOTT ST
LYDGATE ST
JEPHSON ST
COURT ST
GODWIN ST
SQUIRE ST
KNIGHT ST
MILLER ST
GEOFFREY ST
PHILLIPA ST
TOPAZ ST
MELIBEE ST
BATH ST
REEVES ST
TRENTHAM ST
JETTY RD
CAXTON ST
LAW ST
PENMAN ST
COOK ST
WOODLAND CL
SHIPMAN ST
FRIAR ST
CANTERBURY RD
WILDCOAST RD
PEARSE
TIBIR
MIRINO ST
KORRA CT
MUNGALA CT
CARSLAKE AV
DARWIN ST
VERNON ST
TASMAN
Peninsula Coastal Walk
National Park
Dimmicks Beach
The Divide
STRAIT
Number Sixteen Beach
Parks VICTORIA

A B C D E F G H J K L

680

PORT

Rye Jetty

Rye Beach

POINT NEPEAN RD

B110

Foreshore

Reserve

Rye Yacht Club

Rye Bicentennial Park

RYE

CAIN RD
CLIFFS
TAROOK AV
HORNERS LA
WHITE
LIND AV
MINNIMURRA
BRAE CT
VIEW RD
RECREATION RD
WHITES LA
MAORI AV
GILGAN
REX AV
MARVIN AV
BIMBIANG
WEATHERLY CT
R J Rowley Recreation Reserve
Tennis
CR
GEORGE ST
EVA ST
WILLONGA ST
NELSON
DUNDAS ST
Cmnty Hse
MCH
Civic Hall
Snr Cits
RSL
COLLINGWOOD
MAY AV
SINCLAIR AV
Kanasta Karavan Kamp
ROSYTH
BOWEN
Rye Pmy
NAPIER ST
Cemetery
BALLABIL
LYONS ST
SULLIVAN ST
BIMBLE
GRACE
HUNT AV
SAVILLE CT
WEIR
OZONE
HYGEIA
GOVERNMENT
DALY
RICHARDSON
WARATAH
SHEILA
FIELD
SHIRLOW
GRANDVIEW
LOCKSLEY
OBSERVATION
MCDONALD
AMELIA AV
BE AUNA
VISTA DR
KARKAROOK RD
ILUKA RD
YOORALA RD
WAMBA AV
SUNSHINE
CRESTVIEW CT
MONTE VISTA CT
GRANDVIEW
WEEROONA
BRIGHTS RD
VICTOR AV
JACOLYN AV
HILLVIEW AV
RIO VISTA CT
BETHAN
KELLY CL
ALEXANDRA DR
LEAH CT
SUSAN PL
PENINSULA AV
MELBOURNE
RIATTA
TURRANA ST
NOEL ST
CHARLES
ELVIE
MOORONG ST
KIAMA CT
YOOTHA CT
TUERONG
GUNYAH ST
LEAWARRA
BYAHAMEE ST
ALLARA ST
CARRAMAR
WYENA ST
TOAGARA ST
CROANNA ST
LEWANA ST
KIRRI
BURDOO ST
WOOMERA ST
LOATTA ST
WOLLERT
TANDERRA
KOROWA ST
LOONGANA
ORA CT
KOOLYA CT
GOYARRA ST
KANBURRA
BALOOK ST
BARKALA
YARRAYNE ST
VERA
INALA
CR
GAWALLA
NALONG
TARRAWILL ST
YANNUGA ST
BANDA CT
MANNANA ST
ONWARRA
GOORNA CT
ADINA ST
STEWART
ROBERTS
DUNLANE
TIMMINS CR
ALATHEA CT
STRATHMORE
DERWIN LA
COOMBES CT
PIER ST
KANIMBLA CT
HIGHVIEW CT
POE
GOLF LA
PRENTICE AV
HILL ST
PIER
GOLF
QUEENS CT
KENT
GLEN RD
SUSSEX
VALLEY
SHERWOOD DR
OBSERVATION
FAIRHILLS
CREEDMORE
RIDGE CT
TWAKURRA AV
JENKE
KNIGHT PL
DARGO CT
WARGUNDY
MONOMEITH
KALIMNA CR
DARANA DR
MILPA CT
GOTHIC RD
WONDAREE
GLENVUE RD
Proposed Freeway
Glenvue Holiday Park
JOINS 696
BROWNS RD
HEYFIELD RD
STRATFORD
BERYL CT
PAUL ST
DANNY
FORBES
ALWYN ST
GALILEE CT
BRUCE
JILLIAN
EMMAUS
SPURGEON CL
HIGGINS CT
TRINITY CT
AVON
WARWICK CT
LEITH CT
DOUGLAS CT
SYDNEY
BREWSTER RD
LAYNE
ROSLYN ST
ALISON AV
(RYE OCEAN BEACH RD)
The Dunes Golf Course
Clubhouse
18
FINGAL
Mornington Peninsula National Park
Parks Victoria
Peninsula Coastal Walk
BASS STRAIT
(Priv Rd)
SURF RD
WUNDA CT
GUNIDA CT
BANYAN
SANDY RD
(Sandy Tr)
ST ANDREWS BEACH
FOAM
LIMIT OF MAPS

A B C D E F G H J K L

LIMIT OF MAPS
PHILLIP
Tootgarook Foreshore
Beach
POINT NEPEAN RD
B110
80
TOOTGAROOK
ROSEBUD WEST
Tootgarook Sports Reserve
Athletics
Tennis
Netball
Tootgarook Pmy
Quinns Park
Senior Citizens
MCH
Bella Vista
Mornington Peninsula Shire Council Central Tip
TRUEMANS RD
BROWNS RD
BONEO
Golf Driving Range
FINGAL
Proposed Moonah Links Development
DEVONPORT DR
LIMESTONE RD
PLACADENA RD
Freeway
Proposed
CITY
Gate
HISCOCK RD
683
JOINS 699
LIMIT OF MAPS

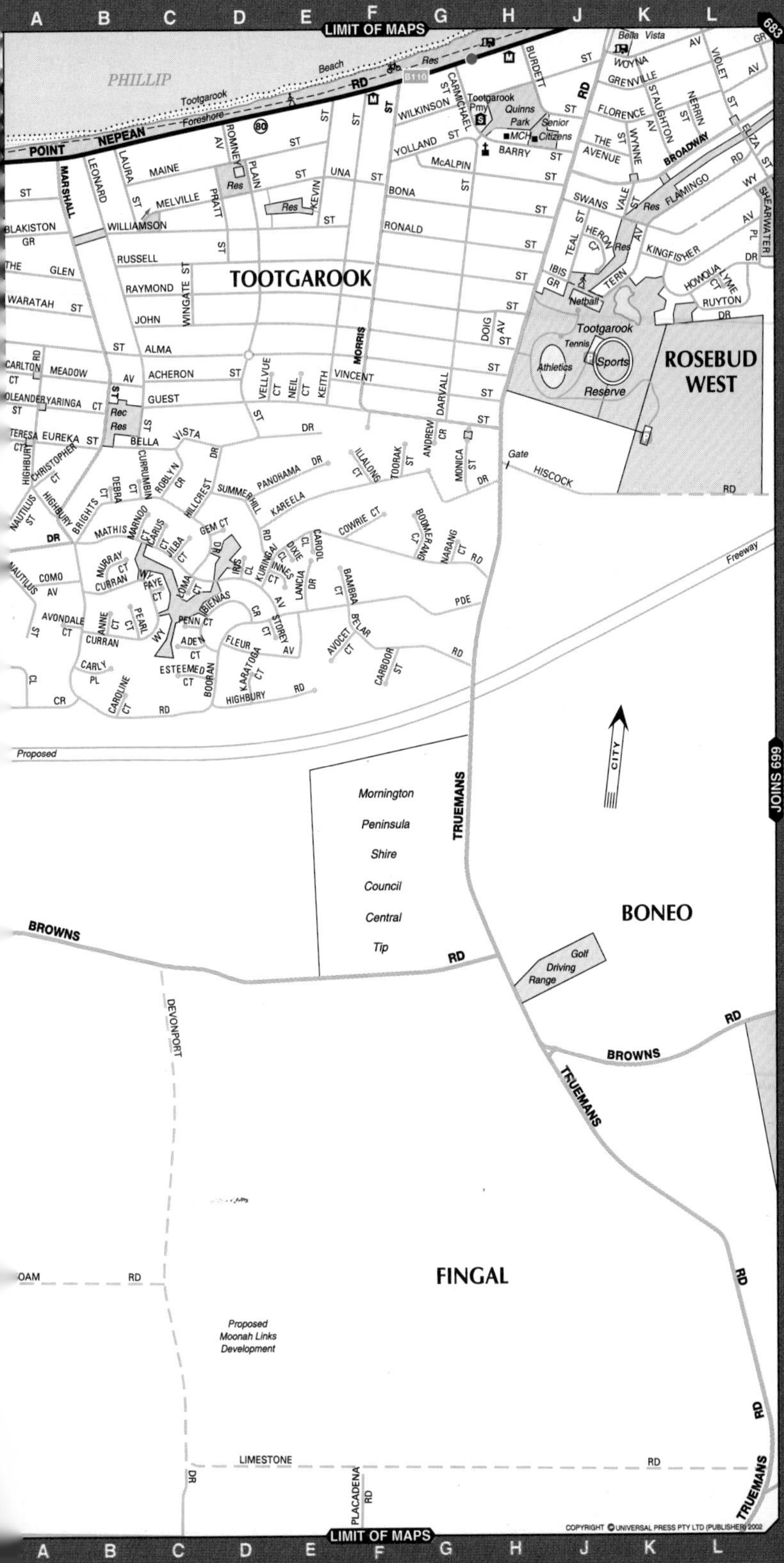

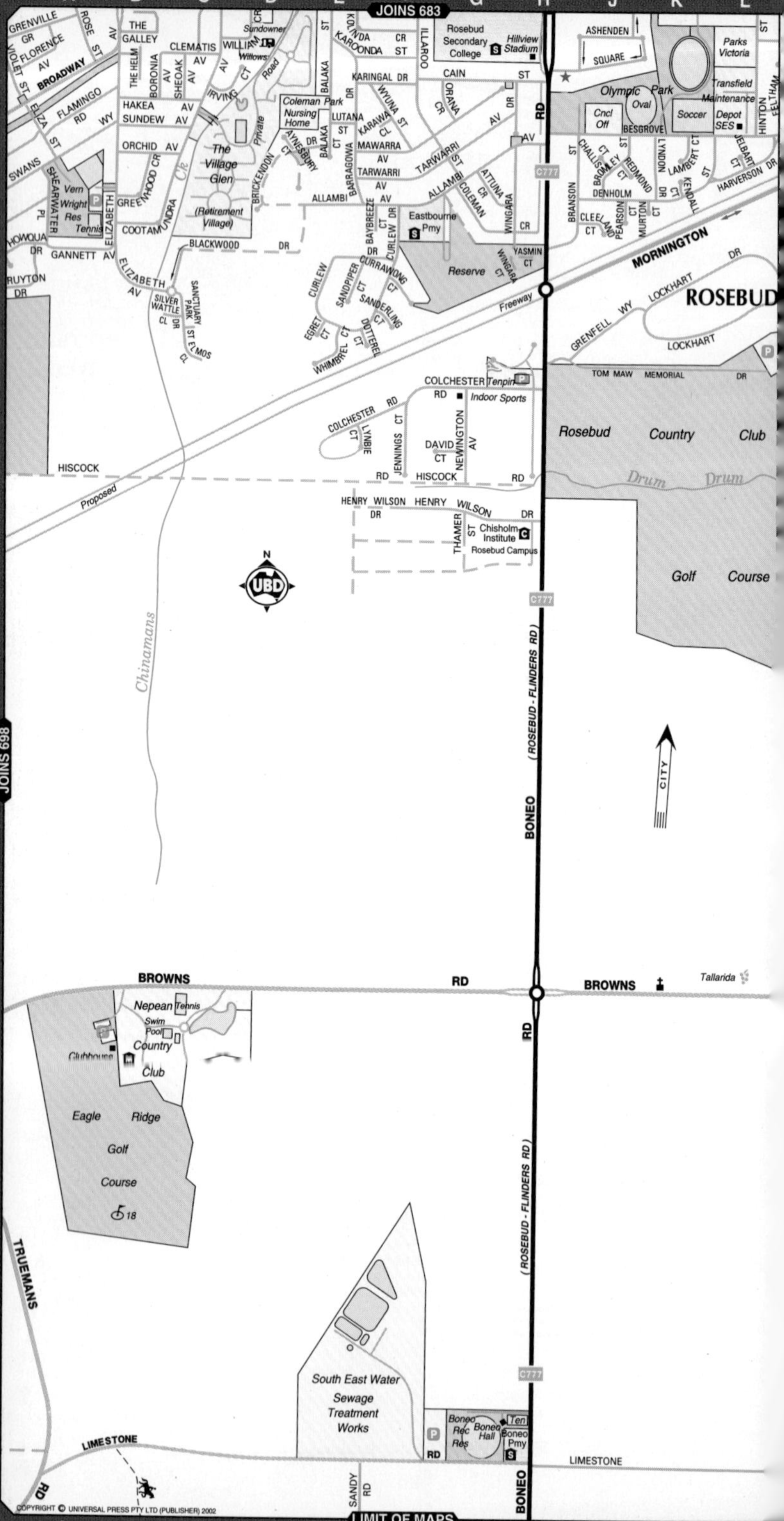

A B C D E F G H J K L

JOINS 683

GRENVILLE GR
ROSE ST
VIOLET ST
FLORENCE AV
BROADWAY
THE GALLEY
THE HELM
BORONIA AV
SHEOAK AV
CLEMATIS AV
WILLIAM CT
IRVING
Road
Sundowner Willows
CR
KOLINDA CR
KAROONDA ST
BALAKA ST
ILLAROO
Rosebud Secondary College
Hillview Stadium
ASHENDEN
SQUARE
Parks Victoria
ST
ELIZA ST
FLAMINGO RD WY
HAKEA AV
SUNDEW AV
ORCHID AV
Private
Coleman Park Nursing Home
LUTANA ST
KARINGAL DR
KARAWA CL
WYUNA ST
ORANA CR
CAIN ST
DR
Olympic Park
Oval
Cncl Off
Soccer
Transfield Maintenance Depot
SES
BESGROVE
HINTON
FELTHAM
RD
AV
SWANS
SHEARWATER PL
Vern Wright Res
Tennis
ELIZABETH
GREENHOOD CR
UNDRA
Ck
The Village Glen (Retirement Village)
BRICKENDON CT
AYNESBURY DR
BALAKA CT
BARRAGOWA DR
MAWARRA AV
TARWARRI
TARWARRI ST
ALLAMBI AV
ATTUNA CR
COLEMAN
C777
BRANSON ST
CHALLIS CT
BROMLEY ST
REDMOND CT
LYNDON DR
LAMBERT CT
KENDALL ST
JELBART CT
HARVERSON DR
DENHOLM
CLEELAND CT
PEARSON CT
MURTON CT
HOWQUA DR
GANNETT AV
COOTAMUNDRA
BLACKWOOD DR
BAYBREEZE DR
CURLEW DR
Eastbourne Pmy
WINGARA CR
YASMIN CT
MORNINGTON DR
RUYTON DR
ELIZABETH AV
SILVER WATTLE CL
SANCTUARY PARK DR
ST ELMOS CL
CURLEW
SANDPIPER CT
CURRAWONG CT
SANDERLING CT
Reserve
WINGARA CT
Freeway
ROSEBUD
LOCKHART DR
GRENFELL WY
LOCKHART
EGRET CT
WHIMBREL CT
DOTTEREL CT
TOM MAW MEMORIAL DR
COLCHESTER RD
Tenpin
Indoor Sports
COLCHESTER CT
LYNBIE
JENNINGS CT
DAVID CT
NEWINGTON AV
Rosebud Country Club
HISCOCK
HISCOCK RD
RD
Drum Drum
Proposed
HENRY WILSON DR
HENRY WILSON DR
THAMER ST
Chisholm Institute Rosebud Campus
UBD
Golf Course
C777
Chinamans
BONEO RD (ROSEBUD - FLINDERS RD)

JOINS 698

CITY
BROWNS RD
BROWNS
Tallarida
Nepean Country Club
Tennis
Swim Pool
Clubhouse
RD
Eagle Ridge Golf Course 18
(ROSEBUD - FLINDERS RD)
TRUEMANS RD
South East Water Sewage Treatment Works
C777
Boneo Rec Res
Boneo Hall
Ten
Boneo Pmy
RD
LIMESTONE
LIMESTONE
SANDY RD
BONEO

1 2 3 4 5 6 7 8 9 10 11 12 13 14 15 16 17 18 19 20

LIMIT OF MAPS

A B C D E F G H J K L

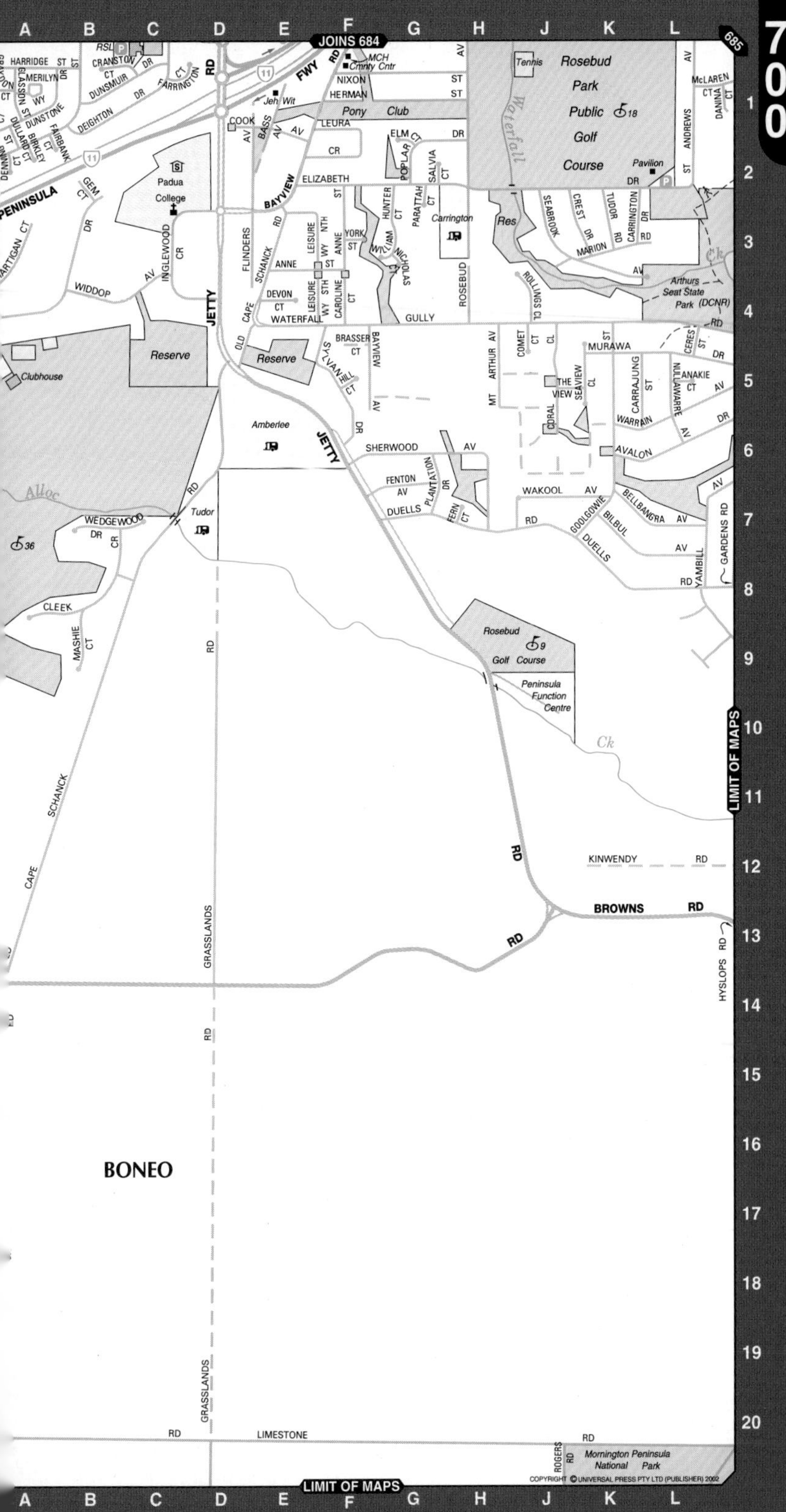

JOINS 684
685
Rosebud Park Public Golf Course
Tennis
Pavilion
Waterfall
Padua College
Pony Club
MCH
Cmnty Cntr
Jeh Wit
Carrington
Res
Arthurs Seat State Park (DCNR)
Reserve
Clubhouse
Amberlee
Tudor
Alloc
Rosebud Golf Course
Peninsula Function Centre
Ck
LIMIT OF MAPS
BONEO
PENINSULA FWY
JETTY RD
BAYVIEW
ELIZABETH
NIXON ST
HERMAN ST
LEURA
COOK
BASS AV
CR
ELM CT
POPLAR
SALVIA CT
PARATTAH CT
HUNTER CT
WILLIAM
NICHOLAS
YORK ST
ANNE ST
LEISURE WY NTH
LEISURE WY STH
CAROLINE CT
DEVON CT
WATERFALL
GULLY
ROSEBUD
FLINDERS
SCHANCK
CAPE
OLD CAPE SCHANCK RD
INGLEWOOD CR
WIDDOP AV
HARRIDGE ST
MERILYN DR
CRANSTON CT
DUNSMUIR DR
FARRINGTON CT
DEIGHTON DR
DUNSTONE WY
GLASSON ST
DULLARD CT
BIRKLEY CT
FAIRBANK CT
DENNING ST
GEM CT
HARTIGAN CT
SEABROOK
CREST DR
TUDOR RD
CARRINGTON DR
MARION
ROLLINGS CL
BRASSER CT
SYLVAN HILL CT
MT ARTHUR AV
COMET CT
MURAWA ST
CERES ST
ANAKIE CT
CARRAJUNG ST
NILLAWARRE AV
WARRAIN DR
AVALON
THE VIEW
SEAVIEW CL
CORAL
SHERWOOD AV
FENTON AV
PLANTATION DR
DUELLS
FERN CT
WAKOOL AV
GOOLGOWIE
BILBUL
BELLBANGRA AV
YAMBILL
GARDENS RD
WEDGEWOOD DR
CLEEK
MASHIE CT
KINWENDY RD
BROWNS RD
HYSLOPS RD
GRASSLANDS RD
LIMESTONE RD
ROGERS RD
Mornington Peninsula National Park
McLAREN CT
DANINA CT
ANDREWS ST

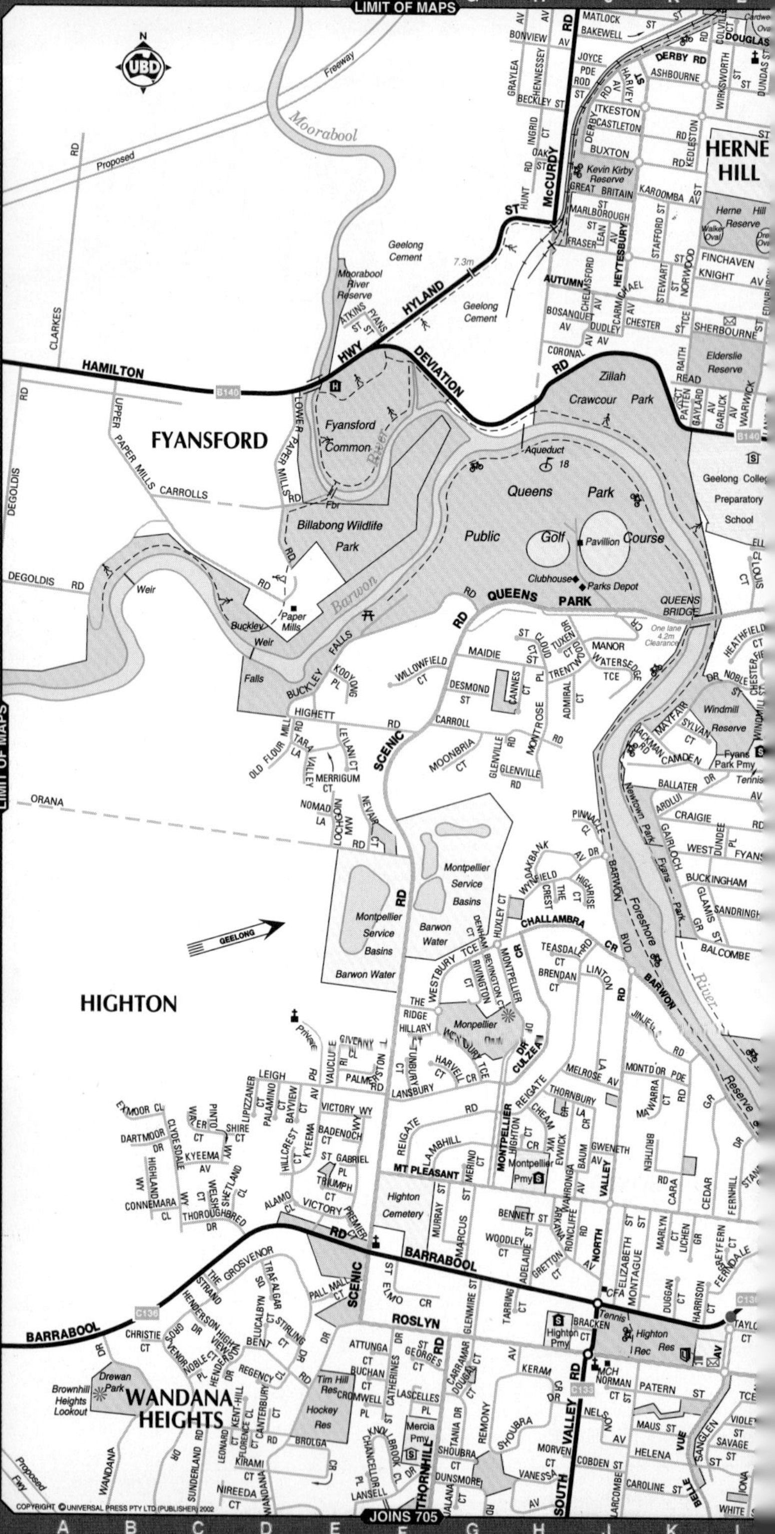
LIMIT OF MAPS
FYANSFORD
HERNE HILL
HIGHTON
WANDANA HEIGHTS
HAMILTON
HYLAND
HWY
DEVIATION
Moorabool
Freeway
Proposed
Geelong Cement
Moorabool River Reserve
Fyansford Common
Billabong Wildlife Park
Paper Mills
Buckley Weir
Falls
Weir
Barwon
Queens Park Public Golf Course
Pavillion
Clubhouse
Parks Depot
Aqueduct
QUEENS PARK RD
QUEENS BRIDGE
Zillah Crawcour Park
Elderslie Reserve
Herne Hill Reserve
Kevin Kirby Reserve
Geelong College Preparatory School
Windmill Reserve
Fyans Park Pmy
Montpellier Service Basins
Barwon Water
Monpellier Reserve
Montpellier Pmy
Hilton Cemetery
Highton Pmy
Highton Rec Res
Tim Hill Res
Hockey Res
Mercia Pmy
Drewan Park
Brownhill Heights Lookout
Newtown Park
Fyans Park
Barwon Foreshore Reserve
GEELONG
SCENIC RD
BARRABOOL RD
ROSLYN RD
MT PLEASANT RD
HIGHETT RD
BARWON BVD
CHALLAMBRA CR
SOUTH VALLEY RD
McCURDY RD
B140
C136
C133
COPYRIGHT © UNIVERSAL PRESS PTY LTD (PUBLISHER) 2002

JOINS 705

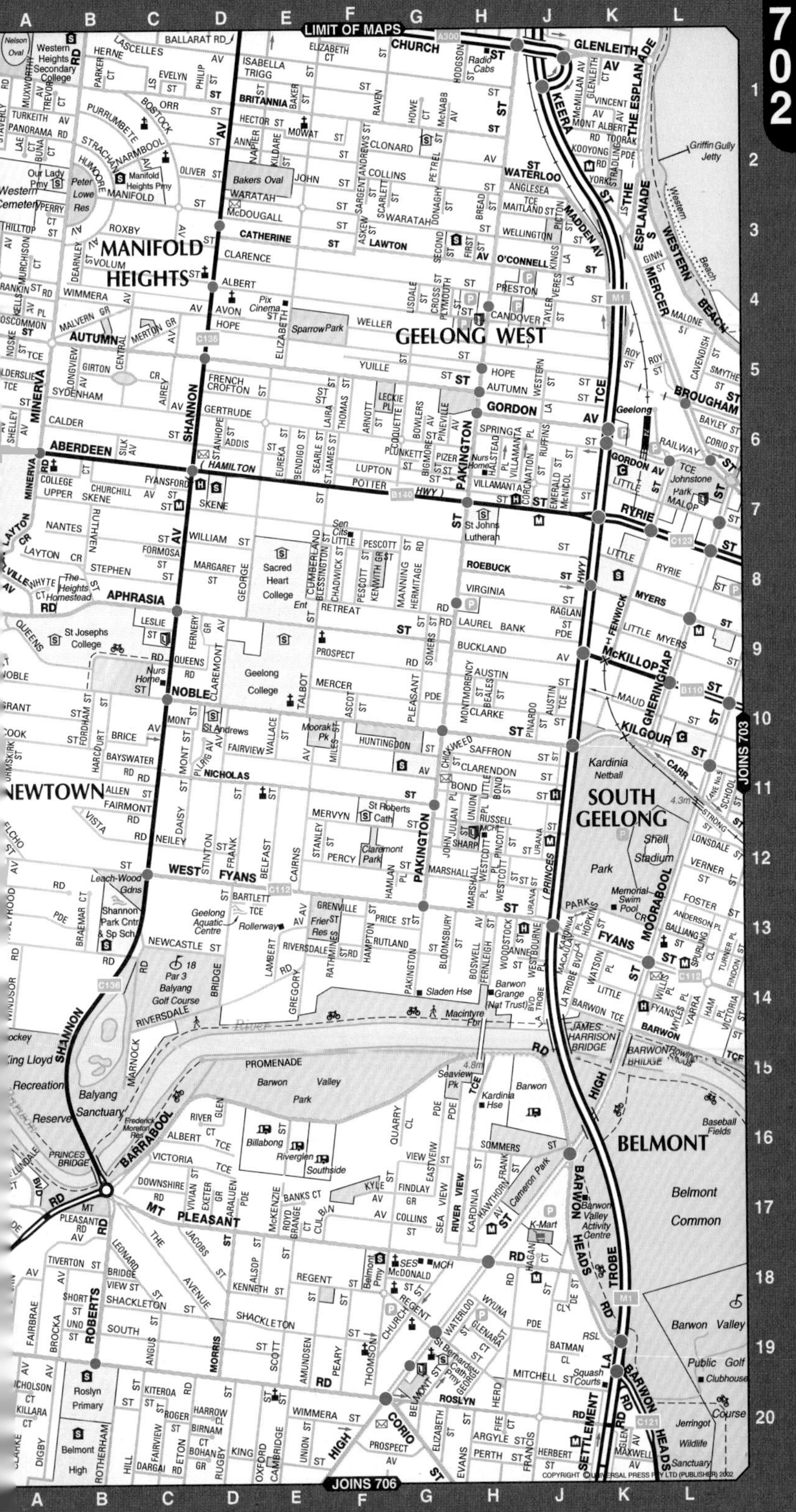
A B C D E F G H J K L
LIMIT OF MAPS
1 2 3 4 5 6 7 8 9 10 11 12 13 14 15 16 17 18 19 20
MANIFOLD HEIGHTS
GEELONG WEST
NEWTOWN
SOUTH GEELONG
BELMONT
JOINS 703
JOINS 706
CHURCH ST
GLENLEITH AV
THE ESPLANADE
WESTERN BEACH
Griffin Gully Jetty
Western Heights Secondary College
Nelson Oval
Western Cemetery
Our Lady Pmy
Manifold Heights Pmy
Peter Lowe Res
Bakers Oval
Sparrow Park
Pix Cinema
Radio Cabs
SHANNON AV
PAKINGTON ST
LATROBE TCE
MERCER ST
AUTUMN ST
ABERDEEN ST
HAMILTON HWY
POTTER ST
RYRIE ST
GORDON AV
Geelong
Johnstone Park
MALOP ST
BROUGHAM ST
St Johns Lutheran
Sacred Heart College
St Josephs College
The Heights Homestead
Geelong College
Moorabool St
KARDINIA PARK
Kardinia Netball
Shell Stadium
Memorial Swim Pool
St Roberts Cath
Claremont Park
Leach-Wood Gdns
Shannon Park Cntr & Sp Sch
Geelong Aquatic Centre
Rollerway
Friend Res
Balyang Par 3 Golf Course
Sladen Hse
Barwon Grange (Nat Trust)
Macintyre Br
JAMES HARRISON BRIDGE
BARWON ROWING CLUB
Barwon River
PROMENADE
Barwon Valley Park
Seaview Pk
Kardinia Hse
Balyang Sanctuary
Recreation Reserve
King Lloyd
PRINCES BRIDGE
Billabong
Riverglen
Southside
Cameron Park
Barwon Valley Activity Centre
K-Mart
Baseball Fields
Belmont Common
Barwon Valley Public Golf Course
Clubhouse
Jerringot Wildlife Sanctuary
Squash Courts
Roslyn Primary
Belmont High
Belmont Pmy
St Bernards Cath Pmy
MT PLEASANT RD
HIGH ST
BARWON HEADS RD
PRINCES HWY
COPYRIGHT © UNIVERSAL PRESS PTY LTD (PUBLISHER) 2002

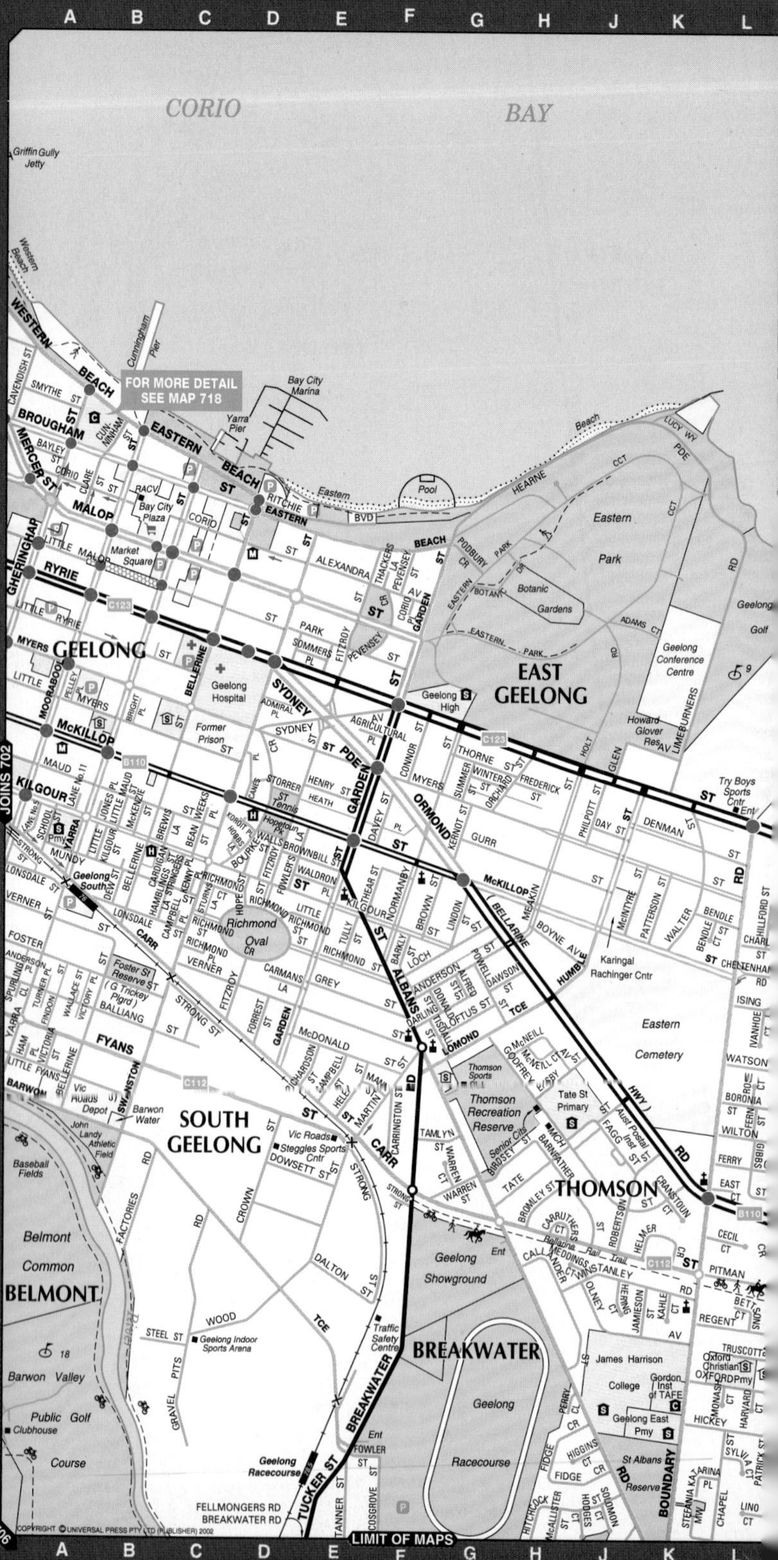

FOR MORE DETAIL SEE MAP 718

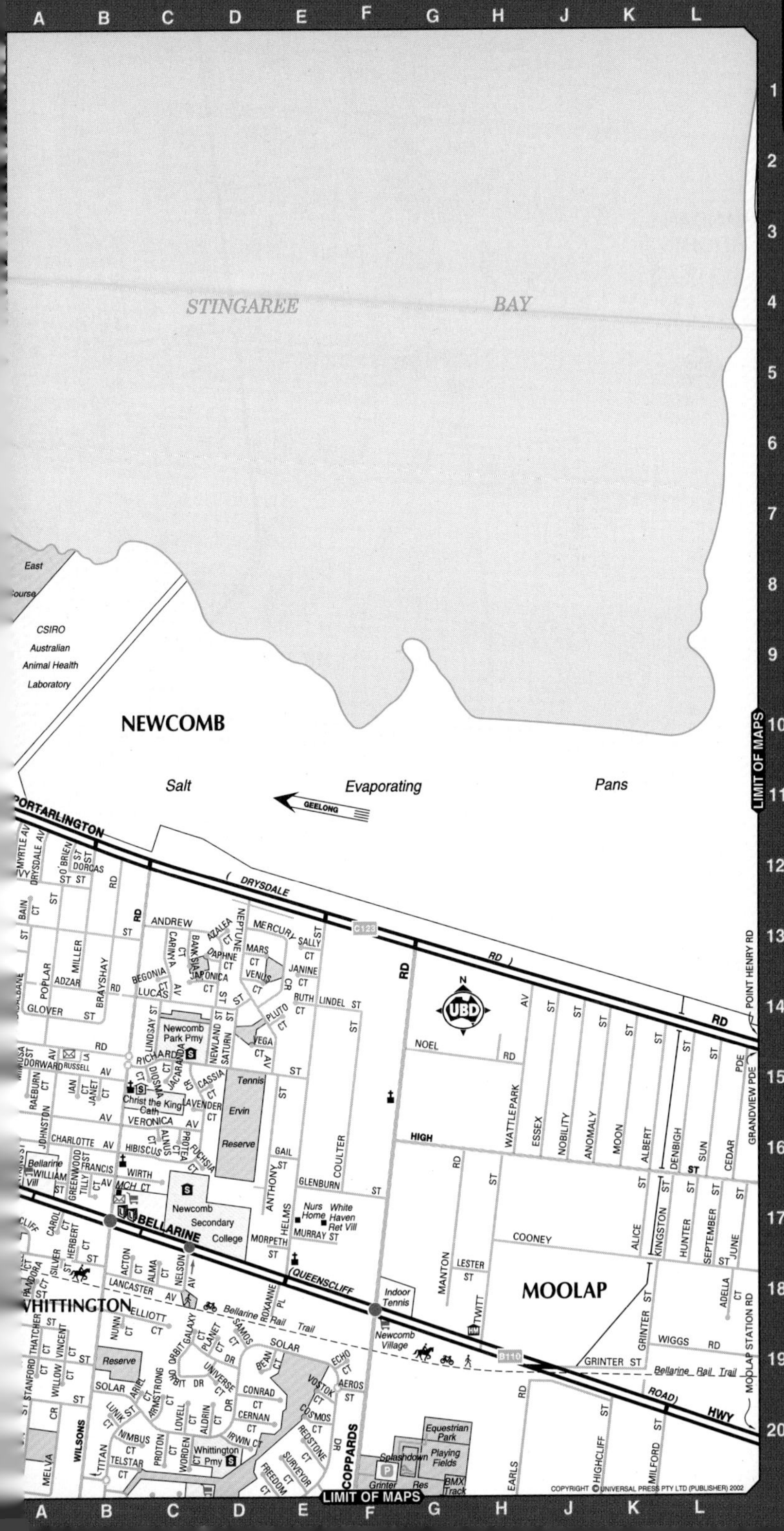

A B C D E F G H J K L

1 2 3 4 5 6 7 8 9 10 11 12 13 14 15 16 17 18 19 20

STINGAREE BAY

East Course

CSIRO Australian Animal Health Laboratory

NEWCOMB

Salt Evaporating Pans

GEELONG

PORTARLINGTON

DRYSDALE RD

C123

POINT HENRY RD

MOOLAP

WHITTINGTON

BELLARINE

QUEENSCLIFF

ROAD HWY

B110

Bellarine Rail Trail

Newcomb Park Pmy

Christ the King Cath

Tennis Ervin Reserve

Newcomb Secondary College

Nurs Home

White Haven Ret Vill

Bellarine Vill

Indoor Tennis

Newcomb Village

Reserve

Whittington Pmy

Equestrian Park

Splashdown

Playing Fields

Grinter Res

BMX Track

MOOLAP STATION RD

GRANDVIEW PDE

COPPARDS RD

WILSONS

LIMIT OF MAPS

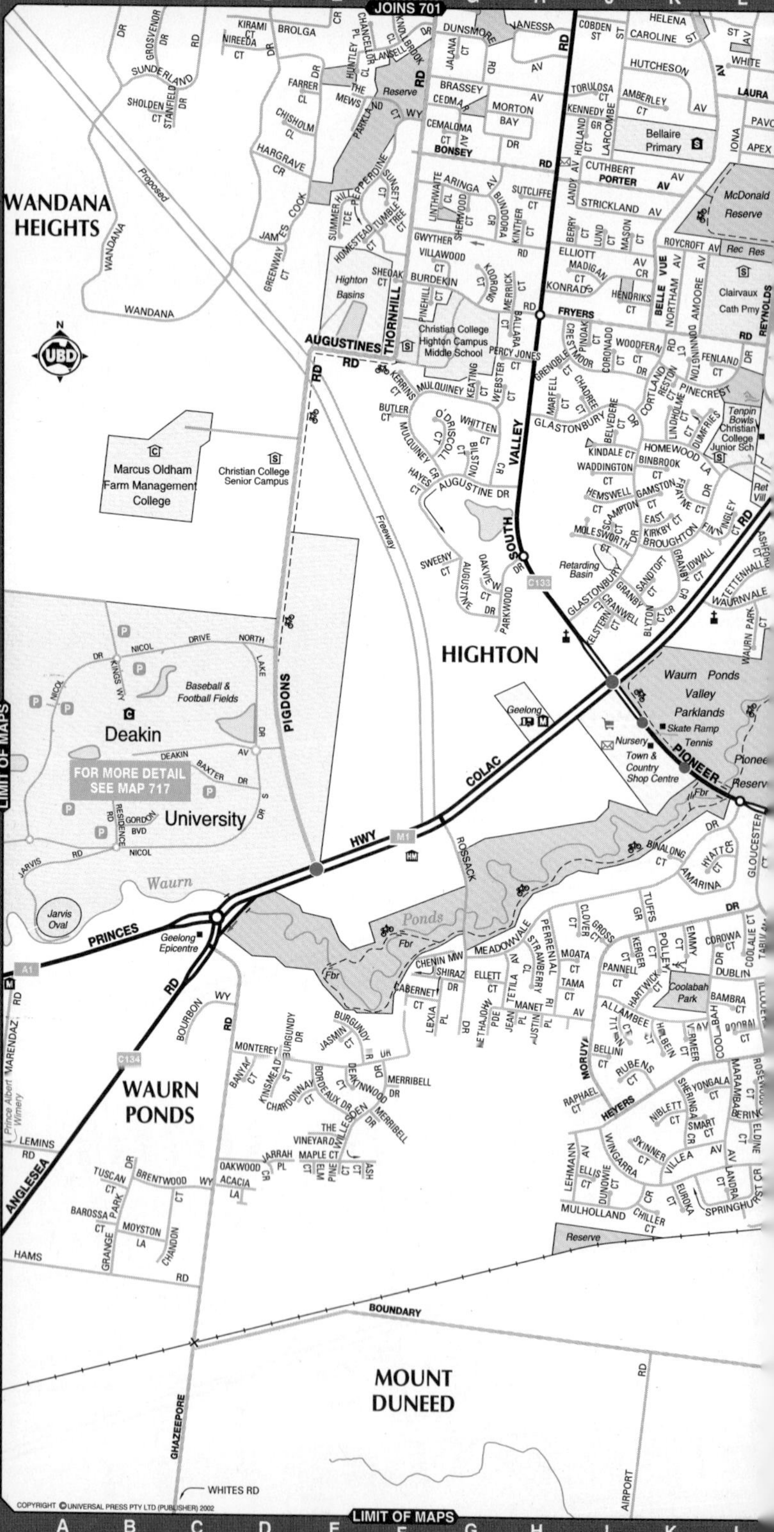

A B C D E F G H J K L

JOINS 701

WANDANA HEIGHTS

HIGHTON

WAURN PONDS

MOUNT DUNEED

GROSVENOR DR
SUNDERLAND DR
SHOLDEN CT
STANFIELD DR
Proposed
WANDANA
WANDANA
KIRAMI CT
NIREEDA CT
BROLGA
FARRER CL
CHISHOLM CL
HARGRAVE CR
JAMES COOK
GREENWAY CT
HUNTLEY PL
CHANCELLOR CL
LANSELL CL
KNOLLBROOK DR
THE MEWS
Reserve
PARKLAND WY
SUMMERHILL TCE
PEPPERDINE
SUNSET CT
HOMESTEAD
TUMBLE TREE
Highton Basins
SHEOAK
THORNHILL RD
AUGUSTINES RD
DUNSMORE RD
JALANA CT
VANESSA AV
BRASSEY AV
CEDMAR
MORTON BAY DR
CEMALOMA CT
BONSEY
ARINGA AV
LINTHWAITE CL
SHERWOOD CT
BUNDOORA
SUTCLIFFE CT
KINTHER CT
GWYTHER
VILLAWOOD CT
BURDEKIN
KOORONG
PINEHILL
MERRICK CT
BALLARA
Christian College Highton Campus Middle School
PERCY JONES CT
COBDEN ST
CAROLINE ST
HELENA
HUTCHESON
TORULOSA CT
KENNEDY
AMBERLEY CT
LARCOMBE
HOLLAND
GR
Bellaire Primary
CUTHBERT
PORTER AV
LANDY
STRICKLAND AV
BERRY CT
LUND CT
MASON CT
ELLIOTT
MADIGAN CR
KONRADS
HENDRIKS CT
BELLE VUE
NORTHAM AV
AMOORE AV
ROYCROFT AV
Rec Res
Clairvaux Cath Pmy
FRYERS RD
REYNOLDS
ST
WHITE
LAURA
PAVO
APEX
IONA
McDonald Reserve
WOODFERN
CORONADO
PINOAK
CRESTMOOR
DONNINGTON
FENLAND CT
PINECREST
GRENOBLE
MARFELL CT
CHADREE
GLASTONBURY DR
BELVEDERE CT
CORTLAND
RESTON
LINDHOLME
DUMFRIES
Tenpin Bowls
Christian College Junior Sch
KINDALE CT
BINBROOK CT
HOMEWOOD LA
WADDINGTON CT
HEMSWELL CT
GAMSTON CT
FAYNE CT
SCAMPTON
EAST
KIRKBY CT
FINNINGLEY CT
MOLESWORTH CT
BROUGHTON
Retarding Basin
SANDTOFT CT
GRANBY CR
UDWALL CT
GLASTONBURY
CRANWELL
KELSTERN CT
BLYTON CT
Ret Vill
ASHFORD
TETTENHALL
WAURNVALE
WAURN PARK
KERRINS
MULQUINEY
BUTLER CT
O'DRISCOLL CT
WHITTEN CT
BILSTON CR
HAYES CT
AUGUSTINE DR
KEATING CT
WEBSTER
SOUTH VALLEY RD
C133
SWEENY CT
OAKVIEW CT
AUGUSTINE DR
PARKWOOD
Marcus Oldham Farm Management College
Christian College Senior Campus
Freeway
PIGDONS RD
NICOL DRIVE NORTH
KINGS WY
LAKE DR
NICOL
Baseball & Football Fields
Deakin University
DEAKIN AV
BAXTER DR
FOR MORE DETAIL SEE MAP 717
RESIDENCE RD
GORDON BVD
NICOL
JARVIS RD
Waurn
Jarvis Oval
LIMIT OF MAPS
Geelong
COLAC HWY
M1
ROSSACK DR
Waurn Ponds Valley Parklands
Skate Ramp
Tennis
Nursery
Town & Country Shop Centre
PIONEER
Pioneer Reserve
Fbr
BINALONG CT
HYATT CR
AMARINA
GLOUCESTER
PRINCES
Geelong Epicentre
A1
Ponds
Fbr
CHENIN MW
SHIRAZ DR
CABERNET CT
LEXIA PL
MEADOWVALE
STRAWBERRY CL
PERRENIAL
ELLETT CT
TETILA AV
MANET
JEAN PL
JUSTIN PL
METHAJOW PDE
MOATA CT
TAMA CT
AV
CLOVER CT
GROSS CT
TUFFS GR
KERGER CT
POLLEY CT
EMMY CT
PANNELL CT
HARTWICK CT
COROWA CT
DR
DUBLIN
COOLALIE CT
Coolabah Park
BAMBRA CT
ALLAMBEE
TITIAN CT
HOLBEIN CT
VERMEER
COOLABAH CT
BOORAL CT
MORUYA
BELLINI CT
RUBENS CT
RAPHAEL CT
HEYERS
NIBLETT CT
SHERINGA CR
YONGALA CT
MARAMBA
SMART CT
BERING
ROSEWOOD CT
ELDINE
SKINNER CT
VILLEA AV
WINGARRA
LEHMANN AV
ELLIS CT
DUNOWIE CT
CHILLER CT
EUROKA CT
LANDRA CT
SPRINGHURST CR
MULHOLLAND
Reserve
RD
BOURBON WY
MONTEREY CT
BURGUNDY DR
JASMIN CT
BURGUNDY
BANYAN CT
KINSMEAD ST
CHARDONNAY
BORDEAUX DR
DEAKINWOOD DR
MERRIBELL DR
MERRIBELL
WILLESDEN
THE VINEYARD
JARRAH PL
MAPLE CT
ELM CT
PINE CT
ASH CT
OAKWOOD CR
ACACIA LA
C134
ANGLESEA RD
MARENDAZ
Prince Albert Wimery
LEMINS RD
TUSCAN CT
BRENTWOOD WY
BAROSSA PARK
MOYSTON LA
GRANGE CT
CHANDON CT
HAMS RD
BOUNDARY
GHAZEEPORE
AIRPORT RD
WHITES RD

LIMIT OF MAPS

A B C D E F G H J K L

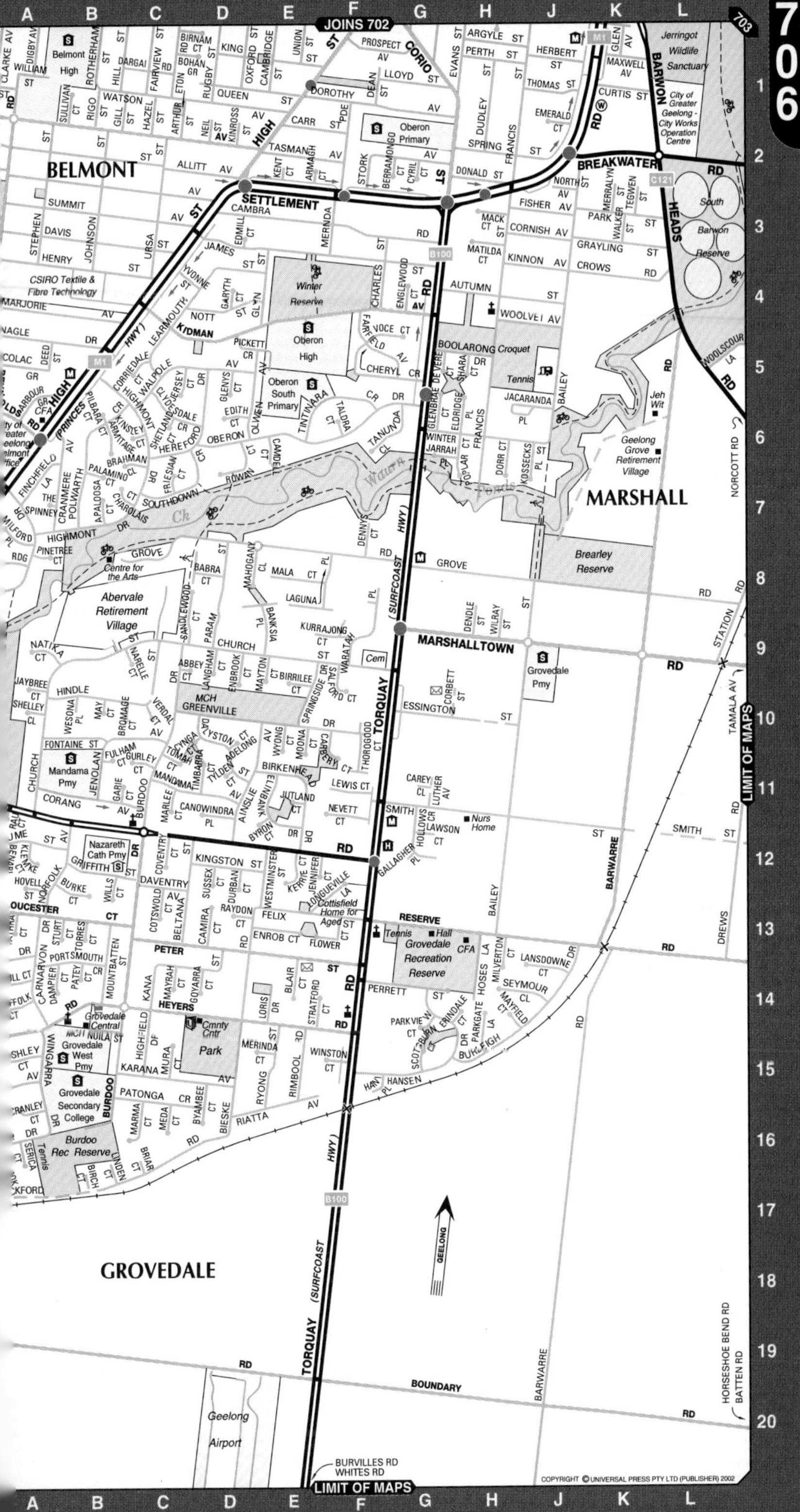
JOINS 702
703
BELMONT
MARSHALL
GROVEDALE
SETTLEMENT RD
BREAKWATER RD
BARWON HEADS RD
PRINCES HWY
HIGH ST
MARSHALLTOWN RD
TORQUAY (SURFCOAST HWY)
BOUNDARY RD
BARWARRE RD
GROVE RD
SMITH ST
CHURCH ST
Jerringot Wildlife Sanctuary
City of Greater Geelong - City Works Operation Centre
South Barwon Reserve
Belmont High
Oberon Primary
Oberon High
Oberon South Primary
Winter Reserve
Boolarong Croquet
Tennis
Jeh Wit
Geelong Grove Retirement Village
Brearley Reserve
Centre for the Arts
Abervale Retirement Village
Waurn Ponds Ck
Grovedale Pmy
MCH GREENVILLE
Mandama Pmy
Nazareth Cath Pmy
Nurs Home
Cottisfield Home for Aged
Grovedale Recreation Reserve
Hall
CFA
Cmnty Cntr
Park
Grovedale Central
MCH
Grovedale West Pmy
Grovedale Secondary College
Burdoo Rec Reserve
CSIRO Textile & Fibre Technology
Geelong Airport
GEELONG
LIMIT OF MAPS
BURVILLES RD
WHITES RD
HORSESHOE BEND RD
BATTEN RD
COPYRIGHT © UNIVERSAL PRESS PTY LTD (PUBLISHER) 2002

A B C D E F G H J K L
LIMIT OF MAPS 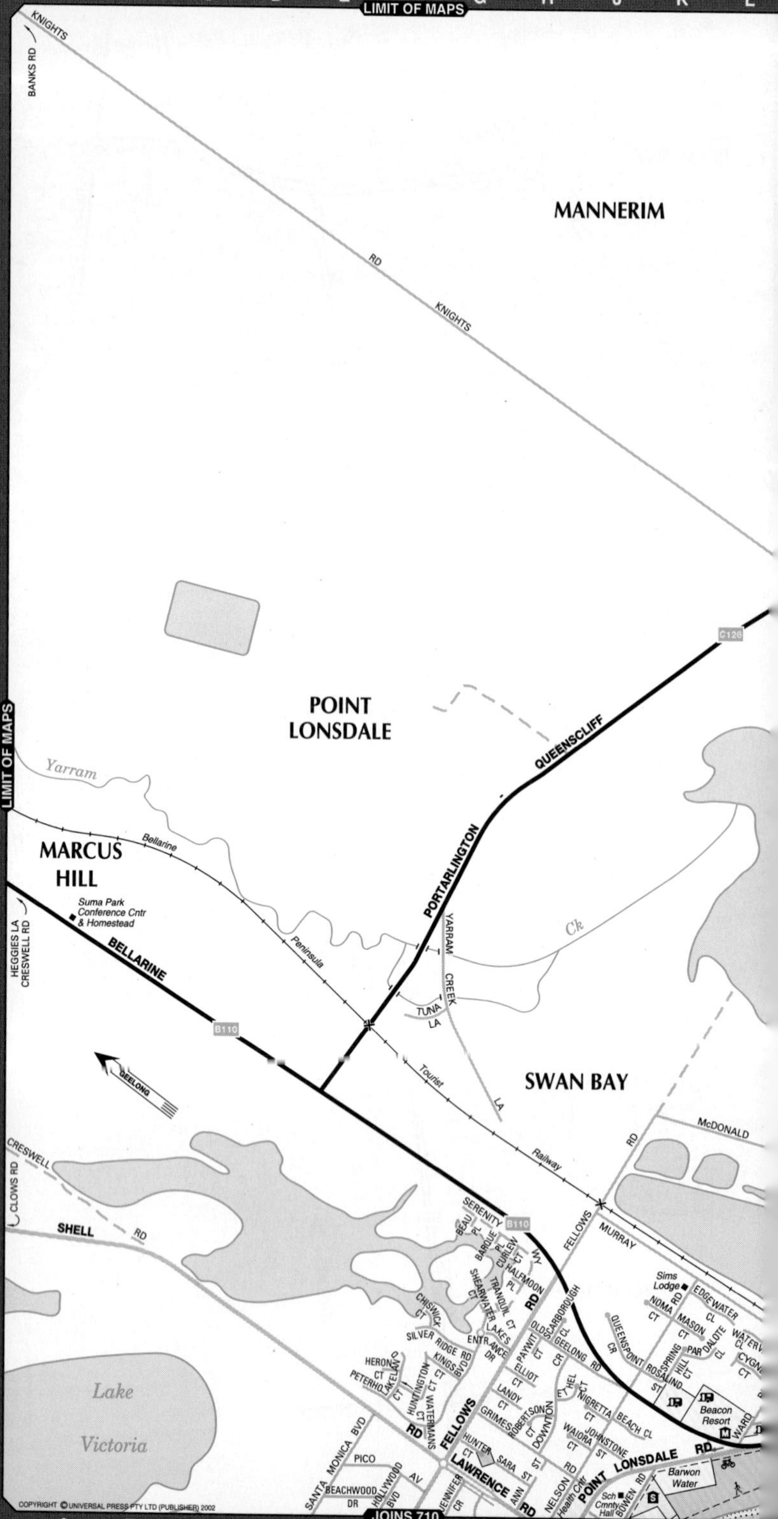
1 2 3 4 5 6 7 8 9 10 11 12 13 14 15 16 17 18 19 20
KNIGHTS
BANKS RD
MANNERIM
RD
KNIGHTS
C126
POINT LONSDALE
QUEENSCLIFF
LIMIT OF MAPS
Yarram
MARCUS HILL
Bellarine
PORTARLINGTON
Ck
Suma Park Conference Cntr & Homestead
HEGGIES LA
CRESWELL RD
BELLARINE
Peninsula
YARRAM
CREEK
TUNA LA
B110
GEELONG
Tourist
LA
SWAN BAY
Railway
RD
McDONALD
CRESWELL
CLOWS RD
SHELL
RD
SERENITY
B110
BEAU PL
BARQUE PL
CURLEW CT
WY
FELLOWS
MURRAY
HALFMOON PL
SHEARWATER CT
TRANQUIL CT
RD
SCARBOROUGH
Sims Lodge
NOMA CT
RD
EDGEWATER CL
CHISWICK CT
LAKES DR
OLD CT
MASON CT
SILVER RIDGE RD
KINGS BVD
ENTRANCE
PAYWIT CT
CR
GEELONG RD
QUEENSPOINT CR
SPRING HILL CT
PARDALOTE CL
WATERV CL
CYGN CT
HERON CT
PETERHO CT
LAKELAND CT
HUNTINGTON CT
WATERMANS CT
ELLIOT CT
LANDY CT
ETHEL CT
ROSALIND ST
Beacon Resort
WARD
GRIMES CT
ROBERTSON CT
DOWNTON ST
NIGRETTA CT
BEACH CL
SANTA MONICA BVD
RD
FELLOWS
HUNTER CT
SARA ST
WAIDRA CT
JOHNSTONE ST
PICO
HOLLYWOOD BVD
AV
LAWRENCE RD
ANN RD
NELSON RD
POINT LONSDALE RD
Barwon Water
BEACHWOOD DR
JENNIFER CR
Health Cntr
Sch Cmnty Hall
BOWEN RD
Lake Victoria
JOINS 710
A B C D E F G H J K L

LIMIT OF MAPS
BLACKGATE RD
HORSESHOE BEND RD
Torquay Sands Golf Course
Clubhouse
THE ESPLANADE
Reserve
Foreshore
Recreation Reserve
Tennis
Taylor Park
ESPLANADE
FISCHER ST
Fishermans Beach
Yellow Bluff
Zeally Bay
Front Beach
Point Danger
Surf Beach
Coast
BASS STRAIT
GRANGE
GOLDEN BEACH
RIVERSIDE
GRANDVIEW
DARIAN RD
GILBERT ST
PEARL ST
WALKER ST
PRIDE ST

A B C D E F G H J K L

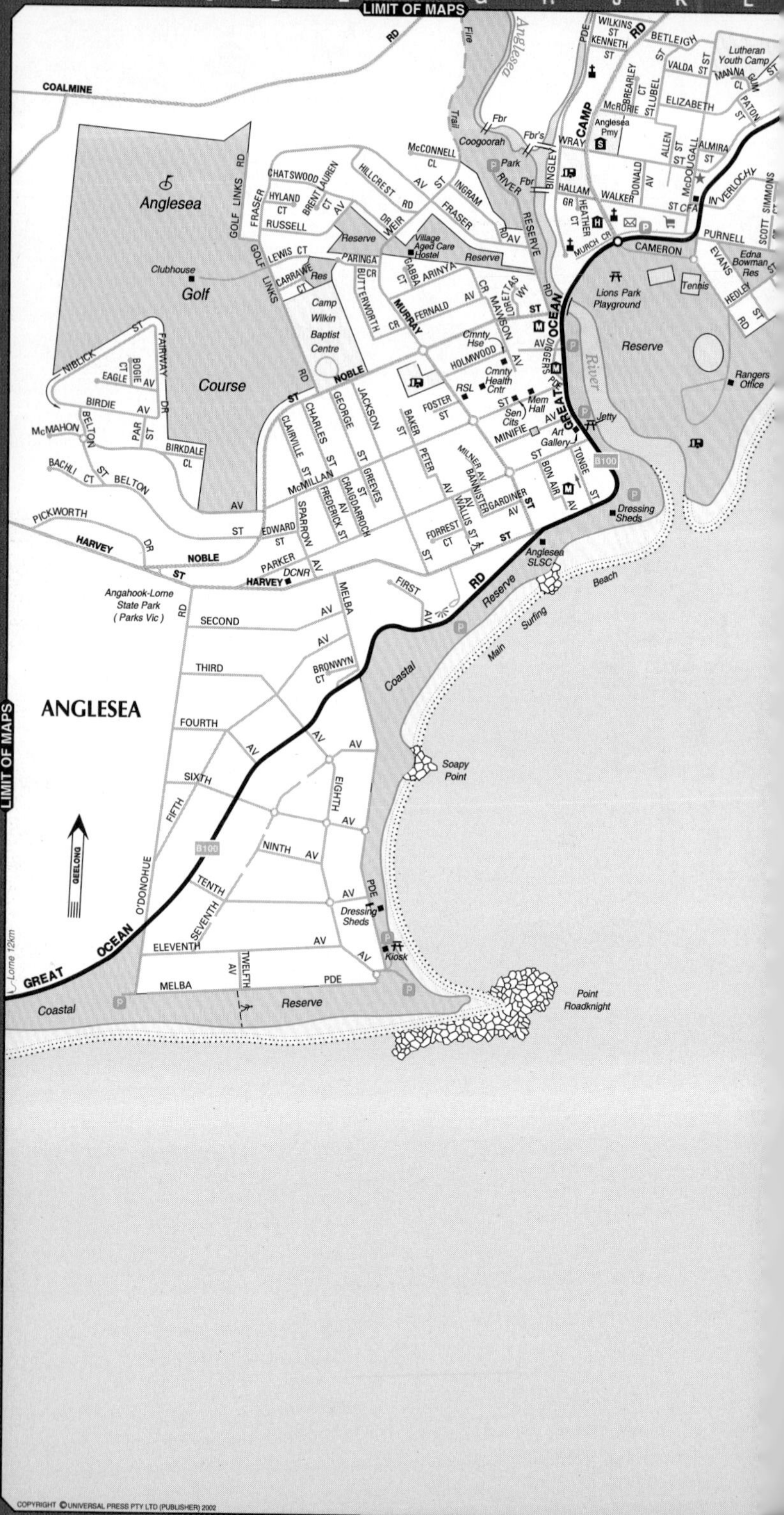

LIMIT OF MAPS

ANGLESEA

COALMINE RD
Anglesea River
Fire Trail
Fbr
Coogoorah Park
Fbr's
Fbr
RIVER RESERVE RD
WILKINS ST
KENNETH ST
PDE
BETLEIGH ST
Lutheran Youth Camp
VALDA ST
MANNA GUM CL
BREARLEY CT
LUBEL ST
ELIZABETH ST
PATON ST
McRORIE ST
CAMP RD
Anglesea Pmy
WRAY ST
ALLEN ST
McDOUGALL ST
ALMIRA ST
INVERLOCHY
SIMMONS
BINGLEY
HALLAM ST
DONALD AV
WALKER
CFA
GR
HEATHER CT
MURCH CR
PURNELL
SCOTT
CAMERON
EVANS
Edna Bowman Res
Lions Park Playground
Tennis
HEDLEY RD
Reserve
Rangers Office
River
Jetty
Art Gallery
TONGE ST
BON AIR AV
Dressing Sheds
Anglesea SLSC
Beach
Main Surfing
Reserve
Coastal
Soapy Point
Point Roadknight
Dressing Sheds
Kiosk
Coastal Reserve
Lorne 12km
GREAT OCEAN RD
B100
GEELONG

Anglesea Golf Course
Clubhouse
GOLF LINKS RD
NIBLICK ST
FAIRWAY DR
EAGLE CT
BOGIE AV
BIRDIE AV
PAR ST
McMAHON
BELTON ST
BIRKDALE CL
BACHLI CT
PICKWORTH
HARVEY DR
NOBLE ST
EDWARD ST
PARKER AV
HARVEY DCNR
Angahook-Lorne State Park (Parks Vic)

McCONNELL CL
CHATSWOOD
LAUREN CT
HYLAND CT
BRENT AV
RUSSELL
HILLCREST RD
WEIR DR
INGRAM
FRASER AV
FRASER
Reserve
Village Aged Care Hostel
Reserve
LEWIS CT
PARINGA
CARRAWE CT
Res
GABBA CT
ARINYA
BUTTERWORTH CR
Camp Wilkin Baptist Centre
MURRAY CR
FERNALD AV
MAWSON CR
LORETTAS WY
DIGGERS PDE
Cmnty Hse
HOLMWOOD
Cmnty Health Cntr
RSL
Mem Hall
Sen Cits
MINIFIE AV
FOSTER ST
BAKER ST
PETER AV
MILNER AV
BANNISTER
WALLIS ST
GARDINER ST
FORREST CT
NOBLE ST
GEORGE ST
JACKSON ST
CHARLES ST
CLAIRVILLE ST
McMILLAN
GREEVES ST
CRAIGDARROCH AV
FREDERICK ST
SPARROW
FIRST AV
MELBA
SECOND AV
THIRD AV
BRONWYN CT
FOURTH AV
SIXTH AV
FIFTH
EIGHTH
NINTH AV
TENTH
SEVENTH
AV
PDE
ELEVENTH AV
TWELFTH AV
O'DONOHUE
MELBA PDE

A B C D E F G H J K L

1 2 3 4 5 6 7 8 9 10

BASS STRAIT

11 12 13 14 15 16 17 18 19 20

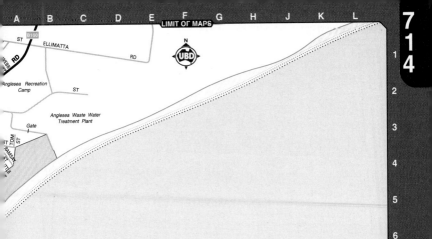

THE UNIVERSITY OF MELBOURNE

THIS MAP IS AN ENLARGEMENT OF A SECTION OF MAP 18 A13

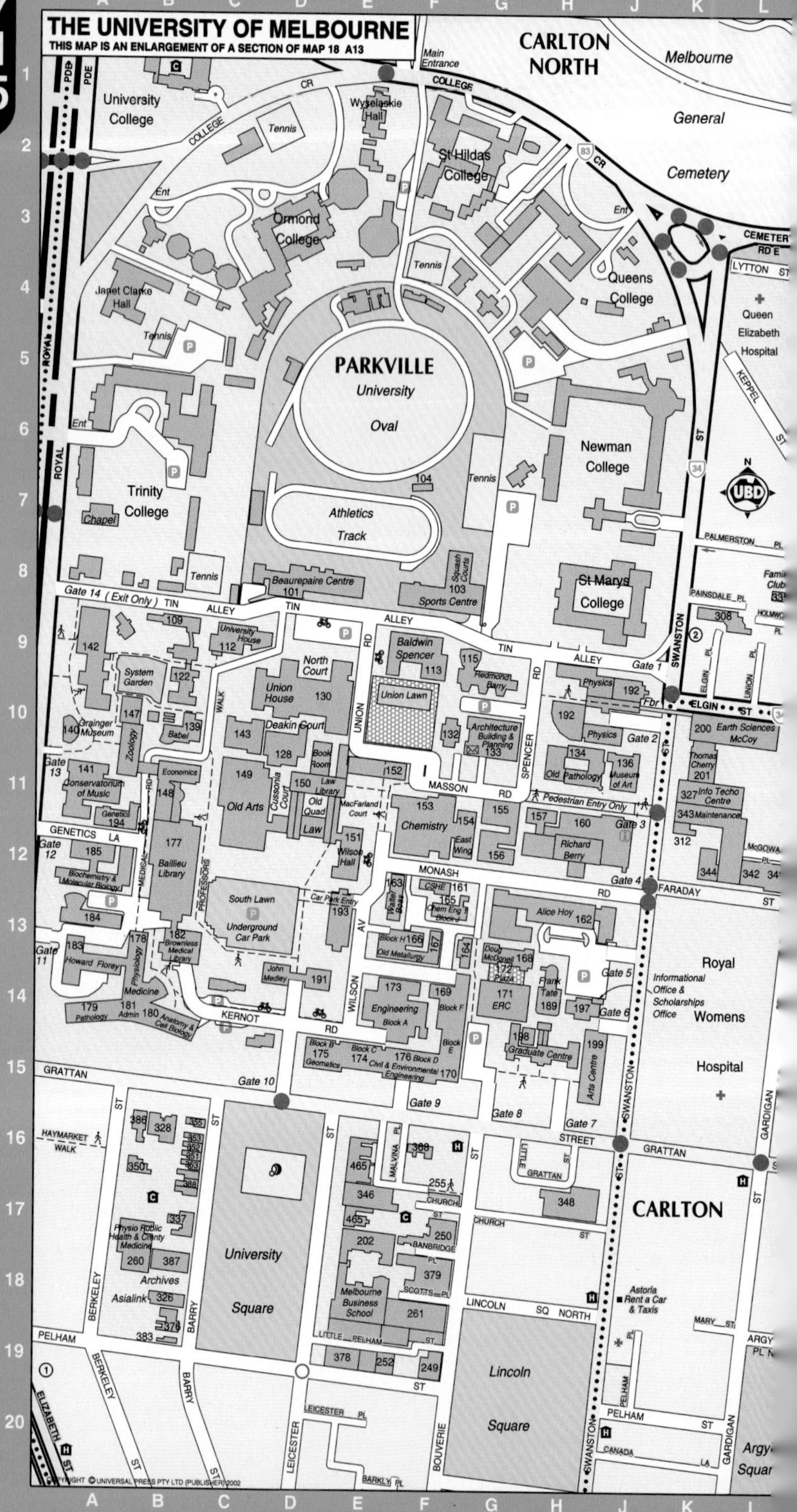

LA TROBE UNIVERSITY

THIS MAP IS AN ENLARGEMENT OF A SECTION OF MAP 284 D11

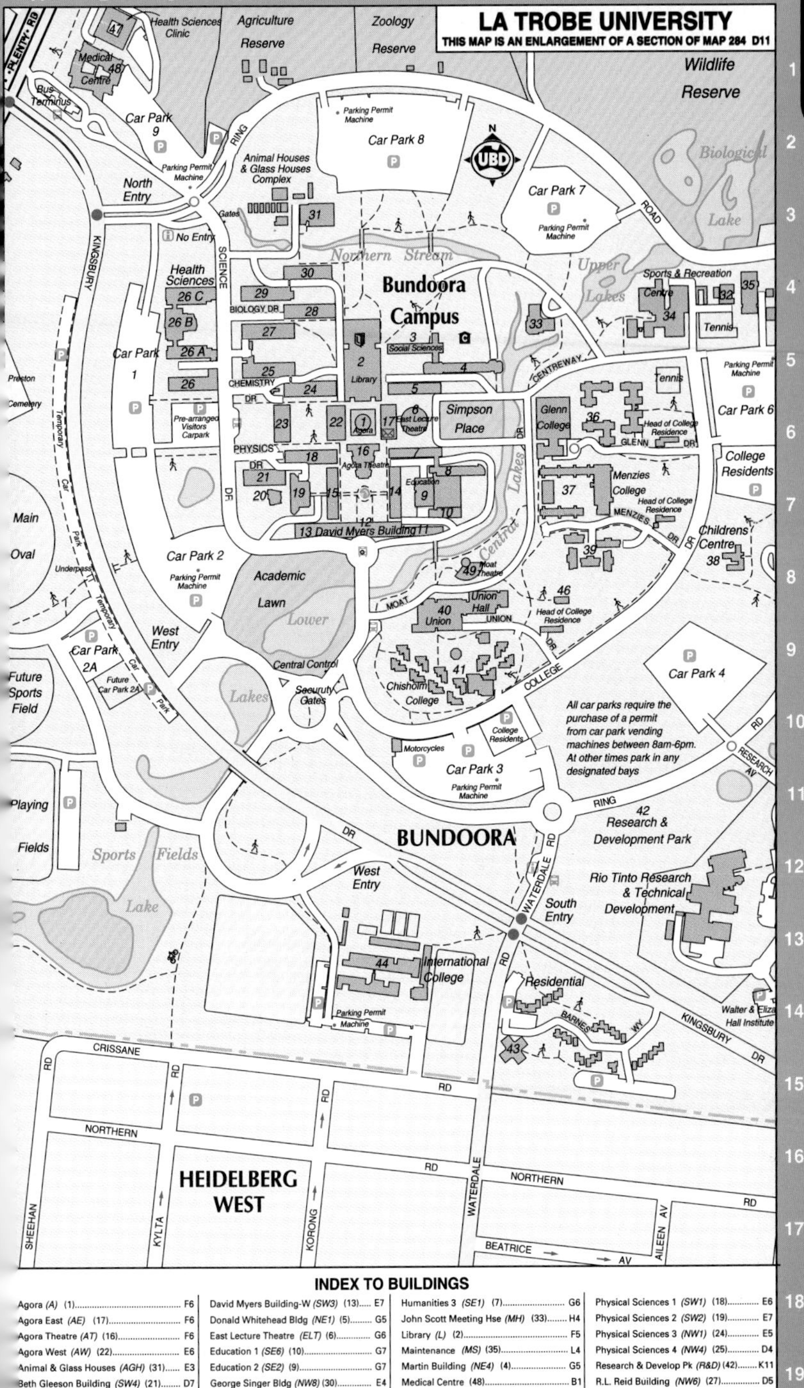

INDEX TO BUILDINGS

- Agora (A) (1) F6
- Agora East (AE) (17) F6
- Agora Theatre (AT) (16) F6
- Agora West (AW) (22) E6
- Animal & Glass Houses (AGH) (31) E3
- Beth Gleeson Building (SW4) (21) D7
- Biological Sciences 1 (NW3) (28) E4
- Biological Sciences 2 (NW7) (29) D4
- Campus Graphics (CS) (32) L4
- Children's Centre (CCR) (38) L8
- Chisholm College (CC) (41) G9
- David Myers Building-Cntr (S) (12) F7
- David Myers Building-E (SE3) (11) G7
- David Myers Building-W (SW3) (13) E7
- Donald Whitehead Bldg (NE1) (5) G5
- East Lecture Theatre (ELT) (6) G6
- Education 1 (SE6) (10) G7
- Education 2 (SE2) (9) G7
- George Singer Bldg (NW8) (30) E4
- Glenn College (GC) (36) J6
- Health Sciences 1 (NW9) (26) C5
- Health Sciences 2 (NW10) (26A) C5
- Health Sciences 3 (NW11) (26C) C4
- Health Sciences Clinic (HSC) (47) B1
- Hooper & Szental Lecture Th (SW5)(5) G5
- Humanities 2 (SE4) (8) G7
- Humanities 3 (SE1) (7) G6
- John Scott Meeting Hse (MH) (33) H4
- Library (L) (2) F5
- Maintenance (MS) (35) L4
- Martin Building (NE4) (4) G5
- Medical Centre (48) B1
- Menzies College (MC) (37) K7
- Menzies Coll Annexe (MCA) (39) J8
- Moat Theatre (MT) (49) H8
- Non-Collegiate Hsg (NCH) (43) H14
- Peribolos East (PE) (14) F7
- Peribolos West (PW) (15) E7
- Physical Sciences 1 (SW1) (18) E6
- Physical Sciences 2 (SW2) (19) E7
- Physical Sciences 3 (NW1) (24) E5
- Physical Sciences 4 (NW4) (25) D4
- Research & Develop Pk (R&D) (42) K11
- R.L. Reid Building (NW6) (27) D5
- Social Sciences (NE2) G5
- Sports & Recreation Cntr (ISC) (34) K4
- Thomas Cherry Building (X1) (23) E6
- Union (U) (40) G9
- Union Children's Co-op (UCC) (46) J8
- West Lecture Th (NW12) (26B) C4

18 19 20

DEAKIN UNIVERSITY

THIS MAP IS AN ENLARGEMENT OF A SECTION OF MAP 705 A10

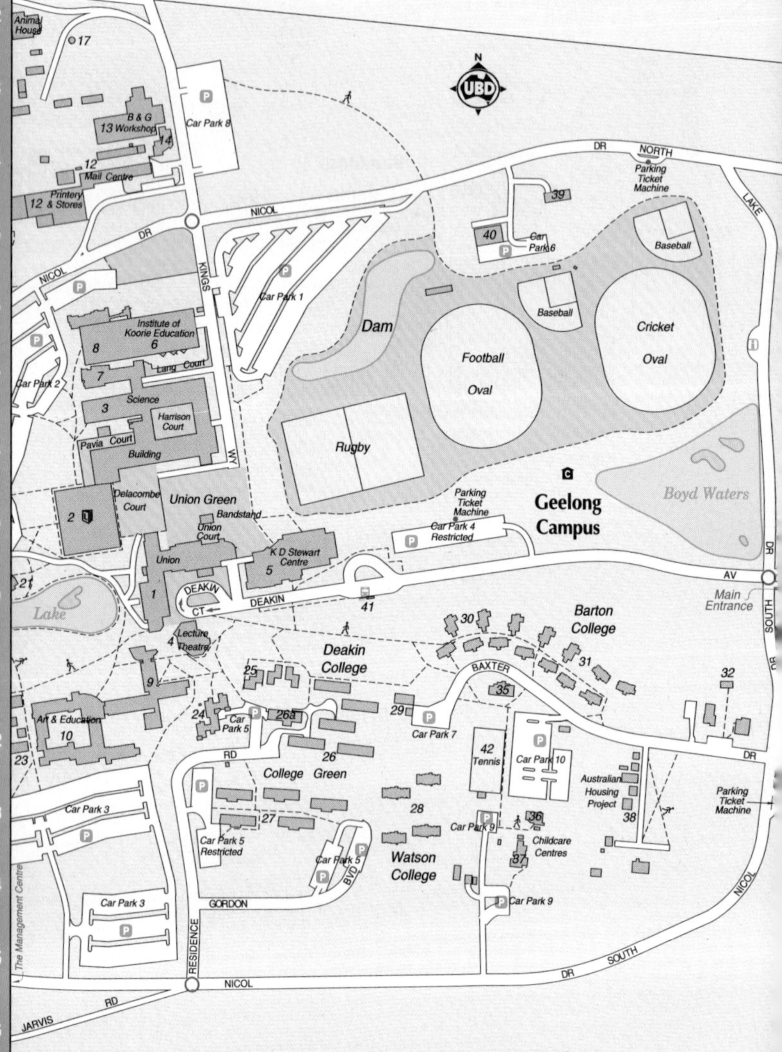

INDEX TO BUILDINGS

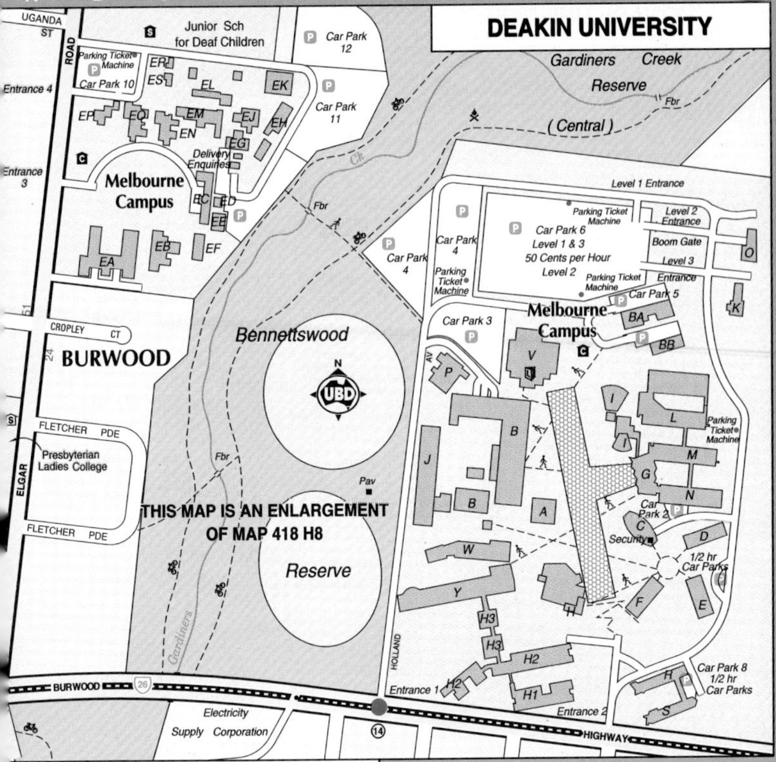

DEAKIN UNIVERSITY

Gardiners Creek Reserve (Central)

Melbourne Campus

BURWOOD

Bennettswood Reserve

THIS MAP IS AN ENLARGEMENT OF MAP 418 H8

INDEX TO BUILDINGS

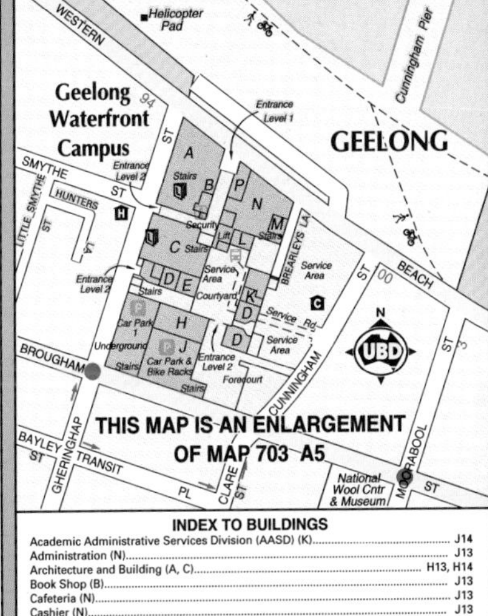

INDEX TO BUILDINGS

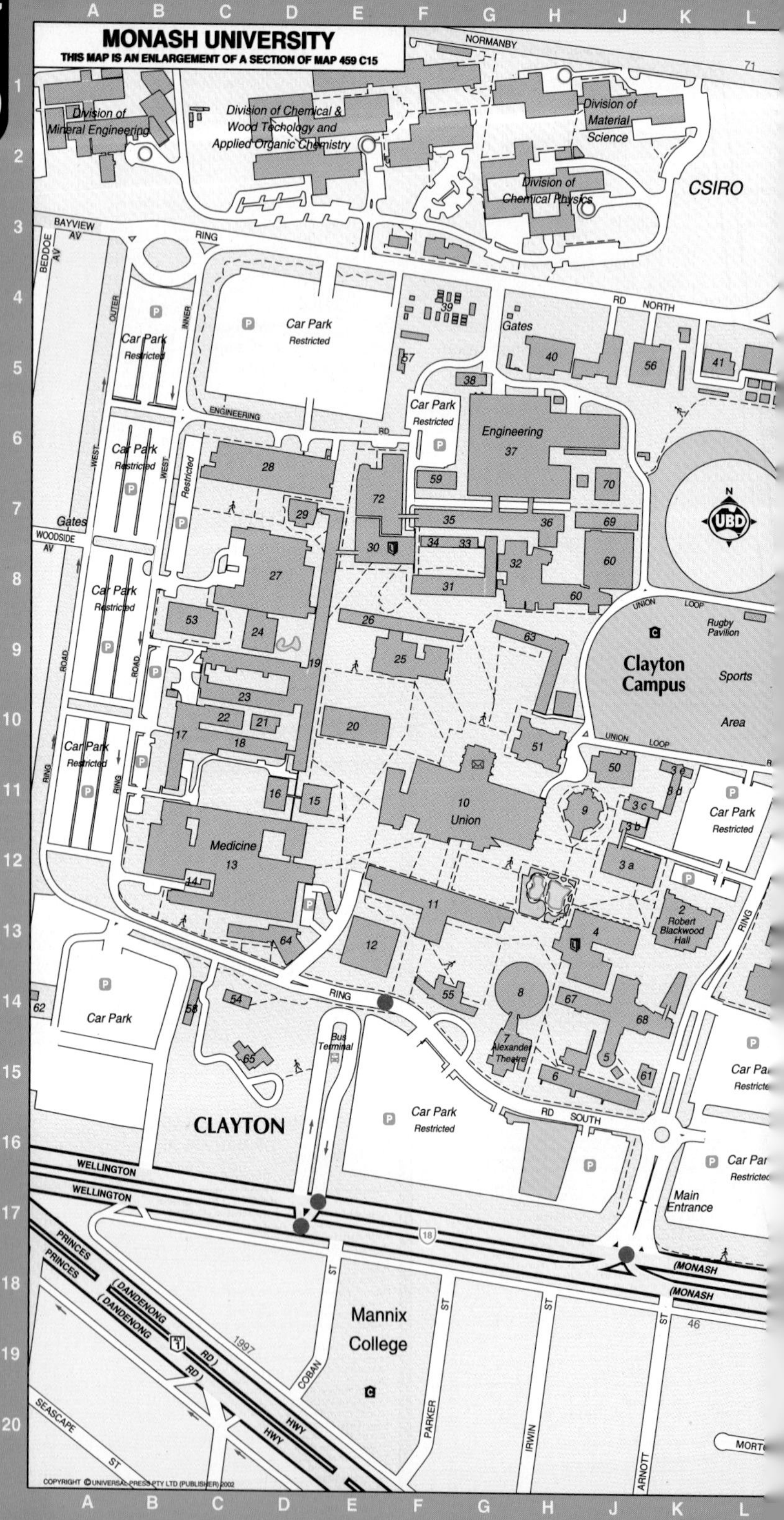
MONASH UNIVERSITY
THIS MAP IS AN ENLARGEMENT OF A SECTION OF MAP 459 C15
NORMANBY
Division of Mineral Engineering
Division of Chemical & Wood Techology and Applied Organic Chemistry
Division of Material Science
Division of Chemical Physics
CSIRO
BAYVIEW AV
RING
BEDDOE AV
Car Park Restricted
OUTER
INNER
RD NORTH
Gates
ENGINEERING RD
Engineering
WEST
Restricted
WOODSIDE AV
ROAD
Medicine
Union
UNION LOOP
Rugby Pavilion
Clayton Campus
Sports Area
Robert Blackwood Hall
Alexander Theatre
Bus Terminal
Car Park
CLAYTON
RD SOUTH
Main Entrance
WELLINGTON
PRINCES
(DANDENONG RD)
HWY
(MONASH
ST
COBAN
Mannix College
PARKER
IRWIN
ARNOTT
SEASCAPE ST
MORT
1997
COPYRIGHT © UNIVERSAL PRESS PTY LTD (PUBLISHER) 2002

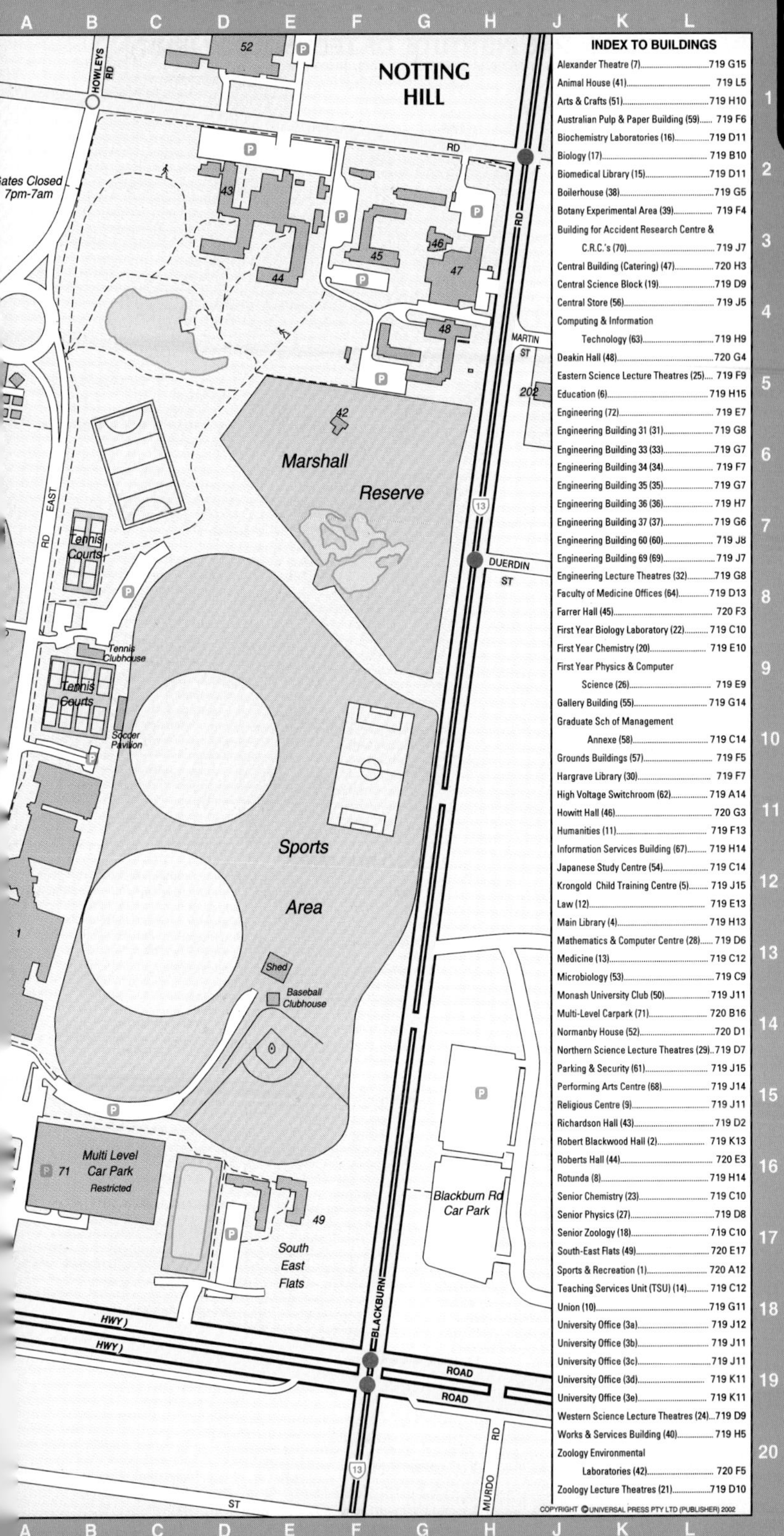

INDEX TO BUILDINGS

ROYAL MELBOURNE INSTITUTE OF TECHNOLOGY (RMIT)

THIS MAP IS AN ENLARGEMENT OF A SECTION OF MAP 2 F2

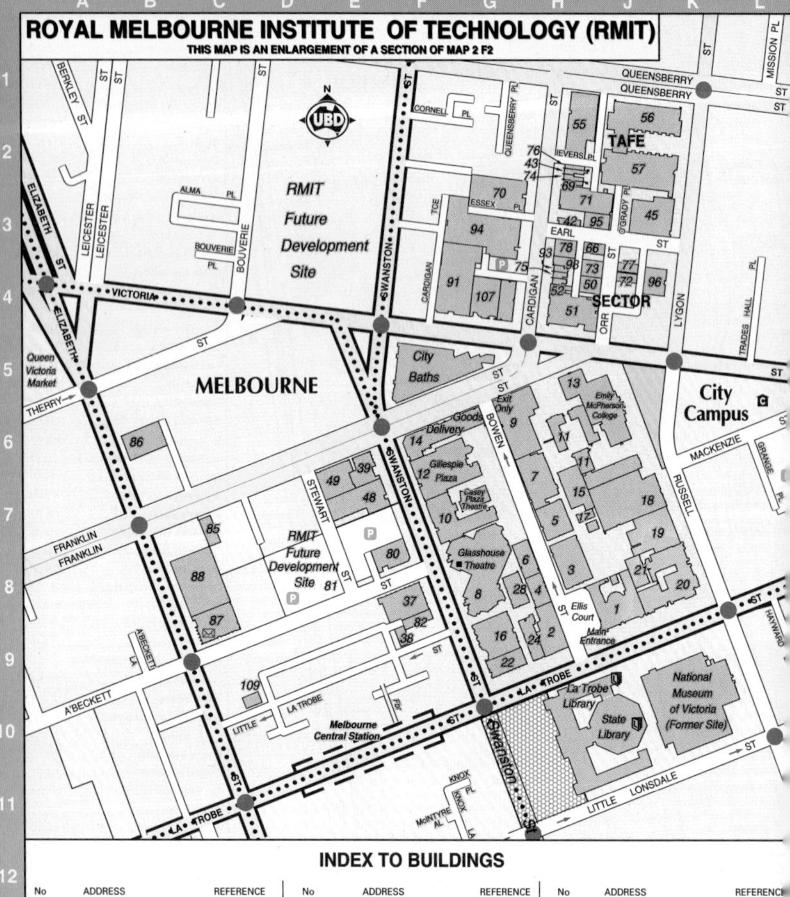

INDEX TO BUILDINGS

No	ADDRESS	REFERENCE
1	124 La Trobe Street	J8
2	124 La Trobe Street	H9
3	124 La Trobe Street	H8
4	124 La Trobe Street	H8
5	124 La Trobe Street	H7
6	124 La Trobe Street	H8
7	124 La Trobe Street	H6
8	368-374 Swanston Street	G8
9	124 La Trobe Street	G6
10	376-392 Swanston Street	F7
11	Corner Russell & Franklin Streets	H6
12	394-412 Swanston Street	F6
13	Corner Russell & Franklin Streets	H5
14	414-418 Swanston Street	F6
15	124 La Trobe Street	H7
16	336-348 Swanston Street	G9
17	124 La Trobe Street	H7
18	Russell Street	J7
19	Russell Street	J7
20	Russell Street	K8
21	Russell Street	J8
22	330-334 Swanston Street	G9
24	124 La Trobe Street	H9
28	124 La Trobe Street	G8
37	411 Swanston Street	F8
38	12-14 La Trobe Street	F9
39	459-469 Swanston Street	E6
42	36-40 Cardigan Street	H3
43	54 Cardigan Street	H2
45	33 Lygon Street	J3
48	449 Swanston Street	E7
49	67 Franklin Street	E7
50	11-15 Orr Street	H4
51	80-92 Victoria Street	H4
52	16 Cardigan Street	H4
55	58 Cardigan Street	H2
56	115 Queensberry Street	J1
57	115 Queensberry Street	J2
66	15-21 Earl Street	H3
69	50 Cardigan Street	H2
70	39-49 Cardigan Street	G3
71	42 Cardigan Street	H3
72	20 Orr Street	J
73	15 Orr Street	J
74	52 Cardigan Street	H
75	20 Cardigan Street	H
76	56 Cardigan Street	H
77	24-26 Orr Street	J
78	26-30 Cardigan Street	H
80	427-433 Swanston Street	F
81	427-433 Swanston Street	E
82	407-409 Swanston Street	[illegible]
85	95-105 Franklin Street	C
86	480 Elizabeth Street	B
87	410 Elizabeth Street	C
88	440 Elizabeth Street	[illegible]
91	110 Victoria Street	
94	23-27 Cardigan Street	[illegible]
95	24-26 Earl Street	
96	17-25 Lygon Street	
107	102 Victoria Street	
109	74-76 Little La Trobe Street	

SWINBURNE UNIVERSITY OF TECHNOLOGY

THIS MAP IS AN ENLARGEMENT OF A SECTION OF MAP 372 A17

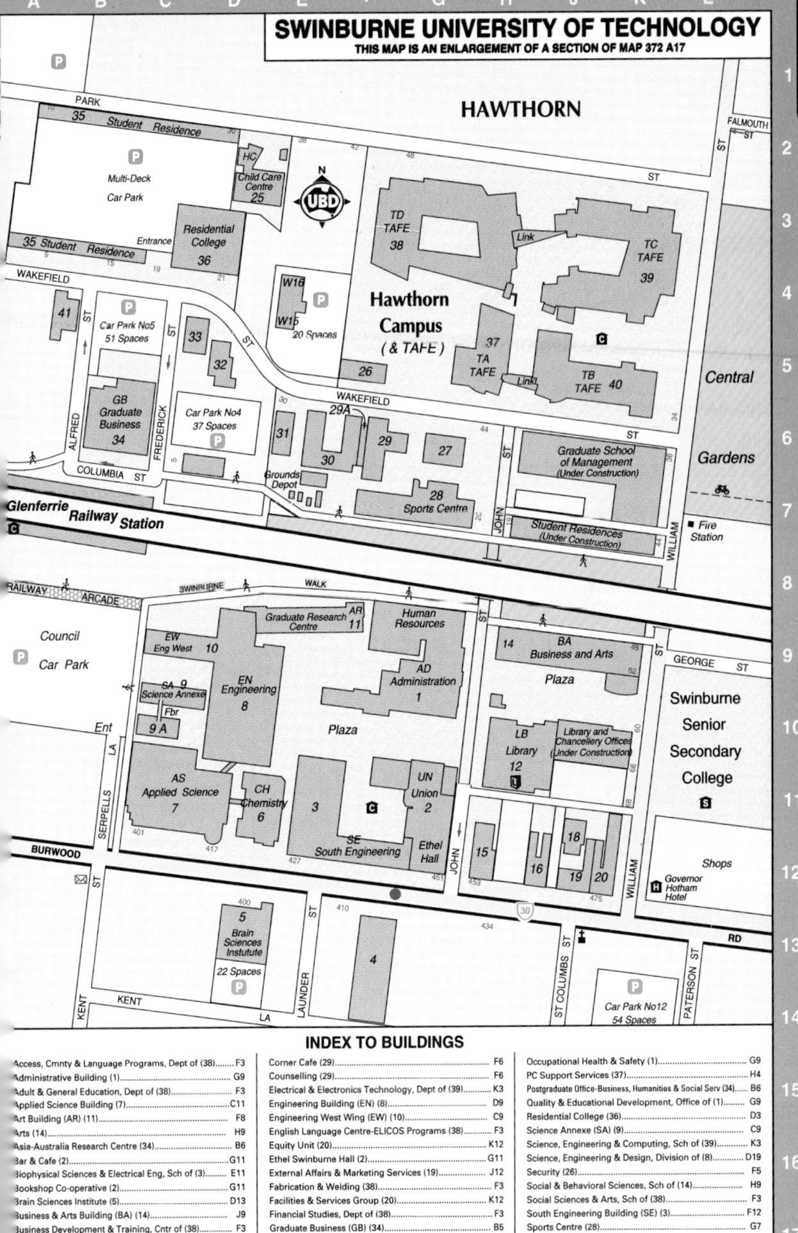

INDEX TO BUILDINGS

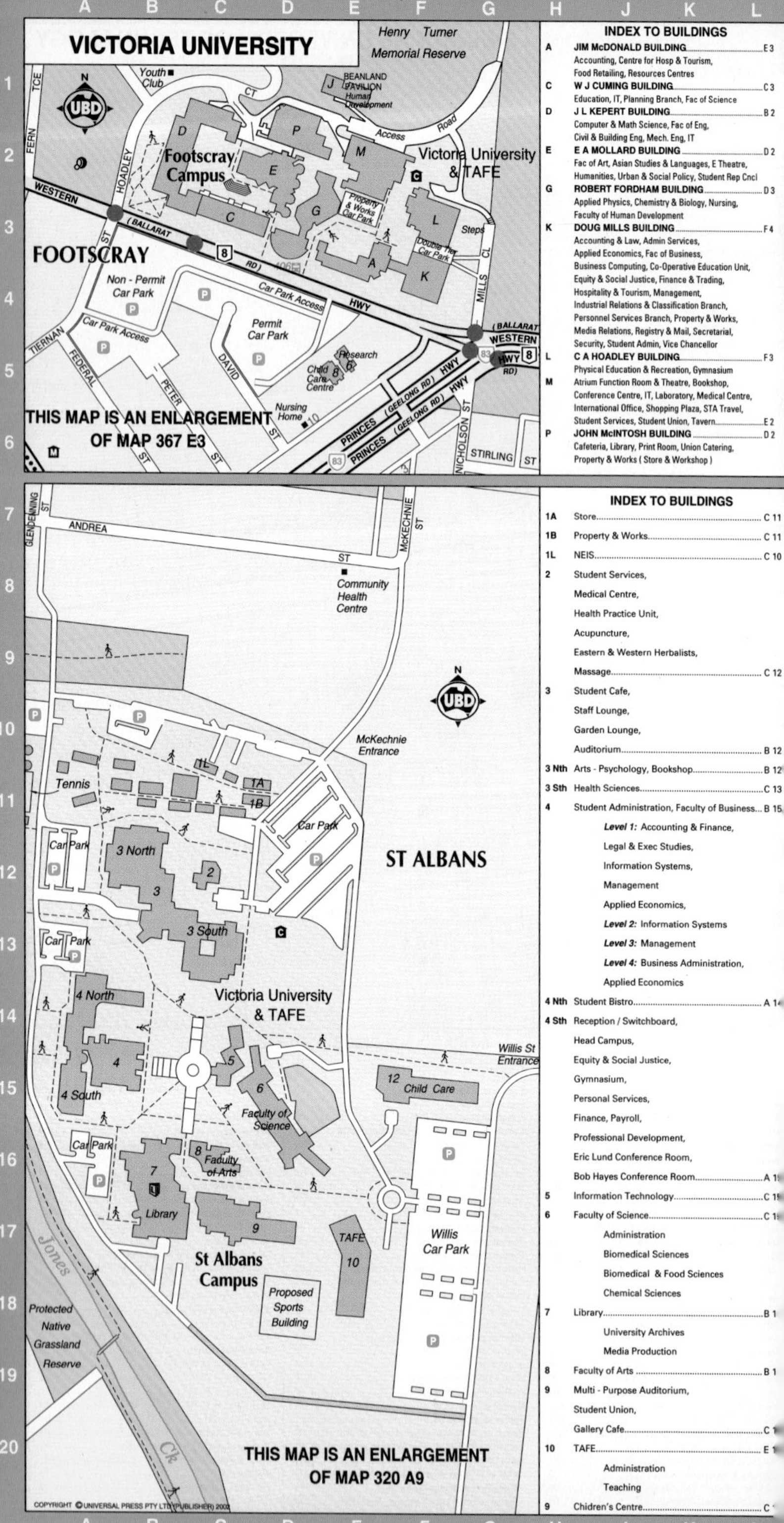
VICTORIA UNIVERSITY
Henry Turner Memorial Reserve
Youth Club
BEANLAND PAVILION Human Development
Footscray Campus
Victoria University & TAFE
FOOTSCRAY
Non - Permit Car Park
Car Park Access
Permit Car Park
Research
Child Care Centre
Nursing Home
Property & Works Car Park
Double Tier Car Park
Steps
WESTERN (BALLARAT RD) HWY
PRINCES (GEELONG RD) HWY
HOADLEY ST
FERN TCE
TIERNAN
FEDERAL ST
PETER ST
DAVID ST
MILLS CL
NICHOLSON ST
STIRLING ST
Access Road
THIS MAP IS AN ENLARGEMENT OF MAP 367 E3
INDEX TO BUILDINGS
A JIM McDONALD BUILDING ... E 3
Accounting, Centre for Hosp & Tourism, Food Retailing, Resources Centres
C W J CUMING BUILDING ... C 3
Education, IT, Planning Branch, Fac of Science
D J L KEPERT BUILDING ... B 2
Computer & Math Science, Fac of Eng, Civil & Building Eng, Mech. Eng, IT
E E A MOLLARD BUILDING ... D 2
Fac of Art, Asian Studies & Languages, E Theatre, Humanities, Urban & Social Policy, Student Rep Cncl
G ROBERT FORDHAM BUILDING ... D 3
Applied Physics, Chemistry & Biology, Nursing, Faculty of Human Development
K DOUG MILLS BUILDING ... F 4
Accounting & Law, Admin Services, Applied Economics, Fac of Business, Business Computing, Co-Operative Education Unit, Equity & Social Justice, Finance & Trading, Hospitality & Tourism, Management, Industrial Relations & Classification Branch, Personnel Services Branch, Property & Works, Media Relations, Registry & Mail, Secretarial, Security, Student Admin, Vice Chancellor
L C A HOADLEY BUILDING ... F 3
Physical Education & Recreation, Gymnasium
M Atrium Function Room & Theatre, Bookshop, Conference Centre, IT, Laboratory, Medical Centre, International Office, Shopping Plaza, STA Travel, Student Services, Student Union, Tavern ... E 2
P JOHN McINTOSH BUILDING ... D 2
Cafeteria, Library, Print Room, Union Catering, Property & Works (Store & Workshop)
GLENDENNING ST
ANDREA ST
McKECHNIE ST
Community Health Centre
McKechnie Entrance
Tennis
Car Park
3 North
3 South
4 North
4 South
ST ALBANS
Victoria University & TAFE
Willis St Entrance
Child Care
Faculty of Science
Faculty of Arts
Library
TAFE
Willis Car Park
St Albans Campus
Proposed Sports Building
Protected Native Grassland Reserve
Jones Ck
THIS MAP IS AN ENLARGEMENT OF MAP 320 A9
COPYRIGHT © UNIVERSAL PRESS PTY LTD (PUBLISHER) 2002
INDEX TO BUILDINGS
1A Store ... C 11
1B Property & Works ... C 11
1L NEIS ... C 10
2 Student Services, Medical Centre, Health Practice Unit, Acupuncture, Eastern & Western Herbalists, Massage ... C 12
3 Student Cafe, Staff Lounge, Garden Lounge, Auditorium ... B 12
3 Nth Arts - Psychology, Bookshop ... B 12
3 Sth Health Sciences ... C 13
4 Student Administration, Faculty of Business ... B 15
Level 1: Accounting & Finance, Legal & Exec Studies, Information Systems, Management, Applied Economics,
Level 2: Information Systems
Level 3: Management
Level 4: Business Administration, Applied Economics
4 Nth Student Bistro ... A 1
4 Sth Reception / Switchboard, Head Campus, Equity & Social Justice, Gymnasium, Personal Services, Finance, Payroll, Professional Development, Eric Lund Conference Room, Bob Hayes Conference Room ... A 1
5 Information Technology ... C 1
6 Faculty of Science ... C 1
Administration
Biomedical Sciences
Biomedical & Food Sciences
Chemical Sciences
7 Library ... B 1
University Archives
Media Production
8 Faculty of Arts ... B 1
9 Multi - Purpose Auditorium, Student Union, Gallery Cafe ... C 1
10 TAFE ... E 1
Administration
Teaching
9 Chidren's Centre ... C

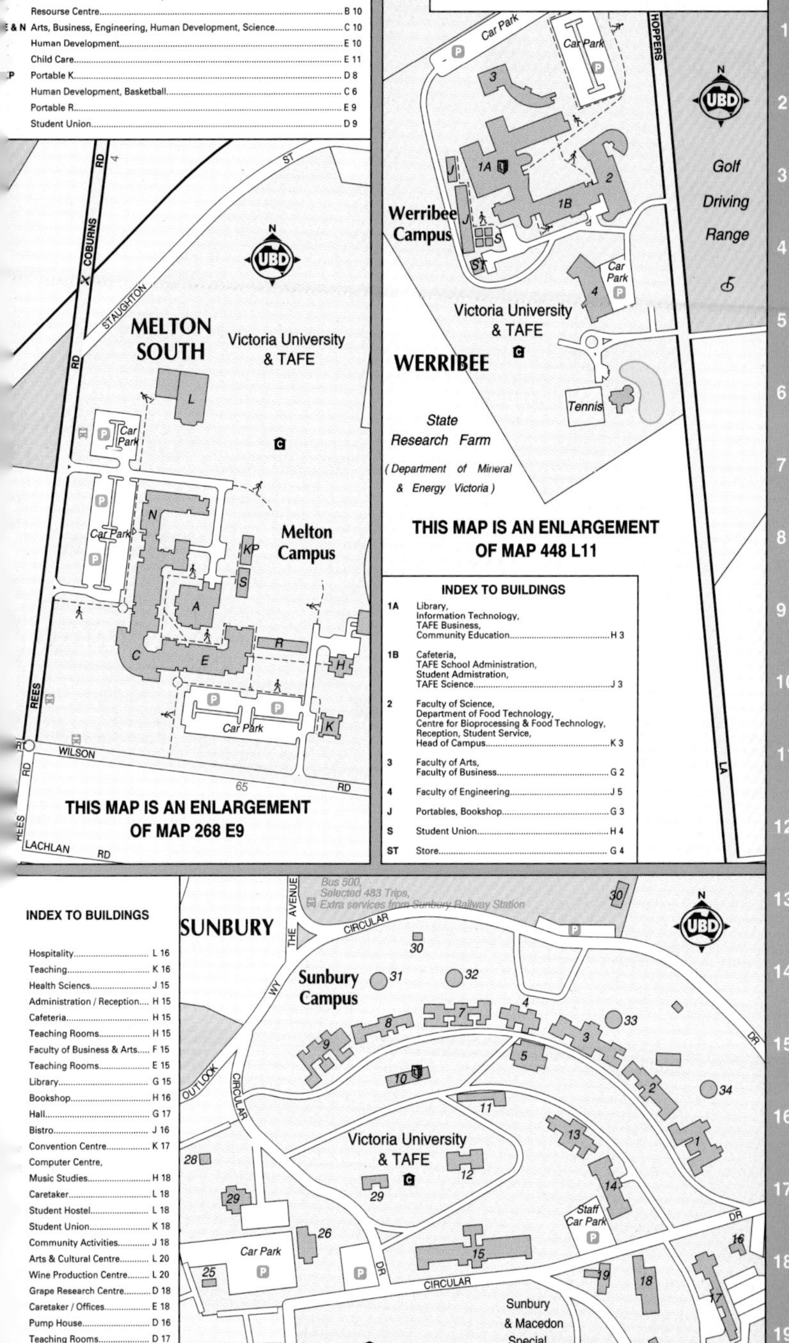
INDEX TO BUILDINGS
Auditorium, Cafeteria, Bookshop .... C 9
Resourse Centre .... B 10
E & N Arts, Business, Engineering, Human Development, Science .... C 10
Human Development .... E 10
Child Care .... E 11
P Portable K .... D 8
Human Development, Basketball .... C 6
Portable R .... E 9
Student Union .... D 9
VICTORIA UNIVERSITY
MELTON SOUTH
Victoria University & TAFE
Melton Campus
STAUGHTON
COBURNS RD
ST
REES RD
WILSON RD
LACHLAN RD
65
Car Park
THIS MAP IS AN ENLARGEMENT OF MAP 268 E9
Werribee Campus
Victoria University & TAFE
WERRIBEE
State Research Farm
(Department of Mineral & Energy Victoria)
HOPPERS LA
Golf Driving Range
Tennis
Car Park
THIS MAP IS AN ENLARGEMENT OF MAP 448 L11
INDEX TO BUILDINGS
1A Library, Information Technology, TAFE Business, Community Education .... H 3
1B Cafeteria, TAFE School Administration, Student Admistration, TAFE Science .... J 3
2 Faculty of Science, Department of Food Technology, Centre for Bioprocessing & Food Technology, Reception, Student Service, Head of Campus .... K 3
3 Faculty of Arts, Faculty of Business .... G 2
4 Faculty of Engineering .... J 5
J Portables, Bookshop .... G 3
S Student Union .... H 4
ST Store .... G 4
INDEX TO BUILDINGS
Hospitality .... L 16
Teaching .... K 16
Health Sciencs .... J 15
Administration / Reception .... H 15
Cafeteria .... H 15
Teaching Rooms .... H 15
Faculty of Business & Arts .... F 15
Teaching Rooms .... E 15
Library .... G 15
Bookshop .... H 16
Hall .... G 17
Bistro .... J 16
Convention Centre .... K 17
Computer Centre, Music Studies .... H 18
Caretaker .... L 18
Student Hostel .... L 18
Student Union .... K 18
Community Activities .... J 18
Arts & Cultural Centre .... L 20
Wine Production Centre .... L 20
Grape Research Centre .... D 18
Caretaker / Offices .... E 18
Pump House .... D 16
Teaching Rooms .... D 17
Recreation .... G 14
Recreation .... K 13
Rotunda .... F 14
Rotunda .... G 14
Rotunda .... K 15
Rotunda .... L 16
SUNBURY
Sunbury Campus
Victoria University & TAFE
Bus 500, Selected 483 Trips, Extra services from Sunbury Railway Station
THE AVENUE
CIRCULAR DR
OUTLOOK DR
WY
Car Park
Staff Car Park
Sunbury Primary
Sunbury & Macedon Special
HILLTOP
FLORENCE LA
CT
SCHOOLHOUSE LA
THE HEIGHTS
THIS MAP IS AN ENLARGEMENT OF MAP 143 J18
COPYRIGHT © UNIVERSAL PRESS PTY LTD (PUBLISHER) 2002

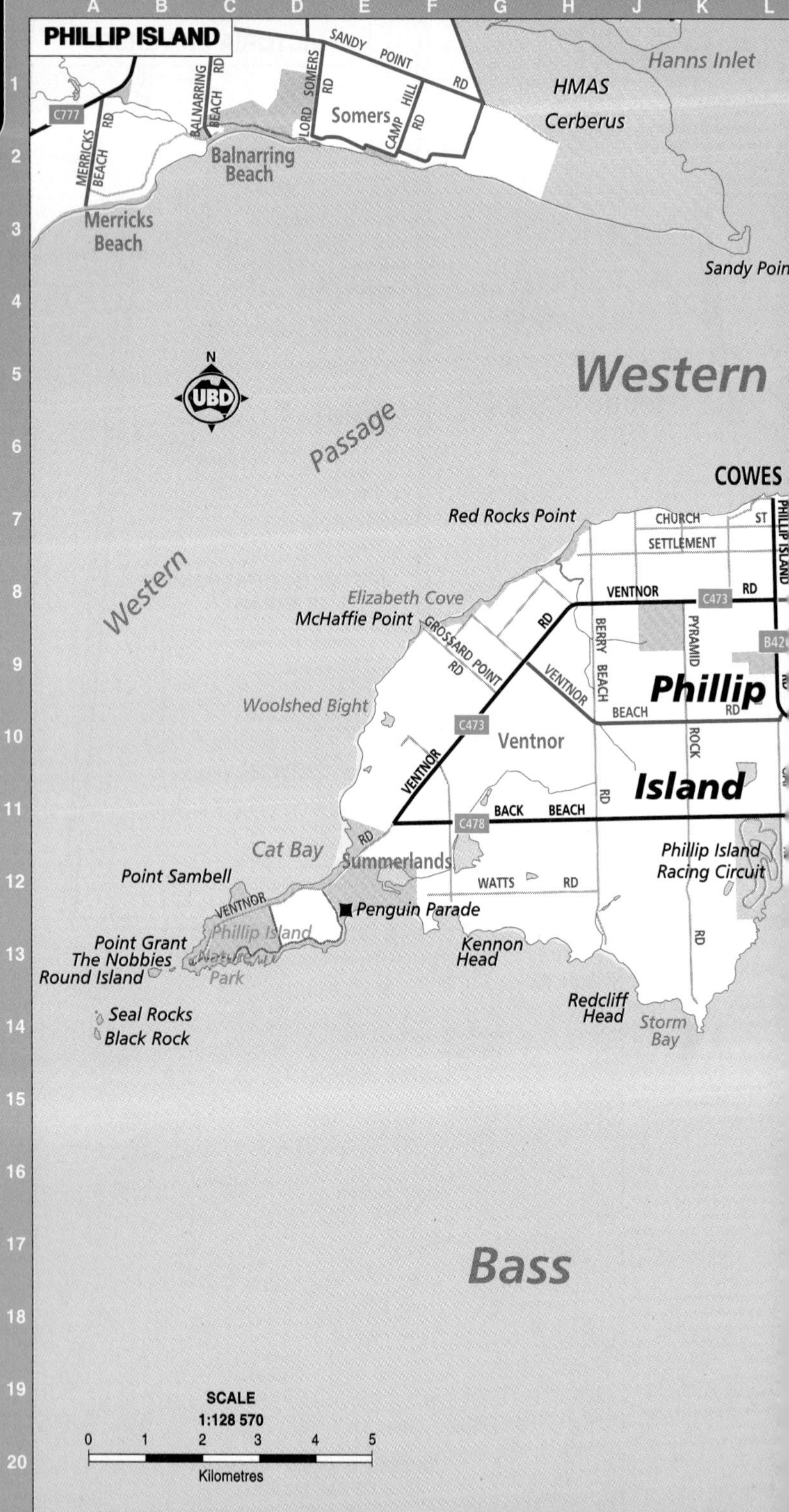
PHILLIP ISLAND
A B C D E F G H J K L
1 2 3 4 5 6 7 8 9 10 11 12 13 14 15 16 17 18 19 20
Hanns Inlet
HMAS
Cerberus
Sandy Point
SANDY POINT RD
Somers
SOMERS RD
LORD
CAMP HILL RD
BALNARRING BEACH RD
MERRICKS BEACH RD
C777
Balnarring
Beach
Merricks
Beach
Western
Passage
Western
COWES
Red Rocks Point
CHURCH ST
SETTLEMENT
PHILLIP ISLAND
VENTNOR RD
C473
Elizabeth Cove
McHaffie Point
GROSSARD POINT RD
BERRY BEACH RD
PYRAMID ROCK RD
B420
Phillip
Island
BEACH RD
Woolshed Bight
C473
Ventnor
VENTNOR
BACK BEACH
C478
Cat Bay
RD
Summerlands
Point Sambell
WATTS RD
Phillip Island
Racing Circuit
VENTNOR
Penguin Parade
Phillip Island
Nature
Park
Point Grant
The Nobbies
Round Island
Kennon
Head
Redcliff
Head
Storm
Bay
Seal Rocks
Black Rock
Bass
SCALE
1:128 570
0 1 2 3 4 5
Kilometres
COPYRIGHT © UNIVERSAL PRESS PTY LTD (PUBLISHER) 2002

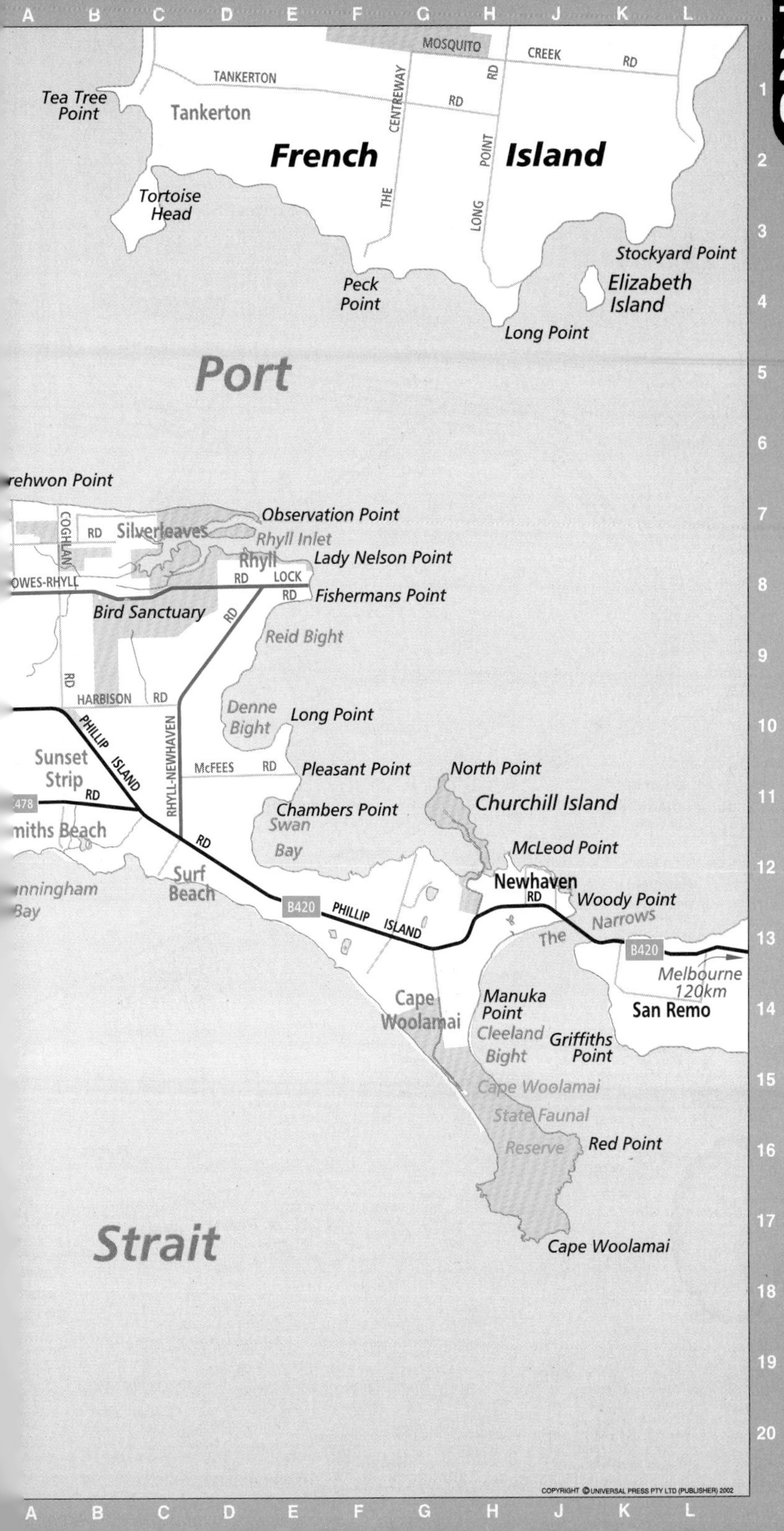

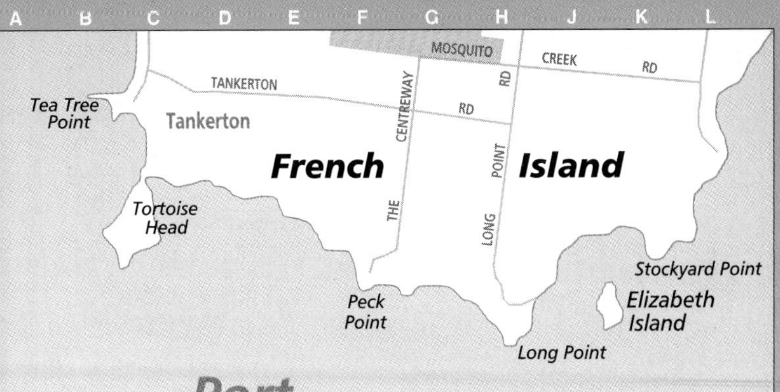
MOSQUITO
CREEK
RD
TANKERTON
RD
Tea Tree Point
Tankerton
French Island
THE CENTREWAY
LONG POINT RD
Tortoise Head
Stockyard Point
Elizabeth Island
Peck Point
Long Point

Port
rehwon Point
Observation Point
COGHLAN RD
Silverleaves
Rhyll Inlet
Rhyll
Lady Nelson Point
OWES-RHYLL
RD
LOCK
RD
Fishermans Point
Bird Sanctuary
RD
Reid Bight
RD
HARBISON RD
Denne Bight
Long Point
PHILLIP ISLAND RD
RHYLL-NEWHAVEN
Sunset Strip
McFEES RD
Pleasant Point
North Point
Churchill Island
478
Chambers Point
Swan Bay
miths Beach
McLeod Point
Newhaven
RD
Woody Point
nningham Bay
Surf Beach
B420
PHILLIP ISLAND
The Narrows
B420
Melbourne 120km
San Remo
Cape Woolamai
Manuka Point
Cleeland Bight
Griffiths Point
Cape Woolamai State Faunal Reserve
Red Point
Strait
Cape Woolamai

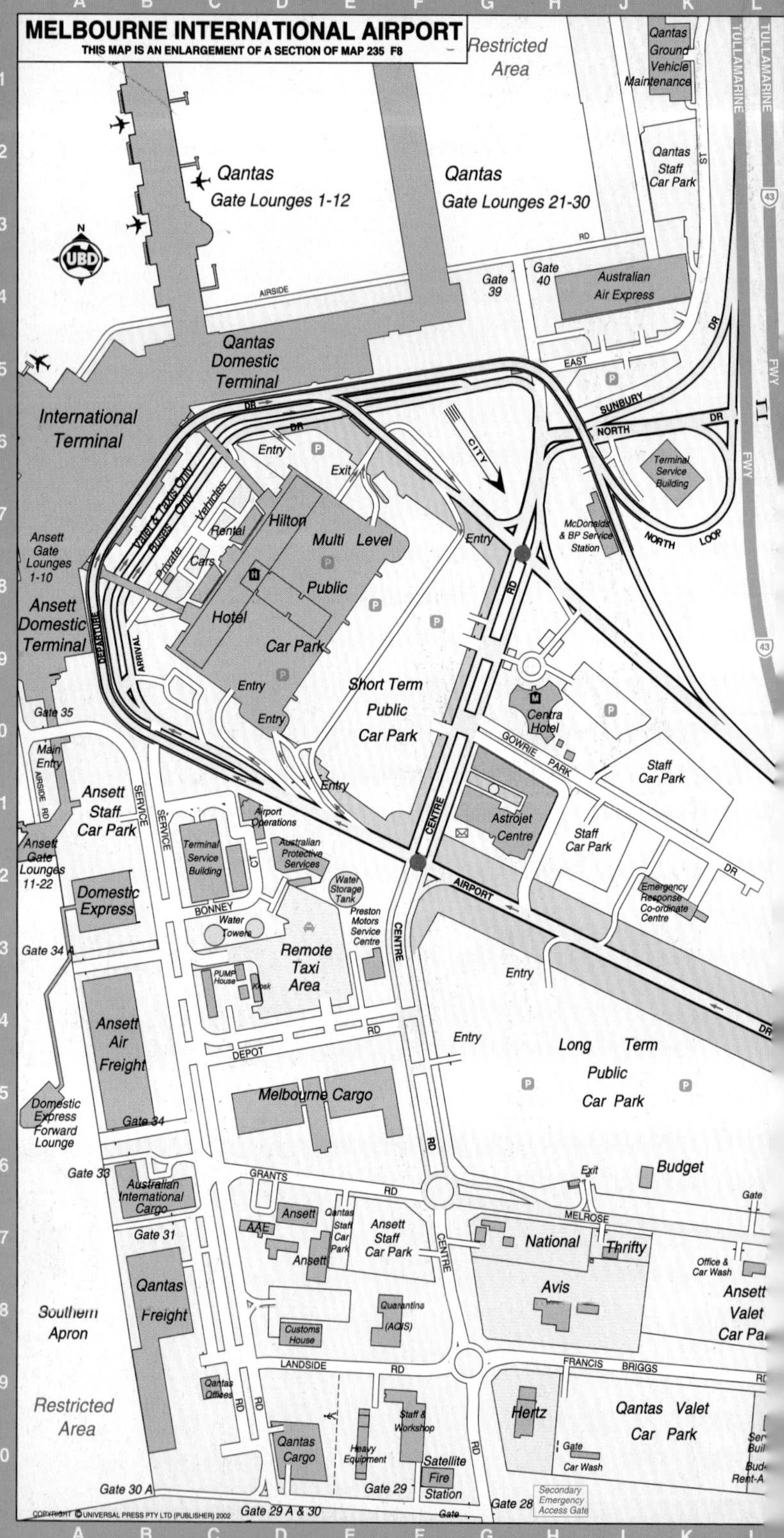

MELBOURNE INTERNATIONAL AIRPORT
THIS MAP IS AN ENLARGEMENT OF A SECTION OF MAP 235 F8
A B C D E F G H J K L
1 2 3 4 5 6 7 8 9 10 11 12 13 14 15 16 17 18 19 20
Restricted Area
Qantas Ground Vehicle Maintenance
TULLAMARINE
Qantas Staff Car Park
Qantas Gate Lounges 1-12
Qantas Gate Lounges 21-30
ST
RD
43
Gate 39
Gate 40
Australian Air Express
AIRSIDE
Qantas Domestic Terminal
EAST
DR
SUNBURY
NORTH
DR
FWY
International Terminal
DR
DR
Entry
Exit
CITY
Terminal Service Building
Valet & Taxis Only
Buses Only
Vehicles
Rental
Private
Cars
Hilton
Multi Level
Public
Hotel
Car Park
Ansett Gate Lounges 1-10
Ansett Domestic Terminal
DEPARTURE
ARRIVAL
Entry
McDonalds & BP Service Station
NORTH
LOOP
RD
Short Term Public Car Park
Centra Hotel
Gate 35
Main Entry
AIRSIDE RD
Ansett Staff Car Park
SERVICE
SERVICE
GOWRIE
PARK
Staff Car Park
Astrojet Centre
Staff Car Park
CENTRE
Airport Operations
Terminal Service Building
CT
Australian Protective Services
Water Storage Tank
Ansett Gate Lounges 11-22
Domestic Express
BONNEY
Water Towers
Preston Motors Service Centre
AIRPORT
DR
Emergency Response Co-ordinate Centre
Gate 34 A
Remote Taxi Area
CENTRE
PUMP House
Kiosk
Entry
RD
DEPOT
Entry
Ansett Air Freight
Long Term Public Car Park
Melbourne Cargo
Domestic Express Forward Lounge
Gate 34
RD
Gate 33
GRANTS
Exit
Budget
Australian International Cargo
RD
MELROSE
Gate
Gate 31
Ansett
AAE
Qantas Staff Car Park
Ansett Staff Car Park
CENTRE
National
Thrifty
Office & Car Wash
Ansett
Avis
Ansett Valet Car Pa
Southern Apron
Qantas Freight
Quarantine (AQIS)
Customs House
LANDSIDE
RD
FRANCIS
BRIGGS
RD
Qantas Offices
RD
RD
Staff & Workshop
Hertz
Qantas Valet Car Park
Restricted Area
Qantas Cargo
Heavy Equipment
Satellite Fire Station
RD
Gate
Car Wash
Gate 30 A
Gate 29
Gate 28
Secondary Emergency Access Gate
Gate 29 A & 30
Gate